英汉双解版工作人员名单

项目负责人：

夏　天

翻译：

王　莹　　魏　博　　夏　天

编辑组成员：

魏　博　　杨书旗　　周子平　　官亚平　　王苗苗

其他编校人员：

高耿松　　董燕萍　　任素琴　　吴　硕　　刘英姣

Little Oxford

ENGLISH-CHINESE

Dictionary

牛津英汉
双解小词典

第 9 版

(英) Sara Hawker 主编

外语教学与研究出版社

FOREIGN LANGUAGE TEACHING AND RESEARCH PRESS

北京 BEIJING

牛津大学出版社

OXFORD UNIVERSITY PRESS

京权图字：01-2007-3157

English text originally published as Little Oxford English Dictionary 9th
Edition by Oxford University Press, Great Clarendon Street, Oxford. ©
Oxford University Press 1969, 1980, 1986, 1994, 1998, 2002, 2006
This English-Chinese edition published in association with Foreign
Language Teaching and Research Press for distribution in the Chinese
mainland only and by Oxford University Press for distribution elsewhere
including Hong Kong SAR, Macau SAR and Taiwan Province
只限中华人民共和国境内销售，不包括香港特别行政区、澳门特
别行政区及台湾省。不得出口。
Copyright © Oxford University Press 2008
Oxford is a registered trademark of Oxford University Press
Foreign Language Teaching and Research Press has made some
changes to the original work in order to make this edition more
appropriate for Chinese readers.
外语教学与研究出版社对原书进行了个别修改，使其更符合中国
读者的需要。

图书在版编目（CIP）数据

即牛津英汉双解小词典 = Little Oxford English-
Chinese Dictionary 9th Edition ／ 英国牛津大学出版社编
著. — 北京：外语教学与研究出版社，2008.6（2017.3
重印）
 ISBN 978-7-5600-7619-5

Ⅰ. ①牛… Ⅱ. ①英… Ⅲ. ①英语—双解词典②双解
词典—英、汉 Ⅳ. ①H316

中国版本图书馆CIP数据核字（2008）第088426号

出版人　蔡剑峰
责任编辑　夏　天
封面设计　袁　璐
出版发行　外语教学与研究出版社
社　　址　北京市西三环北路19号（100089）
网　　址　http://www.fltrp.com
印　　刷　南京爱德印刷有限公司
开　　本　805×1300　1/64
印　　张　19.875
版　　次　2008年6月第1版　2017年3月第22次印刷
书　　号　ISBN 978-7-5600-7619-5
定　　价　31.90元

购书咨询：(010) 88819926　电子邮箱: club@fltrp.com
外研书店：https://waiyants.tmall.com
凡印刷、装订质量问题，请联系我社印制部
联系电话：(010) 61207896　电子邮箱：zhijian@fltrp.com
凡侵权、盗版书籍线索，请联系我社法律事务部
举报电话：(010) 88817519　电子邮箱：banquan@fltrp.com
法律顾问：立方律师事务所　刘旭东律师
　　　　　中咨律师事务所　殷　斌律师

物料号：176190001

出版前言

《牛津英汉双解小词典》自 2002 年出版以来，深受广大英语学习者和英语爱好者的喜爱，赢得了良好的市场口碑。为了继续满足广大读者对便携型英汉双解小词典的需要，紧跟当代英语词汇的发展变化，外研社以牛津大学出版社最新出版的《牛津英语小词典》第 9 版为蓝本推出了这本最新版的《牛津英汉双解小词典》。

《牛津英语小词典》第 9 版保持了以前各版一贯坚持的释义简明、准确的特色，同时对词条释义做了更加符合学习型词典特点的修订，方便读者理解释义。词典收录的词语、短语和释义达到 90,000 余条，所收词目包罗万象，既囊括了近年涌现出来的 blog（博客）、gigabyte（吉字节）、HTML（超文本链接标示语言）、SMS（短信服务）等网络和信息技术用语，又涵盖了政治、经济、体育、文化、文学艺术等诸多学科的常用词汇及义项。为了强化本词典指导英语学习的功能，还特别增加了上百条"拼写指南"（spelling tips）及用法注释。新增的资料速查部分（Factfinder）收录了英语阅读中常见的国家名、人名、地名、货币名称、度量衡单位等，使这本小词典具备了大多数同类型词典所不具备的小型资料手册的功能。为了方便读者查阅，本双解版还对所有一般词目词标注了以第 15 版国际音标为基础的国际音标。

本双解版延续了上一版牛津英汉双解小词典的优秀品质，同时在收词规模、释义简明性、内容丰富性和读者易用性方面都有了显著改进和提升，相信本词典一定会成为广大英语学习者新的良师益友。

外语教学与研究出版社
学术与辞书出版分社

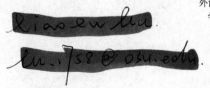

Contents 目录

Introduction

The ninth edition of the *Little Oxford English Dictionary* has been revised, updated, and redesigned. It is part of the range based on the *Concise Oxford English Dictionary* (11th edition), for which we analysed hundreds of millions of words of English taken from books, newspapers, magazines, and the Internet. It provides clear, up-to-date coverage of the core vocabulary of English and reflects how the language is really used today. Extra care has been taken to make the definitions easier to understand than ever before, using everyday English and avoiding the use of difficult or technical vocabulary.

This new edition gives even more help with those words that cause problems in terms of spelling, grammar, or pronunciation. Special notes throughout the dictionary give guidance about words that people often confuse with each other (for example, *accept* and *except* or *pour* and *pore*). There are also notes on words that are difficult to spell (such as *receive*, *harass*, or *indispensable*), and on tricky points of English (for example, whether to use *fewer* or *less*). A handy Factfinder section of the dictionary gives lots of useful lists of factual information, including countries of the world and their capital cities, kings and queens of England and the UK, and member states of the European Union.

Small enough to fit easily into a bag or rucksack, the *Little Oxford English Dictionary* is ideal for adults and school students who require a straightforward, user-friendly guide to the English language of today.

前言

《牛津英语小词典》第 9 版对词条作了修订，更新了内容，进行了重新设计。本词典是以《简明牛津英语词典》（第 11 版）为基础编纂的系列词典之一。为编纂该词典，我们分析了收集自各种书籍、报刊、杂志以及因特网的数以亿计的英文词汇。本词典全面明晰地收录了当代英语的核心词汇，反映了英语的实际用法。为使释义更加明白易懂，本词典的释义词汇格外注意使用日常英语词汇，避免使用难词或术语化的词汇。

新版词典还为容易出现拼写、语法或发音问题的词汇提供了更多帮助信息。对于人们常会弄混的词语（如 accept 与 except, pour 与 pore），在词典各处给出了专门的注释，指导如何区分。对于难于拼写的词汇（如 receive, harass 和 indispensable）和词语用法难点（例如该如何选择使用 fewer 和 less），本词典亦提供了注释文字加以说明。本词典还设置了方便易用的资料速查单元，从中可以查索诸多有用的资料信息。这些资料包括世界各国及首都、英格兰和英国历代君主、欧洲联盟成员国等。

《牛津英语小词典》小巧便携，可以轻松放进口袋或背包，对于需要获得学习当代英语的简明、方便指导的读者，不论是成人还是学生，本词典都称得上是理想之选。

Guide to the dictionary 本词典使用指南

The *Little Oxford English Dictionary* is designed to be as easy to use and understand as possible. Here is an explanation of the main features that you will find in the dictionary. 《牛津英语小词典》以易用、易于理解为基本的编纂理念。下面是对本词典主要体例的说明。

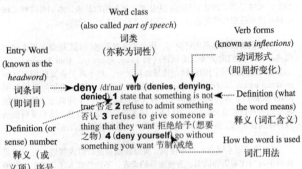

Word class
(also called *part of speech*)
词类
(亦称为词性)

Verb forms
(known as *inflections*)
动词形式
(即屈折变化)

Entry Word
(known as the
headword)
词条词
(即词目)

deny /dɪˈnaɪ/ **verb (denies, denying, denied) 1** state that something is not true 否定 **2** refuse to admit something 否认 **3** refuse to give someone a thing that they want 拒绝给予(想要之物) **4 (deny yourself)** go without something you want 节制;减绝

Definition (or
sense) number
释义(或
义项)序号

Definition (what
the word means)
释义(词汇含义)

How the word is used
词汇用法

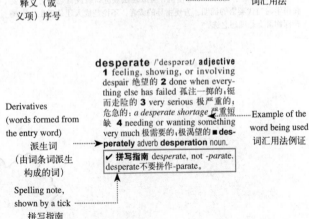

Derivatives
(words formed from
the entry word)
派生词
(由词条词派生
构成的词)

desperate /ˈdespərət/ **adjective
1** feeling, showing, or involving despair 绝望的 **2** done when everything else has failed 孤注一掷的;铤而走险的 **3** very serious 极严重的;危急的: *a desperate shortage* 严重短缺 **4** needing or wanting something very much 极需要的;极渴望的 ■ **desperately** adverb **desperation** noun.

Example of the
word being used
词汇用法例证

✔ 拼写指南 *desperate*, not *-parate*.
desperate不要拼作-parate。

Spelling note,
shown by a tick
拼写指南
(以勾号标示)

Plural form of noun

名词的复数形式

Geographical label showing where the term is used

表示词语使用区域的地域标签

donkey /'dɒŋki/ **noun** (plural **donkeys**) a domesticated animal of the horse family with long ears and a braying call 驴 □ **donkey jacket** Brit. 【英】 a heavy jacket with a patch of waterproof material across the shoulders 风雨衣 **donkey's years** informal 【非正式】 a very long time 很久；猴年马月

Phrases and compounds (terms made up of one or more existing words)

短语及复合词（由一个或多个现有词汇构成的词语）

Label showing the situation in which the word is used

表示词汇使用场合的标签

classy /'klɑːsi/ **adjective** (**classier**, **classiest**) informal 【非正式】 stylish and sophisticated 时髦的；高级的

Adjective forms (the comparative and superlative)

形容词形式（比较级和最高级）

Usage note giving extra information, shown by an exclamation mark

用法注释，提供额外信息（以感叹号标示）

flair /fleə(r)/ **noun 1** a natural ability or talent 天赋；资质 **2** stylishness 时髦

! 注意 don't confuse **flair** with **flare**, which means 'burn' or 'gradually become wider'. 不要混淆flair和flare，后者表示"烧旺"或"逐渐变宽"。

Entry number, given for words that have the same spelling but different meanings (known as homonyms)

词条编号，用于拼写相同但意义不同的词汇（即同形异义词）

bail² **noun** Cricket 【板球】 either of the two small pieces of wood that rest on the stumps 三柱门上的横木

Label showing the subject with which the word is connected

表示词汇相关科目的标签

mackintosh or **macintosh** ◄──── Different spelling
/ˈmækɪntɒʃ/ **noun** Brit. 【英】a full-
length waterproof coat 长雨衣

> Different spelling
> of the entry word
> (both are allowed)
> 词条词的异体拼
> 法（两种拼法均
> 可）

Pronunciation
(how to say the
word)
音标（词汇的
读法）

discotheque /ˈdɪskətek/ = DISCO.

> Cross reference to
> another dictionary
> entry
> 参见词典另一词条

Labels 标签

Most of the words and senses in the dictionary are part of standard English. Some words, however, are only appropriate to certain situations (such as a conversation with friends) or are found only in certain contexts (for example, in poetry or in official documents). Where this is the case a label (or a combination of labels) is used. 本词典中大部分都是标准英语的词汇和意义。但也有部分词汇只适用于特定场合（如与友人的谈话）或语境（如诗歌和官方文件），此情况就用标签（或一组标签）予以说明。

Register labels 语域标签

Register labels refer to a particular level of use in language. They show that a term is informal or formal, old-fashioned or technical, and so on. 语域标签指语言的特定使用层次，标示某词语是正式还是非正式，是过时词汇还是术语，等等。

formal 【正式】:	normally used only in writing, especially in official documents (e.g. *dwelling* or *deceased*) 通常只用于书面文体，尤其用于官方文件中（如 dwelling 和 deceased）
informal 【非正式】:	normally used only in speaking, or in informal writing or email (e.g. *gawp*, *barmy*, or *telly*) 通常只用于口语、非正式文体或电子邮件中（如 gawp, barmy 和 telly）

dated 【废】:	no longer used by most people (e.g. *gramophone*) 大多数人已不再使用（如 gramophone）
old use 【旧】:	not in ordinary use today, though sometimes used to give an old-fashioned effect and also found in the literature of the past (e.g. *farewell* or *maiden*) 现已不常用，偶尔使用会给人一种古雅老派的印象，亦见于旧时的文学作品中（如 farewell 和 maiden）
historical 【历史】:	only used today to refer to things that are no longer part of modern life (e.g. *blunderbuss* or *doublet*) 现只用来描述现代生活中已不存在的事物（如 blunderbuss 和 doublet）
literary 【文】:	found only or mainly in poems, plays, and novels (e.g. *flaxen* or *serpent*) 只用于或主要用于诗歌、戏剧、小说（如 flaxen 和 serpent）
technical 【术语】:	normally used only in technical language (e.g. *node* or *fluvial*) 通常只用于专门术语（如 node 和 fluvial）
humorous 【幽默】:	used to sound funny or playful (e.g. *underwhelmed*) 用以产生可笑或滑稽的效果（如 underwhelmed）
dialect 【方】:	used only in certain local regions of the UK (e.g. *aye* or *bide*) 只用于英国的某些地区（如 aye 和 bide）
disapproving 【贬】:	meant to convey a low opinion or to insult someone (e.g. *pleb*) 表达轻视或羞辱他人（如 pleb）
offensive 【冒犯】:	likely to cause offence, whether the person speaking means to or not 容易冒犯他人，不论说话者是否有意

Geographical labels 地域标签

English is spoken throughout the world, and while most of the words used in standard British English will be the same as those used in other varieties, there are some words which are only found in one type of English. For example, the normal American word for a lift is **elevator**. If a word or phrase has the geographical label Brit. in this dictionary, this means that it is used in standard British English but not in American English, although it may be found in other varieties such as Australian English. The labels US and N. Amer., on the other hand, mean that the word or phrase is typically American and is not standard in

British English, though it may be found elsewhere. 英语是全球通用的语言。标准英式英语和其他英语变体中使用的大多数词汇都是相同的，但也有部分词汇只用于一种英语。例如，美国英语中通常称 lift（电梯）为 elevator。在本词典中，如果某个词汇或短语具有地域标签 Brit.【英】，即表示它只用于标准英式英语，而不用于美式英语，但澳大利亚英语等其他地区的英语中也可能使用。US【美】及 N. Amer.【北美】则表示该词汇或短语通常用于美式而非标准英式英语，但其他地区也可能使用。

Subject labels 学科标签

These are used to show that a word or sense is connected with a particular subject or specialist activity such as Music, Computing, or Rugby. 学科标签表示某词汇或义项与某学科或专门活动相关联，如 Music【音乐】、Computing【计】和 Rugby【英式橄榄球】。

Cross references 参见项

Cross references are pointers to another dictionary entry. They are indicated by an arrow (⇒) or an equals sign (=). The arrow means that the term is an alternative spelling of the one referred to (e.g. **caftan** ⇒ KAFTAN), while the equals sign shows that the term means the same as the one referred to (e.g. **groundnut** = PEANUT). 参见项以箭头（⇒）或等号（=）标示，是指向本词典中另一个词条的标识。箭头表示某词语是所指词语的另一种拼法（如 **caftan** ⇒ KAFTAN），等号则表示某词语与所指词语同义（如 **groundnut** = PEANUT）。

Pronunciation Symbols 发音符号

Vowels 元音	Examples 例词	Vowels 元音	Examples 例词
iː	**meet**	ʌ	**cup**
i	**happy**	ɜː	**her**
ɪ	**pin**	ə	the 'a' in **along**
e	**bed**	eɪ	**say**
æ	**cat**	əʊ	**most**
ɑː	**calm**	aɪ	**cry**
ɒ	**top**	ɔɪ	**boy**
ɔː	**law**	aʊ	**cow**
ʊ	**book**	ɪə(r)	**beer**
u	**actual**	eə(r)	**hair**
uː	**soon**	ʊə(r)	**poor**

Consonants 辅音	Examples 例词	Consonants 辅音	Examples 例词
b	**bat**	r	**red**
d	**day**	s	**sit**
dʒ	**jam**	t	**top**
f	**fat**	tʃ	**chin**
g	**get**	v	**van**
h	**hat**	w	**will**
k	**king**	j	**yes**
kh	**loch**	z	**zebra**
l	**leg**	θ	**thin**
m	**man**	ð	**this**
n	**not**	ʃ	**shop**
ŋ	**singer, finger**	ʒ	**vision**
p	**pen**		

Note 注:

1. Foreign pronunciations are always shown in the way an English speaker would say them, e.g. /ˌkɔːdn ˈblɜː/ (cordon bleu). 外来语的发音以操英语者的发音标示，如：/ˌkɔːdn ˈblɜː/ (cordon bleu)。

2. (r)表示后接辅音时不发音，后接元音时要发音。

Note on trademarks and proprietary status
关于专利名称地位的说明

This dictionary includes some words which have, or are asserted to have, proprietary status as trademarks or otherwise. Their inclusion does not imply that they have acquired for legal purposes a non-proprietary or general significance, nor any other judgement concerning their legal status. In cases where the editorial staff have some evidence that a word has proprietary status this is indicated in the entry for that word by the label trademark, but no judgement concerning the legal status of such words is made or implied thereby. 本词典所收录的词中，有些词具有或据声称具有商标的专利名称地位，而有些词则恰恰相反。收录这些词既不意味着它们在法律上已不再具有专利意义或已经具有了一般意义，也不表示对其法律地位作出了任何判断。词典编纂者有证据表明某词具有专利名称地位时，在词条中使用 trademark【商标】这个标签予以标示，但并不意味着以此对此类词汇的法律地位作出判断或暗示。

A or **a** /eɪ/ noun (plural **As** or **A's**) the first letter of the alphabet 英语字母表的第1个字母 • abbreviation **1** ampere(s). **2** (A) angstroms. □ **A level** (in the UK except Scotland) the higher of the two main levels of the GCE exam (英国除苏格兰以外地区的)高级普通教育文凭考试

a /ə, eɪ/ determiner **1** used when mentioning someone or something for the first time; the indefinite article 一个,某个,任何(不定冠词,用于指第一次提及某人或某物) **2** one single 单个;一 **3** per 每(个)

AA /eɪ 'eɪ/ abbreviation **1** Alcoholics Anonymous 嗜酒者互诫协会 **2** Automobile Association 汽车协会

aardvark /'ɑːdvɑːk/ noun an African animal with a long snout,that eats ants and termites 土豚(非洲动物,有长吻,以蚂蚁和白蚁为食)

aback /ə'bæk/ adverb (**be taken aback**) be shocked or surprised 感到震惊;大吃一惊

abacus /'æbəkəs/ noun (plural **abacuses**) a frame with rows of wires along which you slide beads,used for counting 算盘

abaft /ə'bɑːft/ adverb & preposition at the back of or behind a ship 在船尾;在…尾部

abandon /ə'bændən/ verb **1** leave a place or person permanently 抛弃;遗弃 **2** give up a practice completely 放弃 **3** (**abandon yourself to**) give in to a desire 听任,完全屈从于(欲望) • noun complete lack of self-consciousness or self-control 无所顾忌;放纵 ■ **abandonment** noun

abase /ə'beɪs/ verb (**abases, abasing, abased**) (**abase yourself**) behave

in a very humble way 举止谦卑;卑躬屈膝 ■ **abasement** noun.

abashed /ə'bæʃt/ adjective embarrassed or ashamed 窘迫的;羞愧的

abate /ə'beɪt/ verb (**abates, abating, abated**) become less severe or widespread 减弱;减少;减退 ■ **abatement** noun.

abattoir /'æbətwɑː(r)/ noun Brit. 【英】 a slaughterhouse 屠宰场

abbess /'æbes/ noun a woman who is the head of an abbey of nuns 女修道院(或隐修院)院长

abbey /'æbi/ noun (plural **abbeys**) a building occupied by a community of monks or nuns 修道院;隐修院

abbot /'æbət/ noun a man who is the head of an abbey of monks (男)修道院(或隐修院)院长

abbreviate /ə'briːvieɪt/ verb (**abbreviates, abbreviating, abbreviated**) shorten a word or phrase 缩写(单词或短语)

abbreviation /ə,briːvi'eɪʃn/ noun a shortened form of a word or phrase 缩略形式;缩写词;略语

ABC /eɪ biː 'siː/ noun **1** the alphabet 字母表 **2** the basic facts of a subject 基础知识;入门

abdicate /'æbdɪkeɪt/ verb (**abdicates, abdicating, abdicated**) **1** give up being king or queen (国王或女王)退位,逊位 **2** fail to carry out a duty 未履行(职责) ■ **abdication** noun.

abdomen /'æbdəmən/ noun **1** the part of the body that contains the organs used for digestion and reproduction 腹(部) **2** the rear part of the body of an insect, spider, or crustacean (昆虫、蜘蛛或甲壳纲动物

A

的)腹部 ■ **abdominal** adjective.

abduct /əb'dʌkt, æb-/ **verb** take someone away, especially by force 绑架；劫持 ■ **abduction** noun **abductor** noun

aberrant /æ'berənt/ **adjective** not normal or acceptable 反常的；异常的；脱离常规的

aberration /æbə'reɪʃn/ **noun 1** an action or event which is not normal or acceptable 反常行为；异常现象 **2** an unexpected silly mistake 出乎意料的愚蠢错误

abet /ə'bet/ **verb** (**abets, abetting, abetted**) encourage or help someone to do something wrong 教唆；唆使；怂恿

abeyance /ə'beɪəns/ **noun** (**in** or **into abeyance**) temporarily not occurring or in use 暂时中止；暂时搁置

abhor /əb'hɔː(r)/ **verb** (**abhors, abhorring, abhorred**) feel strong hatred for 厌恶；憎恨

abhorrent /əb'hɒrənt/ **adjective** disgusting or hateful 可恶的；讨厌的 ■ **abhorrence** noun.

abide /ə'baɪd/ **verb** (**abides, abiding, abided**) **1** (**abide by**) accept or obey a rule or decision 遵守，遵循(规定或决定) **2** (**cannot abide**) dislike very much 极其厌恶，无法容忍 **3** (of a feeling or memory) last for a long time (感情或记忆)持久

ability /ə'bɪləti/ **noun** (plural **abilities**) **1** the power or capacity to do something 能力，才干 **2** skill or talent 技能；天分，天资

abject /'æbdʒekt/ **adjective 1** very unpleasant and humiliating 凄苦可怜的；悲惨的 **2** completely without pride or dignity 卑微的；自卑的 ■ **abjectly** adverb.

abjure /əb'dʒʊə(r)/ **verb** (**abjures, abjuring, abjured**) formal 【正式】swear that you will give up a belief or claim 发誓放弃(信仰或要求)

ablaze /ə'bleɪz/ **adjective** burning fiercely 熊熊燃烧的

able /'eɪbl/ **adjective** (**abler, ablest**) **1** having the power, skill, or means to do something 能够…的 **2** skilful and capable 有能力的；有才干的 □ **able-bodied** physically fit and healthy 健康的；健壮的 ■ **ably** adverb.

ablutions /ə'bluːʃnz/ **plural noun** the act of washing yourself 沐浴；洗澡

abnegation /æbnɪ'geɪʃn/ **noun** formal 【正式】the giving up of something wanted or valuable 放弃；拒绝 ■ **abnegate** verb.

abnormal /æb'nɔːml/ **adjective** different from what is usual or expected in a bad or worrying way 反常的；异常的 ■ **abnormality** noun **abnormally** adverb.

aboard /ə'bɔːd/ **adverb & preposition** on or into a ship, train, or other vehicle 在(船、火车等)上；上(船、火车等)

abode /ə'bəʊd/ **noun** a house or home 住所；家

abolish /ə'bɒlɪʃ/ **verb** put an end to a custom or law 废除，废止(习俗或法律)

abolition /æbə'lɪʃn/ **noun** the abolishing of a custom or law (习俗或法律的)废除，废止

abolitionist /æbə'lɪʃənɪst/ **noun** a person who supports the abolition of a custom or law (习俗或法律的)废除主义者

abominable /ə'bɒmɪnəbl/ **adjective 1** very unpleasant and causing disgust 可恶的；讨厌的 **2** informal 【非正式】very bad 极坏的；糟透的 □ **Abominable Snowman** = YETI. ■ **abominably** adverb.

abominate /ə'bɒmɪneɪt/ **verb** (**abominates, abominating, abominated**) feel strong hatred for 厌恶；憎恶

abomination /ə,bɒmɪ'neɪʃn/ **noun 1** something that you hate or find disgusting 令人厌恶的东西 **2** a feeling of hatred 厌恶;憎恶

aboriginal /ˌæbəˈrɪdʒənl/ **adjective 1** existing in a country from the earliest times 土生的;土著的 **2 (Aboriginal)** having to do with the Australian Aborigines 澳大利亚土著居民的 ● **noun (Aboriginal)** an Australian Aborigine 澳大利亚土著居民

Aborigine /ˌæbəˈrɪdʒəni/ **noun** a member of one of the original peoples of Australia 澳大利亚土著居民

abort /əˈbɔːt/ **verb 1** end a pregnancy early to stop the baby from developing and being born 堕胎;使流产 **2** undergo a natural abortion 流产;小产 **3** end something early because of a problem or fault 使中途失败;使夭折

abortion /əˈbɔːʃn/ **noun 1** the deliberate ending of a human pregnancy 堕胎;打胎 **2** the natural ending of a pregnancy before the fetus is able to survive on its own 流产;小产

abortionist /əˈbɔːʃənɪst/ **noun** disapproving 【贬】a person who carries out abortions 为人堕胎者

abortive /əˈbɔːtɪv/ **adjective** failing to achieve the intended result; unsuccessful 无结果的;夭折的;失败的

abound /əˈbaʊnd/ **verb 1** exist in large numbers or amounts 大量存在 **2 (abound in or with)** have a large number or amount of something 充足;多产

about /əˈbaʊt/ **preposition & adverb 1** on the subject of 对于;关于 **2** here and there within a particular area 在(…)各处 **3** approximately 大概;大约 □ **about-turn** Brit.【英】**1** Military 【军事】a turn made so as to face the opposite direction 向后转 **2** a complete change of opinion or policy (观点或政策的)彻底改变

above /əˈbʌv/ **preposition & adverb 1** at a higher level than 在(…)上面;

往(…)上方 **2** rather or more than 先于;多于 **3** (in printed writing) mentioned earlier (文章中)在上文,上述 □ **above board** lawful and honest 光明正大

abracadabra /ˌæbrəkəˈdæbrə/ **exclamation** a word said by magicians when performing a trick (魔术师表演魔术时说的)咒语

abrade /əˈbreɪd/ **verb (abrades, abrading, abraded)** scrape or wear away 擦伤;磨蚀

abrasion /əˈbreɪʒn/ **noun 1** the process of scraping or wearing away 擦伤;磨蚀 **2** an area of scraped skin (皮肤的)擦伤处

abrasive /əˈbreɪsɪv/ **adjective 1** able to polish or clean a surface by rubbing or grinding 有研磨作用的;有磨蚀作用的 **2** harsh or unkind 生硬粗鲁的 ■ **abrasively** adverb.

abreast /əˈbrest/ **adverb 1** side by side and facing the same way 肩并肩地;(朝同一方向)并排地 **2 (abreast of)** up to date with 了解…的最新情况;跟上…的发展

abridge /əˈbrɪdʒ/ **verb (abridges, abridging, abridged)** shorten a book or film 删节(书籍或电影) ■ **abridgement** noun.

abroad /əˈbrɔːd/ **adverb 1** in or to a foreign country or countries 在国外;到国外 **2** felt or talked about by many people 广泛流传

abrogate /ˈæbrəɡeɪt/ **verb (abrogates, abrogating, abrogated)** formal 【正式】cancel or do away with a law or agreement 废除,废止(法律或协议) ■ **abrogation** noun.

abrupt /əˈbrʌpt/ **adjective 1** sudden and unexpected 突然的;意外的 **2** brief to the point of rudeness 唐突的;鲁莽的 ■ **abruptly** adverb **abruptness** noun.

abscess /ˈæbses/ **noun** a swelling that contains pus 脓肿

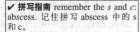

✔ **拼写指南** remember the *s* and *c*: abscess. 记住拼写 abscess 中的 s 和 c。

abscond /əb'skɒnd/ **verb** leave quickly and secretly to escape from custody or avoid arrest 潜逃

abseil /'æbseɪl/ **verb** Brit. 【英】climb down a rock face using a rope wrapped round the body and fixed at a higher point (从高处岩壁)缘绳滑下

absence /'æbsəns/ **noun 1** the state of being away from a place or person 缺席,不在 **2** (**absence of**) the lack of 缺乏,没有

absent adjective /'æbsənt/ **1** not present 缺席的;不在场的 **2** not paying attention 心不在焉的 • **verb** /æb'sent/ (**absent yourself**) go away 缺席;离开 □ **absent-minded** forgetful, or not paying attention 健忘的;心不在焉的 ■ **absently** adverb.

absentee /ˌæbsən'tiː/ **noun** a person who is absent 缺席者;不在者

absenteeism /ˌæbsən'tiːɪzəm/ **noun** frequent absence from work or school without good reason (经常无故的)旷工,旷课

absinthe /'æbsɪnθ/ **noun** a green aniseed-flavoured liqueur 苦艾酒

absolute adjective /'æbsəluːt/ **adjective 1** complete; total 完全的;十足的 **2** having unlimited power 拥有无限权力的;专制独裁的 **3** not related or compared to anything else 绝对的 □ **absolute zero** the lowest temperature theoretically possible (-273.15°C) 绝对零度;开氏温标零度(即-273.15°C) ■ **absolutely** adverb.

absolution /ˌæbsə'luːʃn/ **noun** formal 【正式】forgiveness of a person's sins 赦免;宽恕

absolutism /'æbsəluːtɪzəm/ **noun** the principle that the government or ruler should have unlimited power 专制主义;专制政体论 ■ **absolutist** noun & adjective.

absolve /əb'zɒlv/ **verb** (**absolves, absolving, absolved**) formally declare that someone is free from guilt, blame, or sin 宣告无罪;免除责任

absorb /əb'sɔːb, -'zɔːb/ **verb 1** soak up liquid or another substance 吸收(液体或其他物质) **2** take in information 理解,掌握(信息) **3** take over something less powerful 吞并,同化(较弱势之物) **4** use up time or resources 耗费,消耗(时间或资源) **5** reduce the effect or strength of sound or an impact 吸收(声音);减轻(冲击)的作用 **6** hold someone's attention 吸引…的注意;使全神贯注

absorbent /əb'sɔːbənt, -'zɔː-/ **adjective** able to soak up liquid easily 易吸收(液体)的 ■ **absorbency** noun.

absorption /əb'sɔːpʃn, -'zɔː-/ **noun** the process of absorbing, or of being absorbed 吸收;消化;专心致志

abstain /əb'steɪn/ **verb 1** (**abstain from**) stop yourself from doing something pleasant 克制,戒绝(享乐) **2** purposely choose not to vote 弃权

abstemious /əb'stiːmiəs/ **adjective** not letting yourself have much food, alcohol, or enjoyment (在饮食、娱乐方面)有节制的

abstention /əb'stenʃn/ **noun 1** a deliberate decision not to vote 弃权 **2** abstinence (饮食、娱乐等方面的)禁绝

abstinence /'æbstɪnəns/ **noun** the avoidance of something enjoyable, such as food or alcohol (对食物、酒类等的)禁绝 ■ **abstinent** adjective.

abstract adjective /'æbstrækt/ **1** having to do with ideas or qualities rather than physical or concrete things 抽象的;纯理论的 **2** (of art) using colour and shapes to create an effect rather than attempting to represent real life accurately (艺术)

抽象的 • verb /æb'strækt/ take out or remove 提取;抽取 • noun /'æbstrækt/ a summary of a book or article (书或文章的)摘要;概要 ■ **abstractly** adverb.

abstracted /æb'stræktɪd/ adjective not paying attention to what is happening; preoccupied 心不在焉的;出神的 ■ **abstractedly** adverb.

abstraction /æb'strækʃn/ noun **1** the quality of being abstract 抽象 **2** something which exists only as an idea 抽象概念 **3** the state of being preoccupied 心不在焉;出神

abstruse /əb'struːs/ adjective difficult to understand 深奥的;难懂的

absurd /əb'sɜːd/ adjective completely unreasonable or inappropriate 荒谬的;荒唐的 ■ **absurdity** noun **absurdly** adverb.

abundance /ə'bʌndəns/ noun a very large quantity or amount of something 大量;众多

abundant /ə'bʌndənt/ adjective **1** existing in large quantities; plentiful 大量的;丰富的 **2** (abundant in) having plenty of 富于…的;盛产…的 ■ **abundantly** adverb.

abuse verb /ə'bjuːz/ (abuses, abusing, abused) **1** use something wrongly or badly 滥用;妄用 **2** treat someone cruelly or violently 虐待;伤害 **3** speak to someone in an insulting way 辱骂 • noun /ə'bjuːs/ **1** the wrong or harmful use of something 滥用;妄用 **2** cruel and violent treatment 虐待;伤害 **3** insulting language 辱骂;恶语 ■ **abuser** noun.

abusive /ə'bjuːsɪv/ adjective **1** very insulting 辱骂的;毁谤的 **2** involving cruelty and violence 虐待的 ■ **abusively** adverb.

abut /ə'bʌt/ verb (abuts, abutting, abutted) be next to or touching 邻接;毗邻

abysmal /ə'bɪzməl/ adjective very bad; terrible 极坏的;糟透的 ■ **abysmally** adverb.

abyss /ə'bɪs/ noun a very deep hole 深渊;无底洞

AC /ˌeɪ 'siː/ abbreviation alternating current 交流电

acacia /ə'keɪʃə/ noun a tree or shrub with yellow or white flowers 金合欢属植物

academia /ˌækə'diːmiə/ noun the world of higher education 高等教育界;学术界

academic /ˌækə'demɪk/ adjective **1** having to do with education or study 教学的;学业的;学术的 **2** not related to a real situation; theoretical 学究式的;不切实际的 • noun a teacher or scholar in a university or college 大学教师;学者 ■ **academically** adverb.

academy /ə'kædəmi/ noun (plural academies) **1** a place where people study or are trained in a particular field 学院;专科院校 **2** a society of scholars, artists, or scientists 学会 □ **Academy Award** an Oscar 奥斯卡金像奖(美国电影艺术科学院颁发的电影成就奖)

acanthus /ə'kænθəs/ noun a plant or shrub with spiny leaves 老鼠簕属植物

a cappella /ˌæ kə'pelə/ adjective & adverb (of music) sung without being accompanied by instruments (音乐)无伴奏的(地),清唱的(地)

accede /ək'siːd/ verb (accedes, acceding, acceded) (usu. accede to) formal 【正式】**1** agree to a demand or request 答应,同意(要求或请求) **2** take up a role or position 就任;就职: accede to the throne 即位

accelerate /ək'seləreɪt/ verb (accelerates, accelerating, accelerated) **1** begin to move more quickly 加快;加速 **2** begin to happen more quickly 提早发生 ■ **acceleration** noun.

accelerator /ək'seləreɪtə(r)/ noun **1** a foot pedal which controls the speed of a vehicle (机动车的)油门 **2** Physics 【物理】a machine that makes charged particles move at high speeds (带电粒子)加速器

accent /ˈæksənt/ **noun 1** a way of pronouncing a language 口音;腔调 **2** an emphasis given to a syllable, word, or musical note 重音 **3** a mark on a letter or word that shows how a sound is pronounced or stressed 读音符号;重音符号 **4** a particular emphasis 着重点,强调 • **verb** /ækˈsent/ **1** (accented) spoken with a particular accent 带着…口音讲话 **2** stress or emphasize 着重;强调

accentuate /əkˈsentʃueɪt/ **verb** (accentuates, accentuating, accentuated) make a feature more noticeable 使更明显;使更突出 ■ **accentuation** noun.

accept /əkˈsept/ **verb 1** agree to receive or do something that is offered or suggested 接受;收受;同意 **2** believe that something said is true or correct 相信;接受 **3** admit responsibility for something 承担(责任) **4** come to terms with something unwelcome 忍受;容忍 ■ **acceptance** noun.

！注意 don't confuse **accept** with **except**, which means 'not including'. 不要混淆 accept 和 except,后者意为 "排除"。

acceptable /əkˈseptəbl/ **adjective 1** able to be accepted 可以接受的 **2** good enough; adequate 适当的;尚可的 ■ **acceptability** noun **acceptably** adverb.

access /ˈækses/ **noun 1** a way of approaching or entering a place 通道;入口 **2** the right or opportunity to use something or see someone 享用权;见到…的机会 • **verb 1** approach or enter a place 接近,进入(某处) **2** obtain information stored in a computer 从(计算机)获取(数据)

accessible /əkˈsesəbl/ **adjective 1** able to be reached or used 可到达的;

可使用的 **2** friendly and easy to talk to 友善的;随和的 **3** easily understood or enjoyed 易懂的;易理解的 ■ **accessibility** noun **accessibly** adverb.

accession /ækˈseʃn/ **noun 1** the gaining of an important position or rank (重要职位或级别的)获得 **2** a new item added to a library or museum collection (图书馆的)新增藏书;(博物馆的)新藏品

accessory /əkˈsesəri/ **noun** (plural **accessories**) **1** a thing which can be added to or worn with something else to make it more useful or attractive 附件;配件;(衣服的)配饰 **2** Law 【法律】a person who helps someone commit a crime without taking part in it 同谋;帮凶;从犯

accident /ˈæksɪdənt/ **noun 1** something harmful that happens unexpectedly or without being intended 事故;不测事件 **2** an incident that happens by chance or without apparent cause 偶然事件

accidental /ˌæksɪˈdentl/ **adjective** happening by chance 意外的;偶然发生的 ■ **accidentally** adverb.

acclaim /əˈkleɪm/ **verb** praise enthusiastically and publicly 欢呼,喝彩,称赞 • **noun** enthusiastic public praise 欢呼;喝彩;称赞

acclamation /ˌækləˈmeɪʃn/ **noun** enthusiastic approval or praise 拥护;赞成,欢呼,喝彩

acclimatize or **acclimatise** /əˈklaɪmətaɪz/ **verb** (acclimatizes, acclimatizing, acclimatized) get used to a new climate or conditions 服水土;适应新气候(或新环境) ■ **acclimatization** noun.

accolade /ˈækəleɪd/ **noun** something given as a special honour or as a reward for excellence 荣誉;奖励

accommodate /əˈkɒmədeɪt/ **verb** (accommodates, accommodating, accommodated) **1** provide a room or rooms for someone, or space for something 向…提供住宿；向…提供空间 **2** adapt to or fit in with (使)适应；(使)符合一致

✔ 拼写指南 double *c*, double *m*: acco**mm**odate. accommodate 中有两个 c 和两个 m.

accommodating /ə'kɒmədeɪtɪŋ/ **adjective** willing to fit in with someone's wishes 乐于助人的；与人方便的

accommodation /əˌkɒmə'deɪʃn/ **noun** a room or building where someone may live or stay 住处

accompaniment /ə'kʌmpənimənt/ **noun 1** a musical part which accompanies an instrument, voice, or group 伴奏 **2** something that adds to or improves something else 伴随物

accompany /ə'kʌmpəni/ **verb** (**accompanies, accompanying, accompanied**) **1** go somewhere with someone 陪伴；陪同 **2** be present or happen at the same time as 伴随；和…同时存在(或发生) **3** play musical backing for an instrument or voice 为(乐器或歌唱)伴奏 ■ **accompanist** noun.

accomplice /ə'kʌmplɪs/ **noun** a person who helps another commit a crime 共犯；共同犯罪者

accomplish /ə'kʌmplɪʃ/ **verb** achieve or complete something successfully 实现；完成

accomplished /ə'kʌmplɪʃt/ **adjective** highly trained or skilled 熟练的；有造诣的

accomplishment /ə'kʌmplɪʃmənt/ **noun 1** an activity that you can do well 才艺；技艺 **2** something that has been achieved successfully 成就；成绩 **3** the successful achievement of a task (任务)的完成

accord /ə'kɔːd/ **verb 1** give power or recognition to 授予，给予(权力或认可) **2** (**accord with**) be consistent or in agreement with 与…相符合，

与…相一致 • **noun 1** agreement in opinion or feeling (意见或感觉的)一致 **2** an official agreement or treaty 协议；条约 □ **of your own accord** willingly 出于自愿；主动地

accordance /ə'kɔːdns/ **noun** (**in accordance with**) in a way that fits in with 依照；根据

according /ə'kɔːdɪŋ/ **adverb** (**according to**) **1** as stated by 据…所说，按…所说 **2** in a way that corresponds to 根据；按照

accordingly /ə'kɔːdɪŋli/ **adverb 1** appropriately 照着；相应地 **2** therefore 因此；所以

accordion /ə'kɔːdiən/ **noun** a musical instrument that you play by stretching and squeezing it with your hands and pressing buttons or keys 手风琴 ■ **accordionist** noun.

accost /ə'kɒst/ **verb** approach someone and speak to them, often in a rude or aggressive way (大胆或唐突地)走近与…讲话，和…搭讪

account /ə'kaʊnt/ **noun 1** a description of an event 记述；描述；报告 **2** a record of money that has been spent and received 账目 **3** an arrangement by which you can keep money in a bank or buy things from a business on credit 账户；赊购账；欠欠账 **4** importance 重要性 • **verb** consider in a particular way 把…视作；认为 □ **account for 1** supply or make up an amount 提供，占(一定数量) **2** give an explanation of 为…作出解释 **on account of** because of 因为；由于 **on no account** under no circumstances 决不；绝对不 **take account of** take into consideration 考虑到；顾及

accountable /ə'kaʊntəbl/ **adjective** expected to explain your actions or decisions 应作解释的；需作说明的 ■ **accountability** noun.

accountant /ə'kaʊntənt/ **noun** a person who keeps or inspects financial accounts 会计人员；会计师 ■ **accountancy** noun.

accoutrement /əˈkuːtrəmənt/ (US spelling 【美拼作】 **accouterment**) **noun** an extra item of clothing or equipment 饰物；饰品；装备；配备

accredit /əˈkredɪt/ **verb** (**accredits**, **accrediting**, **accredited**) **1** (**accredit something to**) give someone the credit for something 将(某事)归结于(某人)；认为(某事)是(某人)所为 **2** give official authorization to 信托；委托 ■ **accreditation** noun.

accretion /əˈkriːʃn/ **noun 1** growth or increase by a gradual build-up 生长；增大 **2** something formed or added gradually 生长物；增大物

accrue /əˈkruː/ **verb** (**accrues**, **accruing**, **accrued**) **1** (of money) be received in regular or increasing amounts (钱)增加，增长 **2** collect or receive payments or benefits 积累，获取(支付款或利润) ■ **accrual** noun.

accumulate /əˈkjuːmjəleɪt/ **verb** (**accumulates**, **accumulating**, **accumulated**) **1** gather together a number or quantity of 积累；积聚 **2** increase 增加 ■ **accumulation** noun **accumulative** adjective.

✔ 拼写指南 two cs, one m: accumulate. accumulate 中有两个 c 和一个 m。

accumulator /əˈkjuːmjəleɪtə(r)/ **noun** Brit. 【英】 **1** a large rechargeable electric battery 蓄电池 **2** a bet placed on a series of events, the winnings from each being placed on the next (每赢一次即押于下一events的累计赌注)

accurate /ˈækjərət/ **adjective 1** correct in all details 正确无误的 **2** reaching an intended target 准确的；精确的 ■ **accuracy** noun **accurately** adverb.

accursed /əˈkɜːsɪd/ **adjective** literary 【文】 under a curse 受诅咒的

accusation /ˌækjuˈzeɪʃn/ **noun** a claim that someone has done something illegal or wrong 指控；控告；指责

accusative /əˈkjuːzətɪv/ **noun** Grammar 【语法】 (in some languages) the case used for the object of a verb (某些语言中的)宾格

accuse /əˈkjuːz/ **verb** (**accuses**, **accusing**, **accused**) (often **accuse someone of**) claim that someone has done something wrong or illegal 指控；控告；指责 ■ **accusatory** adjective **accuser** noun.

accustom /əˈkʌstəm/ **verb 1** (**accustom someone/thing to**) make someone or something used to 使习惯于 **2** (**be accustomed to**) be used to 习惯于；适应

accustomed /əˈkʌstəmd/ **adjective** usual or habitual 通常的；惯常的

AC/DC /ˌeɪ siː diː siː/ **adjective** alternating current/direct current 交流电或直流电的；交直流两用的

ace /eɪs/ **noun 1** a playing card with a single spot on it, the highest card in its suit in most games A 纸牌 **2** informal 【非正式】 a person who is very good at a particular activity 精于…的人；善于…的人 **3** Tennis【网球】 a service that an opponent is unable to return 发球得分；爱司球 • **adjective** informal 【非正式】 very good 一流的；杰出的

acerbic /əˈsɜːbɪk/ **adjective** sharp and direct 尖酸的；尖刻的 ■ **acerbically** adverb **acerbity** noun.

acetate /ˈæsɪteɪt/ **noun 1** a kind of chemical compound made from acetic acid 醋酸盐；醋酸酯 **2** fibre or plastic made of cellulose acetate 醋酸纤维；醋酸塑料

acetic acid /əˈsiːtɪk/ **noun** the acid that gives vinegar its taste 醋酸

acetone /ˈæsɪtəʊn/ **noun** a colourless liquid used as a solvent 丙酮(无色液体，用作溶剂)

acetylene /əˈsetəliːn/ **noun** a gas

which burns with a bright flame,used in welding 乙炔，电石气(用于焊接)

ache /eɪk/ *noun* a continuous or long-lasting dull pain (持续或隐隐的)疼痛 • *verb* (**aches, aching, ached**) **1** suffer from an ache 疼，痛 **2** (**ache for** or **to do**) want very much to have or do something 渴望；渴望做 ■ **achy** *adjective.*

achieve /əˈtʃiːv/ *verb* (**achieves, achieving, achieved**) manage to do something by effort, skill, or courage 完成；实现；达到；得到 ■ **achievable** *adjective* **achiever** *noun.*

> ✔ 拼写指南 the usual rule is *i* before *e* except after c: achi*eve*. 通常的规则是 i 在 e 前，在 c 后时除外，如 achieve。

achievement /əˈtʃiːvmənt/ *noun* **1** a thing that is achieved 成就；成绩 **2** the process of achieving something 完成；实现；达到

Achilles heel /əˈkɪliːz/ *noun* a weak point 阿喀琉斯的脚踵；致命的弱点

Achilles tendon *noun* the tendon connecting calf muscles to the heel 跟腱

acid /ˈæsɪd/ *noun* **1** a substance that turns litmus red, neutralizes alkalis, and dissolves some metals 酸 **2** *informal* 【非正式】 the drug LSD 迷幻药 • *adjective* **1** sharp-tasting or sour 酸的；酸味的 **2** (of a remark) bitter or cutting (言语)尖酸的，尖刻的 □ **acid rain** rainfall that has been made acidic by pollution 酸雨 **acid test** a decisive test of something 决定性的试验；严峻的考验 ■ **acidic** *adjective* **acidity** *noun* **acidly** *adverb.*

acidify /əˈsɪdɪfaɪ/ *verb* (**acidifies, acidifying, acidified**) make or become acid (使)酸化；(使)变成酸

acknowledge /əkˈnɒlɪdʒ/ *verb* (**acknowledges, acknowledging, acknowledged**) **1** accept that something exists or is true 承认 **2** confirm that you have received something 确认收到 **3** greet someone with words or gestures 向…打招呼；理会

acknowledgement or **acknowledgment** /əkˈnɒlɪdʒmənt/ *noun* **1** the action of acknowledging 承认；确认 **2** something done or given as thanks to someone 答谢；回报 **3** a mention of someone in a book thanking them for work they have done (书中的)鸣谢，致谢

acme /ˈækmi/ *noun* the highest point of achievement or excellence 顶峰；顶点，极致

acne /ˈækni/ *noun* a skin condition causing red pimples 粉刺；痤疮

acolyte /ˈækəlaɪt/ *noun* an assistant or follower 助手；追随者

acorn /ˈeɪkɔːn/ *noun* the fruit of the oak tree, a smooth oval nut in a cup-like base 橡树果实

acoustic /əˈkuːstɪk/ *adjective* **1** having to do with sound or hearing 声音的；听觉的 **2** not electrically amplified 无电声放大的；原声的 • *noun* (**acoustics**) **1** the aspects of a room or building that affect how well it transmits sound (房间或建筑物的)传声效果，音响效果 **2** the branch of physics concerned with sound 声学 ■ **acoustically** *adverb.*

acquaint /əˈkweɪnt/ *verb* **1** (**acquaint someone with**) make someone aware of or familiar with 使了解；使知晓；使熟悉 **2** (**be acquainted with**) know someone personally 认识；了解

> ✔ 拼写指南 **acquaint, acquiesce, acquire,** and **acquit,** and related words have a *c* before the *qu*: a*c*quaint. acquaint, acquiesce, acquire, acquit 等词在 qu 前有一个 c。

acquaintance /əˈkweɪntəns/ *noun* **1** familiarity with someone or something 认识；了解 **2** a person you know slightly 熟人；泛泛之交

A

acquiesce /ˌækwi'es/ **verb** (acquiesces, acquiescing, acquiesced) accept something without protest 默许;默认。

acquiescent /ˌækwi'esnt/ **adjective** ready to accept or do something without protest 默许的;默认的。■ **acquiescence** noun.

acquire /ə'kwaɪə(r)/ **verb** (acquires, acquiring, acquired) **1** buy or obtain an article 买到;获得 **2** learn or develop a skill or quality 学习,学到,习得(技能或品质)

acquisition /ˌækwɪ'zɪʃn/ **noun 1** something that you have recently obtained 获得物 **2** the action of obtaining or learning something 获得;得到;学会;习得

acquisitive /ə'kwɪzətɪv/ **adjective** too interested in gaining money or material things 渴望得到财物的;贪婪的

acquit /ə'kwɪt/ **verb** (acquits, acquitting, acquitted) **1** formally state that someone is not guilty of a criminal charge 宣判(某人)无罪 **2** (acquit yourself) behave or perform in a particular way 使(自己)作出某种表现,使(自己)履行 ■ **acquittal** noun.

acre /'eɪkə(r)/ **noun** a unit of land area equal to 4,840 square yards (0.405 hectare) 英亩(等于4,840平方码,合0.405公顷) ■ **acreage** noun.

acrid /'ækrɪd/ **adjective** unpleasantly bitter or sharp 辛辣的;苦的;尖刻的

acrimonious /ˌækrɪ'məʊniəs/ **adjective** angry and bitter 尖刻的;讥刺的 ■ **acrimoniously** adverb.

acrimony /'ækrɪməni/ **noun** feelings of anger and bitterness 尖刻;讥刺

acrobat /'ækrəbæt/ **noun** an entertainer who performs spectacular gymnastic feats 杂技演员

acrobatic /ˌækrə'bætɪk/ **adjective** involving or performing spectacular gymnastic feats 杂技的 • **noun** (acrobatics) spectacular gymnastic feats 杂技 ■ **acrobatically** adverb.

acronym /'ækrənɪm/ **noun** a word formed from the first letters of other words (e.g. *Aids*) 首字母缩略词

across /ə'krɒs/ **preposition & adverb** from one side to the other of something 从(…)一边到另一边;穿过;横过 □ **across the board** applying to all 全面的;适用于一切的

acrostic /ə'krɒstɪk/ **noun** a poem or puzzle in which certain letters in each line form a word or words (每一行的某些字母联成词的)离合诗;离合诗形式的字谜

acrylic /ə'krɪlɪk/ **adjective** (of paint, fabric, etc.) made using acrylic acid (an organic acid) (颜料、织物等)含丙烯酸的

act /ækt/ **verb 1** do something 做事;行动 **2** have a particular effect 起作用 **3** behave in a particular way 举止;表现 **4** (act as) perform the function of 担任;充当 **5** (acting) temporarily doing the duties of another person 代理 **6** perform a role in a play or film 扮演(戏剧或电影中的角色) • **noun 1** a thing done 行为;行动 **2** a law passed formally by a parliament 法案;法令 **3** a pretence 假装;装腔作势 **4** a main division of a play, ballet, or opera (戏剧、芭蕾或歌剧的)一幕 **5** a set performance, or a performing group 表演组合;演出组合 □ **act of God** an event caused by natural forces beyond human control 天灾;不可抗力

action /'ækʃn/ **noun 1** the process of doing something to achieve an aim 行动(过程) **2** a thing done 所做之事;行为 **3** the effect of something such as a chemical (化学品等的)作用 **4** a lawsuit 诉讼 **5** fighting in a battle or war 战斗;作战 **6** the way in which something works or moves 功能;动作;动作姿势 • **verb** deal with a particular matter 处理;应付

actionable /'ækʃənəbl/ adjective giving someone grounds to take legal action 可提起诉讼的

activate /'æktɪveɪt/ verb (activates, activating, activated) make something start working 使动动;激活 ■ **activation** noun.

active /'æktɪv/ adjective 1 moving about often or energetically 积极的;活跃的 2 regularly taking part in something 定期进行的;活跃的 3 working; functioning 在活动中的;在起作用的 4 (of a volcano) erupting or having erupted in the past (火山)处于喷发状态的,活跃的 5 Grammar【语法】(of a verb) having as its subject the person or thing doing the action (e.g. *she loved him* as opposed to the passive form *he was loved*) (动词)主动语态的 □ **active service** military service in wartime 现役;战时服役 ■ **actively** adverb.

activist /'æktɪvɪst/ noun a person who campaigns for political or social change 政治或社会变革方面的)积极分子,活跃分子 ■ **activism** noun.

activity /æk'tɪvəti/ noun (plural **activities**) 1 a condition in which things are happening or being done 活跃;热闹(状况) 2 busy or energetic action or movement 繁忙活动;剧烈活动 3 an action, especially one done for interest or pleasure 活动(尤指消遣)

actor /'æktə(r)/ noun a person whose profession is acting 男演员

actress /'æktrəs/ noun a female actor 女演员

actual /'æktʃuəl/ adjective existing in fact or reality 事实上的;真实的;实际的

actuality /ˌæktʃu'æləti/ noun (plural **actualities**) actual reality or fact 现实情况;事实

actualize or **actualise** /'æktʃuəlaɪz/ verb (actualizes, actualizing, actualized) make something real or actual 实行;把…变成现实

actually /'æktʃuəli/ adverb in truth; in reality 事实上,实际上

actuary /'æktʃuəri/ noun (plural **actuaries**) a person who calculates insurance risks (保险)精算师 ■ **actuarial** adjective.

actuate /'æktʃueɪt/ verb 1 cause a machine to function 开动(机器) 2 motivate someone to act in a particular way 激励;驱使

acuity /ə'kjuːəti/ noun sharpness of thought, vision, or hearing 尖锐;敏锐

acumen /'ækjəmən/ noun the ability to make good judgements and take quick decisions 敏锐;精明

acupuncture /'ækjupʌŋktʃə(r)/ noun a medical treatment in which very thin needles are inserted into the skin 针刺疗法 ■ **acupuncturist** noun

acute /ə'kjuːt/ adjective 1 (of something bad) very serious (坏事)严重的 2 intelligent and shrewd 敏锐的;精明的 3 (of a physical sense or faculty) highly developed (感官或官能)灵敏的 4 (of an angle) less than 90° (角)锐角的 □ **acute accent** a mark (′) placed over certain letters in some languages to show pronunciation (e.g. in *fiancée*) (标在字母上方指示发音的)尖音符 ■ **acutely** adverb **acuteness** noun.

AD /ˌeɪ'diː/ abbreviation used to indicate that a date comes a particular number of years after the traditional date of Jesus's birth 公元 [short for【缩写】= *Anno Domini* ('in the year of our Lord' in Latin)]

❗注意 if a date is written in figures, AD should be placed **before** the numerals, e.g. AD 375, but when the date is spelled out, AD should be placed after it, as in *the third century AD*. 当日期用数字表示时, AD 置于数字前,如: AD 375 (公元

375年)。但当日期用单词表示时,应写作: the third century AD (公元3世纪)。

adage /ˈædɪdʒ/ **noun** a popular saying expressing something that most people accept as true 谚语;格言

adagio /əˈdɑːdʒɪəʊ/ **noun** (plural **adagios**) a piece of music to be played in slow time 慢板;慢板乐章

adamant /ˈædəmənt/ **adjective** refusing to be persuaded or to change your mind 坚决的;坚定不移的 ■ **adamantly** adverb.

Adam's apple /ˈædəmz/ **noun** a projection at the front of the neck, more prominent in men than women 喉结

adapt /əˈdæpt/ **verb 1** make something suitable for a new use or purpose 使适应;使适合 **2** become adjusted to new conditions 适应

adaptable /əˈdæptəbl/ **adjective** able to adjust to, or be altered for, new conditions or uses 有适应能力的;能适应的 ■ **adaptability** noun **adaptably** adverb.

adaptation /ˌædæpˈteɪʃn/ or **adaption** /əˈdæpʃn/ **noun 1** the process of adapting 适应;适合 **2** a film or play adapted from a written work 改编本

adaptor or **adapter** /əˈdæptə(r)/ **noun 1** a device for connecting pieces of equipment 适配器 **2** Brit.【英】a device for connecting several electric plugs to one socket 多功能插头

add /æd/ **verb 1** put something together with something else 增加;添加;附加 **2** put together two or more numbers or amounts to find their total value 把…加起来;计算…的总和 **3** (**add up**) increase in amount or number 增加;扩大;**4** say as a further remark 又说;补充说道 **5** (**add up**) informal【非正式】make sense 言之有理;有道理

addendum /əˈdendəm/ **noun** (plural

addenda /əˈdendə/) an extra item added at the end of a book or other publication 补遗;补篇

adder /ˈædə(r)/ **noun** a poisonous snake with a dark zigzag pattern on its back 蝰蛇(一种毒蛇,背部有深色之字形斑纹)

addict /ˈædɪkt/ **noun** a person who is addicted to something 入迷的人;有瘾的人

addicted /əˈdɪktɪd/ **adjective** (usu. **addicted to**) **1** physically dependent on a particular substance 上瘾的 **2** very keen on a particular interest or activity 入迷的

addiction /əˈdɪkʃn/ **noun** the condition of being addicted to something 瘾;入迷;嗜好 ■ **addictive** adjective.

addition /əˈdɪʃn/ **noun 1** the action of adding 添加;增加 **2** a person or thing that is added 增加的人(或事物)

additional /əˈdɪʃnəl/ **adjective** added; extra 添加的;附加的;额外的 ■ **additionally** adverb.

additive /ˈædətɪv/ **noun** a substance added to improve or preserve something 添加剂;添加物

addled /ˈædld/ **adjective 1** humorous【幽默】confused or puzzled 糊涂的 **2** (of an egg) rotten (蛋)变质的,腐坏的

address /əˈdres/ **noun 1** the details of where a building is or where someone lives 地址;住址 **2** a string of characters identifying a destination for email messages (电子邮件)地址 **3** a formal speech (正式)讲话,演说 • **verb 1** write a name and address on an envelope or parcel 在(信封或包裹)上写姓名地址 **2** make a speech or remark to 对…讲话;对…发表演说 **3** think about a task and begin to deal with it 对付;处理

✔ **拼写指南** two ds: address. address 中有两个 d.

adduce /əˈdjuːs/ **verb** (**adduces**,

adducing, adduced) formal【正式】refer to something as evidence 引证

adenoids /ˈædənɔɪdz/ plural noun a mass of tissue between the back of the nose and the throat 腺样增殖体；增殖腺

adept adjective /ˈædept, əˈdept/ very skilled or able 熟练的；擅长的；内行的 • noun /ˈædept/ an adept person 能手；内行 ■ **adeptly** adverb.

adequate /ˈædɪkwət/ adjective satisfactory or acceptable; good enough 令人满意的；可接受的；合格的 ■ **adequacy** noun **adequately** adverb.

adhere /ədˈhɪə(r)/ verb (**adheres, adhering, adhered**) (**adhere to**) 1 stick firmly to 黏附；附着 2 follow or observe 追随；遵守 ■ **adherence** noun.

adherent /ədˈhɪərənt/ noun a person who supports a particular party, person,or set of ideas 信徒；追随者；拥护者 • adjective sticking firmly to an object or surface 黏着的；附着的

adhesion /ədˈhiːʒn/ noun the process of adhering 黏附；附着

adhesive /ədˈhiːsɪv/ noun a substance used to stick things together 黏合剂 • adjective sticky 黏的；黏着的

ad hoc /ˌæd ˈhɒk/ adjective & adverb created or done for a particular purpose only 特别的(地)；专门的(地)

adieu /əˈdjuː/ exclamation old use【旧】goodbye 再见；再会

Adi Granth /ˌɑːdiː ˈɡrʌnt/ noun the main sacred scripture of Sikhism《阿底·格兰特》(锡克教主要经典)

ad infinitum /ˌæd ɪnfɪˈnaɪtəm/ adverb endlessly; forever 无止境地；永远地

adjacent /əˈdʒeɪsnt/ adjective near or next to something else 邻近的；毗连的

adjective /ˈædʒɪktɪv/ noun Grammar【语法】a word used to describe a noun or to make its meaning clearer, such as *sweet* or *red* 形容词 ■ **adjectival** adjective.

adjoin /əˈdʒɔɪn/ verb be next to and joined with 邻接；毗连

adjourn /əˈdʒɜːn/ verb 1 break off a meeting until later 休(会) 2 postpone a decision 推迟(决定) ■ **adjournment** noun.

adjudge /əˈdʒʌdʒ/ verb (**adjudges, adjudging, adjudged**) (of a law court or judge) formally decide (法庭或法官)判决,宣判

adjudicate /əˈdʒuːdɪkeɪt/ verb (**adjudicates, adjudicating, adjudicated**) 1 make a formal judgement 裁定；评定 2 judge a competition 做(比赛)的裁判 ■ **adjudication** noun **adjudicator** noun.

adjunct /ˈædʒʌŋkt/ noun an additional part or thing 附属物；附件

adjure /əˈdʒʊə(r)/ verb (**adjures, adjuring, adjured**) formal【正式】urge someone to do something 要求；恳求

adjust /əˈdʒʌst/ verb 1 alter something slightly 校准,调准；校正 2 become used to a new situation 适应 3 decide the amount to be paid when settling an insurance claim 理算,评定(保险索赔金额) ■ **adjustable** adjective **adjustment** noun.

adjutant /ˈædʒʊtənt/ noun a military officer who helps a senior officer with administrative work (高级军官的)副官

ad-lib /ˌædˈlɪb/ verb (**ad-libs, ad-libbing, adlibbed**) speak or perform in public without preparing first 即兴讲话；即席表演 • noun an unprepared remark or speech 即兴讲话

administer /ədˈmɪnɪstə(r)/ verb (**administers, administering, administered**) 1 organize or put into effect 管理；治理；实施；执行 2 give out or apply a drug or remedy 给予，施用(药品或疗法)

administrate /ədˈmɪnɪstreɪt/ verb

A

(**administrates, administrating, administrated**) manage the affairs of a business or organization 经营；管理 ■ **administrative** adjective **administrator** noun.

administration /ədˌmɪnɪˈstreɪʃn/ **noun 1** the running of a business or system 经营；管理；行政 **2** the action of giving out or applying something 提供；施用 **3** the government in power 政府

admirable /ˈædmərəbl/ **adjective** deserving respect and approval 令人钦佩的；值得赞美的 ■ **admirably** adverb.

admiral /ˈædmərəl/ **noun 1** the most senior commander of a fleet or navy 舰队司令；海军总司令 **2** a naval officer of the second most senior rank 海军上将

admire /ədˈmaɪə(r)/ **verb** (**admires, admiring, admired**) **1** respect or approve of 钦佩；赞赏；仰慕 **2** look at with pleasure 欣赏；观赏 ■ **admiration** noun **admirer** noun.

admissible /ədˈmɪsəbl/ **adjective** acceptable or valid 可接受的；可容许的；可采纳的

admission /ədˈmɪʃn/ **noun 1** the process of being allowed in to a place 准许进入 **2** a confession 承认；供认

admit /ədˈmɪt/ **verb** (**admits, admitting, admitted**) **1** confess that something is true or is the case 承认；供认 **2** allow someone to enter a place 准许(某人)进入 **3** accept that something is valid 接受；确认

admittance /ədˈmɪtns/ **noun** the process of entering, or of being allowed to enter 进入；准许进入

admonish /ədˈmɒnɪʃ/ **verb** firmly tell someone off 责备；告诫 ■ **admonition** noun **admonitory** adjective.

ad nauseam /ˌæd ˈnɔːziæm/ **adverb** to an annoying or boring extent 令人作呕地；讨厌地

ado /əˈduː/ **noun** trouble; fuss 麻烦；纷扰；忙乱

adolescent /ˌædəˈlesnt/ **adjective** in the process of developing from a child into an adult 青春期的 • **noun** an adolescent boy or girl 青少年 ■ **adolescence** noun.

Adonis /əˈdəʊnɪs/ **noun** a very handsome young man 美少年

adopt /əˈdɒpt/ **verb 1** legally take someone else's child and bring it up as your own 领养；收养 **2** choose an option or course of action 采取，采纳(供选择的方案或行动路线) ■ **adoption** noun.

adoptive /əˈdɒptɪv/ **adjective** (of a parent) having adopted a child (父母)收养的

adorable /əˈdɔːrəbl/ **adjective** very lovable or charming 可爱的；迷人的 ■ **adorably** adverb.

adore /əˈdɔː(r)/ **verb** (**adores, adoring, adored**) love deeply 崇拜；敬爱；仰慕 ■ **adoration** noun.

adorn /əˈdɔːn/ **verb** make more attractive; decorate 美化；装饰 ■ **adornment** noun.

adrenal /əˈdriːnl/ **adjective** having to do with the adrenal glands, a pair of glands above the kidneys 肾上腺的

adrenalin or **adrenaline** /əˈdrenəlɪn/ **noun** a hormone produced by the adrenal glands in response to stress, that makes the body's natural processes work more quickly 肾上腺素

adrift /əˈdrɪft/ **adjective & adverb 1** (of a boat) drifting without control (小船)漂流着(的)，漂浮着(的) **2** no longer fixed in position 脱开(的)；松开(的)

adroit /əˈdrɔɪt/ **adjective** clever or skilful 灵巧的；聪明的；精明的 ■ **adroitly** adverb.

adulation /ˌædjuˈleɪʃn/ **noun** excessive admiration 吹捧；谄媚 ■ **adulatory** adjective.

adult /ˈædʌlt/ **noun** a person who is

fully grown and developed 成年人
• adjective **1** fully grown and developed
成 年 的 **2** suitable for or typical of
adults 适宜成年人的;成熟的 ■ **adult-
hood** noun.

adulterate /ə'dʌltəreɪt/ verb (**adul-
terates**, **adulterating**, **adulterated**)
make something worse in quality by
adding another substance 在 … 中掺
杂 ■ **adulteration** noun.

adulterer /ə'dʌltərə(r)/ noun (feminine
【阴性】 **adulteress**) a person who
has committed adultery 奸夫;通奸者

adultery /ə'dʌltəri/ noun sex between
a married person and a person who
is not their husband or wife 通奸
■ **adulterous** adjective.

adumbrate /'ædʌmbreɪt/ verb
(**adumbrates**, **adumbrating**,
adumbrated) formal 【正式】 give a
faint or general idea of 模糊地显示;
模糊地勾划

advance /əd'vɑːns/ verb (**advances**,
advancing, **advanced**) **1** move
forwards 向前移动;前进 **2** put forward a theory or suggestion 提出
(理论或建议) **3** hand over payment
to someone as a loan or before it
is due 贷(款);预 付(款项) ■ noun **1**
a forward movement 前进;行 进 **2**
a development or improvement 进
展;进步 **3** an amount of money
advanced 预付款 **4** an approach
made with the aim of beginning a
sexual or romantic relationship 勾
引;求爱 ■ adjective done, sent, or
supplied beforehand 预先的;事先的

advanced /əd'vɑːnst/ adjective **1** far
on in progress or life 先进的;年迈
的;上年纪的 **2** complex; not basic
复杂的;高级的;高等的 □ **advanced
level** an A level 高级程度

advancement /əd'vɑːnsmənt/ noun
1 the process of helping a cause or
plan to develop or succeed 促进;
推动 **2** the raising of a person to a
higher rank or status 提拔;晋升 **3** a

development or improvement 进展;
进步

advantage /əd'vɑːntɪdʒ/ noun **1**
something that puts you in a good
position 优势 **2** Tennis 【网
球】 a score marking a point between
deuce and winning the game 占先(指
局末平分后一方先得的)分) □ **take
advantage of 1** make unfair use of
someone 利用;占 … 的便宜 **2** make
good use of an opportunity 充分利用
(机会) ■ **advantageous** adjective.

advent /'ædvent/ noun **1** the arrival
of an important person or thing
(重要的人或事物的)出现, 到来 **2**
(**Advent**) (in Christian belief) the
coming or second coming of Jesus
基督降临;耶稣复临 **3** (**Advent**) the
time leading up to Christmas (基督
教)降临节(圣诞节前的时期)

adventitious /ædven'tɪʃəs/ adjective
formal 【正式】 happening by chance
偶然的

adventure /əd'ventʃə(r)/ noun **1**
an unusual, exciting, and daring
experience 冒险经历;冒险活动 **2**
excitement resulting from danger or
risk 冒险性;(危险或冒险带来的)刺
激

adventurer /əd'ventʃərə(r)/ noun **1**
a person willing to take risks or do
dishonest things for personal gain
投机者;投机分子 **2** a person who
looks for adventure 冒险家

adventurous /əd'ventʃərəs/ adjective
1 involving new or daring methods
or experiences 大胆开拓的;新奇刺激
的 **2** willing to take risks and try new
things 爱冒险的 ■ **adventurously**
adverb.

adverb /'ædvɜːb/ noun Grammar 【语法】
a word that gives more information
about an adjective, verb, or other adverb
(e.g. *gently*, *very*) 副词 ■ **adverbial**
adjective.

adversarial /ædvə'seəriəl/ adjective
having to do with conflict or

opposition 对立的;对抗的

adversary /'ædvəsəri/ **noun** (plural **adversaries**) an opponent or enemy 对手;敌手;敌人

adverse /'ædvɜːs/ **adjective** harmful or unfavourable 有害的;不利的 ■ **adversely** adverb.

> **! 注意** don't confuse **adverse** with **averse**, which means 'strongly disliking or opposed to', as in *I am not averse to helping out*. 不要混淆 adverse 和 averse, 后者意为"厌恶的;反对的", 如 I am not averse to helping out (我不是不愿意帮忙).

adversity /əd'vɜːsəti/ **noun** (plural **adversities**) a difficult or unpleasant situation 困境;逆境;灾难

advert /'ædvɜːt/ **noun** Brit. informal 【英,非正式】an advertisement 广告

advertise /'ædvətaɪz/ **verb** (**advertises**, **advertising**, **advertised**) **1** describe a product, service, or event in a publication or on television or radio in order to increase sales 为(产品、服务或活动)做广告;宣传 **2** try to fill a job vacancy by publishing details of it 登(职位)招聘广告 **3** make a fact known 公告;公布 ■ **advertiser** noun.

advertisement /əd'vɜːtɪsmənt/ **noun** a notice or display advertising something 广告

advice /əd'vaɪs/ **noun** guidance or recommendations about what someone should do in the future 劝告;忠告;建议

> **! 注意** don't confuse the noun **advice** and the verb **advise**. 不要混淆名词 advice 和动词 advise。

advisable /əd'vaɪzəbl/ **adjective** sensible; to be recommended 可取的;适当的;明智的 ■ **advisability** noun.

advise /əd'vaɪz/ **verb** (**advises**, **advising**, **advised**) **1** recommend that someone should do something 劝告;忠告;建议 **2** tell someone

about a fact or situation 通知;告知 ■ **adviser** (or **advisor**) noun.

advised /əd'vaɪzd/ **adjective** behaving as someone would recommend; sensible 深思熟虑的;明智的 ■ **advisedly** adverb.

advisory /əd'vaɪzəri/ **adjective** having the power to make recommendations but not to make sure that they are carried out 顾问的;咨询的

advocaat /'ædvəʊkɑː/ **noun** a liqueur made with eggs, sugar, and brandy 蛋黄白兰地酒(用蛋、糖和白兰地混合制成)

advocate **noun** /'ædvəkət/ **1** a person who publicly supports or recommends a cause or policy 拥护者;提倡者 **2** a person who argues a case on someone else's behalf 辩护人 **3** Scottish 【苏格兰】a barrister 律师 • **verb** /'ædvəkeɪt/ (**advocates**, **advocating**, **advocated**) publicly recommend or support 拥护;提倡 ■ **advocacy** noun.

adze /ædz/ (US spelling 【美拼作】**adz**) **noun** a tool like an axe, with an arched blade 扁斧;锛子

aegis /'iːdʒɪs/ **noun** the protection, backing, or support of someone 庇护;支持

aeon /'iːən/ (US spelling 【美拼作】**eon**) **noun** a very long period of time 极漫长的时期;万古

aerate /'eəreɪt/ **verb** bring air into something 使通气 ■ **aeration** noun.

aerial /'eəriəl/ **noun** a wire, rod, etc. that sends out or receives radio or television signals 天线 • **adjective 1** existing or taking place in the air 存在于空气中的;空中的 **2** involving the use of aircraft 航空的

aerie /'eəri/ US spelling of **EYRIE**. eyrie 的美式拼法

aerobatics /ˌeərə'bætɪks/ **noun** exciting and daring flying performed for display 特技飞行 ■ **aerobatic** adjective.

aerobic /eə'rəʊbɪk/ **adjective** (of exercise) intended to increase the amount of oxygen you breathe in and make it move around the body more quickly (锻炼)有氧运动的 ■ **aerobically** adverb.

aerobics /eə'rəʊbɪks/ **noun** exercises intended to strengthen the heart and lungs 有氧运动

aerodrome /'eərədrəʊm/ **noun** Brit. 【英】 an airfield 机场

aerodynamic /ˌeərəʊdaɪ'næmɪk/ **adjective 1** relating to aerodynamics 空气动力学的;气体动力学的 **2** having a shape which moves through the air quickly 流线型的 • **noun** (**aerodynamics**) the science concerned with the movement of objects through the air 空气动力学;气体动力学 ■ **aerodynamically** adverb.

aerofoil /'eərəfɔɪl/ **noun** Brit. 【英】 a curved structure, such as a wing, designed to give an aircraft lift 机翼;翼面

aeronautics /ˌeərə'nɔːtɪks/ **noun** the study or practice of travel through the air 航空学;飞行术 ■ **aeronautical** adjective.

aeroplane /'eərəpleɪn/ **noun** Brit.【英】 a powered flying vehicle with fixed wings 飞机

aerosol /'eərəsɒl/ **noun** a substance sealed in a container under pressure and released as a fine spray 气雾剂

aerospace /'eərəʊspeɪs/ **noun** the technology and industry concerned with flight 航空航天技术;航空航天工业

aesthete /'iːsθiːt/ (US spelling 【美拼作】 esthete) **noun** a person who appreciates art and beauty 美学家;审美家

aesthetic /iːs'θetɪk/ (US spelling 【美拼作】 esthetic) **adjective 1** concerned with beauty 美学的;审美的 **2** having a pleasant appearance 美的

• **noun** a set of principles behind the work of an artist or artistic movement 美学标准 ■ **aesthetically** adverb.

aesthetics /iːs'θetɪks/ (US spelling 【美拼作】 esthetics) **noun 1** a set of principles concerned with beauty 审美标准 **2** the branch of philosophy which deals with questions of beauty and artistic taste 美学

afar /ə'fɑː(r)/ **adverb** at or to a distance 在远处;向远处

affable /'æfəbl/ **adjective** good-natured and friendly 和蔼可亲的;亲切友善的 ■ **affability** noun **affably** adverb.

affair /ə'feə(r)/ **noun 1** an event or series of events 事情;事件 **2** a matter that is a particular person's responsibility 个人的事 **3** a love affair 风流韵事 **4** (**affairs**) matters of public interest and importance 公共事务

affect /ə'fekt/ **verb 1** make a difference to 影响 **2** make someone feel sadness, pity, etc. 打动;感动 **3** pretend to have a particular feeling 假装;佯装 **4** wear something or behave in a particular way in an attempt to impress people 做作地穿戴(或表现)

！注意 don't confuse **affect** and **effect**. **Affect** chiefly means 'make a difference to', as in *the changes will affect everyone*. **Effect** is chiefly a noun meaning 'a result', as in *the effects of ageing*. 不要混淆 affect 和 effect。affect 主要表示 "影响",如 the changes will affect everyone (改变会影响每一个人); effect 主要用作名词,意为 "结果,效果",如 the effects of ageing (上年纪的结果)。

---

affectation /ˌæfek'teɪʃn/ **noun** behaviour that is designed to impress people 做作;矫揉造作

affected /ə'fektɪd/ **adjective** designed to impress people 假装的;做作的 ■ **affectedly** adverb.

affection /əˈfekʃn/ **noun** a feeling of fondness or liking 喜爱；钟爱

affectionate /əˈfekʃənət/ **adjective** readily showing affection 表示关爱的；充满深情的 ■ **affectionately** adverb.

affidavit /ˌæfəˈdeɪvɪt/ **noun** a written statement that a person swears is true and that can be used as evidence in a law court 宣誓书

affiliate verb /əˈfɪlieɪt/ (**affiliates**, **affiliating**, **affiliated**) officially link a person or group to an organization 使隶属于；接纳…为成员(或分支机构) • **noun** /əˈfɪliət/ an affiliated person or group 成员；分支机构 ■ **affiliation** noun.

affinity /əˈfɪnəti/ **noun** (plural **affinities**) **1** a natural liking or understanding 喜好；亲近 **2** a close relationship between people or things with similar qualities 密切关系；类同；近似

affirm /əˈfɜːm/ **verb** state firmly or publicly 坚持声称；公开断言 ■ **affirmation** noun.

affirmative /əˈfɜːmətɪv/ **adjective** agreeing with a statement, or consenting to a request 肯定的；同意的 ■ **affirmatively** adverb.

affix verb /əˈfɪks/ attach or fasten something to something else 粘上；贴上；把…固定 • noun /ˈæfɪks/ Grammar 【语法】 a prefix or suffix 词缀

afflict /əˈflɪkt/ verb cause pain or suffering to 使痛苦；折磨 ■ **affliction** noun.

affluent /ˈæfluənt/ **adjective** wealthy; rich 富裕的；富有的 ■ **affluence** noun.

afford /əˈfɔːd/ **verb 1** have enough money or time for 买得起；有时间做 **2** provide an opportunity or facility 提供，给予(机会或设施) ■ **affordable** adjective.

affray /əˈfreɪ/ **noun** Law, dated 【法律，废】a breach of the peace by fighting in a public place (在公共场所的)闹事，打架

affront /əˈfrʌnt/ **noun** an action or remark that offends someone 冒犯；侮辱 • **verb** offend someone 冒犯；侮辱

Afghan /ˈæfɡæn/ **noun** a person from Afghanistan 阿富汗人 • **adjective** relating to Afghanistan 阿富汗的

aficionado /əˌfɪʃəˈnɑːdəʊ/ **noun** (plural **aficionados**) a person who knows a lot about an activity or subject and is very keen on it 狂热爱好者；迷

afield /əˈfiːld/ **adverb** to or at a distance 向远处；在远处

aflame /əˈfleɪm/ **adjective** in flames 燃烧着的

afloat /əˈfləʊt/ **adjective & adverb 1** floating in water (在水中)漂浮的(地) **2** out of debt or difficulty 摆脱债务(或困难)

afoot /əˈfʊt/ **adverb & adjective** happening; in preparation or progress 在发生(的)；在准备中(的)；在进行中(的)

aforementioned /əˌfɔːˈmenʃənd/ **adjective** previously mentioned 前面提到的

afraid /əˈfreɪd/ **adjective** feeling fear 恐惧的；害怕的

afresh /əˈfreʃ/ **adverb** in a new or different way 重新

African /ˈæfrɪkən/ **noun** a person from Africa 非洲人 • **adjective** relating to Africa or Africans 非洲的；非洲人的

Afrikaans /ˌæfrɪˈkɑːns/ **noun** a language of southern Africa that developed from Dutch 南非荷兰语

aft /ɑːft/ **adverb & adjective** at or towards the rear of a ship or an aircraft 在船尾(或机尾)(的)；向船尾(或机尾)(的)

after /ˈɑːftə(r)/ **preposition 1** in the time following an event or another period of time 以后 **2** next to and following in order or importance (按顺序或重要性)随…之后，次于 **3** behind 在…后面 **4** trying to find or get 追求 **5** in reference to 按照；依

照 • **conjunction & adverb** in the time following an event 在 … 之后;以后;后来 □ **after-effect** an effect that happens some time after its cause 余波;事后影响

afterbirth /'ɑːftəbɜːθ/ **noun** the placenta and other material that passes out of the mother's womb after a birth 胞衣;胎盘胎膜

afterlife /'ɑːftəlaɪf/ **noun** life after death 来生;来世

aftermath /'ɑːftəmæθ/ **noun** the situation that exists as a result of an unpleasant or disastrous event (不愉快事件或灾难的)后果

afternoon /ˌɑːftə'nuːn/ **noun** the time from noon or lunchtime to evening 下午;午后

aftershave /'ɑːftəʃeɪv/ **noun** a scented liquid for men to apply to their skin after shaving 须后水

afterthought /'ɑːftəθɔːt/ **noun** something that is thought of or added later 事后想到的事物;后来添加的东西

afterwards /'ɑːftəwədz/ (US spelling 【美拼作】 **afterward**) **adverb** at a later or future time 以后;将来

again /ə'gen/ **adverb 1** once more 再一次;又一次 **2** returning to a previous position or condition 回到原处;回到原来的状态 **3** in addition 又;另外

against /ə'genst/ **preposition 1** in opposition to 反对;逆着 **2** in resistance to 抵抗 **3** in contrast to 与…相对 **4** in or into contact with 靠;倚;贴

agape /ə'geɪp/ **adjective** (of a person's mouth) wide open (人的嘴)大张着的

agate /'ægət/ **noun** an ornamental stone marked with bands of colour 玛瑙

age /eɪdʒ/ **noun 1** the length of time that a person or thing has existed 年龄;年纪 2 存在时间;生存期 **2** a particular stage in someone's life 一生中的某个阶段 **3** old age 老年 **4** a

distinct period of history 时代;时期 • **verb** (**ages**, **ageing** or **aging**, **aged**) grow old or older 变老;显旧 □ **age of consent** the age at which a person can legally have sex 同意年龄(法律上允许发生性行为的年龄) **come of age** be legally recognized as an adult 成年;满法定年龄

aged adjective 1 /eɪdʒd/ of a specified age 一岁的 **2** /'eɪdʒɪd/ old 年老的;旧的

ageism /'eɪdʒɪzəm/ **noun** prejudice or discrimination on the grounds of a person's age 年龄歧视 ■ **ageist** adjective & noun.

ageless /'eɪdʒləs/ **adjective** not ageing or appearing to age 永不衰老的;永不显老的

agency /'eɪdʒənsi/ **noun 1** an organization providing a particular service 服务机构;专门机构 **2** action or intervention 力量;能动作用

agenda /ə'dʒendə/ **noun 1** a list of items to be discussed at a meeting (会议的)议程表,议事日程 **2** a list of matters to be dealt with 日常工作事项

agent /'eɪdʒənt/ **noun 1** a person who provides a particular service 代理人;代理商 **2** a spy 特工人员;间谍 **3** a person or thing that takes an active role or produces a particular effect 起积极作用(或产生特定效果)的人(或事物)

agent provocateur /ˌæʒɒŋ prəˌvɒkə'tɜː(r)/ **noun** (plural **agents provocateurs** /ˌæʒɒŋ prəˌvɒkə'tɜː(r)/) a person who tempts suspected criminals to commit a crime and therefore be convicted (诱使疑犯犯罪以便将其定罪的)密探,坐探

agglomeration /əˌɡlɒmə'reɪʃn/ **noun** a mass or collection of things 大团;大块

aggrandize or **aggrandise** /ə'grændaɪz/ **verb** (**aggrandizes**, **aggrandizing**, **aggrandized**) make more powerful, important, or

A

aggrandize 扩大…的权势；提高…的地位 ■ **aggrandizement** noun.

aggravate /'ægrəveɪt/ **verb** (**aggravates, aggravating, aggravated**) **1** make worse 加重；加剧，使恶化 **2** informal【非正式】annoy or exasperate 惹恼；激怒 ■ **aggravation** noun.

aggregate noun /'ægrɪgət/ **1** a whole formed by combining several different elements 集合体，总数；合计 **2** the total score of a player or team in a fixture that is made up of more than one game or round (多场或多轮比赛的)总分，总积分 • **adjective** /'ægrɪgət/ formed by combining many separate items 集合的；合计的 • **verb** /'ægrɪgeɪt/ (**aggregates, aggregating, aggregated**) combine into a whole 集合；聚集

aggression /ə'greʃn/ **noun** hostile or violent behaviour or attitudes 侵犯；侵略；挑衅

aggressive /ə'gresɪv/ **adjective 1** very angry or hostile 侵犯的，侵略的；挑衅的 **2** too forceful 咄咄逼人的；强有力的 ■ **aggressively** adverb.

✔ 拼写指南 double *g*, double *s*: *aggressive*. *aggressive* 中有两个 g 和两个 s.

aggressor /ə'gresə(r)/ **noun** a person or country that attacks another without being provoked 侵略者；挑衅者

aggrieved /ə'gri:vd/ **adjective** resentful because you feel you have been treated unfairly 感到委屈的；愤愤不平的

aghast /ə'gɑ:st/ **adjective** filled with horror or shock 吓呆的；惊骇的

agile /'ædʒaɪl/ **adjective 1** able to move quickly and easily (动作)敏捷的，灵活的 **2** able to think quickly and intelligently (思维)机敏的 ■ **agilely** adverb **agility** noun.

agitate /'ædʒɪteɪt/ **verb** (**agitates,** **agitating, agitated**) **1** make someone troubled or nervous 使激动；使紧张 **2** try to arouse public concern about an issue 鼓动，煽动 **3** stir or shake a liquid 摇动，搅动(液体) ■ **agitation** noun.

agitator /'ædʒɪteɪtə(r)/ **noun** a person who urges other people to protest or rebel 鼓动者；煽动者

AGM /ˌeɪ dʒi: 'em/ **abbreviation** Brit. 【英】annual general meeting 年会；年度大会

agnostic /æg'nɒstɪk/ **noun** a person who believes it is impossible to know whether or not God exists 不可知论者 ■ **agnosticism** noun.

ago /ə'gəʊ/ **adverb** before the present 以前

agog /ə'gɒg/ **adjective** very eager to hear or see something 渴望的；期待的

agonize or **agonise** /'ægənaɪz/ **verb** (**agonizes, agonizing, agonized**) **1** worry about something very much 十分焦虑 **2** (**agonizing**) very painful or worrying 极度痛苦的

agony /'ægəni/ **noun** (plural **agonies**) extreme suffering 极度痛苦 □ **agony column** Brit. informal【英，非正式】a column in a newspaper or magazine offering advice on readers' personal problems (报刊的)答读者问专栏

agoraphobia /ˌægərə'fəʊbiə/ **noun** abnormal fear of open or public places 恐旷症；广场恐惧症 ■ **agoraphobic** adjective & noun.

agrarian /ə'greəriən/ **adjective** having to do with agriculture 农业的

agree /ə'gri:/ **verb** (**agrees, agreeing, agreed**) **1** have the same opinion about something 同意；赞同 **2** (**agree to**) say that you will do something that has been suggested by someone else 应允；答应 **3** (**agree with**) be consistent with 与…相符；与…一致 **4** (**agree with**) be good for 相宜；适合

agreeable /əˈgriːəbl/ **adjective 1** pleasant 令人愉快的;惬意的;讨人喜欢的 **2** willing to agree to something 欣然同意的;愿意的 **3** acceptable 可以接受的;适合的 ■ **agreeably** adverb.

agreement /əˈgriːmənt/ **noun 1** the state of sharing the same opinion or feeling 同意;意见一致 **2** an arrangement that has been made between people 协定;协议;契约

agriculture /ˈægrɪkʌltʃə(r)/ **noun** the science or practice of farming 农业;农艺 ■ **agricultural** adjective **agriculturally** adverb.

aground /əˈgraʊnd/ **adjective & adverb** (of a ship) touching the bottom in shallow water (船)搁浅的

ague /ˈeɪgjuː/ **noun** old use 【旧】malaria or some other illness involving fever and shivering 疟疾;寒热病

ahead /əˈhed/ **adverb 1** further forward 在前面 **2** in the lead 领先;占优势

ahoy /əˈhɔɪ/ **exclamation** a call used by people in ships or boats to attract attention 喂,啊嗬(船上人的呼喊以引起注意)

aid /eɪd/ **noun 1** help or support 帮助;援助 **2** food or money given to a country in need of help (食品或钱款)援助 • **verb** give help to 帮助;援助

aide /eɪd/ **noun** an assistant to a political leader (政治领袖的)助手

Aids /eɪdz/ **noun** a disease, caused by the HIV virus and transmitted in body fluids, which breaks down the sufferer's natural defences against infection 艾滋病 [short for 【缩写】 =*acquired immune deficiency syndrome*]

aikido /aɪˈkiːdəʊ/ **noun** a Japanese martial art (日本的)合气道

ail /eɪl/ **verb** old use 【旧】cause someone to suffer or have problems 困扰;使苦恼

ailing /ˈeɪlɪŋ/ **adjective** in bad health 有病的;患病的

ailment /ˈeɪlmənt/ **noun** a minor illness 小病

aim /eɪm/ **verb 1** point a weapon, camera,etc. at a target 对准;瞄准 **2** try to achieve something 力争做到;力求达到 • **noun 1** a purpose or intention 目的;意图 **2** the aiming of a weapon or missile 对准;瞄准

aimless /ˈeɪmləs/ **adjective** having no direction or purpose 无目的的;没有目标的 ■ **aimlessly** adverb.

ain't /eɪnt/ **short form** informal 【非正式】 **1** am not; are not; is not. **2** has not; have not.

! 注意 do not use **ain't** when writing or speaking in a formal situation. 正式写作或谈话中不要使用 ain't。

air /eə(r)/ **noun 1** the invisible mixture of gases surrounding the earth 空气 **2** the open space above the surface of the earth 空中;天空 **3** (**an air of**) an impression of 印象;神态 **4** (**airs**) a pretentious or condescending way of behaving 装腔作势;做作的姿态 **5** a tune 曲调;旋律 • **verb 1** express an opinion or complaint publicly 公开发表(意见或怨言) **2** broadcast a programme on radio or television 播出,播送(节目) **3** expose something to fresh or warm air 晾晒;烘干;使通风 □ **air conditioning** a system that cools the air in a building or vehicle 空调;空调 **air force** the branch of the armed forces concerned with fighting in the air 空军 **air gun** a gun which uses compressed air to fire pellets 气枪 **on the air** being broadcast on radio or television 在播送中 ■ **airing** noun **airless** adjective.

airbase /ˈeəbeɪs/ **noun** a base for military aircraft 空军基地

airborne /ˈeəbɔːn/ **adjective 1** carried or spread through the air 空运的;空气传播的 **2** (of an aircraft) in the air; flying (飞机)在飞行中的

airbrush /ˈeəbrʌʃ/ **noun** a device

A

for spraying paint by means of compressed air (喷颜料用的)气刷，气笔 ■ **verb** paint a picture or alter a photograph with an airbrush 用气笔作(画)；用气笔修改(照片)

aircraft /'eəkrɑ:ft/ **noun** (plural **aircraft**) a plane, helicopter, or other machine that can fly 飞机；航空器
■ **aircraft carrier** a large warship from which aircraft can take off and land 航空母舰

airfield /'eəfi:ld/ **noun** an area of ground where aircraft can take off and land (飞)机场

airlift /'eəlɪft/ **noun** an act of transporting supplies by aircraft 空运

airline /'eəlaɪn/ **noun** a company that provides regular flights for the public to use 航空公司

airliner /'eəlaɪnə(r)/ **noun** a large passenger aircraft 大型客机；班机

airlock /'eəlɒk/ **noun 1** a bubble of air that stops the flow in a pump or pipe 气塞 **2** a compartment which allows people to move between areas that are at different pressures 压差隔离室；密封舱

airmail /'eəmeɪl/ **noun** a system of transporting mail overseas by air 航空邮政

airman /'eəmən/ **noun** (plural **airmen**) a pilot or crew member in a military aircraft 空军飞行员；空军士兵

airplane /'eəpleɪn/ **noun** N. Amer.【北美】a plane 飞机

airport /'eəpɔ:t/ **noun** an area consisting of a set of runways and buildings where non-military aircraft can take off and land 机场；航空站；航空港

airship /'eəʃɪp/ **noun** a large aircraft filled with gas which is lighter than air 飞艇；飞船

airspace /'eəspeɪs/ **noun** the part of the air above a particular country 领空；空域

airstrip /'eəstrɪp/ **noun** a strip of

ground where aircraft can take off and land 简易机场；简便跑道

airtight /'eətaɪt/ **adjective 1** not allowing air to escape or pass through 密封的；气密的；不透气的 **2** unable to be proved false 没有漏洞的；无懈可击的

airwaves /'eəweɪvz/ **plural noun** the radio frequencies used for broadcasting (广播使用的)无线电波，波段

airway /'eəweɪ/ **noun 1** the passage by which air reaches the lungs 气道 **2** a recognized route followed by aircraft 航空路线；航路

airworthy /'eəwɜ:ði/ **adjective** (of an aircraft) safe to fly (飞机)适航的

airy /'eəri/ **adjective** (**airier**, **airiest**) **1** spacious and having plenty of fresh air 宽敞通风的 **2** showing that you feel something is not worth serious consideration 轻率的；漫不经心的
■ **airily** adverb.

airy-fairy /ˌeəri'feəri/ **adjective** informal【非正式】vague and unrealistic or impractical 模糊的；不现实的；不切实际的

aisle /aɪl/ **noun** a passage between rows of seats in a public building, aircraft, or train or between shelves in a shop 通道；过道

ajar /ə'dʒɑ:(r)/ **adverb & adjective** (of a door or window) slightly open (门或窗)半开着的，微开着的

aka /ˌeɪ keɪ 'eɪ, 'ækə/ **abbreviation** also known as 又名；亦称

akimbo /ə'kɪmbəʊ/ **adverb** with hands on the hips and elbows turned outwards 双手叉腰地

akin /ə'kɪn/ **adjective** similar in nature or type 类似的；相似的

alabaster /'æləbɑ:stə(r)/ **noun** a white, semi-transparent mineral that is carved into ornaments 雪花石膏

à la carte /ˌɑ: lɑ: 'kɑ:t/ **adjective & adverb** (of a menu) offering dishes that are separately priced, rather than part of a set meal 按菜单点菜的(地)

alacrity /ə'lækrəti/ *noun* great eagerness or enthusiasm 乐意;欣然同意

alarm /ə'lɑːm/ *noun* **1** anxiety or fear caused by being aware of danger 忧虑;担心;惊恐 **2** a warning of danger 警报 **3** a sound or device that gives a warning of danger 警报声;警报器 • *verb* **1** frighten or disturb 使惊恐;使忧虑;使担心 **2** (**be alarmed**) (of a car or building) be fitted with an alarm (汽车或建筑物)装有警报器 □ **alarm clock** a clock set to sound at a particular time to wake you up 闹钟

alarmist /ə'lɑːmɪst/ *noun* a person who exaggerates a danger and causes unnecessary alarm 大惊小怪的人;危言耸听的人

alas /ə'læs/ *exclamation* literary or humorous 【文或幽默】 an expression of grief, pity, or concern 哎呀,唉(表示悲痛、怜悯或关切)

albatross /'ælbətrɒs/ *noun* (plural **albatrosses**) a very large white seabird with long, narrow wings 信天翁(大型白色海鸟,翼长而窄)

albeit /ɔːl'biːɪt/ *conjunction* though 尽管;即使

albino /æl'biːnəʊ/ *noun* (plural **albinos**) a person or animal born with white skin and hair and pink eyes 患白化病的人(或动物)

album /'ælbəm/ *noun* **1** a blank book for displaying photographs, stamps,etc. 影集;集邮册;集子 **2** a collection of musical recordings issued as a single item 音乐专辑

albumen /'ælbjumɪn/ *noun* egg white 蛋白

alchemy /'ælkəmi/ *noun* a medieval form of chemistry that was chiefly concerned with trying to convert ordinary metals into gold 炼金术 ■ **alchemical** adjective **alchemist** noun.

alcohol /'ælkəhɒl/ *noun* **1** drinks containing a colourless liquid that can make people drunk, such as wine, beer,and spirits 酒精饮料;酒 **2** this liquid 酒精;乙醇

alcoholic /ˌælkə'hɒlɪk/ *adjective* relating to alcohol 酒精的 • *noun* a person suffering from alcoholism 饮酒过度者;酗酒者

alcoholism /'ælkəhɒlɪzəm/ *noun* addiction to alcoholic drink 酗酒

alcove /'ælkəʊv/ *noun* a recess in the wall of a room 凹室;壁龛

alder /'ɔːldə(r)/ *noun* a tree of the birch family,which produces catkins 桤木(桦木科树木,柔荑花序)

alderman /'ɔːldəmən/ *noun* (plural **aldermen**) chiefly historical 【主历史】 a member of a council below the rank of mayor 高级市政官(地位次于市长)

ale /eɪl/ *noun* chiefly Brit. 【主英】 beer, especially bitter 麦芽啤酒

alert /ə'lɜːt/ *adjective* **1** quick to notice and respond to danger or change 警觉的;警惕的 **2** quick-thinking; intelligent 机灵的;机敏的 • *noun* **1** a watchful state 警觉;警惕 **2** a warning of danger 警报 • *verb* warn someone of a danger or problem 使警觉;使警惕 ■ **alertly** adverb **alertness** noun.

alfalfa /æl'fælfə/ *noun* a plant with bluish flowers, used as food for animals 苜蓿(用作饲料)

alfresco /æl'freskəʊ/ *adverb & adjective* in the open air 在户外(的);在露天(的)

algae /'ældʒiː, -gi/ *plural noun* simple plants that do not have true stems, roots, and leaves, such as seaweed 水藻;海藻

algebra /'ældʒɪbrə/ *noun* the branch of mathematics in which letters and other symbols are used to represent numbers and quantities 代数(学) ■ **algebraic** /ˌældʒɪ'breɪk/ adjective.

Algerian /æl'dʒɪəriə/ *noun* a person from Algeria 阿尔及利亚人 • *adjective* relating to Algeria 阿尔及利亚的

algorithm 24

A

algorithm /'ælgərɪðəm/ **noun** a process or set of rules used in calculations 算法;运算规则

alias /'eɪliəs, -æs/ **adverb** also known as 亦叫作;亦称为 • **noun** a false identity 假名;化名

alibi /'æləbaɪ/ **noun** (plural **alibis**) a piece of evidence that a person was somewhere else when a crime was committed 不在犯罪现场的证据

alien /'eɪliən/ **adjective 1** belonging to a foreign country 外国的 **2** unfamiliar and unappealing 不熟悉的;陌生的;格格不入的 **3** from another world 外星球的 • **noun 1** a foreigner 外国人 **2** a being from another world 外星人

alienate /'eɪliəneɪt/ **verb** (**alienates, alienating, alienated**) **1** make someone feel isolated 使疏远 **2** lose the support or sympathy of 失去…的支持;使不同情 ■ **alienation** noun.

alight[1] /ə'laɪt/ **verb 1** get off a train or bus 从车上下来 **2** (of a bird) land on something (鸟)飞落,落下

alight[2] **adverb & adjective 1** on fire 燃烧(的);在着火的(的) **2** shining brightly 闪亮地(的)

align /ə'laɪn/ **verb 1** place something in a straight line or in the right position in relation to other things 使成直线;调准 **2** (**align yourself with**) be on the side of 与…结盟 ■ **alignment** noun.

alike /ə'laɪk/ **adjective** similar 相像的;相似的 • **adverb** in a similar way 相像地;相似地

alimentary canal /ˌælɪ'mentəri/ **noun** the passage along which food passes through the body 消化道

alimony /'ælɪməni/ **noun** chiefly N. Amer. 【主北美】 financial support for a husband or wife after separation or divorce (夫妻分居或离婚后付给对方的)赡养费,生活费

alive /ə'laɪv/ **adjective 1** living; not dead 活着的;在世的 **2** continuing in existence or use 继续存在的;在起作用的 **3** alert and active 有活力的;有生气的 **4** (**alive with**) full of 充满的 **5** (**alive to**) aware of and willing to respond to 意识到;积极应对

alkali /'ælkəlaɪ/ **noun** (plural **alkalis**) a substance whose chemical properties include turning litmus blue and neutralizing acids 碱 ■ **alkaline** adjective.

all /ɔːl/ **determiner 1** the whole quantity or extent of 整个的;全部的 **2** any whatever 任何的 **3** the greatest possible 尽量的;最大限度的 • **pronoun** everything or everyone 全体;每个 • **adverb 1** completely 完全地;很;非常 **2** indicating an equal score (得分)双方相等 各: *one-all* 1平 □ **all and sundry** everyone 全体;每一个人 **the all clear** a signal that danger is over 消除警报(危险解除的信号) **all in** informal 【非正式】exhausted 精疲力竭;疲乏到极点 **all out** trying as hard as you can 竭尽全力;全力以赴 **all-rounder** Brit. 【英】a person with a wide range of skills 多面手 **all told** in total 总共;一共;共计 **on all fours** on hands and knees 四肢并用地;爬行

Allah /'ælə/ **noun** the Arabic name of God 安拉,真主(阿拉伯人信奉的神)

allay /ə'leɪ/ **verb** reduce or end fear, concern, or difficulty 减轻(恐惧、忧虑或困难);使平静

allegation /ˌælə'ɡeɪʃn/ **noun** a claim that someone has done something illegal or wrong 指控;断言

allege /ə'ledʒ/ **verb** (**alleges, alleging, alleged**) claim that someone has done something illegal or wrong 断言;声称;指控 ■ **alleged** adjective **allegedly** adverb.

allegiance /ə'liːdʒəns/ **noun** loyalty to a person,group, or cause 忠诚;效忠;拥戴

allegory /'æləɡəri/ **noun** (plural **allegories**) a story, poem, or picture which contains a hidden meaning 寓言；讽喻作品 ■ **allegorical** adjective.

allegro /ə'legrəʊ/ **noun** (plural **allegros**) a piece of music that is to be played at a brisk speed 快板

alleluia /ˌælɪ'luːjə/ ⟹ 见 HALLELUJAH.

allergic /ə'lɜːdʒɪk/ **adjective 1** caused by an allergy 过敏引起的；过敏性的 **2** having an allergy 过敏的

allergy /'ælədʒi/ **noun** (plural **allergies**) a medical condition that makes you feel ill when you eat or come into contact with a particular substance 过敏(性)

alleviate /ə'liːvieɪt/ **verb** (**alleviates**, **alleviating**, **alleviated**) make a pain or problem less severe 减轻；缓解 ■ **alleviation** noun.

alley /'æli/ **noun** (plural **alleys**) **1** (also **alleyway**) a narrow passageway between or behind buildings (建筑群中间或后面的)小街、小巷 **2** a path in a park or garden (公园或花园里的)小径 **3** a long, narrow area in which skittles and bowling are played (九柱戏和保龄球的)球道

alliance /ə'laɪəns/ **noun 1** the state of being joined or associated 联合；结合 **2** an agreement made between countries or organizations to work together (国家或组织间的)盟约 **3** a relation-ship or connection 联盟；同盟

allied /'ælaɪd/ **adjective 1** joined by an alliance 结盟的；联盟的，同盟的 **2** (**Allied**) relating to Britain and its allies in the First and Second World Wars (第一次世界大战期间)协约国的；(第二次世界大战期间)同盟国的 **3** (**allied to** or **with**) combined with 与…结合的

alligator /'ælɪgeɪtə(r)/ **noun** a large reptile similar to a crocodile 短吻鳄

alliteration /əˌlɪtə'reɪʃn/ **noun** the occurrence of the same letter or sound at the beginning of words that are next to or close to each other 头

韵；头韵法 ■ **alliterative** adjective.

allocate /'æləkeɪt/ **verb** (**allocates**, **allocating**, **allocated**) assign or give to 分配；分派 ■ **allocation** noun.

allot /ə'lɒt/ **verb** (**allots**, **allotting**, **allotted**) give or share out something 分配；分给

allotment /ə'lɒtmənt/ **noun 1** Brit. 【英】a small plot of rented land for growing vegetables or flowers (租借的)小块园地 **2** the action of allotting something, or an amount of something allotted to someone 分配；分派

allow /ə'laʊ/ **verb 1** let someone do something 允许；准许 **2** (**allow for**) take into consideration 考虑到，顾及 **3** provide or set aside 提供；留给 **4** admit that something is true 承认 ■ **allowable** adjective.

> **！注意** don't confuse **allowed**, meaning 'permitted', with **aloud**, meaning 'out loud'. 不要混淆allowed和aloud，前者表示"允许的"，后者意为"大声地"。

allowance /ə'laʊəns/ **noun 1** the amount of something that is allowed 分配额；允给额 **2** a sum of money paid regularly to a person 津贴；补贴 **3** Brit. 【英】an amount of money that can be earned free of tax 免税额 ◻ **make allowances for 1** take into consideration 考虑到；顾及 **2** treat someone less harshly because they are in difficult circumstances 体谅；谅解

alloy noun /'ælɔɪ/ **1** a mixture of two or more metals 合金 **2** an inferior metal mixed with a precious one (与贵重金属熔合的)贱金属 • verb /ə'lɔɪ/ mix metals to make an alloy 将(金属)铸成合金

all right adjective **1** satisfactory; acceptable 令人满意的；可以接受的 **2** allowed 允许的 • adverb fairly well 还好

✔ **拼写指南** use the spelling **all right** rather than **alright**. 应使用 all right，不要拼作 alright。

allude /əˈluːd/ *verb* (**alludes, alluding, alluded**) (**allude to**) **1** mention in passing 顺带提及 **2** hint at 暗指；影射

allure /əˈlʊə(r)/ *noun* the quality of being very attractive or appealing 吸引力；诱惑力；魅力

alluring /əˈlʊərɪŋ/ *adjective* very attractive or tempting 吸引人的；诱人的 ■ **alluringly** *adverb*.

allusion /əˈluːʒn/ *noun* an indirect reference to something 暗指；影射 ■ **allusive** *adjective*.

alluvial /əˈluːviəl/ *adjective* made of clay, silt, and sand that is left by flood water 冲积的；淤积的

ally *noun* /ˈælaɪ/ (plural **allies**) **1** a person, organization, or country that cooperates with another 同盟；同盟者；同盟国 **2** (**the Allies**) the countries that fought with Britain in the First and Second World Wars (第一次世界大战中的)协约国，(第二次世界大战中的)同盟国 • *verb* /əˈlaɪ/ (**allies, allying, allied**) **1** (**ally something to** or **with**) combine one resource with another in a way that benefits both 结合；联合 **2** (**ally yourself with**) side with 站在…一边；拥护；支持

alma mater /ˌælmə ˈmɑːtə(r)/ *noun* the school, college, or university that a person once attended 母校

almanac or **almanack** /ˈɔːlmənæk/ *noun* **1** a calendar that gives important dates and also information about the sun, moon, tides, etc. 历书；年历 **2** a book published yearly and containing useful information for that year 年鉴

almighty /ɔːlˈmaɪti/ *adjective* **1** having unlimited or very great power 全能的；万能的 **2** *informal* 【非正式】

enormous 极大的；非常的 • *noun* (**the Almighty**) God 上帝

almond /ˈɑːmənd/ *noun* an oval nut with a woody shell, growing on a tree found in warm climates 杏仁；扁桃仁

almost /ˈɔːlməʊst/ *adverb* very nearly 几乎；差不多

alms /ɑːmz/ *plural noun* (in the past) money or goods given to the poor (旧用词)施舍，救济

almshouse /ˈɑːmzhaʊs/ *noun* (in the past) a house built for poor people to live in (旧时的)贫民所，救济院

aloe /ˈæləʊ/ *noun* a tropical plant with succulent leaves, whose bitter juice is used in medicine 芦荟(热带植物，叶多汁，味苦，可入药)

aloe vera /ˈvɪərə/ *noun* a jelly-like substance obtained from a kind of aloe, used to soothe the skin 芦荟油(用作润肤剂)

aloft /əˈlɒft/ *adjective & adverb* up in or into the air 在(或向)高处(的)；在(或向)空中(的)

alone /əˈləʊn/ *adjective & adverb* **1** on your own 独自的(地) **2** isolated and lonely 孤独的(地) **3** only; exclusively 单单；仅仅；只

along /əˈlɒŋ/ *preposition & adverb* **1** moving on a surface in a constant direction 沿着；顺着 **2** extending on a surface in a horizontal line (水平)延伸，沿着 **3** in company with other people (与…)一道，(与…)一起

alongside /əˌlɒŋˈsaɪd/ *preposition* **1** close to the side of; next to 沿着…的边；在…旁边 **2** at the same time as 与…同时

aloof /əˈluːf/ *adjective* not friendly or showing an interest in other people 冷漠的；冷淡的 ■ **aloofness** *noun*.

alopecia /ˌæləˈpiːʃə/ *noun* abnormal loss of hair 脱发；秃发

aloud /əˈlaʊd/ *adverb* not silently; out loud 出声地；大声地

! 注意 don't confuse **aloud**, meaning 'out loud', with **allowed**, meaning 'permitted'. 不要混淆 aloud 和 allowed，前者表示"大声地"，后者意为"允许的"。

alp /ælp/ **noun 1** a high mountain 高山 **2** (**the Alps**) a high range of mountains in Switzerland and adjoining countries 阿尔卑斯山脉(位于瑞士及毗邻国家境内)

alpaca /æl'pækə/ **noun** (plural **alpaca** or **alpacas**) a long-haired South American animal related to the llama (南美洲)羊驼

alpha /'ælfə/ **noun** the first letter of the Greek alphabet (A, α) 希腊语字母表的第1个字母 • **adjective** referring to the dominant animal or person in a group (动物或人类群体中)首要的，占主导地位的: *the alpha male* 占主导地位的男性

alphabet /'ælfəbet/ **noun** a set of letters or symbols used to represent the basic speech sounds of a language (一种语言的)全部字母，字母表

alphabetical /ælfə'betɪkl/ **adjective** in the order of the letters of the alphabet 按字母顺序的 ■ **alphabetically** adverb.

alpine /'ælpaɪn/ **adjective 1** relating to or found on high mountains 高山的；高山生长的 **2** (**Alpine**) relating to the Alps 阿尔卑斯山脉的

already /ɔːl'redi/ **adverb 1** before the time in question 早已；已经 **2** as surprisingly soon or early as this 已经，都(表示惊讶)

alright /ɔːl'raɪt/ = ALL RIGHT.

Alsatian /æl'seɪʃn/ **noun** Brit. 【英】a German shepherd dog 德国牧羊犬，阿尔萨斯狼狗

also /'ɔːlsəʊ/ **adverb** in addition 而且(也)；另外(还) ■ **also-ran** a loser in a race or contest (赛跑比赛或竞赛中的)失败者

altar /'ɔːltə(r)/ **noun 1** the table in a Christian church at which bread and wine are made sacred (基督教教堂内的)圣餐台 **2** a table or block on which offerings are made to a god or goddess 圣坛，祭坛

alter /'ɔːltə(r)/ **verb** make or become different; change (使)变样；改变；改动 ■ **alteration** noun.

altercation /ɔːltə'keɪʃn/ **noun** a noisy argument or disagreement 争论；争吵

alter ego **noun 1** another side to a person's normal personality 第二个自我；个性的另一面 **2** a close friend who is very like yourself 知心朋友；知己；密友

alternate **verb** /'ɔːltəneɪt/ (**alternates**, **alternating**, **alternated**) **1** (of two things or people) repeatedly follow one another in turn (两事物或两人)轮流 **2** keep changing between two states (两种状态)交替，更迭 • **adjective** /ɔːl'tɜːnət/ **1** every other 间隔的 **2** (of two things) each following and succeeded by the other in a regular pattern (两事物)交替的，轮流的 ■ **alternating current** an electric current that reverses its direction many times a second 交流电 ■ **alternately** adverb **alternation** noun.

alternative /ɔːl'tɜːnətɪv/ **adjective 1** (of one or more things) available as another possibility (一种或多种事物)供选择的，供替代的 **2** different from what is usual or traditional 非传统的；另类的: *alternative therapy* 非传统疗法 • **noun** one of two or more available possibilities 可供选择的事物 ■ **alternatively** adverb.

alternator /'ɔːltəneɪtə(r)/ **noun** a dynamo that generates an alternating current 交流发电机

although /ɔːl'ðəʊ/ **conjunction 1** in spite of the fact that 虽然；尽管 **2** but 不过；然而

altimeter /'æltɪmiːtə(r)/ **noun** an instrument which indicates the altitude that has been reached 测高仪;高度计

altitude /'æltɪtjuːd/ *noun* the height of an object or point above sea level or ground level 海拔;高度

alto /'æltəʊ/ *noun* (plural **altos**) the highest adult male or lowest female singing voice 男声最高音;女低音

altogether /ˌɔːltə'geðə(r)/ *adverb* **1** completely 完全,全然,全部 **2** in total 共总 **3** on the whole 总的说来;总之,基本上

altruism /'æltruːɪzəm/ *noun* unselfish concern for other people 利他主义;利他;无私 ■ **altruist** *noun* **altruistic** *adjective*.

alum /'æləm/ *noun* a compound of aluminium and potassium, used in dyeing and in making leather 明矾 (用于染色和鞣革)

aluminium /ˌæljə'mɪnɪəm/ (US spelling 【美拼法】 **aluminum** /ə'luːmɪnəm/) *noun* a lightweight silvery-grey metal (金属元素)铝

alumnus /ə'lʌmnəs/ *noun* (plural **alumni** /ə'lʌmnaɪ/) a former student of a particular school, college, or university 校友;毕业生

always /'ɔːlweɪz/ *adverb* **1** at all times 总是 **2** forever 永远,始终,一直 **3** repeatedly 一再;老是 **4** failing all else 总还

Alzheimer's disease /'æltshaɪ-məz/ *noun* a disease of the brain which can affect older people, causing memory loss and confusion 阿尔茨海默氏病;早老性痴呆症

AM /eɪ 'em/ *abbreviation* amplitude modulation 调幅;调幅广播

am /æm, əm/ 1st person singular present of BE.

a.m. /eɪ 'em/ *abbreviation* before noon 上午;早上 [short for Latin 【缩写,拉丁】 =*ante meridiem*.]

amalgam /ə'mælɡəm/ *noun* **1** a mixture or blend of things 混合物 **2** an alloy of mercury with another

metal 汞齐;汞合金

amalgamate /ə'mælɡəmeɪt/ *verb* (**amalgamates, amalgamating, amalgamated**) combine two or more things to form one organization or structure 联合;合并 ■ **amalgamation** *noun*.

amanuensis /əˌmænju'ensɪs/ *noun* (plural **amanuenses** /əˌmænju'ensiːz/) a person who helps a writer with their work (作家的)文书,文书助手

amass /ə'mæs/ *verb* build up over time 积聚;积累

amateur /'æmətə(r)/ *noun* **1** a person who takes part in a sport or other activity without being paid 业余运动员 **2** a person who is not skilled at an activity 外行 • *adjective* **1** non-professional 业余的 **2** not skilful 外行的;不熟练的 ■ **amateurism** *noun*.

> ✔ 拼写指南 *-eur*, not *–uer*: amat**eur**. amateur 中的 -eur 不要拼作 –uer。

amateurish /'æmətɜːrɪʃ/ *adjective* not done or made very well; unskilful 业余的;外行的;不熟练的

amatory /'æmətəri/ *adjective* having to do with love or desire 性爱的;情欲的

amaze /ə'meɪz/ *verb* (**amazes, amazing, amazed**) make someone feel very surprised 使惊愕;使惊异 ■ **amazement** *noun* **amazing** *adjective* **amazingly** *adverb*.

Amazon /'æməzən/ *noun* **1** a member of a legendary race of female warriors (传说中的)亚马孙族女战士 **2** a very tall, strong woman 高大强悍的女人,悍妇 ■ **Amazonian** *adjective*.

ambassador /æm'bæsədə(r)/ *noun* **1** a person sent by a state as its representative in a foreign country 大使 **2** a person who represents or promotes a particular activity 使者;代表

amber /'æmbə(r)/ *noun* **1** a hard,

clear yellowish substance used in jewellery 琥珀 **2** a yellowish colour 琥珀色；黄褐色

ambergris /ˈæmbəɡriːs/ **noun** a wax-like substance produced by sperm whales, used in making perfume 龙涎香(抹香鲸的蜡状分泌物，可制香料)

ambidextrous /ˌæmbɪˈdekstrəs/ **adjective** able to use the right and left hands equally well 左右手都善用的

ambience or **ambiance** /ˈæmbɪəns/ **noun** the character and atmosphere of a place 环境；气氛；氛围

ambient /ˈæmbɪənt/ **adjective 1** relating to the surroundings of something 周围的；围绕的 **2** (of music) quiet and relaxing (音乐)舒缓的

ambiguity /ˌæmbɪˈɡjuːəti/ **noun** (plural **ambiguities**) the quality of having more than one possible meaning 意义含糊；模棱两可

ambiguous /æmˈbɪɡjuəs/ **adjective 1** having more than one possible meaning 有歧义的；模棱两可的 **2** not clear or decided 模糊不清的；不明确的 ■ **ambiguously** adverb.

ambit /ˈæmbɪt/ **noun** the scope or extent of something 范围；界限

ambition /æmˈbɪʃn/ **noun 1** a strong desire to do or achieve something 强烈欲望；渴望 **2** desire for success, wealth, or fame 野心；志向；抱负

ambitious /æmˈbɪʃəs/ **adjective 1** having or showing determination to succeed 有野心的；有志向的；有抱负的 **2** intended to reach a high standard and therefore difficult to achieve 雄心勃勃的；要求高的；费劲的 ■ **ambitiously** adverb.

ambivalent /æmˈbɪvələnt/ **adjective** having mixed feelings about something or someone 有矛盾情感的 ■ **ambivalence** noun **ambivalently** adverb.

amble /ˈæmbl/ **verb** (**ambles**, **ambling**, **ambled**) walk at a leisurely pace 漫步；缓行 • **noun** a leisurely walk 漫步；缓行

ambrosia /æmˈbrəʊziə/ **noun 1** Greek & Roman Mythology【希腊和罗马神话】the food of the gods 神的食物 **2** something very pleasing to taste or smell 美味佳肴

ambulance /ˈæmbjələns/ **noun** a vehicle for taking sick or injured people to and from hospital 救护车

ambulatory /ˈæmbjələtəri/ **adjective** relating to walking, or able to walk or move 步行的；走动的；能走动的

ambush /ˈæmbʊʃ/ **noun** a surprise attack by people lying in wait in a hidden position 伏击；埋伏 • **verb** make a surprise attack on someone from a hidden position 伏击

ameba /əˈmiːbə/ US spelling of AMOEBA. amoeba 的美式拼法

ameliorate /əˈmiːliəreɪt/ **verb** (**ameliorates**, **ameliorating**, **ameliorated**) formal【正式】make something better 改善；改良

amen /ɑːˈmen, eɪ-/ **exclamation** a word said at the end of a prayer or hymn, meaning 'so be it' 阿门(祈祷或赞美诗的结束语，意为"诚心所愿")

amenable /əˈmiːnəbl/ **adjective 1** willing to be persuaded 顺从的 **2** (**amenable to**) able to be affected by 可受…影响的

amend /əˈmend/ **verb** change or make minor improvements to 修改；修订

amendment /əˈmendmənt/ **noun** a minor change or improvement 修改；修订

amends /əˈmendz/ **plural noun** (**make amends**) make up for a wrongdoing 赔偿；补偿

amenity /əˈmiːnəti/ **noun** (plural **amenities**) a useful or desirable feature of a place 生活福利设施；便利设施

American /əˈmerɪkən/ **adjective**

relating to the United States or to the continents of America 美国的；美洲的 • **noun** a person from the United States or any of the countries of North, South, or Central America 美国人；美洲人 □ **American football** a kind of football played with an oval ball on a field marked with parallel lines 美式橄榄球；美式足球 **American Indian** a member of one of the original peoples of America 美洲印第安人

amethyst /'æməθɪst/ **noun** a violet or purple precious stone 紫水晶

amiable /'eɪmɪəbl/ **adjective** friendly and pleasant 和蔼可亲的；亲切友好的 ■ **amiability** noun **amiably** adverb.

amicable /'æmɪkəbl/ **adjective** friendly and without disagreement 友善的；友好的 ■ **amicably** adverb.

amid /ə'mɪd/ or **amidst** /ə'mɪdst/ **preposition** in the middle of 在…中间；在…之中

amidships /ə'mɪdʃɪps/ **adverb & adjective** in the middle of a ship 在船体中部(的)

amino acid /ə'miːnəu/ **noun** any of the natural substances which combine to form proteins 氨基酸

amir /ə'mɪə(r)/ ⇒ 见 EMIR.

amiss /ə'mɪs/ **adjective** not quite right; inappropriate 错误的；出毛病的；不恰当的 □ **take something amiss** be offended by something 对…见怪；对…生气

amity /'æməti/ **noun** formal 【正式】 friendly relations between people or countries 和睦；友好

ammeter /'æmiːtə(r)/ **noun** an instrument for measuring electric current 安培计

ammo /'æməu/ **noun** informal 【非正式】 ammunition 弹药

ammonia /ə'məunɪə/ **noun** a colourless, strong-smelling gas which can be used to make a cleaning fluid 氨(无色气体，有刺激性气味，可用于制配清洁剂)

ammonite /'æmənaɪt/ **noun** an extinct sea creature with a spiral shell 菊石(一种已灭绝的海洋生物，有螺旋状外壳)

ammunition /ˌæmju'nɪʃn/ **noun 1** a supply of bullets and shells 军火；弹药 **2** points used to support your case in an argument 炮弹(指支持自己论点的论据)

amnesia /æm'niːzɪə/ **noun** loss of memory 记忆缺失；遗忘(症) ■ **amnesiac** adjective.

amnesty /'æmnəsti/ **noun** (plural **amnesties**) **1** a pardon given to people who have committed an offence against the government 大赦；赦免 **2** a period during which people who admit to committing an offence are not punished 赦免期限(自首可以免受处罚的期限)

amniocentesis /ˌæmnɪəusen'tiːsɪs/ **noun** (plural **amniocenteses** /ˌæmnɪəusen'tiːsiːz/) a medical procedure in which a sample of amniotic fluid is taken to check for possible abnormalities in the unborn baby 羊膜穿刺术，羊水诊断(对羊水取样检查胎儿发育是否异常)

amniotic fluid /ˌæmni'ɒtɪk/ **noun** the fluid surrounding an unborn baby in the womb 羊水(子宫内胎儿周围的液体)

amoeba /ə'miːbə/ (US spelling 【美拼作】**ameba**) **noun** (plural **amoebas** or **amoebae** /ə'miːbiː/) a microscopic creature that is made up of a single cell and can change its shape 变形虫，阿米巴

amok /ə'mɒk/ or **amuck** /ə'mʌk/ **adverb** (**run amok**) behave in an uncontrolled way 发狂；狂乱

among /ə'mʌŋ/ or **amongst** /ə'mʌŋst/ **preposition 1** surrounded by 被…所环绕 **2** included or occurring in 系…中之一；在…中 **3** shared by; between 为…所共有；在…之间

amoral /ˌeɪˈmɒrəl/ **adjective** not concerned with doing what is right 无道德的；不在意道德准则的，■ **amorality** noun.

amorous /ˈæmərəs/ **adjective** showing or feeling sexual desire 求爱的；表示性爱的，■ **amorously** adverb.

amorphous /əˈmɔːfəs/ **adjective** without a clear shape or form 无固定形状的；不规则的

amount /əˈmaʊnt/ **noun 1** the total number, size, or value of something 总数；总大小；总值 **2** a quantity 数量；数额 • **verb (amount to) 1** add up to 合计，总计 **2** be the same as 相当于；等于

ampere /ˈæmpeə(r)/ **noun** a basic unit of electric current 安，安培(电流基本单位)

ampersand /ˈæmpəsænd/ **noun** the sign &, which means *and*. &号(表示 and)

amphetamine /æmˈfetəmiːn/ **noun** a drug used as a stimulant 苯丙胺,安非他明(用作兴奋剂)

amphibian /æmˈfɪbiən/ **noun** an animal such as a frog or toad, which lives in the water when young and on the land as an adult 两栖动物 ■ **amphibious** adjective.

amphitheatre /ˈæmfɪθɪətə(r)/ (US spelling 【美拼作】 **amphitheater**) **noun** a round building without a roof, in which tiers of seats surround a central space used for performing plays or for sports 圆形露天剧场；圆形露天竞技场

ample /ˈæmpl/ **adjective 1** enough or more than enough; plentiful 足够的；充裕的；丰富的 **2** large 大的 ■ **amply** adverb.

amplifier /ˈæmplɪfaɪə(r)/ **noun** a device that makes sounds or radio signals louder 放大器；扩音器；扬声器

amplify /ˈæmplɪfaɪ/ **verb (amplifies, amplifying, amplified) 1** increase the strength of a sound or an electrical signal 放大(声音或电子信号) **2** explain something in more detail 扩展；进一步阐发 ■ **amplification** noun.

amplitude /ˈæmplɪtjuːd/ **noun 1** the maximum amount by which a vibration such as an alternating current varies from its average level (交流电等的)振幅 **2** great size, range, or extent 广大；广阔

ampoule /ˈæmpuːl/ **noun** a small glass capsule containing liquid used in giving an injection 安瓿(装针剂的小玻璃瓶)

amputate /ˈæmpjuteɪt/ **verb (amputates, amputating, amputated)** cut off a limb in a surgical operation (通过外科手术)切断，截(肢) ■ **amputation** noun.

amputee /ˌæmpjuˈtiː/ **noun** a person who has had a limb amputated 被截肢者

amuck /əˈmʌk/ ⇒ 见AMOK.

amulet /ˈæmjulət/ **noun** a small piece of jewellery worn as protection against evil 护身符

amuse /əˈmjuːz/ **verb (amuses, amusing, amused) 1** make someone laugh or smile 逗乐；逗笑 **2** give someone something enjoyable to do 给…提供娱乐(或消遣)

amusement /əˈmjuːzmənt/ **noun 1** the feeling that you have when something is funny 愉悦；开心 **2** a game or activity that provides entertainment and pleasure 娱乐活动

an /æn, ən/ **determiner** the form of the indefinite article 'a' used before words beginning with a vowel sound (不定冠词,用在以元音开头的单词前代替 a)

anabolic steroid /ˌænəˈbɒlɪk/ **noun** a synthetic hormone used to build up muscle 促蛋白合成类固醇

anachronism /əˈnækrənɪzəm/ **noun 1** something which seems to belong to another time 不合时代的事物 **2**

A

something which is wrongly placed in a particular period 年代误植 ■ **anachronistic** adjective.

anaconda /ˌænə'kɒndə/ **noun** a very large snake of the boa family, found in South America 森蚺(见于南美洲的大蟒蛇)

anaemia /ə'niːmiə/ (US spelling 【美拼作】 **anemia**) **noun** a shortage of red cells or haemoglobin in the blood, making a person pale and tired 贫血(症) ■ **anaemic** adjective.

anaesthetic /ˌænəs'θetɪk/ (US spelling 【美拼作】 **anesthetic**) **noun** a drug or gas that stops you feeling pain 麻醉药;麻醉剂

anaesthetize or **anaesthetise** /ə'niːsθətaɪz/ (US spelling 【美拼作】 **anesthetize**) **verb** (**anaesthetizes, anaesthetizing, anaesthetized**) give an anaesthetic to 使麻醉;对…施行麻醉 ■ **anaesthetist** noun.

anagram /'ænəɡræm/ **noun** a word or phrase formed by rearranging the letters of another 变位词;变位短语

anal /'eɪnl/ **adjective** having to do with the anus 肛门的

analgesic /ˌænl'dʒiːzɪk/ **noun** a pain-relieving drug 止痛药

analogous /ə'næləɡəs/ **adjective** similar to and able to be compared with something else 相似的;类似的;可比拟的

analogue /'ænəlɒɡ/ (US spelling 【美拼作】 **analog**) **adjective** using a variable physical effect, such as voltage or the position of a pointer, to represent information, rather than a digital display 模拟的 • **noun** something that is similar to and can be compared with something else 相似物;类似事情

analogy /ə'nælədʒi/ **noun** (plural **analogies**) a way of explaining something by comparing it to something else 比拟;比喻;类比 ■ **analogical** adjective.

analyse /'ænəlaɪz/ (US spelling 【美拼作】 **analyze**) **verb** (**analyses, analysing, analysed**) **1** examine something in detail to explain it or to find out its structure or composition 分析;细察 **2** psychoanalyse someone 对(某人)作心理分析

analysis /ə'næləsɪs/ **noun** (plural **analyses** /ə'næləsiːz/) **1** a detailed examination of the elements or structure of something 分析;化验 **2** psychoanalysis 心理分析

analyst /'ænəlɪst/ **noun** a person who carries out analysis 分析者;化验员

analytical /ˌænə'lɪtɪkl/ or **analytic** /ˌænə'lɪtɪk/ **adjective** using analysis 分析的 ■ **analytically** adverb.

anarchic /ə'nɑːkɪk/ **adjective** not controlled or governed by any rules or principles 无政府的;无秩序的;混乱的

anarchist /'ænəkɪst/ **noun** a person who believes that all government and laws should be abolished 无政府主义者 ■ **anarchism** noun **anarchistic** adjective.

anarchy /'ænəki/ **noun 1** a situation in which no rules or principles are being followed and there is complete disorder 无政府状态;混乱 **2** a society with no government 无政府社会

anathema /ə'næθəmə/ **noun** something that you hate 令人厌恶的事物

anatomy /ə'nætəmi/ **noun** (plural **anatomies**) **1** the scientific study of the structure of the human body 解剖学 **2** the structure of a person, animal, or plant (人、动植物的)结构 **3** a detailed examination or analysis 剖析;分析 ■ **anatomical** adjective **anatomically** adverb **anatomist** noun.

ancestor /'ænsestə(r)/ **noun 1** a person from whom you are descended 祖宗;祖先 **2** something from which a later species or version has developed 原种;原型;先驱

ancestral /æn'sestrəl/ **adjective** inherited from your ancestors 祖先的；祖宗传下来的

ancestry /'ænsestri/ **noun** (plural **ancestries**) your ancestors or ethnic origins 祖先；世系；血统

anchor /'æŋkə(r)/ **noun** a heavy object that is attached to a boat by a rope or chain and is dropped to the sea bed to stop the boat from drifting 锚 • **verb 1** hold with an anchor 抛锚泊(船) **2** secure or fix firmly in position 固定；扎牢；系牢

anchorage /'æŋkərɪdʒ/ **noun** a place where ships may anchor safely 锚地；停泊处

anchorite /'æŋkəraɪt/ **noun** (in the past) a person who lived alone for religious reasons (旧时的)隐居修道士

anchorman /'æŋkəmæn/ or **anchorwoman** /'æŋkəwʊmən/ **noun** (plural **anchormen** or **anchorwomen**) a person who presents a live television or radio programme (电视或广播节目的)主持人

anchovy /'æntʃəvi/ **noun** (plural **anchovies**) a small fish of the herring family, with a strong flavor 鳀(一种鲱科小鱼，有浓重腥味)

ancien régime /ˌɒnsiæn reɪ'ʒiːm/ **noun** (plural **anciens régimes** /ˌɒnsiæn reɪ'ʒiːm/) a political or social system that has been replaced by a more modern one 旧制度

ancient /'eɪnʃənt/ **adjective 1** belonging to the very distant past 古代的 **2** very old 老旧的 • **noun** (**the ancients**) the people of ancient times 古代人

ancillary /æn'sɪləri/ **adjective 1** providing support 辅助的；补充的 **2** additional; extra 附属的，附加的

and /ænd, ənd, ən/ **conjunction 1** used to connect words, clauses, or sentences (用来连接单词、从句或句子)和，与，及 **2** (connecting two numbers) plus (连接两个数字)加

andante /æn'dænteɪ/ **adverb & adjective** Music【音乐】at a moderately slow pace 徐缓地(的)；用行板的(的)

androgynous /æn'drɒdʒənəs/ **adjective** partly male and partly female 雌雄同体的；半阴阳的 ■ **androgyny** noun.

android /'ændrɔɪd/ **noun** (in science fiction) a robot with a human appearance (科幻小说中的)人形机器人

anecdotal /ˌænɪk'dəʊtl/ **adjective** (of a story) not backed up by facts (故事)轶事的，趣闻的

anecdote /'ænɪkdəʊt/ **noun** a short entertaining story about a real incident or person 轶事；趣闻

anemia /ə'niːmiə/ US spelling of **ANAEMIA**. anaemia 的美式拼法

anemometer /ˌænɪ'mɒmɪtə(r)/ **noun** an instrument for measuring the speed of the wind 风速记录仪；风速计

anemone /ə'neməni/ **noun** a plant with brightly coloured flowers 银莲花

anesthetic /ˌænəs'θetɪk/ US spelling of **ANAESTHETIC**. anaesthetic 的美式拼法

aneurysm or **aneurism** /'ænjʊərɪzəm/ **noun** a swelling of the wall of an artery 动脉瘤

anew /ə'njuː/ **adverb 1** in a new or different way 不同地 **2** once more; again 重新；再一次

angel /'eɪndʒl/ **noun 1** a messenger of God, pictured as being of human form but with wings 天使；神的使者 **2** a very beautiful or good person (美丽、善良的)安琪儿；善人 ■ **angelic** adjective.

angelica /æn'dʒelɪkə/ **noun** a plant whose stalks are preserved in sugar and used in cake decoration 白芷，当归(可糖渍用作糕点配饰)

anger /'æŋgə(r)/ **noun** a strong feeling

of extreme displeasure 愤怒；生气
• **verb** (**angers, angering, angered**) make someone angry 使发怒；激怒

angina /æn'dʒaɪnə/ or **angina pectoris** /'pektərɪs/ **noun** severe pain in the chest caused by an inadequate supply of blood to the heart 心绞痛

angle¹ /ˈæŋgl/ **noun 1** the space between two lines or surfaces that meet 角 **2** a position from which something is viewed 视角；角度 **3** a way of thinking about something 观点；立场；角度
• **verb** (**angles, angling, angled**) **1** place something in a slanting position 使成角度放置；斜置 **2** present information from a particular point of view 从某角度报道；使(信息)带倾向性

angle² **verb** (**angles, angling, angled**) **1** fish with a rod and line 钓鱼；垂钓 **2** try to get something without asking for it directly 谋取；博取 ■ **angler** noun.

Anglican /ˈæŋglɪkən/ **adjective** relating to the Church of England 英格兰圣公会的 • **noun** a member of the Church of England 圣公会教徒 ■ **Anglicanism** noun.

anglicize or **anglicise** /ˈæŋglɪsaɪz/ **verb** (**anglicizes, anglicizing, anglicized**) make something English 使英国化；使英语化 ■ **anglicization** noun.

Anglophile /ˈæŋgləʊfaɪl/ **noun** a person who admires England or Britain 亲英者；崇英者

Anglo-Saxon /ˌæŋgləʊˈsæksn/ **noun 1** a person living in England between the 5th century and the Norman Conquest, whose ancestors came from north and west Europe 盎格鲁-撒克逊人 **2** the Old English language 盎格鲁-撒克逊语；古英语

angora /æŋ'gɔːrə/ **noun 1** a breed of cat, goat, or rabbit with long, soft hair 安哥拉猫；安哥拉山羊；安哥拉兔 **2** fabric made from the hair of the angora goat or rabbit 安哥拉山羊毛(或兔毛)织物

angostura /ˌæŋgə'stjʊərə/ **noun** the bitter bark of a South American tree, used as a flavouring 安古斯图拉树皮(产于南美，味苦，用作调味品)

angry /ˈæŋgri/ **adjective** (**angrier, angriest**) **1** feeling or showing anger 生气的；愤怒的；发怒的 **2** (of a wound or sore) red and swollen (伤口或患处)红肿发炎的 ■ **angrily** adverb.

angst /æŋst/ **noun** a strong feeling of anxiety about life in general (对生活的)忧虑，焦虑

angstrom /ˈæŋstrəm/ **noun** a unit of length equal to one hundred millionth of a centimetre 埃(长度单位,等于一厘米的百万分之一)

anguish /ˈæŋgwɪʃ/ **noun** severe pain or suffering 极度痛苦；剧痛 ■ **anguished** adjective.

angular /ˈæŋgjələ(r)/ **adjective 1** having angles or sharp corners 有角的；有尖角的 **2** (of a person) lean and bony (人)瘦骨嶙峋的 **3** placed or directed at an angle 成角度的 ■ **angularity** noun.

animal /ˈænɪml/ **noun 1** a living being that can move about of its own accord and has specialized sense organs and nervous system 动物 **2** a mammal, as opposed to a bird, reptile, fish, or insect 哺乳动物；兽 • **adjective 1** having to do with animals 动物的 **2** physical rather than spiritual or intellectual 肉体的 ■ **animality** noun.

animate **verb** /ˈænɪmeɪt/ (**animates, animating, animated**) **1** bring life or energy to 使有生命；使有活力 **2** make drawings or models into an animated film 将…制作成动画片 • **adjective** /ˈænɪmət/ living 有生命的 ■ **animator** noun.

animated /ˈænɪmeɪtɪd/ **adjective 1** lively 活生生的；生气勃勃的 **2** (of a film) made using animation (影片)动画的 ■ **animatedly** adverb.

animation /ˌænɪˈmeɪʃn/ **noun 1** liveliness 生气；活力 **2** the technique of filming a sequence of drawings or positions of models to give the appearance of movement 动画片制作技术 **3** the creation of moving images by means of a computer (电脑)动画制作

animism /ˈænɪmɪzəm/ **noun** the belief that all things in nature have a soul 泛灵论；万物有灵论 ■ **animist** noun.

animosity /ˌænɪˈmɒsəti/ **noun** (plural **animosities**) hatred or strong dislike 仇恨；憎恶；敌意

animus /ˈænɪməs/ **noun** hatred or dislike 仇恨；憎恶；敌意

anion /ˈænaɪən/ **noun** an ion with a negative charge 阴离子；带负电荷的离子

aniseed /ˈænɪsiːd/ **noun** the seed of the **anise plant**, used as a flavouring 洋茴香(茴芹种子，用作调味品)

ankle /ˈæŋkl/ **noun** the joint connecting the foot with the leg 踝关节

anklet /ˈæŋklət/ **noun** a chain or band worn round the ankle 脚镯；踝环

annals /ˈænlz/ **plural noun** a historical record of events made year by year 编年史

anneal /əˈniːl/ **verb** heat metal or glass and allow it to cool slowly, so as to toughen it 使(金属或玻璃)退火

annex verb /əˈneks/ **1** take possession of another country's land 吞并，占取(领土) **2** add something as an extra part 附加；添加；附带 • noun (also **annexe**) /ˈæneks/ (plural **annexes**) **1** a building attached to or near to a main building 附属建筑物；配楼 **2** an addition to a document (文件的)附件，附录 ■ **annexation** noun.

annihilate /əˈnaɪəleɪt/ **verb** (annihilates, annihilating, annihilated) destroy completely 毁灭，彻底消灭 ■ **annihilation** noun.

anniversary /ˌænɪˈvɜːsəri/ **noun** (plural **anniversaries**) the date on which an event took place in a previous year 周年纪念日

annotate /ˈænəteɪt/ **verb** (annotates, annotating, annotated) add explanatory notes to 给…加注解 ■ **annotation** noun.

announce /əˈnaʊns/ **verb** (announces, announcing, announced) **1** make a public statement about 宣布；宣告 **2** be a sign of 是…的迹象；显示 ■ **announcer** noun.

announcement /əˈnaʊnsmənt/ **noun** a public statement 通告；布告

annoy /əˈnɔɪ/ **verb** make someone slightly angry 使恼怒；使烦恼 ■ **annoyance** noun.

annual /ˈænjuəl/ **adjective 1** happening once a year 年度的；一年一次的 **2** calculated over or covering a year 全年的 **3** (of a plant) living for a year or less (植物)一年生的 • noun a book published once a year 年报；年刊；年鉴 ■ **annually** adverb.

annuity /əˈnjuːəti/ **noun** (plural **annuities**) a fixed sum of money paid to someone each year 年金

annul /əˈnʌl/ **verb** (annuls, annulling, annulled) declare a law, marriage, or other legal contract to be no longer valid 宣告…无效；废除；取消 ■ **annulment** noun.

annular /ˈænjʊlə(r)/ **adjective** technical 【术语】ring-shaped 环状的

annunciation /əˌnʌnsɪˈeɪʃn/ **noun** (**the Annunciation**) (in Christian belief) the announcement by the angel Gabriel to the Virgin Mary that she was to be the mother of Jesus (基督教信仰中的)天使传报(天使加百列向马利亚传报她将做基督的母亲)

anode /ˈænəʊd/ **noun** an electrode with a positive charge 阳极

anodized or **anodised** /ˈænədaɪzd/ **adjective** (of metal) coated with a protective layer by the action of an electric current (金属)阳极氧化过的

anodyne /ˈænədaɪn/ **adjective**

not likely to cause offence or disagreement 温和的；不得罪人的 • noun a painkilling drug 止痛药；镇痛剂

anoint /ə'nɔɪnt/ verb dab or smear water or oil on someone as part of a religious ceremony (作为宗教仪式的一部分)给…涂油，给…抹油

anomalous /ə'nɒmələs/ adjective differing from what is standard or normal 不规则的；反常的，异常的

anomaly /ə'nɒməli/ noun (plural **anomalies**) something that is different from what is normal or expected 不规则；反常事物；异常事物

anon /ə'nɒn/ adverb old use【旧】soon; shortly 不久；很快

anonymous /ə'nɒnɪməs/ adjective **1** having a name that is not publicly known 匿名的 **2** having no outstanding or individual features 无特色的；无个性特征的 ■ **anonymity** noun **anonymously** adverb.

anorak /'ænəræk/ noun a waterproof jacket with a hood 带风帽的防水夹克

anorexia /ænə'reksiə/ or **anorexia nervosa** /nɜː'vəʊsə/ noun a disorder in which a person refuses to eat because they are afraid of becoming fat 食欲缺乏；厌食 ■ **anorexic** adjective & noun.

another /ə'nʌðə(r)/ determiner & pronoun **1** one more 再一个(的)；又一个(的) **2** different from the one already mentioned 不同的(一个)

answer /'ɑːnsə(r)/ noun **1** something said or written in reaction to a question or statement 回答，答复 **2** the solution to a problem 答案；解决办法 • verb (**answers**, **answering**, **answered**) **1** give an answer 回答；答复 **2** (**answer back**) give a cheeky reply 回嘴；顶嘴 **3** (**answer to**) have to explain your actions or decisions to someone 向(某人)负责 **4** (**answer for**) be responsible for the things you

do 对(某事)负责 **5** meet a need 适应，适合(需要) □ **answering machine** a machine which gives a pre-recorded reply to a telephone call and can record a message from the caller 电话答录机

answerable /'ɑːnsərəbl/ adjective **1** (**answerable to**) having to explain to someone why you have done the things you have done 向(某人)负责的 **2** (**answerable for**) responsible for something 为(某事)承担责任的

ant /ænt/ noun a small insect that lives with many others in an organized group 蚂蚁

antacid /ænt'æsɪd/ adjective (of a medicine) reducing excess acid in the stomach (药物)解酸的，中和酸的

antagonism /æn'tægənɪzəm/ noun the expression of hostile feelings 敌对；敌意；对立

antagonist /æn'tægənɪst/ noun an opponent or enemy 对抗者；对手；敌手 ■ **antagonistic** adjective.

antagonize or **antagonise** /æn'tægənaɪz/ verb (**antagonizes**, **antagonizing**, **antagonized**) make someone feel hostile 使对抗；使对立；引起敌意

Antarctic /æn'tɑːktɪk/ adjective relating to the region surrounding the South Pole 南极的；南极地区的

✔ 拼写指南 remember the c after the r:Antarctic. 记住拼写 Antarctic 中 r 后的 c。

anteater /'ænti:tə(r)/ noun an animal with a long snout and sticky tongue, that feeds on ants and termites 食蚁兽

antecedent /ænti'si:dnt/ noun **1** a thing that exists or comes before another 前事；前情 **2** (**antecedents**) a person's ancestors 祖先；先人 • adjective coming before in time or order 先前的

antedate /ænti'deɪt/ verb (**antedates**,

antedating, antedated) come or exist before something else 先于；早于

antediluvian /ˌæntɪdɪˈluːvɪən/ **adjective 1** belonging to the time before the biblical Flood (《圣经》记载的)大洪水以前的 **2** very old-fashioned 陈旧的；早已过时的

antelope /ˈæntɪləʊp/ **noun** a swift deer-like animal found in Africa and Asia 羚羊

antenatal /ˌæntiˈneɪtl/ **adjective** Brit. 【英】before birth; during pregnancy 产前的；怀孕期的；怀孕的

antenna /ænˈtenə/ **noun 1** (plural **antennae** /ænˈteniː/) each of a pair of long, thin feelers on the heads of some insects and shellfish 触角；触须 **2** (plural **antennae** or **antennas**) an aerial 天线

anterior /ænˈtɪərɪə(r)/ **adjective** at or near the front 位于前部的；前面的；头部附近的

anteroom /ˈæntɪrʊm/ **noun** a small room leading to a more important one (连接正厅的)前厅

anthem /ˈænθəm/ **noun 1** a song chosen by a country to express patriotic feelings 国歌 **2** a musical setting of a religious work that is sung by a choir during a church service (宗教)圣歌

anther /ˈænθə(r)/ **noun** the part of a flower's stamen that contains the pollen 花药

anthill /ˈænthɪl/ **noun** a mound of earth made by ants when they build a nest 蚁冢；蚁垤

anthology /ænˈθɒlədʒi/ **noun** (plural **anthologies**) a collection of poems or other pieces of writing or music (诗歌、文章或乐曲的)选集

anthracite /ˈænθrəsaɪt/ **noun** hard coal that burns without producing much flame and smoke 无烟煤

anthrax /ˈænθræks/ **noun** a serious disease of sheep and cattle, that can be passed to humans 炭疽(牛、羊患的严重疾病，能传染给人)

anthropoid /ˈænθrəpɔɪd/ **adjective** having to do with apes that resemble human beings in form, such as gorillas or chimpanzees (猿猴)类人的，似人的

anthropology /ˌænθrəˈpɒlədʒi/ **noun** the study of human origins, societies, and cultures 人类学 ■ **anthropological** adjective **anthropologist** noun.

anthropomorphic /ˌænθrəpəˈmɔːfɪk/ **adjective** treating a god, animal, or object as if they were human (神、动物或物体)人格化的，拟人的

antibiotic /ˌæntibaɪˈɒtɪk/ **noun** a medicine that kills bacteria 抗菌素；抗生素

antibody /ˈæntibɒdi/ **noun** (plural **antibodies**) a protein produced in the blood to react against harmful substances (血液中的)抗体

Antichrist /ˈæntikraɪst/ **noun** an enemy of Christ that some people believe will appear before the end of the world (某些人认为将在世界末日前出现的)敌基督

anticipate /ænˈtɪsɪpeɪt/ **verb** (**anticipates, anticipating, anticipated**) **1** be aware of and prepared for a future event 预料(某事件) **2** look forward to 期望；期盼 **3** do something earlier than someone else 先于(别人)采取行动；早于(别人)做 ■ **anticipation** noun **anticipatory** adjective.

anticlimax /ˌæntiˈklaɪmæks/ **noun** a disappointing end to an exciting series of events 突降；扫兴的结尾 ■ **anticlimactic** adjective.

anticlockwise /ˌæntiˈklɒkwaɪz/ **adverb & adjective** Brit. 【英】in the opposite direction to the way in which a clock's hands move round 逆时针地(的)

A

antics /'æntɪks/ **plural noun** silly or amusing behaviour 蠢行；滑稽的行为；噱头

anticyclone /ˌænti'saɪkləʊn/ **noun** an area of high atmospheric pressure around which air slowly circulates, usually resulting in calm, fine weather 反气旋；高气压

antidote /'æntɪdəʊt/ **noun** a medicine taken to undo the effect of a poison 解毒药；解毒剂

antifreeze /'æntɪfriːz/ **noun** a liquid added to water to prevent it from freezing, used in car radiators (用在汽车散热器中的)防冻剂，抗凝剂

antigen /'æntɪdʒən/ **noun** a harmful substance which causes the body to produce antibodies 抗原(导致人体产生抗体的有害物质)

anti-hero /'æntihɪərəʊ/ **noun** a central character in a story, film, or play who is either ordinary or unpleasant 非正派主角，反英雄

antihistamine /ˌænti'hɪstəmiːn/ **noun** a drug that is used in treating allergies 抗组胺药(用于治疗过敏)

antimacassar /ˌæntimə'kæsə(r)/ **noun** a decorative piece of cloth put over the back of a chair to protect it from grease and dirt (椅背的)套，罩

antimatter /'æntimætə(r)/ **noun** Physics 【物理】 matter consisting of particles with the same mass as those of normal matter but opposite electric or magnetic properties 反物质

antimony /'æntɪməni/ **noun** a brittle silvery-white metallic element (金属元素)锑

antipathy /æn'tɪpəθi/ **noun** (plural **antipathies**) a strong feeling of dislike 反感；厌恶 ■ **antipathetic** adjective.

antiperspirant /ˌænti'pɜːspərənt/ **noun** a substance applied to the skin to prevent or reduce sweating 止汗剂

antiphonal /æn'tɪfənl/ **adjective** sung or recited alternately by two groups 轮流吟唱的；交替背诵的

Antipodes /æn'tɪpədiːz/ **plural noun** (**the Antipodes**) Australia and New Zealand 澳大利亚和新西兰 ■ **Antipodean** adjective & noun.

antiquarian /ˌænti'kweəriən/ **adjective** relating to the collection or study of antiques or rare books 古文物收藏的；古文物研究的

antiquated /'æntɪkweɪtɪd/ **adjective** very old fashioned or out of date 老式的；过时的

antique /æn'tiːk/ **noun** an object or piece of furniture that is valuable because of its age 古董；古玩；古器 • **adjective** having value because of its age 古董的

antiquity /æn'tɪkwəti/ **noun** (plural **antiquities**) **1** the distant past 古代 **2** an object from the distant past 古物

anti-Semitism /ˌænti'semətɪzəm/ **noun** hostility to or prejudice against Jews 反犹主义；排犹主义；仇犹情绪 ■ **anti-Semite** noun **anti-Semitic** adjective.

antiseptic /ˌænti'septɪk/ **adjective** preventing the growth of germs that cause disease or infection 抗菌的；防腐的 • **noun** an antiseptic substance 抗菌剂；防腐剂

antisocial /ˌænti'səʊʃl/ **adjective** **1** behaving in a way that is unacceptable or annoying to other people 反社会的；令人讨厌的 **2** not wanting to mix with other people 不爱交际的；孤僻的

antithesis /æn'tɪθəsɪs/ **noun** (plural **antitheses** /æn'tɪθəsiːz/) **1** a person or thing that is the direct opposite of another 对立面 **2** the putting together of contrasting ideas or words to produce an effect in writing or speaking 对比法；对偶

antithetical /ˌænti'θetɪkl/ **adjective** opposed to each other 对立的；正相

反的

antler /ˈæntlə(r)/ **noun** each of a pair of branched horns on the head of an adult male deer (雄)鹿角；鹿茸

antonym /ˈæntənɪm/ **noun** a word opposite in meaning to another 反义词

anus /ˈeɪnəs/ **noun** the opening through which solid waste matter leaves the body 肛门

anvil /ˈænvɪl/ **noun** an iron block on which metal is hammered and shaped 铁砧

anxiety /æŋˈzaɪəti/ **noun** (plural **anxieties**) an anxious feeling or state 焦虑；挂虑

anxious /ˈæŋkʃəs/ **adjective 1** feeling worried or nervous 焦虑的；担心的 **2** very eager 渴望的；急切的 ■ **anxiously** adverb.

any /ˈeni/ **determiner & pronoun 1** one or some, no matter how much or how many 一个；一些；若干 **2** whichever or whatever you choose 任何一个 • **adverb** at all 根本

anybody /ˈenibɒdi/ **pronoun** anyone 任何人

anyhow /ˈenihaʊ/ **adverb 1** anyway 不管怎样；无论如何 **2** in a careless or haphazard way 随随便便地；杂乱无章地

anyone /ˈeniwʌn/ **pronoun** any person or people 任何人

anything /ˈeniθɪŋ/ **pronoun** a thing of any kind 任何东西

anyway /ˈeniweɪ/ **adverb 1** said to emphasize something just said or to change the subject (用于强调或改变话题)无论如何，反正 **2** nevertheless 尽管，不过

anywhere /ˈeniweə(r)/ **adverb** in or to any place 在(或往)什么地方，在(或往)任何地方 • **pronoun** any place 任何地方

aorta /eɪˈɔːtə/ **noun** the main artery supplying blood from the heart to the rest of the body 主动脉

apace /əˈpeɪs/ **adverb** literary 【文】 quickly 飞快地；迅速地

apart /əˈpɑːt/ **adverb 1** separated by a distance 相隔；分离 **2** into pieces 成碎片 ▢ **apart from 1** except for 除…外 **2** as well as 除…外(还有)

apartheid /əˈpɑːtheɪt/ **noun** the official system of racial segregation formerly in force in South Africa (南非过去实行的)种族隔离(制度)

apartment /əˈpɑːtmənt/ **noun 1** a flat 公寓套房 **2** (**apartments**) a private set of rooms in a large house (大房子里的)套房

✔ 拼写指南 only one *p*: apartment.
apartment 中只有一个 p。

apathetic /ˌæpəˈθetɪk/ **adjective** not interested or enthusiastic 不感兴趣的；冷淡的，漠然的

apathy /ˈæpəθi/ **noun** general lack of interest or enthusiasm 无兴趣；冷淡；漠然

apatosaurus /ˌæpætəˈsɔːrəs/ **noun** a huge plant-eating dinosaur with a long neck and tail; a brontosaurus 雷龙(大型食草恐龙，长颈长尾)

ape /eɪp/ **noun** an animal related to the monkeys but with no tail, such as a chimpanzee or gorilla 无尾猿，类人猿(如黑猩猩、大猩猩) • **verb** (**apes**, **aping**, **aped**) imitate someone 模仿

aperitif /əˌperəˈtiːf/ **noun** an alcoholic drink taken before a meal (饭前)开胃酒

aperture /ˈæpətʃə(r)/ **noun 1** an opening, hole, or gap 孔；缝隙；缺口 **2** the variable opening by which light enters a camera (照相设备上的)孔径

apex /ˈeɪpeks/ **noun** (plural **apexes** or **apices** /ˈeɪpɪsiːz/) the top or highest point of something 顶；顶点

aphid /ˈeɪfɪd/ **noun** a small insect that feeds on the sap of plants 蚜虫

aphorism /ˈæfərɪzm/ **noun** a short clever phrase which makes a true point 格言；警句

aphrodisiac /ˌæfrəˈdɪziæk/ **noun** a food, drink, or drug that makes people want to have sex 催欲剂；春药

apiary /ˈeɪpɪəri/ **noun** (plural **apiaries**) a place where bees are kept 养蜂场；蜂房

apiece /əˈpiːs/ **adverb** for or by each one 每；各

aplenty /əˈplenti/ **adjective** in large amounts 大量的；充裕的；绰绰有余的

aplomb /əˈplɒm/ **noun** calm self-confidence 镇定；沉着

apocalypse /əˈpɒkəlɪps/ **noun** a terrible event in which everything is destroyed 大动乱，大灾变

apocalyptic /əˌpɒkəˈlɪptɪk/ **adjective** having to do with or resembling the destruction of the world 大动乱的；大灾变的

apocryphal /əˈpɒkrɪfl/ **adjective** (of a story or piece of information) widely known but unlikely to be true (故事或信息)真实性可疑的，杜撰的

apogee /ˈæpədʒiː/ **noun 1** the highest point reached 最高点；顶峰 **2** the point in the orbit of the moon or a satellite at which it is furthest from the earth 远地点(月球或卫星运行轨道上与地球相距最远的点)

apolitical /ˌeɪpəˈlɪtɪkl/ **adjective** not interested or involved in politics 对政治不感兴趣的，不关心政治的，与政治无关的

apologetic /əˌpɒləˈdʒetɪk/ **adjective** showing that you are sorry for making a mistake or doing something wrong 道歉的，认错的 ■ **apologetically adverb.**

apologia /ˌæpəˈləʊdʒiə/ **noun** a formal defence of opinions or actions 辩解；辩护

apologist /əˈpɒlədʒɪst/ **noun** a person who defends something controversial 辩解者；辩护者

apologize or **apologise** /əˈpɒlədʒaɪz/ **verb** (**apologizes**, **apologizing**, **apologized**) say that you are

sorry for making a mistake or doing something wrong 道歉；认错

apology /əˈpɒlədʒi/ **noun** (plural **apologies**) **1** a statement in which someone apologizes for a mistake made or for harm done 道歉，认错 **2** (**an apology for**) a very bad example of …的勉强代用品；…的权充代替物

apoplectic /ˌæpəˈplektɪk/ **adjective 1** very angry 大怒的 **2** old use 【旧】relating to apoplexy (a stroke) 中风的，卒中的

apoplexy /ˈæpəpleksi/ **noun** (plural **apoplexies**) old use 【旧】 a stroke 中风，卒中

apostasy /əˈpɒstəsi/ **noun** the abandoning of a belief or principle 叛教，变节

apostate /əˈpɒsteɪt/ **noun** a person who abandons a belief or principle 叛教者；变节者

apostle /əˈpɒsl/ **noun 1** (**Apostle**) each of the twelve chief disciples of Jesus 使徒(耶稣的十二门徒之一) **2** a person who strongly supports a policy, cause, etc. (某一政策、事业等的)倡导者，热心追随者

apostrophe /əˈpɒstrəfi/ **noun** a punctuation mark (') used to show that something belongs to someone or to show that letters or numbers have been missed out 撇号(表示所有格或省略的记号)

apothecary /əˈpɒθəkəri/ **noun** (plural **apothecaries**) old use 【旧】 a person who prepared and sold medicines 药剂师；药商

apotheosis /əˌpɒθiˈəʊsɪs/ **noun** (plural **apotheoses** /əˌpɒθiˈəʊsiːz/) the highest level in the development of something 极致；顶点

appal /əˈpɔːl/ (US spelling 【美拼作】 **appall**) **verb** (**appals**, **appalling**, **appalled**) **1** make someone feel horror and dismay 使惊恐，使惊骇 **2** (**appalling**) informal 【非正式】 very bad 糟糕的，不像话的 ■ **appallingly**

adverb.

apparatus /ˌæpəˈreɪtəs/ **noun** (plural **apparatuses**) the equipment needed for a particular activity or task 器械；仪器；设备

apparel /əˈpærəl/ **noun** formal 【正式】 clothing 衣服；服饰

apparent /əˈpærənt/ **adjective 1** clearly seen or understood; obvious 显而易见的；明白易懂的；显然的 **2** seeming real, but not necessarily so 表面上的；貌似的；未必真实的 ■ **apparently** adverb.

✔ 拼写指南 -ent, not -ant: appar**ent**. apparent 中的 -ent 不要拼作 -ant。

apparition /ˌæpəˈrɪʃn/ **noun** a remarkable thing making a sudden appearance, especially a ghost 鬼；幽灵；幻影

appeal /əˈpiːl/ **verb 1** ask earnestly or formally for something 呼吁；恳求 **2** be attractive or interesting 有吸引力；有趣 **3** ask a higher court of law to reverse the decision of a lower court 上诉；申诉 ■ **noun 1** an act of appealing 呼吁；恳求；申诉 **2** the quality of being attractive or interesting 吸引力；感染力

appealing /əˈpiːlɪŋ/ **adjective** attractive or interesting 动人的；吸引人的；有感染力的 ■ **appealingly** adverb.

appear /əˈpɪə(r)/ **verb 1** come into view or start to exist 出现；露面；起诉 **2** seem 看来好像；似乎 **3** present yourself as a performer or in a law court 出演；出庭

appearance /əˈpɪərəns/ **noun 1** the way that someone or something looks or seems 外观；外貌；外表 **2** an act of appearing 出现；露面；出演；出庭

appease /əˈpiːz/ **verb** (**appeases, appeasing, appeased**) make someone calm or less hostile by agreeing to their demands (通过满足对方要求来)抚慰，安抚 ■ **appeasement** noun.

appellation /ˌæpəˈleɪʃn/ **noun** formal 【正式】 a name or title 名称；称号；称呼

append /əˈpend/ **verb** add something to the end of a document 附加；增补

appendage /əˈpendɪdʒ/ **noun** a thing that is attached to something larger or more important 附属物；附加物

appendicitis /əˌpendəˈsaɪtɪs/ **noun** inflammation of the appendix 阑尾炎

appendix /əˈpendɪks/ **noun** (plural **appendices** /əˈpendɪsiːz/ or **appendixes**) **1** a small tube of tissue attached to the lower end of the large intestine 阑尾 **2** a section of additional information at the end of a book (书末的)附录

appertain /ˌæpəˈteɪn/ **verb** (**appertain to**) formal 【正式】 relate to 与…有关联

appetite /ˈæpɪtaɪt/ **noun 1** a natural desire and physical need for food 胃口；食欲 **2** a liking or desire for something 喜好；欲望

appetizer or **appetiser** /ˈæpɪtaɪzə(r)/ **noun** a small dish of food or a drink taken before a meal to stimulate the appetite (餐前)开胃小吃，开胃饮料

appetizing or **appetising** /ˈæpɪtaɪzɪŋ/ **adjective** stimulating the appetite 开胃的；刺激食欲的

applaud /əˈplɔːd/ **verb 1** show approval by clapping 鼓掌(表示赞许)；喝彩 **2** say that you approve of or admire something 称赞；赞许；赞成

applause /əˈplɔːz/ **noun** clapping 鼓掌；喝彩

apple /ˈæpl/ **noun** a round fruit with green or red skin and crisp flesh 苹果 □ **the apple of your eye** a person who you are very fond of and proud of 掌上明珠；心肝宝贝

appliance /əˈplaɪəns/ **noun** an electrically operated machine for use in the home 家用电器

applicable /'æplɪkəbl/ adjective relevant to someone or something 相关的；适用的 ■ **applicability** noun.

applicant /'æplɪkənt/ noun a person who applies for something 申请人

application /ˌæplɪ'keɪʃn/ noun **1** a formal request to an authority 申请(书) **2** the action of applying something 申请 **3** practical use or relevance 应用；关联 **4** continued effort 持续的努力；专注

applicator /'æplɪkeɪtə(r)/ noun a device for putting something into or on to something 敷抹器；涂抹器

applied /ə'plaɪd/ adjective (of a subject of study) used in a practical way (学科)实用的，应用的

appliqué /ə'pliːkeɪ/ noun decorative needlework in which fabric shapes are fixed on to a background 针织嵌花

apply /ə'plaɪ/ verb (applies, applying, applied) **1** make a formal request for something 申请；请求 **2** bring into operation or use 应用；使用 **3** be relevant 有关；适用 **4** put a substance on a surface 涂；敷；施 **5** (apply yourself) concentrate on what you are doing 使(自己)专注于

appoint /ə'pɔɪnt/ verb **1** give someone a job or role 任命；委任 **2** decide on a time for something 确定，指定(时间) **3** (appointed) equipped or furnished in a particular way (以特定方式)布置的，陈设的

appointment /ə'pɔɪntmənt/ noun **1** an arrangement to meet 约会；约定 **2** the appointing of someone to a job 任命；委任 **3** (appointments) furniture or fittings 家具；陈设

apportion /ə'pɔːʃn/ verb share out 分配；分摊 ■ **apportionment** noun.

apposite /'æpəzɪt/ adjective appropriate 合适的；恰当的

appraisal /ə'preɪzl/ noun **1** an assessment of the quality or value of something 估量；估计；估价 **2** a formal assessment of an employee's performance (对员工工作表现的)考评，评估

appraise /ə'preɪz/ verb (appraises, appraising, appraised) assess the quality or value of something 估量；估计；估价

appreciable /ə'priːʃəbl/ adjective large or important enough to be noticed (大得)可以觉察到的；足以认为重要的；可观的 ■ **appreciably** adverb.

appreciate /ə'priːʃieɪt/ verb (appreciates, appreciating, appreciated) **1** recognize the value of something 欣赏；赏识 **2** understand a situation fully 充分了解；领会 **3** be grateful for 为…表示感激 **4** rise in value or price 升值；涨价

appreciation /əˌpriːʃi'eɪʃn/ noun **1** recognition of the value of something 欣赏；赏识；重视 **2** gratitude for something 感激；感谢 **3** a piece of writing in which the qualities of a person or their work are discussed (对人或作品的)评论文字，书面评价 **4** an increase in value 升值；增值

appreciative /ə'priːʃətɪv/ adjective feeling or showing gratitude or pleasure 感激的；感谢的；赞赏的 ■ **appreciatively** adverb.

apprehend /ˌæprɪ'hend/ verb **1** arrest someone for doing something wrong 逮捕；拘押 **2** understand something 领会；理解

apprehension /ˌæprɪ'henʃn/ noun **1** a feeling of worry or fear about what might happen 忧虑；担心；恐惧 **2** understanding 理解

apprehensive /ˌæprɪ'hensɪv/ adjective worried or afraid about what might happen 忧虑的；担心的；疑惧的 ■ **apprehensively** adverb.

apprentice /ə'prentɪs/ noun a person learning a skilled trade from an employer 学徒；徒弟 • verb (be apprenticed) be employed as an apprentice 做学徒 ■ **apprenticeship** noun.

apprise /ə'praɪz/ **verb** (**apprises**, **apprising**, **apprised**) (**apprise someone of**) make someone aware of 通知；告知

approach /ə'prəʊtʃ/ **verb 1** come near to 接近，靠近 **2** go to someone with a proposal or request 向…建议；找…要求 **3** deal with something in a certain way (以某种方式)处理，对付 • **noun 1** a way of dealing with something (处理事情的)方式，方法 **2** a proposal or request 建议；要求 **3** the action of approaching 接近，靠近 **4** a way leading to a place 路径；通路

approachable /ə'prəʊtʃəbl/ **adjective 1** friendly and easy to talk to 友好的；易攀谈的 **2** able to be reached from a particular direction 可接近的；可通达的

approbation /ˌæprə'beɪʃn/ **noun** approval 批准；赞成

appropriate adjective /ə'prəʊpriət/ suitable or right in the circumstances 适合的；恰当的 • **verb** /ə'prəʊprieɪt/ (**appropriates**, **appropriating**, **appropriated**) **1** take something for your own use without permission 挪用；侵吞 **2** set money aside for a special purpose 拨(款项)供专用 ■ **appropriately** adverb **appropriation** noun.

approval /ə'pruːvl/ **noun 1** a feeling that something is good or acceptable 赞成；同意 **2** official permission or agreement 批准；认可

approve /ə'pruːv/ **verb** (**approves**, **approving**, **approved**) **1** feel that something is good or acceptable 赞成；同意 **2** officially accept something as satisfactory 批准；认可

approximate adjective /ə'prɒksɪmət/ almost but not completely accurate 近似的；大概的；接近的 • **verb** /ə'prɒksɪmeɪt/ (**approximates**, **approximating**, **approximated**) come close or be similar to 接近；近似 ■ **approximately** adverb **approximation** noun.

appurtenances /ə'pɜːtɪnənsɪz/ **plural noun** the things you need for a particular activity (某种活动的)附属物，附加物

après-ski /ˌæpreɪ'skiː/ **noun** parties and entertainments which take place after a day's skiing 滑雪后的社交娱乐活动

apricot /'eɪprɪkɒt/ **noun** an orange-yellow fruit resembling a small peach 杏

April /'eɪprəl/ **noun** the fourth month of the year 四月

a priori /ˌeɪ praɪ'ɔːraɪ/ **adjective & adverb** using facts that are known to be true in order to decide what an unknown effect or result will be 演绎的；推理的；以演绎方式；经推理

apron /'eɪprən/ **noun 1** a garment tied over the front of clothes to keep them clean 围裙 **2** an area on an airfield used for manoeuvring or parking aircraft 停机坪 **3** a strip of stage extending in front of the curtain 台口(指舞台幕布前的部分)

apropos /ˌæprə'pəʊ/ **preposition** (**apropos of**) with reference to 关于；至于

apse /æps/ **noun** a recess with a domed or arched roof at the end of a church (教堂的)半圆凹室

apt /æpt/ **adjective 1** suitable for the occasion; appropriate 恰当的；适当的 **2** (**apt to**) tending to 易于…的；有…倾向的 **3** quick to learn 聪明的；学得快的 ■ **aptly** adverb.

aptitude /'æptɪtjuːd/ **noun** a natural ability 天资；天赋

aqualung /'ækwəlʌŋ/ **noun** a piece of equipment worn by divers to enable them to breathe underwater (潜水员用的)水肺，水中呼吸器

aquamarine /ˌækwəməˈriːn/ **noun 1** a bluish-green precious stone 海蓝宝石；水蓝宝石 **2** a light bluish-green colour 浅绿色；水绿色

aquaplane /ˈækwəpleɪn/ **verb** (**aquaplanes**, **aquaplaning**, **aquaplaned**) (of a vehicle) slide uncontrollably on a wet surface (车辆)在潮湿路面上打滑

aquarium /əˈkweəriəm/ **noun** (plural **aquaria** /əˈkweəriə/ or **aquariums**) a water-filled glass tank in which fish and other water creatures are kept 水族箱

Aquarius /əˈkweəriəs/ **noun** a sign of the zodiac (the Water Carrier), 21 January–20 February 宝瓶宫(黄道十二宫之一)

aquatic /əˈkwætɪk/ **adjective 1** relating to water 水的 **2** living in or near water 水生的；水栖的

aqueduct /ˈækwɪdʌkt/ **noun** a long channel or bridge-like structure for carrying water across country 高架渠；渡槽；桥管

aqueous /ˈeɪkwɪəs/ **adjective** relating to or containing water 水的；含水的

aquiline /ˈækwɪlaɪn/ **adjective 1** (of a person's nose) curved like an eagle's beak (人的鼻子)钩状的，鹰钩鼻的 **2** like an eagle 似鹰的

Arab /ˈærəb/ **noun** a member of a people inhabiting much of the Middle East and North Africa 阿拉伯人 ■ **Arabian** noun & adjective.

arabesque /ˌærəˈbesk/ **noun 1** a ballet position in which one leg is extended horizontally backwards and the arms are outstretched 阿拉贝斯克舞姿(一种芭蕾舞姿，单腿直立，另一腿向后抬起，双臂伸展) **2** an ornamental design of intertwined flowing lines 涡卷线状图案

Arabic /ˈærəbɪk/ **noun** the language of the Arabs, written from right to left 阿拉伯语(文字从右至左书写) • **adjective** relating to the Arabs or Arabic 阿拉伯人的；阿拉伯语的 □ **Arabic numeral** any of the numerals 0, 1, 2, 3, 4, 5, 6, 7, 8, and 9 阿拉伯数字

arable /ˈærəbl/ **adjective** (of land) able to be used for growing crops (土地)可耕的，适于耕种的

arachnid /əˈræknɪd/ **noun** a creature of a class including spiders, scorpions, mites, and ticks 蛛形纲动物(包括蜘蛛、蝎子、螨、扁虱等)

arachnophobia /əˌræknəˈfəʊbiə/ **noun** extreme fear of spiders 恐蜘蛛症

arbiter /ˈɑːbɪtə(r)/ **noun 1** a person who settles a dispute 仲裁人；公断人 **2** a person who has influence in a particular area (某一领域的)权威人士

arbitrary /ˈɑːbɪtrəri/ **adjective 1** not seeming to be based on any plan or system 任意的；武断的；随心所欲的 **2** (of power) used without restraint (权力)专制的，专断的 ■ **arbitrarily** adverb.

arbitrate /ˈɑːbɪtreɪt/ **verb** (**arbitrates**, **arbitrating**, **arbitrated**) act as an arbitrator to settle a dispute 进行仲裁；作出公断 ■ **arbitration** noun.

arbitrator /ˈɑːbɪtreɪtə(r)/ **noun** a person or organization appointed to settle a dispute 仲裁人；公断人

arboreal /ɑːˈbɔːriəl/ **adjective 1** living in trees 生活在树上的；树栖的 **2** relating to trees 树木的

arboretum /ˌɑːbəˈriːtəm/ **noun** (plural **arboretums** or **arboreta** /ˌɑːbəˈriːtə/) a garden in which trees are grown for study and display to the public 树木园

arbour /ˈɑːbə(r)/ (US spelling 【美拼作】 arbor) **noun** a shady place in a garden, with a canopy of trees or climbing plants 棚架；凉棚

arc /ɑːk/ **noun 1** a curve forming part of the circumference of a circle 弧 **2** a curving movement through the air (空中划过的)弧线 **3** a glowing electrical discharge between two points 电弧;弧光 • verb (arcs, arcing, arced) move in an arc 作弧线运动

arcade /ɑːˈkeɪd/ noun 1 a series of arches supporting a roof or wall 拱廊 2 a covered walk with shops along the sides (旁边设有商店的)拱廊人行道

arcane /ɑːˈkeɪn/ adjective secret and mysterious 秘密的;神秘的

arch¹ /ɑːtʃ/ noun 1 a curved structure spanning an opening or supporting the weight of a bridge or roof 拱;拱门;拱形结构 2 the inner side of the foot 足背;足弓 • verb form an arch 成拱形;成弓形

arch² adjective suggesting in a playful way that you know more than you are revealing 调皮的;淘气的 ■ archly adverb.

archaeology /ˌɑːkiˈɒlədʒi/ (US spelling 【美拼作】 archeology) noun the study of ancient history through the examination of objects, structures,and materials dug up from old sites 考古学 ■ archaeological adjective archaeologist noun.

archaic /ɑːˈkeɪɪk/ adjective 1 very old or old-fashioned 过时的;陈旧的 2 belonging to an earlier period 古代的;古老的 ■ archaism noun.

archangel /ˈɑːkeɪndʒl/ noun an angel of high rank 大天使;天使长

archbishop /ˌɑːtʃˈbɪʃəp/ noun a bishop of the highest rank 大主教

archdeacon /ˌɑːtʃˈdiːkən/ noun a senior Christian priest 会吏长(基督教高级教士)

arch-enemy /ˌɑːtʃˈenɪmɪ/ noun a chief enemy 主要敌人

archer /ˈɑːtʃə(r)/ noun a person who shoots with a bow and arrows 弓箭手;射箭运动员 ■ archery noun.

archetype /ˈɑːkitaɪp/ noun 1 a very typical example 典型 2 an original model which others follow 原型 ■ archetypal adjective.

archipelago /ˌɑːkɪˈpeləɡəʊ/ noun (plural **archipelagos** or **archipelagoes**) a group of many islands and the sea surrounding them 群岛;列岛

architect /ˈɑːkɪtekt/ noun 1 a person who designs buildings 建筑师 2 the person responsible for something 缔造者;创建者: *the architect of the reforms* 改革的设计师

architecture /ˈɑːkɪtektʃə(r)/ noun 1 the design and construction of buildings 建筑学 2 the complex structure of something 结构;架构 ■ architectural adjective.

architrave /ˈɑːkɪtreɪv/ noun 1 (in classical architecture) a beam resting across the tops of columns (古典建筑的)柱顶过梁, 楣梁 2 the frame around a doorway or window (门口或窗的)框缘,嵌线

archive /ˈɑːkaɪv/ noun 1 a collection of historical documents or records 档案 2 a complete record of the data in a computer system (计算机系统中的)归档数据 • verb (archives, archiving, archived) put something in an archive 把⋯⋯存档;把⋯⋯归档 ■ archival adjective.

archivist /ˈɑːkɪvɪst/ noun a person who is in charge of archives of historical material 档案保管员

archway /ˈɑːtʃweɪ/ noun a curved structure forming a passage or entrance 拱道;拱门

Arctic /ˈɑːktɪk/ adjective relating to the regions around the North Pole 北极的;北极区的

> ✔ **拼写指南** remember the first c: Arctic. 记住拼写 Arctic 中的第一个 c。

ardent /ˈɑːdnt/ adjective 1 feeling passionate about something 热情的;热切的;热烈的 2 old use 【旧】 burning; glowing 燃烧的;发光的 ■ ardently adverb.

ardour /ˈɑːdə(r)/ (US spelling 【美拼作】 ardor) noun passionate feelings

热情;热切;激情

arduous /ˈɑːdjuəs/ **adjective** difficult and tiring 艰巨的;费力的;困难的 ■ **arduously** adverb.

are /ɑː(r), ə(r)/ 2nd person singular present and 1st, 2nd, and 3rd person plural present of BE.

!注意 don't confuse **are** with **our**. 不要混淆 are 和 our。

area /ˈeəriə/ **noun 1** a part of a place, object, or surface 地区;区域;场所 **2** the extent or measurement of a surface 面积 **3** a subject or range of activity 领域;范围;方面

arena /əˈriːnə/ **noun 1** a level area surrounded by seating, in which sports and other events are held 圆形运动场;圆形场地 **2** an area of activity 活动场所

aren't /ɑːnt/ **short form 1** are not. **2** am not (only in questions 仅用于疑问句)

areola /əˈriːələ/ **noun** (plural **areolae** /əˈriːəliː/) the circular area of darker skin surrounding a human nipple 乳晕

Argentinian /ˌɑːdʒənˈtɪniən/ or **Argentine** /ˈɑːdʒəntaɪn/ **noun** a person from Argentina 阿根廷人 • **adjective** relating to Argentina 阿根廷的

argon /ˈɑːgɒn/ **noun** an inert gaseous element, present in small amounts in the air (惰性气体元素)氩

argot /ˈɑːgəʊ/ **noun** the jargon or slang of a particular group 行话;俚语

arguable /ˈɑːgjuəbl/ **adjective** able to be argued or disagreed with 可争辩的;可辩驳的 ■ **arguably** adverb.

argue /ˈɑːgjuː/ **verb** (**argues, arguing, argued**) **1** discuss something in a serious or angry way with someone who disagrees with you 争吵;争辩 **2** make statements in support of an action or opinion 说理;论证;主张

argument /ˈɑːgjumənt/ **noun 1** a serious or angry discussion between people who disagree with each other 争论;争辩;辩论 **2** a set of reasons given in support of an action or opinion 理由;论据;论点

✔ 拼写指南 no *e* in the middle: *argument*, not *argue-*. argument 中间没有 e, 不要拼作 argue-。

argumentative /ˌɑːgjuˈmentətɪv/ **adjective** tending to argue 好争论的;好争吵的

aria /ˈɑːriə/ **noun** a song for a solo voice in an opera (歌剧)咏叹调

arid /ˈærɪd/ **adjective** or **1** very dry because having little or no rain 干旱的;干燥的 **2** dull and boring 枯燥的;乏味的 ■ **aridity** noun.

Aries /ˈeəriːz/ **noun** a sign of the zodiac (the Ram), 20 March–20 April 白羊宫(黄道十二宫之一)

arise /əˈraɪz/ **verb** (**arises, arising, arose**; past participle **arisen**) **1** start to exist or be noticed 形成;产生;出现 **2** (**arise from** or **out of**) happen as a result of 由…引起;由…产生;起源于 **3** formal 【正式】 stand up 起立;起身

aristocracy /ˌærɪˈstɒkrəsi/ **noun** (plural **aristocracies**) the highest social class, consisting of people whose families hold a title such as *Lord* or *Duke* 贵族;上层社会 ■ **aristocrat** noun **aristocratic** adjective.

arithmetic /əˈrɪθmətɪk/ **noun** the use of numbers in counting and calculation 算术 ■ **arithmetical** adjective **arithmetically** adverb.

ark /ɑːk/ **noun 1** (in the Bible) the ship built by Noah to save two of every kind of animal from the Flood (《圣经》中的)方舟(挪亚为使一对对的各种动物逃离洪水而造) **2** a chest or cupboard in a synagogue in which the holy scrolls are kept (犹太教堂内藏有经卷的)经柜 **3** (**Ark of the**

Covenant) the chest which contained the laws of the ancient Israelites (内置古以色列人律法的)约柜

arm¹ /ɑːm/ **noun 1** each of the two upper limbs of the human body from the shoulder to the hand 臂；手臂 **2** a side part of a chair supporting a sitter's arm (椅子的)扶手 **3** a strip of water or land 狭长港湾；狭长地带 **4** a branch or division of a company or organization 部门；分部

arm² **verb 1** supply with weapons 以武器装备；武装 **2** provide with essential equipment or information 提供；配备 **3** make a bomb ready to explode 使(炸弹)可随时爆炸

armada /ɑːˈmɑːdə/ **noun** a fleet of warships 舰队

armadillo /ˌɑːməˈdɪləʊ/ **noun** (plural **armadillos**) an insect-eating animal of Central and South America, with a body covered in bony plates 犰狳(产于中美洲和南美洲，以昆虫为食，身上覆盖有骨质甲壳)

Armageddon /ˌɑːməˈɡedən/ **noun 1** (in the Bible) the final battle between good and evil before the Last Judgement (《圣经》中)世界末日前的)善恶大决战 **2** a terrible war with a catastrophic ending 大决战；大规模战争

armament /ˈɑːməmənt/ **noun 1** (also **armaments**) military weapons and equipment 武器；军备 **2** the equipping of military forces 武装；战备

armature /ˈɑːmətʃə(r)/ **noun 1** the rotating coil of a dynamo or electric motor (发电机或电动机的)电枢，转子 **2** a piece of iron placed across the poles of a magnet to preserve its power (磁铁的)衔铁

armchair /ˈɑːmtʃeə(r)/ **noun** a comfortable chair with padded sides on which to rest your arms 扶手椅

armed /ɑːmd/ **adjective** carrying a weapon 武装的；武器的 □ **armed forces** a country's army, navy, and

air force (一国的)武装部队，武装力量

armistice /ˈɑːmɪstɪs/ **noun** an agreement to stop fighting 停战；休战

armorial /ɑːˈmɔːriəl/ **adjective** relating to coats of arms 纹章的

armour /ˈɑːmə(r)/ (US spelling 【美拼作】**armor**) **noun 1** metal coverings worn in the past to protect the body in battle 盔甲；甲胄 **2** (also **armour plate**) the tough metal layer covering a military vehicle or ship 装甲(钢)板 ■ **armoured** adjective.

armourer /ˈɑːmərə(r)/ (US spelling 【美拼作】**armorer**) **noun** a person who makes, supplies,or looks after weapons or armour 武器制造者；武器提供者；军械士

armoury /ˈɑːməri/ (US spelling 【美拼作】**armory**) **noun** (plural **armouries**) a store of arms 军械库；武器库

armpit /ˈɑːmpɪt/ **noun** a hollow under the arm at the shoulder 腋窝；夹肢窝

arms /ɑːmz/ **plural noun 1** guns and other weapons 武器；兵器 **2** the emblems on a coat of arms 纹章；徽章 □ **up in arms** protesting strongly 极力反对

army /ˈɑːmi/ **noun** (plural **armies**) **1** a military force that fights on land 军队；陆军 **2** a large number of people or things 大批；大群

aroma /əˈrəʊmə/ **noun** a pleasant smell 芳香；香味；香气 ■ **aromatic** adjective.

aromatherapy /əˌrəʊməˈθerəpi/ **noun** the use of aromatic oils for healing or to give pleasant feelings 芳香疗法 ■ **aromatherapist** noun.

arose /əˈrəʊz/ past of ARISE.

around /əˈraʊnd/ **adverb & preposition 1** on every side of something 在(…)周围；在(…)四周 **2** in or to many places throughout an area 在(…)各处；到处 • **adverb 1** so as to face in the opposite direction 朝相反方向；

向着对立面 **2** about; approximately 大约 **3** available or present 现有；可用

arouse /əˈrauz/ **verb** (**arouses, arousing, aroused**) **1** bring about a feeling or response in someone 引起，激起(感情或反应) **2** excite someone sexually 激起…的情欲 **3** awaken someone from sleep 唤醒；使醒来 ■ **arousal** noun.

arpeggio /ɑːˈpedʒiəu/ **noun** (plural **arpeggios**) the notes of a musical chord played in rapid succession 琶音(连续快速演奏的和弦音符)

arraign /əˈreɪn/ **verb** call someone before a court to answer a criminal charge 传讯；提讯；提审 ■ **arraignment** noun.

arrange /əˈreɪndʒ/ **verb** (**arranges, arranging, arranged**) **1** put tidily or in a particular order 整理；排列；布置 **2** organize or plan 安排；筹划 **3** adapt a piece of music for performance 改编(乐曲) ■ **arranger** noun.

arrangement /əˈreɪndʒmənt/ **noun** **1** a plan for a future event 安排；筹划 **2** something made up of things arranged in a particular way 整理好的东西 **3** an arranged piece of music 改编曲

arrant /ˈærənt/ **adjective** complete; absolute 完全的；彻底的：*arrant nonsense* 一派胡言

array /əˈreɪ/ **noun** **1** an impressive display or range (显眼的)一系列，大批 **2** an ordered arrangement of troops 阵形；编队 **3** literary 【文】 elaborate clothing 盛装 • **verb** **1** (**be arrayed**) be displayed or arranged in a neat or impressive way 着盛装 **2** (**be arrayed in**) be dressed in 穿戴

arrears /əˈrɪəz/ **plural noun** money owed that should already have been paid 应付欠款；逾期债款 口 **in arrears 1** behind with paying money that is owed 拖欠 **2** (of wages or rent) paid at the end of each period of work

or occupation (工资或租金)后付的

arrest /əˈrest/ **verb** **1** seize someone and take them into custody 逮捕；拘捕 **2** stop the progress of something 使停止；阻止 **3** (**arresting**) attracting attention 引人注意的 • **noun** **1** the action of arresting someone 逮捕；拘捕 **2** a sudden stop (突然的)停止

arrival /əˈraɪvl/ **noun** **1** the process of arriving somewhere 到达；到来 **2** a person or thing that has just arrived 到达者；到达物

arrive /əˈraɪv/ **verb** (**arrives, arriving, arrived**) **1** reach a destination 到达；抵达 **2** (of a particular moment) come about (某时刻)到来 **3** (**arrive at**) reach a conclusion or decision 得出(结论)；作出(决定)

arrogant /ˈærəgənt/ **adjective** behaving in an unpleasant way because you think that you are better than other people 傲慢的；自大的 ■ **arrogance** noun **arrogantly** adverb.

arrogate /ˈærəgeɪt/ **verb** (**arrogates, arrogating, arrogated**) formal 【正式】 take or claim something that you have no right to 僭取；僭称

arrow /ˈærəu/ **noun** **1** a stick with a sharp point, shot from a bow 箭 **2** a symbol resembling this, used to show direction or position (表示方向或位置的)符号，箭头

arrowroot /ˈærəuruːt/ **noun** a starch obtained from a plant and used as a thickener in cookery 竹芋粉(从竹芋根提取的淀粉，烹饪时用于增稠)

arsenal /ˈɑːsənl/ **noun** a store of weapons and ammunition 军火库；武(器)库

arsenic /ˈɑːsnɪk/ **noun** a brittle grey element from which a highly poisonous white powder is obtained (化学元素)砷

arson /ˈɑːsn/ **noun** the criminal act of deliberately setting fire to property 放火罪；纵火罪 ■ **arsonist** noun.

art /ɑːt/ **noun** the expression of

creative skill in a visual form such as painting or sculpture（绘画、雕塑等）视觉艺术，艺术 **2** paintings, drawings, and sculpture as a whole 美术 **3** (the arts) creative activities such as painting, music, and drama 艺术（指绘画、音乐、戏剧等创造性活动）**4** (arts) subjects of study concerned with human culture 人文科学；文科 **5** a skill 技能；技巧

artefact /ˈɑːtɪfækt/ (US spelling【美拼作】artifact) **noun** a useful or decorative man-made object 人工制品；手工艺品

artery /ˈɑːtəri/ **noun** (plural **arteries**) **1** any of the tubes through which blood flows from the heart around the body 动脉 **2** an important transport route 干线；要道 ■ **arterial** adjective.

artesian well /ɑːˈtiːziən/ **noun** a well in which water comes to the surface through natural pressure 自流井

artful /ˈɑːtfl/ **adjective** clever in a cunning way 狡猾的；奸诈的 ■ **artfully** adverb.

arthritis /ɑːˈθraɪtɪs/ **noun** painful inflammation and stiffness of the joints 关节炎 ■ **arthritic** /ɑːˈθrɪtɪk/ adjective & noun.

arthropod /ˈɑːθrəpɒd/ **noun** an animal with a body that is divided into segments, such as an insect, spider, crab, etc. 节肢动物

artichoke /ˈɑːtɪtʃəʊk/ **noun** a vegetable consisting of the unopened flower head of a thistle-like plant 洋蓟；朝鲜蓟

article /ˈɑːtɪkl/ **noun 1** a particular object 物件；物品 **2** a piece of writing in a newspaper or magazine（报刊上的）文章，论文，报道 **3** an item in a legal document（法律文件中的）条款，项 **4** (articles) a period of training in a company as a solicitor, accountant, etc.（律师、会计师等的）实习期 • **verb** (be articled) (of a solicitor, accountant, etc.) be employed as a trainee（律师、会计师等）做实习生

articulate **adjective** /ɑːˈtɪkjələt/ **1** fluent and clear in speech 说话流利的；口齿清楚的 **2** having joints or jointed segments 有关节的；分节的 • **verb** /ɑːˈtɪkjuleɪt/ (**articulates, articulating, articulated**) **1** pronounce words distinctly 清晰地吐字 **2** clearly express an idea or feeling 明确表达（想法或感情）**3** (**articulated**) having sections connected by a flexible joint or joints 由关节连接的；铰接的 ■ **articulacy** noun **articulately** adverb **articulation** noun.

artifact /ˈɑːtɪfækt/ US spelling of ARTEFACT. artefact 的美式拼法

artifice /ˈɑːtɪfɪs/ **noun** the clever use of tricks to deceive someone 狡诈；欺骗

artificer /ɑːˈtɪfɪsə(r)/ **noun** a person skilled in making or planning things 工匠；技工

artificial /ˌɑːtɪˈfɪʃl/ **adjective 1** made as a copy of something natural 人工的；人造的 **2** not sincere 虚假的；不真诚的 □ **artificial insemination** the injection of semen through a syringe into the vagina or womb 人工授精 **artificial intelligence** the performance by computers of tasks that normally need human intelligence 人工智能 **artificial respiration** the forcing of air into and out of a person's lungs to make them begin breathing again 人工呼吸 ■ **artificiality** noun **artificially** adverb.

artillery /ɑːˈtɪləri/ **noun 1** large guns used in warfare on land 火炮；大炮 **2** a branch of the armed forces that uses artillery 炮兵（部队）

artisan /ˌɑːtɪˈzæn/ **noun** a skilled worker who makes things by hand 工匠；手艺人

artist /ˈɑːtɪst/ **noun 1** a person who paints or draws 美术家；画家 **2** a person who practises or performs

A

any of the creative arts 艺术家

artiste /ɑːˈtiːst/ noun a professional singer or dancer 艺人;专业歌唱(或舞蹈)演员

artistic /ɑːˈtɪstɪk/ adjective **1** having creative skill 有艺术才能的 **2** having to do with art or artists 艺术的;艺术家的 ■ **artistically** adverb.

artistry /ˈɑːtɪstri/ noun creative skill or ability 艺术才能

artless /ˈɑːtləs/ adjective straightforward and sincere 天真的;直率的 ■ **artlessly** adverb.

artwork /ˈɑːtwɜːk/ noun illustrations to be included in a publication (出版物中的)插图

arty /ˈɑːti/ (US spelling【美拼作】**artsy**) adjective informal【非正式】displaying an obvious interest in the arts 装作爱好艺术的;附庸风雅的 ■ **artiness** noun.

Aryan /ˈeəriən/ noun **1** a member of an ancient people of Europe and Asia 雅利安人 **2** (in Nazi thinking) a white person not of Jewish descent (纳粹意识形态中)非犹太血统的白种人 • adjective relating to Aryans 雅利安人的

as /æz, əz/ adverb used in comparisons to refer to extent or amount (在程度或数量上)同样地,一样地 • conjunction **1** while 当…时 **2** in the way that 以…的方式;如同…那样 **3** because 因为;由于 **4** even though 虽然;尽管 • preposition **1** in the role of; being 以…的身份;作为 **2** while; when 当…时;在…同时

asap /ˌeɪ es eɪ ˈpiː/ abbreviation as soon as possible 尽快

asbestos /æsˈbestɒs/ noun a fibrous grey-white mineral that does not burn 石棉

asbestosis /ˌæsbesˈtəʊsɪs/ noun a serious lung disease caused by breathing asbestos dust 石棉沉着病;石棉肺

ASBO /ˈæzbəʊ/ abbreviation Brit.【英】antisocial behaviour order 反社会行为规则

ascend /əˈsend/ verb go up; climb or rise 升起;登高

ascendant /əˈsendənt/ adjective **1** rising in power or status (权力或地位)上升的 **2** (of a planet or sign of the zodiac) just above the eastern horizon (行星或黄道宫)刚刚高出东方地平线的 ■ **ascendancy** noun.

ascension /əˈsenʃn/ noun **1** the action of reaching a higher position or status (地位的)上升 **2** (the Ascension) the ascent of Jesus into heaven after the Resurrection (复活后的)耶稣升天

ascent /əˈsent/ noun **1** the action of going up 上升;登高 **2** an upward slope 上坡

ascertain /ˌæsəˈteɪn/ verb find something for certain 查明,弄清;确定 ■ **ascertainable** adjective.

ascetic /əˈsetɪk/ adjective choosing to live without pleasures and luxuries 苦行的;禁欲的 • noun an ascetic person 苦行者;禁欲者 ■ **asceticism** noun.

ascorbic acid /əˈskɔːbɪk/ noun vitamin C 抗坏血酸;维生素C

ascribe /əˈskraɪb/ verb (ascribes, ascribing, ascribed) (ascribe something to) say or believe that something is caused by 把…归因于 ■ **ascription** noun.

aseptic /eɪˈseptɪk/ adjective free from germs 无菌的

asexual /eɪˈsekʃuəl/ adjective **1** without sex or sexual organs 无性的;无性器官的 **2** not having sexual feelings 无性欲的 ■ **asexually** adverb.

ash¹ /æʃ/ noun **1** the powder remaining after something has been burned 灰;灰烬 **2** (ashes) the remains of a human body after cremation 骨灰

ash² noun a tree with winged fruits and hard pale wood 梣,白蜡树(结翅果,木质坚硬平滑)

ashamed /ə'ʃeɪmd/ **adjective** feeling embarrassed or guilty 羞愧的;愧疚的

ashen /'æʃn/ **adjective** very pale from shock, fear, or illness 灰白的;苍白的

ashore /ə'ʃɔː(r)/ **adverb** to or on the shore or land 向岸地;在岸上

ashram /'æʃrəm/ **noun** a Hindu religious retreat or community (印度教的)静修处

ashtray /æʃtreɪ/ **noun** a small container for tobacco ash and cigarette ends 烟灰缸

Asian /'eɪʃn/ **noun** a person from Asia, or whose family originally came from Asia 亚洲人;亚裔 • **adjective** relating to Asia 亚洲的

Asiatic /eɪʃi'ætɪk/ **adjective** relating to Asia 亚洲的

aside /ə'saɪd/ **adverb 1** to one side; out of the way 到旁边;向一边;在旁边 **2** in reserve 留;存 • **noun 1** an actor's remark spoken to the audience 旁白 **2** a remark not directly related to the subject being discussed 离题的话;插入语

asinine /'æsɪnaɪn/ **adjective** very foolish 极度愚蠢的

ask /ɑːsk/ **verb 1** say something so as to get an answer or some information 问;询问 **2** say that you want someone to do, give, or allow something 要求;请求 **3 (ask for)** say that you want to speak to 要求和…说话 **4** expect something of someone 索要 **5** invite someone to a social occasion 邀请

askance /ə'skæns/ **adverb** with a suspicious or disapproving look (表情)怀疑地,不赞同地

askew /ə'skjuː/ **adverb & adjective** not straight or level 歪斜地(的)

aslant /ə'slɑːnt/ **adverb & preposition** at a slant or crossing something at a slant 倾斜地;歪斜地;倾斜地横在…上

asleep /ə'sliːp/ **adjective & adverb 1** in or into a state of sleep 睡着的(的);进

入睡眠状态(的) **2** (of a limb) numb (肢体)麻木的

asp /æsp/ **noun** a small viper 角蝰(一种小毒蛇)

asparagus /ə'spærəgəs/ **noun** a vegetable consisting of the tender young shoots of a tall plant 芦笋;龙须菜

aspect /'æspekt/ **noun 1** a particular part or feature of something 方面;层面 **2** a particular appearance or quality 外观;外表;样子 **3** the side of a building facing a particular direction (建筑物朝某方向的)一面

aspen /'æspən/ **noun** a poplar tree with small rounded leaves 山杨;颤杨;大齿杨

asperity /æ'sperəti/ **noun** harshness in the way you speak to or treat someone (语调或待人态度的)粗暴

aspersion /ə'spɜːʃn/ **noun** (**cast aspersions on**) attack someone's character or reputation 诽谤;中伤

asphalt /'æsfælt/ **noun** a tar-like substance used in surfacing roads or roofs 沥青;柏油

asphyxia /æs'fɪksiə/ **noun** a condition in which someone cannot get enough oxygen and becomes unconscious or dies 窒息

asphyxiate /əs'fɪksieɪt/ **verb** (**asphyxiates, asphyxiating, asphyxiated**) die or cause to die from lack of oxygen (使)窒息;(使)闷死 ■ **asphyxiation** noun.

aspic /'æspɪk/ **noun** a savoury jelly made with meat stock 肉冻

aspidistra /æspɪ'dɪstrə/ **noun** a plant with broad tapering leaves 蜘蛛抱蛋(一种植物,叶宽而尖)

aspirant /'æspərənt/ **noun** a person with ambitions to do or be something 有志向的人;有抱负的人

aspiration /æspə'reɪʃn/ **noun** a hope or ambition 渴望;抱负;志向 ■ **aspirational** adjective.

aspire /ə'spaɪə(r)/ **verb** (**aspires, aspir-**

A

ing, aspired) have a strong desire to achieve or become something 渴望；追求；有志向

aspirin /ˈæspərɪn/ noun (plural **aspirin** or **aspirins**) a medicine used to relieve pain and reduce fever and inflammation 阿司匹林

ass /æs/ noun **1** a donkey or related small wild horse 驴 **2** informal 【非正式】 a stupid person 傻瓜；蠢人

assail /əˈseɪl/ verb **1** attack someone violently 攻击；袭击 **2** (of an unpleasant feeling) come over someone strongly (不悦的情绪)困扰，使苦恼

assailant /əˈseɪlənt/ noun an attacker 攻击者；袭击者

assassin /əˈsæsɪn/ noun a person who assassinates someone 暗杀者；行刺者

assassinate /əˈsæsɪneɪt/ verb (**assassinates, assassinating, assassinated**) murder a political or religious leader 暗杀,行刺(政治或宗教领袖) ■ **assassination** noun.

assault /əˈsɔːlt/ noun **1** a violent attack 攻击；袭击 **2** a determined attempt (坚决的)努力，尝试 • verb make an assault on 攻击；袭击 □ **assault course** Brit. 【英】 an obstacle course used for training soldiers (训练士兵的)障碍训练场

assay /əˈseɪ/ noun the testing of a metal to see how pure it is (对金属纯度的)试验，检验 • verb test a metal 试验，检验(金属)

assemblage /əˈsemblɪdʒ/ noun **1** a collection or gathering of things or people 集聚；聚集 **2** something made of pieces fitted together 组装物；装配成的东西

assemble /əˈsembl/ verb (**assembles, assembling, assembled**) **1** come or bring together 集合；集聚；召集 **2** construct something by fitting parts together 组装；装配

assembly /əˈsembli/ noun (plural

assemblies) **1** a group of people gathered together 集会；聚在一起的一群人 **2** a group of people with powers to make decisions and laws 立法机构；议会 **3** the action of fitting the parts of something together 组装；装配 □ **assembly line** a series of workers and machines in a factory along which identical products pass to be assembled in stages 流水生产线；装配线

assent /əˈsent/ noun approval or agreement 赞成；同意 • verb agree to a request or suggestion 赞成；同意

assert /əˈsɜːt/ verb **1** confidently state that something is true 断言；明确肯定 **2** (**assert yourself**) be confident and forceful 坚持自己的主张；表现坚定

assertion /əˈsɜːʃn/ noun a confident and forceful statement 明确肯定；断言

assertive /əˈsɜːtɪv/ adjective speaking and doing things in a confident and forceful way 坚定自信的；坚决主张的 ■ **assertively** adverb **assertiveness** noun.

assess /əˈses/ verb make a judgement about the value or quality of something 估价；评价；评估 ■ **assessment** noun **assessor** noun.

asset /ˈæset/ noun **1** a useful or valuable thing or person 有用的事物(或人)，有价值的事物(或人) **2** (**assets**) property owned by a person or company 资产

assiduous /əˈsɪdjuəs/ adjective showing great care and thoroughly 勤勉的；刻苦的 ■ **assiduity** noun **assiduously** adverb.

assign /əˈsaɪn/ verb give someone a task or duty 指派；指定

assignation /ˌæsɪɡˈneɪʃn/ noun a secret meeting, especially between lovers 秘密会面(尤指情人间的)幽会

assignment /əˈsaɪnmənt/ noun a

piece of work that someone has been asked to do (分派的)任务

assimilate /ə'sɪmɪleɪt/ **verb (assimilates, assimilating, assimilated) 1** take in and understand information 理解,吸收(信息) **2** absorb people or ideas into a society or culture 使(人)同化;使(思想)融入 ▪ **assimilation** noun.

assist /ə'sɪst/ **verb** help someone 帮助,协助

assistance /ə'sɪstəns/ **noun** help or support 帮助;援助

assistant /ə'sɪstənt/ **noun** a person employed to help someone more senior 助手;助理

assize /ə'saɪz/ or **assizes** /ə'saɪzɪz/ **noun** historical 【历史】 a court which sat at intervals in each county of England and Wales (英格兰和威尔士的)巡回法庭

associate verb /ə'səʊʃɪeɪt/ **(associates, associating, associated) 1 (associate something with)** mentally connect something with something else (在思想上)联系,联想 **2 (associate with)** frequently meet or have dealings with 与…接触;与…交往 **3 (associate yourself with)** be involved with 与…有关联 ▪ **noun** /ə'səʊʃɪət/ a work partner or colleague 伙伴,同事 ▪ **adjective** /ə'səʊʃɪət/ **1** connected with an organization 有关联的 **2** belonging to an association but not having full membership 非正式的;准的

association /ə,səʊʃɪ'eɪʃn/ **noun 1** a group of people organized for a joint purpose 协会;社团;联盟 **2** a connection or link 联合;关联 □ **Association Football** soccer 足球(运动)

assonance /'æsənəns/ **noun** a rhyming of vowel sounds 准押韵;半谐音

assorted /ə'sɔːtɪd/ **adjective** made up of various sorts 各种各样的;混杂的

assortment /ə'sɔːtmənt/ **noun** a varied collection 各种各样

assuage /ə'sweɪdʒ/ **verb (assuages, assuaging, assuaged) 1** make an unpleasant feeling less strong 缓和,减轻(不快) **2** relieve thirst or an appetite or desire 解(渴);充(饥);满足(欲望)

assume /ə'sjuːm/ **verb (assumes, assuming, assumed) 1** think that something must be true but have no proof 假定;假设;臆断 **2** take responsibility or control 承担(责任);取得(控制权) **3** begin to have 呈现;具有 **4** pretend to have or feel 假装;装出

assumption /ə'sʌmpʃn/ **noun 1** a feeling that something must be true 假定;假设 **2** the taking on of responsibility or control (责任的)承担,(控制权的)取得

assurance /ə'ʃʊərəns/ **noun 1** something said to make someone feel confident about something 保证;担保 **2** self-confidence 自信 **3** Brit.【英】 life insurance 人寿保险

assure /ə'ʃʊə(r)/ **verb (assures, assuring, assured) 1** make someone feel confident about something 使确信;向…保证 **2** make certain 使确定;弄清 **3** Brit.【英】 insure a person's life 给…上人寿保险

assured /ə'ʃʊəd/ **adjective 1** confident in yourself and your abilities 自信的;有把握的 **2** certain; guaranteed 确定的;有保证的 □ **assuredly** adverb.

asterisk /'æstərɪsk/ **noun** a symbol (*) used as a pointer to a note 星号

✔ 拼写指南 aster*isk*, not -*ix* (Astérix is a character in a cartoon strip). asterisk 不要拼作 asterix (Astérix 是一部连环画中的人物)。

astern /ə'stɜːn/ **adverb** behind or towards the rear of a ship or aircraft 在船(或飞机)尾部;向船(或飞机)尾部

asteroid /'æstərɔɪd/ **noun** a small rocky planet orbiting the sun 小行星

asthma /'æsmə/ **noun** a medical

condition that causes difficulty in breathing 气喘;哮喘 ■ **asthmatic** adjective & noun.

astigmatism /ə'stɪgmətɪzəm/ noun a fault in the shape of the eye which prevents clear vision 散光

astir /ə'stɜː(r)/ adjective **1** in a state of excited movement 激动的;骚动的 **2** awake and out of bed 起床的

astonish /ə'stɒnɪʃ/ verb surprise someone very much 使惊讶;使大吃一惊 ■ **astonishment** noun.

astound /ə'staʊnd/ verb shock or surprise someone very much 使震惊;使惊骇

astrakhan /ˌæstrə'kæn/ noun the dark curly fleece of young lambs from central Asia, used to make coats and hats (产自中亚的)阿斯特拉罕羔羊毛

astral /'æstrəl/ adjective relating to the stars 星的

astray /ə'streɪ/ adverb away from the correct course 偏离正确的道路;迷路地

astride /ə'straɪd/ preposition & adverb with a leg on each side of (跨)在…上 • adverb (of a person's legs) apart (人的两腿)分开着,跨骑

astringent /ə'strɪndʒənt/ adjective **1** causing body tissue to contract (使肌体组织)收敛的 **2** sharp or severe 尖刻的;辛辣的;严厉的 • noun an astringent lotion 收敛剂;涩剂 ■ **astringency** noun.

astrolabe /'æstrəleɪb/ noun an instrument formerly used in navigation and for measuring the altitude of the stars 星盘(旧时用于航海和测量星体高度)

astrology /ə'strɒlədʒi/ noun the study of the supposed influence of the stars and planets on human affairs 占星术;占星学 ■ **astrologer** noun **astrological** adjective.

astronaut /'æstrənɔːt/ noun a person trained to travel in a spacecraft 宇航员;航天员

astronomical /ˌæstrə'nɒmɪkl/ adjective **1** relating to astronomy 天文学的 **2** informal 【非正式】 very large 天文数字的;极巨大的 ■ **astronomic** adjective **astronomically** adverb.

astronomy /ə'strɒnəmi/ noun the scientific study of stars, planets, and the universe 天文学 ■ **astronomer** noun.

astrophysics /ˌæstrəʊ'fɪzɪks/ noun the study of the physical nature of stars and planets 天体物理学 ■ **astrophysicist** noun.

astute /ə'stjuːt/ adjective good at making accurate judgements 敏锐的;精明的;判断准确的 ■ **astutely** adverb.

asunder /ə'sʌndə(r)/ adverb apart or into pieces 分开;离散;碎

asylum /ə'saɪləm/ noun **1** protection from danger 避难 **2** protection given to someone who has fled their country for political reasons 政治庇护 **3** dated 【废】 an institution for people who are mentally ill 精神病院

asymmetrical /ˌeɪsɪ'metrɪkl/ adjective not symmetrical 不对称的 ■ **asymmetric** adjective

asymmetry /'eɪ'sɪmətri/ noun (plural **asymmetries**) lack of symmetry 不对称

at /æt, ət/ preposition used to express 用于表示: **1** location, arrival, or time (地点、到达或时间)在,于 **2** a value, rate, or point on a scale (等级中的价值、比率或点)以,达 **3** a state or condition in …方面;处于 **4** direction towards (方向)朝,向 **5** the means by which something is done 以…方式

atavistic /ˌætə'vɪstɪk/ adjective inherited from the earliest human beings 返祖性的;隔代遗传的 ■ **atavism** noun.

ate /et, eɪt/ past of EAT.

atheism /'eɪθiɪzəm/ noun 无神论 ■ **atheist** noun **atheistic** adjective.

athlete /'æθliːt/ noun **1** a person who

is good at sports 运动员 **2** a person who competes in track and field events 田径运动员 □ **athlete's foot** a form of ringworm infection affecting the feet 足癣；脚气

athletic /æθ'letɪk/ **adjective 1** fit and good at sport 健壮的 **2** relating to athletics 运动的；体育 • **noun** (**athletics**) Brit.【英】the sport of competing in track and field events 田径运动 ■ **athletically** adverb **athleticism** noun.

athwart /ə'θwɔːt/ **preposition** across from side to side 横跨

Atlantic /ət'læntɪk/ **adjective** having to do with the Atlantic Ocean 大西洋的

atlas /'ætləs/ **noun** a book of maps or charts 地图册；图表集

atmosphere /'ætməsfɪə(r)/ **noun 1** the gases surrounding the earth or another planet (包围地球或其他星体的)大气，大气层 **2** the quality of the air in a place (场所的)空气 **3** an overall tone or mood 环境；气氛 **4** a unit of pressure equal to the pressure of the atmosphere at sea level (标准)大气压

atmospheric /ˌætməs'ferɪk/ **adjective 1** relating to the atmosphere of a planet 大气的；大气层的 **2** creating a distinctive mood 有独特氛围的 • **noun** (**atmospherics**) electrical disturbances in the atmosphere 天电，大气干扰

atoll /'ætɒl/ **noun** a ring-shaped coral reef or chain of islands 环礁，环状珊瑚岛

atom /'ætəm/ **noun 1** the smallest particle of a chemical element that can exist 原子 **2** a very small amount 丝毫；微量 □ **atom bomb** (or **atomic bomb**) a bomb whose explosive power comes from the fission (splitting) of the nuclei of atoms 原子弹

atomic /ə'tɒmɪk/ **adjective 1** relating to an atom or atoms 原子的 **2** relating to nuclear energy or weapons 原子能的；原子武器的

atomize or **atomise** /'ætəmaɪz/ **verb** (**atomizes**, **atomizing**, **atomized**) convert something into very fine particles or droplets 使成为微粒；使粉碎 ■ **atomizer** noun.

atonal /eɪ'təʊnl/ **adjective** not written in any musical key (乐曲)无调的

atone /ə'təʊn/ **verb** (**atones**, **atoning**, **atoned**) (**atone for**) do something to show you are sorry for something that happened in the past 赎罪；弥补 ■ **atonement** noun.

atrium /'eɪtrɪəm/ **noun** (plural **atria** /'eɪtrɪə/ or **atriums**) **1** a central hall rising through several storeys 中央大厅 **2** an open central court in an ancient Roman house (古罗马房屋的)中庭，正厅 **3** each of the two upper cavities of the heart 心房

atrocious /ə'trəʊʃəs/ **adjective 1** horrifyingly wicked 凶恶的；残暴的 **2** very bad or unpleasant 糟透的；恶劣的 ■ **atrociously** adverb.

atrocity /ə'trɒsəti/ **noun** (plural **atrocities**) a very wicked or cruel act 凶恶行为；残暴行为

atrophy /'ætrəfi/ **verb** (**atrophies**, **atrophying**, **atrophied**) (of a part of the body) waste away (身体部位)萎缩，衰退 • **noun** the condition or process of atrophying 萎缩；衰退

attach /ə'tætʃ/ **verb 1** fasten; join 系；固定；连接 **2** believe that something has significance or importance 认为有(意义或重要性) **3** (**be attached to**) be working with a group of people 加入；参与 **4** (**attached to**) very fond of 依恋；酷爱 ■ **attachable** adjective.

✔ **拼写指南** -ach, not -atch: attach. attach 中 -ach 不要拼作 -atch。

attaché /ə'tæʃeɪ/ **noun** a person on an ambassador's staff (大使的)随员

A

□ **attaché case** a small, flat briefcase for carrying documents 公文包

attachment /ə'tætʃmənt/ *noun* **1** an extra part that is attached to something 附属物;附件 **2** a computer file sent with an email (与电子邮件一起发送的)附件

attack /ə'tæk/ *verb* **1** violently hurt or attempt to hurt 攻击;袭击 **2** have a harmful effect on 侵袭;损害 **3** fiercely criticize 抨击 **4** tackle something with determination 奋力对付 **5** (in sport) try to score goals or points (体育比赛中)进攻 • *noun* **1** an instance of attacking 攻击;袭击;进攻 **2** a sudden period of illness (疾病的)突然发作 ■ **attacker** *noun.*

attain /ə'teɪn/ *verb* **1** succeed in doing 获得;达到 **2** reach 到达 ■ **attainable** *adjective.*

attainment /ə'teɪnmənt/ *noun* **1** the achieving of something 获得;得到 **2** an achievement 成就;造诣

attar /'ætə(r)/ *noun* a sweet-smelling oil made from rose petals (从玫瑰花瓣中提炼的)玫瑰油,香精油

attempt /ə'tempt/ *verb* make an effort to do something 企图;试图;尝试 • *noun* an effort to do something 企图;尝试;努力

attend /ə'tend/ *verb* **1** be present at or go regularly to 出席;参加;经常去 **2** (attend to) deal with or pay attention to 处理;对付;致力于 **3** happen at the same time as or as a result of (作为结果)伴随 **4** escort and help someone 护送;侍候

attendance /ə'tendəns/ *noun* **1** the action of attending 出席;参加 **2** the number of people present 出席人数

attendant /ə'tendənt/ *noun* **1** a person employed to help people in a public place 服务员;侍者 **2** an assistant to an important person 侍从;随从 • *adjective* accompanying 伴随的;随之产生的

attention /ə'tenʃn/ *noun* **1** special care, notice, or consideration 关照;注意;关心 **2** (attentions) things done to help someone or to express sexual interest 殷勤 **3** a straight standing position taken by soldiers 立正姿势

attentive /ə'tentɪv/ *adjective* **1** paying close attention 注意的;专心的;留心的 **2** considerate and helpful 关心的;体贴的 ■ **attentively** *adverb.*

attenuate /ə'tenjueɪt/ *verb* (**attenuates, attenuating, attenuated**) **1** make something weaker 使减弱;削弱 **2** make something thin or thinner 使纤细;使稀薄 ■ **attenuation** *noun.*

attest /ə'test/ *verb* **1** provide or act as clear evidence of something 是…的证据;表明 **2** declare something to be true 证明;证实 ■ **attestation** *noun.*

attic /'ætɪk/ *noun* a space or room inside the roof of a building 顶楼;阁楼

attire /ə'taɪə(r)/ *formal* 【正式】 *noun* clothes of a particular kind 服装;衣服 • *verb* (**be attired**) be wearing clothes of a particular kind 穿着…衣服;着装

attitude /'ætɪtjuːd/ *noun* **1** a way of thinking 态度;看法 **2** a position of the body (身体的)姿势,姿态 **3** *informal* 【非正式】 self-confident or aggressive behavior 我行我素的作派

attitudinize or **attitudinise** /ˌætɪ'tjuːdɪnaɪz/ *verb* (**attitudinizes, attitudinizing, attitudinized**) adopt an attitude just for effect 装腔作势;故作姿态

attorney /ə'tɜːni/ *noun* (plural **attorneys**) **1** a person who is appointed to act for someone else in legal matters (法律事务上的)代理人 **2** chiefly US 【主美】 a lawyer 律师

attract /ə'trækt/ *verb* **1** draw someone in by offering something interesting or appealing 吸引;诱惑 **2** cause a particular reaction 引起…反应 **3** draw something closer by an unseen force 吸引;吸

attraction /əˈtrækʃn/ **noun 1** the action or power of attracting 吸引；吸引力；诱惑力 **2** something interesting or appealing 具有吸引力的事物

attractive /əˈtræktɪv/ **adjective 1** very pleasing to look at 妩媚动人的；有魅力的 **2** arousing interest 有吸引力的；引起兴趣的 ■ **attractively** adverb **attractiveness** noun.

attribute verb /əˈtrɪbjuːt/ (**attributes, attributing, attributed**) (**attribute something to**) say or believe that something is the result of or belongs to 把…归因于；认为…属于 • noun /ˈætrɪbjuːt/ a quality or feature 属性；特性；特征 ■ **attributable** adjective **attribution** noun.

attrition /əˈtrɪʃn/ **noun** gradual wearing down through prolonged attack, pressure, or friction 削弱；消耗；磨损

attune /əˈtjuːn/ **verb** (**be attuned**) be receptive to and able to understand someone or something 使合拍；使协调；使适应

atypical /ˌeɪˈtɪpɪkl/ **adjective** not typical 非典型的

aubergine /ˈəʊbəʒiːn/ **noun** a large vegetable with purple skin 茄；茄子

auburn /ˈɔːbən/ **noun** a reddish-brown colour 赤褐色；赭色

auction /ˈɔːkʃn/ **noun** a public sale in which each item is sold to the person who offers most for it 拍卖 • verb sell something at an auction 拍卖

auctioneer /ˌɔːkʃəˈnɪə(r)/ **noun** a person who conducts auctions 拍卖师

audacious /ɔːˈdeɪʃəs/ **adjective** very confident and daring 敢于冒险的；大胆的 ■ **audaciously** adverb **audacity** noun.

audible /ˈɔːdəbl/ **adjective** able to be heard 听得见的 ■ **audibility** noun **audibly** adverb.

audience /ˈɔːdɪəns/ **noun 1** the people gathered to see or listen to a play, concert, film, etc. 观众；听众 **2** a formal interview with a person in authority 觐见；谒见；正式接见

audio tape /ˈɔːdiəʊ/ **noun** magnetic tape on which sound can be recorded 录音带

audit /ˈɔːdɪt/ **noun** an official inspection of an organization's accounts 审计；查账 • verb (**audits, auditing, audited**) inspect the accounts of 对…进行审计 ■ **auditor** noun.

audition /ɔːˈdɪʃn/ **noun** an interview for a performer in which they give a practical demonstration of their skill (对表演者的)面试 • verb assess or be assessed by an audition 对(表演者)进行面试

auditorium /ˌɔːdɪˈtɔːriəm/ **noun** (plural **auditoriums** or **auditoria** /ˌɔːdɪˈtɔːriə/) the part of a theatre or hall in which the audience sits 听众席；观众席

auditory /ˈɔːdətri/ **adjective** relating to hearing 听的；听觉的

au fait /ˌəʊ ˈfeɪ/ **adjective** (**au fait with**) completely familiar with 对…熟悉的；对…精通的

auger /ˈɔːgə(r)/ **noun** a tool for boring holes 螺丝钻；木螺钻

aught /ɔːt/ **pronoun** old use 【旧】anything at all 任何事物

augment /ɔːgˈment/ **verb** increase the amount or value of 扩大；增加；提高 ■ **augmentation** noun.

augur /ˈɔːgə(r)/ **verb** be a sign of a likely outcome 是…的预兆；预示(可能的结果)

augury /ˈɔːgjuri/ **noun** (plural **auguries**) a sign of what will happen in the future 征兆；预兆

August /ˈɔːgəst/ **noun** the eighth month of the year 八月

august /ɔːˈgʌst/ **adjective** inspiring respect and admiration 威严的；令人敬畏的

auk /ɔːk/ **noun** a black and white seabird 海雀

aunt /ɑːnt/ **noun** the sister of your

father or mother or the wife of your uncle 姑母；姨母；伯母；婶母；舅母

au pair /ˌəʊ ˈpeə(r)/ **noun** a foreign girl employed to look after children and help with housework 换工的女孩，"互裨"女生(受雇照看小孩和做家务的外国年轻女孩)

aura /ˈɔːrə/ **noun** (plural **auras**) the distinctive feeling that seems to surround a particular place or person 气味；气息；氛围

aural /ˈɔːrəl/ **adjective** having to do with the ear or hearing 耳的；听觉的；听力的 ■ **aurally** adverb.

aureole /ˈɔːriəʊl/ **noun** a circle of light around the sun or moon (太阳或月亮的)晕

au revoir /ˌəʊ rəˈvwɑː(r)/ **exclamation** goodbye 再见

aurora borealis /ɔːˌrɔːrə ˌbɒriˈeɪlɪs/ **noun** streamers of light sometimes seen in the sky near the North Pole; the Northern Lights 北极光

auspice /ˈɔːspɪs/ **noun** (**under the auspices of**) with the support or protection of 在…的支持下；在…的保护下

auspicious /ɔːˈspɪʃəs/ **adjective** suggesting that there is a good chance of success 吉利的；吉祥的 ■ **auspiciously** adverb.

Aussie /ˈɒzi/ informal【非正式】 **noun** (plural **Aussies**) an Australian 澳大利亚人 • **adjective** Australian 澳大利亚人的

austere /ɒˈstɪə(r)/ **adjective 1** without luxuries or decoration; very simple and plain 苦行的；禁欲的；无华饰的；简朴的 **2** severe or strict in appearance or behaviour 严肃的；严厉的；严酷的 ■ **austerely** adverb **austerity** noun.

Australasian /ˌɒstrəˈleɪʒən/ **adjective** relating to Australasia, a region made up of Australia, New Zealand, and neighbouring islands 澳大拉西亚的(包括澳大利亚、新西兰和附近诸岛)

Australian /ɒˈstreɪliən/ **noun** a

person from Australia 澳大利亚人 • **adjective** relating to Australia 澳大利亚的

Austrian /ˈɒstriən/ **noun** a person from Austria 奥地利人 • **adjective** relating to Austria 奥地利的

authentic /ɔːˈθentɪk/ **adjective** known to be real; genuine 真的；真实的；真正的 ■ **authentically** adverb **authenticity** noun.

authenticate /ɔːˈθentɪkeɪt/ **verb** (**authenticates, authenticating, authenticated**) prove or show that something is authentic 证明…真实；证明…可信 ■ **authentication** noun.

author /ˈɔːθə(r)/ **noun 1** a writer of a book or article 著作者；作家 **2** the inventor of something 创始者；发起人 ■ **authorship** noun.

authoritarian /ɔːˌθɒrɪˈteəriən/ **adjective** demanding strict obedience of authority and rules 独裁的；专断的 • **noun** an authoritarian person 独裁者

authoritative /ɔːˈθɒrətətɪv/ **adjective 1** true or accurate and so able to be trusted 权威的；可信的 **2** commanding and self-confident 命令式的；专断的 **3** official 当局的；官方的 ■ **authoritatively** adverb.

authority /ɔːˈθɒrəti/ **noun** (plural **authorities**) **1** the power to give orders and make people obey you 权威；权力 **2** a person or organization that has official power 当权者；当局；官方 **3** recognized knowledge or expertise 威信；影响力 **4** a person or book that is trusted as a source of knowledge 专家；权威人士；权威典籍

authorize or **authorise** /ˈɔːθəraɪz/ **verb** (**authorizes, authorizing, authorized**) give official permission for 批准；准许；授权 ■ **authorization** noun.

autism /ˈɔːtɪzəm/ **noun** a mental condition in which a person has great difficulty in communicating with other people 自闭症；孤独症 ■ **autistic** adjective.

autobiography /ˌɔ:təbaɪˈɒgrəfi/ **noun** (plural **autobiographies**) an account of a person's life written by that person 自传 ■ **autobiographical** adjective.

autocracy /ɔ:ˈtɒkrəsi/ **noun** (plural **autocracies**) a system of government in which one person has total power 独裁政体；专制制度

autocrat /ˈɔ:təkræt/ **noun 1** a ruler who has total power 独裁者；专制君主 **2** a person who expects obedience 独断专行的人；专横的人 ■ **autocratic** adjective.

autograph /ˈɔ:təgrɑ:f/ **noun** a celebrity's signature written for an admirer (名人的)亲笔签名 • **verb** write an autograph on something 亲笔签名于

automate /ˈɔ:təmeɪt/ **verb** (**automates**, **automating**, **automated**) convert a process or machine so that it can operate automatically 使(过程或机器)自动化 ■ **automation** noun.

automatic /ˌɔ:təˈmætɪk/ **adjective 1** operating by itself without human control 自动的 **2** (of a gun) able to fire continuously until the bullets run out (枪支)自动的 **3** done without conscious thought 无意识的；不假思索的 **4** (of a punishment) applied without question because of a fixed rule (惩罚)必然的，自然的 □ **automatic pilot** a device for keeping an aircraft on course without the pilot having to control it (飞机的)自动驾驶仪 ■ **automatically** adverb.

automaton /ɔ:ˈtɒmətən/ **noun** (plural **automata** /ɔ:ˈtɒmətə/ or **automatons**) a mechanical device that looks like a human being 机器人

automobile /ˈɔ:təməbi:l/ **noun** N. Amer. 【北美】 a car 汽车

automotive /ˌɔ:təˈməʊtɪv/ **adjective**

having to do with motor vehicles 汽车的

autonomous /ɔ:ˈtɒnəməs/ **adjective** self-governing or independent 自治的；独立自主的 ■ **autonomously** adverb.

autonomy /ɔ:ˈtɒnəmi/ **noun 1** self-government 自治 **2** freedom of action 自主权；自由

autopsy /ˈɔ:tɒpsi/ **noun** (plural **autopsies**) an examination of a dead body to discover the cause of death 尸体解剖；验尸

autumn /ˈɔ:təm/ **noun** chiefly Brit. 【主英】 the season after summer and before winter 秋天；秋季 ■ **autumnal** adjective.

auxiliary /ɔ:gˈzɪliəri/ **adjective** providing extra help and support • **noun** (plural **auxiliaries**) an auxiliary person or thing 辅助者；助手；辅助物 □ **auxiliary verb** a verb such as *be*, *do*, and *have*, which is used to form tenses of other verbs 助动词

avail /əˈveɪl/ **verb** (**avail yourself of**) formal 【正式】 use or take advantage of 使用；利用 • **noun** use or benefit 效用；益处

available /əˈveɪləbl/ **adjective 1** able to be used or obtained 可用的；可获得的 **2** not occupied 未占用的；有空的 ■ **availability** noun.

avalanche /ˈævəlɑ:nʃ/ **noun 1** a mass of snow and ice falling rapidly down a mountainside 雪崩 **2** an overwhelming amount of something 大量

avant-garde /ˌævɒnˈgɑ:d/ **adjective** (in the arts) new and experimental (艺术)先锋派的，前卫的

avarice /ˈævərɪs/ **noun** extreme greed for money or material things 贪婪；贪得无厌

avaricious /ˌævəˈrɪʃəs/ **adjective** very greedy for money or material things 贪婪的；贪得无厌的

avenge /əˈvendʒ/ **verb** (**avenges**, **avenging**, **avenged**) repay something bad that has been done to you by harming the person who did it 为…进行报复 ■ **avenger** noun.

avenue /ˈævənjuː/ **noun 1** a broad road or path 大街；林阴道 **2** a way of making progress towards achieving something 途径；方法

aver /əˈvɜː(r)/ **verb** (**avers, averring, averred**) formal【正式】declare that something is the case 断言；坚称

average /ˈævərɪdʒ/ **noun 1** the result obtained by adding several amounts together and then dividing the total by the number of amounts 平均数 **2** a usual amount or level 通常数量；一般水平 • **adjective 1** being an average 平均的 **2** usual or ordinary 平常的；普通的 • **verb** (**averages, averaging, averaged**) **1** amount to a particular figure as an average 平均数为 **2** calculate the average of several amounts 计算…的平均数

averse /əˈvɜːs/ **adjective** (**averse to**) strongly disliking or opposed to 厌恶的；反对的

> **！注意** don't confuse **averse** with **adverse**, which means 'harmful or unfavourable'. 不要混淆 averse 和 adverse, 后者意为"有害的,不利的"。

aversion /əˈvɜːʃn/ **noun** a strong dislike 厌恶

avert /əˈvɜːt/ **verb 1** turn away your eyes 转移(目光) **2** prevent something unpleasant happening 防止，避免(令人不快的事)

avian /ˈeɪviən/ **adjective** having to do with birds 鸟的；关于鸟的

aviary /ˈeɪviəri/ **noun** (plural **aviaries**) a large enclosure for keeping birds in 大型鸟舍；鸟类饲养场

aviation /ˌeɪviˈeɪʃn/ **noun** the activity of operating and flying aircraft 航空，飞行

aviator /ˈeɪvieɪtə(r)/ **noun** dated【废】a pilot 飞行员；飞机驾驶员

avid /ˈævɪd/ **adjective** very interested or enthusiastic 热衷的；渴望的；急切

的 ■ **avidly** adverb.

avionics /ˌeɪviˈɒnɪks/ **plural noun** electronics used in aviation 航空电子学

avocado /ˌævəˈkɑːdəʊ/ **noun** (plural **avocados**) a pear-shaped fruit with pale green flesh and a large stone 鳄梨

avoid /əˈvɔɪd/ **verb 1** keep away from, or stop yourself from doing 避开；躲避 **2** prevent something from happening 避免；防止 **3** manage not to collide with 闪避 ■ **avoidable** adjective **avoidance** noun.

avoirdupois /ˌævədəˈpɔɪz, ˌævwɑːˈdjuːˈpwɑː/ **noun** the system of weights based on a pound of 16 ounces 常衡(以16盎司为1磅)

avow /əˈvaʊ/ **verb** openly state or confess 声明；公开承认 ■ **avowed** adjective.

avuncular /əˈvʌŋkjələ(r)/ **adjective** kind and friendly towards a younger person 慈爱的；慈祥的

await /əˈweɪt/ **verb** wait for 等；等待

awake /əˈweɪk/ **verb** (**awakes, awaking, awoke**; past participle **awoken**) **1** stop sleeping 醒；唤醒 **2** make or become active again (被)唤起；(被)激起 • **adjective** not asleep 醒着的

awaken /əˈweɪkən/ **verb 1** awake 醒；唤醒 **2** stir up a feeling 唤起；激起(感情)

award /əˈwɔːd/ **verb** give an official prize or reward to 授予(奖品) • **noun 1** an official prize or reward 奖；奖品 **2** the action of awarding 授予

aware /əˈweə(r)/ **adjective** (usu. **aware of** or **that**) knowing about a situation or fact 意识到的；知道的 ■ **awareness** noun.

awash /əˈwɒʃ/ **adjective** covered or flooded with water 被水覆盖的；被水淹没的

away /əˈweɪ/ **adverb 1** to or at a distance 向远处；在远处；离开 **2** into a place for storage (放)到某处(保存) **3** out of existence 不存在；消失 **4** constantly or continuously 持续不断地 • **adjective** (of a sports match) played at the opponents'ground (体育比赛)在客场进行的

awe /ɔː/ **noun** a feeling of great respect mixed with fear 敬畏 • **verb** (**awes, awing, awed**) fill someone with awe 使敬畏

awesome /'ɔːsəm/ **adjective 1** inspiring awe 令人敬畏的 **2** informal 【非正式】 excellent 极好的 ■ **awesomely** adverb.

awful /'ɔːfl/ **adjective 1** very bad or unpleasant 极坏的；极讨厌的 **2** used to emphasize something (用于强调) 极大的；非常的: *an awful lot* 非常多 ■ **awfully** adverb.

awhile /ə'waɪl/ **adverb** for a short time 片刻

awkward /'ɔːkwəd/ **adjective 1** hard to do or deal with 棘手的；难处理的；难对付的 **2** causing or feeling embarrassment 令人难堪的；令人尴尬的 **3** inconvenient 不方便的 **4** clumsy 笨拙的；不灵巧的 ■ **awkwardly** adverb.

awl /ɔːl/ **noun** a small pointed tool used for making holes 钻子；尖锥

awning /'ɔːnɪŋ/ **noun** a sheet of canvas on a frame, used for shelter 雨篷；凉篷；遮篷

awoke /ə'wəʊk/ past of AWAKE.

awoken /ə'wəʊkən/ past participle of AWAKE.

AWOL /'eɪwɒl/ **adjective** (**go AWOL**) informal 【非正式】 go missing 擅离职守 [short for 【缩写】 = *absent without official leave*, a military expression.]

awry /ə'raɪ/ **adverb & adjective** away from the expected course or position 偏离预期路线地(的)；歪斜地(的)

axe /æks/ (US spelling 【美拼作】 **ax**) **noun** a tool with a heavy blade, used for chopping wood 斧；斧子 • **verb** (**axes, axing, axed**) suddenly and ruthlessly cancel or dismiss 取消；撤销；裁减 □ **have an axe to grind** have a private reason for doing something 有私心；有个人打算

axiom /'æksɪəm/ **noun** a statement regarded as being obviously true 公理，自明之理 ■ **axiomatic** adjective.

axis /'æksɪs/ **noun** (plural **axes** /'æksiːz/)**1** an imaginary line around which an object or shape rotates 轴；轴线 **2** a fixed line against which points on a graph are measured 参考线轴；坐标轴 **3** (**the Axis**) Germany and its allies in the Second World War (第二次世界大战中的)轴心国

axle /'æksl/ **noun** a rod passing through the centre of a wheel or group of wheels 轴；车轴

ayatollah /ˌaɪə'tɒlə/ **noun** a religious leader in Iran 阿亚图拉(伊朗的宗教领袖)

aye /aɪ/ **exclamation** old use or dialect 【旧或方】 yes 是；对

azalea /ə'zeɪlɪə/ **noun** a shrub with brightly coloured flowers 杜鹃花

azimuth /'æzɪməθ/ **noun** Astronomy 【天文】 the direction of a star measured horizontally as an angle from due north or south 方位；地平经度

azure /'æʒə(r)/ **noun** a bright blue colour like a cloudless sky 天蓝色；蔚蓝色

Bb

B or **b** /biː/ **noun** (plural **Bs** or **B's**) the second letter of the alphabet 英语字母表的第2个字母

BA /ˌbiː ˈeɪ/ **abbreviation** Bachelor of Arts 文学士

baa /bɑː/ **verb** (**baas, baaing, baaed**) (of a sheep or lamb) bleat (羊或羊羔) 发咩声

babble /ˈbæbl/ **verb** talk quickly in a silly or confused way 含糊不清地说话 • **noun** silly or confused talk 含糊不清的话

babe /beɪb/ **noun** 1 literary 【文】a baby 婴儿 2 informal 【非正式】an attractive young woman 宝贝儿(用于称呼娇娆动人的年轻女子)

babel /ˈbeɪbl/ **noun** a confused noise made by many people speaking together (众人讲话的)嘈杂声

baboon /bəˈbuːn/ **noun** a large monkey with a long snout and a pink rump 狒狒(一种大猴,口鼻部长,臀部发红)

baby /ˈbeɪbi/ **noun** (plural **babies**) 1 a child or animal that has recently been born 婴儿;幼畜;幼兽 2 a timid or childish person 胆怯的人;孩子气的人 • **adjective** small or very young 小的;幼小的 • **verb** (**babies, babying, babied**) treat someone too protectively 把(某人)当成婴儿对待;百般呵护 ■ **babyhood** noun **babyish** adjective

babysit /ˈbeɪbisɪt/ **verb** (**babysits, babysitting, babysat**) look after a child or children while the parents are out 代人临时照看小孩 ■ **babysitter** noun

baccalaureate /ˌbækəˈlɔːriət/ **noun** an exam taken in some countries to qualify for higher education (某些国家的)中学毕业会考

baccarat /ˈbækərɑː/ **noun** a gambling card game 巴卡拉纸牌戏(一种赌博游戏)

bacchanalian /ˌbækəˈneɪliən/ **adjective** (of a party or celebration) drunken and wild (聚会或庆祝活动)狂饮闹宴的

bachelor /ˈbætʃələ(r)/ **noun** 1 a man who has never been married 未婚男子;单身汉 2 a person who holds a first degree from a university 学士;获得学士学位的人

bacillus /bəˈsɪləs/ **noun** (plural **bacilli** /bəˈsɪlaɪ/) a type of bacterium 杆菌

back /bæk/ **noun** 1 the rear surface of a person's body, or the upper part of an animal's body (人的)背,背部;(动物的)脊背 2 the side or part of something that is furthest from the front 反面;背面;后部 3 a defending player in a team game 后卫 • **adverb** 1 in the opposite direction from the one in which you are facing or travelling 向后 2 so as to return to an earlier or normal position or state 回原处;回原状 3 into the past 以前 4 in return 还;回 • **adjective** 1 at or towards the back 后面的;向后的 2 in a remote or less important position 边远的;偏僻的 3 relating to the past 过去的 • **verb** 1 give support to 支持;做后盾 2 walk or drive backwards 倒退;后退 3 bet money on a person or animal to win a race or contest 下赌注于(人或动物) 4 (**back on to**) (of a building) have its back facing or next to (建筑物)背向 5 cover the back of an object 覆盖…的背部 6 provide musical backing for a singer or musician 伴奏 □ **the back of beyond** a very remote place 偏僻

地方;边远地区 **back down** give in 放弃(原有立场);打退堂鼓 **back off** stop opposing someone 放弃对抗; 不再反对 **back out** withdraw from something you have promised to do 食言;反悔 **back-pedal** go back on something previously said 出尔反尔;变卦 **back someone/thing up 1** support someone or something 支持(某人或某事) **2** Computing【计】make a spare copy of data or a disk 备份(数据或磁盘) **put someone's back up** annoy someone 使(某人)生气 ■ **backer** noun.

backbencher /ˌbæk'bentʃə(r)/ *noun* an MP who does not hold a government or opposition post (议会下院的)后座议员,普通议员

backbiting /'bækbaɪtɪŋ/ *noun* spiteful talk about a person who is not present 背后中伤;背后诽谤

backbone /'bækbəʊn/ *noun* **1** the spine 脊骨;脊柱 **2** strength of character 骨气,坚毅

backchat /'bæktʃæt/ *noun* Brit. informal 【英,非正式】rude or cheeky remarks 谩骂;傲慢的话

backdate /ˌbæk'deɪt/ *verb* (**backdates, backdating, backdated**) Brit.【英】make something valid from an earlier date 使…的生效日期提前

backdrop /'bækdrɒp/ *noun* **1** a painted cloth hung at the back of a theatre stage as part of the scenery (舞台后部的)背景幕布 **2** the setting or background for a scene or event 背景

backfire /ˌbæk'faɪə(r)/ *verb* (**backfires, backfiring, backfired**) **1** (of an engine) make a banging sound as a result of fuel igniting wrongly (发动机)回火,逆火 **2** produce the opposite effect to what was intended 使事与愿违;发生意外

backgammon /'bækgæmən/ *noun* a board game played with counters and a dice 巴加门;十五子游戏

background /'bækgraʊnd/ *noun* **1** the part of a scene or picture behind the main figures 背景;后景 **2** information or circumstances that influence or explain something 背景资料 **3** a person's education, experience, and early life 出身背景;履历

backhand /'bækhænd/ *noun* (in tennis and similar games) a stroke played with the back of the hand facing in the direction of the stroke (网球等运动中的)反击球

backhanded /ˌbæk'hændɪd/ *adjective* expressed in a way that is indirect or has more than one meaning 拐弯抹角的,讽刺挖苦的: *a backhanded compliment* 隐含讥刺的假恭维

backhander /'bækhændə(r)/ *noun* **1** a backhand stroke or blow 使用手背的一击;反手一击 **2** Brit. informal【英,非正式】a bribe 贿赂

backing /'bækɪŋ/ *noun* **1** support 支持;做后盾 **2** a layer of material that forms or strengthens the back of something 背衬 **3** music or singing accompanying a pop singer (流行歌手演唱时的)伴奏,伴唱

backlash /'bæklæʃ/ *noun* an angry reaction by a large number of people 强烈反应;集体反对

backlog /'bæklɒg/ *noun* a build-up of things needing to be dealt with (事务的)积压

backpack /'bækpæk/ *noun* a rucksack 帆布背包 • *verb* travel carrying your belongings in a rucksack 背包旅行 ■ **backpacker** noun

backside /'bæksaɪd/ *noun* informal 【非正式】a person's bottom 屁股

backslapping /'bækslæpɪŋ/ *noun* the offering of hearty congratulations or praise 热烈祝贺;热情赞扬

backsliding /'bækslaɪdɪŋ/ *noun* a return to bad behaviour after an attempt to improve 退步;倒退;故态

复萌

backstage /ˌbækˈsteɪdʒ/ **adverb & adjective** behind the stage in a theatre 在后台(的)

backstreet /ˈbækstriːt/ **noun** a less important street in a town or city 偏僻街道

backstroke /ˈbækstrəʊk/ **noun** a swimming stroke in which you lie on your back and lift your arms out of the water in a backward circular movement 仰泳

backtrack /ˈbæktræk/ **verb 1** retrace your steps 原路返回；折回 **2** change your opinion to the opposite of what it was 改变观点；出尔反尔

backup /ˈbækʌp/ **noun 1** support 支持 **2** a person or thing kept ready to be used when needed 后备人员；备用物品

backward /ˈbækwəd/ **adjective 1** directed towards the back 向后的 **2** having made less progress than is normal or expected 落后的；进步慢 • **adverb** (also **backwards**) **1** towards the back, or back towards the starting point 向后；往回；回原处 **2** opposite to the usual direction or order 朝反方向；倒；逆

backwash /ˈbækwɒʃ/ **noun** waves flowing outwards behind a ship 船后的反流；尾流

backwater /ˈbækwɔːtə(r)/ **noun 1** a stretch of stagnant water on a river 滞水；壅水 **2** a place where change happens very slowly 死气沉沉的地方；停滞状态

backwoods /ˈbækwʊdz/ **plural noun** a remote area or region 边远地区

bacon /ˈbeɪkən/ **noun** salted or smoked meat from the back or sides of a pig 腌猪肉；熏猪肉

bacteria /bækˈtɪəriə/ **plural noun** (sing. **bacterium**) a group of microscopic organisms, many kinds of which can cause disease 细菌 ■ **bacterial** adjective.

! 注意 bacteria is actually a plural (the singular is **bacterium**), and should always be used with a plural verb, e.g. *the bacteria were multiplying*. bacteria 实际上是复数形式的名词(其单数形式为 bacterium)，应与复数动词连用，如 the bacteria were multiplying(细菌在繁殖)。

bad /bæd/ **adjective** (**worse**, **worst**) **1** low in quality; well below standard 坏的；劣质的 **2** unpleasant 令人不快的；不合格的 **3** severe; serious 厉害的；严重的 **4** wicked or evil 邪恶的；罪恶的 **5** (**bad for**) harmful to 有害的 **6** injured, ill, or diseased 受伤的；不舒服的；有病的 **7** (of food) decayed (食物)腐烂的，腐败的 ■ **badness** noun.

bade /beɪd/ past of **BID**².

badge /bædʒ/ **noun** a small flat object that a person pins to their clothing to show that they belong to an organization, have a particular rank, etc. 徽章；证章

badger /ˈbædʒə(r)/ **noun** an animal with a black and white striped head which lives underground and is active at night 獾 • **verb** (**badgers**, **badgering**, **badgered**) pester someone to do something 纠缠；困扰

badinage /ˈbædɪnɑːʒ/ **noun** witty conversation 戏谑；打趣

badlands /ˈbædlændz/ **plural noun** land where plants or crops will not grow 劣地；荒地

badly /ˈbædli/ **adverb** (**worse**, **worst**) **1** in a way that is not acceptable or satisfactory 坏；差；拙劣地 **2** severely; seriously 厉害地；严重地 **3** very much 很；非常 □ **badly off** poor 贫困的

badminton /ˈbædmɪntən/ **noun** a game in which the players hit a shuttlecock across a high net with rackets 羽毛球(运动)

baffle /ˈbæfl/ **verb** (**baffles**, **baffling**, **baffled**) make someone feel puzzled

使困惑;难住 • **noun** a device for controlling the flow of sound, light, gas, or fluid (控制声音、光传播的)缓冲板,(阻止气体、液体流动的)折流板 ■ **bafflement** noun.

bag /bæg/ **noun 1** a flexible container with an opening at the top 袋;包 **2** (**bags**) loose folds of skin under a person'seyes 眼袋 **3** (**bags of**) Brit. informal【英,非正式】plenty of 许多、大量 **4** informal【非正式】an unpleasant or unattractive woman 丑妇 • **verb** (**bags**, **bagging**, **bagged**) **1** put something in a bag 把…装进袋子 **2** manage to catch an animal 捕杀,猎获(动物) **3** informal【非正式】manage to get 设法获得

bagatelle /ˌbæɡə'tel/ **noun 1** a game in which you hit small balls into numbered holes on a board 巴格代拉桌球戏,小型台球 **2** something unimportant or of little value 小事;琐事

bagel /'beɪɡl/ **noun** a ring-shaped bread roll with a heavy texture 硬面包圈

baggage /'bæɡɪdʒ/ **noun** luggage packed with belongings for travelling 行李

baggy /'bæɡi/ **adjective** (**baggier**, **baggiest**) loose and hanging in folds 宽松下垂的

bagpipe /'bæɡpaɪp/ or **bagpipes** /'bæɡpaɪps/ **noun** a musical instrument with pipes that are sounded by wind squeezed from a bag 风笛 ■ **bagpiper** noun.

baguette /bæ'ɡet/ **noun** a long, narrow French loaf of bread 法国棍子面包

bail[1] /beɪl/ **noun 1** the release of an accused person on condition that a sum of money is left with the court, which will be returned as long as the person attends their trial 保释 **2** money paid to release an accused person 保释金 • **verb** release an accused person on payment of bail 允许保释(被告)

bail[2] **noun** Cricket【板球】either of the two small pieces of wood that rest on the stumps 三柱门上的横木

bail[3] or Brit.【英】**bale verb 1** scoop water out of a ship or boat 从(船)里往外舀水 **2** (**bail out**) make an emergency jump out of an aircraft, using a parachute 紧急跳伞 **3** (**bail someone out**) rescue someone who is in difficulties 使脱离困境

bailey /'beɪli/ **noun** (plural **baileys**) the outer wall of a castle (城堡的)外墙;城郭

bailiff /'beɪlɪf/ **noun** a person who delivers writs and seizes the property of people who owe money for rent 郡副司法长官(负责传唤和查封欠租者财物)

bailiwick /'beɪlɪwɪk/ **noun 1** a district over which a bailiff has authority 郡副司法长官的辖区 **2** a person's area of activity or interest 活动范围;兴趣范围

bait /beɪt/ **noun** food put on a hook or in a trap to attract fish or other animals (诱捕鱼等的)饵,诱饵 • **verb 1** taunt or tease 侮弄;逗弄 **2** (**baiting**) the activity of setting dogs on an animal that is trapped or tied up 纵犬袭击(落入陷阱或被锁住的野兽) **3** put bait on a hook or in a trap 装饵于(钩)上;在(陷阱)中放诱饵

baize /beɪz/ **noun** a thick green material used for covering billiard tables (铺在台球桌上的)台面呢,桌面呢

bake /beɪk/ **verb** (**bakes**, **baking**, **baked**) **1** cook food in an oven (在烤箱里)烘烤(食品) **2** heat something to dry or harden it 烧硬;烘干 **3** (**baking**) informal【非正式】(of weather) very hot (天气)灼热,炎热 □ **baking soda** sodium bicarbonate 小苏打;碳酸氢钠

baker /'beɪkə(r)/ **noun** a person whose job is making bread and cakes 面包

师;糕饼师 □ **baker's dozen** a group of thirteen 一打加一；十三 ■ **bakery** noun (plural **bakeries**)

balaclava /ˌbæləˈklɑːvə/ noun a close-fitting woollen hat covering the head and neck except for the face (罩住头和颈部的)巴拉克拉瓦盔式帽

balalaika /ˌbæləˈlaɪkə/ noun a Russian musical instrument like a guitar, with a triangular body 巴拉莱卡琴，俄式三弦琴

balance /ˈbæləns/ noun **1** a state in which weight is evenly distributed, so that a person or object does not wobble or fall over 平衡，均衡 **2** a situation in which different parts are in the right proportions 均势；协调；和谐 **3** a piece of equipment for weighing 天平，秤 **4** an amount that is the difference between money received and money spent in an account (账户中的)结存 **5** an amount still owed when part of a debt has been paid 余欠之(钱)数 • verb (**balances**, **balancing**, **balanced**) **1** put your body, or an object, in a steady position 使平衡 **2** compare the value of one thing with another 权衡；比较 **3** give equal importance to two or more things 使均衡；使协调 □ **balance of payments** the difference between payments into and out of a country over a period 国际收支差额 **balance sheet** a written statement of what a business owns and what it owes 资产负债表；决算表

balcony /ˈbælkəni/ noun (plural **balconies**) **1** a platform with a railing or low wall, projecting from the outside of a building 阳台 **2** the highest level of seats in a theatre or cinema (剧院或电影院的)楼座，楼厅

bald /bɔːld/ adjective **1** having no hair on the head 秃头的，秃顶的 **2** (of a tyre) having the tread worn away (轮胎)表面磨光的 **3** plain or blunt 明显的；直接的 ■ **baldly** adverb **baldness** noun.

balderdash /ˈbɔːldədæʃ/ noun nonsense 胡说八道；废话

balding /ˈbɔːldɪŋ/ adjective going bald 在脱发的；变秃的

bale[1] /beɪl/ noun a large bundle of paper, hay, or cloth (纸、干草或布的)大捆，大包 • verb (**bales**, **baling**, **baled**) make paper, hay, or cloth into bales 把…打成大捆(或大包)

bale[2] /beɪl/ = 见 BAIL[3].

baleen /bəˈliːn/ noun whalebone 鲸须

baleful /ˈbeɪlfl/ adjective threatening to cause harm 有害的；破坏的 ■ **balefully** adverb.

balk /bɔːk/ US spelling of BAULK. baulk 的美式拼法

ball[1] /bɔːl/ noun **1** a rounded object that is kicked, thrown, or hit in a game (体育运动中用的)球 **2** a single throw or kick of the ball in a game 传球 **3** a rounded part or thing 圆形物 • verb squeeze or form something into a ball 把…捏压成球 □ **ball bearing** a ring of small metal balls which separate moving parts to reduce rubbing 滚珠轴承；球轴承 **2** one of these balls 滚珠，钢球

ball[2] noun a formal gathering for dancing and meeting people (正式的)舞会

ballad /ˈbæləd/ noun **1** a poem or song telling a story 叙事诗歌；民谣，民歌 **2** a slow, sentimental song (节奏缓慢的)抒情歌曲

ballast /ˈbæləst/ noun **1** a heavy substance carried by a ship or hot-air balloon to keep it stable (船或热气球上的)压舱物，压载物 **2** stones used to form the base of a railway track or road (铁路或公路铺路基用的)道砟

ballcock /ˈbɔːlkɒk/ noun a valve which automatically tops up a cistern when liquid is drawn from it (水箱中的)浮球旋塞，浮球阀

ballerina /ˌbæləˈriːnə/ noun a female ballet dancer 芭蕾舞女演员

ballet /'bæleɪ/ **noun** an artistic form of dancing performed to music, using set steps and gestures 芭蕾舞 ■ **balletic** adjective.

ballistic /bə'lɪstɪk/ **adjective** having to do with the flight of missiles, bullets, or similar objects 弹道的;射弹的;发射的 □ **ballistic missile** a missile which is fired into the air and falls on to its target 弹道导弹

balloon /bə'luːn/ **noun 1** a small rubber bag which is blown up and used as a toy or decoration 玩具气球;装饰气球 **2** (also **hot-air balloon**) a large bag filled with hot air or gas to make it rise in the air, with a basket for passengers attached to it (悬有载人吊篮的)热气球 **3** a rounded outline in which the words of characters in a cartoon are written (连环漫画中以线条圈出人物言语的)气球状圆圈,气球状对话框 • **verb 1** swell outward 鼓起;膨胀 **2** increase quickly 激增;飞涨 **3** (**ballooning**) travelling by hot-air balloon 乘热气球旅行

ballot /'bælət/ **noun 1** a way of voting on something secretly by putting paper slips in a box 无记名投票 **2** (**the ballot**) the total number of votes recorded 投票总数 • **verb** (**ballots, balloting, balloted**) ask people to vote secretly about something 要求就…进行无记名投票

ballpoint pen /'bɔːlpɔɪnt/ **noun** a pen with a tiny ball as its writing point 圆珠笔

ballroom /'bɔːlruːm/ **noun** a large room for formal dancing 舞厅 □ **ballroom dancing** formal dancing for couples (两人跳的)交际舞,交谊舞

ballyhoo /ˌbælɪ'huː/ **noun** informal 【非正式】a lot of fuss 大吹大擂;大肆宣传

balm /bɑːm/ **noun 1** a sweet-smelling ointment used to heal or soothe the skin 香膏;镇痛软膏 **2** something that soothes or heals 安慰(物);慰藉(物)

balmy /'bɑːmi/ **adjective** (**balmier, balmiest**) (of the weather) pleasantly warm (天气)温和的,宜人的

baloney /bə'ləʊni/ **noun** informal 【非正式】nonsense 废话;胡扯

balsa /'bɔːlsə/ **noun** very lightweight wood from a tropical American tree, used for making models 轻木(产于美洲热带地区,用于制作模型)

balsam /'bɔːlsəm/ **noun** a scented substance obtained from some trees and shrubs, used in perfumes and medicines 香脂(提取自某些树木和蕴木,用于香水和药物中)

baluster /'bæləstə(r)/ **noun** a short pillar forming part of a series supporting a rail 栏杆柱

balustrade /ˌbælə'streɪd/ **noun** a railing supported by balusters 栏杆;扶手

bamboo /ˌbæm'buː/ **noun** a giant tropical grass with hollow woody stems 竹;竹子

bamboozle /bæm'buːzl/ **verb** (**bamboozles, bamboozling, bamboozled**) informal 【非正式】cheat or deceive 欺骗;哄骗

ban /bæn/ **verb** (**bans, banning, banned**) **1** officially forbid something (以官方命令)禁止 **2** forbid someone to do something 禁止(某人)做 • **noun** an official order forbidding something 禁令

banal /bə'nɑːl/ **adjective** boring through being too ordinary and predictable 陈腐的;乏味的 ■ **banality** noun (plural **banalities**) **banally** adverb.

banana /bə'nɑːnə/ **noun** a long curved fruit of a tropical tree, with yellow skin 香蕉

band¹ /bænd/ **noun 1** a flat, thin strip or loop of material used for fastening, strengthening, or decoration 箍;带;饰带 **2** a stripe or strip that is different from its surroundings 条纹;条带 ■ **banded** adjective.

band² **noun 1** a small group of musicians and singers who play pop, jazz, or rock music 乐队 **2** a group of musicians who play brass, wind, or percussion instruments 管弦乐队 **3** a group of people with the same aim or a shared feature 群；伙；帮 • **verb** form a group with other people 聚集成群

bandage /'bændɪdʒ/ **noun** a strip of material tied round a wound or an injury (包扎伤口的)绷带 • **verb** (**bandages, bandaging, bandaged**) tie a bandage round 用绷带包扎

bandanna /bæn'dænə/ **noun** a square of cloth tied round the head or neck 印花大手帕(系于头部或颈部)

B. & B. /ˌbiː ən 'biː/ **abbreviation** bed and breakfast 住宿及早餐；膳宿

bandit /'bændɪt/ **noun** a member of a gang of armed robbers 强盗；土匪 ■ **banditry** noun.

bandolier /ˌbændə'lɪə(r)/ **noun** a belt with loops or pockets for carrying bullets, worn over the shoulder (挂在肩上的)子弹带

bandstand /'bændstænd/ **noun** a covered outdoor platform for a band to play on (有篷的)室外乐队演奏台

bandwagon /'bændwægən/ **noun** an activity or cause that has suddenly become fashionable or popular 风靡一时的活动；浪潮；时尚

bandwidth /'bændwɪdθ/ **noun 1** a range of frequencies used in telecommunications (电信系统的)频带宽度，带宽 **2** the ability of a computer network to transmit signals (计算机网络或其他电信系统的)带宽

bandy[1] /'bændi/ **adjective** (**bandier, bandiest**) (of a person's legs) curved outwards so that the knees are wide apart (人腿)向外弯曲的，罗圈的

bandy[2] **verb** (**bandies, bandying, bandied**) use an idea or word frequently in casual talk (漫不经心地)随便传播，胡乱散布 □ **bandy words** exchange angry remarks 吵架

bane /beɪn/ **noun** a cause of great distress or annoyance 灾星；祸根；祸害

bang /bæŋ/ **noun 1** a sudden loud noise (突然的)巨响 **2** a sudden painful blow 猛击；猛撞 • **verb 1** hit or put down forcefully and noisily 猛击；猛敲；砸 **2** make a bang (使)砰砰作响 • **adverb** Brit. informal【英,非正式】exactly 正好；恰好：*bang on time* 正好准时

banger /'bæŋə(r)/ **noun** Brit. informal 【英,非正式】**1** a sausage 香肠 **2** an old car 旧汽车 **3** a loud explosive firework 爆竹，鞭炮

Bangladeshi /ˌbæŋglə'deʃi/ **noun** (plural **Bangladeshis**) a person from Bangladesh 孟加拉人 • **adjective** relating to Bangladesh 孟加拉的

bangle /'bæŋgl/ **noun** a bracelet of rigid material worn loosely on the wrist 手镯；臂镯

banish /'bænɪʃ/ **verb 1** make someone leave a place as a punishment 放逐，流放 **2** get rid of; drive away 清除；排除，赶走 ■ **banishment** noun.

banister or **bannister** /'bænɪstə(r)/ **noun 1** the upright posts and handrail at the side of a staircase (楼梯的)栏杆，扶手 **2** a single upright post at the side of a staircase 栏杆柱

banjo /'bændʒəʊ/ **noun** (plural **banjos** or **banjoes**) a musical instrument like a guitar, with a circular body 班卓琴

bank[1] /bæŋk/ **noun 1** the land alongside a river or lake (河,湖的)岸 **2** a long, high slope, mound, or mass 坡；埂；堆 **3** a set of similar things grouped together in rows (类似事物的)一排，一列，一组 • **verb 1** form into a bank (把…)堆积起来 **2** (of an aircraft) tilt sideways in making a turn (飞机)倾斜飞行

bank[2] **noun 1** an organization that makes loans and keeps customers' money for them 银行 **2** a stock or supply of something 库存 **3** a site or container where you can leave something for recycling 库;储藏库 • verb **1** put money in a bank 把(钱)存入银行 **2** have an account at a bank 在银行开户 **3 (bank on)** rely on 依赖;指望 □ **bank holiday** Brit. 【英】a public holiday, when banks are officially closed 银行假日 **break the bank** informal 【非正式】cost more than you can afford 无力负担 ■ **banker** noun **banking** noun.

bankable /'bæŋkəbl/ **adjective** certain to bring profit and success 可获利的;有赚头的

banknote /'bæŋknəʊt/ **noun** a piece of paper money 钞票;纸币

bankroll /'bæŋkrəʊl/ **verb** informal 【非正式】give money to 为…提供资金;资助 • **noun** N. Amer. 【北美】a roll of banknotes 资金

bankrupt /'bæŋkrʌpt/ **adjective** officially declared not to have the money to pay your debts 宣布破产的;破产的 • **noun** a bankrupt person 破产者 • **verb** make someone bankrupt 使破产 ■ **bankruptcy** noun (plural **bankruptcies**)

banner /'bænə(r)/ **noun** a long strip of cloth with a slogan or design, hung up or carried on poles 横幅;旗;旗帜

bannister /'bænɪstə(r)/ ⇒ 见 BANISTER.

banns /bænz/ **plural noun** an announcement of an intended marriage read out in a church (教堂中的)结婚预告

banquet /'bæŋkwɪt/ **noun** an elaborate formal meal for many people 宴会;盛宴 • **verb** (**banquets, banqueting, banqueted**) attend a banquet 赴宴;参加宴会

banshee /bæn'ʃiː/ **noun** (in Irish legend) a female spirit whose wailing warns of a death (爱尔兰民间传说中的)报丧女妖(其哀号预示着有人死亡)

bantam /'bæntəm/ **noun** a kind of small chicken 矮脚鸡

banter /'bæntə(r)/ **noun** friendly teasing (善意的)取笑,逗弄 • **verb** (**banters,** **bantering, bantered**) make friendly teasing remarks (善意地)取笑,逗弄

bap /bæp/ **noun** Brit. 【英】a soft, round, flattish bread roll 软面包卷

baptism /'bæptɪzəm/ **noun** the Christian ceremony of sprinkling a person with water or dipping them in it to show that they have entered the Church (基督教的)浸礼,洗礼 □ **baptism of fire** a difficult new experience 初次考验 ■ **baptismal** adjective.

Baptist /'bæptɪst/ **noun** a member of a Christian group believing that only adults, not babies, should be baptized (基督教)浸礼会教徒(主张成年人才可受洗)

baptize or **baptise** /bæp'taɪz/ **verb** (**baptizes, baptizing, baptized**) **1** perform the baptism ceremony on someone 授洗;施洗 **2** give someone a name or nickname 给…起绰号

bar /bɑː(r)/ **noun 1** a long rigid piece of wood, metal, etc. (木头、金属等的)条,块 **2** a counter, room, or place where alcohol is served (售酒的)柜台 **3** something that stops or delays progress 障碍 **4** any of the short units into which a piece of music is divided (乐谱的)小节 **5 (the bar)** the place in a courtroom where an accused person stands during a trial (法庭上的)被告席 **6 (the Bar)** the profession of barrister 律师业 **7** Brit. 【英】a metal strip added to a medal as an additional honour (奖章上的)金属绶带 • **verb** (**bars, barring, barred**) **1** fasten with a bar or bars 闩上 **2** forbid or prevent 禁止;阻止 • **preposition** except for 除…之外 □ **bar code** a row of printed stripes identifying a product and its price, able to be read by a computer 条形码

barb /bɑːb/ **noun 1** the backward-pointing part of a fish hook, the tip of an arrow, etc. (箭头、鱼钩等的)倒钩,倒刺 **2** a spiteful remark 尖刻伤

人的话;讥讽

barbarian /ba:'beəriən/ **noun 1** (in ancient times) a person who did not belong to the Greek, Roman, or Christian civilizations (古代的)野蛮人,未开化的人 **2** a very uncivilized or cruel person 没有文化的人;残暴的人

barbaric /ba:'bærɪk/ **adjective 1** savagely cruel 残暴的;残忍的 **2** not cultured or civilized 无教养的;粗野的

barbarism /'ba:bərɪzəm/ **noun 1** great cruelty 野蛮;残暴 **2** an uncivilized or primitive state 未开化状态;原始蒙昧状态 ■ **barbarity** noun (plural **barbarities**)

barbarous /'ba:bərəs/ **adjective 1** very cruel 残暴的;残忍的 **2** uncivilized or uncultured 原始的;未开化的

barbecue /'ba:bɪkju:/ **noun 1** an outdoor meal at which food is grilled over a charcoal fire 户外烧烤餐 **2** a grill used at a barbecue (户外烧烤用的)烤架 • **verb** (**barbecues, barbecuing, barbecued**) cook food on a barbecue 烧烤(食物)

barbed /ba:bd/ **adjective 1** having a barb or barbs 有倒刺的;有钩的 **2** (of a remark) spiteful 尖刻的,刺的 ■ **barbed wire** wire with clusters of short, sharp spikes along it 刺丝网;带刺铁丝(网)

barbel /'ba:bl/ **noun 1** a long, thin growth hanging from the mouth or snout of some fish (鱼)触须 **2** a freshwater fish with barbels 鲃(一种带触须的淡水鱼)

barbell /'ba:bel/ **noun** a long metal bar with discs of different weights attached at each end, used for weightlifting (举重用的)杠铃

barber /'ba:bə(r)/ **noun** a person whose job is cutting men's hair and shaving or trimming their beards (为男子理发、修面的)理发师

barbiturate /ba:'bɪtʃʊrət/ **noun** a kind of drug used as a sedative 巴比土酸盐(一种镇静药)

bard /ba:d/ **noun** old use 【旧】a poet 诗人

bare /beə(r)/ **adjective 1** not wearing clothes 没穿衣服的;赤裸的 **2** without the usual covering or contents 光秃的;无遮盖的;无陈设的 **3** without detail; basic 不加修饰的;最基本的 **4** only just enough 刚刚够的;勉强的 • **verb** (**bares, baring, bared**) uncover or reveal 使露出;暴露;揭露 ■ **barely** adverb **bareness** noun

bareback /'beəbæk/ **adverb & adjective** on a horse without a saddle (骑马时)不用鞍的

barefaced /'beəfeɪst/ **adjective** done openly and without shame 露骨的;无耻的

bargain /'ba:gən/ **noun 1** an agreement made between people to do something for each other 协议;交易 **2** a thing sold at a low price 便宜货,廉价货 • **verb 1** discuss the terms of an agreement 讲条件;谈判;讨价还价 (**bargain for** or **on**) expect 预料;指望 **2 into the bargain** as well 此外;而且

> ✔ **拼写指南** remember the second *a*: bar*gain*. 记住拼写 bargain 中的第二个 a。

barge /ba:dʒ/ **noun** a long flat-bottomed boat for carrying goods on canals and rivers 长平底船;驳船 • **verb** (**barges, barging, barged**) **1** move forcefully or roughly 猛撞;乱闯 **2** (**barge in**) burst in on someone rudely 碰上;撞见(某人)

baritone /'bærɪtəʊn/ **noun** a man's singing voice between tenor and bass 男中音

barium /'beəriəm/ **noun** a chemical element that is a soft white metal (化学元素)钡

bark[1] /ba:k/ **noun** the sharp sudden cry of a dog, fox, or seal (狗、狐狸或海

豹的)吠声,叫声 • **verb 1** give a bark 吠;叫 **2** say a command or question suddenly or fiercely 厉声说出(命令或问题) **3** (**barking**) Brit. informal 【英,非正式】completely mad 完全发疯的

bark² **noun** the tough outer covering of the trunk and branches of a tree 树皮 • **verb** scrape the skin off your shin by accidentally hitting it 擦破(胫部)的皮

barley /'bɑːli/ **noun** a type of cereal plant with a bristly head 大麦 ■ **barley sugar** an orange sweet made of boiled sugar 大麦糖;麦芽糖

bar mitzvah /,bɑː 'mɪtsvə/ **noun** a religious ceremony in which a Jewish boy aged 13 takes on the responsibilities of an adult (年满13岁太男孩的)受诫礼

barmy /'bɑːmi/ **adjective** (**barmier**, **barmiest**) Brit. informal【英,非正式】mad 疯疯癫癫的

barn /bɑːn/ **noun** a large farm building used for storing hay or grain or keeping livestock 谷仓;粮仓;牲口棚 □ **barn dance** a party with country dancing 谷仓舞会

barnacle /'bɑːnəkl/ **noun** a small shellfish which fixes itself to things 藤壶(一种附着于物体上的小型外壳动物)

barnstorming /'bɑːnstɔːmɪŋ/ **adjective** done in a very showy, energetic way 炫耀的;气势盛的

barnyard /'bɑːnjɑːd/ **noun** N. Amer.【北美】a farmyard 仓院

barometer /bə'rɒmɪtə(r)/ **noun** an instrument that measures the pressure of the atmosphere, used to forecast the weather 气压表;气压计

baron /'bærən/ **noun 1** a man belonging to the lowest rank of the British nobility 男爵(在英国贵族中等级最低) **2** (in the Middle Ages) a man who held lands or property granted to him by the king or queen or a lord (中世纪的)贵族(由国王或女王敕封领地或财产) **3** a powerful person in business or industry (工商业)巨头,大亨 ■ **baronial** adjective.

baroness /'bærənəs/ **noun 1** the wife or widow of a baron 男爵夫人 **2** a woman holding the rank of baron 女男爵

baronet /'bærənət/ **noun** a man who holds a title below that of baron 准男爵

baroque /bə'rɒk/ **adjective** in a highly decorated style of European architecture, art, and music popular during the 17th and 18th centuries 巴洛克风格(17和18世纪流行于欧洲、涉及建筑、艺术和音乐领域的一种华丽风格)

barrack /'bærək/ **verb** Brit.【英】shout loud insulting comments at a performer or speaker 喝倒彩;起哄

barracks /'bærəks/ **noun** a building or set of buildings for soldiers to live in 营房;兵营

barracuda /,bærə'kjuːdə/ **noun** (plural **barracuda** or **barracudas**) a large predatory fish found in tropical seas 舒,梭鱼(大型掠食性鱼类,产于热带海域)

barrage /'bærɑːʒ/ **noun 1** a continuous attack by heavy guns 火力网;弹幕 **2** an overwhelming number of questions or complaints 一连串的问题;接二连三的抱怨 **3** a barrier placed across a river to control the water level 堰;水坝;拦河坝

barrel /'bærəl/ **noun 1** a large cylindrical container bulging out in the middle and with flat ends 桶 **2** a tube forming part of a gun, pen, etc. 枪管;炮管 □ **barrel organ** a small organ that plays a tune when you turn a handle 手摇风琴

barren /'bærən/ **adjective 1** (of land) not good enough to produce plants or crops (土地)贫瘠的,不毛的 **2** unable to produce children or young animals

不孕的;不生育的 **3** bleak 沉闷无趣的;无生气的

barricade /ˌbærɪˈkeɪd/ **noun** a makeshift barrier used to block a road or entrance 路障;街垒 • **verb** (**barricades, barricading, barricaded**) block or defend with a barricade 设路障于;阻塞;挡住

barrier /ˈbærɪə(r)/ **noun** something that stops people entering a place or making progress 障碍物;屏障

barring /ˈbɑːrɪŋ/ **preposition** except for; if not for 除…之外;除非

barrister /ˈbærɪstə(r)/ **noun** Brit. 【英】 a lawyer qualified to argue a case in court (有资格出席法庭辩护的)出庭律师,辩护律师,高级律师

barrow¹ /ˈbærəʊ/ **noun** Brit. 【英】 a two-wheeled cart pushed by hand and used by street traders (街头小贩用的)两轮手推车,流动售货车

barrow² **noun** a mound of earth built over a grave in ancient times 古坟;古墓

bartender /ˈbɑːtendə(r)/ **noun** a person serving drinks at a bar 酒吧侍者

barter /ˈbɑːtə(r)/ **verb** (**barters, bartering, bartered**) exchange goods or services for other goods or services 以(货物或服务)作交换 • **noun** trade by bartering 易货贸易

basalt /ˈbæsɔːlt/ **noun** a dark volcanic rock 玄武岩(一种深色火山岩)

base¹ /beɪs/ **noun 1** the lowest or supporting part of something 底;底座;基座 **2** the main place where a person works or stays 居所;据点;总部 **3** a centre of operations 基地;根据地;*a military base* 军事基地 **4** a main element to which others are added 基本成分;主要成分 **5** Chemistry 【化学】 a substance able to react with an acid to form a salt and water 碱 **6** Baseball 【棒球】 each of the four points that you must reach in turn to score a run 垒 • **verb** (**bases, basing, based**) **1** (**base something on**) use something

as the foundation for something else 以…为基础 **2** station someone or something at a particular base 驻扎;设立

base² **adjective 1** bad or immoral 卑劣的;卑鄙的 **2** old use 【旧】 of low social class 卑下的;卑贱的 □ **base metal** a common non-precious metal 贱金属

baseball /ˈbeɪsbɔːl/ **noun** a game played with a bat and ball on a diamond-shaped circuit of four bases, which a batsman must run around to score 棒球(运动) □ **baseball cap** a cotton cap with a large peak 棒球帽

baseless /ˈbeɪsləs/ **adjective** not based on fact; untrue 无根据的;不真实的

baseline /ˈbeɪslaɪn/ **noun 1** a starting point for comparisons 基础;起点 **2** (in tennis, volleyball, etc.) the line marking each end of a court (网球场、排球场等的)底线

basement /ˈbeɪsmənt/ **noun** a room or floor below ground level 地下室

bases /ˈbeɪsiːz/ plural of BASE¹ and BASIS.

bash /bæʃ/ informal 【非正式】 **verb** hit hard and violently 猛击;猛撞 • **noun 1** a heavy blow 猛击;猛撞 **2** a party 聚会 **3** Brit. 【英】 an attempt 尝试

bashful /ˈbæʃfʊl/ **adjective** shy and easily embarrassed 扭怩的;羞怯的 ■ **bashfully** adverb.

basic /ˈbeɪsɪk/ **adjective 1** forming an essential foundation; fundamental 基础的;基本的;根本的 **2** of the simplest or lowest kind or standard 最基本需要的;最低水平的 • **noun** (**basics**) essential facts or principles 基本事实;基本原则 ■ **basically** adverb.

basil /ˈbæzl/ **noun** a herb used in cooking 罗勒(用于烹饪的一种香草)

basilica /bəˈzɪlɪkə/ **noun** a large church or hall with two rows of columns inside and a curved end with a dome 巴西利卡;长方形会堂

basilisk /ˈbæzɪlɪsk/ **noun** a mythical

reptile that could kill people by looking at or breathing on them (神话中的)蛇怪(传说其目光或气息可致人死命)

basin /ˈbeɪsɪn/ **noun 1** a large bowl or open container for holding liquid 盆 **2** a circular valley 盆地;凹地 **3** an area drained by a river 流域 **4** an enclosed area of water for mooring boats 内港;内湾;船坞

basis /ˈbeɪsɪs/ **noun** (plural **bases** /ˈbeɪsiːz/) **1** the foundation of a theory or process 基础;根据 **2** the reasons why something is done (做事的)依据,准则

bask /bɑːsk/ **verb 1** lie in the sun for pleasure (舒适地)晒太阳 **2** (**bask in**) take great pleasure in 在…中得到极大乐趣

basket /ˈbɑːskɪt/ **noun 1** a container for carrying things, made from strips of cane or wire 篮;篓;筐 **2** a net fixed on a hoop, used as the goal in basketball (篮球运动中的)篮

basketball /ˈbɑːskɪtbɔːl/ **noun** a team game in which goals are scored by throwing a ball through a hoop 篮球(运动)

bass¹ /beɪs/ **noun 1** the lowest adult male singing voice 男低音 **2** a bass guitar or double bass 低音吉他;低音提琴 **3** the deep, low-frequency part of sound 低音 ▪ **bassist** noun.

bass² /bæs/ **noun** (plural **bass** or **basses**) a fish related to the perch, used for food 鲈鱼(供食用)

basset hound /ˈbæsɪt/ **noun** a breed of hunting dog with a long body, short legs, and long, drooping ears 短脚猎狗(体长腿短,耳长而下垂)

bassoon /bəˈsuːn/ **noun** a large low-pitched woodwind instrument 大管;巴松管 ▪ **bassoonist** noun.

bastard /ˈbɑːstəd/ **noun 1** old use 【旧】a person whose parents were not married 私生子;非婚生子 **2** informal 【非正式】a nasty person 讨厌鬼

bastardize or **bastardise** /ˈbɑːstədaɪz/ **verb** (**bastardizes, bastardizing, bastardized**) make something less good by adding new elements 使变低劣;使退化不纯

baste /beɪst/ **verb** (**bastes, basting, basted**) pour fat or juices over meat while it cooks (烹调时)在(肉)上浇滴油脂(或卤汁)

bastion /ˈbæstɪən/ **noun 1** a part of a fortified building that sticks out 棱堡 **2** something that protects or preserves particular principles or activities 堡垒

bat¹ /bæt/ **noun** a piece of wood with a handle and a solid surface, used in sports for hitting the ball 球棒;球板;球拍 ▪ **verb** (**bats, batting, batted**) **1** (in sport) take the role of hitting rather than throwing the ball (在体育运动中)担任击球手 **2** hit with the flat of your own hand (用手掌)击,打 **off your own bat** Brit. informal 【英,非正式】of your own accord 出于自愿;主动地

bat² **noun 1** a flying animal that is active at night 蝙蝠 **2** (**old bat**) informal 【非正式】an unpleasant woman 讨厌女人;丑妇

bat³ **verb** (**bats, batting, batted**) flutter your eyelashes 眨(眼);扑闪(眼睫毛)

batch /bætʃ/ **noun** a quantity of goods produced or dispatched at one time 一批(生产量或发送量)

bated /ˈbeɪtɪd/ **adjective** (**with bated breath**) in great suspense 屏息以待地;焦虑地

> ✔ 拼写指南 bated, not baited. bated 不要拼作 baited。

bath /bɑːθ/ **noun 1** a large tub that you fill with water and sit or lie in to wash your body 浴缸;浴盆 **2** an act of washing yourself in a bath 浴;洗澡 **3** (also **baths**) Brit. 【英】a building containing a public swimming pool or washing facilities 公共浴室;澡堂

• verb Brit.【英】wash in a bath (在澡堂) 洗澡

bathe /beɪð/ **verb** (**bathes, bathing, bathed**) **1** wash by putting your body in water 洗澡 游泳 **2** Brit.【英】have a swim 游泳 **3** soak or wipe gently with liquid (轻柔地)浸洗, 擦洗 • **noun** Brit.【英】a swim 游泳 ▪ **bather** noun.

bathos /'beɪθɒs/ **noun** (in literature) a change from a serious mood to something trivial (文学中的)突降法 (指由重大严肃突降至平庸琐屑的手法)

bathroom /'bɑːθrʊm/ **noun 1** a room containing a bath and usually also a washbasin and toilet 浴室, 盥洗室 **2** N. Amer.【北美】a room containing a toilet 厕所; 洗手间

batik /'bɑːtiːk/ **noun** a method of producing coloured designs on cloth using wax to cover the areas not to be dyed 蜡防印花法

baton /'bætɒn/ **noun 1** a thin stick used to conduct an orchestra or choir (指挥乐队或合唱队用的)指挥棒 **2** a short stick passed from runner to runner in a relay race (接力赛跑用的)接力棒 **3** a police officer's truncheon (警官用的)警棍

batsman /'bætsmən/ **noun** (plural **batsmen**) a player who bats in cricket (板球运动中的)击球手

battalion /bə'tæliən/ **noun** an army unit forming part of a brigade (军队的)营

batten /'bætn/ **noun** a long wooden or metal strip used for strengthening or securing something 板条, 压条 □ **batten down the hatches** prepare for a crisis 准备面对危机

batter[1] /'bætə(r)/ **verb** (**batters, battering, battered**) hit repeatedly with hard blows 连续猛击

batter[2] **noun** a mixture of flour, egg, and milk or water, used for making pancakes or coating food before frying 面糊(用面粉、鸡蛋和牛奶或水

调制而成)

battery /'bætri/ **noun** (plural **batteries**) **1** a device containing one or more electrical cells, used as a source of power 电池; 电池组 **2** an extensive series 一系列; 一套: *a battery of tests* 一套测验 **3** Brit.【英】a series of small cages for keeping chickens in artificial conditions 层架式家禽饲养笼 **4** Law【法律】an unlawful physical attack on another person 殴打(罪)

battle /'bætl/ **noun 1** a prolonged fight between organized armed forces 战役; 战斗 **2** a long and difficult struggle or conflict 斗争; 冲突 • **verb** (**battles, battling, battled**) fight or struggle with determination 战斗; 斗争; 奋斗

battleaxe /'bætlæks/ **noun 1** a large axe used in ancient warfare (古代战争中使用的)战斧 **2** informal【非正式】an aggressive older woman 悍妇; 母老虎

battledress /'bætldres/ **noun** clothing worn by soldiers for fighting (士兵穿的)战斗服装, 战地服装

battlefield /'bætlfiːld/ **noun** the piece of ground where a battle is fought 战场

battlement /'bætlmənt/ **noun** a wall at the top of a castle with gaps for firing through 城垛, 雉堞

battleship /'bætlʃɪp/ **noun** a heavily armoured warship with large guns 战列舰

batty /'bæti/ **adjective** (**battier, battiest**) informal【非正式】mad 神经错乱的; 疯疯癫癫的

bauble /'bɔːbl/ **noun** a small, showy trinket or decoration (花哨的)小玩意儿, 小装饰品

baulk /bɔːk/ (US spelling【美拼作】**balk**) **verb 1** (**baulk at**) hesitate to accept an idea 对(某想法)犹豫不决 **2** prevent from getting or doing something 妨碍; 阻碍

bauxite /ˈbɔːksaɪt/ **noun** a clay-like rock from which aluminium is obtained 铝土矿；铝土岩

bawdy /ˈbɔːdi/ **adjective** (**bawdier**, **bawdiest**) referring to sex in an amusing way 猥亵的；低级下流的

bawl /bɔːl/ **verb 1** shout out noisily 大声叫嚷 **2** cry noisily 放声痛哭 • **noun** a loud shout 大叫声

bay¹ /beɪ/ **noun** an area of sea and coast forming a broad curve 海湾

bay² **noun** a Mediterranean shrub whose leaves are used in cookery 月桂树(地中海地区灌木，叶用于烹饪)

bay³ **noun 1** a window area that sticks out from a wall (装窗的)房间突出部分 **2** an area for a particular purpose (用于特定用途的)分隔区：*a loading bay* 装卸货区 □ **bay window** a window sticking out from a wall 凸窗

bay⁴ **adjective** (of a horse) mainly reddish-brown in colour (马)枣红色的

bay⁵ **verb** (of a dog) bark or howl loudly (狗)狂吠，大叫 □ **at bay** trapped or cornered 被围；处于走投无路的境地 **hold** (or **keep**) **someone/thing at bay** prevent someone or something from approaching or having an effect 不让…接近；阻止…发生

bayonet /ˈbeɪənət/ **noun** a long blade fixed to a rifle for hand-to-hand fighting (步枪上的)刺刀 • **verb** (**bayonets**, **bayoneting**, **bayoneted**) stab someone with a bayonet 用刺刀刺刷

bazaar /bəˈzɑː(r)/ **noun 1** a market in a Middle Eastern country (中东国家的)市场，集市 **2** a sale of goods to raise funds 义卖

bazooka /bəˈzuːkə/ **noun** a short-range rocket launcher used against tanks 反坦克火箭筒

BBC /ˌbiː biː ˈsiː/ **abbreviation** British Broadcasting Corporation 英国广播公司

BC /ˌbiː ˈsiː/ **abbreviation** before Christ (used to show that a date is before the traditional date of Jesus's birth) 公元前(用于表示基督出生前的日期)

❗注意 write BC **after** the numerals, as in 72 BC. BC应置于年份数字后，如 72 BC (公元前72年)。

be /biː, bi/ **verb** (singular present **am**; **are**; **is**; plural present **are**; 1st and 3rd singular past **was**; 2nd singular past and plural past **were**; present participle **being**; past participle **been**) **1** exist; be present 在；存在 **2** happen 发生 **3** have the specified state, nature, or role (具有某一特定的状态、性质或充当某一角色)是，成为 **4** come, go, or visit 来；去；前往；造访 • **auxiliary verb 1** used with a present participle to form continuous tenses (与现在分词连用构成进行时) **2** used with a past participle to form the passive voice (与过去分词连用构成被动语态) **3** used to show something that is due to, may, or should happen (表示某事预定、可能或应该发生)

beach /biːtʃ/ **noun** a shore of sand or pebbles at the edge of the sea 海滩；沙滩 • **verb** bring something on to a beach from the water 把…拖上岸；使搁浅

beachcomber /ˈbiːtʃkəʊmə(r)/ **noun** a person who searches beaches for valuable things 海滩拾荒者

beacon /ˈbiːkən/ **noun 1** a fire lit on the top of a hill as a signal 烽火 **2** a light acting as a signal for ships or aircraft 灯塔；灯标

bead /biːd/ **noun 1** a small piece of glass, stone, etc., threaded with others to make a necklace (可串起来的)小珠，珠子 **2** a drop of a liquid on a surface 滴 ■ **beaded** adjective

beadle /ˈbiːdl/ **noun** Brit.【英】**1** an official of a church, college, etc. (教堂、学院等的)执事，行政官员 **2** historical 【历史】a parish officer who dealt with minor offenders (处理犯轻罪者的)教区执事

beady /ˈbiːdi/ **adjective** (of a person's

eyes) small, round, and observant (人的眼睛)亮晶晶的

beagle /ˈbiːgl/ *noun* a small short-legged breed of hound 小猎兔犬

beak /biːk/ *noun* a bird's hard projecting jaws 鸟喙

beaker /ˈbiːkə(r)/ *noun* Brit. 【英】**1** a tall plastic cup 高塑料杯 **2** a cylindrical glass container used in laboratories (实验室用的)烧杯

beam /biːm/ *noun* **1** a long piece of timber or metal used as a support in building (建筑物的)横梁 **2** a narrow length of timber for balancing on in gymnastics (体操运动中的)平衡木 **3** a ray of light or particles 光线;光柱;(粒子的)束,柱 **4** a wide, happy smile 笑容;喜色 **5** the width of a ship 船宽;船幅 • *verb* **1** transmit a radio signal 发出(无线电信号) **2** shine brightly 照耀 **3** smile broadly 面露喜色;喜笑颜开

bean /biːn/ *noun* **1** an edible seed growing in long pods on certain plants 豆 **2** the hard seed of a coffee or cocoa plant 咖啡豆,可可豆 □ **full of beans** *informal* 【非正式】in high spirits 精力充沛;兴高采烈

beanbag /ˈbiːnbæg/ *noun* **1** a small bag filled with dried beans and used in children's games (儿童游戏用的)豆子袋 **2** a large cushion filled with polystyrene beads, used as a seat 豆袋椅

bear¹ /beə(r)/ *verb* (**bears**, **bearing**, **bore**; *past participle* **borne**) **1** carry 携带 **2** have a particular quality or visible mark 带有;具有 **3** support a weight 承受,支撑(重量) **4** (**bear yourself**) behave in a particular way (以某种方式)表现 **5** tolerate 忍受;容忍 **6** give birth to a child 生(孩子) **7** (of a tree or plant) produce fruit or flowers (树或草本植物)结(果实),开(花) **8** turn and go in a particular direction 转向;拐弯 □ **bear down on** approach someone in a determined or threatening way 向…逼近;冲向 **bear something in mind** remember and take something into account 记住(某事物) **bear something out** support or confirm something 为…提供支持;证实 **bear up** remain cheerful in difficult circumstances 保持振作;不灰心 **bear with** be patient with 对…有耐心;容忍 ■ **bearable** *adjective* **bearably** *adverb* **bearer** *noun.*

bear² *noun* a large, heavy animal with thick fur 熊

beard /bɪəd/ *noun* a growth of hair on a man's chin and lower cheeks (男子下巴和面颊下部的)胡须,络腮胡子 • *verb* boldly confront or challenge an important or powerful person 公然反对,对抗(权贵) ■ **bearded** *adjective.*

bearing /ˈbeərɪŋ/ *noun* **1** a person's way of standing, moving, or behaving 举止;风度 **2** relevance 关系;关联 **3** (**bearings**) a part of a machine that allows one part to rotate or move in contact with another 轴承 **4** direction or position in relation to a fixed point 方向;方位 **5** (**your bearings**) awareness of where you are 方位感

beast /biːst/ *noun* **1** an animal, especially a large or dangerous mammal 动物;野兽 **2** a very cruel or wicked person 凶残的人;邪恶的人 □ **beast of burden** an animal used for carrying loads 役畜;牲口

beastly /ˈbiːstli/ *adjective* Brit. *informal* 【英,非正式】very unpleasant 令人讨厌的;可恶的 ■ **beastliness** *noun*

beat /biːt/ *verb* (**beats**, **beating**, **beat**; *past participle* **beaten**) **1** hit someone repeatedly and violently (连续,猛烈地)打,击 **2** hit something repeatedly to flatten it or make a noise (反复)敲击,拍打 **3** defeat or be better than 打败;战胜,胜过 **4** *informal* 【非正式】baffle someone 难倒;使困惑不解 **5** (of the heart) throb (心脏)跳动,搏动 **6** (of a bird) move its wings up and down (鸟)扑打,拍打(翅膀) **7** stir cooking ingredients vigorously 搅打，搅拌(烹调用配料) • **noun 1** an act of beating 击打；拍打；跳动 **2** the main rhythm, or a unit of rhythm, in music or poetry (音乐或诗歌的)强音，节拍，音拍 **3** a brief pause 短暂停顿 **4** an area patrolled by a police officer (警察的)巡逻范围 • **adjective** informal 【非正式】completely exhausted 筋疲力尽的 □ **beat about the bush** discuss something without coming to the point 转弯抹角地说；旁敲侧击 **beat it** informal 【非正式】leave 跑掉；溜走 **beat someone up** hit or kick someone repeatedly 痛打；狠揍 **off the beaten track** isolated 偏僻的

beatific /ˌbiːəˈtɪfɪk/ **adjective** feeling or expressing blissful happiness 至福的；极乐的 ■ **beatifically adverb**.

beatify /biˈætɪfaɪ/ **verb** (**beatifies**, **beatifying**, **beatified**) state officially that a dead person is very holy (the first step towards making them a saint) 为(去世的人)行宣福礼

beatnik /ˈbiːtnɪk/ **noun** a young person in the 1950s and early 1960s who rejected conventional society (20世纪50至60年代初的)"垮掉的一代"成员

beau /bəʊ/ **noun** (plural **beaux** or **beaus** /bəʊz, bəʊ/) dated 【废】a young woman's boyfriend (年轻女子的)男友

beautician /bjuːˈtɪʃn/ **noun** a person whose job is to give beauty treatments 美容师

beautiful /ˈbjuːtɪfl/ **adjective 1** very pleasing to the senses 美的；美丽的 **2** of a very high standard; excellent 出色的；很好的 ■ **beautifully adverb**.

> ✔ 拼写指南 remember the *u* before the *t*: bea*u*tiful. 记住拼写 beautiful 中 t 前的 u。

beautify /ˈbjuːtɪfaɪ/ **verb** (**beautifies**, **beautifying**, **beautified**) make someone or something look more attractive 美化；使变美

beauty /ˈbjuːti/ **noun** (plural **beauties**) **1** the quality of being very pleasing to the senses 美；美丽 **2** a beautiful woman 美人；美女 **3** an excellent example of something 榜样；典型例子 **4** an attractive feature or advantage 好处；优点。

beaver /ˈbiːvə(r)/ **noun** (plural **beaver** or **beavers**) a large rodent that lives partly in water 河狸；海狸 • **verb** (**beavers**, **beavering**, **beavered**) (**beaver away**) informal 【非正式】work hard 努力工作

becalmed /bɪˈkɑːmd/ **adjective** (of a sailing ship) unable to move because there is no wind (航行中的船因无风而)无法移动的

because /bɪˈkɒz/ **conjunction** for the reason that; since 因为；由于

beck /bek/ **noun** (**at someone's beck and call**) always having to be ready to obey someone's orders 唯(某人)之命是从；听凭(某人)调遣

beckon /ˈbekən/ **verb 1** make a movement encouraging someone to approach or follow 向…示意；召唤 **2** seem appealing 吸引；引诱

become /bɪˈkʌm/ **verb** (**becomes**, **becoming**, **became**; past participle **become**) **1** begin to be 变得；开始变得 **2** turn into 成为 **3** (**become of**) happen to 发生于 **4** suit or be appropriate to 与…相称；适合

becquerel /ˈbekərel/ **noun** a unit of radioactivity 贝可，贝可勒尔(放射性活度单位)

bed /bed/ **noun 1** a piece of furniture for sleeping on 床 **2** an area of ground where flowers and shrubs are grown 花坛；苗圃 **3** a flat base 基础；基座 • **verb** (**beds**, **bedding**, **bedded**) **1** (**bed down**) sleep in a place where you do not usually sleep 住宿 **2** (**bed something in**) fix something firmly 把…固定

bedclothes /ˈbedkləʊðz/ **plural noun** coverings for a bed, such as sheets and blankets 床上用品

bedding /'bedɪŋ/ **noun 1** bedclothes 床上用品 **2** straw for animals to sleep on (供家畜垫在身下作睡铺的)垫草

bedevil /bɪ'devl/ **verb** (**bedevils, bedevilling, bedevilled**; US spelling 【美拼作】**bedevils, bedeviling, bedeviled**) cause continual trouble to 长期搅扰

bedlam /'bedləm/ **noun** a scene of great confusion and noise 混乱嘈杂的场面

bedpan /'bedpæn/ **noun** a container used as a toilet by a bedridden patient (卧床病人用的)床上便盆

bedraggled /bɪ'drægld/ **adjective** untidy 不整洁的

bedridden /'bedrɪdn/ **adjective** unable to get out of bed because of illness or old age (因生病或年老)卧床不起的

bedrock /'bedrɒk/ **noun 1** a layer of solid rock under soil 基岩 **2** the central principles on which something is based 基本原则;基本原理

bedroom /'bedru:m/ **noun** a room for sleeping in 卧室

bedsit /'bedsɪt/ or **bedsitter** /bed'sɪtə(r)/ **noun** Brit. 【英】a rented room consisting of a combined bedroom and living room, with cooking facilities 卧室兼起居室

bedsore /'bedsɔ:(r)/ **noun** a sore caused by lying in bed in one position for a long time 褥疮

bedspread /'bedspred/ **noun** a decorative cloth used to cover a bed 床罩

bedstead /'bedsted/ **noun** the framework of a bed 床架

bee /bi:/ **noun** a winged insect which collects nectar and pollen from flowers and makes wax and honey 蜜蜂

beech /bi:tʃ/ **noun** a large tree with grey bark and pale wood 山毛榉

beef /bi:f/ **noun** the flesh of a cow, bull, or ox, used as food 牛肉 • **verb** (**beef something up**) informal 【非正式】make something stronger or larger 增强;扩大

beefburger /'bi:fbɜ:gə(r)/ **noun** a fried or grilled cake of minced beef eaten in a bun 牛肉汉堡包

beefy /'bi:fi/ **adjective** (**beefier, beefiest**) informal 【非正式】muscular or strong 肌肉发达的;粗壮的

beehive /'bi:haɪv/ **noun** a structure in which bees are kept 蜂房;蜂箱

beeline /'bi:laɪn/ **noun** (**make a beeline for**) hurry straight to 径直奔向

Beelzebub /bi:'elzɪbʌb/ **noun** the Devil 别西卜(鬼王)

been /bi:n/ past participle of BE.

beep /bi:p/ **noun** a short, high-pitched sound made by electronic equipment or the horn of a vehicle (电子设备或车辆喇叭发出的)哔哔声,嘟嘟声 • **verb** produce a beep 发哔哔声;发嘟嘟声

beer /bɪə(r)/ **noun** an alcoholic drink made from fermented malt flavoured with hops 啤酒

beeswax /'bi:zwæks/ **noun** wax produced by bees to make honeycombs, used for wood polishes and candles 蜂蜡,黄蜡(蜜蜂为筑巢而分泌的蜡质,用于给木器上光和制蜡烛)

beet /bi:t/ **noun** a plant with a fleshy root, grown as food and for making into sugar 甜菜

beetle /'bi:tl/ **noun** an insect with hard, shiny covers over its wings 甲壳虫

beetroot /'bi:tru:t/ **noun** Brit. 【英】the edible dark-red root of a kind of beet 甜菜根

befall /bɪ'fɔ:l/ **verb** (**befalls, befalling, befell**; past participle **befallen**) literary 【文】(of something bad) happen to someone (坏事情)发生在…身上,降临在…头上

befit /bɪ'fɪt/ **verb** (**befits, befitting, befitted**) be appropriate for 适合;对…相称 ■ **befitting** adjective.

before /bɪ'fɔ:(r)/ **preposition, conjunction, & adverb 1** during the time preceding 在…以前;以前;以往 **2** in front of 在…前面;在前 **3** rather than (宁可…而)不愿

beforehand /bɪˈfɔːhænd/ **adverb** in advance 预先;事先;提前

befriend /bɪˈfrend/ **verb** become a friend to 和…交朋友;对…以朋友相待

befuddled /bɪˈfʌdl/ **adjective** confused 糊涂的;迷惑不解的

beg /beg/ **verb** (**begs**, **begging**, **begged**) **1** humbly ask someone for something 请求;恳求 **2** ask for food or money as charity 乞讨;乞求施舍 □ **beg the question 1** (of a fact or action) invite a question or point that has not been dealt with (事实或行动)引起疑问,令人置疑 **2** assume that something is true without discussing it 想当然;以假定作为论据 **go begging** be available because other people do not want it 没人要;没人接

beget /bɪˈget/ **verb** (**begets**, **begetting**, **begot** or **begat**; past participle **begotten**) old use 【旧】 **1** cause something 产生;引起;招致 **2** become the father of a child 做父亲

beggar /ˈbegə(r)/ **noun 1** a person who lives by begging for food or money 乞丐;叫花子 **2** informal 【非正式】a particular type of person 家伙: *lucky beggar!* 幸运的家伙! □ **beggar belief** be too extraordinary to be believed 难以置信 ■ **beggarly** adjective.

begin /bɪˈgɪn/ **verb** (**begins**, **beginning**, **began**; past participle **begun**) **1** carry out or experience the first part of an action or activity 开始;启动 **2** come into being 开始出现;开始存在 **3** have a particular starting point (从…)开始;(以…)为起点 **4** (**begin on**) set to work on 着手 ■ **beginner** noun **beginning** noun.

begonia /bɪˈgəʊniə/ **noun** a plant with brightly coloured flowers 秋海棠

begrudge /bɪˈgrʌdʒ/ **verb 1** feel envious that someone possesses something 妒忌;羡慕 **2** give something resentfully 勉强给予

beguile /bɪˈgaɪl/ **verb** charm or trick 使着迷;诱骗

behalf /bɪˈhɑːf/ **noun** (**on behalf of** or **on someone's behalf**) **1** in the interests of a particular person, group, or principle 为了…的利益 **2** as a representative of 代表

behave /bɪˈheɪv/ **verb 1** act in a certain way 表现 **2** (also **behave yourself**) act in a polite or proper way 举止得体;守规矩

behaved /bɪˈheɪvd/ **adjective** acting in a certain way 表现…的: *a well-behaved child* 听话的孩子

behaviour /bɪˈheɪvjə(r)/ (US spelling 【美拼作】**behavior**) **noun** the way in which someone or something behaves 行为;举止;表现 ■ **behavioural** adjective.

behead /bɪˈhed/ **verb** execute someone by cutting off their head 砍(某人)的头;将(某人)斩首

behemoth /bɪˈhiːmɒθ/ **noun** a huge creature or a very large organization 巨兽;庞然大物

behest /bɪˈhest/ **noun** (**at someone's behest**) in response to someone's order 按照(某人)的命令

behind /bɪˈhaɪnd/ **preposition & adverb 1** at or to the back or far side of (…的)背后;到(…的)背后;在(…的)远端;到(…的)远端 **2** further back than other members of a group 落在(…的)后面 **3** in support of 支持 **4** responsible for an event or plan 对(事件或计划)负责 **5** late in doing something 迟(于);晚(于)

behold /bɪˈhəʊld/ **verb** (**beholds**, **beholding**, **beheld**) old use 【旧】 see or look at 看;瞧;观察

beholden /bɪˈhəʊldən/ **adjective** (**beholden to**) owing something to someone because they have done you a favour 对(某人)感恩的,欠人情的

behove /bɪˈhəʊv/ **verb** (**it behoves someone to do**) formal 【正式】it is right or appropriate for someone to do 对(某人)来说应理应(或合适)做

beige /beɪʒ/ *noun* a pale sandy colour 米色

being /'biːɪŋ/ *noun* **1** existence 存在，生存 **2** the nature of a person (人的)本质,本性 **3** a living creature 生物

bejewelled /bɪ'dʒuːəld/ (US spelling 【美拼作】**bejeweled**) *adjective* decorated with jewels 饰有珠宝的，镶嵌珠宝的

belated /bɪ'leɪtɪd/ *adjective* coming late or too late 来迟的;延误的 ■ **belatedly** *adverb*.

belch /beltʃ/ *verb* **1** noisily expel wind from the stomach through the mouth 打嗝 **2** give out smoke or flames with great force 喷出,喷射(烟或火) • *noun* an act of belching 打嗝;喷吐

beleaguered /bɪ'liːɡəd/ *adjective* **1** in difficulties 处于困境的;受困扰的 **2** under siege 被围困的;受围攻的

belfry /'belfri/ *noun* (plural **belfries**) the place in a bell tower or steeple in which the bells are situated 钟室;钟阁

Belgian /'beldʒən/ *noun* a person from Belgium 比利时人 • *adjective* relating to Belgium 比利时的

belie /bɪ'laɪ/ *verb* (**belies**, **belying**, **belied**) **1** fail to give a true idea of 使人对…产生误解,掩饰 **2** show that something is not true 显示…虚假

belief /bɪ'liːf/ *noun* **1** a feeling that something exists or is true 相信 **2** a firmly held opinion 信念;看法 **3** (**belief in**) trust or confidence in 信任;信心 **4** religious faith 宗教信仰

believe /bɪ'liːv/ *verb* (**believes**, **believing**, **believed**) **1** accept that something is true or someone is telling the truth 相信,确信 **2** (**believe in**) have faith that something is true or exists 相信…的真实性;相信…的存在 **3** think or suppose 认为,猜想,料想 **4** have a religious faith 信奉 ■ **believable** *adjective* **believer** *noun*.

✔ **拼写指南** *i* before *e* except after *c*: bel*ie*ve. i 置于 e 前，在 c 后除外，如 believe.

belittle /bɪ'lɪtl/ *verb* (**belittles**, **belittling**, **belittled**) dismiss as unimportant 轻视,小看;贬低

bell /bel/ *noun* **1** a deep metal cup that sounds a clear musical note when struck 钟 **2** a device that buzzes or rings to give a signal 铃 □ **ring a bell** *informal* 【非正式】sound vaguely familiar 听起来有些许耳熟

belladonna /belə'dɒnə/ *noun* **1** deadly nightshade 颠茄 **2** a drug made from deadly nightshade 颠茄碱(一种药物)

belle /bel/ *noun* a beautiful woman 美女

bellicose /'belɪkəʊs/ *adjective* aggressive and ready to fight 好战的;好斗的

belligerence /bə'lɪdʒərəns/ *noun* aggressive or warlike behaviour 好战性;好斗性

belligerent /bə'lɪdʒərənt/ *adjective* **1** hostile and aggressive 好战的;好斗的 **2** taking part in a war or conflict 交战中的;在斗殴的 ■ **belligerently** *adverb*.

bellow /'beləʊ/ *verb* **1** give a deep roar of pain or anger 怒吼;咆哮;惨叫 **2** shout or sing very loudly 大声叫喊;大声唱 • *noun* a deep shout or noise 大声叫喊;吼叫声

bellows /'beləʊz/ *plural noun* a device consisting of a bag with two handles, used for blowing air into a fire 风箱

belly /'beli/ *noun* (plural **bellies**) **1** the front part of the body below the ribs, containing the stomach and bowels 腹部,肚子 **2** a person's stomach 胃

bellyache /'belieɪk/ *informal* 【非正式】 *noun* a stomach pain 肚子痛 • *verb* complain noisily or often 大声抱怨;时不时地发牢骚

bellyflop /'belɪflɒp/ *noun* *informal* 【非正式】a dive into water in which you

land flat on your front 腹部先触水的跳水动作

belong /bɪˈlɒŋ/ **verb 1 (belong to)** be the property of 属于；是…的财产 **2 (belong to)** be a member of 是…的成员 **3** be rightly put into a particular position or class 应被放置(在某位置)；应归入(某类) **4** feel at ease in a particular place or situation 适应(某地或某情况)

belongings /bɪˈlɒŋɪŋz/ **plural noun** a person's movable possessions 动产；财物

beloved /bɪˈlʌvd/ **adjective** dearly loved 热爱的；钟爱的

below /bɪˈləʊ/ **preposition & adverb 1** at a lower level than 在(…)下面；在(…)以下 **2** (in printed writing) mentioned further down (书面文字中)在下文

belt /belt/ **noun 1** a strip of leather or fabric worn round the waist 腰带 **2** a continuous band in machinery that connects two wheels 传送带 **3** a strip or encircling area (狭长或环形的)地带，地区 • **verb 1** fasten with a belt 用带束紧；用带系牢 **2** hit very hard 狠揍；痛打 **3 (belt something out)** informal 【非正式】 sing or play something loudly 高声唱；大声演奏 **4 (belt up)** Brit. informal 【英, 非正式】 be quiet 保持安静 □ **below the belt** against the rules; unfair 不公正；违反规则

belying /bɪˈlaɪɪŋ/ present participle of BELIE.

bemoan /bɪˈməʊn/ **verb** express sadness or regret about something 哀悼

bemused /bɪˈmjuːzd/ **adjective** confused or bewildered 困惑的；茫然的 ■ **bemusement** noun.

bench /bentʃ/ **noun 1** a long seat for more than one person 长椅；长凳 **2** a long table for working at in a workshop or laboratory 工作台 **3 (the bench)** the office of judge or magistrate 法官(或地方法官)的职位 **4 (the bench)** a seat at the side of a sports field for coaches and reserve players (教练员和替补运动员的)场外席

benchmark /ˈbentʃmɑːk/ **noun** a standard against which things may be compared 基准；基准尺度

bend /bend/ **verb (bends, bending, bent) 1** change from being straight; make or become curved or angled 变弯曲；转弯 **2** lean or curve the body downwards 屈身；俯身 **3** change a rule to suit yourself 歪曲(规则)以适合自身需要) • **noun 1** a place where something bends; a curve or turn 弯曲处；弯曲部分 **2 (the bends)** decompression sickness 减压病 □ **round the bend** informal 【非正式】 mad 疯狂的

beneath /bɪˈniːθ/ **preposition & adverb** extending or directly underneath 在(…)下方；在(…)底下 • **preposition** of lower status or worth than (在地位或价值上)低于，次于

benediction /ˌbenɪˈdɪkʃn/ **noun** the speaking of a blessing 祝福

benefactor /ˈbenɪfæktə(r)/ **noun** a person who gives money or other help 捐助人，赞助人

benefice /ˈbenɪfɪs/ **noun** an arrangement by which a Christian priest is paid and given accommodation for being in charge of a parish (基督教教区牧师的)有俸圣职

beneficent /bɪˈnefɪsnt/ **adjective** doing or resulting in good 行善的；有益的 ■ **beneficence** noun.

beneficial /ˌbenɪˈfɪʃl/ **adjective** having a good effect 效果好的；有益的 ■ **beneficially** adverb.

beneficiary /ˌbenɪˈfɪʃəri/ **noun** (plural **beneficiaries**) a person who benefits from something, especially a trust or will (尤指信托或遗嘱的)受益人，受惠者

benefit /ˈbenɪfɪt/ **noun 1** advantage or profit 益处；好处 **2** payment made by the state to someone in need 补助

费;救济金: *unemployment benefit* 失业救济 **3** a public performance to raise money for a charity 义演 • **verb** (**benefits, benefiting, benefited** or **benefitting, benefitted**) **1** get an advantage; profit 得益;得到好处 **2** bring advantage to 有利于;对…有好处

✔ **拼写指南** there is usually a single *t* in **benefited** and **benefiting**; the spelling with a double *t* is commoner in American English. benefited 和 benefiting 中 t 通常只有一个,双写 t 的拼法在美国英语中更常用。

benevolent /bə'nevələnt/ *adjective* **1** well meaning and kindly 善意的;善心的;仁慈的 **2** (of an organization) charitable rather than profit-making (组织)慈善性质的,非营利的 ■ **benevolence** *noun*.

Bengali /beŋ'gɔ:li/ *noun* (plural **Bengalis**) **1** a person from Bengal in the the Indian subcontinent 孟加拉人 **2** the language of Bangladesh and West Bengal 孟加拉语 • *adjective* relating to Bengal 孟加拉的

benighted /bɪ'naɪtɪd/ *adjective* ignorant or primitive 愚昧的;无知的

benign /bɪ'naɪn/ *adjective* **1** cheerful and kindly 善良的;宽厚的;慈祥的 **2** favourable; not harmful 有利的;无害的 **3** (of a tumour) not malignant (肿瘤)良性的

bent /bent/ past and past participle of **BEND**. • *adjective* **1** Brit. informal 【英,非正式】dishonest or corrupt 不诚实的;不正派的;贪赃枉法的 **2** (**bent on**) determined to do 决心的,执意的 • *noun* a natural talent 天赋;倾向

benzene /'benzi:n/ *noun* a liquid present in coal tar and petroleum 苯

bequeath /bɪ'kwi:ð/ *verb* **1** leave property to someone by a will (按遗嘱)遗赠(财产) **2** hand down or pass on 传给;留给

bequest /bɪ'kwest/ *noun* **1** something that is left to someone by a will 遗赠物;遗产 **2** the action of bequeathing 遗赠

berate /bɪ'reɪt/ *verb* (**berates, berating, berated**) angrily scold or criticize 痛斥;严责

bereave /bɪ'ri:v/ *verb* (**be bereaved**) be deprived of a close relation or friend through their death (因死亡)使丧失亲人(或朋友) ■ **bereavement** *noun*.

bereft /bɪ'reft/ *adjective* **1** (**bereft of**) deprived of; without 丧失…的;没有…的 **2** lonely and abandoned 孤寂的

beret /'bereɪ, bə'reɪ/ *noun* a flat round cap of felt or cloth 贝雷帽

bergamot /'bɜ:gəmɒt/ *noun* an oily substance found in some oranges, used as a flavouring 香柠檬油(用作香料)

beriberi /,beri'beri/ *noun* a disease caused by a lack of vitamin B_1 脚气病

berk /bɜ:k/ *noun* Brit. informal 【英,非正式】a stupid person 傻瓜;笨蛋

berry /'beri/ *noun* (plural **berries**) a small, juicy round fruit without a stone 浆果(多汁的无核小圆果)

berserk /bə'zɜ:k/ *adjective* out of control; wild and frenzied 狂怒的;狂暴的

berth /bɜ:θ/ *noun* **1** a place in a harbour where a boat can stay 锚地;泊位 **2** a bunk on a ship or train (船或火车上的)铺位 • *verb* moor a boat in a berth 使停泊 □ **give a wide berth to** stay well away from 避开;对…敬而远之

beryllium /bə'rɪliəm/ *noun* a hard, grey, lightweight metallic element (金属元素)铍

beseech /bɪ'si:tʃ/ *verb* (**beseeches, beseeching, besought** or **beseeched**) ask in a pleading way 恳求;哀求;乞求

beset /bɪ'set/ *verb* (**besets, besetting, beset**) continually trouble or worry (持续地)困扰,使苦恼

beside /bɪˈsaɪd/ **preposition 1** at the side of 在…旁边；在…附近 **2** compared with 和…相比 **3** (also **besides**) as well as 除…之外(还) • **adverb** (**besides**) as well 此外(还) □ **beside yourself** frantic with worry (因焦虑而)发狂，失常

besiege /bɪˈsiːdʒ/ **verb** (**besieges**, **besieging**, **besieged**) **1** surround a place so that no one can come or go 围困，围攻(某地) **2** overwhelm someone with requests or complaints 烦扰，缠磨

✔ 拼写指南 remember, *i* before *e* except after *c*: bes*ie*ge. 记住 i 置于 e 前，在 c 后时除外，如 besiege。

besmirch /bɪˈsmɜːtʃ/ **verb** damage someone's reputation 玷污，损害(某人的名誉)

besotted /bɪˈsɒtɪd/ **adjective** so much in love that you stop acting sensibly 沉迷的；痴迷的

bespoke /bɪˈspəʊk/ **adjective** Brit.【英】made to a customer's requirements 定做的

best /best/ **adjective 1** of the highest quality 最好的；最优秀的 **2** most suitable or sensible 最适当的；最合理的 • **adverb 1** to the highest degree; most 最 **2** most suitably or sensibly 最适当地；最合理地 • **noun** (**the best**) something which is of the highest quality 最好的东西 □ **best man** a male friend or relative who helps a bridegroom at his wedding (婚礼上的)男傧相 **best-seller** a book or other product that sells in very large numbers 畅销书；畅销产品 **make the best of** get what advantage you can from 充分利用

bestial /ˈbestɪəl/ **adjective** savagely cruel 残忍的，野蛮的；凶残的

bestiality /ˌbestɪˈælətɪ/ **noun 1** savagely cruel behaviour 兽行 **2** sex between a person and an animal 兽奸；兽交

bestir /bɪˈstɜː(r)/ **verb** (**bestirs**, **bestir**-ring, **bestirred**) (**bestir yourself**) make yourself start to do something 发奋；振作起来

bestow /bɪˈstəʊ/ **verb** give an honour, right, or gift 授予(荣誉、权利)；赠与(礼物)

bestride /bɪˈstraɪd/ **verb** (**bestrides**, **bestriding**, **bestrode**; past participle **bestridden**) put a leg on either side of 两腿分跨站于

bet /bet/ **verb** (**bets**, **betting**, **bet** or **betted**) **1** risk money against someone else's on the basis of the outcome of an unpredictable event such as a race 赌；打赌 **2** informal【非正式】feel sure 敢说；确信 • **noun** an act of betting the money betted 打赌；赌金；赌注

beta /ˈbiːtə/ **noun** the second letter of the Greek alphabet (Β, β) 希腊语字母表的第2个字母 □ **beta blocker** a drug used to treat high blood pressure and angina β-受体阻滞药(用于治疗高血压和绞痛)

bête noire /ˌbet ˈnwɑː(r)/ **noun** (plural **bêtes noires**) a person or thing that you greatly dislike 令人厌恶的人(或事物)

betide /bɪˈtaɪd/ **verb** (**betide**, **betiding**, **betided**) literary【文】happen or happen to 发生；降临于

betimes /bɪˈtaɪmz/ **adverb** in good time; early 及时；提早

betoken /bɪˈtəʊkən/ **verb** be a sign of 是…的征兆；预示

betray /bɪˈtreɪ/ **verb 1** harm someone or something by giving information to an enemy 背叛；出卖 **2** be disloyal to someone 对…不忠 **3** reveal a secret without meaning to 无意间暴露(或显露) ■ **betrayal** noun.

betrothed /bɪˈtrəʊðd/ **adjective** engaged to be married 已订婚的 ■ **betrothal** noun.

better /ˈbetə(r)/ **adjective 1** of a higher standard or quality 更好的 **2** partly or fully recovered from illness or injury 健康状况有所好转的；恢复健康的 • **adverb 1** in a more satisfactory way 更好地 **2** to a greater degree; more 较大程度地；更 • **noun (your betters)** people who have greater ability or are more important than you 能力更强的人；更重要者；上级 • **verb 1** improve on something 改善，提高，提高 **2 (better yourself)** improve your social position 提高社会地位 □ **better off** having more money or being in a more desirable situation 境况较好的 **get the better of** defeat 战胜；打败

betterment /'betəmənt/ **noun** improvement 改善；改进；提高

between /bɪ'twiːn/ **preposition & adverb 1** at, into, or across the space separating two things 在(两事物)之间；在(…)中间 **2** in the period separating two points in time 在(两时间点)之间；在(…)中间 **3** indicating a connection or relationship (表示相互关联或关系)在…之间 **4** shared by two or more people or things 由…所共有；由…所分享

betwixt /bɪ'twɪkst/ **preposition & adverb** old use【旧】between 在(…)中间

bevel /'bevl/ **noun** an edge cut at an angle in wood or glass (木头或玻璃的)斜面，斜边 • **verb (bevels, bevelling, bevelled**; US spelling【美拼作】**bevels, beveling, beveled)** cut the edge of wood or glass at an angle 把…切成斜面

beverage /'bevərɪdʒ/ **noun** a drink 饮料

bevy /'bevi/ **noun (plural bevies)** a large group 一(大)群

bewail /bɪ'weɪl/ **verb** be very sorry or sad about 对…而表示遗憾；为…而悲伤

beware /bɪ'weə(r)/ **verb** be aware of danger 注意；当心

bewilder /bɪ'wɪldə(r)/ **verb (bewilders, bewildering, bewildered)** puzzle or confuse 使迷惑；使糊涂

■ **bewilderment** noun.

bewitch /bɪ'wɪtʃ/ **verb 1** put a magic spell on 施魔法于 **2** attract and delight 使着迷；使陶醉

beyond /bɪ'jɒnd/ **preposition & adverb 1** at or to the further side of 在(…的)那一边，向(…的)那一边 **2** outside the range or limits of 超出 **3** happening or continuing after 迟于；晚于 **4** except 除…之外；此外

biannual /baɪ'ænjuəl/ **adjective** happening twice a year 一年两次的；一年两度的 ■ **biannually** adverb.

bias /'baɪəs/ **noun 1** a feeling for or against a person or thing that is based on prejudice rather than reason 偏见；偏心 **2** a direction diagonal to the grain of a fabric (织物的)斜纹

biased /'baɪəst/ **adjective** having a bias; prejudiced 有偏见的

bib /bɪb/ **noun 1** a piece of cloth or plastic fastened under a baby's chin to protect its clothes when it is being fed (小孩的)围嘴 **2** the part of an apron or pair of dungarees that covers the chest 围裙(或工装裤)上部

Bible /'baɪbl/ **noun** the book containing the writings of the Christian Church (基督教的)《圣经》 ■ **biblical** adjective.

bibliography /ˌbɪbli'ɒɡrəfi/ **noun (plural bibliographies)** a list of books in a particular subject 文献目录；书目 ■ **bibliographer** noun **bibliographic** adjective.

bibliophile /'bɪbliəfaɪl/ **noun** a person who collects books 图书收藏者；藏书家；书籍爱好者

bibulous /'bɪbjuləs/ **adjective** fond of drinking alcohol 爱喝酒的；嗜酒的

bicameral /ˌbaɪ'kæmərəl/ **adjective** (of a parliament) having two separate parts (立法机构)有两个议院的，两院制的

bicarbonate of soda /ˌbaɪ'kɑːbənət/ **noun** a soluble white powder used in fizzy drinks and in baking 碳酸氢钠；小苏打

bicentenary /ˌbaɪsen'tiːnəri/ **noun** (plural **bicentenaries**) a two-hundredth anniversary 200周年纪念 ∎ **bicentennial** noun & adjective.

biceps /'baɪseps/ **noun** (plural **biceps**) a large muscle in the upper arm which flexes the arm and forearm 二头肌

bicker /'bɪkə(r)/ **verb** (**bickers**, **bickering**, **bickered**) argue about unimportant things 争吵；口角

bicycle /'baɪsɪkl/ **noun** a two-wheeled vehicle that you ride by pushing the pedals with your feet 自行车；脚踏车 • **verb** (**bicycles**, **bicycling**, **bicycled**) ride a bicycle 骑自行车

bid[1] /bɪd/ **verb** (**bids**, **bidding**, **bid**) **1** offer a price for something 叫(价)；出(价) **2** (**bid for**) offer to do work for a stated price 投标 **3** (**bid for**) try to get 努力争取；试图获得 • **noun** an act of bidding 叫价；出价；争取

bid[2] **verb** (**bids**, **bidding**, **bid** or **bade**; past participle **bid**) **1** say a greeting 向…问候 **2** old use 【旧】command 命令；吩咐

biddable /'bɪdəbl/ **adjective** obedient 顺从的；听话的

biddy /'bɪdi/ **noun** (plural **biddies**) informal 【非正式】an old woman 老太婆

bide /baɪd/ **verb** (**bides**, **biding**, **bided**) old use or dialect 【旧或方】stay in a place 停留；居住 □ **bide your time** wait patiently for an opportunity to do something 等待良机

bidet /'biːdeɪ/ **noun** a low basin that you sit on to wash your bottom (洗下身的)坐浴盆

biennial /baɪ'eniəl/ **adjective** **1** taking place every other year 两年一次的 **2** (of a plant) living for two years (植物) 两年生的

bier /bɪə(r)/ **noun** a platform on which a coffin or dead body is placed before burial 棺材架；停尸架

bifocal /baɪ'fəʊkl/ **adjective** (of a lens) made in two sections, one for distant and one for close vision (镜片)双焦的, 双光的(指分远视和近视两种镜片) • **noun** (**bifocals**) a pair of glasses with bifocal lenses 双光眼镜

big /bɪg/ **adjective** (**bigger**, **biggest**) **1** large in size, amount, or extent 大的；巨大的 **2** very important or serious 重大的；重要的 **3** informal 【非正式】(of a brother or sister) older (兄弟或姊妹) 年龄较大的 □ **Big Bang** the rapid expansion of dense matter which is thought to have started the formation of the universe 创世大爆炸 **big-headed** conceited 傲慢的；自负的 **big top** the main tent in a circus (马戏团的)主帐篷

bigamy /'bɪgəmi/ **noun** the crime of marrying someone when you are already married to someone else 重婚罪 ∎ **bigamist** noun **bigamous** adjective.

bigot /'bɪgət/ **noun** a prejudiced and intolerant person 偏执者 ∎ **bigoted** adjective **bigotry** noun.

bigwig /'bɪgwɪg/ **noun** informal 【非正式】an important person 要人；大人物

bijou /'biːʒuː/ **adjective** small and elegant 小巧玲珑的

bike /baɪk/ informal 【非正式】**noun** a bicycle or motorcycle 自行车；摩托车 • **verb** (**bikes**, **biking**, **biked**) ride a bicycle or motorcycle 骑自行车；骑摩托车 ∎ **biker** noun.

bikini /bɪ'kiːni/ **noun** (plural **bikinis**) a woman's two-piece swimsuit 比基尼泳装

bilateral /baɪ'lætərəl/ **adjective** involving two countries or groups of people 双方的；双边的

bilberry /'bɪlbəri/ **noun** (plural **bilberries**) a small blue edible berry 欧洲越橘(蓝色小浆果，可食)

bile /baɪl/ **noun** **1** a bitter fluid which is produced by the liver and helps digestion 胆汁 **2** anger 怒气；暴躁

bilge /bɪldʒ/ **noun** the bottom of a ship's hull 舱底；底舱

bilingual /ˌbaɪˈlɪŋgwəl/ **adjective 1** speaking two languages fluently 能(流利地)说两种语言的 **2** expressed in two languages 用两种语言表示的；双语的

bilious /ˈbɪlɪəs/ **adjective** feeling sick 恶心的；想呕吐的

bilk /bɪlk/ **verb** informal 【非正式】cheat someone 欺骗

bill¹ /bɪl/ **noun 1** a note saying how much a person owes for something 账单；欠条 **2** a written proposal for a new law, presented to parliament for discussion 议案；法案 **3** a programme of entertainment at a theatre or cinema (剧院或电影院的)剧目单，节目单，放映表 **4** an advertising poster 招贴；海报；广告 **5** N. Amer. 【北美】a banknote 钞票；纸币 • **verb 1** send someone a bill saying what they owe 给…开账单 **2** list someone in a programme of entertainment 将(某人)列入节目单 **3** (**bill someone/thing as**) describe someone or something as 把…宣传为 □ **fit the bill** be suitable 符合要求；适合需要

bill² **noun** a bird's beak 鸟嘴；喙

billboard /ˈbɪlbɔːd/ **noun** a large board for displaying advertising posters 广告牌；告示牌

billet /ˈbɪlɪt/ **noun** a private house where soldiers live temporarily 士兵临时营房 • **verb** (**be billeted**) (of a soldier) stay in a particular place (士兵)临时在(某处)住宿

billet-doux /ˌbɪleɪˈduː/ **noun** (plural **billets-doux** /ˌbɪleɪˈduːz/) a love letter 情书

billhook /ˈbɪlhʊk/ **noun** a tool with a curved blade, used for pruning (修剪树枝用的)钩镰

billiards /ˈbɪlɪədz/ **noun** a game played on a table with pockets at the sides and corners, into which balls are struck with a cue 台球(运动)；撞球(运动)

billion /ˈbɪljən/ **cardinal number** (plural **billions** or (with another word or number) **billion**) a thousand million; 1,000,000,000 十亿 ■ **billionth** ordinal number.

billionaire /ˌbɪljəˈneə(r)/ **noun** a person owning money and property worth at least a billion pounds or dollars 亿万富翁

billow /ˈbɪləʊ/ **verb 1** (of smoke, cloud, or steam) roll outward (烟、云或蒸汽)冒出，涌出，汹涌向前 **2** fill with air and swell out 鼓起 • **noun 1** a large rolling mass of cloud, smoke, or steam 涌动的大块云团，大量冒出的烟(或蒸汽) **2** literary 【文】a large sea wave 巨浪

billy /ˈbɪli/ or **billycan** /ˈbɪlikæn/ **noun** (plural **billies**) Brit. 【英】a metal cooking pot with a lid and handle, used in camping (露营烹饪用的)铁皮罐

billy goat noun a male goat 公山羊

bimbo /ˈbɪmbəʊ/ **noun** (plural **bimbos**) informal 【非正式】an attractive but unintelligent young woman 头脑简单的漂亮女子

bin /bɪn/ Brit. 【英】**noun 1** a container for rubbish 垃圾箱 **2** a large storage container 大容器；箱；柜 • **verb** (**bins**, **binning**, **binned**) throw away 扔掉；丢弃

binary /ˈbaɪnəri/ **adjective 1** composed of or involving two things 由两部分组成的，双重的 **2** relating to a system of numbers which has two as its base and uses only the digits 0 and 1 二进制的

bind /baɪnd/ **verb** (**binds**, **binding**, **bound**) **1** firmly tie, wrap, or fasten 捆绑；捆扎 **2** hold together in a united group or mass 使结合；使联合在一起；使结合 **3** (**be bound by**) be hampered or restricted by 受…阻碍；受…束缚 **4** require someone to do something by law or because of a contract 使(某人)受法律(或合同)约束 **5** (**bind someone over**) (of a court of law) require someone to do something (法庭)令(某人)具结保

证 **6** enclose the pages of a book in a cover 装订(书页) **7** trim the edge of a piece of material with a fabric strip 给 (材料)镶边 • *noun informal* 【非正式】 an annoying or difficult situation 窘境，困境

binder /'baɪndə(r)/ *noun* **1** a cover for holding loose papers together 活页夹 **2** a machine that binds grain into sheaves (谷物)割捆机 **3** a person who binds books (书籍)装订工 ■ **bindery** *noun* (*plural* **binderies**).

bindi /'bɪndi/ *noun* (*plural* **bindis**) a decorative mark worn in the middle of the forehead by some Indian women (某些印度妇女前额中间的)装饰物

binding /'baɪndɪŋ/ *noun* **1** a strong covering holding the pages of a book together (书籍的)封皮 **2** fabric in a strip, used for binding the edges of material 镶边;滚条 • *adjective* (of an agreement) legally compelling someone to do what is stated (协议)有法律约束力的,必须遵守的

bindweed /'baɪndwiːd/ *noun* a plant that twines itself round things 旋花属植物

binge /bɪndʒ/ *informal* 【非正式】 *noun* a short period of uncontrolled eating or drinking 狂饮作乐;大肆吃喝 • *verb* (**binges**, **bingeing**, **binged**) eat or drink in an uncontrolled way 狂饮作乐;大吃大喝

bingo /'bɪŋɡəʊ/ *noun* a game in which players mark off on a card numbers called at random, the winner being the first to mark off all their numbers 宾戈游戏(游戏者在一张卡上标出随机叫出的数字,第一个标出全部数字者胜出)

binocular /bɪ'nɒkjələ(r)/ *adjective* for or using both eyes 双目的;双目并用的 • *noun* (**binoculars**) an instrument with a separate lens for each eye, for viewing distant objects 双目望远镜

biochemistry /ˌbaɪəʊ'kemɪstri/ *noun*

the study of the chemical processes that take place within living things 生物化学 ■ **biochemical** *adjective* **biochemist** *noun*.

biodegradable /ˌbaɪəʊdɪ'ɡreɪdəbl/ *adjective* able to be decomposed by bacteria or other living things 可进行生物降解的

biodiversity /ˌbaɪəʊdaɪ'vɜːsəti/ *noun* the variety of plant and animal life in the world or in a particular environment 生物多样性

biography /baɪ'ɒɡrəfi/ *noun* (*plural* **biographies**) an account of a person's life written by someone else 传记 ■ **biographer** *noun* **biographical** *adjective*.

biological /ˌbaɪə'lɒdʒɪkl/ *adjective* **1** relating to biology or living things 生物学的;生物的 **2** (of a parent or child) related by blood (父母或孩子)亲生的 **3** relating to the use of germs as a weapon in war (战争)使用微生物武器的 **4** (of a detergent) containing enzymes (洗涤剂)含酶的 ■ **biologically** *adverb*.

biology /baɪ'ɒlədʒi/ *noun* the scientific study of the life and structure of plants and animals 生物学 ■ **biologist** *noun*.

bionic /baɪ'ɒnɪk/ *adjective* **1** (of an artificial body part) electronically powered (人造人体器官)仿生的 **2** *informal* 【非正式】 having superhuman powers 超人的;具有非凡能力的

biopsy /'baɪɒpsi/ *noun* (*plural* **biopsies**) an examination of tissue taken from the body, to discover the presence or cause of a disease 活组织检查

biorhythm /'baɪəʊrɪðəm/ *noun* a recurring cycle in the functioning of an animal or plant 生物节律

bioterrorism /ˌbaɪəʊ'terərɪzəm/ *noun* the use of harmful organisms such as viruses or bacteria as weapons of terrorism 生物恐怖活动(以病毒、细菌等有害生物体作为恐怖袭击的武

器）

bipartite /baɪ'pɑːtaɪt/ **adjective** involving two separate groups or parties 双方的；双边的

biped /'baɪped/ **noun** an animal that walks on two feet 二足动物

biplane /'baɪpleɪn/ **noun** an early type of aircraft with two pairs of wings, one above the other 双翼飞机

bipolar /baɪ'pəʊlə(r)/ **adjective** having two poles or outer limits 有两极的；双极的

birch /bɜːtʃ/ **noun 1** a slender tree with thin peeling bark 桦；白桦 **2 (the birch)** (in the past) the punishment of being beaten with a bundle of birch twigs (旧时)用桦木条抽打(的惩罚)

bird /bɜːd/ **noun 1** an animal with feathers, wings, and a beak, that lays eggs and is usually able to fly 鸟；禽 **2** Brit. informal 【英，非正式】a young woman or girlfriend 少女；女朋友 □ **bird of prey** (plural **birds of prey**) a bird that eats small animals or birds, such as an eagle or hawk (鹰、隼等)猛禽 **bird's-eye view** a view of something from high above 俯视；鸟瞰

birdie /'bɜːdi/ **noun** (plural **birdies**) Golf 【高尔夫】a score of one stroke under par at a hole 小鸟球(比标准击球杆数少一杆的得分)

biro /'baɪrəʊ/ **noun** (plural **biros**). Brit. trademark 【英，商标】a ballpoint pen 伯罗圆珠笔

birth /bɜːθ/ **noun 1** the process by which a baby or other young animal comes out of its mother's body 出生；诞生 **2** the beginning of something 创始；起源 **3** a person's family origins 出身；血统 □ **birth control** the use of contraceptives to prevent unwanted pregnancies 节育；避孕 **give birth** produce a baby or young animal 生小孩；产崽

birthday /'bɜːθdeɪ/ **noun** the day in each year which is the same as the day on which a person was born 生日

birthmark /'bɜːθmɑːk/ **noun** an unusual mark on the body which is there from birth 胎记；胎痣

birthright /'bɜːθraɪt/ **noun 1** a right or privilege that a person inherits 因出身而享有的权利(或特权) **2** a basic right belonging to all human beings (所有人)与生俱来的权利

biscuit /'bɪskɪt/ **noun 1** Brit. 【英】a small, flat, crisp cake 饼干 **2** a light brown colour 浅褐色

> ✔ 拼写指南 don't forget the *u*: biscuit. 不要忘记拼写 biscuit 中的 u。

bisect /baɪ'sekt/ **verb** divide into two parts 把…分为两部分

bisexual /baɪ'sekʃuəl/ **adjective 1** sexually attracted to both men and women 双性恋的 **2** Biology 【生物】having both male and female organs 雌雄同体的 • **noun** a bisexual person 双性恋者 ■ **bisexuality** noun.

bishop /'bɪʃəp/ **noun** (in the Christian Church) a senior minister who is in charge of a diocese (a district) (基督教会的)主教

bismuth /'bɪzməθ/ **noun** a brittle reddish-grey metallic element resembling lead (金属元素)铋

bison /'baɪsn/ **noun** (plural **bison**) a wild ox with a humped back and shaggy hair 野牛

bistro /'biːstrəʊ/ **noun** (plural **bistros**) a small, inexpensive restaurant 小饭馆；小酒馆

bit[1] /bɪt/ **noun 1** a small piece or quantity 一小块；一小片；一点儿 **2 (a bit)** a short time or distance 一小会儿；短距离 **3 (a bit)** rather; slightly 相当；有点儿 □ **bit part** a small acting role in a play or a film 小角色；龙套

bit[2] **noun 1** a metal mouthpiece attached to a bridle, used to control a horse (马的)嚼子 **2** a tool or piece for boring or drilling 钻头；钻头

bit[3] **noun** Computing 【计】the smallest unit of information, expressed as either a 0 or 1 比特;二进制位

bitch /bɪtʃ/ **noun 1** a female dog 母狗 **2** informal 【非正式】a spiteful or unpleasant woman 坏女人;令人讨厌的女人 • **verb** informal 【非正式】say spiteful things about someone 说坏话;抱怨

bitchy /ˈbɪtʃi/ **adjective** (**bitchier**, **bitchiest**) informal 【非正式】spiteful 恶毒的;恶意的 ■ **bitchiness** noun.

bite /baɪt/ **verb** (**bites**, **biting**, **bit**; past participle **bitten**) **1** cut into something with your teeth 咬 **2** (of a tool, tyre, etc.) grip a surface (工具、轮胎等)抓紧,卡紧 **3** take effect in an unwelcome way 产生不良影响 • **noun 1** an act of biting or a piece bitten off 咬;咬下的一块 **2** informal 【非正式】a quick snack 快餐 **3** a feeling of cold in the air 寒冷;寒意 □ **bite the bullet** make yourself do something that is difficult or unpleasant 勇敢行动;咬紧牙关

biting /ˈbaɪtɪŋ/ **adjective 1** (of a wind) painfully cold (风)凛冽的,刺骨的 **2** (of something said) cruel (话语)尖酸的,辛辣的

bitter /ˈbɪtə(r)/ **adjective 1** having a sharp or sour taste or smell; not sweet 有苦味的;苦的 **2** feeling or causing resentment or unhappiness 充满怨恨的;令人痛苦的 **3** (of a conflict) intense and full of hatred (冲突)激烈的,充满仇恨的 **4** very cold 严寒的,寒冷刺骨的 • **noun 1** Brit. 【英】bitter-tasting beer that is strongly flavoured with hops 苦啤酒 **2** (**bitters**) bitter alcoholic spirits used in cocktails (用于调制鸡尾酒的)苦味酒 ■ **bitterly** adverb **bitterness** noun.

bittersweet /ˌbɪtəˈswiːt/ **adjective 1** sweet with a bitter aftertaste 又苦又甜的 **2** bringing pleasure mixed with sadness 又苦又乐的;喜忧参半的

bitty /ˈbɪti/ **adjective** (**bittier**, **bittiest**) Brit. informal 【英,非正式】made up of lots of small unrelated parts 零碎的;东拼西凑的

bitumen /ˈbɪtʃəmən/ **noun** a black sticky substance obtained from oil, used for covering roads and roofs 沥青 ■ **bituminous** adjective.

bivalve /ˈbaɪvælv/ **noun** a creature that has a shell divided into two parts, such as an oyster or mussel 双壳类动物(如牡蛎或贻贝)

bivouac /ˈbɪvuæk/ **noun** a makeshift open-air camp without tents 露营;野营 • **verb** (**bivouacs**, **bivouacking**, **bivouacked**) stay overnight in such a camp 露营;露宿

bizarre /bɪˈzɑː(r)/ **adjective** very strange or unusual 怪诞的;异乎寻常的 ■ **bizarrely** adverb.

✔ 拼写指南 one *z*, two *r*s: biz*a*rre. bizarre 中有一个 z 和两个 r。

blab /blæb/ **verb** (**blabs**, **blabbing**, **blabbed**) informal 【非正式】give away a secret 泄密;说漏嘴

blabber /ˈblæbə(r)/ **verb** (**blabbers**, **blabbering**, **blabbered**) informal 【非正式】talk in a silly or annoying way 乱说;胡扯;喋喋不休

black /blæk/ **adjective 1** of the very darkest colour 黑色的 **2** relating to people who have dark-coloured skin 黑人的 **3** (of coffee or tea) without milk (咖啡或茶)不加牛奶的,清的 **4** indicating that bad or unwelcome things are likely to happen 凶险的;不祥的 **5** (of a joke) making something bad or unwelcome seem funny (玩笑)黑色的 **6** full of anger or hatred 怒气冲冲的,充满仇恨的 • **noun 1** black colour 黑色 **2** a black person 黑人 • **verb 1** make something black 使变成黑色 **2** (**black out**) faint 失去知觉;昏厥 **3** (**black something out**) make a building dark by switching off lights and covering windows (关灯)使(建筑物)变黑暗 □ **black belt** a black belt awarded to an expert in judo, karate, and other martial arts (柔道、空手道

等武术运动中高级别选手系的)黑腰带 **black box** a machine that records what is happening to the controls in an aircraft during a flight (飞机上的)黑匣子,飞行记录仪 **black eye** an area of bruising around the eye (被打成的)青肿眼眶 **black hole** an area in space where gravity is so strong that nothing, not even light, can escape (太空中的)黑洞 **black ice** a transparent coating of ice on a road 黑冰;透明薄冰 **black magic** magic in which evil spirits are called on 巫术;妖术 **black market** the illegal trade in goods that are officially controlled or hard to obtain 黑市(交易) **black pudding** a pork sausage containing dried pig's blood (由干猪血制成的)黑香肠 **black sheep** a person who is considered bad or embarrassing by the rest of their family 有辱门楣者;败类;害群之马 **black spot** a place that is dangerous or where problems arise 问题多发区 **black widow** a very poisonous American spider with a black body and red markings 黑寡妇毒蜘(产于美洲,身体黑色带红斑,有剧毒) **in the black** not owing any money 有盈余;有结余 ■ **blackness** noun.

blackball /'blækbɔːl/ **verb** prevent someone from joining a club 拒绝,反对(某人加入俱乐部)

blackberry /'blækbəri/ **noun** (plural **blackberries**) a soft purple-black fruit that grows on a prickly bush 黑莓

blackbird /'blækbɜːd/ **noun** a bird with black feathers and a yellow beak 乌鸫(黑羽黄喙)

blackboard /'blækbɔːd/ **noun** a board with a black surface for writing on with chalk 黑板

blackcurrant /ˌblækˈkʌrənt/ **noun** a small round edible purple-black berry 黑醋栗;黑加仑子

blacken /'blækən/ **verb 1** make or become black (使)变黑;(使)变黑变暗 **2** damage someone's reputation 破坏,败坏(某人的名誉)

blackfly /'blækflaɪ/ **noun** (plural **blackflies**) a small black fly which eats the young shoots of plants 黑蝇

blackguard /'blægɑːd/ **noun** dated 【废】a man who is dishonest or treats other people badly 无赖;恶棍

blackhead /'blækhed/ **noun** a lump of oily matter blocking a pore in the skin 黑头粉刺

blackleg /'blækleg/ **noun** Brit. disapproving 【英,贬】a person who continues working when other workers are on strike 罢工破坏者;工贼

blacklist /'blæklɪst/ **noun** a list of people who cannot be trusted or who are out of favour 黑名单 • **verb** put someone on a blacklist 将…列入黑名单

blackmail /'blækmeɪl/ **noun 1** the demanding of money from someone in return for not giving away secret information about them 敲诈;勒索 **2** the use of threats or other pressure to influence someone 威胁;胁迫 • **verb** use blackmail on someone 敲诈;勒索;胁迫

blackout /'blækaʊt/ **noun 1** a period when all lights must be switched off or covered during an enemy air raid 灯火管制期 **2** a sudden failure of electric lights 断电;停电 **3** a short loss of consciousness 暂时性知觉丧失 **4** an official restriction on the publishing of news 新闻封锁

blacksmith /'blæksmɪθ/ **noun** a person who makes and repairs things made of iron 铁匠

blackthorn /'blækθɔːn/ **noun** a thorny bush that has blue-black fruits (called sloes) 黑刺李

bladder /'blædə(r)/ **noun** a bag-like organ in the abdomen in which urine collects before it is passed from the body 膀胱

blade /bleɪd/ **noun 1** the flat cutting

edge of a knife or other tool or weapon 刀身;刀片;刀刃 **2** the broad flat part of an oar, leaf, or other object 桨叶;叶片 **3** a long, narrow leaf of grass (细长的)草叶,叶片

blag /blæg/ **verb** (**blags**, **blagging**, **blagged**) Brit. informal【英,非正式】get something by clever talk or lying 巧妙得到;骗得 ▪ **blagger** noun.

blame /bleɪm/ **verb** (**blames**, **blaming**, **blamed**) say that someone is responsible for something bad 把…归罪于;责备;指责 • **noun** responsibility for something bad (坏事的)责任 ▪ **blameworthy** adjective.

blameless /'bleɪmləs/ **adjective** having done nothing bad; innocent 无可指责的;无过错的

blanch /blɑːntʃ/ **verb 1** become white or pale 变白;漂白;变苍白 **2** prepare vegetables by putting them briefly in boiling water 用沸水速煮(蔬菜);焯

blancmange /blə'mɒndʒ/ **noun** Brit.【英】a dessert like a milky jelly, made with cornflour and milk 牛奶冻

bland /blænd/ **adjective 1** not having any interesting features or qualities 淡而无味的;枯燥乏味的 **2** showing no emotion or excitement 无动于衷的

blandishments /'blændɪʃmənts/ **plural noun** nice things said to someone in order to persuade them to do something 奉承;哄骗

blank /blæŋk/ **adjective 1** not marked or decorated 空白的;无装饰的 **2** not understanding or reacting 不理解的 • **noun 1** a space in a form left to be filled in (表格的)空白处 **2** a state in which you cannot understand or remember something 茫然;头脑空白 **3** a gun cartridge containing gunpowder but no bullet (有火药但无弹头的)空弹 • **verb 1** (**blank something out**) hide or block out something 遮盖;遮掩;忘掉;抹去 **2** Brit. informal【英,非正式】deliberately ignore someone 故意不

理睬 □ **blank verse** poetry that has a regular rhythm but does not rhyme 无韵诗 ▪ **blankly** adverb **blankness** noun.

blanket /'blæŋkɪt/ **noun 1** a large piece of woollen material used as a warm covering 毯子;毛毯 **2** a thick mass or layer 厚覆盖物;厚覆盖层 • **verb** (**blankets**, **blanketing**, **blanketed**) cover with a thick layer 以厚层覆盖(或笼罩)

blare /bleə(r)/ **verb** (**blares**, **blaring**, **blared**) make a loud, harsh sound 发出响亮刺耳的声音 • **noun** a loud, harsh sound 响亮刺耳的声音

blarney /'blɑːni/ **noun** talk that is friendly and charming but may not be truthful 花言巧语;奉承话

blasé /'blɑːzeɪ/ **adjective** not impressed by something because you have experienced it often before (因司空见惯而)无动于衷的

blaspheme /blæs'fiːm/ **verb** (**blasphemes**, **blaspheming**, **blasphemed**) speak rudely about God or use the name of God as a swear word 亵渎(上帝) ▪ **blasphemous** adjective **blasphemy** noun (plural **blasphemies**).

blast /blɑːst/ **noun 1** an explosion, or the rush of compressed air spreading outwards from it 爆炸;爆炸气浪;冲击波 **2** a strong gust of wind 一阵疾风;一股强劲气流 **3** a single loud note of a horn or whistle (号或哨子的)响声,吹奏声 • **verb 1** blow something up with explosives (用炸药)炸,炸掉 **2** (**blast off**) (of a rocket or spacecraft) take off (火箭或航天器)发射 **3** produce loud music or noise 发出巨响 □ **blast furnace** a furnace for extracting metal from ore, using blasts of hot compressed air (炼铁的)高炉,鼓风炉

blatant /'bleɪtnt/ **adjective** done in an open and unashamed way 公然的;明目张胆的 ▪ **blatancy** noun **blatantly**

adverb.

blather /ˈblæðə(r)/ **verb (blathers, blathering, blathered)** talk without making much sense 喋喋不休地胡说；唠叨 • **noun** rambling talk 废话

blaze /bleɪz/ **noun 1** a very large or fierce fire 烈火；火焰 **2** a very bright light or display of colour 光辉；强烈的光；灿烂色彩 **3** a conspicuous display or outburst of something 进发；爆发：*a blaze of publicity* 完全公开 **4** a white stripe down the face of a horse (马面部的)白斑 • **verb (blazes, blazing, blazed) 1** burn or shine fiercely or brightly 熊熊燃烧；发强光；闪耀 **2** shoot repeatedly or wildly 连续射击；胡乱射击 □ **blaze a trail 1** mark out a path 开辟道路 **2** be the first to do something 倡导；开创

blazer /ˈbleɪzə(r)/ **noun 1** a jacket worn by schoolchildren or sports players as part of a uniform (学生或运动员穿的)上衣 **2** a man's smart jacket (色彩鲜亮的)男式夹克

blazon /ˈbleɪzn/ **verb** display or proclaim something in a way that catches people's attention 炫示；宣传

bleach /bliːtʃ/ **verb** lighten something by using a chemical or leaving it in sunlight 漂白；晒白 • **noun** a chemical used to remove stains and also to sterilize drains, sinks, etc. 漂白剂

bleak /bliːk/ **adjective 1** bare and exposed to the weather 光秃秃的；无遮蔽的；受到风吹雨打的 **2** dreary and unwelcome 沉闷的；阴郁的 **3** (of a situation) not hopeful (局面)没有希望的，暗淡的 ■ **bleakly** adverb **bleakness** noun.

bleary /ˈblɪəri/ **adjective (blearier, bleariest)** (of the eyes) tired and not focusing properly (眼睛)视线模糊的 ■ **blearily** adverb.

bleat /bliːt/ **verb 1** (of a sheep or goat)

make a weak, wavering cry (羊)咩咩叫 **2** speak or complain in a weak or silly way 胡诉；愚蠢地诉讲；抱怨；诉苦 • **noun** a bleating sound 咩咩叫(声)

bleed /bliːd/ **verb (bleeds, bleeding, bled) 1** lose blood from the body 出血；流血 **2** informal【非正式】drain someone of money or resources 榨取…的钱财(或资源) **3** (of dye or colour) seep into an adjoining colour or area (染料或颜色)渗开，渗色 **4** allow fluid or gas to escape from a closed system through a valve 放掉(液体或气体)；抽干 **5** (in the past) take blood from someone as a medical treatment (旧时)给…放血，抽血 • **noun** an instance of bleeding 出血；流血

bleep /bliːp/ **noun** a short, high-pitched sound made by an electronic device 短而尖的声音；哔哔声；嘟嘟声 • **verb** make a bleep 发哔哔声；发嘟嘟声 ■ **bleeper** noun.

blemish /ˈblemɪʃ/ **noun** a small mark or flaw 斑点；疤痕；瑕疵 • **verb** spoil the appearance of 有损…的外观；使…蒙污

blench /blentʃ/ **verb** flinch suddenly out of fear or pain (因恐惧或疼痛)畏缩，畏惧

blend /blend/ **verb 1** mix and combine one thing with something else 混在一起；混合 **2** (blend in) become unnoticeable 混入；融合 • **noun** a mixture 混合物

blender /ˈblendə(r)/ **noun** an electric device for liquidizing or chopping food 食物搅拌器

bless /bles/ **verb 1** make something holy by saying a prayer over it (通过祈祷)使神圣 **2** ask God to protect a person or thing 祈求上帝保佑(或赐福)；祝福 **3** (be blessed with) have or be given something that is desired 享有，被给予(想要的东西)

blessed /ˈblesɪd/ **adjective 1** holy and protected by God 神圣的；上帝庇佑的 **2** bringing welcome pleasure or relief

带来快乐的；使人舒服的 ■ **blessedly** adverb.

blessing /'blesɪŋ/ noun **1** God's approval and protection, or a prayer asking for this (祈求)上帝赐福(祈求)上帝庇佑 **2** something for which you are very grateful 幸事；幸运 **3** a person's approval or support (某人的)同意，允准，支持

blew /bluː/ past of BLOW¹.

blight /blaɪt/ noun **1** a plant disease caused by fungi (植物的)枯萎病(由真菌引起) **2** a thing that spoils or damages something 有害的事物；起破坏作用的因素 • verb spoil or damage something 破坏；摧残

blighter /'blaɪtə(r)/ noun Brit. informal 【英，非正式】an annoying or unfortunate person 讨厌的家伙；倒霉蛋

blind /blaɪnd/ adjective **1** not able to see 瞎的，盲的；失明的 **2** done without being able to see or without certain information 看不见的；盲目的 **3** without awareness or judgement 未察觉的，未加判断的 **4** concealed, closed, or blocked off 隐蔽的；封闭的；堵塞的: a blind alley 死胡同 • verb **1** make someone blind 使瞎，使失明 **2** stop someone thinking clearly or sensibly 使失去理智 **3** (**blind someone with**) confuse someone by presenting them with something hard to understand 用(深奥的事物)迷惑 • noun a screen for a window 窗帘；百叶窗 □ **blind date** a meeting with a person you have not met before, arranged in the hope of starting a romantic relationship 男女初次约会 □ **blind man's buff** a game in which a player tries to catch people while wearing a blindfold 捉迷藏(游戏) **blind spot 1** an area where someone's view is obstructed 看不见的地方；视线盲区 **2** an inability to understand something 不理解；无知 **turn a blind eye** pretend not to notice 视而不见；假装看不见

■ **blindly** adverb **blindness** noun.

blindfold /'blaɪndfəʊld/ noun a piece of cloth covering someone's eyes, so that they cannot see 蒙眼布，眼罩 • verb cover someone's eyes with a blindfold 蒙住…的眼睛；挡住…的视线

blinding /'blaɪndɪŋ/ adjective **1** (of light) very bright (光线)刺眼的，眩目的 **2** (of pain) very severe (疼痛)极其剧烈的 ■ **blindingly** adverb.

bling-bling /'blɪŋ'blɪŋ/ or **bling** /blɪŋ/ noun informal 【非正式】showy, expensive clothes and jewellery 炫目昂贵的时装和珠宝

blink /blɪŋk/ verb **1** shut and open the eyes quickly 眨眼睛 **2** (of a light) flash on and off (光)闪烁 • noun an act of blinking 眨眼；闪烁 □ **on the blink** informal 【非正式】no longer working properly 失灵；出故障

blinkered /'blɪŋkəd/ adjective having a limited point of view 主观狭隘的

blinkers /'blɪŋkəz/ plural noun a pair of flaps used to prevent a horse from seeing sideways 马眼罩

blip /blɪp/ noun **1** a short, high-pitched sound made by an electronic device 尖锐而急促的声音；哔哔声 **2** a small flashing point of light on a radar screen (雷达屏幕上的)光点 **3** a temporary change in a situation or process that is generally steady 小偏差 • verb (**blips**, **blipping**, **blipped**) make a blip 发哔哔声

bliss /blɪs/ noun perfect happiness 极乐，无上幸福

blissful /'blɪsfl/ adjective full of joy and happiness 极其幸福的，极乐的 ■ **blissfully** adverb.

blister /'blɪstə(r)/ noun **1** a small bubble on the skin filled with watery liquid (皮肤上的)水疱 **2** a similar bubble on a surface 气泡 • verb (**blisters**, **blistering**, **blistered**) form blisters (使)起水疱(或气泡)

blistering /'blɪstərɪŋ/ adjective **1** (of

heat) very strong (热度)极强的 **2** very fierce or forceful 猛烈的

blithe /blaɪð/ **adjective 1** without thought or care 漫不经心的，不在意的 **2** very happy 欢乐的，愉快的 ■ **blithely** adverb.

blithering /ˈblɪðərɪŋ/ **adjective** informal【非正式】thoroughly stupid 愚蠢透顶的

blitz /blɪts/ **noun 1** a sudden fierce military attack 闪电战；闪击战 **2** informal【非正式】a sudden and concentrated effort 突击；闪电式行动 • **verb** make a sudden fierce attack on 用闪电战攻击

blizzard /ˈblɪzəd/ **noun** a snowstorm with high winds 暴风雪；雪暴

bloat /bləʊt/ **verb** cause something to swell with fluid or gas 使膨胀，使肿胀 ■ **bloated** adjective.

bloater /ˈbləʊtə(r)/ **noun** a salted and smoked herring 烟熏的鲱鱼

blob /blɒb/ **noun 1** a drop of a thick or sticky liquid (黏稠的)一滴 **2** a roundish mass or shape 圆乎乎的一团；圆乎乎的形状

bloc /blɒk/ **noun** a group of allied countries with similar political systems (政治制度相近的国家结成的)集团

block /blɒk/ **noun 1** a large solid piece of material 大块 **2** Brit.【英】a large building divided into flats or offices 大厦；大楼 **3** a group of buildings with streets on all four sides 街区 **4** an obstacle 障碍(物) • **verb 1** prevent movement or flow in something 堵塞，阻塞 **2** prevent the progress of something 妨碍，阻挡 □ **block capitals** plain capital letters 大写字母

blockade /blɒˈkeɪd/ **noun** a blocking of the way in or out of a place to prevent people or goods from entering or leaving it 封锁 • **verb** (**blockades**, **blockading**, **blockaded**) block the way in or out of a place 封锁

blockage /ˈblɒkɪdʒ/ **noun** an obstruction 阻塞；堵塞

blockbuster /ˈblɒkbʌstə(r)/ **noun** informal【非正式】a film or book that is very successful 极其成功的电影(或书)

blog /blɒg/ **noun** a weblog 网络日志；博客 • **verb** (**blogs**, **blogging**, **blogged**) regularly update a weblog 定期更新网络日志(或博客) ■ **blogger** noun.

bloke /bləʊk/ **noun** Brit. informal【英，非正式】a man 家伙

blonde /blɒnd/ **adjective** (also **blond**) **1** (of hair) pale yellow (头发)金黄色的 **2** having pale yellow hair 金发的 • **noun** a woman with blonde hair 金发女郎

blood /blʌd/ **noun 1** the red liquid that flows through the arteries and veins 血，血液 **2** family background 血统；家世 • **verb** give someone their first experience of an activity 使取得初次经验；使初次尝试 □ **blood-curdling** horrifying 令人毛骨悚然的 **blood pressure** the pressure created by blood as it moves around the body 血压 **blood sport** a sport involving the hunting or killing of animals 猎杀动物的运动 **blood vessel** a vein, artery, or capillary carrying blood through the body 血管 **new** (or **fresh**) **blood** people who join a group and give it new ideas 新鲜血液；新生力量

bloodbath /ˈblʌdbɑːθ/ **noun** an event in which many people are violently killed 血洗；大屠杀

bloodhound /ˈblʌdhaʊnd/ **noun** a large hound used for following scents 大猎犬；大警犬

bloodless /ˈblʌdləs/ **adjective 1** without violence or killing 不流血的；兵不血刃的 **2** (of the skin) drained of colour (皮肤)无血色的，苍白的 **3** lacking emotion or vitality 无感情的；无生气的

bloodletting /ˈblʌdletɪŋ/ **noun 1** violent conflict 暴力冲突；杀戮 **2** (in the past) the removal of some of a patient's blood, as a medical treatment (旧时作为治疗手段的)放血

bloodshed /'blʌdʃed/ **noun** the killing or wounding of people 杀戮；屠杀

bloodshot /'blʌdʃɒt/ **adjective** (of the eyes) having tiny red blood vessels visible in the whites (眼睛)充血的，布满血丝的

bloodstream /'blʌdstriːm/ **noun** the blood circulating through the body 血流；体内循环的血液

bloodthirsty /'blʌdθɜːsti/ **adjective** (**bloodthirstier**, **bloodthirstiest**) taking pleasure in killing and violence 嗜血的；残忍好杀的

bloody /'blʌdi/ **adjective** (**bloodier**, **bloodiest**) **1** covered with or containing blood 染上血的；血淋淋的 **2** involving violence or cruelty 嗜杀的；残忍的 • **verb** (**bloodies**, **bloodying**, **bloodied**) cover or stain with blood 血染 □ **bloody-minded** Brit. informal 【英,非正式】deliberately unhelpful 故意作对的；有意不合作的

bloom /bluːm/ **verb 1** produce flowers; be in flower 开花 **2** be healthy and happy 健康；变得健康 • **noun 1** a flower 花 **2** a state or period of blooming 开花；开花期 **3** a healthy glow in a person's complexion (面色的)健康红润 **4** a powdery coating on the surface of some fruit (水果外皮的)粉衣,粉霜

bloomers /'bluːməz/ **plural noun 1** women's baggy knee-length knickers (长及膝部的)宽松女内裤 **2** historical 【历史】women's loose-fitting trousers (长及膝部或踝部的)女式灯笼裤,裙裤

blossom /'blɒsəm/ **noun** a flower or a mass of flowers on a tree 花；花簇 • **verb 1** produce blossom 开花 **2** become strong and healthy 变得强壮健康

blot /blɒt/ **noun 1** a spot of ink 墨水渍 **2** a thing that spoils something good 有损美的东西；污点 • **verb** (**blots**,

blotting, **blotted**) **1** dry something with an absorbent material 吸干 **2** mark or spoil 弄脏；玷污 **3** (**blot something out**) hide something 掩盖；遮蔽 □ **blotting paper** absorbent paper used for drying ink when writing 吸墨纸 **blot your copybook** Brit.【英】spoil your good reputation 玷污名声

blotch /blɒtʃ/ **noun** an irregular mark (不规则的)斑点,污渍 • **verb** mark something with blotches 弄脏；使…粘上污渍 ■ **blotchy** adjective.

blotter /'blɒtə(r)/ **noun** a pad of blotting paper 吸墨板

blouse /blauz/ **noun** a woman's top that is similar to a shirt (似衬衫的)女式上衣

blouson /'bluːzɒn/ **noun** a short loose-fitting jacket 宽松短上衣

blow¹ /bləu/ **verb** (**blows**, **blowing**, **blew**; past participle **blown**) **1** (of the wind) move (风)吹, 吹动 **2** send out air through pursed lips 吹(气) **3** force air into an instrument through the mouth 吹奏(乐器) **4** sound a horn 按响(喇叭) **5** break something open with explosives (用炸药)炸开 **6** burst through pressure or overheating 使裂开；熔断 **7** informal【非正式】spend money recklessly 挥霍(金钱) **8** informal【非正式】waste an opportunity 浪费掉(机会) • **noun** an act of blowing 吹 □ **blow-dry** style the hair while drying it with a hand-held dryer (用吹风机)吹干(头发)使成型 **blow hot and cold** keep changing your mind 出尔反尔；拿不定主意 **blow over** (of trouble) fade away (麻烦)平息,过去 **blow up** explode 爆炸 **blow something up 1** make something explode 使(某物)爆炸 **2** inflate something 给(某物)充气；使(某物)膨胀

blow² **noun 1** a powerful stroke with a hand or weapon (用手或武器的)重击，捶打 **2** a sudden shock or disappointment 打击；挫折

blowfly /ˈbləʊflaɪ/ **noun** (plural **blow-flies**) a large fly which lays its eggs in meat 丽蝇

blowhole /ˈbləʊhəʊl/ **noun** the nostril of a whale or dolphin on the top of its head (鲸或海豚头顶的)鼻孔

blowout /ˈbləʊaʊt/ **noun** the release of air or gas from a tyre, oil well, etc. 车胎爆裂;井喷

blowsy or **blowzy** /ˈblaʊzi/ **adjective** (of a woman) plump and untidy (女子)肥胖邋遢的

blowtorch /ˈbləʊtɔːtʃ/ or **blowlamp** /ˈbləʊlæmp/ **noun** a portable device producing a hot flame, used to burn off paint 喷灯(用于除油漆)

blowy /ˈbləʊi/ **adjective** windy or wind-swept 有风的;刮风的

blub /blʌb/ **verb** (**blubs, blubbing, blubbed**) informal 【非正式】cry noisily 大哭

blubber¹ /ˈblʌbə(r)/ **noun** the fat of whales and seals 鲸脂;海豹脂 ■ **blubbery** adjective.

blubber² **verb** (**blubbers, blubbering, blubbered**) informal 【非正式】cry noisily 放声哭;号哭

bludgeon /ˈblʌdʒən/ **noun** a thick, heavy stick used as a weapon (作武器用的)大头棒 • **verb 1** hit someone with a thick, heavy stick 用大头棒打 **2** bully someone into doing something 恫吓;胁迫

blue /bluː/ **adjective** (**bluer, bluest**) **1** of the colour of the sky on a sunny day 蓝色的;天蓝色的,蔚蓝的 **2** informal 【非正式】sad or depressed 悲伤的;忧郁的 **3** informal 【非正式】indecent or pornographic 色情的;黄色的 • **noun** a blue colour 蓝色 □ **blue-blooded** from a royal or aristocratic family 有贵族血统的;出身高贵的 **blue cheese** having veins of mould in it 蓝纹奶酪;蓝干酪 **blue-chip** (of an investment) safe and reliable (投资)稳妥可靠的, 蓝筹的 **blue-collar** relating to manual work

蓝领的;体力劳动的 **out of the blue** unexpectedly 出乎意料地

bluebell /ˈbluːbel/ **noun** a woodland plant with clusters of blue bell-shaped flowers 蓝钟花

blueberry /ˈbluːbəri/ **noun** (plural **blueberries**) a blue-black berry that grows on a North American bush 蓝莓,越橘(产于北美洲丛林)

bluebottle /ˈbluːbɒtl/ **noun** a large fly with a bluish body 反吐丽蝇(身体呈蓝色)

blueprint /ˈbluːprɪnt/ **noun 1** a technical drawing or plan 蓝图 **2** a model or prototype 模型;原型

blues /bluːz/ **noun 1** slow, sad music of black American origin 布鲁斯音乐,蓝调(源于美国黑人音乐,节奏缓慢、忧伤) **2** (**the blues**) informal 【非正式】feelings of sadness or depression 忧伤;沮丧 ■ **bluesy** adjective.

bluestocking /ˈbluːstɒkɪŋ/ **noun** a serious intellectual woman 女学者;女才子

bluff¹ /blʌf/ **noun** a pretence that you know or can do something when this is not true 虚张声势;唬人 • **verb** pretend in this way 欺骗;吓唬 □ **call someone's bluff** challenge someone to do something, in the belief that they will not be able to 要(某人)摊牌;向(某人)挑战

bluff² **adjective** frank and direct in a good-natured way 直率的;坦率的

bluff³ **noun** a steep cliff or bank 悬崖;峭壁;陡岸

bluish or **blueish** /ˈbluːɪʃ/ **adjective** having a blue tinge 带蓝色的;有点儿蓝的

blunder /ˈblʌndə(r)/ **noun** a clumsy mistake 愚蠢的错误 • **verb** (**blunders, blundering, blundered**) **1** make a blunder 犯愚蠢的错误;因疏忽犯错 **2** move clumsily or as if unable to see 跌跌撞撞;踉踉跄跄

blunderbuss /ˈblʌndəbʌs/ **noun** historical 【历史】a gun with a short, wide barrel 大口径短枪

blunt /blʌnt/ *adjective* **1** not having a sharp edge or point 钝的；不锋利的 **2** frank and direct 率直的；直言不讳的 • *verb* make or become blunt (使)变钝 ■ **bluntly** *adverb*.

blur /blɜː(r)/ *verb* (**blurs, blurring, blurred**) make or become unclear or less distinct (使)变得模糊不清 • *noun* something that cannot be seen, heard, or remembered clearly 模糊不清的东西 ■ **blurry** *adjective*.

blurb /blɜːb/ *noun* a short description written to promote a book, film, or other product (书、电影等的)简介，推荐说明

blurt /blɜːt/ *verb* (**blurt something out**) say something suddenly and without thinking 脱口说出；不假思索地说

blush /blʌʃ/ *verb* become red in the face from shyness or embarrassment (因害羞或尴尬)脸红 • *noun* a reddening of the face from shyness or embarrassment 脸红

blusher /blʌʃə(r)/ *noun* a cosmetic used to give a reddish tinge to the cheeks 胭脂

bluster /blʌstə(r)/ *verb* (**blusters, blustering, blustered**) **1** talk loudly or aggressively but without having any effect 咆哮；叫嚷；气势汹汹地说话 **2** (of wind or rain) blow or beat fiercely and noisily (风或雨)咆哮 • *noun* loud and aggressive talk that does not have much effect 空洞的叫嚷 ■ **blustery** *adjective*.

boa /bəʊə/ *noun* **1** a large snake which winds itself round and crushes its prey 巨蟒；蟒 **2** a long, thin scarf of feathers or fur (羽毛或毛皮制的)长围巾

boar /bɔː(r)/ *noun* (plural **boar** or **boars**) **1** (also **wild boar**) a wild pig with tusks 野猪 **2** a male pig 公猪

board /bɔːd/ *noun* **1** a long, narrow, flat piece of wood used in building (建筑用的)木板 **2** a rectangular piece of stiff material used as a surface for a particular purpose 板；牌子 **3** the people who control and direct an organization 委员会；理事会；董事会 **4** regular meals provided in return for payment 伙食；膳食 • *verb* **1** get on a ship, aircraft, or other passenger vehicle 上(船、飞机等) **2** (**board something up** or **over**) seal something in with pieces of wood 用木板遮住(或封住) **3** have a bedroom and receive meals in return for payment 付费膳宿 **4** (of a pupil) live in school during term time (学生)在校寄宿 ☐ **board game** a game in which counters are moved around a board 棋类游戏 **boarding house** a private house providing rooms and meals for paying guests 提供膳宿的私人住宅 **boarding school** a school in which the pupils live during term time 寄宿学校 **go by the board** (of a plan or principle) be rejected or abandoned (计划或原则)被废弃，被否决 **on board** on or in a ship, aircraft, or other vehicle 在船(或飞机等)上

boarder /bɔːdə(r)/ *noun* a pupil who lives in school during term time 寄宿生；住校生

boardroom /bɔːdruːm/ *noun* a room in which a board of directors regularly meets 董事会(或委员会、理事会)会议室

boast /bəʊst/ *verb* **1** talk about yourself with too much pride 自吹自擂；自夸 **2** (of a place or organization) have something as an impressive feature (地方或组织)有(值得自豪的特色) • *noun* an act of boasting 自吹自擂；自夸 ■ **boastful** *adjective* **boastfully** *adverb*.

boat /bəʊt/ *noun* a vehicle that travels on water and is smaller than a ship 船；小船 ☐ **be in the same boat** informal 【非正式】 be in the same difficult situation as other people 处于相同的困境

boater /bəʊtə(r)/ *noun* a flat-topped straw hat with a brim (有边的)平顶

草帽

boatswain /ˈbəʊsn/ **noun** an officer in charge of equipment and the crew on a ship 水手长

bob¹ /bɒb/ **verb** (**bobs, bobbing, bobbed**) **1** make a quick, short movement up and down 上下快速移动 **2** curtsy briefly 行屈膝礼；鞠躬 • **noun** a bobbing movement 上下快速移动

bob² **noun** a short hairstyle that hangs evenly all round 短齐发型 • **verb** (**bobs, bobbing, bobbed**) cut hair in a bob 剪短(头发)

bob³ **noun** (plural **bob**) Brit. informal, dated【英，非正式，废】a shilling (five pence) 先令

bobbin /ˈbɒbɪn/ **noun** a reel for holding thread 线轴；绕线筒

bobble /ˈbɒbl/ **noun** a small ball made of strands of wool 小羊毛球；小绒球

bobby /ˈbɒbi/ **noun** (plural **bobbies**) Brit. informal, dated【英，非正式，废】a police officer 警察

bobsleigh /ˈbɒbsleɪ/ **noun** a sledge used for racing down an ice-covered run 大雪橇

bode /bəʊd/ **verb** (**bodes, boding, boded**) (**bode well or ill**) be a sign of a good or bad outcome 预示吉兆(或凶兆)

bodge /bɒdʒ/ **verb** (**bodges, bodging, bodged**) Brit. informal【英，非正式】make or repair something badly or clumsily 拙劣(或笨拙)地制作(或修补)

bodice /ˈbɒdɪs/ **noun 1** the part of a dress above the waist 连衣裙上身 **2** a woman's sleeveless undergarment 妇女紧身胸衣

bodily /ˈbɒdɪli/ **adjective** relating to the body 身体的；躯体的 • **adverb** by taking hold of a person's body with force 用力抓住身体地

bodkin /ˈbɒdkɪn/ **noun** a thick needle with a blunt, rounded end (粗钝的)大针眼缝针

body /ˈbɒdi/ **noun** (plural **bodies**) **1** a person's or animal's physical structure 身体；躯体 **2** the main part of the body, apart from the head and limbs 躯干 **3** the main or central part of something 主干部分；主要部分 **4** a mass or collection 大量；大批 **5** a group of people organized for a particular purpose 团体；群体；机构 **6** Brit.【英】a woman's stretchy garment for the upper body 女紧身衣 口 **body language** the showing of your feelings through the way in which you move or hold your body 身体语言；肢体语言

bodybuilder /ˈbɒdibɪldə(r)/ **noun** a person who enlarges their muscles through exercise 参加健美运动者；健美运动员

bodyguard /ˈbɒdigɑːd/ **noun** a person paid to protect someone rich or famous 保镖；警卫

bodywork /ˈbɒdiwɜːk/ **noun** the metal outer shell of a vehicle 车身；船身

Boer /ˈbəʊə(r)/ **noun** a member of the Dutch people who settled in southern Africa 布尔人(南部非洲早期的荷兰定居者)

boffin /ˈbɒfɪn/ **noun** Brit. informal【英，非正式】a scientist 科学家

bog /bɒg/ **noun** an area of soft, wet ground 泥塘；沼泽 • **verb** (**be/get bogged down**) be prevented from making progress 被阻碍；受妨碍 ■ **boggy** adjective.

bogey or **bogy** /ˈbəʊgi/ **noun** (plural **bogeys**) **1** an evil spirit 恶鬼；妖怪 **2** a cause of fear or alarm 令人惧怕的原因

bogeyman or **bogyman** /ˈbəʊgimæn/ **noun** (plural **bogeymen**) an evil spirit 鬼怪；怪物

boggle /ˈbɒgl/ **verb** (**boggles, boggling, boggled**) informal【非正式】**1** be astonished or baffled 惊奇；困惑 **2** (**boggle at**) hesitate to do 迟疑；犹豫

bogie /ˈbəʊgi/ **noun** (plural **bogies**) a supporting frame with wheels, fitted beneath the end of a railway vehicle (铁路机车尾部下面的)转向架

bogus /ˈbəʊgəs/ *adjective* not genuine or true 假的;伪造的

Bohemian /bəʊˈhiːmɪən/ *noun* an artistic and unconventional person 波希米亚人 • *adjective* unconventional 放荡不羁的;反世俗陈规的

boil¹ /bɔɪl/ *verb* **1** (of a liquid) reach a temperature where it bubbles and turns to vapour (液体)沸腾,烧开 **2** cook food in boiling water 在沸水中煮,烹煮(食物) **3** (**boil down to**) amount to 归结为 • *noun* the process of boiling 煮沸,沸腾

boil² *noun* an inflamed pus-filled swelling on the skin 疖

boiler /ˈbɔɪlə(r)/ *noun* a device for heating water 锅炉 □ **boiler suit** Brit.【英】a pair of overalls worn for dirty work 连衫裤工作服

boiling /ˈbɔɪlɪŋ/ *adjective* **1** (of a liquid) at or near the temperature at which it boils (液体)达到沸点的,接近沸点的 **2** *informal*【非正式】very hot 极热的;炎热的

boisterous /ˈbɔɪstərəs/ *adjective* lively and high-spirited 喧闹的;充满活力的 ■ **boisterously** *adverb*.

bold /bəʊld/ *adjective* **1** brave and confident 自信大胆的;勇敢的 **2** (of a colour or design) strong or vivid (色彩或图案)醒目的,显著的 **3** (of printed words or letters) in thick, dark type (字体)黑体的,粗体的 ■ **boldly** *adverb* **boldness** *noun*.

bole /bəʊl/ *noun* a tree trunk 树干

bolero /bəˈleərəʊ/ *noun* (plural **boleros**) **1** /bəˈleərəʊ/ a Spanish dance 博莱罗舞,波列罗舞(一种西班牙舞蹈) **2** /ˈbɒlərəʊ/ a woman's short open jacket 前襟敞开的女式短上衣

Bolivian /bəˈlɪvɪən/ *noun* a person from Bolivia 玻利维亚人 • *adjective* relating to Bolivia 玻利维亚的

boll /bəʊl/ *noun* the rounded seed capsule of plants such as cotton or flax

(棉、亚麻等的)圆荚,铃

bollard /ˈbɒlɑːd/ *noun* **1** Brit.【英】a short post used to prevent traffic from entering an area (阻止车辆进入某区域的)护柱 **2** a short post on a ship or quayside for securing a rope (船上或码头上的)系船柱,带缆桩

Bolshevik /ˈbɒlʃɪvɪk/ *noun* a member of the group which seized power in the Russian Revolution of 1917 布尔什维克 ■ **Bolshevism** *noun*.

bolshie or **bolshy** /ˈbɒlʃɪ/ *adjective* Brit. *informal*【英,非正式】bad-tempered and uncooperative 敌对的;不合作的

bolster /ˈbəʊlstə(r)/ *noun* a long, firm pillow 长枕;靠枕 • *verb* (**bolsters**, **bolstering**, **bolstered**) support or strengthen 支持;加强

bolt /bəʊlt/ *noun* **1** a heavy metal pin with a head that screws into a nut, used to fasten things together 螺栓 **2** a bar that slides into a socket to fasten a door or window (门或窗的)闩,插销 **3** a short, heavy arrow shot from a crossbow 弩箭 **4** a flash of lightning 闪电;霹雳 **5** a roll of fabric (织物的)一卷,一匹 • *verb* **1** fasten with a bolt 用闩闩上;用螺栓固定 **2** run away suddenly 突然逃跑 **3** eat food quickly 匆匆吞吃(食物) **4** (of a plant) grow quickly upwards and stop flowering as seeds develop (植物)迅速成长结实而不再开花 □ **bolt-hole** a place to escape to and hide in 避难所;藏身处 **bolt upright** with the back very straight 背部笔直地 **make a bolt for** run suddenly towards 突然跑向

bomb /bɒm/ *noun* **1** a device designed to explode and cause damage 炸弹;爆炸装置 **2** (**the bomb**) nuclear weapons 核武器;核弹 **3** (**a bomb**) Brit. *informal*【英,非正式】a large sum of money 大笔钱 • *verb* **1** attack with a bomb or bombs 轰炸 **2** Brit. *informal*【英,非正式】move very quickly 快速移动;疾行 **3** *informal*【非正式】fail badly 惨败

bombard /bɒm'bɑ:d/ **verb 1** attack continuously with bombs or other missiles 轰炸;炮击 **2** direct a continuous flow of questions or information at 连珠炮似地质问;向…一下子提供大量信息 ∎ **bombardment** noun.

bombardier /ˌbɒmbə'dɪə(r)/ **noun 1** a rank of non-commissioned officer in some artillery regiments (炮兵部队中的)军士 **2** a member of a bomber crew in the US air force who is responsible for releasing the bombs (美国空军轰炸机的)投弹手

bombast /'bɒmbæst/ **noun** language that sounds impressive but has little meaning 浮夸之辞;大话 ∎ **bombastic** adjective.

bomber /'bɒmə(r)/ **noun 1** an aircraft designed for dropping bombs 轰炸机 **2** a person who plants bombs 投弹手;放置炸弹的人

bombshell /'bɒmʃel/ **noun 1** a great surprise or shock 出人意料的事物 **2** informal【非正式】a very attractive woman 美女

bona fide /ˌbəʊnə 'faɪdi/ **adjective** genuine; real 真诚的;真正的

bonanza /bə'nænzə/ **noun 1** a situation creating wealth or success 富源;财源 **2** a large amount of something desirable 大量诱人之物

bonbon /'bɒnbɒn/ **noun** a sweet 糖果

bond /bɒnd/ **noun 1** a thing used to tie or fasten things together 捆绑物;捆扎物 **2** (**bonds**) ropes or chains used to hold someone prisoner 镣铐;枷锁 **3** an instinct or feeling that draws people together 结合力;纽带;联系 **4** a legally binding agreement 契约;合同 **5** a certificate issued by a government or public company promising to repay money lent to it at a fixed rate of interest and at a particular time 债券 • **verb 1** join or be joined securely to something else (使)结合,(使)连接 **2** feel connected to someone 感到与…相联系

bondage /'bɒndɪdʒ/ **noun 1** the state of being a slave or of having no freedom 奴役;束缚 **2** sexual activity that involves the tying up of one partner 捆绑式性虐待

bone /bəʊn/ **noun 1** any of the pieces of hard material that make up the skeleton in vertebrates 骨;骨头 **2** the hard material of which bones are made 骨质 • **verb** (**bones**, **boning**, **boned**) remove the bones from meat or fish before cooking 剔去(肉或鱼)的骨(或刺) □ **bone china** white porcelain that contains a mineral obtained from bone 骨灰瓷 **bone dry** completely dry 十分干燥的;干旱的 **bone idle** very lazy 懒透了的 **bone of contention** something argued about 争论的焦点;争议点 **close to the bone 1** (of a remark) accurate to the point of making you feel uncomfortable (话)露骨的 **2** (of a joke or story) rather rude (笑话或故事)近乎下流的 **have a bone to pick with** informal【非正式】have reason to quarrel with someone or to tell them off 有理由与(某人)争吵;有理由责备(某人) **make no bones about** be direct in stating or dealing with 对…直言不讳 ∎ **boneless** adjective.

bonemeal /'bəʊnmiːl/ **noun** ground bones used as a fertilizer 骨粉(用作肥料)

bonfire /'bɒnfaɪə(r)/ **noun** an open-air fire lit to burn rubbish or as a celebration 为焚烧垃圾而燃的)火堆;(为庆祝而燃的)篝火

bongo /'bɒŋɡəʊ/ **noun** (plural **bongos**) each of a pair of small drums that are held between the knees 邦戈鼓;小手鼓

bonhomie /'bɒnəmi/ **noun** good-natured friendliness 温和;友好

bonkers /'bɒŋkəz/ **adjective** informal【非正式】mad 疯狂的

bonnet /'bɒnɪt/ **noun 1** a woman's

or child's hat tied under the chin (有带子系于领下的)女帽 **2** Brit. 【英】the hinged metal cover over the engine of a vehicle (汽车)引擎罩

bonny or **bonnie** /ˈbɒni/ **adjective** (**bonnier**, **bonniest**) chiefly Scottish & N. English 【主苏格兰和英格兰北部】attractive and healthy-looking 漂亮的;好看的;健康的

bonsai /ˈbɒnsaɪ/ **noun** the art of growing miniature ornamental trees 盆景(艺术)

bonus /ˈbəʊnəs/ **noun 1** a sum of money added to a person's wages for good performance 奖金;红利;津贴 **2** an unexpected extra benefit 意想不到的好事

bon voyage /ˌbɒn vɔɪˈɑːʒ/ **exclamation** have a good journey 一路平安

bony /ˈbəʊni/ **adjective** (**bonier**, **boniest**) **1** containing or resembling bones 骨的;含骨的 **2** so thin that the bones can be seen 瘦骨嶙峋的;皮包骨头的

boo /buː/ **exclamation 1** said suddenly to surprise someone 哟(冷不防吓唬人的声音) **2** said to show disapproval or contempt 呸(表示不满或轻蔑) • **verb** (**boos**, **booing**, **booed**) say 'boo' to show disapproval or contempt 发出嘘声;喝倒彩

boob /buːb/ Brit. informal 【英,非正式】**noun** an embarrassing mistake 大错;过失 • **verb** make an embarrassing mistake 犯大错

booby /ˈbuːbi/ **noun** (plural **boobies**) informal 【非正式】a stupid person 笨蛋;傻瓜 □ **booby prize** a prize given to someone who comes last in a contest (给比赛最后一名的)末名奖 **booby trap** an object containing a hidden explosive device 饵雷;诡雷

boogie /ˈbuːɡi/ **verb** (**boogies**, **boogieing**, **boogied**) informal 【非正式】dance to pop music 随着流行音乐跳舞

book /bʊk/ **noun 1** a written or printed work consisting of pages fastened together along one side and bound in covers 书;书本 **2** a main division of a literary work or of the Bible (文学作品或《圣经》的)卷,篇,部 **3** (**books**) a record of financial transactions 记录;账目 • **verb 1** reserve accommodation or a ticket 预订(住宿或票) **2** (**book in**) register your arrival at a hotel 登记入住(旅馆) **3** engage a performer or guest for an event (为某活动)预约(演员或来宾) **4** (**be booked up**) have all places or dates reserved 预订一空;预约已满 **5** make an official note of the name of someone who has broken a law or rule 将(违法或违规者)登记入册;记名警告

bookcase /ˈbʊkkeɪs/ **noun** a cabinet containing shelves on which books are kept 书架;书橱

bookend /ˈbʊkend/ **noun** a support placed at the end of a row of books to keep them upright 书立;书挡

bookie /ˈbʊki/ **noun** (plural **bookies**) informal 【非正式】a bookmaker 赌注登记经纪

bookish /ˈbʊkɪʃ/ **adjective** very interested in reading and studying 喜欢读书的;好学习的

bookkeeping /ˈbʊkkiːpɪŋ/ **noun** the keeping of records of financial transactions 记账;簿记

booklet /ˈbʊklət/ **noun** a small, thin book with paper covers 小册子

bookmaker /ˈbʊkmeɪkə(r)/ **noun** a person who takes bets and pays out winnings 赌注登记经纪人

bookmark /ˈbʊkmɑːk/ **noun 1** a strip of leather or card used to mark a place in a book 书签 **2** a record of the address of a computer file, Internet page, etc., enabling a user to return to it quickly 书签(对计算机文件或因特网网页地址的记录,便于快速查找) • **verb** record the address of a computer file, Internet page, etc. 为(计算机文件或因特网网页地址)加书签

bookworm /'bʊkwɜːm/ **noun** informal 【非正式】 a person who loves reading 极爱读书者；书迷；书虫

boom¹ /buːm/ **noun 1** a deep, loud sound 低沉的响声；隆隆声 **2** a period of fast economic growth 繁荣；迅速发展；兴旺 • **verb 1** make a deep, loud sound 轰鸣；轰响 **2** experience fast economic growth 繁荣；迅速发展

boom² **noun 1** a movable pole to which the bottom of a sail is attached 帆的下桁 **2** a movable arm carrying a microphone or film camera (麦克风的)吊杆；(摄像机的)支臂 **3** a beam used to form a barrier across the mouth of a harbour 水栅；拦障

boomerang /'buːməræŋ/ **noun** a curved flat piece of wood that follows a circle through the air and returns to you when you throw it 回飞镖

boon /buːn/ **noun** a very helpful thing 有裨益的东西

boor /bʊə(r)/ **noun** a rough and bad-mannered person 粗野无礼的人 ■ **boorish** adjective.

boost /buːst/ **verb** help or encourage 推动；促进；激励 • **noun** a source of help or encouragement 推动；促进；激励

booster /'buːstə(r)/ **noun 1** a dose of a vaccine that increases or renews the effect of an earlier one (增强药效的)加强剂量 **2** the part of a rocket or spacecraft used to give acceleration after lift-off (火箭或航天器的)助推器

boot /buːt/ **noun 1** an item of footwear covering the foot and the ankle or lower leg 靴子 **2** Brit. 【英】 a space at the back of a car for carrying luggage (汽车后部的)行李箱 **3** informal 【非正式】 a hard kick 猛踢 **4 (the boot)** informal 【非正式】 dismissal from a job 解雇 • **verb 1** informal 【非正式】 kick someone hard 猛踢 **2 (boot someone out)** informal 【非正式】 force someone to leave 逐出；撵走 **3** start a computer and make it ready to operate 启动(计算机)□ **to boot** as

well 而且；加之

bootee or **bootie** /buː'tiː/ **noun 1** a baby's woollen shoe 婴儿毛绒鞋 **2** a woman's short boot 短筒女靴

booth /buːð/ **noun 1** an enclosed compartment that gives you privacy when telephoning, voting, etc. 封闭的小隔间(指电话亭、投票室等) **2** a small temporary structure used for selling goods or staging shows at a market or fair 货摊；(演出用的)临时棚舍

bootleg /'buːtleg/ **adjective** made or distributed illegally 非法制造的；非法贩卖的 ■ **bootlegger** noun **bootlegging** noun.

booty /'buːti/ **noun** valuable stolen goods 赃物

booze /buːz/ **noun** informal 【非正式】 alcoholic drink 酒；白酒 • **verb** (**boozes, boozing, boozed**) drink a lot of alcohol 大量饮酒；痛饮 ■ **boozer** noun **boozy** adjective

bop /bɒp/ informal 【非正式】 **noun** a dance to pop music 博普舞 • **verb** (**bops, bopping, bopped**) dance to pop music 跳博普舞 ■ **bopper** noun.

boracic /bə'ræsɪk/ **adjective** having to do with boric acid 硼酸的

borage /'bɒrɪdʒ/ **noun** a plant with bright blue flowers and hairy leaves 琉璃苣(开明亮蓝色花，叶多绒毛)

borax /'bɔːræks/ **noun** a white mineral used in making glass 硼砂(白色矿物质，用于制玻璃)

border /'bɔːdə(r)/ **noun 1** a boundary between two countries or areas 边界；边境 **2** a decorative band around the edge of something 镶边；包边 **3** a strip of ground along the edge of a lawn where flowers or shrubs are planted (草坪边缘的)狭长花坛，狭长绿化地带 • **verb** (**borders, bordering, bordered**) **1** form a border around or along 形成…的边界 **2 (of a country or area) be next to)** (国家或地区)毗连，邻接 **3 (border on)** come near to 近似；接近

borderline /ˈbɔːdəlaɪn/ noun a boundary 边缘线；边界线 • adjective on the boundary between two qualities or categories 两可间的；临界的

bore¹ /bɔː(r)/ verb (bores, boring, bored) make a hole in something with a drill or other tool 钻(孔) • noun the hollow part inside a gun barrel or other tube (枪炮或管道的)孔，内径

bore² noun a dull person or activity 令人厌烦的人(或活动) • verb (bores, boring, bored) make someone feel tired and unenthusiastic by being dull 使厌烦；使厌倦 ■ boring adjective.

bore³ past of BEAR¹.

bored /bɔːd/ adjective feeling tired and unenthusiastic because you have nothing interesting to do 厌烦的；厌倦的

> ！注意 use bored by or bored with rather than bored of. 应使用 bored by 或 bored with，不要用 bored of。

boredom /ˈbɔːdəm/ noun the state of feeling bored 厌倦；乏味；无聊

borehole /ˈbɔːhəʊl/ noun a deep hole in the ground made to find water or oil (为找到水或石油而开凿的)钻孔，探孔

boric acid /ˈbɔːrɪk/ noun a substance made from boron, used as an antiseptic 硼酸(用作杀菌剂)

born /bɔːn/ adjective 1 having come out of your mother's body; having started life 出生的；出世的 2 having a particular natural ability 天生的：a born engineer 天生的工程师 3 (born of) existing as a result of a situation or feeling 由于某情形(或情感)而得以存在的；源于…的 □ born-again newly converted to Christianity or some other cause 再生的；皈依的

> ！注意 don't confuse born with borne, which is the past participle of bear and means 'carried'. 不要混淆 born 和 borne，borne 是 bear 的过去分词形式，意为"被携带的"。

borne /bɔːn/ past participle of BEAR¹.

boron /ˈbɔːrɒn/ noun a chemical element used in making alloy steel and in nuclear reactors (化学元素)硼

borough /ˈbʌrə/ noun 1 Brit. 【英】a town with a corporation and privileges granted by a royal charter (获皇家特许的)自治市镇 2 a part of London or New York City which has its own local council (伦敦市或纽约市的)行政区

borrow /ˈbɒrəʊ/ verb take and use something belonging to someone else with the intention of returning it 借；借入

borstal /ˈbɔːstl/ noun Brit. historical 【英，历史】a type of prison for young offenders 青少年犯教养院

Bosnian /ˈbɒznɪən/ noun a person from Bosnia 波斯尼亚人 • adjective relating to Bosnia 波斯尼亚的

bosom /ˈbʊzəm/ noun 1 a woman's breast or chest (女人的)乳房，胸部 2 loving care 关怀；爱护：He went home to the bosom of his family. 他回家投入到家人的温暖怀抱。• adjective (of a friend) very close (朋友)亲密的，知心的

boss¹ /bɒs/ informal 【非正式】noun a person who is in charge of other people at work 老板；上司 • verb tell someone what to do in an arrogant or annoying way 对(某人)发号施令

boss² noun a knob at the centre of a shield, propeller, or similar object (盾牌等的)饰扣；(螺旋桨的)轮毂

bossa nova /ˌbɒsə ˈnəʊvə/ noun a dance like the samba, from Brazil 波萨诺伐舞(一种类似桑巴舞的巴西舞蹈)

boss-eyed /ˈbɒsaɪd/ adjective Brit. informal 【英，非正式】cross-eyed 斜眼的；斜视的

bossy /ˈbɒsi/ adjective (bossier, bossiest) tending to tell people what to do in an arrogant or annoying way 好指挥人的；专横的 ■ bossiness noun.

bosun or **bo'sun** /'bəʊsn/ = BOAT-SWAIN.

botany /'bɒtəni/ noun the scientific study of plants 植物学 ■ **botanical** (or **botanic**) adjective **botanist** noun.

botch /bɒtʃ/ verb informal 【非正式】 do something badly or carelessly 拙劣地做；漫不经心地做

both /bəʊθ/ determiner & pronoun two people or things, considered together 两者；两个人；双方 • adverb applying to each of two alternatives 两方面都；兼而

bother /'bɒðə(r)/ verb (bothers, bothering, bothered) 1 take the trouble to do something 费心；麻烦 2 annoy, worry, or upset someone 使烦恼；打扰，使不安 3 (bother with or about) feel concern about or interest in 焦虑；担心，关心 • noun 1 trouble and fuss 麻烦；烦恼；纷乱 2 (a bother) a cause of trouble or fuss 带来麻烦的人(或事物)

bothersome /'bɒðəsəm/ adjective troublesome 令人烦恼的；麻烦的

bottle /'bɒtl/ noun 1 a container with a narrow neck, used for storing liquids (细颈)瓶子 2 Brit. informal【英，非正式】courage 勇气 • verb (bottles, bottling, bottled) 1 place in bottles for storage 把…放入瓶中 2 (bottle something up) hide your feelings 隐藏(感情) □ **bottle green** dark green 深绿色的

bottleneck /'bɒtlnek/ noun a narrow section of road where the flow of traffic is restricted 瓶颈路段，狭窄路段；交通阻塞点

bottom /'bɒtəm/ noun 1 the lowest or furthest point or part of something 底；底层；底部 2 the lowest position in a competition or ranking 最后名次；最低级别 3 a person's buttocks 屁股，臀部 4 (also **bottoms**) the lower half of a two-piece garment (两件一套衣服的)下半身 • adjective in the lowest or furthest position 最低的；尽头的 • verb (bottom out) (of a situation) reach the lowest point before becoming stable or improving (局势)达最低点 □ **get to the bottom of** find an explanation for 弄清…的起因；寻找…的根源 **the bottom line** informal【非正式】the most important factor 要点；关键 ■ **bottomless** adjective.

botulism /'bɒtjʊlɪzəm/ noun a dangerous form of food poisoning 肉毒中毒

boudoir /'buːdwɑː(r)/ noun a woman's bedroom or small private room 女子卧室；闺房

bouffant /'buːfɒn/ adjective (of hair) styled so as to stand out from the head in a rounded shape (头发)蓬松的，鼓起的

bougainvillea /ˌbuːgən'vɪliə/ noun a tropical climbing plant with brightly coloured flower-like leaves (called bracts) 九重葛属植物；叶子花属植物(热带攀援植物，叶子似花，色彩明亮)

bough /baʊ/ noun a large branch 大树枝；粗树枝

bought /bɔːt/ past and past participle of BUY.

！注意 don't confuse **bought** with **brought**, which is the past of **bring**. 不要混淆 bought 和 brought，后者是 bring 的过去式。

---

boulder /'bəʊldə(r)/ noun a large rock 巨石

boulevard /'buːləvɑːd/ noun a wide street 林阴大道

bounce /baʊns/ verb (bounces, bouncing, bounced) 1 move quickly up or away from a surface after hitting it 弹起；反弹 2 move or jump up and down repeatedly 蹦跳；跳动 3 informal【非正式】(of a cheque) be returned by a bank when there is not enough money in an account for it to be paid (支票)被拒付，被退回 • noun 1 an act of bouncing 弹起；反弹；蹦跳，跳动 2

bouncer /'baʊnsə(r)/ **noun** a person employed by a nightclub to control or keep out troublemakers (夜总会的) 保安人员，保镖

bouncy /'baʊnsi/ **adjective** (**bouncier, bounciest**) **1** able to bounce, or making something bounce 有弹性的；弹力足的 **2** confident and lively 生气勃勃的；精神饱满的

bound¹ /baʊnd/ **verb** move with long, leaping strides 跳跃着前进；蹦蹦跳跳地跑 • **noun** a leaping movement 跳跃

bound² **verb 1** form the boundary of 形成…的边界 **2** restrict 限制；束缚 • **noun** a boundary or restriction 边界；界限 □ **out of bounds 1** (in sport) beyond the field of play (体育运动中)出界的 **2** beyond where you are allowed to go 不准进入的；禁止入内的

bound³ past and past participle of BIND. • **adjective 1** restricted to or by a place or situation 受…束缚的；受…约束的：*His job kept him city-bound.* 他从事的工作决定了他只能呆在城里。**2** going towards somewhere 前往…的：*a train bound for Edinburgh* 驶往爱丁堡的火车 **3** (**bound to**) certain to be, do, or have 一定的；必然的；注定的

boundary /'baʊndri/ **noun** (plural **boundaries**) a line marking the limits of an area 边界；界限；分界线

boundless /'baʊndləs/ **adjective** unlimited 无限的，无边无际的

bounteous /'baʊntiəs/ **adjective** old use 【旧】given or giving generously 慷慨的，无限的

bountiful /'baʊntɪfl/ **adjective 1** existing in large quantities 充足的；丰富的 **2** giving generously 慷慨的；大方的

bounty /'baʊnti/ **noun** (plural **bounties**) **1** literary 【文】generosity, or something given in generous amounts 慷慨；大量给予之物 **2** a reward paid for

killing or capturing someone (杀死或捉住某人的)悬赏金

bouquet /bu'keɪ/ **noun 1** a bunch of flowers 花束 **2** the pleasant smell of a particular wine or perfume (酒或香水的)香味，芬芳

bourbon /'bɜːbən/ **noun** an American whisky made from maize and rye 波旁威士忌酒(用玉米和黑麦酿造的美国威士忌酒)

bourgeois /'bʊəʒwɑː/ **adjective** having to do with the middle class, especially in being concerned with wealth and social status 中产阶级的

bourgeoisie /ˌbʊəʒwɑː'zi/ **noun** the middle class 中产阶级

bout /baʊt/ **noun 1** a short period of great activity, or of illness (大型活动的)一场，一阵，(疾病的)发作期 **2** a wrestling or boxing match 摔跤(或拳击)比赛

boutique /buː'tiːk/ **noun** a small shop selling fashionable clothes (铺面不大的)时装店

bovine /'bəʊvaɪn/ **adjective 1** having to do with cattle 牛的 **2** rather slow and stupid 迟钝的，愚笨的

bow¹ /bəʊ/ **noun 1** a knot tied with two loops and two loose ends 蝴蝶结；环状装饰结 **2** a weapon for shooting arrows, consisting of a string held taut by a strip of bent wood 弓 **3** a rod with horsehair stretched along its length, used for playing some stringed instruments (弦乐器的)弓，琴弓 □ **bow-legged** having legs that curve outwards at the knee 罗圈腿的；弓形腿的 **bow tie** a man's tie that is tied in a bow 蝶形领结

bow² /baʊ/ **verb 1** bend the head and upper body as a sign of respect 低头，鞠躬，欠身(表示尊敬) **2** bend with age or under a heavy weight (因年岁大或负重)弯身，弯腰 **3** give in to pressure 让步；屈服 **4** (**bow out**) withdraw from an activity 撤出；退出；辞职；退休 • **noun** an act of bowing

低头；鞠躬；欠身 □ **bow and scrape** try too hard to please someone 卑躬屈膝

bow³ /bau/ or **bows** /bauz/ *noun* the front end of a ship 船头，艏

bowdlerize or **bowdlerise** /ˈbaud-ləraɪz/ *verb* (**bowdlerizes, bowdlerizing, bowdlerized**) remove parts of a written work that might shock or offend people 删改(文章)的内容

bowel /ˈbauəl/ *noun* 1 (also **bowels**) the intestine 肠 2 (**bowels**) the innermost parts of something 内部；深处 □ **bowel movement** an act of emptying waste matter from the bowels 解大便

bower /ˈbauə(r)/ *noun* a pleasant shady place under trees 树阴处，阴凉处

bowl¹ /bəul/ *noun* 1 a round, deep dish or basin 碗；钵 2 a rounded, hollow part of an object (物体的)碗状部分，凹处

bowl² *verb* 1 roll a round object along the ground 在地上滚(圆形物体) 2 Cricket 【板球】 (of a bowler) throw the ball towards the wicket (投球手)投(球) 3 Brit. 【英】 move along rapidly and smoothly 快速而平稳地移动 • *noun* a heavy ball used in bowls or tenpin bowling (草地滚球游戏或十柱保龄球游戏中使用的)球 □ **bowl someone over** 1 knock someone down 撞倒(某人) 2 *informal* 【非正式】 surprise or impress someone very much 使(某人)大吃一惊；使(某人)印象深刻

bowler¹ /ˈbəulə(r)/ *noun* 1 Cricket 【板球】 a member of the fielding side who bowls 投球手 2 a player at bowls or tenpin bowling 玩草地滚球游戏(或十柱保龄球游戏)的人

bowler² *noun* a man's hard black felt hat that is rounded at the top and has a rim 常礼帽；圆顶硬礼帽

bowling /ˈbəulɪŋ/ *noun* bowls, tenpin bowling, or skittles 草地滚球游戏、十柱保龄球游戏；撞柱游戏

bowls /bəulz/ *noun* a game played with wooden balls called bowls, in which you roll your bowl as close as possible to a small white ball (the jack) 草地滚球游戏

box¹ /bɒks/ *noun* 1 a square or rectangular container with a lid 箱；盒 2 an enclosed area reserved for a group of people in a theatre or sports ground (剧院或体育场的)包厢 3 (**the box**) *informal* 【非正式】 television 电视机 • *verb* 1 put something in a box 把…放于箱(或盒)内 2 (**box someone in**) restrict or confine someone 堵住；困住 □ **box number** a number identifying an advertisement in a newspaper, used as an address for replies (报纸广告用的)信箱号码 **box office** the place at a theatre or cinema where tickets are sold 票房；售票处 **box room** Brit. 【英】 a small room used for storage 窄室；斗室

box² *verb* take part in boxing 参加拳击 • *noun* a slap on the side of a person's head 耳光；巴掌 □ **box someone's ears** slap someone on both sides of the head 打(某人)的耳光

box³ *noun* a shrub with small, round glossy leaves 黄杨(一种灌木，叶小呈圆形，表面有光泽)

boxer /ˈbɒksə(r)/ *noun* 1 a person who boxes as a sport 拳击手；拳击运动员 2 a breed of dog with a smooth brown coat and a flattened face 斗拳狗(皮毛光滑，呈棕色，面部扁平) □ **boxer shorts** men's underpants that look like shorts (男子穿的)平脚短内裤

boxing /ˈbɒksɪŋ/ *noun* a sport in which contestants fight each other wearing big padded gloves 拳击(运动)

Boxing Day *noun* Brit. 【英】 a public holiday on the day after Christmas Day 节礼日(圣诞节后的第一天，为公共假日)

boxy /ˈbɒksi/ *adjective* 1 roughly square in shape 盒形的；箱形的；四四方方的 2 (of a room or space) cramped (房间或空间)狭窄的

boy /bɔɪ/ **noun** a male child or youth 男孩；男青年；小伙子 ■ **boyhood noun** **boyish** adjective.

boycott /ˈbɔɪkɒt/ **verb 1** refuse to have dealings with 拒绝与…交易(或来往) **2** refuse to buy goods as a protest 抵制；拒绝购买 • **noun** an act of boycotting someone or something 抵制

boyfriend /ˈbɔɪfrend/ **noun** a person's regular male companion in a romantic or sexual relationship 男朋友

bra /brɑː/ **noun** a woman's undergarment worn to support the breasts 奶罩；胸罩

brace /breɪs/ **noun 1** a part that strengthens or supports something 托架；支架 **2** (**braces**) Brit.【英】a pair of straps that pass over the shoulders and fasten to the top of trousers to hold them up (裤子的)背带 **3** a wire device used to straighten the teeth 畸齿矫正钢丝架；牙箍 **4** (plural **brace**) a pair 一对；一双 **5** (also **brace and bit**) a drilling tool with a crank handle and a socket to hold a bit 手摇曲柄钻 • **verb** (**braces, bracing, braced**) **1** make something stronger or firmer with a brace (用托架等)加固，支撑 **2** press your body firmly against something to stay balanced 使(身体)抵住，使稳扎 **3** (**brace yourself**) prepare for something difficult or unpleasant (为困难或坏事)作准备，防备

bracelet /ˈbreɪslət/ **noun** an ornamental band or chain worn on the wrist or arm 手镯；臂镯

bracing /ˈbreɪsɪŋ/ **adjective** refreshing; making you feel full of energy 使人心旷神怡的；令人振奋的

bracken /ˈbrækən/ **noun** a tall fern 欧洲蕨

bracket /ˈbrækɪt/ **noun 1** each of a pair of marks ( ) [ ] { } < > used to enclose words or figures 括号 **2** a category of similar people or things 等级；类别；阶层 **3** a right-angled support that sticks out from a wall (成直角凸出墙壁的)支托，托座 • **verb** (**brackets, bracketing, bracketed**) **1** enclose in brackets 把…放在括号内 **2** place in the same category 把…归入同一类

brackish /ˈbrækɪʃ/ **adjective** (of water) slightly salty (水)微咸的，含少量盐分的

bract /brækt/ **noun** a leaf with a flower in the angle where it meets the stem 苞片；苞

brag /bræg/ **verb** (**brags, bragging, bragged**) speak boastfully 自夸；吹嘘；吹牛 • **noun** a simplified form of the card game poker 布莱格牌戏(一种简化扑克牌戏)

braggart /ˈbrægət/ **noun** a boastful person 自夸者；吹牛者

braid /breɪd/ **noun 1** threads woven into a decorative band 穗带；饰带 **2** a length of hair made up of strands plaited together 发辫 • **verb 1** form hair into a braid 将(头发)编织辫子 **2** trim something with braid (用饰带)镶缀

Braille /breɪl/ **noun** a written language for blind people, using raised dots 布莱叶盲文

brain /breɪn/ **noun 1** an organ contained in the skull that controls thought and feeling and is the centre of the nervous system 脑；大脑 **2** intellectual ability 智力；脑力 **3** (**the brains**) informal 【非正式】the main organizer within a group (团体中的)中枢人物，策划组织者 • **verb** informal 【非正式】hit someone hard on the head 猛击(某人)的头部

brainchild /ˈbreɪntʃaɪld/ **noun** informal 【非正式】an idea or invention thought up by a particular person 脑力劳动成果(指想法或发明)

brainless /ˈbreɪnləs/ **adjective** very stupid 愚蠢的；笨的

brainstorm /ˈbreɪnstɔːm/ **noun** Brit. informal 【英，非正式】a moment in which you are suddenly unable to think clearly 一时糊涂;突然神志不清 • verb hold a group discussion to solve a problem or produce new ideas 进行集体讨论;集思广益

brainwash /'breɪnwɒʃ/ **verb** force someone to accept an idea or belief by putting pressure on them or repeating the same thing over and over again 给(某人)洗脑;强行灌输

brainwave /'breɪnweɪv/ **noun 1** an electrical impulse in the brain 脑电波 **2** informal 【非正式】a sudden clever idea 突然想到的妙计

brainy /'breɪni/ **adjective** (**brainier**, **brainiest**) informal 【非正式】intelligent 聪明的;脑子好使的

braise /breɪz/ **verb** (**braises**, **braising**, **braised**) fry food lightly and then stew it slowly in a closed container 将(食物)清炒后用文火炖

brake /breɪk/ **noun** a device for slowing or stopping a moving vehicle 闸;制动器;刹车 • **verb** (**brakes**, **braking**, **braked**) slow or stop a vehicle with a brake 用闸使(车)减速;刹住(车)

> **！注意** don't confuse **brake** with **break** which mainly means 'separate into pieces' or 'a pause or short rest'. 不要混淆 brake 和 break,后者主要含义为"破碎"或"停顿;短暂休息"。

bramble /'bræmbl/ **noun 1** a blackberry bush or similar prickly shrub 黑莓;悬钩子属植物 **2** Brit. 【英】the fruit of the blackberry 黑莓果

bran /bræn/ **noun** pieces of the outer husk left when grain is made into flour 糠;麸皮

branch /brɑːntʃ/ **noun 1** a part of a tree which grows out from the trunk 树枝 **2** a river, road, or railway extending out from a main one 支流;支路;支线 **3** a division of a larger group (大机构的)分支,分部 • **verb 1** divide into one or more branches 分支;分岔 **2** (**branch out**) start doing a different sort of activity 扩大活动

范围;开辟新的领域

brand /brænd/ **noun 1** a type of product made by a company under a particular name (商品的)牌子,商标 **2** (also **brand name**) a name given to a product by its maker 品牌名称 **3** a mark burned on farm animals with a piece of hot metal (牲畜身上的)烙印,火印 **4** a piece of smouldering wood 燃烧的木头 • **verb 1** mark with a piece of hot metal 给…打烙印 **2** mark someone out as being bad in a particular way 加污名于 **3** give a brand name to 加商标于 □ **brand new** completely new 全新的

brandish /'brændɪʃ/ **verb** wave something as a threat or in anger or excitement (表示威胁、愤怒或激动)挥舞,挥动(某物)

brandy /'brændi/ **noun** (plural **brandies**) a strong alcoholic drink made from wine or fermented fruit juice 白兰地(酒)

brash /bræʃ/ **adjective** confident in a rather rude or aggressive way 粗鲁的;莽撞的;自以为是的 ■ **brashly** adverb **brashness** noun.

brass /brɑːs/ **noun 1** a yellowish metal made by mixing copper and zinc 黄铜(铜锌合金) **2** (also **horse brass**) Brit. 【英】a flat brass ornament for a horse's harness 黄铜马饰 **3** Brit. 【英】a brass plate fixed in a church in memory of someone (教堂的)黄铜纪念牌 **4** brass wind instruments forming a section of an orchestra 铜管乐器 □ **brass band** a group of musicians playing brass instruments 铜管乐队 **top brass** informal 【非正式】people in authority 要人

brasserie /'bræsəri/ **noun** (plural **brasseries**) an inexpensive French or French-style restaurant (法国或法式的)小餐馆

brassiere /'bræzɪə(r)/ **noun** a bra 胸罩;奶罩

brassy /'brɑːsi/ **adjective** (**brassier**,

brassiest) 1 resembling brass in colour 黄铜色的 **2** unpleasantly bright or showy 花哨的 **3** harsh or blaring like a brass instrument 响亮刺耳的；喧闹的

brat /bræt/ **noun** informal 【非正式】a badly behaved child 顽童

bravado /brəˈvɑːdəʊ/ **noun** confidence or a show of confidence that is intended to impress 逞能；虚张声势

brave /breɪv/ **adjective** willing to do something that is dangerous or frightening; not afraid 勇敢的；无畏的 • **noun** dated 【废】an American Indian warrior 美洲印第安武士 • **verb** (**braves, braving, braved**) face or deal with something frightening or unpleasant 勇敢面对(困境) ■ **bravely** adverb **bravery** noun.

bravo /brɑːˈvəʊ/ **exclamation** shouted to express approval for a performer 好啊(表示向演员喝彩、叫好)

bravura /brəˈvjʊərə/ **noun 1** great skill; brilliance 精湛技艺；卓越才智 **2** the display of great daring 显示胆量

brawl /brɔːl/ **noun** a noisy fight or quarrel 斗殴；闹事 • **verb** take part in a brawl 斗殴；闹事

brawn /brɔːn/ **noun** physical strength 膂力；体力 ■ **brawny** adjective.

bray /breɪ/ **verb** (of a donkey) make a loud, harsh cry (驴)发出驴叫声 • **noun** the loud, harsh cry of a donkey 驴叫声

brazen /ˈbreɪzn/ **adjective** not caring if other people think you are behaving badly; shameless 厚颜无耻的；恬不知耻的 • **verb** (**brazen it out**) endure an awkward situation without seeming ashamed or embarrassed 厚着脸皮硬挺 ■ **brazenly** adverb.

brazier /ˈbreɪzɪə(r)/ **noun** a portable heater holding lighted coals (取暖用的)便携式火盆，火钵

Brazilian /brəˈzɪlɪən/ **noun** a person from Brazil 巴西人 • **adjective** relating to Brazil 巴西的

brazil nut /brəˈzɪl/ **noun** the large three-sided nut of a South American forest tree 巴西坚果

breach /briːtʃ/ **verb 1** make a hole in; break through 在…上打开缺口；突破；攻破 **2** break a rule or agreement 破坏(规定或协议) • **noun 1** a gap made in a wall or barrier 破口；缺口 **2** an act that breaks a rule or agreement 破坏；违反 **3** a quarrel or disagreement 争吵；分歧 □ **step into the breach** replace someone who is suddenly unable to do a job 代理别人的工作

bread /bred/ **noun 1** food made of flour, water, and yeast mixed together and baked 面包 **2** informal 【非正式】money 钱 □ **bread and butter** a person's main source of income 主要的收入来源

breadcrumb /ˈbredkrʌm/ **noun** a very small fragment of bread 面包屑

breaded /ˈbredɪd/ **adjective** (of food) coated with breadcrumbs and fried (食物)裹着面包屑油炸的

breadline /ˈbredlaɪn/ **noun** (**on the breadline**) Brit. 【英】very poor 极度贫困

breadth /bredθ/ **noun 1** the distance from side to side of something 宽度；幅度 **2** wide range 广泛；广阔

breadwinner /ˈbredwɪnə(r)/ **noun** a person who supports their family with the money they earn 挣钱养家的人

break /breɪk/ **verb** (**breaks, breaking, broke**; past participle **broken**) **1** separate into pieces as a result of a blow or strain 弄碎；打破 **2** stop working 出故障；出毛病 **3** interrupt a sequence or course 打断；中断 **4** fail to obey a rule or agreement 破坏；违反 **5** beat a record 打破(纪录) **6** work out a code 破译(密码) **7** make a rush or dash 急冲；猛闯 **8** soften a fall 减弱(下降的力量) **9** suddenly become public (突然)透露，传开 **10** (of a person's voice) falter and change tone (人的嗓音)突变 **11**

(of a teenage boy's voice) become deeper (男孩的嗓音)变粗 **12** (of the weather) change suddenly (天气)突变 • noun **1** a pause or gap 停顿;间歇 **2** a short rest 短暂休息 **3** an instance of breaking, or the point where something is broken 破碎;破裂;破裂处;裂缝 **4** a sudden rush or dash 急冲;猛闯 **5** informal 【非正式】a chance 机会 **6** Tennis 【网球】the winning of a game against an opponent's serve 破对方发球局 **7** Snooker & Billiards 【斯诺克和台球】a continuous series of successful shots 一次连续得分 **8** a short solo in music 独奏华彩段 □ **break away** escape 逃脱 **break down 1** stop working 停止运转;出故障 **2** lose control of your emotions when upset 感情上失去控制 **break in** force your way into a building 非法强行闯入(建筑物) **break something in** make a horse used to being ridden 驯(马) **break off** stop suddenly 突然停止 **break out 1** (of something unwelcome) start suddenly (不愉快之事)突然发生,爆发 **2** escape 逃离 **break up 1** (of a gathering) end (聚会)结束 **2** (of a couple) end a relationship (夫妇)分手,离婚 **3** end a school term 学期结束;放假 **break wind** release gas from the anus 放屁 ■ **breakable** adjective.

breakage /ˈbreɪkɪdʒ/ **noun** the action of breaking something 破损;毁坏

breakaway /ˈbreɪkəweɪ/ **noun 1** a major change from something established 脱离;分离 **2** (in sport) a sudden attack or forward movement (体育运动中的)突然进攻,猛冲

breakdown /ˈbreɪkdaʊn/ **noun 1** a failure or collapse 损坏;故障;崩溃;垮台 **2** a careful analysis of costs or figures (对费用或数字的)细密分析

breaker /ˈbreɪkə(r)/ **noun 1** a heavy sea wave that breaks on the shore (在海岸上溅开的)碎浪,浪花 **2** a person

that breaks up old machinery 捣毁旧机器者

breakfast /ˈbrekfəst/ **noun** the first meal of the day 早饭;早餐 • **verb** eat breakfast 吃早餐

breakneck /ˈbreɪknek/ **adjective** dangerously fast 飞速惊险的;极快的

breakthrough /ˈbreɪkθruː/ **noun** a sudden important development or success 重大进展;突破

breakwater /ˈbreɪkwɔːtə(r)/ **noun** a barrier built out into the sea to protect a coast or harbour from waves 防波堤;防浪墙

bream /briːm/ **noun** (plural **bream**) a greenish-bronze freshwater fish 欧鳊(一种青褐色淡水鱼)

breast /brest/ **noun 1** either of the two soft organs on a woman's chest which produce milk when she has had a baby (女人的)乳房 **2** a person's or animal's chest (人或动物的)胸部,胸膛 • **verb 1** reach the top of a hill 登上山顶 **2** move forwards while pushing against something 挺胸面对;挺胸迎…而上

breastbone /ˈbrestbəʊn/ **noun** a bone running down the centre of the chest and connecting the ribs 胸骨

breastfeed /ˈbrestfiːd/ **verb** (**breastfeeds, breastfeeding, breastfed**) feed a baby with milk from the breast 用母乳喂养(婴儿);哺乳

breastplate /ˈbrestpleɪt/ **noun** a piece of armour covering the chest 胸铠

breaststroke /ˈbreststrəʊk/ **noun** a swimming stroke in which you push your arms forwards and then sweep them back while kicking your legs out 蛙泳

breath /breθ/ **noun 1** air taken into or sent out of the lungs 气息;呼吸的空气 **2** an instance of breathing in or out 呼吸 **3** a slight movement of air (空气的)微微流动,轻拂 **4** a sign or hint 迹象;暗示 ■ **breathable** adjective.

breathalyser /ˈbreθəlaɪzə(r)/ (US

spelling 【美拼作】 **Breathalyzer** (trademark 【商标】)) **noun** a device for measuring the amount of alcohol in a driver's breath 呼气测醉器 ■ **breathalyse** (US spelling 【美拼作】 **breathalyze**) verb.

breathe /briːð/ **verb** (**breathes, breathing, breathed**) **1** take air into the lungs and send it out again 呼吸 **2** say quietly 低声说 **3** let air or moisture in or out 通气；透气；吸入(或散发)水气

breather /ˈbriːðə(r)/ **noun** informal 【非正式】 a brief pause for rest 短暂休息

breathless /ˈbreθləs/ **adjective 1** gasping for breath 气喘吁吁的；上气不接下气的 **2** feeling or causing great excitement 扣人心弦的；令人喘不过气的 ■ **breathlessly** adverb.

breathtaking /ˈbreθteɪkɪŋ/ **adjective** astonishing or awe-inspiring 惊人的；激动人心的 ■ **breathtakingly** adverb.

breathy /ˈbreθi/ **adjective** (of speech or singing) having a noticeable sound of breathing (讲话或歌唱)带呼吸声的

breech /briːtʃ/ **noun** the back part of a rifle or gun barrel 枪尾；炮尾；(枪炮的)后膛

breech birth noun a birth in which the baby's buttocks or feet are delivered first 臀位分娩

breeches /ˈbrɪtʃɪz/ **plural noun** short trousers fastened just below the knee (裤脚束于膝下的)半长裤，马裤

breed /briːd/ **verb** (**breeds, breeding, bred**) **1** (of animals) mate and then produce young (动物)交配繁殖 **2** keep animals for the young that they produce (为育种目的)饲养(动物) **3** produce or cause 产生；导致 • **noun** a particular type of domestic or farm animal that has been specially developed (家畜或农场动物的)品种 ■ **breeder** noun.

breeding /ˈbriːdɪŋ/ **noun** upper-class good manners 教养

breeze /briːz/ **noun** a gentle wind 微风；和风 • **verb** (**breezes, breezing, breezed**) informal 【非正式】 come or go casually 飘然而行；轻浮地走

breeze block noun Brit. 【英】 a lightweight building brick made from sand, cement, and pieces of partly burnt coal or wood 煤渣砖

breezy /ˈbriːzi/ **adjective** (**breezier, breeziest**) **1** pleasantly windy 有微风的；微风和煦的 **2** relaxed and cheerfully brisk 轻松活泼的

brethren /ˈbreðrən/ **plural noun 1** old-fashioned plural of BROTHER 弟兄们 (brother 的旧用复数形式) **2** fellow Christians or members of group 教友们；同道；同人

breve /briːv/ **noun** Music 【音乐】 a note twice as long as a semibreve 二全音符

brevity /ˈbrevəti/ **noun 1** economical and exact use of words (措词的)简洁，简练 **2** the fact of lasting a short time (时间的)短暂，短促

brew /bruː/ **verb 1** make beer 酿造(啤酒) **2** make tea or coffee by mixing it with hot water 泡(茶)；煮(咖啡) **3** begin to develop 酝酿 • **noun** something brewed 酿造物 ■ **brewer** noun.

brewery /ˈbruːəri/ **noun** (plural **breweries**) a place where beer is made 啤酒厂

briar or **brier** /ˈbraɪə(r)/ **noun** a prickly shrub 多刺灌木

bribe /braɪb/ **verb** (**bribes, bribing, bribed**) pay someone to do something dishonest that helps you 向(某人)行贿；收买 • **noun** an amount of money offered in an attempt to bribe someone 贿赂 ■ **bribery** noun.

bric-a-brac /ˈbrɪkəbræk/ **noun** various objects of little value (不值钱的)小装饰品，小摆设

brick /brɪk/ **noun** a small rectangular block of fired clay, used in building 砖；砖块 • **verb** (**brick something up**) block or enclose something with a wall of bricks 用砖墙堵住；用砖墙

围住

brickbat /'brɪkbæt/ **noun** a critical remark 批评

bricklayer /'brɪkleɪə(r)/ **noun** a person whose job is to build structures with bricks 砌砖工人

bridal /'braɪdl/ **adjective** relating to a bride or a newly married couple 新娘的;新婚夫妇的

bride /braɪd/ **noun** a woman at the time of her wedding 新娘

bridegroom /'braɪdɡruːm/ **noun** a man at the time of his wedding 新郎

bridesmaid /'braɪdzmeɪd/ **noun** a girl or woman who accompanies a bride at her wedding 女傧相;伴娘

bridge /brɪdʒ/ **noun** a structure that allows people or vehicles to cross a river, road, etc. 桥;桥梁 **2** the platform on a ship where the captain and officers stand (舰船的)驾驶台,舰桥,桥楼 **3** the upper bony part of a person's nose 鼻梁 **4** the part on a stringed instrument over which the strings are stretched (弦乐器上的)琴马 **5** a card game played by two teams of two players 桥牌 • **verb** (**bridges**, **bridging**, **bridged**) be or make a bridge over 是…的桥梁;在…上架桥

bridgehead /'brɪdʒhed/ **noun** a strong position gained by an army inside enemy territory 桥头堡;桥头阵地

bridle /'braɪdl/ **noun** the harness used to control a horse 马勒;马笼头;辔头 • **verb** (**bridles**, **bridling**, **bridled**) **1** put a bridle on 给…套笼头 **2** show resentment or anger 恼怒;生气

bridleway /'braɪdlweɪ/ **noun** Brit. 【英】 a path along which horse riders have right of way 马道

brief /briːf/ **adjective 1** lasting a short time 短暂的;短时间的 **2** using few words (措词)简洁的, 简练的 **3** (of clothing) not covering much of the body (衣服)短的,暴露的 • **noun** Brit. 【英】 **1** a set of instructions about a task 任务指示 **2** a summary of the facts in a case given to a barrister to argue in court (向辩护律师提供的)案情摘要 **3** informal 【非正式】 a solicitor or barrister 初级律师;辩护律师 • **verb** give someone information to prepare them for a task 给(某人)任务指示 ■ **briefly** adverb.

briefcase /'briːfkeɪs/ **noun** a flat rectangular case for carrying documents 公事包;公文包

briefing /'briːfɪŋ/ **noun** a meeting for giving information or instructions 吹风会;情况介绍会;传达指示会

briefs /briːfs/ **plural noun** short, close-fitting underpants 紧身内裤

brier /'braɪə(r)/ ⇒ 见 BRIAR.

brig /brɪɡ/ **noun** a sailing ship with two masts 双桅横帆船

brigade /brɪ'ɡeɪd/ **noun 1** a large army unit, forming part of a division 旅(陆军编制单位) **2** disapproving 【贬】 a particular group of people 一伙人: the anti-smoking brigade 反吸烟派

brigadier /ˌbrɪɡə'dɪə(r)/ **noun** a rank of officer in the British army, above colonel (英国陆军)准将

brigand /'brɪɡənd/ **noun** a member of a gang of bandits 土匪;强盗

bright /braɪt/ **adjective 1** giving out light, or filled with light 明亮的 **2** (of colour) strong and eye-catching (色彩)鲜艳的 **3** intelligent and quick-witted 聪明的;机灵的 **4** (of sound) clear and high-pitched (声音)清亮的 **5** cheerfully lively 欢快的 **6** (of prospects) good (前景)光明的 ■ **brightly** adverb **brightness** noun.

brighten /'braɪtn/ **verb** make or become brighter or more cheerful (使)变得更明亮;(使)变得更高兴

brilliant /'brɪlɪənt/ **adjective 1** (of light or colour) very bright or vivid (光线或色彩)光辉的,明亮的,鲜艳的 **2** very clever or talented 极聪明的;才华横溢的 **3** Brit. informal 【英,非正式】 very good; marvellous 卓越的;杰出的 ■ **brilliance** noun **brilliantly** adverb.

brim /brɪm/ **noun 1** the projecting edge around the bottom of a hat 帽檐 **2** the lip of a cup, bowl, etc. (杯、碗等的) 边,边沿 • **verb** (**brims, brimming, brimmed**) be full to the point of over-flowing 注满;充盈;充溢

brimstone /'brɪmstəʊn/ **noun** old use 【旧】sulphur 硫磺

brindle /'brɪndl/ or **brindled** /'brɪndld/ **adjective** (of an animal) brownish with streaks of grey or black (动物) 棕色间杂斑纹的

brine /braɪn/ **noun** water which contains dissolved salt 浓盐水;卤水

bring /brɪŋ/ **verb** (**brings, bringing, brought**) **1** take someone or something to a place 把…带至;带来 **2** cause to be in a particular position or state 导致;引起;使处于…状态 **3** cause someone to receive something 使(某人)得到;给(某人)带来 **4** (**bring yourself to do**) force yourself to do something unpleasant 强迫自己做(令人不快之事) **5** begin legal action 提起(诉讼) □ **bring something about** cause something to happen 导致(某事)发生 **bring something off** achieve something successfully 成功做成(某事) **bring something on** cause something unpleasant to develop 导致,惹来(令人不快之事) **bring something out 1** produce and launch a new product 推出(新产品) **2** emphasize a feature 强调(某特征) **bring someone round 1** make someone conscious again 使(某人)恢复知觉 **2** persuade someone to agree to something 说服(某人) **bring someone/thing up 1** look after a child until it is an adult 抚养,养育(孩子) **2** mention something in order to discuss it 提出(问题) ■ **bringer** noun.

brink /brɪŋk/ **noun 1** the edge of land before a steep slope or an area of water (陡坡或水域的)边,边沿 **2** the stage just before a new situation 边缘;初始状态

brinkmanship /'brɪŋkmənʃɪp/ **noun** the practice of continuing with a dangerous course of action to the limits of safety before stopping 边缘策略

briny /braɪnɪ/ **adjective** salty 咸的 • **noun** (**the briny**) Brit. informal 【英,非正式】the sea 海洋

brio /'briːəʊ/ **noun** energy or liveliness 活力;活泼

brioche /briː'ɒʃ/ **noun** a soft, sweet French roll (法式)奶油鸡蛋卷

brisk /brɪsk/ **adjective 1** quick, active, or energetic 敏捷的;活泼的;生气勃勃的 **2** (of a person's manner) practical and efficient (人的行事方式)务实高效的 ■ **briskly** adverb.

brisket /'brɪskɪt/ **noun** meat from the chest of a cow (牛的)胸脯肉

bristle /'brɪsl/ **noun** a short, stiff hair 短而硬的毛发;刚毛;鬃毛 • **verb** (**bristles, bristling, bristled**) **1** (of hair or fur) stand upright away from the skin (毛发)竖起,耸起 **2** react angrily or defensively 被激怒;进入防备状态 **3** (**bristle with**) be covered with 布满;充满 ■ **bristly** adjective.

British /'brɪtɪʃ/ **adjective** relating to Great Britain 大列颠的;英国的

Briton /'brɪtn/ **noun** a British person 英国人

brittle /'brɪtl/ **adjective 1** hard but likely to break easily 硬而脆的;易碎的 **2** sharp or artificial 尖厉的;假装的：*a brittle laugh* 尖厉的笑声

broach /brəʊtʃ/ **verb 1** raise a subject for discussion 提出(话题) **2** pierce a container 钻孔开启(容器)

broad /brɔːd/ **adjective 1** larger than usual from side to side; wide 宽的;阔的 **2** large in area or range 广阔的;辽阔的 **3** without detail; general 粗略的;概括的 **4** (of a hint) clear and unmistakable (暗示)明确无误的 **5** (of an accent) very strong (口音)浓重的 • **noun** N. Amer. informal 【北美,非正式】a woman 女人 □ **broad bean** a large flat green bean 蚕豆 **broad-minded** not easily shocked; tolerant 豁达的;宽容的 ■ **broadly** adverb.

broadband /'brɔːdbænd/ noun a telecommunications technique which uses a wide range of frequencies, enabling messages to be sent at the same time 宽带,宽带技术(使用大量不同频率传输数据的通信技术)

broadcast /'brɔːdkɑːst/ verb (**broadcasts**, **broadcasting**, **broadcast**; past participle **broadcast** or **broadcasted**) **1** transmit on radio or television(由无线电或电视)广播,播放 **2** tell to a lot of people 散布;传播 • noun a radio or television programme 广播节目;电视节目 ■ **broadcaster** noun.

broaden /'brɔːdn/ verb make or become broader (使)变宽;(使)变阔

broadleaved /'brɔːdliːvd/ or **broadleaf** /'brɔːdliːf/ adjective having fairly wide flat leaves 阔叶的

broadsheet /'brɔːdʃiːt/ noun a newspaper printed on large sheets of paper 宽幅报纸

broadside /'brɔːdsaɪd/ noun **1** a fierce verbal or written criticism 猛烈抨击 **2** historical 【历史】 a firing of all the guns from one side of a warship 舷炮齐射

brocade /brə'keɪd/ noun a rich fabric woven with a raised pattern 锦缎;织锦

broccoli /'brɒkəli/ noun a vegetable with heads of small green or purplish flower buds 花茎甘蓝;花椰菜;西兰花

✔ 拼写指南 two *c*s, one *l*: bro*cc*oli. broccoli 中有两个 c 和一个 l。

brochure /'brəʊʃə(r)/ noun a booklet or magazine containing information about a product or service 小册子

brogue /brəʊg/ noun **1** a strong outdoor shoe with perforated patterns in the leather 拷花皮鞋 **2** a strong regional accent 土腔

broil /brɔɪl/ verb N. Amer.【北美】 cook meat or fish using direct heat 烤,焙,炙(肉或鱼)

broke /brəʊk/ past of BREAK. • adjective informal 【非正式】 having no money 不名一文的;破产的

broken /'brəʊkən/ past participle of BREAK. • adjective (of a language) spoken hesitantly and with many mistakes (语言)蹩脚的,不流利的 □ **broken home** a family in which the parents are divorced or separated (父母离异或分居的)破裂家庭

broker /'brəʊkə(r)/ noun a person who buys and sells things for other people 经纪人;代理人;中间人 • verb arrange a deal or plan (作为中间人)安排,促成

bromide /'brəʊmaɪd/ noun a compound of bromine, used in medicine 溴化物(用于药物中)

bromine /'brəʊmiːn/ noun a dark red liquid chemical element (液态化学元素)溴

bronchial /'brɒŋkiəl/ adjective relating to the tubes leading to the lungs 支气管的

bronchitis /brɒŋ'kaɪtɪs/ noun inflammation of the tubes that lead to the lungs 支气管炎

bronco /'brɒŋkəʊ/ noun (plural **broncos**) a wild or half-tamed horse of the western US 布朗科马(美国西部的野马或半驯化马)

brontosaurus /ˌbrɒntə'sɔːrəs/ former term for APATOSAURUS. apatosaurus 的旧称

bronze /brɒnz/ noun **1** a yellowish-brown metal made by mixing copper and tin 青铜 **2** a yellowish-brown colour 黄褐色;青铜色 **3** (also **bronze medal**) a medal given for third place in a competition 铜牌;铜质奖章 • verb (**bronzes**, **bronzing**, **bronzed**) **1** give something a bronze surface 给…镀铜 **2** make someone suntanned 使呈古铜色 □ **Bronze Age**

an ancient period when weapons and tools were made of bronze, following the Stone Age 青铜(器)时代

brooch /brəʊtʃ/ **noun** an ornament fastened to clothing with a hinged pin 胸针；领针；饰针

brood /bruːd/ **noun** a family of young animals born or hatched at one time (一次生出的)一窝动物；(一次孵出的)一窝小鸟 • **verb 1** think deeply about an unpleasant subject 想，深思(令人不快的问题) **2** (**brooding**) appearing mysterious or menacing 神秘凶险的 **3** (of a bird) sit on eggs to hatch them (鸟)孵(蛋)

broody /ˈbruːdi/ **adjective** (**broodier**, **broodiest**) **1** (of a hen) wanting to hatch eggs (母鸡)要抱窝的 **2** informal 【非正式】(of a woman) having a strong desire to have a baby (女子)急于生育的 **3** thoughtful and unhappy 郁郁沉思的；闷闷不乐的

brook¹ /brʊk/ **noun** a small stream 溪；小河

brook² **verb** formal 【正式】tolerate 容忍；许许

broom /bruːm/ **noun 1** a long-handled brush used for sweeping 扫帚；笤帚 **2** a shrub with yellow flowers 金雀花

broomstick /ˈbruːmstɪk/ **noun** a brush with twigs at one end and a long handle, on which witches are said to fly 扫帚柄(传说中女巫用以飞行)

Bros abbreviation brothers.

broth /brɒθ/ **noun** thin soup or stock, sometimes with chunks of meat or vegetables 肉汤；菜汤

brothel /ˈbrɒθl/ **noun** a house where men visit prostitutes 妓院

brother /ˈbrʌðə(r)/ **noun 1** a man or boy in relation to other children of his parents 兄；弟 **2** a male colleague or friend (男性)同事，伙伴 **3** (plural **brothers** or **brethren**) a male fellow Christian or member of a religious order (基督教的男性)教友；(同一教派的)教友，修士 □ **brother-in-law**

(plural **brothers-in-law**) **1** the brother of a person's wife or husband 内兄；内弟；大伯子；小叔子 **2** the husband of a person's sister or sister-in-law 姐夫；妹夫；连襟 ■ **brotherly** adjective.

brotherhood /ˈbrʌðəhʊd/ **noun 1** the relationship between brothers 兄弟关系；手足之情 **2** a feeling of friendliness and understanding between people 情谊 **3** a group of people linked by a shared interest 兄弟会；同志会

brought /brɔːt/ past and past participle of BRING.

! 注意 don't confuse **brought** with **bought**, which is the past of **buy**. 不要混淆 brought 和 bought, 后者是 buy 的过去式。

brow /braʊ/ **noun 1** a person's forehead 额头 **2** an eyebrow 眉；眉毛 **3** the highest point of a hill 坡顶；山脊

browbeat /ˈbraʊbiːt/ **verb** (**browbeats**, **browbeating**, **browbeat**; past participle **browbeaten**) bully someone with aggressive or threatening words 恫吓；威逼

brown /braʊn/ **adjective 1** of a colour produced by mixing red, yellow, and blue 棕色的；褐色的 **2** dark-skinned or suntanned 肤色深的；皮肤晒黑的 • **noun** a brown colour 棕色；褐色 • **verb 1** make or become brown by cooking (经烹煮)(使)变棕色，(使)变褐色 **2** (**be browned off**) Brit. informal 【英，非正式】be dissatisfied 不满

brownfield /ˈbraʊnfiːld/ **adjective** Brit. 【英】(of a piece of land) having buildings on it already (土地)棕色地带的，已开发建设过的

Brownie /ˈbraʊni/ **noun** (plural **Brownies**) **1** a member of the junior branch of the Guides Association 幼年女童子军 **2** (**brownie**) a small square of rich chocolate cake (小方块)巧克力蛋糕 **3** (**brownie**) a kind elf believed to do people's housework secretly 棕仙(偷偷帮人做家务的小精灵)

browse /brauz/ **verb** (**browses, browsing, browsed**) **1** read or look at something in a leisurely way 随便看看;浏览;翻阅 **2** look at information on a computer (在计算机上)浏览,查看(信息) **3** (of an animal) feed on leaves, twigs, etc. (动物)吃(树叶、细枝等) • **noun** an act of browsing 浏览;查看

browser /brauzə(r)/ **noun 1** a person or animal that browses 浏览者;吃草的牲畜 **2** a computer program for navigating the World Wide Web (浏览万维网的)浏览程序,浏览器

bruise /bruːz/ **noun 1** an area of discoloured skin on the body, caused by a blow 青肿;淤伤 **2** a damaged area on a fruit or vegetable (水果或蔬菜的)碰伤,伤痕 • **verb** (**bruises, bruising, bruised**) make a bruise appear on (使)出现青肿;(使)产生伤痕

bruiser /bruːzə(r)/ **noun** informal 【非正式】 a tough, aggressive person 彪形大汉;好斗之人

brunch /brʌntʃ/ **noun** a late morning meal eaten instead of breakfast and lunch 早午餐(早餐和午餐并作一餐)

brunette /bruːˈnet/ **noun** a woman or girl with dark brown hair 头发深褐色的女子(或女孩)

brunt /brʌnt/ **noun** the chief impact of something bad (坏事的)主要冲力,冲击

brush[1] /brʌʃ/ **noun 1** an object with a handle and a block of bristles, hair, or wire 刷子;毛笔;画笔 **2** an act of brushing 拂;刷;画;写;涂抹 **3** a slight, brief touch 轻触 **4** a brief encounter with something bad 小接触;小冲突 **5** the bushy tail of a fox (狐狸的)毛茸茸的尾巴 • **verb 1** clean, smooth, or apply with a brush 拂;刷 **2** touch lightly 轻触;掠过 **3** (**brush someone/thing off**) dismiss someone or something abruptly 把…打发掉;粗鲁拒绝 **4** (**brush something up**) work to improve a skill you have

not used for a long time 温习,复习(荒疏的技艺)

brush[2] **noun** undergrowth, small trees, and shrubs 灌木丛;小树丛

brushwood /brʌʃwʊd/ **noun** undergrowth, twigs, and small branches 灌木丛;柴枝

brusque /bruːsk/ **adjective** rather rude and abrupt 唐突的;简慢的;无礼的 ■ **brusquely** adverb.

Brussels sprout /ˈbrʌslz/ **noun** a small green vegetable, the bud of a variety of cabbage 汤菜;抱子甘蓝

brutal /ˈbruːtl/ **adjective 1** savagely violent 野蛮的;残忍的;粗暴的 **2** not attempting to hide something unpleasant 直截了当的;冷酷的: brutal honesty 冷酷的诚实 ■ **brutality** noun **brutally** adverb.

brutalize or **brutalise** /ˈbruːtəlaɪz/ **verb** (**brutalizes, brutalizing, brutalized**) **1** make someone cruel or violent by frequently exposing them to violence 使变残忍 **2** treat someone in a violent way 残酷对待

brute /bruːt/ **noun** a violent or savage person, or a large and uncontrollable animal 残忍的人;大野兽 • **adjective** involving physical strength rather than reasoning 蛮干而不动脑筋的;无理性的: brute force 暴力 ■ **brutish** adjective.

BSE /ˌbiː es ˈiː/ **abbreviation** bovine spongiform encephalopathy, a fatal brain disease in cattle 牛脑海绵体病;疯牛病

BST /ˌbiː es ˈtiː/ **abbreviation** British Summer Time 英国夏令时

bubble /ˈbʌbl/ **noun 1** a thin ball of liquid enclosing a gas 泡;水泡 **2** a ball filled with gas in a liquid or a material such as glass (液体、玻璃等物质中的)气泡 **3** a transparent dome 透明圆罩 • **verb** (**bubbles, bubbling, bubbled**) **1** (of a liquid) contain rising bubbles of gas (液体)起泡,冒泡 **2** (**bubble with**) be filled with 充满;充溢

bubblegum /'bʌblgʌm/ noun chewing gum that can be blown into bubbles 泡泡糖

bubbly /'bʌbli/ adjective (bubblier, bubbliest) 1 containing bubbles 多泡沫的 2 cheerful and high-spirited 欢快的；欢欣的 ■ noun informal【非正式】champagne 香槟酒

bubonic plague /bju:'bɒnɪk/ noun a form of plague passed on by rat fleas 腺鼠疫；腹股沟淋巴结鼠疫

buccaneer /ˌbʌkə'nɪə(r)/ noun 1 historical【历史】a pirate 海盗 2 a recklessly adventurous person 无所顾忌的冒险家 ■ **buccaneering** adjective.

buck¹ /bʌk/ noun 1 the male of some animals, e.g. deer and rabbits 雄性动物(如雄鹿、公兔) 2 a vertical jump performed by a horse (马的)弓背跃起 3 old use【旧】a fashionable young man 花花公子；纨绔子弟 ■ verb 1 (of a horse) perform a buck (马)弓背跃起 2 go against something 抵抗；反对: Don't try to buck the system. 不要试图反对体制。 3 (buck up or buck someone up) informal【非正式】become or make someone more cheerful (使)振奋；(使)打起精神 □ **buck teeth** teeth that stick out 龅牙

buck² noun N. Amer. & Austral./NZ【北美和澳/新西兰】informal【非正式】a dollar (一)元；(一)块

buck³ noun an object placed in front of a poker player whose turn it is to deal 培克(扑克牌游戏中的庄家标记) □ **pass the buck** informal【非正式】shift responsibility to someone else 推诿责任

bucket /'bʌkɪt/ noun 1 an open container with a handle, used to carry liquids 水桶；吊桶 2 (buckets) informal【正式】large quantities 大量 ■ verb (buckets, bucketing, bucketed) (bucket down) Brit. informal【英，非正式】rain very heavily 下倾盆大雨

buckle /'bʌkl/ noun a flat frame with a hinged pin, used as a fastener 搭扣；搭钩 ■ verb (buckles, buckling, buckled) 1 fasten with a buckle 搭扣扣住 2 bend and give way under pressure (在压力下)弯曲，屈服 3 (buckle down) tackle a task with determination 认真做；努力干

buckwheat /'bʌkwiːt/ noun a grain used for flour or animal feed 荞麦

bucolic /bju:'kɒlɪk/ adjective relating to country life 乡村生活的；田园的

bud /bʌd/ noun a growth on a plant which develops into a leaf, flower, or shoot 芽；苞；花蕾 ■ verb (buds, budding, budded) form a bud or buds 发芽

Buddhism /'budɪzəm/ noun a religion based on the teachings of Buddha (real name Siddartha Gautama, c.563–c.460 BC) 佛教 ■ **Buddhist** noun & adjective.

budding /'bʌdɪŋ/ adjective beginning and showing signs of promise 发展中的；崭露头角的

buddy /'bʌdi/ noun (plural buddies) informal, chiefly N. Amer.【非正式，主北美】a close friend 密友；好朋友

budge /bʌdʒ/ verb (budges, budging, budged) 1 move very slightly 微微移动 2 change an opinion 改变主意

budgerigar /'bʌdʒərɪɡɑː(r)/ noun a small Australian parakeet 虎皮鹦鹉 (澳大利亚长尾小鹦鹉)

budget /'bʌdʒɪt/ noun 1 an estimate of income and spending for a set period of time 预算 2 the amount of money needed or available for a purpose (供某种用途的)专款，预算拨款 3 (Budget) a regular estimate of national income and spending put forward by a finance minister (由政府财政部长提交的)年度预算 ■ verb (budgets, budgeting, budgeted) plan to spend a particular amount of money 编预算；安排开支 ■ **adjective** inexpensive 低廉的；便宜的 ■ **budgetary** adjective.

budgie /'bʌdʒi/ noun a budgerigar 虎皮鹦鹉

buff¹ /bʌf/ noun a yellowish-beige colour

浅黄色；米色 • **verb** polish something with a soft cloth (用软布)擦亮 □ **in the buff** informal 【非正式】 naked 裸体的；一丝不挂的

buff² **noun** informal 【非正式】 a person who knows a lot about a particular subject 行家；爱好者；迷

buffalo /ˈbʌfələʊ/ **noun** (plural **buffalo** or **buffaloes**) **1** a heavily built wild ox with backward-curving horns 水牛 **2** the North American bison 北美野牛

buffer /ˈbʌfə(r)/ **noun 1** (**buffers**) Brit. 【英】 shock absorbers at the end of a railway track or on a railway vehicle (铁轨或火车的)减震器，缓冲器 **2** a person or thing that lessens the impact of harmful effects 起缓冲作用的人(或物)

buffet¹ /ˈbʊfeɪ/ **noun 1** a meal made up of several dishes from which you serve yourself 自助餐 **2** a counter at which snacks are sold 快餐部；餐饮柜台

buffet² **verb** (**buffets**, **buffeting**, **buffeted**) (especially of wind or waves) strike repeatedly (尤指风或波浪)反复敲打，猛烈撞击

buffoon /bəˈfuːn/ **noun** a ridiculous but amusing person 丑角；滑稽的人 ■ **buffoonery** noun.

bug /bʌg/ **noun 1** a small insect 臭虫；小虫 **2** informal 【非正式】 a germ, or an illness caused by one 病菌；病菌引起的疾病 **3** informal 【非正式】 an enthusiasm for something 热；癖好：*the sailing bug* 航海热 **4** a microphone used for secret recording 窃听器 **5** an error in a computer program or system (计算机程序或系统的)缺陷，漏洞 • **verb** (**bugs**, **bugging**, **bugged**) **1** hide a microphone in a room or telephone 在(房间或电话机)中装窃听器 **2** informal 【非正式】 annoy someone 使恼怒

bugbear /ˈbʌgbeə(r)/ **noun** something that causes anxiety or irritation 使人

焦虑(或恼怒)的根由

buggery /ˈbʌgəri/ **noun** anal sex 鸡奸；肛交

buggy /ˈbʌgi/ **noun** (plural **buggies**) **1** a kind of pushchair 婴儿车 **2** a small motor vehicle with an open top 小型无篷汽车 **3** historical 【历史】 a light horse-drawn vehicle 轻便马车

bugle /ˈbjuːgl/ **noun** a brass instrument like a small trumpet 军号；喇叭 ■ **bugler** noun.

build /bɪld/ **verb** (**builds**, **building**, **built**) **1** make something by putting parts together 建筑；建造；修建 **2** (**build up**) increase over time 增长；增加 **3** (**build on**) use as a basis for further development 在……基础上发展；把……建立于 • **noun** the size or form of someone or something 体格；体形；构造 □ **build-up 1** a gradual increase 逐渐的增长 **2** a period of preparation before an event 准备期；准备时间 ■ **builder** noun.

building /ˈbɪldɪŋ/ **noun 1** a structure with a roof and walls 建筑物；房屋 **2** the process or trade of building houses and other structures 建筑业 □ **building society** Brit. 【英】 a financial organization which pays interest on members' investments and lends money for mortgages 建屋互助会(向会员的存款支付利息并提供房屋按揭贷款的金融机构)

built /bɪlt/ past and past participle of BUILD. • **adjective** of a particular physical build 有……体格的 □ **built-in** included as part of a larger structure 嵌入式的；内置的 **built-up** covered by many buildings 布满建筑物的；建筑物多的

bulb /bʌlb/ **noun 1** the rounded base of the stem of some plants, from which the roots grow 球茎；鳞茎 **2** (also **light bulb**) a glass ball filled with gas, which provides light when an electric current is passed through it 电灯泡

bulbous /'bʌlbəs/ **adjective 1** round or bulging in shape 圆鼓鼓的 **2** (of a plant) growing from a bulb (植物)由球茎(或鳞茎)长出的

Bulgarian /bʌl'geəriə/ **noun 1** a person from Bulgaria 保加利亚人 **2** the language of Bulgaria 保加利亚语 • **adjective** relating to Bulgaria 保加利亚的

bulge /bʌldʒ/ **noun** a rounded swelling on a flat surface 膨胀；肿块 • **verb** (**bulges, bulging, bulged**) **1** swell or stick out unnaturally 膨胀；凸出 **2** (**bulge with**) be full of 装满；塞满

bulimia /bu'lɪmiə/ **noun** a disorder marked by bouts of overeating, followed by fasting or vomiting 食欲过盛；贪食症；暴食症 ■ **bulimic** adjective & noun.

bulk /bʌlk/ **noun 1** the mass or size of something large (大的)体积 **2** the greater part of something 主体；大部分 **3** a large mass or shape 大团；大块 • **adjective** large in quantity 大量的；大批的 □ **in bulk** (of goods) in large quantities (货物)大批量(的)

bulkhead /'bʌlkhed/ **noun** an internal wall or barrier in a ship or aircraft (船或飞机的)舱壁，隔板，隔离壁

bulky /'bʌlki/ **adjective** (**bulkier, bulkiest**) large and unwieldy 庞大的；笨重的

bull¹ /bʊl/ **noun 1** an adult male animal of the cattle group 公牛 **2** a large male animal, e.g. a whale or elephant (大型动物的)雄兽 □ **take the bull by the horns** deal decisively with a difficult situation 勇敢面对困境；不畏艰险

bull² **noun** an order or announcement issued by the Pope 教皇诏书；教皇训谕

bulldog /'bʊldɒg/ **noun** a breed of dog with a flat wrinkled face and a broad chest 斗牛犬

bulldoze /'bʊldəʊz/ **verb** (**bulldozes, bulldozing, bulldozed**) clear or destroy with a bulldozer (用推土机)清除，推倒

bulldozer /'bʊldəʊzə(r)/ **noun** a tractor with a broad curved blade at the front for clearing ground 推土机

bullet /'bʊlɪt/ **noun** a small piece of metal fired from a gun 子弹

bulletin /'bʊlətɪn/ **noun 1** a short official statement or summary of news 公告；公报 **2** a regular newsletter or report 通讯；会刊；简报 □ **bulletin board** a site on a computer system where any user can read or write messages (计算机系统中的)公告板

bullfighting /'bʊlfaɪtɪŋ/ **noun** the sport of tormenting and killing bulls as a public entertainment 斗牛 ■ **bullfight** noun **bullfighter** noun.

bullfinch /'bʊlfɪntʃ/ **noun** a finch (songbird) with a reddish breast 红腹灰雀

bullfrog /'bʊlfrɒg/ **noun** a very large frog with a deep croak 牛蛙

bullion /'bʊliən/ **noun** gold or silver in bulk before being made into coins (铸币用的)金(或银)块，金(或银)条

bullish /'bʊlɪʃ/ **adjective** aggressively confident 有信心的；乐观的

bullock /'bʊlək/ **noun** a castrated bull 阉公牛

bullring /'bʊlrɪŋ/ **noun** an arena where bullfights are held 斗牛场

bullseye /'bʊlzaɪ/ **noun** the centre of the target in sports such as archery and darts 靶心；鹄的

bully /'bʊli/ **noun** (plural **bullies**) a person who frightens or persecutes weaker people 恃强凌弱者；横行霸道者 • **verb** (**bullies, bullying, bullied**) frighten or persecute a weaker person 恐吓；胁迫

bulrush or **bullrush** /'bʊlrʌʃ/ **noun** a tall reed-like waterside plant 宽叶香蒲；灯心草

bulwark /'bʊlwək/ **noun 1** a defensive wall 堡垒；壁垒 **2** a person or thing that acts as a defence 人墙 **3** an extension of a ship's sides above deck level (船的)舷墙

bum¹ /bʌm/ **noun** Brit. informal 【英,非正式】 a person's bottom 屁股

bum² N. Amer. informal 【北美,非正式】 **noun 1** a homeless person or beggar 流浪汉;流浪乞丐 **2** a lazy or worthless person 懒汉;无用的人 • **verb** (bums, bumming, bummed) **1** get something by asking or begging 乞求;乞讨 **2** (bum around) laze around 闲荡;无所事事 • **adjective** bad 劣质的;蹩脚的

bumble /ˈbʌmbl/ **verb** (bumbles, bumbling, bumbled) act or speak in an awkward or confused way 笨手笨脚地行动;语无伦次地说

bumblebee /ˈbʌmblbiː/ **noun** a large hairy bee with a loud hum 熊蜂;大黄蜂

bumf or **bumph** /bʌmf/ **noun** Brit. informal 【英,非正式】 printed information 印刷品

bump /bʌmp/ **noun 1** a light blow or collision 轻击;轻撞 **2** a hump or projection on a level surface 肿块;隆起物;凸块 • **verb 1** knock or run into with a jolt 碰;撞 **2** move with a lot of jolting 颠簸着行进 **3** (bump into) meet by chance 偶然遇见;碰见 **4** (bump someone off) informal 【非正式】 murder someone 杀害 **5** (bump something up) informal 【非正式】 increase something 提高;增加 ■ **bumpy** (bumpier, bumpiest) adjective.

bumper /ˈbʌmpə(r)/ **noun** a bar fixed across the front or back of a vehicle to reduce damage in a collision (汽车的)保险杠 • **adjective** exceptionally large or successful 特大的;极成功的

bumpkin /ˈbʌmpkɪn/ **noun** an unsophisticated person from the countryside 乡下佬;土包子

bumptious /ˈbʌmpʃəs/ **adjective** irritatingly confident and self-important 狂妄的;自以为是的

bun /bʌn/ **noun 1** a small cake or bread roll 小圆蛋糕;小圆面包 **2** a tight coil of hair at the back of the head (盘在脑后的)圆发髻

bunch /bʌntʃ/ **noun 1** a number of things grouped or held together 束;串;捆 **2** informal 【非正式】 a group of people 一群人 • **verb** collect or form into a bunch (使)成一束(或一群)

bundle /ˈbʌndl/ **noun** a group of things tied or wrapped up together 束;捆;包;一大堆;一大批 • **verb** (bundles, bundling, bundled) **1** tie or roll up in a bundle 把…扎成一捆(或一包) **2** (be bundled up) be dressed in a lot of warm clothes 穿得暖和 **3** informal 【非正式】 push or carry forcibly 推搡;打发走

bunfight /ˈbʌnfaɪt/ **noun** humorous 【英,幽默】 a grand party or other large social event 盛大聚会(或其他社交活动)

bung /bʌŋ/ **noun** a stopper for a hole in a container (容器的)塞子 • **verb 1** (bung something up) block something 堵塞;塞住 **2** Brit. informal 【英,非正式】 put or throw something somewhere casually or carelessly 丢;扔

bungalow /ˈbʌŋɡələʊ/ **noun** a house with only one storey 平房

bungee jumping /ˈbʌndʒi/ **noun** the sport of jumping from a high place to which you are attached with a long elastic cord tied to your ankles 蹦极(运动)

bungle /ˈbʌŋɡl/ **verb** (bungles, bungling, bungled) fail in performing a task 失败;失败 • **noun** a mistake or failure 失误;失败 ■ **bungler** noun.

bunion /ˈbʌnjən/ **noun** a painful swelling on the big toe 大趾囊肿

bunk¹ /bʌŋk/ **noun** a narrow shelf-like bed 床铺;铺位

bunk² **verb** (bunk off) Brit. informal 【英,非正式】 play truant from school 逃学 □ **do a bunk** leave hurriedly 匆忙离开

bunker /ˈbʌŋkə(r)/ **noun 1** a large container for storing fuel 燃料箱；燃料舱 **2** an underground shelter for use in wartime 地下掩体；地堡 **3** a hollow filled with sand on a golf course (高尔夫球场上的)沙坑

bunkum /'bʌŋkəm/ noun informal, dated 【非正式，废】nonsense 胡说八道

bunny /'bʌni/ noun (plural **bunnies**) informal 【非正式】a rabbit 兔子

Bunsen burner /bʌnsn/ noun a small gas burner used in laboratories 本生灯(实验室用的煤气灯)

bunting[1] /'bʌntɪŋ/ noun a small bird with brown streaked feathers 鹀(有棕色条纹状羽毛的小鸟)

bunting[2] noun flags and streamers used as decorations (装饰用)彩旗，旗帜

buoy /bɔɪ/ noun an anchored float used to mark an area of water 浮标；航标 • verb (**be buoyed** or **buoyed up**) be cheered up and made more confident 情绪高涨；鼓舞

✔ **拼写指南** the *u* comes before the *o* in b*uo*y and b*uo*yant. buoy 和 buoyant 中的 u 在 o 前。

buoyant /'bɔɪənt/ adjective **1** able to keep afloat 能浮起的；有浮力的 **2** cheerful and optimistic 轻快愉快的；乐观的 ■ **buoyancy** noun.

burble /'bɜːbl/ verb (**burbles**, **burbling**, **burbled**) **1** make a continuous murmuring noise 汩汩作响 **2** speak for a long time in a way that is hard to understand 喋喋嚷嚷地说；语无伦次地说 • noun a continuous murmuring noise 汩汩声

burden /'bɜːdn/ noun **1** a heavy load 重负 **2** something that causes hardship, worry, or grief 精神负担 **3** the main responsibility for a task 重担 • verb **1** load heavily 使负重 **2** cause someone worry, hardship, or grief 使背负精神重担

burdensome /'bɜːdnsəm/ adjective causing worry or difficulty 令人担心

的；麻烦的

bureau /'bjʊərəʊ/ noun (plural **bureaux** /'bjʊərəʊz/ or **bureaus**) **1** Brit. 【英】a writing desk with a sloping top 书桌；写字台 **2** N. Amer. 【美】a chest of drawers 五斗橱 **3** an office for carrying out particular business 办事处；机构 **4** a government department (政府部门的)局，处，署

bureaucracy /bjʊə'rɒkrəsi/ noun (plural **bureaucracies**) **1** administrative procedures that are too complicated 官僚主义；官僚作风 **2** a system of government in which most decisions are taken by state officials 官僚体制；官僚制度

bureaucrat /'bjʊərəkræt/ noun a government official, especially one who follows guidelines rigidly 官僚主义者；机械刻板的官吏 ■ **bureaucratic** adjective.

burgeon /'bɜːdʒən/ verb grow or increase rapidly 迅速发展；激增

burger /'bɜːgə(r)/ noun a hamburger 汉堡包

burgher /'bɜːgə(r)/ noun old use 【旧】a citizen of a town or city (某城镇的)居民，市民

burglar /'bɜːglə(r)/ noun a person who burgles a building 入室窃贼

burglary /'bɜːgləri/ noun (plural **burglaries**) the action of burgling a building 入室盗窃

burgle /'bɜːgl/ verb (**burgles**, **burgling**, **burgled**) go into a building illegally to steal its contents 入室盗窃

burgundy /'bɜːgəndi/ noun (plural **burgundies**) **1** a red wine from Burgundy in France (法国)勃艮第红葡萄酒 **2** a deep red colour 深红色；紫红色

burial /'beriəl/ noun the burying of a dead body 埋葬；掩埋

burlesque /bɜː'lesk/ noun **1** a comically exaggerated imitation of something 滑稽模仿；诙谐模仿 **2** N. Amer. 【北美】a variety show 滑稽歌舞杂剧

burly /'bɜːli/ **adjective** (**burlier**, **burliest**) (of a man) large and strong (人)高大壮实的, 魁梧的

burn¹ /bɜːn/ **verb** (**burns**, **burning**, **burned** or chiefly Brit. 【主英】**burnt**) **1** (of a fire) produce flames and heat while using up a fuel (火)燃烧, 烧着 **2** harm or damage by fire 烧掉; 烧毁; 烧伤; 灼伤 **3** (**be burning with**) experience a very strong desire or emotion 充满(欲望或情感) **4** (**burn out**) become exhausted through working too hard 精疲力竭 **5** produce a CD by copying from an original or master copy 刻录(光盘) • **noun** an injury caused by burning 烧伤; 灼伤; 晒伤 □ **burn your boats** (or **bridges**) do something which makes turning back impossible 不留退路, 破釜沉舟

burn² **noun** Scottish 【苏格兰】a small stream 小河; 小溪

burner /'bɜːnə(r)/ **noun** a part of a cooker, lamp, etc. that puts out a flame 灯头; 煤气头 □ **on the back burner** given a low priority 居于次要地位

burning /'bɜːnɪŋ/ **adjective 1** very hot 极热的 **2** deeply felt 热烈的, 强烈的 **3** important and urgent 紧急的; 十分重要的

burnish /'bɜːnɪʃ/ **verb** polish something by rubbing it 抛光; 擦亮

burnout /'bɜːnaʊt/ **noun** physical or mental collapse 精疲力竭

burp /bɜːp/ informal 【非正式】**verb** belch 打嗝 • **noun** a belch 嗝; 饱嗝

burr /bɜː(r)/ **noun 1** a strong pronunciation of the letter *r* 颤动小舌的 r 音; 粗重的 r 音 **2** a prickly seed case or flower head that clings to clothing and animal fur 刺果; 刺球状花序

burrow /'bʌrəʊ/ **noun** a hole or tunnel dug by a small animal to live in (小动物掘出的)地洞, 地道 • **verb 1** make a burrow 掘地洞 **2** hide underneath or search inside something 钻到下面; 钻入

bursar /'bɜːsə(r)/ **noun** a person who

manages the financial affairs of a college or school (大学或中学的)财务主管, 司库

bursary /'bɜːsəri/ **noun** (plural **bursaries**) Brit. 【英】a grant for studying 奖学金

burst /bɜːst/ **verb** (**bursts**, **bursting**, **burst**) **1** break suddenly and violently apart (使)爆炸, (使)爆裂, (使)破裂 **2** (**be bursting**) be very full 爆满, 充满 **3** move or be opened suddenly and forcibly 猛冲; 突然打开 **4** (**be bursting with**) feel full of an emotion 充满(情感) **5** (**burst out** or **into**) suddenly do something as a result of strong emotion 突发 • **noun 1** an instance of bursting 爆炸; 爆裂; 破裂 **2** a sudden brief outbreak 爆发; 进发 **3** a period of continuous effort 一阵猛劲

bury /'beri/ **verb** (**buries**, **burying**, **buried**) **1** place or hide something underground 埋藏 **2** make something disappear or be hidden 使退隐; 使湮没 **3** (**bury yourself**) involve yourself deeply in something 专心致志

bus /bʌs/ **noun** (plural **buses**; US 【美】also **busses**) a large motor vehicle that carries customers along a fixed route 公共汽车; 公交车 • **verb** (**buses**, **busing**, **bused** or **busses**, **bussing**, **bussed**) transport or travel in a bus 用公共汽车载送; 乘公共汽车 □ **a busman's holiday** leisure time spent doing the same thing that you do at work 做日常工作的假日

busby /'bʌzbi/ **noun** (plural **busbies**) a tall fur hat worn by certain military regiments (某些士兵戴的)毛皮高顶帽

bush /bʊʃ/ **noun 1** a shrub or clump of shrubs 灌木; 灌木丛 **2** (**the bush**) (in Australia and Africa) wild or uncultivated country (澳大利亚和非洲)未开发的荒野地区, 丛林地带

bushbaby /'bʊʃbeɪbi/ **noun** (plural **bushbabies**) a small African animal with very large eyes (非洲的)丛猴, 夜猴

bushel /ˈbʊʃl/ **noun 1** Brit.【英】a measure of capacity equal to 8 gallons (36.4 litres) 蒲式耳(容量单位, 等于8加仑, 合36.4升) **2** US【美】a measure of capacity equal to 64 US pints (35.2 litres) 蒲式耳(容量单位, 等于64美制品脱, 合35.2升)

bushy /ˈbʊʃi/ **adjective (bushier, bushiest) 1** growing thickly 浓密的 **2** covered with bushes 灌木丛生的

business /ˈbɪznəs/ **noun 1** a person's regular occupation 工作;职业 **2** commercial activity 商业;生意 **3** a commercial organization 工商企业 **4** work to be done or things to be attended to 事务;事情 **5** a person's concern 所关心的事: *It's none of your business.* 不关你的事.

✔ 拼写指南 remember the *i*: busi-ness. 记住拼写 business 中的 i。

businesslike /ˈbɪznəslaɪk/ **adjective** efficient and practical 效率高的;讲究实际的

businessman /ˈbɪznəsmæn/ or **businesswoman** /ˈbɪznəswʊmən/ **noun (plural businessmen** or **businesswomen)** a person who works in business 商人

busk /bʌsk/ **verb** play music in the street in the hope of being given money by passers-by 街头卖艺 ■ **busker** noun.

bust¹ /bʌst/ **noun 1** a woman's breasts (女子的)胸部 **2** a sculpture of a person's head, shoulders, and chest 胸像;半身像

bust² informal **verb (busts, busting, busted** or **bust) 1** break, split, or burst 打碎;(使)破裂;(使)爆裂 **2** chiefly N. Amer.【主北美】raid or search a building, or arrest someone 突袭, 搜查(建筑物);逮捕(某人) • **noun 1** a period of economic difficulty (经济上的)崩溃,不景气 **2** a police raid (警方的)突袭 • **adjective 1** Brit.【英】damaged;

broken 损坏的;破裂的 **2** bankrupt 破产的 □ **bust-up** a serious quarrel or fight 激烈争吵;扭打

bustle¹ /ˈbʌsl/ **verb (bustles, bustling, bustled) 1** move energetically or noisily 奔忙;忙乱 **2** (of a place) be full of activity (场所)熙熙攘攘, 繁忙 • **noun** excited activity and movement 热闹的活动;忙乱

bustle² noun a pad or frame formerly worn by women under a skirt to puff it out behind (撑裙子用的)衬垫, 裙撑

busy /ˈbɪzi/ **adjective (busier, busiest) 1** having a lot to do 忙的;忙碌的 **2** occupied with an activity 忙于…的 **3** crowded or full of activity 繁华的;热闹的 • **verb (busies, busying, busied) (busy yourself)** keep yourself occupied 忙于 ■ **busily** adverb.

busybody /ˈbɪzibɒdi/ **noun (plural busybodies)** an interfering or nosy person 好管闲事的人;爱打听消息的人

but /bət, bʌt/ **conjunction 1** nevertheless 但是;可是 **2** on the contrary 而;相反 **3** other than; otherwise than 除了 **4** old use【旧】without it being the case that 若不 • **preposition** except; apart from 除了;除…之外 • **adverb** only 只;仅仅 □ **but for 1** except for 除了…外 **2** if it were not for 倘没有;要不是

butane /ˈbjuːteɪn/ **noun** a flammable gas present in petroleum and natural gas and used as a fuel 丁烷

butch /bʊtʃ/ **adjective** informal【非正式】aggressively masculine 男子气的

butcher /ˈbʊtʃə(r)/ **noun 1** a person who cuts up and sells meat as a trade 肉商;肉贩 **2** a person who kills animals for food 屠夫 **3** a person who kills brutally 刽子手;凶手 • **verb (butchers, butchering, butchered) 1** kill or cut up an animal for food 屠宰,宰杀(牲畜) **2** kill someone brutally 屠杀;残杀 ■ **butchery** noun.

butler /ˈbʌtlə(r)/ **noun** the chief male

servant of a house 男管家

butt¹ /bʌt/ **verb 1** hit with the head or horns 用头(或角)顶撞 **2** (**butt in**) interrupt a conversation 插嘴 • **noun** a rough push with the head (用头的)顶撞

butt² **noun 1** an object of criticism or ridicule (批评或嘲弄的)对象 **2** a target in archery or shooting (射箭或射击的)靶

butt³ **noun 1** the thicker end of a tool or a weapon (工具或武器的)粗大的一头 **2** the stub of a cigar or a cigarette (雪茄烟或香烟的)烟蒂 **3** N. Amer. informal 【北美,非正式】a person's bottom 屁股 • **verb** meet end to end 毗连;紧靠

butt⁴ **noun** a cask used for wine, beer, or water 酒桶;水桶

butter /ˈbʌtə(r)/ **noun** a pale yellow fatty substance made by churning cream 黄油 • **verb** (**butters, buttering, buttered**) **1** spread with butter 涂黄油于 **2** (**butter someone up**) informal 【非正式】flatter someone 奉承(某人) □ **butter bean** Brit. 【英】a large flat edible bean 利马豆

buttercream /ˈbʌtəkriːm/ **noun** a mixture of butter and icing sugar used to ice cakes 奶油蛋糕

buttercup /ˈbʌtəkʌp/ **noun** a plant with small bright yellow flowers 毛茛

butterfly /ˈbʌtəflaɪ/ **noun** (plural **butterflies**) **1** an insect with two pairs of large wings, which feeds on nectar 蝴蝶 **2** (**butterflies**) informal 【非正式】a fluttering sensation in the stomach when you are nervous (紧张引起的)要呕吐的感觉 **3** a stroke in swimming in which you raise both arms out of the water together 蝶泳

buttermilk /ˈbʌtəmɪlk/ **noun** the slightly sour liquid left after butter has been churned 脱脂乳;乳酪

butterscotch /ˈbʌtəskɒtʃ/ **noun** a sweet made with butter and brown sugar 黄油硬糖

buttery /ˈbʌtəri/ **adjective** containing, resembling, or covered with butter 含有黄油的;有黄油味道的;涂有黄油的 • **noun** (plural **butteries**) Brit. 【英】a room in a college where food is sold to students (大学里的)饮食服务部

buttock /ˈbʌtək/ **noun** either of the two round fleshy parts of the human body that form the bottom (人的)半边臀部

button /ˈbʌtn/ **noun 1** a small disc sewn on to a garment to fasten it by being pushed through a buttonhole 纽扣;扣子 **2** a knob on a piece of equipment which is pressed to operate it 按钮 • **verb** fasten a garment with buttons 用纽扣扣住;扣上纽扣

buttonhole /ˈbʌtnhəʊl/ **noun 1** a slit in a piece of clothing through which a button is pushed to fasten it 扣眼 **2** Brit. 【英】a flower worn in a buttonhole of a lapel 别在翻领扣眼上的花 • **verb** (**buttonholes, buttonholing, buttonholed**) informal 【非正式】stop someone and hold them in conversation 强留(某人)谈话

buttress /ˈbʌtrəs/ **noun 1** a projecting support built against a wall 扶壁 **2** a projecting part of a hill or mountain 山的扶壁状凸出部 • **verb** support or strengthen 支持;加强

buxom /ˈbʌksəm/ **adjective** (of a woman) attractively plump and large-breasted (女子)胸部丰满的

buy /baɪ/ **verb** (**buys, buying, bought**) **1** get something in return for payment 买;购买 **2** informal 【非正式】accept that something is true 接受;相信 • **noun** informal 【非正式】something that has been bought 购买的东西 □ **buy someone out** pay someone to give up a share in something 买断(某人)的股份 ■ **buyer** noun.

buzz /bʌz/ **noun 1** a low continuous humming sound 嗡嗡声 **2** the sound of a buzzer or telephone (蜂鸣器或电

话的)蜂鸣声, 嘟嘟声 **3** an atmosphere of excitement and activity 骚动;闹哄哄 **4** informal 【非正式】a thrill 兴奋 • **verb 1** make a humming sound 发出嗡嗡声 **2** call someone with a buzzer 用蜂鸣器唤(某人) **3** move quickly 急行 **4** (**buzz off**) informal 【非正式】go away 走开;离去 **5** have an air of excitement or activity 闹哄哄;忙乱;忙碌

buzzard /'bʌzəd/ **noun** a large bird of prey 鵟;秃鹫

buzzer /'bʌzə(r)/ **noun** an electrical device that makes a buzzing noise to attract attention 蜂鸣器

buzzword /'bʌzwɜːd/ **noun** informal 【非正式】a technical word or phrase that has become fashionable 时髦术语;流行行话

by /baɪ/ **preposition 1** through the action of 由;被;凭借;通过 **2** indicating an amount or the size of a margin (表示相差的数量或大小) **3** indicating the end of a time period 在…之前;不迟于 **4** beside 在…旁边;靠近 **5** past and beyond 经过 **6** during 在…期间 **7** according to 根据;按照 • **adverb** so as to go past (由旁边)经过 □ **by and by** before long 不久 **by the by** in passing 顺便提一句 **by and large** on the whole 大体上;总的来说

bye[1] /baɪ/ **noun 1** the moving of a competitor straight to the next round of a competition because they have no opponent 轮空(参赛者因无对手而直接进入下一轮比赛) **2** Cricket 【板球】a run scored from a ball that passes the batsman without being hit 漏击得分

bye[2] **exclamation** informal 【非正式】goodbye 再见;再会

by-election /'baɪɪlekʃn/ **noun** Brit. 【英】an election held during a government's term of office to fill a vacant seat 补缺选举;补选

bygone /'baɪɡɒn/ **adjective** belonging to an earlier time 过去的;以往的 □ **let bygones be bygones** decide to forget past disagreements 过去的事就让它过去;捐弃前嫌

by-law or **bye-law** /'baɪlɔː/ **noun 1** Brit. 【英】a rule made by a local authority 地方法规 **2** a rule made by a company or society (公司或社团的)内部章程

byline /'baɪlaɪn/ **noun 1** a line in a newspaper bearing the writer of an article (报纸文章的)作者署名行 **2** (in soccer) the part of the goal line to either side of the goal (足球运动中的)球门线

bypass /'baɪpɑːs/ **noun 1** a road passing round a town (绕过城镇的)旁路, 旁道 **2** an operation to help the circulation of blood by directing it through a new passage (帮助血液循环的)旁流术, 搭桥术 • **verb** go past or round 绕过;绕…走

by-product /'baɪprɒdʌkt/ **noun** a product produced in the process of making something else 副产品

byre /baɪə(r)/ **noun** Brit. 【英】a cow-shed 牛棚

bystander /'baɪstændə(r)/ **noun** a person who is present at an event but does not take part 旁观者

byte /baɪt/ **noun** a unit of information stored in a computer, equal to eight bits 字节(计算机信息存储单位)

byway /'baɪweɪ/ **noun** a minor road or path 旁道;小路

byword /'baɪwɜːd/ **noun 1** a notable example of something 典范 **2** a saying 俗语;谚语

Byzantine /bɪ'zæntaɪn, baɪ-/ **adjective 1** relating to Byzantium (now Istanbul) or the Eastern Orthodox Church 拜占庭(今伊斯坦布尔)的;拜占庭帝国的;东正教的 **2** very complicated and detailed 错综复杂的

Cc

C or **c** /siː/ *noun* (plural **Cs** or **C's**) **1** the third letter of the alphabet 英语字母表的第3个字母 **2** the Roman numeral for 100 (罗马数字)一百 • **abbreviation 1** Celsius or centigrade. **2** (©) copyright. **3** (c) cents. **4** (c or ca.) circa. **5** (c.) century or centuries.

cab /kæb/ *noun* **1** a taxi 出租车 **2** the driver's compartment in a truck, bus, or train (卡车、公共汽车或火车的)司机驾驶室

cabal /kə'bæl/ *noun* a secret political group (政治)阴谋集团，秘密组织

cabaret /'kæbəreɪ/ *noun* entertainment held in a nightclub or restaurant while the audience sit at tables 卡巴莱(夜总会或餐馆的娱乐表演)

cabbage /'kæbɪdʒ/ *noun* a vegetable with thick green or purple leaves 卷心菜；洋白菜

caber /'keɪbə(r)/ *noun* a tree trunk used in the Scottish Highland sport of tossing the caber (苏格兰高地抛掷树干运动中使用的)长树干

cabin /'kæbɪn/ *noun* **1** a private compartment on a ship 船舱；客舱 **2** the passenger compartment in an aircraft (飞机的)座舱 **3** a small wooden shelter or house 小棚屋；小木屋

cabinet /'kæbɪnət/ *noun* **1** a cupboard with drawers or shelves for storing things 储藏柜 **2** a piece of furniture enclosing a radio, speaker, etc. (放收音机、扬声器等的)机箱，机壳 **3** (**Cabinet**) a committee of senior government ministers (政府)内阁

cabinetmaker /'kæbɪnətmeɪkə(r)/ *noun* a person who makes fine wooden furniture as a job 家具工人；细木工人

cable /'keɪbl/ *noun* **1** a thick rope of wire or fibre 钢索；绳缆 **2** a wire for transmitting electricity or telecommunication signals 电缆 □ **cable car** a small carriage that hangs from a moving cable and travels up and down the side of a mountain (上下山乘坐的)缆车，索车 **cable television** a system in which programmes are transmitted by cable 有线电视

caboodle /kə'buːdl/ *noun* (**the whole caboodle**) informal 【非正式】 the whole number of people or things in question 全部；全体

caboose /kə'buːs/ *noun* N. Amer. 【北美】 a guards' van on a goods train (货运)火车守车

cabriolet /'kæbriəʊleɪ/ *noun* **1** a car with a roof that folds down 篷式汽车 **2** a horse-drawn carriage with a hood (带篷的)单马双轮轻便车

cacao /kə'kaʊ/ *noun* the seeds of a tropical American tree, from which cocoa and chocolate are made 可可豆(美洲热带可可树的种子，可可粉和巧克力的制作原料)

cache /kæʃ/ *noun* a hidden store of things 隐藏物；贮藏物

cachet /'kæʃeɪ/ *noun* the state of being respected or admired; prestige 威望；声望

cackle /'kækl/ *verb* (**cackles**, **cackling**, **cackled**) **1** laugh noisily 咯咯笑 **2** (of a hen) make a noisy clucking cry (母鸡)咯咯叫，发出咯咯声 • *noun* a noisy cry or laugh 咯咯声

cacophony /kə'kɒfəni/ *noun* (plural **cacophonies**) a mixture of loud and unpleasant sounds 刺耳的嘈杂声 ■ **cacophonous** adjective.

cactus /'kæktəs/ **noun** (plural **cacti** /'kæktaɪ/ or **cactuses**) a plant with a thick fleshy stem that has spines but no leaves 仙人掌

cad /kæd/ **noun** dated or humorous 【废 或幽默】 a man who is dishonest or treats other people badly 无赖;行为 不端的男子 ▪ **caddish** adjective.

cadaver /kə'dævə(r)/ **noun** Medicine 【医】 a dead body 尸体

cadaverous /kə'dævərəs/ **adjective** very pale and thin 惨白的;枯槁的

caddie or **caddy** /'kædi/ **noun** (plural **caddies**) a person who carries a golfer's clubs (高尔夫球)球童 ▪ **verb** (**caddies**, **caddying**, **caddied**) work as a caddie 做球童

caddy /'kædi/ **noun** (plural **caddies**) a small storage container 小容器;小罐

cadence /'keɪdns/ **noun 1** the rise and fall in pitch of the voice (话音 的)抑扬顿挫 **2** the close of a musical phrase (乐章的)收束,终止

cadenza /kə'denzə/ **noun** a difficult solo passage in a piece of music (独 奏或独唱的)华彩段

cadet /kə'det/ **noun** a young trainee in the armed services or police (军校或 警校的)学员

cadge /kædʒ/ **verb** (**cadges**, **cadging**, **cadged**) informal 【非正式】 ask for or get something without paying or working for it 乞求;求得

cadmium /'kædmiəm/ **noun** a silvery-white metallic element (金属元素)镉

cadre /'kɑːdə(r)/ **noun** a small group of people trained for a particular purpose or at the centre of a political organization (政治组织的)骨干队伍, 核心团子

Caesar /'siːzə(r)/ **noun** a title of Roman emperors 恺撒(罗马帝国皇 王的称号)

✔ 拼写指南 -ae-, not -ea-: Caesar. Caesar 中 -ae- 不要拼作 -ea-。

Caesarean /sɪ'zeərɪən/ or **Cae-**

sarean section **noun** an operation for delivering a child by cutting through the wall of the mother's abdomen 剖腹产手术

cafe • **café** /'kæfeɪ/ **noun** a small restaurant selling light meals and drinks 小餐 馆;茶室;咖啡馆

cafeteria /ˌkæfə'tɪəriə/ **noun** a self-service restaurant 自助餐厅

cafetière /ˌkæfə'tjeə(r)/ **noun** a coffee pot containing a plunger to push the grounds to the bottom 滤压式咖啡壶

caffeine /'kæfiːn/ **noun** a stimulating substance found in tea and coffee 咖 啡因;咖啡碱

caftan ⇒ 见 KAFTAN.

cage /keɪdʒ/ **noun** a structure of bars or wires used for confining animals 笼子 ▪ **verb** (**cages**, **caging**, **caged**) confine an animal in a cage 把…关 在笼中

cagey /'keɪdʒi/ **adjective** informal 【非 正式】 cautiously reluctant to speak 吞吞吐吐的;守口如瓶的 ▪ **cagily** adverb.

cagoule /kə'guːl/ **noun** Brit. 【英】 a lightweight hooded waterproof jacket (防水的)连帽薄外衣

cahoots /kə'huːts/ **plural noun** (**in cahoots**) informal 【非正式】 making secret plans together (与…)勾结的

caiman /'keɪmən/ **noun** a tropical American reptile similar to an alligator 凯门鳄(产于美洲热带地区, 与短吻鳄类似)

cairn /keən/ **noun** a mound of rough stones built as a memorial or land-mark (作墓碑或路标用的)堆石标

cajole /kə'dʒəʊl/ **verb** (**cajoles**, **cajoling**, **cajoled**) persuade someone to do something by flattering them (用甜言蜜语)哄,劝诱

cake /keɪk/ **noun 1** an item of soft sweet food made from baking a mixture of flour, fat, eggs, and sugar 蛋糕 **2** a flat round item of savoury food 饼;饼状食物 ▪ **verb** (**cakes**, **caking**, **caked**) (of a thick or sticky substance) cover and become encrusted on something (厚实或黏稠的物质)涂, 覆盖

calabrese /'kæləbriːs/ **noun** a bright green variety of broccoli 花茎甘蓝

calamine /'kæləmaɪn/ **noun** a pink powder used to make a soothing lotion or ointment 炉甘石, 异极石(一种用于制作安抚洗剂或药膏的粉红色粉末)

calamity /kə'læməti/ **noun** (plural **calamities**) an event causing great and sudden damage or distress 灾难, 灾祸 ■ **calamitous** adjective.

calcified /'kælsɪfaɪd/ **adjective** hardened by the addition of calcium salts 硬化的, 钙化的

calcium /'kælsɪəm/ **noun** a soft grey metallic substance (金属元素)钙 □ **calcium carbonate** a white compound found as chalk, limestone, and marble 碳酸钙

calculate /'kælkjuleɪt/ **verb** (**calculates**, **calculating**, **calculated**) **1** work out a number or amount using mathematics 计算 **2** intend an action to have a particular effect 想要, 意欲 ■ **calculable** adjective.

calculated /'kælkjuleɪtɪd/ **adjective** done with awareness of the likely effect 精心设计的, 蓄意的

calculating /'kælkjuleɪtɪŋ/ **adjective** craftily planning things so as to benefit yourself 精于算计的, 精明的

calculation /ˌkælkju'leɪʃn/ **noun 1** a count or assessment done using mathematics 计算 **2** an assessment of the risks or effects of a course of action 预测, 估计

calculator /'kælkjuleɪtə(r)/ **noun** a small electronic device used for making mathematical calculations 计算器

calculus /'kælkjələs/ **noun** the branch of mathematics concerned with problems involving rates of change (数学中的)微积分

caldron /'kɔːldrən/ US spelling of **CAULDRON**. cauldron 的美式拼法

calendar /'kælɪndə(r)/ **noun 1** a chart showing the days, weeks, and months of a particular year 日历, 历书 **2** a system by which the beginning and end of a year are fixed 历法 **3** a list of special days or events 日程表, 记事录

calf¹ /kɑːf/ **noun** (plural **calves**) **1** a young cow or bull 小牛, 牛犊 **2** the young of some other large animals, e.g. elephants (象等大型动物的)幼兽, 崽

calf² **noun** (plural **calves**) the fleshy part at the back of a person's leg below the knee 腓肠, 腿肚

calibrate /'kælɪbreɪt/ **verb** (**calibrates**, **calibrating**, **calibrated**) **1** mark a gauge or instrument with units of measurement 标定(仪器)的刻度 **2** compare the readings of an instrument with those of a standard 调整, 校准(仪器) ■ **calibration** noun.

calibre /'kælɪbə(r)/ (US spelling 【美拼法】**caliber**) **noun 1** the diameter of the inside of a gun barrel, or of a bullet or shell (枪炮等的)口径, (子弹或炮弹的)直径, 弹径 **2** a person's quality or ability (人的)品质, 能力

calico /'kælɪkəʊ/ **noun** (plural **calicoes** or US 【美】**calicos**) **1** Brit. 【英】a type of plain white cotton cloth (本色白的)白棉布 **2** N. Amer. 【北美】printed cotton fabric 印花棉布

caliper or **calliper** /'kælɪpə(r)/ **noun 1** (also **calipers**) a measuring instrument with two hinged legs 弯脚圆规 **2** a metal support for a person's leg 双脚规形夹(支撑腿的金属支架)

caliph /'keɪlɪf/ **noun** (in the past) the chief Muslim ruler 哈里发(旧时伊斯兰国家的统治者)

calk /kɔːk/ US spelling of **CAULK**. caulk 的美式拼法

call /kɔːl/ **verb 1** shout to someone to attract their attention or ask them to come somewhere 传唤；招呼；叫喊 **2** telephone someone 给(某人)打电话 **3** (of a bird or animal) make its characteristic cry (鸟或兽)鸣，啼，叫 **4** pay a brief visit (短暂地)拜访，访问 **5** name or describe someone or something 给…取名；把…说成是 **6** predict the result of a vote or contest 预测(投票或比赛)的结果 • **noun 1** an act of calling someone 打电话 **2** an act of telephoning someone 打电话 **3** the cry of a bird or animal (鸟或兽的)鸣，啼，叫 **4** a brief visit 拜访 **5** (**call for**) demand or need for 要求；需要 □ **call centre** an office in which large numbers of telephone calls are handled for an organization 呼叫中心；电话服务中心 **call for** require 要求；需要 **call something off** cancel something 取消(某事) **call on** turn to for help 求助 **call the shots** (or **tune**) be in charge of how something should be done 掌控局势 **call someone up** summon someone to serve in the army or to play in a team 征召(某人)入伍(或入队) ■ **caller** noun.

calligraphy /kə'lɪɡrəfi/ **noun** decorative handwriting 书法 ■ **calligrapher** noun **calligraphic** adjective.

calling /'kɔːlɪŋ/ **noun 1** a profession or occupation 职业；行业 **2** a strong feeling that you are suitable for a particular occupation; a vocation 天职；神召

callisthenics /ˌkælɪs'θenɪks/ (US spelling 【美拼法】 **calisthenics**) **plural noun** gymnastic exercises 健美操；健身操

callous /'kæləs/ **adjective** insensitive and cruel 无感觉的；麻木不仁的 ■ **callously** adverb.

callow /'kæləʊ/ **adjective** young and inexperienced (年轻人)无经验的，不成熟的

callus or **callous** /'kæləs/ **noun** an area of thickened and hardened skin 老茧；硬皮

calm /kɑːm/ **adjective 1** not nervous, angry, or excited 镇静的；平静的 **2** peaceful and undisturbed 宁静的；无干扰的 • **noun** a calm state or period 平静的状态(或时期) • **verb** (often **calm down** or **calm someone down**) become or make someone calm (使)镇静；(使)平静 ■ **calmly** adverb **calmness** noun.

calorie /'kæləri/ **noun** (plural **calories**) **1** a unit for measuring how much energy food will produce 大卡，千卡(食物的热量单位) **2** a unit of heat 卡路里，小卡(热量单位)

calorific /ˌkælə'rɪfɪk/ **adjective** relating to the amount of energy contained in food or fuel 含热量的；热卡的

calumny /'kæləmni/ **noun** (plural **calumnies**) formal 【正式】 the making of false and damaging statements about someone 诽谤；诋毁

calve /kɑːv/ **verb** (**calves, calving, calved**) give birth to a calf 生小牛；产牛犊

calves /kɑːvz/ plural of CALF¹, CALF².

calypso /kə'lɪpsəʊ/ **noun** (plural **calypsos**) a kind of West Indian song with improvised words on a topical theme 卡利普索民歌(西印度群岛一种以时事为主题、歌词即兴创作的歌曲)

calyx /'keɪlɪks/ **noun** (plural **calyces** /'keɪlɪsiːz/ or **calyxes**) the ring of small leaves (sepals) which form a layer around the bud of a flower 花萼

cam /kæm/ **noun 1** a projecting part on a wheel or shaft, which comes into contact with another part while rotating and makes it move 凸轮(轮或轴上的凸出部件，通过旋转或移动与其他部件相接触) **2** a camshaft 凸轮轴

camaraderie /ˌkæmə'rɑːdəri/ **noun** trust and friendship between people 同志情谊；友谊

camber /'kæmbə(r)/ **noun** a slightly

curved shape of a horizontal surface such as a road (道路等表面的)中凸形,反拱

Cambodian /kæm'bəudiən/ **noun** a person from Cambodia 柬埔寨人 • **adjective** relating to Cambodia 柬埔寨的

cambric /'kæmbrɪk/ **noun** a light-weight white linen or cotton fabric 细麻纱,细棉纱

camcorder /'kæmkɔːdə(r)/ **noun** a portable combined video camera and video recorder (便携式)摄像机

came /keɪm/ past tense of **COME**.

camel /'kæml/ **noun** a large long-necked animal with either one or two humps on its back 骆驼

camellia /kə'miːliə/ **noun** an evergreen shrub with bright flowers and shiny leaves 山茶(常绿灌木,花朵艳丽,叶子有光泽)

cameo /'kæmiəu/ **noun** (plural **cameos**) **1** a piece of jewellery consisting of a carving of a head against a differently coloured background 多彩浮雕宝石 **2** a short piece of writing giving a good description of a person or thing 小品文;描写片段 **3** a small part played by a well-known actor (由著名演员出演的)客串小角色

camera /'kæmərə/ **noun** a device for taking photographs or recording moving images 照相机;摄影机 □ **in camera** Law【法律】in a judge's private rooms, without the press and public being present 在法官的私室里;不公开地

camisole /'kæmɪsəul/ **noun** a woman's loosefitting undergarment for the upper body 宽松女内衣

camomile or **chamomile** /'kæməmaɪl/ **noun** a plant with white and yellow flowers, used in herbal preparations 洋甘菊,春黄菊(开白色和黄色花,用于配制草药)

camouflage /'kæməflɑːʒ/ **noun 1** the painting or covering of soldiers and military equipment to make them blend in with their surroundings (士兵和军事装备的)伪装 **2** clothing or materials used for this purpose 伪装物 **3** the natural appearance of an animal which allows it to blend in with its surroundings (动物的)保护色,保护性 • **verb** (**camouflages**, **camouflaging**, **camouflaged**) disguise using camouflage 用伪装隐藏(或掩饰)

camp¹ /kæmp/ **noun 1** a place where soldiers, refugees, etc. live temporarily in tents, huts, or cabins (临时的)营地 **2** a complex of buildings for holidaymakers 露营地 **3** the supporters of a particular party or set of beliefs (某一党派或信仰体系的)阵营 • **verb** live in a tent while on holiday 露营;宿营 □ **camp bed** Brit.【英】a folding portable bed 行军床;折叠床 **camp follower** a person who associates with a group without being a full member 随军杂役 ■ **camper** noun.

camp² informal【非正式】**adjective 1** (of a man) effeminate in an exaggerated way (男子)忸怩的,女子气的 **2** deliberately exaggerated and theatrical in style 矫揉造作的;惺惺作态的 □ **camp it up** behave in a camp way 举止做作

campaign /kæm'peɪn/ **noun 1** a series of military operations in a particular area (军事)战役 **2** an organized course of action to achieve a goal (有组织的)运动 • **verb** work towards a goal 参加运动 ■ **campaigner** noun.

campanology /ˌkæmpə'nɒlədʒi/ **noun** the art of bell-ringing 鸣钟术

campfire /'kæmpfaɪə(r)/ **noun** an open-air fire in a camp 篝火;营火

camphor /'kæmfə(r)/ **noun** a strong-smelling white substance, used in medicine and in insect repellents 樟脑,茨酮(气味浓烈的白色物质,用于制药及驱虫)

campus /'kæmpəs/ **noun** (plural **campuses**) the grounds and buildings of a university or college 校园

camshaft /'kæmʃɑːft/ **noun** a shaft with one or more cams attached to it 凸轮轴

can[1] /kæn, kən/ **modal verb** (3rd singular present **can**; past **could**) **1** be able to 能;能够 **2** be allowed to 可以;允许

> ! 注 意 when you're asking to be allowed to do something, it is more polite to say **may** rather than **can** (*May we leave now?* rather than *Can we leave now?*). 当请求许可做某事时,用 may 比用 can 更加礼貌。例如,说 May we leave now? (我们现在可以离开吗?)比 Can we leave now? 更客气。

can[2] /kæn/ **noun** a cylindrical metal container (金属)罐,听 • **verb** (**cans**, **canning**, **canned**) preserve food in a can 用罐(或听)保存 □ **a can of worms** a complicated matter that will prove difficult to manage (隐藏着许多问题的)麻烦事,棘手的事情

Canadian /kə'neɪdɪən/ **noun** a person from Canada 加拿大人 • **adjective** relating to Canada 加拿大的

canal /kə'næl/ **noun 1** a water-filled channel made for boats to travel on or to convey water to fields 运河 **2** a passage in a plant or animal carrying food, liquid, or air (动植物体内的)管,道

canapé /'kænəpeɪ/ **noun** a small piece of bread or pastry with a savoury topping 开胃面包;油酥点心

canard /kæ'nɑːd/ **noun** a false rumour or story 谣言;虚假报道

canary /kə'neəri/ **noun** (plural **canaries**) a small bright yellow bird with a tuneful song 金丝雀

canasta /kə'næstə/ **noun** a card game using two packs and usually played by two pairs of partners 凯纳斯特纸牌戏;塔牌

cancan /'kænkæn/ **noun** a lively, high-kicking stage dance 康康舞,坎坎舞(高高踢腿的欢快的舞台舞蹈)

cancel /'kænsl/ **verb** (**cancels**, **cancelling**, **cancelled**; US spelling 【美拼作】**cancels**, **canceling**, **canceled**) **1** decide that a planned event will not take place 取消(计划) **2** withdraw from or end an arrangement 撤销,终止(安排) **3** (**cancel something out**) (of one thing) have an equal but opposite effect on another thing 抵消 **4** mark a stamp, ticket, etc. to show that it has been used 盖销(邮票、票据等) ■ **cancellation** noun.

Cancer /'kænsə(r)/ **noun** a sign of the zodiac (the Crab), 21 June–20 July 巨蟹宫(黄道十二宫之一)

cancer /'kænsə(r)/ **noun 1** a disease caused by an uncontrolled growth of abnormal cells in a part of the body 癌症 **2** a tumour 恶性肿瘤 **3** something evil or destructive that is hard to contain or destroy (难以控制或消除的)毒瘤,弊端 ■ **cancerous** adjective.

candela /kæn'diːlə/ **noun** the basic unit of luminous intensity 堪德拉(发光强度基本单位)

candelabrum /kændə'lɑːbrəm/ **noun** (plural **candelabra** /kændə'lɑːbrə/) a large branched holder for several candles or lamps 枝形大烛台;枝形大吊灯

candid /'kændɪd/ **adjective** truthful and straightforward; frank 直言不讳的;坦率的 ■ **candidly** adverb.

candidate /'kændɪdət/ **noun 1** a person who applies for a job or is nominated for election (职位或选举的)候选人 **2** Brit. 【英】a person taking an exam 应试者;投考者 ■ **candidacy** noun.

candied /'kændɪd/ **adjective** (of fruit)

preserved in a sugar syrup (水果)糖渍保存的,蜜饯的

candle /'kændl/ **noun** a stick of wax with a central wick which is lit to produce light as it burns 蜡烛

candlestick /'kændlstɪk/ **noun** a support or holder for a candle 蜡扦; 烛台

candlewick /'kændlwɪk/ **noun** a thick, soft cotton fabric with a tufted pattern 烛芯纱

candour /'kændə(r)/ (US spelling 【美拼作】 **candor**) **noun** the quality of being open and honest 直率;坦诚

candy /'kændi/ **noun** (plural **candies**) N. Amer. 【北美】 sweets 糖果

candyfloss /'kændiflɒs/ **noun** Brit. 【英】 a mass of pink or white fluffy spun sugar wrapped round a stick 棉花糖

cane /keɪn/ **noun 1** the hollow stem of tall reeds, grasses, etc. (芦苇、禾本植物等的)茎 **2** a length of cane used as a walking stick, for beating someone, etc. 竹竿;手杖;答条 • **verb** (**canes**, **caning**, **caned**) beat someone with a cane as a punishment 用答杖打

canine /'keɪnaɪn/ **adjective** relating to or resembling a dog 犬的, 似犬的 • **noun** a pointed tooth next to the incisors 犬齿(位于门齿旁侧)

canister /'kænɪstə(r)/ **noun** a round or cylindrical container (圆形或圆柱形)小盒,小罐

canker /'kæŋkə(r)/ **noun 1** a disease of trees and plants (树木和植株的)枯枝病,溃疡病 **2** a condition in animals that causes open sores (动物的)溃疡, 疮

cannabis /'kænəbɪs/ **noun** a drug made from the hemp plant 大麻

canned /kænd/ **adjective** preserved in a sealed can 装罐保存的

cannelloni /ˌkænə'ləʊni/ **plural noun** rolls of pasta stuffed with a meat or vegetable mixture and cooked in a cheese sauce 肉馅面卷;菜馅面卷

cannery /'kænəri/ **noun** (plural **canneries**) a factory where food is canned 罐头食品厂

cannibal /'kænɪbl/ **noun** a person who eats the flesh of human beings 食人肉者 ■ **cannibalism noun cannibalistic** adjective.

cannibalize or **cannibalise** /'kænɪbəlaɪz/ **verb** (**cannibalizes**, **cannibalizing**, **cannibalized**) use a machine as a source of spare parts for others 拆用机器部件(修配其他机器)

cannon /'kænən/ **noun** (plural **cannon** or **cannons**) **1** a large, heavy gun formerly used in warfare (旧时战争中使用的)大炮 **2** an automatic heavy gun that fires shells from an aircraft or tank (飞机或坦克上的)自动机关炮 • **verb** (**cannons**, **cannoning**, **cannoned**) (**cannon into** or **off**) chiefly Brit. 【主英】 collide with 碰撞 □ **cannon fodder** soldiers seen merely as a resource to be used up in war 炮灰(在战争中充当牺牲品的士兵)

cannonball /'kænənbɔːl/ **noun** a metal or stone ball fired from a cannon 炮弹

cannot /'kænɒt, -ət/ **short form** cannot.

canny /'kæni/ **adjective** (**cannier**, **canniest**) shrewd, especially in financial matters (尤指在金融事务方面)精明的 ■ **cannily** adverb.

canoe /kə'nuː/ **noun** a narrow boat with pointed ends, propelled with a paddle 小划子;独木舟 • **verb** (**canoes**, **canoeing**, **canoed**) travel in a canoe 乘坐独木舟 ■ **canoeist** noun.

canon /'kænən/ **noun 1** a general rule or principle by which something is judged 规则;标准;原则 **2** a Church decree or law 教令;教规 **3** the works of a particular author or artist that are recognized as genuine (某一作家或艺术家的)真迹,真作 **4** a list of literary works considered as being of the highest quality (文学)经典作品 **5** a member of the clergy on the staff of a cathedral 大教堂教士 **6** a piece of music in which a theme is taken up by two or more parts that overlap 卡农曲(一种复调乐曲) □ **canon law** the laws of the Christian Church 教会法规

canonical /kə'nɒnɪkl/ **adjective 1** accepted as authentic or as a standard 权威性的;标准的 **2** according to the laws of the Christian Church 按照基督教会教规的

canonize or **canonise** /'kænənaɪz/ **verb** (**canonizes, canonizing, canonized**) officially declare a dead person to be a saint 正式宣布(死者)为圣徒 ∎ **canonization** noun.

canoodle /kə'nuːdl/ **verb** (**canoodles, canoodling, canoodled**) informal 【非正式】 kiss and cuddle lovingly 亲吻;搂抱

canopy /'kænəpi/ **noun** (plural **canopies**) **1** a cloth covering over a throne or bed (宝座或床等上方的)华盖,罩篷 **2** a roof-like covering or shelter 顶篷;天篷 **3** the expanding, umbrella-like part of a parachute (降落伞的)伞衣 ∎ **canopied** adjective.

cant[1] /kænt/ **noun 1** insincere talk about moral or religious matters (关于道德或宗教问题的)言不由衷的话,伪善的言辞 **2** disapproving 【贬】 the language typical of a particular group (某个群体的)行话

cant[2] **verb** tilt or slope 倾斜 • **noun** a slope or tilt 斜坡;倾斜

can't /kɑːnt/ **short form** cannot.

cantaloupe /'kæntəluːp/ **noun** a small melon with orange flesh 罗马甜瓜

cantankerous /kæn'tæŋkərəs/ **adjective** bad-tempered and uncooperative 脾气坏的;不合作的

cantata /kæn'tɑːtə/ **noun** a musical work with a solo voice and usually a

chorus and orchestra 康塔塔(通常有合唱团伴唱、乐队伴奏的音乐作品)

canteen /kæn'tiːn/ **noun 1** a restaurant in a workplace, school, or college (工作地点或学校的)食堂,餐厅 **2** Brit. 【英】a case containing a set of cutlery 餐具盒 **3** a small water bottle used by soldiers or campers (士兵或露营者用的)小水壶

canter /'kæntə(r)/ **noun** a pace of a horse between a trot and a gallop (马介于小跑和疾奔之间的)中速跑 • **verb** (**canters, cantering, cantered**) move at this pace 骑马中速跑

canticle /'kæntɪkl/ **noun** a hymn or chant forming part of a church service 赞美诗,圣歌(教堂礼拜仪式的组成部分)

cantilever /'kæntɪliːvə(r)/ **noun** a long beam or girder fixed at only one end, used for supporting a bridge 大梁,悬臂梁(用于支撑桥梁、一端固定) ∎ **cantilevered** adjective.

canto /'kæntəʊ/ **noun** (plural **cantos**) a division of a long poem 诗章(长诗的一个篇章)

canton /'kæntɒn/ **noun** a political or administrative subdivision of a country, especially in Switzerland 小行政区;(尤指瑞士的)州

canvas /'kænvəs/ **noun** (plural **canvases** or **canvasses**) **1** a strong, coarse cloth used to make sails, tents, etc. (制作船帆、帐篷等的)帆布 **2** an oil painting on canvas 帆布油画

canvass /'kænvəs/ **verb 1** visit someone to ask for their vote in an election (向选民)拉选票 **2** question someone to find out their opinion 调查(民意);征求(意见) ∎ **canvasser** noun.

canyon /'kænjən/ **noun** a deep gorge (很深的)峡谷

cap /kæp/ **noun 1** a soft flat hat with a peak (带帽舌的)软帽,便帽 **2** Brit. 【英】a cap awarded to members of a national sports team (国家运动队的)队员帽 **3** a lid or cover 盖;罩;套 **4** an upper limit on spending or borrowing (花费或借款的)上限,限额 **5** a small amount of explosive powder in a case that explodes when you hit it 火帽;火药帽 **6** a contraceptive diaphragm (避孕用)子宫帽 ▪ verb **(caps, capping, capped) 1** put a cap on 给…戴帽子(或加盖,加罩) **2** be a fitting end to 使圆满结束 **3** put a limit on 给…定限额 **4 (be capped)** Brit.【英】be chosen as a member of a national sports team 入选(国家运动队) □ **cap in hand** humbly asking for a favour 谦卑地讨要

capability /ˌkeɪpəˈbɪləti/ **noun** (plural **capabilities**) the power or ability to do something 能力;才能

capable /ˈkeɪpəbl/ **adjective 1 (capable of)** having the ability to do something 具备…能力的 **2** able to achieve what you need to do; competent 无所不能的;能力强的 ▪ **capably** adverb.

capacious /kəˈpeɪʃəs/ **adjective** having a lot of space inside; roomy 容量大的;宽敞的

capacitance /kəˈpæsɪtəns/ **noun** the ability to store electric charge 电流容量;电容

capacitor /kəˈpæsɪtə(r)/ **noun** a device used to store electric charge 电容器

capacity /kəˈpæsəti/ **noun** (plural **capacities**) **1** the maximum amount that something can contain or produce 最大容量;最大产量 **2** the ability or power to do something 才能;能力 **3** a role or position 职责;地位;职位

cape[1] /keɪp/ **noun** a short cloak 披肩

cape[2] **noun** a piece of land that sticks out into the sea 海角;岬

caper[1] /ˈkeɪpə(r)/ **verb** (**capers, capering, capered**) skip or dance about in a lively or playful way 蹦

跳;雀跃 ▪ **noun** informal【非正式】a light-hearted or dishonest activity 恶作剧;欺诈行为

caper[2] **noun** the flower bud of a shrub, pickled and used in cooking 刺山柑花蕾(用于烹饪)

capillarity /ˌkæpɪˈlærəti/ **noun** capillary action 毛细作用

capillary /kəˈpɪləri/ **noun** (plural **capillaries**) **1** a very small blood vessel 毛细血管 **2** a tube with a very narrow diameter 毛细管 □ **capillary action** the force which acts on a liquid in a narrow tube to push it up or down 毛细作用

capital /ˈkæpɪtl/ **noun 1** the most important city or town of a country or region 首都;首府;省会 **2** wealth that is owned or invested, lent, or borrowed 资本;本钱 **3** a capital letter 大写字母 **4** the top part of a pillar 柱顶;柱头 ▪ **adjective** informal, dated【非正式,废】excellent 极好的 □ **capital letter** a large size of letter used to begin sentences and names 大写字母 **capital offence** an offence that is punished by death 死罪 **capital punishment** the punishment of a crime by death 死刑 **make capital out of** use to your own advantage 利用…牟利

capitalism /ˈkæpɪtəlɪzəm/ **noun** a system in which a country's trade and industry are controlled by private owners for profit 资本主义 ▪ **capitalist** noun & adjective.

capitalize or **capitalise** /ˈkæpɪtəlaɪz/ **verb** (**capitalizes, capitalizing, capitalized**) **1 (capitalize on)** take advantage of 利用;从…获利 **2** convert into or provide with financial capital 使资本化;为…提供资本 **3** write in capital letters or with a capital first letter 用大写字母书写;把…首字母大写 ▪ **capitalization** noun.

capitulate /kəˈpɪtjuleɪt/ **verb**

(**capitulates**, **capitulating**, **capitulated**) give in to an opponent 投降；让步；屈从 ■ **capitulation** noun.

capon /'keɪpɒn, -pən/ noun a male chicken that has been fattened up for eating (养肥供食用的)阉鸡

cappuccino /ˌkæpu'tʃiːnəʊ/ noun (plural **cappuccinos**) coffee made with milk that has been frothed up with pressurized steam 卡普契诺咖啡(加牛奶用蒸汽煮出的多泡咖啡)

caprice /kə'priːs/ noun a sudden change of mood or behaviour (情绪或行为的)突然变化

capricious /kə'prɪʃəs/ adjective having sudden changes of mood 变化无常的；善变的 ■ **capriciously** adverb.

Capricorn /'kæprɪkɔːn/ noun a sign of the zodiac (the Goat), 21 December–20 January 摩羯宫(黄道十二宫之一)

capsicum /'kæpsɪkəm/ noun (plural **capsicums**) a sweet pepper or chilli pepper 甜椒；辣椒

capsize /kæp'saɪz/ verb (**capsizes**, **capsizing**, **capsized**) (of a boat) overturn in the water (小船)倾覆

capstan /'kæpstən/ noun a broad revolving cylinder for winding a heavy rope or cable (缠绕绳索或缆绳的)绞盘

capsule /'kæpsjuːl/ noun 1 a small gelatin container with a dose of medicine inside, swallowed whole (装药物的)胶囊 2 a small case or compartment 小盒；小隔间

captain /'kæptɪn/ noun 1 the person in command of a ship or commercial aircraft 船长；(商用飞机的)机长 2 the rank of naval officer above commander 海军上校 3 the rank of army officer above lieutenant 陆军上尉 4 the leader of a team 队长 • verb be the captain of 率领；指挥 ■ **captaincy** noun.

caption /'kæpʃn/ noun 1 a title or explanation accompanying an illustration or cartoon (插图或漫画的)标题, 说明文字 2 a piece of writing appearing as part of a film or television broadcast (电影或电视的)字幕 • verb provide a caption for 给…加标题；给…加字幕

captivate /'kæptɪveɪt/ verb (**captivates**, **captivating**, **captivated**) attract and hold the interest of; charm 迷住；使着迷

captive /'kæptɪv/ noun a person who has been captured 俘虏；囚徒 • adjective unable to escape 被关押的 ■ **captivity** noun.

captor /'kæptə(r)/ noun a person who captures another 俘获(他人)者；劫持者

capture /'kæptʃə(r)/ verb (**captures**, **capturing**, **captured**) 1 take prisoner, or forcibly get possession of 俘获;(用武力)夺取, 获得 2 record accurately in words or pictures (用语言或图画)记录；刻画 3 cause data to be stored in a computer 采集(数据);将(数据)存入计算机 • noun the action of capturing 俘获；俘虏

capybara /ˌkæpɪ'bɑːrə/ noun (plural **capybara** or **capybaras**) a large South American rodent 水豚(大型啮齿动物,产于南美洲)

car /kɑː(r)/ noun 1 a powered road vehicle designed to carry a small number of people 小汽车；轿车 2 a railway carriage or wagon 火车车厢；四轮运货马车 □ **car park** Brit. 【英】an area or building where cars may be left temporarily 停车场；停车库

carafe /kə'ræf/ noun a wide-necked glass bottle for serving wine 卡拉夫瓶(餐厅里盛酒的喇叭口玻璃瓶)

caramel /'kærəməl/ noun 1 sugar or syrup heated until it turns brown 焦糖(浆) 2 soft toffee made with sugar and butter 卡拉梅尔糖(一种乳脂软糖)

carapace /'kærəpeɪs/ noun the hard

upper shell of a tortoise, lobster, etc. (龟、龙虾等的)硬壳

carat /ˈkærət/ **noun 1** a unit of weight for precious stones and pearls 克拉 (珍贵宝石和珍珠的重量单位) **2** a measure of the purity of gold 开(黄金纯度单位)

caravan /ˈkærəvæn/ **noun 1** a vehicle equipped for living in, designed to be towed by a car or a horse (用汽车或马匹拖拽的)活动住房 **2** *historical* 【历史】 a group of people travelling together across a desert 沙漠旅行车队

caraway /ˈkærəweɪ/ **noun** a plant whose seeds are used as a spice 葛缕子籽(用作调料)

carbide /ˈkɑːbaɪd/ **noun** a compound of carbon with a metal or other element 碳化物

carbine /ˈkɑːbaɪn/ **noun** a light automatic rifle 卡宾枪

carbohydrate /ˌkɑːbəʊˈhaɪdreɪt/ **noun** a substance (e.g. sugar and starch) containing carbon, hydrogen, and oxygen, found in food and used to give energy 碳水化合物

carbolic /kɑːˈbɒlɪk/ or **carbolic acid** **noun** a kind of disinfectant (消毒用)石炭酸，苯酚

carbon /ˈkɑːbən/ **noun** a chemical element with two main pure forms (diamond and graphite), found in all organic compounds (化学元素)碳 □ **carbon copy 1** a copy made with carbon paper 复写本 **2** a person or thing identical to another 一模一样的人(或物) **carbon dating** a method of finding out how old something is by measuring the amount of radioactive carbon-14 in it 碳-14年代测定法 **carbon dioxide** a gas produced by people and animals breathing out, and also by burning carbon, which is absorbed by plants in photosynthesis 二氧化碳 **carbon monoxide** a poisonous gas formed when carbon is not completely burned 一氧化碳 **carbon paper** thin paper coated with carbon, used for making a copy of a document 复写纸

carbonaceous /ˌkɑːbəˈneɪʃəs/ **adjective** consisting of or containing carbon or its compounds 由碳(化合物)组成的；含碳(化合物)的

carbonate /ˈkɑːbəneɪt/ **noun** a compound containing carbon and oxygen together with a metal 碳酸盐

carbonated /ˈkɑːbəneɪtɪd/ **adjective** (of a drink) fizzy because it contains small bubbles of carbon dioxide (饮料)含二氧化碳的

carbonic acid /kɑːˈbɒnɪk/ **noun** a very weak acid formed from carbon dioxide and water 碳酸

carborundum /ˌkɑːbəˈrʌndəm/ **noun** a very hard black substance used for grinding and polishing 金刚砂，氧化硅(用作研磨料)

carbuncle /ˈkɑːbʌŋkl/ **noun 1** a large abscess or boil in the skin 痈，疔 **2** a polished red gem 红宝石；红榴石

carburettor /ˌkɑːbəˈretə(r)/ (US spelling 【美拼作】 **carburetor**) **noun** a device in an engine that mixes the fuel with air (发动机中的)汽化器，化油器

carcass or **carcase** /ˈkɑːkəs/ **noun** the dead body of an animal 动物尸体

carcinogen /kɑːˈsɪnədʒən/ **noun** a substance that can cause cancer 致癌物 ■ **carcinogenic** adjective.

carcinoma /ˌkɑːsɪˈnəʊmə/ **noun** (plural **carcinomas**) a cancer of the skin or of the internal organs 癌

card[1] /kɑːd/ **noun 1** thick, stiff paper or thin cardboard 厚纸片；薄纸板 **2** a piece of card printed with information, greetings, etc. 卡片；贺帖 **3** a small rectangular piece of plastic used for obtaining money from a bank or paying for goods 银行卡；购物卡 **4** a playing card 纸牌 **5** (**cards**) a game played with playing cards 纸

牌游戏 □ **card sharp** a person who cheats at cards 玩牌作弊者；老千 **on the cards** possible or likely 可能的

card² verb disentangle the fibres of raw wool by combing it with a sharp-toothed instrument (用梳理机)梳理(羊毛)

cardamom /'kɑːdəməm/ noun the seed and pods of a SE Asian plant, used as a spice 豆蔻籽(产于东南亚，用作调料)

cardboard /'kɑːdbɔːd/ noun thin board made from paper pulp 卡纸板；薄纸板

cardiac /'kɑːdiæk/ adjective having to do with the heart 心脏的

cardigan /'kɑːdɪɡən/ noun a sweater with buttons down the front 开襟毛衣

cardinal /'kɑːdɪnl/ noun an important Roman Catholic priest, having the power to elect the Pope (罗马天主教的)红衣主教 • adjective most important; chief 最重要的，主要的 □ **cardinal number** a number expressing quantity (one, two, three, etc.) 基数

cardiograph /'kɑːdiəɡrɑːf/ noun an instrument for recording heart movements 心电图仪

cardiology /ˌkɑːdi'ɒlədʒi/ noun the branch of medicine concerned with the heart 心脏病学

cardiovascular /ˌkɑːdiəʊ'væskjulə(r)/ adjective having to do with the heart and blood vessels 心血管的

care /keə(r)/ noun 1 special attention or effort made to avoid damage, risk, or error 小心；谨慎 2 the process of looking after and protecting someone or something 照看；保护 3 a cause for anxiety, or a worried feeling 挂念；忧虑；烦心事 4 the responsibility of a local authority to look after children, rather than their parents (地方当局对儿童的)收养，监护 • verb (cares, caring, cared) 1 feel concern or interest 关注；感兴趣 2 feel affection or liking 喜欢；在意 3 (care for or to do) like to have or be willing to do 希望拥有；愿意做 4 (care for) look after 照顾；抚养 □ **care of** at the address of someone who will look after or pass on mail 由(某人)转交 **take care of** look after or deal with 照顾；照管；处理

careen /kə'riːn/ verb (of a ship) tilt to one side (船)倾斜，倾侧

career /kə'rɪə(r)/ noun an occupation which is undertaken for a long period of a person's life 事业；职业 • verb (careers, careering, careered) move very fast and in an uncontrolled way 疾驰；猛冲

careerist /kə'rɪərɪst/ noun a person whose only concern is to make progress in their career 一味追求事业的人；工作狂 ■ **careerism** noun.

carefree /'keəfriː/ adjective free from anxiety or responsibility 无忧无虑的；无责任的

careful /'keəfl/ adjective 1 taking care to avoid harm; cautious 谨慎的；小心的 2 showing a lot of thought and attention 周到的；注意的；精心的 ■ **carefully** adverb **carefulness** noun.

careless /'keələs/ adjective not giving enough attention to avoiding harm or mistakes 粗心的；疏忽的；草率的 ■ **carelessly** adverb **carelessness** noun.

carer /'keərə(r)/ noun someone who looks after a sick, elderly, or disabled person (照看病人、老人或残疾人的)家人，护工

caress /kə'res/ verb touch or stroke gently or lovingly 轻拍；抚摸 • noun a gentle or loving touch 轻拍；抚摸

caretaker /'keəteɪkə(r)/ noun a person employed to look after a public building (公共建筑的)看门人，门卫

careworn /'keəwɔːn/ adjective showing signs of prolonged worry 忧心忡忡的；忧虑憔悴的

cargo /'kɑːgəʊ/ **noun** (plural **cargoes** or **cargos**) goods carried on a ship, aircraft, etc. (船、飞机等装载的)货物

Caribbean /ˌkærɪ'biːən/ **adjective** relating to the Caribbean Sea and its islands 加勒比海的；加勒比海诸岛的

> ✔ **拼写指南** one *r* and two *bs*: *Caribbean*. caribbean 中有一个 r 和两个 b。

caribou /'kærɪbuː/ **noun** (plural **caribou**) N. Amer. 【北美】a reindeer 驯鹿

caricature /'kærɪkətjʊə(r)/ **noun** a picture in which a person's distinctive features are amusingly exaggerated 漫画；讽刺画 • **verb** (**caricatures**, **caricaturing**, **caricatured**) make a caricature of 把…画成漫画

caries /'keəriːz/ **noun** decay of a tooth or bone 龋齿；骨疡

carmine /'kɑːmaɪn/ **noun** a vivid crimson colour 胭脂红色

carnage /'kɑːnɪdʒ/ **noun** the killing of a large number of people 大屠杀

carnal /'kɑːnl/ **adjective** relating to sexual needs and activities 性欲的；性行为的 ■ **carnality** noun.

carnation /kɑː'neɪʃn/ **noun** a plant with pink, white, or red flowers 康乃馨

carnelian /kɑː'niːliən/ **noun** a dull red or pink semi-precious stone 红玉髓；光玉髓

carnival /'kɑːnɪvl/ **noun** a festival involving processions, music, and dancing 狂欢节；嘉年华会

carnivore /'kɑːnɪvɔː(r)/ **noun** an animal that eats meat 食肉动物

carnivorous /kɑː'nɪvərəs/ **adjective** eating a diet of meat 食肉的

carob /'kærəb/ **noun** a substitute for chocolate made from the pod of an Arabian tree 角豆荚(可用于制作巧克力的替代品)

carol /'kærəl/ **noun** a religious song associated with Christmas 赞美诗；圣诞颂歌 • **verb** (**carols**, **carolling**, **carolled**; US spelling 【美拼作】 **carols**, **caroling**, **caroled**) **1** sing carols in the streets (在街上)唱圣诞颂歌 **2** sing or say happily 欢快地唱(或说)

carotene /'kærətiːn/ **noun** an orange or red substance found in carrots and other plants, important in the formation of vitamin A 胡萝卜素

carotid artery /kə'rɒtɪd/ **noun** either of two main arteries carrying blood to the head 颈动脉

carouse /kə'raʊz/ **verb** (**carouses**, **carousing**, **caroused**) drink alcohol and enjoy yourself with other people in a noisy, lively way 痛饮狂欢；狂欢作乐

carousel /ˌkærə'sel/ **noun** **1** a merry-go-round at a fair 旋转木马 **2** a rotating device for baggage collection at an airport (机场运送旅客行李的)旋转式传送带

carp¹ /kɑːp/ **noun** (plural **carp**) an edible freshwater fish 鲤鱼

carp² **verb** complain or find fault 抱怨；挑剔

carpal /'kɑːpl/ **adjective** relating to the bones in the wrist 腕骨的

carpel /'kɑːpl/ **noun** the female reproductive organ of a flower 心皮

carpenter /'kɑːpəntə(r)/ **noun** a person who makes objects and structures out of wood 木匠；木工 ■ **carpentry** noun.

carpet /'kɑːpɪt/ **noun** **1** a floor covering made from thick woven fabric 地毯 **2** a thick or soft layer of something (某物)地毯状的一层 • **verb** (**carpets**, **carpeting**, **carpeted**) **1** cover with a carpet 在…上铺地毯 **2** informal 【非正式】tell someone off severely 训斥；责骂 □ **carpet-bomb** bomb an area intensively 对(某区域)进行地毯式轰炸

carport /'kɑːpɔːt/ **noun** an open-sided shelter for a parked car 汽车棚

carriage /'kærɪdʒ/ noun **1** a four-wheeled horse-drawn vehicle for passengers (用于载客的)四轮马车 **2** a passenger vehicle in a train (火车)客车厢 **3** the carrying of goods from one place to another (货物)运输 **4** a person's way of standing or moving 仪态；举止 **5** a wheeled support for moving a gun (有轮的)炮架 □ **carriage clock** a portable clock with a handle on top 旅行钟

carriageway /'kærɪdʒweɪ/ noun **1** each of the two sides of a dual carriageway or motorway 单向行车道 **2** the part of a road intended for vehicles 车行道

carrier /'kærɪə(r)/ noun **1** a person or thing that carries or holds something 搬运者；携带者；运输工具 **2** a company that transports goods or people for payment 运输公司 □ **carrier bag** a plastic or paper bag with handles (塑料或纸制的)手提袋 **carrier pigeon** a homing pigeon trained to carry messages 信鸽

carrion /'kærɪən/ noun the decaying flesh of dead animals (动物尸体的)腐肉

carrot /'kærət/ noun **1** a tapering orange root vegetable 胡萝卜 **2** something tempting offered as a means of persuasion 诱饵

carry /'kæri/ verb (**carries**, **carrying**, **carried**) **1** move or take from one place to another 运送；运载 **2** support the weight of 支撑；承载 **3** take on or accept responsibility or blame 承担(责任)；承受(批评) **4** have a particular feature or result 带有；具有 **5** approve a proposal by a majority of votes (以多数票)通过，接受(提议) **6** publish or broadcast something 刊载；播出 **7** (of a sound or voice) travel a long way (声音)传送 **8** (**carry yourself**) stand and move in a particular way 保持姿态 **9** be pregnant with 怀孕 □ **be** (or **get**) **carried away** lose self-control 冲昏头脑；失去自我控制 **carry the can** informal 【非正式】 take responsibility for a mistake 承担责任 **carry something off** succeed in doing something 成功处理(某事) **carry on 1** continue with something 继续 **2** informal 【非正式】 have a love affair 有男女关系 **carry-on** informal 【非正式】 **1** a fuss 大惊小怪 **2** (also 亦作 **carryings-on**) improper behaviour 不当行为；不得体的举止 **carry something out** perform a task 执行(任务) **carry something through** manage to complete something 完成(某事)

carrycot /'kærikɒt/ noun a baby's small portable cot 便携式婴儿床

cart /kɑːt/ noun **1** an open horse-drawn vehicle for carrying goods or people (马拉的)大车 **2** a shallow open container on wheels, pulled or pushed by hand 小车；手推车 • verb **1** carry in a cart or similar vehicle 用大车运送 **2** informal 【非正式】 carry a heavy object with difficulty 费力地运送(重物)

carte blanche /ˌkɑːt 'blɑːnʃ/ noun complete freedom to act as you wish 全权；自由处置权

cartel /kɑː'tel/ noun an association of manufacturers or suppliers formed to keep prices high 卡特尔，同业联盟(制造商或供应商为维持高价格而组成的联盟)

carthorse /'kɑːθɔːs/ noun a large, strong horse suitable for heavy work (适于干重活的)拉车大马

cartilage /'kɑːtɪlɪdʒ/ noun firm, flexible tissue which covers the ends of joints and forms structures such as the external ear 软骨组织 ■ **cartilaginous** adjective.

cartography /kɑː'tɒɡrəfi/ noun the science or practice of drawing maps 地图学；地图绘制 ■ **cartographer** noun **cartographic** adjective.

carton /'kɑːtn/ noun a light cardboard

box or container 纸板盒；纸板箱

cartoon /kɑːˈtuːn/ **noun 1** a humorous drawing in a newspaper or magazine (报刊上的)漫画，幽默画 **2** (also **cartoon strip**) a sequence of cartoon drawings that tell a story 连环漫画 **3** a film made from a sequence of drawings, using animation techniques to give the appearance of movement 动画片，卡通片 **4** a fullsize drawing made as a preliminary design for a work of art (艺术品的)草图，底图 ■ **cartoonist** noun.

cartridge /ˈkɑːtrɪdʒ/ **noun 1** a container holding film, ink, etc., designed to be inserted into a mechanism such as a camera or printer (装胶卷的)暗盒；墨水囊；笔芯 **2** a casing containing explosives and a bullet or shot for a gun 弹壳，弹药筒 □ **cartridge paper** thick paper for drawing on (用于绘画的)厚纸

cartwheel /ˈkɑːtwiːl/ **noun** a sideways somersault performed with the arms and legs extended 侧手翻 ■ **verb** perform cartwheels 做侧手翻

carve /kɑːv/ **verb** (**carves**, **carving**, **carved**) **1** cut into a hard material to produce an object or design 刻，雕刻 **2** cut cooked meat into slices for eating (熟肉)切成片 **3** (**carve something out**) develop a career, reputation, etc. through great effort 奋斗取得(事业、名声等) **4** (**carve something up**) divide something up ruthlessly (无情地)瓜分，分割

carvery /ˈkɑːvəri/ **noun** (plural **carveries**) a restaurant where cooked joints of meat are carved as required 熟肉餐馆(按顾客要求现切熟肉的餐馆)

carving /ˈkɑːvɪŋ/ **noun** an object or design carved from wood or stone 雕刻品；雕刻图案

Casanova /ˌkæsəˈnəʊvə/ **noun** a man known for seducing many women 乱搞男女关系的男子；滥交的男子

casbah /ˈkæzbɑː/ ⇒ 见 **KASBAH**.

cascade /kæˈskeɪd/ **noun 1** a small waterfall 小瀑布 **2** a mass of something falling or hanging down 瀑布状物 ■ **verb** (**cascades**, **cascading**, **cascaded**) pour downwards in large quantities 瀑布般落下；倾泻而下

case[1] /keɪs/ **noun 1** an instance of something happening 事例，实例 **2** an incident being investigated by the police (警方正在调查的)案件 **3** a legal action decided in a court of law 诉讼；讼案 **4** a set of facts or arguments supporting one side of a debate or lawsuit (辩论或诉讼一方的)论据，事实 **5** a person or problem being given the attention of a doctor, social worker, etc. 患者；病症；(社会福利工作者的)帮助对象 **6** Grammar 【语法】 a form of a noun, adjective, or pronoun expressing the relationship of the word to others in the sentence 格 □ **in case** so as to allow for the possibility of something happening 以防万一；免得

case[2] **noun 1** a container or protective covering 箱；罩；保护性外壳 **2** a suitcase 衣箱；行李箱 **3** a box containing twelve bottles of wine (12瓶装的)酒箱 ■ **verb** (**cases**, **casing**, **cased**) **1** enclose in a case 把…装箱；把…装盒 **2** informal 【非正式】 examine a place before robbing it (实施抢劫前)探察，去…踩点

casement /ˈkeɪsmənt/ **noun** a window hinged at the side so that it opens like a door 门扇窗

cash /kæʃ/ **noun 1** money in coins or notes 硬币；纸币 **2** money available for use 现金；现钞 ■ **verb 1** give or receive notes or coins for a cheque or money order 把(支票或汇票)兑换成现金 **2** (**cash something in**) convert an insurance policy, savings account, etc. into money 把(保险单、账户存款等)兑换成现金 **3** (**cash in on**) informal 【非正式】 take advantage of

从…获利;利用 □ **cash crop** a crop produced for sale rather than for use by the grower 经济作物(用于出售而非种植者自己食用的农作物) **cash flow** the total amount of money passing into and out of a business 现金流;现金周转 **cash register** a machine used in shops for adding up and recording the amount of each sale and storing the money received (商店里使用的)现金出纳机,现金收出记录机

cashew /ˈkæʃuː/ *noun* an edible kidneyshaped nut 腰果

cashier /kæˈʃɪə(r)/ *noun* a person responsible for paying out and receiving money in a shop, bank, etc.(商店、银行等的)出纳员,收银员 • *verb* (**cashiers, cashiering, cashiered**) dismiss someone from the armed forces 革除…的军职

cashmere /ˈkæʃmɪə(r)/ *noun* fine, soft wool from a breed of Himalayan goat 开士米;山羊绒

casing /ˈkeɪsɪŋ/ *noun* a cover that protects or encloses something (保护或封用用的)套,罩,壳

casino /kəˈsiːnəʊ/ *noun* (plural **casinos**) a public building or room for gambling 赌场

cask /kɑːsk/ *noun* a large barrel for storing alcoholic drinks 大酒桶

casket /ˈkɑːskɪt/ *noun* **1** a small ornamental box or chest for holding valuable objects (放珠宝、带装饰的)小盒,小箱 **2** chiefly N. Amer.【北美】a coffin 棺;柩;骨灰盒

cassava /kəˈsɑːvə/ *noun* the root of a tropical American tree, used as food (用作食物的)木薯根茎

casserole /ˈkæsərəʊl/ *noun* **1** a large dish with a lid, used for cooking food slowly in an oven (文火烹制食物用的)炖锅,砂锅焙盘 **2** a kind of stew cooked slowly in an oven 炖烧菜;砂锅菜 • *verb* (**casseroles, casseroling, casseroled**) cook food in

a casserole 用焙盘烧;用砂锅煮

cassette /kəˈset/ *noun* a sealed plastic case containing audio tape, videotape, film, etc., designed to be inserted into a player or camera (内有磁带、录像带或胶卷等的)封闭小盒

cassock /ˈkæsək/ *noun* a long garment worn by Christian priests and members of church choirs (基督教牧师穿的)法衣;(教堂唱诗班成员穿的)长袍

cassowary /ˈkæsəwəri/ *noun* (plural **cassowaries**) a very large bird that cannot fly, found in New Guinea 鹤驼,食火鸡(不会飞的大型禽鸟,产于新几内亚)

cast /kɑːst/ *verb* (**casts, casting, cast**) **1** throw forcefully (用力)投,掷,抛 **2** make light or shadow appear on a surface 投射(光线或阴影) **3** direct your eyes or thoughts 把(目光或思绪)投向 **4** give a vote 投出(选票) **5** make a magic spell take effect 使(魔咒)应验 **6** throw a fishing line out into the water 抛渔线 **7** shed or discard 抛开;摆脱;打 消 **8** shape metal by pouring it into a mould while molten 浇铸(金属) **9** give a part to an actor, or allocate parts in a play or film 分派(演员)扮演角色;为(戏剧或电影)选角 • *noun* **1** the actors taking part in a play or film 演员;演员阵容 **2** (also **casting**) an object made by casting metal 铸件;铸造品 **3** a bandage stiffened with plaster of Paris to support and protect a broken limb (固定断骨用的)石膏绷带 **4** the appearance or character of a person or thing 容貌;特征;气质 **5** a slight squint (轻微的)斜视 □ **cast about** (or **around** or **round**) search far and wide 四处搜寻 **casting vote** an extra vote used by a chairperson to decide an issue when votes on each side are equal (当双方票数相同时由主席投出的)决定票 **cast iron** a hard alloy of iron and carbon which can be cast in a mould 铸铁 **cast off** release a boat or ship from its moorings 给(船只)解缆;解(船) **cast-off** abandoned or discarded 被抛弃的;被丢弃的

castanets /ˌkæstə'nets/ **plural noun** a pair of small curved pieces of wood, clicked together by the fingers to accompany Spanish dancing 响板(由一对弧形木片组成,通过用手指叩击为西班牙舞蹈伴奏)

castaway /'kɑːstəweɪ/ **noun** a person who has been shipwrecked in an isolated place (船只失事后)漂流到荒地的人

caste /kɑːst/ **noun** each of the classes of Hindu society (印度社会的)种姓,世袭等级

castellated /'kæstəleɪtɪd/ **adjective** having battlements 有城垛的;有雉堞的

castigate /'kæstɪgeɪt/ **verb** (**castigates, castigating, castigated**) tell someone off severely 谴责;训斥;严厉批评 ■ **castigation noun**.

castle /'kɑːsl/ **noun 1** a large fortified building of the medieval period (中世纪时期的)城堡,堡垒 **2** Chess【国际象棋】a rook 车 □ **castles in the air** dreams or plans that will never be achieved 空中楼阁;无法实现的计划

castor or **caster** /'kɑːstə(r)/ **noun 1** a small swivelling wheel fixed to the legs or base of a piece of furniture (安装在家具腿上或底部的)小脚轮 **2** a small container with holes in the top, used for sprinkling salt, sugar, etc. (用于撒盐、糖等的)调味瓶 □ **castor oil** oil from the seeds of an African shrub, used as a laxative 蓖麻油(用作轻泻剂) **castor sugar** white sugar in fine granules 精白砂糖

castrate /kæ'streɪt/ **verb** (**castrates, castrating, castrated**) **1** remove the testicles of 阉割 **2** make something less powerful or strong 使失去力量

■ **castration noun**.

casual /'kæʒuəl/ **adjective 1** relaxed and unconcerned 漠不关心的;不感兴趣的 **2** done without enough attention or proper planning 随意的;未经考虑的 **3** occasional or temporary 不定期的;偶发的;临时的: *casual work* 临时工作 **4** happening by chance; accidental 偶然的 **5** (of clothes) informal (服装)非正式的,休闲的 ■ **casually** adverb.

casualty /'kæʒuəlti/ **noun** (plural **casualties**) **1** a person killed or injured in a war or accident (战争或事故中的)伤亡人员 **2** a person or thing badly affected by an event or situation 受害者;受损物

casuistry /'kæʒuɪstri/ **noun** the use of clever but false reasoning 诡辩

cat /kæt/ **noun 1** a small furry animal kept as a pet 猫 **2** a wild animal related to this, such as a lion or tiger 猫科动物(如狮、虎) □ **cat burglar** a thief who enters a building by climbing to an upper storey 跃墙攀屋的窃贼;飞贼 **cat's paw** a person used by another to carry out an unpleasant task 被他人利用者 **the cat's whiskers** informal【非正式】an excellent person or thing 很好的人(或物) **let the cat out of the bag** reveal a secret by mistake (无意中)泄露秘密

cataclysm /'kætəklɪzəm/ **noun** a violent upheaval or disaster 大动乱;大灾难 ■ **cataclysmic** adjective.

catacomb /'kætəkuːm/ **noun** an underground cemetery consisting of tunnels with recesses for tombs (带地下走廊的)地下墓地

catalepsy /'kætəlepsi/ **noun** a condition in which a person becomes unconscious and goes rigid 强直性昏厥;僵住症

catalogue /'kætəlɒg/ (US spelling【美拼法】**catalog**) **noun 1** a list of items arranged in order (按顺序排列

的)目录 **2** a publication containing details of items for sale 商品目录册 **3** a series of bad things 一系列(坏事): *a catalogue of failures* 一系列失败 • verb (**catalogues, cataloguing, catalogued**; US spelling【美拼法】**catalogs, cataloging, cataloged**) list in a catalogue 把…编入目录

catalyse /ˈkætəlaɪz/ (US spelling【美拼法】**catalyze**) verb (**catalyses, catalysing, catalysed**) cause or speed up a reaction by acting as a catalyst 催化;促进

catalysis /kəˈtæləsɪs/ noun the speeding up of a chemical reaction by a catalyst 催化作用 ■ **catalytic** /kætəˈlɪtɪk/ adjective.

catalyst /ˈkætəlɪst/ noun **1** a substance that increases the rate of a chemical reaction while remaining unchanged itself 催化剂 **2** a person or thing that causes something to happen 触发事件的人(或事物);刺激因素

catalytic converter /kætəˈlɪtɪk/ noun a device in a motor vehicle which converts pollutant exhaust gases into less harmful ones (机动车辆排气装置上的)催化转化器, 催化式排气净化器

catamaran /kætəməˈræn/ noun a boat with twin parallel hulls 双体船; 双连船

catapult /ˈkætəpʌlt/ noun **1** a forked stick with elastic fastened to the two prongs, used for shooting small stones (叉杆等样式的)弹弓 **2** a device for launching a glider or aircraft (发射滑翔机或飞机的)弹射器 • verb **1** throw forcefully 猛掷;用力扔 **2** move suddenly or very fast 突然移动;快速移动

cataract /ˈkætərækt/ noun **1** a large waterfall 大瀑布 **2** a condition in which the lens of the eye becomes cloudy, resulting in blurred vision 白内障

catarrh /kəˈtɑː(r)/ noun excessive mucus in the nose or throat 鼻喉部黏液

catastrophe /kəˈtæstrəfi/ noun a sudden event that causes great damage or suffering 大灾难 ■ **catastrophic** adjective **catastrophically** adverb.

catatonia /kætəˈtəʊniə/ noun a condition in which a person experiences both periods of near unconsciousness and periods of overactivity 紧张症;紧张性精神分裂症 ■ **catatonic** adjective.

catcall /ˈkætkɔːl/ noun a shrill whistle or shout of mockery or disapproval (表示嘲笑或反对的)嘘声, 尖叫声 • verb make a catcall 发出嘘声;发出尖叫声

catch /kætʃ/ verb (**catches, catching, caught**) **1** seize and hold something moving 接住, 截住(运动物体) **2** capture a person or animal 捕获, 捉住(人或动物) **3** be in time to get on a vehicle or to see a person or event 及时赶上;来得及看 **4** entangle or become entangled (被)缠住 **5** surprise someone in the act of doing something wrong or embarrassing 当场发现, 撞见(做坏事或令人尴尬的事) **6** (**be caught in**) unexpectedly find yourself in an unwelcome situation 突然发现(自己处于困境) **7** see, hear, or understand 看见;听到;理解 **8** hit or strike 击打;击中 **9** become infected with an illness 染上 (疾病) **10** (**catching**) infectious (疾病)传染性的 • noun **1** an act of catching 接;抓;捉 **2** a device for fastening a door, window, etc. 门闩;窗钩 **3** a hidden problem 隐藏的问题 **4** a break in a person's voice caused by emotion (嗓音的)停顿, 哽塞 **5** an amount of fish caught (鱼的)捕获量 □ **catch on** informal 【非正式】 **1** become popular 流行起来;受欢迎 **2** understand 理解;领

悟 **catch someone out** discover that someone has done something wrong 发觉(某人)做错事 **catch-22** a difficult situation from which there is no escape because it involves conditions which conflict with each other 不可逾越的障碍；无法摆脱的困境 **catch up** do tasks which you should have done earlier 赶做(早就应该做的事情) **catch someone up** succeed in reaching a person ahead of you 赶上，追上(前面的人)

catchment area /'kætʃmənt/ **noun 1** the area from which a hospital's patients or a school's pupils are drawn (医院的)病人收治区；(学校的)生源区 **2** the area from which rainfall flows into a river, lake, or reservoir (河流或水库的)集水区，汇水盆地

catchphrase /'kætʃfreɪz/ **noun** a well-known sentence or phrase 流行语；时髦话

catchword /'kætʃwɜːd/ **noun** a word or phrase frequently used to sum something up 标语；口号

catchy /'kætʃi/ **adjective** (**catchier, catchiest**) (of a tune or phrase) appealing and easy to remember (曲调或短语)易记的

catechism /'kætəkɪzəm/ **noun** a summary of the principles of Christian religion in the form of questions and answers, used for teaching (基督教的)教理问答

categorical /ˌkætə'ɡɒrɪkl/ **adjective** completely clear and direct 非常明确的，直截了当的 ■ **categorically** adverb.

categorize or **categorise** /'kætəɡəraɪz/ **verb** (**categorizes, categorizing, categorized**) place in a category 把…归类 ■ **categorization** noun.

category /'kætəɡəri/ **noun** (plural **categories**) a class or group of people or things with shared char-

acteristics 种类；类别

cater /'keɪtə(r)/ **verb 1** (**cater for**) Brit. 【英】 provide food and drink at a social event 为…提供饮食；为…承办酒席 **2** (**cater for**) provide someone with what is needed 满足(需求) **3** (**cater to**) satisfy a need or demand 迎合，投合(需要) ■ **caterer** noun.

caterpillar /'kætəpɪlə(r)/ **noun** a creature like a small worm with legs, which develops into a butterfly or moth 毛虫(蝶或蛾的幼虫)

caterwaul /'kætəwɔːl/ **verb** make a shrill howling or wailing noise 号叫；尖叫

catgut /'kætɡʌt/ **noun** material used for the strings of musical instruments, made of the dried intestines of sheep or horses (制琴弦或缝合伤口的)肠线

catharsis /kə'θɑːsɪs/ **noun** the process of releasing strong but pent-up emotions in such a way as to free yourself of them (被压抑感情的)宣泄，释放 ■ **cathartic** adjective.

cathedral /kə'θiːdrəl/ **noun** the most important church of a diocese (district) 教区总教堂；大教堂

Catherine wheel /'kæθrɪn/ **noun** Brit. 【英】 a firework in the form of a spinning coil 凯瑟琳车轮式焰火

catheter /'kæθɪtə(r)/ **noun** a tube that is inserted into a body cavity to drain fluid (插入体腔排液用的)导管

cathode /'kæθəʊd/ **noun** an electrode with a negative charge 阴极；负极 ▫ **cathode ray tube** a tube in which beams of electrons produce a luminous image on a screen, as in a television 阴极射线管

catholic /'kæθlɪk/ **adjective 1** including a wide variety of things 包罗万象的；无所不包的 **2** (**Catholic**) Roman Catholic 天主教的 ● **noun** (**Catholic**) a Roman Catholic 天主教教徒 ■ **Catholicism** noun.

cation /'kætaɪən/ **noun** an ion with a

positive charge 阳离子

catkin /'kætkɪn/ **noun** a spike of small, soft flowers hanging from trees such as willow and hazel 柔荑花序(垂于柳树、榛树等枝头的软毛花穗)

catnap /'kætnæp/ **noun** a short sleep during the day (日间的)小睡、瞌睡、打盹儿

catseye /'kætsaɪ/ **noun** Brit. trademark 【英,商标】each of a series of reflective studs marking the lanes or edges of a road "猫眼"反光镜

catsuit /'kætsuːt/ **noun** a woman's close-fitting one-piece garment with trouser legs 女式紧身连衣裤

cattery /'kætərɪ/ **noun** (plural **catteries**) a place where cats are kept while their owners are away (主人不在家时临时寄养猫的)猫屋、猫窝

cattle /'kætl/ **plural noun** cows, bulls, and oxen 牛

catty /'kætɪ/ **adjective** (**cattier**, **cattiest**) spiteful 恶毒的

catwalk /'kætwɔːk/ **noun 1** a narrow platform along which models walk to display clothes (时装模特走的)T型舞台 **2** a narrow raised walkway 狭窄通道

Caucasian /kɔː'keɪʒən/ **adjective 1** relating to peoples from Europe, western Asia, and parts of India and North Africa 高加索人的 **2** white-skinned 白种人的 • **noun** a Caucasian person 高加索人

caucus /'kɔːkəs/ **noun** (plural **caucuses**) **1** a meeting of a policymaking group of a political party (政党的)决策委员会会议 **2** a group of people within a larger organization who have similar interests (大机构内部的)核心成员、核心小组

caught /kɔːt/ past and past participle of **CATCH**.

caul /kɔːl/ **noun** a membrane that encloses an unborn baby in the womb 胎头羊膜

cauldron /'kɔːldrən/ (US spelling 【美拼作】 **caldron**) **noun** a large metal cooking pot (用于烹饪的)大锅

cauliflower /'kɒlɪflaʊə(r)/ **noun** a vegetable with a large white edible flower head 花椰菜；花菜

caulk /kɔːk/ (US spelling 【美拼作】 **calk**) **noun** a waterproof substance used to fill cracks and seal joins 防水填料；防渗漏剂

causal /'kɔːzl/ **adjective** relating to or being a cause 原因的；构成原因的 ■ **causally** adverb **causality** noun.

causation /kɔː'zeɪʃn/ **noun** the process of causing an effect 引起结果；产生效果 ■ **causative** adjective.

cause /kɔːz/ **noun 1** a person or thing that produces an effect 引起结果的人(或事物)；起因 **2** a good reason for thinking or doing something 原因；理由 **3** a principle or movement 事业；运动 • **verb** (**causes**, **causing**, **caused**) make something happen 使发生

causeway /'kɔːzweɪ/ **noun** a raised road or track across low or wet ground (穿过低地或湿地的)堤道

caustic /'kɔːstɪk/ **adjective 1** able to burn through or wear away something by chemical action 腐蚀性的 **2** sarcastic in a hurtful way 尖刻的；讽刺的 □ **caustic soda** sodium hydroxide, used in industrial processes, such as soapmaking 苛性钠；烧碱 ■ **caustically** adverb.

cauterize or **cauterise** /'kɔːtəraɪz/ **verb** (**cauterizes**, **cauterizing**, **cauterized**) burn the area round a wound to stop bleeding or prevent infection (为止血或防止感染)烧灼(伤口)

caution /'kɔːʃn/ **noun 1** care taken to avoid danger or mistakes 慎重；谨慎 **2** a warning to the public (对公众的)警告 **3** Brit. 【英】an official or legal warning given to someone who has committed a minor offence (正式给予的)警告 • **verb 1** warn or advise someone 警告；劝告 **2** give someone a legal caution 给予法律警告

cautionary /'kɔːʃənəri/ **adjective** acting as a warning 警告的；告诫的

cautious /'kɔːʃəs/ **adjective** taking care to avoid possible problems or dangers 谨慎的；小心的 ■ **cautiously** adverb.

cavalcade /ˌkævl'keɪd/ **noun** a procession of vehicles or people on horseback 车队；骑手队列

cavalier /ˌkævə'lɪə(r)/ **noun** (**Cavalier**) a supporter of King Charles I in the English Civil War (英国内战时期支持查理一世的)保王党成员 • **adjective** showing a lack of proper concern 不在乎的；漫不经心的

cavalry /'kævlri/ **noun** (plural **cavalries**) (in the past) the part of the army that fought on horseback (旧时的)骑兵(部队) ■ **cavalryman** noun.

cave /keɪv/ **noun** a large natural hollow in the side of a hill or cliff, or underground 山洞；洞穴；地穴 • **verb** (**caves**, **caving**, **caved**) **1** (**cave in**) give way or collapse 塌落；坍塌 **2** (**cave in**) give in to demands 放弃；屈服 **3** (**caving**) the exploring of caves as a sport 探察洞穴(运动)

caveat /'kæviæt/ **noun** a warning 警告；告诫

cavern /'kævən/ **noun** a large cave 大洞穴

cavernous /'kævənəs/ **adjective** huge, spacious, or gloomy 深邃的；宽敞的；幽暗的

caviar or **caviare** /'kæviɑː(r)/ **noun** the pickled roe of the sturgeon (a large fish) (鲟鱼子制作的)鱼子酱

cavil /'kævl/ **verb** (**cavils**, **cavilling**, **cavilled**; US spelling【美拼作】**cavils**, **caviling**, **caviled**) make unnecessary complaints 吹毛求疵；挑剔 • **noun** an unnecessary complaint 吹毛求疵的意见

cavity /'kævəti/ **noun** (plural **cavities**)

1 a hollow space inside something solid (固体内的)洞，穴 **2** a decayed part of a tooth (牙齿的)龋洞

cavort /kə'vɔːt/ **verb** jump or dance around excitedly 乱跳乱蹦；雀跃

caw /kɔː/ **verb** make a harsh cry 呱呱地叫

cayenne /keɪ'en/ **noun** a hot-tasting red powder made from dried chillies 红辣椒粉

CBE /ˌsiː biː 'iː/ **abbreviation** Commander of the Order of the British Empire 二等高级英帝国勋爵士

cc or **c.c.** /ˌsiː 'siː/ **abbreviation 1** carbon copy. **2** cubic centimeters 立方厘米

CCTV /ˌsiː siː tiː 'viː/ **abbreviation** closed-circuit television.

CD /ˌsiː 'diː/ **abbreviation** compact disc.

CD-ROM /ˌsiː diː 'rɒm/ **abbreviation** a compact disc storing large amounts of information, used in a computer (ROM stands for 'read-only memory') (计算机的)光盘只读存储器

CDT /ˌsiː diː 'tiː/ **abbreviation** craft, design, and technology (as a school subject) 设计和技术(课程)

cease /siːs/ **verb** (**ceases**, **ceasing**, **ceased**) come or bring to an end; stop 终止；停止

ceasefire /'siːsfaɪə(r)/ **noun** a temporary period during a conflict when fighting stops (暂时的)停战期，停火期

ceaseless /'siːsləs/ **adjective** not stopping 不停的；无休止的 ■ **ceaselessly** adverb.

cedar /'siːdə(r)/ **noun** a tall evergreen tree with sweet-smelling wood 雪松

cede /siːd/ **verb** (**cedes**, **ceding**, **ceded**) give up power or territory 放弃(权力)；割让(领土)

cedilla /sɪ'dɪlə/ **noun** a mark (¸) written under the letter c to show that it is pronounced like an *s* (e.g. soupçon) 下加符(加在字母 c 下面，表示该字母读 /s/)

ceilidh /'keɪli/ **noun** a party with Scottish or Irish folk music and dancing 同乐会(有苏格兰或爱尔兰歌舞的社交聚会)

ceiling /'siːlɪŋ/ **noun 1** the top surface of a room 天花板 **2** a top limit set on prices, wages, or spending (价格、工资或花费等的)最高限额，上限

✔ 拼写指南 *i* before *e* except after *c*: ceiling. *i* 置于 e 前，在 c 后时除外，如 ceiling.

celebrate /'selɪbreɪt/ **verb** (**celebrates, celebrating, celebrated**) mark an important occasion by doing something special 歌颂；颂扬 ■ **celebration noun celebratory adjective.**

celebrity /sə'lebrəti/ **noun** (plural **celebrities**) **1** a famous person 名人，名流 **2** the state of being famous 著名，有名

celeriac /sə'leriæk/ **noun** a vegetable with a large edible root 块根芹(根部可食用)

celerity /sə'lerəti/ **noun** old use 【旧】 speed of movement 迅速

celery /'seləri/ **noun** a vegetable with crisp juicy stalks 芹菜

celestial /sə'lestiəl/ **adjective 1** relating to heaven 天国的 **2** relating to the sky or outer space 天空的；太空的

celibate /'selɪbət/ **adjective** not married or in a sexual relationship 独身的；禁欲的 ■ **celibacy noun.**

cell /sel/ **noun 1** a small room for a prisoner, monk, or nun (关押囚犯的)单人牢房；(修士或修女住的)小房间 **2** the smallest unit of a living thing 细胞 **3** a small political group that is part of a larger organization (政治组织的)基层单位 **4** a device for producing electricity by chemical action or light 电池

cellar /'selə(r)/ **noun 1** a room below ground level, used for storage 地窖；地下室 **2** a stock of wine 窖藏的酒

cello /'tʃeləʊ/ **noun** (plural **cellos**) an instrument like a large violin, held upright on the floor between the legs of the seated player 大提琴 ■ **cellist noun.**

cellophane /'seləfeɪn/ **noun** trademark 【商标】 a thin transparent wrapping material 赛璐玢；玻璃纸

cellphone /'selfəʊn/ **noun** a mobile phone 蜂窝电话；移动电话；手机

cellular /'seljələ(r)/ **adjective 1** relating to or made up of cells 细胞的；由细胞构成的 **2** (of a mobile phone system) using a number of short-range radio stations to cover the area it serves (移动电话系统)蜂窝式的(由许多短程无线通信基站覆盖服务区)

cellulite /'seljulaɪt/ **noun** fat that builds up under the skin, causing a dimpled effect (皮下)脂肪团

celluloid /'seljulɔɪd/ **noun** a kind of transparent plastic formerly used for cinema film 赛璐珞，明胶(一种透明塑料，曾用于制作电影胶片)

cellulose /'seljuləʊs/ **noun** a substance found in all plant tissues, used in making paint, plastics, and fibres 植物纤维素(用于制作涂料、塑料和人造纤维)

Celsius /'selsiəs/ **noun** a scale of temperature on which water freezes at 0° and boils at 100° 摄氏温标

Celt /kelt/ **noun** a member of a people who lived in Britain and elsewhere in Europe before the Romans arrived 凯尔特人(在罗马人之前居住于英国和欧洲其他地区)

Celtic /'keltɪk/ **noun** a group of languages including Irish, Scottish Gaelic, and Welsh 凯尔特语 • **adjective** relating to Celtic languages or to the Celts 凯尔特语的；凯尔特人的

cement /sɪ'ment/ **noun** a powdery substance made by heating lime and clay, used in making mortar and concrete 水泥 • **verb 1** fix with cement 用水泥固定 **2** make something stronger 加固；巩固

cemetery /'semətri/ **noun** (plural **cemeteries**) a large burial ground 大墓地；公墓

> ✔ **拼写指南** -*tery*, not -*try* or -*tary*: ceme*tery*. cemetery 中，-tery 不要拼作 -try 或 -tary.

cenotaph /'senətɑːf/ **noun** a monument built to honour soldiers killed in a war (为阵亡战士立的)纪念碑

censer /'sensə(r)/ **noun** a container in which incense is burnt 香炉

censor /'sensə(r)/ **noun** a person who examines films, books, or documents and bans unacceptable parts (电影、书籍或文件的)审查者，检查员 • **verb** ban unacceptable parts of a film, book, or document 修改，删节(电影、书籍或文件中不适宜的内容) ■ **censorship** noun.

censorious /sen'sɔːriəs/ **adjective** very critical 严厉批评的

censure /'senʃə(r)/ **verb** (**censures**, **censuring**, **censured**) criticize strongly 严厉批评；谴责 • **noun** strong disapproval or criticism 强烈反对；严厉批评

census /'sensəs/ **noun** (plural **censuses**) an official count of a population (官方的)人口普查，人口调查

cent /sent/ **noun** a unit of money equal to one hundredth of a dollar, euro, or other decimal currency unit 分(美元、欧元或其他十进制货币单位的1/100)

centaur /'sentɔː(r)/ **noun** (in Greek mythology) a creature with a man's head, arms, and upper body and a horse's lower body and legs (希腊神话中的)半人半马怪物

centenarian /ˌsentɪ'neəriən/ **noun** a person who has reached one hundred years of age 百岁老人

centenary /sen'tiːnəri/ **noun** (plural **centenaries**) Brit. 【英】the hundredth anniversary of an event 一百周年纪念(日)

centennial /sen'teniəl/ **adjective** relating to a hundredth anniversary 百年纪念的 • **noun** a hundredth anniversary 一百周年纪念(日)

center /'sentə(r)/ US spelling of CENTRE. centre 的美式拼法

centigrade /'sentɪɡreɪd/ **adjective** measured by the Celsius scale of temperature 摄氏温度的

centilitre /'sentɪliːtə(r)/ (US spelling 【美拼作】**centiliter**) **noun** a metric unit equal to one hundredth of a litre 厘升(公制容量单位，等于1/100升)

centime /'sɒntiːm/ **noun** a unit of money equal to one hundredth of a franc 分(等于1/100法郎)

centimetre /'sentɪmiːtə(r)/ (US spelling 【美拼作】**centimeter**) **noun** a metric unit equal to one hundredth of a metre 厘米(公制长度单位，等于1/100米)

centipede /'sentɪpiːd/ **noun** an insect-like creature with a long, thin body and many legs 百足虫，蜈蚣

central /'sentrəl/ **adjective 1** in or near the centre 中央的；接近中心的 **2** very important 极其重要的；至关重要的 □ **central heating** heating conducted from a boiler through pipes and radiators 中央供暖系统；集中供暖系统 **central nervous system** the system of nerve tissues in the brain and spinal cord in vertebrates 中枢神经系统 ■ **centrally** adverb.

centralize or **centralise** /'sentrəlaɪz/ **verb** (**centralizes**, **centralizing**, **centralized**) bring under the control of a central authority 使处于中央集权下 ■ **centralization** noun.

centre /'sentə(r)/ (US spelling 【美拼作】**center**) **noun 1** a point in the middle of something 中点；中心；中央 **2** a place where a particular activity takes place (某种活动的)中心(地区) **3** a point from which something spreads or to which something is directed 核心；发源地 • verb (**centres, centring, centred**；US spelling【美拼式】**centers, centering, centered**) **1** place in the centre 把…置于中心 **2** (**centre on** or **around**) have as a main concern or theme 使成为中心 □ **centre back** (or **centre half**) (in soccer) a defender who plays in the middle of the field (足球运动中的) 中后卫，中前卫 **centre forward** (in soccer) an attacker who plays in the middle of the field (足球运动中的) 中锋 **centre of gravity** the central point in an object, around which its mass is evenly distributed 重心

centrefold /ˈsentəfəʊld/ **noun** the two middle pages of a magazine, usually containing a special feature (杂志的) 中间跨页，折叠插页

centrepiece /ˈsentəpiːs/ **noun** an item that is designed to have people's attention focused on it 引人注目的事物

centrifugal force /ˈsentrɪˈfjuːgl/ **noun** a force which appears to cause something travelling round a central point to fly outwards from its circular path 离心力

centurion /senˈtjʊəriən/ **noun** a commander of one hundred men in the army of ancient Rome (古罗马军队的)百夫长，百人队队长

century /ˈsentʃəri/ **noun** (plural **centuries**) **1** a period of one hundred years 世纪，百年 **2** a batsman's score of a hundred runs in cricket (板球击球手的)一百分 **3** a unit of a hundred men in the army of ancient Rome (古罗马军队的)百人队

ceramic /səˈræmɪk/ **adjective** made of fired clay 陶制的 • **noun** (**ceramics**) the art of making ceramic articles 制陶工艺

cereal /ˈsɪəriəl/ **noun 1** a grass producing an edible grain, such as wheat, oats, maize, or rye (食用的)

谷类植物 **2** a breakfast food made from the grain of cereals 谷物早餐食品

cerebellum /ˌserəˈbeləm/ **noun** (plural **cerebellums** or **cerebella** /ˌserəˈbelə/) the part of the brain at the back of the skull 小脑

cerebral /ˈserəbrəl/ **adjective 1** relating to the brain 脑的；大脑的 **2** intellectual rather than emotional or physical 智力的；用脑筋的 □ **cerebral palsy** a condition in which a person has difficulty in controlling their muscles 大脑性麻痹

cerebrum /ˈserɪbrəm/ **noun** (plural **cerebra**) the main part of the brain, in the front of the skull 大脑

ceremonial /ˌserɪˈməʊniəl/ **adjective** relating to or used in ceremonies 礼节的；仪式的 ■ **ceremonially** adverb.

ceremonious /ˌserɪˈməʊniəs/ **adjective** done in a formal and grand way 讲究礼仪的；隆重的 ■ **ceremoniously** adverb.

ceremony /ˈserəməni/ **noun** (plural **ceremonies**) a formal occasion during which a set of special acts are performed 典礼；仪式 □ **stand on ceremony** behave formally 坚持礼节；拘礼

cerise /səˈriːs/ **noun** a light pinkish-red colour 鲜红色；樱桃红

cerium /ˈsɪəriəm/ **noun** a silvery-white metallic element (金属元素)铈

certain /ˈsɜːtn/ **adjective 1** able to be relied on to happen or be the case 肯定的；无可争议的 **2** completely sure about something 确信的；有把握的 **3** specific but not directly named or stated 某个；某些 • **pronoun** some but not all 有些；某些

certainly /ˈsɜːtnli/ **adverb 1** without doubt; definitely 无疑地；肯定地 **2** yes 当然；行

certainty /ˈsɜːtnti/ **noun** (plural **certainties**) **1** the state of being certain 确信；肯定 **2** a fact that is true or an event that is definitely going to take place 肯定无疑的事实；必然的事

certifiable /ˈsɜːtɪfaɪəbl/ **adjective** able or needing to be officially declared insane 可证明患有精神病的；需要证明患有精神病的

certificate /səˈtɪfɪkət/ **noun 1** an official document recording a particular fact, event, or achievement 证明；证书 **2** an official classification given to a cinema film, saying which age group it is suitable for (电影的)官方分级 ■ **certification** noun.

certify /ˈsɜːtɪfaɪ/ **verb** (**certifies**, **certifying**, **certified**) **1** declare or confirm in a certificate or other official document (用证书)证明，证实 **2** officially declare someone insane 正式证明(某人)精神失常

certitude /ˈsɜːtɪtjuːd/ **noun** a feeling of complete certainty 确信；深信

cervical /ˈsɜːvɪkl/ **adjective** relating to the cervix 子宫颈的 □ **cervical smear** a specimen of cells taken from the neck of the womb and examined for signs of cancer 子宫颈涂片(取自子宫颈上的细胞样本，用以检测癌细胞)

cervix /ˈsɜːvɪks/ **noun** (plural **cervices** /ˈsɜːvɪsiːz/) the narrow neck-like passage between the lower end of the womb and the vagina 子宫颈

Cesarean /sɪˈzeərɪən/ US spelling of CAESAREAN. Caesarean 的美式拼法

cessation /seˈseɪʃn/ **noun** the stopping of something 停止；休止

cession /ˈseʃn/ **noun** the giving up of rights or territory by a state (权利的)放弃；(领土的)割让

cesspool /ˈsespuːl/ or **cesspit** /ˈsespɪt/ **noun** an underground tank or covered pit where sewage is collected 污水池；化粪池

cetacean /sɪˈteɪʃn/ **noun** the name in zoology for a whale or dolphin 鲸目动物(包括鲸、海豚)

cf. /ˌsiː ˈef/ **abbreviation** compare with 比较；参见 [short for Latin 【缩写，拉丁】 = confer, meaning 'compare'.]

CFC /ˌsiː ef ˈsiː/ **abbreviation** chlorofluorocarbon, a gas used in fridges and aerosols that is harmful to the ozone layer 含氯氟烃(用于冰箱和气雾剂中，对大气臭氧层具有破坏作用)

CFE /ˌsiː ef ˈiː/ **abbreviation** College of Further Education 继续教育学院；进修学院

chador /ˈtʃɑːdɔː(r)/ **noun** a piece of dark cloth worn by Muslim women around the head and upper body (穆斯林妇女裹住头部和上半身的)黑色披风

chafe /tʃeɪf/ **verb** (**chafes**, **chafing**, **chafed**) **1** make something sore or worn by rubbing against it 擦痛，擦破 **2** rub a part of the body to warm it 擦热(身体部位) **3** become impatient because of restrictions (因受限制而)烦躁，生气

chaff[1] /tʃɑːf/ **noun** husks of grain that have been separated from the seed 谷壳；糠

chaff[2] **verb** tease someone 戏弄；取笑

chaffinch /ˈtʃæfɪntʃ/ **noun** a small finch (songbird) with a pink breast 苍头燕雀(胸部粉红色)

chagrin /ˈʃæɡrɪn/ **noun** a feeling of disappointment or annoyance 失望，烦恼 ■ **verb** (**be chagrined**) feel disappointed or annoyed 觉得失望，觉得烦恼

chain /tʃeɪn/ **noun 1** a series of connected metal links 链条；链子 **2** a connected series, set, or sequence 一系列；一套；一连串 ■ **verb** fasten or restrain with a chain 用链条固定；用链子束缚 □ **chain mail** armour made of small metal rings linked together 锁子甲 **chain reaction** a series of events, each caused by the previous one (事件的)连锁反应 **chain-smoke** smoke cigarettes one after the other

一支接一支地抽(烟) **chain store** each of a series of shops owned by one firm 连锁店

chainsaw /'tʃeɪnsɔː/ **noun** a power-driven saw with teeth set on a moving chain 链锯

chair /tʃeə(r)/ **noun 1** a seat for one person, with a back and four legs 椅子;座椅 **2** a person in charge of a meeting or an organization (会议或机构的)主席 **3** a post as professor 教授职位 • **verb** be in charge of a meeting 担任(会议的)主席;主持(会议)

chairlift /'tʃeəlɪft/ **noun** a lift for carrying skiers up and down a mountain, consisting of a series of chairs hung from a moving cable (运送滑雪者上下山的)架空吊椅,升降椅

chairman /'tʃeəmən/ or **chairwoman** /'tʃeəwʊmən/ **noun** (plural **chairmen** or **chairwomen**) a person in charge of a meeting or organization (会议或机构的)主席

chairperson /'tʃeəpɜːsn/ **noun** a person in charge of a meeting (会议的)主席

chaise longue /ˌʃeɪz 'lɒŋ/ **noun** (plural **chaises longues** /ˌʃeɪz 'lɒŋ/) a sofa with a backrest at only one end 睡椅;躺椅

chalet /'ʃæleɪ/ **noun 1** a wooden house with overhanging eaves, found in the Swiss Alps (见于瑞士阿尔卑斯山、带悬垂屋檐的)木屋 **2** a wooden cabin used by holiday-makers (度假者住的)小木屋

chalice /'tʃælɪs/ **noun** a large cup or glass for wine (高脚)酒杯

chalk /tʃɔːk/ **noun 1** a soft white limestone 白垩 **2** a similar substance made into sticks and used for drawing or writing 粉笔 • **verb** draw or write with chalk 用粉笔画(或写) □ **by a long chalk** by far 远远地 **chalk something up** achieve something noteworthy 达到;获得 ■ **chalkiness**

noun chalky adjective.

challenge /'tʃælɪndʒ/ **noun 1** an interesting but difficult task or situation 具挑战性的任务;艰巨的任务 **2** an invitation to someone to take part in a contest or to prove something 比赛邀请;质疑 • **verb** (**challenges**, **challenging**, **challenged**) **1** raise doubt as to whether something is true or genuine 对…提出质疑 **2** call on someone to fight or do something difficult 向…挑战 **3** (of a guard) call on someone to prove their identity (警卫)查问…的身份 ■ **challenger** noun.

challenging /'tʃælɪndʒɪŋ/ **adjective** testing your abilities in an interesting way 挑战性的

chamber /'tʃeɪmbə(r)/ **noun 1** a large room used for formal or public events 大厅;会议厅 **2** each of the houses of a parliament (议会的)议院 **3** (**chambers**) rooms used by a barrister 律师事务所 **4** old use 【旧】a bedroom 卧室;寝室 **5** a hollow space inside something 洞穴;空隙 **6** the part of a gun bore that contains the explosive (枪的)弹膛,药室 □ **chamber music** classical music played by a small group of musicians 室内乐(由小型乐团演奏的古典乐曲) **chamber pot** a bowl kept in a bedroom and used as a toilet 夜壶

chamberlain /'tʃeɪmbəlɪn/ **noun** (in the past) a person who looked after the household of a king or queen, or a noble (旧时的)王宫内侍,贵族管家

chambermaid /'tʃeɪmbəmeɪd/ **noun** a woman who cleans rooms in a hotel (旅馆中的)客房女服务员

chameleon /kə'miːliən/ **noun** a small lizard that is able to change colour to fit in with its surroundings 变色蜥蜴;变色龙

chamfer /'tʃæmfə(r)/ **verb** (**chamfers**, **chamfering**, **chamfered**) (in carpentry) cut an angled edge on a piece of wood (木工工艺中)将…削角,将…切成斜面

chamois /'ʃæmwɑː/ noun (plural **chamois** /'ʃæmwɑː, 'ʃæmwɑːz/) an antelope that lives in the mountains of southern Europe (南欧山区的)岩羚羊 □ **chamois leather** very soft leather made from the skin of sheep, goats, or deer 软羊皮;软鹿皮;麂皮

chamomile /'kæməmaɪl/ ➾ 见 CAMO-MILE.

champ /tʃæmp/ verb munch noisily 大声咀嚼 □ **champ at the bit** be very impatient 烦躁不安;迫不及待

champagne /ʃæm'peɪn/ noun a white sparkling wine from the Champagne region of France 香槟酒

champion /'tʃæmpɪən/ noun 1 a person who has won a contest (竞赛的)冠军 2 a person who argues or fights for a cause 捍卫者;拥护者;斗士 • verb argue or fight in support of a cause 捍卫;拥护 • adjective informal or dialect 【非正式或方】excellent 极好的;出众的

championship /'tʃæmpɪənʃɪp/ noun a competition for the position of champion (体育)锦标赛

chance /tʃɑːns/ noun 1 (also **chances**) a possibility of something happening 可能;机会 2 an opportunity 机会 3 the way that things happen without any obvious plan or cause 偶然性: They met by chance. 他们是偶然相遇的。• verb (**chances, chancing, chanced**) 1 happen to do something 偶然发生;碰巧做 2 informal【非正式】do something even though it is risky 冒险做 □ **on the off chance** just in case 对…抱有一线希望

chancel /'tʃɑːnsl/ noun the part of a church near the altar, where the choir sits (教堂的)圣坛

chancellor /'tʃɑːnsələ(r)/ noun 1 a senior state or legal official 大臣;大法官 2 (**Chancellor**) the head of

the government in some European countries (一些欧洲国家的)总理 □ **Chancellor of the Exchequer** (in the UK) the government minister in charge of the country's finances (英国的)财政大臣

chancer /'tʃɑːnsə(r)/ noun informal 【非正式】a person who makes the most of any opportunity 冒险家;机会主义者

chancy /'tʃɑːnsi/ adjective (**chancier, chanciest**) informal 【非正式】uncertain and risky 不确定的;有风险的

chandelier /ʃændə'lɪə(r)/ noun an ornamental hanging light with holders for several candles or light bulbs 枝形吊灯

chandler /'tʃɑːndlə(r)/ noun a person who buys and sells supplies and equipment for ships and boats 船具商 ■ **chandlery** noun.

change /tʃeɪndʒ/ verb (**changes, changing, changed**) 1 make or become different (使)变化;(使)改变 2 exchange one thing for something else 交换 3 (**change over**) move from one system or situation to another 改换;变更 4 exchange a sum of money for the same sum in a different currency or different units 兑换(外币) • noun 1 a process through which something becomes different 改变;变化;变更 2 money returned as the balance of the amount paid or given in exchange for the same amount in larger units 零钱;找头 3 coins as opposed to banknotes (与纸币相对的)硬币 4 a clean set of clothes (干净的)衣物 □ **change hands** pass to a different owner 转手;易主

changeable /'tʃeɪndʒəbl/ adjective 1 likely to change in an unpredictable way 易变的;不确定的 2 able to be changed 可改变的

changeling /'tʃeɪndʒlɪŋ/ noun a child believed to have been left by fairies in exchange for the parents' real child (被仙女) 偷换后留下的孩子

changeover /'tʃeɪndʒəʊvə(r)/ **noun** a change from one system or situation to another (制度或情况的) 改变, 变更

channel /'tʃænl/ **noun 1** a band of frequencies used in radio and television broadcasting (广播或电视的) 波段, 频道 **2** a means of communication 交际手段; 沟通渠道 **3** a wide stretch of water joining two seas 海峡 **4** a passage along which liquid flows (液体流通的) 管道, 水道 **5** a passage that boats can pass through in a stretch of water 河床; 河槽 **6** an electric circuit which acts as a path for a signal (信号传输的) 信道 • **verb** (**channels**, **channelling**, **channelled**; US spelling 【美拼作】 **channels**, **channeling**, **channeled**) **1** direct something towards a particular purpose 引导; 把…导向 **2** pass along or through a particular channel (通过某种渠道) 输送, 传送

chant /tʃɑːnt/ **noun 1** a repeated rhythmic phrase that is called out or sung to music 反复吟诵的话语; 反复呼唱的歌曲 **2** a tune to which the words of psalms are fitted by singing several syllables or words to the same note 圣歌 • **verb** say, shout, or sing in a chant 反复说; 反复喊; 反复唱

Chanukkah /'hɑːnukɑː, -nəkə/ ⇒ 见 **HANUKKAH**.

chaos /'keɪɒs/ **noun** complete confusion and disorder 混乱; 紊乱

chaotic /keɪ'ɒtɪk/ **adjective** in a state of complete confusion and disorder 混乱的; 紊乱的 ■ **chaotically** adverb.

chap /tʃæp/ **noun** informal 【非正式】 a man or boy 男人; 男孩

chapatti /tʃə'pɑːti/ **noun** (plural **chapattis**) (in Indian cookery) a flat round piece of unleavened bread (印度烹饪中的) 薄煎饼

chapel /'tʃæpl/ **noun 1** a small building or room used for prayers 小教堂; 祈祷室 **2** a part of a large church with its own altar (带祭坛的大教堂的) 礼拜堂

chaperone /'ʃæpərəʊn/ **noun 1** a person who accompanies and looks after another person or group of people 陪伴者 **2** dated 【废】 an older woman in charge of an unmarried girl at social occasions (在社交场合陪伴未婚少女的) 年长女伴 • **verb** (**chaperones**, **chaperoning**, **chaperoned**) go with and look after 陪伴; 监护

chaplain /'tʃæplɪn/ **noun** a minister of the church attached to a chapel in an institution or military unit, or a private house (机构或军队、私人家庭的) 牧师 ■ **chaplaincy** noun.

chapped /tʃæpt/ **adjective** (of the skin) cracked and sore through exposure to cold weather (皮肤) 皲裂的

chapter /'tʃæptə(r)/ **noun 1** a main division of a book (书的) 章, 篇 **2** a particular period in history or in a person's life (历史或人生的) 时代, 时期 **3** the group of people in charge of a cathedral or other religious community (大教堂或其他宗教团体的) 教士会 **4** chiefly N. Amer. 【主北美】 a local branch of a society (社团的) 地方分会, 支部

char[1] /tʃɑː(r)/ **verb** (**chars**, **charring**, **charred**) partially burn something so as to blacken the surface 把…烧焦

char[2] **noun** informal 【非正式】 a woman employed as a cleaner in a private house 打杂女工; 女勤杂工

char[3] **noun** informal 【非正式】 tea 茶

character /'kærəktə(r)/ **noun 1** the particular qualities that make a person or thing an individual and different from others 性格; 特点, 特色 **2** strong personal qualities such as courage and determination 勇气; 决心 **3** a person's good reputation (好

的)名誉,名声 **4** a person in a novel, play, or film (小说、戏剧或电影中的)人物,角色 **5** informal【非正式】an eccentric or amusing person 古怪的人;有趣的人 **6** a printed or written letter or symbol (印刷或书写的)字体,符号 ■ **characterful** adjective **characterless** adjective.

characteristic /ˌkærəktəˈrɪstɪk/ **noun** a quality typical of a person or thing 特点;特征;特色 • **adjective** typical of a particular person or thing 典型的,特有的 ■ **characteristically** adverb.

characterize or **characterise** /ˈkærəktəraɪz/ **verb** (**characterizes, characterizing, characterized**) **1** describe the character of 描绘…的特征 **2** be typical of 是…的特征;以…为特征 ■ **characterization** noun.

charade /ʃəˈrɑːd/ **noun 1** a pretence that something is true when it is clearly not 装模作样 **2** (**charades**) a game of guessing a word or phrase from clues that are acted out 字谜游戏;猜字游戏

charcoal /ˈtʃɑːkəʊl/ **noun 1** a form of carbon obtained when wood is burned slowly with little air 木炭 **2** a dark grey-black colour 深灰色

chard /tʃɑːd/ **noun** a vegetable with large leaves and thick leaf stalks 瑞士甜菜;厚皮菜

charge /tʃɑːdʒ/ **verb** (**charges, charging, charged**) **1** ask an amount as a price 要…价;收费 **2** formally accuse someone of something (正式)指控,控告 **3** rush forward in an attack 进攻;冲锋 **4** (**charge someone with**) give someone a task or responsibility 委派(任务);使承担(责任) **5** store electrical energy in a battery 使(电池)充电 **6** load or fill a container, gun, etc. 把(容器)装满;给(枪)装弹药 **7** fill with an emotion or quality 使充满: *The air was charged with menace.* 空气中充斥着危险。 • **noun 1** a price asked 要价;价钱 **2** a formal

accusation (正式的)指控,控告 **3** responsibility for the care or control of a person or thing 责任;职责 **4** a person or thing handed over to someone's care 被照管的人(或物) **5** a headlong rush forward 猛冲;冲锋 **6** the electricity naturally existing in a substance 电荷 **7** energy stored chemically in a battery (电池中的)电量 **8** a quantity of explosive needed to fire a gun (枪的)火药量 □ **charge card** a kind of credit card issued by a large shop (由大型商店发行的)信用卡 ■ **chargeable** adjec-tive.

chargé d'affaires /ˌʃɑːʒeɪ dæˈfeə(r)/ **noun** (plural **chargés d'affaires** /ˌʃɑːʒeɪ dæˈfeə(r)/) **1** an ambassador's deputy 代办(代理大使的外交官) **2** the diplomatic representative in a country to which an ambassador has not been sent 派驻未设大使国家的外交使节,公使

charger /ˈtʃɑːdʒə(r)/ **noun 1** a device for charging a battery (电池的)充电器 **2** a strong horse formerly ridden by a knight or mounted soldier (骑士或骑兵的)战马,军马

chargrill /ˈtʃɑːgrɪl/ **verb** grill food quickly at a very high heat (用高温)快速烤(食物)

chariot /ˈtʃærɪət/ **noun** a two-wheeled horsedrawn vehicle, used in ancient warfare and racing (古代的)双轮战车,双轮赛马车 ■ **charioteer** noun.

charisma /kəˈrɪzmə/ **noun** attractiveness that inspires admiration and enthusiasm in other people (能激发钦慕或热情的)领袖气质,非凡的个人魅力 ■ **charismatic** adjective.

charitable /ˈtʃærətəbl/ **adjective 1** relating to help given to people in need 慈善的;慷慨的 **2** showing kindness and understanding when judging other people 宽容的;宽厚的 ■ **charitably** adverb.

charity /ˈtʃærəti/ **noun** (plural **charities**) **1** an organization set up to help people in need 慈善机构 **2** the giving of money or other help to people in need 慈善捐助 **3** kindness and understanding shown when judging other people 宽容；宽厚

charlatan /ˈʃɑːlətən/ noun a person who claims to have skills or knowledge that they do not really have 假内行；江湖骗子

charm /tʃɑːm/ noun **1** the power or quality of delighting or fascinating other people 魅力；吸引力 **2** a small ornament worn on a necklace or bracelet (项链或手镯上的)小装饰物 **3** an object or saying believed to have magic power 魔力；魔法；魔咒 • verb **1** make someone feel great pleasure or delight 使喜悦；使陶醉 **2** use your charm in order to influence someone 用魅力影响；哄诱 **3** (**charmed**) unusually lucky as if protected by magic 似有魔法保护的 ■ **charmer** noun **charmless** adjective.

charming /ˈtʃɑːmɪŋ/ adjective **1** delightful; attractive 令人高兴的；迷人的 **2** very likeable 讨人喜欢的 ■ **charmingly** adverb.

charnel house /ˈtʃɑːnl/ noun a place formerly used for keeping dead bodies and bones in 停尸房；藏骸所

chart /tʃɑːt/ noun **1** a sheet of paper on which information is displayed in the form of a table, graph, or diagram 图表；曲线图 **2** a map used for navigation by sea or air (用于航海或航空的)地图，海图，航图 **3** (**the charts**) a weekly listing of the current best-selling pop records 每周流行歌曲唱片排行榜 • verb **1** make a map of 绘制…的地图 **2** follow progress or record something on a chart 在地图上标示；用图表说明

charter /ˈtʃɑːtə(r)/ noun **1** an official document stating that a ruler or government allows an institution to exist and setting out its rights (统治者或政府颁发的)特许状，许可证，授予特权的法令 **2** a document listing and describing the functions of an organization (组织)的章程，纲领 **3** the hiring of an aircraft, ship, or vehicle (飞机、船只或机动车辆的)包租 • verb **1** hire an aircraft, ship, or vehicle 包租(飞机、船只或机动车辆) **2** grant a charter to an institution 授予…特权；准许 □ **charter flight** a flight by an aircraft that has been hired for a specific journey 包机飞行

chartered /ˈtʃɑːtəd/ adjective (of an accountant, engineer, etc.) qualified as a member of a professional institution that has a royal charter (会计、工程师等)合格的，持有特许状的

chary /ˈtʃeəri/ adjective (**charier, chariest**) cautious about doing something 谨慎的

chase[1] /tʃeɪs/ verb (**chases, chasing, chased**) **1** go after someone in order to catch them 追逐；追赶 **2** rush or hurry (使)匆忙 **3** try to make contact with or get hold of 追索；试图获得 • noun **1** an act of chasing 追逐；追赶 **2** (**the chase**) hunting as a sport 狩猎(运动)

chase[2] verb (**chases, chasing, chased**) engrave metal 镂刻(金属)

chaser /ˈtʃeɪsə(r)/ noun informal 【非正式】 a strong alcoholic drink taken after a weaker one (饮淡味酒后喝的)烈酒

chasm /ˈkæzəm/ noun **1** a deep crack in the earth (地上的)裂缝，深坑 **2** a very big difference between two people or their opinions (人与人之间的)显著差别，显著分歧

chassis /ˈʃæsi/ noun (plural **chassis** /ˈʃæsɪz/) the framework forming the base of a vehicle (车辆的)底盘，车架

chaste /tʃeɪst/ adjective **1** having sex only with your husband or wife, or not at all 忠贞的；禁欲的 **2** not expressing sexual interest; demure and modest 纯洁的；高雅的；正派的

■ **chastely** adverb.

chasten /ˈtʃeɪsn/ **verb** make someone feel subdued and less confident about something 使缓和；使不自信

chastise /tʃæˈstaɪz/ **verb** (**chastises, chastising, chastised**) **1** tell someone off in a very strict way 严厉训斥；责骂

chastity /ˈtʃæstɪti/ **noun** the practice of having sex only with your husband or wife, or not at all 忠贞；禁欲

chasuble /ˈtʃæzjʊbl/ **noun** a long sleeveless garment worn by a priest over other robes 十字褡(牧师穿在外面的无袖长袍)

chat /tʃæt/ **verb** (**chats, chatting, chatted**) **1** talk informally 闲聊；聊天 **2** (**chat someone up**) informal【非正式】talk flirtatiously to someone 与…调情 • **noun** an informal conversation 闲聊；聊天 □ **chat room** an area on the Internet where users can communicate (因特网上的)聊天室 ■ **chatty** adjective.

chateau /ˈfætəʊ/ **noun** (plural **chateaux** /ˈʃætəʊz/ or **chateaus**) a large French country house or castle 法国庄园；法国城堡

chattel /ˈtʃætl/ **noun** a personal possession 个人财产

chatter /ˈtʃætə(r)/ **verb** (**chatters, chattering, chattered**) **1** talk informally about unimportant things 喋喋不休地讲(琐事)；饶舌 **2** (of a person's teeth) click together continuously from cold or fear (人的牙齿因寒冷或恐惧而)打战 • **noun** informal or unimportant talk 唠叨的话

chatterbox /ˈtʃætəbɒks/ **noun** informal【非正式】a person who likes to chatter 唠叨的人；饶舌者

chauffeur /ˈʃəʊfə(r)/ **noun** a person who is employed to drive someone around in a car (受雇的)汽车司机 • **verb** be a driver for someone 为…开车

chauvinism /ˈʃəʊvɪnɪzəm/ **noun 1** a strong and unreasonable belief that your own country or group is better than others 沙文主义；本国至上主义 **2** the belief held by some men that men are superior to women 大男子主义 ■ **chauvinist** adjective & noun **chauvinistic** adjective.

cheap /tʃiːp/ **adjective 1** low in price, or charging low prices 廉价的；便宜的；要价低的 **2** low in price and of bad quality 劣质的；低劣的 **3** having no value because achieved in a bad way 无价值的；不值钱的 ■ **cheaply** adverb **cheapness** noun.

cheapen /ˈtʃiːpən/ **verb** lower the quality or value of something 降低…的价格；贬低…的价值

cheapskate /ˈtʃiːpskeɪt/ **noun** informal【非正式】a person who hates to spend money 小气鬼；吝啬鬼

cheat /tʃiːt/ **verb 1** act dishonestly or unfairly to gain an advantage 行骗；作弊 **2** deprive someone of something by tricking them 欺骗；骗取 • **noun** a person who cheats 行骗者；作弊者

check[1] /tʃek/ **verb 1** examine the accuracy, quality, or condition of 核对；检查 **2** make sure that something is the case 确保 **3** stop or slow the progress of 阻止；抑制 • **noun 1** an act of checking accuracy, quality, or condition 核对；检查 **2** a control or restraint 控制；限制 **3** Chess【国际象棋】a position in which a king is directly threatened 将军 **4** N. Amer.【北美】the bill in a restaurant (餐馆的)账单 □ **check in** register at a hotel or airport (在酒店)登记入住；(在机场)办理登机 **check out** pay your hotel bill before leaving (从酒店)结账离开 **check something out** find out about something 查阅(某事) **check-up** an examination by a doctor or dentist (医生或牙医做的)

检查 **check up on** investigate 调查
in check under control 受控制

check² noun a pattern of small
squares 格子图案；格子花样 • adjec-
tive (also **checked**) having a pattern
of small squares 带格子图案的

check³ US spelling of CHEQUE.
cheque 的美式拼法

checker /'tʃekə(r)/ US spelling of
CHEQUER. chequer 的美式拼法

checklist /'tʃeklɪst/ noun a list of
items to be considered or things to
be done (要考虑或要做的事情的)一
览表，清单

checkmate /'tʃekmeɪt/ Chess【国际
象棋】noun a position of check from
which a king cannot escape 将死
• verb put a king into checkmate 将死

checkout /'tʃekaʊt/ noun a point
at which goods are paid for in a
supermarket or large shop (超市或大
型商店的)收银台，付款台

checkpoint /'tʃekpɔɪnt/ noun a
barrier where security checks are
carried out on travellers (对旅行者进
行安全检查的)关卡，检查站

Cheddar /'tʃedə(r)/ noun a kind of
firm, smooth cheese 切达干酪

cheek /tʃiːk/ noun 1 the area on either
side of the face below the eye 面颊；
脸蛋 2 either of the buttocks 半边屁
股 3 rude or disrespectful behaviour
鲁莽的行为；大胆的行为 • verb
informal【非正式】speak to someone
rudely or disrespectfully 粗鲁地对…
讲话 □ **cheek by jowl** close together
紧密在一起，亲密地 **turn the other
cheek** stop yourself from fighting
back (被打后)把另一面颊凑过去；甘
受侮辱

cheekbone /'tʃiːkbəʊn/ noun the
rounded bone below the eye 颧骨

cheeky /'tʃiːki/ adjective (**cheekier**,
cheekiest) showing a cheerful lack
of respect 厚颜无耻的，■ **cheekily**
adverb.

cheep /tʃiːp/ noun a squeaky cry

made by a young bird (小鸟)吱吱的
叫声 • verb make a cheep 发出吱吱
声

cheer /tʃɪə(r)/ verb 1 shout for joy or
in praise or encouragement 欢呼；喝
彩 2 praise or encourage a person
or group to …喝彩；用欢呼声鼓励
3 (**cheer up** or **cheer someone
up**) become or make someone less
miserable (使)振作 4 give comfort to
someone 安慰 • noun 1 a shout of joy,
encouragement, or praise 欢呼；喝彩
2 (also **good cheer**) cheerfulness；
optimism 欢欣；快活；乐观

cheerful /'tʃɪəfl/ adjective 1 noticeably happy and optimistic 欢欣鼓舞
的；兴高采烈的 2 bright and pleasant 明亮的；令人愉快的 ■ **cheer-
fully** adverb **cheerfulness** noun.

cheerleader /'tʃɪəliːdə(r)/ noun (in
North America) a girl belonging to
a group that performs organized
chanting and dancing at sports
events (北美体育赛事中的)拉拉队队
员

cheerless /'tʃɪələs/ adjective
gloomy; depressing 阴郁的；沉闷的

cheers /tʃɪəz/ exclamation informal
【非正式】1 said before having an
alcoholic drink with other people
干杯 2 said to express thanks or on
parting 谢谢；再见

cheery /'tʃɪəri/ adjective (**cheerier**,
cheeriest) happy and optimistic 兴
高采烈的；欢快的 ■ **cheerily** adverb.

cheese¹ /tʃiːz/ noun a food made
from the pressed curds of milk 奶酪；
干酪 □ **cheese-paring** very careful
about spending money; mean 吝啬
的；小气的

cheese² verb (**be cheesed off**)
informal【非正式】be irritated or bored
被激怒；觉得无聊

cheesecake /'tʃiːzkeɪk/ noun a rich,
sweet tart having a thick topping
made with cream cheese 奶酪饼

cheesecloth /'tʃiːzklɒθ/ noun thin,

loosely woven cotton cloth 薄纱织物

cheesy /'tʃi:zi/ **adjective** (**cheesier**, **cheesiest**) **1** like cheese 像奶酪的 **2** informal 【非正式】 sentimental or of bad quality 脆弱的；劣质的

cheetah /'tʃi:tə/ **noun** a large spotted cat that can run very fast, found in Africa and parts of Asia 猎豹(产于非洲和亚洲部分地区，体形大，奔跑速度很快)

chef /ʃef/ **noun** a professional cook in a restaurant or hotel (餐馆或酒店里的)厨师

chemical /'kemɪkl/ **adjective** relating to chemistry or chemicals 化学的；化学制品的 • **noun** a substance which has been artificially prepared or purified 化学制品 ■ **chemically** adverb.

chemise /ʃəˈmi:z/ **noun** a woman's loose-fitting dress, nightdress, or petticoat 女式宽松连衣裙(或睡衣、内衣)

chemist /'kemɪst/ **noun 1** a person who is authorized to give out or sell medicines 药剂师；药商 **2** a shop where medicines, toiletries, and cosmetics are sold 药店；化妆品店 **3** a person who studies chemistry 化学家

chemistry /'kemɪstri/ **noun 1** the branch of science concerned with the nature of substances and how they react with each other 化学 **2** attraction or interaction between two people (人与人之间的)吸引力；人际感情

chemotherapy /ˌki:məʊˈθerəpi/ **noun** the treatment of cancer with drugs (对癌症的)化学治疗，化疗

chenille /ʃəˈni:l/ **noun** a fabric with a thick velvety pile 绳绒线；绳绒织物

cheque /tʃek/ (US spelling 【美拼作】 **check**) **noun** a written order to a bank to pay a stated sum from an account to a named person 支票 □ **cheque card** a card issued by a bank to guarantee payment of a customer's

cheques (银行发放的)支票保付卡

chequer /'tʃekə(r)/ (US spelling 【美拼作】 **checker**) **noun 1** (**chequers**) a pattern of alternately coloured squares (颜色交错的方格图案 **2** (**checkers**) N. Amer. 【北美】 the game of draughts 西洋跳棋

chequered /'tʃekəd/ **adjective 1** divided into or marked with chequers 方格图案的 **2** having successful and unsuccessful periods 好运与厄运交替的；盛衰无常的 • *a chequered career* 变化无常的职业生涯

cherish /'tʃerɪʃ/ **verb 1** protect and care for someone lovingly 爱护；珍爱 **2** keep a thought or memory in your mind 怀念；怀有

cheroot /ʃəˈru:t/ **noun** a cigar with both ends open 方头雪茄烟

cherry /'tʃeri/ **noun** (plural **cherries**) **1** a small, round red fruit with a stone 樱桃 **2** a bright red colour 樱桃色，鲜红色

cherub /'tʃerəb/ **noun 1** (plural **cherubim** or **cherubs**) a type of angel, shown in art as a plump child with wings 小天使(艺术品中带翅膀的孩童图像) **2** (plural **cherubs**) a beautiful or innocent-looking child 漂亮的儿童；天真的小孩 ■ **cherubic** /tʃəˈru:bɪk/ adjective.

chervil /'tʃɜ:vɪl/ **noun** a herb with an aniseed flavour 细叶芹；雪维菜

chess /tʃes/ **noun** a board game for two players, the object of which is to put the opponent's king under a direct attack, leading to checkmate 国际象棋

chest /tʃest/ **noun 1** the front of a person's body between the neck and the stomach 胸部 **2** a large, strong box for storing or transporting things 大箱子；大盒子 □ **chest of drawers** a piece of furniture fitted with a set of drawers 五斗橱

chesterfield /'tʃestəfi:ld/ **noun** a sofa with a back of the same height as the arms (靠背与扶手高度相同的)沙发，坐卧两用长沙发

chestnut /'tʃesnʌt/ **noun 1** an edible nut with a glossy brown shell 栗子；板栗 **2** a deep reddish-brown colour 深红棕色；栗色 **3** (**old chestnut**) a joke, story, or subject that has become boring through being repeated too often 陈词滥调；陈腐的笑话(或故事)

chesty /'tʃesti/ **adjective** informal 【非正式】having a lot of catarrh in the lungs 有肺炎的；有肺病的

chevron /'ʃevrən/ **noun** a V-shaped line or stripe, worn on the sleeve of a military uniform to show rank or length of service (军服衣袖上表示衔级的)V形臂章

chew /tʃuː/ **verb 1** grind food with the teeth to make it easier to swallow 嚼，咀嚼(食物) **2** (**chew something over**) discuss or consider something at length 详细讨论；商谈；深思 • **noun** a sweet meant for chewing 供咀嚼的糖果 □ **chewing gum** flavoured gum for chewing 口香糖

chewy /'tʃuːi/ **adjective** needing a lot of chewing 需要多嚼的，难嚼的

chic /ʃiːk/ **adjective** (**chicer, chicest**) smart and fashionable 雅致的；时髦的

chicane /ʃɪ'keɪn/ **noun** a sharp double bend in a motor-racing track 赛车道上的双急转弯

chicanery /ʃɪ'keɪnəri/ **noun** the use of cunning tricks to get what you want 耍诡计；诈骗

chick /tʃɪk/ **noun 1** a newly hatched young bird (刚孵出的)小鸟，小鸡 **2** informal 【非正式】a young woman 年轻女子；少妇

chicken /'tʃɪkɪn/ **noun 1** a large domestic bird kept for its eggs or meat (用于生蛋或食用的)家禽，鸡 **2** informal 【非正式】a coward 胆小鬼；懦夫 • **adjective** informal 【非正式】cowardly 胆小的；畏缩的 • **verb** (**chicken out**) informal 【非正式】be

too scared to do something 畏缩

chickenpox /'tʃɪkɪnpɒks/ **noun** a disease causing itchy inflamed pimples 水痘

chickpea /'tʃɪkpiː/ **noun** a yellowish seed eaten as a vegetable (作蔬菜食用的)鹰嘴豆

chickweed /'tʃɪkwiːd/ **noun** a small white-flowered plant that grows as a garden weed 卷耳，繁缕(生长于花园中，开白色小花)

chicory /'tʃɪkəri/ **noun** (plural **chicories**) a plant whose leaves are eaten and whose root can be used instead of coffee 菊苣(根部可用作咖啡替代品)

chide /tʃaɪd/ **verb** (**chides, chiding, chided**) tell someone off 责备；责骂

chief /tʃiːf/ **noun** a leader or ruler 领袖；首领 • **adjective 1** having the highest rank or authority 职位最高的 **2** most important 最重要的；首要的

chiefly /'tʃiːfli/ **adverb** mainly; mostly 主要地；大部分

chieftain /'tʃiːftən/ **noun** the leader of a people or clan 首领；酋长；族长

chiffon /'ʃɪfɒn/ **noun** a light, see-through fabric 雪纺绸；薄绸

chignon /'ʃiːnjɒn/ **noun** a knot or coil of hair arranged on the back of a woman's head (女子盘在脑后的)发髻

chihuahua /tʃɪ'wɑːwə/ **noun** a very small breed of dog with smooth hair 奇瓦瓦小狗

chilblain /'tʃɪlbleɪn/ **noun** a painful, itchy swelling on a hand or foot caused by exposure to cold (手脚上的)冻疮

child /tʃaɪld/ **noun** (plural **children** /'tʃɪldrən/) **1** a young human being below the age of full physical development 小孩；儿童 **2** a son or daughter of any age (任何年龄的)子女，孩子 ■ **childhood noun childless** adjective.

childbirth /'tʃaɪldbɜːθ/ **noun** the process of giving birth to a baby 分

娩；生孩子

childish /'tʃaɪldɪʃ/ **adjective 1** silly and immature 幼稚的，不成熟的，愚蠢的 **2** like a child 像小孩的；适合小孩的

childlike /'tʃaɪldlaɪk/ **adjective** (of an adult) innocent and unsuspecting like a child (成年人)孩子般的，单纯的，天真的

childminder /'tʃaɪldˌmaɪndə(r)/ **noun** Brit. 【英】a person who is paid to look after other people's children 受雇照看孩子的人；保育员

Chilean /'tʃɪlɪən/ **noun** a person from Chile 智利人 • **adjective** relating to Chile 智利的

chill /tʃɪl/ **noun 1** an unpleasant feeling of coldness 严寒；寒冷 **2** a feverish cold 风寒；寒战 • **verb 1** make cold 使变冷 **2** frighten or horrify 使恐惧；使惊吓 **3** (usu. chill out) informal 【非正式】relax 放松；休息 • **adjective** unpleasantly cold 凉飕飕的

chilli /'tʃɪli/ (US spelling 【美拼作】**chili**) **noun** (plural **chillies**) a small hot-tasting pepper, used in cookery and as a spice (烹饪中用作调味品的)红辣椒 □ **chilli con carne** a stew of minced beef and beans flavoured with chilli 辣味牛肉末儿炖菜豆

chilly /'tʃɪli/ **adjective** (**chillier**, **chilliest**) **1** too cold to be comfortable 酷寒的；极冷的 **2** unfriendly 不友好的；冷漠的

chime /tʃaɪm/ **noun 1** a tuneful ringing sound 和谐的钟声；悦耳的音调 **2** a bell, bar, or tube used in a set to produce chimes when struck 钟；编钟；排钟 • **verb** (**chimes**, **chiming**, **chimed**) **1** (of a bell or clock) make a tuneful ringing sound (钟表)鸣响 **2** (**chime in**) interrupt a conversation with a remark 插嘴；插话

chimera or **chimaera** /kaɪ'mɪərə/ **noun 1** (in Greek mythology) a female monster with a lion's head, a goat's body, and a snake's tail (希腊神话中的)喀迈拉(狮头、羊身、蛇尾的女怪) **2** an unrealistic hope or dream 妄想；幻想

chimerical /kaɪ'merɪkl/ **adjective** not real or possible 空想的；幻想的；异想天开的

chimney /'tʃɪmni/ **noun** (plural **chimneys**) a pipe or channel which takes smoke and gases up from a fire or furnace 烟囱；烟道 □ **chimney breast** the part of an inside wall that surrounds a chimney 壁炉腔

chimpanzee /ˌtʃɪmpæn'ziː/ **noun** an ape native to west and central Africa (产于西非和中非的)黑猩猩

chin /tʃɪn/ **noun** the part of the face below the mouth 下巴；颏

china /'tʃaɪnə/ **noun 1** a delicate white ceramic material 瓷器，陶器 **2** household objects made from china (家用的)陶瓷用品

chinchilla /tʃɪn'tʃɪlə/ **noun** a small South American rodent with soft grey fur and a long bushy tail 绒鼠，毛丝鼠(产于南美洲的小型啮齿动物，毛皮柔软，呈灰色，有毛茸茸的长尾巴)

Chinese /tʃaɪ'niːz/ **noun** (plural **Chinese**) **1** the language of China 中文；汉语 **2** a person from China 中国人 • **adjective** relating to China 中国的

chink[1] /tʃɪŋk/ **noun 1** a narrow opening or crack 裂口；缝隙 **2** a beam of light entering through a chink (透过缝隙的)一缕光

chink[2] /tʃɪŋk/ **verb** make a high-pitched ringing sound (使)叮当响 • **noun** a high-pitched ringing sound 叮当声

chinos /'tʃiːnəʊz/ **plural noun** casual trousers made from a smooth cotton fabric 斜纹棉布休闲裤

chintz /tʃɪnts/ **noun** patterned cotton fabric with a glazed finish, used for curtains and upholstery (制作窗帘和室内装饰用的)轧光印花棉布

chintzy /'tʃɪntsi/ **adjective 1** like

chintz 像轧光印花棉布的的 **2** colourful but fussy and tasteless 艳俗的；花哨的；无品位的

chip /tʃɪp/ **noun 1** a small piece cut or broken off from something hard (削、凿硬物时落下的) 碎屑，碎片 **2** Brit. 【英】a long, thin piece of deepfried potato 油炸薯条 **3** (also **potato chip**) chiefly N. Amer. 【主北美】a potato crisp 油炸薯条 **4** a microchip 微型集成电路片；芯片 **5** a counter used in some gambling games to represent money (一些赌博游戏中代表钱的) 筹码 • **verb** (**chips**, **chipping**, **chipped**) **1** cut or break off a small piece from something hard 削下(屑片)；凿下(碎屑) **2** (**chip away**) gradually make something smaller or weaker 使逐渐变小；使逐渐变弱 **3** (**chip in**) add a contribution 做贡献 □ a **chip on your shoulder** informal 【非正式】a long-held feeling of resentment 宿怨

chipboard /'tʃɪpbɔːd/ **noun** a building material made from chips of wood pressed and stuck together 刨花板；胶合板

chipmunk /'tʃɪpmʌŋk/ **noun** a burrowing squirrel with light and dark stripes running down the body 金花鼠(有深浅两色条纹)

chipolata /ˌtʃɪpə'lɑːtə/ **noun** Brit. 【英】a small, thin sausage 蔡珀拉特小香肠

chipping /'tʃɪpɪŋ/ **noun** a small fragment of stone, wood, or similar material (石头、木头或类似材料的) 碎片，碎屑

chiropody /kɪ'rɒpədi/ **noun** care and treatment of the feet 足疗；足医术 ■ **chiropodist** noun.

chiropractic /ˌkaɪərəʊ'præktɪk/ **noun** a system of complementary medicine based on the manipulation of the joints, especially those of the spinal column (尤指对脊柱的) 按摩疗法 ■ **chiropractor** noun.

chirp /tʃɜːp/ **verb** (of a small bird) make a short, high-pitched sound (小鸟) 唧唧叫，喞啾 • **noun** a chirping sound 唧唧声；喞啾声

chirpy /'tʃɜːpi/ **adjective** (**chirpier**, **chirpiest**) informal 【非正式】cheerful and lively 轻松愉快的；活泼快活的

chisel /'tʃɪzl/ **noun** a hand tool with a narrow blade, used with a hammer to cut or shape wood, stone, or metal 凿子；凿刀 • **verb** (**chisels**, **chiselling**, **chiselled**；US spelling 【美拼作】**chisels**, **chiseling**, **chiseled**) **1** cut or shape something with a chisel (用凿子)凿，雕，刻 **2** (**chiselled**) (of a man's facial features) clear and strong (男子面部)似雕刻的，轮廓鲜明的

chit /tʃɪt/ **noun** a short note recording a sum of money owed 欠款字据；欠条

chivalrous /'ʃɪvlrəs/ **adjective** acting in a polite and charming way towards women (对女子)彬彬有礼的，有绅士风度的 ■ **chivalrously** adverb.

chivalry /'ʃɪvəlri/ **noun 1** an honourable code of behaviour which knights in medieval times were expected to follow (中世纪的)骑士制度 **2** polite behaviour by a man towards women (男子对女子的)彬彬有礼，绅士风度

chives /tʃaɪvz/ **plural noun** a plant with long, thin leaves that are used as a herb (用于烹饪中调味的)细香葱

chivvy /'tʃɪvi/ **verb** (**chivvies**, **chivvying**, **chivvied**) keep telling someone to do something 催促；唠叨

chloride /'klɔːraɪd/ **noun** a compound of chlorine with another substance 氯化物

chlorinate /'klɔːrɪneɪt/ **verb** (**chlorinates**, **chlorinating**, **chlorinated**) treat water with chlorine 用氯浸渍；用氯处理 ■ **chlorination** noun.

chlorine /'klɔːriːn/ **noun** a chemical

element in the form of a green gas, sometimes added to water as a disinfectant (化学元素)氯

chloroform /'klɔːrəfɔːm/ **noun** a liquid used to dissolve things and formerly as an anaesthetic 氯仿,三氯甲烷(用作溶剂,旧时曾用作麻醉剂)

chlorophyll /'klɔːrəfɪl/ **noun** a green pigment in plants which allows them to absorb sunlight and use it in photosynthesis 叶绿素

chock /tʃɒk/ **noun** a wedge or block placed against a wheel to prevent it from moving (防止轮子移动的)楔子,垫块 □ **chock-a-block** crammed full 挤满的,塞满的

chocolate /'tʃɒklət/ **noun 1** a dark brown sweet food made from roasted cacao seeds 巧克力 **2** a drink made by mixing milk or water with powdered chocolate 巧克力饮料

choice /tʃɔɪs/ **noun 1** an act of choosing 选择;抉择 **2** the right or ability to choose 选择权;选择能力 **3** a range from which to choose 供选择的范围 **4** something that has been chosen 被选中的东西 • **adjective** of very good quality 上等的;优质的

choir /'kwaɪə(r)/ **noun 1** an organized group of singers 合唱团 **2** the part of a church between the altar and the nave, used by the choir 唱诗班

choirboy /'kwaɪəbɔɪ/ **noun** a boy who sings in a church choir 唱诗班男童歌手

choke /tʃəʊk/ **verb** (**chokes**, **choking**, **choked**) **1** prevent someone from breathing by blocking their throat or depriving them of air 使窒息;掐住(某人)的脖子 **2** have trouble breathing 呼吸困难 **3** (**be choked with**) be blocked or filled with (空间)塞满,堵塞 • **noun** a valve used to reduce the amount of air in the fuel mixture of a petrol engine (控制汽油发动机进气量的)阻气门

choker /'tʃəʊkə(r)/ **noun** a close-fitting necklace (贴颈的)项链;(装饰用的)项圈

cholera /'kɒlərə/ **noun** an infectious disease causing severe vomiting and diarrhoea 霍乱

choleric /'kɒlərɪk/ **adjective** literary 【文】bad-tempered 易怒的;暴躁的

cholesterol /kə'lestərɒl/ **noun** a substance in the body which is believed to cause disease of the arteries when there is too much of it in the blood 胆固醇

chomp /tʃɒmp/ **verb** munch or chew food noisily 大声咀嚼

choose /tʃuːz/ **verb** (**chooses**, **choosing**, **chose**; past participle **chosen**) pick something out as being the closest to what you want or need 挑选;选择

choosy /'tʃuːzi/ **adjective** (**choosier**, **choosiest**) informal 【非正式】very careful in making a choice 爱挑剔的;过分讲究的

chop /tʃɒp/ **verb** (**chops**, **chopping**, **chopped**) **1** cut something into pieces with a knife or axe (用斧头或刀子)劈,砍 **2** hit with a short downward stroke 削击;切击 • **noun 1** a thick slice of meat cut from or including the rib bone 肋条肉;排骨 **2** a downward cutting movement 劈,砍 **3** (**the chop**) Brit. informal 【英,非正式】the cancellation or end of something 取消;结束 □ **chop and change** Brit. informal 【英,非正式】keep changing your mind 变化无常

chopper /'tʃɒpə(r)/ **noun 1** a short axe with a large blade 斧头 **2** informal 【非正式】a helicopter 直升机

choppy /'tʃɒpi/ **adjective** (of the sea) having many small waves (海洋)波浪滔滔的

chopstick /'tʃɒpstɪk/ **noun** each of a pair of thin sticks used by the Chinese and Japanese to eat with 筷子

chop suey /ˌtʃɒp 'suːi/ *noun* a Chinese-style dish of meat with bean sprouts, bamboo shoots, and onions 炒杂碎(用豆芽、竹笋、洋葱和肉等烹制的中式菜肴)

choral /ˈkɔːrəl/ *adjective* sung by a choir or chorus 合唱的

chorale /kɒˈrɑːl/ *noun* a simple, stately hymn tune 赞美诗曲调

chord /kɔːd/ *noun* a group of three or more musical notes sounded together in harmony 和弦；和音

> **! 注意** don't confuse **chord** with **cord**, which means 'thin string or rope'. 不要混淆 chord 和 cord，后者意为"细绳"。

chore /tʃɔː(r)/ *noun* a boring or routine job or task 杂务；琐事

choreograph /ˈkɒriəɡrɑːf/ *verb* compose the sequence of steps for a ballet or dance routine 为(舞蹈表演)设计舞蹈动作 ■ **choreographer** *noun* **choreography** *noun*.

chorister /ˈkɒrɪstə(r)/ *noun* a member of a church choir 唱诗班歌手

chortle /ˈtʃɔːtl/ *verb* (**chortles, chortling, chortled**) chuckle happily 咯咯地笑

chorus /ˈkɔːrəs/ *noun* (plural **choruses**) **1** a part of a song which is repeated after each verse (歌曲的)副歌，叠句 **2** a group of singers or dancers performing together in a supporting role in an opera, musical, etc. 伴唱团；伴舞团 **3** something said at the same time by many people 齐声说的话 • *verb* (**choruses, chorusing, chorused**) (of a group of people) say the same thing at the same time (一群人)齐声说

chose /tʃəʊz/ past of CHOOSE.

chosen /ˈtʃəʊzn/ past participle of CHOOSE.

choux pastry /ʃuː/ *noun* very light pastry made with egg 鸡蛋松软面团

chow mein /ˌtʃaʊ 'meɪn/ *noun* a Chinese-style dish of fried noodles served with shredded meat or seafood and vegetables 炒面(用肉丝、海鲜、蔬菜和面条炒制的中式菜肴)

Christ /kraɪst/ *noun* the title given to Jesus 基督(耶稣的头衔)

christen /ˈkrɪsn/ *verb* give a name to a baby while it is being baptized (施洗礼时)给…取名

Christian /ˈkrɪstʃən/ *adjective* based on or believing in Christianity 基督教的；基督教教义的；信仰基督教的 • *noun* a person who believes in Christianity 受过洗礼的人；基督教徒 □ **Christian name** a person's first name 受洗礼名

Christianity /ˌkrɪsti'ænəti/ *noun* the religion based on the life and teaching of Jesus 基督教

Christmas /ˈkrɪsməs/ *noun* (plural **Christmases**) the annual Christian festival celebrating the birth of Jesus, held on 25 December 圣诞节(12月25日) □ **Christmas tree** an evergreen tree decorated with lights and ornaments at Christmas 圣诞树

chromatic /krəˈmætɪk/ *adjective* **1** Music 【音乐】 using notes that do not belong to the key in which the passage is written 使用临时记号的 **2** Music 【音乐】 going up or down by semitones (音阶)半音阶的，半音变化的 **3** relating to or produced by colour 颜色的；色彩产生的

chrome /krəʊm/ *noun* a hard, bright metal coating made from chromium 铬合金

chromium /ˈkrəʊmiəm/ *noun* a hard white metallic element (金属元素)铬

chromosome /ˈkrəʊməsəʊm/ *noun* a thread-like structure found in the nuclei of most living cells, carrying genetic information in the form of genes (细胞核中的)染色体

chronic /ˈkrɒnɪk/ *adjective* **1** (of an illness or problem) lasting for a long time (疾病)慢性的；(问题)长期的 **2**

having a long-lasting illness or bad habit 患慢性病的；积习难改的 **3** Brit. informal【英，非正式】very bad 糟糕透顶的；非常坏的 ■ **chronically** adverb.

chronicle /ˈkrɒnɪkl/ **noun** a record of historical events made in the order in which they happened 编年史 • **verb** (**chronicles, chronicling, chronicled**) record a series of events in detail 详细记录(一系列事件) ■ **chronicler** noun.

chronological /ˌkrɒnəˈlɒdʒɪkl/ **adjective** (of a record of events) starting with the earliest and following the order in which they happened (事件)按年代顺序编排的 ■ **chronologically** adverb.

chronology /krəˈnɒlədʒi/ **noun** (plural **chronologies**) the arrangement of events or dates in the order in which they happened 按年代顺序的排列

chronometer /krəˈnɒmɪtə(r)/ **noun** an instrument for measuring time 精密计时仪；天文钟

chrysalis /ˈkrɪsəlɪs/ **noun** (plural **chrysalises**) a butterfly or moth when it is changing from a larva to the adult form, inside a hard case 昆虫蛹；蝶蛹；蛾蛹

chrysanthemum /krɪˈsænθəməm/ **noun** (plural **chrysanthemums**) a garden plant with brightly coloured flowers 菊花

chub /tʃʌb/ **noun** a thick-bodied river fish 圆鳍雅罗鱼

chubby /ˈtʃʌbi/ **adjective** (**chubbier, chubbiest**) plump and rounded 圆胖的；丰满的

chuck¹ /tʃʌk/ **verb** informal【非正式】throw something carelessly or casually (胡乱或随意地)扔，抛

chuck² **verb** touch someone playfully under the chin 抚弄…的下巴

chuckle /ˈtʃʌkl/ **verb** (**chuckles, chuckling, chuckled**) laugh quietly 窃笑；暗自笑 • **noun** a quiet laugh 窃笑；悄悄的笑

chuff /tʃʌf/ **verb** (of a steam engine) move with a regular puffing sound (蒸汽机)噗噗地运转

chuffed /tʃʌft/ **adjective** Brit. informal【英，非正式】very pleased 高兴的；愉快的

chug /tʃʌg/ **verb** (**chugs, chugging, chugged**) (of a vehicle) move slowly with a loud, regular sound (车辆)发着突突声缓慢移动

chum /tʃʌm/ **noun** informal【非正式】a close friend 密友；好朋友 ■ **chummy** adjective.

chump /tʃʌmp/ **noun** informal【非正式】a silly person 傻瓜；笨蛋

chunk /tʃʌŋk/ **noun** a thick, solid piece 厚块 ■ **chunky** adjective.

church /tʃɜːtʃ/ **noun 1** a building where Christians go to worship (基督教)教堂，礼拜堂 **2** (**Church**) a particular Christian organization 基督教会 **3** (**the Church**) people within the Christian faith 基督教徒

churchyard /ˈtʃɜːtʃjɑːd/ **noun** an enclosed area surrounding a church 教堂庭院

churlish /ˈtʃɜːlɪʃ/ **adjective** unfriendly and rude 粗鲁的；脾气暴躁的 ■ **churlishly** adverb.

churn /tʃɜːn/ **noun 1** a machine for making butter by shaking milk or cream 搅乳器；黄油制造机 **2** a large metal milk can (金属)大奶罐 • **verb 1** (of liquid) move about vigorously (液体)剧烈沸腾 **2** (**churn something out**) produce something in large quantities and without much thought 大量粗制滥造 **3** shake milk or cream in a churn to produce butter 用搅乳器搅乳(以制作黄油)

chute /ʃuːt/ **noun 1** a sloping channel for moving things to a lower level (将物品运送到较低位置的)斜槽，倾斜槽 **2** a slide into a swimming pool (通往游泳池的)滑道

chutney /'tʃʌtnɪ/ **noun** (plural **chutneys**) a spicy sauce made of fruits or vegetables with vinegar, spices, and sugar 酸辣酱

chutzpah /'hʊtspə/ **noun** informal 【非正式】 extreme self-confidence 肆无忌惮

CIA /si: aɪ 'eɪ/ **abbreviation** (in the US) Central Intelligence Agency (美国的) 中央情报局

ciabatta /tʃə'bɑːtə/ **noun** a flat Italian bread made with olive oil (加橄榄油制作的)意大利扁面包

cicada /sɪ'kɑːdə/ **noun** an insect which makes a shrill droning noise 蝉;知了

CID /si: aɪ 'diː/ **abbreviation** Criminal Investigation Department 犯罪调查科

cider /'saɪdə(r)/ **noun** an alcoholic drink made from apple juice 苹果酒

cigar /sɪ'gɑː(r)/ **noun** a cylinder of tobacco rolled in tobacco leaves for smoking 雪茄烟

cigarette /ˌsɪgə'ret/ **noun** a cylinder of finely cut tobacco rolled in paper for smoking 香烟;烟卷

cilium /'sɪliəm/ **noun** (plural **cilia** /'sɪliə/) a microscopic hair-like structure, found on the surface of certain cells (某些细胞表面的)纤毛

cinch /sɪntʃ/ **noun** informal 【非正式】 1 a very easy task 轻而易举之事 2 a certainty 必然之事

cinder /'sɪndə(r)/ **noun** a piece of partly burnt coal or wood (未燃尽的)煤渣,炭屑

cine /'sɪni/ **adjective** relating to or used for the making of films 电影;电影制作的

cinema /'sɪnəmə/ **noun** Brit. 【英】1 a place where films are shown 电影院 2 the production of films as an art or industry 电影制作;电影业

cinematic /ˌsɪnɪ'mætɪk/ **adjective** relating to the cinema, or like a film 电影院的;电影的;像电影的

cinematography /ˌsɪnɪmə'tɒgrəfi/ **noun** the skilled use of the camera in film-making 电影制片术;电影摄影术 ■ **cinematographer** noun.

cinnamon /'sɪnəmən/ **noun** a spice made from the bark of an Asian tree 桂皮香料,肉桂皮(产于亚洲)

cipher or **cypher** /'saɪfə(r)/ **noun** 1 a code 密码;暗号 2 a key to a code 密码检索;密码索引 3 an unimportant person or thing 无足轻重的人(或物)

circa /'sɜːkə/ **preposition** approximately 大约

circadian /sɜː'keɪdɪən/ **adjective** relating to processes in the body that happen regularly every twenty-four hours (生理过程)昼夜节律的,以二十四小时为周期的

circle /'sɜːkl/ **noun** 1 a round flat shape whose edge is at the same distance from the centre all the way round 圆;圆圈 2 a group of people with shared interests, friends, etc. (有共同兴趣、朋友等的一群人行成的)圈子 3 Brit. 【英】a curved upper tier of seats in a theatre (剧院的)弧形梯级座位 • **verb** (**circles**, **circling**, **circled**) 1 move or be placed all the way round 环行;盘旋;绕绕 2 draw a line round 在…上画圈;圈出

circuit /'sɜːkɪt/ **noun** 1 a roughly circular line, route, or movement (戴在头上的)环形饰物 2 Brit. 【英】a track used for motor racing 汽车赛道 3 a system of components forming a complete path for an electric current 电路 4 a series of sports events or entertainments (体育)巡回比赛,(娱乐)巡回表演

circuitous /sɜː'kjuːɪtəs/ **adjective** (of a route) long and indirect (路线)迂回的,绕行的

circuitry /'sɜːkɪtri/ **noun** (plural **circuitries**) a system of electric circuits 电路系统

circular /'sɜːkjələ(r)/ **adjective** 1 having the form of a circle 环形的 2 (of a letter or advertisement) for distribution to a large number of people (信件或广告)供阅读的 • **noun** a circular letter or advertisement 传阅的信件(或广告)

circulate /'sɜːkjəleɪt/ **verb** (**circulates, circulating, circulated**) **1** move continuously through a system or area 循环；流通 **2** pass from place to place or person to person 传播；散布

circulation /ˌsɜːkjə'leɪʃn/ **noun 1** movement through a system or area 环行流通 **2** the continuous movement of blood round the body (血液的)循环 **3** the spreading or passing of something from one person or place to another 传播；流通 **4** the number of copies of a newspaper or magazine sold (报刊的)发行量

circumcise /'sɜːkəmsaɪz/ **verb** (**circumcises, circumcising, circumcised**) **1** cut off a boy's or man's foreskin 为(男子)切除包皮 **2** cut off a girl's or woman's clitoris 为(女子)切除阴蒂 ■ **circumcision** noun.

circumference /sə'kʌmfərəns/ **noun 1** the boundary which encloses a circle 圆周；周线 **2** the distance around something 周长

circumflex /'sɜːkəmfleks/ **noun** a mark (^) placed over a vowel in some languages to show a change in its sound (某些语言中标在元音上方表示读音变化的)音调符号

circumlocution /ˌsɜːkəmlə'kjuːʃn/ **noun** a way of saying something which uses more words than are necessary 迂回的说法；累赘的说法

circumnavigate /ˌsɜːkəm'nævɪgeɪt/ **verb** (**circumnavigates, circumnavigating, circumnavigated**) sail all the way around 环绕航行 ■ **circumnavigation** noun.

circumscribe /'sɜːkəmskraɪb/ **verb** (**circumscribes, circumscribing, circumscribed**) restrict the freedom or power of 限制；约束

circumspect /'sɜːkəmspekt/ **adjective** not wanting to take risks; cautious 小心谨慎的；考虑周全的

circumstance /'sɜːkəmstəns/ **noun 1** a fact or condition that is connected with an event or action 事实；条件；情况 **2** things that happen that are beyond your control (人为无法控制的)外部条件，形势 **3** (**circumstances**) the practical things that affect a person's life 生活状况；境遇

circumstantial /ˌsɜːkəm'stænʃl/ **adjective** (of evidence) consisting of facts that make something seem likely but do not prove it (证据)间接的，旁证的 ■ **circumstantially** adverb.

circumvent /ˌsɜːkəm'vent/ **verb** find a way of avoiding a problem or obstacle 绕过，避开(障碍)

circus /'sɜːkəs/ **noun** (plural **circuses**) a travelling group of entertainers, including acrobats, clowns, and people who perform with trained animals (流动演出的)马戏团

cirrhosis /sɪ'rəʊsɪs/ **noun** a disease of the liver 肝硬化

cirrus /'sɪrəs/ **noun** (plural **cirri** /'sɪraɪ/) cloud forming wispy streaks high in the sky 卷云

CIS /ˌsiː aɪ 'es/ **abbreviation** Commonwealth of Independent States 独立国家联盟

cistern /'sɪstən/ **noun** a tank connected to a toilet, in which the water used for flushing it is stored (抽水马桶的)水箱

citadel /'sɪtədəl/ **noun** a fortress protecting or overlooking a city (用于保护或俯瞰城市的)城堡，堡垒

citation /saɪ'teɪʃn/ **noun 1** a quotation from a book or author 引文；引语 **2** an official mention of someone who has done something deserving praise 表彰；嘉奖

cite /saɪt/ **verb** (**cites, citing, cited**)

quote a book or author as evidence for an argument (在论据中)引证，引用(书籍或作者)

citizen /ˈsɪtɪzn/ **noun 1** a person who is legally recognized as being a member of a country 公民 **2** an inhabitant of a town or city 城镇居民 ■ **citizenship** noun.

citric acid /ˈsɪtrɪk/ **noun** a sharp-tasting acid present in the juice of lemons and other sour fruits 柠檬酸

citrus /ˈsɪtrəs/ **noun** (plural **citruses**) a fruit of a group that includes the lemon, lime, orange, and grapefruit 柑橘属水果(包括柠檬、酸橙、橘子和葡萄柚)

city /ˈsɪti/ **noun** (plural **cities**) **1** a large town, in particular (Brit.【英】) a town that has been created a city by charter, usually containing a cathedral 城市；(尤指英国特许建立并带有大教堂的)特别市 **2** (**the City**) the part of London that is a centre of finance and business 伦敦城(尤指其金融和商业机构) □ **city state** a city that forms an independent state (组成独立国家的)城邦；城市国家

civet /ˈsɪvɪt/ **noun 1** a cat native to Africa and Asia (产于非洲和亚洲的)灵猫 **2** a strong perfume obtained from the civet 灵猫香

civic /ˈsɪvɪk/ **adjective** having to do with a city or town 城市的；城镇的

civil /ˈsɪvl/ **adjective 1** relating to the lives of ordinary people rather than to military or church matters 平民的；非军事的；非教会的 **2** (of a court) dealing with personal legal matters rather than criminal offences (法庭)民事的 **3** polite 有礼貌的；文明的 □ **civil engineer** an engineer who designs roads, bridges, dams, etc. 土木工程师 **civil liberties** a person's rights to freedom of action and speech (while staying within the law) 公民自由权 **civil servant** a person who works in the civil service 公务员；文职人员

civil service the departments that carry out the work of the government (国家的)行政机构，文职部门 **civil war** a war between groups of people within the same country (国家的)内战 ■ **civilly** adverb.

civilian /sɪˈvɪlɪən/ **noun** a person who is not a member of the armed services or the police force 平民(与军人或警察相对) • **adjective** relating to a civilian 平民的

civility /sɪˈvɪləti/ **noun** (plural **civilities**) polite behaviour or speech 礼貌；客气；客套

civilization or **civilisation** /ˌsɪvɪlaɪˈzeɪʃn/ **noun 1** an advanced stage of human development in which people in a society behave well towards each other and share a common culture 文明；文明阶段 **2** the society, culture, and way of life of a particular area or period (特定地区和时期的)社会文明

civilize or **civilise** /ˈsɪvɪlaɪz/ **verb** (**civilizes, civilizing, civilized**) **1** bring a person or group to an advanced stage of social development 使文明；使开化 **2** (**civilized**) polite and good-mannered 有礼貌的；举止文明的

CJD /ˌsiː dʒeɪ ˈdiː/ **abbreviation** Creutzfeldt–Jakob disease, a fatal disease affecting the brain, possibly linked to BSE 克罗伊茨费尔特–雅各布病，克–雅二氏病(一种致命的脑部疾病)

cl abbreviation centilitre.

clack /klæk/ **verb** make a sharp sound like that of one hard object hitting another 发出尖厉的撞击声；发出咔嗒声 • **noun** a clacking sound 咔嗒声

clad /klæd/ **adjective 1** clothed 穿…衣服的 **2** fitted with cladding 有包层的；有镀层的

cladding /ˈklædɪŋ/ **noun** a protective or insulating covering or coating 包层；镀层

claim /kleɪm/ **verb 1** say that some-

thing is true although you are not able to prove it 断言；宣称 **2** request something that you believe you have a right to 要求(拥有)；认领；索取 **3** cause the loss of someone's life 夺去(生命) **4** ask for money under the terms of an insurance policy 索取(保险赔偿) **5** call for someone's attention 需要；要求(关注) • noun **1** a statement that something is true 断言；宣称 **2** a statement requesting something that you believe you have a right to 认领；索取 **3** a request for compensation under the terms of an insurance policy (保险)索赔
■ **claimant** noun.

clairvoyant /kleə'vɔɪənt/ noun a person who claims that they are able to see into the future or communicate mentally with people who are dead or far away 先知；能预知未来的人；通灵的人 • adjective able to see into the future 能预知未来的 ■ **clairvoyance** noun.

clam /klæm/ noun a large shellfish with a hinged shell 蛤蜊 • verb (**clams**, **clamming**, **clammed**) (**clam up**) informal 【非正式】 suddenly stop talking about something 突然闭口不言

clamber /'klæmbə(r)/ verb (**clambers**, **clambering**, **clambered**) climb or move using your hands and feet 攀登；爬

clammy /'klæmi/ adjective (**clammier**, **clammiest**) **1** unpleasantly damp and sticky 黏湿的 **2** (of air) cold and damp (空气)湿冷的

clamour /'klæmə(r)/ (US spelling 【美拼作】 **clamor**) noun **1** a loud and confused noise 喧闹声；吵闹声 **2** a loud protest or demand 大声抗议(或要求)；要求 • verb shout or demand something loudly 吵闹；大声要求
■ **clamorous** adjective.

clamp /klæmp/ noun **1** a brace, band, or clasp for holding something tightly 夹具 **2** a device attached to

the wheel of an illegally parked car to prevent it being driven away 用于锁住违章停放车辆的夹钳，车轮夹锁 • verb **1** fasten or hold with a clamp 用夹具固定；夹住 **2** (**clamp down**) suppress or prevent something 严格限制；取缔 **3** fit a wheel clamp to a car 用夹钳锁住(汽车)

clan /klæn/ noun a group of families, especially in the Scottish Highlands (尤指苏格兰高地人的)宗族，家族

clandestine /klæn'destɪn/ adjective done secretly 秘密的；偷偷摸摸的
■ **clandestinely** adverb.

clang /klæŋ/ noun a loud metallic sound 铿锵声 • verb make a clang 发出铿锵声

clank /klæŋk/ noun a sharp sound like that of pieces of metal being struck together (金属撞击的)当啷声 • verb make a clank 发出当啷声

clannish /'klænɪʃ/ adjective (of a group) tending to exclude people from outside the group (群体)排外的，小集团的

clap /klæp/ verb (**claps**, **clapping**, **clapped**) **1** bring the palms of your hands together loudly and repeatedly to show that you approve of something 拍手；鼓掌 **2** slap someone encouragingly on the back 拍击(某人)背部(以示鼓励) **3** suddenly place a hand over a part of your face as a gesture of dismay (突然用手)捂住(脸)(以示惊恐) • noun **1** an act of clapping 鼓掌；拍手 **2** a sudden loud sound of thunder (雷的)轰隆声
□ **clapped-out** Brit. informal 【英，非正式】 worn out from age or heavy use 用旧了的；破旧的

clapper /'klæpə(r)/ noun the moving part inside a bell 钟锤；钟舌

clapperboard /'klæpəbɔːd/ noun a pair of hinged boards that are struck together at the beginning of filming so that the picture and sound can be matched (拍摄电影时用的)场记板

claret /'klærət/ noun a red wine from Bordeaux in France (产自法国波尔多的)红葡萄酒

clarify /'klærɪfaɪ/ verb (**clarifies, clarifying, clarified**) **1** make something easier to understand 使易懂;阐明 **2** melt butter to separate out the impurities 纯化,净化(黄油) ■ **clarification** noun.

clarinet /ˌklærə'net/ noun a woodwind instrument with holes that are stopped by keys 单簧管;黑管 ■ **clarinettist** (US spelling【美拼作】**clarinetist**) noun.

clarion /'klærɪən/ noun historical【历史】a war trumpet 号角 □ **clarion call** a loud, clear call for action 号召;召唤

clarity /'klærəti/ noun **1** the quality of being clear and easily understood 清晰;易懂 **2** transparency or purity 透明;纯净

clash /klæʃ/ verb **1** come into violent conflict 发生冲突 **2** disagree or be at odds 意见不一;不和 **3** (of colours) look unpleasant together (色彩)不协调 **4** (of events) happen inconveniently at the same time (活动)相冲突 **5** strike metal objects together, producing a loud harsh sound 发出刺耳的撞击声 • noun an act or sound of clashing 冲突,不协调;刺耳的撞击声

clasp /klɑːsp/ verb **1** grasp tightly with your hand 握紧 **2** place your arms tightly around 拥抱;抱紧 **3** fasten with a clasp 扣住;钩住 • noun **1** a device with interlocking parts used for fastening 钩子;扣子 **2** an act of clasping 握紧;抱紧 □ **clasp knife** a knife with a blade that folds into the handle 折刀

class /klɑːs/ noun **1** a set or category of things that have something in common 种类;类别 **2** the division of people into different groups according to their social status 等级 **3** a group of people of the same social status

阶级;阶层 **4** a group of students or pupils who are taught together 班级 **5** a school or college lesson 课;课程 **6** informal【非正式】impressive stylishness 优雅;典雅 • verb place something in a particular category 把…归类 ■ **classless** adjective.

classic /'klæsɪk/ adjective **1** judged over a period of time to be of the highest quality 第一流的;最优秀的 **2** typical 典型的 • noun (**Classics**) the study of ancient Greek and Latin language and culture 古典学研究(指古希腊语言、文化及拉丁学研究)

classical /'klæsɪkl/ adjective **1** relating to the cultures of ancient Greece and Rome 与古希腊和古罗马文化相关的;古典文化的 **2** representing the highest standard within a long-established form 经典的 **3** (of music) written in the tradition of formal European music (音乐)古典乐派的 ■ **classically** adverb.

classicism /'klæsɪsɪzəm/ noun the use of a simple and elegant style characteristic of the art, architecture, or literature of ancient Greece and Rome 古典主义(指在艺术、建筑及文学领域采用古希腊和古罗马的简约、典雅风格)

classicist /'klæsɪsɪst/ noun a person who studies Classics 古典主义者;古典学家

classification /ˌklæsɪfɪ'keɪʃn/ noun **1** the arrangement of things in categories 分级;归类 **2** a category into which something is put 类别

classified /'klæsɪfaɪd/ adjective **1** (of newspaper or magazine advertisements) organized in categories (报刊广告)分类的 **2** (of information or documents) officially secret (信息或文件)机密的,保密的

classify /'klæsɪfaɪ/ verb (**classifies, classifying, classified**) **1** arrange things in groups according to features that they have in common 把…分级

C

把…归类 **2** put in a particular class or category 把…归入(某类)

classroom /'klɑːsrʊm/ **noun** a room in which a class of pupils or students is taught 教室

classy /'klɑːsi/ **adjective** (**classier**, **classiest**) informal 【非正式】 stylish and sophisticated 时髦的；高级的

clatter /'klætə(r)/ **noun** a loud rattling sound like that of hard objects hitting each other (硬物相撞时发出的)哐当声 • **verb** (**clatters**, **clattering**, **clattered**) make a clatter 发出哐当声

clause /klɔːz/ **noun 1** a group of words that includes a subject and a verb and forms part of a sentence 从句；分句 **2** a part of a treaty, bill, or contract (条约、法案或合同的)条款

claustrophobia /ˌklɔːstrə'fəʊbiə/ **noun** an extreme fear of being in a small or enclosed space 幽闭恐怖(症) ■ **claustrophobic** adjective.

clavicle /'klævɪkl/ **noun** the collarbone 锁骨

claw /klɔː/ **noun 1** each of the horny nails on the feet of birds, lizards, and some mammals (鸟、蜥蜴和一些哺乳动物的)爪 **2** the pincer of a shellfish (甲壳动物的)螯 • **verb** scratch or tear at something with the claws or fingernails (用爪或手指甲)抓，撕

clay /kleɪ/ **noun** sticky earth that can be moulded when wet and baked to make bricks and pottery (用于制砖和陶器的)黏土

clean /kliːn/ **adjective 1** free from dirt or harmful substances 一尘不染的，洁净的；无病菌的 **2** not yet used or marked 未使用过的，无痕迹的 **3** not obscene 不猥亵的；正派的 **4** having no record of offences or crimes 清白的；无违章记录的；无犯罪记录的 **5** (of an action) smoothly and skilfully done (动作)顺畅娴熟的 • **verb** make something free from dirt or harmful substances 使洁净；使清洁 • **noun** an act of cleaning 清扫；扫除 □ **clean-**

cut (of a person) clean and neat (人)干净整洁的 **clean-shaven** (of a man) without a beard or moustache (男子)不蓄胡子的，胡子刮净的 **come clean** informal 【非正式】 fully confess something 和盘托出；全部招供 ■ **cleaner** noun **cleanly** adverb.

cleanliness /'klenlinəs/ **noun** the quality of being clean 干净

cleanse /klenz/ **verb** (**cleanses**, **cleansing**, **cleansed**) make something thoroughly clean or pure 彻底清洁；净化 ■ **cleanser** noun.

clear /klɪə(r)/ **adjective 1** easy to see, hear, or understand 清楚的；清晰的；明白易懂的 **2** leaving or feeling no doubt 无疑的 **3** 确信的 transparent 透明的；清澈的 **4** free of obstructions or unwanted objects 无阻碍的；无多余物的 **5** (of a period of time) free of commitments (一段时间)空闲的 **6** free from disease or guilt 无病的；无罪的 **7** (clear of) not touching 不接触的 • **verb 1** make or become clear (使)变清楚；(使)变清晰 **2** get past or over something safely or without touching it 无阻碍地越过；不接触地越过 **3** show or state that someone is innocent 证明…无罪；宣告…无罪 **4** give official approval to (正式)批准 **5** make people leave a place 疏散(场所)中的人；使人撤离(场所) **6** (of a cheque) be paid into someone's account (支票)兑现 □ **clear-cut** sharply defined; easy to see or understand 清晰易见的；明白易懂的 **clear off** informal 【非正式】 go away 离开 **clear up 1** (of an illness) become cured (疾病)被治愈 **2** stop raining 停雨；转晴 **clear something up 1** tidy something 整理(某物) **2** solve or explain a mystery or misunderstanding 解开(谜团)；消除(误会) **in the clear** no longer in danger or under suspicion 无危险的；无嫌疑的 ■ **clearly** adverb.

clearance /'klɪərəns/ **noun 1** the

action of clearing 清除；清理 **2** official permission for someone to take place (官方的)许可，批准 **3** clear space allowed for a thing to move past or under another 净空；间隙

clearing /ˈklɪərɪŋ/ **noun** an open space in a wood or forest 林中空地

clearway /ˈklɪəweɪ/ **noun** Brit. 【英】a main road other than a motorway on which vehicles are not allowed to stop 禁停公路

cleat /kliːt/ **noun 1** a projection to which a rope may be attached (系绳用的)系索耳 **2** a projecting wedge on a tool, the sole of a boot, etc., to prevent it slipping (工具、鞋底等的)防滑橡胶，防滑钉

cleavage /ˈkliːvɪdʒ/ **noun 1** the space between a woman's breasts (女子两乳间的)乳沟 **2** a sharp difference or division between people (人与人之间的)显著差异，分歧

cleave[1] /kliːv/ **verb** (**cleaves, cleaving, clove** or **cleft** or **cleaved**; past participle **cloven** or **cleft** or **cleaved**) divide or split in two 分开；裂开

cleave[2] **verb** (**cleaves, cleaving, cleaved**) (**cleave to**) literary 【文】stick to something 粘住；紧贴

cleaver /ˈkliːvə(r)/ **noun** a tool with a broad, heavy blade, for chopping meat 切肉刀

clef /klef/ **noun** Music【音乐】a symbol placed next to the notes on a stave, to show their pitch 谱号

cleft /kleft/ past and past participle of CLEAVE[1]. • **adjective** split or divided into two 劈开的；半裂开的 • **noun** a split or indentation 裂缝；裂口口 **cleft lip** an upper lip with an abnormal split in the centre 裂唇 **cleft palate** a split in the roof of the mouth 腭裂

clematis /ˈklemətɪs/ **noun** an ornamental climbing plant 铁线莲(装饰性攀缘植物)

clemency /ˈklemənsi/ **noun** kind or merciful treatment 宽大；仁慈

clement /ˈklemənt/ **adjective** (of weather) mild (天气)温和的

clementine /ˈkleməntiːn/ **noun** a small citrus fruit with bright orange-red skin 克莱门氏小柑橘

clench /klentʃ/ **verb 1** close your fist or hold your teeth or muscles together tightly in response to stress or anger 攥紧(拳头)；咬紧(牙齿) **2** grasp something tightly 握紧；紧紧抓住

clerestory /ˈklɪəstɔːri/ **noun** (plural **clerestories**) a row of windows in the upper part of the wall of a church or other large building (教堂或其他大型建筑顶端采光用的)天窗

clergy /ˈklɜːdʒi/ **noun** (plural **clergies**) the priests and ministers of a religion, especially those of the Christian Church (尤指基督教会的)天职人员

clergyman /ˈklɜːdʒimən/ or **clergywoman** /ˈklɜːdʒiwʊmən/ **noun** (plural **clergymen** or **clergywomen**) a Christian priest or minister (基督教的)牧师

cleric /ˈklerɪk/ **noun** a priest or religious leader 教士；牧师；宗教领袖

clerical /ˈklerɪkl/ **adjective 1** relating to the normal work of an office clerk 文职的；文书工作的 **2** relating to the priests and ministers of the Christian Church (基督教)神职人员的

clerk /klɑːk/ **noun 1** a person employed in an office or bank to keep records or accounts and do other routine work (办公室或银行的)职员 **2** a person in charge of the records of a local council or court (地方议会或法庭的)文书，书记员

clever /ˈklevə(r)/ **adjective** (**cleverer, cleverest**) **1** quick to understand and learn 聪明的；机灵的 **2** skilled at doing something 灵巧的，熟练的 ■ **cleverly** adverb **cleverness** noun.

cliché /ˈkliːʃeɪ/ **noun** a phrase or idea that has been used too much and is no longer fresh or interesting 陈词滥调；陈腐观念 ▪ **clichéd** adjective.

click /klɪk/ **noun** a short, sharp sound as of two hard objects coming into contact (两硬物相碰发出的)咔嗒声 ▪ **verb 1** make a click 发出咔嗒声 **2** move or become secured with a click 咔嗒移动；咔嗒固定 **3** Computing 【计】 press a mouse button 点击(鼠标键) **4** informal 【非正式】 become suddenly clear or understood 豁然开朗；突然明白

client /'klaɪənt/ **noun** a person who uses the services of a professional person or organization (聘请专业人士或机构的)委托人，当事人，客户

clientele /ˌkliːɒn'tel/ **noun** the clients or customers of a shop, restaurant, or professional service 顾客；客户；委托人

cliff /klɪf/ **noun** a steep rock face at the edge of the sea (海边的)悬崖，峭壁

cliffhanger /'klɪfhæŋə(r)/ **noun** a situation in a story which is exciting because you do not know what is going to happen next (故事中扣人心弦的)悬念

climacteric /klaɪ'mæktrɪk/ **noun** the period in a person's life when their fertility has started to decline 更年期

climactic /klaɪ'mæktɪk/ **adjective** forming an exciting climax 形成高潮的

climate /'klaɪmət/ **noun 1** the general weather conditions in an area over a long period 气候 **2** a general attitude or feeling among people 趋势；风气，思潮 ▪ **climatic** adjective.

climax /'klaɪmæks/ **noun 1** the most intense, exciting, or important point of something 高潮 **2** an orgasm 性高潮 ▪ **verb** reach a climax 达到高潮

climb /klaɪm/ **verb 1** go or come up to a higher position 攀升；爬高 **2** go up a hill, rock face, etc. 登(山)；攀(岩) **3** move somewhere, especially with effort or difficulty (尤指费力地向某处)爬 **4**

increase in value or amount 增值；增长 ▪ **noun 1** an act of climbing 攀登，攀爬 **2** a route up a mountain or cliff 攀爬路线 □ **climb down** admit that you are wrong about something 认错 ▪ **climber** noun.

clime /klaɪm/ **noun** literary 【文】 a place considered in terms of its climate (气候)带：*sunnier climes* 阳光较充足的气候带

clinch /klɪntʃ/ **verb 1** settle a contract or contest 达成(合同)；解决(争端) **2** settle something that has been uncertain or undecided 确定，决定 ▪ **noun 1** a tight hold in a fight or struggle (拳击或格斗中的)扭抱 **2** informal 【非正式】 a tight embrace 紧紧的拥抱

cling /klɪŋ/ **verb** (**clings, clinging, clung**) (**cling to** or **on to**) **1** hold on tightly to 紧握 **2** stick to 粘住 **3** unwilling to give up a belief or hope 执著于(信仰或希望) **4** be emotionally dependent on (感情上)依赖，依附 □ **cling film** Brit. 【英】 thin plastic film used to wrap or cover food 食品保鲜膜 ▪ **clingy** adjective.

clinic /'klɪnɪk/ **noun** a place where medical treatment or advice is given 门诊部；诊所

clinical /'klɪnɪkl/ **adjective 1** relating to the observation and treatment of patients 临床(治疗)的 **2** (of a place) very clean and plain (场所)简朴的 **3** efficient and showing no emotion 冷静的；超然的 ▪ **clinically** adverb.

clink /klɪŋk/ **noun** a sharp ringing sound (刺耳的)叮当声 ▪ **verb** make a clink 发出叮当声

clinker /'klɪŋkə(r)/ **noun** the stony remains from burnt coal or from a furnace 煤渣；炉渣

clip¹ /klɪp/ **noun 1** a flexible or spring-loaded device for holding objects together or in place 曲别针；弹簧夹 **2** a piece of jewellery that is fastened to a garment with a clip 饰物别针 ▪ **verb** (**clips, clipping, clipped**) fasten with a clip 用夹子夹住；用别针别住

clip² /klɪp/ **verb** (**clips, clipping, clipped**) **1** cut or trim with shears or scissors (用剪刀)修剪 **2** trim the hair or wool of an animal 给(动物)修剪毛发 **3** hit quickly or lightly 猛击；痛打 • **noun 1** an act of clipping 修剪 **2** a short sequence taken from a film or broadcast (电影或广播电视的)剪辑片段 **3** informal 【非正式】 a quick or light blow 猛击；抽打

clipboard /'klɪpbɔːd/ **noun** a board with a clip at the top, for holding papers and writing on 带夹子的写字板；写字夹板

clipped /klɪpt/ **adjective** (of speech) having short, sharp vowel sounds and clear pronunciation (说话)发音短促清脆的

clipper /'klɪpə(r)/ **noun 1** (**clippers**) an instrument for clipping 剪具；剪子 **2** (in the past) a type of fast sailing ship (旧时的)快速帆船

clipping /'klɪpɪŋ/ **noun 1** a small piece trimmed from something 剪下物 **2** an article cut from a newspaper or magazine 剪报；杂志剪materials文章

clique /kliːk/ **noun** a small group of people who do not allow other people to join them 小集团；小圈子；派系 ■ **cliquey** adjective.

clitoris /'klɪtərɪs/ **noun** the small sensitive organ just in front of the vagina 阴蒂

cloak /kləʊk/ **noun** an outer garment that hangs loosely from the shoulders to the knees or ankles 斗篷；披风 • **verb** cover or hide something 覆盖；遮掩 □ **cloak-and-dagger** involving secret activities 涉及阴谋活动的

cloakroom /'kləʊkrʊm/ **noun 1** a room where coats and bags may be left 衣帽间；存包处 **2** Brit. 【英】 a room that contains a toilet 洗手间，卫生间

clobber /'klɒbə(r)/ informal 【非正式】 **verb** (**clobbers, clobbering, clobbered**) hit someone hard 狠揍；猛揍 • **noun** Brit. 【英】 clothing and personal belongings 衣物；随身物品

cloche /klɒʃ/ **noun 1** a small cover for protecting young or tender plants (保护植物幼苗的)玻璃罩，塑料罩 **2** a woman's close-fitting bell-shaped hat 钟形女帽

clock /klɒk/ **noun 1** an instrument that indicates the time (时)钟 **2** informal 【非正式】 a measuring device resembling a clock, such as a speedometer 计量仪表 • **verb** informal 【非正式】 **1** reach a particular speed or distance 达到(特定速度或距离) **2** (**clock in** or **out** or **on** or **off**) register the time you are arriving at or leaving work 记录上班(或下班)时间 **3** (**clock something up**) reach a total 总计

clockwise /'klɒkwaɪz/ **adverb & adjective** in the direction of the movement of the hands of a clock 顺时针方向地(的)

clockwork /'klɒkwɜːk/ **noun** a mechanism which has a spring and a system of interlocking wheels, used to make a mechanical clock or other device work 发条齿轮装置 □ **like clockwork** very smoothly and easily 一帆风顺地；轻松地

clod /klɒd/ **noun 1** a lump of earth 土块；泥块 **2** informal 【非正式】 a stupid person 傻子；笨蛋

clodhopper /'klɒdhɒpə(r)/ **noun** informal 【非正式】 **1** a large, heavy shoe 笨重的大鞋子 **2** a clumsy person 笨拙的人

clog /klɒg/ **noun** a shoe with a thick wooden sole 木屐 • **verb** (**clogs, clogging, clogged**) (often **clog something up**) block something up 阻塞

cloister /'klɔɪstə(r)/ **noun** a covered passage round an open courtyard in a convent, monastery, cathedral, etc. (修道院、寺院、大教堂等庭院周围的)

回廊,走廊

cloistered /ˈklɔɪstəd/ **adjective 1** having a cloister 带回廊的;回廊围住的 **2** protected from the outside world 与世隔绝的;隐居的

clomp /klɒmp/ **verb** walk with a heavy tread 重踏着走 • **noun** the sound of a heavy tread 重踏声

clone /kləʊn/ **noun** an animal or plant created from the cells of another, to which it is genetically identical (动植物的)克隆,无性繁殖 • **verb** (**clones, cloning, cloned**) **1** create something as a clone 无性繁殖;克隆 **2** make an identical copy of something 复制

close[1] /kləʊs/ **adjective 1** only a short distance away or apart in space or time (空间或时间上)近的 **2** (of a connection or likeness) strong (联系)紧密的,(相似程度)很大的 **3** (of two people) very affectionate and friendly (两人)亲近的,亲密的 **4** (of observation or examination) done in a careful and thorough way (观察或检查)仔细彻底的,缜密的 • **adverb** so as to be very near; with very little space between 接近地;靠近地 • **noun** Brit. 【英】a street of houses that is closed at one end 死胡同,死路 □ **close-knit** (of a group of people) united by strong relationships (一群人)紧密团结的,关系密切的 **at close quarters** (or **range**) from a position close to someone or something 近距离地 **close shave** (or **close call**) informal 【非正式】a narrow escape from danger or disaster 死里逃生;侥幸脱险 **close-up** a photograph or sequence in a film that is taken from a very short distance 特写照片;(电影的)特写镜头 ■ **closely** adverb.

close[2] /kləʊz/ **verb** (**closes, closing, closed**) **1** move something so as to cover an opening 盖;封闭 **2** (also **close something up**) bring two parts of something together 关;关闭;合上 **3** (**close on** or **in on**) gra-

dually surround or get nearer to 靠拢;围拢 **4** (**close around** or **over**) encircle and hold 环抱;抱住 **5** come or bring something to an end (使)结束 **6** finish speaking or writing 结束(讲话) **7** (often **close down**) stop trading or working 停业;关闭 **8** bring a deal or arrangement to a conclusion 达成(交易);商定(协议) • **noun** the end of an event or of a period of time or activity (一段时间或活动的)结束,终止 □ **close season** (or **closed season**) a period in the year when fishing or hunting is officially forbidden, or when a sport is not played 禁渔季节;禁猎季节

closed /kləʊzd/ **adjective 1** not open or allowing people to go in 关闭的;不准通行的 **2** not communicating with or influenced by other people 封闭的;闭关自守的 □ **closed-circuit television** a television system used to watch people within a building, shopping centre, etc. 闭路电视 **closed shop** a place of work where all employees must belong to a particular trade union 只雇用工会会员的企业

closet /ˈklɒzɪt/ **noun** chiefly N. Amer.【主北美】**1** a tall cupboard or wardrobe 橱柜;衣柜 **2** a small room 小房间 • **verb** (**closets, closeting, closeted**) shut yourself in a private room 把…关进房间(独处) □ **in** (or **out of**) **the closet** not open (or open) about being homosexual 不公开(或公开)同性恋身份

closure /ˈkləʊʒə(r)/ **noun 1** the closing of something 关闭;结束 **2** a feeling that an upsetting experience has been resolved 如释重负

clot /klɒt/ **noun 1** a lump that is formed when a thick liquid substance dries or becomes thicker 凝结块 **2** Brit. informal 【英,非正式】a stupid person 傻子;蠢货 • **verb** (**clots, clotting, clotted**) form into clots 凝结成块 □ **clotted**

cream thick cream obtained by heating and cooling milk slowly 浓缩奶油

cloth /klɒθ/ noun (plural **cloths**) **1** fabric made from a soft fibre such as wool or cotton 织物;布料 **2** a piece of cloth used for a particular purpose (用于特定用途的)一块布片 **3** (**the cloth**) ministers of the Church (统称)牧师,神父

clothe /kləʊð/ verb (**clothes, clothing, clothed**) **1** provide with clothes 为…提供衣服 **2** (**be clothed in**) be dressed in 穿着…衣服

clothes /kləʊðz/ plural noun things worn to cover the body 衣服;服装 □ **clothes horse** a frame on which washed clothes are hung to dry 晾衣架

clothing /kləʊðɪŋ/ noun clothes 衣服 (总称)

cloud /klaʊd/ noun **1** a mass of vapour floating in the atmosphere 云;云雾 **2** a mass of smoke, dust, etc. in the air 烟雾;烟尘 **3** a state or cause of anxiety or worry 忧郁;焦虑;令人忧虑的事 • verb **1** (**cloud over**) (of the sky) become full of clouds (天空)布满乌云,阴云密布 **2** become less clear 变模糊;变得不清晰 **3** (of someone's face or eyes) show sadness, anxiety, or anger (某人的脸或眼睛)显得悲伤(或忧虑、愤怒) □ **cloud cuckoo land** a state of unrealistic fantasy (脱离现实的)理想世界;幻境 **on cloud nine** very happy 极为幸福;非常快乐 **under a cloud** out of favour or suspected of having done wrong 不受欢迎;有嫌疑 ■ **cloudless** adjective **cloudy** adjective.

cloudburst /ˈklaʊdbɜːst/ noun a sudden fall of very heavy rain 大暴雨

clout /klaʊt/ informal 【非正式】noun **1** a heavy blow 重击;猛击 **2** influence or power 影响;权力 • verb hit someone hard 重击;猛击

clove¹ /kləʊv/ noun the dried flower bud of a tropical tree, used as a spice 干丁香花苞(用作香料)

clove² noun any of the segments making up a bulb of garlic 小鳞茎;小球茎

clove³ past of CLEAVE¹. □ **clove hitch** a knot used to fasten a rope to a spar or another rope 卷结;酒瓶结

cloven /ˈkləʊvn/ past participle of CLEAVE¹. □ **cloven hoof** the divided hoof of animals such as cattle, sheep, and deer (牛、羊、鹿等动物的)分趾蹄,偶蹄

clover /ˈkləʊvə(r)/ noun a plant with white or pink flowers and a leaf with three lobes 三叶草;苜蓿 □ **in clover** in ease and luxury 安逸奢侈;养尊处优

clown /klaʊn/ noun **1** an entertainer who does silly things to make people laugh (马戏团的)小丑,滑稽演员 **2** a playful or silly person 爱开玩笑的人;笨人 • verb **1** perform as a clown 扮演小丑 **2** behave in a funny or silly way (像小丑般)开玩笑,逗趣 ■ **clownish** adjective.

cloying /ˈklɔɪɪŋ/ adjective **1** too sweet and making you feel slightly sick 甜得发腻的 **2** too sentimental 多愁善感的

club¹ /klʌb/ noun **1** a group of people who meet regularly for a particular activity 社团;联合会 **2** a place where members can relax, eat meals, or stay overnight 俱乐部 **3** a nightclub with dance music 夜总会 • verb (**clubs, clubbing, clubbed**) **1** (**club together**) combine with other people to do something 联合起来,合伙(做事) **2** informal 【非正式】go out to nightclubs 去夜总会 ■ **clubber** noun.

club² noun **1** a heavy stick used as a weapon (用作武器的)大头棒,棍棒 **2** a heavy stick with a thick head, used to hit the ball in golf (高尔夫球

运动中的)球杆 **3** (**clubs**) one of the four suits in a pack of playing cards, represented by a design of three black clover leaves on a short stem (纸牌中的)梅花牌 • verb (**clubs**, **clubbing**, **clubbed**) beat someone with a heavy stick 用大头棒打;用棍棒打 □ **club foot** a deformed foot which is twisted so that the sole cannot be placed flat on the ground 畸形足;内弯足

clubhouse /ˈklʌbhaʊs/ noun a building having a bar and other facilities for club members (为会员提供酒吧和其他设施的)俱乐部会所

cluck /klʌk/ verb (of a hen) make a short, throaty sound (母鸡)咯咯声 • noun the short, throaty sound made by a hen (母鸡的)咯咯叫声

clue /kluː/ noun a fact or piece of evidence that helps to clear up a mystery or solve a problem 线索 □ **not have a clue** informal【非正式】have no idea about something 毫无头绪;一无所知 **clued up** informal【非正式】well informed 消息灵通的

clueless /ˈkluːləs/ adjective not able to understand or do something 一无所知的;无能的

clump /klʌmp/ noun **1** a small group of trees or plants growing closely together (树或草本植物的)丛,簇 **2** a mass or lump of something 一团,一堆 **3** the sound of a heavy tread 重踏声 • verb **1** form into a clump or mass 形成一丛,结成团 **2** walk heavily 重步走

clumpy /ˈklʌmpi/ adjective (of shoes or boots) thick and heavy (鞋或靴子)笨重的

clumsy /ˈklʌmzi/ adjective (**clumsier**, **clumsiest**) **1** awkward and badly coordinated 笨拙的 **2** tactless 不老练的;不圆滑的 ■ **clumsily** adverb **clumsiness** noun.

clung /klʌŋ/ past and past participle of CLING.

clunk /klʌŋk/ noun a dull, heavy sound 嘟嘟声 • verb make a clunk 发嘟嘟声

cluster /ˈklʌstə(r)/ noun a group of similar things placed or occurring closely together 丛;簇;团;群 • verb (**cluster**, **clustering**, **clustered**) form a cluster 丛生;群聚

clutch[1] /klʌtʃ/ verb grasp something tightly 紧紧握住 • noun **1** a tight grasp 紧握 **2** (**clutches**) power and control 势力;控制 **3** a mechanism in a vehicle that connects the engine with the axle and wheels (车辆的)离合器

clutch[2] noun **1** a group of eggs fertilized at the same time and laid in a single session 一窝蛋 **2** a group of chicks hatched from the same clutch of eggs 一窝小鸡

clutter /ˈklʌtə(r)/ verb (**clutters**, **cluttering**, **cluttered**) cover or fill with an untidy assortment of things 胡乱堆满;塞满 • noun things lying about untidily 杂乱的东西

cm abbreviation centimetres.

Co. /kəʊ/ abbreviation **1** company. **2** county.

co- /kəʊ/ prefix joint; mutual; together with another or others 联合;相互的;和……一起: coexist 共存 | costar 共同主演

c/o /siː ˈəʊ/ abbreviation care of (信件)由……转交

coach[1] /kəʊtʃ/ noun **1** Brit.【英】a comfortable single-decker bus used for longer journeys (单层)长途汽车 **2** a railway carriage 火车车厢 **3** a large horse-drawn carriage 大马车

coach[2] noun **1** a person who trains someone in a sport (运动)指导,教练 **2** a person who gives private lessons in a subject 私人教师;家庭教师 • verb give private lessons or training to someone 辅导;训练

coagulate /kəʊˈæɡjuleɪt/ verb (**coagulates**, **coagulating**, **coagulated**) (of a liquid) thicken or become solid (液体)凝固，凝结 ■ **coagulant** noun **coagulation** noun.

coal /kəʊl/ **noun** a black rock used as fuel, consisting mainly of carbon formed from the remains of ancient plants 煤 □ **coal tar** a thick black liquid produced when gas is made from coal 煤焦油(干馏煤时获得的黑色黏稠液体)

coalesce /ˌkəʊəˈles/ **verb** (**coalesces, coalescing, coalesced**) come or bring together to form a single mass or whole (使)合并；(使)结合

coalface /ˈkəʊlfeɪs/ **noun** an exposed surface of coal in a mine 采煤工作面

coalfield /ˈkəʊlfiːld/ **noun** a large area where there is a lot of coal underground 煤田

coalition /ˌkəʊəˈlɪʃn/ **noun** a government made up of two political parties who have agreed to work together (两个政党组成的)联合政府

coarse /kɔːs/ **adjective 1** having a rough texture (质地)粗的，粗糙的 **2** consisting of large grains or particles 由大颗粒构成的 **3** rude or vulgar 无礼的；粗俗的 □ **coarse fish** Brit. 【英】any freshwater fish other than salmon and trout (除鲑鱼和鳟鱼之外的)淡水鱼 ■ **coarsely** adverb.

! **注意** don't confuse **coarse** with **course**, which means 'a direction', as in *the plane changed course*. 不要混淆 coarse 和 course，后者意为"方向"，如 the plane changed course(飞机改变了航向)

coarsen /ˈkɔːsn/ **verb** make or become coarse (使)变粗的；(使)变粗俗

coast /kəʊst/ **noun** a stretch of land next to or near the sea 沿海地区；海滨 • **verb 1** move easily without using power 溜；靠惯性移动 **2** do something without making much effort 毫不费力地做事 □ **the coast is clear** there is no danger of being

seen or caught 没有被发现(或抓到)的危险；危险已过 ■ **coastal** adjective.

coaster /ˈkəʊstə(r)/ **noun 1** a small mat for a glass 小杯垫 **2** a ship that sails along the coast from port to port 沿海岸航行的船只

coastguard /ˈkəʊstɡɑːd/ **noun** an organization or person that keeps watch over coastal waters 海岸警卫队(队员)

coastline /ˈkəʊstlaɪn/ **noun** the shape or appearance of the land along a coast 海岸线

coat /kəʊt/ **noun 1** a full-length outer garment with sleeves 外套；大衣 **2** an animal's covering of fur or hair (动物的)毛皮 **3** an outer layer or covering 覆盖层；掩体 **4** a single layer of paint (油漆的)涂层 • **verb** form or provide with a layer or covering 涂抹；覆盖 □ **coat of arms** a design used as a special symbol of a family, city, or organization 作为家庭、城市或机构象征的纹章,盾形徽章

coax /kəʊks/ **verb 1** gently persuade someone to do something 劝诱;哄 **2** gently guide or move something 小心

coaxial /kəʊˈæksɪəl/ **adjective** (of a cable) having two wires, one wrapped round the other but separated by insulation (电缆)同轴的

cob /kɒb/ **noun 1** Brit. 【英】a loaf of bread 一块面包 **2** the central part of an ear of maize 玉米穗轴；玉米棒子芯 **3** (also **cobnut**) a hazelnut or filbert 榛子 **4** a sturdily built horse 壮马

cobalt /ˈkəʊbɔːlt/ **noun** a silvery-white metallic element (金属元素)钴

cobber /ˈkɒbə(r)/ **noun** Austral./NZ informal 【澳/新西兰,非正式】a companion or friend 同伴;朋友

cobble[1] /ˈkɒbl/ or **cobblestone** /ˈkɒblstəʊn/ **noun** a small round stone used to cover road surfaces (铺

路用的)鹅卵石，小圆石 ■ **cobbled** adjective.

cobble² verb (**cobbles, cobbling, cobbled**) (**cobble something together**) make up something roughly from materials that happen to be available 胡乱拼凑

cobbler /'kɒblə(r)/ noun **1** a person whose job is mending shoes 修鞋匠 **2** chiefly N. Amer.【主北美】a fruit pie with a cake-like crust 脆皮面水果馅饼

cobra /'kəʊbrə/ noun a highly poisonous snake native to Africa and Asia 眼镜蛇(产于非洲和亚洲的，有剧毒)

cobweb /'kɒbweb/ noun a spider's web 蜘蛛网

cocaine /kəʊ'keɪn/ noun an addictive drug made from the leaves of a tropical plant 可卡因；古柯碱

coccyx /'kɒksɪks/ noun (plural **coccyges** /'kɒksɪdʒi:z/ or **coccyxes**) a small triangular bone at the base of the spine (人体脊椎底部的)尾骨

cochineal /ˌkɒtʃɪ'ni:l/ noun a bright red dye used for colouring food (用于食品染色的)胭脂虫红

cochlea /'kɒkliə/ noun (plural **cochleae** /'kɒkliː/) the spiral cavity of the inner ear 耳蜗(内耳的螺旋形腔)

cock /kɒk/ noun a male chicken or game bird 公鸡；雄禽 • verb **1** tilt or bend something in a particular direction 使翘起；使弯曲 **2** raise the firing lever of a gun to make it ready to shoot 扳起(枪)的扳机 **3** (**cock something up**) Brit. informal【英，非正式】spoil something by doing it badly 搞砸；弄糟 □ **cock-a-hoop** very pleased 极其高兴的；得意洋洋的 **cock and bull story** a very unlikely story 荒诞故事

cockade /kɒ'keɪd/ noun a rosette or knot of ribbons worn on a hat as part of a uniform 帽子上的花结；帽章

cockatiel /ˌkɒkə'ti:l/ noun a small Australian parrot with a crest (澳大利亚产的)鸡尾鹦鹉

cockatoo /ˌkɒkə'tu:/ noun a kind of parrot with a crest 凤头鹦鹉

cockcrow /'kɒkkrəʊ/ noun literary【文】dawn 黎明

cockerel /'kɒkərəl/ noun a young cock 小公鸡

cocker spaniel /'kɒkə(r)/ noun a small breed of spaniel with a silky coat 可卡犬(一种小型獚，皮毛柔软光洁)

cockeyed /'kɒkaɪd/ adjective informal【非正式】**1** crooked 弯曲的 **2** stupid and impractical 荒谬的；不切实际的

cockle /'kɒkl/ noun an edible shellfish with a ribbed shell 鸟蛤，海扇(可食用贝类，外壳有罗纹)

cockney /'kɒkni/ noun (plural **cockneys**) **1** a person who was born in the East End of London 伦敦东区佬 **2** the dialect or accent used in this area 伦敦东区方言；伦敦东区口音

cockpit /'kɒkpɪt/ noun **1** a compartment for the pilot and crew in an aircraft or spacecraft (飞机或航天器的)驾驶舱，机务人员座舱 **2** the driver's compartment in a racing car (赛车的)驾驶座

cockroach /'kɒkrəʊtʃ/ noun a beetle-like insect with long antennae and legs 蟑螂

cocksure /ˌkɒk'ʃʊə(r)/ adjective arrogantly confident 自以为是的

cocktail /'kɒkteɪl/ noun **1** an alcoholic drink consisting of a spirit mixed with other ingredients 鸡尾酒 **2** a mixture 混合物

cocky /'kɒki/ adjective (**cockier, cockiest**) too self-confident 趾高气扬的；狂妄自大的 ■ **cockily** adverb **cockiness** noun.

cocoa /'kəʊkəʊ/ noun a drink made from powdered cacao seeds, mixed with hot milk 可可茶(可可粉与热奶

混合调制的饮料)

coconut /ˈkəʊkənʌt/ **noun 1** the large brown seed of a kind of palm tree, consisting of a woody husk lined with edible white flesh 椰子 **2** the white flesh of a coconut 椰子肉 □ **coconut shy** a sideshow at a fair, in which you throw balls at a coconut and win it if you knock it off a stand (游乐场中以椰子为靶子的)投靶游戏

✔ 拼写指南 just *-o-*, not *-oa-*: coconut. coconut 中只有 -o-, 不要拼作 -oa-。

cocoon /kəˈkuːn/ **noun 1** a silky case spun by the larva of many insects, which protects it while it is turning into an adult (昆虫的)茧 **2** something that envelops you in a protective or comforting way 防护层；保护膜 • **verb** wrap in a cocoon 给…加上保护层；把…包住

cod /kɒd/ **noun** (plural **cod**) a large sea fish used for food 鳕鱼(一种大型海鱼，可食用) □ **cod liver oil** oil obtained from the liver of cod, rich in vitamins D and A (鳕)鱼肝油(富含维生素D和A)

coda /ˈkəʊdə/ **noun** an extra passage marking the end of a piece of music (乐曲的)尾声

coddle /ˈkɒdl/ **verb** (**coddles**, **coddling**, **coddled**) give someone too much care and attention 娇纵；溺爱

code /kəʊd/ **noun 1** a system of words, figures, or symbols used to represent others secretly or briefly (保密的)代码，暗号 **2** (also **dialling code**) a sequence of numbers dialled to connect a telephone line with another exchange 电话区域号码；电话区号 **3** instructions for a computer program (程序)编码 **4** a set of laws or rules 法规；准则 • **verb** (**codes**, **coding**, **coded**) **1** convert into a code 把…编成代码 **2** (**coded**)

expressed in an indirect way 间接表达的；隐讳表达的

codeine /ˈkəʊdiːn/ **noun** a painkilling drug obtained from morphine 可待因(从吗啡中提取的一种镇痛药物)

codger /ˈkɒdʒə(r)/ **noun** informal 【非正式】an elderly man 老家伙

codicil /ˈkəʊdɪsɪl/ **noun** a part added to a will that explains or alters an earlier part 遗嘱附件(对遗嘱进行解释或修改)

codify /ˈkəʊdɪfaɪ/ **verb** (**codifies**, **codifying**, **codified**) arrange a set of rules as a formal code 将(规则)编集成典 ■ **codification** noun.

codpiece /ˈkɒdpiːs/ **noun** (in the past) a pouch worn by a man over his trousers, covering the groin (旧时男子裤子上盖住私处的)遮阴袋

codswallop /ˈkɒdzwɒləp/ **noun** Brit. informal 【英,非正式】nonsense 胡说八道

co-education /ˌkəʊedʒʊˈkeɪʃn/ **noun** the teaching of boys and girls together in the same schools 男女同校(教育) ■ **co-educational** adjective.

coefficient /ˌkəʊɪˈfɪʃnt/ **noun 1** 【数学】a quantity which is placed before another which it multiplies (e.g. 4 in $4x^2$) 系数 **2** Physics 【物理】a multiplier or factor that measures some property 系数

coerce /kəʊˈɜːs/ **verb** (**coerces**, **coercing**, **coerced**) force someone to do something 强迫；胁迫 ■ **coercion** noun **coercive** adjective.

coexist /ˌkəʊɪɡˈzɪst/ **verb 1** exist at the same time or in the same place (同时或同地)共存 **2** be together in harmony 和平共处 ■ **coexistence** noun.

C. of E. /ˌsiː əv ˈiː/ **abbreviation** Church of England 英国国教会；英格兰圣公会

coffee /ˈkɒfi/ **noun** a hot drink made from the seeds of a tropical shrub 咖啡 □ **coffee table** a small low table for putting cups, books, etc. on 咖啡桌;矮茶几

coffer /'kɒfə(r)/ **noun** a small chest for holding money or valuable items (装钱或贵重物品的)小箱,小柜

coffin /'kɒfɪn/ **noun** a long box in which a dead body is buried or cremated 棺材;灵柩

cog /kɒg/ **noun 1** (also **cogwheel**) a wheel or bar with projections on its edge, which transfers motion by engaging with projections on another wheel or bar 齿轮;嵌齿轮 **2** a projection on a cog 轮齿;轮牙;齿

cogent /'kəʊdʒənt/ **adjective** (of an argument) clear, logical, and convincing (论点)合乎逻辑的,令人信服的 ■ **cogency noun cogently** adverb.

cogitate /'kɒdʒɪteɪt/ **verb** (**cogitates, cogitating, cogitated**) formal【正式】think carefully about something 仔细思考;慎重考虑 ■ **cogitation noun.**

cognac /'kɒnjæk/ **noun** brandy made in Cognac in western France (产于法国西部科涅克的)科涅克白兰地,干邑

cognition /kɒg'nɪʃn/ **noun** the process of gaining knowledge through thought, experience, and the senses 认知;感知 ■ **cognitive adjective.**

cognizance or **cognisance** /'kɒgnɪzəns/ **noun** formal【正式】knowledge or awareness 认识;觉察;感知 ■ **cognizant adjective.**

cognoscenti /ˌkɒnjə'ʃenti/ **plural noun** people who are well informed about a particular subject (某一学科的)专家

cohabit /kəʊ'hæbɪt/ **verb** (**cohabits, cohabiting, cohabited**) live together and have a sexual relationship without being married (未婚)同居 ■ **cohabitation noun.**

cohere /kəʊ'hɪə(r)/ **verb** (**coheres, cohering, cohered**) hold firmly together; form a whole 黏合;凝聚

coherent /kəʊ'hɪərənt/ **adjective 1** (of an argument or theory) logical and consistent (论点或理论)合乎逻辑的,前后一致的 **2** able to speak clearly and logically (说话)条理清楚的,合乎逻辑的 ■ **coherence noun coherently** adverb.

cohesion /kəʊ'hiːʒn/ **noun** the fact of holding firmly together 黏合;凝聚

cohesive /kəʊ'hiːsɪv/ **adjective** holding or making something hold together 凝聚的;团结的

cohort /'kəʊhɔːt/ **noun 1** a large group of people 一大群人 **2** an ancient Roman military unit equal to one tenth of a legion (古罗马的)步兵队(相当于一个军团的1/10)

coif noun /kɔɪf/ a close-fitting cap worn by nuns under a veil (修女戴在头巾下面的)贴头帽 ■ **verb** /kwɑːf/ (**coifs, coiffing, coiffed**) arrange someone's hair 给(某人)做发型

coiffure /kwɑː'fjʊə(r)/ **noun** a person's hairstyle 发型 ■ **coiffured adjective.**

coil /kɔɪl/ **noun 1** a length of something wound in loops 圈;匝;卷 **2** a contraceptive in the form of a small coil, fitted into the womb 子宫节育环;避孕环 ■ **verb** arrange or form something into a coil 盘绕;盘成环

coin /kɔɪn/ **noun** a flat disc or piece of metal used as money 硬币;钱币 ■ **verb 1** invent a new word or phrase 创造,杜撰(新词或短语) **2** make coins by stamping metal (冲压金属)铸造(硬币)

coinage /'kɔɪnɪdʒ/ **noun 1** coins of a particular type (某种类型的)硬币,钱币 **2** a newly invented word or phrase 新造的词语

coincide /ˌkəʊɪn'saɪd/ **verb** (**coincides, coinciding, coincided**) **1** happen at the same time or place (时间或地点上)巧合;同时 **2** be the same or similar; tally 相符;一致

coincidence /kəʊ'ɪnsɪdəns/ **noun**

1 a remarkable instance of things happening at the same time by chance 巧合;巧事 **2** the fact of things being the same or similar 符合;一致 ■ **coincidental** adjective **coincidentally** adverb.

coitus /'kɔɪɪtəs/ **noun** technical 【术语】 sexual intercourse 性交 ■ **coital** adjective.

coke[1] /kəʊk/ **noun** a solid fuel made by heating coal in the absence of air 焦炭

coke[2] **noun** informal 【非正式】 cocaine 可卡因;古柯碱

colander /'kʌləndə(r)/ **noun** a bowl with holes in it, used to strain off liquid from food (淘洗食物的)滤盆, 滤器

cold /kəʊld/ **adjective 1** at a low temperature 寒冷的;温度低的 **2** not feeling or showing emotion 冷漠的; 无感情的 **3** (of a colour) containing a lot of blue or grey and giving no impression of warmth (色彩)灰色调的,冷色的 **4** (of a scent or trail) no longer fresh and easy to follow (气味或痕迹)隐秘的,不易追踪的 **5** without preparation 无准备的;出其不意的 ● **noun 1** cold weather 寒冷的天气 **2** an infection causing a streaming nose and sneezing 感冒;伤风 □ **cold-blooded 1** (of reptiles and fish) having a body that is the same temperature as the surrounding air (爬行动物和鱼类)冷血的 **2** heartless and cruel 无情的;残酷的 **the cold shoulder** deliberately unfriendly behaviour 冷淡;冷漠 **cold sore** an inflamed blister near the mouth, caused by a virus (病毒引起的)唇疮疹,嘴边疱疹 **cold snap** a brief period of cold weather 寒潮 **cold turkey** unpleasant feelings experienced by someone who has suddenly stopped taking a drug to which they are addicted (瘾君子)突然戒毒引起的难受感 **cold war** a

state of hostility between the Soviet Union and its allies and the Western powers after the Second World War 冷战(二战后苏联阵营和西方大国之间的敌对状态) **get cold feet** lose your nerve 临阵退缩 **in cold blood** deliberately cruel 冷血的;残忍的 ■ **coldly** adverb **coldness** noun.

coleslaw /'kəʊlslɔː/ **noun** a dish of shredded raw cabbage and carrots mixed with mayonnaise 丝(用生圆白菜丝、胡萝卜丝、蛋黄酱拌制)

colic /'kɒlɪk/ **noun** severe pain in the abdomen caused by wind or an obstruction in the intestines 腹绞痛 ■ **colicky** adjective.

collaborate /kə'læbəreɪt/ **verb** (**collaborates**, **collaborating**, **collaborated**) **1** work together on an activity 合作;协作 **2** cooperate with your country's enemy (与敌人)勾结 ■ **collaboration** noun **collaborative** adjective **collaborator** noun.

collage /'kɒlɑːʒ/ **noun** a form of art in which various materials are arranged and stuck to a backing 拼图艺术

collapse /kə'læps/ **verb** (**collapses**, **collapsing**, **collapsed**) **1** suddenly fall down or give way 倒塌;坍塌 **2** fail and come to a sudden end 崩溃;垮掉 ● **noun 1** the falling down or giving way of a structure 倒塌;坍塌 **2** a sudden failure 崩溃;瓦解

collapsible /kə'læpsəbl/ **adjective** able to be folded down 可折叠的

collar /'kɒlə(r)/ **noun 1** a band of material around the neck of a shirt or other garment 衣领;领子 **2** a band put around the neck of a dog or cat (狗或猫的)脖圈,颈圈 ● **verb** informal 【非正式】 seize someone 抓住;揪住;逮捕

collarbone /'kɒləbəʊn/ **noun** either of the pair of bones joining the breastbone to the shoulder blades 锁骨

collate /kə'leɪt/ **verb** (**collates**,

collating, collated) collect and combine documents or information 收集并组合(文件或信息) ∎ **collation** noun.

collateral /kə'lætərəl/ **noun** something that you promise to give to someone if you cannot repay a loan (贷款的)抵押品, 担保品 • **adjective** additional but less important; secondary 附属的; 次要的

colleague /'kɒli:g/ **noun** a person that you work with 同事; 同僚

collect /kə'lekt/ **verb 1** bring or gather things together 收集 **2** come together and form a group 聚集 **3** go somewhere to fetch someone or something 拿走; 收走; 领取 **4** buy or find and keep items of a particular kind as a hobby (作为爱好而)收藏, 搜集 ∎ **collectable** (or **collectible**) adjective **collector** noun.

collected /kə'lektɪd/ **adjective 1** calm 冷静的; 镇定的 **2** brought together in one volume or edition 结集成卷(或册)的

collection /kə'lekʃn/ **noun 1** the action of collecting 收集; 收藏 **2** a group of things that have been collected (一批)收集物; (一批)收藏品 **3** a time when mail is picked up from a post-box, or when rubbish is taken away (信件的)定时取走; (垃圾)定期清除

collective /kə'lektɪv/ **adjective 1** done by or belonging to all the members of a group 共同(完成)的; 集体(所有)的 **2** taken as a whole 总的 • **noun** a small business or project owned by all the people who work for it 集体企业 □ **collective noun** a noun that refers to a group of people or things (e.g. staff or herd) 集合名词 ∎ **collectively** adverb.

college /'kɒlɪdʒ/ **noun 1** a place providing higher education or specialized training 大学; 专科学校; 职业学院 **2** (in Britain) any of the independent institutions into which

some universities are separated (英国大学中独立的)学院

collegiate /kə'li:dʒiət/ **adjective 1** having to do with a college or college students 大学的; 学院的; 大学生的 **2** (of a university) composed of different colleges (大学)由学院组成的

collide /kə'laɪd/ **verb** (**collides, colliding, collided**) move or bump into something 碰撞

collie /'kɒli/ **noun** (plural **collies**) a breed of sheepdog with long hair 柯利牧羊犬(毛长)

collier /'kɒliə(r)/ **noun** a coal miner 煤矿工人; 矿工

colliery /'kɒliəri/ **noun** (plural **collieries**) a coal mine 煤矿

collision /kə'lɪʒn/ **noun** an instance when two or more things collide 碰撞; 冲突

colloquial /kə'ləʊkwiəl/ **adjective** (of language) used in ordinary conversation (语言)用于日常对话的, 口语的, 口头的 ∎ **colloquialism** noun **colloquially** adverb.

colloquy /'kɒləkwi/ **noun** (plural **colloquies**) formal【正式】a conference or conversation 会议; 交谈

collude /kə'lu:d/ **verb** (**colludes, colluding, colluded**) make a secret plan with someone to do something illegal or dishonest 密谋; 共谋; 勾结 ∎ **collusion** noun.

collywobbles /'kɒliwɒblz/ **plural noun** informal【非正式】nervousness or anxiety 紧张; 焦虑

cologne /kə'ləʊn/ **noun** a type of light perfume 古龙香水; 科隆香水

Colombian /kə'lɒmbiən/ **noun** a person from Colombia 哥伦比亚人 • **adjective** relating to Colombia 哥伦比亚的

colon[1] /'kəʊlən, -lɒn/ **noun** a punctuation mark (:) used before a list of items, a quotation, or an expansion or explanation 冒号

colon² /noun/ the main part of the large intestine, which leads to the rectum 结肠 ■ **colonic** adjective.

colonel /ˈkɜːnl/ *noun* a rank of officer in the army and in the US air force, above a lieutenant colonel (陆军)上校;(美国)空军上校

colonial /kəˈləʊnɪəl/ *adjective* having to do with a colony or with colonialism 殖民地的;殖民主义的 • *noun* a person who lives in a colony 殖民地居民

colonialism /kəˈləʊnɪəlɪzəm/ *noun* the practice of gaining control over other countries and occupying them with settlers 殖民主义;殖民政策 ■ **colonialist** noun & adjective.

colonist /ˈkɒlənɪst/ *noun* an inhabitant of a colony 殖民者;殖民地居民

colonize or **colonise** /ˈkɒlənaɪz/ *verb* (**colonizes, colonizing, colonized**) **1** make a colony in… 在…建立殖民地 **2** take over a place for your own use 接管(某地) ■ **colonization** noun.

colonnade /ˌkɒləˈneɪd/ *noun* a row of evenly spaced columns supporting a roof (支撑屋顶、间隔均匀的)列柱,柱廊

colony /ˈkɒlənɪ/ *noun* (plural **colonies**) **1** a country or area under the control of another country and occupied by settlers from that country 殖民地;属国(或地区) **2** a group of people of one nationality or race living in a foreign place 聚居的同国侨民;(在外地或外国)聚居的同种族人 **3** a place where a group of people with a common interest live together (拥有共同兴趣的人群的)聚居地 **4** a community of animals or plants living close together (动植物的)集群,群落

coloration or **colouration** /ˌkʌləˈreɪʃn/ *noun* the colours and markings of a plant or animal (动植物的)颜色,色泽

colossal /kəˈlɒsl/ *adjective* very large 庞大的 ■ **colossally** adverb.

colossus /kəˈlɒsəs/ *noun* (plural **colossi** /kəˈlɒsaɪ/) a person or thing that is very important or large in size 巨人;庞然大物

colostomy /kəˈlɒstəmɪ/ *noun* (plural **colostomies**) a surgical operation in which the colon is shortened and the cut end is moved to a new opening made in the wall of the abdomen 结肠切开术

colour /ˈkʌlə(r)/ (US spelling【美拼作】**color**) *noun* **1** an object's property of producing different sensations on the eye as a result of the way it reflects or gives out light 色;颜色 **2** one of the parts into which light can be separated (光谱中的)色彩,色调 **3** the use of all colours in photography or television (摄影或电视中运用的)彩色 **4** the natural colouring of the skin as an indication of someone's race (作为种族标志的)肤色 **5** redness of the complexion (脸色的)红润 **6** interest and excitement 趣味;刺激 *verb* **1** change the colour of something 给…着色 **2** blush 脸红 **3** influence something 影响 □ **colour-blind** not able to see certain colours 色盲的

coloured /ˈkʌləd/ (US spelling【美拼作】**colored**) *adjective* **1** having a colour or colours 有颜色的;彩色的 **2** offensive【冒犯】not having white skin 有色人种的 **3** (in South Africa) having parents who are of different races (南非)混血的 • *noun* **1** offensive【冒犯】a non-white person 有色人种 **2** (in South Africa) a person with parents of different races (南非的)混血儿

colourful /ˈkʌləfl/ (US spelling【美拼作】**colorful**) *adjective* **1** having many or varied colours 色彩缤纷的;色彩丰富的 **2** lively and exciting; vivid 活泼的;生动的 ■ **colourfully**

adverb.

colouring /'kʌlərɪŋ/ (US spelling 【美拼作】 **coloring**) noun 1 the process or art of applying colour 着色(法) 2 visual appearance in terms of colour 色彩;色调 3 a substance used to colour something 着色剂;色素

colourist /'kʌlərɪst/ (US spelling 【美拼作】 **colorist**) noun an artist or designer who uses colour in a special or skilful way 色彩画家;色彩设计师

colourless /'kʌlələs/ (US拼作 【美拼作】 **colorless**) adjective 1 without colour 无色的 2 without character or interest; dull 无特色的;平淡无奇的;无趣味的

colt /kəʊlt/ noun a young male horse 雄马驹

coltish /'kəʊltɪʃ/ adjective energetic but awkward in movement or behaviour 充满活力但行动笨拙的

column /'kɒləm/ noun 1 an upright pillar supporting a structure or standing alone as a monument 柱;支柱 2 a line of people or vehicles moving in the same direction (人或车辆的)队,行 3 a vertical division of a page or piece of writing (页面的)列,栏 4 a regular section of a newspaper or magazine on a particular subject or by a particular person (报刊的)专栏

columnist /'kɒləmnɪst/ noun a journalist who writes a column in a newspaper or magazine (报刊的)专栏作家

coma /'kəʊmə/ noun a state of long-lasting deep unconsciousness (长时间的)深度昏迷

comatose /'kəʊmətəʊs/ adjective in a coma 昏迷的

comb /kəʊm/ noun 1 an object with a row of narrow teeth, used for smoothing and neatening the hair 梳;梳子 2 a device for separating and smoothing the fibres of raw wool or cotton 精梳机 3 the red fleshy crest on the head of a chicken (鸡冠)肉冠 • verb 1 neaten the hair with a comb 梳理(头发);梳刷(毛发) 2 search systematically through something 彻底搜寻 3 prepare wool or cotton for manufacture with a comb 精梳(羊毛或棉)

combat /'kɒmbæt/ noun fighting, especially between armed forces 格斗;(尤指)战斗 • verb (combats, combating, combated or combats, combatting, combatted) take action to prevent something undesirable 与…抗争;与…斗争

combatant /'kɒmbətənt/ noun a person or group that is fighting a battle or war 参战者;参战国

combative /'kɒmbətɪv/ adjective ready or eager to fight or argue 好斗的;爱争吵的

combe /kuːm/ noun Brit. 【英】 a short valley or hollow on a hillside or coastline 山谷;崖谷;海岸谷

combination /ˌkɒmbɪ'neɪʃn/ noun 1 something that is made up of distinct parts 混合物 2 the action of combining different things 结合;组合;联合 □ **combination lock** a lock that is opened using a sequence of letters or numbers 暗码锁;密码锁

combine verb /kəm'baɪn/ (combines, combining, combined) 1 join or mix together 结合;混合 2 join together to do something 加入(做某事) • noun /'kɒmbaɪn/ a group acting together for a commercial purpose 联合企业;康拜因 □ **combine harvester** a farming machine that cuts a crop and separates out the grain in one process 联合收割机

combust /kəm'bʌst/ verb catch fire or burn 着火;燃烧 ■ **combustion** noun.

combustible /kəm'bʌstəbl/ adjective able to catch fire and burn easily 易燃的

come /kʌm/ verb (comes, coming, came; past participle come) 1 move towards or into a place near to the speaker 来;来到 **3** arrive 到达 **3** happen; take place 发生 **4** have or achieve a certain position 居···位置;取得···名次 **5** be sold or available in a particular form 出售;可得到 **6** (**coming**) likely to be successful in the future 可能成功的 □ **come about** happen 发生;产生 **come across 1** give a particular impression 留下···印象 **2** meet or find by chance 偶遇;偶然发现 **come by** manage to get 获得;得到 **come into** inherit 继承 **come off** succeed 成功 **come on 1** (of a state or condition) begin (状况)开始 **2** (also **come upon**) meet or find by chance 偶遇;偶然发现 **come out 1** (of a fact) become known (事实)显现,暴露 **2** declare publicly that you are homosexual 公开宣布是同性恋 **come round** Brit. 【英】 **1** recover consciousness 苏醒;恢复知觉 **2** be converted to another person's opinion 改变观点;改变立场 **come to 1** recover consciousness 苏醒;清醒 **2** (of an expense) amount to (费用)总计为 **come up** happen 出现;发生

comeback /'kʌmbæk/ **noun 1** a return to fame or popularity 恢复声望;再度走红 **2** informal 【非正式】 a quick reply to a remark (对评价的话)迅速作出的反驳,回应

comedian /kə'miːdiən/ **noun** (feminine 【阴性】 **comedienne**) an entertainer whose act is intended to make people laugh 滑稽演员;小丑

comedown /'kʌmdaʊn/ **noun** informal 【非正式】 **1** a loss of status or importance 潦泊;落泊;失势 **2** a feeling of disappointment or depression 沮丧;失望

comedy /'kɒmədi/ **noun** (plural **comedies**) **1** a film, play, or other entertainment intended to make people laugh 滑稽表演 **2** a light-hearted play in which the characters find happiness after experiencing difficult situations 喜剧

comely /'kʌmli/ **adjective** old use 【旧】 pleasant to look at 标致的;好看的

comestibles /kə'mestɪblz/ **plural noun** formal 【正式】 items of food 食物;食品

comet /'kɒmɪt/ **noun** a mass of ice and dust with a long tail, moving around the solar system 彗星

comeuppance /kʌm'ʌpəns/ **noun** (**get your comeuppance**) informal 【非正式】 get the punishment or fate that you deserve 受到应得的惩罚;遭报应

comfort /'kʌmfət/ **noun 1** a pleasant state of ease and relaxation 舒适;安逸 **2** (**comforts**) things that contribute to comfort 带来舒适安逸的事物 **3** consolation for unhappiness or anxiety 安慰;慰藉 • **verb** make someone less unhappy 安慰;慰藉 ■ **comforter** noun.

comfortable /'kʌmftəbl/ **adjective 1** giving or enjoying physical comfort 舒服的;舒适的 **2** free from financial worry 无经济负担的;宽裕的 **3** (of a victory) easily achieved (胜利)轻松取得的 ■ **comfortably** adverb.

comfy /'kʌmfi/ **adjective** (**comfier**, **comfiest**) informal 【非正式】 comfortable 舒适的;舒服的

comic /'kɒmɪk/ **adjective 1** making people laugh; amusing 使人发笑的;滑稽的 **2** having to do with comedy 喜剧的 • **noun 1** a comedian 喜剧演员 **2** a children's magazine that contains comic strips (儿童)连环漫画册 □ **comic strip** a sequence of drawings that tell an amusing story (内容诙谐的)连环漫画

comical /'kɒmɪkl/ **adjective** causing laughter, especially through being ridiculous 滑稽的;(尤指)荒唐可笑的 ■ **comically** adverb.

comma /ˈkɒmə/ noun a punctuation mark (,) showing a pause between parts of a sentence or separating items in a list 逗号

command /kəˈmɑːnd/ verb 1 give an order 命令;指示 2 be in charge of a military unit 统率;指挥(部队) • noun 1 an order 命令;指示 2 authority 指挥权 3 a group of officers in control of a particular group or operation 指挥部;司令部 4 the ability to use or control something 掌握;控制能力 5 an instruction which makes a computer carry out one of its basic functions (计算机操作的)指令

commandant /ˈkɒməndænt/ noun an officer in charge of a force or institution 司令官;指挥官

commandeer /ˌkɒmənˈdɪə(r)/ verb (**commandeers**, **commandeering**, **commandeered**) officially take possession of something for military purposes (为军事目的)强征,强占

commander /kəˈmɑːndə(r)/ noun 1 a person in command 指挥官;司令官 2 the rank of naval officer below captain 海军中校 □ **commander-in-chief** (plural **commanders-in-chief**) an officer in charge of all of the armed forces of a country (一国所有武装力量的)总司令,最高统帅

commanding /kəˈmɑːndɪŋ/ adjective 1 having or showing authority 威严的;权威的 2 having greater strength 居高临下的;支配的;权力大的

commandment /kəˈmɑːndmənt/ noun a divine rule, especially one of the Ten Commandments (上帝的)戒律;(尤指十诫中的)诫条

commando /kəˈmɑːndəʊ/ noun (plural **commandos**) a soldier trained for carrying out raids 突击队员

commemorate /kəˈmeməreɪt/ verb (**commemorates**, **commemorating**, **commemorated**) honour the memory of 纪念 ■ **commemoration** noun **commemorative** adjective.

✔ **拼写指南** the first *m* is double, but not the second: co*mm*emorate. commemorate中第一处 m 双写,第二处不双写。

commence /kəˈmens/ verb (**commences**, **commencing**, **commenced**) begin 开始;着手

commencement /kəˈmensmənt/ noun the beginning of something 开始;起始;开端

commend /kəˈmend/ verb 1 praise formally or officially 表扬;称赞 2 recommend someone or something 推荐;举荐 ■ **commendation** noun.

commendable /kəˈmendəbl/ adjective deserving praise 值得表扬的;值得称赞的 ■ **commendably** adverb.

commensurable /kəˈmenʃərəbl/ adjective formal 【正式】 able to be measured by the same standard 可用同一标准衡量的

commensurate /kəˈmenʃərət/ adjective (often **commensurate with**) matching something else in size, value, etc. 与…大小相称的;与…价值相当的

comment /ˈkɒment/ noun 1 a remark expressing an opinion or reaction 意见;评论 2 discussion of an issue or event 讨论;谈论 • verb express an opinion or reaction 发表意见;评论

commentary /ˈkɒməntri/ noun (plural **commentaries**) 1 a broadcast account of a sports match or other event as it happens (体育比赛等的)实况解说 2 the expression of opinions about an event or situation 评论;发表意见 3 a set of explanatory notes on a written work (对文本的)系统注释;评注

commentate /ˈkɒmənteɪt/ verb (**commentates**, **commentating**, **commentated**) give a commentary on an event 对…作实况解说;作报道 ■ **commentator** noun.

commerce /'kɒmɜːs/ **noun** the activity of buying and selling; trade 买卖;商业;贸易

commercial /kə'mɜːʃl/ **adjective 1** concerned with commerce 商业的 **2** making or intended to make a profit 商业化的;营利性的 • **noun** a television or radio advertisement (电视或电台的)商业广告 ■ **commercially** adverb.

commercialism /kə'mɜːʃəlɪzəm/ **noun** emphasis on making as much profit as possible 商业主义;营利主义

commercialize or **commercialise** /kə'mɜːʃəlaɪz/ **verb** (**commercializes**, **commercializing**, **commercialized**) manage something in a way designed to make a profit 使商业化;利用…牟利 ■ **commercialization** noun.

commiserate /kə'mɪzəreɪt/ **verb** (**commiserates**, **commiserating**, **commiserated**) express sympathy or pity; sympathize 同情;怜悯 ■ **commiseration** noun.

commissar /'kɒmɪ'sɑː(r)/ **noun** an official of the Communist Party responsible for political education 政委

commission /kə'mɪʃn/ **noun 1** an instruction, command, or duty 委托;授权;任务 **2** a formal request for something to be produced 委托制作 **3** a group of people given official authority to do something 委员会 **4** payment made to someone for selling goods or services 佣金;回扣 **5** the position of officer in the armed forces 军官职务 • **verb 1** order something to be made or produced 委托制作;授权制造 **2** bring something into working order 将…投入运行;开始使用 (**commissioned**) having the rank of a military officer (军官)现役的 ❑ **out of commission** not in working order 运转不正常

commissionaire /kə,mɪʃə'neə(r)/ **noun** Brit. 【英】a uniformed door attendant at a hotel, theatre, etc. (酒店、剧院等处的)穿制服的看门人

commissioner /kə'mɪʃənə(r)/ **noun 1** a member of an official commission 特派员;委员 **2** a representative of the highest authority in an area 地区最高代表;专员

commit /kə'mɪt/ **verb** (**commits**, **committing**, **committed**) **1** do something wrong or bad 做(错事或坏事) **2** set aside something for a particular use (为特定用途)拨出,留出(某物) **3** (**commit yourself**) say that you will definitely do something 作出保证;承诺 **4** put something in a safe place 把…放置于妥善地点 **5** send someone to prison or a psychiatric hospital 把(某人)送入监狱(或精神病院)

commitment /kə'mɪtmənt/ **noun 1** the time, work, and loyalty that someone devotes to a cause, activity, or job 奉献;献身 **2** a promise 承诺;诺言 **3** an engagement or duty that limits your freedom of action 义务;责任

✔ 拼写指南 there's a single *t* in the middle: commi*t*ment. commitment 中间只有一个 t。

committal /kə'mɪtl/ **noun** the sending of someone to prison or a psychiatric hospital, or for trial 收监;送入精神病院;送审判

committed /kə'mɪtɪd/ **adjective** devoting a lot of time and hard work to a cause, activity, or job 奉献的;忠诚的;兢兢业业的

committee /kə'mɪti/ **noun** a group of people appointed for a particular function by a larger group 委员会

✔ 拼写指南 double *m*, double *t*: co*mm*i*tt*ee. committee 中有两个 m 和两个 t。

commode /kə'məud/ **noun** a piece

of furniture containing a concealed chamber pot 便桶箱

commodious /kə'məʊdiəs/ **adjective** formal 【正式】 roomy and comfortable 宽敞舒适的

commodity /kə'mɒdəti/ **noun** (plural **commodities**) **1** a raw material or agricultural product that can be bought and sold 原料产品；农产品 **2** something useful or valuable 有用物品；有价值的东西

commodore /'kɒmədɔ:(r)/ **noun 1** the naval rank above captain 海军准将 **2** the president of a yacht club 游艇俱乐部主席

common /'kɒmən/ **adjective** (**commoner, commonest**) **1** happening, found, or done often; not rare 常见的；通常的 **2** without special qualities or position; ordinary 普通的；一般的；平凡的 **3** of the most familiar type 最常见的；通俗的 **4** shared by two or more people or things 共同的；共有的 **5** belonging to or affecting the whole of a community 公共的；公众的 **6** Brit. 【英】 not well mannered or tasteful, in a way supposedly typical of lower-class people 粗俗的；下层社会的 • **noun 1** a piece of open land for the public to use 公用土地 **2** (**the Commons**) the House of Commons 下院；众议院 □ **common denominator 1** Maths 【数学】 a number that can be divided exactly by all the numbers below the line in a set of fractions 公分母 **2** a feature shared by all members of a group 共性；共同点 **the common market** the European Union 欧洲经济共同体；欧洲联盟 **common noun** a noun referring to a class of things (e.g. *plant, sea*) as opposed to a particular person or thing 普通名词(与人名、地名相对) **common or garden** Brit. informal 【英，非正式】 of the usual or ordinary type 常见的；普通的 **common room** a room in a school or college for students or staff to use outside teaching hours (学校师生的)公共休息室 **common sense** good sense and judgement in practical matters 常识；判断力 **in common** shared 共有的 ■ **commonly** adverb.

commoner /'kɒmənə(r)/ **noun** an ordinary person as opposed to an aristocrat 平民

commonplace /'kɒmənpleɪs/ **adjective** ordinary 普通的；平凡的 • **noun** a remark that is not new or interesting 平淡无奇的言语；老生常谈

commonsensical /kɒmən'sensɪkl/ **adjective** having common sense 有常识的；通情达理的

commonwealth /'kɒmənwelθ/ **noun 1** (**the Commonwealth**) an association consisting of the UK together with countries that used to be part of the British Empire 英联邦 **2** an independent state or community 独立的国家(或集体)

commotion /kə'məʊʃn/ **noun** a state of confused and noisy disturbance 混乱；骚乱；骚动

communal /kə'mju:nl/ **adjective** shared or done by all members of a community 公有的；共有的；集体的 ■ **communally** adverb.

commune¹ /'kɒmju:n/ **noun** a group of people living together and sharing possessions 群居团体

commune² /kə'mju:n/ **verb** (**communes, communing, communed**) (**commune with**) share your intimate thoughts or feelings with 与…亲密交谈(或谈心)

communicable /kə'mju:nɪkəbl/ **adjective** (of a disease) able to be passed on to other people (疾病)传染性的

communicant /kə'mju:nɪkənt/ **noun** a person who receives Holy Communion 领受圣餐者

communicate /kə'mju:nɪkeɪt/ **verb**

(**communicates, communicating, communicated**) share or exchange information or ideas 传达，交流(信息) **2** pass on or convey an emotion, disease, etc. 表达(感情)；传播(疾病) **3** (**communicating**) (of two rooms) having a connecting door (两个房间)相通的，相连的

communication /kəˌmjuːnɪˈkeɪʃn/ **noun 1** the action of communicating 传达；传递；交流 **2** a letter or message 书信；消息 **3** (**communications**) means of sending information or travelling 通信；通讯

communicative /kəˈmjuːnɪkətɪv/ **adjective** willing or eager to talk or pass on information 爱说话的；健谈的；愿意提供信息的

communion /kəˈmjuːniən/ **noun 1** the sharing of intimate thoughts and feelings 沟通；交流；谈心 **2** (also **Holy Communion**) the service of Christian worship at which bread and wine are made holy and shared; the Eucharist 圣餐；领受圣餐

communiqué /kəˈmjuːnɪkeɪ/ **noun** an official announcement or statement 公报

communism /ˈkɒmjunɪzəm/ **noun 1** a political system in which all property is owned by the community 共产主义制度 **2** a system of this kind based on Marxism 共产主义 ■ **communist** noun & adjective.

community /kəˈmjuːnəti/ **noun** (plural **communities**) **1** a group of people living together in one place or having the same religion, race, etc. 团体；社团；界 **2** (**the community**) the people of an area or country considered as a group (某一地区或国家的)全体居民 □ **community service** socially useful work that an offender is sentenced to do instead of going to prison 社区服务(要求违法者从事有益于社会的工作以代替坐牢)

commute /kəˈmjuːt/ **verb** (**commutes, commuting, commuted**) **1** regularly travel some distance between your home and place of work (定时)往返(于住所和工作地点) **2** reduce a sentence given to an offender to a less severe one 减轻(刑罚) ■ **commuter** noun.

compact[1] **adjective** /kəmˈpækt/ **1** closely and neatly packed together; dense 紧密的；密集的 **2** having all the necessary parts fitted into a small space 小巧的；紧凑的 ● **verb** /kəmˈpækt/ press something together into a small space 把…压实；把…压紧 ● **noun** /ˈkɒmpækt/ a small case containing face powder, a mirror, and a powder puff 带镜小粉盒 □ **compact disc** a small disc on which music or other digital information is stored 激光唱盘；光盘

compact[2] /ˈkɒmpækt/ **noun** a formal agreement between two or more parties 协定；协议；合同；契约

companion /kəmˈpæniən/ **noun 1** a person that you spend time or travel with 同伴；旅伴 **2** each of a pair of things intended to match each other, or that can be used together 成对物之一；相配物 ■ **companionship** noun.

companionable /kəmˈpæniənəbl/ **adjective** friendly and sociable 友善的 ■ **companionably** adverb.

company /ˈkʌmpəni/ **noun** (plural **companies**) **1** a commercial business 公司；商号 **2** the fact of being with other people 陪伴；交往 **3** a guest or guests 客人；宾客 **4** a number of people gathered together 一群人 **5** a unit of soldiers (步兵的)连 **6** a group of actors, singers, or dancers who perform together 剧团；演出团

comparable /ˈkɒmpərəbl/ **adjective** similar to someone or something else and able to be compared 可比较的；比得上的；类似的 ■ **comparably**

adverb.

comparative /kəm'pærətɪv/ **adjective 1** measured or judged by comparing one thing with another 相比较而言的；相对的 **2** involving comparison between two or more subjects 比较的；用比较方法的 **3** (of an adjective or adverb) expressing a higher degree of a quality, but not the highest possible (e.g. *braver*) (形容词或副词)比较级的 ■ **comparatively** adverb.

✔ 拼写指南 compar*ative*, not -*itive*. comparative 不要拼作 -itive.

compare /kəm'peə(r)/ **verb** (**compares, comparing, compared**) **1** (often **compare something to** or **with**) estimate or measure the ways in which one person or thing is similar to or unlike another 比较，对照 **2** (**compare something to**) point out the ways in which one person or thing is similar to another 把…比作 **3** (usu. **compare with**) be similar to another thing or person (与…)类似，比得上

comparison /kəm'pærɪsn/ **noun 1** the action of comparing 比较；对照 **2** the quality of being similar 相似；可比性

compartment /kəm'pɑːtmənt/ **noun** a separate section of a structure or container 分隔的空间

compartmentalize or **compartmentalise** /ˌkɒmpɑːt'mentəlaɪz/ **verb** (**compartmentalizes, compartmentalizing, compartmentalized**) divide into categories or sections 划分；分类；分隔

compass /'kʌmpəs/ **noun 1** an instrument containing a pointer which shows the direction of magnetic north 罗盘；指南针 **2** (also **compasses**) an instrument for drawing circles, consisting of two arms linked by a movable joint 圆规

3 range or scope 范围；界限

compassion /kəm'pæʃn/ **noun** sympathetic pity and concern for the sufferings of other people 同情；怜悯

compassionate /kəm'pæʃənət/ **adjective** feeling or showing compassion 有同情心的；怜悯的 ■ **compassionately** adverb.

compatible /kəm'pætəbl/ **adjective 1** able to exist or be used together 可以并存的；兼容的 **2** (of two people) able to have a good relationship; well suited (两个人)和睦相处的，合得来的 **3** (usu. **compatible with**) consistent or in keeping 协调的；一致的 ■ **compatibility** noun.

✔ 拼写指南 compat*ible*, not -*able*. compatible 不要拼作 -able.

compatriot /kəm'pætriət/ **noun** a person from the same country; a fellow citizen 同国人

compel /kəm'pel/ **verb** (**compels, compelling, compelled**) **1** force someone to do something 强迫；迫使 **2** make something happen 使发生；引起反应

compelling /kəm'pelɪŋ/ **adjective** powerfully gaining people's attention or admiration 有吸引力的；令人羡慕的 ■ **compellingly** adverb.

compendium /kəm'pendiəm/ **noun** (plural **compendiums** or **compendia** /kəm'pendiə/) **1** a collection of information about a subject 概要；纲要 **2** a collection of similar items 集合

compensate /'kɒmpenseɪt/ **verb** (**compensates, compensating, compensated**) **1** give someone something to reduce or balance the bad effect of loss, suffering, or injury 补偿；赔偿 **2** (**compensate for**) reduce or balance something bad by having an opposite force or effect 抵消；弥补 ■ **compensatory** adjective.

compensation /ˌkɒmpen'seɪʃn/ **noun 1** something given to compensate for loss, suffering, or injury 赔偿物；赔偿金 **2** something that compensates for something bad 补偿

compère /'kɒmpeə(r)/ Brit.【英】 **noun** a person who introduces the different acts that are performing in one show 节目主持人 • **verb** (**compères**, **compèring**, **compèred**) act as a compère for 做节目主持人

compete /kəm'piːt/ **verb** (**competes**, **competing**, **competed**) try to gain or win something by defeating other people 竞争；争夺

competent /'kɒmpɪtənt/ **adjective 1** having the necessary skill or knowledge to do something successfully 能胜任的；称职的 **2** satisfactory, though not outstanding 令人满意的 ■ **competence** (or **competency**) noun **competently** adverb.

competition /ˌkɒmpə'tɪʃn/ **noun 1** the activity of competing against other people 竞争 **2** an event or contest in which people compete 竞赛；比赛 **3** the person or people that you are competing against 竞争对手

competitive /kəm'petətɪv/ **adjective 1** involving competition 竞争的 **2** strongly wanting to be more successful than other people 好胜的 **3** as good as or better than others of a similar nature 有竞争力的 ■ **competitively** adverb.

competitor /kəm'petɪtə(r)/ **noun 1** a person who takes part in a sports contest (体育比赛的)选手，参赛者 **2** an organization that competes with others in business (商业上的)竞争者，对手

compilation /ˌkɒmpɪ'leɪʃn/ **noun 1** a book, record, etc. compiled from different sources (书籍、唱片等的)选集，选辑 **2** the process of compiling something 编集；编写

compile /kəm'paɪl/ **verb** (**compiles**, **compiling**, **compiled**) produce a book, record, etc. by bringing

together material from different sources 汇编(书、唱片等) ■ **compiler** noun.

complacent /kəm'pleɪsnt/ **adjective** smugly satisfied with yourself 沾沾自喜的；自鸣得意的 ■ **complacency** noun **complacently** adverb.

complain /kəm'pleɪn/ **verb 1** express dissatisfaction or annoyance 抱怨；投诉 **2** (**complain of**) state that you are suffering from a particular symptom 主诉；诉说(病症)

complainant /kəm'pleɪnənt/ **noun** Law【法律】 a plaintiff 原告；控诉人

complaint /kəm'pleɪnt/ **noun 1** an act of complaining 抱怨；投诉 **2** a reason to be dissatisfied 不满的理由 **3** a minor illness or medical condition (轻微的)疾病

complaisant /kəm'pleɪzənt/ **adjective** willing to please other people or to accept their behaviour without protest 殷勤的；顺从的

complement noun /'kɒmplɪmənt/ **1** a thing that contributes extra features to something else so as to improve it 补充物；补足物 **2** the number or quantity that makes something complete 足额；全数 **3** Grammar【语法】 a word or words used with a verb to complete the meaning (e.g. *happy* in *we are happy*) 补语 • **verb** /'kɒmplɪment/ add to something in a way that improves it 补足；补充

> **！注意** don't confuse **complement** and **compliment**. **Complement** means 'add to something in a way that improves it', while **compliment** means 'politely congratulate or praise'. 不要混淆 complement 和 compliment。complement 意为"补充"，而 compliment 意为"祝贺；赞美"。

complementary /ˌkɒmplɪ'mentri/ **adjective** combining so as to form a complete whole or to improve each

other's qualities 补足的；互补的
■ **complementary medicine** medical therapy that is not part of scientific medicine, e.g. acupuncture 辅助性疗法；非正统疗法

complete /kəmˈpliːt/ **adjective 1** having all the necessary parts 完整的；完全的 **2** having run its course; finished 完成的；结束的 **3** to the greatest extent or degree; total 绝对的；十足的；彻底的 **4** skilled at every aspect of an activity 全才的 • **verb (completes, completing, completed) 1** finish making or doing something 完成；结束 **2** make something complete 使完整；使圆满 **3** write the required information on a form 填写(表格) ■ **completely** adverb **completion** noun.

complex /ˈkɒmpleks/ **adjective 1** consisting of many different and connected parts 组合的 **2** not easy to understand; complicated 费解的；复杂的 • noun **1** a group of similar buildings or facilities on the same site 建筑群 **2** a network of linked things 相关联的一组事物；体系 **3** a group of subconscious ideas or feelings that influence a person's mental state or behaviour 情结(由潜意识的思想感情引起的心理状态或行为) ■ **complexity** noun (plural **complexities**).

complexion /kəmˈplekʃn/ **noun 1** the natural condition of the skin of a person's face 面色，气色 **2** the general character of something 性质

compliance /kəmˈplaɪəns/ **noun** the action of complying 遵守；顺从；服从

compliant /kəmˈplaɪənt/ **adjective 1** meeting rules or standards 遵守(规则)的；符合(标准)的 **2** too ready to do what other people want 顺从的；屈从的

complicate /ˈkɒmplɪkeɪt/ **verb (complicates, complicating, complicated)** make something less

easy to understand or deal with 使复杂化

complicated /ˈkɒmplɪkeɪtɪd/ **adjective 1** consisting of many connected elements; intricate 复杂的 **2** involving many different and confusing aspects 费解的；复杂的

complication /ˌkɒmplɪˈkeɪʃn/ **noun 1** a circumstance that complicates something; a difficulty 纠葛，难题 **2** an involved or confused state 复杂的状况；混乱 **3** an extra disease or condition which makes an existing one worse 并发症

complicit /kəmˈplɪsɪt/ **adjective** involved with other people in an unlawful activity 共谋的；串通的

complicity /kəmˈplɪsəti/ **noun** involvement with other people in an unlawful activity 共谋；串通

compliment noun /ˈkɒmplɪmənt/ **1** a remark that expresses praise or admiration 赞美；恭维 **2** (**compliments**) formal greetings (正式的)问候，祝贺 • verb /ˈkɒmplɪment/ politely congratulate or praise 祝贺；赞美

! **注意** don't confuse **compliment** and **complement**: see the note at COMPLEMENT. 不要混淆 compliment 和 complement，参见词条 complement 处注释。

complimentary /ˌkɒmplɪˈmentri/ **adjective 1** praising or approving 表扬的；赞赏的 **2** given free of charge 免费赠送的

comply /kəmˈplaɪ/ **verb (complies, complying, complied) (comply with) 1** do what someone wants or tells you to do 遵从；顺从 **2** meet specified standards 符合(特定标准)

component /kəmˈpəʊnənt/ **noun** a part of a larger whole 组成部分；部件

comport /kəmˈpɔːt/ **verb (comport yourself)** formal 【正式】 behave in a particular way 举止；表现

compose /kəm'pəuz/ *verb* (**composes, composing, composed**) **1** make up a whole 构成(整体) **2** create a work of art, especially music or poetry 创作(艺术作品，尤指音乐或诗歌) **3** arrange in an orderly or artistic way (整齐地或有艺术性地)安排 **4** (**composed**) calm and in control of your feelings 平静的；镇定的 ■ **composer** noun.

composite /'kɒmpəzɪt/ *adjective* made up of several parts 合成的 • *noun* a thing made up of several parts 合成物；混合物

composition /ˌkɒmpə'zɪʃn/ *noun* **1** the way in which something is made up 构成；结构 **2** a work of music, literature, or art (音乐、文学或艺术)作品 **3** an essay written by a school pupil (学生的)作文 **4** the action of composing 组合；构成

compositor /kəm'pɒzɪtə(r)/ *noun* a person who arranges type or keys material for printing 排版工人

compos mentis /ˌkɒmpɒs 'mentɪs/ *adjective* having full control of your mind 精神正常的；心智健全的

compost /'kɒmpɒst/ *noun* decayed organic material added to soil as a fertilizer 有机肥料

composure /kəm'pəuʒə(r)/ *noun* the state of being calm and self-controlled 沉着；镇静

compound¹ *noun* /'kɒmpaund/ **1** a thing made up of two or more separate elements 复合物；混合物 **2** a substance formed from two or more elements chemically united in fixed proportions 化合物 • *adjective* /'kɒmpaund/ made up or consisting of several parts 混合的；组合的 • *verb* /kəm'paund/ **1** make up a whole from several elements 构成(整体) **2** make something bad worse 使恶化 □ **compound fracture** an injury in which a broken bone pierces the skin 开放性骨折；哆开骨折

compound² /'kɒmpaund/ *noun* a large open area enclosed by a fence 带围栏的大块场地；院子

comprehend /ˌkɒmprɪ'hend/ *verb* understand something 领会；理解

comprehensible /ˌkɒmprɪ'hensəbl/ *adjective* able to be understood 可理解的

comprehension /ˌkɒmprɪ'henʃn/ *noun* **1** the action of understanding 领会；理解 **2** the ability to understand 理解力

comprehensive /ˌkɒmprɪ'hensɪv/ *adjective* **1** including or dealing with all or nearly all aspects of something 广泛的；综合的；无所不包的 **2** Brit. 【英】(of secondary education) in which children of all abilities are educated in one school (中学教育)综合性的，招收不同资质学生的 **3** (of a victory or defeat) by a large margin (输赢)差距大的 • *noun* Brit. 【英】 a comprehensive school 综合中学 ■ **comprehensively** *adverb*.

compress *verb* /kəm'pres/ **1** flatten by pressure; force into less space 压缩 **2** squeeze or press two things together 挤压；压紧 **3** alter the form of computer data so that it takes up less space on a disk or magnetic tape 压缩(计算机数据) • *noun* /'kɒmpres/ an absorbent pad pressed on to part of the body to relieve inflammation or stop bleeding (用于消炎或止血的)敷布，压布 ■ **compression** noun.

compressor /kəm'presə(r)/ *noun* a machine used to supply air at increased pressure 压气机

comprise /kəm'praɪz/ *verb* (**comprises, comprising, comprised**) **1** be made up of; consist of 由…构成；包含 **2** (also **be comprised of**) make up a whole 由…构成；由…组成

compromise /'kɒmprəmaɪz/ *noun* **1** an agreement reached by each side giving way on some points

妥协方案；折中方案 **2** something that is midway between different or conflicting elements 妥协；折中：*a compromise between price and quality of output* 价格与产品质量之间的折中 • **verb** (**compromises, compromising, compromised**) **1** give way on some points in order to settle a dispute 达成妥协；通过互让解决 **2** accept something that is less good than you would like 妥协；让步 **3** cause someone danger or embarrassment by behaving in an indiscreet or reckless way 使名誉受损；危及；损害

comptroller /kənˈtrəʊlə(r), kɒmpˈtrəʊlə(r)/ **noun** a person in charge of the financial affairs of an organization 审计员；会计主任

compulsion /kəmˈpʌlʃn/ **noun 1** pressure to do something 强制力；强迫力 **2** an irresistible urge to do something 强烈的冲动；不可抑制的欲望

compulsive /kəmˈpʌlsɪv/ **adjective 1** done because of an irresistible urge 由冲动造成的 **2** unable to stop yourself doing something 不由自主的；禁不住的 **3** irresistibly exciting 极度迷恋的；引人入胜的 ■ **compulsively** adverb.

compulsory /kəmˈpʌlsəri/ **adjective** required by law or a rule; obligatory 法律规定的；强制的；义务的

compunction /kəmˈpʌŋkʃn/ **noun** a feeling of guilt about doing something wrong 内疚；自责；悔恨

computation /ˌkɒmpjuˈteɪʃn/ **noun 1** mathematical calculation (数学)计算 **2** the use of computers 使用计算机 ■ **computational** adjective.

compute /kəmˈpjuːt/ **verb** (**computes, computing, computed**) calculate a figure or amount 计算；估算

computer /kəmˈpjuːtə(r)/ **noun** an electronic device capable of storing and processing information according to a set of instructions 计算机；电脑 ■ **computing** noun.

computerize or **computerise** /kəmˈpjuːtəraɪz/ **verb** (**computerizes, computerizing, computerized**) convert to a system controlled by or stored on computer 使计算机化；使电脑化

comrade /ˈkɒmreɪd/ **noun 1** (among men) a person who shares your activities or is a fellow member of an organization (男性)同事，伙伴 **2** a fellow soldier 战友 ■ **comradeship** noun.

con[1] /kɒn/ informal 【非正式】 **verb** (**cons, conning, conned**) deceive someone into doing or believing something 哄骗；欺骗 • **noun** a deception of this kind 哄骗；欺骗 □ **con man** a man who cheats people after gaining their trust 骗子

con[2] **noun** (usu. in **pros and cons** 中) a disadvantage of or argument against something 弊端；反对…的理由

concatenation /kənˌkætəˈneɪʃn/ **noun** a series of interconnected things 一系列相互关联的事物

concave /ˈkɒnkeɪv/ **adjective** having an outline or surface that curves inwards 凹的；凹面的 ■ **concavity** noun.

conceal /kənˈsiːl/ **verb 1** stop someone or something being seen 遮掩 **2** keep something secret 隐瞒 ■ **concealment** noun.

concede /kənˈsiːd/ **verb** (**concedes, conceding, conceded**) **1** finally admit that something is true 承认(事实) **2** give up a possession, advantage, or right 让与，放弃(所有权、优势或权利) **3** admit defeat in a match or contest (在比赛或竞争中)认输 **4** fail to prevent an opponent scoring a goal or point 让(对手)进球(或得分)

conceit /kənˈsiːt/ **noun 1** too much

pride in yourself 自负；自满 **2** an artistic effect 美感 **3** a complicated metaphor 巧妙的比喻

conceited /kən'si:tɪd/ **adjective** too proud of yourself 自负的；自满

conceivable /kən'si:vəbl/ **adjective** able to be imagined or understood 可想象的；可理解的 ■ **conceivably** adverb.

conceive /kən'si:v/ **verb** (**conceives, conceiving, conceived**) **1** become pregnant with a child 怀胎；怀孕 **2** form an idea in your mind 想象，构想

✔ **拼写指南** i before e except after c: conceive. i 置于 e 前，在 c 后时除外，如 conceive。

concentrate /'kɒnsntreɪt/ **verb** (**concentrates, concentrating, concentrated**) **1** focus all your attention on something 集中注意力；全神贯注 **2** gather together in numbers or a mass at one point 聚集；凝聚 **3** (**concentrated**) (of a solution) strong (溶液)浓缩的 • **noun** a concentrated substance or solution 浓缩物；浓缩液

concentration /ˌkɒnsn'treɪʃn/ **noun** **1** the action or power of concentrating 专注；注意力 **2** a close gathering of people or things 聚集；集中 **3** the amount of a particular substance in a solution or mixture 浓度 □ **concentration camp** a camp for holding political prisoners (关押政治犯的)集中营

concentric /kɒn'sentrɪk/ **adjective** (of circles or arcs) sharing the same centre (圆或弧)同心的

concept /'kɒnsept/ **noun** an abstract idea 观念；概念

conception /kən'sepʃn/ **noun** **1** the conceiving of a child 妊娠；怀孕 **2** the forming of a plan or idea 构想；设想 **3** an idea or concept 想法；概念 **4** ability to imagine or understand 想

象力；理解力

conceptual /kən'septʃuəl/ **adjective** having to do with concepts 观念的；概念的 ■ **conceptually** adverb.

conceptualize or **conceptualise** /kən'septʃuəlaɪz/ **verb** (**conceptualizes, conceptualizing, conceptualized**) form an idea of something in your mind 使概念化；使形成概念

concern /kən'sɜːn/ **verb** **1** relate to; be about 和…有关；关于 **2** affect or involve 影响到；涉及 **3** make someone worried 使忧虑；使挂念 • **noun 1** worry; anxiety 挂念；忧虑 **2** a matter of interest or importance 感兴趣的事；重要的事 **3** a business 公司；企业

concerned /kən'sɜːnd/ **adjective** worried 挂念的；忧虑的

concerning /kən'sɜːnɪŋ/ **preposition** about 关于

concert /'kɒnsət/ **noun** a musical performance given in public 音乐会 □ **in concert** acting together 共同；一起

concerted /kən'sɜːtɪd/ **adjective 1** jointly arranged or carried out 一致的；联合的 **2** done in a determined way 坚决的

concertina /ˌkɒnsə'tiːnə/ **noun** a small musical instrument which you play by stretching and squeezing it and pressing buttons 六角手风琴 • **verb** (**concertinas, concertinaing, concertinaed**) compress in folds like those of a concertina (像六角手风琴般)折叠

concerto /kən'tʃɜːtəʊ/ **noun** (plural **concertos** or **concerti** /kən'tʃɜːti/) a musical work for an orchestra and one or more solo instruments 协奏曲

concession /kən'seʃn/ **noun 1** something done or given up in order to settle a dispute 让与物；让步 **2** a reduction allowed in the price of something 减价；优惠 **3** the right to use land or other property for a particular purpose (使用土地或财产的)特许权 **4** a stall, bar, or small shop selling things within a larger business or shop (大公司或商场内的)销售场地，摊位 ■ **concessionary** adjective.

conch /kɒntʃ/ noun (plural **conches**) a shellfish with a spiral shell 海螺

concierge /kɒnsiˈeəʒ/ noun a resident caretaker of a block of flats or small hotel (公寓区或小旅馆的)看门人

conciliate /kənˈsɪlieɪt/ verb (**conciliates**, **conciliating**, **conciliated**) **1** make someone calm and content 使平静，安抚 **2** try to bring the two sides in a dispute together 调解，使和解 ■ **conciliation** noun **conciliatory** adjective.

concise /kənˈsaɪs/ adjective giving a lot of information clearly and in few words 简明的；言简意赅的 ■ **concisely** adverb **concision** noun.

conclave /ˈkɒŋkleɪv/ noun a private meeting 秘密会议，秘密集会

conclude /kənˈkluːd/ verb (**concludes**, **concluding**, **concluded**) **1** bring or come to an end (使)结束 **2** arrive at an opinion by reasoning 断定，推断出 **3** formally settle or arrange a treaty or agreement 缔结，议定(协议)

conclusion /kənˈkluːʒn/ noun **1** an end or finish 结束，完结 **2** the summing up of an argument or written work (文章等的)结论，结尾 **3** a decision reached by reasoning (推理得出的)结论，推论

conclusive /kənˈkluːsɪv/ adjective decisive or convincing 决定性的；有说服力的 ■ **conclusively** adverb.

concoct /kənˈkɒkt/ verb **1** make a dish by combining ingredients 调制，配制(菜肴) **2** think up a story or plan 捏造，虚构(故事)；策划 ■ **concoction** noun.

concomitant /kənˈkɒmɪtənt/ adjective formal【正式】naturally accompanying or connected with something else 相伴的；伴随的

concord /ˈkɒŋkɔːd/ noun literary【文】agreement; harmony 一致；和谐

concordance /kənˈkɔːdəns/ noun an alphabetical list of the important words in a written work (按字母顺序排列的)重要词语索引

concordat /kənˈkɔːdæt/ noun an agreement or treaty 协议；契约

concourse /ˈkɒŋkɔːs/ noun a large open area inside or in front of a public building (公共建筑内部的)大厅；(公共建筑前方的)广场

concrete /ˈkɒŋkriːt/ noun a building material made from gravel, sand, cement, and water 混凝土 • adjective **1** existing in a physical form; not abstract 有形的，具体的 **2** definite or certain 确定的，确实的：concrete proof 确凿的证据 • verb (**concretes**, **concreting**, **concreted**) cover with concrete 用混凝土覆盖

concretion /kənˈkriːʃn/ noun a hard solid mass 凝结物；凝固物

concubine /ˈkɒŋkjʊbaɪn/ noun (in some societies) a woman who lives with a man but has lower status than his wife or wives (某些社会中男子的)妾，小老婆

concur /kənˈkɜː(r)/ verb (**concurs**, **concurring**, **concurred**) (often **concur with**) agree 同意，赞同

concurrent /kənˈkʌrənt/ adjective existing or happening at the same time 并存的；同时发生的 ■ **concurrently** adverb.

concussion /kənˈkʌʃn/ noun temporary unconsciousness or confusion caused by a blow on the head (头部被击打造成的)暂时性昏迷，脑震荡 ■ **concussed** adjective.

condemn /kənˈdem/ verb **1** express complete disapproval of 谴责；指责 **2** (usu. **condemn someone to**) sentence someone to a punishment 判(某人)刑 **3** (**condemn someone to**) force someone to endure something unpleasant 迫使(某人)忍受(不快之事) **4** officially declare something to be unfit for use 宣告…不适用 ■ **condemnation** noun.

condensation /ˌkɒndenˈseɪʃn/ *noun* **1** water from humid air collecting as droplets on a cold surface 冷凝物;凝结物 **2** the conversion of a vapour or gas to a liquid 冷凝;凝结

condense /kənˈdens/ *verb* (**condenses, condensing, condensed**) **1** change from a gas or vapour to a liquid (由气体)冷凝,(使气体)凝结 **2** make a liquid thicker or more concentrated 使(液体)浓缩 **3** express a piece of writing or a speech in fewer words 缩写;使简洁 □ **condensed milk** milk that has been thickened and sweetened 炼乳

condescend /ˌkɒndɪˈsend/ *verb* **1** behave as if you were better than someone else 有优越感;表现出高人一等的样子 **2** do something even though you think it is beneath your dignity 俯就;屈尊 **3** (**condescending**) behaving as if you are better than other people 有优越感的;屈尊俯就的

condescension /ˌkɒndɪˈsenʃn/ *noun* a patronizing attitude or way of behaving 带有优越感;屈尊俯就

condiment /ˈkɒndɪmənt/ *noun* something such as salt or mustard that is added to food to bring out its flavour 调味品;佐料

condition /kənˈdɪʃn/ *noun* **1** the state that someone or something is in as regards appearance, fitness, or working order 状况;状态 **2** (**conditions**) circumstances that affect the way something works or exists 环境;形势 **3** a situation that must exist before something else is possible 前提;先决条件 **4** an illness or medical problem 疾病;健康问题 • *verb* **1** train or influence someone to behave

in a certain way 制约;影响 **2** (**be conditioned by**) be influenced or determined by 受…的影响;受…的制约 **3** bring something into a good condition 使处于良好的状态

conditional /kənˈdɪʃənl/ *adjective* **1** depending on one or more conditions being fulfilled 视…而定的 **2** Grammar 【语法】 expressing something that must happen or be true before something else can happen or be true 条件的 ■ **conditionally** *adverb*.

conditioner /kənˈdɪʃənə(r)/ *noun* a liquid added when washing hair or clothing, to make them softer 护发剂;(洗衣用的)柔顺剂

condo /ˈkɒndəʊ/ = CONDOMINIUM.

condolence /kənˈdəʊləns/ *noun* an expression of sympathy 慰问;慰唁

condom /ˈkɒndəm/ *noun* a rubber sheath that a man wears on his penis during sex to stop the woman getting pregnant or to protect against infection 避孕套;安全套

condominium /ˌkɒndəˈmɪniəm/ *noun* (plural **condominiums**) N. Amer. 【北美】 a building containing a number of individually owned flats 公寓楼

condone /kənˈdəʊn/ *verb* (**condones, condoning, condoned**) accept or forgive an offence or wrong 容忍;原谅

condor /ˈkɒndɔː(r)/ *noun* a very large South American vulture 大秃鹫(产于南美洲)

conducive /kənˈdjuːsɪv/ *adjective* (**conducive to**) contributing or helping towards 有助于…的;有益于…的

conduct *noun* /ˈkɒndʌkt/ **1** the way in which a person behaves 举止;言行 **2** management or direction 管理;指挥 • *verb* /kənˈdʌkt/ **1** organize and carry out 组织;实施 **2** direct the performance of a piece of music 指挥(音乐表演) **3** guide or lead someone to a place 引导;带领 **4**

(**conduct yourself**) behave in a particular way 表现；为人 **5** transmit heat or electricity directly through a substance 传导(热或电) ■ **conduction** noun.

conductance /kən'dʌktəns/ noun the degree to which a material conducts electricity 导电性

conductive /kən'dʌktɪv/ adjective conducting heat or electricity 导热的；导电的 ■ **conductivity** noun.

conductor /kən'dʌktə(r)/ noun **1** a person who conducts musicians (乐队的)指挥 **2** a material or device that conducts heat or electricity 导体 **3** a person who collects fares on a bus (公共汽车的)售票员

conduit /'kɒndjuɪt/ noun **1** a channel for moving water from one place to another 渠道；引水道 **2** a tube protecting electric wiring 导线管；导线槽

cone /kəʊn/ noun **1** an object which tapers from a circular base to a point 锥形物；圆锥体 **2** the hard, dry fruit of a pine or fir tree 松球；球果

coney /'kəʊni/ noun (plural **coneys**) a rabbit 兔；野兔

confection /kən'fekʃn/ noun **1** an elaborate sweet dish 甜食 **2** something put together in an elaborate or complicated way 精制工艺品

confectionery /kən'fekʃənəri/ noun (plural **confectioneries**) sweets and chocolates 糖果；甜食

✔ **拼写指南** the ending is -ery, not -ary: confection*ery*. confectionery 词末拼作 -ery, 不要拼作 -ary。

confederacy /kən'fedərəsi/ noun (plural **confederacies**) **1** an alliance of states or groups 邦联；联盟；同盟 **2** (**the Confederacy**) the Confederate states of the US 美国联邦各州

confederate adjective /kən'fedərət/ **1** joined by an agreement or treaty 联合的；结盟的 **2** (**Confederate**)

having to do with the southern states which separated from the US in 1860-1861 (1860-1861 年期间脱离美国联邦的)南部邦联的 ● verb /kən'fedəreɪt/ (**confederates**, **confederating**, **confederated**) unite in an alliance 使联合；使结盟

confederation /kən.fedə'reɪʃn/ noun an alliance of states or groups 同盟；联盟

confer /kən'fɜ:(r)/ verb (**confers**, **conferring**, **conferred**) **1** formally give a title, benefit, or right to someone 授予(称号、好处或权利) **2** have discussions 商谈；讨论 ■ **conferment** noun.

conference /'kɒnfərəns/ noun a formal meeting to discuss something 协商会；讨论会

confess /kən'fes/ verb **1** admit that you have done something criminal or wrong 供认，坦白(罪行) **2** acknowledge something reluctantly 勉强承认 **3** formally declare your sins to a priest (向神父)忏悔，告罪

confession /kən'feʃn/ noun **1** an act of confessing 供认；坦白 **2** formal 【正式】 declaration of your sins to a priest (向神父的)忏悔，告罪

confessional /kən'feʃnl/ noun **1** an enclosed box in a church, in which a priest sits to hear confessions (教堂里神父聆听告罪的)告解室 **2** a confession 忏悔；告罪

confessor /kən'fesə(r)/ noun a priest who hears confessions 听忏悔的神父

confetti /kən'feti/ noun small pieces of coloured paper traditionally thrown over a bride and groom after a marriage ceremony (婚礼后向新郎和新娘抛撒的)五彩纸屑

confidant /'kɒnfɪdænt/ noun (feminine 【阴性】 **confidante**) a person you trust and confide in 知己；密友

confide /kən'faɪd/ verb (**confides**, **confiding**, **confided**) (often **confide in**) tell someone about a secret or private matter 吐露(秘密或心事)

confidence /'kɒnfɪdəns/ noun **1** faith in someone or something 信任;信赖 **2** a positive feeling gained from a belief in your own ability to do things well 自信;信心 **3** a feeling of certainty about something 肯定;确定 □ **confidence trick** an act of cheating someone after gaining their trust 骗局 **in confidence** as a secret 秘密地

confident /'kɒnfɪdənt/ adjective **1** feeling confidence in yourself 自信的;有信心的 **2** feeling certain about something 确定的;肯定的 ■ **confidently** adverb.

confidential /ˌkɒnfɪ'denʃl/ adjective intended to be kept secret 机密的;秘密的 ■ **confidentiality** noun **confidentially** adverb.

configuration /kənˌfɪɡə'reɪʃn/ noun a particular arrangement of parts 构造;配置

configure /kən'fɪɡə(r)/ verb (con-figures, configuring, configured) **1** arrange or set up in a particular way 安排;布局 **2** arrange a computer system so that it is able to do a particular task 配置(计算机系统)

confine verb /kən'faɪn/ (confines, confining, confined) **1** (confine someone/thing to) keep someone or something within certain limits 把…限限于;把…限制于 **2** (be confined to) be unable to leave a place due to illness or disability (由于疾病或残疾)无法离开 • noun /'kɒnfaɪn/ (confines) limits, boundaries, or restrictions 界限;边界;限制

confined /kən'faɪnd/ adjective (of a space) small and enclosed (空间)小而闭塞的,局促的

confinement /kən'faɪnmənt/ noun **1** the state of being confined 局限;限制 **2** dated 【废】 the time around which a woman gives birth to a baby (妇女的)分娩,产褥期

confirm /kən'fɜːm/ verb **1** state or establish that something is definitely true or correct 证实;验证 **2** make something definite or valid 使明确;使有效 **3** (be confirmed) go through the religious ceremony of confirmation 给…施坚信礼

confirmation /ˌkɒnfə'meɪʃn/ noun **1** the action of confirming 证实;确定 **2** the ceremony at which a baptized person is admitted as a full member of the Christian Church (基督教会的)坚信礼

confirmed /kən'fɜːmd/ adjective firmly established in a habit, belief, etc. 成习惯的,根深蒂固的

confiscate /'kɒnfɪskeɪt/ verb (confis-cates, confiscating, confiscated) officially take or seize someone's property 没收;征用

conflagration /ˌkɒnflə'greɪʃn/ noun a large and destructive fire (毁灭性的)大火

conflate /kən'fleɪt/ verb (conflates, conflating, conflated) combine into one 合并 ■ **conflation** noun.

conflict noun /'kɒnflɪkt/ **1** a serious disagreement 争执;冲突 **2** a long-lasting armed struggle (长期的)战斗,战争 **3** a difference of opinions, principles, etc. 分歧;抵触 • verb /kən'flɪkt/ (of opinions, stories, etc.) disagree or be different (观点、报道等)不一致,存在差异

confluence /'kɒnfluəns/ noun the junction of two rivers (两条河流的)交汇处,汇流处

conform /kən'fɔːm/ verb (often **conform to**) **1** obey a rule 遵守(规则) **2** behave in an expected or conventional way 因循守旧;墨守成规 **3** be similar in form or type 相似;一致 ■ **conformity** noun.

conformist /kən'fɔːmɪst/ noun a person who behaves in an expected or conventional way 因循守旧者;墨守成规者

confound /kən'faʊnd/ **verb 1** surprise or bewilder someone 使惊讶;使困惑;使不知所措 **2** prove a person, theory, or expectation wrong 驳倒;驳斥 **3** (**confounded**) informal, dated 【非正式,废】used to express annoyance (用于表示恼怒)讨厌的,该死的

confront /kən'frʌnt/ **verb 1** meet an enemy or opponent face to face 对抗;遭遇;面临 **2** face up to and deal with a problem 勇敢面对,应对(问题) **3** make someone face up to a problem 使对质;使面临

confrontation /ˌkɒnfrʌn'teɪʃn/ **noun** a situation of angry disagreement or hostility 对抗,对峙;冲突 ■ **confrontational** adjective.

confuse /kən'fjuːz/ **verb** (**confuses, confusing, confused**) **1** make someone bewildered or puzzled 使困惑;使茫然 **2** make something less easy to understand 使模糊不清;使含糊 **3** mistake one thing or person for another 混淆;搞错

confused /kən'fjuːzd/ **adjective 1** bewildered 困惑的;茫然的 **2** difficult to understand or distinguish 混乱的;分不清的

confusion /kən'fjuːʒn/ **noun 1** uncertainty or bewilderment 困惑;茫然 **2** a situation of panic or disorder 混乱;无秩序 **3** the mistaking of one person or thing for another 混淆;误认

confute /kən'fjuːt/ **verb** (**confutes, confuting, confuted**) formal 【正式】prove a person or argument to be wrong 驳斥;驳倒

conga /'kɒŋɡə/ **noun** a Latin American dance performed by people in single file (舞蹈者站成一排跳的)康茄舞

congeal /kən'dʒiːl/ **verb** become semi-solid 凝结;凝固

congenial /kən'dʒiːniəl/ **adjective** suited to or pleasing to your tastes 适宜的;合意的 ■ **congeniality** noun.

congenital /kən'dʒenɪtl/ **adjective 1** (of a disease or abnormality) present from birth (疾病或畸形)先天性的,天生的 **2** having a particular characteristic as part of your character 生性的;生就的: *a congenital liar* 生性好说谎者 ■ **congenitally** adverb.

conger eel /'kɒŋɡə(r)/ **noun** a large eel found in coastal waters 康吉鳗(见于沿海水域的大型鳗)

congested /kən'dʒestɪd/ **adjective 1** so crowded that it is difficult to move freely 拥挤不堪的 **2** abnormally full of blood 充血的 **3** blocked with mucus 被黏液堵塞的 ■ **congestion** noun.

conglomerate noun /kən'ɡlɒmərət/ **1** a large corporation formed by the merging of separate firms 联合大企业;企业集团 **2** something consisting of a number of different and distinct things 聚合物;混合体 ■ **conglomeration** noun.

congratulate /kən'ɡrætʃuleɪt/ **verb** (**congratulates, congratulating, congratulated**) **1** tell someone that you are pleased at their success or good fortune 祝贺;道贺 **2** (**congratulate yourself**) think that you are fortunate or clever (为自己)庆幸 ■ **congratulatory** adjective.

congratulation /kənˌɡrætʃu'leɪʃn/ **noun 1** (**congratulations**) good wishes given to someone who has had success or good fortune 祝贺;恭喜 **2** the action of congratulating someone 道贺

congregate /'kɒŋɡrɪɡeɪt/ **verb** (**congregates, congregating, congregated**) gather into a crowd or mass 集合;聚集

congregation /ˌkɒŋɡrɪ'ɡeɪʃn/ **noun 1** a group of people assembled for religious worship (参加宗教仪式的)会众 **2** a gathering or collection of people or things (人或物的)一群;聚集的人(或物)

congress /'kɒŋɡres/ **noun 1** a formal

meeting or series of meetings between representatives of different groups 代表大会 **2** (**Congress**) (in the US and some other countries) the group of people elected to pass laws (美国等国家的)立法机构, 国会 ■ **congressional** adjective.

congruent /'kɒŋgruənt/ **adjective 1** in agreement or harmony 一致的, 和谐的 **2** Geometry 【几何】(of figures) identical in form (图形)叠合的, 全等的 ■ **congruence** noun.

conical /'kɒnɪkl/ **adjective** shaped like a cone 圆锥形的

conifer /'kɒnɪfə(r)/ **noun** a tree that produces hard dry fruit (cones) and evergreen needle-like leaves 针叶树 ■ **coniferous** adjective.

conjecture /kən'dʒektʃə(r)/ **noun** an opinion based on incomplete information; a guess 推测; 猜测 • **verb** (**conjectures, conjecturing, conjectured**) form a conjecture; guess 推测; 猜测 ■ **conjectural** adjective.

conjoin /kən'dʒɔɪn/ **verb** formal 【正式】join; combine 连接; 结合

conjugal /'kɒndʒəɡl/ **adjective** having to do with marriage 婚姻的

conjugate /'kɒndʒəɡeɪt/ **verb** (**conjugates, conjugating, conjugated**) Grammar 【语法】give the different forms of a verb 列举(动词)的词形变化 ■ **conjugation** noun.

conjunction /kən'dʒʌŋkʃn/ **noun 1** a word used to connect words or clauses (e.g. *and, if*) 连词 **2** an instance of two or more things happening at the same time or being in the same place (事件的)同时发生, 在同一地点发生

conjunctivitis /kən,dʒʌŋktɪ'vaɪtɪs/ **noun** inflammation of the eye 结膜炎

conjure /'kʌndʒə(r)/ **verb** (**conjures, conjuring, conjured**) (usu. **conjure something up**) **1** make something appear by magic, or as if by magic 变出; 使(魔术般)出现 **2** make something appear as an image in your mind 使想起

conjuring /'kʌndʒərɪŋ/ **noun** entertainment in the form of seemingly magical tricks 变戏法; 魔术 ■ **conjuror** (or **conjurer**) noun.

conk /kɒŋk/ informal 【非正式】**verb** (**conk out**) **1** (of a machine) break down (机器)发生故障, 出毛病 **2** faint or go to sleep 昏倒; 入睡 • **noun** a person's nose (人的)鼻子

conker /'kɒŋkə(r)/ **noun** Brit. 【英】the dark brown nut of a horse chestnut tree 七叶树果

connect /kə'nekt/ **verb 1** join or bring together; link 连接 **2** (**be connected**) be related in some way 有关联

connection or Brit. 【英】 **connexion** /kə'nekʃn/ **noun 1** a link or relationship 联系; 关系 **2** the action of linking one thing with another 连接 **3** (**connections**) influential people that you know or are related to (有影响力的)社会关系, 熟人, 关系户 **4** a train, bus, etc. that you can catch to continue a journey 联运火车(或公共汽车等)

connective /kə'nektɪv/ **adjective** connecting one thing to another 连接的; 联结的 • **noun** a word or phrase that links parts of a sentence 连接词(或词组)

connive /kə'naɪv/ **verb** (**connives, conniving, connived**) **1** (**connive at** or **in**) secretly allow something wrong to be done 默许(不正当行为); 纵容 **2** (often **connive with**) conspire to do something wrong 共谋; 串通 ■ **connivance** noun.

connoisseur /,kɒnə'sɜː(r)/ **noun** a person with great knowledge and appreciation of something 鉴赏家; 鉴定家

connotation /,kɒnə'teɪʃn/ **noun** an idea or feeling that is suggested by a word in addition to its main meaning (词语的)内涵意义, 隐含意义

connote /kə'nəʊt/ **verb** (**connotes**, **connoting**, **connoted**) (of a word) suggest something in addition to its main meaning (词语)暗示，意味着

connubial /kə'njuːbiəl/ **adjective** having to do with marriage 婚姻的；夫妻关系的

conquer /'kɒŋkə(r)/ **verb** (**conquers**, **conquering**, **conquered**) **1** take control of a country or its people by military force (以军事力量)征服，攻取，占领 **2** successfully overcome a problem 解决(问题) ■ **conqueror** noun.

conquest /'kɒŋkwest/ **noun 1** the action of conquering 征服；攻取；克服 **2** a place that has been conquered 被攻占的领土；占领地 **3** a person whose affection you have won (爱情的)俘房

conscience /'kɒnʃəns/ **noun** a person's moral sense of right and wrong 良心；道德心；是非感

conscientious /ˌkɒnʃi'enʃəs/ **adjective** careful and thorough in carrying out your work or duty 尽责的；一丝不苟的 □ **conscientious objector** a person who refuses to serve in the armed forces for moral reasons (出于道德原因的)拒服兵役者 ■ **conscientiously** adverb.

conscious /'kɒnʃəs/ **adjective 1** aware of and responding to your surroundings 神志清醒的 **2** (usu. **conscious of**) aware 意识到的；觉察到的 **3** deliberate; intentional 故意的；存心的 ■ **consciously** adverb **consciousness** noun.

conscript **verb** /kən'skrɪpt/ call someone up for compulsory military service 征募(某人)服兵役 • **noun** /'kɒnskrɪpt/ a person who has been conscripted 应征入伍者 ■ **conscription** noun.

consecrate /'kɒnsɪkreɪt/ **verb** (**consecrates**, **consecrating**, **consecrated**) **1** make or declare something holy 使神圣；祝圣；圣化 **2** officially make someone a bishop 任命(某人)就圣职；祝圣神职人员 ■ **consecration** noun.

consecutive /kən'sekjʊtɪv/ **adjective** following one after another in unbroken sequence 连续不断的 ■ **consecutively** adverb.

consensual /kən'senʃuəl/ **adjective** relating to or involving consent or consensus 赞同的；一致同意的

consensus /kən'sensəs/ **noun** general agreement 一致同意；共识

✔ **拼写指南** con*sen*sus, not -*cen*-. consensus 不要拼作 -cen-。

---

consent /kən'sent/ **noun** permission or agreement 准许；同意 • **verb 1** give permission 准许 **2** agree to do something 同意

consequence /'kɒnsɪkwəns/ **noun 1** a result or effect 结果；后果 **2** importance or relevance 重要性；相关性

consequent /'kɒnsɪkwənt/ **adjective** following as a consequence 作为结果的；随之发生的 ■ **consequently** adverb.

conservation /ˌkɒnsə'veɪʃn/ **noun 1** preservation or restoration of the natural environment (对自然环境的)保护(或恢复) **2** preservation of historical sites and objects (对历史遗址及文物的)保护，修复 **3** careful use of a resource (对资源的)节约使用 ■ **conservationist** noun.

conservative /kən'sɜːvətɪv/ **adjective 1** opposed to change and holding traditional values 反对变革的，因循守旧的 **2** (in politics) favouring free enterprise and private ownership (政治上)赞成自由企业制度的，提倡私有化的 **3** (**Conservative**) relating to the Conservative Party, a British right-wing political party favouring free enterprise and private ownership (英国)保守党的 **4** (of an estimate) deliberately low for the sake of caution (估计)保守的，谨慎的 • **noun 1** a conservative person 保守主义者；因循守旧者 **2** (**Conservative**) a supporter or member of the Conservative Party 保守党支持者；保守党成员 ■ **conservatism** noun **conservatively** adverb.

conservatory /kən'sɜːvətri/ **noun** (plural **conservatories**) Brit. 【英】 a room with a glass roof and walls, attached to a house (与住宅相连的)温室，暖房

conserve verb /kən'sɜːv/ (**conserves, conserving, conserved**) protect something from being harmed or overused 保护；保存；贮藏 • **noun** /'kɒnsɜːv/ fruit jam 果酱

consider /kən'sɪdə(r)/ verb (**considers, considering, considered**) **1** think carefully about 考虑；细想；斟酌 **2** believe or think 相信；认为 **3** take into account when making a judgement 顾及；考虑到

considerable /kən'sɪdərəbl/ **adjective** great in size, amount, or importance 相当大的；相当多的；相当重要的 ■ **considerably** adverb.

considerate /kən'sɪdərət/ **adjective** careful not to harm or inconvenience other people 体贴的；考虑周到的 ■ **considerately** adverb.

consideration /kən,sɪdə'reɪʃn/ **noun 1** careful thought 考虑；细想；斟酌 **2** a fact taken into account when making a decision 所考虑的事；需考虑的事 **3** thoughtfulness towards other people 体贴

considering /kən'sɪdərɪŋ/ **preposition & conjunction** taking something into account 考虑到；就…而论

consign /kən'saɪn/ verb **1** deliver something to someone 把…交付给；把…委托给 **2** (**consign someone/thing to**) put someone or something in a place so as to be rid of them 把…丢弃(在某地)；打发

consignment /kən'saɪnmənt/ **noun** a batch of goods that are delivered 托运物

consist /kən'sɪst/ verb **1** (**consist of**) be composed or made up of 由…组成 **2** (**consist in**) have as an essential feature 在于；存在于

consistency /kən'sɪstənsi/ **noun** (plural **consistencies**) **1** the state of being consistent 一致性；连贯性 **2** the thickness of a liquid or semi-liquid substance 黏稠度；浓度

consistent /kən'sɪstənt/ **adjective 1** always behaving in the same way; unchanging 始终如一的；一贯的 **2** (usu. **consistent with**) in agreement 一致的；和谐的 ■ **consistently** adverb.

consolation /,kɒnsə'leɪʃn/ **noun 1** comfort received after a loss or disappointment 安慰；慰藉 **2** a source of such comfort 起安慰作用的人(或事物) □ **consolation prize** a prize given to a competitor who just fails to win 安慰奖；鼓励奖

console¹ /kən'səʊl/ verb (**consoles, consoling, consoled**) comfort someone who is unhappy or disappointed about something 安慰；抚慰

console² /'kɒnsəʊl/ **noun 1** a panel or unit containing a set of controls 仪表板；控制台 **2** a small machine for playing computerized video games (玩计算机游戏用的)操纵器

consolidate /kən'sɒlɪdeɪt/ verb (**consolidates, consolidating, consolidated**) **1** make stronger or more solid 加强；巩固；使坚固 **2** combine into a single unit 联合；合并 ■ **consolidation** noun.

consommé /kən'sɒmeɪ/ **noun** a clear soup made with concentrated stock 清炖肉汤

consonance /'kɒnsənəns/ **noun** formal 【正式】 agreement or compatibility 一致；和谐；协调

consonant /'kɒnsənənt/ **noun** a letter

of the alphabet representing a sound in which the breath is completely or partly obstructed 辅音 • **adjective** (**consonant with**) formal 【正式】in agreement or harmony with 一致的；和谐的

consort noun /ˈkɒnsɔːt/ formal 【正式】a wife, husband, or companion 配偶；伙伴 • **verb** /kənˈsɔːt/ (**consort with**) habitually associate with 结交；交往

consortium /kənˈsɔːtɪəm/ noun (plural **consortia** /kənˈsɔːtɪə/ or **consortiums**) an association of several companies 联营企业

conspicuous /kənˈspɪkjuəs/ **adjective 1** clearly visible 显眼的；显而易见的 **2** attracting notice 惹人注目的 ∎ **conspicuously** adverb.

conspiracy /kənˈspɪrəsi/ noun (plural **conspiracies**) a secret plan by a group to do something unlawful or harmful 犯罪图谋；阴谋计划

conspire /kənˈspaɪə(r)/ verb (**conspires, conspiring, conspired**) **1** jointly make secret plans to commit a wrongful act 密谋；搞阴谋 **2** (of circumstances) seem to be working together to bring about something bad (各种情况)共同导致(不良后果) ∎ **conspirator** noun **conspiratorial** adjective.

constable /ˈkʌnstəbl/ noun Brit.【英】a police officer of the lowest rank (级别最低的)警察

constabulary /kənˈstæbjələri/ noun (plural **constabularies**) Brit.【英】a police force 警察部队

constant /ˈkɒnstənt/ **adjective 1** occurring continuously 不断的；持续的 **2** remaining the same 始终如一的；持久不变的 **3** faithful and dependable 忠实的；可靠的 • **noun 1** an unchanging situation 恒定不变 **2** Maths & Physics【数学和物理】a number or quantity that does not change its value 常数；常量；恒量 ∎ **constancy** noun **constantly** adverb.

constellation /ˌkɒnstəˈleɪʃn/ noun a group of stars forming a recognized pattern 星座

consternation /ˌkɒnstəˈneɪʃn/ noun anxiety or dismay 焦虑；惊愕；惊慌

constipated /ˈkɒnstɪpeɪtɪd/ **adjective** suffering from constipation 便秘的

constipation /ˌkɒnstɪˈpeɪʃn/ noun difficulty in emptying the bowels 便秘

constituency /kənˈstɪtjuənsi/ noun (plural **constituencies**) chiefly Brit.【主英】an area that elects a representative to a parliament 选区

constituent /kənˈstɪtjuənt/ **adjective** being a part of a whole 组成的；构成的 • **noun 1** a member of a constituency 选民 **2** a part of a whole 成分；要素

constitute /ˈkɒnstɪtjuːt/ verb (**constitutes, constituting, constituted**) **1** be a part of a whole 组成；构成 **2** be equivalent to 相当于；等于 **3** establish by law 合法地设立

constitution /ˌkɒnstɪˈtjuːʃn/ noun **1** a set of principles according to which a state or organization is governed 宪法 **2** the composition or formation of something 构成；形成 **3** a person's physical or mental state 体质；心理素质

constitutional /ˌkɒnstɪˈtjuːʃənl/ **adjective 1** relating or according to a constitution 宪法的；符合宪法的 **2** relating to a person's physical or mental state 体质的；心理素质的 • **noun** dated【废】a walk taken regularly so as to stay healthy 保健散步 ∎ **constitutionally** adverb.

constrain /kənˈstreɪn/ verb **1** force someone to do something 强迫；迫使 **2** (**constrained**) appearing forced or unnatural 勉强的；不自然的 **3** severely restrict or limit 约束；限制

constraint /kənˈstreɪnt/ noun a limitation or restriction 约束；限制

constrict /kənˈstrɪkt/ verb **1** make or

become narrower; tighten 使变紧，使收缩；压缩；压紧 **2** stop someone moving or acting freely 剥夺…的行动自由 ■ **constriction** noun.

constrictor /kən'strɪktə(r)/ noun a snake that kills by squeezing and choking its prey 蟒，大蛇

construct verb /kən'strʌkt/ build or put together 建造；构筑；建立 • noun /'kɒnstrʌkt/ an idea or theory containing various elements 构想，构建的理论

construction /kən'strʌkʃn/ noun **1** the process of constructing something 建造；构筑；建立 **2** a building or other structure 建筑物；建造物 **3** an interpretation of something 解释；释义

constructive /kən'strʌktɪv/ adjective having a useful and helpful effect 建设性的；有助益的 ■ **constructively** adverb.

construe /kən'struː/ verb (**construes, construing, construed**) interpret something in a particular way 把…理解为；把…解释成

consul /'kɒnsl/ noun **1** an official who is based in a foreign city and protects their country's citizens and interests there 领事 **2** (in ancient Rome) each of two elected officials who ruled the republic jointly for a year (古罗马的)二执政官之一 ■ **consular** adjective.

consulate /'kɒnsjələt/ noun the place where a consul works 领事馆

consult /kən'sʌlt/ verb **1** try to get advice or information from 向…咨询；请教 **2** ask someone for permission or approval 请求(某人)批准 ■ **consultation** noun **consultative** adjective.

consultancy /kən'sʌltənsi/ noun (plural **consultancies**) a company that gives expert advice in a particular field 咨询公司

consultant /kən'sʌltənt/ noun **1** a person who provides expert advice

professionally (提供专业咨询的)顾问 **2** Brit.【英】a senior hospital doctor (高级)顾问医生，会诊医师

consume /kən'sjuːm/ verb (**consumes, consuming, consumed**) **1** eat or drink 吃；喝 **2** use up 消耗，耗尽；用完 **3** (of a fire) completely destroy (大火)毁灭，烧毁 **4** (of a feeling) absorb someone wholly (感情)充满，使着迷

consumer /kən'sjuːmə(r)/ noun a person who buys a product or uses a service 消费者

consumerism /kən'sjuːmərɪzəm/ noun the preoccupation of society with buying goods 消费主义 ■ **consumerist** adjective.

consummate verb /'kɒnsəmeɪt/ (**consummates, consummating, consummated**) **1** make a marriage or relationship complete by having sex (通过同房)使完婚，使关系圆满 **2** complete a transaction 完成(交易) • adjective /kən'sʌmət/ showing great skill and flair 技艺高超的；才能出众的 ■ **consummation** noun.

consumption /kən'sʌmpʃn/ noun **1** the process of consuming, or an amount consumed 消费；消耗 **2** dated 【废】tuberculosis 痨病；肺结核 ■ **consumptive** adjective (dated【废】).

contact /'kɒntækt/ noun **1** physical touching 触摸 **2** communicating or meeting 联系；交往 **3** a person whom you can ask for information or help 联系人；联络人 **4** a connection for an electric current to pass from one thing to another 接头；触点 • verb get in touch with 与…联系；与…接触 □ **contact lens** a plastic lens placed on the surface of the eye to help you see better 隐形眼镜

contagion /kən'teɪdʒən/ noun the passing of a disease from one person to another by close contact (疾病的)接触性传染

contagious /kən'teɪdʒəs/ adjective

1 (of a disease) spread by contact between people (疾病)接触传染的 **2** having a contagious disease 患接触性传染病的

contain /kən'teɪn/ **verb 1** have or hold something inside 包含；容纳 **2** control or restrain 控制；抑制；克制 **3** prevent a problem from becoming worse 阻止(问题)恶化

container /kən'teɪnə(r)/ **noun 1** a box or similar object for holding something 容器 **2** a large metal box for transporting goods 集装箱

containment /kən'teɪnmənt/ **noun** the keeping of something harmful under control 遏制；抑制

contaminate /kən'tæmɪneɪt/ **verb** (**contaminates, contaminating, contaminated**) make something dirty or poisonous by allowing it to come into contact with harmful substances 污染；弄脏 ■ **contamination** noun.

contemplate /'kɒntəmpleɪt/ **verb** (**contemplates, contemplating, contemplated**) **1** look at thoughtfully 凝视；注视 **2** think about 思考；思忖 **3** think deeply and at length 沉思，冥想；深思熟虑 ■ **contemplation** noun **contemplative** adjective.

contemporaneous /kən,tempə'reɪnɪəs/ **adjective** existing at or happening in the same period of time 同时存在的；同时发生的

contemporary /kən'temprəri/ **adjective 1** living or happening at the same time 生活在同时代的，发生于同时代的 **2** belonging to or happening in the present 当代的 **3** modern in style (风格)现代的 • **noun** (plural **contemporaries**) a person living or working in the same period as another 同时代的人

✔ 拼写指南 contem*porary*, not -*pory*. contemporary 不要拼作 -pory。

contempt /kən'tempt/ **noun 1** the feeling that someone or something is worthless 轻视；鄙视，蔑视 **2** (also **contempt of court**) the offence of disobeying or being disrespectful to a court of law 藐视法庭(罪)

contemptible /kən'temptəbl/ **adjective** deserving contempt 可鄙的；卑鄙的 ■ **contemptibly** adverb.

contemptuous /kən'temptjuəs/ **adjective** showing contempt 表示轻蔑的；鄙视的 ■ **contemptuously** adverb.

contend /kən'tend/ **verb 1** (**contend with** or **against**) struggle to deal with a difficulty 与(困难)斗争 **2** (**contend for**) struggle to achieve 争夺；争夺 **3** put forward a view in an argument 声称；主张；认为 ■ **contender** noun.

content[1] /kən'tent/ **adjective** peacefully happy or satisfied 满足的；满意的 • **verb** satisfy or please 使满足；使满意 • **noun** a state of happiness or satisfaction 满足；满意 ■ **contentment** noun.

content[2] /'kɒntent/ **noun 1** (**contents**) the things that are contained in something 所含之物；内容 **2** the amount of a particular thing occurring in a substance 含量 **3** (**contents**) a list of chapters given at the front of a book or magazine (书刊的)目录 **4** the material in a piece of writing, as opposed to its form or style (文章的)实质内容，要旨

contented /kən'tentɪd/ **adjective** happy or satisfied 惬意的；满足的；满意的 ■ **contentedly** adverb.

contention /kən'tenʃn/ **noun 1** heated disagreement 争论；争执 **2** a point of view that is expressed 主张；论点 □ **in contention** having a good chance of success in a contest (在竞赛中)很有希望获胜的

contentious /kən'tenʃəs/ **adjective** causing disagreement or controversy; controversial 引起争论的；有争议的

contest noun /'kɒntest/ an event in which people compete to see who is the best 竞赛；比赛 • **verb** /kən'test/ **1** take part in a competition or election 参加(比赛或选举) **2** challenge or dispute a decision or theory 对(决定或理论)提出质疑；争辩

contestant /kən'testənt/ **noun** a person who takes part in a contest 参赛者；竞赛者

context /'kɒntekst/ **noun 1** the circumstances surrounding an event, statement, or idea 来龙去脉；背景 **2** the parts that come immediately before and after a word or passage and make its meaning clearer 上下文；语境 ■ **contextual** adjective.

contiguous /kən'tɪgjuəs/ **adjective** sharing a border 接壤的

continent[1] /'kɒntɪnənt/ **noun 1** any of the world's main continuous expanses of land (Europe, Asia, Africa, North and South America, Australia, Antarctica) 大陆，洲(指欧洲、亚洲、非洲、南北美洲、大洋洲和南极洲) **2** (**the Continent**) the mainland of Europe as distinct from the British Isles (除不列颠群岛之外的)欧洲大陆

continent[2] **adjective 1** able to control movements of the bowels and bladder 有大小便自控能力的 **2** restrained; selfdisciplined 自我节制的；自我约束的 ■ **continence** noun.

continental /ˌkɒntɪ'nentl/ **adjective 1** forming or belonging to a continent 大洲的 **2** coming from or like mainland Europe 欧洲大陆(性)的 • **noun** a person from mainland Europe 欧洲大陆人 □ **continental breakfast** a light breakfast of coffee and bread rolls (以咖啡和面包卷为主的)欧洲大陆式早餐，清淡早餐

contingency /kən'tɪndʒənsi/ **noun** (plural **contingencies**) a future event which may happen but cannot be predicted with certainty 可能发生的事；不测事件

contingent /kən'tɪndʒənt/ **noun** a group of people forming part of a larger group 分遣队；小分队 • **adjective 1** (**contingent on**) dependent on 取决于…的 **2** depending on chance 偶然的；意外的

continual /kən'tɪnjuəl/ **adjective** happening constantly or often, with intervals in between 连续的；频繁的：*He met with continual delays.* 他遭遇多番延误。■ **continually** adverb.

> **!注意** note that **continual** and **continuous** don't mean exactly the same thing. 注意 continual 和 continuous 意思不完全相同。

continuation /kənˌtɪnju'eɪʃn/ **noun 1** the action of continuing 继续；持续 **2** a part that is attached to something else and is an extension of it 附加部分；延长部分；扩展部分

continue /kən'tɪnjuː/ **verb** (**continues, continuing, continued**) **1** keep doing something; carry on with 继续；坚持下去 **2** keep existing or happening 连续；持续 **3** carry on travelling in the same direction 继续(沿同一方向)行进 **4** start doing something again 重新开始；接着做

continuity /ˌkɒntɪ'njuːəti/ **noun** (plural **continuities**) **1** the fact of not stopping or changing 坚持；持续 **2** an unbroken connection or line of development 延续；连接 **3** organization of a film or television programme so that the plot makes sense and clothing, scenery, etc. remain the same in different scenes (电影和电视节目的)各场景串联

continuous /kən'tɪnjuəs/ **adjective** forming an unbroken whole or sequence without interruptions or exceptions 持续的；不断的：*a day of continuous rain* 雨下个不停的一天 ■ **continuously** adverb.

continuum /kən'tɪnjuəm/ **noun** (plural **continua** /kən'tɪnjuə/) a continuous sequence in which the elements change gradually 统一体；连续体

contort /kən'tɔ:t/ **verb** twist or bend something out of its normal shape (使)扭曲，(使)弯曲 ■ **contortion** noun.

contortionist /kən'tɔ:ʃənɪst/ **noun** an entertainer who twists and bends their body into unnatural positions 柔体杂技演员

contour /'kɒntuə(r)/ **noun 1** an outline of the shape or form of something 外形；轮廓 **2** (also **contour line**) a line on a map joining points of equal height (地图上的)等高线 ■ **contoured** adjective.

contraband /'kɒntrəbænd/ **noun** goods that have been imported or exported illegally 走私货；违禁品

contraception /ˌkɒntrə'sepʃn/ **noun** the use of contraceptives 避孕；节育

contraceptive /ˌkɒntrə'septɪv/ **noun** a device or drug used to prevent a woman becoming pregnant 避孕器，避孕药 ● **adjective** preventing a woman becoming pregnant 避孕用的；阻止怀孕的

contract noun /'kɒntrækt/ **1** an official, legally binding agreement 合同 **2** informal 【非正式】 an arrangement for someone to be murdered by a hired killer (与雇佣杀手达成的)暗杀协议 ● **verb** /kən'trækt/ **1** make or become smaller (使)缩小，(使)缩减；缩紧 **2** become shorter and tighter 收缩；缩紧 **3** shorten a word or phrase 缩写(单词或短语) **4** make a formal and legally binding agreement to do something 订契约，立合同 **5** catch or develop a disease 感染(疾病) ■ **contractual** adjective.

contraction /kən'trækʃn/ **noun 1** the process of contracting 缩小，缩减 **2** a shortening of the muscles of the womb happening at intervals during childbirth (分娩时的)子宫肌肉收缩，牵缩 **3** a shortened form of a word or words (词语的)缩略形式

contractor /kən'træktə(r)/ **noun** a

person or firm that undertakes to provide materials or labour for a job 承包人，承包商

contradict /ˌkɒntrə'dɪkt/ **verb** deny the truth of a statement made by someone by saying the opposite 反驳；驳斥

contradiction /ˌkɒntrə'dɪkʃn/ **noun 1** a combination of statements, ideas, or features which are opposed to one another 矛盾，对立 **2** saying the opposite to something already said 否认；反驳

contradictory /ˌkɒntrə'dɪktəri/ **adjective 1** inconsistent with or opposing each other 抵触的，对立的 **2** containing inconsistent elements 自相矛盾的

contradistinction /ˌkɒntrədɪ'stɪŋkʃn/ **noun** distinction made by contrasting two things 对比，区别

contraflow /'kɒntrəfləʊ/ **noun** Brit. 【英】 an arrangement by which the lanes of a dual carriageway normally carrying traffic in one direction become two-directional (通常为一幅单向行驶的车道临时改为双向的)一侧双向行驶，逆道行驶

contralto /kən'træltəʊ/ **noun** (plural **contraltos**) the lowest female singing voice 女低音

contraption /kən'træpʃn/ **noun** a machine or device that appears strange or unnecessarily complicated 奇异的机械；过于复杂的装置

contrapuntal /ˌkɒntrə'pʌntl/ **adjective** Music 【音乐】 relating to or in counterpoint 对位的，复调的

contrariwise /'kɒntrəriwaɪz/ **adverb** in the opposite way 相反地；反之

contrary /'kɒntrəri/ **adjective 1** opposite in nature, direction, or meaning (性质、方向或意义)相反的 **2** /'kɒntrəri/ (of two or more statements, beliefs, etc.) opposed to one another (两种或两种以上的陈述、信仰等)对立的 **3** /kən'treəri/ deliberately inclined to do the opposite of what is expected or wanted 对抗的；逆反的；倔强的 • **noun (the contrary)** the opposite 反面；对立面 ■ **contrariness** noun.

contrast noun /'kɒntrɑːst/ **1** the state of being noticeably different from something else 对比；对照 **2** a thing or person noticeably different from another 对照物（或人） **3** the amount of difference between tones in a television picture, photograph, etc. (电视画面、照片等的)色调对比，反差 • **verb** /kən'trɑːst/ **1** be noticeably different 形成对照；形成对比 **2** compare two things to emphasize their differences 对比；对照

contravene /ˌkɒntrə'viːn/ **verb** (**contravenes, contravening, contravened**) **1** do something that breaks a law, treaty, etc. 违犯，违反(法律、协定等) **2** conflict with a right, principle, etc. 与(权利、原则等)相抵触 ■ **contravention** noun.

contretemps /'kɒntrətɒn/ **noun** (plural **contretemps** /'kɒntrətɒnz/) a minor disagreement 争论；小争执

contribute /kən'trɪbjuːt/ **verb** (**contributes, contributing, contributed**) **1** give something in order to help an undertaking or effort 捐献；捐助 **2** (**contribute to**) help to cause or bring about 有助于；促成 ■ **contribution** noun **contributor** noun.

contributory /kən'trɪbjətəri/ **adjective 1** playing a part in bringing something about 促成的，作出贡献的 **2** (of a pension or insurance scheme) operated by means of a fund into which people pay (退休金或保险金计划)需受益人出资支付的

contrite /'kɒntraɪt, kən'traɪt/ **adjective** sorry for something that you have done 悔悔的；悔悟的 ■ **contritely** adverb **contrition** noun.

contrivance /kən'traɪvəns/ **noun 1** a clever device or scheme 巧妙的装

置；妙计 **2** the action of contriving something 设计

contrive /kən'traɪv/ **verb** (**contrives, contriving, contrived**) **1** plan or achieve something in a clever or skilful way 谋划；设计 **2** manage to do something foolish 设法做成(蠢事)

contrived /kən'traɪvd/ **adjective** deliberately created and seeming artificial; not natural or spontaneous 人为的；不自然的

control /kən'trəʊl/ **noun 1** the power to influence people's behaviour or the course of events 支配；控制 **2** the restriction of something 遏制；抑制：*crime control* 遏制犯罪 **3** a way of regulating or limiting something 管制手段；调节手段；抑制手段：*controls on local spending* 本地花费控制 **4** a person or thing used as a standard of comparison for checking the results of a survey or experiment (调查或实验的)对照物，对照标准 • **verb** (**controls, controlling, controlled**) **1** have control or command of 支配；控制 **2** limit or regulate 管制；调节 □ **control tower** a tall building at an airport from which the movements of aircraft are controlled (空中交通的)指挥调度台 ■ **controllable** adjective **controller** noun.

controversial /ˌkɒntrə'vɜːʃl/ **adjective** causing or likely to cause controversy 引起争论的；有争议的 ■ **controversially** adverb.

controversy /'kɒntrəvɜːsi/ **noun** (plural **controversies**) debate or disagreement about a subject which arouses strong opinions 争论；争议

contumely /'kɒntjuːmli/ **noun** (plural **contumelies**) old use 【旧】 insulting language or treatment 侮辱性的言语；傲慢

contusion /kən'tjuːʒn/ **noun** a bruise 擦伤

conundrum /kə'nʌndrəm/ **noun**

(plural **conundrums**) **1** a difficult problem or question 疑难问题 **2** a riddle 谜语

conurbation /ˌkɒnɜːˈbeɪʃn/ **noun** an area consisting of several towns merging together or with a city (由中心城市及卫星城镇构成的)大都市圈,集合城市

convalesce /ˌkɒnvəˈles/ **verb** (**convalesces, convalescing, convalesced**) gradually get better after an illness or injury 康复;恢复

convalescent /ˌkɒnvəˈlesnt/ **adjective** recovering from an illness or injury 康复的;恢复的 ■ **convalescence** noun.

convection /kənˈvekʃn/ **noun** the process by which heat moves through a gas or liquid as the warmer part rises and the cooler part sinks 对流

convector /kənˈvektə(r)/ **noun** a heater that circulates warm air by convection 对流加热器;换流器

convene /kənˈviːn/ **verb** (**convenes, convening, convened**) **1** call people together for a meeting 召集,组织(会议) **2** come together for a meeting (为会议而)聚集,集合 ■ **convener** (or **convenor**) noun.

convenience /kənˈviːniəns/ **noun 1** freedom from effort or difficulty 方便;便利 **2** a useful or helpful device or situation 便利设施;便利处境 **3** Brit. 【英】a public toilet 公共厕所

convenient /kənˈviːniənt/ **adjective 1** fitting in well with a person's needs, activities, and plans 舒适的;合适的,方便的 **2** involving little trouble or effort 便利的;简便的 ■ **conveniently** adverb.

convent /ˈkɒnvənt/ **noun** a building where nuns live together 女修道院

convention /kənˈvenʃn/ **noun 1** a way in which something is usually done 惯例;常规 **2** socially acceptable behaviour 社会行为准则 **3** a large meeting or conference 大会;会议 **4** an agreement between countries (国家间的)公约,协定

conventional /kənˈvenʃənl/ **adjective 1** based on or following what is generally done 惯例的;常规的 **2** not individual or adventurous 无个人创新的;墨守成规的,因袭传统的 **3** (of weapons or power) non-nuclear (武器或动力)常规的,非核的 ■ **conventionally** adverb.

converge /kənˈvɜːdʒ/ **verb** (**converges, converging, converged**) **1** come together from different directions 会合;集中 **2** (**converge on**) come from different directions and meet at 相交于;汇集于 ■ **convergent** adjective.

conversant /kənˈvɜːsnt/ **adjective** (**conversant with**) familiar with or knowledgeable about 熟悉的;精通的

conversation /ˌkɒnvəˈseɪʃn/ **noun** an informal talk between two or more people (非正式的)交谈,谈话 ■ **conversational** adjective **conversationalist** noun.

converse[1] /kənˈvɜːs/ **verb** (**converses, conversing, conversed**) hold a conversation 交谈;进行谈话

converse[2] /ˈkɒnvɜːs/ **noun** something that is the opposite of another 反面;对立面 ■ **adjective** opposite 相反的 ■ **conversely** adverb.

conversion /kənˈvɜːʃn/ **noun 1** the action of converting 改变;转化 **2** Brit. 【英】a building that has been converted to a new purpose 改建的房屋 **3** Rugby 【英式橄榄球】a successful kick at goal after a try (以球触地得分后的)再踢定位球得分

convert verb /kənˈvɜːt/ **1** change the form, character, or function of something 改变;转变;转换 **2** change money or units into others of a different kind 兑换(货币);折算(单位) **3** adapt a building for a new purpose 改建(房屋) **4** change your religious faith 改变

(宗教信仰) • noun /kɒnvɜːt/ a person who has changed their religious faith 改变宗教信仰者

convertible /kən'vɜːtəbl/ **adjective 1** able to be converted 可转换的;可转化的 **2** (of a car) having a folding or detachable roof (汽车)有折叠(或可拆卸)车篷的 • noun a convertible car 活动顶篷式汽车

convex /'kɒnveks/ **adjective** having an outline or surface that curves outwards 凸出的;凸面的

convey /kən'veɪ/ **verb 1** transport or carry to a place 运送;运输 **2** communicate an idea or feeling 传达,表达 (想法或感情)

conveyance /kən'veɪəns/ **noun 1** the action of conveying 运输;表达 **2** formal 【正式】 a means of transport 运输工具 **3** the legal process of transferring property from one owner to another 产权转让 ■ **conveyancing** noun.

conveyor belt /kən'veɪə(r)/ **noun** a continuous moving band used for transporting objects from one place to another 传送带

convict verb /kən'vɪkt/ officially declare that someone is guilty of a criminal offence 判定(某人)有罪 • noun /'kɒnvɪkt/ a person in prison after being convicted of a criminal offence 已决犯;服刑犯

conviction /kən'vɪkʃn/ **noun 1** an instance of being convicted of a criminal offence 定罪;判罪 **2** a firmly held belief or opinion 坚定的信念(或看法) **3** the quality of showing that you believe strongly in what you are saying or doing 信服;确信

convince /kən'vɪns/ **verb** (**convinces, convincing, convinced**) **1** cause someone to believe firmly that something is true 使确信,使信服 **2** persuade someone to do something 说服;劝服

convincing /kən'vɪnsɪŋ/ **adjective 1** able to convince someone 有说服力的;使人信服的 **2** (of a victory or a winner) leaving no margin of doubt (胜利或获胜者)毫无悬念的,确定无疑的 ■ **convincingly** adverb.

convivial /kən'vɪviəl/ **adjective 1** (of an atmosphere or event) friendly and lively (气氛或活动)欢快友好的 **2** (of a person) cheerfully sociable (人)好交际的 ■ **conviviality** noun.

convoluted /'kɒnvəluːtɪd/ **adjective 1** (of an argument or account) very complex (论点或陈述)错综复杂的,晦涩难懂的 **2** folded or twisted in an elaborate way 盘绕的;卷曲的

convolution /ˌkɒnvə'luːʃn/ **noun 1** a coil or twist 盘绕;卷曲 **2** (**convolutions**) something complex and difficult to follow 复杂费解的事物

convoy /'kɒnvɔɪ/ **noun** a group of ships or vehicles travelling together under armed protection 护航舰队;护送车队

convulse /kən'vʌls/ **verb** (**convulses, convulsing, convulsed**) **1** suffer convulsions 痉挛;抽搐 **2** (**be convulsed**) make sudden, uncontrollable movements because of emotion, laughter, etc. (因激动、发笑等)全身抖动 ■ **convulsive** adjective.

convulsion /kən'vʌlʃn/ **noun 1** a sudden, irregular movement of the body caused by muscles contracting uncontrollably (肌肉不由自主收缩造成的)惊厥,抽搐 **2** (**convulsions**) uncontrollable laughter 狂笑;大笑 **3** a violent upheaval 大骚乱;动乱

coo /kuː/ **verb** (**coos, cooing, cooed**) **1** (of a pigeon or dove) make a soft murmuring sound (鸽子)咕咕叫,发咕咕声 **2** speak in a soft, gentle voice (人)语调轻柔地说 • noun a cooing sound 咕咕声;轻柔低语声

cook /kuk/ **verb 1** prepare food or a meal by heating the ingredients 烹调(食物);做(饭菜) **2** (of food) be heated so as to become edible (食物)

被烧煮,在烹调中 **3** informal【非正式】alter accounts dishonestly 篡改;伪造 **4 (cook something up)** informal【非正式】invent a story or plan 捏造,编造(故事或计划) ∎ noun a person who cooks 厨师

cooker /'kʊkə(r)/ noun Brit.【英】an appliance for cooking food 厨具,炊具

cookery /'kʊkəri/ noun the practice or skill of preparing and cooking food 烹调;厨艺

cookie /'kʊki/ noun (plural **cookies**) **1** N. Amer.【北美】a sweet biscuit 甜饼干;曲奇饼 **2** informal【非正式】a person of a particular kind 特别的人:*She's a tough cookie.* 她是个很强硬的人。

cool /kuːl/ adjective **1** fairly cold 温度低的;凉的 **2** stopping you from becoming too hot 凉爽的;凉快的 **3** unfriendly or unenthusiastic 不友好的;冷淡的;冷漠的 **4** not anxious or excited 沉着的;冷静的 **5** informal【非正式】fashionably attractive or impressive 时髦的;酷的 **6** informal【非正式】excellent 极好的;绝妙的 ∎ noun the state of being calm and self-controlled 沉着;冷静 ∎ verb (**cools, cooling, cooled**) make or become cool (使)变凉,(使)冷却 ∎ **cooler** noun **coolly** adverb **coolness** noun.

coolant /'kuːlənt/ noun a fluid used to cool an engine or other device (用于发动机或其他装置的)冷却剂

coolie /'kuːli/ noun (plural **coolies**) dated【废】an unskilled labourer in an Asian country (亚洲国家的)无技能劳动力,苦力

coon /kuːn/ noun N. Amer.【北美】a raccoon 黑鬼

coop /kuːp/ noun a cage or pen for poultry 禽舍;笼子 ∎ verb (**coop someone/thing up**) confine a person or animal in a small space 把…关(或拘禁)起来

cooper /'kuːpə(r)/ noun a person who makes or repairs casks and barrels 制桶匠;修桶匠

cooperate or **co-operate** /kəʊ-'ɒpəreɪt/ verb (**cooperates, co-operating, cooperated**) **1** work together towards the same end 合作;协作 **2** do what someone wants 配合;协助 ∎ **cooperation** noun.

cooperative or **co-operative** /kəʊ'ɒpərətɪv/ adjective **1** involving cooperation 合作的;协助的 **2** willing to help 愿意合作的;配合的 **3** (of a business) owned and run jointly by its members (企业)共同拥有的,合作经营的 ∎ noun a cooperative organization 合作机构 ∎ **cooperatively** adverb.

co-opt /kəʊ'ɒpt/ verb **1** appoint someone as a member of a committee or other body 选派(某人)为…的成员 **2** adopt an idea or policy for your own use 接受,借鉴(观念或政策)

coordinate or **co-ordinate** verb /kəʊ'ɔːdɪneɪt/ (**coordinates, coordinating, coordinated**) **1** bring the different elements of something together so that it works well 使协调;调节 **2 (coordinate with)** negotiate with other people to work together effectively 与…协调;配合 **3** (of different things) match or look attractive together (不同事物)协调,搭配 ∎ noun /kəʊ'ɔːdɪnət/ Maths【数学】each of a group of numbers used to indicate the position of a point, line, or plane 坐标 ∎ **coordinator** noun.

coordination or **co-ordination** /kəʊ,ɔːdɪ'neɪʃn/ noun **1** the process of coordinating 协调;搭配 **2** the ability to move different parts of the body smoothly and at the same time (身体各部分的)协调能力

coot /kuːt/ noun a waterbird with black feathers and a white bill 白骨顶(一种黑羽水鸟,喙为白色)

cop /kɒp/ informal【非正式】noun

a police officer 警察 • **verb** (**cops, copping, copped**) **1** arrest an offender 抓获, 逮捕(罪犯) **2** receive or experience something unwelcome 遭受, 忍受(不快之事) **3** (**cop out**) avoid doing something that you ought to do 逃避, 回避(应做的事) □ **cop it** Brit. 【英】get into trouble 陷入麻烦 **not much cop** Brit. 【英】not very good 不太好的

cope[1] /kəʊp/ **verb** (**copes, coping, coped**) deal effectively with something difficult (有效地)应对, 处理

cope[2] **noun** a long cloak worn by a priest on ceremonial occasions (牧师主持仪式时穿的)长袍, 法衣

copier /'kɒpɪə(r)/ **noun** a machine that makes exact copies of something 复印机

co-pilot /'kəʊpaɪlət/ **noun** a second pilot in an aircraft (飞机的)副驾驶员

coping /'kəʊpɪŋ/ **noun** the top line of bricks or stones in a wall (砖墙或石墙的)护顶, 盖顶

copious /'kəʊpɪəs/ **adjective** in large amounts; plentiful 大量的; 充裕的; 丰富的 ■ **copiously** adverb.

copper[1] /'kɒpə(r)/ **noun 1** a reddish-brown metal (金属元素)铜 **2** (**coppers**) Brit. 【英】coins made of copper or bronze 铜币 **3** a reddish-brown colour 红棕色 □ **copper-bottomed** Brit. 【英】thoroughly reliable 绝对可靠的

copper[2] **noun** Brit. informal 【英, 非正式】a police officer 警察

copperplate /'kɒpəpleɪt/ **noun** an elaborate style of handwriting 工整手写体; 铜版体

coppice /'kɒpɪs/ **noun** an area of woodland in which the trees or shrubs are periodically cut back to ground level (定期修剪的)矮林, 萌生林

copse /kɒps/ **noun** a small group of trees 萌生林

copulate /'kɒpjʊleɪt/ **verb** (**copulates, copulating, copulated**) mate or have sex 交配; 性交; 交媾 ■ **copulation** noun.

copy /'kɒpi/ **noun** (plural **copies**) **1** a thing made to be similar or identical to another 仿制物; 复制品 **2** a single example of a particular book, record, etc. 一册; 一本; 一份 **3** material for a newspaper or magazine article (报刊的)稿件, 文字材料 • **verb** (**copies, copying, copied**) **1** make a copy of 仿制; 复制 **2** imitate the behaviour or style of 模仿; 仿效 □ **copy-edit** check that written material is consistent and accurate 编辑, 修改(稿件) ■ **copyist** noun.

copyright /'kɒpɪraɪt/ **noun** the exclusive right to publish, perform, film, or record literary, artistic, or musical material 版权; 著作权

copywriter /'kɒpɪraɪtə(r)/ **noun** a person who writes advertisements or publicity material (广告或宣传材料的)文字撰稿人

coquette /kɒ'ket/ **noun** a flirtatious woman 卖弄风情的女子 ■ **coquetry** noun **coquettish** adjective.

coracle /'kɒrəkl/ **noun** a small round boat made of wickerwork covered with a watertight material 科拉克尔小艇(一种小圆船, 用柳条编制, 涂有防水材料)

coral /'kɒrəl/ **noun 1** a hard substance found in warm seas which consists of the skeletons of small animals living together as a stationary mass 珊瑚 **2** a pinkish-red colour 珊瑚色; 粉红色

cor anglais /ˌkɔːr 'ɒŋɡleɪ/ **noun** (plural **cors anglais** /ˌkɔːr 'ɒŋɡleɪ/) a woodwind instrument of the oboe family 英国管; 次中音双簧管

corbel /'kɔːbl/ **noun** a projection jutting out from a wall to support a structure above it (墙上的)托臂, 梁托

cord /kɔːd/ **noun 1** thin string or rope

made from several twisted strands 细绳；索；带 **2** an electric flex 电线 **3** corduroy 灯芯绒 **4 (cords)** trousers made of corduroy 灯芯绒裤子 ■ **cordless** adjective.

！注意 don't confuse **cord** with **chord**, which means 'a group of musical notes'. 不要混淆 cord 和 chord, 后者意为 "和弦，和音"。

cordial /ˈkɔːdiəl/ **adjective 1** warm and friendly 热情友好的 **2** sincere 真诚的；诚挚的 ■ **noun 1** Brit. 【英】a sweet fruit-flavoured drink, sold in concentrated form (浓缩的)甜果汁饮料 **2** chiefly N. Amer. 【主北美】a liqueur 烈酒 ■ **cordiality** noun **cordially** adverb.

cordite /ˈkɔːdaɪt/ **noun** a kind of explosive 科达无烟火药

cordon /ˈkɔːdn/ **noun** a line or circle of police, soldiers, or guards forming a barrier 警戒线；哨兵线；包围圈 ■ **verb (cordon something off)** close somewhere off by means of a cordon 设置警戒线围起(或封锁)

cordon bleu /ˈkɔːdɒn ˈblɜː/ **adjective** Cookery 【烹饪】of the highest class 烹饪手艺高超的；厨艺一流的

corduroy /ˈkɔːdərɔɪ/ **noun** a thick cotton fabric with velvety ridges 灯芯绒

core /kɔː(r)/ **noun 1** the tough central part of a fruit 果核 **2** the central or most important part of something 核心；精髓；最重要部分 ■ **verb (cores, coring, cored)** remove the core from a fruit 除去(水果)的核

co-respondent /ˌkəʊrɪˈspɒndənt/ **noun** a person named in a divorce case as having committed adultery with the respondent (离婚诉讼的)共同被告(指与被告通奸的人)

corgi /ˈkɔːgi/ **noun (plural corgis)** a breed of dog with short legs and a pointed face 威尔士矮脚狗；柯吉犬

coriander /ˌkɒriˈændə(r)/ **noun** a

plant used as a herb in cookery 芫荽，香菜(用于烹饪)

cork /kɔːk/ **noun 1** a light, soft brown substance obtained from the bark of a tree 栓皮；软木 **2** a bottle stopper made of cork 软木瓶塞 ■ **verb 1** seal a bottle with a cork (用软木瓶塞)塞住，封堵 **2 (corked)** (of wine) spoilt by a faulty cork (酒由于软木塞腐朽)味道不佳的，带瓶塞味的

corker /ˈkɔːkə(r)/ **noun** informal 【非正式】an excellent person or thing 非凡的人(或事物) ■ **corking** adjective.

corkscrew /ˈkɔːkskruː/ **noun** a device used for pulling corks from bottles (拔软木塞的)瓶塞钻，螺丝起子 ■ **verb** move or twist in a spiral 作螺旋式移动；扭曲

corm /kɔːm/ **noun** an underground part of certain plants 球茎

cormorant /ˈkɔːmərənt/ **noun** a diving seabird with a long hooked bill and black feathers 鸬鹚(会潜水的海鸟，喙呈长钩状，羽毛黑色)

corn¹ /kɔːn/ **noun 1** Brit. 【英】the chief cereal crop of a district (in England, wheat) 谷物(在英格兰指小麦) **2** N. Amer. & Austral./NZ 【北美和澳/新西兰】maize 玉米 □ **corn on the cob** maize cooked and eaten straight from the cob (熟的)玉米棒子

corn² **noun** a painful area of thickened skin on the toes or foot (脚趾或脚上的)鸡眼，钉胼

cornea /ˈkɔːniə/ **noun** the transparent layer forming the front of the eye (眼睛的)角膜

corned beef /ˈkɔːnd/ **noun** beef preserved with salt, often sold in tins (通常罐装出售的)咸牛肉

corner /ˈkɔːnə(r)/ **noun 1** a place or angle where two or more sides or edges meet 角；角落 **2** a place where two streets meet 街角 **3** a secluded or remote area 隐秘处；偏僻处 **4** a difficult or awkward position 困境；窘境 **5** Soccer 【足球】a free kick taken by the attacking side from a corner of the field 角球 • verb (**corners, cornering, cornered**) **1** force someone into a place or situation from which it is hard to escape 使走投无路；使..陷入绝境 **2** go round a bend in a road 转弯 **3** control the trade in a particular type of goods 垄断(某种货品的交易)

cornerstone /ˈkɔːnəstəʊn/ **noun 1** a vital part 基础；核心 **2** a stone that forms the base of a corner of a building (建筑物的)奠基石

cornet /ˈkɔːnɪt/ **noun 1** a brass instrument resembling a trumpet but shorter and wider 短号(铜管乐器) **2** Brit.【英】a cone-shaped wafer for holding ice cream (盛冰激凌的)圆锥形蛋筒

cornflour /ˈkɔːnflaʊə(r)/ **noun** Brit.【英】ground maize flour, used for thickening sauces (用于使调味品变黏稠的)玉米粉，玉米面

cornflower /ˈkɔːnflaʊə(r)/ **noun** a plant with deep blue flowers 矢车菊(花为深蓝色)

cornice /ˈkɔːnɪs/ **noun** a decorative border round the wall of a room just below the ceiling (室内墙壁与天花板邻接处的)檐口，楣

cornucopia /ˌkɔːnjuˈkəʊpɪə/ **noun** a plentiful supply of good things 丰盛，富饶

corny /ˈkɔːni/ **adjective** (**cornier, corniest**) informal【非正式】sentimental or unoriginal 伤感的；陈腐的

corolla /kəˈrɒlə/ **noun** the petals of a flower 花冠

corollary /kəˈrɒləri/ **noun** (plural **corollaries**) **1** a direct consequence or result 直接结果；直接后果 **2** a logical conclusion 逻辑推论；必然结论

corona /kəˈrəʊnə/ **noun** (plural **coronae** /kəˈrəʊniː/) **1** the gases surrounding the sun or a star 日冕；(恒星的)冕 **2** a small circle of light around

the sun or moon 日华；月华

coronary /ˈkɒrənri/ **adjective** having to do with the heart, in particular with the arteries which supply it with blood 心脏冠状动脉的 • **noun** (plural **coronaries**) (also **coronary thrombosis**) a blockage of the flow of blood to the heart 冠状动脉血栓；冠心病

coronation /ˌkɒrəˈneɪʃn/ **noun** the ceremony of crowning a king or queen (国王或女王的)加冕典礼

coroner /ˈkɒrənə(r)/ **noun** an official who holds inquests into violent, sudden, or suspicious deaths 验尸官；法医

coronet /ˈkɒrənet/ **noun 1** a small or simple crown 小冠冕 **2** a decorative band put around the head 冠状头带

corpora /ˈkɔːpərə/ plural of CORPUS.

corporal[1] /ˈkɔːpərəl/ **noun** a rank of officer in the army, below sergeant (陆军)下士

corporal[2] **adjective** relating to the human body 人体的；身体的 □ **corporal punishment** physical punishment, such as caning 体罚

corporate /ˈkɔːpərət/ **adjective 1** relating to a business corporation 公司的；企业的 **2** relating to or shared by all members of a group 集体的；共有的

corporation /ˌkɔːpəˈreɪʃn/ **noun 1** a large company, or a group of companies acting as a single unit 大公司；企业集团 **2** Brit.【英】a group of people elected to govern a city, town, or borough 市政委员会

corporeal /kɔːˈpɔːriəl/ **adjective** relating to a person's body; physical rather than spiritual 肉体的；(区别于精神的)物质的

corps /kɔː(r)/ **noun** (plural **corps** /kɔːz/) **1** a large unit of an army 军，兵团(陆军编制单位) **2** a branch of an army with a particular kind of work 特种部队；特殊兵种 **3** a group of people involved in a particular activity (从事某项活动的)集体、团队

corpse /kɔːps/ **noun** a dead body 尸体

corpulent /'kɔːpjʊlənt/ **adjective** (of a person) fat (人)肥胖的 ■ **corpulence** noun.

corpus /'kɔːpəs/ **noun** (plural **corpora** /'kɔːpərə/ or **corpuses**) a collection of written works 文集；语料库

corpuscle /'kɔːpʌsl/ **noun** a red or white blood cell 血细胞；红细胞；白细胞

corral /kə'rɑːl/ **noun** N. Amer. 【北美】 a pen for animals on a farm or ranch (农场或牧场的)畜栏 • **verb** (**corrals**, **corralling**, **corralled**) **1** N. Amer. 【北美】 drive animals into a corral 把(牲畜)关进畜栏 **2** gather a group together 把(群体)集中起来

correct /kə'rekt/ **adjective 1** free from mistakes; true or right 无误的；正确的 **2** following accepted social standards 得体的；合乎礼节的 • **verb 1** put something right 改正；纠正 **2** mark the mistakes in a piece of writing 批改 **3** tell someone that they are wrong 指出(某人)的错误 ■ **correctly** adverb **correctness** noun.

correction /kə'rekʃn/ **noun 1** the process of correcting 改正，纠正 **2** a change that corrects a mistake or inaccuracy 修改

corrective /kə'rektɪv/ **adjective** designed to put something right 改正的；纠正的

correlate /'kɒrəleɪt/ **verb** (**correlates**, **correlating**, **correlated**) place things together so that one thing depends on another and vice versa 使相互影响，使相互依存

correlation /ˌkɒrə'leɪʃn/ **noun 1** a situation in which one thing depends on another and vice versa 相互影响；相互依存 **2** the process of correlating two or more things 相关；发生联系

correspond /ˌkɒrə'spɒnd/ **verb 1** match or agree almost exactly 相符合，一致 **2** be similar or the same 类似；相当于 **3** communicate by exchanging letters 通信

correspondence /ˌkɒrə'spɒndəns/ **noun 1** letters sent or received 通信；信件 **2** a close connection or similarity 相关；相似 □ **correspondence course** a course of study in which student and tutors communicate by post 函授课程

✔ 拼写指南 the ending is -ence, not -ance: correspond*ence*. correspond*ence* 词末拼作 -ence，不要拼作 -ance。

correspondent /ˌkɒrə'spɒndənt/ **noun 1** a journalist who reports on a particular subject 通讯员；记者 **2** a person who writes letters 通信者

corridor /'kɒrɪdɔː(r)/ **noun 1** a passage in a building or train, with doors leading into rooms or compartments (建筑物的)走廊，过道，(火车的)车厢走廊 **2** a strip of land linking two other areas (连接两个区域的)走廊地带

✔ 拼写指南 -dor, not -door: corri*dor*. corridor 中 -dor 不要拼作 -door。

corroborate /kə'rɒbəreɪt/ **verb** (**corroborates**, **corroborating**, **corroborated**) confirm or give support to a statement or theory 证实，支持(陈述或理论) ■ **corroboration** noun.

corrode /kə'rəʊd/ **verb** (**corrodes**, **corroding**, **corroded**) **1** slowly wear away a hard material by the action of a chemical (通过化学作用)腐蚀(硬物) **2** gradually weaken or destroy 逐渐削弱；侵蚀

corrosion /kə'rəʊʒn/ **noun** the process of corroding, or damage caused by it 腐蚀；侵蚀

corrosive /kə'rəʊsɪv/ **adjective** tending to cause corrosion 腐蚀性的

corrugated /'kɒrəgeɪtɪd/ **adjective** shaped into alternate ridges and grooves 起皱的；起波纹的 ■ **corrugation** noun.

corrupt /kə'rʌpt/ **adjective 1** willing to act dishonestly in return for money or other reward 腐败的；贪污受贿的 **2** evil or immoral 邪恶的；不道德的 **3** (of a written work or computer data) unreliable because of mistakes or alterations (文本或计算机数据)有讹误的 • **verb** make corrupt 使腐败；使道德败坏；使讹误 ■ **corruptly** adverb.

corruption /kə'rʌpʃn/ **noun 1** dishonest or illegal behaviour 欺诈行为；违法行为 **2** the action of corrupting 腐化；腐败

corsage /kɔː'sɑːʒ/ **noun** a small bunch of flowers worn pinned to a woman's clothes (女装上佩戴的)装饰花束

corset /'kɔːsɪt/ **noun** a tight-fitting undergarment worn to shape a woman's figure or to support a person's back (女子穿的)紧身内衣 (用以束腰或支撑背部)

cortège /kɔː'teʒ, -'teɪʒ/ **noun** a funeral procession 送葬队列

cortex /'kɔːteks/ **noun** (plural **cortices** /'kɔːtɪsiːz/) the outer layer of an organ or structure, especially the outer layer of the brain 皮质；皮层；(尤指)大脑皮层

coruscating /'kɒrəskeɪtɪŋ/ **adjective** literary 【文】 flashing or sparkling 闪光的；闪烁的

corvette /kɔː'vet/ **noun** a small warship designed for escorting convoys 轻型护卫舰

cos **abbreviation** cosine.

cosh /kɒʃ/ **noun** a thick, heavy stick or bar used as a weapon (用作武器的)短棍，粗棒 • **verb** hit someone on the head with a cosh 用短棍(或粗棒)击打(头部)

cosine /'kəʊsaɪn/ **noun** Maths 【数学】 (in a right-angled triangle) the ratio of the side next to a particular acute angle to the longest side (直角三角形中的)余弦

cosmetic /kɒz'metɪk/ **adjective 1** (of treatment) intended to improve a person's appearance (治疗)整容的 **2** improving something only outwardly 装点门面的 • **noun** (**cosmetics**) substances put on the face and body to make them more attractive 化妆品；护肤品

cosmic /'kɒzmɪk/ **adjective** relating to the universe 宇宙的

cosmonaut /'kɒzmənɔːt/ **noun** a Russian astronaut (俄罗斯)宇航员，航天员

cosmopolitan /ˌkɒzmə'pɒlɪtən/ **adjective 1** made up of people from many different countries and cultures 世界性的；全球各地的 **2** familiar with many different countries 通晓多国知识的；见多识广的

cosmos /'kɒzmɒs/ **noun** the universe 宇宙

Cossack /'kɒsæk/ **noun** a member of a people of Russia and Ukraine famous for being good riders 哥萨克人(居住于俄罗斯和乌克兰，善骑术)

cosset /'kɒsɪt/ **verb** (**cossets**, **cosseting**, **cosseted**) look after and protect someone in a way that is too indulgent 宠爱；溺爱；娇纵

cost /kɒst/ **verb** (**costs, costing, cost**) **1** be able to be bought or done for a specific price 价钱为；需花费 **2** involve the loss of 使付出(代价)；使损失 **3** (**costs, costing, cost**) estimate the cost of work that needs to be done 估计…的成本 • **noun 1** an amount given or required as payment 成本；价格 **2** the effort or loss necessary to achieve something 代价；损失 **3** (**costs**) legal expenses 诉讼费 □ **cost-effective** effective or productive in relation to its cost 成本效益好的；合算的

co-star noun /ˈkəʊstɑː(r)/ a performer appearing with another or others of equal importance 联合主演 • verb /kəʊˈstɑː(r)/ **1** appear in a film or play as a co-star 联袂主演 **2** (of a film or play) include someone as a co-star (影片或戏剧)由…联袂主演

Costa Rican /ˈkɒstə ˈriːkən/ noun a person from Costa Rica 哥斯达黎加人 • adjective relating to Costa Rica 哥斯达黎加的

costermonger /ˈkɒstəˌmʌŋgə(r)/ noun dated 【废】a person who sells fruit and vegetables in the street (沿街叫卖水果蔬菜的)小贩

costly /ˈkɒstli/ adjective (**costlier, costliest**) **1** expensive 昂贵的 **2** causing suffering, loss, or disadvantage 造成损失的；代价高的 ■ **costliness** noun.

costume /ˈkɒstjuːm/ noun **1** a set of clothes in a style typical of a particular country or historical period (特定国家或历史时期的)服装,服式样 **2** a set of clothes worn by an actor or performer for a role (演员穿的)戏装 □ **costume jewellery** jewellery made with inexpensive materials or imitation gems (廉价的)珠宝饰物

costumier /kɒsˈtjuːmɪə(r)/ noun a person who makes or supplies theatrical or fancy-dress costumes (戏剧服装或化装服的)服装制造商(或供应商)

cosy /ˈkəʊzi/ (US spelling 【美拼作】**cozy**) adjective (**cosier, cosiest**) **1** comfortable, warm, and secure 温暖舒适的;安逸的 **2** not difficult or demanding 轻松的;不费力的 • noun (plural **cosies**) a cover to keep a teapot or a boiled egg hot (茶壶或煮熟鸡蛋的)保暖罩 ■ **cosily** adverb **cosiness** noun.

cot /kɒt/ noun a small bed with high barred sides for a baby or very young child (有高栏杆的)婴儿床,幼儿床 □ **cot death** the unexplained death of a baby in its sleep 婴儿猝死

coterie /ˈkəʊtəri/ noun (plural **coteries**) a small, close-knit group of people 小圈子;小集团

cottage /ˈkɒtɪdʒ/ noun a small house in the country (乡村)农舍;村屋 □ **cottage cheese** soft, lumpy white cheese 农家乳酪

cotter pin /ˈkɒtə(r)/ noun a metal pin used to fasten two parts of a mechanism together 开尾销;扁销

cotton /ˈkɒtn/ noun **1** soft white fibres surrounding the seeds of a plant that grows in warm climates 棉;棉花 **2** cloth or thread made from these fibres 棉料;棉线 • verb (**cotton on**) informal 【非正式】begin to understand 明白;领会 □ **cotton wool** fluffy soft material used for cleaning the skin or a wound 药棉,脱脂棉(用于清洁皮肤或伤口)

cotyledon /ˌkɒtɪˈliːdən/ noun the first leaf that grows from a seed (种子发芽长出的)子叶

couch /kaʊtʃ/ noun a long padded piece of furniture for sitting or lying on 长沙发 • verb (**couch something in**) express something in language of a particular style (以某种方式)表达 □ **couch potato** informal 【非正式】a person who watches a lot of television 总泡在电视机前的人

cougar /ˈkuːgə(r)/ noun N. Amer. 【北美】a puma 美洲狮

cough /kɒf/ verb **1** send out air from the lungs with a sudden sharp sound 咳嗽 **2** (**cough something up**) informal 【非正式】reluctantly give money or information 勉强交出(钱);勉强提供(信息) • noun **1** an act of coughing 咳嗽 **2** an illness of the throat or lungs causing coughing 咳嗽(病)

could /kʊd, kəd/ modal verb past of **CAN¹**.

couldn't /ˈkʊdnt/ short form could

not.

coulomb /'ku:lɒm/ noun a unit of electric charge 库仑(电量单位)

council /'kaʊnsl/ noun **1** a group of people that meet regularly to discuss or organize something 委员会 **2** a group of people elected to manage the affairs of a city, county, or district (市、郡、区的)政务委员会 □ **council house** a house owned by a local council and rented to tenants 由地方政务会提供的出租房 **council tax** (in the UK) a tax charged on households by local authorities (英国依据财产估价征收的)市政税

councillor /'kaʊnsələ(r)/ noun a member of a council 政务会委员;议员

!注意 note the difference between **councillor** and **counsellor**. 注意 councillor 与 counsellor 之间的区别。

counsel /'kaʊnsl/ noun **1** advice 忠告;劝告 **2** (plural **counsel**) a barrister or other lawyer involved in a case 辩护律师;法律顾问 • verb (**counsels**, **counselling**, **counselled**; US spelling【美拼作】**counsels**, **counseling**, **counseled**) **1** advise or recommend 建议;劝告 **2** give professional help and advice to someone with psychological or personal problems (就心理或个人问题)辅导,引导(某人)

counsellor /'kaʊnsələ(r)/ (US spelling【美拼作】**counselor**) noun a person trained to give advice on personal or psychological problems (个人或心理问题的)咨询顾问,辅导员

count[1] /kaʊnt/ verb **1** find the total number of 计数;清点(数目) **2** recite numbers in ascending order (按顺序)数数 **3** take into account 把…算入;包括 **4** regard as being 认为;看作: *people she counted as her friends* 被她当作朋友的人 **5** be important 重要 **6** (**count on** you) rely on 依靠;指望 **7** (**count someone in** or **out**) include (or not include) someone in an activity 包括(或不包括);算入(或不算入) • noun **1** an act of counting 数数;计数;点数 **2** a total found by counting (计算出的)总数 **3** a point to be discussed or considered (讨论或考虑的)事项 **4** Law【法律】each of the charges against an accused person (被指控的)罪状 □ **out for the count** Boxing【拳击】defeated by being knocked to the ground and unable to get up within ten seconds (被击倒的10秒钟以内无法站起来而)被判失败的 **2** informal【非正式】unconscious or asleep 无知觉的;睡着的

count[2] noun a foreign nobleman (国外的)贵族

countdown /'kaʊntdaʊn/ noun an act of counting backwards to zero 倒计时;倒读数

countenance /'kaʊntənəns/ noun a person's face or expression 脸;面容;面部表情 • verb (**countenances**, **countenancing**, **countenanced**) tolerate or allow 容忍;认可;允许

counter[1] /'kaʊntə(r)/ noun **1** a long flat surface over which goods are sold or served or across which business is conducted with customers 柜台 **2** a small disc used in board games or to represent a coin (棋盘游戏的)记分圆盘;硬币 **3** a person or thing that counts something 计算者;计算器;计数器 □ **under the counter** bought or sold secretly and illegally (买卖货物)秘密地,非法地

counter[2] verb (**counters**, **countering**, **countered**) **1** argue against or reply to 反驳;驳斥 **2** try to stop or prevent 阻止;防止 • adverb (**counter to**) **1** in the opposite direction to 相反地;在相反方向 **2** in opposition to 反对地

counteract /ˌkaʊntə'rækt/ verb do

something to reduce or prevent the bad effects of 阻止；抵消；抵制

counter-attack /'kaʊntərə,tæk/ **noun** an attack made in response to an attack 还击；反攻 • **verb** attack in response 还击；反攻

counterbalance /'kaʊntəbæləns/ **noun 1** a weight that balances another 平衡重；砝码；平衡力 **2** something that has an equal but opposite effect to something else 平衡因素 • **verb** (**counterbalances, counterbalancing, counterbalanced**) have an equal but opposite effect on 抵消；使平衡

counter-espionage /,kaʊntər-'espɪənɑːʒ/ **noun** activities designed to prevent spying by an enemy 反间谍活动

counterfeit /'kaʊntəfɪt/ **adjective** made in exact imitation of something valuable so as to deceive or cheat people 伪造的；仿制的 • **noun** a forgery 伪造物；仿制物；赝品 • **verb** imitate something dishonestly 伪造；仿制

counterfoil /'kaʊntəfɔɪl/ **noun** the part of a cheque, ticket, etc. that you keep when you give the other part up (支票、票据等的)存根，票根

countermand /,kaʊntə'mɑːnd/ **verb** cancel an order 撤销(命令)，取消(订单)

countermeasure /'kaʊntəmeʒə(r)/ **noun** something done to deal with a danger or threat (应对危险或威胁的)对策，反措施

counterpane /'kaʊntəpeɪn/ **noun** dated 【废】 a bedspread 床罩；床单

counterpart /'kaʊntəpɑːt/ **noun** a person or thing that corresponds to another 对应的人(或事物)

counterpoint /'kaʊntəpɔɪnt/ **noun 1** the playing of two or more tunes at the same time (演奏中的)对位法，对位 **2** a tune played at the same time as another 对位旋律；复调

counterproductive /,kaʊntəprə-'dʌktɪv/ **adjective** having the opposite effect to the one intended 适得其反的

countersign /'kaʊntəsaɪn/ **verb** sign a document that has already been signed by another person 副署，会签(文件)

countersink /'kaʊntəsɪŋk/ **verb** (**countersinks, countersinking, countersunk**) insert a screw or bolt so that the head lies flat with the surface 钻埋头孔

countertenor /,kaʊntə'tenə(r)/ **noun** the highest male adult singing voice 男最高音歌手

counterterrorism /,kaʊntə'terərɪzəm/ **noun** political or military activities designed to prevent terrorism 反恐怖主义；反恐行动

countervailing /,kaʊntə'veɪlɪŋ/ **adjective** having an equal but opposite effect 与…抗衡的；抵消的

countess /'kaʊntəs/ **noun 1** the wife or widow of a count or earl 伯爵夫人 **2** a woman holding the rank of count or earl 女伯爵

counting /'kaʊntɪŋ/ **preposition** taking account of; including 考虑到；包括

countless /'kaʊntləs/ **adjective** too many to be counted; very many 数不胜数的；非常多的

countrified /'kʌntrɪfaɪd/ **adjective** characteristic of the country or country life 乡村的；乡村生活的

country /'kʌntri/ **noun** (plural **countries**) **1** a nation with its own government 国家 **2** areas outside large towns and cities 农村；乡下 **3** an area of land with particular physical features (具有某种自然特征的)区域，地区: *hilly country* 丘陵地带 □ **country music** (or **country and western**) a kind of popular music from country areas of the southern US 乡村音乐(源于美国南部乡村地

区的一种流行音乐)

countryside /ˈkʌntrɪsaɪd/ **noun** land and scenery outside towns and cities 乡下;农村

county /ˈkaʊnti/ **noun** (plural **counties**) each of the main areas into which some countries are divided for the purposes of local government 郡;县 □ **county town** the main town of a county, where its council is based 郡治;县城

coup /kuː/ **noun** (plural **coups** /kuːz/) **1** (also **coup d'état** /kuː deɪˈtɑː/) a sudden violent seizing of power from a government 政变 **2** a successful move or action 成功的举动

coupe /kuːp/ **noun** a sports car with a fixed roof and a sloping rear (斜背) 双门跑车

couple /ˈkʌpl/ **noun 1** two individuals of the same sort considered together 一对;一双 **2** two people who are married or in a romantic or sexual relationship 夫妻;情侣 **3** informal 【非正式】an unspecified small number 一些;几个 • **verb** (**couples, coupling, coupled**) **1** connect or combine 连接;结合 **2** have sex 性交;交配

couplet /ˈkʌplət/ **noun** a pair of rhyming lines of poetry one after another 对句(指两行尾韵相谐的诗句)

coupling /ˈkʌplɪŋ/ **noun** a device for connecting railway vehicles or parts of machinery together (连接火车的)车钩,挂钩;(机器部件的)连接器

coupon /ˈkuːpɒn/ **noun 1** a voucher that gives you the right to claim a discount or buy something (购物)优惠券 **2** a form that can be sent off to ask for information or to enter a competition 信息索取单;参赛表格

courage /ˈkʌrɪdʒ/ **noun 1** the ability to do something frightening; bravery 胆量 **2** strength when faced with pain or grief 勇气

courageous /kəˈreɪdʒəs/ **adjective**

having courage; brave 勇敢的;无畏的 • **courageously** adverb.

courgette /kʊəˈʒet/ **noun** Brit. 【英】a long, thin vegetable with green skin 密生西葫芦

courier /ˈkʊriə(r)/ **noun 1** a person employed to deliver goods or documents quickly 送货的人;信差 **2** a person employed to guide and help a group of tourists 导游

course /kɔːs/ **noun 1** a direction that is taken or intended 行动方向;方针 **2** the way in which something progresses or develops 进展;进程 **3** (also **course of action**) a way of dealing with a situation 途径;做法 **4** a dish forming one of the stages of a meal 一道菜 **5** a series of lectures or lessons in a particular subject 课程 **6** a series of repeated treatments or doses of a drug 疗程 **7** an area prepared for racing, golf, or another sport (赛跑、高尔夫球等运动的)比赛场地 • **verb** (**courses, coursing, coursed**) **1** (of liquid) flow (液体)流动 **2** (**coursing**) the activity of hunting animals, especially hares, with greyhounds 追猎,狩猎(尤指野兔)□ **of course 1** as expected 当然;诚然 **2** certainly; yes 肯定

> **! 注意** don't confuse **course** with **coarse**, which means 'having a rough texture'. 不要混淆 course 和 coarse, 后者意为"质地粗糙的"。

court /kɔːt/ **noun 1** the judge, jury, and lawyers who sit and hear legal cases 全体审判人员 **2** the place where a law court meets 法院;法庭 **3** an area marked out for ball games such as tennis (网球等球类运动的)比赛场地,球场 **4** a courtyard 院子;庭院 **5** the home, advisers, and staff of a king or queen 宫廷;朝廷;朝臣 • **verb 1** try to win someone's support 寻求…的支持 **2** behave in a way that might lead to something bad happening 招致；招惹 **3** dated 【废】 try to win the love of someone you want to marry 向(某人)求婚 □ **court shoe** a woman's plain shoe with a low-cut upper and no fastening (低帮、无鞋后的)女式便鞋 **hold court** be the centre of attention 成为关注的焦点

courteous /ˈkɜːtɪəs/ **adjective** polite and considerate 温文尔雅的；彬彬有礼的 ■ **courteously** adverb.

courtesan /ˌkɔːtɪˈzæn/ **noun** a prostitute with wealthy clients (接待富有嫖客的)高级妓女，交际花

courtesy /ˈkɜːtəsi/ **noun** (plural **courtesies**) **1** polite and considerate behaviour 谦恭有礼 **2** a polite speech or action 礼貌的言辞(或行为) □ **courtesy of** given or allowed by 承蒙…的允许

courtier /ˈkɔːtɪə(r)/ **noun** a companion or adviser of a king or queen 侍臣；廷臣

courtly /ˈkɔːtli/ **adjective** (**courtlier**, **courtliest**) very dignified and polite 端庄有礼的

court martial **noun** (plural **courts martial**) a court for trying people accused of breaking military law 军事法庭 ■ **verb** (**court-martial**) (**courtmartials**, **court-martialling**, **courtmartialled**) try someone in a court martial 使受军事法庭审判

courtship /ˈkɔːtʃɪp/ **noun 1** a period during which a couple develop a romantic relationship 恋爱期；求爱期 **2** the process of trying to win someone's love or support 求爱；寻求支持

courtyard /ˈkɔːtjɑːd/ **noun** an open area enclosed by walls or buildings 庭院

couscous /ˈkuskus/ **noun** a North African dish of steamed or soaked semolina (北非的)蒸粗麦粉食物

cousin /ˈkʌzn/ **noun** (also **first cousin**) a child of your uncle or aunt 堂兄弟(或姐妹)；表兄弟(或姐妹) □ **second cousin** a child of your mother's or father's first cousin 远房堂兄弟(或姐妹)；远房表兄弟(或姐妹)

couture /kuˈtjʊə(r)/ **noun** the design and making of fashionable clothes, especially for a particular customer (尤指为特定顾客的)时装设计制作

couturier /kuˈtjʊəriei/ **noun** a person who designs couture clothes 时装设计师

cove /kəʊv/ **noun** a small sheltered bay 小海湾

coven /ˈkʌvn/ **noun** a group of witches who meet regularly (定期聚会的)女巫团

covenant /ˈkʌvənənt/ **noun 1** a formal agreement 契约；盟约；合同 **2** an agreement to make regular payments to a charity (向慈善机构定期捐款的)契约书

cover /ˈkʌvə(r)/ **verb** (**covers**, **covering**, **covered**) **1** put something over or in front of a person or thing so as to protect or hide them 保护；掩护；遮蔽 **2** spread or extend over an area 盖；覆盖 **3** deal with a subject 涉及；论及 **4** travel a particular distance 行走(一段距离) **5** (of money) be enough to pay for something (钱)足以支付 **6** (of insurance) protect against a loss or accident (保险)给…保险，承保 **7** (**cover something up**) try to hide or deny a mistake or crime 掩盖，否认错误或罪行 **8** (**cover for**) temporarily take over someone's job 顶替，暂时接替(某人的工作) **9** perform a cover version of a song 翻唱 ■ **noun 1** something that covers or protects 覆盖物；遮盖物；保护物 **2** a thick protective outer part or page of a book or magazine (书刊的)封面，封皮 **3** shelter 躲避处；掩蔽处 **4** a means of hiding an illegal or secret activity (非法或秘密行动的)掩护，幌子 **5** protection by insurance 保险 **6** (also **cover version**) a performance of a song previously recorded by a different artist 翻唱歌曲 □ **break cover** suddenly leave shelter when being chased (被追逐时)突然从隐藏处出来 **cover charge** a charge per person added to the bill in a restaurant (饭店的)服务费 **covering letter** a letter sent with a document or parcel to explain what it is 附信 **cover-up** an attempt to hide a mistake or crime (对错误或罪行的)掩饰,掩盖

coverage /ˈkʌvərɪdʒ/ **noun** the extent to which something is covered 覆盖范围

coverlet /ˈkʌvələt/ **noun** a bedspread 床罩

covert adjective /ˈkʌvət, ˈkəʊvɜːt/ not done openly; secret 隐蔽的,不公开的;秘密的 • **noun** /ˈkʌvət/ an area of bushes and undergrowth where game birds and animals can hide (猎物藏身的)丛林 ■ **covertly** adverb.

covet /ˈkʌvət/ **verb** (**covets, coveting, coveted**) long to possess something belonging to someone else 垂涎,觊觎(他人之物) ■ **covetous** adjective.

covey /ˈkʌvi/ **noun** (plural **coveys**) a small flock of game birds (作为猎物对象的鸟的)一小群,一窝

cow[1] /kaʊ/ **noun 1** a mature female animal of a domesticated breed of ox (成年的)母牛,奶牛 **2** the female of certain other large animals 母兽 **3** informal 【非正式】 a nasty woman (令人厌恶的)婆娘,娘儿们

cow[2] **verb** frighten someone so much that they do what you want 恐吓,胁迫

coward /ˈkaʊəd/ **noun** a person who is too scared to do dangerous or unpleasant things 懦夫;胆小鬼 ■ **cowardliness** noun **cowardly** adjective.

cowardice /ˈkaʊədɪs/ **noun** lack of bravery 懦弱;胆小

cowboy /ˈkaʊbɔɪ/ **noun 1** a man on

horseback who herds cattle in the western US (美国西部骑马放牧的)牛仔 **2** informal 【非正式】 a dishonest or unqualified tradesman 奸商;无营业资质的商人

cower /ˈkaʊə(r)/ **verb** (**cowers, cowering, cowered**) crouch down or shrink back in fear (因恐惧而)蜷缩,退缩

cowl /kaʊl/ **noun 1** a large, loose hood forming part of a monk's garment (修道士袍服的)大兜帽 **2** a hoodshaped covering for a chimney or ventilation shaft 烟囱帽;通风帽

cowling /ˈkaʊlɪŋ/ **noun** a removable cover for a vehicle or aircraft engine (车辆或飞机发动机可拆卸的)罩,外壳

cowrie /ˈkaʊri/ **noun** (plural **cowries**) a shellfish whose glossy shell has a long, narrow opening 宝贝(一种贝类动物,壳光滑明亮,有狭长壳口)

cowslip /ˈkaʊslɪp/ **noun** a wild plant with clusters of yellow flowers 黄花九轮草

cox /kɒks/ **noun** the person who steers a rowing boat 舵手

coxcomb /ˈkɒkskəʊm/ **noun** old use 【旧】 a vain and conceited man 自命不凡的家伙

coxswain /ˈkɒksn/ = **cox**.

coy /kɔɪ/ **adjective** (**coyer, coyest**) **1** pretending to be shy or modest 故作腼腆的;忸怩作态的 **2** reluctant to give details about something 含糊其词的 ■ **coyly** adverb.

coyote /kɔɪˈəʊti, kaɪ-/ **noun** (plural **coyote** or **coyotes**) a wolf-like wild dog found in North America (产于北美的)郊狼,丛林狼

coypu /ˈkɔɪpuː/ **noun** (plural **coypus**) a large South American rodent resembling a beaver 河狸鼠(一种产于南美、形似海狸的啮齿动物)

cozy /ˈkəʊzi/ US spelling of **cosy**. cosy 的美式拼法

crab /kræb/ **noun** a sea creature with

a broad shell and five pairs of legs 蟹；螃蟹 □ **crab apple** a small, sour kind of apple 沙果

crabbed /'kræbɪd, kræbd/ *adjective* **1** (of writing) hard to read or understand (字迹)潦草的，难以辨认的 **2** bad-tempered 脾气坏的

crabby /'kræbi/ *adjective* (**crabbier, crabbiest**) informal【非正式】 bad-tempered 脾气坏的

crack /kræk/ *noun* **1** a narrow opening between two parts of something which has split or been broken 裂缝；裂口 **2** a sudden sharp noise 爆裂声，噼啪声 **3** a sharp blow 猛击；重击 **4** informal【非正式】a joke 玩笑；俏皮话 **5** informal【非正式】an attempt to do something 尝试 **6** (also **crack cocaine**) a very strong form of cocaine 强效纯可卡因 • *verb* **1** break without dividing into separate parts 开裂；破裂 **2** give way under pressure or strain (因承受压力或紧张)崩溃，瓦解 **3** make a sudden sharp sound 发出爆裂声，发出噼啪声 **4** hit hard 猛击；重击 **5** (of a person's voice) suddenly change in pitch (人的嗓子)突然变音 **6** informal【非正式】solve or decipher 解决；破译 • *adjective* very good or skilful 极好的；技艺高超的：*a crack shot* 精彩的射门 □ **crack down on** informal【非正式】deal severely with 对……采取严厉措施 **crack of dawn** daybreak 破晓 **crack a joke** tell a joke 讲笑话 **crack up** informal【非正式】suffer an emotional breakdown (感情上)垮掉，崩溃 **2** (**be cracked up to be**) be said to be 被说成

crackdown /'krækdaʊn/ *noun* a series of severe measures against undesirable or illegal behaviour 镇压；取缔；制裁

cracker /'krækə(r)/ *noun* **1** a paper cylinder which makes a sharp noise and releases a small toy when it is pulled apart 彩包爆竹 **2** a firework

that explodes with a crack 爆竹 **3** a thin, dry biscuit 薄脆饼干 **4** informal 【非正式】a very good example of something 典范；典型

crackers /'krækəz/ or **cracked** /krækt/ *adjective* informal【非正式】 mad 疯狂的

cracking /'krækɪŋ/ *adjective* informal 【非正式】**1** excellent 极好的，绝妙的 **2** fast 迅速的：*a cracking pace* 快步

crackle /'krækl/ *verb* (**crackles, crackling, crackled**) make a series of slight cracking noises 发出噼啪声 • *noun* a crackling sound 噼啪声 ■ **crackly** *adjective*.

crackling /'kræklɪŋ/ *noun* the crisp fatty skin of roast pork (烤猪肉的)脆皮

crackpot /'krækpɒt/ *noun* informal【非正式】an eccentric or foolish person 怪人；蠢人

cradle /'kreɪdl/ *noun* **1** a baby's bed on rockers 摇篮 **2** a place or period in which something originates or flourishes 发源地；发祥地：*the cradle of civilization* 文明的发祥地 **3** a supporting framework 支架；托架 • *verb* (**cradles, cradling, cradled**) hold gently and protectively 轻轻抱着

craft /krɑːft/ *noun* **1** an activity involving skill in making things by hand 手工艺 **2** skill in carrying out work 手艺；技艺 **3** (**crafts**) things made by hand 手工艺品 **4** (plural **craft**) a boat, ship, or aircraft 船；飞机，飞行器 **5** skill in deceiving people 骗术；诡计 • *verb* make something skilfully 精心制作

craftsman /'krɑːftsmən/ *noun* (plural **craftsmen**) a worker who is skilled in a particular craft 工匠；手艺人 ■ **craftsmanship** *noun*.

crafty /'krɑːfti/ *adjective* (**craftier, craftiest**) clever at deceiving people; cunning 诡计多端的；狡诈的 ■ **craftily** *adverb*.

crag /kræg/ **noun** a steep or rugged cliff or rock face 悬崖;峭壁 ■ **craggy** adjective.

cram /kræm/ **verb** (**crams, cramming, crammed**) **1** force too many people or things into a space 把…塞入;挤满 **2** fill something to the point of overflowing 塞满;把…装满 **3** study hard just before an exam (考试前)突击学习,临时抱佛脚

crammer /ˈkræmə(r)/ **noun** a college that prepares students for exams (应付考试的)补习学校

cramp /kræmp/ **noun 1** pain caused by a muscle or muscles tightening 抽筋;痛性痉挛 **2** a tool for clamping two objects together 夹钳 • **verb** restrict the development of 限制;束缚

cramped /kræmpt/ **adjective 1** uncomfortably small or crowded 狭小的;拥挤的 **2** (of hand-writing) small and difficult to read (字迹)小而难辨认的

crampon /ˈkræmpɒn/ **noun** a spiked plate fixed to a boot for climbing on ice or rock (在冰上行走或攀岩的)带钉快鞋底

cranberry /ˈkrænbəri/ **noun** (plural **cranberries**) a small sour-tasting red berry 越橘;小红莓

crane /kreɪn/ **noun 1** a tall machine used for moving heavy objects by suspending them from a projecting arm 起重机;吊车 **2** a wading bird with long legs and a long neck 鹤;仙鹤 • **verb** (**cranes, craning, craned**) stretch out your neck to see something 伸长(脖子);探头去看 □ **crane fly** a flying insect with very long legs (长腿)大蚊

cranium /ˈkreɪniəm/ **noun** (plural **craniums** or **crania** /ˈkreɪniə/) the part of the skull that encloses the brain 头颅;颅 ■ **cranial** adjective.

crank /kræŋk/ **noun 1** a part of an axle or shaft that is bent at right angles, turned to produce motion 曲柄;曲轴 **2** an eccentric person 怪人 • **verb 1** start an engine by turning a crankshaft 用曲柄启动;用曲柄转动 **2** (**crank something up**) informal 【非正式】make something more intense 提高…的强度 **3** (**crank something out**) informal 【非正式】produce something regularly and routinely 机械地制造

crankshaft /ˈkræŋkʃɑːft/ **noun** a shaft driven by a crank 曲轴

cranky /ˈkræŋki/ **adjective** (**crankier, crankiest**) informal 【非正式】**1** strange or eccentric 古怪的 **2** bad-tempered 坏脾气的

cranny /ˈkræni/ **noun** (plural **crannies**) a small, narrow space or opening 裂缝;隙隙;裂口

crape /kreɪp/ **noun** black silk, formerly used for mourning clothes (旧时丧服用的)黑皱绸

craps /kræps/ **noun** a North American gambling game played with two dice (北美)双骰子赌博游戏

crash /kræʃ/ **verb 1** (of a vehicle) collide violently with an obstacle or another vehicle (车辆)猛烈碰撞 **2** (of an aircraft) fall from the sky and hit the land or sea (飞机)坠毁,坠落 **3** move or fall with a sudden loud noise (移动或下落时)发出巨响 **4** (of shares) fall suddenly in value (股票)暴跌 **5** Computing 【计】fail suddenly 突然死机;崩溃 **6** (also **crash out**) informal 【非正式】fall deeply asleep 睡熟 **7** (**crashing**) informal 【非正式】complete; total 彻底的;完全的,十足的:a crashing bore 无聊透顶的人 • **noun 1** an instance of crashing 猛撞;坠落;暴跌 **2** a sudden loud, deep noise 突然的巨响 • **adjective** rapid and concentrated 速成的:a crash course in Italian 意大利语速成课程 □ **crash helmet** a helmet worn by a motorcyclist to protect the head (摩托车手戴的)防撞头盔,安全帽 **crash-land** (of an aircraft) land roughly in an emergency (飞机)紧急着陆，强行着陆

crass /kræs/ **adjective** very thoughtless and stupid 非常愚钝的；极其愚蠢的 ■ **crassly** adverb.

crate /kreɪt/ **noun 1** a wooden case for transporting goods (装运货物的)板条箱，货箱 **2** a square container divided into individual units for holding bottles (放置瓶子的)分格箱

crater /ˈkreɪtə(r)/ **noun** a large hollow caused by an explosion or impact or forming the mouth of a volcano (爆炸或冲击造成的)坑，火山口

cravat /krəˈvæt/ **noun** a strip of fabric worn by men round the neck and tucked inside a shirt (男子的)圆领巾

crave /kreɪv/ **verb** (**craves**, **craving**, **craved**) **1** feel a very strong desire for 渴望；热望 **2** old use 【旧】ask for 恳求；请求

craven /ˈkreɪvn/ **adjective** cowardly 胆小的；懦弱的

craving /ˈkreɪvɪŋ/ **noun** a very strong desire for something 渴望；热望

craw /krɔː/ **noun** dated 【废】the part of a bird's throat where food is prepared for digestion (鸟的)嗉囊

crawl /krɔːl/ **verb 1** move forward on the hands and knees or with the body close to the ground 爬；爬行 **2** move very slowly along 缓慢行进 **3** (**be crawling with**) be unpleasantly covered or crowded with 爬满；挤满 **4** feel an unpleasant sensation like that of something moving over the skin 起鸡皮疙瘩 **5** informal 【非正式】be too friendly or obedient in order to make someone like you 卑躬屈膝；奉承；巴结 • **noun 1** an act of crawling 爬；爬行 **2** a very slow rate of movement 缓慢移动；徐行 **3** a swimming stroke involving alternate overarm movements and rapid kicks of the legs 爬泳；自由泳

crayfish /ˈkreɪfɪʃ/ **noun** (plural **crayfish** or **crayfishes**) a shellfish like a small lobster 淡水螯虾；小龙虾

crayon /ˈkreɪən/ **noun** a stick of coloured chalk or wax, used for drawing 彩色粉笔；彩色蜡笔 • **verb** draw with a crayon or crayons 用彩色粉笔(或蜡笔)画

craze /kreɪz/ **noun** a widespread but short-lived enthusiasm for something (一时的)狂热，激情

crazed /kreɪzd/ **adjective 1** behaving in a wild or mad way 疯狂的 **2** covered with fine cracks (表面)布满细纹的

crazy /ˈkreɪzi/ **adjective** (**crazier**, **craziest**) **1** mad 疯狂的 **2** (**crazy about**) informal 【非正式】very enthusiastic about or fond of 狂热的；痴迷的 **3** foolish or ridiculous 愚蠢的；荒唐的 □ **crazy paving** paving made of irregular pieces of flat stone 用不规则石块铺的路面 ■ **crazily** adverb **craziness** noun.

creak /kriːk/ **verb** make a harsh, high sound 嘎吱作响 • **noun** a creaking sound 嘎吱声 ■ **creaky** adjective.

cream /kriːm/ **noun 1** the thick fatty liquid which rises to the top when milk is left to stand 奶油；乳脂 **2** a food containing cream or having a creamy texture 奶油食品；奶油状食品 **3** a thick liquid substance that is applied to the skin 护肤霜 **4** the very best of a group 精华 **5** a very pale yellow or off-white colour 浅黄色；米色 • **verb 1** mash a cooked vegetable with milk or cream (加入牛奶或奶油)将(煮熟的蔬菜)搅成糊状 **2** (**cream someone/thing off**) take away the best of a group 提取(精华)；选取(最好的部分) □ **cream cheese** a soft, rich kind of cheese 奶油干酪 ■ **creamy** adjective.

crease /kriːs/ **noun 1** a line or ridge produced on paper or cloth by folding or pressing it 折痕；皱褶 **2** Cricket 【板球】any of a number of lines marked on the pitch 区域线

界线 • verb (**creases**, **creasing**, **creased**) make creases in 使起皱

create /kri'eɪt/ verb (**creates**, **creating**, **created**) 1 bring into existence 创造;产生 2 cause something to happen 使发生;引起;产生 3 informal 【非正式】make a fuss; complain 发牢骚;抱怨

creation /kri'eɪʃn/ noun 1 the action of creating 创造 2 a thing which has been made or invented 产物;创造物;作品 3 (**Creation**) literary 【文】the universe 宇宙;天地万物

creative /kri'eɪtɪv/ adjective involving the use of the imagination in order to create something 创造的;创造性的 ■ **creatively** adverb **creativity** noun.

creator /kri'eɪtə(r)/ noun 1 a person or thing that creates 创造者;创造物 2 (**the Creator**) God 上帝

creature /'kri:tʃə(r)/ noun a living being, in particular an animal rather than a person 生物;(区别于人的)动物 □ **creature comforts** things that make life comfortable 物质享受

crèche /kreʃ/ noun a place where babies and young children are looked after while their parents are at work 托儿所

credence /'kri:dns/ noun belief that something is true 信任;信念

credential /krə'denʃl/ noun 1 a qualification, achievement, or quality used to indicate how suitable a person is for something 资历;资格 2 (**credentials**) documents that prove a person's identity or qualifications 证件;资格证书

credible /'kredəbl/ adjective able to be believed; convincing 可信的;令人信服的 ■ **credibility** noun **credibly** adverb.

! 注意 don't confuse **credible** with **creditable**: **credible** means 'believable or convincing', whereas **creditable** means 'deserving recognition

and praise'. 不要混淆 credible 和 creditable，前者意为"可信的;令人信服的"，而后者意为"应当认可的;值得赞扬的"。

credit /'kredɪt/ noun 1 the system of doing business by trusting that a customer will pay at a later date for goods or services supplied 赊购;赊欠 2 public recognition or praise given for an achievement or quality 信誉;声望;赞扬 3 (**a credit to**) a source of pride to 值得…骄傲的人(或事物);为…增光的人(或事物) 4 (**credits**) a list of the people who worked on a film or television programme, displayed at the end (电影或电视节目的)制作人员名单 5 a unit of study counting towards a degree or diploma (获取学位的)学分 6 an entry in an account recording an amount received (账户的)存款数额 • verb (**credits**, **crediting**, **credited**) 1 (**credit someone with**) feel that someone is responsible for something good 把…归功于(某人) 2 believe something surprising 相信(令人惊奇的事) 3 add an amount of money to an account 把(钱款)存入账户 □ **be in credit** (账户)有余额 **credit card** a plastic card that allows you to buy things and pay for them later 信用卡

creditable /'kredɪtəbl/ adjective deserving recognition and praise 应当认可的;值得赞扬的 ■ **creditably** adverb.

creditor /'kredɪtə(r)/ noun a person or company to whom money is owed 债权人;债主

credo /'kri:dəʊ/ noun (plural **credos**) a statement of a person's beliefs or aims 信条

credulous /'kredjələs/ adjective too ready to believe things 轻信的 ■ **credulity** noun.

creed /kri:d/ noun 1 a system of

religious belief; a faith 宗教信仰 **2** a set of beliefs or principles 信条；原则

creek /kriːk/ **noun 1** a narrow stretch of water running inland from the coast 小海湾；小海港 **2** N. Amer. & Austral./NZ【北美和澳/新西兰】a stream or small river 溪流；小河 □ **up the creek** informal【非正式】in severe difficulty 处于困境

creel /kriːl/ **noun** a large basket for carrying fish 鱼篓；鱼笼

creep /kriːp/ **verb** (**creeps, creeping, crept**) **1** move slowly and cautiously 缓慢而谨慎地移动；蹑手蹑脚地走 **2** progress or develop gradually 逐渐发展 • **noun** informal【非正式】a person who is insincerely friendly or respectful 献媚者；奴颜婢膝的人 □ **give you the creeps** make you feel disgust or fear 使起鸡皮疙瘩，令人毛骨悚然

creeper /ˈkriːpə(r)/ **noun** a plant that grows along the ground or another surface 匍匐植物；攀缘植物

creepy /ˈkriːpi/ **adjective** (**creepier, creepiest**) informal【非正式】causing an unpleasant feeling of fear or unease 令人毛骨悚然的，使人起鸡皮疙瘩的

cremate /krəˈmeɪt/ **verb** (**cremates, cremating, cremated**) dispose of a dead body by burning it 火化（尸体） ■ **cremation** noun.

crematorium /ˌkreməˈtɔːriəm/ **noun** (plural **crematoria** /ˌkreməˈtɔːriə/ or **crematoriums**) a building where dead people are cremated 火葬场

crème de la crème /ˌkrem də lɑː ˈkrem/ **noun** the best person or thing of a particular kind 最优秀分子；精英，精华部分

crenellations /ˌkrenəˈleɪʃnz/ **plural noun** battlements 雉堞；城垛 ■ **crenellated** adjective.

Creole /ˈkriːəʊl/ **noun 1** a person of mixed European and black descent 克里奥耳人（欧洲人和黑人的混血儿） **2** a descendant of French settlers in

the southern US 克里奥耳人（美国南部的法国移民的后裔） **3** a combination of a European language and an African Language 克里奥耳语（欧洲语言和非洲语言的混合语）

creosote /ˈkriːəsəʊt/ **noun** a dark brown oil painted on to wood to preserve it 杂酚油（深褐色，涂于木材表面防腐）

crêpe or **crepe** /kreɪp/ **noun 1** a light, thin fabric with a wrinkled surface 绉织物 **2** hard-wearing wrinkled rubber used for the soles of shoes（用于鞋底的）绉胶 **3** /kreɪp, krep/ a thin pancake 薄烤饼 □ **crêpe paper** thin, crinkled paper 绉纸

crept /krept/ past and past participle of CREEP.

crepuscular /krɪˈpʌskjələ(r)/ **adjective** literary【文】resembling twilight; dim and shadowy 昏暗的；蒙胧的

crescendo /krəˈʃendəʊ/ **noun** (plural **crescendos** or **crescendi** /krəˈʃendi/) **1** a gradual increase in loudness in a piece of music（音乐的）渐强 **2** a climax 高潮；顶点

crescent /ˈkresnt/ **noun** a narrow curved shape tapering to a point at each end 新月形；月牙形

cress /kres/ **noun** a plant with hot-tasting leaves 水芹（叶味辣）

crest /krest/ **noun 1** a tuft or growth of feathers, fur, or skin on the head of a bird or animal 鸟冠；羽冠；肉冠 **2** a plume of feathers on a helmet（头盔上的）羽饰 **3** the top of a ridge, wave, etc. 山顶；浪尖 **4** a distinctive design in heraldry representing a family or organization（代表某个家族或机构的）饰章 • **verb** reach the top of 到达…的顶点 ■ **crested** adjective.

crestfallen /ˈkrestfɔːlən/ **adjective** sad and disappointed 沮丧的，垂头丧气的

cretin /ˈkretɪn/ **noun** a stupid person 蠢人；傻瓜 ■ **cretinous** adjective.

crevasse /krəˈvæs/ **noun** a deep open

crack in a glacier (冰川的)裂口

crevice /'krevɪs/ **noun** a narrow opening or crack in a rock or wall (岩石或墙壁的)裂缝, 缺口

crew¹ /kru:/ **noun 1** a group of people who work on a ship, aircraft, or train 全体船员; 全体机组人员; 列车乘务组 **2** the members of a crew other than the officers (除船长、机长和列车长外的)船员, 机务人员, 列车员 **3** a group of people who work together 一组工作人员: *a film crew* 电影摄制组 • **verb** act as a member of a crew 充当船员(或机务人员、列车员) □ **crew cut** a very short haircut for men and boys (男子的)平头发型 **crew neck** a close-fitting round neckline 圆紧衣领; 水手领

crew² past of CROW².

crib /krɪb/ **noun 1** chiefly N. Amer. 【主北美】 a child's cot 儿童床 **2** informal 【非正式】 a list of answers or other information used, for example, by students to cheat in a test 抄袭的答案; 剽窃的作品 **3** the card game cribbage 克里比奇纸牌戏 • **verb** (**cribs, cribbing, cribbed**) informal 【非正式】 copy something dishonestly 抄袭; 剽窃

cribbage /'krɪbɪdʒ/ **noun** a card game for two players (两人玩的)克里比奇纸牌戏

crick /krɪk/ **noun** a painful stiff feeling in the neck or back (颈或背的)痛性痉挛 • **verb** twist or strain the neck or back 引起(颈或背)痛性痉挛

cricket¹ /'krɪkɪt/ **noun** a team game played with a bat, ball, and wickets 板球(运动) ■ **cricketer** noun.

cricket² **noun** an insect like a grasshopper, the male of which produces a shrill chirping sound 蟋蟀

cried /kraɪd/ past and past participle of CRY.

crime /kraɪm/ **noun 1** an action that is against the law 罪; 罪行 **2** illegal actions as a whole 犯罪活动 **3** some-thing disgraceful or very unfair 羞愧的事; 憾事

criminal /'krɪmɪnl/ **noun** a person who has committed a crime 罪犯 • **adjective 1** relating to crime or a crime 犯罪的; 罪行的 **2** informal 【非正式】 disgraceful or very unfair 可耻的; 令人遗憾的 ■ **criminality** noun **criminally** adverb.

crimp /krɪmp/ **verb** press into small folds or ridges 把⋯压成褶, 使有褶

crimson /'krɪmzn/ **noun** a deep red colour 深红色

cringe /krɪndʒ/ **verb** (**cringes, cringing, cringed**) **1** shrink back or cower in fear 畏缩; 退缩 **2** have a sudden feeling of embarrassment or disgust 感到难堪(或厌恶)

crinkle /'krɪŋkl/ **verb** (**crinkle, crinkling, crinkled**) form small creases or wrinkles 起皱; 出褶 • **noun** a small crease or wrinkle 折痕, 皱褶 ■ **crinkly** adjective.

crinoline /'krɪnəlɪn/ **noun** a petticoat stiffened with hoops, formerly worn to make a long skirt stand out (旧时的)裙衬, 裙撑

cripple /'krɪpl/ **noun** old use or offensive 【旧或冒犯】 a person who is unable to walk or move properly because they are disabled or injured 跛子; 瘸子 • **verb** (**cripples, crippling, crippled**) **1** make someone unable to move or walk properly 使跛; 使瘸 **2** severely damage or weaken 严重损害; 严重削弱

crisis /'kraɪsɪs/ **noun** (plural **crises**) **1** a time of severe difficulty or danger 危机; 危急关头 **2** a time when a difficult decision must be made 决定性时刻

crisp /krɪsp/ **adjective 1** firm, dry, and brittle 松脆的; 易碎的 **2** (of the weather) cool and fresh (天气)清新凉爽的 **3** brisk and decisive 干脆利落的 • **noun** a thin, crisp slice of fried potato 油炸薯片 ■ **crisply** adverb

crispy adjective.

crispbread /'krɪspbred/ **noun** a thin, crisp biscuit made from rye or wheat (黑麦或小麦制成的)薄脆饼干

criss-cross /'krɪskrɒs/ **adjective** with a pattern of crossing lines 十字形的;纵横交错的 • **verb 1** form a criss-cross pattern on 交叉;成十字 **2** repeatedly go back and forth around a place 重复往来于;不断奔波于

criterion /kraɪ'tɪərɪən/ **noun** (plural **criteria** /kraɪ'tɪərɪə/) a standard by which something may be judged (判断的)标准,原则

> **! 注意** the singular form is **criterion** and the plural form is **criteria**. It's wrong to use **criteria** as a singular: say *further criteria need to be considered* not *a further criteria needs to be considered.* criterion 为单数形式,其复数形式为 criteria, 把 criteria 当成单数使用是错误的。应说 further criteria need to be considered(需要考虑进一步的标准),不要说 a further criteria needs to be considered。

critic /'krɪtɪk/ **noun 1** a person who finds fault with someone or something 批评家 **2** a person who assesses literary or artistic works (文艺作品的)评论家

critical /'krɪtɪkl/ **adjective 1** expressing disapproving comments 批评的;批判的 **2** assessing a literary or artistic work (对文艺作品)批评的,评论的 **3** very important in terms of the success or failure of something 决定性的;关键性的 **4** at a point of danger or crisis 危急的;紧要关头的 ∎ **critically** adverb.

criticism /'krɪtɪsɪzəm/ **noun 1** expression of disapproval 批评;批判 **2** the assessment of literary or artistic works (对文艺作品的)评论

criticize or **criticise** /'krɪtɪsaɪz/ **verb** (**criticizes**, **criticizing**, **criticized**) **1** express disapproval of 批评;批判 **2** assess a literary or artistic work 评论(文艺作品)

critique /krɪ'tiːk/ **noun** a critical assessment 评论

croak /krəʊk/ **noun** a deep, hoarse sound, like that made by a frog (青蛙似的)呱呱声;低沉而沙哑的声音 • **verb** make a croak 呱呱地叫;用沙哑声说话 ∎ **croaky** adjective.

Croatian /krəʊ'eɪʃən/ **noun** (also **Croat** /'krəʊt/) **1** a person from Croatia 克罗地亚人 **2** the language of Croatia 克罗地亚语 • **adjective** relating to Croatia or Croatian 克罗地亚的;克罗地亚人的;克罗地亚语的

crochet /'krəʊʃeɪ/ **noun** a craft in which yarn is made into fabric with a hooked needle 钩针编织 • **verb** (**crochets**, **crocheting**, **crocheted**) make an article by means of crochet 用钩针编织

crock¹ /krɒk/ **noun** informal 【非正式】 a feeble and useless old person 老朽的人;年老体衰者

crock² **noun** an earthenware pot or jar 瓦罐

crockery /'krɒkəri/ **noun** plates, dishes, cups, etc. made of earthenware or china 陶器;瓷器

crocodile /'krɒkədaɪl/ **noun 1** a large reptile with long jaws, a long tail, and a thick skin 鳄;鳄鱼 **2** Brit. informal 【英,非正式】a line of schoolchildren walking in pairs (学生)两人一排的纵列 ◻ **crocodile tears** insincere tears or sorrow 鳄鱼眼泪;假慈悲

crocus /'krəʊkəs/ **noun** (plural **crocuses** or **croci** /'krəʊkiː/) a small plant with bright yellow, purple, or white flowers 藏红花;番红花

croft /krɒft/ **noun** a small rented farm in Scotland or northern England (苏格兰或英格兰北部供租赁的)小农场 ∎ **crofter** noun.

croissant /'krwæsɒn/ **noun** a flaky

crescent-shaped bread roll 羊角面包 (新月形酥皮面包卷)

crone /krəʊn/ **noun** an ugly old woman 丑陋的老太婆

crony /ˈkrəʊnɪ/ **noun** (plural **cronies**) informal【非正式】close friend or companion 密友；亲密伙伴

crook /krʊk/ **noun 1** a shepherd's or bishop's hooked staff (牧羊人或主教的)曲柄杖 **2** a bend at a person's elbow 肘弯 **3** informal【非正式】a criminal or dishonest person 罪犯；骗子 • **verb** bend a finger or leg 弯曲 (手指或腿)

crooked /ˈkrʊkɪd/ **adjective 1** bent or twisted out of shape or position 弯曲的；扭曲的 **2** informal【非正式】dishonest or illegal 不诚实的；非法的

croon /kruːn/ **verb** hum, sing, or speak in a soft, low voice 低声哼唱；低声诉说 ■ **crooner** noun.

crop /krɒp/ **noun 1** a plant grown in large quantities, especially as food 庄稼；作物 **2** an amount of a crop harvested at one time (庄稼的)收成，产量 **3** a very short hairstyle 平头；短发 **4** a pouch in a bird's throat where food is stored or prepared for digestion (鸟的)嗉囊 **5** a short flexible whip used by horse riders (骑手的)短马鞭 • **verb** (**crops**, **cropping**, **cropped**) **1** cut something very short 把…剪得很短 **2** (of an animal) bite off and eat the tops of plants (动物)啃食(植物)的顶部 **3** (**crop up**) appear or happen unexpectedly 意外地出现(或发生)

cropper /ˈkrɒpə(r)/ **noun** (**come a cropper**) informal【非正式】fall or fail heavily 重重摔倒；惨败

croquet /ˈkrəʊkeɪ/ **noun** a game in which wooden balls are hit through hoops with a mallet 槌球游戏(用木槌击木球使之穿过拱门)

croquette /krəʊˈket/ **noun** a small cake or roll of vegetables, meat, or fish, fried in breadcrumbs 炸丸子(蔬菜、肉、鱼等弄成丸状外裹面包屑油

炸而成)

cross /krɒs/ **noun 1** a mark, object, or shape formed by two short intersecting lines or pieces (+ or ×) 交叉符号；叉形物；叉形；十字形 **2** a cross-shaped medal or monument 十字形勋章(或纪念碑) **3** (**the Cross**) the wooden cross on which Jesus was crucified (耶稣受难的)十字架 **4** an animal or plant resulting from cross-breeding 杂种；杂交植物 **5** a mixture of two things 混合物 • **verb 1** go or extend across or to the other side of 横穿；越过 **2** pass in an opposite or different direction 和…错过；与…对面而过 **3** place crosswise 使交叉 **4** draw a line or lines across 在…上画线；在…上画十字 **5** Brit.【英】mark a cheque with a pair of parallel lines to indicate that it must be paid into a named bank account 在(支票)上画两条平行线；签注(支票) **6** Soccer【足球】pass the ball across the field towards the centre 横传(球) **7** oppose or stand in the way of 反对；阻挠 **8** make an animal breed with another of a different species 使(动物)杂交 • **adjective** annoyed 生气的；恼怒的 □ **at cross purposes** misunderstanding or having different aims from one another 误解的；目标不同的 **cross-breed** produce an animal or plant by making two different species, breeds, or varieties breed 使杂交 **cross-check** check figures or information by using a different source or method 交叉检查；(从多方面)核对(数字或信息) **cross-country 1** across fields or countryside 越野的 **2** across a region or country 横跨地区的；横穿全国的 **cross-dressing** the wearing of clothes usually worn by the opposite sex 穿异性服装 **cross-examine** question a witness called by the other party in a court of law (在法庭上)盘诘，盘问(证人) **cross-eyed** having one or both eyes turned inwards towards the nose 内斜视眼的;斗鸡眼的 **cross-fertilize** fertilize a plant using pollen from another plant of the same species 使(植物)异花受粉 **cross something off** remove an item from a list 删除、划去(单子上的项目) **cross something out** remove a word or phrase by drawing a line through it 画线删去(词语) **cross-question** question in great detail 盘问 **cross reference** a reference to another written work, or part of one, given to provide further information 相互参照条目 **cross section 1** a surface exposed by making a straight cut through a solid object at right angles to its length 横断面;截面;剖面 **2** a sample of a larger group 典型;实例 **cross swords** have an argument or dispute 争辩;交锋 ■ **crossly** adverb.

crossbar /'krɒsbɑː(r)/ **noun 1** a horizontal bar between the two upright posts of a football goal (足球球门的)横梁 **2** a bar between the handlebars and saddle on a bicycle (自行车的)车架横梁

crossbow /'krɒsbəʊ/ **noun** a bow with a mechanism for drawing and releasing the string 弩

crossfire /'krɒsfaɪə(r)/ **noun** gunfire from two or more directions passing through the same area 交叉火力

cross-hatch /'krɒshætʃ/ **verb** shade an area with many intersecting parallel lines 用交叉平行线给(某区域)加上阴影

crossing /'krɒsɪŋ/ **noun 1** a place where roads or railway lines cross (公路或铁路线的)交叉路口 **2** a place to cross a street or railway line 人行横道

crossroads /'krɒsrəʊdz/ **noun** a place where two or more roads cross each other 十字路口

crosswise /'krɒswaɪz/ or **cross-ways** /'krɒsweɪz/ **adverb 1** in the form of a cross 交叉地 **2** diagonally 对角地;斜穿地

crossword /'krɒswɜːd/ **noun** a puzzle in which words crossing each other vertically and horizontally are written as answers to clues 纵横字谜

crotch /krɒtʃ/ **noun** the part of the human body between the legs (人体的)胯部

crotchet /'krɒtʃɪt/ **noun** a musical note that lasts half as long as a minim 四分音符

crotchety /'krɒtʃəti/ **adjective** irritable 急躁的;易怒的

crouch /kraʊtʃ/ **verb** bend the knees and bring the upper body forward and down 蹲;蹲伏 • **noun** a crouching position 蹲伏;蜷伏

croup[1] /kruːp/ **noun** an illness of children, with coughing and breathing difficulties 哮吼,格鲁布(儿童疾病,伴有咳嗽和呼吸困难)

croup[2] **noun** a horse's hindquarters (马的)臀部

croupier /'kruːpieɪ/ **noun** the person in charge of a gambling table in a casino 赌台管理员;赌资收付人

crouton /'kruːtɒn/ **noun** a small piece of fried or toasted bread served with soup 油炸面包小块(浸在汤里食用)

crow[1] /krəʊ/ **noun** a large black bird with a harsh call 鸦;乌鸦 □ **as the crow flies** in a straight line across country 笔直地;成直线地 **crow's feet** wrinkles at the outer corner of a person's eye 眼角皱纹 **crow's-nest** a platform at the top of a ship's mast to watch from (船的)桅杆瞭望台

crow[2] **verb** (**crows, crowing, crowed** or **crew**) **1** (of a cock) make its loud, shrill cry (公鸡)啼叫,打鸣 **2** boastfully express pride or triumph 洋洋得意 • **noun** the cry of a cock 鸡啼声

crowbar /'krəʊbɑː(r)/ **noun** an iron bar with a flattened end, used as a lever 铁撬;撬棍

crowd /kraʊd/ **noun 1** a large number

of people gathered together 人群 **2** informal 【非正式】 a group of people with a shared quality (有共同特点的)一群人，一伙人 • **verb 1** fill a space almost completely 塞满，挤满 (某处) **2** move or come together as a crowd 群集；聚集 **3** move or stand too close to 逼近；挤；靠近

crown /kraʊn/ **noun 1** a circular head-dress worn by a king or queen 王冠；冕 **2** (**the Crown**) the reigning king or queen 国王；女王；君主 **3** a wreath of leaves or flowers worn as an emblem of victory 花冠(用树叶或花朵做成，象征胜利) **4** an award gained by a victory 冠军称号 **5** the top or highest part of something 顶部；最高部 **6** an artificial replacement or covering for the upper part of a tooth 假齿冠 **7** a former British coin worth five shillings (25 pence) 克朗(英国旧时硬币，面值5先令或25便士) • **verb 1** place a crown on the head of someone to declare them to be king or queen 为(某人)加冕；立(某人)为君主 **2** rest on or form the top of 位于…的顶部；形成…的顶部

crozier /ˈkrəʊziə(r)/ **noun** a hooked staff carried by a bishop (主教的)权杖

crucial /ˈkruːʃl/ **adjective** very important, especially in terms of the success or failure of something 决定性的，关键性的 ∎ **crucially** adverb.

crucible /ˈkruːsɪbl/ **noun** a container in which metals or other substances may be melted or heated (熔化金属等的)坩埚，熔炉

crucifix /ˈkruːsəfɪks/ **noun** a small cross with a figure of Jesus on it (有耶稣像的)小十字架

crucifixion /ˌkruːsəˈfɪkʃn/ **noun 1** the execution of a person by crucifying them 钉死十字架 **2** (**the Crucifixion**) the crucifixion of Jesus 耶稣受难

cruciform /ˈkruːsɪfɔːm/ **adjective** having the shape of a cross 十字形的

crucify /ˈkruːsɪfaɪ/ **verb** (**crucifies, crucifying, crucified**) **1** kill someone by nailing or tying them to a cross 把(某人)钉(或绑)在十字架上处死 **2** informal 【非正式】 criticize someone severely 严厉批评

crude /kruːd/ **adjective 1** in a natural state; not yet processed 天然的；未加工的 **2** rough or simple 粗糙的；简陋的 **3** coarse or vulgar 粗鄙的；粗俗的 ∎ **crudely** adverb **crudity** noun.

cruel /ˈkruːəl/ **adjective** (**crueller, cruellest** or **crueler, cruelest**) **1** taking pleasure in the suffering of other people 残忍的，残暴的 **2** causing pain or suffering 令人痛苦的 ∎ **cruelly** adverb.

cruelty /ˈkruːəlti/ **noun** (plural **cruelties**) cruel behaviour or treatment 残忍行为；残暴

cruet /ˈkruːɪt/ **noun** a small container or set of containers for salt, pepper, oil, or vinegar 调味品小瓶

cruise /kruːz/ **verb** (**cruises, cruising, cruised**) **1** move slowly around without a definite destination 漫游 **2** travel smoothly at a moderate speed 以中速巡行 • **noun** a voyage on a ship taken as a holiday 度假航游

cruiser /ˈkruːzə(r)/ **noun 1** a large, fast warship 巡洋舰 **2** a yacht or motorboat with passenger accommodation 游艇

crumb /krʌm/ **noun 1** a small fragment of bread, cake, or biscuit (面包、蛋糕或饼干的)碎屑 **2** a very small amount 少许；一点儿

crumble /ˈkrʌmbl/ **verb** (**crumbles, crumbling, crumbled**) **1** break or fall apart into small fragments 把…弄碎；(使)破碎 **2** gradually decline or fall apart 逐渐崩溃；瓦解 • **noun** Brit. 【英】 a baked pudding made with fruit and a crumbly topping 酥皮水果点心 ∎ **crumbly** adjective.

crummy /ˈkrʌmi/ **adjective** (**crummier, crummiest**) informal 【非正式】

bad or unpleasant 糟糕的;令人不快
的

crumpet /ˈkrʌmpɪt/ noun **1** a soft,
flat cake with an open texture, eaten
toasted and buttered (涂上黄油食用
的)烤面饼 **2** Brit. informal【英,非正式】
sexually attractive women 性感女郎

crumple /ˈkrʌmpl/ verb (**crumples,
crumpling, crumpled**) **1** crease
something by crushing it 弄皱;使起
皱 **2** collapse 崩溃;垮掉

crunch /krʌntʃ/ verb **1** crush
something hard or brittle with the
teeth 嘎吱嘎吱地咀嚼 **2** move with a
noisy grinding sound 嘎吱嘎吱地移
动 • noun **1** a crunching sound 嘎吱
声 **2** (**the crunch**) informal【非正式】
the crucial point of a situation 关键
时刻;危急关头 ■ **crunchy** adjective.

crusade /kruːˈseɪd/ noun **1** (**the
Crusades**) a series of medieval
military expeditions made by
Europeans against Muslims in the
Middle East (中世纪的)十字军东征
2 an energetic organized campaign
(积极、有组织的)运动 • verb (**crusades, crusading, crusaded**) take
part in a crusade 从事,参与(某项运
动) ■ **crusader** noun.

crush /krʌʃ/ verb **1** squash, crease, or
break up something by pressing it 压
扁;压皱;压碎 **2** defeat completely
(彻底)打败, 征服 • noun **1** a crowd
of people pressed closely together
拥挤的人群 **2** informal【非正式】a
strong, short-lived feeling of love for
someone 迷恋;热恋

crust /krʌst/ noun **1** the tough outer
part of a loaf of bread 面包皮 **2** a
hardened layer, coating, or deposit
硬外皮;坚硬外壳;表面沉积物 **3** the
outermost layer of the earth (地球的)
地壳 **4** a layer of pastry covering a
pie 馅饼皮 • verb form into a crust,
or cover with a crust 结成硬皮;以硬
壳覆盖

crustacean /krʌˈsteɪʃn/ noun a hard-

shelled creature such as a crab or
lobster, usually living in water 甲壳
纲动物(通常水生,包括蟹、龙虾等)

crusty /ˈkrʌsti/ adjective (**crustier,
crustiest**) **1** having or consisting of
a crust 有外壳的 **2** easily irritated 暴
躁的,易怒的

crutch /krʌtʃ/ noun **1** a long stick
with a bar at the top, used as a
support by a lame person T字形拐杖
2 a person's crotch (人的)胯部

crux /krʌks/ noun (**the crux**) the
most important point that is being
discussed (讨论的)关键,核心

cry /kraɪ/ verb (**cries, crying, cried**)
1 shed tears 流泪,哭泣 **2** shout or
scream loudly 大声叫喊,尖叫 **3** (of
an animal) make a distinctive call (动
物)鸣, 叫 **4** (**cry out for**) demand or
need 迫切需要 **5** (**cry off**) informal【非
正式】fail to keep to an arrangement
未遵守(约定);打退堂鼓 • noun (plural
cries) **1** a period of shedding tears
一阵哭泣 **2** a loud shout or scream
大声喊叫,尖叫 **3** an animal's distinctive call (动物的)鸣声,叫声 □ **a
crying shame** a very unfortunate
situation 奇耻大辱

cryogenics /ˌkraɪəˈdʒenɪks/ noun
the branch of physics concerned
with very low temperatures 低温学
■ **cryogenic** adjective.

crypt /krɪpt/ noun an underground
room beneath a church, used as a
chapel or burial place (用作礼拜堂或
墓穴的)教堂地下室

cryptic /ˈkrɪptɪk/ adjective mysterious
or obscure in meaning 神秘的;含义
模糊的 ■ **cryptically** adverb.

crystal /ˈkrɪstl/ noun **1** a transparent
mineral, especially quartz 水晶;(尤
指)石英 **2** a piece of a solid substance that is formed naturally and
has flat sides arranged symmetrically
结晶体 **3** very clear glass 水晶玻璃
□ **crystal ball** a globe of glass or
crystal, used for predicting the future

(占卜用的)水晶球

crystalline /ˈkrɪstəlaɪn/ **adjective 1** resembling a crystal 晶体结构的；晶状的 **2** literary 【文】very clear 清澈透明的；晶莹剔透的

crystallize or **crystallise** /ˈkrɪstəlaɪz/ **verb** (**crystallizes, crystallizing, crystallized**) **1** form crystals 结晶 **2** become definite and clear 明确；变得朗3**3** (**crystallized**) (of fruit) coated with and preserved in sugar (水果)糖渍的，蜜饯的

cu. abbreviation cubic.

cub /kʌb/ **noun 1** the young of a fox, bear, lion, or other meat-eating mammal (狐狸、熊、狮等食肉哺乳动物的)幼崽，幼兽 **2** (also **Cub Scout**) a member of the junior branch of the Scout Association 幼童军成员

Cuban /ˈkjuːbən/ **noun** a person from Cuba 古巴人 • **adjective** relating to Cuba 古巴的

cubbyhole /ˈkʌbihəʊl/ **noun** a small enclosed space or room 小壁橱；鸽笼式小房间

cube /kjuːb/ **noun 1** a three-dimensional shape with six equal square faces 立方体 **2** the result obtained when a number is multiplied by itself twice 立方；三次幂 • **verb 1** cut food into small cubes 把(食物)切成小方块 **2** find the cube of a number 求(某数)的立方 □ **cube root** the number which produces a given number when cubed 立方根

cubic /ˈkjuːbɪk/ **adjective 1** having the shape of a cube 立方形的 **2** involving the cube of a quantity 立方的：*a cubic metre* 立方米

cubicle /ˈkjuːbɪkl/ **noun** a small area of a room that is separated off for privacy (出于隐私而隔开的)小单间，小隔间

cubism /ˈkjuːbɪzəm/ **noun** a style of painting featuring regular lines and shapes 立体派，立体主义(一种绘画风格，把物体表现为规则的线条和图形) ■ **cubist** noun & adjective.

cubit /ˈkjuːbɪt/ **noun** an ancient measure of length, approximately equal to the length of a forearm 腕尺，肘尺(古时长度单位，约等于前臂的长度)

cuckoo /ˈkʊkuː/ **noun** a bird known for laying its eggs in the nests of other birds 杜鹃，布谷鸟 • **adjective** informal 【非正式】crazy 疯狂的

cucumber /ˈkjuːkʌmbə(r)/ **noun** a long green fruit with watery flesh, eaten in salads 黄瓜

cud /kʌd/ **noun** (usu. in 通常用于 **chew the cud**) partly digested food that cows and similar animals bring back from the first stomach to the mouth for further chewing 反刍的食物

cuddle /ˈkʌdl/ **verb** (**cuddles, cuddling, cuddled**) **1** hold closely and lovingly in your arms 拥抱；搂抱 **2** (often **cuddle up to**) lie or sit close 依偎 • **noun** an affectionate hug (深情的)拥抱

cuddly /ˈkʌdli/ **adjective** (**cuddlier, cuddliest**) pleasantly soft or plump 软乎乎的，胖嘟嘟的

cudgel /ˈkʌdʒl/ **noun** a short, thick stick used as a weapon (用作武器的)粗短棍，短棒 • **verb** (**cudgels, cudgelling, cudgelled**; US spelling 【美拼作】**cudgels, cudgeling, cudgeled**) beat with a cudgel 用棍棒打；棒打

cue¹ /kjuː/ **noun 1** a signal for an actor to enter or to begin their speech or performance (提醒演员进场或开始说话或表演的)提示，暗示 **2** a signal or prompt for action 行动信号 • **verb** (**cues, cueing** or **cuing, cued**) **1** give a cue 给⋯提示；向⋯提白 **2** set a piece of audio or video equipment to play a particular part of a recording 使(录音或录像设备)准备播放(录制材料的特定部分)

cue² **noun** a long rod for hitting the ball in snooker, billiards, or pool (台

球等的)球杆

cuff¹ /kʌf/ **noun 1** the end part of a sleeve, where the material of the sleeve is turned back or a separate band is sewn on 袖口 **2** chiefly N. Amer. 【主北美】a trouser turn-up (裤脚的)翻边口 **off the cuff** informal 【非正式】without preparation 未作准备地;即兴地

cuff² /kʌf/ **verb** hit with an open hand 掌击;用巴掌打 • **noun** a blow with an open hand 掌击;一巴掌

cufflink /ˈkʌflɪŋk/ **noun** a device for fastening together the sides of a shirt cuff (衬衫的)袖口链扣

cuisine /kwɪˈziːn/ **noun** a particular style of cooking (某种)烹饪风格

cul-de-sac /ˈkʌldəsæk/ **noun** (plural **culs-de-sac** /ˈkʌldəsæk/) a street or passage closed at one end 死胡同;死巷

culinary /ˈkʌlɪnəri/ **adjective** having to do with cooking 烹饪的,烹调的

cull /kʌl/ **verb 1** kill a selected number of a certain kind of animal to reduce its population (通过有选择宰杀)剔除宰杀(动物) **2** choose a few things from a wide range 选用;挑选 • **noun** a selective killing of a certain kind of animal (对动物的)选择性宰杀

culminate /ˈkʌlmɪneɪt/ **verb** (**culminates**, **culminating**, **culminated**) reach a climax or point of highest development 达到高潮;达到顶点 ■ **culmination** noun.

culottes /kjuːˈlɒts/ **plural noun** women's wide-legged knee-length trousers 女用裙裤

culpable /ˈkʌlpəbl/ **adjective** deserving blame 应受责备的;该受惩处的 ■ **culpability** noun.

culprit /ˈkʌlprɪt/ **noun** the person responsible for an offence 罪犯;犯法者;犯过失的人

cult /kʌlt/ **noun 1** a system of religious worship directed towards a particular person or object 宗教膜拜 **2** a small, unconventional religious group 异教团体 **3** something popular or fashionable among a particular group of people (特定人群中)被狂热喜爱(或崇尚)的事物

cultivate /ˈkʌltɪveɪt/ **verb** (**cultivates**, **cultivating**, **cultivated**) **1** prepare and use land for crops or gardening 耕;耕作 **2** grow plants or crops 栽培,种植 **3** try to develop or gain a particular quality 培养,养成(某种素质) **4** try to win the friendship or support of 结交(朋友);培养(好感) **5** (**cultivated**) well educated and having good taste 有修养的;品位高雅的 ■ **cultivation** noun **cultivator** noun.

cultural /ˈkʌltʃərəl/ **adjective 1** relating to the culture of a society 文化的 **2** relating to the arts and intellectual achievements 人文艺术 ■ **culturally** adverb.

culture /ˈkʌltʃə(r)/ **noun 1** the arts, customs, and institutions of a nation, people, or group (国家、民族或群体的)文化,文明 **2** the arts and intellectual achievements regarded as a whole (总称)文化,人文艺术 **3** a refined understanding or appreciation of culture 文化修养 **4** a preparation of cells or bacteria grown for medical or scientific study (细胞或细菌的)培养

cultured /ˈkʌltʃəd/ **adjective 1** well educated and having good taste 有修养的;有教养的;有品位的 **2** (of a pearl) formed round a foreign body inserted into an oyster (珍珠)人工培养的

culvert /ˈkʌlvət/ **noun** a tunnel carrying a stream or open drain under a road or railway (道路或铁路下的)涵洞,涵洞管道

cum /kʌm/ **preposition** combined with 和;与;附有;连同

cumbersome /ˈkʌmbəsəm/ **adjective 1** difficult to carry or use because of its size or weight 笨重的；难使用的，不方便的 **2** complicated and time-consuming 繁琐的；耗时的

cumin /'kʌmɪn/ **noun** the seeds of a plant, used as a spice 小茴香，欧蒔萝籽(用作调料)

cummerbund /'kʌməbʌnd/ **noun** a sash worn round the waist as part of a man's formal evening suit (男式晚礼服的)宽腰带

cumulative /'kju:mjələtɪv/ **adjective** increasing by successive additions 累积的，渐增的 • **cumulatively** adverb.

cuneiform /'kju:nɪfɔ:m/ **adjective** (of ancient writing systems) using wedge-shaped characters (古代书写)使用楔形文字的

cunning /'kʌnɪŋ/ **adjective 1** skilled at deceiving people 狡猾的；狡诈的 **2** skilful or clever 熟练的，灵巧的 • **noun** craftiness 狡诈；熟练，灵巧 ■ **cunningly** adverb.

cup /kʌp/ **noun 1** a small bowl-shaped drinking container with a handle 杯子 **2** a trophy in the shape of a cup on a stem, awarded as a prize in a sports contest (体育比赛的)奖杯，优胜杯 **3** a sports contest in which the winner is awarded a cup (体育)锦标赛，杯赛 **4** either of the two parts of a bra shaped to contain one breast 乳罩窝，罩杯 • **verb** (**cups, cupping, cupped**) **1** form your hand or hands into the curved shape of a cup 把(手)合成杯状 **2** place your curved hand or hands around 用手拢住；用手捧着

cupboard /'kʌbəd/ **noun** a piece of furniture, or a recess in a wall with a door, used for storage 橱柜，壁橱 □ **cupboard love** affection shown to someone in order to obtain something (有所企图的)假装亲热

Cupid /'kju:pɪd/ **noun 1** the Roman god of love 丘比特(罗马爱神) **2** (also **cupid**) a picture or statue of a naked winged child carrying a bow 丘比特画像(或塑像)

cupidity /kju:'pɪdəti/ **noun** greed for money or possessions 贪财；贪婪

cupola /'kju:pələ/ **noun** a rounded dome that forms or decorates a roof 圆屋顶；穹顶

cur /kɜ:(r)/ **noun** an aggressive mongrel dog 恶狗

curate /'kjʊərət/ **noun** an assistant to a parish priest 助理牧师

curative /'kjʊərətɪv/ **adjective** able to cure disease 有疗效的；能治疗的

curator /kjʊə'reɪtə(r)/ **noun** a keeper of a museum or other collection (博物馆等的)馆长，管理人

curb /kɜ:b/ **verb** control or put a limit on 抑制；约束 • **noun 1** a control or limit on something 抑制；约束 **2** a type of bit with a strap or chain which passes under a horse's lower jaw 马勒；马嚼子 **3** US spelling of **KERB**. kerb 的美式拼法

curd /kɜ:d/ or **curds** /kɜ:dz/ **noun** a soft, white substance formed when milk coagulates 凝乳

curdle /'kɜ:dl/ **verb** (**curdles, curdling, curdled**) form curds or lumps 结成凝乳；凝固

cure /kjʊə(r)/ **verb** (**cures, curing, cured**) **1** make a person who is ill well again 治愈；使痊愈 **2** end a disease, condition, or problem by treatment or appropriate action 解除(病痛)；解决(问题) **3** preserve meat, fish, etc. by salting, drying, or smoking (用腌、晒干、熏等方法)保存(肉、鱼等) • **noun 1** something that cures; a remedy 药剂；疗法 **2** the healing of a person who is ill 治愈；痊愈 ■ **curable** adjective.

curfew /'kɜ:fju:/ **noun 1** a regulation requiring people to remain indoors between specific hours of the night 宵禁(令) **2** the time at which a curfew begins 宵禁时间

curie /'kjʊəri/ **noun** (plural **curies**) a unit of radioactivity 居里(放射性强度单位)

curio /'kjuəriəu/ noun (plural **curios**) an object that is interesting because it is rare or unusual 古玩；珍品

curiosity /ˌkjuəri'ɒsəti/ noun (plural **curiosities**) 1 a strong desire to know or learn something 好奇心；求知欲 2 an unusual or interesting object or fact 珍品；奇物

curious /'kjuəriəs/ adjective 1 eager to know or learn something 好奇的；求知欲强的 2 strange; unusual 奇特的；不同寻常的 ■ **curiously** adverb.

curl /kɜːl/ verb form a curved or spiral shape 弯曲；成螺旋形 • noun something in the shape of a spiral or coil 螺旋状物；卷曲物 ■ **curly** adjective.

curler /'kɜːlə(r)/ noun a roller or clasp around which you wrap hair to curl it 卷发夹

curlew /'kɜːljuː/ noun (plural **curlew** or **curlews**) a large wading bird with a long curved bill 麻鹬(大型涉禽，喙长而弯)

curling /'kɜːlɪŋ/ noun a game played on ice, in which you slide large circular flat stones towards a mark 冰壶(运动)；冰上溜石(运动)

curmudgeon /kɜː'mʌdʒən/ noun a bad-tempered person 脾气坏的人 ■ **curmudgeonly** adjective.

currant /'kʌrənt/ noun a dried fruit made from a small seedless variety of grape 无核小葡萄干；加仑子

currency /'kʌrənsi/ noun (plural **currencies**) 1 a system of money used in a country (一国流通的)货币 2 the state or period of being current 流行(时期)

current /'kʌrənt/ adjective 1 happening or being used or done now 现时的；当前的 2 in common or general use 通用的；流通的 • noun 1 a flow of water or air in a particular direction 水流；气流 2 a flow of electrically charged particles 电流 □ **current account** Brit. 【英】a bank or building society account from which you may withdraw money at any time 活期存款账户 ■ **currently** adverb.

! 注意 don't confuse **current** with **currant**, which means 'a dried grape'. 不要混淆 current 和 currant，后者意为"葡萄干"。

curriculum /kə'rɪkjələm/ noun (plural **curricula** /kə'rɪkjələ/ or **curriculums**) the subjects that make up a course of study in a school or college (学校的)全部课程 □ **curriculum vitae** /kə,rɪkjələm 'viːtaɪ/ a written account of a person's qualifications and previous jobs, sent with a job application (用于求职的)个人履历，简历 ■ **curricular** adjective.

curry¹ /'kʌri/ noun (plural **curries**) an Indian dish of meat, vegetables, or fish, cooked in a hot, spicy sauce (印度的)咖喱食品，咖喱菜肴

curry² verb (**curry favour**) try to win someone's approval by flattering them and being very helpful 奉承；讨好

curry comb noun a hand-held rubber device used for grooming horses 马梳

curse /kɜːs/ noun 1 an appeal to a supernatural power to harm someone or something 诅咒；咒语 2 a cause of harm or misery 祸因；祸根 3 an offensive word or phrase used to express anger or annoyance 骂人话；咒骂 • verb (**curses, cursing, cursed**) 1 use a curse against 诅咒 2 (**be cursed with**) continuously suffer from or be affected by 受…之苦；受…之害 3 say offensive words; swear 咒骂

cursor /'kɜːsə(r)/ noun a mark on a computer screen identifying the point where typing or other input will take effect (计算机屏幕上的)光标

✔ 拼写指南 *-or* at the end, not *-er*: cur*sor*. cursor 词末拼作 -or，不要拼作 -er。

cursory /ˈkɜːsəri/ **adjective** hasty and therefore not thorough 仓促的；粗略的；草率的 ■ **cursorily** adverb.

curt /kɜːt/ **adjective** (of a person's speech) rudely brief (人的言语)简短失礼的 ■ **curtly** adverb.

curtail /kɜːˈteɪl/ **verb** cut short or restrict 减少；缩短 ■ **curtailment** noun.

curtain /ˈkɜːtn/ **noun** a piece of material hung up to form a screen at a window or between the stage and the audience in a theatre 窗帘；幕布；帷幕 • **verb** provide or screen something with a curtain or curtains 给…装帘子；为…挂帷幕 □ **curtain call** the appearance of a performer on stage after a performance to acknowledge applause (演员的)谢幕 **curtain-raiser** an event happening just before a longer or more important one (事件的)序曲，前奏

curtsy or **curtsey** /ˈkɜːtsi/ **noun** (plural **curtsies** or **curtseys**) a woman's or girl's respectful greeting, made by bending the knees with one foot in front of the other (女子的)屈膝礼 • **verb** (**curtsies**, **curtsying**, **curtsied** or **curtseys**, **curtseying**, **curtseyed**) perform a curtsy 行屈膝礼

curvaceous /kɜːˈveɪʃəs/ **adjective** having an attractively curved shape 有曲线美的

curvature /ˈkɜːvətʃə(r)/ **noun** the fact of being curved; a curved shape 弯曲；曲度

curve /kɜːv/ **noun** a line which gradually turns from a straight course 曲线；弧线 • **verb** (**curves**, **curving**, **curved**) form a curve 弯曲；成曲线 ■ **curvy** adjective.

cushion /ˈkʊʃn/ **noun 1** a bag of cloth stuffed with soft material, used to provide comfort when sitting 垫子；靠垫；坐垫 **2** something that gives protection against impact or something unpleasant 缓冲垫；减震器；起缓解作用的东西 **3** the inner sides of a billiard table (台球桌的)弹性衬边 • **verb 1** soften the effect of an impact on 缓和…的冲击；减少…的震动 **2** lessen the bad effects of 减轻…的影响

cushy /ˈkʊʃi/ **adjective** (**cushier**, **cushiest**) informal 【非正式】 easy and undemanding 容易的；不费劲儿的

cusp /kʌsp/ **noun 1** a pointed end where two curves meet (两曲线相交的)尖点，会切点 **2** a point in between two different states (两种状态的)转变点

custard /ˈkʌstəd/ **noun 1** a sweet sauce made with milk and eggs, or milk and flavoured cornflour 蛋奶沙司 **2** a baked dessert made from eggs and milk 蛋奶糕；蛋挞

custodian /kʌˈstəʊdiən/ **noun** a person responsible for looking after something 监护人；看守人；保管人

custody /ˈkʌstədi/ **noun 1** protective care 守卫；保护 **2** imprisonment 监禁；拘留 ■ **custodial** adjective.

custom /ˈkʌstəm/ **noun 1** a traditional way of behaving or doing something 风俗；习俗 **2** regular dealings with a shop or business by customers 光顾；惠顾 □ **custom-built** (or **custom-made**) made to a particular customer's order (按照顾客要求)定制的

customary /ˈkʌstəməri/ **adjective** usual or habitual 通常的；惯例的 ■ **customarily** adverb.

customer /ˈkʌstəmə(r)/ **noun 1** a person who buys goods or services from a shop or business 顾客；主顾；客户 **2** a person or thing that you have to deal with (不得不应对的)家伙，东西：*a tough customer* 难缠的家伙

customize or **customise**
/'kʌstəmaɪz/ **verb** (**customizes**, **customizing**, **customized**) modify something to suit a person or task (按要求)改制,定制,定做

customs /'kʌstəmz/ **plural noun 1** charges made by a government on imported goods 关税;进口税 **2** the official department that administers and collects customs charges 海关

cut /kʌt/ **verb** (**cuts**, **cutting**, **cut**) **1** make an opening or wound with something sharp 割破;划伤 **2** shorten, divide, or remove with something sharp 剪;切;割;截 **3** make or design a garment in a particular way 裁剪(衣服) **4** reduce the amount or quantity of 削减;裁减 **5** go across or through an area 斜穿;横穿;穿过 **6** stop filming or recording 停止拍片(或录音) **7** divide a pack of playing cards by lifting a portion from the top 切(牌);把(牌)分成 • **noun 1** a wound or opening resulting from cutting 伤口;切口;破口;裂口 **2** a reduction 削减;降低 **3** the style in which a garment or a person's hair is cut (服装的)款式,式样;发型;发式 **4** a piece of meat cut from a carcass 切下的肉 **5** informal 【非正式】 a share of profits 利润份额 **6** a version of a film after editing (电影)剪辑后的版本 □ **cut and dried** already decided 已成定局的 **cut and thrust** a competitive atmosphere or environment 刀光剑影;激烈交锋 **cut corners** do something badly to save time or money (为了节省时间或金钱而)敷衍了事 **cut glass** glass with decorative patterns cut into it 雕花玻璃;刻花玻璃 **cut in 1** interrupt 打断 **2** pull in too closely in front of another vehicle 超车抢道 **3** (of a machine) begin operating automatically (机器)自动启动,发动 **cut the mustard** informal 【非正式】 reach the required standard 达到规定标

准;达标 **cut no ice** informal 【非正式】 have no influence or effect 没有影响;不起作用 **cut someone/thing off 1** make it impossible to reach a place 封锁,阻断,隔断(通路) **2** deprive someone of a supply 切断(某人)的…供应 **3** break a telephone connection with someone 中断与(某人)的通话 **cut out** (of an engine) suddenly stop operating (发动机)突然熄火 **cut someone out** exclude someone 把(某人)排除在外 **cut-throat** ruthless and fierce 残酷无情的;激烈的

cutaneous /kju:'teɪnɪəs/ **adjective** having to do with the skin 皮肤的

cutback /'kʌtbæk/ **noun** a reduction 削减;减少

cute /kju:t/ **adjective 1** charmingly pretty; sweet 妩媚动人的;漂亮的;可爱的 **2** N. Amer. informal 【北美,非正式】 clever; shrewd 机灵的;精明的 ■ **cutely** adverb.

cuticle /'kju:tɪkl/ **noun** the dead skin at the base of a fingernail or toenail (手指甲或脚趾甲根部的)死皮

cutlass /'kʌtləs/ **noun** a short sword with a slightly curved blade, formerly used by sailors (旧时水手用的)短弯刀

cutlery /'kʌtləri/ **noun** knives, forks, and spoons used for eating or serving food (刀、叉、匙等)餐具

cutlet /'kʌtlət/ **noun 1** a lamb or veal chop from just behind the neck 羊颈(或牛颈)排骨 **2** a flat cake of minced meat, nuts, etc., covered in breadcrumbs and fried (用肉末、坚果末等裹面包屑做成的)炸饼

cutter /'kʌtə(r)/ **noun 1** a person or thing that cuts something 切割工;裁剪者;切割(或剪裁)工具 **2** a light, fast patrol boat or sailing boat 巡逻快艇

cutting /'kʌtɪŋ/ **noun 1** an article cut from a newspaper 剪报 **2** a piece cut from a plant to grow a new one (植物的)插枝,插条 **3** a way dug through higher ground for a railway, road, etc. (为修铁路、公路等从高地开凿出的)路堑 • **adjective** hurtful 尖刻的；伤人的：*a cutting remark* 尖酸刻薄的话 □ **the cutting edge** the most advanced or modern stage; the forefront 尖端；领先阶段；最前沿

cuttlefish /'kʌtlfɪʃ/ **noun** (plural **cuttlefish** or **cuttlefishes**) a sea creature resembling a squid 乌贼；墨鱼

CV /si: 'vi:/ **abbreviation** curriculum vitae.

cwt. abbreviation hundredweight.

cyan /'saɪən/ **noun** a greenish-blue colour 蓝绿色；青色

cyanide /'saɪənaɪd/ **noun** a highly poisonous compound containing a metal combined with carbon and nitrogen atoms 氰化物(一种剧毒化合物)

cybernetics /ˌsaɪbə'netɪks/ **noun** the science of communications and control in machines (e.g. computers) and living things (e.g. by the nervous system) 控制论；神经机械学(研究信息在机器和生物体中的传递和控制的科学) ■ **cybernetic** adjective.

cyberspace /'saɪbəspeɪs/ **noun** the hypothetical place in which communication over computer networks takes place 计算机空间；虚拟空间

cyclamen /'sɪkləmən/ **noun** a plant having pink, red, or white flowers with backward-curving petals 仙客来(一种植物，开粉色、红色或白色花，花瓣反折)

cycle /'saɪkl/ **noun 1** a series of events that are regularly repeated in the same order 循环；周而复始 **2** a complete sequence of changes associated with something recurring such as an alternating electric current 循环；变化周期 **3** a series of musical or literary works composed around a particular theme (表现某一特定主题的)组歌，全套文学作品，组诗 **4** a bicycle 自行车 • **verb** (**cycles, cycling, cycled**) ride a bicycle 骑自行车 ■ **cyclist** noun.

cyclic /'saɪklɪk/ or **cyclical** /'saɪklɪkl/ **adjective** happening in cycles 循环的；反复出现的

cyclone /'saɪkləʊn/ **noun 1** a system of winds rotating inwards to an area of low atmospheric pressure 气旋 **2** a violent tropical storm 热带风暴，旋风 ■ **cyclonic** adjective.

cygnet /'sɪgnɪt/ **noun** a young swan 幼天鹅

cylinder /'sɪlɪndə(r)/ **noun 1** a three-dimensional shape with straight parallel sides and circular or oval ends 圆柱(体) **2** a chamber in which a piston moves in an engine (发动机的)汽缸 ■ **cylindrical** adjective.

cymbal /'sɪmbl/ **noun** a musical instrument consisting of a round brass plate which is either struck against another one or hit with a stick 钹(一种打击乐器)

cynic /'sɪnɪk/ **noun 1** a person who believes that people always act from selfish motives 愤世嫉俗者；认为人皆自私的人 **2** a person who raises doubts about something 怀疑者；悲观者 ■ **cynicism** noun.

cynical /'sɪnɪkl/ **adjective 1** believing that people always act from selfish motives 愤世嫉俗的；认为人皆自私的 **2** doubtful or sneering 怀疑的；冷嘲热讽的 **3** concerned only with your own interests 自私的，不顾及他人的 ■ **cynically** adverb.

cypher /'saɪfə(r)/ ⟹ 见 **CIPHER**.

cypress /'saɪprəs/ **noun** an evergreen coniferous tree with small dark leaves 柏树

Cypriot /'sɪpriət/ **noun** a person from Cyprus 塞浦路斯人 • **adjective** relating to Cyprus 塞浦路斯的

Cyrillic /sə'rɪlɪk/ **noun** the alphabet

used for Russian and related languages 西里尔字母(俄语及相关语言的字母)

cyst /sɪst/ **noun** an abnormal cavity in the body which contains fluid (肌体内的)囊肿;囊

cystic /ˈsɪstɪk/ **adjective 1** having to do with cysts 囊肿的 **2** relating to the bladder or the gall bladder 膀胱的;胆囊的 □ **cystic fibrosis** an inherited disease which causes too much mucus to be produced and often leads to blockage of tubes in the body 囊性纤维化,囊性纤维变性

(一种遗传性疾病,黏液的大量分泌常导致人体管道阻塞)

cystitis /sɪˈstaɪtɪs/ **noun** inflammation of the bladder 膀胱炎

cytoplasm /ˈsaɪtəʊplæzəm/ **noun** the material of a living cell, excluding the nucleus (除细胞核之外的)细胞质,细胞浆

czar etc. /zɑː(r)/ ⇒ 见 TSAR etc.

Czech /tʃek/ **noun 1** a person from the Czech Republic or (formerly) Czechoslovakia 捷克人;(旧时的)捷克斯洛伐克人 **2** the language spoken in the Czech Republic 捷克语

Dd

SPELLING TIP 拼写指南 Some words which sound as if they might begin with the letters 'di' are spelled with 'de' instead, for example **deter** or **dessert**. 某些根据发音似乎是以字母组合di开头的词实际应拼作de,如deter和dessert。

D or d /diː/ **noun** (plural **Ds** or **D's**) **1** the fourth letter of the alphabet 英语字母表的第4个字母 **2** the Roman numeral for 500 (罗马数字)五百 • **abbreviation** (**d**) (before decimal currency was brought in) penny or pence (改用十进位货币前的)旧便士

'd /d/ **short form** had or would.

DA /diː'eɪ/ **abbreviation** (in the US) district attorney (美国的)地方检察官

dab /dæb/ **verb** (**dabs**, **dabbing**, **dabbed**) **1** press lightly with something absorbent (用吸水性物质)轻触,轻按 **2** apply with light, quick strokes 轻涂;轻敷;轻搽 • **noun** a small amount of something applied lightly 少量;一点点 □ **dab hand** Brit. informal 【英,非正式】a person who is very good at something 能手;行家

dabble /'dæbl/ **verb** (**dabbles**, **dabbling**, **dabbled**) **1** gently move your hands or feet around in water 用(手或脚)玩水 **2** take part in an activity in a casual way 涉猎;浅尝 ■ **dabbler** noun.

dace /deɪs/ **noun** (plural **dace**) a small freshwater fish related to the carp 雅罗鱼,代斯鱼(一种小型淡水鱼)

dachshund /'dæksnd/ **noun** a breed of dog with a long body and very short legs (体长腿短的)猎獾狗,腊肠狗

dad /dæd/ **or daddy** /'dædi/ **noun** (plural **dads** or **daddies**) informal 【非正式】your father 爸爸;爹爹

daddy-long-legs /ˌdædi'lɒŋlegz/ **noun** Brit. informal 【英,非正式】a crane fly 大蚊

daffodil /'dæfədɪl/ **noun** a plant that has bright yellow flowers with a long trumpet-shaped centre 黄水仙

daft /dɑːft/ **adjective** informal 【非正式】silly; foolish 愚蠢的

dagger /'dægə(r)/ **noun** a short pointed knife, used as a weapon 匕首;短剑

daguerreotype /də'gerətaɪp/ **noun** an early kind of photograph produced using a silver-coated plate 用达盖尔银版法拍的照片

dahlia /'deɪliə/ **noun** a garden plant with brightly coloured flowers 大丽花;大丽菊

daily /'deɪli/ **adjective & adverb** every day or every weekday 每日(的);每工作日的(的)

dainty /'deɪnti/ **adjective** (**daintier**, **daintiest**) delicately small and pretty 小巧的;精致的 • **noun** (plural **dainties**) a small, tasty item of food 美味食物;珍馐 ■ **daintily** adverb.

dairy /'deəri/ **noun** (plural **dairies**) a building where milk and milk products are produced 牛奶场,乳品场;乳品间 • **adjective 1** made from milk 牛奶的,奶制的,乳品的 **2** involved in milk production 乳品生产的

dais /'deɪs/ **noun** a low platform that supports a throne, or that people stand on to make a speech (放置宝座的)平台;讲台

daisy /'deɪzi/ noun (plural **daisies**) a small plant that has flowers with a yellow centre and white petals 雏菊

dale /deɪl/ noun (in northern England) a valley（英格兰北部的）山谷，峪

dalliance /'dæliəns/ noun a casual relationship 调情

dally /'dæli/ verb (**dallies, dallying, dallied**) **1** do something in a leisurely way 慢悠悠地做事；磨蹭 **2** (**dally with**) have a casual relationship with 调情；玩弄

Dalmatian /dæl'meɪʃn/ noun a breed of large dog with short white hair and dark spots 达尔马提亚狗(一种白色黑斑的短毛大狗)

dam¹ /dæm/ noun a barrier constructed across a river to hold back water 坝；堤 • verb (**dams, damming, dammed**) build a dam across 在⋯上筑堤坝

dam² noun the female parent of an animal 母兽

damage /'dæmɪdʒ/ noun **1** physical harm that makes something less valuable or effective 损害；损坏；毁坏 **2** harmful effects 不良后果 **3** (**damages**) money paid to compensate for a loss or injury 损害赔偿金 • verb (**damages, damaging, damaged**) cause harm to 损害；损坏；毁坏

damask /'dæməsk/ noun a rich, heavy fabric with a pattern woven into it 花缎；锦缎

dame /deɪm/ noun **1** (**Dame**) (in the UK) the title of a woman awarded a knighthood, equivalent to *Sir*（英国的）女爵士 **2** N. Amer. informal 【北美，非正式】 a woman 女人 **3** Brit. 【英】 a comic female character in pantomime, played by a man（哑剧中由男子扮演的）滑稽女角色

damn /dæm/ verb **1** (**be damned**) (in Christian belief) be condemned by God to eternal punishment in hell 基督教信仰中)被罚入地狱 **2** harshly condemn 强烈指责；谴责 **3** curse 诅咒

damnable /'dæmnəbl/ adjective very bad or unpleasant 糟透的；讨厌的

damnation /dæm'neɪʃn/ noun the fate of being condemned to eternal punishment in hell 罚入地狱；天谴

damned /dæmd/ adjective said to emphasize anger or frustration（用于强调愤怒或受挫)该死的，可恶的

damp /dæmp/ adjective slightly wet 潮湿的；微湿的 • noun moisture in the air, on a surface, or in a solid substance 潮湿；潮气；湿气 • verb **1** make something damp 使潮湿 **2** (**damp something down**) control a feeling or situation 抑制(感情)；控制(局面)；给⋯泼冷水口

damp course a layer of waterproof material in a wall near the ground, to prevent rising damp 防潮层 **damp squib** Brit. 【英】 something that turns out to be a lot less impressive than expected 无成效的事；落空；失败

dampen /'dæmpən/ verb **1** make something damp 使潮湿 **2** make a feeling or reaction less strong or intense 抑制，减弱(感情或反应)

damper /'dæmpə(r)/ noun **1** a pad for silencing a piano string（钢琴的）制音器，减音器 **2** a movable metal plate for controlling the air flow in a chimney（烟囱的）挡板，调节风门 □ **put a damper on** informal 【非正式】 make something less enjoyable or lively 抑制；使扫兴

damsel /'dæmzl/ noun old use 【旧】 a young unmarried woman 未婚少女

damson /'dæmzn/ noun a small purple-black fruit resembling a plum 布拉姆李子；西洋李子

dance /dɑːns/ verb (**dances, dancing, danced**) **1** move rhythmically to music 跳舞 **2** move in a quick and lively way 跳跃；轻快

移动 • **noun 1** a series of steps and movements performed to music 舞蹈 **2** a social gathering at which people dance 舞会 ■ **dancer** noun.

dandelion /'dændɪlaɪən/ **noun** a weed with large bright yellow flowers 蒲公英

dander /'dændə(r)/ **noun** (**get your dander up**) informal 【非正式】lose your temper 发怒

dandle /'dændl/ **verb** (**dandles, dandling, dandled**) gently bounce a young child on your knees or in your arms 在膝上或怀抱中摇晃(小孩)

dandruff /'dændrʌf/ **noun** flakes of dead skin on a person's scalp and in the hair 头皮屑

dandy /'dændi/ **noun** (plural **dandies**) a man who is too concerned with looking stylish and fashionable 花花公子；纨绔子弟 • **adjective** (**dandier, dandiest**) N. Amer. informal 【北美，非正式】excellent 极好的；第一流的 ■ **dandified** adjective.

Dane /deɪn/ **noun** a person from Denmark 丹麦人

danger /'deɪndʒə(r)/ **noun 1** the possibility of suffering harm or of experiencing something unpleasant 危险；风险 **2** a cause of harm 危险的起因；危害

dangerous /'deɪndʒərəs/ **adjective** likely to cause harm or injury 有危险的；不安全的 ■ **dangerously** adverb.

dangle /'dæŋgl/ **verb** (**dangles, dangling, dangled**) **1** hang or swing freely 悬挂；悬荡 **2** offer something to someone to persuade them to do something. 以……诱惑

Danish /'deɪnɪʃ/ **adjective** relating to Denmark or the Danes 丹麦的；丹麦人的 • **noun** the language of Denmark 丹麦语

dank /dæŋk/ **adjective** damp and cold 阴冷潮湿的；湿冷的

dapper /'dæpə(r)/ **adjective** (of a man) neat in appearance；smart (男子)衣着整齐的，衣冠楚楚的

dapple /'dæpl/ **verb** (**dapples, dappling, dappled**) mark with patches of colour or of light and shadow 使有斑点，使呈驳杂 □ **dapple grey** (of a horse) grey with darker ring-shaped markings (马)灰色并带有深色斑点的，菊花青色的

dare /deə(r)/ **verb** (**dares, daring, dared**) **1** have the courage to do something 敢；敢于 **2** challenge someone to do something 激；挑战 • **noun** a challenge to do something brave or risky 挑战

daredevil /'deədevl/ **noun** a person who enjoys doing dangerous things 鲁莽大胆的人，蛮勇的人

daring /'deərɪŋ/ **adjective** willing to do dangerous or risky things 大胆的；勇敢的；敢于冒险的 • **noun** the courage to do dangerous or risky things 勇敢；勇气；胆量 ■ **daringly** adverb.

dark /dɑːk/ **adjective 1** with little or no light 黑暗的；阴暗的 **2** of a deep colour 深色的；暗色的 **3** depressing or gloomy 忧郁的；暗淡的 **4** evil；wicked 邪恶的；坏的 **5** mysterious 隐秘的；神秘的：*a dark secret* 深藏的秘密 • **noun 1** (**the dark**) the absence of light 黑暗 **2** nightfall 傍晚；黄昏 □ **the Dark Ages** the period c. 500 – 1100 in Europe, seen as lacking culture or learning 黑暗时代(欧洲约公元500年至1100年被认为文化、学术式微的时代) **dark horse** a person about whom little is known 黑马；深藏不露的人 **in the dark** knowing nothing about a situation or matter 不知情；蒙在鼓里 **a shot in the dark** a wild guess 瞎猜；乱猜 ■ **darkly** adverb **darkness** noun.

darken /'dɑːkən/ **verb 1** make or become darker (使)变暗 **2** become unhappy or angry 不快;生气

darkroom /'dɑːkruːm/ **noun** a darkened room for developing photographs (冲洗照片的)暗室

darling /'dɑːlɪŋ/ **noun 1** an affectionate form of address (用作昵称)亲爱的, 宝贝 **2** a lovable person 可爱的人 • **adjective 1** much loved 心爱的 **2** charming 可爱的,迷人的

darn[1] /dɑːn/ **verb** mend a hole in a knitted garment by weaving yarn across it 织补(织物)

darn[2] **or darned** /dɑːnd/ **adjective** informal 【非正式】 another way of saying DAMNED (damned的另一说法)

dart /dɑːt/ **noun 1** a small pointed missile fired as a weapon or thrown in the game of darts (用作武器或用于投掷游戏的)飞镖 **2** (**darts**) an indoor game in which you throw darts at a circular board marked with numbers 掷镖游戏 **3** a sudden rapid movement 猛冲;飞奔 **4** a tapered tuck stitched into a garment to make it fit better 缝褶 • **verb** move suddenly or rapidly 猛冲;飞奔

dash /dæʃ/ **verb 1** run or travel in a great hurry 猛冲;飞奔 **2** hit or throw with great force猛击;猛掷 **3** destroy 毁灭:*His hopes were dashed* 他的希望破灭了。**4** (**dash something off**) write something hurriedly 匆忙地写 • **noun 1** an act of dashing 猛冲;飞奔;猛击 **2** a small amount added to something (添加的)少量, 少许 **3** a horizontal stroke in writing (一)破折号

dashboard /'dæʃbɔːd/ **noun** the panel of instruments and controls facing the driver of a vehicle (车辆上的)仪表板

dashing /'dæʃɪŋ/ **adjective** (of a man) attractive, stylish, and confident (男子)有魅力的,时髦的,自信的

dastardly /'dæstədli/ **adjective** old

use 【旧】 wicked and cruel 邪恶的;残忍的

data /'deɪtə/ **noun 1** facts, statistics, or other information 资料;材料;统计数据 **2** information stored by a computer (计算机存储的)数据

! 注意 data is the plural of the Latin word **datum**. Scientists use it as a plural noun, taking a plural verb (as in *the data were classified*). In everyday use, however, **data** is usually treated as a singular noun with a singular verb (as in *here is the data*). data是拉丁语datum的复数,科人员把它视为复数名词,接复数动词(如 the data were classified 数据已经分了类)。但在日常用法中,data 常被视为单数名词(如 here is the data 数据在这里)。

database /'deɪtəbeɪs/ **noun** a set of data held in a computer (存放在计算机中的)数据库,资料库

date[1] /deɪt/ **noun 1** the day of the month or year as specified by a number 日期;日子 **2** a day or year when a particular event happened or will happen (事件发生的)日期,年份 **3** a social or romantic appointment 约定;约会 **4** a musical or theatrical performance 音乐演出;戏剧演出 • **verb** (**dates, dating, dated**) **1** mark something with a date 给…注明日期 **2** establish the date when something existed or was made 确定…的年代 **3** (**date from** or **back to**) have existed since a particular time in the past 追溯到(过去某一时间) **4** informal 【非正式】 go on a date or regular dates with…约会 □ **to date** until now 迄今为止 ■ **datable** (or **dateable**) adjective.

date[2] **noun** the sweet, dark brown, oval fruit of a palm tree 海枣

dated /'deɪtɪd/ **adjective** old-fashioned

过时的；废弃的

dative /ˈdeɪtɪv/ **noun** Grammar【语法】(in Latin, Greek, German, etc.) the case of nouns and pronouns that indicates an indirect object or the person or thing affected by a verb (拉丁语、希腊语、德语等中的)与格

datum /ˈdeɪtəm/ **noun** (plural **data**) a piece of information 资料；信息；数据

daub /dɔːb/ **verb** smear something with a thick substance 在…上厚涂抹 • **noun 1** plaster, clay, or a similar substance, used in building(建筑用的)灰泥 **2** a smear of a thick substance(厚厚的)涂抹物

daughter /ˈdɔːtə(r)/ **noun 1** a girl or woman in relation to her parents 女儿 **2** a female descendant 女性后裔 □ **daughter-in-law** (plural **daughters-in-law**) the wife of a person's son 儿媳妇

daunt /dɔːnt/ **verb** make someone feel nervous or discouraged 使胆怯；使气馁 ■ **daunting adjective**.

dauntless /ˈdɔːntləs/ **adjective** brave and determined 无所畏惧的；吓不倒的；勇敢的

dawdle /ˈdɔːdl/ **verb** (**dawdles**, **dawdling**, **dawdled**) move slowly；take your time 游荡；拖延；磨蹭

dawn /dɔːn/ **noun 1** the first appearance of light in the sky in the morning 黎明；破晓；拂晓 **2** the beginning of something new 开端；起始 • **verb 1** (of a day) begin (天)破晓 **2** come into existence 产生；出现 **3** (**dawn on**) (of a fact) become clear to(对事实)被理解，被领悟 □ **dawn chorus** the early-morning singing of birds 破晓鸟鸣声

day /deɪ/ **noun 1** a period of twenty-four hours, reckoned from midnight to midnight 一天，一日 **2** the time between sunrise and sunset 白昼；白天 **3** (usu. **days**) a particular period

of the past 过去的日子 **4** (**the day**) the present time or the time in question 现在；当前 □ **call it a day** decide to stop doing something 停止；到此为止

daybreak /ˈdeɪbreɪk/ **noun** dawn 黎明；拂晓

daydream /ˈdeɪdriːm/ **noun** a series of pleasant thoughts that distract your attention from the present 白日梦；幻想；空想 • **verb** have a daydream 做白日梦；幻想；空想

daylight /ˈdeɪlaɪt/ **noun 1** the natural light of the day 日光 **2** dawn 黎明；拂晓 □ **daylight robbery** Brit. informal【英，非正式】the fact of charging far too much for something 漫天要价，敲竹杠

daze /deɪz/ **noun** a state of stunned confusion or bewilderment 茫然，迷乱；困惑 ■ **dazed adjective**.

dazzle /ˈdæzl/ **verb** (**dazzles**, **dazzling**, **dazzled**) **1** (of a bright light) blind someone temporarily (强光)使目眩，使眼花 **2** amaze someone by being very impressive 使倾倒；使赞叹不已 • **noun** blinding brightness 耀眼；眩目 ■ **dazzling adjective**.

dB abbreviation decibels.

DC /diːˈsiː/ **abbreviation 1** direct current. **2** District of Columbia 哥伦比亚特区

deacon /ˈdiːkən/ **noun 1** a Christian minister just below the rank of priest (基督教的)执事 **2** (in some Protestant Churches) a person who helps a minister but is not a member of the clergy (某些基督教新教教会会)助祭 ■ **deaconess noun**.

deactivate /diːˈæktɪveɪt/ **verb** (**deactivates**, **deactivating**, **deactivated**) stop equipment from working by disconnecting or destroying it 使(设备)不能使用

dead /ded/ **adjective 1** no longer alive 死亡的 **2** (of a part of the body) numb (身体部位)麻木的，失去知

觉的 **3** showing no emotion 无感情的；冷漠的 **4** without activity or excitement 无活力的，无生气的，呆滞的 **5** complete 全然的；绝对的：*dead silence* 寂静无声 • adverb **1** absolutely, exactly, or directly 绝对地；准确地；直接地：*You're dead right.* 你完全正确。 **2** Brit. informal 【英，非正式】very 非常；十分 □ **dead end** a road or passage that is closed at one end 一头封死的道路（或通道）；死巷 **dead heat** a result in a race in which two or more competitors finish at exactly the same time 同时到达终点的比赛结果 **dead loss** a useless person or thing 无用的人（或物）**dead reckoning** a way of finding out your position by estimating the direction and distance travelled 航位推算；航位推测法 **dead ringer** informal 【非正式】a person or thing very like another 酷似的人；看上去一模一样的东西

deadbeat /'dedbiːt/ noun informal 【非正式】a lazy or aimless person 游手好闲的人；二流子

deaden /'dedn/ verb **1** make a noise or sensation less strong or intense 缓和，减弱 **2** make something numb 使麻木

deadhead /'dedhed/ verb remove dead flower heads from a plant 摘去（植物）的枯花

deadline /'dedlam/ noun the time or date by which you have to complete something 最后期限

deadlock /'dedlɒk/ noun **1** a situation in which no one can make any progress 僵局；僵持；停顿 **2** Brit. 【英】a lock operated by a key 单门锁 • verb (**be deadlocked**) be unable to make any progress 使陷入僵局；使停顿

deadly /'dedli/ adjective (**deadlier**, **deadliest**) **1** causing or able to cause death 致命的；致死的 **2** (of a

voice, glance, etc.) filled with hate （说话声、扫视等）充满仇恨的 **3** very accurate or effective 极精确的；极有效的 **4** informal 【非正式】very boring 沉闷的，枯燥的 • adverb very 非常；极其：*She was deadly serious.* 她极其认真。 □ **deadly nightshade** a plant with purple flowers and poisonous black berries 颠茄（开紫色花，结有毒黑色浆果）

deadpan /'dedpæn/ adjective not showing any emotion; expressionless 不带感情色彩的；面无表情的

deadweight /,ded'weit/ noun **1** the weight of a motionless person or thing （人或物的）静止重量 **2** the total weight which a ship can carry （船的）总载重量

deaf /def/ adjective **1** unable to hear 聋的 **2** (**deaf to**) unwilling to listen to 不愿听的 □ **deaf mute** offensive 【冒犯】a person who is deaf and unable to speak 聋哑人 ■ **deafness** noun.

deafen /'defn/ verb **1** make deaf 使聋 **2** (**deafening**) very loud 震耳欲聋的；极喧闹的 ■ **deafeningly** adverb.

deal[1] /diːl/ verb (**deals**, **dealing**, **dealt**) **1** (**deal something out**) distribute something 分配；分给 **2** buy and sell a product commercially 经营，买卖（产品）**3** buy and sell illegal drugs 非法买卖（毒品）**4** give out cards to players of a card game 发（纸牌）• noun **1** an agreement between two or more people or groups 协议；交易 **2** a particular form of treatment received 待遇 □ **deal with 1** do business with 与…做生意 **2** do things to put a problem right 处理 **3** cope with 对付；对待 **4** have something as a subject 论述；讨论 **a good** (or **great**) **deal** a lot 许多 ■ **dealer** noun.

deal[2] noun fir or pine wood 冷杉木；

松木

dealer /'di:lə(r)/ noun 1 a person who buys and sells goods 商人 2 a person who buys and sells shares directly (rather than as a broker or agent) 买卖证券者 3 a player who deals cards in a card game 发牌者

dean /di:n/ noun 1 the head of a cathedral's governing body (大教堂的)座堂主任牧师 2 the head of a university department or medical school (大学里的)系主任,医学院院长

dear /dɪə(r)/ adjective 1 much loved 亲爱的;心爱的;被热爱的 2 used in the polite introduction to a letter 亲爱的(用作书信抬头的礼貌称呼) 3 expensive 昂贵的 • noun a lovable person 可爱的人

dearly /'dɪəli/ adverb 1 very much 非常;很 2 at great cost 以高价;昂贵地

dearth /dɜ:θ/ noun a lack of something 缺乏,不足

death /deθ/ noun 1 an instance of a person or an animal dying 死亡事件 2 the end of life; the state of being dead 死亡 3 the end of something 终止;结束;灭亡 □ **at death's door** so ill that you may die 病人膏肓;命在旦夕 **death knell** an event that signals the end of something 丧钟 **death penalty** punishment by being executed 死刑 **death row** a block of cells for prisoners who have been sentenced to death (监狱的)死囚区,死囚牢房 **death-watch beetle** a beetle that makes a ticking sound which people used to think was an omen of death 红毛窃蠹(发出的嘀嗒声被视为死亡的征兆)

deathly /'deθli/ adjective suggesting death 死一般的: *a deathly hush* 死一般的寂静

debacle /deɪ'bɑ:kl/ noun an utter failure or disaster 溃败;崩溃;大灾难

debar /dɪ'bɑ:(r)/ verb (**debars, debarring, debarred**) officially prevent someone from doing something (正式)阻止,禁止

debase /dɪ'beɪs/ verb (**debases, debasing, debased**) make something worse in quality, value, or character 贬损…的质量(或价值,特点) ■ **debasement** noun.

debatable /dɪ'beɪtəbl/ adjective open to discussion or argument 可争辩的;可争论的

debate /dɪ'beɪt/ noun 1 a formal discussion in which people present opposing arguments 辩论;讨论 2 an argument 争论 • verb (**debates, debating, debated**) 1 discuss or argue about 辩论;讨论;争论 2 consider a possible course of action 考虑,思考(行动方式)

debauched /dɪ'bɔ:tʃt/ adjective indulging in a lot of pleasures in a way considered to be immoral 放荡的;道德败坏的 ■ **debauchery** noun.

debilitate /dɪ'bɪlɪteɪt/ verb (**debilitates, debilitating, debilitated**) severely weaken 削弱;使衰弱

debility /dɪ'bɪləti/ noun (plural **debilities**) physical weakness 体弱;虚弱;衰弱

debit /'debɪt/ noun 1 an entry in an account recording a sum owed (账户的)借项 2 a payment that has been made or that is owed 借方金额 • verb (**debits, debiting, debited**) (of a bank) remove money from a customer's account (银行)把(钱)记入账户的借方 □ **debit card** a card that lets you take money from your bank account electronically when buying something 借记卡

debonair /ˌdebə'neə(r)/ adjective (of a man) confident, stylish, and charming (男子)温文尔雅的,时髦的,有魅力的

debrief /ˌdiːˈbriːf/ **verb** question someone in detail about a mission they have completed (就执行任务的情况)盘问(某人)

debris /ˈdebriː/ **noun 1** scattered items or pieces of rubbish 垃圾;碎片;残骸 **2** loose broken pieces of rock 岩屑

debt /det/ **noun 1** a sum of money owed 欠款;债务 **2** a situation where you owe someone money 负债状态 **3** gratitude for a favour or service 恩义;恩情

debtor /ˈdetə(r)/ **noun** a person who owes money 债务人;借方

debug /ˌdiːˈbʌg/ **verb** (**debugs, debugging, debugged**) remove errors from computer hardware or software 排除(计算机硬件或软件)中的错误

debunk /ˌdiːˈbʌŋk/ **verb** show that something believed in by many people is false or exaggerated 揭穿,揭露(虚假或被夸大的事物)

debut /ˈdeɪbjuː/ **noun** a person's first appearance in a role 首次登台演出;首次露面 • **verb** make a debut 首次登台演出;首次露面

debutant /ˈdebjutɒnt/ **noun** a person making a debut 首次登台演出(或露面)的人

debutante /ˈdebjutɑːnt/ **noun** a young upper-class woman making her first appearance in society 首次进入社交界的上层社会青年女子

decade /ˈdekeɪd/ **noun** a period of ten years 十年;十年期

decadent /ˈdekədənt/ **adjective 1** immoral and interested only in pleasure 堕落的;颓废的;贪图享乐的 **2** luxuriously self-indulgent 奢侈放纵的 ■ **decadence** noun **decadently** adverb.

decaffeinated /ˌdiːˈkæfɪneɪtɪd/ **adjective** (of tea or coffee) having had most or all of its caffeine removed (茶或咖啡)脱咖啡因的

decagon /ˈdekəgən/ **noun** a figure with ten straight sides and angles 十边形;十角形

decahedron /ˌdekəˈhiːdrən/ **noun** (plural **decahedra** /ˌdekəˈhiːdrə/ or **decahedrons**) a solid figure with ten sides 十面体

decamp /dɪˈkæmp/ **verb** depart suddenly or secretly 匆忙逃走;秘密逃走

decant /dɪˈkænt/ **verb** pour liquid from one container into another 倒出(液体)

decanter /dɪˈkæntə(r)/ **noun** a glass container with a stopper, for wine or spirits (带塞子的)玻璃酒瓶

decapitate /dɪˈkæpɪteɪt/ **verb** (**decapitates, decapitating, decapitated**) cut off the head of 杀…的头;斩首 ■ **decapitation** noun.

decathlon /dɪˈkæθlɒn/ **noun** an athletic event in which each competitor takes part in the same ten events (田径)十项全能运动 ■ **decathlete** noun.

decay /dɪˈkeɪ/ **verb 1** (of plant or animal material) rot (植物或动物器官)腐烂,腐朽 **2** become weaker or less good 衰退;衰落 • **noun 1** the state or process of decaying 腐烂;腐朽;衰败;衰退 **2** rotten matter or tissue 腐烂物质;腐烂组织

decease /dɪˈsiːs/ **noun** formal or Law 【正式或法律】death 死亡

deceased /dɪˈsiːst/ formal or Law 【正式或法律】noun (**the deceased**) the recently dead person in question (刚刚去世的)死者 • **adjective** recently dead 已死的;死去的

deceit /dɪˈsiːt/ **noun** behaviour intended to make someone believe something that is not true 欺骗行为

deceitful /dɪˈsiːtfl/ **adjective** deliberately deceiving other people

欺骗的；骗人的 ■ **deceitfully** adverb.

deceive /dɪ'siːv/ **verb (deceives, deceiving, deceived)1** deliberately make someone believe something that is not true 欺骗；诓骗；蒙骗 **2** (of a thing) give a mistaken impression (事物) 使人误解，误导 ■ **deceiver** noun.

✔ 拼写指南 *i* before *e* except after *c*: dece*i*ve. i 置于 e 前，在 c 后时除外，如 deceive。

---

decelerate /ˌdiː'seləreɪt/ **verb (decelerates, decelerating, decelerated)** slow down 减速；降低速度 ■ **deceleration** noun.

December /dɪ'sembə(r)/ **noun** the twelfth month of the year 十二月

decency /'diːsnsi/ **noun (plural decencies) 1** decent behaviour 正派；庄重；得体 **2 (decencies)** standards of acceptable behaviour 礼仪；行为准则

decennial /dɪ'seniəl/ **adjective** happening every ten years 每十年一次的

decent /'diːsnt/ **adjective 1** having good moral standards 正派的；正直的 **2** of an acceptable quality 过得去的；尚可的；还好的 **3** Brit. informal 【英，非正式】kind or generous 和气的；大方的 ■ **decently** adverb.

decentralize or **decentralise** /ˌdiː'sentrəlaɪz/ **verb (decentralizes, decentralizing, decentralized)** transfer authority from central to local government 分散，下放 (权力) ■ **decentralization** noun.

deception /dɪ'sepʃn/ **noun 1** the action of deceiving 欺骗；诓骗；蒙骗 **2** a thing that deceives 骗人的东西

deceptive /dɪ'septɪv/ **adjective** giving a false impression 骗人的；造成假象的 ■ **deceptively** adverb.

decibel /'desɪbel/ **noun** a unit for measuring the loudness of a sound or the power of an electrical signal 分贝 (声音强度和电子信号强度单位)

decide /dɪ'saɪd/ **verb (decides, deciding, decided) 1** think about something and make a judgement or decision 决定；拿定主意 **2** settle an issue or contest 解决 (问题)；决定 (比赛) 的胜负

decided /dɪ'saɪdɪd/ **adjective** definite；clear 明确的；明显的 ■ **decidedly** adverb.

decider /dɪ'saɪdə(r)/ **noun** a contest that settles the winner of a series of contests 决胜局；决赛

deciduous /dɪ'sɪdʒuəs/ **adjective** (of a tree or shrub) shedding its leaves annually (树或灌木) 每年落叶的

decimal /'desɪml/ **adjective** having to do with a system of numbers based on the number ten 十进位的 • **noun** a fractional number in the decimal system, written with figures either side of a full point 小数 □ **decimal place** the position of a digit to the right of a decimal point 小数点后的位数 **decimal point** a full point placed after the figure representing units in a decimal fraction 小数点

decimate /'desɪmeɪt/ **verb (decimates, decimating, decimated) 1** kill or destroy a large proportion of 大批杀死；大量毁灭 **2** drastically reduce in strength 大大削弱 ■ **decimation** noun.

decipher /dɪ'saɪfə(r)/ **verb (deciphers, deciphering, deciphered) 1** convert something from code into normal language 破译 **2** succeed in understanding something that is hard to interpret 理解 (难以解释的事)

decision /dɪ'sɪʒn/ **noun 1** a choice or judgement made after considering something 决定；决议；结论 **2** the ability to decide things quickly 决断力

decisive /dɪ'saɪsɪv/ **adjective 1** having great importance for the outcome of a situation 决定性的 **2** able to make decisions quickly 坚定的;果断的 ■ **decisively** adverb **decisiveness** noun.

deck /dek/ **noun 1** a floor of a ship 甲板;舱面 **2** a floor or platform 层面;平台 **3** chiefly N. Amer. 【主北美】 a pack of cards 一副纸牌 **4** a player or recorder for discs or tapes (光碟或磁带的)播放机,录放机 • **verb** decorate something 装饰;打扮

deckchair /'dektʃeə(r)/ **noun** a folding chair with a wooden frame and a canvas seat 折叠帆布躺椅

decking /'dekɪŋ/ **noun** material used in making a deck 甲板敷层;甲板板

declaim /dɪ'kleɪm/ **verb** speak or recite in a dramatic or passionate way 慷慨陈词;朗诵

declamation /deklə'meɪʃn/ **noun** the action of declaiming something 慷慨陈词;朗诵 ■ **declamatory** adjective.

declaration /deklə'reɪʃn/ **noun 1** a formal statement or announcement 宣言;公告;声明 **2** the action of declaring 宣告;宣告;公布

declare /dɪ'kleə(r)/ **verb** (**declares, declaring, declared**) **1** announce something solemnly or officially 宣布;宣告;声明 **2** (**declare yourself**) reveal your intentions or identity 表明意图(或身份) **3** acknowledge that you have income or goods on which tax or duty should be paid 申报(应纳税收入或物品) **4** Cricket 【板球】 voluntarily close an innings before all the players have batted (在还有未出局击球员的情况下)自愿宣布结束(赛局)

declassify /di:'klæsɪfaɪ/ **verb** (**declassifies, declassifying, declassified**) officially declare information or documents to be no longer secret 将(信息或文件)解密

declension /dɪ'klenʃn/ **noun** Grammar 【语法】 the changes in the form of a noun, pronoun, or adjective that identify its case, number, and gender 词形变化;变格

decline /dɪ'klaɪn/ **verb** (**declines, declining, declined**) **1** become smaller, weaker, or worse 减少;下降;衰退;衰落 **2** politely refuse 婉辞;谢绝 **3** Grammar 【语法】 form a word according to its case, number, and gender 使发生词性变化;使变格 • **noun** a gradual loss of strength, numbers, or value 减少;下降;衰退;衰落

declivity /dɪ'klɪvəti/ **noun** (plural **declivities**) formal 【正式】 a downward slope 斜坡

decode /di:'kəʊd/ **verb** (**decodes, decoding, decoded**) convert a coded message into understandable language 破译(密码文电)■ **decoder** noun.

décolletage /deɪkɒl'tɑːʒ/ **noun** a low neckline on a woman's dress or top (女服的)低领,露胸

décolleté /deɪ'kɒlteɪ/ **adjective** having a low neckline 低领的;露肩的

decommission /di:kə'mɪʃn/ **verb** take a nuclear reactor or weapon out of use and make it safe 关闭(核反应堆);拆除(核武器)

decompose /di:kəm'pəʊz/ **verb** (**decomposes, decomposing, decomposed**) decay; rot 腐烂;变腐败 ■ **decomposition** noun.

decompress /di:kəm'pres/ **verb 1** reduce the pressure on 给…减压;给…卸压 **2** expand compressed computer data to its normal size 将(压缩的计算机数据)恢复到原大小;使解压缩

decompression /di:kəm'preʃn/ **noun 1** reduction in air pressure 减

压;卸压 **2** the decompressing of computer data (对计算机数据的)解压压缩 □ **decompression sickness** a serious condition that results when a deep-sea diver surfaces too quickly (潜水员浮出水面太急造成的)减压病

decongestant /ˌdiːkənˈdʒestənt/ **noun** a medicine used to relieve a blocked nose 减轻鼻塞的药物

deconstruct /ˌdiːkənˈstrʌkt/ **verb** reduce something to its basic elements in order to interpret it in a different way 解构 ■ **deconstruction** noun.

decontaminate /ˌdiːkənˈtæmɪneɪt/ **verb** (**decontaminates**, **decontaminating**, **decontaminated**) remove dangerous substances from 清除…的有害物质; 净化 ■ **decontamination** noun.

decor /ˈdeɪkɔː(r)/ **noun** the furnishing and decoration of a room (房间的)装饰, 布置

decorate /ˈdekəreɪt/ **verb** (**decorates**, **decorating**, **decorated**) **1** make something more attractive by adding extra items 装饰; 装潢 **2** apply paint or wallpaper to the walls of a room or house 粉刷; 油漆; 裱糊 **3** give someone an award or medal 授予(某人)奖章(或勋章) ■ **decorator** noun.

decoration /ˌdekəˈreɪʃn/ **noun 1** the process or art of decorating 装饰; 装潢 **2** a decorative object or pattern 装饰品; 装饰图案 **3** the way in which something is decorated 装饰风格 **4** a medal or award given as an honour 勋章; 奖章

decorative /ˈdekərətɪv/ **adjective 1** making something look more attractive 装饰性的; 作装饰用的 **2** having to do with decoration 装饰的 ■ **decoratively** adverb.

decorator /ˈdekəreɪtə(r)/ **noun** a person who decorates, in particular

(Brit. 【英】) a person whose job is to paint interior walls or hang wallpaper 装修工; (英国尤指)油漆匠, 裱糊匠

decorous /ˈdekərəs/ **adjective** in good taste; polite and restrained 得体的; 端庄稳重的 ■ **decorously** adverb.

decorum /dɪˈkɔːrəm/ **noun** polite and socially acceptable behaviour 礼貌得体, 端庄稳重

decoy **noun** /ˈdiːkɔɪ/ **1** a real or imitation bird or animal, used by hunters to lure game (诱捕猎物的)假鸟, 假兽 **2** a person or thing used to mislead or lure someone into a trap 用作诱饵的人; 诱惑物; 诱饵 • **verb** /dɪˈkɔɪ/ lure by means of a decoy 引诱; 诱骗

decrease **verb** /dɪˈkriːs/ (**decreases**, **decreasing**, **decreased**) make or become smaller or fewer 减小; 减少 • **noun** /ˈdiːkriːs/ the process of decreasing, or the amount by which something decreases 减小; 减少; 减少量

decree /dɪˈkriː/ **noun 1** an official order that has the force of law 法令; 政令 **2** a judgement of certain law courts 判决; 裁定 • **verb** (**decrees**, **decreeing**, **decreed**) order something officially 下令; 颁布

decrepit /dɪˈkrepɪt/ **adjective** worn out or ruined because of age or neglect 破旧的; 年久失修的 ■ **decrepitude** noun.

decriminalize or **decriminalise** /ˌdiːˈkrɪmɪnəlaɪz/ **verb** (**decriminalizes**, **decriminalizing**, **decriminalized**) change the law to make something no longer illegal 使合法化 ■ **decriminalization** noun.

decry /dɪˈkraɪ/ **verb** (**decries**, **decrying**, **decried**) publicly declare something to be wrong or bad (公开)反对, 谴责

decrypt /ˌdiːˈkrɪpt/ **verb** convert

a coded or unclear message into understandable language 破译(密码文电等)

dedicate /'dedɪkeɪt/ verb (**dedicates, dedicating, dedicated**) **1** give time or effort to a particular subject, task, or purpose 把…奉献给 **2** address a book to someone as a sign of respect or affection 题献词于(书)上;把(书)献给

dedicated /'dedɪkeɪtɪd/ adjective **1** devoting a lot of time and attention to a particular task or subject 献身的;专心致志的 **2** exclusively given over to a particular purpose 专用的

dedication /ˌdedɪ'keɪʃn/ noun **1** devotion to a particular task or subject 奉献精神;献身精神 **2** the action of dedicating 奉献;献身 **3** the words with which a book is dedicated to someone 题词;献词

deduce /dɪ'djuːs/ verb (**deduces, deducing, deduced**) reach a conclusion by thinking about the information or evidence that is available 演绎出;推论出;推断出

deduct /dɪ'dʌkt/ verb take an amount away from a total (从总量中)扣除,减去 ■ **deductible** adjective.

deduction /dɪ'dʌkʃn/ noun **1** the action of deducting something 扣除;减除 **2** an amount that is or may be deducted 扣除额;减除数 **3** the process of deducing something 演绎 ■ **deductive** adjective.

deed /diːd/ noun **1** something that is done deliberately 行为;行动 **2** (usu. **deeds**) a legal document 契约;证书 □ **deed poll** Law 【法律】a legal deed made by one party only 片务契约;单务契约(指由一方订立的契约)

deem /diːm/ verb formal 【正式】 consider in a particular way 认为;视为;以为

deep /diːp/ adjective **1** extending far down or in from the top or surface 深的;厚的 **2** extending a specified distance from the top or surface 有…深的 **3** (of sound) not shrill (声音)深沉的,低沉的 **4** (of colour) dark (色彩)深的,暗的 **5** very intense or extreme 强烈的;严重的;极度的: *He was in deep trouble.* 他深陷困境。**6** difficult to understand 深奥的;难懂的 **7** (in ball games) far down or across the field (球类运动中)靠近对方端线的,打得深的 • noun (**the deep**) literary 【文】the sea 海洋 □ **deep freeze** (or **deep freezer**) a freezer 深冻冰箱;冷冻柜 **deep-fry** fry food in enough fat or oil to cover it completely 油炸(食物) ■ **deeply** adverb.

deepen /'diːpən/ verb make or become deep or deeper (使)变深,深化

deer /dɪə(r)/ noun (plural **deer**) a grazing animal with hooves, the male of which usually has antlers 鹿

deerstalker /'dɪəstɔːkə(r)/ noun a soft cloth cap, with peaks in front and behind and ear flaps which can be tied together over the top 猎鹿帽(一种软布帽,前后都有帽舌,护耳可系在帽顶)

deface /dɪ'feɪs/ verb (**defaces, defacing, defaced**) spoil the surface or appearance of 破坏…的表面(或外貌)

de facto /ˌdeɪ 'fæktəʊ/ adjective & adverb existing or happening in fact, whether it is supposed to or not 实际存在的(地)

defame /dɪ'feɪm/ verb (**defames, defaming, defamed**) damage the good reputation of 破坏…的名誉;诽谤;中伤 ■ **defamation** noun **defamatory** adjective.

default /dɪ'fɔːlt/ noun **1** failure to do something that is required by law 未履行义务;违约 **2** an option adopted by a computer program or other mechanism when no alternative is specified (计算机程序等的)默认选项,缺省值 • **verb 1** fail to do something that is required by law 未履行义务;违约 **2** (**default to**) go back automatically to a default option 默认(预设选项) □ **by default** because there is no opposition or positive action 因没有异议;因未采取积极行动 ■ **defaulter** noun.

defeat /dɪˈfiːt/ **verb 1** win a victory against; beat 击败;战胜 **2** prevent someone from achieving an aim 挫败;使落空 **3** reject or block a proposal or motion 否决(议案或动议) • **noun** an instance of defeating or of being defeated 战胜;失败

defeatist /dɪˈfiːtɪst/ **noun** a person who gives in to difficulty or failure too easily 失败主义者 ■ **defeatism** noun.

defecate /ˈdefəkeɪt/ **verb** expel waste matter from the bowels 排便;通大便 ■ **defecation** noun.

defect[1] /ˈdiːfekt/ **noun** a fault or imperfection 缺点;毛病;缺陷;瑕疵

defect[2] /dɪˈfekt/ **verb** abandon your country or cause in favour of an opposing one 背叛;叛变 ■ **defection** noun **defector** noun.

defective /dɪˈfektɪv/ **adjective** not perfect; faulty 有缺陷的;有缺点的;有毛病的

defence /dɪˈfens/ (US spelling【美拼作】defense) **noun 1** the action of defending something 防御;保卫;保护 **2** something that protects a building, country, etc. against attack 防御工事 **3** an attempt to justify something 辩解;辩护 **4** the case presented by the person being accused or sued in a lawsuit 被告方;辩方 **5** (**the defence**) the lawyer or lawyers acting for the person being sued in a lawsuit 辩护律师 **6** (in sport) the action of defending the goal or wicket, or the players who perform this role (体育比赛中的)防守队员

defenceless /dɪˈfensləs/ (US spelling【美拼作】defenseless) **adjective** completely vulnerable 无防卫能力的

defend /dɪˈfend/ **verb 1** protect from harm or danger 防御;保卫;保护 **2** argue in support of the person being accused or sued in a lawsuit 为(被告)辩护 **3** attempt to justify 为…辩解;为…辩白 **4** compete to hold on to a title or seat in a contest or election 捍卫(称号或席位) **5** (in sport) protect your goal or wicket rather than attempt to score against your opponents (体育比赛中)防守 ■ **defender** noun.

defendant /dɪˈfendənt/ **noun** a person sued or accused in a court of law 被告

defensible /dɪˈfensəbl/ **adjective 1** able to be justified by argument 可辩解的;正当有理的 **2** able to be protected 能防御的;能保护的

defensive /dɪˈfensɪv/ **adjective 1** used or intended to defend or protect 防御的;保卫的;保护的 **2** very anxious to defend yourself against criticism 自卫的;怀有戒心的 ■ **defensively** adverb **defensiveness** noun.

defer[1] /dɪˈfɜː(r)/ **verb** (**defers, deferring, deferred**) put something off to a later time 推迟;拖延 ■ **deferment** noun **deferral** noun.

defer[2] **verb** (**defers, deferring, deferred**) (**defer to**) give in to or agree to accept 遵从;听从

deference /ˈdefərəns/ **noun** polite respect 敬重;尊敬

deferential /ˌdefəˈrenʃl/ **adjective** polite and respectful 尊敬的;恭敬的 ■ **deferentially** adverb.

defiance /dɪˈfaɪəns/ **noun** open refusal to obey someone or something 违抗;反抗;蔑视 ■ **defiant** adjective **defiantly** adverb.

deficiency /dɪˈfɪʃnsi/ **noun** (plural **deficiencies**) **1** a lack or shortage of something 缺乏;缺少;不足 **2** a failing or shortcoming 缺点;缺陷

deficient /dɪˈfɪʃnt/ **adjective 1** not having enough of a particular quality or ingredient 缺乏的;缺少的;不足的 **2** inadequate in amount or quantity 数量不足的

deficit /ˈdefɪsɪt/ **noun 1** the amount by which a total falls short of that required 不足额 **2** the amount by which money spent is greater than money earned in a particular period of time 赤字;逆差;亏损

defile[1] /dɪˈfaɪl/ **verb** (**defiles, defiling, defiled**) **1** make dirty 弄脏;玷污 **2** treat something sacred with disrespect 亵渎(神圣的事物) ■ **defilement** noun.

defile[2] **noun** a narrow steep-sided gorge or mountain pass 峡谷;隘口

define /dɪˈfaɪn/ **verb** (**defines, defining, defined**) **1** describe the exact nature or scope of 明确;确定 **2** give the meaning of a word or phrase 解释;下定义 **3** mark out the limits or outline of 限定;确定…的界限;标出…的轮廓 ■ **definable** adjective.

definite /ˈdefɪnət/ **adjective 1** clearly stated or decided 清楚的;明显的 **2** (of a person) certain about something (人)肯定的,有把握的 **3** known to be true or real 确切的;确切的 **4** having exact and measurable physical limits 限定的;有界限的 □ **the definite article** Grammar【语法】the word *the* 定冠词(the) ■ **definitely** adverb.

✔ 拼写指南 *-ite*, not *-ate*: defi*nite*. definite中的-ite不要拼作-ate。

definition /ˌdefɪˈnɪʃn/ **noun 1** a statement of the exact meaning of a word or the nature or scope of something 定义;释义 **2** the degree of sharpness in outline of an object or image (物体的)清晰度;(图像的)分辨率

definitive /dɪˈfɪnətɪv/ **adjective 1** (of a conclusion or agreement) final and not able to be changed (结论或协议)最后的,决定性的 **2** (of a written work) the most accurate of its kind (书面作品)最精确的,权威性的 ■ **definitively** adverb.

deflate /dɪˈfleɪt/ **verb** (**deflates, deflating, deflated**) **1** let air or gas out of a tyre, balloon, etc. 放掉,抽掉(轮胎、气球等)的气 **2** make someone feel suddenly depressed 使泄气;挫锐气 **3** reduce price levels in an economy 紧缩(通货)

deflation /ˌdiːˈfleɪʃn/ **noun 1** the action of deflating something 放气;抽气;泄气 **2** reduction of the general level of prices in an economy 通货紧缩 ■ **deflationary** adjective.

deflect /dɪˈflekt/ **verb 1** turn something aside from a straight course 使转向;使偏斜;使转移 **2** make someone change their mind about doing something 使改变想法 ■ **deflection** noun.

deflower /ˌdiːˈflaʊə(r)/ **verb** literary【文】have sex with a woman who is a virgin 使(女子)失去童贞

defoliate /ˌdiːˈfəʊlieɪt/ **verb** (**defoliates, defoliating, defoliated**) remove the leaves from trees or plants 使落叶;除掉…的叶子 ■ **defoliant** noun **defoliation** noun.

deforest /ˌdiːˈfɒrɪst/ **verb** clear an area of trees 砍掉(某地区)的树林 ■ **deforestation** noun.

deform /dɪˈfɔːm/ **verb** change or spoil the usual shape of 使变形;损毁…的外观 ■ **deformed** adjective.

deformity /dɪˈfɔːmətɪ/ **noun** (plural **deformities**) **1** a deformed part 畸形部位 **2** the state of being deformed 畸形;变形

defraud /dɪˈfrɔːd/ **verb** obtain money from someone by deception 骗取,诈取钱财

defray /dɪˈfreɪ/ **verb** provide money to pay a cost 支付(费用)

defrock /diːˈfrɒk/ **verb** remove the official status of a Christian priest 免去(基督教教士)的圣职

defrost /diːˈfrɒst/ **verb 1** remove ice from something 除冰霜 **2** thaw frozen food 使(冷冻食物)解冻

deft /deft/ **adjective** quick and skilful 灵巧的;熟练的 ∎ **deftly** adverb **deftness** noun.

defunct /dɪˈfʌŋkt/ **adjective** no longer existing or functioning 已不存在的;已灭绝的;不再使用的;不再活动的

defuse /ˌdiːˈfjuːz/ **verb** (**defuses**, **defusing**, **defused**) **1** make a situation less tense or difficult 缓和(局面) **2** remove the fuse from an explosive device to prevent it from exploding 拆除(爆炸装置)的引信

> ! **注意** don't confuse defuse with diffuse, which means 'spread over a wide area'. 不要混淆defuse和diffuse,后者意为"传播;散布"。

defy /dɪˈfaɪ/ **verb** (**defies**, **defying**, **defied**)**1** openly resist or refuse to obey (公然)反抗,藐视 **2** challenge someone to do or prove something 向…挑战;激

degenerate verb /dɪˈdʒenəreɪt/ (**degenerates**, **degenerating**, **degenerated**) deteriorate physically or morally; get worse 变坏,堕落,衰退 • **adjective** /dɪˈdʒenərət/ having very low moral standards 堕落的 •**noun** /dɪˈdʒenərət/ a person with very low moral standards 堕落者 ∎ **degeneracy** noun **degeneration** noun.

degenerative /dɪˈdʒenərətɪv/ **adjective** (of a disease) becoming progressively worse (疾病)恶化的

degrade /dɪˈɡreɪd/ **verb** (**degrades**, **degrading**, **degraded**) **1** cause someone to lose dignity or self-respect 侮辱…的人格;使丢脸 **2** make worse in character or quality削弱,使降低品质 **3** make something break down or deteriorate chemically使降解;使分解 ∎ **degradable** adjective **degradation** noun.

degree /dɪˈɡriː/ **noun 1** the amount, level, or extent to which something happens or is present 程度;量 **2** a unit for measuring angles, equivalent to one ninetieth of a right angle 度,度数(角的度量单位) **3** a stage in a scale, e.g. of temperature or hardness (温度、硬度等的)度数,等级 **4** a qualification awarded to someone who has successfully completed a course at a university 学位

dehumanize or **dehumanise** /diːˈhjuːmənaɪz/ **verb** (**dehumanizes**, **dehumanizing**, **dehumanized**) remove the positive human qualities from 使失去人性;使非人化

dehumidify /ˌdiːhjuːˈmɪdɪfaɪ/ **verb** (**dehumidifies**, **dehumidifying**, **dehumidified**) remove moisture from the air or a gas 从(空气或气体)中除湿;使干燥 ∎ **dehumidifier** noun.

dehydrate /diːˈhaɪdreɪt/ **verb** (**dehydrates**, **dehydrating**, **dehydrated**) **1** make someone lose a lot of water from their body 使(某人)脱水 **2** remove water from food to preserve it 使(食物)脱水 ∎ **dehydration** noun.

de-ice /diːˈaɪs/ **verb** (**de-ices**, **de-icing**, **de-iced**) remove ice from 除去…上的冰 ∎ **de-icer** noun.

deify /ˈdeɪɪfaɪ/ **verb** (**deifies**, **deifying**, **deified**) treat or worship someone as a god 把…神化;把…奉若神明;崇拜

■ **deification** noun.

deign /deɪn/ **verb (deign to do)** do something that you think you are too important to do 降低身份做；屈尊做

deity /'deɪəti/ **noun (plural deities)** a god or goddess 神；女神

déjà vu /ˌdeɪʒɑː 'vuː/ **noun** a feeling of having already experienced the present situation 似曾经历的感觉

dejected /dɪ'dʒektɪd/ **adjective** sad and in low spirits 沮丧的；垂头丧气的；情绪低落的 ■ **dejection** noun.

delay /dɪ'leɪ/ **verb 1** make someone late or slow 使延误，使耽搁 **2** hesitate or be slow 耽搁，延误 **3** put off or postpone 延期，延迟，推迟 • **noun** the period or length of time that someone or something is delayed 延误期，耽搁的时间

delectable /dɪ'lektəbl/ **adjective** lovely, delightful, or delicious 令人愉快的，使人高兴的；美味的 ■ **delectably** adverb.

delectation /ˌdiːlek'teɪʃn/ **noun** formal 【正式】 pleasure and delight 享受；愉快

delegate **noun** /'delɪgət/ **1** a person sent to represent other people 代表 **2** a member of a committee 委员会成员 • **verb** /'delɪgeɪt/ **(delegates, delegating, delegated) 1** give a task or responsibility to someone else, especially someone more junior （尤指向下级）派遣任务 **2** authorize someone to act as a representative 委派（某人）为代表

delegation /ˌdelɪ'geɪʃn/ **noun 1** a group of delegates 代表团 **2** the process of delegating something 委托；委派

delete /dɪ'liːt/ **verb (deletes, deleting, deleted)** cross out or remove something written or printed or stored in a computer's memory 删除；删去，划掉 ■ **deletion** noun.

deleterious /ˌdelə'tɪəriəs/ **adjective** formal 【正式】 causing harm or damage 有害的；造成伤害的

deli /'deli/ **noun (plural delis)** informal 【非正式】 a delicatessen 熟食店

deliberate **adjective** /dɪ'lɪbərət/ **1** done on purpose; intentional 故意的；蓄意的 **2** careful and unhurried 慎重的；不慌不忙的；从容的 • **verb** /dɪ'lɪbəreɪt/ **(deliberates, deliberating, deliberated)** think about something carefully and for a long time 仔细考虑，思考 ■ **deliberately** adverb.

deliberation /dɪˌlɪbə'reɪʃn/ **noun 1** long and careful consideration 仔细考虑，思考 **2** slow and careful movement or thought 审慎；从容

deliberative /dɪ'lɪbərətɪv/ **adjective** having to do with consideration or discussion 仔细考虑的；思考的；审议的

delicacy /'delɪkəsi/ **noun (plural delicacies) 1** intricate or fragile texture or structure 精细（或脆弱）的质地（或结构） **2** discretion and tact 谨慎；周到 **3** a tasty, expensive food 美味昂贵的食物；佳肴

delicate /'delɪkət/ **adjective 1** attractively light and intricate in texture or structure （质地或结构）轻巧的，精细的 **2** easily broken or damaged 脆的；易碎的 **3** tending to become ill easily 纤弱的；娇弱的 **4** needing or showing careful handling 需要小心处理的，微妙的，棘手的：a delicate issue 棘手的问题 **5** (of colour or flavour) subtle and pleasant （色彩或味道）柔和的，清淡的 ■ **delicately** adverb.

delicatessen /ˌdelɪkə'tesn/ **noun** a shop selling unusual or foreign prepared foods 熟食店

delicious /dɪ'lɪʃəs/ **adjective** having a very pleasant taste or smell 美味的；可口的 ■ **deliciously** adverb.

delight /dɪ'laɪt/ **verb 1** please someone very much 使高兴；使愉快；使快乐

2 (delight in) take great pleasure in 以…为乐 • **noun** great pleasure, or something that causes it 高兴；愉快；乐事

delighted /dɪˈlaɪtɪd/ **adjective** very pleased 高兴的；愉快的 ■ **delightedly** adverb.

delightful /dɪˈlaɪtfl/ **adjective** causing delight; very pleasing 令人高兴的；使人愉快的 ■ **delightfully** adverb.

delineate /dɪˈlɪnieɪt/ **verb** (**delineates, delineating, delineated**) describe or indicate something precisely 描述；描写；刻画 ■ **delineation** noun.

delinquency /dɪˈlɪŋkwənsi/ **noun** (plural **delinquencies**) minor crime 轻度违法行为

delinquent /dɪˈlɪŋkwənt/ **adjective** tending to commit crime 有违法倾向的 • **noun** a delinquent person 罪犯；违法者

deliquesce /ˌdelɪˈkwes/ **verb** (**deliquesces, deliquescing, deliquesced**) (of a solid) become liquid by absorbing moisture （固体）溶化，潮解 ■ **deliquescence** noun **deliquescent** adjective.

delirious /dɪˈlɪriəs/ **adjective 1** suffering from delirium 谵妄的；神志不清的；说胡话的 **2** very excited or happy 极度兴奋的；狂喜的 ■ **deliriously** adverb.

✔ 拼写指南 note there's an *i*, not an *e* in the middle: deli**ri**ous. 注意 delirious 中间有一个i，而不是e。

delirium /dɪˈlɪriəm/ **noun** a disturbed state of mind in which a person becomes very restless, has illusions, and is unable to think clearly 谵妄；神志不清；说胡话

deliver /dɪˈlɪvə(r)/ **verb 1** bring something and hand it over to the person who is supposed to receive it 投递；送交 **2** provide something promised or expected 履行（诺言）；兑现 **3** give a speech 发表（讲话）**4**

launch or aim a blow or attack 给予（打击）**5** save or set free 解救；释放 **6** assist in the birth of a baby 给…接生 **7** give birth to a baby 分娩；生孩子

deliverance /dɪˈlɪvərəns/ **noun** the process of being rescued or set free 解救；释放

delivery /dɪˈlɪvəri/ **noun** (plural **deliveries**) **1** the action of delivering something 投递；送交 **2** the process of giving birth 分娩 **3** an act of throwing or bowling a ball 投球

dell /del/ **noun** literary 【文】 a small valley 小山谷

delphinium /delˈfɪniəm/ **noun** (plural **delphiniums**) a garden plant that has tall spikes of blue flowers 翠雀，飞燕草（高株园艺植物，开蓝花）

delta /ˈdeltə/ **noun 1** an area of land where the mouth of a river has split into several channels 三角洲 **2** the fourth letter of the Greek alphabet (Δ, δ) 希腊语字母表的第4个字母

delude /dɪˈluːd/ **verb** (**deludes, deluding, deluded**) persuade someone to believe something that is not true 欺骗；哄骗

deluge /ˈdeljuːdʒ/ **noun 1** a severe flood or very heavy fall of rain 洪水；大雨；暴雨 **2** a great quantity of something arriving at the same time 蜂拥而至的事物：*a deluge of complaints* 大量投诉 • **verb** (**deluges, deluging, deluged**) **1** overwhelm someone with a great quantity of something 使充满 **2** flood a place 使泛滥；淹没

delusion /dɪˈluːʒn/ **noun** a mistaken belief or impression 谬见；错觉 ■ **delusional** adjective.

de luxe /də ˈlʌks/ **adjective** of a higher quality than usual 高级的；豪华的

delve /delv/ **verb** (**delves, delving, delved**) **1** reach inside a container and search for something（在容器中）翻找 **2** research something very thoroughly 探索；钻研

demagnetize or **demagnetise** /ˌdiːˈmægnətaɪz/ **verb** (**demagnetizes**, **demagnetizing**, **demagnetized**) stop something being magnetic 使去磁；使消磁

demagogue /ˈdeməgɒg/ **noun** a political leader who appeals to people's desires and prejudices rather than using reasoned arguments 蛊惑民心的政客；煽动家

demand /dɪˈmɑːnd/ **noun 1** a very firm request for something（坚决的）要求，请求 **2** (**demands**) tasks or requirements that are urgent or difficult（迫切或困难的）任务，要求 **3** the desire of consumers for a particular product or service（顾客对产品或服务的）需要，需求 • **verb 1** ask very firmly（坚决）要求 **2** insist on having 坚持要拥有 **3** require; need 要求；需要 □ **in demand** wanted by many people 需求大的

demanding /dɪˈmɑːndɪŋ/ **adjective** needing a lot of skill or effort 需要技能；费力的

demarcate /ˈdiːmɑːkeɪt/ **verb** (**demarcates**, **demarcating**, **demarcated**) set the boundaries of 给…划界 ■ **demarcation** noun.

dematerialize or **dematerialise** /ˌdiːməˈtɪərɪəlaɪz/ **verb** (**dematerializes**, **dematerializing**, **dematerialized**) stop being physically present 非物质化；消失

demean /dɪˈmiːn/ **verb** make someone lose dignity or respect 使失去尊严；贬损

demeanour /dɪˈmiːnə(r)/ (US spelling 【美拼作】**demeanor**) **noun** the way a person behaves or looks 行为；举止；外表；风度

demented /dɪˈmentɪd/ **adjective 1** suffering from dementia 痴呆的 **2** informal 【非正式】wild and irrational 发狂的；精神错乱的

dementia /dɪˈmenʃə/ **noun** a disorder in which a person is unable to remember things or think clearly 痴呆；精神错乱

demerara sugar /ˌdeməˈreərə/ **noun** a type of light brown sugar 德麦拉拉蔗糖

demerit /diːˈmerɪt/ **noun** a fault or disadvantage 过失；缺点

demigod /ˈdemigɒd/ **noun** a being that is partly a god and partly a human 半神半人

demilitarize or **demilitarise** /ˌdiːˈmɪlɪtəraɪz/ **verb** (**demilitarizes**, **demilitarizing**, **demilitarized**) remove all military forces from an area 从…撤军；使（某地区）非军事化 ■ **demilitarization** noun.

demi-monde /ˌdemiˈmɒnd/ **noun** a group of people on the fringes of respectable society 名声不好的一群人

demise /dɪˈmaɪz/ **noun 1** a person's death 死亡 **2** the end or failure of something 终止；失败

demo /ˈdeməʊ/ **noun** (plural **demos**) informal 【非正式】**1** a political demonstration 政治示威 **2** a tape or disc containing a demonstration of a performer's music or a piece of software 录音样带；试样唱片；试用软件

demob /ˌdiːˈmɒb/ **verb** (**demobs**, **demobbing**, **demobbed**) Brit. informal 【英，非正式】demobilize 遣散（部队）；使退伍

demobilize or **demobilise** /ˌdiːˈməʊbəlaɪz/ **verb** (**demobilizes**, **demobilizing**, **demobilized**) take troops out of active service 遣散（部队）；使退伍 ■ **demobilization** noun.

democracy /dɪˈmɒkrəsi/ **noun** (plural **democracies**) **1** a form of government in which the people can vote for representatives to govern the state on their behalf 民主制度; 民主政体 **2** a state governed in this way 民主国家

democrat /'deməkræt/ **noun 1** a supporter of democracy 民主主义者; 民主人士 **2** (**Democrat**) (in the US) a member of the Democratic Party (美国的)民主党党员,民主党人

democratic /ˌdeməˈkrætɪk/ **adjective 1** relating to or supporting democracy 民主的;支持民主的 **2** based on the principle that everyone in society is equal 有民主原则的,平等的 **3** (**Democratic**) (in the US) relating to or supporting the Democratic Party (美国)民主党的,支持民主党的 ■ **democratically** adverb.

democratize or **democratise** /dɪˈmɒkrətaɪz/ **verb** (**democratizes**, **democratizing**, **democratized**) introduce a democratic system or democratic ideas to 使民主化 ■ **democratization** noun.

demography /dɪˈmɒgrəfi/ **noun** the study of changes in human populations using records of the numbers of births, deaths, etc. in a particular area 人口学;人口统计学 ■ **demographic** adjective.

demolish /dɪˈmɒlɪʃ/ **verb 1** knock down a building 拆除,拆毁(建筑物) **2** show that a theory is completely wrong 推翻(某理论) **3** humorous【幽默】 eat up food quickly 狼吞虎咽地吃(食物) ■ **demolition** noun

demon /'diːmən/ **noun** an evil spirit or devil 恶魔,鬼魅 • **adjective** very forceful or skilful 强有力的;技艺出众的: *a demon cook* 技艺高超的厨师

demoniac /dɪˈməʊniæk/ or **demoniacal** /ˌdiːməʊˈnaɪəkl/ **adjective** demonic 恶魔的;魔鬼的

demonic /diːˈmɒnɪk/ **adjective** having to do with demons or evil spirits 恶魔的;魔鬼的 ■ **demonically** adverb.

demonize or **demonise** /ˈdiːmənaɪz/ **verb** (**demonizes**, **demonizing**, **demonized**) portray someone as wicked and threatening 妖魔化;丑化

demonstrable /dɪˈmɒnstrəbl/ **adjective** clearly apparent or able to be proved 显而易见的;可证明的;可论证的 ■ **demonstrably** adverb.

demonstrate /ˈdemənstreɪt/ **verb** (**demonstrates**, **demonstrating**, **demonstrated**) **1** clearly show that something exists or is true 论证,证明 **2** show and explain how something works 示范;演示 **3** express a feeling or quality by your actions 显示,表露(情感或品质) **4** take part in a public demonstration 游行示威 ■ **demonstrator** noun.

demonstration /ˌdemənˈstreɪʃn/ **noun 1** the action of demonstrating 论证,证明;演示 **2** a public meeting or march expressing an opinion on an issue 示威集会,示威游行

demonstrative /dɪˈmɒnstrətɪv/ **adjective 1** tending to show your feelings openly 公开表露感情的;感情外露的 **2** demonstrating something 论证的,证明的 ■ **demonstratively** adverb.

demoralize or **demoralise** /dɪˈmɒrəlaɪz/ **verb** (**demoralizes**, **demoralizing**, **demoralized**) make someone lose confidence or hope 使士气低落;使泄气 ■ **demoralization** noun.

demote /diːˈməʊt/ **verb** (**demotes**, **demoting**, **demoted**) move someone to a less senior position 使降级;使降低地位 ■ **demotion** noun.

demotivate /ˌdiːˈməʊtɪveɪt/ **verb** make someone less eager to work or make an effort 使失去动力;使变得

消极

demur /dɪ'mɜː(r)/ **verb** (**demurs**, **demurring**, **demurred**) show reluctance 不愿 □ **without demur** without objecting or hesitating 毫无异议地；毫不犹豫地 ■ **demurral** noun.

demure /dɪ'mjʊə(r)/ **adjective** (of a woman) reserved, modest, and shy (女子)矜持的、娴静的、端庄的 ■ **demurely** adverb.

demystify /ˌdiː'mɪstɪfaɪ/ **verb** (**demystifies**, **demystifying**, **demystified**) make a subject less difficult to understand 使浅显易懂

den /den/ **noun 1** a wild animal's lair or home 兽穴；兽窝 **2** informal【非正式】a person's private room 私室 **3** a place where people meet to do something immoral or forbidden (从事邪恶或非法活动的)巢穴，窝点：*an opium den* 鸦片烟窟

denationalize or **denationalise** /ˌdiː'næʃnəlaɪz/ **verb** (**denationalizes**, **denationalizing**, **denationalized**) transfer an industry or business from public to private ownership 使非国有化；使私有化

denial /dɪ'naɪəl/ **noun 1** a statement that something is not true 否认；否定 **2** the refusal to acknowledge or accept something unpleasant 拒绝承认；拒绝接受：*He's still in denial.* 他仍然拒绝接受。

denier /'deniə(r)/ **noun** a unit for measuring the fineness of nylon or silk 旦尼尔，旦(纱线的纤度单位)

denigrate /'denɪɡreɪt/ **verb** (**denigrates**, **denigrating**, **denigrated**) criticize someone unfairly 诋毁；诽谤 ■ **denigration** noun.

denim /'denɪm/ **noun 1** a hard-wearing cotton fabric 粗斜棉布；牛仔布 **2** (**denims**) jeans or other clothes made of denim 牛仔裤；劳动布衣服

denizen /'denɪzn/ **noun** formal【正式】an inhabitant or occupant 居民；居住者

denominate /dɪ'nɒmɪneɪt/ **verb** (**denominates**, **denominating**, **denominated**) formal【正式】call; name 称呼；命名

denomination /dɪˌnɒmɪ'neɪʃn/ **noun 1** a recognized branch of a Church or religion 教派；宗派 **2** the face value of a banknote, coin, postage stamp, etc. (纸币、硬币、邮票等的)面额，面值 **3** formal【正式】a name or designation 名称；称谓 ■ **denominational** adjective.

denominator /dɪ'nɒmɪneɪtə(r)/ **noun** Maths【数学】the number below the line in a fraction, for example 4 in 1/4 (分数的)分母

denote /dɪ'nəʊt/ **verb** (**denotes**, **denoting**, **denoted**) **1** be a sign of 表示；标志；预示；象征 **2** (of a word) have something as a main meaning (单词)意思是

denouement /deɪ'nuːmɒn/ **noun** the final part of a play, film, or story, in which matters are explained or settled (戏剧、电影或小说的)结局，收场

denounce /dɪ'naʊns/ **verb** (**denounces**, **denouncing**, **denounced**) publicly declare that someone is wrong or evil 谴责；指责；痛斥

dense /dens/ **adjective 1** containing many people or things crowded closely together 拥挤的；稠密的 **2** having a thick or closely packed texture 密集的；密度大的 **3** informal【非正式】stupid 愚蠢的；迟钝的 ■ **densely** adverb.

density /'densəti/ **noun** (plural **densities**) **1** the degree to which something is dense 密集；稠密；密度 **2** the quantity of people or things in a given area (某区域内人或物的)密度

dent /dent/ **noun** a slight hollow in a surface made by a blow or pressure

凹痕；凹坑 • verb 1 mark with a dent 使凹陷；使产生凹痕 2 have a bad effect on 削弱；损害

dental /'dentl/ **adjective** relating to the teeth or to dentistry 牙齿的；牙科学的

dentine /'denti:n/ **noun** the hard, bony tissue that teeth are made of 牙质；牙本质

dentist /'dentɪst/ **noun** a person who is qualified to treat the diseases and conditions that affect the teeth and gums 牙科医生；牙医 ■ **dentistry** noun.

denture /'dentʃə(r)/ **noun** a removable plate or frame fitted with one or more false teeth 义齿；托牙

denude /dɪ'nju:d/ **verb** (**denudes, denuding, denuded**) make something bare or empty 使裸露；使光秃

denunciation /dɪ,nʌnsɪ'eɪʃn/ **noun** the action of denouncing 谴责；指责

deny /dɪ'naɪ/ **verb** (**denies, denying, denied**) 1 state that something is not true 否定 2 refuse to admit something 否认 3 refuse to give someone a thing that they want 拒绝给予（想要之物）4 (**deny yourself**) go without something you want 节制；戒绝

deodorant /di'əʊdərənt/ **noun** a substance which prevents unpleasant bodily odours（除体臭的）除臭剂，解臭剂

deodorize or **deodorise** /di'əʊdəraɪz/ **verb** (**deodorizes, deodorizing, deodorized**) prevent an unpleasant smell in 除去…的臭味;脱去…的臭味

depart /dɪ'pɑ:t/ **verb** 1 leave; go away 离开；离去 2 (**depart from**) do something different from the usual or accepted thing 违反；背离

departed /dɪ'pɑ:tɪd/ **adjective** deceased; dead 死去的；已故的

department /dɪ'pɑ:tmənt/ **noun** 1 a division of a large organization or building 部；系；科；部门 2 an administrative district in some countries, e.g. France（某些国家的）行政区 3 informal【非正式】 a person's area of special knowledge or responsibility（某人的）专长，责任范围 □ **department store** a large shop that stocks many types of goods in different departments 百货商店；百货公司 ■ **departmental** adjective **departmentally** adverb.

departure /dɪ'pɑ:tʃə(r)/ **noun** 1 the action of leaving 离开；离去 2 a change from the usual way of doing something 违反；背离

depend /dɪ'pend/ **verb** (**depend on**) 1 be determined by 取决于 2 rely on 依靠；依赖

dependable /dɪ'pendəbl/ **adjective** trustworthy and reliable 可靠的；可信赖的 ■ **dependability** noun **dependably** adverb.

dependant or **dependent** /dɪ'pendənt/ **noun** a person who relies on another for financial support 受抚养者；靠他人生活者

! 注意 the noun can be spelled **dependant** or **dependent**. The adjective is always spelled **dependent**. 该词的名词形式可拼作 dependant 或 dependent，形容词形式总是拼作 dependent。

dependency /dɪ'pendənsi/ **noun** (plural **dependencies**) 1 a country or province controlled by another 附属国；附属地 2 the state of being dependent 依赖；依赖

dependent /dɪ'pendənt/ **adjective** 1 (**dependent on**) determined by 取决于…的 2 relying on someone or something for support 依赖的；依赖 3 (**dependent on**) unable to do without 对…有瘾的 • **noun** ⇨ 见 DEPENDANT. ■ **dependence** noun **dependently** adverb.

depict /dɪˈpɪkt/ **verb 1** represent something by a drawing, painting, or other art form 描画；描绘 **2** portray in words 描写；描述 ■ **depiction** noun.

depilate /ˈdepɪleɪt/ **verb** (**depilates, depilating, depilated**) remove the hair from 除毛；使脱毛 ■ **depilation** noun **depilatory** adjective.

deplete /dɪˈpliːt/ **verb** (**depletes, depleting, depleted**) reduce the number or quantity of 减少 ■ **depletion** noun.

deplorable /dɪˈplɔːrəbl/ **adjective** shockingly bad 糟糕的；悲惨的 ■ **deplorably** adverb.

deplore /dɪˈplɔː(r)/ **verb** (**deplores, deploring, deplored**) strongly disapprove of 强烈反对；谴责

deploy /dɪˈplɔɪ/ **verb 1** bring or move forces into position for military action 部署，调度(军队) **2** use a resource or quality effectively (充分)利用 ■ **deployment** noun.

depopulate /ˌdiːˈpɒpjuleɪt/ **verb** (**depopulates, depopulating, depopulated**) greatly reduce the population of a place 使人口剧减 ■ **depopulation** noun.

deport /dɪˈpɔːt/ **verb** expel a foreigner or immigrant from a country 把(外国人或移民)驱逐出境 ■ **deportation** noun **deportee** noun.

deportment /dɪˈpɔːtmənt/ **noun 1** the way a person stands and walks 仪态；风度 **2** N. Amer. 【北美】 a person's behaviour or manners 行为；举止

depose /dɪˈpəʊz/ **verb** (**deposes, deposing, deposed**) remove someone from office suddenly and forcefully 罢免；废黜

deposit /dɪˈpɒzɪt/ **noun 1** a sum of money placed in an account 存款 **2** a payment made as a first instalment in buying something 订金；首付款 **3** a returnable sum paid when renting something, to cover possible loss or damage 押金 **4** a layer of a substance that has built up (一层)沉积物 ● **verb** (**deposits, depositing, deposited**) **1** put something down in a particular place 放下；放置 **2** store something somewhere for safe-keeping 存放；寄存 **3** pay a sum as a deposit 支付(订金)；付(押金) **4** lay down a layer of a substance 使沉淀，使沉积

deposition /ˌdepəˈzɪʃn/ **noun 1** the action of deposing someone from office 罢免；废黜 **2** Law 【法律】 a sworn statement to be used as evidence in a court of law 证词；证言 **3** the action of depositing 存放；沉淀；沉积

depository /dɪˈpɒzɪtri/ **noun** (plural **depositories**) a place where things are stored 仓库；储藏处

depot /ˈdepəʊ/ **noun 1** a place where large quantities of goods are stored (大宗商品的)储藏处，仓库 **2** a place where vehicles are kept and maintained 车库；修车厂 **3** N. Amer. 【北美】 /ˈdiːpəʊ/ a railway or bus station 火车站；公共汽车站

deprave /dɪˈpreɪv/ **verb** (**depraves, depraving, depraved**) make someone morally bad; corrupt someone 使道德败坏；使堕落；使腐化

depravity /dɪˈprævəti/ **noun** immoral behaviour or character 道德败坏，堕落，腐化

deprecate /ˈdeprəkeɪt/ **verb** (**deprecates, deprecating, deprecated**) express disapproval of 不赞成；反对 ■ **deprecation** noun.

depreciate /dɪˈpriːʃieɪt/ **verb** (**depreciates, depreciating, depreciated**) **1** decrease in value over a period of time 跌价；贬值 **2** dismiss something as being unimportant 轻视，贬低 ■ **depreciation** noun.

depredations /ˌdeprəˈdeɪʃnz/ **plural**

noun acts that cause harm or damage 劫掠；蹂躏；破坏

depress /dɪ'pres/ **verb 1** make someone feel very unhappy 使抑郁；使沮丧 **2** make something less active 降低；削弱 **3** push or pull down 按下；压下

depressant /dɪ'presnt/ **noun** a drug or other substance that slows down the natural processes of the body（药物等物质）起抑制作用的

depressed /dɪ'prest/ **adjective 1** feeling very unhappy and without hope 抑郁的；意志消沉的 **2** suffering the damaging effects of an economic slump 不景气的；萧条的

depression /dɪ'preʃn/ **noun 1** a mental state in which a person has feelings of great unhappiness and hopelessness 抑郁；消沉 **2** a long and severe slump in an economy or market 不景气；萧条 **3** the action of depressing 降低；按下 **4** a sunken or hollow place 洼地；凹地；凹陷 **5** an area of low pressure which may bring rain 低气压带

depressive /dɪ'presɪv/ **adjective** tending to cause or feel depression 令人抑郁的；令人沮丧的

deprivation /ˌdeprɪ'veɪʃn/ **noun 1** hardship resulting from not having enough of the things necessary for life 匮乏；贫困 **2** the action of depriving someone of something 夺去；剥夺

deprive /dɪ'praɪv/ **verb** (**deprives, depriving, deprived**) prevent someone from having or using something 剥夺；使丧失；使不能享有

deprived /dɪ'praɪvd/ **adjective** not having enough of the things necessary for life 贫困的；匮乏的

Dept **abbreviation** Department.

depth /depθ/ **noun 1** the distance from the top or surface down, or from front to back 深度；纵深 **2** complex or meaningful thought（思想的）深刻，深奥 **3** extensive and detailed study 渊博 **4** strength of emotion（情感的）深厚，深切 **5** (**the depths**) the deepest, lowest, or innermost part of something 最低处；最里面 □ **depth charge** a device designed to explode under water, used for attacking submarines 深水炸弹

deputation /ˌdepju'teɪʃn/ **noun** a group of people who are sent to do something on behalf of a larger group 代表团

depute /dɪ'pjuːt/ **verb** (**deputes, deputing, deputed**) instruct someone to do something that you are responsible for 委派（某人）；把（任务）交托给

deputize or **deputise** /'depjutaɪz/ **verb** (**deputizes, deputizing, deputized**) temporarily act on behalf of someone else 担任代表；充当代理人

deputy /'depjuti/ **noun** (plural **deputies**) a person appointed to do the work of a more senior person in that person's absence 代表；代理人

derail /dɪ'reɪl/ **verb 1** make a train leave the tracks 使（火车）出轨，使脱轨 **2** prevent a process from following its intended course 使离开正常进程；干扰 ■ **derailment** noun.

deranged /dɪ'reɪndʒd/ **adjective** mad; insane 发疯的；发狂的 ■ **derangement** noun.

derby /'dɑːbi/ **noun** (plural **derbies**) a sports match between two rival teams from the same area（两支本地参赛队的）同城比赛，德比比赛

deregulate /ˌdiː'regjuleɪt/ **verb** (**deregulates, deregulating, deregulated**) remove regulations or restrictions from 撤销对…的管制；解除对…的限制 ■ **deregulation** noun.

derelict /'derəlɪkt/ **adjective** in a very bad condition as a result of disuse and neglect 荒废的；被弃置的；破败的 • **noun** a person without a home, job, or property 无家可归者；社会弃儿

dereliction /ˌderəˈlɪkʃn/ **noun 1** an abandoned and run-down state 荒废；被弃置，破败不堪 **2** (usu. **dereliction of duty**) shameful failure to do something you are supposed to do 玩忽职守；渎职

deride /dɪˈraɪd/ **verb** (**derides**, **deriding**, **derided**) express contempt for; ridicule 嘲笑；取笑；嘲弄

de rigueur /də rɪˈɡɜː(r)/ **adjective** necessary if you want to be accepted socially 合乎礼节的；按照时尚的

derision /dɪˈrɪʒn/ **noun** scornful ridicule or mockery 嘲笑；嘲弄

derisive /dɪˈraɪsɪv/ **adjective** expressing contempt or ridicule 嘲笑的 ■ **derisively** adverb.

derisory /dɪˈraɪsəri/ **adjective 1** ridiculously small or inadequate 少得可怜的；微不足道的 **2** expressing contempt or ridicule; derisive 嘲笑的，嘲弄的

derivation /ˌderɪˈveɪʃn/ **noun 1** the obtaining of something from a source 得到；溯源 **2** the formation of a word from another word （词的）派生

derivative /dɪˈrɪvətɪv/ **adjective** imitating the work of another artist, writer, etc.; not original 模仿他人的；缺乏独创性的 • **noun** something which comes from or is based on another source 派生物；衍生物

derive /dɪˈraɪv/ **verb** (**derives**, **deriving**, **derived**) **1** (**derive something from**) obtain something from a source 从…得到，从…获得 **2** (**derive from**) originate or develop from 起源于；来自

dermatitis /ˌdɜːməˈtaɪtɪs/ **noun** inflammation of the skin as a result of irritation or an allergic reaction 皮炎

dermatology /ˌdɜːməˈtɒlədʒi/ **noun** the branch of medicine concerned with skin disorders 皮肤病学 ■ **dermatological** adjective **dermatologist** noun.

derogatory /dɪˈrɒɡətri/ **adjective** critical or disrespectful 贬低的，不敬的

derrick /ˈderɪk/ **noun 1** a type of crane 转臂起重机 **2** the framework over an oil well for holding the drilling machinery （油井的）井架

derring-do /ˌderɪŋˈduː/ **noun** old use 【旧】heroic actions 大胆的行动；英勇行为

dervish /ˈdɜːvɪʃ/ **noun** a member of a Muslim religious group, some orders of which are known for their wild rituals （伊斯兰教的）托钵僧，苦行僧

descant /ˈdeskænt/ **noun** an independent melody sung or played above a basic melody 高于主音的旋律

descend /dɪˈsend/ **verb 1** move down or downwards 下来；下降 **2** slope or lead downwards 下倾；下斜 **3** (**descend to**) do something very shameful 降低身份去做，堕落到去做（可耻之事）**4** (**descend on**) make a sudden attack on or unwelcome visit to 突然袭击；贸然造访 **5** (**be descended from**) have a particular person as an ancestor 是…的后裔

descendant /dɪˈsendənt/ **noun** a person that is descended from a particular ancestor 后裔；后代

> ✔ 拼写指南 the correct spelling of the noun **descendant** is with *-ant*, not *-ent*, at the end. 名词 descendant 词末的正确拼法是-ant，而不是-ent。

descent /dɪˈsent/ **noun 1** an act of descending 下降 **2** a downward slope 斜坡；坡道 **3** a person's origin or nationality 血统；世系

describe /dɪˈskraɪb/ **verb** (**describes**, **describing**, **described**) **1** give a detailed account of something in words 描写;描述;形容 **2** mark out or draw a shape 画出(图形)

description /dɪˈskrɪpʃn/ **noun 1** a spoken or written account (口头或书面)描述,叙述 **2** the process of describing 描写;描述;形容 **3** a sort, kind, or class 种类;类型: *people of any description* 各色人等

descriptive /dɪˈskrɪptɪv/ **adjective** describing something, especially in a vivid style 描写的;叙述的 ■ **descriptively** adverb.

descry /dɪˈskraɪ/ **verb** (**descries**, **descrying**, **descried**) literary 【文】 catch sight of 看见,发现

desecrate /ˈdesɪkreɪt/ **verb** (**desecrates**, **desecrating**, **desecrated**) damage something sacred or treat it with great disrespect 亵渎(圣物) ■ **desecration** noun.

desegregate /ˌdiːˈseɡrɪɡeɪt/ **verb** (**desegregates**, **desegregating**, **desegregated**) end a policy by which people of different races are kept separate 废除种族隔离 ■ **desegregation** noun.

deselect /ˌdiːsɪˈlekt/ **verb** Brit.【英】 (of a local branch of a political party) reject an existing MP as a candidate in a forthcoming election (政党的地方分支机构)否决(现任议员)担任下届候选人 ■ **deselection** noun.

desensitise or **desensitise** /ˌdiːˈsensətaɪz/ **verb** (**desensitizes**, **desensitizing**, **desensitized**) make less sensitive 使不敏感

desert[1] /dɪˈzɜːt/ **verb 1** leave someone without help or support 抛弃,遗弃(某人) **2** leave a place, making it seem empty 舍弃,离开(某地) **3** illegally leave the armed forces 擅自离开(军队);从(军队)开小差 ■ **deserter** noun **desertion** noun.

desert[2] /ˈdezət/ **noun** an empty, waterless area of land with very few plants 沙漠 □ **desert island** an uninhabited tropical island (热带)荒岛

! 注意 don't confuse **desert** (a waterless area) with **dessert** (the sweet course)! 不要混淆 desert (沙漠)和 dessert (甜点)!

deserts /dɪˈzɜːts/ **plural noun** (**get your just deserts**) get the reward or punishment that you deserve 得到应得的奖赏(或惩罚)

deserve /dɪˈzɜːv/ **verb** (**deserves**, **deserving**, **deserved**) do something worthy of a particular reward or punishment 应受,应得(奖赏或惩罚) ■ **deservedly** adverb.

deserving /dɪˈzɜːvɪŋ/ **adjective** worthy of being treated well or helped 应得的;值得的

déshabillé /ˌdeɪzæˈbiːjeɪ/ **noun** the state of being only partly clothed 衣着仅部分蔽体

desiccate /ˈdesɪkeɪt/ **verb** (**desiccates**, **desiccating**, **desiccated**) remove the moisture from 使干燥;脱去…的水分 ■ **desiccation** noun.

design /dɪˈzaɪn/ **noun 1** a plan or drawing produced before something is made 图样;草图 **2** the production of such plans or drawings (图样或草图)的)设计,构思 **3** purpose or deliberate planning 意图;目的;计划;规划 **4** a decorative pattern 装饰图案 • **verb 1** produce a design for 设计;构思 **2** (**be designed**) be intended for a purpose 计划;打算 □ **have designs on** aim to obtain 图谋得到

designate /ˈdezɪɡneɪt/ **verb** (**designates**, **designating**, **designated**) **1** officially give a particular status or name to something 命名 **2** appoint someone to a job or position 选派;委任 • **adjective** /ˈdezɪɡnət/ appointed to a position but not yet having taken it up 已被任命

而未就职的;候任的: the Director designate 候任局长

designation /ˌdezɪɡˈneɪʃn/ **noun 1** the action of designating 指定;命名;选派;委任 **2** an official title or description 名称;称号

designer /dɪˈzaɪnə(r)/ **noun** a person who designs things 设计者 • **adjective** made by a famous fashion designer由著名时装设计师设计的: designer jeans 著名时装设计师设计的牛仔裤

desirable /dɪˈzaɪərəbl/ **adjective 1** wished for as being attractive, useful, or necessary 值得拥有的;吸引人的;必要的 **2** (of a person) sexually attractive (人)引起性欲的,性感的 ■ **desirability** noun.

desire /dɪˈzaɪə(r)/ **noun** a strong feeling of wanting to have something or wishing for something to happen 渴望;欲望;愿望 • **verb** (**desires, desiring, desired**) **1** strongly wish for or want 渴望;盼望 **2** 非常想要 **2** find someone attractive 被(某人)吸引

desirous /dɪˈzaɪərəs/ **adjective** (**desirous of** or **to do**) wanting a particular thing 渴望的

desist /dɪˈzɪst/ **verb** stop doing something 停止;中止

desk /desk/ **noun 1** a piece of furniture with a flat or sloping surface for writing on 书桌;写字台;办公桌 **2** a counter in a hotel, bank, etc. (旅馆、银行等的)问讯处,服务台

desktop /ˈdesktɒp/ **noun 1** a computer suitable to be used at a desk 台式计算机 **2** the area of a computer screen that you can work in (计算机屏幕的)桌面

desolate adjective /ˈdesələt/ **1** (of a place) bleak and empty (地方)荒凉的,荒无人烟的 **2** very unhappy 忧伤的 • **verb** /ˈdesəleɪt/ (**be desolated**) be very unhappy 极度伤心 ■ **desolation** noun.

despair /dɪˈspeə(r)/ **noun** the complete loss or absence of hope 绝望 • **verb** lose hope, or be without hope 绝望;失去希望

✔ 拼写指南 des-, not dis-: despair. despair 中的des-不要拼作dis-。

despatch /dɪˈspætʃ/ ⇒见 DISPATCH.

desperado /ˌdespəˈrɑːdəʊ/ **noun** (plural **desperadoes** or **desperados**) a reckless and dangerous criminal 暴徒;亡命徒

desperate /ˈdespərət/ **adjective 1** feeling, showing, or involving despair 绝望的 **2** done when everything else has failed 孤注一掷的;铤而走险的 **3** very serious 极严重的;危急的: a desperate shortage 严重短缺 **4** needing or wanting something very much 极需要的;极渴望的 ■ **desperately** adverb **desperation** noun.

✔ 拼写指南 desperate, not -parate. desperate不要拼作-parate。

despicable /dɪˈspɪkəbl/ **adjective** deserving hatred and contempt 令人厌恶的;卑鄙的;可耻的 ■ **despicably** adverb.

despise /dɪˈspaɪz/ **verb** (**despise, despising, despised**) hate or feel disgusted by 鄙视;藐视;看不起

despite /dɪˈspaɪt/ **preposition** in spite of 不管;尽管;任凭

despoil /dɪˈspɔɪl/ **verb** literary 【文】 steal valuable possessions from a place 掠夺;劫掠

despondent /dɪˈspɒndənt/ **adjective** very sad and without much hope 沮丧的;泄气的 ■ **despondency** noun **despondently** adverb.

despot /ˈdespɒt/ **noun** a ruler with unlimited power 专制统治者;极权君主 ■ **despotic** adjective **despotism** noun.

dessert /dɪˈzɜːt/ **noun** the sweet course eaten at the end of a meal (餐

后吃的)甜点,甜食

dessertspoon /dɪˈzɜːtspuːn/ **noun** a spoon smaller than a tablespoon and larger than a teaspoon 点心匙(比汤匙小,比茶匙大)

! 注意 don't confuse **dessert** (the sweet course) with **desert** (a waterless area)! 不要混淆 dessert (甜点)和 desert (沙漠)!

destabilize or **destabilise** /ˌdiːˈsteɪbəlaɪz/ **verb** (**destabilizes, destabilizing, destabilized**) make a country or government less stable 使(国家或政府)不稳定;破坏…的稳定

destination /ˌdestɪˈneɪʃn/ **noun** the place to which someone or something is going or being sent 目的地;终点

destine /ˈdestɪn/ **verb 1** (**be destined for** or **to**) be intended for a particular purpose, or certain to do or be a particular thing 注定;指定 **2** (**be destined for**) be on the way to a particular place 开往;前往

destiny /ˈdestəni/ **noun** (plural **destinies**) **1** the things that will happen to a person 命运;天命;定数 **2** the hidden power believed to control what will happen in the future 主宰命运的力量;命运之神

destitute /ˈdestɪtjuːt/ **adjective** very poor and without a home or other things necessary for life 穷困的;赤贫的 ■ **destitution** noun.

destroy /dɪˈstrɔɪ/ **verb 1** make something stop existing by damaging or attacking it 破坏;毁灭;摧毁 **2** kill a sick or unwanted animal using a humane method (人道地)消灭,杀死(动物)

destroyer /dɪˈstrɔɪə(r)/ **noun 1** a person or thing that destroys 破坏者;毁灭者;起破坏作用的东西 **2** a small, fast warship 驱逐舰

destruction /dɪˈstrʌkʃn/ **noun** the destroying of something 破坏;毁灭;消灭

destructive /dɪˈstrʌktɪv/ **adjective 1** causing destruction 破坏性的;毁灭性的 **2** negative and unhelpful 负面的;无用的 ■ **destructively** adverb.

desultory /ˈdesəltri/ **adjective** lacking enthusiasm or a definite plan 无目的的;散漫的 ■ **desultorily** adverb.

detach /dɪˈtætʃ/ **verb 1** remove something that is attached to something larger 拆卸;使分开;使分离 **2** (**be detached**) Military 〖军事〗 be sent on a mission 被派遣;被分遣 ■ **detachable** adjective.

✔ 拼写指南 **-ach**, not **-atch**: det**ach**. detach中的-ach不要拼作-atch.

detached /dɪˈtætʃt/ **adjective 1** separate or disconnected 独立的;分离的;不连接的 **2** not involved or interested; aloof 客观的;公正的;超然的

detachment /dɪˈtætʃmənt/ **noun 1** a feeling of being uninvolved or aloof 超然;超脱 **2** a group of troops, ships, etc. sent away on a mission 分遣队;独立小分队;特遣舰队

detail /ˈdiːteɪl/ **noun 1** a small individual item or fact 枝节;细节 **2** small items or facts as a group 详情;细节: *attention to detail* 对细节的关注 **3** a small part of a picture reproduced separately (图画的)细部, 局部 **4** a small group of troops or police officers given a special duty 特遣队;小分队 • **verb 1** describe something item by item 详述;说明 **2** instruct someone to undertake a particular task 派遣;指派

detailed /ˈdiːteɪld/ **adjective** having many details 详细的;详尽的

detain /dɪˈteɪn/ **verb 1** keep someone back 留住;阻止离开 **2** keep someone in custody 拘留;扣押

detainee /ˌdiːteɪˈniː/ **noun** a person who is kept in custody 被拘留者；被扣押者

detect /dɪˈtekt/ **verb 1** discover or notice that something is present 查出；察觉；发现 **2** discover or investigate a crime or criminal 侦查出；查明 ■ **detectable** adjective **detection** noun.

detective /dɪˈtektɪv/ **noun** a person whose job is investigating crimes 侦探

detector /dɪˈtektə(r)/ **noun** a device designed to detect that something, e.g. smoke or gas, is present 探测器

détente /deɪˈtɑːnt/ **noun** the easing of hostility or strained relations between countries（国家间紧张关系的）缓和

detention /dɪˈtenʃn/ **noun 1** the state of being kept in custody 拘留；扣押 **2** the punishment of being kept in school after hours（惩罚学生的）课后留校，留堂

deter /dɪˈtɜː(r)/ **verb** (**deters, deterring, deterred**) **1** make someone decide not to do something because they are afraid of the consequences 威慑住；吓住 **2** prevent something happening 阻止；制止；防止

detergent /dɪˈtɜːdʒənt/ **noun** a chemical substance used for removing dirt and grease 洗涤剂；去垢剂

deteriorate /dɪˈtɪəriəreɪt/ **verb** (**deteriorates, deteriorating, deteriorated**) become gradually worse 恶化；衰退 ■ **deterioration** noun.

determination /dɪˌtɜːmɪˈneɪʃn/ **noun 1** persistence in continuing to do something even when it is difficult 坚定；果断；决心 **2** the process of establishing something exactly 决定；确定；规定

determine /dɪˈtɜːmɪn/ **verb 1** make

something develop in a particular way or be of a particular type 决定；确定（发展方式或类型）**2** discover the facts about something by research or calculation 查明；确定；测定 **3** firmly decide 决定；下决心

determined /dɪˈtɜːmɪnd/ **adjective** persisting in doing something even when it is difficult; resolute 已下决心的；坚定的；坚决的 ■ **determinedly** adverb.

determiner /dɪˈtɜːmɪnə(r)/ **noun 1** a person or thing that determines 决定者；起决定作用的人（或事物）**2** Grammar【语法】a word that comes before a noun to show how the noun is being used, e.g. a, the, every 限定词

deterrent /dɪˈterənt/ **noun** a thing that deters or is intended to deter 威慑物 ■ **deterrence** noun.

detest /dɪˈtest/ **verb** feel strong dislike for 厌恶；憎恶 ■ **detestable** adjective **detestation** noun.

dethrone /ˌdiːˈθrəʊn/ **verb** (**dethrones, dethroning, dethroned**) remove a ruler from power 废黜（君主）

detonate /ˈdetəneɪt/ **verb** (**detonates, detonating, detonated**) explode, or make something explode（使）爆炸 ■ **detonation** noun.

detonator /ˈdetəneɪtə(r)/ **noun** a device used to detonate an explosive 起爆装置；雷管

detour /ˈdiːtʊə(r)/ **noun** a long or roundabout route taken to avoid something or to visit something along the way 绕行的路；迂回路线

detoxify /ˌdiːˈtɒksɪfaɪ/ **verb** (**detoxifies, detoxifying, detoxified**) remove poisonous substances from 给…解毒

detract /dɪˈtrækt/ **verb** (**detract from**) make something seem less valuable or impressive 减损；诋毁；贬低

detractor /dɪˈtræktə(r)/ **noun** a person

who is critical about someone or something 贬低者

detriment /'detrɪmənt/ **noun** harm or damage 伤害；损害 ■ **detrimental** adjective **detrimentally** adverb.

detritus /dɪ'traɪtəs/ **noun** debris or waste material 瓦砾；废物

deuce /dju:s/ **noun 1** Tennis【网球】the score of 40 all in a game, at which two consecutive points are needed to win the game 局末平分(即40平) **2 (the deuce)** informal【非正式】said instead of 'devil' when making an exclamation (用于替代 devil 表示惊叹)到底，究竟

Deutschmark /'dɔɪtʃmɑːk/ **noun** the former basic unit of money in Germany 马克(德国以前的基本货币单位)

devalue /diː'væljuː/ **verb (devalues, devaluing, devalued) 1** make something seem less important than it is 降低…的价值；贬低 **2** reduce the value of a currency in relation to other currencies 使(货币)贬值 ■ **devaluation** noun.

devastate /'devəsteɪt/ **verb (devastates, devastating, devastated) 1** destroy or ruin 破坏；毁灭；摧毁 **2 (be devastated)** be overwhelmed with shock or grief 感到极为震惊；伤心欲绝 ■ **devastation** noun.

devastating /'devəsteɪtɪŋ/ **adjective 1** highly destructive 毁灭性的 破坏力极大的 **2** very distressing 令人极为悲伤的 **3** informal【非正式】very impressive or attractive 令人印象深刻的；极漂亮的 ■ **devastatingly** adverb.

develop /dɪ'veləp/ **verb (develops, developing, developed) 1** make or become larger or more advanced (使)成长；(使)发展 **2** start to exist; come into being 产生；形成 **3** start to experience or possess something

开始经历；获得 **4** convert land to a new purpose 开发(土地) **5** treat a photographic film with chemicals to make a visible image 冲洗(胶卷)；使(胶卷)显影 ■ **developer** noun.

✔ **拼写指南** there is no e at the end: deve*lop*. develop末尾没有e。

development /dɪ'veləpmənt/ **noun 1** the action of developing 成长；发展；开发；冲洗 **2** a new product or idea 新产品；新想法 **3** a new stage in a changing situation 新情况；进展 **4** an area of land with new buildings on it 新建住宅区；开发地 ■ **developmental** adjective.

deviant /'diːviənt/ **adjective** different from what is considered normal 偏常的；不正常的；离经叛道的 • **noun** disapproving【贬】a deviant person 偏常者；不正常者；离经叛道者 ■ **deviance** noun.

deviate /'diːvieɪt/ **verb (deviates, deviating, deviated)** depart from an established course or from normal standards 背离；偏离；越轨 ■ **deviation** noun.

device /dɪ'vaɪs/ **noun 1** a piece of equipment made for a particular purpose 装置；设备；器械 **2** a plan or method with a particular aim 计谋；策略；方法 **3** an emblem or design 图形；图案 □ **leave someone to their own devices** let someone do as they wish 听任(某人)自行其是

devil /'devl/ **noun 1 (the Devil)** (in Christian and Jewish belief) the most powerful spirit of evil (基督教和犹太教信仰中的)魔鬼 **2** an evil spirit 魔鬼；恶鬼 **3** a very wicked or cruel person 恶棍；残酷的人 **4** informal【非正式】a person of a particular sort 人；家伙：*the poor devil* 可怜的家伙 □ **devil-may-care** cheerful and reckless 漫不经心的；漫不经心的 **devil's advocate** a person who expresses an opinion that they do not really hold in order to provoke discussion 故意唱反调的人；为引起争辩而故意持不同意见的人

devilish /'devəlɪʃ/ **adjective 1** like a devil in evil and cruelty 邪恶的；恶毒的 **2** mischievous 调皮的；淘气的 **3** very difficult to deal with 难缠的；不好对付的 ■ **devilishly** adverb.

devilment /'devlmənt/ **noun** mischievous behaviour 恶作剧；捣蛋

devilry /'devlri/ **noun 1** wicked activity 恶行 **2** mischievous behaviour 恶作剧；捣蛋

devious /'di:viəs/ **adjective 1** behaving in a cunning way to get what you want 不光明正大的；阴险的；狡猾的 **2** (of a route or journey) indirect（路线或旅行）迂回的，绕道的 ■ **deviously** adverb **deviousness** noun.

devise /dɪ'vaɪz/ **verb** (**devises, devising, devised**) plan or invent a complex procedure or device 设计（复杂步骤）；发明（复杂装置）

devoid /dɪ'vɔɪd/ **adjective** (**devoid of**) entirely without 毫无的，没有的

devolution /,di:və'lu:ʃn/ **noun** the transfer of power by central government to local or regional governments（中央政府向地方政府的）权力下放

devolve /dɪ'vɒlv/ **verb** (**devolves, devolving, devolved**) **1** transfer power to a lower level 下放（权力）**2** (**devolve on or to**) (of responsibility) pass to（职责）移交给

devote /dɪ'vəʊt/ **verb** (**devotes, devoting, devoted**) (**devote something to**) give time or resources to 把(时间或资源)用于

devoted /dɪ'vəʊtɪd/ **adjective** very loving or loyal 挚爱的，忠诚的 ■ **devotedly** adverb.

devotee /,devə'ti:/ **noun 1** a person who is very enthusiastic about someone or something 爱好者；热心人士 **2** a follower of a particular religion or god 宗教信徒

devotion /dɪ'vəʊʃn/ **noun 1** great love or loyalty 挚爱；热爱；忠诚；忠实 **2** religious worship 宗教崇拜 **3** (**devotions**) prayers or other religious practices 祈祷；宗教仪式 ■ **devotional** adjective.

devour /dɪ'vaʊə(r)/ **verb 1** eat something greedily 吞食；狼吞虎咽地吃 **2** (of a force) destroy something completely（力量）吞没，席卷 **3** read something quickly and eagerly 如饥似渴地读

devout /dɪ'vaʊt/ **adjective 1** deeply religious 虔诚的，虔敬的 **2** earnestly sincere 真诚的；诚挚的；诚恳的：a devout hope 真诚的希望 ■ **devoutly** adverb.

dew /dju:/ **noun** tiny drops of moisture that form on cool surfaces at night, when water vapour in the air condenses 露；露水 ■ **dewy** adjective.

dewlap /'dju:læp/ **noun** a fold of loose skin hanging from the neck or throat of an animal or bird（动物或鸟类颈部或喉部下面的）垂皮，垂肉

dexterity /dek'sterəti/ **noun** skill in performing tasks 灵巧；熟练

dexterous or **dextrous** /'dekstrəs/ **adjective** showing skill, especially with the hands 灵巧的；熟练的；敏捷的 ■ **dexterously** adverb.

dhoti /'dəʊti/ **noun** (plural **dhotis**) a long piece of cloth tied around the waist, worn by some Hindu men (印度教男子系的)腰布

diabetes /,daɪə'bi:ti:z/ **noun** an illness in which the body cannot absorb sugar and starch properly because it does not have enough of the hormone insulin 糖尿病

diabetic /,daɪə'betɪk/ **adjective** having to do with diabetes 糖尿病的 ■ **noun** a person with diabetes 糖尿病患者

diabolical /,daɪə'bɒlɪkl/ **adjective 1** (also **diabolic**) relating to or like the Devil 魔鬼的，魔鬼似的 **2** informal 【非正式】 very bad 糟透的 ■ **diabolically** adverb.

diadem /'daɪədem/ noun a crown 王冠

diagnose /'daɪəgnəʊz/ verb (**diagnoses**, **diagnosing**, **diagnosed**) identify which illness or problem a person is suffering from by examining the symptoms 诊断(疾病)；判断(问题)的性质 ■ **diagnostic** adjective.

diagnosis /daɪəg'nəʊsɪs/ noun (plural **diagnoses**) the identification of which illness or problem a person is suffering from by examining the symptoms (疾病的)诊断；(问题原因的)判断

diagonal /daɪ'ægənl/ adjective **1** (of a straight line) joining opposite corners of a rectangle, square, or other figure (直线)对角线的 **2** straight and at an angle; slanting (线条)斜的 ■ noun a diagonal line 对角线；斜线 ■ **diagonally** adverb.

diagram /'daɪəgræm/ noun a simplified drawing showing the appearance or structure of something 示意图；简图；图表 ■ **diagrammatic** adjective.

dial /'daɪəl/ noun **1** a disc marked to show the time or to indicate a measurement 表盘；钟盘；标度盘；刻度盘 **2** a disc with numbered holes on a telephone, turned to make a call (电话机的)拨号盘，转盘 **3** a disc turned to choose a setting on a radio, cooker, etc. (收音机、灶具等的)调谐指示板 ■ verb (**dials**, **dialling**, **dialled**; US spelling 【美拼作】 **dials**, **dialing**, **dialed**) call a telephone number by turning a dial or pressing numbered keys 拨(电话号码)

dialect /'daɪəlekt/ noun a form of a language used in a particular region or by a particular social group 地方

话；方言；土话 ■ **dialectal** adjective.

dialectic /daɪə'lektɪk/ or **dialectics** /daɪə'lektɪks/ noun a way of discovering whether ideas are true by discussion and logical argument 辩证法 ■ **dialectical** adjective.

dialogue /'daɪəlɒg/ (US spelling 【美拼作】 **dialog**) noun **1** conversation between two or more people in a book, play, or film (书、戏剧或电影中的)对话，对白 **2** a discussion intended to explore a subject or solve a problem 对话；讨论；交换意见

dialysis /daɪ'ælɪsɪs/ noun the use of a machine to purify the blood of a person whose kidneys do not work properly 渗析；透析

diamanté /di:ə'mɒnteɪ/ adjective decorated with glass that is cut to look like diamonds 饰以人工钻石的

diameter /daɪ'æmɪtə(r)/ noun a straight line passing from side to side through the centre of a circle or sphere 直径

diametrical /daɪə'metrɪkl/ adjective **1** complete 截然的；完全的：the diametrical opposite 完全相反的对立面 **2** having to do with a diameter 直径的 ■ **diametrically** adverb.

diamond /'daɪəmənd/ noun **1** a clear precious stone, the hardest naturally occurring substance 金刚石；钻石 **2** a figure with four straight sides of equal length forming two opposite acute angles and two opposite obtuse angles 菱形 □ **diamond jubilee** the sixtieth anniversary of a notable event 六十周年纪念 **diamond wedding** Brit. 【英】 the sixtieth anniversary of a wedding 钻石婚(结婚六十周年)

diaper /'daɪəpə(r)/ noun N. Amer. 【北美】 a baby's nappy 尿布

diaphanous /daɪ'æfənəs/ adjective light, delicate, and semitransparent 轻柔的；精致的；半透明的

diaphragm /'daɪəfræm/ **noun 1** a layer of muscle between the lungs and the stomach 膈；膈膜 **2** a piece of flexible material in mechanical or sound systems 膜片；膜件；振动膜 **3** a thin rubber or plastic contraceptive device worn over the cervix（避孕用的）子宫帽

diarist /'daɪərɪst/ **noun** a person who writes a diary 记日记者

diarrhoea /ˌdaɪə'rɪə/ (US spelling【美拼作】**diarrhea**) **noun** a condition in which a person has frequent liquid bowel movements 腹泻

> ✔ 拼写指南 two *r*s, and *-hoea* at the end: dia*r*rhoea. diarrhoea 中有两个 r，词末拼作 -hoea。

diary /'daɪərɪ/ **noun** (plural **diaries**) a book in which you keep a daily record of events and experiences, or note down future appointments 日记；日志

diatonic /ˌdaɪə'tɒnɪk/ **adjective** Music【音乐】involving only the notes of the appropriate major or minor scale 自然音阶的

diatribe /'daɪətraɪb/ **noun** a speech or piece of writing forcefully attacking someone（口头或书面的）抨击，谴责

dice /daɪs/ **noun** (plural **dice**) a small cube whose sides are marked with one to six spots, used in games of chance 骰子 • **verb** (**dices**, **dicing**, **diced**) **1** cut food into small cubes 把（食物）切成小方块 **2** (**dice with**) take great risks with 拿 … 冒险；冒 … 风险: *dicing with death* 拿生命冒险

dicey /'daɪsɪ/ **adjective** (**dicier**, **diciest**) informal【非正式】difficult or risky 困难的；冒险的

dichotomy /daɪ'kɒtəmɪ/ **noun** (plural **dichotomies**) a separation or contrast between two things 一分为二；对分

dicky /'dɪkɪ/ **adjective** Brit. informal

【英，非正式】not strong, healthy, or working properly 虚弱的；不结实的；有病的；出毛病的

dictate **verb** /dɪk'teɪt/ (**dictates**, **dictating**, **dictated**) **1** give orders with great authority 强行规定；命令 **2** control or influence 支配；影响 **3** speak words for someone else to type or write down 口授；口述 • **noun** /'dɪkteɪt/ an order or principle that must be obeyed 命令；规定 ■ **dictation** noun.

dictator /dɪk'teɪtə(r)/ **noun** a ruler who has total power over a country 独裁者；专政者 ■ **dictatorial** adjective

dictatorship /ˌdɪk'teɪtəʃɪp/ **noun 1** government by a dictator 独裁政治；专政 **2** a country governed by a dictator 独裁国家；专制国家

diction /'dɪkʃn/ **noun 1** the choice and use of words in speech or writing 措词；用语 **2** a person's way of pronouncing words 咬字；发音

dictionary /'dɪkʃənrɪ/ **noun** (plural **dictionaries**) a book that lists the words of a language and gives their meaning, or their equivalent in a different language 字典；词典

dictum /'dɪktəm/ **noun** (plural **dicta** /'dɪktə/ or **dictums**) **1** a formal announcement made by someone in authority 宣言；正式声明 **2** a short statement that expresses a general principle 名言；格言

did /dɪd/ past of **do**.

didactic /daɪ'dæktɪk/ **adjective** intended to teach or give moral instruction 用于教学的；教诲的；道德说教的 ■ **didactically** adverb.

diddle /'dɪdl/ **verb** (**diddles**, **diddling**, **diddled**) informal【非正式】cheat or swindle 欺骗；哄骗

didgeridoo /ˌdɪdʒərɪ'duː/ **noun** an Australian Aboriginal musical instrument in the form of a long wooden tube, which produces a deep sound when blown 迪吉里杜管(澳大利亚土著使用的一种管乐器)

didn't /dɪdnt/ short form did not.

die¹ /daɪ/ verb (**dies, dying, died**) **1** stop living 死;死亡 **2** (**die out**) become extinct 消失;灭绝 **3** become less loud or strong 减弱;变微弱 **4** (**be dying for** or **to do**) informal 【非正式】be very eager to have or do 渴望;极想

die² noun **1** a dice 骰子 **2** (plural **dies**) a device for cutting or moulding metal or for stamping a design on to coins or medals 模具;冲模,压模 □ **die-cast** formed by pouring molten metal into a mould 压铸的

diehard /ˈdaɪhɑːd/ noun a person who stubbornly continues to support something in spite of opposition or changing circumstances 顽固分子;死硬派

diesel /ˈdiːzl/ noun **1** a type of engine in which heat produced by compressing air is used to ignite the fuel 柴油机;内燃机 **2** a form of petroleum used as fuel in diesel engines 柴油

diet /ˈdaɪət/ noun **1** the kinds of food that a person or animal usually eats 日常饮食;日常食物 **2** a limited range or amount of food, eaten in order to lose weight or for medical reasons (用于减肥或医疗目的的)特种饮食,规定饮食 • verb (**diets, dieting, dieted**) keep to a special diet in order to lose weight (为减肥而)节食,进特种饮食

dietary /ˈdaɪətri/ adjective **1** having to do with diets or dieting 饮食的;节食的 **2** provided by the food you eat 由饮食提供的

dietitian or **dietician** /ˌdaɪəˈtɪʃn/ noun an expert on diet and nutrition 饮食学家;膳食学家

differ /ˈdɪfə(r)/ verb (**differs, differing, differed**) **1** be different

不同;有区别 **2** disagree 产生分歧,持不同看法

difference /ˈdɪfrəns/ noun **1** a way in which people or things are unlike each other 差异;不同之处 **2** a disagreement or dispute 意见分歧;不和;争执 **3** what is left when one number or amount is subtracted from another 差;差额

different /ˈdɪfrənt/ adjective **1** not the same as another or each other 有差别的;不同的 **2** separate 分别的,各别的 **3** informal 【非正式】new and unusual 独特的;不平常的;与众不同的 ■ **differently** adverb.

> **！注意** say **different from**, not **different to** in British English; **different than** is American. 英式英语中使用different from,而不说different to,美式英语用different than.

differential /ˌdɪfəˈrenʃl/ adjective involving a difference 差别的;依差别而定的 • noun **1** Brit. 【英】a difference in wages between industries or between categories of worker (不同行业或不同工种之间的)工资级差 **2** Maths 【数学】a minute difference between successive values of a variable 微分 **3** a gear that allows a vehicle's wheels to revolve at different speeds when going around corners 差动齿轮;差速齿轮

differentiate /ˌdɪfəˈrenʃieɪt/ verb (**differentiates, differentiating, differentiated**) **1** recognize things as being different from each other; distinguish 区分;区别;鉴别 **2** make things appear different from each other 使不同;使有差别 ■ **differentiation** noun.

difficult /ˈdɪfɪkəlt/ adjective **1** needing a lot of effort or skill to do or understand; hard 困难的;费劲的 **2** causing or involving problems 麻烦的;问题多的 **3** not easy to please or satisfy; awkward 难以取悦的;难以满足的。

difficulty /ˈdɪfɪkəlti/ **noun** (plural **difficulties**) **1** the state of being difficult 困难;艰难;深奥 **2** a difficult or dangerous situation; a problem 难事;困境;难题

diffident /ˈdɪfɪdənt/ **adjective** not having much self-confidence 胆怯的;缺乏自信的 ■ **diffidence** noun **diffidently** adverb.

diffract /dɪˈfrækt/ **verb** cause a beam of light to be spread out as a result of passing through a narrow opening or across an edge 使(光线)分散;使衍射 ■ **diffraction** noun.

diffuse verb /dɪˈfjuːz/ (**diffuses, diffusing, diffused**) **1** spread over a wide area 传播;普及;散布 **2** (of a gas or liquid) become mingled with a substance (气体或液体)扩散,弥漫 • **adjective** /dɪˈfjuːs/ **1** spread out over a large area; not concentrated 弥漫的;扩散的 **2** not clearly or concisely expressed 不清楚的;冗长的 ■ **diffusely** adverb **diffusion** noun.

> **! 注意** don't confuse **diffuse** with **defuse**, which means 'make a situation less tense or difficult' or 'remove the fuse from'. 不要混淆 diffuse 和 defuse，后者意为"缓和局面"或"拆除…的引信"。

dig /dɪg/ **verb** (**digs, digging, dug**) **1** cut into earth in order to turn it over or move it 挖;掘 **2** remove or produce something by digging 挖得;掘出 **3** push or poke sharply 戳;刺;捅 **4** (**dig into** or **through**) search or rummage in 搜寻;寻找 **5** (**dig something out** or **up**) discover facts 发掘,发现(事实) **6** (**dig in**) start eating heartily 开始大吃 **7** informal, dated 【非正式，废】 like 喜欢 • **noun 1** an act of digging 挖;掘;挖掘 **2** an investigation of a site by archaeologists 考古发掘 **3** a sharp push or poke 戳;

刺;捅 **4** informal 【非正式】 a critical remark 批评 **5** (**digs**) informal 【非正式】 temporary accommodation 寄宿舍;住所 ■ **digger** noun.

digest verb /daɪˈdʒest/ **1** break down food in the stomach and intestines so that it can be absorbed by the body 消化(食物) **2** reflect on and absorb information 吸收,领悟,理解(信息) • **noun** /ˈdaɪdʒest/ a summary or collection of material or information 摘要;概要;汇编;文摘 ■ **digestible** adjective.

digestion /daɪˈdʒestʃən/ **noun 1** the process of digesting food 消化 **2** a person's ability to digest food 消化力

digestive /daɪˈdʒestɪv/ **adjective** relating to the digestion of food 消化的 • **noun** Brit. 【英】 a semi-sweet biscuit made with wholemeal flour 消化饼干;粗面饼干

digit /ˈdɪdʒɪt/ **noun 1** any of the numerals from 0 to 9 (从0到9的任何一个)数字,数位 **2** a finger or thumb 手指;拇指

digital /ˈdɪdʒɪtl/ **adjective 1** having to do with information represented as a series of binary digits, as in a computer 数字的;数码的 **2** having to do with computer technology 计算机技术的 **3** (of a clock or watch) showing the time by displaying numbers electronically, rather than having a clock face (钟表或表)数字显示的 **4** having to do with a finger or fingers 手指的 ■ **digitally** adverb.

digitize or **digitise** /ˈdɪdʒɪtaɪz/ **verb** (**digitizes, digitizing, digitized**) convert pictures or sound into a digital form 使(图片或声音)数字化

dignified /ˈdɪgnɪfaɪd/ **adjective** having or showing dignity 庄重的;庄严的;有尊严的;高贵的

dignify /ˈdɪgnɪfaɪ/ **verb** (**dignifies, dignifying, dignified**) make something impressive or worthy of respect 使有尊严，使高贵

dignitary /'dɪɡnɪtəri/ **noun** (plural **dignitaries**) a very important or high-ranking person 显贵；要人

dignity /'dɪɡnəti/ **noun** (plural **dignities**) **1** the quality of being worthy of respect 尊贵；高贵 **2** a calm or serious manner 庄重；庄严 **3** pride in yourself 自尊；尊严

digress /daɪ'ɡres/ **verb** temporarily leave the main subject in speech or writing（讲话或写作）离题，偏离主题 ■ **digression** noun.

dike /daɪk/ ⇒ 见 DYKE.

diktat /'dɪktæt/ **noun** an order given by someone in power 勒令；强制命令

dilapidated /dɪ'læpɪdeɪtɪd/ **adjective** old and in bad condition 年久失修的；破旧的；破烂的 ■ **dilapidation** noun.

✔ 拼写指南 **dil**-, not **del**-: **dil**apidated. dilapidated 中的dil-不要拼作del-。

dilate /daɪ'leɪt/ **verb** (**dilates**, **dilating**, **dilated**) become wider, larger, or more open 膨胀；扩大 ■ **dilation** noun.

dilatory /'dɪlətəri/ **adjective** **1** slow to act 迟缓的；拖拉的 **2** intended to cause delay 拖延的

dilemma /dɪ'lemə/ **noun** a difficult situation in which you have to make a choice between alternatives 左右为难的处境，进退两难的窘境

dilettante /dɪlɪ'tænti/ **noun** (plural **dilettanti** /dɪlɪ'tænti/ or **dilettantes**) a person who does or studies something for enjoyment but does not take it very seriously 浅薄的涉猎者

diligent /'dɪlɪdʒənt/ **adjective** showing care and effort in a task or duty 勤奋的；刻苦的 ■ **diligence** noun **diligently** adverb.

dill /dɪl/ **noun** a herb used in cookery and medicine 莳萝；小茴香

dilly-dally /'dɪlɪdæli/ **verb** (**dilly-dallies**, **dillydallying**, **dilly-dallied**) informal【非正式】be slow or indecisive 游荡；闲混；犹豫

dilute **verb** /daɪ'ljuːt/ (**dilutes**, **diluting**, **diluted**) **1** make a liquid thinner or weaker by adding water or other liquid 稀释，冲淡（液体）**2** weaken something by modifying it or adding other elements 削弱，减轻 ● **adjective** /'daɪljuːt/ (of a liquid) diluted；weak（液体）稀释了的，冲淡了的 ■ **dilution** noun.

dim /dɪm/ **adjective** (**dimmer**, **dimmest**) **1** not bright or well lit 暗淡的；昏暗的 **2** not clearly seen or remembered 不分明的，不清楚的；（记忆）不清晰的，模糊的 **3** not able to see clearly（视力）差的，看不清的 **4** informal【非正式】stupid 迟钝的；愚笨的 ● **verb** (**dims**, **dimming**, **dimmed**) make or become dim（使）变暗淡；（使）变模糊 □ **take a dim view of** disapprove of 对…持不赞成态度 ■ **dimly** adverb **dimness** noun.

dime /daɪm/ **noun** N. Amer.【北美】a ten-cent coin 十分硬币；十分钱

dimension /daɪ'menʃn/ **noun** **1** a measure of how long, broad, high, etc. something is（长、宽、高等的）量度，维度，尺寸 **2** an aspect or feature 方面；特征；特点 ■ **dimensional** adjective.

diminish /dɪ'mɪnɪʃ/ **verb** make or become smaller, weaker, or less（使）变小，（使）变弱，（使）变少

diminution /dɪmɪ'njuːʃn/ **noun** a reduction 减小；减少；缩减

diminutive /dɪ'mɪnjʊtɪv/ **adjective** very or unusually small 极小的；微小的 ● **noun** a shortened form of a person's name（人名的）简称

dimmer /'dɪmə(r)/ **noun** a device for varying the brightness of an electric light 变光器；调光器

dimple /'dɪmpl/ **noun** a small hollow

formed in the cheeks when you smile 酒窝；笑靥 ■ **dimpled** adjective.

dimwit /'dɪmwɪt/ noun informal 【非正式】 a stupid person 笨蛋；傻子 ■ **dim-witted** adjective.

din /dɪn/ noun a prolonged loud and unpleasant noise 喧嚣；喧闹声；嘈杂声 • verb (**dins**, **dinning**, **dinned**) (**din something into**) teach something to someone by constantly repeating it 再三叮嘱，反复告诫

dine /daɪn/ verb (**dines**, **dining**, **dined**) eat dinner 进餐；吃饭

diner /'daɪnə(r)/ noun 1 a person who dines 就餐者 2 a carriage providing meals on a train（火车上的）餐车 3 N. Amer. 【北美】a small, cheap restaurant 小餐馆

dinghy /'dɪŋgi/ noun (plural **dinghies**) 1 a small open boat with a mast and sails 小舢板；小艇；敞篷小船 2 a small inflatable rubber boat 橡皮筏；橡皮艇

dingo /'dɪŋgəʊ/ noun (plural **dingoes** or **dingos**) a wild or semi-domesticated Australian dog 澳洲野犬

dingy /'dɪndʒi/ adjective (**dingier**, **dingiest**) gloomy and drab 暗淡的，无光泽的 ■ **dinginess** noun.

dinky /'dɪŋki/ adjective (**dinkier**, **dinkiest**) Brit. informal 【英，非正式】attractively small and neat 小巧的，小而精致的

dinner /'dɪnə(r)/ noun 1 the main meal of the day, eaten either around midday or in the evening（中午或晚上吃的）正餐，主餐 2 a formal evening meal 晚宴 □ **dinner jacket** a black or white jacket worn by men for formal evening occasions（男子的）晚礼服，无尾礼服

dinosaur /'daɪnəsɔ:(r)/ noun an extinct reptile that lived millions of years ago, some kinds of which were very large 恐龙

dint /dɪnt/ noun a dent 凹；凹痕 □ **by**

dint of by means of 借助；凭借

diocese /'daɪəsɪs/ noun (plural **dioceses** /'daɪəsi:z, -sɪ:zɪz/) a district under the control of a bishop in the Christian Church（基督教会的）主教辖区

diode /'daɪəʊd/ noun an electrical device that has two terminals and allows current to flow in one direction only 二极管

dioxide /daɪ'ɒksaɪd/ noun an oxide with two atoms of oxygen to one of a metal or other element 二氧化物

dip /dɪp/ verb (**dips**, **dipping**, **dipped**) 1 (**dip something in** or **into**) put or lower something briefly in or into 浸；蘸 2 sink, drop, or slope downwards 下沉；落下；倾斜 3 (of a level or amount) temporarily become lower or smaller（水平或数量）下降，减少 4 lower something briefly（短暂地）放低，使下降 5 (**dip into**) reach into a container to take something out 从（容器）中取出 • noun 1 an act of dipping 浸，蘸 2 a thick sauce in which you dip pieces of food before eating them 调味酱；沙司 3 a brief swim 游一游，泡一泡 4 a brief downward slope followed by an upward one 斜坡

diphtheria /dɪf'θɪəriə/ noun a serious illness that causes inflammation of the mucous membranes, especially in the throat 白喉

diphthong /'dɪfθɒŋ/ noun a sound formed by the combination of two vowels in a single syllable (as in coin) 二合元音，复合元音；双元音

diploma /dɪ'pləʊmə/ noun a certificate awarded to someone who has successfully completed a course of study 毕业文凭

diplomacy /dɪ'pləʊməsi/ noun 1 the management of relations between countries 外交 2 skill and tact in dealing with people（处理人际关系

的)手段,手腕

diplomat /'dɪpləmæt/ **noun** an official who represents a country abroad 外交官

diplomatic /ˌdɪplə'mætɪk/ **adjective 1** having to do with diplomacy 外交的 **2** tactful 有手腕的;策略的;圆通的 • **diplomatically** adverb.

dipper /'dɪpə(r)/ **noun 1** a bird that dives into fast-flowing streams to feed 河乌(一种鸟,会潜入湍急溪流中觅食) **2** a ladle 长柄勺

dipsomania /ˌdɪpsə'meɪnɪə/ **noun** alcoholism 嗜酒狂 ■ **dipsomaniac** noun.

dipstick /'dɪpstɪk/ **noun** a rod for measuring the depth of a liquid 浸量尺;测深尺

dire /'daɪə(r)/ **adjective 1** very serious or urgent 极严重的;极紧迫的 **2** informal【非正式】 of very bad quality 极糟的;极差的

direct /də'rekt/ **adjective 1** going from one place to another without changing direction or stopping 笔直的;径直的;最近的 **2** with nothing or no one in between 直接的;亲自的 **3** saying exactly what you mean; frank 直率的;坦率的 **4** clear and explicit 直白的 • **adverb** in a direct way or by a direct route 直接地;径直地 • **verb 1** aim something towards 把…对准 **2** tell or show someone the way 给…指路 **3** control the operations of 管理;监督;指导 **4** supervise the production of a film, play, etc. 导演(电影、戏剧等) **5** give an order to 指示;命令 ▫ **direct current** an electric current that flows in one direction only 直流电 **direct debit** Brit.【英】 an arrangement by which a bank transfers money from your account to pay a particular person or organization 直接借记 **direct speech** the actual words of a speaker quoted in writing 直接引语

direction /də'rekʃn/ **noun 1** a course along which someone or something moves, or which leads to a destination 路线;道路 **2** a point to or from which someone or something moves or faces 方向;方位 **3** the direc-ting or managing of people 管理;监督;指导 **4** (**directions**) instructions on how to reach a destination or how to do something (行路的)指引;(用法、操作的)说明 ■ **directional** adjective.

directive /də'rektɪv/ **noun** an official instruction 指示;命令

directly /də'rektli/ **adverb 1** in a direct way 直接地;径直地;坦率地 **2** exactly in a particular position 正好地: *the house directly opposite* 正对面的房子 **3** immediately 立即;马上 • **conjunction** Brit.【英】 as soon as 一…就

director /də'rektə(r)/ **noun 1** a person who is in charge of an organization or activity 负责人;主管 **2** a member of the board which manages a business 董事;理事;经理 **3** a person responsible for directing a film, play, etc. (电影、戏剧等的)导演 ▫ **director general** (plural **directors general**) the chief executive of a large organization (大机构的)主任,署长,局长,总督 ■ **directorial** adjective.

directory /də'rektəri/ **noun** (plural **directories**) a book that lists individuals or organizations and gives their addresses, telephone numbers, etc. 电话号码簿;公司名录

dirge /dɜːdʒ/ **noun 1** a piece of music expressing sadness for someone's death 哀乐;挽歌 **2** a slow, boring song or piece of music 单调缓慢的歌曲(或乐曲)

dirigible /'dɪrɪdʒəbl/ **noun** an airship 飞船

dirk /dɜːk/ **noun** a kind of short dagger formerly carried by Scottish

Highlanders（旧时苏格兰高地人佩带的）短剑，匕首

dirt /dɜːt/ *noun* **1** a substance that makes something dirty 污物，灰尘 **2** soil or earth 泥土 **3** *informal*【非正式】 scandalous or damaging information about someone 恶意中伤的闲话

dirty /'dɜːti/ *adjective* (**dirtier, dirtiest**) **1** covered or marked with mud, dust, grease, etc.; not clean 肮脏的；污秽的 **2** obscene 下流的；色情的 **3** unfair or dishonest 卑鄙的；不诚实的 • *verb* (**dirties, dirtying, dirtied**) make something dirty 弄脏 □ **dirty look** *informal*【非正式】a look expressing disapproval, disgust, or anger 不赞成的神情；厌恶的表情；生气的表情

disability /ˌdɪsə'bɪləti/ *noun* (plural **disabilities**) **1** a physical or mental condition that restricts your movements, senses, or activities 残疾；伤残；缺陷 **2** a disadvantage or handicap 不利，障碍

disable /dɪs'eɪbl/ *verb* (**disables, disabling, disabled**) **1** cause someone to be disabled 使残疾；使伤残 **2** put something out of action 使无效，使不能正常运转 ■ **disablement** *noun*.

disabled /dɪs'eɪbld/ *adjective* having a disability 有残疾的，有缺陷的

disabuse /ˌdɪsə'bjuːz/ *verb* (**disabuses, disabusing, disabused**) (**disabuse someone of**) persuade someone that an idea or belief is mistaken 消除（某人）的错误想法，使省悟

disadvantage /ˌdɪsəd'vɑːntɪdʒ/ *noun* something that causes a problem or reduces the chances of success 不利因素；不利条件 • *verb* (**disadvantages, disadvantaging, disadvantaged**) **1** put someone in an unfavourable position 使处于不利地位 **2** (**disadvantaged**) having less money and fewer opportunities than most

people 弱势的；处于不利地位的；贫困的 ■ **disadvantageous** *adjective*.

disaffected /ˌdɪsə'fektɪd/ *adjective* unhappy with the people in authority or with the organization you belong to, and no longer willing to support them 不满的；不忠的 ■ **disaffection** *noun*.

disagree /ˌdɪsə'ɡriː/ *verb* (**disagrees, disagreeing, disagreed**) **1** have a different opinion 持不同意见；不同意；有分歧 **2** be inconsistent 不一致；不符 **3** (**disagree with**) make someone slightly unwell 对（某人）不适宜；使（某人）不舒服 ■ **disagreement** *noun*.

disagreeable /ˌdɪsə'ɡriːəbl/ *adjective* **1** unpleasant 令人不快的；讨厌的 **2** bad-tempered 脾气坏的

disallow /ˌdɪsə'laʊ/ *verb* declare that something is not valid 宣布…无效；驳回

disappear /ˌdɪsə'pɪə(r)/ *verb* **1** stop being visible 消失；不见 **2** cease to exist 不复存在；灭绝；消亡 ■ **disappearance** *noun*.

✔ 拼写指南 one *s*, two *p*s: *disappear*. disappear中有一个s和两个p。

disappoint /ˌdɪsə'pɔɪnt/ *verb* **1** make someone sad or upset through failing to fulfil their hopes or expectations 使失望 **2** prevent hopes or expectations being fulfilled 使（希望）破灭 ■ **disappointed** *adjective*.

✔ 拼写指南 one *s*, two *p*s: *disappoint*. disappoint中有一个s和两个p。

disappointment /ˌdɪsə'pɔɪntmənt/ *noun* **1** sadness felt when hopes or expectations are not fulfilled 失望，沮丧 **2** a person or thing that causes disappointment 令人失望的人（或事物）

disapprobation /ˌdɪsæprə'beɪʃn/ *noun* strong disapproval 强烈反对；非难

disapprove /ˌdɪsəˈpruːv/ **verb** (disapproves, disapproving, disapproved) feel that someone or something is bad or immoral 不赞成；反对 ■ disapproval noun.

disarm /dɪsˈɑːm/ **verb 1** take a weapon or weapons away from someone 缴…的械；解除…的武装 **2** (of a country) reduce the size of its armed forces or give up its weapons (国家) 裁军，裁减军备 **3** win over a hostile or suspicious person, especially through being charming (尤指通过施展魅力) 消除敌意，消释疑心 **4** remove the fuse from a bomb 拆除(炸弹)的引信

disarmament /dɪsˈɑːməmənt/ **noun** the reduction or withdrawal of military forces and weapons 裁军，裁减军备

disarrange /ˌdɪsəˈreɪndʒ/ **verb** (disarranges, disarranging, disarranged) make something untidy or disordered 使紊乱；弄乱

disarray /ˌdɪsəˈreɪ/ **noun** a state of disorder or confusion 紊乱；混乱

disassemble /ˌdɪsəˈsembl/ **verb** (disassembles, disassembling, disassembled) take to pieces 解开；分解；拆卸

disassociate /ˌdɪsəˈsəʊʃɪeɪt/ = DISSOCIATE.

disaster /dɪˈzɑːstə(r)/ **noun 1** a sudden accident or natural event that causes great damage or loss of life 灾难；灾祸；灾害 **2** a sudden misfortune 不幸

disastrous /dɪˈzɑːstrəs/ **adjective 1** causing great damage 灾难性的；造成灾害的 **2** informal 【非正式】 very unsuccessful 完全失败的 ■ disastrously adverb.

✔ 拼写指南 no *e*: disa*s*trous, not *-erous*. disastrous中没有e, 不要拼作-erous。

---

disavow /ˌdɪsəˈvaʊ/ **verb** deny that

you are responsible for or in favour of something 拒绝对…承担责任；拒绝支持 ■ disavowal noun.

disband /dɪsˈbænd/ **verb** (of an organized group) break up (有组织的团体)解散

disbar /dɪsˈbɑː(r)/ **verb** (disbars, disbarring, disbarred) stop a barrister from working as a lawyer 取消律师执业资格

disbelief /ˌdɪsbɪˈliːf/ **noun 1** inability or refusal to accept that something is true or real 不信；怀疑 **2** lack of faith 不忠实

disbelieve /ˌdɪsbɪˈliːv/ **verb** (disbelieves, disbelieving, disbelieved) be unable to believe 不信；怀疑

disburse /dɪsˈbɜːs/ **verb** (disburses, disbursing, disbursed) pay out money from a fund (从基金中)支付，支出(款项)■ disbursement noun.

disc /dɪsk/ (US spelling 【美拼作】 disk) **noun 1** a flat, thin, round object 圆盘；盘状物 **2** (disk) a device on which computer data is stored (计算机) 磁盘，光盘 **3** a layer of cartilage that separates vertebrae in the spine 椎间盘 **4** a compact disc or record 唱片；碟片 □ disc jockey a DJ 唱片节目主持人

discard **verb** /dɪsˈkɑːd/ get rid of something useless or unwanted 丢弃，抛弃 • **noun** /ˈdɪskɑːd/ something that has been discarded 被抛弃的东西

discern /dɪˈsɜːn/ **verb 1** recognize or be aware of 认出；觉察出 **2** see or hear something with difficulty (依稀)看出，听出 ■ discernible adjective.

discerning /dɪˈsɜːnɪŋ/ **adjective** having or showing good judgement 有识别力的；有眼力的 ■ discernment noun.

discharge **verb** /dɪsˈtʃɑːdʒ/ (discharges, discharging, discharged) **1** dismiss or allow to leave 开除；允许离开；释

放 **2** send out a liquid, gas, or other substance 排出；放出；流出 **3** fire a gun or missile 击发(枪、炮)；发射(导弹) **4** fulfil a responsibility 履行(责任) • **noun 1** the action of discharging 开除；允许离开；释放；排出；发射；履行 **2** a substance that has been discharged 流出物；排出物

disciple /dɪ'saɪpl/ **noun 1** a person who followed Jesus during his life, especially one of the twelve Apostles 耶稣的信徒(尤指十二使徒之一) **2** a follower of a teacher, leader, or philosophy 信徒；门徒；追随者；信奉者

disciplinarian /ˌdɪsɪplɪ'neəriən/ **noun** a person who enforces firm discipline 严格执行纪律者

disciplinary /'dɪsəplɪnəri/ **adjective** having to do with discipline 训练的；纪律的；学科的

discipline /'dɪsəplɪn/ **noun 1** the training of people to obey rules or a code of behaviour 训练；训导 **2** controlled behaviour resulting from such training 纪律；风纪 **3** a branch of academic study 学科；科目 • **verb** (**disciplines, disciplining, disciplined**) **1** train someone to be obedient or self-controlled 训练；训导；管教 **2** formally punish someone for an offence 惩罚；处罚 **3** (**disciplined**) behaving in a controlled way 遵守纪律的

✔ **拼写指南** there's a *c* in the middle: *disc*ipline. discipline 中间有一个c。

disclaim /dɪs'kleɪm/ **verb** refuse to acknowledge that you are responsible for or interested in something 拒绝承认；否认

disclaimer /dɪs'kleɪmə(r)/ **noun** a statement disclaiming responsibility for something 不承担责任的声明

disclose /dɪs'kləʊz/ **verb** (**discloses, disclosing, disclosed**) **1** make information known 揭露；透露；泄露 **2** allow to be seen 使显露

disclosure /dɪs'kləʊʒə(r)/ **noun 1** the disclosing of information 揭露；透露；泄露 **2** a secret that is disclosed 被揭露的秘密

disco /'dɪskəʊ/ **noun** (plural **discos**) a club or party at which people dance to pop music 迪斯科舞厅；迪斯科舞会

discolour /dɪs'kʌlə(r)/ (US spelling 【美拼作】 **discolor**) **verb** make something stained or unattractive in colour 损坏…的色彩；使变色；使褪色 ■ **discoloration** (or **discolouration**) **noun**.

discomfit /dɪs'kʌmfɪt/ **verb** (**discomfits, discomfiting, discomfited**) make someone uneasy or embarrassed 使不安；使窘迫；使尴尬 ■ **discomfiture noun**.

discomfort /dɪs'kʌmfət/ **noun 1** slight pain 轻微的病痛 **2** slight anxiety or embarrassment 不安；不自在；尴尬 • **verb** cause someone discomfort 使不舒服；使不安；使尴尬

discompose /ˌdɪskəm'pəʊz/ **verb** (**discomposes, discomposing, discomposed**) make someone feel worried or disturbed 扰乱；使不安；使心乱

disconcert /ˌdɪskən'sɜːt/ **verb** make someone feel worried, confused, or uneasy 使心绪不宁；使困惑

disconnect /ˌdɪskə'nekt/ **verb 1** break the connection between two things 使不连接；使分离 **2** detach an electrical device from a power supply 切断(电器)的电源 ■ **disconnection noun**.

disconsolate /dɪs'kɒnsələt/ **adjective** very unhappy and unable to be consoled 忧郁的；郁郁寡欢的

discontent /ˌdɪskən'tent/ **noun** a feeling of unhappiness or dissatisfaction 不满；不满足 ■ **discontented adjective discontentment noun**.

discontinue /ˌdɪskən'tɪnjuː/ **verb**

(**discontinues**, **discontinuing**, **discontinued**) stop doing, providing, or making 停止；中断；终止 ■ **discontinuation** noun.

discontinuous /ˌdɪskən'tɪnjuəs/ **adjective** having intervals or gaps; not continuous 不连续的；间断的；断续的 ■ **discontinuity** noun.

discord /'dɪskɔːd/ noun **1** lack of agreement or harmony 不和；不一致；纷争 **2** lack of harmony between musical notes sounding together (音调的)不和谐

discordant /dɪs'kɔːdənt/ **adjective 1** not in harmony or agreement 不和的；不一致的；相冲突的 **2** (of a sound or sounds) harsh and unpleasant (声音)不和谐的，刺耳的

discotheque /'dɪskətek/ = **DISCO**

discount noun /'dɪskaʊnt/ an amount by which the usual cost of something is reduced 折扣 • **verb** /dɪs'kaʊnt/ **1** reduce the usual price of something 打折扣 **2** decide not to believe something because you think it is unlikely 不相信；漠视

discourage /dɪs'kʌrɪdʒ/ **verb** (**discourages**, **discouraging**, **discouraged**) **1** cause someone to lose confidence or enthusiasm 使灰心；使泄气 **2** try to persuade someone not to do something 阻止；阻拦；劝阻 ■ **discouragement** noun.

discourse noun /'dɪskɔːs/ **1** written or spoken communication or debate 论文；谈话；争论 **2** a formal discussion of a topic 论述；著述 • **verb** /dɪs'kɔːs/ (**discourses**, **discoursing**, **discoursed**) speak or write about something with authority 论述；著述

discourteous /dɪs'kɜːtiəs/ **adjective** rude and without consideration for other people 不礼貌的；失礼的；粗鲁的

discourtesy /dɪs'kɜːtəsi/ noun (plural **discourtesies**) behaviour that is rude and inconsiderate 无礼；粗鲁

discover /dɪ'skʌvə(r)/ **verb** (**discovers**, **discovering**, **discovered**) **1** find something unexpectedly or in the course of a search (出乎意料地)发现，找到，发觉 **2** gain knowledge about, or become aware of 认识到；了解到 **3** be the first to find or observe something (第一个)发现，观察到

discovery /dɪ'skʌvəri/ noun (plural **discoveries**) **1** the action of discovering 发现；发觉 **2** a person or thing discovered 被发现的人(或事物)

discredit /dɪs'kredɪt/ **verb** (**discredits**, **discrediting**, **discredited**) **1** make someone seem less trustworthy or honourable 败坏…的名誉；使丧失信誉 **2** make something seem false or unreliable 证实…虚假；使不可信 • **noun** damage to someone's reputation 名声的败坏；信誉的丧失

discreditable /dɪs'kredɪtəbl/ **adjective** causing damage to someone's reputation; shameful 有损名誉的；可耻的；丢脸的

discreet /dɪ'skriːt/ **adjective** careful not to attract attention or give offence 谨慎的；慎重的 ■ **discreetly** adverb.

> **！注意** don't confuse **discreet** with **discrete**, which means 'separate'. 不要混淆discreet和discrete，后者意为"分离的"。

discrepancy /dɪs'krepənsi/ noun (plural **discrepancies**) a difference between things that should be the same 差异；不符合；不一致

discrete /dɪ'skriːt/ **adjective** separate and distinct 分离的；截然不同的

discretion /dɪ'skreʃn/ noun **1** the quality of being discreet 谨慎；慎重 **2** the freedom to decide what should be done in a particular situation 酌情决定权

discretionary /dɪˈskreʃənəri/ **adjective** done or used according to the judgement of a particular person 酌情行事的；便宜行事的；可随意使用的

discriminate /dɪˈskrɪmɪneɪt/ **verb** (**discriminates**, **discriminating**, **discriminated**) **1** recognize a difference between one thing and another 区分；区别；辨别 **2** treat people unfairly on the grounds of race, sex, or age 区别对待；歧视

discriminating /dɪˈskrɪmɪneɪtɪŋ/ **adjective** having or showing good taste or judgement 有鉴赏力的；有识别力的

discrimination /dɪˌskrɪmɪˈneɪʃn/ **noun 1** unfair treatment of people on the grounds of race, sex, or age（对人的）区别对待，歧视 **2** recognition of the difference between one thing and another 区分；区别；辨别 **3** good judgement or taste 识别力；鉴赏力

discriminatory /dɪˈskrɪmɪnətəri/ **adjective** showing discrimination or prejudice 歧视的；有偏见的

discursive /dɪsˈkɜːsɪv/ **adjective** (of writing) moving from subject to subject（写作）东拉西扯的，离题的

discus /ˈdɪskəs/ **noun** (plural **discuses**) a heavy disc thrown in athletic contests 铁饼

discuss /dɪˈskʌs/ **verb 1** talk about something in order to reach a decision 讨论；谈论 **2** talk or write about a topic in detail（口头或书面）论述，详述

discussion /dɪˈskʌʃn/ **noun 1** conversation or debate about something 讨论；谈论 **2** a detailed treatment of a topic in writing（书面的）论述，详述

disdain /dɪsˈdeɪn/ **noun** the feeling that someone or something does not deserve respect 鄙视；蔑视 • **verb** treat with disdain 鄙视；蔑视 ■ **disdainful**

adjective **disdainfully** adverb.

disease /dɪˈziːz/ **noun** an illness in a human, animal, or plant 病；疾病 ■ **diseased** adjective.

disembark /ˌdɪsɪmˈbɑːk/ **verb** leave a ship, aircraft, or train 下船；下飞机；下火车 ■ **disembarkation** noun.

disembodied /ˌdɪsɪmˈbɒdid/ **adjective 1** separated from the body, or existing without a body 脱离躯体的 **2** (of a sound) not having any obvious physical source（声音）看不到的声源发出的

disembowel /ˌdɪsɪmˈbaʊəl/ **verb** (**disembowels**, **disembowelling**, **disembowelled**; US spelling【美拼作】**disembowels**, **disemboweling**, **disemboweled**) cut open and remove the internal organs of 取出…的内脏；开…的膛

disempower /ˌdɪsɪmˈpaʊə(r)/ **verb** (**disempowers**, **disempowering**, **disempowered**) make someone less powerful or confident 使权力削弱；使信心下降

disenchant /ˌdɪsɪnˈtʃɑːnt/ **verb** make someone disillusioned 使不抱幻想 ■ **disenchantment** noun.

disenfranchise /ˌdɪsɪnˈfræntʃaɪz/ **verb** (**disenfranchises**, **disenfranchising**, **disenfranchised**) **1** deprive someone of the right to vote 剥夺（某人）的选举权 **2** deprive someone of a right or privilege 剥夺（某人）的权利（或特权）

disengage /ˌdɪsɪnˈgeɪdʒ/ **verb** (**disengages**, **disengaging**, **disengaged**) **1** release or detach 使松开；使脱离 **2** remove troops from an area of conflict 使（军队）脱离接触，使撤出战斗 ■ **disengagement** noun.

disentangle /ˌdɪsɪnˈtæŋgl/ **verb** (**disentangles**, **disentangling**, **disentangled**) stop something being tangled 使摆脱；使解脱

disestablish /ˌdɪsɪˈstæblɪʃ/ **verb** end the official status of a national

Church 废除(国教)的法定地位

disfavour /dɪsˈfeɪvə(r)/ (US spelling 【美排作】disfavor) noun disapproval or dislike 不赞成;不喜欢

disfigure /dɪsˈfɪɡə(r)/ verb (disfigures, disfiguring, disfigured) spoil the appearance of 毁损…的外形 ■ disfigurement noun.

disgorge /dɪsˈɡɔːdʒ/ verb (disgorges, disgorging, disgorged) 1 cause something to pour out 涌出;倾泻出 2 bring up food from the stomach 吐出,呕出(食物)

disgrace /dɪsˈɡreɪs/ noun 1 the loss of other people's respect as the result of behaving badly 丢脸;耻辱 2 a shamefully bad person or thing 丢脸的人(或事) • verb (disgraces, disgracing, disgraced) bring disgrace to 使丢脸;使蒙受耻辱

disgraceful /dɪsˈɡreɪsfl/ adjective shockingly unacceptable 不光彩的;耻辱的;丢脸的 ■ disgracefully adverb.

disgruntled /dɪsˈɡrʌntld/ adjective angry or dissatisfied 生气的,不满的 ■ disgruntlement noun.

disguise /dɪsˈɡaɪz/ verb (disguises, disguising, disguised) 1 change the appearance of someone or something so they cannot be recognized 假扮;化装;伪装 2 hide a feeling or situation 掩饰,掩盖(感情或情况) • noun 1 a way of disguising yourself 化装(或伪装)方式 2 the state of being disguised 假扮;伪装

disgust /dɪsˈɡʌst/ noun a strong feeling that something is unpleasant, offensive, or unacceptable 厌恶;憎恶 • verb give someone a feeling of disgust 使厌恶,使憎恶 ■ disgusting adjective.

dish /dɪʃ/ noun 1 a shallow container for cooking or serving food 盘;碟 2 (the dishes) all the crockery and utensils used for a meal（就餐时使用的）所有餐具 3 a particular kind of food 一道菜;一种食品 4 a shallow concave object 盘状物 5 informal 【非正式】an attractive person 有吸引力的人;性感的人 • verb (dish something out or up) put food on to plates before a meal（餐前）把(食物)装盘

disharmony /dɪsˈhɑːməni/ noun lack of harmony 不协调;不和谐;不一致

dishearten /dɪsˈhɑːtn/ verb make someone lose determination or confidence 使沮丧;使失去决心(或信心)

dishevelled /dɪˈʃevld/ (US spelling 【美排作】disheveled) adjective untidy in appearance 不整洁的,衣冠不整的

dishonest /dɪsˈɒnɪst/ adjective not honest, trustworthy, or sincere 不诚实的;不老实的,不诚恳的 ■ dishonestly adverb dishonesty noun.

dishonour /dɪsˈɒnə(r)/ (US spelling 【美排作】dishonor) noun shame or disgrace 不名誉;耻辱;丢脸 • verb 1 bring shame or disgrace to 使丢脸;使蒙受耻辱 2 fail to keep an agreement 不遵守,违反(协议)

dishonourable /dɪsˈɒnərəbl/ (US spelling 【美排作】dishonorable) adjective bringing shame or disgrace 不名誉的;不光彩的;可耻的

dishwasher /ˈdɪʃwɒʃə(r)/ noun a machine for washing dishes automatically 洗碗机

dishy /ˈdɪʃi/ adjective (dishier, dishiest) informal 【非正式】good-looking 漂亮的

disillusion /ˌdɪsɪˈluːʒn/ verb make someone realize that a belief they hold is mistaken or unrealistic 使醒悟;使幻想破灭 • noun disappointment caused by discovering that your beliefs are mistaken or unrealistic 醒悟;不抱幻想;幻想破灭 ■ disillusionment noun.

disincentive /ˌdɪsɪnˈsentɪv/ **noun** a factor that discourages someone from doing a particular thing 起抑制作用的因素；遏制因素

disinclination /ˌdɪsɪnklɪˈneɪʃn/ **noun** a reluctance to do something 不愿；勉强

disinclined /ˌdɪsɪnˈklaɪnd/ **adjective** reluctant; unwilling 不愿意的；不情愿的；勉强的

disinfect /ˌdɪsɪnˈfekt/ **verb** clean with a disinfectant in order to destroy bacteria (用消毒剂)消毒，杀菌 ■ **disinfection noun.**

disinfectant /ˌdɪsɪnˈfektənt/ **noun** a chemical liquid that destroys bacteria 消毒剂；杀菌剂

disinformation /ˌdɪsɪnfəˈmeɪʃn/ **noun** information which is intended to mislead people 假情报；假消息

disingenuous /ˌdɪsɪnˈdʒenjuəs/ **adjective** not sincere, especially in pretending ignorance about something 不真诚的；不诚实的；(尤指)故意装聋作哑的

disinherit /ˌdɪsɪnˈherɪt/ **verb** (**disinherits, disinheriting, disinherited**) prevent a person from inheriting something 剥夺(某人)的继承权

disintegrate /dɪsˈɪntɪɡreɪt/ **verb** (**disintegrates, disintegrating, disintegrated**) break up into small parts as a result of impact or decay 碎裂；分裂；粉碎 ■ **disintegration** noun.

disinter /ˌdɪsɪnˈtɜː(r)/ **verb** (**disinters, disinterring, disinterred**) dig up something buried 掘出，挖出(埋藏物)

disinterest /dɪsˈɪntrəst/ **noun 1** impartiality 公正；不偏不倚 **2** lack of interest 无兴趣；不关心；冷漠

disinterested /dɪsˈɪntrəstɪd/ **adjective** not influenced by personal feelings; impartial 客观的；公正无私的

| ! 注意 don't confuse **disinterested** and **uninterested**. Disinterested means 'impartial', while **uninterested** means 'not interested'. 不要混淆disinterested和uninterested。disinterested意为"不偏不倚的"，而uninterested意为"不感兴趣的"。 |

disjointed /dɪsˈdʒɔɪntɪd/ **adjective** not having a logical sequence or clear connection; disconnected 不连贯的；支离破碎的

disjunction /dɪsˈdʒʌŋkʃn/ **noun** a difference or lack of agreement between things that you might expect to be the same 分离；分裂

disk /dɪsk/ ⇒ 见 DISC. □ **disk drive** a device which allows a computer to read from and write on to computer disks 磁盘驱动器

diskette /dɪsˈket/ **noun** a floppy disk 软盘

dislike /dɪsˈlaɪk/ **verb** (**dislikes, disliking, disliked**) find someone or something unpleasant or offensive 不喜欢；讨厌 • **noun 1** a feeling that someone or something is unpleasant or offensive 不喜欢；讨厌 **2** a person or thing that you dislike 不喜欢的人(或物)

dislocate /ˈdɪsləkeɪt/ **verb** (**dislocates, dislocating, dislocated**) **1** put a bone out of its proper position in a joint 使(骨头)脱位；使脱臼 **2** stop something from working properly; disrupt 扰乱；使混乱 ■ **dislocation** noun.

dislodge /dɪsˈlɒdʒ/ **verb** (**dislodges, dislodging, dislodged**) remove something from its position (从所在位置)去除，移动

disloyal /dɪsˈlɔɪəl/ **adjective** not loyal or faithful to someone 不忠诚的；不忠实的 ■ **disloyalty** noun.

dismal /ˈdɪzməl/ **adjective 1** causing or showing gloom or depression 令人忧郁的；阴暗的；阴沉的；忧郁的

2 informal 【非正式】disgracefully bad 极差劲的；极糟糕的 ■ **dismally** adverb.

dismantle /dɪsˈmæntl/ **verb** (**dismantles, dismantling, dismantled**) take something to pieces 拆卸；拆开

dismay /dɪsˈmeɪ/ **noun** a feeling of unhappiness and discouragement 气馁；苦恼 • **verb** cause someone to feel dismay 使气馁；使苦恼

dismember /dɪsˈmembə(r)/ **verb** (**dismembers, dismembering, dismembered**) **1** tear or cut the limbs from 分割…的肢体；肢解 **2** divide up a territory or organization 分割（领土或机构）■ **dismemberment** noun.

dismiss /dɪsˈmɪs/ **verb 1** order or allow someone to leave 让(某人)离开；打发走；解散 **2** order an employee to leave a job 解雇；开除 **3** treat something as not being worthy of serious consideration 对…不予考虑 **4** refuse to allow a legal case to continue 驳回，不受理(案件) **5** Cricket 【板球】end the innings of a batsman or side 迫使(击球员或一方)退场 ■ **dismissal** noun.

dismissive /dɪsˈmɪsɪv/ **adjective** showing that you feel something is not worth serious consideration 轻蔑的；蔑视的 ■ **dismissively** adverb.

dismount /dɪsˈmaʊnt/ **verb** get off a horse or bicycle 下马；下自行车

disobedient /ˌdɪsəˈbiːdiənt/ **adjective** failing or refusing to be obedient 不服从的；不顺从的；违抗命令的 ■ **disobedience** noun.

disobey /ˌdɪsəˈbeɪ/ **verb** fail or refuse to obey 不服从，不顺从；违抗

disorder /dɪsˈɔːdə(r)/ **noun 1** untidiness or disorganization 杂乱；混乱；凌乱 **2** the breakdown of peaceful and law-abiding behaviour 骚乱；动乱 **3** an illness or disease 失调；不适；

疾病 ■ **disordered** adjective.

disorderly /dɪsˈɔːdəli/ **adjective 1** involving a breakdown of peaceful behaviour 骚乱的；动乱的 **2** untidy or disorganized 杂乱的；凌乱的；无秩序的

disorganized or **disorganised** /dɪsˈɔːgənaɪzd/ **adjective 1** not well planned and controlled 计划不周的；管理不善的 **2** not able to plan your activities efficiently 杂乱无章的；无条理的 ■ **disorganization** noun.

disorientate /dɪsˈɔːriənteɪt/ or **disorient** /dɪsˈɔːriənt/ **verb** (**disorientates, disorientating, disorientated**) make someone lose their bearings or feel confused 使迷失方向；使迷惘；使无所适从 ■ **disorientation** noun.

disown /dɪsˈəʊn/ **verb** show or decide that you no longer want to have anything to do with someone 与(某人)断绝关系

disparage /dɪˈspærɪdʒ/ **verb** (**disparages, disparaging, disparaged**) speak critically or negatively about 贬低；轻视

disparate /ˈdɪspərət/ **adjective 1** very different from one another 根本不同的；迥然不同的 **2** containing elements that are very different from one another 由不同成分组成的

disparity /dɪˈspærəti/ **noun** (plural **disparities**) a great difference 巨大差异；悬殊

dispassionate /dɪsˈpæʃənət/ **adjective** not influenced by strong feelings; impartial 不带感情的；冷静的；无偏见的；公正的 ■ **dispassionately** adverb.

dispatch or **despatch** /dɪˈspætʃ/ **verb 1** send to a destination, especially for a particular purpose 派遣；调遣 **2** send a letter or parcel somewhere 发送(信件或包裹) **3**

deal with a task or problem quickly and efficiently 迅速完成(任务);迅速处理(问题) **4** kill a person or animal 杀死(人或动物) • noun **1** the action of dispatching 派遣;调遣;发送;迅速完成;迅速处理 **2** a report on the latest situation in state or military affairs 新闻报道 **3** speed and efficiency 迅速;利索

dispel /dɪˈspel/ verb (**dispels, dispelling, dispelled**) make a doubt, feeling, or belief disappear 驱散;消除

dispensable /dɪˈspensəbl/ adjective able to be replaced or done without 非必要的;可有可无的;不重要的

dispensary /dɪˈspensəri/ noun (plural **dispensaries**) a room where medicines are prepared and provided 药房

dispensation /ˌdɪspenˈseɪʃn/ noun **1** special permission not to obey a rule 豁免;免除 **2** the religious system of a particular time (某一特定时期的)教规 **3** the action of dispensing 分配;分发

dispense /dɪˈspens/ verb (**dispenses, dispensing, dispensed**) **1** distribute something to a number of people 分配;分发 **2** (of a chemist) prepare and supply medicine according to a prescription (药剂师)配药,发药 **3** (**dispense with**) get rid of or manage without 摒弃;省掉;不用 ■ **dispenser** noun.

disperse /dɪˈspɜːs/ verb (**disperses, dispersing, dispersed**) **1** move apart and go in different directions 分散;散开;疏散 **2** (of gas, smoke, etc.) thin out and eventually disappear (气体、烟等)消散,消失 ■ **dispersal** noun **dispersion** noun.

dispirited /dɪˈspɪrɪtɪd/ adjective discouraged or depressed 沮丧的;气馁的 ■ **dispiriting** adjective.

displace /dɪsˈpleɪs/ verb (**displaces,**

displacing, displaced) **1** move something from its proper or usual position 移动…的位置;挪动 **2** take over the position or role of 取代;替代 **3** force someone to leave their home 使背井离乡

displacement /dɪsˈpleɪsmənt/ noun **1** the action of displacing something, or the amount by which something is displaced 移位;取代;排量;转移量 **2** the volume or weight of water displaced by a floating ship, used as a measure of the ship's size (船的)排水量

display /dɪˈspleɪ/ verb **1** put something on show in a noticeable and attractive way 陈列;展出;展示 **2** show a quality or feeling 显露;表露(特性或感情) **3** show data or an image on a screen (在屏幕上)显示(数据或图像) • noun **1** a performance, show, or event for public entertainment 表演;陈列;展览 **2** the displaying of a quality or feeling 显露;表露 **3** a collection of objects being displayed 陈列品;展品 **4** the data or image shown on a screen (屏幕上)显示出的数据(或图像)

displease /dɪsˈpliːz/ verb (**displeases, displeasing, displeased**) annoy or upset 使不快;得罪;惹怒

displeasure /dɪsˈpleʒə(r)/ noun annoyance or dissatisfaction 不快;生气;不满

disport /dɪˈspɔːt/ verb (**disport yourself**) old use 【旧】enjoy yourself in an unrestrained way 自娱;玩乐

disposable /dɪˈspəʊzəbl/ adjective **1** intended to be used once and then thrown away 一次性的;用完即丢弃的 **2** (of money) available to be used (钱款)可动用的,可支配的

disposal /dɪˈspəʊzl/ noun the action of disposing of something 丢掉;清除;布置;安排 □ **at your disposal**

available to be used whenever or however you wish 供…使用；任…处理

dispose /dɪˈspəʊz/ *verb* (**disposes, disposing, disposed**) **1** (**dispose of**) get rid of 除掉；丢掉；清除 **2** (**be disposed to**) be inclined to do or think something 倾向于 **3** (**disposed**) having a particular attitude 抱有…态度的：*They were favourably disposed towards him.* 他们对他很友好。 **4** arrange something in a particular position 排列；布置；安排

disposition /ˌdɪspəˈzɪʃn/ *noun* **1** the natural qualities of a person's character 性格；性情 **2** an inclination or tendency 意向；倾向 **3** the way in which something is arranged 排列；布置；安排

dispossess /ˌdɪspəˈzes/ *verb* deprive someone of a possession 剥夺，夺去 (某人的财产) ▪ **dispossession** *noun*.

disproportionate /ˌdɪsprəˈpɔːʃənət/ *adjective* too large or too small in comparison with something else 不成比例的；不相称的；太大 (或太小) 的 ▪ **disproportionately** *adverb*.

disprove /ˌdɪsˈpruːv/ *verb* (**disproves, disproving, disproved**) prove something to be false 证明…为虚假

disputation /ˌdɪspjuˈteɪʃn/ *noun* debate or argument 辩论；争论

disputatious /ˌdɪspjuˈteɪʃəs/ *adjective* fond of arguing 爱争论的；好辩的

dispute *verb* /dɪˈspjuːt/ (**disputes, disputing, disputed**) **1** argue about … 发生争论 **2** question whether something is true or valid 对…表示异议 (或怀疑) **3** compete for 争夺；竞争 ▪ *noun* /dɪˈspjuːt, ˈdɪspjuːt/ an argument or disagreement 争论；争吵 ▪ **disputable** *adjective*.

disqualify /dɪsˈkwɒlɪfaɪ/ *verb* (**disqualifies, disqualifying, disqualified**) prevent someone performing an activity or taking an office because they have broken a rule or are not suitable 取消…的资格 ▪ **disqualification** *noun*.

disquiet /dɪsˈkwaɪət/ *noun* a feeling of anxiety 焦虑；担心 ▪ **disquieting** *adjective*.

disquisition /ˌdɪskwɪˈzɪʃn/ *noun* a long or complex discussion of a topic 专题演讲；专题论文；专题讨论

disregard /ˌdɪsrɪˈɡɑːd/ *verb* pay no attention to 不理会；不顾；漠视 ▪ *noun* the action of disregarding something 忽视；漠视

disrepair /ˌdɪsrɪˈpeə(r)/ *noun* (**in disrepair**) in a bad condition as a result of being neglected 失修；破败

disreputable /dɪsˈrepjətəbl/ *adjective* not respectable in appearance or character 外表不体面的；名声不好的

disrepute /ˌdɪsrɪˈpjuːt/ *noun* the state of having a bad reputation 不名誉；坏名声

disrespect /ˌdɪsrɪˈspekt/ *noun* lack of respect or courtesy 不尊敬；无礼 ▪ **disrespectful** *adjective* **disrespectfully** *adverb*.

disrobe /dɪsˈrəʊb/ *verb* (**disrobes, disrobing, disrobed**) take off your clothes 脱去…的衣服

disrupt /dɪsˈrʌpt/ *verb* interrupt or disturb an activity or process 扰乱；使中断 ▪ **disruption** *noun*.

disruptive /dɪsˈrʌptɪv/ *adjective* causing disruption 扰乱性的；捣乱的

dissatisfied /dɪsˈsætɪsfaɪd/ *adjective* not content or happy 不满的；不悦的 ▪ **dissatisfaction** *noun*.

dissect /dɪˈsekt/ *verb* **1** cut up the dead body of a person or animal to study its internal parts 解剖 **2** analyse in great detail 仔细分析；剖析 ▪ **dissection** *noun*.

✔ 拼写指南 **dissect** has a double *s*. dissect 中有两个 *s*。

dissemble /dɪ'sembl/ **verb (dissembles, dissembling, dissembled)** hide or disguise your motives or feelings 掩盖，掩饰(动机或感情)

disseminate /dɪ'semɪneɪt/ **verb (disseminates, disseminating, disseminated)** spread information widely 散布，传播(消息) ■ **dissemination** noun.

dissension /dɪ'senʃn/ **noun** disagreement that causes trouble within a group (内部的)意见分歧，争吵，不和

dissent /dɪ'sent/ **verb 1** express disagreement with a widely held view (对普遍持有的看法)不同意，持异议 **2** disagree with the doctrine of an established Church (对国教教义)不赞成，反对 **3** (in sport) disagree with the referee's decision (在体育比赛中)对判罚有异议 • **noun** disagreement with a widely held view (对普遍持有看法的)不同意见，异议 ■ **dissenter** noun.

dissertation /ˌdɪsə'teɪʃn/ **noun** a long essay, especially one written for a university degree (尤指为取得大学学位而写的)论文

disservice /dɪs'sɜːvɪs/ **noun** a harmful action 损害；危害

dissident /'dɪsɪdənt/ **noun** a person who opposes official policy 持不同政见者 • **adjective** opposing official policy 持不同政见的 ■ **dissidence** noun.

dissimilar /dɪ'sɪmɪlə(r)/ **adjective** not similar; different 不一样的；不同的 ■ **dissimilarity** noun.

dissimulate /dɪ'sɪmjuleɪt/ **verb (dissimulates, dissimulating, dissimulated)** hide or disguise your thoughts or feelings 掩饰，掩盖(思想或感情) ■ **dissimulation** noun.

dissipate /'dɪsɪpeɪt/ **verb (dissipates, dissipating, dissipated) 1** disappear or disperse 消失；消散；驱散 **2** waste money, energy, or resources 挥霍，浪费(钱财、精力或资源) **3** (dissipated) indulging too much in alcohol and other physical pleasures 放荡的；花天酒地的 ■ **dissipation** noun.

dissociate /dɪ'səʊʃieɪt/ **verb (dissociates, dissociating, dissociated) 1** disconnect or separate (使)分开；(使)分离 **2** (dissociate yourself from) say publicly that you are not connected with 否认同…有联系；声明断绝和…的关系 ■ **dissociation** noun.

dissolute /'dɪsəluːt/ **adjective** indulging too much in physical pleasures 放纵的；放荡的

dissolution /ˌdɪsə'luːʃn/ **noun 1** the formal closing down or ending of an official body or agreement (官方机构的)解散；(协议的)结束，终止 **2** the action of dissolving or decomposing 溶解；分解；腐朽

dissolve /dɪ'zɒlv/ **verb (dissolves, dissolving, dissolved) 1** (of a solid) mix with a liquid and form a solution (固体)溶解 **2** close down or end an assembly or agreement 解散(议会)；结束，终止(协议) **3** (dissolve into or in) give way to strong emotion 陷于(强烈情感)

dissonant /'dɪsənənt/ **adjective** without harmony; discordant 不和谐的；不协调的；不悦耳的；刺耳的 ■ **dissonance** noun.

dissuade /dɪ'sweɪd/ **verb (dissuades, dissuading, dissuaded)** persuade or advise someone not to do something 劝阻 ■ **dissuasion** noun.

distaff /'dɪstɑːf/ **noun** a stick or spindle on to which wool or flax is wound for spinning 绕线杆；纺纱杆

□ **distaff side** the female side of a family (家族的)母系,女系

distance /'dɪstəns/ **noun 1** the length of the space between two points 距离;间距 **2** the state of being distant 远;遥远 **3** a far-off point or place 远处;远方 **4** the full length or time of a race (赛跑的)全程,全部时间 ▪ **verb** (**distances**, **distancing**, **distanced**) (**distance yourself**) become less friendly or supportive 变疏远

distant /'dɪstənt/ **adjective 1** far away in space or time 在远处的;远离的;久远的 **2** at a specified distance …距离的 **3** far apart in terms of resemblance or relationship 不相似的;(关系)远的 **4** aloof or reserved 冷淡的;疏远的 ▪ **distantly** adverb.

distaste /dɪs'teɪst/ **noun** the feeling that something is unpleasant or offensive 不喜欢;反感;厌恶

distasteful /dɪs'teɪstfl/ **adjective** unpleasant or disliked 使人不愉快的;令人反感的;讨厌的 ▪ **distastefully** adverb.

distemper /dɪ'stempə(r)/ **noun 1** a kind of paint used on walls 刷墙水粉;水浆涂料 **2** a disease of dogs, causing fever and coughing 犬热病

distend /dɪ'stend/ **verb** swell because of internal pressure (使)膨胀;(使)肿胀 ▪ **distension** noun.

distil /dɪ'stɪl/ (US spelling 【美拼writing】 **distill**) **verb** (**distils**, **distilling**, **distilled**) **1** purify a liquid by heating it until it vaporizes, then condensing the vapour and collecting the resulting liquid 蒸馏,用蒸馏法提取(液体) **2** make alcoholic spirits such as whisky in this way 用蒸馏法酿造(烈酒) **3** extract the most important aspects of 吸取…的精华;提炼;浓缩 ▪ **distiller** noun **distillation** noun.

distillery /dɪ'stɪləri/ **noun** (plural **distilleries**) a factory that makes alcoholic spirits 酿酒厂

distinct /dɪ'stɪŋkt/ **adjective 1** recognizably different 截然不同的 **2** able to be perceived clearly by the senses 清楚的;清晰的;明显的 ▪ **distinctly** adverb.

distinction /dɪ'stɪŋkʃn/ **noun 1** a noticeable difference 差别;不同 **2** outstanding excellence 优秀;杰出;卓越 **3** a special honour or recognition 荣誉;殊荣

distinctive /dɪ'stɪŋktɪv/ **adjective** characteristic of a person or thing and distinguishing them from others 独特的;特别的;有特色的 ▪ **distinctively** adverb.

distinguish /dɪ'stɪŋgwɪʃ/ **verb 1** recognize the difference between two people or things 区分;分清 **2** manage to see or hear 看清;认出;听出 **3** be a characteristic that makes two people or things different 成为…的特征;使有别于 **4** (**distinguish yourself**) do something very well 使与众不同;使优秀 ▪ **distinguishable** adjective.

distinguished /dɪ'stɪŋgwɪʃt/ **adjective 1** successful and greatly respected 卓越杰出的;受人尊敬的 **2** having a dignified appearance 高贵的;气度不凡的

distort /dɪ'stɔːt/ **verb 1** pull or twist out of shape 扭歪;扭曲;使变形 **2** give a misleading account of 歪曲;曲解 ▪ **distortion** noun.

distract /dɪ'strækt/ **verb 1** prevent someone from giving their full attention to something 分散(某人)的注意力;使分心 **2** take attention away from something 转移(注意力)

distracted /dɪ'stræktɪd/ **adjective** unable to concentrate on something 分散注意力的;分心的

distraction /dɪ'strækʃn/ **noun 1** a thing that distracts someone's attention 分散注意力的事物;使人分心的事物 **2** something that provides entertainment 娱乐;消遣 **3** the state of being distracted 注意力分散;分心

distraught /dɪˈstrɔːt/ **adjective** very worried and upset 心烦意乱的;心神不定的

distress /dɪˈstres/ **noun 1** extreme unhappiness, pain, or suffering 苦恼;忧虑;疼痛;痛苦 **2** the state of a ship or aircraft when in danger or difficulty (船或飞机的)遇险,遇难 • **verb** cause distress to 使苦恼;使忧虑;使疼痛;使痛苦

distribute /dɪˈstrɪbjuːt/ **verb (distributes, distributing, distributed) 1** hand or share out to a number of people 分发;分配 **2 (be distributed)** be spread over an area 散布;分布 **3** supply goods to retailers 分销(货物)

distribution /ˌdɪstrɪˈbjuːʃn/ **noun 1** the action of distributing 分发;分配;散布;分布 **2** the way in which something is distributed 分配方式;分布方式

distributor /dɪˈstrɪbjətə(r)/ **noun 1** a company that supplies goods to retailers 分销商 **2** a device in a petrol engine for passing electric current to each spark plug in turn 配电器;配电盘

district /ˈdɪstrɪkt/ **noun** a particular area of a town or region 管区;行政区;地区

distrust /dɪsˈtrʌst/ **noun** lack of trust 不信任;怀疑 have little trust in 不信任;怀疑 ■ **distrustful** adjective.

disturb /dɪˈstɜːb/ **verb 1** interrupt the sleep, relaxation, or privacy of 打扰;扰乱 **2** move something from its normal position 搞乱;弄乱 **3** make someone anxious 使焦虑;使烦恼 **4 (disturbed)** having emotional or mental problems 有精神病的;精神不正常的

disturbance /dɪˈstɜːbəns/ **noun 1** the interruption of a normal or settled condition 打扰;干扰 **2** a riot or other breakdown of peaceful behaviour 骚乱;混乱

disunited /ˌdɪsjuˈnaɪtɪd/ **adjective** not united 不统一的;不团结的;分离的;分裂的 ■ **disunity** noun.

disuse /dɪsˈjuːs/ **noun** the state of not being used; neglect 不用;废弃 ■ **disused** adjective.

ditch /dɪtʃ/ **noun** a narrow channel dug to hold or carry water 沟;渠 • **verb 1** informal 【非正式】 abandon or get rid of 抛弃;丢弃 **2** (of an aircraft) come down in a forced landing on the sea (飞机)在海上迫降

dither /ˈdɪðə(r)/ **verb (dithers, dithering, dithered)** be indecisive 犹豫;踌躇

ditto /ˈdɪtəʊ/ **noun 1** the same thing again (used in lists) (用于表单中) 同上,同前,上述事物 **2** a symbol consisting of two apostrophes (″) placed under the item to be repeated 表示同上(或同前)的符号

ditty /ˈdɪti/ **noun (plural ditties)** a short, simple song 小曲;小调

diuretic /ˌdaɪjʊˈretɪk/ **adjective** (of a drug) making you pass more urine (药物)利尿的

diurnal /daɪˈɜːnl/ **adjective 1** relating to or during the daytime 白昼的;白天的 **2** daily 每天的

diva /ˈdiːvə/ **noun** a famous female opera singer 著名歌剧女主角

Divali /dɪˈvɑːli/ ⟹ 见 **DIWALI**.

divan /dɪˈvæn/ **noun 1** a bed consisting of a base and mattress but no headboard (有床体和床垫、无床头板的)床 **2** a long, low sofa without a back or arms (无靠背或扶手的)矮长沙发

dive /daɪv/ **verb (dives, diving, dived;** US 【美】 past and past participle also **dove** /dəʊv/) **1** plunge head first into water 跳水 **2** (of a submarine or swimmer) go under water (潜

艇或游泳者)潜水,下潜 **3** plunge steeply downwards through the air 俯冲 **4** move quickly or suddenly in a downward direction or under cover 扑;冲;奔 • **noun 1** an act of diving 跳水;潜水;扑;冲;奔 **2** informal 【非正式】a disreputable nightclub or bar 低级夜总会;低级酒吧 □ **dive-bomb** bomb a target while diving steeply in an aircraft 俯冲轰炸(目标)

diver /ˈdaɪvə(r)/ **noun 1** a person who dives under water 跳水员;潜水员 **2** a large diving waterbird 潜鸟

diverge /daɪˈvɜːdʒ/ **verb** (**diverges, diverging, diverged**) **1** (of a route or line) separate from another route and go in a different direction (路线或线条)分岔,岔开 **2** be different 与…有分歧;与…相异 ■ **divergence** noun **divergent** adjective.

diverse /daɪˈvɜːs, dɪ-/ **adjective** widely varied 多种多样的;形形色色的

diversify /daɪˈvɜːsɪfaɪ/ **verb** (**diversifies, diversifying, diversified**) **1** make or become more varied (使)多样化 **2** (of a company) expand its range of products or area of operation (公司)从事多种经营,扩大业务范围 ■ **diversification** noun.

diversion /daɪˈvɜːʃn/ **noun 1** the action of diverting something from its course 转向;改道 **2** Brit.【英】an alternative route used when a road is closed (正常道路封闭后的)临时绕行路 **3** something intended to distract attention 转移注意力的事物 **4** a pastime or other pleasant activity 消遣;娱乐 ■ **diversionary** adjective.

diversity /daɪˈvɜːsəti/ **noun** (**plural diversities**) **1** the state of being varied 多样性 **2** a range of different things 差异;差异性;不同点

divert /daɪˈvɜːt/ **verb 1** change the direction or course of 使转向,使改道 **2** distract a person or their attention

使(某人)分心;转移(注意力) **3** amuse or entertain 娱乐;使得到消遣

divest /daɪˈvest/ **verb 1** (**divest someone/thing of**) deprive someone or something of 剥夺 **2** (**divest yourself of**) remove or get rid of 使摆脱;处理掉;丢弃

divide /dɪˈvaɪd/ **verb** (**divides, dividing, divided**) **1** separate into parts 分开;分割 **2** share out 分配;分享 **3** cause disagreement between people or groups 使产生分歧 **4** form a boundary between 是…的分界线;分隔 **5** find how many times one number contains another 除(某数) • **noun** a difference or disagreement between two groups 不同;差异;分歧

dividend /ˈdɪvɪdend/ **noun 1** a sum of money that is divided among a number of people, such as the part of a company's profits paid to its shareholders 红利;股息;股利 **2** (**dividends**) benefits 益处;好处

divider /dɪˈvaɪdə(r)/ **noun 1** a screen that divides a room into separate parts 分隔房间的屏风 **2** (**dividers**) a measuring compass 分线规;两脚规

divination /ˌdɪvɪˈneɪʃn/ **noun** the use of supernatural means to find out about the future or the unknown 占卜;预言

divine¹ /dɪˈvaɪn/ **adjective 1** having to do with God or a god 上帝的;神的 **2** informal【非正式】excellent 绝妙的;极好的 ■ **divinely** adverb.

divine² /dɪˈvaɪn/ **verb** (**divines, divining, divined**) **1** discover by guesswork or intuition 猜出;(凭直觉)发现,悟得 **2** have supernatural insight into the future 占卜;预测(未来)■ **diviner** noun.

divinity /dɪˈvɪnəti/ **noun** (**plural divinities**) **1** the state of being divine 神性 **2** a god or goddess 神;女神 **3** the study of religion; theology 神学

divisible /dɪˈvɪzəbl/ **adjective 1**

capable of being divided 可分的 **2** (of a number) containing another number a number of times without a remainder (数字)可除(尽)的

division /dɪˈvɪʒn/ **noun 1** the action of dividing, or the state of being divided 分开;分割;分隔;分配;分享 **2** each of the parts into which something is divided (分出来的)部分 **3** a major section of an organization (机构的)主要部门 **4** a number of sports teams or competitors grouped to compete against each other (体育运动中的)级 **5** a partition 分隔物;隔断 □ **division sign** the sign ÷, placed between two numbers showing that the first is to be divided by the second, as in 6 ÷ 3 = 2 除号 ■ **divisional** adjective.

divisive /dɪˈvaɪsɪv/ **adjective** causing disagreement or hostility between people 造成不和的;引起分歧的;制造分裂的

divorce /dɪˈvɔːs/ **noun** the legal ending of a marriage 离婚 • **verb** (**divorces, divorcing, divorced**) **1** legally end your marriage with 与…离婚 **2** (**divorce something from**) separate something from 脱离;分离

divorcee /dɪˌvɔːˈsiː/ **noun** a divorced person 离了婚的人

divot /ˈdɪvət/ **noun** a piece of turf cut out of the ground 削起的一块草皮

divulge /daɪˈvʌldʒ/ **verb** (**divulges, divulging, divulged**) reveal information 泄露,透露(消息)

Diwali /diːˈwɑːliː/ or **Divali** /diːˈvɑːli/ **noun** a Hindu festival at which lights, candles, etc. are lit, held in October and November 排灯节(印度教节日，每年10月和11月间庆祝)

DIY /diː aɪ ˈwaɪ/ **abbreviation** Brit. 【英】do it yourself 自己动手

dizzy /ˈdɪzi/ **adjective** (**dizzier, dizziest**) having a sensation of spinning around and losing your balance 头晕目眩的;眩晕的 • **verb** (**dizzies, dizzying, dizzied**) make unsteady or confused 使头晕;使困惑 ■ **dizzily** adverb **dizziness** noun.

DJ /ˌdiː ˈdʒeɪ/ **noun** a person who introduces and plays recorded pop music on radio or at a club (电台或俱乐部的)唱片节目主持人

DNA /ˌdiː en ˈeɪ/ **noun** a substance carrying genetic information that is found in the cells of nearly all animals and plants 脱氧核糖核酸 [short for 【缩写】= deoxyribonucleic acid.]

do /duː, də, du/ **verb** (**does, doing, did**; past participle **done**) **1** carry out or complete an action, duty, or task 履行;执行;完成 **2** have a specified amount of success 做;表现:The team did well. 该队表现不错。**3** make or provide something 制作;提供 **4** have a particular result or effect on 对…有效果 **5** work at for a living or take as a subject of study 从事;攻读;学习;研究 **6** be suitable or acceptable 适合;可接受;行 **7** informal 【非正式】swindle someone 欺骗 • **auxiliary verb 1** used before a verb in questions and negative statements (用于动词前,构成疑问句和否定句) **2** used to refer back to a verb already mentioned (用于替代已提及的动词) **3** used in commands, or to give emphasis to a verb (用于命令或强调某动词) • **noun** (plural **dos** or **do's**) Brit. informal 【英,非正式】a party or other social event 聚会;社交活动 □ **do away with** informal 【非正式】put an end to or kill 结束;杀死;干掉 **do something up 1** fasten or wrap something 捆;扎;包 **2** informal 【非正式】renovate or redecorate a room or building 整修;重新装饰

docile /ˈdəʊsaɪl/ **adjective** quiet and easy to control 驯服的;易控制的 ■ **docilely** adverb **docility** noun.

dock¹ /dɒk/ **noun** an enclosed area of water in a port for loading, unloading, and repairing ships 码头；船坞 • **verb 1** (of a ship) come into a dock (船)停靠码头 **2** (of a spacecraft) join with a space station or another spacecraft in space（航天器）与(太空站或另一航天器)在太空对接

dock² **noun** the enclosure in a criminal court for a person on trial (刑事法庭的)被告席，犯人栏

dock³ **noun** a weed with broad leaves 酸模(一种阔叶野草)

dock⁴ **verb 1** take away money from a person's wages before they are paid（工资）**2** cut short an animal's tail 剪短(动物的尾巴)

docker /ˈdɒkə(r)/ **noun** a person employed in a port to load and unload ships 码头工人

docket /ˈdɒkɪt/ **noun** Brit. 【英】 a document accompanying a batch of goods that lists its contents, shows that duty has been paid, etc. 货物单据；货物标签

dockyard /ˈdɒkjɑːd/ **noun** an area with docks and equipment for repairing and building ships 修船厂；造船厂

doctor /ˈdɒktə(r)/ **noun 1** a person who is qualified to practise medicine 医生；大夫 **2** (**Doctor**) a person who holds the highest university degree 博士 • **verb 1** change something in order to deceive people 篡改；伪造 **2** add a harmful or strong ingredient to food or drink 把有害（或味重）的调料加入(食品或饮料)中 **3** Brit. 【英】 remove the sexual organs of an animal 阉割(动物)

doctoral /ˈdɒktərəl/ **adjective** relating to a doctorate 博士学位的；博士的

doctorate /ˈdɒktərət/ **noun** the highest degree awarded by a university 博士学位

doctrinaire /ˌdɒktrɪˈneə(r)/ **adjective** very strict in applying beliefs or principles 教条主义的；空谈理论的

doctrine /ˈdɒktrɪn/ **noun** a set of beliefs or principles held by a religious or political group 教义；信条；主义；学说 ■ **doctrinal** /dɒkˈtraɪnl/ adjective.

document **noun** /ˈdɒkjumənt/ a piece of written, printed, or electronic material that provides information or evidence 文件 • **verb** /ˈdɒkjument/ record something in written or other form 记录；记载

documentary /ˌdɒkjuˈmentri/ **noun** (plural **documentaries**) a film or television or radio programme giving a factual report, using film, photographs, and sound recordings of real events 纪录影片；(电视或广播)纪实节目 ■ **adjective** consisting of documents 文件的；文献的：*documentary evidence* 文献证据

documentation /ˌdɒkjumenˈteɪʃn/ **noun** documents providing official information, evidence, or instructions 文献资料；证明文件

dodder /ˈdɒdə(r)/ **verb** be slow and unsteady 摇摇晃晃；蹒跚 ■ **doddery** adjective.

doddle /ˈdɒdl/ **noun** Brit. informal 【英，非正式】 a very easy task 轻而易举的任务

dodecagon /dəʊˈdekəgɒn/ **noun** a figure with twelve straight sides and angles 十二边形；十二角形

dodecahedron /ˌdəʊdekəˈhiːdrən/ **noun** (plural **dodecahedra** /ˌdəʊdekəˈhiːdrə/ or **dodecahedrons**) a three-dimensional shape with twelve faces 十二面体

dodge /dɒdʒ/ **verb** (**dodges, dodging, dodged**) **1** avoid something by a sudden quick movement 闪身躲开 **2** avoid something in a cunning or dishonest way（以欺诈的方式）逃避，躲避 ■ **noun** an act of avoiding something 躲闪;躲避 ■ **dodger** noun.

dodgem /'dɒdʒəm/ **noun** a small electric car driven at a funfair with the aim of bumping other such cars (游乐场的)碰碰车

dodgy /'dɒdʒi/ **adjective** Brit. informal 【英,非正式】 **1** dishonest 不诚实的; 狡猾的 **2** risky 冒险的 **3** not good or reliable 状况不佳的;不可靠的

dodo /'dəʊdəʊ/ **noun** (plural **dodos** or **dodoes**) a large extinct bird that could not fly, formerly found on Mauritius 渡渡鸟(原产于毛里求斯, 现已灭绝)

doe /dəʊ/ **noun 1** a female deer or reindeer 雌鹿;雌驯鹿 **2** the female of some other animals, such as a rabbit or hare 雌性动物(如雌兔、雌野兔)

does /dʌz/ 3rd person singular present of **do**.

doesn't /'dʌznt/ **short form** does not.

doff /dɒf/ **verb** remove your hat when greeting someone 脱(帽)致意

dog /dɒg/ **noun 1** a four-legged meat-eating animal, kept as a pet or used for work or hunting 狗;犬 **2** any member of the dog family, such as the wolf or fox 犬科动物 **3** the male of an animal of the dog family 犬科雄兽 ● **verb** (**dogs**, **dogging**, **dogged**) **1** follow someone closely and persistently 跟踪;尾随 **2** cause continual trouble for 困扰;折磨 □ **a dog in the manger** a person who stops other people having things that they do not need themselves 占马槽的狗;占着茅坑不拉屎的人 **dog collar** informal 【非正式】a white upright collar worn by Christian priests (基督教神职人员穿的)白色立领,牧师领 **dog-eared** (of a book) having the corners of the pages curled or folded over from constant use (书)卷角的,旧了的 **dog-end**

informal 【非正式】a cigarette end 烟蒂;烟头 **dog-leg** a sharp bend 急转弯 **go to the dogs** informal 【非正式】get much worse 每况愈下;日趋衰败

dogfight /'dɒgfaɪt/ **noun** a close combat between military aircraft (战斗机的)近距离格斗

dogfish /'dɒgfɪʃ/ **noun** (plural **dogfish** or **dogfishes**) a small shark with a long tail 锹鲨

dogged /'dɒgɪd/ **adjective** very persistent 顽强的;坚持不懈的 ■ **doggedly** adverb.

doggerel /'dɒgərəl/ **noun** badly written verse 打油诗;蹩脚诗

doggo /'dɒgəʊ/ **adverb** (**lie doggo**) informal 【非正式】hide by keeping still and quiet 隐蔽;隐伏

doggy-paddle /'dɒgipædl/ **noun** a simple swimming stroke like that of a dog 狗刨式游泳

doghouse /'dɒghaʊs/ **noun** N. Amer. 【北美】a dog's kennel 狗窝;犬舍 □ **in the doghouse** informal 【非正式】in disgrace 丢脸的;失体面的

dogma /'dɒgmə/ **noun** a firm set of principles 教义;教理;信条

dogmatic /dɒg'mætɪk/ **adjective** firmly putting forward your own opinions and not willing to accept those of other people 武断的;固执己见的 ■ **dogmatically** adverb.

dogsbody /'dɒgzbɒdi/ **noun** (plural **dogsbodies**) Brit. informal 【英,非正式】a person who is given boring tasks that no one else wants to do 勤杂工;杂役

doily /'dɔɪli/ **noun** (plural **doilies**) a small decorative mat made of lace or paper 小装饰垫

doings /'duːɪŋz/ **plural noun** a person's actions or activities (某人的)所作所为,行动,活动

doldrums /'dɒldrəmz/ **plural noun** (**the doldrums**) a state of being inactive or feeling depressed 停滞;

萧条;忧郁;消沉

dole /dəʊl/ **noun** Brit. informal【英,非正式】money paid by the state to unemployed people (政府发放的) 失业救济金 ▪ **verb (doles, doling, doled)** distribute something 发放

doleful /ˈdəʊlfl/ **adjective** sad or depressing 悲伤的;忧郁的 ▪ **dolefully** adverb.

doll /dɒl/ **noun** a small model of a human figure, used as a child's toy 玩偶;玩具娃娃 ▪ **verb (be dolled up)** informal【非正式】be dressed in smart or fancy clothes 打扮得花枝招展;打扮得漂漂亮亮

dollar /ˈdɒlə(r)/ **noun** the chief unit of money in the US, Canada, Australia, and some other countries 元(美国、加拿大、澳大利亚等国的基本货币单位)

dollop /ˈdɒləp/ informal【非正式】**noun** a shapeless mass or lump (无形状的)一团,一块 ▪ **verb (dollops, dolloping, dolloped)** casually add or serve out a mass of something 掺和;分发

dolour /ˈdɒlə(r)/ (US spelling【美拼作】**dolor**) **noun** literary【文】great sorrow or distress 悲痛;忧伤 ▪ **dolorous** adjective.

dolphin /ˈdɒlfɪn/ **noun** a small whale with a beak-like snout and a curved fin on the back 海豚

dolphinarium /ˌdɒlfɪˈneəriəm/ **noun** (plural **dolphinariums** or **dolphinaria** /ˌdɒlfɪˈneəriə/) an aquarium in which dolphins are kept and trained for public entertainment 海豚馆

dolt /dəʊlt/ **noun** a stupid person 笨蛋,傻瓜

domain /dəˈmeɪn/ **noun 1** an area controlled by a ruler or government 领土;领地 **2** an area of activity or knowledge (活动或知识的)领域,范围 **3** a set of websites whose addresses end with the same group of letters (因特网网站的)域

dome /dəʊm/ **noun 1** a rounded roof with a circular base 圆屋顶;穹顶 **2** a stadium or other building with a rounded roof 圆顶体育场;圆顶建筑物 ▪ **domed** adjective.

domestic /dəˈmestɪk/ **adjective 1** relating to a home or family 家的;家庭的 **2** for use in the home 家用的 **3** (of an animal) tame and kept by humans (动物)驯养的,非野生的 **4** existing or occurring within a country; not foreign 国内的;本国的 ▪ **domestically** adverb.

domesticate /dəˈmestɪkeɪt/ **verb (domesticates, domesticating, domesticated)** tame an animal and keep it as a pet or on a farm 驯养,驯化(动物) ▪ **domestication** noun.

domesticity /ˌdɒmeˈstɪsəti/ **noun** home life 家庭生活

domicile /ˈdɒmɪsaɪl/ formal or Law【正式或法律】**noun 1** the country in which a person lives permanently 定居国 **2** a person's home 住处;住所;住宅 ▪ **verb (be domiciled)** be living in a particular country or place 居住

dominant /ˈdɒmɪnənt/ **adjective 1** most important, powerful, or influential 支配的;统治的 **2** (of a gene) appearing in offspring even if a contrary gene is also inherited (基因)显性的 ▪ **dominance** noun **dominantly** adverb.

dominate /ˈdɒmɪneɪt/ **verb (dominates, dominating, dominated) 1** have a very strong influence over 支配;控制 **2** be the most important or noticeable person or thing in 在…中占首要地位;在…中最显眼 ▪ **domination** noun.

domineering /ˌdɒmɪˈnɪərɪŋ/ **adjective** arrogantly trying to control other people 专横的;盛气凌人的

dominion /də'mɪnɪən/ **noun 1** supreme power or control 统治；管辖；支配 **2** the territory of a ruler or government 领土；版图

domino /'dɒmɪnəʊ/ **noun** (plural **dominoes**) any of twenty-eight small oblong pieces marked with 0–6 pips in each half, used in the game of dominoes 多米诺骨牌

don[1] /dɒn/ **noun** a university teacher 大学教师

don[2] **verb** (**dons, donning, donned**) put on an item of clothing 披上，穿上（衣服）

donate /dəʊ'neɪt/ **verb** (**donates, donating, donated**) give something to a charity or other good cause 捐赠；赠送

donation /dəʊ'neɪʃn/ **noun** something given to a charity or other good cause（给慈善机构的）捐赠物，捐款

done /dʌn/ past participle of DO. • **adjective 1** cooked thoroughly 煮熟的 **2** no longer happening or existing 已了结的；结束的 **3** informal【非正式】socially acceptable 合乎规矩的；得体的：*the done thing* 得体的事情

doner kebab /'dɒnə(r), 'dʊ-/ **noun** a Turkish dish of spiced lamb cooked on a spit and served in slices（土耳其）烤羊肉串

donkey /'dɒŋki/ **noun** (plural **donkeys**) a domesticated animal of the horse family with long ears and a braying call 驴 □ **donkey jacket** Brit.【英】a heavy jacket with a patch of waterproof material across the shoulders 风雨衣 **donkey's years** informal【非正式】a very long time 很久，猴年马月

donor /'dəʊnə(r)/ **noun** a person who donates something 捐赠者；赠送者

don't /dəʊnt/ **short form** do not.

donut /'dəʊnʌt/ US spelling of DOUGHNUT. doughnut 的美式拼法

doodle /'du:dl/ **verb** (**doodles, doodling, doodled**) scribble absent-mindedly（心不在焉地）乱涂，乱写乱画 • **noun** a drawing made absentmindedly 涂抹的画作

doom /du:m/ **noun** death, destruction, or another terrible fate 死亡；毁灭；厄运；劫数 • **verb** (**be doomed**) be fated to fail or be destroyed 注定失败；注定毁灭

doomsday /'du:mzdeɪ/ **noun 1** the last day of the world's existence 世界末日 **2** (in religious belief) the day of the Last Judgement（宗教信仰中的）最后审判日

door /dɔ:(r)/ **noun** a movable barrier at the entrance to a building, room, vehicle, etc. 门 □ **out of doors** in or into the open air 在户外；在露天；到户外

doorman /'dɔ:mən/ **noun** (plural **doormen**) a man who is on duty at the entrance to a large building 看门人，门卫

doormat /'dɔ:mæt/ **noun 1** a mat placed in a doorway for wiping your shoes 门口擦鞋垫 **2** informal【非正式】a person who lets other people control them 逆来顺受的可怜虫；受气包

doorstep /'dɔ:step/ **noun** a step leading up to the outer door of a house 门阶

doorstop /'dɔ:stɒp/ **noun** an object that keeps a door open or in place 门挡；门吸

doorway /'dɔ:weɪ/ **noun** an entrance with a door 门口

dope /dəʊp/ **noun 1** informal【非正式】an illegal drug , especially cannabis 麻醉剂；毒品；(尤指)大麻 **2** a drug used to improve the performance of an athlete, racehorse, or greyhound 兴奋剂 **3** informal【非正式】a stupid person 笨蛋；呆子 • **verb** (**dopes, doping, doped**) give a drug to 给⋯⋯

服麻醉剂(或毒品);给…服兴奋剂

dopey or **dopy** /ˈdəʊpi/ **adjective** informal【非正式】**1** in a semiconscious state from sleepiness or a drug 迷迷糊糊的;昏昏沉沉的 **2** stupid 迟钝的;愚笨的

doppelgänger /ˈdɒplɡæŋə(r)/ **noun** a ghost or double of a living person 活人的幽灵;面貌极相似的人

Doppler effect /ˈdɒplə(r)/ **noun** an apparent change in the frequency of sound or light waves as the source and the observer move towards or away from each other 多普勒效应

dormant /ˈdɔːmənt/ **adjective 1** (of an animal) in a deep sleep (动物) 冬眠的,蛰伏的 **2** (of a plant or bud) alive but not growing (植物或蓓蕾) 休眠的 **3** (of a volcano) temporarily inactive (火山)暂时停止活动的,休眠的 ■ **dormancy** noun.

dormer window /ˈdɔːmə(r)/ **noun** a window set vertically into a sloping roof 老虎窗;屋顶窗

dormitory /ˈdɔːmətri/ **noun** (plural **dormitories**) a bedroom for a number of people in an institution 大寝室;集体宿舍 • **adjective** (of a town) from which people travel to work in a nearby city (城镇)郊外住宅区的

dormouse /ˈdɔːmaʊs/ **noun** (plural **dormice**) a small mouse-like rodent with a bushy tail 睡鼠

dorsal /ˈdɔːsl/ **adjective** relating to the upper side or back 背部的;背侧的

dose /dəʊs/ **noun 1** a quantity of a medicine taken at one time (药物的)一剂,一服 **2** an amount of radiation absorbed at one time (辐射的)吸收量 • **verb** (**doses, dosing, dosed**) give a dose of medicine to (按剂量)给…服药 ■ **dosage** noun.

dosh /dɒʃ/ **noun** Brit. informal【英,非正式】money 钱

doss /dɒs/ **verb** Brit. informal【英,非

正式】**1** sleep in an uncomfortable place or without a proper bed (在简陋的地方)过夜 **2** spend time in a lazy or aimless way 混日子 ■ **dosser** noun.

dossier /ˈdɒsieɪ/ **noun** a collection of documents about a person or subject 材料汇编;卷宗;档案

dot /dɒt/ **noun** a small round mark or spot 点;小圆点 • **verb** (**dots, dotting, dotted**) **1** mark with a dot or dots 打点于;以小圆点标出 **2** cover an area with a scattering of something 星罗棋布于,散布于(某区域) □ **dot-com** a company that carries out its business on the Internet 网络公司 **on the dot** informal【非正式】exactly on time 准时地

dotage /ˈdəʊtɪdʒ/ **noun** the period of life in which a person is old and weak 衰老期

dote /dəʊt/ **verb** (**dotes, doting, doted**) (**dote on**) love someone very much, ignoring their faults 溺爱;过分宠爱

dotty /ˈdɒti/ **adjective** Brit. informal【英,非正式】slightly mad or eccentric 疯疯癫癫的;古怪的

double /ˈdʌbl/ **adjective 1** consisting of two equal, identical, or similar parts or things 双的;成双的;成对的 **2** having twice the usual size, quantity, or strength 双倍的;加倍的 **3** designed to be used by two people 供两人用的;双人的 **4** having two different roles or meanings 双重的;双关的 • **adverb** twice the amount or quantity 两倍地 • **noun 1** a thing which is twice as large as usual or is made up of two parts 两倍物;由两部分组成的事物 **2** a person who looks exactly like another 酷似的人 **3** (**doubles**) a game involving sides made up of two players 双打比赛 • **verb** (**doubles, doubling,**

doubled) **1** make or become double (使)加倍;(使)增一倍 **2** fold or bend over on itself 把…对折;折叠 **3** (double up) curl up with pain or laughter (因疼痛或大笑)弯着身子 **4** (double as) be used in or play a different role 兼作;兼任 □ **at the double** very fast 迅速地 **double agent** an agent who pretends to act as a spy for one country while in fact acting for its enemy 双重间谍 **double back** go back in the direction you have come from 循原路折回 **double-barrelled** Brit.【英】(of a surname) having two parts joined by a hyphen (姓氏)由两部分组成的 **double bass** the largest and lowest-pitched instrument of the violin family 低音大提琴 **double-breasted** (of a jacket or coat) having a large overlap at the front and two rows of buttons (上衣或大衣)双排纽扣的 **double chin** a roll of flesh below a person's chin 双下巴 **double cream** Brit.【英】thick cream with a high fat content 高脂稠奶油 **double-cross** betray a person that you are supposed to be helping 贩卖,出卖(本该帮助的人) **double-dealing** deceitful behaviour 口是心非;两面派行为 **double-decker** a bus with two floors 双层公共汽车 **double Dutch** Brit. informal【英,非正式】language that is hard to understand 难以理解的语言 **double glazing** windows having two layers of glass with a space between them 双层玻璃窗 **double-jointed** (of a person) having unusually flexible joints (人)有双关节的,关节可作异常弯曲的 **double standard** a rule or principle applied unfairly in different ways to different people 双重标准 **double take** a second reaction to something unexpected, immediately after your first one (对出乎意料的

事的)第二反应,过一阵后才恍然大悟的反应 • **doubly** adverb.

double entendre /ˌduːbl ɒnˈtɒndrə/ **noun** (plural **double entendres** /ˌduːbl ɒnˈtɒndrə/) a word or phrase with two meanings, one of which is usually rude (通常有粗鲁含意的)双关语

doublet /ˈdʌblət/ **noun** historical【历史】a man's short close-fitting padded jacket (男子穿的)紧身短上衣

doubloon /dʌˈbluːn/ **noun** historical【历史】a Spanish gold coin 达布隆(一种西班牙金币)

doubt /daʊt/ **noun** a feeling of uncertainty 疑惑;疑问;不确定 • **verb 1** feel uncertain about something 不能肯定 **2** disbelieve or mistrust someone 怀疑;不相信 □ **no doubt** certainly; probably 无疑;确实地;很可能

doubtful /ˈdaʊtfl/ **adjective 1** feeling uncertain 疑惑的;怀疑的 **2** causing uncertainty 可疑的;令人生疑的 **3** not likely or probable 未必的;不大可能的 • **doubtfully** adverb.

doubtless /ˈdaʊtləs/ **adverb** very probably 很可能

douche /duːʃ/ **noun** a jet of water applied to part of the body 冲洗;灌洗

dough /dəʊ/ **noun 1** a thick mixture of flour and liquid, for baking into bread or pastry (制作面包或糕点的)生面团 **2** informal【非正式】money 钱 • **doughy** adjective.

doughnut /ˈdəʊnʌt/ (US spelling【美拼作】**donut**) **noun** a small fried cake or ring of sweetened dough 炸面圈;甜面圈

doughty /ˈdaʊti/ **adjective** old use【旧】brave and determined 勇敢坚决的

dour /ˈdaʊə(r)/ **adjective** very severe, stern, or gloomy 严厉的;严峻的;阴郁的

douse or **dowse** /daʊs/ **verb** (**douses**, **dousing**, **doused**) **1**

drench with liquid 把…浸在液体里；向…泼水 **2** extinguish a fire 熄灭，浇灭(火)

dove[1] /dʌv/ **noun 1** a bird with a cooing voice, very similar to a pigeon 鸽子 **2** (in politics) a person who is in favour of a policy of peace and negotiation (政治上的)鸽派人物，温和派人物

dove[2] /dəʊv/ US 【美】 past and past participle of DIVE.

dovecote /ˈdʌvkɒt, -kəʊt/ or **dovecot** /ˈdʌvkɒt/ **noun** a shelter with nest holes for domesticated pigeons 鸽房；鸽棚

dovetail /ˈdʌvteɪl/ **verb** fit together neatly 吻合 • **noun** a wedge-shaped joint formed by interlocking two pieces of wood 鸠尾榫接头

dowager /ˈdaʊədʒə(r)/ **noun 1** a widow who holds a title that belonged to her late husband (承袭亡夫头衔的)寡妇 **2** a dignified elderly woman 老年贵妇人

dowdy /ˈdaʊdi/ **adjective** unfashionable and dull in appearance 不时髦的，相貌平平的

dowel /ˈdaʊəl/ **noun** a peg used to hold together parts of a structure 木钉；暗榫

down[1] /daʊn/ **adverb 1** towards, in, or at a lower place, position, or level 向下；在下面；在低处；处于低水平 **2** to a smaller amount or size (数量或尺寸)减少，减小，降低 **3** in or into a weaker or worse position or condition 处于(或进入)更差的状况 **4** away from a central place or the north 中不心心；离开中心；在南方；向南方 **5** from an earlier to a later point in time or order (时间或顺序上)直至，下至 **6** in or into writing (写)下；(记)下 **7** (of a computer system) out of action (计算机系统)停止运行 • **preposition 1** from a higher to a lower point of 从(高处)向…下方 **2** at or

to a point further along the course of 在(或向)…的远端 • **adjective 1** directed or moving downwards 向下的 **2** unhappy or depressed 沮丧的；情绪低落的 • **verb** informal 【非正式】 drink something quickly 迅速喝下 □ **down and out** homeless and without money 无家可归的；穷困潦倒的 **down at heel** shabby because of a lack of money 潦倒的，寒酸的 **down payment** an initial payment made when buying something on credit (分期付款的)首付款 **down-to-earth** practical and realistic 务实的；实际的 **down under** informal 【非正式】 Australia and New Zealand 对跖地；澳大利亚和新西兰地区

down[2] **noun** fine, soft feathers or hairs 绒羽；绒毛；软毛；汗毛

downbeat /ˈdaʊnbiːt/ **adjective 1** gloomy 忧郁的；令人沮丧的 **2** relaxed and low-key 放松的，低调的

downcast /ˈdaʊnkɑːst/ **adjective 1** (of eyes) looking downwards (眼睛)向下的，低垂的 **2** unhappy; discouraged 沮丧的；垂头丧气的

downer /ˈdaʊnə(r)/ **noun** informal 【非正式】 **1** a tranquillizing or depressant drug 镇静药；抑制药 **2** a depressing experience 令人沮丧的经历

downfall /ˈdaʊnfɔːl/ **noun** a loss of power, wealth, or status 垮台；衰落

downgrade /ˌdaʊnˈɡreɪd/ **verb** (**downgrades**, **downgrading**, **downgraded**) bring someone down to a lower rank or level of importance 使降级；使降职，贬低；降低

downhearted /ˌdaʊnˈhɑːtɪd/ **adjective** unhappy; discouraged 闷闷不乐的，沮丧的

downhill /ˌdaʊnˈhɪl/ **adverb & adjective 1** towards the bottom of a slope 向山下(的)；向坡下(的) **2** into a steadily worsening situation

每况愈下地(的);走下坡路地(的)

download /ˌdaʊn'ləʊd/ **verb** copy data from one computer system to another (计算机)下载(数据) • **noun** data that has been downloaded 下载的数据

downmarket /ˌdaʊn'mɑːkɪt/ **adjective** chiefly Brit. 【主英】cheap and of low quality 价廉质次的;低档的

downplay /ˌdaʊn'pleɪ/ **verb** make something appear less important than it really is 对…轻描淡写,贬低;低估

downpour /'daʊnpɔː(r)/ **noun** a heavy fall of rain 倾盆大雨

downright /'daʊnraɪt/ **adjective** utter; complete 彻头彻尾的,完全的;十足的 • **adverb** extremely 极其;简直

downs /daʊnz/ **noun** gently rolling hills (起伏平缓的)小丘

downside /'daʊnsaɪd/ **noun** the negative aspect of something 负面;不利方面

Down's syndrome noun a medical condition in which a person is born with physical abnormalities and an intellectual ability that is lower than average 唐氏综合征(患者先天生理发育异常,智力低下)

downstairs /ˌdaʊn'steəz/ **adverb & adjective** on or to a lower floor 在楼下(的);顺楼梯下下(的);往楼下的(的)

downstream /ˌdaʊn'striːm/ or **downriver** /ˌdaʊn'rɪvə(r)/ **adverb** in the direction in which a stream or river flows 顺流地

downtown /ˌdaʊn'taʊn/ **adjective & adverb** chiefly N. Amer. 【主北美】in, to, or towards the central or main business area of a city 在城镇中心(的);往城镇中心的

downtrodden /'daʊntrɒdn/ **adjective** treated badly by those in power 受压迫的;受践踏的

downward /'daʊnwəd/ **adjective & adverb** towards a lower point or level 向下的(的);下降地(的) ■ **downwards**

adverb.

downwind /ˌdaʊn'wɪnd/ **adverb** in the direction in which the wind is blowing 顺风地

downy /'daʊni/ **adjective** covered with fine soft hair or feathers 毛茸茸的;长着绒毛的;绒可覆盖的

dowry /'daʊri/ **noun** (plural **dowries**) property or money brought by a bride to her husband on their marriage 嫁妆;陪嫁

dowse[1] /daʊz/ **verb** (**dowses**, **dowsing**, **dowsed**) search for underground water or minerals with a pointer which is supposedly moved by unseen influences 用占卜杖探水源(或矿产)

dowse[2] /daʊs/ ⇒ 见 DOUSE.

doyen /'dɔɪən/ **noun** (feminine 【阴性】 **doyenne** /dɔɪ'en/) the most respected or prominent person in a field (某领域的)资格最老者,老前辈,元老

doze /dəʊz/ **verb** (**dozes**, **dozing**, **dozed**) sleep lightly 打瞌睡;打盹儿 • **noun** a short, light sleep 瞌睡;小睡 ■ **dozy** adjective.

dozen /'dʌzn/ **noun 1** (plural **dozen**) a group or set of twelve (一)打;十二个 **2** (**dozens**) a lot 许多;好多

DPhil /ˌdiː 'fɪl/ **abbreviation** Doctor of Philosophy 哲学博士

Dr abbreviation Doctor.

drab /dræb/ **adjective** (**drabber**, **drabbest**) dull and uninteresting 单调乏味的 ■ **drabness** noun.

drachma /'drækmə/ **noun** (plural **drachmas** or **drachmae** /'drækmiː/) the former basic unit of money in Greece 德拉克马(希腊以前的基本货币单位)

draconian /drə'kəʊniən/ **adjective** (of laws) very harsh and severe (法律)严苛的,严酷的

draft /drɑːft/ **noun 1** a rough early version of a piece of writing 草稿;草案 **2** a written order requesting a bank to pay a specific sum of money 汇票

3 (the draft) US【美】compulsory recruitment for military service 征兵；服役 **4** US spelling of DRAUGHT. draught 的美式拼法 ▪ **verb 1** prepare a rough version of a piece of writing 草拟，起草（文本）**2** select someone for a particular purpose 挑选；选派 **3 (be drafted)** US【美】recruit someone for compulsory military service 征募；征召（某人）入伍

drafty /'drɑːfti/ US spelling of DRAUGHTY. draughty 的美式拼法

drag /dræg/ **verb (drags, dragging, dragged) 1** pull along forcefully, roughly, or with difficulty（用力地，粗鲁地或困难地）拖，拉，扯，拽 **2** trail along the ground（在地上）拖着行进 **3** (of time) pass slowly（时间）过得慢，慢吞吞地过去 **4 (drag something out)** make something last longer than necessary 使拖延 **5** move an image across a computer screen using a mouse（用鼠标）拖动（图像）**6** search the bottom of an area of water with hooks or nets 用抓钩（或网）搜寻（水域）的底部 ▪ **noun 1** informal【非正式】a boring or annoying person or thing 令人厌烦的人；乏味无聊的东西 **2** a person or thing that makes progress difficult 阻滞进步的人（或物）**3** informal【非正式】an act of inhaling smoke from a cigarette 吸烟；抽烟 **4** the force exerted by air or water to slow down a moving object（作用于空中和水下运动体的）阻力，抗力 □ **drag race** a short race between two cars from a standstill 短程高速汽车赛 **in drag** (of a man) wearing women's clothes（男子）男扮女装的，着女装的

dragnet /'drægnet/ **noun** a net drawn through water or across ground to trap fish or game（捕鱼的）拖网；捕猎网

dragon /'drægən/ **noun** a mythical monster that can breathe out fire 龙

dragonfly /'drægənflaɪ/ **noun** (plural **dragonflies**) an insect with a long body and two pairs of large transparent wings 蜻蜓

dragoon /drə'guːn/ **noun** a member of any of several British cavalry regiments（英国骑兵团的）骑兵，龙骑兵 ▪ **verb** force someone into doing something 强迫；迫使

drain /dreɪn/ **verb 1** make something empty or dry by removing the liquid from it 排去…的液体 **2** (of liquid) run off or out（液体）流去，流掉 **3** make someone feel weak or tired 使精疲力竭 **4** use up a resource 消耗；耗尽 **5** drink the entire contents of a glass or cup 喝光 ▪ **noun 1** a channel or pipe for carrying off rainwater or liquid waste 下水道；排水沟；排水管 **2** a thing that uses up a resource or strength 消耗；耗竭 □ **draining board** Brit.【英】a surface next to a sink, on which crockery is left after it has been washed（洗涤池边上控干餐具的）滴水板 ▪ **drainage** noun.

drainpipe /'dreɪnpaɪp/ **noun 1** a pipe for carrying off rainwater from a building 雨水管；排水管 **2** (**drainpipes**) trousers with very narrow legs 瘦腿紧身裤

drake /dreɪk/ **noun** a male duck 公鸭；雄鸭

dram /dræm/ **noun** a small drink of spirits 少量烈酒

drama /'drɑːmə/ **noun 1** a play（一部）戏，剧 **2** plays as a literary form 戏剧 **3** an exciting series of events 戏剧性事件

dramatic /drə'mætɪk/ **adjective 1** relating to drama 戏剧的；有关戏剧的 **2** sudden and striking 戏剧性的；突然的；引人注目的 **3** exciting or impressive 激动人心的；给人深刻印象的 ▪ **noun** (**dramatics**) the practice of acting and presenting plays 戏剧艺术 ▪ **dramatically** adverb.

dramatist /'dræmətɪst/ **noun** a person who writes plays 戏剧家；编剧

dramatize or **dramatise**
/'dræmətaɪz/ **verb** (**dramatizes,
dramatizing, dramatized**) **1**
present a novel or story as a play
把…改编成戏剧;用戏剧形式表现 **2**
make something seem more exciting
or serious than it really is 戏剧性地
表现;夸张 ■ **dramatization** noun.

drank /dræŋk/ past of DRINK.

drape /dreɪp/ **verb** (**drapes, draping,
draped**) **1** arrange cloth or clothing
loosely on or round something 将
(布或衣服)悬挂(或披)在…上 **2** rest
part of your body on something in a
relaxed way 使(身体部位)放松地搭
在…上 ■ **noun** (**drapes**) 《北
美》long curtains (长的)窗帘,帷幕

draper /'dreɪpə(r)/ **noun** Brit. dated 《英,
废》a person who sells fabrics 布商;
纺织品商

drapery /'dreɪpəri/ **noun** (plural
draperies) curtains or fabric
hanging in loose folds 打褶悬挂的窗
帘(或织物)

drastic /'dræstɪk/ **adjective** having a
strong or far-reaching effect 激烈的;
猛烈的 ■ **drastically** adverb.

draught /drɑːft/ (US spelling 《美拼作》
draft) **noun 1** a current of cool air
indoors 穿堂风;通风气流 **2** an act
of drinking or breathing in 饮;吸
入 **3** old use 《旧》a quantity of a
medicinal liquid (药水的)剂量 **4**
the depth of water needed to float
a particular ship (船的)吃水深度
5 (**draughts**) Brit. 《英》a game
played on a chequered board 国际跳棋
■ **verb** = DRAFT. ■ **adjective 1** (of beer)
served from a cask (啤酒)散装的 **2**
(of an animal) used for pulling heavy
loads (动物)役用的,拖载重物的

draughtsman /'drɑːftsmən/ **noun**
(plural **draughtsmen**) **1** a person
who makes detailed technical plans
or drawings 制图员 **2** an artist skilled
in drawing 画师

draughty /'drɑːfti/ (US spelling 《美拼
作》 **drafty**) **adjective** uncomfortable
because of draughts of cold air 有穿
堂风的;有冷风吹过的

draw /drɔː/ **verb** (**draws, drawing,
drew**; past participle **drawn**) **1**
produce a picture or diagram by
making lines and marks on paper
画;描绘 **2** pull or drag a vehicle 拖,
牵引(车辆) **3** move in a particular
direction 移动;行进 **4** pull curtains
shut or open 拉上,拉开(窗帘) **5**
arrive at a point in time 达到(某时
间) **6** take from a container or source
拔出;抽出;取出 **7** be the cause of
a particular response 产生,引起(某
种反应) **8** attract people to a place
or an event 吸引;招引 **9** persuade
someone to reveal something 使说
出;使吐露 **10** reach a conclusion
得出,推断出(结论) **11** finish a
contest or game with an even score
以平局结束(比赛) **12** take in a
breath 吸(气) ■ **noun 1** a game or match
that ends with the scores even 平局;
不分胜负的比赛 **2** an act of choosing
names at random for prizes, sports
fixtures, etc. 抽彩;抽奖;抽签 **3** a
person or thing that is very attractive
or interesting 有吸引力的人(或
物);有趣的人(或事物) **4** an act of
inhaling smoke from a cigarette 吸
烟;抽烟 □ **draw the line at** refuse to
do or tolerate 拒绝做;拒不容忍 **draw
something out** make something
last longer 使(某事物)变长,延长(某
事) **draw up** (of a vehicle) come to
a halt (车辆)停下来,停住 **draw
something up** prepare a plan or
document 制定,起草(计划或文件)

| ! 注意 don't confuse **draw** with
drawer, which means 'a sliding
storage compartment'. 不要混淆
draw和drawer,后者意为"抽屉"。

drawback /'drɔːbæk/ **noun** a

disadvantage or problem 缺点；不利条件

drawbridge /'drɔːbrɪdʒ/ noun a bridge which is hinged at one end so that it can be raised 吊桥；开合桥

drawer noun 1 /drɔː/ a compartment for storage that slides horizontally in and out of a desk or chest 抽屉 2 /drɔːz/ (**drawers**) dated 【废】 knickers or underpants 内裤 3 /'drɔːə(r)/ a person who draws something 制图员

drawing /'drɔːɪŋ/ noun a picture or diagram made with a pencil, pen, or crayon 图画；素描；草图 □ **drawing pin** Brit. 【英】 a short flatheaded pin for fastening paper to a surface 图钉 **drawing room** a sitting room 起居室

drawl /drɔːl/ verb speak in a slow, lazy way with long vowel sounds 慢吞吞说话；拉长调子讲话 • noun a drawling accent 拖腔；拉长调子讲话的语音

drawn /drɔːn/ past participle of DRAW. • adjective looking strained from illness or exhaustion（因生病或劳累）憔悴的

drawstring /'drɔːstrɪŋ/ noun a string in the seam of a garment or bag, which can be pulled to tighten or close it（衣服缝口或袋口的）束带，拉绳

dray /dreɪ/ noun a low truck or cart for delivering barrels or other loads（无围边的）板车，大车

dread /dred/ verb think about something with great fear or anxiety 畏惧；担忧 • noun great fear or anxiety 畏惧；担忧

dreadful /'dredfl/ adjective 1 very bad or serious 糟透了的 2 used for emphasis（用于强调）极度的：*He's a dreadful flirt.* 他是个打情骂俏的老手。 ■ **dreadfully** adverb.

dreadlocks /'dredlɒks/ plural noun a Rastafarian hairstyle in which the hair is twisted into tight braids or ringlets "骇人"长发绺（拉斯塔法里教派成员蓄的一种发式，头发被编成小辫或发卷）

dream /driːm/ noun 1 a series of images and feelings that happen in your mind while you are asleep 梦；睡梦 2 an ambition or wish 梦想；理想；愿望 3 【非正式】 a wonderful or perfect person or thing 美好的人（或事物）• verb (**dreams, dreaming, dreamed** or **dreamt** /dremt/) 1 experience dreams during sleep 做梦 2 have daydreams 空想；幻想 3 think of something as possible 想到；料到 4 (**dream something up**) imagine or invent something 虚构；编造 ■ **dreamer** noun.

dreamy /'driːmi/ adjective 1 tending to daydream 喜做白日梦的，爱空想的 2 having a magical or pleasantly unreal quality 似梦的，模糊的；蒙眬的 ■ **dreamily** adverb.

dreary /'drɪəri/ adjective (**drearier, dreariest**) dull, bleak, and depressing 沉闷的；阴郁的；令人沮丧的 ■ **drearily** adverb **dreariness** noun.

dredge /dredʒ/ verb (**dredges, dredging, dredged**) 1 use a machine to scoop out mud and objects from the bed of a river, canal, etc.（用机器）疏浚（河流、沟渠等） 2 (**dredge something up**) mention something unpleasant that people have forgotten 重提，翻出（令人不快或已遗忘的事物）■ **dredger** noun.

dregs /dregz/ noun 1 the last remaining amount of a liquid left in a cup, bottle, etc. together with any sediment 残渣；渣滓 2 the most worthless parts 无用之物：渣滓：*the dregs of society* 社会渣滓

drench /drentʃ/ verb wet thoroughly; soak 使湿透；浸透

dress /dres/ **verb 1** (also **get dressed**) put on your clothes 穿衣服 **2** put clothes on someone 给…穿衣服 **3** clean or apply a dressing to a wound 清洗并包扎（伤口）**4** prepare food for cooking or eating（烹调前）收拾，处理；（食用前）加工，备办 **5** decorate or arrange in an artistic or attractive way 装饰；布置 • **noun 1** a woman's garment that covers the body and extends down over the legs 连衣裙 **2** clothing of a particular kind 服装 □ **dress rehearsal** a final rehearsal in which costumes are worn and things are done as if it is a real performance（正式表演前的）彩排 **dress up** dress in smart clothes or in a special costume 穿上光鲜讲究的衣服；精心打扮

dressage /'dresɑːʒ/ **noun** the training of a horse to perform a series of precise movements at the rider's command 花式骑术训练

dresser /'dresə(r)/ **noun** a sideboard with shelves above it 餐具柜；碗橱

dressing /'dresɪŋ/ **noun 1** a sauce for salads, usually consisting of oil and vinegar with flavourings（拌制色拉用的）调料 **2** a piece of material placed on a wound to protect it（保护伤口的）敷料 □ **dressing-down** informal【非正式】a severe telling-off or reprimand 严厉训斥；痛斥 **dressing gown** a long, loose garment worn after getting out of bed 晨衣；浴衣 **dressing room** a room in which performers change their clothes（演艺人员的）化装间 **dressing table** a table with a mirror, used while dressing or putting on make-up 梳妆台

dressmaker /'dresmeɪkə(r)/ **noun** a person who makes women's clothes（制作女装的）裁缝 ■ **dressmaking** noun.

dressy /'dresi/ **adjective** (**dressier,** **dressiest**) (of clothes) smart or formal（衣服）光鲜讲究的，正式的

drew /druː/ past of DRAW.

dribble /'drɪbl/ **verb** (**dribbles,** **dribbling, dribbled**) **1** (of a liquid) fall slowly in drops or a thin stream（液体）一点一滴地落下；细流 **2** let saliva run from the mouth 流口水 **3** (in sport) take the ball forward with slight touches（在体育运动中）运球，带球 • **noun** a thin stream of liquid 细流；小滴

dribs and drabs plural noun (**in dribs and drabs**) informal【非正式】in small amounts over a period of time 点点滴滴地；少量地

dried /draɪd/ past and past participle of DRY.

drier¹ /'draɪə(r)/ ⇒见 DRYER.

drier² comparative of DRY.

drift /drɪft/ **verb 1** be carried slowly by a current of air or water 飘；漂流 **2** walk or move slowly or casually 慢慢行走；随意移动；漂泊 **3** (of snow, leaves, etc.) be blown into heaps by the wind（雪、叶子等）被吹积 • **noun 1** a continuous slow movement from one place to another 缓慢移动；流动 **2** the general meaning of someone's remarks（话语的）主旨，大意 **3** a large mass of snow, leaves, etc. piled up by the wind 吹积物；堆积物

drifter /'drɪftə(r)/ **noun** a person who moves from place to place, with no fixed home or job 漂泊者；流浪汉

driftwood /'drɪftwʊd/ **noun** pieces of wood floating on the sea or washed ashore（海上漂浮或冲到岸边的）漂流木；浮木

drill /drɪl/ **noun 1** a tool or machine used for boring holes 钻头；钻床；钻机 **2** training in military exercises（军事）操练，演习 **3** (**the drill**) informal【非正式】the correct procedure 正确步骤；常规 **4** a machine for sowing seed in rows 条播机 • **verb 1** bore a hole with a drill 钻孔;打眼 **2** give someone military training or other strict instruction 操练;练习;训练

drily or **dryly** /'draɪli/ **adverb** in a matter-of-fact or ironically humorous way 冷冰冰地;不动感情地;冷面滑稽地

drink /drɪŋk/ **verb** (**drinks**, **drinking**, **drank**; past participle **drunk**) **1** take a liquid into the mouth and swallow it 喝;饮 **2** drink alcohol 喝酒 • **noun 1** a liquid for drinking 饮料 **2** a quantity of liquid swallowed at one time 一杯(或一份)饮料 **3** alcohol, or an alcoholic drink 酒;酒精饮料 □ **drink-driving** Brit. 【英】 the crime of driving a vehicle after drinking too much alcohol 酒后驾车 ■ **drinkable** adjective **drinker** noun.

drip /drɪp/ **verb** (**drips**, **dripping**, **dripped**) fall in small drops of liquid 滴下 • **noun 1** a small drop of a liquid (液体的)一滴 **2** a device which slowly passes a liquid substance into a patient's body through a vein (静脉)滴注器 **3** informal 【非正式】 a weak person 软弱的人 □ **drip-feed** give a patient liquid nourishment through a drip给(病人)滴注输液 ■ **drippy** adjective.

dripping /'drɪpɪŋ/ **noun** Brit. 【英】 fat that has dripped from roasting meat (烤肉上滴下的)油滴 • **adjective** very wet 湿淋淋的

drive /draɪv/ **verb** (**drives**, **driving**, **drove**; past participle **driven**) **1** operate a motor vehicle 驾驶;开车 **2** take someone somewhere in a motor vehicle 驾车送(人) **3** make someone or something move in a particular direction 赶;驱赶 **4** make someone behave in a particular way 逼迫;迫使 **5** provide energy to make an engine or machine work 推动,驱动(发动机或机器) • **noun 1** a journey in a car 驾车行程;驱车旅行 **2** (also **driveway**)

a short private road leading to a house (私人)车道 **3** a natural urge 欲望;冲动 **4** an organized effort to achieve something (为达到某一目的而开展的)运动 **5** determination and ambition 干劲儿;魄力 ■ **driver** noun.

drivel /'drɪvl/ **noun** nonsense 胡言;废话

drizzle /'drɪzl/ **noun** light rain falling in fine drops 毛毛雨;细雨 • **verb** (it **drizzles**, it is **drizzling**, it **drizzled**) rain lightly 下毛毛雨 ■ **drizzly** adjective.

droll /drəʊl/ **adjective** amusing in a strange or unusual way 古怪有趣的;离奇可笑的

dromedary /'drɒmədəri/ **noun** (plural **dromedaries**) a kind of camel with one hump 单峰驼

drone /drəʊn/ **verb** (**drones**, **droning**, **droned**) **1** make a low continuous humming sound 嗡嗡叫;嗡嗡响 **2** talk for a long time in a boring way 唠唠叨叨地说 • **noun 1** a low continuous humming sound 嗡嗡声 **2** a male bee which does no work but can fertilize a queen 雄蜂

drool /druːl/ **verb** (**drools**, **drooling**, **drooled**) **1** drop saliva uncontrollably from the mouth 垂涎;淌口水 **2** (often **drool over**) informal 【非正式】 show great pleasure or desire 对…垂涎欲滴;痴迷

droop /druːp/ **verb** bend, hang, or sag downwards limply or wearily 低垂;垂下 ■ **droopy** adjective.

droopy /'druːpi/ **adjective** (**droopier**, **droopiest**) **1** hanging down limply 低垂的,下垂的 **2** not having much strength or spirit 沮丧的,消沉的

drop /drɒp/ **verb** (**drops**, **dropping**, **dropped**) **1** fall, or let something fall (使)落下; (使)掉下 **2** make or become lower or less (使)降低;(使)减少; (使)变弱 **3** abandon a course of action 放弃;终止 **4** (often **drop someone/thing off**) set down or unload a passenger or goods 停下让(乘客)下去；停车卸下(货物) **5** (in sport) lose a point or match (体育比赛中)丢分，输掉比赛 • noun **1** a small round or pear-shaped amount of liquid (液体的)珠，滴 **2** a small drink 一点儿饮料 **3** an abrupt fall or slope 急降；陡坡 **4** a type of sweet 糖果 □ **drop kick** a kick made by dropping a ball and kicking it as it bounces 抛踢球 **drop off** fall asleep 睡着；入睡 **drop out 1** stop taking part in something 不再参加；退出 **2** start living an alternative lifestyle 逃避现实生活；寻求另类生活方式

droplet /ˈdrɒplət/ **noun** a very small drop of a liquid 小滴

dropout /ˈdrɒpaʊt/ **noun** a person who has started living an alternative lifestyle, or abandoned a course of study 逃避现实社会的人；辍学者

droppings /ˈdrɒpɪŋz/ **plural noun** the excrement of animals (动物的)粪便

dross /drɒs/ **noun** rubbish 废物；垃圾

drought /draʊt/ **noun** a very long period of abnormally low rainfall 长期干旱；旱灾

drove[1] /drəʊv/ past of DRIVE.

drove[2] **noun 1** a flock of animals being moved along (被驱赶的)畜群 **2** a large number of people doing the same thing (做同一件事的)一大群人

drown /draʊn/ **verb 1** die through taking water into the lungs, or kill someone in this way (使)淹死，(使)溺死 **2** flood an area 淹没(某地区) **3** (usu. **drown something out**) make something impossible to hear by being much louder (以更大的声音)压过，盖过

drowsy /ˈdraʊzi/ **adjective** (**drowsier, drowsiest**) sleepy 困倦的，昏昏欲睡的 ■ **drowsily** adverb **drowsiness** noun.

drub /drʌb/ **verb** (**drubs, drubbing, drubbed**) beat repeatedly 连续击打 ■ **drubbing** noun.

drudge /drʌdʒ/ **noun** a person who is made to do hard or dull work 做苦工的人；贱役的人，做艰苦工作的人

drudgery /ˈdrʌdʒəri/ **noun** hard or dull work 苦活；贱役；单调乏味的工作

drug /drʌg/ **noun 1** a substance used as a medicine 药；药物 **2** an illegal substance taken for the effects it has on the body 麻醉药；毒品 • verb (**drugs, drugging, drugged**) make a person or animal unconscious or sleepy by giving them a drug 用药使(人或动物)麻醉

drugstore /ˈdrʌgstɔː(r)/ **noun** N. Amer. 【北美】a shop which sells medicines and also cosmetics and other articles (兼售化妆品和其他物品的)药店，杂货店

Druid /ˈdruːɪd/ **noun** a priest in the ancient Celtic religion 德鲁伊特(古代凯尔特宗教的教士)

drum /drʌm/ **noun 1** a percussion instrument which you play by hitting it with sticks or the hands 鼓 **2** a cylindrical object or part 鼓状物；圆桶 • verb (**drums, drumming, drummed**) **1** play on a drum 击鼓；敲鼓 **2** make a continuous rhythmic noise 有节奏地持续敲击 **3** (**drum something into**) teach something to someone by constantly repeating it 反复强调；反复灌输 **4** (**drum something up**) try hard to get support or business 竭力争取(支持)；兜揽(生意) □ **drum and bass** a type of dance music consisting largely of electronic drums and bass 鼓和贝司(一种舞曲，主要由电子鼓和电声贝司演奏) ■ **drummer** noun.

drumstick /ˈdrʌmstɪk/ **noun 1** a stick used for beating a drum 鼓槌 **2** the lower joint of the leg of a cooked chicken 熟鸡腿的下半部分；琵琶腿

drunk /drʌŋk/ past participle of DRINK.
• **adjective** having drunk so much alcohol that you cannot think or speak clearly 醉的；喝醉的 • **noun** a person who is drunk or who often drinks too much 醉酒者；酗酒者

drunkard /ˈdrʌŋkəd/ **noun** a person who is often drunk 醉汉；酒鬼

drunken /ˈdrʌŋkən/ **adjective 1** drunk 醉酒的 **2** caused by or showing the effects of drink 醉酒引起的 ■ **drunkenly** adverb **drunkenness** noun.

drupe /druːp/ **noun** Botany 【植物】a fruit with a central stone, e.g. a plum or olive 核果(如李子或橄榄)

dry /draɪ/ **adjective** (**drier**, **driest**) **1** free from moisture 干的；干燥的 **2** dull and serious 干巴巴的；枯燥的 **3** (of humour) subtle and expressed in a matter-of-fact way (幽默)巧妙而不露声色的 **4** (of wine) not sweet(葡萄酒)无甜味的，干的 • **verb** (**dries**, **drying**, **dried**) **1** make or become dry (使)变干；弄干；擦干 **2** preserve something by evaporating the moisture 使脱水；风干 **3** (**dry up**) (of a supply) decrease and stop (补给品)停止提供 □ **dry-clean** clean a garment with a chemical rather than by washing it 干洗(衣服) **dry rot** a fungus that causes wood to decay (造成木材腐烂的)干腐菌 **dry run** a rehearsal 排练；预演 ■ **dryness** noun.

dryer or **drier** /ˈdraɪə(r)/ **noun** a machine or device for drying something 烘干机；干燥机

dryly /ˈdraɪli/ ⇒ 见 DRILY.

drystone /ˈdraɪstəʊn/ **adjective** Brit. 【英】(of a stone wall) built without using mortar (石墙)干砌的

dual /ˈdjuːəl/ **adjective** consisting of two parts or aspects 两部分的；双重的 □ **dual carriageway** Brit. 【英】a road with two or more lanes in each direction 双幅车行道；复式车行道

dualism /ˈdjuːəlɪzəm/ **noun 1** division

into two contrasted aspects, such as good and evil 二元论 **2** duality 两重性；二元性 ■ **dualist** noun & adjective.

duality /djuːˈæləti/ **noun** (plural **dualities**) the state of having two parts or aspects 两重性；二元性

dub¹ /dʌb/ **verb** (**dubs**, **dubbing**, **dubbed**) **1** give an unofficial name to 把…戏称为 **2** knight someone by touching their shoulder with a sword in a special ceremony (以剑触肩)封(某人)为爵士

dub² **verb** (**dubs**, **dubbing**, **dubbed**) **1** give a film a soundtrack in a different language from the original 为(影片)译制(影片) **2** add sound effects or music to a film or recording 为影片(或唱片)配入(音响或音乐)

dubbin /ˈdʌbɪn/ **noun** Brit. 【英】a grease used for softening and waterproofing leather (皮革用)软化防水油脂

dubious /ˈdjuːbiəs/ **adjective 1** hesitating or doubting 迟疑的；犹豫不决的 **2** probably not honest 不老实的；靠不住的 **3** of uncertain quality or value 不确定的；可疑的 ■ **dubiously** adverb.

ducal /ˈdjuːkl/ **adjective** relating to a duke or dukedom 公爵的；公爵领地的

ducat /ˈdʌkət/ **noun** a gold coin formerly used in Europe 达克特(欧洲旧时通用的金币)

duchess /ˈdʌtʃəs/ **noun 1** the wife or widow of a duke 公爵夫人 **2** a woman holding a rank equivalent to duke 女公爵

duchy /ˈdʌtʃi/ **noun** (plural **duchies**) the territory of a duke or duchess 公爵(或女公爵)领地，公国

duck¹ /dʌk/ **noun** (plural **duck** or **ducks**) **1** a waterbird with a broad blunt bill, short legs, and webbed feet 鸭；鸭子 **2** a female duck 母鸭 □ **duck-billed platypus** ⇒见 PLATYPUS.

duck² /dʌk/ **verb 1** lower yourself quickly to avoid being hit or seen (迅速)低下头,弯下身 **2** push someone under water 把…按入水中 **3** informal 【非正式】 avoid an unwelcome duty 回避,逃避(职责)

duck³ noun Cricket【板球】a batsman's score of nought 零分

duckboards /'dʌkbɔːdz/ **plural noun** wooden slats joined together to form a path over muddy ground (泥地上铺的)板道,垫路板

duckling /'dʌklɪŋ/ **noun** a young duck 小鸭,幼鸭

duct /dʌkt/ **noun 1** a tube or passageway for air, cables, etc. (输送气体、铺设电缆等的)管道,沟,槽 **2** a tube in the body through which fluid passes (人体内的)导管,排泄管

ductile /'dʌktaɪl/ **adjective** (of a metal) able to be drawn out into a thin wire (金属)可伸展的,有延性的

dud /dʌd/ informal 【非正式】 **noun** a thing that fails to work properly 不中用的东西,废物 • **adjective** failing to work properly 出故障的

dude /duːd/ **noun** N. Amer. informal【北美,非正式】a man (男)人,家伙

dudgeon /'dʌdʒən/ **noun** deep resentment 愤怒,强烈不满

due /djuː/ **adjective 1** expected at a certain time 预定的,预计的 **2** owing; needing to be paid or given 欠款的;应支付的 **3** (of a person) owed or deserving something (人)应有的,应得的 **4** proper or adequate 适当的,合适的 • **noun 1** (**someone's due** or **dues**) what someone deserves or is owed (某人)应得的东西 **2** (**dues**) fees 费;会费 • **adverb** directly 正对着: *head due south* 向正南行进 □ **due to 1** caused by 由…引起 **2** because of 因为;由于

duel /'djuːəl/ **noun 1** historical 【历史】a contest with deadly weapons between two people to settle a point of

honour 决斗 **2** a contest between two parties (双方的)竞争 • **verb** (**duels, duelling, duelled;** US spelling 【美拼作】**duels, dueling, dueled**) fight a duel 决斗 ■ **duellist** (US spelling【美拼作】**duelist**) noun.

duet /dju'et/ **noun 1** a performance by two singers or musicians 二重唱;二重奏 **2** a piece of music for two performers 二重唱曲;二重奏曲

duff /dʌf/ Brit. informal 【英,非正式】 **adjective** of very bad quality; useless 劣质的,无用处的 • **verb** (**duff someone up**) beat someone up 痛打,毒打(某人)

duffel bag or **duffle bag** /'dʌfl/ **noun** a cylinder-shaped canvas bag closed by a drawstring (圆筒状的)帆布包,旅行包

duffel coat or **duffle coat noun** a hooded coat made of a rough woollen material 连帽粗呢大衣

duffer /'dʌfə(r)/ **noun** informal【非正式】 an incompetent or stupid person 无能的人,蠢货

dug¹ /dʌg/ past and past participle of DIG.

dug² **noun** the udder, teat, or nipple of a female animal 雌性动物的乳房(或乳头)

dugout /'dʌgaʊt/ **noun 1** a trench that is roofed over as a shelter for troops 防空洞;地下掩体 **2** a low shelter at the side of a sports field for a team's coaches and substitutes 休息处(设在运动场边供教练和替补队员用) **3** a canoe made from a hollowed-out tree trunk 独木舟

duke /djuːk/ **noun 1** the highest rank of nobleman in Britain and certain other countries (英国及其他一些国家的)公爵 **2** historical 【历史】 (in parts of Europe) a male ruler of a small independent state (欧洲部分地区小公国的)君主,亲王 ■ **dukedom** noun.

dulcet /'dʌlsɪt/ **adjective** (of a sound)

dulcimer /ˈdʌlsɪmə(r)/ **noun** a musical instrument which you play by hitting the strings with small hammers 扬琴

dull /dʌl/ **adjective 1** not very interesting 乏味的,单调的 **2** not vivid or bright 不鲜明的;无光泽的 **3** (of the weather) overcast (天气) 阴沉的,昏暗的 **4** slow to understand 愚钝的,愚蠢的;笨的 • **verb** make or become dull (使)变乏味;(使)变得无光泽;(使)变阴沉;(使)变愚钝 ■ **dullness** noun **dully** adverb.

dullard /ˈdʌlɑːd/ **noun** a slow or stupid person 愚钝的人,蠢人;笨蛋

duly /ˈdjuːli/ **adverb** in the proper or expected way 适当地;恰当地

dumb /dʌm/ **adjective 1** offensive 【冒犯】 unable to speak; not having the power of speech 哑的;不能说话的 **2** temporarily unable or unwilling to speak 说不出话的,沉默的;不愿说话的 **3** N. Amer. informal 【北美,非正式】stupid 愚蠢的;笨的 • **verb** (**dumb something down**) informal 【非正式】make something less intellectually challenging 使降低难度;使简单化 □ **dumbbell** a short bar with a weight at each end, used for exercise 哑铃 **dumb waiter** a small lift for carrying food and crockery between floors (楼层间运送食物和餐具的)升降机

dumbfounded /dʌmˈfaʊndɪd/ **adjective** greatly astonished 目瞪口呆的

dumbstruck /ˈdʌmstrʌk/ **adjective** so shocked or surprised that you cannot speak 震惊得说不出话的,惊呆的

dumdum bullet /ˈdʌmdʌm/ **noun** a kind of soft-nosed bullet that expands on impact 达姆弹;柔头弹

dummy /ˈdʌmi/ **noun** (plural **dummies**) **1** a model of a human being 人体模型 **2** an object designed to resemble and take the place of the real one 仿制品;仿造物 **3** Brit. 【英】a rubber or plastic teat for a baby to suck on 橡皮(或塑料)奶头 **4** (in sport) a movement made to deceive an opponent into thinking that you are going to kick or pass the ball (体育比赛中的)假传球,假踢球 **5** informal 【非正式】a stupid person 蠢货;笨蛋 □ **dummy run** a practice or trial 演习;试用;试演

dump /dʌmp/ **noun 1** a place where rubbish or waste is left 垃圾场 **2** a temporary store of weapons or military provisions 武器(或军用补给品)的临时存放处 **3** informal 【非正式】an unpleasant or boring place 脏地方;邋遢场所 • **verb 1** get rid of something unwanted 扔掉,倾倒(垃圾) **2** put down something carelessly 随便堆放,乱放(某物) **3** informal 【非正式】abandon someone 丢下,抛弃(某人)

dumpling /ˈdʌmplɪŋ/ **noun** a small savoury ball of dough boiled in water or in a stew 汤团;饺子

dumps /dʌmps/ **plural noun** (**down in the dumps**) informal 【非正式】depressed or unhappy 闷闷不乐的;忧郁的

dumpy /ˈdʌmpi/ **adjective** short and stout 矮胖的

dun /dʌn/ **noun** a dull greyish-brown colour 暗褐色;灰褐色

dunce /dʌns/ **noun** a person who is slow at learning 智力迟钝的人;愚笨的人

dune /djuːn/ **noun** a mound or ridge of sand formed by the wind (风吹积成的)沙丘

dung /dʌŋ/ **noun** manure 粪;粪肥

dungarees /ˌdʌŋɡəˈriːz/ **noun** a garment consisting of trousers held up by straps over the shoulders 工装裤;背带裤

dungeon /ˈdʌndʒən/ **noun** a strong underground prison cell 地牢

dunk /dʌŋk/ **verb 1** dip food into a

drink or soup before eating it（吃前在饮料或汤里）浸、蘸（食物）**2** put something in water 浸；泡

dunnock /'dʌnək/ **noun** a small bird with a grey head and a reddish-brown back 林岩鹨（一种小鸟，头部灰色，背部呈红褐色）

duo /'dju:əʊ/ **noun** (plural **duos**) **1** a pair of people or things, especially in music or entertainment（尤指音乐或娱乐表演中的）一对表演者，双人组合 **2** Music【音乐】a duet 二重唱；二重奏

duodenum /ˌdju:ə'di:nəm/ **noun** (plural **duodenums** or **duodena** /ˌdju:ə'di:nə/) the first part of the small intestine immediately beyond the stomach 十二指肠

dupe /dju:p/ **verb** (**dupes, duping, duped**) deceive; trick 欺骗；诈骗；愚弄 • **noun** a person who is tricked or deceived 受骗上当者

duple /'dju:pl/ **adjective** Music【音乐】(of rhythm) based on two main beats to the bar（节奏）双拍子的

duplex /'dju:pleks/ N. Amer.【北美】**noun 1** a building divided into two flats 联式房屋 **2** a flat on two floors 复式住宅；跃层住宅

duplicate **adjective** /'dju:plɪkət/ **1** exactly like something else 完全一样的；复制的 **2** having two corresponding parts 成对的 • **noun** /'dju:plɪkət/ each of two or more identical things 完全一样的东西 • **verb** /'dju:plɪkeɪt/ (**duplicates, duplicating, duplicated**) **1** make or be an exact copy of 复印；复制；复写 **2** multiply by two 使加倍 **3** do something again unnecessarily（不必要地）重复 ■ **duplication** noun ■ **duplicator** noun.

duplicity /dju:'plɪsəti/ **noun** deceitful behaviour 欺骗行为 ■ **duplicitous** adjective.

durable /'djʊərəbl/ **adjective 1** hard-wearing 耐穿的；结实的 **2** (of goods) not for immediate consumption and

so able to be kept（商品）耐用的 ■ **durability** noun.

duration /dju'reɪʃn/ **noun** the time during which something continues 持续时间

duress /dju'res/ **noun** threats or violence used to force a person to do something 胁迫；强迫

during /'djʊərɪŋ/ **preposition 1** throughout the course of 在…期间 **2** at a particular point in the course of 在…期间的某个时候

dusk /dʌsk/ **noun** the darker stage of twilight 黄昏；薄暮

dusky /'dʌski/ **adjective** dark, or darkish in colour 颜色暗淡的

dust /dʌst/ **noun** fine, dry powder, especially tiny particles of earth, sand, etc. 灰尘；尘土 • **verb 1** remove dust from the surface of 除去…的尘土 **2** cover lightly with a powdered substance 撒粉末于 □ **dust-up** informal【非正式】a fight 打架；吵架；争吵 ■ **dusty** adjective.

dustbin /'dʌstbɪn/ **noun** Brit.【英】a large container for household rubbish 垃圾箱

dustcart /'dʌstkɑ:t/ **noun** Brit.【英】a vehicle used for collecting household rubbish 垃圾车

duster /'dʌstə(r)/ **noun** a cloth for dusting furniture 抹布

dustman /'dʌstmən/ **noun** (plural **dustmen**) Brit.【英】a man employed to remove rubbish from dustbins 垃圾清理工；清道夫

dustpan /'dʌstpæn/ **noun** a hand-held container into which you sweep dust and waste 簸箕

Dutch /dʌtʃ/ **adjective** relating to the Netherlands or its language 荷兰的；荷兰语的 • **noun** the language of the Netherlands 荷兰语 □ **Dutch courage** confidence gained from drinking alcohol 酒后之勇 **go Dutch** share the cost of a meal equally 各人付各人的账；平摊费用

dutiable /ˈdjuːtiəbl/ *adjective* on which duty needs to be paid 应征税的

dutiful /ˈdjuːtɪfl/ *adjective* carrying out all your obligations; doing your duty 尽职的;尽责的 ■ **dutifully** *adverb*.

duty /ˈdjuːti/ *noun* (plural **duties**) **1** a moral or legal obligation 责任;本分;义务 **2** a person's regular work, or a task required as part of their job 职责;任务 **3** a charge made when some goods are imported, exported, or sold 税;关税 □ **duty-bound** morally or legally obliged 责无旁贷的;义不容辞的 **duty-free** not requiring duty to be paid 免税的

duvet /ˈduːveɪ/ *noun* chiefly Brit.【主英】 a thick quilt used instead of an upper sheet and blankets 羽绒被

DVD /ˌdiː viː ˈdiː/ *abbreviation* digital versatile disc 数字激光视盘;数字多功能光碟

dwarf /dwɔːf/ *noun* (plural **dwarfs** or **dwarves**) **1** a member of a mythical race of short human-like creatures (神话中的)小矮人 **2** a person who is unusually small 矮子;侏儒 • *verb* make something seem small in comparison 使显得矮小

dwell /dwel/ *verb* (**dwells**, **dwelling**, past and past participle **dwelt** or **dwelled**) **1** formal【正式】live in or at a place 居住 **2** (**dwell on**) think about something at length 老想着

dwelling /ˈdwelɪŋ/ *noun* formal【正式】 a house or home 住处;住宅;寓所

dwindle /ˈdwɪndl/ *verb* (**dwindles**, **dwindling**, **dwindled**) gradually become smaller or weaker 逐渐减少;缩小;衰退

dye /daɪ/ *noun* a substance used to colour something 染料 • *verb* (**dyes**, **dyeing**, **dyed**) make something a particular colour with dye 给…染色;染 □ **dyed in the wool** having firm beliefs that never change (信仰)根

深蒂固的

dying /ˈdaɪɪŋ/ present participle of DIE¹.

dyke or **dike** /daɪk/ *noun* **1** a barrier built to prevent flooding from the sea 堤;坝;堰 **2** a ditch or water-filled channel 沟;渠;水道 **3** informal【非正式】 a lesbian 女同性恋者

dynamic /daɪˈnæmɪk/ *adjective* **1** full of energy, enthusiasm, and new ideas 充满活力的;精力充沛的;有创新思想的 **2** (of a process or system) constantly changing and developing (过程或制度)不断变化的,动态的 **3** Physics【物理】relating to forces that produce motion 力的;动力的 ■ **dynamically** *adverb*.

dynamics /daɪˈnæmɪks/ *plural noun* **1** the study of the forces involved in movement 力学;动力学 **2** forces which stimulate change 动力 **3** the varying levels of sound in a musical performance (音乐的)力度,力度变化

dynamism /ˈdaɪnəmɪzəm/ *noun* the quality of being full of energy, enthusiasm, and new ideas 活力;干劲儿

dynamite /ˈdaɪnəmaɪt/ *noun* a kind of high explosive 达纳炸药;氨爆炸药 • *verb* (**dynamites**, **dynamiting**, **dynamited**) blow up something with dynamite (用炸药)炸毁,爆破

dynamo /ˈdaɪnəməʊ/ *noun* (plural **dynamos**) a machine for converting mechanical energy into electrical energy 发电机

dynasty /ˈdɪnəsti, ˈdaɪ-/ *noun* (plural **dynasties**) a series of rulers or powerful people who belong to the same family 王朝

dysentery /ˈdɪsəntri/ *noun* a disease of the intestines which results in severe diarrhea 痢疾

dysfunctional /dɪsˈfʌŋkʃənl/ *adjective* **1** not operating properly 机能障碍的;不能正常运转的 **2** unable to deal with normal social relations

不能处理一般社会关系的；有缺陷的

dyslexia /dɪsˈleksiə/ noun a disorder involving difficulty in learning to read words and letters 诵读困难

■ **dyslexic** adjective & noun.

dyspepsia /dɪsˈpepsiə/ noun indigestion 消化不良

dyspeptic /dɪsˈpeptɪk/ adjective **1** suffering from indigestion 消化不良的 **2** irritable 脾气坏的

Ee

SPELLING TIP 拼写指南 Some words sound as if they should begin with 'e' but actually begin with 'ae' or 'oe' instead, for example **aesthetic**, **aeon**, **oestrogen**, or **oesophagus**. 有些词根据发音似乎是以e开头，但实际上是以 ae 或oe 开头，如 aesthetic, aeon, oestrogen 和 oesophagus。

E or **e** /iː/ **noun 1** (plural **Es** or **E's**) the fifth letter of the alphabet 英语字母表的第5个字母 **2** (€) euro or euros. • **abbreviation 1** East or Eastern. **2** informal 【非正式】the drug Ecstasy 迷幻药 □ **E-number** Brit. 【英】a code number starting with the letter E, given to food additives according to European Union instructions E 数 (根据欧洲联盟的规定加于食品添加剂的以E开头的编码数字)

each /iːtʃ/ **determiner & pronoun** every one of two or more people or things, regarded separately 各个；每个个 • **adverb** to, for, or by every one of a group 对各个；为每个；由每个

eager /ˈiːgə(r)/ **adjective** very much wanting to do or have something 渴望的；热切的 ■ **eagerly** adverb.

eagle /ˈiːgl/ **noun** a large bird of prey with long, broad wings 雕；鹰 □ **eagle-eyed** very observant 目光锐利的；观察敏锐的

ear /ɪə(r)/ **noun 1** the organ of hearing in humans and animals 耳；耳朵 **2** an ability to recognize and appreciate music or language 听力 **3** the spike of seeds at the top of the stalk of a cereal plant 穗 □ **within** (or **out of**) **earshot** near enough (or too far away) to be heard 在(或不在)听力所及范围内

earache /ˈɪəreɪk/ **noun** pain inside the ear 耳痛

eardrum /ˈɪədrʌm/ **noun** a membrane in the ear which vibrates in response to sound waves 鼓膜；耳膜

earl /ɜːl/ **noun** a British nobleman ranking above a viscount (英国的)伯爵 ■ **earldom** noun.

early /ˈɜːli/ **adjective** (**earlier**, **earliest**) & **adverb 1** before the expected time 早(的)；提早(的) **2** at the beginning of a particular time, period, or sequence 在初期(的)；在早期(的)

earmark /ˈɪəmɑːk/ **verb** choose or set aside for a particular purpose 指定…的用途；留作…用

earmuffs /ˈɪəmʌfs/ **plural noun** a pair of fabric coverings worn over the ears to protect them from cold or noise (御寒或防噪声用的)耳套

earn /ɜːn/ **verb 1** be given money in return for work or services 挣得，赚得(钱) **2** gain a reward for hard work or good qualities 获得；赢得 ■ **earner** noun.

earnest /ˈɜːnɪst/ **adjective** very serious 认真的；严肃的；诚挚的 □ **in earnest** sincere and serious about your intentions 认真的；严肃；诚挚 ■ **earnestly** adverb.

earnings /ˈɜːnɪŋz/ **plural noun** money or income earned 收益；收入

earphones /ˈɪəfəʊnz/ **plural noun** devices worn on the ears to listen to radio, recorded sound, etc. 耳机；耳塞

earpiece /ˈɪəpiːs/ **noun** the part of a telephone or other device that is held to or put inside the ear during use (电话)听筒；耳机；耳塞

earplug /ˈɪəplʌg/ **noun** a piece of wax, cotton wool, etc., placed in the ear as protection against noise or water (防噪声或防水的)耳塞

earring /ˈɪərɪŋ/ **noun** a piece of jewellery worn on the lobe or edge of the ear 耳环；耳饰

earth /ɜːθ/ **noun 1** (also **Earth**) the planet on which we live 地球 **2** the ground 地面 **3** soil 泥土；土壤 **4** Brit. 【英】a wire that connects an electrical circuit to the ground and makes it safe 地线 **5** the underground lair of a badger or fox 獾穴；狐穴 • **verb** Brit. 【英】connect an electrical device to earth 把(电器)接地

earthen /ˈɜːθn/ **adjective** made of earth or baked clay 泥土做的；陶制的

earthenware /ˈɜːθnweə(r)/ **noun** pottery made of fired clay 陶器；瓦器

earthling /ˈɜːθlɪŋ/ **noun** (in science fiction) a person from the earth (科幻小说中的)地球人

earthly /ˈɜːθli/ **adjective 1** having to do with the earth or human life 地球的；世俗的；尘世的 **2** remotely possible 可能性极小的：*no earthly reason* 根本没有理由

earthquake /ˈɜːθkweɪk/ **noun** a sudden violent shaking of the ground, caused by movements within the earth's crust 地震

earthwork /ˈɜːθwɜːk/ **noun** a large man-made bank of soil 土方

earthworm /ˈɜːθwɜːm/ **noun** a burrowing worm that lives in the soil 蚯蚓

earthy /ˈɜːθi/ **adjective** (**earthier**, **earthiest**) **1** like soil 泥土似的 **2** direct and unembarrassed about sexual subjects or bodily functions 粗俗的；下流的

earwig /ˈɪəwɪɡ/ **noun** a small insect with a pair of pincers at its rear end 蠼螋

ease /iːz/ **noun 1** lack of difficulty or effort 容易；不费力 **2** freedom from problems 安适；自在 • **verb** (**eases**, **easing**, **eased**) **1** make or become less serious or severe (使)缓和；(使)减轻 **2** move carefully or gradually

小心(或逐渐)地移动；挪动

easel /ˈiːzl/ **noun** a wooden frame on legs used by artists for holding the picture they are working on (木制)画架

east /iːst/ **noun 1** the direction in which the sun rises 东；东方 **2** the eastern part of a place 东部；东部地区 • **adjective & adverb 1** towards or facing the east 向东的；朝东的 **2** (of a wind) blowing from the east (风)从东面吹来的，从东面的 ■ **eastward** adjective & adverb **eastwards** adverb.

Easter /ˈiːstə(r)/ **noun** the Christian festival celebrating the resurrection of Jesus (基督教纪念耶稣复活的)复活节 □ **Easter egg** a chocolate egg given as a gift at Easter 复活节巧克力彩蛋

easterly /ˈiːstəli/ **adjective & adverb 1** facing or moving towards the east 朝东(的)；向东(的) **2** (of a wind) blowing from the east (风)从东面吹来的，从东面

eastern /ˈiːstən/ **adjective 1** situated in or facing the east 位于东方的；面朝东方的 **2** (**Eastern**) having to do with the part of the world to the east of Europe 欧洲以东地区的

easterner /ˈiːstənə(r)/ **noun** a person from the east of a region 东部人

easy /ˈiːzi/ **adjective** (**easier**, **easiest**) **1** able to be done without great effort 容易的；不费力的 **2** free from worry or problems 安逸的；安心的 □ **easy chair** a comfortable armchair 安乐椅 **easy-going** having a relaxed and tolerant attitude 心平气和的；脾气随和的 ■ **easily** adverb.

eat /iːt/ **verb** (**eats**, **eating**, **ate**; past participle **eaten**) **1** put food into the mouth and chew and swallow it 吃(食物) **2** (**eat something away**) gradually wear away or destroy something 侵蚀；消耗；逐渐毁坏 **3** (**eat something up**) use resources in very large quantities (大量)

用(资源);用光 □ **eat your words** admit that what you previously said was wrong 收回前言；承认说错 ■ **eatable** adjective.

eatery /'iːtəri/ noun (plural **eateries**) informal 【非正式】a restaurant or cafe 餐馆；快餐店

eau de cologne /ˌəʊ də kə'ləʊn/ = COLOGNE.

eaves /iːvz/ plural noun the part of a roof that meets or overhangs the walls of a building 屋檐

eavesdrop /'iːvzdrɒp/ verb (**eavesdrops, eavesdropping, eavesdropped**) secretly listen to a conversation 偷听；窃听

ebb /eb/ noun the movement of the tide out to sea 落潮，退潮 • verb **1** (of the tide) move away from the land (潮)落，退 **2** (**ebb away**) gradually become less or weaker (逐渐)减少，衰减 □ **at a low ebb** in a weakened or depressed state 处于低潮；处于衰退状态

ebony /'ebəni/ noun **1** heavy dark wood from a tree of tropical and warm regions 乌木 **2** a very dark brown or black colour 棕黑色；乌黑色

ebullient /ɪ'bʌliənt/ adjective cheerful and full of energy 奔放的；热情洋溢的；兴高采烈的 ■ **ebullience** noun.

EC /ˌiː 'siː/ abbreviation European Community 欧洲共同体

eccentric /ɪk'sentrɪk/ adjective unconventional and slightly strange 异乎寻常的，古怪的 • noun an eccentric person 怪人 ■ **eccentrically** adverb **eccentricity** noun.

ecclesiastical /ɪˌkliːzi'æstɪkl/ adjective relating to the Christian Church or its clergy (基督教)教会的，传教士的

echelon /'eʃəlɒn/ noun a level or rank in an organization, profession, or society (组织、行业或社会的)等级，阶层

echo /'ekəʊ/ noun (plural **echoes**) **1** a sound caused by the reflection of sound waves from a surface back to the listener 回声；回音 **2** a reflected radio or radar beam (无线电或雷达的)反射波，回波 • verb (**echoes, echoing, echoed**) **1** (of a sound) reverberate or be repeated after the original sound has stopped (声音)回响，回荡，被重复 **2** repeat someone's words or opinions 重复(某人的话或观点) ■ **echoey** adjective.

eclair /ɪ'kleə(r)/ noun a cake of light pastry filled with cream and topped with chocolate icing 狭长形松饼(以奶油为馅，用巧克力做糖衣)

éclat /eɪ'klɑː/ noun a notably brilliant or successful effect 显赫；显著成就

eclectic /ɪ'klektɪk/ adjective taking ideas from a wide range of sources 博采众长的；兼收并蓄的

eclipse /ɪ'klɪps/ noun **1** an occasion when one planet, the moon, etc. passes between another and the observer, or in front of a planet's source of light (行星、月亮等的)食 **2** a sudden loss of significance or power (重要性、权势的)消失，黯然失色 • verb (**eclipses, eclipsing, eclipsed**) **1** (of a planet, the moon, etc.) obscure the light coming from or shining on another (行星、月亮等)食，遮蔽(天体)的光 **2** make less significant or powerful 使失去重要性(或权势)；使失色

eco-friendly /ˌiːkəʊ'frendli/ adjective not harmful to the environment 环保的；对生态无害的

ecology /i'kɒlədʒi/ noun the study of how animals and plants relate to one another and to their surroundings 生态学 ■ **ecological** adjective **ecologically** adverb **ecologist** noun.

economic /ˌiːkə'nɒmɪk/ adjective **1** relating to economics or the economy of a country or region 经济学的；经济的 **2** profitable, or concerned with profitability 有利可图的

economical /ˌiːkəˈnɒmɪkl/ **adjective 1** giving good value in relation to the resources used or money spent 经济的；经济实惠的 **2** careful in the use of resources or money 节约的；节俭的 ∎ **economically** adverb

economics /ˌiːkəˈnɒmɪks/ **plural noun** the study of the production, consumption, and transfer of wealth 经济学

economist /ɪˈkɒnəmɪst/ **noun** an expert in economics 经济学家

economize or **economise** /ɪˈkɒnəmaɪz/ **verb** (**economizes**, **economizing**, **economized**) spend less; be economical 节省；节俭

economy /ɪˈkɒnəmi/ **noun** (plural **economies**) **1** the state of a country or region in terms of the production and consumption of goods and services and the supply of money 经济(状况) **2** careful management of resources 节约；节俭 **3** a financial saving (财政)节余

ecosystem /ˈiːkəʊsɪstəm/ **noun** all the plants and animals of a particular area considered in terms of how they interact with their environment 生态系统

ecstasy /ˈekstəsi/ **noun** (plural **ecstasies**) **1** an overwhelming feeling of great happiness 狂喜；欣喜若狂 **2** (**Ecstasy**) an illegal drug that produces feelings of excitement and happiness 迷幻药；摇头丸

✔ 拼写指南 no *x*: there is a *-cs-* at the beginning and an *s* at the end: ec*s*ta*s*y. ecstasy 的拼写中没有字母 x，开头有一个 *-cs-* 字母组合，词末有一个字母 s。

---

ecstatic /ɪkˈstætɪk/ **adjective** very happy or enthusiastic 狂喜的；热情极高的 ∎ **ecstatically** adverb

ectoplasm /ˈektəʊplæzm/ **noun** a substance that is thought by some people to come out of the body of a

medium during a seance 灵的外质

Ecuadorean or **Ecuadorian** /ˌekwəˈdɔːriən/ **noun** a person from Ecuador 厄瓜多尔人 ∎ **adjective** relating to Ecuador 厄瓜多尔的

ecumenical /ˌiːkjuˈmenɪkl/ **adjective 1** representing a number of different Christian Churches 代表不同基督教教会的 **2** wishing for the world's Christian Churches to be united 主张全世界基督教会联合的

eczema /ˈeksɪmə/ **noun** a condition in which patches of skin become rough and inflamed 湿疹

eddy /ˈedi/ **noun** (plural **eddies**) a circular movement of water causing a small whirlpool 漩涡；涡流 ∎ **verb** (**eddies**, **eddying**, **eddied**) (of water, air, etc.) move in a circular way (水、空气等)旋转，起漩涡

edelweiss /ˈeɪdlvaɪs/ **noun** a mountain plant with small flowers 高山火绒草

edema /ɪˈdiːmə/ US spelling of **oedema**. oedema 的美式拼法

Eden /ˈiːdn/ **noun 1** (also **Garden of Eden**) the place where Adam and Eve lived in the story of the Creation in the Bible (《圣经》中记载的)伊甸园 **2** a place of happiness or unspoilt beauty 乐园；圣洁之地

edge /edʒ/ **noun 1** the outside limit of an object, area, or surface 边缘；边界 **2** the sharpened side of a blade 刀口；刃 **3** the line along which two surfaces meet 棱；边 **4** a slight advantage over close rivals (对劲敌的)微弱优势 ∎ **verb** (**edges**, **edging**, **edged**) **1** provide with an edge 加边于 **2** move slowly and carefully 徐徐移动 ❑ **on edge** tense or irritable 紧张的；烦躁的；恼怒的

edgeways /ˈedʒweɪz/ or **edgewise** /ˈedʒwaɪz/ **adverb** with the edge uppermost or towards the viewer 边朝上(或朝前) ❑ **get a word in edgeways** manage to break into a conversation 插话；插嘴

edgy /'edʒi/ **adjective** (**edgier, edgiest**) tense, nervous, or irritable 紧张的；烦躁的；易怒的

edible /'edəbl/ **adjective** fit to be eaten 可以吃的；可食用的

edict /'i:dɪkt/ **noun** an official order or announcement 法令；布告

edifice /'edɪfɪs/ **noun** formal【正式】a large, impressive building (巨大而雄伟的)建筑

edify /'edɪfaɪ/ **verb** (**edifies, edifying, edified**) teach someone something that is educational or morally improving 教诲；启迪；教化 ■ **edification** noun.

edit /'edɪt/ **verb** (**edits, editing, edited**) **1** prepare written material for publication by correcting or shortening it 编辑(文字) **2** prepare material for a recording or broadcast 剪辑(录音或广播) **3** be editor of a newspaper or magazine 做(报刊)的编辑

edition /ɪ'dɪʃn/ **noun 1** a particular form of a published written work 版本 **2** the total number of copies of a book, newspaper, etc. that are issued (书报等的)一版印数，一次发行数 **3** a particular example of a regular programme or broadcast (广播电视定期节目的)一次，一期

editor /'edɪtə(r)/ **noun 1** a person who is in charge of a newspaper or magazine (报刊的)主 **2** a person who prepares material for publication or broadcasting (出版物或广播电视节目的)编辑

editorial /ˌedɪ'tɔːriəl/ **adjective** relating to the editing of material 编辑的 • **noun** a newspaper article giving the editor's opinion 社论

educate /'edʒukeɪt/ **verb** (**educates, educating, educated**) train or instruct someone to improve their mind or character 训练；教育；培养

education /ˌedʒu'keɪʃn/ **noun 1** the process of teaching or learning 教育 **2** the theory and practice of teaching 教育学 **3** training in a particular subject (特定科目的)培养，训练 ■ **educational** adjective **educationally** adverb.

Edwardian /ed'wɔːdiən/ **adjective** relating to the reign of King Edward VII (1901–1910)爱德华七世(时代)的

EEC /ˌiː iː 'siː/ **abbreviation** European Economic Community 欧洲经济共同体

eel /iːl/ **noun** a snake-like fish with a slender body 鳗，鳗鱼

eerie /'ɪəri/ **adjective** (**eerier, eeriest**) strange and frightening 怪异的；可怕的 ■ **eerily** adverb.

efface /ɪ'feɪs/ **verb** (**effaces, effacing, effaced**) **1** rub off a mark from a surface 擦掉，抹去(痕迹) **2** make something disappear 使消失 **3** (**efface yourself**) make yourself appear unimportant 使(自己)显得微不足道；不露锋芒

effect /ɪ'fekt/ **noun 1** a change that something causes in something else; a result 结果；效果 **2** operation or effectiveness 实行；生效；起作用 **3** the extent to which something succeeds 效力(范围)；作用(范围) **4** (**effects**) personal belongings (个人)财产 **5** (**effects**) the lighting, sound, or scenery used in a play or film (戏剧或电影中运用的光、声、景等)效果 • **verb** make something happen 使生效；实现 □ **in effect** in practice, even if not formally acknowledged 实质上；实际上

! 注意 don't confuse **effect** and **affect**. **Effect** chiefly means 'a result', while **affect** is a verb whose main meaning is 'make a difference to'. 不要混淆 effect 和 affect。effect 的主要含义为"结果"，而 affect 用作动词，主要含义为"影响"。

effective /ɪ'fektɪv/ **adjective 1**

producing a desired or intended result; successful 产生预期结果的；有效的 **2** (of a law or policy) in operation (法律或政策)生效的，起作用的 **3** existing in fact, though not formally acknowledged as such 实际(存在)的 ■ **effectively** adverb **effectiveness** noun.

effectual /ɪ'fektʃʊəl/ **adjective** producing the intended result; effective 有效的；生效的

effeminate /ɪ'femɪnət/ **adjective** disapproving 【贬】(of a man) looking, behaving, or sounding like a woman (男子)女人气的，无男子汉气概的 ■ **effeminacy** noun.

effervescent /ˌefə'vesnt/ **adjective 1** (of a liquid) giving off bubbles; fizzy (液体)起沫的，冒泡的 **2** lively and enthusiastic 活泼的，欢腾的；兴高采烈的 ■ **effervesce** verb **effervescence** noun.

effete /ɪ'fiːt/ **adjective 1** weak; feeble 衰弱的，虚弱的 **2** (of a man) effeminate (男子)女人气的

efficacious /ˌefɪ'keɪʃəs/ **adjective** formal 【正式】effective 有效的；灵验的

efficacy /'efɪkəsi/ **noun** formal 【正式】effectiveness 效力；效验

efficient /ɪ'fɪʃnt/ **adjective** working well with no waste of money or effort 效率高的；收效大的 ■ **efficiency** noun **efficiently** adverb.

effigy /'efɪdʒi/ **noun** (plural **effigies**) a sculpture or statue of a person (人的)雕像，塑像

effluent /'efluənt/ **noun** liquid waste or sewage that flows into a river or the sea 废水；污水

effluvium /ɪ'fluːvɪəm/ **noun** (plural **effluvia** /ɪ'fluːvɪə/) an unpleasant or harmful smell 臭气；恶臭

effort /'efət/ **noun 1** a determined attempt to do something 不懈的尝试 **2** the physical or mental energy needed to do something 努力；勉力

effortless /'efətləs/ **adjective** done or achieved without effort; natural and easy 不费劲的；轻松自如的 ■ **effortlessly** adverb.

effrontery /ɪ'frʌntəri/ **noun** rude and disrespectful behaviour 厚颜无耻；放肆

effusion /ɪ'fjuːʒn/ **noun** an act of talking or writing in an unrestrained way (讲话或文章中思想感情的)迸发，倾泻

effusive /ɪ'fjuːsɪv/ **adjective** expressing pleasure or approval in a warm and emotional way 奔放的 ■ **effusively** adverb.

e.g. /ˌiː'dʒiː/ **abbreviation** for example 比如，例如 [short for Latin 【缩写，拉丁】= *exempli gratia*, meaning 'for the sake of example'.]

egalitarian /ɪˌgælɪ'teəriən/ **adjective** believing that all people are equal and deserve equal rights and opportunities 平等主义的 • **noun** an egalitarian person 平等主义者 ■ **egalitarianism** noun.

egg[1] /eg/ **noun 1** a small oval or round object laid by a female bird, reptile, fish, etc., and containing a cell which can develop into a new creature 蛋；卵 **2** a female reproductive cell; an ovum 卵子；卵细胞

egg[2] **verb** (**egg someone on**) urge someone to do something foolish 怂恿，煽动(做傻事)

egghead /'eghed/ **noun** informal 【非正式】a very intelligent and hard-working person 好学的人；用功的人

eggplant /'egplɑːnt/ **noun** N. Amer. 【北美】an aubergine 茄子

ego /'iːgəʊ/ **noun** (plural **egos**) **1** a person's sense of their own value and importance 自尊心；自负 **2** the part of the mind that is responsible for a person's sense of who they are 自我；自我心智

egocentric /ˌiːgəʊ'sentrɪk/ **adjective** self-centred 自我中心的

egomania /ˌiːɡəʊˈmeɪnɪə/ **noun** an obsessive concern with yourself 极端自我主义;利己狂

egotism /ˈiːɡətɪzəm/ or **egoism** /ˈiːɡəʊɪzəm/ **noun** the quality of being very conceited or self-absorbed 自负;自大;念念不忘自我 ■ **egotist** (or **egoist**) **noun egotistical** (or **egoistical**) adjective.

egregious /ɪˈɡriːdʒɪəs/ **adjective** formal 【正式】 very bad 极坏的

egress /ˈiːɡres/ **noun** formal 【正式】 **1** the action of going out of a place 外出;出去 **2** a way out 出口;出路

egret /ˈiːɡrət/ **noun** a kind of heron with white feathers 白鹭

Egyptian /ɪˈdʒɪpʃn/ **noun 1** a person from Egypt 埃及人 **2** the language used in ancient Egypt 古埃及语 • **adjective** relating to Egypt 埃及的

Eid or **Id** /iːd/ **noun 1** the Muslim festival marking the end of the fast of Ramadan (伊斯兰教的)开斋节 **2** the Muslim festival marking the end of the annual pilgrimage to Mecca (伊斯兰教的)朝圣节

eider /ˈaɪdə(r)/ **noun** (plural **eider** or **eiders**) a black and white duck that lives in northern countries 绒鸭(毛色黑白,生活在北方国家)

eiderdown /ˈaɪdədaʊn/ **noun** Brit. 【英】 a quilt filled with down or another soft material 鸭绒被

eight /eɪt/ **cardinal number 1** one more than seven; 8 八 (Roman numeral 罗马数字: **viii** or **VIII**.) **2** a rowing boat with eight oars 八桨划船

eighteen /eɪˈtiːn/ **cardinal number** one more than seventeen; 18 十八 (Roman numeral 罗马数字: **xviii** or **XVIII**.) ■ **eighteenth** ordinal number.

eighth /eɪtθ/ **ordinal number 1** at number eight in a sequence; 8th 第八 **2** (**an eighth** or **one eighth**) each of eight equal parts of something 八分之一

✔ 拼写指南 there are two *h*s: eigh*th*. eighth 中有两个 h。

eighty /ˈeɪtɪ/ **cardinal number** (plural **eighties**) ten less than ninety; 80 八十 (Roman numeral 罗马数字: **lxxx** or **LXXX**.) ■ **eightieth** ordinal number.

eisteddfod /aɪˈsteðvɒd/ **noun** a Welsh festival with music and poetry competitions 艾斯特福德(威尔士音乐及诗歌大会)

either /ˈaɪðə(r), ˈiː-/ **conjunction & adverb 1** used before the first of two alternatives specified 或者;要么 **2** used to indicate a similarity or link with a statement just made 也 **3** for that matter; moreover 而且;此外 • **determiner & pronoun 1** one or the other of two people or things (两者之中的)任何一个 **2** each of two (两者之中的)每一个

ejaculate /ɪˈdʒækjuleɪt/ **verb** (**ejaculates**, **ejaculating**, **ejaculated**) **1** (of a man or male animal) eject semen from the penis at the moment of orgasm (男子或雄性动物)射精 **2** dated 【废】 say something suddenly 突然说出 ■ **ejaculation** noun.

eject /ɪˈdʒekt/ **verb 1** force or throw out violently or suddenly 用力扔出 **2** force someone to leave a place 逐出,撵出(某人) **3** (of a pilot) escape from an aircraft by means of an ejection seat (飞行员)弹射出来 □ **ejection seat** (or **ejector seat**) a seat that can throw the pilot out of the aircraft in an emergency 弹射坐椅 ■ **ejection** noun.

eke /iːk/ **verb** (**ekes**, **eking**, **eked**) (**eke something out**) **1** make a supply of something last a long time 省着用 **2** make a living with difficulty 艰难维持(生计)

elaborate **adjective** /ɪˈlæbərət/ involving many carefully arranged parts; complicated 精心计划的(精心安排的;复杂的 • **verb** /ɪˈlæbəreɪt/

(**elaborates**, **elaborating**, **elaborated**) develop something in more detail 详尽阐述 ■ **elaborately** adverb **elaboration** noun.

elan /er'læn/ noun energy and stylishness 活力;干劲;热情

elapse /ɪ'læps/ verb (**elapses**, **elapsing**, **elapsed**) (of time) pass (时间) 流逝, 消逝

elastic /ɪ'læstɪk/ adjective 1 able to go back to its normal shape being stretched or squeezed 有弹性的;有弹力的 2 flexible 灵活的 ● noun cord or fabric which returns to its original length or shape after being stretched 弹性绳;松紧带;弹性织物 □ **elastic band** a rubber band 橡皮筋;橡皮带 ■ **elasticity** noun.

elasticated /ɪ'læstɪkeɪtɪd/ adjective Brit. 【英】(of a garment or part of a garment) made elastic with rubber thread or tape (服装或材料中)织入橡皮筋的

elated /i'leɪtɪd/ adjective very happy and excited 兴高采烈的;得意洋洋的

elation /i'leɪʃn/ noun great happiness and excitement 兴高采烈;得意洋洋

elbow /'elbəʊ/ noun the joint between the forearm and the upper arm 肘 ● verb push someone with your elbow 用肘挤推 □ **elbow grease** informal 【非正式】hard work in cleaning something (清扫类的)重活儿

elder[1] /'eldə(r)/ adjective older 年龄较大的 ● noun 1 (**your elder**) a person who is older than you are 比自己年长的人 2 a leader or senior figure in a tribe 头领;元老;前辈;长者

elder[2] noun a small tree or shrub with white flowers and bluish-black or red berries (**elderberries**) 接骨木(小乔木或灌木, 开白花, 果实黑紫色或红色)

elderly /'eldəli/ adjective old or ageing 年老的;渐老的

eldest /'eldɪst/ adjective oldest 年龄最大的;最年长的

elect /ɪ'lekt/ verb 1 choose someone to hold a position by voting for them (投票)选举 2 choose to do something 选择 ● adjective elected to a position but not yet in office 当选而尚未就职的;候任的: *the President-Elect* 候任总统

election /ɪ'lekʃn/ noun 1 a procedure by which a person is elected 选举(程序) 2 the action of electing 选举;推选

electioneering /ɪ,lekʃə'nɪərɪŋ/ noun the action of campaigning to be elected 竞选活动;拉选票

elective /ɪ'lektɪv/ adjective 1 using or chosen by election 选举的;选任的 2 (of study, treatment, etc.) chosen; not compulsory 选修的;(治疗等)可选择的,非必需的

elector /ɪ'lektə(r)/ noun a person who has the right to vote in an election 选举人;选民

electoral /ɪ'lektərəl/ adjective relating to elections or electors 选举的;选民的 □ **electoral roll** (or **electoral register**) an official list of the people in a district who are entitled to vote in an election 选民登记册

electorate /ɪ'lektərət/ noun the people who are entitled to vote in an election (全体)选举人,选民

electric /ɪ'lektrɪk/ adjective 1 of, worked by, or producing electricity 电的;用电的;发电的 2 very exciting 高度刺激的 ● noun (**electrics**) Brit. 【英】the system of electric wiring in a house or vehicle (房屋或车辆中的)电路,电力系统 □ **electric chair** a chair in which convicted criminals are executed by electrocution 电椅 (用以处决死刑犯) **electric shock** a sudden discharge of electricity through a part of the body 触电;电击

electrical /ɪ'lektrɪkl/ adjective concerned with, operating by, or producing electricity 电的;用电的;发电的 ■ **electrically** adverb.

electrician /ɪˌlek'trɪʃn/ **noun** a person who installs and maintains electrical equipment 电工；电气工程师

electricity /ɪˌlek'trɪsəti/ **noun 1** a form of energy resulting from charged particles 电；电能 **2** the supply of electric current to a building for heating, lighting, etc. 供电

electrify /ɪ'lektrɪfaɪ/ **verb** (**electrifies**, **electrifying**, **electrified**) **1** charge something with electricity 使通电；使带电 **2** convert something to use electrical power 使电气化 **3** (**electrifying**) very exciting 令人极度兴奋的

electroconvulsive /ɪˌlektrəʊkən'vʌlsɪv/ **adjective** (of therapy for mental illness) using electric shocks applied to the brain (精神疾病治疗法)电休克疗法的，电惊厥疗法的

electrocute /ɪ'lektrəkjuːt/ **verb** (**electrocutes**, **electrocuting**, **electrocuted**) injure or kill by electric shock 电伤；电死 ■ **electrocution** noun.

electrode /ɪ'lektrəʊd/ **noun** a conductor through which electric current enters or leaves something 电极

electrolysis /ɪˌlek'trɒləsɪs/ **noun 1** the separation of a liquid into its chemical parts by passing an electric current through it 电解 **2** the removal of hair roots or small blemishes on the skin by means of an electric current 电解美容；电除斑

electrolyte /ɪ'lektrəlaɪt/ **noun** a liquid or gel that an electric current can pass through, e.g. in a battery 电解液，电解质

electromagnet /ɪˌlektrəʊ'mæɡnɪt/ **noun** a metal core made into a magnet by passing electric current through a surrounding coil 电磁体；电磁铁

electromagnetic /ɪˌlektrəʊmæɡ'netɪk/ **adjective** relating to electric currents and magnetic fields 电磁(场)的 ■ **electromagnetism** noun.

electromotive /ɪˌlektrəʊ'məʊtɪv/ **adjective** tending to produce an electric current 电动势的

electron /ɪ'lektrɒn/ **noun** Physics 【物理】 a subatomic particle with a negative charge, found in all atoms 电子 □ **electron microscope** a powerful microscope using electron beams instead of light 电子显微镜

electronic /ɪˌlek'trɒnɪk/ **adjective 1** having parts such as microchips and transistors that control and direct electric currents 电子操作的；电子件的 **2** relating to electrons or electronics 电子的；电子学的 **3** carried out by means of a computer 由计算机完成的 □ **electronic mail** email 电子邮件 ■ **electronically** adverb.

electronics /ɪˌlek'trɒnɪks/ **plural noun 1** the use or study of electronic devices 电器应用；电器学 **2** the study of the behaviour and movement of electrons 电子学 **3** circuits or devices using transistors, microchips, etc. 电子电路；电子仪器

electroplate /ɪ'lektrəpleɪt/ **verb** (**electroplates**, **electroplating**, **electroplated**) coat a metal object with another metal using electrolysis 电镀

elegant /'elɪɡənt/ **adjective** attractive, graceful, and stylish 优美的；雅致的；典雅的 ■ **elegance** noun **elegantly** adverb.

elegiac /ˌelɪ'dʒaɪək/ **adjective** expressing sadness, especially about the past or a person who has died 忧伤的；(尤指)哀悼过去的，伤逝的

elegy /'elədʒi/ **noun** (plural **elegies**) a poem expressing sadness, especially for a person who has died 挽歌；挽诗

element /'elɪmənt/ **noun 1** a basic part of something 基本组成部分；要素 **2** each of more than one hundred substances that cannot be changed or broken down 元素 **3** any of the four substances (earth, water, air, and fire) which were formerly believed to make up all matter 要素(指旧时认为构成一切物质的四大要素土、水、风、火) **4** a trace 迹象；痕迹 **5** a distinct group within a larger group (团体中独特的)一组人，一群人 **6** (**the elements**) weather conditions such as rain, wind, and cold 天气 **7** a part in an electric device through which an electric current is passed to provide heat 电热丝；电热元件

elemental /ˌelɪˈmentl/ **adjective 1** fundamental 基础的 **2** having to do with or like the primitive forces of nature (似)自然力的

elementary /ˌelɪˈmentri/ **adjective 1** relating to the most basic aspects of a subject 基本的；基础的；初级的 **2** straightforward and uncomplicated 容易的；简单的

elephant /ˈelɪfənt/ **noun** (plural **elephant** or **elephants**) a very large animal with a trunk, long curved tusks, and large ears, found in Africa and Asia 象(产于非洲和亚洲)

elephantine /ˌelɪˈfæntaɪn/ **adjective** resembling an elephant 似象的

elevate /ˈelɪveɪt/ **verb** (**elevates**, **elevating**, **elevated**) **1** lift to a higher position 举起；抬 高；使上升 **2** raise to a higher level or status 提高；提升；晋升

elevated /ˈelɪveɪtɪd/ **adjective** of a high intellectual or moral level 睿智的；高尚的

elevation /ˌelɪˈveɪʃn/ **noun 1** the action of elevating 提高；抬起；提升；晋升 **2** height above a given level, especially sea level 高度；(尤指)海拔 **3** the angle of something with the horizontal 仰角

elevator /ˈelɪveɪtə(r)/ **noun** N. Amer. 【北美】a lift in a building 电梯

eleven /ɪˈlevn/ **cardinal number 1** one more than ten; 11 十一(Roman numeral 罗马数字 : **xi** or **XI**). **2** a sports team of eleven players (体育)十一人队 □ **the eleventh hour** the

latest possible moment 最后时刻；最后一刻 ■ **eleventh** ordinal number

elevenses /ɪˈlevnzɪz/ **plural noun** Brit. informal 【英，非正式】a mid-morning snack 午前茶点

elf /elf/ **noun** (plural **elves**) (in folk tales) a creature resembling a small human figure with pointed ears (民间故事中的)小精灵(具人形，尖耳朵)

elfin /ˈelfɪn/ **adjective** (of a person) small and delicate (人)小精灵似的，小巧玲珑的

elicit /iˈlɪsɪt/ **verb** (**elicits**, **eliciting**, **elicited**) produce or draw out a response or reaction 引出；探出

elide /iˈlaɪd/ **verb** (**elides**, **eliding**, **elided**) **1** omit a sound or syllable when speaking (音或音节) **2** join together 连接；接合

eligible /ˈelɪdʒəbl/ **adjective 1** meeting the conditions to do or receive something 有资格的；符合条件的 **2** desirable as a husband or wife (做丈夫或妻子)合适的，中意的 ■ **eligibility** noun.

eliminate /ɪˈlɪmɪneɪt/ **verb** (**eliminates**, **eliminating**, **eliminated**) **1** completely remove or get rid of 消除；根除 **2** exclude someone from a competition by beating them (体育赛中)淘汰(选手) ■ **elimination** noun.

elision /ɪˈlɪʒn/ **noun** the omission of a sound or syllable in speech 省音

elite /eɪˈliːt/ **noun** a group of people regarded as the best in a particular society or organization 杰出人物；精英

elitism /eɪˈliːtɪzəm/ **noun 1** the belief that a society should be run by an elite 杰出人物统治论；精英主义 **2** the superior attitude associated with an elite 高人一等的优越感 ■ **elitist** adjective & noun.

elixir /ɪˈlɪksə(r)/ **noun** a drink believed to make people live for ever or have other magical effects 灵丹妙药，长生不老药

Elizabethan /ɪˌlɪzəˈbiːθn/ **adjective** relating to the reign of Queen Elizabeth I (1558–1603) 伊丽莎白一世时期的

elk /elk/ **noun** (plural **elk** or **elks**) a kind of large deer 驼鹿，麋

ellipse /ɪˈlɪps/ **noun** a regular oval shape 椭圆

ellipsis /ɪˈlɪpsɪs/ **noun** (plural **ellipses** /ɪˈlɪpsiːz/) **1** the omission of words from speech or writing 省略 **2** a set of dots indicating such an omission 省略号

elliptical /ɪˈlɪptɪkl/ **adjective 1** (of speech or writing) having a word or words deliberately left out (讲话或写作中)有意省略的 **2** (also **elliptic**) having the shape of an ellipse 椭圆的

elm /elm/ **noun** a tall tree with rough leaves 榆树

elocution /ˌeləˈkjuːʃn/ **noun** the skill of speaking clearly 演讲技巧；演说术

elongate /ˈiːlɒŋɡeɪt/ **verb** (**elongates**, **elongating**, **elongated**) make or become longer (使)伸长，(使)延长 ■ **elongation** noun.

elope /ɪˈləʊp/ **verb** (**elopes**, **eloping**, **eloped**) run away secretly to get married 私奔

eloquence /ˈeləkwəns/ **noun** fluent or persuasive speaking or writing 流利；雄辩

eloquent /ˈeləkwənt/ **adjective 1** fluent or persuasive in speech or writing 口才流利的；雄辩的 **2** clearly expressive 表达清楚的；明白显示的 ■ **eloquently** adverb.

else /els/ **adverb 1** in addition 此外；另外 **2** different; instead 不同的；另外的 □ **or else** if not; otherwise 否则；要不然

elsewhere /ˌelsˈweə(r)/ **adverb** in, at, or to some other place or other places 在别处；到别处

elucidate /ɪˈluːsɪdeɪt/ **verb** (**elucidates**, **elucidating**, **elucidated**) make clear; explain 阐明，解释 ■ **elu-cidation** noun.

elude /ɪˈluːd/ **verb** (**eludes**, **eluding**, **eluded**) **1** cleverly escape from or avoid 逃避，躲避；避开 **2** fail to be understood or achieved by 不为…所理解；把…难倒

elusive /ɪˈluːsɪv/ **adjective** difficult to find, catch, or achieve 难以发现(或抓住、获得)的

elver /ˈelvə(r)/ **noun** a young eel 幼鳗

elves /elvz/ plural of ELF.

emaciated /ɪˈmeɪʃieɪtɪd/ **adjective** abnormally thin and weak 消瘦的；憔悴的，■ **emaciation** noun.

email or **e-mail** /ˈiːmeɪl/ **noun** the sending of electronic messages from one computer user to another via a network, or a message sent in this way (发送)电子邮件 • **verb** send someone a message using email 发送电子邮件；用电子邮件传递

emanate /ˈeməneɪt/ **verb** (**emanates**, **emanating**, **emanated**) **1** (**emanate from**) come out from a place or source 发源于；从…发出 **2** give out a feeling or quality 显露出；散发出 ■ **emanation** noun.

emancipate /ɪˈmænsɪpeɪt/ **verb** (**emancipates**, **emancipating**, **eman-cipated**) **1** set free from restrictions 使不受束缚 **2** free from slavery 使摆脱奴役；解放 ■ **emancipation** noun.

emasculate /ɪˈmæskjuleɪt/ **verb** (**emasculates**, **emasculating**, **emasculated**) **1** make weaker or less effective 使柔弱，使无力；使效力减弱 **2** deprive a man of his male role or identity 阉割；使无男子气 ■ **emasculation** noun.

embalm /ɪmˈbɑːm/ **verb** treat a dead body to preserve it from decay 对(尸体)进行防腐处理

embankment /ɪmˈbæŋkmənt/ **noun 1** a wall or bank built to prevent flooding by a river 堤；堤岸 **2** a bank of earth or stone built to carry a road or railway over an area of low ground (公路或铁路的)路堤

embargo /ɪmˈbɑːɡəʊ/ **noun** (plural **embargoes**) an official ban, especially on trade with a particular country (尤指对某国贸易的)禁运 • **verb** (**embargoes, embargoing, embargoed**) put an embargo on 禁止…的贸易;禁运

embark /ɪmˈbɑːk/ **verb 1** go on board a ship or aircraft 上船;登机 **2** (**embark on**) begin a new project or course of action 开始,着手,从事(新项目或行动) ■ **embarkation** noun.

embarrass /ɪmˈbærəs/ **verb** make someone feel awkward or ashamed 使窘迫;使尴尬 ■ **embarrassment** noun.

✔ 拼写指南 double *r*, double *s*: em*barrass*. embarrass 中有两个 r 和两个 s。

embassy /ˈembəsi/ **noun** (plural **embassies**) the official residence or offices of an ambassador 大使馆

embattled /ɪmˈbætld/ **adjective 1** facing a lot of difficulties 陷入困境的 **2** surrounded by enemy forces 被敌军包围的

embed or **imbed** /ɪmˈbed/ **verb** (**embeds, embedding, embedded**) fix something firmly in a surrounding mass 把…嵌入

embellish /ɪmˈbelɪʃ/ **verb 1** make more attractive; decorate 美化;装饰;修饰 **2** add extra details to a story 给(故事)添加细节;润饰

ember /ˈembə(r)/ **noun** a piece of burning wood or coal in a dying fire 余火未尽的木块(或煤块)

embezzle /ɪmˈbezl/ **verb** (**embezzles, embezzling, embezzled**) steal money that you have been given responsibility for 侵吞,盗用(钱款) ■ **embezzlement** noun.

embittered /ɪmˈbɪtəd/ **adjective** angry or resentful 怨愤的;不满的

emblazon /ɪmˈbleɪzn/ **verb** display

a design on something in a very noticeable way 炫示(设计图案)

emblem /ˈembləm/ **noun** a design or symbol as a badge of a nation, organization, or family (代表国家、组织或家族的)徽章,纹章(图案)

emblematic /ˌembləˈmætɪk/ **adjective** representing a particular quality or idea 象征(性)的;标志的

embody /ɪmˈbɒdi/ **verb** (**embodies, embodying, embodied**) **1** give a tangible or visible form to an idea or quality 使(思想或品质)具体化;体现 **2** include or contain 包括;包含 ■ **embodiment** noun.

embolden /ɪmˈbəʊldən/ **verb** make someone braver or more confident 使有胆量;使有信心

embolism /ˈembəlɪzəm/ **noun** obstruction of an artery by a clot of blood or an air bubble 栓塞

emboss /ɪmˈbɒs/ **verb** carve a raised design on 浮雕压印;凹凸印

embrace /ɪmˈbreɪs/ **verb** (**embraces, embracing, embraced**) **1** hold someone closely in your arms 拥抱;怀抱 **2** include or contain 包括;包含 **3** willingly accept or support a belief or change 自愿接受;信奉;乐意支持(变化) • **noun** an act of embracing 拥抱;接受;支持

embrocation /ˌembrəˈkeɪʃn/ **noun** a liquid medication rubbed on the body to relieve pain from strains 擦剂

embroider /ɪmˈbrɔɪdə(r)/ **verb** (**embroiders, embroidering, embroidered**) **1** sew decorative needlework patterns on 在…上刺绣 **2** add false or exaggerated details to 渲染;对…添油加醋

embroidery /ɪmˈbrɔɪdəri/ **noun** (plural **embroideries**) **1** the art of embroidering 刺绣;绣花 **2** embroidered cloth 绣花布;刺绣制品

embroil /ɪmˈbrɔɪl/ **verb** (**embroil someone in**) involve someone in a conflict or difficult situation 使卷入

(冲突);使陷入(困境)

embryo /'embriəʊ/ **noun** (plural **embryos**) an unborn or unhatched baby or animal in the early stages of development 胚胎

embryonic /ˌembri'ɒnɪk/ **adjective 1** relating to an embryo 胚的;胚胎的 **2** in a very early stage of development 初期的;萌芽阶段的

emend /i'mend/ **verb** correct and revise a piece of writing 校订,修改(文稿)

emerald /'emərəld/ **noun 1** a green precious stone 祖母绿;绿宝石;翡翠 **2** a bright green colour 翠绿色,鲜绿色

emerge /i'mɜːdʒ/ **verb** (**emerges**, **emerging**, **emerged**) **1** become gradually visible 浮现;逐渐显现 **2** (of facts) become known (事实)暴露,被知晓 **3** recover from a difficult situation or experience (从困苦中)摆脱出来 ■ **emergence** noun.

emergency /i'mɜːdʒənsi/ **noun** (plural **emergencies**) a serious and unexpected situation requiring immediate action 紧急情况;不测事件;非常时刻

emergent /i'mɜːdʒənt/ **adjective** new and still developing 新兴的;处于发展初期的

emeritus /i'merɪtəs/ **adjective** having retired but allowed to keep a title as an honour 荣誉退休的;退休后保留头衔的: *an emeritus professor* 荣誉退休教授

emery board /'eməri/ **noun** a strip of thin wood or card coated with a rough material and used as a nail file 指甲砂锉

emetic /i'metɪk/ **adjective** causing vomiting 催吐的

emigrant /'emɪɡrənt/ **noun** a person who emigrates 移居外国的人;移民

emigrate /'emɪɡreɪt/ **verb** (**emigrates**, **emigrating**, **emigrated**) leave your own country and settle permanently in another 移居外国 ■ **emigration** noun.

émigré /'emɪɡreɪ/ **noun** a person who has emigrated 移居外国的人;移民

eminence /'emɪnəns/ **noun 1** the quality of being very famous and respected in a particular area of activity 出众;卓越;显赫 **2** an important or distinguished person 要人;权威;名家

eminent /'emɪnənt/ **adjective 1** very famous and respected; distinguished 著名的;卓越的;显赫的 **2** outstanding or obvious 突出的;显著的 ■ **eminently** adverb.

emir /e'mɪə(r)/ or **amir** /ə'mɪə(r)/ **noun** a title of some Muslim rulers. 埃米尔(对伊斯兰国家统治者的称呼)

emissary /'emɪsəri/ **noun** (plural **emissaries**) a person sent as a diplomatic representative on a mission 使者

emission /i'mɪʃn/ **noun 1** the action of emitting 发出;射出;散发 **2** a substance which is emitted 发射物;散发物

emit /i'mɪt/ **verb** (**emits**, **emitting**, **emitted**) **1** give out light, heat, gas, etc. 发出,射出,散发(光、热、气体等) **2** make a sound (声音)

emollient /i'mɒliənt/ **adjective 1** softening or soothing the skin 使皮肤柔软的;润肤的 **2** attempting to avoid conflict; calming 试图避免冲突的;使平静的 ■ **emollience** noun.

emolument /i'mɒljumənt/ **noun** formal 【正式】 a salary or fee 薪水,工资;报酬

emotion /i'məʊʃn/ **noun 1** a strong feeling, such as joy or anger 强烈的情感;激情;情绪 **2** instinctive feeling as opposed to reasoning (与理智相对的)情感

emotional /i'məʊʃənl/ **adjective 1** relating to the emotions 情绪(上)的;情感(上)的 **2** arousing or showing emotion 激起感情的;令人激动的 ■ **emotionally** adverb.

emotive /ɪˈməʊtɪv/ **adjective** arousing strong feeling 激起感情的；令人激动的

empathize or **empathise** /ˈempəθaɪz/ **verb** (**empathizes, empathizing, empathized**) understand and share the feelings of someone else 神入；感情移入；有同感

empathy /ˈempəθi/ **noun** the ability to understand and share the feelings of someone else 感情移入；同情；同感

emperor /ˈempərə(r)/ **noun** the ruler of an empire 皇帝

emphasis /ˈemfəsɪs/ **noun** (plural **emphases** /ˈemfəsiːz/) **1** special importance or value given to something 重要性 **2** stress put on a word or words in speaking (讲话时对个别词的)强调，着重

emphasize or **emphasise** /ˈemfəsaɪz/ **verb** (**emphasizes, emphasizing, emphasized**) give special importance or prominence to 强调；着重

emphatic /ɪmˈfætɪk/ **adjective 1** showing or giving emphasis 强调的；着重的 **2** definite and clear 确切的；清楚的。■ **emphatically** adverb.

emphysema /ˌemfɪˈsiːmə/ **noun** a condition that affects the lungs, causing breathlessness 肺气肿

empire /ˈempaɪə(r)/ **noun 1** a large group of countries under a single authority or ruler 帝国 **2** a large commercial organization under the control of one person or group (由一人或一个集团控制的)大企业

empirical /ɪmˈpɪrɪkl/ **adjective** based on observation or experience rather than theory or logic 以观察(或经验)为依据的 ■ **empirically** adverb. **empiricism** noun **empiricist** noun.

emplacement /ɪmˈpleɪsmənt/ **noun** a structure or platform where a gun is placed for firing 炮位；炮台

employ /ɪmˈplɔɪ/ **verb 1** give work to someone and pay them for it 雇用 **2** make use of 使用；利用 **3** keep someone occupied 使忙碌；使从事

employee /ɪmˈplɔɪiː/ **noun** a person who is employed by a company or individual 雇员；受雇者

employer /ɪmˈplɔɪə(r)/ **noun** a company or individual that employs people 雇主；老板

employment /ɪmˈplɔɪmənt/ **noun 1** the state of having paid work 受雇 **2** a person's work or profession 工作；职业

emporium /emˈpɔːriəm/ **noun** (plural **emporia** /emˈpɔːriə/ or **emporiums**) a large store selling a wide variety of goods 大型百货商场；大商店

empower /ɪmˈpaʊə(r)/ **verb** (**empowers, empowering, empowered**) **1** give authority or power to 授权；给…权力 **2** give strength and confidence to 给…力量和信心 ■ **empowerment** noun.

empress /ˈemprəs/ **noun 1** a female emperor 女皇 **2** the wife or widow of an emperor 皇后

empty /ˈempti/ **adjective** (**emptier, emptiest**) **1** containing nothing; not filled or occupied 空的，无人的 **2** (of words or gestures) having no real meaning (词语或姿势)空虚的，无意义的: *empty promises* 空洞的许诺 • **verb** (**empties, emptying, emptied**) **1** make or become empty 使空；变空 **2** (of a river) flow into the sea or a lake (河流)汇入(海或湖) ■ **emptiness** noun.

emu /ˈiːmjuː/ **noun** a large Australian bird which is unable to fly, similar to an ostrich 鸸鹋(一种不会飞的大型鸟,产于澳大利亚,形似鸵鸟)

emulate /ˈemjuleɪt/ **verb** (**emulates, emulating, emulated**) try to do as well as or be better than 努力赶上(或超过) ■ **emulation** noun.

emulsify /ɪˈmʌlsɪfaɪ/ **verb** (**emulsifies, emulsifying, emulsified**) combine two liquids into a smooth mixture 使乳化 ■ **emulsifier** noun.

emulsion /ɪˈmʌlʃn/ noun 1 a mixture of two liquids in which particles of one are evenly distributed in the other 乳状液；乳浊液 2 a type of paint for walls and ceilings 乳胶漆 3 a light-sensitive coating for photographic film 感光乳剂

enable /ɪˈneɪbl/ verb (**enables, enabling, enabled**) 1 provide with the ability or means to do something 使有能力做；使能够 2 make something possible 使可能

enact /ɪˈnækt/ verb 1 pass a law 使(法律)通过 2 act out a role or play 扮演(角色)；上演(戏) ■ **enactment** noun.

enamel /ɪˈnæml/ noun 1 a coloured glassy substance applied to metal, glass, or pottery for decoration or protection 瓷釉；搪瓷；珐琅 2 the hard substance that covers the crown of a tooth (牙齿的)珐琅质，釉质 3 a paint that dries to give a hard coat 瓷漆；亮漆 • verb (**enamels, enamelling, enamelled**; US spelling 【美拼作】 **enamels, enameling, enameled**) coat or decorate with enamel 给…上珐琅(或瓷漆)

enamour /ɪˈnæmə(r)/ (US spelling 【美拼作】 **enamor**) verb (**be enamoured of** or **with**) be filled with love or admiration for 喜爱；崇拜；迷恋

en bloc /ˌɒn ˈblɒk/ adverb all together, or all at once 整个；全部；一起

encamp /ɪnˈkæmp/ verb settle in or set up a camp 扎营；露营

encampment /ɪnˈkæmpmənt/ noun a place where a camp is set up 营地

encapsulate /ɪnˈkæpsjuleɪt/ verb (**encapsulates, encapsulating, encapsulated**) summarize clearly and in few words 把…装入胶囊；用胶囊装；封装

encase /ɪnˈkeɪs/ verb (**encases, encasing, encased**) enclose or cover in a case 把…装入箱(或盒)内

encephalitis /ˌensefəˈlaɪtəs/ noun inflammation of the brain 脑炎

enchant /ɪnˈtʃɑːnt/ verb 1 delight; charm 使入迷；使陶醉 2 put under a spell 使着魔；对…施魔法 ■ **enchanter** noun **enchantment** noun **enchantress** noun.

enchanting /ɪnˈtʃɑːntɪŋ/ adjective delightfully charming or attractive 令人陶醉的；迷人的

encircle /ɪnˈsɜːkl/ verb (**encircles, encircling, encircled**) form a circle around 环绕；围绕；包围

enclave /ˈenkleɪv/ noun a small area of one country's territory which is surrounded by another country 飞地 (某国被他国领土所包围的小块领土)

enclose /ɪnˈkləʊz/ verb (**encloses, enclosing, enclosed**) 1 surround or close off on all sides 围住；包住 2 put a document or object in an envelope along with a letter 把…随信装入信封；随信附上

enclosure /ɪnˈkləʊʒə(r)/ noun 1 an enclosed area 围场；圈地 2 a document or object put in an envelope along with a letter (信中的)附件，装入物

encode /ɪnˈkəʊd/ verb (**encodes, encoding, encoded**) convert into a coded form 把…译成电码(或密码)

encompass /ɪnˈkʌmpəs/ verb 1 include a wide range of things 包含，包括(广泛事物) 2 surround or cover 围绕；包围；覆盖

encore /ˈɒŋkɔː(r)/ noun a short extra performance given at the end of a concert in response to calls by the audience (应观众要求)加演的节目

encounter /ɪnˈkaʊntə(r)/ verb (**encounters, encountering, encountered**) unexpectedly meet or be faced with 意外遇见；邂逅 • noun 1 an unexpected or casual meeting 意外遇见；邂逅 2 a confrontation 冲突；交战

encourage /ɪnˈkʌrɪdʒ/ verb (**encour-**

ages, encouraging, encouraged) **1** give support, confidence, or hope to 鼓励;激励 **2** help the development of 促进;促长;激发 ■ **encouragement** noun encouraging adjective.

encroach /ɪnˈkrəʊtʃ/ verb **1** (encroach on) gradually intrude on a person's territory, rights, etc. (逐渐)侵犯,侵占(某人的领土、权利等) **2** gradually advance beyond expected or acceptable limits (逐渐)超出可接受的界限;侵蚀 ■ **encroachment** noun.

encrust /ɪnˈkrʌst/ verb cover with a hard crust 在…上包硬壳

encrypt /ɪnˈkrɪpt/ verb convert into code 把…编码;把…译成密码(或电码) ■ **encryption** noun.

encumber /ɪnˈkʌmbə(r)/ verb (encumbers, encumbering, encumbered) prevent someone from moving or acting freely 拖累;妨碍;阻碍

encumbrance /ɪnˈkʌmbrəns/ noun a thing that prevents someone from moving or acting freely 累赘;阻碍

encyclopedia or **encyclopaedia** /ɪnˌsaɪkləˈpiːdiə/ noun a book or set of books giving information on many subjects 百科全书 ■ **encyclopedic** adjective.

end /end/ noun **1** the final part of something 最后部分;末尾 **2** the furthest or most extreme part 端;尽头 **3** the stopping of a state or situation 结束;终止 **4** a person's death or downfall 死亡;毁灭 **5** a goal or desired result 目标;目的 • verb **1** come or bring to an end (使)结束;(使)终结 **2** (end in) have a particular result 以…为结果;以…告终 **3** (end up) eventually reach or come to a particular state or place 最终达到;最终取得 □ **make ends meet** earn just enough money to live on 勉强维持生计

endanger /ɪnˈdeɪndʒə(r)/ verb (endangers, endangering, endangered) put in danger 危及;使遭遇危

险

endangered /ɪnˈdeɪndʒəd/ adjective in danger of extinction 有灭绝危险的;濒于灭绝的

endear /ɪnˈdɪə(r)/ verb (endear someone to) make someone popular with or liked by 使受欢迎;使爱喜

endearing /ɪnˈdɪərɪŋ/ adjective inspiring affection; lovable 惹人喜爱的;令人倾心的 ■ **endearingly** adverb.

endearment /ɪnˈdɪəmənt/ noun **1** a word or phrase expressing affection 表达爱慕的言语 **2** love or affection 爱慕;倾心

endeavour /ɪnˈdevə(r)/ (US spelling 【美拼作】**endeavor**) verb try hard to achieve something 努力;尽力 • noun **1** an attempt to achieve something 努力;尽力 **2** concentrated hard work and effort 努力工作

endemic /enˈdemɪk/ adjective **1** (of a disease or condition) regularly found among particular people or in a certain area (疾病或情况)地方性的,某群体特有的,某地流行的 **2** (of a plant or animal) native to a certain area (动植物)土生的,特有的

ending /ˈendɪŋ/ noun an end or final part 结尾;结局

endive /ˈendaɪv/ noun a plant with bitter leaves, eaten in salads 菊苣(一种植物,叶苦,拌色拉食用)

endless /ˈendləs/ adjective having or seeming to have no end or limit 无止境的;无穷尽的;无垠的 ■ **endlessly** adverb.

endocrine /ˈendəkrɪn/ adjective (of a gland) secreting hormones or other products directly into the blood (腺体)内分泌的

endorphin /enˈdɔːfɪn/ noun a painkilling hormone within the brain and nervous system 内啡肽(有止痛作用的激素,存在于脑部和神经系统中)

endorse /ɪnˈdɔːs/ verb (endorses,

endorsing, endorsed) **1** publicly state that you approve of something (公开)支持，赞同 **2** sign a cheque on the back so that it can be paid into an account 在(支票)背面签字；背书 **3** Brit. 【英】 mark details of a driving offence on a driving licence 在(驾驶执照上)记录违章情况 ■ **endorsement** noun.

endow /ɪn'daʊ/ **verb 1** give someone your property, or leave it to them in your will 遗嘱赠予 **2** donate a large sum of money to an institution, from which they will be able to receive a regular income 捐赠 **3** (be endowed with) have as a natural quality or characteristic 给予，赋予(与生俱来的品质或特点)

endowment /ɪn'daʊmənt/ **noun 1** property or a regular income that has been given or left to a person or an institution 捐赠；资助 **2** a quality or ability that you are born with 天赋；天资；才能 □ **endowment mortgage** Brit. 【英】 a mortgage linked to an insurance policy, in which the sum received when the policy matures is used to pay back the money borrowed 定期人寿保险按揭

endpaper /'endˌpeɪpə(r)/ **noun** a sheet of paper at the beginning or end of a book, fixed to the inside of the cover (书籍卷首和卷尾的)衬页，环衬

endurance /ɪn'djʊərəns/ **noun** the ability to do or cope with something painful or difficult for a long time 忍耐；忍耐力

endure /ɪn'djʊə(r)/ **verb (endures, enduring, endured) 1** experience and be able to cope with prolonged pain or difficulty 忍受；忍耐 **2** last for a long time 持续；持久

enema /'enəmə/ **noun** a process in which liquid is injected into the rectum to clean it out 灌肠

enemy /'enəmi/ **noun (plural enemies) 1** a person who is hostile to you 敌人；反对者 **2 (the enemy)** a country that your own is fighting in a war (战争中的)敌国

energetic /ˌenə'dʒetɪk/ **adjective** having a lot of energy 精力充沛的；充满活力的 ■ **energetically** adverb.

energize or **energise** /'enədʒaɪz/ **verb (energizes, energizing, energized)** give energy and enthusiasm to 使精力充沛；使有活力；激发

energy /'enədʒi/ **noun (plural energies) 1** the strength and vitality that you need in order to be active 活力 **2 (energies)** a person's physical and mental powers 精力；力量 **3** power obtained from physical or chemical resources to provide light and heat or to work machines 能源

enervate /'enəˌveɪt/ **verb (enervates, enervating, enervated)** cause someone to feel deprived of energy 使衰弱；使无力；使失去活力

enfant terrible /ˌɒnfɒn te'riːbl/ **noun (plural enfants terribles** /ˌɒnfɒn-te'riːbl/) a person who is known for behaving in an unconventional or controversial way 行事莽撞的人；肆无忌惮的人

enfeeble /ɪn'fiːbl/ **verb (enfeebles, enfeebling, enfeebled)** make someone weak 使衰弱；使无力

enfold /ɪn'fəʊld/ **verb** envelop someone 包住；裹住

enforce /ɪn'fɔːs/ **verb (enforces, enforcing, enforced) 1** make sure a law or rule is obeyed 使(法律或规定)生效；强制执行(法律或规定) **2** force something to happen 迫使…发生 ■ **enforceable** adjective **enforcement** noun **enforcer** noun.

enfranchise /ɪn'fræntʃaɪz/ **verb (enfranchises, enfranchising, enfranchised) 1** give a person or group the right to vote 给予…选举权 **2** historical 【历史】 free a slave 解放(奴隶)；使(奴隶)恢复自由 ■ **enfran-**

chisement noun.

engage /ɪnˈgeɪdʒ/ **verb (engages, engaging, engaged) 1** attract or involve someone's interest or attention 吸引(某人的兴趣或注意); 使关注 **2** (**engage in** or **with**) become involved in 忙于; 从事 **3** employ or hire someone 雇用; 聘用 **4** move a part of a machine or engine into position 使(机器或引擎部件)接合

engaged /ɪnˈgeɪdʒd/ **adjective 1** occupied 忙的 **2** Brit. 【英】(of a telephone line) unavailable because already in use (电话线)被占用的, 使用中的 **3** having formally agreed to get married 已订婚的

engagement /ɪnˈgeɪdʒmənt/ **noun 1** a formal agreement to get married 订婚; 婚约 **2** an appointment 约会 **3** the state of being involved in something 从事 **4** fighting between armed forces 交战; 遭遇战

engaging /ɪnˈgeɪdʒɪŋ/ **adjective** charming and attractive 迷人的; 有吸引力的, ■ **engagingly** adverb.

engender /ɪnˈdʒendə(r)/ **verb (engenders, engendering, engendered)** give rise to 使发生; 使出现; 引起

engine /ˈendʒɪn/ **noun 1** a machine with moving parts that converts power into motion 发动机; 引擎 **2** a railway locomotive 机车; 火车头

engineer /ˌendʒɪˈnɪə(r)/ **noun 1** a person who is qualified in engineering 工程师 **2** a person who maintains or controls an engine or machine 机械师 • **verb (engineers, engineering, engineered) 1** design and build 设计; 建造 **2** arrange for something to happen 操纵; 策划

engineering /ˌendʒɪˈnɪərɪŋ/ **noun** the study of the design, building, and use of engines, machines, and structures 工程学

English /ˈɪŋglɪʃ/ **noun** the language of England, used in many varieties

throughout the world 英语 • **adjective** relating to England 英格兰的; 英国的

engorged /ɪnˈgɔːdʒd/ **adjective** swollen 肿胀的

engrained /ɪnˈgreɪnd/ ⇒ 见 INGRAINED.

engrave /ɪnˈgreɪv/ **verb (engraves, engraving, engraved) 1** carve words or a design on a hard surface or object (在坚硬表面或物体上)雕刻(文字或图案) **2** (**be engraved on** or **in**) be fixed in a person's mind 在(记忆中)留下深刻印象; 深深印入(脑海) ■ **engraver** noun.

engraving /ɪnˈgreɪvɪŋ/ **noun 1** a print made from an engraved plate or block 雕版印刷品; 版画 **2** the process of engraving 雕刻

engross /ɪnˈgrəʊs/ **verb** (often **be engrossed in**) absorb all of someone's attention 使全神贯注

engulf /ɪnˈgʌlf/ **verb** (of a natural force) sweep over someone or something and completely surround or cover them (自然力)吞没

enhance /ɪnˈhɑːns/ **verb (enhances, enhancing, enhanced)** increase the quality, value, or extent of something 提高(质量、价值); 增大(范围) ■ **enhancement** noun.

enigma /ɪˈnɪgmə/ **noun** a mysterious or puzzling person or thing 神秘的人; 费解的事物 ■ **enigmatic** adjective **enigmatically** adverb.

enjoin /ɪnˈdʒɔɪn/ **verb** instruct or urge someone to do something 吩咐; 责令; 敦促

enjoy /ɪnˈdʒɔɪ/ **verb 1** get pleasure from 喜爱; 乐于 **2** (**enjoy yourself**) have a good time 得到乐趣; 过得快活 **3** have and benefit from 享有; 享受 ■ **enjoyment** noun.

enjoyable /ɪnˈdʒɔɪəbl/ **adjective** giving pleasure 有乐趣的; 使人快乐的 ■ **enjoyably** adverb.

enlarge /ɪnˈlɑːdʒ/ **verb (enlarges, enlarging, enlarged) 1** make or become bigger (使)扩大;(使)变大 **2 (enlarge on)** speak or write about something in greater detail 细说;详述

enlargement /ɪnˈlɑːdʒmənt/ **noun 1** the state of being enlarged 扩大；变大 **2** a photograph that is larger than the original negative or than an earlier print 放大的照片

enlighten /ɪnˈlaɪtn/ **verb 1** give someone greater knowledge and understanding 启迪;开导;教育 **2 (enlightened)** well informed and able to make good judgements 有见识的;开明的 ■ **enlightenment** noun.

enlist /ɪnˈlɪst/ **verb 1** join the armed services 应募;入伍 **2** ask for someone's help in doing something 请求(帮助) ■ **enlistment** noun.

enliven /ɪnˈlaɪvn/ **verb 1** make something more interesting 使有趣 **2** make someone more cheerful or animated 使生活泼,使愉快

en masse /ˌɒn ˈmæs/ **adverb** all together 全体;一起

enmesh /ɪnˈmeʃ/ **verb (be enmeshed in)** be involved in a complicated situation 陷入,卷入(复杂局面)

enmity /ˈenməti/ **noun (plural enmities)** hostility 敌意,仇恨

ennoble /ɪˈnəʊbl/ **verb (ennobles, ennobling, ennobled)** give greater dignity to 使变尊贵;使更崇高

ennui /ɒnˈwiː/ **noun** a feeling of listlessness, boredom, and dissatisfaction 厌倦;无聊

enormity /ɪˈnɔːməti/ **noun (plural enormities) 1 (the enormity of)** the extreme seriousness of something bad 穷凶极恶;凶暴 **2** great size or scale 巨大;广大 **3** a serious crime or sin 滔天大罪;暴行

enormous /ɪˈnɔːməs/ **adjective** very large 巨大的;极大的 ■ **enormously** adverb.

enough /ɪˈnʌf/ **determiner & pronoun** as much or as many as is necessary or desirable 足够(的) • **adverb 1** to the required degree 足够地;充分地 **2** to a moderate degree 相当;尚

enquire /ɪnˈkwaɪə(r)/ **verb (enquires, enquiring, enquired) 1** ask for information 询问 **2 (enquire after)** ask how someone is 问候 **3 (enquire into)** investigate 调查

enquiry /ɪnˈkwaɪəri/ **noun (plural enquiries) 1** an act of asking for information 询问 **2** an official investigation (官方)调查

enrage /ɪnˈreɪdʒ/ **verb (enrages, enraging, enraged)** make someone very angry 激怒,使狂怒

enrapture /ɪnˈræptʃə(r)/ **verb (enraptures, enrapturing, enraptured)** make someone feel great pleasure or joy 使狂喜;使着迷

enrich /ɪnˈrɪtʃ/ **verb 1** improve the quality or value of 提高(质量),增加(价值) **2** improve something by adding an extra item or ingredient 充实,强化 ■ **enrichment** noun.

enrol /ɪnˈrəʊl/ **(US spelling 【美拼作】enroll) verb (enrols, enrolling, enrolled)** officially register or recruit someone as a member or student (正式)吸收(成员);招(生) ■ **enrolment** noun.

en route /ɒn ˈruːt/ **adverb** on the way 在途中

ensconce /ɪnˈskɒns/ **verb (ensconces, ensconcing, ensconced)** establish in a comfortable, safe, or secret place (舒适、安全或秘密地)安顿,安置

ensemble /ɒnˈsɒmbl/ **noun 1** a group of musicians, actors, or dancers who perform together 乐团;剧团;舞蹈队 **2** a group of items viewed as a whole 全体;整体;全套

enshrine /ɪnˈʃraɪn/ **verb (enshrines, enshrining, enshrined)** preserve a right, tradition, or idea in a form that ensures it will be respected 把(权利、传统或思想)奉为神圣

enshroud /ɪnˈʃraʊd/ **verb** completely

envelop something and hide it from view 遮盖;掩盖

ensign /'ensən/ **noun** a flag 旗;旗帜

enslave /ɪn'sleɪv/ **verb** (**enslaves, enslaving, enslaved**) **1** make someone a slave 使成为奴隶 **2** make someone dependent on something 使依赖;使受控制 ■ **enslavement** noun.

ensnare /ɪn'sneə(r)/ **verb** (**ensnares, ensnaring, ensnared**) **1** catch an animal in a trap (用陷阱)诱捕 **2** keep someone in a situation from which they cannot escape 使陷入圈套

ensue /ɪn'sju:/ **verb** (**ensues, ensuing, ensued**) happen afterwards or as a result 接着发生;接踵而来;因而产生

en suite /ɒn 'swi:t/ **adjective & adverb** Brit.【英】(of a bathroom) leading directly off a bedroom (浴室)与卧室构成一体的(地)

ensure /ɪn'ʃʊə(r)/ **verb** (**ensures, ensuring, ensured**) **1** make certain that something will turn out in a particular way 确保;担保 **2** (**ensure against**) make sure that a problem does not happen 保证…(不会发生)

entail /ɪn'teɪl/ **verb** involve something as an inevitable part or result 使成为必要

entangle /ɪn'tæŋɡl/ **verb** (**entangles, entangling, entangled**) **1** cause something to become tangled 缠住;套住 **2** involve someone in complicated circumstances 使卷入,使陷入(复杂局面) ■ **entanglement** noun.

entente /ɒn'tɒnt/ or **entente cordiale** /ɒntɒnt kɔ:di'ɑ:l/ **noun** a friendly understanding between people or countries (人与人或国家间的)谅解

enter /'entə(r)/ **verb** (**enters, entering, entered**) **1** come or go into 进来;进入 **2** (often **enter into**) begin to be involved in or do 开始;开始从事 **3** join an institution or profession 参加,加入(机构或行业) **4** register as a participant in a competition or contest 报名参加(竞赛) **5** (**enter into**) undertake to be bound by an agreement 开始受(协议)约束 **6** record information in a book, computer, etc. (在书本、计算机中)记录(信息)

enterprise /'entəpraɪz/ **noun 1** a business or company 企业;公司 **2** a large project 大型项目 **3** the ability to think of and set up new projects 事业心;进取心

enterprising /'entəpraɪzɪŋ/ **adjective** having the ability to think of and set up new projects 有事业心的;有进取心的;有魄力的

entertain /ˌentə'teɪn/ **verb 1** provide someone with interest or amusement 给…娱乐;使快乐 **2** receive someone as a guest and provide them with food and drink 招待;款待 **3** give consideration to 考虑 ■ **entertainer** noun.

entertaining /ˌentə'teɪnɪŋ/ **adjective** providing amusement or enjoyment 使人得到娱乐的;有趣的 ■ **entertainingly** adverb.

entertainment /ˌentə'teɪnmənt/ **noun 1** the action of entertaining 娱乐;表演 **2** an event or activity designed to entertain other people 文娱节目;表演会

enthral /ɪn'θrɔ:l/ (US spelling 【美拼作】**enthrall**) **verb** (**enthrals, enthralling, enthralled**) fascinate someone and hold their attention 迷住;吸引住

> ✔ **拼写指南** one *l* in **enthral** and **enthrals**, two in **enthralled** and **enthralling**. enthral 和 enthrals 中有一个 l, enthralled 和 enthralling 有两个 l。

enthrone /ɪn'θrəʊn/ **verb** (**enthrones, enthroning, enthroned**) mark the new reign of a king or queen by a ceremony in which they sit on a throne 使登基;使即位 ■ **enthronement** noun.

enthuse /ɪnˈθjuːz/ **verb** (**enthuses, enthusing, enthused**) **1** express enthusiasm about something 表现出热情 **2** make someone enthusiastic 使充满热情；使热心

enthusiasm /ɪnˈθjuːziæzəm/ **noun** excited interest in and enjoyment of something 热心；热情；巨大兴趣

enthusiast /ɪnˈθjuːziæst/ **noun** a person who is very interested in a particular activity 热衷…者；热心人

enthusiastic /ɪnˌθjuːziˈæstɪk/ **adjective** feeling very interested in and happy about something 满腔热情的；热心的；极感兴趣的 ■ **enthusiastically** adverb.

entice /ɪnˈtaɪs/ **verb** (**entices, enticing, enticed**) attract someone by offering them something desirable 诱惑；吸引 ■ **enticingly** adverb.

entire /ɪnˈtaɪə(r)/ **adjective** with no part left out; whole 全部的；整个的；完全的

entirely /ɪnˈtaɪəli/ **adverb** wholly; completely 全部地；完全地；彻底地

entirety /ɪnˈtaɪərəti/ **noun** (**the entirety**) the whole 整体；总体 口 **in its entirety** as a whole 作为一个整体；整个地

entitle /ɪnˈtaɪtl/ **verb** (**entitles, entitling, entitled**) **1** give someone a right to do or have something 使享有权利；使获得资格 **2** give a title to a book, play, etc. 给(书、戏剧等)题名 ■ **entitlement** noun.

entity /ˈentəti/ **noun** (plural **entities**) a thing that exists independently 实体；独立存在物

entomb /ɪnˈtuːm/ **verb** **1** place someone in a tomb 下葬 **2** bury or completely cover 埋葬；完全覆盖

entomology /ˌentəˈmɒlədʒi/ **noun** the study of insects 昆虫学 ■ **entomological** adjective **entomologist** noun.

entourage /ˈɒntʊrɑːʒ/ **noun** a group of people who accompany and assist an important person 随行人员；随员

entrails /ˈentreɪlz/ **plural noun** a person's or animal's intestines or internal organs (人或动物的)肠，内脏

entrance[1] /ˈentrəns/ **noun** **1** a door or passageway into a place 入口；入口处 **2** an act of entering 进入 **3** the right or opportunity to go into a place 进入权；进入机会

entrance[2] /ɪnˈtrɑːns/ **verb** (**entrances, entrancing, entranced**) **1** fill someone with wonder and delight 使狂喜；使着迷 **2** cast a spell on 使神志恍惚

entrant /ˈentrənt/ **noun** a person who joins or takes part in something 参加者；新成员

entrap /ɪnˈtræp/ **verb** (**entraps, entrapping, entrapped**) **1** catch a person or animal in a trap 诱捕；诱入陷阱 **2** trick someone into committing a crime in order to have them prosecuted 诱使(某人)犯罪；诱捕 ■ **entrapment** noun.

entreat /ɪnˈtriːt/ **verb** ask earnestly or anxiously to do something 恳求；祈求；请求

entreaty /ɪnˈtriːti/ **noun** (plural **entreaties**) an earnest request 恳求；祈求；请求

entrée /ˈɒntreɪ/ **noun** **1** the main course of a meal (一餐的)主菜 **2** Brit. 【英】 a dish served between the first and main courses at a formal dinner 小菜(正式宴会上首道菜和主菜之间上的菜) **3** the right to enter a place or social group 入场权；入场许可

entrench /ɪnˈtrentʃ/ **verb** **1** establish a military force in fortified positions 使(军队)进入(固防地) **2** (**be entrenched**) be so firmly established that change is difficult 确立；使处于牢固地位 ■ **entrenchment** noun.

entrepreneur /ˌɒntrəprəˈnɜː(r)/ **noun** a person who is successful in setting up businesses 企业家 ■ **entrepreneurial** /ˌɒntrəprəˈnɜːriəl/ adjective.

entropy /ˈentrəpi/ **noun** Physics 【物理】

a quantity expressing how much of a system's thermal energy is not available for conversion into mechanical work 熵(热力系统中不能做功的一定量的热能)

entrust /ɪn'trʌst/ **verb** make someone responsible for doing or looking after something 托;委托;交托

entry /'entrɪ/ **noun** (plural **entries**) **1** an act of entering 进入 **2** a door or passageway into a place 入口 **3** the right or opportunity to enter 进入权;进入机会 **4** an item included in a list, reference book, etc. 条目;词目;词条

entwine /ɪn'twaɪn/ **verb** (**entwines**, **entwining**, **entwined**) wind or twist together 盘绕;缠绕

enumerate /ɪ'njuːmərət/ **verb** (**enumerates**, **enumerating**, **enumerated**) mention a number of things one by one 列举;枚举 ■ **enumeration** noun.

enunciate /ɪ'nʌnsɪeɪt/ **verb** (**enunciates**, **enunciating**, **enunciated**) **1** say or pronounce clearly 清楚地念(字);清晰地发(音) **2** set something out clearly and precisely (准确地)阐明,阐述 ■ **enunciation** noun.

envelop /ɪn'veləp/ **verb** (**envelops**, **enveloping**, **enveloped**) wrap up, cover, or surround completely 包住;盖住;围绕

> ✔ 拼写指南 unlike the noun *envelope*, the verb **envelop** has no *e* on the end. 与名词envelope不同,动词envelop 词末没有e。

envelope /'envələʊp/ **noun** a flat paper container with a flap, used to enclose a letter or document 信封

enviable /'enviəbl/ **adjective** offering something desirable 引起妒忌的;惹人羡慕的 ■ **enviably** adverb.

envious /'enviəs/ **adjective** feeling discontented because you want something that someone else has 妒忌的;羡慕的 ■ **enviously** adverb.

environment /ɪn'vaɪrənmənt/ **noun 1** the surroundings in which a person, animal, or plant lives or operates 环境;周围状况 **2** (**the environment**) the natural world 生态环境;自然环境 ■ **environmental** adjective **environmentally** adverb.

> ✔ 拼写指南 remember the *n*: environment. 记住拼写 environment 中的n。

environmentalist /ɪn,vaɪrən'mentəlɪst/ **noun** a person who is concerned with the protection of the environment 环保主义者;环境保护论者 ■ **environmentalism** noun.

environs /ɪn'vaɪrənz/ **plural noun** the surrounding area or district 周围的区域;郊区

envisage /ɪn'vɪzɪdʒ/ **verb** (**envisages**, **envisaging**, **envisaged**) **1** see something as a possibility 展望;设想 **2** form a mental picture of 想象

envoy /'envɔɪ/ **noun** a messenger or representative 使者;代表

envy /'envi/ **noun** (plural **envies**) **1** a feeling of wanting something that belongs to someone else 妒忌;羡慕 **2** (**the envy of**) a thing that is wanted by other people 妒忌(或羡慕)的对象 • **verb** (**envies**, **envying**, **envied**) wish that you had the same possessions or opportunities as someone 妒忌;羡慕

enzyme /'enzaɪm/ **noun** a substance produced by an animal or plant which helps a chemical change happen without being changed itself 酶

eon /'iːən/ US spelling of AEON. 的美式拼法

epaulette /'epəlet/ (US spelling 【美拼作】 **epaulet**) **noun** a flap attached to the shoulder of a coat or jacket 肩章;肩饰

ephemera /ɪ'femərə/ **plural noun** things that people use or are interested in for only a short time 昙

花一现的事物；短期内有用(或引人关注)之物

ephemeral /ɪˈfemərəl/ **adjective** lasting only for a short time 极短的；短暂的

epic /ˈepɪk/ **noun 1** a long poem about the actions of great men or women or about a nation's history 史诗 **2** a long film or book dealing with a long period of time 史诗般的电影(或书籍) • **adjective 1** having to do with an epic 史诗的；叙事诗的 **2** great and impressive in scale or character 宏伟的；壮丽的；英雄的

epicentre /ˈepɪsentə(r)/ (US spelling 【美拼作】 **epicenter**) **noun** the point on the earth's surface where the effects of an earthquake are felt most strongly (地震的)震中

epicure /ˈepɪkjʊə(r)/ **noun** a person who enjoys and is interested in good food and drink 讲究饮食的人；饮食鉴赏家；美食家 ■ **epicurean** noun & adjective.

epidemic /ˌepɪˈdemɪk/ **noun** a situation in which a large number of people have caught the same infectious disease (疾病的)流行，广泛传播

epidermis /ˌepɪˈdɜːmɪs/ **noun 1** the surface layer of an animal's skin, on top of the dermis (动物的)表皮 **2** the outer layer of tissue in a plant (植物的)表皮 ■ **epidermal** adjective.

epidural /ˌepɪˈdjʊərəl/ **noun** an anaesthetic injected into the space around the spinal cord, especially during childbirth 硬脊膜外麻醉

epiglottis /ˌepɪˈɡlɒtɪs/ **noun** a flap of cartilage in the throat that descends during swallowing to cover the opening of the windpipe 会厌

epigram /ˈepɪɡræm/ **noun 1** a concise and witty saying 警句；隽语 **2** a short witty poem 机敏诙谐的短诗 ■ **epigrammatic** adjective.

epigraph /ˈepɪɡrɑːf/ **noun 1** an inscription on a building, statue, or coin (建筑物、塑像或钱币上的)刻文，铭文 **2** a short quotation introducing a book or chapter (卷首或章节前的)引语

epilepsy /ˈepɪlepsi/ **noun** a disorder of the nervous system that causes convulsions and loss of consciousness 癫痫；羊痫风 ■ **epileptic** adjective & noun.

epilogue /ˈepɪlɒɡ/ (US spelling 【美拼作】 **epilog**) **noun** a section at the end of a book or play which comments on what has happened (书的)后记，跋；(戏剧的)结尾部分，尾声

epiphany /ɪˈpɪfəni/ **noun** (plural **epiphanies**) **1** (**Epiphany**) (in the Bible) the time when the Magi visited the baby Jesus in Bethlehem (《圣经》中的)耶稣显现 **2** a sudden and inspiring revelation 顿悟；突然领悟

episcopacy /ɪˈpɪskəpəsi/ **noun** (plural **episcopacies**) **1** government of a Church by bishops (教会的)主教制 **2** (**the episcopacy**) the bishops of a region or Church as a group (总称)主教

episcopal /ɪˈpɪskəpəl/ **adjective** having to do with a bishop or bishops 主教的

episcopalian /ɪˌpɪskəˈpeɪliən/ **adjective** having to do with the government of a Church by bishops 主教制的 • **noun** a supporter of this type of Church government 主教制拥护者

episode /ˈepɪsəʊd/ **noun 1** an event or group of events happening as part of a sequence (一连串事件中的)一个(或一组)事件 **2** each of the separate parts into which a serialized story or programme is divided (连载小说或系列节目的)一节，一集，一部分

episodic /ˌepɪˈsɒdɪk/ **adjective 1** made up of a series of separate events 由一系列独立事件组成的 **2** happening at irregular intervals 偶尔发生的；变化无常的

epistemology /ɪˌpɪstəˈmɒlədʒi/ **noun** the branch of philosophy that deals with knowledge 认识论

epistle /ɪˈpɪsl/ **noun 1** formal 【正式】 a letter **2** (**Epistle**) a book of the New Testament in the form of a letter from an Apostle (《圣经·新约》中的)使徒书信

epistolary /ɪˈpɪstələri/ **adjective 1** relating to the writing of letters 与书信有关的 **2** (of a literary work) in the form of letters (文学作品)书信体的

epitaph /ˈepɪtɑːf/ **noun** words written in memory of a person who has died 悼文；祭文

epithet /ˈepɪθet/ **noun** a word or phrase describing someone or something's character or most important quality (描述人或事物最重要特性的)表述词语

epitome /ɪˈpɪtəmi/ **noun** (**the epitome of**) a perfect example of something 典型

epitomize or **epitomise** /ɪˈpɪtəmaɪz/ **verb** (**epitomizes**, **epitomizing**, **epitomized**) be a perfect example of 代表，象征；为…的典型

epoch /ˈiːpɒk/ **noun** a long and distinct period of time 时期；时代

eponym /ˈepənɪm/ **noun 1** a person after whom something is named 名祖(姓名被用来命名某物的人) **2** a word or phrase based on someone's name 人名名称(以某人的名字命名的词或短语)

eponymous /ɪˈpɒnɪməs/ **adjective 1** (of a person) giving their name to something (人)以自己名使(某物)得名的 **2** (of a thing) named after a particular person (某物)以(某人之名)命名的

equable /ˈekwəbl/ **adjective 1** calm and even-tempered 冷静的；沉着的；平和的 **2** (of a climate) not changing very much (气候)稳定的，变化小的 ■ **equably** adverb.

equal /ˈiːkwəl/ **adjective 1** the same in quantity, size, value, or status (在数量、大小、价值或地位上)相等的，同样的 **2** evenly balanced 均衡的；均等的 **3** (**equal to**) able to face a challenge 可应对(挑战)的 • **noun** a person or thing that is equal to another 匹敌者；可相比拟的东西 • **verb** (**equals**, **equalling**, **equalled**; US spelling 【美拼作】 **equals**, **equaling**, **equaled**) **1** be equal to 等于；跟…相同 **2** be as good as 比得上；敌得过 ■ **equally** adverb.

equality /ɪˈkwɒləti/ **noun** the state of having the same rights, opportunities, or advantages as others 相等；相同；平等

equalize or **equalise** /ˈiːkwəlaɪz/ **verb** (**equalizes**, **equalizing**, **equalized**) **1** make things equal 使平等；使相等 **2** level the score in a match by scoring a goal 打成平局；扳平 ■ **equalization noun equalizer** noun.

equanimity /ˌekwəˈnɪməti/ **noun** calmness of temper 冷静；稳重；平和

equate /ɪˈkweɪt/ **verb** (**equates**, **equating**, **equated**) consider one thing as equal to another 认为与…相同(或相等)

equation /ɪˈkweɪʒn/ **noun 1** the process of equating one thing with another 等同；平衡 **2** Maths 【数学】 a statement that the values of two mathematical expressions are equal (indicated by the sign =) 等式；方程(式) **3** Chemistry 【化学】 a formula representing the changes which happen in a chemical reaction 反应式；化学方程式

equator /ɪˈkweɪtə(r)/ **noun** an imaginary line around the earth at an equal distance from the two poles, dividing the earth into northern and southern hemispheres 赤道

equatorial /ˌekwəˈtɔːriəl/ **adjective** having to do with the equator 赤道的

equerry /ˈekwəri/ **noun** (plural **equerries**) a male officer of the

British royal household who acts as an attendant to a member of the royal family 英国王室侍卫官

equestrian /ɪˈkwestriən/ **adjective** relating to horse riding 骑马的 • **noun** a person on horseback 骑马者; 骑师

equestrianism /ɪˈkwestriənɪzəm/ **noun** the skill or sport of horse riding (骑)马术

equidistant /ˌiːkwɪˈdɪstənt/ **adjective** at equal distances 等距(离)的

equilateral /ˌiːkwɪˈlætərəl/ **adjective** having all its sides of the same length 等边的;等面的

equilibrium /ˌiːkwɪˈlɪbriəm/ **noun** (plural **equilibria**) **1** a state in which opposing forces are balanced 均势 **2** the state of being physically balanced 平衡;均衡 **3** a calm state of mind 平静;冷静

equine /ˈekwaɪn/ **adjective 1** relating to horses 马的;马科的 **2** resembling a horse 似马的

equinoctial /ˌiːkwɪˈnɒkʃl/ **adjective 1** having to do with the equinox 二分时刻的;昼夜平分时的 **2** at or near the equator (近)赤道的

equinox /ˈiːkwɪnɒks/ **noun** the time or date (twice each year, about 22 September and 20 March) when day and night are of equal length 二分时刻,昼夜平分时(每年两次,在9月22日和3月20日前后)

equip /ɪˈkwɪp/ **verb** (**equips**, **equipping**, **equipped**) **1** supply someone with the things they need for a particular activity 配备;装备 **2** prepare someone for a situation or task 使有准备;训练

equipment /ɪˈkwɪpmənt/ **noun** the items needed for a particular activity 设备;器械;用具

equitable /ˈekwɪtəbl/ **adjective** fair and impartial 公平的;公正的 ■ **equitably** adverb.

equity /ˈekwəti/ **noun** (plural **equities**) **1** the quality of being fair and impartial 公平;公正 **2** the value of the shares issued by a company (公司的)股票值;股本 **3** the value of a mortgaged property after all charges and debts have been paid 抵押资产净值

equivalent /ɪˈkwɪvələnt/ **adjective** (often **equivalent to**) **1** equal in value, amount, function, meaning, etc. (价值、数量、功能、意义等)相等的,等值的 **2** having the same effect 等效的 • **noun** a person or thing that is equivalent to another 对等的人;相等物;等价物 ■ **equivalence** noun.

equivocal /ɪˈkwɪvəkl/ **adjective** (of words or intentions) not clear because they can be interpreted in more than one way (言语或意图)有歧义的,模棱两可的 ■ **equivocally** adverb.

equivocate /ɪˈkwɪvəkeɪt/ **verb** (**equivocates**, **equivocating**, **equivocated**) use language that can be interpreted in more than one way in order to hide the truth or avoid committing yourself 用模棱两可的话回避;含糊其词 ■ **equivocation** noun.

era /ˈɪərə/ **noun** a long and distinct period of history 时代;历史时期

eradicate /ɪˈrædɪkeɪt/ **verb** (**eradicates**, **eradicating**, **eradicated**) remove or destroy completely 根除;消灭;杜绝 ■ **eradication** noun.

erase /ɪˈreɪz/ **verb** (**erases**, **erasing**, **erased**) **1** rub out something written in pencil 擦掉;抹去 **2** remove all traces of something 消除…的痕迹

eraser /ɪˈreɪzə(r)/ **noun** a piece of rubber or plastic used to rub out something written in pencil 擦除器;橡皮

ere /eə(r)/ **preposition & conjunction** old use【旧】before (in time) (时间上)在…之前,在…以前

erect /ɪˈrekt/ **adjective 1** rigidly upright 竖直的;挺直的 **2** (of the penis) enlarged and stiffened (阴茎)勃起的

• **verb 1** put up a structure or object 建造;竖立 **2** create or establish something 创造;建立

erectile /ɪˈrektaɪl/ **adjective** able to become erect 可竖立的;可勃起的

erection /ɪˈrekʃn/ **noun 1** the action of erecting a structure or object 竖立;建造;建立 **2** a building or other upright structure 建筑物;竖立物 **3** an erect state of the penis (阴茎的)勃起

ergo /ˈɜːɡəʊ/ **adverb** therefore 因此

ergonomics /ˌɜːɡəˈnɒmɪks/ **noun** the study of people's efficiency in their working environment 工效学;人类工程学 ■ **ergonomic adjective**.

ermine /ˈɜːmɪn/ **noun** (plural **ermine** or **ermines**) **1** a stoat 白鼬;扫雪 **2** the white winter fur of the stoat (白鼬在冬季变白的)白色毛皮

erode /ɪˈrəʊd/ **verb** (**erodes, eroding, eroded**) **1** gradually wear away 腐蚀;侵蚀;磨去 **2** gradually destroy 逐渐破坏;逐渐损害

erogenous /ɪˈrɒdʒənəs/ **adjective** (of a part of the body) giving pleasure in a sexual way when it is touched (身体部位)对性刺激敏感的

erosion /ɪˈrəʊʒn/ **noun** the process of eroding 腐蚀;侵蚀;磨损

erotic /ɪˈrɒtɪk/ **adjective** having to do with sexual desire or excitement 性爱的;性欲的 ■ **erotically adverb**.

erotica /ɪˈrɒtɪkə/ **noun** literature or art that is intended to make people feel sexually excited 色情文学;色情艺术

eroticism /ɪˈrɒtɪsɪzəm/ **noun 1** the use of images that are intended to be sexually exciting 性诱惑;性刺激 **2** sexual desire or excitement 性欲;性冲动

err /ɜː(r)/ **verb 1** make a mistake 犯错误;出差错 **2** do wrong 犯罪;犯过错

errand /ˈerənd/ **noun** a short journey made to deliver or collect something (短程的)差事,差使

errant /ˈerənt/ **adjective 1** doing something wrong or unacceptable 犯错误的;离开正道的 **2** old use 【旧】 travelling in search of adventure 漫游的;游侠的

erratic /ɪˈrætɪk/ **adjective** happening, moving, or acting in an irregular or uneven way 不规律的;不稳定的 ■ **erratically adverb**.

erratum /eˈrɑːtəm/ **noun** (plural **errata** /eˈrɑːtə/) a mistake in a book or printed document (书本或打印文件中的)错误

erroneous /ɪˈrəʊniəs/ **adjective** incorrect 错误的;不正确的 ■ **erroneously adverb**.

error /ˈerə(r)/ **noun 1** a mistake 错误;差错 **2** the state of being wrong 犯错误;出错

ersatz /ˈeəzæts/ **adjective** (of a product) artificial and not as good as the real thing (产品)假的,代用的

erstwhile /ˈɜːstwaɪl/ **adjective** former 从前的;过去的

erudite /ˈeruːdaɪt/ **adjective** having or showing knowledge gained from reading and study 博学的;有学问的 ■ **erudition noun**.

erupt /ɪˈrʌpt/ **verb 1** (of a volcano) become active and eject lava, ash, and gases (火山)喷发 **2** break out suddenly 突然发生;爆发 **3** show or express your feelings in a sudden and noisy way 宣泄感情 **4** (of a spot, rash, etc.) suddenly appear on the skin (丘疹等)突然出现;(皮肤上)发疹 ■ **eruption noun**.

erythrocyte /ɪˈrɪθrəʊsaɪt/ **noun** technical【术语】a red blood cell 红(血)细胞;红血球

escalate /ˈeskəleɪt/ **verb** (**escalates, escalating, escalated**) **1** increase rapidly 迅速上升;迅速增加 **2** become more serious 升级;变得更严重 ■ **escalation noun**.

escalator /ˈeskəleɪtə(r)/ **noun** a moving staircase consisting of a circulating belt of steps driven by a motor 自动扶梯

escalope /ˈeskəlɒp/ **noun** a thin slice of meat coated in breadcrumbs and fried (外裹面包屑、油煎的)薄肉片

escapade /ˈeskəpeɪd/ **noun** an adventure 越轨行为;恶作剧

escape /ɪˈskeɪp/ **verb (escapes, escaping, escaped) 1** break free from captivity or control 逃跑;逃走 **2** succeed in avoiding something bad 避 免(坏事) **3** fail to be noticed or remembered by 未被注意;未被想起 • **noun 1** an act of escaping 逃跑;逃脱;逃离 **2** a means of escaping 逃跑(或逃脱、逃避)的方法 ■ **escapee** noun **escaper** noun.

escapism /ɪˈskeɪpɪzəm/ **noun** the habit of doing enjoyable things to stop you thinking about unpleasant realities (沉湎于消遣的)逃避现实 ■ **escapist** noun & adjective.

escapologist /ˌeskəˈpɒlədʒɪst/ **noun** an entertainer whose act consists of breaking free from ropes and chains 脱身术表演者 ■ **escapology** noun.

escarpment /ɪˈskɑːpmənt/ **noun** a long, steep slope at the edge of an area of high land 陡坡;悬崖

eschew /ɪsˈtʃuː/ **verb** deliberately avoid doing or having something (有意)回避,避开

escort noun /ˈeskɔːt/ **1** a person, vehicle, or group accompanying someone to protect or honour them 护送者;护卫车辆;护卫队 **2** a person who accompanies a member of the opposite sex to a social event 陪伴异性赴社交场合的人 • **verb** /ɪˈskɔːt/ accompany someone as an escort 护送

escudo /eˈskuːdəʊ/ **noun (plural escudos)** the former basic unit of money in Portugal 埃斯库多(葡萄牙旧货币基本单位)

escutcheon /ɪˈskʌtʃən/ **noun** a shield on which a coat of arms is depicted 有武器纹饰的盾牌(或徽章)

Eskimo /ˈeskɪməʊ/ **noun (plural Eskimo or Eskimos)** a member of a people inhabiting northern Canada, Alaska, Greenland, and eastern Siberia 爱斯基摩人

！注意 many of the peoples traditionally called **Eskimos** now prefer to call themselves **Inuit**. 传统上被称作 Eskimos (爱斯基摩人)的人中很多更愿意被称作 Inuit (伊努伊特人)。

esophagus /iːˈsɒfəgəs/ US spelling of **OESOPHAGUS**. oesophagus 的美式拼法

esoteric /ˌesəˈterɪk/ **adjective** intended for or understood by only a small number of people with a specialized knowledge 秘传的;只有内行才懂的

ESP /iː es ˈpiː/ **abbreviation** extra-sensory perception 超感知觉

espadrille /ˈespədrɪl/ **noun** a light canvas shoe with a plaited fibre sole 帆布便鞋

especial /ɪˈspeʃ/ **adjective 1** special 特别的;特殊的 **2** for or belonging chiefly to one person or thing (某人或某事物)特有的,独有的

especially /ɪˈspeʃəli/ **adverb 1** in particular 专门地;特地 **2** to a great extent 在很大程度上

espionage /ˈespɪənɑːʒ/ **noun** the practice of spying 间谍行为;间谍活动

esplanade /ˌespləˈneɪd/ **noun** a long, open, level area where people may walk for pleasure 空地

espouse /ɪˈspauz/ **verb (espouses, espousing, espoused)** support or choose a particular belief or way of doing things 信奉(信仰);采纳(行为方式) ■ **espousal** noun.

espresso /eˈspresəʊ/ **noun (plural espressos)** strong black coffee made by forcing steam through ground coffee beans (用蒸汽加压煮出的)浓咖啡

✔ **拼写指南 espresso** is an Italian word (from *caffè espresso*, meaning 'pressed out freshly') and should be spelled the Italian way, with an *s*, not an *x*. expresso 是意大利语词(源自caffè espresso, 意为"压出的咖啡"), 应按意大利语拼写规则拼写, 不要将 s 写作 x.

esprit de corps /eˌspriː də ˈkɔː(r)/ **noun** a feeling of pride and loyalty that unites the members of a group 集体荣誉感; 团结精神

espy /eˈspaɪ/ **verb** (**espies**, **espying**, **espied**) literary 【文】 catch sight of 窥见; 望见; 看见

Esq. abbreviation Esquire.

Esquire /ɪˈskwaɪə(r)/ **noun** Brit. 【英】 a polite title placed after a man's name when no other title is used 先生(在没有其他称谓时, 用在男子姓名前的礼貌称呼)

essay **noun** /ˈeseɪ/ **1** a piece of writing on a particular subject 论说文; 散文; 随笔 **2** formal 【正式】 an attempt 尝试; 企图 • **verb** /eˈseɪ/ formal 【正式】 attempt to do something 试图 ■ **essayist** noun.

essence /ˈesns/ **noun 1** the quality which is most important in making something what it is 本质; 实质; 精髓 **2** an extract obtained from a plant or other substance and used for flavouring or scent 香精; 香料

essential /ɪˈsenʃl/ **adjective 1** absolutely necessary 必不可少的; 绝对必要的 **2** relating to the most important part or basic nature of something 本质的; 实质的 • **noun** (**essentials**) **1** things that are absolutely necessary 必不可少的东西; 必需品 **2** things that are part of the basic nature of something 基本要素 □ **essential oil** a natural oil extracted from a plant (香)精油 ■ **essentially** adverb.

establish /ɪˈstæblɪʃ/ **verb 1** set something up on a firm or permanent basis 建造; 设立; 确立 **2** make someone or something accepted, recognized, or respected by other people 使被接受; 使被承认; 使受尊敬 **3** show something to be true 证实

establishment /ɪˈstæblɪʃmənt/ **noun 1** the action of establishing something 建立; 确立; 确定 **2** a business, public institution, or household 企业; 机构; 家庭 **3** (**the Establishment**) the group in society who have control over policy and resist change (反对变革的)当权派, 权势集团

estate /ɪˈsteɪt/ **noun 1** a property consisting of a large house with grounds 地产; 房地产 **2** Brit. 【英】 a group of modern houses, or of buildings used by businesses 现代住宅区; 商业区 **3** a property where crops such as coffee or grapes are grown (咖啡、葡萄等的)种植园, 庄园 **4** all the money and property owned by a person at the time of their death 遗产 □ **estate agent** a person who sells or rents out houses or flats for clients 房地产经纪人 **estate car** Brit. 【英】 a car with a large storage area behind the seats and an extra door at the rear 旅行轿车; 客货两用轿车

esteem /ɪˈstiːm/ **noun** respect and admiration 尊重; 敬重; 崇拜 • **verb** respect and admire someone 尊重; 敬重; 崇拜

ester /ˈestə(r)/ **noun** Chemistry 【化学】 an organic compound formed by a reaction between an acid and an alcohol 酯

esthetic /iːsˈθetɪk/ US spelling of **AESTHETIC**. aesthetic的美式拼法

estimable /ˈestɪməbl/ **adjective** deserving respect and admiration 值得敬重的; 令人钦佩的

estimate **verb** /ˈestɪmeɪt/ (**estimates**, **estimating**, **estimated**) roughly calculate the value, number, or amount of something 估计; 估算 • **noun** /ˈestɪmət/ **1** a rough calculation

估计；估算 **2** a written statement giving the likely price that will be charged for work 估价单；投标 **3** an opinion 看法；评价；判断 ■ **estimation** noun.

Estonian /ɪˈstəʊnɪən/ noun a person from Estonia 爱沙尼亚人 • adjective relating to Estonia 爱沙尼亚的

estranged /ɪˈstreɪndʒd/ adjective **1** no longer friendly or in contact with someone 疏远的 **2** (of someone's husband or wife) no longer living with them (某人的丈夫或妻子与其)分居的，■ **estrangement** noun.

estrogen /ˈiːstrədʒən/ US spelling of OESTROGEN. oestrogen的美式拼法

estuary /ˈestjʊərɪ/ noun (plural estuaries) the mouth of a large river where it becomes affected by tides 河口

et al. /et ˈæl/ abbreviation and others 以及其他；等等 [Latin, short for【拉丁，缩写】= et alii.]

etc. abbreviation et cetera.

et cetera or **etcetera** /et ˈsetərə/ adverb and other similar things; and so on 和其他类似之物；等等

etch /etʃ/ verb **1** engrave metal, glass, or stone by applying a coating, drawing on it with a needle, and then covering the surface with acid to attack the exposed parts 在(金属、玻璃或石头)上蚀刻；浸蚀 **2** cut words or a design on a surface 雕刻(文字或图案) **3** (be etched on or in) be fixed permanently in someone's mind 铭记(在心)

etching /ˈetʃɪŋ/ noun **1** the process of etching 蚀刻(艺术) **2** a print produced by etching 蚀刻版印刷品；蚀刻画

eternal /ɪˈtɜːnl/ adjective lasting or existing forever 永久的；无休止的；永存的 ■ **eternally** adverb.

eternity /ɪˈtɜːnətɪ/ noun (plural eternities) **1** unending time 永恒；永久 **2** (an eternity) informal 【非正式】an

undesirably long period of time 无穷无尽的一段时间；(令人不快的)漫长时间

ethane /ˈiːθeɪn/ noun a flammable gas present in petroleum and natural gas 乙烷

ether /ˈiːθə(r)/ noun **1** a highly flammable liquid used as an anaesthetic and a solvent 乙醚 **2** literary【文】the upper regions of the air 天空；苍穹

ethereal /ɪˈθɪərɪəl/ adjective **1** very delicate and light 精致的，微妙的；轻飘的；缥缈的 **2** heavenly or spiritual 上苍的；苍天的；精神上的

ethic /ˈeθɪk/ noun **1** (also ethics) a set of principles concerning right and wrong and how people should behave 伦理标准；道德规范；道德体系 **2** (ethics) the branch of philosophy concerned with moral principles 伦理学；道德学

ethical /ˈeθɪkl/ adjective **1** having to do with principles about right and wrong 道德标准的 **2** morally correct 道德的；合乎道德的 ■ **ethically** adverb.

Ethiopian /ˌiːθiˈəʊpɪən/ noun a person from Ethiopia 埃塞俄比亚人 • adjective relating to Ethiopia 埃塞俄比亚的

ethnic /ˈeθnɪk/ adjective **1** having to do with people from the same national or cultural background 民族的；种族的 **2** referring to a person's origins rather than their present nationality …种族的；…后裔的 **3** belonging to a non-Western cultural tradition 非西方文化传统的 □ **ethnic cleansing** the removal or killing of members of one ethnic or religious group in an area by those of another 种族驱逐；种族清洗；种族灭绝 **ethnic minority** a group which has a different ethnic origin from the main population 少数民族 ■ **ethnically** adverb **ethnicity** noun.

ethos /'iːθɒs/ **noun** the characteristic spirit of a culture, period, etc. (某一文化、时期等的)精神特质, 气质

ethyl /'eθɪl, 'iːθaɪl/ **noun** Chemistry【化学】a radical obtained from ethane, present in alcohol and ether 乙烯

etiquette /'etɪket/ **noun** the rules of polite or correct behaviour in a society 礼节; 礼仪

etymology /etɪ'mɒlədʒi/ **noun** (plural **etymologies**) an account of the origins and the developments in meaning of a word 阐述词源, 词源说明 ■ **etymological** adjective.

EU /iː 'juː/ **abbreviation** European Union.

eucalyptus /juːkə'lɪptəs/ **noun** (plural **eucalyptuses** or **eucalypti** /juːkə'lɪptaɪ/) an evergreen Australasian tree whose leaves produce a strong-smelling oil 桉树

Eucharist /'juːkərɪst/ **noun 1** the Christian ceremony commemorating the Last Supper, in which consecrated bread and wine are consumed 圣餐仪式; 感恩祭 **2** the consecrated bread and wine used in this ceremony (经过祝圣的)圣餐面包及酒

eugenics /juː'dʒenɪks/ **noun** the study of ways to increase the occurrence of desirable characteristics in a population by choosing which people become parents 优生学; 人种改良学

eulogize or **eulogise** /'juːlədʒaɪz/ **verb** (**eulogizes**, **eulogizing**, **eulogized**) praise highly 称赞; 歌颂; 赞美

eulogy /'juːlədʒi/ **noun** (plural **eulogies**) a speech or piece of writing that praises someone or something highly 颂词; 颂文

eunuch /'juːnək/ **noun** a man who has had his testicles removed 阉人; 去掌者; 宦官

euphemism /'juːfəmɪzəm/ **noun** a less direct word used instead of one that is blunt or offensive 委婉说法; 委婉语 ■ **euphemistic** adjective **euphemistically** adverb.

euphonious /juː'fəʊnɪəs/ **adjective** sounding pleasant 悦耳的; 动听的 ■ **euphoniously** adverb.

euphonium /juː'fəʊnɪəm/ **noun** a brass musical instrument like a small tuba 上低音大号; 次中音号

euphony /'juːfəni/ **noun** (plural **euphonies**) the quality of sounding pleasant 声音和谐; 声音悦耳

euphoria /juː'fɔːrɪə/ **noun** a feeling of great happiness 心情愉快; 情绪高涨; 兴奋 ■ **euphoric** adjective.

Eurasian /juː'reɪʒn/ **adjective 1** of mixed European and Asian parentage 欧亚混血的 **2** relating to Eurasia (the land mass of Europe and Asia together) 欧亚大陆的

eureka /juː'riːkə/ **exclamation** a cry of joy or satisfaction when you discover something 我发现了(找到或发现某物时的惊呼语)

euro /'jʊərəʊ/ **noun** the basic unit of money in fifteen states of the European Union 欧元

European /jʊərə'piːən/ **noun 1** a person from Europe 欧洲人 **2** a person who is of European parentage 欧洲人后裔 • **adjective** having to do with Europe or the European Union 欧洲的; 欧盟的 □ **European Union** an economic and political association of certain European countries 欧洲联盟; 欧盟

euthanasia /juːθə'neɪzɪə/ **noun** the painless killing of a patient suffering from an incurable disease 安乐死术; 无痛苦致死术

evacuate /ɪ'vækjueɪt/ **verb** (**evacuates**, **evacuating**, **evacuated**) **1** remove someone from a place of danger to a safer place 疏散; 使从(危险地点)撤离; 撤出 **2** leave a dangerous place 撤离, 离开(危险地点) **3** empty the bowels 排空(肠胃)

■ **evacuation** noun.

evacuee /ɪˌvækjuˈiː/ noun a person who is evacuated from a place of danger 撤离者;被疏散者

evade /ɪˈveɪd/ verb (**evades**, **evading**, **evaded**) 1 escape or avoid 逃脱;躲开 2 avoid giving a direct answer to a question 回避(问题)

evaluate /ɪˈvæljueɪt/ verb (**evaluates**, **evaluating**, **evaluated**) form an idea of the amount or value of 给…估量;给…估值 ■ **evaluation** noun.

evanescent /ˌiːvəˈnesnt/ adjective soon passing out of existence; fleeting 很快消失的;瞬息的;短暂的 ■ **evanescence** noun.

evangelical /ˌiːvænˈdʒelɪkl/ adjective 1 having to do with a tradition within Protestant Christianity which emphasizes the authority of the Bible and salvation through personal faith in Jesus 基督教福音派的 2 having to do with the teaching of the gospel or Christianity 按福音书教义的;按基督教教义的 3 showing passionate support for something 狂热的;热衷的 • noun a member of the evangelical tradition in the Christian Church 福音会教徒;新教徒 ■ **evangelicalism** noun.

evangelist /ɪˈvændʒəlɪst/ noun 1 a person who sets out to convert other people to Christianity (基督教)福音传道者 2 the writer of one of the four Gospels 四《福音书》作者(马太、马可、路加、约翰)之一 3 a passionate supporter of something 狂热鼓吹者 ■ **evangelism** noun **evangelistic** adjective.

evangelize or **evangelise** /ɪˈvændʒəlaɪz/ verb (**evangelizes**, **evangelizing**, **evangelized**) 1 set out to convert people to Christianity 使皈依基督教 2 preach the gospel 宣讲福音

evaporate /ɪˈvæpəreɪt/ verb (**eva-porates**, **evaporating**, **evaporated**)

1 turn from liquid into vapour 蒸发;挥发 2 cease to exist 消失;失踪;逝去 □ **evaporated milk** thick sweetened milk from which some of the liquid has been evaporated 淡炼乳 ■ **evaporation** noun.

evasion /ɪˈveɪʒn/ noun the action of avoiding something 躲避;逃避;回避

evasive /ɪˈveɪsɪv/ adjective 1 avoiding committing yourself or revealing things about yourself 回避的;推托的 2 (of an action) intended to avoid or escape something (行动)躲避的,逃避的 ■ **evasively** adverb.

eve /iːv/ noun 1 the day or period of time immediately before an event or occasion 前夜;前夕 2 evening 傍晚

even[1] /ˈiːvn/ adjective 1 flat and smooth; level 平坦的;光滑的;水平的 2 equal in number, amount, or value 相等的;均等的 3 regular 均匀的;规律的 4 equally balanced 平衡的;均衡的 5 placid; calm 平静的;平和的 6 (of a number) able to be divided by two without a remainder (数字)双数的,偶数的 • verb (**evens**, **evening**, **evened**) make or become even 使平坦;使相等;使平衡;变平 • adverb used for emphasis (用于强调)甚至,更,还：He knows even less than I do. 他知道的还没我多。□ **even-handed** fair and impartial 不偏不倚的;公正的;无偏见的 ■ **evenly** adverb **evenness** noun.

even[2] noun old use 【旧】evening 傍晚;晚上

evening /ˈiːvnɪŋ/ noun the period of time at the end of the day 傍晚;晚上

evensong /ˈiːvnsɒŋ/ noun a Christian service of evening prayers, psalms, and hymns (基督教)晚祷

event /ɪˈvent/ noun 1 a thing that happens or takes place 发生的事情;事件 2 a public or social occasion 公众场合;社交场合;活动 3 each of several contests making up a sports competition 比赛项目

eventful /ɪ'ventfl/ **adjective** marked by interesting or exciting events 多姿多彩的

eventual /ɪ'ventʃuəl/ **adjective** occurring at the end of or resulting from a process or period of time 最终发生的；最后的；结果的 ■ **eventually** adverb.

eventuality /ɪˌventʃu'æləti/ **noun** (plural **eventualities**) a possible event or outcome 可能发生的事情；可能出现的结果

ever /'evə(r)/ **adverb 1** at any time 在任何时候；从来 **2** used for emphasis in comparisons and questions (用于比较，表示强调)以往任何时候，曾经；*better than ever* 比以往任何时候都好 **3** always 总是；永远 **4** increasingly 渐增地，越来越多地

evergreen /'evəɡriːn/ **adjective** (of a plant) having green leaves throughout the year (植物)常绿的

everlasting /ˌevə'lɑːstɪŋ/ **adjective** lasting forever or a very long time 永久的；无穷无尽的 ■ **everlastingly** adverb.

evermore /ˌevə'mɔː(r)/ **adverb** always; forever 始终；永远

every /'evri/ **determiner 1** used to refer to all the individual members of a set without exception 每个；每一 **2** used to indicate how often something happens 每一次的；每隔的；*every thirty minutes* 每隔30分钟 **3** all possible 所有可能的；完全的；*Every effort was made.* 尽了全力。

everybody /'evribɒdi/ **pronoun** every person 每人；人人

everyday /'evrideɪ/ **adjective 1** daily 每天的；天天的 **2** happening regularly 日常的

everyone /'evriwʌn/ **pronoun** every person 每人；人人

everything /'evriθɪŋ/ **pronoun 1** all things, or all the things of a group 每件事；每样事物；所有事物；一切 **2**

the most important thing 最重要的东西

everywhere /'evriweə(r)/ **adverb 1** in or to all places 无论何处；到处；各处 **2** in many places 在很多地方

evict /ɪ'vɪkt/ **verb** legally force someone to leave a property (依法)驱逐(某人) ■ **eviction** noun.

evidence /'evɪdəns/ **noun 1** information indicating whether something is true or valid 根据；证明 **2** information used to establish facts in a legal investigation (法律上的)证据 • **verb** (**evidences**, **evidencing**, **evidenced**) be or show evidence of 证明；表明 □ **in evidence** noticeable 可看见的；明显的

evident /'evɪdənt/ **adjective** easily seen or understood; obvious 明显的；明白的 ■ **evidently** adverb.

evil /'iːvl/ **adjective 1** deeply immoral and wicked 邪恶的；罪恶的 **2** very unpleasant 讨厌的；使人不舒服的 • **noun 1** extreme wickedness 邪恶；罪恶 **2** something harmful or undesirable 坏事；恶行 ■ **evilly** adverb.

evince /ɪ'vɪns/ **verb** (**evinces**, **evincing**, **evinced**) formal【正式】reveal the presence of 表明；表现；显示出

eviscerate /ɪ'vɪsəreɪt/ **verb** (**eviscerates**, **eviscerating**, **eviscerated**) formal【正式】remove the intestines of 除去……的内脏 ■ **evisceration** noun.

evocative /ɪ'vɒkətɪv/ **adjective** bringing strong images, memories, or feelings to mind 使形象再现的；引起记忆的；使情感共鸣的

evoke /ɪ'vəʊk/ **verb** (**evokes**, **evoking**, **evoked**) **1** bring a feeling or memory into someone's mind 唤起(感情或记忆)；使想起 **2** obtain a response 使产生(反应) ■ **evocation** noun.

evolution /ˌiːvə'luːʃn/ **noun 1** the process by which different kinds of animals and plants develop from earlier forms (生物的)演变,进化 **2** gradual development (逐步的)发展, 演化 ■ **evolutionary** adjective.

evolve /iˈvɒlv/ **verb** (**evolves**, **evolving**, **evolved**) **1** develop gradually (逐步)发展,进化,演化 **2** (of an animal or plant) develop and change over many generations by evolution (动植物)进化,成长,发育

ewe /juː/ **noun** a female sheep 母羊, 雌羊

ewer /ˈjuːə(r)/ **noun** a large jug with a wide mouth 大口水壶;广口水罐

ex /eks/ **noun** informal 【非正式】a former husband, wife, boyfriend, or girlfriend 前夫;前妻;前男友(或女友) • **prefix** (**ex-**) **1** out 出;向外; *exclude* 排除 **2** former 以前的;前任: *ex-husband* 前夫

exacerbate /ɪgˈzæsəbeɪt/ **verb** (**exacerbates**, **exacerbating**, **exacerbated**) make something that is already bad worse 使恶化;使加剧 ■ **exacerbation** noun.

exact /ɪgˈzækt/ **adjective 1** precise 精确的;恰好的 **2** accurate in all details 确切的;准确的 • **verb 1** demand and obtain something from someone 索取;强求 **2** take revenge on someone 报(仇) ■ **exactness** noun.

exacting /ɪgˈzæktɪŋ/ **adjective** (of a task) making you concentrate or work very hard (任务)苛求的,严格的

exactitude /ɪgˈzæktɪtjuːd/ **noun** the quality of being exact 正确(性);精确(性)

exactly /ɪgˈzæktli/ **adverb 1** in an exact way 精确地;确切地 **2** used to agree with what has just been said 正是如此;一点儿不错

exaggerate /ɪgˈzædʒəreɪt/ **verb** (**exaggerates**, **exaggerating**, **exaggerated**) make something seem larger, more important, etc. than it really is 夸张;夸大 ■ **exaggeration** noun.

✔ 拼写指南 two gs: exaggerate. exaggerate 中有两个 g.

exalt /ɪgˈzɔːlt/ **verb 1** praise someone or something highly 颂扬;吹捧 **2** give someone or something a higher rank or status 提升;提拔

exaltation /ˌegzɔːlˈteɪʃn/ **noun 1** extreme happiness 兴高采烈;兴奋 **2** the action of exalting 晋升;提高

exalted /ɪgˈzɔːltɪd/ **adjective 1** having high rank or status 地位高的 **2** very grand or noble; high-flown 崇高的; 高尚的

exam /ɪgˈzæm/ **noun** an examination in a subject or skill 考试

examination /ɪgˌzæmɪˈneɪʃn/ **noun 1** a detailed inspection (仔细的)检查,检验;审查 **2** a formal test of knowledge or ability in a subject or skill 考试 **3** the action of examining 考查;调查; 讯究

examine /ɪgˈzæmɪn/ **verb** (**examines**, **examining**, **examined**) **1** inspect something closely 调查;检查 **2** (of a doctor or dentist) look closely at a part of a person's body to detect any problems (医生或牙医)诊察,检查 **3** test someone's knowledge or ability 对 … 考查;测验 ■ **examinee** noun **examiner** noun.

example /ɪgˈzɑːmpl/ **noun 1** a thing that is typical of or represents a particular group 典型 **2** something that shows or supports a general rule 实例;例证 **3** a person or thing seen in terms of how suitable they are to be copied 榜样;楷模

exasperate /ɪgˈzæspəreɪt/ **verb** (**exasperates**, **exasperating**, **exasperated**) irritate someone very much 激怒;使气恼 ■ **exasperation** noun.

excavate /ˈekskəveɪt/ **verb** (**excavates**, **excavating**, **excavated**) **1** make a hole by digging 开凿;挖掘 **2** carefully remove earth from an area in

E

order to find buried remains 发掘 (遗迹等) **3** dig material out of the ground (从地下)挖出 ■ **excavation** noun.

exceed /ɪk'siːd/ **verb 1** be greater in number or size than (在数量或尺寸上)超过,大于 **2** go beyond a set limit 越出(限度) **3** go beyond what is expected 超出(预期)

exceedingly /ɪk'siːdɪŋli/ **adverb** extremely 极其;非常

excel /ɪk'sel/ **verb** (**excels, excelling, excelled**) **1** be very good at something 擅长;善于 **2** (**excel yourself**) do something exceptionally well 超常;突出

Excellency /'eksələnsi/ **noun** (plural **Excellencies**) (**His, Your,** etc. **Excellency**) a form of address for certain high officials of state or of the Roman Catholic Church 阁下(对国家高官或罗马天主教会居要职者的称呼)

excellent /'eksələnt/ **adjective** very good; outstanding 优秀的;卓越的;杰出的 ■ **excellence** noun **excellently** adverb.

except /ɪk'sept/ **preposition** not including 除…外 • **conjunction** used before a statement that forms an exception to one just made 除了 • **verb** exclude 把…除外;排除

✔ 拼写指南 don't forget the c in **except** and related words. Also, don't confuse **except** and **accept**, which means 'agree to receive or do something'. 不要忘记拼写 except 及有关词中的 c,也不要混淆 except 和 accept,后者意为"接受"。

excepting /ɪk'septɪŋ/ **preposition** except for 除…外

exception /ɪk'sepʃn/ **noun** a person or thing that is excluded or that does not follow a rule 除外的;除外的人;例外的事物 □ **take exception to** object strongly to 对…强烈反对

exceptionable /ɪk'sepʃənəbl/ **adjective** formal 【正式】causing disapproval or offence 引起反对(或冒犯)的

exceptional /ɪk'sepʃənl/ **adjective 1** unusual 例外的;罕见的;独特的 **2** unusually good 优越的;杰出的 ■ **exceptionally** adverb.

excerpt /'eksɜːpt/ **noun** a short extract from a film or piece of music or writing (电影、乐曲或文章的)摘录,片段,节录

excess noun **1** an amount that is too much 超过部分;过多的量 **2** (**excesses**) extreme or outrageous behaviour 过分的行为;暴行 **3** Brit. 【英】a part of an insurance claim to be paid by the person insured (保险中的)免赔偿金额 • adjective /'ekses/ going beyond an allowed or desirable amount 过量的;超额的

excessive /ɪk'sesɪv/ **adjective** more than is necessary, normal, or desirable 过多的;过分的 ■ **excessively** adverb.

exchange /ɪks'tʃeɪndʒ/ **noun 1** an act of giving something and receiving something else in return 交换;互换 **2** a short conversation or argument (短暂的)交谈,争吵 **3** the changing of money to its equivalent in another currency 兑换货币;换汇 **4** a building used for financial trading 交易所 **5** a set of equipment that connects telephone lines during a call (电话)交换机 • verb (**exchanges, exchanging, exchanged**) give something and receive something else in return 交换;互换 □ **exchange rate** the value at which one currency may be exchanged for another 汇率;兑换率;汇价

exchequer /ɪks'tʃekə(r)/ **noun 1** a royal or national treasury 国库;金库 **2** (**Exchequer**) Brit. 【英】the account at the Bank of England into which public money is paid 国库账

户(英格兰银行的公共资金账户)

excise[1] /'eksaɪz/ **noun** a tax charged on certain goods produced or sold within a country 消费税;商品税

excise[2] /ɪk'saɪz/ **verb** (**excises**, **excising**, **excised**) **1** cut something out surgically (手术)切除，割去 **2** remove a section from a written work or piece of music 删除(文章或音乐的一段) ▪ **excision** noun.

excitable /ɪk'saɪtəbl/ **adjective** easily excited 易激动的;易兴奋的 ▪ **excitability** noun **excitably** adverb.

excite /ɪk'saɪt/ **verb** (**excites**, **exciting**, **excited**) **1** make someone feel very enthusiastic and eager 使兴奋；刺激 **2** make someone feel sexually aroused 激起(性欲) **3** give rise to 引起;激起 **4** increase the energy or activity in a physical or biological system 刺激(生理系统)的活动 ▪ **excitation** noun **exciting** adjective **excitingly** adverb.

✔ 拼写指南 don't forget the *c*: excite. 不要忘记拼写excited中的c。

---

excitement /ɪk'saɪtmənt/ **noun 1** a feeling of great enthusiasm and eagerness 激动;兴奋 **2** something that arouses such a feeling 令人兴奋(或激动)的事物 **3** sexual arousal 性刺激

exclaim /ɪk'skleɪm/ **verb** cry out suddenly (突然)呼喊,大叫

exclamation /ˌeksklə'meɪʃn/ **noun** a sudden cry or remark (突然的)呼喊，大叫 □ **exclamation mark** a punctuation mark (!) indicating an exclamation 感叹号(!) ▪ **exclamatory** adjective.

exclude /ɪk'sklu:d/ **verb** (**excludes**, **excluding**, **excluded**) **1** choose not to include something in what you are counting or considering 对…不予考虑 **2** prevent someone from being a part of something 阻止…进入;把…排除在外

exclusion /ɪk'sklu:ʒn/ **noun** the process of excluding, or the state of being excluded 排除;被排除在外的状态

exclusive /ɪk'sklu:sɪv/ **adjective 1** restricted to the person, group, or area concerned (人、团体或地区)专有的, 独有的 **2** high-quality and expensive 高级的；奢华的 **3** not including other things 排斥的;排他的 **4** not published or broadcast elsewhere 独家发表的;独家报道的 ▪ **noun** a story or film that has not been published or broadcast elsewhere 独家新闻,独家报道 ▪ **exclusively** adverb **exclusivity** noun.

excommunicate /ˌekskə'mju:nɪkeɪt/ **verb** (**excommunicates**, **excommunicating**, **excommunicated**) officially bar someone from membership of the Christian Church 开除(某人)的教籍，把(某人)逐出教会 ▪ **excommunication** noun.

excoriate /eks'kɔ:rɪeɪt/ **verb** (**excoriates**, **excoriating**, **excoriated**) **1** formal 【正式】criticize severely 严厉指责;痛斥 **2** Medicine 【医】damage or remove part of the surface of the skin 擦破(皮肤);剥去(皮) ▪ **excoriation** noun.

excrement /'ekskrɪmənt/ **noun** waste material passed from the body through the bowels 排泄物;粪便

excrescence /ɪk'skresns/ **noun** an abnormal growth or lump on a part of the body or a plant 赘疣;瘤

excreta /ɪk'skri:tə/ **noun** waste material that is passed out of the body 排泄物

excrete /ɪk'skri:t/ **verb** (**excretes**, **excreting**, **excreted**) pass waste material from the body 排泄 ▪ **excretion** noun **excretory** adjective.

excruciating /ɪk'skru:ʃɪeɪtɪŋ/ **adjective 1** very painful 极痛苦的；剧痛的 **2** very embarrassing, awkward, or boring 极尴尬的；极笨拙的;极乏味的 ▪ **excruciatingly** adverb.

exculpate /'ekskʌlpeɪt/ **verb**

(exculpates, exculpating, exculpated) formal 【正式】 say that someone is not guilty of doing something wrong 声称⋯无罪

excursion /ɪkˈskɜːʃn/ **noun** a short journey or trip taken for pleasure 短途旅行

excuse verb /ɪkˈskjuːz/ **(excuses, excusing, excused) 1** give reasons why something that someone has done wrong may be justified 为⋯辩解；为⋯开脱 **2** forgive someone for something they have done wrong 原谅；宽恕 **3** allow someone to not do something that is usually required 使免除(责任) **4** allow someone to leave a room or meeting 准许离开；放走 • **noun** /ɪkˈskjuːs/ **1** a reason put forward to justify a fault or wrongdoing (开脱的)理由 **2** something said to conceal the real reason for an action 借口 **3** informal 【非正式】 a very bad example of something (某物品的)拙劣样品，蹩脚货 ■ **excusable** adjective.

ex-directory /ˌeksdɪˈrektəri/ **adjective** Brit. 【英】 not listed in a telephone directory at your own request (应本人的要求)未列入电话簿的

execrable /ˈeksɪkrəbl/ **adjective** very bad or unpleasant 恶劣的；讨厌的

execrate /ˈeksɪkreɪt/ **verb (execrates, execrating, execrated)** feel or express great hatred for 憎恶；咒骂；痛斥 ■ **execration** noun.

execute /ˈeksɪkjuːt/ **verb (executes, executing, executed) 1** carry out a plan, order, etc. 实施；执行(命令) **2** carry out an activity or manoeuvre 实施(行动)；施行(策略) **3** kill a condemned person as a legal punishment 处死；处决

execution /ˌeksɪˈkjuːʃn/ **noun 1** the carrying out of something 实行；实施；执行 **2** the killing of a person who has been condemned to death 执行死刑；处决

executioner /ˌeksɪˈkjuːʃənə(r)/ **noun** an official who executes condemned criminals 行刑人

executive /ɪgˈzekjʊtɪv/ **noun 1** a senior manager in a business 高级经理 **2** a group of people who run an organization or business (机构或组织的)行政人员；(企业中的)管理者 **3** (**the executive**) the branch of a government responsible for putting plans, actions, or laws into effect (政府的)行政部门 • **adjective** having the power to put plans, actions, or laws into effect 执行的；实施的

executor /ɪgˈzekjʊtə(r)/ **noun** a person appointed by someone to carry out the terms of their will 遗嘱执行人

exegesis /ˌeksɪˈdʒiːsɪs/ **noun (plural exegeses** /ˌeksɪˈdʒiːsiːz/**)** an explanation or interpretation of a written work 注释；评注

exemplar /ɪgˈzemplɑː(r)/ **noun** a person or thing that is a good or typical example of something 典型；模范；榜样

exemplary /ɪgˈzempləri/ **adjective 1** giving a good example to other people 模范的；典范的 **2** (of a punishment) acting as a warning (惩罚)警诫性的，惩戒性的

exemplify /ɪgˈzemplɪfaɪ/ **verb (exemplifies, exemplifying, exemplified)** be or give a typical example of 是⋯的典型；举例证明 ■ **exemplification** noun.

exempt /ɪgˈzempt/ **adjective** not having to do or pay something that other people have to do or pay 免除的；豁免的 • **verb** make someone exempt 免除；豁免 ■ **exemption** noun.

exercise /ˈeksəsaɪz/ **noun 1** physical activity done to stay healthy or become stronger 运动；锻炼 **2** a set of movements, activities, or questions that test your ability or help you practise a skill 练习；习题 **3** an activity carried out for a specific purpose (为某目的所进行的)活动 **4**

the putting into practice of a power or right 运用；行使 • **verb (exercises, exercising, exercised) 1** use or apply a power or right 运用，行使(权力或权利) **2** do physical exercise 训练；锻炼 **3** worry or puzzle someone 使担忧；使迷惑不解 ☐ **exercise book** Brit. 【英】a booklet with blank pages for students to write in 练习本

exert /ɪgˈzɜːt/ **verb 1** use a force, influence, or quality to make something happen 运用(力量)；施加(影响)；发挥(某素质) **2 (exert yourself)** make a physical or mental effort 用力；尽力 ■ **exertion** noun.

exeunt /ˈeksiʌnt/ **verb** (in a play) a stage direction telling actors to leave the stage (戏剧中的)退场，下场(指示演员退场的舞台说明语)

exfoliate /eksˈfəʊlɪeɪt/ **verb (exfoliates, exfoliating, exfoliated)** wash or rub the skin with a grainy substance to remove dead cells (为除去死皮用粗糙物)擦(皮肤) ■ **exfoliation** noun.

exhale /eksˈheɪl/ **verb (exhales, exhaling, exhaled) 1** breathe out 呼(气) **2** give off vapour or fumes 散出(蒸气或烟) ■ **exhalation** noun.

exhaust /ɪgˈzɔːst/ **verb 1** tire someone out 使精疲力竭 **2** use up all of something 用完；花光；耗尽 **3** talk about a subject so thoroughly that there is nothing left to say 详尽谈论，穷尽(某话题) • **noun 1** waste gases that are expelled from the engine of a car or other machine (引擎排出的)废气 **2** the system through which these gases are expelled 排气系统；排气管；排气口 ■ **exhaustible** adjective.

exhaustion /ɪgˈzɔːstʃən/ **noun** the state of being exhausted 精疲力竭；耗尽，穷尽

exhaustive /ɪgˈzɔːstɪv/ **adjective** thoroughly covering all aspects of something 全面彻底的；详尽无遗的 ■ **exhaustively** adverb.

exhibit /ɪgˈzɪbɪt/ **verb 1** display an item in an art gallery or museum (在美术馆或博物馆)展出，展览，陈列 **2** show a particular quality 表现；显示 • **noun 1** an object or collection on display in an art gallery or museum 展览品；陈列品 **2** an object produced in a court of law as evidence (当庭出示的)证据，物证 ■ **exhibitor** noun.

exhibition /ˌeksɪˈbɪʃn/ **noun 1** a public display of items in an art gallery or museum 展览；展览会 **2** a display or demonstration of a skill or quality (技能、特性的)展示，表现

exhibitionism /ˌeksɪˈbɪʃənɪzəm/ **noun** behaviour that is intended to make people notice you 表现癖；表现狂 ■ **exhibitionist** noun.

exhilarate /ɪgˈzɪləreɪt/ **verb (exhilarates, exhilarating, exhilarated)** make someone feel very happy and full of energy 使高兴；使活跃 ■ **exhilaration** noun.

> ✔ 拼写指南 the middle is -lar-, not -ler-: exhilarate. exhilarate 中间应拼作 -lar-，不要拼作 -ler-。

exhort /ɪgˈzɔːt/ **verb** strongly urge someone to do something 敦促；激励 ■ **exhortation** noun.

exhume /eksˈhjuːm/ **verb (exhumes, exhuming, exhumed)** dig out from the ground something that has been buried 挖出，发掘(埋葬品) ■ **exhumation** noun.

exigency /ˈeksɪdʒənsi/ **noun (plural exigencies)** formal 【正式】an urgent need 急切需要；迫切要求

exigent /ˈeksɪdʒənt/ **adjective** formal 【正式】needing urgent action; pressing 紧急的；急迫的

exiguous /egˈzɪgjʊəs/ **adjective** formal 【正式】very small 微小的；细微的

exile /ˈeksaɪl/ **noun 1** the state of being forbidden to live or spend time in your own country 流放；放逐；流亡 **2** a person who lives in exile 被流放者；流亡国外者；背井离乡者 • **verb**

(**exiles, exiling, exiled**) expel and bar someone from their own country 将(某人)流放(到国外)

exist /ɪgˈzɪst/ **verb 1** be present in a place or situation 存在;实有 **2** live 生存;生活

existence /ɪgˈzɪstəns/ **noun 1** the fact or state of existing 存在;实有 **2** a way of living 生存方式: *a rural existence* 农村生活

✔ 拼写指南 *-ence*, not *-ance*: exis*tence*. existence 中的 -ence 不要拼作 -ance。

existential /ˌegzɪˈstenʃəl/ **adjective 1** having to do with existence 存在的;实有的 **2** Philosophy【哲学】concerned with existentialism 存在主义的

existentialism /ˌegzɪˈstenʃəlɪzəm/ **noun** a theory in philosophy which says that people are free individuals, responsible for their own actions 存在主义(一种哲学理论,主张人是自由的个体,对其行为负责) ▪ **existentialist** noun & adjective.

exit /ˈeksɪt/ **noun 1** a way out of a place 出口 **2** an act of leaving 出去;离开 ▪ **verb** (**exits, exiting, exited**) go out of or leave a place 出去;离开 □ **exit poll** an opinion poll in which people leaving a polling station are asked how they voted 出口民调(在投票者离开投票站时对其投票情况的调查)

exodus /ˈeksədəs/ **noun** a mass departure of people (人)大批离开

exonerate /ɪgˈzɒnəreɪt/ **verb** (**exonerates, exonerating, exonerated**) officially state that someone has not done something wrong or illegal (正式)使免除责备,宣布…无罪 ▪ **exoneration** noun.

exorbitant /ɪgˈzɔːbɪtənt/ **adjective** (of an amount charged) unreasonably high (收费)过高的 ▪ **exorbitantly** adverb.

✔ 拼写指南 no *h*: ex*orbitant*. exorbitant 中没有 h。

exorcize or **exorcise** /ˈeksɔːsaɪz/ **verb** (**exorcizes, exorcizing, exorcizes**) drive an evil spirit from a person or place (从某人身上或某地)驱除(妖魔) ▪ **exorcism** noun **exorcist** noun.

exotic /ɪgˈzɒtɪk/ **adjective 1** coming from or characteristic of a distant foreign country 外来的;异国情调的 **2** strikingly colourful or unusual 极富特色的;异乎寻常的 ▪ **exotically** adverb **exoticism** noun.

expand /ɪkˈspænd/ **verb 1** make or become larger or more extensive (使)扩大;(使)扩展;(使)变大 **2** (**expand on**) give a fuller account of something 详尽;更充分地阐述 ▪ **expandable** adjective **expansion** noun.

expanse /ɪkˈspæns/ **noun** a wide continuous area of something 广阔区域;大片地区

expansive /ɪkˈspænsɪv/ **adjective 1** covering a wide area 广阔的;辽阔的 **2** relaxed, friendly, and communicative 放松的;友善的;健谈的 ▪ **expansively** adverb.

expat /ˈeksˌpæt/ ⇒ 见 EXPATRIATE.

expatiate /ɪkˈspeɪʃieɪt/ **verb** (**expatiates, expatiating, expatiated**) (**expatiate on**) speak or write in detail about something 细说;详述;阐述

expatriate /ˌeksˈpætriət/ **noun** a person who lives outside their own country 侨居国外者

expect /ɪkˈspekt/ **verb 1** think something is likely to happen 预计…可能发生;预料 **2** think someone is likely to do or be something 预期…做;预期…成为 **3** believe that someone will arrive soon 等待;盼望(某人) **4** assume or demand that someone will do something because it is their duty or responsibility 认为,要求(应履行

职责或承担责任) **5 (be expecting)** informal 【非正式】 be pregnant 怀孕; 有喜

expectancy /ɪkˈspektənsi/ **noun** (plural **expectancies**) the belief or hope that something will happen 期待;期望;预期

expectant /ɪkˈspektənt/ **adjective 1** believing or hoping that something is about to happen 期待的;预期的; 期望的 **2 (of a woman)** pregnant (女子)怀孕的 ■ **expectantly** adverb.

expectation /ˌekspekˈteɪʃn/ **noun 1** belief that something will happen or be the case 期待;预期;预料 **2** a thing that is expected to happen 预期的事物

expectorant /ɪkˈspektərənt/ **noun** a medicine which helps to bring up phlegm from the air passages, used to treat a cough 祛痰止咳药

expectorate /ɪkˈspektəreɪt/ **verb** (**expectorates, expectorating, expectorated**) cough or spit out phlegm from the throat or lungs 咳出(痰)

expedient /ɪkˈspiːdiənt/ **adjective 1** useful or helpful for a particular purpose 有用的;有益的 **2** useful in achieving something, rather than morally correct 权宜 • **noun** a means of achieving something 权宜 之计;应急手段 ■ **expediency** (or **expedience**) noun.

expedite /ˈekspədaɪt/ **verb** (**expedites, expediting, expedited**) make something happen more quickly 促进;加速

expedition /ˌekspəˈdɪʃn/ **noun** a journey with a particular purpose, made by a group of people 远征;探险 ■ **expeditionary** adjective.

expeditious /ˌekspəˈdɪʃəs/ **adjective** quick and efficient 迅速而有效的 ■ **expeditiously** adverb.

expel /ɪkˈspel/ **verb** (**expels, expelling, expelled**) **1** force someone to leave a school, organization, or place 开除; 驱逐 **2** force something out 赶出去; 赶走

expend /ɪkˈspend/ **verb** spend or use up a resource 花费;耗费

expendable /ɪkˈspendəbl/ **adjective** able to be sacrificed in order to gain or achieve something (为获取某物或实现某目的)可被牺牲的

expenditure /ɪkˈspendɪtʃə(r)/ **noun 1** the action of spending money (金钱的)花费,支出 **2** the amount of money spent 支出额;消耗量

expense /ɪkˈspens/ **noun 1** the amount something costs 价钱;费用 **2** something on which money must be spent 必须花钱的事物 **3 (expenses)** money spent in doing a particular thing 支出 **4 (expenses)** money paid for meals, fares, etc. by an employee in the course of their work, which they can claim back from their employer 开销

expensive /ɪkˈspensɪv/ **adjective** costing a lot of money 昂贵的;花钱多的 ■ **expensively** adverb.

experience /ɪkˈspɪəriəns/ **noun 1** the fact of being present at or taking part in something 经历;阅历;体验 **2** knowledge or skill gained over time 经验 **3** an event which affects you in some way (对某人产生某种影响的)事件,经历 • **verb** (**experiences, experiencing, experienced**) **1** be present at or be affected by something 经历;体验 **2** feel an emotion 体验到(某种感情)

experienced /ɪkˈspɪəriənst/ **adjective** having gained a lot of knowledge or skill in a job or activity over time 经验丰富的,熟练的

experiment /ɪkˈsperɪmənt/ **noun 1** a scientific procedure carried out to make a discovery, test a theory, or demonstrate a fact 实验 **2** a new course of action that you try out without being sure of the outcome

试验 • verb 1 perform a scientific experiment 做实验 2 try out new things 进行试验 ■ experimentation noun.

experimental /ɪkˌsperɪ'mentl/ adjective 1 based on a new idea and not yet fully tested 试验(性)的，根据试验的 2 having to do with scientific experiments 科学实验的 3 (of art, music, etc.) new and unconventional (美术、音乐等)独创的，不因袭传统的 ■ experimentally adverb.

expert /'eksps:t/ noun a person who has great knowledge or skill in a particular field 专家，高手 • adjective having or involving great knowledge or skill 知识丰富的，熟练的 ■ expertly adverb.

expertise /ˌeksps:'ti:z/ noun great skill or knowledge in a particular field 专门技能，专业知识

expiate /'ekspɪeɪt/ verb (expiates, expiating, expiated) do something to make up for having done something wrong 赎(罪)；为(过失)作出补偿 ■ expiation noun.

expire /ɪk'spaɪə(r)/ verb (expires, expiring, expired) 1 (of a document or agreement) cease to be valid (文件或协议)失效 2 (of a period of time) come to an end 期满，终止；期满 3 (of a person) die (人)死亡 4 breathe out air from the lungs 呼出(空气)

expiry /ɪk'spaɪəri/ noun the end of the period for which something is valid (期限的)终止；期满

explain /ɪk'spleɪn/ verb 1 describe something in a way that makes it easy to understand 讲解，阐明 2 give a reason for something 解释，说明 3 (explain yourself) say why you are doing something in order to justify or excuse it 为自己的行为作解释 ■ explanation noun.

explanatory /ɪk'splænətri/ adjective giving the reason for something, or making something clear 解释的，说明的；辩明的

expletive /ɪk'spli:tɪv/ noun a swear word 咒骂语；秽语

explicable /ɪk'splɪkəbl/ adjective able to be explained 可解释的，可说明的；可辩明的

explicit /ɪk'splɪsɪt/ adjective 1 clear, detailed, and easy to understand 明晰的；明确的；易懂的 2 showing or describing sexual activity openly and clearly (表现或描述性行为时)清晰露骨的 ■ explicitly adverb.

explode /ɪk'spləʊd/ verb (explodes, exploding, exploded) 1 burst or shatter violently as a result of the release of internal energy 爆炸，爆破 2 show sudden violent emotion (感情)爆发，迸发 3 increase suddenly in number or extent 激增；迅速扩大 4 show a belief to be false 破除；戳穿

exploit verb /ɪk'splɔɪt/ 1 make use of someone unfairly (不公平地)利用(某人)；剥削 2 make good use of a resource 利用(资源) • noun /'eksplɔɪt/ a daring act 英勇行为 ■ exploitation noun exploitative adjective.

explore /ɪk'splɔ:(r)/ verb (explores, exploring, explored) 1 travel through an unfamiliar area in order to learn about it 勘探；勘查；探测 2 examine or discuss something in detail 研究；探究 3 investigate 调查 ■ exploration noun exploratory adjective explorer noun.

explosion /ɪk'spləʊʒn/ noun an instance of exploding 爆炸；迸发；激增

explosive /ɪk'spləʊsɪv/ adjective 1 able or likely to explode 会爆炸的；可能爆炸的 2 likely to cause anger or controversy 爆炸性的；极有争议的 3 (of an increase) sudden and dramatic (增长)突然的，剧烈的 • noun a substance which can be made to explode 炸药 ■ explosively adverb.

exponent /ɪk'spəʊnənt/ noun 1 a promoter of an idea or theory(思想

或理论的)倡导者,拥护者 **2** a person who does a particular thing skilfully 内行;能手 **3** Maths 【数学】 a raised figure beside a number indicating how many times that number is to be multiplied by itself (e.g.³ in $2^3 = 2 \times 2 \times 2$) 指数

exponential /ˌekspəˈnenʃl/ **adjective 1** (of an increase) becoming more and more rapid (增长)越来越快的 **2** Maths 【数学】 having to do with a mathematical exponent 指数的 ■ **exponentially** adverb.

export verb /ɪkˈspɔːt/ send goods or services to another country for sale 出口,输出(商品或服务) • noun /ˈekspɔːt/ **1** the exporting of goods or services 出口,输出 **2** an exported item 输出品 ■ **exportation** noun **exporter** noun.

expose /ɪkˈspəʊz/ verb (**exposes, exposing, exposed**) **1** uncover something and make it visible 暴露;显露,使无遮蔽 **2** show the true nature of someone or something 揭露…的真相;揭露 **3** (**exposed**) not protected from the weather 暴露(在空气中)的;无遮蔽的 **4** (**expose someone to**) make someone vulnerable to 使易受影响;使易受伤害 **5** subject photographic film to light 使(胶卷)曝光 **6** (**expose yourself**) show your sexual organs in public (在公共场所)祖露,裸露(性器官)

exposé /ekˈspəʊzeɪ/ noun a report in the news revealing shocking information about someone (媒体对丑事的)揭发,曝光

exposition /ˌekspəˈzɪʃn/ noun **1** a careful setting out of the facts or ideas involved in something 说明;讲解 **2** an exhibition 展览会;博览会 **3** Music 【音乐】 the part of a movement in which the main themes are first presented (乐章的)呈示部

expostulate /ɪkˈspɒstʃuleɪt/ verb (**expostulates, expostulating, expostulated**) express strong disapproval or disagreement 表示强烈反对;规劝 ■ **expostulation** noun.

exposure /ɪkˈspəʊʒə(r)/ noun **1** the state of being exposed to something harmful (对有害物质的)接触;暴露 **2** a physical condition resulting from being exposed to severe weather conditions 暴露;日晒雨淋 **3** the revealing of the true facts about someone or something 揭露;揭发 **4** the fact of being discussed or mentioned on television, in newspapers, etc. (在电视、报纸等上的)曝光 **5** the quantity of light reaching a photographic film (胶片的)曝光量

expound /ɪkˈspaʊnd/ verb set out and explain the facts or ideas involved in something 阐述;详细说明;解释

express¹ /ɪkˈspres/ verb **1** show by words or actions what you are thinking or feeling (用语言或行动)表达(思想或情感) **2** squeeze out liquid or air 榨,挤,压出(液体或空气)

express² adjective operating or delivered very quickly 快的;高速的 • adverb by express train or delivery service 由快速列车;用特快专递 • noun **1** a train that travels quickly and stops at few stations 快速列车 **2** a special delivery service 特快专递

express³ adjective **1** stated very clearly 表达清楚的;明确的 **2** excluding anything else 专门的;特别的 ■ **expressly** adverb.

expression /ɪkˈspreʃn/ noun **1** the action of expressing 表达;陈述 **2** the look on someone's face 表情 **3** a word or phrase expressing an idea (表达思想的)词语 **4** Maths 【数学】 a collection of symbols expressing a quantity 式;表达式 ■ **expressionless** adjective.

expressionism /ɪkˈspreʃənɪzəm/ noun a style in art, music, or drama in which the artist or writer shows the inner world of emotion rather than external reality 表现主义(美术、音乐或戏剧的一种形式,艺术家或作家试图表达内在的情感世界而非外在现实) ■ **expressionist** noun & adjective.

expressive /ɪkˈspresɪv/ **adjective** clearly showing thoughts or feelings 富于表现力的 ■ **expressively** adverb **expressiveness** noun.

expropriate /eksˈprəʊprieɪt/ **verb** (**expropriates**, **expropriating**, **expropriated**) (of the state or an authority) take property from its owner (国家或权力机构)征用,没收(财产) ■ **expropriation** noun.

expulsion /ɪkˈspʌlʃn/ **noun** the action of expelling 驱逐;开除

expunge /ɪkˈspʌndʒ/ **verb** (**expunges**, **expunging**, **expunged**) remove something completely (彻底)除去,删去

expurgate /ˈekspəɡeɪt/ **verb** (**expurgates**, **expurgating**, **expurgated**) remove unsuitable material from a written work 删除(文章)中的不当之处 ■ **expurgation** noun.

exquisite /ɪkˈskwɪzɪt, ˈekskwɪzɪt/ **adjective 1** very beautiful and delicate 精美的;精致的 **2** showing great sensitivity or refinement 敏锐的;精湛的;高雅的 **3** strongly felt (感觉)剧烈的,强烈的 ■ **exquisitely** adverb.

extant /ekˈstænt/ **adjective** still in existence 尚存的;现存的

extempore /ekˈstempəri/ **adjective & adverb** spoken or done without preparation 即兴(地);无准备的(地);临时的(地)

extemporize or **extemporise** /ɪkˈstempəraɪz/ **verb** (**extemporizes**, **extemporizing**, **extemporized**) make something up as you go along 即兴创作;即兴表演

extend /ɪkˈstend/ **verb 1** make something larger in area 扩展,扩大(面积)

2 make something last longer 延长(时间),延期 **3** occupy a particular area or continue for a particular distance 占据(某地区);延伸(一定距离) **4** stretch out a part of your body 伸出,伸展(身体部位) **5** offer something to someone 提供;给予 □ **extended family** a family group consisting of parents and children and close relatives living nearby (包括近亲的)大家庭,大家族 ■ **extendable** (or **extendible**) adjective **extensible** adjective.

extension /ɪkˈstenʃn/ **noun 1** the action of extending something 扩展;延长;伸出 **2** a part added to a building to make it bigger (建筑的)扩建部分 **3** an additional period of time 附加时间;延长的时间,放宽的期限 **4** an extra telephone on the same line as the main one 电话分机 □ **extension lead** a length of electric cable which can be plugged into a socket and has another socket on the end 延长引线

extensive /ɪkˈstensɪv/ **adjective 1** covering a large area 广阔的;广大的 **2** large in amount or scale 数量大的;规模大的 ■ **extensively** adverb.

extent /ɪkˈstent/ **noun 1** the area covered by something 覆盖面积 **2** size or scale 大小;范围;规模 **3** the degree to which something is the case 程度

extenuating /ɪkˈstenjueɪtɪŋ/ **adjective** serving to make an offence less serious by partially excusing it 情有可原的;可减轻罪过的: extenuating circumstances 可减轻罪责的情况 ■ **extenuation** noun.

exterior /ɪkˈstɪəriə(r)/ **adjective** having to do with the outside of something 外部的;外面的;外表的 • **noun** the outer surface or structure of something 外部;外面;外表

exterminate /ɪkˈstɜːmɪneɪt/ **verb** (**exterminates**, **exterminating**,

exterminated) destroy something completely 根除;灭绝;消灭 ■ **extermination** noun **exterminator** noun.

external /ɪkˈstɜːnl/ **adjective 1** having to do with the outside of something 外面的;外部的 **2** coming from outside an organization or situation 外来的;外界的 **3** having to do with another country or institution 与外国有关的;和其他机构有关的 ■ **externally** adverb.

externalize or **externalise** /ɪkˈstɜːnəlaɪz/ **verb** (**externalizes, externalizing, externalized**) express a thought or feeling in words or actions (用言语或行动)表达(思想或感情)

extinct /ɪkˈstɪŋkt/ **adjective 1** no longer in existence 消亡的;不复存在的 **2** (of a volcano) not having erupted in recorded history (火山)死的,不再喷发的 ■ **extinction** noun.

extinguish /ɪkˈstɪŋɡwɪʃ/ **verb 1** put out a fire (将火)扑灭;熄灭 **2** put an end to 使终结;使消亡 ■ **extinguisher** noun.

extirpate /ˈekstəpeɪt/ **verb** (**extirpates, extirpating, extirpated**) search out and destroy something completely 根除;毁灭 ■ **extirpation** noun.

extol /ɪkˈstəʊl/ **verb** (**extols, extolling, extolled**) praise enthusiastically 颂扬;赞颂;赞美

extort /ɪkˈstɔːt/ **verb** obtain something by force, threats, or other unfair means 强求;勒索 ■ **extortion** noun.

extortionate /ɪkˈstɔːʃənət/ **adjective** (of a price) much too high (价格)过高的 ■ **extortionately** adverb.

extra /ˈekstrə/ **adjective** added to an existing or usual amount or number 额外的;外加的 • **adverb 1** to a greater extent than usual 特别地;非常 **2** in addition 额外地;另外 • **noun 1** an additional item, for which an extra charge is made 另外收费的物件 **2** a person employed to take part in a crowd scene in a film or play (电

影或戏剧中的)临时演员,群众演员 • **prefix (extra-)** outside; beyond 外面的;外部的:*extramarital* 婚外的

extract **verb** /ɪkˈstrækt/ **1** remove something with care or effort (小心或费力地)取出,移出 **2** obtain something from someone unwilling to give it 索得;强取 **3** separate out a substance by a special method (用特殊方法)提取,榨取,采掘 • **noun** /ˈekstrækt/ **1** a short passage taken from a written work, film, or piece of music 摘录;引文;选段;选曲 **2** an extracted substance 提取(或榨取,采掘)的物质 □ **extractor fan** a device that removes steam and smells from a room 抽油烟机

extraction /ɪkˈstrækʃn/ **noun 1** the action of extracting 提取;榨取;采掘 **2** the ethnic origin of someone's family 血统;祖系

extradite /ˈekstrədaɪt/ **verb** (**extradites, extraditing, extradited**) hand over a person accused or convicted of committing a crime in a foreign state to the legal authority of that state 引渡(罪犯) ■ **extradition** noun.

extramarital /ˌekstrəˈmærɪtl/ **adjective** happening outside marriage 婚外的

extramural /ˌekstrəˈmjʊərəl/ **adjective** Brit. 【英】(of a course of study) for people who are not full-time members of an educational establishment (课程)为非在校生开设的

extraneous /ɪkˈstreɪniəs/ **adjective 1** unrelated to the subject being dealt with 无关的 **2** of external origin 外来的

extraordinaire /ɪkˌstrɔːdɪˈneə(r)/ **adjective** outstanding in a particular capacity 非凡的,出色的:*She was a gardener extraordinaire.* 她是一名出色的园艺师。

extraordinary /ɪkˈstrɔːdnri/ **adjective 1** very unusual or remarkable 非同寻常的;非常优秀的 **2** (of a

meeting) held for a particular reason rather than being one of a regular series (会议)非惯例的,特别召开的
■ **extraordinarily** adverb.

✔ 拼写指南 the beginning is *extra-*, not just *extr-*: *extra*ordinary. extraordinary 以 extra- 开头,而不仅仅是 extr-

extrapolate /ɪkˈstræpəleɪt/ **verb** (**extrapolates, extrapolating, extrapolated**) use a fact or conclusion that is valid for one situation and apply it to a larger or different one 推断;推知 ■ **extrapolation** noun.

extrasensory perception /ˌekstrə-ˈsensəri/ **noun** the supposed ability to perceive things by means other than the known senses, e.g. by telepathy 超感知觉;超感觉力

extraterrestrial /ˌekstrətəˈrestriəl/ **adjective** having to do with things that come from beyond the earth or its atmosphere 地球以外的;大气圈外的 • **noun** a fictional being from outer space (小说中的)天外来客,外星生物

extravagant /ɪkˈstrævəgənt/ **adjective 1** spending or using more than is necessary or more than you can afford 奢侈的;铺张的,浪费的 **2** very expensive 昂贵的 **3** going beyond what is reasonable 过度的;过分的 ■ **extravagance** noun **extravagantly** adverb.

extravaganza /ɪkˌstrævəˈɡænzə/ **noun** an elaborate and spectacular entertainment 铺张华丽的演出

extreme /ɪkˈstriːm/ **adjective 1** to the highest degree 极度的;极大的 **2** highly unusual 极端的 **3** very severe or serious 极严厉的 **4** not moderate 偏激的;过分的 **5** furthest from the centre or a given point (离中心)最远的;末端的,尽头的 • **noun 1** either of two abstract things that are as different from each other as possible 极端不同的(抽象)事物 **2**

the most extreme degree 极度;极端
■ **extremely** adverb.

extremist /ɪkˈstriːmɪst/ **noun** a person who holds extreme political or religious views (政治或宗教上的)极端主义者,极端分子 ■ **extremism** noun.

extremity /ɪkˈstreməti/ **noun** (plural **extremities**) **1** the furthest point or limit 末端;尽头 **2** (**extremities**) a person's hands and feet 手脚 **3** extreme hardship 绝境;极其艰难的境地

extricate /ˈekstrɪkeɪt/ **verb** (**extricates, extricating, extricated**) **1** free someone from a difficult situation 解救(某人) **2** free something that is trapped 使(某物)脱离(困境)

extrinsic /eksˈtrɪnsɪk/ **adjective** coming from outside; not part of something's basic nature 外来的;非本质的

extrovert /ˈekstrəvɜːt/ **noun** an outgoing, lively person 性格外向者;好交际者 • **adjective** outgoing and lively 性格外向的;好交际的

✔ 拼写指南 *extro-*, not *extra-*: *extro*vert. extrovert 中的 extro 不要拼作 extra。

extrude /ɪkˈstruːd/ **verb** (**extrudes, extruding, extruded**) thrust or force something out 挤压;伸出;使突出

exuberant /ɪɡˈzjuːbərənt/ **adjective 1** lively and cheerful 生气勃勃的;兴高采烈的 **2** growing thickly 茂盛的 ■ **exuberance** noun **exuberantly** adverb.

exude /ɪɡˈzjuːd/ **verb** (**exudes, exuding, exuded**) **1** send out or give off a liquid or smell slowly and steadily 慢慢流出 **2** display an emotion or quality strongly and openly 充分显露(感情或特质)

exult /ɪɡˈzʌlt/ **verb** show or feel triumphant joy 狂喜;欢欣鼓舞 ■ **exultant**

adjective **exultantly** adverb **exultation** noun.

eye /aɪ/ **noun 1** the organ of sight in humans and animals 眼睛 **2** the small hole in a needle through which the thread is passed 针眼 **3** a small metal loop into which a hook is fitted as a fastener on a garment(衣服上的)钩眼 **4** a person's opinion or feelings 眼力;鉴赏力 **5** the calm region at the centre of a storm (风)眼 **6** a dark spot on a potato from which a new shoot grows (马铃薯的)芽眼 • verb (**eyes**, **eyeing** or **eying**, **eyed**) look at closely or with interest 看;审视;(有兴趣地)注视 □ **see eye to eye** be in complete agreement 看法完全一致

eyeball /'aɪbɔːl/ **noun** the round part of the eye of a vertebrate, within the eyelids 眼球;眼珠

eyebrow /'aɪbraʊ/ **noun** the strip of hair growing on the ridge above a person's eye socket 眉;眉毛

eyeglass /'aɪglɑːs/ **noun** a single lens for correcting eyesight 镜片;单片眼镜

eyelash /'aɪlæʃ/ **noun** each of the short hairs growing on the edges of the eyelids 睫;睫毛

eyelet /'aɪlət/ **noun** a small round hole with a metal ring around it, for threading a lace or cord through 圆孔眼

eyelid /'aɪlɪd/ **noun** each of the upper and lower folds of skin which cover the eye when it is closed 睑;眼睑;眼皮

eyeliner /'aɪlaɪnə(r)/ **noun** a cosmetic applied as a line round the eyes 眼线笔;眼线膏

eyeshadow /'aɪʃædəʊ/ **noun** a cosmetic applied to the skin around the eyes 眼睑膏;眼影

eyesight /'aɪsaɪt/ **noun** a person's ability to see 视力;目力

eyesore /'aɪsɔː(r)/ **noun** a thing that is very ugly 丑东西

eyewitness /'aɪwɪtnəs/ **noun** a person who has seen something happen 目击者;见证人

eyrie /'ɪəri, 'aɪəri/ (US spelling 【美拼作】 aerie) **noun** a large nest of a bird of prey 猛禽的大巢

Ff

SPELLING TIP 拼写指南 Certain words which sound as if they begin with 'f' are spelled with a 'ph' instead, for example **phrase**, **phantom**, or **phobia**. 某些根据发音似乎是以f开头的词实际以ph开头，如 phrase, phantom 和 phobia。

F or **f** /ef/ **noun** (plural **Fs** or **F's**) the sixth letter of the alphabet 英语字母表的第6个字母 • **abbreviation** Fahrenheit.

FA /ˌef ˈeɪ/ **abbreviation** Football Association 足球总会

fable /ˈfeɪbl/ **noun 1** a short story, often about animals, which teaches about right and wrong behaviour 寓言 **2** a story about mythical characters or events 传说；神话

fabled /ˈfeɪbld/ **adjective 1** famous 著名的 **2** described in myths and legends 神话式的；虚构的；杜撰的

fabric /ˈfæbrɪk/ **noun 1** cloth 布；织物 **2** the walls, floor, and roof of a building (建筑)的架构，结构 (指墙、地板和屋顶)**3** the basic structure of a system or organization (系统或组织的)构造，结构

fabricate /ˈfæbrɪkeɪt/ **verb** (**fabricates**, **fabricating**, **fabricated**) **1** make up facts that are not true 捏造；编造 **2** make an industrial product 制造 (工业产品)■ **fabrication noun**.

fabulous /ˈfæbjələs/ **adjective 1** great; extraordinary 巨大的，惊人的；非常的 **2** informal 【非正式】wonderful 极好的；绝妙的 **3** existing in myths and legends 神话式的；传说中的 ■ **fabulously** adverb.

facade /fəˈsɑːd/ **noun 1** the front of a building (建筑物的)正面 **2** a misleading outward appearance (给人假象的)表面，外观

face /feɪs/ **noun 1** the front part of the head from the forehead to the chin 脸；面孔 **2** an expression on someone's face 面部表情 **3** the surface of a thing 表面 **4** a vertical or sloping side of a mountain or cliff 陡面；斜坡；山坡 **5** an aspect of something 方面 • **verb** (**faces**, **facing**, **faced**) **1** be positioned with the face or front towards something 面朝；面向；正对 **2** confront and deal with 正视；对付 **3** have a difficulty ahead of you 面临(困难) **4** cover the surface of something with a layer of material 用…抹盖；用…覆盖 □ **face pack** Brit. 【英】a cream or gel spread over the face to improve the skin (护理皮肤的乳状或胶状)面膜 **face the music** be confronted with the unpleasant results of your actions 自食其果；自吞苦果 **face value 1** the value stated on a coin or postage stamp (钱币或邮票的)面值，面额 **2** the value that something seems to have before you look at it closely 表面价值；字面意义 **lose** (or **save**) **face** suffer (or avoid) humiliation 丢(或保全)面子

facecloth /ˈfeɪsklɒθ/ **noun** a small towelling cloth for washing your face 洗脸毛巾

faceless /ˈfeɪsləs/ **adjective** without character or individuality; impersonal 无个性的；冷漠的

facelift /ˈfeɪslɪft/ **noun** an operation to remove wrinkles in the face by tightening the skin 去皱整容手术；面部拉皮手术

facet /ˈfæsɪt/ **noun 1** one of the sides of a cut gemstone (宝石的)刻面，面 **2** an aspect of something 方面

■ **faceted** adjective.

facetious /fəˈsiːʃəs/ **adjective**
trying to be funny or clever about
something that should be treated
seriously 开玩笑的；诙谐的 ■ **face-
tiously** adverb.

facia /ˈfeɪʃə/ ⇒ 见 FASCIA.

facial /ˈfeɪʃl/ **adjective 1** having to
do with the face 面部的；表面的；面部用
的 • **noun** a beauty treatment for the
face (面部)美容 ■ **facially** adverb.

facile /ˈfæsaɪl/ **adjective 1** produced
without careful thought 轻率的；欠
考虑的 **2** too simple, or too easily
achieved 轻易获得的；容易做到的

facilitate /fəˈsɪlɪteɪt/ **verb** (**facilitates,
facilitating, facilitated**) make
something possible or easier 使(更)
容易；使(更)便利 ■ **facilitation** noun
facilitator noun.

facility /fəˈsɪləti/ **noun** (plural **facilities**)
1 a building, service, or piece of
equipment provided for a particular
purpose 设备；设施 **2** a natural ability
to do something well and easily 天资；
天赋

facing /ˈfeɪsɪŋ/ **noun 1** a strip of material sewn inside the neck, armhole,
etc. of a piece of clothing to strengthen it (衣服领口、袖口等处的)镶边，
贴条 **2** an outer layer covering the
surface of a wall (墙的)面层，饰面

facsimile /fækˈsɪməli/ **noun** an exact
copy of written or printed material
摹本；复制本

fact /fækt/ **noun 1** a thing that is definitely the case 事实；真相 **2** (**facts**)
information used as evidence or as
part of a report 证据；论据 □ **the
facts of life** information explaining
things relating to sex 性知识

faction /ˈfækʃn/ **noun** a small group
within a larger one (集团内的)小团
体，派系 ■ **factional** adjective.

factious /ˈfækʃəs/ **adjective** having
opposing views 反对的；持歧见的

factitious /fækˈtɪʃəs/ **adjective** made

up; not genuine 人为的；虚假的；杜撰
的

factor /ˈfæktə(r)/ **noun 1** a circumstance, fact, or influence that helps
to bring about a result 因素；要素 **2**
Maths【数学】a number by which a
larger number can be divided exactly
因子；因数 **3** the amount by which
something increases or decreases 系
数 **4** any of a number of substances
in the blood which are involved in
clotting 凝血因子 • **verb** (**factor
something in** or **out**) consider (or
ignore) something when making a
decision 考虑(或忽略)…因素

factory /ˈfæktri/ **noun** (plural **factories**)
a building where goods are made or
assembled in large numbers 工厂；制
造厂 □ **factory farming** the rearing
of poultry, pigs, or cattle indoors
under strictly controlled conditions
工厂化饲养法

factotum /fækˈtəʊtəm/ **noun** (plural
factotums) an employee who does
all kinds of jobs 杂工；勤杂工

factual /ˈfæktʃuəl/ **adjective** based on
or concerned with facts 根据事实的；
真实的 ■ **factually** adverb.

faculty /ˈfæklti/ **noun** (plural **faculties**)
1 a basic mental or physical power
官能；天赋 **2** a talent 能力；才能 **3**
a department or group of related
departments in a university (大学的)
院，系

fad /fæd/ **noun 1** a craze 一时的狂热；
一时的风尚 **2** a fussy like or dislike
of something 挑剔 ■ **faddish** adjective
faddy adjective.

fade /feɪd/ **verb** (**fades, fading, faded**)
1 gradually grow faint and disappear
(逐渐)变弱，变暗；逐渐消失 **2** lose
colour 褪色 **3** (**fade something in**
or **out**) make a film or video image
or sound more or less clear or loud
使(画面)淡入(或淡出)；使(声音)渐
强(或渐弱)

faeces /ˈfiːsiːz/ (US spelling【美拼

作】feces) **plural noun** waste matter passed out of the body from the bowels 粪便;排泄物 ■ **faecal** /ˈfiːkl/ adjective.

fag¹ /fæg/ **noun** Brit. informal 【英,非正式】a cigarette 香烟

fag² Brit. informal 【英,非正式】**noun** **1** a tiring or boring task 苦差事 **2** a junior schoolboy at a public school who does minor chores for an older one (被高年级生使唤的)低年级生

faggot /ˈfægət/ **noun 1** Brit. 【英】a ball of seasoned chopped liver which is baked or fried 丸子(用烤或炸过并加入调料的碎肝末做成) **2** a bundle of sticks bound together as fuel 柴把;柴捆

Fahrenheit /ˈfærənhaɪt/ **noun** a scale of temperature on which water freezes at 32° and boils at 212° 华氏温标

fail /feɪl/ **verb 1** not succeed in achieving something 失败 **2** be unable to meet the standards by a test 未通过(考试);不及格 **3** not do something that you should have done 忽视;漏做 **4** stop working properly 失灵;失去作用 **5** become weaker or less good 变弱;衰退;变差 **6** let someone down 使失望;有负于 • **noun** a mark which is not high enough to pass an exam (考试)不及格 □ **fail-safe 1** (of machinery) going back to a safe condition if it is faulty (机器)故障安全的,自动防止故障危害的 **2** unlikely or unable to fail 不会失败的;万全的 **without fail** whatever happens 必定;务必

failing /ˈfeɪlɪŋ/ **noun** a weakness in a person's character 缺点;(性格)弱点 • **preposition** if not 如果没有;若不…时

failure /ˈfeɪljə(r)/ **noun 1** lack of success 失败 **2** an unsuccessful person or thing 失败的人(或事) **3** a situation in which something stops working properly 故障;失灵 **4** an instance of

not doing something that is expected 未履行;未做(应做之事)

faint /feɪnt/ **adjective 1** not clearly seen, heard, or smelt 不清楚的;模糊的;隐约的 **2** slight 微小的 **3** close to losing consciousness 晕眩的;行将昏厥的 • **verb** briefly lose consciousness 昏厥;晕倒 • **noun** a sudden loss of consciousness 昏厥 □ **faint-hearted** timid 胆怯的;懦弱的 ■ **faintly** adverb.

fair¹ /feə(r)/ **adjective 1** treating people equally 公正的;公平的 **2** reasonable or appropriate 合理的;适当的 **3** quite large in size or amount 相当大的;颇多的 **4** quite good 不错的;尚可的 **5** (of hair or complexion) light; blonde (头发或皮肤)淡色的,白皙的 **6** (of weather) fine and dry (天气)晴朗的 **7** old use 【旧】beautiful 美丽的 □ **fair game** a person or thing that people feel they can criticize or exploit 该受批评(或利用)的对象 **fair-weather friend** a person who stops being a friend when you have problems 不能共患难的朋友;酒肉朋友

fair² **noun 1** a gathering of sideshows and amusements for public entertainment 公共游乐场 **2** an event held to promote or sell goods 商品展览会;博览会: an antiques fair 古玩展

fairground /ˈfeəɡraʊnd/ **noun** an outdoor area where a fair is held 露天游乐场;露天展览会场地

fairing /ˈfeərɪŋ/ **noun** a structure added to make a vehicle, boat, or aircraft more streamlined (车辆、船或飞机的)整流片,整流罩

fairly /ˈfeəli/ **adverb 1** in a fair way 公平地;公正地 **2** to some extent; quite 一定地;相当地

fairway /ˈfeəweɪ/ **noun** the part of a golf course between a tee and a green (高尔夫球场上的)平坦球道

fairy /ˈfeəri/ **noun** (plural **fairies**) a small imaginary being that has magical powers 小仙子；小精灵 □ **fairy godmother** a female character in fairy stories who brings good fortune to the hero or heroine (在神话中帮助主人公的)女恩人，仙女 **fairy lights** small electric lights used to decorate a Christmas tree (装饰圣诞树的)彩灯 **fairy tale** (or **fairy story**) **1** a children's story about magical beings and lands 神话；童话 **2** a lie 谎言

fait accompli /ˌfeɪt əˈkɒmpliː/ **noun** something that has been done and cannot be changed 既成事实；无可辩驳的事

faith /feɪθ/ **noun 1** complete trust or confidence 信赖；信心 **2** belief in a religion 宗教信仰 **3** a system of religious belief 宗教 □ **faith healing** healing achieved by religious faith, rather than by medical treatment (靠宗教信仰治病的)信仰疗法

faithful /ˈfeɪθfʊl/ **adjective 1** remaining loyal and committed 忠实的；忠诚的 **2** accurate; true to the facts 如实的；真实的 • **noun** (**the faithful**) the people who believe in a particular religion (特定宗教的)信徒，信众 ■ **faithfully** adverb.

faithless /ˈfeɪθləs/ **adjective** unable to be trusted; disloyal 不守信的；不忠诚的

fake /feɪk/ **adjective** not genuine 假的；伪造的 • **noun** a person or thing that is not genuine 骗子；冒充者；假货 • **verb** (**fakes, faking, faked**) **1** make a copy or imitation of something in order to deceive 伪造；捏造 **2** pretend to have an emotion or illness 装出(某种感情)；佯装(生病)

fakir /ˈfeɪkɪə(r)/ **noun** a Muslim or Hindu holy man who lives by asking people for money or food (伊斯兰教的)托钵僧，(印度教的)苦行者

falcon /ˈfɔːlkən/ **noun** a fast-flying bird of prey with long pointed wings 隼；猎鹰

falconry /ˈfɔːlkənri/ **noun** the keeping and training of birds of prey 猎鹰饲养；猎鹰训练 ■ **falconer** noun.

fall /fɔːl/ **verb** (**falls, falling, fell**; past participle **fallen**) **1** move downwards quickly and without control 落下；降落；跌落 **2** collapse to the ground 跌倒；摔倒；坍倒 **3** slope down 下垂；倾斜 **4** become less or lower 减少；降低 **5** become 变得；变成 **6** happen; come about 发生；产生 **7** (of someone's face) show dismay (人的面部)变阴沉；被击败 • **noun 1** an act of falling 落下；跌倒；坍塌；下垂 **2** a thing which falls or has fallen 下落之物；跌落之物 **3** (**falls**) a waterfall 瀑布 **4** a drop in size or number 变小；减少 **5** a defeat or downfall 失败；垮台 **6** N. Amer. 【北美】autumn 秋天 □ **fall back** retreat 后退；退却 **fall back on** turn to something for help 借助于；转而依靠 **fall for** informal 【非正式】**1** fall in love with 对…倾心；迷恋 **2** be tricked by 受…骗；上…的当 **fall foul of** come into conflict with 与…发生冲突 **fall guy** informal 【非正式】a person who is blamed for something that is not their fault 替罪羊；替死鬼 **fall out** have an argument 吵架；争吵 **fall short** fail to reach a required standard 未达标准；达不到要求 **fall through** fail to happen or be completed 失败；落空

fallacious /fəˈleɪʃəs/ **adjective** based on a mistaken belief 谬误的

fallacy /ˈfæləsi/ **noun** (plural **fallacies**) **1** a mistaken belief 谬论；谬见；谬误 **2** a false or misleading argument 谬误观点；误导性论点

fallback /ˈfɔːlbæk/ **noun** an alternative plan for use in an emergency 应变计划；退路

fallible /ˈfæləbl/ **adjective** capable of making mistakes 易犯错的；会做错的 ■ **fallibility** noun.

Fallopian tube /fəˈləʊpiən/ **noun**

either of a pair of tubes along which eggs travel from the ovaries to the uterus of a female mammal 输卵管

fallout /'fɔːlaʊt/ **noun 1** radioactive particles that are spread over a wide area after a nuclear explosion (核 爆炸后的)放射性坠尘 **2** the bad effects of a situation 负面影响;余波

fallow /'fæləʊ/ **adjective** (of farmland) ploughed but left for a period without being planted with crops (耕地)犁过而未播种的

false /fɔːls/ **adjective 1** not correct or true; wrong 不正确的;错误的;不真实的 **2** fake; artificial 假的;伪造的;人造的 **3** based on something that is not true or correct 虚假的: a false sense of security 虚假的安全感 **4** disloyal 不忠诚的 □ **false alarm** a warning given about something that does not happen 假警报 **false pretences** behaviour that is intended to deceive 欺诈行为 ■ **falsely** adverb **falsity** noun.

falsehood /'fɔːlshʊd/ **noun 1** the state of being untrue 虚假;虚妄 **2** a lie 谎言

falsetto /fɔːl'setəʊ/ **noun** (plural **falsettos**) a high-pitched voice used by male singers (男歌手的)假声

falsify /'fɔːlsɪfaɪ/ **verb** (**falsifies**, **falsifying**, **falsified**) alter something in order to mislead people 篡改;伪造 ■ **falsification** noun.

falter /'fɔːltə(r)/ **verb** (**falters**, **faltering**, **faltered**) **1** lose strength or momentum 变弱;衰退 **2** move or speak hesitantly 犹豫;畏缩;结巴地说

fame /feɪm/ **noun** the state of being famous 名望;声誉;鼎鼎大名

famed /feɪmd/ **adjective** famous; well known 有名的;著名的

familial /fə'mɪliəl/ **adjective** having to do with a family 家庭的;家族的

familiar /fə'mɪliə(r)/ **adjective 1** well known 熟知的;熟悉的 **2** frequently encountered; common 常见的;普

通的 **3** (**familiar with**) having a good knowledge of 通晓的;熟悉的 **4** friendly or informal 亲昵的;随便的 ● **noun** a spirit believed to accompany a witch (女巫身边的)妖精 ■ **familiarity** noun **familiarly** adverb.

> ✔ 拼写指南 remember that **familiar** is spelled with only one *l*. 记住 familiar 中只有一个 l。

familiarize or **familiarise** /fə'mɪliəraɪz/ **verb** (**familiarizes**, **familiarizing**, **familiarized**) (**familiarize someone with**) give someone knowledge of something 使通晓;使熟悉 ■ **familiarization** noun.

family /'fæməli/ **noun** (plural **families**) **1** a group of parents and their children 家;家庭 **2** a group of people related by marriage or through having the same ancestors 家族;氏族 **3** the children of a person or couple 子女 **4** a group of things that are alike in some way (有相似之处的)一组东西,一类物品 **5** a group of related plants or animals (动植物的)科 ● **adjective** designed to be suitable for children as well as adults 老少咸宜的 □ **family planning** control of the number of children in a family by using contraceptives 计划生育 **family tree** a diagram showing the relationship between people in a family 家谱(图)

famine /'fæmɪn/ **noun** a period when there is a severe shortage of food in a region 饥荒

famished /'fæmɪʃt/ **adjective** informal 【非正式】 very hungry 非常饥饿的

famous /'feɪməs/ **adjective 1** known about by many people 著名的;出名的 **2** informal 【非正式】 very good or impressive 极好的 ■ **famously** adverb.

fan[1] /fæn/ **noun 1** a device which uses rotating blades to create a current of air 风扇;鼓风机 **2** a semicircular object that you wave to cool yourself 扇子 • **verb** (**fans**, **fanning**, **fanned**) **1** make a current of air blow towards 扇(风) **2** make a belief or emotion stronger 煽动;激起 **3** (**fan out**) spread out from a central point 成扇形展开 □ **fan belt** a belt driving the fan that cools the radiator of a motor vehicle (汽车散热风扇上的)风扇皮带

fan² **noun** a person who is very interested in a sport, celebrity, etc. 狂热爱好者;…迷

fanatic /fəˈnætɪk/ **noun** a person who is too enthusiastic about something 狂热者;入迷者 ■ **fanatical** adjective **fanatically** adverb **fanaticism** noun.

fancier /ˈfænsɪə(r)/ **noun** a person who keeps or breeds a particular type of animal (某种动物的)驯养者: *a pigeon fancier* 喜欢养鸽子的人

fanciful /ˈfænsɪfl/ **adjective 1** existing only in the imagination 想象中的;空想的 **2** very unusual or creative 想象奇特的;富有创意的 ■ **fancifully** adverb.

fancy /ˈfænsi/ **verb** (**fancies**, **fancying**, **fancied**) **1** Brit. informal 【英,非正式】 want or want to do 想要(做) **2** Brit. informal 【英,非正式】 find someone attractive 爱慕;喜欢 **3** imagine; think 想象;认为 • **adjective** (**fancier**, **fanciest**) elaborate or highly decorated 精致的;花哨的 • **noun** (plural **fancies**) **1** a brief feeling of attraction (一时的)爱好,迷恋 **2** the ability to imagine things 想象力 **3** a belief or idea that may not be true 幻想;空想 □ **fancy dress** an unusual costume or disguise worn at a party 化装服 **fancy-free** not in a serious relationship (感情方面)自由的,无恋爱对象的

fandango /fænˈdæŋɡəʊ/ **noun** (plural **fandangoes** or **fandangos**) a lively Spanish dance for two people 方丹戈舞 (一种欢快的西班牙双人舞)

fanfare /ˈfænfeə(r)/ **noun** a short tune played on brass instruments to announce someone or something 号角齐鸣(用铜管乐器吹奏的短曲,宣布某人到达或某事开始)

fang /fæŋ/ **noun 1** a long, pointed tooth of a dog or wolf (狗或狼的)尖牙,犬齿 **2** a tooth with which a snake injects poison (毒蛇的)毒牙

fanlight /ˈfænlaɪt/ **noun** a small semicircular window over a door or window 扇形窗

fantasize or **fantasise** /ˈfæntəsaɪz/ **verb** (**fantasizes**, **fantasizing**, **fantasized**) daydream about something that you would like to do, or that you would like to happen 幻想;想象

fantastic /fænˈtæstɪk/ **adjective 1** hard to believe 难以置信的;想象中的 **2** strange or exotic 奇异的;古怪的 **3** informal 【非正式】 very good or large 极好的;极大的 ■ **fantastical** adjective **fantastically** adverb.

fantasy /ˈfæntəsi/ **noun** (plural **fantasies**) **1** the imagining of things that do not exist in reality 想象;幻想 **2** an imagined situation or event that is desirable but unlikely to happen 幻想情境;虚幻事件 **3** a type of fiction that involves magic and adventure 奇幻小说

fanzine /ˈfænziːn/ **noun** a magazine for fans of a particular performer, team, etc. 爱好者杂志

far /fɑː(r)/ **adverb** (**further**, **furthest** or **farther**, **farthest**) **1** at, to, or by a great distance in space or time 遥远地;久远地 **2** by a great deal 很大程度上;远远 • **adjective 1** distant in space or time 遥远的;久远的 **2** extreme 极度的 □ **far-fetched** exaggerated or unlikely 夸大的;不太可能的 **far-flung** widely spread out; scattered 分布广的;分散的 **the Far East** China, Japan, and other countries of east Asia 远东(指中国、日本和其他东亚

国家) **far-off** distant in space or time 遥远的；久远的

farad /'færæd/ **noun** the basic unit of electrical capacitance 法拉(电容基本单位)

faraway /'fɑːrəweɪ/ **adjective 1** remote or distant 遥远的；远方的 **2** lost in thought; dreamy 心不在焉的；恍惚的

farce /fɑːs/ **noun 1** a comedy based on situations which are ridiculous and improbable 闹剧；笑剧；滑稽戏 **2** an absurd event 荒诞可笑的事

farcical /'fɑːsɪkl/ **adjective** absurd or ridiculous 荒诞的；荒谬的；可笑的 ■ **farcically** adverb.

fare /feə(r)/ **noun 1** the money which a passenger pays to travel on public transport 公共交通费；车费，船费，飞机票价 **2** a range of food 饭菜 • **verb** (**fares**, **faring**, **fared**) get on in a particular situation (在某情况下)进行，做：*The party fared badly in the elections.* 该党在竞选中表现很差。

farewell /ˌfeə'wel/ **exclamation** old use 【旧】goodbye 再见；再会 • **noun** an act of leaving 告别；离别

farm /fɑːm/ **noun 1** an area of land and buildings used for growing crops and rearing animals 农场 **2** a farmhouse 农庄住宅 • **verb 1** make a living by growing crops or keeping animals 经营农场为生；务农；从事畜牧业 **2** (**farm something out**) give work to other people to do 包出(活计)

farmer /'fɑːmə(r)/ **noun** a person who owns or manages a farm 农场主；牧场主

farmhouse /'fɑːmhaʊs/ **noun** a house attached to a farm 农庄住宅

farmyard /'fɑːmjɑːd/ **noun** a yard or enclosure surrounded by farm buildings 农场庭院；农场空地

farrago /fə'rɑːgəʊ/ **noun** (plural **farragos** or **farragoes**) a confused mixture 混杂物；大杂烩

farrier /'færɪə(r)/ **noun** a person who

shoes horses 蹄铁工

farrow /'færəʊ/ **noun** a litter of pigs 一窝仔猪 • **verb** (of a sow) give birth to piglets (母猪)产(仔猪)

farther /'fɑːðə(r)/ ⇒ 见 FURTHER.

farthest /'fɑːðɪst/ ⇒ 见 FURTHEST.

farthing /'fɑːðɪŋ/ **noun** a former UK coin, worth a quarter of an old penny 法寻(英国旧时值1/4便士的硬币)

fascia or Brit. 【英】 **facia** /'feɪʃə/ **noun 1** a board covering the ends of rafters or other fittings (椽头等上的)挑口饰板 **2** Brit. 【英】a board above the entrance of a shop, displaying the shop's name (商店门面上的)招牌 **3** the dashboard of a motor vehicle (汽车上的)仪表板 **4** a detachable cover for the front of a mobile phone (移动电话的)可更换外壳

fascinate /'fæsɪneɪt/ **verb** (**fascinates**, **fascinating**, **fascinated**) interest or charm someone greatly 使感兴趣；强烈吸引；迷住 ■ **fascination** noun.

> ✔ 拼写指南 spell **fascinate** and **fascination** with an *s* before the *c*. fascinate 和 fascination 中在c前有一个字母s。

fascism /'fæʃɪzəm/ **noun 1** a right-wing system of government with extreme nationalistic beliefs 法西斯主义 **2** an attitude which is very intolerant or right-wing 偏狭观念；极右态度 ■ **fascist** noun & adjective.

fashion /'fæʃn/ **noun 1** a popular style of clothes, way of behaving, etc. 流行样式；时尚 **2** a way of doing something 方式；风格 • **verb** make or shape something 制作；使成形

fashionable /'fæʃnəbl/ **adjective** in a style that is currently popular 流行的；时髦的 ■ **fashionably** adverb.

fast¹ /fɑːst/ **adjective 1** moving or capable of moving very quickly 快的；迅速的 **2** taking place quickly 迅速发生的；动作敏捷的 **3** (of a clock or watch) ahead of the correct time

(钟表)快的 **4** firmly fixed or attached 缚牢的；系牢的 **5** (of a dye) not fading (染料)不褪色的 • adverb **1** quickly 快速地；迅速地 **2** firmly or securely 紧紧地；牢牢地

fast² verb go without food or drink 禁食；绝食 • noun a period of fasting 禁食期；斋戒期

fasten /'fɑːsn/ verb **1** close or do up securely 扎牢；系牢 **2** fix or hold in place 使牢固；使固定 **3** (fasten on) pick out and concentrate on 集中注意力于；全神贯注于 ■ **fastener** noun **fastening** noun.

fastidious /fæ'stɪdɪəs/ adjective **1** paying a lot of attention to detail 一丝不苟的；严谨的；挑剔的 **2** very concerned about cleanliness 讲究整洁的；有洁癖的 ■ **fastidiously** adverb.

fastness /'fɑːstnəs/ noun **1** a place that is secure and well protected 要塞；堡垒 **2** the ability of a dye to keep its colour (染料)不褪色(性)

fat /fæt/ noun **1** an oily substance found in animals (动物的)脂肪，油脂 **2** a substance used in cooking made from the fat of animals, or from plants (用于烹饪的)动物油，植物油 • adjective (**fatter**, **fattest**) **1** having too much fat 高脂肪的；油腻的 **2** informal 【非正式】 large; substantial 肥大的；丰富的 □ **fat cat** disapproving 【贬】 a wealthy and powerful businessman 大亨；财阀 ■ **fatness** noun.

fatal /'feɪtl/ adjective **1** causing death 致命的；毁灭性的 **2** leading to disaster 灾难性的；毁灭性的 ■ **fatally** adverb.

fatalism /'feɪtəlɪzəm/ noun the belief that all events are decided in advance by a supernatural power 宿命论 ■ **fatalist** noun **fatalistic** adjective.

fatality /fə'tæləti/ noun (plural **fatalities**) a death occurring in a war, or caused by an accident or disease (战争、事故或疾病造成的)死亡

fate /feɪt/ noun **1** a supernatural power

believed to control all events 天命；天数 **2** the things that will inevitably happen to someone or something 命运 • verb (**be fated**) be destined to happen in a particular way 注定；命定

fateful /'feɪtfl/ adjective having important, often unpleasant, consequences 有深远影响的；造成不良后果的

father /'fɑːðə(r)/ noun **1** a male parent 父亲 **2** an important figure in the early history of something 创始人；鼻祖；先驱 **3** literary 【文】a male ancestor 祖先；祖宗 **4** a priest 神父 **5** (**the Father**) God 上帝 • verb (**fathers**, **fathering**, **fathered**) be the father of 是…的父亲 □ **father-in-law** (plural **fathers-in-law**) the father of a person's husband or wife 岳父；公公 ■ **fatherhood** noun.

fatherland /'fɑːðəlænd/ noun a person's native country 祖国

fatherly /'fɑːðəli/ adjective protective and affectionate 保护的；爱护的；慈爱的

fathom /'fæðəm/ noun a measure of the depth of water, equal to six feet (1.8 metres) 英寻(测量水深使用的长度单位，等于6英尺，合1.8米) • verb understand after a lot of thought (深思后)理解，透彻了解

fatigue /fə'tiːɡ/ noun **1** great tiredness 疲劳；劳累 **2** weakness in metals caused by repeated stress (金属)疲劳 **3** (**fatigues**) loose-fitting clothing worn by soldiers (士兵穿的)宽松工作服，劳动服 • verb (**fatigues**, **fatiguing**, **fatigued**) make someone very tired 使极度疲劳

fatten /'fætn/ verb make or become fat or fatter (使)长肥；(使)长胖

fatty /'fæti/ adjective (**fattier**, **fattiest**) containing a lot of fat 肥胖的；富含脂肪的

fatuity /fə'tjuːəti/ noun **1** a silly remark 愚蠢的话 **2** foolishness 愚昧；愚蠢

fatuous /'fætʃuəs/ adjective silly and

pointless 愚昧的;蠢的 ■ **fatuously** adverb.

fatwa /ˈfætwɑ/ **noun** a ruling on a point of Islamic law given by a recognized authority (伊斯兰律法中的)判decision,裁决令

faucet /ˈfɔːsɪt/ **noun** N. Amer.【北美】 a tap 水龙头

fault /fɔːlt/ **noun 1** a defect or mistake 缺点,毛病;错误 **2** responsibility for an accident or unfortunate event (对事故或不幸所负的)责任 **3** (in tennis) a service that is against the rules (网球运动中的)发球失误 **4** a break in the layers of rock of the earth's crust (地壳岩层的)断层 • **verb** find a defect or mistake in someone or something 挑错;找岔子 ■ **faultless** adjective.

faulty /ˈfɔːlti/ **adjective** (**faultier**, **faultiest**) having faults 有错误的;有缺点的

faun /fɔːn/ **noun** (in Roman mythology) a god of woods and fields, with a human body and a goat's horns, ears, legs, and tail (罗马神话中的)农牧神(呈人身,长有羊角、羊耳、羊腿和羊尾)

fauna /ˈfɔːnə/ **noun** the animals of a particular region or period (某地区或时期的)动物群

faux pas /ˌfəʊ ˈpɑː/ **noun** (plural **faux pas**) a mistake which causes embarrassment in a social situation 有失检点;失言;失态

favour /ˈfeɪvə(r)/ (US spelling【美拼作】**favor**) **noun 1** approval or liking 赞同;喜爱 **2** a kind or helpful act 恩惠;善意行为 **3** special treatment of one person or group 特殊照顾;偏爱;偏袒 • **verb 1** view or treat with favour 赞同;喜爱;偏爱;偏袒 **2** work to the advantage of 有利于;有助于 **3** (**favour someone with**) give someone something they wish for 赐予;给予 □ **in favour of 1** to be replaced by 看中;选择 **2** in support of 支持;

赞同

favourable /ˈfeɪvərəbl/ (US spelling 【美拼作】**favorable**) **adjective 1** expressing approval or consent 支持的;赞同的 **2** advantageous or helpful 有利的;有益的 ■ **favourably** adverb.

favourite /ˈfeɪvərɪt/ (US spelling【美拼作】**favorite**) **adjective** preferred to all other people or things of the same kind 最受喜爱的 • **noun 1** a favourite person or thing 最受喜爱的人(或物) **2** the competitor thought most likely to win 最有希望的获胜者

favouritism /ˈfeɪvərɪtɪzəm/ (US spelling 【美拼作】**favoritism**) **noun** the unfair favouring of one person or group 偏爱;偏袒

fawn[1] /fɔːn/ **noun 1** a young deer 幼鹿 **2** a light brown colour 浅黄褐色

fawn[2] **verb** try to please someone by flattering them and being too attentive 奉承;讨好

fax /fæks/ **noun 1** a copy of a document which has been scanned and transmitted electronically 传真件 **2** a machine for transmitting and receiving faxes 传真机 • **verb** send a document by fax 发传真

faze /feɪz/ **verb** (**fazes**, **fazing**, **fazed**) informal【非正式】shock or confuse 打扰;烦扰

FBI /ˌef biː ˈaɪ/ **abbreviation** (in the US) Federal Bureau of Investigation (美国)联邦调查局

FC /ˌef ˈsiː/ **abbreviation** Football Club 足球俱乐部

fear /fɪə(r)/ **noun 1** an unpleasant emotion caused by the threat of danger 害怕;恐惧 **2** the likelihood of something unwelcome happening (发生不愉快事情的)可能性 • **verb 1** be afraid of 害怕;畏惧 **2** (**fear for**) be anxious about 为…忧虑;为…担心

fearful /ˈfɪəfl/ **adjective 1** feeling afraid 惧怕的;胆怯的 **2** causing fear

可怕的;吓人的 **3** informal 【非正式】
very great 非常的;极大的 ■ **fearfully**
adverb.

fearless /'fɪələs/ **adjective** having no
fear; brave 无畏的,勇敢的 ■ **fear-
lessly** adverb.

fearsome /'fɪəsəm/ **adjective** very
impressive and frightening 可怕的;
吓人的

feasible /'fiːzəbl/ **adjective 1** able
to be done easily 容易做的;可行的
2 likely 可能的 ■ **feasibility** noun
feasibly adverb.

> **！注意** some people say **feasible**
> should not be used to mean 'likely',
> but this sense has been in the lan-
> guage for centuries and is generally
> considered to be acceptable. 有些人
> 认为 **feasible** 不应取其"可能的"之
> 义,但该含义在英语中已经使用了
> 数个世纪,普遍视为可以接受。

feast /fiːst/ **noun 1** a large meal
marking a special occasion 盛宴;筵
席 **2** an annual religious celebration
(一年一度的)宗教庆典 • **verb 1** have
a feast 设宴 **2** (**feast on**) eat large
quantities of 尽情吃,饱餐

feat /fiːt/ **noun** an achievement requiring great courage, skill, or strength
功绩;业绩;英勇事迹

feather /'feðə(r)/ **noun** any of the
structures growing from a bird's skin,
consisting of a hollow shaft fringed
with fine strands 羽;羽毛 • **verb**
(**feathers**, **feathering**, **feathered**)
turn an oar so that the blade passes
through the air edgeways 划(桨)
□ **a feather in your cap** an achievement to be proud of 引以自豪的成
就 **feather your nest** make money
dishonestly 中饱私囊 ■ **feathery** adjective.

feature /'fiːtʃə(r)/ **noun 1** a distinctive
element or aspect 特点,特征 **2** a part
of the face 面容的一部分 **3** a special
article in a newspaper or magazine

(报纸或杂志的)特写,专题文章 **4**
(also **feature film**) the main film
showing at a cinema (电影院上放映
的)正片,故事片 • **verb** (**features**,
featuring, **featured**) **1** have as
a feature 以…为特色 **2** have an
important part in something 在…中
起重要作用;在…中占重要地位
■ **featureless** adjective.

febrile /'fiːbraɪl/ **adjective 1** having
the symptoms of a fever 发热的;发
烧的 **2** overactive and excitable 狂热
的;兴奋的

February /'februəri/ **noun** (plural
Februaries) the second month of
the year 二月

> **✔ 拼写指南** *-ruary*, not *-uary*: Feb-
> *ruary*. February 中 -ruary 不要拼作
> -uary.

feces /'fiːsiːz/ US spelling of FAECES.
faeces的美式拼法

feckless /'fekləs/ **adjective** irresponsible and without strength of
character 不负责任的;无能的;软弱
的

fecund /'fiːkənd/ **adjective** very fertile
肥沃的;丰饶的;多产的 ■ **fecundity**
noun.

fed /fed/ past and past participle of
FEED. □ **fed up** informal 【非正式】
annoyed or bored 厌烦的;厌恶的;厌
倦的

federal /'fedərəl/ **adjective 1** having
a system of government in which
several states unite under a central
authority 联邦(制)的 **2** having to
do with the central government of a
federation 联邦政府的 **3** (**Federal**)
US historical 【美,历史】having to do
with the Northern States in the Civil
War (美国内战时期)北方联邦政府的
■ **federalism** noun **federalist** noun &
adjective **federally** adverb.

federate /'fedəreɪt/ **verb** (**federates**,
federating, **federated**) join as a
federation 结成联邦;加入联邦

federation /ˌfedəˈreɪʃn/ *noun* **1** a group of states united under a central authority in which individual states keep control of their internal affairs 联邦 **2** a group organized like a federation 同盟；联盟

fee /fiː/ *noun* **1** a payment given for professional advice or services 咨询费；服务费 **2** a sum paid to be allowed to do something (为获准做某事支付的)费用

feeble /ˈfiːbl/ *adjective* (**feebler, feeblest**) **1** weak 虚弱的；衰弱的 **2** not convincing or effective 无说服力的；无效的 ■ **feebleness** *noun* **feebly** *adverb*.

feed /fiːd/ *verb* (**feeds, feeding, fed**) **1** give food to 喂；给…食物 **2** provide enough food for 为…提供(足够的)食物 **3** (of an animal or baby) eat (动物或婴儿)吃，进食 **4** supply with material or information 供给，提供(材料或信息) **5** pass something gradually through a confined space 把…塞进(狭窄空间) ● *noun* **1** an act of feeding 喂食；进食 **2** food for domestic animals (家畜的)饲料

feedback /ˈfiːdbæk/ *noun* **1** comments made in response to something you have done 反馈意见 **2** the return of part of the output of an amplifier to its input, causing a whistling sound (音频系统的)反馈噪声

feeder /ˈfiːdə(r)/ *noun* **1** a thing that feeds or supplies something 进料器；供给装置 **2** a minor route that links outlying areas with the main route 支线；支路

feel /fiːl/ *verb* (**feels, feeling, felt**) **1** be aware of, examine, or search by touch (通过触摸)察觉到，检查，搜查 **2** give a particular sensation when touched 摸上去，给人…的手感 **3** experience an emotion or sensation 感受到 **4** be affected by 受到…的影响 **5** have a belief or opinion 认为，相信 ● *noun* **1** an act of feeling 触；摸 **2** the sense of touch 触觉 **3** a sensation or impression 感受；印象 **4** a sensitive appreciation of 对…的敏锐鉴赏力

feeler /ˈfiːlə(r)/ *noun* **1** an organ used by certain animals for testing things by touch 触角；触须 **2** a cautious proposal intended to find out someone's opinion 试探

feeling /ˈfiːlɪŋ/ *noun* **1** an emotional state or reaction 心情；情绪 **2** (**feelings**) the emotional side of a person's character 感情；情感 **3** strong emotion 激动；激情；强烈情绪 **4** the ability to feel 感受力；鉴赏力 **5** the sensation of touching or being touched 触觉 **6** a belief or opinion 看法；意见 **7** (**feeling for**) an understanding of 对…的理解

feet /fiːt/ plural of FOOT.

feign /feɪn/ *verb* pretend to feel or have 假装；装作；佯作

feint /feɪnt/ *noun* a movement made to deceive an opponent, especially in boxing or fencing (尤指拳击或击剑运动中的)虚击 ● *verb* make a feint 佯攻

feisty /ˈfaɪsti/ *adjective* (**feistier, feistiest**) lively and spirited 活跃的；精力充沛的

felicitations /fɪˌlɪsɪˈteɪʃnz/ *plural noun* formal 【正式】congratulations 祝贺；恭喜

felicitous /fəˈlɪsɪtəs/ *adjective* well chosen or appropriate 恰当的；贴切的

felicity /fəˈlɪsəti/ *noun* (plural **felicities**) **1** great happiness (极大的)幸福，快乐 **2** the ability to express yourself in an appropriate way (措词的)恰当，得体 **3** a pleasing feature of an artistic work (艺术作品的)精妙之处

feline /ˈfiːlaɪn/ *adjective* having to do with a cat or cats 猫的；猫科的 ● *noun* a cat or other animal of the cat family 猫；猫科动物

fell[1] /fel/ past of FALL.

fell² verb **1** cut down a tree 砍伐，砍倒(树木) **2** knock someone down 击倒；打倒

fell³ noun a hill or stretch of high moorland in northern England (英格兰北部的)小山，高沼地

fellow /'feləʊ/ noun **1** a man or boy 男人；男孩 **2** a person in the same situation as you 同伙；同事 **3** a thing of the same kind as another 同类 **4** a member of a learned society (学术团体的)会员 **5** Brit.【英】a senior member of certain universities or collegess (某些大学或学院的)董事 • adjective in the same situation 处境相同的：*a fellow sufferer* 共患难的人

fellowship /'feləʊʃɪp/ noun **1** friendship between people who share an interest 伙伴关系；友谊 **2** a group of people who share an interest (有共同利益的)团体，协会 **3** the position of a fellow of a college or society (学院的)董事职位；(学会的)公员资格

felon /'felən/ noun a person who has committed a felony 重罪犯 ■ **felonious** adjective.

felony /'feləni/ noun (plural **felonies**) (in the US and formerly also in English Law) a serious crime (美国法律及旧时英国法律中的)重罪

felt¹ /felt/ noun cloth made from wool that has been rolled and pressed 毛毡 □ **felt tip pen** a pen with a writing point made of felt or tightly packed fibres 毡尖笔

felt² past and past participle of FEEL.

female /'fiːmeɪl/ adjective **1** of the sex that can give birth to offspring or produce eggs 雌的；母的 **2** having to do with women 女(人)的；女性的 **3** (of a plant or flower) having a pistil but no stamens (植物或花)雌性的 **4** (of a fitting) having a hollow or part that a corresponding part can be inserted (设备)阴的，内凹的 • noun a female person, animal, or plant 女子；雌性动物；雌性植物；雌株

feminine /'femɪnɪn/ adjective **1** having qualities associated with women 有女子气质的 **2** female 女性的 **3** Grammar【语法】(of nouns and adjectives in some languages) having a gender regarded as female (某些语言中的名词和形容词)阴性的 ■ **femininity** noun.

feminism /'femɪnɪzəm/ noun a movement or theory that supports the rights of women 女权运动；女权主义 ■ **feminist** noun & adjective.

feminize or **feminise** /'femənaɪz/ verb (**feminizes**, **feminizing**, **feminized**) make more feminine or female 使女性化；使有女子气

femme fatale /ˌfæm fə'taːl/ noun (plural **femmes fatales** /ˌfæm fə'taːl/) an attractive and seductive woman 妖妇；祸水红颜

femur /'fiːmə(r)/ noun (plural **femurs** or **femora** /'femərə/) the bone of the thigh 股骨 ■ **femoral** adjective.

fen /fen/ noun a low and marshy or frequently flooded area of land 沼地；沼泽

fence /fens/ noun **1** a barrier made of wire or wood that encloses an area of land 栅栏；篱笆 **2** an obstacle for horses to jump over in a competition (障碍赛马中的)障碍物 **3** informal【非正式】a person who buys and resells stolen goods 买卖赃物者 • verb (**fences**, **fencing**, **fenced**) **1** surround or protect with a fence 用栅栏(或篱笆)围起 **2** take part in the sport of fencing 击剑 □ **sit on the fence** avoid making a decision 采取骑墙态度；保持中立 ■ **fencer** noun.

fencing /'fensɪŋ/ noun **1** the sport of fighting with blunted swords 击剑(运动) **2** fences or material for making fences 筑栅栏(或篱笆)的材料

fend /fend/ verb **1** (**fend for yourself**) look after yourself without help from other people 照料自己；自谋生计 **2**

(**fend someone/thing off**) defend yourself from an attack or attacker 挡开；避开

fender /'fendə(r)/ *noun* **1** a low frame around a fireplace to stop coals from falling out 壁炉围栏 **2** a soft object that is hung over the side of a ship to protect it from collisions (舰船的)碰垫，护舷木 **3** N. Amer.【北美】the mudguard or area around the wheel of a vehicle (车辆的)挡泥板

feng shui /ˌfeŋ 'fuːi/ *noun* an ancient Chinese system of designing buildings and arranging objects in rooms to achieve a good flow of energy and so bring happiness or good luck 风水

fennel /'fenl/ *noun* a plant whose leaves and seeds are used as a herb or vegetable 茴香(其叶和籽用作草药，茎作蔬菜)

feral /'ferəl/ *adjective* **1** (of an animal) wild, especially after having been tame or kept as a pet (尤指经驯化的动物)变野的，恢复野生习性的 **2** savage or fierce 野蛮的，凶残的

ferment *verb* /fə'ment/ **1** undergo a chemical change by the action of yeast or bacteria 发酵 **2** stir up disorder 使骚动；激起，煽动 • *noun* /'fɜːment/ a state of widespread unrest or excitement 骚动，动乱 ■ **fermentation** *noun*.

fern /fɜːn/ *noun* (plural **fern** or **ferns**) a plant which has feathery fronds and no flowers 蕨；蕨类植物

ferocious /fə'rəʊʃəs/ *adjective* very fierce or violent 凶恶的；残忍的，凶猛的 ■ **ferociously** *adverb*.

ferocity /fə'rɒsəti/ *noun* the state of being ferocious 凶恶；残忍，凶猛

ferret /'ferɪt/ *noun* a small, fierce animal with a long thin body, used for catching rabbits 白鼬，雪貂(身体细长的小型猛兽，用于捕兔) • *verb* (**ferrets**, **ferreting**, **ferreted**) **1**

search among a lot of things 搜索；找 **2** (**ferret something out**) discover something by searching thoroughly 搜出；查获 **3** (**ferreting**) hunting with ferrets 用雪貂猎取

Ferris wheel /'ferɪs/ *noun* a fairground ride consisting of a large upright revolving wheel 费里斯转轮；摩天轮

ferrous /'ferəs/ *adjective* (of a metal) containing iron (金属)含铁的

ferrule /'feruːl/ *noun* a metal cap which protects the end of a stick or umbrella (手杖或伞的)金属箍，金属包头

ferry /'feri/ *noun* (plural **ferries**) a boat or ship that transports passengers and goods as a regular service 渡船 • *verb* (**ferries**, **ferrying**, **ferried**) carry by ferry or other transport 渡运；渡送，运送

fertile /'fɜːtaɪl/ *adjective* **1** (of soil or land) producing a lot of plants or crops (土壤或土地)肥沃的，富饶的 **2** (of a person, animal, or plant) able to produce offspring or seeds (人、动物或植物)能生育的，可繁殖的 **3** producing a lot of good results or ideas 点子多的；想象力丰富的 ■ **fertility** *noun*.

fertilize or **fertilise** /'fɜːtəlaɪz/ *verb* (**fertilizes**, **fertilizing**, **fertilized**) **1** introduce sperm or pollen into an egg or plant so that a new individual develops 使受精；使受粉；使受孕 **2** add fertilizer to soil 施肥于 ■ **fertilization** *noun*.

fertilizer or **fertiliser** /'fɜːtəlaɪzə(r)/ *noun* a chemical or natural substance added to soil to make it more fertile 化肥，肥料

fervent /'fɜːvənt/ *adjective* showing strong or passionate feeling 热情的；热烈的 ■ **fervently** *adverb*.

fervid /'fɜːvɪd/ *adjective* fervent 炽热的；热情的

fervour /'fɜːvə(r)/ (US spelling 【美拼作】**fervor**) **noun** strong or passionate feeling 热情；热诚；热烈

festal /'festl/ **adjective** relating to a festival 节日的；假日的

fester /'festə(r)/ **verb** (**festers, festering, festered**) **1** (of a wound or sore) become septic (伤口或疮)化脓，溃烂 **2** become rotten 腐败，腐烂 **3** become worse or more strongly felt 恶化

festival /'festɪvl/ **noun** **1** a time when people celebrate a special occasion 节日；喜庆日 **2** an organized series of concerts, films, etc. (音乐会、电影等的)汇演，节

festive /'festɪv/ **adjective** relating to a period of celebration 节日的

festivity /fe'stɪvəti/ **noun** (plural **festivities**) **1** joyful celebration 欢庆 **2** (**festivities**) activities or events celebrating a special occasion 庆典，庆祝活动

festoon /fe'stuːn/ **verb** decorate with chains of flowers, ribbons, etc. 饰以花彩 • **noun** a decorative chain of flowers, ribbons, etc. 花彩

feta /'fetə/ **noun** a salty Greek cheese made from the milk of sheep or goats (希腊的)羊奶干酪

fetal or Brit. 【英】**foetal** /'fiːtl/ **adjective** relating to a fetus 胎的；胎儿的

fetch /fetʃ/ **verb** **1** go for something and bring it back 拿来，取来 **2** be sold for a particular price 售得，卖得 (某价) **3** (**fetching**) attractive 吸引人的，迷人的

fete or **fête** /feɪt/ **noun** Brit. 【英】an outdoor event to raise funds for a special purpose 义卖游乐会 • **verb** (**fetes, feting, feted**) praise or entertain someone lavishly 表彰；热情招待

fetid or **foetid** /'fetɪd/ **adjective** smelling very unpleasant 恶臭的

fetish /'fetɪʃ/ **noun** **1** a form of sexual desire in which pleasure is gained from a particular object or part of the body (从某物或身体某部位获得性快感的)恋物 **2** an object worshipped for its supposed magical powers 奉若神明之物；物神 ▪ **fetishism** **noun** **fetishist** **noun**.

fetlock /'fetlɒk/ **noun** a joint of a horse's leg between the knee and the hoof (马膝部与蹄之间的)球节

fetter /'fetə(r)/ **verb** (**fetters, fettering, fettered**) **1** limit the freedom of 束缚，桎梏；控制 **2** restrain with chains or shackles 给…上脚镣 • **noun** **1** (**fetters**) restraints or controls 束缚，桎梏；控制 **2** a chain placed around a prisoner's ankles 脚镣

fettle /'fetl/ **noun** condition 条件；状况

fettuccine /ˌfetə'tʃiːni/ **plural noun** pasta made in long flat strips 意大利宽面条

fetus or Brit. 【英】**foetus** /'fiːtəs/ **noun** (plural **fetuses**) an unborn baby of a mammal 胎；胎儿

feud /fjuːd/ **noun** a long and bitter dispute 长期不和；世仇 • **verb** take part in a feud 长期争斗；结世仇

feudal /'fjuːdl/ **adjective** having to do with feudalism 封建的

feudalism /'fjuːdəlɪzəm/ **noun** the social system in medieval Europe, in which people worked and fought for a nobleman in return for land 封建主义；封建制度

fever /'fiːvə(r)/ **noun** **1** an abnormally high body temperature 发热；发烧 **2** a state of nervous excitement 高度兴奋；激动不安 ▪ **feverish** **adjective**.

fevered /'fiːvəd/ **adjective** **1** having a fever 发热的；发烧的 **2** nervously excited 高度兴奋的；激动的

few /fjuː/ **determiner, pronoun, & adjective** **1** (**a few**) a small number of; some 少数；几个 **2** not many 很少；不多 • **noun** (**the few**) a select minority 少数人；特权集团

! 注意 make sure you distinguish between **fewer** and **less**. Use **fewer** with plural nouns, as in *there were fewer tourists this year*; use **less** with nouns referring to things that can't be counted, as in *there is less blossom on this tree*. It's wrong to use **less** with a plural noun (as in *there were less tourists*). 注意区分 fewer 和 less 的用法。fewer 与复数名词连用，如 there were fewer tourists this year（今年游客比较少）；less 与不可数名词连用，如 there is less blossom on this tree（这棵树上的花比较少）。less 与复数名词连用是错误的，如：there were less tourists。

fey /feɪ/ **adjective** seeming vague or mysterious and unaware of the realities of life 神秘兮兮的；不食人间烟火的

fez /fez/ **noun** (plural **fezzes**) a conical red hat with a flat top, worn by men in some Muslim countries 非斯帽，土耳其帽(某些伊斯兰国家男子戴的红色平顶圆筒帽)

ff. **abbreviation** following pages 及以后各页

fiancé /fiˈɒnseɪ/ **noun** (feminine **fiancée** /fiˈɒnseɪ/) a person to whom you are engaged to be married 未婚夫；未婚妻

fiasco /fiˈæskəʊ/ **noun** (plural **fiascos**) a ridiculous or humiliating failure 可笑的失败；可耻的失败

fiat /ˈfiːæt/ **noun** an official order (官方的)命令，法令

fib /fɪb/ **noun** a trivial lie 小谎；无关紧要的谎话 • **verb** (**fibs, fibbing, fibbed**) tell a fib 撒小谎 ■ **fibber** noun.

fibre /ˈfaɪbə(r)/ (US spelling 【美拼作】**fiber**) **noun 1** each of the thin threads which form plant or animal tissue, cloth, or minerals (动植物组织、布料或矿物质的)纤维 **2** a material

made from fibres 纤维制品 **3** the part of some foods that is difficult to digest and which helps food to pass through the body (食物中的)纤维素 **4** strength of character 品质；骨气 □ **fibre optics** the use of glass fibres to send information in the form of light 纤维光学 ■ **fibrous** adjective.

fibreboard /ˈfaɪbəbɔːd/ (US spelling 【美拼作】**fiberboard**) **noun** a building material made of compressed wood fibres 纤维板

fibreglass /ˈfaɪbəglɑːs/ (US spelling 【美拼作】**fiberglass**) **noun 1** a strong plastic material containing glass fibres 强化塑料 **2** a material made from woven glass fibres 玻璃纤维

fibula /ˈfɪbjələ/ **noun** (plural **fibulae** /ˈfɪbjəliː/ or **fibulas**) the outer of the two bones between the knee and the ankle 腓骨

fickle /ˈfɪkl/ **adjective** changeable in your loyalties (忠诚度)不坚定的，易变的

fiction /ˈfɪkʃn/ **noun 1** literature describing imaginary events and people 小说 **2** something that is invented and not true 虚构；想象 ■ **fictional** adjective.

fictionalize or **fictionalise** /ˈfɪkʃənəlaɪz/ **verb** (**fictionalizes, fictionalizing, fictionalized**) make into a fictional story 把…编成小说

fictitious /fɪkˈtɪʃəs/ **adjective** imaginary or invented; not real 想象的；虚构的；不真实的

fiddle /ˈfɪdl/ **noun** informal 【非正式】**1** a violin 小提琴 **2** something done dishonestly in order to obtain money (以获取钱财为目的的)欺骗，诈骗 • **verb** (**fiddles, fiddling, fiddled**) **1** touch or move something restlessly or nervously (不安或紧张地)拨弄，摆弄 **2** informal 【非正式】change the details of something dishonestly 篡改；伪造 □ **play second fiddle** take a less important role 居次要地位；当

副手 ■ **fiddler** noun.

fiddly /'fɪdli/ **adjective** Brit. 【英】complicated and awkward to do or use 复杂的;难弄的;难用的

fidelity /fɪ'delɪti/ **noun 1** faithfulness to a person or belief 忠诚;忠实;忠贞 **2** the accuracy with which something is copied or reproduced 精确度;准确性

fidget /'fɪdʒɪt/ **verb (fidgets, fidgeting, fidgeted)** make small movements because you are nervous or impatient 坐立不安;烦躁 ■ **noun** a person who fidgets 坐立不安的人;烦躁的人 ■ **fidgety** adjective.

fief /fiːf/ **noun** historical 【历史】a piece of land held under the feudal system 采邑;封地;领地 ■ **fiefdom** noun.

field /fiːld/ **noun 1** an enclosed area of land for growing crops or keeping animals 田地;牧场 **2** a piece of land used for a sport or game 运动场;比赛场 **3** a subject of study or area of activity 研究领域;活动范围 **4** an area within which a force has an effect 场: *a magnetic field* 磁场 **5 (the field)** all the people taking part in a contest or sport (参加比赛或体育运动的)全体运动员 ■ **verb 1** Cricket & Baseball 【板球和棒球】attempt to catch or stop the ball after it has been hit 接(球);截(球) **2** try to deal with something 处理;应付 **3** choose someone to play in a game or to stand in an election 派(某人)上场;使参加比赛;使参加竞选 □ **field day** a good opportunity to do something 大干一番的机会 **field events** athletic sports other than races 田赛项目 **field marshal** the highest rank of officer in the British army (英国的)陆军元帅 **field sports** hunting, shooting, and fishing 野外运动(指打猎、射击和钓鱼) **play the field** informal 【非正式】have a series of casual sexual relationships 滥交;乱搞男女关系 ■ **fielder** noun.

fiend /fiːnd/ **noun 1** an evil spirit 魔鬼;恶魔 **2** a very wicked or cruel person 邪恶的人;残忍的人 **3** informal 【非正式】a person who is very enthusiastic about something …迷;…狂;…爱好者: *an exercise fiend* 健身狂

fiendish /'fiːndɪʃ/ **adjective 1** very cruel or unpleasant 极度残酷的;使人很不愉快的 **2** informal 【非正式】very difficult 极为困难的 ■ **fiendishly** adverb.

fierce /fɪəs/ **adjective 1** violent or aggressive 凶猛的;好斗的 **2** strong or powerful 强大的 ■ **fiercely** adverb **fierceness** noun.

✔ **拼写指南** *i* before *e* except after *c*: fierce. i 应置于 e 前,在 c 后时除外,如 fierce.

fiery /'faɪəri/ **adjective (fierier, fieriest) 1** consisting of or resembling fire 含火的;似火的 **2** quick-tempered or passionate 性情急躁的;充满激情的

fiesta /fi'estə/ **noun** (in Spanish-speaking countries) a religious festival (西班牙语国家的)宗教节日

fife /faɪf/ **noun** a small, high-pitched flute used in military bands (军乐队使用的)小横笛

fifteen /fɪf'tiːn/ **cardinal number** one more than fourteen; 15 十五 (Roman numeral 罗马数字: **xv** or **XV**.) ■ **fifteenth** ordinal number.

fifth /fɪfθ/ **ordinal number 1** being number five in a sequence; 5th 第五 **2 (a fifth** or **one fifth)** each of five equal parts of something 五分之一 □ **fifth column** a group within a country at war who are working for its enemies 第五纵队 (战时为所在国家的敌人效力的群体)

fifty /'fɪfti/ **cardinal number** (plural **fifties**) ten less than sixty; 50 五十 (Roman numeral 罗马数字: **l** or **L**.) □ **fifty-fifty** with equal shares or chances 各半(的);平分(的) ■ **fiftieth**

fig 376

ordinal number

fig /fɪg/ **noun** a soft, sweet fruit with many small seeds 无花果

fight /faɪt/ **verb** (**fights, fighting, fought**) **1** take part in a violent struggle involving physical force 战斗;搏斗;打架 **2** (**fight someone off**) defend yourself against an attacker 抵抗;击退 **3** struggle to overcome or prevent 同…斗争;极力防止 • **noun** a period of fighting 战斗;搏斗;打架;斗殴 □ **fighting chance** a possibility of succeeding if you make an effort 要努力奋斗才能获得的成功机会 **fighting fit** in very good health 非常健康的;非常强健的 **fight shy of** be unwilling to do or accept 畏缩;避开

fighter /'faɪtə(r)/ **noun 1** a person or animal that fights 战士;斗士;斗争的动物 **2** a fast military aircraft designed for attacking other aircraft 战斗机;歼击机

figment /'fɪgmənt/ **noun** a thing that exists only in the imagination 虚构的事物;臆造的事物

figurative /'fɪgərətɪv/ **adjective 1** not using words in their literal sense; metaphorical 比喻的;借喻的 **2** (of art) representing things as they appear in real life (艺术)形象的 ■ **figuratively** adverb.

figure /'fɪgə(r)/ **noun 1** a number or numerical symbol 数字;数字符号 **2** the shape of a person's body, especially that of a woman (尤指女性的)体形,身材,身段 **3** an important or distinctive person (重要或特殊)人物 **4** a shape defined by one or more lines 几何图形 **5** a diagram or drawing 图表;插图 • **verb** (**figures, figuring, figured**) **1** play a significant part 是重要部分;发挥重要作用 **2** (**figure something out**) informal 【非正式】 understand something 理解;弄明白 **3** N. Amer. informal 【北美,非正式】 think; consider 认为;考虑 □ **figure**

of speech a word or phrase used in a way different from its usual sense 修辞格;比喻 **figure skating** ice skating in set patterns 花样滑冰

figurehead /'fɪgəhed/ **noun 1** a leader without real power 有名无实的首脑;傀儡 **2** a wooden statue of a person at the front of a sailing ship (帆船上的)艏饰像

figurine /'fɪgəriːn/ **noun** a small statue of a human form 小雕像;小塑像

filament /'fɪləmənt/ **noun 1** a long, thin threadlike piece of something 细丝;细线;丝状物 **2** a metal wire in a light bulb, which glows when an electric current is passed through it (电灯泡的)灯丝

filbert /'fɪlbət/ **noun** a type of hazelnut 欧洲榛实;榛子

filch /fɪltʃ/ **verb** informal 【非正式】 steal something 偷

file[1] /faɪl/ **noun 1** a folder or box for keeping loose papers together 文件夹;文件箱 **2** a collection of computer data stored under a single name (计算机)文件 **3** a line of people or things one behind another 成纵列的人(或物) • **verb** (**files, filing, filed**) **1** place in a file 把…归档 **2** officially present a legal document, application, etc. so that it can be dealt with 将(法律文件、申请等)登记备案 **3** walk one behind the other 排成纵列行进

file[2] **noun** a tool with a roughened surface, used for smoothing or shaping 锉;锉刀 • **verb** (**files, filing, filed**) smooth or shape with a file 锉;用锉刀锉光(或平);用锉刀使成形

filial /'fɪliəl/ **adjective** having to do with a son or daughter 子女的

filibuster /'fɪlɪbʌstə(r)/ **noun** (in parliament) a very long speech made to prevent the passing of a new law (在议会为阻挠通过新法律所作的)冗长演说

filigree /'fɪlɪɡriː/ **noun** delicate ornamental work of thin wire 细工饰

品

filings /ˈfaɪlɪŋz/ **plural noun** small particles rubbed off by a file 锉屑

fill /fɪl/ **verb 1** make or become full 装满;注满;充满 **2** block up a hole or gap 堵塞,填塞(洞或豁口) **3** appoint a person to a vacant post 指派人填补(职位空缺) **4** hold a particular position or role 充任 • **noun** (**your fill**) as much as you want or can bear 所要的最大量;能忍受的最大限度 □ **fill in** act as a substitute 代替;临时补缺 **fill something in** complete a form 填写(表格) **fill someone in** give someone information 向(某人)提供详情

filler /ˈfɪlə(r)/ **noun** something used to fill a hole or gap, or to increase bulk 填塞物;填充物

fillet /ˈfɪlɪt/ **noun 1** a piece of meat without bones 里脊 **2** a piece of fish with the bones taken out 去骨鱼片 **3** a decorative band or ribbon worn round the head 头带;束发带 • **verb** (**fillets, filleting, filleted**) take the bones out of a piece of fish 将(鱼)去骨

filling /ˈfɪlɪŋ/ **noun** a quantity or piece of material used to fill something 填补物;填料 • **adjective** (of food) giving you a pleasantly full feeling (食物)能填饱肚子的

fillip /ˈfɪlɪp/ **noun** a stimulus or boost 刺激;激励

filly /ˈfɪli/ **noun** (plural **fillies**) **1** a young female horse 小牝马 **2** humorous 【幽默】a lively girl or young woman 活泼的女孩(或年轻姑娘)

film /fɪlm/ **noun 1** a thin flexible strip coated with light-sensitive material, used in a camera to make photographs or motion pictures 胶片;胶卷 **2** a story or event recorded by a camera and shown in a cinema or on television 电影;影片 **3** material in the form of a very thin flexible sheet 薄膜;膜 **4** a thin layer of something

on a surface (覆盖表面的)薄层,薄皮 • **verb** make a film of; record on film 拍摄;把…拍成电影

filmy /ˈfɪlmi/ **adjective** (**filmier**, **filmiest**) thin and almost transparent 薄而几乎透明的

filter /ˈfɪltə(r)/ **noun 1** a device or substance that lets liquid or gas pass through but holds back solid particles 滤器;过滤物质 **2** a screen, plate, or layer that absorbs some of the light passing through it 滤光器;滤色镜 **3** Brit. 【英】(at a junction) a set of lights that lets vehicles turn but stops traffic waiting to go straight ahead (路口的)分流指示灯 • **verb** (**filters, filtering, filtered**) **1** pass through a filter 过滤 **2** move gradually in or out of somewhere 缓行;渗入;透过

filth /fɪlθ/ **noun 1** disgusting dirt 污秽;污物 **2** obscene and offensive language or material 下流言辞;淫秽书刊

filthy /ˈfɪlθi/ **adjective** (**filthier**, **filthiest**) **1** disgustingly dirty 肮脏的;污秽的 **2** obscene and offensive 淫秽的;猥亵的 **3** informal 【非正式】very unpleasant 恶劣的;讨厌的

filtrate /ˈfɪltreɪt/ **noun** a liquid which has passed through a filter 滤液

filtration /fɪlˈtreɪʃn/ **noun** the action of passing something through a filter 过滤

fin /fɪn/ **noun 1** a flattened projection on the body of a fish or whale, used for swimming and balancing (鱼或鲸的)鳍 **2** an underwater swimmer's flipper (潜水者用的)脚蹼,橡皮脚掌 **3** a projection on an aircraft, rocket, etc., for making it more stable (飞机的)垂直尾翼;(火箭的)舵,尾翅

final /ˈfaɪnl/ **adjective 1** coming at the end; last 最后的;最终的 **2** allowing no further doubt or dispute 决定性的;确定的 • **noun 1** the last game in a tournament, which will decide the overall winner 决赛 **2** (**finals**) Brit.

[英] a series of exams at the end of a degree course 期终考试;课程终结考试 ■ **finally** adverb.

finale /fɪˈnɑːli/ noun the last part of a piece of music or entertainment 终曲;末乐章;终场;最后一幕

finalist /ˈfaɪnəlɪst/ noun a person or team competing in a final 参加决赛者

finality /faɪˈnæləti/ noun the fact or quality of being final 终结;定局

finalize or **finalise** /ˈfaɪnəlaɪz/ verb (**finalizes, finalizing, finalized**) complete or agree on the last part of a plan, agreement, etc. 最后定下,完成(计划、协议等)

finance /ˈfaɪnæns/ noun 1 the management of large amounts of money by governments or large companies 财政;财务;金融 2 money to support an enterprise (对企业的)资金支持 3 (**finances**) the money held by a state, organization, or person (国家、组织或个人的)财源,财力 ● verb (**finances, financing, financed**) provide funding for 为…提供资金

financial /faɪˈnænʃl/ adjective relating to finance 财政的;金融的 ■ **financially** adverb.

financier /faɪˈnænsɪə(r)/ noun a person who manages money for large organizations 金融家;理财家

finch /fɪntʃ/ noun a small bird with a short, stubby bill 雀科小鸟

find /faɪnd/ verb (**finds, finding, found**) 1 discover by chance or by searching (偶然)发现;(经过搜寻)发现,找到 2 discover that something is the case 发觉…存在;发现…的实情 3 work out or confirm by research or calculation 找到;查明;(通过计算)求得 4 (of a law court) officially declare that a defendant is guilty or not guilty (法庭对被告)作出裁决 ● noun a valuable or interesting discovery (有价值或有趣的)发现

□ **find someone/thing out 1** discover information 查明,弄清(情况) **2** discover that someone has lied or been dishonest 查出,识破(某人) ■ **finder** noun.

finding /ˈfaɪndɪŋ/ noun a conclusion reached as a result of an inquiry or trial 调查结论;判决

fine¹ /faɪn/ adjective 1 of very high quality 极好的;高质量的 2 satisfactory 令人满意的 3 in good health and feeling well 健康的;舒适的 4 (of the weather) bright and clear (天气)晴朗的 5 (of a thread, strand, or hair) thin (线、绳或头发)纤细的 6 consisting of small particles 微小颗粒组成的 7 delicate or complex 精致的;精密的 8 difficult to distinguish or describe accurately 细微的;难以区分(或描述)的 □ **fine art** such as painting or sculpture 美术(如绘画或雕塑) **fine-tune** make small adjustments to 对(某物)进行微调 **with a fine-tooth comb** (or **fine-toothed comb**) with a very thorough search or examination 仔细彻底地(进行搜索或检查) ■ **finely** adverb **fineness** noun.

fine² noun a sum of money that has to be paid as a punishment 罚金;罚款 ● verb (**fines, fining, fined**) make a person, company, etc. pay a fine 对…处以罚金

finery /ˈfaɪnəri/ noun smart, colourful clothes or decoration 华丽的衣服(或装饰)

finesse /fɪˈnes/ noun 1 elegant or delicate skill (雅致或精湛的)技巧 2 subtle skill in handling people or situations 手腕;手段;策略

finger /ˈfɪŋɡə(r)/ noun 1 each of the four long, thin parts attached to either hand (or five, if the thumb is included) 手指 2 an object shaped like a finger 指状物 3 an amount of alcohol in a glass equivalent to the width of a finger 一指之宽(杯内酒

的深度的测量单位) • verb (fingers, fingering, fingered) touch or feel with the fingers 用手指触碰 (或感觉)

fingerboard /'fɪŋgəbɔːd/ noun a flat strip on the neck of a stringed instrument, against which you press the strings (弦乐器的)指板

fingering /'fɪŋgərɪŋ/ noun a way of using the fingers to play a musical instrument 用指弹奏；指法

fingernail /'fɪŋgəneɪl/ noun the nail on the upper surface of the tip of each finger 手指甲

fingerprint /'fɪŋgəprɪnt/ noun a mark made on a surface by a person's fingertip, which can be used to identify the person 指纹 • verb record the fingerprints of 取下…的指纹

finial /'fɪnɪəl/ noun a decorative part at the top of a roof, wall, or other structure (屋顶、墙壁等的)尖顶饰，顶端装饰物

finicky /'fɪnɪki/ adjective fussy and hard to please 过分讲究的；爱挑剔的

finish /'fɪnɪʃ/ verb 1 bring or come to an end 结束；完成 2 (finish with) have nothing more to do with 与…断绝关系 3 reach the end of a race or other competition (赛跑等比赛中)到达终点 4 (finish someone off) kill or completely defeat someone 杀死；彻底击败 5 give an article an attractive surface appearance 加工润饰；给(表面)抛光 • noun 1 an end or final stage 结束；最后阶段 2 the place at which a race or competition ends 赛跑等比赛的终点 3 the way in which a manufactured article is finished 最后工序 □ finishing school a college where girls are taught how to behave in fashionable society 精修学校(青年女子接受社交礼仪修养教育的私立学校) ■ finisher noun.

finite /'faɪnaɪt/ adjective limited in size or extent 有限的；有限制的

Finn /fɪn/ noun a person from Finland 芬兰人

Finnish /'fɪnɪʃ/ noun the language of the Finns 芬兰语 • adjective relating to Finland or the Finns 芬兰的；芬兰人的

fiord /fjɔːd/ ⇒ 见 FJORD.

fir /fɜː(r)/ noun an evergreen coniferous tree with needle-shaped leaves 冷杉(松科常绿树,叶呈针形)

fire /faɪə(r)/ noun 1 the light, heat, and smoke produced when something burns 火 2 an occasion in which a building is damaged or destroyed by a fire 火灾；失火 3 wood or coal that is burning for heating or cooking 柴火；炉火；灶火 4 a heater for a room that uses electricity or gas as fuel 电暖装置；煤气取暖器 5 passionate emotion or enthusiasm 激情；热情 6 the firing of guns 射击 • verb (fires, firing, fired) 1 send a bullet, shell, etc. from a gun or other weapon 射出(子弹、炮弹等) 2 direct a rapid series of questions or statements towards someone 向(某人)提出一连串问题；向(某人)发表连珠炮似的声明 3 informal 【非正式】 dismiss an employee from a job 解雇；开除 4 supply a furnace or power station with fuel 给(炉子)加燃料；为(电站)供应燃料 5 stimulate 激起；唤起 6 bake or dry pottery or bricks in a kiln (在窑内)烧制(陶器或砖) 7 old use 【旧】 set fire to 点燃；使燃烧 □ fire brigade Brit. 【英】 a team of people employed to put out fires 消防队 fire door a strong door for preventing the spread of fire 防火安全门 fire drill a practice of the emergency procedures to be used in case of fire 消防演习 fire engine a vehicle carrying firefighters and their equipment 救火车；消防车 fire escape a staircase or ladder for escaping from a burning building (失火时从建筑物中逃生用的)太平梯 fire extinguisher a device that sprays a jet of liquid, foam, or gas to put out a fire 灭火器 **the firing line 1** the front line of troops in a battle (战斗中部队的)射击前线, 火线 **2** a situation where you are likely to be criticized 易受批评的位置 **firing squad** a group of soldiers ordered to shoot a condemned person 行刑队

firearm /ˈfaɪrɑːm/ **noun** a rifle, pistol, or other portable gun 火器 (指步枪、手枪或其他轻便枪支)

fireball /ˈfaɪəbɔːl/ **noun** a ball of flames 火球

firebomb /ˈfaɪəbɒm/ **noun** a bomb intended to cause a fire 燃烧弹

firebrand /ˈfaɪəbrænd/ **noun** a person who passionately supports a particular cause 狂热分子

firebreak /ˈfaɪəbreɪk/ **noun** a strip of open space cleared in a forest to stop a fire from spreading 防火障 (森林中防止火势蔓延的带状空地)

firecracker /ˈfaɪəkrækə(r)/ **noun** a firework that makes a loud bang 爆竹；鞭炮

firefighter /ˈfaɪəfaɪtə(r)/ **noun** a person whose job is to put out fires 消防队员

firefly /ˈfaɪəflaɪ/ **noun** (plural **fireflies**) a kind of beetle which glows in the dark 萤火虫

fireguard /ˈfaɪəgɑːd/ **noun** a protective screen or grid in front of an open fire 炉栏；炉挡

fireman /ˈfaɪəmən/ **noun** (plural **firemen**) a male firefighter (男性)消防队员

fireplace /ˈfaɪəpleɪs/ **noun** a space at the base of a chimney for lighting a fire 壁炉；火炉

firepower /ˈfaɪəpaʊə(r)/ **noun** the destructive capacity of guns, missiles, or forces 火力

fireproof /ˈfaɪəpruːf/ **adjective** able to withstand fire or great heat 防火的；耐火的

firestorm /ˈfaɪəstɔːm/ **noun** a very fierce fire fanned by strong currents of air 风暴性大火

firewall /ˈfaɪəwɔːl/ **noun** a part of a computer system that prevents people from seeing the information stored in it unless they are authorized to do so (计算机系统的)防火墙

firewood /ˈfaɪəwʊd/ **noun** wood that is burnt as fuel 木柴；柴火

firework /ˈfaɪəwɜːk/ **noun 1** a device consisting of a small container of chemicals that produces spectacular effects and explosions when it is lit 烟花火 **2 (fireworks)** an outburst of anger or a display of skill (怒火的)迸发；(技能的)炫示

firm[1] /fɜːm/ **adjective 1** not giving way under pressure 坚固的；坚硬的；结实的 **2** solidly in place and stable 稳固的；牢固的 **3** having steady power or strength 强有力的 **4** showing determination and strength of character 坚定的；坚决的；坚强的 **5** fixed or definite 确定的；明确的 ● **verb** make firm 使坚实；使牢固；加强 ■ **firmly** adverb **firmness** noun.

firm[2] **noun** a business organization 商行；商号；公司

firmament /ˈfɜːməmənt/ **noun** literary 【文】the heavens; the sky 天穹；苍穹

first /fɜːst/ **ordinal number 1** coming before all others in time, order, or importance 最早的；最先的；最前面的；首要的 **2** before doing something else 首先；第一 **3** Brit.【英】a place in the top grade in an exam for a degree (学位考试的)最高成绩，优等成绩 **4** informal 【非正式】something that has never happened or been done before 前所未有的事；从未做过的事 □ **first aid** emergency medical help given to a sick or injured person (对病人或伤者的)急救 **first class 1** the best accommodation in a train, ship, etc. (火车的)头等车厢；(轮船等的)头等舱 **2** very good 优等的；一流的 **first-degree** (of burns) causing only reddening of the skin

(烧伤)一度的,最轻的 **first-hand** from the original source or personal experience; direct 第一手的;直接的 **first lady** the wife of the President of the United States (美国的)第一夫人,总统夫人 **first name** a name given to someone when they are born or baptized 名字;教名 **first-rate** very good 优秀的;一流的 ■ **firstly** adverb.

firstborn /ˈfɜːstbɔːn/ **noun** the first child to be born to someone 头胎;长子,长女

firth /fɜːθ/ **noun** a narrow channel of the sea that runs inland 河口狭长海湾;港湾

fiscal /ˈfɪskl/ **adjective** relating to the income received by a government, especially from taxes 财政收入的;国家岁入的 ■ **fiscally** adverb.

fish /fɪʃ/ **noun** (plural **fish** or **fishes**) **1** a cold-blooded animal with a backbone, gills and fins, living in water 鱼 **2** the flesh of fish as food 鱼肉 • **verb 1** try to catch fish 捕(鱼);钓(鱼) **2** (**fish something out**) take something out of water or a container (从水或容器中)取出, 捞出 **3** (**fish for**) search or feel for something hidden 寻找;摸索 **4** (**fish for**) try to get something 谋取: *fishing for compliments* 博取恭维

fisherman /ˈfɪʃəmən/ **noun** (plural **fishermen**) a person who catches fish for a living or as a sport 渔民;渔夫;钓鱼者

fishery /ˈfɪʃəri/ **noun** (plural **fisheries**) a place where fish are reared for food, or caught in large quantities 渔场;养鱼场

fisheye lens /ˈfɪʃaɪ lenz/ **noun** a highly curved lens for a camera, covering a very wide angle of view 鱼眼镜头;超广角镜头

fishmonger /ˈfɪʃmʌŋɡə(r)/ **noun** a person who sells fish for food 鱼贩;鱼商

fishnet /ˈfɪʃnet/ **noun** an open mesh fabric resembling a fishing net 网眼织物

fishwife /ˈfɪʃwaɪf/ **noun** (plural **fishwives**) a woman with a loud, coarse voice 说话粗声大气的女人

fishy /ˈfɪʃi/ **adjective** (**fishier**, **fishiest**) **1** resembling fish 像鱼的 **2** informal 【非正式】 causing feelings of doubt or suspicion 可疑的;靠不住的

fissile /ˈfɪsaɪl/ **adjective 1** able to undergo nuclear fission 可产生核裂变的 **2** (of rock) easily split (岩石)易裂的

fission /ˈfɪʃn/ **noun 1** the action of splitting into two or more parts 分裂 **2** a reaction in which an atomic nucleus splits in two, releasing a great deal of energy (原子核的)裂变, 分裂 **3** reproduction by means of a cell dividing into two or more new cells (细胞的)分裂,分裂生殖

fissure /ˈfɪʃə(r)/ **noun** a long, narrow crack (狭长的)裂缝,裂隙

fist /fɪst/ **noun** a person's hand when the fingers are bent in towards the palm and held there tightly 拳;拳头 ■ **fistful** noun.

fisticuffs /ˈfɪstɪkʌfs/ **plural noun** fighting with the fists 拳斗;互殴

fit¹ /fɪt/ **adjective** (**fitter**, **fittest**) **1** of a suitable quality, standard, or type 合适的;适合的;恰当的 **2** in good health 健康的;强健的 • **verb** (**fits**, **fitting**, **fitted**) **1** be the right shape and size for 合身;合适 **2** be able to occupy a particular position or space 可容纳;装下 **3** fix in place 安装;安置 **4** provide with a part or attachment; equip 给…安装配件;装备 **5** be in harmony with; match 与…相协调;符合;与…相称 **6** (**fit in**) be well suited 相合;相处融洽 • **noun** the way in which something fits 合身;合适 ■ **fitness** noun **fitter** noun.

fit² **noun 1** a sudden attack when a person makes violent, uncontrolled movements （肢体剧烈反应症状的）突发，发作 **2** a sudden attack of coughing, fainting, etc. （咳嗽，昏厥等的）发作，阵发 **3** a sudden burst of strong feeling （强烈感情的）突发，迸发 • verb (**fits, fitting, fitted**) have a fit or convulsion 突然发作；痉挛 □ **in fits and starts** with irregular bursts of activity 间歇地；一阵一阵地

fitful /ˈfɪtfʊl/ **adjective** not steady or continuous 间歇的，断断续续的，一阵一阵的 ■ **fitfully** adverb.

fitment /ˈfɪtmənt/ **noun** Brit. 【英】 a fixed item of furniture or piece of equipment （位置固定不能移动的）家具，设备

fitted /ˈfɪtɪd/ **adjective** made to fill a space or to cover something closely 尺寸合适的；刚好的

fitting /ˈfɪtɪŋ/ **noun 1** a small part attached to furniture or equipment 配件，附件 **2** (**fittings**) items which are fixed in a building but can be removed when the owner moves 可拆除装置 **3** a time when someone tries on an item of clothing that is being made or altered 试穿；试衣 • **adjective** appropriate 适合的；恰当的 ■ **fittingly** adverb.

five /faɪv/ **cardinal number** one more than four; 5 五 (Roman numeral 罗马数字: **v** or **V**.) • **noun** (**fives**) a game in which a ball is hit with a gloved hand or a bat against a wall 墙手球 (运动)

fiver /ˈfaɪvə(r)/ **noun** Brit. informal 【英，非正式】 a five-pound note 五英镑钞票

fix /fɪks/ **verb 1** attach or position securely 使固定；安装 **2** mend or repair 修理；修复；整理 **3** decide or settle on 确定；决定 **4** make arrangements for 安排 **5** make something unchanging or permanent 使经久不变；使永恒 **6** informal 【非正式】 dishonestly influence the outcome of 操纵；作弊 • **noun** informal 【非正式】

1 a difficult or awkward situation 困境；窘境 **2** a dose of an addictive drug （毒品的）一次用量 **3** an act of fixing something 定位；维修；操纵 ■ **fixer** noun.

fixate /ˈfɪkseɪt/ **verb** (**fixates, fixating, fixated**) (**fixate on** or **be fixated on**) be obsessed with 对…迷恋；固恋

fixation /fɪkˈseɪʃn/ **noun** an obsessive interest in someone or something 迷恋；固恋；癖

fixative /ˈfɪksətɪv/ **noun** a substance used to fix or protect something 固定剂；定影液；定色剂

fixity /ˈfɪksəti/ **noun** the state of being unchanging or permanent 固定性；稳定性

fixture /ˈfɪkstʃə(r)/ **noun 1** a piece of equipment or furniture which is fixed in position 固定装置；固定家具 **2** (**fixtures**) articles attached to a house that normally remain in place when the owner moves （房屋中的）固定装置 **3** Brit. 【英】 a sports event arranged to take place on a particular date （定期举行的）体育活动

fizz /fɪz/ **verb** make a hissing sound, like gas escaping in bubbles from a liquid 起泡发嘶嘶声 • **noun** the sound of fizzing or the quality of being fizzy 气泡嘶嘶声；起泡发嘶嘶声(的特性)

fizzle /ˈfɪzl/ **verb** (**fizzles, fizzling, fizzled**) **1** make a weak hissing sound 发（微弱的）嘶嘶声 **2** (**fizzle out**) end or fail in a weak or disappointing way 失败；结果不妙；终成泡影

fizzy /ˈfɪzi/ **adjective** (**fizzier, fizziest**) (of a drink) containing bubbles of gas （饮料）起泡的

fjord or **fiord** /ˈfjɔːd/ **noun** a long, narrow inlet of the sea between high cliffs, especially in Norway （尤指挪威两岸峭壁间的）峡湾

fl. abbreviation fluid.

flab /flæb/ **noun** informal 【非正式】

excess fat on a person's body (人体的)多余脂肪

flabbergasted /ˈflæbəgɑːstɪd/ **adjective** informal 【非正式】 very surprised 大吃一惊的；目瞪口呆的

flabby /ˈflæbi/ **adjective** (flabbier, flabbiest) (of a part of a person's body) fat and floppy (人的身体某部位)肥胖的，肌肉松垂的 ■ **flabbiness** noun.

flaccid /ˈflæsɪd/ **adjective** soft and limp 软弱的；松弛的 ■ **flaccidity** noun.

flack /flæk/ ⇨ 见 FLAK.

flag[1] /flæg/ **noun** a piece of cloth that is attached to a pole or rope and used as a symbol of a country or organization or as a signal 旗，旗帜 • **verb** (flags, flagging, flagged) **1** mark something as needing attention 标示(以引起注意) **2** (flag someone down) signal to a driver to stop 打信号使(司机)停下

flag[2] or **flagstone** /ˈflæɡstəʊn/ **noun** a flat stone slab used for paving (铺路用的)石板，板石

flag[3] **verb** (flags, flagging, flagged) become tired or less enthusiastic 变得疲乏；热情衰减

flagellate /ˈflædʒəleɪt/ **verb** whip someone as a form of religious punishment or for sexual pleasure (作为宗教惩罚或为获得性快感)鞭打，鞭笞 ■ **flagellation** noun.

flagon /ˈflæɡən/ **noun** a large bottle or jug for wine, cider, or beer 大酒壶；大肚酒瓶

flagpole /ˈflæɡpəʊl/ or **flagstaff** /ˈflæɡstɑːf/ **noun** a pole used for flying a flag 旗杆

flagrant /ˈfleɪɡrənt/ **adjective** very obvious and unashamed 极端明显的；明目张胆的 ■ **flagrantly** adverb.

flagship /ˈflæɡʃɪp/ **noun 1** the ship in a fleet which carries the admiral in command (舰队的)旗舰 **2** the best or most important thing owned or

produced by an organization (某组织机构)最好的东西，最重要产品

flail /fleɪl/ **verb 1** swing something wildly (狂乱地)摆动，摇动 **2** (flail **around** or **about**) move around in an uncontrolled way 挣扎 • **noun** a tool or machine that is swung to separate grains of wheat from the husks 连枷(脱粒农具)

flair /fleə(r)/ **noun 1** a natural ability or talent 天赋；资质；才华 **2** stylishness 时髦；雅致

> **!注意** don't confuse **flair** with **flare**, which means 'burn' or 'gradually become wider'. 不要混淆flair和flare, 后者意为"烧旺"或"逐渐变宽"。

flak or **flack** /flæk/ **noun 1** anti-aircraft fire 高射炮火 **2** strong criticism 严厉批评；抨击

flake /fleɪk/ **noun** a small, flat, very thin piece of something 小薄片 • **verb** (flakes, flaking, flaked) **1** come away from a surface in flakes (成片)剥离，脱落 **2** separate into flakes 使成薄片 **3** (flake out) informal 【非正式】 fall asleep or drop from exhaustion 入睡；(因疲倦而)倒下 ■ **flaky** adjective.

flambé /ˈflɒmbeɪ/ **verb** (flambés, flambéing, flambéed) cover food with spirits and set it on fire briefly 在(食物)上浇酒点燃

flamboyant /flæmˈbɔɪənt/ **adjective 1** very confident and lively 卖弄的；炫耀的 **2** brightly coloured or highly decorated 颜色鲜艳的；装饰华丽的 ■ **flamboyance** noun **flamboyantly** adverb.

flame /fleɪm/ **noun 1** a glowing stream of burning gas produced by something on fire 火焰；火舌 **2** a brilliant orange-red colour 火红色；橘红色 • **verb** (flames, flaming, flamed) **1** give off flames 发火焰；燃烧 **2** set on fire 点燃 **3** (of a strong emotion) appear suddenly and fiercely (强烈感情)进

发,爆发 4 informal 【非正式】send insulting email messages to 给…发辱骂邮件 □ **old flame** informal 【非正式】a former lover 旧情人

flamenco /fləˈmeŋkəʊ/ noun a lively style of Spanish guitar music accompanied by singing and dancing 弗拉门科乐曲(一种西班牙吉他曲子,风格活泼,伴有歌舞)

flamingo /fləˈmɪŋgəʊ/ noun (plural **flamingos** or **flamingoes**) a wading bird with mainly pink or red feathers and a long neck and legs 红鹳,火烈鸟(一种涉禽,羽毛主要为粉色或红色,长颈长腿)

flammable /ˈflæməbl/ adjective easily set on fire 易燃的;可燃的;速燃的

flan /flæn/ noun a baked dish consisting of an open pastry case with a savoury or sweet filling 果馅饼

flange /flændʒ/ noun a projecting flat rim for strengthening an object or attaching it to something 凸缘;法兰

flank /flæŋk/ noun **1** the side of the body between the ribs and the hip 胁,胁腹 **2** the side of something such as a mountain (山等的)侧面 **3** the left or right side of a group of people (一群人的)侧旁 • verb be on the side of 在…的侧面

flannel /ˈflænl/ noun **1** a kind of soft woollen or cotton fabric 法兰绒;绒布 **2** (**flannels**) men's trousers made of woollen flannel 法兰绒男裤 **3** Brit. 【英】a small piece of towelling for washing yourself (擦洗身体用的)毛巾 **4** Brit. informal 【英,非正式】talk that does not have much meaning, used to avoid a difficult subject 空洞的话;兜圈子的话语

flannelette /ˌflænəˈlet/ noun a cotton fabric resembling flannel 绒布;棉法兰绒

flap /flæp/ verb (**flaps**, **flapping**, **flapped**) **1** move up and down or from side to side 摆动;飘动 **2** Brit. informal 【英,非正式】be very anxious; panic 焦急;恐慌 • noun **1** a flat piece of paper, cloth, or metal that is attached to one side of something and covers an opening (一侧附于某物、用以覆盖开口的)片状悬垂物,封盖 **2** a movable section of an aircraft wing, used to control upward movement (飞机的)襟翼,副翼 **3** a flapping movement 摆动;飘动 **4** informal 【非正式】a panic 恐慌

flapjack /ˈflæpdʒæk/ noun **1** Brit. 【英】a soft biscuit made from oats and butter 甜燕麦饼 **2** N. Amer. 【北美】a pancake 薄煎饼

flapper /ˈflæpə(r)/ noun informal 【非正式】a fashionable young woman of the 1920s (20世纪20年代的)时尚女郎

flare /fleə(r)/ noun **1** a sudden brief burst of flame or light 摇曳的火焰;闪烁;闪光 **2** a device that produces a very bright flame as a signal or marker 闪光装置;闪光信号灯;照明弹 **3** (**flares**) trousers whose legs widen from the knees down 喇叭裤 • verb (**flares**, **flaring**, **flared**) **1** burn or shine suddenly and strongly (突然)烧旺,闪耀 **2** (usu. **flare up**) suddenly become intense or violent 突然增强(或加剧) **3** gradually become wider at one end (一端)逐渐变宽

!注意 don't confuse **flare** with **flair**, which means 'a natural ability or talent'. 不要混淆 flare 和 flair, 后者意为"天赋;资质"。

flash /flæʃ/ verb **1** shine with a bright but brief or irregular light 闪光;闪耀 **2** move quickly 飞驰;掠过 **3** display words or images briefly or repeatedly (短暂或反复地)闪现,亮出 **4** informal 【非正式】display something in an obvious way to impress people 炫耀;卖弄 **5** informal 【非正式】(of a man) show his genitals in public (男子)露阴 • **noun 1** a sudden brief burst of bright light 闪光;闪烁 **2** a camera attachment that produces a flash of light, for taking photographs in bad light (照相机的)闪光灯 **3** a sudden or brief occurrence 闪现;突发 **4** Brit. 【英】 a coloured patch on a uniform, used to identify a regiment, country, etc. 徽章;臂章;肩章 • **adjective** informal 【非正式】 stylish or expensive in a showy way 亮丽时尚的;奢华的 □ **flash flood** sudden local flood resulting from very heavy rainfall 骤发的洪水;暴洪 **flash in the pan** a sudden but brief success 昙花一现 ■ **flasher** noun.

flashback /ˈflæʃbæk/ **noun 1** a scene in a film or novel set in a time earlier than the main story (电影的)闪回镜头;(小说的)倒叙情节 **2** a sudden vivid memory of a past event (往事在记忆中的)突然重现

flashgun /ˈflæʃɡʌn/ **noun** a device which gives a brief flash of intense light, used for taking photographs in bad light (摄影用的)闪光枪

flashing /ˈflæʃɪŋ/ **noun** a strip of metal used to seal the join of a roof with another surface (屋顶与其他平面接合处的)金属防雨板, 盖片

flashlight /ˈflæʃlaɪt/ **noun 1** an electric torch with a strong beam 手电筒 **2** a flashgun 闪光枪

flashpoint /ˈflæʃpɔɪnt/ **noun** a point or place at which anger or violence flares up (愤怒或暴力的)爆发点,发生点

flashy /ˈflæʃi/ **adjective** (**flashier**, **flashiest**) attractive in a showy or cheap way 俗艳的;华而不实的

flask /flɑːsk/ **noun 1** a bottle with a narrow neck 细颈瓶 **2** Brit. 【英】 a container that keeps a substance hot or cold by means of a double wall that encloses a vacuum 保温瓶;热水瓶

flat¹ /flæt/ **adjective** (**flatter**, **flattest**) **1** having a level and even surface 平的;平坦的 **2** not sloping; horizontal 水平的 **3** with a level surface and little height or depth 扁平的;平而浅的 **4** not lively or interesting 无生气的;无趣的 **5** (of a sparkling drink) no longer fizzy (起泡饮料)不起泡的,走了气的 **6** (of something inflated) having lost its air (充气物)瘪了的,漏了气的 **7** Brit. 【英】 (of a battery) having used up its charge (电池)电用完的 **8** (of a charge or price) fixed (收费或价格)固定的 **9** definite and firm 明确的;坚决的 **10** (of a musical sound) below the proper pitch (音乐声)偏低的,降音的 **11** (of a note or key) lower by a semitone than a stated note or key (音符或调)降半音的 • **adverb** informal 【非正式】 completely; absolutely 完全地;彻底地 • **noun 1** the flat part of something 平坦部分;平面部分 **2** (**flats**) low level ground near water (水边的)平地,低洼地 **3** informal 【非正式】 a flat tyre 漏气轮胎 **4** (**the Flat**) Brit. 【英】 flat racing 平地赛马 **5** a musical note that is a semitone lower than the named note, shown by the sign ♭. 降半音的记号;降音;降号 □ **flat feet** feet with arches that are lower than usual (扁)平足 **flat out** as fast or as hard as possible 用全速;竭尽全力 **flat race** a horse race over a course with no jumps (无障碍物的)平地赛马 ■ **flatly** adverb **flatness** noun.

flat² **noun** Brit. 【英】 a set of rooms on one floor forming a separate home within a larger building 一套房间;单元房;公寓

flatfish /ˈflætfɪʃ/ **noun** (plural **flatfish** or **flatfishes**) a sea fish, such as a plaice, that has both eyes on the upper side of its flattened body 比目鱼

flatmate /ˈflætmeɪt/ **noun** Brit. 【英】 a person that you share a flat with 公

寓合住者

flatten /ˈflætn/ **verb** make or become flat or flatter 弄平；变平

flatter /ˈflætə(r)/ **verb** (**flatters, flattering, flattered**) **1** compliment someone too much or in an insincere way 向(某人)谄媚；奉承；讨好 **2** (**be flattered**) feel honoured and pleased 感到荣幸；感到高兴 **3** make someone appear attractive 使(某人)显得漂亮

flattery /ˈflætəri/ **noun** excessive or insincere praise 谄媚；奉承；讨好

flatulent /ˈflætjʊlənt/ **adjective** suffering from a build-up of gas in the intestines or stomach 肠胃气胀的
■ **flatulence** noun.

flatworm /ˈflætwɜːm/ **noun** a type of worm with a simple flattened body 扁虫

flaunt /flɔːnt/ **verb** display proudly or obviously 炫耀；夸耀；夸示

> **！注意** don't confuse **flaunt** with **flout**, which means 'ignore a rule'. 不要混淆flaunt和flout，后者意为"无视规则"。

flautist /ˈflɔːtɪst/ **noun** a flute player 长笛手

flavour /ˈfleɪvə(r)/ (US spelling 【美拼写】 **flavor**) **noun 1** the distinctive taste of a food or drink 滋味；味道 **2** a particular quality 特色；风味 • **verb** give flavour to 加味于；给…增添风味 ■ **flavouring** noun **flavourless** adjective.

flaw /flɔː/ **noun 1** a mark or fault that spoils something 缺陷；缺点；瑕疵 **2** a weakness or mistake 弱点；错误
■ **flawed** adjective **flawless** adjective.

flax /flæks/ **noun** a blue-flowered plant that is grown for its seed (linseed) and for its stalks, from which thread is made 亚麻

flaxen /ˈflæksn/ **adjective** literary 【文】 (of hair) pale yellow (头发)亚麻色的，浅黄色的

flay /fleɪ/ **verb 1** strip the skin from a body 剥…的皮 **2** whip or beat very harshly 狠狠鞭打；毒打

flea /fliː/ **noun** a small wingless jumping insect which feeds on the blood of mammals and birds 蚤；跳蚤
□ **flea market** a street market selling second-hand goods (卖二手货的)跳蚤市场

fleapit /ˈfliːpɪt/ **noun** Brit. informal 【英，非正式】 a run-down cinema 蚤窝(指破败的电影院)

fleck /flek/ **noun 1** a very small patch of colour or light 色斑；光斑 **2** a very small piece of something 微粒 • **verb** mark or dot with flecks 使有斑点；使斑驳

fledged /fledʒd/ **adjective** (of a young bird) having developed wing feathers that are large enough for it to fly (小鸟)羽翼已丰的

fledgling or **fledgeling** /ˈfledʒlɪŋ/ **noun** a young bird that has just learned to fly 刚长出羽毛的小鸟

flee /fliː/ **verb** (**flees, fleeing, fled**) run away 逃走；逃掉

fleece /fliːs/ **noun 1** the wool coat of a sheep 羊毛 **2** a soft, warm fabric with a pile, or a jacket made from this (带绒面的)柔软暖和的织物，绒头织物；羊毛呢衫 • **verb** (**fleeces, fleecing, fleeced**) informal 【非正式】 swindle someone 向(某人)漫天索价；对…敲竹杠 ■ **fleecy** adjective.

fleet[1] /fliːt/ **noun 1** a group of ships travelling together 舰队；船队 **2** a group of vehicles or aircraft with the same owner 车队；机群

fleet[2] **adjective** literary 【文】 fast in movement 快速的；敏捷的

fleeting /ˈfliːtɪŋ/ **adjective** lasting for a very short time 飞逝的；短暂的
■ **fleetingly** adverb.

flesh /fleʃ/ **noun 1** the soft substance in the body consisting of muscle and fat 肉(包括肌肉和脂肪) **2** the edible part of a fruit or vegetable 果肉；蔬菜的可食部分 **3** (**the flesh**) the physical aspects and needs of the body 肉体；肉欲 • **verb (flesh something out)** make something more detailed 使更详细；用细节充实 □ **in the flesh** in person 本人；亲自；活生生地

fleshly /'fleʃli/ **adjective** relating to the body and its needs 肉体的；肉欲的

fleshpots /'fleʃpɒts/ **plural noun** humorous 【幽默】 places with a lot of nightlife and lively entertainment 声色场所

fleshy /'fleʃi/ **adjective (fleshier, fleshiest) 1** plump 肥胖的；丰满的 **2** soft and thick 肉质的

fleur-de-lis or **fleur-de-lys** /ˌflɜːdə'liː/ **noun (plural fleurs-de-lis** /ˌflɜːdə'liː/) a design showing a lily made up of three petals bound together at the bottom 鸢尾花饰；百合花饰

flew /fluː/ past of **FLY**[1].

flex /fleks/ **verb 1** bend a limb or joint 屈曲，弯曲(四肢或关节) **2** tighten a muscle 收紧(肌肉) • **noun** Brit. 【英】 a cable for carrying electric current to an appliance (向设备输电的)花线，皮线

flexible /'fleksəbl/ **adjective 1** able to bend easily without breaking 柔韧的；易弯曲的；有弹性的 **2** able to adapt to different circumstances 可变通的，易适应的；灵活的 ■ **flexibility** noun **flexibly** adverb.

flexitime /'fleksitaɪm/ **noun** a system that lets you vary your working hours 弹性工作时间制

flick /flik/ **verb 1** hit or remove with a quick light movement 轻弹；轻拂 **2** make a sudden quick movement 突然快速移动 **3 (flick through)** look quickly through a book, magazine, etc. 浏览，草草翻阅(书、杂志等) • **noun 1** a sudden quick movement 突然快速的移动 **2** informal 【非正式】 a cinema film

电影 □ **flick knife** Brit. 【英】 a knife with a blade that springs out from the handle when you press a button 弹簧折刀

flicker /'flikə(r)/ **verb (flickers, flickering, flickered) 1** shine or burn unsteadily 摇曳；闪烁 **2** appear briefly 忽隐忽现；闪现 **3** make small, quick movements 抖动 • **noun 1** a flickering movement or light 快速的小动作；摇曳的光；闪烁的光 **2** a brief occurrence of a feeling (感情的)闪现，一闪而过

flier /'flaɪə(r)/ ⇨ 见 **FLYER**.

flight /flaɪt/ **noun 1** the action of flying 飞翔 **2** a journey made in an aircraft or in space 空中旅行；太空旅行 **3** the path of something through the air 飞行路线 **4** the action of running away 逃跑 **5** a group of birds or aircraft flying together (飞行中的)鸟群，机群 **6** a series of steps between floors or levels 一段楼梯；一段阶梯 **7** the tail of an arrow or dart 箭尾；镖尾 □ **flight deck 1** the cockpit of a large aircraft (大型飞机的)驾驶舱 **2** the deck of an aircraft carrier (航空母舰上的)飞行甲板 **flight of fancy** a very imaginative idea or story 异想天开；奇思怪想 ■ **flightless** adjective.

flighty /'flaɪti/ **adjective** unreliable and uninterested in serious things 靠不住的；不可信赖的；轻浮的

flimsy /'flimzi/ **adjective (flimsier, flimsiest) 1** weak and fragile 不牢固的；易损坏的 **2** (of clothing) light and thin (衣服)轻而薄的 **3** unconvincing 没有说服力的；不足信的：*a flimsy excuse* 站不住脚的借口

flinch /flintʃ/ **verb 1** make a quick, nervous movement as a reaction to fear or pain (因害怕或疼痛而)退缩，畏缩 **2 (flinch from)** avoid something because you are scared or anxious (因害怕或焦虑而)逃避，躲避

fling /flɪŋ/ **verb (flings, flinging, flung)** throw or move forcefully (用力) 扔,掷,抛;猛动 • **noun 1** a short period of enjoyment or wild behaviour 一时的放纵;尽情行乐的一阵 **2** a short sexual relationship 短暂的风流韵事

flint /flɪnt/ **noun 1** a hard grey rock 燧石;火石 **2** a piece of flint or a metal alloy, used to produce a spark in a cigarette lighter 打火石;(打火机的) 电石

flintlock /'flɪntlɒk/ **noun** an old-fashioned type of gun fired by a spark from a flint (老式)燧发机,明火枪

flip /flɪp/ **verb (flips, flipping, flipped) 1** turn over with a quick, smooth movement (快速)翻动,翻转 **2** move or throw with a sudden sharp movement 突然急速地动(或抛) **3** informal【非正式】suddenly become very angry or lose your self-control 暴怒;失去自我控制 • **noun** a flipping action or movement (快速的)翻动,翻转;急动;突然的动作,轻抛 • **adjective** not serious or respectful; flippant 鲁莽的,无礼的,轻率的 □ **flip-flop** a light sandal with a thong that passes between the big and second toes 平底人字拖鞋 **flip side** informal【非正式】the reverse and less welcome aspect of a situation (形势的)反面,不利的一面

flippant /'flɪpənt/ **adjective** not properly serious or respectful 轻率的;无礼的 ■ **flippancy** noun **flippantly** adverb.

flipper /'flɪpə(r)/ **noun 1** a broad, flat limb used for swimming by sea creatures such as turtles (海龟等的)鳍状肢,前肢,鳍足 **2** a flat rubber attachment worn on each foot for swimming underwater (潜水时缚在脚上的)脚蹼,鸭脚板,橡皮脚掌

flirt /flɜːt/ **verb 1** behave as if you are trying to attract someone sexually, but without serious intentions 调情;卖俏 **2** (**flirt with**) show a casual interest in (不认真地)对…感兴趣 **3** (**flirt with**) deliberately risk danger or death 故意冒(险);玩(命) • **noun** a person who likes to flirt 调情者;卖俏者 ■ **flirtation** noun **flirty** adjective.

flirtatious /flɜː'teɪʃəs/ **adjective** liking to flirt 爱调情的;卖弄风情的

flit /flɪt/ **verb (flits, flitting, flitted)** move quickly and lightly 轻快地移动

flitter /'flɪtə(r)/ **verb** move quickly here and there 飞来飞去;奔忙

float /fləʊt/ **verb 1** rest on the surface of a liquid without sinking 漂;浮 **2** move or be held up in a liquid or the air 浮动;飘动 **3** put forward a suggestion 提出(建议) **4** (**floating**) not having fixed opinions or living in a fixed location 不固定的;流动的;浮动的 **5** put shares in a company on sale for the first time (首次)发行(股票)上市 • **noun 1** a lightweight object designed to float on water 漂浮物;漂浮装置 **2** a vehicle that carries a display in a procession (游行时装载展品的)彩车 **3** Brit.【英】a sum of money available for minor expenses 备用零钱 ■ **floaty** adjective.

floatation /fləʊ'teɪʃn/ ⇒ 见 **FLOTATION**.

flock¹ /flɒk/ **noun 1** a number of birds, sheep, or goats together (鸟、羊等的)一群 **2** (**a flock or flocks**) a large number or crowd 一大群人 **3** a Christian congregation 全体基督教教徒 • **verb** gather or move in a flock 群集;成群结队;蜂拥

flock² /flɒk/ **noun 1** a soft material for stuffing cushions and quilts (填塞垫子、被子用的)软填料 **2** powdered wool or cloth, used to give a raised pattern on wallpaper (用来制作有浮雕效果壁纸的)绒屑

floe /fləʊ/ **noun** a sheet of floating ice 浮冰块

flog /flɒg/ **verb (flogs, flogging, flogged) 1** beat with a whip or stick as a punishment (作为惩罚)鞭打,棒

打 2 Brit. informal 【英,非正式】sell 出售

flood /flʌd/ **noun 1** an overflow of a large amount of water over dry land (洪水的)泛滥;水灾 **2** an overwhelming quantity or amount 大量;大片;大批 **3** the rising of the tide 涨潮 • **verb 1** cover with water in a flood 淹没 **2** (of a river) overflow its banks (河流)泛滥 **3** arrive in very large numbers 大量涌来;纷至沓来 □ **flood plain** an area of low ground next to a river that is regularly flooded 洪泛区;涝原;漫滩 **flood tide** an incoming tide 涨潮;升潮

floodgate /flʌdɡeɪt/ **noun 1** a gate that can be opened or closed to control a flow of water 水闸;防洪闸门 **2** (floodgates) controls that hold back something powerful 控制物;制约物

floodlight /flʌdlaɪt/ **noun** a large, powerful lamp used to light up a sports ground (运动场的)泛光灯 • **verb** (floodlights, floodlighting, floodlit) light up with floodlights 用泛光灯照明

floor /flɔː(r)/ **noun 1** the lower surface of a room (房间的)地面,地板 **2** a storey of a building (楼房的)层 **3** the bottom of the sea, a cave, etc. (海洋、山洞等的)底 **4** (the floor) the part of a parliament or other law-making assembly in which members sit and from which they speak (立法机构成员的)席位 • **verb** informal 【非正式】 **1** knock someone to the ground 把…打倒在地 **2** surprise or confuse someone 使吃惊;使困惑 □ **floor show** an entertainment presented on the floor of a nightclub or restaurant (夜总会或餐馆里的)娱乐表演 ■ **floored** adjective.

floorboard /flɔːbɔːd/ **noun** a long plank making up part of a wooden floor 木地板

floozy or **floozie** /fluːzi/ **noun** (plural floozies) informal 【非正式】a girl or woman who has many sexual partners (有很多性伙伴的)放荡女子

flop /flɒp/ **verb** (flops, flopping, flopped) **1** hang or swing loosely (松弛地悬挂(或摆动) **2** sit or lie down heavily 重重地坐下(或躺下) **3** informal 【非正式】fail totally 彻底失败 • **noun 1** a heavy and clumsy fall (笨重的)摔倒 **2** informal 【非正式】a total failure 彻底失败

floppy /flɒpi/ **adjective** not firm or rigid 松软的;松松垮垮的,松垂的 □ **floppy disk** a flexible disk used for storing computer data 软(磁)盘

flora /flɔːrə/ **noun** the plants of a particular area or period (某一地区或时期的)植物群

floral /flɔːrəl/ **adjective** having to do with flowers 花的

floret /flɒrət/ **noun 1** each of the small flowers making up a flower head (花序中的)小花 **2** each of the flowering stems making up a head of cauliflower or broccoli (花椰菜或球茎甘蓝的)花茎

florid /flɒrɪd/ **adjective 1** having a red or flushed complexion (肤色)红润的;脸发红的 **2** too elaborate 绚丽的;过分华丽的

florin /flɒrɪn/ **noun** a former British coin worth two shillings (ten pence) 弗罗林(英国旧币,合两先令)

florist /flɒrɪst/ **noun** a person who sells cut flowers 花商

floss /flɒs/ **noun 1** (also **dental floss**) soft thread used to clean between the teeth 牙线(用于清洁牙缝) **2** silk thread used in embroidery 绣花(丝)线 • **verb** clean between the teeth with dental floss 用牙线清洁(牙缝)

flotation or **floatation** /fləʊˈteɪʃn/ **noun 1** the action of floating 漂浮 **2** the offering of a company's shares for sale for the first time (公司股份的)首次发行

flotilla /fləˈtɪlə/ **noun** a small fleet of ships or boats 小舰队;小船队

flotsam /ˈflɒtsəm/ **noun** wreckage found floating on the sea (海上遇难船只的)漂浮残骸

flounce /flaʊns/ **verb** (flounces, flouncing, flounced) move in an angry or impatient way (因愤怒或不耐烦)走动,急动 • **noun 1** an exaggerated action expressing annoyance or impatience (因愤怒或不耐烦作出的)夸张动作 **2** a wide strip of material sewn to a skirt or dress (衣裙上的)荷叶边

flounder¹ /ˈflaʊndə(r)/ **verb** (flounders, floundering, floundered) **1** stagger clumsily in mud or water (笨拙地在泥或水中)挣扎,踉跄,蹒跚 **2** have trouble doing or understanding something 力不从心地做;举步维艰,苦于无法理解

flounder² **noun** a small flatfish 鲆;鲽

flour /ˈflaʊə(r)/ **noun** a powder produced by grinding grain, used to make bread, cakes, and pastry 谷物磨成的粉;面粉 ■ **floury** adjective.

flourish /ˈflʌrɪʃ/ **verb 1** grow or develop well; thrive 茁壮成长;茂盛 **2** be successful 成功;繁荣;兴旺 **3** wave something about in a noticeable way 挥舞 • **noun 1** a dramatic or exaggerated movement or gesture 大胆放纵的动作;夸张动作 **2** a decorative flowing curve in handwriting (手写花体字的)花饰 **3** a fanfare played by brass instruments 响亮的铜管乐声;喇叭齐鸣

flout /flaʊt/ **verb** openly fail to follow a rule, law, or custom 公然蔑视(规则、法律或习俗)

> **！注意** don't confuse **flout** with **flaunt**, which means 'display proudly or obviously'. 不要混淆flout和flaunt,后者意为"炫耀;夸耀"。

flow /fləʊ/ **verb 1** move steadily and continuously in a current or stream 流;流动;流淌 **2** hang loosely and elegantly 飘垂;飘拂 • **noun 1** a steady, continuous stream 一连串 □ **flow chart** a diagram that shows the sequence of stages making up a complex process (复杂过程的)流程图

flower /ˈflaʊə(r)/ **noun 1** the part of a plant from which the seed or fruit develops, usually having brightly coloured petals 花;花朵 **2** (the flower of) the best of a group 精华;最好的部分 • **verb** (flowers, flowering, flowered) **1** produce flowers 开花 **2** develop fully and well 发育;成熟;繁荣;兴旺

flowerpot /ˈflaʊəpɒt/ **noun** a container for growing plants in 花盆

flowery /ˈflaʊəri/ **adjective 1** full of or decorated with flowers 多花的;饰以花卉的 **2** (of speech or writing) elaborate (讲话或文章)词藻华丽的

flown /fləʊn/ past participle of FLY¹.

flu /fluː/ **noun** influenza or fever, milder infection 流行性感冒;流感

fluctuate /ˈflʌktʃueɪt/ **verb** (fluctuates, fluctuating, fluctuated) rise and fall irregularly in number or amount (数字或数量)波动,上下浮动,起伏 ■ **fluctuation** noun.

flue /fluː/ **noun** a pipe that takes smoke and gases away from a chimney, heater, etc. (烟囱的)烟道

fluent /ˈfluːənt/ **adjective 1** able to use a language in a clear and natural way (语言使用)流利的,娴熟的 **2** smoothly graceful and easy 优美自然的;流畅的 ■ **fluency** noun **fluently** adverb.

fluff /flʌf/ **noun 1** soft fibres gathered in small, light clumps (结成小团的)线毛 **2** the soft fur or feathers of a young animal or bird (幼兽或雏鸟的)软毛 • **verb 1** (fluff something up) make something fuller and softer by shaking or patting it 抖松;拍松 **2** informal 【非正式】fail to do something properly 把…搞糟

fluffy /'flʌfi/ **adjective** (**fluffier,
fluffiest**) **1** covered with fluff 覆有
绒毛的 **2** (of food) light in texture (食
物)松软的

flugelhorn /'flu:glhɔ:n/ **noun** a brass
musical instrument like a cornet but
with a broader tone 翼号，活塞军号
(类似短号，但音调更宽)

fluid /'flu:ɪd/ **noun** a liquid or gas 流
体；流质；液 ■ **adjective 1** able to flow
easily 能流动的 **2** not fixed or stable
不固定的；不稳定的 **3** graceful 优
美的 □ **fluid ounce** Brit. 【英】one
twentieth of a pint (approximately
0.028 litre) 液盎司，液量盎司(1/20
品脱，约 0.028升) ■ **fluidity** noun
fluidly adverb.

fluke /flu:k/ **noun** something lucky
that happens by chance 侥幸；偶然机
会 ■ **fluky** adjective

flume /flu:m/ **noun 1** an artificial
channel for carrying water (人工)引
水槽 **2** a water slide at a swimming
pool or amusement park (游泳池或
游乐场的)滑水槽

flummery /'flʌməri/ **noun** (plural **flum-
meries**) empty talk or compliments
废话；空洞的恭维话

flummox /'flʌməks/ **verb** informal 【非
正式】baffle someone completely 使
困惑；彻底难住

flung /flʌŋ/ past and past participle of
FLING.

flunk /flʌŋk/ **verb** informal, chiefly N.
Amer. 【非正式，主北美】fail an exam
未通过(考试)

flunkey or **flunky** /'flʌŋki/ **noun**
(plural **flunkeys** or **flunkies**) **1** a
uniformed male servant (穿制服的)
男仆 **2** a person who does menial
tasks for someone else 干粗活的人

fluoresce /ˌflʊə'res/ **verb** (**fluores-
ces, fluorescing, fluoresced**)
shine or glow brightly 发荧光

fluorescent /flʊə'resnt/ **adjective 1**
giving off bright light when exposed

to radiation such as ultraviolet
light 有荧光的；发荧光的 **2** vividly
colourful 发亮的 ■ **fluorescence**
noun.

✔ 拼写指南 *fluor*-, not *flour*-: *fluor*-
escent. fluorescent 中 fluor- 不要拼
作 flour-。

fluoridate /'flʊərɪdeɪt/ **verb** (**fluori-
dates, fluoridating, fluoridated**)
add fluoride to a water supply 在(供
水)中加入氟化物 ■ **fluoridation** noun.

fluoride /'flʊəraɪd/ **noun** a compound
of fluorine that is added to water
supplies or toothpaste to reduce
tooth decay (加到供水或牙膏中以减
少龋齿的)含氟盐

fluorine /'flʊəriːn/ **noun** a poisonous
pale yellow gas 氟(有毒的浅黄色气
体)

fluorite /'flʊəraɪt/ **noun** a mineral
found in the form of crystals 萤石；
氟石

fluorspar /'flʊəspɑ:(r)/ = FLUORITE.

flurry /'flʌri/ **noun** (plural **flurries**) **1** a
small swirling mass of snow, leaves,
etc. moved by a gust of wind (被一
阵风吹起、打着旋的)一团雪花(或
树叶等) **2** a sudden short period of
activity or excitement 一阵忙乱；一
阵兴奋 **3** a number of things arriving
suddenly and at the same time 突然
同时发生的一连串事情

flush¹ /flʌʃ/ **verb 1** (of a person's skin
or face) become red and hot (人的
皮肤或脸)发红，发热 **2** (**be flushed
with**) be very pleased by 因…而得意
3 clean something by passing large
quantities of water through it (用水)
冲洗 **4** force a person or animal out
into the open 把(人或动物)驱赶出
来 ● **noun 1** a reddening of the face
or skin 脸红；潮红 **2** a sudden rush
of strong emotion 一阵强烈情感 **3** a
period of freshness and energy 一段
生气勃勃的时期；旺盛时期: *the first
flush of youth* 青春活力旺盛时期 **4**

an act of flushing 冲洗

flush² **adjective 1** completely level with another surface 同平面的;齐平的 **2** informal 【非正式】 having plenty of money 很有钱的;富裕的

flush³ **noun** (in poker) a hand of cards all of the same suit (扑克牌戏中的)同花

fluster /ˈflʌstə(r)/ **noun** an agitated and confused state 慌乱;激动;紧张不安

flustered /ˈflʌstəd/ **adjective** agitated and confused state 慌乱的;激动的,紧张不安的

flute /fluːt/ **noun 1** a high-pitched wind instrument that you hold sideways and play by blowing across a hole at one end 长笛 **2** a tall, narrow wine glass 细而高的酒杯

fluted /ˈfluːtɪd/ **adjective** decorated with a series of gently rounded grooves 有装饰性凹槽(或沟槽)的

flutter /ˈflʌtə(r)/ **verb** (flutters, fluttering, fluttered) **1** fly unsteadily by flapping the wings quickly and lightly (轻快地)拍翅而飞 **2** move or fall with a light trembling motion 颤动;振动;飘落 **3** (of a pulse or heartbeat) beat feebly or irregularly (脉搏或心脏)微弱地跳动,不规则地跳动 • **noun 1** a state of nervous excitement 紧张不安;激动 **2** Brit. informal 【英,非正式】 a small bet 小赌 ■ **fluttery** adjective.

fluvial /ˈfluːviəl/ **adjective** technical 【术语】 having to do with a river 河的;河流的

flux /flʌks/ **noun 1** continuous change (不断的)变动 **2** a flow 流;涌流

fly¹ /flaɪ/ **verb** (flies, flying, flew; past participle flown) **1** (of a winged creature or aircraft) move through the air (有翼动物或飞机)飞,飞翔 **2** control the flight of an aircraft 驾驶(飞机) **3** move quickly through the air (在空中)疾飞,飞行 **4** go or move quickly 疾行;飞跑;冲 **5** (of a

flag) be displayed on a flagpole (旗)飘扬 **6** (**fly at**) attack 扑向;攻击 **7** old use 【旧】 run away 逃跑 • **noun** (plural **flies**) **1** (Brit. 【英】 also **flies**) an opening at the crotch of a pair of trousers, closed with a zip or buttons (裤子前部的)拉锁盖,纽扣盖 **2** a flap of material covering the opening of a tent (帐篷的)门帘 **3** (**the flies**) the space over the stage in a theatre (戏院舞台的)吊景区 □ **fly-by-night** unreliable or untrustworthy 不可靠的;不值得信赖的 **flypost** Brit. 【英】 put up advertising posters without permission (未经许可)张贴(广告) **flying saucer** a disc-shaped flying spacecraft supposedly piloted by aliens 飞碟;不明飞行物 **flying squad** a division of a police force which is capable of reaching an incident quickly (警察)闪电行动队,快速特警队 **flying start** a good beginning that gives an advantage over competitors 占优势的有利开端;良好的开端 **fly in the face of** do the opposite of what is usual or expected 与(通常情况或预期)完全相悖 **fly off the handle** informal 【非正式】 lose your temper 发怒 **with flying colours** with distinction 出色地

fly² **noun** (plural **flies**) **1** a flying insect with transparent wings 苍蝇;家蝇 **2** an artificial fly used as a fishing bait (用作钓饵的)假蝇 □ **a fly in the ointment** a small irritation that spoils the enjoyment of something 使人扫兴的小事;煞风景的事物 **a fly on the wall** an unnoticed observer 未被注意的观察者

fly³ **adjective** (**flyer**, **flyest**) Brit. informal 【英,非正式】 knowing and clever 精明的;机灵的

flyaway /ˈflaɪəweɪ/ **adjective** (of hair) fine and difficult to control (头发)细软且难梳理的

flyblown /ˈflaɪbləʊn/ **adjective**

contaminated by contact with flies 被苍蝇污染的

flycatcher /ˈflaɪkætʃə(r)/ **noun** a small bird that catches flying insects 鹟(捕食飞虫的鸟)

flyer or **flier** /ˈflaɪə(r)/ **noun 1** a person or thing that flies 飞行员;飞鸟;飞行物;航空者 **2** a small printed advertisement 小(广告)传单

flyleaf /ˈflaɪliːf/ **noun** (plural **flyleaves**) a blank page at the beginning or end of a book (书籍前后的)空白页,衬页

flyover /ˈflaɪəʊvə(r)/ **noun** Brit. 【英】a bridge carrying one road or railway line over another 立交桥

flysheet /ˈflaɪʃiːt/ **noun** Brit. 【英】a cover over a tent for keeping the rain out (帐篷外面的)篷顶,防雨布

flywheel /ˈflaɪwiːl/ **noun** a heavy revolving wheel in a machine that helps it to work smoothly 飞轮;惯性轮

FM /ˌef ˈem/ **abbreviation** frequency modulation 调频

foal /fəʊl/ **noun** a young horse or related animal 马(或马科动物)的幼畜;驹子 • **verb** give birth to a foal (母马)产(崽),产(驹)

foam /fəʊm/ **noun 1** a mass of small bubbles formed on the surface of liquid 泡沫 **2** a liquid substance containing many small bubbles 泡沫剂 **3** a lightweight form of rubber or plastic that is full of small holes 泡沫橡胶;泡沫塑料 • **verb** form or produce foam (使)起泡沫 ■ **foamy** adjective.

fob¹ /fɒb/ **noun 1** a chain attached to a watch for carrying in a pocket 怀表表链 **2** a tab on a key ring 钥匙环上的)小饰物

fob² **verb** (**fobs**, **fobbing**, **fobbed**) **1** (**fob someone off**) try to deceive someone into accepting excuses or something inferior 哄骗(某人)接受借口(或低劣的东西) **2** (**fob something off on**) give something inferior to 用

欺骗手段脱手(劣质品)

focaccia /fəˈkætʃə/ **noun** a type of flat Italian bread made with olive oil 弗卡切面包(用橄榄油制作的意式面包)

focal /ˈfəʊkl/ **adjective** relating to a focus 焦点的 □ **focal point 1** the point at which rays or waves of light, sound, etc. meet, or from which they seem to come 焦点;聚光点;聚波点 **2** the centre of interest or activity (兴趣或活动的)中心,焦点

fo'c's'le /ˈfəʊksl/ ⇒ 见 FORECASTLE.

focus /ˈfəʊkəs/ **noun** (plural **focuses** or **foci** /ˈfəʊsaɪ/) **1** the centre of interest or activity (兴趣或活动的)中心,焦点 **2** the state of having or producing a clear image 清晰;清楚: *His face is out of focus.* 他的脸模糊了。**3** the point at which an object must be situated for a lens or mirror to produce a clear image of it 成像清晰点 **4** a focal point 焦点;聚光点;聚波点 • **verb** (**focuses**, **focusing** or **focussing**, **focused** or **focussed**) **1** adapt to the amount of light available and become able to see clearly (逐渐适应光线亮度而)看清 **2** (**focus on**) pay particular attention to 集中注意力于 **3** adjust the focus of a telescope, camera, etc. 调节(望远镜、照相机等的)焦距 **4** (of rays or waves) meet at a single point (光束或波)聚焦 □ **focus group** a group of people brought together to give their opinions of a new product, political campaign, etc. 焦点小组(集中在一起对新产品、政治运动等发表评论的一组人)

fodder /ˈfɒdə(r)/ **noun 1** food for cattle and other livestock (牛等牲畜的)饲料,秣 **2** a person or thing viewed only as material to satisfy a particular need (人或物)只能是…的料

foe /fəʊ/ **noun** an enemy or opponent 敌人;仇敌,反对者

foetid /ˈfiːtɪd/ ⇒ 见 FETID.

foetus /ˈfiːtəs/ ⇒ 见 FETUS.

fog /fɒg/ **noun** a thick cloud of water droplets which is difficult to see through 雾 • **verb** (**fogs, fogging, fogged**) **1** become covered with steam 被雾笼罩 **2** confuse 使困惑；使迷惘

fogey /ˈfəʊgi/ **noun** (plural **fogeys** or **fogies**) a very old-fashioned or conservative person 守旧者；老保守；老顽固

foggy /ˈfɒgi/ **adjective** (**foggier, foggiest**) **1** full of fog 多雾的；雾茫茫的 **2** confused or unclear 糊涂的；不清楚的

foghorn /ˈfɒghɔːn/ **noun** a device that makes a loud, deep sound as a warning to ships in fog (向雾中的船只发警告的)雾角，雾喇叭

foible /ˈfɔɪbl/ **noun** a slight peculiarity in a person's character or habits 怪癖

foil¹ /fɔɪl/ **verb 1** prevent something from happening 挫败 **2** stop someone from doing something 阻止；制止

foil² **noun 1** metal in the form of a thin flexible sheet 箔；金属薄片 **2** a person or thing that contrasts with and so emphasizes the qualities of another 陪衬物；陪衬者

foil³ **noun** a light, blunt-edged fencing sword (击剑运动中的)花剑，轻剑

foist /fɔɪst/ **verb** (**foist someone/ thing on**) make someone accept an unwelcome person or thing 将(不受欢迎的人或物)强加于

fold¹ /fəʊld/ **verb 1** bend something over on itself so that one part of it covers another 折叠；对折 **2** be able to be folded into a flatter shape 可以折叠；可叠平 **3** clasp someone in your arms 抱；拥抱 **4** informal【非正式】(of a company) stop trading as a result of financial problems (公司)倒闭 **5** (**fold something in** or **into**) mix one ingredient gently with another 把(食品配料)调入(另一种

配料) • **noun 1** a folded part 折叠部分 **2** a line or crease produced by folding 折痕；折缝；折线

fold² **noun 1** a pen or enclosure for livestock 牲畜栏；牲畜圈 **2** (**the fold**) a group or community 群体；社群

folder /ˈfəʊldə(r)/ **noun** a folding cover or wallet for storing loose papers 文件夹；纸夹

foliage /ˈfəʊliɪdʒ/ **noun** the leaves of plants 叶；叶子

folic acid /ˈfɒlɪk/ **noun** a vitamin found especially in green vegetables, liver, and kidney 叶酸

folio /ˈfəʊliəʊ/ **noun** (plural **folios**) **1** a sheet of paper folded once to form four pages of a book 对折纸；对开纸 **2** a large-sized book made up of such sheets 对开本

folk /fəʊk/ **plural noun 1** (also **folks**) informal【非正式】people in general (泛指)人们 **2** (**your folks**) informal, chiefly N. Amer.【非正式，主北美】your family 家属；亲属 **3** (also **folk music**) traditional music whose composer is unknown, passed on through performances 民间音乐 □ **folk tale** a traditional story passed on by word of mouth 民间故事；民间传说

folklore /ˈfəʊklɔː(r)/ **noun** the traditional stories and customs of a community 民间传说；民俗

folksy /ˈfəʊksi/ **adjective** traditional and homely 传统的；朴实的

follicle /ˈfɒlɪkl/ **noun** one of the small holes in the skin that hair grows out of (皮肤上长出毛发的)小囊

follow /ˈfɒləʊ/ **verb 1** go after or move along behind 跟随；跟踪 **2** go along a route 沿着(线路)行进 **3** come after in time or order (在时间或顺序上)接在…之后，跟着 **4** be a result or consequence 是…的结果 **5** act according to advice or an instruction 按照(建议或指示)行事；遵照 **6** understand or pay attention to 领会;关注 **7** (**follow something through**) continue an action or task to its end (行动或任务)进行到底; 坚持完成 **8** (**follow something up**) pursue something further 进一步追击;继续进行 □ **follow suit** do the same as someone else 效仿(别人);照着做

follower /'fɒləʊə(r)/ **noun 1** a supporter, fan, or disciple 拥护者;追随者;崇拜者;信徒 **2** a person who follows 跟在后面的人

following /'fɒləʊɪŋ/ **preposition** coming after or as a result of 在…以后;由于 • **noun** a group of supporters 拥护者; 崇拜者 • **adjective 1** next in time or order (在时间或顺序上)接着的,其次的 **2** about to be mentioned 将提及的

folly /'fɒli/ **noun** (plural **follies**) **1** foolishness 愚笨;愚蠢 **2** a foolish act 愚蠢行为 **3** an ornamental building with no practical purpose 装饰性建筑

foment /fəʊ'ment/ **verb** stir up revolution or conflict 激起,引发(革命或冲突)

fond /fɒnd/ **adjective 1** (**fond of**) having a liking or affection for 喜欢的;喜爱的 **2** affectionate 深情的 **3** hoped for but unlikely to be fulfilled 不大可能实现的 ■ **fondly** adverb **fondness** noun.

fondant /'fɒndənt/ **noun** a thick paste made of sugar and water, used in making sweets and icing cakes 软糖料(用于制作糖果或糕饼糖霜)

fondle /'fɒndl/ **verb** (**fondles**, **fondling**, **fondled**) stroke or caress lovingly or in a sexual way 爱抚;抚弄

fondue /'fɒndju:/ **noun** a dish in which you dip small pieces of food into melted cheese or a hot sauce (将食物放入融化的乳酪或辣调料中的)涮制菜肴,乳酪火锅,辣火锅

font /fɒnt/ **noun 1** a large stone bowl in a church for the water used in baptizing people 洗礼盆;圣水盂 **2** (Brit. 【英】also **fount**) a set of printed letters of a particular size and design (某一字号、字体的)一副铅字

food /fu:d/ **noun** any substance that people or animals eat to stay alive 食物 □ **food chain** a series of creatures in which each depends on the next as a source of food 食物链 **food for thought** something that makes you think carefully about an issue 引人深思的事 **food poisoning** illness caused by food contaminated by bacteria 食物中毒

foodstuff /'fu:dstʌf/ **noun** a substance that can be eaten as food 食物;食品

fool¹ /fu:l/ **noun 1** a person who behaves in a silly or stupid way 蠢人;傻子;笨蛋 **2** historical 【历史】a jester or clown 弄臣;小丑 • **verb 1** trick or deceive 愚弄;欺骗 **2** (**fool about** or **around**) act in a joking or silly way 干傻事;出洋相 □ **fool's gold** a yellowish mineral that can be mistaken for gold 愚人金(指黄铁矿或黄铜矿') **fool's paradise** a happy state that is based on ignoring possible trouble 虚幻的幸福

fool² **noun** Brit. 【英】a cold dessert made of puréed fruit and cream or custard 奶油拌果子泥(一种甜点)

foolhardy /'fu:lhɑ:di/ **adjective** recklessly daring 有勇无谋的;鲁莽的

foolish /'fu:lɪʃ/ **adjective** silly or stupid 愚蠢的;傻的 ■ **foolishly** adverb **foolishness** noun.

foolproof /'fu:lpru:f/ **adjective** incapable of going wrong or being wrongly used 不会出毛病的;不会误用的

foolscap /'fu:lskæp/ **noun** Brit. 【英】a size of paper, about 330 × 200 (or 400) mm 大裁(一种纸的规格,约为330×200或330×400毫米)

foot /fʊt/ **noun** (plural **feet**) **1** the part of the leg below the ankle, on which

a person walks 脚;足 **2** the bottom of something vertical (垂直物体的)底座,底部 **3** the end of a bed (床的)床脚,下端 **4** a unit of length equal to 12 inches (30.48 cm) 英尺(等于12英寸,合30.48厘米) **5** a group of syllables making up a basic unit of rhythm in poetry (诗歌中的)音步
• **verb** informal 【非正式】pay a bill 支付(账单) □ **foot-and-mouth disease** a disease of cattle and sheep, causing ulcers on the hoofs and around the mouth (牛羊的)口蹄疫

footage /'fʊtɪdʒ/ **noun** a length of film made for cinema or television (电影院或电视上放映的)电影片断

football /'fʊtbɔːl/ **noun 1** a team game involving kicking a ball, in particular (in the UK) soccer or (in the US) American football (英国的)足球运动;(美国的)橄榄球运动 **2** a large inflated ball used in football 足球;橄榄球 ■ **footballer** noun.

footbridge /'fʊtbrɪdʒ/ **noun** a bridge for pedestrians 人行桥;步行桥

footfall /'fʊtfɔːl/ **noun** the sound of a footstep or footsteps 脚步声,脚步

foothill /'fʊthɪl/ **noun** a low hill at the base of a mountain 山麓小丘

foothold /'fʊthəʊld/ **noun 1** a place where you can put a foot down securely while climbing (攀登时可踩脚的)立脚处 **2** a secure position from which to make further progress 稳固的地位

footing /'fʊtɪŋ/ **noun 1** a secure grip with the feet 站稳 **2** the basis on which something is established or operates (创建或运行的)基础

footlights /'fʊtlaɪts/ **plural noun** a row of spotlights along the front of a stage at the level of the actors' feet (舞台上的)脚灯

footling /'fuːtlɪŋ/ **adjective** unimportant and irritating 无足轻重的;恼人的

footloose /'fʊtluːs/ **adjective** free to do as you please 自由自在的;行动无拘束的

footman /'fʊtmən/ **noun** (plural **footmen**) a servant who lets in visitors and serves food at the table 男仆;侍者

footnote /'fʊtnəʊt/ **noun** an additional piece of information printed at the bottom of a page (书页上的)脚注

footpad /'fʊtpæd/ **noun** (in the past) a highwayman who operated on foot (旧时)徒步的拦路强盗

footpath /'fʊtpɑːθ/ **noun** a path for people to walk along 人行小径

footprint /'fʊtprɪnt/ **noun** the mark left by a foot or shoe on the ground 脚印,足迹

footsore /'fʊtsɔː(r)/ **adjective** having sore feet from walking 脚痛的;脚酸的

footstep /'fʊtstep/ **noun** a step taken in walking 脚步

footstool /'fʊtstuːl/ **noun** a low stool for resting the feet on when sitting (坐时搁脚的)脚凳

fop /fɒp/ **noun** a man who is too concerned with his clothes and appearance 纨绔子弟;花花公子 ■ **foppish** adjective.

for /fɔː(r), fə(r)/ **preposition 1** affecting or relating to 影响…;关于 **2** in favour of 赞成 **3** on behalf of 代表 **4** because of 因为;由于 **5** so as to get, have, or do为了;以便 **6** in place of 取代;替 **7** in exchange for 换取 **8** in the direction of 往;向 **9** over a distance or during a period 经过(一段距离或时间) **10** so as to happen at 在…时
• **conjunction** literary 【文】because 因为

fora /'fɔːrə/ plural of FORUM.

forage /'fɒrɪdʒ/ **verb** (**forages**, **foraging**, **foraged**) search for food 搜寻食物 • **noun** food for horses and cattle (马和牛的)草料,饲料

foray /'fɒreɪ/ **noun 1** a sudden attack or move into enemy territory 突袭;闪

电式侵袭 **2** a brief but spirited attempt to become involved in a new activity (对新活动短暂而勇敢的)尝试

forbear¹ /fɔːˈbeə(r)/ *verb* (**forbears, forbearing, forbore**; past participle **forborne**) stop yourself from doing something 克制;自制

forbear² 见 FOREBEAR.

forbearance /fɔːˈbeərəns/ *noun* patient self-control (耐心的)克制,自制

forbearing /fɔːˈbeərɪŋ/ *adjective* patient and self-controlled 有耐心的;克制的;自制的

forbid /fəˈbɪd/ *verb* (**forbids, forbidding, forbade** or **forbad**; past participle **forbidden**) **1** refuse to allow something 不允许,禁止(某事) **2** order someone not to do something 不准,禁止(某人做某事)

forbidding /fəˈbɪdɪŋ/ *adjective* appearing unfriendly or threatening 冷峻的;令人生畏的 ■ **forbiddingly** adverb.

force /fɔːs/ *noun* **1** physical strength or energy that makes something move 力;力量 **2** violence used to obtain or achieve something 武力;暴力 **3** effect or influence 效果;影响 **4** a person or thing that has influence 有影响的人(或事物) **5** an organized group of soldiers, police, or workers (有组织的)一群人 **6** (**the forces**) Brit. 【英】the army, navy, and air force 武装力量(陆海空三军) • *verb* (**forces, forcing, forced**) **1** make someone do something against their will 强迫,逼迫(某人) **2** use physical strength to move something 用力移动(某物) **3** achieve something by making an effort 勉力获得;勉强作出: *He forced a smile.* 他勉强作笑脸。 **4** (**force something on**) impose something on 把…强加于 □ **force-feed** force someone to eat food 强使进食;强制喂养 **in force 1** in great strength or numbers 大量地;大批地

2 (of a law or rule) in effect (法律或规则)有效,在实施中

forceful /ˈfɔːsfl/ *adjective* powerful and confident 强有力的;自信的 ■ **forcefully** adverb.

forcemeat /ˈfɔːsmiːt/ *noun* chopped meat or vegetables used as a stuffing (作馅儿的)加料碎肉(或蔬菜)

forceps /ˈfɔːseps/ *plural noun* a pair of pincers used in surgery (手术用的)镊子,钳子

forcible /ˈfɔːsəbl/ *adjective* done by force 强迫的;用暴力的 ■ **forcibly** adverb.

ford /fɔːd/ *noun* a shallow place in a river or stream where it can be crossed (河或小溪中可涉水而过的)浅滩,浅水处 • *verb* cross a river or stream at a ford 涉过(浅水)

fore /fɔː(r)/ *adjective* found or placed in front 在前部的;在前的 • *noun* the front part of something 前部 • **combining form (fore-)** **1** in front 在…前 **2** in advance 先于;预先 **3** coming before 先前的: *forefather* 祖先 • **exclamation** called out as a warning to people in the path of a golf ball 前面当心(打高尔夫球时喊的警告语)

forearm¹ /ˈfɔːrɑːm/ *noun* the part of a person's arm from the elbow to the wrist or the fingertips (人的)前臂

forearm² /ˌfɔːrˈɑːm/ *verb* (**be forearmed**) be prepared in advance for danger or attack 预先准备,预先武装(以防危险或攻击)

forebear or **forbear** /ˈfɔːbeə(r)/ *noun* an ancestor 祖宗;祖先

foreboding /fɔːˈbəʊdɪŋ/ *noun* a feeling that something bad will happen (对不祥之事的)预感

forecast /ˈfɔːkɑːst/ *verb* (**forecasts, forecasting, forecast** or **forecasted**) predict what will happen in the future 预言;预测;预报 • *noun* a prediction 预言;预测;预报 ■ **forecaster** noun.

forecastle or **fo'c's'le** /ˈfəʊksl/

noun the front part of a ship below the deck 艏楼

foreclose /fɔːˈkləuz/ **verb** (**forecloses, foreclosing, foreclosed**) take possession of a property because the occupant has not kept up their mortgage payments (因按揭人未如期还贷)取消抵押品赎回权 ■ **foreclosure** noun.

forecourt /ˈfɔːkɔːt/ **noun 1** an open area in front of a large building or petrol station (大型建筑物的)前院，前庭；(加油站前的)大片空地 **2** Tennis 【网球】the part of the court between the service line and the net 前场

forefather /ˈfɔːfɑːðə(r)/ **noun** an ancestor 祖先；祖宗

forefinger /ˈfɔːfɪŋɡə(r)/ **noun** the finger next to the thumb 食指

forefoot /ˈfɔːfʊt/ **noun** (plural **forefeet**) each of the two front feet of a four-legged animal (四足动物的)前足

forefront /ˈfɔːfrʌnt/ **noun** the leading position 最重要的位置

forego¹ /fɔːˈɡəu/ ⇒ 见 FORGO.

forego² **verb** (**foregoes, foregoing, forewent**; past participle **foregone**) old use 【旧】come before in place or time 走在…之前；发生于…之前 □ **foregone conclusion** a result that can be easily predicted 可轻易料到的结果

foregoing /fɔːˈɡəuɪŋ/ **adjective** previously mentioned 前述的

foreground /ˈfɔːɡraund/ **noun 1** the part of a view or image nearest to the observer (景物或图像的)前景 **2** the most important position 最重要的地位

forehand /ˈfɔːhænd/ **noun** (in tennis and similar games) a stroke played with the palm of the hand facing in the direction of the stroke (网球及类似运动中的)正手击球，正拍

forehead /ˈfɔːhed, ˈfɒrɪd/ **noun** the part of the face above the eyebrows

额；前额

foreign /ˈfɒrən/ **adjective 1** having to do with a country or language other than your own 外国的 **2** coming from outside 外来的；来自外部的 **3** (**foreign to**) not familiar to or typical of 陌生的；非典型的 □ **foreign body** a small piece of material that has entered the body from outside (进入人体的)异物

✔ 拼写指南 -*eign*, not -*igen*: for*eign*. foreign 中的 -eign 不要拼作 -iegn.

foreigner /ˈfɒrənə(r)/ **noun 1** a person from a foreign country 外国人 **2** informal 【非正式】a stranger 陌生人；外来者

foreknowledge /fɔːˈnɒlɪdʒ/ **noun** awareness of something before it happens 预知；事先知道

foreleg /ˈfɔːleg/ **noun** either of the front legs of a four-legged animal (四足动物的)前腿，前足

forelock /ˈfɔːlɒk/ **noun** a lock of hair growing just above the forehead 额发；前发

foreman /ˈfɔːmən/ **noun** (plural **foremen**) **1** a worker who supervises other workers 工头；领班 **2** (in a law court) a person who is head of a jury (法庭上的)陪审团团长

foremast /ˈfɔːmɑːst/ **noun** the mast of a ship nearest the bow 前桅

foremost /ˈfɔːməust/ **adjective** highest in rank, importance, or position 首要的；最重要的；最前的 • **adverb** in the first place 在最前；首先

forename /ˈfɔːneɪm/ **noun** a person's first name 名字；教名

forensic /fəˈrensɪk/ **adjective 1** having to do with the use of scientific methods in investigating crime 法医的 **2** having to do with courts of law 法庭的

foreplay /ˈfɔːpleɪ/ **noun** activities such as kissing and touching that people may engage in before having sex (性交前的)前戏

forerunner /ˈfɔːrʌnə(r)/ **noun** a person or thing which exists before another comes or is developed 前驱；先驱；先行者；先导

foresee /fɔːˈsiː/ **verb** (**foresees, foreseeing, foresaw**; past participle **foreseen**) be aware of something before it happens; predict 预见；预知 ■ **foreseeable** adjective.

foreshadow /fɔːˈʃædəʊ/ **verb** be a warning or indication of a future event 预示；是…的预兆

foreshore /ˈfɔːʃɔː(r)/ **noun** the part of a shore between the highest and lowest levels reached by the sea (高潮线和低潮线之间的)前滩，滩头

foreshorten /fɔːˈʃɔːtn/ **verb 1** portray something as being closer or shallower than it really is 将…按透视法缩短(或缩小) **2** end something before the usual or intended time (时间上)提前结束

foresight /ˈfɔːsaɪt/ **noun** the ability to predict future events and needs 预见；先见之明

foreskin /ˈfɔːskɪn/ **noun** the roll of skin covering the end of the penis 包皮

forest /ˈfɒrɪst/ **noun 1** a large area covered thickly with trees and plants 林区；森林 **2** a large number of tangled or upright objects 林立之物 ■ **forested** adjective.

forestall /fɔːˈstɔːl/ **verb** prevent or delay something by taking action in advance 预先阻止(或推迟)

forestry /ˈfɒrɪstri/ **noun** the science or practice of planting and taking care of forests 林学；林业 ■ **forester** noun.

foretaste /ˈfɔːteɪst/ **noun** a sample of something that is to come 预示；征象

foretell /fɔːˈtel/ **verb** (**foretells, foretelling, foretold**) predict 预言；预测

forethought /ˈfɔːθɔːt/ **noun** careful consideration of what will be necessary or may happen in the future 事先的考虑；事先的筹划

forever /fərˈevə(r)/ **adverb 1** (also **for ever**) for all future time 永远 **2** a very long time 长久地 **3** continually 老是；不断地

forewarn /fɔːˈwɔːn/ **verb** warn in advance 预先警告；预先告诫

forewent /fɔːˈwent/ past of FOREGO[1], FOREGO[2].

foreword /ˈfɔːwɜːd/ **noun** a short introduction to a book (书的)前言，序言

forfeit /ˈfɔːfɪt/ **verb** (**forfeits, forfeiting, forfeited**) lose property or a right as a punishment for doing wrong (因犯错)丧失，失去(财产或权利) • **noun** a punishment for doing wrong (因犯错而得到的)惩罚

forge[1] **verb** (**forges, forging, forged**) **1** shape a metal object by heating and hammering it 锻造 **2** create something through effort 创造；创建 **3** produce a copy of a banknote, signature, etc. to deceive people 伪造(钞票、签名等) • **noun 1** a blacksmith's workshop 铁匠铺 **2** a furnace for melting or refining metal 锻造炉 ■ **forger** noun **forgery** noun.

forge[2] **verb** (**forges, forging, forged**) **1** move forward gradually or steadily 缓缓向前；稳步前进 **2** (**forge ahead**) make progress 取得进展

forget /fəˈget/ **verb** (**forgets, forgetting, forgot**; past participle **forgotten** or chiefly US【主美】**forgot**) **1** be unable to remember 忘；忘记 **2** fail to remember to do something 忘记做 **3** stop thinking of 不再想；不再把…放在心上 **4** (**forget yourself**) behave in an inappropriate or unacceptable way 行为举止失检 □ **forget-me-not** a plant with light blue flowers 勿忘我，勿忘草(开淡蓝色花) ■ **forgettable** adjective.

forgetful /fə'getfl/ **adjective** tending to forget things 健忘的 ■ **forgetfully** adverb.

forgive /fə'gɪv/ **verb** (**forgives**, **forgiving**, **forgave**; past participle **forgiven**) **1** stop feeling angry or resentful towards a person who has done something hurtful or wrong 宽恕，饶恕(某人) **2** excuse an offence or mistake 原谅(冒犯或错误) ■ **forgivable** adjective.

forgiveness /fə'gɪvnəs/ **noun** the action of forgiving, or the state of being forgiven (被)原谅；(被)宽恕

forgo or **forego** /fɔː'gəʊ/ **verb** (**forgoes**, **forgoing**, **forwent**; past participle **forgone**) go without something that you want 放弃，抛弃(想要之物)

fork /fɔːk/ **noun 1** an object with two or more prongs used for lifting or holding food 餐叉 **2** a similar-shaped farm or garden tool used for digging or lifting 叉；耙 **3** the point where a road, river, etc. divides into two parts (路的)岔口；(河流的)分流处 **4** either of two such parts 岔路；支流 • **verb 1** divide into two parts 分岔 **2** take one route or the other at a fork 在岔路口拐弯 **3** dig or lift with a fork (用叉、耙)挖，起 **4** (**fork something out**) informal 【非正式】pay money 为…付钱

forked /fɔːkt/ **adjective 1** having a divided or fork-shaped end 叉状的；有叉的；分岔的 **2** in the shape of a zigzag 之字形的

forklift truck /'fɔːklɪft/ **noun** a vehicle with a device on the front for lifting and carrying heavy loads 铲车；叉车

forlorn /fə'lɔːn/ **adjective 1** pitifully sad and lonely 愁苦的；孤苦伶仃的 **2** unlikely to succeed or be fulfilled 不大可能成功的；难以实现的: *a forlorn hope* 几乎无法实现的愿望 ■ **forlornly** adverb.

form /fɔːm/ **noun 1** the shape or arrangement of something 形状；外形；轮廓 **2** a particular way in which a thing exists (事物的)存在形式，形态 **3** a type 种类；类型 **4** a printed document with blank spaces for information to be filled in 表格 **5** the current standard of play of a sports player or team (运动员或运动队的)竞技状态 **6** a person's mood and state of health 情绪；健康状况 **7** the way something is usually done 惯例；常规 **8** Brit. 【英】a class or year in a school 年级 • **verb 1** create something by shaping material or bringing together parts 制作 **2** go to make up 构成 **3** establish or develop 建立；形成 ■ **formless** adjective.

formal /'fɔːml/ **adjective 1** suitable for or referring to official or important occasions 正式的；官方的 **2** officially recognized 经官方认可的 **3** arranged in a regular way, according to an exact plan 整齐的；布置井然的；有条理的 ■ **formally** adverb.

formaldehyde /fɔː'mældɪhaɪd/ **noun** a strong-smelling gas mixed with water and used as a preservative and disinfectant 甲醛(有强烈气味的气体，可溶于水中作防腐剂和消毒剂)

formalin /'fɔːməlɪn/ **noun** a solution of formaldehyde in water 甲醛溶液；福尔马林

formality /fɔː'mæləti/ **noun** (plural **formalities**) **1** a thing done to follow rules or usual customs 手续；俗套 **2** correct and formal behaviour 遵守礼节 **3** (**a formality**) a thing done or happening as a matter of course 例行公事

formalize or **formalise** /'fɔːməlaɪz/ **verb** (**formalizes**, **formalizing**, **formalized**) make an arrangement official 使正式

format /'fɔːmæt/ **noun 1** the way in which something is arranged or presented (安排或呈现的)方式，样式 **2** the shape, size, and presentation of a book, document, etc. (书、文件等的)形状,开本,版式 • verb (**formats**, **formatting**, **formatted**) give something a particular format 为…安排版式;为…编排格式

formation /fɔːˈmeɪʃn/ noun **1** the action of forming 形成;组成 **2** something that has been formed 形成物;组成物 **3** a particular structure or arrangement 结构;排列

formative /ˈfɔːmətɪv/ adjective having a strong influence in the way something is formed (对…的形成)有重大影响的

former¹ /ˈfɔːmə(r)/ adjective **1** having been previously 前任的;一度的: *her former boyfriend* 她的前男友 **2** in the past 以前的;先前的;旧时的 **3** (**the former**) referring to the first of two things mentioned (两者中)前面的,前者的

former² noun **1** a person or thing that forms something 起形成作用的人(或事物) **2** Brit. 【英】 a person in a particular school year 某一年级的学生

formerly /ˈfɔːməli/ adverb in the past 以前;从前

Formica /fɔːˈmaɪkə/ noun trademark 【商标】 a hard plastic material used for worktops, cupboard doors, etc. 福米加(用作贴面板的硬塑料)

formic acid /ˈfɔːmɪk/ noun an acid present in the fluid produced by some ants 甲酸;蚁酸

formidable /ˈfɔːmɪdəbl/ adjective frightening or intimidating through being very large, powerful, or capable 可怕的;令人敬畏的 ■ **formidably** adverb.

formula /ˈfɔːmjələ/ noun (plural **formulae** /ˈfɔːmjəliː/ or **formulas**) **1** a mathematical relationship or rule expressed in symbols (数学)公式,方程式 **2** a set of chemical symbols showing what elements are present in a compound (化学)分子式 **3** a

method for achieving something 方案;方法 **4** a fixed form of words used in particular situations (特定场合的)惯用语,套话 **5** a list of ingredients with which something is made 配方;处方 **6** a powder-based milky drink for babies (婴儿饮用的)配方奶

formulaic /ˌfɔːmjuˈleɪɪk/ adjective **1** containing a set form of words 含有固定套话的 **2** made by closely following a rule or style 公式化的

formulate /ˈfɔːmjuleɪt/ verb (**formulates**, **formulating**, **formulated**) **1** create or prepare something methodically (条理清楚地)制作,准备,规划 **2** express an idea clearly and briefly (清楚简要地)表达(想法) ■ **formulation** noun.

fornicate /ˈfɔːnɪkeɪt/ verb (**fornicates**, **fornicating**, **fornicated**) formal 【正式】 have sex with someone you are not married to (与某人)私通,通奸 ■ **fornication** noun **fornicator** noun.

forsake /fəˈseɪk/ verb (**forsakes**, **forsaking**, **forsook**; past participle **forsaken**) literary 【文】 **1** abandon 遗弃;抛弃 **2** give up 放弃;摒弃

forsooth /fəˈsuːθ/ adverb old use 【旧】 indeed 真正地;确实

forswear /fɔːˈsweə(r)/ verb (**forswears**, **forswearing**, **forswore**; past participle **forsworn**) formal 【正式】 agree to give up or do without 同意放弃(或抛弃)

forsythia /fɔːˈsaɪθɪə/ noun a shrub with bright yellow flowers 连翘,金钟花(开鲜亮黄花)

fort /fɔːt/ noun a building constructed to defend a place against attack 堡垒,城堡;碉堡 □ **hold the fort** be responsible for something while a person is away 临时代为负责

forte /ˈfɔːteɪ/ noun a thing for which someone has a particular talent 特长;专长

forth /fɔːθ/ adverb old use 【旧】 **1**

forwards or into view 向前；露出着 **2** onwards in time 以后

forthcoming /fɔːˈθkʌmɪŋ/ **adjective 1** about to happen or appear 即将发生的；即将出现的 **2** made available when required 随要随有的；(需要时)现成的 **3** willing to reveal information 乐于提供信息的

forthright /ˈfɔːθraɪt/ **adjective** direct and outspoken 直率的；直截了当的

forthwith /ˌfɔːθˈwɪθ/ **adverb** without delay 立即；毫不拖延地

fortify /ˈfɔːtɪfaɪ/ **verb** (fortifies, fortifying, fortified) **1** strengthen a place to protect it against attack 筑防御工事于；设防于 **2** give strength or energy to 激励；鼓舞 **3** add alcohol or vitamins to food or drink (加入酒精或维生素)提高(食物或饮料)的营养价值 ■ **fortification** noun.

fortissimo /fɔːˈtɪsɪməʊ/ **adverb & adjective** Music【音乐】very loud or loudly 非常响地(的)；极强地(的)

fortitude /ˈfɔːtɪtjuːd/ **noun** courage and strength when facing pain or trouble 坚忍；刚毅

fortnight /ˈfɔːtnaɪt/ **noun** Brit.【英】a period of two weeks 两星期；两周

fortnightly /ˈfɔːtnaɪtli/ Brit.【英】 **adjective & adverb** happening or produced every two weeks 两星期一次的(地)；每两周的(地)

fortress /ˈfɔːtrəs/ **noun** a building or town which has been strengthened against attack 要塞；堡垒

fortuitous /fɔːˈtjuːɪtəs/ **adjective 1** happening by chance 偶然(发生)的 **2** lucky 幸运的；吉祥的 ■ **fortuitously** adverb.

fortunate /ˈfɔːtʃənət/ **adjective 1** involving good luck 幸运的；交好运的 **2** advantageous or favourable 有利的；吉利的 ■ **fortunately** adverb.

fortune /ˈfɔːtʃuːn/ **noun 1** chance or luck as it affects human affairs (影响人生的)机会，运气 **2** (fortunes)

the success or failure of a person or undertaking (人或事业的)际遇，命运 **3** a large amount of money or property 大笔钱；大量财产

forty /ˈfɔːti/ **cardinal number** (plural **forties**) ten less than fifty; 40 四十 (Roman numeral 罗马数字：**xl** or **XL**.) □ **forty winks** informal【非正式】a short daytime sleep 打盹；小睡 ■ **fortieth** ordinal number.

✔ 拼写指南 for-, not four-: forty. forty 中的 for- 不要拼作 four-。

forum /ˈfɔːrəm/ **noun** (plural **forums**) **1** a meeting or opportunity for exchanging views 论坛；讨论机会 **2** (plural **fora**) (in ancient Roman cities) a square or marketplace used for public business (古罗马城市的)公共广场(或市场)

forward /ˈfɔːwəd/ **adverb & adjective 1** in the direction that you are facing or travelling 向前的；朝前的 **2** towards a successful end 前进的 **3** ahead in time 向将来的；往后的 **4** in or near the front of a ship or aircraft 在(或靠近)船头的；在(或靠近)机首的 • **adjective** behaving in a way that is too confident or friendly 鲁莽的；冒失的；无礼的 • **noun** an attacking player in sport (体育比赛中的)前锋 • **verb** send a letter, especially on to a further destination 转寄，转交(信件) ■ **forwards** adverb.

forwent /fɔːˈwent/ past of FORGO.

fossil /ˈfɒsl/ **noun** the remains of a prehistoric plant or animal that have become hardened into rock 化石 □ **fossil fuel** a fuel such as coal or gas that is formed from the remains of animals and plants 矿物燃料

fossilize or **fossilise** /ˈfɒsəlaɪz/ **verb** (fossilizes, fossilizing, fossilized) preserve an animal or plant so that it becomes a fossil 使(动植物)成化石；使石化 ■ **fossiliza-**

tion noun.

foster /'fɒstə(r)/ *verb* (fosters, fostering, fostered) **1** encourage the development of 促进;鼓励;助长 **2** bring up a child that is not your own by birth 养育,抚育(非亲生子女)

fought /fɔːt/ past and past participle of FIGHT.

foul /faʊl/ *adjective* **1** having a disgusting smell or taste 难闻的;恶臭的 **2** very unpleasant 很令人不快的;极讨厌的 **3** wicked or obscene 邪恶的;下流的;猥亵的 **4** polluted 被污染的 • *noun* (in sport) a piece of play that is not allowed by the rules (体育比赛中的)犯规 • *verb* **1** make foul or dirty 弄脏;弄污;污染 **2** (in sport) commit a foul against (体育比赛中)犯规 **3** (foul something up) make a mistake with something 把…搞糟 **4** make a cable or anchor become entangled or jammed 使(缆绳或锚)缠结;使壅塞 ▪ **foul-mouthed** using bad language 出言不逊的;口出恶言的 **foul play 1** unfair play in sport (体育比赛中的)犯规行为 **2** criminal or violent activity 犯罪活动;暴力行为 ▪ **foully** *adverb*.

found[1] /faʊnd/ past and past participle of FIND.

found[2] *verb* **1** establish an institution or organization 建立,创建(机构或组织) **2** (be founded on) be based on a particular concept 基于(某种观念)

found[3] *verb* melt and mould metal to make an object 熔铸;铸造

foundation /faʊn'deɪʃn/ *noun* **1** the lowest part of a building, which supports the weight 地基;地脚 **2** an underlying basis or reason 基础;原因 **3** an institution or organization 机构 **4** the action of founding something 建立;创建 **5** a cream or powder applied to the face as a base for other make-up 粉底(霜)

founder[1] /'faʊndə(r)/ *noun* a person who founds an institution or

settlement 奠基人;创建者;缔造者

founder[2] *verb* (founders, foundering, foundered) **1** (of a plan or undertaking) fail; come to nothing (计划)失败;(企业)倒闭 **2** (of a ship) fill with water and sink (船)进水沉没

foundling /'faʊndlɪŋ/ *noun* a child that has been abandoned by its parents and is discovered and cared for by other people 弃婴;弃儿

foundry /'faʊndri/ *noun* (plural foundries) a workshop or factory for casting metal 铸造车间;铸造厂

fount /faʊnt/ *noun* **1** a source of a desirable quality 源;源头 **2** literary【文】a spring or fountain 泉;源泉 **3** ⇒ 见 FONT.

fountain /'faʊntən/ *noun* **1** a decorative structure in a pool or lake from which a jet of water is pumped into the air (装饰性)喷泉 **2** literary【文】a natural spring of water (天然)喷泉 ▪ **fountain pen** a pen with a container from which ink flows to the nib 自来水笔

fountainhead /'faʊntənhed/ *noun* an original source of something 源头;来源;根源

four /fɔː(r)/ *cardinal number* **1** one more than three; 4 四 (Roman numeral 罗马数字: **iv** or **IV**.) **2** Cricket【板球】a hit that reaches the boundary after first hitting the ground, scoring four runs 得四分的一击 □ **four-poster bed** a bed with a post at each corner holding up a canopy 有四根帷柱的床 **four-square** having a square shape and solid appearance 方形坚固的;方方正正的

foursome /'fɔːsəm/ *noun* a group of four people 四人组

fourteen /ˌfɔː'tiːn/ *cardinal number* one more than thirteen; 14 十四 (Roman numeral 罗马数字: **xiv** or **XIV**.) ▪ **fourteenth** *ordinal number*.

fourth /fɔːθ/ *ordinal number* **1** number four in a sequence; 4th 第四

2 (a fourth or **one fourth)** a quarter 四分之一 ■ **fourthly** adverb.

fowl /faʊl/ **noun** (plural **fowl** or **fowls**) **1** a bird kept for its eggs or meat, such as a chicken or turkey 家禽 **2** birds as a group (总称)鸟

fox /fɒks/ **noun** an animal with a pointed muzzle, bushy tail, and a reddish coat 狐;狐狸 • **verb** informal 【非正式】 baffle or deceive 使迷惑; 欺骗

foxglove /'fɒksɡlʌv/ **noun** a tall plant with spikes of flowers shaped like the fingers of gloves 毛地黄(一种高大植物,所开花形似五指手套上的指套)

foxhole /'fɒkshəʊl/ **noun** a hole in the ground used by troops as a shelter against the enemy or as a place to fire from 散兵坑(用于躲避敌方炮火或用作射击点)

foxhound /'fɒkshaʊnd/ **noun** a breed of dog trained to hunt foxes in packs 猎狐犬

foxtrot /'fɒkstrɒt/ **noun** a ballroom dance which involves switching between slow and quick steps 狐步舞

foxy /'fɒksi/ **adjective** (**foxier**, **foxiest**) **1** like a fox 似狐的 **2** crafty or sly 狡猾的;诡计多端的

foyer /'fɔɪeɪ/ **noun** a large entrance hall in a hotel or theatre (旅馆或剧院的)门厅

fracas /'fræka:/ **noun** (plural **fracas** /'fræka:z/) a noisy disturbance or quarrel 喧闹的骚乱;高声争吵

fraction /'frækʃn/ **noun 1** a number that is not a whole number (e.g. 1/2, 0.5) 分数;小数 **2** a very small part or amount 小部分;些微

fractional /'frækʃənl/ **adjective 1** having to do with a fraction 分数的; 小数的 **2** very small in amount 少量的;不足道的 ■ **fractionally** adverb.

fractious /'frækʃəs/ **adjective 1** bad-tempered 暴躁的;易怒的 **2** difficult

to control 难控制的;难驾驭的

fracture /'fræktʃə(r)/ **noun 1** a crack or break 裂缝;断裂 **2** the cracking or breaking of a hard object or material 破裂;断裂;折断 • **verb** (**fractures**, **fracturing**, **fractured**) **1** crack or break 破裂; 断裂;折断 **2** (of a group) break up (团体)解散

fragile /'frædʒaɪl/ **adjective 1** easily broken or damaged 易碎的;脆的; 易损坏的 **2** (of a person) delicate and vulnerable (人)脆弱的,虚弱的 ■ **fragility** noun.

fragment noun /'fræɡmənt/ a small part that has broken off or come from something larger 碎片;片断 • **verb** /fræɡ'ment/ break into fragments 打碎;打破;分裂 ■ **fragmentary** adjective **fragmentation** noun.

fragrance /'freɪɡrəns/ **noun 1** a pleasant, sweet smell 芳香;香味;香气 **2** a perfume or aftershave 香水; 剃须后的润肤香水

fragrant /'freɪɡrənt/ **adjective** having a pleasant, sweet smell 香的;芬芳的

frail /freɪl/ **adjective 1** weak and delicate 虚弱的;脆弱的 **2** easily damaged or broken 易损坏的;不坚实的

frailty /'freɪlti/ **noun** (plural **frailties**) the condition of being frail; weakness 脆弱;虚弱

frame /freɪm/ **noun 1** a rigid structure surrounding a picture, door, etc. or giving support to a building or vehicle. (画、门等的)框架,边框; (建筑)的构架;(车辆的)车架 **2** the structure of a person's body (人的)体形,体格 **3** a single picture in a series forming a cinema or video film (电影或录像中的)镜头,画面 **4** a single game of snooker (斯诺克台球的)一局 • **verb** (**frames**, **framing**, **framed**) **1** put a picture in a frame 把(画)装入框内 **2** create or develop a plan or system 制定,开发(计划或体系) **3** informal 【非正式】 produce false evidence against someone to make them appear guilty of a crime (作伪证)诬陷(无辜者) □ **frame of mind** a particular mood 心态;心绪

framework /ˈfreɪmwɜːk/ noun a supporting or underlying structure 构架;体系;结构

franc /fræŋk/ noun the basic unit of money of Switzerland and some other countries, and formerly also of France, Belgium, and Luxembourg 法郎(瑞士等国家的基本货币单位,也曾是法国、比利时和卢森堡的基本货币单位)

franchise /ˈfræntʃaɪz/ noun 1 a licence allowing a person or company to use or sell certain products 特许经销权;特别经营权 2 a business that has been given a franchise 获特许权的公司 3 the right to vote in elections 选举权

frank¹ /fræŋk/ adjective 1 honest and direct 真诚的;坦白的 2 open or undisguised 公开的;不加掩饰的 ■ **frankly** adverb **frankness** noun.

frank² /fræŋk/ verb stamp a mark on a letter or parcel to indicate that postage has been paid or does not need to be paid (在信件或包裹上)盖邮资已付印记,盖免付邮资印记

frankfurter /ˈfræŋkfɜːtə(r)/ noun a seasoned smoked sausage made of beef and pork 法兰克福熏肠

frankincense /ˈfræŋkɪnsens/ noun a kind of sweet-smelling gum that is burnt as incense 乳香(从非洲一种树木中提取的芳香物质,可作香燃烧)

frantic /ˈfræntɪk/ adjective 1 agitated because of fear, anxiety, etc. (因恐惧、焦虑等)发狂的 2 done in a hurried and chaotic way 紧张纷乱的;手忙脚乱的 ■ **frantically** adverb.

fraternal /frəˈtɜːnl/ adjective 1 brotherly 兄弟般的 2 having to do with a fraternity 兄弟会的

fraternity /frəˈtɜːnəti/ noun (plural **fraternities**) 1 a group of people sharing a common profession or interests (有相同职业或兴趣爱好的)一群人,同人 2 N. Amer. 【北美】a male students' society in a university or college (大学或学院的)男大学生联谊会 3 friendship and support within a group 友爱;博爱;兄弟般的友谊

fraternize or **fraternise** /ˈfrætənaɪz/ verb (**fraternizes, fraternizing, fraternized**) be on friendly terms 友善;亲如兄弟 ■ **fraternization** noun.

fratricide /ˈfrætrɪsaɪd/ noun 1 the killing by someone of their brother or sister 杀兄弟(或姐妹)行为 2 the accidental killing of your own forces in war (战争中)误杀自己人

fraud /frɔːd/ noun 1 the crime of deceiving someone in order to get money or goods 欺诈罪;诈骗罪 2 a person who deceives other people by claiming to be something they are not 骗子

fraudster /ˈfrɔːdstə(r)/ noun a person who commits fraud 诈骗者

fraudulent /ˈfrɔːdjələnt/ adjective 1 involving fraud 诈骗的;骗人的 2 deceitful or dishonest 欺骗性的;不诚实的 ■ **fraudulently** adverb.

fraught /frɔːt/ adjective 1 (**fraught with**) filled with something undesirable 充满(不合意之事)的 2 causing or feeling anxiety or stress (使人)焦虑的;(使人)忧虑的

fray¹ /freɪ/ verb 1 (of a fabric or rope) unravel or become worn at the edge (织物或绳索)磨散,磨损 2 (of a person's nerves or temper) show the effects of strain (人的情绪或脾气)烦躁起来

fray² /freɪ/ noun (**the fray**) 1 a battle or fight 战斗;打架 2 a very competitive situation 竞争激烈的情况

frazzle /ˈfræzl/ noun (**a frazzle**) informal 【非正式】1 an exhausted state 疲惫 2 a charred or burnt state 烧焦 ■ **frazzled** adjective.

freak /friːk/ **noun 1** informal 【非正式】 a person who is obsessed with a particular interest 狂热爱好者: *a fitness freak* 狂热的健身爱好者 **2** a very unusual and unexpected event 不寻常的事;出乎意料的事 **3** a person, animal, or plant with a physical abnormality 畸形(可指人、动物或植物) ▪ **verb** (**freak out**) informal 【非正式】 behave in a wild, excited, or shocked way 躁动不安;发狂 ▪ **freakish** adjective **freaky** adjective.

freckle /frekl/ **noun** a small light brown spot on the skin 雀斑 ▪ **freckled** adjective **freckly** adjective.

free /friː/ **adjective** (**freer, freest**) **1** not under the control of someone else 不受约束的;自由的;随心所欲的 **2** not confined, obstructed, or fixed 不受限制的;不受阻碍的;未固定的 **3** not being used 未使用的;空着的 **4** (**free of** or **from**) not affected by 不受…影响的 **5** given or available without charge 免费的;不收费的 **6** (**free with**) giving something generously 慷慨的 ▪ **adverb** without cost or payment 免费地;无偿地 ▪ **verb** (**frees, freeing, freed**) make free 使自由;解放 □ **free enterprise** a system in which private businesses compete with each other 自由企业制 **free fall** unrestricted downward movement under the force of gravity 自由下落 **free-for-all** a disorganized situation in which everyone may take part 自由放任 **free-form** not in a regular or formal structure 结构不规则的 **a free hand** freedom to do exactly what you want 放手干的自由 **free house** Brit.【英】 a pub not controlled by a brewery (不受某酒厂控制的)酒馆,酒吧 **free kick** (in soccer and rugby) an unopposed kick of the ball awarded when the opposition have broken the rules (足球和橄榄球运动中的)任意球 **the free market** a system in which prices are determined by unrestricted competition between privately owned businesses 自由市场 **free-range** referring to farming in which animals are kept in natural conditions where they can move around freely (牲畜)自由放养的 **free-standing** not supported by another structure 独立(式)的;非附属的 **free trade** unrestricted international trade without taxes or regulations on imports and exports 自由贸易 **free will** the power to act according to your own wishes 自由意志 **free verse** poetry that does not rhyme or have a regular rhythm (不押韵或无固定格律的)自由诗 ▪ **freely** adverb.

freebie /friːbi/ **noun** informal 【非正式】 a thing given free of charge 免费物

freedom /friːdəm/ **noun 1** the right to act or speak freely 自主权 **2** the state of not being a prisoner or slave 自由(状态) **3** (**freedom from**) not being affected by something undesirable 不受(讨厌之事)影响的 **4** unrestricted use of something 自由使用权 **5** Brit.【英】 a special honour given to someone by a city (某城市授予某人的)荣誉自由权

freehand /friːhænd/ **adjective & adverb** drawn by hand without a ruler or other aid 徒手画的;不用仪器画的

freehold /friːhəʊld/ **noun** permanent ownership of land or property with the freedom to sell it whenever you wants (不动产的)自由保有,终身保有,完全保有 ▪ **freeholder** noun.

freelance /friːlɑːns/ **adjective** self-employed and working for different companies on particular assignments 自由职业(者)的 ▪ **noun** (also **freelancer**) a freelance worker 自由职业者 ▪ **verb** (**freelances, freelancing, freelanced**) work as a freelance 做自由职业者

freeloader /friːləʊdə(r)/ **noun** informal

【非正式】 a person who takes advantage of other people's generosity 占便宜的人

freeman /'fri:mən/ **noun** (plural **freemen**) **1** Brit. 【英】a person who has been given the freedom of a city 荣誉市民 **2** historical 【历史】a person who was not a slave or serf 自由民

Freemason /'fri:meɪsn/ **noun** a member of an organization whose members help each other and hold secret ceremonies 共济会成员 ■ **Freemasonry** noun.

freesia /'fri:ʒə/ **noun** a plant with sweet-smelling, colourful flowers 小苍兰(花有香味, 颜色多样)

freestyle /'fri:staɪl/ **adjective** (of a contest or sport) having few restrictions on the technique that competitors use (竞赛或体育项目)自由式的

freethinker /ˌfri:'θɪŋkə(r)/ **noun** a person who questions or rejects accepted opinions 自由思想者

freeway /'fri:weɪ/ **noun** N. Amer. 【北美】a dual-carriageway main road (车道为复式车行道的)高速公路, 高速干道

freewheel /ˌfri:'wi:l/ **verb** ride a bicycle without using the pedals (骑自行车时不踩脚蹬)靠惯性滑行

freeze /fri:z/ **verb** (**freezes**, **freezing**, **froze**; past participle **frozen**) **1** (of a liquid) turn into a solid as a result of extreme cold (液体)冻结, 结冰, 凝固 **2** become blocked or rigid with ice 被冰堵塞; 冻僵 **3** be very cold 极冷 **4** preserve something by storing it at a very low temperature 冷藏; 冷冻贮藏 **5** suddenly become motionless with fear, shock, etc. (因恐惧、震惊等)呆住 **6** (of a computer screen) suddenly become locked (计算机屏幕)定格; 卡住 **7** keep or hold at a fixed level 固定; 稳定 • **noun 1** an act of freezing 结冰 **2** a period of very cold

weather 冰冻期; 严寒期 □ **freeze-dry** preserve something by rapidly freezing it and then drying it in a vacuum 冷冻干燥保存 **freeze-frame** the stopping of a film or videotape to obtain a single still image (电影或录像带的)定格, 定帧

freezer /'fri:zə(r)/ **noun** a refrigerated cabinet or room for preserving food at very low temperatures 冷冻柜; 冰柜; 冷冻室

freezing /'fri:zɪŋ/ **adjective 1** having a temperature below 0°C 冰冻的; 冰点以下的 **2** very cold 极冷的

freight /freɪt/ **noun** goods transported by truck, train, ship, or aircraft (以卡车、火车、船只或飞机运送的)货物 • **verb** transport goods by truck, train, etc. 运送(货物)

freighter /'freɪtə(r)/ **noun** a large ship or aircraft designed to carry freight 货船; 运输机

French /frentʃ/ **adjective** having to do with France or its language 法国的; 法语的 • **noun** the language of France, also used in parts of Belgium, Switzerland, Canada, etc. 法语 □ **French dressing** a salad dressing of vinegar, oil, and seasonings (由醋、油和香料制成的)法式色拉调料 **French fries** chiefly N. Amer. 【主北美】chips 炸薯条 **French horn** a brass instrument with a coiled tube and a wide opening at the end 法国号; 圆号 **French kiss** a kiss with contact between tongues (舌头接触的)法式接吻 **French polish** a kind of polish used on wood to give it a very glossy finish 罩光漆 **French windows** glazed doors in an outside wall 落地窗

frenetic /frə'netɪk/ **adjective** fast and energetic in a rather wild and uncontrolled way 发狂似的; 疯狂的 ■ **frenetically** adverb.

frenzy /'frenzi/ **noun** (plural **frenzies**) a state of uncontrolled excitement or wild behaviour 极度激动；疯狂；狂乱 ■ **frenzied** adjective **frenziedly** adverb.

frequency /'fri:kwənsi/ noun (plural **frequencies**) **1** the rate at which something happens 发生率；出现率；重复率 **2** the state of being frequent 频繁 **3** the number of cycles per second of a sound, light, or radio wave (声波、光波或无线电波的)频率，周率 **4** the particular waveband at which radio signals are transmitted (无线电信号传输的)频率

frequent adjective /'fri:kwənt/ **1** happening or done many times at short intervals 时常发生的 **2** doing something often 经常的，惯常的 • verb /fri'kwent/ visit a place often 常到，常去(某地) ■ **frequently** adverb.

fresco /'freskəʊ/ noun (plural **frescoes** or **frescos**) a painting that is done on wet plaster on a wall or ceiling 湿壁画

fresh /freʃ/ adjective **1** new or different 新的；不同的 **2** (of food) recently made or obtained (食物)新做的，新鲜的 **3** recently created and not faded 新制的；未凋谢的 **4** pleasantly clean and cool 清新的；清爽的：*fresh air* 清新的空气 **5** (of the wind) cool and fairly strong (风)冷而强劲的 **6** (of water) not salty (水)淡的 **7** full of energy 精神饱满的；精力充沛的 **8** informal 【非正式】too familiar with someone 过分随便的；放肆的 ■ **freshly** adverb **freshness** noun.

freshen /'freʃn/ verb **1** make or become fresh 使新鲜；变新鲜；使精神饱满 **2** (**freshen up**) wash and tidy yourself 洗浴后精神振作

fresher /'freʃə(r)/ noun Brit. 【英】a first-year student at college or university 大学一年级新生

freshman /'freʃmən/ noun (plural

freshmen) a first-year student at university or (N. Amer. 【北美】) at high school 大学一年级新生；(北美)中学一年级新生

fret¹ /fret/ verb (**frets, fretting, fretted**) be anxious and restless 焦虑；烦躁

fret² noun each of the ridges on the neck of guitars and similar instruments (吉他等乐器指板上定音的)品

fretful /'fretfl/ adjective anxious and restless 苦恼的；烦躁的 ■ **fretfully** adverb.

fretwork /'fretwɜːk/ noun decorative designs cut into in wood 凹纹饰

friable /'fraɪəbl/ adjective easily crumbled 易碎的；脆的

friar /'fraɪə(r)/ noun a member of certain religious orders of men 托钵修会修士

friary /'fraɪəri/ noun (plural **friaries**) a building or community occupied by friars 托钵修院；托钵修会

fricassée /'frɪkəseɪ, -'si:/ noun a dish of stewed or fried pieces of meat served in a thick white sauce 原汁煨(或炸)肉块

friction /'frɪkʃn/ noun **1** the resistance that one surface or object encounters when moving over another 摩擦力 **2** the action of one surface or object rubbing against another 摩擦 **3** conflict or disagreement 不和；分歧

Friday /'fraɪdeɪ, -di/ noun the day of the week before Saturday and following Thursday 星期五；周五

fridge /frɪdʒ/ noun an appliance in which food and drink are stored at a low temperature 冰箱

fried /fraɪd/ past and past participle of FRY¹.

friend /frend/ noun **1** a person that you know well and like 友人；朋友；2 a supporter of a cause or organization (事业或组织的)支持者 **3** (**Friend**) a Quaker 公谊会教友 ■ **friendless**

adjective **friendship** noun.

✔ 拼写指南 -ie-, not -ei-: friend. friend 中 -ie- 不要拼作 -ei。

friendly /'frendli/ adjective (friendlier, friendliest) **1** treating someone as a friend; on good terms 朋友般的；和睦的 **2** kind and pleasant 友善的；友好的 **3** not harmful to a particular thing 无害的: *environment-friendly* 对环境无害的 • noun (plural **friendlies**) Brit. 【英】a game not forming part of a serious competition 友谊赛 ■ **friendliness** noun.

frieze /friːz/ noun a broad horizontal band of sculpted or painted decoration 壁缘；饰带

frigate /'frɪgət/ noun a kind of fast warship 护卫舰

fright /fraɪt/ noun **1** a sudden strong feeling of fear 惊吓；恐惧 **2** a shock 令人震惊的事物

frighten /'fraɪtn/ verb make someone afraid 使惊恐；吓唬 ■ **frightening** adjective **frighteningly** adverb.

frightful /'fraɪtfl/ adjective **1** very unpleasant, serious, or shocking 讨厌的；严重的；令人震惊的 **2** informal 【非正式】terrible; awful 可怕的；骇人的 ■ **frightfully** adverb.

frigid /'frɪdʒɪd/ adjective **1** literary 【文】very cold 极冷的 **2** disapproving 【贬】(of a woman) not interested in sex (女子)性冷淡的 ■ **frigidity** noun.

frill /frɪl/ noun **1** a decorative strip of gathered or pleated cloth attached to the edge of clothing or material 褶边；荷叶边 **2** (frills) unnecessary extra features 不必要的装饰；虚饰 ■ **frilled** adjective **frilly** adjective.

fringe /frɪndʒ/ noun **1** a decorative border of threads or tassels attached to the edge of clothing or material 穗；缘饰；流苏 **2** Brit. 【英】a part of someone's hair that hangs over the forehead (头发的)刘海儿 **3** the outer part of an area, group, etc. 边缘；外围 • verb (fringes, fringing, fringed) add a fringe to something 加穗于 □ **fringe benefit** something extra given to someone as well as wages 附加福利；附带好处

frippery /'frɪpəri/ noun (plural **fripperies**) showy or unnecessary decoration 俗丽的装饰

frisbee /'frɪzbi/ noun trademark 【商标】a plastic disc that you skim through the air as an outdoor game (户外投掷游戏用的)飞碟

frisk /frɪsk/ verb **1** pass your hands over someone in a search for hidden weapons or drugs (用手搜(某人)的)身 **2** skip or move playfully 欢跃；蹦跳 • noun a playful skip or leap 欢跃；蹦跳

frisky /'frɪski/ adjective (friskier, friskiest) playful and full of energy 活跃的；活泼的；精力旺盛的

frisson /'friːsɒn/ noun a sudden shiver of excitement 颤抖；战栗

fritillary /frɪ'tɪləri/ noun (plural **fritillaries**) **1** a plant with hanging bell-like flowers 贝母(开悬钟形花) **2** a butterfly with orange-brown wings 豹纹蝶；豹蛱蝶

fritter¹ /'frɪtə(r)/ verb (fritters, frittering, frittered) (fritter something away) waste time or money on unimportant matters (在微不足道的事情上)浪费(时间或金钱)

fritter² noun a piece of food that is coated in batter and deep-fried (裹面糊的)油炸馅饼

frivolous /'frɪvələs/ adjective **1** not having any serious purpose or value 琐屑的；无意义的；不重要的 **2** (of a person) not treating things seriously (人)轻浮的，不严肃的 ■ **frivolity** noun **frivolously** adverb.

frizz /frɪz/ verb (of hair) form into a mass of tight curls (头发)紧紧卷曲，卷成小卷儿 • noun a mass of tightly curled hair 一团卷紧的头发 ■ **frizzy** adjective.

frock /frɒk/ **noun 1** a dress 女式礼服;连衣裙 **2** a loose outer garment, worn by priests 僧袍;教士服 □ **frock coat** a man's long, double-breasted coat, worn on formal occasions (双排扣的)男礼服大衣

frog /frɒg/ **noun** an amphibian with a short body, very long hind legs for leaping, and no tail 蛙;蛙类动物 □ **have a frog in your throat** informal 【非正式】be hoarse 嗓音嘶哑

frogman /'frɒgmən/ **noun** (plural **frogmen**) a diver equipped with a rubber suit, flippers, and breathing equipment (使用蛙式潜水装备的)蛙人

frogmarch /'frɒgmɑːtʃ/ **verb** force someone to walk forward by holding their arms from behind 蛙式押送(将人双臂反扣后强推行走)

frogspawn /'frɒgspɔːn/ **noun** a mass of frogs' eggs surrounded by transparent jelly 蛙卵

frolic /'frɒlɪk/ **verb** (**frolics, frolicking, frolicked**) play or move about in a cheerful and lively way 嬉戏;闹着玩;作乐 • **noun** a playful action or movement 嬉戏;嬉闹

frolicsome /'frɒlɪksəm/ **adjective** lively and playful 嬉戏的;爱闹着玩的;欢乐的

from /frəm,frɒm/ **preposition 1** indicating the point at which a journey, process, or action starts 从…起;始于 **2** indicating the source of something 来自;源于 **3** indicating separation, removal, or prevention (表示分离,去除或防止) **4** indicating a cause 由于;因为 **5** indicating a difference 与…(不同)

fromage frais /,frɒmɑːʒ 'freɪ/ **noun** a type of smooth, soft cheese 新鲜软干酪

frond /frɒnd/ **noun** the leaf of a palm, fern, or similar plant (棕榈、蕨类等植物的)叶

front /frʌnt/ **noun 1** the part of an object that faces forwards or that is normally seen first 正面;前面 **2** the position directly ahead 前面;正前方 **3** the furthest position that an army has reached 前线;最前沿 **4** a particular situation or area of activity 某种局面,某一领域 **5** (in weather forecasting) the forward edge of an advancing mass of air (天气预报用语)锋 **6** a false appearance or way of behaving (伪装的)外表,行为 **7** a person or organization that is a cover for secret or illegal activities (秘密或非法活动的)掩护者(或组织) **8** a very confident manner 勇敢;自信 • **adjective** having to do with the front 正面的;前面的;前部的 • **verb 1** have the front facing towards 面向 **2** be at the front of 位于…的前面 **3** (**be fronted with**) have the front covered with 以…作正面 be the leader or presenter of 领导;主持 □ **the front line** the part of an army that is closest to the enemy 前线;火 线 **front runner** the leader in a competition 领跑者(竞争中的领先者)

frontage /'frʌntɪdʒ/ **noun 1** the front of a building (建筑物的)正面,前方 **2** a strip of land next to a street or waterway 临街地;临水地

frontal /'frʌntl/ **adjective** having to do with the front 前面的;正面的 ■ **frontally** adverb.

frontier /'frʌntɪə(r)/ **noun 1** a border separating two countries 边境;边界 **2** the furthest part of land that has been settled 开发地区边缘 **3** the limit of what is known about a subject or area of activity (某学科或活动区域的)最前沿,边缘

frontispiece /'frʌntɪspiːs/ **noun** an illustration facing the title page of a book (书籍的)卷首插图,扉页

frontman /'frʌntmæn/ **noun** (plural **frontmen**) a person who represents an illegal organization to make it seem respectable (合法组织的)代表

frost /frɒst/ **noun 1** white ice crystals that form on surfaces when the temperature falls below freezing 白霜 **2** a period of cold weather when frost forms 冰冻期

frostbite /'frɒstbaɪt/ **noun** injury to parts of the body caused by exposure to extreme cold 冻伤;冻疮 ■ **frostbitten** adjective.

frosted /'frɒstɪd/ **adjective 1** covered with frost 上霜的,结霜的 **2** (of glass) having a semitransparent textured surface (玻璃)毛面的,有霜状态面的 **3** N. Amer. 【北美】 (of a cake) covered with icing (蛋糕)覆糖霜的

frosting /'frɒstɪŋ/ **noun** N. Amer. 【北美】 icing 糖霜;糖衣

frosty /'frɒsti/ **adjective (frostier, frostiest) 1** (of the weather) very cold with frost forming on surfaces (天气)严寒的,霜冻的 **2** cold and unfriendly 冷淡的;冷若冰霜 ■ **frostily** adverb.

froth /frɒθ/ **noun 1** a mass of small bubbles in liquid 泡;泡沫 **2** appealing but trivial ideas or activities 空洞的想法;无价值的行为 • **verb** produce or contain froth 起泡沫;含泡沫 ■ **frothy** adjective.

frown /fraʊn/ **verb 1** make an angry or worried expression by bringing your eyebrows together so that lines appear on your forehead 皱眉,蹙额 **2** (**frown on**) disapprove of 不赞同;反对 • **noun** a frowning expression 皱眉;蹙额

frowsty /'fraʊsti/ **adjective** Brit. 【英】 warm and stuffy 闷热的;霉臭的

frowzy or **frowsy** /'fraʊzi/ **adjective** scruffy and neglected in appearance 肮脏的;邋遢的;不整洁的

froze /frəʊz/ past of **FREEZE**.

frozen /'frəʊzn/ past participle of **FREEZE**.

fructose /'frʌktəʊs/ **noun** a kind of sugar found in honey and fruit 果糖

左旋糖

frugal /'fruːgl/ **adjective 1** careful in the use of money or food 节约的;俭省的 **2** (of a meal) plain and cheap (饭食)简单的,便宜的 ■ **frugality** noun **frugally** adverb.

fruit /fruːt/ **noun 1** a fleshy part of a plant that contains seed and can be eaten as food 水果 **2** Botany 【植物】 the part of a plant in which seeds develop, e.g. an acorn 果实 **3** the result of work or activity 成果;结果 • **verb** produce fruit 结果实 □ **fruit machine** Brit. 【英】 a coin-operated gambling machine 吃角子老虎机(一种投币赌博机)

fruiterer /'fruːtərə(r)/ **noun** a person who sells fruit 水果商

fruitful /'fruːtfl/ **adjective 1** producing a lot of fruit 果实结得多的 **2** producing good results 有收益的;富有成果的 ■ **fruitfully** adverb **fruitfulness** noun.

fruition /fruˈɪʃn/ **noun** the fulfilment of a plan or project 完成计划;取得成果

fruitless /'fruːtləs/ **adjective** failing to achieve the desired results 无结果的;徒劳的 ■ **fruitlessly** adverb.

fruity /'fruːti/ **adjective (fruitier, fruitiest) 1** having to do with fruit 水果的 **2** (of someone's voice) mellow, deep, and rich (嗓音)圆润的

frump /frʌmp/ **noun** an unattractive woman who wears unfashionable clothes 衣着过时的女人 ■ **frumpy** adjective.

frustrate /frʌˈstreɪt/ **verb (frustrates, frustrating, frustrated) 1** prevent a plan or action from succeeding 挫败,阻挠(计划或行动) **2** prevent someone from doing or achieving something 阻挠(某人);使受挫折 **3** make someone feel dissatisfied or unfulfilled 使不满 ■ **frustrating** adjective **frustration** noun.

fry¹ /fraɪ/ **verb (fries, frying, fried)**

cook in hot fat or oil 油煎;油炸;油炒 ■ noun (fries) French fries; chips 炸薯条 □ **frying pan** a shallow pan used for frying food 油炸锅 ■ **fryer** (or **frier**) noun.

fry² plural noun young fish 鱼苗;鱼秧

ft abbreviation foot or feet.

fuchsia /'fju:ʃə/ noun a shrub with drooping purplish-red flowers 倒挂金钟(灌木,开紫红色悬垂状花)

fuddled /'fʌdld/ adjective not able to think clearly 迷惑的;糊涂的;晕眩的

fuddy-duddy /'fʌdidʌdi/ noun (plural **fuddy-duddies**) informal 【非正式】 a person who is very old-fashioned and pompous 守旧的人;老保守;自命不凡的人

fudge /fʌdʒ/ noun 1 a soft sweet made from sugar, butter, and milk or cream 乳脂软糖 2 an attempt to present an issue in a vague way 回避态度 • verb (**fudges**, **fudging**, **fudged**) present something in a vague or deceptive way 模糊地呈现;篡改

fuel /fju:əl/ noun 1 material such as coal, gas, or oil that is burned to produce heat or power 燃料 2 something that stirs up argument or strong emotion 激起争论或强烈情感的刺激因素 • verb (**fuels**, **fuelling**, **fuelled**; US spelling 【美拼作】 **fuels**, **fueling**, **fueled**) 1 supply or power with fuel 给…加油,用燃料为…提供动力 2 stir up strong feeling 激起;刺激 □ **fuel injection** the direct introduction of fuel into the cylinders of an engine 燃料喷射;喷油

fug /fʌg/ noun Brit. informal 【英,非正式】 a warm, stuffy atmosphere 闷热的空气

fugitive /'fju:dʒətɪv/ noun a person who has escaped from captivity or is in hiding 逃亡者;亡命者

fugue /fju:g/ noun a piece of music in which a short melody is introduced and then successively taken up by other instruments or voices 赋格曲

führer or **fuehrer** /'fjʊərə(r)/ noun the title that Hitler held as leader of Germany "元首"(纳粹统治时期对希特勒的称呼)

fulcrum /'fʌlkrəm/ noun the point on which a lever turns or is supported (杠杆的)支点

fulfil /fʊl'fɪl/ (US spelling 【美拼作】 **fulfill**) verb (**fulfils**, **fulfilling**, **fulfilled**) 1 do or achieve something that was desired, promised, or predicted 履行;实现 2 meet a requirement 满足(要求) 3 (**fulfil yourself**) fully develop your abilities 充分发挥(能力) ■ **fulfilment** noun.

full /fʊl/ adjective 1 holding as much or as many as possible 满的;装满的;充满的 2 (**full of**) having a large number or quantity of 大量的;丰富的 3 (also **full up**) filled to capacity 填满的 4 complete 完整的;full details 详情 5 plump or rounded 丰满的;圆鼓鼓的 6 (of flavour, sound, or colour) strong or rich (味道)浓郁的;(声音)圆润的;(色彩)浓浓的 • adverb straight; directly 正好;直接地 □ **full back** (in soccer and similar sports) a defender who plays at the side (足球及类似运动中的)防守后卫 **full-blooded** wholehearted and enthusiastic 一心一意的;热情的 **full-blown** fully developed 完全成熟的;充分发展的 **full board** Brit. 【英】 accommodation at a hotel or guest house which includes all meals 全食宿(指住宿及全部伙食均由旅馆提供) **full-bodied** rich and satisfying in flavour or sound (味道)浓的;(音质)圆润的 **full-frontal** fully exposing the front of the body 正面全裸的 **full house 1** a theatre that is filled to capacity (观众人数达到最大限度的)满员剧院 **2** a poker hand with three of a kind and a pair 满堂红,满贯(指有三张同点和两张同点的一手扑克

牌) **3** a winning card at bingo (宾戈游戏中的)赢牌 **full moon** the moon when its whole disc is illuminated 满月(期) **full-scale 1** (of a model or plan) of the same size as the thing represented (模型或平面图)原尺寸的 **2** complete and thorough 完全的；彻底的 **full stop** a punctuation mark (.) used at the end of a sentence or abbreviation 句点，句号 **full time** the end of a sports match (体育比赛的)结束时间，终场 **full-time** working for the whole of the available time 全日地；作为全职 ■ **fullness (or fulness)** noun.

fuller /ˈfʊlə(r)/ noun historical 【历史】 a person whose job was treating cloth to make it thicker 缩绒工；漂洗工

fully /ˈfʊli/ adverb **1** completely 完全地；彻底地 **2** no less or fewer than 至少；整整 □ **fully fledged** Brit. 【英】completely developed or established 成熟的；充分发展的

fulminate /ˈfʌlmɪneɪt/ verb (fulminates, fulminating, fulminated) protest strongly 大声斥责；怒喝 ■ **fulmination** noun.

fulsome /ˈfʊlsəm/ adjective **1** too flattering or complimentary 过分恭维的；谄媚的 **2** of large size or quantity 巨大的；大量的 ■ **fulsomely** adverb.

fumble /ˈfʌmbl/ verb (fumbles, fumbling, fumbled) **1** use the hands clumsily while doing something 乱摸，摸索 **2** deal with something clumsily 笨拙地做 **3** fail to catch a ball cleanly 失球；漏接球 • noun an act of fumbling 乱摸；摸索；笨拙的处理；失球

fume /fjuːm/ noun a gas or vapour that smells strongly or is dangerous to breathe in (气味浓烈或有毒的)烟，气，汽 • verb (fumes, fuming, fumed) **1** send out fumes 冒烟(或气，汽) **2** be very angry 发怒，大怒

fumigate /ˈfjuːmɪɡeɪt/ verb (fumigates, fumigating, fumigated) disinfect an area using chemical fumes 烟

熏，熏蒸(以消毒) ■ **fumigation** noun.

fun /fʌn/ noun **1** light-hearted pleasure, or something that provides it 享乐；乐趣；快乐 **2** playfulness 嬉戏，戏谑；玩笑 □ **make fun of** laugh at in a mocking way 取笑；拿⋯⋯开玩笑

function /ˈfʌŋkʃn/ noun **1** a purpose or natural activity of a person or thing 用途；官能；功能 **2** a large social event 重大社交活动 **3** a basic task of a computer (计算机的)功能 **4** Maths 【数学】 a quantity whose value depends on the varying values of others 函数 • verb **1** work or operate 工作；运转 □ **function (as)** fulfil the purpose of 行使职责；起作用

functional /ˈfʌŋkʃənl/ adjective **1** having to do with a functionn 官能的；功能的 **2** designed to be practical and useful 为实用而设计的；实用的 **3** working or operating 起作用的；工作的；运转的 ■ **functionality** noun **functionally** adverb.

functionary /ˈfʌŋkʃənəri/ noun (plural functionaries) an official 官员；公务员

fund /fʌnd/ noun **1** a sum of money saved or made available for a purpose 基金；专款 **2 (funds)** financial resources 资金；财源 **3** a large stock 储备；贮存 • verb provide money for 为⋯⋯提供资金；资助

fundamental /ˌfʌndəˈmentl/ adjective of basic importance 基本的；根本的 • noun a basic rule or principle 基本原则；根本法则 ■ **fundamentally** adverb.

fundamentalism /ˌfʌndəˈmentəlɪzəm/ noun strict following of the basic teachings of a religion 原教旨主义(主张严格遵守某宗教的基本教义) ■ **fundamentalist** noun & adjective.

funeral /ˈfjuːnərəl/ noun a ceremony in which a dead person is buried or cremated 葬礼；丧礼 □ **funeral**

director an undertaker 丧葬承办者；殡仪员

funerary /ˈfjuːnərəri/ **adjective** having to do with a funeral or other rites in which dead people are remembered 殡仪馆

funereal /fjuːˈnɪəriəl/ **adjective** solemn, in a way appropriate to a funeral 肃穆的；适于丧葬的

funfair /ˈfʌnfeə(r)/ **noun** Brit. 【英】 a fair consisting of rides, sideshows, etc. 露天游乐场

fungicide /ˈfʌŋɡɪsaɪd/ **noun** a chemical that destroys fungus 杀真菌剂

fungus /ˈfʌŋɡəs/ **noun** (plural **fungi** /ˈfʌŋɡaɪ/) an organism, such as a mushroom, that has no leaves or flowers and grows on plants or decaying vegetable matter and reproduces by spores 真菌,真菌类植物(如蘑菇) ■ **fungal** adjective.

funicular railway /fjuːˈnɪkjələ(r)/ **noun** a railway on a steep slope which is operated by cable (登山铁路)用缆索运转的

funk¹ /fʌŋk/ **noun** a style of popular dance music with a strong rhythm 乡土爵士乐(一种节奏强劲的流行舞曲)

funk² **noun** informal 【非正式】 a state of panic or anxiety 恐慌,焦虑

funky /ˈfʌŋki/ **adjective** (**funkier**, **funkiest**) informal 【非正式】 1 (of music) having a strong dance rhythm (音乐)节奏感强烈的 2 modern and stylish 时髦独特的

funnel /ˈfʌnl/ **noun** 1 an object that is wide at the top and narrow at the bottom, used for guiding liquid or powder into a small opening 漏斗 2 a chimney on a ship or steam engine (轮船或蒸汽机的)烟囱 • **verb** (**funnels**, **funnelling**, **funnelled**; US spelling 【美拼作】 **funnels**, **funneling**, **funneled**) guide through a funnel or narrow space 流经漏斗；通过狭窄空间

funny /ˈfʌni/ **adjective** (**funnier**, **funniest**) 1 causing laughter or amusement 滑稽的；有趣的,逗人发笑的 2 strange; odd 奇怪的；不寻常的 3 suspicious or illegal 可疑的,非法的 4 informal 【非正式】 slightly unwell 稍有不适的 □ **funny bone** informal 【非正式】 the part of the elbow over which a very sensitive nerve passes (尺骨肘部的)鹰嘴突 ■ **funnily** adverb.

fur /fɜː(r)/ **noun** 1 the short, soft hair of certain animals (动物的)柔毛, 软毛 2 the skin of an animal with fur on it, or a coat made from this 动物毛皮；毛皮外衣 3 Brit. 【英】 a coating formed by hard water on the inside surface of a pipe, kettle, etc. (管道、水壶等的)水锈 ■ **furred** adjective.

furbelow /ˈfɜːbɪləʊ/ **noun** 1 a strip of gathered or pleated material sewn on a skirt or petticoat (女裙或衬裙的)褶边, 皱襞裙饰 2 (**furbelows**) showy decorations or ornaments 俗艳浮华的装饰

furious /ˈfjʊəriəs/ **adjective** 1 very angry 狂怒的,暴怒的 2 with great energy or speed 激烈的；飞速的 ■ **furiously** adverb.

furl /fɜːl/ **verb** roll or fold up neatly 卷起；折拢

furlong /ˈfɜːlɒŋ/ **noun** an eighth of a mile, 220 yards 浪, 弗隆(合1/8英里或220码)

furlough /ˈfɜːləʊ/ **noun** a time when you have permission to be away from your work or duties 休假许可

furnace /ˈfɜːnɪs/ **noun** 1 an enclosed space for heating material to very high temperatures 火炉,熔炉 2 a very hot place 火炉；极闷热的地方

furnish /ˈfɜːnɪʃ/ **verb** 1 provide a room or building with furniture and fittings 为…配备家具 2 supply or provide 供给；提供

furnishings /ˈfɜːnɪʃɪŋz/ **noun** furniture and fittings in a room or building 家具；室内陈设；装备

furniture /ˈfɜːnɪtʃə(r)/ **noun** the movable articles that make a room or building suitable for living or working in 家具

furore /fjʊˈrɔːri/ (US spelling 【美拼作】 **furor** /ˈfjʊərɔː(r)/) **noun** an outbreak of public anger or excitement (公愤或骚乱的)爆发

furrier /ˈfʌriə(r)/ **noun** a person who deals in clothes made of fur 皮毛加工者；皮货商

furrow /ˈfʌrəʊ/ **noun 1** a long, narrow trench made in the ground by a plough 犁沟 **2** a deep wrinkle on a person's face 皱纹 • **verb** make a furrow in 犁；使起皱纹

furry /ˈfɜːri/ **adjective (furrier, furriest)** covered with or like fur 毛皮覆盖的；似毛皮的

further /ˈfɜːðə(r)/ **adverb (also farther)** **1** at, to, or by a greater distance (距离上)更远地 **2** at or to a more advanced stage 进一步；在更大程度上 **3** in addition 此外；而且 • **adjective 1** (also **farther**) more distant in space 更远的较远的 **2** additional 附加的，另外的 • **verb (furthers, furthering, furthered)** help the progress of 促进；推进；助长 □ **further education** Brit.【英】education below degree level for people older than school age 继续教育；进修

furtherance /ˈfɜːðərəns/ **noun** the process of helping something to develop or succeed 促进；推进

furthermore /ˌfɜːðəˈmɔː(r)/ **adverb** in addition 此外；而且

furthest or **farthest** /ˈfɜːðɪst/ **adverb & adjective** at or to the greatest distance (距离)最远地(的)

furtive /ˈfɜːtɪv/ **adjective** secretively trying to avoid being noticed 偷偷摸摸的;鬼鬼祟祟的 ■ **furtively** adverb.

fury /ˈfjʊəri/ **noun (plural furies) 1** extreme anger 狂怒；暴怒 **2** extreme strength or violence 狂暴 **3** (**the Furies**) Greek Mythology【希腊神话】three

goddesses who punished people for their crimes 复仇三女神

furze /fɜːz/ = GORSE.

fuse¹ /fjuːz/ **verb (fuses, fusing, fused) 1** join or combine to form a whole 熔合；融合；结合 **2** melt something so it joins with something else 熔化；熔接 **3** Brit.【英】(of an electrical appliance) stop working when a fuse melts (电器因保险丝熔断而)中断工作 **4** fit a circuit or electrical appliance with a fuse 给(电路或电器)装保险丝 • **noun 1** a safety device consisting of a strip of wire that melts and breaks an electric circuit if the current goes beyond a safe level 保险丝，熔线 **2** a length of material which is lit to explode a bomb or firework 导火线；导火索 **3** a device in a bomb that controls the timing of the explosion 引信；引管

fuselage /ˈfjuːzəlɑːʒ/ **noun** the main body of an aircraft (飞机的)机身

fusible /ˈfjuːzəbl/ **adjective** able to be melted easily 易熔的；可熔的

Fusilier /ˌfjuːzəˈlɪə(r)/ **noun** a member of a British regiment formerly armed with muskets called **fusils** (英国的)燧发枪团士兵

fusillade /ˌfjuːzəˈleɪd/ **noun** a series of shots fired at the same time or quickly one after the other (枪炮的)连放齐射

fusion /ˈfjuːʒn/ **noun 1** the joining of two or more things together to form a whole 熔合；联合；合并 **2** a reaction in which the nuclei of atoms fuse to form a heavier nucleus, releasing a great deal of energy 核聚变

fuss /fʌs/ **noun 1** unnecessary excitement or activity 大惊小怪；小题大做 **2** a protest or complaint 抗议；抱怨 • **verb (usu. fuss over)** show unnecessary concern about something 过于忧虑；大惊小怪

fussy /ˈfʌsi/ **adjective (fussier, fussiest) 1** hard to please 难以取悦

的；爱挑剔的 **2** full of unnecessary detail 细节过多的；过分重视细节的 ■ **fussily** adverb **fussiness** noun.

fusty /ˈfʌsti/ adjective **1** smelling stale or damp 发霉味的；朽霉的 **2** old-fashioned 过时的；守旧的

futile /ˈfjuːtaɪl/ adjective pointless 无用的；无效的；无益的 ■ **futilely** adverb **futility** noun.

futon /ˈfuːtɒn/ noun a padded mattress that can be rolled up 蒲团

future /ˈfjuːtʃə(r)/ noun **1 (the future)** time that is still to come 未来；将来 **2** a prospect of success or happiness (成功或幸福的)前景，前途 • adjective **1** existing or happening in the future 未来的；将来的 **2** Grammar【语法】(of

a verb) expressing an event yet to happen (动词)将来时的

futuristic /ˌfjuːtʃəˈrɪstɪk/ adjective **1** having very modern technology or design (技术或设计)极现代的，极先进的 **2** (of a film or book) set in the future (电影或书)想象的，幻想的

futurity /fjuːˈtjʊərəti/ noun the future time 将来；未来

fuzz /fʌz/ noun **1** a frizzy mass of hair or fibre 绒毛；茸毛 **2 (the fuzz)** informal【非正式】the police 警察；警方

fuzzy /ˈfʌzi/ adjective (**fuzzier**, **fuzziest**) **1** having a frizzy texture or appearance 茸毛的；绒毛状的 **2** blurred; not clear 模糊的；不清楚的

Gg

G or **g** /dʒiː/ **noun** (plural **Gs** or **G's**) the seventh letter of the alphabet 英语字母表的第7个字母 ▪ **abbreviation 1** grams. **2** gravity. □ **G-string** a pair of knickers consisting of a narrow strip of cloth attached to a waistband (当作三角裤用的)G带，遮羞布

gab /gæb/ **verb** (**gabs, gabbing, gabbed**) informal 【非正式】 talk at length 喋喋不休 □ **the gift of the gab** the ability to speak in a fluent and persuasive way 口才；辩才

gabble /'gæbl/ **verb** (**gabbles, gabbling, gabbled**) talk very quickly and in a way that is difficult to understand 急促而含混地说 ▪ **noun** talk that is fast and difficult to understand 急促而含混的话语

gaberdine or **gabardine** /ˌgæbə'diːn, 'gæbədiːn/ **noun** a smooth, hard-wearing cloth used for making raincoats 华达呢，轧别丁（用来制雨衣的结实光滑的布料）

gable /'geɪbl/ **noun** the triangular upper part of a wall at the end of a roof 山墙；三角墙

gad /gæd/ **verb** (**gads, gadding, gadded**) (**gad about**) informal 【非正式】 enjoy yourself by visiting many different places 闲逛；游荡

gadfly /'gædflaɪ/ **noun** (plural **gadflies**) **1** a fly that bites cattle 牛虻 **2** annoying person 讨厌的人

gadget /'gædʒɪt/ **noun** a small mechanical device 小装置；小机械

▪ **gadgetry** noun.

Gaelic /'geɪlɪk/ **noun** a language spoken in parts of Ireland and western Scotland (爱尔兰部分地区和苏格兰西部使用的)盖尔语

gaff¹ /gæf/ **noun** a stick with a hook for landing large fish (拉大鱼上岸的)手钩，挽钩

gaff² **noun** (**blow the gaff**) Brit. informal 【英,非正式】 reveal a secret 泄露秘密

gaffe /gæf/ **noun** an embarrassing mistake made in a social situation 出丑；失态

gaffer /'gæfə(r)/ **noun** informal 【非正式】 **1** Brit. 【英】 a person's boss 工头 **2** an old man 老头

gag¹ /gæg/ **noun** a piece of cloth put over a person's mouth to stop them speaking (使人不能说话的)塞口物，包口物 ▪ **verb** (**gags, gagging, gagged**) **1** put a gag on 塞住…的嘴 **2** choke or retch 窒息；作呕

gag² **noun** a joke or funny story 笑话；噱头

gaga /'gɑːgɑː/ **adjective** informal 【非正式】 rambling in speech or thought, especially as a result of old age (尤指由于年老)糊涂的

gage /geɪdʒ/ US spelling of GAUGE. gauge 的美式拼写

gaggle /'gægl/ **noun 1** a flock of geese 一群鹅 **2** informal 【非正式】 a noisy group of people 吵吵嚷嚷的一群人

gaiety /'geɪəti/ (US spelling【美拼

作】**gayety**) **noun** (plural **gaieties**) light-hearted and cheerful mood or behaviour 欢乐;愉悦

gaily /'geɪli/ **adverb 1** in a light-hearted and cheerful way 欢乐地;愉快地 **2** without thinking of the effect of your actions 草率地;欠考虑地 **3** with a bright appearance 鲜艳地;艳丽地

gain /geɪn/ **verb 1** obtain or secure something 获得;得到 **2** reach a place 到达 **3** (**gain on**) get closer to a person or thing that you are chasing 接近,逼近 (追赶的人或物) **4** increase in weight or speed 增加,提高(重量或速度) **5** (**gain in**) improve or progress in some respect (在…方面)提高,进步 **6** (of a clock or watch) become fast (钟表)走快 ■ **noun 1** a thing that is gained 获取物;收益 **2** an increase in wealth or resources (财富或资源)的增值,增加

gainful /'geɪnfl/ **adjective** (of employment) paid; profitable (工作)有报酬的,有收益的 ■ **gainfully** adverb.

gainsay /ˌgeɪn'seɪ/ **verb** (**gainsays, gainsaying, gainsaid**) formal【正式】 deny or contradict 否认;反驳

gait /geɪt/ **noun** a way of walking 步态

gaiter /'geɪtə(r)/ **noun** a covering of cloth or leather for the ankle and lower leg (布或皮制的)绑腿

gala /'gɑːlə/ **noun 1** a social occasion with special entertainments 欢庆盛典;特别演出 **2** Brit.【英】a special sports event, especially a swimming competition 体育盛会;(尤指)游泳比赛

galactic /gə'læktɪk/ **adjective** relating to a galaxy 星系的;银河系的

galaxy /'gæləksi/ **noun** (plural **galaxies**) **1** a large system of stars 星系 **2** (**the Galaxy**) the system of stars that includes the sun and the earth; the Milky Way (包括太阳和地球在内的)银河系,银河

gale /geɪl/ **noun 1** a very strong wind 大风;强风 **2** an outburst of laughter 一阵大笑

gall¹ /gɔːl/ **noun** disrespectful or rude behaviour 粗鲁;厚颜无耻 □ **gall bladder** a small organ beneath the liver, in which bile is stored 胆囊

gall² **noun 1** annoyance; irritation 烦恼;恼怒 **2** a sore on the skin made by rubbing 擦痛处;擦伤处 ● **verb** annoy; irritate 使烦恼;使恼怒 ■ **galling** adjective.

gallant **adjective 1** /'gælənt/ brave or heroic 勇敢的,英勇的 **2** /gə'lænt/ (of a man) polite and charming to women (男子)迷人的,有风度的 ● **noun** /gə'lænt/ a man who is polite and charming to women (对女子殷勤的)迷人男子 ■ **gallantly** adverb.

gallantry /'gæləntri/ **noun** (plural **gallantries**) **1** courageous behaviour 英勇行为 **2** polite attention given by men to women (男子对女子的)殷勤

galleon /'gæliən/ **noun** historical【历史】a large sailing ship with three or more decks and masts 大帆船

gallery /'gæləri/ **noun** (plural **galleries**) **1** a room or building in which works of art are displayed or sold (艺术品的)陈列室,展览馆 **2** a balcony at the back of a large hall (大厅或教堂的)楼座,廊台 **3** the highest part of a theatre (剧院的)顶层楼座

galley /'gæli/ **noun** (plural **galleys**) **1** historical【历史】a low, flat ship with one or more sails and up to three banks of oars 桨帆船 **2** a narrow kitchen in a ship or aircraft (船或飞机上的)厨房

Gallic /'gælɪk/ **adjective** having to do with France or the French 高卢(人)的;法国(人)的

gallivant /'gælɪvænt/ **verb** informal 【非正式】go from place to place enjoying yourself 游荡;闲逛

gallon /'gælən/ **noun** a unit of volume for measuring liquids, equal to eight pints (4.55 litres) 加仑(液量单位,等于8品脱,合4.55升) **2**

(**gallons**) informal【非正式】large quantities 大量

gallop /ˈɡæləp/ **noun 1** the fastest speed a horse can run (马的)飞奔，疾驰 **2** a ride on a horse at its fastest speed 骑马奔驰 • **verb** (**gallops, galloping, galloped**) **1** go at the speed of a gallop 飞奔，疾驰 **2** proceed very quickly 飞速发展

gallows /ˈɡæləʊz/ **plural noun 1** a structure used for hanging a person 绞刑架 **2** (**the gallows**) execution by hanging 绞刑

gallstone /ˈɡɔːlstəʊn/ **noun** a hard mass of crystals formed in the gall bladder or bile ducts, causing pain and obstruction 胆(结)石

galore /ɡəˈlɔː(r)/ **adjective** in large numbers or amounts 很多的，大量的

galoshes /ɡəˈlɒʃɪz/ **plural noun** rubber shoes worn over normal shoes in wet weather 橡胶套鞋 (雨天套在平常穿的鞋上)

galumph /ɡəˈlʌmf/ **verb** informal【非正式】move in a clumsy or noisy way 笨拙地移动，吵吵嚷嚷地行进

galvanic /ɡælˈvænɪk/ **adjective** relating to electric currents produced by chemical action (由化学作用)产生电流的

galvanize or **galvanise** /ˈɡælvənaɪz/ **verb** (**galvanizes, galvanizing, galvanized**) **1** shock or excite someone into doing something 刺激；使兴奋 **2** (**galvanized**) (of iron or steel) coated with a protective layer of zinc (钢铁)镀锌的

galvanometer /ˌɡælvəˈnɒmɪtə(r)/ **noun** an instrument for measuring small electric currents 电流计；电流测定器

Gambian /ˈɡæmbiən/ **noun** a person from Gambia 冈比亚人 • **adjective** relating to Gambia 冈比亚的

gambit /ˈɡæmbɪt/ **noun** something that somebody says or does that is meant to give them an advantage (意图占得

先机的)开场白，策略

gamble /ˈɡæmbl/ **verb** (**gambles, gambling, gambled**) **1** play games of chance for money 赌博 **2** bet a sum of money 赌钱 **3** risk losing something in the hope that you will be successful 碰运气；冒险 • **noun** a risky action 冒险 ■ **gambler** noun.

gambol /ˈɡæmbl/ **verb** (**gambols, gambolling, gambolled**; US spelling 【美拼法】**gambols, gamboling, gamboled**) run or jump about playfully 蹦跳；嬉戏

game[1] /ɡeɪm/ **noun 1** an activity that you take part in for amusement 游戏 **2** a competitive activity or sport played according to rules 竞赛；体育比赛 **3** a period of play, ending in a final result (游戏、比赛的)一场 **4** a section of a tennis match, forming a unit in scoring (网球比赛的)一局 **5** (**games**) a meeting for sporting competitions 运动会 **6** informal【非正式】a type of activity or business regarded as a game (竞争性的)行业，行当 **7** wild animals or birds that people hunt for food or as a sport 猎物；野味 • **adjective** eager and willing to do something new or challenging 有勇气的；有冒险精神的 • **verb** (**games, gaming, gamed**) play at games of chance for money 赌博；赌钱 ■ **gamely** adverb.

game[2] **adjective** dated【废】(of a person's leg) lame (人的腿)残疾的，瘸的，跛的

gamekeeper /ˈɡeɪmkiːpə(r)/ **noun** a person employed to breed and protect game for a large country estate 猎场看守人

gamesmanship /ˈɡeɪmzmənʃɪp/ **noun** the ability to win games by making your opponent feel less confident 克敌制胜术；比赛策略

gamete /ˈɡæmiːt/ **noun** Biology【生物】a cell which is able to unite with another one of the opposite sex in sexual reproduction to form a zygote 配子

gamine /'gæmiːn/ **adjective** (of a girl) having a mischievous, boyish charm (女孩)淘气的,男孩子气的

gamma /'gæmə/ **noun** the third letter of the Greek alphabet (Γ, γ)希腊语字母表的第3个字母 □ **gamma rays** (or **gamma radiation**) electromagnetic radiation of shorter wavelength than X-rays 伽马射线

gammon /'gæmən/ **noun** Brit.【英】 **1** ham which has been cured like bacon 腌猪后腿 **2** the part of a side of bacon that includes the hind leg (连带后腿的)腌猪肋肉

gammy /'gæmi/ **adjective** Brit. informal 【英,非正式】(of a person's leg) injured or painful (人的腿)受伤的,疼的

gamut /'gæmət/ **noun** the complete range or scope of something 全部,整个范围 □ **run the gamut** experience or perform the complete range of something 体验全部过程

gander /'gændə(r)/ **noun 1** a male goose 公鹅 **2** informal【非正式】a look 一瞥;一眼

gang /gæŋ/ **noun 1** an organized group of criminals or rowdy young people 一帮,一伙(罪犯或刁民) **2** informal 【非正式】a group of people who regularly meet and do things together (定期聚会的)一伙 **3** an organized group of people doing manual work (体力劳动者的)一队,一组 • **verb 1** (**gang together**) form a group or gang 成群;结伙 **2** (**gang up**) join together to oppose or intimidate someone 拉帮结派(反对或威胁某人)

gangling /'gæŋɡlɪŋ/ or **gangly** /'gæŋɡli/ **adjective** (of a person) tall, thin, and awkward (人)瘦高且笨拙的

ganglion /'gæŋɡliən/ **noun** (plural **ganglia** or **ganglions**) **1** a mass of nerve cells 神经节 **2** a swelling in a tendon 腱鞘囊肿

gangmaster /'gæŋmɑːstə(r)/ **noun** Brit.【英】a person who organizes and supervises the work of manual labourers employed on a casual basis 监工

gangplank /'gæŋplæŋk/ **noun** a movable plank used as a bridge between a boat and the shore (船和岸间的)跳板,步桥

gangrene /'gæŋɡriːn/ **noun** the decay of tissue in a part of the body, caused by an obstructed blood supply or by infection 坏疽 ■ **gangrenous** adjective.

gangster /'gæŋstə(r)/ **noun** a member of an organized gang of violent criminals 歹徒;匪徒

gangway /'gæŋweɪ/ **noun 1** Brit.【英】 a passage between rows of seats (两排座位之间的)过道 **2** a bridge placed between a ship and the shore (放在船和岸之间的)步桥,跳板

gannet /'gænɪt/ **noun 1** a large seabird 鲣鸟,塘鹅(大型海鸟) **2** Brit. informal 【英,非正式】a greedy person 贪婪的人

gantry /'gæntri/ **noun** (plural **gantries**) a bridge-like structure used as a support 起重龙门架

gaol /dʒeɪl/ ⇒ 见 JAIL.

gap /gæp/ **noun 1** a hole in an object or between two objects 裂口;裂缝,缝隙 **2** an empty space or period of time; a break in something 空隙;间隔;缺口 ■ **gappy** adjective.

gape /ɡeɪp/ **verb** (**gapes**, **gaping**, **gaped**) **1** stare with your mouth open wide in amazement 目瞪口呆地凝视;张口结舌地看 **2** be or become wide open 张开;裂开

garage /'gærɑːʒ/ **noun 1** a building in which a car or other vehicle is kept 车库;车房 **2** a business which sells fuel or which repairs and sells motor vehicles 加油站;汽车修理厂;汽车销售点 **3** a type of music with elements of drum and bass, house, and soul 车库乐(融合了鼓和贝司舞曲、豪斯音乐和灵乐等音乐元素)• verb (**garages, garaging, garaged**) keep a vehicle in a garage把机动车放入(或存入)车库

garb /gɑːb/ **noun** unusual or distinctive clothes (特定的)服装,制服 • **verb** (**be garbed in**) be dressed in distinctive clothes 穿着(特定)服装

garbage /'gɑːbɪdʒ/ **noun** chiefly N. Amer. 【主北美】 **1** domestic rubbish or waste (家庭)垃圾 **2** something worthless or meaningless 无价值的事物;无聊的东西

garble /gɑːbl/ **verb** (**garbles, garbling, garbled**) confuse or distort a message or transmission 使(传达的信息)混乱不清;曲解

garden /'gɑːdn/ **noun 1** a piece of ground next to or around a house (房屋旁边或周围的)园圃,花园 **2** (**gardens**) a public park 公园 • **verb** work in a garden 种植花草;从事园艺 ■ **gardener** noun.

gargantuan /gɑːˈɡæntjuən/ **adjective** enormous 巨大的;庞大的

gargle /'gɑːgl/ **verb** (**gargles, gargling, gargled**) hold liquid in your mouth and throat while slowly breathing out through it 含漱;漱喉 • **noun 1** an act of gargling 含漱;漱 **2** a liquid used for gargling 漱口液

gargoyle /'gɑːgɔɪl/ **noun** a spout in the form of an ugly person or animal that carries water away from the roof of a building (建筑物屋顶的)滴水嘴(形状为丑陋人形或怪兽)

garish /'geərɪʃ/ **adjective** unpleasantly bright and showy 俗艳的;花哨的 ■ **garishly** adverb.

garland /'gɑːlənd/ **noun** a wreath of flowers and leaves 花环,花冠 • **verb** crown or decorate with a garland 用花环装饰;给…饰以花冠

garlic /'gɑːlɪk/ **noun** a plant of the onion family with a strong taste and smell 蒜;大蒜

garment /'gɑːmənt/ **noun** a piece of clothing 衣服

garner /'gɑːnə(r)/ **verb** (**garners, garnering, garnered**) gather or collect 积累;收集

garnet /'gɑːnɪt/ **noun** a red semi-precious stone 石榴石(红色半宝石)

garnish /'gɑːnɪʃ/ **verb** decorate food 给(食物)加装饰,加饰菜于 • **noun** a decoration for food (食物的)装饰菜

garret /'gærət/ **noun** a room in the roof of a house 顶楼;阁楼

garrison /'gærɪsn/ **noun** a group of troops stationed in a fortress or town to defend it 卫戍部队,警卫部队 • **verb** provide a place with a garrison 驻防;驻守

garrotte /gəˈrɒt/ (US spelling 【美拼作】 **garrote**) **verb** (**garrottes, garrotting, garrotted**) strangle someone with a wire or cord 勒死;绞杀 • **noun** a wire or cord used for garrotting 用于绞杀的金属丝(或绳索)

garrulous /'gærələs/ **adjective** very talkative 滔滔不绝的;喋喋不休的 ■ **garrulity** noun.

garter /'gɑːtə(r)/ **noun** a band worn around the leg to keep up a stocking or sock 袜带

gas /gæs/ **noun** (plural **gases** or chiefly US 【主美】 **gasses**) **1** an air-like substance that expands to fill any available space 气体 **2** a type of gas used as a fuel 气体燃料;天然气,煤气 **3** a type of gas that stops you feeling pain, used during a medical operation 麻醉气 **4** N. Amer. 【北美】 gasoline 汽油 • **verb** (**gases, gassing, gassed**) **1** attack with, expose to, or kill with gas 用毒气伤害,使吸入毒气;用毒气杀死 **2** informal 【非正式】 talk or chat at length 闲聊;空谈 □ **gas chamber** an airtight room that can be filled with poisonous gas to kill people or animals 毒气室 **gas mask** a mask used as protection against poisonous gas 防毒面罩

✔ **拼写指南** in British English, the spelling of the plural is *gases*: no double *s*. 英式英语中 gas 的复数形式拼作 gases, 不是双写 s。

gaseous /'gæsɪəs/ **adjective** relating to or like a gas 气体的, 似气体的

gash /gæʃ/ **noun** a long deep cut or wound 深长的切痕(或伤口) • **verb** make a gash in… 在…上划深长的切口

gasket /'gæskɪt/ **noun** a rubber seal at the junction between two surfaces in an engine (橡胶)密封垫, 垫圈

gaslight /'gæslaɪt/ **noun** light from a gas lamp 煤气灯 ■ **gaslit** adjective.

gasoline /'gæsəliːn/ **noun** N. Amer. 【北美】 petrol 汽油

gasometer /gæ'sɒmɪtə(r)/ **noun** a large tank for the storage of gas (大型)储气罐

gasp /gɑːsp/ **verb 1** take a quick breath with your mouth open, because you are surprised or in pain (由于惊讶或痛苦而)喘气, 喘息, 倒抽气 **2 (gasp for)** struggle for air 急促地吸(气) • **noun** a sudden quick breath 深吸气; 急促的喘息

gassy /'gæsi/ **adjective (gassier, gassiest)** full of gas 充满气体的

gastric /'gæstrɪk/ **adjective** having to do with the stomach 胃部的

gastro-enteritis /ˌgæstrəʊˌentə'raɪtɪs/ **noun** inflammation of the stomach and intestines 胃肠炎

gastronomy /gæ'strɒnəmi/ **noun** the practice or art of cooking and eating good food 烹饪法, 美食学 ■ **gastronomic** adjective.

gasworks /'gæswɜːks/ **plural noun** a place where gas is processed 煤气厂

gate /geɪt/ **noun 1** a hinged barrier used to close an opening in a wall, fence, or hedge 门; 栅栏门; 篱笆门 **2** an exit from an airport building to an aircraft (机场的)登机口 **3** a barrier that controls the flow of water on a river or canal 闸门, 闸门 **4** the number of people who pay to attend a sports event (体育赛事的)观众人数

gateau /'gætəʊ/ **noun (plural gateaus or gateaux** /'gætəʊ/) Brit. 【英】 a cake 蛋糕

gatecrash /'geɪtkræʃ/ **verb** go to a party without an invitation or ticket (未经邀请或无票)擅自参加, 闯入(聚会) ■ **gatecrasher** noun.

gatefold /'geɪtfəʊld/ **noun** an oversized page in a book or magazine, intended to be opened out for reading (书刊的)大张折叠插页

gatehouse /'geɪthaʊs/ **noun** a house standing by the gateway to a country estate (乡间宅邸的)门房, 门楼

gatekeeper /'geɪtkiːpə(r)/ **noun** an attendant at a gate 看门人

gatepost /'geɪtpəʊst/ **noun** a post on which a gate is hinged or against which it shuts 门柱

gateway /'geɪtweɪ/ **noun 1** an opening that can be closed by a gate 通道, 门径 **2 (gateway to)** a means of entering somewhere or achieving something 途径; 方法

gather /'gæðə(r)/ **verb (gathers, gathering, gathered) 1** come or bring together 聚集; 集合; 收集 **2** increase in force, speed, etc. 增加(力量、速度等) **3** understand something to be the case 理解; 推断 **4** collect plants or fruits for food 采集(植物或水果) **5** harvest a crop 收割(庄稼) **6** draw together or towards yourself 拉紧 **7** pull fabric into folds by drawing thread through it 给(织物)打褶 • **noun (gathers)** a part of a piece of clothing that is gathered (衣物上的)褶

gathering /'gæðərɪŋ/ **noun** a group of people who have come together for a purpose 集会; 聚会

gauche /gəʊʃ/ **adjective** awkward in social situations 不善交际的

gaucho /'gautʃəu/ **noun** (plural **gauchos**) a cowboy from the South American plains 加乌乔(南美洲大草原的牛仔)

gaudy /'gɔːdi/ **adjective** (**gaudier, gaudiest**) tastelessly bright and showy 过于明亮的;花哨而俗气的
■ **gaudily** adverb.

gauge /geidʒ/ (US spelling 【美拼作】**gage**) **noun 1** an instrument for measuring the amount or level of something 测量仪表;量规 **2** the thickness or size of a wire, tube, bullet, etc. 厚度;大小;直径 **3** the distance between the rails of a railway track (铁轨的)轨距 • **verb 1** judge a situation or mood 判断,估计(形势或情绪) **2** estimate or measure something 计量;测量

✔ 拼写指南 spell gauge with -au-in the middle (the spelling gage is American). gauge 中间拼作 -au-(gage 为美式英语拼法)。

gaunt /gɔːnt/ **adjective** (of a person) looking thin and exhausted (人)消瘦的,疲惫的

gauntlet /'gɔːntlət/ **noun 1** a strong glove with a long loose wrist 长手套;防护手套 **2** a glove worn as part of medieval armour (中世纪甲胄的)铁手套 □ **run the gauntlet** have to face criticism or hostility from a large number of people 面对众人的攻击;成为众矢之的 **throw down the gauntlet** set a challenge 发出挑战

gauze /gɔːz/ **noun 1** a thin transparent fabric 薄纱;纱罗 **2** a fine wire mesh 网纱 ■ **gauzy** adjective.

gave /geiv/ past of **GIVE**.

gavel /'gævl/ **noun** a small hammer with which a judge or auctioneer hits a surface in order to get people's attention (法官或拍卖者使用的)小木槌

gavotte /gə'vɒt/ **noun** a French dance, popular in the 18th century 加伏特舞(流行于18世纪的法国)

gawk /gɔːk/ **verb** stare in a stupid or rude way 呆头呆脑地凝望;无礼地盯看

gawky /'gɔːki/ **adjective** awkward and clumsy 笨手笨脚的

gawp /gɔːp/ **verb** Brit. informal 【英,非正式】 gawk 呆头呆脑地凝望;无礼地盯看

gay /gei/ **adjective** (**gayer, gayest**) **1** (especially of a man) homosexual (尤指男子)同性恋的 **2** relating to homosexuals 与同性恋者有关的 **3** dated 【废】 light-hearted and carefree 轻松愉快的 **4** dated 【废】 brightly coloured 色彩鲜艳的;艳丽的 • **noun** a homosexual person, especially a man 同性恋者;(尤指)男同性恋

gayety /'geiəti/ US spelling of **GAIETY**. gaiety 的美式拼法

gaze /geiz/ **verb** (**gazes, gazing, gazed**) look steadily 凝视;注视 • **noun** a steady look 凝视;注视

gazebo /gə'ziːbəu/ **noun** (plural **gazebos**) a summer house with a pleasant view 凉亭;观景亭

gazelle /gə'zel/ **noun** a small antelope 瞪羚(一种小羚羊)

gazette /gə'zet/ **noun** a journal or newspaper 报;报纸

gazetteer /ˌgæzə'tɪə(r)/ **noun** a list of place names 地名索引;地名词典

gazump /gə'zʌmp/ **verb** Brit. informal 【英,非正式】 offer or accept a higher price for a house after a lower offer has already been accepted (向接受议定价格的购房者)抬价敲诈

GB /ˌdʒiː'biː/ **abbreviation 1** Great Britain 大不列颠;英国 **2** (also **Gb**) Computing 【计】 gigabytes.

GBH /ˌdʒiː biː 'eitʃ/ **abbreviation** Brit. 【英】 grievous bodily harm.

GC /ˌdʒiː 'siː/ **abbreviation** George Cross 乔治勋章

GCE /dʒi: si: 'i:/ **abbreviation** General Certificate of Education 普通教育证书

GCSE /dʒi: si: es 'i:/ **abbreviation** (in the UK except Scotland) General Certificate of Secondary Education (the lower of the two main levels of the GCE exam) (英国除苏格兰以外的)普通中等教育证书

gear /gɪə(r)/ **noun 1 (gears)** a set of machinery that connects the engine to the wheels of a vehicle and controls its speed 齿轮传动装置,排挡 **2** a particular position of gears in a vehicle 档位;挡: *fifth gear* 五档 **3** informal 【非正式】equipment or clothing 设备;装备,衣物 ● **verb 1** adapt something for a particular purpose 使适合 **2** adjust the gears in a vehicle to a particular level 调整挡位;换挡 **3 (gear up)** get prepared for something 为…做好准备 □ **gear lever** Brit.【英】a lever used to change gear in a vehicle (汽车的)变速杆,换挡杆

gearbox /'gɪəbɒks/ **noun** a set of gears with its casing 齿轮箱

gecko /'gekəʊ/ **noun (plural geckos** or **geckoes)** a lizard with adhesive pads on the feet, active at night 壁虎

gee /dʒi:/ **exclamation 1 (gee up)** a command to a horse to go faster 驾 (驱马快跑的吆喝语) **2 (also gee whiz)** N. Amer. informal【北美,非正式】a mild expression of surprise, enthusiasm, or sympathy (表示惊讶、热心或同情)哎呀,哇

geek /gi:k/ **noun** informal【非正式】**1** an awkward or unfashionable person 呆子;土包子 **2** a person who is obsessed with something 极客(对某事物)痴狂者: *a computer geek* 电脑极客 ■ **geeky** adjective.

geese /gi:s/ **plural of** GOOSE.

geezer /'gi:zə(r)/ **noun** informal【非正式】a man 男人;人

Geiger counter /'gaɪgə(r)/ **noun** a device for measuring radioactivity 盖格计数器(测量放射性的仪器)

geisha /'geɪʃə/ **noun (plural geisha** or **geishas)** a Japanese woman who is paid to accompany and entertain men (日本的)艺妓

gel¹ /dʒel/ **noun** a jelly-like substance used on the hair or skin (用于头发或护肤的)发胶,凝胶 ● **verb (gels, gelling, gelled)** smooth your hair with gel 涂抹发胶于

gel² **(gels, gelling, gelled) 1** (of jelly or a similar substance) set or become firmer (胶状物)胶凝,胶化 **2** take definite form or begin to work well 成型;起作用

gelatin /'dʒelətɪn/ or **gelatine** /'dʒeləti:n/ **noun** a clear substance made from animal bones and used to make jelly, glue, and photographic film 明胶;骨胶(提取自动物骨头,用于制肉冻、胶水和摄影胶卷) ■ **gelatinous** /dʒə'lætɪnəs/ adjective.

geld /geld/ **verb** castrate a male animal 阉割(雄性动物)

gelding /'geldɪŋ/ **noun** a castrated male horse 阉割的公马

gelignite /'dʒelɪgnaɪt/ **noun** a powerful explosive made from nitroglycerine 葛里炸药,硝铵炸药

gem /dʒem/ **noun 1** a precious stone 宝石 **2** an outstanding person or thing 杰出人物;宝物;美妙事物

Gemini /'dʒemɪnaɪ, -ni/ **noun** a sign of the zodiac (the Twins), 21 May–20 June 双子宫(黄道十二宫之一)

gemstone /'dʒemstəʊn/ **noun** a gem used in a piece of jewellery (珠宝首饰上的)宝石

gen /dʒen/ Brit. informal【英,非正式】**noun** information 信息,情报 ● **verb (gens, genning, genned) (gen up on)** obtain information about something 获取(情报)

gendarme /'ʒɒndɑ:m/ **noun** a member of the French police force (法国的)警察,宪兵

gender /'dʒendə(r)/ noun 1 Grammar 【语法】 each of the classes into which nouns and pronouns are divided in some languages, usually referred to as masculine, feminine, and neuter (某些语言中名词和代词的)性 2 the state of being male or female (in terms of social or cultural differences rather than biological ones) 性别(偏重社会或文化方面的差异) 3 the members of one or other sex 男性；女性

gene /dʒiːn/ noun Biology 【生物】 a distinct sequence of DNA forming part of a chromosome, by which offspring inherit characteristics from a parent 基因

genealogy /dʒiːniˈælədʒi/ noun (plural **genealogies**) 1 a line of descent traced from an ancestor 家谱；宗谱 2 the study of lines of descent 家谱研究；家谱学 ■ **genealogical** adjective **genealogist** noun.

genera /'dʒenərə/ plural of GENUS.

general /'dʒenrəl/ adjective 1 affecting or concerning all or most people or things 普遍的；一般的 2 involving only the main features of something; not detailed 大致的；概括的 3 chief or principal 首席的；主要的: the general manager 总经理 ● noun a commander of an army, or an army officer ranking above lieutenant general 将军；上将 □ **general anaesthetic** an anaesthetic that affects the whole body and causes a loss of consciousness 全身麻醉 **general election** the election of representatives to a parliament by all the people of a country (全国范围的)普选，大选 **general practitioner** a doctor who treats patients in a local community rather than at a hospital 普通医师；全科医生

generality /dʒenəˈræləti/ noun (plural **generalities**) 1 a general statement rather than one that is specific or detailed 概论；概述 2 the quality or state of being general 一般性；普遍性；笼统；概括

generalize or **generalise** /'dʒenrəlaɪz/ verb (**generalizes, generalizing, generalized**) 1 make a general or broad statement 归纳；概括 2 make something more common or more widely applicable 推广；普及 ■ **generalization** noun.

generally /'dʒenrəli/ adverb 1 in most cases 普遍地；广泛地 2 without discussing the details of something 大体上；大致 3 widely 广泛地

generate /'dʒenəreɪt/ verb (**generates, generating, generated**) create or produce something 产生；引起 ■ **generative** adjective.

generation /dʒenəˈreɪʃn/ noun 1 all the people born and living at about the same time 一代人；同代人；同辈人 2 the average period in which a person grows up and has children of their own 代；一代；一辈 3 a single stage in the history of a family (家史中的)一代 4 a stage in the development of a product (产品的)代 5 the producing or creating of something 产生；发生

generator /'dʒenəreɪtə(r)/ noun a machine for producing electricity 发电机

generic /dʒəˈnerɪk/ adjective 1 referring to a class or group of things 属的；类的 2 (of goods) having no brand name (货物)无商标的，无品牌的 ■ **generically** adverb.

generous /'dʒenərəs/ adjective 1 freely giving more than is necessary or expected 慷慨的；大方的 2 kind towards other people 宽厚的，宽宏大量的 3 larger or more plentiful than is usual 大量的；丰富的 ■ **generosity** noun.

genesis /'dʒenəsɪs/ noun the origin or development of something 起源；开端

genetic /dʒəˈnetɪk/ adjective 1

relating to genes 基因的；遗传的 **2** relating to genetics 遗传学的 ■ **genetically** adverb. □ **genetically modified** (of an animal or plant) containing genetic material that has been altered in order to produce a desired characteristic (动植物)转基因的 **genetic engineering** the changing of the characteristics of an animal or plant by altering its genetic material 遗传工程 **genetic fingerprinting** the analysis of genetic material in order to identify individual people 遗传指纹分析

genetics /dʒə'netɪks/ **plural noun** the study of the way characteristics are passed from one generation to another 遗传学 ■ **geneticist** noun.

genial /'dʒiːnɪəl/ **adjective** friendly and cheerful 友好的；欢快的 ■ **geniality** noun **genially** adverb.

genie /'dʒiːni/ **noun** (in Arabian folklore) a spirit (阿拉伯传说中的)神怪，妖怪

genital /'dʒenɪtl/ **adjective** referring to the external reproductive organs of a person or animal 生殖器官的 • **noun** (**genitals**) the external reproductive organs 外生殖器

genitalia /ˌdʒenɪ'teɪlɪə/ **plural noun** formal or technical 【正式或术语】the genitals 外生殖器

genitive /'dʒenətɪv/ **adjective** Grammar【语法】the form of a noun, pronoun, or adjective used to show possession. 属格；所有格

genius /'dʒiːnɪəs/ **noun** (plural **geniuses**) **1** exceptional natural ability 天才；天赋；天资 **2** an exceptionally intelligent or able person 天才人物；奇才

genocide /'dʒenəsaɪd/ **noun** the deliberate killing of a very large number of people from a particular ethnic group or nation 种族灭绝 ■ **genocidal** adjective.

genre /'ʒɒnrə/ **noun** a type or style of art or literature (艺术或文学的)样式，体裁

gent /dʒent/ **noun** informal 【非正式】a gentleman 绅士

genteel /dʒen'tiːl/ **adjective** polite and refined in an affected or exaggerated way 显得彬彬有礼的；假斯文的 ■ **gentility** noun.

Gentile /'dʒentaɪl/ **adjective** not Jewish 非犹太人的 • **noun** a person who is not Jewish 非犹太人

gentle /'dʒentl/ **adjective** (**gentler**, **gentlest**) **1** (of a person) mild and kind (人)慈祥的，和蔼的 **2** moderate; not harsh or severe 温和的；和缓的 ■ **gentleness** noun **gently** adverb.

gentleman /'dʒentlmən/ **noun** (plural **gentlemen**) **1** a polite or honourable man 彬彬有礼的男士 **2** a man of good social position 贵族出身的人；社会地位高的人 **3** (in polite or formal use) a man (礼貌或正式用法)男士，先生

gentry /'dʒentri/ **noun** (**the gentry**) people of good social position 绅士阶层；上流社会人士

genuflect /'dʒenjuflekt/ **verb** lower your body as a sign of respect by bending one knee 屈膝；单膝跪拜 ■ **genuflection** noun.

genuine /'dʒenjuɪn/ **adjective 1** truly what it is said to be 名副其实的；真正的 **2** honest 真诚的；诚实的 ■ **genuinely** adverb.

genus /'dʒiːnəs/ **noun** (plural **genera** /'dʒenərə/) a category in the classification of animals and plants (动植物的)属

geodesic /ˌdʒiːəʊ'desɪk/ **adjective** relating to a method of construction based on straight lines between points on a curved surface (曲面上两点之间)最短距离线的

geographical /ˌdʒiːə'ɡræfɪkl/ or **geographic** /ˌdʒiːə'ɡræfɪk/ **adjective** relating to geography 地理学的 ■ **geographically** adverb.

geography /dʒiˈɒgrəfi/ **noun 1** the study of the physical features of the earth and how people relate to them 地理(学) **2** the way in which places and physical features are arranged 地形；地势 ■ **geographer** noun.

geology /dʒiˈɒlədʒi/ **noun 1** the scientific study of the physical structure and substance of the earth 地质学 **2** the geological features of a particular area (某地区的)地质情况 ■ **geological** adjective **geologist** noun.

geometric /dʒiːəˈmetrɪk/ **adjective 1** relating to geometry 几何的；几何学的 **2** (of a design) featuring regular lines and shapes (设计)几何图形的 ■ **geometrical** adjective **geometrically** adverb.

geometry /dʒiˈɒmətri/ **noun** (plural **geometries**) **1** the branch of mathematics that deals with the properties and relationships of lines, angles, surfaces, and solids 几何(学) **2** the shape and relationship of the parts of something 几何形状

Geordie /ˈdʒɔːdi/ **noun** Brit. informal 【英，非正式】 a person from Tyneside in NE England (英格兰东北部的)泰恩赛德人

Georgian /ˈdʒɔːdʒən/ **adjective** relating to the reigns of the British kings George I–IV (1714–1830) 乔治一世至四世统治时期的；乔治王朝的

geranium /dʒəˈreɪniəm/ **noun** a plant with red, pink, or white flowers 天竺葵(开红色，粉色或白色花)

gerbil /ˈdʒɜːbɪl/ **noun** a small rodent, often kept as a pet 沙鼠(常被当作宠物饲养)

geriatric /ˌdʒeriˈætrɪk/ **adjective** relating to old people 老年人的 ● **noun** an old person, especially one receiving special care (尤指接受特殊护理的)老年人，老年病人

germ /dʒɜːm/ **noun 1** a microorganism, especially one which causes disease 微生物，(尤指)病菌 **2** a part of an organism that is able to develop into a new one 胚芽；萌芽 **3** an initial stage from which something may develop 发端；起源

German /ˈdʒɜːmən/ **noun 1** a person from Germany 德国人 **2** the language of Germany, Austria, and parts of Switzerland 德语 ● **adjective** relating to Germany or German 德国的；德国人的；德语的 □ **German measles** = RUBELLA. **German shepherd** a large breed of dog often used as guard dogs; an Alsatian 德国牧羊犬；阿尔萨斯狼狗

germane /dʒɜːˈmeɪn/ **adjective** (**germane to**) relevant or appropriate to 有关的；适合的

Germanic /dʒɜːˈmænɪk/ **adjective 1** of the language family that includes English, German, Dutch, and the Scandinavian languages (族)的 **2** characteristic of Germans or Germany 有德国人(或德国)特点的

germicide /ˈdʒɜːmɪsaɪd/ **noun** a substance which destroys germs 杀菌剂 ■ **germicidal** adjective.

germinal /ˈdʒɜːmɪnl/ **adjective 1** relating to a gamete or embryo 胚芽的；胚胎的 **2** in the earliest stage of development 处于萌芽状态的；初级阶段的

germinate /ˈdʒɜːmɪneɪt/ **verb** (**germinates, germinating, germinated**) (of a seed) begin to grow (种子)发芽，开始生长 ■ **germination** noun.

gerontology /ˌdʒerɒnˈtɒlədʒi/ **noun** the scientific study of old age and old people 老年学

gerrymander /ˈdʒerɪmændə(r)/ **verb** (**gerrymanders, gerrymandering, gerrymandered**) change the boundaries of a constituency so as to give an unfair advantage to one party in an election (为使某个党派获

取优势而)改划,不公正地划分(选区)

gerund /'dʒerənd/ **noun** Grammar 【语法】a verb form which functions as a noun (e.g. *asking* in *do you mind my asking?*) 动名词

Gestapo /ge'stɑːpəʊ/ **noun** the German secret police under Nazi rule 盖世太保(纳粹德国的秘密警察)

gestation /dʒe'steɪʃn/ **noun 1** the growth of a baby inside its mother's body 怀孕;妊娠 **2** the development of a plan or idea over a period of time (计划或想法的)形成,构思

gesticulate /dʒe'stɪkjuleɪt/ **verb** (**gesticulates**, **gesticulating**, **gesticulated**) make gestures instead of speaking or in order to emphasize what you are saying 做手势示意(或强调) ■ **gesticulation** noun.

gesture /'dʒestʃə(r)/ **noun 1** a movement of part of the body to express an idea or meaning 手势;示意动作 **2** an action performed to convey your feelings or intentions (表达感情或意图的)姿态,表示 • **verb** (**gestures**, **gesturing**, **gestured**) make a gesture 做手势;用动作示意

get /get/ **verb** (**gets**, **getting**, **got**; past participle **got**, N. Amer. or old use 【北美或旧】**gotten**) **1** come to have or hold; receive 获得,收到 **2** succeed in achieving or experiencing 实现;达到 **3** experience or suffer 经历;遭受 **4** fetch 拿来;取来 **5** reach a particular state or condition 进入(某种状态): *It's getting late.* 天晚了。**6** move to or from a particular place 到达,离开(某处) **7** travel by or catch a form of transport 乘坐,搭乘(某种交通工具) **8** begin to be or do something 开始(做) □ **get away with** escape blame or punishment for 逃脱…的罪责(或惩罚) **get by** manage to live or do something with the things that you have 勉强度日;勉强做成 **get off** informal 【非

正式】escape a punishment 逃脱惩罚 **get on 1** make progress with a task 取得进展 **2** have a friendly relationship 和睦相处 **3** (**be getting on**) informal 【非正式】be old 变老 **get over** recover from an illness or an unpleasant experience 从(疾病或不愉快的经历)中恢复过来 **get something over** manage to communicate an idea 把(想法)讲清楚 **get your own back** informal 【非正式】have your revenge 报复 **get-together** an informal social gathering (非正式的)聚会 **get-up** informal 【非正式】an unusual style of clothes (特殊的)服装,穿戴

getaway /'getəweɪ/ **noun** an escape 逃跑

geyser /'giːzə(r)/ **noun** a hot spring that sometimes sprays water and steam into the air 间歇(喷)泉

Ghanaian /gɑː'neɪən/ **noun** a person from Ghana 加纳人 • **adjective** relating to Ghana 加纳的

ghastly /'gɑːstli/ **adjective** (**ghastlier**, **ghastliest**) **1** causing great horror or fear 可怕的;恐怖的 **2** informal 【非正式】very unpleasant 令人不快的;令人反感的 **3** looking very pale and ill 面色苍白的;面露病容的 ■ **ghastliness** noun.

ghee /giː/ **noun** a kind of butter used in Indian cooking (印度烹饪用的)酥油,黄油

gherkin /'gɜːkɪn/ **noun** a small pickled cucumber 腌小黄瓜

ghetto /'getəʊ/ **noun** (plural **ghettos** or **ghettoes**) a part of a city lived in by people of a particular race, nationality, or ethnic group (某一种族或民族人口的)聚居区 □ **ghetto blaster** informal 【非正式】a large portable radio and cassette or CD player 大型便携式收录机(或CD播放机)

ghost /gəʊst/ **noun 1** a spirit of a dead person which is believed to appear to the living 鬼；幽灵 **2 (a or the ghost of)** a faint trace of 隐约的痕迹；一丝，一点 □ **ghost town** a town in which no one lives any more 废弃的城镇 **ghost writer** a person who writes something for someone else who is named as the author 捉刀人；代笔者

ghostly /ˈgəʊstli/ *adjective* like a ghost; eerie 鬼似的，怪异恐怖的

ghoul /guːl/ *noun* **1** an evil spirit or phantom 恶鬼；幽灵 **2** a person who is too interested in death or disaster 对死亡(或灾难)有变态兴趣的人 ■ **ghoulish** *adjective*.

GI /dʒiː ˈaɪ/ *noun* (plural **GIs**) a private soldier in the US army 美国兵

giant /ˈdʒaɪənt/ *noun* **1** (in stories) a person of superhuman size and strength (传说中的)巨人 **2** an unusually large person, animal, or plant 巨人；巨兽；巨型植物 ■ *adjective* unusually large巨大的；巨型的

gibber /ˈdʒɪbə(r)/ *verb* speak quickly in a way that is difficult to understand 急促不清地说 ■ **gibbering** *adjective*.

gibberish /ˈdʒɪbərɪʃ/ *noun* speech or writing that is impossible to understand; nonsense 令人费解的话(或文字)；胡话

gibbet /ˈdʒɪbɪt/ *noun* (in the past) a post and beam used for hanging people, or for displaying the bodies of those who had been executed (旧时的)绞刑架，示众架

gibbon /ˈgɪbən/ *noun* a small ape with long, powerful arms, native to SE Asia 长臂猿(小型类类，臂长而有力，产于东南亚)

gibe /dʒaɪb/ *noun* 见 JIBE.

giblets /ˈdʒɪblɪts/ *plural noun* the liver, heart, gizzard, and neck of a chicken or other bird (禽类的)内脏，杂碎

giddy /ˈgɪdi/ *adjective* (**giddier**, **giddiest**) **1** having the feeling that everything is moving and that you are going to fall 眩晕的；令人目眩的 **2** excitable and silly 易激动的；爱犯傻的 ■ **giddily** *adverb* **giddiness** *noun*.

gift /gɪft/ *noun* **1** a thing that you give to someone; a present 赠品；礼物 **2** a natural ability or talent 天赋；天资 ■ *verb* **1** give something as a gift 赠送，送出 **2 (gifted)** having exceptional talent or ability 有天赋的；有天分的

gig¹ /gɪg/ *noun* (in the past) a light two wheeled carriage pulled by one horse (旧时的)轻便两轮马车

gig² /gɪg/ *noun* informal 【非正式】 a live performance by a musician 现场音乐会

gigabyte /ˈgɪgəbaɪt/ *noun* Computing 【计】 a unit of information equal to one thousand million (10^9) bytes 千兆字节；十亿字节；吉字节

gigantic /dʒaɪˈgæntɪk/ *adjective* of very great size or extent 巨大的；庞大的

giggle /ˈgɪgl/ *verb* (**giggles**, **giggling**, **giggled**) laugh lightly in a nervous or silly way 咯咯笑；傻笑 ■ *noun* **1** a laugh of this kind 咯咯笑；傻笑 **2** Brit. informal 【英，非正式】 an amusing person or thing 可笑的人(或事物) ■ **giggly** *adjective*.

gigolo /ˈdʒɪgələʊ/ *noun* (plural **gigolos**) a young man paid to be the companion or lover of an older woman 面首，舞男(年长女子供养的年轻男性或情人)

gild /gɪld/ *verb* **1** cover thinly with gold 给…镀金 **2 (gilded)** wealthy and privileged 富有的，有特权的 ■ **gilding** *noun*.

gilet /ˈʒɪleɪ/ *noun* a light sleeveless padded jacket 背心，马甲

gill¹ /gɪl/ *noun* **1** the breathing organ in fish and some amphibians (鱼类和一些两栖动物的)鳃 **2** the plates on the underside of mushrooms and many toadstools (蘑菇和伞菌的)菌褶

gill² /dʒɪl/ *noun* a unit for measuring

liquids, equal to a quarter of a pint 吉耳(液量单位,等于1/4品脱)

gillie /ˈgɪli/ **noun** (in Scotland) a man or boy who helps someone who is on a shooting or fishing trip (苏格兰的)渔猎随从

gilt /gɪlt/ **adjective** covered thinly with gold 镀金的;漆金的 • **noun** a thin layer of gold on a surface 镀金表层;金色涂层 □ **gilt-edged** (of investments) safe and reliable (投资)安全的,可靠的

gimlet /ˈgɪmlət/ **noun** a T-shaped tool with a screw-tip for boring holes 螺丝锥;手钻

gimmick /ˈgɪmɪk/ **noun** a trick or device intended to attract attention rather than fulfil a useful purpose 噱头;花招 ■ **gimmicky** adjective.

gin[1] /dʒɪn/ **noun** a strong, clear alcoholic drink flavoured with juniper berries 杜松子酒(无色烈酒,有杜松子味道)

gin[2] **noun 1** a machine for separating cotton from its seeds 轧棉机 **2** a trap for catching small wild animals or birds (诱捕小型兽类或鸟类的)陷阱,罗网

ginger /ˈdʒɪndʒə(r)/ **noun 1** a hot spice made from the stem of an Asian plant 姜 **2** a light reddish-yellow colour 姜黄色 □ **ginger ale** (or **ginger beer**) a fizzy drink flavoured with ginger 姜汁汽水

gingerbread /ˈdʒɪndʒəbred/ **noun** cake made with treacle and flavoured with ginger 姜饼

gingerly /ˈdʒɪndʒəli/ **adverb** in a careful or cautious way 小心地;谨慎地

gingham /ˈgɪŋəm/ **noun** lightweight cotton cloth, typically checked 方格棉布

gingivitis /ˌdʒɪndʒɪˈvaɪtəs/ **noun** inflammation of the gums 牙龈炎

ginormous /dʒaɪˈnɔːməs/ **adjective** Brit. informal 【英,非正式】 very large 巨大的;庞大的

ginseng /ˈdʒɪnseŋ/ **noun** the root of an east Asian and North American plant, used in some medicines 人参

Gipsy /ˈdʒɪpsi/ ⇒ 见 GYPSY.

giraffe /dʒəˈrɑːf/ **noun** (plural **giraffe** or **giraffes**) a large African animal with a very long neck and legs 长颈鹿

gird /gɜːd/ **verb** (**girds, girding, girded**; past participle **girded** or **girt**) literary 【文】 encircle with a belt or band 束;缠 □ **gird your loins** get ready to do something 准备行动

girder /ˈgɜːdə(r)/ **noun** a large metal beam 大梁;主梁

girdle /ˈgɜːdl/ **noun 1** a belt or cord worn round the waist 腰带 **2** a corset encircling the body from waist to thigh 紧身褡 • **verb** (**girdles, girdling, girdled**) encircle with a girdle or belt 缠绕;围裹

girl /gɜːl/ **noun 1** a female child 女孩;小姑娘 **2** a young woman 年轻女子;少女 ■ **girlish** adjective.

girlfriend /ˈgɜːlfrend/ **noun 1** a person's regular female romantic or sexual partner 女朋友 **2** a woman's female friend (女子的)女性朋友

giro /ˈdʒaɪrəʊ/ **noun** (plural **giros**) **1** a system in which money is transferred electronically from one bank or post office account to another (银行或邮局的)直接转账系统 **2** a cheque or payment by giro 直接转账支票(或汇款)

girt /gɜːt/ past participle of GIRD.

girth /gɜːθ/ **noun 1** the measurement around the middle of something 周长;围长;腰围 **2** a strap attached to a saddle and fastened round a horse's belly (马的)肚带

gist /dʒɪst/ **noun** the main or general meaning of a speech or piece of writing (发言或文章的)主旨,要点

give /gɪv/ **verb** (**gives, giving, gave**; past participle **given**) **1** make someone

have, get, or experience something
给；交给；给予；使经历 **2** carry out an
action or make a sound 实施(行动)；
发出(声音) **3** show 呈现；显出: *He
gave no sign of life.* 他没有任何生命
迹象。**4** state information 提供，报
告(信息) **5** (**give something off** or
out) send out a smell, heat, etc. 发
出，散发(气味、热量等) **6** bend under
pressure (在压力下)弯曲，支撑不住
• **noun** the ability of something to
bend under pressure (压力下的)伸展
性，弹性 □ **give something away**
reveal something secret 泄露(秘密)
give in stop opposing something 屈
服；让步 **give out** stop operating 停
止运转 **give rise to** make happen
使发生；引起 **give up** stop making
an effort and accept that you have
failed 放弃；认输 **give something
up** stop doing, eating, or drinking
something regularly 戒除(习惯)

given /'gɪvn/ past participle of GIVE.
• **adjective 1** already named or stated
特定的；指定的；规定的 **2** (**given to**)
inclined to 倾向于…的 • **preposition**
taking into account 考虑到；鉴于
□ **given name** a person's first name
名；名字

gizmo /'gɪzməʊ/ **noun** (plural **gizmos**)
informal 【非正式】a gadget 小玩意
儿

gizzard /'gɪzəd/ **noun** a muscular part
of a bird's stomach for grinding food
(禽类的)砂囊，胗

glacé /'glæseɪ/ **adjective** (of fruit)
preserved in sugar (水果)糖渍的，蜜
饯的

glacial /'gleɪʃl/ **adjective 1** relating to
ice and glaciers 冰的；冰川的；冰河
的 **2** very cold 冷冰冰的

glaciation /ˌgleɪsi'eɪʃn/ **noun** the
formation of glaciers 冰川作用

glacier /'glæsiə(r)/ **noun** a slowly
moving mass of ice formed by the
accumulation of snow on mountains
冰川

glad /glæd/ **adjective** (**gladder**,
gladdest) **1** pleased; delighted 高兴
的；愉快的 **2** (often **glad of**) grateful
感激的 **3** giving pleasure 使人愉快
的；令人高兴的 □ **glad rags** informal
【非正式】clothes for a party or
special occasion (聚会或特殊场合穿
的)盛装，礼服 ■ **gladly** adverb.

gladden /'glædn/ **verb** make glad 使
高兴；使愉快

glade /gleɪd/ **noun** an open space in a
forest 林中空地

gladiator /'glædieɪtə(r)/ **noun** (in
ancient Rome) a man trained to
fight other men or animals in a
public arena (古罗马的)角斗士
■ **gladiatorial** adjective.

gladiolus /ˌglædi'əʊləs/ **noun** (plural
gladioli /ˌglædi'əʊlaɪ/) a plant with
tall stems and brightly coloured
flowers 剑兰，唐菖蒲(茎高大，花色鲜
艳)

glamorize or **glamorise**
/'glæməraɪz/ **verb** (**glamorizes**,
glamorizing, **glamorized**) often
disapproving 【常贬】make something
seem attractive or desirable 使迷人；
使有吸引力；美化

glamorous /'glæmərəs/ **adjective**
excitingly attractive 富有魅力的；有
吸引力的 ■ **glamorously** adverb.

✔ 拼写指南 **glamorous** drops the *u* of
glamour: glam*or*ous. 拼写 glamorous
要去掉 glamour 中 o 和 r 之间的 u。

glamour /'glæmə(r)/ (US spelling 【美
拼作】**glamor**) **noun** an attractive
and exciting quality 魅力；诱惑力

glance /glɑːns/ **verb** (**glances**,
glancing, **glanced**) **1** look briefly
扫视；匆匆一瞥 **2** (**glance off**) hit
something at an angle and bounce off
擦过；掠过 • **noun** a brief or hurried
look 一瞥 ■ **glancing** adjective.

gland /glænd/ **noun** an organ of the
body which produces a particular
chemical substance 腺

glandular /'glændjʊlə(r)/ **adjective** relating to a gland or glands 腺的，与腺有关的 □ **glandular fever** Brit.【英】an infectious disease which causes swelling of the lymph glands and a persistent lack of energy 腺热，传染性单核细胞增多症

glare /gleə(r)/ **verb** (**glares, glaring, glared**) **1** stare in an angry way 怒视 **2** shine with a dazzling light 闪耀，发出刺眼强光 **3** (**glaring**) very obvious 极为明显的，显而易见的 ■ **noun 1** a fierce or angry stare 怒视 **2** strong and dazzling light 耀眼的强光

glasnost /'glæznɒst/ **noun** (in the former Soviet Union) the policy of more open government (前苏联政府的)透明化(政策)，公开化(政策)

glass /glɑːs/ **noun 1** a hard transparent substance made by fusing sand with soda and lime 玻璃 **2** a drinking container made of glass 玻璃杯 **3** a mirror 镜子 □ **glass-blowing** the craft of making glass objects by blowing semi-liquid glass through a long tube 玻璃吹制(工艺) ■ **glassy** adjective.

glasses /'glɑːsɪz/ **plural noun** a pair of lenses set in a frame that rests on the nose and ears, used to correct eyesight 眼镜

glasshouse /'glɑːshaʊs/ **noun** Brit.【英】a greenhouse 温室；暖房

glaucoma /glɔːˈkəʊmə/ **noun** a condition of increased pressure within the eyeball, causing gradual loss of sight 青光眼

glaze /gleɪz/ **verb** (**glazes, glazing, glazed**) **1** fit panes of glass into a window frame or similar structure 给(窗框等)镶玻璃 **2** enclose or cover with glass 用玻璃罩住；用玻璃覆盖 **3** cover with a glaze 给…上釉 **4** glaze over) (of a person's eyes) lose brightness and liveliness (人的眼睛)失去神采，变得呆滞 ■ **noun 1** a glass-like substance fused on to the surface of pottery to form a hard coating 釉；光油 **2** a liquid such as milk or beaten egg, used to form a shiny coating on food (涂在食物表面增加光泽的)浆汁

glazier /'gleɪzɪə(r)/ **noun** a person who fits glass into windows and doors 镶玻璃匠

gleam /gliːm/ **verb** shine brightly, especially with reflected light (尤指反射光)闪烁，发光 ■ **noun 1** a faint or brief light 微光 **2** a brief or faint show of a quality or emotion (品质或感情的)闪现，隐现: *a gleam of hope* 一线希望

glean /gliːn/ **verb 1** collect information from various sources 四处搜集(信息) **2** gather leftover grain after a harvest (收获后)拾(落穗)

glee /gliː/ **noun** great delight 欣喜

gleeful /'gliːfl/ **adjective** very happy, usually in a smug or gloating way 欣喜若狂的，欢天喜地的 ■ **gleefully** adverb.

glen /glen/ **noun** Scottish & Irish【苏格兰和爱尔兰】a narrow valley 峡谷

glib /glɪb/ **adjective** using words easily but without much thought or sincerity 油嘴滑舌的，油腔滑调的 ■ **glibly** adverb.

glide /glaɪd/ **verb** (**glides, gliding, glided**) **1** move with a smooth, quiet, continuous motion 滑动，滑行 **2** fly without power or in a glider 滑翔；乘滑翔机飞行 ■ **noun** an instance of gliding 滑行；滑动；滑翔

glider /'glaɪdə(r)/ **noun** a light aircraft that flies without an engine 滑翔机

glimmer /'glɪmə(r)/ **verb** (**glimmers, glimmering, glimmered**) shine faintly with a wavering light 隐约地闪烁，发出闪烁的微光 ■ **noun 1** a faint or wavering light 微光；闪光 **2** a faint sign of a feeling or quality (感情或品质的)闪现，隐现

glimpse /glɪmps/ **noun** a brief look at something 一瞥；瞥见 • **verb** (**glimpses, glimpsing, glimpsed**) see something briefly or partially 瞥见

glint /glɪnt/ **verb** give off small flashes of light 闪烁；闪光 • **noun** a sudden flash of light 闪烁；闪光

glisten /ˈglɪsn/ **verb** (of something wet) shine or sparkle (湿物)闪光, 发亮

glitch /glɪtʃ/ **noun** informal【非正式】a sudden problem or fault 故障，错误

glitter /ˈglɪtə(r)/ **verb 1** shine with a shimmering reflected light 闪烁；闪闪发光 **2** (**glittering**) impressively successful or glamorous 极其辉煌的；光彩夺目的 • **noun 1** shimmering reflected light 闪光；光亮 **2** tiny pieces of sparkling material used for decoration 闪亮的小装饰品 **3** an attractive but superficial quality (表面的)吸引力，魅力 ■ **glittery** adjective.

glitz /glɪts/ **noun** superficial glamour 浮华；眩目 ■ **glitzy** adjective.

gloaming /ˈgləʊmɪŋ/ **noun** (**the gloaming**) literary【文】twilight; dusk 黄昏；薄暮

gloat /gləʊt/ **verb** be smug or pleased about your own success or another person's failure 沾沾自喜，幸灾乐祸

global /ˈgləʊbl/ **adjective 1** relating to the whole world; worldwide 全世界的；全球的 **2** relating to all the parts of something 整体的，综合的 □ **global warming** a gradual increase in the temperature of the earth's atmosphere due to the increase of gases such as carbon dioxide 全球变暖(由于二氧化碳等气体的增加造成的地球气温的逐渐上升) ■ **globally** adverb.

globalization or **globalisation** /ˌgləʊbəlaɪˈzeɪʃn/ **noun** the process by which businesses start to operate on a global scale 全球化 ■ **globalize** verb.

globe /gləʊb/ **noun 1** a spherical or rounded object 球体；球状物 **2** (**the globe**) the earth 地球 **3** a model of the earth with a map on its surface 地球仪

globetrotter /ˈgləʊbtrɒtə(r)/ **noun** informal【非正式】a person who travels widely 环游旅行者；周游世界者 ■ **globetrotting** noun & adjective.

globular /ˈglɒbjələ(r)/ **adjective 1** shaped like a globe; spherical 球形的；球体的 **2** consisting of globules 由小球组成的

globule /ˈglɒbjuːl/ **noun** a small drop or ball of a substance 小球；滴

glockenspiel /ˈglɒkənʃpiːl/ **noun** a musical instrument made of metal bars that you hit with small hammers (用小槌敲击的)钟琴

gloom /gluːm/ **noun 1** darkness 黑暗 **2** a feeling of sadness and hopelessness 沮丧；消沉

gloomy /ˈgluːmi/ **adjective** (**gloomier, gloomiest**) **1** dark or badly lit 黑暗的，昏暗的 **2** sad or depressed 忧郁的；沮丧的 ■ **gloomily** adverb **gloominess** noun.

glorify /ˈglɔːrɪfaɪ/ **verb** (**glorifies, glorifying, glorified**) **1** represent something as admirable 赞美，颂扬 **2** (**glorified**) made to appear more important than in reality 被美化的；被夸张的 **3** praise and worship God 赞美，崇拜(上帝)

glorious /ˈglɔːriəs/ **adjective 1** having or bringing glory 光荣的；荣耀的 **2** very beautiful or impressive 美丽的；壮丽的 ■ **gloriously** adverb.

glory /ˈglɔːri/ **noun** (plural **glories**) **1** fame and honour 荣誉；光荣 **2** magnificence; great beauty 辉煌；壮丽 **3** a very beautiful or impressive thing 壮美景色；荣耀的事 **4** worship and praise of God (对上帝的)崇拜，赞颂 • **verb** (**glories, glorying, gloried**) (**glory in**) take great pride or pleasure in 为…而自豪；因…而喜悦

gloss¹ /glɒs/ **noun 1** the shine on a smooth surface (平滑表面的)光泽 **2** a type of paint which dries to a bright shiny surface 光漆;釉 **3** an attractive appearance that hides something ordinary or less attractive 虚饰;虚假外表 • **verb 1** give a glossy appearance to 给…加光泽;给…上釉 **2** (**gloss over**) give only brief or misleading details about something 掩饰;掩盖

gloss² **noun** a translation or explanation of a word, phrase, or passage 注释;注解 • **verb** provide a gloss for 给…作注释

glossary /'glɒsəri/ **noun** (plural **glossaries**) a list of words and their meanings 注释词汇表;术语汇编

glossy /'glɒsi/ **adjective** (**glossier**, **glossiest**) **1** shiny and smooth 有光泽的;光滑的 **2** appearing attractive and stylish 虚饰的

glottal /'glɒtl/ **adjective** having to do with the glottis 声门的 □ **glottal stop** a speech sound made by opening and closing the glottis, sometimes used instead of a properly sounded t 声门(闭)塞音

glottis /'glɒtɪs/ **noun** the part of the larynx made up of the vocal cords and the narrow opening between them 声门

glove /glʌv/ **noun 1** a covering for the hand having separate parts for each finger (分指)手套 **2** a padded covering for the hand used in boxing and other sports (拳击等运动中戴的)手套 □ **glove compartment** a small storage compartment in the dashboard of a car (汽车仪表盘上的)杂物箱

glow /gləʊ/ **verb 1** give out a steady light 燃烧 **2** have flushed skin, especially after exercising (尤指锻炼后)容光焕发,气色红润 **3** look very happy 喜形于色 • **noun** a steady light or heat 发亮;光辉;灼热 □ **glow-worm** a kind of beetle which gives out light 发光虫

glower /ˈglaʊə(r)/ **verb** have an angry or sullen expression 怒目而视;愠然作色 • **noun** an angry or sullen look 怒视;阴沉的表情

glowing /ˈgləʊɪŋ/ **adjective** expressing great praise 热烈赞扬的: *a glowing report* 充满赞美之词的报道

glucose /ˈgluːkəʊs/ **noun** a type of sugar that is easily changed into energy by the body 葡萄糖

glue /gluː/ **noun** a sticky substance used for joining things together 胶;胶水 • **verb** (**glues**, **gluing** or **glueing, glued**) **1** join something with glue 用胶水粘贴;胶合 **2** (**be glued to**) informal【非正式】be paying very close attention to 全神贯注于

glum /glʌm/ **adjective** sad or miserable 闷闷不乐的;忧郁的 ■ **glumly** adverb.

glut /glʌt/ **noun** more of something than is needed 供应过剩;供过于求 • **verb** (**gluts**, **glutting**, **glutted**) supply or provide with too much of something 过量供应;使充斥

gluten /ˈgluːtn/ **noun** a substance containing protein, found in wheat and other cereal plants 谷胶, 麸质(含有蛋白质成分,存在于小麦等谷物中)

glutinous /ˈgluːtənəs/ **adjective** like glue in texture; sticky 似胶的;黏的

glutton /ˈglʌtn/ **noun 1** a very greedy eater 贪食者;吃得过多的人 **2** a person who is very eager for something difficult or challenging 吃苦耐劳的人;任劳任怨的人: *a glutton for punishment* 不怕吃苦的人

gluttony /ˈglʌtəni/ **noun** the habit of eating too much 暴饮暴食;贪食

glycerine /ˈglɪsəriːn/ (US spelling【美拼】**glycerin**) **noun** a liquid made from fats and oils, used in medicines and cosmetics 甘油;丙三醇

GM /ˌdʒiː ˈem/ **abbreviation** genetically modified 转基因的;基因变异的

gm abbreviation grams.

GMO /ˌdʒiː em 'əʊ/ **abbreviation** genetically modified organism 转基因生物体

GMT /ˌdʒiː em 'tiː/ **abbreviation** Greenwich Mean Time 格林尼治标准时间

gnarled /nɑːld/ **adjective** knobbly or twisted 多节的；扭曲的

gnash /næʃ/ **verb** grind your teeth together, especially as a sign of anger (尤指因愤怒而)咬(牙)，咬牙切齿

gnat /næt/ **noun** a small two-winged fly 小飞虫

gnaw /nɔː/ **verb 1** bite at or nibble something persistently 咬；啃；啃 **2** cause persistent anxiety or pain 折磨；使痛苦；使烦恼

gnome /nəʊm/ **noun** (in stories) a creature like a tiny man, who lives underground and guards treasure (传说中的)地下宝藏守护神，地精

gnomic /'nəʊmɪk/ **adjective** clever but hard to understand 睿智深奥的

GNP /ˌdʒiː en 'piː/ **abbreviation** gross national product 国民生产总值

gnu /nuː/ **noun** a large African antelope with a long head and a mane 牛羚，角马(产于非洲的大型羚羊，头部长有鬃毛)

GNVQ /ˌdʒiː en viː 'kjuː/ **abbreviation** General National Vocational Qualification 国家国民职业资格证书

go /gəʊ/ **verb** (**goes**, **going**, **went**; past participle **gone**) **1** move to or from a place 去；走 **2** pass into or be in a particular state 进入，处于(某状态) **3** lie or extend in a certain direction (向某方向)伸展，延伸 **4** come to an end 结束；停止 **5** disappear or be used up 消失；耗尽；用完 **6** (of time) pass (时间)流逝，过去 **7** take part in a particular activity 去参加(某活动) **8** have a particular outcome 结果(为…) **9** (**be going to** be or do) used to express a future tense (用于表示将来时态) **10**

function or operate 运行；运转 **11** be harmonious or matching 适合；相配 **12** be acceptable or allowed 被接受；获得允许 **13** fit into or be regularly kept in a particular place 被放置；被摆放 **14** make a particular sound 发出(某种声音) • **noun** (plural **goes**) informal 【非正式】 **1** an attempt 尝试 **2** a turn to do or use something 轮到的机会 **3** spirit or energy 精力；活力；干劲 □ **the go-ahead** informal 【非正式】permission to proceed 准许，许可 **go along with** agree to find 同意；赞成 **go back on** fail to keep a promise 违背(诺言) **go-between** a person who acts as a messenger or negotiator 中间人 **go-cart** (or **go-kart**) a small racing car with a lightweight body 微型赛车 **go for 1** decide on 选择 **2** try to gain 试图得到；争取获得 **3** attack 攻击；抨击 **go in for 1** enter a contest 参加(比赛) **2** like or habitually take part in 喜欢；爱好 **go into 1** investigate or enquire into调查；研究 **2** (of a whole number) be capable of dividing another (整数)能除尽 **go off 1** (of a gun or bomb) explode or fire (枪、炮或炸弹)开火，爆炸 **2** Brit.【英】(of food) begin to decompose (食物)变质，腐烂 **3** Brit. informal【英，非正式】begin to dislike 不再喜欢；开始讨厌 **go on** continue 继续 **go out 1** stop shining or burning 熄灭 **2** have a regular romantic relationship with someone (与某人)谈恋爱 **go over** examine or check the details of 仔细查看 **go through 1** undergo a difficult experience 经历；遭受 **2** examine carefully 仔细检查 **go without** suffer lack or hardship 没有…而勉强支撑；遭受没有…的困苦 **have a go at** attack or criticize 抨击；批评 ■ **goer** noun.

goad /gəʊd/ **verb** keep annoying or criticizing someone until they react 刺激；招惹 • **noun 1** a thing that makes someone do something (促使某人做某事的)刺激,激励 **2** a spiked stick used for driving cattle (赶牛用的)尖棒

goal /ɡəʊl/ **noun 1** (in soccer, rugby, etc.) a wooden frame into or over which the ball has to be sent to score (足球、英式橄榄球等运动中的)球门 **2** an instance of sending the ball into or over a goal 进球 **3** an aim or desired result 目标;意图 ■ **goalless** adjective.

goalkeeper /ˈɡəʊlkiːpə(r)/ **noun** (in soccer, hockey, etc.) a player whose role is to stop the ball from entering the goal (足球、曲棍球等运动中的)守门员,门将

goalpost /ˈɡəʊlpəʊst/ **noun** either of the two upright posts of a goal 球门柱

goat /ɡəʊt/ **noun** an animal with horns and a hairy coat, often kept for milk 山羊

goatee /ɡəʊˈtiː/ **noun** a small pointed beard like that of a goat 山羊胡子

goatherd /ˈɡəʊthɜːd/ **noun** a person who looks after goats 牧羊人,羊倌

gob /ɡɒb/ **noun** Brit. informal【英,非正式】a person's mouth (人的)嘴

gobbet /ˈɡɒbɪt/ **noun** a piece of flesh, food, or other matter (肉、食物等的)片,块

gobble /ˈɡɒbl/ **verb** (**gobbles**, **gobbling**, **gobbled**) **1** eat hurriedly and noisily 狼吞虎咽 **2** (of a turkey) make a swallowing sound in the throat (火鸡)发吞咽声,咯咯叫

gobbledegook or **gobbledygook** /ˈɡɒbldɪɡuːk/ **noun** informal【非正式】complicated language that is difficult to understand 费解的语言

goblet /ˈɡɒblət/ **noun** a drinking glass with a foot and a stem (玻璃制的)高脚杯

goblin /ˈɡɒblɪn/ **noun** (in stories) a small, ugly, mischievous creature (传说中捉弄人的)小妖精,丑妖怪

gobsmacked /ˈɡɒbsmækt/ **adjective** Brit. informal【英,非正式】utterly astonished 震惊的;大吃一惊的

gobstopper /ˈɡɒbstɒpə(r)/ **noun** a hard round sweet 大块硬糖

goby /ˈɡəʊbi/ **noun** (plural **gobies**) a small sea fish 虾虎鱼(一种小海鱼)

God /ɡɒd/ **noun 1** (in Christianity and some other religions) the creator and supreme ruler of the universe (基督教等宗教信仰的)上帝天主,真主 **2** (**god**) a superhuman being or spirit 神;神灵 □ **God-fearing** earnestly religious 虔诚的,敬畏上帝的

godchild /ˈɡɒdtʃaɪld/ **noun** (plural **godchildren**) a person in relation to a godparent 教子;教女

god-daughter /ˈɡɒddɔːtə(r)/ **noun** a female godchild 教女

goddess /ˈɡɒdes/ **noun** a female deity 女神

godfather /ˈɡɒdfɑːðə(r)/ **noun 1** a male godparent 教父 **2** the male leader of an illegal organization 教父(犯罪组织的男性头目)

godforsaken /ˈɡɒdfəseɪkən/ **adjective** (of a place) remote, unattractive, or depressing (地方)荒芜的,凄凉的

godhead /ˈɡɒdhed/ **noun 1** (**the Godhead**) God 上帝 **2** divine nature 神性

godless /ˈɡɒdləs/ **adjective 1** not believing in God or a god 无神的;不信神的,不信奉上帝的 **2** wicked 邪恶的

godly /ˈɡɒdli/ **adjective** very religious 虔诚的;敬神的;崇敬上帝的

godmother /ˈɡɒdmʌðə(r)/ **noun** a female godparent 教母

godparent /ˈɡɒdpeərənt/ **noun** a person who promises to be responsible for a child's religious education 教父;教母

godsend /ˈɡɒdsend/ **noun** something that is very helpful or welcome 天赐之物;意外的好运

godson /ˈɡɒdsʌn/ **noun** a male godchild 教子

goes /gəʊz/ 3rd person singular present of **go**.

goggle /ˈgɒgl/ **verb** (**goggles**, **goggling**, **goggled**) **1** look with wide open eyes 瞪大眼睛看；瞪着眼睛看 **2** (of the eyes) stick out or open wide (眼睛)鼓出，睁大 • **noun** (**goggles**) close-fitting protective glasses 护目镜

going /ˈgəʊŋ/ **noun 1** the condition of the ground in terms of its suitability for horse racing or walking (赛马或步行的)场地状况, 路面状况 **2** conditions for an activity (某活动的)情况: *The going gets tough.* 形势变得艰难起来。• **adjective 1** existing or available 现存的；可得的 **2** (of a price) normal or current (价格)现行的, 当前的 □ **going concern** a thriving business 兴隆的生意 **goings-on** informal 【非正式】 activities that are strange or dishonest 异常行为；不正当行为

goitre /ˈgɔɪtə(r)/ **noun** a swelling of the neck which is caused by enlargement of the thyroid gland (颈部)甲状腺肿大

gold /gəʊld/ **noun 1** a yellow precious metal 金；黄金 **2** a deep yellow or yellow-brown colour 金(黄)色 **3** things made of gold 黄金制品 □ **gold leaf** gold beaten into a very thin sheet 金叶；金箔 **gold medal** a medal awarded for first place in a race or competition 金牌 **gold rush** a rapid movement of people to a place where gold has been discovered 淘金热

golden /ˈgəʊldən/ **adjective 1** made of or resembling gold 金制的；似金的 **2** (of a period) very happy and prosperous (时期)极其幸福的, 黄金般的 **3** excellent 绝好的 □ **golden age** the period when something is very successful 黄金时期；鼎盛时期 **golden eagle** a large eagle with yellow-tipped head feathers 金雕(头顶有黄色羽毛) **golden handshake** informal 【非正式】 a payment given to

someone who is made redundant or retires early遣散费；退职金 **golden jubilee** the fiftieth anniversary of an important event 五十周年纪念 **golden rule** a principle which should always be followed 处世准则；金科玉律 **golden wedding** Brit. 【英】the fiftieth anniversary of a wedding 金婚纪念(结婚五十周年)

goldfinch /ˈgəʊldfɪntʃ/ **noun** a brightly coloured finch with a yellow patch on each wing 金翅雀

goldfish /ˈgəʊldfɪʃ/ **noun** (plural **goldfish** or **goldfishes**) a small orange carp, often kept in ponds 金鱼

goldsmith /ˈgəʊldsmɪθ/ **noun** a person who makes things out of gold 金匠

golf /gɒlf/ **noun** a game played on an outdoor course, the aim of which is to hit a small ball into a series of small holes using a set of special clubs 高尔夫球(运动) ■ **golfer** noun.

golliwog /ˈgɒlɪwɒg/ **noun** a soft doll with a black face and fuzzy hair 黑脸黑发布娃娃

gonad /ˈgəʊnæd/ **noun** an organ in the body that produces gametes; a testis or ovary 性腺；睾丸；卵巢

gondola /ˈgɒndələ/ **noun** a light flat-bottomed boat used on canals in Venice, worked by one oar at the stern (威尼斯的)凤尾船, 贡多拉

gondolier /ˌgɒndəˈlɪə(r)/ **noun** a person who propels a gondola 凤尾船船夫

gone /gɒn/ past participle of **go**. • **adjective** no longer present or in existence 消失了的；不存在的 • **preposition** Brit. 【英】 **1** (of time) past (时间)过了…以后 **2** (of age) older than (年龄)高于, 过了…岁

goner /ˈgɒnə(r)/ **noun** informal 【非正式】 a person or thing that cannot be saved 无法挽救的人(或事物)

gong /gɒŋ/ **noun 1** a metal disc that makes a deep ringing sound when struck 锣 **2** Brit. informal 【英, 非正式】

a medal or other award 奖章;勋章

gonorrhoea /ˌgɒnəˈriːə/ (US spelling 【美拼作】**gonorrhea**) noun a disease caused by bacteria that are passed on during sex 淋病

goo /guː/ noun informal【非正式】 a soft, sticky substance 黏性物质

good /gʊd/ adjective **1** having the right qualities; of a high standard 合格的;良好的 **2** of high quality 优质的 **2** behaving in a way that is right, polite, or obedient 规矩的;礼貌的 **3** enjoyable or satisfying 让人高兴的;令人满意的 **4** suitable or appropriate 适宜的;适当的 **5** (**good for**) having a useful or helpful effect on 对…有益的 **6** thorough 彻底的;充分的 • noun (**goods**) **1** products or possessions 产品;个人财产 **2** Brit.【英】freight 货物 □ **as good as** very nearly 几乎 **for good** forever 永远 **good faith** honest or sincere intentions 诚实;真挚 **good-for-nothing** worthless 毫无价值的;一无是处 **Good Friday** the Friday before Easter Sunday, on which Christians commemorate the Crucifixion of Jesus 耶稣受难日(复活节前的星期五) **good-looking** attractive 漂亮的;吸引人的 **good-natured** kind and unselfish 善良无私的 **make something good 1** compensate for loss or damage 弥补,赔偿(损失) **2** fulfil a promise or claim 履行(诺言);满足(要求)
■ **goodness** noun.

goodbye /ˌgʊdˈbaɪ/ exclamation used to express good wishes when parting or ending a conversation 再见;再会 • noun (plural **goodbyes**) a parting 分别

goodly /ˈgʊdli/ adjective (**goodlier**, **goodliest**) quite large in size or quantity 相当大的;相当多的

goodwill /ˌgʊdˈwɪl/ noun friendly or helpful feelings towards other people 友好;好意

goody or **goodie** /ˈgʊdi/ noun (plural **goodies**) informal【非正式】**1** Brit.【英】a good person, especially a hero in a story or film 好人;(尤指故事或电影中的)英雄好汉 **2** (**goodies**) tasty things to eat 美味 □ **goody-goody** informal【非正式】a person who behaves well in order to impress other people 假正经的人;伪善的人

gooey /ˈguːi/ adjective informal【非正式】soft and sticky 柔软黏稠的

goof /guːf/ noun informal, chiefly N. Amer.【非正式,主北美】verb **1** make a mistake 犯错误 **2** fool around 闲荡;混日子 • noun a mistake 错误;差错

goofy /ˈguːfi/ adjective informal【非正式】**1** chiefly N. Amer.【主北美】silly 愚蠢的;犯傻的 **2** having front teeth that stick out 龅牙的

goon /guːn/ noun informal【非正式】**1** a silly person 笨蛋;傻瓜 **2** N. Amer.【北美】a thug 暴徒;打手

goose /guːs/ noun (plural **geese**) **1** a large waterbird with a long neck and webbed feet 鹅 **2** a female goose 雌鹅 **3** informal【非正式】a silly person 笨蛋;傻瓜 □ **goose pimples** little raised bumps on your skin, caused by feeling cold or frightened (因寒冷或恐惧而在皮肤上起的)鸡皮疙瘩 **goose step** a way of marching in which the legs are kept straight 正步走

gooseberry /ˈgʊzbəri/ noun (plural **gooseberries**) **1** an edible yellowish-green berry with a hairy skin 醋栗 **2** Brit. informal【英,非正式】a third person in the company of two lovers (夹在情侣间的)"电灯泡",不知趣者

gopher /ˈgəʊfə(r)/ noun a burrowing rodent found in North America 囊地鼠,金花鼠(见于北美洲)

gore[1] /gɔː(r)/ noun blood that has been shed (流出的)血

gore[2] verb (**gores**, **goring**, **gored**) (of an animal such as a bull) pierce with a horn or tusk (公牛等动物用角或长牙)抵刺,戳

gore³ noun a triangular piece of material used in making a garment, sail, or umbrella 三角形布料(用于制作衣服、船帆或雨伞)

gorge /ɡɔːdʒ/ noun a narrow valley or ravine 峡谷；溪谷 • verb (**gorges**, **gorging**, **gorged**) eat a large amount greedily 狼吞虎咽地吃

gorgeous /ˈɡɔːdʒəs/ adjective **1** beautiful 华丽的；美丽的 **2** informal 【非正式】 very pleasant 令人愉快的

gorgon /ˈɡɔːɡən/ noun Greek Mythology 【希腊神话】 each of three sisters with snakes for hair, who had the power to turn anyone who looked at them to stone 戈耳工(蛇发三女妖之一，人见之即变成石头)

gorilla /ɡəˈrɪlə/ noun a powerfully built ape of central Africa 大猩猩(产于非洲中部)

gormless /ˈɡɔːmləs/ adjective Brit. informal 【英，非正式】 stupid 愚蠢的；傻的

gorse /ɡɔːs/ noun a yellow-flowered shrub with spiny leaves 荆豆(开黄花的灌木，叶多刺)

gory /ˈɡɔːri/ adjective **1** involving violence and bloodshed 充满暴力的；血腥的 **2** covered in blood 沾满鲜血的

gosling /ˈɡɒzlɪŋ/ noun a young goose 小鹅；幼鹅

gospel /ˈɡɒspl/ noun **1** the teachings of Jesus (基督的)教导，教诲 **2** (**the Gospel**) the record of Jesus's life and teaching in the first four books of the New Testament (《圣经·新约别的)四福音书 **3** (**Gospel**) each of these books 四福音书之一 **4** (also **gospel truth**) something absolutely true 绝对真理 **5** (also **gospel music**) a style of black American religious singing 福音音乐(美国黑人的一种宗教歌唱音乐)

gossamer /ˈɡɒsəmə(r)/ noun a fine substance consisting of cobwebs spun by small spiders 蛛丝 • adjective very fine and flimsy 极轻薄的

gossip /ˈɡɒsɪp/ noun **1** casual conversation about other people 说长道短；闲言碎语 **2** disapproving 【贬】 a person who likes talking about other people 喜欢说长道短的人 • verb (**gossips**, **gossiping**, **gossiped**) talk about other people 说长道短；说三道四

got /ɡɒt/ past and past participle of GET.

Gothic /ˈɡɒθɪk/ adjective **1** of the style of architecture common in western Europe in the 12th to 16th Centuries (建筑风格)哥特式的 **2** very gloomy or horrifying 阴森的；恐怖的

gotten /ˈɡɒtn/ N. Amer. or old use 【北美或旧】 past participle of GET.

gouache /ɡuˈɑːʃ, ɡwɑːʃ/ noun **1** a method of painting using watercolours thickened with glue 水粉画法 **2** paint used in this method 水粉画颜料

gouge /ɡaʊdʒ/ verb (**gouges**, **gouging**, **gouged**) **1** make a rough hole in a surface 凿(洞)；挖(洞) **2** (**gouge something out**) cut something out roughly 抠出；挖出 • noun **1** a chisel with a concave blade 半圆凿；弧口凿 **2** a hole or groove made by gouging 凿出的洞；开出的槽

goulash /ˈɡuːlæʃ/ noun a rich Hungarian stew of meat and vegetables 匈牙利红烩肉，菜炖肉

gourd /ɡʊəd/ noun a fruit with a hard skin, usually used as a container rather than as food 葫芦

gourmand /ˈɡʊəmənd/ noun a person who enjoys eating 贪食者

gourmet /ˈɡʊəmeɪ/ noun a person who knows a lot about good food 美食家 • adjective suitable for a gourmet 适合供美食家享用的

gout /ɡaʊt/ noun a disease causing the joints to swell and become painful 痛风(引发关节肿痛的疾病)

govern /'gʌvn/ **verb 1** control the laws and affairs of a state, organization, or community 统治，管理(国家、组织或社区) **2** control or influence 控制；影响

governance /'gʌvənəns/ **noun** the action or style of governing 统治(方式)；管理(方法)

governess /'gʌvənəs/ **noun** a woman employed to teach the children of a family in their home 家庭女教师

government /'gʌvənmənt/ **noun 1** the group of people who govern a state 政府 **2** the system by which a state, organization, or community is governed 政体；体制 ■ **governmental** adjective.

✔ **拼写指南** remember that **government** is spelled with an *n* before the *m*. 记住拼写 government 中 m 前的 n。

governor /'gʌvənə(r)/ **noun 1** an official appointed to govern a town or region 地方长官 **2** the head of a public institution (公共机构的)主管，负责人 **3** a member of a governing body 理事；董事

gown /gaʊn/ **noun 1** a long dress worn on formal occasions 长礼服 **2** a protective garment worn in hospital by surgeons or patients (医院的外科工作人员或患者穿的)罩衣 **3** a loose cloak showing your profession or status, worn by a lawyer, academic, or university student (律师、学者或大学生穿的)长袍

GP /ˌdʒiː 'piː/ **abbreviation** general practitioner.

gr. abbreviation 1 grains. **2** grams. **3** gross.

grab /græb/ **verb** (**grabs**, **grabbing**, **grabbed**) **1** seize someone or something suddenly and roughly 抓住，夺取 **2** informal 【非正式】take the opportunity to get something 抓住，把握(机会) • **noun** a sudden attempt to seize someone or something 抓取；

抢夺

grace /greɪs/ **noun 1** attractive smoothness of movement (动作的)优雅，优美 **2** polite respect 彬彬有礼 **3** (**graces**) attractive qualities or behaviour 风度；魅力 **4** (in Christian belief) the unearned favour of God (基督教信仰中的)上帝的恩惠 **5** the condition of being trusted and respected by someone (某人的)信任，尊敬 **6** a period officially allowed to do something 宽限(期)：*three days' grace* 3天的宽限期 **7** a short prayer of thanks said at a meal (用餐时的)感恩祷告 **8** (**His**, **Her**, or **Your Grace**) used as a way of addressing a duke, duchess, or archbishop 阁下，夫人，大人(对公爵、公爵夫人或女公爵、大主教的称呼) • **verb** (**graces**, **gracing**, **graced**) **1** bring honour to someone or something by your presence (某人的出席)给…带来荣耀 **2** make something more attractive 修饰；美化 □ **grace note** Music 【音乐】an extra note which is not needed for the harmony or melody 装饰音

graceful /'greɪsfl/ **adjective** having or showing grace or elegance 优美的；优雅的 ■ **gracefully** adverb.

graceless /'greɪsləs/ **adjective** without grace or charm 不雅的；难看的

gracious /'greɪʃəs/ **adjective 1** kind, pleasant, and polite 有礼貌的，亲切的，和蔼的 **2** showing the elegance associated with high social status or wealth 高雅的；雍容华贵的 **3** (in Christian belief) showing divine grace (基督教信仰)显示恩典的 ■ **graciously** adverb.

gradation /grə'deɪʃn/ **noun 1** a scale of gradual change from one thing to another 渐变 **2** a stage in such a scale 阶段；等级

grade /greɪd/ **noun 1** a level of rank or ability 等级；级别 **2** a mark indicating the quality of a student's work (学生的)分数，成绩 **3** N. Amer. 【北美】

a class of school students grouped according to age or ability 年级 • verb (**grades**, **grading**, **graded**) **1** arrange people or things in groups according to quality, ability, etc. 将…分级 **2** N. Amer.【北美】give a grade to a student or their work 打分 □**make the grade** informal【非正式】 succeed 成功

gradient /'greɪdɪənt/ noun **1** a sloping part of a road or railway (公路或铁路的)斜坡,坡道 **2** the degree to which something slopes 坡度

gradual /'grædʒuəl/ adjective **1** taking place in stages over a long period of time 逐步的,逐渐的 **2** (of a slope) not steep (斜坡)不陡的,平缓的 ■ **gradually** adverb.

graduate noun /'grædʒuət/ a person who has been awarded a university degree 大学毕业生;学士学位获得者 • verb /'grædʒueɪt/ (**graduates**, **graduating**, **graduated**) **1** successfully complete a degree or course 完成学业;毕业 **2** (**graduate to**) move up to something more advanced 逐渐发展;逐步上升 **3** change something gradually 渐变 ■ **graduation** noun.

graffiti /grə'fi:ti/ noun writing or drawings on a wall in a public place (在公共场所的)乱涂乱画,涂鸦

✔ 拼写指南 double *f*, single *t*: gra*ffi*ti. graffiti 有两个 f,一个 t。

graft[1] /grɑ:ft/ noun **1** a shoot from one plant inserted into another to form a new growth (嫁接用的)接穗,嫩枝 **2** a piece of body tissue that is transplanted from one part of the body to another part that has been damaged (从人体)移植的组织 • verb **1** insert or transplant as a graft 嫁接(嫩枝);移植 **2** add something to something else, especially in a way that seems inappropriate (尤指不适当地)添加

graft[2] Brit. informal【英,非正式】noun hard work 艰苦的工作 • verb work hard 努力工作

graft[3] informal【非正式】noun bribery and other illegal methods used to gain advantage in politics or business 行贿;贿赂

Grail /greɪl/ noun (in medieval legend) the cup or dish used by Jesus at the Last Supper (中世纪传说中的)圣杯,圣盘(耶稣在最后晚餐上所用)

grain /greɪn/ noun **1** wheat or another cereal plant grown for food 谷物;谷类 **2** a single seed or fruit of a cereal plant 谷粒 **3** a small, hard particle of a substance such as sand (沙等的)颗粒 **4** the smallest unit of weight in the troy and avoirdupois systems 格令(金衡制和常衡制中的重量单位) **5** the smallest possible amount 微量;一丁点儿 **6** the arrangement of fibres in wood, fabric, etc. (木头、织物等的)纹理 □**against the grain** conflicting with your nature or instinct 违背本性的;非本意的 ■ **grainy** adjective.

gram or Brit.【英】**gramme** /græm/ noun a metric unit of mass equal to one thousandth of a kilogram 克(公制质量单位,等于 1/1000 千克)

grammar /'græmə(r)/ noun **1** the whole system and structure of a language 语法;语法规则 **2** knowledge and use of the rules of Grammar 语法知识 **3** a book on grammar 语法书 □**grammar school** (in the UK, especially formerly) a state secondary school to which pupils are admitted on the basis of their ability (尤指英国旧时的)文法学校

✔ 拼写指南 -*ar*, not -*er*: gramm*ar*. grammar 中的 -ar 不要拼作 -er。

grammatical /grə'mætɪkl/ adjective **1** having to do with grammar 语法的 **2** conforming to the rules of grammar 符合语法规则的 ■ **grammatically**

adverb.

gramophone /'græməfəʊn/ **noun** dated 【废】 a record player 唱机；留声机

grampus /'græmpəs/ **noun** (plural **grampuses**) a killer whale or other animal of the dolphin family 虎鲸；逆戟鲸；灰海豚

gran /græn/ **noun** Brit. informal 【英，非正式】 your grandmother 奶奶；外婆

granary /'grænəri/ **noun** (plural **granaries**) a storehouse for grain 谷仓

grand /grænd/ **adjective 1** magnificent and impressive 宏伟的，壮丽的 **2** large or ambitious in scale 宏大的；有气派的 **3** of the highest importance or rank 最重要的；(级别)最高的 **4** dignified, noble, or proud 高贵的；崇高的；傲慢的 **5** informal 【非正式】 excellent 极好的 • **noun** (plural **grand**) informal 【非正式】 a thousand dollars or pounds 一千美元(或英镑) □ **grand piano** a large piano which has the strings arranged horizontally 大钢琴；三角钢琴 **grand slam** the winning of each of a group of major sports championships or matches in the same year 大满贯(指赢得某项运动同年中所有重大赛事的冠军) **grand total** the final amount after everything is added up 总计；总共 ■ **grandly** adverb.

grandad or **granddad** /'grændæd/ **noun** informal 【非正式】 your grandfather 爷爷；姥爷；外公

grandchild /'græntʃaɪld/ **noun** (plural **grandchildren**) the child of a person's son or daughter 孙子；孙女；外孙；外孙女

granddaughter /'grændɔːtə(r)/ **noun** the daughter of a person's son or daughter 孙女；外孙女

grandee /græn'diː/ **noun** a person of high status and social rank 显贵；要人

grandeur /'grændʒə(r)/ **noun 1** the quality of being grand and impressive 宏伟；壮丽 **2** high status and social rank 显赫；高贵

grandfather /'grænfɑːðə(r)/ **noun** the father of a person's father or mother 祖父；外祖父 □ **grandfather clock** a large clock in a tall wooden case (立于高木匣中的)落地式大摆钟

grandiloquent /græn'dɪləkwənt/ **adjective** pompous in style and using long and fancy words 卖弄词藻的；言语晦涩的

grandiose /'grændiəʊs/ **adjective** (of a plan or building) very large and ambitious and intended to impress 冠冕堂皇的；过分华丽的

grandma /'grænmɑː/ **noun** informal 【非正式】 your grandmother 奶奶；姥姥；外婆

grandmother /'grænmʌðə(r)/ **noun** the mother of a person's father or mother 祖母；外祖母

grandpa /'grænpɑː/ **noun** informal 【非正式】 your grandfather 爷爷；姥爷；外公

grandparent /'grænpeərənt/ **noun** a grandmother or grandfather (外)祖母；(外)祖父

Grand Prix /ˌgrɒn 'priː/ **noun** (plural **Grands Prix** /ˌgrɒn 'priː/) a race forming part of a motor-racing or motorcycling world championship 国际汽车(或摩托车)大奖赛

grandson /'grænsʌn/ **noun** the son of a person's son or daughter 孙子；外孙

grandstand /'grænstænd/ **noun** the main stand at a racecourse or sports ground (跑道或体育比赛场地旁的)大看台

grange /greɪndʒ/ **noun** Brit. 【英】 a country house with farm buildings attached 庄园大宅

granite /'grænɪt/ **noun** a hard grey rock 花岗岩

granny or **grannie** /'græni/ **noun** (plural **grannies**) informal 【非正式】 your grandmother 奶奶；外婆 □ **granny flat** a small flat that is part of or attached to a house, in which an elderly relative can live 老奶奶 套间(指住宅中供老人居住的一套房间) **granny knot** a reef knot with the ends crossed the wrong way and therefore liable to slip 老奶奶结(反向打的结,容易松开)

grant /grɑ:nt/ **verb 1** agree to give something to someone or to allow them to do something 同意;允许 **2** give something formally or legally (正式或依照法律)授予 **3** admit to someone that something is true (向某人)承认 ▪ **noun** a sum of money given by a government or public body for a particular purpose (政府或公共机构的)拨款

granted /grɑ:ntɪd/ **adverb** admittedly; it is true 的确;当然

granulated /ˈɡrænjuleɪtɪd/ **adjective** in the form of granules 颗粒状的 ▪ **granulation** noun.

granule /ˈɡrænju:l/ **noun** a small compact particle of a substance 小颗粒;细粒 ▪ **granular** adjective.

grape /greɪp/ **noun** a green or purple-black berry growing in clusters on a vine, eaten as fruit and used in making wine 葡萄

grapefruit /ˈɡreɪpfru:t/ **noun** (plural **grapefruit**) a large yellow citrus fruit with a slightly bitter taste 西柚;葡萄柚

grapeshot /ˈɡreɪpʃɒt/ **noun** (in the past) ammunition consisting of a number of small iron balls fired together from a cannon (旧时的)葡萄弹,霰弹

grapevine /ˈɡreɪpvaɪn/ **noun 1** a vine which produces grapes 葡萄藤 **2** (**the grapevine**) the spreading of information through talk or rumour 谣言的传播;道听途说

graph /grɑ:f, græf/ **noun** a diagram showing how two or more sets of numbers relate to each other 图表;曲线图 □ **graph paper** paper printed with small squares, used for graphs

and diagrams 坐标纸;方格纸;标绘纸

graphic /ˈɡræfɪk/ **adjective 1** relating to visual art, especially involving drawing and the design of printed material 视觉艺术的;(尤指)绘画的,图样的 **2** giving vivid details 生动的;清楚详细的 ▪ **noun 1** a pictorial image or symbol on a computer screen (计算机屏幕上的)图形,图表,图像 **2** (**graphics**) the use of designs or pictures to illustrate books, magazines, etc. 图样;图案 □ **graphic design** the design of books, posters, and other printed material (书籍、海报等印刷品的)平面造型设计 ▪ **graphically** adverb.

graphite /ˈɡræfaɪt/ **noun** a grey form of carbon used as pencil lead and as a lubricant in machinery 石墨(用作铅笔芯和机器润滑剂)

graphology /ɡræˈfɒlədʒi/ **noun** the study of handwriting as a guide to personality 笔迹学 ▪ **graphologist** noun.

grapnel /ˈɡræpnəl/ **noun** or **grappling hook** noun a device with iron claws, used for dragging or grasping things 多爪锚;抓钩

grapple /ˈɡræpl/ **verb** (**grapples**, **grappling**, **grappled**) **1** struggle or fight physically with someone 扭打;揪斗 **2** (**grapple with**) struggle to deal with or understand 努力解决;尽力理解

grasp /grɑ:sp/ **verb 1** seize and hold something firmly 抓牢;握紧 **2** understand something 领会;理解 ▪ **noun 1** a firm grip 紧抓;紧握 **2** a person's ability to understand something 能力;理解力

grasping /grɑ:spɪŋ/ **adjective** greedy 贪婪的;贪心的

grass /grɑ:s/ **noun 1** plants with long narrow leaves and stalks 草 **2** ground covered with grass 草地;草皮;草坪 **3** informal 【非正式】

cannabis 大麻 **4** Brit. informal【英，非正式】a police informer (警察的线人 • **verb 1** cover an area with grass 用草覆盖 **2** Brit. informal【英，非正式】inform the police about someone's criminal activity (向警方)告发，检举 □ **grass roots** the ordinary people in an organization or society, rather than the leaders 普通群众；草根阶层 ■ **grassy** adjective.

grasshopper /'grɑːshɒpə(r)/ **noun** an insect with long hind legs which it uses for jumping and for producing a chirping sound 蚱蜢，蝗虫

grate¹ /greɪt/ **verb** (**grates**, **grating**, **grated**) **1** shred food by rubbing it on a grater (用磨碎机)磨碎(食物) **2** make an unpleasant rasping sound 发出刺耳的摩擦声 **3** have an irritating effect 使烦躁，使气恼

grate² **noun** a metal frame or basket in a fireplace in which the coals or wood are placed 金属炉架

grateful /'greɪtfl/ **adjective** feeling thankful and appreciative 感激的，表示感谢的 ■ **gratefully** adverb.

✔ 拼写指南 *grate*ful, not *great*ful. grateful 不要拼作 greatful.

grater /'greɪtə(r)/ **noun** a device having a surface covered with sharp-edged holes, used for grating food (食物)磨碎机

gratify /'grætɪfaɪ/ **verb** (**gratifies**, **gratifying**, **gratified**) **1** give someone pleasure or satisfaction 使…高兴，使满足 **2** indulge or satisfy a desire 纵容，满足(欲望) ■ **gratification** noun.

grating¹ /'greɪtɪŋ/ **adjective 1** sounding harsh and unpleasant (声音)刺耳的 **2** irritating 恼人的；令人讨厌的

grating² **noun** a grid of metal bars used as a barrier (金属)格栅，栅栏

gratis /'grætɪs/ **adverb & adjective** free of charge 免费地(的)

gratitude /'grætɪtjuːd/ **noun** the feeling of being grateful 谢意，感激

gratuitous /grə'tjuːɪtəs/ **adjective** having no justifiable reason or purpose 无正当理由的；不必要的 ■ **gratuitously** adverb.

gratuity /grə'tjuːəti/ **noun** (plural **gratuities**) formal【正式】a sum of money given to someone who has provided a service; a tip 赏钱，小费

grave¹ /greɪv/ **noun** a hole dug in the ground for a coffin or dead body 坟墓；墓地

grave² **adjective 1** giving cause for alarm or concern 严重的；重大的 **2** solemn 严肃的 ■ **gravely** adverb.

grave accent /grɑːv/ **noun** a mark (`) placed over a vowel in some languages to indicate a change in its sound quality 钝重音符；沉音符

gravel /'grævl/ **noun** a loose mixture of small stones used for paths and roads 碎石，沙砾(用于铺路)

gravelly /'grævəli/ **adjective 1** resembling or containing gravel 像沙砾的；含沙砾的 **2** (of a voice) deep and rough (声音)粗重沙哑的

graven image /'greɪvn/ **noun** a carved figure 雕像

gravestone /'greɪvstəʊn/ **noun** a stone slab marking a grave 墓碑；墓石

graveyard /'greɪvjɑːd/ **noun** a burial ground 墓地；坟场

gravitas /'grævɪtæs/ **noun** a serious and dignified manner 庄重；严肃

gravitate /'grævɪteɪt/ **verb** (**gravitates**, **gravitating**, **gravitated**) (**gravitate to/towards**) be drawn towards 被吸引

gravitation /ˌgrævɪ'teɪʃn/ **noun** movement towards a centre of gravity 下沉，引力作用 ■ **gravitational** adjective.

gravity /'grævəti/ **noun 1** the force that attracts a body towards the centre of the earth, or towards any other physical body having mass 地心引力，重力 **2** extreme importance or seriousness 重大，严重 **3** a solemn manner 严肃；庄重

gravy /ˈɡreɪvi/ **noun** (plural **gravies**) a sauce made from the fat and juices that come out of meat during cooking 肉汁 □ **gravy boat** a long, narrow jug used for serving gravy 船形肉汁盘

gray /ɡreɪ/ US spelling of GREY. grey 的美式拼法

graze¹ /ɡreɪz/ **verb** (**grazes**, **grazing**, **grazed**) (of cattle, sheep, etc.) eat grass (牛、羊等)吃草

graze² /ɡreɪz/ **verb** (**grazes**, **grazing**, **grazed**) **1** scrape the skin on a part of your body 擦破(皮肤) **2** touch something lightly in passing 掠过；擦过 • **noun** an area where the skin has been scraped 皮肤擦伤；破皮

grazing /ˈɡreɪzɪŋ/ **noun** grassland suitable for use as pasture (用于放牧的)草场，牧场

grease /ɡriːs/ **noun 1** a thick oily substance used as a lubricant 油腻物；脂膏；润滑油 **2** animal fat used or produced in cooking 动物油脂 • **verb** (**greases**, **greasing**, **greased**) smear or lubricate something with grease 给…涂油脂；给…加润滑油 ■ **greasy** adjective.

greasepaint /ˈɡriːspeɪnt/ **noun** a waxy substance used as make-up by actors (演员化妆用的)油彩

greaseproof /ˈɡriːspruːf/ **adjective** not allowing grease to pass through it 防油的；耐油的

great /ɡreɪt/ **adjective 1** considerably above average in extent, amount, or strength 大的；众多的；巨大的 **2** considerably above average in ability or quality 伟大的；杰出的，非常的 **3** informal 〖非正式〗 excellent 出色的；极好的 **4** used to emphasize something (用于强调)：*He's a great cricket fan.* 他是个板球发烧友。 □ **great-aunt** (or **great-uncle**) an aunt (or uncle) of your mother or father 姑婆(或姑爷)；姨婆(或姨爷)

■ **greatness** noun.

greatcoat /ˈɡreɪtkəʊt/ **noun** a long heavy overcoat 厚长大衣

greatly /ˈɡreɪtli/ **adverb** very much 非常；很

grebe /ɡriːb/ **noun** a diving bird with a long neck 䴙䴘(一种长颈潜水鸟)

Grecian /ˈɡriːʃn/ **adjective** relating to ancient Greece 古希腊的

greed /ɡriːd/ **noun 1** a strong and selfish desire for possessions, wealth, or power 贪婪；贪欲 **2** a desire to eat more food than you need 贪食

greedy /ˈɡriːdi/ **adjective** (**greedier**, **greediest**) having or showing greed 贪婪的；贪心的 ■ **greedily** adverb.

Greek /ɡriːk/ **noun 1** a person from Greece 希腊人 **2** the ancient or modern language of Greece 古希腊语；现代希腊语 • **adjective** relating to Greece 希腊的

green /ɡriːn/ **adjective 1** of a colour between blue and yellow, like that of grass 绿色的 **2** covered with grass or other plants 长满青草的；绿油油的 **3** (**Green**) concerned with or supporting protection of the environment 绿党的；关心环保的 **4** inexperienced or naive 无经验的；天真的 • **noun 1** a green colour 绿色 **2** a piece of grassy land for public use 草坪；草地 **3** an area of smooth grass used for cricket or bowls, or surrounding a hole on a golf course (高尔夫球场的)球穴区，果岭 **4** (**greens**) cabbage or other green vegetables 绿色蔬菜 **5** (**Green**) a supporter of a Green political party 绿党支持者；支持环保者 □ **green belt** an area of open land around a city, on which building is restricted (城市周围的)绿化带 **green card** (in the US) a permit allowing a foreigner to live and work permanently in the US (美国的)绿卡，永久居留证 **green fingers** Brit. 〖英〗 natural ability in growing plants 园艺技能 **green light** permission to go ahead with a project

(对项目的)许可 **green pepper** an unripe sweet green pepper 青椒；甜椒
■ **greenness** noun.

greenery /ˈgriːnəri/ **noun** green leaves or plants 绿叶；绿色植物

greenfield /ˈgriːnfiːld/ **adjective** (of a site) previously undeveloped (地区)未开发的

greenfinch /ˈgriːnfɪntʃ/ **noun** a large finch with green and yellow feathers 绿金翅雀(有绿色和黄色羽毛)

greenfly /ˈgriːnflaɪ/ **noun** (plural **greenflies**) a green aphid 蚜虫

greengage /ˈgriːngeɪdʒ/ **noun** a sweet greenish fruit like a small plum 西洋李；青梅

greengrocer /ˈgriːnɡrəʊsə(r)/ **noun** Brit. 【英】 a person who has a shop selling fruit and vegetables 水果蔬菜商

greenhouse /ˈgriːnhaʊs/ **noun** a glass structure in which plants are kept to protect them from cold weather 温室；暖房 □ **greenhouse effect** the tendency of atmospheric temperature to rise because certain gases absorb infrared radiation from the earth 温室效应(由于某些气体吸收地球红外辐射造成大气温度上升) **greenhouse gas** a gas that contributes to the greenhouse effect by absorbing infrared radiation 温室气体

greet /griːt/ **verb 1** give a word or sign of welcome when meeting someone 问候；致意；打招呼 **2** acknowledge or react to someone or something in a particular way (以某种方式)接受，对…作出反应

greeting /ˈgriːtɪŋ/ **noun 1** a word or sign of welcome when meeting someone 问候；欢迎；招呼 **2** (**greetings**) a formal expression of good wishes 问候语，贺词

gregarious /grɪˈgeəriəs/ **adjective 1** enjoying being with people; sociable 喜人陪伴的；爱交际的 **2** (of animals) living in flocks or colonies (动物)群居的

Gregorian chant /grɪˈgɔːriən/ **noun** medieval church music for voices 格列高利圣咏

gremlin /ˈgremlɪn/ **noun** an imaginary mischievous creature regarded as responsible for unexplained mechanical or electrical faults (假想的)小妖精(被认为造成原因不明的机械或电路故障)

grenade /grəˈneɪd/ **noun** a small bomb that is thrown by hand 手榴弹；枪榴弹

grenadier /ˌɡrenəˈdɪə(r)/ **noun 1** historical 【历史】 a soldier armed with grenades 掷弹兵 **2** (**Grenadiers** or **Grenadier Guards**) a regiment of the royal household infantry (英国)近卫步兵团

grew /gruː/ past of GROW.

grey /greɪ/ (US spelling 【美拼作】 **gray**) **adjective 1** of a colour between black and white, like that of ashes or lead 灰色的；灰白色的 **2** (of hair) turning grey or white with age (头发)灰白的，花白的 **3** (of the weather) cloudy and dull (天气)灰暗的，阴沉的 ● **noun** a grey colour 灰色；灰白色 ● **verb** (of hair) become grey with age (头发)变白，发白 □ **grey area** a subject or area of activity that does not easily fit into existing categories 灰色区域；中间地带 **grey matter** informal 【非正式】 the brain 头脑

greyhound /ˈɡreɪhaʊnd/ **noun** a swift, slender breed of dog used in racing 灵缇，灰狗(身体瘦长、行动敏捷，用于赛狗)

grid /grɪd/ **noun 1** a set of bars lying parallel to or crossing each other 格栅；格子 **2** a network of lines that cross each other to form a series of squares or rectangles 格网；坐标方格 **3** a network of cables or pipes for distributing power 输电网；输气网

griddle /ˈɡrɪdl/ **noun** a heavy iron

plate that is heated and used for cooking food (烹饪用的)烤盘

gridiron /ˈɡrɪdaɪən/ **noun** a frame of metal bars used for grilling food over an open fire (烤制食物的)烤架，铁丝格子

gridlock /ˈɡrɪdlɒk/ **noun** a traffic jam affecting a whole network of intersecting streets 交通全面大堵塞 ■ **gridlocked** adjective.

grief /ɡriːf/ **noun 1** great sorrow and sadness, especially caused by someone's death (尤指因某人去世而引起的)悲伤 **2** informal 【非正式】trouble or annoyance 麻烦；烦恼

grievance /ˈɡriːvəns/ **noun** a cause for complaint 牢骚；不满；怨恨

grieve /ɡriːv/ **verb** (grieves, grieving, grieved) **1** feel great sorrow and sadness 感到悲伤 **2** cause someone distress 使悲痛

grievous /ˈɡriːvəs/ **adjective** formal 【正式】(of something bad) very severe or serious (不幸之事)极其严重的 □ **grievous bodily harm** Law, Brit. 【法律，英】serious physical injury deliberately inflicted on someone 严重人身伤害 ■ **grievously** adverb.

griffin /ˈɡrɪfɪn/ or **gryphon** /ˈɡrɪfən/ **noun** a mythical creature with the head and wings of an eagle and the body of a lion (神话中的)狮身鹰首兽

griffon /ˈɡrɪfən/ **noun** a small breed of dog 布鲁塞尔小种犬

grill /ɡrɪl/ **noun** Brit. 【英】**1** a device on a cooker that radiates heat downwards for cooking food (炊具、烤炉内的)烤架，铁板 **2** a frame of metal bars used for cooking food on an open fire 烧烤架 **3** a dish of food cooked using a grill 一盘烤制的菜 **4** ⇨ 见 GRILLE. • **verb 1** cook food with a grill 烤；烧 **2** informal 【非正式】question someone in a relentless or aggressive way 严厉盘问；审问

grille or **grill** /ɡrɪl/ **noun** a framework of metal bars or wires (金属)格栅，

隔板

grim /ɡrɪm/ **adjective** (grimmer, grimmest) **1** very serious and stern or forbidding 严峻的，阴森的 **2** horrifying or depressing 恐怖的；令人沮丧的 ■ **grimly** adverb.

grimace /ɡrɪˈmeɪs, ˈɡrɪməs/ **noun** a twisted expression on a person's face, showing disgust, pain, or wry amusement (由于厌恶、痛苦等的)脸部扭曲；鬼脸；怪相 • **verb** (grimaces, grimacing, grimaced) make a grimace 扭曲脸部；做鬼脸；扮怪相

grime /ɡraɪm/ **noun** dirt ingrained on a surface 污垢，尘垢 ■ **grimy** adjective.

grin /ɡrɪn/ **verb** (grins, grinning, grinned) smile broadly 咧嘴笑；露齿笑 • **noun** a broad smile 咧嘴笑；露齿笑

grind /ɡraɪnd/ **verb** (grinds, grinding, ground) **1** reduce something to small particles or powder by crushing it 磨碎，碾碎；把…磨成粉 **2** make something sharp or smooth by rubbing it against a hard or abrasive tool or surface 使锋利；磨快；磨光 **3** rub together or move gratingly 刺耳地磨擦(或移动) **4** (grind someone down) wear someone down with continuous harsh treatment 压榨，折磨(某人) **5** (grind something out) produce something slowly and with effort 缓慢而费力地弄出 **6** (grinding) (of an unpleasant situation) seemingly endless (困境)似无止境的 • **noun 1** an act or process of grinding 磨碎；碾碎 **2** hard dull work 艰苦乏味的工作

grindstone /ˈɡraɪndstəʊn/ **noun 1** a revolving disc of abrasive material used for sharpening or polishing metal objects 砂轮；磨石 **2** a millstone 里程碑 □ **keep your nose to the grindstone** keep working hard 埋头苦干

grip /ɡrɪp/ **verb** (grips, gripping, gripped) **1** hold something tightly

握紧;抓牢 **2** deeply affect someone 深刻影响 **3** hold someone's attention 吸引住…的注意 • **noun 1** a firm hold on something 握紧;抓牢 **2** understanding of something 理解 (力) **3** a part or attachment by which something is held in the hand 把手;柄 **4** a travelling bag 旅行袋 □ **come (or get) to grips with** begin to deal with or understand 着手处理;开始理解

gripe /graɪp/ **verb** (**gripes, griping, griped**) **1** informal 【非正式】 grumble 抱怨;发牢骚 **2** (**griping**) (of pain in the stomach or intestines) sudden and sharp (肠胃疼痛)绞痛的, 急腹的 • **noun 1** informal 【非正式】 a trivial complaint 怨言;牢骚 **2** pain in the stomach or intestines 胃痛;肚子痛

gripping /ˈgrɪpɪŋ/ **adjective** very interesting or exciting 引人入胜的;扣人心弦的

grisly /ˈgrɪzli/ **adjective** (**grislier, grisliest**) causing horror or disgust 恐怖的;令人厌恶的

! 注意 don't confuse **grisly** with **grizzly**, as in *grizzly bear*. 不要混淆 grisly 和 grizzly, 如 grizzly bear 中 grizzly 不要拼作 grisly。

grist /grɪst/ **noun** corn that is ground to make flour 制粉用谷物 □ **grist to the mill** useful experience or knowledge 有用的经历(或知识)

gristle /ˈgrɪsl/ **noun** tough inedible cartilage in meat (肉中的)软骨 ■ **gristly adjective**.

grit /grɪt/ **noun 1** small loose particles of stone or sand 细石;沙砾 **2** (also **gritstone**) a coarse sandstone 粗砂岩 **3** courage and determination 勇气;毅力 • **verb** (**grits, gritting, gritted**) spread grit on an icy road 在(结冰的)路面上铺沙路 □ **grit your teeth** resolve to do something difficult 咬紧牙关

gritty /ˈgrɪti/ **adjective** (**grittier,**

grittiest) **1** containing or covered with grit 含沙砾的;铺满沙砾的 **2** brave and determined 勇敢的,刚毅的 **3** showing something unpleasant as it really is (展示令人不快的事物)逼真的,实事求是的 ■ **grittily adverb**.

grizzle /ˈgrɪzl/ **verb** (**grizzles, grizzling, grizzled**) Brit. informal 【英, 非正式】 cry fretfully 啜泣;呜咽

grizzled /ˈgrɪzld/ **adjective** having grey or grey-streaked hair 有灰白色头发的;发色斑白的

grizzly bear /ˈgrɪzli/ **noun** a large brown bear, often with white-tipped fur 灰熊

groan /grəʊn/ **verb** make a deep sound of pain or despair 呻吟;发哼声 • **noun** a groaning sound 呻吟声;哼哼声

groat /grəʊt/ **noun** historical 【历史】 an English silver coin worth four old pence 格罗特(英格兰的4便士古银币)

grocer /ˈgrəʊsə(r)/ **noun** a person who sells food and small household goods 食品杂货商

grocery /ˈgrəʊsəri/ **noun** (plural **groceries**) **1** a grocer's shop or business 食品杂货店;食品杂货业 **2** (**groceries**) items of food sold in a grocer's shop or supermarket (杂货店及超市场出售的)食品

grog /grɒg/ **noun** spirits mixed with water 掺水的烈酒

groggy /ˈgrɒgi/ **adjective** (**groggier, groggiest**) dazed and unsteady 眩晕的;不稳的 ■ **groggily adverb**.

groin /grɔɪn/ **noun 1** the area between the stomach and the thigh 腹股沟 **2** US spelling of GROYNE. groyne 的美式拼法

grommet /ˈgrɒmɪt/ **noun 1** a protective metal ring or eyelet (起保护作用的)金属环(或孔眼) **2** Brit.【英】 a tube fitted in the eardrum to drain fluid from the middle ear 中耳引流管

groom /gruːm/ **verb 1** brush and

clean the coat of a horse or dog 刷洗 (马或狗的)毛 **2** keep yourself neat and tidy in appearance 使自己整洁；打扮 **3** train someone for a particular activity (为某活动)训练，培训 • **noun 1** a person employed to take care of horses 马夫 **2** a bridegroom 新郎

groove /gruːv/ **noun 1** a long, narrow cut in a hard surface (坚硬表面的)凹槽 **2** a spiral track cut in a music record (唱片上的)纹路 **3** a routine or habit 常规，惯例 • **verb** (**grooves, grooving, grooved**) **1** make a groove or grooves in 在…上开槽 **2** informal 【非正式】listen or dance to jazz or pop music 听爵士乐(或流行音乐)；在爵士乐(或流行音乐)的伴奏下跳舞

groovy /ˈgruːvi/ **adjective** (**groovier, grooviest**) informal, dated 【非正式，废】fashionable and exciting 时髦的，刺激的

grope /grəʊp/ **verb** (**gropes, groping, groped**) **1** feel about with your hands 摸索，探寻 **2** ease your way forward using your hands to guide you 摸索，前行 **3** informal 【非正式】feel someone's body for sexual pleasure (为获得性快感而)摸索，抚摸

gross /grəʊs/ **adjective 1** unattractively large 臃肿的，粗大的 **2** very obvious and unacceptable 严重的 **3** informal 【非正式】very unpleasant 非常讨厌的 **4** rude or vulgar 粗俗的；不雅的 **5** (of income, profit, or interest) before tax has been deducted (收入，利润或利息)税前的，毛的 **6** (of weight) including contents or other variable items (重量)毛的，总的 • **adverb** in total 总地 • **verb** earn a particular amount of money as gross profit or income 总收入为，总共赚得 • **noun 1** (plural **gross**) twelve dozen; 144 一罗，罗(等于12打或144个) **2** (plural **grosses**) a gross profit or income 总利润，总收入 ▪ **grossly** adverb.

grotesque /grəʊˈtesk/ **adjective 1** ugly or distorted in a way that is funny or frightening 丑陋的；奇形怪状的，怪诞骇人的 **2** shocking 令人震惊的 • **noun** a grotesque figure or image 怪异的人(或形象) ▪ **grotesquely** adverb.

grotto /ˈgrɒtəʊ/ **noun** (plural **grottoes** or **grottos**) a small cave, especially an artificial one (尤指人工的)小洞穴

grotty /ˈgrɒti/ **adjective** (**grottier, grottiest**) Brit. informal 【英，非正式】**1** unpleasant and of bad quality 令人讨厌的；劣质的 **2** unwell 不舒服的

grouch /graʊtʃ/ **noun** informal 【非正式】**1** a grumpy person 爱发牢骚的人 **2** a complaint 抱怨，牢骚 ▪ **grouchy** adjective.

ground¹ /graʊnd/ **noun 1** the solid surface of the earth 地面，地表 **2** land or soil of a particular kind 土地；土壤 **3** an area of land or sea with a particular use (有特定用途的)场地，海域 **4** (**grounds**) an area of enclosed land surrounding a large house (大宅周围的)庭院 **5** (**grounds**) good reasons for doing or believing something 理由，依据 **6** (**grounds**) small pieces of solid matter in a liquid which settle at the bottom 渣滓；沉淀物 • **verb 1** ban or prevent a pilot or aircraft from flying 禁止(飞行员或飞机)飞行 **2** run a ship aground 使(船)搁浅 **3** (**be grounded in** or **on**) have as a foundation or basis 把…作为依据 □ **ground control** the people who direct the flight and landing of aircraft or spacecraft (飞机或航天器的)地面导航人员 **ground floor** the floor of a building at ground level (建筑物的)一层，一楼 **ground rent** Brit. 【英】rent paid by the owner of a building to the owner of the land on which it is built 地租 **ground rules** basic rules controlling the way in which something is done 基本原则

ground² past and past participle of GRIND.

groundbreaking /'graʊnbreɪkɪŋ/ **adjective** involving completely new methods or discoveries 全新的；开创性的

grounding /'graʊndɪŋ/ **noun** basic training or instruction in a subject (某一学科的)基础训练，基础知识教授

groundless /'graʊndləs/ **adjective** not based on any good reason 无根据的；无理由的

groundnut /'graʊndnʌt/ = PEANUT.

groundsel /'graʊnsl/ **noun** a plant with small yellow flowers 千里光(一种植物，开黄色小花)

groundsheet /'graʊndʃiːt/ **noun** a waterproof sheet spread on the ground inside a tent (帐篷内铺地用的)防潮布

groundsman /'graʊndzmən/ **noun** (plural **groundsmen**) Brit. 【英】a person who maintains a sports ground or the grounds of a large building 体育场地(或大型建筑物周围场地)管理员

groundswell /'graʊndswel/ **noun 1** a large swell in the sea (海里的)大浪 **2** a build-up of public opinion (公众舆论的)迅速高涨

groundwork /'graʊndwɜːk/ **noun** preliminary or basic work 准备工作，基础工作

group /gruːp/ **noun 1** a number of people or things placed or classed together (人或物的)组，群 **2** a band of pop musicians 流行乐团 • **verb** put into a group (把…)分组

groupie /'gruːpi/ **noun** informal 【非正式】a fan who follows a pop group or celebrity around 追星族

grouse¹ /graʊs/ **noun** (plural **grouse**) a game bird with a plump body 松鸡

grouse² **verb** (**grouses**, **grousing**, **groused**) complain; grumble 发牢骚；诉苦 • **noun** a grumble or complaint 牢骚；抱怨

grout /graʊt/ **noun** a substance used for filling the gaps between tiles (填补瓦片间缝隙的)水泥浆，灰泥 • **verb** fill between tiles with grout 给…灌浆

grove /grəʊv/ **noun** a small wood, orchard, or group of trees 小果园；小树林

grovel /'grɒvl/ **verb** (**grovels**, **grovelling**, **grovelled**; US spelling 【美拼作】**grovels**, **groveling**, **groveled**) **1** crouch or crawl on the ground 趴下；匍匐 **2** act very humbly towards someone to make them forgive you or treat you favourably 低声下气，卑躬屈膝

grow /grəʊ/ **verb** (**grows**, **growing**, **grew**; past participle **grown**) **1** (of a living thing) develop and get bigger (生物)成长，发育 **2** (**grow up**) become an adult 长大成人 **3** become larger or greater over a period of time 发展；壮大 **4** become gradually or increasingly 逐渐变成：*We grew braver.* 我们逐渐变得勇敢起来。**5** (**grow on**) become gradually more appealing to 对…越来越有吸引力；愈来愈讨…喜欢 □ **grown-up 1** adult 成年的 **2** informal 【非正式】an adult 成年人 ■ **grower** noun.

growl /graʊl/ **verb 1** (of a dog) make a low hostile sound in the throat (狗)低吼 **2** say something in a low grating voice 小声说；低声说 **3** make a low or harsh rumbling sound 发隆隆声 • **noun** a growling sound 低吼声；隆隆声

growth /grəʊθ/ **noun 1** the process of growing 生长；发育；成长 **2** something that has grown or is growing 产物；生长物 **3** a tumour 肿瘤；赘生物

groyne /grɔɪn/ (US spelling 【美拼作】**groin**) **noun** a low wall built out into the sea from a beach to prevent the beach from shifting or being eroded (海岸的)防沙堤，折流坝

grub /grʌb/ **noun 1** the larva of an

insect（昆虫的）幼虫 **2** informal【非正式】food 食物 • verb (**grubs, grubbing, grubbed**) **1** dig or poke about in soil 掘；挖 **2 (grub something up)** dig up 挖出（某物）

grubby /'grʌbi/ adjective (**grubbier, grubbiest**) **1** rather dirty 肮脏的 **2** dishonest or immoral 不诚实的；不道德的

grudge /grʌdʒ/ noun a persistent feeling of anger or dislike resulting from a past insult or injury 宿怨；嫌隙 • verb (**grudges, grudging, grudged**) **1** be unwilling to give or allow something 不情愿地给；勉强准许 **2** feel resentful that someone has achieved something 忌妒

grudging /'grʌdʒɪŋ/ adjective reluctantly given or allowed 勉强的；不情愿的
■ **grudgingly** adverb.

gruel /'gru:əl/ noun a thin liquid food of oatmeal boiled in milk or water 稀粥；燕麦粥

gruelling /'gru:əlɪŋ/ (US spelling【美拼作】**grueling**) adjective very tiring and demanding 令人筋疲力尽的；极费力的

gruesome /'gru:səm/ adjective causing disgust or horror 令人反感的；让人恐惧的

gruff /grʌf/ adjective **1** (of a voice) rough and low (嗓音) 粗哑的 **2** abrupt in manner (态度) 生硬的 ■ **gruffly** adverb.

grumble /'grʌmbl/ verb (**grumbles, grumbling, grumbled**) **1** complain in a quiet but bad-tempered way 发牢骚；抱怨 **2** make a low rumbling sound 发隆隆声 • noun a complaint 抱怨；牢骚

grumpy /'grʌmpi/ adjective (**grumpier, grumpiest**) bad-tempered and sulky 脾气暴躁的；乖戾的 ■ **grumpily** adverb.

grunge /grʌndʒ/ noun a style of rock music with a raucous guitar sound (以刺耳的吉他声伴奏的)垃圾摇滚乐

■ **grungy** adjective.

grunt /grʌnt/ verb **1** (of an animal) make a short, low sound (动物)发出咕噜声 **2** (of a person) make a low sound because of physical effort or to show agreement (人)发出嘟哝声；嘟哝着表示 • noun a grunting sound 咕噜声；嘟哝声

gryphon /'grɪfən/ ⇒ 见 **GRIFFIN**.

guano /'gwa:nəʊ/ noun the excrement of seabirds, used as fertilizer 海鸟粪(用作肥料)

guarantee /ˌgærən'ti:/ noun **1** a promise that certain things will be done 保证；担保 **2** a promise that a product will remain in working order for a particular length of time (产品)保修单，保用证书 **3** something that makes a particular outcome certain 保证，起保证作用的事物 **4** an undertaking to pay or do something on behalf of someone if they fail to do it 担保 • verb (**guarantees, guaranteeing, guaranteed**) **1** provide a guarantee for something 担保；保证 **2** promise something with certainty 许诺；允诺 **3** provide financial security for 为…提供经济担保

✔ **拼写指南** *gua-*, not *gau-*: *gua*rantee guarantee 中的 gua- 不要拼作 gau-。

guarantor /ˌgærən'tɔ:(r)/ noun a person or organization that gives a guarantee 保证人；担保人

guard /ga:d/ verb **1** watch over in order to protect or control 守卫；看守 **2 (guard against)** take precautions against 预防；防备 • noun **1** a person who guards or keeps watch 守卫者；看守者 **2** a group of soldiers guarding a place or person 卫兵；警卫 **3** a state of looking out for possible danger 警戒状态；警惕: *She was on guard.* 她存有戒心。 **4** a device worn or fitted to prevent injury or damage 防护装置 **5** Brit.【英】an official in charge of a train 列车长 **6** N. Amer. 【北美】 a prison warder 监狱看守

✔ 拼写指南 *gua-*, not *gau-*: g**ua**rd. guard 中的 gua- 不要拼作 gau-。

guarded /'gɑːdɪd/ **adjective** cautious 小心谨慎的

guardian /'gɑːdɪən/ **noun 1** a person who defends and protects something 保卫者;保护者;保管者 **2** a person who is legally responsible for someone who cannot take care of their own affairs (无独立行为能力者)的监护人 □ **guardian angel** a spirit who is believed to watch over and protect you (某人的)守护天使 ■ **guardianship** noun.

Guatemalan /ˌgwɑːtɪˈmɑːlən/ **noun** a person from Guatemala 危地马拉人 • **adjective** relating to Guatemala 危地马拉的

guava /'gwɑːvə/ **noun** a tropical fruit with pink juicy flesh 番石榴

gudgeon /'gʌdʒən/ **noun** a small freshwater fish 鮈鱼(一种小型淡水鱼)

guerrilla or **guerilla** /gə'rɪlə/ **noun** a member of a small independent group fighting against the government or regular forces 游击队员

guess /ges/ **verb 1** estimate or suppose something without having the information you need to be sure 推测;猜想 **2** correctly estimate or suppose 猜对;猜中 • **noun** an attempt to guess something 猜测;估计

guesswork /'geswɜːk/ **noun** the process or results of guessing 猜测;猜测的结果

guest /gest/ **noun 1** a person who is invited to someone's house or to a social occasion 客人;宾客 **2** a person invited to take part in a broadcast or entertainment 特邀嘉宾 **3** a person staying at a hotel 旅馆房客 □ **guest house** a kind of small hotel 家庭旅馆;小旅馆

guffaw /gə'fɔː/ **noun** a loud, deep laugh 哄笑;大笑 • **verb** give a loud, deep laugh 哄笑;大笑

guidance /'gaɪdns/ **noun** advice and information given by an experienced or skilled person 指导;咨询

guide /gaɪd/ **noun 1** a person who advises or shows the way to other people 向导;指路者 **2** a thing that helps you to form an opinion or make a decision 导引的事物;指针 **3** a book providing information on a subject 指南;手册 **4** a structure or marking which directs the movement or positioning of something 路标;指向牌 **5** (**Guide**) a member of the Guides Association, a girls' organization corresponding to the Scouts 女童子军 • **verb** (**guides, guiding, guided**) **1** show someone the way 指引;引导 **2** direct the movement or positioning of something 指导;支配;操纵 **3** (**guided**) directed by remote control or internal equipment 遥控的;制导的 □ **guide dog** a dog trained to lead a blind person 导盲犬

guidebook /'gaɪdbʊk/ **noun** a book containing information about a place for visitors 旅游手册;旅游指南

guideline /'gaɪdlaɪn/ **noun** a general rule, principle, or piece of advice 准则;指导原则;指导准则

guild /gɪld/ **noun 1** a medieval association of craftsmen or merchants (中世纪的)行会,同业公会 **2** an association of people who do the same work or have the same interests 协会;联合会

guilder /'gɪldə(r)/ **noun** (plural **guilder** or **guilders**) the former basic unit of money in the Netherlands 荷兰盾(荷兰以前的基本货币单位)

guildhall /'gɪldhɔːl/ **noun 1** the meeting place of a guild or corporation (行会或同业公会的)会馆,会议厅 **2** Brit. 【英】 a town hall 市政厅

guile /gaɪl/ **noun** clever but dishonest

or deceitful behaviour 狡猾；诡诈

guileless /'gaɪlləs/ **adjective** innocent and honest 老实厚道的

guillemot /'gɪlɪmɒt/ **noun** a seabird with a narrow pointed bill 海鸠(喙窄而尖)

guillotine /'gɪləti:n/ **noun 1** a machine with a heavy blade, used for beheading people 断头台 **2** a piece of equipment with a descending or sliding blade used for cutting paper or sheet metal 切纸机；(金属)截切机 • **verb** (**guillotines, guillotining, guillotined**) behead someone with a guillotine 把(某人)送上断头台

guilt /gɪlt/ **noun 1** the fact of having committed an offence or crime 有罪 **2** a feeling of having done something wrong 内疚；自责 ■ **guiltless** adjective.

guilty /'gɪlti/ **adjective** (**guiltier, guiltiest**) **1** responsible for doing something wrong 有罪的；有过失的 **2** having or showing a feeling of guilt 内疚的；自责的 ■ **guiltily** adverb.

guinea /'gɪni/ **noun** a former British gold coin worth 21 shillings (￡1.05) 几尼(英国旧时的金币，价值21先令，合1.05英镑)

guineafowl /'gɪnifaʊl/ **noun** (plural **guineafowl**) a large African bird with grey, white-spotted feathers 珠鸡(产于非洲的大型禽鸟，羽毛灰色，带白斑点)

guinea pig noun 1 a South American rodent without a tail 豚鼠，天竺鼠(产于南美洲，无尾) **2** a person or thing used as a subject for experiment 实验对象；实验品

guise /gaɪz/ **noun** an outward form, appearance, or manner 外形；外表；表现形式

guitar /gɪ'tɑ:(r)/ **noun** a stringed musical instrument which you play by plucking or strumming 吉他 ■ **guitarist** noun.

Gujarati /ˌguːdʒə'rɑːti/ **noun** (plural **Gujaratis**) **1** a person from the Indian state of Gujarat (印度的)古吉拉特人 **2** the language of the Gujaratis 古吉拉特语

gulch /gʌltʃ/ **noun** N. Amer. 【北美】 a narrow ravine 沟壑；急流峡谷

gulf /gʌlf/ **noun 1** a deep inlet of the sea with a narrow mouth 海湾 **2** a deep ravine 深渊；深坑 **3** a large difference in opinion between two people or groups 鸿沟；巨大分歧

gull¹ /gʌl/ **noun** a white seabird with long wings and a grey or black back 海鸥

gull² **verb** fool or deceive 愚弄；欺骗

gullet /'gʌlɪt/ **noun** the passage by which food passes from the mouth to the stomach 食管；食道

gullible /'gʌləbl/ **adjective** easily believing what people tell you 轻信的；易受欺骗的 ■ **gullibility** noun.

gully or **gulley** /'gʌli/ **noun** (plural **gullies** or **gulleys**) a ravine or channel formed by running water (流水冲刷形成的)沟壑，溪谷

gulp /gʌlp/ **verb 1** swallow food or drink quickly or in large mouthfuls 快速吞咽；大口饮；狼吞虎咽 **2** swallow with difficulty because you are upset or nervous (由于难过或紧张而)倒吸气 • **noun 1** an act of gulping 吞咽 **2** a large mouthful of liquid hastily drunk (匆忙饮下的)一大口

gum¹ /gʌm/ **noun 1** a sticky substance produced by some trees 树胶；树脂 **2** glue used for sticking paper or other light materials together 黏胶 **3** chewing gum 口香糖；泡泡糖

gum² **noun** the firm area of flesh around the roots of the teeth 牙龈；牙床

gumboot /'gʌmbuːt/ **noun** Brit. dated 【英，废】 a tall rubber boot; a wellington 橡胶靴；威灵顿长筒靴

gumdrop /'gʌmdrɒp/ **noun** a firm, jelly-like sweet 橡皮糖；胶皮糖

gummy¹ /'gʌmi/ **adjective** sticky 黏

gummy² adjective toothless 无牙的

gumption /'ɡʌmpʃn/ noun informal【非正式】initiative and resourcefulness 进取心；机智，足智多谋

gun /ɡʌn/ noun **1** a weapon with a metal tube from which bullets or shells are fired by means of a small explosion 枪；炮 **2** a device using pressure to send out a substance or object 喷射器；喷枪 • verb (guns, gunning, gunned) (gun someone down) shoot someone with a gun 用枪射击 □ jump the gun act before the proper or right time 过早行动 stick to your guns refuse to compromise 坚持己见，拒绝妥协

gunboat /'ɡʌnbəʊt/ noun a small ship armed with guns 炮舰艇

gunfire /'ɡʌnfaɪə(r)/ noun the repeated firing of a gun or guns 连续开炮，连续开枪

gunge /ɡʌndʒ/ (N. Amer.【北美】also **gunk**) noun informal【非正式】an unpleasantly sticky or messy substance 黏稠物质

gung-ho /ˌɡʌŋ'həʊ/ adjective too eager to take part in fighting or warfare (对战斗或战争)盲目热情的，狂热的

gunman /'ɡʌnmən/ noun (plural **gunmen**) a man who uses a gun to commit a crime 持枪歹徒；持枪杀手

gunmetal /'ɡʌnmetl/ noun **1** a grey form of bronze containing zinc (含锌的)炮铜，炮合金 **2** a dull bluish-grey colour 炮铜色；暗灰色

gunnel /'ɡʌnl/ ⇨ 见 GUNWALE.

gunner /'ɡʌnə(r)/ noun **1** a person who operates a gun 炮手 **2** a British artillery soldier (英国)炮兵

gunnery /'ɡʌnəri/ noun the design, manufacture, or firing of heavy guns 重炮设计制造；重炮射击

gunpoint /'ɡʌnpɔɪnt/ noun (at **gunpoint**) while threatening someone or being threatened with a gun 在枪口的威逼下

gunpowder /'ɡʌnpaʊdə(r)/ noun an explosive consisting of a powdered mixture of saltpetre, sulphur, and charcoal 火药

gunrunner /'ɡʌnrʌnə(r)/ noun a person involved in the illegal sale or importing of firearms 走私军火者，私运军火者 ■ gunrunning noun.

gunship /'ɡʌnʃɪp/ noun a heavily armed helicopter 武装直升机

gunwale or **gunnel** /'ɡʌnl/ noun the upper edge or planking of the side of a boat 船舷上缘；舷缘

guppy /'ɡʌpi/ noun (plural **guppies**) a small colourful fish 古比鱼，虹鳉(一种彩色小鱼)

gurdwara /ɡɜː'dwɑːrə/ noun a Sikh place of worship 谒师所(锡克教徒的礼拜场所)

gurgle /'ɡɜːɡl/ verb (gurgles, gurgling, gurgled) make a hollow bubbling sound 发汩汩声 • noun a hollow bubbling sound 汩汩声

Gurkha /'ɡɜːkə/ noun a member of a Nepalese regiment in the British army 廓尔喀兵(英国军队中的尼伯尔军人)

gurn or **girn** /ɡɜːn/ verb Brit.【英】pull a grotesque face 扮鬼脸；做怪相

guru /'ɡuːruː/ noun **1** a Hindu spiritual teacher 古鲁(印度教的宗师) **2** a person who is an expert on a subject and has a lot of followers 专家；大师

gush /ɡʌʃ/ verb **1** flow in a strong, fast stream 喷出；涌出 **2** express approval very enthusiastically 过分称赞 • noun a strong, fast stream 涌流；激流 ■ gushing adjective.

gusset /'ɡʌsɪt/ noun a piece of material sewn into a garment to strengthen or enlarge a part of it 衬料(缝于衣服内用以加固或加大的)衬料

gust /ɡʌst/ noun **1** a brief, strong rush of wind 一阵狂风 **2** a burst of sound or emotion (声音或情感的)爆发，迸发 • verb blow in gusts 劲吹；狂刮

■ **gusty** adjective.

gusto /ˈɡʌstəʊ/ **noun** enthusiasm and energy 热情;精力

gut /ɡʌt/ **noun 1** the stomach or intestine 胃;肠 **2** (**guts**) internal organs that have been removed or exposed (取出或露出的)内脏 **3** (**guts**) the inner or most important part of something 核心;实质 **4** (**guts**) informal【非正式】courage and determination 勇气;决心 • **verb** (**guts, gutting, gutted**) **1** take out the internal organs of a fish before cooking (烹饪前)取出(鱼)的内脏 **2** remove or destroy the internal parts of something 除去…的核心部分;毁掉…的内部

gutless /ˈɡʌtləs/ **adjective** informal 【非正式】not showing courage or determination 缺乏勇气的;怯懦的

gutsy /ˈɡʌtsi/ **adjective** (**gutsier, gutsiest**) informal【非正式】brave and determined 勇敢的;有决心的

gutted /ˈɡʌtɪd/ **adjective** Brit. informal【英,非正式】bitterly disappointed or upset 极其失望的;心烦意乱的

gutter /ˈɡʌtə(r)/ **noun 1** a shallow trough beneath the edge of a roof, or a channel at the side of a street, for carrying off rainwater (屋檐下的)排水檐沟;(街道旁的)排水沟,阴沟 **2** (**the gutter**) a very poor or unpleasant environment 极其恶劣的环境 • **verb** (**gutters, guttering, guttered**) (of a flame) flicker and burn unsteadily (火焰)摇曳不定,忽明忽暗

guttering /ˈɡʌtərɪŋ/ **noun** the gutters of a building (建筑物的)排水系统

guttersnipe /ˈɡʌtəsnaɪp/ **noun** disapproving【贬】a scruffy, badly behaved child 脏兮兮的坏小孩

guttural /ˈɡʌtərəl/ **adjective** (of a speech sound) produced in the throat (讲话声)喉部发出的

guy¹ /ɡaɪ/ **noun 1** informal【非正式】a man 男人;家伙 **2** (**guys**) informal,

chiefly N. Amer.【非正式,主北美美】people of either sex 伙计们;兄弟(或姐妹)们 **3** Brit.【英】a stuffed figure that is traditionally burnt on a bonfire on 5 November 盖伊(盖伊·福克斯的模拟像,作为传统每年11月5日点起篝火将其焚烧) • **verb** make fun of someone 嘲弄

guy² **noun** a rope or line fixed to the ground to secure a tent (固定帐篷用的)拉绳,牵索

guzzle /ˈɡʌzl/ **verb** (**guzzles, guzzling, guzzled**) eat or drink greedily 狼吞虎咽;狂饮

gym /dʒɪm/ **noun 1** a gymnasium 体操馆;健身房 **2** a private club with equipment for improving physical fitness 健身俱乐部 **3** gymnastics 体操

gymkhana /dʒɪmˈkɑːnə/ **noun** a horse-riding event consisting of a series of competitions 赛马(会);马术比赛

gymnasium /dʒɪmˈneɪziəm/ **noun** (plural **gymnasiums** or **gymnasia** /dʒɪmˈneɪziə/) a hall or building equipped for gymnastics and other sports 体操馆;健身房

gymnast /ˈdʒɪmnæst/ **noun** a person trained in gymnastics 体操运动员

gymnastics /dʒɪmˈnæstɪks/ **plural noun** exercises involving physical agility and coordination 体操(运动)
■ **gymnastic** adjective.

gymslip /ˈdʒɪmslɪp/ **noun** Brit.【英】a pinafore dress reaching from the shoulder to the knee, formerly worn by schoolgirls 束腰无袖外衣

gynaecology /ˌɡaɪnəˈkɒlədʒi/ (US spelling【美拼作】**gynecology**) **noun** the branch of medicine concerned with conditions and diseases experienced by women 妇科学;妇科 ■ **gynaecological** adjective **gynaecologist** noun.

gypsum /ˈdʒɪpsəm/ **noun** a soft white or grey mineral used to make plaster of Paris and in the building industry

石膏

Gypsy or **Gipsy** /ˈdʒɪpsi/ noun (plural **Gypsies**) a member of a travelling people 吉卜赛人

gyrate /dʒaɪˈreɪt/ verb (**gyrates, gyrating, gyrated**) move in a circle or spiral 旋转；回旋；环动 ■ **gyration** noun.

gyroscope /ˈdʒaɪrəskəʊp/ noun a device, used to provide stability or maintain a fixed direction, consisting of a wheel or disc spinning rapidly about an axis which is itself free to alter in direction 陀螺仪；回转仪

Hh

SPELLING TIP 拼写指南 Some words sound as if they might begin with 'h' but actually begin with 'wh' instead, for example **whole** or **whom**. 有些词根据发音似乎是以 h 开头，实际是以 wh 开头，如 whole 和 whom。

H or **h** /eɪtʃ/ *noun* (plural **Hs** or **H's**) the eighth letter of the alphabet 英语字母表的第8个字母 • *abbreviation* (**h**) hours. □ **H-bomb** a hydrogen bomb 氢弹

ha *abbreviation* hectares.

habeas corpus /ˌheɪbɪəs ˈkɔːpəs/ *noun* Law 【法律】 a written order saying that a person must come before a judge or court 人身保护令(受拘押者须移送法庭的书面令状)

haberdashery /ˌhæbəˈdæʃəri/ *noun* Brit. 【英】 materials used in dressmaking and sewing 缝纫用品

habit /ˈhæbɪt/ *noun* **1** a thing you do regularly and repeatedly 习惯 **2** informal 【非正式】 an addiction to a drug 毒瘾 **3** a long, loose garment worn by a monk or nun (修道士或修女穿的)修道服，长袍

habitable /ˈhæbɪtəbəl/ *adjective* suitable to live in 适合居住的

habitat /ˈhæbɪtæt/ *noun* the natural home or environment of a plant or animal (动物的)栖息地；(植物的)产地

habitation /ˌhæbɪˈteɪʃn/ *noun* **1** the fact of living somewhere 居住 **2** formal 【正式】 a house or home 住宅，住处

habitual /həˈbɪtʃuəl/ *adjective* **1** done constantly or as a habit 经常做的，习以为常的 **2** regular 惯常的，通常的 ■ **habitually** *adverb*.

habituate /həˈbɪtʃueɪt/ *verb* (**habituates**, **habituating**, **habituated**) make or become accustomed to something (使)习惯于

habitué /həˈbɪtjueɪ/ *noun* a frequent visitor to a place 常客

hacienda /ˌhæsɪˈendə/ *noun* (in Spanish-speaking countries) a large estate with a house (西班牙语国家的)大农庄，大庄园

hack¹ /hæk/ *verb* **1** cut or hit at something with rough or heavy blows 乱劈；用刀砍 **2** use a computer to read or alter information in another computer system without permission 非法侵入(计算机)以窃取(或改动)信息 ■ **hacker** *noun*.

hack² *noun* **1** a journalist producing dull, unoriginal work 平庸记者 **2** do a horse for ordinary riding 普通坐骑，驽马

hackles /ˈhæklz/ *plural noun* hairs along an animal's back which raise when it is angry or alarmed (动物的)颈背毛(发怒或警觉时能竖起)

hackney /ˈhækni/ *noun* (plural **hackneys**) (in the past) a horse-drawn vehicle kept for hire (旧时的)出租马车 □ **hackney carriage** a taxi 出租车

hackneyed /ˈhæknid/ *adjective* (especially of a phrase) not original or interesting (尤指词语)陈腐的，老一套的

hacksaw /ˈhæksɔː/ *noun* a saw with a narrow blade set in a frame 钢锯；弓锯

had /hæd, həd/ past and past participle of HAVE.

haddock /ˈhædək/ *noun* (plural **haddock**) a silvery-grey sea fish used for food 黑线鳕(一种银灰色食用海鱼)

hadn't /'hædnt/ **short form** had not.

haematology /ˌhiːmə'tɒlədʒi/ (US spelling 【美拼作】 **hematology**) **noun** the branch of medicine concerned with the blood 血液学

haemoglobin /ˌhiːmə'gləʊbɪn/ (US spelling 【美拼作】 **hemoglobin**) **noun** a red protein in the blood that carries oxygen 血红蛋白

haemophilia /ˌhiːmə'fɪliə/ (US spelling 【美拼作】 **hemophilia**) **noun** a condition in which the ability of the blood to clot is reduced, causing severe bleeding from even a small injury 血友病 ■ **haemophiliac** noun.

haemorrhage /'hemərɪdʒ/ (US spelling 【美拼作】 **hemorrhage**) **noun** an escape of blood from a burst blood vessel 出血；失血 • **verb** (**haemorrhages, haemorrhaging, haemorrhaged**) have a haemorrhage 出血；失血

haemorrhoid /'hemərɔɪd/ (US spelling 【美拼作】 **hemorrhoid**) **noun** a swollen vein in the region of the anus 痔

haft /hɑːft/ **noun** the handle of a knife, axe, or spear (刀、斧或矛的)柄

hag /hæg/ **noun** an ugly old woman 老丑妇

haggard /'hægəd/ **adjective** looking exhausted and ill 憔悴的；形容枯槁的

haggis /'hægɪs/ **noun** (plural **haggis**) a Scottish dish consisting of the internal organs of a sheep or calf mixed with suet and oatmeal 肚包羊(或牛)杂碎(一种苏格兰菜肴)

haggle /'hægl/ **verb** (**haggles, haggling, haggled**) argue or negotiate with someone about the price of something 讨价还价 • **noun** a period of haggling 讨价还价时期

hagiography /ˌhægi'ɒgrəfi/ **noun 1** writing which is about the lives of saints 圣徒传记 **2** a biography that presents its subject as better than in reality 理想化传记

ha-ha /'hɑːhɑː/ **noun** a trench which forms a boundary to a park or garden without interrupting the view (筑于界沟中不遮挡视线的)暗墙，隐篱

haiku /'haɪkuː/ **noun** (plural **haiku** or **haikus**) a Japanese poem of three lines and seventeen syllables (日本的)俳句，十七音诗

hail[1] /heɪl/ **noun 1** pellets of frozen rain falling in showers 雹子；冰雹 **2** a large number of things hurled forcefully through the air 冰雹般袭来的大量事物 • **verb** (**it hails, it is hailing, it hailed**) hail falls 下冰雹

hail[2] **verb 1** call out to someone to attract their attention 大声招呼(某人) **2** (**hail someone/thing as**) enthusiastically describe someone or something as 称赞；赞颂 **3** (**hail from**) have your home or origins in 出生于；来自

hailstone /'heɪlstəʊn/ **noun** a pellet of hail 冰雹；雹块

hair /heə(r)/ **noun 1** each of the thread-like strands growing from the skin of animals, or from plants (动植物的)毛发，茸毛 **2** strands of hair 头发 □ **hair-raising** very alarming or frightening 令人毛骨悚然的；极其恐怖的 **hair shirt** (in the past) a shirt made of very rough cloth worn as a way of punishing yourself (旧时苦修者穿的)刚毛衬衣，苦衣 **hair trigger** a firearm trigger set for release at the slightest pressure (枪的)微力扳机 **let your hair down** informal 【非正式】 behave wildly or in a very relaxed way 无拘无束；不拘礼节 **split hairs** make small and unnecessary distinctions 吹毛求疵；过分纠缠细节

hairband /'heəbænd/ **noun** a band worn on the head to keep the hair off the face 发带；发箍

haircut /'heəkʌt/ **noun 1** the style in which someone's hair is cut 发型；发式 **2** an act of cutting someone's hair 理发

hairdo /'heədu:/ **noun** (plural **hairdos**) informal 【非正式】 the style of a person's hair 发型；发式

hairdresser /'heədresə(r)/ **noun** a person who cuts and styles hair 理发师，美发师 ■ **hairdressing** noun.

hairdryer or **hairdrier** /'heədraɪə(r)/ **noun** an electrical device for drying the hair with warm air (吹干头发用的)吹风机

hairgrip /'heəgrɪp/ **noun** Brit. 【英】 a hairpin 发夹

hairline /'heəlaɪn/ **noun** the edge of a person's hair 发际线；头发轮廓线 • **adjective** very thin or fine 非常细的；细微的

hairnet /'heənet/ **noun** a fine net for holding the hair in place (固定头发用的)发网

hairpiece /'heəpi:s/ **noun** a piece of false hair worn with your own hair to make it look thicker 假发

hairpin /'heəpɪn/ **noun** a U-shaped pin for fastening the hair (U 形)发卡，发针 □ **hairpin bend** a sharp U-shaped bend in a road (道路的)U 形急转弯

hairspray /'heəspreɪ/ **noun** a solution sprayed on to hair to keep it in place 喷发胶;喷发定型剂

hairstyle /'heəstaɪl/ **noun** a way in which a person's hair is cut or arranged 发型；发式 ■ **hairstylist** noun.

hairy /'heəri/ **adjective** (**hairier**, **hairiest**) **1** covered with or like hair 长满毛的；似毛的 **2** informal【非正式】 dangerous or frightening 危险的；可怕的

Haitian /'heɪʃn/ **noun** a person from Haiti 海地人 • **adjective** relating to Haiti 海地的

hajj or **haj** /hædʒ/ **noun** the pilgrimage to Mecca which all Muslims are expected to make at least once if they can afford to (伊斯兰教徒的)麦加朝觐

hake /heɪk/ **noun** a long-bodied sea fish used for food 狗鳕，无须鳕(一种长体食用海鱼)

halal /hə'lɑ:l/ **adjective** (of meat) prepared according to Muslim law (肉)按伊斯兰教规制备的

halberd /'hælbɜ:d/ **noun** historical 【历史】 a combined spear and battleaxe 戟(一种枪钺两用武器)

halcyon /'hælsɪən/ **adjective** (of a past time) very happy and peaceful (往昔)平安幸福的

hale /heɪl/ **adjective** (of an old person) strong and healthy (老人)矍铄的，硬朗的

half /hɑ:f/ **noun** (plural **halves**) **1** either of two equal parts into which something is or can be divided 半；一半 **2** Brit. informal【英，非正式】 half a pint of beer 半品脱啤酒 • **pronoun** an amount equal to a half 半数；一半 • **adverb 1** to the extent of half 到一半程度 **2** partly 部分地 □ **at half mast** (of a flag) flown halfway down its mast, as a mark of respect for a person who has died (旗)降半旗(以示哀悼) **half-and-half** in equal parts 相等;对等 **half-baked** informal 【非正式】 not well planned or considered 计划不周的；考虑不缜密的 **half board** Brit. 【英】 a type of accommodation at a hotel or guest house which includes breakfast and one main meal 半食宿(旅馆或家庭旅馆提供早餐和一顿主餐的住宿) **half-brother** (or **half-sister**) a brother (or sister) with whom you have one parent in common 同父异母(或同母异父)兄弟(或姐妹) **half-caste** offensive【冒犯】 a person whose parents are of different races 混血儿 **half-crown** (or **half a crown**) a former British coin equal to two shillings and sixpence (12½p) 半克朗(英国旧时使用的硬币，等于2

先令6便士) **half-dozen** (or **half a dozen**) a group of six 半打;六个 **half-hearted** without enthusiasm or energy 缺乏热情的;不尽力的 **half-hour** (or **half an hour**) a period of thirty minutes 半小时;三十分钟 **half-life** the time taken for the radioactivity of a substance to fall to half its original value 半衰期(指物质的放射性降至其原值的一半所用的时间) **half measures** actions or policies that are not forceful or decisive enough 不彻底的行动;执行不力的政策 **half nelson** a hold in wrestling in which you pass one arm under your opponent's arm from behind while applying your other hand to their neck 单臂扼颈(摔跤动作,指从对手背后以一臂穿过腋下反扣其颈背) **half-term** Brit.【英】 a short holiday halfway through a school term (学校的)期中假 **half-timbered** having walls with a timber frame and a brick or plaster filling 露明木架的 **half-time** (in sport) a short gap between two halves of a match (体育比赛中的)中场休息 **not half 1** not nearly 远非;差得多 **2** Brit. informal【英,非正式】to an extreme degree 非常;极其

halfback /ˈhɑːfbæk/ noun a player in a ball game whose position is between the forwards and fullbacks (球类比赛中的)前卫

halfpenny or **ha'penny** /ˈheɪpnɪ/ noun (plural **halfpennies** or **halfpence** /ˈheɪpns/) a former British coin equal to half an old penny (英国旧时使用的)半便士硬币

halfway /hɑːfˈweɪ/ adverb & adjective **1** at or to a point equal in distance between two others 在中途(的);半路上(的) **2** to some extent 一定程度上(的)

halfwit /ˈhɑːfwɪt/ noun informal【非正式】a stupid person 傻瓜;笨蛋 ■ **half-witted** adjective.

halibut /ˈhælɪbət/ noun (plural **halibut**) a large flat sea fish used for food 大比目鱼,庸鲽(大型食用海鱼)

halitosis /ˌhælɪˈtəʊsɪs/ noun bad-smelling breath 口臭

hall /hɔːl/ noun **1** also **hallway**) a room or space inside a front door, or between a number of rooms (住宅的)门厅;(正门入口处的)过道,走廊 **2** a large room for meetings, concerts, etc. (用于开会、举办音乐会等的)大厅,礼堂 **3** (also **hall of residence**) Brit.【英】a university building in which students live (大学的)学生宿舍 **4** Brit.【英】a large country house 乡间大庄园;府第

hallelujah /ˌhælɪˈluːjə/ or **alleluia** /ˌælɪˈluːjə/ **exclamation** God be praised 哈利路亚(赞美上帝用语)

hallmark /ˈhɔːlmɑːk/ noun **1** an official mark stamped on objects made of pure gold, silver, or platinum (金、银或铂金制品的)纯度印记 **2** a distinctive feature 特征;特点 • verb stamp an object with a hallmark 给…打上纯度印记

hallo /həˈləʊ/ → 见 HELLO.

hallowed /ˈhæləʊd/ adjective **1** made holy 神圣化的 **2** very honoured and respected 受尊崇的;深受敬重的

Halloween or **Hallowe'en** /ˌhæləʊˈiːn/ noun the night of 31 October, the evening before All Saints' Day 万圣节前夕(10月31日晚上)

hallucinate /həˈluːsɪneɪt/ verb (**hallucinates**, **hallucinating**, **hallucinated**) see something which is not actually there 产生幻觉 ■ **hallucination** noun **hallucinatory** adjective.

hallucinogen /həˈluːsɪnədʒən/ noun a drug causing hallucinations 致幻药 ■ **hallucinogenic** adjective.

halo /ˈheɪləʊ/ noun (plural **haloes** or **halos**) **1** (in a painting) a circle of light surrounding the head of a holy person (绘画中圣人头上的)光轮,光环 **2** a circle of light round the sun or moon (环绕日、月的)晕、晕圈

halogen /ˈhælədʒən/ **noun** any of a group of elements including fluorine, chlorine, bromine, and iodine 卤素

halt¹ /hɔːlt/ **verb** come or bring to a sudden stop (使)停住;(使)暂停 • **noun 1** a stopping of movement or activity 停止;停住;暂停 **2** Brit.【英】a minor stopping place on a railway line (铁路沿线上的)小站

halt² **adjective** old use【旧】lame 瘸的;跛足的

halter /ˈhɔːltə(r)/ **noun** a rope or strap placed around the head of an animal and used to lead it (牵动物的)笼头、缰绳 □ **halter neck** a style of woman's top that is fastened behind the neck, leaving the shoulders, upper back, and arms bare 绕颈系带式领口

halting /ˈhɔːltɪŋ/ **adjective** slow and hesitant 犹豫不决的;迟疑的

halve /hɑːv/ **verb** (halves, halving, halved) **1** divide into two halves 分为两半 **2** reduce or be reduced by half (把…)对半分

halves /hɑːvz/ **plural of** HALF.

halyard /ˈhæljəd/ **noun** a rope used for raising and lowering a sail, yard, or flag on a ship (用于升降船帆、帆桁或旗帜的)吊索,升降索

ham¹ /hæm/ **noun 1** meat from the upper part of a pig's leg which is salted and dried or smoked 火腿(肉) **2** (hams) the back of the thighs 大腿后部;股臀 □ **ham-fisted** clumsy 笨拙的;笨手笨脚的

ham² **noun 1** an actor who overacts (表演过火的)蹩脚演员 **2** (also **radio ham**) informal【非正式】an amateur radio operator 业余无线电爱好者 • **verb** (hams, hamming, hammed) informal【非正式】overact 表演过火 ■ **hammy** adjective.

hamburger /ˈhæmbɜːgə(r)/ **noun** a small cake of minced beef, fried

or grilled and typically served in a bread roll 汉堡包

hamlet /ˈhæmlət/ **noun** a small village 小村庄

hammer /ˈhæmə(r)/ **noun 1** a tool with a heavy metal head and a wooden handle, for driving in nails 锤子;榔头 **2** an auctioneer's mallet, tapped to indicate a sale (拍卖者用的)小木槌 **3** a part of a mechanism that hits another 击铁;击锤 **4** a heavy metal ball attached to a wire for throwing in an athletic contest (田径比赛中投掷的)链球 • **verb** (hammers, hammering, hammered) **1** hit repeatedly with a hammer 反复敲打;锤打 **2** (**hammer away**) work hard and persistently 辛勤工作;不懈努力 **3** (**hammer something in** or **into**) make something stick in someone's mind by constantly repeating it 灌输;反复强调 **4** (**hammer something out**) work out the details of a plan or agreement 作出(详细计划);推敲(协议细节)

hammerhead /ˈhæməhed/ **noun** a shark with flattened extensions on either side of the head 槌头双髻鲨

hammock /ˈhæmək/ **noun** a wide strip of canvas or rope mesh suspended at both ends, used as a bed (帆布或绳网做的)吊床

hamper¹ /ˈhæmpə(r)/ **noun** a basket used for food and other items needed for a picnic (野餐上用来盛食物等的)篮子

hamper² **verb** (hampers, hampering, hampered) slow down or prevent the movement or progress of 牵制;阻碍

hamster /ˈhæmstə(r)/ **noun** a burrowing rodent with a short tail and large cheek pouches 仓鼠(短尾,有颊囊)

> ✔ 拼写指南 no p: *hamster*, not *hamp-*. hamster 中没有 p,不要拼作 hamp-。

hamstring /ˈhæmstrɪŋ/ **noun** any of

five tendons at the back of a person's knee 腘绳肌腱 • verb (**hamstrings**, **hamstringing**, past and past participle **hamstrung**) **1** cripple by cutting the hamstrings (割断肌腱)使腘腿, 使残疾 **2** severely restrict 严重限制

hand /hænd/ noun **1** the end part of the arm beyond the wrist, with four fingers and a thumb 手 **2** a pointer on a clock or watch indicating the passing of time (钟表的)指针 **3** (**hands**) a person's power or control (人的)权力, 控制 **4** an active role 积极作用 **5** help in doing something 帮助;协助 **6** a person who does physical work 劳动力;体力劳动者 **7** a round of applause 鼓掌 **8** the set of cards dealt to a player in a card game (牌戏中的)一手牌 **9** a unit of measurement of a horse's height, equal to 4 inches (10.16 cm) 一手之宽(用以量马的高度, 等于4英寸, 合10.16厘米) • verb give or pass something to 传递;交给 □ **at hand** (or **on** or **to hand**) near; easy to reach 在附近;在手边 **from hand to mouth** meeting only your immediate needs 仅够糊口的;勉强度日的 **hand grenade** a grenade that is thrown by hand 手榴弹 **hand in glove** very closely together 密切合作 **hand-me-down** a piece of clothing that has been passed on from another person (别人穿过的)旧衣服 **hand-pick** choose carefully 精选;仔细挑选 **hands-on** involving direct participation in something 积极参与的;亲身体验的 **hand-to-hand** (of fighting) involving physical contact (搏斗)直接交手的;肉搏的 **in hand** in progress 在进行中 **out of hand 1** not under control 失控地 **2** without taking time to think 不假思索地

handbag /hændbæg/ noun Brit. 【英】a small bag used by a woman to carry everyday personal items (女用)小手提包;坤包

handball /hændbɔːl/ noun **1** a game in which the ball is hit with the hand in a walled court 墙手球(运动) **2** Soccer 【足球】unlawful touching of the ball with the hand or arm 手球犯规

handbill /hændbɪl/ noun a small printed advertisement handed out in the street 广告单;传单

handbook /hændbʊk/ noun a book giving basic information or instructions 手册;便览;指南

handbrake /hændbreɪk/ noun a brake operated by hand, used to hold an already stationary vehicle 手刹车;手闸

handcuff /hændkʌf/ noun (**handcuffs**) a pair of lockable linked metal rings for securing a prisoner's wrists 手铐 • verb put handcuffs on 给…戴手铐

handful /hændfʊl/ noun **1** a quantity that fills the hand 一把 **2** a small number or amount 少数;少量 **3** informal 【非正式】a person who is difficult to deal with or control 难应付的人;难控制的人

handgun /hændɡʌn/ noun a gun designed for use with one hand 手枪

handhold /hændhəʊld/ noun something for a hand to grip on 可以抓握的东西

handicap /hændikæp/ noun **1** a condition that limits a person's ability to function physically, mentally, or socially 残疾 **2** something that makes progress or success difficult 困难;障碍 **3** a disadvantage given to a leading competitor in a sport in order to make the chances of winning more equal, such as the extra weight given to certain racehorses (体育比赛中给强者设置的)不利条件, 障碍 **4** the number of strokes by which a golfer normally exceeds par for a course (高尔夫球手)超过标准杆数的击球数 • verb (**handicaps**, **handicapping**, **handicapped**) make it difficult for someone to do something 妨碍;使处于不利境地

handicapped /'hændikæpt/ **adjective** having a handicap or disability 残疾的;弱智的

> **！注意** when used to refer to people with physical and mental disabilities, the word **handicapped** sounds old-fashioned and may cause offence; it is better to use **disabled**, or, when referring to mental disability, **having learning difficulties**. 当指人有身体残疾或智力缺陷时, handicapped 有些过时而且可能冒犯他人, 最好用 disabled, 当指人有智力缺陷时, 最好用 having learning difficulties.

handicraft /'hændikrɑːft/ **noun 1** the skilled making of decorative objects by hand 手艺;手工工艺 **2** an object made in this way 手工艺品

handiwork /'hændiwɜːk/ **noun 1** (**your handiwork**) something that you have made or done 手工制品 **2** the making of things by hand 手工制作

handkerchief /'hæŋkətʃɪf/ **noun** (plural **handkerchiefs** or **handkerchieves**) a square of material for wiping or blowing the nose on 手绢;手帕

handle /'hændl/ **verb** (**handles**, **handling**, **handled**) **1** feel or move something with the hands 触;摸;拿;搬 **2** control an animal, vehicle, or tool 控制(动物);操纵(车辆或工具) **3** deal with a situation 处理;应对 **4** control, manage, or deal in something commercially 负责;经销 **5** (**handle yourself**) behave 行事;表现 • **noun 1** the part by which a thing is held, carried, or controlled 把手;手柄 **2** a means of understanding or approaching a person or situation 理解途径;控制手段 ▪ **handler** noun.

handlebar /'hændlbɑː(r)/ or **handlebars** /'hændlbɑːz/ **noun** the steering bar of a bicycle or motor-bike (自行

车或摩托车的)车把

handmade /hænd'meɪd/ **adjective** made by hand rather than machine 手工制作的

handmaid /'hændmeɪd/ or **handmaiden** /'hændmeɪdn/ **noun** old use 【旧】 a female servant 侍女;女仆

handout /'hændaʊt/ **noun 1** a parcel of food, clothes, or money given to a person in need 捐赠品;救济品;救济金 **2** a piece of printed information provided free of charge (免费分发的)宣传品,传单

handset /'hændset/ **noun 1** the part of a telephone that is spoken into and listen to 电话听筒 **2** a hand-held control device for a piece of electronic equipment (电子设备的)手控装置,遥控器

handshake /'hændʃeɪk/ **noun** an act of shaking a person's hand 握手

handsome /'hænsəm/ **adjective** (**handsomer**, **handsomest**) **1** (of a man) good-looking (男子)英俊的, 漂亮的 **2** (of a woman) striking and impressive rather than pretty (女子)健美的,标致的 **3** (of a thing) impressive and of good quality (物品)制作精良的,优质的 **4** (of an amount) large (数量)相当大的,可观的 ▪ **handsomely** adverb.

handspring /'hændsprɪŋ/ **noun** a jump through the air on to your hands followed by another on to your feet 前手翻腾越;手翻

handstand /'hændstænd/ **noun** an act of balancing on your hands with your legs in the air 手倒立

handwriting /'hændraɪtɪŋ/ **noun 1** writing with a pen or pencil rather than by typing or printing 书写;手写 **2** a person's particular style of writing 书写风格;书法;笔迹 ▪ **handwritten** adjective.

handy /'hændi/ **adjective** (**handier**, **handiest**) **1** convenient to handle or use 方便的;便于使用的;有用的 **2**

close by and ready for use 近便的；附近的 ■ **handily** adverb.

handyman /ˈhændimæn/ **noun** (plural **handymen**) a person employed to do general building repairs (做房屋维修工作的)杂务工，工匠

hang /hæŋ/ **verb** (**hangs**, **hanging**, past and past participle **hung** except in sense 2) **1** suspend or be suspended from above with the lower part dangling freely (被)悬挂 **2** (past and past participle **hanged**) kill someone by suspending them from a rope tied around the neck 绞死，吊死(某人) **3** (of a piece of clothing) fall or drape in a particular way (衣服)垂落，下垂 □ **get the hang of** informal 【非正式】 learn how to do something 掌握…的要领 **hang-glider** a simple aircraft consisting of a framework from which a person is suspended while they glide through the air 悬挂式滑翔机 **hang out** informal 【非正式】 spend time relaxing or enjoying yourself 放松；享乐 **hang-up** informal 【非正式】 an emotional problem 感情困扰；苦恼

! 注意 hang has two past tense and past participle forms, **hanged** and **hung**: use **hung** in general situations, as in *they hung out the washing*, and **hanged** when talking about execution by hanging, as in *the prisoner was hanged*. hang 的过去式和过去分词有两种形式：hanged 和 hung。在通常情况下用后一种形式 hung，如 they hung out the washing(把洗好的衣服晾出去)；而谈论对某人实施绞刑时则用 hanged，如 the prisoner was hanged(该犯被施以绞刑)。

hangar /ˈhæŋə(r)/ **noun** a large building in which aircraft are kept 飞机库

✔ 拼写指南 -ar, not -er: hang*ar*; hangar 中的 -ar 不要拼作 -er。

hangdog /ˈhæŋdɒg/ **adjective** having a sad or guilty appearance (表情)悲哀的，内疚的

hanger /ˈhæŋə(r)/ **noun 1** a person who hangs something 挂东西的人 **2** (also **coat hanger**) a curved frame with a hook at the top, for hanging clothes from a rail 衣架 □ **hanger-on** (plural **hangers-on**) a person who tries to be friendly with someone of higher status 攀附权贵者；钻营拍马的人

hanging /ˈhæŋɪŋ/ **noun** a decorative piece of fabric hung on the wall of a room or around a bed 墙幔；围幔

hangman /ˈhæŋmən/ **noun** (plural **hangmen**) an executioner who hangs condemned people 执行绞刑者

hangnail /ˈhæŋneɪl/ **noun** a piece of torn skin at the root of a fingernail (指甲根部的)倒刺，甲刺

hangover /ˈhæŋəʊvə(r)/ **noun 1** a headache or other after-effects caused by drinking too much alcohol 宿醉(饮酒过量引起的严重头痛或其他不良反应) **2** a thing that has survived from the past 残存物；遗留物

hank /hæŋk/ **noun** a coil or length of wool, hair, or other material (毛线、头发等的)一束，一卷，一绺

hanker /ˈhæŋkə(r)/ **verb** (**hanker after** or **for** or **to do**) feel a desire for or to do 渴望；热切期望

hanky or **hankie** /ˈhæŋki/ **noun** (plural **hankies**) informal 【非正式】 a handkerchief 手绢；手帕

hanky-panky /ˌhæŋkiˈpæŋki/ **noun** informal 【非正式】 naughty behaviour 不老实的行为；骗人的把戏

hansom /ˈhænsəm/ or **hansom cab noun** (in the past) a horsedrawn carriage with two wheels and a hood, for two passengers (旧时的)双轮式双座马车

Hanukkah or **Chanukkah** /ˈhænʊkə/ *noun* a Jewish festival of lights held in December (犹太人每年12月过的)光明节,献殿节

haphazard /hæpˈhæzəd/ *adjective* having no particular order or plan 无秩序的,随意的,无计划的 ■ **haphazardly** *adverb*.

hapless /ˈhæpləs/ *adjective* unlucky 不幸的,运气不好的

happen /ˈhæpən/ *verb* 1 take place without being planned or as the result of something (偶然)发生 2 (**happen to do**) do by chance 碰巧做 3 (**happen on**) come across by chance 偶遇;偶然发现 4 (**happen to**) be experienced by 使经历;使遭遇到 5 (**happen to**) become of 发生于

happening /ˈhæpənɪŋ/ *noun* an event or occurrence 事件;发生的事情 ● *adjective informal* 【非正式】 fashionable 流行的;时髦的

happy /ˈhæpi/ *adjective* (**happier**, **happiest**) 1 feeling or showing pleasure 高兴的;愉快的 2 willing to do something 乐意的;愿意的 3 fortunate and convenient 幸运的;运气好的 □ **happy-go-lucky** cheerfully unconcerned about the future 无忧无虑的;乐天的 **happy hour** a period of the day when drinks are sold at reduced prices in a bar 快乐折扣,优惠时间(酒吧一天中降价出售饮品的时间段) ■ **happily** *adverb* **happiness** *noun*.

hara-kiri /ˌhærəˈkɪri/ *noun* a Japanese method of ritual suicide in which a person cuts open their stomach with a sword (日本人的)剖腹自尽

harangue /həˈræŋ/ *verb* (**harangues**, **haranguing**, **harangued**) use loud and aggressive language in criticizing someone or trying to persuade them to do something 呵斥;大声训诉 ● *noun* an act of haranguing 呵斥;大声训诉

harass /ˈhærəs, həˈræs/ *verb* 1 torment someone by putting constant pressure on them or by being unpleasant 烦扰;使苦恼 2 (**harassed**) tired or tense as a result of having too many demands made on you 疲惫而焦虑的 3 make repeated small-scale attacks on an enemy in order to wear down resistance 骚扰,袭扰(敌人) ■ **harassment** *noun*.

✔ 拼写指南 only one *r*: harass. harass 中只有一个 r.

harbinger /ˈhɑːbɪndʒə(r)/ *noun* a person or thing that announces or signals the approach of something 通报者;前兆;预示

harbour /ˈhɑːbə(r)/ (US spelling 【美拼作】 **harbor**) *noun* a sheltered area of coast, where ships can be moored 港口;港湾 ● *verb* 1 keep a thought or feeling secretly in your mind 心怀(想法或感情) 2 give a refuge or shelter to 庇护;窝藏 3 carry the germs of a disease 携带(病菌)

hard /hɑːd/ *adjective* 1 solid, firm, and rigid 坚硬的;结实的 2 needing a lot of endurance or effort; difficult 艰难的;费力的 3 (of a person) not showing any signs of weakness (人)强硬的,坚强的 4 (of information) precise and definitely true (信息)确实的,可靠的 5 harsh or unpleasant to the senses 刺耳的;刺目的 6 done with a lot of force or strength 大力的,猛烈的 7 (of drink) strongly alcoholic (饮料)烈性的,酒精含量高的 8 (of a drug) very addictive (药物)易上瘾的 ● *adverb* 1 with a lot of effort or force 大力地;猛烈地 2 so as to be solid or firm 坚硬地,坚实地 □ **hard-boiled** 1 (of an egg) boiled until the yolk is firm (蛋)煮硬的,煮老的 2 (of a person) tough and cynical (人)顽强的,坚韧的 **hard cash** coins and banknotes as opposed to other forms of payment 现金;现钞 **hard copy** a printed version of data held in a computer 硬拷贝,打印文本(打印出的计算机储存数据) **hard core 1** the most committed or uncompromising members of a group 中坚分子;铁杆分子 **2** very explicit pornography 赤裸裸的色情作品 **3** pop music that is loud and aggressive in style 狂躁的流行音乐 **hard disk** (or **hard drive**) (in a computer) a rigid magnetic disk on which a large amount of data can be stored (计算机中的)硬盘 **hard done by** Brit.【英】harshly or unfairly treated 被…虐待的,受到…不公平对待的 **hard feelings** feelings of resentment 愤怒;憎恨 **hard-headed** tough and realistic 讲求实际的;不感情用事的 **hard line** a strict policy or attitude 强硬政策;强硬态度 **hard-nosed** realistic and tough-minded 讲求实际的,不妥协的 **hard shoulder** Brit.【英】a strip of road alongside a motorway for use in an emergency (高速公路旁供车辆紧急停车的)硬质路肩 **hard up** informal【非正式】short of money 缺钱的,■ **harden** verb **hardness** noun.

hardback /'hɑːdbæk/ noun a book bound in stiff covers 精装书

hardbitten /ˌhɑːd'bɪtn/ adjective tough and cynical 顽强的,坚韧的

hardboard /'hɑːdbɔːd/ noun stiff board made of compressed wood pulp 硬质纤维板

hardly /'hɑːdli/ adverb **1** scarcely; barely 几乎不 **2** only with great difficulty 勉强;好不容易

> **!注意** don't use **hardly** in a negative sentence, such as I can't hardly wait; say I can hardly wait instead. 在否定句中不用 hardly, 不能说 I can't hardly wait; 正确说法应为 I can hardly wait; (我几乎等不了了)。

hardship /'hɑːdʃɪp/ noun severe suffering 困苦;艰难

hardware /'hɑːdweə(r)/ noun **1** tools and other items used in the home and in activities such as gardening (家用或园艺用的)金属用具,五金制品 **2** the machines, wiring, and other parts of a computer (计算机的)硬件 **3** heavy military equipment such as tanks and missiles (坦克、导弹等)重型军事装备,重型武器

hardwood /'hɑːdwʊd/ noun the wood from a broadleaved tree as distinguished from that of conifers 硬木;硬材;阔叶材

hardy /'hɑːdi/ adjective (hardier, hardiest) capable of surviving difficult conditions 能吃苦耐劳的 ■ **hardiness** noun.

hare /heə(r)/ noun a fast-running animal like a large rabbit, with long hind legs 野兔 • verb (hares, haring, hared) run very fast 飞跑;疾跑 □ **hare-brained** foolish and unlikely to succeed 愚蠢的;轻率的

harebell /'heəbel/ noun a plant with pale blue bell-shaped flowers 圆叶风铃草(开淡蓝色钟形花)

harelip /'heəlɪp/ noun offensive【冒犯】a cleft lip 兔唇;三瓣嘴

harem /'hɑːriːm/ noun **1** the separate part of a Muslim household reserved for women (伊斯兰教徒家中女眷的)内室,闺房 **2** the women living in a harem (伊斯兰教徒家中的)女眷

haricot /'hærɪkəʊ/ noun a round white bean 菜豆;扁豆

hark /hɑːk/ verb **1** literary【文】listen 倾听 **2** (hark back to) recall or remind you of something in the past 回忆起;使想起

harken /'hɑːkən/ ⇒ 见 HEARKEN.

harlequin /'hɑːləkwɪn/ noun (Harlequin) (in traditional pantomime) a character who wears a mask and a diamond-patterned costume 哈乐根(传统哑剧中戴面具、穿饰有菱形图案花衣的滑稽角色) • adjective in varied colours 五颜六色的

harlot /'hɑːlət/ noun old use【旧】a prostitute 妓女;娼妓

harm /hɑːm/ **noun 1** hurt or injury to a person 伤害 **2** damage done to a thing 损害;损坏 **3** a bad effect on something 害处;坏处 • **verb 1** hurt or injure someone 伤害(某人) **2** damage or have a bad effect on something 损害;对…产生不良影响

harmful /ˈhɑːmfl/ **adjective** causing or likely to cause harm 有害的;导致损害的 ■ **harmfully** adverb.

harmless /ˈhɑːmləs/ **adjective** not able or likely to cause harm 无害的;不会导致损害的 ■ **harmlessly** adverb.

harmonic /hɑːˈmɒnɪk/ **adjective** relating to harmony 和声的;泛音的

harmonica /hɑːˈmɒnɪkə/ **noun** a small rectangular wind instrument with a row of metal reeds that produce different notes 口琴

harmonious /hɑːˈməʊniəs/ **adjective 1** tuneful 音调和谐的;悦耳的 **2** arranged in a pleasing way so that each part goes well with the others 协调的;和谐的 **3** free from conflict 融洽的;和睦的 ■ **harmoniously** adverb.

harmonium /hɑːˈməʊniəm/ **noun** a keyboard instrument in which the notes are produced by air driven through metal reeds by foot-operated bellows 簧风琴,脚踏式风琴(键盘乐器,通过脚踏风箱产生气流使簧片振动发声)

harmonize or **harmonise** /ˈhɑːmənaɪz/ **verb** (**harmonizes, harmonizing, harmonized**) **1** add notes to a melody to produce harmony 给(乐曲)配和音 **2** make or be harmonious (使)和谐,(使)协调

harmony /ˈhɑːməni/ **noun** (plural **harmonies**) **1** the combination of musical notes sounded at the same time to produce chords with a pleasing effect 和声 **2** a pleasing quality when things are arranged together well 和谐;协调 **3** agreement 一致;融洽

harness /ˈhɑːnɪs/ **noun 1** a set of straps by which a horse or other animal is fastened to a cart, plough, etc. 马具;挽具 **2** an arrangement of straps used for attaching a person's body to something (系在人身上的)背带,牵索 • **verb 1** fit a person or animal with a harness 给…上挽具;给…系绳索 **2** control and make use of resources 控制并利用(资源)

harp /hɑːp/ **noun** a musical instrument consisting of a frame supporting a series of strings of different lengths, played by plucking with the fingers 竖琴 • **verb** (**harp on**) keep talking about something in a boring way 唠叨;喋喋不休 ■ **harpist** noun.

harpoon /hɑːˈpuːn/ **noun** a barbed spear-like missile used for catching whales and other large sea creatures 渔猎标枪;鱼叉 • **verb** spear with a harpoon 用渔猎标枪刺

harpsichord /ˈhɑːpsɪkɔːd/ **noun** a keyboard instrument with horizontal strings plucked by points operated by pressing the keys 拨弦键琴

harpy /ˈhɑːpi/ **noun** (plural **harpies**) **1** Greek & Roman Mythology 【希腊和罗马神话】 a cruel creature with a woman's head and body and a bird's wings and claws 哈比;鸟身女妖 **2** an unpleasant woman 泼妇;恶妇

harridan /ˈhærɪdən/ **noun** a bossy or aggressive old woman 老泼妇;母夜叉

harrier /ˈhæriə(r)/ **noun 1** a hound used for hunting hares 猎兔犬 **2** a bird of prey 鹞(一种猛禽)

harrow /ˈhærəʊ/ **noun** a piece of equipment consisting of a heavy frame set with teeth which is dragged over ploughed land to break up or spread the soil 耙;耙子 • **verb** draw a harrow over 用耙子耙

harrowing /ˈhærəʊɪŋ/ **adjective** very distressing 令人痛苦的

harry /ˈhæri/ **verb** (**harries, harrying,**

harried 1) carry out repeated attacks on an enemy 不断袭扰(敌人) 2 pester continuously 不断烦扰

harsh /hɑːʃ/ **adjective 1** unpleasantly rough or jarring to the senses 粗糙的, 刺耳的; 刺目的; 刺鼻的 2 cruel or severe 无情的; 严厉的 3 (of climate or conditions) difficult to survive in; hostile (气候或条件)恶劣的, 艰苦的 ■ **harshly** adverb **harshness** noun.

hart /hɑːt/ **noun** an adult male deer (成年)雄鹿

harvest /ˈhɑːvɪst/ **noun 1** the process or period of gathering in crops 收割; 收获, 收获季节 2 the season's yield or crop 收成; 收获量 • **verb** gather in a crop 收割; 收获 ■ **harvester** noun.

has /hæz, həz/ 3rd person singular present of HAVE. □ **has-been** informal 【非正式】 a person who is no longer important 过时(或不再重要)的人

hash /hæʃ/ **noun** a dish of chopped cooked meat reheated with potatoes 回锅肉末土豆泥 □ **make a hash of** informal 【非正式】 make a mess of 把…搞糟

hash = HASHISH.

hash **noun** Brit. 【英】the symbol # 符号 #

hashish /ˈhæʃiːʃ/ **noun** cannabis 大麻麻醉剂; 大麻

hasn't /ˈhæznt/ **short form** has not.

hasp /hɑːsp/ **noun** a hinged metal plate that is fitted over a metal loop and secured by a pin or padlock to fasten something (金属)搭扣, 锁扣

hassle /ˈhæsl/ informal 【非正式】 **noun 1** annoying inconvenience 麻烦; 不便 2 a situation involving argument or disagreement 烦扰; 骚扰 • **verb** (**hassles, hassling, hassled**) harass or pester someone 烦扰; 骚扰

hassock /ˈhæsək/ **noun** a cushion for kneeling on in church (教堂里的)跪垫

haste /heɪst/ **noun** speed or urgency of action 匆忙; 仓促

hasten /ˈheɪsn/ **verb 1** move or act quickly 急忙行动; 赶往 2 make something happen sooner than expected 使加速; 催促

hasty /ˈheɪsti/ **adjective (hastier, hastiest)** hurried; rushed 匆忙; 仓促的 ■ **hastily** adverb.

hat /hæt/ **noun** a covering for the head 帽子 □ **hat-trick** three successes of the same kind 帽子戏法(连续三次成功)

hatch /hætʃ/ **noun 1** a small opening in a floor, wall, or roof allowing access to an area (地板、墙或屋顶上的)开口, 活板口 2 a door in an aircraft, spacecraft, or submarine (飞机、航天器或潜水艇的)舱口, 出口

hatch **verb 1** (of a young bird, fish, or reptile) come out of its egg (小鸟、鱼或爬行动物)孵出, 破壳而出 2 (of an egg) open and produce a young animal (蛋)孵化 3 form a plot or plan 策划(阴谋); 拟订(计划)

hatch **verb** (in drawing) shade an area with closely drawn parallel lines (绘画中)给…加影线

hatchback /ˈhætʃbæk/ **noun** a car with a door that opens upwards across the full width at the back end 掀背式轿车; 舱门式汽车

hatchet /ˈhætʃɪt/ **noun** a small axe with a short handle 短柄小斧 □ **bury the hatchet** end a quarrel 结束争吵

hatchling /ˈhætʃlɪŋ/ **noun** a newly hatched young animal 新孵出的小动物

hate /heɪt/ **verb** (**hates, hating, hated**) feel very strong dislike for 憎恶; 痛恨 • **noun 1** very strong dislike 憎恶; 厌恶 2 informal 【非正式】 a disliked person or thing 所憎恶的人(或事物)

hateful /ˈheɪtfl/ **adjective** very unkind or unpleasant 可恨的; 令人厌恶的

hatred /ˈheɪtrɪd/ **noun** very strong dislike; hate 仇恨; 憎恶

haughty /ˈhɔːti/ **adjective (haughtier,**

haughtiest) arrogant and superior towards other people 高傲自大的，傲慢的 ■ **haughtily** adverb.

haul /hɔːl/ verb **1** pull or drag something with a lot of effort (用力)拖，拉 **2** transport something in a lorry or cart (用卡车或马车)运送 • noun **1** a quantity of something obtained, especially illegally 非法获得的数量 **2** a number of fish caught at one time 一网渔获量

haulage /'hɔːlɪdʒ/ noun Brit. 【英】the commercial transport of goods 货运

haulier /'hɔːliə(r)/ noun Brit. 【英】a person or company employed in the commercial transport of goods by road 货运承运人；货运公司

haulm /hɔːm/ noun a plant stalk (植物的)茎，秆

haunch /hɔːntʃ/ noun **1** a person's or animal's buttock and thigh (人的)臀部；(动物的)腰腿 **2** the leg and loin of an animal, as food (动物可食用的)腰腿肉

haunt /hɔːnt/ verb **1** (of a ghost) appear regularly in a place (鬼魂)常出没于(某处) **2** (of a person) visit a place frequently (人)常去(某处) **3** keep coming into someone's mind in a disturbing way 萦绕在…心头；不断缠扰 • noun a place where a particular type of person frequently goes (某人的)常去之处

haunted /'hɔːntɪd/ adjective **1** visited by a ghost 闹鬼的；鬼魂出没的 **2** showing signs of mental suffering 忧虑的；烦恼的

haunting /'hɔːntɪŋ/ adjective making someone feel sad or thoughtful 难以忘怀的；萦绕于心的 ■ **hauntingly** adverb.

haute couture /ˌəʊt kuˈtjʊə(r)/ noun the designing and making of high-quality clothes by leading fashion houses 高级时装设计和制作

haute cuisine /ˌəʊt kwiˈziːn/ noun high-quality cooking in the traditional

French style (法国传统的)高级烹饪

have /hæv, həv/ verb (**has**, **having**, **had**) **1** possess or own 有；拥有 **2** experience 经历；遭受 **3** be able to make use of 能利用 **4** (**have to**) be obliged to；must 必须；不得不 **5** perform an action 进行(活动) **6** show a personal characteristic 显示出(个性) **7** suffer from an illness or disability 患(病)；有(残疾) **8** cause something to be or be done 使成为；使完成 **9** place, hold, or keep something in a particular position 把…放置(或保持)于(某处) **10** eat or drink something 吃；喝 • **auxiliary verb** used with a past participle to form the perfect, pluperfect, and future perfect tenses, and the conditional mood (与过去分词连用构成现在完成时，过去完成时，将来完成时以及虚拟语气)

> **!注意** be careful not to write **of** when you mean **have** or **'ve**: I could've told you that not I could of told you that. 本意是要用 have 或 've 时当心不要误写作 of, 如 I could've told you that (我本该告诉你)不要写成 I could of told you that。

haven /'heɪvn/ noun **1** a place of safety 安全之处；避难所 **2** a harbour or small port 港口；小港

haven't /'hævnt/ short form have not.

haver /'heɪvə(r)/ verb (**havers**, **havering**, **havered**) **1** Scottish 【苏格兰】talk foolishly 胡说；说傻话 **2** Brit.【英】be indecisive 迟疑；犹豫

haversack /'hævəsæk/ noun a small, sturdy bag carried on the back or over the shoulder 背包

havoc /'hævək/ noun great destruction, confusion, or disorder 大破坏；浩劫；混乱 □ **play havoc with** completely disrupt 完全破坏

Hawaiian /hə'waɪən/ noun a person from Hawaii 夏威夷人 • **adjective** relating to Hawaii 夏威夷的

hawk¹ /hɔːk/ *noun* **1** a fast-flying bird of prey with a long tail 鹰 **2** a person in favour of aggressive policies in foreign affairs 鹰派人物；强硬分子 • *verb* hunt with a trained hawk 带鹰狩猎 ■ **hawkish** *adjective*.

hawk² *verb* offer goods for sale in the street (沿街)兜售，叫卖 ■ **hawker** *noun*.

hawk³ *verb* clear the throat noisily 大声清嗓子

hawser /ˈhɔːzə(r)/ *noun* a thick rope for mooring or towing a ship (系船或拖船的)粗绳，缆索

hawthorn /ˈhɔːθɔːn/ *noun* a thorny shrub or tree with small dark red fruits called **haws** 山楂树

hay /heɪ/ *noun* grass that has been mown and dried for use as animal feed (用作饲料的)干草 □ **hay fever** an allergy to pollen or dust, causing sneezing and watery eyes 枯草热，花粉症(对花粉或尘埃过敏、引起打喷嚏或流泪的病症)

haystack /ˈheɪstæk/ or **hayrick** /ˈheɪrɪk/ *noun* a large packed pile of hay 干草堆

haywire /ˈheɪwaɪə(r)/ *adjective* informal 【非正式】 out of control 失控的

hazard /ˈhæzəd/ *noun* **1** a danger 危险 **2** an obstacle, such as a bunker, on a golf course (高尔夫球场上的)障碍 • *verb* **1** dare to say 大胆说出；斗胆提出 **2** put at risk 使遭受危险

hazardous /ˈhæzədəs/ *adjective* dangerous 危险的

haze /heɪz/ *noun* **1** a thin mist caused by fine particles of dust, water, etc. 薄雾；烟霭 **2** a state of mental confusion 糊涂；困惑

hazel /ˈheɪzl/ *noun* **1** a shrub or small tree which produces round nuts called **hazelnuts** 榛木，榛树 **2** a rich reddish-brown colour 赤褐色

hazy /ˈheɪzi/ *adjective* (**hazier**, **haziest**) **1** covered by a haze 雾蒙蒙的；有薄雾的 **2** vague or unclear 模糊的；不清楚的 ■ **hazily** *adverb*.

he /hiː/ *pronoun* **1** used to refer to a man, boy, or male animal previously mentioned or easily identified 他；它(雄性动物) **2** used to refer to a person or animal whose sex is not specified (不论性别的)人，动物

> **!注意** until recently, **he** was used to refer to any person, male or female (as in *every child needs to know that he is loved*), but many people now think that this is old-fashioned and sexist. One solution is to use **he or she**; another is to use **they**, as in *everyone needs to feel that they matter*. 过去当某人性别未确定时，he 既用于指代男性也用于指代女性，如 every child needs to know that he is loved (每个孩子都需要知道自己受到关爱)，但是现在许多人认为这种用法已经过时且存在性别歧视。一种解决办法是使用 he or she，另外一个办法是使用 they，如 everyone needs to feel that they matter (每个人都需要感觉到自己很重要)。

head /hed/ *noun* **1** the upper part of the body, containing the brain, mouth, and sense organs 头；头部 **2** a person in charge 主管人；领导；头目 **3** the front, forward, or upper part of something 前部；上端 **4** a person considered as a unit 一人；每人：*fifty pounds per head* 每人50英镑 **5** a particular number of cattle or sheep (牛或羊的)头数 **6** a compact mass of leaves or flowers at the top of a stem (茎顶端的)叶球，头状花序 **7** a part of a computer or a tape or video recorder which transfers information to and from a tape or disk (计算机、录音机或录像机的)磁头 **8** the source of a river or stream (河流或溪流的)源头 **9** the foam on top of a glass of beer (一杯啤酒顶端的)泡沫 **10** (**heads**) the side of a coin showing the image of a head (硬币的)人头面 pressure of water or steam in an enclosed space (水或蒸汽的)压力 • **adjective** chief 主要的；最重要的 • **verb 1** be the head of 位于…之首；带领 **2** move in a particular direction 朝(某方向)行进 **3** (**head someone/thing off**) intercept someone or something and force them to change direction 拦截…使改变方向 **4** give a heading to 给…加标题 **5** Soccer【足球】hit the ball with the head 用头顶(球) □ **come to a head** reach a crisis 濒临危急关头 **head-on 1** with the front of a vehicle (车辆)迎面地 **2** involving direct confrontation 正面冲突的 **head start** an advantage gained at the beginning of something 起步前的优势 ■ **headless** adjective

headship noun.

headache /'hedeɪk/ **noun 1** a continuous pain in the head (持续的)头痛 **2** informal【非正式】something that causes worry 令人忧虑的事物

headband /'hedbænd/ **noun** a band of fabric worn around the head 束发带；头带

headboard /'hedbɔːd/ **noun** an upright panel at the head of a bed 床头板

headbutt /'hedbʌt/ **verb** attack someone by hitting them with the head (用头)撞(人)

headdress /'heddres/ **noun** a decorative covering for the head 头巾；头饰

header /'hedə(r)/ **noun 1** Soccer【足球】a shot or pass made with the head 头球 **2** a line of writing at the top of each page of a book or document 页眉；题头

headhunt /'hedhʌnt/ **verb** approach someone already employed elsewhere to fill a vacant post 猎头；延揽人才

heading /'hedɪŋ/ **noun 1** a title at the head of a page or section of a book 标题；题目 **2** a direction or bearing 方向；方位

headland /'hedlənd/ **noun** a narrow piece of land that sticks out into the sea 海角；陆岬

headlight /'hedlaɪt/ or **headlamp** /'hedlæmp/ **noun** a powerful light at the front of a motor vehicle (机动车的)前灯，头灯

headline /'hedlaɪn/ **noun 1** a heading at the top of a newspaper or magazine article (报刊文章的)标题，题目 **2** (**the headlines**) a summary of the most important items of news 新闻提要 • **verb** (**headlines, headlining, headlined**) **1** give an article a headline 给…加标题 **2** appear as the star performer at a concert 成为(音乐会)的主角

headlong /'hedlɒŋ/ **adverb & adjective 1** with the head first 头朝前地(的) **2** in a rush 匆忙地(的)

headmaster /ˌhed'mɑːstə(r)/ or **headmistress** /ˌhed'mɪstrəs/ **noun** a teacher in charge of a school 校长；女校长

headphones /'hedfəʊnz/ **plural noun** a pair of earphones joined by a band placed over the head 耳机；头戴式受话器

headquarters /ˌhed'kwɔːtəz/ **noun** the place from which an organization or military operation is directed 总部；司令部

headset /'hedset/ **noun** a set of headphones with a microphone attached (带麦克风的)耳机，头戴式受话器

headstone /'hedstəʊn/ **noun** a stone slab set up at the head of a grave 墓碑

headstrong /'hedstrɒŋ/ **adjective** very independent and determined to have your own way 任性的；固执的

headway /'hedweɪ/ **noun** (**make headway**) make progress 进展；进步

headwind /'hedwɪnd/ **noun** a wind blowing from directly in front, towards someone or something 逆风；顶头风

headword /ˈhedwɜːd/ **noun** a word which begins a separate entry in a dictionary or encyclopedia (词典或百科全书中的)词目，词条

heady /ˈhedi/ **adjective** (**headier, headiest**) **1** having a strong or exciting effect 令人陶醉的；使人兴奋的 **2** (of alcohol) strong (酒)上头的，烈性的

heal /hiːl/ **verb 1** make or become healthy again (使)痊愈；(使)康复 **2** put right 使恢复正常 ■ **healer** noun.

health /helθ/ **noun 1** the state of being free from illness or injury 健康 **2** a person's mental or physical condition (人的精神或身体的)健康状况 □ **health club** a private club where exercise facilities and health and beauty treatments are available 健身俱乐部 **health farm** a place where people stay in order to try to become healthier through dieting, exercise, and special treatments 健身庄(通过节食、锻炼和特殊治疗改善健康状况的场所) **health food** natural food that is believed to be good for your health 绿色食物，保健食品

healthful /ˈhelθfʊl/ **adjective** good for the health 健康的，有益健康的

healthy /ˈhelθi/ **adjective** (**healthier, healthiest**) **1** in good health, or helping towards good health 健康的；有益健康的 **2** normal, sensible, or desirable 正常的，明智的；合意的 **3** of a very satisfactory size or amount 可观的，相当多的 ■ **healthily** adverb.

heap /hiːp/ **noun 1** a pile of a substance or of a number of objects 堆 **2** informal 【非正式】 a large amount or number 大量，许多 **3** informal 【非正式】 an old vehicle in bad condition 破旧车辆 ■ **verb 1** put in or form a heap (使)成堆，堆积 **2** (**heap something with**) load something heavily with 装满，盛满 **3** (**heap something on**) give

a lot of praise, criticism, etc. to 大量给予(赞扬、批评等)

hear /hɪə(r)/ **verb** (**hears, hearing, heard**) **1** be aware of a sound with the ears 听见 **2** be told of 听说；得知 **3** (**have heard of**) be aware of the existence of 知道；了解 **4** (**hear from**) receive a letter, phone call, or email from 收到…的来信；接到…的电话 **5** listen to 注意听；聆听 **6** listen to and judge a case in a law court 审理(案件) ■ **hearer** noun.

hearing /ˈhɪərɪŋ/ **noun 1** the ability to hear sounds 听觉；听力 **2** the range within which sounds can be heard 听力所及的范围 **3** an opportunity to state your case 申辩机会 **4** an act of listening to evidence 听证；听审 □ **hearing aid** a small device worn by a partially deaf person to make them hear better 助听器

hearken or **harken** /ˈhɑːkən/ **1 verb** (usu. **hearken to**) old use 【旧】 listen 倾听

hearsay /ˈhɪəseɪ/ **noun** information received from other people which is possibly unreliable 传闻，道听途说

hearse /hɜːs/ **noun** a vehicle for carrying the coffin to a funeral 灵车，柩车

heart /hɑːt/ **noun 1** the organ in the chest that pumps the blood around the body 心；心脏 **2** the central or innermost part of something 中心，核心 **3** a person's ability to feel love or compassion 爱心；心肠；心地 **4** mood or feeling 心情；心境 **5** courage or enthusiasm 勇气；热情 □ **heart attack** a sudden failure of the heart to work properly 心脏病突发 **heart-rending** very sad or upsetting 令人心碎的，使人悲痛的 **heart-searching** thorough examination of your feelings and motives 反省；省察 **heart-throb** a very good-looking famous man 漂亮迷人的出名男子 **heart-to-heart** (of a conversation) very intimate and personal (谈话)交心的 **heart-warming** arousing feelings of happiness or pleasure 暖人心房的；令人欣喜的 **wear your heart on your sleeve** show your feelings openly 流露自己的感情

heartache /ˈhɑːteɪk/ **noun** emotional suffering or grief 苦恼；悲痛；心痛

heartbeat /ˈhɑːtbiːt/ **noun** a pulsation of the heart 心跳；心搏

heartbreak /ˈhɑːtbreɪk/ **noun** extreme distress 心碎；极度悲伤 ■ **heart-breaking** adjective **heartbroken** adjective.

heartburn /ˈhɑːtbɜːn/ **noun** a form of indigestion felt as a burning sensation in the chest (消化不良引起的)胃灼热，烧心

hearten /ˈhɑːtn/ **verb** make more cheerful or confident 使振奋；激励 ■ **heartening** adjective.

heartfelt /ˈhɑːtfelt/ **adjective** deeply and strongly felt 由衷的；诚挚的

hearth /hɑːθ/ **noun** the floor or surround of a fireplace 壁炉前的地面；壁炉边

hearthrug /ˈhɑːθrʌg/ **noun** a rug laid in front of a fireplace 壁炉前的地毯

heartily /ˈhɑːtɪli/ **adverb 1** in a hearty way 热心地；尽情地 **2** very 非常

heartless /ˈhɑːtləs/ **adjective** feeling no pity for other people 冷酷的；无情的

hearty /ˈhɑːti/ **adjective** (**heartier**, **heartiest**) **1** enthusiastic and friendly 热忱的；友好的 **2** strong and healthy 强健的 **3** heartfelt 由衷的；诚挚的 **4** (of a meal) large and filling (饭菜)丰盛的

heat /hiːt/ **noun 1** the quality of being hot 热；高温 **2** hot weather or high temperature 热天气；高温 **3** strength of feeling (感情的)强烈 **4** (**the heat**) informal【非正式】pressure to do or achieve something 压力；紧张 **5** one of a series of races or contests held to decide who will take part in the next stage of a competition 预赛 • **verb 1** make or become hot or warm (使)变热；给…加热 **2** (**heat up**) become more intense and exciting 加剧；激化 **3** (**heated**) passionate 激烈的 □ **on heat** (of a female mammal) ready for mating (雌性哺乳动物)在发情期的 ■ **heatedly** adverb.

heater /ˈhiːtə(r)/ **noun** a device for heating something 加热器；加热装置

heath /hiːθ/ **noun** an area of open uncultivated land covered with heather, gorse, etc. 荒野；荒原

heathen /ˈhiːðn/ **noun** old use【旧】a person who does not belong to a widely held religion (主要宗教教徒以外的)异教徒

heather /ˈheðə(r)/ **noun** a shrub with small purple flowers, found on moors and heaths 帚石楠，开紫色小花，见于荒野地带

heating /ˈhiːtɪŋ/ **noun** equipment used to provide heat 供热装置

heatstroke /ˈhiːtstrəʊk/ **noun** a feverish condition caused by being exposed to very high temperatures 中暑

heatwave /ˈhiːtweɪv/ **noun** a period of abnormally hot weather 热浪；酷热时期

heave /hiːv/ **verb** (**heaves**, **heaving**, **heaved** or chiefly Nautical【主航海】**hove**) **1** lift or move with great effort (用力)推，举，拉 **2** produce a sigh noisily (沉重地)发出(叹息) **3** rise and fall 起伏；升降 **4** try to vomit 呕吐；恶心 **5** (**heave to**) Nautical【航海】come to a stop 停航 **6** (**heaving**) Brit. informal【英，非正式】very crowded 非常拥挤的 □ **heave in sight** (or **into view**) Nautical【航海】come into view 进入视野

heaven /ˈhevn/ **noun 1** (in Christianity and some other religions) the place where God or the gods live and where good people go when they die (基督教等宗教中认为存在的)天国，

天堂 **2 (the heavens)** literary 【文】 the sky 天空;苍穹 **3** a place or state of great happiness 极乐世界;极乐 □ **in seventh heaven** very happy 极乐的;非常幸福的

heavenly /ˈhevnli/ **adjective 1** having to do with heaven 天国的 **2** having to do with the sky 天空的 **3** informal 【非正式】 wonderful 美妙的 □ **heavenly body** a planet, star, etc. 天体

heavy /ˈhevi/ **adjective (heavier, heaviest) 1** of great weight 重的;沉的 **2** thick or dense 浓密的;密集的 **3** of more than the usual size, amount, or force (规模、数量或力量)超出一般的 **4** hard or forceful 大力的;用力的 **5** needing a lot of physical effort 费力的;繁重的 **6** informal 【非正式】 very important or serious 非常重要的;很严肃的 • **noun (plural heavies)** informal 【非正式】 **1** a large, strong man 壮汉 **2** an important person 要人 □ **heavy-duty** designed to withstand a lot of use or wear 耐用的;经久的 **heavy-handed** clumsy, insensitive, or too forceful 笨拙的;迟钝的;粗鲁的 **heavy industry** large-scale production of large, heavy articles and materials 重工业 **heavy metal** very loud, forceful rock music 重金属摇滚乐 ■ **heavily** adverb **heaviness** noun.

heavyweight /ˈheviweɪt/ **noun 1** the heaviest weight in boxing (拳击运动中)最重量级 **2** informal 【非正式】 an influential person 大腕;大牌;重量级人物

Hebrew /ˈhiːbruː/ **noun** an ancient language still spoken in Israel 希伯来语

heckle /ˈhekl/ **verb (heckles, heckling, heckled)** interrupt a public speaker with comments or abuse 诘难(公开演讲者);对(公开演讲者)起哄 ■ **heckler** noun.

hectare /ˈhekteə(r)/ **noun** a unit of area equal to 10,000 square metres

(2.471 acres) 公顷(等于10,000平方米,合2.471英亩)

hectic /ˈhektɪk/ **adjective** full of frantic activity 忙碌的;手忙脚乱的 ■ **hectically** adverb.

hector /ˈhektə(r)/ **verb** talk to someone in a bullying way 吓唬;威胁

he'd /hiːd/ **short form 1** he had. **2** he would.

hedge /hedʒ/ **noun** a fence formed by bushes growing closely together (灌木)树篱 • **verb (hedges, hedging, hedged) 1** surround with a hedge 用树篱围起 **2** avoid making a definite statement or decision 回避;规避 □ **hedge your bets** avoid committing yourself 避免明确立场;脚踏两只船

hedgehog /ˈhedʒhɒg/ **noun** a small animal with a spiny coat, which can roll itself into a ball for defence 刺猬

hedgerow /ˈhedʒrəʊ/ **noun** a hedge of wild shrubs and trees bordering a field 灌木篱墙;树篱

hedonism /ˈhiːdənɪzəm/ **noun** behaviour based on the belief that pleasure is the most important thing in life 享乐主义 ■ **hedonist** noun **hedonistic** adjective.

heebie-jeebies /ˌhiːbiˈdʒiːbiz/ **plural noun (the heebie-jeebies)** informal 【非正式】 a state of nervous fear or anxiety 神经紧张;焦虑不安

heed /hiːd/ **verb** pay attention to 留意;注意 □ **pay (or take) heed** pay careful attention 注意;留心

heedless /ˈhiːdləs/ **adjective** showing a reckless lack of care or attention 欠考虑的;忽视的;掉以轻心的

heel[1] /hiːl/ **noun 1** the back part of the foot below the ankle 脚跟;踵 **2** the part of a shoe or boot supporting the heel 鞋跟 • **verb** renew the heel on a shoe 给(鞋)换鞋跟 □ **take to your heels** run away 溜掉;逃走

heel[2] **verb** (of a ship) lean over to one side (船)倾侧

heft /heft/ **verb** lift or carry something heavy 举起，运送(重物)

hefty /'hefti/ **adjective (heftier, heftiest) 1** large, heavy, and powerful 大而重的 **2** (of a number or amount) considerable (数目或数量)可观的，巨大的

hegemony /hɪ'dʒeməni, -'ge-/ **noun** formal 【正式】 leadership or dominance 领导权；支配权；霸权

Hegira or **Hejira** /'hedʒɪrə/ **noun** Muhammad's departure from Mecca to Medina in AD 622 穆罕默德从麦加到麦地那的逃亡

heifer /'hefə(r)/ **noun** a young cow 小母牛

height /haɪt/ **noun 1** measurement from head to foot or from base to top 高度；身高 **2** distance above sea level or the ground 海拔；(距地面的)高度 **3** the quality of being tall or high 高 **4** a high place 高处；高地 **5** the most intense or extreme part 最激烈的部分；高潮；顶点

heighten /'haɪtn/ **verb 1** make or become more intense (使)增强；(使)加强 **2** make higher 使变高；提高

heinous /'heɪnəs/ **adjective** very wicked 极邪恶的；令人发指的

heir /eə(r)/ **noun 1** a person who will inherit the property or rank of another when that person dies 继承人 **2** a person who continues someone else's work 接班人；后继者 □ **heir apparent** (plural **heirs apparent**) **1** an heir whose rights cannot be taken away by the birth of another heir 当然继承人；法定继承人 **2** someone who is most likely to take the job or role of another person (职位等的)最可能接替者

heiress /'eəres, -rəs/ **noun** a female heir 女继承人

heirloom /'eəluːm/ **noun** a valuable object that has belonged to a family for several generations 传家宝

heist /haɪst/ **noun** informal 【非正式】 a robbery 抢劫

held /held/ past and past participle of HOLD.

helical /'helɪkl/ **adjective** in the shape of a helix 螺旋形的

helicopter /'helɪkɒptə(r)/ **noun** a type of aircraft which is powered and lifted by horizontally revolving blades 直升机

helium /'hiːliəm/ **noun** a light colourless gas that does not burn (气体元素)氦

helix /'hiːlɪks/ **noun** (plural **helices** /'hiːlɪsiːz/) an object in the shape of a spiral 螺旋状物

hell /hel/ **noun 1** (in Christianity and some other religions) a place of evil and suffering where wicked people are sent after death (基督教等宗教中认为存在的)地狱，阴间 **2** a state or place of great suffering 苦境；受苦的地方 □ **hell-bent** determined to achieve something 不顾一切的；破釜沉舟的

he'll /hiːl/ **short form 1** he shall. **2** he will.

Hellenic /he'lenɪk/ **adjective** Greek 希腊的

hellhole /'helhəʊl/ **noun** a very unpleasant place 地狱般可怕的地方；魔窟

hellish /'helɪʃ/ **adjective** informal 【非正式】 very difficult or unpleasant 地狱般的；地狱的 ■ **hellishly** adverb.

hello /hə'ləʊ/, **hallo**, or **hullo** **exclamation 1** used as a greeting (用作问候语)你好 **2** Brit. 【英】 used to express surprise or to attract someone's attention (用于表示惊讶或吸引某人的注意)嘿，喂

hellraiser /'helreɪzə(r)/ **noun** a person who causes trouble by drunken or outrageous behaviour 惹是生非者；爱惹麻烦的人

helm /helm/ **noun 1** a wheel or tiller for steering a ship or boat 舵轮；舵柄 **2** (the helm) the position of leader

领导地位

helmet /'helmɪt/ noun a hard or padded protective hat 头盔；安全帽；防护帽

helmsman /'helmzmən/ noun (plural **helmsmen**) a person who steers a boat 掌舵者；舵手

help /help/ verb 1 make it easier for someone to do something 帮助；协助 2 improve a situation or problem 改善(状况)；促进(问题解决) 3 (**help yourself**) take something without asking for it first 随意拿取；自取 4 (**cannot help**) be unable to stop yourself doing 忍不住，无法克制 • noun a person or thing that helps someone 有帮助的人(或事物) ■ **helper** noun.

helpful /'helpfl/ adjective 1 ready to give help 提供帮助的；乐于助人的 2 useful 有用的；有益的 ■ **helpfully** adverb.

helping /'helpɪŋ/ noun a portion of food served to one person at one time (食物的)一份，一客

helpless /'helpləs/ adjective 1 unable to defend yourself or to act without help 无法自我保护的；不能独立的 2 uncontrollable 无法控制的 ■ **helplessly** adverb.

helpmate /'helpmeɪt/ or **helpmeet** /'helpmiːt/ noun a helpful companion 助手；伴侣；伙伴

helter-skelter /ˌheltə'skeltə(r)/ adjective & adverb in a hasty and confused or disorganized way 慌张的(地)；忙乱的(地) • noun Brit. 【英】 a tall slide winding around a tower at a fair (游乐场里的)螺旋滑梯

hem /hem/ noun the edge of a piece of cloth or clothing which has been turned under and sewn (布或衣服的)褶边，卷边 • verb (**hems, hemming, hemmed**) 1 give something a hem 给…缝褶边 2 (**hem someone/thing in**) surround someone or something and restrict their movement 包围；限

hematology /ˌhiːmə'tɒlədʒi/ etc. US spelling of HAEMATOLOGY etc. haematology 等的美式拼法

hemisphere /'hemɪsfɪə(r)/ noun 1 a half of a sphere 半球；球体的一半 2 a half of the earth (地球的)半球 ■ **hemispherical** adjective.

hemline /'hemlaɪn/ noun the level of the lower edge of a skirt or coat (裙子或外套的)底边

hemlock /'hemlɒk/ noun a poison made from a plant with small white flowers 由毒芹提炼的毒药

hemp /hemp/ noun 1 the cannabis plant, the fibre of which is used to make rope, fabrics, etc. 大麻(其纤维可用于制绳索、织物等) 2 the drug cannabis 大麻毒品

hen /hen/ noun a female bird, especially of a domestic fowl 雌禽(尤指家禽) □ **hen night** Brit. informal【英，非正式】an all-female celebration for a woman who is about to get married 女性婚前庆祝会(为准新娘举行的庆祝会，只有女性参加)

hence /hens/ adverb 1 for this reason 因此；所以 2 from now 从此时；从现在起

henceforth /ˌhens'fɔːθ/ or **henceforward** /ˌhens'fɔːwəd/ adverb from this time on 从此以后；今后

henchman /'hentʃmən/ noun (plural **henchmen**) chiefly disapproving【主贬】a faithful follower or assistant 党羽；走狗；心腹

henna /'henə/ noun a reddish-brown dye made from the powdered leaves of a tropical shrub 散沫花染剂(棕红色，提取自一种热带灌木叶) ■ **hennaed** adjective.

henpecked /'henpekt/ adjective (of a man) continually nagged or criticized by his wife (男子)惧内的，妻管严的

hepatitis /ˌhepə'taɪtɪs/ noun a serious disease of the liver, mainly transmitted by viruses 肝炎

heptagon /'heptəgən/ **noun** a figure with seven straight sides and angles 七边形；七角形 ■ **heptagonal** adjective.

heptathlon /hep'tæθlɒn/ **noun** an athletic contest for women that consists of seven separate events (女子田径中的)七项全能运动 ■ **heptathlete** noun.

her /hə(r), ɜː(r)/ **pronoun** used as the object of a verb or preposition to refer to a female person or animal previously mentioned 她(用作宾语) • **possessive determiner** belonging to or associated with a female person or animal previously mentioned 她的

herald /'herəld/ **noun 1** (in the past) a person who carried official messages and supervised tournaments (旧时的)传令官，使节，通报者 **2** a sign that something is about to happen or arrive 预兆 • **verb 1** be a sign that something is about to happen or arrive 预示…的到来；预告 **2** describe in enthusiastic terms 热烈宣布

heraldic /he'rældɪk/ **adjective** having to do with heraldry 纹章学的

heraldry /'herəldri/ **noun** the system by which coats of arms are organized and controlled 纹章学

herb /hɜːb/ **noun 1** a plant used for flavouring food or in medicine 草药；芳草 **2** Botany 【植物】a plant which dies down to the ground after flowering 草本植物 ■ **herbal** adjective.

herbaceous /hɜː'beɪʃəs/ **adjective** relating to herbs (in the botanical sense) (植物)草本的 □ **herbaceous border** a garden border containing plants which flower every year (栽种多年生开花植物的)花园边缘花草带

herbalism /'hɜːblɪzəm/ **noun** the use of plants in medicine and cookery 草药学；药膳学 ■ **herbalist** noun.

herbivore /'hɜːbɪvɔː(r)/ **noun** an animal that feeds on plants 食草动物

■ **herbivorous** /hɜː'bɪvərəs/ adjective.

Herculean /hɜːkju'liːən/ **adjective** needing great strength or effort 费力的；艰巨的：*a Herculean task* 艰巨的任务

herd /hɜːd/ **noun 1** a large group of animals that live or are kept together 兽群；牧群 **2** disapproving 【贬】a large group of people 人群 • **verb** make animals or people move in a large group 使成群移动；放牧

here /hɪə(r)/ **adverb** in, at, or to this place or position 在这里；向这里

hereabouts /'hɪərəbaʊts/ or **hereabout** /'hɪərəbaʊt/ **adverb** near this place 在这附近；在这一带

hereafter /hɪər'ɑːftə(r)/ **adverb** formal 【正式】from now on or at some time in the future 此后；今后 • **noun (the hereafter)** life after death 死后的生命；来世

hereby /hɪə'baɪ/ **adverb** formal 【正式】as a result of this 由此；兹

hereditary /hə'redɪtri/ **adjective 1** passed on by parents to their children or young 世袭的；继承的 **2** having to do with inheritance 遗传的；遗传性的

heredity /hə'redəti/ **noun 1** the passing on of characteristics from one generation to another 遗传 **2** the inheriting of a title, office, etc. 继承；世袭

herein /hɪər'ɪn/ **adverb** formal 【正式】in this document, book, or matter 于此；此中

heresy /'herəsi/ **noun (plural heresies)** **1** belief which goes against traditional religious teachings 宗教异端 **2** opinion which is very different from what is generally accepted 非主流观点；离经叛道

heretic /'herətɪk/ **noun** a person who is guilty of heresy 异教徒；犯异端罪者 ■ **heretical** adjective.

hereto /hɪə'tuː/ **adverb** formal 【正式】to this matter or document 于此；至此

heretofore /ˌhɪətuˈfɔː(r)/ **adverb** formal 【正式】 before now 在此之前；直至此时

herewith /hɪəˈwɪð/ **adverb** formal 【正式】 with this 随此

heritable /ˈherɪtəbl/ **adjective** able to be inherited 可遗传的；可继承的

heritage /ˈherɪtɪdʒ/ **noun** valued things such as historic buildings that have been passed down from previous generations 遗产；继承物

hermaphrodite /hɜːˈmæfrədaɪt/ **noun** a person, animal, or plant with both male and female sex organs or characteristics 两性人；雌雄同体的动物；雌雄同株的植物

hermetic /hɜːˈmetɪk/ **adjective** (of a seal or closure) complete and airtight (封闭物或闭合物)密封的，不透气的 ■ **hermetically** adverb.

hermit /ˈhɜːmɪt/ **noun** a person who lives completely alone, especially for religious reasons 独居修道士；隐修士

hernia /ˈhɜːniə/ **noun** a condition in which part of an organ pushes through the wall of the cavity containing it (脏器的)疝，突出

hero /ˈhɪərəʊ/ **noun** (plural **heroes**) **1** a person who is admired for their courage or outstanding achievements 英雄；杰出人物 **2** the chief male character in a book, play, or film 男主人公；男主角 □ **hero worship** extreme admiration for someone 偶像崇拜

heroic /həˈrəʊɪk/ **adjective 1** very brave 非常英勇的 **2** very grand or ambitious in scale (规模)宏大的 • **noun** (**heroics**) brave or dramatic behaviour or talk 豪壮行为；豪言壮语 ■ **heroically** adverb.

heroin /ˈherəʊɪn/ **noun** a very addictive painkilling drug 海洛因

heroine /ˈherəʊɪn/ **noun 1** a woman admired for her courage or outstanding achievements 女英雄；女豪杰 **2** the chief female character in a book, play, or film 女主人公；女主角

heroism /ˈherəʊɪzəm/ **noun** great bravery 英勇；大无畏

heron /ˈherən/ **noun** a large fish-eating bird with long legs, a long neck, and a long pointed bill 鹭；苍鹭

herpes /ˈhɜːpiːz/ **noun** an infectious disease that causes blisters on the skin 疱疹

herring /ˈherɪŋ/ **noun** a silvery fish which is found in shoals and is used for food 鲱；鲱鱼(近海水域盛产的一种银色食用鱼)

herringbone /ˈherɪŋbəʊn/ **noun** a zigzag pattern consisting of columns of short slanting parallel lines 人字形图案；鲱骨式图案

hers /hɜːz/ **possessive pronoun** used to refer to something belonging to or associated with a female person or animal previously mentioned 她的(所有物)

✔ 拼写指南 no apostrophe: **hers**. hers 没有撇号。

herself /hɜːˈself, həˈself/ **pronoun 1** used as the object of a verb or preposition to refer to a female person or animal previously mentioned as the subject of the clause 她自己(用作宾语) **2** she or her personally 她本人；她亲自

hertz /hɜːts/ **noun** (plural **hertz**) the basic unit of frequency, equal to one cycle per second 赫兹(频率单位，等于1周/秒)

he's short form **1** /hiːz/ he is. **2** /hiːz/ he has.

hesitant /ˈhezɪtənt/ **adjective** slow to act or speak through indecision or reluctance 迟疑的；犹豫的；优柔寡断的 ■ **hesitancy** noun **hesitantly** adverb.

hesitate /ˈhezɪteɪt/ **verb** (**hesitates**, **hesitating**, **hesitated**) **1** pause indecisively 犹豫；迟疑 **2** be reluctant to do something 不愿意 ■ **hesitation** noun.

hessian /'hesɪən/ **noun** a strong, coarse fabric 粗麻布

heterogeneous /ˌhetərə'dʒiːnɪəs/ **adjective** varied 各种各样的；混杂的 ■ **heterogeneity** /ˌhetərədʒə'niːəti/ noun.

heterosexual /ˌhetərə'sekʃuəl/ **adjective** sexually attracted to people of the opposite sex 被异性吸引的 • **noun** a heterosexual person 异性恋者 ■ **heterosexuality** noun.

het up adjective informal 【非正式】 angry and agitated 生气的，激动的；烦躁不安的

hew /hjuː/ **verb** (**hews, hewing, hewed**; past participle **hewn** or **hewed**) chop wood, coal, etc. with an axe or other tool (用斧头等)劈砍

hex /heks/ N. Amer. 【北美】 **verb** cast a spell on 施魔法 • **noun** a magic spell 魔法

hexagon /'heksəgən/ **noun** a figure with six straight sides and angles 六边形；六角形 ■ **hexagonal** adjective.

hexameter /hek'sæmɪtə(r)/ **noun** a line of verse made up of six groups of syllables 六韵步诗体

heyday /'heɪdeɪ/ **noun** (**your heyday**) the period when you are most successful or active 鼎盛时期；全盛时期

HGV /ˌeɪtʃ dʒiː 'viː/ **abbreviation** Brit. 【英】 heavy goods vehicle 大型货运卡车

hiatus /haɪ'eɪtəs/ **noun** (plural **hiatuses**) a pause or gap in a series or sequence 间断；裂隙

hibernate /'haɪbəneɪt/ **verb** (**hibernates, hibernating, hibernated**) (of an animal) spend the winter in a state like deep sleep (动物)冬眠 ■ **hibernation** noun.

hibiscus /hɪ'bɪskəs/ **noun** a plant with large brightly coloured flowers

木槿

hiccup or **hiccough** /'hɪkʌp/ **noun** **1** a sudden gulping sound caused by an involuntary spasm of the diaphragm 打嗝声 **2** a minor setback 小挫折 • **verb** (**hiccups, hiccuping, hiccuped**) make the sound of a hiccup 发打嗝声；打嗝

hick /hɪk/ **noun** informal, chiefly N. Amer. 【非正式,主北美】 an unsophisticated country person 乡下人；土包子

hickory /'hɪkəri/ **noun** a tree with edible nuts 山核桃木(果实可食用)

hide¹ /haɪd/ **verb** (**hides, hiding, hid**; past participle **hidden**) **1** put or keep something out of sight 隐藏；把…藏起来 **2** get into a place where you cannot be seen 隐藏 **3** keep secret 隐瞒；掩盖 • **noun** Brit. 【英】 a concealed shelter used to watch wild animals or birds 隐蔽观察处(用于近距离观察野生鸟类或鸟类) □ **hide-and-seek** a game in which one player hides and the others have to look for them 捉迷藏

hide² **noun** the skin of an animal 兽皮

hideaway /'haɪdəweɪ/ **noun** a hiding place 隐藏处；藏身处

hidebound /'haɪdbaʊnd/ **adjective** unwilling to give up old-fashioned ideas in favour of new ways of thinking 思想偏狭的；墨守成规的

hideous /'hɪdɪəs/ **adjective 1** very ugly 非常丑陋的 **2** very unpleasant 令人极其厌恶的 ■ **hideously** adverb.

hideout /'haɪdaʊt/ **noun** a hiding place 隐藏处；藏身之处

hiding /'haɪdɪŋ/ **noun** a physical beating 痛打

hierarchy /'haɪərɑːki/ **noun** (plural **hierarchies**) **1** a system in which people are ranked one above the other according to status or authority 等级制度 **2** a classification of things according to their relative importance (按重要性划分的)等级 ■ **hierarchical** adjective.

✔ 拼写指南 -ie-, not -ei-, and remember the second r: hie*rarchy.* hierarchy 中的 -ie- 不要拼作 -ei-，记住拼写第二个 r。

hieroglyphics /ˌhaɪərəˈɡlɪfɪks/ **plural noun** writing in which a picture represents a word, syllable, or sound, as used in ancient Egypt 象形文字

hi-fi /ˈhaɪfaɪ/ **noun** (plural **hi-fis**) a set of equipment for reproducing high-fidelity sound 高保真音响设备 • **adjective** having to do with high-fidelity sound 高保真的

higgledy-piggledy /ˌhɪɡldɪˈpɪɡldɪ/ **adverb & adjective** in confusion or disorder 乱七八糟(的)；杂乱无章(的)

high /haɪ/ **adjective 1** extending far upwards 高 的 **2** of a particular height 有…高的 **3** far above ground or sea level 远离地面(或海面)的 **4** large in amount, size, or intensity (数量或规模大的，强烈的 **5** (of a period or movement) at its peak (时期或运动)处于顶点的，全盛的 **6** great in status; important (地位)高的；重要的 **7** (of a sound or note) not deep or low (声音或音调)高的，尖厉的 **8** informal 【非正式】 under the influence of drugs or alcohol 被毒品麻醉了的；喝醉的 **9** (of food) beginning to go bad 食物(发馊的，开始变质的 • **noun 1** a high point, level, or figure 高点，高水平，高数值 **2** an area of high atmospheric pressure 高(气)压带 **3** informal 【非正式】 a state of high spirits 兴奋状态 • **adverb** (of a sound) at a high pitch (声音)高调地，尖地 ▢ **High Church** the section of the Church of England which gives an important place to ritual and the authority of bishops and priests (英国国教的)高教会派 **high commission** an embassy of one Commonwealth country in another (英联邦中一国派驻另一国的)高级专员公署 **higher education** education

to degree level or its equivalent, provided at universities and colleges 高等教育 **high explosive** powerful chemical explosive used in shells and bombs 烈性炸药，高爆炸药 **high fidelity** the reproduction of sound with little distortion (声音的)高保真 **high-flown** grand-sounding 言过其实的；夸张的 **high-flyer** (or **high-flier**) a very successful person 非常成功的人 **high-handed** using authority without considering the feelings of other people 专横的，高压的；霸道的 **high jinks** high-spirited fun 狂欢作乐 **high jump** an athletic event in which competitors try to jump over a bar 跳高(运动) **high-rise** (of a building) having many storeys (建筑物)高层的 **high school** a secondary school 中学 **the high seas** the areas of the sea that are not under the control of any one country 公海 **high-spirited** lively and cheerful 活泼的；愉快的 **high tea** Brit. 【英】 a meal eaten in the late afternoon or early evening 下午茶；傍晚茶 **high-tech** (also **hi-tech**) using advanced technology 高技术的 **high technology** advanced technology 高技术；高科技 **high tide** the time when the sea is closest to the land 高潮，满潮

highbrow /ˈhaɪbraʊ/ **adjective** very intellectual or refined in taste 文化层次高的；品位高雅的

highfalutin /ˌhaɪfəˈluːtɪn/ **adjective** informal 【非正式】 grand or self-important in a pretentious way 傲慢的；妄自尊大的

highland /ˈhaɪlənd/ or **highlands** /ˈhaɪləndz/ **noun 1** an area of high or mountainous land 高地；高原 **2** (**the Highlands**) the mountainous northern part of Scotland 苏格兰高地 ▪ **highlander** noun.

highlight /ˈhaɪlaɪt/ **noun 1** an outstanding part of an event or period of time 精彩部分；重要时刻 **2** a bright area in a picture (图片中的)强光部分，亮部 **3** (highlights) bright tints in hair, created by bleaching or dyeing (漂染而成的)头发上发亮的浅色 • verb **1** draw attention to 使注意力集中于；强调 **2** create highlights in hair 将(头发)挑染出光亮的浅色 ■ highlighter noun.

highly /'haɪli/ adverb **1** to a high degree or level 高度地；非常 **2** favourably 赞许地 □ highly strung Brit.【英】very nervous and easily upset 易紧张不安的；神经质的；十分敏感的

Highness /'haɪnəs/ noun (His, Her, Your Highness) a title given to a person of royal rank 殿下，阁下(对皇室成员的尊称)

highway /'haɪweɪ/ noun **1** chiefly N. Amer.【主北美】a main road 干道 **2** a public road 公路

highwayman /'haɪweɪmən/ noun (plural highwaymen) (in the past) a man who held up and robbed travellers (旧时的)拦路强盗，公路响马

hijack /'haɪdʒæk/ verb **1** illegally seize control of an aircraft while it is travelling somewhere 劫持(飞机) **2** take over something and use it for a different purpose 接管(以用于其他目的) • noun an act of hijacking 劫持 ■ hijacker noun.

hike /haɪk/ noun **1** a long walk or walking tour 徒步旅行；远足 **2** a sharp increase 激增 • verb (hikes, hiking, hiked) **1** go on a hike 作徒步旅行；远足 **2** pull or lift up clothing 拉上，提起(衣服) **3** increase a price sharply 大幅提高(价格) ■ hiker noun.

hilarious /hɪ'leərɪəs/ adjective very amusing 狂欢的；欢闹的 ■ hilariously adverb hilarity noun.

hill /hɪl/ noun **1** a naturally raised area of land, not as high as a mountain 小山；山丘 □ over the hill informal【非正式】old and past your best 已过巅

峰期的；不再年轻的

hillbilly /'hɪlbɪli/ noun (plural hillbillies) N. Amer. informal【北美，非正式】an unsophisticated country person 乡巴佬

hillock /'hɪlək/ noun a small hill or mound 小山丘；土堆

hilly /'hɪli/ adjective (hillier, hilliest) having many hills 多小山的；丘陵的

hilt /hɪlt/ noun the handle of a sword, dagger, or knife (剑、匕首或刀的)柄 □ to the hilt completely 完全地

him /hɪm/ pronoun used as the object of a verb or preposition to refer to a male person or animal previously mentioned 他(用作宾语)

himself /hɪm'self/ pronoun **1** used as the object of a verb or preposition to refer to a male person or animal previously mentioned as the subject of the clause 他自己(用作宾语) **2** he or him personally 他本人；他亲自

hind[1] /haɪnd/ adjective situated at the back 后面的；后部的

hind[2] noun a female deer 雌鹿

hinder /'hɪndə(r)/ verb (hinders, hindering, hindered) delay or obstruct 耽搁；妨碍

Hindi /'hɪndi/ noun a language of northern India (印度北部的)印地语

hindmost /'haɪndməʊst/ adjective furthest back 最后面的

hindquarters /haɪnd'kwɔːtəz/ plural noun the rear part and hind legs of a four-legged animal (四足动物的)臀部及后腿

hindrance /'hɪndrəns/ noun a thing that hinders someone or something 障碍物

✔ 拼写指南 no *e*: h*i*ndr*a*nce, not h*i*nd*e*rance. hindrance 中间没有 e，不要拼作 hinderance。

hindsight /'haɪndsaɪt/ noun understanding of a situation or event after it has happened 事后聪明；事后的认识

Hindu /'hɪnduː/ noun (plural Hindus)

a follower of Hinduism 印度教教徒

Hinduism /'hɪndu:ɪzəm/ noun a religion of the Indian subcontinent, with a large number of gods and goddesses 印度教(印度大陆的宗教,信奉多位天神)

hinge /hɪndʒ/ noun a movable joint or mechanism by which a door, gate, or lid opens and closes (门等的)铰链, 合页 • verb (hinges, hingeing or hinging, hinged) 1 attach or join with a hinge 给…装铰链;用铰链接合 2 (hinge on) depend entirely on 完全依赖;取决于

hint /hɪnt/ noun 1 a slight or indirect suggestion 暗示;示意 2 a very small trace of something 细微迹象;线索 3 a small piece of practical information 指点,忠告 • verb suggest indirectly 暗示;示意

hinterland /'hɪntəlænd/ noun 1 the areas of a country away from the coast 内地;腹地 2 the area around or beyond a major town (重要城镇的)外围地区,周围地区

hip[1] /hɪp/ noun a projection formed by the pelvis and upper thigh bone on each side of the body 臀部,屁股

hip[2] noun the fruit of a rose 蔷薇果

hip[3] adjective (hipper, hippest) informal 【非正式】fashionable 时髦的,流行的 ■ hipness noun.

hip hop noun a style of pop music featuring rap with an electronic backing 嬉蹦乐(以电子乐伴奏、以说唱为特色的流行音乐)

hippo /'hɪpəʊ/ = HIPPOPOTAMUS.

hippopotamus /ˌhɪpə'pɒtəməs/ noun (plural hippopotamuses or hippopotami /ˌhɪpə'pɒtəmaɪ/) a large African animal with massive jaws, living partly on land and partly in water 河马

hippy or **hippie** /'hɪpɪ/ noun (plural hippies) a young person who rejects traditional social values and dresses in an unconventional way 嬉皮士(反对传统价值观、穿奇装异服的年轻人)

hipsters /'hɪpstəz/ plural noun Brit. 【英】trousers cut to fit and fasten at the hips 低腰裤

hire /'haɪə(r)/ verb (hires, hiring, hired) 1 pay to be allowed to use something temporarily 租用 2 (hire something out) allow something to be used temporarily in return for payment 租出 3 pay someone to work for you 雇用(某人) • noun the action of hiring 租用;雇用 □ hire purchase Brit. 【英】a system by which you pay for a thing in regular instalments while having the use of it 分期付款购物

hireling /'haɪəlɪŋ/ noun a person who is willing to do any kind of work as long as they are paid 雇工;受雇听人使唤者

hirsute /'hɜːsjuːt/ adjective hairy 多毛的

his /hɪz/ possessive determiner & pronoun belonging to or associated with a male person or animal previously mentioned 他的(所有物)

Hispanic /hɪ'spænɪk/ adjective having to do with Spain or other Spanish-speaking countries 西班牙的;西班牙语国家的

hiss /hɪs/ verb 1 make a sharp sound like that made when pronouncing the letter s 发出嘶嘶声 2 whisper something in an urgent or angry way 急速(或生气)地低声说出 • noun a hissing sound 嘶嘶声;嘘声

histamine /'hɪstəmiːn/ noun a substance which is released by cells in response to an injury or allergy 组胺

historian /hɪ'stɔːrɪən/ noun an expert in history 历史学家

historic /hɪ'stɒrɪk/ adjective famous or important in history, or likely to be seen as such in the future 历史上著名的;有重大历史意义的

historical /hɪ'stɒrɪkl/ adjective 1 having to do with history 历史的 2

belonging to or set in the past 属于历史的;历史上的 ■ **historically** adverb.

history /ˈhɪstrɪ/ *noun* (plural **histories**) **1** the study of past events 历史学;历史研究 **2** the past considered as a whole (总 称)历 史 **3** the past events connected with someone or something 经历;过去;来历 **4** a continuous record of past events or trends 历史记载;沿革

histrionic /ˌhɪstrɪˈɒnɪk/ *adjective* too theatrical or dramatic 过分戏剧化的;装腔作势的;做作的 ■ *noun* (**histrionics**) exaggerated behaviour intended to attract attention 装腔作势;矫揉造作

hit /hɪt/ *verb* (**hits, hitting, hit**) **1** bring your hand or a tool, weapon, bat, etc. against someone or something quickly and with force 击;击中 **2** (of something moving) come into contact with someone or something quickly and forcefully 运动物体碰撞;撞击 **3** reach a target 击中(目标) **4** cause harm or distress to 伤害;打击 **5** be suddenly realized by 使突然意识到 **6** (**hit out**) criticize or attack strongly 严厉批评;猛烈抨击 **7** *informal* 【非正式】 reach 达到 **8** (**hit on**) suddenly discover or think of 突然发现(或想到) ■ *noun* **1** an instance of hitting or being hit 打;被击打 **2** a successful film, pop record, etc. 风靡一时的电影(或流行音乐唱片等) **3** an instance of a website being accessed or a word being found in an Internet search 对因特网网址或搜索词的)点击 **4** *informal, chiefly N. Amer.*【非正式,主北美】 a murder carried out by a criminal organization (犯罪组织实施的)谋杀 **5** *informal* 【非正式】 a dose of an addictive drug 一剂毒品 □ **hit-and-miss** not done in a careful, planned way 漫不经心的;随意的 **hit-and-run** (of a road accident) in which the driver responsible leaves rapidly without helping the other

people involved (道路交通事故)肇事后逃逸的 **hit it off** *informal* 【非正式】 get on well with someone 合得来

hitch /hɪtʃ/ *verb* **1** move into a different position with a jerk 猛地移动 **2** fasten with a rope (用绳子)系住,套住 **3** travel by hitchhiking 搭免费便车旅行 ■ *noun* a temporary difficulty 暂时的困难;障碍 ■ **hitcher** noun.

hitchhike /ˈhɪtʃhaɪk/ *verb* travel by getting free lifts in passing vehicles 免费搭便车旅行 ■ **hitchhiker** noun.

hither /ˈhɪðə(r)/ *adverb* old use 【旧】 to or towards this place 到这儿;向这儿

hitherto /ˌhɪðəˈtuː/ *adverb* until this time 迄今;至今

HIV /ˌeɪtʃ aɪ ˈviː/ *abbreviation* human immunodeficiency virus (the virus causing Aids)人体免疫缺损病毒;艾滋病病毒

hive /haɪv/ *noun* **1** a beehive 蜂房;蜂箱 **2** a place full of people working hard 繁忙的场所 □ **hive something off** transfer part of a business to new ownership 把(部分业务)分离;移交

hives /haɪvz/ *plural noun* a rash of red, itchy marks on the skin, caused by an allergy 荨麻疹

HM /ˌeɪtʃ ˈem/ *abbreviation* Her (or His) Majesty's 陛下

HMS /ˌeɪtʃ em ˈes/ *abbreviation* Her or His Majesty's Ship 皇家军舰

HND /ˌeɪtʃ en ˈdiː/ *abbreviation* Higher National Diploma 国家高级文凭

hoard /hɔːd/ *noun* a store of money, valued objects, or useful information 储藏;积存;宝库 ■ *verb* build up a store of something 聚藏;囤积 ■ **hoarder** noun.

! 注意 don't confuse **hoard** with **horde**: a **hoard** is a store of something valuable; a **horde** is a large group of people. 不要混淆 hoard 和 horde:a hoard 指储存的一批有价值的东西,a horde 指一大群人。

hoarding /ˈhɔːdɪŋ/ noun Brit. 【英】 a large board used to display advertisements 大幅广告牌

hoar frost /hɔː(r)/ noun a feathery greyish-white deposit of frost 白霜

hoarse /hɔː(r)s/ adjective (of a voice) rough and harsh (嗓音)嘶哑的,沙哑的 ■ **hoarsely** adverb.

hoary /ˈhɔːri/ adjective (**hoarier**, **hoariest**) **1** greyish-white 灰白的 **2** having grey hair 头发花白的 **3** old and unoriginal 古老的;陈旧的;老套的

hoax /həʊks/ noun a humorous or cruel trick 恶作剧;骗局 • verb deceive with a hoax 戏弄;欺骗 ■ **hoaxer** noun.

hob /hɒb/ noun Brit. 【英】 the flat top part of a cooker, with hotplates or burners 炉盘

hobble /ˈhɒbl/ verb (**hobbles**, **hobbling**, **hobbled**) **1** walk awkwardly 蹒跚;跛行 **2** strap together the legs of a horse to stop it wandering away 捆绑(马)的腿(以防走失)

hobby /ˈhɒbi/ noun (plural **hobbies**) an activity that you do regularly in your leisure time for pleasure 业余爱好;消遣 □ **hobby horse 1** a child's toy consisting of a stick with a model of a horse's head at one end (儿童玩的)竹马,马头杆 **2** something that a person talks about very often 喜爱的话题

hobgoblin /hɒbˈɡɒblɪn/ noun a mischievous imp 淘气的小精灵

hobnail /ˈhɒbneɪl/ noun a short nail used to strengthen the soles of boots (钉在靴底起加固作用的)平头钉 ■ **hobnailed** adjective.

hobnob /ˈhɒbnɒb/ verb (**hobnobs**, **hobnobbing**, **hobnobbed**) informal 【非正式】 spend time with rich or important people 与(富人或要人)交往密切

hobo /ˈhəʊbəʊ/ noun (plural **hoboes** or **hobos**) N. Amer. 【北美】 a homeless person 无家可归者;流浪者

Hobson's choice /ˈhɒbsnz/ noun a choice of taking what is offered or nothing at all 无选择余地的选择

hock¹ /hɒk/ noun the middle joint in an animal's back leg (四足动物后腿的)跗关节

hock² noun Brit. 【英】 a dry white wine from Germany 霍克酒(德国产的干白葡萄酒)

hock³ verb informal 【非正式】 pawn an object 抵押;典当 □ **in hock** in debt 负债

hockey /ˈhɒki/ noun a team game played using hooked sticks to drive a small, hard ball towards a goal 曲棍球(运动)

hocus-pocus /ˌhəʊkəs ˈpəʊkəs/ noun **1** meaningless talk used to deceive people 骗人的鬼话 **2** a form of words used by a magician 魔术师的话

hod /hɒd/ noun **1** a builder's V-shaped open trough attached to a short pole, used for carrying bricks (建筑工人用以运砖的)砖斗 **2** a metal container for storing coal 煤斗

hoe /həʊ/ noun a long-handled gardening tool with a thin metal blade 锄头;长柄锄 • verb (**hoes**, **hoeing**, **hoed**) break up soil or dig up weeds with a hoe 锄(地);锄(草)

hoedown /ˈhəʊdaʊn/ noun N. Amer. 【北美】 a lively folk dance (热烈的)方形舞

hog /hɒɡ/ noun a castrated male pig reared for its meat (供食用的)阉公猪 • verb (**hogs**, **hogging**, **hogged**) informal 【非正式】 take or hoard selfishly 独占;自私地占用 □ **go the whole hog** informal 【非正式】 do something fully 全力以赴做

Hogmanay /ˈhɒɡməneɪ/ noun (in Scotland) New Year's Eve (苏格兰的)除夕

hogshead /ˈhɒɡzhed/ noun a large cask 大桶

hogwash /ˈhɒɡwɒʃ/ noun informal 【非正式】 nonsense 胡说;废话

hoick /hɔɪk/ **verb** Brit. informal 【英,非正式】lift or pull with a jerk 猛地提起(或拉起)

hoi polloi /ˌhɔɪ pəˈlɔɪ/ **plural noun** disapproving 【贬】the common people 民众;乌合之众

hoist /hɔɪst/ **verb 1** raise with ropes and pulleys (用绳子和滑轮)吊起,提起 **2** haul or lift up 拉起;举起 • **noun** a piece of equipment for hoisting something 起重机;升降机

hoity-toity /ˌhɔɪtiˈtɔɪti/ **adjective** informal 【非正式】snobbish 势利的

hokey-cokey /ˌhəʊkiˈkəʊki/ **noun** a group song and dance performed in a circle, involving the shaking of each limb in turn 集体歌舞

hokum /ˈhəʊkəm/ **noun** informal 【非正式】**1** nonsense 胡说;废话 **2** unoriginal or sentimental material in a film, book, etc. (电影、书等中的)俗套(或煽情)的惯用法

hold /həʊld/ **verb (holds, holding, held) 1** grasp, carry, or support 抓住;托住;支撑 **2** contain or be able to contain 包含;可容纳 **3** have, own, or occupy 拥有;占据 **4** keep or detain someone 保留;扣留;拘留 **5** stay or keep at a certain level 保持,维持(在某一水平) **6** (**hold someone to**) make someone keep a promise 使遵守(承诺) **7** (**hold someone/thing in**) have a particular attitude to someone or something 对(某人或事物)抱有…态度 • **noun 1** a grip 抓;握;抱 **2** a place to grip while climbing (攀爬时的)抓握点 **3** a degree of control 控制力 **4** a storage space in the lower part of a ship or aircraft (轮船或飞机底部的)存储空间 □ **hold back** hesitate 犹豫;踌躇 **hold fast 1** remain tightly secured 保持稳固 **2** stick to a principle 坚持原则 **hold forth** talk at length 滔滔不绝地讲 **hold someone/thing off** resist an attacker 抵挡(进攻者) **hold on 1** wait 等着 **2** keep going in difficult circumstances (在困境中)

坚持下去 **hold out 1** resist difficult circumstances 抵御(困境) **2** continue to be enough; last 维持;坚持 **hold something over** postpone something 推迟;拖延 **hold someone/thing up 1** delay someone or something 阻碍;延误 **2** rob someone using the threat of violence 抢劫 **hold-up 1** a cause of delay 耽误原因;延误原因 **2** a robbery carried out with the threat of violence (暴力)抢劫 **no holds barred** without restrictions 无限制地;无约束地 **on hold** waiting to be dealt with or connected by telephone 等待处理;等待接通电话 ■ **holder** noun.

holdall /ˈhəʊldɔːl/ **noun** Brit. 【英】a large bag with handles and a shoulder strap 大手提袋

holding /ˈhəʊldɪŋ/ **noun 1** an area of land held by lease 租借的土地 **2** (**holdings**) stocks and property owned by a person or organization (持有的)股份;(拥有的)财产

hole /həʊl/ **noun 1** a hollow space or opening in a solid object or surface 洞;孔 **2** (in golf) a hollow in the ground which you try to hit the ball into (高尔夫球运动中的)球穴,球洞 **3** 【非正式】an awkward or unpleasant place or situation 窘境;困境 • **verb** (**holes, holing, holed**) **1** make a hole or holes in 在…上打洞;在…穿孔 **2** (in golf) hit the ball into a hole (高尔夫球)击球入洞 **3** (**hole up**) informal 【非正式】hide yourself 躲藏;隐藏 ■ **holey** adjective.

Holi /ˈhəʊli/ **noun** a Hindu spring festival (印度教的)胡里节,春节

holiday /ˈhɒlədeɪ/ **noun 1** Brit. 【英】a time spent away from home for rest or enjoyment 假期 **2** a day when most people do not have to work 公众假日;宗教假日 • **verb** spend a holiday 度假

holidaymaker /ˈhɒlədeɪmeɪkə(r)/ **noun** Brit. 【英】a tourist 度假者;游

客

holiness /ˈhəʊlɪnəs/ noun **1** the state of being holy 神圣 **2** (**His or Your Holiness**) the title of the Pope and some other religious leaders 圣座(对教皇和其他宗教领袖的尊称)

holistic /həʊˈlɪstɪk/ adjective treating the whole person rather than just the symptoms of a disease (治疗)整体性的 ■ **holism** noun.

holler /ˈhɒlə(r)/ informal 【非正式】 verb (**hollers, hollering, hollered**) give a loud shout 叫喊 • noun a loud shout 大叫;大嚷

hollow /ˈhɒləʊ/ adjective **1** having empty space inside 中空的;空心的 **2** curving inwards 凹陷的 **3** (of a sound) echoing (声音)低沉的,有回音的 **4** worthless or not sincere 无价值的;缺乏诚意的 • noun **1** a hole 洞;孔 **2** a small valley 小山谷 • verb (usu. **hollow something out**) form by making a hole 挖洞形成(某物)

holly /ˈhɒli/ noun an evergreen shrub with prickly dark green leaves and red berries 冬青(常绿灌木,叶多刺,深绿色,结红色浆果)

hollyhock /ˈhɒlihɒk/ noun a tall plant with large showy flowers 蜀葵(高大植物,花大而鲜艳)

holocaust /ˈhɒləkɔːst/ noun **1** destruction or killing on a very large scale 大破坏;大屠杀 **2** (**the Holocaust**) the mass murder of Jews under the German Nazi regime in World War II (第二次世界大战期间德国纳粹对犹太人的)大屠杀

hologram /ˈhɒləɡræm/ noun a picture that looks three-dimensional when it is lit up (立体)全息图,全息影像 ■ **holographic** adjective.

holster /ˈhəʊlstə(r)/ noun a holder for carrying a handgun 手枪套

holy /ˈhəʊli/ adjective (**holier, holiest**) **1** dedicated to God or a religious purpose 献身于上帝(或宗教事业)的 **2** morally and spiritually good 至善的;圣洁的 □ **the holy of holies** a very sacred place 神圣之处 **Holy Spirit** (or **Holy Ghost**) (in Christianity) God as a spirit that is active in the world (基督教中的)圣灵 **Holy Week** the week before Easter 圣周(复活节前一周)

homage /ˈhɒmɪdʒ/ noun honour shown to someone in public (向某人公开表示的)敬意,崇敬

homburg /ˈhɒmbɜːɡ/ noun a man's felt hat with a narrow curled brim 霍姆堡毡帽(男用毡帽,帽边狭窄卷曲)

home /həʊm/ noun **1** the place where you live 家;住所 **2** a place where people who need special care live (为进行特殊护理开设的)收容所,疗养所,休养所 **3** a place where something flourishes or where it started 发祥地,发源地 • adjective **1** relating to your home 家的 **2** relating to your own country 祖国的;本国的 **3** (of a sports match) played at a team's own ground (体育比赛)主场的 • adverb **1** to or at your home 到家,在家 **2** to the intended position 正中目标;至意欲到达的位置 • verb (**homes, homing, homed**) **1** (of an animal) return by instinct to its territory (动物)回窝,回巢 **2** (**home in on**) move or be aimed towards 朝…运动;对准;针对 □ **home economics** the study of cookery and household management 家政学 **home page** the main page of an individual's or organization's Internet site (因特网上个人或机构的)主页 **home rule** the government of a place by its own citizens 地方自治 **home run** Baseball 【棒球】 a hit that allows the batter to make a run around all the bases 本垒打;全垒打 **home truth** an unpleasant fact about yourself that someone else tells you (关于自己的)令人不快的事实 ■ **homeless** adjective **homeward** adjective & adverb **homewards** adverb.

homeland /ˈhəʊmlænd/ **noun** a person's native land 祖国；家乡

homely /ˈhəʊmli/ **adjective** (**homelier, homeliest**) **1** Brit. 【英】 simple but comfortable 家常的；简朴舒适的 **2** Brit.【英】unsophisticated 质朴的；朴实的 **3** N. Amer.【北美】(of a person) unattractive (人) 长相一般的

homeopathy or **homoeopathy** /ˌhəʊmiˈɒpəθi/ **noun** a system of treating diseases by tiny doses of substances that would normally produce symptoms of the disease 顺势疗法 ■ **homeopath** noun **homeopathic** adjective.

homesick /ˈhəʊmsɪk/ **adjective** feeling upset because you are missing your home 思乡的；想家的

homespun /ˈhəʊmspʌn/ **adjective** simple and unsophisticated 朴实的；单纯的

homestead /ˈhəʊmsted/ **noun** a farmhouse with surrounding land and outbuildings (包括周围土地和附近房屋的)宅宅，农庄

homework /ˈhəʊmwɜːk/ **noun 1** school work that you are expected to do at home (学生的)家庭作业 **2** preparation for an event 准备工作

homicide /ˈhɒmɪsaɪd/ **noun** chiefly N. Amer.【主北美】the killing of another person 谋杀，杀人 ■ **homicidal** adjective.

homily /ˈhɒmɪli/ **noun** (plural **homilies**) **1** a talk on a religious subject 布道；讲道 **2** a dull talk on a moral issue (乏味的)道德说教

homoeopathy /ˌhəʊmiˈɒpəθi/ ⇒ 见 **HOMEOPATHY**.

homogeneous /ˌhɒməˈdʒiːniəs/ **adjective 1** alike 相像的；相似的 **2** made up of parts which are all of the same kind 由同类部分(或成分)组成的 ■ **homogeneity** /ˌhɒmədʒəˈniːəti/ noun.

✔ 拼写指南 the ending is *-eous*, with

an *e*, not *-ous*: homogen*eous*. homo-geneous 词末拼作 -eous，有一个 e，不要拼作 -ous.

homogenize or **homogenise** /həˈmɒdʒənaɪz/ **verb** (**homogenizes, homogenizing, homogenized**) **1** treat milk so that the cream is mixed in 使(牛奶)均质 **2** make different things more alike 使类同，使相似

homograph /ˈhɒməɡrɑːf/ **noun** a word that is spelled the same as another but has a different meaning (e.g. *bat* 'a flying animal' and *bat* 'a piece of wood for hitting a ball') 同形异义词

homonym /ˈhɒmənɪm/ **noun** a word that is spelled or pronounced the same as another but has a different meaning 同音同形异义词

homophobia /ˌhɒməˈfəʊbiə/ **noun** extreme hatred or fear of homosexuality and homosexuals 对同性恋的憎恨(或恐惧) ■ **homophobic** adjective.

homophone /ˈhɒməfəʊn/ **noun** a word that is pronounced the same as another but has a different meaning or spelling (e.g. *new* and *knew*) 同音异义词；同音异形词

Homo sapiens /ˌhəʊməʊ ˈsæpienz/ **noun** the species to which modern humans belong 人类；智人(现代人的学名)

homosexual /ˌhəʊməˈsekʃuəl/ **adjective** sexually attracted to people of your own sex 同性恋的 • **noun** a homosexual person 同性恋者 ■ **homosexuality** noun.

Hon. /ɒn/ **abbreviation** Honorary or Honourable 名誉的；尊敬的

hone /həʊn/ **verb** (**hones, honing, honed**) **1** make better or more efficient 使更好；使高效 **2** sharpen a tool with a stone (在磨石上)把(工具)磨锋利

honest /ˈɒnɪst/ **adjective 1** truthful

and sincere 诚实的；正直的 **2** fairly earned 以正当的方式挣得的 **3** simple and straightforward 简单的 ■ **honest-ly** adverb.

honesty /'ɒnəsti/ **noun** the quality of being honest 诚实；正直

honey /'hʌni/ **noun** (plural **honeys**) a sweet, sticky yellowish-brown fluid made by bees from flower nectar 蜂蜜

honeybee /'hʌnibiː/ **noun** the common bee 蜜蜂

honeycomb /'hʌnikəʊm/ **noun** a structure of six-sided wax compartments made by bees to store honey and eggs 蜂巢

honeydew /'hʌnidjuː/ **noun** a sweet, sticky substance produced by small insects feeding on the sap of plants (小昆虫分泌的)蜜露，蜜汁 □ **honeydew melon** a variety of melon with sweet green flesh 蜜瓜，白兰瓜

honeyed /'hʌnid/ **adjective 1** containing or coated with honey 含有蜂蜜的；涂有蜂蜜的 **2** (of words) soothing and soft (言语)甜蜜的，中听的

honeymoon /'hʌnimuːn/ **noun 1** a holiday taken by a newly married couple 蜜月 **2** an initial period of enthusiasm or goodwill 初期的热情，蜜月时期 • **verb** spend a honey-moon somewhere 度蜜月

honeypot /'hʌnipɒt/ **noun** a place that many people are attracted to 非常吸引人的地方；胜地

honeysuckle /'hʌnisʌkl/ **noun** a climbing shrub with sweet-smelling flowers 忍冬(蔓生灌木，所开花气味芳香)

honk /hɒŋk/ **noun 1** the cry of a goose 鹅叫声 **2** the sound of a car horn (汽车)鸣笛声，喇叭声 • **verb** make a honk 发出鹅叫似的声音；按(喇叭)；鸣(笛)

honky-tonk /'hɒŋkitɒŋk/ **noun** informal 【非正式】 **1** N. Amer. 【北美】 a bar 酒吧 **2** ragtime piano music 雷

格泰姆钢琴乐

honorary /'ɒnərəri/ **adjective 1** (of a title or position) given as an honour (头衔或职位)名誉的，荣誉的 **2** Brit. 【英】unpaid 无报酬的；义务的

> ✔ 拼写指南 honor-, not honour-: honorary. honorary 中的 honor- 不要拼作 honour-。

honorific /ˌɒnə'rɪfɪk/ **adjective** given as a mark of respect 表示尊敬的

honour /'ɒnə(r)/ (US spelling 【美拼作】 **honor**) **noun 1** great respect 崇敬；敬意 **2** a privilege 特权 **3** a clear sense of what is right 正义感；道义 **4** a person or thing that brings credit 带来荣誉的人；增光的事物 **5** an award or title given as a reward for achievement 荣誉；名声；荣誉称号 **6** (**honours**) a university course of a higher level than an ordinary one (大学的)荣誉学位课程，高级课程 **7** (**His, Your**, etc. **Honour**) a title for a judge 阁下，大人(对法官的尊称) • **verb 1** regard or treat with great respect 敬重；尊敬 **2** fulfil an obligation or keep an agreement 履行(义务)；遵守(协议)

honourable /'ɒnərəbl/ (US spelling 【美拼作】 **honorable**) **adjective 1** deserving honour 光荣的；增光的；值得尊敬的 **2** having high moral standards 品格高尚的 **3** (**Honourable**) a title for MPs, nobles, etc. 尊敬的(对议员、贵族等的称呼) ■ **honourably** adverb.

hooch /huːtʃ/ **noun** informal 【非正式】 alcoholic drink 烈酒

hood¹ /hʊd/ **noun 1** a covering for the head and neck with an opening for the face 风帽；兜帽 **2** Brit. 【英】 a folding waterproof cover of a vehicle (车辆可防水的)折式车篷 **3** N. Amer. 【北美】the bonnet of a vehicle 汽车发动机罩 **4** a protective canopy 护罩 ■ **hooded** adjective.

hood² **noun** N. Amer. informal 【北美，非

正式】a gangster or violent criminal 恶棍;暴徒

hoodlum /'huːdləm/ **noun** a gangster or violent criminal 恶棍;暴徒

hoodoo /'huːduː/ **noun 1** a run or cause of bad luck 不祥之物;厄运 **2** voodoo 伏都教

hoodwink /'hudwɪŋk/ **verb** deceive or trick 哄骗;欺诈

hoody or **hoodie** /'hudi/ **noun** (plural **hoodies**) a hooded sweatshirt or other top 带风帽的衬衫;带风帽的上衣

hoof /huːf/ **noun** (plural **hoofs** or **hooves**) the horny part of the foot of a horse, cow, etc. (马、牛 等的)蹄
• **verb** informal 【非正式】**1** kick a ball powerfully 用力踢(球) **2** (**hoof it**) go on foot 步行 ■ **hoofed** adjective.

hook /huk/ **noun 1** a curved object for catching hold of things or hanging things on 挂钩;吊钩 **2** a punch made with the elbow bent and rigid 勾拳 **3** a catchy passage in a song (歌曲中)旋律优美的段落 • **verb 1** catch or fasten with a hook 用钩抓;约 **2** (**hook someone/thing up**) link someone or something to electronic equipment 把…与电子设备接通 **3** (**be hooked**) informal 【非正式】be very interested or addicted (吸毒)成瘾;非常感兴趣的 **4** (in sport) hit the ball in a curving path (体育比赛中)击出曲线球 □ **by hook or by crook** by any possible means 千方百计地;不择手段地 **hook, line, and sinker** completely 完全地;全部地 ■ **hooked** adjective.

hookah /'hukə/ **noun** a kind of tobacco pipe in which the smoke is drawn through water to cool it 水烟筒;水烟袋

hooker /'hukə(r)/ **noun 1** informal 【非正式】a prostitute 妓女 **2** Rugby 【英式橄榄球】the player in the middle of the front row of the scrum (并列争球时前排中间的)钩球队员

hookworm /'hukwɜːm/ **noun** a worm which can infest the intestines (肠道内滋生的)钩虫

hooligan /'huːlɪɡən/ **noun** a violent young troublemaker 小流氓;阿飞 ■ **hooliganism** noun.

hoop /huːp/ **noun 1** a rigid circular band 箍;圈;环 **2** a large ring used as a toy or for circus performers to jump through (用作玩具的)大环;(杂技团演员跳跃用的)大圆 **3** a metal arch through which you hit the balls in croquet (槌球戏中的)拱门 **4** a contrasting horizontal band on a sports shirt (运动衫上对比分明的)水平线条 ■ **hooped** adjective.

hoopla /'huːplɑː/ **noun** Brit. 【英】a game in which you try to throw rings over a prize 套圈游戏

hooray /hu'reɪ/ **exclamation** hurrah 好哇;万岁

hoot /huːt/ **noun 1** a low sound made by owls, or a similar sound made by a horn, siren, etc. 猫头鹰的叫声;喇叭(或汽笛等)的鸣响声 **2** a shout of scorn or disapproval 嗤笑;哄笑 **3** an outburst of laughter 大笑 **4** (**a hoot**) informal 【非正式】an amusing person or thing 可笑的人(或事物) • **verb** make a hoot 发出猫头鹰般的叫声;鸣响 ■ **hooter** noun.

Hoover /'huːvə(r)/ Brit. 【英】**noun** trademark 【商标】a vacuum cleaner 胡佛牌吸尘器 • **verb** (**hoover**) (**hoovers, hoovering, hoovered**) clean with a vacuum cleaner 用吸尘器吸干净

hooves /huːvz/ plural of HOOF.

hop /hɒp/ **verb** (**hops, hopping, hopped**) **1** move by jumping on one foot 单足跳跃 **2** (of a bird or animal) move by jumping (鸟或兽)单足跳跃 **3** (**hop it**) Brit. informal 【英、非正式】go away 移动 • **noun 1** a hopping movement 单足跳;齐足跳 **2** an informal dance (非正式)舞会 □ **on the hop** Brit. informal 【英、非正

式】 unprepared 全无准备的

hope /həʊp/ **noun 1** a feeling that something you want may happen 希望，期望，指望 **2** a cause for hope 寄予希望的事 **3** something that you wish for 希望得到的事物 • **verb** (**hopes, hoping, hoped**) **1** expect and want something to happen 期望，盼望 **2** intend if possible to do something 想望

hopeful /ˈhəʊpfl/ **adjective** feeling or inspiring hope 抱有希望的；给人希望的 • **noun** a person likely or hoping to succeed 有成功希望的人；希望获得成功的人

hopefully /ˈhəpfəli/ **adverb 1** in a hopeful way 抱有希望地 **2** it is to be hoped that 但愿

！注意 although the meaning 'it is to be hoped that' (as in *hopefully we'll see you tomorrow*) is now the more common one, some people feel that it is wrong and so it is best avoided in formal writing. 尽管 hopefully 表示"但愿"的意思现在更常用，如 hopefully we'll see you tomorrow（希望明天能见到你），但有些人觉得这种用法是错误的，因此在正式书面语中最好避免该用法。

hopeless /ˈhəʊpləs/ **adjective 1** feeling or causing despair 不抱希望的；令人绝望的 **2** not at all skilful 非常糟糕的；无能的 ∎ **hopelessly** adverb.

hopper /ˈhɒpə(r)/ **noun** a container that tapers downwards and empties its contents at the bottom 漏斗；送料斗

hops /hɒps/ **plural noun** the dried flowers of a climbing plant, used to give beer a bitter flavour 忽布；啤酒花（干燥后可用于酿酒，使啤酒有苦味）

hopscotch /ˈhɒpskɒtʃ/ **noun** a children's game in which you hop over squares marked on the ground 跳房子，跳间（儿童游戏）

horde /hɔːd/ **noun** chiefly disapproving 【主贬】a large group of people （人的）一大群，一大帮

！注意 don't confuse **horde** with **hoard**: a **horde** is a large group of people, whereas a **hoard** is a store of something valuable. 不要混淆 horde 和 hoard，a horde 是指一大群人，而 a hoard 是指储存的一批有价值的东西。

horizon /həˈraɪzn/ **noun 1** the line at which the earth's surface and the sky appear to meet 地平线 **2** (**horizons**) the limits of a person's understanding, experience, or interest （理解力、经历或兴趣的）范围，界限

horizontal /ˌhɒrɪˈzɒntl/ **adjective** parallel to the horizon 平行的；水平的 • **noun** a horizontal line or surface 水平线；水平面 ∎ **horizontally** adverb.

hormone /ˈhɔːməʊn/ **noun** a substance produced in the body that controls the action of particular cells or tissues 荷尔蒙；激素 ∎ **hormonal** adjective.

horn /hɔːn/ **noun 1** a hard bony growth on the heads of cattle, sheep, and other animals （牛、羊等头上的）角 **2** the substance that horns are made of 角质；角质物 **3** a wind instrument shaped like a cone or wound into a spiral 号（管乐器） **4** an instrument sounding a signal 喇叭；警报器 ∎ **horned** adjective.

hornblende /ˈhɔːnblend/ **noun** a dark brown, black, or green mineral 角闪石（深棕色、黑色或绿色矿石）

hornet /ˈhɔːnɪt/ **noun** a kind of large wasp 大黄蜂

hornpipe /ˈhɔːnpaɪp/ **noun** a lively solo dance traditionally performed by sailors 角笛舞（生动活泼的水手传统单人舞）

horny /ˈhɔːni/ **adjective** (**hornier, horniest**) **1** made of or resembling horn 角质的；角状的 **2** hard and rough 坚硬而粗糙的

horology /hɒˈrɒlədʒi/ **noun 1** the study and measurement of time 计时学；测时法 **2** the art of making clocks and watches 钟表制造术

horoscope /ˈhɒrəskəʊp/ **noun** a forecast of a person's future based on the positions of the stars and planets at the time of their birth 占星术

horrendous /hɒˈrendəs/ **adjective** very unpleasant or horrifying 极讨厌的；很可怕的；骇人的 ■ **horrendously** adverb.

horrible /ˈhɒrɪbl/ **adjective 1** causing horror 可怕的；令人恐惧的 **2** very unpleasant 极讨厌的；令人极不愉快的 ■ **horribly** adverb.

horrid /ˈhɒrɪd/ **adjective** horrible 可怕的

horrific /həˈrɪfɪk/ **adjective** causing horror 令人恐惧的 ■ **horrifically** adverb.

horrify /ˈhɒrɪfaɪ/ **verb** (**horrifies**, **horrifying**, **horrified**) fill with horror 使充满恐惧

horror /ˈhɒrə(r)/ **noun 1** a strong feeling of fear, shock, disgust, or dismay 恐惧；震惊；憎恶 **2** a thing causing such a feeling 令人恐惧(或震惊、憎恶)的事物

hors d'oeuvre /ɔː ˈdɜːv/ **noun** (plural **hors d'oeuvre** or **hors d'oeuvres** /ɔː ˈdɜːv/) a small savoury first course of a meal (餐前的)开胃小吃

horse /hɔːs/ **noun 1** a large four-legged animal used for riding and for pulling loads 马 **2** cavalry 骑兵 • **verb** (**horses**, **horsing**, **horsed**) (**horse around**) informal 【非正式】 fool about 胡混；胡闹 ▢ **horse chestnut 1** a large tree that produces nuts (conkers) in a spiny case 七叶树 **2** a conker 七叶树坚果 **horse sense** common sense 常识 ■ **horsey** (or **horsy**) adjective.

horseback /ˈhɔːsbæk/ **noun** (on

horseback) mounted on a horse 骑着马

horsebox /ˈhɔːsbɒks/ **noun** Brit. 【英】 a vehicle or trailer for transporting horses 运马棚车

horsefly /ˈhɔːsflaɪ/ **noun** (plural **horse-flies**) a large fly that bites horses and other large animals (叮咬马等的)虻，马蝇

horseman /ˈhɔːsmən/ or **horse-woman** /ˈhɔːswʊmən/ **noun** (plural **horsemen** or **horsewomen**) a rider on horseback 骑马者

horseplay /ˈhɔːspleɪ/ **noun** rough, highspirited play 喧闹嬉戏

horsepower /ˈhɔːspaʊə(r)/ **noun** (plural **horsepower**) a unit measuring the power of an engine 马力(发动机功率单位)

horseradish /ˈhɔːsrædɪʃ/ **noun** a plant with strong-tasting roots which are made into a sauce 辣根(一种植物，根部味道浓重，常制成酱料)

horseshoe /ˈhɔːsʃuː/ **noun** a U-shaped iron band attached to the base of a horse's hoof 马蹄铁

horticulture /ˈhɔːtɪkʌltʃə(r)/ **noun** the cultivation of gardens 园艺；园艺术 ■ **horticultural** adjective.

hosanna /həʊˈzænə/ **noun** an exclamation of praise or joy used in the Bible 和散那(《圣经》中赞美和快乐的呼喊声)

hose /həʊz/ **noun 1** (Brit. 【英】 also **hosepipe**) a flexible tube that conveys water 软管；水龙带 **2** historical 【历史】 men's breeches 男式紧身裤 • **verb** (**hoses**, **hosing**, **hosed**) spray with a hose 用软管冲洗

hosiery /ˈhəʊziəri/ **noun** socks, tights, and stockings 长筒袜；短袜；裤袜

hospice /ˈhɒspɪs/ **noun** a home for people who are very ill or dying (患病者或临终病人的)安养所

hospitable /ˈhɒspɪtəbl/ **adjective 1** friendly and welcoming to strangers or guests 热情友好的；好客的 **2**

H

(of an environment) pleasant and favourable for living in (环境)适宜居住的 ■ **hospitably** adverb.

hospital /ˈhɒspɪtl/ **noun** a place where sick or injured people are looked after 医院

hospitality /ˌhɒspɪˈtæləti/ **noun** the friendly and generous treatment of guests or strangers 热情友好的；殷勤好客的

hospitalize or **hospitalise** /ˈhɒspɪtəlaɪz/ **verb** (**hospitalizes, hospitalizing, hospitalized**) admit someone to hospital 接纳(某人)入院治疗；收治 ■ **hospitalization** noun.

Host /həʊst/ **noun** (**the Host**) the bread used in the Christian ceremony of Holy Communion (基督教圣餐中食用的)圣饼

host¹ /həʊst/ **noun 1** a person who receives or entertains guests (待客的)主人 **2** the presenter of a television or radio programme (电视或广播节目的)主持人 **3** the place that holds an event to which others are invited 主办人；主办地；主办机构 **4** Biology 【生物】 an animal or plant on or in which a parasite lives 寄主，宿主(寄生物所寄生的动植物) • **verb** act as host at 当…东道主，做…主持人

host² **noun** (**a host or hosts of**) a large number of 大量；许多

hostage /ˈhɒstɪdʒ/ **noun** a person held prisoner in an attempt to make other people give in to a demand 人质

hostel /ˈhɒstl/ **noun** a place which provides cheap food and accommodation for a particular group of people (提供廉价食宿的)招待所

hostelry /ˈhɒstəlri/ **noun** (plural **hostelries**) old use or humorous 【旧或幽默】 a pub 客栈；旅栈

hostess /ˈhəʊstəs/ **noun 1** a female host 女主人人 **2** a woman employed to welcome customers at a nightclub or bar (夜总会或酒吧里的)

女招待

hostile /ˈhɒstaɪl/ **adjective 1** aggressively unfriendly 不友好的，怀有敌意的 **2** having to do with a military enemy 敌人的；敌方的

hostility /hɒˈstɪləti/ **noun** (plural **hostilities**) **1** hostile behaviour 敌对；对抗 **2** (**hostilities**) acts of warfare 战斗；战争

hot /hɒt/ **adjective** (**hotter, hottest**) **1** having a high temperature 热的；烫的 **2** feeling or producing an uncomfortable sensation of heat 感到热的，发烧的 **3** informal 【非正式】 currently popular or interesting 流行的；热门的 **4** informal 【非正式】 (of goods) stolen (物品)偷来的 **5** (**hot on**) informal 【非正式】 knowing a lot about 对…了如指掌的；有见识的 **6** (**hot on**) informal 【非正式】 strict about 对…严格的 • **verb** (**hots, hotting, hotted**) (**hot up**) Brit. informal 【英，非正式】 become more exciting 变得更加兴奋 □ **hot air** informal 【非正式】 empty or boastful talk 空话；夸夸其谈 **hot-blooded** passionate 热情的 **hot cross bun** a bun marked with a cross, eaten on Good Friday 十字面包(耶稣受难时吃的传统食物) **hot dog** a hot sausage served in a long, soft roll 热狗(夹有热香肠的长面包) **hot rod** a car specially adapted to be fast (改装的)高速汽车 **hot-water bottle** a container filled with hot water and used for warming a bed 热水袋 **hot-wire** informal 【非正式】 start a vehicle without using the ignition switch (不用点火开关而)热线发动(汽车) ■ **hotly** adverb.

hotbed /ˈhɒtbed/ **noun** a place where a lot of a particular activity is happening (某种活动滋生发展的)温床

hotchpotch /ˈhɒtʃpɒtʃ/ **noun** a confused mixture 乱七八糟的混杂物；大杂烩

hotel /həʊˈtel/ **noun** a place providing accommodation and meals for travellers (提供膳宿的)酒店，宾馆，旅馆

hotelier /həʊˈteliə(r)/ **noun** a person who owns or manages a hotel 酒店(或旅馆)老板；酒店(或旅馆)经营者

hotfoot /ˈhɒtfʊt/ **adverb** quickly and eagerly 火速地；急匆匆地 □ **hotfoot it** hurry eagerly 急行；急走

hothead /ˈhɒthed/ **noun** an impetuous or quick-tempered person 性急的人；急躁的人

hothouse /ˈhɒthaʊs/ **noun** a heated greenhouse 温室；暖房

hotplate /ˈhɒtpleɪt/ **noun** a flat heated surface on an electric cooker (电炉的)加热板

hotpot /ˈhɒtpɒt/ **noun** Brit. 【英】 a casserole of meat and vegetables with a covering layer of sliced potato 罐焖土豆烧肉

hotshot /ˈhɒtʃɒt/ **noun** informal 【非正式】 an important or very skilled person 要人；高手；能人

houmous /ˈhuːməs/ **noun** ⇒ 见 HUMMUS.

hound /haʊnd/ **noun** a hunting dog 猎狗；猎犬 • **verb** harass someone 烦扰；纠缠

hour /ˈaʊə(r)/ **noun 1** a twenty-fourth part of a day and night; 60 minutes 小时 **2** (**hours**) a period set aside for a particular purpose 一段时间 **3** a particular point in time 时刻；点钟 **4** (**hours**) informal 【非正式】 a very long time 很长一段时间

hourglass /ˈaʊəglɑːs/ **noun** an object consisting of two connected glass bulbs containing sand that takes an hour to fall from the upper to the lower bulb (计时用的)沙漏

hourly /ˈaʊəli/ **adverb & adjective 1** every hour 每小时一次地(的) **2** by the hour 按钟点计算地(的)

house **noun** /haʊs/ **1** a building for people to live in 房屋；住宅 **2** a firm or institution 公司；机构；商行 **3** a group of pupils living in the same building at a boarding school (学校)寄宿生 **4** a long-established and powerful family 世家；望族 **5** (also **house music**) a style of popular dance music 豪斯音乐(一种流行舞шин) • **verb** /haʊz/ (**houses, housing, housed**) **1** provide with accommodation 给…提供住宿 **2** provide space for 给…空间 **3** enclose something 覆盖；把…装箱 □ **house arrest** the state of being kept as a prisoner in your own house 软禁(在家) **House of Commons** the chamber of the UK Parliament whose members are elected (英国议会的)下议院 **House of Lords** the chamber of the UK Parliament whose members are peers and bishops (英国议会的)上议院 **house-proud** very concerned with the appearance of your home 注重家居整洁的 **house-train** train a pet to urinate and defecate outside the house 训练(宠物)在室外便溺 **house-warming** a party held to celebrate moving into a new home 庆祝迁入新居的聚会；乔迁宴 **on the house** at the management's expense 由主者出钱的；免费的

houseboat /ˈhaʊsbəʊt/ **noun** a boat that people can live in 船屋；居住船

housebound /ˈhaʊsbaʊnd/ **adjective** unable to leave your house 离不了家的；出不了门的

housebreaking /ˈhaʊsbreɪkɪŋ/ **noun** the action of breaking into a building to commit a crime 破门入室(犯罪)

household /ˈhaʊshəʊld/ **noun** a house and all the people living in it 一家子；家庭；同住一所房子的人 ■ **householder** noun.

housekeeper /ˈhaʊskiːpə(r)/ **noun** a person employed to shop, cook, and clean the house (雇来的)管家 ■ **housekeeping** noun.

housemaid /ˈhaʊsmeɪd/ **noun** a female servant in a house (做家务的)

女佣, 女工

housemaster /ˈhaʊsmɑːstə(r)/ or **housemistress** /ˈhaʊsmɪstrəs/ **noun** a teacher in charge of a house at a boarding school (寄宿学校的)舍监

housemate /ˈhaʊsmeɪt/ **noun** a person with whom you share a house 同住一所房子的人

housewife /ˈhaʊswaɪf/ **noun** (plural **housewives**) a woman whose main occupation is looking after her family and the home 家庭妇女

housework /ˈhaʊswɜːk/ **noun** cleaning, cooking, etc. done in running a home 家务(劳动)

housing /ˈhaʊzɪŋ/ **noun 1** houses and flats as a whole (总称)住房 **2** a hard cover for a piece of equipment (机器设备的)外壳, 外罩

hove /həʊv/ chiefly Nautical 【主航海】 past tense of **HEAVE**.

hovel /ˈhɒvl/ **noun** a small house that is dirty and run-down 肮脏(或破败)的住所

hover /ˈhɒvə(r)/ **verb** (**hovers, hovering, hovered**) **1** remain in one place in the air (在空中)盘旋 **2** wait about uncertainly 徘徊 **3** remain near a particular level or between two states 维持在…水平; 停留在…水平附近

hovercraft /ˈhɒvəkrɑːft/ **noun** (plural **hovercraft**) a vehicle that travels over land or water on a cushion of air 气垫运载工具; 气垫船

how /haʊ/ **adverb 1** in what way or by what means 怎样; 如何 **2** in what condition 情况如何 **3** to what extent or degree 多么; 多少 **4** the way in which 怎么; 怎么样

howdah /ˈhaʊdə/ **noun** a seat for riding on the back of an elephant 象轿(置于象背供人骑坐)

however /haʊˈevə(r)/ **adverb 1** used to begin a statement that contrasts with something that has just been

said 然而; 不过 **2** in whatever way or to whatever extent 无论如何; 不管怎样

howitzer /ˈhaʊɪtsə(r)/ **noun** a short gun for firing shells at a high angle 榴弹炮

howl /haʊl/ **noun 1** a long wailing cry made by an animal (动物的)嗥叫, 长嚎 **2** a loud cry of pain, amusement, etc. (表达痛苦、快乐等的)高声叫喊 • **verb** make a howl 嗥叫; 长嚎; 吼叫

howler /ˈhaʊlə(r)/ **noun** informal 【非正式】a stupid mistake 愚蠢的错误

h.p. or **HP** /ˌeɪtʃ ˈpiː/ **abbreviation 1** Brit. 【英】hire purchase. **2** horsepower.

HQ /ˌeɪtʃ ˈkjuː/ **abbreviation** headquarters.

HRH /ˌeɪtʃ ɑːr ˈeɪtʃ/ **abbreviation** Brit. 【英】Her (or His) Royal Highness 殿下

HTML /ˌeɪtʃ tiː em ˈel/ **abbreviation** Computing 【计】Hypertext Markup Language 超文本链接标示语言

hub /hʌb/ **noun 1** the central part of a wheel 轮毂 **2** the centre of an activity or region (活动或区域的)中心, 枢纽

hubbub /ˈhʌbʌb/ **noun** a loud confused noise caused by a crowd (人群的)喧闹声, 嘈杂声

hubris /ˈhjuːbrɪs/ **noun** excessive pride or self-confidence 傲慢; 自大

huckster /ˈhʌkstə(r)/ **noun 1** a person who sells things forcefully 兜售者 **2** a person who sells small items in the street (沿街叫卖的)小贩

huddle /ˈhʌdl/ **verb** (**huddles, huddling, huddled**) **1** crowd together 聚集在一起 **2** curl your body into a small space 蜷缩; 缩成一团 • **noun** a number of people or things crowded together 挤成一团的人; 聚成一堆的物品

hue /hjuː/ **noun 1** a colour or shade 颜色; 色彩 **2** a particular aspect of something 方面

hue and cry **noun** a strong public outcry (公众的)强烈抗议

huff /hʌf/ **verb** (often **huff and puff**) breathe out noisily 气喘吁吁 • **noun** a bad mood 发怒；气恼 ■ **huffy** adjective.

hug /hʌg/ **verb** (**hugs, hugging, hugged**) **1** hold tightly in your arms 紧紧抱住；拥抱 **2** keep close to 紧挨；紧靠 • **noun** an act of hugging 紧抱；拥抱

huge /hjuːdʒ/ **adjective** (**huger, hugest**) very large 巨大的，庞大的 ■ **hugely** adverb **hugeness** noun.

hugger-mugger /ˈhʌgəmʌgə(r)/ **adjective** confused or disorderly 混乱的

hula /ˈhuːlə/ **noun** a dance performed by Hawaiian women, in which the dancers sway their hips (夏威夷女子跳的)草裙舞，呼啦舞 □ **hula hoop** (also US trademark【美，商标】**Hula-Hoop**) a large hoop that you spin around your body by moving your hips 呼啦圈

hulk /hʌlk/ **noun 1** an old ship stripped of fittings and no longer used 废弃旧船体 **2** a large or clumsy person or thing 高大笨拙的人；庞然大物

hulking /ˈhʌlkɪŋ/ **adjective** informal【非正式】very large or clumsy 巨大的；笨重的

hull[1] /hʌl/ **noun** the main body of a ship 船体；船身

hull[2] **noun 1** the outer covering of a fruit or seed (水果或种子的)外壳 **2** the cluster of leaves and stalk on a strawberry or raspberry (草莓或悬钩子的)花萼 • **verb** remove the hulls from 除去…的外壳(或花萼)

hullabaloo /ˌhʌləbəˈluː/ **noun** informal【非正式】an uproar 喧嚣；骚动

hullo /həˈləʊ/ → 见 HELLO.

hum /hʌm/ **verb** (**hums, humming, hummed**) **1** make a low continuous sound like that of a bee 发嗡嗡声 **2** sing a tune with closed lips 哼唱 **3** informal【非正式】be in a state of great activity 忙碌；活跃 • **noun** a low continuous sound 低沉而持续的声

音；嗡嗡声

human /ˈhjuːmən/ **adjective 1** having to do with men, women, or children 人的；人类的 **2** showing the better qualities of people 通人情的，有人情味的 • **noun** (also **human being**) a man, woman, or child 人 □ **human rights** basic rights which belong to all people, such as freedom 人权 ■ **humanly** adverb.

humane /hjuːˈmeɪn/ **adjective** showing concern and kindness towards other people 人道的；仁慈的 ■ **humanely** adverb.

humanism /ˈhjuːmənɪzəm/ **noun** a system of thought that sees people as able to live their lives without the need for religious beliefs 人本主义 ■ **humanist** noun & adjective **humanistic** adjective.

humanitarian /hjuːˌmænɪˈteərɪən/ **adjective** concerned with the welfare of people 人道主义的 • **noun** a humanitarian person 人道主义者

humanity /hjuːˈmænəti/ **noun 1** people as a whole (总称)人类 **2** the condition of being human 人性 **3** sympathy and kindness towards other people 仁慈；博爱 **4** (**humanities**) studies concerned with human culture, such as literature or history 人文学科

humanize or **humanise** /ˈhjuːmənaɪz/ **verb** (**humanizes, humanizing, humanized**) make more pleasant or suitable for people 使人性化

humankind /ˌhjuːmənˈkaɪnd/ **noun** people as a whole (总称)人类

humanoid /ˈhjuːmənɔɪd/ **adjective** like a human in appearance 人形的；类人的 • **noun** a humanoid being 类人生物

humble /ˈhʌmbl/ **adjective** (**humbler, humblest**) **1** having a modest or low opinion of your own importance 谦虚的；谦逊的 **2** of low rank (地

位)低下的，卑微的 **3** not large or important 不大的；微不足道的 • **verb** (**humbles**, **humbling**, **humbled**) make someone seem less important 贬低 □ **eat humble pie** make a humble apology 低声下气地道歉 ■ **humbly** adverb.

humbug /ˈhʌmbʌg/ **noun 1** false or misleading talk or behaviour 谎话；花招 **2** a person who is not sincere or honest 虚伪的人；骗子 **3** Brit. 【英】a boiled peppermint sweet 薄荷硬糖

humdrum /ˈhʌmdrʌm/ **adjective** ordinary; dull 平淡的；无变化的；单调乏味的

humerus /ˈhjuːmərəs/ **noun** (plural **humeri** /ˈhjuːməraɪ/) the bone of the upper arm, between the shoulder and the elbow 肱骨

humid /ˈhjuːmɪd/ **adjective** (of the air or weather) damp and warm (空气或天气)温暖潮湿的，湿热的 ■ **humidity** noun.

humiliate /hjuːˈmɪlieɪt/ **verb** (**humiliates**, **humiliating**, **humiliated**) make someone feel ashamed or stupid 使蒙羞；使丢脸 ■ **humiliation** noun.

humility /hjuːˈmɪləti/ **noun** the quality of being humble 谦虚；谦逊

hummingbird /ˈhʌmɪŋbɜːd/ **noun** a small bird able to hover by beating its wings very fast 蜂鸟(一种小鸟，能够极速振动翅膀盘旋)

hummock /ˈhʌmək/ **noun** a small hill or mound 小山；小土堆

hummus or **houmous** /ˈhʊməs/ **noun** a Middle Eastern dip made from chickpeas, sesame seeds, etc. (中东的)鹰嘴豆调味酱

humorist /ˈhjuːmərɪst/ **noun** a writer or speaker who is known for being amusing 幽默作家；谈吐诙谐的人

humorous /ˈhjuːmərəs/ **adjective 1** causing amusement 幽默的；诙谐的 **2** showing a sense of humour 有幽默感的 ■ **humorously** adverb.

✔ 拼写指南 *-or-* not *-our-*: hum*or*ous. humorous 中 -or- 不要拼作 -our-。

humour /ˈhjuːmə(r)/ (US spelling 【美拼作】 humor) **noun 1** the quality of being amusing 幽默；诙谐 **2** a state of mind 心境；情绪 • **verb** do as someone wishes in order to keep them happy 迎合；迁就 ■ **humourless** adjective.

hump /hʌmp/ **noun 1** a rounded mass of earth or land 土墩；小丘 **2** a round part projecting from the back of a camel or other animal, or as an abnormal feature on a person's back 驼峰；(人的)驼背 • **verb** informal 【非正式】 lift or carry with difficulty 费劲地举起(或搬运) ■ **humped** adjective.

humus /ˈhjuːməs/ **noun** a substance found in soil, made from dead leaves and plants (土壤中的)腐殖质

hunch /hʌntʃ/ **verb** raise your shoulders and bend the top part of your body forward 耸肩；弓背 • **noun** an idea based on a feeling rather than evidence 直觉；预感

hunchback /ˈhʌntʃbæk/ **noun** offensive 【冒犯】 a person with an abnormal hump on their back 驼背的人；罗锅

hundred /ˈhʌndrəd/ **cardinal number 1** ten more than ninety; 100 百；一百 (Roman numeral 罗马数字：**c** or **C.**) **2** (**hundreds**) informal 【非正式】 a large number 大量；许多 ■ **hundredth** ordinal number.

hundredweight /ˈhʌndrədweɪt/ **noun** (plural **hundredweight** or **hundredweights**) **1** Brit. 【英】 a unit of weight equal to 112 lb (about 50.8kg) 英担(重量单位，等于112磅，约合50.8千克) **2** US 【美】 a unit of weight equal to 100 lb (about 45.4 kg) 英担(重量单位，等于100磅，约合45.4千克)

hung /hʌŋ/ past and past participle of HANG. • **adjective 1** having no political party with an overall majority 各党派势均力敌的 **2** (of a jury) unable to agree on a verdict (陪审团)无法作出裁定的 **3** (**hung up**) informal【非正式】emotionally confused or disturbed 困惑的；烦恼的

Hungarian /hʌŋ'geəriən/ **noun 1** a person from Hungary 匈牙利人 **2** the language of Hungary 匈牙利语 • **adjective** relating to Hungary 匈牙利的

hunger /'hʌŋgə(r)/ **noun 1** a feeling of discomfort caused by a lack of food 饥饿 **2** a strong desire 渴望 • **verb** (**hungers**, **hungering**, **hungered**) (**hunger after** or **for**) have a strong desire for 渴望；渴求 □ **hunger strike** a refusal to eat for a long period, carried out as a protest about something 绝食抗议

hungover /ˌhʌŋ'əʊvə(r)/ **adjective** suffering from a hangover 因宿醉而感到不适的

hungry /'hʌŋgri/ **adjective** (**hungrier**, **hungriest**) **1** feeling that you want to eat something 饥饿的 **2** having a strong desire for something 渴望的 ■ **hungrily** adverb.

hunk /hʌŋk/ **noun 1** a large piece cut or broken from something larger 大块；大片 **2** informal【非正式】a good-looking man 美男子 ■ **hunky** adjective.

hunky-dory /ˌhʌŋki'dɔːri/ **adjective** informal【非正式】fine; satisfactory 满意的；极好的；顶呱呱的

hunt /hʌnt/ **verb 1** chase and kill a wild animal for food or as a sport 追猎，猎杀(野生动物) **2** search for something 搜寻；寻找 **3** (**hunt someone down**) chase and capture someone 追捕(某人) **4** (**hunted**) looking worried and as if you are being chased 焦虑的；惊惧的 • **noun 1** an act of hunting 狩猎；打猎 **2** a group of people who meet regularly to hunt animals as a sport 打猎队伍 ■ **hunter** noun.

huntsman /'hʌntsmən/ **noun** (plural **huntsmen**) a person who hunts 狩猎者；猎人

hurdle /'hɜːdl/ **noun 1** each of a series of upright frames that an athlete jumps over in a race (跨栏比赛中的)栏架 **2** a frame used as a temporary fence 临时围栏 **3** an obstacle or difficulty 障碍；困难 • **verb** (**hurdles**, **hurdling**, **hurdled**) jump over an obstacle while running (跑步时)跨越栏架 ■ **hurdler** noun.

hurdy-gurdy /'hɜːdigɜːdi/ **noun** (plural **hurdygurdies**) a musical instrument played by turning a handle 手摇风琴

hurl /hɜːl/ **verb 1** throw something with great force 用力扔；猛投 **2** shout insults 大声辱骂

hurling /'hɜːlɪŋ/ or **hurley** /'hɜːli/ **noun** an Irish game resembling hockey 爱尔兰曲棍球

hurly-burly /'hɜːlibɜːli/ **noun** busy and noisy activity 繁忙；喧闹

hurrah /hə'rɑː/, **hooray** /hu'reɪ/, or **hurray** /hə'reɪ/ **exclamation** used to express joy or approval (用于表示喜悦或赞许)好哇，万岁

hurricane /'hʌrɪkən/ **noun** a severe storm with a violent wind 飓风

hurry /'hʌri/ **verb** (**hurries**, **hurrying**, **hurried**) **1** move or act quickly 赶紧；匆忙 **2** do something quickly or too quickly 迅速地做；仓促地做 • **noun** great haste 匆忙；急忙；急促 ■ **hurriedly** adverb.

hurt /hɜːt/ **verb** (**hurts**, **hurting**, **hurt**) **1** make someone feel physical pain 弄疼；使受伤 **2** feel pain 感到疼痛 **3** upset someone 使(某人)伤心；伤害(某人) • **noun** injury, pain, or unhappiness 创伤；疼痛

hurtful /'hɜːtfl/ **adjective** upsetting; unkind 使人痛苦的；伤感情的 ■ **hurtfully** adverb.

hurtle /'hɜːtl/ **verb** (**hurtles**, **hurtling**, **hurtled**) move very fast 飞速移动；

猛冲

husband /'hʌzbənd/ **noun** the man that a woman is married to 丈夫 • **verb** use something carefully without wasting it 节约使用(资源)

husbandry /'hʌzbəndri/ **noun 1** farming 农业；饲养业；农牧业 **2** careful management of resources 节约资源

hush /hʌʃ/ **verb 1** make or become quiet (使)变安静 **2** (hush something up) stop something from becoming known 阻止…张扬；遮掩 • **noun** a silence 安静，寂静

husk /hʌsk/ **noun** the dry outer covering of some fruits or seeds (某些水果或种子的)外壳，外皮 • **verb** remove the husk from 除去…的外壳(或外皮)

husky¹ /'hʌski/ **adjective** (huskier, huskiest) **1** (of a voice) deep and rough (嗓音)沙哑的，嘶哑的 **2** big and strong 高大强壮的 ■ **huskily** adverb.

husky² **noun** (plural huskies) a powerful dog used for pulling sledges (用于拉雪橇的)爱斯基摩犬

hussar /hə'zɑː(r)/ **noun** historical 【历史】 a soldier in a light cavalry regiment 轻骑兵

hussy /'hʌsi/ **noun** (plural hussies) a girl or woman who behaves in an immoral or cheeky way 轻佻的女子；荡妇；粗野的女子

hustings /'hʌstɪŋz/ **noun** the political meetings and speeches that take place before an election (选举前的)竞选活动(指政治集会和演讲)

hustle /'hʌsl/ **verb** (hustles, hustling, hustled) **1** push or move roughly 推搡；挤撞 **2** informal, chiefly N. Amer. 【非正式，主北美】obtain something dishonestly 非法获得 • **noun** busy movement and activity 忙碌；奔忙 ■ **hustler** noun.

hut /hʌt/ **noun** a small, simple house or shelter 简陋的小屋；棚屋；茅舍

hutch /hʌtʃ/ **noun** a box with a front made of wire, used for keeping rabbits (用于饲养兔子的)铁笼

hyacinth /'haɪəsɪnθ/ **noun** a plant with bell-shaped flowers 风信子(开钟形花)

hyaena /haɪ'iːnə/ ⇒ 见 HYENA.

hybrid /'haɪbrɪd/ **noun 1** the offspring of two plants or animals of different species or varieties 杂交种；混合种 **2** something made by combining two different things (两种不同东西的)混合物，合成物

hydrangea /haɪ'dreɪndʒə/ **noun** a shrub with white, blue, or pink clusters of flowers 绣球花(灌木，开白色、蓝色和粉红色花)

hydrant /'haɪdrənt/ **noun** a water pipe with a nozzle for attaching a fire hose 消防栓；消防龙头

hydrate /haɪ'dreɪt/ **verb** (hydrates, hydrating, hydrated) make something absorb or combine with water 水合物；水化物 ■ **hydration** noun.

hydraulic /haɪ'drɔːlɪk/ **adjective** operated by a liquid moving through pipes under pressure 水力的，液压的 • **noun** (hydraulics) the branch of science concerned with the use of liquids moving under pressure to provide mechanical force 水力学 ■ **hydraulically** adverb.

hydrocarbon /ˌhaɪdrə'kɑːbən/ **noun** any of the compounds of hydrogen and carbon 碳氢化合物；烃

hydrocephalus /ˌhaɪdrə'sefələs/ **noun** a condition in which fluid collects in the brain 脑积水；脑水肿

hydrochloric acid /ˌhaɪdrə'klɒrɪk/ **noun** an acid containing hydrogen and chlorine 盐酸；氢氯酸

hydroelectric /ˌhaɪdrəʊɪ'lektrɪk/ **adjective** having to do with the use of flowing water to generate electricity 水力发电的

hydrofoil /'haɪdrəfɔɪl/ **noun** a boat designed to rise above the water when it is travelling fast 水翼船

hydrogen /'haɪdrədʒən/ **noun** a highly flammable gas which is the lightest of the chemical elements (气体元素)氢 □ **hydrogen bomb** a very powerful nuclear bomb 氢弹 **hydrogen sulphide** a poisonous gas with a smell of bad eggs 硫化氢

hydrophobia /ˌhaɪdrə'fəʊbɪə/ **noun** **1** extreme fear of water, especially as a symptom of rabies 恐水(症); 畏水(症) **2** rabies 狂犬病;恐水病 ■ **hydrophobic** adjective.

hydroplane /'haɪdrəpleɪn/ **noun** a light, fast motorboat designed to skim over the surface of water 水上滑艇

hydrous /'haɪdrəs/ **adjective** containing water 含水的,水合的,水化的

hydroxide /haɪ'drɒksaɪd/ **noun** a compound containing oxygen and hydrogen together with a metallic element 氢氧化合物

hyena or **hyaena** /haɪ'iːnə/ **noun** a doglike African animal 鬣狗(产于非洲)

hygiene /'haɪdʒiːn/ **noun** the practice of keeping yourself and your surroundings clean in order to prevent illness and disease 卫生

hygienic /haɪ'dʒiːnɪk/ **adjective** clean and not likely to spread disease 卫生的,保健的 ■ **hygienically** adverb.

> ✔ **拼写指南** remember, *i* before *e* except after *c*: hyg*ie*nic. 记住 i 置于 e 前,在 c 后则除外,如 hygienic.

hygienist /haɪ'dʒiːnɪst/ **noun** a dental worker who specializes in oral hygiene 牙科保健员

hymen /'haɪmən/ **noun** a membrane which partially closes the opening of the vagina and is usually broken when a woman or girl first has sex 处女膜

hymn /hɪm/ **noun** a religious song of praise, especially a Christian one

(尤指基督教的)赞美诗,圣歌 • **verb** praise or celebrate 赞美;称颂

hymnal /'hɪmnəl/ **noun** a book of hymns 赞美诗集;圣歌集

hype /haɪp/ *informal* 【非正式】 **noun** extravagant publicity given to a product 夸张的宣传;言过其实的宣传 • **verb** (hypes, hyping, hyped) **1** publicize a product in an extravagant way 大肆宣传 **2** (be hyped up) be very excited or tense 感到兴奋;变得紧张

hyper /'haɪpə(r)/ **adjective** *informal* 【非正式】 having a lot of nervous energy 亢奋的;高度紧张的

hyperactive /ˌhaɪpər'æktɪv/ **adjective** very active; unable to keep still 多动的;极度活跃的

hyperbola /haɪ'pɜːbələ/ **noun** (plural **hyperbolas**) a symmetrical curve formed when a cone is cut by a plane nearly parallel to the cone's axis 双曲线

hyperbole /haɪ'pɜːbəlɪ/ **noun** a way of speaking or writing that exaggerates things and is not meant to be understood literally 夸张(法)

hyperbolic /ˌhaɪpə'bɒlɪk/ **adjective** **1** deliberately exaggerated 夸张的 **2** relating to a hyperbola 双曲线的

hyperlink /'haɪpəlɪŋk/ **noun** *Computing* 【计】 a link from a hypertext document to another location 超文本链接

hypermarket /'haɪpəmɑːkɪt/ **noun** *Brit.* 【英】 a very large supermarket 超大型超级市场

hypersensitive /ˌhaɪpə'sensətɪv/ **adjective** too sensitive 过度敏感的

hypersonic /ˌhaɪpə'sɒnɪk/ **adjective** **1** relating to speeds of more than five times the speed of sound 高超音速(超过音速5倍以上)的 **2** relating to sound frequencies above about a thousand million hertz 特超声频(声频超过1,000兆赫)的

hypertension /ˌhaɪpə'tenʃn/ **noun**

H

abnormally high blood pressure 高血压

hypertext /ˈhaɪpətekst/ **noun** Computing 【计】 a system that lets you move quickly between documents or sections of data 超文本

hyperventilate /ˌhaɪpəˈventɪleɪt/ **verb** (**hyperventilates**, **hyperventilating**, **hyperventilated**) breathe at an abnormally rapid rate 换气过度；强力呼吸 ■ **hyperventilation** noun.

hyphen /ˈhaɪfn/ **noun** the sign (-) used to join words together or to divide a word into parts between one line and the next 连字符

hyphenate /ˈhaɪfəneɪt/ **verb** (**hyphenates**, **hyphenating**, **hyphenated**) join or divide words with a hyphen 用连字符书写(或隔开) ■ **hyphenation** noun.

hypnosis /hɪpˈnəʊsɪs/ **noun** the practice of causing a person to enter a state in which they respond very readily to suggestions or commands 催眠(术)

hypnotherapy /ˌhɪpnəʊˈθerəpi/ **noun** the use of hypnosis to treat physical or mental problems 催眠疗法

hypnotic /hɪpˈnɒtɪk/ **adjective 1** having to do with hypnosis 催眠术的 **2** making you feel very relaxed or sleepy 使放松的；引起睡眠的 ■ **hypnotically** adverb.

hypnotism /ˈhɪpnətɪzəm/ **noun** the study or practice of hypnosis 催眠；催眠术；催眠术研究 ■ **hypnotist** noun.

hypnotize or **hypnotise** /ˈhɪpnətaɪz/ **verb** (**hypnotizes**, **hypnotizing**, **hypnotized**) put someone into a state of hypnosis 对…施催眠术；使进入催眠状态

hypoallergenic /ˌhaɪpəʊæləˈdʒenɪk/ **adjective** unlikely to cause an allergic reaction 低变应原的

hypochondria /ˌhaɪpəˈkɒndriə/ **noun** extreme anxiety about your health 疑病(症)

hypochondriac /ˌhaɪpəˈkɒndriæk/ **noun** a person who is too anxious about their health 疑病症患者

hypocrisy /hɪˈpɒkrəsi/ **noun** behaviour in which a person pretends to have higher standards than they really have 伪善；虚伪

hypocrite /ˈhɪpəkrɪt/ **noun** a person who pretends to have higher standards than they really have 伪善者；伪君子 ■ **hypocritical** adjective.

hypodermic /ˌhaɪpəˈdɜːmɪk/ **adjective** (of a needle or syringe) used to inject a drug or other substance beneath the skin (针头或注射器)用于皮下注射的 • **noun** a hypodermic syringe or injection 皮下注射(器)

hypotension /ˌhaɪpəʊˈtenʃn/ **noun** abnormally low blood pressure 低血压

hypotenuse /haɪˈpɒtənjuːz/ **noun** the longest side of a right-angled triangle, opposite the right angle (直角三角形的)斜边，弦

hypothermia /ˌhaɪpəʊˈθɜːmiə/ **noun** the condition of having an abnormally low body temperature 体温过低；低体温

hypothesis /haɪˈpɒθəsɪs/ **noun** (plural **hypotheses** /haɪˈpɒθəsiːz/) an idea that has not yet been proved to be true or correct 假设；假说

hypothesize or **hypothesise** /haɪˈpɒθəsaɪz/ **verb** (**hypothesizes**, **hypothesizing**, **hypothesized**) put forward as a hypothesis 假设；假定

hypothetical /ˌhaɪpəˈθetɪkl/ **adjective** based on a situation which is imagined rather than true 假设的；假定的 ■ **hypothetically** adverb.

hysterectomy /ˌhɪstəˈrektəmi/ **noun** (plural **hysterectomies**) a surgical operation to remove all or part of the womb 子宫切除(术)

hysteria /hɪˈstɪəriə/ **noun 1** wild or uncontrollable emotion 歇斯底里；情绪失控 **2** dated 【废】 a medical condition in which a person loses control of their emotions 癔病

hysterical /hɪ'sterɪkl/ **adjective 1** affected by wild or uncontrolled emotion 歇斯底里的,情绪失控的 **2** informal 【非正式】very funny 非常滑稽的 ■ **hysterically** adverb.

hysterics /hɪ'sterɪks/ **plural noun 1** wildly emotional behaviour 狂热举动 **2** informal 【非正式】uncontrollable laughter 狂笑

Hz abbreviation hertz.

I¹ or **i** /aɪ/ **noun** (plural **Is** or **I's**) **1** the ninth letter of the alphabet 英语字母表的第 9 个字母 **2** the Roman numeral for one (罗马数字)一

I² **pronoun** used by a speaker to refer to himself or herself 我(说话者自称)

iambic /aɪˈæmbɪk/ **adjective** (of rhythm in poetry) having one unstressed syllable followed by one stressed syllable (诗歌韵律)抑扬格的,短长格的

ibex /ˈaɪbeks/ **noun** (plural **ibexes**) a wild mountain goat with long horns 北山羊(一种长角野山羊)

ibid. /ˈɪbɪd/ **adverb** in the same book as the one that has just been mentioned (引文)出处同上 [short for Latin【缩写,拉丁】 = *ibidem*, meaning 'in the same place']

ibis /ˈaɪbɪs/ **noun** (plural **ibises**) a large wading bird with a long curved bill 鹮(一种大型涉禽,喙长而弯)

ice /aɪs/ **noun 1** water that has frozen and become solid 冰;冰块 **2** Brit.【英】an ice cream 冰激凌 • **verb** (**ices, icing, iced**) **1** decorate a cake with icing 用糖霜装饰 **2** (**ice up** or **over**) become covered with ice 被冰封住;被冰覆盖 □ **ice age** a period of time when ice covered much of the earth's surface 冰川期 **ice cap** a large area that is permanently covered with ice, especially at the North and South Poles (尤指南北极的)冰盖,冰冠 **ice cream** a frozen dessert made with sweetened milk fat 冰激凌 **ice hockey** a form of hockey played on an ice rink 冰球(运动);冰上曲棍球(运动) **ice pack** a bag filled with ice and held against part of the body to reduce swelling or lower temperature (消肿或降温用的)冰袋 **ice skate** a boot with a blade attached to the sole, used for skating on ice 溜冰鞋 **on thin ice** in a risky situation 如履薄冰;处于危险境地

iceberg /ˈaɪsbɜːɡ/ **noun** a large mass of ice floating in the sea 冰山

icebox /ˈaɪsbɒks/ **noun 1** a chilled container for keeping food cold 冰箱;冰柜 **2** Brit.【英】a compartment in a fridge for making and storing ice (冰箱的)冷冻室

iced /aɪst/ **adjective 1** cooled or mixed with ice 冰镇的;混有冰块的 **2** decorated with icing 饰有糖霜的

Icelandic /aɪsˈlændɪk/ **noun** the language of Iceland 冰岛语 • **adjective** relating to Iceland 冰岛的 ■ **Icelander** noun.

ichthyology /ˌɪkθiˈɒlədʒi/ **noun** the branch of zoology concerned with fish 鱼类学;鱼类研究 ■ **ichthyologist** noun.

icicle /ˈaɪsɪkl/ **noun** a hanging piece of ice formed when dripping water freezes (滴水形成成的)冰锥,冰柱

icing /ˈaɪsɪŋ/ **noun** Brit.【英】a mixture of sugar and water or fat, used to cover cakes (覆于糕饼上的)糖霜 □ **icing sugar** finely powdered sugar used to make icing (做糖霜用的)糖粉

icon /ˈaɪkɒn/ **noun 1** (also **ikon**) (in the Orthodox Church) a painting of a holy person that is also regarded as holy (东正教会的)圣像 **2** a person or thing that is seen as a symbol of something 偶像;象征 **3** Computing【计】a symbol on a computer screen that represents a program (计算机屏幕上的)图标 ■ **iconic** adjective.

iconify /ɪˈkɒnɪfaɪ/ **verb (iconifies, iconifying, iconified)** Computing 【计】 reduce a window to an icon 把(计算机屏幕上的窗口)图标化

iconoclast /aɪˈkɒnəklæst/ **noun** a person who attacks established customs and values 抨击传统习俗和价值观者 ■ **iconoclasm** noun **iconoclastic** adjective.

iconography /ˌaɪkəˈnɒɡrəfi/ **noun** 1 the use or study of pictures or symbols in visual arts 图示法；象征手法；图像学 2 the pictures or symbols associated with a person or movement 图像；符号；意象 ■ **iconographic** adjective.

ICT /aɪ siː ˈtiː/ **abbreviation** information and computing technology 信息与计算技术

icy /ˈaɪsi/ **adjective (icier, iciest)** 1 covered with ice 冰覆盖的；冰封的 2 very cold 非常冷的 3 very unfriendly; hostile 极不友好的；充满敌意的 ■ **icily** adverb.

ID /aɪ ˈdiː/ **abbreviation** identification or identity.

Id /ɪd/ ⇒ 见 **EID**.

I'd /aɪd/ **short form** 1 I had. 2 I should or I would.

id /ɪd/ **noun** the part of the mind that consists of a person's unconscious instincts and feelings 本我(个人的本能冲动和情感)

idea /aɪˈdɪə/ **noun** 1 a thought or suggestion about a possible course of action 想法；建议 2 a mental picture or impression 印象；概念 3 a belief 信仰；信念 4 **(the idea)** the aim or purpose 目的；目标

ideal /aɪˈdiːəl/ **adjective** 1 most suitable; perfect 最合适的；理想的；完美的 2 existing only in the imagination 想象的；不切实际的 ● **noun** 1 a person or thing regarded as perfect 完美的人(或物) 2 a principle or standard that is worth trying to achieve 理想；理想规范(或标准) ■ **ideally** adverb.

idealism /aɪˈdɪəlɪzəm/ **noun** 1 the belief that ideals can be achieved 理想主义 2 the representation of things as better than they really are 理想化描述；理想化 ■ **idealist** noun **idealistic** adjective.

idealize or **idealise** /aɪˈdiːəlaɪz/ **verb (idealizes, idealizing, idealized)** represent someone or something as better than they really are 将…理想化 ■ **idealization** noun.

identical /aɪˈdentɪkl/ **adjective** 1 exactly alike 极相似的 2 the same 完全一致的；相同的 3 (of twins) very similar in appearance (双胞胎)非常相像的 ■ **identically** adverb.

identification /aɪˌdentɪfɪˈkeɪʃn/ **noun** 1 the action of identifying 识别；验明 2 an official document or other proof of your identity 身份证明

identify /aɪˈdentɪfaɪ/ **verb (identifies, identifying, identified)** 1 prove or recognize that someone or something is a specified person or thing 识别；认出 2 recognize as being worthy of attention 意识到；注意到 3 **(identify with)** feel that you understand or share the feelings of 有同感；产生共鸣 4 **(identify someone/thing with)** associate someone or something closely with 使与…紧密相关 ■ **identifiable** adjective.

identity /aɪˈdentəti/ **noun (plural identities)** 1 the fact of being who or what a person or thing is 身份；本身；本体 2 a close similarity or feeling of understanding 同一性；认同感 □ **identity parade** Brit. 【英】 a group of people assembled so that an eyewitness may identify someone suspected of a crime from among them (证人从中指认犯罪嫌疑人的)辨认行列

ideology /ˌaɪdiˈɒlədʒi/ **noun (plural ideologies)** 1 a system of ideas that an economic or political theory is based on 思想体系;意识形态 **2** the set of beliefs held by a particular group 思想观念 ■ **ideological** adjective **ideologically** adverb.

idiocy /'ɪdɪəsɪ/ noun (plural **idiocies**) very stupid behaviour 极其愚蠢的行为

idiom /'ɪdɪəm/ noun **1** a group of words whose overall meaning is different from the meanings of the individual words (e.g. *over the moon*) 习语;成语 **2** a form of language used by a particular group of people (特定人群的)语言,用语 **3** a style of music or art (音乐或艺术的)风格

idiomatic /ɪdɪə'mætɪk/ adjective using expressions that are natural to a native speaker of a language (表达方式)符合(某语言)习惯的,地道的

idiosyncrasy /ɪdɪə'sɪŋkrəsɪ/ noun (plural **idiosyncrasies**) a person's particular way of behaving or thinking (某人特有的)行事方式,思维方法 ■ **idiosyncratic** adjective

✔ 拼写指南 the ending is -*asy*, not -*acy*: idiosyncr*asy*. idiosyncrasy 词末拼作 -asy,不要拼作 -acy。

idiot /'ɪdɪət/ noun a stupid person 笨蛋;傻子 ■ **idiotic** adjective **idiotically** adverb.

idle /'aɪdl/ adjective (**idler**, **idlest**) **1** avoiding work; lazy 不愿工作的;懒惰的 **2** not working or in use 不做事的;不用的;闲置的 **3** having no purpose or effect 无目的的;无效果的 • verb (**idles**, **idling**, **idled**) **1** spend time doing nothing 无所事事,虚度时光 **2** (of an engine) run slowly while out of gear (发动机)空转,挂空挡 ■ **idleness** noun **idler** noun **idly** adverb.

idol /'aɪdl/ noun **1** a statue or picture of a god that is worshipped (被崇拜的)神像 **2** a person who is very much admired 受到极度崇拜的人;偶像

idolatry /aɪ'dɒlətrɪ/ noun worship of idols 偶像崇拜

idolize or **idolise** /'aɪdəlaɪz/ verb (**idolizes**, **idolizing**, **idolized**) admire or love someone very much极度崇拜;宠爱

idyll /'ɪdɪl/ noun **1** a very happy or peaceful time or situation 快乐宁静的时期;幸福安宁的情景 **2** a short piece of writing describing a peaceful scene of country life (描绘乡村恬静安宁情景的)短文,田园诗

idyllic /ɪ'dɪlɪk/ adjective very happy, peaceful, or beautiful 幸福的;恬静的;美丽的 ■ **idyllically** adverb.

i.e. /aɪ'iː/ abbreviation that is to say 即;就是说 [short for Latin 【缩写,拉丁】= *id est*, meaning 'that is'.]

if /ɪf/ conjunction **1** on the condition or in the event that 假如;如果;倘若 **2** despite the possibility that 即使;纵然 **3** whether 是否 **4** whenever 无论何时

igloo /'ɪgluː/ noun a dome-shaped Eskimo house built from blocks of solid snow (爱斯基摩人用雪块砌的)圆顶小冰屋

igneous /'ɪgnɪəs/ adjective (of rock) formed when molten rock is solidified (岩石)火成的

ignite /ɪg'naɪt/ verb (**ignites**, **igniting**, **ignited**) **1** catch fire, or set on fire 着火;使燃烧,点燃 **2** provoke or stir up 激起

ignition /ɪg'nɪʃn/ noun **1** the action of igniting 点火;点燃 **2** the mechanism in a vehicle that ignites the fuel to start the engine (车辆的)点火装置,点火器

ignoble /ɪg'nəʊbl/ adjective not good or honest; dishonourable 卑鄙的;不诚实的;不光彩的

ignominious /ɪgnə'mɪnɪəs/ adjective deserving or causing disgrace or shame 可耻的;耻辱的 ■ **ignominiously** adverb.

ignominy /'ɪgnəmɪnɪ/ **noun** public shame or disgrace 耻辱；不光彩

ignoramus /ɪgnə'reɪməs/ **noun** (plural **ignoramuses**) an ignorant or stupid person 白痴；傻子

ignorance /'ɪgnərəns/ **noun** lack of knowledge or information 无知；不了解

ignorant /'ɪgnərənt/ **adjective 1** lacking knowledge or information 无知的；不了解情况的 **2** informal【非正式】not polite; rude 无礼的；粗鲁的

ignore /ɪg'nɔː(r)/ **verb** (**ignores**, **ignoring**, **ignored**) **1** deliberately take no notice of 不顾；不理睬 **2** fail to consider something important 未考虑；忽视

iguana /ɪg'gwɑːnə/ **noun** a large tropical American lizard with a spiny crest along the back 鬣蜥(美洲热带地区之大型蜥蜴，背部有棘刺状突起)

ikon /'aɪkɒn/ ⇒ 见 ICON.

ilk /ɪlk/ **noun** a type 种类；类型

I'll /aɪl/ **short form 1** I shall. **2** I will.

ill /ɪl/ **adjective 1** not in good health; unwell 有病的；不舒服的 **2** bad or harmful 有害的；不利的 • **adverb 1** badly or wrongly 恶劣地；错误地 **2** only with difficulty 艰难地；勉强地 • **noun 1** a problem or misfortune 麻烦；不幸 **2** evil or harm 邪恶；伤害 □ **ill-advised** not sensible or well thought out 不明智的；考虑不周的 **ill at ease** uncomfortable or embarrassed 不舒服的；不自在的；尴尬的 **ill-fated** destined to fail or be unlucky 注定失败的；注定要倒霉的 **ill-favoured** unattractive 不吸引人的；丑陋的 **ill-gotten** obtained by illegal or unfair means 非法获得的；来路不正的 **ill-starred** unlucky 不幸的；倒霉的 **ill-treat** treat in a cruel or unkind way 虐待；折磨 **ill will** hostility 恶意；敌意

illegal /ɪ'liːgl/ **adjective** against the law 违法的；非法的 ■ **illegality noun illegally** adverb.

illegible /ɪ'ledʒəbl/ **adjective** not clear enough to be read 难以辨认的；模糊的 ■ **illegibility** noun.

illegitimate /ɪlɪ'dʒɪtəmət/ **adjective 1** not allowed by law or rules 违法的；违规的 **2** (of a child) born to parents who are not married to each other (孩子)私生的 ■ **illegitimacy** noun.

illiberal /ɪ'lɪbərəl/ **adjective** not allowing freedom of thought or behaviour 限制思想(或行为)自由的

illicit /ɪ'lɪsɪt/ **adjective** forbidden by law, rules, or standards 违法的；违禁的；不正当的 ■ **illicitly** adverb.

illiterate /ɪ'lɪtərət/ **adjective 1** unable to read or write 文盲的；不会读写的 **2** not knowing very much about a particular subject (对某领域)了解不多的，外行的 ■ **illiteracy** noun.

illness /'ɪlnəs/ **noun** a disease, or a period of being ill 疾病；患病期

illogical /ɪ'lɒdʒɪkl/ **adjective** not sensible or based on sound reasoning 悖理的；不合逻辑的 ■ **illogicality** noun **illogically** adverb.

illuminate /ɪ'luːmɪneɪt/ **verb** (**illuminates**, **illuminating**, **illuminated**) **1** light something up 照明；照亮 **2** help to explain something 阐明；解释；说明 **3** decorate a manuscript with coloured designs (用彩色图案)装饰(手稿)

illumination /ɪˌluːmɪ'neɪʃn/ **noun 1** lighting or light 照明；光亮 **2** (**illuminations**) lights used in decorating a building for a special occasion (建筑物的)灯彩，灯饰 **3** understanding 理解；领悟

illumine /ɪ'luːmɪn/ **verb** literary【文】light up; illuminate 照明；照亮

illusion /ɪ'luːʒn/ **noun 1** a false idea or belief 错误观念；幻想 **2** a thing that seems to be something that is not 幻想的事物；幻觉，错觉

illusionist /ɪ'luːʒənɪst/ **noun** a magician or conjuror 魔术师；幻术师

illusory /ɪˈluːsəri/ or **illusive** /ɪˈluːsɪv/ **adjective** not real, although seeming to be 不真实的；幻觉的

illustrate /ˈɪləstreɪt/ **verb** (**illustrates, illustrating, illustrated**) **1** provide a book or magazine with pictures 给(书或杂志)配插图 **2** make something clear by using examples, charts, etc. (用例子、图表等)解释，说明 **3** act as an example of 作为例证说明 ■ **illustrative** adjective **illustrator** noun.

illustration /ˌɪləˈstreɪʃn/ **noun 1** a picture illustrating a book or magazine (书籍或杂志的)插图 **2** the action of illustrating 图解；图示 **3** an example that helps to explain something 例证；实例

illustrious /ɪˈlʌstriəs/ **adjective** famous and admired for what you have achieved 著名的；杰出的

I'm /aɪm/ **short form** I am.

image /ˈɪmɪdʒ/ **noun 1** a picture or statue of someone or something 肖像，塑像 **2** a picture seen on a television or computer screen, through a lens, or reflected in a mirror 映像；图像；影像；镜像 **3** a picture in the mind (头脑中的)形象 **4** the impression that a person or group gives to the public 形象，印象 **5** (**the image of**) a person or thing that looks very similar to another 酷似的人(或物) **6** a word or phrase describing something in an imaginative way; a simile or metaphor 意象；明喻；隐喻 • **verb** (**images, imaging, imaged**) make or form an image of 画(或造)…的像

imagery /ˈɪmɪdʒəri/ **noun 1** language that produces images in the mind 形象的语言；意象 **2** pictures as a whole (总称)图象，照片

imaginary /ɪˈmædʒɪnəri/ **adjective** existing only in the imagination 想象中的；假想的；幻想的

✔ **拼写指南** the ending is -ary not -ery: imagin*ary*. imaginary 词末拼作 -ary，不要拼作 -ery。

imagination /ɪˌmædʒɪˈneɪʃn/ **noun 1** the part of the mind that imagines things 想象力 **2** the ability to be creative or solve problems 想象力；创造力

imaginative /ɪˈmædʒɪnətɪv/ **adjective** using the imagination in a creative or inventive way 富于想象力的；有创造力的 ■ **imaginatively** adverb.

imagine /ɪˈmædʒɪn/ **verb** (**imagines, imagining, imagined**) **1** form a mental picture of 想象；设想 **2** think that something is probable 料想；认为 **3** believe that something unreal exists 误认为；臆测 ■ **imaginable** adjective.

imam /ɪˈmɑːm/ **noun** the person who leads prayers in a mosque (清真寺主持礼拜的)伊玛目

imbalance /ɪmˈbæləns/ **noun** a lack of proportion or balance 失调；失衡

imbecile /ˈɪmbəsiːl/ **noun** informal 【非正式】a stupid person 傻瓜；笨蛋 ■ **imbecilic** adjective **imbecility** noun.

imbed /ɪmˈbed/ ⇒ 见 EMBED.

imbibe /ɪmˈbaɪb/ **verb** (**imbibes, imbibing, imbibed**) **1** formal 【正式】drink alcohol 喝(酒) **2** absorb ideas or knowledge 吸收，吸取(观念或知识)

imbroglio /ɪmˈbrəʊliəʊ/ **noun** (plural **imbroglios**) a very confused or complicated situation 错综复杂的形势

imbue /ɪmˈbjuː/ **verb** (**imbues, imbuing, imbued**) fill with a feeling or quality 使充满(感情或品质)

imitate /ˈɪmɪteɪt/ **verb** (**imitates, imitating, imitated**) **1** follow as a model; copy 模仿；效法 **2** copy the way that a person speaks or behaves in order to amuse people (为逗人开心)模仿(某人的言谈或举止) ■ **imitator** noun.

imitation /ˌɪmɪˈteɪʃn/ **noun 1** a

copy 仿造品；赝品 **2** the action of imitating 模仿；仿效

imitative /'ɪmɪtətɪv/ **adjective** imitating or copying something 模仿的；仿效的

immaculate /ɪ'mækjələt/ **adjective 1** completely clean or tidy 纯洁的；整洁的 **2** free from mistakes; perfect 无瑕疵的；无误的、完美的 ■ **immaculately** adverb.

immanent /'ɪmənənt/ **adjective** present within or throughout something 内在的；无所不在的 ■ **immanence** noun.

immaterial /ˌɪmə'tɪərɪəl/ **adjective 1** unimportant under the circumstances 不重要的；无关紧要的 **2** spiritual rather than physical 精神的；非物质的；无形的

immature /ˌɪmə'tjʊə(r)/ **adjective 1** not fully developed 未发育全的；未成熟的 **2** behaving in a way that is typical of someone younger 不成熟的；幼稚的 ■ **immaturity** noun.

immeasurable /ɪ'meʒərəbl/ **adjective** too large or extreme to measure 不可计量的；无限的 ■ **immeasurably** adverb.

immediate /ɪ'miːdɪət/ **adjective 1** happening or done at once 立即的 **2** nearest in time, space, or relationship 最接近的；紧接的 **3** most urgent; current 最紧急的，迫切的；当前的 **4** without anything coming between; direct 直接的 ■ **immediacy** noun.

immediately /ɪ'miːdɪətli/ **adverb 1** at once 立即；马上 **2** very close in time, space, or relationship 紧接；接近 • **conjunction** chiefly Brit.【主英】as soon as 一⋯⋯就；即刻

✔ 拼写指南 -tely, not -tly: immediately. immediately 中 -tely 不要拼作 -tly。

immemorial /ˌɪmə'mɔːrɪəl/ **adjective** existing for longer than people can remember 远古的；无法追忆的

immense /ɪ'mens/ **adjective** very large or great 极大的；巨大的；广大的 ■ **immensely** adverb **immensity** noun.

immerse /ɪ'mɜːs/ **verb** (**immerses, immersing, immersed**) **1** dip or cover completely in a liquid 浸入；沉浸 **2** (**immerse yourself in**) involve yourself deeply in an activity 使专注于；使沉浸在

immersion /ɪ'mɜːʃn/ **noun 1** the action of immersing 浸入；浸没 **2** deep involvement in an activity 专注；陷入 □ **immersion heater** an electric device in a water tank which heats water for a house 浸没式热水器

immigrant /'ɪmɪgrənt/ **noun** a person who comes to live permanently in a foreign country (外来)移民

immigration /ˌɪmɪ'greɪʃn/ **noun** the action of coming to live permanently in a foreign country 移居；移民 ■ **immigrate** verb.

imminent /'ɪmɪnənt/ **adjective** about to happen 即将发生的；临近的 ■ **imminence** noun **imminently** adverb.

immiscible /ɪ'mɪsəbl/ **adjective** (of liquids) not able to be mixed together (液体)不能混合的，不能溶合的

immobile /ɪ'məʊbaɪl/ **adjective** not moving or able to move 不活动的；静止的 ■ **immobility** noun.

immobilize or **immobilise** /ɪ'məʊbəlaɪz/ **verb** (**immobilizes, immobilizing, immobilized**) prevent from moving or operating normally 使不动；使固定；使无法运作 ■ **immobilization** noun.

immoderate /ɪ'mɒdərət/ **adjective** not sensible or controlled; excessive 不明智的；不节制的；过度的

immodest /ɪ'mɒdɪst/ **adjective 1** conceited or boastful 不客气的；不谦

虚的；傲慢的 **2** showing too much of the body 不雅的；下流的

immolate /'ɪməleɪt/ **verb** kill or sacrifice by burning 烧死；(以焚烧)献祭 ■ **immolation** noun.

immoral /ɪ'mɒrəl/ **adjective** not following accepted standards of morality 不道德的；伤风败俗的 ■ **immorality** noun.

immortal /ɪ'mɔːtl/ **adjective 1** living forever 永生的；不朽的 **2** deserving to be remembered forever 流芳百世的；永垂不朽的 • **noun 1** an immortal god 神仙 **2** a person who will be famous for a very long time 流芳百世的人 ■ **immortality** noun.

immortalize or **immortalise** /ɪ'mɔːtəlaɪz/ **verb** (**immortalizes, immortalizing, immortalized**) prevent someone or something from being forgotten for a very long time 使不朽；使永生

immovable /ɪ'muːvəbl/ **adjective 1** not able to be moved 不可移动的 **2** unable to be changed or persuaded 不动摇的；无法说服的

immune /ɪ'mjuːn/ **adjective 1** having a natural ability to resist a particular infection 有免疫力的；免疫的 **2** not affected by something 不受影响的 **3** exempt or protected from something 免除的；豁免的；受保护的

immunity /ɪ'mjuːnəti/ **noun** (plural **immunities**) **1** the body's ability to resist a particular infection 免疫；免疫力 **2** freedom from a duty or punishment 免除；豁免

immunize or **immunise** /'ɪmjunaɪz/ **verb** (**immunizes, immunizing, immunized**) make immune to infection 使免疫 ■ **immunization** noun.

immunology /ˌɪmjuˈnɒlədʒi/ **noun** the branch of medicine and biology concerned with immunity to infection 免疫学 ■ **immunological** adjective **immunologist** noun.

immure /ɪ'mjʊə(r)/ **verb** (**immures, immuring, immured**) literary【文】shut someone up in a place 紧闭；囚禁；监禁

immutable /ɪ'mjuːtəbl/ **adjective** not changing or able to be changed 不变的；不可改变的

imp /ɪmp/ **noun 1** (in stories) a small, mischievous devil (传说中的)小魔鬼，小精灵 **2** a mischievous child 顽童，小淘气

impact noun /'ɪmpækt/ **1** an instance of one object hitting another 碰撞；冲击 **2** a noticeable effect or influence (显著的)效果，影响 • **verb** /ɪm'pækt/ **1** hit another object with force 碰；撞 **2** (**impact on**) have a strong effect on 产生强烈影响 **3** (**impacted**) (of a tooth) wedged between another tooth and the jaw (牙齿)阻生的

impair /ɪm'peə(r)/ **verb** weaken or damage 削弱；损害 ■ **impairment** noun.

impale /ɪm'peɪl/ **verb** (**impales, impaling, impaled**) pierce with a sharp instrument (用尖利工具)刺破，刺穿

impalpable /ɪm'pælpəbl/ **adjective 1** unable to be felt by touch 触摸不到的；感觉不到的 **2** not easily understood 难以理解的；晦涩难懂的

impart /ɪm'pɑːt/ **verb 1** communicate information 通知；透露 **2** give a particular quality to 把(某品质)赋予

impartial /ɪm'pɑːʃl/ **adjective** not favouring one person or thing more than another 不偏不倚的；无偏见的 ■ **impartiality** noun **impartially** adverb.

impassable /ɪm'pɑːsəbl/ **adjective** impossible to travel along or over 不能通行的；不可逾越的

impasse /'æmpɑːs/ **noun** a situation in which no progress is possible 绝境；僵局

impassioned /ɪm'pæʃnd/ **adjective**

filled with or showing great emotion 充满激情的;热烈的

impassive /ɪmˈpæsɪv/ **adjective** not feeling or showing emotion 麻木的;无动于衷的,没有表情的 ■ **impassively** adverb.

impasto /ɪmˈpɑːstəʊ/ **noun** the technique of laying on paint thickly so that it stands out from the surface of a painting 厚涂法(一种绘画技法)

impatient /ɪmˈpeɪʃnt/ **adjective 1** not having much patience or tolerance 无耐心的,不耐烦的 **2** restlessly eager 迫不及待的;热切的 ■ **impatience** noun **impatiently** adverb.

impeach /ɪmˈpiːtʃ/ **verb** chiefly US 【美】charge a person who holds an important public office with a serious crime 控告,弹劾(显要政府官员) ■ **impeachment** noun.

impeccable /ɪmˈpekəbl/ **adjective** without faults or mistakes 无缺点的;无错误的;完美的 ■ **impeccably** adverb.

impecunious /ˌɪmpɪˈkjuːnɪəs/ **adjective** having little or no money 一文不名的;一贫如洗的

impedance /ɪmˈpiːdns/ **noun** the total resistance of an electric circuit to the flow of alternating current 阻抗;全电阻

impede /ɪmˈpiːd/ **verb** (**impedes**, **impeding**, **impeded**) delay or block the progress of 耽误;妨碍;阻碍

impediment /ɪmˈpedɪmənt/ **noun 1** something that delays or blocks progress 妨碍;阻碍;障碍物 **2** (also **speech impediment**) a defect in a person's speech, such as a stammer 言语障碍;口吃

impel /ɪmˈpel/ **verb** (**impels**, **impelling**, **impelled**) force to do something 驱使;促成;激励

impending /ɪmˈpendɪŋ/ **adjective** be about to happen 即将发生的;逼近的

impenetrable /ɪmˈpenɪtrəbl/ **adjective 1** impossible to get through

or into 不能通过的;无法进入的 **2** impossible to understand 不可理解的

impenitent /ɪmˈpenɪtənt/ **adjective** not feeling shame or regret 不知羞耻的;不知悔改的

imperative /ɪmˈperətɪv/ **adjective 1** of vital importance 至关重要的 **2** giving a command 命令的;强制的 **3** Grammar【语法】(of a verb) expressing a command, as in *come here!* (动词)祈使语气的 ● **noun** an essential or urgent thing 必要的事,紧急的事

imperceptible /ˌɪmpəˈseptəbl/ **adjective** too slight or gradual to be seen or felt (因细小或渐变)看不见的,感觉不到的 ■ **imperceptibly** adverb.

imperfect /ɪmˈpɜːfɪkt/ **adjective 1** faulty or incomplete 有缺陷的;不完全的;不完美的 **2** Grammar【语法】(of a verb) referring to a past action that is not yet completed (动词)过去未完成时的 ■ **imperfection** noun **imperfectly** adverb.

imperial /ɪmˈpɪərɪəl/ **adjective 1** relating to an empire or an emperor 帝国的;帝王的 **2** (of weights and measures) in a nonmetric system formerly used in the UK (度量衡)英制的

imperialism /ɪmˈpɪərɪəlɪzm/ **noun** a system in which one country extends its power and influence by defeating other countries in war, forming colonies, etc. 帝国统治 ■ **imperialist** noun & adjective.

imperil /ɪmˈperəl/ **verb** (**imperils**, **imperiling**, **imperilled**; US spelling 【美拼作】**imperils**, **imperiling**, **imperiled**) put into danger 使陷入危险;危及

imperious /ɪmˈpɪərɪəs/ **adjective** expecting to be obeyed 专横的;飞扬跋扈的 ■ **imperiously** adverb.

impermanent /ɪmˈpɜːmənənt/ **adjective** not permanent 非永久的;暂时的

■ **impermanence** noun.

impermeable /ɪmˈpɜːmiəbl/ **adjective** not allowing a liquid or gas to pass through 无法渗透的；不透水的；不透气的

impersonal /ɪmˈpɜːsənl/ **adjective** **1** not influenced by or involving personal feelings 不受个人感情影响的；客观的 **2** lacking human feelings or atmosphere 没有人情味的，冷淡的 **3** Grammar 【语法】 (of a verb) used only with *it* as a subject (as in *it is snowing*) (动词)非人称的，无人称的 ■ **impersonality** noun **impersonally** adverb.

impersonate /ɪmˈpɜːsəneɪt/ **verb** (**impersonates, impersonating, impersonated**) pretend to be another person in order to entertain or deceive people（为取乐或骗人）装扮，冒充 ■ **impersonation** noun **impersonator** noun.

impertinent /ɪmˈpɜːtɪnənt/ **adjective** not showing proper respect 无礼的；不敬的 ■ **impertinence** noun.

imperturbable /ˌɪmpəˈtɜːbəbl/ **adjective** not easily upset or excited 不易生气的；不易激动的；沉着的

impervious /ɪmˈpɜːviəs/ **adjective** **1** not allowing a liquid or a gas to pass through 不能渗透的；不透水的；不透气的 **2** (**impervious to**) unable to be affected by 不受影响的

impetuous /ɪmˈpetʃuəs/ **adjective** acting quickly and without thinking or being careful 鲁莽的；冲动的 ■ **impetuously** adverb.

impetus /ˈɪmpɪtəs/ **noun 1** the force or energy with which something moves 动量；冲力 **2** the force that makes something happen 推动力

impinge /ɪmˈpɪndʒ/ **verb** (**impinges, impinging, impinged**) (**impinge on**) have an effect or impact on 起作用；影响

impious /ˈɪmpiəs/ **adjective** not showing respect or reverence 不敬的；

不恭的

implacable /ɪmˈplækəbl/ **adjective** **1** unwilling to stop being hostile towards someone or something 不愿和解的，不饶恕的 **2** (of strong negative feelings) unable to be changed (强烈的消极感情)无法改变的，不可平息的 ■ **implacably** adverb.

implant verb /ɪmˈplɑːnt/ **1** put tissue or an artificial object into someone's body, by means of a surgical operation (通过手术)植入，移植(组织或人造器官) **2** fix an idea firmly in someone's mind 灌输(观念) • noun /ˈɪmplɑːnt/ a thing that is implanted 植入物 ■ **implantation** noun.

implausible /ɪmˈplɔːzəbl/ **adjective** not seeming reasonable or probable 似乎不合情理的；看似不可能的 ■ **implausibility** noun **implausibly** adverb.

implement noun /ˈɪmplɪmənt/ a tool that is used for a particular purpose 工具；用具；器具 • verb /ˈɪmplɪment/ put something into effect 实施；执行；贯彻 ■ **implementation** noun.

implicate /ˈɪmplɪkeɪt/ **verb** (**implicates, implicating, implicated**) **1** show that someone is involved in a crime 牵连；涉及；卷入 **2** (**be implicated in**) be partly responsible for 对…负有责任；与…有牵连

implication /ˌɪmplɪˈkeɪʃn/ **noun 1** a conclusion that can be drawn from something 含意；暗示 **2** a possible effect 可能的影响(或作用) **3** involvement in something 牵连；涉及；卷入

implicit /ɪmˈplɪsɪt/ **adjective 1** suggested without being directly expressed 含着的，不直接言明的 **2** (**implicit in**) forming part of something (某物)内含的，固有的 **3** not doubted or questioned 无疑的；绝对的 ■ **implicitly** adverb.

implode /ɪmˈpləʊd/ **verb** (**implodes, imploding, imploded**) collapse violently inwards 内爆 ■ **implosion**

noun.

implore /ɪmˈplɔː(r)/ **verb (implores, imploring, implored)** beg earnestly or desperately 恳求；央求；乞求

imply /ɪmˈplaɪ/ **verb (implies, implying, implied) 1** suggest rather than state directly 暗指；暗示 **2** suggest as a possible effect 意味着；表明

> **！注意** don't confuse the words **imply** and **infer**. They can describe the same situation, but from different points of view. If you **imply** something, it means that you are suggesting something though not saying it directly. If you **infer** something from what has been said, you come to the conclusion that this is what the speaker really means, although they are not saying it directly. 不要混淆 imply 和 infer。两者均可描述相同的情形，但描述的角度不同。imply 指某人暗示但没有直接说出某事。infer 指从某人所说的话中推论出(他没有直接说明的)真实意思。

impolite /ˌɪmpəˈlaɪt/ **adjective** not having good manners 不礼貌的；失礼的

impolitic /ɪmˈpɒlətɪk/ **adjective** unwise 不明智的

imponderable /ɪmˈpɒndərəbl/ **noun** something that is difficult or impossible to assess 难以(或无法)估量的事物 • **adjective** difficult or impossible to assess 难以(或无法)估量的

import **verb** /ɪmˈpɔːt/ **1** bring goods into a country from abroad 进口 **2** transfer computer data into a file 输入(计算机数据) • **noun** /ˈɪmpɔːt/ **1** an imported article 进口商品 **2** the action of importing 进口；输入 **3** the implied meaning of something 含意 **4** importance 重要性 ■ **importation** noun **importer** noun.

important /ɪmˈpɔːtnt/ **adjective 1** having a great effect or value 重要的；重大的；非常有价值的 **2** (of a person) having great authority or influence (人)有权威的，有影响的 ■ **importance** noun **importantly** adverb.

importunate /ɪmˈpɔːtʃənət/ **adjective** very persistent 非常执着的；纠缠不休的

importune /ˌɪmpɔːˈtjuːn/ **verb (importunes, importuning, importuned)** ask someone persistently for something 再三要求；纠缠

impose /ɪmˈpəʊz/ **verb (imposes, imposing, imposed) 1** force something to be accepted 把…强加于；迫使 **2** (often **impose on**) take unfair advantage of someone 利用(某人)

imposing /ɪmˈpəʊzɪŋ/ **adjective** grand and impressive 壮观的；给人深刻印象的

imposition /ˌɪmpəˈzɪʃn/ **noun 1** the action of imposing something 强加；强迫 **2** an unreasonable thing that you are asked or expected to do or accept (强加的)不合理要求

impossible /ɪmˈpɒsəbl/ **adjective 1** not able to exist or be done 不可能存在的；不可能的；办不到的 **2** very difficult to deal with 难对付的 ■ **impossibility** noun **impossibly** adverb.

impostor or **imposter** /ɪmˈpɒstə(r)/ **noun** a person who pretends to be someone else in order to deceive other people 冒充者；冒名顶替者

imposture /ɪmˈpɒstʃə(r)/ **noun** an act of pretending to be someone else in order to deceive 冒名行骗

impotent /ˈɪmpətənt/ **adjective 1** helpless or powerless 无助的；无能的 **2** (of a man) unable to achieve an erection (男子)阳痿的 ■ **impotence** noun.

impound /ɪmˈpaʊnd/ **verb 1** officially seize something 没收，扣押(某物)

2 shut up domestic animals in an enclosure 将(家畜)关入栏内

impoverish /ɪmˈpɒvərɪʃ/ **verb 1** make someone poor 使贫困 **2** make something worse in quality 使(品质)变差 ■ **impoverishment** noun

impracticable /ɪmˈpræktɪkəbl/ **adjective** not able to be done 不可行的；行不通的

impractical /ɪmˈpræktɪkl/ **adjective** not sensible or realistic 不明智的；不现实的

imprecation /ˌɪmprɪˈkeɪʃn/ **noun** formal【正式】a spoken curse 咒骂语

imprecise /ˌɪmprɪˈsaɪs/ **adjective** not exact 不精确的；不准确的 ■ **imprecision** noun.

impregnable /ɪmˈpregnəbl/ **adjective 1** (of a building) unable to be captured or broken into (建筑物)坚不可摧的，牢不可破的 **2** unable to be defeated 无法战胜的

impregnate /ˈɪmpregneɪt/ **verb** (**impregnates, impregnating, impregnated**) **1** soak with a substance 浸渍 **2** fill with a feeling or quality 灌输；注入 **3** make pregnant 使怀孕，使受孕 ■ **impregnation** noun.

impresario /ˌɪmprəˈsɑːrɪəʊ/ **noun** (plural **impresarios**) a person who organizes plays, concerts, or operas (戏剧、音乐会、歌剧演出等的)主办人，舞台监督

impress /ɪmˈpres/ **verb 1** make someone feel admiration and respect 使敬佩；给(某人)留下好印象 **2** (**impress something on**) make someone aware of something important 使意识到…的重要性 **3** make a mark or design using a stamp or seal 压印，盖(印记或图案)

impression /ɪmˈpreʃn/ **noun 1** an idea, feeling, or opinion 想法；感受；感想 **2** the effect that something has on someone 印象 **3** an imitation of the way that a person speaks or behaves done in order to entertain people (对某人言语举止的)滑稽模仿 **4** a mark made by pressing on a surface 压印；压痕；印记

impressionable /ɪmˈpreʃənəbl/ **adjective** easily influenced 易受影响的

Impressionism /ɪmˈpreʃənɪzəm/ **noun** a style of painting concerned with showing the visual impression of a particular moment 印象主义,印象派(一种绘画风格,注重表现某个时刻的视觉印象) ■ **Impressionist** noun & adjective.

impressionist /ɪmˈpreʃənɪst/ **noun** an entertainer who impersonates famous people (模仿名人的)滑稽模仿演员

impressionistic /ɪmˌpreʃəˈnɪstɪk/ **adjective** based on personal ideas or feelings 凭个人印象的；主观的

impressive /ɪmˈpresɪv/ **adjective** arousing admiration through size, quality, or skill 令人赞叹的；印象深刻的 ■ **impressively** adverb.

imprimatur /ˌɪmprɪˈmɑːtə(r)/ **noun** the authority or approval of someone 批准；认可；同意

imprint verb /ɪmˈprɪnt/ make a mark on an object by pressing something on to it 压(印)；盖(印) • **noun** /ˈɪmprɪnt/ **1** a mark made by pressing something on to an object 印痕；印记 **2** a publisher's name and other details printed in a book (出版物上的)出版商信息

imprison /ɪmˈprɪzn/ **verb** put or keep in prison 关押；监禁 ■ **imprisonment** noun.

improbable /ɪmˈprɒbəbl/ **adjective** not likely to be true or to happen 不大可能的 ■ **improbability** noun **improbably** adverb.

impromptu /ɪmˈprɒmptjuː/ **adjective & adverb** done without being planned or rehearsed 即兴的(地)；事先无准备的(地)

improper /ɪmˈprɒpə(r)/ **adjective 1**

not fitting in with accepted standards of behaviour 不适当的；不得体的 **2** not modest or decent 不成体统的；不雅的；不体面的

impropriety /ˌɪmprə'praɪəti/ **noun** (plural **improprieties**) improper behaviour 不合适举止；不当行为

improve /ɪm'pruːv/ **verb** (**improves**, **improving**, **improved**) **1** make or become better (使)改善,(使)改进 **2** (**improve on**) produce something better than 改进；改良 ■ **improvement** noun.

improvident /ɪm'prɒvɪdənt/ **adjective** not preparing for the future 不顾将来的；没有长远打算的

improvise /'ɪmprəvaɪz/ **verb** (**improvises**, **improvising**, **improvised**) **1** invent and perform music or drama without planning it in advance 即兴创作；即兴表演 **2** make something from whatever is available 临时凑成 ■ **improvisation** noun.

imprudent /ɪm'pruːdnt/ **adjective** not sensible or careful 不明智的；不谨慎的

impudent /'ɪmpjədənt/ **adjective** not showing respect for another person 不恭敬的；无礼的 ■ **impudence** noun **impudently** adverb.

impugn /ɪm'pjuːn/ **verb** formal 【正式】express doubts about whether something is true or honest 对…表示怀疑；置疑

impulse /'ɪmpʌls/ **noun** **1** a sudden urge to do something 冲动 **2** a force that makes something happen 推动力

impulsive /ɪm'pʌlsɪv/ **adjective** acting without thinking ahead 冲动的 ■ **impulsively** adverb.

impunity /ɪm'pjuːnəti/ **noun** freedom from being punished or hurt 不受惩罚；免受伤害

impure /ɪm'pjʊə(r)/ **adjective** **1**

mixed with unwanted substances 不纯的；掺杂的 **2** morally wrong 不道德的

impurity /ɪm'pjʊərəti/ **noun** (plural **impurities**) **1** the state of being impure 不纯；掺杂 **2** a thing which makes something less pure 杂质；使不纯之物

impute /ɪm'pjuːt/ **verb** (**imputes**, **imputing**, **imputed**) (**impute something to**) believe that something has been done or caused by 把…归因于；归咎于 ■ **imputation** noun.

in /ɪn/ **preposition 1** expressing the position of something that is enclosed or surrounded 在…内；在…中 **2** expressing movement which results in something being enclosed or surrounded 进入 **3** expressing a period of time before or during which something happens 在(一段时间)内 **4** expressing a state or quality (表示状态或性质)处于…中 **5** indicating that something is included or involved 参与；涉及 **6** indicating the language or material used by someone 用,以(某种语言或材料) **7** used to express a value as a proportion of a whole (表示与整体的比例)每,以,按 • **adverb 1** expressing the state of being enclosed or surrounded 在里面；在内 **2** expressing movement which results in being enclosed or surrounded 进入 **3** present at your home or office 在家；在办公室 **4** having arrived at a destination 到达 **5** (of the tide) rising or at its highest level (潮水)在上涨,位于最高点 • **adjective** informal 【非正式】fashionable 流行的；时髦的 □ **in-depth** thorough and detailed 彻底的；深入的 **in-house** within an organization 内部的 **in-joke** a joke shared only by a small group 小圈子里的笑话；内部笑话 **the ins and outs** informal 【非正式】all the details

详情；所有细节

in. abbreviation inches.

inability /ˌɪnəˈbɪləti/ noun the state of being unable to do something 无能；无力；不能

in absentia /ˌɪn æbˈsenʃiə/ adverb while not present 不在；缺席

inaccessible /ˌɪnækˈsesəbl/ adjective **1** unable to be reached or used 达不到的；不能使用的 **2** difficult to understand 难以理解的

inaccurate /ɪnˈækjərət/ adjective not accurate 不准确的；不精确的 ■ inaccuracy noun (plural inaccuracies) inaccurately adverb.

inactive /ɪnˈæktɪv/ adjective not active or working 不活跃的；不运转的 ■ inaction noun inactivity noun.

inadequate /ɪnˈædɪkwət/ adjective **1** not enough or not good enough 不足的；不够好的 **2** unable to deal with a situation 不能胜任的 ■ inadequacy noun (plural inadequacies) inadequately adverb.

inadmissible /ˌɪnədˈmɪsəbl/ adjective (of evidence in court) not accepted as valid (法庭证据)不能采纳的，无效的

inadvertent /ˌɪnədˈvɜːtənt/ adjective not deliberate or intentional 非故意的；无心的 ■ inadvertently adverb.

✔ 拼写指南 -ent, not -ant: inadvertent. inadvertent 中 -ent 不要拼作 -ant。

inadvisable /ˌɪnədˈvaɪzəbl/ adjective likely to have unfortunate results 不可取的；失策的

inalienable /ɪnˈeɪliənəbl/ adjective unable to be taken away or given away 不可剥夺的；不可分割的；不能让与的

inane /ɪˈneɪn/ adjective silly or stupid 愚蠢的；无聊的 ■ inanely adverb inanity noun.

inanimate /ɪnˈænɪmət/ adjective not alive 无生气的；死气沉沉的

inapplicable /ˌɪnəˈplɪkəbl/ adjective

not relevant or appropriate 不相关的；不适当的

inappropriate /ˌɪnəˈprəupriət/ adjective not suitable or appropriate 不适当的；不妥的 ■ inappropriately adverb.

inarticulate /ˌɪnɑːˈtɪkjələt/ adjective **1** unable to express your ideas clearly 表达不清的；不善辞令的 **2** not expressed in words 未表达出来的

inasmuch /ˌɪnəzˈmʌtʃ/ adverb (inasmuch as) **1** to the extent that 在…限度内 **2** considering that; since 鉴于；考虑到；由于

inattentive /ˌɪnəˈtentɪv/ adjective not paying attention 不关注的；漫不经心的 ■ inattention noun.

inaudible /ɪnˈɔːdəbl/ adjective unable to be heard 听不见的 ■ inaudibly adverb.

inaugural /ɪˈnɔːgjərəl/ adjective marking the start of something important 开幕的；成立的；创立的

inaugurate /ɪˈnɔːgjəreɪt/ verb (inaugurates, inaugurating, inaugurated) **1** begin or introduce a system or project 开始；引进 **2** mark the beginning of an organization or the opening of a building with a ceremony 为…举行创建仪式，为…举行落成典礼 ■ inauguration noun.

inauspicious /ˌɪnɔːˈspɪʃəs/ adjective not likely to lead to success 凶兆的；不祥的

inauthentic /ˌɪnɔːˈθentɪk/ noun not genuine or sincere 不真实的；不真诚的

inborn /ˌɪnˈbɔːn/ adjective existing from birth 天生的；先天的

inbred /ˌɪnˈbred/ adjective **1** produced by breeding from closely related people or animals 近亲繁殖的，同系交配的 **2** existing from birth; inborn 天生的；先天的

inbreeding /ˈɪnbriːdɪŋ/ noun breeding from closely related people or animals 近亲繁殖；同系交配

inbuilt /'ɪnbɪlt/ **adjective** existing as an original or important part 固有的；核心的

Inc. /ɪŋk/ **abbreviation** N. Amer.【北美】 Incorporated 公司

incalculable /ɪn'kælkjʊləbl/ **adjective** too great to be calculated or estimated 无法计算的；不可估量的

incandescent /ˌɪnkæn'desnt/ **adjective** glowing as a result of being heated 炽热的；白热的 ■ **incandescence** noun.

incantation /ˌɪnkæn'teɪʃn/ **noun** a magic spell or charm 咒语；符咒 ■ **incantatory** adjective.

incapable /ɪn'keɪpəbl/ **adjective** 1 (**incapable of**) not able to do something 无能力的；不能胜任的 2 not able to look after yourself 不能自理的

incapacitate /ˌɪnkə'pæsɪteɪt/ **verb** (**incapacitates, incapacitating, incapacitated**) prevent from working in a normal way 使无法正常工作 ■ **incapacitation** noun.

incapacity /ˌɪnkə'pæsəti/ **noun** (plural **incapacities**) inability to do something 无能力

incarcerate /ɪn'kɑːsəreɪt/ **verb** (**incarcerates, incarcerating, incarcerated**) imprison 监禁；关押 ■ **incarceration** noun.

incarnate /ɪn'kɑːnət/ **adjective** in human form 人形的；拟人化的

incarnation /ˌɪnkɑː'neɪʃn/ **noun** 1 a god, spirit, or quality in human form (神，精神或品质的)化身 2 (**the Incarnation**) (in Christian belief) God taking human form as Jesus (基督教信仰中的)道成肉身(指上帝化身为耶稣)

incautious /ɪn'kɔːʃəs/ **adjective** not concerned about possible problems 不慎重的；鲁莽的

incendiary /ɪn'sendiəri/ **adjective** 1 (of a bomb) designed to cause fires (炸弹)能引起燃烧的 2 tending to cause strong feelings 煽动性的；易引起冲突的 • **noun** (plural **incendiaries**) an incendiary bomb 燃烧弹

incense[1] /'ɪnsens/ **noun** a substance that produces a sweet smell when you burn it (焚烧时散发香气的)香

incense[2] /ɪn'sens/ **verb** (**incenses, incensing, incensed**) make very angry 使震怒；使大发雷霆

incentive /ɪn'sentɪv/ **noun** something that influences or encourages you to do something 动机；刺激；鼓励

inception /ɪn'sepʃn/ **noun** the beginning of an organization or activity (组织或活动的)开始，开端

incessant /ɪn'sesnt/ **adjective** never stopping 永不停止的；不断的 ■ **incessantly** adverb.

incest /'ɪnsest/ **noun** sex between people who are very closely related in a family 乱伦；血亲相奸

incestuous /ɪn'sestjuəs/ **adjective** 1 involving incest 乱伦的 2 involving a group of people who are very close and do not want to include others 小集团的；排外的

inch /ɪntʃ/ **noun** 1 a unit of length equal to one twelfth of a foot (2.54 cm) 英寸(等于 1/12 英尺，合 2.54 厘米) 2 a very small amount or distance (数量或距离)一点儿，少许 • **verb** move along slowly and carefully 小心翼翼地移动；缓慢移动

incidence /'ɪnsɪdəns/ **noun** 1 the extent to which something happens 发生率 2 Physics【物理】the meeting of a line or ray with a surface 入射

incident /'ɪnsɪdənt/ **noun** 1 something that happens 事件 2 a violent event 暴力事件

incidental /ˌɪnsɪ'dentl/ **adjective** 1 occurring in connection with something else 伴随…发生的；由…引起的 2 relatively unimportant 相对次要的；附带的 □ **incidental**

music background music in a film or play (电影或戏剧的)配乐,背景音乐 ■ **incidentally** adverb.

incinerate /ɪnˈsɪnəreɪt/ verb (**incinerates, incinerating, incinerated**) destroy by burning 烧毁;焚毁 ■ **incineration** noun.

incinerator /ɪnˈsɪnəreɪtə(r)/ noun a device for burning rubbish (垃圾)焚化炉

incipient /ɪnˈsɪpiənt/ adjective beginning to happen or develop 刚出现的;早期的

incise /ɪnˈsaɪz/ verb (**incises, incising, incised**) mark a surface by cutting into it (在表面)切,割,刻

incision /ɪnˈsɪʒn/ noun 1 a cut made as part of a surgical operation (外科手术中的)切口 2 the action of cutting into something 切入;切开

incisive /ɪnˈsaɪsɪv/ adjective 1 showing clear thought and good understanding 锐利的;深刻的 2 quick and direct 干脆的;直截了当的

incisor /ɪnˈsaɪzə(r)/ noun a narrow-edged tooth at the front of the mouth 切牙;门齿

incite /ɪnˈsaɪt/ verb (**incites, inciting, incited**) encourage someone to do something violent or unlawful 煽动,教唆(某人) ■ **incitement** noun.

incivility /ˌɪnsəˈvɪləti/ noun rude speech or behaviour 粗鲁的言语;无礼的举动

inclement /ɪnˈklemənt/ adjective (of the weather) unpleasantly cold or wet (天气)严寒的,极潮湿的 ■ **inclemency** noun.

inclination /ˌɪnklɪˈneɪʃn/ noun 1 a tendency to do things in a particular way 倾向;意向 2 (**inclination for** or **to do**) an interest in or liking for 兴趣;爱好 3 a slope or slant 斜坡;斜面

incline verb /ɪnˈklaɪn/ (**inclines, inclining, inclined**) 1 (**incline to** or **be inclined to**) tend to do or think in a particular way 倾向于;乐于 2 lean or bend 倾斜;曲身;弯腰 ● noun /ˈɪnklaɪn/ a slope 斜坡

include /ɪnˈkluːd/ verb (**includes, including, included**) 1 have something as part of a whole 包括;包含 2 make part of a whole 使成为一部分;把…列为一部分

including /ɪnˈkluːdɪŋ/ preposition having as part of the whole 包括

inclusion /ɪnˈkluːʒn/ noun 1 the act of including 包括;包含 2 a person or thing that is included 包括在内的人(或物)

inclusive /ɪnˈkluːsɪv/ adjective 1 including everything expected or required 包括的;包含的 2 between the limits stated 包括界限的

incognito /ˌɪnkɒɡˈniːtəʊ/ adjective & adverb having your true identity concealed 隐姓埋名的(地)

incoherent /ˌɪnkəʊˈhɪərənt/ adjective 1 hard to understand; not clear 难理解的;不清楚的 2 not logical or well organized 不合逻辑的;无条理的 ■ **incoherence** noun **incoherently** adverb.

incombustible /ˌɪnkəmˈbʌstəbl/ adjective (of a material) that does not burn (材料)不燃(烧)的

income /ˈɪnkʌm/ noun money received for work or from investments 收入;收益 □ **income tax** tax that must be paid on personal income 所得税

incomer /ˈɪnkʌmə(r)/ noun Brit. 【英】 a person who has come to live in an area in which they have not grown up 新迁居者;移民

incoming /ˈɪnkʌmɪŋ/ adjective 1 coming in or arriving 进来的;正来临的 2 (of a public official) having just been chosen to replace someone (政府官员)新任的,继任的

incommensurable /ˌɪnkəˈmenʃərəbl/ adjective not able to be compared 不能比较的;无法相比的

incommode /ˌɪnkəˈməʊd/ verb

(**incommodes, incommoding, incommoded**) formal【正式】cause someone difficulties or problems 给…带来不便；妨碍

incommunicado /ˌɪnkəˌmjuːmɪˈkɑːdəʊ/ **adjective & adverb** not able to communicate with other people 不能与他人接触(的)

incomparable /ɪnˈkɒmprəbl/ **adjective** so good that nothing can be compared to it 无与伦比的；无双的 ■ **incomparably** adverb.

incompatible /ˌɪnkəmˈpætəbl/ **adjective 1** (of two things) not able to exist or be used together (两物)不相容的，不兼容的 **2** (of two people) unable to live or work together without disagreeing (两人)无法融洽相处的，合不来的 ■ **incompatibility** noun.

incompetent /ɪnˈkɒmpɪtənt/ **adjective** not having the skill to do something well 不胜任的；无能力的 ■ **incompetence** noun **incompetently** adverb.

incomplete /ˌɪnkəmˈpliːt/ **adjective** not complete 不完全的；不完整的 ■ **incompletely** adverb.

incomprehensible /ɪnˌkɒmprɪˈhensəbl/ **adjective** not able to be understood 无法理解的，难于领悟的 ■ **incomprehension** noun.

inconceivable /ˌɪnkənˈsiːvəbl/ **adjective** not able to be imagined or believed 无法想象的，不可思议的 ■ **inconceivably** adverb.

inconclusive /ˌɪnkənˈkluːsɪv/ **adjective** not leading to a firm conclusion 非结论性的；非决定性的 ■ **inconclusively** adverb.

incongruous /ɪnˈkɒŋɡruəs/ **adjective** out of place 不适当的，不相称的 ■ **incongruity** noun **incongruously** adverb.

inconsequential /ɪnˌkɒnsɪˈkwenʃl/ **adjective** not important 不重要的；琐屑的 ■ **inconsequentially** adverb.

inconsiderable /ˌɪnkənˈsɪdərəbl/ **adjective** small in size or amount 小的；微不足道的

inconsiderate /ˌɪnkənˈsɪdərət/ **adjective** not thinking about other people's feelings 不体谅人的；考虑不周的

inconsistent /ˌɪnkənˈsɪstənt/ **adjective 1** having parts that contradict each other 矛盾的；不一致的 **2** (**inconsistent with**) not in keeping with 与…不一致的；与…不协调的 ■ **inconsistency** noun (plural **inconsistencies**).

inconsolable /ˌɪnkənˈsəʊləbl/ **adjective** not able to be comforted 无法安慰的；不能慰藉的

inconspicuous /ˌɪnkənˈspɪkjuəs/ **adjective** not noticeable 不显眼的，不引人注目的 ■ **inconspicuously** adverb.

inconstant /ɪnˈkɒnstənt/ **adjective 1** formal【正式】not faithful or dependable 不忠实的；不可靠的 **2** frequently changing 多变的；不定的

incontestable /ˌɪnkənˈtestəbl/ **adjective** not able to be disputed 无可争辩的

incontinent /ɪnˈkɒntɪnənt/ **adjective 1** unable to control your bladder or bowels (大小便)失禁的 **2** lacking self-control 缺乏自制的；不受控制的 ■ **incontinence** noun.

incontrovertible /ˌɪnkɒntrəˈvɜːtəbl/ **adjective** not able to be denied or disputed 不可否认的；无可辩驳的 ■ **incontrovertibly** adverb.

inconvenience /ˌɪnkənˈviːnɪəns/ **noun** slight trouble or difficulty 小麻烦，小困难 • **verb** (**inconveniences, inconveniencing, inconvenienced**) cause someone inconvenience 给(某人)带来不便 ■ **inconvenient** adjective **inconveniently** adverb.

incorporate /ɪnˈkɔːpəreɪt/ **verb** (**incorporates, incorporating, incorporated**) include something as part of a whole 使成为一部分；把…包括在内 ■ **incorporation** noun.

incorporated /ɪnˈkɔːpəreɪtɪd/ **adjective** (of a company) formed into a legal corporation (公司)组成法人组织的

incorporeal /ˌɪnkɔːˈpɔːriəl/ **adjective** without a body or form 无形体的；无形的

incorrect /ˌɪnkəˈrekt/ **adjective** not true or accurate 不真实的；不正确的；不准确的 ■ **incorrectly** adverb.

incorrigible /ɪnˈkɒrɪdʒəbl/ **adjective** having bad habits that cannot be changed (坏习惯)屡教不改的，无法改变的

incorruptible /ˌɪnkəˈrʌptəbl/ **adjective** too honest to be corrupted by taking bribes 廉洁的；不接受贿赂的

increase verb /ɪnˈkriːs/ (**increases, increasing, increased**) make or become greater in size, amount, or strength (使)增大，(使)增多，使增长 • noun /ˈɪnkriːs/ a rise in amount, size, or strength 增大；增多；增长

increasingly /ɪnˈkriːsɪŋli/ **adverb** more and more 渐增地；越来越多地

incredible /ɪnˈkredəbl/ **adjective 1** impossible or hard to believe 无法相信的，难以置信的 **2** informal 【非正式】very good 极好的 ■ **incredibly** adverb.

incredulity /ˌɪnkrəˈdjuːləti/ **noun** unwillingness or inability to believe something 不轻信；不相信

incredulous /ɪnˈkredjələs/ **adjective** unwilling or unable to believe something 不轻信的，不相信的 ■ **incredulously** adverb.

increment /ˈɪŋkrəmənt/ **noun** an increase in a number or amount 增加量；增加额 ■ **incremental** adjective.

incriminate /ɪnˈkrɪmɪneɪt/ **verb** (**incriminates, incriminating, incriminated**) make it look as though someone has done something wrong or illegal 使显得有罪；牵连；连累 ■ **in-**crimination noun.

incubate /ˈɪŋkjubeɪt/ **verb** (**incubates, incubating, incubated**) **1** (of a bird) sit on eggs to keep them warm so that they hatch (鸟)孵(卵) **2** keep bacteria and cells at a suitable temperature so that they develop 培养(细菌、细胞) **3** (of an infectious disease) develop slowly without obvious signs (传染病)潜伏 ■ **incubation** noun **incubator** noun.

inculcate /ˈɪnkʌlkeɪt/ **verb** (**inculcates, inculcating, inculcated**) fix ideas in someone's mind by repeating them 反复灌输；谆谆教诲 ■ **inculcation** noun.

incumbency /ɪnˈkʌmbənsi/ **noun** (plural **incumbencies**) the period during which an official position is held 任期

incumbent /ɪnˈkʌmbənt/ **adjective 1** (**incumbent on**) necessary for someone as a duty (某人)有职责的，不能推卸的 **2** currently holding an official position 现任的；在职的 • noun the holder of an official position 现任者；在职者

incur /ɪnˈkɜː(r)/ **verb** (**incurs, incurring, incurred**) make something unwelcome happen 招致；引起

incurable /ɪnˈkjuərəbl/ **adjective** not able to be cured 无法治愈的；无可救治的 ■ **incurably** adverb.

incurious /ɪnˈkjuəriəs/ **adjective** not curious 不好奇的；不感兴趣的

incursion /ɪnˈkɜːʃn/ **noun** a sudden invasion or attack 入侵；侵犯；袭击

indebted /ɪnˈdetɪd/ **adjective 1** feeling grateful to someone 感谢的；感激的 **2** owing money 欠债的

indecent /ɪnˈdiːsnt/ **adjective 1** causing offence by showing too much of the body or involving sex 下流的；猥亵的 **2** not appropriate 不当的；不合适的 ■ **indecency** noun **indecently** adverb.

indecipherable /ˌɪndɪˈsaɪfrəbl/

adjective not able to be read or understood 无法辨认的；无法理解的

indecisive /ˌɪndɪˈsaɪsɪv/ **adjective 1** not able to make decisions quickly 优柔寡断的；无决断力的 **2** not settling an issue 非决定性的；不解决问题的 ■ **indecision** noun **indecisively** adverb **indecisiveness** noun.

indeed /ɪnˈdiːd/ **adverb 1** used to emphasize a statement 确实，的确 **2** used to introduce a further and stronger point (用于进一步引出更有力的论点)实际上，其实

indefatigable /ˌɪndɪˈfætɪɡəbl/ **adjective** never tiring 不倦的；不懈的

indefensible /ˌɪndɪˈfensəbl/ **adjective** not able to be justified or defended 站不住脚的；无法防御的

indefinable /ˌɪndɪˈfaɪnəbl/ **adjective** not able to be defined or described exactly 难下定义的；不能精确描述的

indefinite /ɪnˈdefɪnət/ **adjective 1** not clearly stated, seen, or heard; vague 表达不明确的；模糊的，不清楚的 **2** lasting for an unknown length of time (持续时间)不确定的，无限期的 □ **indefinite article** Grammar【语法】 the word *a* or *an* 不定冠词 ■ **indefinitely** adverb.

indelible /ɪnˈdeləbl/ **adjective 1** (of ink or a mark) unable to be removed (墨水或印记)无法消除的 **2** unable to be forgotten 不能忘记的 ■ **indelibly** adverb.

indelicate /ɪnˈdelɪkət/ **adjective** likely to be thought rude or embarrassing 粗俗的；不得体的

indemnify /ɪnˈdemnɪfaɪ/ **verb** (**indemnifies, indemnifying, indemnified**) **1** pay money to someone to compensate for harm or loss 赔偿；补偿 **2** insure someone against legal responsibility for their actions 使免负法律责任；保障

indemnity /ɪnˈdemnəti/ **noun** (plural **indemnities**) **1** insurance against legal responsibility for your actions

免罚；免罪 **2** a sum of money paid to compensate for damage or loss 赔款；补偿金

indent verb /ɪnˈdent/ **1** form hollows or notches in 造成凹痕于 **2** begin a line of writing further from the margin than the other lines 将(书写的一行)缩格;缩排 • noun /ˈɪndent/ Brit.【英】an official order for goods 订货单 ■ **indentation** noun.

indenture /ɪnˈdentʃə(r)/ **noun** a formal agreement or contract 契约

independent /ˌɪndɪˈpendənt/ **adjective 1** free from the control or influence of others 不受控制的；不受影响的 **2** (of a country) self-governing (国家)自治的，独立的 **3** having or earning enough money to support yourself 经济独立的；自食其力的 **4** not connected with another; separate 单独的；分开的 • noun an independent person or body 独立自主者；自立者；独立机构 ■ **independence** noun **independently** adverb.

> ✔ 拼写指南 -*ent*, not -*ant*: independ*ent*. independent 中 -ent 不要拼作 -ant。

indescribable /ˌɪndɪˈskraɪbəbl/ **adjective** too extreme or unusual to be described 难以描述的；无法形容的 ■ **indescribably** adverb.

indestructible /ˌɪndɪˈstrʌktəbl/ **adjective** not able to be destroyed 毁灭不了的；不可摧毁的

indeterminate /ˌɪndɪˈtɜːmɪnət/ **adjective** not certain; vague 不确定的；模糊的

index /ˈɪndeks/ **noun** (plural **indexes** or **indices** /ˈɪndɪsiːz/) **1** a list of names or subjects referred to in a book, arranged in alphabetical order (书中人名、主题等的)索引 **2** an alphabetical list or catalogue of books or documents (书或文件的)索引，列表 **3** a sign or measure of something 标志；指标；量度 • **verb**

record in or provide with an index 将…编入索引；为…编索引 □ **index finger** the forefinger 食指

Indian /'ɪndɪən/ **noun 1** a person from India 印第安人 **2** an American Indian 印第安人 • **adjective 1** relating to India 印度的 **2** relating to American Indians 印第安人的 □ **Indian ink** deep black ink used in drawing 墨；墨汁 **Indian summer** a period of dry, warm weather in late autumn 印第安夏(深秋干燥、暖和的一段时间)

indicate /'ɪndɪkeɪt/ **verb** (**indicates, indicating, indicated**) **1** point something out 指出；指示 **2** be a sign of 表明；象征；暗示 **3** mention briefly 简述 **4** (**be indicated**) formal 【正式】be necessary or recommended 有必要；应该 ■ **indication** noun.

indicative /ɪn'dɪkətɪv/ **adjective 1** acting as a sign 暗示的；指示的 **2** Grammar 【语法】(of a verb) expressing a simple statement of fact (e.g. *she left*) (动词形式)陈述的，直陈的

indicator /'ɪndɪkeɪtə(r)/ **noun 1** a thing that shows the state or level of something 指示物 **2** a light on a vehicle that flashes to show that it is about to turn left or right (车辆的)转向指示灯

indict /ɪn'daɪt/ **verb** formally accuse someone of a serious crime 起诉；指控 ■ **indictable** adjective.

indictment /ɪn'daɪtmənt/ **noun 1** a formal accusation that someone has committed a serious crime 起诉；指控 **2** an indication that something is bad and deserves to be condemned (事物的)腐败迹象

indifferent /ɪn'dɪfrənt/ **adjective 1** not interested in or caring about something 没有兴趣的；无同情心的 **2** not very good; mediocre 不太好的，一般的 ■ **indifference** noun **indifferently** adverb.

indigenous /ɪn'dɪdʒənəs/ **adjective**

belonging to a place; native 本地的；本土的

indigent /'ɪndɪdʒənt/ **adjective** poor; needy 贫穷的；困厄的

indigestible /ˌɪndɪ'dʒestəbl/ **adjective** difficult or impossible to digest 难以消化的；不能消化的

indigestion /ˌɪndɪ'dʒestʃən/ **noun** pain or discomfort caused by difficulty in digesting food 消化不良

indignant /ɪn'dɪgnənt/ **adjective** feeling or showing indignation 愤怒的；愤慨的 ■ **indignantly** adverb.

indignation /ˌɪndɪg'neɪʃn/ **noun** anger caused by something that you consider to be unfair 愤怒；义愤

indignity /ɪn'dɪgnəti/ **noun** (plural **indignities**) a thing that causes you to feel ashamed or embarrassed 侮辱

indigo /'ɪndɪgəʊ/ **noun** a dark blue colour or dye 靛蓝；靛青

indirect /ˌɪndə'rekt/ **adjective 1** not going in a straight line 不走直线的 **2** not saying something in a straightforward way 间接的 **3** happening as a secondary effect or consequence 间接发生的；间接影响的 □ **indirect speech** reported speech 间接引语 ■ **indirectly** adverb.

indiscipline /ɪn'dɪsɪplɪn/ **noun** lack of discipline 无纪律

indiscreet /ˌɪndɪ'skri:t/ **adjective** too ready to reveal things that should remain secret or private 言行失检的；(说话)欠考虑的；轻率的 ■ **indiscreetly** adverb.

indiscretion /ˌɪndɪ'skreʃn/ **noun 1** indiscreet behaviour 有失检点的行为 **2** an indiscreet act or remark 轻率的言行

indiscriminate /ˌɪndɪ'skrɪmɪnət/ **adjective** done or acting without careful judgement 行事欠考虑的；随意的 ■ **indiscriminately** adverb.

indispensable /ˌɪndɪ'spensəbl/ **adjective** absolutely necessary 必不可少的；必要的

✔ 拼写指南 -able, not -ible: indispens*able*. indispensable 中 -able 不要拼作 -ible。

indisposed /ˌɪndɪ'spəʊzd/ **adjective 1** slightly unwell 不舒服的 **2** unwilling 不情愿的；不愿意的

indisposition /ˌɪndɪspə'zɪʃn/ **noun** a slight illness 小病；微恙

indisputable /ˌɪndɪ'spjuːtəbl/ **adjective** unable to be challenged or denied 无可争辩的；不容否认的 ■ **disputably** adverb.

indissoluble /ˌɪndɪ'sɒljəbl/ **adjective** unable to be destroyed; lasting 无法毁损的；牢不可破的；持久的

indistinct /ˌɪndɪ'stɪŋkt/ **adjective** not clear or sharply defined 不清楚的；模糊的 ■ **indistinctly** adverb.

indistinguishable /ˌɪndɪ'stɪŋgwɪʃəbl/ **adjective** not able to be distinguished 无法辨认的；不能区别的 ■ **indistinguishably** adverb.

individual /ˌɪndɪ'vɪdʒuəl/ **adjective 1** considered separately; single 个别的；单独的 **2** having to do with one particular person 一个人的；个人的 **3** striking or unusual; original 有个性的；独特的 • **noun 1** a single person or item as distinct from a group 个人；个体 **2** a distinctive or original person 与众不同的人；特立独行者 ■ **individually** adverb.

individualism /ˌɪndɪ'vɪdʒuəlɪzm/ **noun 1** the quality of doing things in your own way; independence 独立性；独创性 **2** the belief that individual people should have freedom of action 个人主义 ■ **individualist** noun & adjective **individualistic** adjective.

individuality /ˌɪndɪvɪdʒu'æləti/ **noun** the quality or character of a person or thing that makes them different from other people or things 个性；独特性

individualize or **individualise** /ˌɪndɪ'vɪdʒuəlaɪz/ **verb** (individu-

dualizes, individualizing, individualized) give something an individual character 使个性化

indivisible /ˌɪndɪ'vɪzəbl/ **adjective** unable to be divided or separated 不能分开的；不可分割的

indoctrinate /ɪn'dɒktrɪneɪt/ **verb** (indoctrinates, indoctrinating, indoctrinated) force someone to accept a set of beliefs 向(某人)强行灌输(信仰) ■ **indoctrination** noun.

Indo-European /ˌɪndəʊ jʊərə'piːən/ **noun** the family of languages spoken over most of Europe and Asia as far as northern India 印欧语系 • **adjective** relating to Indo-European 印欧语系的

indolent /'ɪndələnt/ **adjective** lazy 懒惰的 ■ **indolence** noun.

indomitable /ɪn'dɒmɪtəbl/ **adjective** impossible to defeat or subdue 不可战胜的；不屈不挠的

Indonesian /ˌɪndəʊ'niːʒən/ **noun 1** a person from Indonesia 印度尼西亚人 **2** the group of languages spoken in Indonesia 印度尼西亚语 • **adjective** relating to Indonesia 印度尼西亚的

indoor /'ɪndɔː(r)/ **adjective** situated, done, or used inside a building 室内的；屋内的 • **adverb** (indoors) into or inside a building 到室内；在屋里

indubitable /ɪn'djuːbɪtəbl/ **adjective** impossible to doubt; certain 不容置疑的；明确无误的 ■ **indubitably** adverb.

induce /ɪn'djuːs/ **verb** (induces, inducing, induced) **1** persuade or influence someone to do something 劝说；劝诱 **2** bring about or cause 引起；导致 **3** make a woman begin to give birth to her baby by means of special drugs (用特殊药物)为(产妇)引产

inducement /ɪn'djuːsmənt/ **noun** a thing that persuades someone to do something 引诱物(物)

induct /ɪn'dʌkt/ **verb** formally

admit someone to an organization or establish them in a position of authority 使正式就职;使正式加入

inductance /ɪn'dʌktəns/ **noun** a process by which a change in the current of an electric circuit produces an electromotive force 电感; 感应

induction /ɪn'dʌkʃn/ **noun 1** introduction to a post or organization 就职;入会 **2** the action of inducing 引起;招致 **3** a method of reasoning in which a general rule or conclusion is drawn from particular facts or examples 归纳论证 **4** the passing of electricity or magnetism from one object to another without them touching (电磁)感应 ■ **inductive** adjective.

indulge /ɪn'dʌldʒ/ **verb** (**indulges, indulging, indulged**) **1** (**indulge in**) allow yourself to do something that you enjoy 沉迷于;沉溺于 **2** satisfy a desire or interest 满足(欲望或兴趣) **3** allow someone to do or have whatever they wish 迁就;放纵

indulgence /ɪn'dʌldʒəns/ **noun 1** the action of indulging in something 沉迷;沉溺 **2** a thing that is indulged in; a luxury 嗜好;爱好;享受品 **3** willingness to tolerate someone's faults 迁就;放纵

indulgent /ɪn'dʌldʒənt/ **adjective** allowing someone to do or have whatever they want or overlooking their faults 迁就的;溺爱的;纵容的 ■ **indulgently** adverb.

industrial /ɪn'dʌstriəl/ **adjective** having to do with industry 工业的; 产业的 □ **industrial action** Brit. 【英】a strike or other action taken by workers as a protest 劳工行动; 罢工 **industrial estate** Brit. 【英】an area of land developed as a site for factories 工业区 ■ **industrially** adverb.

industrialist /ɪn'dʌstriəlɪst/ **noun** a person who owns or controls a large

factory or manufacturing business 工厂主;工业家;实业家

industrialize or **industrialise** /ɪn'dʌstriəlaɪz/ **verb** (**industrializes, industrializing, industrialized**) develop industries in a country or region on a wide scale (使)工业化 ■ **industrialization** noun.

industrious /ɪn'dʌstriəs/ **adjective** hard-working 勤劳的;勤奋的 ■ **industriously** adverb.

industry /'ɪndəstri/ **noun** (plural **industries**) **1** the manufacture of goods in factories 工业 **2** a branch of economic or commercial activity 行业;产业 **3** hard work 勤劳;勤奋

inebriated /ɪ'niːbrieɪtɪd/ **adjective** drunk 喝醉的 ■ **inebriation** noun.

inedible /ɪn'edəbl/ **adjective** not fit for eating 不宜食用的

ineffable /ɪn'efəbl/ **adjective** too great or extreme to be expressed in words 难用语言表达的

ineffective /ˌɪnɪ'fektɪv/ **adjective** not having any effect or achieving what you want 不起作用的;无效果的 ■ **ineffectively** adverb.

ineffectual /ˌɪnɪ'fektʃuəl/ **adjective 1** ineffective 无效的 **2** not forceful enough to do something well 无能的 ■ **ineffectually** adverb.

inefficient /ˌɪnɪ'fɪʃnt/ **adjective** failing to make the best use of time or resources 效率不高的;利用率不高的 ■ **inefficiency** noun **inefficiently** adverb.

inelegant /ɪn'elɪɡənt/ **adjective** not elegant or graceful 粗俗的;不雅的

ineligible /ɪn'elɪdʒəbl/ **adjective** not qualified to have or do something 无资格的;不胜任的;不适合的

ineluctable /ˌɪnɪ'lʌktəbl/ **adjective** rare unable to be resisted or avoided 不可抗拒的;不可避免的

inept /ɪ'nept/ **adjective** lacking skill 缺乏技巧的;笨拙的 ■ **ineptitude** noun **ineptly** adverb.

inequality /ˌɪnɪˈkwɒləti/ noun (plural **inequalities**) lack of equality 不平等；不公允

inequitable /ɪnˈekwɪtəbl/ adjective unfair; unjust 不公平的；不公正的

inequity /ɪnˈekwəti/ noun (plural **inequities**) lack of fairness or justice 不公平；不公正

ineradicable /ˌɪnɪˈrædɪkəbl/ adjective unable to be rooted out or destroyed 无法根除的；不能消除的

inert /ɪnˈɜːt/ adjective **1** lacking the ability or strength to move or act 不能动的；无活动能力的 **2** without active chemical properties (化学特性)惰性的，不活泼的

inertia /ɪnˈɜːʃə/ noun **1** a tendency to do nothing or to remain unchanged 惰性，保守 **2** Physics【物理】a property by which matter remains still or continues moving unless acted on by an external force 惯性

inescapable /ˌɪnɪˈskeɪpəbl/ adjective unable to be avoided or denied 不可避免的；不容否认的

inessential /ˌɪnɪˈsenʃl/ adjective not absolutely necessary 非必要的；可有可无的

inestimable /ɪnˈestɪməbl/ adjective too great to be measured 难以计量的；无法估量的

inevitable /ɪnˈevɪtəbl/ adjective certain to happen; unavoidable 必定发生的；不可避免的 ■ **inevitability** noun **inevitably** adverb.

inexact /ˌɪnɪɡˈzækt/ adjective not quite accurate 不精确的

inexcusable /ˌɪnɪkˈskjuːzəbl/ adjective too bad to be justified or tolerated 无可原谅的；不可容忍的

inexhaustible /ˌɪnɪɡˈzɔːstəbl/ adjective (of a supply) never ending because available in unlimited quantities (供给)用不完的，无穷尽的

inexorable /ɪnˈeksərəbl/ adjective **1** impossible to stop or prevent 无法阻止的；不可阻挡的 **2** unable to be

persuaded 劝不动的；无动于衷的 ■ **inexorably** adverb.

inexpensive /ˌɪnɪkˈspensɪv/ adjective not costing a lot of money 不贵的；廉价的

inexperience /ˌɪnɪkˈspɪəriəns/ noun lack of experience 缺乏经验 ■ **inexperienced** adjective.

inexpert /ɪnˈekspɜːt/ adjective lacking skill or knowledge in a particular field 不熟练的；非内行的

inexplicable /ˌɪnɪkˈsplɪkəbl/ adjective unable to be explained 无法解释的 ■ **inexplicably** adverb.

inexpressive /ˌɪnɪkˈspresɪv/ adjective showing no feelings 无表情的，不露感情的

in extremis /ˌɪn ɪkˈstriːmɪs/ adverb **1** in a very difficult situation 在极困难情况下；在危急关头 **2** at the point of death 在弥留之际

inextricable /ˌɪnɪkˈstrɪkəbl/ adjective impossible to untangle or separate 解不开的；分不开的 ■ **inextricably** adverb.

infallible /ɪnˈfæləbl/ adjective incapable of making mistakes or being wrong 不可能犯错的；一贯正确的 ■ **infallibility** noun **infallibly** adverb.

infamous /ˈɪnfəməs/ adjective well known for some bad quality or act 臭名昭著的；声名狼藉的 ■ **infamously** adverb **infamy** noun.

infancy /ˈɪnfənsi/ noun **1** the state or period of early childhood or babyhood 幼儿期 **2** an early stage of development (事物发展的)初期，早期

infant /ˈɪnfənt/ noun **1** a very young child or baby 幼儿；婴儿 **2** Brit.【英】a schoolchild between the ages of about four and seven (5 至 7 岁的)学童

infanticide /ɪnˈfæntɪsaɪd/ noun the killing of a child 杀婴(罪)

infantile /ˈɪnfəntaɪl/ adjective **1** relating to infants 婴幼儿的 **2** disapproving【贬】childish 孩子气的;幼稚的

infantry /ˈɪnfəntri/ **noun** soldiers who fight on foot 步兵(部队)

infatuate /ɪnˈfætʃueɪt/ **verb** (**be infatuated with**) have a strong but short-lived feeling of love for 对…着迷;热恋 ∎ **infatuation** noun.

infect /ɪnˈfekt/ **verb 1** pass a germ that causes disease to a person, animal, or plant 传染;使感染 **2** contaminate with something harmful 污染;施加不良影响

infection /ɪnˈfekʃn/ **noun 1** the process of infecting 传染;感染 **2** an infectious disease 传染病

infectious /ɪnˈfekʃəs/ **adjective 1** (of a disease or germ) able to be passed on through the environment (疾病或病菌)传染性的 **2** liable to spread infection 易传播疾病的 **3** likely to spread to or influence other people 易传播的,有感染力的 ∎ **infectiously** adverb.

infer /ɪnˈfɜː(r)/ **verb** (**infers**, **inferring**, **inferred**) work something out from the information you have available 推断;推定

> ! 注意 on the difference between the words **imply** and **infer**, see the note at **IMPLY**. 关于 imply 和 infer 的区别见词条 imply 处注释。

inference /ˈɪnfərəns/ **noun 1** a conclusion drawn from the information available to you 结论;推断结果 **2** the process of inferring 推断;推理

inferior /ɪnˈfɪəriə(r)/ **adjective** lower in quality or status 劣质的;差的,地位低的 • **noun** a person who is lower in status or less good at doing something 地位低的人;不如别人的人 ∎ **inferiority** noun.

infernal /ɪnˈfɜːnl/ **adjective 1** having to do with hell or the underworld 地狱的;阴间的 **2** informal【非正式】very annoying 极恼人的;极讨厌的

inferno /ɪnˈfɜːnəʊ/ **noun** (plural **infernos**) a large uncontrollable fire 无法控制的大火

infertile /ɪnˈfɜːtaɪl/ **adjective 1** unable to have babies or other young 不能生育的 **2** (of land) unable to produce crops or plants (土地)贫瘠的,不毛的 ∎ **infertility** noun.

infest /ɪnˈfest/ **verb** (especially of insects or rats) be present in large numbers so as to cause damage or disease (尤指昆虫或老鼠)群集于,大批出没于 ∎ **infestation** noun.

infidel /ˈɪnfɪdəl/ **noun** old use【旧】a person who has no religion or whose religion is not that of the majority 不信教者;异教徒;不信奉正统宗教者

infidelity /ˌɪnfɪˈdeləti/ **noun** (plural **infidelities**) the action or state of not being faithful to your sexual partner (对性伴侣的)不忠行为,不忠

infighting /ˈɪnfaɪtɪŋ/ **noun** conflict within a group or organization (集团或组织内的)争斗,内讧

infiltrate /ˈɪnfɪltreɪt/ **verb** enter or gain access to an organization or place secretly and gradually 潜入,渗入 ∎ **infiltration** noun **infiltrator** noun.

infinite /ˈɪnfɪnət/ **adjective 1** having no limits and impossible to measure 无限的;无穷的 **2** very great in amount or degree (数量或程度)极大的 ∎ **infinitely** adverb.

infinitesimal /ˌɪnfɪnɪˈtesɪml/ **adjective** very small 极微小的;极少的 ∎ **infinitesimally** adverb.

infinitive /ɪnˈfɪnətɪv/ **noun** the basic form of a verb, normally occurring in English with the word **to** (as in **to see**, **to ask**) (动词的)原形,不定式

infinity /ɪnˈfɪnəti/ **noun** (plural **infinities**) **1** the state or quality of being infinite 无限;无穷 **2** very great number or amount 无穷大(的数);无限大(的量)

infirm /ɪnˈfɜːm/ **adjective** physically

weak 体弱的；虚弱的

infirmary /ɪnˈfɜːməri/ **noun** (plural **infirmaries**) a place where sick people are cared for 医院；医务室

infirmity /ɪnˈfɜːməti/ **noun** (plural **infirmities**) physical or mental weakness 虚弱；体弱；意志薄弱

inflame /ɪnˈfleɪm/ **verb** (**inflames**, **inflaming**, **inflamed**) 1 make someone feel something passionately 激起(某人)的强烈情感；使激动 2 make a difficult situation worse 使恶化；加剧 3 (**inflamed**) (of a part of the body) red, swollen, and hot as a result of infection or injury (身体部位)红肿的，发炎的

inflammable /ɪnˈflæməbl/ **adjective** easily set on fire 易燃的

!注意 inflammable and flammable both mean 'easily set on fire'. It's safer to use flammable, however, because inflammable is sometimes thought to mean 'non-flammable'. inflammable 和 flammable 都表示"易燃的"，但最好使用 flammable，因为 inflammable 有时会使人误以为该词意为"不可燃的"。

inflammation /ˌɪnfləˈmeɪʃn/ **noun** a condition in which an area of the skin is red, swollen, and hot (皮肤局部的)炎症，发炎

inflammatory /ɪnˈflæmətri/ **adjective** 1 making people feel angry 使人激愤的 2 relating to or causing inflammation 发炎的；引起炎症的

inflatable /ɪnˈfleɪtəbl/ **adjective** capable of being inflated 可充气的，可充气的 ▪ **noun** an inflatable plastic or rubber boat 充气小艇

inflate /ɪnˈfleɪt/ **verb** (**inflates**, **inflating**, **inflated**) 1 expand something by filling it with air or gas 使充气；使膨胀 2 increase the cost or price of something by a large amount 使成本上涨；使涨价；使(通

贷)膨胀 3 (**inflated**) exaggerated 夸张的；言过其实的

inflation /ɪnˈfleɪʃn/ **noun** 1 the action of inflating 充气；膨胀 2 a general increase in prices and fall in the value of money 物价上涨；通货膨胀 ▪ **inflationary** adjective.

inflect /ɪnˈflekt/ **verb** Grammar 【语法】 (of a word) be changed by inflection (词)产生屈折变化 2 vary the tone or pitch of your voice 使(语调)抑扬顿挫

inflection /ɪnˈflekʃn/ **noun** 1 Grammar 【语法】a change in the form of a word to show its grammatical function, number, or gender 词的屈折变化；屈折形式 2 a variation in the tone or pitch of a voice (语调的)抑扬变化

inflexible /ɪnˈfleksəbl/ **adjective** 1 not able to be altered or adapted 不可改变的；缺乏弹性的 2 unwilling to change or compromise 死板的，不愿妥协的 3 not able to be bent 不可弯曲的；刚性的 ▪ **inflexibility** noun.

inflict /ɪnˈflɪkt/ **verb** (**inflict something on**) make someone experience something unpleasant or painful 使遭受；使承受 ▪ **infliction** noun.

influence /ˈɪnfluəns/ **noun** 1 the power or ability to affect someone's beliefs or actions 影响(力)；作用 2 a person or thing with such ability or power 有影响的人(或物) 3 the power arising out of status, contacts, or wealth (地位、社会关系或财富带来的)影响力 ▪ **verb** (**influences**, **influencing**, **influenced**) have an influence on 施加影响于；对…起作用

influential /ˌɪnfluˈenʃl/ **adjective** having great influence 有很大影响的

influenza /ˌɪnfluˈenzə/ **noun** a disease spread by a virus and causing fever, aching, and catarrh 流行性感冒

influx /ˈɪnflʌks/ **noun** the arrival or entry of large numbers of people or things (人或事物的)大量到来，涌入，流入

inform /ɪnˈfɔːm/ **verb 1** give facts or information to 通知；告知 **2** (**inform on**) give information about someone's involvement in a crime to the police 告发；检举

informal /ɪnˈfɔːml/ **adjective 1** relaxed and friendly, and not following strict rules of behaviour 放松的；友好的；不拘礼节的 **2** (of clothes) suitable for wearing when relaxing (衣服)休闲风格的，随便的 **3** (of language) used in everyday speech and writing, rather than official contexts (语言)日常使用的，非正式的 ■ **informality** noun **informally** adverb.

informant /ɪnˈfɔːmənt/ **noun** a person who gives information to another 信息提供者；提供情报者

information /ˌɪnfəˈmeɪʃn/ **noun** facts or details supplied to or learned by someone 信息；情报；消息；资料 □ **information technology** the use of computers and telecommunications for storing, retrieving, and sending information 信息技术

informative /ɪnˈfɔːmətɪv/ **adjective** providing useful information 提供有用信息的

informed /ɪnˈfɔːmd/ **adjective 1** having or showing knowledge 有学问的；有见识的 **2** (of a judgement) based on a sound understanding of the facts (判断)以事实为依据的

informer /ɪnˈfɔːmə(r)/ **noun** a person who informs on another person to the police 告密者；线人

infraction /ɪnˈfrækʃn/ **noun** a breaking of a law or agreement 违法；违约

infra dig /ˌɪnfrə ˈdɪg/ **adjective** informal 【非正式】beneath your dignity 有失尊严的；有失身份的

infrared /ˌɪnfrəˈred/ **adjective** (of electromagnetic radiation) having a wavelength just greater than that of red light (电磁辐射)红外线的

infrastructure /ˈɪnfrəstrʌktʃə(r)/ **noun** the basic things (e.g. buildings, roads, power supplies) needed for the operation of a society or enterprise (社会或企业的)基础设施

infrequent /ɪnˈfriːkwənt/ **adjective** not happening often 不常发生的；罕见的 ■ **infrequency** noun **infrequently** adverb.

infringe /ɪnˈfrɪndʒ/ **verb 1** break a law or agreement 违反(法律或协议) **2** restrict a right or privilege 限制(权利或特权) ■ **infringement** noun.

infuriate /ɪnˈfjʊərieɪt/ **verb** (**infuriates, infuriating, infuriated**) make someone angry 使愤怒；激怒 ■ **infuriating** adjective.

infuse /ɪnˈfjuːz/ **verb** (**infuses, infusing, infused**) **1** spread throughout something 使弥漫；充满 **2** soak tea or herbs to extract the flavour or healing properties 泡(茶)；泡(草药)

infusion /ɪnˈfjuːʒn/ **noun 1** a drink prepared by soaking tea or herbs 泡成的饮料；泡制的饮料 **2** the action of infusing 浸泡；泡制

ingenious /ɪnˈdʒiːniəs/ **adjective** clever, original, and inventive 聪明灵巧的；新颖独特的；善于发明创造的 ■ **ingeniously** adverb.

ingénue /ˈænʒeɪnjuː/ **noun** a naive young woman 天真少女

ingenuity /ˌɪndʒəˈnjuːəti/ **noun** the quality of being ingenious 聪明才智；心灵手巧

ingenuous /ɪnˈdʒenjuəs/ **adjective** innocent and unsuspecting 天真无邪的；单纯的；不城府的

ingest /ɪnˈdʒest/ **verb** take food or drink into the body by swallowing it 摄取；咽下(食物或饮料) ■ **ingestion** noun.

inglenook /ˈɪŋglnʊk/ **noun** a space on either side of a large fireplace 壁炉边

inglorious /ɪnˈglɔːrɪəs/ **adjective** not making you feel proud; rather shameful 羞耻的；不光彩的；丢脸的

ingoing /ˈɪngəʊɪŋ/ **adjective** going towards or into 迎来来的，进人的

ingot /ˈɪŋgət/ **noun** a rectangular block of steel, gold, or other metal (钢铁、金等金属的)锭，铸块

ingrained or **engrained** /ɪnˈgreɪnd/ **adjective 1** (of a habit or belief) firmly established (习惯或信仰)根深蒂固的 **2** (of dirt) deeply embedded (污垢)深嵌着的

ingratiate /ɪnˈgreɪʃɪeɪt/ **verb** (**ingratiates**, **ingratiating**, **ingratiated**) (**ingratiate yourself**) do things in order to make someone like you 讨好；巴结

ingratitude /ɪnˈgrætɪtjuːd/ **noun** a lack of appropriate gratitude 忘恩负义

ingredient /ɪnˈgriːdɪənt/ **noun 1** any of the substances that are combined to make a particular dish (做菜用的)原料，材料 **2** a component part or element 成分；要素

ingress /ˈɪngres/ **noun 1** the action of entering or coming in 进人 **2** a place or means of access 入口；进人方式

ingrown /ˈɪngrəʊn/ or **ingrowing** /ˈɪngrəʊɪŋ/ **adjective** (of a toenail) having grown into the flesh (脚趾甲)向内生长的，长入肉内的

inhabit /ɪnˈhæbɪt/ **verb** (**inhabits**, **inhabiting**, **inhabited**) live in or occupy 居住于；栖居于；占据 ■ **inhabitable** adjective.

inhabitant /ɪnˈhæbɪtənt/ **noun** a person or animal that lives in or occupies a place 居民；住户；(栖居于某处的)动物

inhale /ɪnˈheɪl/ **verb** (**inhales**, **inhaling**, **inhaled**) breathe in air, smoke, etc. 吸人(空气、烟等) ■ **inhalation** noun.

inhaler /ɪnˈheɪlə(r)/ **noun** a portable device used for inhaling a drug (药物)吸人器

inherent /ɪnˈhɪərənt/ **adjective** existing in something as a permanent or essential quality 固有的；内在的；生来就有的 ■ **inherently** adverb.

inherit /ɪnˈherɪt/ **verb** (**inherits**, **inheriting**, **inherited**) **1** receive money or property from someone when they die 继承(金钱或财产) **2** have a quality or characteristic passed on to you from your parents or ancestors 因遗传而获得(品质或性格) **3** be left with something previously belonging to someone else (从他人处)接受，接收

inheritance /ɪnˈherɪtəns/ **noun 1** a thing that is inherited 继承物；遗产 **2** the action of inheriting 继承

inhibit /ɪnˈhɪbɪt/ **verb** (**inhibits**, **inhibiting**, **inhibited**) **1** prevent or slow down a process 抑制；阻止 **2** make someone unable to act in a relaxed and natural way 使拘谨；使不自然

inhibition /ˌɪnhɪˈbɪʃn/ **noun** a feeling that makes you unable to act in a relaxed and natural way 拘谨；压抑

inhospitable /ˌɪnhɒˈspɪtəbl/ **adjective** (of an environment) harsh and difficult to live in (环境)不适合居住的

inhuman /ɪnˈhjuːmən/ **adjective 1** lacking positive human qualities; cruel and barbaric 无人性的；残忍的；野蛮的 **2** not human in nature or character 非人的

inhumane /ˌɪnhjuːˈmeɪn/ **adjective** without pity; cruel 没有同情心的；残忍的

inhumanity /ˌɪnhjuːˈmænəti/ **noun** (plural **inhumanities**) cruel and brutal behaviour 残酷行径；兽行

inimical /ɪˈnɪmɪkl/ **adjective** having a harmful effect on something; not helpful 有害的；不利的

inimitable /ɪˈnɪmɪtəbl/ **adjective** impossible to imitate; unique 无法

模仿的；独一无二的 ■ **inimitably** adverb.

iniquity /ɪˈnɪkwətɪ/ noun (plural **iniquities**) great injustice or unfairness 极不公正；很不正当 ■ **iniquitous** adjective.

initial /ɪˈnɪʃl/ adjective existing or occurring at the beginning 开始的；最初的 • noun the first letter of a name or word (名字或单词的)首字母 • verb (**initials**, **initialling**, **initialled**; N. Amer. 【北美】 **initials**, **initialing**, **initialed**) mark something with your initials as a sign of approval or agreement 用姓名的首字母作标记 (以示同意) ■ **initially** adverb.

initiate /ɪˈnɪʃɪeɪt/ verb (**initiates**, **initiating**, **initiated**) **1** make a process or action start 开始；发起 **2** admit someone into a society or group with a formal ceremony (通过正式仪式) 接纳，使加入 **3** introduce someone to a new activity 使入门 ■ **initiation** noun.

initiative /ɪˈnɪʃətɪv/ noun **1** the ability to act independently and with a fresh approach 自主性；主动性 **2** the power or opportunity to act before other people do 主动权；先机 **3** a new development or approach to a problem (解决问题的)新方法，新方案.

inject /ɪnˈdʒekt/ verb **1** put a drug or other substance into the body with a syringe 注射 **2** add a new or different quality 增加，增添(新特色) ■ **injection** noun.

injudicious /ˌɪndʒuˈdɪʃəs/ adjective unwise 不明智的.

injunction /ɪnˈdʒʌŋkʃn/ noun **1** Law 【法律】an order saying that someone must or must not carry out a certain action 禁令；禁制令 **2** a strong warning 强烈警告.

injure /ˈɪndʒə(r)/ verb (**injures**, **injuring**, **injured**) **1** do physical harm to; wound 伤害；使受伤 **2** have a bad effect on; damage 损坏；毁损.

injurious /ɪnˈdʒʊərɪəs/ adjective causing or likely to cause injury (可能)造成伤害的.

injury /ˈɪndʒərɪ/ noun (plural **injuries**) **1** harm done to the body (对身体的) 伤害，损伤 **2** hurt feelings (感情上的)伤害，挫伤.

injustice /ɪnˈdʒʌstɪs/ noun **1** lack of justice 不公平；不公正 **2** an unjust act 不公平(或不公正)行为.

ink /ɪŋk/ noun **1** a coloured fluid used for writing, drawing, or printing 墨水；墨汁；印油 **2** a black liquid produced by a cuttlefish, octopus, or squid (乌贼、章鱼或鱿鱼分泌的)墨汁 ■ **inky** adjective.

inkling /ˈɪŋklɪŋ/ noun a slight suspicion; a hint 猜疑；暗示.

inland /ˈɪnlænd/ adjective & adverb in or into the interior of a country 在内地(的)；向内陆(的) □ **inland revenue** Brit. 【英】the government department responsible for collecting income tax 国内税务局.

in-law /ˈɪnlɔː/ noun a relative by marriage 姻亲.

inlay verb /ɪnˈleɪ/ (**inlays**, **inlaying**, **inlaid**) fix pieces of a different material into a surface as a form of decoration 镶嵌；把…镶(或嵌)入 • noun /ˈɪnleɪ/ decoration of this type 镶嵌装饰.

inlet /ˈɪnlet/ noun **1** a small arm of the sea, a lake, or a river 小海湾；湖湾，河湾 **2** a place or means of entry 进口；入口.

in loco parentis /ɪn ˌləʊkəʊ pəˈrentɪs/ adverb having the same responsibility for a child or young person as a parent has 代替家长责任.

inmate /ˈɪnmeɪt/ noun a person living in an institution such as a prison or hospital (监狱、医院等机构的)被收容者，同住者.

inn /ɪn/ noun a pub, especially in the country (尤指乡下的)小酒店 ■ **inn-**

keeper noun (old use【旧】)

innards /'ɪnədz/ **plural noun** informal 【非正式】 **1** internal organs 内脏 **2** the internal workings of a machine (机器的)内部构造

innate /ɪ'neɪt/ **adjective** natural or inborn 先天的；天生的 ■ **innately** adverb.

inner /'ɪnə(r)/ **adjective 1** situated inside or close to the centre 内部的；里面的；靠近中心的 **2** private; not expressed 内心的，私密的；未表达出来的 **3** mental or spiritual 心灵的；精神的 □ **inner city** an area in or near the centre of a large city 市中心区 **inner tube** a separate inflatable tube inside a tyre (轮胎的)内胎

innermost /'ɪnəməʊst/ **adjective 1** furthest in; closest to the centre 最里面的；最靠近中心的 **2** (of thoughts) most private (思想)内心深处的，最隐秘的

innings /'ɪnɪŋz/ **noun** (plural **innings**) Cricket【板球】 each of the divisions of a game during which one side has a turn at batting 局；回合

innocent /'ɪnəsnt/ **adjective 1** not guilty of a crime or offence 无罪的；清白的 **2** having little experience of life 天真无邪的；阅世不深的 **3** not intended to cause offence 无意冒犯的；没有恶意的 • **noun** an innocent person 无辜者；天真单纯的人 ■ **innocence** noun **innocently** adverb.

innocuous /ɪ'nɒkjuəs/ **adjective** not harmful or offensive 无害的；不冒犯人的

innovate /'ɪnəveɪt/ **verb** (**innovates**, **innovating**, **innovated**) introduce new ideas or products 创新；革新 ■ **innovative** adjective **innovator** noun.

innovation /ˌɪnə'veɪʃn/ **noun 1** the introduction of new ideas or products 革新；创新 **2** a new idea or product 新想法；新产品

innuendo /ˌɪnju'endəʊ/ **noun** (plural **innuendoes** or **innuendos**) a remark which makes a vague and indirect reference to something 暗指；影射

innumerable /ɪ'nju:mərəbl/ **adjective** too many to be counted 无数的；数不清的

innumerate /ɪ'nju:mərət/ **adjective** without a basic knowledge of mathematics and arithmetic 不懂数学的；不懂算术的

inoculate /ɪ'nɒkjuleɪt/ **verb** treat someone with a vaccine to stop them getting a disease 给(某人)接种疫苗 ■ **inoculation** noun.

> ✔ 拼写指南 one *n*, one *c*: *inoculate*. *inoculate* 中有一个 n 和一个 c。

inoffensive /ˌɪnə'fensɪv/ **adjective** causing no offence or harm 不会冒犯人的；无害的

inoperable /ɪn'ɒpərəbl/ **adjective 1** (of an illness) not able to be cured by an operation (疾病)手术不能治愈的 **2** not able to be used or operated 不能使用的；无法运转的

inoperative /ɪn'ɒpərətɪv/ **adjective** not working or taking effect 不起作用的；不生效的

inopportune /ɪn'ɒpətjuːn/ **adjective** happening at an inconvenient time 不合时宜的

inordinate /ɪn'ɔːdɪnət/ **adjective** much greater than is usual or expected; excessive 过度的；超出预期的；过分的 ■ **inordinately** adverb.

inorganic /ˌɪnɔː'gænɪk/ **adjective 1** not consisting of or coming from living matter 无生物的 **2** (of a chemical compound) not containing carbon (化合物)无机的

inpatient /'ɪnpeɪʃnt/ **noun** a patient who is staying day and night in a hospital 住院病人

input /'ɪnpʊt/ **noun 1** what is put or taken into a system or process 投入(物)；投资 **2** the putting or feeding in of something 投入；输入 **3** a person's contribution (某人的)捐献,捐资 • verb (**inputs, inputting, input** or **inputted**) put data into a computer 把(数据)输入计算机

inquest /'ɪŋkwest/ noun **1** a legal inquiry to gather the facts relating to an incident (收集事故信息的)质询,调查 **2** Brit. 【英】an inquiry by a coroner's court into the cause of a death (对死亡原因的)调查;验尸

inquire /ɪn'kwaɪə(r)/ = ENQUIRE.

inquiry /ɪn'kwaɪəri/ = ENQUIRY.

inquisition /ˌɪŋkwɪ'zɪʃn/ noun a long period of questioning or investigation (长时间的)盘问,调查

inquisitive /ɪn'kwɪzətɪv/ adjective **1** eager to find things out 爱钻研的;好奇的 **2** prying 爱打听他人私事的 ■ **inquisitively** adverb.

inquisitor /ɪn'kwɪzɪtə(r)/ noun a person conducting an inquisition 审讯人,调查人

inroad /'ɪnrəʊd/ noun a gradual entry into or effect on a place or situation 侵蚀;消耗

inrush /'ɪnrʌʃ/ noun a sudden inward rush or flow (突然的)流入,涌入

insalubrious /ˌɪnsə'luːbriəs/ adjective unpleasant because not clean or well kept (因不卫生或存放不善)令人不适的,有损健康的

insane /ɪn'seɪn/ adjective **1** seriously mentally ill 精神失常的,精神错乱的 **2** very foolish 极其愚蠢的;荒唐的 ■ **insanely** adverb **insanity** noun.

insanitary /ɪn'sænətri/ adjective so dirty as to be a danger to health 不卫生的;有害健康的

insatiable /ɪn'seɪʃəbl/ adjective always wanting more and not able to be satisfied 无法满足的;贪得无厌的 ■ **insatiably** adverb.

inscribe /ɪn'skraɪb/ verb (**inscribes, inscribing, inscribed**) **1** write or carve something on a surface (在表面上)题写,刻 **2** write a dedication to someone in a book 题赠,题献(书)

inscription /ɪn'skrɪpʃn/ noun words or symbols written or carved on a surface or in a book 铭刻,刻印符号;题词

inscrutable /ɪn'skruːtəbl/ adjective impossible to understand or interpret 不可理解的;无法解释的 ■ **inscrutably** adverb.

insect /'ɪnsekt/ noun a small animal with six legs and no backbone 昆虫

insecticide /ɪn'sektɪsaɪd/ noun a substance used for killing insects 杀虫剂;杀虫药

insectivore /ɪn'sektɪvɔː(r)/ noun an animal that eats insects 食虫动物 ■ **insectivorous** adjective.

insecure /ˌɪnsɪ'kjʊə(r)/ adjective **1** not confident or assured 不自信的;不确信的;无把握的 **2** not firm or firmly fixed 不牢固的;动摇的 ■ **insecurity** noun (plural **insecurities**).

inseminate /ɪn'semɪneɪt/ verb (**inseminates, inseminating, inseminated**) introduce semen into a woman or a female animal 使受精;授精 ■ **insemination** noun.

insensate /ɪn'senseɪt/ adjective lacking physical sensation 无感觉的;无知觉的

insensible /ɪn'sensəbl/ adjective **1** unconscious 意识不到的;未发觉的 **2** numb; without feeling 麻木的;无感觉的

insensitive /ɪn'sensətɪv/ adjective **1** showing or feeling no concern for the feelings of other people 不顾及他人感受的;冷漠的 **2** not sensitive to physical sensation 无感觉的;失去知觉的 **3** not aware of or able to respond to something 感觉迟钝的;麻木的 ■ **insensitively** adverb **insensitivity** noun.

inseparable /ɪn'seprəbl/ adjective unable to be separated or treated separately 分不开的;不能分别对待的 ■ **inseparably** adverb.

insert verb /ɪn'sɜːt/ place, fit, or incorporate something into something else 插入；嵌入 • **noun** /'ɪnsɜːt/ a loose page or section in a magazine (杂志的)插页 ■ **insertion** noun.

inset noun /'ɪnset/ a thing inserted 插入物；嵌入物 • **verb** /ɪn'set/ (**insets**, **insetting**, **inset** or **insetted**) insert 插入；嵌入

inshore /ˌɪn'ʃɔː(r)/ **adjective & adverb 1** at sea but close to the shore 接近海岸的(地) **2** towards the shore 向海岸(的)

inside /ˌɪn'saɪd/ **noun 1** the inner side or surface of a thing 里面；内侧；内部 **2** the inner part; the interior 内部 **3** (**insides**) informal【非正式】a person's stomach and bowels (人的)肠胃 • **adjective** situated on or in the inside 里面的，内侧的；内部的 • **preposition & adverb 1** situated or moving within 在(…)里面；向(…)里面 **2** informal【非正式】in prison 在监牢里 **3** within a particular time (时间)在…以内，少于 □ **inside out** with the inner surface turned outwards 里面朝外

insider /ˌɪn'saɪdə(r)/ **noun** a person working within an organization 内部人士

insidious /ɪn'sɪdiəs/ **adjective** proceeding in a gradual and harmful way 逐渐恶化的；潜伏的 ■ **insidiously** adverb.

insight /'ɪnsaɪt/ **noun 1** the ability to understand the truth about people and situations 洞察力；领悟力 **2** understanding of this kind 洞悉；深刻见解 ■ **insightful** adjective.

insignia /ɪn'sɪɡniə/ **noun** (plural **insignia**) a badge or symbol showing someone's rank, position, or membership of an organization (表明级别、地位或成员身份的)徽章，标志，标记

insignificant /ˌɪnsɪɡ'nɪfɪkənt/ **adjective** having very little importance or value 无足轻重的；不重要的；无价值

的 ■ **insignificance** noun **insignificantly** adverb.

insincere /ˌɪnsɪn'sɪə(r)/ **adjective** saying or doing things that you do not mean 言不由衷的，虚伪的 ■ **insincerely** adverb **insincerity** noun.

insinuate /ɪn'sɪnjueɪt/ **verb** (**insinuates**, **insinuating**, **insinuated**) **1** suggest or hint at something bad in an indirect way 暗示；含沙射影地说(不好的事) **2** (**insinuate yourself into**) move yourself gradually into a favourable position 钻营；活动

insinuation /ɪnˌsɪnju'eɪʃn/ **noun** an unpleasant hint or suggestion 影射；旁敲侧击；暗示

insipid /ɪn'sɪpɪd/ **adjective 1** having almost no flavour 无味道的；淡而无味的 **2** not interesting or lively 无趣的；无生气的

insist /ɪn'sɪst/ **verb 1** demand forcefully that something is done 坚持；执意要求 **2** firmly state that something is the case, without letting anyone disagree 强烈主张 **3** (**insist on**) persist in doing something 坚持(做)

insistent /ɪn'sɪstənt/ **adjective 1** insisting that someone does something or that something is the case 坚持的；固执的 **2** continuing for a long time and demanding attention 持续不断的；再三的 ■ **insistence** noun **insistently** adverb.

> ✔ 拼写指南 -*ent*, not -*ant*: insist**ent**. insistent 中 -ent 不要拼作 -ant。

in situ /ɪn 'sɪtjuː/ **adverb & adjective** in the natural or original place 在原处(的)；在原地的

insole /'ɪnsəʊl/ **noun** the inner sole of a boot or shoe (靴或鞋的)内底

insolent /'ɪnsələnt/ **adjective** rude and disrespectful 粗鲁的；不敬的 ■ **insolence** noun **insolently** adverb.

insoluble /ɪn'sɒljəbl/ **adjective 1** impossible to solve 无法解决的 **2**

(of a substance) incapable of being dissolved (物质)不溶的

insolvent /ɪnˈsɒlvənt/ **adjective** not having enough money to pay your debts 无偿还能力的 ■ **insolvency** noun.

insomnia /ɪnˈsɒmniə/ **noun** inability to sleep 失眠 ■ **insomniac** noun & adjective.

insouciant /ɪnˈsuːsiənt/ **adjective** carefree and unconcerned 漠不关心的;漫不经心的;无忧无虑的 ■ **insouciance** noun.

inspect /ɪnˈspekt/ **verb 1** look at something closely 检查,审视 **2** make an official visit to a school, factory, etc. to check on standards 视察 ■ **inspection** noun.

inspector /ɪnˈspektə(r)/ **noun 1** an official who makes sure that regulations are obeyed 检查员;视察员 **2** a police officer ranking below a chief inspector (警察)巡官

inspiration /ˌɪnspəˈreɪʃn/ **noun 1** the process of being inspired 灵感 **2** a person or thing that inspires 启发灵感的人(或事物);鼓舞人心的人(或事物) **3** a sudden clever idea (突然想到的)好主意,妙计 ■ **inspirational** adjective.

inspire /ɪnˈspaɪə(r)/ **verb** (**inspires, inspiring, inspired**) **1** fill someone with the urge or ability to do something 启发;激励;鼓舞 **2** create a feeling in a person 激起;唤起(感情) **3** give rise to 引起;使产生

inspired /ɪnˈspaɪəd/ **adjective** showing great creativity or imagination 有灵感的

instability /ˌɪnstəˈbɪləti/ **noun** (plural **instabilities**) lack of stability 不稳定;不稳固

install /ɪnˈstɔːl/ **verb** (**installs, installing, installed**) **1** place or fix equipment in position ready for use 安装(设备) **2** establish someone in a new place or role 安顿;安置

✔ 拼写指南 **install** is spelled with two *l*s, while **instalment** is spelled with only one in British English. install 中有两个 l,而 instalment 在英式英语拼写中只有一个 l.

installation /ˌɪnstəˈleɪʃn/ **noun 1** the installing of something 安装;设置 **2** a large piece of equipment installed for use 大型设备;装备 **3** a military or industrial establishment 军事设施;工业设施 **4** a large piece of art constructed within a gallery (美术馆内的)装置艺术品

instalment /ɪnˈstɔːlmənt/ (US spelling 【美拼作】**installment**) **noun 1** each of several payments made over a period of time (分期付款的)一期付款 **2** each of several parts of something published or broadcast at intervals (分期连载的)一部分;(连续播出节目的)一集

instance /ˈɪnstəns/ **noun** a particular example or occurrence of something 实例;例证 • **verb** (**instances, instancing, instanced**) mention something as an example 举⋯为例 □ **for instance** as an example 例如

instant /ˈɪnstənt/ **adjective 1** happening immediately 立即的;立刻的 **2** (of food) processed so that it can be prepared very quickly (食品)速食的,即食的 • **noun 1** a precise moment of time 某一刻 **2** a very short time 瞬间;刹那 ■ **instantly** adverb.

instantaneous /ˌɪnstənˈteɪniəs/ **adjective** happening or done immediately or at the same time 即时的;瞬间的;同时的 ■ **instantaneously** adverb.

instead /ɪnˈsted/ **adverb 1** as an alternative 作为替代 **2** (**instead of**) in place of 代替;而不是

instep /ˈɪnstep/ **noun** the part of a person's foot between the ball and the ankle 脚背;足弓

instigate /ˈɪnstɪɡeɪt/ **verb** (**instigates,**

instigating, instigated) make something happen or come about 使发生;使开始 ■ **instigation** noun **instigator** noun.

instil or **instill** /ɪnˈstɪl/ **verb** (**instils, instilling, instilled**) gradually but firmly establish an idea or attitude in someone's mind (逐步)灌输,培养(观念或态度)

instinct /ˈɪnstɪŋkt/ **noun 1** an inborn tendency to behave in a certain way 天性;本能 **2** a natural ability or skill 天资;天分 ■ **instinctual** adjective.

instinctive /ɪnˈstɪŋktɪv/ **adjective** based on instinct rather than thought or training 基于本能的,出于天性的 ■ **instinctively** adverb.

institute /ˈɪnstɪtjuːt/ **noun** an organization for the promotion of science, education, or a profession 科研机构;学会;学院 • **verb** (**institutes, instituting, instituted**) set up or establish 开始;建立;设立

institution /ˌɪnstɪˈtjuːʃn/ **noun 1** an important organization or public body (重要的)机构,公共组织 **2** an organization providing residential care for people who have special needs 慈善机构;福利机构 **3** an established law or custom 法规;制度;惯例 ■ **institutional** adjective.

institutionalize or **institutionalise** /ˌɪnstɪˈtjuːʃənəlaɪz/ **verb** (**institutionalizes, institutionalizing, institutionalized**) **1** establish something as a feature of an organization or culture 使成惯例;使制度化 **2** place someone in a residential institution 把(某人)送进收容机构 **3** (**become institutionalized**) lose your individuality as a result of staying for a long time in a residential institution (因长期生活在收容机构)失去个性

instruct /ɪnˈstrʌkt/ **verb 1** tell or order someone to do something 指示;命令 **2** teach 教授;讲授 **3** inform someone of a fact or situation 通知;通报

instruction /ɪnˈstrʌkʃn/ **noun 1** an order 指示;命令 **2** a piece of information about how something should be done 用法说明;操作指南 **3** teaching or education 教学;教育 ■ **instructional** adjective.

instructive /ɪnˈstrʌktɪv/ **adjective** useful and informative 有用的;给予知识的;富有教益的

instructor /ɪnˈstrʌktə(r)/ **noun** a teacher 教师

instrument /ˈɪnstrəmənt/ **noun 1** a tool or piece of equipment used for delicate or scientific work 仪器;器具 **2** a measuring device (量度用的)仪表 **3** (also **musical instrument**) a device for producing musical sounds 乐器

instrumental /ˌɪnstrəˈmentl/ **adjective 1** important in making something happen 起重要作用的 **2** (of music) performed on instruments (音乐)用乐器演奏的 • **noun** a piece of music performed by instruments, with no vocals (乐器演奏的)器乐曲

instrumentalist /ˌɪnstrəˈmentəlɪst/ **noun** a player of a musical instrument 乐器演奏者

instrumentation /ˌɪnstrəmenˈteɪʃn/ **noun 1** the instruments used in a piece of music (演奏某乐曲使用的)乐器 **2** the arrangement of a piece of music for particular instruments 乐谱写

insubordinate /ˌɪnsəˈbɔːdɪnət/ **adjective** disobedient 不服从的;不听话的 ■ **insubordination** noun.

insubstantial /ˌɪnsəbˈstænʃl/ **adjective** not strong or solid 不坚固的;非实体的

insufferable /ɪnˈsʌfrəbl/ **adjective** unbearable 不能忍受的;难以忍受的 ■ **insufferably** adverb.

insufficient /ˌɪnsəˈfɪʃnt/ **adjective** not enough 不够的;不足的;不充分的 ■ **insufficiency** noun **insufficiently**

adverb.

insular /'ɪnsjələ(r)/ **adjective 1** narrow-minded through being isolated from outside influences 思想偏狭的；保守的 **2** relating to an island 岛屿的 ■ **insularity** noun.

insulate /'ɪnsjuleɪt/ **verb (insulates, insulating, insulated) 1** place material between one thing and another to prevent loss of heat or intrusion of sound 使隔热，使隔音 **2** cover something with non-conducting material to prevent the passage of electricity 使绝缘 **3** protect from something unpleasant 保护 ■ **insulation** noun **insulator** noun.

insulin /'ɪnsjəlɪn/ **noun** a hormone which regulates glucose levels in the blood 胰岛素

insult **verb** /ɪn'sʌlt/ say or do hurtful or disrespectful things to someone 辱骂；侮辱 • **noun** /'ɪnsʌlt/ an insulting remark or action 辱骂；侮辱

insuperable /ɪn'sjuːpərəbl/ **adjective** impossible to overcome 不能克服的；不可逾越的

insupportable /ˌɪnsə'pɔːtəbl/ **adjective 1** unable to be justified 不正当的 **2** unbearable 无法忍受的

insurance /ɪn'ʃʊərəns/ **noun 1** an arrangement by which you make regular payments to a company who pay an agreed amount if something is lost or damaged or someone is hurt or killed 保险 **2** money paid by or to an insurance company 保险赔偿金，保费 **3** a thing that provides protection in case anything bad happens 安全措施；安全保障

insure /ɪn'ʃʊə(r)/ **verb (insures, insuring, insured) 1** pay money in order to receive financial compensation if something is lost or damaged or someone is hurt or killed 给……保险；为……投保 **2** (**insure against**) provide protection in case anything bad happens 采取预防措施 **3** = ENSURE.

insurgent /ɪn'sɜːdʒənt/ **noun** a rebel or revolutionary 叛乱者；革命者 • **adjective** fighting against a system or authority 反叛的；造反的 ■ **insurgency** noun.

insurmountable /ˌɪnsə'maʊntəbl/ **adjective** too great to be overcome 难以克服的；不可逾越的

insurrection /ˌɪnsə'rekʃn/ **noun** a violent uprising against authority 起义；暴动

intact /ɪn'tækt/ **adjective** not damaged 未受损伤的；完好的

intake /'ɪnteɪk/ **noun 1** an amount or quantity of something that is taken in 吸入量；接受量；摄取量 **2** a set of people entering a school or college at a particular time (某一时期学校的)招生人数，入学人数

intangible /ɪn'tændʒəbl/ **adjective 1** not solid or real 触摸不到的；无形的 **2** vague and abstract 模糊的；抽象的 • **noun** an intangible thing 触摸不到的东西；无形的事物 ■ **intangibly** adverb.

integer /'ɪntɪdʒə(r)/ **noun** a whole number 整数

integral /'ɪntɪɡrəl, ɪn'teɡrəl/ **adjective 1** necessary to make a whole complete; fundamental 必需的；不可或缺的；基本的 **2** included as part of a whole 作为组成部分的

integrate /'ɪntɪɡreɪt/ **verb (integrates, integrating, integrated) 1** combine with something to form a whole (使)合并；(使)成为一体 **2** make someone accepted within a social group 使融入；使成为集体一员 ■ **integration** noun.

integrity /ɪn'teɡrəti/ **noun 1** the quality of being honest, fair, and good 诚实；正直 **2** the state of being whole or unified 完整；统一

intellect /'ɪntəlekt/ **noun** the power of using your mind to think logically and understand things 逻辑领悟能力；智力

intellectual /ˌɪntəˈlektʃuəl/ **adjective 1** relating or appealing to the intellect 智力的；脑力的；需要智力的 **2** having a highly developed intellect 智力发达的 • **noun** a person with a highly developed intellect 才智出众者；高智商者 ■ **intellectually** adverb.

intellectualize or **intellectualise** /ˌɪntəˈlektʃuəlaɪz/ **verb** (**intellectualizes, intellectualizing, intellectualized**) talk or write in an intellectual way 作理性探讨

intelligence /ɪnˈtelɪdʒəns/ **noun 1** the ability to gain and apply knowledge and skills 智力；才智；悟性 **2** the secret gathering of information about an enemy or opponent 情报搜集；情报工作 **3** information of this sort 情报；机密

intelligent /ɪnˈtelɪdʒənt/ **adjective** good at learning, understanding, and thinking 有才智的；聪明的 ■ **intelligently** adverb.

intelligentsia /ɪnˌtelɪˈdʒentsiə/ **noun** intellectuals or highly educated people 知识分子；高学历阶层

intelligible /ɪnˈtelɪdʒəbl/ **adjective** able to be understood 能领悟的；可理解的 ■ **intelligibly** adverb.

intemperate /ɪnˈtempərət/ **adjective** lacking self-control 缺乏自制力的；放纵的 ■ **intemperance** noun.

intend /ɪnˈtend/ **verb 1** have something as your aim or plan 打算；计划 **2** plan that something should be, do, or mean something 意图；意指 **3** (**intend something for** or **to do**) design or plan something for a particular purpose 专为…设计(或计划)

intense /ɪnˈtens/ **adjective** (**intenser, intensest**) **1** of great force or strength 强烈的；极端的 **2** very earnest or serious 非常热切的；极严肃的 ■ **intensely** adverb **intensity** noun (plural **intensities**).

intensify /ɪnˈtensɪfaɪ/ **verb** (**intensifies, intensifying, intensified**) make or become more intense (使)增强；(使)强化

intensive /ɪnˈtensɪv/ **adjective 1** involving a lot of effort over a short time 集中的；密集的 **2** (of agriculture) aiming to produce the highest possible yields (农业)精耕细作的；集约的 □ **intensive care** special medical treatment given to a dangerously ill patient 重病特别护理；重症监护 ■ **intensively** adverb.

intent /ɪnˈtent/ **noun** intention or purpose 意图；目的 • **adjective 1** (**intent on**) determined to do 下定决心的 **2** (**intent on**) giving all your attention to 专注的；投入的 **3** showing great interest and attention 极感兴趣的；极为关心的 □ **to all intents and purposes** in all important respects 几乎完全 ■ **intently** adverb.

intention /ɪnˈtenʃn/ **noun 1** an aim or plan 目的；计划 **2** the fact of intending something 打算；计划 **3** (**intentions**) a man's plans about getting married (男子的)求婚意图

intentional /ɪnˈtenʃənl/ **adjective** deliberate 有意的；故意的 ■ **intentionally** adverb.

inter /ɪnˈtɜː(r)/ **verb** (**inters, interring, interred**) place a dead body in a grave or tomb 掩埋，埋葬(尸体)

interact /ˌɪntərˈækt/ **verb** (of two people or things) do things which have an effect on each other (两人或两物)互相作用，互相影响 ■ **interaction** noun.

interactive /ˌɪntərˈæktɪv/ **adjective 1** influencing each other 相互影响的；相互作用的 **2** (of a computer or other electronic device) allowing a two-way flow of information between it and a user (计算机等电子设备) 交互式的，人机对话的

interbreed /ˌɪntəˈbriːd/ **verb** (**interbreeds, interbreeding, interbred**) breed with an animal of a different species 异种交配；杂交繁殖

intercede /ˌɪntəˈsiːd/ **verb** intervene on behalf of someone else (为某人) 说情

intercept /ˌɪntəˈsept/ **verb** stop someone or something and prevent them from continuing to a destination 拦截；截住；截击 ▪ **interceptor** noun **interception** noun.

intercession /ˌɪntəˈseʃn/ **noun 1** the action of interceding 代人说情 **2** the saying of a prayer on behalf of another person 代祷

interchange verb /ˌɪntəˈtʃeɪndʒ/ (**interchanges**, **interchanging**, **interchanged**) **1** (of two people) exchange things with each other (两人)互换(物品) **2** put each of two things in the place of the other 使(两物)相互易位 ▪ noun /ˈɪntətʃeɪndʒ/ **1** the action of interchanging things 互换 **2** an exchange of words 争论 **3** a road junction built on several levels 立体交叉道 ▪ **interchangeable** adjective **interchangeably** adverb.

intercity /ˌɪntəˈsɪti/ **adjective** existing or travelling between cities 城市间的；城际的；来往于城市间的

intercom /ˈɪntəkɒm/ **noun** a system of communication by telephone or radio inside a building or group of buildings (建筑物的)内部通话设备

interconnect /ˌɪntəkəˈnekt/ **verb** (of two things) connect with each other (两物)互相连接

intercontinental /ˌɪntəˌkɒntɪˈnentl/ **adjective** relating to or travelling between continents 洲际的；跨洲的

intercourse /ˈɪntəkɔːs/ **noun 1** communication or dealings between people (人与人之间的)交往，沟通 **2** sexual intercourse 性交

intercut /ˌɪntəˈkʌt/ **verb** (**intercuts**, **intercutting**, **intercut**) alternate scenes with contrasting scenes in a film 使(电影场景)交切

interdependent /ˌɪntədɪˈpendənt/

adjective (of two or more people or things) dependent on each other (两个或两个以上的人或事物)互相依存的

interest /ˈɪntrəst/ **noun 1** the state of wanting to know about something or someone 兴趣；好奇 **2** the quality of making someone curious or holding their attention 趣味性 **3** a subject about which you are concerned or enthusiastic 关心的事；感兴趣的事 **4** money that is paid for the use of money lent 利息 **5** a person's advantage or benefit 利益；好处 **6** a share, right, or stake in property or a financial undertaking 股份；股权 ▪ **verb 1** make someone curious or attentive 使感兴趣；使关注 **2** (**interested**) not impartial 有偏见的 ▪ **interesting** adjective **interestingly** adverb.

interface /ˈɪntəfeɪs/ **noun 1** a point where two things meet and interact 交接点 **2** a device or program enabling a user to communicate with a computer, or for connecting two items of hardware or software 接口；接口程序 ▪ **verb** (**interfaces**, **interfacing**, **interfaced**)(**interface with**) connect with another computer by an interface (通过接口)连接

interfere /ˌɪntəˈfɪə(r)/ **verb** (**interferes**, **interfering**, **interfered**) **1** (**interfere with**) prevent something from continuing or being carried out properly 妨碍；阻止 **2** (**interfere with**) handle or adjust something without permission 擅自处理；擅自调整 **3** become involved in something without being asked 干预；干涉 **4** (**interfere with**) Brit. [英] sexually molest someone 强奸；侮辱

interference /ˌɪntəˈfɪərəns/ **noun 1** the action of interfering 干涉；介入 **2** disturbance to radio signals caused by unwanted signals from other sources (无线电信号的)干扰

interferon /ˌɪntə'fɪərɒn/ **noun** a protein released by animal cells which prevents a virus from reproducing itself 干扰素(动物细胞产生的一种蛋白质,能阻止病毒复制)

intergalactic /ˌɪntəgə'læktɪk/ **adjective** relating to or situated between galaxies 星系的;星系际的

interim /'ɪntərɪm/ **noun** (**in the interim**) the time between two events (两起事件的)间隙,期间 • **adjective** lasting for a short time, until a replacement is found 短暂的;临时的

interior /ɪn'tɪəriə(r)/ **adjective 1** situated within or inside; inner 位于里面的,内部的 **2** remote from the coast or frontier; inland 内陆的,内地的 • **noun 1** the interior part 内部;里面 **2** the internal affairs of a country (一国的)内政,内务

interject /ˌɪntə'dʒekt/ **verb** say something suddenly as an interruption 突然插(话)

interjection /ˌɪntə'dʒekʃn/ **noun** an exclamation (e.g. *ah!*)感叹词,感叹语

interlace /ˌɪntə'leɪs/ **verb** (**interlaces**, **interlacing**, **interlaced**) weave together 编织;交错

interleave /ˌɪntə'liːv/ **verb 1** insert between the pages of a book 夹(或插)入(书页间) **2** place between the layers of something else 将…插入;将…夹入

interlock /ˌɪntə'lɒk/ **verb** (of two parts, fibres, etc.) engage with each other by overlapping or fitting together (两部分、两织物等)连锁,扣紧,紧密相连

interlocutor /ˌɪntə'lɒkjətə(r)/ **noun** formal【正式】a person who takes part in a conversation 对话者;参与谈话者

interloper /'ɪntələʊpə(r)/ **noun** a person who is in a place or situation where they are not wanted or do not belong 干涉者;闯入者

interlude /'ɪntəluːd/ **noun 1** a period

of time that contrasts with what goes before and after 间歇,间隔 **2** a pause between the acts of a play (戏剧)的幕间休息 **3** a piece of music played between other pieces 插曲

intermarry /ˌɪntə'mæri/ **verb** (**intermarries, intermarrying, intermarried**) (of people of different races or religions) marry each other (种族或宗教信仰不同的人)通婚 ■ **intermarriage** noun.

intermediary /ˌɪntə'miːdiəri/ **noun** (plural **intermediaries**) a person who tries to settle a dispute between other people 调解人;中间人

intermediate /ˌɪntə'miːdiət/ **adjective 1** coming between two things in time, place, character, etc. 中间的;居中的 **2** having more than basic knowledge or skills but not yet advanced 中等程度的;中级水平的 • **noun** an intermediate person or thing 中间人;中间事物

interment /ɪn'tɜːmənt/ **noun** the burial of a dead body 埋葬;安葬

intermezzo /ˌɪntə'metsəʊ/ **noun** (plural **intermezzi** /ˌɪntə'metsiː/ or **intermezzos**) a short piece of music connecting parts of an opera or other work 间奏曲

interminable /ɪn'tɜːmɪnəbl/ **adjective** lasting a very long time and therefore boring 冗长的;没完没了的 ■ **interminably** adverb.

intermingle /ˌɪntə'mɪŋgl/ **verb** (**intermingles, intermingling, intermingled**) mix or mingle together (使)混合

intermission /ˌɪntə'mɪʃn/ **noun 1** a pause or break in something 中断;停顿 **2** an interval between parts of a play or film (戏剧或电影的)幕间休息

intermittent /ˌɪntə'mɪtənt/ **adjective** stopping and starting at irregular intervals 断断续续的;间歇的 ■ **intermittently** adverb.

intern **verb** /ɪn'tɜːn/ confine someone as a prisoner 拘留;扣押 • **noun** /'ɪntɜːn/ N. Amer. 【北美】**1** a recent medical graduate receiving supervised training in a hospital 实习医生 **2** a student or trainee doing a job to gain work experience 实习生 ■ **internment** noun.

internal /ɪn'tɜːnl/ **adjective 1** relating to or situated on the inside 内部的;里面的 **2** inside the body 体内的 **3** relating to affairs and activities within a country 内政的 **4** existing or used within an organization (机构)内部的 **5** within the mind 内心的;心灵的 □ **internal-combustion engine** an engine in which power is generated by the expansion of hot gases from the burning of fuel with air inside the engine 内燃机 ■ **internally** adverb.

internalize or **internalise** /ɪn'tɜːnəlaɪz/ **verb** (**internalizes**, **internalizing**, **internalized**) make a feeling or belief part of the way you think 使(情感或信仰)成为思想的一部分;使内在化

international /ˌɪntə'næʃnəl/ **adjective 1** existing or happening between nations 国际的;世界性的 **2** agreed on or used by all or many nations 国际间认可(或使用)的 • **noun** Brit. 【英】a game or contest between teams representing different countries 国际比赛 ■ **internationally** adverb.

internationalism /ˌɪntə'næʃnə-lɪzəm/ **noun** belief in the value of cooperation between nations 国际主义

internationalize or **internationalise** /ˌɪntə'næʃnəlaɪz/ **verb** (**internationalizes**, **internationalizing**, **internationalized**) make something international 使国际化

internecine /ˌɪntə'niːsaɪn/ **adjective** (of fighting) taking place between members of the same country or group (冲突)发生在内部的;内讧的

Internet /'ɪntənet/ **noun** a very large international computer network 互联网;因特网

interpersonal /ˌɪntə'pɜːsənl/ **adjective** having to do with relationships or communication between people 人际(关系)的

interplanetary /ˌɪntə'plænɪtri/ **adjective** situated or travelling between planets 行星间的;行星间航行的

interplay /'ɪntəpleɪ/ **noun** the way in which things interact 相互作用

interpolate /ɪn'tɜːpəleɪt/ **verb** (**interpolates**, **interpolating**, **interpolated**) **1** add a remark to a conversation 插话;插嘴 **2** add something to a piece of writing (在文字间)插入 ■ **interpolation** noun.

interpose /ˌɪntə'pəʊz/ **verb** (**interposes**, **interposing**, **interposed**) **1** place something between two other things 使介入(两者之间);使插入(某物) **2** say something as an interruption 斡旋;调停

interpret /ɪn'tɜːprɪt/ **verb** (**interprets**, **interpreting**, **interpreted**) **1** explain the meaning of 解释;阐释 **2** translate aloud the words of a person speaking a different language 口译 **3** understand something as having a particular meaning 理解 ■ **interpretation** noun **interpreter** noun.

interracial /ˌɪntə'reɪʃl/ **adjective** existing between or involving different races 不同种族间的;涉及不同种族的

interregnum /ˌɪntə'reɡnəm/ **noun** (plural **interregnums** or **interregna** /ˌɪntə'reɡnə/) a period between regimes when normal government is suspended 政权空白期;空位期

interrelate /ˌɪntərɪ'leɪt/ **verb** (**interrelates**, **interrelating**, **interrelated**) (of two people or things) relate or connect to one other (两人或事物)相

互关联 ■ **interrelation** noun.

interrogate /ɪnˈterəɡeɪt/ **verb 1** (**interrogates, interrogating, interrogated**) ask someone a lot of questions, often in an aggressive way 盘问;讯问;审问 ■ **interrogation** noun **interrogator** noun.

interrogative /ˌɪntəˈrɒɡətɪv/ **adjective** in the form of or used in a question 疑问式的;用于提问的 • noun a word used in questions, e.g. how or what 疑问词

interrupt /ˌɪntəˈrʌpt/ **verb 1** stop the continuous progress of 中断;中止 **2** stop a person who is speaking by saying or doing something 打断(讲话者) **3** break the continuity of a line, surface, or view 阻断(连续线条、平面或景观) ■ **interruption** noun.

✔ 拼写指南 double **r** in the middle: inter**r**upt. interrupt 中间有两个 **r**。

intersect /ˌɪntəˈsekt/ **verb 1** divide something by passing or lying across it 横断;横穿;贯穿 **2** (of lines, roads, etc.) cross or cut each other (线路、道路等的)相交,交叉

intersection /ˌɪntəˈsekʃn/ **noun 1** a point or line where lines or surfaces intersect 交叉点;交线 **2** a point where roads intersect 交叉路口

intersperse /ˌɪntəˈspɜːs/ **verb** (**intersperses, interspersing, interspersed**) place or scatter among or between other things 散布;散置;点缀

interstate /ˈɪntəsteɪt/ **adjective** existing or carried on between states 州际的

interstellar /ˌɪntəˈstelə(r)/ **adjective** occurring or situated between stars 星际的

interstice /ɪnˈtɜːstɪs/ **noun** a small crack or space in something 空隙;裂缝

intertwine /ˌɪntəˈtwaɪn/ **verb** (**intertwines, intertwining, intertwined**)

twist or twine together 缠绕;缠结

interval /ˈɪntəvl/ **noun 1** a period of time between two events 间隔;间歇 **2** a pause or break 暂停 **3** Brit. 【英】a pause between parts of a play, concert, etc (戏剧、音乐会等的)幕间休息,休息时间 **4** the difference in pitch between two sounds 音程

intervene /ˌɪntəˈviːn/ **verb** (**intervenes, intervening, intervened**) **1** become involved in a situation in order to improve or control it 斡旋;介入 **2** happen in the time or space beween other things 介于…之间 ■ **intervention** noun.

interview /ˈɪntəvjuː/ **noun 1** a meeting at which a journalist asks someone questions about their work or their opinions (记者对某人的)采访 **2** a formal meeting at which someone is asked questions to judge whether they are suitable for a job, college place, etc. (对求职者或投考者的)面试 • **verb** ask someone questions in an interview 对…进行面试(或面谈);访问;采访 ■ **interviewee** noun **interviewer** noun.

interweave /ˌɪntəˈwiːv/ **verb** (**interweaves, interweaving, interwove**; past participle **interwoven**) weave two or more fibres or strands together 交织;编织;编结

intestate /ɪnˈtesteɪt/ **adjective** (of someone who has died) not having made a will (死者)未留遗嘱的

intestine /ɪnˈtestɪn/ or **intestines** /ɪnˈtestɪnz/ **noun** the long tube leading from the stomach to the anus 肠 ■ **intestinal** adjective.

intimacy /ˈɪntɪməsi/ **noun** (plural **intimacies**) **1** close familiarity or friendship 亲密;友谊 **2** an intimate act or remark 亲密的行为(或言语)

intimate¹ /ˈɪntɪmət/ **adjective 1** familiar 亲密的;友好的 **2** private and personal 私下的;个人的 **3** (of two people) having a sexual relationship (两人)有性关系的 **4** involving very close connection 有紧密联系的 **5** (of knowledge) detailed (知识)详尽的 **6** having a friendly, informal atmosphere (气氛)轻松友好的 • noun a very close friend 密友；知己 ∎ **intimately** adverb.

intimate² /'ɪntɪmeɪt/ verb (intimates, intimating, intimated) say or suggest that something is the case 暗示；提示 ∎ **intimation** noun.

intimidate /ɪn'tɪmɪdeɪt/ verb (intimidates, intimidating, intimidated) frighten or threaten someone, especially to force them to do something 恐吓；威慑 ∎ **intimidation** noun.

into /'ɪntuː, 'ɪntu, 'ɪntə/ preposition **1** expressing motion or direction to a point on or within 进入；到…里面 **2** expressing a change of state or the result of an action 变成；成为；转为 **3** indicating the direction towards which something is turned 朝…方向 **4** indicating an object of interest 关于；有关 **5** expressing division 除

intolerable /ɪn'tɒlərəbl/ adjective unable to be endured 不能忍受的 ∎ **intolerably** adverb.

intolerant /ɪn'tɒlərənt/ adjective not willing to accept ideas or ways of behaving that are different from your own (观点或行为)偏狭的，不容忍的 ∎ **intolerance** noun.

intonation /ɪntə'neɪʃn/ noun the rise and fall of the voice in speaking 声调；语调

intone /ɪn'təʊn/ verb (intones, intoning, intoned) say or recite something with your voice hardly rising or falling 以平直的音调说(或背诵)

intoxicate /ɪn'tɒksɪkeɪt/ verb (intoxicates, intoxicating, intoxicated) **1** (of alcoholic drink or a drug) make someone lose control of themselves (酒或毒品)使失去自制, 使麻醉 **2**

(be intoxicated) be excited or exhilarated by something 激动；兴奋 ∎ **intoxication** noun.

intractable /ɪn'træktəbl/ adjective **1** hard to solve or deal with 难应付的 **2** stubborn 顽固的

intranet /'ɪntrənet/ noun a computer network for use within an organization (机构的)内联网

intransigent /ɪn'trænsɪdʒənt/ adjective refusing to change your views or behaviour 拒不让步的，不妥协的 ∎ **intransigence** noun.

intransitive /ɪn'trænsətɪv/ adjective (of a verb) not taking a direct object, e.g. look in look at the sky (动词)不及物的

intrauterine /ˌɪntrə'juːtəraɪn/ adjective within the womb 子宫内的

intravenous /ˌɪntrə'viːnəs/ adjective within or into a vein 静脉内的，进入静脉的

intrepid /ɪn'trepɪd/ adjective not afraid of danger or difficulties 无畏的，勇敢的 ∎ **intrepidly** adverb.

intricacy /'ɪntrɪkəsi/ noun (plural intricacies) **1** the quality of being intricate 错综复杂；复杂精细 **2** (intricacies) details 细节

intricate /'ɪntrɪkət/ adjective very complicated or detailed 非常复杂的；极为详细的 ∎ **intricately** adverb.

intrigue verb /ɪn'triːg/ (intrigues, intriguing, intrigued) **1** arouse great curiosity in someone 激起…的好奇心；使产生兴趣 **2** plot something illegal or harmful 耍阴谋；施诡计 • noun /'ɪntriːg/ **1** the plotting of something illegal or harmful 阴谋，诡计 **2** a secret plan or relationship 密谋；秘密关系 ∎ **intriguing** adjective **intriguingly** adverb.

intrinsic /ɪn'trɪnsɪk/ adjective forming part of the real and fundamental nature of something 本质的；固有的 ∎ **intrinsically** adverb.

introduce /ˌɪntrə'djuːs/ verb (intro-

duces, introducing, introduced)
1 bring something into use or operation for the first time 引进；推行 **2** present someone by name 介绍，引荐 (某人) **3** (introduce something to) bring a subject to someone's attention for the first time 使初次了解；使尝试 **4** insert or bring something into 插入，带入 **5** happen at the start of 作为…的开头 **6** provide an opening announcement for 宣布…开始；为…作开场白

introduction /ˌɪntrəˈdʌkʃn/ **noun 1** the action of introducing or being introduced 引进；推行 **2** a thing which introduces another, such as a section at the beginning of a book (书等的) 引言，导言 **3** a thing newly brought in 新引进之物；新采用的东西 **4** a book or course intended to introduce a newcomer to a subject of study 入门书；初级课程 **5** a person's first experience of a subject or activity 初次经历；首次体验

introductory /ˌɪntrəˈdʌktəri/ **adjective** forming an introduction; basic 介绍的；引言的；基本的

introspection /ˌɪntrəˈspekʃn/ **noun** concentration on your own thoughts or feelings 内省；反思 ■ **introspective** adjective.

introvert /ˈɪntrəvɜːt/ **noun** a shy, quiet person who is focused on their own thoughts and feelings 内向的人 ● **adjective** (also **introverted**) characteristic of an introvert 性格内向的

intrude /ɪnˈtruːd/ **verb** (intrudes, intruding, intruded) come into a place or situation where you are unwelcome or uninvited 擅自进入，闯入，侵入

intruder /ɪnˈtruːdə(r)/ **noun 1** a person who intrudes 不速之客 **2** a person who goes into a building or an area illegally 闯入者；侵入者

intrusion /ɪnˈtruːʒn/ **noun 1** the action of intruding 闯入；侵入 **2** a

thing that has intruded 闯入物；侵入物

intrusive /ɪnˈtruːsɪv/ **adjective** having a disturbing and unwelcome effect 侵扰的；不受欢迎的

intuit /ɪnˈtjuːɪt/ **verb** understand or work something out by intuition 凭直觉知道；凭直觉解决

intuition /ˌɪntjuˈɪʃn/ **noun** the ability to understand or know something without conscious reasoning 直觉

intuitive /ɪnˈtjuːɪtɪv/ **adjective** able to understand or know something without conscious reasoning 有直觉力的 ■ **intuitively** adverb.

Inuit /ˈɪnjuɪt/ **noun** (plural **Inuit** or **Inuits**) a member of a people of northern Canada and parts of Greenland and Alaska; an Eskimo 伊努伊特人

! 注意 **Inuit** is the official term in Canada, and many of the peoples traditionally called **Eskimos** prefer it. Inuit (伊努伊特人) 一词是加拿大的官方称谓，很多传统上被称作 Eskimos (爱斯基摩人) 的人更喜欢这个称谓。

inundate /ˈɪnʌndeɪt/ **verb** (inundates, inundating, inundated) **1** give or send someone so many things that they cannot deal with them all 使不胜负荷；使应接不暇 **2** flood a place 淹没 ■ **inundation** noun.

inure /ɪˈnjʊə(r)/ **verb** (be inured to) make someone used to something unpleasant 使习惯于(令人不愉快的事物)

invade /ɪnˈveɪd/ **verb** (invades, invading, invaded) **1** enter a country so as to conquer or occupy it 侵略；入侵 **2** enter a place in large numbers 大量涌入 **3** intrude on 侵犯 **4** (of a parasite or disease) spread into (寄生虫或疾病)侵袭 ■ **invader** noun.

invalid[1] /ˈɪnvəlɪd/ **noun** a person

suffering from an illness or injury 病弱者 • verb (be invalided) be removed from active military service because of injury or illness (因伤病)退役

invalid² /ɪnˈvælɪd/ **adjective 1** not legally or officially recognized 无法律效力的 **2** not correct because based on a mistake 不真实的；站不住脚的

invalidate /ɪnˈvælɪdeɪt/ **verb (invalidates, invalidating, invalidated)** make something invalid 使无效；证明…错误

invalidity /ˌɪnvəˈlɪdəti/ **noun 1** Brit. 【英】the condition of being an invalid 病弱 **2** the fact of not being valid 无法律效力；不真实

invaluable /ɪnˈvæljʊəbl/ **adjective** very useful 极有用的

invariable /ɪnˈveəriəbl/ **adjective 1** never changing 恒常不变的；始终如一 **2** Maths【数学】(of a quantity) constant (量)常数的，非变量的

invariably /ɪnˈveəriəbli/ **adverb** always 总是

invasion /ɪnˈveɪʒn/ **noun 1** an act of invading a country 侵略 **2** the arrival of a large number of unwelcome people or things (人或物的)大量涌入

invasive /ɪnˈveɪsɪv/ **adjective 1** tending to invade or intrude 侵入的；侵袭的 **2** (of medical procedures) involving the introduction of instruments or other objects into the body (医疗)开刀的，切入的

invective /ɪnˈvektɪv/ **noun** strongly abusive or critical language 咒骂，辱骂

inveigh /ɪnˈveɪ/ **verb (inveigh against)** speak or write about someone or something with great hostility 痛斥；猛烈抨击

inveigle /ɪnˈveɪgl/ **verb (inveigles, inveigling, inveigled) (inveigle someone into)** cleverly persuade someone to do something 哄骗；诱骗

invent /ɪnˈvent/ **verb 1** create or design a new device or process 创造，发明 **2** make up a false story, name, etc. 编造，虚构(故事、姓名等) ■ **inventor** noun.

invention /ɪnˈvenʃn/ **noun 1** the action of inventing 发明；创造 **2** a thing that has been invented 发明物；创造物 **3** a false story 虚构的故事 **4** creative ability 创造能力

inventive /ɪnˈventɪv/ **adjective** having or showing creativity or original thought 有发明创造才能的；显示创造力的 ■ **inventively** adverb.

inventory /ˈɪnvəntri/ **noun (plural inventories) 1** a complete list of items 货物清单 **2** a quantity of goods in stock 库存货物

inverse /ɪnˈvɜːs/ **adjective** opposite in position, direction, order, or effect (位置、方向、顺序或效果)相反的 • **noun 1** a thing that is the opposite or reverse of another 相反的事物，颠倒的事物 **2** Maths【数学】a reciprocal quantity 反数；倒数 ■ **inversion** noun.

invert /ɪnˈvɜːt/ **verb** put something upside down or in the opposite position, order, or arrangement 使颠倒；使(位置或顺序)倒置 □ **inverted comma** a quotation mark 引号

invertebrate /ɪnˈvɜːtɪbrət/ **noun** an animal that has no backbone 无脊椎动物

invest /ɪnˈvest/ **verb 1** put money into financial schemes, shares, or property in the hope of making a profit (为盈利)投资 **2** put time or energy into something in the hope of worthwhile results 投入，付出(时间或精力) **3** (invest in) buy something expensive 买进(某物) **4** (invest something with) give something a particular quality 赋予(某品质) **5** give someone a rank, honour, official title, etc. in a special ceremony (在特别仪式上)授予 ■ **investor** noun.

investigate /ɪnˈvestɪgeɪt/ **verb 1**

carry out a systematic inquiry so as to establish the truth of something 调查(事件或指控) **2** carry out research into a subject 研究(某个学科) ■ **investigation** noun **investigative** adjective **investigator** noun.

investiture /ɪn'vestɪtʃə(r)/ **noun 1** the action of formally giving a person a rank, honour, or special title 授予(荣誉、特殊头衔等);授爵;授职 **2** a ceremony at which this takes place 授衔仪式;授爵仪式

investment /ɪn'vestmənt/ **noun 1** the process of investing in something 投资 **2** a thing worth buying because it may be profitable or useful in the future 值得买的东西;有用的投资物

inveterate /ɪn'vetərət/ **adjective 1** having done a particular thing so often that you are now unlikely to stop doing it 有…瘾的;积习难改的 **2** (of a feeling or habit) firmly established (感情或习惯)根深蒂固的

invidious /ɪn'vɪdiəs/ **adjective** unfair and likely to arouse resentment or anger in other people 不公平而招致怨恨的;引起不满的

invigilate /ɪn'vɪdʒɪleɪt/ **verb** (**invigilates**, **invigilating**, **invigilated**) Brit. 【英】supervise candidates during an exam 监考 ■ **invigilation** noun **invigilator** noun.

invigorate /ɪn'vɪɡəreɪt/ **verb** (**invigorates**, **invigorating**, **invigorated**) give strength or energy to 使精力充沛

invincible /ɪn'vɪnsəbl/ **adjective** too powerful to be defeated or overcome 不可战胜的;不可征服的

inviolable /ɪn'vaɪələbl/ **adjective** that must be respected; never to be broken or attacked 不可侵犯的;不可亵渎的

inviolate /ɪn'vaɪələt/ **adjective** free from injury or violation 不受破坏(或侵犯)的

invisible /ɪn'vɪzəbl/ **adjective** not able to be seen 看不见的;隐形的 ■ **invisibility** noun **invisibly** adverb.

invitation /ˌɪnvɪ'teɪʃn/ **noun 1** a request that someone should join you in going somewhere or doing something 邀请 **2** the action of inviting 邀请(行为) **3** a situation or action that is likely to provoke a particular outcome or response 引来;招致

invite /ɪn'vaɪt/ **verb** (**invites**, **inviting**, **invited**) **1** ask someone to join you in going somewhere or doing something 邀请;约请 **2** ask formally or politely for a response to something (正式或礼貌地)要求,请求 **3** tend to provoke a particular outcome or response 招致,引起(结果或反应) • **noun** informal 【非正式】an invitation 邀请

inviting /ɪn'vaɪtɪŋ/ **adjective** tempting or attractive 诱人的;吸引人的 ■ **invitingly** adverb.

in vitro /ɪn 'viːtrəʊ/ **adjective & adverb** taking place in a test tube, culture dish, or elsewhere outside a living animal or plant (生物过程)在试管内进行的(地);在生物体外进行的(地)

invocation /ˌɪnvə'keɪʃn/ **noun 1** the action of invoking 祈祷;祈求 **2** an appeal to a god or supernatural being 祈求神助

invoice /'ɪnvɔɪs/ **noun** a list of goods or services provided, with a statement of the payment that is due 发货清单;发票 • **verb** (**invoices**, **invoicing**, **invoiced**) send an invoice to someone 给…开发票

invoke /ɪn'vəʊk/ **verb** (**invokes**, **invoking**, **invoked**) **1** appeal to someone or something as an authority or in support of an argument 援引 **2** call on a god or supernatural being 祈求(神灵) **3** call earnestly for 热切要求;唤起

involuntary /ɪn'vɒləntri/ **adjective 1** done without conscious control 不受

意识控制的 **2** (especially of muscles or nerves) unable to be consciously controlled (尤指肌肉或神经)无知觉的，无法控制的 **3** done against someone's will 违背意愿的；出于无奈的 ■ **involuntarily** adverb.

involve /ɪnˈvɒlv/ verb (**involves, involving, involved**) **1** (of a situation or event) include something as a necessary part or result (形势或事件)包括，使成为必然部分(或结果) **2** make someone experience or take part in something 使经历；使参与 ■ **involvement** noun.

involved /ɪnˈvɒlvd/ adjective **1** connected with someone or something on an emotional or personal level (感情上或个人)有关的，有牵扯的 **2** complicated 复杂的

invulnerable /ɪnˈvʌlnərəbl/ adjective impossible to harm or damage 不能伤害的；不能损坏的

inwards /ˈɪnwədz/ or **inward** /ˈɪnwəd/ adverb **1** towards the inside 向内；向内 **2** into or towards the mind, spirit, or soul 向内心深处；精神上 ■ **inwardly** adverb.

iodine /ˈaɪədiːn/ noun **1** a black, non-metallic chemical element (非金属化学元素)碘 **2** a solution of iodine in alcohol used as an antiseptic 碘酒

ion /ˈaɪən/ noun an atom or molecule with a net electric charge through loss or gain of electrons 离子 ■ **ionic** adjective.

ionize or **ionise** /ˈaɪənaɪz/ verb convert an atom, molecule, or substance into an ion or ions 使(原子、分子或物质)离子化 ■ **ionization** noun.

ionizer /ˈaɪənaɪzə(r)/ noun a device which produces ions, used to improve the quality of the air in a room (用于净化室内空气的)离子发生器

ionosphere /aɪˈɒnəsfɪə(r)/ noun the layer of the atmosphere above the mesosphere 电离层

iota /aɪˈəʊtə/ noun a very small amount 极少量

IOU /ˌaɪ əʊ ˈjuː/ noun a signed document acknowledging a debt 借据

ipso facto /ˌɪpsəʊ ˈfæktəʊ/ adverb by that very fact or act 根据事实本身；根据该行为

IQ /ˌaɪ ˈkjuː/ abbreviation intelligence quotient, a number representing a person's ability to reason, calculated from the results of special tests 智商

IRA /ˌaɪ ɑː ˈreɪ/ abbreviation Irish Republican Army 爱尔兰共和军

Iranian /ɪˈreɪniən/ noun a person from Iran 伊朗人 • adjective relating to Iran 伊朗的

Iraqi /ɪˈrɑːki/ noun (plural **Iraqis**) a person from Iraq 伊拉克人 • adjective relating to Iraq 伊拉克的

irascible /ɪˈræsəbl/ adjective hot-tempered; irritable 脾气暴躁的；易怒的

irate /aɪˈreɪt/ adjective very angry 非常生气的，大怒的

ire /ˈaɪə(r)/ noun literary [文] anger 愤怒

iridescent /ˌɪrɪˈdesnt/ adjective showing bright colours that seem to change when seen from different angles 色彩斑斓闪耀的 ■ **iridescence** noun.

> ✔ 拼写指南 just one *r*: iridescent. iridescent 中只有一个 r。

iris /ˈaɪrɪs/ noun **1** the round coloured part of the eye, with the pupil in the centre 虹膜 **2** a plant with sword-shaped leaves and purple, yellow, or white flowers 鸢尾属植物(叶呈剑形，开紫色、黄色或白色的花)

Irish /ˈaɪrɪʃ/ noun (also **Irish Gaelic**) the language of Ireland 爱尔兰语 • adjective relating to Ireland or Irish 爱尔兰的；爱尔兰语的

irk /ɜːk/ verb irritate; annoy 使愤怒；使厌烦

irksome /ˈɜːksəm/ adjective irritating；

annoying 使人愤怒的；使人厌烦的

iron /'aɪən/ **noun 1** a strong magnetic silvery-grey metal 铁 **2** a tool made of iron 铁器 **3** a hand-held piece of equipment with a heated steel base, used to smooth clothes 熨斗 **4** a golf club used for hitting the ball at a high angle (高尔夫)铁头球杆 **5** (**irons**) handcuffs or chains used as a restraint 脚镣；手铐 • **verb 1** smooth clothes with an iron (用熨斗)熨(衣服) **2** (**iron something out**) settle a difficulty or problem 解决(困难或问题) □ **Iron Age** an ancient period when weapons and tools were made of iron 铁器时代 **Iron Curtain** an imaginary barrier separating the communist countries of the former Soviet bloc and western Europe 铁幕(前苏联阵营与西方之间的一道无形的屏障)

ironic /aɪ'rɒnɪk/ **adjective 1** using irony 冷嘲的；讽刺的 **2** happening in the opposite way to what is expected 具有反讽意味的 ■ **ironically** adverb.

ironmonger /'aɪənmʌŋɡə(r)/ **noun** Brit. 【英】a person who sells tools and other hardware 小五金商 ■ **ironmongery** noun.

ironworks /'aɪənwɜːks/ **noun** a place where iron is smelted or iron goods are made 钢铁厂

irony /'aɪrəni/ **noun** (plural **ironies**) **1** the use of words that say the opposite of what you really mean in order to be funny or to make a point 反语 **2** aspects of a situation that are opposite to what are expected 与预期相反的情况

irradiate /ɪ'reɪdieɪt/ **verb** (**irradiates, irradiating, irradiated**) **1** expose to radiation 使受辐射 **2** shine light on 照亮；照耀 ■ **irradiation** noun.

irrational /ɪ'ræʃənl/ **adjective** not logical or reasonable 不合逻辑的，不合理的 ■ **irrationality** noun **irrationally** adverb.

irreconcilable /ɪ'rekənsaɪləbl/ **adjective 1** incompatible 不相容的 **2** (of differences) not able to be settled (分歧)不能调和的

irrecoverable /ˌɪrɪ'kʌvərəbl/ **adjective** not able to be recovered 不能回复的

irredeemable /ˌɪrɪ'diːməbl/ **adjective** not able to be saved, improved, or corrected 不能挽救的；无法改善的；不能改正的

irreducible /ˌɪrɪ'djuːsəbl/ **adjective** not able to be reduced or simplified 不能减缩的；不可简化的

irrefutable /ˌɪrɪ'fjuːtəbl/ **adjective** impossible to deny or disprove 不可否认的；无可辩驳的

irregular /ɪ'reɡjələ(r)/ **adjective 1** not regular in shape, arrangement, or occurrence (形状、排列或发生之事)无规则的，不规律的 **2** against a rule, standard, or convention 不合规则的；不按标准的 **3** not belonging to regular army units 非正规军的 **4** Grammar【语法】(of a word) having inflections that do not conform to the usual rules (单词)不规则变化的 ■ **irregularity** noun (plural **irregularities**).

irrelevant /ɪ'reləvənt/ **adjective** not relevant 不相关的 ■ **irrelevance** noun **irrelevantly** adverb.

✔ 拼写指南 *-ant*, not *-ent*: irrelevant. irrelevant 中 -ant 不要拼作 -ent.
---

irreligious /ˌɪrɪ'lɪdʒəs/ **adjective** indifferent or hostile to religion 漠视宗教的；敌视宗教的

irremediable /ˌɪrɪ'miːdiəbl/ **adjective** impossible to cure or put right 不可治愈的，不能补救的；无法纠正的

irreparable /ɪ'repərəbl/ **adjective** impossible to put right or repair 不能矫正的；无法修理的 ■ **irreparably** adverb.

irreplaceable /ˌɪrɪ'pleɪsəbl/ **adjective**

impossible to replace if lost or damaged 不可替代的

irrepressible /ˌɪrɪˈpresəbl/ **adjective** not able to be restrained 压抑不住的；十分强烈的

irreproachable /ˌɪrɪˈprəʊtʃəbl/ **adjective** very good and unable to be criticized 无懈可击的；无可指责的

irresistible /ˌɪrɪˈzɪstəbl/ **adjective** too tempting or powerful to be resisted 十分诱人的；无法抗拒的 ■ **irresistibly** adverb.

✔ 拼写指南 -ible, not -able: irresistible. irresistible 中 -ible 不要拼作 -able。

irresolute /ɪˈrezəluːt/ **adjective** uncertain 踌躇的；犹豫不决的

irrespective /ˌɪrɪˈspektɪv/ **adjective** (**irrespective of**) regardless of 不顾；不管

irresponsible /ˌɪrɪˈspɒnsəbl/ **adjective** not showing a proper sense of responsibility 无责任感的；不负责任的 ■ **irresponsibility** noun **irresponsibly** adverb.

irretrievable /ˌɪrɪˈtriːvəbl/ **adjective** not able to be brought back or made right 不能挽回的；不能纠正的 ■ **irretrievably** adverb.

irreverent /ɪˈrevərənt/ **adjective** disrespectful 无礼的；不尊敬的 ■ **irreverence** noun **irreverently** adverb.

irreversible /ˌɪrɪˈvɜːsəbl/ **adjective** impossible to be reversed or altered 不可逆的；不可改变的 ■ **irreversibly** adverb.

irrevocable /ɪˈrevəkəbl/ **adjective** not able to be changed or reversed 不可改变的；不能逆转的；不能恢复的 ■ **irrevocably** adverb.

irrigate /ˈɪrɪɡeɪt/ **verb** (**irrigates**, **irrigating**, **irrigated**) supply water to land or crops through channels 灌溉(土地或庄稼) ■ **irrigation** noun.

irritable /ˈɪrɪtəbl/ **adjective 1** easily annoyed or angered 暴躁的；易怒的

2 Medicine 【医】unusually sensitive 过敏的 ■ **irritability** noun **irritably** adverb.

irritant /ˈɪrɪtənt/ **noun 1** a substance that irritates the skin or a part of the body 刺激物 **2** a source of continual annoyance 令人烦恼的事物

irritate /ˈɪrɪteɪt/ **verb** (**irritates**, **irritating**, **irritated**) **1** make someone annoyed or angry 使恼怒 **2** cause soreness, itching, or inflammation 使(身体某部位)发炎 ■ **irritation** noun.

is /ɪz/ 3rd person singular present of BE.

ISA /ˌaɪ es ˈeɪ/ **abbreviation** individual savings account 个人储蓄账户

Islam /ˈɪzlɑːm/ **noun 1** the religion of the Muslims, revealed through Muhammad as the Prophet of Allah 伊斯兰教 **2** the Muslim world 伊斯兰世界 ■ **Islamic** adjective.

island /ˈaɪlənd/ **noun 1** a piece of land surrounded by water 岛(屿) **2** a thing that is isolated, detached, or surrounded 岛状物 ■ **islander** noun.

isle /aɪl/ **noun** literary 【文】an island 岛

islet /ˈaɪlət/ **noun** a small island 小岛

isn't /ˈɪznt/ **short form** is not.

isobar /ˈaɪsəbɑː(r)/ **noun** a line on a map connecting points having the same atmospheric pressure(地图上的)等压线

isolate /ˈaɪsəleɪt/ **verb** (**isolates**, **isolating**, **isolated**) **1** place something or someone apart from others and on their own 孤立；使脱离 **2** extract a substance in a pure form 离析；提纯 ■ **isolation** noun.

isolated /ˈaɪsəleɪtɪd/ **adjective 1** (of a place) remote (地方)遥远的 **2** (of a person) cut off from other people; lonely (人)孤独的，孤立的 **3** single; exceptional 单独的；例外的

isolationism /ˌaɪsəˈleɪʃnɪzəm/ **noun** a policy of remaining apart from the political affairs of other countries (政

治上的)孤立主义

isomer /'aɪsəmə(r)/ **noun** Chemistry 【化学】each of two or more compounds with the same formula but a different arrangement of atoms (同分)异构体；(同分)异构物

isometric /ˌaɪsə'metrɪk/ **adjective** having equal dimensions 等量的；等尺寸的

isosceles /aɪ'sɒsəli:z/ **adjective** (of a triangle) having two sides of equal length (三角形)等腰的

isotope /'aɪsətəʊp/ **noun** each of two or more forms of the same element that contain equal numbers of protons but different numbers of neutrons in their nuclei 同位素

ISP /ˌaɪ es 'pi:/ **abbreviation** Internet service provider 因特网服务供应商

Israeli /ɪz'reɪli/ **noun** (plural **Israelis**) a person from Israel 以色列人 • **adjective** relating to the modern country of Israel 以色列的

Israelite /'ɪzriəlaɪt/ **noun** a member of the people of ancient Israel 古以色列人

issue /'ɪʃu:/ **noun 1** an important topic to be discussed or settled 争论的问题；待解决的问题 **2** a problem or difficulty 问题；困难 **3** each of a regular series of publications 一期；期号 **4** the action of supplying something 提供；分发 • **verb** (**issues, issuing, issued**) **1** supply or give out 提供；分发 **2** formally send out or make known 正式颁发；发布 **3** (**issue from**) come, go, or flow out from 从…中出来(或流出) □ **take issue with** challenge someone 向(某人)提出异议

isthmus /'ɪsməs/ **noun** (plural **isthmuses**) a narrow strip of land with sea on either side, linking two larger areas of land 地峡

IT /ˌaɪ 'ti:/ **abbreviation** information technology.

it /ɪt/ **pronoun 1** used to refer to a thing previously mentioned or easily identified 它(用于指先前提到的某物或易认定之物) **2** referring to an animal or child whose sex is not specified 它(指动物或未确定性别的小孩) **3** used in the normal subject position in statements about time, distance, or weather (用于谈论时间、距离或天气时作主语) **4** the situation or circumstances (用于指情形或状况)

Italian /ɪ'tæliən/ **noun 1** a person from Italy 意大利人 **2** the language of Italy 意大利语 • **adjective** relating to Italy or Italian 意大利的；意大利人的；意大利语的

italic /ɪ'tælɪk/ **adjective** (of a typeface) sloping to the right, used especially for emphasis and for foreign words 印刷字体斜体的(尤用于强调或表示外来语) • **noun** (also **italics**) an italic typeface or letter 斜体；斜体字 ■ **italicize** (or **italicise**) verb.

itch /ɪtʃ/ **noun 1** an uncomfortable sensation that makes you want to scratch your skin (皮肤)瘙痒 **2** informal 【非正式】an impatient desire 渴望；热望 • **verb 1** experience an itch 发痒 **2** informal 【非正式】feel an impatient desire to do something 渴望；热望 ■ **itchy** adjective.

it'd /'ɪtəd/ **short form 1** it had. **2** it would.

item /'aɪtəm/ **noun** an individual article or unit 项目；单元

itemize or **itemise** /'aɪtəmaɪz/ **verb** (**itemizes, itemizing, itemized**) present a quantity as a list of individual items or parts 逐条登录；列出清单

itinerant /aɪ'tɪnərənt/ **adjective** travelling from place to place 巡游的；流动的 • **noun** an itinerant person 流浪者；巡回旅游者

itinerary /aɪ'tɪnərəri/ **noun** (plural **itineraries**) a planned route or journey 预定行程；旅行日程

✔ 拼写指南 itine*rar*y, not -*ery*.
itinerary 不要拼作 -ery。

it'll /ɪtl/ **short form 1** it shall. **2** it will.

its /ɪts/ **possessive determiner 1** belonging to or associated with a thing previously mentioned or easily identified 它的(指先前提及或认定的事物) **2** belonging to or associated with a child or animal whose sex is not specified 它的(指性别未确定的孩子或动物)

! 注意 don't confuse the possessive **its** (as in *turn the camera on its side*) with the form **it's** (short for either **it is** or **it has**, as in *it's my fault* or *it's been a hot day*). 不要混淆所有格形式的 its(如 turn the camera on its side 把照相机侧立起来)和 it's,后者是 it is 或 it has 的缩略形式,如 it's my fault (是我的错) 或 it's been a hot day (今天是个大热天)。

it's /ɪts/ **short form 1** it is. **2** it has.

itself /ɪt'self/ **pronoun 1** used to refer to something previously mentioned as the subject of the clause 自身;它自己 **2** used to emphasize a particular thing mentioned (用于强调已提及的事物)

ITV /ˌaɪ tiː ˈviː/ **abbreviation** Independent Television 独立电视(台)

IUD /ˌaɪ juː ˈdiː/ **abbreviation** intrauterine device 宫内避孕器

I've /aɪv/ **short form** I have.

IVF /ˌaɪ viː ˈef/ **abbreviation** in vitro fertilization 体外受精;试管内受精

ivory /ˈaɪvəri/ **noun** (plural **ivories**) **1** the hard creamy-white substance which elephants' tusks are made of 象牙 **2** the creamy-white colour of ivory 象牙色 □ **ivory tower** a situation in which someone leads a privileged life and does not have to face normal difficulties 象牙塔(指脱离现实生活的小天地)

ivy /ˈaɪvi/ **noun** an evergreen climbing plant 常春藤

Jj

J or **j** /dʒeɪ/ noun (plural **Js** or **J's**) the tenth letter of the alphabet 英语字母表的第10个字母 • abbreviation joules.

jab /dʒæb/ verb (**jabs, jabbing, jabbed**) poke someone with something sharp or pointed 猛戳; 捅; 刺; 扎 • noun **1** a quick, sharp poke or blow 猛 戳; 捅; 扎; 猛击 **2** Brit. informal 【英, 非正式】 a vaccination 接种

jabber /'dʒæbə(r)/ verb (**jabbers, jabbering, jabbered**) talk quickly and excitedly but without making much sense 急促而含糊不清地说

jack /dʒæk/ noun **1** a device for lifting a vehicle off the ground so that a wheel can be changed or the underside examined 起重器; 千斤顶 **2** a playing card ranking next below a queen (牌戏中的) J牌, 杰克 **3** a connection between two pieces of electrical equipment 插座 **4** (in bowls) a small white ball at which players aim the bowls (草地滚球戏中作靶子的) 小白球 • verb (**jack something up**) **1** raise something with a jack 用千斤顶托起; 用起重器举起 **2** informal 【非正式】 increase something by a large amount 猛增; 激增 ☐ **jack-in-the-box** a toy consisting of a box containing a figure on a spring, which pops up when the lid is opened 玩偶匣 (内装掀开盒盖即跳起的玩偶)

jackal /'dʒækɔːl/ noun a wild dog that often hunts or scavenges in packs 豺, 胡狼 (常常成群捕猎或觅食的野狗)

jackass /'dʒækæs/ noun **1** a stupid

person 傻瓜; 笨蛋 **2** a male ass or donkey 公驴

jackdaw /'dʒækdɔː/ noun a small crow with a grey head 寒鸦

jacket /'dʒækɪt/ noun **1** an outer garment reaching to the waist or hips, with sleeves 夹克衫; (带袖) 短 上 衣 **2** a covering placed around something for protection or insulation 保护罩; 绝缘罩; 隔热罩 **3** Brit. 【英】 the skin of a potato 马铃薯皮; 土豆皮 ☐ **jacket potato** Brit. 【英】 a potato that is baked and served with the skin on 带皮烤的马铃薯

jackknife /'dʒæknaɪf/ noun (plural **jackknives**) a large knife with a folding blade 大折刀; 折叠刀 • verb (**jackknifes, jackknifing, jackknifed**) (of an articulated lorry or truck) bend into a V-shape in an uncontrolled skidding movement (铰接式卡车) 突然弯折

jackpot /'dʒækpɒt/ noun a large cash prize in a game or lottery (游戏或抽彩中设置的) 巨额奖金 ☐ **hit the jackpot** have great or unexpected success 大获成功; 意外获胜

Jacobean /ˌdʒækəʊ'biːən/ adjective having to do with the reign of James I of England (1603–1625) 英王詹姆斯一世时期的 • noun a person who lived in the Jacobean period 詹姆斯一世时期的人

Jacobite /'dʒækəbaɪt/ noun a supporter of the deposed James II and his descendants in their claim to the British throne 詹姆斯党 (拥护詹姆斯二世及其后裔复辟者)

jacquard /ˈdʒækɑːd/ **noun** a fabric with a woven pattern 提花织物

jacuzzi /dʒəˈkuːzi/ **noun** (plural **jacuzzis**) trademark 【商标】 a large, wide bath with jets of water to massage the body "极可意"浴缸(一种水力按摩浴缸)

jade /dʒeɪd/ **noun** a hard bluish-green precious stone 碧玉；翡翠

jaded /ˈdʒeɪdɪd/ **adjective** tired out or lacking enthusiasm after having had too much of something 精疲力竭的；厌倦的

jagged /ˈdʒægɪd/ **adjective** with rough, sharp points or edges sticking out 有尖突的；参差不齐的；凹凸不平的

jaguar /ˈdʒægjuə(r)/ **noun** a large cat with a spotted coat, found in Central and South America 美洲豹；美洲虎

jail or Brit. 【英】 **gaol** /dʒeɪl/ **noun** a place for holding people who are accused or convicted of a crime 看守所；监狱 • **verb** put someone in jail 关押；监禁 ■ **jailer** (or Brit. 【英】 **gaoler**) **noun**.

jalopy /dʒəˈlɒpi/ **noun** (plural **jalopies**) informal 【非正式】 an old car 破旧汽车；老爷车

jam[1] /dʒæm/ **verb** (**jams, jamming, jammed**) **1** squeeze or pack tightly into a space 挤压；塞满，塞人 **2** push something roughly and forcibly into a position 用力挤进 **3** block something through crowding 堵塞 **4** make or become unable to function because a part is stuck (使)卡住而无法运转 **5** (**jam something on**) apply a brake suddenly and with force 突然制动；猛地刹车 **6** interrupt a radio transmission by causing interference 干扰(无线电传输) **7** informal 【非正式】 improvise with other musicians 即兴演奏 • **noun 1** an instance of something being jammed 堵塞；阻塞 **2** informal 【非正式】 a difficult

situation 困境；窘境 **3** informal 【非正式】 an improvised performance by a group of musicians 即兴演奏会

jam[2] **noun** chiefly Brit. 【主英】 a spread made from fruit and sugar 果酱

Jamaican /dʒəˈmeɪkən/ **noun** a person from Jamaica 牙买加人 • **adjective** relating to Jamaica 牙买加的

jamb /dʒæm/ **noun** a side post of a doorway, window, or fireplace 门窗边框；壁炉框

jamboree /ˌdʒæmbəˈriː/ **noun** a large celebration or party 大型聚会；庆祝会

jammy /ˈdʒæmi/ **adjective** (**jammier, jammiest**) **1** covered or filled with jam 涂着果酱的；装满果酱的 **2** Brit. informal 【英，非正式】 lucky 幸运的

jangle /ˈdʒæŋgl/ **verb** (**jangles, jangling, jangled**) **1** make a ringing metallic sound 发出丁零当啷声 **2** (of your nerves) be set on edge (神经)紧张；焦躁不安 • **noun** a ringing metallic sound 丁零当啷声 ■ **jangly** adjective.

janitor /ˈdʒænɪtə(r)/ **noun** a caretaker of a building 门房；看楼人

January /ˈdʒænjuəri/ **noun** (plural **Januaries**) the first month of the year 一月

Japanese /ˌdʒæpəˈniːz/ **noun** (plural **Japanese**) **1** a person from Japan 日本人 **2** the language of Japan 日语 • **adjective** relating to Japan 日本的

jape /dʒeɪp/ **noun** a practical joke 玩笑；恶作剧

jar[1] /dʒɑː(r)/ **noun** a cylindrical container made of glass or pottery 罐子；坛子

jar[2] **verb** (**jars, jarring, jarred**) **1** send a painful shock through a part of the body 撞击，撞击(身体部位) **2** hit something with an unpleasant vibration or jolt 震动；摇动 **3** have an unpleasant or strange effect 产生不快的影响 • **noun** an instance of jarring 撞击;震动;摇动;不快

jargon /'dʒɑːgən/ **noun** words or phrases used by a particular group that are difficult for other people to understand 行话;术语

jasmine /'dʒæzmɪn/ **noun** a shrub or climbing plant with sweet-smelling flowers 素馨;茉莉

jasper /'dʒæspə(r)/ **noun** a reddish-brown variety of quartz 碧玉

jaundice /'dʒɔːndɪs/ **noun 1** a condition in which the skin takes on a yellow colour 黄疸病 **2** bitterness or resentment 痛苦;怨恨 ■ **jaundiced** adjective.

jaunt /dʒɔːnt/ **noun** a short trip or journey taken for pleasure 短途旅行;远足

jaunty /'dʒɔːnti/ **adjective (jauntier, jauntiest)** lively and self-confident 活泼的;自信的 ■ **jauntily** adverb.

javelin /'dʒævlɪn/ **noun** a long spear thrown in a competitive sport or as a weapon (竞技体育中使用的)标枪;(用作武器的)投枪

jaw /dʒɔː/ **noun** each of the upper and lower bony structures forming the framework of the mouth and containing the teeth 颌;颚 • **verb** informal 【非正式】talk at length 喋喋不休;唠叨

jawbone /'dʒɔːbəʊn/ **noun** the lower jaw, or the lower part of the face 下颌骨

jay /dʒeɪ/ **noun** a noisy bird of the crow family with brightly coloured feathers 松鸦(羽毛鲜艳,喜鸣叫)

jaywalk /'dʒeɪwɔːk/ **verb** chiefly N. Amer. 【主北美】walk in or across a road without paying proper attention to the traffic 不遵守交通规则乱走(或乱穿马路)■ **jaywalker** noun.

jazz /dʒæz/ **noun** a type of music that is mainly instrumental, in which the players often improvise 爵士乐 • **verb (jazz something up)** make something more lively 使更活泼

jazzy /'dʒæzi/ **adjective (jazzier, jazziest) 1** in the style of jazz 爵士乐的 **2** bright, colourful,and showy 鲜亮的,鲜艳的;花哨的

jealous /'dʒeləs/ **adjective 1** envious of someone else's achievements or advantages 羡慕的;妒忌的 **2** resentful of someone who you think is a sexual rival 爱吃醋的;嫉妒的 **3** very protective of your rights or possessions (对权利或财产)极力守护的,唯恐失去的 ■ **jealously** adverb **jealousy** noun.

jeans /dʒiːnz/ **noun** casual trousers made of denim 牛仔裤

jeep /dʒiːp/ **noun** trademark 【商标】a sturdy motor vehicle with four-wheel drive 吉普车

jeer /dʒɪə(r)/ **verb (jeers, jeering, jeered)** shout rude and mocking remarks at someone 奚落;嘲笑 • **noun** a rude and mocking remark 奚落;嘲笑的话

Jehovah /dʒɪˈhəʊvə/ **noun** a form of the Hebrew name of God used in some translations of the Bible 耶和华(一些《圣经》译本中对上帝的希伯来语称呼)

jejune /dʒɪˈdʒuːn/ **adjective 1** naive and simplistic 天真的;幼稚的 **2** not interesting 枯燥无味的;干巴巴的

jell /dʒel/ **verb** ⇒ 见 GEL².

jelly /'dʒeli/ **noun (plural jellies) 1** Brit. 【英】a dessert consisting of a fruit-flavoured liquid set with gelatin to form a semi-solid mass 果冻 **2** a substance with a similar semisolid consistency 胶状物 ■ **jellied** adjective.

jellyfish /'dʒelifɪʃ/ **noun (plural jellyfish or jellyfishes)** a sea creature with a soft jelly-like body that has stinging tentacles around the edge 水母;海蜇

jemmy /'dʒemi/ **noun (plural jemmies)** a short crowbar 短撬棍

je ne sais quoi /ʒə nə seɪ ˈkwɑː/ **noun**

a quality that cannot be easily identified 难以辨别的品质

jenny /'dʒeni/ noun (plural **jennies**) a female donkey or ass 母驴

jeopardize or **jeopardise** /'dʒepədaɪz/ verb (**jeopardizes**, **jeopardizing**, **jeopardized**) risk harming or destroying something 危及；损害

jeopardy /'dʒepədi/ noun danger of loss, harm, or failure 危险；危害

jerboa /dʒɜː'bəʊə/ noun a desert rodent with very long hind legs 跳鼠 (见于沙漠地区，后腿特长)

jerk /dʒɜːk/ noun 1 a quick, sharp, sudden movement 猛拉；猛扯 2 informal 【非正式】 a stupid person 傻瓜，笨蛋 • verb move or raise with a jerk 猝然一动；猛举

jerkin /'dʒɜːkɪn/ noun a sleeveless jacket 无袖短上衣；坎肩

jerky /'dʒɜːki/ adjective (**jerkier**, **jerkiest**) moving in sudden stops and starts 忽动忽停的；颠簸的 ■ **jerkily** adverb.

jerry-built /'dʒerɪbɪlt/ adjective badly or quickly built, using cheap materials 建筑质量差的，仓促建成的

jerrycan or **jerrican** /'dʒerɪkæn/ noun a large flat-sided metal container for liquids 扁平大容器(盛放或运送液体)

jersey /'dʒɜːzi/ noun (plural **jerseys**) 1 a knitted garment with long sleeves 长袖针织衫 2 a distinctive shirt worn by people who play certain sports (某些运动员穿的)运动衫 3 a soft knitted fabric 针织织物 4 (**Jersey**) a breed of light brown dairy cattle 泽西乳牛(一种浅褐色奶牛)

Jerusalem artichoke /dʒə'ruːsələm/ noun a knobbly root vegetable with white flesh 菊芋；洋姜

jest /dʒest/ noun a joke 玩笑 • verb speak or behave in a joking way 讲

笑话；开玩笑；逗弄

jester /'dʒestə(r)/ noun a man who entertained people in a medieval court (中世纪宫廷中的)弄臣，逗乐小丑

Jesuit /'dʒezjuɪt/ noun a member of the Society of Jesus, a Roman Catholic order (罗马天主教)耶稣会会士

Jesus /'dʒiːzəs/ or **Jesus Christ** noun the central figure of the Christian religion, considered by Christians to be the son of God 耶稣 (基督教的核心人物，被基督教徒奉为上帝之子)

jet[1] /dʒet/ noun 1 a rapid stream of liquid or gas forced out of a small opening (液体或气体的)喷射流 2 an aircraft powered by jet engines 喷气式飞机 • verb (**jets**, **jetting**, **jetted**) 1 spurt out in a jet 喷射；喷发；喷出 2 travel by jet aircraft 乘喷气式飞机飞行 □ **jet engine** an aircraft engine which gives propulsion by sending out a highspeed jet of gas obtained by burning fuel 喷气发动机 **jet lag** extreme tiredness felt after a long flight across different time zones 时差综合征(跨时区飞行引起的极度疲劳) **the jet set** informal 【非正式】 wealthy people who frequently travel abroad for pleasure 喷气机阶层，喷气一族(经常乘飞机四处旅游的富人阶层) **jet ski** trademark【商标】 a small vehicle which skims across the surface of water 喷气式滑水车

jet[2] noun 1 a hard black semiprecious mineral 煤玉；黑色大理石 2 (also **jet black**) a glossy black colour 乌黑色

jetsam /'dʒetsəm/ noun unwanted material thrown overboard from a ship and washed ashore (从船舶上丢弃并被冲上岸的)投弃物品

jettison /'dʒetɪsn/ verb 1 throw or drop something from an aircraft or ship (从飞机或船只上)投弃 2

abandon or get rid of something 抛弃;除去

jetty /'dʒeti/ **noun** (plural **jetties**) a landing stage or small pier where boats can be moored 登岸码头,突堤;小码头

Jew /dʒuː/ **noun** a member of the people whose religion is Judaism and who trace their origins to the Hebrew people of ancient Israel 犹太教徒;犹太人 □ **Jew's harp** a small musical instrument like a U-shaped harp, held between the teeth and struck with a finger 单簧口琴(含在齿间用指拨奏的小型乐器,形似U形竖琴)

jewel /'dʒuːəl/ **noun 1** a precious stone 宝石 **2** (**jewels**) pieces of jewellery 首饰 **3** a highly valued person or thing 难能可贵的人;珍贵之物 ■ **jewelled** (US spelling 【美拼作】 **jeweled**) adjective.

jeweller /'dʒuːələ(r)/ (US spelling 【美拼作】 **jeweler**) **noun** a person who makes or sells jewellery 宝石匠;珠宝商

jewellery /'dʒuːəlri/ (US spelling 【美拼作】 **jewelry**) **noun** objects such as necklaces, rings, or bracelets worn on the body for decoration 珠宝;首饰

Jewish /'dʒuːɪʃ/ **adjective** having to do with Jews or Judaism 犹太人的;犹太教的 ■ **Jewishness** noun.

Jewry /'dʒuəri/ **noun** Jews as a group (总称)犹太人

Jezebel /'dʒezəbel/ **noun** an immoral woman 淫妇;荡妇

jib[1] /dʒɪb/ **noun 1** Sailing 【航行】a triangular sail in front of the mast 艏三角帆 **2** the projecting arm of a crane (起重机的)悬臂,挺杆

jib[2] **verb** (**jibs**, **jibbing**, **jibbed**) **1** (**jib at**) be unwilling to do or accept something 不愿做;不愿接受 **2** (of a horse) stop and refuse to go on (马)

却步,逡巡不前

jibe or **gibe** /dʒaɪb/ **noun** an insulting remark 嘲讽;嘲弄;奚落 • **verb** (**jibes**, **jibing**, **jibed**) make insulting remarks 嘲讽;嘲弄;奚落

jiffy /'dʒɪfi/ or **jiff** /dʒɪf/ **noun** informal 【非正式】a moment片刻;瞬间

jig /dʒɪg/ **noun 1** a lively dance 吉格舞 **2** a device that holds something in position and guides the tools working on it 夹具;钻模 • **verb** (**jigs**, **jigging**, **jigged**) move up and down with a quick, jerky motion 上下急动

jiggle /'dʒɪgl/ **verb** (**jiggles**, **jiggling**, **jiggled**) move lightly and quickly from side to side or up and down 左右晃动;上下颠簸 • **noun** a quick, light shake (快速)轻摇 ■ **jiggly** adjective.

jigsaw /'dʒɪgsɔː/ **noun 1** a picture printed on cardboard or wood and cut into many interlocking shapes that have to be fitted together (用板子或木头做的)拼图玩具 **2** a machine saw with a fine blade allowing it to cut curved lines in a sheet of wood, metal, etc. 线锯;钢线锯;镂花锯

jihad /dʒɪ'hɑːd/ **noun** (in Islam) a war or struggle against non-Muslims (伊斯兰教的)护教圣战

jilt /dʒɪlt/ **verb** abruptly break off a relationship with a lover 抛弃(情人)

jingle /'dʒɪŋgl/ **noun 1** a light ringing sound 叮当声 **2** a short easily remembered slogan, verse, or tune (易记的)短口号,短诗,短曲 • **verb** (**jingles**, **jingling**, **jingled**) make a jingle 发出叮当声 ■ **jingly** adjective.

jingoism /'dʒɪŋgəʊɪzəm/ **noun** too much pride in your country 极端爱国主义 ■ **jingoistic** adjective.

jinx /dʒɪŋks/ **noun** a person or thing that brings bad luck 不祥的人(或事物)• **verb** bring bad luck to 给…带来厄运

jitterbug /'dʒɪtəbʌg/ **noun** a fast

dance performed to swing music, popular in the 1940s 吉特巴舞(随摇摆音乐起舞的快节奏舞蹈,流行于20世纪40年代)

jitters /'dʒɪtəz/ **noun** informal【非正式】a feeling of being very nervous 极度紧张 ▪ **jittery** adjective.

jive /dʒaɪv/ **noun** a style of lively dance popular in the 1940s and 1950s, performed to swing music or rock and roll 摇摆舞(流行于20世纪40年代和50年代的快节奏舞蹈,随摇摆乐或摇滚乐起舞)• **verb** (**jives, jiving, jived**) dance the jive 跳摇摆舞

job /dʒɒb/ **noun 1** a paid position of regular employment 工作;活计 **2** a task 任务 **3** informal【非正式】a crime 罪行 **4** informal【非正式】a procedure to improve the appearance of something 整容手术 • **verb** (**jobs, jobbing, jobbed**) do casual or occasional work 打零工;做杂活 □ **job lot** a batch of articles sold or bought at one time (一次出售或购买的)成批杂货 **jobshare** (of two part-time employees) share a single full-time job (两名兼职员工)分摊工作,轮岗分担一份工作 ▪ **jobless** adjective.

jobcentre /'dʒɒbsentə(r)/ **noun** (in the UK) a government office which gives out information about available jobs to unemployed people (英国政府的)职业介绍所,就业服务中心

jockey /'dʒɒki/ **noun** (plural **jockeys**) a professional rider in horse races 职业赛马骑师 • **verb** (**jockeys, jockeying, jockeyed**) struggle to gain or achieve something 努力奋斗,努力争取

jockstrap /'dʒɒkstræp/ **noun** a support or protection for the male genitals (男子的)下体护身

jocose /dʒə'kəʊs/ **adjective** formal【正式】playful or humorous 滑稽的;幽默的

jocular /'dʒɒkjələ(r)/ **adjective** humorous 幽默的。▪ **jocularity** noun **jocularly** adverb.

jocund /'dʒɒkənd/ **adjective** formal【正式】cheerful and light-hearted 愉快的;开心的

jodhpurs /'dʒɒdpəz/ **plural noun** trousers worn for horse riding that are close-fitting below the knee (骑马穿的)马裤

jog /dʒɒg/ **verb** (**jogs, jogging, jogged**) **1** run at a steady, gentle pace 慢跑 **2** (**jog along or on**) continue in a steady, uneventful way 平稳继续 **3** knock or nudge slightly 轻触;轻碰 • **noun 1** a period of jogging (一段时间的)慢跑 **2** a gentle running pace 平缓的跑步步伐 **3** a slight knock or nudge 轻触;轻碰 □ **jog someone's memory** make someone remember something 唤起(某人的)记忆 ▪ **jogger** noun.

joggle /'dʒɒgl/ **verb** (**joggles, joggling, joggled**) move with repeated small jerks 颠摇

joie de vivre /ˌʒwʌ də 'viːvrə/ **noun** lively and cheerful enjoyment of life 生活的乐趣

join /dʒɔɪn/ **verb 1** connect things together, or become connected 连接;与…相连 **2** come together to form a whole 结合;联合 **3** become a member or employee of 成为…的一员;成为…的雇员 **4** (also **join in**) take part in an activity 参加(活动) **5** (**join up**) become a member of the armed forces 参军;从军 **6** do something or go somewhere with someone else 与(某人)一起做 • **noun** a place where two or more things are joined 连接处;接合点

joiner /'dʒɔɪnə(r)/ **noun** a person who puts together the wooden parts of a building 细木工

joinery /'dʒɔɪnəri/ **noun 1** the wooden

parts of a building 细木作(建筑物的木结构部分) **2** the work of a joiner 细木的制品

joint /dʒɔɪnt/ **noun 1** a point at which parts are joined 连接点,接合处 **2** a structure in a body which joins two bones (骨)关节 **3** the part of a plant stem from which a leaf or branch grows (植物的)节 **4** Brit.【英】a large piece of meat 大块肉 **5** informal【非正式】a particular kind of place (特定的)地方,场所: *a burger joint* 汉堡店 **6** informal【非正式】a cannabis cigarette 大麻烟卷 • **adjective 1** shared, held, or made by two or more people 分享的;共有的;共同制作的 **2** sharing in an achievement or activity (成就或活动)与他人合作的 • **verb** cut the body of an animal into joints 把(动物)切成大块肉 ■ **jointed** adjective **jointly** adverb.

joist /dʒɔɪst/ **noun** a length of timber or steel supporting the floor or ceiling of a building 托梁;桁

jojoba /həʊˈhəʊbə/ **noun** an oil extracted from the seeds of a North American shrub 加州希蒙得木籽油

joke /dʒəʊk/ **noun 1** a thing that someone says to cause amusement or laughter 玩笑;笑话 **2** a trick played for fun 恶作剧 **3** informal【非正式】a person or thing that is ridiculously inadequate 荒唐可笑的人(或事物);差劲的人(或物) • **verb** (**jokes, joking, joked**) make jokes 开玩笑 ■ **jokey** (or **joky**) adjective.

joker /ˈdʒəʊkə(r)/ **noun 1** a person who likes making or playing jokes 爱开玩笑的人;爱逗乐的人 **2** a playing card with the figure of a jester, used as a wild card 百搭牌

jollification /ˌdʒɒlɪfɪˈkeɪʃn/ **noun** time spent having fun 作乐;狂欢

jollity /ˈdʒɒləti/ **noun 1** lively and cheerful activity 狂欢活动 **2** the quality of being cheerful 愉快;欢乐

jolly /ˈdʒɒli/ **adjective** (**jollier, jolliest**) **1** happy and cheerful 兴高采烈的;快活的 **2** lively and entertaining 生动的;逗乐的 • **verb** (**jollies, jollying, jollied**) (**jolly someone along**) informal【非正式】encourage someone in a friendly way 友好地鼓励 • **adverb** Brit. informal【英,非正式】very 非常

jolt /dʒəʊlt/ **verb 1** push or shake abruptly and roughly 摇动;震动;颠簸 **2** shock someone into taking action 使震惊 • **noun 1** an act of jolting 摇动;震动;颠簸 **2** a shock 震惊

josh /dʒɒʃ/ **verb** informal【非正式】tease playfully 戏弄;开玩笑

joss stick /dʒɒs/ **noun** a thin stick covered with a substance that produces a sweet smell when you burn it 香;香柱

jostle /ˈdʒɒsl/ **verb** (**jostles, jostling, jostled**) **1** push or bump against someone roughly 推;撞 **2** (**jostle for**) struggle for 竞争;争夺

jot /dʒɒt/ **verb** (**jots, jotting, jotted**) write something quickly 快速记下;草草记下 • **noun** a very small amount 少量;一点儿

jotter /ˈdʒɒtə(r)/ **noun** Brit.【英】a small notebook 便笺簿;便条簿

joule /dʒuːl, dʒaʊl/ **noun** a unit of work or energy 焦耳(功或能量单位)

journal /ˈdʒɜːnl/ **noun 1** a newspaper or magazine dealing with a particular subject 报纸;期刊;杂志 **2** a diary or daily record 日记;日志

journalese /ˌdʒɜːnəˈliːz/ **noun** informal【非正式】a bad writing style thought to be typical of that used in newspapers 新闻文体

journalism /ˈdʒɜːnəlɪzəm/ **noun** the activity or profession of being a journalist 新闻工作;新闻业

journalist /ˈdʒɜːnəlɪst/ **noun** a person who writes for newspapers or magazines or prepares news to be broadcast 新闻记者；新闻工作者 ■ **journalistic** adjective.

journey /'dʒɜːni/ **noun** (plural **journeys**) an act of travelling from one place to another 旅行 • **verb** (**journeys, journeying, journeyed**) travel 旅游 **noun jovially** adverb.

journeyman /'dʒɜːnɪmən/ **noun** (plural **journeymen**) a worker who is reliable but not outstanding 可靠但不出色的工人

joust /dʒaʊst/ **verb** (of medieval knights) fight each other with lances while on horseback（中世纪骑士）进行马上长矛比武 • **noun** a jousting contest 马上长矛比武

jovial /'dʒəʊviəl/ **adjective** cheerful and friendly 愉快的；友好的 ■ **joviality** noun **jovially** adverb.

jowl /dʒaʊl/ **noun** the lower part of a person's or animal's cheek 下颌；下巴 ■ **jowly** adjective.

joy /dʒɔɪ/ **noun 1** great pleasure and happiness 快乐；喜悦；欣喜 **2** something that brings joy 愉快的事；乐事 **3** Brit. informal 【英，非正式】 success or satisfaction 成功；满意 ■ **joyless** adjective.

joyful /'dʒɔɪfl/ **adjective** feeling or causing joy 感到高兴的，令人愉快的 ■ **joyfully** adverb.

joyous /'dʒɔɪəs/ **adjective** full of happiness and joy 幸福快乐的 ■ **joyously** adverb.

joyriding /'dʒɔɪraɪdɪŋ/ **noun** informal 【非正式】 the crime of stealing a vehicle and driving it in a fast and dangerous way（驾驶偷来汽车的）开车兜风(指开快车、危险驾驶) ■ **joyride** noun **joyrider** noun.

joystick /'dʒɔɪstɪk/ **noun** informal 【非正式】 **1** the rod used for controlling an aircraft（飞机的）操纵杆，驾驶杆 **2** a lever for controlling the movement of an image on a computer screen（控制计算机屏幕上图像活动的）控制杆

JP /ˌdʒeɪ 'piː/ **abbreviation** Justice of the Peace

jubilant /'dʒuːbɪlənt/ **adjective** happy and triumphant 幸福的；胜利的；成功的 ■ **jubilantly** adverb.

jubilation /ˌdʒuːbɪˈleɪʃn/ **noun** a feeling of great happiness and triumph 幸福感；成就感

jubilee /'dʒuːbɪliː/ **noun** a special anniversary（具有特殊意义的）周年纪念

Judaism /'dʒuːdeɪɪzəm/ **noun** the religion of the Jews, based on the Old Testament and the Talmud 犹太教 ■ **Judaic** adjective.

Judas /'dʒuːdəs/ **noun** a person who betrays a friend 出卖朋友者；叛徒

judder /'dʒʌdə(r)/ **verb** (**judders, juddering, juddered**) shake rapidly and violently 剧烈震动；震颤 ■ **juddery** adjective.

judge /dʒʌdʒ/ **noun 1** a public official who has the authority to decide cases in a law court 法官；审判员 **2** a person who decides the results of a competition（竞赛的）裁判 **3** a person who is qualified to give an opinion 鉴定人；鉴赏家 • **verb** (**judges, judging, judged**) **1** form an opinion about something 判断；断定 **2** give a verdict on a case or person in a law court 审判(案件)；判决(某人) **3** decide the results of a competition 裁决，裁判(比赛)

judgement or **judgment** /'dʒʌdʒmənt/ **noun 1** the ability to make good decisions or form sensible opinions 判断力；鉴别力 **2** an opinion or conclusion 看法；结论 **3** a decision of a law court or judge 判决；裁决 □ **Judgement Day** the time of the Last Judgement 世界末日；最后审判日

judgemental or **judgmental** /dʒʌdʒˈmentl/ **adjective 1** having to do with the use of judgement 判断的 **2** too critical of other people 批判性的；苛责的

judicature /'dʒuːdɪkətʃə(r)/ **noun** the organization and putting into practice of justice 司法；司法系统

judicial /dʒuˈdɪʃl/ **adjective** having to do with a law court or judge 法庭的；法官的，■ **judicially** adverb.

judiciary /dʒuˈdɪʃəri/ **noun** (**the judiciary**) judges as a group (总称)审判人员

judicious /dʒuˈdɪʃəs/ **adjective** having or done with good judgement 明断的；有见地的，■ **judiciously** adverb.

judo /'dʒuːdəʊ/ **noun** a kind of unarmed combat performed as a sport 柔道

jug /dʒʌg/ **noun** a cylindrical container with a handle and a lip, for holding and pouring liquids (有柄有嘴的)罐，壶 □ **jugged hare** a dish made with hare that has been cooked slowly in a covered container 焖炖野兔

juggernaut /'dʒʌgənɔːt/ **noun** Brit. 【英】a large, heavy lorry 重型卡车

juggle /'dʒʌgl/ **verb** (**juggles, juggling, juggled**) **1** continuously toss and catch a number of objects so as to keep at least one in the air at any time 玩杂耍(连续抛接多个物体) **2** do several things at the same time 同时应付(几件事) **3** present facts or figures in a way that makes them seem good 篡改(事实或数字) ■ **juggler** noun.

jugular /'dʒʌgjələ(r)/ or **jugular vein noun** any of several large veins in the neck, carrying blood from the head 颈静脉

juice /dʒuːs/ **noun 1** the liquid present in fruit and vegetables (水果或蔬菜的)汁液 **2** a drink made from this liquid 果汁；蔬菜汁 **3** (**juices**) fluid produced by the stomach 胃液 **4** (**juices**) liquid coming from food during cooking (烹饪时食物里的)汁，液 • **verb** (**juices, juicing, juiced**) extract the juice from 榨取…的汁液

juicy /'dʒuːsi/ **adjective** (**juicier, juiciest**) **1** full of juice 多汁的 **2** informal 【非正式】(of gossip) very interesting (流言)生动有趣的

ju-jitsu /dʒuːˈdʒɪtsuː/ **noun** a Japanese system of unarmed combat 柔术

jukebox /'dʒuːkbɒks/ **noun** a machine that plays a selected musical recording when a coin is inserted (投进硬币后可选听唱片的)自动唱机

julep /'dʒuːlep/ **noun** a sweet drink made from sugar syrup (糖浆做的)甜饮料

July /dʒuˈlaɪ/ **noun** (plural **Julys**) the seventh month of the year 七月

jumble /'dʒʌmbl/ **noun 1** an untidy collection of things 一堆杂乱之物 **2** Brit. 【英】articles collected for a jumble sale 出售的旧货 • **verb** (**jumbles, jumbling, jumbled**) mix things up in a confused way 使杂乱；使混乱 □ **jumble sale** Brit. 【英】a sale of second-hand items 旧货出售

jumbo /'dʒʌmbəʊ/ informal 【非正式】 **noun** (plural **jumbos**) **1** a very large person or thing 体形巨大的人；庞然大物 **2** (also **jumbo jet**) a very large airliner 巨型喷气式飞机 • **adjective** very large 巨型的；庞大的

jump /dʒʌmp/ **verb 1** push yourself off the ground using the muscles in your legs and feet 跳；跃 **2** move over something by jumping 跳过；跃过 **3** make a sudden involuntary movement in surprise 不由自主地跳动；惊跳 **4** (**jump at** or **on**) accept something eagerly 急切地接受；欣然应承 **5** (often **jump on**) informal 【非正式】attack someone suddenly 突然袭击 **6** pass abruptly from one subject or state to another 跳过，略去(话题或状态) • **noun 1** an act or action of jumping 跳；跃 **2** a large or sudden increase 大增；激增；暴涨 **3** an obstacle to be jumped by a horse (马要跳过的)障碍物 □ **jumped-up** informal

【非正式】 considering yourself to be more important than you really are 自以为是的；自认为重要的 **jump jet** a jet aircraft that can take off and land without a runway 垂直起降喷气机 **jump leads** 【英】 a pair of cables used to recharge a battery in a vehicle by connecting it to the battery of a vehicle whose engine is running 跨接电缆线(用于从一辆汽车向另一辆汽车的蓄电池充电) **jump the queue** move ahead of your proper place in a queue 插队 **jump ship** (of a sailor) leave a ship without permission (水手)擅自弃船 **jump-start** start a car with jump leads or by a sudden release of the clutch while it is being pushed 用跨接电缆线(或助推启动法)启动(汽车)

jumper /'dʒʌmpə(r)/ **noun 1** Brit. 【英】 a pullover or sweater (套头)毛衣 **2** N. Amer. 【北美】 a pinafore dress 无袖连衣裙 **3** a person or animal that jumps 跳跃的人(或动物)

jumpsuit /'dʒʌmpsuːt/ **noun** a one-piece garment incorporating trousers and a sleeved top 连衫裤

jumpy /'dʒʌmpi/ **adjective (jumpier, jumpiest)** informal 【非正式】 anxious and uneasy 担心的；紧张不安的

junction /'dʒʌŋkʃn/ **noun 1** a point where things meet or are joined 连接点，汇合处；交叉口 **2** a place where roads or railway lines meet (公路或铁路的)会合点，交叉口，枢纽

juncture /'dʒʌŋktʃə(r)/ **noun 1** a particular point in time 时刻，时间点 **2** a place where things join 接合点；交接处

June /dʒuːn/ **noun** the sixth month of the year 六月

jungle /'dʒʌŋɡl/ **noun 1** an area of land with thick forest and tangled vegetation 丛林，密林 **2** a very bewildering or competitive situation 令人困惑的情形；竞争激烈的形势

junior /'dʒuːniə(r)/ **adjective 1** having to do with young or younger people 年轻人的；较年幼的 **2** Brit. 【英】 having to do with schoolchildren aged 7-11 (学校)七至十一岁儿童的 **3** (after a name) referring to the younger of two with the same name in a family 小(置于姓名后，表示同一家庭中名字相同的两人中较年幼的一个) **4** low or lower in status 地位低的；地位较低的 • **noun 1** a person who is a stated number of years younger than someone else 年少者；较年幼者: *He's five years her junior.* 他比她小5岁。 **2** Brit. 【英】 a child at a junior school 初中生 **3** a person with low status 地位低下者

juniper /'dʒuːnɪpə(r)/ **noun** an evergreen shrub with sweet-smelling berries 桧，杜松(常绿灌木，结有香味的浆果)

junk¹ /dʒʌŋk/ **noun** informal 【非正式】 useless or worthless articles 无用之物；破烂；垃圾 □ **junk food** unhealthy food 垃圾食品；不健康食品 **junk mail** unwanted advertising material sent to you in the post 垃圾邮件

junk² **noun** a flat-bottomed sailing boat used in China and the East Indies 中国式平底帆船

junket /'dʒʌŋkɪt/ **noun 1** informal 【非正式】 a trip or excursion made by government officials and paid for using public funds (政府官员的)奢华旅行 **2** a dish of sweetened curds of milk 凝乳食品；乳冻甜食

junkie or **junky** /'dʒʌŋki/ **noun** informal 【非正式】 a drug addict 吸毒成瘾者；瘾君子

junta /'dʒʌntə/ **noun** a group ruling a country after taking power by force (靠武力上台的)军政府

Jupiter /'dʒuːpɪtə(r)/ **noun** the largest planet in the solar system 木星(太阳

系中最大的行星)

jurisdiction /ˌdʒʊərɪsˈdɪkʃn/ **noun 1** the official power to make legal decisions 司法权；审判权 **2** the area over which the legal authority of a court or other institution extends 管辖范围；管辖区域

jurisprudence /ˌdʒʊərɪsˈpruːdns/ **noun** the study of law 法学；法理学

jurist /ˈdʒʊərɪst/ **noun** an expert in law 法学家；法律学者

juror /ˈdʒʊərə(r)/ **noun** a member of a jury 陪审员

jury /ˈdʒʊəri/ **noun** (plural **juries**) **1** a group of people who are required to attend a legal case and come to a verdict based on the evidence given in court 陪审团 **2** a group of people judging a competition（竞赛的）评审团，评判委员会

just /dʒʌst/ **adjective 1** right and fair 正义的；公正的 **2** deserved 应得的 **3** (of an opinion) based on good evidence or reasons（观点）有充分根据（或理由）的 • **adverb 1** exactly or at this moment 恰恰正是 **2** exactly or nearly at that moment 刚刚；方才 **3** very recently 最近 **4** barely 很少 **5** only 只是；仅仅 ■ **justly** adverb.

justice /ˈdʒʌstɪs/ **noun 1** just behaviour or treatment 公正的行为；公正对待 **2** the quality of being fair and reasonable 公平；合理 **3** a judge or magistrate 法官；地方法院法官 □ **Justice of the Peace** (in the UK) a non-professional magistrate appointed to hear minor cases（英国处理小案件的）地方执法官，治安法官

justifiable /ˈdʒʌstɪfaɪəbl/ **adjective** able to be shown to be right or reasonable 可证明为正当的；无可非议的 ■ **justifiably** adverb.

justify /ˈdʒʌstɪfaɪ/ **verb** (**justifies**, **justifying**, **justified**) **1** prove something to be right or reasonable 证明正确;证明合理 **2** be a good reason for 是…的正当理由 **3** adjust lines of type so that they form straight edges at both sides 使齐行；对齐 ■ **justification** noun.

jut /dʒʌt/ **verb** (**juts**, **jutting**, **jutted**) extend out beyond the main body or line of something 凸出;伸出

jute /dʒuːt/ **noun** rough fibre made from the stems of a tropical plant, used for making rope or woven into sacking（可织成绳或麻袋的）黄麻纤维

juvenile /ˈdʒuːvənaɪl/ **adjective 1** having to do with young people, birds, or animals 少年的;幼小动物的 **2** childish 孩子气的 • **noun 1** a young person, bird, or animal 少年;幼小动物 **2** Law【法律】a person below the age at which they have adult status in law (18 in most countries) 青少年，未成年人(大多数国家以18岁为限) □ **juvenile delinquent** a young person who regularly commits crimes 少年犯

juxtapose /ˈdʒʌkstəpəʊz/ **verb** (**juxtaposes**, **juxtaposing**, **juxtaposed**) place two things close together 把…并置;把…并列 ■ **juxtaposition** noun.

Kk

Justifiable /ˈdʒʌstɪfaɪəbl/ adjective
able to be shown to be right or
reasonable 可辩护的；有道理的

SPELLING TIP 拼写指南 Some words sound as if they begin with 'k' but actually begin with the letters 'ch', for example **chorus** or **chrysalis**. 有些根据发音似乎以k开头的词实际是以ch开头，如chorus和chrysalis。

K or **k** /keɪ/ **noun** (plural **Ks** or **K's**) the eleventh letter of the alphabet 英语字母表的第11个字母 • **abbreviation** informal【非正式】a thousand 一千

kaftan or **caftan** /ˈkæftæn/ **noun 1** a woman's long, loose dress or top 宽大女袍(或上衣) **2** a man's long tunic, worn in the East (东方人穿的)男式长衫

kaiser /ˈkaɪzə(r)/ **noun** historical【历史】the German or Austrian Emperor (德国或奥地利的)皇帝

kale /keɪl/ **noun** a type of cabbage with large curly leaves 羽衣甘蓝；无头甘蓝

kaleidoscope /kəˈlaɪdəskəʊp/ **noun 1** a tube containing mirrors and pieces of coloured glass or paper, whose reflections produce changing patterns when the tube is turned 万花筒 **2** a constantly changing pattern 千变万化的图案 ■ **kaleidoscopic** adjective.

kameez /kəˈmiːz/ **noun** (plural **kameez** or **kameezes**) a long tunic worn by people from the Indian subcontinent 克米兹(南亚次大陆居民穿的长罩衫)

kamikaze /ˌkæmɪˈkɑːzi/ **noun** (in the Second World War) a Japanese aircraft loaded with explosives and deliberately crashed on to an enemy target in a suicide mission (第二次世界大战中日军使用的自杀性)神风突击机 • **adjective** potentially causing death or harm to yourself 自杀性的；有自残倾向的

kangaroo /ˌkæŋɡəˈruː/ **noun** a large Australian animal with a long powerful tail and strong hind legs that enable it to travel by leaping 袋鼠 □ **kangaroo court** a court set up unofficially with the aim of finding someone guilty "袋鼠法庭"(为给某人定罪而私设的法庭)

kaolin /ˈkeɪəlɪn/ **noun** a fine soft white clay, used for making china and in medicine 高岭土，瓷土(用于制作瓷器和药品)

kapok /ˈkeɪpɒk/ **noun** a substance resembling cotton wool which grows around the seeds of a tropical tree, used as padding 木棉(类似棉絮的物质,用作填充料)

kaput /kæˈpʊt/ **adjective** informal【非正式】broken and useless 坏了的；破损无用的

karaoke /ˌkæriˈəʊki/ **noun** a form of entertainment in which people sing popular songs over prerecorded backing tracks 卡拉OK

karate /kəˈrɑːti/ **noun** a Japanese system of fighting using the hands and feet rather than weapons 空手道

karma /ˈkɑːmə/ **noun** (in Hinduism and Buddhism) a person's actions in this and previous lives, seen as affecting their future fate (印度教和佛教中的)业,羯磨(指个人今生和前世的行为,可决定来世的命运)

karst /kɑːst/ **noun** a limestone region with underground streams and many cavities in the rock 喀斯特地区，岩溶区

kart /kɑːt/ **noun** a small racing car

with no suspension and having the engine at the back 卡丁车(一种微型赛车，发动机后置)

kasbah or **casbah** /'kæzbɑː/ **noun** a fortress in the old part of a North African city, and the narrow streets that surround it 卡斯巴(北非的城堡及周边窄旧街道)

kayak /'kaɪæk/ **noun** a canoe made of a light frame with a watertight covering 独木舟；单人划子 • **verb** (**kayaks**, **kayaking**, **kayaked**) travel in a kayak 乘独木舟(或单人划子)旅行

kazoo /kə'zuː/ **noun** a simple musical instrument consisting of a pipe that produces a buzzing sound when you hum into it 卡祖笛(一种简单乐器)

kebab /kɪ'bæb/ **noun** a dish of pieces of meat, fish, or vegetables roasted or grilled on a skewer or spit 烤串

kedgeree /'kedʒəriː/ **noun** a dish of smoked fish, rice, and hardboiled eggs 鱼蛋烩饭

keel /kiːl/ **noun** a structure running along the length of the base of a ship (船的)龙骨 • **verb** (**keel over**) **1** (of a boat or ship) turn over on its side (舰船)翻转，倾覆 **2** fall over 翻倒

keelhaul /'kiːlhɔːl/ **verb** (in the past) punish someone by dragging them through the water from one side of a boat to the other (旧时)以拖刑惩罚(某人)

keen¹ /kiːn/ **adjective 1** eager and enthusiastic 热切的；热衷的 **2** (of a blade) sharp (刀刃)锋利的，尖利的 **3** quick to understand 领悟力强的 **4** (of a sense) highly developed (感觉)灵敏的，敏锐的 **5** Brit. 【英】(of prices) very low (价格)非常低的 ■ **keenly** adverb **keenness** noun.

keen² **verb 1** wail in grief for a person who has died 哀号；恸哭了 **2** make an eerie wailing sound 发出哀号声

keep /kiːp/ **verb** (**keeps**, **keeping**, **kept**) **1** continue to have something 保有；保存 **2** save something for use in the future 保管，存放(以备用) **3** store something in a regular place 存放；储藏 **4** continue in a particular condition, position, or activity 保持(特定状态、位置或活动)：*She kept quiet.* 她默不作声。**5** do something that you have promised or agreed to do 遵循，恪守(承诺) **6** (of food) remain in good condition (食物)保存得好，持久不坏 **7** make a note about something 记(笔记) **8** provide accommodation and food for someone 为…提供食宿 **9** (**kept**) dated 【废】supported financially in return for sex 被包养的 • **noun 1** food, clothes, and other essentials for living 生活必需品 **2** the strongest or central tower of a castle 城堡中最坚固的塔楼；城堡主楼 □ **keep-fit** regular exercises done to improve fitness 健身(运动) **keep up** move at the same rate as someone or something else 保持同步；不落后 **keep something up** continue a course of action 继续(行动)

keeper /'kiːpə(r)/ **noun 1** a person who manages or looks after something or someone 看护人，领养人 **2** a goalkeeper or wicketkeeper (足球或板球的)守门员

keeping /'kiːpɪŋ/ **noun** (**in** (or **out of**) **keeping with**) in (or not in) harmony or agreement with 与…一致(或不一致)

keepsake /'kiːpseɪk/ **noun** a small item kept in memory of the person who gave it or originally owned it 纪念品

keg /keg/ **noun** a small barrel 小桶

kelim /kə'liːm/ **noun** ⇒ **KILIM**.

kelp /kelp/ **noun** a very large brown seaweed 大型褐藻

kelvin /'kelvɪn/ **noun** a unit of temperature, equal to one degree Celsius

开(开尔文温标的计量单位)

ken /ken/ **noun (your ken)** the range of your knowledge and experience 知识范围；眼界 • **verb (kens, kenning, kenned or kent)** Scottish & N. English 【苏格兰和英格兰北部】know or recognize 认出；辨出

kennel /'kenl/ **noun 1** a small shelter for a dog 狗窝 **2 (kennels)** a place where dogs are looked after or bred 养狗场

Kenyan /'kenjən/ **noun** a person from Kenya 肯尼亚人 • **adjective** relating to Kenya 肯尼亚的

kept /kept/ past and past participle of KEEP.

keratin /'kerətɪn/ **noun** a protein forming the basis of hair, feathers, hoofs, claws, and horns（构成毛发、羽毛、蹄、爪和角的）角蛋白

kerb /kɜːb/ (US spelling【美拼作】**curb**) **noun** a stone edging to a pavement 路缘石；路边镶边石 □ **kerb-crawling** Brit.【英】driving slowly along the edge of the road in search of a prostitute（驾车者为寻找娼妓）沿路缘缓慢行驶的

kerbstone /'kɜːbstəʊn/ **noun** a long, narrow stone or concrete block, laid end to end with others to form a kerb 路缘石

kerchief /'kɜːtʃɪf/ **noun 1** a piece of fabric used to cover the head 方头巾；方围巾 **2** dated【废】a handkerchief 手帕

kerfuffle /kə'fʌfl/ **noun** Brit. informal 【英，非正式】a fuss or commotion 吵闹；混乱；骚乱

kernel /'kɜːnl/ **noun 1** the softer part inside the shell of a nut, seed, or fruit stone（坚果、种子或果核的）仁 **2** the seed and hard husk of a cereal（谷物的）颗粒，种子 **3** the central part of something 核心；要点

✔ 拼写指南 -el, not -al: kernel. kernel 中的-el不要拼作-al。

kerosene /'kerəsiːn/ **noun** N. Amer.【北美】paraffin 煤油；火油

kestrel /'kestrəl/ **noun** a small falcon that hovers in the air with rapidly beating wings 红隼（一种小型猎鹰）

ketch /ketʃ/ **noun** a small sailing boat with two masts 双桅帆船

ketchup /'ketʃəp/ **noun** a spicy sauce made from tomatoes and vinegar 番茄酱；番茄沙司

kettle /'ketl/ **noun** a container with a spout and handle, used for boiling water（烧水用的）水壶

kettledrum /'ketldrʌm/ **noun** a large drum shaped like a bowl 定音鼓；铜鼓

key /kiː/ **noun (plural keys) 1** a small piece of shaped metal which is inserted into a lock and turned to open or close it 钥匙 **2** a lever pressed down by the finger in playing an instrument such as the organ, piano, or flute（风琴、钢琴、长笛等乐器的）键 **3** each of several buttons on a panel for operating a computer or typewriter（计算机或打字机键盘的）键 **4** a list explaining the symbols used in a map or table（地图、图表的）略语表，符号表，凡例 **5** a word or system for solving a code 密码；密码系统 **6** Music【音乐】a group of notes making up a scale 调；主音 • **adjective** of great importance 重要的 • **verb (keys, keying, keyed) 1** enter data using a computer keyboard 用键盘输入(数据) **2 (be keyed up)** be nervous, tense, or excited 变得提心吊胆(或激动)

keyboard /'kiːbɔːd/ **noun 1** a panel of keys for use with a computer or typewriter（计算机或打字机的）键盘 **2** a set of keys on a musical instrument（乐器的）键盘 **3** an electronic musical instrument with keys arranged as on a piano 键盘式电子乐器；电子琴 • **verb** enter data by means of a keyboard 用键盘输入(数

据）■ **keyboarder** noun.

keyhole /'kiːhəʊl/ **noun** a hole in a lock into which the key is inserted 锁眼;钥匙孔 □ **keyhole surgery** surgery carried out through a very small cut in the patient's body 小切口外科手术;"匙孔"手术

keynote /'kiːnəʊt/ **noun 1** a central theme of a book, speech, etc. (书,演讲等的)基调,要旨 **2** Music 【音乐】 the note on which a key is based 主音 • **adjective** (of a speech) setting out the theme of a conference (发言)确定会议基调的

keypad /'kiːpæd/ **noun** a small keyboard or set of buttons for operating a portable electronic device or telephone (移动电子装置或电话的)小型键盘,袖珍键盘

keystone /'kiːstəʊn/ **noun 1** the most important part of a policy or system (政策或体系的)主旨,核心 **2** a central stone at the top of an arch 拱顶石

keystroke /'kiːstrəʊk/ **noun** a single act of pressing a key on a keyboard (在键盘上的)一次敲击

keyword /'kiː wɜːd/ **noun 1** a significant word mentioned in an index (索引中的)关键词 **2** a word used in a computer system to indicate the content of a document (计算机系统中用于指示文件内容的)关键词

kg abbreviation kilograms.

khaki /'kɑːki/ **noun** (plural **khakis**) **1** a dull greenish- or yellowish-brown colour 暗褐黄色;卡其黄;土黄色 **2** a cotton or wool fabric of this colour (暗褐黄色的)卡其布,卡其毛料

khan /kɑːn/ **noun** a title given to rulers and officials in central Asia, Afghanistan, and certain other Muslim countries 可汗(中亚、阿富汗及其他一些伊斯兰国家的统治者的称号)

kHz abbreviation kilohertz 千赫(兹)

kibbutz /kɪ'bʊts/ **noun** a farming settlement in Israel in which work is shared between all of its members. 基布兹(以色列的合作农场,其成员共同劳动)

kibosh /'kaɪbɒʃ/ **noun (put the kibosh on)** informal 【非正式】 firmly put an end to 坚决结束;断然终止

kick /kɪk/ **verb 1** hit or propel something forcibly with the foot 踢;踹 **2** hit out with the foot or feet 踢出 **3** informal 【非正式】 succeed in giving up a habit 戒除(习惯) **4 (kick off)** start or restart with a kick of the ball from the centre (足球比赛)开赛,中圈开球 **5 (kick someone out)** informal 【非正式】 force someone to leave 迫使离开 **6** (of a gun) spring back when fired (枪,炮)反冲,后坐 • **noun 1** an instance of kicking 踢 **2** informal 【非正式】 a thrill of excitement 激动;兴奋 **3** informal 【非正式】 the strong effect of alcohol or a drug (酒或毒品的)强烈作用 □ **kick-boxing** a form of martial art which combines boxing with kicking with bare feet 搏击 **kickoff** the start of a football match (足球比赛的)开赛,中圈开球 **kick-start 1** start a motorcycle engine with a downward thrust of a lever 用脚踏启动器启动(摩托车) **2** take action to make something start or develop more quickly 刺激 **kick the bucket** informal 【非正式】 die 死掉;蹬腿儿 ■ **kicker** noun.

kickback /'kɪkbæk/ **noun 1** informal 【非正式】 an underhand payment to someone who has helped in a business deal (非法的)酬金,回扣 **2** an instance of a gun springing back when fired (枪,炮的)强烈反冲,后坐

kid¹ /kɪd/ **noun 1** informal 【非正式】 a child or young person 小孩;小伙子 **2** a young goat 小山羊

kid² **verb** (**kids, kidding, kidded**)

informal【非正式】fool someone into believing something 欺骗；哄骗

kidnap /'kɪdnæp/ **verb** (**kidnaps, kidnapping, kidnapped**; US spelling【美拼作】**kidnaps, kidnaping, kidnaped**) take someone by force and hold them captive 绑架；劫持 • **noun** an instance of kidnapping someone 绑架；劫持 ■ **kidnapper** noun.

kidney /'kɪdni/ **noun** (plural **kidneys**) **1** each of a pair of organs that remove waste products from the blood and produce urine 肾；肾脏 **2** the kidney of a sheep, ox, or pig as food（可食用的羊、牛或猪的）腰子 □ **kidney bean** an edible dark red bean shaped like a kidney 菜豆；芸豆 **kidney machine** a device that performs the functions of a kidney, used if a person has a damaged kidney 人工肾；血液透析器 **kidney stone** a hard mass formed in the kidneys 肾结石

kilim or **kelim** /kɪ'liːm/ **noun** a carpet or rug of a kind made in Turkey and neighbouring areas 基里姆地毯（产于土耳其及其周边地区）

kill /kɪl/ **verb 1** cause the death of 杀死；杀害 **2** put an end to 使结束；使终止 **3** informal【非正式】cause someone pain 使痛苦 **4** pass time 消磨，打发(时间) • **noun 1** an act of killing 杀死；捕杀 **2** an animal or animals killed by a hunter or another animal 被捕杀的动物；猎获物

killer /'kɪlə(r)/ **noun 1** a person or thing that kills 杀手；导致死亡的人(或事物) **2** informal【非正式】something that is very difficult or very impressive 极难之事；动人的事物 □ **killer whale** = ORCA.

killing /'kɪlɪŋ/ **noun** an act of causing death 杀害；谋杀 • **adjective** informal【非正式】exhausting 令人筋疲力尽的 □ **make a killing** make a lot of money out of something 发财；挣大钱

killjoy /'kɪldʒɔɪ/ **noun** a person who spoils the enjoyment of other people 令人扫兴的人

kiln /kɪln/ **noun** a furnace for baking or drying things 窑

kilo /'kiːləʊ/ **noun** (plural **kilos**) a kilogram 千克；公斤

kilobyte /'kɪləbaɪt/ **noun** Computing【计】a unit of memory or data equal to 1,024 bytes 千字节(存储单位,等于1024字节)

kilogram or **kilogramme** /'kɪləgræm/ **noun** a unit of mass, equal to 1,000 grams (approximately 2.205 lb) 千克，公斤(约合2.205磅)

kilometre /'kɪləmiːtə(r)/ (US spelling【美拼作】**kilometer**) **noun** a metric unit of measurement equal to 1,000 metres (0.62 miles) 千米，公里(约合0.62英里)

kiloton or **kilotonne** /'kɪlətʌn/ **noun** a unit of explosive power equivalent to 1,000 tons of TNT 千吨(爆炸当量单位,相当于1000吨TNT炸药的爆炸力)

kilovolt /'kɪləvəʊlt/ **noun** 1,000 volts 千伏

kilowatt /'kɪləwɒt/ **noun** 1,000 watts 千瓦 □ **kilowatt-hour** a measure of electrical energy equivalent to one kilowatt operating for one hour 千瓦时；一度(电)

kilt /kɪlt/ **noun** a skirt of pleated tartan cloth, traditionally worn by men as part of Scottish Highland dress 苏格兰褶裥短裙(苏格兰高地男子的传统服装,由格子花呢制成)

kilter /'kɪltə(r)/ **noun** (**out of kilter**) out of balance 失去平衡

kimono /kɪ'məʊnəʊ/ **noun** (plural **kimonos**) a long, loose Japanese robe with wide sleeves, tied with a sash (日本)和服

kin /kɪn/ **plural noun** your family and relations 家属；亲属

kind[1] /kaɪnd/ **noun** a class or type of similar people or things 种；类 □ **in**

kind 1 in the same way 同样地;以同样方式 **2** (of payment) in goods or services instead of money (偿付)以实物(或劳务)

> **！注意** use **this kind of** to refer to a singular noun (e.g. *this kind of behaviour is not acceptable*), and **these kinds of** to refer to a plural noun (e.g. *these kinds of questions are not relevant*). this kind of 用于修饰单数名词(如 *this kind of behaviour is not acceptable* 这种行为是不可接受的);these kinds of 用于修饰复数名词(如 *these kinds of questions are not relevant* 这些问题与主题无关)。

kind 2 adjective considerate and generous 宽厚的;善良的;仁慈的

kindergarten /'kɪndəgɑːtn/ noun a nursery school 幼儿园

kindle /'kɪndl/ verb (**kindles**, **kindling**, **kindled**) **1** light a flame; make a fire start burning 点着;点燃 **2** arouse an emotion 激起(某种情感)

kindling /'kɪndlɪŋ/ noun small sticks used for lighting fires 引火柴

kindly /'kaɪndli/ adverb **1** in a kind way 友好地;亲切地 **2** please (used in a polite request) 请(用于客气的请求) • adjective (**kindlier**, **kindliest**) kind 宽厚的;善良的;仁慈的 □ **not take kindly to** be not pleased by 不喜欢 ■ **kindliness** noun.

kindness /'kaɪndnəs/ noun **1** the quality of being kind 和蔼;仁慈;好心 **2** a kind act 仁慈(或好心)的行为

kindred /'kɪndrəd/ plural noun your family and relations 家属;亲属 • adjective having similar qualities 同类的;类似的 □ **kindred spirit** a person whose interests or attitudes are similar to your own 志同道合的人

kinetic /kɪ'netɪk, kaɪ-/ adjective relating to or resulting from motion 运动的;运动引起的 ■ **kinetically** adverb.

king /kɪŋ/ noun **1** the male ruler of an independent state 国王;君主 **2** the best or most important person or thing of their kind 最优秀者;最重要者;王者 **3** a playing card ranking next below an ace (牌戏中的)老 K **4** the most important chess piece, which the opponent has to checkmate in order to win (国际象棋中的)王 □ **kingsized** (or **king-size**) of a larger than normal size 大号的;特大的 ■ **kingly** adjective **kingship** noun.

kingdom /'kɪŋdəm/ noun **1** a country, state, or territory ruled by a king or queen 王国 **2** each of the three divisions (animal, vegetable, and mineral) in which natural objects are classified (动物、植物和矿物的)界

kingfisher /'kɪŋfɪʃə(r)/ noun a colourful bird with a long sharp beak which dives to catch fish in streams and ponds 翠鸟(一种食鱼鸟,喙长而尖,羽毛绚丽,可从空中俯冲入水捕鱼)

kingpin /'kɪŋpɪn/ noun **1** a person or thing that is essential to the success of an organization or operation 关键的人(或物) **2** a large bolt in a central position 主销

kink /kɪŋk/ noun **1** a sharp twist in something long and narrow (细长物的)扭结,绞缠 **2** a flaw or difficulty 缺点;难点 **3** a peculiar habit or characteristic 怪癖 • verb form a kink 扭结;绞缠

kinky /'kɪŋki/ adjective (**kinkier**, **kinkiest**) **1** informal 非正式 having to do with unusual sexual behaviour 性变态的 **2** having kinks or twists 扭结的;绞缠的

kinsfolk /'kɪnzfəʊk/ or **kinfolk** /'kɪnfəʊk/ plural noun your family and relations 家属;亲属

kinship /'kɪnʃɪp/ noun **1** the relationship between members of the same family 亲属关系 **2** a state of having similar characteristics or origins（特点或起源的）类似，近似

kinsman /ˈkɪnzmən/ or **kinswoman** /ˈkɪnzwʊmən/ **noun** (plural **kinsmen** or **kinswomen**) one of your relations 亲属；亲戚

kiosk /ˈkiːɒsk/ **noun 1** a small open-fronted hut from which newspapers, refreshments, or tickets are sold（出售报刊、点心饮料、车票等的）小摊棚，售货亭 **2** Brit.【英】a public telephone booth 公共电话亭

kip /kɪp/ Brit. informal【英，非正式】**noun** a sleep 睡眠 • **verb** (**kips**, **kipping**, **kipped**) sleep 睡觉

kipper /ˈkɪpə(r)/ **noun** a herring that has been split open, salted, and dried or smoked 腌晒（或熏制）的鲱鱼 □ **kipper tie** a very wide tie 宽领带

kirk /kɜːk/ **noun** Scottish & N. English【苏格兰和英格兰北部】a church 教堂，教会

kismet /ˈkɪzmet/ **noun** fate 命运；天命

kiss /kɪs/ **verb** touch someone or something with the lips as a sign of love, affection, or greeting 吻；亲吻 • **noun** an act of kissing 吻；亲吻 □ **kiss curl** a small curl of hair on the forehead or in front of the ear 垂于额前（或耳前）的一小绺卷发 **the kiss of life** mouth-to-mouth resuscitation 口对口人工呼吸

kit /kɪt/ **noun 1** a set of equipment or clothes for a specific purpose（满足特定需要的）成套物品，成套设备 **2** a set of drums, cymbals, and other percussion instruments 成套打击乐器 • **verb** (**kits**, **kitting**, **kitted**) (**kit someone out**) provide someone with the clothes or equipment needed for a particular activity 使装备

kitbag /ˈkɪtbæg/ **noun** a long canvas bag for carrying a soldier's possessions（士兵用的）大圆筒形背包，行囊

kitchen /ˈkɪtʃɪn/ **noun 1** a room where food is prepared and cooked 厨房；

灶房 **2** a set of fittings and units installed in a kitchen 厨房设备；炊具 □ **kitchen garden** a part of a garden where vegetables, fruit, and herbs are grown 家庭菜园

kitchenette /ˌkɪtʃɪˈnet/ **noun** a small kitchen or cooking area 小厨房

kite /kaɪt/ **noun 1** a toy consisting of a light frame with thin material stretched over it, flown in the wind at the end of a long string 风筝 **2** a long-winged bird of prey with a forked tail 鸢（食肉猛禽，翼长，尾部呈叉状）**3** Geometry【几何】a four-sided figure having two pairs of equal sides next to each other 平行四边形

kith /kɪθ/ **noun** (**kith and kin**) your family and relations 亲属；亲戚

kitsch /kɪtʃ/ **noun** art, objects, or design that are thought to be unpleasantly bright and showy or too sentimental 庸俗花哨的艺术作品；过分感伤的作品 ■ **kitschy** adjective.

kitten /ˈkɪtn/ **noun** a young cat 小猫

kittenish /ˈkɪtnɪʃ/ **adjective** playful, lively, or flirtatious 嬉耍的；活泼的；卖弄风情的

kitty¹ /ˈkɪti/ **noun** (plural **kitties**) **1** a fund of money for use by a number of people（一群人共同使用的）资金钱 **2** a pool of money in some card games（纸牌戏中的）全部赌注

kitty² **noun** (plural **kitties**) informal【非正式】a cat 小猫

kiwi /ˈkiːwiː/ **noun** (plural **kiwis**) **1** a bird from New Zealand that cannot fly 几维（新西兰的一种不能飞的鸟）**2** (**Kiwi**) informal【非正式】a person from New Zealand 新西兰人 □ **kiwi fruit** the fruit of an Asian plant, with green flesh and black seeds 猕猴桃

klaxon /ˈklæksn/ **noun** trademark【商标】a vehicle horn or warning hooter 汽车喇叭；高音警报器

kleptomania /ˌkleptəˈmeɪniə/ **noun** a compulsive urge to steal 盗窃癖

■ **kleptomaniac** noun & adjective.

km abbreviation kilometres.

knack /næk/ noun **1** a skill at performing a task 技能;本领 **2** a habit of doing something 习惯;癖好

knacker /'nækə(r)/ verb (knackers, knackering, knackered) Brit. informal【英,非正式】 **1** damage or injure something 损害;伤害 **2** (knackered) very tired 筋疲力尽的

knacker's yard noun Brit. informal【英,非正式】 a place where old or injured animals are taken to be killed 老弱动物屠宰场

knapsack /'næpsæk/ noun a bag with shoulder straps, carried on the back 背包

knave /neɪv/ noun **1** old use【旧】 a dishonest man 不诚实的人;骗子 **2** (in cards) a jack（牌戏中的）J牌,杰克 ■ **knavish** adjective.

knead /niːd/ verb **1** work dough or clay with the hands 揉,捏(面团或制陶黏土）**2** massage something as if kneading it 按摩

knee /niː/ noun **1** the joint between the thigh and the lower leg 膝关节;膝盖 **2** the upper surface of your thigh when you are in a sitting position（人坐着时的）大腿面 • verb (knees, kneeing, kneed) hit someone with your knee 用膝盖顶 □ **knee-jerk** done automatically and without thinking 自动的;不假思索的 **knees-up** Brit. informal【英,非正式】 a lively party 欢乐的聚会

kneecap /'niːkæp/ noun the bone in front of the knee joint 髌;膝盖骨 • verb (kneecaps, kneecapping, kneecapped) shoot someone in the knee 用枪击穿(某人)的膝盖骨

kneel /niːl/ verb (kneels, kneeling, knelt or kneeled) be in a position in which you rest your weight on your knees 跪下

knell /nel/ noun literary【文】 the sound of a bell ringing to mark a person's death 丧钟

knew /njuː, nuː/ past of KNOW.

knickerbockers /'nɪkəbɒkəz/ plural noun loosefitting trousers or knickers gathered at the knee or calf（膝盖或小腿部收紧的）九分灯笼裤

knickers /'nɪkəz/ plural noun Brit.【英】 women's or girls' underpants 女用短衬裤

knick-knack /'nɪknæk/ noun a small worthless object（不值钱的）小物件

knife /naɪf/ noun (plural knives) a cutting tool consisting of a blade fixed into a handle 刀 • verb (knifes, knifing, knifed) **1** stab someone with a knife 用刀刺（或扎）**2** cut through or into something like a knife 刀切似地穿过(或扎入) □ **at knifepoint** under threat of injury from a knife 在刀子的威胁下 **knife-edge** a very tense or dangerous situation 非常紧张的状态;十分危险的情形

knight /naɪt/ noun **1** (in the Middle Ages) a man of noble rank with a duty to fight for his king（中世纪的）骑士 **2** (in the UK) a man awarded a title by the king or queen and entitled to use 'Sir' in front of his name（英国的）爵士 **3** a chess piece that moves by jumping to the opposite corner of a rectangle two squares by three（国际象棋中的）马 • verb give a man the title of knight 授予(某人)爵士头衔;封(某人)为爵士 ■ **knighthood** noun.

knit /nɪt/ verb (knits, knitting, knitted or knit) **1** make a garment by looping yarn together with knitting needles or on a machine 针织,编织(衣服) **2** make a plain stitch in knitting 织(平针) **3** join together 接合;连接 **4** tighten your eyebrows in a frown 皱紧(眉头)

knitwear /'nɪtweə(r)/ noun knitted clothes 针织衣物

knob /nɒb/ noun **1** a rounded lump at the end or on the surface of something 球形凸出物；瘤；疙瘩 **2** a ball-shaped handle 球形把手 **3** a round button on a machine（机器上的）旋钮 **4** a small lump of something 小块

knobble /'nɒbl/ **noun** Brit.【英】a small lump on something 小球形突起 ■ **knobbly** adjective.

knock /nɒk/ **verb 1** hit a surface noisily to attract attention 敲击，打（表面）**2** collide with 撞击；碰撞 **3** hit someone or something so that they move or fall 使移动；使掉落 **4** make a hole, dent, etc. in something by hitting it 敲出，击出（洞、凹痕等）**5** informal【非正式】criticize 批评 **6** (of a motor) make a thumping or rattling noise（马达）发出爆震声 • **noun 1** a sound of knocking 碰撞声 **2** a blow or collision 敲击；碰撞 **3** a setback 挫折 □ **knock-kneed** having legs that curve inward at the knee 膝外翻 **knock off** informal【非正式】stop work 停止工作 **knock something off** informal【非正式】produce a piece of work quickly and easily 轻快地完成（一件作品）**knock-on effect** an effect or result that causes a series of other things to happen 撞击效应；连锁反应 **knock someone out 1** make someone unconscious 击昏（某人）**2** eliminate a person or team from a knockout competition（在淘汰赛中）淘汰（某人或某运动员）

knockabout /'nɒkəbaʊt/ **adjective** (of comedy) lively and involving deliberately clumsy or rough actions（喜剧）喧闹的，打闹的

knocker /'nɒkə(r)/ **noun** a hinged object fixed to a door and rapped by visitors to attract attention 门环

knockout /'nɒkaʊt/ **noun 1** an act of knocking someone out 击昏 **2** Brit.【英】a competition in which the loser in each round is eliminated 淘汰赛 **3**

informal【非正式】a very impressive person or thing 令人印象深刻的人（或事物）

knoll /nəʊl/ **noun** a small hill or mound 小山丘；土墩

knot /nɒt/ **noun 1** a fastening made by looping a piece of string or rope and tightening it（线或绳的）结 **2** a tangled mass in hair, wool, etc. 绞成一团的头发(或毛线等) **3** a hard mass in wood at the point where the trunk and a branch join（树干与树枝连接处的）节疤 **4** a hard lump of muscle or muscle tissue（身体上的）肿块，硬结，瘤 **5** a small group of people 一小群人 **6** a unit of speed of a ship, aircraft, or the wind, equivalent to one nautical mile per hour 节(船、飞机或风的速度单位，即1海里/小时) • **verb** (**knots, knotting, knotted**) **1** fasten with a knot 使打结；把…结牢 **2** tangle 纠缠；缠结 **3** make a muscle tense and hard 使(肌肉)绷紧 □ **tie the knot** informal【非正式】get married 结婚；结为连理

knotty /'nɒti/ **adjective** (**knottier, knottiest**) **1** full of knots 多节的 **2** very complex 极其复杂的

know /nəʊ/ **verb** (**knows, knowing, knew; past participle known**) **1** be aware of something as a result of observing, asking, or being told 知道；懂得 **2** be absolutely sure of something 确信 **3** be familiar with 熟悉；认识 **4** have a good grasp of a subject or language 精通，掌握（某学科或语言）**5** have personal experience of 经历过；体验过 **6** (**be known as**) be thought of as having a particular quality or title 被认为具有…特点（或头衔）□ **be in the know** informal【非正式】be aware of a something known only to a few people 知情；了解内幕 **know-all** informal【非正式】a person who behaves as if they know everything

自以为无所不知者 **know-how**
practical knowledge or skill 实用知
识；技能；技术 **know the ropes** have
experience of the right way of doing
something 懂行；在行；精通业务
■ **knowable** adjective.

knowing /ˈnəʊɪŋ/ **adjective** suggesting
that you know something that is
meant to be secret 心照不宣的；会意
的 ■ **knowingly** adverb.

knowledge /ˈnɒlɪdʒ/ **noun 1**
information and awareness gained
through experience or education
(通过经验或教育获得的)知识，技
能 **2** the state of knowing about
something 了解；熟悉；知晓

✔ 拼写指南 remember the *d*: knowledge. 记住拼写knowledge中的d。

knowledgeable or **knowledg-
able** /ˈnɒlɪdʒəbl/ **adjective** intelligent
and well informed 知识渊博的；有见
识的 ■ **knowledgeably** adverb.

known /nəʊn/ past participle of KNOW.
• **adjective 1** identified as being 已
知的；闻名的：*a known criminal* 出
了名的罪犯 **2** Maths 【数学】(of a
quantity or variable) having a value
that can be stated (量或变量)已知的

knuckle /ˈnʌkl/ **noun 1** each of the
joints of a finger 指关节 **2** a knee
joint of a fourlegged animal, or the
part joining the leg to the foot (四
足动物的)膝关节，肘关节 • **verb**
(**knuckles, knuckling, knuckled**)
1 (**knuckle down**) apply yourself
seriously to a task 开始认真工作；干
劲十足地工作 **2** (**knuckle under**)
accept someone's authority 屈服

knuckleduster /ˈnʌkldʌstə(r)/
noun a metal fitting worn over the
knuckles in fighting to increase the
effect of blows 指节套(戴在指关节
上的金属套，打斗时增加击打效果)

koala /kəʊˈɑːlə/ **noun** a bear-like
Australian animal that lives in trees
考拉，树袋熊(产于澳大利亚的树栖

有袋动物)

kohl /kəʊl/ **noun** a black powder used
as eye make-up 眼圈粉(用作眼部化
妆品的黑色粉末)

kohlrabi /ˌkəʊlˈrɑːbi/ **noun** a variety
of cabbage with an edible thick,
round stem 苤蓝(球形茎可食用)

kookaburra /ˈkʊkəbʌrə/ **noun** a
very large, noisy kingfisher found in
Australia and New Zealand 笑翠鸟
(产于澳大利亚和新西兰的一种大型
翠鸟，喜鸣叫)

Koran /kɔːˈrɑːn/ **noun** the sacred book
of Islam, believed to be the word
of God as told to Muhammad and
written down in Arabic(伊斯兰教的)
《古兰经》，《可兰经》

Korean /kəˈriːən/ **noun 1** a person
from Korea 朝鲜人，韩国人 **2** the
language of Korea 朝鲜语；韩语 • **adjective** relating to Korea 朝鲜的；韩
国的

kosher /ˈkəʊʃə(r)/ **adjective 1** (of
food) prepared according to the
requirements of Jewish law (食物)
符合犹太教规的 **2** informal【非正式】
genuine and legitimate 真正的；合法
的

kowtow /ˌkaʊˈtaʊ/ **verb 1** be too
meek and obedient towards someone
对…卑躬屈膝；对…极其恭顺 **2** (in
the past, as part of Chinese custom)
kneel and touch the ground with the
forehead, in worship or as a sign of
respect 叩头，磕头(中国旧时的习俗，
表示崇拜或尊敬)

kraal /krɑːl/ **noun** S. African【南非】**1**
a traditional African village of huts
栅栏村落 **2** an enclosure for sheep
and cattle 羊栏；牛栏

krill /krɪl/ **plural noun** small shrimp-
like crustaceans which are the main
food of baleen whales 磷虾

krona /ˈkrəʊnə/ **noun 1** (plural **kronor**)
the basic unit of money of Sweden
瑞典克朗(瑞典的基本货币单位) **2**

(plural **kronur**) the unit of money of Iceland 冰岛克朗(冰岛货币单位)

krone /ˈkrəʊnə/ **noun** (plural **kroner**) the basic unit of money of Denmark and Norway 克朗(丹麦和挪威的基本货币单位)

krypton /ˈkrɪptɒn/ **noun** a gaseous chemical element used in some kinds of electric light (气体元素)氪

kudos /ˈkjuːdɒs/ **noun** praise and honour 赞扬;荣誉

! 注意 kudos is a singular word and it is wrong to use it as if it were a plural; for example, you should say *he received much kudos for his work*, not *he received many kudos for his work*. kudos是一个单数词,不能将其当作复数词使用,例如,应该说 *he received much kudos for his work* (他因其工作获得了很多赞誉),而不能说 *he received many kudos for his work*。

---

kumquat /ˈkʌmkwɒt/ **noun** a very small orange-like fruit 金橘;金柑

kung fu /ˌkʊŋ ˈfuː/ **noun** a Chinese martial art resembling karate 功夫;中国武术

Kurd /kɜːd/ **noun** a member of a mainly Islamic people living in Kurdistan, a region in the Middle East 库尔德人(居住在中东的库尔德斯坦地区,主要信仰伊斯兰教)

Kuwaiti /kuˈweɪti/ **noun** a person from Kuwait 科威特人 • **adjective** relating to Kuwait 科威特的

L or **l** /el/ **noun** (plural **Ls** or **L's**) **1** the twelfth letter of the alphabet 英语字母表的第12个字母 **2** the Roman numeral for 50 (罗马数字)五十 • **abbreviation 1** Brit 【英】learner driver 见习汽车司机：*L-plate* 见习汽车司机车牌 **2** (l) litres. **3** (l.) old use 【旧】pounds 英镑

£ abbreviation pounds 英镑

lab /læb/ **noun** informal 【非正式】a laboratory 实验室

label /'leɪbl/ **noun 1** a small piece of paper, fabric, etc. attached to an object and giving information about it 标签；签条；标记 **2** the name or trademark of a fashion company (时装公司的)名称，商标 **3** a company that produces recorded music 唱片公司 **4** a classifying name given to a person or thing (人或物的)绰号，称号 • **verb** (**labels**, **labelling**, **labelled**; US spelling【美拼作】**labels**, **labeling**, **labeled**) **1** attach a label to 贴标签于；用标签标明 **2** put someone or something in a category 把…归类

> ✔ 拼写指南 *-el*, not *-le*: label. label 中的 -el 不要拼作 -le。

labia /'leɪbɪə/ **plural noun** (singular **labium**) the inner and outer folds of a woman's genitals 阴唇 ■ **labial** adjective.

labor /'leɪbə(r)/ etc. US spelling of **LABOUR** etc. labour 等的美式拼法

laboratory /lə'bɒrətri/ **noun** (plural **laboratories**) a room or building for scientific research or teaching, or for the making of drugs or chemicals 实验室；实验大楼

laborious /lə'bɔːrɪəs/ **adjective 1** needing a lot of time and effort 费时的；费力的；费力的；辛劳的 **2** showing obvious signs of effort 吃力的 ■ **laboriously** adverb.

labour /'leɪbə(r)/ (US spelling【美拼作】**labor**) **noun 1** work 工作；劳动 **2** workers as a group (总称)劳工，工人 **3** (**Labour** or **the Labour Party**) a left-wing political party formed to represent ordinary working people 工党(代表普通劳动人民利益的左翼政党) **4** the process of giving birth 分娩 • **verb 1** do hard physical work 辛苦劳动；做重活 **2** have difficulty doing something in spite of working hard 费劲做 **3** move with difficulty and effort 费力移动 **4** (**labour under**) believe something that is not true 为…所蒙蔽 □ **labour camp** a prison camp where prisoners have to do hard physical work (强制因犯劳动的)劳动营 **labour force** the members of a population who are able to work 劳动力 **labour-intensive** needing a lot of work 劳动密集型的 **labour the point** repeat something that has already been said and understood 一再重复；反复解释

laboured /'leɪbəd/ (US spelling【美拼作】**labored**) **adjective 1** done with great difficulty 吃力的，费劲的 **2** not spontaneous or natural 不自然的；矫揉造作的

labourer (US spelling【美拼作】**laborer**) /'leɪbərə(r)/ **noun** a person who does hard physical work that does not need any special skill or training 工人，力夫

Labrador /'læbrədɔː(r)/ **noun** a breed of dog with a black or yellow coat, used as a retriever and as a guide dog 拉布拉多猎狗(皮毛黑色或黄色，

用作寻回犬和导盲犬)

laburnum /ləˈbɜːnəm/ *noun* a small tree with hanging clusters of yellow flowers 金链花树(开成串黄花)

labyrinth /ˈlæbərɪnθ/ *noun* a complicated network of passages 迷宫；曲径 ■ **labyrinthine** /ˌlæbəˈrɪnθaɪn/ *adjective*.

lace /leɪs/ *noun* 1 a delicate open fabric made by looping, twisting, or knitting thread in patterns 网眼织物；花边 2 a cord used to fasten a shoe or garment 鞋带；(衣服的)束带 • *verb* (**laces, lacing, laced**) 1 fasten something with a lace or laces (用鞋带或束带)系牢 2 add an ingredient to a drink or dish to make it stronger or improve the flavour 在(饮料或菜肴)中搀入

lacerate /ˈlæsəreɪt/ *verb* (**lacerates, lacerating, lacerated**) tear or deeply cut the flesh or skin 撕裂，划破(肉或皮) ■ **laceration** *noun*.

lachrymal or **lacrimal** /ˈlækrɪml/ *adjective* connected with weeping or tears 哭泣的；流泪的；眼泪的

lachrymose /ˈlækrɪməʊs/ *adjective* literary 【文】 tearful 含泪的；眼泪汪汪的

lack /læk/ *noun* the state of being without or not having enough of something 没有；缺乏；不足 • *verb* (also **lack for**) be without or without enough of 没有；缺少；短缺

lackadaisical /ˌlækəˈdeɪzɪkl/ *adjective* not showing enthusiasm or thoroughness 无精打采的；懒散的

lackey /ˈlæki/ *noun* (plural **lackeys**) 1 a servant 仆人；用人 2 a person who is too willing to serve or obey other people 走狗；卑躬屈膝者

lacklustre /ˈlæklʌstə(r)/ (US spelling 【美拼作】 **lackluster**) *adjective* 1 not exciting or interesting 无活力的；无生气的 2 (of the hair or eyes) not shining (头发)无光泽的；(眼睛)无神

采的

laconic /ləˈkɒnɪk/ *adjective* using very few words 简短的；精炼的 ■ **laconically** *adverb*.

lacquer /ˈlækə(r)/ *noun* 1 a liquid applied to wood or metal to give it a hard, glossy surface (涂于木头或金属表面的)漆 2 decorative wooden goods coated with lacquer (木质)漆器 3 hairspray 定型发胶 ■ **lacquered** *adjective*.

lacrimal /ˈlækrɪml/ ⇒ 见 **LACHRYMAL**.

lacrosse /ləˈkrɒs/ *noun* a team game in which a ball is thrown, caught, and carried with a long-handled stick which has a net at one end 长曲棍球(运动)(用带网兜的球棍传球、接球和带球)

lactate /lækˈteɪt/ *verb* (**lactates, lactating, lactated**) (of a woman or female animal) produce milk in the breasts or mammary glands, for feeding babies or young (妇女或雌性动物)泌乳，喂奶，哺乳 ■ **lactation** *noun*.

lactic /ˈlæktɪk/ *adjective* relating to or obtained from milk 乳的；从乳中提取的 □ **lactic acid** an acid present in sour milk, and produced in the muscles during strenuous exercise 乳酸

lactose /ˈlæktəʊs/ *noun* a sugar present in milk 乳糖

lacuna /ləˈkjuːnə/ *noun* (plural **lacunae** /ləˈkjuːniː/ or **lacunas**) a gap or missing part 空隙；空白；脱漏

lacy /ˈleɪsi/ *adjective* (**lacier, laciest**) made of, resembling, or trimmed with lace 网眼织物的，网眼状的，有花边的

lad /læd/ *noun* informal 【非正式】 a boy or young man 男孩；少年；小伙子

ladder /ˈlædə(r)/ *noun* 1 a structure consisting of a series of bars or steps between two uprights, used for climbing up or down 梯子 **2** a series of stages by which progress can be made 梯级;(发展的)途径: *the career ladder* 职业阶梯 **3** Brit 【英】 a hole in tights or stockings where the threads have come undone (连裤袜或长筒袜的)抽丝 • **verb (ladders, laddering, laddered)** Brit 【英】cause a ladder to develop in a pair of tights or a stocking 使(连裤袜或长筒袜)抽丝

laddish /ˈlædɪʃ/ **adjective** behaving in a way thought to be typical of young men, especially in being rowdy or drinking too much 小伙子的;有小伙子特征的

laden /ˈleɪdn/ **adjective** heavily loaded or weighed down 装满的;满载的;压弯的

la-di-da or **lah-di-dah** /ˌlɑːdɪˈdɑː/ **adjective** informal 【非正式】affected or snobbish 装腔作势的;自命不凡的

ladle /ˈleɪdl/ **noun** a large spoon with a cupshaped bowl and a long handle, for serving soup, stew, etc. 长柄勺 • **verb (ladles, ladling, ladled)** serve or transfer soup, stew, etc. with a ladle (用勺)舀,盛

lady /ˈleɪdi/ **noun (plural ladies) 1** (in polite or formal use) a woman (礼貌或正式用语)夫人,小姐,女士 **2** a well-mannered woman, or a woman of high social position 举止文雅的女子;淑女;贵妇人 **3** (**Lady**) a title used by peeresses, female relatives of peers, and the wives and widows of knights 小姐,夫人(对女贵族、贵族女眷、爵士夫人或遗孀的称呼) ▫ **lady-in-waiting** (**plural ladies-in-waiting**) a woman who accompanies and looks after a queen or princess (女王、王后或公主的)女侍臣,女官

ladybird /ˈleɪdɪbɜːd/ **noun** a small beetle that has a red back with black spots 瓢虫

ladykiller /ˈleɪdɪkɪlə(r)/ **noun** informal

【非正式】a man who is successful in seducing women 善于勾引女子的男人

ladylike /ˈleɪdilaɪk/ **adjective** typical of a well-mannered woman or girl 合乎妇女(或淑女)身份的;端庄的;优雅的

Ladyship /ˈleɪdiʃɪp/ **noun** (**Her/Your Ladyship**) a respectful way of referring to or addressing a Lady 夫人,小姐(对女贵族、贵族女眷、爵士夫人或遗孀的尊称)

lag[1] /læg/ **verb (lags, lagging, lagged)** fall behind 落后;落后于 • **noun** (also **time lag**) a period of time between two events (两事件之间的)间隔,间歇

lag[2] **verb (lags, lagging, lagged)** cover a water tank or pipes with material designed to prevent heat loss 给(水箱或管道)覆盖绝热层

lager /ˈlɑːɡə(r)/ **noun** a light fizzy beer 拉格啤酒,贮藏啤酒(一种起泡沫的淡啤酒)

laggard /ˈlæɡəd/ **noun** a person who falls behind other people 落后者

lagging /ˈlæɡɪŋ/ **noun** material wrapped round a water tank and pipes to prevent heat loss 绝热材料;绝热层

lagoon /ləˈɡuːn/ **noun** a stretch of salt water separated from the sea by a low sandbank or coral reef 潟湖;环礁湖

lah-di-dah ⇒ 见 **LA-DI-DA**.

laid /leɪd/ past and past participle of **LAY**[1]. ▫ **laid-back** informal 【非正式】relaxed and easy-going 松弛的;悠闲的

lain /leɪn/ past participle of **LIE**[1].

lair /leə(r)/ **noun 1** a wild animal's resting place 兽穴;兽窝 **2** a person's secret den (人的)躲藏处,藏身处

laird /leəd/ **noun** (in Scotland) a person who owns a large estate (苏格兰的)地主,领主

laissez-faire /ˌleseɪˈfeə(r)/ **noun** a policy of leaving things to take their own course, without interfering 自由放任政策；不干涉政策

laity /ˈleɪəti/ **noun** (**the laity**) people who are not priests or ministers of the Church; ordinary people 平信徒；俗人

lake /leɪk/ **noun** a large area of water surrounded by land 湖；湖泊

lama /ˈlɑːmə/ **noun 1** a title given to a religious leader in Tibetan Buddhism 喇嘛(对藏传佛教宗教领袖的称呼) **2** a Buddhist monk in Mongolia or Tibet, China 喇嘛(藏传佛教或蒙古佛教的僧侣)

lamb /læm/ **noun 1** a young sheep 羔羊 **2** a gentle or innocent person 温顺的人 • **verb** (of a female sheep) give birth to lambs (母 羊)产羊羔 ■ **lambing** noun.

lambada /læmˈbɑːdə/ **noun** a fast Brazilian dance 兰巴达舞(巴西的一种快节奏舞)

lambaste or **lambast** /læmˈbeɪst/ **verb** (**lambastes** or **lambasts**, **lambasting**, **lambasted**) criticize someone harshly 严厉批评

lambent /ˈlæmbənt/ **adjective** literary 【文】lit up or flickering with a soft glow 闪烁的；摇曳的

lame /leɪm/ **adjective 1** walking with difficulty because of an injury or illness affecting the leg or foot 瘸的；跛的 **2** (of an explanation or excuse) unconvincing and feeble (解释或理由)无说服力的，站不住脚的 **3** (of something meant to be entertaining) dull (笑话)索然无味的 • **verb** (**lames**, **laming**, **lamed**) make a person or animal lame 把…弄瘸 □ **lame duck** an unsuccessful person or thing 不成功的人(或事物) ■ **lamely** adverb **lameness** noun.

lamé /ˈlɑːmeɪ/ **noun** fabric with interwoven gold or silver threads 金银锦缎

lament /ləˈment/ **noun 1** a passionate expression of grief 悲痛;哀诉 **2** a song or poem expressing grief or regret 挽歌；哀诗 • **verb 1** mourn a person's death 哀悼 **2** express regret or disappointment about 为…感到遗憾;对…感到失望 ■ **lamentation** noun.

lamentable /ˈlæməntəbl/ **adjective** very bad or disappointing 极糟糕的；令人惋惜的 ■ **lamentably** adverb

laminate **verb** /ˈlæmɪneɪt/ (**laminates**, **laminating**, **laminated**) **1** cover a flat surface with a layer of protective material 在(平面)上覆保护层 **2** make something by sticking layers of material together 用薄片粘贴叠成;层压出 **3** split into layers or leaves 分割成薄层(或薄片) **4** beat or roll metal into thin plates 将(金属)锻打(或辗压)成薄片 • **noun** /ˈlæmɪnət/ a laminated product or material 薄片制品;层压材料 ■ **lamination** noun.

lamp /læmp/ **noun** a device using electricity, oil, or gas to give light 灯；电灯；油灯；煤气灯

lampoon /læmˈpuːn/ **verb** mock or ridicule 嘲笑；嘲弄 • **noun** a mocking attack 讽刺性抨击

lamprey /ˈlæmpri/ **noun** (plural **lampreys**) a fish like an eel, having a round sucking mouth with horny teeth 七鳃鳗，八目鳗(形似鳗鱼，嘴呈圆形，有吸盘和粗硬牙齿)

lance /lɑːns/ **noun** (in the past) a weapon with a long shaft and a pointed steel head, used by people on horseback (旧时)骑马者进攻时使用的)长矛 • **verb** (**lances**, **lancing**, **lanced**) Medicine【医】prick or cut open a boil or wound with a sharp instrument 刺破,切开(脓肿或伤口) □ **lance corporal** a rank of non-commissioned officer in the army, below corporal (陆军)一等兵

lancer /ˈlɑːnsə(r)/ **noun** (in the past) a soldier armed with a lance (旧时的)

长矛骑兵

lancet /ˈlɑːnsɪt/ **noun** a small two-edged knife with a sharp point, used in surgery 柳叶刀(尖头双刃，用作手术刀)

land /lænd/ **noun 1** the part of the earth's surface that is not covered by water 陆地 **2** an area of ground 地带；土地 **3 (the land)** ground or soil used for farming 田地；耕地 **4** a country or state 国家；国土 • **verb 1** put or go ashore (使)靠岸；(使)上岸 **2** come or bring something down to the ground (使)登陆；(使)着陆 **3** bring a fish out of the water with a net or rod 捕上(鱼)；钓到(鱼) **4** informal 【非正式】 succeed in obtaining or achieving something 赢得；获得 **5 (land up)** reach a particular place or destination 抵达；到达 **6 (land someone in)** informal 【非正式】 put someone in a difficult situation 使陷入(困境) **7 (land someone with)** inflict something unwelcome on someone 把(苦差事)推给(某人) **8** informal 【非正式】 inflict a blow on someone (向某人)打(一拳)

landau /ˈlændɔː/ **noun** an enclosed horse-drawn carriage (封闭式)四轮马车

landed /ˈlændɪd/ **adjective** owning a lot of land 拥有大量土地的

landfall /ˈlændfɔːl/ **noun** arrival on land after a sea journey 到岸；登陆

landfill /ˈlændfɪl/ **noun 1** the disposal of rubbish by burying it 废弃物填埋法 **2** buried rubbish 填埋的废弃物

landing /ˈlændɪŋ/ **noun 1** a level area at the top of a staircase 楼梯顶部平台 **2** a place where people and goods can be landed from a boat 登陆处；码头 □ **landing gear** the undercarriage of an aircraft (飞机的)起落架

landless /ˈlændləs/ **adjective** owning no land 无地的

landlocked /ˈlændlɒkt/ **adjective** (of a place) surrounded by land (地方)陆

围的

landlord /ˈlændlɔːd/ or **landlady** /ˈlændleɪdi/ **noun 1** a person who rents out property or land 地主；房东 **2** Brit 【英】 a person who runs a pub (酒馆的)老板

landlubber /ˈlændlʌbə(r)/ **noun** informal 【非正式】 a person who is not familiar with the sea or sailing "旱鸭子"，不谙航海者

landmark /ˈlændmɑːk/ **noun 1** an object or feature that is easily seen from a distance 地标；路标 **2** an important stage or turning point 里程碑；转折点

landmine /ˈlændmaɪn/ **noun** an explosive mine laid on or just under the surface of the ground 地雷

landscape /ˈlændskeɪp/ **noun 1** all the visible features of an area of land (陆上)风景，景色 **2** a picture of an area of countryside 风景画 • **verb** (**landscapes**, **landscaping**, **landscaped**) improve the appearance of land by changing its contours, planting trees and shrubs, etc. 对(土地)作景观美化

landslide /ˈlændslaɪd/ **noun 1** (Brit 【英】 also **landslip**) a mass of earth or rock that slides down a mountain or cliff 山崩；塌方 **2** an overwhelming majority of votes for one party in an election (选举中的)压倒多数票

lane /leɪn/ **noun 1** a narrow road 小路，小巷，胡同 **2** a division of a road for a single line of traffic 车道 **3** a strip of track or water for each of the competitors in a race (田径比赛中的)分道；(游泳比赛中的)泳道 **4** a course followed by ships or aircraft 航道；航空线

language /ˈlæŋgwɪdʒ/ **noun 1** human communication through the use of spoken or written words (人与人之间用以交流沟通的)语言 **2** a particular system or style of spoken or written communication 语言；语言文字 **3**

a system of symbols and rules for writing computer programs 计算机语言

✔ **拼写指南** -*guage*, not -*gauge*: lan*guage*. language 中的 -guage 不要拼作 -gauge。

languid /'læŋgwɪd/ **adjective** relaxed and not inclined to be physically active 懒散的 ■ **languidly** adverb.

languish /'læŋgwɪʃ/ **verb 1** become weak or faint 变得虚弱;衰弱无力 **2** be kept in an unpleasant place or situation 受苦;受折磨

languor /'læŋgə(r)/ **noun** a pleasant feeling of being tired or without energy 倦怠;懒散 ■ **languorous** adjective.

lank /læŋk/ **adjective** (of hair) long, limp, and straight (毛发)蓬松平直的

lanky /'læŋki/ **adjective** (**lankier**, **lankiest**) tall, thin, and moving in an awkward or ungraceful way 瘦长且行动笨拙(或难看)的

lanolin /'lænəlɪn/ **noun** a fatty substance from sheep's wool, used in skin cream 羊毛脂

lantern /'læntən/ **noun** a lamp enclosed in a metal frame with glass panels 灯笼

lanthanum /'lænθənəm/ **noun** a silvery-white metallic element (金属元素)镧

lanyard /'lænjəd/ **noun 1** a rope used on a ship (用于船上的)收紧索,绞收索 **2** a cord around the neck or shoulder for holding a whistle or similar object (用于系哨子等的)颈带,项带

lap[1] /læp/ **noun** the flat area between the waist and knees of a seated person (坐着时的)大腿部

lap[2] **noun 1** one circuit of a track or racetrack (轨道或跑道的)一圈 **2** an overlapping part 重叠部分 • **verb** (**laps**, **lapping**, **lapped**) overtake a competitor in a race to become a lap ahead (比赛中)超越(对手)一圈

lap[3] **verb** (**laps**, **lapping**, **lapped**) **1** (of an animal) take up liquid with the tongue (动物)舔,舔饮 **2** (**lap something up**) accept something with obvious pleasure 欣然接受 **3** (of water) wash against something with a gentle rippling sound (水)轻轻拍打

lapdog /'læpdɒg/ **noun 1** a small pampered pet dog 宠物狗;叭儿狗 **2** a person who is completely under the influence of someone else 仰人鼻息者

lapel /lə'pel/ **noun** the part which is folded back at the front opening of a jacket or coat (夹克或上衣的)翻领

lapidary /'læpɪdəri/ **adjective 1** relating to the engraving, cutting, or polishing of stone or gems 玉石雕刻的;玉石雕琢的 **2** (of language) elegant and concise (语言)优雅简洁的

lapis lazuli /ˌlæpɪs 'læzjuli/ **noun** a bright blue stone used in jewellery 天青石,青金石(用于珠宝制作)

Lapp /læp/ **noun** a member of a people of the extreme north of Scandinavia 拉普人(居住在斯堪的纳维亚最北部)

!注意 the people themselves prefer to be called *Sami*. 拉普人更喜欢被称作萨米人。

lapse /læps/ **noun 1** a brief failure of concentration, memory, or judgement 疏忽;小错;失误 **2** a decline from previously high standards (水准的)下降,滑坡 **3** an interval of time (时间的)间隔 • **verb** (**lapses**, **lapsing**, **lapsed**) **1** (of a right, agreement, etc.) become invalid because it is not used or renewed (权利、协议等)丧失,失效 **2** stop following a religion or doctrine 背弃,放弃(宗教信仰或信条) **3** (**lapse into**) pass gradually into a different state (逐渐)进入,陷入(某状态)

laptop /'læptɒp/ **noun** a portable computer 便携式电脑;笔记本电脑

lapwing /'læpwɪŋ/ **noun** a black and

white bird with a crest on the head 凤头鹦鹉

larboard /ˈlɑːbəd/ = PORT³.

larceny /ˈlɑːsəni/ **noun** (plural **larcenies**) theft of personal property 盗窃(罪)

larch /lɑːtʃ/ **noun** a coniferous tree with needles that fall in winter 落叶松

lard /lɑːd/ **noun** fat from a pig, used in cooking 猪油 • **verb 1** insert strips of fat or bacon in meat before cooking (烹饪前)把肥肉(或咸肉)条嵌入(肉)中 **2** add technical or obscure expressions to talk or writing (把专业术语或晦涩的词句)夹杂于(讲话或文章中)

larder /ˈlɑːdə(r)/ **noun** a room or large cupboard for storing food 食品贮藏室;食品柜

large /lɑːdʒ/ **adjective 1** of relatively great size, extent, or capacity (规模、程度或容量)大的,巨大的 **2** of wide range or scope (范围)广大的, 广泛的 □ **at large 1** escaped or not yet captured 逃脱的;逍遥法外的 **2** as a whole 整个;总体

largely /ˈlɑːdʒli/ **adverb** on the whole; mostly 大体上;主要地

largesse /lɑːˈdʒes/ **noun 1** generosity 慷慨 **2** money or gifts given generously 大额赏金;慷慨赠予

largo /ˈlɑːgəʊ/ **adverb & adjective** Music【音乐】in a slow tempo and dignified style 缓慢而庄严地(的)

lariat /ˈlæriət/ **noun** a rope used as a lasso or for tying an animal to a post 套索;(系牲畜用的)系绳

lark¹ /lɑːk/ **noun** a brown bird that sings while flying 百灵鸟;云雀

lark² /lɑːk/ **noun** informal【非正式】**1** something done for fun or as a joke 玩乐;嬉闹;玩笑 **2** Brit【英】an activity viewed as foolish or a waste of time (被视为愚蠢或浪费时间的)事情,行当 • **verb** (**lark about** or **around**) behave in a playful and mischievous

way 嬉闹;闹着玩

larva /ˈlɑːvə/ **noun** (plural **larvae** /ˈlɑːviː/) an immature form of an insect that looks very different from the adult creature, e.g. a caterpillar 幼虫;幼体

laryngitis /ˌlærɪnˈdʒaɪtɪs/ **noun** inflammation of the larynx 喉炎

larynx /ˈlærɪŋks/ **noun** (plural **larynxes** or **larynges** /ləˈrɪndʒiːz/) the area at the top of the throat forming an air passage to the lungs and containing the vocal cords 喉

lasagne /ləˈzænjə/ **noun** pasta in the form of sheets, baked in layers with meat or vegetables and a cheese sauce 意大利宽面条(以多层面条夹以肉或蔬菜并浇干酪汁制成)

lascivious /ləˈsɪviəs/ **adjective** showing strong or inappropriate sexual desire 好色的;淫荡的 ■ **lasciviously** adverb **lasciviousness** noun.

laser /ˈleɪzə(r)/ **noun** a device that produces an intense narrow beam of light 激光器

laserdisc /ˈleɪzədɪsk/ **noun** a disc resembling a large compact disc, used for high-quality video and multimedia 光盘;光碟

lash /læʃ/ **verb 1** beat with a whip or stick (用鞭子或棍子)鞭打,抽打 **2** beat strongly against 猛烈打击 **3** (**lash out**) attack someone verbally or physically 抨击;猛击 **4** (of an animal) move its tail quickly and violently (动物)猛地甩动(尾巴) **5** fasten securely with a cord or rope 栓牢;缚紧 • **noun 1** an eyelash 睫毛 **2** a sharp blow with a whip or stick 鞭打;抽打 **3** the flexible part of a whip 鞭梢

lashings /ˈlæʃɪŋz/ **plural noun** Brit. informal【英,非正式】a large amount of something 大量;许多

lass /læs/ or **lassie** /ˈlæsi/ **noun** Scottish & N. English【苏格兰和英格兰北部】a girl or young woman 少女;

姑娘；年轻妇女

lassitude /'læsɪtjuːd/ **noun** lack of energy 疲倦，倦怠；无精打采

lasso /læ'suː/ **noun** (plural **lassos** or **lassoes**) a rope with a noose at one end, used for catching cattle (用以捕牛的)套索 • **verb** (**lassoes**, **lassoing**, **lassoed**) catch with a lasso 用套索套捕

last[1] /lɑːst/ **adjective 1** coming after all others in time or order 最后的；末了的 **2** most recent in time 最近的 **3** lowest in importance or rank 最不重要的；等级最低的 **4** (**the last**) the least likely or suitable 最不可能的；最不合适的 **5** only remaining from 仅剩的 • **adverb** on the last occasion before the present 最末地；上一次 • **noun** (plural **last**) **1** the last person or thing 最后的人(或事物) **2** (**the last of**) the only remaining part of 仅剩的部分 □ **Last Judgement** (in some religions) the judgement of humankind expected to take place at the end of the world (某些宗教信仰的)最后审判，末日审判 **last rites** a Christian religious ceremony performed for a person who is about to die (基督教的)临终圣礼 ■ **lastly** adverb.

last[2] **verb 1** continue for a particular period of time 延续；持续 **2** remain operating for a considerable or particular length of time 维持；持久 **3** be enough for someone to use for a particular length of time 够用，维持(一定的时间)

last[3] **noun** a block used by a shoemaker for shaping or repairing shoes (制鞋或修鞋用的)鞋楦

latch /lætʃ/ **noun 1** a bar with a catch and lever used for fastening a door or gate 门闩 **2** a type of door lock which can be opened from the outside only with a key 碰锁，弹簧锁 • **verb 1** fasten a door or gate with a latch 用门闩闩上 **2** (**latch on to**)

associate yourself enthusiastically with 缠住不放

latchkey /'lætʃkiː/ **noun** (plural **latchkeys**) a key to an outer door of a house (大门的)碰锁钥匙，弹簧锁钥匙

late /leɪt/ **adjective 1** acting, arriving, or happening after the proper or usual time 迟的；晚的 **2** far on in a period (时间)晚的；(时期)晚期的，后期的 **3** far on in the day or night 近日暮的；近深夜的 **4** (**the late**) (of a person) recently dead (人)已故的，过世的 **5** (**latest**) of most recent date or origin 新近的；最近的 • **adverb 1** after the proper or usual time 迟，晚 **2** towards the end of a period 接近末期 **3** far on in the day or night 近日暮；近深夜 **4** (**later**) afterwards or in the near future 过后；以后 □ **of late** recently 最近 ■ **lateness** noun.

lately /'leɪtli/ **adverb** recently; not long ago 最近；近来；不久

latent /'leɪtnt/ **adjective** existing but not yet developed, showing, or active 潜在的；不易觉察的；隐伏的 ■ **latency** noun.

lateral /'lætərəl/ **adjective** of, at, towards, or from the side or sides 横向的；朝侧面的，横侧的 □ **lateral thinking** chiefly Brit. 【主英】 the solving of a problem by thinking of new ways to approach it 横向思维(指通过思考不同的方法解决问题) ■ **laterally** adverb.

latex /'leɪteks/ **noun 1** a milky fluid in some plants which thickens when exposed to the air (某些植物分泌的)胶乳 **2** a synthetic product resembling this, used to make paints, coatings, etc. 合成胶乳

lath /lɑːθ/ **noun** (plural **laths**) a thin, flat strip of wood 木板条；条板

lathe /leɪð/ **noun** a machine that shapes pieces of wood or metal by turning them against a cutting tool 车床

lather /ˈlɑːðə(r)/ *noun* **1** a frothy mass of bubbles produced by soap when mixed with water (肥皂水的)泡沫 **2** heavy sweat visible on a horse's coat as a white foam (马的)汗沫 • *verb* (**lathers, lathering, lathered**) **1** cover with or form a lather 用皂沫覆盖；起泡沫 **2** cover or spread generously with a substance (用某物质)覆盖(或涂满)

Latin /ˈlætɪn/ *noun* the language of ancient Rome and its empire 拉丁语 • *adjective* relating to the Latin language 拉丁语的 □ **Latin America** the parts of the American continent where Spanish or Portuguese is spoken 拉丁美洲

Latino /læˈtiːnəʊ/ *noun* (plural **Latinos**) N. Amer 【北美】 a Latin American inhabitant of the United States (美国)拉丁族裔的人

latitude /ˈlætɪtjuːd/ *noun* **1** the distance of a place north or south of the equator 纬度 **2** (**latitudes**) regions at a particular distance from the equator 纬度地区 **3** scope for freedom of action or thought (行动或想法的)自由，回旋余地

latrine /ləˈtriːn/ *noun* a communal toilet, especially a temporary one in a camp (尤指营地中临时的)公共厕所

latter /ˈlætə(r)/ *adjective* **1** nearer to the end than to the beginning 后半部分的 **2** recent 近来的；最近的 **3** (**the latter**) referring to the second-mentioned of two people or things (二者中的)后者 □ **latter-day** modern or contemporary 现代的；当代的 ■ **latterly** *adverb*.

lattice /ˈlætɪs/ *noun* a structure or pattern of strips crossing each other with square or diamond-shaped spaces left between 格子架；斜条格构；斜格图案

Latvian /ˈlætvɪən/ *noun* a person from Latvia 拉脱维亚人 • *adjective* relating to Latvia 拉脱维亚的

laud /lɔːd/ *verb* formal 【正式】 praise highly 颂扬；高度赞美

laudable /ˈlɔːdəbl/ *adjective* deserving praise 值得称赞的；值得赞扬的

laudanum /ˈlɔːdənəm/ *noun* a liquid containing opium, formerly used as a sedative 鸦片酊，劳丹酊(旧时用作镇静剂)

laudatory /ˈlɔːdətəri/ *adjective* formal 【正式】 expressing praise 表示赞美的；赞扬的

laugh /lɑːf/ *verb* **1** make sounds and movements that express amusement 笑；发笑 **2** (**laugh at**) make fun of 取笑；嘲笑 **3** (**laugh something off**) dismiss something by treating it light-heartedly 对…一笑置之 • *noun* **1** an act of laughing 笑 **2** (**a laugh**) informal 【非正式】 someone or something that makes people laugh 笑柄；笑料；引人发笑的事 □ **laughing gas** nitrous oxide, used as an anaesthetic 笑气(一氧化二氮的俗称，用作麻醉剂) **laughing stock** a person who is made fun of 笑柄；笑料

laughable /ˈlɑːfəbl/ *adjective* ridiculous or absurd; deserving to be laughed at 荒唐可笑的；滑稽有趣的 ■ **laughably** *adverb*.

laughter /ˈlɑːftə(r)/ *noun* the action or sound of laughing 笑；笑声

launch[1] /lɔːntʃ/ *verb* **1** move a boat or ship from land into the water 使(船)下水 **2** send a rocket or missile on its course 发射，投射(火箭或导弹) **3** begin an enterprise or introduce a new product 开创，创办(企业)；投放(新产品) **4** (**launch into**) begin something energetically and enthusiastically (积极热情地)开始，着手 • *noun* an act of launching something 下水；发射；创办；投放市场 ■ **launcher** *noun*.

launch[2] *noun* a large motorboat 大汽艇

launder /ˈlɔːndə(r)/ *verb* (**launders**,

laundering, laundered) 1 wash and iron clothes, sheets, etc. 洗熨(衣物) 2 informal 【非正式】 pass illegally obtained money through a bank or business to conceal its origins 洗(钱)

launderette or **laundrette** /lɔːnˈdret/ *noun* Brit 【英】 a place with coin-operated washing machines and dryers for public use 投币式自助洗衣店

laundry /ˈlɔːndri/ *noun* (plural **laundries**) 1 clothes, sheets, etc. that need to be washed or that have been newly washed 待洗衣物;刚洗好的衣物 2 a room or building where clothes, sheets, etc. are washed 洗衣房;洗衣店

laurel /ˈlɒrəl/ *noun* 1 an evergreen shrub or small tree with dark green glossy leaves 月桂树 2 (**laurels**) a crown of bay leaves awarded as a mark of honour in classical times 桂冠(古时用月桂叶编成的王冠,象征荣誉) 3 (**laurels**) honour or praise 荣誉;赞美 ◻ **rest on your laurels** be so satisfied with what you have achieved that you make no more effort 满足于既得成就;固步自封

lava /ˈlɑːvə/ *noun* hot molten rock that erupts from a volcano, or solid rock formed when this cools 熔岩;火山岩

lavatorial /ˌlævəˈtɔːriəl/ *adjective* (of humour) referring to bodily functions in a rude way (幽默)粗俗的,低级下流的

lavatory /ˈlævətri/ *noun* (plural **lavatories**) a toilet 厕所;抽水马桶

lavender /ˈlævəndə(r)/ *noun* 1 a strong-smelling shrub with bluish-purple flowers 熏衣草(灌木,气味浓烈,开淡紫色花) 2 a pale bluish-purple colour 淡紫色

lavish /ˈlævɪʃ/ *adjective* 1 very rich, elaborate, or luxurious 极其丰富的;过分复杂的;异常奢侈的 2 giving or given in large amounts 慷慨给予的;大量的 • *verb* give something in large or generous quantities 慷慨给予;滥施 ■ **lavishly** adverb.

law /lɔː/ *noun* 1 a rule or system of rules that regulates the actions of the people in a country or community 法律;法令;法规 2 a rule laying down the correct procedure or behaviour in a sport (体育)规则 3 a statement of fact to the effect that a particular phenomenon always occurs if certain conditions are present 定律;定理;法则

lawful /ˈlɔːfl/ *adjective* allowed by or obeying law or rules 合法的;法定的;依法的;守法的 ■ **lawfully** adverb.

lawless /ˈlɔːləs/ *adjective* not governed by or obeying laws 无法律的;不守法的 ■ **lawlessness** noun.

lawn /lɔːn/ *noun* 1 an area of mown grass in a garden or park 草坪;草地 2 a fine linen or cotton fabric 上等细麻布(或棉布)

lawnmower /ˈlɔːnməʊə(r)/ *noun* a machine for cutting the grass on a lawn 割草机

lawsuit /ˈlɔːsuːt, -sjuːt/ *noun* a claim brought to a law court to be decided 诉讼;起诉

lawyer /ˈlɔːjə(r)/ *noun* a person who practises or studies law 律师

lax /læks/ *adjective* 1 not strict, severe, or careful enough 不严格的;马虎的;疏忽的 2 (of limbs or muscles) relaxed (肌体或肌肉)松弛的 ■ **laxity** noun.

laxative /ˈlæksətɪv/ *adjective* tending to make someone empty their bowels 轻泻的;通便的 • *noun* a laxative drug or medicine 轻泻药;通便剂

lay[1] /leɪ/ *verb* (**lays**, **laying**, past and past participle **laid**) 1 put something down gently or carefully (轻轻地或小心地)放下,安置 2 put something down in position for use 铺;铺放 3 assign or place 把…归于;把…加诸于 4 (of a female bird, reptile, etc.) produce an egg from inside the body

(雌鸟、雌性爬行动物等)产(卵)，下(蛋) **5** stake an amount of money in a bet 赌(钱)，押(赌注) □ **lay-by** (plural **lay-bys**) Brit【英】an area at the side of a road where vehicles may stop 路侧停车带 **lay off** informal【非正式】stop doing something 停止活动 **lay someone off** dismiss a worker because of a shortage of work (因工作不多而)解雇(某人) **lay something on** provide food or entertainment 提供(食物或娱乐) **lay something out** arrange something according to a plan 布置，安排(计划项目)

> **！注意** don't confuse lay and lie. You *lay* something, as in *they are going to lay the carpet*, but you *lie* down on a bed or other flat surface. The past tense and past participle of *lay* is *laid*, as in *they laid the groundwork*; the past tense of *lie* is *lay* (*he lay on the floor*) and the past participle is *lain* (*she had lain on the bed for hours*). 不要混淆 lay 和 lie。lay something 指放下某物，如 they are going to lay the carpet (他们要铺地毯)，而 lie 指躺在床上或者某一平面上。lay 的过去式和过去分词为 laid，如 they laid the groundwork (他们打下了基础)；lie 的过去式是 lay (如 he lay on the floor 他躺在地板上)，过去分词是 lain (如 she had lain on the bed for hours 她在床上躺了几个小时了)。

lay² adjective **1** not having an official position in the Church 世俗的；非神职的 **2** not having professional qualifications or expert knowledge 外行的；非专业的

lay³ noun a short poem intended to be sung (供吟唱的)短诗

lay⁴ past of LIE¹.

layabout /ˈleɪəbaʊt/ noun disapproving【贬】a person who does little or no work 懒汉；游手好闲者

layer /ˈleɪə(r)/ noun a sheet or thickness of material covering a surface 层 • verb arrange or cut in a layer or layers 把⋯分层摆放(或切)割

layman /ˈleɪmən/ or **laywoman** /ˈleɪwʊmən/ noun (plural **laymen** or **laywomen**) **1** a member of a Church who is not a priest or minister 平信徒；在俗教徒 **2** a person without professional or specialized knowledge 外行；门外汉

layout /ˈleɪaʊt/ noun the way in which something is laid out 布局；设计；布局

laze /leɪz/ verb (**lazes, lazing, lazed**) spend time relaxing or doing very little 懒散；闲混

lazy /ˈleɪzi/ adjective (**lazier, laziest**) **1** unwilling to work or use energy 懒惰的，懒散的 **2** showing a lack of effort or care 没下工夫的；马虎的 ■ **lazily** adverb **laziness** noun.

lazybones /ˈleɪzɪbəʊnz/ noun informal【非正式】a lazy person 懒骨头；懒人

lb abbreviation pounds (in weight) (重量单位)磅 [short for Latin【缩写，拉丁】= *libra* 'pound, balance'.]

lbw /ˌel biː ˈdʌbljuː/ abbreviation Cricket【板球】leg before wicket (击球手)腿碰球

lea /liː/ noun literary【文】an area of grassy land 草地；牧场

leach /liːtʃ/ verb (of chemicals or minerals) be removed from soil by water passing through it (化学品或矿物质)过滤，渗滤，滤掉

lead¹ /liːd/ verb (**leads, leading, led**) **1** cause a person or animal to go with you 带领；引领 **2** be a route or means of access 通达；通向 **3** (**lead to**) result in 引起；导致 **4** cause someone to do or believe something 影响；引导；使得 **5** be in charge of 领导，带领 **6** have the advantage in a race or game (在比赛中)跑在前面，领先 **7** have a particular way of life 过着(某种生活) **8** (**lead up**

to) come before or result in 为…的先导;导致 **9** (**lead someone on**) deceive someone into believing they you are attracted to them 使误信(自己被其吸引) • noun **1** an example for other people to copy 实例;榜样 **2** a position of advantage in a contest (竞争中的)领导地位,领先地位 **3** the chief part in a play or film (戏剧或电影中的)主角 **4** a clue to follow when trying to solve a problem (解决问题的)线索 **5** Brit 【英】a strap or cord for controlling and guiding a dog (牵狗的)绳索,皮带 **6** a wire conveying electric current 电线;导线

lead² /led/ **noun 1** a heavy bluish-grey metal 铅 **2** the part of a pencil that makes a mark 铅笔芯

leaded /'ledɪd/ **adjective 1** framed or covered with lead 有铅框的;包铅的,灌铅的 **2** (of petrol) containing lead (汽油)含铅的

leaden /'ledn/ **adjective 1** dull, heavy, or slow 沉闷的;沉重的;迟钝的 **2** dull grey in colour 铅灰色的

leader /'li:də(r)/ **noun 1** a person or thing that leads 领导;首领;引导者;引导物 **2** the most successful or advanced person or thing in a particular area 领先者;榜样 **3** the main player in a music group 领奏者 **4** a newspaper article giving the editor's opinion (报纸的)社论 ■ **leadership** noun.

leading /'li:dɪŋ/ **adjective** most important, or in first place 最重要的;首位的 □ **leading light** a prominent or influential person 重要人物;有影响的人物 **leading question** a question that encourages someone to give the answer that you want 诱导性问题

leaf /li:f/ **noun** (plural **leaves**) **1** a flat green part of a plant that is attached to a stem 叶子;叶片 **2** a single sheet of paper in a book (书的)页,张 **3** gold or silver in the form of a very thin sheet 金箔;银箔 **4** a hinged or detachable part of a table (桌子的)活动面板 • **verb** (**leaf through**) turn over pages or papers, reading them quickly or casually 匆匆翻阅;随意浏览 □ **turn over a new leaf** start to behave in a better way 揭开新的一页;重新开始;改过自新 ■ **leafy** adjective.

leaflet /'li:flət/ **noun 1** a printed sheet of paper containing information or advertising 传单;小册子 **2** a small leaf 小叶;嫩叶 • **verb** (**leaflets**, **leafleting**, **leafleted**) distribute leaflets to 向…散发传单(或小册子)

league¹ /li:g/ **noun 1** a collection of people, countries, or groups that combine to help or protect each other 联盟;同盟;联合会 **2** a group of sports clubs that play each other over a period for a championship (体育)联合会,联赛 **3** a class of quality or excellence 级别;等级 □ **in league** (of two or more people) making secret plans (两个或两个以上的人)密谋的,勾结的

league² noun a former measure of distance, of about three miles 里格(旧时距离单位,约合3英里)

leak /li:k/ **verb 1** accidentally allow contents to escape or enter through a hole or crack 漏;渗漏 **2** (of liquid, gas, etc.) escape or enter accidentally through a hole or crack (液体、气体等)渗入,漏出 **3** deliberately give out secret information 泄露;透露(机密) • noun **1** a hole or crack through which contents leak 漏洞;罅隙;裂缝 **2** an instance of leaking 漏;渗漏;透露 ■ **leakage** noun **leaky** adjective.

lean¹ /li:n/ **verb** (**leans**, **leaning**, past and past participle **leaned** or Brit. 【英】**leant**) **1** be in a sloping position 倾侧;倾斜 **2** (**lean against** or **on**) rest against 靠;倚 **3** (**lean on**) rely on for support 依靠;依赖 **4** (**lean to** or **towards**) favour a particular

point of view 赞同，倾向于(某观点)
□ **lean-to** (plural **lean-tos**) a small building sharing a wall with a larger building 披屋；单坡顶屋

lean² adjective **1** (of a person) having little fat；thin (人)瘦的 **2** (of meat) containing little fat (肉)脂肪少的，瘦的 **3** (of a period of time) unproductive (时期)不景气的，产品产量少的

leaning /ˈliːnɪŋ/ noun a tendency or preference 倾向；爱好

leap /liːp/ verb (**leaps**, **leaping**, past and past participle **leaped** or **leapt**) **1** jump high or a long way 跳；跳跃 **2** move quickly and suddenly 突然快速移动 **3** (**leap at**) accept something eagerly 迫不及待地接受 **4** increase dramatically 激增；猛涨 • noun an act of leaping 跳；跳跃 □ **leap year** a year with 366 days, occurring every four years 闰年

leapfrog /ˈliːpfrɒɡ/ noun a game in which players in turn jump over others who are bending down 跳背游戏(双腿分开一次从弯背站立的人身上跳过) • verb (**leapfrogs**, **leapfrogging**, **leapfrogged**) **1** jump over someone in leapfrog 做跳背动作 **2** overtake others to move into a leading position 跃居首位

learn /lɜːn/ verb (**learns**, **learning**, past and past participle **learned** or **learnt**) **1** gain knowledge or skill through study or experience 学；学习；学到；学会 **2** become aware of something through observing or hearing about it 获悉；得知；发现；觉察到 **3** memorize 记住 ► **learner** noun.

learned /ˈlɜːnɪd/ adjective having gained a lot of knowledge by studying 知识渊博的；有学问的

learning /ˈlɜːnɪŋ/ noun knowledge or skills gained by studying 学问；学识

lease /liːs/ noun an agreement by which one person uses land, property, etc. which belongs to another person for a stated time in return for payment 租约；租契 • verb (**leases**, **leasing**, **leased**) let out or rent land, property, etc. by a lease 出租(土地、资产等)

leasehold /ˈliːshəʊld/ noun the holding of property by a lease 租赁权

leash /liːʃ/ noun a dog's lead (系狗的)皮带，绳子，链条

least /liːst/ determiner & pronoun (usu. **the least**) smallest in amount, extent, or significance 最小(的)；最少(的)；程度最轻的；最不重要(的) • adverb to the smallest extent or degree 最少；最小；微不足道 □ **at least 1** not less than 至少 **2** if nothing else 起码 **3** anyway 无论如何；不管怎样

leather /ˈleðə(r)/ noun a material made from the skin of an animal by tanning or a similar process 皮革

leathery /ˈleðəri/ adjective tough and hard like leather 坚韧粗糙的；似皮革的

leave¹ /liːv/ verb (**leaves**, **leaving**, **left**) **1** go away from 离开 **2** stop attending or working for 搬离(住所)；脱离；离职 **3** go away without taking someone or something 留下；丢下 **4** (**be left**) remain to be used or dealt with 留给；遗留 **5** let someone do something without interfering 任由(某人做某事) **6** put something somewhere to be collected or dealt with 留；留下 **7** give something to someone in a will 遗赠；遗留 **8** (**leave someone/thing out**) fail to include someone or something 遗漏 ► **leaver** noun.

leave² noun **1** (also **leave of absence**) time when you have permission to be absent from work or duty 假期；休假 **2** formal 【正式】permission 准许；同意 □ **take your leave** formal 【正式】say goodbye 告别

leaven /ˈlevn/ noun a substance added to dough to make it ferment and rise 发酵剂；酵母 • verb make something less serious or dull by adding something 改善；使改观

leaves /li:vz/ plural of LEAF.

Lebanese /ˌlebə'ni:z/ noun (plural **Lebanese**) a person from Lebanon 黎巴嫩人 • **adjective** relating to Lebanon 黎巴嫩的

lecher /'letʃə(r)/ noun a lecherous man 好色之徒；淫棍 ■ **lechery** noun.

lecherous /'letʃərəs/ adjective (of a man) showing sexual desire in an offensive way (男子)好色的，纵欲的，淫荡的

lectern /'lektən/ noun a tall stand with a sloping top from which a speaker can read while standing up (面板倾斜的)讲台

lecture /'lektʃə(r)/ noun **1** an educational talk to an audience 讲座；讲课 **2** a long telling-off or critical talk 冗长的训斥 • verb (**lectures**, **lecturing**, **lectured**) **1** give a lecture, or a series of lectures 作讲座；讲课 **2** give someone a long telling-off (长时间地)批评，训斥 ■ **lecturer** noun.

led /led/ past and past participle of LEAD¹.

ledge /ledʒ/ noun a narrow horizontal surface sticking out from a wall, cliff, etc. 壁架；岩架；架状突出物

ledger /'ledʒə(r)/ noun a book in which financial accounts are kept 分类账；分户账

lee /li:/ noun the side of something that provides shelter from wind or weather 隐蔽处

leech /li:tʃ/ noun **1** a worm that sucks the blood of animals or people 水蛭；蚂蟥 **2** a person who lives off other people 榨取他人脂膏者；寄生虫

leek /li:k/ noun a plant with a long cylindrical bulb which is eaten as a vegetable 韭葱

leer /lɪə(r)/ verb look or smile at someone in a lustful or unpleasant way (对某人)色迷迷地看(或笑) • noun a lustful or unpleasant look or smile 色迷迷的目光；奸笑

leery /'lɪəri/ adjective informal 【非正式】 wary 谨慎的；警惕的

lees /li:z/ plural noun the sediment left in the bottom of a bottle or barrel of wine 沉淀物；渣滓

leeward /'li:wəd, 'lu:əd/ adjective & adverb on or towards the side that is sheltered from the wind 背风的(地)；下风的(地)

leeway /'li:wei/ noun the amount of freedom to move or act that is available (活动的)自由度，余地，灵活性

left¹ /left/ adjective **1** on or towards the side of a person or thing which is to the west when the person or thing is facing north 左边的；在面的；朝左的 **2** left-wing 左翼的；左派的 • adverb on or to the left side 在左面向；往左；向左 • noun **1** (the left) the left-hand part, side, or direction 左边，左侧；左方 **2** a left turn 左转弯 **3** (often the Left) a left-wing group or party (团体、政党的)左派，左翼 □ **left-field** unconventional or experimental 不依惯例的；非常规的；实验性的 • **left wing** socialist, or supporting political or social change 左翼的；左派

left² past and past participle of LEAVE¹.

leftovers /'leftəuvəz/ plural noun food remaining after the rest has been eaten 残羹剩饭 • adjective (**leftover**) remaining after the rest of something has been used 剩余的

leg /leg/ noun **1** each of the limbs on which a person or animal moves and stands (人或动物的)腿 **2** each of the parts of a table, chair, etc. that rest on the floor and support its weight 细长支撑物；椅子腿；桌腿 **3** a section of a journey, race, etc. (旅程、比赛等的)一段 **4** (in sport) each of two or more games making up a round of a competition (体育比赛的)一场，一轮，一局 • verb (**legs**, **legging**, **legged**) (**leg it**) informal 【非正式】

run away 逃跑

legacy /'legəsi/ **noun** (plural **legacies**) **1** an amount of money or property left to someone in a will 遗赠的财物;遗产 **2** something handed down by a predecessor 祖传的东西;(祖先的)遗产

legal /'liːgl/ **adjective 1** having to do with the law 法律的;法律上的 **2** permitted by law 法律许可的;合法的 □ **legal aid** money given to people who cannot afford to pay for a lawyer 法律援助 **legal tender** accepted methods of payment such as coins or banknotes 法定货币 ■ **legality** noun **legally** adverb.

legalize or **legalise** /'liːgəlaɪz/ **verb** (**legalizes**, **legalizing**, **legalized**) make something legal 使合法化;使得到法律认可 ■ **legalization** noun.

legate /'legət/ **noun** a representative of the Pope (教皇的)使节,使者

legation /lɪ'geɪʃn/ **noun 1** a diplomat below the rank of ambassador, and their staff 公使馆全体人员(指公使及其随员) **2** the official residence of a diplomat 公使馆

legato /lɪ'gɑːtəʊ/ **adverb & adjective** Music【音乐】in a smooth, flowing way 连奏地(的);连音地(的)

legend /'ledʒənd/ **noun 1** a traditional story from long ago which is not definitely true 传说;传奇 **2** a very famous person 传奇人物 **3** an inscription, caption, or list explaining the symbols used in a map or table 铭文;(图片等的)说明文字;(地图的)图例

legendary /'ledʒəndri/ **adjective 1** described in legends 传说中的;与传说有关的 **2** remarkable enough to be famous 传奇式的;传奇般的

leggings /'legɪŋz/ **plural noun 1** women's tight-fitting stretchy trousers (女式)紧身弹力裤 **2** strong protective coverings for the legs, worn over trousers 绑腿;裹腿

leggy /'legi/ **adjective** (**leggier**, **leggiest**) long-legged 腿长的

legible /'ledʒəbl/ **adjective** (of handwriting or print) clear enough to read (手写或印刷文字)字迹清楚的,易读的 ■ **legibility** noun **legibly** adverb.

legion /'liːdʒən/ **noun 1** a division of 3,000 to 6,000 men in the army of ancient Rome (古罗马的)军团 **2** (a **legion** or **legions of**) a vast number of 大量;大批;众多 • **adjective** literary【文】great in number 众多的;大量的

legionnaire /ˌliːdʒə'neə(r)/ **noun** a member of a legion 军团成员 □ **legionnaire's disease** a form of pneumonia 军团病(一种肺部疾病)

legislate /'ledʒɪsleɪt/ **verb** (**legislates**, **legislating**, **legislated**) **1** make laws 立法;制定法律 **2** (**legislate for** or **against**) prepare for or try to prevent a situation 为…立法(或为防止…立法) ■ **legislator** noun.

legislation /ˌledʒɪs'leɪʃn/ **noun** laws 法律

legislative /'ledʒɪslətɪv/ **adjective 1** having the power to make laws 有立法权的 **2** relating to laws 法律的;立法的

legislature /'ledʒɪsleɪtʃə(r)/ **noun** the group of people who make a country's laws 立法机构;立法机关

legitimate adjective /lɪ'dʒɪtɪmət/ allowed by the law or rules 法规许可的;合法的 **2** able to be defended;reasonable 合理的;合乎逻辑的 **3** (of a child) born to parents who are married to each other (孩子)婚生的;嫡出的 • **verb** /lɪ'dʒɪtɪmeɪt/ (**legitimates**, **legitimating**, **legitimated**) make something legitimate 使合法;使得到法律认可 ■ **legitimacy** noun **legitimately** adverb.

✔ 拼写指南 leg-, not lig-: *legitimate*. legitimate 中 leg- 不要拼作 lig-。

legitimize or **legitimise** /lɪˈdʒɪtəmaɪz/ **verb** (**legitimizes, legitimizing, legitimized**) make something legitimate 使合法;使得到法律认可

legume /ˈlegjuːm/ **noun** a plant with seeds in pods, such as the pea 豆科植物 ■ **leguminous** adjective.

leisure /ˈleʒə(r)/ **noun** time for relaxation or enjoyment 空闲时间;闲暇 □ **at leisure 1** not occupied; free 空闲的;有空的 **2** in an unhurried way 不慌不忙;从容

leisurely /ˈleʒəli/ **adjective** relaxed and unhurried 从容的;不慌不忙的 ● **adverb** without hurry 从容地;不慌不忙地

lemming /ˈlemɪŋ/ **noun** a small Arctic rodent, some kinds of which periodically migrate in large numbers (they are popularly believed to run headlong into the sea and drown) 旅鼠(见于北极地区的小型啮齿动物,定期成群大批迁徙)

lemon /ˈlemən/ **noun 1** a pale yellow citrus fruit with thick skin and acidic juice 柠檬 **2** a pale yellow colour 淡黄色;柠檬色 □ **lemon curd** a sweet spread made with lemons 柠檬乳

lemonade /ˌleməˈneɪd/ **noun** a sweet drink made with lemon juice or flavouring 柠檬汽水

lemur /ˈliːmə(r)/ **noun** an animal resembling a monkey, found only in Madagascar 狐猴(仅见于马达加斯加)

lend /lend/ **verb** (**lends, lending, lent**) **1** allow someone to use something on the understanding that they will return it 把…借给;借出 **2** give someone money on condition that they will pay it back later 贷(款) **3** add or contribute a particular quality 提供;贡献;增添 **4** (**lend itself to**) be suitable for something 适合于 ■ **lender** noun.

length /leŋθ/ **noun** the measurement or extent of something from end to end 长;长度 **2** the amount of time that something lasts 时间长度;一段时间 **3** the quality of being long 长(指性质) **4** a stretch or piece of something (某物的)长度 **5** the extent to which someone does something (某人的)努力程度: *going to great lengths* 竭尽全力

lengthen /ˈleŋθən/ **verb** make or become longer (使)延长;(使)变长

lengthways /ˈleŋθweɪz/ or **lengthwise** /ˈleŋθwaɪz/ **adverb** in a direction parallel with a thing's length 纵向地;纵长地

lengthy /ˈleŋθi/ **adjective** (**lengthier, lengthiest**) lasting a long time 很长的 ■ **lengthily** adverb.

lenient /ˈliːniənt/ **adjective** not strict; merciful or tolerant 不严格的;温和的;仁慈的;宽厚的 ■ **leniency** noun **leniently** adverb.

lens /lenz/ **noun 1** a piece of transparent curved material that concentrates or spreads out light rays, used in cameras, glasses, etc. 透镜 **2** the transparent part of the eye that focuses light on to the retina (眼球的)晶状体

Lent /lent/ **noun** (in the Christian Church) the period immediately before Easter (基督教复活节前的)大斋期

lent /lent/ past and past participle of **LEND**.

lentil /ˈlentl/ **noun** an edible seed with one flat and one curved side 小扁豆;兵豆

lento /ˈlentəʊ/ **adverb & adjective** Music 【音乐】 slow or slowly 缓慢地(的)

Leo /ˈliːəʊ/ **noun** a sign of the zodiac (the Lion), 23 July–22 August 狮子宫(黄道十二宫之一)

leonine /ˈliːənaɪn/ **adjective** relating to or like a lion or lions 狮子的;狮子般的

leopard /ˈlepəd/ **noun** (feminine 【阴性】

leopardess) a large cat with a spotted coat, found in Africa and southern Asia 豹

leotard /'li:əta:d/ **noun** a close-fitting, stretchy one-piece garment covering the body to the top of the thighs, worn for dance, exercise, etc. 紧身连衣裤

leper /'lepə(r)/ **noun 1** a person who has leprosy 麻风病人 **2** someone who is rejected or avoided by other people 被排斥的人；大家躲避的人

leprechaun /'leprəkɔ:n/ **noun** (in Irish folklore) a mischievous elf (爱尔兰民间传说中的)矮妖精

leprosy /'leprəsi/ **noun** a contagious disease that affects the skin and can cause deformities 麻风病 ■ **leprous** adjective.

lesbian /'lezbiən/ **noun** a woman who is sexually attracted to other women 女同性恋者 • **adjective** relating to lesbians 女同性恋的 ■ **lesbianism** noun.

lesion /'li:ʒn/ **noun** an area of skin or part of the body which has been damaged (皮肤或器官的)损伤，损坏

less /les/ **determiner & pronoun 1** a smaller amount of; not as much (数量)较少的，较少量 **2** fewer in number (数目)较小的；较小数目 • **adverb** to a smaller extent; not so much 较少地；较小地 • **preposition** minus 减去

> **！注意** make sure you distinguish between **less** and **fewer**. Use **fewer** with plural nouns, as in there are fewer tourists this year; use **less** with nouns referring to things that cannot be counted, as in there is less blossom on this tree. Using **less** with a plural noun (less tourists) is wrong. 一定要了解 less 和 fewer 的区别：fewer 与复数名词连用，如 there are fewer tourists this year (今年游客较少)；less 与不可数名词连用，如 there is less blossom on this

tree (这棵树上开的花少)。less 与复数名词连用(如 less tourists)是错误的。

lessee /le'si:/ **noun** a person who holds the lease of a property 承租人，租户

lessen /'lesn/ **verb** make or become less (使)减少；(使)缩小；(使)变少

lesser /'lesə(r)/ **adjective** not so great, large, or important as the other or the rest 较轻的；较小的；次要的

lesson /'lesn/ **noun 1** a period of learning or teaching 一堂课；一节课 **2** a thing that has been learned 所学的功课；课 **3** a thing that acts as a warning or encouragement 教训；经验 **4** a passage from the Bible read aloud during a church service (礼拜时的)经书选读

lessor /le'sɔ:(r)/ **noun** a person who lets a property to someone else 出租人

lest /lest/ **conjunction** formal 【正式】**1** with the intention of preventing; to avoid the risk of 免得；以免 **2** because of the possibility of 因为有…的可能

let /let/ **verb** (**lets**, **letting**, **let**) **1** allow 允许；让 **2** used to express an intention, suggestion, or order (用于表示意图、建议或命令)让：Let's have a drink. 我们喝一杯吧。**3** allow someone to use a room or property in return for payment 出租(房间或房屋) • **noun 1** Brit. 【英】a period during which a room or property is rented 出租期 **2** (in racket sports) a situation in which a point is not counted and is played for again (执拍运动项目中的)重新发球 ▢ **let alone** not to mention 更不用说 **let someone down** fail to support or help someone 不能帮助(某人)；不能支持(某人)；使(某人)失望 **let someone go** allow someone to go free 释放(某人) **let yourself go 1** act in a relaxed way 放松；随心所

欲 **2** become careless in your habits or appearance 变得不修边幅 **let someone off 1** choose not to punish someone 放过，宽恕(某人) **2** excuse someone from a task 免除(某人)的任务;准许(某人)不工作 **let something off** cause a gun, firework, etc. to fire or explode 放(枪、烟火等);引爆(炸弹) **let up** informal 【非正式】 become less strong or severe 减弱;减轻;缓和

lethal /ˈliːθl/ adjective **1** able to cause death 可致死的;能致命的 **2** very harmful or destructive 极有害的;危害极大的 ■ **lethally** adverb.

lethargic /ləˈθɑːdʒɪk/ adjective lacking energy or enthusiasm 没精打采的;无活力的;无热情的 ■ **lethargically** adverb.

lethargy /ˈleθədʒi/ noun a lack of energy and enthusiasm 没精打采;无活力;无热情

let's /lets/ short form let us.

letter /ˈletə(r)/ noun **1** any of the symbols of an alphabet 字母 **2** a written communication, usually sent by post 信 **3** (letters) old use 【旧】 knowledge of literature 文学 • verb (letters, lettering, lettered) **1** write something with letters 用字母书写 **2** (lettered) old use 【旧】 able to read and write 识字的;能读会写的 □ **letter bomb** an explosive device hidden in a small package, which explodes when the package is opened 邮件炸弹 **letter box** a slot in a door through which letters are delivered (门上的)邮箱;信箱 **the letter of the law** the precise terms of a law or rule 法律法规的精确条款

letterhead /ˈletəhed/ noun a printed heading on stationery 信笺抬头

lettuce /ˈletɪs/ noun a plant whose leaves are eaten in salads 莴苣;生菜

leucocyte or **leukocyte** /ˈluːkəsaɪt/ noun technical 【术语】 a white blood cell 白细胞

leukaemia /luːˈkiːmiə/ (US spelling 【美拼作】 leukemia) noun a serious disease in which too many white blood cells are produced 白血病

levee /ˈlevi/ noun an embankment built to stop a river overflowing 防洪堤

level /ˈlevl/ noun **1** a position on a scale (秤的)水平位置 **2** the amount of something that is present 水平 **3** a horizontal line or surface 水平线;水平面 **4** height in relation to the ground 水平高度 **5** a particular floor in a building (建筑物的)层 • adjective **1** having a flat horizontal surface 平的;平坦的;水平的 **2** having the same relative height or position as someone or something else 等高的;位置(或地位)相同的 • verb (levels, levelling, levelled; US spelling 【美拼作】 levels, leveling, leveled) **1** make or become level 使水平;使平坦;达到水平状态;变平坦 **2** aim or direct a weapon, criticism, or accusation 把(武器)对准;使(批评、指控)针对 **3** (level with) informal 【非正式】 be honest with 对…诚实 □ **level crossing** Brit. 【英】 a place where a road crosses a railway at the same level (公路与铁路的)平面交叉处,交叉道口 **level-headed** calm and sensible 头脑冷静的;清醒的 ■ **levelly** adverb.

lever /ˈliːvə(r)/ noun **1** a bar used to move a load with one end when pressure is applied to the other 杆;撬棒;杠杆 **2** an arm or handle that is moved to operate a mechanism (机械装置的)控制杆,柄 • verb (levers, levering, levered) lift or move with a lever (用杠杆)撬起,撬动

leverage /ˈliːvərɪdʒ/ noun **1** the application of force with a lever 杠杆作用 **2** the power to influence other people 影响力

leveret /ˈlevərɪt/ noun a young hare 小野兔

leviathan /lɪˈvaɪəθən/ noun **1** (in the

Bible) a sea monster (《圣经》中的)海中怪兽 **2** a very large or powerful thing 庞然大物

levitate /'levɪteɪt/ **verb** (**levitates, levitating, levitated**) rise and hover in the air 升空；空中漂浮 ■ **levitation** noun.

levity /'levəti/ **noun** the treatment of a serious matter with humour or lack of respect 轻率；轻浮

levy /'levi/ **verb** (**levies, levying, levied**) make a person, organization, etc. pay a tax or fine 征税；收费；罚款 ● **noun** (plural **levies**) **1** a sum of money paid as a tax 税款；征收额 **2** old use【旧】 a group of enlisted troops 征募的军队

lewd /luːd/ **adjective** referring to sex in a crude and offensive way 下流的；猥亵的

lexical /'leksɪkl/ **adjective** relating to the words of a language 词汇的

lexicography /ˌleksɪ'kɒɡrəfi/ **noun** the writing of dictionaries 词典编纂 ■ **lexicographer** noun.

lexicon /'leksɪkən/ **noun 1** the vocabulary of a person, language, or branch of knowledge 词汇 **2** a dictionary 词典；辞典

ley line /leɪ/ **noun** a line of energy believed by some people to connect some ancient sites (被认为连接古代遗址的)假想线

liability /ˌlaɪə'bɪləti/ **noun** (plural **liabilities**) **1** the state of being liable 责任；义务 **2** an amount of money that a person or company owes 负债；债务 **3** a person or thing likely to cause you embarrassment or trouble 可能使人陷入尴尬境地(或惹麻烦)的人(或事物)

liable /'laɪəbl/ **adjective 1** responsible by law 负有法律责任的 **2** (**liable to**) able to be punished by law for something 会受法律惩处的 **3** (**liable to do**) likely to do or to be affected

by 可能做…的；可能受…影响的

liaise /li'eɪz/ **verb** (**liaises, liaising, liaised**) **1** (of two or more people or groups) cooperate with each other and share information (两个或两个以上的人或群体)联络，联系 **2** (**liaise between**) act as a link between two or more people or groups 充当联络人；做联系人

> ✔ **拼写指南** remember the second *i* in **liaise** and **liaison**. 记住拼写 liaise 和 liaison 中的第2个 i。

liaison /li'eɪzn/ **noun 1** communication or cooperation between people or organizations 联络；联系 **2** a sexual relationship (男女之间的)私通

liana /li'ɑːnə/ **noun** a tropical climbing plant that hangs from trees (热带)藤本植物

liar /'laɪə(r)/ **noun** a person who tells lies 说谎者

libation /laɪ'beɪʃn/ **noun** (in the past) a drink poured as an offering to a god (旧时的)祭酒，奠酒

libel /'laɪbl/ **noun** the crime of publishing something false that is damaging to a person's reputation (文字)诽谤罪 ● **verb** (**libels, libelling, libelled**; US spelling【美拼作】 **libels, libeling, libeled**) publish something false about 以文字诽谤 ■ **libellous** (US spelling【美拼作】 **libelous**) adjective.

liberal /'lɪbərəl/ **adjective 1** willing to respect and accept behaviour or opinions different from your own 开明的；心胸开阔的 **2** (in politics) supporting the freedom of individuals and in favour of moderate political reform (政治上)自由主义的 **3** (**Liberal**) relating to the Liberal or Liberal Democrat Party 自由党；自由民主党 **4** generous in applying or adding something 慷慨的；大方的 ● **noun 1** a person with liberal views 自由主义者 **2** (**Liberal**) a supporter of the Liberal or Liberal Democrat Party 自由党人；自由民主党人 ■ **liberalism** noun **liberality** noun **liberally** adverb.

liberalize or **liberalise** /'lɪbrəlaɪz/ **verb (liberalizes, liberalizing, liberalized)** remove or loosen restrictions on 使自由化；放开对…的限制 ■ **liberalization** noun.

liberate /'lɪbəreɪt/ **verb (liberates, liberating, liberated) 1** set free 解放；释放 **2 (liberated)** free from traditional ideas about social behaviour 解放的；不受传统观念束缚的 ■ **liberation** noun **liberator** noun.

libertine /'lɪbəti:n/ **noun** a man who is immoral and indulges too much in sexual pleasure 浪荡子；淫荡的男子

liberty /'lɪbəti/ **noun (plural liberties) 1** the state of being free 自由 **2** a right or privilege 权利；特权 **3** the ability to act as you please 自主权；自由权 **4** 〔非正式〕 a rude remark or disrespectful act 失礼；放肆的话(或行为) □ **take liberties** behave in a disrespectful or overfamiliar way 举止放肆

libidinous /lɪ'bɪdɪnəs/ **adjective** having a strong sexual drive 好色的；淫荡的

libido /lɪ'bi:dəʊ/ **noun (plural libidos)** sexual desire 性欲

Libra /'li:brə/ **noun** a sign of the zodiac (the Scales or Balance), 23 September–22 October 天秤宫(黄道十二宫之一)

librarian /laɪ'breəriən/ **noun** a person who works in a library 图书馆馆长；图书馆管理员

library /'laɪbrəri/ **noun (plural libraries) 1** a building or room containing a collection of books which people can read or borrow 图书馆；书库；藏书室 **2** a private collection of books 私人藏书

libretto /lɪ'bretəʊ/ **noun (plural libretti** /lɪ'breti/ or **librettos)** the words of an opera or musical (歌剧或音乐剧的)歌词 ■ **librettist** noun.

lice /laɪs/ plural of LOUSE.

licence /'laɪsns/ (US spelling 【美拼作】 **license) noun 1** an official permit to own, use, or do something 许可证；执照 **2** the freedom to do or say what you want (行为或言论的)自由，放纵 □ **license plate** N. Amer. 【北美】 a number plate 车牌

✔ **拼写指南** licence is the spelling for the noun, and license for the verb; in American English the -ense spelling is used for both. licence 是用作名词时的拼法，license 是用作动词时的拼法，美式英语中无论用作名词还是动词都拼作 -ense。

license /'laɪsns/ **verb (licenses, licensing, licensed) 1** grant a licence to 给…发许可证 **2** authorize or permit 准许；授权

licensee /ˌlaɪsn'si:/ **noun** a person who holds a licence to sell alcoholic drinks 售酒执照持有者

licentious /laɪ'senʃəs/ **adjective** behaving in a sexually immoral way 放荡的；淫荡的

lichen /'laɪkən/ **noun** a plant resembling moss which grows on rocks, walls, and trees 地衣

lick /lɪk/ **verb 1** pass the tongue over something 舔 **2** move lightly and quickly (舔噬般地)快速运动 • **noun 1** an act of licking 舔 **2** informal 【非正式】 a small amount or quick application of something 少量

licorice /'lɪkərɪʃ/ US spelling of LIQUORICE. liquorice 的美式拼法

lid /lɪd/ **noun 1** a removable or hinged cover for the top of a container 盖；盖子 **2** an eyelid 眼睑；眼皮

lido /'li:dəʊ/ **noun (plural lidos)** a public open-air swimming pool 露天公共游泳池

lie[1] /laɪ/ **verb (lies, lying, lay; past participle lain) 1** be in a horizontal position on a supporting surface 平卧；躺 **2** be in a particular state 处于…状态 **3** be situated or found 位于 □ **the lie of the land 1** the features or characteristics of an area 地形；地貌 **2** the current situation 当前形势

！注意 don't confuse lay and lie: see the note at **LAY**[1]. 不要混淆 lay 和 lie：见 lay[1]处用法说明。

lie[2] **noun** a false statement made deliberately by someone who knows it is not true 谎言；假话 • **verb** (**lies, lying, lied**) tell a lie or lies 说谎

liege /liːdʒ/ **noun** historical 【历史】**1** (also **liege lord**) a lord under the feudal system 封建领主；郡主 **2** a person who served a feudal lord 臣属；臣民

lieu /luː/ **noun** (**in lieu of**) instead of 替代

lieutenant /lefˈtenənt/ **noun 1** a deputy or substitute acting for a superior 副职官员；代理官员，助理官员 **2** a rank of officer in the army and navy 陆军中尉；海军上尉

life /laɪf/ **noun** (plural **lives**) **1** the condition of being alive 生命；性命 **2** the existence of an individual human being or animal 生存 **3** a particular type or aspect of existence 生活 **4** living things and their activity 生活经历 **5** vitality or energy 生气；活力 **6** informal 【非正式】a sentence of imprisonment for life 无期徒刑 □ **life insurance** (or **life assurance**) insurance that pays out money either when the insured person dies or after a set period 人身保险 **life jacket** a jacket for keeping a person afloat in water 救生衣 **life peer** (in the UK) a peer whose title cannot be inherited (英国的)终身贵族(爵位不能世袭) **life raft** an inflatable raft used in an emergency at sea 救生筏，充气救生船

lifebelt /ˈlaɪfbelt/ **noun** a ring used to help a person who has fallen into water to stay afloat 救生圈

lifeblood /ˈlaɪfblʌd/ **noun** a vital factor or force 生命线；命脉

lifeboat /ˈlaɪfbəʊt/ **noun** a boat which is launched from land to rescue people at sea, or which is kept on a ship for use in an emergency 救生船

lifeguard /ˈlaɪfɡɑːd/ **noun** a person employed to rescue people who get into difficulty at a beach or swimming pool 救生员

lifeless /ˈlaɪfləs/ **adjective 1** dead or apparently dead 死的；无生命的 **2** not containing living things 无生物的 **3** lacking energy or excitement 无活力的；无生气的

lifelike /ˈlaɪflaɪk/ **adjective** accurate in its representation of a living person or thing 栩栩如生的；逼真的

lifeline /ˈlaɪflaɪn/ **noun 1** a thing on which someone or something depends 生命线 **2** a rope thrown to rescue someone in difficulties in water 救生索

lifelong /ˈlaɪflɒŋ/ **adjective** lasting or remaining throughout a person's life 终身的；一生的；毕生的

lifespan /ˈlaɪfspæn/ **noun** the length of time that a person or animal is likely to live (人或动物的)寿命

lifestyle /ˈlaɪfstaɪl/ **noun** the way in which a person lives 生活方式

lifetime /ˈlaɪftaɪm/ **noun** the length of time that a person lives or a thing functions 一生；终身；(事物的)存在期，使用期，有效期

lift /lɪft/ **verb 1** raise to a higher position 举起；抬起；提起 **2** pick up and move to a different position 移至；搬动 **3** formally end a restriction 撤销，解除，中止(限制) **4** (**lift off**) (of an aircraft, spacecraft, etc.) take off (飞机、航天器等)起飞，发射 • **noun 1** Brit. 【英】a device for moving people or things between different levels of a building 电梯；升降梯 **2** a free ride in another person's vehicle 免费

搭车 **3** a device for carrying people up or down a mountain (上下山载人用的)缆车 **4** a feeling of increased cheerfulness 鼓舞;振奋 **5** upward force exerted by the air on an aircraft wing or similar structure 提升力;升力

ligament /'lɪgəmənt/ **noun** a band of tissue which connects two bones or holds together a joint 韧带

ligature /'lɪgətʃə(r)/ **noun** a thing used for tying something tightly, especially a cord used to stop the flow of blood from a bleeding artery (尤指用于动脉止血的)结扎线,缚线

light¹ /laɪt/ **noun 1** the natural energy that makes things visible 光;光线 **2** a device that uses electricity, oil, or gas to give light 点火装置 **3** a match or cigarette lighter 火柴;打火机 **4** understanding or enlightenment 理解;领会 • **verb** (**lights, lighting, lit**; past participle **lit** or **lighted**) **1** provide an area or object with light 照亮,照耀 **2** make something start burning 点燃 **3** (**light up**) become lively or happy 使欢快;变欢快 **4** (**light on**) discover by chance 偶然发现 • **adjective 1** having a lot of light 明亮的 **2** pale in colour 浅色的 □ **in the light of** taking something into consideration 考虑到;鉴于;由于 **light-fingered** informal 【非正式】 tending to steal things 惯偷的;喜扒窃的 **light-headed** dizzy and slightly faint 眩晕的 **light-hearted 1** amusing and entertaining 轻松愉快的;逗乐的 **2** cheerful and carefree 开心的;愉快的 **light year** the distance that light travels in one year, nearly 6 million million miles 光年(约合6万亿英里)

light² **adjective 1** of little weight; not heavy 不重的;轻的 **2** not heavy enough 不沉的 **3** not strongly or heavily built 轻型的;轻便的 **4** relatively low in density, amount, or strength 轻薄的;稀少的;少量的;

轻度的 **5** gentle or delicate 轻巧的;精致的 **6** not profound or serious 不严肃的;轻率的 ■ **lightly** adverb **lightness** noun.

lighten /'laɪtn/ **verb 1** make or become lighter in weight (使)变轻;(使)减轻 **2** make or become brighter 使明亮;变得明亮

lighter¹ /'laɪtə(r)/ **noun** a device producing a small flame, used to light cigarettes 打火机

lighter² **noun** a barge used to transfer goods to and from ships in harbour 驳船

lighthouse /'laɪthaʊs/ **noun** a tower containing a powerful light to guide ships at sea 灯塔

lighting /'laɪtɪŋ/ **noun 1** equipment for producing light 照明设备 **2** the arrangement or effect of lights 布光;灯光效果

lightning /'laɪtnɪŋ/ **noun** a flow of high-voltage electricity between a cloud and the ground or within a cloud, accompanied by a bright flash 闪电 • **adjective** very quick 闪电般的;飞快的 □ **lightning conductor** (or N. Amer. 【北美】 **lightning rod**) a rod or wire fixed to a high place to divert lightning into the ground 避雷针;避雷导线

✔ 拼写指南 the spelling is **lightning**, not -tening. lightning 不要拼作 -tening.

lights /laɪts/ **plural noun** the lungs of sheep, pigs, or bullocks as food 牲畜肺脏(用作食品)

lightweight /'laɪtweɪt/ **noun 1** a weight in boxing between featherweight and welterweight (拳击运动的)轻量级 **2** informal 【非正式】 a person who is not very important 无足轻重的人

ligneous /'lɪgnɪəs/ **adjective** consisting of, or resembling, wood 木质的;似木的

like¹ /laɪk/ **preposition 1** similar to 像 **2** in a similar way to 像…一样 **3** in a way appropriate to 以与…相称的方式 **4** such as 比如;例如 • **conjunction** informal **1** in the same way that 如同 **2** as though 好像 • **noun** (**the like**) things of the same kind 同类事物 • **adjective** having similar characteristics to someone or something else 相似的;相像的

> **! 注意** don't use like to mean 'as if', as in *he's behaving like he owns the place*. Use **as if** or **as though** instead. 不要用 like 表示 as if 的意思,例如,不能说 he's behaving like he owns the place (他表现得就像他是这个地方的主人),而要用 as if 或 as though。

like² **verb** (**likes, liking, liked**) **1** find pleasant or satisfactory 喜欢;喜爱 **2** wish for; want 希望;想;要 • **noun** (**likes**) the things that you like 爱好;喜欢的事物

likeable or **likable** /ˈlaɪkəbl/ **adjective** pleasant; easy to like 可爱的;讨人喜欢的

likelihood /ˈlaɪklihʊd/ **noun** the state of being likely; probability 可能

likely /ˈlaɪkli/ **adjective** (**likelier, likeliest**) **1** probable 很可能的 **2** promising 有希望的;有指望的;有前途的 • **adverb** probably 很可能

liken /ˈlaɪkən/ **verb** (**liken someone/ thing to**) point out the resemblance of someone or something to 把…比作;指出…与…相似

likeness /ˈlaɪknəs/ **noun 1** resemblance 相似 **2** outward appearance 外表 **3** a portrait or representation 肖像;画像

likewise /ˈlaɪkwaɪz/ **adverb 1** also; moreover 也;亦;而且 **2** similarly 同样地;照样地

liking /ˈlaɪkɪŋ/ **noun 1** a fondness for someone or something 喜爱 **2** (**your liking**) your taste 兴趣;爱好:*The coffee was just to her liking.* 这份咖啡正合她的口味。

lilac /ˈlaɪlək/ **noun 1** a shrub or small tree with sweet-smelling violet, pink, or white blossom 丁香 **2** a pale pinkish-violet colour 丁香紫;淡紫色

lilo /ˈlaɪləʊ/ **noun** (plural **lilos**) an inflatable mattress used for floating on water 充气床;气垫

lilt /lɪlt/ **noun 1** a rising and falling of the voice when speaking (说话时)抑扬顿挫的声调 **2** a gentle rhythm in a tune (乐曲的)轻快节奏 ■ **lilting** adjective.

lily /ˈlɪli/ **noun** (plural **lilies**) a plant with large trumpet-shaped flowers on a tall, slender stem 百合 □ **lily-livered** cowardly 胆怯的;懦弱的 **lily of the valley** a plant with broad leaves and white bell-shaped flowers 铃兰(叶阔大,开白色钟形花)

limb /lɪm/ **noun 1** an arm, leg, or wing 肢;臂;腿;翼;翅膀 **2** a large branch of a tree (树的)大枝 □ **out on a limb** not supported by other people 处于孤立地位

limber /ˈlɪmbə(r)/ **verb** (**limbers, limbering, limbered**) (**limber up**) warm up in preparation for exercise or activity (锻炼或活动前)做准备活动 • **adjective** supple; flexible 柔软的;灵活的

limbo¹ /ˈlɪmbəʊ/ **noun** an uncertain period of waiting 不确定的等待时间

limbo² **noun** (plural **limbos**) a West Indian dance in which you bend backwards to pass under a horizontal bar 林宝舞(西印度群岛的一种舞蹈,舞者向后弯腰,钻过水平横杆)

lime¹ /laɪm/ **noun** a white alkaline substance used as a building material or fertilizer 生石灰;熟石灰;钙盐;钙碱

lime² **noun 1** a green citrus fruit similar to a lemon 酸橙 **2** a bright light green colour 酸橙绿色;浅亮绿色

lime³ noun a deciduous tree with heart-shaped leaves and yellowish blossom 椴树(叶呈心形,开黄花)

limelight /'laɪmlaɪt/ noun (**the limelight**) the focus of public attention 公众瞩目的中心;公众关注的焦点

limerick /'lɪmərɪk/ noun a humorous five-line poem with a rhyme scheme *aabba* 五行打油诗(一种幽默短诗,韵式为aabba)

limestone /'laɪmstəʊn/ noun a hard rock composed mainly of calcium carbonate 石灰岩

limit /'lɪmɪt/ noun **1** a point beyond which something does not or may not pass 限度;限制 **2** a restriction on the size or amount of something 限额;限量 • verb (**limits, limiting, limited**) put a limit on 限制;限定 □ **off limits** out of bounds 不准进入;禁止入内 ■ **limitless** adjective.

limitation /lɪmɪ'teɪʃn/ noun **1** a restriction 限制 **2** a fault or failing 弱点;缺点

limited /'lɪmɪtɪd/ adjective restricted in size, amount, extent, or ability 有限的;能力有限的 □ **limited company** Brit. 【英】a company whose owners have only a limited responsibility for its debts 有限(责任)公司

limo /'lɪməʊ/ noun (plural **limos**) informal 【非正式】a limousine 豪华轿车

limousine /'lɪməziːn/ noun a large, luxurious car (大型)豪华轿车

limp¹ /lɪmp/ verb walk with difficulty because of an injured leg or foot 跛行;一瘸一拐地走 **2** (of a damaged ship or aircraft) proceed with difficulty (受损的船只或飞机)艰难地前进 • noun a limping walk 跛行

limp² adjective **1** not stiff or firm 柔软的;松垮的 **2** without energy or strength 无生气的;无活力的;意志薄弱的 ■ **limply** adverb.

limpet /'lɪmpɪt/ noun a shellfish with a muscular foot for clinging tightly to rocks 帽贝(足部发达,可牢固吸附于岩石上)

limpid /'lɪmpɪd/ adjective (of a liquid or the eyes) clear (液体或眼睛)清澈的,透明的

linchpin or **lynchpin** /'lɪntʃpɪn/ noun **1** a very important person or thing 极为重要的人(或事物) **2** a pin through the end of an axle keeping a wheel in position 制轮楔;车轴销

linctus /'lɪŋktəs/ noun Brit. 【英】thick liquid medicine, especially cough mixture 药糖剂;(尤指)止咳糖浆

line¹ /laɪn/ noun **1** a long, narrow mark or band 线;线条 **2** a length of cord, wire, etc. 绳;索;线 **3** a row or series of people or things (人或物的)行,列,排 **4** a row of written or printed words 字行 **5** a direction, course, or channel 方向;路线;方针;渠道 **6** a telephone connection 电话线 **7** a railway track or route 铁路轨道;铁路线路 **8** a series of military defences facing an enemy force 防线;前线 **9** a wrinkle in the skin 皱纹 **10** a range of commercial products 成套商品;系列商品 **11** an area of activity 行业;行当;活动范围:*their line of work* 他们从事的行业 **12** (**lines**) a way of doing or thinking about something (行事或思考的)方式 **13** (**lines**) the words of an actor's part (演员的)台词 **14** (**lines**) Brit. 【英】a school punishment in which you have to write out the same sentence a stated number of times (学校惩罚学生的)重复抄写的句子 • verb (**lines, lining, lined**) **1** be positioned at intervals along a route (按一定间隔)沿…站立,沿…边放置 **2** (**line someone/thing up**) arrange people or things in a row 使排列成行 **3** (**line something up**) have something prepared 使安排就绪 **4** (**lined**) marked or covered with lines

用线条画出；勾勒出 □ **in line under control** 在控制之下 **in line for** likely to receive 有可能获得 **line dancing** country and western dancing in which a line of dancers follow a set pattern of steps 队列舞 **line-up 1** a group of people or things assembled for a particular purpose 一组人；一队人；一批东西 **2** an identity parade 排队辨认嫌疑人 **on the line** at serious risk 冒极大的危险 **out of line** informal 【非正式】 behaving badly or wrongly 出格；举止不当

line² verb (**lines**, **lining**, **lined**) cover the inner surface of something with different material 给…加衬里

lineage /ˈlɪnɪdʒ/ noun ancestry or pedigree 世系；血统；家谱；谱系

lineal /ˈlɪnɪəl/ adjective in a direct line of descent or ancestry 直系的；嫡系的

lineament /ˈlɪnɪəmənt/ noun literary 【文】 a distinctive feature, especially of the face 特征；(尤指)面部特征

linear /ˈlɪnɪə(r)/ adjective **1** arranged in or extending along a straight line 成一直线的；线的；直线的 **2** consisting of lines or outlines 线构的；有轮廓的 **3** involving one dimension only 单维的 **4** progressing from one stage to another in a series of steps 按顺序的 ■ **linearity** noun.

linen /ˈlɪnɪn/ noun **1** cloth woven from flax 亚麻服装 **2** articles such as sheets, pillowcases, and duvet covers 亚麻制品

liner¹ /ˈlaɪnə(r)/ noun **1** a large passenger ship 大型客轮；班轮 **2** a cosmetic for outlining or emphasizing a facial feature 眼线膏；眼线笔；描唇笔

liner² noun a lining of a garment, container, etc. (服装、容器等的)衬里

linesman /ˈlaɪnzmən/ noun (plural **linesmen**) (in sport) an official who helps the referee or umpire to decide whether the ball is out of play (体育比赛中的)边线裁判，巡边员，司线员

ling¹ /lɪŋ/ noun a long-bodied sea fish 鳕鱼(一种长体海鱼)

ling² noun heather 帚石楠

linger /ˈlɪŋɡə(r)/ verb **1** be slow or reluctant to leave 徘徊；留恋不舍 **2** (**linger over**) spend a long time over 拖延；磨蹭 **3** be slow to fade, disappear, or die 苟延残喘

lingerie /ˈlænʒəri/ noun women's underwear and nightclothes 女式内衣裤；女睡衣

lingo /ˈlɪŋɡəʊ/ noun (plural **lingos** or **lingoes**) informal 【非正式】 **1** a foreign language 外国语；外语 **2** the jargon of a particular subject or group 术语；行话；隐语

lingua franca /ˌlɪŋɡwə ˈfræŋkə/ noun (plural **lingua francas**) a language used as a common language between speakers whose native languages are different (讲不同语言的人用作共同语言的)混合语，通用语，交际语

linguine /lɪŋˈɡwiːni/ plural noun small ribbons of pasta 扁面条

linguist /ˈlɪŋɡwɪst/ noun **1** a person who is good at foreign languages 通晓数国语言的人 **2** a person who studies linguistics 语言学家

linguistic /lɪŋˈɡwɪstɪk/ adjective relating to language or linguistics 语言的；语言学的

linguistics /lɪŋˈɡwɪstɪks/ plural noun the scientific study of language 语言学

liniment /ˈlɪnəmənt/ noun an ointment rubbed on the body to relieve pain or bruising 擦剂；搽剂

lining /ˈlaɪnɪŋ/ noun a layer of material covering or attached to the inside of something 衬里；里子；衬料

link /lɪŋk/ noun **1** a relationship or connection between people or things 关系；联系；纽带 **2** something that lets people communicate 通讯装置 **3** a means of contact or transport between two places (两地间的)通讯线

路，交通线路 **4** a code or instruction that connects one part of a computer program, website, etc. to another (计算机间的)连接 **5** a loop in a chain (链的)一环，环节 • verb connect or join 连接；联系

linkage /'lɪŋkɪdʒ/ noun **1** the action of linking or the state of being linked 连接，关联；联系 **2** a system of links 连接装置

links /lɪŋks/ plural noun a golf course, especially one near the sea (尤指海边的)高尔夫球场

linnet /'lɪnɪt/ noun a type of finch (songbird) 赤胸朱顶雀

lino /'laɪnəʊ/ noun Brit. informal 【英，非正式】 linoleum 油地毡，漆布

linoleum /lɪ'nəʊlɪəm/ noun a floor covering made from a mixture of linseed oil and powdered cork (亚麻)油地毡；漆布

linseed /'lɪnsiːd/ noun the seeds of the flax plant, which are crushed to make an oil used in paint, varnish, etc. 亚麻籽

lint /lɪnt/ noun **1** short, fine fibres which separate from cloth when it is being made 棉绒，飞花 **2** a fabric used for dressing wounds (包扎伤口用的)绒布，软麻布

lintel /'lɪntl/ noun a horizontal support across the top of a door or window (门窗的)过梁

lion /'laɪən/ noun (feminine 【阴性】 **lioness**) a large cat of Africa and NW India, the male of which has a shaggy mane 狮；狮子 □ **the lion's share** the largest part of something 最大的部分

lionize or **lionise** /'laɪənaɪz/ verb (**lionizes, lionizing, lionized**) treat as a celebrity 把…视作名人

lip /lɪp/ noun **1** either of the two fleshy parts forming the edges of the mouth opening 嘴唇 **2** the edge of a hollow container or an opening (容器的)嘴；(开口的)边缘 **3** informal 【非正式】

cheeky talk 唐突无礼的话 □ **lip-read** understand speech from watching a speaker's lip movements 唇读，观唇辨义

liposuction /'lɪpəʊsʌkʃn/ noun a technique in cosmetic surgery for sucking out excess fat from under the skin (美容手术中的)脂肪抽吸术，吸脂术

lippy /'lɪpi/ adjective informal 【非正式】 cheeky 厚脸皮的；无耻的；无礼的；莽撞的

lipstick /'lɪpstɪk/ noun coloured cosmetic applied to the lips from a small solid stick 口红；唇膏

liquefy /'lɪkwɪfaɪ/ verb (**liquefies, liquefying, liquefied**) make or become liquid (使)液化 ■ **liquefaction** noun.

✔ 拼写指南 lique*fy*, not -*ify*. liquefy 不要拼作 -ify.

liqueur /lɪ'kjʊə(r)/ noun a strong, sweet alcoholic drink 利口酒；烈性甜酒

liquid /'lɪkwɪd/ noun a substance such as water or oil that flows freely 液体；液态物 • adjective **1** in the form of a liquid 液体的；液态的 **2** clear, like water 清澈的；明亮的 **3** (of assets) held in cash, or easily converted into cash (资金)现金的，易变为现金的

liquidate /'lɪkwɪdeɪt/ verb (**liquidates, liquidating, liquidated**) **1** close a business and sell what it owns so as to pay its debts 清算，清盘(公司) **2** convert assets into cash 将(资产)变换成现金；变卖 **3** pay off a debt 清偿(债务) **4** informal 【非正式】 kill 杀戮 ■ **liquidation** noun.

liquidity /lɪ'kwɪdəti/ noun the state of owning assets that are held in or easily converted to cash 资产流动性

liquidize or **liquidise** /'lɪkwɪdaɪz/ verb (**liquidizes, liquidizing, liquidized**) Brit. 【英】 convert solid food into a liquid or purée 使(固体食

物)液化(或成泥状) ■ **liquidizer** noun.

liquor /ˈlɪkə(r)/ **noun 1** alcoholic drink, especially spirits 含酒精饮料;(尤指)酒 **2** liquid that has been produced in cooking (产生于烹煮的)液,汁水

liquorice /ˈlɪkərɪs/ (US spelling 【美拼作】 **licorice**) **noun** a black substance made from the juice of a root and used as a sweet and in medicine 甘草;甘草糖

lira /ˈlɪərə/ **noun** (plural **lire** /ˈlɪərə/) the basic unit of money of Turkey and formerly also of Italy 里拉(土耳其基本货币单位和意大利以前的基本货币单位)

lisp /lɪsp/ **noun** a speech defect in which the sound *s* is pronounced like *th* 咬舌;口齿不清 • **verb** speak with a lisp 咬舌;口齿不清地说

lissom or **lissome** /ˈlɪsəm/ **adjective** slim, supple, and graceful 苗条柔美的

list¹ /lɪst/ **noun** a number of connected items or names written one after the other 一览表;目录;清单 • **verb 1** make a list of 把…编成一览表(或目录、清单) **2** include in a list 把…列入一览表(或目录、清单)

list² **verb** (of a ship) lean over to one side (船)倾斜,倾侧

listed /ˈlɪstɪd/ **adjective** (of a building in the UK) officially protected because of its historical importance (英国建筑物作为文物)登录入册(受保护)

listen /ˈlɪsn/ **verb 1** give your attention to a sound 听;倾听 **2** make an effort to hear something (努力地)听 **3** pay attention to advice or a request 认真听(建议或要求) • **noun** an act of listening 听 ■ **listener** noun.

listeria /lɪˈstɪəriə/ **noun** a type of bacterium which infects humans and animals through contaminated food 利斯特氏菌(一种通过受污染的食品使人和动物受感染的细菌)

listing /ˈlɪstɪŋ/ **noun 1** a list or catalogue 一览表;名单;目录 **2** an entry in a list (表单上的)项目

listless /ˈlɪstləs/ **adjective** lacking energy or enthusiasm 无精打采的;缺乏热情的 ■ **listlessly** adverb.

lit /lɪt/ past and past participle of **LIGHT¹**.

litany /ˈlɪtəni/ **noun** (plural **litanies**) **1** a series of prayers to God used in church services (教堂礼拜中的)连祷 **2** a long, boring list of complaints, reasons, etc. 枯燥冗长的叙述

liter /ˈliːtə(r)/ US spelling of **LITRE**. litre 的美式拼法

literacy /ˈlɪtərəsi/ **noun** the ability to read and write 读写能力

literal /ˈlɪtərəl/ **adjective 1** using or interpreting words in their usual or most basic sense 字面意义的;原义的 **2** (of a translation) representing the exact words of the original piece of writing (翻译)直译的 **3** not exaggerated or distorted 完全按照原文的

literally /ˈlɪtərəli/ **adverb 1** in a literal way 逐字地;按字面意义地 **2** informal 【非正式】 used to emphasize what you are saying (用于强调)简直: *We were literally killing ourselves laughing.* 我们自己简直要笑死了。

literary /ˈlɪtərəri/ **adjective 1** having to do with literature 文学的;有关文学的 **2** (of language) characteristic of literature or formal writing (语言)书卷气的,书面体的

literate /ˈlɪtərət/ **adjective 1** able to read and write 能读写的;识字的 **2** knowledgeable in a particular field (对某领域)通晓的,精通的: *computer-literate* 精通计算机

literati /ˌlɪtəˈrɑːti/ **plural noun** educated people who are interested in literature 文人学士

literature /ˈlɪtrətʃə(r)/ **noun 1** written

works that are regarded as having artistic merit 文学作品 **2** books and printed information on a particular subject (某学科的)文献，图书资料

lithe /laɪð/ **adjective** slim, supple, and graceful 苗条柔美的

lithium /ˈlɪθiəm/ **noun** a silver-white metallic element (金属元素)锂

lithograph /ˈlɪθəɡrɑːf/ **noun** a print made by lithography 石印品；平版印刷品

lithography /lɪˈθɒɡrəfi/ **noun** printing from a flat metal surface which has been prepared so that ink sticks only where it is required 石印术；平版印刷术

Lithuanian /ˌlɪθjuˈeɪniən/ **noun** a person from Lithuania 立陶宛人 • **adjective** relating to Lithuania 立陶宛的

litigation /ˌlɪtɪˈɡeɪʃn/ **noun** the process of taking a dispute to a law court 起诉；诉讼

litigious /lɪˈtɪdʒəs/ **adjective** frequently choosing to go to a law court to settle a dispute 好诉讼的；好打官司的

litmus /ˈlɪtməs/ **noun** a dye that is red under acid conditions and blue under alkaline conditions 石蕊(一种在酸性环境下变红，在碱性环境下变蓝的颜料) □ **litmus paper** paper stained with litmus, used as a test for acids or alkalis 石蕊试纸 **litmus test** a reliable test of the quality or truth of something 试金石；检验真伪的办法

litre /ˈliːtə(r)/ (US spelling 【美拼作】 **liter**) **noun** a metric unit of capacity equal to 1,000 cubic centimetres (about 1.75 pints) 升(公制容量单位，等于1,000立方厘米，合1.75品脱)

litter /ˈlɪtə(r)/ **noun 1** rubbish left in an open or public place (丢弃在公共场所的)垃圾，废物 **2** an untidy collection of things 一堆杂乱的东西 **3** a number of young born to an animal at one time 一窝幼崽 **4** (also

cat litter) absorbent material that is put into a tray for a cat to use as a toilet indoors 猫砂(吸水性物质，置于盘内，供猫室内便溺用) **5** straw or other material used as bedding for animals (用作动物睡铺的)褥草 **6** (also **leaf litter**) decomposing leaves forming a layer on top of soil (覆盖土壤的)腐叶层 **7** (in the past) an enclosed chair or bed carried by men or animals (旧时的)轿，舆 • **verb** (**litters**, **littering**, **littered**) make a place untidy by dropping litter 使凌乱；弄乱

little /ˈlɪtl/ **adjective 1** small in size, amount, or degree (尺寸、数量或程度)小的，少的 **2** (of a person) young or younger (人)幼小的，年幼的 **3** (of distance or time) short (距离或时间)短的 • **determiner & pronoun** not much 少量；一点儿 • **adverb** hardly, or not at all 几乎没有；一点也不 □ **a little 1** a small amount of 少量；一点儿 **2** a short time or distance 很短的时间(或距离) **3** to a limited extent 稍微

liturgy /ˈlɪtədʒi/ **noun** (plural **liturgies**) a set form of public worship used in the Christian Church (基督教的)礼拜仪式 ■ **liturgical** adjective.

live¹ /lɪv/ **verb** (**lives**, **living**, **lived**) **1** remain alive 活着 **2** be alive at a particular time 生存 **3** spend your life in a particular way 生活；过活 **4** have your home in a particular place 居住 **5** obtain the things necessary for staying alive 维持生活 □ **live something down** manage to make other people forget something embarrassing 使他人忘却(尴尬的事) **live rough** live outdoors with no home (因无家可归而)风餐露宿，流浪街头 ■ **liveable** (or **livable**) adjective.

live² /laɪv/ **adjective 1** living 有生命的；活的 **2** (of music) played in front of an audience; not recorded (音乐)现场演奏的 **3** (of a broadcast) transmitted at the time it happens, rather than recorded (广播电视)实况转播的，现场直播的 **4** (of a wire or device) connected to a source of electric current (电线或设备)带电的，通电的 **5** containing explosive that can be detonated (弹药)能引爆的，未爆炸的 • *adverb* as a live performance 以现场直播方式 □ **live wire** *informal* 【非正式】an energetic and lively person 精力旺盛的人；富有活力的人

livelihood /ˈlaɪvlihʊd/ *noun* a way of earning enough money to live on 生计；生存手段

lively /ˈlaɪvli/ *adjective* (**livelier**, **liveliest**) **1** full of life and energy 充满活力的；精力充沛的 **2** (of a place) full of activity (地方)热闹的 ■ **liveliness** *noun*.

liven /ˈlaɪvn/ *verb* (**liven someone/thing up** or **liven up**) make or become more lively or interesting (使)变得有生气；(使)变得有趣

liver /ˈlɪvə(r)/ *noun* **1** a large organ in the abdomen that produces bile 肝脏 **2** the liver of some animals used as food (动物供食用的)肝

livery /ˈlɪvəri/ *noun* (plural **liveries**) **1** a special uniform worn by a servant or official (仆人或官员穿的)制服 **2** a distinctive design and colour scheme used on the vehicles or products of a company (公司车辆或产品上印的)标志性图案及色彩 ■ **liveried** *adjective*.

lives /laɪvz/ plural of LIFE.

livestock /ˈlaɪvstɒk/ *noun* farm animals 牲畜；家畜

livid /ˈlɪvɪd/ *adjective* **1** furiously angry 大怒的；狂怒的 **2** dark bluish grey in colour 青肿的；乌青发炎的

living /ˈlɪvɪŋ/ *noun* **1** being alive 生活 **2** an income which is enough to live on 生活收入；生计 • *adjective* alive 活着的；有生命的 □ **living room** a room in a house used for relaxing in 起居室；客厅

lizard /ˈlɪzəd/ *noun* a small four-legged reptile with a long body and tail 蜥蜴

llama /ˈlɑːmə/ *noun* a South American animal related to the camel 美洲驼；亚美利加驼

lo /ləʊ/ *exclamation* old use 【旧】used to draw attention to something (用于唤起注意)看，瞧

loach /ləʊtʃ/ *noun* a small freshwater fish 泥鳅

load /ləʊd/ *noun* **1** a heavy or bulky thing that is being carried 负载物；负荷 **2** a weight or source of pressure 负担；担子；重任 **3** the total number or amount carried in a vehicle or container 装载量 **4** (**a load** or **loads of**) *informal* 【非正式】a lot of 许多；大量 • *verb* **1** put a load on or in (把货物)装上，装入 **2** put ammunition into a gun 把(弹药)装入(枪炮) **3** put something into a device so that it will operate 把…装入设备中

loaded /ˈləʊdɪd/ *adjective* **1** carrying or supporting a load 装满的；有负荷的；载货的 **2** biased towards a particular outcome 偏袒性的；诱导性的 **3** having an underlying meaning 有隐含意思的；含蓄的：*a loaded question* 话里有话的问题 **4** *informal* 【非正式】wealthy 富有的

loaf¹ /ləʊf/ *noun* (plural **loaves**) a quantity of bread that is shaped and baked in one piece (一条)面包

loaf² *verb* spend your time in a lazy or aimless way 虚度光阴；闲逛

loafer /ˈləʊfə(r)/ *noun* **1** a person who spends their time in a lazy or aimless way 游手好闲者；闲荡者 **2** a casual leather shoe with a flat heel 懒汉鞋；平跟便鞋

loam /ləʊm/ *noun* a fertile soil of clay and sand containing hummus 沃土；土壤

loan /ləʊn/ *noun* **1** a sum of money that is lent to someone 贷款 **2** the action of lending something 出借

• **verb** give something as a loan 贷款 给;贷与 □ **loan shark** informal 【非正式】 a moneylender who charges very high rates of interest 放高利贷者

loath /ləʊð/ or **loth** /ləʊθ/ **adjective** (**loath to do**) reluctant or unwilling to do 勉强的;不愿意的;不情愿的

> **! 注意** don't confuse **loath** with **loathe**, which means 'feel hatred for'. 不要混淆 loath 和 loathe, 后者意为"憎恨"。

loathe /ləʊð/ **verb** (**loathes, loathing, loathed**) feel hatred or disgust for 憎恨;厌恶

loathsome /ˈləʊðsəm/ **adjective** causing hatred or disgust 令人憎恨的;令人厌恶的

loaves /ləʊvz/ plural of LOAF¹.

lob /lɒb/ **verb** (**lobs, lobbing, lobbed**) throw or hit something in a high arc 以高弧线抛出(或击打) • **noun** (in soccer or tennis) a ball lobbed over an opponent (足球或网球运动中的)高弧线球

lobby /ˈlɒbi/ **noun** (plural **lobbies**) 1 an open area inside the entrance of a public building (公共建筑入口处的)大厅, 前厅 2 any of several large halls in the Houses of Parliament in which MPs meet members of the public (议院的)民众接待厅 3 each of two corridors in the Houses of Parliament where MPs vote (议院的)议员分组投票厅 4 a group of people who try to influence politicians on a particular issue (就某问题试图影响政界人士的)院外游说集团 • **verb** (**lobbies, lobbying, lobbied**) try to influence a politician on an issue (就某问题)游说(政界人士) ■ **lobbyist** noun.

lobe /ləʊb/ **noun** 1 a roundish and flattish part that projects from or divides something (物体的)扁圆状部分 2 the rounded fleshy part at the lower edge of the ear 耳垂 3 each of the sections of the main part of the brain 脑叶

lobelia /ləʊˈbiːliə/ **noun** a garden plant with blue or red flowers 半边莲(园艺植物, 开蓝色或红色花)

lobotomy /ləʊˈbɒtəmi/ **noun** (plural **lobotomies**) an operation that involves cutting into part of the brain, formerly used to treat mental illness 脑白质切断术;脑叶切断术

lobster /ˈlɒbstə(r)/ **noun** a large edible shellfish with large pincers 龙虾 □ **lobster pot** a basket-like trap in which lobsters are caught (捕)龙虾笼

local /ˈləʊkl/ **adjective** having to do with a particular area, or with the place where you live 当地的;本地的;地方性的 • **noun** 1 a person who lives in a particular place 当地居民;本地人 2 Brit. informal 【英, 非正式】 a pub near where you live (住所附近的)小酒馆 □ **local anaesthetic** an anaesthetic that causes a loss of feeling in a particular part of the body 局部麻醉 ■ **locally** adverb.

locale /ləʊˈkɑːl/ **noun** a place where something happens 事发现场;事发地点

locality /ləʊˈkæləti/ **noun** (plural **localities**) 1 an area or neighbourhood 地区;街区 2 the position or site of something (某事发生的)地点, 场所

localize or **localise** /ˈləʊkəlaɪz/ **verb** (**localizes, localizing, localized**) restrict to a particular place 使局部化;使地方化 ■ **localization** noun.

locate /ləʊˈkeɪt/ **verb** (**locates, locating, located**) 1 discover the exact place or position of 找到…的确切地点(或位置) 2 (**be located**) be situated in a particular place 坐落于

location /ləʊˈkeɪʃn/ **noun** 1 a place where something is located 地点;位置;场所 2 the action of locating someone or something 定位;寻找;安

置 **3** an actual place in which a film or broadcast is made, as distinct from a studio (制作电影或广播电视的)外景地,实景拍摄地

loch /lɒkh/ *noun* Scottish【苏格兰】a lake, or a narrow strip of sea that is almost surrounded by land 湖;狭长海湾

loci /ˈləʊsaɪ/ plural of LOCUS.

lock¹ /lɒk/ *noun* **1** a mechanism for keeping a door or container fastened, operated by a key 锁 **2** a similar device used to prevent a vehicle or other machine from operating 锁定器;制轮楔 **3** a short section of a canal or river with gates at each end which can be opened or closed to change the water level, used for raising and lowering boats (运河或河流的)船闸,水闸 **4** a hold in wrestling that prevents an opponent from moving a limb (摔跤中的)抱,夹 **5** the maximum extent that the front wheels of a vehicle can be turned (车辆的)前轮转向角 • *verb* **1** fasten with a lock 锁;锁上 **2** shut in or imprison by locking a door 把…关起来;把…锁在屋里 **3** become fixed in one position 拴住;被锁 □ **lock, stock, and barrel** including everything 全部;所有 **lock-up 1** a place used as a temporary jail 把…关进监狱 **2** Brit.【英】a small shop or rented garage that is separate from other premises (与住宅区分离可上锁的)小商店,车库 ■ **lockable** adjective.

lock² *noun* **1** a coil or hanging piece of a person's hair 一绺头发 **2 (locks)** literary【文】a person's hair 头发

locker /ˈlɒkə(r)/ *noun* a small cupboard or compartment that can be locked 有锁存物柜

locket /ˈlɒkɪt/ *noun* a piece of jewellery in the form of a small case on a chain, worn round a person's neck and used to hold a tiny photograph, a lock of hair, etc. (装小照片、头发等的)盒式

项链锁

lockjaw /ˈlɒkdʒɔː/ *noun* a form of disease tetanus in which the jaws become stiff and tightly closed 破伤风;牙关紧闭(破伤风的症状)

lockout /ˈlɒkaʊt/ *noun* a situation in which an employer refuses to allow employees to enter their place of work until they agree to certain conditions 闭厂,停工(指雇主不允许雇员进入工作场所直到其同意某些条件)

locksmith /ˈlɒksmɪθ/ *noun* a person who makes and repairs locks 锁匠

locomotion /ˌləʊkəˈməʊʃn/ *noun* movement from one place to another 运动(力);移动(力);运转(力)

locomotive /ˌləʊkəˈməʊtɪv/ *noun* a powered railway vehicle used for pulling trains 火车头;机车 • *adjective* relating to locomotion 运动的;活动的;移动的

locum /ˈləʊkəm/ *noun* a doctor or priest standing in for another who is temporarily away 代班医生;代班牧师

locus /ˈləʊkəs/ *noun* (plural **loci** /ˈləʊsaɪ/) technical【术语】a particular position, point, or place 地点;所在;点

locust /ˈləʊkəst/ *noun* a large tropical grasshopper which migrates in vast swarms 蝗虫

locution /ləˈkjuːʃn/ *noun* **1** a word or phrase 单词;短语 **2** a person's particular way of speaking (某人的)讲话风格

lode /ləʊd/ *noun* a vein of metal ore in the earth 矿脉;矿藏

lodestone /ˈləʊdstəʊn/ *noun* a piece of magnetic iron ore used as a magnet 天然磁石

lodge /lɒdʒ/ *noun* **1** a small house at the gates of a large house with grounds (宅第大门口的)小屋 **2** a room for a porter at the entrance of a large building (大楼入口处

的)门房 **3** a small country house where people stay while hunting and shooting (狩猎时住的)村舍 **4** a branch of an organization such as the Freemasons (共济会等组织的)分会 **5** a beaver's den (海狸或河狸的)穴，窝 • verb (**lodges, lodging, lodged**) **1** formally present a complaint, appeal, etc. 提交(投诉书、呼吁书等) **2** firmly fix something in a place 使固定；卡住 **3** rent accommodation in another person's house 借宿；租住 **4** leave something valuable in a safe place or with someone reliable 寄放；存放

lodger /ˈlɒdʒə(r)/ **noun** a person who pays rent to live in a house or flat with the owner 租住者；房客

lodging /ˈlɒdʒɪŋ/ **noun 1** temporary accommodation 借宿；寄宿 **2** (usu. **lodgings**) a rented room or rooms, usually in the same house as the owner 租住的房间；公寓房间

loft /lɒft/ **noun 1** a room or storage space directly under the roof of a house 阁楼；顶楼 **2** a large, open flat in a converted warehouse or factory (仓库或工厂改建成的)公寓 **3** a gallery in a church or hall (教堂或大厅的)楼厢 • **verb** kick, hit, or throw a ball high into the air 吊高(球)；将(球)踢(或击、投)高

lofty /ˈlɒfti/ **adjective** (**loftier, loftiest**) **1** tall and impressive 高耸的；巍峨的 **2** morally good; noble 崇高的；高尚的 **3** proud and superior 高傲的，傲慢的 ■ **loftily** adverb.

log¹ /lɒg/ **noun 1** a part of the trunk or a large branch of a tree that has fallen or been cut off (伐倒的)原木 **2** an official record of the voyage of a ship or aircraft 航海日志；飞行日志 • **verb** (**logs, logging, logged**) **1** record facts in a log 把…载入航海(或飞行)日志 **2** achieve a certain distance, speed, or time 达到(某一距离、速度或时间) **3** (**log in/on** or **out/off**) begin or finish using a computer

system 登录(或退出)计算机系统 **4** cut down an area of forest to use the wood commercially 采伐(森林)；伐木 ■ **logger** noun.

log² noun a logarithm 对数

loganberry /ˈləʊɡənbəri/ **noun** (plural **loganberries**) an edible red soft fruit, similar to a raspberry 罗甘莓

logarithm /ˈlɒɡərɪðəm/ **noun** each of a series of numbers which allow you to do calculations by adding and subtracting rather than multiplying and dividing 对数 ■ **logarithmic** adjective.

logbook /ˈlɒgbʊk/ **noun 1** a log of a ship or aircraft 航海日志；飞行日志 **2** Brit. 【英】a document recording details about a vehicle and its owner 机动车辆行车日志

loggerheads /ˈlɒgəhedz/ **plural noun** (**at loggerheads**) in strong disagreement 不和；相争

loggia /ˈləʊdʒə/ **noun** a long room with one or more open sides 凉廊

logic /ˈlɒdʒɪk/ **noun 1** the science of reasoning 逻辑学 **2** clear, sound reasoning 合乎逻辑；合理 **3** a set of principles used in preparing a computer or electronic device to perform a task (计算机或电子设备的)逻辑程序，逻辑原理 ■ **logician** noun.

logical /ˈlɒdʒɪkl/ **adjective 1** following the rules of logic 遵循逻辑原则的 **2** using clear, sound reasoning 符合逻辑的 **3** expected or reasonable under the circumstances 可推想而知的；合情合理的 ■ **logically** adverb.

logistics /ləˈdʒɪstɪks/ **noun** the detailed organization of a large and complex project or event 后勤；物流 • **adjective** relating to logistics 后勤的；物流的 ■ **logistic** adjective **logistical** adjective.

logjam /ˈlɒgdʒæm/ **noun** a situation in which progress is difficult or impossible 僵局

logo /ˈləʊgəʊ/ **noun (plural logos)** a design or symbol used by an organization to identify its products (组织机构的)徽标, 标识

loin /lɔɪn/ **noun 1** the part of the body between the ribs and the hip bones 腰(部) **2** a joint of meat from this part of an animal (动物的)腰肉, 脊肉 **3 (loins)** literary【文】a person's sexual organs (人的)生殖器官

loincloth /ˈlɔɪnkləʊθ/ **noun** a piece of cloth wrapped round the hips, worn by men in some hot countries 腰布 (一些热带国家男子用来蔽体)

loiter /ˈlɔɪtə(r)/ **verb (loiters, loitering, loitered)** stand around without any obvious purpose 闲荡; 徘徊

loll /lɒl/ **verb 1** sit, lie, or stand in a lazy, relaxed way 懒洋洋地坐(或躺、站)着 **2** hang loosely 垂下

lollipop /ˈlɒlipɒp/ **noun** a large, flat, rounded boiled sweet on the end of a stick 棒棒糖

lollop /ˈlɒləp/ **verb (lollops, lolloping, lolloped)** move in a series of clumsy bounding steps 跌跌撞撞地走

lolly /ˈlɒli/ **noun (plural lollies)** Brit. informal【英, 非正式】**1** a lollipop 棒棒糖 **2 (also ice lolly)** a piece of flavoured ice or ice cream on a stick 冰棍 **3** money 钱

lone /ləʊn/ **adjective 1** having no companions 孤独无伴的; 独自的 **2** not having the support of other people 孤立的 □ **lone wolf** a person who prefers to be alone 喜欢单独行动的人

lonely /ˈləʊnli/ **adjective (lonelier, loneliest) 1** sad because of having no friends or company 孤苦的; 孤寂的 **2** (of time) spent alone (时间)独自度过的 **3** (of a place) remote (地方)遥远的, 偏僻的 ■ **loneliness** noun.

loner /ˈləʊnə(r)/ **noun** a person who prefers to be alone 好独处的人

lonesome /ˈləʊnsəm/ **adjective** N. Amer.【北美】lonely 孤独的; 孤寂的; 偏远的

long¹ /lɒŋ/ **adjective (longer, longest) 1** of great length in space or time 间距长的; 时间久的 **2** having or lasting a particular length, distance, or time (长度、距离或时间…)长的 **3** (of odds in betting) reflecting a low level of probability (打赌的胜算)可能性低的 ● **adverb (longer, longest) 1** for a long time 长久地; 长期地 **2** at a distant time 很久地 **3** throughout a stated period of time 始终; 整个 □ **long-haul** involving transport over a long distance 长途运输 **long in the tooth** rather old 年长的 **long johns** informal【非正式】underpants with close-fitting legs extending to the ankles (长及脚踝的)长内裤, 长衬裤 **long jump** an athletic event in which competitors jump as far as possible 跳远 **long-lived** living or lasting a long time 长寿的 **long shot** a scheme or guess that has only the slightest chance of succeeding 成功希望极小的计划; 准确性很低的猜测 **long-sighted** unable to see things clearly if they are close to the eyes 远视的 **long-suffering** patiently putting up with problems or annoying behaviour (对问题、恼人的行为)长期忍受的 **long-winded** long and boring 冗长乏味的

long² /lɒŋ/ **verb (long for** or **to do)** have a strong wish to do or have something 盼望; 渴望

longboat /ˈlɒŋbəʊt/ **noun 1** historical【历史】the largest boat carried by a sailing ship (大帆船上的)大艇 **2** = LONGSHIP.

longbow /ˈlɒŋbəʊ/ **noun** a large bow formerly used for shooting arrows (旧时用于射箭的)长弓, 大弓

longevity /lɒnˈdʒevəti/ **noun** long life 长寿; 长命

longhand /ˈlɒŋhænd/ **noun** ordinary handwriting (as opposed to shorthand,

typing, or printing) 普通书写(与速记、打字或印刷相对)

longing /ˈlɒŋɪŋ/ *noun* a strong wish to do or have something 渴望；企盼 • *adjective* strongly wishing for something 渴望的；企盼 ■ **longingly** *adverb*.

longitude /ˈlɒndʒɪtjuːd/ *noun* the distance of a place east or west of the Greenwich meridian, measured in degrees 经度

longitudinal /ˌlɒndʒɪˈtjuːdɪnl/ *adjective* **1** extending lengthwise 纵向的；纵的 **2** relating to longitude 经度的 ■ **longitudinally** *adverb*.

longship /ˈlɒŋʃɪp/ *noun* a long, narrow warship with oars and a sail, used by the Vikings (北欧海盗使用的)狭长快速战船

longways /ˈlɒŋweɪz/ *adverb* lengthways 纵向地；纵长地

loo /luː/ *noun* Brit. informal 【英，非正式】 a toilet 厕所

loofah /ˈluːfə/ *noun* a long, rough object used to wash yourself with in the bath, consisting of the dried inner parts of a tropical fruit 丝瓜络，丝瓜筋(用于擦澡)

look /lʊk/ *verb* **1** direct your eyes in a particular direction 看；瞧 **2** have the appearance of being; seem 看上去；显得 **3** face in a particular direction 面向；朝向 • *noun* **1** an act of looking 看；瞧 **2** appearance 外表，外观 **3** (**looks**) a person's facial appearance 容貌；表情；脸色 **4** a style or fashion 流行式样；时尚 **look after** take care of 照顾；照料，照看 **look down on** think that you are better than 轻视；看不起 **look for** try to find 寻找 **looking glass** a mirror 镜子 **look into** investigate 调查 **look on** watch without getting involved 旁观 **look out** be alert for possible trouble 警惕；注意；留神 **look up** improve 改善；好转 **look someone/thing up 1** search for information in a reference

book (在参考书中)查阅，查找(信息) **2** informal 【非正式】 visit or contact a friend 拜访，联系(朋友) **look up to** have a lot of respect for 尊敬；敬仰

lookalike /ˈlʊkəlaɪk/ *noun* a person who looks very similar to another 长得极像的人

lookout /ˈlʊkaʊt/ *noun* **1** a place from which you can keep watch or view landscape 瞭望台；观景台 **2** a person who keeps watch for danger or trouble 守望者；监视者

loom¹ /luːm/ *noun* a machine for weaving cloth 织布机

loom² *verb* **1** appear as a vague and threatening shape 隐约出现；赫然耸现 **2** (of something bad) seem about to happen (坏事)逼近

loony /ˈluːni/ *informal* 【非正式】 *noun* (plural **loonies**) a mad or silly person 疯子；傻子 • *adjective* mad or silly 发疯的；愚蠢的

loop /luːp/ *noun* **1** a shape produced by a curve that bends round and crosses itself 圈，环 **2** a strip of tape or film with the ends joined, allowing sounds or images to be continuously repeated 环形磁带；环形胶片 **3** a complete circuit for an electric current (电流)回路 • *verb* form into or have the shape of a loop (使)成环，(使)绕成圈 □ **loop the loop** (of an aircraft) fly in a vertical circle (飞机)翻跟头飞行

loophole /ˈluːphəʊl/ *noun* a mistake or piece of vague wording that lets someone avoid obeying a law or keeping to a contract (法律或合同的)空子，漏洞

loopy /ˈluːpi/ *adjective informal* 【非正式】 mad or silly 发疯的，傻的

loose /luːs/ *adjective* **1** not firmly or tightly fixed in place 松的；松动的 **2** not fastened or packaged together 未固定在一起的；散装的；零散的 **3** not tied up or shut in 不受约束的；自由的 **4** (of a garment) not fitting tightly (衣服)宽松的 **5** not exact 不严格的；不严谨的；不准确的：*a loose translation* 不准确的翻译 **6** careless and indiscreet 随便的，轻率的，欠考虑的 **7** dated 【废】immoral 不道德的 • verb (**looses, loosing, loosed**) **1** unfasten or set free 松开；释放；使不受束缚 **2** (**loose something off**) fire a shot, bullet, etc. 射出，发射(子弹等) □ **be at a loose end** have nothing definite to do 无事可做；无所事事 **loose cannon** a person who behaves in an unpredictable and potentially harmful way 炮筒子(指因行事出人意料而带来危害的人) **loose-leaf** (of a folder) having sheets of paper that can be added or removed (文件夹)活页的 ■ **loosely** adverb **looseness** noun.

！注意 don't confuse **loose** with **lose**, which means 'no longer have' or 'become unable to find'. 不要混淆 loose 和 lose，后者意为"不再有"或"找不到"。

loosen /ˈluːsn/ verb **1** make or become loose (使)变松；(使)松开 **2** (**loosen up**) warm up in preparation for an activity 做准备活动；做热身运动

loot /luːt/ verb steal goods from empty buildings during a war, riot, etc. (战争、暴乱中)抢劫，掠夺(物品) • noun **1** goods stolen from empty buildings during a war, riot, etc. 战利品；掠夺物 **2** goods stolen by a thief 被盗物；赃物 **3** informal 【非正式】money 钱 ■ **looter** noun.

lop /lɒp/ verb (**lops, lopping, lopped**) cut off a branch or limb from a tree or body 剪去，砍掉(树枝)；截(肢) □ **lop-eared** (of an animal) having drooping ears (动物)垂耳的

lope /ləʊp/ verb (**lopes, loping, loped**) run with long, relaxed strides 轻松地大步跑

lopsided /ˌlɒpˈsaɪdɪd/ adjective with one side lower or smaller than the other 向一侧倾斜的；不对称的；不平衡的

loquacious /ləˈkweɪʃəs/ adjective formal 【非正式】talkative 话多的，过于健谈的 ■ **loquacity** noun.

lord /lɔːd/ noun **1** a nobleman 贵族 **2** (**Lord**) a title given to certain British peers or high officials 勋爵(英国授予某些贵族的称号)；大人，阁下(英国对某些高级官员的尊称) **3** (**the Lords**) the House of Lords 上议院 **4** a master or ruler 主人；君主；统治者 **5** (**Lord**) a name for God or Jesus 上帝；耶稣基督；主 □ **lord it over** act in an arrogant and bullying way towards someone 耍威风；摆架子 **Lord Mayor** the title of the mayor in London and some other large cities 市长大人(对英国伦敦及其他几个大城市市长的称呼)

lordly /ˈlɔːdli/ adjective proud or superior 高傲的；贵族气派的

Lordship /ˈlɔːdʃɪp/ noun (**His/Your Lordship**) a form of address to a judge, bishop, or nobleman 阁下，大人，爵爷(对法官、主教或贵族的尊称)

lore /lɔː(r)/ noun all the traditions and knowledge relating to a particular subject (某一方面的)传统，知识

lorgnette /lɔːˈnjet/ or **lorgnettes** /lɔːˈnjets/ noun a pair of glasses held by a long handle at one side (一侧有握柄的)长柄眼镜

lorry /ˈlɒri/ noun (plural **lorries**) Brit. 【英】a large motor vehicle for transporting goods 卡车

lose /luːz/ verb (**loses, losing, lost**) **1** have something or someone taken away from you; no longer have 失去；丧失 **2** become unable to find 遗失；丢失 **3** fail to win a game or contest 输掉，未赢得(比赛或竞赛) **4** earn less money than you are spending 亏损；亏蚀 **5** waste an opportunity 浪费(机会) **6** (**be lost**) be destroyed or killed 毁灭；丧命 **7** escape from 摆脱；逃离

8 (lose yourself in or **be lost in)** be or become deeply involved in 沉湎于;专注于 **9** (of a clock or watch) become slow (时钟或表)走慢,慢 □ **lose out** not get a fair chance or share 失去好机会;损失

! 注意 don't confuse **lose** with **loose**, which means 'not fixed in place or tied up'. 不要混淆 lose 和 loose, 后者意为"松动的;不受约束的"。

loser /ˈluːzə(r)/ **noun 1** the person who loses a contest 输家;败者 **2** informal 【非正式】 a person who is generally unsuccessful in life 总是失败的人

loss /lɒs/ **noun 1** the losing of something or someone 遗失;丧失 **2** a person or thing that is lost 损失的人(或物) **3** the feeling of sadness after losing a valued person or thing (失去珍视的人或物后的)悲痛,失落感 □ **at a loss 1** uncertain or puzzled 不知所措的;困惑的 **2** losing more money than is being made 亏损的 **loss-leader** a product sold at a very low price to attract customers 为吸引顾客而亏本出售的产品

lost /lɒst/ past and past participle of LOSE. □ **be lost for words** be so surprised or upset that you cannot think what to say (惊讶或生气得)说不出话来,一时语塞 **be lost on** not be noticed or understood by 未被…注意(或理解) **lost cause** something that has no chance of success 无望成功的事

lot /lɒt/ **pronoun & adverb (a lot** or informal 【非正式】 **lots)** a large number or amount 许多;大量 • **noun 1** an item or set of items for sale at an auction (拍卖品的)一件,一套 **2** informal 【非正式】a particular group of people (特定的)一群人 **3 (the lot)** informal 【非正式】the whole number or quantity 总量;总数 **4** a method of deciding something by chance in which one

piece is chosen from a number of marked pieces of paper 抽签;抓阄 **5** a person's luck or situation in life (人的)命运,境遇 **6** chiefly N. Amer. 【主北美】 a plot of land 小块地

✔ 拼写指南 **a lot** is a two-word phrase; don't spell it as one word. a lot 是两个词组成的短语,不要把它拼成一个词。

loth /ləʊθ/ ⇒ see LOATH.

Lothario /ləˈθeəriəʊ/ **noun** (plural **Lotharios)** a man who has many casual sexual relationships with women 专事勾引妇女者

lotion /ˈləʊʃn/ **noun** a creamy liquid put on the skin as a medicine or cosmetic (医用或化妆用的)乳液

lottery /ˈlɒtəri/ **noun** (plural **lotteries) 1** a way of raising money by selling numbered tickets and giving prizes to the holders of numbers drawn at random 抽奖筹款法 **2** something whose success is controlled by luck 碰运气的事

lotus /ˈləʊtəs/ **noun** a kind of large water lily 莲花 □ **lotus position** a cross-legged position with the feet resting on the thighs, used in meditation 莲花坐姿;盘腿打坐

louche /luːʃ/ **adjective** having a bad reputation but still attractive 名声坏但不乏魅力的

loud /laʊd/ **adjective 1** producing a lot of noise 吵闹的;喧闹的 **2** expressed forcefully 大声疾呼的;强烈表达的 **3** very brightly coloured and in bad taste 花哨的;俗艳的 ■ **loudly** adverb **loudness** noun.

loudhailer /ˌlaʊdˈheɪlə(r)/ **noun** an electronic device for making the voice louder 扩音器;麦克风

loudspeaker /ˌlaʊdˈspiːkə(r)/ **noun** a device that converts electrical impulses into sound 扬声器

lough /lɒk/ **noun** Irish 【爱尔兰】 a loch 湖;狭长海湾

lounge /laʊndʒ/ **verb** (**lounges, lounging, lounged**) lie, sit, or stand in a relaxed way 懒洋洋地躺(或坐、站)着 • **noun 1** Brit. 【英】a sitting room 起居室 **2** a room in a hotel, airport, etc. in which people can relax or wait (宾馆、机场等的)休息室 □ **lounge bar** Brit. 【英】a bar in a pub or hotel that is more comfortable than the public bar 雅座酒吧 **lounge suit** Brit. 【英】a man's ordinary suit (男子的)日常西服

lounger /laʊndʒə(r)/ **noun** an outdoor chair that you can lie back in 户外躺椅

lour or **lower** /laʊə/ **verb 1** (of the sky) look dark and threatening (天空)显得阴沉 **2** scowl 皱眉头；怒目而视

louse /laʊs/ **noun 1** (plural **lice**) a small insect which lives as a parasite on animals or plants 虱 **2** (plural **louses**) informal 【非正式】an unpleasant person 讨厌的人

lousy /laʊzi/ **adjective** (**lousier, lousiest**) informal 【非正式】very bad 极糟糕的；极差的

lout /laʊt/ **noun** a rude or aggressive man or boy 粗鲁(或好斗)的男子 ■ **loutish adjective**.

louvre /luːvə(r)/ (US spelling 【美拼作】**louver**) **noun** each of a set of slanting slats fixed at intervals in a door, shutter, etc. to allow air or light through 百叶窗板

lovable or **loveable** /lʌvəbl/ **adjective** easy to love or feel affection for 可爱的；讨人喜欢的

lovage /lʌvɪdʒ/ **noun** a herb used in cookery 拉维纪草(用于烹饪)

love /lʌv/ **noun 1** a very strong feeling of affection 爱；热爱 **2** a strong feeling of affection linked with sexual attraction 【英】爱情；恋爱；性爱 **3** a great interest and pleasure in something 热爱；爱好 **4** a person or thing that you love 喜爱的人(或事物) **5** (in tennis, squash, etc.) a score of zero (网球、壁球等运动中的)零分 • **verb** (**loves, loving, loved**) **1** feel love for 爱；热爱 **2** like very much 喜爱 □ **love affair** a romantic or sexual relationship between two people who are not married to each other 风流韵事；(非夫妻之间的)性关系 **love child** a child born to parents who are not married to each other 私生子 **make love** have sex 做爱 ■ **loveless adjective lover noun**.

lovelorn /lʌvlɔːn/ **adjective** unhappy because you love someone who does not feel the same way about you 受单相思折磨的；失恋的

lovely /lʌvli/ **adjective** (**lovelier, loveliest**) **1** very beautiful 十分漂亮的；秀美的 **2** very pleasant 令人愉快的；悦人的 ■ **loveliness noun**.

lovemaking /lʌvmeɪkɪŋ/ **noun** sex and other sexual activity 做爱；发生性关系

lover /lʌvə(r)/ **noun 1** a person having a sexual or romantic relationship with someone 爱人；情人 **2** a person who enjoys a particular thing 爱好者；热爱者

lovesick /lʌvsɪk/ **adjective** unable to think clearly or act normally as a result of being in love 害相思病的；因爱情而憔悴的

low¹ /ləʊ/ **adjective 1** not high or tall or far above the ground 低的；矮的 **2** below average in amount, extent, or strength (数量、程度或力量)低的，少的，弱的 **3** not good or important 低微的；低等的；差的 **4** (of a sound) deep or quiet (声音)低的，轻的 **5** depressed or without energy 消沉的；精神不振的；没有活力的 **6** not honest or moral 不诚实的；不道德的；卑鄙的 • **noun** a low point or level 低点；低水平 **2** an area of low atmospheric pressure 低气压区 **3** (of a sound) at a low pitch (声音)低的；以低音调 □ **Low Church** the section of the Church of England that places little emphasis on ritual and the authority of bishops and priests 低教会派(英国国教会的一派,不太注重仪式及主教和牧师的权威地位) **the low-down** informal 【非正式】 the important facts about something (某事的)真相,实情 **lowest common denominator** the lowest number that the bottom number of a group of fractions can be divided into exactly 最小公分母 **low-key** not elaborate or showy 克制的;低调的;谦虚的 **low life** dishonest or immoral people or activities 卑鄙的人(或活动) **low tide** the time when the sea is furthest out 低潮

low² verb (of a cow) moo (牛)哞哞叫

lowbrow /'ləʊbraʊ/ adjective not intellectual or interested in culture 没有知识的;对文化不感兴趣的

lower¹ /'ləʊə(r)/ adjective **1** less high 较低的;较下的 **2** (in place names) situated to the south (用于地名)南部的 • verb (lowers, lowering, lowered) **1** make or become lower 降低;(使)变低;(使)下降 **2** move downwards 往下落;下沉 **3** (lower yourself) behave in a way that makes other people lose respect for you 降低身份 □ **lower case** small letters as opposed to capitals 小写字母

lower² ⇒ 见 LOUR.

lowland /'ləʊlənd/ or **lowlands** /'ləʊləndz/ noun **1** lowlying country 低地国家 **2** (**the Lowlands**) the part of Scotland lying south and east of the Highlands 苏格兰低地 ■ **lowlander** noun.

lowly /'ləʊli/ adjective (**lowlier, lowliest**) low in status or importance 地位低的;低微的 ■ **lowliness** noun.

loyal /'lɔɪəl/ adjective firm and faithful in your support for a person, organization, etc. 忠诚的;忠心的 ■ **loyally** adverb.

loyalist /'lɔɪəlɪst/ noun **1** a person who remains loyal to the established ruler or government 忠君者;忠于政府者 **2** (**Loyalist**) a person who believes that Northern Ireland should remain part of Great Britain 效忠派,忠英分子(支持北爱尔兰仍为英国一部分的人) ■ **loyalism** noun.

loyalty /'lɔɪəlti/ noun (plural **loyalties**) **1** the state of being loyal 忠诚 **2** a strong feeling of support 忠心

lozenge /'lɒzɪndʒ/ noun **1** a tablet of medicine that is sucked to soothe a sore throat 锭剂,糖锭(用于缓解嗓子痛) **2** a diamond-shaped figure 菱形

LP /ˌel 'piː/ abbreviation long-playing (record) (慢转)密纹唱片

LSD /ˌel es 'diː/ noun lysergic acid diethylamide, a drug that causes hallucinations 麦角酸酰二乙胺;致幻药

Ltd abbreviation Brit. 【英】 Limited 有限(责任)公司

lubricant /'luːbrɪkənt/ noun a substance, e.g. oil, for lubricating part of a machine 润滑剂;润滑油

lubricate /'luːbrɪkeɪt/ verb (**lubricates, lubricating, lubricated**) apply oil or grease to machinery so that it moves easily 使(机器)润滑;给(机器)加润滑油 ■ **lubrication** noun.

lubricious /luːˈbrɪʃəs/ adjective formal 【正式】 referring to sexual matters in a rude or offensive way 下流的;淫荡的;好色的

lucid /'luːsɪd/ adjective **1** easy to understand; clear 易懂的;清楚的 **2** able to think clearly 头脑清楚的;神智清醒的 ■ **lucidity** noun **lucidly** adverb.

Lucifer /'luːsɪfə(r)/ noun the Devil 魔鬼;撒旦

luck /lʌk/ noun **1** good things that happen by chance 好运;幸运 **2** chance considered as a force that causes good or bad things to happen 运气;命运

luckily /'lʌkɪli/ adverb it is fortunate that 幸运的是;幸好

luckless /'lʌkləs/ **adjective** unlucky 运气不好的;不幸的

lucky /'lʌki/ **adjective** (**luckier, luckiest**) having, bringing, or resulting from good luck 有好运的;带来好运的;幸运的 □ **lucky dip** Brit. 【英】a game in which prizes are hidden in a container for people to pick out at random 摸彩游戏

lucrative /'lu:krətɪv/ **adjective** making a large profit 获利多的;赚大钱的

lucre /'lu:kə(r)/ **noun** money 金钱

Luddite /'lʌdaɪt/ **noun** a person who is opposed to new technology 反对采用新技术者

ludicrous /'lu:dɪkrəs/ **adjective** absurd; ridiculous 荒唐的;荒谬的 ■ **ludicrously** adverb.

ludo /'lu:dəʊ/ **noun** Brit. 【英】a board game in which players move counters according to throws of a dice 鲁多(根据掷骰子的点数移动棋子的棋盘游戏)

lug¹ /lʌg/ **verb** (**lugs, lugging, lugged**) carry or drag with great effort 吃力地搬;用力地拖;使劲拉

lug² **noun 1** informal 【非正式】an ear 耳朵 **2** a projection on an object for carrying it or fixing it in place (物体上的)柄,把手,突出物

luggage /'lʌgɪdʒ/ **noun** suitcases or other bags for a traveller's belongings 行李

lugubrious /lə'gu:briəs/ **adjective** sad and gloomy 悲哀的;忧郁的

lukewarm /ˌlu:k'wɔ:m/ **adjective 1** only slightly warm 微温的;温热的 **2** unenthusiastic 不热情的;冷淡的

lull /lʌl/ **verb 1** make someone relaxed or calm 使放松;使平静 **2** make someone feel safe or confident, even if they are at risk of something bad 使放松警惕 • **noun** a quiet period between times of activity 暂时的平静;间歇

lullaby /'lʌləbaɪ/ **noun** (plural **lullabies**) a soothing song sung to send a child to sleep 摇篮曲;催眠曲

lumbago /lʌm'beɪgəʊ/ **noun** pain in the lower back 腰痛

lumbar /'lʌmbə(r)/ **adjective** relating to the lower back 腰的;腰部的

lumber /'lʌmbə(r)/ **noun 1** Brit. 【英】disused furniture 废旧家具 **2** chiefly N. Amer. 【主北美】timber sawn into rough planks 锯板材;木料 • **verb** (**lumbers, lumbering, lumbered**) **1** Brit. informal 【英,非正式】give someone an unwanted responsibility 给(某人)添麻烦;拖累 **2** move in a heavy, awkward way 缓慢笨拙地移动

lumberjack /'lʌmbədʒæk/ **noun** a person who cuts down trees and saws them into logs 伐木工;运木工

luminary /'lu:mɪnəri/ **noun** (plural **luminaries**) an important or influential person 杰出人物;名人

luminescence /ˌlu:mɪ'nesns/ **noun** light given off by a substance that has not been heated, e.g. fluorescent light 发冷光 ■ **luminescent** adjective.

luminous /'lu:mɪnəs/ **adjective** bright or shining, especially in the dark (尤指在黑暗中)明亮的,发光的 ■ **luminosity** noun **luminously** adverb.

lump /lʌmp/ **noun 1** an irregularly shaped piece of something hard or solid (坚硬结实物质不定形的)团,块 **2** a swelling under the skin 皮下肿块 • **verb** (**lump together**) casually group different people or things together 把……归并在一起 □ **lump it** informal 【非正式】put up with something whether you like it or not 勉强忍受 **lump sum** a single payment as opposed to a number of smaller payments 一次付款 ■ **lumpy** adjective.

lumpen /'lʌmpən/ **adjective 1** lumpy and misshapen 疙疙瘩瘩的;奇形怪状的 **2** stupid or loutish 愚蠢的;粗鲁的

lunacy /'lu:nəsi/ **noun 1** insanity; mental illness 精神错乱；精神失常 **2** great stupidity 极度愚蠢

lunar /'lu:nə(r)/ **adjective** having to do with the moon 月的；月亮的；似月亮的 □ **lunar eclipse** an eclipse in which the moon is hidden by the earth's shadow 月食

lunatic /'lu:nətɪk/ **noun 1** a person who is mentally ill 精神错乱的人 **2** a very foolish person 极其愚蠢的人

lunch /lʌntʃ/ **noun** a meal eaten in the middle of the day 午餐 • **verb** eat lunch 吃午餐

luncheon /'lʌntʃən/ **noun** formal 【正式】lunch 午餐

lung /lʌŋ/ **noun** each of a pair of organs in the chest into which humans and animals draw air when breathing 肺

lunge /lʌndʒ/ **noun** a sudden forward movement of the body 冲；扑 • **verb** (**lunges, lunging** or **lungeing, lunged**) make a sudden forward movement 突然向前冲(或扑)

lupin /'lu:pɪn/ **noun** a plant with spikes of tall flowers 羽扇豆，鲁冰花(穗状花序，高株)

lupine /'lu:paɪn/ **adjective** resembling a wolf 狼似的；凶残的

lurch /lɜːtʃ/ **verb** make a sudden, unsteady movement 踉跄；突然晃动 • **noun** a sudden, unsteady movement 突然的晃动 □ **leave someone in the lurch** leave someone in a difficult situation without help or support 弃(某人)于困境中

lurcher /'lɜːtʃə(r)/ **noun** Brit. 【英】a dog that is a cross between a greyhound and a retriever, collie, or sheepdog 杂种猎犬，混血狗

lure /ljʊə(r)/ **verb** (**lures, luring, lured**) tempt someone to do something by offering a reward 吸引；引诱 • **noun 1** the attractive and tempting qualities of something 吸引力；魅力；诱惑力 **2** a type of bait used in fishing or hunting (钓鱼或打猎用的)诱饵

lurex /'ljʊəreks/ **noun** trademark 【商标】yarn or fabric containing a glittering metallic thread 卢勒克斯金银纱(或织物)

lurid /'ljʊərɪd/ **adjective 1** unpleasantly bright in colour (色彩)花哨的，俗丽的 **2** (of a description) deliberately containing many shocking details (描述)过分渲染的，骇人听闻的 ■ **luridly** adverb.

lurk /lɜːk/ **verb** wait in hiding to attack someone 潜伏；埋伏

luscious /'lʌʃəs/ **adjective 1** having a pleasantly rich, sweet taste 甘甜的；香甜的 **2** (of a woman) very attractive (女子)性感的，迷人的

lush /lʌʃ/ **adjective 1** (of plants) growing thickly and strongly (植物)繁茂的，茂盛的 **2** rich or luxurious 富裕的；奢华的 • **noun** N. Amer. Informal 【北美，非正式】a drunkard 酒鬼；醉汉 ■ **lushly** adverb **lushness** noun.

lust /lʌst/ **noun 1** strong sexual desire 强烈的性欲；淫欲 **2** a passionate desire for something 渴望；强烈的欲望 • **verb** feel lust or a strong desire 渴望；贪求 ■ **lustful** adjective.

lustre /'lʌstə(r)/ (US spelling 【美拼作】**luster**) **noun 1** a soft glow or shine 光泽；光辉；光彩 **2** prestige or honour 声望；名望；荣誉；光荣 ■ **lustrous** adjective.

lusty /'lʌsti/ **adjective** (**lustier, lustiest**) healthy and strong 壮健的；精力充沛的 ■ **lustily** adverb.

lute /lu:t/ **noun** a stringed instrument with a long neck and a rounded body, which you play by plucking 诗琴，鲁特琴(一种拨弦乐器)

luxuriant /lʌg'ʒʊəriənt/ **adjective** growing thickly and strongly 茂盛的；浓密的 ■ **luxuriance** noun **luxuriantly** adverb.

luxuriate /lʌg'ʒʊərieɪt/ **verb** (**luxuriates, luxuriating, luxuriated**) (**luxuriate in**) relax and enjoy something very pleasant 尽情享受

luxurious /lʌgˈʒʊəriəs/ **adjective** very comfortable or elegant and expensive 奢华的,豪华的 ■ **luxuriously** adverb.

luxury /ˈlʌkʃəri/ **noun** (plural **luxuries**) **1** comfortable and expensive living or surroundings 奢侈,豪华 **2** something that is expensive and enjoyable but not essential 奢侈品

lychee /ˈlaɪtʃiː/ **noun** a small, sweet fruit with thin, rough skin 荔枝

lychgate /ˈlɪtʃgeɪt/ **noun** a roofed gateway to a churchyard 停枢门(通向墓地,有顶盖)

Lycra /ˈlaɪkrə/ **noun** trademark 【商标】 an elastic fabric used for close-fitting clothing 莱卡(一种使衣服紧身的弹性织物)

lye /laɪ/ **noun** an alkaline solution used for washing or cleaning 碱液(用于洗涤或清洁)

lying /ˈlaɪɪŋ/ present participle of LIE¹, LIE².

lymph /lɪmf/ **noun** a colourless fluid in the body that contains white blood cells 淋巴;淋巴液 □ **lymph node** (or **lymph gland**) each of a number of small swellings where lymph is filtered 淋巴结;淋巴腺 ■ **lymphatic** adjective.

lynch /lɪntʃ/ **verb** (of a group) kill

someone believed to be guilty of a crime without a legal trial (团体)用私刑处死(某人)

lynchpin /ˈlɪntʃpɪn/ ⇨ 见 LINCHPIN.

lynx /lɪŋks/ **noun** a wild cat with a short tail and tufted ears 猞猁

lyre /ˈlaɪə(r)/ **noun** a stringed instrument like a small harp, used in ancient Greece 里尔琴(古希腊的一种形似小型竖琴的弦乐器)

lyric /ˈlɪrɪk/ **noun 1** (also **lyrics**) the words of a song 歌词 **2** a poem that expresses the writer's thoughts and emotions 抒情诗歌 • **adjective** (of poetry) expressing the writer's thoughts and emotions (诗歌)抒情的

lyrical /ˈlɪrɪkl/ **adjective 1** (of writing or music) expressing the writer's emotions in an imaginative and beautiful way (写作或音乐)优美抒情的 **2** relating to the words of a popular song (流行歌曲)歌词的 □ **wax lyrical** talk about something in a very enthusiastic way 热情洋溢地谈论 ■ **lyrically** adverb.

lyricism /ˈlɪrɪsɪzəm/ **noun** expression of emotion in writing or music in an imaginative and beautiful way (写作或音乐的)抒情

lyricist /ˈlɪrɪsɪst/ **noun** a person who writes the words to popular songs (流行歌曲的)词作者

Mm

M or **m** /em/ **noun** (plural **Ms** or **M's**) **1** the thirteenth letter of the alphabet 英语字母表的第13个字母 **2** the Roman numeral for 1,000 (罗马数字) 一千 • **abbreviation 1** Monsieur. **2** motorway. **3** (m) metres. **4** (m) miles. **5** (m) millions.

MA /em'eɪ/ **abbreviation** Master of Arts 文科硕士

ma'am /mæm/ **noun** madam 夫人；女士

mac /mæk/ **noun** Brit. informal 【英，非正式】a mackintosh 雨衣

macabre /mə'kɑːbrə/ **adjective** disturbing and horrifying because concerned with death and injury (因与死亡和伤害有关系的) 可怕的，骇人的

macadam /mə'kædəm/ **noun** broken stone used for surfacing roads and paths (铺路面用的) 碎石

macadamia /ˌmækə'deɪmɪə/ **noun** the round edible nut of an Australian tree 澳洲坚果

macaroni /ˌmækə'rəʊni/ **noun** pasta in the form of narrow tubes 通心粉；通心面

macaroon /ˌmækə'ruːn/ **noun** a light biscuit made with ground almonds or coconut 蛋白杏仁饼干；蛋白椰子饼干

macaw /mə'kɔː/ **noun** a brightly coloured parrot found in Central and South America 金刚鹦鹉 (色彩艳丽，产于中南美洲)

mace¹ /meɪs/ **noun 1** a decorated stick carried by an official such as a mayor 权杖 **2** (in the past) a heavy club with a spiked metal head (旧时的) 狼牙棒

mace² **noun** a spice made from the dried outer covering of nutmeg 肉豆蔻干皮 (一种香料)

macerate /'mæsəreɪt/ **verb** (**macerates, macerating, macerated**) soften food by soaking it in a liquid 把(食物)浸软 ■ **maceration** noun.

Mach /mæk/ **noun** (**Mach 1, Mach 2,** etc.) the speed of sound, twice the speed of sound, etc. 马赫(速度单位，1 马赫等于声速)

machete /mə'ʃeti/ **noun** a broad, heavy knife used as a tool or weapon 大砍刀

Machiavellian /ˌmækɪə'velɪən/ **adjective** using cunning and underhand methods to get what you want 诡计多端的；不择手段的

machinations /ˌmæʃɪ'neɪʃnz/ **plural noun** plots and scheming 阴谋；诡计

machine /mə'ʃiːn/ **noun 1** a mechanical device for performing a particular task 机器 装置 **2** an efficient group of influential people 核心集体；核心组织 • **verb** (**machines, machining, machined**) make or work on something with a machine 用机器制造(或加工) □ **machine gun** a gun that fires many bullets in rapid succession 机关枪 **machine-readable** in a form that a computer can process 机器可读的；计算机可读的

machinery /mə'ʃiːnəri/ **noun 1** machines as a whole, or the parts of a machine (总称)机器，机械 **2** an organized system or structure 系统；体制；机构

machinist /mə'ʃiːnɪst/ **noun** a person who operates a machine or makes machinery 机工；机械师；机器制造者

machismo /mə'tʃɪzməʊ/ **noun** strong or aggressive male pride 大男子气概；男子汉的自信

macho /ˈmætʃəʊ/ **adjective** showing aggressive pride in being male 大男子气的；男子气概的

mackerel /ˈmækrəl/ **noun** an edible sea fish 鲭鱼，鲐鱼(一种可食用的海鱼)

mackintosh or **macintosh** /ˈmækɪntɒʃ/ **noun** Brit. 【英】a full-length waterproof coat 长雨衣

macramé /məˈkrɑːmi/ **noun** the craft of knotting cord to make decorative articles 装饰编结术

macrobiotic /ˌmækrəʊbaɪˈɒtɪk/ **adjective** (of diet) consisting of foods grown or produced without the use of chemicals (饮食)由有机绿色食物组成的，延年益寿的

macrocosm /ˈmækrəʊkɒzm/ **noun** the whole of a complex structure, contrasted with a small or representative part of it (a microcosm) 复杂而完整的结构；宏观世界

mad /mæd/ **adjective** (**madder**, **maddest**) **1** seriously mentally ill 疯的，精神不正常的 **2** very foolish 愚蠢的 **3** done without thought or control 不理智的；失控的 **4** informal 【非正式】very enthusiastic about something 狂热的；着迷的 **5** informal 【非正式】very angry 异常愤怒的，十分恼火的 □ **mad cow disease** BSE 疯牛病 ■ **madly** adverb **madness** noun.

madam /ˈmædəm/ **noun** **1** a polite form of address for a woman (对妇女的敬称)夫人，女士，太太 **2** Brit. informal 【英，非正式】a bossy or cheeky girl 傲慢(或放肆)的年轻女子 **3** a woman who runs a brothel (妓院的)鸨母

Madame /məˈdæm/ **noun** (plural **Mesdames** /meɪˈdæm/) a form of address for a French woman (对讲法语女性的称呼)夫人，太太，女士

madcap /ˈmædkæp/ **adjective** acting without thought; reckless 鲁莽的

madden /ˈmædn/ **verb** make someone mad or very annoyed 使恼怒；使发火

madder /ˈmædə(r)/ **noun** a red dye obtained from the roots of a plant 茜草染料；红色染料

made /meɪd/ past and past participle of MAKE.

Madeira /məˈdɪərə/ **noun** a strong sweet white wine from the island of Madeira 马德拉白葡萄酒 □ **Madeira cake** Brit. 【英】a rich kind of sponge cake 马德拉海绵蛋糕

Mademoiselle /ˌmædəmwɑːˈzel/ **noun** (plural **Mesdemoiselles** /ˌmeɪdəmwæˈzel/) a form of address for an unmarried French woman (对讲法语的未婚妇女的称呼)小姐

Madonna /məˈdɒnə/ **noun** (**the Madonna**) the Virgin Mary 圣母马利亚

madrigal /ˈmædrɪɡl/ **noun** a 16th- or 17th-century song for several voices without instrumental accompaniment (16或17世纪的)无伴奏合唱歌曲，牧歌

maelstrom /ˈmeɪlstrɒm/ **noun** **1** a situation of confusion or upheaval 混乱；动乱；激变 **2** a powerful whirlpool 大旋涡

maestro /ˈmaɪstrəʊ/ **noun** (plural **maestros**) a famous and talented man, especially a classical musician (男性)大师，名师；(尤指)古典音乐大师

Mafia /ˈmæfiə/ **noun** **1** (**the Mafia**) an international criminal organization originating in Sicily 黑手党(源于意大利西西里岛) **2** (**mafia**) a powerful group who secretly influence matters 势力集团；小集团

Mafioso /ˌmæfiˈəʊsəʊ/ **noun** (plural **Mafiosi** /ˌmæfiˈəʊsiː/) a member of the Mafia 黑手党成员

magazine /ˌmæɡəˈziːn/ **noun** **1** a weekly or monthly publication that contains articles and pictures 杂志；期刊 **2** the part of a gun that holds bullets before they are fired (枪的)弹仓,弹盒,弹盘 **3** a store for weapons, ammunition, and explosives 军火库,弹药库,炸药库

magenta /mə'dʒentə/ **noun** a light crimson colour 品红色,洋红色

maggot /'mægət/ **noun** the soft-bodied larva of a fly or other insect (苍蝇或其他昆虫的)蛆

Magi /'meɪdʒaɪ/ **plural noun** the three wise men from the East who brought gifts to the infant Jesus 东方三博士 (来自东方的三贤人,他们给初生的耶稣带来了礼物)

magic /'mædʒɪk/ **noun 1** the use of mysterious or supernatural forces to influence events 魔法;法术 **2** conjuring tricks performed to entertain people 魔术;戏法;幻术 **3** a mysterious or wonderful quality 魔力 • **adjective 1** having supernatural powers 有魔力的 **2** informal【非正式】wonderful 极好的,极妙的 • **verb** (**magics**, **magicking**, **magicked**) use magic to make something happen 施加魔法

magical /'mædʒɪkl/ **adjective 1** relating to or using magic 魔法的;魔术的 **2** wonderful; very enjoyable 绝妙的;有趣的 ■ **magically adverb**.

magician /mə'dʒɪʃn/ **noun 1** a person with magic powers 魔法师;巫师 **2** a conjuror 魔术师

magisterial /,mædʒɪ'stɪəriəl/ **adjective 1** having or showing great authority 有权威的;威严的 **2** relating to a magistrate 地方行政官的

magistrate /'mædʒɪstreɪt/ **noun** an official who judges minor cases and holds preliminary hearings 地方行政官;地方法官 ■ **magistracy** noun (plural **magistracies**).

magma /'mægmə/ **noun** very hot fluid or semi-fluid rock under the earth's crust 岩浆

magnanimous /mæg'nænɪməs/ **adjective** generous or forgiving towards a rival or enemy 宽宏的,气量大的 ■ **magnanimity** noun.

magnate /'mægneɪt/ **noun** a wealthy and influential person, especially in business 富豪;权贵;(尤指商业领域的)巨头,…大王

magnesium /mæg'ni:ziəm/ **noun** a silvery-white substance which burns with a brilliant white flame 镁

magnet /'mægnət/ **noun 1** a piece of iron that attracts objects containing iron and that points north and south when suspended 磁铁;磁石 **2** (in the Indian subcontinent and SE Asia) a person, place, etc. that someone or something is strongly attracted to (印度次大陆和东南亚的)有吸引力的人 (或地方,事物)

magnetic /mæg'netɪk/ **adjective 1** having the property of magnetism 有磁性的 **2** very attractive 吸引人的;有魅力的 □ **magnetic pole** each of the points near the geographical North and South Poles, which the needle of a compass points to 磁极 **magnetic tape** tape used in recording sound, pictures, or computer data (记录声音、图像或计算机数据的)磁带 ■ **magnetically** adverb.

magnetism /'mægnətɪzəm/ **noun 1** the property displayed by magnets of attracting or pushing away metal objects 磁性 **2** the ability to attract and charm people 吸引力;魅力

magnetize or **magnetise** /'mægnətaɪz/ **verb** (**magnetizes**, **magnetizing**, **magnetized**) make magnetic 使磁化

magneto /mæg'ni:təʊ/ **noun** (plural **magnetos**) a small generator that uses a magnet to produce pulses of electricity (小型的)磁电机

magnification /,mægnɪfɪ'keɪʃn/ **noun 1** the action of magnifying something 放大;扩大 **2** the degree to which something is magnified 放大率;放大倍数

magnificent /mæg'nɪfɪsnt/ **adjective 1** very attractive and impressive; splendid 壮观的；壮丽的；宏伟的 **2** very good 极好的；顶呱呱的 ■ **magnificence** noun **magnificently** adverb

magnify /'mægnɪfaɪ/ **verb** (**magnifies**, **magnifying**, **magnified**) **1** make something appear larger than it is with a lens or microscope 使放大；使扩大 **2** make larger or stronger 使更大；使更强 **3** old use 【旧】 praise 赞美 □ **magnifying glass** a lens used to help you see something very small by magnifying it 放大镜

magnitude /'mægnɪtjuːd, -tuːd/ **noun 1** great size or importance 巨大；广大；重要(性) **2** size 大小

magnolia /mæg'nəʊliə/ **noun** a tree or shrub with large white or pale pink flowers 木兰树，木兰(开白色或淡粉色花)

magnum /'mægnəm/ **noun** (plural **magnums**) a wine bottle of twice the standard size, normally 1½ litres (容量两倍于普通瓶子的)大酒瓶(容积通常为1.5升)

magpie /'mægpaɪ/ **noun 1** a black and white bird with a long tail 喜鹊 **2** a person who collects things of little use or value 爱收集零碎东西的人

maharaja or **maharajah** /ˌmɑːhəˈrɑːdʒə/ **noun** (in the past) an Indian prince (旧时印度的)土邦主，王公

mah-jong or **mah-jongg** /ˌmɑːˈdʒɒŋ/ **noun** a Chinese game played with small rectangular tiles 麻将牌，麻将

mahogany /məˈhɒɡəni/ **noun 1** hard reddish-brown wood from a tropical tree 红木 **2** a rich reddish-brown colour 红褐色

mahout /məˈhaʊt/ **noun** (in the Indian subcontinent and SE Asia) a person who works with elephants (印度次大陆和东南亚的)管象人，赶象人

maid /meɪd/ **noun 1** a female servant 女佣；保姆；侍女；女仆 **2** old use 【旧】 a girl or young unmarried woman 少女；年轻姑娘

maiden /'meɪdn/ **noun 1** old use 【旧】 a girl or young unmarried woman 少女；年轻姑娘 **2** (also **maiden over**) Cricket 【板球】 an over in which no runs are scored 未得分的一轮投球 • **adjective** first of its kind 初次的；首次的: *a maiden voyage* 首航 □ **maiden name** the surname of a married woman before her marriage (已婚女子的)婚前姓，娘家姓

maidenhead /'meɪdnhed/ **noun** old use 【旧】 a girl's or woman's virginity 处女身份；童贞

mail¹ /meɪl/ **noun 1** letters and parcels sent by post 邮件；邮包 **2** the postal system 邮政(系统) **3** email 电子邮件 • **verb 1** send by post 邮寄 **2** send post or email to 给…寄送邮件；给…发电子邮件 □ **mail order** the buying or selling of goods by post 邮购；函购

mail² **noun** (in the past) armour made of metal rings or plates (旧时的)锁子甲，铠甲

maim /meɪm/ **verb** inflict a permanent injury on 使永久性伤残；使终身残疾

main /meɪn/ **adjective** greatest or most important 最大的，主要的；最重要的 • **noun 1** a chief water or gas pipe or electricity cable (水、气、电的)总管，主管道 **2** (**the mains**) Brit. 【英】 the network of pipes and cables supplying water, gas, and electricity (公共用水、煤气、电的)供给网，干线 □ **in the main** on the whole 大体上；基本上

mainframe /'meɪnfreɪm/ **noun** a large highspeed computer supporting a network of workstations (大型计算机的)主机；(支持网络工作站的)主计算机

mainland /'meɪnlænd/ **noun** the main area of land of a country, not including islands and separate territories (不包括

附近岛屿及本土外领土的)国土主体,大陆

mainly /'meɪnli/ **adverb** for the most part; chiefly 主要地;大部分地

mainspring /'meɪnsprɪŋ/ **noun** the most important or influential part of something 最重要部分;最具影响的部分

mainstay /'meɪnsteɪ/ **noun** a thing on which something depends or is based 主要依靠;支柱

mainstream /'meɪnstriːm/ **noun** the ideas, attitudes, or activities that are shared by most people 主流思想;主流倾向

maintain /meɪn'teɪn/ **verb** keep something in the same state or at the same level 保持;维持 **2** regularly check and repair a building, machine, etc. 维修,保养,养护(建筑物、机器等) **3** provide someone with financial support (经济上)援助 **4** strongly state that something is the case 断言;极力主张;坚持

maintenance /'meɪntənəns/ **noun 1** the action of maintaining something 维持;保养;保持 **2** Brit. 【英】financial support that someone gives to their former husband or wife after divorce (离婚后给前夫或前妻的)生活费

> ✔ 拼写指南 -**ten**-, not -*tain*-: main**ten**ance. maintenance 中 -ten-不要拼成 -tain-。

maisonette /ˌmeɪzə'net/ **noun** a flat on two storeys of a larger building (占有两层楼的)公寓套房

maize /meɪz/ **noun** Brit. 【英】a cereal plant whose large yellow grains are eaten as a vegetable 玉蜀黍;玉米

majestic /mə'dʒestɪk/ **adjective** impressively grand or beautiful 壮丽的;雄伟的;壮观的 ■ **majestically adverb**.

majesty /'mædʒəsti/ **noun** (plural **majesties**) **1** impressive beauty or grandeur 壮丽;雄伟 **2** (His,

Your, etc. **Majesty**) a title given to a king or queen or their wife or widow 陛下(对帝王、王后等的尊称)

major /'meɪdʒə(r)/ **adjective 1** important or serious 重要的;重大的 **2** greater or more important; main 较重要的;主要的 **3** Music 【音乐】(of a scale) having intervals of a semitone between the third and fourth, and seventh and eighth notes (音阶)大音阶的,大调的 • **noun 1** the rank of army officer above captain 陆军少校 **2** N. Amer. 【北美】a student specializing in a particular subject (某专业的)主修学生 • **verb** (**major in**) N. Amer. & Austral./NZ 【北美和澳/新西兰】specialize in a particular subject at college or university (在学院或大学中)主修(某专业) □ **major general** the rank of army officer above brigadier 陆军少将

major-domo /ˌmeɪdʒə'dəʊməʊ/ **noun** (plural **major-domos**) a person employed to manage a large household (大户人家的)总管家

majority /mə'dʒɒrəti/ **noun** (plural **majorities**) **1** the greater number 多数;过半数;大半 **2** Brit. 【英】the number of votes by which one party or candidate in an election defeats the opposition (选举获胜者的)多数票 **3** the age when a person is legally an adult, usually 18 or 21 成年,法定年龄(通常为18或21岁)

make /meɪk/ **verb** (**makes**, **making**, **made**) **1** form something by putting parts together or mixing substances 做;制造;组装 **2** cause something to happen or come into existence 使产生;使出现;引起 **3** force someone to do something 迫使;逼迫 **4** add up to 总计;等于 **5** be suitable as 宜用作;适合 **6** estimate as or decide on 估计;推测 **7** earn money or profit 挣、赚(钱或利润) **8** arrive at or achieve 抵达;达到 **9** prepare to go in a particular direction or to do something (准备)赶往;准备做 (某事) • noun the manufacturer or trade name of a product (产品的)品牌, 牌子 □ make-believe fantasy or pretence 虚幻;假想;假装 make do manage with something that is not satisfactory 凑合着用;设法应付 make for move towards 走向;向…行进 make it become successful 成功 make off leave hurriedly 匆忙离开 make off with steal 偷走 make out claim or pretend to be 说成;装作 make something out manage with difficulty to see, hear, or understand something (勉强)看出, 听出, 理解(某事物) make up be friendly again after a quarrel (吵嘴后)和解, 言归于好 make someone up apply cosmetics to someone 为(某人)化妆 make something up 1 put something together from parts or ingredients 配制, 合成(某物) 2 invent a story 编造, 虚构(故事) make-up cosmetics applied to the face 化妆品 make up for compensate for 弥补;补救 make up your mind make a decision 下定决心;拿定主意 on the make informal 【非正式】trying to make money or gain an advantage 谋取利益的 ■ maker noun.

makeover /'meɪkəʊvə(r)/ noun a transformation of someone's appearance with cosmetics, hairstyling, and clothes (通过化妆、发型、服饰实现的)改头换面

makeshift /'meɪkʃɪft/ adjective temporary and improvised 临时凑合的;权宜之计的

makeweight /'meɪkweɪt/ noun an unimportant person or thing that is only added or included to make up the correct number, amount, etc. 充数之人(或物)

malachite /'mæləkaɪt/ noun a bright green mineral 孔雀石

maladjusted /ˌmælə'dʒʌstɪd/ adjective not able to cope well with normal life 不适应社会环境的

maladroit /ˌmælə'drɔɪt/ adjective clumsy 笨拙的;不灵巧的

malady /'mælədi/ noun (plural maladies) literary 【文】a disease or illness 疾病;毛病

malaise /mə'leɪz/ noun 1 a general feeling of illness or low spirits 心神不宁;不适;不愉快 2 a long-standing problem that is difficult to identify 难以捉摸的问题

malapropism /'mæləprɒpɪzəm/ noun the mistaken use of a word in place of a similar-sounding one 近义词误用

malaria /mə'leəriə/ noun a disease that causes fever and is transmitted by the bite of some mosquitoes 疟疾 ■ malarial adjective.

malarkey /mə'lɑːki/ noun informal 【非正式】nonsense 胡说;废话

Malaysian /mə'leɪziən/ noun a person from Malaysia 马来西亚人 • adjective relating to Malaysia 马来西亚的

malcontent /'mælkəntent/ noun a person who is dissatisfied and rebellious 不满者;反叛者

male /meɪl/ adjective 1 of the sex that can fertilize or inseminate the female 男性的;雄性的;公的 2 to do with men 男人的;男子的 3 (of a plant or flower) having stamens but not a pistil (植物或花卉)只具雄蕊的 4 (of a fitting) made to fit inside a corresponding part (配件)凸形的, 插入的 • noun a male person, animal, or plant 男人;雄性动物;雄性植物

malediction /ˌmælɪ'dɪkʃn/ noun formal 【正式】a curse 诅咒;咒骂

malefactor /'mælɪfæktə(r)/ noun formal 【正式】a criminal or wrongdoer 犯罪分子;坏人

malevolent /mə'levələnt/ adjective wishing to harm other people 怀恶意的;心肠坏的 ■ malevolence noun.

malformation /ˌmælfɔː'meɪʃn/ noun the state of being abnormally shaped or formed 畸形 ■ **malformed** adjective.

malfunction /ˌmælˈfʌŋkʃn/ **verb** (of equipment or machinery) fail to function normally (设备或机器)发生故障，运转失常，失灵 ■ **noun** a failure to function normally 功能障碍，机能失灵；故障

malice /ˈmælɪs/ **noun** the desire to harm someone 恶意；恶念；害人之心

malicious /məˈlɪʃəs/ **adjective** meaning to harm other people 恶意的；存心不良的；蓄意谋害的 ■ **maliciously** adverb.

malign /məˈlaɪn/ **adjective** harmful or evil 有害的；邪恶的 ■ **verb** say unpleasant things about 诬蔑，诽谤；中伤 ■ **malignity** noun.

malignancy /məˈlɪɡnənsi/ **noun** (plural **malignancies**) **1** a cancerous growth 癌；恶性肿瘤 **2** the quality of being harmful or evil 有害；恶意，恶毒

malignant /məˈlɪɡnənt/ **adjective 1** (of a tumour) cancerous (肿瘤)癌的，恶性的 **2** having or showing a desire to harm other people 有害的；邪恶的；恶毒的

malinger /məˈlɪŋɡə(r)/ **verb** (**malingers**, **malingering**, **malingered**) pretend to be ill in order to avoid work 装病(以逃避工作) ■ **malingerer** noun.

mall /mɔːl, mæl/ **noun 1** a large enclosed shopping area 商业区；大型商业中心 **2** a sheltered walk 林阴道

mallard /ˈmælɑːd/ **noun** a kind of duck, the male of which has a dark green head 绿头鸭（一种野鸭，雄性头部呈深绿色）

malleable /ˈmæliəbl/ **adjective 1** able to be hammered or pressed into shape 有延展性的；可锻的；有韧性的 **2** easily influenced 易受外界影响的

mallet /ˈmælɪt/ **noun 1** a hammer with a large wooden head 大头锤(锤头木制) **2** a wooden stick with a head like a hammer, for hitting a croquet or polo ball (槌球的)木槌；(马球的)球棍

mallow /ˈmæləʊ/ **noun** a plant with pink or purple flowers 锦葵(开粉色或紫色花)

malnourished /ˌmælˈnʌrɪʃt/ **adjective** suffering from malnutrition 营养不良的

malnutrition /ˌmælnjuːˈtrɪʃn/ **noun** bad health caused by not having enough food, or not enough of the right food 营养不良

malodorous /ˌmælˈəʊdərəs/ **adjective** smelling very unpleasant 恶臭的；难闻的

malpractice /ˌmælˈpræktɪs/ **noun** illegal, corrupt, or careless behaviour by a professional person 营私舞弊，渎职；玩忽职守

malt /mɔːlt/ **noun** barley or other grain that has been soaked in water and then dried 麦芽 ■ **malted** adjective.

maltreat /ˌmælˈtriːt/ **verb** treat badly or cruelly 虐待；苛待 ■ **maltreatment** noun.

mama or **mamma** /ˈmæmə/ **noun** dated or N. Amer. 【废或北美】your mother 妈妈

mamba /ˈmæmbə/ **noun** a large, highly poisonous African snake 树眼镜蛇，曼巴(一种体大、剧毒的非洲蛇)

mammal /ˈmæml/ **noun** a warm-blooded animal that has hair or fur, produces milk, and gives birth to live young 哺乳动物 ■ **mammalian** adjective.

mammary /ˈmæməri/ **adjective** relating to the breasts or the milk-producing organs of other mammals 乳房的；乳腺的

Mammon /ˈmæmən/ **noun** money thought of as being worshipped like a god (被视为崇拜偶像的)财富，钱财

mammoth /ˈmæməθ/ **noun** a large extinct form of elephant with a hairy coat and long curved tusks (已灭绝

的)猛犸,毛象 • **adjective** huge 巨大的;庞大的

man /mæn/ **noun** (plural **men**) **1** an adult human male (成年)男子,男人 **2** a person 人;任何人 **3** human beings in general (泛指)人,人类 **4** a figure or token used in a board game (棋类游戏的)棋子 • **verb** (**mans**, **manning**, **manned**) provide a place or machine with people to operate or defend it 给(场所或机器)配置人员(或兵力) □ **man-made** made or caused by human beings 人造的;人为的 **man-of-war** historical【历史】an armed sailing ship 军舰 ■ **manhood** noun.

manacle /'mænəkl/ **noun** a metal band fastened round a person's hands or ankles to restrict their movement 手铐;镣铐 • **verb** (**manacles**, **manacling**, **manacled**) restrict someone with manacles 给…上手铐(或镣铐)

manage /'mænɪdʒ/ **verb** (**manages**, **managing**, **managed**) **1** be in charge of people or an organization 管理,掌管(人员或机构) **2** succeed in doing 成功做到;设法完成 **3** be able to cope despite difficulties 能应付;能对付;能处理 **4** control the use of money or other resources 合理使用(钱财或其他资源) ■ **manageable** adjective.

management /'mænɪdʒmənt/ **noun 1** the action of managing 管理;经营 **2** the managers of an organization (机构的)管理人员,管理者

manager /'mænɪdʒə(r)/ **noun 1** a person who manages staff, an organization, or a sports team (员工、机构或运动队的)经理,管理者,教练 **2** a person in charge of the business affairs of a performer, group of musicians, etc. (演员、音乐人等的)经纪人 ■ **managerial** adjective.

manageress /ˌmænɪdʒə'res/ **noun** a woman who manages a business 女经理;女管理者;女经纪人

manatee /'mænəti:/ **noun** a large plant-eating animal that lives in tropical seas 海牛(大型食草动物,生活在热带海域)

mandarin /'mændərɪn/ **noun 1** (**Mandarin**) the official form of the Chinese language (中国的)普通话,官话 **2** (in the past) a high-ranking Chinese official (旧时中国的)高级官吏 **3** a powerful official 官僚政要 **4** a small citrus fruit with a loose yellow-orange skin 柑橘;橘子

mandate **noun** /'mændeɪt/ **1** an official order or permission to do something 命令;训令;许可;批准 **2** the authority to carry out a policy that is given by voters to the winner of an election (执行某项政策的)授权(指选举民赋予选举获胜者的权力) • **verb** /.mæn'deɪt/ (**mandates**, **mandating**, **mandated**) give someone authority to do something 授权(某人)做

mandatory /'mændətəri/ **adjective** required by law or rules; compulsory 法定的;强制的;必须履行的

mandible **noun** /'mændɪbl/ **noun 1** the lower jawbone in mammals or fish (哺乳动物或鱼类的)下颌骨 **2** either of the upper and lower parts of a bird's beak 鸟喙的上(或下)部 **3** either of the parts of an insect's mouth that crush its food (昆虫咀嚼食物的)颚

mandolin /'mændəlɪn/ **noun** a musical instrument with a rounded back and metal strings 曼陀林琴

mandrake /'mændreɪk/ **noun** a plant whose root is used in herbal medicine and magic 曼德拉草(用作草药或用于法术)

mandrill /'mændrɪl/ **noun** a large baboon with a red and blue face 山魈(一种大型狒狒,面部有红蓝两种颜色)

mane /meɪn/ **noun 1** a growth of long hair on the neck of a horse, lion, etc.

(马、狮等的)鬃毛 **2** a person's long hair (人的)长发

maneuver /məˈnuːvə(r)/ US spelling of MANOEUVRE. manoeuvre 的美式拼法

manful /ˈmænfl/ **adjective** brave and determined 勇敢的；果敢的；坚决的 ■ **manfully** adverb.

manganese /ˈmæŋɡəniːz/ **noun** a hard grey metallic element (金属元素)锰

mange /meɪndʒ/ **noun** a skin disease of some animals that causes itching and hair loss 兽疥癣

mangel-wurzel /ˈmæŋɡl.wɜːzl/ **noun** a variety of beet grown as feed for farm animals (作饲料用的)甜菜

manger /ˈmeɪndʒə(r)/ **noun** a long trough from which horses or cattle eat (马或牛的)食槽

mangetout /ˈmɒnʒtuː/ **noun** (plural **mangetout** or **mangetouts** /ˈmɒnʒtuː/) chiefly Brit. 【主英】 a variety of pea with an edible pod 嫩豌豆；荷兰豆

mangle /ˈmæŋɡl/ **verb** (**mangles, mangling, mangled**) destroy or severely damage by crushing or twisting 压碎；撕烂；毁损 • **noun** a machine with rollers for squeezing wet laundry to remove the water 轧布机；轧干机

mango /ˈmæŋɡəʊ/ **noun** (plural **mangoes** or **mangos**) a tropical fruit with yellow flesh 芒果

mangrove /ˈmæŋɡrəʊv/ **noun** a tropical tree or shrub found in coastal swamps 红树属植物(热带树木或灌木，产于沿海沼泽地带)

mangy /ˈmeɪndʒi/ **adjective 1** (of an animal) having mange (动物)患(兽)疥癣的 **2** in bad condition; shabby 状况不佳的；破旧的；褴褛的

manhandle /ˈmænhændl/ **verb** (**manhandles, manhandling, manhandled**) **1** move a heavy object with effort 用力移动(重物) **2** push or drag someone roughly (粗暴地)推搡，拉拉

manhole /ˈmænhəʊl/ **noun** a covered opening giving access to a sewer or other underground structure (下水道或其他地下建筑供人出入的)人孔，检修孔

mania /ˈmeɪniə/ **noun 1** mental illness in which a person imagines things and has periods of wild excitement 躁狂症 **2** an extreme enthusiasm 狂热；癖好

maniac /ˈmeɪniæk/ **noun 1** a person who behaves in a very wild or violent way 躁狂者；疯子 **2** informal 【非正式】 a person who is very enthusiastic about something 入迷的人；有癖者 ■ **maniacal** /məˈnaɪəkl/ adjective.

manic /ˈmænɪk/ **adjective 1** having to do with mania 躁狂的；疯狂的 **2** showing wild excitement and energy 狂热的；激动的 □ **manic depression** a mental disorder with alternating periods of excitement and depression 躁狂抑郁症 ■ **manically** adverb.

manicure /ˈmænɪkjʊə(r)/ **noun** treatment to improve the appearance of the hands and nails 修指甲；指甲护理 ■ **manicured** adjective **manicurist** noun.

manifest /ˈmænɪfest/ **adjective** clear and obvious 明了的；显然的 • **verb 1** show or display 表明；表露；显示 **2** appear; become apparent 显现；变得明显 • **noun** a document listing the cargo, crew, and passengers of a ship or aircraft (船或飞机的)货物清单；船员(或机组人员)名单，乘客名单 ■ **manifestly** adverb.

manifestation /ˌmænɪfeˈsteɪʃn/ **noun 1** a sign or evidence of something 显示；表明；证明 **2** an appearance of a ghost or spirit (鬼怪等的)显灵

manifesto /ˌmænɪˈfestəʊ/ **noun** (plural **manifestos**) a public declaration of the policy and aims of a political party (政党的)宣言,声明,政纲

manifold /'mænɪfəʊld/ **adjective** of many kindss 多种多样的;繁多的 • **noun** a pipe with several openings, especially in a car engine 多支管;(尤指汽车发动机的)歧管

manikin /'mænɪkɪn/ **noun** a very small person 矮子;侏儒

manioc /'mænɪɒk/ = CASSAVA.

manipulate /mə'nɪpjuleɪt/ **verb** (**manipulates, manipulating, manipulated**) **1** handle skilfully (熟练地)处理 **2** control or influence in a clever or underhand way (用巧妙或不正当的手段)操纵,控制,摆布 ■ **manipulation** noun **manipulator** noun.

manipulative /mə'nɪpjələtɪv/ **adjective** manipulating other people in a clever or underhand way 善于操纵他人的;会摆布人的;会控制的

mankind /mæn'kaɪnd/ **noun** human beings as a whole 人类

manky /'mæŋki/ **adjective** Brit. informal 【英,非正式】 dirty or of bad quality 肮脏的;劣质的

manly /'mænli/ **adjective** (**manlier, manliest**) **1** having good qualities associated with men, such as courage and strength 具有男子气概的 **2** suitable for a man 适合男子的 ■ **manliness** noun.

manna /'mænə/ **noun 1** (in the Bible) the substance supplied by God as food to the Israelites in the wilderness (《圣经》中记载的)吗哪(以色列人在荒野中获得的神赐食物) **2** something unexpected and beneficial 意外收获

mannequin /'mænɪkɪn/ **noun** a dummy used to display clothes in a shop window (商店展示服装用的)人体模型

manner /'mænə(r)/ **noun 1** a way in which something is done or happens 方式;做法 **2** a person's outward behaviour 举止;态度;姿态

3 (**manners**) polite social behaviour 礼貌;礼仪 **4** literary【文】a kind or sort 种类

mannered /'mænəd/ **adjective 1** behaving in a particular way 举止…的: *a well-mannered girl* 彬彬有礼的姑娘 **2** artificial and exaggerated 不自然的;矫揉造作的

mannerism /'mænərɪzəm/ **noun** a distinctive gesture or way of speaking 独特的举止(或说话方式)

mannerly /'mænəli/ **adjective** well mannered; polite 彬彬有礼的;礼貌的

mannish /'mænɪʃ/ **adjective** (of a woman) like a man in appearance or behaviour (女子)像男人的,男子气的

manoeuvre /mə'nuːvə(r)/ (US spelling【美拼作】 **maneuver**) **noun 1** a movement or series of moves needing skill and care 机动动作(巧妙的)部署,调动 **2** a carefully planned scheme 策略;花招 **3** (**manoeuvres**) a large-scale military exercise 大规模军事演习 • **verb** (**manoeuvres, manoeuvring, manoeuvred**) **1** make a movement or series of moves skilfully and carefully (巧妙、谨慎地)移动,运动,调动,部署 **2** cleverly influence someone or something in order to achieve an aim (巧妙地)操纵,控制 ■ **manoeuvrable** adjective.

✔ 拼写指南 the British spelling has -oeu- in the middle and -re at the end: man*oeu*vre. manoeuvre 为英式拼法,中间拼作 -oeu-,词末拼作 -re.

manometer /mə'nɒmɪtə(r)/ **noun** an instrument for measuring the pressure of fluids (流体)压力计,压力表

manor /'mænə(r)/ **noun** a large country house with lands 大庄园 ■ **manorial** adjective.

manpower /'mænpaʊə(r)/ **noun** the number of people working or available for work 劳动力

manse /mæns/ **noun** the house provided

M

for a minister of certain Christian Churches(基督教会的)牧师住宅

mansion /'mænʃn/ noun a large, impressive house 宅第;公馆;大厦

manslaughter /'mænslɔːtə(r)/ noun the crime of killing a person without meaning to do so 过失杀人

mantel /'mæntl/ noun a mantelpiece or mantelshelf 壁炉架;壁炉台

mantelpiece /'mæntlpiːs/ noun 1 a structure surrounding a fireplace 壁炉架 2 (also **mantelshelf**) a shelf forming the top of a mantelpiece 壁炉台

mantilla /mæn'tɪlə/ noun a lace or silk scarf worn by Spanish women over the hair and shoulders (西班牙妇女用的)披肩头巾

mantis /'mæntɪs/ or **praying mantis** noun (plural **mantis** or **mantises**) a large insect that waits for its prey with its forelegs folded like hands in prayer 螳螂

mantle /'mæntl/ noun 1 a woman's loose sleeveless cloak (妇女的)小披风,短斗篷 2 a close covering, e.g. of snow (紧密的)覆盖层 3 a cover around a gas jet that produces a glowing light when heated (煤气灯的)白炽罩 4 a role or responsibility that passes from one person to another (由一人传给另一人的)衣钵,责任,职分 5 the region of very hot, dense rock between the earth's crust and its core 地幔

mantra /'mæntrə/ noun a word or sound repeated to aid concentration when meditating (冥想时重复念的)曼特罗,祷文,符咒;念咒声

manual /'mænjuəl/ adjective 1 having to do with the hands 手的;手动的;手工操作的 2 operated by or using the hands 手工的;体力的 • noun a book giving instructions or information 说明书;使用手册;便览;指南 ■ **manually** adverb

manufacture /ˌmænjuˈfæktʃə(r)/ verb (**manufactures**, **manufacturing**, **manufactured**) 1 make something on a large scale using machinery (使用机器大规模地)制造,生产 2 invent evidence or a story 编造,捏造(证据或故事) • noun the manufacturing of things (大规模的)制造,生产 ■ **manufacturer** noun.

manure /məˈnjuə(r)/ noun animal dung used for fertilizing land 肥料;粪肥

manuscript /'mænjuskrɪpt/ noun 1 a handwritten book, document, etc. (书籍、文件等的)手写本,手稿 2 an author's handwritten or typed work, before printing and publication 手稿;打字稿

Manx /mæŋks/ adjective relating to the Isle of Man 马恩岛的 □ **Manx cat** a breed of cat that has no tail 马恩岛猫(一种无尾猫)

many /'meni/ determiner, pronoun, & adjective a large number of 多的;许多的;大量的 • noun (**the many**) the majority of people 大多数人

Maori /'mauri, 'mɑːri/ noun (plural **Maori** or **Maoris**) a member of the aboriginal people of New Zealand 毛利人(新西兰土著居民)

map /mæp/ noun a flat diagram of an area showing physical features, cities, roads, etc. 地图 • verb (**maps**, **mapping**, **mapped**) 1 show something on a map 在地图上标示 2 (**map something out**) plan something in detail 详细筹划

maple /'meɪpl/ noun a tree with five-pointed leaves 枫树

mar /mɑː(r)/ verb (**mars**, **marring**, **marred**) spoil the appearance or quality of 损坏;损毁;玷污

maraca /məˈrækə/ noun a container filled with small beans or stones, shaken as a musical instrument 响葫芦,沙球(内装豆子、石子等作为乐器摇动)

marathon /'mærəθən/ noun 1 a long-distance running race, strictly one

of 26 miles 385 yards (42.195 km)
马拉松长跑(全程为26英里385码,
合42.195公里) **2** a long-lasting and
difficult task 持久而困难的任务

maraud /məˈrɔːd/ **verb** go about a
place in search of things to steal or
people to attack 抢夺;抢掠;劫夺
■ **marauder** noun.

marble /ˈmɑːbl/ **noun 1** a hard stone,
usually white with coloured streaks,
which can be polished and used in
sculpture and building 大理石 **2** a
small ball of coloured glass used as
a toy (用作玩具的)彩色玻璃弹球

marbled /ˈmɑːbld/ **adjective** patterned
with coloured streaks 具有大理石花
纹的

March /mɑːtʃ/ **noun** the third month
of the year 三月

march /mɑːtʃ/ **verb 1** walk in time
and with regular paces, like a soldier
行军;齐步前进 **2** walk quickly and
with determination (坚定地快步)
前进,行进 **3** force someone to walk
quickly 迫使(某人)快步行进 **4** take
part in an organized procession to
make a protest 游行抗议 • **noun 1**
an act of marching 行军;行进;前
进;行走 **2** a procession organized
as a protest 游行示威 **3** (**Marches**)
land on the border between two territories 边界;边境
■ **marcher** noun.

marchioness /ˌmɑːʃəˈnes/ **noun 1**
the wife or widow of a marquess 侯
爵夫人 **2** a woman who holds the
rank of marquess 女侯爵

Mardi Gras /ˌmɑːdi ˈɡrɑː/ **noun** a
carnival held in some countries on
Shrove Tuesday 肥美星斯二(某些国
家在忏悔星期二举办的狂欢节)

mare /meə(r)/ **noun** the female of a
horse or related animal 母马;雌性马
科动物

margarine /ˌmɑːdʒəˈriːn/ **noun** a butter
substitute made from vegetable oils
or animal fats 人造黄油

margin /ˈmɑːdʒɪn/ **noun 1** an edge or
border 边缘;边沿 **2** the blank border
on each side of the print on a page
(页边的)空白,白边 **3** an amount by
which something is won 差额;差数;
幅度 □ **margin of** (or **for**) **error** a
small amount allowed for or included
so as to be sure of success or safety
(允许的)误差幅度

marginal /ˈmɑːdʒɪnl/ **adjective 1** in a
margin 页边的;边缘的 **2** slight, or of
minor importance 不重要的;微不足
道的 **3** Brit. 【英】(of a parliamentary
seat) held by only a small majority
(议会席位)以微弱多数获得的,边缘
的 ■ **marginality** noun **marginally**
adverb.

marginalize or **marginalise** /
ˈmɑːdʒɪnəlaɪz/ **verb** (**marginalizes,
marginalizing, marginalized**)
reduce the power or importance of
使边缘化;排斥 ■ **marginalization**
noun.

marigold /ˈmærɪɡəʊld/ **noun** a plant
of the daisy family with yellow or
orange flowers 万寿菊;金盏花

marijuana /ˌmærəˈwɑːnə/ **noun**
cannabis 大麻

marina /məˈriːnə/ **noun** a purpose-
built harbour with moorings for
yachts and small boats (供游艇及小
船停泊的)码头,船坞

marinade noun /ˌmærɪˈneɪd/ a
mixture of ingredients in which food
is soaked before cooking to flavour
or soften it (给食物增加风味或使
其软化的)腌泡汁 • **verb** /ˈmærɪneɪd/
(**marinades, marinading,
marinaded**) = MARINATE.

marinate /ˈmærɪneɪt/ **verb** (**marinates,
marinating, marinated**) soak food
in a marinade 腌泡,浸泡(食物)

marine /məˈriːn/ **adjective 1** relating
to the sea (洋)**2** relating to
shipping or matters concerning a
navy 海运(或航海)的;船舰的 • **noun**
a soldier trained to serve on land or

sea 海军陆战队士兵

mariner /'mærɪnə(r)/ **noun** literary 【文】 a sailor 海员；水手

marionette /ˌmæriə'net/ **noun** a puppet worked by strings 牵线木偶

marital /'mærɪtl/ **adjective** having to do with marriage 婚姻的

maritime /'mærɪtaɪm/ **adjective 1** relating to shipping or other activity taking place at sea 船舶的；海上的；航海的；海事的 **2** living or found in or near the sea 滨海居住的；近海的 **3** (of a climate) moist and having a mild temperature due to the influence of the sea (气候)海洋性的，暖湿的

marjoram /'mɑːdʒərəm/ **noun 1** a sweet-smelling plant of the mint family, used as a herb in cooking 牛至；墨角兰 **2** = OREGANO.

mark¹ /mɑːk/ **noun 1** a small area on a surface having a different colour from its surroundings 痕迹，斑点，污迹 **2** something that indicates position or acts as a pointer 标志；标记 **3** a line, figure, or symbol made to identify or record something 符号；记号 **4** a sign of a quality or feeling (品质或感情的)迹象，标志 **5** a characteristic feature of something 特征，特点 **6** a point awarded for a correct answer or for a piece of work 分数；评价 **7** a particular model of a vehicle or machine (车辆、机器的)型，型号 • **verb 1** make a mark on 在…上作记号；留痕迹于 **2** write a word or symbol on an object in order to identify it 标明，标示 **3** indicate the position of 标示…的位置 **4** (mark someone/thing out) show someone or something to be different or special 区分；区别 **5** do something to celebrate or remember a significant event 庆祝，纪念(重要事件) **6** (mark something up or down) increase or reduce the price of an item 提高(或降低)价格 **7** assess and give a mark

to a piece of work 给…评等级；给…打分 **8** pay careful attention to 注意，留心 **9** Brit.【英】(in team games) stay close to an opponent in order to prevent them getting or passing the ball (在集体比赛中)盯住(对方球员) □ **mark time 1** fill in time with routine activities 消极怠工 **2** (of troops) march on the spot without moving forward (部队)原地踏步 on **your marks** be ready to start (used to instruct competitors in a race) 各就各位(用于赛跑口令) up to the **mark** up to the required standard 达到要求，符合标准

mark² **noun** the former basic unit of money in Germany 马克(德国以前的基本货币单位)

marked /mɑːkt/ **adjective 1** having an identifying mark 打上标记的；有记号的 **2** clearly noticeable 明显的；显著的 **3** singled out as a target for attack 被列为袭击对象的 ■ **markedly** adverb.

marker /'mɑːkə(r)/ **noun 1** an object used to indicate a position, place, or route (位置、地点或线路的)标记，示物 **2** a felt-tip pen with a broad tip 记号笔 **3** (in team games) a player who marks an opponent (集体比赛中的)盯防队员

market /'mɑːkɪt/ **noun 1** a regular gathering for the buying and selling of food, livestock, or other goods 集市 **2** an outdoor space or large hall where traders offer their goods for sale 市场 **3** a particular area of trade or competitive activity 交易市场；商业区 **4** demand for a particular product or service (产品或服务的)销路，市场 • **verb** (markets, marketing, marketed) advertise or promote a product 宣传推销；促销 □ **market garden** a place where vegetables and fruit are grown to be sold (种植蔬菜和水果供出售的)商品果蔬园 **market research**

the gathering of information about what people choose to buy 市场调研 **market town** a medium-sized town where a regular market is held 集镇(定期举行集市贸易的中等城镇) **market value** the amount for which something can be sold 市场价值;市值 **on the market** available for sale 在出售;可买到 ■ **marketable** adjective.

marketing /'mɑːkɪtɪŋ/ **noun** the promoting and selling of products or services 市场营销

marketplace /'mɑːkɪtpleɪs/ **noun 1** an open space where a market is held 市场 **2** the world of trade and commerce 贸易市场;商业界

marking /'mɑːkɪŋ/ **noun 1** an identification mark 标识;记号 **2** (also **markings**) a pattern of marks on an animal's fur, feathers, or skin (动物毛皮、羽毛或皮肤上的)斑纹,斑点

marksman /'mɑːksmən/ **noun** (plural **marksmen**) a person skilled in shooting 神射手;射击能手 ■ **marksmanship** noun.

markup /'mɑːkʌp/ **noun** the difference between the basic cost of producing something and the amount it is sold for 加价;标高售价

marl¹ /mɑːl/ **noun** a rock or soil consisting of clay and lime 泥灰岩;泥灰土

marl² **noun** a type of yarn or fabric with differently coloured threads 夹花纱线织物

marmalade /'mɑːməleɪd/ **noun** a thick spread made from oranges 橘子果酱

marmoreal /mɑː'mɔːrɪəl/ **adjective** literary 【文】 made of or resembling marble 大理石的;似大理石的

marmoset /'mɑːməzet/ **noun** a small tropical American monkey with a long tail 狨(产于美洲热带地区的小型长尾猴)

marmot /'mɑːmət/ **noun** a heavily built burrowing rodent 旱獭;土拨鼠

maroon¹ /mə'ruːn/ **noun** a dark brownish-red colour 栗色;褐红色

maroon² **verb** (**be marooned**) be abandoned or isolated in a place which cannot be reached 被放逐到偏远地方;陷入孤立无援境地

marque /mɑːk/ **noun** a make of car, as distinct from a specific model (汽车的)型号,牌子

marquee /mɑː'kiː/ **noun 1** chiefly Brit. 【主英】 a large tent used for special events (用于特别活动的)大帐篷,大营帐 **2** N. Amer. 【北美】 a roof-like canopy over the entrance to a building (建筑物入口处的)门罩

marquess /'mɑːkwɪs/ **noun** a British nobleman ranking above an earl and below a duke (英国的)侯爵

marquetry /'mɑːkɪtrɪ/ **noun** patterns or pictures made from small pieces of coloured wood inlaid into a surface, used to decorate furniture 镶嵌细工,镶嵌艺术(以著色小木片镶制,用于装饰家具)

marquis /'mɑːkwɪs/ **noun** (in some European countries) a nobleman ranking above a count and below a duke (某些欧洲国家的)侯爵

marquise /mɑː'kiːz/ **noun** the wife or widow of a marquis, or a woman holding the rank of marquis in her own right 侯爵夫人;女侯爵

marriage /'mærɪdʒ/ **noun 1** the formal union of a man and woman, by which they become husband and wife 婚姻 **2** the relationship between a husband and wife 婚姻关系 ■ **marriageable** adjective.

marrow /'mærəʊ/ **noun 1** Brit. 【英】 a long vegetable with a green skin and white flesh 西葫芦;食用葫芦 **2** (also **bone marrow**) a soft fatty substance inside bones, in which blood cells are produced 骨髓

marrowbone /'mærəʊbəʊn/ **noun** a bone containing edible bone marrow (含可食用骨髓的)髓骨

marry /'mæri/ **verb** (**marries**, **marrying**, **married**) **1** become the husband or wife of 结婚；娶；嫁 **2** join two people in marriage 使成婚 **3** join two things together 使结合

Mars /mɑːz/ **noun** the fourth planet from the sun in the solar system and the nearest to the earth 火星

marsh /mɑːʃ/ **noun** an area of low-lying land which usually remains waterlogged 沼泽；湿地 ■ **marshy** adjective.

marshal /'mɑːʃl/ **noun 1** an officer of the highest rank in the armed forces of some countries (某些国家武装力量的)最高指挥官；元帅 **2** (in the US) a type of law enforcement officer (美国的)司法官员 **3** an official responsible for supervising public events (主持公众活动的)典礼官，司仪 • **verb** (**marshals**, **marshalling**, **marshalled**; US spelling 【美拼作】 **marshals**, **marshaling**, **marshaled**) **1** assemble a group of people in order 集结，整顿安排(一群人) **2** bring facts together in an organized way 整理

marshmallow /mɑː'ʃmæləʊ/ **noun** a spongy sweet made from sugar, egg white, and gelatin 软糖(由糖、蛋白和凝胶混合制成)

marsupial /mɑː'suːpiəl/ **noun** a mammal whose young are carried and suckled in a pouch on the mother's belly 有袋动物(将幼畜带在母畜腹部袋中哺乳的动物)

mart /mɑːt/ **noun 1** N. Amer. 【北美】 a shop 商店 **2** a trade centre or market 贸易中心；集市

marten /'mɑːtɪn/ **noun** a forest animal resembling a weasel 貂(形似鼬鼠的森林动物)

martial /'mɑːʃl/ **adjective** having to do with war 战争的 □ **martial arts** sports which started as forms of self-defence or attack, such as judo and karate 武术(如柔道和空手道) **martial law** government by the military

forces of a country 军事管制；戒严

Martian /'mɑːʃn/ **noun** a supposed inhabitant of the planet Mars (假想的)火星人，火星生物 • **adjective** relating to Mars 火星的

martin /'mɑːtɪn/ **noun** a small short-tailed swallow 圣马丁鸟，紫崖燕(一种小型短尾燕)

martinet /mɑːtɪ'net/ **noun** a person who is very strict and insists on being obeyed 严格执行纪律者

martyr /'mɑːtə(r)/ **noun 1** a person who is killed because of their beliefs 殉教者；殉道者；烈士 **2** a person who exaggerates their difficulties in order to obtain sympathy or admiration 夸大困难以博取同情或赞赏的乞怜者，假圣人 • **verb** make a martyr of 使殉难；使殉道 ■ **martyrdom** noun.

marvel /'mɑːvl/ **verb** (**marvels**, **marvelling**, **marvelled**; US spelling 【美拼作】 **marvels**, **marveling**, **marveled**) be filled with wonder 感到惊讶 • **noun** a person or thing that causes a feeling of wonder 非凡的人；令人惊奇之物

marvellous /'mɑːvələs/ (US spelling 【美拼作】 **marvelous**) **adjective** wonderful; very good 极好的；极妙的；了不起的 ■ **marvellously** adverb.

Marxism /'mɑːksɪzəm/ **noun** the political and economic theories of Karl Marx and Friedrich Engels, which formed the basis for communism 马克思主义 ■ **Marxist** noun & adjective.

marzipan /'mɑːzɪpæn/ **noun** a sweet paste of ground almonds, sugar, and egg whites 杏仁蛋白软糖

mascara /mæ'skɑːrə/ **noun** a cosmetic for darkening the eyelashes 睫毛膏

mascot /'mæskət/ **noun** a person, animal, or object that is supposed to bring good luck 福星；吉祥动物；吉祥物

masculine /'mæskjəlɪn/ **adjective 1** relating to men 男性的；男子的 **2** having the qualities or appearance traditionally associated with men 有男子特征的; 男子气概的 **3** Grammar 【语法】 referring to a gender of nouns and adjectives seen as male (名词和形容词)阳性的 ■ **masculinity** noun.

mash /mæʃ/ **verb** crush or beat something into a soft mass 将…捣成泥状; 捣烂; 捣碎 • **noun 1** a soft mass made by crushing a substance 糊状物 **2** Brit. informal 【英,非正式】 boiled and mashed potatoes 土豆泥

mask /mɑːsk/ **noun 1** a covering for all or part of the face, worn for protection, as a disguise, or for theatrical effect 脸部遮盖物; 面具; 面罩 **2** a likeness of a person's face moulded in clay or wax 面模 • **verb 1 (masked)** wearing a mask 戴面具的 **2** conceal or disguise 隐瞒; 掩饰; 掩盖

masochism /ˈmæsəkɪzəm/ noun enjoyment felt in being hurt or humiliated by someone 受虐狂 ■ **masochist** noun **masochistic** adjective.

mason /ˈmeɪsn/ **noun 1** a person who works with stone 石匠; 石工 **2 (Mason)** a Freemason 石工工会会员; 共济会会员

Masonic /məˈsɒnɪk/ **adjective** relating to Freemasons 石工工会会员的; 共济会会员的

masonry /ˈmeɪsənri/ **noun** the parts of a building that are made of stone 石建筑

masque /mɑːsk/ **noun** (in the past) a form of entertainment consisting of dancing and acting performed by masked players (旧时的)假面剧

masquerade /ˌmæskəˈreɪd/ **noun 1** a pretence 假装; 掩饰 **2** a ball at which people wear masks 假面舞会; 化装舞会 • **verb (masquerades, masquerading, masqueraded)** pretend to be someone or something else 假扮; 假冒

Mass /mæs/ **noun 1** the Christian service of the Eucharist or Holy Communion 弥撒(基督教的圣餐仪式) **2** a musical setting of parts of this service 弥撒曲

mass /mæs/ **noun 1** an amount of matter with no definite shape (物质的)团, 块 **2** a large number of people or objects gathered together 大量, 众多(指聚集的人或物) **3 (the masses)** the ordinary people 群众; 平民 **4 (a mass of)** a large amount of 大量的 **5** Physics 【物理】 the quantity of matter which something contains 质量 • **verb** gather together in a mass 集中; 聚集 □ **mass-market** (of goods) produced in large quantities and appealing to a large number of people (货物)销量大的, 畅销的 **mass-produce** produce goods in large quantities in a factory (工厂)大规模生产, 大批量生产

massacre /ˈmæsəkə(r)/ **noun** a brutal killing of a large number of people 大屠杀; 残杀 • **verb (massacres, massacring, massacred)** brutally kill a large number of people 屠杀, 杀戮(大批民众)

massage /ˈmæsɑːʒ/ **noun** the rubbing and kneading of parts of the body with the hands to relieve tension or pain 按摩术; 推拿法 • **verb (massages, massaging, massaged) 1** give a massage to 给…按摩 **2** alter facts or figures to make them seem better than they really are 美化(事实); 虚报(数字)使能过关 □ **massage parlour 1** a place where massage is provided 按摩院 **2** a brothel 妓院

masseur /mæˈsɜː(r)/ **noun (feminine 【阴性】 masseuse** /mæˈsɜːz/) a person who gives massages professionally 职业按摩师

massif /mæˈsiːf/ **noun** a compact group of mountains 山峦; 群山

massive /ˈmæsɪv/ **adjective 1** large and heavy or solid 大而重的; 厚实的 **2** very large, powerful, or severe 巨大的; 强烈的 ■ **massively** adverb.

mast¹ /mɑːst/ **noun 1** a tall upright post on a boat carrying a sail or sails 船桅 **2** any tall upright post or structure 杆;柱

mast² **noun** nuts and other fruit that has fallen from trees (树上落下的)饲料坚果

mastectomy /mæˈstektəmi/ **noun** (plural **mastectomies**) an operation to remove a breast 乳房切除术

master /ˈmɑːstə(r)/ **noun 1** a man in a position of authority, control, or ownership 有控制权的人;(男)主人 **2** a person skilled in a particular art or activity 能手;师傅 **3** the head of a college or school (学院的)院长;(中小学的)校长 **4** chiefly Brit. 【主英】 a male schoolteacher 男教师 **5** a person who holds a second or further degree 硕士 **6** an original film, recording, or document from which copies can be made (电影胶片的)母版;(录音或录像的)原版;(文件的)原件 • **verb** (**masters, mastering, mastered**) **1** gain great knowledge of or skill in 掌握;精通 **2** gain control of 控制;统治 □ **master key** a key that opens several locks, each of which has its own key 万能钥匙 **master of ceremonies** a person in charge of proceedings at a special event 司仪;典礼官;主持人

masterclass /ˈmɑːstəklɑːs/ **noun** a class given to students by a leading musician 高级音乐讲习班

masterful /ˈmɑːstəfl/ **adjective 1** powerful and able to control other people 好支配人的;善于控制人的 **2** performed or performing very skilfully (表演)熟练的,老练高明的 ■ **masterfully** adverb.

masterly /ˈmɑːstəli/ **adjective** performed or performing very skilfully (表演)精湛的,老练高明的

mastermind /ˈmɑːstəmaɪnd/ **noun** a person who plans and directs a complex scheme or project 出谋划策者 • **verb** plan and direct a complex scheme or project 策划(复杂计划)

masterpiece /ˈmɑːstəpiːs/ **noun** a work of outstanding skill 杰作;名作;最佳作品

mastery /ˈmɑːstəri/ **noun 1** complete knowledge or command of a subject or skill 精通;掌握;熟练 **2** control or superiority 控制;支配

masthead /ˈmɑːsthed/ **noun 1** the highest part of a ship's mast (船只桅杆的)桅顶,桅头 **2** the name of a newspaper or magazine printed at the top of the first page 报刊(或杂志)名称;刊头

mastic /ˈmæstɪk/ **noun 1** a gum from the bark of a Mediterranean tree, used in making varnish and chewing gum 乳香,玛琋脂(用于制作清漆和口香糖) **2** a waterproof substance like putty, used in building 胶黏剂;胶泥

masticate /ˈmæstɪkeɪt/ **verb** (**masticates, masticating, masticated**) chew food 咀嚼(食物) ■ **mastication** noun.

mastiff /ˈmæstɪf/ **noun** a dog of a large, strong breed with drooping ears and lips 獒;大驯犬

mastodon /ˈmæstədɒn/ **noun** a large extinct elephant-like mammal 乳齿象(一种已灭绝的大型哺乳动物)

mastoid /ˈmæstɔɪd/ **noun** a part of the bone behind the ear, which has air spaces linked to the middle ear 乳突

masturbate /ˈmæstəbeɪt/ **verb** (**masturbates, masturbating, masturbated**) stimulate your genitals with your hand for sexual pleasure 手淫;自慰 ■ **masturbation** noun.

mat /mæt/ **noun 1** a thick piece of material placed on the floor, used for decoration or to protect the floor 地垫;地席;蒲席 **2** a piece of springy material for landing on in gymnastics or similar sports (体操等体育项目中用的)垫子,厚软垫 **3** a small piece of material placed on a surface to protect it (保护表面的)护垫 **4** a thick layer of hairy or woolly material 小地毯

matador /'mætədɔ:(r)/ **noun** a bullfighter 斗牛士

match¹ /mætʃ/ **noun 1** an event at which two people or teams compete against each other 比赛 **2** a person or thing that can compete with another as an equal in quality or strength 对手；敌手 **3** an exact equivalent 相配的人(或物) **4** a pair of things which correspond or are very similar 配对物；相同(或相似)的一对 • **verb 1** correspond or fit with something 与…一致；与…相符 **2** be equal to 与…相匹配；与…相称 **3** place a person or team in competition with another 使与…较量 □ **match point** (in sports) a point which if won by one of the players will also win them the match (体育比赛中再赢得一分即能胜出的)决胜分，赛点

match² **noun** a short, thin stick tipped with a substance that ignites when rubbed against a rough surface 火柴

matchbox /'mætʃbɒks/ **noun** a small box in which matches are sold 火柴盒

matchless /'mætʃləs/ **adjective** so good that nothing is an equal 无比的,无对手的,无敌的

matchmaker /'mætʃmeɪkə(r)/ **noun** a person who tries to bring about marriages or relationships between other people 媒人

matchstick /'mætʃstɪk/ **noun** the stem of a match 火柴杆

mate /meɪt/ **noun 1** Brit. informal 【英，非正式】 a friend 伙伴 **2** the sexual partner of an animal (动物的)配偶 **3** an assistant to a skilled worker 助手 • **verb** (**mates, mating, mated**) (of animals or birds) come together for breeding (兽或鸟)交配，交尾

matelot /'mætləʊ/ **noun** Brit. informal

【英，非正式】a sailor 水手；海员

material /mə'tɪəriəl/ **noun 1** the matter from which something is or can be made 原料 **2** items needed for doing or creating something 材料；设备；用具 **3** cloth 布料 • **adjective 1** having to do with physical things rather than the mind or spirit 物质的；有形的 **2** essential or relevant 实质的；关联的 ■ **materially** adverb.

materialism /mə'tɪəriəlɪzəm/ **noun** a strong interest in possessions and physical comfort rather than spiritual values 实利主义；物质主义 ■ **materialist** adjective & noun **materialistic** adjective.

materialize or **materialise** /mə'tɪəriəlaɪz/ **verb** (**materialize, materializing, materialized**) **1** happen 实现；发生 **2** appear suddenly 突然出现

maternal /mə'tɜ:nl/ **adjective 1** having to do with a mother 母亲的；母性的 **2** related through the mother's side of the family 母系的 ■ **maternally** adverb.

maternity /mə'tɜ:nəti/ **noun** motherhood 母性；母亲身份

matey /'meɪti/ **adjective** (**matier, matiest**) Brit. informal 【英，非正式】very friendly 平易近人的；友好的

mathematics /mæθə'mætɪks/ **noun** the branch of science concerned with numbers, quantities, and space 数学 ■ **mathematical** adjective **mathematically** adverb **mathematician** noun.

maths /mæθs/ or N. Amer. 【北美】**math** /mæθ/ **noun** mathematics 数学

matinee /'mætɪneɪ/ **noun** an afternoon performance in a theatre or cinema (剧场或影院的)午后演出，午场

matins /'mætɪnz/ **noun** a Christian service of morning prayer 晨祷

matriarch /'meɪtriɑ:k/ **noun** a woman who is the head of a family or tribe

女家长;女族长

matriarchy /ˈmeɪtrɪɑːki/ **noun** a society led or controlled by women 母系社会 ■ **matriarchal** adjective.

matricide /ˈmætrɪsaɪd/ **noun 1** the killing by someone of their own mother 弑母 **2** a person who kills their mother 弑母者

matriculate /məˈtrɪkjuleɪt/ **verb** (**matriculates, matriculating, matriculated**) enrol or be enrolled at a college or university 录取(或被录取)进学院(或大学) ■ **matriculation** noun.

matrimony /ˈmætrɪməni/ **noun** the state of being married 结婚;已婚 ■ **matrimonial** adjective.

matrix /ˈmeɪtrɪks/ **noun** (plural **matrices** /ˈmeɪtrɪsiːz/ or **matrixes**) **1** an environment or material in which something develops 母体;基质;摇篮;策源地 **2** a mould in which something is cast or shaped 铸模;铸型;模子;型板 **3** a grid-like arrangement of elements 网状物

matron /ˈmeɪtrən/ **noun 1** a woman in charge of medical and living arrangements at a boarding school (寄宿学校的)女舍监 **2** Brit. dated 【英,废】a woman in charge of nursing in a hospital 女护士长 **3** an older married woman 上年纪的已婚妇女 □ **matron of honour** a married woman attending the bride at a wedding (婚礼上的)已婚女傧相 ■ **matronly** adjective.

matt or **matte** /mæt/ **adjective** not shiny 无光泽的;暗淡的

matted /ˈmætɪd/ **adjective** (of hair or fur) tangled into a thick mass (头发或毛发)缠结在一起的,乱成一团的

matter /ˈmætə(r)/ **noun 1** physical substance or material 物质 **2** a subject or situation to be considered or dealt with 课题;事情 **3** (**the matter**) the reason for a problem 毛病;差错 • **verb** (**matters, mattering, mattered**) be

important 重要;要紧 □ **matter-of-fact** unemotional and practical 不带感情的;实事求是的

mattock /ˈmætək/ **noun** a farming tool similar to a pickaxe 鹤嘴锄

mattress /ˈmætrəs/ **noun** a fabric case filled with soft or firm material and sometimes incorporating springs, used for sleeping on 床垫;褥垫

mature /məˈtʃʊə(r)/ **adjective 1** fully grown (发育)成熟的,成年的 **2** like a sensible adult (像成人一样)明白事理的,明智的 **3** (of certain foods or drinks) developed over a long period in order to achieve a full flavour (某些食物或饮料)成熟的,酿熟的 • **verb** (**matures, maturing, matured**) **1** become mature 变成熟 **2** (of an insurance policy) reach the end of its term and so become payable (保险单)到期 ■ **maturation** noun **maturely** adverb.

maturity /məˈtʃʊərəti/ **noun 1** the state or period of being mature 成熟;成熟期 **2** the time when an insurance policy matures (保险单的)到期日

maudlin /ˈmɔːdlɪn/ **adjective** sentimental in a self-pitying way 伤感的;自我怜悯的

maul /mɔːl/ **verb 1** wound by scratching and tearing 抓伤;撕伤 **2** treat roughly 粗暴对待

maunder /ˈmɔːndə(r)/ **verb** (**maunders, maundering, maundered**) move, talk, or act in a rambling way 闲逛;胡说;随意行事

mausoleum /ˌmɔːsəˈliːəm/ **noun** (plural **mausolea** /ˌmɔːsəˈliːə/ or **mausoleums**) a building containing a tomb or tombs 陵墓

mauve /məʊv/ **noun** a pale or reddish-purple colour 淡紫色

maverick /ˈmævərɪk/ **noun** an unconventional and independent-minded person 思想与众不同者;有独立见解者

maw /mɔː/ **noun** the jaws or throat 腭;

咽喉

mawkish /'mɔːkɪʃ/ **adjective** foolishly sentimental 多愁善感的；无病呻吟的

max /mæks/ **abbreviation** maximum.

maxim /'mæksɪm/ **noun** a short statement expressing a general truth or rule of behaviour 箴言；格言；座右铭

maximize or **maximise** /'mæksɪmaɪz/ **verb** (**maximizes, maximizing, maximized**) **1** make something as large or great as possible 使达到最大限度地利用 **2** make the best use of 最大限度地利用

maximum /'mæksɪməm/ **noun** (plural **maxima** or **maximums**) the greatest amount, size, or strength that is possible or that has been gained 最大数量；最大规格；最大力量 • **adjective** greatest in amount, size, or strength 最大数量的；最大规格的；最大力量的 ■ **maximal** adjective.

May /meɪ/ **noun 1** the fifth month of the year 五月 **2** (**may**) the hawthorn or its blossom 山楂属植物；山楂花

may /meɪ/ **modal verb** (3rd singular present **may**; past **might**) **1** expressing possibility 可能；也许 **2** expressing permission 可以 **3** expressing a wish or hope 祝愿

maybe /'meɪbi/ **adverb** perhaps 可能

Mayday /'meɪdeɪ/ **noun** an international distress signal used by ships and aircraft (船只和飞机用的)无线电求救信号

mayfly /'meɪflaɪ/ **noun** (plural **mayflies**) an insect which lives as an adult for only a very short time 蜉蝣

mayhem /'meɪhem/ **noun** violent disorder 动乱；大混乱

mayn't /meɪnt/ **short form** may not.

mayonnaise /ˌmeɪə'neɪz/ **noun** a creamy dressing made from egg yolks, oil, and vinegar 蛋黄酱

mayor /meə(r)/ **noun** the elected head of a city or borough council 市长 ■ **mayoral** adjective.

mayoralty /'meərəlti/ **noun** (plural

mayoralties) the period of office of a mayor 市长任期

mayoress /meə'res/ **noun 1** the wife of a mayor 市长夫人 **2** a woman elected as mayor 女市长

maypole /'meɪpəʊl/ **noun** a decorated pole with long ribbons attached to the top, traditionally used for dancing round on the first day of May 五月柱(按照传统习俗，人们在五朔节围着它跳舞)

maze /meɪz/ **noun** a complicated network of paths and walls or hedges designed as a challenge to find a way through 迷宫；迷魂阵

mazurka /mə'zɜːkə/ **noun** a lively Polish dance 玛祖卡舞(一种活泼的波兰舞蹈)

MBA /ˌem biː 'eɪ/ **abbreviation** Master of Business Administration 工商管理硕士

MBE /ˌem biː 'iː/ **abbreviation** Member of the Order of the British Empire 英帝国勋章获得者

MC /ˌem 'siː/ **abbreviation 1** master of ceremonies 司仪；典礼官 **2** Military Cross 军功十字勋章

MD /ˌem 'diː/ **abbreviation 1** Doctor of Medicine 医学博士 **2** Brit. 【英】 Managing Director 总经理；总裁

ME /ˌem 'iː/ **abbreviation** myalgic encephalomyelitis, a medical condition causing aching and prolonged tiredness 肌痛性脑脊髓炎

me /miː, mi/ **pronoun** used as the object of a verb or preposition or after 'than', 'as', or the verb 'to be', to refer to the speaker himself or herself 我(用作动词或介词的宾语，或用于 than、as 或 be 动词之后，指说话者自己)

! 注意 it is wrong to use *me* as the subject of a verb, as in *John and me went to the shops*; in this case use *I* instead. me 不可用作动词主语，如：John and me went to the shops (约翰和我去逛了商店)中 me 应改作 I。

M

mead /miːd/ **noun** an alcoholic drink made from fermented honey and water 蜂蜜酒

meadow /'medəʊ/ **noun** an area of grassland 草地；牧场

meagre /'miːgə(r)/ (US spelling 【美拼作】**meager**) **adjective** small in quantity and of bad quality 贫乏的；不足的；劣质的 ■ **meagreness** noun.

meal¹ /miːl/ **noun 1** any of the regular daily occasions when food is eaten 进餐；一顿饭 **2** the food eaten on such an occasion 一餐所吃的食物

meal² **noun** the edible part of any grain or pulse ground to powder (谷物或豆类磨成的)粗粉 ■ **mealy** adjective.

mealy-mouthed /ˌmiːli'maʊðd/ **adjective** not wanting to speak honestly or frankly 不直率的；说话拐弯抹角的

mean¹ /miːn/ **verb** (**means, meaning, meant**) **1** intend to say or show something 意谓；意思是说 **2** (of a word) have as its explanation (in the same language) or its equivalent in another language (词语)表示…的意思，作…解 **3** intend something to happen or be the case 意欲；打算 **4** have something as a result 引起；导致；造成 **5** intend something for a particular purpose 企图 **6** have a particular level of importance 具有重要性：*Animals mean more to him than people.* 动物对他来说比人更重要。

mean² **adjective 1** unwilling to give or share things 吝啬的；小气的；不大方的 **2** unkind or unfair 不善良的；不公平的 **3** N. Amer.【北美】vicious or aggressive 刻毒的；恶意的 **4** (of a place) poor and dirty in appearance (场所)破旧的，简陋的 ■ **meanly** adverb **meanness** noun.

mean³ **noun 1** the average value of a set of quantities 平均值；平均数 **2** something in the middle of two extremes 中间；中庸 • **adjective 1** calculated as a mean 以中项计算的 **2** equally far from two extremes 中间的；中庸的

meander /mi'ændə(r)/ **verb** (**meanders, meandering, meandered**) **1** follow a winding course 蜿蜒；迂回曲折地前进 **2** wander in a leisurely way 漫步；闲逛 • **noun** a winding bend of a river or road 曲流；河流；曲径

meaning /'miːnɪŋ/ **noun 1** the thing or idea that a word, signal, or action represents (词语、信号或行动的)意思，含义 **2** a sense of purpose 意图；用意

meaningful /'miːnɪŋfl/ **adjective 1** having meaning 有意义的 **2** worthwhile 值得的 **3** expressive 富有意味的 ■ **meaningfully** adverb.

meaningless /'miːnɪŋləs/ **adjective** having no meaning or significance 无意义的；不重要的 ■ **meaninglessly** adverb.

means /miːnz/ **noun 1** a thing or method used to achieve a result 工具；方法；手段 **2** money or wealth 钱财；财富 □ **by all means** of course 当然可以 **by no means** certainly not 一点也不；决不 **means test** an official investigation into how much money or income a person has, to find out whether they qualify for welfare benefits 经济状况调查(用以确定是否给予福利救济金)

meant /ment/ past and past participle of MEAN¹.

meantime /'miːntaɪm/ **adverb** (**in the meantime**) meanwhile 同时

meanwhile /'miːnwaɪl/ **adverb 1** in the period of time between two events 间隔地 **2** at the same time 同时

measles /'miːzlz/ **noun** an infectious disease causing fever and a red rash 麻疹；风疹

measly /'miːzli/ **adjective** informal

【非正式】 ridiculously small or few 微不足道的；少得可怜的

measure /'meʒə(r)/ **verb (measures, measuring, measured) 1** find out what the size, amount, or degree of something is in standard units 量；测量；计量 **2** be of a particular size, amount, or degree 有…(大小、数量或程度) **3 (measure something out)** take an exact quantity of 量出；量取…的确切数量 **4 (measure up)** reach the required standard 合格；达到标准 ■ **noun 1** a course of action taken to achieve a purpose (达到目的的)措施，手段 **2** a proposal for a new law 议案 **3** a standard unit used to express size, amount, or degree 计量单位；度量单位 **4** a measuring device marked with such units 计量仪器；度量器具 **5 (a measure of)** an indication of the extent or quality of …的程度；…的质量 □ **for good** measure as an amount or item that is additional to what is strictly necessary 作为额外的量，作为外加的东西 **have the measure of** understand the character of 估量…的品质 ■ **measurable** adjective **measurably** adverb.

measured /'meʒəd/ **adjective 1** slow and regular in rhythm 节奏缓慢整齐的 **2** carefully considered 仔细考虑的，几经斟酌的

measurement /'meʒəmənt/ **noun 1** the action of measuring 测量；丈量；度量 **2** an amount, size, or extent found by measuring (量得的)数量，尺寸，面积

meat /miːt/ **noun** the flesh of an animal used as food (供食用动物的)肉

meatball /'miːtbɔːl/ **noun** a ball of minced or chopped meat 肉丸

meaty /'miːti/ **adjective (meatier, meatiest) 1** full of meat 多肉的 **2** fleshy or muscular 肉鼓鼓的；强壮的 **3** substantial or challenging 内容充实的；有挑战性的

Mecca /'mekə/ **noun 1** the holiest city for Muslims, in Saudi Arabia 麦加 (沙特阿拉伯一城市，伊斯兰信徒心目中的圣地) **2** a place which attracts many people 热门地方

mechanic /mə'kænɪk/ **noun** a skilled worker who repairs and maintains machinery 机械工；技工；机修工

mechanical /mə'kænɪkl/ **adjective 1** relating to or operated by a machine or machinery 机械的；机械操作的 **2** done without thought 机械的；呆板的 **3** relating to physical forces or movement 力学(或物理运动)的 ■ **mechanically** adverb.

mechanics /mə'kænɪks/ **noun 1** the branch of study concerned with the forces producing movement 力学 **2** machinery or working parts 机械；工作部件 **3** the practical aspects of something 方法；技巧

mechanism /'mekənɪzəm/ **noun 1** a piece of machinery 机械装置；机件 **2** the way in which something works or is made to happen 工作方式；运行机制

mechanize or **mechanise** /'mekənaɪz/ **verb (mechanizes, mechanizing, mechanized)** equip with machines or automatic devices 使机械化；用机械(或自动化装置)装备 ■ **mechanization** noun.

medal /'medl/ **noun** a metal disc with an inscription or design on it, awarded to someone for a special achievement (金属)奖牌，奖章

medallion /mə'dæliən/ **noun 1** a piece of jewellery in the shape of a medal, worn as a pendant (项链上的)奖牌形坠饰 **2** a decorative oval or circular painting, panel, or design 椭圆形装饰；圆形图案

medallist /'medəlɪst/ (US spelling 【美拼作】 **medalist**) **noun** a person who has been awarded a medal 奖牌获得者

meddle /'medl/ **verb (meddles, meddling, meddled)** interfere in something that is not your concern 干预；干涉；管闲事 ■ **meddler** noun.

meddlesome /'medlsəm/ **adjective** fond of interfering in other people's affairs 好干预的；好干涉的；爱管闲事的

media /'miːdiə/ **noun 1** television, radio, and newspapers as providers of information 媒体；传媒 **2** plural of MEDIUM.

> **!注意** the word **media** comes from the Latin plural of **medium**. In its normal sense, 'television, radio, and newspapers', it can be used with either a singular or a plural verb. 单词 media 源自拉丁词 medium 的复数，表示通常的"媒体"这一含义时，可以和单数动词或复数动词连用。

mediaeval /medi'iːvl/ ⟹ 见 MEDIEVAL.

median /'miːdiən/ **adjective** technical 【术语】situated in the middle 中间的；中央的；居中的 • **noun 1** a median value 中位数；中值 **2** Geometry 【几何】a straight line drawn from one of the angles of a triangle to the middle of the opposite side (三角形的)中线

mediate /'miːdieɪt/ **verb (mediates, mediating, mediated)** try to settle a dispute between other people or groups 调解；调停；斡旋 ■ **mediation** noun **mediator** noun.

medic /'medɪk/ **noun** informal【非正式】a doctor or medical student 医生；医科学生

medical /'medɪkl/ **adjective** relating to the science or practice of medicine 医学的；医疗的；医用的 • **noun** an examination to see how healthy someone is 体格检查；体检 ■ **medically** adverb.

medicament /mə'dɪkəmənt/ **noun** a medicine 药物；药品

medicate /'medɪkeɪt/ **verb (medicates, medicating, medicated) 1** give medicine or a drug to 给…服药 **2**

(**medicated**) containing a substance that has healing properties 含药物的

medication /medɪ'keɪʃn/ **noun 1** a medicine or drug 药物 **2** treatment with medicines 药物治疗

medicinal /mə'dɪsɪnl/ **adjective 1** having healing properties 药用的；治病的；有疗效的 **2** relating to medicines 药物的 ■ **medicinally** adverb.

medicine /'medsn/ **noun 1** the science or practice of the treatment and prevention of disease 医学；医术 **2** a substance taken by mouth in order to treat or prevent disease (内服的)药，药品 □ **medicine man** a person believed to have supernatural healing powers 巫医

medieval or **mediaeval** /medi'iːvl/ **adjective** relating to the Middle Ages, the period between about 1000 and 1450 中世纪的

medievalist or **mediaevalist** /medi'iːvlɪst/ **noun** a person who studies medieval history or literature 中世纪历史(或文学)学者

mediocre /miːdi'əʊkə(r)/ **adjective** of only average or fairly low quality 普通的；平庸的；不够好的 ■ **mediocrity** noun.

meditate /'medɪteɪt/ **verb (meditates, meditating, meditated) 1** focus your mind and free it of uncontrolled thoughts, as a spiritual exercise or for relaxation 默念；默想 **2** (**meditate on** or **about**) think carefully about 沉思；深思 ■ **meditation** noun **meditative** adjective **meditatively** adverb.

Mediterranean /medɪtə'reɪniən/ **adjective** relating to the Mediterranean Sea or the countries around it 地中海的；地中海沿岸国家的

> ✔ 拼写指南 one **d**, one **t**, double **r**: Me**diterr**anean. Mediterranean 中有一个 d，一个 t 和两个 r。

medium /'miːdiəm/ **noun** (plural **media** or **mediums**) **1** a means by which something is communicated or achieved 媒介；手段 **2** a substance that something lives or exists in, or through which it travels 媒质；媒介物 **3** the type of material used by an artist (艺术家使用的)材料 **4** (plural **mediums**) a person who claims to be able to communicate with the spirits of dead people 灵媒；巫师 **5** the middle state between two extremes 中间；中庸 • **adjective** between two extremes 中间的；中庸的

medlar /'medlə(r)/ **noun** a fruit resembling a small brown apple 欧楂 (形似棕色小苹果)

medley /'medli/ **noun** (plural **medleys**) a varied mixture 混合物；大杂烩

meek /miːk/ **adjective** quiet, gentle, and obedient 温顺的；谦恭的，驯服的 ■ **meekly** adverb.

meerkat /'mɪəkæt/ **noun** a small southern African mongoose (南非的)笔尾獴

meet /miːt/ **verb** (**meets**, **meeting**, **met**) **1** come together with someone at the same place and time 遇见，和…会面 **2** be introduced to or come across someone for the first time 相识，结识 **3** touch or join 相触；连接 **4** come across a situation 经历 (某情形) **5** (**meet with**) receive a particular reaction 得到(某反应) **6** fulfil or satisfy a requirement 满足 (要求) • **noun** a gathering or meeting 聚会；集会

meeting /'miːtɪŋ/ **noun** **1** an occasion when people meet to discuss or decide something 会议；集会 **2** a situation in which people come together 相会；聚集；汇合

mega /'megə/ **adjective** informal 【非正式】 **1** very large 极大的 **2** excellent 优秀的；杰出的

megabyte /'megəbaɪt/ **noun** Computing 【计】 a unit of information equal to one million bytes 兆字节(信息单位，

等于100万字节)

megalith /'megəlɪθ/ **noun** a large stone that forms a prehistoric monument or part of one (史前建造纪念物用的)巨石 ■ **megalithic** adjective.

megalomania /ˌmegələ'meɪniə/ **noun** **1** the false belief that you are very powerful and important 妄自尊大；自大狂 **2** a strong desire for power 权力狂 ■ **megalomaniac** noun & adjective.

megaphone /'megəfəʊn/ **noun** a cone-shaped device for making the voice sound louder 扩音器；喇叭筒；话筒

megapixel /'megəpɪksl/ **noun** a unit for measuring the resolution of a digital image, equal to one million pixels 百万像素(数码图像分辨率单位，等于100万像素)

megaton /'megətʌn/ **noun** a unit for measuring the power of an explosive, equivalent to one million tons of TNT 百万吨级(爆炸能量单位，相当于100万吨梯恩梯炸药)

megawatt /'megəwɒt/ **noun** a unit of power equal to one million watts 兆瓦(功率单位，等于100万瓦)

melamine /'meləmiːn/ **noun** a hard plastic used to coat the surfaces of tables or worktops 蜜胺树脂

melancholia /ˌmelən'kəʊliə/ **noun** great sadness or depression 忧郁症

melancholy /'melənkəli/ **noun** deep and long-lasting sadness 忧郁；伤悲 • **adjective** sad or depressed 忧郁的；忧愁的 ■ **melancholic** adjective.

melanin /'melənɪn/ **noun** a dark pigment in the hair and skin, responsible for the tanning of skin exposed to sunlight 黑色素

melanoma /ˌmelə'nəʊmə/ **noun** a form of skin cancer 黑素瘤(一种皮肤癌)

meld /meld/ **verb** blend 混合

melee /'meleɪ/ **noun** **1** a confused fight or scuffle 混战；混乱 **2** a

M

disorderly crowd of people 混乱的人群

mellifluous /me'lɪfluəs/ **adjective** pleasingly smooth and musical to hear 声音甜美的；悦耳的

mellow /'meləʊ/ **adjective 1** pleasantly smooth or soft in sound, taste, or colour (声音或色彩) 柔和的；(味道) 醇和的 **2** relaxed and good-humoured 轻松随和的；愉快的 • **verb** make or become mellow (使) 变得柔和；(使) 变得醇和；(使) 变得轻松愉快

melodic /mə'lɒdɪk/ **adjective 1** relating to melody 旋律的 **2** sounding pleasant 优美动听的 ■ **melodically** adverb.

melodious /mə'ləʊdɪəs/ **adjective** tuneful 旋律优美的；悦耳的

melodrama /'melədrɑːmə/ **noun 1** a play full of exciting events, in which the characters seem too exaggerated to be realistic 传奇剧；情节剧 **2** behaviour or events that are very dramatic 夸张的行为；戏剧性事件

melodramatic /melədrə'mætɪk/ **adjective** too dramatic and exaggerated 过于戏剧性的；过于夸张的 ■ **melodramatically** adverb.

melody /'melədɪ/ **noun** (plural **melodies**) **1** a piece of music with a clear or simple tune 旋律；曲调 **2** the main tune in a piece of music 主调；主旋律

melon /'melən/ **noun** a large round fruit with sweet pulpy flesh 瓜

melt /melt/ **verb 1** make or become liquid by heating (使) 融化；(使) 熔化 **2** (**melt away**) gradually disappear 逐渐消失 **3** become more tender or loving 心软，变得温柔 □ **melting pot** a place where different peoples, ideas, or styles are mixed together 大熔炉 (不同民族、想法或风格等相互交融的地方)

meltdown /'meltdaʊn/ **noun** an accident in a nuclear reactor in which the fuel overheats and melts the reactor core (核反应堆堆芯的) 熔毁

member /'membə(r)/ **noun 1** a person or organization belonging to a group or society 会员；成员 **2** old use 【旧】 a part of the body 身体部位 ■ **membership** noun.

membrane /'membreɪn/ **noun 1** a skin-like tissue that connects, covers, or lines cells or parts of the body 细胞膜；膜 **2** a layer of thin, skin-like material 膜状物 ■ **membranous** adjective.

memento /mə'mentəʊ/ **noun** (plural **mementos** or **mementoes**) an object kept as a reminder 纪念品；引人联想的事物

memo /'meməʊ/ **noun** (plural **memos**) a written note sent from one person to another within an organization 备忘录

memoir /'memwɑː(r)/ **noun 1** a historical account or biography written from personal knowledge 回忆录；传记 **2** (**memoirs**) an account written by a public figure of their life and experiences (公众人物的) 自传

memorabilia /memərə'bɪliə/ **plural noun** objects kept or collected because of their associations with people or events (与值得纪念的人或事件有关的) 纪念品

memorable /'memərəbl/ **adjective** worth remembering or easily remembered 值得纪念的；难忘的 ■ **memorably** adverb.

memorandum /memə'rændəm/ **noun** (plural **memoranda** or **memorandums**) **1** formal 【正式】 a memo 备忘录 **2** a note recording something for future use 备忘便条

memorial /mə'mɔːriəl/ **noun** a column or other structure made or built in memory of a person or event 纪念物；纪念碑；纪念馆 • **adjective** created or done in memory of someone 纪念某人的；纪念性的

memorize or **memorise** /'meməraɪz/ **verb** (**memorizes**,

memorizing, memorized) learn and remember exactly 记住

memory /ˈmeməri/ **noun** (plural **memories**) **1** the power that the mind has to store and remember information 记忆力 **2** a thing remembered 记忆中的事物 **3** the length of time over which you can remember things 记忆范围;记忆所及年限 **4** a computer's equipment or capacity for storing data (计算机的)存储器,内存

men /men/ plural of MAN.

menace /ˈmenəs/ **noun 1** a dangerous or troublesome person or thing 危险的人(或事物);令人讨厌的人(或事物) **2** a threatening quality 威胁性 • **verb** (**menaces, menacing, menaced**) threaten 威胁;威吓

ménage à trois /ˌmeɪnɑːʒ ɑː ˈtrwɑː/ **noun** an arrangement in which a married couple and the lover of one of them live together 三角家庭(一对夫妇与其中一方的情人住在一起)

menagerie /məˈnædʒəri/ **noun** a small zoo (小型)动物园

mend /mend/ **verb 1** restore something so that it is no longer broken, torn, or out of action 修理;修补 **2** improve an unpleasant situation 改善;改进 • **noun** a repair 修理;修补

mendacious /menˈdeɪʃəs/ **adjective** untruthful; lying 不真实的;虚假的 ■ **mendacity** noun.

mendicant /ˈmendɪkənt/ **adjective 1** living by begging 行乞的 **2** (of a religious order) originally dependent on charitable donations (修道会)化缘的,依赖捐助生存的 • **noun 1** a beggar 乞丐 **2** a member of a mendicant religious order 托钵僧

menhir /ˈmenhɪə(r)/ **noun** a tall upright prehistoric stone erected as a monument (史前的)竖石纪念物,巨石

menial /ˈmiːniəl/ **adjective** (of work) needing little skill and lacking status (工作)对技术要求低的,卑下的 • **noun**

a person with a menial job 做卑下工作的人

meningitis /ˌmenɪnˈdʒaɪtɪs/ **noun** an infectious disease in which the membranes enclosing the brain and spinal cord become inflamed 脑(脊)膜炎

meniscus /məˈnɪskəs/ **noun** (plural **menisci** /məˈnɪsaɪ/) **1** the curved upper surface of a liquid in a tube 弯(月)液面 **2** a thin lens curving outwards on one side and inwards on the other 弯月形透镜;凹凸透镜

menopause /ˈmenəpɔːz/ **noun** the time when a woman gradually stops having menstrual periods, on average around the age of 50 绝经期;更年期 ■ **menopausal** adjective.

menorah /mɪˈnɔːrə/ **noun** a large candlestick with several branches, used in Jewish worship (犹太教礼拜仪式中用的)大烛台

menstrual /ˈmenstruəl/ **adjective** having to do with menstruation 月经的;行经的;月经来潮的

menstruate /ˈmenstrueɪt/ **verb** (**menstruates, menstruating, menstruated**) (of a woman) have a flow of blood from the lining of the womb each month (女性)行经,月经来潮 ■ **menstruation** noun.

mental /ˈmentl/ **adjective 1** having to do with the mind 精神的;心理的;思想上的;脑力的 **2** relating to disorders of the mind 精神不正常的 **3** informal【非正式】mad 发疯的 ■ **mentally** adverb.

mentality /menˈtæləti/ **noun** (plural **mentalities**) a characteristic way of thinking 心态;心性;思想方法

menthol /ˈmenθɒl/ **noun** a substance found in peppermint oil, used in medicines and as a flavouring 薄荷醇 ■ **mentholated** adjective.

mention /ˈmenʃn/ **verb** refer to something or someone briefly 提及;说起 • **noun 1** a brief reference to someone or something 提及；说起 **2** a formal acknowledgement that someone has done something well 提名表扬

mentor /ˈmentɔː(r)/ *noun* an experienced person who advises you over a period of time 导师；指导者；顾问

menu /ˈmenjuː/ *noun* **1** a list of dishes available in a restaurant 菜单 **2** the food to be served in a restaurant or at a meal (端上来的)菜肴，饭菜 **3** Computing 【计】 a list of commands or facilities displayed on screen (屏幕上的)指令选择单，菜单

meow /miːˈaʊ/ ⇒ 见 MIAOW.

MEP /ˌem iː ˈpiː/ *abbreviation* Member of the European Parliament 欧洲议会议员

mercantile /ˈmɜːkəntaɪl/ *adjective* relating to trade or commerce 贸易的；商业的

mercenary /ˈmɜːsənəri/ *adjective* wanting to do only things that make you money 以金钱为目的的；唯利是图的 • *noun* (plural **mercenaries**) a professional soldier who is hired to serve in a foreign army 外国雇佣兵

merchandise /ˈmɜːtʃəndaɪs/ *noun* goods for sale 商品；货物

merchant /ˈmɜːtʃənt/ *noun* a trader who sells goods in large quantities 商人；(大宗货物的)批发商 • *adjective* (of ships, sailors, or shipping activity) involved with commerce (船只、船员或船运)与商业有关的 □ **merchant bank** a bank whose customers are large businesses 商业银行 **merchant navy** a country's commercial shipping (一国的)全部商船，商船队

merchantable /ˈmɜːtʃəntəbl/ *adjective* suitable for sale 适销的；有销路的

merciful /ˈmɜːsɪfl/ *adjective* **1** showing mercy 慈悲的；仁慈的 **2** giving relief from suffering 结束痛苦的 ■ **mercifully** *adverb*.

merciless /ˈmɜːsɪləs/ *adjective* showing no mercy 无情的；冷酷的

■ **mercilessly** *adverb*.

mercurial /mɜːˈkjʊəriəl/ *adjective* **1** tending to change mood suddenly 情绪多变的；反复无常的 **2** having to do with the element mercury 汞的；水银的

mercury /ˈmɜːkjəri/ *noun* **1** a heavy silvery-white liquid metallic element used in some thermometers and barometers (金属元素)汞，水银 **2** (**Mercury**) the planet closest to the sun in the solar system 水星

mercy /ˈmɜːsi/ *noun* (plural **mercies**) **1** kindness or forgiveness shown towards someone who is in your power 仁慈；慈悲；宽恕 **2** something to be grateful for 恩惠；幸运 □ **at the mercy of** in the power of 受…的支配

mere /mɪə(r)/ *adjective* **1** being no more than what is stated or described 仅仅的；只不过的 **2** (**the merest**) the smallest or slightest 极少的；微不足道的

merely /ˈmɪəli/ *adverb* only 仅仅

meretricious /ˌmerəˈtrɪʃəs/ *adjective* superficially attractive but having no real value 华而不实的；金玉其外的

merge /mɜːdʒ/ *verb* (**merges**, **merging**, **merged**) **1** combine or be combined into a whole (使)合并 **2** blend gradually into something else 渐渐合为一体；融合

merger /ˈmɜːdʒə(r)/ *noun* a merging of two organizations into one (机构的)合并

meridian /məˈrɪdiən/ *noun* a circle passing at the same longitude through a given place on the earth's surface and the two poles 子午线；经线

meringue /məˈræŋ/ *noun* beaten egg whites and sugar baked until crisp 蛋白酥；蛋糖脆皮

merino /məˈriːnəʊ/ *noun* (plural **merinos**) a soft wool obtained from a breed of sheep with a long fleece 美利奴羊毛

merit /'merɪt/ **noun 1** the quality of being good and deserving praise 优秀;卓越 **2** a good point or feature 优点;长处 • verb (**merits, meriting, merited**) deserve 值得;应得

meritocracy /ˌmerɪ'tɒkrəsi/ **noun** (plural **meritocracies**) a society in which power is held by those people who have the greatest ability 精英管理的社会 ■ **meritocratic** adjective.

meritorious /ˌmerɪ'tɔːriəs/ **adjective** deserving reward or praise 值得奖励的;值得称赞的

mermaid /'mɜːmeɪd/ **noun** a mythical sea creature with a woman's head and body and a fish's tail instead of legs (神话中的)美人鱼

merriment /'merɪmənt/ **noun** fun 欢乐;快乐

merry /'meri/ **adjective** (**merrier, merriest**) **1** cheerful and lively 欢乐的;兴高采烈的 **2** informal【非正式】slightly drunk 微醉的 ● **merry-go-round** a revolving platform fitted with model horses or cars, on which people ride for fun 旋转木马;旋转平台 ■ **merrily** adverb.

merrymaking /'merimeɪkɪŋ/ **noun** lively celebration and fun 欢庆活动;狂欢;寻欢作乐

Mesdames /meɪ'dæm/ **plural of** **MADAME**.

Mesdemoiselles /ˌmeɪdəmwɑːˈzel/ **plural of** **MADEMOISELLE**.

mesh /meʃ/ **noun 1** material made of a network of wire or thread 网;网状(织)物 **2** the spacing of the strands of a net 网孔 • verb **1** fit together or be in harmony 吻合;相配 **2** (of a gearwheel) lock together with another (齿轮)相啮合

mesmeric /mez'merɪk/ **adjective** hypnotic 催眠的;易受催眠的

mesmerism /'mezmərɪzəm/ **noun** hypnotism 催眠;催眠术

mesmerize or **mesmerise** /'mezmərɑɪz/ **verb** (**mesmerizes,**

mesmerizing, mesmerized) capture someone's attention so that they are completely enthralled 完全吸引住;迷住

mess /mes/ **noun 1** a dirty or untidy state 肮脏;凌乱 **2** a state of confusion or difficulty 混乱局面;困境 **3** a portion of semi-solid food (半流质的)一份食物 **4** a dog or cat's excrement (猫狗等的)粪便 **5** a place where members of the armed forces eat and relax 军人食堂 • verb **1** make something untidy or dirty 弄乱;弄脏 **2** (**mess about** or **around**) behave in a silly or playful way 胡闹;开玩笑 **3** (**mess with**) informal【非正式】meddle with 干涉;干预

message /'mesɪdʒ/ **noun 1** a spoken, written, or electronic communication (口头、书面或电子)信息 **2** a significant point or central theme 要点;中心思想;要旨 • verb (**messages, messaging, messaged**) send a message to 向…发送信息

messenger /'mesɪndʒə(r)/ **noun** a person who carries a message 报信者;信使

messiah /mə'sɑɪə/ **noun 1** (**the Messiah**) (in Judaism) the person who will be sent by God as the saviour of the Jewish people (犹太教的)弥赛亚(犹太人的复国救主) **2** (**the Messiah**) (in Christianity) Jesus, regarded as this saviour (基督教的)救世主耶稣 **3** a great leader seen as the saviour of a country, group, etc. 领袖;救星

messianic /ˌmesi'ænɪk/ **adjective** relating to a messiah 弥赛亚的

Messieurs /mes'jɜː/ **plural of** **MONSIEUR**.

Messrs /'mesəz/ **plural of** **MR**.

messy /'mesi/ **adjective** (**messier, messiest**) **1** untidy or dirty 凌乱的;肮脏的 **2** confused and difficult to deal with 棘手的;难办的 ■ **messily** adverb **messiness** noun.

met /met/ past and past participle of MEET.

metabolism /mə'tæbəlɪzəm/ **noun** the process by which food is used for the growth of tissue or the production of energy 新陈代谢 ■ **metabolic** adjective.

metabolize or **metabolise** /mə'tæbəlaɪz/ **verb** (**metabolizes, metabolizing, metabolized**) process by metabolism 进行新陈代谢

metal /metl/ **noun 1** a hard, solid, shiny material which conducts electricity and heat 金属 **2** (also **road metal**) broken stone used in making road surfaces (筑路用的)碎石

metalled /metld/ **adjective** Brit.【英】 (of a road) having a hard surface (道路)铺有硬质路面的

metallic /mə'tælɪk/ **adjective 1** having to do with metal 金属的 **2** (of sound) sharp and ringing (声音)尖厉清脆的

metallurgy /mə'tælədʒi/ **noun** the scientific study of metals 冶金学 ■ **metallurgical** adjective **metallurgist** noun.

metamorphic /metə'mɔːfɪk/ **adjective** (of rock) having been changed by heat and pressure (岩石)变质的

metamorphosis /metə'mɔːfəsɪs/ **noun** (plural **metamorphoses** /metə'mɔːfəsiːz/) **1** the transformation of an insect or amphibian from an immature form or larva to an adult form (昆虫或两栖动物的)变态 **2** a change in form or nature 形变；质变 ■ **metamorphose** verb.

metaphor /metəfə(r)/ **noun** a word or phrase used in an imaginative way to represent or stand for something else (e.g. *the long arm of the law*) 隐喻

metaphorical /metə'fɒrɪkl/ or **metaphoric** /metə'fɒrɪk/ **adjective** having to do with metaphor 隐喻的 ■ **metaphorically** adverb.

metaphysical /metə'fɪzɪkl/ **adjective 1** relating to metaphysics 形而上学的；玄学的 **2** beyond physical matter 非实体的；无形的 ■ **metaphysically** adverb.

metaphysics /metə'fɪzɪks/ **noun** the branch of philosophy dealing with the nature of existence, truth, and knowledge 形而上学；玄学

mete /miːt/ **verb** (**metes, meting, meted**) (**mete something out**) give someone a punishment, or subject them to harsh treatment 施以，给予(惩罚，苛待等)

meteor /miːtiə(r)/ **noun** a small body of matter from space that glows as a result of friction with the earth's atmosphere, and appears as a shooting star 流星；流星体

meteoric /miːti'ɒrɪk/ **adjective 1** relating to meteors or meteorites 流星的；陨石的 **2** rapid in achieving success or promotion (成功或晋升)迅疾的，神速的

meteorite /miːtiəraɪt/ **noun** a piece of rock or metal that has fallen to the earth from space 陨星；陨石

meteorology /miːtiə'rɒlədʒi/ **noun** the study of conditions in the atmosphere, especially for weather forecasting 气象学 ■ **meteorological** adjective **meteorologist** noun.

meter[1] /miːtə(r)/ **noun** a device that measures and records the quantity, degree, or rate of something 计量仪表；计量器 • **verb** (**meters, metering, metered**) measure something with a meter 用仪表计量

meter[2] US spelling of METRE[1], METRE[2]. metre[1], metre[2]的美式拼法

methadone /meθədəʊn/ **noun** a powerful painkiller, used as a substitute for morphine and heroin in treating people addicted to those drugs 美沙酮(一种强效止痛药，在戒毒中用作吗啡和海洛因的替代品)

methane /miːθeɪn/ **noun** a flammable

gas which is the main constituent of natural gas 甲烷;沼气

methanol /'meθənɒl/ **noun** a poisonous flammable alcohol, used to make methylated spirit 甲醇

methinks /mɪ'θɪŋks/ **verb** (past **methought**) old use 【旧】 it seems to me 在我看来;我想

method /'meθəd/ **noun 1** a way of doing something 方法;办法 **2** the quality of being well planned and organized 条理性

methodical /mə'θɒdɪkl/ or **methodic adjective** done or doing something in a well-organized and systematic way 有条理的;有条不紊的 ■ **methodically** adverb.

Methodist /'meθədɪst/ **noun** a member of a Christian Protestant group which separated from the Church of England in the 18th century (基督教)循道宗信徒 ● **adjective** relating to Methodists or their beliefs 循道宗信徒的;循道宗教义的 ■ **Methodism** noun.

methodology /ˌmeθə'dɒlədʒi/ **noun** (plural **methodologies**) a particular system of methods 一套方法 ■ **methodological** adjective.

meths /meθs/ **noun** Brit. informal 【英,非正式】 methylated spirit 甲基化酒精

methylated spirit or **methylated spirits** /'meθəleɪtɪd/ **noun** alcohol for use as a solvent or fuel, made unfit for drinking by the addition of methanol and a violet dye 甲基化酒精

meticulous /mə'tɪkjələs/ **adjective** very careful and precise 一丝不苟的;严谨的 ■ **meticulously** adverb.

métier /'metieɪ/ **noun** a person's trade, profession, or special ability 行业;职业;专长

metre¹ /'miːtə(r)/ (US spelling 【美拼作】 **meter**) **noun** the basic unit of length in the metric system, equal

to 100 centimetres (approximately 39.37 inches) 米(公制长度的基本单位,等于100厘米,约合39.37英寸)

metre² (US spelling 【美拼作】 **meter**) **noun** the rhythm of a piece of poetry (诗歌的)韵律,格律

metric /'metrɪk/ **adjective** relating to or using the metric system (采用)公制的;(采用)米制的 □ **metric system** the decimal measuring system based on the metre, litre, and gram 公制;米制 **metric ton** (or **metric tonne**) a unit of weight equal to 1,000 kilograms (2,205 lb) 公吨,米制吨(重量单位,等于1,000千克,合2,205磅)

metrical /'metrɪkl/ **adjective** having to do with poetic metre 韵律的;格律的 ■ **metrically** adverb.

metricate /'metrɪkeɪt/ **verb** (**metricates**, **metricating**, **metricated**) convert a system of measurement to the metric system 改用公制(或米制) ■ **metrication** noun.

metro /'metrəʊ/ **noun** (plural **metros**) an underground railway system in a city 地铁

metronome /'metrənəʊm/ **noun** a device that marks time at a selected rate by giving a regular tick, used by musicians 节拍器 ■ **metronomic** adjective.

metropolis /mə'trɒpəlɪs/ **noun** the main city of a country or region 大城市;大都会

metropolitan /ˌmetrə'pɒlɪtən/ **adjective** relating to the main city of a country or region 大城市的;大都会的

mettle /'metl/ **noun** spirit and strength of character 精神;勇气

mew /mjuː/ **verb** (of a cat or gull) make a soft, high-pitched sound like a cry (猫或海鸥)喵喵叫,喳喳叫

mewl /mjuːl/ **verb 1** cry feebly 低声哭;呜咽 **2** mew 喵喵叫

mews /mjuːz/ **noun** (plural **mews**) Brit. 【英】 a row of houses or flats converted from stables in a small street or square 马厩改建的住房

Mexican /'meksɪkən/ **noun** a person from Mexico 墨西哥人 • **adjective** relating to Mexico 墨西哥的

mezzanine /'metsəniːn, 'mezə-/ **noun** a floor extending over only part of the full area of a building, built between two full floors 夹楼;夹层楼面

mezzo /'metsəu/ or **mezzo-soprano** /ˌmetsəu sə'prɑːnəu/ **noun** (plural **mezzos**) a female singer with a voice pitched between soprano and contralto 女中音

mg abbreviation milligrams.

MHz abbreviation megahertz 兆赫兹;兆赫

miaow or **meow** /mi'au/ **noun** the cry of a cat 猫(猫的叫声) • **verb** make a miaow 喵喵叫

miasma /mi'æzmə/ **noun** an unpleasant or unhealthy atmosphere 不良气氛

mica /'maɪkə/ **noun** a mineral found as tiny shiny scales in rocks 云母

mice /maɪs/ plural of MOUSE.

mickey /'mɪki/ **noun** (**take the mickey**) Brit. informal 【英,非正式】tease or mock someone 取笑;嘲笑

microbe /'maɪkrəub/ **noun** a bacterium; a germ 微生物 ■ **microbial** adjective.

microbiology /ˌmaɪkrəubaɪ'ɒlədʒi/ **noun** the scientific study of living creatures that are so tiny that they can only be seen using a microscope 微生物学

microchip /'maɪkrəutʃɪp/ **noun** a miniature electronic circuit made from a tiny wafer of silicon 微晶片;芯片

microclimate /'maɪkrəuklaɪmɪt/ **noun** the climate of a very small or restricted area 小气候(极小或有限区域内的气候)

microcosm /'maɪkrəukɒzəm/ **noun** a thing that has the features and qualities of something much larger 微观世界;缩影

microfiche /'maɪkrəufiːʃ/ or **microfilm** /'maɪkrəufɪlm/ **noun** a piece of film containing very small-sized photographs of the pages of a newspaper, book, etc. 缩微胶卷

microlight /'maɪkrəulaɪt/ **noun** Brit. 【英】a very small, light, one- or two-seater aircraft (载一至两人的)微型飞机

micrometer /maɪ'krɒmɪtə(r)/ **noun** an instrument which measures small distances or thicknesses 测微计;千分尺

microorganism /ˌmaɪkrəu'ɔːɡənɪzəm/ **noun** an organism that is so small that it can only be seen using a microscope 微生物

microphone /'maɪkrəfəun/ **noun** an instrument for changing sound waves into electrical energy which is then amplified and transmitted or recorded 扩音器;麦克风;话筒

microprocessor /ˌmaɪkrəu'prəusesə(r)/ **noun** an integrated circuit which can function as the main part of a computer 微处理机

microscope /'maɪkrəskəup/ **noun** an instrument for magnifying very small objects 显微镜

microscopic /ˌmaɪkrə'skɒpɪk/ **adjective** so small as to be visible only with a microscope 极小的;需用显微镜观察的 ■ **microscopically** adverb.

microscopy /maɪ'krɒskəpi/ **noun** the use of a microscope 显微镜使用

microsurgery /ˌmaɪkrəu'sɜːdʒəri/ **noun** surgery performed using very small instruments and a microscope 显微手术;显微外科

microwave /'maɪkrəuweɪv/ **noun** 1 an electromagnetic wave with a wavelength in the range 0.001–0.3 m 微波(波长在0.001–0.3米之间的电磁波) 2 (also **microwave oven**) an oven that uses microwaves to cook or heat food 微波炉 • **verb (microwaves, microwaving, microwaved)** cook food in a microwave oven 用微波炉烹调(食物)

mid /mɪd/ **adjective** having to do with the middle position of a range 中部的;中间的;中央的 • **preposition** literary 【文】 amid; in the middle of 在…中间

Midas touch /'maɪdəs/ **noun** the ability to make a lot of money out of anything you do 点石成金的才能;事事能赚大钱的本领

midday /mɪd'deɪ/ **noun** twelve o'clock in the day; noon 中午;正午

midden /mɪdn/ **noun** a heap of dung 粪堆

middle /'mɪdl/ **adjective 1** positioned at an equal distance from the edges or ends of something 中部的;中间的 **2** medium in rank, quality, or ability 中等的;中级的 • **noun 1** a middle point or position 中间;中间 **2** informal 【非正式】 a person's waist and stomach 身体中部;腰部 □ **middle age** the period when a person is between about 45 and 60 in age 中年(大约45岁至60岁之间) **Middle Ages** the period of European history between about 1000 and 1450 中世纪(欧洲历史上约公元1000年至1450年的一段时期) **middle class** the social group between the aristocracy and the working class 中产阶级 **middle ear** the air-filled central cavity of the ear, behind the eardrum 中耳;鼓室 **Middle East** an area of SW Asia and northern Africa, stretching from the Mediterranean to Pakistan 中东 **middle-of-the-road 1** (of views) not extreme (观点)走中间路线的, 中间派的 **2** (of music) generally popular but rather unadventurous (音乐)大众化的, 不标新立异的

middleman /'mɪdlmæn/ **noun (plural middlemen) 1** a person who buys goods from the company who makes them and sells them on to shops or consumers 中间商;经销商 **2** a person who arranges business or political deals between other people 经纪人;掮客

middling /'mɪdlɪŋ/ **adjective** average in size, amount, or rank 中等的;普通的;一般的

midfield /'mɪdfiːld/ **noun** the central part of a sports field (运动场的)中场 ■ **midfielder** noun.

midge /mɪdʒ/ **noun** a small fly that breeds near water 蠓,摇蚊(一种在水边产卵的小飞虫)

midget /'mɪdʒɪt/ **noun** a very small person 侏儒;矮人 • **adjective** very small 极小的

midland /'mɪdlənd/ **noun 1** the middle part of a country 中部地区 **2 (the Midlands)** the inland counties of central England 英格兰中部地区

midnight /'mɪdnaɪt/ **noun** twelve o'clock at night 午夜;子夜

midriff /'mɪdrɪf/ **noun** the front of the body between the chest and the waist 上腹部

midship /'mɪdʃɪp/ **noun** the middle part of a ship or boat 船身中部

midshipman /'mɪdʃɪpmən/ **noun (plural midshipmen)** a low-ranking officer in the Royal Navy 海军候补少尉

midships = AMIDSHIPS.

midst /mɪdst/ old use 【旧】 **preposition** in the middle of 在…之中 • **noun** the middle point or part 中间;中部

midstream /mɪd'striːm/ **noun** the middle of a stream or river 中游

midsummer /mɪd'sʌmə(r)/ **noun 1** the middle part of summer 仲夏 **2** the summer solstice 夏至 □ **Midsummer Day (or Midsummer's Day)** 24 June 施洗约翰节(6月24日)

midterm /mɪd'tɜːm/ **noun** the middle of a period of office, an academic term, or a pregnancy (任期、学期或孕期的)中期

midway /ˈmɪdweɪ/ **adverb & adjective** in or towards the middle 在中间的; 在中途的

midweek /ˈmɪdwiːk/ **noun** the middle of the week 周中 • **adjective & adverb** in the middle of the week 周中的; 在周中

midwife /ˈmɪdwaɪf/ **noun** (plural **midwives**) a nurse who is trained to help women during childbirth 助产士; 接生员 ■ **midwifery noun**.

midwinter /mɪdˈwɪntə(r)/ **noun 1** the middle part of winter 仲冬 **2** the winter solstice 冬至

mien /miːn/ **noun** a person's look or manner (人的)外表, 风度

miffed /mɪft/ **adjective** informal 【非正式】 slightly angry or upset 有点恼火的; 有点不高兴的

might¹ /maɪt/ **modal verb** (3rd singular present **might**) past of MAY. **1** used to express possibility or make a suggestion (用于表示可能或建议)可能, 也许, 可以 **2** used politely in questions and requests (用于问句和请求以表示礼貌)可以

might² **noun** great power or strength 威力; 强大力量

mightn't /ˈmaɪtnt/ **short form** might not.

mighty /ˈmaɪti/ **adjective** (**mightier**, **mightiest**) very strong or powerful 强大的, 强有力的 • **adverb** informal 【非正式】 very 极其; 非常 ■ **mightily adverb**.

migraine /ˈmiːɡreɪn, ˈmaɪ-/ **noun** a severe headache which is accompanied by symptoms such as nausea and disturbed vision 偏头痛

migrant /ˈmaɪɡrənt/ **noun 1** a worker who moves from one place to another to find work 流动工人 **2** an animal that migrates 迁徙动物 • **adjective** tending to migrate or having migrated 迁徙的; 移居的

migrate /maɪˈɡreɪt/ **verb** (**migrates**, **migrating**, **migrated**) **1** (of an animal) move to warmer regions in the winter and to colder regions in the summer (动物)迁徙, 移栖 **2** move to settle in a new area in order to find work 移居 ■ **migration noun migratory adjective**.

mike /maɪk/ **noun** informal 【非正式】 a microphone 话筒; 扩音器; 麦克风

milch /mɪltʃ/ **adjective** (of an animal) giving or kept for milk (动物)产奶的, 为挤奶而饲养的

mild /maɪld/ **adjective 1** not severe or harsh 不严重的; 轻微的, 和缓的 **2** (of weather) fairly warm (天气)温暖的, 暖和的 **3** not sharp or strong in flavour 味淡的 **4** (of a person or their behaviour) calm and gentle (人或其行为)温和的, 平和的 • **noun** Brit. 【英】 a kind of dark beer not strongly flavoured with hops 淡味啤酒 ■ **mildly adverb mildness noun**.

mildew /ˈmɪldjuː/ **noun** a coating of tiny fungi on plants or damp material such as paper or leather 霉; 霉菌 ■ **mildewed adjective**.

mile /maɪl/ **noun 1** a unit of length equal to 1,760 yards (approximately 1.609 kilometres) 英里(约合1.609公里) **2** (**miles**) informal 【非正式】 a very long way 很远的路

mileage /ˈmaɪlɪdʒ/ **noun 1** a number of miles covered 英里数; 英里里程 **2** informal 【非正式】 advantage 好处; 利益

mileometer /maɪˈlɒmɪtə(r)/ ⇒ 见 MILOMETER.

milestone /ˈmaɪlstəʊn/ **noun 1** a stone set up beside a road, marking the distance in miles to a place further along the road (路边的)里程碑, 里程标 **2** an event marking a significant new development or stage (标志新发展或新阶段的)重大事件, 转折点

milieu /miːˈljɜː/ **noun** (plural **milieux** /miːˈljɜː/ or **milieus** /miːˈljɜːz/) the social environment that you live or

work in 社会环境；社会背景

militant /ˈmɪlɪtənt/ **adjective** supporting a cause in a forceful and aggressive way 好战的；好斗的；激进的 • **noun** a militant person 好斗分子；激进分子 ■ **militancy** noun **militantly** adverb.

militarism /ˈmɪlɪtərɪzəm/ **noun** a belief in the value of military strength 军国主义 ■ **militarist** noun & adjective **militaristic** adjective.

militarized or **militarised** /ˈmɪlɪtəraɪzd/ **adjective** supplied with soldiers and military equipment 军事化的

military /ˈmɪlɪtri/ **adjective** having to do with soldiers or armed forces 军人的；军队的；军事的 • **noun** (**the military**) the armed forces of a country (国家的)军队，军事力量 ■ **militarily** adverb.

militate /ˈmɪlɪteɪt/ **verb** (**militates, militating, militated**) (**militate against**) make it very difficult for something to happen or exist 极大妨碍(某事的发生或存在)

> **！注意** don't confuse **militate** with **mitigate**, which means 'make something bad less severe'. 不要混淆 militate 和 mitigate，后者意为"减轻；缓解"。

militia /məˈlɪʃə/ **noun 1** a group of people who are not professional soldiers but who act as an army 民兵队伍 **2** a rebel force opposing a regular army 叛军

milk /mɪlk/ **noun 1** a white fluid produced by female mammals to feed their young 奶 **2** the milk of cows as a food and drink for humans 牛奶 **3** the milk-like juice of certain plants (某些植物的)汁液 • **verb 1** draw milk from an animal 挤(动物)的奶 **2** take money from someone dishonestly and over a period of time 榨取，勒索(钱财) **3** take full advantage of a situation 充分利用(某局面) □ **milk**

chocolate solid chocolate made with milk 奶油巧克力 **milk float** Brit. 【英】 an electrically powered van with open sides, used for delivering milk to houses 送奶车 **milk tooth** a temporary tooth in a child or young mammal 乳牙；乳齿

milkmaid /ˈmɪlkmeɪd/ **noun** old use 【旧】 a girl or woman who worked in a dairy 挤奶女工；牛奶场女工

milkman /ˈmɪlkmən/ **noun** (plural **milkmen**) a man who delivers milk to houses 送奶工

milkshake /ˈmɪlkʃeɪk/ **noun** a cold drink made from milk whisked with ice cream or a flavouring 奶昔

milksop /ˈmɪlksɒp/ **noun** a timid person 懦弱的人

milky /ˈmɪlki/ **adjective 1** containing milk 含牛奶的；含乳的 **2** having a soft white colour or clouded appearance 乳白色的；面带愁容的 □ **Milky Way** the galaxy of which our solar system is a part, visible at night as a faint band of light crossing the sky 银河 ■ **milkily** adverb **milkiness** noun.

mill /mɪl/ **noun 1** a building equipped with machinery for grinding grain into flour 磨坊；磨粉厂 **2** a device for grinding coffee beans, peppercorns, etc. 研磨器；磨粉机 **3** a building fitted with machinery for a manufacturing process 制造厂；工厂 • **verb 1** grind something in a mill 磨，碾 **2** cut or shape metal with a rotating tool 滚压，碾压(金属) **3** (**milled**) (of a coin) having ribbed markings on the edge (硬币)压有凸缘 **4** (**mill about** or **around**) move around in a confused mass 绕圈子；乱转 □ **mill wheel** a wheel used to drive a watermill (驱动水磨的)水车轮

millennium /mɪˈlenɪəm/ **noun** (plural **millennia** /mɪˈlenɪə/ or **millenniums**) **1** a period of a thousand years 一千年；千年期 **2** (**the millennium**) the point at which one period of a thousand years ends and another begins 千禧年 **3** an anniversary of a thousand years 千周年纪念日 ■ **millennial** adjective.

✔ 拼写指南 double l, double n: mil*lenn*ium. millennium 中有两个 1 和两个 n。

miller /ˈmɪlə(r)/ **noun** a person who owns or works in a grain mill 磨坊主；碾磨工

millet /ˈmɪlɪt/ **noun** a cereal plant used to make flour or alcoholic drinks 黍类；小米

millibar /ˈmɪlibɑː(r)/ **noun** a unit for measuring the pressure of the atmosphere 毫巴(大气压强单位)

milligram or **milligramme** / ˈmɪligræm/ **noun** one thousandth of a gram 毫克

millilitre /ˈmɪlɪliːtə(r)/ (US spelling 【美拼作】**milliliter**) **noun** one thousandth of a litre 毫升

millimetre /ˈmɪlimiːtə(r)/ (US spelling 【美拼作】**millimeter**) **noun** one thousandth of a metre 毫米

milliner /ˈmɪlinə(r)/ **noun** a person who makes or sells women's hats 女帽制造者；女帽商 ■ **millinery** noun.

million /ˈmɪljən/ **cardinal number** (plural **millions** or (with another word or number) **million**) **1** a thousand times a thousand; 1,000,000 一百万 **2** (also **millions**) informal 【非正式】a very large number or amount 许多；大量 ■ **millionth** ordinal number.

millionaire /ˌmɪljəˈneə(r)/ **noun** a person whose money and property are worth one million pounds or dollars or more 百万富翁

✔ 拼写指南 just one n: millio*n*aire. millionaire 中只有一个 n。

millipede /ˈmɪlipiːd/ **noun** an insect-like creature with a long body and a lot of legs 马陆，千足虫

millisecond /ˈmɪlisekənd/ **noun** one thousandth of a second 毫秒

millpond /ˈmɪlpɒnd/ **noun 1** a pool created to provide the water that turns the wheel of a watermill 磨坊水池 **2** a very still and calm stretch of water (平静的)池塘，水池

millstone /ˈmɪlstəʊn/ **noun 1** each of a pair of circular stones used for grinding grain 磨石；磨盘 **2** a heavy responsibility that you cannot escape from 重负；重担

milometer or **mileometer** /maɪˈlɒmɪtə(r)/ **noun** Brit.【英】an instrument on a vehicle for recording the number of miles travelled (车辆上的)计程器，里程表

mime /maɪm/ **noun** the use of silent gestures and facial expressions to tell a story or show feelings 手势；哑语 ● **verb** (**mimes, miming, mimed**) **1** use mime to tell a story or show feelings 用手势陈述；以哑语表达 **2** pretend to sing or play an instrument as a recording is being played 假唱；假吹奏(或弹奏)

mimic /ˈmɪmɪk/ **verb** (**mimics, mimicking, mimicked**) **1** imitate the voice or actions of someone else 模仿(某人) **2** (of an animal or plant) take on the appearance of another in order to hide or for protection (动植物)模拟(另一生物)，拟态 ● **noun** a person skilled in mimicking others 善于模仿的人 ■ **mimicry** noun.

mimosa /mɪˈməʊzə/ **noun** an acacia tree with delicate leaves and yellow flowers 含羞草属植物(叶嫩，开黄花)

minaret /ˌmɪnəˈret/ **noun** a slender tower of a mosque, with a balcony from which Muslims are called to prayer (清真寺的)宣礼塔

minatory /ˈmɪnətəri/ **adjective** formal 【正式】threatening 威吓的；威胁性的

mince /mɪns/ **verb 1** cut or grind meat into very small pieces 切碎，剁碎(肉) **2** walk with short, quick steps and swinging hips 扭捏捏捏地小步

快走 • noun Brit【英】minced meat
剁碎的肉;肉末 □ mince pie a small
tart containing mincemeat, eaten at
Christmas 肉馅饼 not mince your
words speak plainly 直言不讳;毫不
遮掩地说

mincemeat /'mɪnsmiːt/ noun a
mixture of dried fruit, candied peel,
sugar, spices, and suet 甜馅(由果
干、蜜饯果皮、糖、香料和板油制成)

mind /maɪnd/ noun 1 the faculty of
consciousness and thought 头脑 2 a
person's intellect or memory 智力;
记忆力 3 a person's attention or will
注意力;心思;意愿 • verb 1 be upset
or annoyed by 因…烦恼;对…介意
2 remember or take care to do 记
住;留心 3 watch out for 当心;留神
4 temporarily take care of 照料;照
看 5 (be minded) be inclined to do
想要;意欲 □ out of your mind not
thinking sensibly; crazy 精神错乱;
发狂

minded /'maɪndɪd/ adjective inclined
to think in a particular way 有…思想
的;有…观念的

minder /'maɪndə(r)/ noun a person
whose job is to take care of or protect
someone or something 照料人员;看
管人员

mindful /'maɪndfl/ adjective (mindful
of or that) aware of or recognizing
that 意识到…的;注意…的

mindless /'maɪndləs/ adjective
1 acting or done without good
reason and with no concern for the
consequences 没头脑的;不理智的;不
计后果的 2 (of an activity) simple and
repetitive (活动)简单重复的,无须动
脑子的 ■ mindlessly adverb.

mindset /'maɪndset/ noun a person's
particular way of thinking and set of
beliefs 思维倾向;观念模式

mine[1] /maɪn/ possessive pronoun
referring to a thing or things
belonging to or associated with the
person speaking 我的(东西);与我有

关的(事物) • possessive determiner
old use【旧】my 我的

mine[2] noun 1 a hole or channel dug in
the earth for extracting coal or other
minerals 矿;矿井 2 an abundant
source 源泉;宝库 3 a type of bomb
placed on or in the ground or water,
which explodes on contact 地雷;水
雷 • verb (mines, mining, mined) 1
obtain coal or other minerals from a
mine (从矿井中)开采 2 lay explosive
mines on or in 布…布雷

minefield /'maɪnfiːld/ noun 1 an
area planted with explosive mines 雷
区 2 a subject or situation presenting
unseen dangers 危险的主题;危险形
势

miner /'maɪnə(r)/ noun a person who
works in a mine 矿工

mineral /'mɪnərəl/ noun 1 a solid
substance occurring naturally, such
as copper and silicon (天然)矿物 2
an inorganic substance needed by the
human body for good health, such as
calcium and iron (人体所需的)无机矿
物质 □ mineral water water from a
natural spring, containing dissolved
mineral salts 矿泉水

mineralogy /ˌmɪnəˈrælədʒi/ noun 矿
物学 ■ mineralogical adjective
mineralogist noun.

mineshaft /'maɪnʃɑːft/ noun a deep,
narrow shaft that gives access to a
mine 矿井

minestrone /ˌmɪnəˈstrəʊni/ noun an
Italian soup containing vegetables
and pasta 意大利蔬菜浓汤

minesweeper /'maɪnswiːpə(r)/ noun
a warship equipped for detecting and
removing or destroying explosive
mines 扫雷舰

mingle /'mɪŋgl/ verb (mingles,
mingling, mingled) mix together 混
合起来;相混合

mingy /'mɪndʒi/ adjective informal
【非正式】not generous 吝啬的;小气

的

mini /'mɪni/ **adjective** very small of its kind 小型的 • **noun** (plural **minis**) a very short skirt 超短裙

miniature /'mɪnətʃə(r)/ **adjective** of a much smaller size than normal 小型的；小于通常尺寸的 • **noun 1** a thing that is much smaller than normal 小型物；微小模型 **2** a tiny, detailed portrait or picture 微型画；袖珍画

✔ 拼写指南 -ia- in the middle: min*ia*ture. miniature 中间的字母组合是 -ia-。
---

miniaturist /'mɪnətʃərɪst/ **noun** an artist who paints miniatures 微型画画家

miniaturize or **miniaturise** /'mɪnətʃəraɪz/ **verb** (**miniaturizes**, **miniaturizing**, **miniaturized**) make a smaller version of 使小型化；使微型化

minibar /'mɪnibɑː(r)/ **noun** a small fridge in a hotel room containing a selection of drinks (宾馆客房内放有饮料的)小冰箱

minibus /'mɪnibʌs/ **noun** a small bus for about ten to fifteen passengers 小型公共汽车，小巴(可载约10至15名乘客)

minicab /'mɪnikæb/ **noun** Brit. 【英】 a taxi that you order by telephone but cannot hail in the street 小型出租汽车(需预约，但不能在街上截停)

minidisc /'mɪnidɪsk/ **noun** a disc similar to a small CD but able to record sound or data as well as play it back 小型磁盘；迷你光碟

minim /'mɪnɪm/ **noun** a musical note that lasts as long as two crotchets 二分音符

minimal /'mɪnɪməl/ **adjective** of a minimum amount, quantity, or degree 最少的；最低限度的 ■ **minimally** adverb.

minimalist /'mɪnɪməlɪst/ **adjective 1** (of art) using simple forms and structures (艺术)极简抽象派的 **2** deliberately simple or basic in design (设计)极简风格的 • **noun** an artist who uses simple forms and structures 极简抽象派艺术家 ■ **minimalism** noun.

minimize or **minimise** /'mɪnɪmaɪz/ **verb** (**minimizes**, **minimizing**, **minimized**) **1** make something as small as possible 使最小化 **2** represent something as less important or significant than it really is 贬低；轻视

minimum /'mɪnɪməm/ **noun** (plural **minima** or **minimums**) the smallest amount, extent, or strength possible 最小量；最低限度；最小力量 • **adjective** smallest in amount, extent, or strength 最小量的；最低限度的；最小力量的

minion /'mɪniən/ **noun** a worker or assistant who has a low or unimportant status 僚属；小卒

miniskirt /'mɪniskɜːt/ **noun** a very short skirt 超短裙；迷你裙

minister /'mɪnɪstə(r)/ **noun 1** a head of a government department 部长；大臣 **2** a person who represents their government in a foreign country 公使；外交使节 **3** a person who carries out religious duties in the Christian Church (基督教的)牧师，教士 • **verb** (**ministers**, **ministering**, **ministered**) (**minister to**) attend to the needs of 照顾；服侍 ■ **ministerial** adjective.

ministrations /ˌmɪnɪ'streɪʃnz/ **plural noun** the providing of help or care 帮助；照顾；服侍

ministry /'mɪnɪstri/ **noun** (plural **ministries**) **1** a government department headed by a minister (政府的)部 **2** a period of government under one Prime Minister 一届政府的任期 **3** the work of a minister in the Christian Church (基督教的)神职

mink /mɪŋk/ **noun** a small stoat-like

animal that is farmed for its fur (以获取皮毛为目的而饲养的)水貂

minnow /ˈmɪnəʊ/ **noun** a small freshwater fish 米诺鱼(小型淡水鱼)

minor /ˈmaɪnə(r)/ **adjective 1** not important or serious 次要的；轻微的 **2** Music【音乐】(of a scale) having intervals of a semitone between the second and third, fifth and sixth, and seventh and eighth notes (音阶)小调的，小音阶的 • **noun** a person under the age of full legal responsibility未成年人

minority /maɪˈnɒrəti/ **noun** (plural **minorities**) **1** the smaller number or part 少数；少数部分 **2** a relatively small group of people differing from the majority in race, religion, etc. 少数民族；少数派；少数群体

minster /ˈmɪnstə(r)/ **noun** Brit.【英】a large or important church 大教堂

minstrel /ˈmɪnstrəl/ **noun** a medieval singer or musician (中世纪的)游方艺人

mint¹ /mɪnt/ **noun 1** a sweet-smelling plant, used as a herb in cookery 薄荷 **2** the flavour of mint 薄荷味 **3** a peppermint sweet 薄荷糖 ■ **minty** adjective.

mint² **noun 1** a place where money is made 造币厂 **2 (a mint)** informal【非正式】a large sum of money 巨款 • **verb** make a coin by stamping metal 铸造(硬币) □ **in mint condition** new, or as good as new 崭新的；完好的

minuet /ˌmɪnjuˈet/ **noun** a ballroom dance popular in the 18th century 米奴哀舞，小步舞(盛行于18世纪)

minus /ˈmaɪnəs/ **preposition 1** with the subtraction of 减(去)；除(去) **2** (of temperature) falling below zero by (温度)零下 **3** informal【非正式】lacking 少；缺少 • **adjective 1** (before a number) below zero (用于数字前)零以下的，负的 **2** (after a grade) slightly below (用于成绩后)略低的，稍差的 **3** having a negative

electric charge 阴性的；负电的 • **noun 1** (also **minus sign**) the symbol –, indicating subtraction or a negative value 减号；负号 **2** informal【非正式】a disadvantage 不利条件；缺点

minuscule /ˈmɪnəskjuːl/ **adjective** very tiny 极微小的

✔ 拼写指南 -u-, not -i-, in the middle: minuscule. minuscule 中间的 -u- 不要拼作 -i-。

---

minute¹ /ˈmɪnɪt/ **noun 1** a period of time equal to sixty seconds or a sixtieth of an hour 分钟 **2 (a minute)** informal【非正式】a very short time 一会儿 **3** a measurement of an angle equal to one sixtieth of a degree 分(角度单位，等于1/60度)

minute² /maɪˈnjuːt/ **adjective** (**minutest**) **1** very small 微小的；细微的 **2** precise and careful 细致入微的；缜密的 ■ **minutely** adverb.

minute³ /ˈmɪnɪt/ **noun 1** (**minutes**) a written summary of the points discussed at a meeting 会议纪要；议事录 **2** an official written message 备忘录 • **verb** (**minutes, minuting, minuted**) record the points discussed at a meeting 记录(会议要点)

minutiae /maɪˈnjuːʃiiː/ **plural noun** small or precise details 细枝末节；细小细节

minx /mɪŋks/ **noun** a cheeky, cunning, or flirtatious girl or young woman 狡猾轻佻的女子

miracle /ˈmɪrəkl/ **noun 1** a welcome event that is so extraordinary that it is thought to be the work of God or a saint 神迹；奇迹 **2** an outstanding example or achievement 令人惊叹的事例(或成就)；杰作 ■ **miracle play** a medieval play based on stories from the Bible (《圣经》中记载的)圣迹剧，奇迹剧

miraculous /mɪˈrækjələs/ **adjective** like a miracle; very surprising and welcome 奇迹般的；不可思议的；非

凡的 ■ **miraculously** adverb.

mirage /ˈmɪrɑːʒ/ noun **1** an effect caused by hot air, in which a sheet of water seems to appear in a desert or on a hot road 幻景；海市蜃楼 **2** something that appears real or possible but is not in fact so 幻象；虚幻的事物

mire /ˈmaɪə(r)/ noun **1** a stretch of swampy or boggy ground 沼泽；泥潭 **2** a difficult situation from which it is hard to escape 困境 • verb (be mired) **1** become stuck in mud 陷入泥沼 **2** be in a difficult situation 陷入困境

mirror /ˈmɪrə(r)/ noun **1** a surface which reflects a clear image 镜子；反射面 **2** something that accurately represents something else 真实反映；写照 • verb reflect 反射；映照 □ **mirror image** an image which is identical in form to another but is reversed, as if seen in a mirror 镜像；映像；反像

mirth /mɜːθ/ noun laughter 欢笑 ■ **mirthful** adjective.

misadventure /ˌmɪsədˈventʃə(r)/noun **1** (also **death by misadventure**) Law 【法律】death caused accidentally and not involving crime 意外致死（与犯罪无关）**2** a mishap 厄运；不幸遭遇

misalliance /ˌmɪsəˈlaɪəns/ noun an unsuitable or unhappy relationship or marriage 不合适的情爱关系；不般配（或不幸福）的婚姻

misanthrope /ˈmɪsənθrəʊp/ or **misanthropist** /mɪsˈænθrəʊpɪst/ noun a person who dislikes and avoids other people 憎恨世人者；不愿与人交往者 ■ **misanthropic** adjective **misanthropy** noun.

misapprehension /ˌmɪsæprɪˈhenʃn/ noun a mistaken belief 误解；误会

misappropriate /ˌmɪsəˈprəʊprɪeɪt/ verb (**misappropriates**, **misappropriating**, **misappropriated**) dishonestly take something for your own use 盗用；侵吞；挪用 ■ **misappropriation** noun.

misbegotten /ˌmɪsbɪˈɡɒtn/ adjective badly thought out or planned 考虑（或计划）不周密的

misbehave /ˌmɪsbɪˈheɪv/ verb (**misbehaves**, **misbehaving**, **misbehaved**) behave badly 举止失礼；行为不端 ■ **misbehaviour** noun.

miscalculate /ˌmɪsˈkælkjuleɪt/ verb (**miscalculates**, **miscalculating**, **miscalculated**) calculate or assess wrongly 误算；错误估计 ■ **miscalculation** noun.

miscarriage /ˈmɪskærɪdʒ/ noun the birth of a baby or fetus before it is able to survive outside the mother's womb 流产；小产 □ **miscarriage of justice** a situation in which a court of law fails to achieve justice 误判；审判不公

miscarry /mɪsˈkæri/ verb (**miscarries**, **miscarrying**, **miscarried**) **1** (of a pregnant woman) have a miscarriage （孕妇）流产，小产 **2** (of a plan) fail (计划)失败

miscast /ˌmɪsˈkɑːst/ verb (be **miscast**) (of an actor) be given an unsuitable role (演员)被分配不合适的角色

miscellaneous /ˌmɪsəˈleɪniəs/ adjective consisting of many different kinds 混杂的

miscellany /mɪˈseləni/ noun (plural **miscellanies**) a collection of different things 大杂烩；杂集

mischance /mɪsˈtʃɑːns/ noun bad luck 厄运；不幸

mischief /ˈmɪstʃɪf/ noun **1** playful bad behaviour that does not cause serious damage or harm 恶作剧；捣蛋 **2** harm caused by someone or something 伤害；危害；麻烦

mischievous /ˈmɪstʃɪvəs/ adjective **1** causing mischief 恶作剧的；有害的 **2** intended to cause trouble 恶意的 ■ **mischievously** adverb.

✔ **拼写指南** the ending is *-ous*, not *-ious*. mischie*vous*. mischievous 词末的 -ous 不要拼作 -ious。

miscible /'mɪsəbl/ **adjective** (of liquids) able to be mixed together (液体)相溶的,可溶混的

misconceived /,mɪskən'siːvd/ **adjective** badly judged or planned 判断错误的;计划不周的

misconception /,mɪskən'sepʃn/ **noun** a failure to understand something correctly 错误的认识;误解

misconduct /,mɪs'kɒndʌkt/ **noun** bad behaviour 不端行为

misconstruction /,mɪskən'strʌkʃn/ **noun** a failure to interpret something correctly 错误阐释

misconstrue /,mɪskən'struː/ **verb** (**misconstrues, misconstruing, misconstrued**) interpret something wrongly 误解;错误阐释

miscreant /'mɪskriənt/ **noun** a person who behaves badly or unlawfully 行为不端者;不法之徒

misdeed /,mɪs'diːd/ **noun** a bad or evil act 恶行

misdemeanour /,mɪsdɪ'miːnə(r)/ (US spelling 【美拼法】**misdemeanor**) **noun** an action that is bad or unacceptable, but does not amount to a serious crime 不正当行为;轻罪

misdiagnose /,mɪs'daɪəgnəʊz/ **verb** (**misdiagnoses, misdiagnosing, misdiagnosed**) diagnose something incorrectly 误诊 ▪ **misdiagnosis** noun.

misdirect /,mɪsdə'rekt/ **verb** direct or instruct wrongly 给…指错方向;误导 ▪ **misdirection** noun.

miser /'maɪzə(r)/ **noun** a person who hoards wealth and spends as little as possible 守财奴;吝啬鬼

miserable /'mɪzrəbl/ **adjective 1** very unhappy or depressed 痛苦的;难过的 **2** causing unhappiness or discomfort 使人痛苦的;令人难过的 **3** (of a person) gloomy and humourless (人)郁郁寡欢的 **4** very small or inadequate 少得可怜的;不足的 ▪ **miserably** adverb.

misericord /mɪ'zerɪkɔːd/ **noun** a ledge projecting from the underside of a hinged seat in the choir of a church, giving support to someone standing when the seat is folded up 凸出托板(教堂唱诗班席位的活动座椅底面伸出的支架,在座椅折起时为站立的人提供支撑)

miserly /'maɪzəli/ **adjective 1** not willing to spend money 不爱花钱的;吝啬的 **2** (of a quantity) too small (数量)极少的 ▪ **miserliness** noun.

misery /'mɪzəri/ **noun** (plural **miseries**) **1** great unhappiness 痛苦;悲惨 **2** a cause of this 不幸;痛苦的事 **3** Brit. informal 【英,非正式】a person who is constantly miserable 老是愁眉苦脸的人

misfire /mɪs'faɪə(r)/ **verb** (**misfires, misfiring, misfired**) **1** (of a gun) fail to fire properly (枪)不发火 **2** (of an internal combustion engine) fail to ignite the fuel correctly (内燃机)不启动 **3** fail to produce the intended result 不奏效

misfit /'mɪsfɪt/ **noun** a person whose attitudes and actions set them apart from other people (态度和行为)怪异的人

misfortune /mɪs'fɔːtʃuːn/ **noun 1** bad luck 厄运;不幸 **2** an unfortunate event 不幸之事

misgivings /,mɪs'gɪvɪŋz/ **plural noun** feelings of doubt or worry 疑虑;忧虑

misguided /,mɪs'gaɪdɪd/ **adjective** badly judged 判断错误的

mishandle /,mɪs'hændl/ **verb** (**mishandles, mishandling, mishandled**) handle a situation badly or wrongly 对…处理不当;错误处理

mishap /'mɪshæp/ **noun** an unlucky accident 事故;倒霉的事

mishear /ˌmɪsˈhɪə(r)/ **verb** (mishears, mishearing, misheard) hear incorrectly 听错

mishit /ˌmɪsˈhɪt/ **verb** (mishits, mishitting, mishit) hit or kick a ball badly 误击;把(球)打歪(或踢歪)

mishmash /ˈmɪʃmæʃ/ **noun** a confused mixture 混杂物;大杂烩

misinform /ˌmɪsɪnˈfɔːm/ **verb** give someone false or inaccurate information 向(某人)传达错误(或不准确)信息 ■ **misinformation** noun.

misinterpret /ˌmɪsɪnˈtɜːprɪt/ **verb** (misinterprets, misinterpreting, misinterpreted) interpret something wrongly 误解;误释 ■ **misinterpretation** noun.

misjudge /ˌmɪsˈdʒʌdʒ/ **verb** (misjudges, misjudging, misjudged) 1 form a wrong opinion about 错看;对…有错误认识 2 estimate wrongly 错误估计 ■ **misjudgement** (or **misjudgment**) noun.

mislay /ˌmɪsˈleɪ/ **verb** (mislays, mislaying, mislaid) lose something because you have forgotten where you put it (因一时忘记放置何处而)丢失

mislead /ˌmɪsˈliːd/ **verb** (misleads, misleading, misled) give someone a wrong impression or wrong information 使产生错误印象;误导

mismanage /ˌmɪsˈmænɪdʒ/ **verb** (mismanages, mismanaging, mismanaged) manage something badly or wrongly 对…管理不善;对…处置失当 ■ **mismanagement** noun.

mismatch noun /ˈmɪsmætʃ/ a combination of things or people that do not go together well 误配;错误的结合 • **verb** /ˌmɪsˈmætʃ/ match people or things unsuitably or incorrectly 将…搭配不当;错配

misnomer /ˌmɪsˈnəʊmə(r)/ **noun** 1 a name or term that is wrong or inaccurate 错误的名称;不准确的名称

2 the wrong use of a name or term 名称误用;用词不当

misogynist /mɪˈsɒdʒɪnɪst/ **noun** a man who hates women 厌恶女人的男人 ■ **misogynistic** adjective **misogyny** noun.

misplace /ˌmɪsˈpleɪs/ **verb** (misplaces, misplacing, misplaced) put in the wrong place 把…放错地方

misplaced /ˌmɪsˈpleɪst/ **adjective** 1 wrongly placed 放错的 2 unwise or inappropriate 不明智的;不适当的

misprint /ˈmɪsprɪnt/ **noun** a mistake in printed material 印刷错误

mispronounce /ˌmɪsprəˈnaʊns/ **verb** (mispronounces, mispronouncing, mispronounced) pronounce wrongly 发错(音);读错;念错 ■ **mispronunciation** noun.

misquote /ˌmɪsˈkwəʊt/ **verb** (misquotes, misquoting, misquoted) quote inaccurately 不当引用

misread /ˌmɪsˈriːd/ **verb** (misreads, misreading, misread) read or interpret wrongly 读误;误解

misrepresent /ˌmɪsreprɪˈzent/ **verb** give a false or misleading account of 误报;误传;歪曲 ■ **misrepresentation** noun.

misrule /ˌmɪsˈruːl/ **noun** 1 bad government 治理不善 2 disorder 混乱;无序

miss[1] /mɪs/ **verb** 1 fail to hit, reach, or come into contact with 未击中;未达到;未接触到 2 be too late for 错过;未赶上 3 fail to notice, hear, or understand 未注意;未听到;未理解 4 fail to be present at 未出席;缺席 5 avoid something unpleasant 避开(令人不快的事物) 6 (miss someone/thing out) fail to include someone or something 漏掉 7 feel sad because of the absence of 怀念;思念 • **noun** a failure to hit, catch, or reach something 未击中;未抓住;未达到

miss[2] **noun** 1 (Miss) a title coming

before the name of an unmarried woman or girl (用在未婚女子姓名前)小姐 **2 (Miss)** used as a form of address to a teacher (对女教师的称呼)老师 **3** a girl or young woman 小姐;(小)姑娘;年轻女子

missal /'mɪsl/ **noun** a book containing the prayers and responses used in the Catholic Mass (天主教的)弥撒书

misshapen /ˌmɪs'ʃeɪpən/ **adjective** not having the normal or natural shape 畸形的;变形的

missile /'mɪsaɪl/ **noun** an object or weapon that is thrown or fired at a target 投掷物;投射物;导弹

missing /'mɪsɪŋ/ **adjective 1** absent and unable to be found 缺失的;丢失的 **2** not present when expected to be 缺席的;不在的

mission /'mɪʃn/ **noun 1** an important assignment, typically involving travel abroad (需出国执行的)任务,使命 **2** an organization involved in a long-term assignment abroad 使团;代表团 **3** a military or scientific expedition 军事远征;科学考察 **4** the work of teaching people about Christianity (基督教团体的)传教 **5** a strongly felt aim or calling 使命;天职

missionary /'mɪʃənri/ **noun** (plural **missionaries**) a person sent on a religious mission 传教士 • **adjective** having to do with a religious mission 传教的

missive /'mɪsɪv/ **noun** formal 【正式】a letter 信件;信函

misspell /ˌmɪs'spel/ **verb** (**misspells, misspelling**, past and past participle **misspelt** or **misspelled**) spell wrongly 拼错;写错

misspend /ˌmɪs'spend/ **verb** (**misspends, misspending, misspent**) spend time or money foolishly 滥用,浪费(时间或金钱)

mist /mɪst/ **noun** a thin cloud of tiny water droplets that makes it difficult

to see (薄)雾 • **verb** cover or become covered with mist (使)雾气笼罩

mistake /mɪ'steɪk/ **noun 1** a thing that is incorrect 错误;不正确之事 **2** an error of judgement 错误判断;失策 • **verb** (**mistakes, mistaking, mistook**; past participle **mistaken**) **1** be wrong about 弄错;误解 **2** (**mistake someone/thing for**) confuse someone or something with 将(某人或某物)错当成或,混淆

mistaken /mɪ'steɪkən/ **adjective 1** wrong in your opinion or judgement 观点错误的;判断失误的 **2** based on a misunderstanding 被误解的;基于错误判断的 ■ **mistakenly adverb**.

mister /'mɪstə(r)/ **noun 1 (Mister)** = **Mr. 2** informal 【非正式】a form of address to a man (对男子的称呼)先生

mistime /ˌmɪs'taɪm/ **verb** (**mistimes, mistiming, mistimed**) choose an inappropriate moment to do or say something 在不适当的时机做(或说)

mistletoe /'mɪsltəʊ/ **noun** a plant which grows as a parasite on trees, producing white berries in winter 槲寄生(寄生于树木上的植物,冬季结白色浆果)

mistreat /ˌmɪs'triːt/ **verb** treat badly or unfairly 虐待;不公正地对待 ■ **mistreatment noun**.

mistress /'mɪstrəs/ **noun 1** a woman in a position of authority 有权势的女子 **2** a woman who is very skilled in something 女强人;女能人 **3** a woman having a sexual relationship with a man who is married to someone else 情妇 **4** Brit.【英】a female schoolteacher 女教师 **5 (Mistress)** old use【旧】Mrs. 夫人

mistrial /ˌmɪs'traɪəl/ **noun** a trial that is not considered valid because of a mistake in proceedings (因诉讼程序错误造成的)无效审判

mistrust /ˌmɪs'trʌst/ **verb** have no

trust in 不信任；猜疑 • noun lack of trust 不信任；猜疑

misty /'mɪsti/ adjective (**mistier, mistiest**) **1** covered with mist 薄雾弥漫的；雾气笼罩的 **2** having an outline that is not clear 模糊的；不清晰的

misunderstand /ˌmɪsʌndə'stænd/ verb (**misunderstands, misunderstanding, misunderstood**) fail to understand correctly 误解；误会 ■ **misunderstanding** noun.

misuse /ˌmɪs'juːz/ verb (**misuses, misusing, misused**) **1** use wrongly 误用；错用；滥用 **2** treat badly or unfairly 虐待；不公正地对待 • noun the action of misusing 误用；滥用

mite /maɪt/ noun **1** a tiny insect-like creature 螨 **2** a small child or animal 小孩；小动物 **3** a very small amount 极少量

mitigate /'mɪtɪɡeɪt/ verb (**mitigates, mitigating, mitigated**) make something bad less severe or serious 减轻；缓和 ■ **mitigation** noun.

> **！注意** don't confuse **mitigate** with **militate**: **militate against** means 'make it very difficult for something to happen or exist'. 不要混淆 **mitigate** 和 **militate**: **militate against** 意为"严重影响某事物"。

mitre /'maɪtə(r)/ (US spelling【美拼作】 **miter**) noun **1** a tall headdress that tapers to a point at the front and back, worn by bishops 主教冠；牧冠 **2** a joint made between two pieces of wood cut at an angle in order to form a corner of 90° 斜接头；阳角接

mitt /mɪt/ noun **1** a mitten 连指手套 **2** informal【非正式】 a person's hand 手

mitten /'mɪtn/ noun a glove having a single section for all four fingers, with a separate section for the thumb 连指手套

mix /mɪks/ verb **1** combine or be combined to form a whole 使混合 **2** make by mixing ingredients 调制；配制 **3** combine different recordings to form one piece of music 混录 **4** (**mix something up**) spoil the arrangement of something 搅乱；弄混 **5** (**mix someone/thing up**) confuse one person or thing with another 混淆 **6** meet different people socially 交际；交往 • noun **1** a mixture 混合物 **2** the proportion of different people or things making up a mixture (组成混合体的)不同人群；(混合物的)配料，成分 **3** a version of a piece of music mixed in a different way from the original 混录音乐 □ **mix-up** informal【非正式】 a misunderstanding or mistake 误会；误解

mixed /mɪkst/ adjective **1** made up of different qualities or things 混合的；混杂的 **2** having to do with males and females 男女混合的 □ **mixed bag** an assortment of people or things of very different types 大杂烩；混合体

mixer /'mɪksə(r)/ noun **1** a machine or device for mixing things 混合器；搅拌器 **2** a soft drink that can be mixed with alcohol 调酒用饮料

mixture /'mɪkstʃə(r)/ noun **1** a substance made by mixing other substances together 混合物 **2** (a **mixture of**) a combination of different things in which each thing is distinct 混合体

mizzen /'mɪzn/ or **mizzenmast** /'mɪznmɑːst/ noun the mast behind a ship's mainmast 后桅

ml abbreviation **1** miles. **2** millilitres.

mm abbreviation millimetres.

mnemonic /nɪ'mɒnɪk/ noun a pattern of letters or words used to help remember something 帮助记忆的词句；助记符号 • adjective designed to help remember something 助记的

moan /məʊn/ **noun 1** a low mournful sound, usually expressing suffering (痛苦的)呻吟声 **2** informal【非正式】a complaint 牢骚；抱怨 • **verb 1** make a moan 呻吟 **2** complain; grumble 发牢骚；抱怨

moat /məʊt/ **noun** a wide defensive ditch surrounding a castle or town 护城河；城壕

mob /mɒb/ **noun 1** a disorderly crowd of people 乱民；乌合之众 **2** Brit. informal【英，非正式】a group of people 人群 **3 (the Mob)** N. Amer.【北美】the Mafia 黑手党 **4 (the mob)** disapproving【贬】the ordinary people 平民；百姓 • **verb (mobs, mobbing, mobbed)** (of a large group of people) crowd round someone (大群人)聚集

mobile /ˈməʊbaɪl/ **adjective 1** able to move or be moved freely or easily 可移动的；易于移动的 **2** (of a shop, library, etc.) set up inside a vehicle and able to travel around (商店、图书馆等)车载的，流动的 **3** able to change your occupation, social class, or where you live 易于变换工作(社会阶层或住处)的；流动的 **4** (of a person's face) easily changing expression (面部)表情多变的 • **noun 1** a decoration that is hung so as to turn freely in the air 悬垂饰物；挂件 **2** (also **mobile phone**) a portable telephone 移动电话；手机

mobility /məʊˈbɪlɪti/ **noun** the quality of being mobile 移动能力；流动性

mobilize or **mobilise** /ˈməʊbəlaɪz/ **verb (mobilizes, mobilizing, mobilized) 1** organize troops for active service 调动(军队) **2** organize people or resources for a particular task 动员，组织(人或资源) ■ **mobilization** noun.

mobster /ˈmɒbstə(r)/ **noun** informal【非正式】a gangster 匪徒；歹徒

moccasin /ˈmɒkəsɪn/ **noun** a soft leather shoe with the sole turned up and sewn to the upper, originally worn by North American Indians 莫卡辛鞋；软帮皮鞋

mocha /ˈmɒkə/ **noun 1** a type of fine-quality coffee 摩卡咖啡(一种优质咖啡) **2** a drink made with coffee and chocolate (加巧克力的)摩卡咖啡饮料

mock /mɒk/ **verb** tease or imitate someone in an unkind way 挖苦；嘲弄 • **adjective 1** not genuine or real 假的；不真实的 **2** (of an exam, battle, etc.) arranged for training or practice (考试、战斗等)模拟的 • **noun (mocks)** Brit. informal【英，非正式】exams taken in school as a practice for public exams 模拟考试 □ **mock-up** a model of a machine or structure that is used for teaching or testing (用于教学或实验的) 实体模型

mockery /ˈmɒkəri/ **noun (plural mockeries) 1** unkind teasing; ridicule 嘲笑；愚弄 **2 (a mockery of)** an absurd or worthless version of something 荒谬的事物，无价值的事物 □ **make a mockery of** make something seem ridiculous or useless 取笑；愚弄；嘲笑

mockingbird /ˈmɒkɪŋbɜːd/ **noun** a long-tailed American songbird, noted for copying the calls of other birds 嘲鸫(美洲长尾鸣禽，善于模仿其他鸟的叫声)

modal verb /ˈməʊdl/ **noun** Grammar【语法】an auxiliary verb expressing necessity or possibility, e.g. *must, shall, will* 情态动词

mode /məʊd/ **noun 1** a way in which something occurs or is done 形式；方式 **2** a style in clothes, art, etc. (服装、艺术等的)风格

model /ˈmɒdl/ **noun 1** a three-dimensional representation of something 模型 **2** something used as an example 范例；样本 **3** a person or thing seen as an excellent example of a quality 典范；榜样：*He was a model of self-control.* 他是严于律

己的楷模。 **4** a person whose job is to display clothes by wearing them 服装模特儿 **5** a person who poses for an artist or photographer 美术模特儿;摄影模特儿 **6** a particular design or version of a product 型号;样式 **7** a simplified mathematical description of a system or process 数学模型 • verb (**models, modelling, modelled**; US spelling【美拼作】**models, modeling, modeled**) **1** make a figure in clay, wax, etc. (用陶、蜡等)模塑, 塑造 **2** (**model something on**) design or plan something using another thing as an example 以…为样板;模仿 **3** work as a fashion model 做时装模特儿 **4** devise a mathematical model of 设计…的数学模型

modem /'məʊdem/ **noun** a device that connects a computer to a telephone line (连接计算机和电话线的)调制解调器

moderate adjective /'mɒdərət/ **1** average in amount, strength, or degree 中等的;适度的;普通的 **2** (of a political position) not extreme (政治立场)温和的, 中庸的 • noun /'mɒdərət/ a person with moderate views 持温和观点者 • verb /'mɒdəreɪt/ (**moderates, moderating, moderated**) **1** make or become less extreme or strong (使)缓和;(使)变温和 **2** check exam papers to ensure that they have been marked consistently (为确保评分标准一致而)审核(试卷)■ **moderately** adverb.

moderation /ˌmɒdə'reɪʃn/ **noun 1** the avoidance of extremes in your actions or opinions (行为或观点的)温和, 中庸, 适度 **2** the process of moderating 缓和;评分审核

moderator /'mɒdəreɪtə(r)/ **noun 1** a person who helps others to solve a dispute 调解人;仲裁人 **2** a chairman of a debate 辩论会主席 **3** a person who moderates exam papers 评卷监督

modern /'mɒdn/ **adjective 1** relating to the present or to recent times 现代的;近代的 **2** using the most up-to-date techniques or equipment (技术或设备)现代化的, 最新的 **3** (of art, architecture, music, etc.) new and intended to be different from traditional styles (美术、建筑、音乐等)现代的, 非传统的 ■ **modernity** noun.

modernism /'mɒdənɪzəm/ **noun 1** modern ideas, methods, or styles 现代观念 **2** a movement in the arts or religion that aims to break with traditional forms or ideas 现代派, 现代主义(旨在打破传统形式或观念) ■ **modernist** noun & adjective.

modernize or **modernise** /'mɒdənaɪz/ **verb** (**modernizes, moder-nizing, modernized**) bring up to date with modern equipment, techniques, etc. 使现代化 ■ **modern-ization** noun.

modest /'mɒdɪst/ **adjective 1** not boasting about your abilities or achievements 谦虚的, 谦恭的 **2** relatively moderate, limited, or small 适中的;有限的;较小的 **3** not showing off the body; decent 端庄的;朴素的 ■ **modestly** adverb **modesty** noun.

modicum /'mɒdɪkəm/ **noun** a small quantity of something 少量;一点点

modification /ˌmɒdɪfɪ'keɪʃn/ **noun 1** the action of modifying something 更改;修改 **2** a change made 改变;变化

modifier /'mɒdɪfaɪə(r)/ **noun 1** a person or thing that modifies 改造者;修改者 **2** Grammar【语法】a word that qualifies the sense of a noun (e.g. *family* in *a family house*) 修饰语(如:a family house 中的 family)

modify /'mɒdɪfaɪ/ **verb** (**modifies, modifying, modified**) make partial changes to 更改;修改

modish /'məʊdɪʃ/ **adjective** fashionable 时髦的

modular /'mɒdjələ(r)/ **adjective** made up of separate units 组件的;组合的

modulate /'mɒdjuleɪt/ **verb** (**modulates, modulating, modulated**) **1** adjust, change, or control something 调节;改变;控制 **2** vary the strength, tone, or pitch of your voice 调整(嗓音强度、音调或音高) **3** Music【音乐】change from one key to another 转调;变调 ■ **modulation** noun.

module /'mɒdjuːl/ **noun 1** each of a set of parts or units that can be used to create a more complex structure 组件;部件 **2** a unit forming part of a course 模块 **3** an independent unit of a spacecraft (航天器独立的)舱

moggie or **moggy** /'mɒgi/ **noun** (plural **moggies**) Brit. informal【英,非正式】a cat 猫咪

mogul /'məʊgl/ **noun** informal【非正式】an important or powerful person 大人物;有权势的人

mohair /'məʊheə(r)/ **noun** a yarn or fabric made from the hair of the angora goat 马海毛;安哥拉山羊毛;马海毛织物

Mohican /məʊ'hiːkən/ **noun** a hair style in which the sides of the head are shaved and a central strip of hair is made to stand up 莫希干发型(两侧剃光,中间留下一道直立的头发)

moiety /'mɔɪəti/ **noun** (plural **moieties**) formal【正式】a half 一半

moist /mɔɪst/ **adjective** slightly wet; damp 微湿的;湿润的 ■ **moisten** verb.

moisture /'mɔɪstʃə(r)/ **noun** tiny droplets of water making something damp 水汽,湿气

moisturize or **moisturise** /'mɔɪstʃəraɪz/ **verb** (**moisturizes, moisturizing, moisturized**) make something, especially the skin, less dry 使滋润;(尤指)使(皮肤)湿润 ■ **moisturizer** noun.

molar /'məʊlə(r)/ **noun** a grinding tooth at the back of the mouth 臼齿;磨牙

molasses /mə'læsɪz/ **noun** a thick brown liquid obtained from raw sugar 糖浆;糖蜜

mold /məʊld/ US spelling of MOULD[1], MOULD[2]. mould[1], mould[2]的美式拼法

mole[1] /məʊl/ **noun 1** a small burrowing mammal with dark fur, a long muzzle, and very small eyes 鼹鼠 **2** someone within an organization who secretly passes confidential information to another organization or country 内奸

mole[2] **noun** a dark brown mark on the skin 痣

mole[3] **noun 1** a pier, breakwater, or causeway 突堤;防波堤 **2** a harbour formed by a mole 筑有防波堤的港湾

mole[4] **noun** Chemistry【化学】the amount of a particular substance which contains as many atoms or molecules as there are atoms in a standard amount of carbon 摩尔;克分子量

molecule /'mɒlɪkjuːl/ **noun** a group of atoms forming the smallest unit into which a substance can be divided 分子 ■ **molecular** adjective.

molehill /'məʊlhɪl/ **noun** a small mound of earth thrown up by a burrowing mole 鼹鼠丘

moleskin /'məʊlskɪn/ **noun 1** the skin of a mole used as fur 鼹鼠毛皮 **2** a thick cotton fabric with a soft surface 斜纹厚绒布

molest /mə'lest/ **verb 1** sexually assault someone 对⋯⋯进行性骚扰;调戏 **2** dated【废】pester someone in a hostile way 骚扰;干扰 ■ **molestation** noun **molester** noun.

moll /mɒl/ **noun** informal【非正式】a gangster's girlfriend 匪徒的女帮凶

mollify /'mɒlɪfaɪ/ **verb** (**mollifies, mollifying, mollified**) make someone feel less angry 安抚；平息

mollusc /ˈmɒləsk/ (US spelling 【美拼作】 **mollusk**) noun an animal of a group with a soft unsegmented body and often an external shell, such as slugs and snails 软体动物

mollycoddle /ˈmɒlikɒdl/ verb (**mollycoddles**, **mollycoddling**, **mollycoddled**) treat someone too indulgently or protectively 娇惯，溺爱；娇宠

molt /məʊlt/ US spelling of MOULT. moult 的美式拼法

molten /ˈməʊltən/ adjective (especially of metal and glass) made liquid by heat (尤指金属和玻璃)熔化的

molto /ˈmɒltəʊ/ adverb Music 【音乐】 very 极；非常；甚

molybdenum /məˈlɪbdənəm/ noun a brittle silver-grey metallic element (金属元素)钼

mom /mɒm/ N. Amer. 【北美】= MUM[1].

moment /ˈməʊmənt/ noun 1 a brief period of time 片刻；一会儿 2 an exact point in time 某一时刻 3 formal 【正式】importance 重要

momentarily /ˈməʊməntrəli/ adverb 1 for a very short time 顷刻间 2 N. Amer. 【北美】very soon 立刻；马上

momentary /ˈməʊməntri/ adjective very brief or short-lived 瞬间的，稍纵即逝的

momentous /məˈmentəs/ adjective of great importance or significance 重大的；非常重要的

momentum /məˈmentəm/ noun (plural **momenta**) 1 the force gained by a moving object 动力 2 the force caused by the development of something (事物发展的)势头

mommy /ˈmɒmi/ N. Amer. 【北美】= MUMMY[1].

monarch /ˈmɒnək/ noun a king, queen, or emperor 君主 ■ **monarchical** adjective.

monarchist /ˈmɒnəkɪst/ noun someone who believes a country

should be ruled by a king or queen 拥护君主制者 ■ **monarchism** noun.

monarchy /ˈmɒnəki/ noun (plural **monarchies**) 1 government by a monarch 君主政体 2 a state with a monarch 君主国

monastery /ˈmɒnəstri/ noun (plural **monasteries**) a community of monks living under religious vows 隐修院；修道院；寺院

monastic /məˈnæstɪk/ adjective 1 relating to monks or nuns 僧侣的；尼姑的，修士的；修女的 2 resembling monks or their way of life 僧侣般的；修士般的

Monday /ˈmʌndeɪ, -di/ noun the day of the week before Tuesday and following Sunday 星期一；周一

monetarism /ˈmʌnɪtərɪzəm/ noun the theory that inflation is best controlled by limiting the supply of money 货币主义(认为限制货币供给是控制通货膨胀最有效的手段) ■ **monetarist** noun & adjective.

monetary /ˈmʌnɪtri/ adjective having to do with money 钱的，货币的

money /ˈmʌni/ noun 1 a means of paying for things in the form of coins and banknotes 货币；钱币；钞票 2 wealth 财富；财产 3 payment or financial gain 报酬；收入，薪水 4 (**moneys** or **monies**) formal 【正式】sums of money 款项；汇款 ■ **money order** a postal order 汇票；汇款单 ■ **money spider** a very small black spider 华盖蛛(一种体型极小的黑蜘蛛)

moneyed or **monied** /ˈmʌnid/ adjective having a lot of money 有钱的；富有的

Mongol /ˈmɒŋɡəl/ noun 1 a person from Mongolia 蒙古人 2 (**mongol**) offensive 【冒犯】a person with Down's syndrome 唐氏综合征患者；伸佳样痴呆患者 ■ **Mongolian** noun & adjective.

mongoose /ˈmɒŋɡuːs/ noun (plural

mongooses) a small meat-eating animal with a long body and tail, native to Africa and Asia 獴(一种体长长的小型食肉哺乳动物, 原产于非洲和亚洲)

mongrel /ˈmʌŋgrəl/ **noun** a dog of no definite breed 杂种狗

moniker /ˈmɒnɪkə(r)/ **noun** informal 【非正式】a name 姓名;名字

monitor /ˈmɒnɪtə(r)/ **noun 1** a person or device that monitors something 监视员;监控器 **2** a television used to view a picture from a particular camera or a display from a computer 监视器;显示器 **3** a school pupil with special duties 班长;班代表 **4** (also **monitor lizard**) a large tropical lizard 巨蜥 • **verb** keep under observation 监视;监测;监控

monk /mʌŋk/ **noun** a man belonging to a religious community typically living under vows of poverty, chastity, and obedience 僧侣;修道士

monkey /ˈmʌŋki/ **noun** (plural **monkeys**) a primate typically having a long tail and living in trees in tropical countries 猴 • **verb** (**monkeys**, **monkeying**, **monkeyed**) **1** (**monkey about** or **around**) behave in a silly or playful way 胡闹;捣蛋 **2** (**monkey with**) tamper with 瞎摆弄;乱拆脐 ■ **monkey nut** Brit.【英】a peanut 花生 **monkey puzzle** a coniferous tree with branches covered in spirals of tough spiny leaves 猴谜树(一种针叶树,叶坚硬,顶端呈针状,在树枝上螺旋排列) **monkey wrench** a spanner with large adjustable jaws 活动扳手

mono /ˈmɒnəʊ/ **noun** sound reproduction which uses only one transmission channel 单声道录制

monochrome /ˈmɒnəkrəʊm/ **adjective** (of a photograph or picture) produced in black and white or in varying tones of one colour (照片或图画)黑白的, 单色的 ■ **monochromatic** adjective.

monocle /ˈmɒnəkl/ **noun** a single lens worn at one eye 单片眼镜

monogamy /məˈnɒgəmi/ **noun** the practice of having only one wife or husband at any one time 一夫一妻制 ■ **monogamous** adjective.

monogram /ˈmɒnəgræm/ **noun** a motif of two or more interwoven letters, typically a person's initials 交织字母, 花押字(一般由姓名首字母组成) ■ **monogrammed** adjective.

monograph /ˈmɒnəgrɑːf/ **noun** a book or academic paper written on a single subject 专著;专论

monolingual /ˌmɒnəˈlɪŋgwəl/ **adjective** speaking or expressed in only one language 单语的;一种语言的

monolith /ˈmɒnəlɪθ/ **noun** a large single upright block of stone 独石柱

monolithic /ˌmɒnəˈlɪθɪk/ **adjective 1** formed of a single large block of stone 整块巨石构成的;独块巨石的 **2** very large and impersonal 庞大的;巨大无情的

monologue /ˈmɒnəlɒg/ **noun 1** a long speech by one actor in a play or film (戏剧或电影中的)独白 **2** a long, boring speech by one person (一个人的)长篇大论, 滔滔不绝的话

monomania /ˌmɒnəˈmeɪniə/ **noun** an obsession with one thing (对某一事物的)偏执, 狂热 ■ **monomaniac** noun.

monomer /ˈmɒnəmə(r)/ **noun** Chemistry【化学】a molecule that can be linked to other identical molecules to form a polymer 单体

monophonic /ˌmɒnəˈfɒnɪk/ **adjective** (of sound reproduction) using only one channel (录音)单声道的

monoplane /ˈmɒnəpleɪn/ **noun** an aircraft with one pair of wings 单翼飞机

monopolize or **monopolise** /məˈnɒpəlaɪz/ **verb** (**monopolizes**, **monopolizing**, **monopolized**) dominate or take control of 垄断;控制

M

monopoly /mə'nɒpəli/ **noun** (plural **monopolies**) the complete control of the supply of a product or service by one person or organization 垄断；独占；完全掌控

monorail /'mɒnəʊreɪl/ **noun** a railway in which the track consists of a single rail 单轨铁路

monosyllabic /ˌmɒnəsɪ'læbɪk/ **adjective 1** (of a word) having one syllable (词)单音节的 **2** (of a person) saying very little (人)寡言少语的

monosyllable /'mɒnəsɪləbl/ **noun** a word of one syllable 单音节词

monotheism /'mɒnəʊθiɪzəm/ **noun** the belief that there is only one god 一神教 ■ **monotheistic** adjective.

monotone /'mɒnətəʊn/ **noun** a continuing sound that does not change pitch 单一声调

monotonous /mə'nɒtənəs/ **adjective** boring and unchanging 重复而乏味的 ■ **monotonously** adverb **monotony** noun.

monoxide /mə'nɒksaɪd/ **noun** Chemistry【化学】an oxide containing one atom of oxygen 一氧化物

Monsieur /mə'sjɜː(r)/ **noun** (plural **Messieurs** /mes'jɜː(r)/) a title for a French man, corresponding to Mr or sir 先生(法语国家对男士的称呼，相当于 Mr 或 sir)

Monsignor /mɒn'siːnjə(r)/ **noun** (plural **Monsignori** /ˌmɒnsiː'njɔːri/) the title of a senior Roman Catholic priest 阁下(罗马天主教会高级神职人员的称呼)

monsoon /ˌmɒn'suːn/ **noun 1** a seasonal wind in the Indian subcontinent and SE Asia 季风(盛行于印度次大陆和东南亚) **2** the rainy season accompanying the monsoon 季风雨季

monster /'mɒnstə(r)/ **noun 1** a frightening imaginary creature 怪物；怪兽 **2** a cruel or wicked person 凶恶至极者；非常邪恶的人 **3** something

that is very large 庞然大物；a monster of a book 一本大书

monstrosity /mɒn'strɒsəti/ **noun** (plural **monstrosities**) something that is very large and ugly 丑陋的巨物

monstrous /'mɒstrəs/ **adjective 1** very large, ugly, or frightening 巨大且丑陋的；巨大而骇人的 **2** shocking and morally wrong 丑恶的；极端错误的 ■ **monstrously** adverb.

montage /mɒn'tɑːʒ/ **noun** a picture or film made by putting together pieces from other pictures or films 蒙太奇；剪辑

month /mʌnθ/ **noun 1** each of the twelve periods of time into which a year is divided 月；月份 **2** a period of time between a date in one month and the same date in the next month 一个月 **3** a period of 28 days or four weeks 一个月的时间(28天或4个星期)

monthly /'mʌnθli/ **adjective & adverb** happening or produced once a month 每月的(地)

monty /'mɒnti/ **noun** (**the full monty**) Brit. informal【英，非正式】the full amount or extent 一切；全部

monument /'mɒnjumənt/ **noun 1** a statue or structure built in memory of a person or event 纪念碑；纪念性建筑 **2** a site of historical importance 历史遗迹 **3** a lasting example of something 丰碑；不朽的典范；a monument to good taste 高雅品位的不朽典范

monumental /ˌmɒnju'mentl/ **adjective 1** very large or impressive 巨大的；给人深刻印象的 **2** forming a monument 纪念碑的；纪念性的 ■ **monumentally** adverb.

moo /muː/ **verb** (**moos, mooing, mooed**) (of a cow) make a long, deep sound (母牛)哞哞叫

mooch /muːtʃ/ **verb** Brit. informal【英，

非正式】stand or walk around in a bored way 闲逛；溜达

mood /muːd/ **noun 1** the way you feel at a particular time 情绪；心情 **2** a period of being bad-tempered 一时的坏脾气；低落的情绪 **3** the atmosphere of a work of art (艺术作品的)氛围，气氛 **4** Grammar 【语法】a form of a verb expressing fact, command, question, wish, or a condition (动词的)语气

moody /ˈmuːdi/ **adjective (moodier, moodiest) 1** having moods that change quickly 喜怒无常的 **2** gloomy or bad-tempered 情绪低落的；脾气不好的

moon /muːn/ **noun 1** (also **Moon**) the natural satellite of the earth 月亮 **2** a natural satellite of any planet 卫星 **3** literary 【文】a month 月份 • **verb 1** (**moon about** or **around**) behave or walk about in a dreamy way 闲混；闲逛；精神恍惚 **2** informal 【非正式】expose your buttocks to someone as an insult or joke (作为侮辱或玩笑)对…亮光屁股，向…露出光腚 □ **over the moon** informal 【非正式】delighted 非常高兴；快活

moonlight /ˈmuːnlaɪt/ **noun** the light of the moon 月光 • **verb (moonlights, moonlighting, moonlighted)** informal 【非正式】do a second job without declaring it for tax purposes (为避税)暗中兼职，做第二份工作 ■ **moonlit** adjective.

moonscape /ˈmuːnskeɪp/ **noun** a landscape that is rocky and barren like the moon 月亮表面般崎岖荒凉的地带

moonshine /ˈmuːnʃaɪn/ **noun** informal 【非正式】**1** foolish talk or ideas 蠢话；愚蠢的想法 **2** N. Amer.【北美】alcohol that is made and sold illegally 私酿酒；走私酒

moonstone /ˈmuːnstəʊn/ **noun** a white semi-precious mineral 月长石

moony /ˈmuːni/ **adjective** dreamy as a result of being in love 因恋爱而神情恍惚的

Moor /mɔː(r)/ **noun** a member of a NW African Muslim people 莫尔人 (非洲西北部的穆斯林) ■ **Moorish** adjective.

moor¹ /mɔː(r)/ **noun** a high open area of land that is not cultivated 荒野；漠泽

moor² **verb** fasten a boat to the shore or to an anchor 使(小船)停泊；系泊

moorhen /ˈmɔːhen/ **noun** a waterbird with black feathers 泽鸡；墨水鸡

mooring /ˈmɔːrɪŋ/ or **moorings** **noun** a place where a boat is moored, or the ropes used to moor it 系泊区；停泊处

moose /muːs/ **noun** = ELK.

moot /muːt/ **adjective** uncertain or undecided 未定的：a moot point 未决定的问题 • **verb** put forward a topic for discussion 提出…供讨论

mop /mɒp/ **noun 1** a bundle of thick strings or a sponge attached to a handle, used for wiping floors 拖把 **2** a thick mass of hair 蓬乱的头发 • **verb (mops, mopping, mopped) 1** clean or soak up by wiping 拖净；抹净；擦净 **2** (**mop something up**) complete something by dealing with the things that remain 清理；完成；使结束

mope /məʊp/ **verb (mopes, moping, moped)** be listless and gloomy 无精打采；闷闷不乐

moped /ˈməʊped/ **noun** a motorcycle with a small engine 机动自行车；机动脚踏车

moraine /məˈreɪn/ **noun** rocks and stones deposited by a glacier 冰碛

moral /ˈmɒrəl/ **adjective 1** concerned with the principles of right and wrong behaviour 道德的 **2** conforming to accepted standards of behaviour 合乎道德的；品行端正的 • **noun 1** a lesson about right or wrong that you learn from a story or experience (由

故事或经历引出的)道德教训,寓意 **2** (morals) standards of good behaviour 品行;道德规范 ■ **morally** adverb.

morale /mə'rɑːl/ noun a feeling of confidence and satisfaction 士气;精神面貌

moralist /'mɒrəlɪst/ noun a person with strict views about morals 道德说教者 ■ **moralistic** adjective.

morality /mə'ræləti/ noun (plural **moralities**) **1** principles concerning the difference between right and wrong or good and bad behaviour 道德准则;道德规范 **2** moral behaviour 德行;品行 **3** the extent to which an action is right or wrong 合乎道德的程度;道德性

moralize or **moralise** /'mɒrəlaɪz/ verb (**moralizes**, **moralizing**, **moralized**) comment on moral issues, usually in a disapproving way 进行道德说教

morass /mə'ræs/ noun **1** an area of muddy or boggy ground 泥泞;沼泽 **2** a complicated or confused situation 困境;陷阱

moratorium /ˌmɒrə'tɔːriəm/ noun (plural **moratoriums** or **moratoria**) a temporary ban on an activity 暂时禁止;暂停

morbid /'mɔːbɪd/ adjective **1** having a strong interest in unpleasant subjects, especially death and disease 病态的;(尤指)对死亡与疾病感兴趣的 **2** Medicine 【医】 having to do with disease 和疾病有关的 ■ **morbidity** noun **morbidly** adverb.

mordant /'mɔːdnt/ adjective (of humour) sharply sarcastic (幽默)尖刻的,挖苦的,讥讽的

more /mɔː(r)/ determiner & pronoun a greater or additional amount or degree (数量或程度)更多的,更大的 • adverb **1** forming the comparative of adjectives and adverbs (构成形容词和副词的比较级)更 **2** to a greater

extent 更大程度地 **3** again 再次 **4** (**more than**) very 极其

morello /mə'reləʊ/ noun (plural **morellos**) a kind of sour dark cherry 欧洲酸樱桃

moreover /mɔːr'əʊvə(r)/ adverb in addition to what has been said already 而且;此外

mores /'mɔːreɪz/ plural noun the customs of a community 风俗;传统

morgue /mɔːg/ noun a mortuary 太平间;停尸房

moribund /'mɒrɪbʌnd/ adjective **1** at the point of death 濒临死亡的;垂死的 **2** about to come to an end 行将消亡的

Mormon /'mɔːmən/ noun a member of the Church of Jesus Christ of Latter-Day Saints 摩门教教徒(耶稣基督末世圣徒教会的成员) ■ **Mormonism** noun.

morn /mɔːn/ noun literary 【文】 morning 清晨

morning /'mɔːnɪŋ/ noun **1** the period of time between midnight and noon, especially from sunrise to noon 早晨;(尤指)上午 **2** sunrise 日出 □ **morning sickness** nausea felt by a woman when she is pregnant 孕妇晨吐;孕妇恶心

Moroccan /mə'rɒkən/ noun a person from Morocco 摩洛哥人 • adjective relating to Morocco 摩洛哥的

moron /'mɔːrɒn/ noun informal 【非正式】 a stupid person 傻瓜;蠢货 ■ **moronic** adjective.

morose /mə'rəʊs/ adjective unhappy and bad-tempered 阴郁的;脾气坏的 ■ **morosely** adverb.

morph /mɔːf/ verb (in computer animation) change smoothly and gradually from one image to another (计算机动画中)变换图像

morphine /'mɔːfiːn/ noun a drug made from opium and used to relieve pain 吗啡

morris dancing /'mɒrɪs/ noun

traditional English folk dancing 莫里斯舞(传统英格兰民间舞蹈)

morrow /ˈmɒrəʊ/ **noun (the morrow)** old use【旧】the next day 次日；翌日

Morse /mɔːs/ or **Morse code** **noun** a code in which letters are represented by combinations of long and short sounds or flashes of light 莫尔斯电码(用长短不同的声音或光信号的组合代表不同字母)

morsel /ˈmɔːsl/ **noun** a small piece of food (食物的)一丁点儿，一小块

mortal /ˈmɔːtl/ **adjective 1** having to die at some time 终将死亡的；有生有死的 **2** causing death 致命的；致死的 **3** (of a battle or enemy) lasting until death (战斗或敌人)至死方休的，不共戴天的 • **noun** a human being 人类；凡人 □ **mortal sin** (in Christian belief) a sin so serious as to result in damnation (基督教信仰中的)不可饶恕的罪孽 ■ **mortally** adverb.

mortality /mɔːˈtæləti/ **noun 1** the state of being mortal 必死性 **2** death 死亡 **3** (also **mortality rate**) the number of deaths in a particular area or period of time 死亡数；死亡率

mortar /ˈmɔːtə(r)/ **noun 1** a mixture of lime with cement, sand, and water, used to stick bricks or stones together 砂浆；灰浆 **2** a cup-shaped container in which substances are crushed with a pestle 研钵；臼 **3** a short cannon for firing shells at high angles 迫击炮 □ **mortar board** an academic cap with a flat square top and a tassel 学位帽；方顶帽

mortgage /ˈmɔːɡɪdʒ/ **noun 1** a legal agreement by which a bank or building society lends you money, using your house as security 抵押；按揭 **2** an amount of money borrowed or lent under such an agreement 按揭借款；按揭贷款 • **verb (mortgages, mortgaging, mortgaged)** give a bank or building society the right to

hold your house as security for the money they agree to lend you 抵押

mortician /mɔːˈtɪʃn/ **noun** N. Amer.【北美】an undertaker 承办丧葬者；殡葬业者

mortify /ˈmɔːtɪfaɪ/ **verb (mortifies, mortifying, mortified)** make someone feel embarrassed or ashamed 使难堪；使受辱 □ **mortification** noun.

mortise or **mortice** /ˈmɔːtɪs/ **noun** a slot cut in a piece of wood in order to hold the end of another piece of wood 榫眼；铆 □ **mortise lock** a lock fitted into a hole in a door (嵌入门里的)插锁，嵌锁

mortuary /ˈmɔːtʃəri/ **noun** (plural **mortuaries**) a room or building in which dead bodies are kept until they are buried or cremated 太平间；停尸房

mosaic /məʊˈzeɪɪk/ **noun** a picture or pattern made by fitting together small coloured pieces of stone, tile, or glass 镶嵌画；镶嵌图案

mosey /ˈməʊzi/ **verb (moseys, moseying, moseyed)** informal【非正式】walk in a leisurely way 漫步；溜达

Moslem /ˈmɒzləm/ ⇒ 见 **MUSLIM**.

mosque /mɒsk/ **noun** a Muslim place of worship 清真寺

mosquito /məˈskiːtəʊ/ **noun** (plural **mosquitoes**) a small long-legged fly, some kinds of which transmit diseases through their bite 蚊子

moss /mɒs/ **noun** a very small green spreading plant which grows in damp places 苔藓 ■ **mossy** adjective.

most /məʊst/ **determiner & pronoun 1** greatest in amount or degree (数量或程度)最多，最大 **2** the majority of 大多数；大部分 • **adverb 1** to the greatest extent 最大程度 **2** forming the superlative of adjectives and adverbs (构成形容词和副词的最高级)最 **3** very 非常；十分；很

mostly /ˈməʊstli/ **adverb 1** on the

whole; mainly 大体上;主要地;多半 **2** usually 通常

mote /məʊt/ **noun** a speck 瑕疵;污点;微粒

motel /məʊˈtel/ **noun** a roadside hotel designed for motorists 汽车旅馆

motet /məʊˈtet/ **noun** a short piece of choral music 经文歌

moth /mɒθ/ **noun** an insect like a butterfly, which is active at night 蛾;飞蛾 □ **moth-eaten 1** eaten by the larvae of moths 虫蛀的 **2** shabby and worn 褴褛的;破旧的

mothball /ˈmɒθbɔːl/ **noun** a small ball of camphor, placed among stored clothes to deter moths 卫生球;樟脑丸

mother /ˈmʌðə(r)/ **noun 1** a female parent 母亲;妈妈 **2** (**Mother**) (especially as a title or form of address) the head of a convent (尤作为称谓或敬称)嬷嬷,女修道院院长 • **verb** look after somebody protectively 给…以母亲般的照顾 □ **mother-in-law** (plural **mothers-in-law**) the mother of a person's husband or wife 婆婆;岳母 **mother-of-pearl** a smooth pearly substance lining the shells of oysters 珠母层;珍珠母 **mother tongue** a person's native language 母语;本国语;本族语 ■ **motherhood** noun **motherly** adjective.

motherland /ˈmʌðəlænd/ **noun** your native country 祖国

motif /məʊˈtiːf/ **noun 1** a pattern or design 图案 **2** a theme that is repeated in a work of literature or piece of music (文学作品或音乐的)主题,主旨

motion /ˈməʊʃn/ **noun 1** the action of moving 移动;动力 **2** a movement or gesture 运动;动作;手势 **3** a formal proposal that is discussed at a meeting 提议;动议 **4** Brit.【英】an emptying of the bowels 大便 • **verb** direct

someone with a gesture 做动作示意 ■ **motion picture** N. Amer.【北美】a cinema film 电影 ■ **motionless** adjective.

motivate /ˈməʊtɪveɪt/ **verb** (**motivates, motivating, motivated**) **1** provide someone with a motive for doing something 使具有…的动机 **2** make someone want to do something 激发 ■ **motivator** noun.

motivation /ˌməʊtɪˈveɪʃn/ **noun 1** the reason for your actions or behaviour 动机;理由 **2** enthusiasm 热情;兴趣 ■ **motivational** adjective.

motive /ˈməʊtɪv/ **noun** something that makes someone act in a particular way 动机;原因 • **adjective** causing motion 引起运动的;发动的

motley /ˈmɒtli/ **adjective** made up of a variety of different things 混杂的

motocross /ˈməʊtəʊkrɒs/ **noun** cross-country racing on motorcycles 摩托车越野赛

motor /ˈməʊtə(r)/ **noun 1** a device that produces power and movement for a vehicle or machine 发动机;马达 **2** Brit. informal【英,非正式】a car 汽车 • **adjective** giving or producing motion 发动的;引起运动的 • **verb** travel in a car 乘汽车旅行;驾车旅行 □ **motor vehicle** a road vehicle powered by an engine 机动车 ■ **motorized** adjective.

motorbike /ˈməʊtəbaɪk/ **noun** a motorcycle 摩托车

motorboat /ˈməʊtəbəʊt/ **noun** a boat powered by a motor 摩托艇

motorcade /ˈməʊtəkeɪd/ **noun** a procession of motor vehicles 机动车队

motorcycle /ˈməʊtəsaɪkl/ **noun** a two-wheeled vehicle powered by a motor 摩托车 ■ **motorcycling** noun **motorcyclist** noun.

motorist /ˈməʊtərɪst/ **noun** the driver of a car 汽车司机

motorway /ˈməʊtəweɪ/ **noun** Brit.

【英】 a road designed for fast traffic, typically with three lanes in each direction 高速公路

mottled /'mɒtld/ **adjective** marked with patches of a different colour 斑驳的；杂色的

motto /'mɒtəʊ/ **noun** (plural **mottoes** or **mottos**) a short sentence or phrase that expresses a belief or aim 箴言；座右铭；格言

mould¹ /məʊld/ (US spelling 【美拼作】 mold) **noun 1** a container into which you pour hot liquid in order to produce a solid object of a desired shape when it cools 模子；模具 **2** a distinctive style or character 类型；风格；特点 ● **verb 1** form an object of a particular shape out of a soft substance 使(柔软物)成形；为(柔软物)塑型 **2** influence the development of something 对…的形成施加影响

mould² (US spelling 【美拼作】 mold) **noun** a furry growth of tiny fungi that occurs in moist warm conditions 霉；霉菌 ■ **mouldy** adjective.

moulder /'məʊldə(r)/ (US spelling 【美拼作】 molder) **verb** (**moulders**, **mouldering**, **mouldered**) slowly decay (逐渐)腐烂

moulding /'məʊldɪŋ/ (US spelling 【美拼作】 molding) **noun** a carved or moulded strip of wood, stone, or plaster as a decorative feature on a building 装饰线条；线脚

moult /məʊlt/ (US spelling 【美拼作】 molt) **verb** shed old feathers, hair, or skin 换羽、蜕毛、蜕皮 ● **noun** a period of moulting 换羽(或蜕毛、蜕皮)期

mound /maʊnd/ **noun 1** a raised mass of earth or other material 土墩；丘 **2** a small hill 小山丘 **3** a heap or pile 堆；垛 ● **verb** heap up into a mound 积成堆；把…堆成堆

mount¹ /maʊnt/ **verb 1** climb up or on to something 攀登；爬上 **2** get up on an animal or bicycle to ride it 骑上；跨上；乘上 **3** increase in size, number, or strength 增加 **4** organize a campaign, bid, etc. 组织；安排 **5** put or fix something in place 安置；安放 ● **noun 1** (also **mounting**) something on which an object is mounted for support or display 支架；底座 **2** a horse used for riding 坐骑

mount² **noun** old use 【旧】 a mountain or hill 山峦；小山

mountain /'maʊntən/ **noun 1** a very high and steep hill 高山；山岳 **2** a large pile or quantity 大堆；大量

mountaineering /ˌmaʊntə'nɪərɪŋ/ **noun** the sport or activity of climbing mountains 登山(运动) ■ **mountaineer** noun.

mountainous /'maʊntənəs/ **adjective 1** having many mountains 多山的 **2** huge 巨大的

mountebank /'maʊntɪbæŋk/ **noun** a person who tricks people in order to get money from them 骗子

mourn /mɔːn/ **verb** feel deep sorrow following the death or loss of 哀悼；感到痛心

mourner /'mɔːnə(r)/ **noun** a person who attends a funeral 参加葬礼者；吊唁者；送葬者

mournful /'mɔːnfl/ **adjective** very sad or depressing 悲痛的；消沉的 ■ **mournfully** adverb.

mourning /'mɔːnɪŋ/ **noun 1** the expression of deep sorrow for someone who has died 哀痛；哀悼 **2** black clothes worn in a period of mourning 丧服

mouse /maʊs/ **noun** (plural **mice**) **1** a small rodent with a pointed snout and a long thin tail 老鼠；耗子 **2** a timid and quiet person 羞怯而胆小的人；胆小的人 **3** (plural also **mouses**) Computing 【计】 a small hand-held device which controls the cursor on a computer screen 鼠标

moussaka /muː'sɑːkə/ **noun** a Greek dish of minced lamb layered with aubergines and tomatoes and topped with a cheese sauce 肉糜茄子饼(由羊羔肉末、茄子、番茄、奶酪酱汁制成的希腊菜肴)

mousse /muːs/ **noun 1** a dish made from whipped cream and egg whites 奶油冻; **2** a light substance used to style hair 摩丝(用于头发定型)

moustache /məˈstɑːʃ/ (US spelling 【美拼作】 **mustache**) **noun** a strip of hair above a man's upper lip 髭(上嘴唇上的胡子)

mousy or **mousey** /ˈmaʊsɪ/ **adjective 1** (of hair) of a light brown colour (毛发)灰褐色的 **2** timid and shy 胆怯的

mouth /maʊθ/ **noun 1** the opening in the body through which food is taken and sounds are made 口;嘴 **2** an opening or entrance to something 开口;入口 **3** the place where a river enters the sea 入海口 • **verb 1** move your lips as if you were saying something 作出说…的口形;用口形无声地说 **2** say something in a pompous way 装腔作势地说 □ **mouth organ** a harmonica 口琴 **mouth-watering** smelling or looking delicious 令人垂涎欲滴的

mouthful /ˈmaʊθfʊl/ **noun 1** an amount of food or drink that fills your mouth 一口的量;满嘴的量 **2** a long or complicated word or phrase 长词(或词组);复杂的词(或词组)

mouthpiece /ˈmaʊθpiːs/ **noun** a part of a musical instrument, telephone, etc. that is put in or against the mouth (乐器的)吹口;(电话的)话筒;咬嘴

mouthwash /ˈmaʊθwɒʃ/ **noun** an antiseptic liquid for rinsing the mouth or gargling 漱口水;漱口液

mouthy /ˈmaʊðɪ/ **adjective** informal【非正式】 inclined to talk a lot 话多的;嘴碎的

move /muːv/ **verb** (**moves**, **moving**, **moved**) **1** go or make something go in a particular direction or way 动;使移动;搬动 **2** change or make

something change position (使)改变位置 **3** change the place where you live 搬家 **4** change from one state or activity to another 改变状态(或活动) **5** take action 采取行动 **6** make progress 进步;发展 **7** provoke a strong feeling in someone 激起(强烈感情);使感动 • **noun 1** an instance of moving 动;移动;搬动 **2** an action taken towards achieving a purpose 行动;步骤 **3** a player's turn during a board game (棋手的)一步,一着 ■ **movable** (or **moveable**) adjective.

movement /ˈmuːvmənt/ **noun 1** an act of moving 移动;运动 **2** the process of moving 运行;行进 **3** a group of people who share the same aims (有共同目标的)团体 **4** a trend or development 趋势;动向 **5** (**movements**) a person's activities during a particular period of time (某人某段时间的)行动,活动 **6** a main division of a piece of music 乐章

movie /ˈmuːvi/ **noun** N. Amer.【北美】a cinema film 电影

moving /ˈmuːvɪŋ/ **adjective 1** in motion 运动中的;活动的 **2** arousing strong emotion 感动人的 ■ **movingly** adverb.

mow /məʊ/ **verb** (**mows**, **mowing**, **mowed**; past participle **mowed** or **mown**) **1** cut down or trim grass, hay, etc. 修剪(草坪);割(草) **2** (**mow someone down**) kill someone with a gun or by knocking them down with a vehicle 枪杀;(用机动车)撞死 ■ **mower** noun.

mozzarella /ˌmɒtsəˈrelə/ **noun** a firm white Italian cheese made from buffalo's or cow's milk 莫萨里拉干酪(一种白色意大利干酪,由水牛乳或奶牛乳制成)

MP /ˌem ˈpiː/ **abbreviation** Member of Parliament 下院议员

Mr /ˈmɪstə(r)/ **noun** a title used before a man's surname or full name 先生(用于男子的姓或全名前)

Mrs /'mɪsɪz/ **noun** a title used before a married woman's surname or full name 夫人，太太(用于已婚女性的姓或全名前)

MS /ˌem 'es/ **abbreviation 1** manuscript **2** multiple sclerosis

Ms /mɪz/ **noun** a title used before a married or unmarried woman's surname or full name 女士(用于已婚或未婚女性的姓或全名前)

MSc abbreviation Master of Science 理科硕士

Mt abbreviation Mount.

much /mʌtʃ/ **determiner & pronoun** a large amount 许多；大量 • **adverb 1** to a great extent 十分；非常 **2** often 常常；经常

muck /mʌk/ **noun 1** dirt or rubbish 污物；垃圾 **2** manure 粪肥 • **verb** chiefly Brit.【主英】**1** (**muck something up**) informal 【非正式】spoil something 破坏；弄糟 **2** (**muck about or around**) informal 【非正式】behave in a silly way 胡闹 **3** (**muck about with or around with**) interfere with 干涉 **4** (**muck in**) informal 【非正式】share a task 一起干活 **5** (**muck something out**) remove manure and dirt from a stable 打扫(马厩) • **mucky adjective** (**muckier, muckiest**).

mucous /'mjuːkəs/ **adjective** having to do with mucus 布满黏液的 □ **mucous membrane** a tissue that produces mucus, lining the nose, mouth, and other organs 黏膜

mucus /'mjuːkəs/ **noun** a slimy substance produced by the mucous membranes (黏膜分泌的)黏液

mud /mʌd/ **noun** soft, wet, sticky earth 烂泥；泥浆

muddle /'mʌdl/ **verb** (**muddles, muddling, muddled**) **1** put things in the wrong order or mix them up 弄乱；弄糟 **2** confuse someone 使糊涂；使迷惑 **3** (**muddle something up**) confuse two or more things with

each other 把…混淆 **4** (**muddle along or through**) manage to cope in spite of a lack of skill, knowledge, etc. 胡乱应付过去 • **noun** a muddled state 混乱状态；糟糕局面

muddy /'mʌdi/ **adjective** (**muddier, muddiest**) **1** covered in mud 沾满烂泥的;满是泥的 **2** not bright or clear 暗淡的;灰暗的;模糊的 • **verb** (**muddies, muddying, muddied**) make something muddy 使沾上烂泥;使发暗,使模糊

mudflap /'mʌdflæp/ **noun** a flap hung behind the wheel of a vehicle to protect against mud and stones thrown up from the road (悬挂在机动车车轮后的)挡泥板

mudflat /'mʌdflæt/ **noun** a stretch of muddy land left uncovered at low tide 淤泥滩;潮泥滩

mudguard /'mʌdɡɑːd/ **noun** a curved strip fitted over a wheel of a bicycle or motorcycle to protect against water and dirt thrown up from the road (自行车或摩托车车轮上的)挡泥板

muesli /'mjuːzli/ **noun** (plural **mueslis**) a mixture of oats, dried fruit, and nuts, eaten with milk 穆兹利(一种燕麦、干果、坚果混合的早餐,与牛奶同食)

muezzin /muː'ezɪn/ **noun** a man who calls Muslims to prayer (召唤穆斯林祷告的)宣礼员

muff¹ /mʌf/ **noun** a short tube made of fur or other warm material into which you place your hands for warmth (保暖用的)手笼,手筒

muff² **verb** informal 【非正式】handle something clumsily or badly 笨拙地处理;搞糟

muffin /'mʌfɪn/ **noun 1** a type of flat bread roll, usually eaten toasted with butter 英式松饼(通常烘烤后涂黄油食用) **2** a type of small cake 圆顶小松糕

muffle /'mʌfl/ **verb** (**muffles, muffling, muffled**) **1** wrap or cover for warmth

M

(为取暖)裹住,蒙住 **2** make a sound quieter 使(声音)减弱

muffler /'mʌflə(r)/ **noun** a scarf 围巾

mufti /'mʌfti/ **noun** (plural **muftis**) **1** a Muslim legal expert allowed to give rulings on religious matters 穆夫提(伊斯兰教法典说明官) **2** civilian clothes when worn by military or police staff (军队或警方人员穿的)便服,便衣

mug[1] /mʌɡ/ **noun 1** a large cylindrical cup with a handle 圆筒形有柄大杯 **2** informal【非正式】 a person's face (人的)脸 **3** Brit. informal【英,非正式】 a stupid or gullible person 蠢人;易上当受骗者 • **verb** (**mugs, mugging, mugged**) attack and rob someone in a public place (在公共场所)行凶抢劫

mug[2] **verb** (**mugs, mugging, mugged**) (**mug something up**) Brit. informal【英,非正式】 learn as much as you can about a subject in a short time 突击学习(课程)

mugger /'mʌɡə(r)/ **noun** a person who attacks and robs someone in a public place (公共场所的)行凶抢劫者

muggins /'mʌɡɪnz/ **noun** (plural **muggins** or **mugginses**) Brit. informal【英,非正式】 a foolish person 蠢人;傻子

muggy /'mʌɡi/ **adjective** (of the weather) unpleasantly warm and humid (天气)闷热潮湿的

mugshot /'mʌɡʃɒt/ **noun** informal【非正式】 a photograph of a person's face made for an official purpose (作正式用途的)脸部照片

mulatto /mju'lætəʊ/ **noun** (plural **mulattoes** or **mulattos**) offensive【冒犯】 a person with one white and one black parent 穆拉托人(父母一方为白人一方为黑人的混血儿)

mulberry /'mʌlbəri/ **noun** (plural **mulberries**) **1** a dark red or white fruit resembling the loganberry 桑椹 **2** a dark red or purple colour 暗红色;深紫色

mulch /mʌltʃ/ **noun** a mass of leaves or compost, used to protect the base of a plant or to enrich the soil (为保护植物或增肥土壤撒在植物周围的)覆盖料 • **verb** cover with mulch 用覆盖料覆盖

mule /mjuːl/ **noun** the offspring of a male donkey and a female horse 骡;骡子

mulish /'mjuːlɪʃ/ **adjective** stubborn 执拗的;固执的

mull[1] /mʌl/ **verb** (**mull something over**) think about something at length 仔细考虑

mull[2] **verb** warm wine or beer and add sugar and spices to it 将(葡萄酒或啤酒)烫热后加入糖和香料

mullah /'mʌlə/ **noun** a Muslim who is an expert in Islamic theology and sacred law 毛拉(精通伊斯兰神学和圣法的伊斯兰教徒)

mullet /'mʌlɪt/ **noun** a sea fish that is caught for food 鲻鱼(一种食用海鱼)

mulligatawny /ˌmʌlɪɡə'tɔːni/ **noun** a spicy meat soup originally made in India (源自印度的)咖喱肉汤

mullion /'mʌlɪən/ **noun** a vertical bar between the panes of glass in a window (窗扇间的)竖框 ■ **mullioned** adjective.

multicoloured or **multicolour** /ˌmʌlti'kʌləd/ (US spelling【美拼作】 **multicolored** or **multicolor**) **adjective** having many colours 多色的;五颜六色的

multicultural /ˌmʌlti'kʌltʃərəl/ **adjective** relating to or made up of several cultural or ethnic groups 多元文化的;融合多种文化的 ■ **multiculturalism** noun.

multifaceted /ˌmʌlti'fæsɪtɪd/ **adjective** having many sides or aspects 多面的;多方面的

multifarious /ˌmʌlti'feəriəs/ **adjective** having great variety 多种多样的;五花八门的

multilateral /ˌmʌlti'lætərəl/ **adjective**

involving three or more participants 多方的；多边的

multilingual /ˌmʌltiˈlɪŋɡwəl/ **adjective** in or using several languages 多种语言的；使用多种语言的

multimedia /ˌmʌltiˈmiːdiə/ **noun** the use of sound and pictures as well as text on a computer screen 多媒体

multinational /ˌmʌltiˈnæʃnəl/ **adjective** involving several countries 多国的 • **noun** a company operating in several countries 跨国公司

multiple /ˈmʌltɪpl/ **adjective 1** having or involving several parts or elements 多重的；多元素的 **2** (of a disease or injury) affecting several parts of the body (疾病)多发性的，(伤情)多处的 • **noun** a number that may be divided by another number without a remainder 倍数 □ **multiple-choice** (of a question in an exam) giving several possible answers, from which you must choose one (试题)多项选择的 **multiple sclerosis** ⇒ 见 SCLEROSIS.

multiplex /ˈmʌltipleks/ **noun** a cinema with several separate screens 多剧场影剧院

multiplication /ˌmʌltɪplɪˈkeɪʃn/ **noun** the process of multiplying 乘法运算；相乘 □ **multiplication sign** the symbol ×, indicating that one number is to be multiplied by another 乘号

multiplicity /ˌmʌltɪˈplɪsəti/ **noun** (plural **multiplicities**) a large number or variety of something 大量；多种多样

multiply /ˈmʌltɪplaɪ/ **verb** (**multiplies, multiplying, multiplied**) **1** add a number to itself a stated number of times 乘；使 相乘 **2** increase in number or quantity 增加 **3** increase in number by reproducing 繁殖 ■ **multiplier** noun.

multiracial /ˌmʌltiˈreɪʃl/ **adjective** having to do with people of many races 多种族的；多人种的

multi-storey /ˌmʌltiˈstɔːri/ **adjective** (of a building) having several storeys (建筑物)多层的 • **noun** Brit. 【英】a multi-storey car park 多层停车场

multitask /ˌmʌltiˈtɑːsk/ **verb 1** Computing 【计】operate more than one program at the same time 进行多任务处理 **2** do several things at the same time 同时做多项工作

multitude /ˈmʌltɪtjuːd/ **noun 1** a large number of people or things 众多的人(或物)；大量；大批 **2** (**the multitude**) the mass of ordinary people 大众；民众

multitudinous /ˌmʌltɪˈtjuːdɪnəs/ **adjective** very numerous 极多的；众多的

mum¹ /mʌm/ **noun** Brit. informal 【英，非正式】your mother 妈妈

mum² **adjective** (**keep mum**) informal 【非正式】stay silent so as not to reveal a secret 保持沉默；保密 □ **mum's the word** it's a secret 要保密；别声张

mumble /ˈmʌmbl/ **verb** (**mumbles, mumbling, mumbled**) say something in a quiet voice that is difficult to hear or understand 含糊地说；咕哝 • **noun** quiet speech that is difficult to hear or understand 喃喃自语；咕哝

mumbo-jumbo /ˌmʌmbəʊˈdʒʌmbəʊ/ **noun** informal 【非正式】language that sounds mysterious but has no real meaning 难懂而无实际意义的语言

mummify /ˈmʌmɪfaɪ/ **verb** (**mummifies, mummifying, mummified**) preserve a body as a mummy 将(尸体)制成木乃伊保存 ■ **mummification** noun.

mummy¹ /ˈmʌmi/ **noun** (plural **mummies**) Brit. informal 【英，非正式】your mother 妈妈

mummy² **noun** (plural **mummies**) (especially in ancient Egypt) a body that has been embalmed and wrapped in bandages in order to preserve it (尤指古埃及的)木乃伊

mumps /mʌmps/ **plural noun** a disease causing swelling of the glands at the sides of the face 流行性腮腺炎

munch /mʌntʃ/ **verb** eat something steadily and often noisily 用力咀嚼；出声地咀嚼

mundane /mʌn'deɪn/ **adjective** lacking interest or excitement 平淡的；乏味的

municipal /mju:'nɪsɪpl/ **adjective** relating to a municipality 市政的；地方政府的

municipality /mju:,nɪsɪ'pæləti/ **noun** (plural **municipalities**) a town or district with its own local government 自治市；自治区；地方政府

munificent /mju:'nɪfɪsnt/ **adjective** very generous 慷慨的；大方的 ■ **munificence** noun.

munitions /mju:'nɪʃnz/ **plural noun** military weapons, ammunition, and equipment 军火；军需品

mural /'mjʊərəl/ **noun** a painting done directly on a wall 壁画

murder /'mɜ:də(r)/ **noun** the unlawful planned killing of one person by another 谋杀 • **verb** (**murders, murdering, murdered**) kill someone unlawfully, having planned to in advance 谋杀 ■ **murderer** noun **murderess** noun.

murderous /'mɜ:dərəs/ **adjective** capable of murdering someone or being very violent 杀人的；蓄意谋杀的；极端暴力的

murk /mɜ:k/ **noun** darkness or fog 黑暗；昏暗

murky /'mɜ:ki/ **adjective** (**murkier, murkiest**) **1** dark and gloomy 黑暗的，阴暗的 **2** (of water) dirty or cloudy (水)肮脏的，浑浊的 **3** suspicious and kept hidden 可疑的；不可告人的

murmur /'mɜ:mə(r)/ **verb 1** say something quietly 小声说 **2** make a low continuous sound 持续发出轻声 • **noun 1** the sound made by a person speaking quietly 低语；喃喃声 **2** a low continuous background noise (持续的)背景细声

muscle /'mʌsl/ **noun 1** a band of body tissue that can be tightened or relaxed in order to move a part of the body 肌肉 **2** power or strength 实力；力量；力气 • **verb** (**muscle in**) informal 【非正式】involve yourself in something that does not concern you 强行干预(他人事务) ■ **muscly** adjective.

muscular /'mʌskjələ(r)/ **adjective 1** having to do with the muscles 肌肉的 **2** having well-developed muscles 肌肉发达的 □ **muscular dystrophy** an inherited condition in which the muscles gradually become weaker 肌营养不良症

musculature /'mʌskjələtʃə(r)/ **noun** the arrangement of muscles in a body 肌肉系统

muse¹ /mju:z/ **noun 1** (**Muse**) (in Greek and Roman mythology) each of nine goddesses representing or associated with a particular art or science (希腊和罗马神话中的)缪斯(司文艺和科学的九位女神之一) **2** a woman who is the inspiration for a creative artist 女神(给艺术家灵感的女性)

muse² **verb** (**muses, musing, mused**) **1** be absorbed in thought 沉思；默想 **2** say something to yourself in a thoughtful way 若有所思地自语

museum /mju:'zi:əm/ **noun** a building in which objects of interest are kept and shown to the public 博物馆；博物院

mush /mʌʃ/ **noun 1** a soft, wet, pulpy mass 烂糊状东西 **2** something that is too sentimental 过度的伤感 ■ **mushy** adjective.

mushroom /'mʌʃrʊm/ **noun** a fungus in the form of a domed cap on a short stalk, many kinds of which are edible 蘑菇 • **verb** increase or

develop quickly迅速增长；快速发展
■ **mushroom cloud** a mushroom-shaped cloud of dust formed after a nuclear explosion (核爆炸后形成的)蘑菇云

music /ˈmjuːzɪk/ **noun 1** the sounds of voices or instruments arranged in a pleasing way 音乐；乐曲 **2** the art of writing or playing music 音乐艺术 **3** the written or printed signs representing a piece of music 乐谱 □ **music hall 1** (in the past) a popular form of entertainment involving singing, dancing, and comedy (旧时的)歌舞杂耍表演 **2** a theatre where such entertainment took place 歌舞杂耍剧场

musical /ˈmjuːzɪkl/ **adjective 1** relating to or accompanied by music 音乐的；配乐的 **2** fond of or skilled in music 喜爱音乐的；精通音乐的 **3** having a pleasant sound 悦耳的；好听的 • **noun** a play or film which involves singing or dancing 音乐剧；音乐影片 ■ **musically** adverb.

musician /mjuˈzɪʃn/ **noun** a person who plays a musical instrument or writes music 音乐家；乐师；作曲家 ■ **musicianship** noun.

musicology /ˌmjuːzɪˈkɒlədʒi/ **noun** the study of the history and theory of music 音乐学

musk /mʌsk/ **noun** a strong-smelling substance produced by the male of a small breed of deer, used as an ingredient in perfume 麝香 ■ **musky** adjective.

musket /ˈmʌskɪt/ **noun** (in the past) a light gun with a long barrel (旧时的)火枪，滑膛枪

musketeer /ˌmʌskɪˈtɪə(r)/ **noun** (in the past) a soldier armed with a musket (旧时的)火枪手，滑膛枪手

muskrat /ˈmʌskræt/ **noun** a large North American rodent with a musky smell 麝鼠(产于北美的大型啮齿动物，可发出类似麝香的香味)

Muslim /ˈmʊzlɪm/ or **Moslem** noun a follower of Islam 伊斯兰教徒；穆斯林 • **adjective** relating to Muslims or Islam 穆斯林的；伊斯兰教的

muslin /ˈmʌzlɪn/ **noun** lightweight cotton cloth in a plain weave 麦斯林纱；平纹细布

musquash /ˈmʌskwɒʃ/ **noun** Brit. 【英】the fur of the muskrat 麝鼠毛皮

mussel /ˈmʌsl/ **noun** a small shellfish with a dark brown or purplish-black shell 贻贝；淡菜

must[1] /mʌst, məst/ **modal verb** (past **had to** or in reported speech **must**) **1** be obliged to; should 必须 **2** used to insist on something 务必；一定要 **3** used to say that something is very likely 谅必；一定：*You must be tired.* 你一定累了。• **noun** informal 【非正式】something that should not be missed 必不可少的事物

must[2] /mʌst/ **noun** grape juice before it is fermented (发酵前的)葡萄汁

mustache /məˈstɑːʃ/ US spelling of MOUSTACHE. moustache的美式拼法

mustang /ˈmʌstæŋ/ **noun** a small wild horse of the south-western US (美国西南部的)小野马

mustard /ˈmʌstəd/ **noun 1** a hot-tasting yellow or brown paste made from the crushed seeds of a plant 芥末 **2** a brownish-yellow colour 芥末色；暗黄色 ■ **mustard gas** a liquid whose vapour causes severe irritation and blistering of the skin, used in chemical weapons 芥子气(用作化学武器)

muster /ˈmʌstə(r)/ **verb** (**musters, mustering, mustered**) **1** summon up a feeling or attitude 激起(感情或态度) **2** bring troops together in preparation for battle 召集，集合(部队) **3** (of people) gather together (人)聚集 • **noun** an instance of mustering troops (部队的)集合，集结 ■ **pass muster** be accepted as satisfactory

被认为合格；被认为可以接受

mustn't /ˈmʌsnt/ **short form** must not.

musty /ˈmʌsti/ **adjective** having a stale or mouldy smell 不新鲜的；变味的；有霉味的 ■ **mustiness** noun.

mutable /ˈmjuːtəbl/ **adjective** able or tending to change 易变的；无常的 ■ **mutability** noun.

mutant /ˈmjuːtənt/ **adjective** resulting from or showing the effect of mutation 突变产生的；突变的 • **noun** a mutant form 突变体

mutate /mjuːˈteɪt/ **verb** (**mutates, mutating, mutated**) undergo mutation 突变

mutation /mjuːˈteɪʃn/ **noun** **1** the process of changing 变化；改变 **2** a change in genetic structure which may be passed on to subsequent generations (基因)突变 **3** a distinct form resulting from such a change 突变体

mute /mjuːt/ **adjective** **1** not speaking 缄默的，不说话的 **2** unable to speak 哑的；不会说话的 **3** (of a letter) not pronounced (字母)不发音的 • **noun 1** dated 【废】 a person who is unable to speak 哑巴 **2** a device used to make the sound of a musical instrument quieter or softer 弱音器 • **verb** (**mutes, muting, muted**) **1** make the sound of something quieter or softer 减弱…的声音 **2** reduce the strength or intensity of 减弱…的强度 ■ **mutely** adverb.

mutilate /ˈmjuːtɪleɪt/ **verb** (**mutilates, mutilating, mutilated**) severely injure or damage 使严重伤；严重破坏 ■ **mutilation** noun.

mutineer /ˌmjuːtəˈnɪə(r)/ **noun** a person who takes part in a mutiny 反叛者；叛乱者

mutinous /ˈmjuːtənəs/ **adjective** rebellious 反叛的，叛乱的

mutiny /ˈmjuːtəni/ **noun** (plural **mutinies**) an open rebellion against authority, especially by soldiers or sailors against their officers (尤指士兵或水手的)反叛，叛乱，哗变 • **verb** (**mutinies, mutinying, mutinied**) take part in a mutiny; rebel 参加叛乱；反叛

mutt /mʌt/ **noun** informal 【非正式】 a mongrel dog 杂种狗

mutter /ˈmʌtə(r)/ **verb** (**mutters, muttering, muttered**) **1** say something in a voice which can barely be heard 悄声说；嘀咕 **2** talk or grumble in private 私下里说，私下发牢骚 • **noun** speech that can barely be heard 小声说出的话；嘀咕

mutton /ˈmʌtn/ **noun** the flesh of a fully grown sheep used as food 羊肉

mutual /ˈmjuːtʃuəl/ **adjective 1** experienced by two or more people equally 相互的；彼此的 **2** shared by two or more people 共同的，共有的：*a mutual friend* 共同的朋友 ■ **mutuality** noun **mutually** adverb.

muzzle /ˈmʌzl/ **noun 1** the nose and mouth of an animal (动物的)鼻口部 **2** a guard fitted over an animal's muzzle to stop it biting (动物的)口套 **3** the open end of the barrel of a gun 枪口；炮口 • **verb** (**muzzles, muzzling, muzzled**) **1** put a muzzle on an animal 给(动物)套上口套 **2** prevent someone speaking freely 钳制…的言论

muzzy /ˈmʌzi/ **adjective 1** dazed or confused 茫然的，糊涂的；困惑的 **2** blurred or indistinct 模糊不清的；轮廓不分明的

my /maɪ/ **possessive determiner** belonging to or associated with the speaker 我的

myalgia /maɪˈældʒiə/ **noun** pain in a muscle 肌痛

mycology /maɪˈkɒlədʒi/ **noun** the scientific study of fungi 真菌学

mynah bird /ˈmaɪnə/ **noun** an Asian or Australasian bird, some kinds of which can mimic human speech 八哥；鹩哥

myopia /maɪˈəʊpiə/ **noun** shortsightedness 近视；目光短浅 ■ **myopic** adjective.

myriad /ˈmɪriəd/ **noun** (also **myriads**) a countless or very great number 无数；极大数量 • **adjective** countless 无数的；数不清的

myrrh /mɜː(r)/ **noun** a sweet-smelling substance obtained from certain trees, used in perfumes and incense 没药（一种芳香树脂，用于制香水和香料）

myrtle /ˈmɜːtl/ **noun** an evergreen shrub with white flowers and purpleblack berries 香桃木；爱神木

myself /maɪˈself/ **pronoun 1** used by a speaker to refer to himself or herself as the object of a verb or preposition when he or she is the subject of the clause 我自己 **2** I or me personally 我亲自；我本人

mysterious /mɪˈstɪəriəs/ **adjective** difficult or impossible to understand or explain 神秘的；难以理解的；不可思议的 ■ **mysteriously** adverb.

mystery /ˈmɪstri/ **noun** (plural **mysteries**) **1** something that is difficult or impossible to understand or explain 神秘的事物；难以理解的事物；谜 **2** secrecy 秘密 **3** a novel, film, etc. dealing with a puzzling crime 疑案（或推理、侦探）作品 □ **mystery play** a medieval play based on biblical stories or the lives of the saints 神秘剧，神迹剧，圣史剧(中世纪根据《圣经》故事中圣徒的生活创作的戏剧)

mystic /ˈmɪstɪk/ **noun** a person who seeks to know God through prayer and contemplation 神秘主义者 • **adjective** mystical 神秘主义(者)的；神秘的

mystical /ˈmɪstɪkl/ **adjective 1** relating

to mystics or mysticism 神秘主义者的；神秘主义的 **2** having a spiritual significance that goes beyond human understanding 神秘的；玄妙的 **3** inspiring a sense of spiritual mystery and awe 引发神秘感的

mysticism /ˈmɪstɪsɪzəm/ **noun 1** the belief that knowledge of God can be found through prayer and contemplation 神秘主义 **2** vague or ill-defined religious or spiritual belief 模糊的信念，虚构的信念

mystify /ˈmɪstɪfaɪ/ **verb** (**mystifies, mystifying, mystified**) **1** completely bewilder someone 使困惑不解；完全难住 **2** make something uncertain or mysterious 使不确定；使神秘 ■ **mystification** noun.

mystique /mɪˈstiːk/ **noun** a quality of mystery, glamour, or power that makes someone or something seem impressive or attractive 神秘性

myth /mɪθ/ **noun 1** a traditional story that describes the early history of a people or explains a natural event 神话(故事) **2** a widely held but false belief (广泛持有的)错误信念 **3** an imaginary person or thing 虚构的人(或事物)

mythical /ˈmɪθɪkl/ **adjective 1** found in or characteristic of myths or folk tales 神话的；民间故事的 **2** imaginary or not real 想象出来的，虚构的

mythology /mɪˈθɒlədʒi/ **noun** (plural **mythologies**) **1** a collection of myths 神话集 **2** a set of widely held but exaggerated or false beliefs (广泛持有的)夸大的说法，错误观念 ■ **mythological** adjective.

myxomatosis /ˌmɪksəməˈtəʊsɪs/ **noun** a highly infectious and usually fatal disease of rabbits (兔)黏液瘤病，多发性黏液瘤病

Nn

N or **n** /en/ *noun* (plural **Ns** or **N's**) the fourteenth letter of the alphabet 英语字母表的第 14 个字母 • *abbreviation* North or Northern.

n/a *abbreviation* not applicable 不适用的

naan /nɑːn/ ⇒ 见 NAN².

nab /næb/ *verb* (**nabs, nabbing, nabbed**) informal【非正式】catch a wrongdoer 抓住(做坏事的人)

nacho /'nɑːtʃəʊ/ *noun* (plural **nachos**) a small piece of tortilla topped with melted cheese, peppers, etc. 烤干酪辣味玉米片

nadir /'neɪdɪə(r)/ *noun* **1** the lowest or most unsuccessful point 最低点；最差点 **2** the point in space directly opposite the zenith and below an observer 天底

naff /næf/ *adjective* Brit. informal【英，非正式】lacking taste or style 缺乏品位的;缺乏风度的

nag¹ /næg/ *verb* (**nags, nagging, nagged**) **1** constantly tell someone they should be doing something 唠叨;絮烦 **2** be constantly worrying or painful 不断烦扰 • *noun* **1** a person who nags 爱唠叨的人 **2** a persistent feeling of anxiety (持续不休的)焦虑,烦躁

nag² *noun* informal【非正式】an old horse 老马;驽马

naiad /'naɪæd/ *noun* (in classical mythology) a water nymph (古典神话中的)水泽神女

nail /neɪl/ *noun* **1** a small metal spike with a flat head, used for joining pieces of wood together 钉子 **2** a thin hard layer covering the upper part of the tip of the finger and toe 指甲;趾甲 • *verb* **1** fasten with a nail or nails 钉住;钉牢 **2** informal【非正式】catch a criminal 抓住(罪犯) □ **nail-biting** making you feel great anxiety or tension 令人焦虑的;令人紧张的

naive or **naïve** /naɪ'iːv/ *adjective* lacking experience or judgement 缺乏经验的;缺乏判断力的 ■ **naively** *adverb*.

naivety /naɪ'iːvəti/ or **naiveté** /naɪ'iːvəter/ *noun* lack of experience, wisdom, or judgement 天真;幼稚;轻信

naked /'neɪkɪd/ *adjective* **1** without clothes 裸体的;赤裸的 **2** (of an object) without the usual covering or protection (物品)无覆盖的,裸露的 **3** (of feelings) not hidden; open (感情)不加掩饰的,无伪装的 **4** vulnerable 脆弱的 □ **the naked eye** the normal power of the eyes, without using a telescope, microscope, etc. 肉眼 ■ **nakedly** *adverb* **nakedness** *noun*.

namby-pamby /'næmbi'pæmbi/ *adjective* lacking strength or courage; feeble 没有活力的;虚弱的;缺乏勇气的

name /neɪm/ **noun 1** a word or words by which someone or something is known (人或事物的)名字 **2** a famous person 名人 **3** a reputation 名誉；名望. *He made a name for himself.* 他使自己出了名. • **verb** (**names, naming, named**) **1** give a name to 给…取名；为…命名 **2** identify or mention by name 通过名称识别；提及…的名字 **3** specify a sum of money, time, or place 确定(款额、时间或地点) □ **name-dropping** mentioning the names of famous people as if you know them, in order to impress other people 抬出名人以标榜自己

nameless /ˈneɪmləs/ **adjective 1** having no name 没有名字的 **2** having a name that is kept secret 不标姓名的；匿名的

namely /ˈneɪmli/ **adverb** that is to say 即；换句话说

namesake /ˈneɪmseɪk/ **noun** a person or thing with the same name as another 同名人；同名物

nan[1] /næn/ **noun** Brit. informal 【英,非正式】 your grandmother 祖母；外祖母

nan[2] or **naan** /nɑːn/ **noun** a type of soft flat Indian bread 馕(一种松软扁平的印度面包)

nanny /ˈnæni/ **noun** (plural **nannies**) **1** a woman employed to look after a child in its own home (照顾孩子的)保姆 **2** (also **nanny goat**) a female goat 母山羊；雌山羊

nanosecond /ˈnænəʊsekənd/ **noun** one thousand millionth of a second 毫微秒

nap[1] /næp/ **noun** a short sleep 小睡；瞌睡 • **verb** (**naps, napping, napped**) have a nap 打瞌睡；打盹

nap[2] **noun** short raised fibres on the surface of certain fabrics (某些织物表面的)短纤维

napalm /ˈneɪpɑːm/ **noun** a highly flammable form of petrol, used in firebombs 凝固汽油(用于燃烧弹)

nape /neɪp/ **noun** the back of the neck 脖颈

naphtha /ˈnæfθə/ **noun** a flammable oil extracted from coal and petroleum (从煤和石油中提取的)轻油,石脑油

napkin /ˈnæpkɪn/ **noun** a piece of cloth or paper used at a meal to wipe the fingers or lips and to protect clothes 餐巾；餐巾纸

nappy /ˈnæpi/ **noun** (plural **nappies**) Brit. 【英】a piece of material wrapped round a baby's bottom and between its legs to absorb urine and faeces 尿布

narcissism /ˈnɑːsɪsɪzəm/ **noun** too much interest in yourself and your appearance 自我陶醉；自恋 ■ **narcissist** noun **narcissistic** adjective.

narcissus /nɑːˈsɪsəs/ **noun** (plural **narcissi** or **narcissuses**) a daffodil with a flower that has pale outer petals and an orange or yellow centre 水仙花

narcotic /nɑːˈkɒtɪk/ **noun 1** an addictive drug which affects mood or behaviour 致幻毒品 **2** a drug which causes drowsiness or unconsciousness, or relieves pain 麻醉药；麻醉剂 • **adjective** relating to narcotics 致幻毒品的；麻醉剂的

nark /nɑːk/ Brit. informal 【英,非正式】 **noun** a police informer (警方的)线人 • **verb** annoy 惹恼；烦扰

narrate /nəˈreɪt/ **verb** (**narrates, narrating, narrated**) **1** give an account of something 叙述；讲述 **2** provide a commentary for a film, television programme, etc. 对(电影、电视节目等)作解说；作实况评述 ■ **narration** noun **narrator** noun.

narrative /ˈnærətɪv/ **noun** an account of connected events; a story 叙述；故事 • **adjective** having to do with stories or the telling of stories 叙事的；讲述故事的

narrow /ˈnærəʊ/ **adjective** (**narrower,**

narrowest) **1** of small width in comparison to length 狭窄的；**2** limited in extent, amount, or scope 有限的；受限制的；狭隘的 **3** only just achieved 刚好达到的: *a narrow escape* 死里逃生 • **verb 1** become or make narrower (使)变窄；(使)变小 **2** (**narrow something down**) reduce the number of possibilities of something 减少，降低(可能性) • **noun** (**narrows**) a narrow channel connecting two larger areas of water (连接两大片水域的)狭窄海峡 □ **narrow-minded** unwilling to listen to or accept the views of other people 气量小的；思想偏狭的；不愿意听取他人意见的 ■ **narrowly** adverb **narrowness** noun.

narrowboat /'nærəʊbəʊt/ **noun** Brit. 【英】a canal boat less than 7 ft (2.1 metres) wide (宽不足 7 英尺即 2.1 米的)运河船

NASA /'næsə/ **abbreviation** (in the US) National Aeronautics and Space Administration (美国)国家航空航天局

nasal /'neɪzl/ **adjective** relating to the nose 鼻(子)的 ■ **nasally** adverb.

nascent /'næsnt/ **adjective** just coming into existence and beginning to develop 新生的；萌芽的

nasturtium /nə'stɜːʃəm/ **noun** a garden plant with bright orange, yellow, or red flowers 旱金莲(一种园艺植物，开鲜艳的橙色、黄色或红色花)

nasty /'nɑːsti/ **adjective** (**nastier**, **nastiest**) **1** unpleasant or disgusting 令人不快的；令人厌恶的 **2** spiteful, violent, or bad-tempered 恶意的；暴力的；脾气坏的 **3** painful or harmful 引起疼痛的；有害的: *a nasty bang on the head* 头部重重地碰了一下 ■ **nastily** adverb **nastiness** noun.

natal /'neɪtl/ **adjective** relating to the place or time of your birth 出生地的；出生时的

nation /'neɪʃn/ **noun** a large group of people sharing the same language, culture, or history and inhabiting a particular territory 国民；民族

national /'næʃnəl/ **adjective 1** having to do with a nation 国家的；民族的 **2** owned, controlled, or financially supported by the state 国有的；国家控制的；国家出资的 • **noun** a citizen of a particular country 国民 □ **national curriculum** a programme of study that must be taught in state schools 全国统一课程(规定公立学校须开设的课程) **national debt** the total amount of money which a country's government has borrowed 国债 **national grid** Brit.【英】**1** the network of power lines between major power stations (主要电站之间的)全国高压输电线路网 **2** the system of geographical coordinates used in maps of the British Isles (英国不列颠群岛地图上使用的)坐标方格 **National Insurance** (in the UK) a system of payments made by employees and employers to provide help for people who are ill, unemployed, or retired (英国的)国民保险制度(由雇员和雇主缴费为生病、失业或退休人员提供帮助) **national park** an area of countryside that is protected by the state 国家公园 **national service** a period of compulsory service in the armed forces during peacetime (和平时期的)义务兵役 ■ **nationally** adverb.

nationalism /'næʃnəlɪzəm/ **noun 1** very strong feelings of support for and pride in your own country 爱国心；爱国主义 **2** belief in independence for a particular country 民族主义；国家主义 ■ **nationalist** noun & adjective **nationalistic** adjective.

nationality /ˌnæʃə'næləti/ **noun** (plural **nationalities**) **1** the status of belonging to a particular nation 国籍 **2** an ethnic group 种族

nationalize or **nationalise** /'næ∫nəlaɪz/ **verb** (**nationalizes, nationalizing, nationalized**) put an industry or business under the control of the government 把(工业或商业)收归国有;使(工业或商业)国有化 ■ **nationalization** noun.

nationwide /ˌneɪ∫n'waɪd/ **adjective & adverb** throughout the whole nation 全国范围的(地);全国性的(地)

native /'neɪtɪv/ **noun 1** a person born in a particular place 本地人 **2** a local inhabitant 当地居民 **3** an animal or plant that lives or grows naturally in a particular area 本地的动物(或植物) **4** dated, offensive 【废,冒犯】a non-white person living in a country before the arrival of white colonists or settlers 土人，土著(殖民地国家中当地的非白色人种) ■ **adjective 1** associated with the place where you were born 出生地的 **2** (of a plant or animal) living or growing naturally in a place (植物或动物)土生土长的 **3** having to do with the original inhabitants of a place 土著的;土著人的 **4** in a person's character 生来就有的;先天的: *his native wit* 他天生的才智 □ **native speaker** a person who has spoken a particular language from earliest childhood 说本族语的人 **Native American** a member of any of the original peoples of North and South America (南北美洲的)土著印第安人

nativity /nə'tɪvəti/ **noun** (plural **nativities**) **1** (**the Nativity**) the birth of Jesus 耶稣诞生 **2** formal 【正式】a person's birth 诞生;出生

NATO or **Nato** /'neɪtəʊ/ **abbreviation** North Atlantic Treaty Organization 北大西洋公约组织

natter /'nætə(r)/ informal 【非正式】**verb** (**natters, nattering, nattered**) chat for a long time 唠叨;喋喋不休地闲聊 ■ **noun** a long chat 聊天;长谈

natty /'næti/ **adjective** (**nattier,**

nattiest) informal 【非正式】smart and fashionable 漂亮的;时髦的 ■ **nattily** adverb.

natural /'næt∫rəl/ **adjective 1** existing in or obtained from nature; not made or caused by people 天然的;自然的;非人工的 **2** as you would expect; normal 自然如此的;正常的 **3** born with a particular skill or quality 天生的: *a natural leader* 天生的领袖 **4** having a relaxed, easy manner 放松的;不娇揉造作的 **5** (of a parent or child) related by blood (父母或孩子)有血缘关系的 **6** Music【音乐】(of a note) not sharp or flat (音符)本位音的,还原的 ■ **noun 1** a person with a particular gift or talent 有天赋的人 **2** Music【音乐】a natural note or a sign (♮) denoting one 本位音;还原符号 □ **natural gas** gas that is found underground and used as fuel 天然气 **natural history** the scientific study of animals or plants 博物学 **natural selection** the evolutionary process by which creatures better adapted to their environment tend to survive and produce more offspring 自然选择 ■ **naturally** adverb.

naturalism /'næt∫rəlɪzəm/ **noun** a style in art or literature that shows things how they are in everyday life (艺术或文学中的)自然主义

naturalist /'næt∫rəlɪst/ **noun** a person who studies animals or plants 博物学家

naturalistic /ˌnæt∫rə'lɪstɪk/ **adjective 1** having to do with real life or nature 仿现实生活的;模仿自然的 **2** based on the theory of naturalism 自然主义的

naturalize or **naturalise** /'næt∫rəlaɪz/ **verb** (**naturalizes, naturalizing, naturalized**) **1** make a foreigner a citizen of a country 接受(外国人)入籍;使归化 **2** introduce a plant or animal into a region where it is not native 使(植物或动物)在异域生长

N

nature /ˈneɪtʃə(r)/ **noun 1** the physical world, including plants, animals, and all things that are not made by people 自然界；大自然 **2** the typical qualities or character of a person, animal, or thing (人、动物或事物的)本性，性质 **3** a type or kind of something 种类；品种；类别

naturism /ˈneɪtʃərɪzəm/ **noun** nudism 裸体主义 ■ **naturist** noun & adjective.

naught /nɔːt/ **pronoun** old use 【旧】 nothing 无；零；没有

naughty /ˈnɔːti/ **adjective** (**naughtier**, **naughtiest**) **1** (of a child) disobedient; badly behaved (孩子)淘气的，顽皮的 **2** informal 【非正式】rude or indecent 下流的，不礼貌的 ■ **naughtily** adverb **naughtiness** noun.

nausea /ˈnɔːziə/ **noun** a feeling of sickness and wanting to vomit 反胃；恶心

nauseate /ˈnɔːzieɪt/ **verb** (**nauseates**, **nauseating**, **nauseated**) make someone feel sick or disgusted 使恶心；使厌恶

nauseous /ˈnɔːziəs/ **adjective 1** suffering from nausea 恶心的；不舒服的 **2** causing nausea 令人作呕的；令人厌恶的

nautical /ˈnɔːtɪkl/ **adjective** having to do with sailors or navigation 水手的；航海的；海事的 □ **nautical mile** a unit used to measure distances at sea, equal to 1,852 metres (approximately 2,025 yards) 海里(等于 1,852 米，约合 2,025 码)

naval /ˈneɪvl/ **adjective** having to do with a navy or navies 海军的

nave /neɪv/ **noun** the central part of a church (教堂的)中殿

navel /ˈneɪvl/ **noun** the small hollow in the centre of a person's belly where the umbilical cord was cut at birth 肚脐；脐

navigable /ˈnævɪɡəbl/ **adjective** able to be used by boats and ships 可航行的；可通航的

navigate /ˈnævɪɡeɪt/ **verb** (**navigates**, **navigating**, **navigated**) **1** plan and direct the route of a ship, aircraft, etc. 领航；导航 **2** guide a boat or vehicle over a particular route 驾驶(船只或车辆) ■ **navigator** noun.

navigation /ˌnævɪˈɡeɪʃn/ **noun 1** the activity of navigating 航海；驾驶 **2** the movement of ships (船)的航行 ■ **navigational** adjective.

navvy /ˈnævi/ **noun** (plural **navvies**) Brit. dated 【英，废】a labourer employed in building a road, railway, or canal (筑路、修建铁路或开凿运河的)苦工

navy /ˈneɪvi/ **noun** (plural **navies**) **1** the branch of a country's armed forces which fights at sea 海军 **2** (also **navy blue**) a dark blue colour 藏青色

nay /neɪ/ **adverb** old use or dialect 【旧或方】no 否；不；反对

Nazi /ˈnɑːtsi/ **noun** (plural **Nazis**) historical 【历史】a member of the far-right National Socialist German Workers' Party 纳粹分子(德国极右政党国家社会主义工人党成员) ■ **Nazism** noun.

NB /ˌen ˈbiː/ **abbreviation** note well 注意；留心；请看以下注意事项 [short for Latin 【缩写，拉丁】= *nota bene*.]

NE /ˌen ˈiː/ **abbreviation** north-east or northeastern.

Neanderthal /niˈændətɑːl/ **noun** an extinct human living in Europe between about 120,000 and 35,000 years ago 尼安德特人(曾生活于欧洲，现已灭绝)

neap tide /niːp/ **noun** the tide when there is least difference between high and low water 小潮；最低潮

near /nɪə(r)/ **adverb 1** at or to a short distance in space or time (在空间或时间上)接近，在附近，在近处 **2** almost 几乎；差不多 • **preposition** (also **near to**) **1** at or to a short distance in space or time from (在空间或时间上)在…附近，在…近

处 **2** close to 近平；接近 • **adjective 1** at a short distance away 接近的；靠近的 **2** close to being 马上就要发生的 • **verb** approach 接近；靠近 □ **Near East** the countries of SW Asia between the Mediterranean and India (including the Middle East) 近东(地中海和印度之间的西南亚国家，包括中东) ■ **nearness** noun.

nearby /ˈnɪəbaɪ/ **adjective & adverb** not far away 附近的；近旁的；在附近

nearly /ˈnɪəli/ **adverb** very close to; almost 非常接近；几乎

nearside /ˈnɪəsaɪd/ **noun** the side of a vehicle nearest the kerb (车辆的)左边，靠路缘的一边

nearsighted /ˌnɪəˈsaɪtɪd/ **adjective** chiefly N. Amer. 【主北美】short-sighted 近视的

neat /niːt/ **adjective 1** tidy or carefully arranged 整洁的；仔细布置的 **2** clever but simple 简单巧妙的 **3** (of a drink of spirits) not diluted (饮料或烈酒)未稀释的，未掺水的 **4** N. Amer. informal 【美，非正式】excellent 极好的；绝佳的 ■ **neatly** adverb.

neaten /ˈniːtn/ **verb** make something neat 使整齐，使整洁

nebula /ˈnebjʊlə/ **noun** (plural **nebulae** /ˈnebjuliː/ or **nebulas**) a cloud of gas or dust in outer space 星云

nebulous /ˈnebjʊləs/ **adjective** not clearly defined; vague 不清楚的；模糊的

necessarily /ˈnesəsərəli/ **adverb** as a necessary result; unable to be avoided 必然地；不可避免地

necessary /ˈnesəsəri/ **adjective 1** needing to be present, or to be done or achieved 必须的；必要的 **2** unavoidable 必然的，不可避免的

> ✔ 拼写指南 one *c*, double *s*: necessary.
> necessary 中有一个 c 和两个 s。

necessitate /nəˈsesɪteɪt/ **verb** (**necessitates**, **necessitating**, **necessitated**) make something

necessary 使成为必要

necessity /nəˈsesəti/ **noun** (plural **necessities**) **1** the fact of being necessary 必要；必须 **2** a thing that it is essential to have 必要的事物；必需品

neck /nek/ **noun 1** the part connecting the head to the rest of the body 颈项；脖子 **2** the part of a bottle near the mouth 瓶颈 **3** the part of a violin, guitar, etc. to which the fingerboard is fixed (小提琴、吉他等的)琴颈 • **verb** informal 【非正式】kiss and caress 搂颈亲吻 □ **neck and neck** level in a race or other competition (在赛跑或其他竞赛中)并驾齐驱

neckerchief /ˈnekətʃiːf/ **noun** a square of cloth worn round the neck 方围巾；围脖儿

necklace /ˈnekləs/ **noun** a piece of jewellery consisting of a chain, string of beads, etc., worn round the neck 项链

necklet /ˈneklɪt/ **noun** a close-fitting ornament worn round the neck (紧戴在脖子上的)短项链

neckline /ˈneklaɪn/ **noun** the edge of a dress or top at or below the neck 领口

necromancy /ˈnekrəʊmænsi/ **noun 1** attempted communication with dead people in order to predict the future 召亡魂问卜 **2** witchcraft or black magic 巫术；魔法 ■ **necromancer** noun.

necrophilia /ˌnekrəˈfɪliə/ **noun** sexual activity with or interest in dead bodies 奸尸；恋尸癖 ■ **necrophiliac** noun.

necropolis /nəˈkrɒpəlɪs/ **noun** a cemetery 坟场；墓地

necrosis /neˈkrəʊsɪs/ **noun** the death of cells in an organ or tissue (器官或组织细胞的)坏死

nectar /ˈnektə(r)/ **noun 1** a fluid produced by flowers and made into honey by bees 花蜜 **2** (in Greek and

Roman mythology) the drink of the gods (希腊和罗马神话中的)琼浆玉液,神酒

nectarine /'nektəri:n/ noun a variety of peach with smooth skin 蜜桃

née /neɪ/ adjective born (used in giving a married woman's maiden name) 出生于…的(用于表示已婚妇女的娘家姓)

need /ni:d/ verb 1 require something because it is essential or very important 需要;必须 2 used to express what should or must be done 有必要 • noun 1 a situation in which something is necessary or must be done 需要;必须 2 a thing that is needed 需要之物;必需品 3 the state of being very poor 贫困,艰难

needful /'ni:dfl/ adjective formal 【正式】 necessary 必要的;必需的

needle /'ni:dl/ noun 1 a very thin pointed piece of metal with a hole or eye for thread at the blunter end, used in sewing (用于缝纫的)针 2 a long, thin rod used in knitting 编结针 3 the pointed hollow end of a hypodermic syringe (注射器的)针头 4 a stylus used to play records (播放唱片的)唱针 5 a thin pointer on a dial, compass, etc. (刻度盘、指南针等的)指针 6 the thin, stiff leaf of a fir or pine tree (杉树或松树的)针叶 • verb (needles, needling, needled) informal 【非正式】 deliberately annoy someone 刺激;激怒;挑逗

needlecord /'ni:dlkɔ:d/ noun Brit. 【英】 a lightweight corduroy fabric with narrow ridges 细灯芯绒;细条纹光面呢

needlepoint /'ni:dlpɔɪnt/ noun closely stitched embroidery done on canvas 帆布刺绣品

needless /'ni:dləs/ adjective unnecessary; avoidable 不需要的,不必要的;可避免的 ■ **needlessly** adverb.

needlework /'ni:dlwɜ:k/ noun sewing

or embroidery 缝纫;刺绣;针线活

needn't /'ni:dnt/ short form need not.

needy /'ni:di/ adjective (needier, neediest) very poor 极贫穷的;极穷困的

ne'er /neə(r)/ short form old use or dialect 【旧或方】 never 从不 □ **ne'er-do-well** a useless or lazy person 无用之人;懒虫

nefarious /nɪ'feəriəs/ adjective bad or illegal 邪恶的;不合法的

negate /nɪ'geɪt/ verb (negates, negating, negated) 1 stop or undo the effect of 使无效 2 say that something does not exist 拒绝;否认 ■ **negation** noun.

negative /'negətɪv/ adjective 1 showing the absence rather than the presence of something 阴性的 2 expressing denial, disagreement, or refusal 否定的;不同意的;拒绝的 3 not hopeful or favourable 无望的;不利的 4 (of a quantity) less than zero (数量)小于零的,负的 5 having to do with the kind of electric charge carried by electrons (电)负的,负极的 6 (of a photograph) showing light and shade or colours reversed from those of the original (照片)反转的,负的 • noun 1 a negative word or statement 否定词;否定句 2 a negative photograph, from which positive prints may be made 底片;负片 ■ **negatively** adverb **negativity** noun.

neglect /nɪ'glekt/ verb 1 fail to give enough care or attention to 疏忽;疏漏 2 fail to do 漏做;忽略 • noun the action of neglecting 疏忽(行为)

neglectful /nɪ'glektfl/ adjective failing to give enough care or attention 疏忽的;疏漏的

negligee /'neglɪʒeɪ/ noun a woman's dressing gown made of a very light, thin fabric (轻薄衣料制作的)女便服

negligence /'neglɪdʒəns/ noun a

failure to give someone or something enough care or attention 忽视；疏忽 ■ **negligent** adjective.

negligible /'neglɪdʒəbl/ **adjective** so small or unimportant as to be not worth considering 可以忽略的；无关紧要的

negotiate /nɪ'gəʊʃɪeɪt/ **verb** (**negotiates, negotiating, negotiated**) **1** reach an agreement by discussion 谈判；商谈；协商 **2** bring something about by discussion 商定；达成 **3** find a way through a difficult path or route 通过，越过(难走的路) ■ **negotiable** adjective **negotiation** noun **negotiator** noun.

> ✔ 拼写指南 -*tiate*, not -*ciate*: nego-*tiate*. negotiate 中 -tiate 不要拼作 -ciate。

Negro /'niːgrəʊ/ **noun** (plural **Negroes**) a black person 黑人

> ！注意 the term **Negro** is now regarded as old-fashioned or even offensive. Negro 一词现已过时甚至具有冒犯意味。

neigh /neɪ/ **noun** a high-pitched cry made by a horse 马嘶声 • **verb** make this cry (马)嘶；发马嘶般的声音

neighbour /'neɪbə(r)/ (US spelling 【美拼作】 **neighbor**) **noun** a person who lives next door to you, or very close by 邻居 ■ **neighbourly** adjective.

neighbourhood /'neɪbəhʊd/ (US spelling 【美拼作】 **neighborhood**) **noun 1** a district within a town or city 地区；地段；居民点 **2** the area surrounding a place, person, or object 邻近地区；邻里

neighbouring /'neɪbərɪŋ/ **adjective** situated next to or very near something 邻近的；接近的

neither /'naɪðə(r), 'niː-/ **determiner & pronoun** not either 两者都不 • **adverb** used to show that a negative statement is true of two things, or also true of something else 也不

> ✔ 拼写指南 **neither** is spelled with the *e* before the *i*. neither 中 e 在 i 之前。

nemesis /'neməsɪs/ **noun** (plural **nemeses** /'neməsiːz/) something that brings about someone's deserved and unavoidable downfall 天谴；报应

neoclassical /ˌniːəʊ'klæsɪkl/ **adjective** relating to the revival of a classical style in the arts 新古典主义的 ■ **neoclassicism** noun.

Neolithic /ˌniːə'lɪθɪk/ **adjective** relating to the later part of the Stone Age 新石器时代的

neologism /ni'ɒlədʒɪzəm/ **noun** a new word or expression 新词；新表达法

neon /'niːɒn/ **noun** a gas that glows when electricity is passed through it, used in fluorescent lighting (气体元素)氖(电流通过时会发光，用于荧光照明)

neonatal /ˌniːəʊ'neɪtl/ **adjective** relating to birth and newborn children 新生儿的

neophyte /'niːəfaɪt/ **noun 1** a person who is new to a subject, skill, or belief 新手；初学者；新人 **2** a novice in a religious order, or a newly ordained priest 新入教者；新受圣职的神父

nephew /'nefjuː, -vjuː/ **noun** a son of your brother or sister 侄子；外甥

nephritis /nɪ'fraɪtɪs/ **noun** inflammation of the kidneys 肾炎

nepotism /'nepətɪzəm/ **noun** favouritism shown to relatives or friends 任人唯亲；裙带关系；重用亲朋

Neptune /'neptjuːn/ **noun** the eighth planet from the sun in the solar system 海王星

nerd /nɜːd/ **noun** informal 【非正式】 an unfashionable person who is obsessed with a particular subject or interest 怪人

nerve /nɜːv/ **noun 1** a fibre or bundle of fibres in the body along which impulses of sensation pass 神经 **2** steadiness and courage in a difficult situation 坚定；勇气；魄力 **3** (**nerves**) nervousness 精神紧张；情绪不安 **4** informal 【非正式】 cheekily disrespectful or inappropriate behavior 厚颜无耻 • **verb** (**nerves, nerving, nerved**) (**nerve yourself**) brace yourself for a difficult situation 使(自己)振奋 □ **get on someone's nerves** informal 【非正式】 irritate someone 激怒(某人) **nerve cell** a neuron 神经细胞 **nerve gas** a poisonous gas which affects the nervous system 神经性毒气 **nerve-racking** (or **nerve-wracking**) causing nervousness or fear 压力大的；令人恐惧的

nerveless /ˈnɜːvləs/ **adjective 1** lacking strength or feeling 无力气的；麻木的 **2** confident 有信心的

nervous /ˈnɜːvəs/ **adjective 1** easily frightened or worried 神经质的；焦虑的 **2** anxious 担忧的 **3** having to do with the nerves 神经的；神经性的 □ **nervous breakdown** a period of mental illness resulting from severe depression or stress 神经失常 **nervous system** the network of nerves which transmits nerve impulses between parts of the body 神经系统 ■ **nervously** adverb **nervousness** noun.

nervy /ˈnɜːvi/ **adjective** (**nervier, nerviest**) Brit. 【英】 nervous or tense 紧张的；神经紧绷的

nest /nest/ **noun 1** a structure made by a bird in which it lays eggs and shelters its young 鸟巢 **2** a place where an animal or insect breeds or shelters (兽类或昆虫的)窝，穴 **3** a set of similar objects that are designed to fit inside each other (可套叠的类

似物件的)一组，一套 • **verb 1** use or build a nest 筑巢；筑巢 **2** fit an object inside a larger one 使套入 □ **nest egg** a sum of money saved for the future 储备金

nestle /ˈnesl/ **verb** (**nestles, nestling, nestled**) **1** settle comfortably within or against something (舒适地)安卧，依偎 **2** (of a place) lie in a sheltered position (场所)位于隐蔽处

nestling /ˈnestlɪŋ/ **noun** a bird that is too young to leave the nest 雏鸟

net[1] /net/ **noun 1** a material made of strands of cord or string that are knotted together to form small open squares 网 **2** a piece or structure of net for catching fish or insects, surrounding a goal, etc. (打鱼或捕捉昆虫的)网；球门网 **3** a thin fabric with a very open weave 网状物 **4** (**the Net**) the Internet 因特网；互联网 • **verb** (**nets, netting, netted**) **1** catch something in a net 捕获；抓获 **2** earn or obtain something 赚得；获取

net[2] or Brit. 【英】 **nett adjective 1** (of a sum of money) remaining after tax or expenses have been deducted (总钱数)税后的，净的，纯的 **2** (of a weight) not including the packaging (重量)净的，不含皮重的 **3** (of an effect or result) overall (效果或结果)整体的，全面的 • **verb** (**nets, netting, netted**) gain a sum of money as clear profit 净赚(利润)

netball /ˈnetbɔːl/ **noun** a team game in which goals are scored by throwing a ball through a net hanging from a hoop 无挡板篮球(运动)

nether /ˈneðə(r)/ **adjective** lower in position (位置)低的，下面的

nettle /ˈnetl/ **noun** a plant with leaves that are covered with stinging hairs 荨麻 • **verb** (**nettles, nettling, nettled**) annoy 使恼火；使烦恼

network /ˈnetwɜːk/ **noun 1** an arrangement of intersecting horizontal and vertical lines 网;网络 **2** a complex system of railways, roads, etc., that cross or connect with each other (铁路、公路等等的)网状系统 **3** a group of radio or television stations that connect to broadcast a programme at the same time 广播网;电视网 **4** a number of interconnected computers, operations, etc. (计算机)互联网;(操控)网络 **5** a group of people who keep in contact with each other to exchange information 关系网 • **verb** keep in contact with other people to exchange information 交际;交流 ■ **networker** noun.

neural /ˈnjʊərəl/ **adjective** relating to a nerve or the nervous system 神经的;神经系统的

neuralgia /njʊəˈrældʒə/ **noun** severe pain along a nerve in the head or face (头部或面部的)神经痛 ■ **neuralgic** adjective.

neurology /njʊəˈrɒlədʒɪ/ **noun** the branch of medicine concerned with the nervous system 神经学;神经病学 ■ **neurological** adjective **neurologist** noun.

neuron or **neurone** /ˈnjʊərɒn/ **noun** a cell that transmits nerve impulses 神经细胞;神经元

neurosis /njʊəˈrəʊsɪs/ **noun** (plural **neuroses** /njʊəˈrəʊsiːz/) a mild mental illness in which a person feels depressed or anxious, or behaves in an obsessive way 神经官能症;神经机能病

neurotic /njʊəˈrɒtɪk/ **adjective 1** having to do with neurosis 神经官能症的;神经机能病的 **2** informal 【非正式】obsessive, or too sensitive or anxious 神经质的;极其敏感的;焦虑的

neuter /ˈnjuːtə(r)/ **adjective 1** (of a noun) neither masculine nor feminine (名词)中性的 **2** having no sexual or reproductive organs 无性器官的;无生殖器官的 • **verb** (**neuters**,

neutering, **neutered**) operate on an animal so that it cannot produce young 阉割(动物);切除(动物)的卵巢

neutral /ˈnjuːtrəl/ **adjective 1** not supporting either side in a dispute or war (在纠纷或战争中)中立的 **2** lacking noticeable or strong qualities 缺乏显著特征的;无明显特质的 **3** Chemistry 【化学】neither acid nor alkaline; having a pH of about 7 酸碱平衡的;中性的 • **noun** a position of a gear mechanism in which the engine is disconnected from the driven parts (排挡装置的)空挡 ■ **neutrality** noun **neutrally** adverb.

neutralize or **neutralise** /ˈnjuːtrəlaɪz/ **verb** (**neutralizes**, **neutralizing**, **neutralized**) **1** stop something from having an effect 使无效;使失去作用 **2** make neutral 使呈中性;使平衡 ■ **neutralization** noun.

neutrino /njuːˈtriːnəʊ/ **noun** (plural **neutrinos**) a subatomic particle with a mass close to zero and no electric charge 中微子

neutron /ˈnjuːtrɒn/ **noun** a subatomic particle of about the same mass as a proton but without an electric charge 中子

never /ˈnevə(r)/ **adverb 1** not ever 决不;从来不 **2** not at all 一点也不 □ **the never-never** Brit. informal【英,非正式】hire purchase 分期付款

nevermore /ˌnevəˈmɔː(r)/ **adverb** never again 永不再;决不再

nevertheless /ˌnevəðəˈles/ **adverb** in spite of that 仍然;不过

new /njuː/ **adjective 1** made, introduced, discovered, or experienced recently 新的 **2** not previously used or owned 未使用过的;新有的 **3** (**new to**) not experienced in 无经验的 **4** different from a recent previous one 新接触的 **5** better than before; renewed or reformed 比以前好的;更新的;新型的 • **adverb** newly 新近 □ **New Age**

an alternative movement concerned with spirituality, care for the environment, etc. 新时代运动 **new moon** the phase of the moon when it first appears as a thin crescent 新月；朔 **New Testament** the second part of the Christian Bible, recording the life and teachings of Jesus《圣经·新约》 **New World** North and South America 新大陆(即南北美洲) **new year** the calendar year that has just begun or is about to begin, following 31 December 新年

newborn /'nju:bɔ:n/ **adjective** recently born 新生的

newcomer /'nju:kʌmə(r)/ **noun 1** a person who has recently arrived 新来的人；新到者 **2** a person who is new to an activity or situation 新手；初学者

newel /'nju:əl/ **noun** the post at the top or bottom of a stair rail (楼梯围栏顶端或底部的)端柱

newfangled /,nju:'fæŋgld/ **adjective** disapproving 【贬】 newly developed and unfamiliar 新开发的；新奇的

newly /'nju:li/ **adverb** recently 最近；新近 □ **newly-wed** a person who has recently married 新婚者；新人

news /nju:z/ **noun 1** new information about recent events 新闻；消息；新情况 **2 (the news)** a broadcast or published news report 新闻广播；新闻报道

newsagent /'nju:zeidʒənt/ **noun** Brit. 【英】 a shopkeeper who sells newspapers and magazines 报刊经售人

newscast /'nju:zkɑ:st/ **noun** N. Amer. 【北美】 a broadcast news report 新闻广播 ■ **newscaster** noun.

newsflash /'nju:zflæʃ/ **noun** a brief item of important news, interrupting other radio or television programmes (中断其他广播或电视节目而播出的)简明新闻

newsgroup /'nju:zgru:p/ **noun** a group of Internet users who exchange information about a particular subject online 新闻组，话题群(在因特网上就共同感兴趣的话题进行讨论的群组)

newsletter /'nju:zletə(r)/ **noun** a bulletin issued on a regular basis to the members of a society or organization (社团或组织定期出版的)内部通讯，简讯

newspaper /'nju:speipə(r), 'nju:z-/ **noun** a daily or weekly publication containing news and articles on current affairs 报纸；报

newsprint /'nju:zprint/ **noun** cheap, low-quality paper used for newspapers 新闻纸

newsreader /'nju:zri:də(r)/ **noun** Brit. 【英】 a person who reads the news on radio or television (电台或电视台的)新闻广播员，新闻播音员

newsreel /'nju:zri:l/ **noun** a short cinema film showing news and current affairs 新闻短片

newsroom /'nju:zru:m/ **noun** the area in a newspaper or broadcasting office where news is processed 新闻编辑室

newsworthy /'nju:zwɜ:ði/ **adjective** important enough to be mentioned as news 有新闻价值的，值得报道的

newt /nju:t/ **noun** a small animal with a slender body and a long tail, that can live in water or on land 蝾螈(一种小型两栖动物,体几尾长)

newton /'nju:tn/ **noun** Physics 【物理】 a unit of force 牛顿(力的单位)

next /nekst/ **adjective 1** coming immediately after the present one in time, space, or order 接下来的；下一个的；邻近的 **2** (of a day of the week) nearest (or the nearest but one) after the present (一周中的一天)紧接在后的，隔了一天的 • **adverb** immediately afterwards 紧接着 □ **next door** in or to the next house or room 在隔壁；到隔壁 **next of kin**

a person's closest living relative or relatives 最近亲

nexus /'neksəs/ **noun** (plural **nexus** or **nexuses**) a connection or series of connections 联结；联系

NHS /en eɪtʃ'es/ **abbreviation** National Health Service 国民保健制度

nib /nɪb/ **noun** the pointed end part of a pen 钢笔尖

nibble /'nɪbl/ **verb** (**nibbles, nibbling, nibbled**) **1** take small bites out of 啃；小口咬 **2** bite gently 轻咬 • **noun** **1** a small piece of food bitten off 少量食物；咬一小口的量 **2** (**nibbles**) informal 【非正式】 small savoury snacks 点心；小吃

Nicaraguan /ˌnɪkə'ræɡjuən/ **noun** a person from Nicaragua 尼加拉瓜人 • **adjective** relating to Nicaragua 尼加拉瓜的

nice /naɪs/ **adjective** **1** enjoyable or attractive; pleasant 令人愉快的，吸引人的 **2** goodnatured; kind 好心的；和蔼的；友好的 **3** involving a very small detail or difference 细微的；细致的；精细的；微妙的 ■ **nicely** adverb **niceness** noun.

nicety /'naɪsəti/ **noun** (plural **niceties**) **1** a very small detail or difference 细节；细微区别 **2** accuracy 准确；精确

niche /niːtʃ, niː/ **noun** **1** a small hollow in a wall 壁龛 **2** (**your niche**) a role or job that suits you 合适的工作

nick /nɪk/ **noun** **1** a small cut 小切口 **2** (**the nick**) Brit. informal 【英，非正式】 prison or a police station 监牢；班房；警察局 **3** Brit. informal 【英，非正式】 condition 情形；状况 • **verb** **1** make a nick or nicks in 使有破损；划痕于 **2** Brit. informal 【英，非正式】 steal 偷；盗窃 **3** Brit. informal 【英，非正式】 arrest 逮捕 □ **in the nick of time** only just in time 刚好；恰好；及时

nickel /'nɪkl/ **noun** **1** a silvery-white metallic element 镍 **2** N. Amer. 【北美】 a five-cent coin 五分镍币

nickname /'nɪkneɪm/ **noun** another name by which someone is known 昵称；绰号；诨名 • **verb** (**nicknames, nicknaming, nicknamed**) give a nickname to 给…起绰号；以昵称称呼

nicotine /'nɪkətiːn/ **noun** a poisonous oily liquid found in tobacco 尼古丁；烟碱

niece /niːs/ **noun** a daughter of your brother or sister 侄女；甥女

> ✔ 拼写指南 *i* before *e* except after *c*: nie*ce*. i 置于 e 前，在 c 后则除外，如 nie*ce*。

nifty /'nɪfti/ **adjective** (**niftier, niftiest**) informal 【非正式】 very skilful, effective, or useful 极好的；极快的；非常有用的

Nigerian /naɪ'dʒɪəriən/ **noun** a person from Nigeria 尼日利亚人 • **adjective** relating to Nigeria 尼日利亚的

niggardly /'nɪɡədli/ **adjective** not generous; mean 吝啬的；小气的

nigger /'nɪɡə(r)/ **noun** offensive 【冒犯】 a black person 黑人

niggle /'nɪɡl/ **verb** (**niggles, niggling, niggled**) slightly worry or annoy 使担心；使烦恼 • **noun** a minor worry or criticism 小烦恼；微不足道的批评

nigh /naɪ/ **adverb, preposition, & adjective** old use 【旧】 near 接近的；靠近的

night /naɪt/ **noun** **1** the time from sunset to sunrise 夜；夜晚 **2** an evening 晚上

nightcap /'naɪtkæp/ **noun** **1** a hot or alcoholic drink taken at bedtime 睡前热饮；睡前酒 **2** (in the past) a soft hat worn in bed 旧时的睡帽

nightclub /'naɪtklʌb/ **noun** a club that is open at night, with a bar and music 夜总会

nightdress /'naɪtdres/ or **nightgown** /'naɪtɡaʊn/ **noun** a light, loose garment worn by a woman or girl in bed 女式睡袍

nightfall /'naɪtfɔːl/ **noun** dusk 黄昏

N

傍晚；日暮

nightie /'naɪti/ **noun** informal 【非正式】 a nightdress 女式睡袍

nightingale /'naɪtɪŋgeɪl/ **noun** a small bird with a tuneful song, often heard at night 夜莺

nightlife /'naɪtlaɪf/ **noun** social activities or entertainment available at night 夜生活

nightly /'naɪtli/ **adjective & adverb** happening or done every night 每夜的(地)；每晚的(地)

nightmare /'naɪtmeə(r)/ **noun 1** a frightening or unpleasant dream 梦魇；噩梦 **2** a very unpleasant experience 极不愉快的经历 ■ **nightmarish** adjective.

nightshirt /'naɪtʃɜːt/ **noun** a long shirt worn in bed 衬衫式长睡衣

nightspot /'naɪtspɒt/ **noun** informal【非正式】 a nightclub 夜总会

nihilism /'naɪɪlɪzəm/ **noun** the belief that nothing has any value 虚无主义 ■ **nihilist** noun **nihilistic** adjective.

nil /nɪl/ **noun** nothing; zero 无；零

nimble /'nɪmbl/ **adjective** (**nimbler**, **nimblest**) **1** quick and light in movement (行动)迅速的，敏捷的 **2** able to think and understand quickly 机敏的 ■ **nimbly** adverb.

nimbus /'nɪmbəs/ **noun** (plural **nimbi** /'nɪmbaɪ/ or **nimbuses**) a large grey rain cloud 雨云

nincompoop /'nɪnkəmpuːp, 'nɪŋ-/ **noun** a stupid person 傻子；笨蛋

nine /naɪn/ **cardinal number** one less than ten; 9 九 (Roman numeral 罗马数字: **ix** or **IX.**)

nineteen /naɪn'tiːn/ **cardinal number** one more than eighteen; 19 十九 (Roman numeral 罗马数字: **xix** or **XIX.**) ■ **nineteenth** ordinal number.

ninety /'naɪnti/ **cardinal number** (plural **nineties**) ten less than one hundred; 90 九十 (Roman numeral 罗马数字: **xc** or **XC.**) ■ **ninetieth** ordinal number.

ninny /'nɪni/ **noun** (plural **ninnies**)

informal【非正式】 a silly person 蠢人；傻子

ninth /naɪnθ/ **ordinal number 1** at number nine in a sequence; 9th 第九 **2** (a ninth or one ninth) each of nine equal parts into which something is divided 九分之一

nip¹ /nɪp/ **verb** (**nips**, **nipping**, **nipped**) **1** pinch, squeeze, or bite sharply 紧紧夹住；挤；紧咬 **2** Brit. informal【英，非正式】 go quickly 快走；一溜烟地跑 • **noun 1** a sharp bite or pinch 夹；掐；咬 **2** a sharp feeling of coldness (严寒的)刺骨，刺痛

nip² **noun** a small quantity or sip of spirits 少量酒；一小口酒

nipper /'nɪpə(r)/ **noun** informal【非正式】 a child 小孩；儿童

nipple /'nɪpl/ **noun** a small projection in the centre of each breast, from which (in a woman who has recently had a baby) a baby is able to suck milk 乳头

nippy /'nɪpi/ **adjective** (**nippier**, **nippiest**) informal【非正式】 **1** able to move quickly 轻快的；敏捷的 **2** chilly 寒冷的

nirvana /nɪə'vɑːnə/ **noun** (in Buddhism) a state of perfect happiness (佛教的)涅槃，极乐世界

nit /nɪt/ **noun** informal【非正式】 **1** the egg of a human head louse 虱子卵 **2** Brit.【英】 a stupid person 傻瓜；笨蛋 □ **nit-picking** criticism of small or unimportant details 找茬儿；挑剔

nitrate /'naɪtreɪt/ **noun** a salt or ester of nitric acid 硝酸盐；硝酸酯

nitric acid /'naɪtrɪk/ **noun** a very corrosive acid 硝酸

nitrite /'naɪtraɪt/ **noun** a salt or ester of nitrous acid 亚硝酸盐；亚硝酸酯

nitrogen /'naɪtrədʒən/ **noun** a gas forming about 78 per cent of the earth's atmosphere (气体元素)氮

nitroglycerine /ˌnaɪtrəʊ'glɪsəriːn, -rɪn/ (US spelling【美拼作】 **nitroglycerin**) **noun** an explosive liquid

used in dynamite 硝化甘油;甘油三硝酸酯

nitrous oxide /ˌnaɪtrəs ˈɒksaɪd/ **noun** a colourless gas used as an anaesthetic 氧化亚氮,笑气(用作麻醉剂)

nitty-gritty /ˌnɪtiˈɡrɪti/ **noun** informal 【非正式】the most important details 重要细节

nitwit /ˈnɪtwɪt/ **noun** informal 【非正式】a stupid person 傻子;笨蛋

no /nəʊ/ **determiner** not any 没有;无 • **exclamation** used to refuse or disagree with something (用于表示拒绝或不赞成)不,不对 • **adverb** not at all 一点也不 • **noun** (plural **noes**) a decision or vote against something 反对;反对票 □ **no-claims bonus** Brit.【英】a reduction in an insurance premium when no claim has been made over an agreed period 无索赔奖励,无赔偿优惠(在合同期内未向保险公司提出索赔者享受到的保险金优惠) **no-ball** a ball in cricket that is unlawfully bowled, counting as an extra run to the batting side (板球比赛中的)违规投球

no. abbreviation number.

nob /nɒb/ **noun** Brit. informal【英,非正式】an upper-class person 社会地位高的人;上层人士

nobble /ˈnɒbl/ **verb** (**nobbles, nobbling, nobbled**) Brit. informal【英,非正式】**1** try to influence someone using unfair or illegal methods 暗中影响;收买 **2** stop someone and talk to them (为了交谈)使(某人)停下

nobility /nəʊˈbɪləti/ **noun 1** the quality of being noble 高尚;崇高 **2** the aristocracy 贵族阶层

noble /ˈnəʊbl/ **adjective** (**nobler, noblest**) **1** belonging to the aristocracy 贵族的 **2** having personal qualities that people admire, such as courage and honesty 高尚的;崇高的 **3** magnificent; impressive 宏伟的;壮观的;给人深刻印象的 • **noun** a

nobleman or noblewoman 贵族;出身高贵的人 ■ **nobly** adverb.

nobleman /ˈnəʊblmən/ or **noble-woman** /ˈnəʊblwʊmən/ **noun** (plural **noblemen** or **noblewomen**) a member of the aristocracy 贵族;出身高贵的人

nobody /ˈnəʊbədi, -bɒdi/ **pronoun** no person 没有人;无人 • **noun** (plural **nobodies**) a person who is not considered important 无名小辈;小人物

nocturnal /nɒkˈtɜːnl/ **adjective** done or active at night 夜间做的;夜晚活动的 ■ **nocturnally** adverb.

nocturne /ˈnɒktɜːn/ **noun** a short piece of music in a dreamy, romantic style 夜曲;梦幻曲

nod /nɒd/ **verb** (**nods, nodding, nodded**) **1** lower and raise your head briefly to show agreement or as a greeting or signal 点头 **2** let your head fall forward when you are drowsy or asleep 垂着头打瞌睡;昏昏欲睡 **3** (**nod off**) informal【非正式】fall asleep 打瞌睡;打盹 • **noun** an act of nodding 点头

node /nəʊd/ **noun** technical 【术语】**1** a point in a network at which lines cross or branch (网络的)结点 **2** the part of a plant stem from which one or more leaves grow 茎节(植物茎上长叶的部位) **3** a small mass of tissue in the body (人体的)结节,结

nodule /ˈnɒdjuːl/ **noun** a small swelling or lump 小瘤;小块 ■ **nodular** adjective.

Noel /nəʊˈel/ **noun** Christmas 圣诞节

noggin /ˈnɒɡɪn/ **noun** a small quantity of alcoholic drink 少量含酒精饮料

Noh /nəʊ/ **noun** a type of traditional Japanese theatre with dance and song 能剧(日本传统歌舞剧)

noise /nɔɪz/ **noun 1** a sound or series of sounds, especially an unpleasant one 噪声;杂音 **2** disturbances that accompany and interfere with an electrical signal 干扰;电子干扰信号 ■ **noiseless** adjective.

noisome /'nɔɪsəm/ adjective literary 【文】 having a very unpleasant smell 恶臭的

noisy /'nɔɪzi/ adjective (noisier, noisiest) full of or making a lot of noise 充满噪声的;吵吵嚷嚷的 ■ **noisily** adverb.

nomad /'nəʊmæd/ noun a member of a people that travels from place to place to find fresh pasture for its animals 游牧部落成员

nomadic /nəʊ'mædɪk, nɒ-/ adjective having the life of a nomad; wandering 游牧的;漫游的;流浪的

nom de plume /ˌnɒm də 'pluːm/ noun (plural noms de plume /ˌnɒm də 'pluːm/) a name used by a writer instead of their real name; a pen name 笔名

nomenclature /nəʊ'menklətʃə(r)/ noun a system of names used in a particular subject 专门术语

nominal /'nɒmɪnl/ adjective 1 in name but not in reality 名义上的;有名无实的 2 (of a sum of money) very small (钱款)些微的,象征性的 ■ **nominally** adverb.

nominate /'nɒmɪneɪt/ verb (nominates, nominating, nominated) 1 put someone forward as a candidate for a job or award 提名(候选人) 2 arrange a time, date, or place 确定,指定(时间、日期或地点) ■ **nomination** noun **nominee** noun.

nominative /'nɒmɪnətɪv/ noun Grammar 【语法】 the case used for the subject of a verb 主格

non- /nɒn/ prefix not 不;非: non-existent 不存在的

nonagenarian /ˌnəʊnədʒə'neəriən, ˌnɒn-/ noun a person between 90 and 99 years old 90 多岁的人

nonchalant /'nɒnʃələnt/ adjective relaxed and unconcerned 若无其事的;漠不关心的 ■ **nonchalance** noun

nonchalantly adverb.

non-commissioned /ˌnɒnkə'mɪʃnd/ adjective (of a military officer) appointed from the lower ranks (军官)无委任状的,未授军官衔的

non-committal /ˌnɒnkə'mɪtl/ adjective not showing what you think or which side you are on 不表态的;不表明意见的 ■ **noncommittally** adverb.

non compos mentis /ˌnɒn ˌkɒmpəs 'mentɪs/ adjective not in your right mind; distracted or mad 精神失常的;发疯的

nonconformist /ˌnɒnkən'fɔːmɪst/ noun 1 a person who does not follow accepted ideas or behavior 不遵守常规的人 2 (Nonconformist) a member of a Protestant Church which does not follow the beliefs of the established Church of England 不信奉英国国教的新教徒 ■ **nonconformity** noun.

nondescript /'nɒndɪskrɪpt/ adjective having no interesting or special features 缺乏特色的;无趣味的

none /nʌn/ pronoun 1 not any 没有一点儿;毫无 2 no one 没有人(或物) • adverb (none the) not at all 一点也不;毫不

nonentity /nɒ'nentəti/ noun (plural nonentities) an unimportant person or thing 无足轻重的人(或事物)

nonetheless or **none the less** /ˌnʌnðə'les/ adverb in spite of that; nevertheless 尽管如此;不过;然而

non-event /ˌnɒnɪ'vent/ noun a very disappointing or uninteresting event 令人失望的事;无趣的事

non-existent /ˌnɒnɪg'zɪstənt/ adjective not real or present 不真实的;不在场的

no-nonsense /ˌnəʊ'nɒnsns/ adjective simple and straightforward; sensible 率直的;直截了当的;明智的

nonplussed /ˌnɒn'plʌst/ adjective surprised and confused 惊讶不已的;

困惑的；不知所措的

non-proliferation /ˌnɒnprəˌlɪfəˈreɪʃn/ **noun** the prevention of an increase in the number of nuclear weapons that are produced 防止核武器扩散

nonsense /ˈnɒnsns/ **noun 1** words or statements that make no sense 无意义的话；胡话 **2** silly behaviour 愚蠢的行为

nonsensical /nɒnˈsensɪkl/ **adjective** making no sense; ridiculous 荒谬的；愚蠢的

non sequitur /ˌnɒn ˈsekwɪtə(r)/ **noun** a statement that does not follow on logically from what has just been said 不合逻辑的推理

non-starter /ˌnɒnˈstɑːtə(r)/ **noun** informal【非正式】something that has no chance of succeeding 不可能成功的事

non-stick /ˌnɒnˈstɪk/ **adjective** (of a pan) covered with a substance that prevents food sticking to it during cooking (锅)不粘的

non-stop /ˌnɒnˈstɒp/ **adjective & adverb 1** continuing without stopping 不停的(地) **2** having no stops on the way to a destination 直达的(地)；中途不停的(地)

noodles /ˈnuːdlz/ **plural noun** thin, long strips of pasta 面条

nook /nʊk/ **noun** a place that is sheltered or hidden 角落；隐蔽处

noon /nuːn/ **noun** twelve o'clock in the day; midday 正午；中午

noonday /ˈnuːndeɪ/ **adjective** taking place or appearing in the middle of the day 中午

no one **pronoun** no person 没有人；无人

noose /nuːs/ **noun** a loop with a knot which tightens as the rope or wire is pulled, used to hang people or trap animals (用于绞死人的)绞索，套索；(诱捕动物的)绳套

nor /nɔː(r)/ **conjunction & adverb** and not; and not either 不；也不

Nordic /ˈnɔːdɪk/ **adjective** relating to Scandinavia, Finland, and Iceland 斯堪的纳维亚的；北欧国家的

norm /nɔːm/ **noun 1 (the norm)** the usual or standard thing 寻常之事；常态 **2** a standard that is required or acceptable 标准；规则

normal /ˈnɔːml/ **adjective** usual and typical; what you would expect 平常的；典型的；预期的 • **noun** the normal state or condition 正常状态(或条件) ■ **normality** noun **normally** adverb.

normalize or **normalise** /ˈnɔːməlaɪz/ **verb (normalizes, normalizing, normalized)** make or become normal 使正常化；变得正常 ■ **normalization** noun.

Norman /ˈnɔːmən/ **noun** a member of a people from Normandy in northern France who conquered England in 1066 诺曼人(来自法国北部的诺曼底，于 1066 年征服了英格兰) • **adjective** relating to the Normans or Normandy 诺曼人的；诺曼底的

normative /ˈnɔːmətɪv/ **adjective** relating to or setting a standard or norm 标准的；规范的；设立标准(或规范)的

Norse /nɔːs/ **noun** ancient or medieval Norwegian or another Scandinavian language 古挪威语；中世纪挪威语；斯堪的纳维亚语 • **adjective** relating to ancient or medieval Norway or Scandinavia 古挪威的；中世纪挪威的；斯堪的纳维亚的

north /nɔːθ/ **noun 1** the direction which is on your left-hand side when you are facing east 北；北方 **2** the northern part of a place 北部；北部地区 • **adjective 1** lying towards or facing the north 向北的；朝北的 **2** (of a wind) blowing from the north (风)来自北方的 • **adverb** to or towards the north 向北；朝北 ■ **northward** adjective & adverb **northwards** adverb.

north-east /ˌnɔːθˈiːst/ **noun** the direction or region halfway between north and east 东北方向；东北地区 • **adjective & adverb 1** towards or facing the north-east 向东北的；东北的 **2** (of a wind) blowing from the north-east (风)来自东北的，从东北 ■ **north-eastern** adjective.

north-easterly /ˌnɔːθˈiːstəli/ **adjective & adverb 1** facing or moving towards the north-east 朝东北的；向东北的 **2** (of a wind) blowing from the north-east (风)来自东北的，从东北

northerly /ˈnɔːðəli/ **adjective & adverb 1** facing or moving towards the north 朝北的；向北的 **2** (of a wind) blowing from the north (风)来自北方的，从北方

northern /ˈnɔːðən/ **adjective 1** situated in or facing the north 位于北方的；朝北的 **2** coming from or characteristic of the north 来自北方的；具有北方特征的 □ **Northern Lights** the aurora borealis 北极光

northerner /ˈnɔːðənə(r)/ **noun** a person from the north of a region 北方人

north-west /ˌnɔːθˈwest/ **noun** the direction or region halfway between north and west 西北方向；西北地区 • **adjective & adverb 1** towards or facing the north-west 向西北的；西北的 **2** (of a wind) blowing from the north-west (风)来自西北的，从西北 ■ **north-western** adjective.

north-westerly /ˌnɔːθˈwestəli/ **adjective & adverb 1** facing or moving towards the north-west 朝西北的；向西北的 **2** (of a wind) blowing from the north-west (风)来自西北的，从西北

Norwegian /nɔːˈwiːdʒən/ **noun 1** a person from Norway 挪威人 **2** the language spoken in Norway 挪威语 • **adjective** relating to Norway 挪威的

nose /nəʊz/ **noun 1** the part of the face containing the nostrils and used in breathing and smelling 鼻子 **2** the front end of an aircraft, car, or other vehicle (飞机、汽车或其他交通工具的)前部 **3** a talent for finding something 发现事物的能力；嗅觉 **4** the characteristic smell of a wine (酒的)气味 • **verb (noses, nosing, nosed) 1** make your way slowly forward 缓慢前行 **2** look around or pry into something 四处察看；窥探；打听 **3** (of an animal) push its nose against or into (动物用鼻子)拱，探入

nosebag /ˈnəʊzbæɡ/ **noun** a bag containing fodder, hung from a horse's head (挂在马颈上的)饲料袋

nosebleed /ˈnəʊzbliːd/ **noun** an instance of bleeding from the nose 鼻出血

nosedive /ˈnəʊzdaɪv/ **noun 1** a sudden dramatic decline 猛跌；暴降 **2** a steep downward plunge by an aircraft (飞机的)俯冲 • **verb (nosedives, nosediving, nosedived) 1** fall or decline suddenly 俯冲；猛跌；暴降 **2** (of an aircraft) make a nosedive (飞机)俯冲

nosegay /ˈnəʊzɡeɪ/ **noun** a small bunch of flowers 一小束花

nosh /nɒʃ/ informal 【非正式】 **noun** food 食物 • **verb** eat enthusiastically 津津有味地吃；贪婪地吃

nostalgia /nɒˈstældʒə/ **noun** longing for a happier or better time in the past 恋旧；怀旧 ■ **nostalgic** adjective **nostalgically** adverb.

nostril /ˈnɒstrəl/ **noun** either of the two openings of the nose through which air passes to the lungs 鼻孔

nostrum /ˈnɒstrəm/ **noun 1** a favourite method for improving something 妙方；良策 **2** an ineffective medicine 无效的药

nosy or **nosey** /ˈnəʊzi/ **adjective (nosier, nosiest)** informal 【非正式】 too inquisitive about other people's affairs 爱管闲事的；好打听的

not /nɒt/ **adverb 1** used to express a negative 不；不是 **2** less than 少于；

低于

notable /ˈnəʊtəbl/ **adjective** deserving to be noticed or given attention 值得关注的;值得注意的 • **noun** a famous or important person 名人;要人 ■ **notably** adverb.

notary /ˈnəʊtəri/ **noun** (plural **notaries**) a lawyer who is authorized to be a witness when people sign documents 公证人;公证员

notation /nəʊˈteɪʃn/ **noun** a system of symbols used in music, mathematics, etc. (音乐、数学等中的)符号,记号

notch /nɒtʃ/ **noun 1** a V-shaped cut on an edge or surface (V字形)槽口,凹口 **2** a point or level on a scale (刻度尺上的)刻点,刻痕 • **verb 1** make notches in 刻痕于 **2** (**notch something up**) score or achieve something 得分;完成;达到

note /nəʊt/ **noun 1** a brief written record of something 笔记;记录 **2** a short written message 短笺;便条 **3** Brit. 【英】a banknote 钞票;纸币 **4** a single sound of a particular pitch and length made by a musical instrument or voice, or a symbol representing this 单音;音调;音符 • **verb** (**notes**, **noting**, **noted**) **1** pay attention to 注意;留意 **2** record something in writing 记录;记下 □ **of note** important 重要的 **take note** pay attention 注意;留意

notebook /ˈnəʊtbʊk/ **noun 1** a small book for writing notes in 笔记本 **2** a portable computer smaller than a laptop 便携式电脑;笔记本电脑

noted /ˈnəʊtɪd/ **adjective** well known 著名的;知名的

notepaper /ˈnəʊtpeɪpə/ **noun** paper for writing letters on 信笺

noteworthy /ˈnəʊtwɜːði/ **adjective** interesting or important 有趣的;重要的

nothing /ˈnʌθɪŋ/ **pronoun 1** not anything 没有什么;没有事情 **2** something that is not important or interesting 微不足道的事;无趣的事 **3** nought 零 • **adverb** not at all 一点儿也不;根本不

nothingness /ˈnʌθɪŋnəs/ **noun** a state of not existing, or in which nothing exists 空;没有;虚无

notice /ˈnəʊtɪs/ **noun 1** the fact of being aware of or paying attention to something 察觉;注意 **2** warning that something is going to happen 征兆;预兆 **3** a formal statement that you are going to leave a job or end an agreement 辞呈;(终止协议的)正式声明 **4** a sheet of paper displaying information 告示;通知 **5** a small published announcement or advertisement in a newspaper (报纸上的)声明,广告 **6** a short published review of a new film, play, or book (对新电影、戏剧或图书的)短评 • **verb** (**notices**, **noticing**, **noticed**) become aware of 意识到;察觉到

noticeable /ˈnəʊtɪsəbl/ **adjective** easily seen or noticed 显而易见的;易于察觉的 ■ **noticeably** adverb.

✔ 拼写指南 remember the *e* in the middle: notic*e*able. 记住拼写 noticeable 中间的 e。

notifiable /ˈnəʊtɪfaɪəbl/ **adjective** (of an infectious disease) that must be reported to the health authorities (传染病)须报告卫生主管部门的

notify /ˈnəʊtɪfaɪ/ **verb** (**notifies**, **notifying**, **notified**) formally tell someone about something 正式通知;告知 ■ **notification** noun.

notion /ˈnəʊʃn/ **noun 1** an idea or belief 想法;信念 **2** an understanding 理解

notional /ˈnəʊʃənl/ **adjective** based on an idea rather than reality 以理论为基础的;假定的 ■ **notionally** adverb.

notoriety /ˌnəʊtəˈraɪəti/ **noun** the state of being notorious 臭名;恶名

notorious /nəʊˈtɔːriəs/ **adjective**

famous for something bad 臭名昭著的 ■ **notoriously** adverb.

notwithstanding /ˌnɒtwɪθˈstændɪŋ, -wɪð-/ preposition in spite of 虽然；尽管 • adverb nevertheless 尽管；然而；还是

nougat /ˈnuːɡɑː, ˈnʌɡət/ noun a sweet made from sugar or honey, nuts, and egg white 牛轧糖

nought /nɔːt/ noun the figure 0 (数字) 零 • pronoun nothing 无；乌有

noun /naʊn/ noun a word (other than a pronoun) that refers to a person, place, or thing 名词

nourish /ˈnʌrɪʃ/ verb 1 give a person, animal, or plant the food and other substances they need in order to grow and be healthy 养育；培养；供给 2 keep a feeling or belief in your mind for a long time (长期)怀有(某种感情或信念)

nourishment /ˈnʌrɪʃmənt/ noun the food and other substances necessary for life, growth, and good health 食物；营养品

nous /naʊs/ noun Brit. informal【英，非正式】common sense 常识

nouveau riche /ˌnuːvəʊ ˈriːʃ/ noun people who have recently become rich and who display their wealth in an obvious or tasteless way 暴发户；新近发财的人

nova /ˈnəʊvə/ noun (plural novae /ˈnəʊviː/ or novas) a star that suddenly becomes very bright for a short period (短期内突然变得很亮的)新星

novel¹ /ˈnɒvl/ noun a story of book length about imaginary people and events 小说

novel² adjective new in an interesting or unusual way 新颖的；新奇的

novelist /ˈnɒvəlɪst/ noun a person who writes novels 小说家

novella /nəˈvelə/ noun a short novel or long short story 短篇小说；中篇小说

novelty /ˈnɒvlti/ noun (plural novelties) 1 the quality of being new and unusual 新奇；新颖 2 a new or unfamiliar thing 新事物；不熟悉的事物 3 a small toy or ornament 小玩具；小装饰品

November /nəʊˈvembə(r)/ noun the eleventh month of the year 十一月

novice /ˈnɒvɪs/ noun 1 a person who is new to and lacks experience in a job or situation 新手；生手；初学者 2 a person who has entered a religious community but has not yet taken their vows 见习修士；见习修女

novitiate or **noviciate** /nəˈvɪʃiət/ noun a period of being a novice in a religious community 修士(或修女)的见习期

now /naʊ/ adverb 1 at the present time 现在；目前 2 immediately 即刻；立即 • conjunction as a result of the fact 既然；由于

nowadays /ˈnaʊədeɪz/ adverb at the present time, in contrast with the past 现今；现在；当今

nowhere /ˈnəʊweə(r)/ adverb not anywhere 到处都不 • pronoun no place 无处

noxious /ˈnɒkʃəs/ adjective harmful or very unpleasant 有害的；非常讨厌的

nozzle /ˈnɒzl/ noun a spout used to control a stream of liquid or gas 喷口；喷嘴；管嘴

nuance /ˈnjuːɑːns/ noun a very slight difference in meaning, expression, sound, etc. (意思、表达、声音等方面的)细微差别

nub /nʌb/ noun 1 (the nub) the central point of a matter (事情的)核心 2 a small lump 小块

nubile /ˈnjuːbaɪl/ adjective (of a girl or young woman) sexually attractive (女孩或年轻妇女)性感的，漂亮的

nuclear /ˈnjuːkliə(r)/ adjective 1 relating to the nucleus of an atom or cell 原子核的；细胞核的 2 using energy released in the fission (splitting) or fusion of atomic nuclei 使用核能的 **3** possessing or involving nuclear weapons 拥有核武器的;有关核武器的 □ **nuclear family** a couple and their children 核心家庭(由一对夫妻及其子女组成) **nuclear physics** the science of atomic nuclei and the way they interact 核物理

nucleic acid /njuːˈkliːɪk/ **noun** either of two substances, DNA and RNA, that are present in all living cells 核酸

nucleus /ˈnjuːklɪəs/ **noun** (plural **nuclei** /ˈnjuːklɪaɪ/) **1** the central and most important part of an object or group 中心;核心 **2** Physics 【物理】 the positively charged central core of an atom 原子核 **3** Biology 【生物】 a structure present in most cells, containing the genetic material 细胞核

nude /njuːd/ **adjective** wearing no clothes 未穿衣服的;裸体的 • **noun** a painting or sculpture of a naked human figure 裸体人像画(或雕塑) ■ **nudity** noun.

nudge /nʌdʒ/ **verb** (**nudges**, **nudging**, **nudged**) **1** prod someone with your elbow to attract their attention 用肘轻推(以引起注意) **2** touch or push something gently 轻触;轻推 • **noun** a light prod or push 轻戳;轻推

nudist /ˈnjuːdɪst/ **noun** a person who prefers to wear no clothes 裸体主义者 ■ **nudism** noun.

nugatory /ˈnjuːɡətəri/ **adjective** formal 【正式】 having no purpose or value 无目的的;无价值的

nugget /ˈnʌɡɪt/ **noun** a small lump of precious metal found in the earth (天然)金块,贵金属块

nuisance /ˈnjuːsns/ **noun** a person or thing that causes annoyance or difficulty 讨厌的人(或事物);引起麻烦的人(或事物)

nuke /njuːk/ informal 【非正式】 **noun** a nuclear weapon 核武器 • **verb** (**nukes**, **nuking**, **nuked**) attack with nuclear weapons 用核武器攻击

null /nʌl/ **adjective** (**null and void**) having no legal force; invalid 无用的;无价值的

nullify /ˈnʌlɪfaɪ/ **verb** (**nullifies**, **nullifying**, **nullified**) **1** make something legally invalid 使无效;废除 **2** cancel out the effect of 抵消…的效果 ■ **nullification** noun.

nullity /ˈnʌlɪti/ **noun** the state of being legally invalid (法律上的)无效

numb /nʌm/ **adjective 1** (of a part of the body) having no sensation (身体某部位)无知觉的 **2** lacking the power to feel, think, or react 麻木的；失去知觉的 • **verb** make something numb 使失去知觉;使麻木 ■ **numbly** adverb **numbness** noun.

number /ˈnʌmbə(r)/ **noun 1** a quantity or value expressed by a word or symbol 数;数字 **2** a quantity or amount 数量 **3** (**a number of**) several 几个 **4** a single issue of a magazine (杂志)一期 **5** a song, dance, or piece of music 一首歌(或一支舞、一首曲子) **6** a grammatical classification of words depending on whether one or more people or things are being referred to (语法的)数 • **verb** (**numbers**, **numbering**, **numbered**) **1** amount to 总计;共计 **2** give a number to each thing in a series 给…编号;把…标号 **3** count 计数;计算 **4** include as a member of a group 把…纳入;把…算作 □ **number plate** Brit. 【英】 a sign on the front and rear of a vehicle showing its registration number 车号牌

numberless /ˈnʌmbələs/ **adjective** too many to be counted 无数的;数不清的

numbskull or **numskull** /ˈnʌmskʌl/ **noun** informal 【非正式】 a stupid person 傻子；蠢材

numeral /'nju:mərəl/ **noun** a symbol or word representing a number 数字

numerate /'nju:mərət/ **adjective** having a good basic knowledge of arithmetic 掌握算术基础知识的；识数的 ■ **numeracy** noun.

numeration /ˌnju:mə'reɪʃn/ **noun** the action of numbering or calculating 计数；计算

numerator /'nju:məreɪtə(r)/ **noun** Maths 【数】 the number above the line in a fraction (分数的)分子

numerical /nju:'merɪkl/ **adjective** having to do with numbers 数字的 ■ **numerically** adverb.

numerous /'nju:mərəs/ **adjective 1** many 许多的；大量的 **2** consisting of many members 成员众多的

numinous /'nju:mɪnəs/ **adjective** having a strong religious or spiritual quality 宗教的；精神的

numismatic /ˌnju:mɪz'mætɪk/ **adjective** having to do with coins or medals 硬币的；奖章的 • **noun** (**numismatics**) the study or collection of coins, banknotes, and medals 硬币(或钞票、奖章的)研究(或搜集) ■ **numismatist** noun.

numskull /'nʌmskʌl/ ⟹见 NUMBSKULL.

nun /nʌn/ **noun** a member of a female religious community who has taken vows of chastity and obedience 修女；尼姑

nuncio /'nʌnsɪəʊ/ **noun** (plural **nuncios**) a person who represents the Pope in a foreign country 教皇使节；教廷大使

nunnery /'nʌnəri/ **noun** (plural **nunneries**) a convent 女修道院

nuptial /'nʌpʃl/ **adjective** having to do with marriage or weddings 婚姻的；婚礼的 • **noun** (**nuptials**) a wedding 婚礼

nurse /nɜ:s/ **noun 1** a person who is trained to care for sick or injured people 护士；护理员 **2** dated 【废】 a person employed to look after young children (照顾孩子的)保姆 • **verb** (**nurses**, **nursing**, **nursed**) **1** look after a sick person 护理，照料(病人) **2** treat or hold carefully or protectively 培育；悉心照料；小心持有 **3** feed a baby from the breast 母乳喂养(婴儿) **4** hold on to a belief or feeling for a long time 怀有(信念或感情) □ **nursing home** a place providing accommodation and health care for old people 疗养院

nursemaid /'nɜ:smeɪd/ **noun** dated 【废】 a woman or girl employed to look after a young child (照顾孩子的)保姆

nursery /'nɜ:səri/ **noun** (plural **nurseries**) **1** a room in a house where young children sleep or play (私人家庭的)儿童房 **2** a nursery school 托儿所；幼儿园 **3** a place where young plants and trees are grown for sale or for planting elsewhere 苗圃 □ **nursery rhyme** a simple traditional song or poem for children 儿歌；童谣 **nursery school** a school for young children between the ages of three and five (接收3至5岁儿童的)幼儿园

nurture /'nɜ:tʃə(r)/ **verb** (**nurtures**, **nurturing**, **nurtured**) **1** care for and protect a child or young plant while they are growing and developing 培养，培育(孩子、植物等) **2** have a feeling or belief for a long time (长期)怀有(某种感情或信念) • **noun** the state of being nurtured 受培养；养育

nut /nʌt/ **noun 1** a fruit consisting of a hard shell around an edible kernel 坚果；干果 **2** the kernel of such a fruit 坚果仁 **3** a small flat piece of metal with a hole through the centre, for screwing on to a bolt 螺母；螺帽 **4** (also **nutcase**) informal 【非正式】 a crazy person 疯子 **5** (**nuts**) informal 【非正式】 mad 发疯的 **6** informal 【非正式】 a person's head 脑袋；

脑壳 □ **in a nutshell** in the fewest possible words 简明扼要地;概括地 **nuts and bolts** informal 【非正式】 basic facts or practical details 基本要点 ■ **nutty** adjective.

nutcrackers /ˈnʌtkrækəz/ **plural noun** a device for cracking nuts 坚果钳

nutmeg /ˈnʌtmeg/ **noun** a spice made from the seed of a tropical tree 肉豆蔻(一种香料,提取自一种热带树种子)

nutrient /ˈnjuːtriənt/ **noun** a substance that provides nourishment 食物;营养品

nutriment /ˈnjuːtrɪmənt/ **noun** nourishment 食物;营养品

nutrition /njuˈtrɪʃn/ **noun** the process of eating or taking nourishment (营养物的)吸收过程 ■ **nutritional** adjective **nutritionist** noun.

nutritious /njuˈtrɪʃəs/ **adjective** full of nourishing things; good for you 有营养的;滋养的

nutritive /ˈnjuːtrətɪv/ **adjective 1** having to do with nutrition 与营养有关的 有营养的;滋养的

nutter /ˈnʌtə(r)/ **noun** Brit. informal【英,非正式】a mad person 疯子

nuzzle /ˈnʌzl/ **verb (nuzzles, nuzzling, nuzzled)** gently rub or push against someone or something with the nose 用鼻子轻擦(或推)

NVQ /ˌen viː ˈkjuː/ **abbreviation** National Vocational Qualification 国家职业资格证书;国家职业资格认证

NW /ˌen ˈdʌbljuː/ **abbreviation** north-west or northwestern.

nylon /ˈnaɪlɒn/ **noun 1** a strong, lightweight synthetic material 尼龙 **2 (nylons)** nylon stockings or tights 尼龙长袜;尼龙紧身衣

nymph /nɪmf/ **noun 1** (in Greek and Roman mythology) a spirit in the form of a beautiful young woman (希腊和罗马神话中的)仙女 **2** an immature form of an insect such as a dragonfly (昆虫的)蛹

nymphet /ˈnɪmfet/ **noun** an attractive and sexually mature young girl 性感少女

nymphomania /ˌnɪmfəˈmeɪniə/ **noun** uncontrollable or abnormally strong sexual desire in a woman 女性性欲亢奋 ■ **nymphomaniac** noun.

Oo

O or **o** /əʊ/ **noun** (plural **Os** or **O's**) **1** the fifteenth letter of the alphabet 英语字母表的第15个字母 **2** zero 零 □ **O level** (in the past) the lower of the two main levels of the GCE exam (旧时的)普通教育文凭考试

oaf /əʊf/ **noun** a stupid, rude, or clumsy man 蠢人；粗笨的人 ■ **oafish** adjective.

oak /əʊk/ **noun** a large tree which produces acorns and a hard wood used in building and for furniture 橡树；栎树

oaken /'əʊkən/ **adjective** literary【文】made of oak 栎木制的

OAP /əʊ eɪ 'piː/ **abbreviation** Brit.【英】old-age pensioner 领取养老金者

oar /ɔː(r)/ **noun** a pole with a flat blade, used for rowing a boat 桨

oarsman /'ɔːzmən/ or **oarswoman** /'ɔːzwʊmən/ **noun** (plural **oarsmen** or **oarswomen**) a rower 桨手

oasis /əʊ'eɪsɪs/ **noun** (plural **oases**) a fertile place in a desert where water rises to ground level (沙漠中的)绿洲

oast house /əʊst/ **noun** a building containing a kiln for drying hops (烘啤酒花用的)烘(炉)房

oat /əʊt/ **noun 1** a cereal plant grown in cool climates 燕麦 **2** (**oats**) the grain of this plant 燕麦谷粒

oatcake /'əʊtkeɪk/ **noun** an oatmeal biscuit 燕麦饼

oath /əʊθ/ **noun** (plural **oaths**) **1** a solemn promise to do something or that something is true 誓言；誓约 **2** a swear word 咒骂；诅咒语

oatmeal /'əʊtmiːl/ **noun** ground oats, used in making porridge and oatcakes 燕麦粉(用于制作燕麦粥和燕麦饼)

obdurate /'ɒbdjərət/ **adjective** refusing to change your mind; stubborn 顽固的；执拗的 ■ **obduracy** noun.

OBE /əʊ biː 'iː/ **abbreviation** Officer of the Order of the British Empire 英帝国官佐勋章

obedient /ə'biːdiənt/ **adjective** willingly doing what you are told 顺从的；听话的 ■ **obedience** noun **obediently** adverb.

obeisance /əʊ'beɪsns/ **noun 1** respect for someone and willingness to obey them 谦恭，尊敬 **2** a gesture expressing this, such as a bow 表示尊敬的姿势

obelisk /'ɒbəlɪsk/ **noun** a stone pillar that tapers to a point, set up as a monument (作为纪念碑的)方尖碑

obese /əʊ'biːs/ **adjective** very fat 肥胖的 ■ **obesity** noun.

obey /ə'beɪ/ **verb** do what a person or a rule tells you to do 服从；遵守

obfuscate /'ɒbfʌskeɪt/ **verb** (**obfuscates**, **obfuscating**, **obfuscated**) make something unclear or hard to understand 使模糊；使费解 ■ **obfuscation** noun.

obituary /ə'bɪtʃuəri/ **noun** (plural **obituaries**) a short piece of writing about a person and their life which is published in a newspaper when they die (在报纸上发布的)讣告

object **noun** /'ɒbdʒɪkt/ **1** a thing that you can see and touch 物体；实物 **2** a person or thing to which an action or feeling is directed (行为或情感的)对象 **3** a purpose 目的；宗旨 **4** Grammar【语法】a noun acted on by a transitive verb or by a preposition 宾语
• **verb** /əb'dʒekt/ say that you disagree

with or disapprove of something 反对;不赞成 ■ **objector** noun.

objectify /əb'dʒektɪfaɪ/ **verb** (**objectifies, objectifying, objectified**) **1** refer to something abstract as if it has a physical form 使(抽象的东西)具体化 **2** treat someone as an object rather than a person 对待(某人)如物体;使(某人)物化 ■ **objectification** noun.

objection /əb'dʒekʃn/ **noun** a statement of disagreement or disapproval 反对;不赞成

objectionable /əb'dʒekʃənəbl/ **adjective** unpleasant or offensive 使人不愉快的;讨厌的

objective /əb'dʒektɪv/ **adjective 1** considering the facts about something without being influenced by personal feelings or opinions 客观的;不带感情的 **2** having actual existence outside the mind (在意识之外)客观存在的 • **noun** a goal or aim 目的;目标 ■ **objectively** adverb **objectivity** noun.

objet d'art /ˌɒbʒeɪ 'dɑː(r)/ **noun** (plural **objets d'art** /ˌɒbʒeɪ 'dɑː(r)/) a small decorative object or piece of art 小装饰品;小艺术品

oblation /ə'bleɪʃn/ **noun** a thing presented or offered to a god (给神的)供物,祭品

obligate /'ɒblɪgeɪt/ **verb** (**be obligated**) having a moral or legal duty to do something (在道义上或法律上)有责任(做某事)

obligation /ˌɒblɪ'geɪʃn/ **noun 1** something you must do in order to keep to an agreement or fulfil a duty (履行协议、承诺等的)义务,责任 **2** the state of having to do something of this kind 负有责任

obligatory /ə'blɪgətri/ **adjective** required by a law, rule, or custom; compulsory 受(法律、规则或习俗)约束的;强制性的

oblige /ə'blaɪdʒ/ **verb** (**obliges,**

obliging, obliged) **1** make someone do something because it is a law, a necessity, or their duty (法律必要性或责任)强迫,迫使 **2** do something to help someone 效劳;帮忙 **3** (**be obliged**) be grateful 感激

obliging /ə'blaɪdʒɪŋ/ **adjective** willing to help 乐于助人的 ■ **obligingly** adverb.

oblique /ə'bliːk/ **adjective 1** at an angle; slanting 倾斜的;斜的 **2** not done in a direct way 间接的 ■ **obliquely** adverb.

obliterate /ə'blɪtəreɪt/ **verb** (**obliterates, obliterating, obliterated**) destroy or remove all signs of something 彻底毁灭;擦掉(某事物的)痕迹 ■ **obliteration** noun.

oblivion /ə'blɪviən/ **noun 1** the state of being unaware of what is happening around you 无感觉;无知觉 **2** the state of being forgotten or destroyed 被遗忘;被毁灭

oblivious /ə'blɪviəs/ **adjective** not aware of what is happening around you 不注意的;不知不觉的

oblong /'ɒblɒŋ/ **adjective** rectangular in shape 长方形的 • **noun** an oblong shape 长方形

obloquy /'ɒbləkwi/ **noun 1** strong public criticism 公开的猛烈抨击;辱骂 **2** disgrace 耻辱

obnoxious /əb'nɒkʃəs/ **adjective** very unpleasant and offensive 令人不快的;可憎的

oboe /'əʊbəʊ/ **noun** a woodwind instrument of treble pitch, that you play by blowing through a reed 双簧管(一种木管乐器,音调高,通过吹簧片演奏) ■ **oboist** noun.

obscene /əb'siːn/ **adjective 1** dealing with sex in an offensive way 淫秽的;下流的 **2** (of a payment, pay rise, etc.) unacceptably large (报酬、加薪等)大得惊人的 ■ **obscenely** adverb.

obscenity /əb'senəti/ **noun** (plural **obscenities**) obscene language or behaviour, or an obscene action or word 淫秽语言；下流行为

obscure /əb'skjʊə(r)/ **adjective 1** not discovered or known about 未被发现的；未知的 **2** hard to understand or see 晦涩的；模糊的 • **verb** (**obscures**, **obscuring**, **obscured**) make something difficult to see, hear, or understand 使变模糊；使费解 ■ **obscurely** adverb.

obscurity /əb'skjʊərəti/ **noun** (plural **obscurities**) **1** the state of being unknown or forgotten 默默无闻；被遗忘 **2** the quality of being hard to understand 晦涩；费解

obsequies /'ɒbsɪkwiz/ **plural noun** funeral ceremonies 葬礼；丧礼

obsequious /əb'siːkwiəs/ **adjective** too attentive and respectful towards someone 巴结的；卑躬屈膝的；奉承拍马的 ■ **obsequiously** adverb **obsequiousness** noun.

observance /əb'zɜːvəns/ **noun 1** the obeying of a rule or following of a custom (对规则、习俗的)遵守，奉行 **2** (**observances**) acts performed for religious or ceremonial reasons (宗教或礼仪性的)仪式，典礼

observant /əb'zɜːvənt/ **adjective** quick to notice things 善于观察的；观察力敏锐的

observation /ˌɒbzə'veɪʃn/ **noun 1** the close watching of someone or something 观察；监视 **2** the ability to notice important details 观察力 **3** a comment 评论；言论 ■ **observational** adjective.

observatory /əb'zɜːvətri/ **noun** (plural **observatories**) a building containing a telescope used for looking at the stars and planets 天文台；观象台；观测台

observe /əb'zɜːv/ **verb** (**observes**, **observing**, **observed**) **1** notice 注意到；察觉到 **2** watch something carefully 观察；监视 **3** make a remark 说；评论 **4** obey a rule 遵守，服从

(规则) **5** celebrate or take part in a particular festival 庆祝(节日)；参加(庆典) ■ **observable** adjective **observer** noun.

obsess /əb'ses/ **verb** preoccupy someone to a disturbing extent 使着迷；使心神不宁

obsession /əb'seʃn/ **noun 1** the state of being obsessed 着迷；困扰 **2** something that you cannot stop thinking about 困扰人的想法 ■ **obsessional** adjective.

obsessive /əb'sesɪv/ **adjective** unable to stop thinking about someone or something 着迷的 ■ **obsessively** adverb **obsessiveness** noun.

obsidian /ɒb'sɪdiən/ **noun** a dark glass-like volcanic rock 黑曜岩(形似玻璃的深色灿岩)

obsolescent /ˌɒbsə'lesnt/ **adjective** becoming obsolete 逐步废弃的；即将过时的 ■ **obsolescence** noun.

obsolete /'ɒbsəliːt/ **adjective** no longer produced or used; out of date 废弃的；淘汰的；过时的

obstacle /'ɒbstəkl/ **noun** a thing that blocks the way or makes it difficult to do something 障碍(物)

obstetrician /ˌɒbste'trɪʃn/ **noun** a doctor who is trained in obstetrics 产科医师

obstetrics /əb'stetrɪks/ **noun** the branch of medicine concerned with childbirth 产科学 ■ **obstetric** adjective.

obstinate /'ɒbstɪnət/ **adjective 1** refusing to change your mind or stop what you are doing 顽固的；固执的；倔强的 **2** hard to deal with 难对付的；棘手的 ■ **obstinacy** noun **obstinately** adverb.

obstreperous /əb'strepərəs/ **adjective** noisy and difficult to control 喧闹的；难控制的

obstruct /əb'strʌkt/ **verb** be in the way or stop the progress of 阻塞；妨碍；阻挠

obstruction /əb'strʌkʃn/ *noun* **1** a thing that is in the way; an obstacle or blockage 阻塞(物);障碍(物) **2** the obstructing of someone or something 阻塞;阻挠

obstructive /əb'strʌktɪv/ *adjective* deliberately causing a delay or difficulty 阻挠的;妨碍的

obtain /əb'teɪn/ *verb* **1** get possession of 得到;获得 **2** formal 【正式】be established or usual 得到公认;通用 ■ **obtainable** adjective.

obtrude /əb'truːd/ *verb* (**obtrudes**, **obtruding**, **obtruded**) become noticeable in an unpleasant or unwelcome way 闯入;打扰

obtrusive /əb'truːsɪv/ *adjective* noticeable in an unwelcome way 扎眼的,过于突出的

obtuse /əb'tjuːs/ *adjective* **1** annoyingly slow to understand 迟钝的;愚钝的 **2** (of an angle) more than 90° and less than 180° (角)钝的;钝角的 **3** not sharp or pointed; blunt 钝的;不锋利的

obverse /'ɒbvɜːs/ *noun* **1** the side of a coin or medal showing the head or main design (硬币、奖章的)正面 **2** the opposite of something 对立面;对应物

obviate /'ɒbvieɪt/ *verb* (**obviates**, **obviating**, **obviated**) remove or prevent a need or difficulty 排除(困难),避免(问题)

obvious /'ɒbviəs/ *adjective* easily seen or understood; clear 显然的,明显的;无疑的 ■ **obviously** adverb.

ocarina /ˌɒkə'riːnə/ *noun* a small egg-shaped wind instrument with holes for the fingers 奥卡里那笛(一种蛋形管乐器)

occasion /ə'keɪʒn/ *noun* **1** a particular event, or the time at which it happens 事件;时刻 **2** a special event or celebration (特殊)事件;庆典 **3** a suitable time for something 时机;机会 **4** formal 【正式】reason or cause 理由 • *verb* formal 【正式】

cause 引起

✔ 拼写指南 two *c*s and one *s*: *oc-casion*. occasion 中有两个 c 和一个 s。

occasional /ə'keɪʒənl/ *adjective* happening or done from time to time 偶尔的;间或的 ■ **occasionally** adverb.

occidental /ˌɒksɪ'dentl/ *adjective* relating to the countries of the West 西方国家的

occlude /ə'kluːd/ *verb* (**occludes**, **occluding**, **occluded**) technical 【术语】close up; block 使闭塞;堵塞

occult /'ɒkʌlt/ *noun* (**the occult**) the world of magic and supernatural beliefs and practices 神秘信仰(或习俗) • *adjective* relating to the occult 超自然的;神秘的 ■ **occultism** noun **occultist** noun.

occupancy /'ɒkjəpənsi/ *noun* **1** the action of occupying a place 占有;占用 **2** the proportion of accommodation that is occupied (住所的)占用比例

occupant /'ɒkjəpənt/ *noun* a person who occupies a place (某地的)占有人,占用者

occupation /ˌɒkju'peɪʃn/ *noun* **1** a job or profession 工作;职业 **2** a way of spending time 消遣 **3** the occupying of a place 占领;占据

occupational /ˌɒkju'peɪʃnl/ *adjective* having to do with a job or profession 工作的;职业的 □ **occupational therapy** the use of certain activities and crafts to help someone recover from an illness (借助特定活动以帮助康复的)职业疗法

occupy /'ɒkjupaɪ/ *verb* (**occupies**, **occupying**, **occupied**) **1** live or work in a building 在…居住(或工作) **2** fill or take up a space, time, or position 占用(空间、时间);承担(职务) **3** keep someone busy 使忙碌 **4** enter and take control of a place 侵占,占领(某地) ■ **occupier** noun.

occur /əˈkɜː(r)/ **verb** (**occurs, occurring, occurred**) **1** happen 发生 **2** be found or present 被发现;存在;出现 **3** (**occur to**) come into someone's mind 被想起;被想到

✔ 拼写指南 double *c*, and there is a double *r* in **occurred, occurring**, and **occurrence**. 在 occurred、occurring 和 occurrence 中有两个 c 和两个 r。

occurrence /əˈkʌrəns/ **noun 1** a thing that happens or exists 发生的事情;存在的事物 **2** the fact of something happening or existing 发生;存在

ocean /ˈəʊʃn/ **noun** a very large area of sea (海)洋

oceanic /ˌəʊʃiˈænɪk/ **adjective** relating to the ocean 海洋的;大洋的

oceanography /ˌəʊʃəˈnɒɡrəfi/ **noun** the study of the sea 海洋学 ■ **oceanographer** noun.

ocelot /ˈɒsəlɒt/ **noun** a medium-sized striped and spotted wild cat, found in South and Central America 豹猫 (野生猫科动物,产于中南美洲,有条纹和斑点)

ochre /ˈəʊkə(r)/ (US spelling【美拼作】**ocher**) **noun** a type of light yellow or reddish earth, used as a pigment 赭石(用作颜料)

o'clock /əˈklɒk/ **adverb** used to say which hour it is when telling the time …点钟

octagon /ˈɒktəɡən/ **noun** a figure with eight straight sides and eight angles 八边形;八角形 ■ **octagonal** adjective.

octahedron /ˌɒktəˈhedrən/ **noun** (plural **octahedra** or **octahedrons**) a three-dimensional shape with eight flat faces 八面体

octane /ˈɒkteɪn/ **noun** a liquid hydrocarbon present in petroleum 辛烷

octave /ˈɒktɪv/ **noun 1** a series of eight musical notes occupying the interval between (and including) two notes 八度音程;八度音阶 **2** the interval between two such notes 八度

octavo /ɒkˈteɪvəʊ/ **noun** (plural **octavos**) a size of book page that results from folding each printed sheet into eight leaves (sixteen pages) (书的)八开本

octet /ɒkˈtet/ **noun 1** a group of eight musicians 八重奏演出团体;八重唱演出小组 **2** a piece of music for an octet 八重奏;八重唱

October /ɒkˈtəʊbə(r)/ **noun** the tenth month of the year 十月

octogenarian /ˌɒktədʒəˈneəriən/ **noun** a person who is between 80 and 89 years old 八旬老人;80到89岁的人

octopus /ˈɒktəpəs/ **noun** (plural **octopuses**) a sea creature with a soft body and eight long tentacles 章鱼

ocular /ˈɒkjələ(r)/ **adjective** having to do with the eyes 眼(睛)的;视力的

OD /ˌəʊ ˈdiː/ **verb** (**OD's, OD'ing, OD'd**) informal【非正式】take an overdose of a drug 过量使用毒品

odd /ɒd/ **adjective 1** unusual or unexpected; strange 不寻常的;意料之外的;奇特的 **2** (of whole numbers such as 3 and 5) having one left over as a remainder when divided by two (3、5之类的整数)奇数的,单数的 **3** occasional 偶尔的;可用的 **4** separated from a pair or set 单只的;不成对的;零散的 **5** separated from a pair or set 单只的;不成对的;零散的 **6** in the region of 在…左右的;大约的 ■ **oddly** adverb **oddness** noun.

oddball /ˈɒdbɔːl/ **noun** informal【非正式】a strange or eccentric person 奇怪的人;古怪的人

oddity /ˈɒdəti/ **noun** (plural **oddities**) **1** the quality of being strange 奇特;古怪 **2** a strange person or thing 怪人;怪事;奇特的东西

oddment /ˈɒdmənt/ **noun** an item or piece left over from a larger piece or set 残剩物

odds /ɒdz/ **plural noun 1** the ratio between the amount placed as a bet and the money which would be received if the bet was won 投注赔率 **2 (the odds)** the chances of something happening 可能性 **3 (the odds)** the advantage thought to be possessed by one person or side compared to another 优势 □ **at odds** in conflict or disagreement 不和的；有分歧的 **odds-on** (of a horse) with betting odds in favour of winning (马)非常有希望赢的 **2** very likely to happen or succeed 极有可能发生(或成功)的

ode /əʊd/ **noun** a poem addressed to a person or thing or celebrating an event 颂诗

odious /ˈəʊdiəs/ **adjective** very unpleasant 可憎的；令人厌恶的

odium /ˈəʊdiəm/ **noun** widespread hatred or disgust 憎恨；厌恶

odoriferous /ˌəʊdəˈrɪfərəs/ **adjective** smelly 散发气味的；发臭味的

odour /ˈəʊdə(r)/ (US spelling 【美拼作】**odor**) **noun** a smell 气味 ■ **odorous** adjective **odourless** adjective.

odyssey /ˈɒdəsi/ **noun** (plural **odysseys**) a long, eventful journey 漫长坎坷的旅程

oedema /ɪˈdiːmə/ (US spelling 【美拼作】**edema**) **noun** a build-up of watery fluid in the tissues of the body 水肿

oesophagus /iːˈsɒfəɡəs/ (US spelling 【美拼作】**esophagus**) **noun** (plural **oesophagi** /iːˈsɒfəɡaɪ/) the muscular tube which connects the throat to the stomach 食管

oestrogen /ˈiːstrədʒən/ (US spelling 【美拼作】**estrogen**) **noun** a hormone which produces female physical and sexual characteristics 雌激素

oeuvre /ˈɜːvrə/ **noun** all the works of a particular artist, composer, or author (一位艺术家、作曲家、作家等的)全部作品

of /ɒv, əv/ **preposition 1** expressing the relationship between a part and a whole (表示部分与整体的关系) **2** belonging to; coming from 属于…；出自… **3** used in expressions of measurement, value, or age (表示计量、价值或年龄) **4** made from 由…制成 **5** used to show position (表示方位) **6** used to show that something belongs to a category (表示属于某一范畴)

!注意 it's wrong to write **of** instead of **have** in sentences such as *I could have told you* (don't write *I could of told you*). 在 I could have told you (我本来能告诉你)这类句子中，用 of 代替 have 是错误的(不要写作 I could of told you)。

off /ɒf/ **adverb 1** away from a place 离(开)；距 **2** so as to be removed or separated 拿掉；脱离 **3** starting a journey or race 开始(旅行或赛跑) **4** so as to finish or be discontinued 终止；中断 **5** (of an electrical appliance or power supply) not working or connected (电器)停止运行；(供电)断开 **6** having a particular level of wealth 有…富裕程度 • **preposition 1** away from 离开(某处)… **2** situated or leading in a direction away from 离；从…离开；距 **3** so as to be removed or separated from 从…除去；分开 **4** having a temporary dislike of (暂时)不喜好 • **adjective** (of food) no longer fresh (食物)变质的，不新鲜的 • **noun** Brit. informal 【英，非正式】the start of a race or journey (竞速赛或旅行的)开始 □ **off-colour** Brit. 【英】slightly unwell 身体不适的 **off-licence** Brit. 【英】a shop selling alcoholic drink to be drunk elsewhere 外卖酒店 **off-peak** at a time when demand is less 在非高峰时期 **off-putting** unpleasant or unsettling 讨厌的，令人不安的 **off white** a white colour with a grey or yellowish tinge 灰白色；黄白色

! 注意 use **off**, not **off of**, in a sentence like *the cup fell off the table*. 在 the cup fell off the table (杯子从桌上掉了下去)这样的句子中，应该用 off 而不要用 off of。

offal /'ɒfl/ **noun** the internal organs of an animal used as food (供食用的)动物内脏，下水

offbeat /ˌɒf'biːt/ **adjective** unconventional; unusual 非常规的;不落俗套的;异常的

offcut /'ɒfkʌt/ **noun** a piece of wood, fabric, etc. left behind after a larger piece has been cut off (木材、布等的)边料，下脚料

offence /ə'fens/ **noun** (US spelling【美拼法】offense) **noun 1** an act that breaks a law or rule 犯法行为;违规行为 **2** a feeling of hurt or annoyance 伤感情;冒犯

offend /ə'fend/ **verb 1** make someone feel upset, insulted, or annoyed 冒犯;侮辱;得罪 **2** seem unpleasant to 使不快;使讨厌 **3** do something illegal 犯罪;犯法 ■ **offender** noun.

offensive /ə'fensɪv/ **adjective 1** causing someone to feel upset, insulted, or annoyed 侮辱性的;冒犯性的 **2** used in attack 进攻性的;攻击性的 • **noun** a campaign to attack or achieve something 攻击;进取 ■ **offensively** adverb.

offer /'ɒfə(r)/ **verb** (**offers**, **offering**, **offered**) **1** present something for a person to accept or reject as they wish 出示;提供 **2** say you are willing to do something for someone 表示愿意(为某人做某事) **3** provide 提供 • **noun 1** an expression of readiness to do or give something 愿意的表示 **2** an amount of money that someone is willing to pay for something 报价 **3** a specially reduced price 削价 □ **on offer 1** available 提供的;可获得的 **2** for sale at a reduced price 削价出售的

offering /'ɒfərɪŋ/ **noun** something that is offered; a gift or contribution 礼物;捐献物

offertory /'ɒfətri/ **noun** (plural **offertories**) **1** the offering of the bread and wine at the Christian service of Holy Communion (基督教圣餐礼中的)奉献仪式 **2** a collection of money made at a Christian church service (基督教礼拜时的)献金

offhand /ˌɒf'hænd/ **adjective** rudely casual or cool in manner 随便的;鲁莽的 • **adverb** without previous thought 不假思索地

office /'ɒfɪs/ **noun 1** a room, set of rooms, or building where people work at desks 办公室;办事处 **2** a position of authority 公职;官职 **3** (**offices**) formal【正式】things done for other people 为别人做的事;服务

officer /'ɒfɪsə(r)/ **noun 1** a person holding a position of authority, especially in the armed forces 官员;(尤指)军官 **2** a policeman or policewoman 警察;警官

official /ə'fɪʃl/ **adjective 1** relating to an authority or public organization 官方的 **2** agreed or done by a person or group in a position of authority 官方批准的;官方实施的 • **noun** a person holding public office or having official duties 官员 ■ **officialdom** noun **officially** adverb.

officiate /ə'fɪʃieɪt/ **verb** (**officiates**, **officiating**, **officiated**) **1** act as an official in charge of something 行使职权;担任职务 **2** perform a religious service or ceremony 主持宗教仪式

officious /ə'fɪʃəs/ **adjective** using your authority or interfering in a bossy way 盛气凌人的;强行干预的

offing /'ɒfɪŋ/ **noun** (**in the offing**) likely to happen or appear soon 即将发生(或出现)的

offline /ˌɒf'laɪn/ **adjective** not connected to a computer (计算机)脱机的,离线的

offload /ˈɒfˈləʊd/ **verb 1** unload a cargo 卸(货) **2** get rid of 卸去(责任等)

offset /ˈɒfset/ **verb** (**offsets, offsetting, offset**) cancel out something with an equal and opposite force or effect 抵消

offshoot /ˈɒfʃuːt/ **noun** a thing that develops from something else 衍生物

offshore /ˌɒfˈʃɔː(r)/ **adjective & adverb 1** at sea some distance from the shore 离岸一定距离的(地) **2** (of the wind) blowing towards the sea from the land (风)向海的(地), 离岸的(地) **3** situated or registered abroad 在国外的(的)

offside /ˌɒfˈsaɪd/ **adjective & adverb** (in games such as football) occupying a position on the field where playing the ball is not allowed (足球等比赛中)越位的, 处于越位位置

offspring /ˈɒfsprɪŋ/ **noun** (plural **offspring**) a person's child or children 子女; 后代

offstage /ˌɒfˈsteɪdʒ/ **adjective & adverb** (in a theatre) not on the stage (剧院里)不在舞台上的(的), 在幕后的(的)

often /ˈɒfn/ **adverb 1** frequently 经常 **2** in many instances 通常

ogle /ˈəʊgl/ **verb** (**ogles, ogling, ogled**) stare at someone in a lecherous way (挑逗地)注视, 盯着看

ogre /ˈəʊgə(r)/ **noun 1** (in stories) a man-eating giant (传说中的)吃人妖魔 **2** a cruel or terrifying person 残忍的人, 可怕的人

ohm /əʊm/ **noun** the basic unit of electrical resistance 欧姆(电阻基本单位)

oik /ɔɪk/ **noun** informal 【非正式】 a rude person 粗鲁的人; 讨厌鬼

oil /ɔɪl/ **noun 1** a thick, sticky liquid obtained from petroleum 石油; 燃料油 **2** a thick liquid which cannot be dissolved in water and is obtained from plants 植物油 **3** (also **oils**) oil paint 油画颜料; 油性涂料 • **verb** treat or coat with oil 用油处理; 给…涂油 □ **oil paint** artist's paint made from powder mixed with linseed or other oil 油画颜料

oilfield /ˈɔɪlfiːld/ **noun** an area where oil is found beneath the ground or seabed 油田

oilskin /ˈɔɪlskɪn/ **noun 1** heavy cotton cloth waterproofed with oil 防水油布 **2** (**oilskins**) a set of clothes made of oilskin 油布衣裤; 防水服装

oily /ˈɔɪli/ **adjective** (**oilier, oiliest**) **1** containing, covered with, or like oil 含油的; 涂油的 **2** (of a person) insincerely polite and flattering (人)谄媚的, 讨好的 ■ **oiliness** noun.

oink /ɔɪŋk/ **noun** the grunting sound made by a pig (猪的)呼噜声 • **verb** make such a sound 发出呼噜声

ointment /ˈɔɪntmənt/ **noun** a smooth substance that is rubbed on the skin to heal a wound or sore place 油膏; 软膏

OK or **okay** /ˌəʊˈkeɪ/ informal 【非正式】 **exclamation** said to express agreement or acceptance (表示同意或接受)行, 好 • **adjective 1** satisfactory, but not especially good 满意的; 可以的 **2** allowed 允许的 • **adverb** in a satisfactory way 不错; 尚可 • **noun** permission to do something 允许; 批准 • **verb** (**OK's, OK'ing, OK'd**) approve or authorize 同意; 批准

okapi /əʊˈkɑːpi/ **noun** (plural **okapi** or **okapis**) a large plant-eating African animal with stripes on the hindquarters and upper legs 霍加皮 (大型非洲食草动物, 后臀及大腿等处有条纹)

okra /ˈəʊkrə/ **noun** the long seed pods of a tropical plant, eaten as a vegetable 秋葵; 羊角豆

old /əʊld/ **adjective** (**older, oldest**) **1** having lived for a long time 年老的 **2** made, built, or originating long ago 很久以前制造的; 历史悠久的

3 owned or used for a long time 旧的;用旧的 **4** former 过去的;旧时的 **5** of a stated age …岁的 □ **old age** the later part of normal life 老年 **Old English** the language spoken in England until about 1150 古英语(约公元1150年以前英格兰使用的语言) **old-fashioned** no longer current or modern 老式的;过时的 **the old guard** the long-standing members of a group, who are often unwilling to accept change 保守派 **old hand** a very experienced person 富有经验的人;老手 **old hat** informal 【非正式】boringly familiar or out of date 陈腐的;过时的 **old maid** disapproving 【贬】a single woman thought of as too old for marriage 老处女;老姑娘 **old master** a great painter of former times (古时的)大艺术家,大画家 **Old Nick** the Devil 魔王;魔鬼 **Old Testament** the first part of the Christian Bible《圣经·旧约》 **old wives' tale** a widely held traditional belief that is incorrect 无稽之谈;荒诞故事;迷信 **Old World** Europe, Asia, and Africa 旧世界(指欧洲、亚洲和非洲)

olden /ˈəʊldən/ **adjective** of a former age 古时的;往昔的

oleaginous /ˌəʊliˈædʒɪnəs/ **adjective 1** oily 油的;含油的;油质的 **2** insincerely flattering 甜言蜜语的;阿谀奉承的

olfactory /ɒlˈfæktəri/ **adjective** relating to the sense of smell 嗅觉的

oligarch /ˈɒlɪɡɑːk/ **noun** a ruler in an oligarchy 寡头政治家

oligarchy /ˈɒlɪɡɑːki/ **noun** (plural **oligarchies**) **1** a small group of people having control of a state 寡头政治集团;寡头统治集团 **2** a state governed by a small group of people 寡头统治的国家 ■ **oligarchic** adjective.

olive /ˈɒlɪv/ **noun 1** a small oval fruit with a hard stone and bitter flesh 橄榄 **2** (also **olive green**) a greyish-green colour like that of an unripe olive 橄榄(绿)色;灰绿色 • **adjective** (of a person's complexion) yellowish brown (人的肤色)黄褐色的 □ **olive branch** an offer to restore friendly relations 橄榄枝;和解建议 **olive oil** oil obtained from olives, used in cookery and salad dressing 橄榄油

Olympiad /əˈlɪmpiæd/ **noun** a staging of the Olympic Games 奥林匹克运动会;奥运会

Olympian /əˈlɪmpiən/ **adjective 1** relating to the Olympic Games 奥运会的;有关奥运会的 **2** having to do with Mount Olympus, traditional home of the Greek gods (希腊)奥林匹斯山的 • **noun 1** a competitor in the Olympic Games 奥林匹克运动会选手 **2** any of the twelve main Greek gods 奥林匹斯山十二神之一

Olympic /əˈlɪmpɪk/ **adjective** relating to the Olympic Games 奥运会的;有关奥运会的 • **noun** (**the Olympics** or **the Olympic Games**) a sports competition held every four years, or the ancient Greek festival of sport and arts that it was based on 奥林匹克运动会;奥运会

ombudsman /ˈɒmbʊdzmən/ **noun** (plural **ombudsmen**) an official who investigates people's complaints against companies or the government 调查官(调查公民对公司或政府的投诉)

omega /ˈəʊmɪɡə/ **noun** the last letter of the Greek alphabet (Ω, ω) 希腊语字母表的最后一个字母

omelette /ˈɒmlət/ (US spelling 【美拼作】 **omelet**) **noun** a dish of beaten eggs cooked in a frying pan, usually with a savoury filling 煎蛋卷;煎蛋饼

omen /ˈəʊmən/ **noun** an event seen as a sign of future good or bad luck 预兆;征兆

ominous /ˈɒmɪnəs/ **adjective** giving the worrying impression that something bad is going to happen 不祥的；不吉利的 ■ **ominously** adverb.

omission /ə'mɪʃ(ə)n/ **noun 1** the action of leaving something out 省略；删节；排除 **2** a failure to do something 遗漏；疏忽 **3** something that has been left out or not done 省略的东西；遗漏的东西

omit /ə'mɪt/ **verb** (**omits**, **omitting**, **omitted**) **1** leave out or exclude 省略；删节；排除 **2** fail to do 遗漏；疏忽

✔ 拼写指南 just one *m*: *omit*. omit 中只有一个 m。

omni- /'ɒmnɪ-/ **combining form 1** of all things 全部；全：*omniscient* 无所不知的；博学的 **2** in all ways or places 总；遍：*omnipresent* 无所不在的

omnibus /'ɒmnɪbəs/ **noun 1** a volume containing several works previously published separately（分开出版的）几部著作的）汇编，选集 **2** a single edition of two or more programmes previously broadcast separately（由分别播出的几期节目组成的）综合电视（或广播）节目 **3** dated【废】a bus 公共汽车

omnipotent /ɒm'nɪpətənt/ **adjective** having unlimited or very great power 全能的；有无限权力的 ■ **omnipotence** noun.

omnipresent /ˌɒmnɪ'preznt/ **adjective 1** (of God) present everywhere at the same time（上帝）无所不在的 **2** widespread 广泛的；普遍的 ■ **omnipresence** noun.

omniscient /ɒm'nɪsɪənt/ **adjective** knowing everything 无所不知的；博学的 ■ **omniscience** noun.

omnivore /'ɒmnɪvɔː(r)/ **noun** an animal that eats both plants and meat 杂食动物

omnivorous /ɒm'nɪvərəs/ **adjective** eating both plants and meat 杂食性的；荤素俱食的

on /ɒn/ **preposition & adverb** in contact with and supported by a surface（表示接触、支撑）在…上 • **preposition 1** (also **on to**) into contact with a surface, **on to**, or aboard a vehicle 到（表面、车辆）上 **2** about; concerning 关于 **3** as a member of 是…的成员 **4** stored in or broadcast by 储存在…里；由…广播 **5** in the course of 在…期间 **6** indicating a day or date when something takes place 在…时候 **7** engaged in 从事… **8** regularly taking a drug or medicine 经常性服用(毒品或药物) **9** informal【非正式】paid for by 由…支付 • **adverb 1** with continued movement or action 继续 **2** (of clothing) being worn (衣服)穿着 **3** taking place or being presented 发生；呈现 **4** (of an electrical appliance or power supply) functioning (电器)开着；(电源)接通

once /wʌns/ **adverb 1** on one occasion or for one time only 一次；一回 **2** formerly 曾经；一度 **3** multiplied by one 乘以一 • **conjunction** as soon as 一…(就…)，一旦…(就…) □ **at once 1** immediately 立刻；马上 **2** at the same time 同时 □ **once-over** informal【非正式】a quick inspection, or act of cleaning something 匆匆的检查(或调查)；草草了事

oncoming /'ɒnˌkʌmɪŋ/ **adjective** moving towards you 迎面而来的

one /wʌn/ **cardinal number 1** the lowest cardinal number 1 ； (Roman numeral 罗马数字：**i** or **I**.) **2** single, or a single person or thing 单个；一个人；一件物 **3** (before a person's name) a certain (用于人名前)某个 **4** the same 同一 • **pronoun 1** used to refer to a person or thing previously mentioned or easily identified (指先前提到或易于辨认的)某人，某物 **2** used to refer to the speaker, or to represent people in general (说话人)自己；(泛指)任何人 □ **one-armed bandit** informal【非正式】a fruit machine operated by pulling a long handle at the side (侧面有一长柄操纵

的吃角子老虎机 **one-liner** informal 【非正式】a short joke or witty remark 小笑话；俏皮话 **one-off** Brit. informal 【英,非正式】done, made, or happening only once 一次性的 **one-upmanship** informal 【非正式】the technique of gaining an advantage over someone else 胜人一筹的本事；占上风的技巧

oneness /ˈwʌnnɪs/ **noun** the state of being whole or in agreement 一体；完整；一致

onerous /ˈəʊnərəs/ **adjective** involving a lot of effort and difficulty 繁重的；麻烦的；困难的

oneself /wʌnˈself/ **pronoun 1** used as the object of a verb or preposition when this is the same as the subject of the clause and the subject is 'one' (反身代词)自己, 自身 **2** used to emphasize that one is doing something individually or without help (用于强调)亲自, 本人 **3** in one's normal state of body or mind (身心)处于正常状态

ongoing /ˈɒnɡəʊɪŋ/ **adjective** still in progress 进行中的

onion /ˈʌnjən/ **noun** a vegetable consisting of a round bulb with a strong taste and smell 洋葱

online /ˌɒnˈlaɪn/ **adjective & adverb 1** controlled by or connected to a computer 联机的；连线的(地) **2** available on or carried out via the Internet 联网的(地)；在线的(地)

onlooker /ˈɒnlʊkə(r)/ **noun** a spectator 旁观者

only /ˈəʊnli/ **adverb 1** and no one or nothing more besides 只；仅仅 **2** no longer ago than 在⋯前不久；刚刚 **3** not until (直到)⋯才 **4** with the negative result that 不料；结果却 • **adjective 1** single or solitary 单独的；唯一的 **2** alone deserving consideration 独一无二的；无可匹敌的 • **conjunction** informal 【非正式】except that 要不是；若非

onomatopoeia /ˌɒnəˌmætəˈpiːə/ **noun** the use of words that sound like the thing they refer to (e.g. sizzle) 拟声法构词 ■ **onomatopoeic** adjective.

onrush /ˈɒnrʌʃ/ **noun** a surging rush forward 奔流；猛冲；急冲 ■ **onrushing** adjective.

onset /ˈɒnset/ **noun** the beginning of something 开始

onshore /ˈɒnʃɔː(r)/ **adjective & adverb 1** situated on land 在岸上的(的) **2** (of the wind) blowing from the sea towards the land (风)向岸的(的)

onside /ˌɒnˈsaɪd/ **adjective & adverb** (in sport) not offside (体育运动中)不越位的(的)，非越位的(的)

onslaught /ˈɒnslɔːt/ **noun 1** a fierce or destructive attack 猛攻；猛击 **2** an overwhelmingly large quantity of people or things 大量的人(或物)

onstage /ˌɒnˈsteɪdʒ/ **adjective & adverb** (in a theatre) on the stage (剧院里)在舞台上的(的)

onto /ˈɒntuː/ ⇨ 见 **on to** (see ON).

ontology /ɒnˈtɒlədʒi/ **noun** philosophy concerned with the nature of being (哲学中的)本体论, 实体论 ■ **ontological** adjective.

onus /ˈəʊnəs/ **noun** a duty or responsibility 责任；义务

onward /ˈɒnwəd/ **adjective & adverb** in a forward direction 向前(的) ■ **onwards** adverb.

onyx /ˈɒnɪks/ **noun** a semi-precious stone with layers of different colours 缟玛瑙

oodles /ˈuːdlz/ **plural noun** informal 【非正式】a very great number or amount 大量；许多

oomph /ʊmf/ **noun** informal 【非正式】excitement or energy 热情；活力

ooze /uːz/ **verb** (**oozes, oozing, oozed**) slowly seep out 渗出；慢慢冒出 • **noun** the very slow flow of a liquid (液体的)细流 ■ **oozy** adjective.

opacity /əʊˈpæsəti/ **noun** the condition of being opaque 不透明；晦涩

opal /'əʊpl/ **noun** a semi-transparent gemstone in which small points of shifting colour can be seen 蛋白石；猫眼石

opalescent /ˌəʊpə'lesnt/ **adjective** having small points of shifting colour 蛋白石色的；色彩变幻的

opaque /əʊ'peɪk/ **adjective 1** not able to be seen through 不透明的 **2** difficult or impossible to understand 晦涩的；费解的

op. cit. /ˌɒp 'sɪt/ **adverb** in the work already cited 在前面所引的书中 [short for Latin 【缩写，拉丁】 = *opere citato*.]

open /'əʊpən/ **adjective 1** not closed, fastened, or restricted 开着的；未系扎的；无限制的 **2** not covered or protected 无遮盖的；无保护的 **3** (**open to**) likely to suffer from or be affected by 可能遭受…的；易受…影响的 **4** spread out, expanded, or unfolded 摊开的；铺开的；展开的 **5** accessible or available 可进入的；可利用的；可获得的 **6** not hiding thoughts and feelings 坦率的 **7** not disguised or hidden 无伪装的，不掩盖的 **8** not finally settled 尚未决定的；悬而未决的 • **verb 1** make or become open 打开；张开；展开 **2** formally begin or establish (正式)开始，开设 **3** (**open on to** or **into**) give access to 通向 **4** (**open out** or **up**) begin to talk freely 畅谈 • **noun** (**the open**) fresh air or open countryside 新鲜空气；野外 □ **the open air** an unclosed space outdoors 野外；露天 **open-and-shut** straightforward 一目了然的；明显的 **open-heart surgery** surgery in which the heart is exposed 心内直视外科 **open house** a place or situation in which all visitors are welcome 接待处；招待会 **open letter** a letter addressed to a particular person but intended to be published 公开信 **open market** a situation in which companies can trade without restrictions (交易无限制的)公开市场 **open-minded** willing to consider new ideas 思想开明的 **open-plan** having large rooms with few or no dividing walls 开敞式平面布置的(房间大，极少或没有隔墙) **open verdict** Law 【法律】 a verdict that a person's death is suspicious but that the cause is not known 死因未详的裁决 ■ **opener** noun **openly** adverb **openness** noun.

opencast /'əʊpənkɑːst/ **adjective** Brit. 【英】 (of mining) in which coal or ore is extracted from a level near the earth's surface, rather than from shafts (采矿)露天(开采)的

opening /'əʊpənɪŋ/ **noun 1** a gap 口子；缝隙 **2** the beginning of something 开始；开端 **3** a ceremony at which a building, show, etc. is declared to be open 落成典礼；首场演出 **4** an opportunity to achieve something 机会 **5** an available job or position (职位的)空缺 • **adjective** coming at the beginning 开始的；最初的

opera¹ /'ɒprə/ **noun** a dramatic work that is set to music for singers and musicians 歌剧 □ **opera glasses** small binoculars used at the opera or theatre 观剧镜(指观看歌剧或戏剧用的小型双筒望远镜)

opera² plural of OPUS.

operable /'ɒpərəbl/ **adjective 1** able to be used 可使用的 **2** able to be treated by a surgical operation 可进行手术的

operate /'ɒpəreɪt/ **verb** (**operates**, **operating**, **operated**) **1** function or work 起作用；运转 **2** use or control a machine 使用；操控(机器) **3** (of an organization or armed force) carry out activities (机构)采取行动；(武装部队)作战 **4** be in effect 在实行；见效 **5** carry out a surgical operation 动手术

operatic /ˌɒpə'rætɪk/ **adjective** having to do with opera 歌剧的

operation /ˌɒpəˈreɪʃn/ **noun 1** the action of operating 操作；运转 **2** an act of cutting into a patient's body to remove or repair a damaged part 手术 **3** an organized action involving a number of people 活动；行动 **4** a business organization 企业；公司

operational /ˌɒpəˈreɪʃənl/ **adjective 1** ready for use, or being used 可使用的；在用的 **2** relating to the functioning of an organization 经营的；运营的 ∎ **operationally** adverb.

operative /ˈɒpərətɪv/ **adjective 1** working or functioning 起作用的 **2** (of a word) having the most significance in a phrase (词)最重要的，关键的 **3** relating to surgery 手术的 ∎ **noun** a worker 工人

operator /ˈɒpəreɪtə(r)/ **noun 1** a person who operates equipment or a machine 操作员 **2** a person who works at the switchboard of a telephone exchange 话务员 **3** a person or company that runs a business or enterprise 经营者；公司 **4** informal 【非正式】 a person who acts in a particular way 以特定方式行事的人：*a smooth operator* 圆滑的人

operetta /ˌɒpəˈretə/ **noun** a short opera on a light or humorous theme 小歌剧；轻歌剧

ophthalmic /ɒfˈθælmɪk/ **adjective** relating to the eye and its diseases 眼的；眼疾的

ophthalmology /ˌɒfθælˈmɒlədʒi/ **noun** the study and treatment of disorders and diseases of the eye 眼科学 ∎ **ophthalmologist** noun.

opiate /ˈəʊpiət/ **noun** a drug containing opium 鸦片剂

opine /əʊˈpaɪn/ **verb** (**opines, opining, opined**) formal 【正式】 say something as your opinion 认为；发表意见

opinion /əˈpɪnjən/ **noun 1** a personal view not necessarily based on fact or knowledge 意见；看法；见解 **2** the views of people in general 舆论 **3** a formal statement of advice by an expert 专家意见；鉴定 ☐ **opinion poll** the questioning of a small number of people in order to assess the views of people in general 民意测验

opinionated /əˈpɪnjəneɪtɪd/ **adjective** having strong opinions that you are not willing to change 固执己见的；武断的

opium /ˈəʊpiəm/ **noun** an addictive drug made from the juice of a poppy 鸦片

opossum /əˈpɒsəm/ **noun 1** an American animal with a tail which it can use for grasping 负鼠 **2** Austral./NZ 【澳/新西兰】 a possum 袋貂

opponent /əˈpəʊnənt/ **noun 1** a person who competes with another in a contest or argument 对手；敌手 **2** a person who disagrees with a proposal or practice 反对者

opportune /ˈɒpətjuːn/ **adjective** happening at a good or convenient time (时间)恰好的，适宜的

opportunist /ˌɒpəˈtjuːnɪst/ **noun** a person who takes advantage of opportunities without worrying about whether or not they are right to do so 机会主义者 ∎ **adjective** (also **opportunistic**) taking advantage of opportunities when they come up 机会主义的 ∎ **opportunism** noun.

opportunity /ˌɒpəˈtjuːnəti/ **noun** (plural **opportunities**) **1** a good time or set of circumstances for doing something 机会；时机 **2** a chance for employment or promotion 就业机会；提升机会

> ✔ 拼写指南 two *ps*: opportunity. opportunity 中有两个 p。

oppose /əˈpəʊz/ **verb** (**opposes, opposing, opposed**) **1** (also **be opposed to**) disapprove of and try to prevent or resist 反对；阻挡；抵抗

2 compete with or fight 与…竞争；对抗 **3 (opposed)** (of two or more things) contrasting or conflicting (两个或两个以上的事物)对立的,对抗的 **4 (opposing)** opposite 相反的

opposite /'ɒpəzɪt/ **adjective 1** facing 对面的 **2** completely different 截然相反的;全然不同的 **3** being the other of a contrasted pair 对应的: *the opposite sex* 异性 • **noun** an opposite person or thing 对立者;对立物;对立面 • **adverb** in an opposite position 在对面;过对 • **preposition** in a position opposite to 在…的对面

opposition /ˌɒpə'zɪʃn/ **noun 1** resistance or disagreement 反抗;抵抗;分歧 **2** a group of opponents 反对派 **3 (the Opposition)** Brit. 【英】 the main party in parliament that is opposed to the one in government 反对党 **4** a contrast or direct opposite 对比;对立 ■ **oppositional** adjective.

oppress /ə'pres/ **verb 1** treat in a harsh and unfair way 压迫;压制 **2** make someone feel distressed or anxious 使苦恼;使忧虑 ■ **oppression** noun **oppressor** noun.

✔ 拼写指南 double *p*, double *s*: o*p*pre*ss*. oppress 中有两个 p 和两个 s。

oppressive /ə'presɪv/ **adjective 1** harsh and unfair 压迫的;压制的;苛严的 **2** causing depression or anxiety 压抑的;令人苦恼的 **3** (of weather) hot and airless (天气)闷热的 ■ **oppressively** adverb.

opprobrious /ə'prəʊbriəs/ **adjective** formal 【正式】 very critical or scornful 申斥的

opprobrium /ə'prəʊbriəm/ **noun** formal 【正式】 **1** harsh criticism or scorn 申斥;辱骂 **2** public disgrace as a result of bad behaviour 耻辱;不光彩

opt /ɒpt/ **verb** make a choice 选择;作出抉择 □ **opt out** choose not to take part 决定不参加;决定退出

optic /'ɒptɪk/ **adjective** relating to the eye or vision 眼的;视力的;视觉的 • **noun** Brit. trademark 【英,商标】 a device fastened to the neck of an upsidedown bottle for measuring out spirits 奥普蒂克量杯(一种系在倒置酒瓶的瓶颈上的烈酒量杯)

optical /'ɒptɪkl/ **adjective** relating to vision, light, or optics 视力的;视觉的;光的;光学的 □ **optical fibre** a thin glass fibre through which light can be transmitted 光学纤维 **optical illusion** something that deceives the eye by appearing to be different from what it really is 视错觉;错视;光幻觉 ■ **optically** adverb.

optician /ɒp'tɪʃn/ **noun** a person qualified to examine people's eyes and to prescribe glasses and contact lenses 光学眼镜配镜师

optics /'ɒptɪks/ **noun** the study of vision and the behaviour of light 光学

optimal /'ɒptɪml/ **adjective** best or most favourable 最优的;最佳的;最适宜的 ■ **optimally** adverb.

optimism /'ɒptɪmɪzəm/ **noun** hopefulness and confidence about the future or success of something 乐观 ■ **optimist** noun.

optimistic /ˌɒptɪ'mɪstɪk/ **adjective** hopeful and confident about the future 乐观的 ■ **optimistically** adverb.

optimize or **optimise** /'ɒptɪmaɪz/ **verb** (**optimizes, optimizing, optimized**) make the best use of 充分利用

optimum /'ɒptɪməm/ **adjective** most likely to lead to a favourable outcome 最优的;最佳的;最适宜的 • **noun** (plural **optima** or **optimums**) the most favourable conditions for growth or success 最佳条件;最适宜条件

option /'ɒpʃn/ **noun 1** a thing that you may choose 选择 **2** the freedom or right to choose 选择自由;选择权 **3**

a right to buy or sell something at a stated price within a set time (未来的)购买权，出售权

optional /'ɒpʃənl/ **adjective** available to be chosen, but not compulsory 可选择的；非强制的 ■ **optionally** adverb.

optometry /ɒp'tɒmətri/ **noun** the occupation of measuring people's eyesight, prescribing lenses, and detecting eye disease 验光配镜业 ■ **optometrist** noun.

opulent /'ɒpjələnt/ **adjective** expensive and luxurious 豪华的；奢侈的 ■ **opulence** noun **opulently** adverb.

opus /'əʊpəs/ **noun** (plural **opuses** or **opera**) **1** a musical work or set of works 一首乐曲；一组作品 **2** a literary work 文学作品

or /ɔː(r)/ **conjunction 1** used to link alternatives 或；或者 **2** introducing a word that means the same as a preceding word or phrase, or that explains it 即；那就是；或者说 **3** otherwise 否则；要不然

oracle /'ɒrəkl/ **noun** (in ancient Greece or Rome) a priest or priestess through whom the gods were believed to give prophecies about the future (在古希腊或古罗马的)传神谕牧师，神使

oracular /ə'rækjələ(r)/ **adjective** having to do with an oracle 神谕的；哲人的

oral /'ɔːrəl/ **adjective 1** spoken rather than written 口头的；口述的 **2** relating to the mouth 口的；嘴的 **3** done or taken by the mouth 用口的 • **noun** a spoken exam 口试 ■ **orally** adverb.

orange /'ɒrɪndʒ/ **noun 1** a large round citrus fruit with a tough reddish-yellow rind 柑橘 **2** a bright reddish-yellow colour 橙红色；橘黄色

orangeade /'ɒrɪndʒ'eɪd/ **noun** Brit. 【英】a fizzy soft drink flavoured with orange 橘子汁(不含酒精的橘味充汽饮料)

orang-utan /ɒ'ræŋuː'tæn/ or

orang-utang /ə'ræŋuː'tæŋ/ **noun** a large ape with long reddish hair 猩猩；褐猿

oration /ɔː'reɪʃn/ **noun** a formal speech (正式的)演讲，演说

orator /'ɒrətə(r)/ **noun** a person who is good at public speaking 演说家；雄辩家

oratorio /ɒrə'tɔːriəʊ/ **noun** (plural **oratorios**) a large-scale musical work on a religious theme for orchestra and voices (以宗教为主题的)大型清唱剧，神剧

oratory[1] /'ɒrətri/ **noun** (plural **oratories**) a small chapel 小礼拜堂

oratory[2] **noun 1** formal public speaking 演讲 **2** exciting and inspiring speech 慷慨激昂的演说 ■ **oratorical** adjective.

orb /ɔːb/ **noun 1** an object shaped like a ball 球状物；球形 **2** a golden globe with a cross on top, carried by a king or queen (国王或女王所持的)王权宝球

orbit /'ɔːbɪt/ **noun 1** the regularly repeated course of a moon, spacecraft, etc. around a star or planet (卫星、宇宙飞船等环绕恒星或行星运行的)轨道 **2** a particular area of activity or influence (活动或影响的)范围 • **verb** (**orbits**, **orbiting**, **orbited**) move in orbit round a star or planet 在环绕(恒星或行星)的轨道上运行

orbital /'ɔːbɪtl/ **adjective 1** relating to an orbit or orbits 轨道的 **2** Brit. 【英】(of a road) passing round the outside of a town (公路)环城的

orca /'ɔːkə/ **noun** a large whale with teeth and black and white markings 逆戟鲸

orchard /'ɔːtʃəd/ **noun** a piece of enclosed land planted with fruit trees 果园

orchestra /'ɔːkɪstrə/ **noun 1** a large group of musicians with string, woodwind, brass, and percussion sections 管弦乐队 **2** (also **orchestra pit**) the part of a theatre where the orchestra plays 乐池 ■ **orchestral** adjective.

orchestrate /'ɔːkɪstreɪt/ **verb** (**orchestrates**, **orchestrating**, **orchestrated**) **1** arrange music to be performed by an orchestra 把…谱写成管弦乐曲 **2** organize a situation to produce a particular effect 引导(形势)以达预期效果 ■ **orchestration** noun.

orchid /'ɔːkɪd/ **noun** a plant with bright, unusually shaped flowers 兰花

ordain /ɔː'deɪn/ **verb 1** make someone a priest or minister 委任(某人)为牧师;授(某人)以圣职 **2** order officially (正式)命令

ordeal /ɔː'diːl/ **noun** a prolonged painful or horrific experience 苦难经历;煎熬

order /'ɔːdə(r)/ **noun 1** the arrangement of people or things according to a particular sequence or method 次序;顺序 **2** a situation in which everything is in its correct place 整齐;有条理 **3** a situation in which the law is being obeyed and no one is behaving badly 治安;秩序 **4** a statement telling someone to do something 命令 **5** a request for something to be made, supplied, or served 指示;吩咐 **6** the procedure followed in a meeting, court, or religious service (会议、法庭或宗教仪式的)程序,规程 **7** quality or class 质量,级别 **8** a social class or system 阶层 **9** a classifying category of plants and animals (动植物分类的)目 **10** (**orders** or **holy orders**) the rank of an ordained Christian minister (基督教牧师的)品级,神品 **11** a group of people living in a religious community 宗教团体 **12** an institution founded by a ruler to honour people (统治者设立的)勋位: *the Order of the Garter* 嘉德勋位

• **verb** (**orders**, **ordering**, **ordered**) **1** tell someone to do something 命令 **2** request that something be made, supplied, or served 指示;吩咐 **3** organize or arrange 布置;安排 □ (or **in**) **the order of** approximately 大约 **out of order 1** not functioning 不正常的;出故障的 **2** Brit. informal 【英,非正式】 unacceptable 不可接受的;不妥当的

orderly /'ɔːdəli/ **adjective 1** arranged in a neat, organized way 整齐的,有条理的 **2** well behaved 守规矩的;有秩序的 • **noun** (plural **orderlies**) **1** a hospital attendant responsible for various non-medical tasks (医院的)护理员,勤杂工 **2** a soldier who carries orders or performs minor tasks 传令兵;通信员;勤务兵 ■ **orderliness** noun.

ordinal /'ɔːdɪnl/ **adjective** relating to order in a series 顺序的 □ **ordinal number** a number defining a thing's position in a series, such as 'first' or 'second' 序数

ordinance /'ɔːdɪnəns/ **noun** formal 【正式】 **1** an official order 法令;条例 **2** a religious rite 宗教仪式

ordinary /'ɔːdnri/ **adjective 1** normal or usual 正常的;通常的 **2** not interesting or exceptional 平淡的;平凡的 □ **out of the ordinary** unusual 不同寻常的 ■ **ordinarily** adverb **ordinariness** noun.

ordination /ˌɔːdɪ'neɪʃn/ **noun** the ordaining of someone as a priest or minister 授圣职(礼)

ordnance /'ɔːdnəns/ **noun 1** mounted guns 火炮;大炮 **2** US 【美】 military equipment and stores 军械;军用器材;军需品

ordure /'ɔːdjʊə(r)/ **noun** formal 【正式】 dung; excrement 粪便;排泄物

ore /ɔː(r)/ **noun** a naturally occurring material from which a metal or mineral can be extracted 矿石

oregano /ˌɒrɪ'gɑːnəʊ/ **noun** a sweet-

smelling plant used in cooking 牛至
(有芳香气味,可用于烹饪)

organ /ˈɔːgən/ **noun 1** a part of the
body that has a particular function,
e.g. the heart or kidneys 器官 **2** a
musical keyboard instrument with
rows of pipes supplied with air from
bellows, or one that produces similar
sounds electronically 管风琴;电风琴
3 a newspaper which puts forward
particular views 报刊;宣传工具
■ **organist** noun.

organic /ɔːˈgænɪk/ **adjective 1** having
to do with living matter 生物体的;
有机体的 **2** produced without the
aid of artificial chemicals such as
fertilizers 施用有机肥料的 **3** (of
chemical compounds) containing
carbon (化合物)有机的 **4** having to
do with an organ of the body 器官
的 **5** (of development or change)
continuous or natural (发展或变化)
连续的,自然的 ■ **organically** adverb.

organism /ˈɔːgənɪzm/ **noun 1** an
individual animal, plant, or life form
生物,有机体(指动植物、植物或其他生
物) **2** a whole made up of parts which
are dependent on each other 有机体;
有机组织

organization or **organisation**
/ˌɔːgənaɪˈzeɪʃn/ **noun 1** an organized
group of people, e.g. a business 组织;
机构 **2** the action of organizing 组织
(行为) **3** a systematic arrangement
or approach 系统安排;有条理的方法
■ **organizational** adjective.

organize or **organise** /ˈɔːgənaɪz/
verb (**organizes, organizing, organized**) **1** arrange in a particular order
or structure 使有条理;组织 **2** make
arrangements for an event or activity
为…作安排 ■ **organizer** noun.

orgasm /ˈɔːgæzəm/ **noun** an intensely
pleasurable sensation that is felt as
the climax of sexual activity 性高潮
• **verb** have an orgasm 达到性高潮
■ **orgasmic** adjective.

orgiastic /ˌɔːdʒiˈæstɪk/ **adjective** like
an orgy 狂欢的;纵酒的,纵欲的

orgy /ˈɔːdʒi/ **noun** (plural **orgies**) **1**
a wild party with a lot of drinking
and sexual activity (酗酒纵欲的)狂
欢聚会 **2** an excessive amount of a
particular activity 放纵;无节制

oriel /ˈɔːriəl/ **noun** a projecting part of
an upper storey with a window 凸肚
窗

orient /ˈɔːriənt/ **noun** (**the Orient**)
literary【文】the countries of the East
东方国家 • **verb** (also **orientate**) **1**
position something in relation to the
points of a compass or other points
给…定方位 **2** (**orient yourself**)
find your position in relation to your
surroundings 确定(自己的)方位 **3**
adapt something to meet particular
needs 以…为目的;使适应

oriental /ˌɔːriˈentl/ **adjective** having to
do with the Far East 远东的;东方的
• **noun** dated or offensive【废或冒犯】
a person of Far Eastern descent 远东
人;东方人

orientation /ˌɔːriənˈteɪʃn/ **noun 1** the
action of orienting 定向;定位 **2** a
position in relation to something else
方向;方位 **3** a person's attitude or
natural tendency (人的)态度,倾向

orienteering /ˌɔːriənˈtɪərɪŋ/ **noun**
the sport of finding your way across
country using a map and compass 定
向越野比赛;越野运动比赛

orifice /ˈɒrɪfɪs/ **noun** an opening 孔;
穴;腔

origami /ˌɒrɪˈgɑːmi/ **noun** the Japanese
art of folding paper into decorative
shapes 日本折纸(术)

origin /ˈɒrɪdʒɪn/ **noun 1** the point
where something begins 起源;来源
2 a person's background or ancestry
出身;血统

original /əˈrɪdʒənl/ **adjective 1**
existing from the beginning 起初的;
原先的 **2** not a copy 原创的 **3** new
in an interesting or unusual way 新

颖的；独特地 • **noun** the earliest form of something, from which copies can be made 原型；原件；原文 □ **original sin** (in Christian belief) the tendency to be sinful that is thought to be present in all people (基督教信仰中的)原罪(指人与生俱来的罪恶倾向) ■ **originality** noun **originally** adverb.

originate /əˈrɪdʒəneɪt/ **verb** (**originates**, **originating**, **originated**) **1** begin in a particular place or situation 发源；来自 **2** create 创始；开创 ■ **origination** noun **originator** noun.

ormolu /ˈɔːməluː/ **noun** a gold-coloured alloy of copper, zinc, and tin 金色铜(铜锌锡合金)

ornament /ˈɔːnəmənt/ **noun 1** an object used as a decoration 装饰品；点缀品 **2** decorative items considered together 装饰；点缀 ■ **ornamental** adjective **ornamentation** noun.

ornate /ɔːˈneɪt/ **adjective** elaborately decorated 装饰华丽的；过分修饰的 ■ **ornately** adverb.

ornithology /ˌɔːnɪˈθɒlədʒi/ **noun** the scientific study of birds 鸟类学 ■ **ornithological** adjective **ornithologist** noun.

orphan /ˈɔːfn/ **noun** a child whose parents are dead 孤儿 • **verb** (**be orphaned**) (of a child) be made an orphan (孩子)成为孤儿

orphanage /ˈɔːfənɪdʒ/ **noun** a place where orphans are looked after 孤儿院

orthodontist /ˌɔːθəˈdɒntɪst/ **noun** a dentist who treats irregularities in the position of the teeth and jaws 正牙医生

orthodox /ˈɔːθədɒks/ **adjective 1** in keeping with generally accepted beliefs 传统的；符合社会习俗的 **2** normal 正统的；通常的 **3** (**Orthodox**) relating to the Orthodox Church 正统派的；东正教的 □ **Orthodox Church** a branch of the Christian Church in Greece and eastern Europe (希腊和东欧的)正教

orthodoxy /ˈɔːθədɒksi/ **noun** (plural **orthodoxies**) **1** the traditional beliefs or practices of a religion 正统信仰；正统做法 **2** a generally accepted idea 正统观念

orthography /ɔːˈθɒɡrəfi/ **noun** (plural **orthographies**) the spelling system of a language 正字法；拼字法 ■ **orthographic** adjective.

orthopaedics /ˌɔːθəˈpiːdɪks/ (US spelling 【美拼作】 **orthopedics**) **noun** the branch of medicine concerned with bones and muscles 矫形外科 ■ **orthopaedic** adjective.

Oscar /ˈɒskə(r)/ **noun** a gold statuette given annually for achievement in various fields of film-making; an Academy award (电影制作方面的)奥斯卡金像奖

oscillate /ˈɒsɪleɪt/ **verb** (**oscillates**, **oscillating**, **oscillated**) **1** move back and forth in a regular rhythm (匀速)来回摆动 **2** waver in your opinions or emotions 动摇；犹豫 ■ **oscillation** noun **oscillator** noun.

osier /ˈəʊziə(r)/ **noun** a type of willow tree with long, flexible shoots that are used for making baskets 青刚柳，杞柳(枝条长而柔韧,用于编柳条筐)

osmium /ˈɒzmiəm/ **noun** a hard, dense silverywhite metallic element (金属元素)锇

osmosis /ɒzˈməʊsɪs/ **noun 1** a process by which molecules pass through a membrane from a less concentrated solution to a more concentrated one 渗透(作用) **2** the gradual absorbing of ideas 潜移默化；耳濡目染 ■ **osmotic** adjective.

osprey /ˈɒspreɪ/ **noun** (plural **ospreys**) a large fish-eating bird of prey 鹗(一种大型食鱼鸟)

osseous /ˈɒsiəs/ **adjective** consisting of bone 由骨构成的

ossify /ˈɒsɪfaɪ/ **verb** (**ossifies**, **ossifying**, **ossified**) **1** turn into bone or bony tissue 骨化；成骨 **2** stop developing or progressing 僵化;停止发展 ■ **ossification** noun.

ostensible /ɒ'stensəbl/ **adjective** apparently true, but not necessarily so 似乎真实的 ■ **ostensibly** adverb.

ostentation /ˌɒsten'teɪʃn/ **noun** a showy display of wealth, knowledge, etc. which is intended to impress 炫耀;夸示;卖弄

ostentatious /ˌɒsten'teɪʃəs/ **adjective** expensive or showy in a way that is designed to impress 炫耀的;夸示的;卖弄的 ■ **ostentatiously** adverb.

osteoarthritis /ˌɒstiəʊɑː'θraɪtɪs/ **noun** a disease that causes pain and stiffness in the joints of the body 骨关节炎

osteopathy /ˌɒsti'ɒpəθi/ **noun** a system of complementary medicine involving manipulation of the bones and muscles 按骨术;整骨术 ■ **osteopath** noun.

osteoporosis /ˌɒstiəʊpə'rəʊsɪs/ **noun** a medical condition in which the bones become brittle 骨质疏松(症)

ostinato /ˌɒstɪ'nɑːtəʊ/ **noun** (plural **ostinatos** or **ostinati** /ˌɒstɪ'nɑːti/) a continually repeated musical phrase or rhythm 固定音型(持续重复的乐句或节奏)

ostler /'ɒslə/ **noun** (in the past) a man employed at an inn to look after customers' horses (旧时旅店的)马夫

ostracize or **ostracise** /'ɒstrəsaɪz/ **verb** (**ostracizes**, **ostracizing**, **ostracized**) exclude someone from a society or group 排斥 ■ **ostracism** noun.

ostrich /'ɒstrɪtʃ/ **noun** a large African bird with a long neck and long legs which is unable to fly 鸵鸟

other /'ʌðə(r)/ **adjective & pronoun**
1 used to refer to a person or thing that is different from one already mentioned or known 别的;其他的 **2** additional 另外的;额外的 **3** the alternative of two (两个中的)另一个

4 those not already mentioned 别的人(或物);其他的人(或物) □ **other-worldly 1** relating to an imaginary or spiritual world 非现实世界的 **2** not aware of the realities of life 不谙世事的

otherness /'ʌðənɪs/ **noun** the quality of being different or unusual 另一(性);不同(性)

otherwise /'ʌðəwaɪz/ **adverb 1** in different circumstances 在不同的情况下 **2** in other respects 在其他方面 **3** in a different way 以不同的方式 **4** alternatively 或;非此即彼

otiose /'əʊtiəʊs/ **adjective** serving no practical purpose 没有用处的;没有实用价值的

otter /'ɒtə(r)/ **noun** a fish-eating animal with a long body, living partly in water and partly on land 水獭

ottoman /'ɒtəmən/ **noun** (plural **ottomans**) a low padded seat without a back or arms (无靠背或扶手的)软垫椅子,褥榻

oubliette /ˌuːblɪ'et/ **noun** a secret dungeon with access only through a trapdoor in its ceiling (出入口在顶部的)地下土牢

ought /ɔːt/ **modal verb** (3rd singular present and past **ought**) **1** used to indicate duty or correctness (表示义务或正确性)应当,应该 **2** used to indicate something that is probable (表示可能性)该 **3** used to indicate a desirable or expected state (表示愿望或期望)该,应该 **4** used to give or ask advice (表示提供建议或征求意见)该

!注意 when using **ought** in a negative sentence, say, for example, *he ought not to have gone* rather than *he didn't/hadn't ought to have gone.* 当用 ought 构成否定句应该用 he ought not to have gone (他本不应该去),而不用 he didn't/hadn't ought to have gone.

oughtn't /'ɔ:tnt/ **short form** ought not.

Ouija board /'wi:dʒə/ **noun** trademark 【商标】 a board marked with letters, used at a seance supposedly to receive messages from dead people 灵应牌，灵乩板(刻有字母，降神会时被认为可以从死者处获得讯息)

ounce /aʊns/ **noun 1** a unit of weight of one sixteenth of a pound (approximately 28 grams) 盎司(1/16磅，约合28克) **2** a very small amount 少量

our /'aʊə(r)/ **possessive determiner 1** belonging to or associated with the speaker and one or more other people 我们的 **2** belonging to or associated with people in general 所有人的；大家的

ours /'aʊəz/ **possessive pronoun** used to refer to something belonging to or associated with the speaker and one or more other people 我们的

✔ 拼写指南 no apostrophe: **ours**. ours 没有撇号。

ourselves /ˌaʊə'selvz/ **pronoun 1** used as the object of a verb or preposition when this is the same as the subject of the clause and the subject is the speaker and one or more other people 我们自己 **2** we or us personally 我们亲自；我们本人

oust /aʊst/ **verb** force someone out from a job or position 罢黜；革职

out /aʊt/ **adverb 1** away from a place 出来；向外 **2** away from your home or office 不在家；不在工作场所 **3** outdoors 在室外 **4** so as to be revealed, heard, or known 显露；被听知；为人所知 **5** to an end 在最后；结束 **6** not possible or worth considering 不可能的；不值得考虑的 **7** (of the tide) falling or at its lowest level (潮汐)退去 **8** (of the ball in tennis, squash, etc.) not in the playing area (网球、壁球等运动中的球)界外的 **9** (in cricket, baseball, etc.) no longer batting (板球、棒球等运动中)出局的
• **verb** informal 【非正式】 reveal that someone is homosexual 公开(某人)为同性恋 □ **out of 1** from 从 **2** not having a supply of something 没有(某物) **out of date 1** old-fashioned 过时的 **2** no longer valid 失效的；废弃的

❗注意 you should say **out of** rather than just **out** in sentences such as *he threw it out of the window*. 在 he threw it out of the window 之类的句子中应该用 out of 而不要只用 out。

outback /'aʊtbæk/ **noun (the outback)** the part of Australia that is remote and has few inhabitants (澳大利亚的)内地，内陆地区

outbid /ˌaʊt'bɪd/ **verb (outbids, outbidding, outbid)** bid more than 出价高于

outboard /'aʊtbɔ:d/ **adjective & adverb** on, towards, or near the outside of a ship or aircraft 在(船或飞机)外侧(的)；靠近(船或飞机)外侧(的) □ **outboard motor** a motor attached to the outside of a boat 舷外发动机

outbreak /'aʊtbreɪk/ **noun** a sudden occurrence of war, disease, etc. (战争、疾病等的)爆发，突发

outbuilding /'aʊtbɪldɪŋ/ **noun** a smaller building in the grounds of a main building 附属建筑；附楼

outburst /'aʊtbɜ:st/ **noun 1** a sudden release of strong emotion (感情的)迸发 **2** a sudden or violent occurrence of something 爆发

outcast /'aʊtkɑ:st/ **noun** a person who is rejected by their social group 被(社会团体)抛弃的人

outclass /ˌaʊt'klɑ:s/ **verb** be far better than 远远好于

outcome /'aʊtkʌm/ **noun** a result or effect 结果

outcrop /'aʊtkrɒp/ **noun** a part of a rock formation that is visible on the surface 露头(岩石露出地面的部分)

outcry /'aʊtkraɪ/ **noun** (plural **outcries**) a strong expression of public disapproval 强烈反对；强烈抗议

outdated /ˌaʊt'deɪtɪd/ **adjective** no longer used or fashionable 废弃的；过时的

outdistance /ˌaʊt'dɪstəns/ **verb** (**outdistances**, **outdistancing**, **outdistanced**) leave a competitor or pursuer far behind 把(竞争者或追随者)远远抛在后面

outdo /ˌaʊt'duː/ **verb** (**outdoes**, **outdoing**, **outdid**; past participle **outdone**) do better than someone else 比(其他人)做得更好

outdoor /'aʊtdɔː(r)/ **adjective** done, situated, or used outdoors 户外的；室外的

outdoors /ˌaʊt'dɔːz/ **adverb** in or into the open air 在户外；往户外 • **noun** any area outside buildings or shelter 户外；野外

outer /'aʊtə(r)/ **adjective 1** outside 外面的；外部的 **2** further from the centre or the inside 远离中心的；远离内部的

outermost /'aʊtəməʊst/ **adjective** furthest from the centre 最外面的；最远的

outface /ˌaʊt'feɪs/ **verb** (**outfaces**, **outfacing**, **outfaced**) unsettle or defeat someone by confronting them in a brave or confident way (通过勇敢或自信地面对)压倒，吓倒

outfall /'aʊtfɔːl/ **noun** the place where a river or drain empties into the sea, a river, or a lake 河口；排水口

outfit /'aʊtfɪt/ **noun 1** a set of clothes worn together 套服 **2** informal【非正式】a group of people working together as a business, team, etc. (共事的)一组人 • **verb** (**outfits**, **outfitting**, **outfitted**) provide someone with an outfit of clothes 为(某人)配备(一套衣服) ■ **outfitter** noun.

outflank /ˌaʊt'flæŋk/ **verb 1** surround in order to attack 侧翼包围 **2** defeat

打败；战胜

outgoing /'aʊtɡəʊɪŋ/ **adjective 1** friendly and confident 友好自信的 **2** leaving an office or position 即将离职的 **3** going out or away from a place 往外去的；离去的 • **noun** (**outgoings**) Brit.【英】money that you spend regularly 支出；开销

outgrow /ˌaʊt'ɡrəʊ/ **verb** (**outgrows**, **outgrowing**, **outgrew**; past participle **outgrown**) **1** grow too big for 长得穿不下；增得容不进 **2** stop doing something as you grow older 因长大而不再做(某事)

outhouse /'aʊthaʊs/ **noun** a smaller building attached or close to a house 附属建筑

outing /'aʊtɪŋ/ **noun** a short trip made for pleasure 短途旅游；远足

outlandish /aʊt'lændɪʃ/ **adjective** bizarre or unfamiliar 奇特的；陌生的；不熟悉的

outlast /ˌaʊt'lɑːst/ **verb** last longer than 比⋯持久；比⋯活得长

outlaw /'aʊtlɔː/ **noun** a person who has broken the law and remains at large 逃犯；亡命之徒 • **verb** make something illegal 使在法律上失效；使不合法

outlay /'aʊtleɪ/ **noun** an amount of money spent 花费；支出额

outlet /'aʊtlet/ **noun 1** a pipe or hole through which water or gas may escape 出水管 **2** a point from which goods are sold or distributed (商品的)经销处 **3** a way of expressing your talents, energy, or emotions (才智、精力或感情的)表现途径，发泄出路

outline /'aʊtlaɪn/ **noun 1** a sketch or diagram showing the shape of an object 轮廓画；草图 **2** the outer edges of an object 外形；轮廓 **3** a general description of something, with no detail 概要；梗概；要点 • **verb** (**outlines**, **outlining**, **outlined**) **1** draw the outer edge or shape of

描…的外形; 画…的轮廓 **2** give a summary of 概述; 概括

outlive /aʊt'lɪv/ **verb** live or last longer than 比…活得长; 比…持久

outlook /'aʊtlʊk/ **noun 1** a person's attitude to life (对待生活的)观点, 看法 **2** a view 景色; 景致; 风光 **3** what is likely to happen in the future 展望; 前景

outlying /'aʊtlaɪɪŋ/ **adjective** situated far from a centre 远离中心的; 边远的

outmanoeuvre /ˌaʊtmə'nuːvə(r)/ **verb** (**outmanoeuvres, outmanoeuvring, outmanoeuvred**) gain an advantage over an opponent by using skill and cunning 巧胜; 智取

outmoded /ˌaʊt'məʊdɪd/ **adjective** old-fashioned 过时的

outnumber /ˌaʊt'nʌmbə(r)/ **verb** (**outnumbers, outnumbering, outnumbered**) be more numerous than 比…多

outpace /ˌaʊt'peɪs/ **verb** (**outpaces, outpacing, outpaced**) go faster than 比…走得快; 在速度上超过

outpatient /'aʊtpeɪʃnt/ **noun** a patient attending a hospital for treatment without staying overnight 门诊病人

outperform /ˌaʊtpə'fɔːm/ **verb** perform better than 做得比…好; 胜过

outplay /ˌaʊt'pleɪ/ **verb** play better than 打得比…好; 击败

outpost /'aʊtpəʊst/ **noun 1** a small military camp at a distance from the main army 前哨基地 **2** a remote part of a country or empire 边远地区

outpouring /'aʊtpɔːrɪŋ/ **noun 1** something that streams out rapidly 倾泻物; 涌出物 **2** an outburst of strong emotion (强烈感情的)迸发

output /'aʊtpʊt/ **noun 1** the amount of something produced 产量 **2** the process of producing something 生产 **3** the power, energy, etc. supplied by a device or system 输出功率; 输出量 **4** a place where power, informa-

tion, etc. leaves a system (电能、信息的)输出端

outrage /'aʊtreɪdʒ/ **noun 1** a very strong reaction of anger or annoyance 愤慨; 震惊 **2** a very immoral or shocking act 暴行; 恶行 • **verb** (**outrages, outraging, outraged**) make someone feel outrage 激怒

outrageous /aʊt'reɪdʒəs/ **adjective 1** shockingly bad or unacceptable 极其糟糕的; 极过分的 **2** very unusual and slightly shocking 令人震惊的; 令人愤慨的 ■ **outrageously** adverb.

outran /aʊt'ræn/ past of OUTRUN.

outrank /aʊt'ræŋk/ **verb** have a higher rank than 比…级别高

outré /'uːtreɪ/ **adjective** unusual and rather shocking 怪诞的; 吓人的

outreach /'aʊtriːtʃ/ **noun** an organization's involvement with the community (某一组织为社区提供的)外展服务

outrider /'aʊtraɪdə(r)/ **noun** a person in a vehicle or on horseback who escorts another vehicle 摩托车警卫; 骑马侍从

outrigger /'aʊtrɪgə(r)/ **noun** a structure fixed to a boat's side to help keep it stable (使船保持稳定的)舷外浮材, 舷外浮体

outright /'aʊtraɪt/ **adverb 1** altogether 全部地; 完全地 **2** openly 公开地; 无保留地 **3** immediately 立即; 当场 • **adjective 1** open and direct 公开的; 直接的 **2** complete 全部的; 完全的

outrun /aʊt'rʌn/ **verb** (**outruns, outrunning, outran**; past participle **outrun**) run or travel faster or further than 跑(或行进)得比…快(或远)

outsell /aʊt'sel/ **verb** (**outsells, outselling, outsold**) be sold in greater quantities than 卖得比…多

outset /'aʊtset/ **noun** the beginning 开始; 开端

outshine /aʊt'ʃaɪn/ **verb** (**outshines, outshining, outshone**) **1** shine more brightly than 比…更亮 **2** be much better than 比…好得多;比…更优异

outside /aʊt'saɪd/ **noun 1** the external side or surface of something 外面;外部 **2** the external appearance of someone or something 外表 **3** the side of a curve where the edge is longer (曲线的)外缘、外道 • **adjective 1** situated on or near the outside 位于外面的;靠近外面的 **2** not belonging to a particular group 局外的 • **preposition & adverb 1** situated or moving beyond the boundaries of 在(…的)外面;向(…的)外面 **2** beyond the limits of 超出(…的)局限 **3** not being a member of 不属于

outsider /aʊt'saɪdə(r)/ **noun 1** a person who does not belong to a particular group 外人;局外人 **2** a competitor thought to have little chance of success 无取胜希望者;冷门

outsize /'aʊtsaɪz/ or **outsized** /'aʊt-saɪzd/ **adjective** very large 极大的

outskirts /'aʊtskɜːts/ **plural noun** the outer parts of a town or city 郊区;市郊

outsmart /aʊt'smɑːt/ **verb** defeat someone by being cleverer than them 智胜(某人)

outsold /aʊt'səʊld/ past and past participle of **OUTSELL**.

outspoken /aʊt'spəʊkən/ **adjective** stating your opinions in an open and direct way 直言的;坦率的

outstanding /aʊt'stændɪŋ/ **adjective 1** exceptionally good 极好的;杰出的 **2** clearly noticeable 显眼的 **3** not yet dealt with or paid 未解决的;未偿付的 ■ **outstandingly** adverb.

outstay /aʊt'steɪ/ **verb** stay for longer than the expected or allowed time 逗留得比…更久

outstrip /aʊt'strɪp/ **verb** (**outstrips**, **outstripping**, **outstripped**) **1** move faster than 行动快于;超越 **2** surpass

胜过;超越

outvote /aʊt'vəʊt/ **verb** (**outvotes**, **outvoting**, **outvoted**) defeat by gaining more votes 以多数票击败

outward /'aʊtwəd/ **adjective & adverb 1** on or from the outside 在外面的;从外面(的) **2** out or away from a place 朝外面(的);向外(的) ■ **outwardly** adverb **outwards** adverb.

outweigh /aʊt'weɪ/ **verb** be more significant than 在重要性上超过

outwit /aʊt'wɪt/ **verb** (**outwits**, **outwitting**, **outwitted**) deceive someone through being cleverer than them 智胜;骗过

ouzo /'uːzəʊ/ **noun** an aniseed-flavoured Greek spirit (希腊)茴香烈酒

ova /'əʊvə/ plural of **OVUM**.

oval /'əʊvl/ **adjective** having a rounded and slightly elongated outline 椭圆形的;卵形的 • **noun** an oval object or design 椭圆形物(或图案);卵形物(或图案)

ovary /'əʊvəri/ **noun** (plural **ovaries**) **1** a female reproductive organ in which eggs are produced 卵巢 **2** the base of the reproductive organ of a flower (花的)子房 ■ **ovarian** adjective.

ovation /əʊ'veɪʃn/ **noun** a long, enthusiastic round of applause (持久的)热烈鼓掌

oven /'ʌvn/ **noun 1** an enclosed compartment in which food is cooked or heated 烤箱;烤炉 **2** a small furnace or kiln 小炉;小窑

ovenproof /'ʌvnpruːf/ **adjective** suitable for use in an oven 适用于烤箱的;能耐烤箱温度的

over /'əʊvə(r)/ **preposition & adverb 1** expressing movement across an area 穿过;越过 **2** beyond and falling or hanging from a point 越过(某点)下落(或悬垂) • **preposition 1** extending upwards from or above 从…向上;向…上方 **2** above so as to cover or protect 覆盖在…上面 **3** expressing length of time 在…期间

4 higher or more than 比…高；比…多 **5** expressing authority or control (表示有权威或控制支配) • adverb **1** in or to the place indicated 在，去(某处) **2** expressing action and result (表示动作和结果) **3** finished 完毕 **4** expressing repetition of a process 再三地；重复地 • noun Cricket【板球】a sequence of six balls bowled by a bowler from one end of the pitch 一轮投球(一位投球手连续投出的6个球)

overact /ˌəʊvərˈækt/ **verb** act a role in an exaggerated way 演得过于夸张；表演过火

overactive /ˌəʊvərˈæktɪv/ **adjective** more active than is normal or desirable 过于活跃的

overall /ˈəʊvərɔːl/ **adjective & adverb** including everything; taken as a whole 全部(的)；总体上(的) • **noun** (also **overalls**) Brit.【英】a loose-fitting garment worn over ordinary clothes to protect them 工作服；防护服

overarching /ˌəʊvərˈɑːtʃɪŋ/ **adjective** covering or dealing with everything 包罗万象的

overarm /ˈəʊvərɑːm/ **adjective & adverb** done with the hand brought forward and down from above shoulder level 举手过肩的(地)

overawe /ˌəʊvərˈɔː/ **verb** (**overawes**, **overawing**, **overawed**) impress someone so much that they are nervous or silent 吓服；吓倒

overbalance /ˌəʊvərˈbæləns/ **verb** (**overbalances**, **overbalancing**, **overbalanced**) fall due to loss of balance 失去平衡；跌倒

overbearing /ˌəʊvərˈbeərɪŋ/ **adjective** trying to control other people; domineering 专横的；傲慢的；盛气凌人的

overblown /ˌəʊvərˈbləʊn/ **adjective** made to seem more important or impressive than it really is 夸张的；做作的；炫耀的

overboard /ˈəʊvərbɔːd/ **adverb** from a ship into the water 向舷外；从船上落下 □ **go overboard** be very enthusiastic 非常热衷；着迷

overcast /ˈəʊvəkɑːst/ **adjective** cloudy 多云的；阴的

overcharge /ˌəʊvərˈtʃɑːdʒ/ **verb** (**overcharges**, **overcharging**, **overcharged**) charge too high a price 要价过高

overcoat /ˈəʊvərkəʊt/ **noun 1** a long, warm coat 外套；大衣 **2** a top layer of paint or varnish (油漆或清漆)保护层

overcome /ˌəʊvərˈkʌm/ **verb** (**overcomes**, **overcoming**, **overcame**; past participle **overcome**) **1** succeed in dealing with a problem 解决，克服(难题) **2** defeat; overpower 战胜；制服

overcompensate /ˌəʊvərˈkɒmpenseɪt/ **verb** (**overcompensates**, **overcompensating**, **overcompensated**) do too much when trying to correct a problem 补偿过多；赔偿过多

overcrowded /ˌəʊvərˈkraʊdɪd/ **adjective** filled beyond what is usual or comfortable 过度拥挤的；塞得太满的

overdo /ˌəʊvərˈduː/ **verb** (**overdoes**, **overdoing**, **overdid**; past participle **overdone**) **1** do something excessively or in an exaggerated way 把…做得过分；夸张 **2** (**overdone**) cooked too much 烹煮过度的

overdose /ˈəʊvərdəʊs/ **noun** an excessive and dangerous dose of a drug (药物等的)过量 • **verb** (**overdoses**, **overdosing**, **overdosed**) take an overdose 用药过量

overdraft /ˈəʊvərdrɑːft/ **noun** an arrangement with a bank that lets you take out more money than your account holds 透支

overdrawn /ˌəʊvərˈdrɔːn/ **adjective** having taken out more money than

overdressed /ˌəʊvəˈdrest/ **adjective** dressed too elaborately or formally 穿着过于讲究的；打扮太正式的

overdrive /ˈəʊvədraɪv/ **noun 1** a mechanism in a motor vehicle providing an extra gear above the usual top gear (机动车的)超速挡 **2** a state of high activity 高度活跃状态

overdue /ˌəʊvəˈdjuː/ **adjective** not having arrived, happened, or been done at the expected or required time 迟到的，延误的，过期的

overestimate /ˌəʊvəˈrestɪmeɪt/ **verb** (**overestimates, overestimating, overestimated**) estimate that something is larger or better than it really is 过高估计；过高评价 • **noun** an estimate which is too high 过高的估计；过高的评价

overexpose /ˌəʊvərɪkˈspəʊz/ **verb** (**overexposes, overexposing, overexposed**) **1** subject photographic film to too much light 使曝光过度 **2** (**overexposed**) seen too much on television, in the newspapers, etc. (在电视、报纸等上)报道过度的

overflow /ˌəʊvəˈfləʊ/ **verb 1** flow over the edge of a container (从容器边沿)流出，溢出 **2** be too full or crowded 充满；拥挤 **3** (**overflow with**) be very full of an emotion (感情)洋溢 • **noun 1** the number of people or things that do not fit into a particular space 过剩的人(或物) **2** an outlet for excess water 溢出；漫出口

overground /ˈəʊvəɡraʊnd/ **adverb & adjective** on or above the ground 在地面上(的)；在地面上方(的)

overgrown /ˌəʊvəˈɡrəʊn/ **adjective 1** covered with plants that have grown wild 植被蔓生的 **2** having grown too large 长得过大的

overhang /ˌəʊvəˈhæŋ/ **verb** (**overhangs, overhanging, overhung**) project outwards over 悬于…之上；凸出于…之上 • **noun** an overhanging part 悬垂(或凸出)的部分

overhaul /ˌəʊvəˈhɔːl/ **verb 1** examine and repair or improve something 检修 **2** Brit.【英】overtake 超过 • **noun** an act of overhauling something 检修

overhead /ˈəʊvəhed/ **adverb & adjective** above your head 在头上方(的) • **noun** (**overheads**) regular expenses involved in running a business or organization 经常性开支；运营费用；管理费用

overhear /ˌəʊvəˈhɪə(r)/ **verb** (**overhears, overhearing, overheard**) hear something accidentally 无意中听到；偶然听到

overheat /ˌəʊvəˈhiːt/ **verb** make or become too hot 使过热；变得过热

overindulge /ˌəʊvərɪnˈdʌldʒ/ **verb** (**overindulges, overindulging, overindulged**) **1** have too much of something enjoyable 过分沉溺于 **2** give in to the wishes of someone too easily 过分纵容 ■ **overindulgence** noun.

overjoyed /ˌəʊvəˈdʒɔɪd/ **adjective** very happy 极为高兴的；欣喜若狂的

overkill /ˈəʊvəkɪl/ **noun** too much of something 过度；过多；过分

overland /ˈəʊvəlænd/ **adjective & adverb** by land 经由陆路(的)

overlap /ˌəʊvəˈlæp/ **verb** (**overlaps, overlapping, overlapped**) **1** extend over something so as to cover it partially 与…互搭；与…交叠 **2** (of two events) happen at the same time for part of their duration (两件事在时间上)部分重叠 • **noun** an overlapping part or amount 交叠部分；重叠量

overlay verb /ˌəʊvəˈleɪ/ (**overlays, overlaying, overlaid**) **1** coat the surface of 覆盖；铺；涂 **2** add a quality, feeling, etc. to (以品质、感情等)装点，撒满 • **noun** /ˈəʊvəleɪ/ a covering 覆盖物

overleaf /ˈəʊvəliːf/ **adverb** on the other side of the page 在本页背面；

在背面

overload verb /ˌəʊvə'ləʊd/ **1** load too heavily 使超载；使过载 **2** put too great a demand on 使负担过重 • noun /'əʊvələʊd/ too much of something 超载量；超负荷

overlook /ˌəʊvə'lʊk/ verb **1** fail to notice 未注意到 **2** ignore or disregard 忽视；不理会 **3** have a view of something from above 眺望；俯瞰

overlord /'əʊvəlɔːd/ noun a ruler 统治者；霸主

overly /'əʊvəli/ adverb excessively 过度地

overmuch /ˌəʊvə'mʌtʃ/ adverb & pronoun too much 过多(地)；过量(地)

overnight /'əʊvənaɪt/ adverb & adjective **1** during or for a night 在(整个)夜间 **2** happening suddenly or very quickly 一夜之间；突然(发生)

overpass /'əʊvəpɑːs/ noun a bridge by which a road or railway line passes over another 立交桥；天桥

overplay /ˌəʊvə'pleɪ/ verb give too much importance to 过分强调

overpower /ˌəʊvə'paʊə(r)/ verb (**overpowers, overpowering, overpowered**) **1** defeat through having greater strength 以较强力量击败 **2** overwhelm 制服；压倒

overpriced /ˌəʊvə'praɪst/ adjective too expensive 定价过高的

overqualified /ˌəʊvə'kwɒlɪfaɪd/ adjective too highly qualified 资历过高的

overrated /ˌəʊvə'reɪtɪd/ adjective rated more highly than is deserved 高估的；评价过高的

overreach /ˌəʊvə'riːtʃ/ verb (**overreach yourself**) fail through being too ambitious or trying too hard (因野心过大或努力过度而)失败

overreact /ˌəʊvəri'ækt/ verb react more strongly than is justified 反应过火；反应过激 ■ **overreaction** noun.

override /ˌəʊvə'raɪd/ verb (**overrides, overriding, overrode**; past participle **overridden**) **1** use your authority to reject someone else's decision or order (利用权威)驳回，否决，推翻 **2** be more important than 比…更重要 **3** interrupt the action of an automatic device 超驰控制(自动装置) • noun a device on a machine for overriding an automatic process 超驰控制装置

overrule /ˌəʊvə'ruːl/ verb (**overrules, overruling, overruled**) use your authority to reject someone else's decision or order (利用权威)驳回，否决，推翻

overrun /ˌəʊvə'rʌn/ verb (**overruns, overrunning, overran**; past participle **overrun**) **1** occupy a place in large numbers 覆盖；蔓延；泛滥 **2** use more time or money than expected 超过(时限或费用限制)

overseas /ˌəʊvə'siːz/ adverb & adjective in or to a foreign country 在国外(的)；在海外(的)

oversee /ˌəʊvə'siː/ verb (**oversees, overseeing, oversaw**; past participle **overseen**) supervise 监督；监视；指导 ■ **overseer** noun.

oversexed /ˌəʊvə'sekst/ adjective having unusually strong sexual desires 性欲过强的

overshadow /ˌəʊvə'ʃædəʊ/ verb **1** appear more important or successful than 在重要性上超过；比…更成功；使相形见绌 **2** make something sad or less enjoyable 使伤心；使不快 **3** tower above and cast a shadow over 将…遮暗；使阴暗

overshoot /ˌəʊvə'ʃuːt/ verb (**overshoots, overshooting, overshot**) go past the place you intended to stop at 越过(预定地点)

oversight /'əʊvəsaɪt/ noun an unintentional failure to notice or do something 失察；疏忽

oversimplify /ˌəʊvə'sɪmplɪfaɪ/ verb (**oversimplifies, oversimplifying, oversimplified**) simplify something so much that an inaccurate impression of it is given 将…过于简单化

oversized /ˈəʊvəsaɪzd/ or **oversize** /ˈəʊvəsaɪz/ **adjective** bigger than the usual size 过大的；超大型的

oversleep /ˌəʊvəˈsliːp/ **verb** (**oversleeps**, **oversleeping**, **overslept**) sleep later than you intended to 睡得过久；睡过头

overspend /ˌəʊvəˈspend/ **verb** (**overspends**, **overspending**, **overspent**) spend too much 花钱过多；超支

overspill /ˈəʊvəspɪl/ **noun** Brit. 【英】people who move from an overcrowded area to live elsewhere 迁出的过剩人口

overstate /ˌəʊvəˈsteɪt/ **verb** (**overstates**, **overstating**, **overstated**) state too strongly; exaggerate 过分强调；夸大 ■ **overstatement noun.**

overstay /ˌəʊvəˈsteɪ/ **verb** stay longer than is allowed by 逗留太久

overstep /ˌəʊvəˈstep/ **verb** (**oversteps**, **overstepping**, **overstepped**) go beyond a limit 超越(限度)

overstretch /ˌəʊvəˈstretʃ/ **verb** make too many demands on a resource 使…超负荷运转

oversubscribed /ˌəʊvəsəbˈskraɪbd/ **adjective** offering too few places to satisfy demand (场所)供不应求的

overt /ˈəʊvɜːt/ **adjective** done or shown openly 公开的；明显的 ■ **overtly adverb.**

overtake /ˌəʊvəˈteɪk/ **verb** (**overtakes**, **overtaking**, **overtook**; past participle **overtaken**) 1 pass while travelling in the same direction 赶超 2 suddenly affect 突然降临；突然影响

overthrow /ˌəʊvəˈθrəʊ/ **verb** (**overthrows**, **overthrowing**, **overthrew**; past participle **overthrown**) remove from power by force 推翻；打倒 ● **noun** a removal from power 推翻；打倒

overtime /ˈəʊvətaɪm/ **noun** time worked in addition to normal working hours 加班时间

overtone /ˈəʊvətəʊn/ **noun** a subtle or secondary quality or implication 弦外之音；言外之意；暗示

overture /ˈəʊvətjʊə(r)/ **noun** 1 an orchestral piece at the beginning of a musical work 前奏曲 2 an orchestral composition in one movement 序曲 3 (**overtures**) approaches made with the aim of opening negotiations or establishing a relationship (为开启谈判或建立关系而作出的)主动表示，友好姿态

overturn /ˌəʊvəˈtɜːn/ **verb** 1 turn over and come to rest upside down 翻倒；翻转 2 abolish or reverse a decision, system, etc. 废除，推翻(决定、体系等)

overuse **verb** /ˌəʊvəˈjuːz/ (**overuses**, **overusing**, **overused**) use too much 过度使用；滥用 ● **noun** /ˌəʊvəˈjuːs/ excessive use 过度使用；滥用

overview /ˈəʊvəvjuː/ **noun** a general review or summary 纵览；综述；概观

overweening /ˌəʊvəˈwiːnɪŋ/ **adjective** showing too much confidence or pride 过于自信的；过于傲慢的

overweight /ˌəʊvəˈweɪt/ **adjective** heavier or fatter than is usual or desirable 超重的；过重的

overwhelm /ˌəʊvəˈwelm/ **verb** 1 have a strong emotional effect on 使感情充溢 2 overpower 征服；压倒 3 bury or drown beneath a huge mass 覆盖；淹没

overwork /ˌəʊvəˈwɜːk/ **verb** 1 work too hard 工作过度 2 use a word or idea too much 过度使用，滥用(某个词语或观点) ● **noun** too much work 劳累过度

overwrite /ˌəʊvəˈraɪt/ **verb** (**overwrites**, **overwriting**, **overwrote**; past participle **overwritten**) destroy computer data by entering new data in its place 重写，覆盖(指向计算机中输入新数据以覆盖旧数据)

overwrought /ˌəʊvəˈrɔːt/ **adjective** 1 in a state of nervous excitement or anxiety 过度兴奋的;过于焦虑的 **2** too elaborate or complicated 过度修饰的;过于复杂的

ovulate /ˈɒvjuleɪt/ **verb (ovulates, ovulating, ovulated)** (of a woman or female animal) release ova (reproductive cells) from the ovary (女子或雌性动物)排卵,产卵 ■ **ovulation** noun.

ovum /ˈəʊvəm/ **noun (plural ova)** a female reproductive cell, which can develop into an embryo if fertilized by a male cell 卵;卵细胞

owe /əʊ/ **verb (owes, owing, owed) 1** be required to give money or goods to someone in return for something received 欠(钱款或物品) **2** be obliged to show someone gratitude, respect, etc. 欠,应给予(感谢、尊敬等) **3 (owe something to)** have something because of 把…归因于

owing /ˈəʊɪŋ/ **adjective** yet to be paid or supplied 未付的;拖欠的;未提供的 □ **owing to** because of 因为;由于

owl /aʊl/ **noun** a bird of prey with large eyes, which is active at night 猫头鹰

owlish /ˈaʊlɪʃ/ **adjective** resembling an owl 像猫头鹰的

own /əʊn/ **adjective & pronoun** belonging to or done by the person specified 自己(的);本人(的) • **verb 1** have something as your property 有,拥有 **2** formal 【正式】 admit that something is the case 承认 **3 (own up)** admit that you have done something wrong or embarrassing 承认(做了错事或丢脸的事) □ **come into your own** become fully effective 开始完全发挥效用;开始充分施展 **hold your own** remain in a strong position (在困境中)坚守

owner /ˈəʊnə(r)/ **noun** a person who owns something 物主;业主;所有权

人 ■ **ownership** noun.

ox /ɒks/ **noun (plural oxen) 1** a cow or bull 牛 **2** a castrated bull (被阉割的)公牛

Oxbridge /ˈɒksbrɪdʒ/ **noun** Oxford and Cambridge universities classed together 牛津大学和剑桥大学

oxidation /ˌɒksɪˈdeɪʃn/ **noun** the process of oxidizing, or the result of being oxidized 氧化(过程)

oxide /ˈɒksaɪd/ **noun** a compound of oxygen with another substance 氧化物

oxidize or **oxidise** /ˈɒksɪdaɪz/ **verb (oxidizes, oxidizing, oxidized)** cause to combine with oxygen 使氧化 ■ **oxidization** noun.

oxtail /ˈɒksteɪl/ **noun** the tail of an ox, used in making soup 牛尾(用于做汤)

oxygen /ˈɒksɪdʒən/ **noun** a colourless, odourless gas that forms about 20 per cent of the earth's atmosphere 氧;氧气

oxygenate /ɒkˈsɪdʒəneɪt/ **verb (oxygenates, oxygenating, oxygenated)** supply or treat with oxygen 供氧;充氧

oxymoron /ˌɒksɪˈmɔːrɒn/ **noun** a figure of speech in which apparently contradictory terms appear together (e.g. bittersweet) 矛盾修辞法;逆喻

oyster /ˈɔɪstə(r)/ **noun 1** a shellfish with two hinged shells, some kinds of which are edible 牡蛎;蚝 **2** a shade of greyish white 牡蛎白;灰白色

oz /ɒz/ **abbreviation** ounces.

ozone /ˈəʊzəʊn/ **noun 1** a strong-smelling, poisonous form of oxygen 臭氧 **2** informal 【非正式】 fresh air blowing from the sea 清新空气 □ **ozone layer** a layer in the stratosphere containing a lot of ozone, which protects the earth from the sun's ultraviolet radiation 臭氧层

Pp

P or **p** /piː/ **noun** (plural **Ps** or **P's**) the sixteenth letter of the alphabet 英语字母表的第16个字母 • **abbreviation 1** page. **2** Brit. 【英】penny or pence.

PA /piː'eɪ/ **abbreviation 1** Brit. 【英】personal assistant 私人助理 **2** public address 有线广播系统;扩音系统

p.a. abbreviation per year 每年 [short for Latin 缩写,拉丁] = *per annum*.]

pace /peɪs/ **noun 1** a single step taken when walking or running (一)步 **2** the rate at which something happens or develops (某事物发生或发展的)速度,节奏 • **verb** (**paces, pacing, paced**) **1** walk to and fro in a small area 来回踱步;走来走去 **2** measure a distance by counting the number of steps taken to cover it 步测 **3** (**pace yourself**) do something at a controlled and steady rate 调整自己的节奏;控制做事的节奏 □ **keep pace with** progress at the same speed as 与…步调一致 **put someone through their paces** make someone demonstrate their abilities 考察(某人)的能力,使(某人)展示能力

pacemaker /'peɪsmeɪkə(r)/ **noun** a device for stimulating and regulating the heart muscle 心脏起搏器

pachyderm /'pækɪdɜːm/ **noun** an elephant or other very large mammal with thick skin (大象等)厚皮动物

pacific /pə'sɪfɪk/ **adjective 1** formal 【正式】peaceful 平静的;和平的 **2** (**Pacific**) having to do with the Pacific Ocean 太平洋的

pacifism /'pæsɪfɪzəm/ **noun** the belief that disputes should be settled by peaceful means and that violence should never be used 和平主义;反战主义 ■ **pacifist** noun & adjective.

pacify /'pæsɪfaɪ/ **verb** (**pacifies, pacifying, pacified**) **1** make someone less angry or upset 使平静;抚慰 **2** make a country peaceful 使(国家)实现和平,平息战争 ■ **pacification** noun.

pack /pæk/ **noun 1** a cardboard or paper container and the items inside it 包裹 **2** Brit. 【英】a set of playing cards (纸牌的)一副 **3** a group of animals that live and hunt together (野兽的)一群 **4** chiefly disapproving 【主贬】a group of similar things or people (相似物的)一堆,(同类人的)一伙 **5** (**the pack**) the main group of competitors following the leader in a race (赛跑时领先者之后的)一群选手 **6** Rugby 【英式橄榄球】a team's forwards (球队的)前锋 **7** (**Pack**) an organized group of Cub Scouts or Brownies (童子军的)一队 **8** a rucksack (旅行)背包 **9** an absorbent pad used for treating an injury (用于处理伤口的)裹布,敷料 • **verb 1** fill a bag with items needed for travel (旅行前)收拾(行李) **2** put something in a container for transport or storage 装(箱);包裹;包装 **3** cram a large number of things into 塞满;填满 **4** (**packed**) crowded 挤满的 **5** cover, surround, or fill 包装,填充 □ **pack ice** a mass of ice floating in the sea 大片浮冰;流冰群 **pack something in** informal 【非正式】give up an activity or job 停止(活动);放弃(工作) **pack someone off** informal 【非正式】send someone somewhere without much notice (匆忙)把(某人)打发走 **pack up** Brit. informal 【英,非正式】(of a machine) break down (机器)停止运转,失灵 **send someone**

packing informal 【非正式】 dismiss someone abruptly 突然解雇(某人)

package /'pækɪdʒ/ noun 1 an object or group of objects wrapped in paper or packed in a box 包裹；包 2 N. Amer. 【北美】 a packet 小包；小盒 3 a set of proposals or terms as a whole 一套建议，一揽子协议 • verb (packages, packaging, packaged) 1 put into a box or wrapping 把…打包 2 present in an attractive way to catch people's attention 以吸引人的方式呈现；包装

packet /'pækɪt/ noun 1 a paper or cardboard container or parcel (小)纸袋；(小)硬纸板盒 2 (a packet) informal 【非正式】 a lot of money 一大笔钱

packhorse /'pækhɔ:s/ noun a horse that is used to carry loads 驮马

pact /pækt/ noun a formal agreement between two or more people, groups, or countries 条约；协议

pacy /'peɪsi/ adjective fast-moving 节奏快的；速度快的

pad /pæd/ noun 1 a thick piece of soft or absorbent material 垫；衬垫 2 a number of sheets of blank paper fastened together at one edge 拍纸簿；便笺本 3 the fleshy underpart of an animal's foot or of a human finger (动物的)爪垫；(人的)指印 4 a protective guard worn by a sports player (运动员的)防护垫 5 a structure or area used for helicopter take-off and landing or for launching rockets (直升机)起落坪；(火箭)发射台 6 informal 【非正式】 a person's home 住处；公寓 • verb (pads, padding, padded) 1 fill or cover with padding 用(软垫)填充(或覆盖)；给…装衬垫 2 (pad something out) add unnecessary material to a speech, article, or book to make it longer (用不必要的内容)充(讲话、文章或书籍)的篇幅 3 walk with quiet, steady steps 放轻脚步走

padding /'pædɪŋ/ noun 1 soft material used to pad or stuff something (柔软的)垫料，填料 2 unnecessary material added to make a speech, article, or book longer (讲话、文章或书籍中的)凑篇幅的废话，冗词赘句

paddle /'pædl/ noun 1 a short pole with a broad end, used to propel a small boat (小船的)桨，短桨 2 a paddle-shaped tool for stirring or mixing 桨状搅拌器 3 a short-handled bat used e.g. in table tennis (短柄)球拍 • verb (paddles, paddling, paddled) 1 walk with bare feet in shallow water (赤脚)涉水，趟水 2 propel a boat with a paddle or paddles 用桨划(小船) □ **paddle steamer** a boat powered by steam and propelled by large wheels which move the water as they turn 明轮船

paddock /'pædək/ noun 1 a small field or enclosure for horses (养马的)小围场 2 an enclosure where horses or cars are displayed before a race 赛前马匹检阅场；(赛车前的)车辆检阅场

paddy¹ /'pædi/ noun (plural **paddies**) a field where rice is grown 稻田

paddy² noun Brit. 【英，非正式】 a fit of temper 发脾气；发火

padlock /'pædlɒk/ noun a detachable lock which is attached by a hinged hook 挂锁 • verb secure with a padlock 用挂锁锁上

paean /'pi:ən/ noun formal 【正式】 a song of praise or triumph 赞歌；凯歌

paediatrics /,pi:di'ætrɪks/ (US spelling 【美拼作】 **pediatrics**) noun the branch of medicine concerned with children and their diseases 儿科学 ■ **paediatric** adjective **paediatrician** noun.

paedophile /'pi:dəʊfaɪl/ (US spelling 【美拼作】 **pedophile**) noun a person who is sexually attracted to children 恋童癖患者 ■ **paedophilia** noun.

paella /paɪˈelə/ **noun** a Spanish dish of rice, chicken, seafood, etc. 西班牙肉菜烩饭

pagan /ˈpeɪgən/ **noun** a person who holds religious beliefs other than those of the main world religions 异教徒 • **adjective** relating to pagans or their beliefs 异教(徒)的 ■ **paganism** noun.

page[1] /peɪdʒ/ **noun 1** one side of a sheet of paper in a book, magazine, etc. (书籍、杂志等的)页 **2** both sides of such a sheet of paper considered as a single unit (书籍、杂志等的)页，张(包括两面) **3** a section of data displayed on a computer screen 页面(指计算机屏幕上一屏显示的数据) • **verb** (**pages, paging, paged**) (**page through**) turn the pages of a book, magazine, etc. 翻阅；浏览

page[2] **noun 1** a boy or young man employed in a hotel to run errands, open doors, etc. (旅馆的)听差，门童 **2** a young boy who attends a bride at a wedding (婚礼上新娘的)侍童，小男傧相 **3** historical 【历史】a boy in training for knighthood 见习小骑士 • **verb** (**pages, paging, paged**) summon someone over a public address system or with a pager (通过扩音系统)呼叫，(用寻呼机)传呼

pageant /ˈpædʒənt/ **noun** an entertainment performed by people in elaborate or historical costumes 盛装游行庆典；露天历史剧表演

pageantry /ˈpædʒəntri/ **noun** elaborate display or ceremonial events 盛况；盛大庆典

pager /ˈpeɪdʒə(r)/ **noun** a small device which bleeps or vibrates to inform you that it has received a message 寻呼机，传呼机；BP机

paginate /ˈpædʒɪneɪt/ **verb** (**paginates, paginating, paginated**) give numbers to the pages of a book, magazine, etc. 为(书籍、杂志等)编页码 ■ **pagination** noun.

pagoda /pəˈgəʊdə/ **noun** a Hindu or Buddhist temple or other sacred building (印度教或佛教的)塔，宝塔

paid /peɪd/ past and past participle of PAY. □ **put paid to** informal 【非正式】stop something abruptly 使突然停止

pail /peɪl/ **noun** a bucket 桶；水桶

pain /peɪn/ **noun 1** a strongly unpleasant physical sensation caused by illness or injury (因疾病或受伤引起的)疼，痛 **2** mental suffering (精神上的)痛苦 **3** (**pains**) great care or trouble 辛苦；操心；苦恼 **4** informal 【非正式】an annoying or boring person or thing 令人讨厌的人(或物)；乏味的人(或物) • **verb 1** cause pain to 使疼痛；使痛苦 **2** (**pained**) showing that you are annoyed or upset 显露烦恼的，表示心烦的 □ **on** (or **under**) **pain of** with the threat of being punished by 违者以…论处

painful /ˈpeɪnfl/ **adjective** suffering or causing pain 疼痛的；引起痛苦的 ■ **painfully** adverb.

painkiller /ˈpeɪnkɪlə(r)/ **noun** a medicine for relieving pain 镇痛剂；止痛药

painless /ˈpeɪnləs/ **adjective 1** not causing pain 无痛的；不痛苦的 **2** involving little effort or stress 不费力的；轻松的 ■ **painlessly** adverb.

painstaking /ˈpeɪnzteɪkɪŋ/ **adjective** very careful and thorough 十分仔细的；费尽心思的 ■ **painstakingly** adverb.

paint /peɪnt/ **noun** a coloured substance which is spread over a surface to give a thin decorative or protective coating 油漆；涂料 • **verb 1** put paint on something 给…上油漆(或涂料) **2** produce a picture with paint 用颜料画 **3** give a description of 描写；描绘

painter[1] /ˈpeɪntə(r)/ **noun 1** an artist who paints pictures 画家 **2** a person who paints buildings 油漆工

painter[2] **noun** a rope attached to the

bow of a boat for tying it to a quay 缆索；系船缆

painting /'peɪntɪŋ/ **noun 1** the action of painting 作画；绘画 **2** a painted picture 油画

paintwork /'peɪntwɜːk/ **noun** painted surfaces in a building or on a vehicle (建筑物或车辆表面的)漆层，漆面

pair /peə(r)/ **noun 1** a set of two things used together or seen as a unit 一对，一双，一副(两个一起使用或作为一组的物件) **2** an article consisting of two joined or corresponding parts 一把，一条，一副(由两个相连接或相对应的部分组成的物件) **3** two people or animals related in some way or considered together 一对(相互有关联或被认为相称的两个人或动物) • **verb 1** join or connect to form a pair (使)成对；(使)配成一对 **2 (pair off** or **up)** form a couple 结婚；结成一对

paisley /'peɪzli/ **noun** an intricate pattern of curved teardrop-shaped figures 佩斯利(羽状)花纹图案

pajamas /pə'dʒɑːməz/ US spelling of PYJAMAS. pyjamas 的美式拼法

Pakistani /ˌpɑːkɪ'stɑːni, ˌpækɪ'stæni/ **noun** a person from Pakistan 巴基斯坦人 • **adjective** relating to Pakistan 巴基斯坦的

pal /pæl/ informal 【非正式】 **noun** a friend 朋友；伙伴 • **verb (pals, palling, palled) (pal up)** form a friendship 交友；成为朋友

palace /'pæləs/ **noun** a large building where a king, queen, president, etc. lives 皇宫；王宫；(总统等的)官邸

palaeontology /ˌpæliɒn'tɒlədʒi, ˌpeɪ-/ (US spelling 【美拼作】 **paleontology) noun** the study of fossil animals and plants 古生物学 ■ **palaeontologist noun.**

palatable /'pælətəbl/ **adjective 1** pleasant to taste 美味的；可口的 **2** acceptable 合意的；可接受的

palate /'pælət/ **noun 1** the roof of the mouth 腭 **2** a person's ability to distinguish between different flavours 味觉

palatial /pə'leɪʃl/ **adjective** large and impressive, like a palace 宏伟壮观的；宫殿似的

palaver /pə'lɑːvə(r)/ **noun** informal 【非正式】 a lot of fuss about something 冗长的空谈；啰唆

pale¹ /peɪl/ **adjective 1** of a light shade or colour (颜色)浅的，淡的 **2 (of a person's face)** having little colour, especially as a result of illness or shock (人的面色因震惊或疾病)无血色的，苍白的 • **verb (pales, paling, paled) 1** become pale in your face (面色)变得苍白；失色 **2** seem or become less important 显得逊色；相形见绌

pale² **noun 1** a wooden stake used with others to form a fence 组成围栏的桩，尖板条 **2** a boundary 边界；界限 □ **beyond the pale** (of behaviour) considered by most people to be unacceptable (行为)出格的，越轨的

Palestinian /ˌpælə'stɪniən/ **adjective** relating to Palestine 巴勒斯坦的 • **noun** a member of the native Arab population of Palestine 巴勒斯坦人

palette /'pælət/ **noun 1** a thin board on which an artist lays and mixes paints (画家用的)调色板 **2** the range of colours used by an artist (画家用的)一副颜色 □ **palette knife** a blunt knife with a flexible blade, for applying or removing paint (画家用的)调色刀

palimpsest /'pælɪmpsest/ **noun** an ancient sheet of parchment from which the original writing has been removed to make room for new writing (刮去文字后另行书写的)再生羊皮纸

palindrome /'pælɪndrəʊm/ **noun** a word or phrase that reads the same backwards as forwards, e.g. *madam* 回文(正反读都相同的单词或短语)

paling /'peɪlɪŋ/ **noun 1** a fence made

from stakes 围篱；栅栏 **2** a stake used in such a fence (作栅栏用的)桩，尖板条

palisade /ˌpælɪ'seɪd/ *noun* a fence of stakes or iron railings (用木桩或铁条围成的)栅栏，围篱

pall¹ /pɔːl/ *noun* **1** a cloth spread over a coffin, hearse, or tomb 棺罩；柩衣；墓布 **2** a dark cloud of smoke or dust 阴暗的笼罩物(指烟幕或灰尘) **3** a general atmosphere of gloom or fear 忧郁(或恐惧)的气氛 □ **pall-bearer** a person helping to carry a coffin at a funeral (出殡时的)抬棺者，扶灵人

pall² *verb* become less appealing through being too familiar (因过于熟悉而)失去吸引力，变得乏味

palladium /pə'leɪdiəm/ *noun* a rare silvery-white metallic element (稀有金属元素)钯

pallet /'pælət/ *noun* **1** a portable platform on which goods can be moved, stacked, and stored (运输、堆放或储存货物的)运货架，集装架 **2** a straw mattress 草垫

palliate /'pælɪeɪt/ *verb* (**palliates, palliating, palliated**) **1** reduce the pain or bad effects of a disease, though not curing it 减轻，缓解(症状) **2** make something bad easier to cope with 掩饰，粉饰(坏事) ▪ **palliative** *adjective*.

pallid /'pælɪd/ *adjective* **1** pale, especially because of bad health (尤指因身体欠佳)苍白的，无血色的 **2** (of colours or light) not strong or bright (色彩或光线)暗淡的

pallor /'pælə(r)/ *noun* an unhealthy pale appearance 苍白面色

pally /'pæli/ *adjective* informal 【非正式】having a close, friendly relationship 亲密的；要好的

palm¹ /pɑːm/ *noun* an evergreen tree of warm regions, with a crown of large feathered or fan-shaped leaves 棕榈树(温带常绿树，叶宽大，呈羽状或蒲扇形)

palm² *noun* the inner surface of the hand between the wrist and fingers 手掌；手心 • *verb* informal 【非正式】**1** (**palm something off**) sell or dispose of something in a way that is dishonest or unfair 骗卖；(用欺骗手段)处理掉 **2** (**palm someone off with**) persuade someone to accept something that is unwanted or has no value 哄骗(某人)接受(不需要或无价值之物)

palmistry /'pɑːmɪstri/ *noun* the activity of interpreting a person's character or predicting their future by examining the palm of their hand 手相术 ▪ **palmist** *noun*.

palmtop /'pɑːmtɒp/ *noun* a computer small and light enough to be held in one hand 掌上电脑

palmy /'pɑːmi/ *adjective* comfortable and prosperous 兴旺的；繁荣的

palomino /ˌpælə'miːnəʊ/ *noun* (plural **palominos**) a tan-coloured horse with a white mane and tail 帕洛米诺马(体色棕黄、鬃毛和尾毛为白色的)

palpable /'pælpəbl/ *adjective* **1** able to be touched or felt 可触知的；可感知的 **2** (of a feeling or quality) very strong or obvious (感觉或品质)强烈的，明显的，易察觉的 ▪ **palpably** *adverb*.

palpate /pæl'peɪt/ *verb* (**palpates, palpating, palpated**) (of a doctor or nurse) examine a part of the body by touching it (医生或护士)触诊，触摸检查(身体部位)

palpitate /'pælpɪteɪt/ *verb* (**palpitates, palpitating, palpitated**) **1** (of the heart) beat fast or irregularly (心脏)急速(或不规则)地跳动，悸动 **2** shake; tremble 颤动；颤抖

palpitations /ˌpælpɪ'teɪʃns/ *plural noun* a noticeably fast, strong, or irregular heartbeat 心悸；心跳过速；心跳不规则

palsy /'pɔːlzi/ *noun* (plural **palsies**) dated 【废】paralysis 麻痹；瘫痪

■ **palsied** adjective.

paltry /ˈpɔːltri/ **adjective (paltrier, paltriest)** (of an amount) very small (数量)很少的

pampas /ˈpæmpəs/ **noun** large treeless plains in South America (南美洲的)无树大草原

pamper /ˈpæmpə(r)/ **verb (pampers, pampering, pampered)** give someone a great deal of care and attention 对…关怀备至；娇惯

pamphlet /ˈpæmflət/ **noun** a small booklet or leaflet 小册子

pan¹ /pæn/ **noun 1** a metal container for cooking food in 平底锅 **2** a bowl fitted at either end of a pair of scales (天平的)秤盘 **3** Brit. 【英】 the bowl of a toilet 马桶；瓷便池 **4** a hollow in the ground in which water collects 洼地 • **verb (pans, panning, panned) 1** informal 【非正式】 criticize harshly 严厉批评；抨击 **2** (pan out) informal 【非正式】 end up or conclude 结果(是)；结束 **3** wash gravel in a pan to separate out gold (用淘洗盘)淘洗(金子)

pan² **verb (pans, panning, panned)** swing a video or film camera to give a wide view or follow a subject (为拍摄全景或追踪物体)摇摄，追拍，移动拍摄

pan- /pæn-/ **combining form** including everyone or everyone 全；整个：*pan-African* 泛非洲的

panacea /ˌpænəˈsiːə/ **noun** something that will cure all diseases or solve all difficulties 万全之策；万灵药

panache /pəˈnæʃ, pæˈn-/ **noun** impressive skill and confidence 非凡技艺；神气十足

panama /ˈpænəmɑː/ **noun** a man's wide-brimmed hat made of straw-like material 巴拿马草帽

panatella /ˌpænəˈtelə/ **noun** a long, thin cigar pancake noun a thin, flat cake of batter, cooked in a frying pan 细长雪茄烟

pancreas /ˈpæŋkriəs/ **noun (plural pancreases)** a large gland behind the stomach which produces insulin and a liquid used in digestion 胰(腺)

■ **pancreatic** adjective.

panda /ˈpændə/ **noun 1** (also **giant panda**) a large black and white bear-like animal native to bamboo forests in China 大熊猫 **2** (also **red panda**) a Himalayan animal like a raccoon, with thick reddish-brown fur and a bushy tail 小熊猫(产于喜马拉雅山区，似浣熊，毛浓密，呈红棕色，长有茸尾)

pandemic /pænˈdemɪk/ **adjective** (of a disease) widespread over a whole country or large part of the world (疾病)全国(或全世界)流行的，广泛蔓延的 • **noun** an outbreak of such a disease (广泛蔓延的)流行病

pandemonium /ˌpændəˈməʊniəm/ **noun** a state of uproar and confusion 喧嚣；混乱

pander /ˈpændə(r)/ **verb (panders, pandering, pandered) (pander to)** indulge someone in an unreasonable desire or bad habit 纵容，迎合(不合理的欲望或恶习)

pane /peɪn/ **noun** a single sheet of glass in a window or door (一片)窗格玻璃，门框玻璃

panegyric /ˌpænəˈdʒɪrɪk/ **noun** a speech or piece of writing praising someone or something 颂扬的演说；颂文

panel /ˈpænl/ **noun 1** a section in a door, vehicle, garment, etc. (门等的)嵌板，镶板；(衣服上的)镶片，饰条 **2** a flat board on which instruments or controls are fixed 仪表盘；控制板 **3** a small group of people brought together to investigate a matter, or to take part in a broadcast quiz or game 专门小组；评判小组；(参加电视或广播节目答问比赛或游戏的)答问小组，游戏小组 ■ **panelled** (US spelling 【美拼

作】 **paneled**) adjective **panellist** (US spelling【美拼法】 **panelist**) noun.

pang /pæŋ/ noun a sudden sharp pain or painful emotion 一阵剧痛；(感情上的)一阵痛苦

panic /ˈpænɪk/ noun **1** sudden uncontrollable fear or anxiety 恐慌，惊慌失措 **2** frenzied hurry to do something 极度匆忙；慌乱 • verb (**panics**, **panicking**, **panicked**) feel sudden uncontrollable fear or anxiety (突然)感到恐慌 ■ **panicky** adjective.

pannier /ˈpæniə(r)/ noun each of a pair of bags, boxes, or baskets fitted on either side of a bicycle or motorcycle, or carried by a horse or donkey (自行车、摩托车后座两侧或驴马等背上的)挂包，挂篮，驮篮

panoply /ˈpænəpli/ noun a large and impressive collection or number of things 全副装备；全套物品

panorama /ˌpænəˈrɑːmə/ noun **1** a broad view of a surrounding region 全景；全貌 **2** a complete survey of a subject or sequence of events 概论；概述 ■ **panoramic** adjective.

pan pipes plural noun a musical instrument made from a row of short pipes fixed together 排箫(由一排短管组成的乐器)

pansy /ˈpænzi/ noun **1** a garden plant with brightly coloured flowers 三色堇 **2** informal 【非正式】 a homosexual man 同性恋男子

pant /pænt/ verb breathe with short, quick breaths 气喘；喘息 • noun a short, quick breath 气喘；喘息

pantaloons /ˌpæntəˈluːnz/ plural noun **1** women's baggy trousers gathered at the ankles 女式灯笼裤 **2** (in the past) men's close-fitting trousers fastened below the calf or at the foot (旧时的)男式马裤，紧身裤

pantechnicon /pænˈteknɪkən/ noun Brit. dated 【英，废】 a large van for transporting furniture 厢式家具运输车

pantheism /ˈpænθiːɪzəm/ noun the belief that God is all around us and is present in all things 泛神论 ■ **pantheist** noun **pantheistic** adjective.

pantheon /ˈpænθiən/ noun **1** all the gods of a people or religion (某一民族或宗教信奉的)众神，诸神 **2** an ancient temple dedicated to all the gods 万神殿 **3** a group of particularly famous or important people (一批)名人，要人

panther /ˈpænθə(r)/ noun **1** a black leopard 黑豹 **2** N. Amer. 【北美】 a puma or a jaguar 美洲狮；美洲豹

panties /ˈpæntiz/ plural noun knickers (女式)短衬裤，内裤

pantile /ˈpæntaɪl/ noun a curved roof tile, fitted to overlap its neighbour 波形瓦；筒瓦

panto /ˈpæntəʊ/ noun (plural **pantos**) Brit. informal 【英，非正式】 a pantomime 童话剧

pantomime /ˈpæntəmaɪm/ noun Brit. 【英】 an entertainment in the theatre involving music and slapstick comedy (包含音乐和打闹逗乐的)童话剧

pantry /ˈpæntri/ noun (plural **pantries**) a small room or cupboard for storing food 餐具室(或柜)；食物储藏室(或柜)

pants /pænts/ plural noun **1** Brit. 【英】 underpants or knickers 短内裤；短衬裤 **2** chiefly N. Amer. 【主北美】 trousers 裤子

pantyhose /ˈpæntihəʊz/ plural noun N. Amer. 【北美】 women's thin nylon tights (女式)连裤袜

pap /pæp/ noun **1** bland soft or semi-liquid food suitable for babies or invalids (婴儿或病人食用的)软食，半流质食物 **2** trivial books, television programmes, etc. 消遣性读物；娱乐节目

papa /pəˈpɑː, ˈpæpə/ noun N. Amer. or dated 【北美或废】 your father 爸爸

papacy /ˈpeɪpəsi/ noun (plural **papacies**) the position or role of the

Pope 教皇职位；教皇职权

papal /'peɪpl/ **adjective** relating to the Pope or the papacy 教皇的；教皇职位的

paparazzo /ˌpæpə'rætsəʊ/ **noun** (plural **paparazzi** /ˌpæpə'rætsi/) a photographer who follows celebrities to get photographs of them 追踪拍摄名人的摄影师；狗仔队

papaya /pə'paɪə/ **noun** a tropical fruit like a long melon, with orange flesh and small black seeds 番木瓜；木瓜

paper /'peɪpə(r)/ **noun 1** material manufactured in thin sheets from the pulp of wood, used for writing or printing on or as wrapping material 纸 **2** (**papers**) sheets of paper covered with writing or printing 文件 **3** a newspaper 报纸 **4** a government report or policy document 公文；政策文献 **5** an academic article read at a conference or published in a journal 论文；学术文章 **6** a set of exam questions 试卷；考卷 • **verb** (**papers**, **papering**, **papered**) **1** cover a wall with wallpaper 用墙纸裱糊 **2** (**paper something over**) conceal or disguise an awkward problem instead of resolving it 掩饰，掩盖(尴尬的问题) □ **on paper 1** in writing 以书面形式 **2** in theory rather than in reality 理论上 **paper clip** a piece of bent wire or plastic used for holding sheets of paper together 回形针 **paper tiger** a person or thing that appears threatening but is actually weak 纸老虎；外强中干者 ■ **papery** adjective.

paperback /'peɪpəbæk/ **noun** a book bound in stiff paper or thin cardboard 平装本

paperknife /'peɪpənaɪf/ **noun** a blunt knife used for opening envelopes 拆信刀

paperweight /'peɪpəweɪt/ **noun** a small, heavy object for keeping loose papers in place 镇纸；压纸器

paperwork /'peɪpəwɜːk/ **noun** routine work involving written documents 文书工作

papier mâché /ˌpæpieɪ 'mæʃeɪ/ **noun** a mixture of paper and glue that becomes hard when dry 纸和胶质混合而成的)制型纸板

papist /'peɪpɪst/ **noun** disapproving【贬】a Roman Catholic 天主教徒

paprika /pə'priːkə, 'pæprɪkə/ **noun** a powdered spice made from sweet red peppers 辣椒粉

papyrus /pə'paɪrəs/ **noun** (plural **papyri** /pə'paɪriː/ or **papyruses**) a material made in ancient Egypt from the stem of a water plant, used for writing or painting on (古埃及人用于书写或绘画的)纸莎草纸

par /pɑː(r)/ **noun** Golf【高尔夫】the number of strokes a first-class player normally requires for a particular hole or course (一洞或一场球的)标准杆数 □ **above** (or **below** or **under**) **par** above (or below) the usual or expected level or amount 高于(或低于)一般水平(或标准) **on a par with** equal to 与…相同

parable /'pærəbl/ **noun** a simple story that teaches a moral or spiritual lesson 寓言

parabola /pə'ræbələ/ **noun** (plural **parabolas** or **parabolae** /pə'ræbəliː/) a curve of the kind formed by the intersection of a cone with a plane parallel to its side 抛物线 ■ **parabolic** adjective.

paracetamol /ˌpærə'siːtəmɒl, -'set-/ **noun** (plural **paracetamol** or **paracetamols**) Brit.【英】a drug used to relieve pain and reduce fever 扑热息痛(一种解热镇痛药)

parachute /'pærəʃuːt/ **noun** a cloth canopy which allows a person or heavy object attached to it to descend slowly when dropped from a high position 降落伞 • **verb** (**parachutes**, **parachuting**, **parachuted**) drop by

P

parachute 伞降；空投 ■ **parachutist** noun.

parade /pə'reɪd/ **noun 1** a public procession 游行 **2** a formal occasion when soldiers march or stand in line in order to be inspected or for display 阅兵行进；阅兵分列式 **3** a series or succession 一系列 **4** Brit. 【英】a row of shops 一排商店 • **verb** (**parades, parading, paraded**) **1** walk, march, or display in a parade 列队行进；游行 **2** display something publicly in order to impress people or attract attention 公开展示；炫耀

paradigm /'pærədaɪm/ **noun** a typical example, pattern, or model of something 范例；样式 ■ **paradigmatic** adjective.

paradise /'pærədaɪs/ **noun 1** (in some religions) heaven (某些宗教中所指的)天堂，天国 **2** the Garden of Eden 伊甸园 **3** an ideal place or state 天堂；乐土；福地

paradox /'pærədɒks/ **noun 1** a statement that sounds absurd or seems to contradict itself, but is in fact true 似矛盾(可能)正确的说法；似非而是的隽语 **2** a person or thing that combines two contradictory features or qualities 矛盾的人(或事物) ■ **paradoxical** adjective **paradoxically** adverb.

paraffin /'pærəfɪn/ **noun 1** Brit. 【英】an oily liquid obtained from petroleum, used as a fuel 煤油 **2** a waxy substance obtained from petroleum, used for sealing and waterproofing and in candles 石蜡

paragliding /'pærəglaɪdɪŋ/ **noun** a sport in which a person glides through the air attached to a wide parachute after jumping from a high place 翼伞滑翔(运动)

paragon /'pærəgɒn/ **noun** a model of excellence or of a particular quality 典范；完人

paragraph /'pærəgrɑːf/ **noun** a distinct section of a piece of writing, beginning on a new line 段落

Paraguayan /'pærəgwaɪən/ **noun** a person from Paraguay 巴拉圭人 • **adjective** relating to Paraguay 巴拉圭的

parakeet or **parrakeet** /'pærəkiːt/ **noun** a small parrot with green feathers and a long tail 长尾小鹦鹉

parallax /'pærəlæks/ **noun** the apparent difference in the position of an object when viewed from different positions (因观察位置改变而引起的)视差

parallel /'pærəlel/ **adjective 1** (of lines or surfaces) side by side and having the same distance continuously between them (线或面)平行的 **2** happening or existing at the same time or in a similar way; corresponding 同时发生的，并存的；类似的，相对应的 • **noun 1** a person or thing that is similar to or can be compared to another 相似的人(或物)；可相比拟的人(或物) **2** a similarity or comparison 相似处；比拟 **3** each of the imaginary parallel circles of latitude on the earth's surface 纬线；纬圈 • **verb** (**parallels, paralleling, paralleled**) correspond to or happen at the same time as 与…相似；与…同时发生

✔ 拼写指南 double *l* in the middle: para*ll*el. parallel 中间有两个 l。

parallelogram /'pærə'leləgræm/ **noun** a figure with four straight sides and opposite sides parallel 平行四边形

paralyse /'pærəlaɪz/ (US spelling 【美拼作】**paralyze**) **verb** (**paralyses, paralysing, paralysed**) **1** make someone unable to move a part of their body 使瘫痪；使麻痹 **2** prevent something from functioning normally 使陷入瘫痪；使无法运行

paralysis /pə'ræləsɪs/ **noun** (plural **paralyses** /pə'ræləsiːz/) **1** the loss of

paralytic /ˌpærəˈlɪtɪk/ **adjective 1** relating to paralysis 瘫痪的；麻痹的 **2** informal【非正式】very drunk 酩酊大醉的

paramedic /ˌpærəˈmedɪk/ **noun** a person who is trained to do medical work but is not a fully qualified doctor 医务辅助人员

parameter /pəˈræmɪtə(r)/ **noun** a thing which decides or limits the way in which something can be done 限定因素；界限；范围

paramilitary /ˌpærəˈmɪlətri/ **adjective** organized on similar lines to a military force 准军事的 • **noun** (plural **paramilitaries**) a member of a paramilitary organization 准军事组织成员

paramount /ˈpærəmaʊnt/ **adjective 1** more important than anything else 最重要的 **2** having the highest position or the greatest power 至高无上的；拥有最高权力的

paramour /ˈpærəmʊə(r)/ **noun** old use 【旧】a person's lover 爱人；情人

paranoia /ˌpærəˈnɔɪə/ **noun** a mental condition in which someone wrongly believes that other people want to harm them, or that they are very important 偏执狂；妄想狂

paranoid /ˈpærənɔɪd/ **adjective 1** wrongly believing that other people want to harm you 偏执狂的；妄想狂的 **2** having to do with paranoia 类似妄想狂的

paranormal /ˌpærəˈnɔːml/ **adjective** beyond the scope of scientific knowledge 科学无法解释的；超自然的

parapet /ˈpærəpɪt/ **noun** a low wall along the edge of a roof, bridge, or balcony (屋顶、桥梁或阳台边缘的)低矮护墙，女儿墙

paraphernalia /ˌpærəfəˈneɪliə/ **noun** the objects needed for a particular activity (某一活动所需的)各种装备

paraphrase /ˈpærəfreɪz/ **verb** (**paraphrases**, **paraphrasing**, **paraphrased**) express the meaning of something using different words (用另外的说法)释义，意译 • **noun** a rewording of something written or spoken (对文字或话语的)释义，意译

paraplegia /ˌpærəˈpliːdʒə/ **noun** paralysis of the legs and lower body 截瘫；下身麻痹 ■ **paraplegic** adjective & noun.

paraquat /ˈpærəkwɒt/ **noun** a powerful weedkiller 百草枯(一种强效除草剂)

parasite /ˈpærəsaɪt/ **noun 1** an animal or plant which lives on or inside another, and gets its food from it 寄生生物 **2** a person who relies on or benefits from someone else but gives nothing in return 靠他人为生者；寄生虫 ■ **parasitic** adjective **parasitism** noun.

parasol /ˈpærəsɒl/ **noun** a light umbrella used to give shade from the sun 阳伞；遮阳伞

paratroops /ˈpærətruːps/ **plural noun** troops trained to be dropped by parachute from aircraft 伞兵部队；空降部队 ■ **paratrooper** noun.

parboil /ˈpɑːbɔɪl/ **verb** boil something until it is partly cooked 把…煮至半熟

parcel /ˈpɑːsl/ **noun** an object or collection of objects wrapped in paper in order to be carried or sent by post 包裹；邮包 • **verb** (**parcels**, **parcelling**, **parcelled**; US spelling 【美拼作】**parcels**, **parceling**, **parceled**) **1** (**parcel something up**) make something into a parcel 将…打包 **2** (**parcel something out**) divide something between several people 分发；分配

parch /pɑːtʃ/ **verb 1** make something

dry through strong heat (通过高温) 使干透 **2 (parched)** informal【非正式】very thirsty 极干渴的

parchment /'pɑːtʃmənt/ noun **1** (in the past) a stiff material made from the skin of a sheep or goat and used for writing on (旧时书写用的)羊皮纸 **2** thick paper resembling parchment 仿羊皮纸

pardon /'pɑːdn/ noun **1** forgiveness for a mistake, sin, or crime 宽恕;原谅 **2** a cancellation of the punishment for a crime 赦免 • verb **1** forgive or excuse a person, mistake, or crime 宽恕;原谅 **2** give an offender a pardon 赦免(犯法者) • exclamation used to ask a speaker to repeat something because you did not hear or understand it 对不起,请原谅(用于礼貌地请求讲话者重复自己没听清或不理解的话) ■ **pardonable** adjective.

pare /peə(r)/ verb **(pares, paring, pared) 1** trim something by cutting away the outer edges 削去…的皮 **2 (pare something away** or **down)** gradually reduce the amount of something 逐步削减

parent /'peərənt/ noun **1** a father or mother 父亲;母亲;父母 **2** an animal or plant from which young or new ones are produced (动植物的)亲代,亲本 **3** an organization or company which owns or controls a number of smaller organizations or companies 母公司;总公司 • verb be or act as a parent to 做…的父亲(或母亲) ■ **parental** adjective **parenthood** noun.

parentage /'peərəntɪdʒ/ noun the identity and origins of your parents 家世;出身

parenthesis /pə'renθəsɪs/ noun (plural **parentheses** /pə'renθəsiːz/) **1** a word or phrase added as an explanation or afterthought, indicated in writing by brackets, dashes, or commas 插入词,插入成分(以括号、破折号或逗号隔开) **2 (parentheses)** a pair of round brackets ( ) surrounding a word or phrase 圆括号 ■ **parenthetic** (or **parenthetical**) adjective.

par excellence /ˌpɑːr 'eksəlɑːns/ adjective better or more than all others of the same kind 卓越的;出类拔萃的: a designer par excellence 杰出的设计师

pariah /pə'raɪə/ noun a person who is rejected by other people; an outcast 受排斥者;被遗弃者

parings /'peərɪŋz/ plural noun thin strips pared off from something 削下的皮;削下物

parish /'pærɪʃ/ noun **1** (in the Christian Church) a district with its own church and church ministers (基督教会的)堂区,教区 **2** Brit.【英】the smallest unit of local government in country areas 行政堂区(乡村的基层行政单位)

parishioner /pə'rɪʃənə(r)/ noun a person who lives in a particular Church parish 堂区居民

parity /'pærəti/ noun the quality of being equal with or equivalent to something 相等;同等;对等

park /pɑːk/ noun **1** a large public garden in a town 公园 **2** a large area of land attached to a country house (乡村住宅的)庭院,园林 **3** an area used for a particular purpose 专用场地 • verb leave a vehicle somewhere for a time (暂时)停放(车辆),泊(车)

parka /'pɑːkə/ noun a windproof hooded jacket (带风帽的)风雪大衣,派克大衣

Parkinson's disease /'pɑːkɪnsnz/ noun a disease of the brain and nervous system marked by trembling, stiffness in the muscles, and slowness of movement 帕金森病(脑部和神经系统疾病,患者肌肉僵直、肢体颤动、行动迟缓)

parky /'pɑːki/ adjective Brit. informal

【英,非正式】chilly 寒冷的

parlance /ˈpɑːləns/ **noun** a way of speaking 术语;说法;用语

parley /ˈpɑːli/ **noun** (plural **parleys**) a meeting between enemies to discuss terms for a truce (敌对双方讨论停战条款的)谈判,和谈 • **verb** (**parleys, parleying, parleyed**) hold a parley 举行谈判;举行和谈

parliament /ˈpɑːləmənt/ **noun 1** (**Parliament**) (in the UK) the assembly that makes laws, consisting of the king or queen, the House of Lords, and the House of Commons (英国的)议会(包括英王、上议院和下议院) **2** a similar assembly in other countries (其他国家的)议会,国会 ■ **parliamentary** adjective.

> ✔ 拼写指南 *-lia-* in the middle, not *-la-*: parliament. parliament 中间的 *-lia-* 不要拼作 *-la-*。

parliamentarian /ˌpɑːləmənˈteərɪən/ **noun** a member of a parliament 议员

parlour /ˈpɑːlə(r)/ (US spelling 【美拼作】**parlor**) **noun 1** dated 【废】 a sitting room 起居室;客厅 **2** a shop providing particular goods or services 店铺;小店

parlous /ˈpɑːləs/ **adjective** old use 【旧】 dangerously uncertain; precarious 危险的;不稳的

Parmesan /ˈpɑːmɪzæn/ **noun** a hard, dry Italian cheese 帕尔马干酪(一种意大利硬干酪)

parochial /pəˈrəʊkɪəl/ **adjective 1** relating to a parish 堂区的 **2** having a narrow outlook 偏狭的;狭隘的 ■ **parochialism** noun.

parody /ˈpærədi/ **noun** (plural **parodies**) a piece of writing, art, or music that deliberately copies the style of someone or something, in order to be funny (文章、艺术、音乐等的)该谐模仿作品 • **verb** (**parodies, parodying, parodied**) produce a parody of 滑稽地模仿

parole /pəˈrəʊl/ **noun** the temporary or permanent release of a prisoner before the end of their sentence, on the condition that they behave well 假释 • **verb** (**paroles, paroling, paroled**) release a prisoner on parole 假释(犯人)

paroxysm /ˈpærəksɪzəm/ **noun** a sudden attack of pain, coughing, etc., or a sudden feeling of overwhelming emotion (病痛、咳嗽等的)发作,阵发;(感情的)一阵突发

parquet /ˈpɑːkeɪ/ **noun** flooring consisting of wooden blocks arranged in a geometric pattern 镶木地板;拼花地板

parrakeet /ˈpærəkiːt/ ⇒ 见 PARAKEET.

parricide /ˈpærɪsaɪd/ **noun** the killing by someone of their own parent or other close relative 弑父;弑母;弑近亲

parrot /ˈpærət/ **noun** a tropical bird with brightly coloured feathers and a hooked bill, some kinds of which can copy human speech 鹦鹉 • **verb** (**parrots, parroting, parroted**) repeat something without thought or understanding 鹦鹉学舌似地重复;机械模仿 □ **parrot-fashion** repeated without thought or understanding 鹦鹉学舌似地;机械重复地

parry /ˈpæri/ **verb** (**parries, parrying, parried**) **1** ward off a weapon or attack 避开,挡开(武器或攻击) **2** say something in order to avoid answering a question directly 回避(问题)

parse /pɑːz/ **verb** analyse a sentence in terms of grammar 对(句子)作语法分析

parsimony /ˈpɑːsɪmənɪ/ **noun** the fact of being very unwilling to spend money 极度节俭;吝啬 ■ **parsimonious** adjective.

parsley /ˈpɑːsli/ **noun** a herb with crinkly or flat leaves, used in cooking 欧芹(香草类植物,有卷叶或平叶,用于烹饪)

parsnip /ˈpɑːsnɪp/ **noun** a long tapering cream-coloured root vegetable 欧洲防风；欧洲萝卜

parson /ˈpɑːsn/ **noun** (in the Church of England) a parish priest (英国国教的)堂区牧师

parsonage /ˈpɑːsənɪdʒ/ **noun** a house provided by the Church for a parson 堂区牧师寓所

part /pɑːt/ **noun 1** a piece or section which is combined with others to make up a whole 组成部分 **2** some but not all of something 部分；局部 **3** a role played by an actor or actress 角色 **4** a person's contribution to an action or situation 参与；作用 **5** (**parts**) informal 【非正式】a region 地区；区域 • **verb 1** move apart or divide to leave a central space 分离；分开 **2** (of two or more people) leave each other (两个或两个以上的人)分离，分别 **3** (**part with**) give up possession of; hand over 放弃；交出 • **adverb** partly 部分地 □ **part company** go in different directions 分手；各奔东西 **part of speech** a category in which a word is placed according to its function in grammar, e.g. noun, adjective, and verb 词类；词性 **part song** a song with three or more voice parts and no musical accompaniment (无伴奏的)多声部合唱曲 **part-time** for only part of the usual working day or week 兼职 **take part** join in or be involved in an activity 参加；参与 **take someone's part** support someone in an argument 支持(某人)；站在(某人)一边

partake /pɑːˈteɪk/ **verb** (**partakes**, **partaking**, past **partook**; past participle **partaken**) formal 【正式】**1** (**partake of**) eat or drink 吃；喝 **2** (**partake in**) participate in 参加

partial /ˈpɑːʃl/ **adjective 1** not complete or whole 部分的；不完全的 **2** favouring one side in a dispute 偏袒的；偏心的 **3** (**partial to**) liking something 偏爱⋯的 ■ **partiality** noun **partially** adverb.

participate /pɑːˈtɪsɪpeɪt/ **verb** (**participates**, **participating**, **participated**) join in something; take part 参与；参加 ■ **participant** noun **participation** noun **participatory** adjective.

participle /ˈpɑːtɪsɪpl/ **noun** Grammar 【语法】a word such as *going* or *burnt* that is formed from a verb and used as an adjective or noun (as in *burnt toast* or *the going was good*), or to make compound verb forms (as in *was going*) 分词

particle /ˈpɑːtɪkl/ **noun 1** a tiny portion of matter 微粒；颗粒 **2** a minute piece of matter smaller than an atom, e.g. an electron 粒子

particular /pəˈtɪkjʊlə(r)/ **adjective 1** relating to an individual member of a group or class 特定的；特指的；某一的 **2** more than is usual 特殊的；不寻常的 **3** very careful or concerned about something 讲究的；挑剔的 • **noun** a detail 细节 □ **in particular** especially 尤其，特别

particularly /pəˈtɪkjələli/ **adverb 1** more than is usual 特殊地 **2** in particular; especially 特别，格外；尤其

> ✔ 拼写指南 particu*lar*ly, not -*culy*. particularly 不要拼作 -culy。

parting /ˈpɑːtɪŋ/ **noun 1** an act of leaving someone and going away 离别；分别 **2** Brit. 【英】a line of scalp which is visible when the hair is combed in different directions (头发的)分缝

partisan /ˌpɑːtɪˈzæn/ **noun 1** a committed supporter of a cause, group, or person 党徒；坚定支持者 **2** a member of an armed group fighting secretly against an occupying force 游击队员 • **adjective** prejudiced 有偏

见的；偏袒的

partition /pɑːˈtɪʃn/ **noun 1** a structure that divides a space into separate areas 隔断；分隔物 **2** division into parts 分割；划分 • **verb 1** divide into parts 分割；将…分成部分 **2** divide a room with a partition (用隔板等)隔开，分隔(房间)

partly /ˈpɑːtli/ **adverb** not completely but to some extent 部分地；不完全地；一定程度上

partner /ˈpɑːtnə(r)/ **noun 1** each of two people involved in doing something as a pair (两人一组中的)伙伴，搭档 **2** the person you are having a sexual relationship with 配偶；性伴侣 **3** each of two or more people who are involved in a project or undertaking or who own a business (生意上的)合伙人，搭档 • **verb** (**partners, partnering, partnered**) be the partner of 成为…的伙伴，做…的搭档 ■ **partnership noun.**

partook /pɑːˈtʊk/ past of PARTAKE.

partridge /ˈpɑːtrɪdʒ/ **noun** (plural **partridge** or **partridges**) a game bird with brown feathers and a short tail 鹧鸪，山鹑(供猎捕鸟类，羽毛褐色，短尾)

parturition /ˌpɑːtjʊəˈrɪʃn/ **noun** formal or technical 【正式或术语】 the action of giving birth 分娩；生产

party /ˈpɑːti/ **noun** (plural **parties**) **1** a social event with food and drink and sometimes dancing 社交聚会 **2** an organized political group that puts forward candidates for election to government 党；政党 **3** a group of people taking part in an activity or trip 队；组；群 **4** a person or group forming one side in an agreement or dispute (协议或争论中的)一方，当事人 • **verb** (**parties, partying, partied**) informal 【非正式】 enjoy yourself at a party 寻欢作乐 □ **be party to** be involved in 参与；牵涉在内 **party**

line a policy officially adopted by a political party 政党政策；政党路线 **party wall** a wall between two adjoining houses or rooms (房屋或房间之间的)界墙

parvenu /ˈpɑːvənjuː/ **noun** disapproving 【贬】 a person from a poor background who has recently joined a group of wealthy or famous people 暴发户；新贵

pascal /ˈpæskl/ **noun** a unit of pressure 帕斯卡(压强单位)

pass¹ /pɑːs/ **verb 1** move or go onward, past, through, or across 走过；通过 **2** change from one state or condition to another 改变；转变 **3** transfer something to someone 传递；转移 **4** kick, hit, or throw the ball to a teammate 传(球) **5** (of time) go by (时间)流逝 **6** spend time 度过，消磨(时间) **7** be done or said 做出；说出 **8** come to an end 结束；终结 **9** be successful in an exam or test 通过(考试或测试) **10** declare something to be satisfactory 表示满意；接受 **11** approve a proposal or law by voting 批准，通过(提案或法律) **12** express an opinion or judgement 发表(意见)；作出(判断) • **noun 1** an act of passing 经过；通过 **2** a success in an exam 合格，通过 **3** an official document which allows you to go somewhere or use something 通行证；出入证 **4** informal 【非正式】 a sexual advance 调情；勾引 **5** a particular situation 境况；处境 □ **pass away** die 去世 **pass off** happen in a particular way (以某种方式)进行，发生 **pass something off as** pretend that something is something else 把(某物)冒充成 **pass out** become unconscious 昏迷；失去知觉 **pass something up** choose not to take up an opportunity 拒绝，放弃(机会)

pass² **noun** a route over or through mountains 山道；山口；关口

passable /ˈpɑːsəbl/ **adjective 1** acceptable, but not outstanding 凑合的; 过得去的 **2** able to be travelled along or on 可通行的; 畅通的 ■ **passably** adverb.

passage /ˈpæsɪdʒ/ **noun 1** the passing of someone or something 通过; 经过 **2** a way through or across something 通道; 通路 **3** a journey by sea or air (乘船或飞机的)航程, 旅行 **4** the right to pass through a place 通行权 **5** a short section from a book, document, or musical work (书籍、文件或音乐作品的)段, 节

passageway /ˈpæsɪdʒweɪ/ **noun** a corridor or other narrow passage between buildings or rooms 走廊; 通道

passé /ˈpɑːseɪ/ **adjective** no longer fashionable 过时的, 陈旧的

passenger /ˈpæsɪndʒə(r)/ **noun** a person travelling in a car, bus, train, ship, or aircraft, other than the driver, pilot, or crew 乘客; 旅客

passer-by /ˌpɑːsəˈbaɪ/ **noun** (plural **passers-by**) a person who happens to be walking past something or someone 过路人; 路人

passim /ˈpæsɪm/ **adverb** used to show that a reference appears at various places throughout a document (引文)多处, 各处

passing /ˈpɑːsɪŋ/ **adjective 1** done quickly and casually 仓促的; 随意的 **2** (of a similarity) slight (相似性)略微的 ● **noun 1** the ending of something 结束 **2** a person's death 去世; 故去

passion /ˈpæʃn/ **noun 1** very strong emotion 强烈的情感; 热情 **2** strong sexual love (两性之间)热烈的情爱, 激情 **3** a strong enthusiasm for something 极度喜爱; 酷爱 **4** (**the Passion**) Jesus's suffering and death on the Cross 耶稣受难 □ **passion flower** a climbing plant with distinctive flowers 西番莲(一种攀缘植物) **passion fruit** the edible fruit of some species of passion flower 西番莲果 **passion play** a play about Jesus's crucifixion 耶稣受难剧

passionate /ˈpæʃənət/ **adjective** showing or caused by passion 热情的; 情绪激昂的 ■ **passionately** adverb.

passive /ˈpæsɪv/ **adjective 1** accepting what happens without resisting or trying to change anything 被动的; 消极的 **2** Grammar 【语法】 (of a verb) having the form used when the subject is affected by the action of the verb (e.g. *they were killed* as opposed to the active form *he killed them*) (动词)被动的, 被动语态的 □ **passive smoking** the inhaling of smoke from other people's cigarettes 被动吸烟 ■ **passively** adverb **passivity** noun.

Passover /ˈpɑːsəʊvə(r)/ **noun** the major Jewish spring festival, commemorating the liberation of the Israelites from slavery in Egypt 逾越节(犹太教春季的主要节日, 纪念古以色列人摆脱埃及人的奴役, 获得自由)

passport /ˈpɑːspɔːt/ **noun** an official document that identifies you as a citizen of a particular country and is required in order to enter and leave other countries 护照

password /ˈpɑːswɜːd/ **noun** a secret word or phrase used to enter a place or use a computer (进入某地或使用计算机的)口令, 密码

past /pɑːst/ **adjective 1** gone by in time and no longer existing 以前的; 不复存在的 **2** (of time) that has gone by (时间)过去的 **3** Grammar 【语法】 (of a tense of a verb) expressing a past action or state (动词时态)过去时的 ● **noun 1** a past period or the events in it 过去; 昔日 **2** a person's or thing's history or earlier life 往事; 经历 ● **preposition 1** beyond in time or space (时间上)晚于, 超过; (空间上)

在…的更远处 **2** in front of or from one side to the other of 经过；越过 **3** beyond the scope or power of 超出(范围或能力) • **adverb 1** so as to pass from one side to the other 经过；越过 **2** used to indicate the passage of time (时间)流逝，过去 □ **past master** an expert in a particular activity 行家；能手 **past participle** Grammar 【语法】 the form of a verb which is used in perfect tenses (e.g. *have you looked?*), to form passive sentences (e.g. *it was broken*), and sometimes as an adjective (e.g. *lost property*) 过去分词

pasta /ˈpæstə/ **noun** a type of food made from flour and water, formed into various shapes and cooked in boiling water 意大利面食

paste /peɪst/ **noun 1** a soft, moist substance 糊状物 **2** a glue made from water and starch 糨糊 **3** a hard substance used in making imitation gems (做人造宝石用的)铅制玻璃 • **verb** (**pastes, pasting, pasted**) **1** coat or stick with paste 用糨糊粘贴 **2** (in computing) insert a section of text (into a document) (计算机应用中)粘贴，插入(文本)

pastel /ˈpæstl/ **noun 1** a soft coloured chalk or crayon used for drawing 彩色粉笔；蜡笔 **2** a pale shade of a colour 淡雅色调；柔和颜色 • **adjective** (of a colour) pale (色彩)淡雅的，柔和的

pasteurize or **pasteurise** /ˈpæstʃəraɪz/ **verb** (**pasteurizes, pasteurizing, pasteurized**) destroy the germs in milk by a process of heating and cooling 用巴氏杀菌法给(牛奶)消毒 ■ **pasteurization** noun.

pastiche /pæˈstiːʃ/ **noun** a piece of writing or work of art produced in a style which imitates that of another work, artist, or period (艺术)模仿作品

pastille /ˈpæstəl/ **noun** a small sweet or throat lozenge 含片；锭剂；润喉糖

pastime /ˈpɑːstaɪm/ **noun** an activity done regularly for enjoyment 消遣；娱乐

pastor /ˈpɑːstə(r)/ **noun** a minister in charge of a Christian church or group 牧师

pastoral /ˈpɑːstərəl/ **adjective 1** relating to or portraying country life 田园式的；田园生活的 **2** relating to the farming or grazing of sheep or cattle 畜牧的 **3** relating to the work of a Christian minister in giving personal and spiritual guidance 牧师职责的；牧灵的 **4** relating to a teacher's responsibility for the well-being of students 教师职责的 • **noun** a pastoral poem, picture, or piece of music 田园诗；田园风格的绘画；田园音乐

pastrami /pəˈstrɑːmi/ **noun** highly seasoned smoked beef 五香熏牛肉

pastry /ˈpeɪstri/ **noun** (plural **pastries**) **1** dough made from flour, fat, and water, used in baked dishes such as pies (用于制馅饼等的)油酥面团 **2** a cake consisting of sweet pastry with a filling 油酥点心

pasture /ˈpɑːstʃə(r)/ **noun** land covered with grass, suitable for grazing cattle or sheep 牧草地；牧场 • **verb** (**pastures, pasturing, pastured**) put animals to graze in a pasture 放牧(牲畜) ■ **pasturage** noun.

pasty¹ or **pastie** /ˈpæsti/ **noun** (plural **pasties**) Brit. 【英】 a folded pastry case filled with seasoned meat and vegetables 馅饼

pasty² /ˈpeɪsti/ **adjective** (**pastier, pastiest**) (of a person's skin) unhealthily pale (人的肤色)不健康的，苍白的

pat¹ /pæt/ **verb** (**pats, patting, patted**) tap quickly and gently with the flat of your hand (以手掌)轻拍 • **noun 1** an act of patting 轻拍 **2** a compact mass of a soft substance 小

块软物

pat² adjective (of something said) too quick or easy; not convincing (话语)随意说出的, 不令人信服的 □ **have something off pat** know facts or words perfectly so that you can repeat them without hesitation 对…烂熟于胸, 对…了如指掌

patch /pætʃ/ noun **1** a small area differing in colour or texture from its surroundings (与周围不同的)斑, 块 **2** a piece of material used to mend a hole or strengthen a weak point 补丁; 补片 **3** a cover worn over an injured eye (保护受伤眼睛的)眼罩 **4** a small plot of land 一小块地 **5** Brit. informal【英, 非正式】a period of time 一段时间 **6** Brit. informal【英, 非正式】an area for which someone is responsible or in which they operate 管辖区 • verb **1** mend, strengthen, or protect with a patch 补缀; 修补; 加固 **2** (patch something up) treat injuries or repair damage quickly or temporarily 草草处理(伤口); 临时修补 □ **not a patch on** Brit. informal【英, 非正式】much less good than 远比…不上

patchwork /ˈpætʃwɜːk/ noun needlework in which small pieces of cloth of different colours are sewn edge to edge 拼缝物; 拼缀物

patchy /ˈpætʃi/ adjective (patchier, patchiest) **1** existing or happening in small, isolated areas 散落的; 局部地区的 **2** uneven in quality; inconsistent 质量不一的; 参差不齐的

pate /peɪt/ noun old use【旧】a person's head 头; 脑袋

pâté /ˈpæteɪ/ noun a rich savoury paste made from meat, fish, etc. 肉酱; 鱼肉酱

patella /pəˈtelə/ noun (plural **patellae** /pəˈteliː/) the kneecap 膑骨; 膝盖骨

patent noun /ˈpeɪtnt, ˈpæt-/ a government licence giving someone the sole right to make, use, or sell their invention for a set period 专利证书; 专利权 • verb /ˈpeɪtnt, ˈpæt-/ obtain a patent for 获得…的专利权 • adjective /ˈpeɪtnt/ **1** easily recognizable; obvious 显而易见的; 明显的 **2** made and marketed under a patent 特许的; 专卖的 □ **patent leather** shiny varnished leather 漆皮; 漆革 ■ **patently** adverb.

paterfamilias /ˌpeɪtəfəˈmɪliæs/ noun the man who is the head of a family or household 男性家长; 男性户主

paternal /pəˈtɜːnl/ adjective **1** having to do with or like a father 父亲的; 父亲般的 **2** related through the father 父系的; 父方的 ■ **paternally** adverb.

paternalism /pəˈtɜːnəlɪzəm/ noun the policy of protecting the people you have control over but also of restricting their freedom 家长式管理 ■ **paternalist** noun & adjective **paternalistic** adjective.

paternity /pəˈtɜːnəti/ noun **1** the state of being a father 父亲身份 **2** descent from a father 父系; 父亲血统

paternoster /ˌpætəˈnɒstə(r)/ noun (in the Roman Catholic Church) the Lord's Prayer (罗马天主教的)主祷文

path /pɑːθ/ noun **1** a way or track laid down for walking or made by repeated treading 道路; 小路 **2** the direction in which a person or thing moves (人或物移动的)方向 **3** a course of action 途径; 行动路线

pathetic /pəˈθetɪk/ adjective **1** arousing pity or sadness 令人同情的; 可怜的 **2** informal【非正式】weak or inadequate 差劲的; 低劣的; 不够格的 ■ **pathetically** adverb.

pathological /ˌpæθəˈlɒdʒɪkl/ adjective **1** relating to or caused by a disease 疾病的; 疾病引起的 **2** informal【非正式】unable to stop yourself doing something; compulsive 无法控制的; 强迫性的 ■ **pathologically** adverb.

pathology /pəˈθɒlədʒi/ noun **1** the study of the causes and effects of diseases 病理学 **2** the typical behaviour of a disease 病征;病状 ■ **pathologist** noun.

pathos /ˈpæɪθɒs/ noun a quality that arouses pity or sadness 激起悲悯的因素;感染力

pathway /ˈpɑːθweɪ/ noun a path or route 小路;小径;路线

patience /ˈpeɪʃns/ noun **1** the ability to accept delay, trouble, or suffering without becoming angry or upset (对迟延、麻烦或苦难的)容忍,忍耐 **2** Brit. 【英】 a card game for one player 单人纸牌戏

patient /ˈpeɪʃnt/ adjective having or showing patience 容忍的;忍耐的 • noun a person receiving or registered to receive medical treatment 病人 ■ **patiently** adverb.

patina /ˈpætɪnə/ noun **1** a green or brown film on the surface of old bronze 铜锈;铜绿 **2** a soft glow on wooden furniture produced by age and polishing (木质家具因长期使用而在表面产生的)光泽

patio /ˈpætɪəʊ/ noun (plural patios) a paved area outside a house 露台;平台

patisserie /pəˈtiːsəri/ noun a shop where pastries and cakes are sold 糕点店

patois /ˈpætwɑː/ noun (plural patois /ˈpætwɑːz/) the dialect of a region 方言;土语

patriarch /ˈpeɪtrɪɑːk/ noun **1** a man who is the head of a family or tribe (男性)家长,族长 **2** a biblical figure regarded as a father of the human race (《圣经》中的)人类祖先 **3** a respected older man 德高望重的长者

patriarchy /ˈpeɪtrɪɑːki/ noun (plural patriarchies) a society led or controlled by men 男性统治的社会 ■ **patriarchal** adjective.

patrician /pəˈtrɪʃn/ noun an aristocrat 贵族 • adjective relating to or characteristic of aristocrats 贵族的

patricide /ˈpætrɪsaɪd/ noun **1** the

killing by someone of their own father 弑父 **2** a person who kills their father 弑父者

patrimony /ˈpætrɪməni/ noun (plural patrimonies) property inherited from your father or male ancestor 祖传财产;世袭财产

patriot /ˈpætrɪət, ˈpeɪ-/ noun a person who strongly supports their country and is prepared to defend it 爱国者 ■ **patriotic** adjective **patriotism** noun.

patrol /pəˈtrəʊl/ noun **1** a person or group sent to keep watch over an area 巡逻兵;巡逻队 **2** the action of patrolling an area 巡逻;巡查 • verb (patrols, patrolling, patrolled) keep watch over an area by regularly walking or travelling around it (定时)巡逻,巡查

patron /ˈpeɪtrən/ noun **1** a person who gives financial support to a person or organization 资助人;赞助者 **2** a regular customer of a restaurant, hotel, etc. (餐馆、酒店等的)常客 ❑ **patron saint** a saint who is believed to protect a particular place or group of people 主保圣人;守护神

patronage /ˈpætrənɪdʒ/ noun **1** support given by a patron 赞助;资助 **2** custom attracted by a restaurant, hotel, etc. (对餐馆、酒店等的)光顾,惠顾

patronize or **patronise** /ˈpætrənaɪz/ verb (patronizes, patronizing, patronized) **1** treat someone as if they lack experience or are not very intelligent 屈尊俯就地对待 **2** go regularly to a restaurant, hotel, etc. 经常光顾(餐馆、酒店等);是(餐馆、酒店等的)常客

patter¹ /ˈpætə(r)/ verb (patters, pattering, pattered) make a repeated light tapping sound 反复轻拍 • noun a repeated light tapping sound 反复轻拍声

patter² noun fast continuous talk 急口词;顺口溜

pattern /'pætn/ noun **1** a repeated decorative design 图案;花样 **2** a regular form or order in which a series of things happen 模式;形式 **3** a model, design, or set of instructions for making something 模型;样式;模式 **4** an example for other people to follow 模范;典范

patterned /'pætənd/ adjective decorated with a pattern 以图案装饰的

patty /'pæti/ noun (plural **patties**) a small pie or pasty 小馅饼

paucity /'pɔːsəti/ noun a very small or inadequate amount of something 少量;缺乏

paunch /pɔːntʃ/ noun an abdomen or stomach that is large and sticks out 大肚子;啤酒肚 ■ **paunchy** adjective.

pauper /'pɔːpə(r)/ noun a very poor person 穷人;贫民

pause /pɔːz/ verb (**pauses, pausing, paused**) stop talking or doing something for a short time before continuing again 暂停(谈话或做事);停顿 • noun a temporary stop 暂停;间歇

pave /peɪv/ verb (**paves, paving, paved**) cover a piece of ground with flat stones (以石板)铺,铺砌(地面) ■ **paving** noun.

pavement /'peɪvmənt/ noun Brit. 【英】a raised path for pedestrians at the side of a road 人行道

pavilion /pə'vɪliən/ noun **1** Brit. 【英】a building at a sports ground used for changing and taking refreshments (运动场边上的)运动员更衣室,休息室 **2** a summer house in a park or large garden (公园或大型花园中的)亭,凉亭,阁 **3** a temporary display stand at a trade exhibition (贸易博览会上的)临时展台

pavlova /pæv'ləʊvə, 'pævləʊvə/ noun a dessert consisting of a meringue base covered with whipped cream and fruit 奶油水果蛋白饼

paw /pɔː/ noun an animal's foot that has claws and pads (动物的)爪子 • verb **1** feel or scrape something with a paw or hoof (用爪或蹄)抓,扒 **2** informal 【非正式】touch someone in a way that is clumsy or unwanted (笨拙或令人厌恶地)摸,动手动脚

pawn[1] /pɔːn/ noun **1** a chess piece of the smallest size and value (国际象棋中的)兵,卒 **2** a person used by more powerful people for their own purposes 爪牙;走卒

pawn[2] verb leave an object with a pawnbroker in exchange for money 典当;抵押

pawnbroker /'pɔːnbrəʊkə(r)/ noun a person who is licensed to lend money in exchange for an object that is left with them, and which they can sell if the borrower fails to pay the money back 典当商;当铺老板

pawnshop /'pɔːnʃɒp/ noun a pawnbroker's shop 典当行;当铺

pawpaw /'pɔːpɔː/ noun Brit. 【英】a papaya 番木瓜

pay /peɪ/ verb (**pays, paying, paid**) **1** give someone money for work or goods 付钱;付酬 **2** give a sum of money that is owed 支付;偿还 **3** be profitable, or result in an advantage 值得;有利;有好处 **4** suffer something as a result of an action 吃苦头;付出代价 **5** give someone attention, respect, or a compliment 给予(注意或尊敬);致以(敬意或问候) **6** make a visit or a call to 进行(访问或拜访) • noun money that you get for work that you have done 报酬;薪水 ❑ **pay someone back** take revenge on someone 报复(某人) **pay-off** informal 【非正式】a payment made to someone as a bribe or so that they will not cause trouble 贿赂 ■ **payable** adjective.

PAYE /piː eɪ waɪ 'iː/ abbreviation pay as you earn, a system by which employers pay their employees' income tax directly to the government 所得税预扣(指从薪水中扣除所得税)

payee /peɪˈiː/ **noun** a person to whom money is paid 受款人；收款人

paymaster /ˈpeɪmɑːstə(r)/ **noun** an official who pays troops or workers (负责发薪饷的)军需官；工资出纳员

payment /ˈpeɪmənt/ **noun 1** the process of paying someone or of being paid 支付；付款 **2** an amount that is paid 支付款项

payola /peɪˈəʊlə/ **noun** N. Amer. 【北美】the illegal payment of money to someone in return for their promoting a product in the media (为在媒体上推销产品所付的)贿赂

payroll /ˈpeɪrəʊl/ **noun** a list of a company's employees and the amount of money they are to be paid 职员工资表；员工工资单

PC /ˌpiː ˈsiː/ **abbreviation 1** personal computer 个人计算机 **2** police constable 警员 **3** politically correct, or political correctness 政治上正确的；政治上正确

PDF /ˌpiː diː ˈef/ **noun** Computing 【计】a kind of electronic file which can be sent by any system and displayed on any computer 可移植文档格式文件；PDF文件

PE /ˌpiː ˈiː/ **abbreviation** physical education.

pea /piː/ **noun** an edible round green seed growing in pods on a climbing plant 豌豆(粒)

peace /piːs/ **noun 1** freedom from disturbance, noise, or anxiety 安静；安宁 **2** freedom from war, or the ending of war 和平

peaceable /ˈpiːsəbl/ **adjective 1** wanting to avoid war 爱好和平的 **2** free from conflict; peaceful 太平的；和平的 ■ **peaceably** adverb.

peaceful /ˈpiːsfl/ **adjective 1** free from disturbance or noise 安静的；安宁的 **2** not involving war or violence

和平的；和平方式的 **3** wanting to avoid conflict; peaceful 息事宁人的 ■ **peacefully** adverb.

peach /piːtʃ/ **noun 1** a round fruit with yellow and red skin and juicy yellow flesh, with a rough stone inside 桃；桃子 **2** a pinkish-orange colour 桃红色

peacock /ˈpiːkɒk/ **noun** a large, colourful bird with very long tail feathers that can be fanned out in display 孔雀；雄孔雀

peahen /ˈpiːhen/ **noun** the female of the peacock 雌孔雀

peak /piːk/ **noun 1** the pointed top of a mountain, or a mountain with a pointed top 山顶；山巅 **2** a stiff brim at the front of a cap 帽舌 **3** the point of highest strength, activity, or achievement (力量、活动或成就的)顶峰，顶点，巅峰 • **verb** reach a maximum or the highest point 达到最大值；达到顶点 • **adjective 1** greatest; maximum 最高的，最大程度的 **2** involving the greatest number of people; busiest 人数最多的；最繁忙的

peaked¹ /piːkt/ **adjective** (of a cap) having a peak (帽子)有帽舌的

peaked² or **peaky** /ˈpiːki/ **adjective** pale from illness or tiredness (因生病或疲劳)苍白的

peal /piːl/ **noun 1** the loud ringing sound of a bell or bells (响亮的)钟声 **2** a loud sound of thunder or laughter 隆隆雷声；响亮笑声 **3** a set of bells 一组钟；编钟 • **verb** ring or sound loudly 鸣响；隆隆响

peanut /ˈpiːnʌt/ **noun 1** an oval edible seed that develops in a pod underground 花生 **2** (**peanuts**) informal【非正式】a very small sum of money 数量极少的钱 □ **peanut butter** a spread made from ground roasted peanuts 花生酱

pear /peə(r)/ **noun** a green edible fruit which has a narrow top and rounded base 梨

pearl /pɜːl/ **noun 1** a small hard, shiny white ball that sometimes forms inside the shell of an oyster and has great value as a gem 珍珠 **2** a thing that is highly valued 宝贵的东西；珍品 □ **pearl barley** barley that is reduced to small round grains by grinding 珍珠大麦 ■ **pearly** adjective.

pearlescent /pɜːˈlesnt/ **adjective** seeming to shine with many soft colours, like mother-of-pearl 有珍珠般光泽的，珠母般闪亮的

peasant /ˈpeznt/ **noun** (in the past, or in poor countries) an agricultural worker (旧时或贫穷国家的)农民 ■ **peasantry** noun.

peat /piːt/ **noun** a soft brown or black substance formed in damp areas from decayed plants 泥煤；泥炭 ■ **peaty** adjective.

pebble /ˈpebl/ **noun** a small, smooth round stone 卵石；小圆石 □ **pebble-dash** mortar mixed with small pebbles, used to coat the outside of houses (涂抹房屋外墙的)小卵石灰浆，(涂)卵石涂层 ■ **pebbly** adjective.

pecan /piːˈkæn/ **noun** the smooth edible nut of a hickory tree of the southern US 美洲山核桃

peccadillo /ˌpekəˈdɪləʊ/ **noun** (plural **peccadilloes** or **peccadillos**) a small sin or fault 小过失；小错

peck¹ /pek/ **verb 1** (of a bird) hit or bite something with its beak (鸟) 啄，啄食 **2** kiss someone lightly or casually 轻轻地吻；漫不经心地吻 ● **noun 1** an act of pecking 啄 **2** a light or casual kiss 轻轻的一吻；漫不经心的一吻 □ **pecking order** the order of importance that people and animals give each other within a group (人或动物群体中的)长幼尊卑制度，权势等级

peck² **noun** a measure of dry goods, equal to a quarter of a bushel 配克(干量单位，等于1/4蒲式耳)

pecker /ˈpekə(r)/ **noun** (**keep your pecker up**) Brit. informal【英，非正式】 remain cheerful 保持乐观，振作精神

peckish /ˈpekɪʃ/ **adjective** informal【非正式】 hungry 饥饿的

pectin /ˈpektɪn/ **noun** a substance present in ripe fruits, used as a setting agent in jams and jellies 果胶

pectoral /ˈpektərəl/ **adjective** relating to the breast or chest 胸的，胸部的 ● **noun** each of four large paired muscles which cover the front of the ribcage 胸肌

peculiar /pɪˈkjuːliə(r)/ **adjective 1** strange or odd 古怪的，不寻常的 **2** (**peculiar to**) belonging only to 特有的，独具的 ■ **peculiarly** adverb.

✔ 拼写指南 -ar, not -er: peculiar.
peculiar 中 -ar 不要拼作 -er。

peculiarity /pɪˌkjuːliˈærəti/ **noun** (plural **peculiarities**) **1** a feature or habit that is strange or unusual, or that belongs only to a particular person, thing, or place 特性；特质 **2** the state of being peculiar 怪异；奇特

pecuniary /pɪˈkjuːniəri/ **adjective** formal【正式】 relating to money 与金钱有关的

pedagogue /ˈpedəgɒg/ **noun** formal【正式】 a teacher 教师 ■ **pedagogy** noun.

pedal /ˈpedl/ **noun 1** each of a pair of levers that you press with your foot to make a bicycle move along (自行车的)踏板，脚蹬子 **2** a lever that you press with your foot to operate an accelerator, brake, or clutch in a motor vehicle (机动车的)踏板 **3** a similar lever on a piano or organ used to sustain or soften the tone (钢琴或管风琴的)踏板，脚踏键 ● **verb** (**pedals, pedalling, pedalled**; US spelling【美拼作】**pedals, pedaling, pedaled**) work the pedals of a bicycle to move along 蹬(自行车)

！注意 don't confuse **pedal** with **peddle**, which means 'sell goods'. 不要混淆 pedal 和 peddle, 后者意为"兜售"。

pedalo /'pedələʊ/ **noun** (plural **pedalos** or **pedaloes**) Brit. 【英】 a small pedal-operated pleasure boat 脚踏小游船

pedant /'pednt/ **noun** a person who cares too much about small details or rules 过分注重细节的人；迂腐的人 ■ **pedantic** adjective **pedantry** noun.

peddle /'pedl/ **verb** (**peddles**, **peddling**, **peddled**) **1** sell goods by going from house to house (挨家挨户)叫卖, 兜售 **2** sell an illegal drug or stolen item 非法贩卖(毒品或赃物) **3** disapproving 【贬】 spread an idea or view widely or persistently 宣扬, 传播(思想)

！注意 don't confuse **peddle** with **pedal**. 不要混淆 peddle 和 pedal。

peddler /'pedlə(r)/ ⟹ 见 PEDLAR.

pederast /'pedəræst/ **noun** a man who has sexual intercourse with a boy 鸡奸者 ■ **pederasty** noun.

pedestal /'pedɪstl/ **noun 1** the base or support on which a statue or column is mounted (雕塑的)底座；柱脚 **2** the supporting column of a washbasin or toilet (洗脸盆的)支柱, (抽水马桶的)底座

pedestrian /pə'destriən/ **noun** a person who is walking rather than travelling in a vehicle 步行者；行人 • **adjective** dull 平淡的, 乏味的

pediatrics /ˌpiːdi'ætrɪks/ US spelling of PAEDIATRICS. paediatrics 的美式拼法

pedicure /'pedɪkjʊə(r)/ **noun** treatment to improve the appearance of the feet and toenails 足疗；修脚

pedigree /'pedɪgriː/ **noun 1** the record of an animal's origins, showing that all the animals from which it is descended are of the same breed (动物的)系谱 **2** a person's family history and background 血统；出身

pediment /'pedɪmənt/ **noun** the triangular upper part of the front of a classical building, above the columns (古典建筑前部上方的)山花饰, 三角檐饰

pedlar or **peddler** /'pedlə(r)/ **noun 1** a trader who sells goods by going from house to house 流动小贩, 货郎 **2** a person who sells illegal drugs or stolen goods 毒贩, (贩卖赃物的)不法商贩

pedometer /pe'dɒmɪtə(r)/ **noun** an instrument for estimating how far you are walking by recording the number of steps you take 计步器；步程器

peek /piːk/ **verb 1** look quickly or secretly 瞥；窥视 **2** be just visible 隐约可见 • **noun** a quick look 一瞥

peel /piːl/ **verb 1** remove the skin or rind from a fruit or vegetable 削…的皮；剥…的皮 **2** remove a thin covering or layer from 除去…的外皮 **3** (of a surface) come off in small pieces (表面)脱皮 • **noun** the outer covering or rind of a fruit or vegetable (水果或蔬菜的)外皮, 壳

peep[1] /piːp/ **verb 1** look quickly and secretly 瞥；窥视 **2** (**peep out**) be just visible 微露出；探出 • **noun 1** a quick or secret look 一瞥；窥视 **2** a momentary or partial view of something 短暂景象；隐约显现 □ **peeping Tom** a person who likes to spy on people undressing or having sex 窥视者汤姆；有窥裸癖者 **peep show** a series of pictures in a box which you look at through a small opening (通过小孔观看的)西洋景, 拉洋片

peep[2] **noun** a short, high-pitched sound 吱吱声；啾啾声 • **verb** make a short, high-pitched sound 发出吱吱声(或啾啾声)

peephole /'piːphəʊl/ **noun** a small hole in a door or wall which you can look through 窥视孔；猫眼

peer¹ /pɪə(r)/ **verb (peers, peering, peered) 1** look at something with difficulty or concentration 费劲地看；端详；凝视 **2** be just visible 隐现；微现

peer² noun **1** a member of the nobility in Britain or Ireland (英国或爱尔兰的)贵族 **2** a person who is the same age or has the same social status as you 同辈；同等地位者 □ **peer group** a group of people of approximately the same age, status, and interests 同辈群体(年龄、地位和兴趣爱好基本相同)

peerage /'pɪərɪdʒ/ noun **1** the title and rank of peer or peeress 贵族爵位 **2 (the peerage)** all the peers in Britain or Ireland (英国或爱尔兰的)贵族(统称)

peeress /'pɪəres/ noun **1** a woman holding the rank of a peer in her own right 女贵族 **2** the wife or widow of a peer 贵族夫人；贵族遗孀

peerless /'pɪələs/ adjective better than all others 无可匹敌的；杰出的

peeved /piːvd/ adjective informal 【非正式】 annoyed; irritated 恼怒的；生气的

peevish /'piːvɪʃ/ adjective irritable 脾气暴躁的；乖戾的

peewit /'piːwɪt/ noun Brit. 【英】 a lapwing 凤头麦鸡

peg /peg/ noun **1** a pin or bolt used for hanging things on, securing something in place, or marking a position 钉；栓；桩 **2** a clip for holding things together or hanging up clothes (晾衣服用的)衣夹 • verb (pegs, pegging, pegged) **1** fix, attach, or mark something with a peg or pegs 用钉(或栓、桩)固定(或标出) **2** fix a price, rate, etc. at a particular level 使(价格、汇率等)固定在特定水平 □ **off the peg** (of clothes) not made to order; ready-made (衣服)成品的，现成的

peignoir /'peɪnwɑː(r)/ noun a woman's light dressing gown or negligee 女式化妆衣；女式睡衣

pejorative /pɪ'dʒɒrətɪv/ adjective expressing contempt or disapproval 表示轻蔑的；贬损的 ■ **pejoratively** adverb.

Pekinese /ˌpiːkɪ'niːz/ noun (plural **Pekinese**) a small dog with long hair and a snub nose 北京狗；狮子狗

pelican /'pelɪkən/ noun a large waterbird with a bag of skin hanging from a long bill 鹈鹕；塘鹅 □ **pelican crossing** (in the UK) a pedestrian crossing with traffic lights that are operated by the pedestrians (英国的)自控人行横道

pellagra /pə'lægrə/ noun a disease caused by an inadequate diet, whose symptoms include inflamed skin and diarrhoea 糙皮病；陪拉格病

pellet /'pelɪt/ noun **1** a small compressed mass of a substance (压成的)小团，小丸 **2** a lightweight bullet or piece of small shot 小弹丸，轻型子弹

pell-mell /'pel'mel/ adjective & adverb in a confused or rushed way 混乱的(地)；忙乱的(地)

pellucid /pe'luːsɪd/ adjective translucent or transparent; clear 透明的；清澈的

pelmet /'pelmɪt/ noun a structure or strip of fabric fitted across the top of a window to conceal the curtain fittings (用来遮挡窗帘杆的)窗帘盒，布帷幔

pelt¹ /pelt/ verb **1** hurl missiles at 向…投掷 **2 (pelt down)** fall very heavily 倾盆而下；倾泻 □ **(at) full pelt** as fast as possible 尽快；全速

pelt² noun the skin of an animal with the fur, wool, or hair still on it (动物的)生皮，带毛兽皮

pelvis /'pelvɪs/ noun the large bony frame at the base of the spine to which the legs are attached 骨盆；盆腔 ■ **pelvic** adjective.

pen[1] /pen/ **noun** an instrument for writing or drawing with ink (使用墨水的)笔 • **verb** (**pens**, **penning**, **penned**) write or compose 写;写作 □ **pen name** a name used by a writer that is not his real name 笔名

pen[2] **noun** a small enclosure for farm animals (圈养家畜的)圈,栏 • **verb** (**pens**, **penning**, **penned**) **1** put or keep animals in a pen (将家畜)关在圈中;圈养(家畜) **2** (**pen someone/thing up or in**) shut a person or animal up in a small space 将…关入狭小空间中

penal /ˈpiːnl/ **adjective 1** relating to the use of punishment as part of the legal system 刑罚的;处罚的 **2** very severe 严重的;苛刻的

penalize or **penalise** /ˈpiːnəlaɪz/ **verb** (**penalizes**, **penalizing**, **penalized**) **1** give someone a penalty or punishment 对…处以刑罚 **2** put in an unfavourable position 使处于不利地位

penalty /ˈpenəlti/ **noun** (plural **penalties**) **1** a punishment given to someone for breaking a law, rule, or contract 处罚;刑罚 **2** something unpleasant suffered as a result of an action or circumstance 不利;弊端 **3** (also **penalty kick**) Soccer【足球】a free shot at the goal awarded to the attacking team after a foul within the area around the goal (the **penalty area**) 罚点球

penance /ˈpenəns/ **noun 1** something that you yourself do or that a priest gives you to do as punishment for having done wrong (表示赎罪的)苦行,自我惩罚 **2** a religious act in which someone confesses their sins to a priest and is given penance or formal forgiveness 忏悔;悔罪

pence /pens/ plural of PENNY.

！注意 it is wrong to use **pence** in the singular to mean 'penny'; say

one penny not *one pence*. 不能用单数形式的 pence 表示 penny,可以说 one penny,而不能说 one pence。

penchant /ˈpɒnʃɒn/ **noun** a strong liking for something 嗜好;偏爱

pencil /ˈpensl/ **noun** an instrument for writing or drawing, consisting of a thin stick of graphite enclosed in a wooden case 铅笔 • **verb** (**pencils**, **pencilling**, **pencilled**; US spelling 【美拼作】**pencils**, **penciling**, **penciled**) **1** write or draw something with a pencil 用铅笔写(或画) **2** (**pencil something in**) enter a time or date in your diary on the understanding that it might have to be changed later (在日记中)暂时记下(时间或日期)

pendant /ˈpendənt/ **noun 1** a piece of jewellery worn hanging from a chain around the neck (项链的)垂饰,挂件 **2** a light designed to hang from the ceiling 吊灯 • **adjective** (also **pendent**) hanging downwards 吊着的;下垂的

pending /ˈpendɪŋ/ **adjective 1** waiting to be decided or settled 未定的;待决的 **2** about to happen 即将发生的;迫近的 • **preposition** awaiting the outcome of 在等待…之际

pendulous /ˈpendjələs/ **adjective** hanging down; drooping 下垂的;松垂的

pendulum /ˈpendjələm/ **noun** a weight hung from a fixed point so that it can swing freely, used in regulating the mechanism of a clock 钟摆

penetrate /ˈpenɪtreɪt/ **verb** (**penetrates**, **penetrating**, **penetrated**) **1** force a way into or through (强力)进入,刺入,穿透 **2** gain access to an enemy organization or a competitor's market 打进,渗透进(敌对组织或竞争者市场) **3** understand something 洞察;看穿 **4** (**penetrating**) (of a sound) clearly heard through or above other sounds (声音)响亮的，尖锐的 **5** (of a man) insert the penis into the vagina or anus of a sexual partner (男子)把阴茎插入 ■ **penetration** noun **penetrative** adjective.

penfriend /'penfrend/ noun a person with whom you form a friendship through exchanging letters 笔友

penguin /'peŋgwɪn/ noun a black and white seabird living in the Antarctic and unable to fly 企鹅

penicillin /ˌpenɪ'sɪlɪn/ noun a type of antibiotic 青霉素；盘尼西林

peninsula /pə'nɪnsjələ(r)/ noun a long, narrow piece of land projecting into the sea 半岛 ■ **peninsular** adjective.

penis /'piːnɪs/ noun the male organ used for urinating and having sex 阴茎

penitent /'penɪtənt/ adjective feeling sorrow and regret for having done wrong 悔过的;忏悔的 • noun a person who is doing penance 悔过者;忏悔者 ■ **penitence** noun **penitential** adjective.

penitentiary /ˌpenɪ'tenʃəri/ noun (plural **penitentiaries**) N. Amer. 【北美】a prison for people convicted of serious crimes (关押重罪犯人的)监狱

penknife /'pennaɪf/ noun a small knife with a blade which folds into the handle 折叠小刀

pennant /'penənt/ noun a long, narrow pointed flag 三角旗

penne /'peneɪ/ plural noun pasta in the form of short wide tubes (短粗的)空心面

penniless /'peniləs/ adjective having no money 身无分文的;一贫如洗的

penny /'peni/ noun (plural **pennies** (for separate coins); **pence** (for a sum of money)) **1** a British bronze coin worth one hundredth of a pound 便士(英国铜币,价值百分之一英镑) **2** (in the past) a British coin worth one twelfth of a shilling and 240th of

a pound (英国旧时的)便士(价值十二分之一先令、二百四十分之一英镑) □ **penny-farthing** an early type of bicycle with a very large front wheel and a small rear wheel (早期)前轮大后轮小的自行车 **penny-pinching** unwilling to spend money 小气的;吝啬的

pension¹ /'penʃn/ noun a regular payment made to retired people, widows, etc., either by the state or from an investment fund 养老金;退休金;抚恤金 • verb (**pension someone off**) dismiss someone from employment and pay them a pension 使…退休 ■ **pensionable** adjective **pensioner** noun.

pension² /'pɒnsjɒn/ noun a small hotel in France and other European countries (法国及其他欧洲国家的)小旅馆

pensive /'pensɪv/ adjective thinking deeply about something 沉思的 ■ **pensively** adverb.

pentacle /'pentəkl/ noun a pentagram 五角形图案

pentagon /'pentəgən/ noun **1** a figure with five straight sides and five angles 五边形;五角形 **2** (**the Pentagon**) the headquarters of the US Department of Defense 五角大楼(美国国防部所在地)

pentagram /'pentəgræm/ noun a five-pointed star used as a magical symbol (象征魔力的)五角形符号

pentameter /pen'tæmɪtə(r)/ noun a line of poetry with five stressed syllables 五音步诗行

Pentateuch /'pentətjuːk/ noun the first five books of the Old Testament and Hebrew Scriptures 《摩西五经》(《圣经·旧约》和希伯来《圣经》的头五卷)

pentathlon /pen'tæθlən/ noun an athletic event consisting of five different activities 五项全能运动 ■ **pentathlete** noun.

Pentecost /'pentɪkɒst/ **noun 1** the Christian festival celebrating the coming of the Holy Spirit to the disciples of Jesus after his Ascension (基督教的)圣灵降临节 **2** a Jewish festival that takes place fifty days after the second day of Passover (犹太教的)五旬节(逾越节次日之后的第50日)

Pentecostal /pentɪ'kɒstl/ **adjective** having to do with a Christian movement which emphasizes the gifts of the Holy Spirit, e.g. the healing of the sick (基督教)五旬节派教会的(强调圣灵恩赐,比如治愈疾病)

penthouse /'penthaʊs/ **noun** a flat on the top floor of a tall building (高层建筑的)楼顶套房,顶层公寓

pent-up /'pent'ʌp/ **adjective** not expressed or released 不表现出来的;未释放的;压抑的

penultimate /pen'ʌltɪmət/ **adjective** last but one 倒数第二的

penumbra /pɪ'nʌmbrə/ **noun** the partially shaded outer part of a shadow 半阴影;半影

penurious /pə'njʊəriəs/ **adjective** formal 【正式】 very poor 极贫困的

penury /'penjəri/ **noun** extreme poverty 极度贫困

peony /'pi:əni/ **noun** a plant with large red, pink, or white flowers 牡丹;芍药

people /'pi:pl/ **plural noun 1** human beings in general (总称)人,人们 **2** (**the people**) all those living in a country or society 国民;民众 **3** (plural **peoples**) the members of a particular nation, community, or ethnic group 民族;种族 • **verb** (**peoples, peopling, peopled**) live in a place or fill it with people 住在(某地);使…住满人

pep /pep/ informal 【非正式】 **verb** (**peps, pepping, pepped**) (**pep someone/thing up**) make someone or something more lively 使更加充满活力 • **noun** liveliness 活力 □ **pep talk** a talk given to someone to make them feel braver or more enthusiastic 鼓舞士气的讲话

pepper /'pepə(r)/ **noun 1** a hot-tasting powder made from peppercorns, used to flavour food 胡椒粉 **2** the fruit of a tropical American plant, of which sweet peppers and chilli peppers are varieties 甜椒;辣椒 • **verb** (**peppers, peppering, peppered**) **1** season food with pepper 用胡椒粉调味 **2** (**pepper something with**) scatter large amounts of something over an area 在…上撒满;使布满 **3** hit a place repeatedly with small missiles or gunshot 密集射击 ■ **pepperiness** noun **peppery** adjective.

peppercorn /'pepəkɔ:n/ **noun** the dried berry of a climbing vine, used whole as a spice or crushed to make pepper 胡椒粒;干胡椒籽 □ **peppercorn rent** a very low rent 极少的租金;象征性的租金

peppermint /'pepəmɪnt/ **noun 1** a plant of the mint family whose leaves and oil are used as a flavouring in food 胡椒薄荷 **2** a sweet flavoured with peppermint oil 胡椒薄荷糖

pepperoni /pepə'rəʊni/ **noun** a dried sausage made from beef and pork and seasoned with pepper 意大利辣味香肠

peptic /'peptɪk/ **adjective** relating to digestion 消化性的 □ **peptic ulcer** an ulcer in the lining of the stomach or small intestine 消化性溃疡

per /pɜ:(r)/ **preposition 1** for each 每;每一 **2** by means of 通过;经;由 **3** (**as per**) according to 按照;根据

perambulate /pə'ræmbjuleɪt/ **verb** (**perambulates, perambulating, perambulated**) formal 【正式】 walk or travel from place to place 到处走;漫步;漫游 ■ **perambulation** noun.

perambulator /pə'ræmbjuleɪtə(r)/ **noun** dated 【废】 a pram 婴儿车

per annum /pər 'ænəm/ *adverb* for each year 每年

per capita /pə 'kæpɪtə/ *adverb & adjective* for each person 人均(的); 每人(的)

perceive /pə'siːv/ *verb* (**perceives, perceiving, perceived**) **1** become aware of something through starting to see, smell, or hear it 感知；察觉；意识到 **2** (**perceive something as**) understand or interpret something in a particular way 把…看作；认为 ▪ **perceivable** *adjective*.

✔ **拼写指南** remember, *i* before *e* except after *c*: perc*ei*ve. 记住 i 置于 e 前，在 c 后时除外，如 perceive。

per cent or US 【美】 **percent** /pə'sent/ *adverb* by a stated amount in or for every hundred 百分之…地；每一百中有…地 • *noun* one part in every hundred 百分之一

percentage /pə'sentɪdʒ/ *noun* **1** a rate, number, or amount in each hundred 百分比；百分率 **2** a proportion or share of a whole (全部中的)所占比例，部分

percentile /pə'sentaɪl/ *noun* Statistics 【统计】 each of 100 equal groups into which a population can be divided 百分位数；百分位数之一

perceptible /pə'septəbl/ *adjective* able to be noticed or felt 可感知的；可察觉的 ▪ **perceptibly** *adverb*.

perception /pə'sepʃn/ *noun* **1** the ability to see, hear, or become aware of something 感觉；知觉；察觉 **2** a particular understanding of something 认识；观念；看法 **3** the process of perceiving 知觉过程；感知过程

perceptive /pə'septɪv/ *adjective* having a good understanding of people and situations 有感知能力的；有洞察力的 ▪ **perceptively** *adverb*.

perceptual /pə'septʃuəl/ *adjective* relating to the ability to perceive 感觉的；知觉的

perch[1] /pɜːtʃ/ *noun* **1** a branch, bar, or ledge on which a bird rests or roosts (鸟的)栖枝，栖木 **2** a high or narrow seat or resting place (高处或狭窄的)座位，歇脚处 • *verb* **1** sit or rest somewhere 坐在；栖息在 **2** place or balance something somewhere 置于…上；使在…上保持平衡

perch[2] *noun* (plural **perch** or **perches**) a freshwater fish with a spiny fin on its back 鲈；河鲈

perchance /pə'tʃɑːns/ *adverb* old use 【旧】 perhaps 可能

percipient /pə'sɪpiənt/ *adjective* having good insight or understanding 有洞察力的；有认识能力的

percolate /'pɜːkəleɪt/ *verb* (**percolates, percolating, percolated**) **1** filter through a porous surface or substance 渗透；渗流；过滤 **2** (of information or ideas) spread gradually through a group of people (信息或想法)逐渐扩散 **3** prepare coffee in a percolator 用渗滤式咖啡壶滤煮(咖啡) ▪ **percolation** *noun*.

percolator /'pɜːkəleɪtə(r)/ *noun* a machine for making coffee, consisting of a pot in which boiling water is circulated through a small chamber that holds the ground beans 渗滤式咖啡壶

percussion /pə'kʌʃn/ *noun* musical instruments that you play by hitting or shaking them 打击乐器 ▪ **percussionist** *noun*.

perdition /pə'dɪʃn/ *noun* (in Christian thinking) a state of eternal damnation into which people who have sinned and not repented pass when they die (基督教信仰中的)永劫，恶报

peregrinations /ˌperəgrɪ'neɪʃnz/ *plural noun* old use 【旧】 journeys or wanderings from place to place 旅行；漫游

peregrine /'perɪgrɪn/ *noun* a powerful falcon with a bluish-grey back and wings 游隼

peremptory /pə'remptri/ **adjective** insisting on immediate attention or obedience 专横的；霸道的 ■ **peremptorily** adverb.

perennial /pə'reniəl/ **adjective** **1** lasting or doing something for a very long time 长久的；不断的 **2** (of a plant) living for several years (植物)多年生的 ■ **noun** a perennial plant 多年生植物 ■ **perennially** adverb.

perestroika /ˌperə'strɔɪkə/ **noun** (in the former Soviet Union) the economic and political reforms introduced during the 1980s (苏联在20世纪80年代进行的)经济政治改革，重建

perfect **adjective** /'pɜːfɪkt/ **1** having all the parts and qualities that are needed or wanted, and no flaws or weaknesses 完善的；完备的；理想的 **2** total; complete 十足的，完全的：*It made perfect sense.* 这非常合理。 **3** Grammar【语法】(of a verb) referring to a completed action or to a state in the past (动词)完成时的，完成体的 ■ **verb** /pə'fekt/ make something perfect 使完美；使完善 ■ **perfectly** adverb.

perfection /pə'fekʃn/ **noun** the process of perfecting, or the state of being perfect 完善；完备

perfectionism /pə'fekʃənɪzəm/ **noun** the refusal to be satisfied with something unless it is done perfectly 完美主义；求全思想 ■ **perfectionist** noun & adjective.

perfidious /pə'fɪdiəs/ **adjective** deceitful and disloyal 背信弃义的；不忠诚的

perfidy /'pɜːfədi/ **noun** literary【文】deceit; disloyalty 背信弃义；不忠诚

perforate /'pɜːfəreɪt/ **verb** (**perforates, perforating, perforated**) pierce and make a hole or holes in 在…上打孔(或穿孔) ■ **perforation** noun.

perforce /pə'fɔːs/ **adverb** formal【正式】necessarily; inevitably 必定；必然；无可避免地

perform /pə'fɔːm/ **verb** **1** carry out an action, task, or function 实施，执行；履行，完成 **2** work, function, or do something to a particular standard 运转；表现 **3** entertain an audience by playing a piece of music, acting in a play, etc. 表演；演出 ■ **performer** noun.

performance /pə'fɔːməns/ **noun** **1** an act of performing a play, piece of music, etc. 演出；演奏；表演 **2** the process of performing 实施，执行；履行 **3** informal【非正式】a fuss 大惊小怪；吵闹 **4** the capabilities of a machine or product (机器或产品的)性能 □ **performance art** an art form that combines visual art with drama 表演艺术；舞台艺术

perfume **noun** /'pɜːfjuːm/ **1** a sweet-smelling liquid put on the body 香水 **2** a pleasant smell 芳香；香味 ■ **verb** /pə'fjuːm/ (**perfumes, perfuming, perfumed**) **1** give a pleasant smell to 使带有香味 **2** put perfume on or in 喷洒香水于 ■ **perfumery** noun.

perfunctory /pə'fʌŋktəri/ **adjective** carried out without much care or effort 随便便便的，敷衍的；马虎的 ■ **perfunctorily** adverb.

pergola /'pɜːɡələ/ **noun** an arched structure forming a framework for climbing plants (藤本植物的)藤架，棚架

perhaps /pə'hæps/ **adverb** possibly；maybe 或许，可能

peril /'perəl/ **noun** a situation of serious and immediate danger (迫在眼前的)险境，险情

perilous /'perələs/ **adjective** full of danger or risk 充满危险的；多险的 ■ **perilously** adverb.

perimeter /pə'rɪmɪtə(r)/ **noun** the boundary or outside edge of something 周；周边；边缘

period /'pɪəriəd/ **noun** **1** a length or

P

portion of time 一段时间；时期 **2** a lesson in a school 学时；课时 **3** (also **menstrual period**) a flow of blood each month from the lining of a woman's womb 月经(期) **4** N. Amer. 【北美】 a full stop 句号 • **adjective** belonging to or characteristic of a past historical time 属于特定时期的，具有特定时期特点的 □ **period piece** an object made or a book or play set in an earlier period (具有特定历史时期特点的)古物，文物，古代作品，古装戏剧

periodic /ˌpɪəriˈɒdɪk/ **adjective** appearing or happening at intervals 周期的；周期性的；定期的 □ **periodic table** a table of all the chemical elements (元素)周期表

periodical /ˌpɪəriˈɒdɪkl/ **adjective 1** happening or appearing at intervals 周期的，周期性的，定期的 **2** (of a magazine or newspaper) published at regular intervals (杂志或报纸)定期出版的，定期发行的 • **noun** a periodical magazine or newspaper (定期出版或发行的)期刊，报纸 ■ **periodically** adverb.

peripatetic /ˌperipəˈtetɪk/ **adjective** travelling from place to place 到处走的；漫游的

peripheral /pəˈrɪfərəl/ **adjective 1** relating to or situated on an edge or boundary 外围的；边缘的 **2** outside the most important part of something; marginal 外围的；次要的 ■ **peripherally** adverb.

periphery /pəˈrɪfəri/ **noun** (plural **peripheries**) **1** the outside edge or boundary of something 外围，边缘 **2** an area of activity that is outside the most important part of something 边缘地带

periscope /ˈperiskəʊp/ **noun** a device consisting of a tube attached to a set of mirrors, through which you can see things that are above or behind something else 潜望镜

perish /ˈperɪʃ/ **verb 1** die 死亡 **2** be completely ruined or destroyed 毁灭；被摧毁 **3** (of rubber or a similar material) become weak or rot (橡胶或类似材料)老化，腐败 **4** (**be perished**) Brit. informal 【英，非正式】 feel very cold 感到冰冷 **5** (**perishing**) Brit. informal 【英，非正式】 very cold 极冷的；酷寒的

perishable /ˈperɪʃəbl/ **adjective** (of food) not able to be kept beyond a certain time because it will rot or decay (食物)易腐的，易坏的

peristalsis /ˌperiˈstælsɪs/ **noun** the contraction and relaxation of muscles in the digestive system and intestines, creating wave-like movements which push food through the body 蠕动

peritoneum /ˌperitəˈniəm/ **noun** (plural **peritoneums** or **peritonea** /ˌperitəˈniə/) a membrane lining the inside of the abdomen 腹膜 ■ **peritoneal** adjective.

peritonitis /ˌperitəˈnaɪtɪs/ **noun** inflammation of the peritoneum 腹膜炎

periwinkle /ˈperiwɪŋkl/ **noun 1** a plant with purple flowers and glossy leaves 长春花 **2** = WINKLE.

perjure /ˈpɜːdʒə(r)/ **verb** (**perjures, perjuring, perjured**) (**perjure yourself**) tell a lie in court after swearing to tell the truth 作伪证；发假誓

perjury /ˈpɜːdʒəri/ **noun** the offence of deliberately telling a lie in court after swearing to tell the truth 伪证罪；假誓罪

perk¹ /pɜːk/ **verb** (**perk up**) become more cheerful or lively 活跃起来；振作起来

perk² **noun** informal 【非正式】 an extra benefit given to an employee in addition to their wages (雇员的)补贴，津贴

perky /ˈpɜːki/ **adjective** (**perkier,**

perkiest) cheerful and lively 活跃的;生气勃勃的

perm /pɜːm/ **noun** (also **permanent wave**) a method of setting the hair in waves or curls and treating it with chemicals so that the style lasts for several months 烫发 • **verb** treat hair in such a way 烫(发)

permafrost /'pɜːməfrɒst/ **noun** a layer of soil beneath the surface that remains below freezing point throughout the year 永久冻土

permanent /'pɜːmənənt/ **adjective** lasting for a long time or forever 长久的;永久的 ■ **permanence** noun **permanently** adverb.

> ✔ 拼写指南 perman**ent**, not -*ant*. permanent 不要拼作 -ant。

permeable /'pɜːmiəbl/ **adjective** allowing liquids or gases to pass through 可渗透的;具渗透性的

permeate /'pɜːmieit/ **verb** (permeates, permeating, permeated) spread throughout 遍布;弥漫

permissible /pə'mɪsəbl/ **adjective** permitted 允许的

permission /pə'mɪʃn/ **noun** the act of allowing someone to do something 许可;准许

permissive /pə'mɪsɪv/ **adjective** allowing someone a lot of freedom of behaviour 宽容的;放任的 ■ **permissiveness** noun.

permit verb /pə'mɪt/ (permits, permitting, permitted) **1** say that someone is allowed to do something 许可;允许;同意 **2** make something possible 使成为可能 • **noun** /'pɜːmɪt/ an official document saying that someone is allowed to do something or go somewhere 许可证

permutation /ˌpɜːmju'teɪʃn/ **noun** each of several possible ways in which a number of things can be ordered or arranged 排列组合

pernicious /pə'nɪʃəs/ **adjective**

having a harmful effect 有害的;恶性的

pernickety /pə'nɪkəti/ **adjective** fussy 爱挑剔的;吹毛求疵的

peroration /ˌperə'reɪʃn/ **noun** the concluding part of a speech (演讲的)结束语,总结语

peroxide /pə'rɒksaɪd/ **noun** (also **hydrogen peroxide**) a chemical that is used as a bleach or disinfectant 过氧化物

perpendicular /ˌpɜːpən'dɪkjələ(r)/ **adjective** at an angle of 90° to the ground, or to another line or surface 垂直的;成直角的 • **noun** a perpendicular line 垂线

perpetrate /'pɜːpətreɪt/ **verb** (perpetrates, perpetrating, perpetrated) carry out a bad or illegal action 做(坏事);犯(罪) ■ **perpetration** noun **perpetrator** noun.

perpetual /pə'petʃuəl/ **adjective** **1** never ending or changing 永恒的;永久的 **2** so frequent as to seem continual 连续不断的;无休止的 ■ **perpetually** adverb.

perpetuate /pə'petʃueɪt/ **verb** (perpetuates, perpetuating, perpetuated) cause something to continue indefinitely 使持久,使长存 ■ **perpetuation** noun.

perpetuity /ˌpɜːpə'tjuːəti/ **noun** (plural **perpetuities**) the state of lasting forever 永恒;永久;长存

perplex /pə'pleks/ **verb** puzzle someone very much 使困惑;使茫然

perplexity /pə'pleksəti/ **noun** (plural **perplexities**) **1** the state of being puzzled 困惑;茫然 **2** a puzzling situation or thing 令人费解的情况(或事物)

perquisite /'pɜːkwɪzɪt/ **noun** formal 【正式】 a special right or privilege 特权;特殊待遇

per se /ˌpɜː 'seɪ/ **adverb** in itself 本身;自身

persecute /'pɜːsɪkjuːt/ **verb** (**persecutes, persecuting, persecuted**) **1** treat badly over a long period (长期)迫害，虐待 **2** harass 困扰；纠缠 ■ **persecution** noun **persecutor** noun.

persevere /ˌpɜːsɪ'vɪə(r)/ **verb** continue doing something in spite of difficulty or lack of success 坚持不懈，锲而不舍 ■ **perseverance** noun.

Persian /'pɜːʃn/ **noun 1** a person from Persia (now Iran) 波斯人 **2** the language of ancient Persia or modern Iran 波斯语 **3** a breed of cat with long hair 波斯猫 • **adjective** relating to Persia or Iran 波斯的；伊朗的

persimmon /pə'sɪmən/ **noun** a fruit that looks like a large tomato but is very sweet 柿子

persist /pə'sɪst/ **verb 1** continue doing something in spite of difficulty or opposition 坚持不懈；执意 **2** continue to exist 持续；存留

persistent /pə'sɪstənt/ **adjective 1** continuing to do something in spite of difficulty or opposition 坚持不懈的，执意的 **2** continuing or recurring over a long period 持续的，反复出现的 ■ **persistence** noun **persistently** adverb.

✔ 拼写指南 persist*ent*, not -*ant*. persistent 不要拼作 -ant.

person /'pɜːsn/ **noun** (plural **people** or **persons**) **1** an individual human being 人 **2** a person's body 身体 **3** Grammar【语法】a category used in classifying pronouns and verb forms according to whether they indicate the speaker (**first person**), the person spoken to (**second person**), or a third party (**third person**) 人称 □ **in person** physically present 亲自；本人

persona /pə'səʊnə/ **noun** (plural **personas** or **personae** /pɜː'səʊniː/) the part of a person's character that

is revealed to other people 表面形象；面具人格

personable /'pɜːsənəbl/ **adjective** having a pleasant appearance and manner 动人的；有风度的；讨人喜欢的

personage /'pɜːsənɪdʒ/ **noun** a person of importance or high status 要人；名人

personal /'pɜːsənl/ **adjective 1** having to do with or belonging to a particular person 个人的；私人的 **2** done by a particular person themselves, rather than someone acting for them 亲自的 **3** concerning a person's private rather than professional or public life 隐私的；私人的 **4** referring to someone's character or appearance in a way that is offensive 针对个人的；人身攻击的 **5** relating to a person's body 身体的 □ **personal pronoun** Grammar【语法】each of the pronouns that show person, gender, number, and case (such as *I, you, he, she*, etc.) 人称代词 **personal stereo** a small portable cassette or compact disc player, used with headphones 便携式磁带(或光盘)播放机；随身听 ■ **personally** adverb.

personality /ˌpɜːsə'næləti/ **noun** (plural **personalities**) **1** the qualities that form a person's character 个性；人格 **2** qualities that make someone interesting or popular 人格魅力 **3** a celebrity 名人

personalize or **personalise** /'pɜːsənəlaɪz/ **verb** (**personalizes, personalizing, personalized**) **1** design or produce something to meet someone's individual requirements 使(设计或产品)符合个人需求；使个性化 **2** cause an issue or argument to become concerned with personalities or feelings 使(论题或论点)针对个人

persona non grata /pəˌsəʊnə nɒn 'grɑːtə/ **noun** a person who is not welcome in a place 不受欢迎的人

personify /pə'sɒnɪfaɪ/ **verb (personifies, personifying, personified) 1** give human characteristics to something that is not human 把…拟人化；把…人格化 **2** be an example of a quality or characteristic 是…的化身；体现 ■ **personification** noun.

personnel /ˌpɜːsə'nel/ **plural noun** people employed in an organization 职员；员工

perspective /pə'spektɪv/ **noun 1** the art of representing things in a picture so that they seem to have height, width, depth, and relative distance 透视(画)法 **2** a way of seeing something 视角；观点 **3** understanding of how important things are in relation to others 洞察力

perspex /'pɜːspeks/ **noun** trademark 【商标】 a tough transparent plastic 珀斯佩有机玻璃

perspicacious /ˌpɜːspɪ'keɪʃəs/ **adjective** quickly gaining insight into things 睿智的；敏锐的；洞察力强的 ■ **perspicacity** noun.

perspicuous /pə'spɪkjuəs/ **adjective 1** clearly expressed and easily understood 表达得清楚的；易懂的 **2** (of a person) expressing things clearly (人)善于表达的，表述清楚的

perspiration /ˌpɜːspə'reɪʃn/ **noun 1** sweat 汗；汗水 **2** the process of sweating 流汗；出汗

perspire /pə'spaɪə(r)/ **verb (perspires, perspiring, perspired)** produce sweat through the pores of your skin 排汗；出汗

persuade /pə'sweɪd/ **verb (persuades, persuading, persuaded)** use reasoning or argument to make someone do or believe something 说服；劝服；使信服

persuasion /pə'sweɪʒn/ **noun 1** the process of persuading or of being persuaded 说服；劝说 **2** a belief or set of beliefs 信仰；信念

persuasive /pə'sweɪsɪv/ **adjective 1** good at persuading someone to do or believe something 雄辩的；善于说服别人的 **2** providing evidence or reasoning that makes you believe something 有说服力的；令人信服的 ■ **persuasively** adverb.

pert /pɜːt/ **adjective 1** attractively lively or cheeky 活泼的；无礼的；唐突的 **2** (of a bodily feature) attractively small and firm (身体部位)雅致的，小巧玲珑的

pertain /pə'teɪn/ **verb (pertain to)** be appropriate, related, or relevant to 适合；与…相关；涉及

pertinacious /ˌpɜːtɪ'neɪʃəs/ **adjective** formal 【正式】 persistent 坚持的；固执的 ■ **pertinacity** noun.

pertinent /'pɜːtɪnənt/ **adjective** relevant or appropriate 恰当的；有关的 ■ **pertinence** noun **pertinently** adverb.

perturb /pə'tɜːb/ **verb** make someone worried or anxious 使心绪不宁；使不安 ■ **perturbation** noun.

peruse /pə'ruːz/ **verb (peruses, perusing, perused)** formal 【正式】 read or examine thoroughly or carefully 仔细阅读；仔细观察 ■ **perusal** noun.

Peruvian /pə'ruːvɪən/ **noun** a person from Peru 秘鲁人 • **adjective** relating to Peru 秘鲁的

pervade /pə'veɪd/ **verb (pervades, pervading, pervaded)** spread or be present throughout 弥漫；渗透；遍及

pervasive /pə'veɪsɪv/ **adjective** spreading widely through something 到处弥漫的；充斥的；遍布的 ■ **pervasively** adverb **pervasiveness** noun.

perverse /pə'vɜːs/ **adjective 1** deliberately choosing to behave in a way that other people find unacceptable 故意作对的；任性的；执拗的 **2** contrary to what is accepted or expected 有悖常情的；不合人意的 ■ **perversely** adverb **perversity** noun.

perversion /pə'vɜːʃn/ **noun 1** the action of perverting 曲解 **2** abnormal or unacceptable sexual behaviour 性欲倒错;性欲反常;性变态

pervert verb /pə'vɜːt/ **1** change the form or meaning of something in a way that distorts it 歪曲;曲解 **2** make someone perverted 使误入歧途;使反常;使错乱 • noun /'pɜːvɜːt/ a person whose sexual behaviour is abnormal and unacceptable 性欲反常者;性变态者

perverted /pə'vɜːtɪd/ **adjective** sexually abnormal or unacceptable 性欲反常的,性变态的

pervious /'pɜːviəs/ **adjective** allowing water to pass through 可渗透的;能透过的

peseta /pə'seɪtə/ **noun** the former basic unit of money in Spain 比塞塔(西班牙以前的基本货币单位)

pesky /'peski/ **adjective** informal【非正式】annoying 恼人的,讨厌的

pessary /'pesəri/ **noun** (plural **pessaries**) a solid medical preparation designed to dissolve after being inserted into the vagina, used to treat infection or as a contraceptive 阴道栓(剂);子宫托

pessimism /'pesɪmɪzəm/ **noun** a tendency to expect the worst to happen 悲观;悲观情绪 ■ **pessimist** noun **pessimistic** adjective **pessimistically** adverb.

pest /pest/ **noun 1** a destructive insect or other animal that attacks plants, crops, or livestock (侵害植物、庄稼或牲畜的)害虫,害虫 **2** informal【非正式】an annoying person or thing 讨厌的人(或物)

pester /'pestə(r)/ **verb** (**pesters**, **pestering**, **pestered**) annoy someone with repeated questions or requests (不断提出问题或要求)纠缠;不断打扰

pesticide /'pestɪsaɪd/ **noun** a substance for destroying insects or other pests 杀虫剂

pestilence /'pestɪləns/ **noun** old use【旧】a disease that spreads widely and causes many deaths 瘟疫 ■ **pestilent** adjective.

pestilential /ˌpestɪ'lenʃl/ **adjective 1** old use【旧】relating to or causing a pestilence 瘟疫的,引起瘟疫的 **2** informal【非正式】annoying 讨厌的,烦人的

pestle /'pesl/ **noun** a small, heavy tool with a rounded end, used for grinding substances in a mortar (捣研用的)杵,捣槌,碾槌

pesto /'pestəʊ/ **noun** a sauce of crushed basil leaves, pine nuts, garlic, Parmesan cheese, and olive oil, served with pasta 香蒜沙司,香蒜酱(由碾碎的香草叶、松果、大蒜、帕尔马干酪和橄榄油制成,浇在意大利面食上)

pet /pet/ **noun 1** an animal or bird that you keep for pleasure 玩赏动物;宠物 **2** a person treated with special favour 得宠的人;宠儿 • **adjective** favourite 宠爱的,最珍爱的 • **verb** (**pets**, **petting**, **petted**) **1** stroke or pat an animal 抚摸,轻拍(动物) **2** caress someone sexually (两性间)爱抚,抚摸 □ **pet name** a name used to express fondness or familiarity 昵称;爱称

petal /'petl/ **noun** each of the segments forming the outer part of a flower 花瓣

peter /'piːtə(r)/ **verb** (**peters**, **petering**, **petered**) (**peter out**) gradually come to an end 逐渐消失

petite /pə'tiːt/ **adjective** (of a woman) small and dainty (女子)娇小的,小巧玲珑的

petit four /ˌpeti/ **noun** (plural **petits fours** /ˌpeti 'fɔː(r)z/) a very small fancy cake, biscuit, or sweet 花色小蛋糕(或小甜饼、小糖果)

petition /pə'tɪʃn/ **noun 1** an appeal or request, especially a written one signed by a large number of people and presented formally to someone in authority 请愿书 **2** Law【法律】an application to a court for a writ, legal action, etc. 上诉；申请；请求 • verb make or present a petition to 向…请愿；向…请求

petrel /'petrəl/ noun a seabird that flies far from land 海燕

Petri dish /'petri, 'pi:-/ noun a shallow transparent dish with a flat lid, used in laboratories 皮氏培养皿 (有扁平盖的透明浅盆，用于实验室中)

petrify /'petrɪfaɪ/ verb (petrifies, petrifying, petrified) **1** make someone so frightened that they cannot move 使吓呆，使惊呆 **2** change organic matter into stone 使(有机物)石化

petrochemical /ˌpetrəʊ'kemɪkl/ adjective relating to petroleum and natural gas 石油化学的；石油化学制品的 • noun a chemical obtained from petroleum and natural gas 石油化学制品

petrol /'petrəl/ noun Brit.【英】a liquid obtained by refining petroleum, used as fuel in motor vehicles 汽油 □ **petrol bomb** a simple firebomb consisting of a bottle containing petrol and a cloth wick 汽油弹；燃烧弹

petroleum /pə'trəʊliəm/ noun an oil that is refined to produce fuels including petrol, paraffin, and diesel oil 石油

petticoat /'petɪkəʊt/ noun a woman's light undergarment in the form of a skirt or dress (女子的)衬裙

pettifogging /'petɪfɒgɪŋ/ adjective petty; trivial 琐碎的，微不足道的

pettish /'petɪʃ/ adjective childishly sulky 任性的；易怒的 ■ **pettishly** adverb.

petty /'peti/ adjective (pettier, pettiest) **1** of little importance 不重要的；琐碎的 **2** too concerned with unimportant things 小心眼儿的；偏狭的 **3** minor 小的；下级的 □ **petty cash** a store of money that is available for spending on small items 小额现金；小额备用金 **petty officer** a rank of naval officer 海军军士 ■ **pettiness** noun.

petulant /'petjʊlənt/ adjective childishly sulky or bad-tempered 任性的；脾气坏的 ■ **petulance** noun **petulantly** adverb.

petunia /pə'tju:niə/ noun a plant with white, purple, or red funnel-shaped flowers 矮牵牛(花)

pew /pju:/ noun **1** a long wooden bench with a back, arranged with others in rows to provide seating in a church (教堂内带靠背的)长椅 **2** Brit. informal【英，非正式】a seat 座位

pewter /'pju:tə(r)/ noun a metal made by mixing tin with copper and antimony 白镴；锡镴

pfennig /'fenɪg/ noun a former unit of money in Germany, equal to one hundredth of a mark 芬尼(德国旧时货币单位，等于0.01马克)

PG /ˌpi: 'dʒi:/ abbreviation Brit.【英】(in film classification) parental guidance (电影分级)宜在家长指导下观看的

pH /ˌpi: 'eɪtʃ/ noun a figure expressing how acid or alkaline a substance is pH值；酸碱度

phalanx /'fælæŋks/ noun (plural **phalanxes**) a group of people standing or moving forward closely together 密集队形；方阵

phallic /'fælɪk/ adjective relating to or resembling a penis 阴茎的；阴茎形状的

phallus /'fæləs/ noun (plural **phalli** /'fælaɪ/ or **phalluses**) a penis 阴茎

phantasm /'fæntæzəm/ noun literary【文】a thing that exists only in the imagination 幻象；幻觉

phantasmagoria /ˌfæntæzmə'gɒrɪə/ noun a sequence of real or imaginary images like that seen in a dream 一连串梦幻般的情景

phantom /'fæntəm/ noun **1** a ghost

幽灵；鬼魂 **2** a thing that exists only in the imagination 幻象；幻觉 • **adjective** not really existing 虚幻的；幻觉的

pharaoh /ˈfeərəʊ/ **noun** a ruler in ancient Egypt 法老(古埃及的统治者)

> ✔ **拼写指南** remember, -aoh, not -oah: phar*aoh*. 记住 pharaoh 中 -aoh 不要拼作 -oah.

Pharisee /ˈfærɪsiː/ **noun** a member of an ancient Jewish sect who followed religious laws very strictly 法利赛人(严格遵守传统犹太法规的古犹太教法利赛派成员)

pharmaceutical /ˌfɑːməˈsjuːtɪkl/ **adjective** relating to medicinal drugs 药物的；药用的 • **noun** a medicinal drug 药物；药品

pharmacist /ˈfɑːməsɪst/ **noun** a person who is qualified to prepare and dispense medicinal drugs 药师；药剂师

pharmacology /ˌfɑːməˈkɒlədʒi/ **noun** the branch of medicine concerned with drugs 药理学；药物学 ■ **pharmacological** adjective **pharmacologist** noun.

pharmacy /ˈfɑːməsi/ **noun** (plural **pharmacies**) **1** a place where medicinal drugs are prepared or sold 药房；药店 **2** the science or practice of preparing and dispensing medicinal drugs 药学；配药学；配药

pharynx /ˈfærɪŋks/ **noun** (plural **pharynges** /fæˈrɪndʒiːz/) the cavity connecting the nose and mouth to the throat 咽

phase /feɪz/ **noun** a distinct period or stage in a process of change or development (变化或发展的)时期，阶段 • **verb** (**phases, phasing, phased**) **1** carry something out in gradual stages 分阶段进行；逐步实行 **2** (**phase something in** or **out**) gradually introduce or withdraw something 逐步采用(或淘汰)

PhD /ˌpiː eɪtʃ ˈdiː/ **abbreviation** Doctor of Philosophy (哲学)博士

pheasant /ˈfeznt/ **noun** a large long-tailed game bird 雉；野鸡

phenomenal /fəˈnɒmɪnl/ **adjective** remarkable or outstanding 非凡的；杰出的 ■ **phenomenally** adverb.

phenomenon /fəˈnɒmɪnən/ **noun** (plural **phenomena**) **1** a fact or situation that is known to exist or happen 现象 **2** a remarkable person or thing 杰出人才；奇观；奇迹

> **!** **注意** the word **phenomenon** comes from Greek, and its plural form is **phenomena**. Don't use **phenomena** as a singular form: say *this is a strange phenomenon*, not *this is a strange phenomena*. phenomenon 一词源自希腊语，其复数形式为 phenomena. 不要将 phenomena 用作单数形式，应说 this is a strange phenomenon (这是个奇怪的现象)，而不能说 this is a strange phenomena.

pheromone /ˈferəməʊn/ **noun** a chemical substance released by an animal and causing a response in others of its species (动物释放的)信息素，外激素

phial /ˈfaɪəl/ **noun** a small cylindrical glass bottle 小玻璃瓶

philander /fɪˈlændə(r)/ **verb** (**philanders, philandering, philandered**) (of a man) have many casual sexual relationships with women (男子)玩弄女性 ■ **philanderer** noun.

philanthropy /fɪˈlænθrəpi/ **noun** the practice of helping people in need 慈善；慈善事业 ■ **philanthropic** adjective **philanthropist** noun.

philately /fɪˈlætəli/ **noun** the hobby of collecting postage stamps 集邮 ■ **philatelist** noun.

philharmonic /ˌfɪlɑːˈmɒnɪk/ **adjective** devoted to music (used in the names of orchestras) 爱乐的(用于交响乐团名称中)

philippic /fɪ'lɪpɪk/ **noun** a verbal attack 言语抨击

Philistine /'fɪlɪstaɪn/ **noun 1** a member of a people of ancient Palestine who fought with the Israelites 非利士人(居住在古巴勒斯坦地区的民族, 曾与以色列人发生冲突) **2** (**philistine**) a person who is not interested in culture and the arts 对文化艺术不感兴趣的人; 庸俗之人; 市侩 ■ **philistinism** noun.

philology /fɪ'lɒlədʒi/ **noun** the study of the structure and development of language and the relationships between languages 语文学 ■ **philological** adjective **philologist** noun.

philosopher /fɪ'lɒsəfə(r)/ **noun 1** a person who is engaged in philosophy 哲学家 **2** a person who thinks deeply about things 哲人; 深思的人

philosophical /fɪlə'sɒfɪkl/ **adjective 1** relating to the study of philosophy 哲学的 **2** having a calm attitude when things are difficult (逆境中)处之泰然的, 豁达的 ■ **philosophically** adverb.

philosophize or **philosophise** /fɪ'lɒsəfaɪz/ **verb** (**philosophizes**, **philosophizing**, **philosophized**) talk about serious issues, especially in a boring way (尤指枯燥地)谈论(严肃问题), 理性谈论

philosophy /fɪ'lɒsəfi/ **noun** (plural **philosophies**) **1** the study of the fundamental nature of knowledge, reality, and existence 哲学 **2** a set or system of beliefs 观念体系; 思想体系

phlegm /flem/ **noun** mucus in the nose and throat 黏液; 痰

phlegmatic /fleg'mætɪk/ **adjective** calm and reasonable, and tending not to get upset 冷静的; 镇定的; 不易冲动的

phobia /'fəʊbiə/ **noun** a strong irrational fear of something (极端不合理的)恐惧, 憎恶 ■ **phobic** adjective.

phoenix /'fiːnɪks/ **noun** (in classical mythology) a bird that lived for hundreds of years before burning itself to death and being born again from its ashes (古典神话中的)不死鸟, 凤凰(在火焰中自焚而死, 又从灰烬中重生)

> ✔ 拼写指南 *-oe-*, not *-eo-*: phoenix. phoenix 中 -oe- 不要拼作 -eo-。

phone /fəʊn/ **noun** a telephone 电话 • **verb** (**phones, phoning, phoned**) make a telephone call to someone 打电话 □ **phone-in** a radio or television programme in which listeners or viewers participate over the telephone 电台(或电视)直播节目(听众或观众通过打电话参与)

phonecard /'fəʊnkɑːd/ **noun** a card which you can use instead of cash to make calls on a public telephone 电话卡

phonetic /fəʊ'netɪk/ **adjective 1** having to do with speech sounds 语音的 **2** (of a system of writing) using symbols that represent sounds (拼写系统)与发音一致的 • **noun** (**phonetics**) the study of speech sounds 语音学 ■ **phonetically** adverb.

phoney or **phony** /'fəʊni/ informal 【非正式】 **adjective** (**phonier, phoniest**) not genuine 虚假的; 伪造的 • **noun** (plural **phoneys** or **phonies**) a person or thing that is not genuine 冒充者; 赝品

phonic /'fɒnɪk, 'fəʊ-/ **adjective** relating to speech sounds 发声的, 语音的 • **noun** (**phonics**) a way of teaching people to read based on the sounds that letters represent (看字)读音法

phonograph /'fəʊnəgrɑːf/ **noun 1** Brit. 【英】an early form of record player that could record as well as reproduce sound (早期可录、放音的)蜡筒式留声机 **2** N. Amer. 【北美】a record player 留声机

phosphate /'fɒsfeɪt/ **noun** a salt or ester of phosphoric acid 磷酸盐; 磷

酯酯
phosphorescence /ˌfɒsfəˈresns/ **noun** a faint light that is given out by a substance with little or no heat 磷光 ■ **phosphorescent** adjective.

phosphorus /ˈfɒsfərəs/ **noun** a yellowish waxy solid which can ignite spontaneously and which glows in the dark 磷 ■ **phosphorous** adjective.

photo /ˈfəʊtəʊ/ **noun** (plural **photos**) a photograph 照片 □ **photo finish** a close finish of a race in which the winner can be identified only from a photograph of competitors crossing the line 摄影定名次(指参赛者到达终点时非常接近,需借照片判定获胜者)

photocall /ˈfəʊtəʊkɔːl/ **noun** Brit. 【英】 a prearranged occasion when famous people pose for photographers (名人)接受媒体拍照时间

photocopy /ˈfəʊtəʊkɒpɪ/ **noun** (plural **photocopies**) a photographic copy of something produced by a process involving the action of light on a specially prepared surface 复印件, 摄影复制品 • verb (**photocopies, photocopying, photocopied**) make a photocopy of 复印; 影印 ■ **photocopier** noun.

photoelectric /ˌfəʊtəʊɪˈlektrɪk/ **adjective** involving the production of electrons as a result of the action of light on a surface 光电(效应)的

photofit /ˈfəʊtəʊfɪt/ **noun** Brit. 【英】 a picture of a person made up from photographs of parts of other people's faces 拼describe像(以面部特征不同的多张照片拼成)

photogenic /ˌfəʊtəʊˈdʒenɪk/ **adjective** looking attractive in photographs 上相的; 上镜的

photograph /ˈfəʊtəɡrɑːf/ **noun** a picture made with a camera 照片; 相片 • verb take a photograph of 拍照; 拍摄 ■ **photographer** noun **photographic** adjective.

photography /fəˈtɒɡrəfɪ/ **noun** the taking and processing of photographs 摄影

photometer /fəʊˈtɒmɪtə(r)/ **noun** an instrument measuring the strength of light 测光仪; 曝光表

photon /ˈfəʊtɒn/ **noun** a particle representing a quantum of light or other electromagnetic radiation 光子; 光量子

photosensitive /ˌfəʊtəʊˈsensɪtɪv/ **adjective** responding to light 光敏的; 感光的

photostat /ˈfəʊtəʊstæt/ **noun** trademark 【商标】 **1** a type of machine for making photocopies on special paper (直接)复印机, 影印机 **2** a copy made by a photostat 直接复印件; 直接影印件 • verb (**photostats, photostatting, photostatted**) copy something with a photostat (用直接复印机或影印机)复印, 影印

photosynthesis /ˌfəʊtəʊˈsɪnθəsɪs/ **noun** the process by which green plants use sunlight to form nutrients from carbon dioxide and water 光合作用

phrase /freɪz/ **noun 1** a group of words forming a unit within a sentence 短语; 词组 **2** Music 【音乐】 a group of notes forming a unit within a longer passage 短句; 乐句 • verb (**phrases, phrasing, phrased**) put an idea into a particular form of words 用言语表达; 措词 □ **phrase book** a book listing and translating useful phrases in a foreign language 外语常用语对照手册 ■ **phrasal** adjective.

phraseology /ˌfreɪzɪˈɒlədʒɪ/ **noun** (plural **phraseologies**) a form of words used to express an idea 措词; 特殊用语; 术语

phrenology /frəˈnɒlədʒɪ/ **noun** (mainly in the past) the study of the shape and size of the skull in the belief that this can indicate

someone's character（主要指旧时的）颅相学

phylum /ˈfaɪləm/ **noun** (plural **phyla** /ˈfaɪlə/) a category used in the classification of animals（动物分类中的）门

physical /ˈfɪzɪkl/ **adjective 1** relating to the body rather than the mind 身体的;肉体的 **2** relating to things that you can see, hear, or feel 物质的;有形的 **3** involving bodily contact or activity 包含身体接触(或活动)的 **4** relating to physics and natural forces such as heat, light, sound, etc. 物理(学)的 • **noun** a medical examination to find out the state of someone's health 体检;体格检查 □ **physical education** instruction in physical exercise, sports, and games 体育;体育课 ■ **physicality** noun **physically** adverb.

physician /fɪˈzɪʃn/ **noun** a person qualified to practise medicine 医生

physics /ˈfɪzɪks/ **noun** the branch of science concerned with the nature and properties of matter and energy 物理学 ■ **physicist** noun.

physiognomy /ˌfɪzɪˈɒnəmi/ **noun** (plural **physiognomies**) a person's face or facial expression 面相;容貌

physiology /ˌfɪzɪˈɒlədʒi/ **noun** the scientific study of the way in which living things function 生理学 ■ **physiological** adjective **physiologist** noun.

physiotherapy /ˌfɪzɪəʊˈθerəpi/ **noun** Brit.【英】the treatment of disease and injury by massage and exercise 物理疗法;理疗 ■ **physiotherapist** noun.

physique /fɪˈziːk/ **noun** the shape and size of a person's body 体形;体格

pi /paɪ/ **noun** the numerical value of the ratio of the circumference of a circle to its diameter (approximately 3.14159) 圆周率(近似值为3.14159)

pianissimo /ˌpɪəˈnɪsɪməʊ/ **adverb & adjective** Music【音乐】very soft or

softly 非常轻柔地(的)

piano¹ /piˈænəʊ/ **noun** (plural **pianos**) a musical instrument which you play by pressing black or white keys on a large keyboard, the sound being produced by small hammers hitting metal strings 钢琴 ■ **pianist** noun.

piano² /ˈpjɑːnəʊ/ **adverb & adjective** Music【音乐】soft or softly 轻柔地(的)

pianoforte /piˌænəʊˈfɔːti/ formal【正式】a piano 钢琴

piazza /piˈætsə/ **noun** a public square or marketplace 公共广场;露天市场

picador /ˈpɪkədɔː(r)/ **noun** (in bullfighting) a person on horseback who goads the bull with a lance (斗牛运动中骑马斗牛的)长矛手

picaresque /ˌpɪkəˈresk/ **adjective** (of fiction) dealing with the adventures of a dishonest but appealing hero (小说)以不诚实但招人喜欢的主人公的冒险事迹为题材的

piccalilli /ˈpɪkəlɪli/ **noun** a pickle of chopped vegetables, mustard, and hot spices 辣泡菜

piccaninny /ˈpɪkəˈnɪni/ **noun** (plural **piccaninnies**) offensive【冒犯】a small black child 黑人小孩

piccolo /ˈpɪkələʊ/ **noun** (plural **piccolos**) a small flute sounding an octave higher than the ordinary flute 短笛

pick¹ /pɪk/ **verb 1** choose from a number of alternatives 挑选;选择 **2** (often **pick something up**) take hold of something and lift or move it 提起;拿起;捡起 **3** remove a flower or fruit from where it is growing 采、摘(花或水果) • **noun 1** an act of choosing something 挑选;选择 **2** (**the pick of**) the best person or thing in a particular group (一组里)最佳的人(或物);精华 □ **pick at 1** repeatedly pull at something with your fingers (用手指)反复拉扯 **2** eat food in small amounts 吃一点点;挑挑拣拣地吃 **pick a fight** provoke an argument or fight 寻衅吵架(或打架) **pick holes in** criticize 挑…的毛病;找…的茬儿 **pick a lock** open a lock with something other than the proper key 撬锁 **pick on** single someone out for unfair treatment 跟…找别扭,故意刁难 **pick someone's pockets** steal something from a person's pocket 扒窃(某人);掏(某人)的包儿 **pick up** improve or increase 改进;好转;增长 **pick someone/thing up 1** go to collect someone 接(某人) **2** informal 【非正式】 flirtatiously start talking to a stranger with the aim of having a sexual relationship with them 勾搭;搭讪;调情 **3** detect or receive a signal or sound 接收到(信号或声音) **4** obtain or learn something 得到;学会 ▪ **picker** noun.

pick² noun **1** (also **pickaxe**) a tool consisting of a curved iron bar with pointed ends and a wooden handle, used for breaking up hard ground or rock 镐;鹤嘴锄 **2** a plectrum (乐器的)拨子

picket /ˈpɪkɪt/ noun **1** a group of people standing outside a workplace and trying to persuade others not to work during a strike (罢工期间劝阻工人上班的)纠察队 **2** a pointed wooden stake driven into the ground (钉入地下的)尖木桩,尖板桩 ▪ verb (**pickets, picketing, picketed**) act as a picket outside a workplace 在…外担任纠察

pickings /ˈpɪkɪŋz/ plural noun **1** profits or gains 利润;收益 **2** scraps or leftovers 残余物;剩余物

pickle /ˈpɪkl/ noun **1** Brit. 【英】 a thick, spicy, cold sauce made from chopped vegetables and fruit 腌菜;泡菜 **2** a preserve of vegetables or fruit in vinegar or salt water 腌渍蔬菜(或水果) **3** (**a pickle**) informal 【非正式】 a difficult situation 困境 ▪ verb (**pickles, pickling, pickled**) preserve food in vinegar or salt water 腌制;腌渍

pickpocket /ˈpɪkpɒkɪt/ noun a person who steals from people's pockets 扒手;小偷

pickup /ˈpɪkʌp/ noun **1** a small truck with low sides 小卡车;敞篷小货车 **2** the part of a record player that holds the stylus (电唱机的)唱头,唱臂 **3** a device on an electric guitar which converts sound vibration into electrical signals for amplification (电吉他的)拾音器

picky /ˈpɪki/ adjective informal 【非正式】 fussy 吹毛求疵的,爱挑剔的

picnic /ˈpɪknɪk/ noun a meal that is eaten outdoors and away from home 野餐 ▪ verb (**picnics, picnicking, picnicked**) have a picnic 去野餐;参加野餐 ▪ **picnicker** noun.

Pict /pɪkt/ noun a member of an ancient people inhabiting northern Scotland in Roman times 皮克特人 (古罗马时代居住在苏格兰北部)

pictograph /ˈpɪktəɡrɑːf/ or **pictogram** /ˈpɪktəɡræm/ noun a small image or picture representing a word or phrase 图画文字

pictorial /pɪkˈtɔːriəl/ adjective having to do with or expressed in pictures 图画的;配有插图的;图示的

picture /ˈpɪktʃə(r)/ noun **1** a painting, drawing, or photograph 绘画;图画;照片 **2** an image on a television screen (电视屏幕上的)图像 **3** a cinema film 电影 **4** (**the pictures**) the cinema 电影院 **5** an image formed in the mind (头脑中的)形象 ▪ verb (**pictures, picturing, pictured**) **1** represent in a picture 绘画;拍摄 **2** form an image of something in your mind 想象;构想 ▫ **picture window** a large window consisting of a single pane of glass (由一整块玻璃构成的)观景窗

picturesque /ˌpɪktʃəˈresk/ adjective (of a place) very pleasant to look at (地方)景色如画的,优美的

pidgin /ˈpɪdʒɪn/ **noun** a simple form of a language with elements taken from local languages 混杂语；洋泾浜语

pie /paɪ/ **noun** a baked dish of meat, vegetables, fruit, etc. inside a pastry case 馅饼；派 □ **pie chart** a diagram in which a circle is divided into segments to show the size of particular amounts in relation to the whole 饼状图，圆形分析图(用圆的扇形面积表示数量)

piebald /ˈpaɪbɔːld/ **adjective** (of a horse) having irregular patches of two colours (马)杂色的，有斑纹的

piece /piːs/ **noun 1** a portion that is separated or seen separately from the whole (整体的)部分，碎片，碎块 **2** an item used in building something or forming part of a set (构成整体的)部分，部件；(成套物品的)一件 **3** a musical or written work (音乐作品或文字作品的)一篇，一部 **4** a token used to make moves in a board game 棋子 **5** a coin of a particular value (一定面值的)硬币 • **verb** (**pieces, piecing, pieced**) (**piece something together**) assemble something from individual parts 拼合(部件)

pièce de résistance /ˌpjes də reˈzɪstɒns/ **noun** the most important or impressive part of something 最重要特点，最引人注目之处

piecemeal /ˈpiːsmiːl/ **adjective & adverb** done in stages over a period of time 逐步的(地)；零散的(地)

piecework /ˈpiːswɜːk/ **noun** work that is paid for by the amount done and not the hours worked 计件工作

pied /paɪd/ **adjective** having two or more different colours 斑驳的；杂色的

pied-à-terre /ˌpjeɪdɑːˈteə(r)/ **noun** (plural **pieds-à-terre** /ˌpjeɪdɑːˈteə(r)/) a small flat or house kept for occasional use (备用)小公寓；临时住所

pier /pɪə(r)/ **noun 1** a structure leading out to sea or into a lake, used as a landing stage for boats 凸式码头；突堤码头 **2** a pillar supporting an arch or bridge 支柱；桥墩

pierce /pɪəs/ **verb** (**pierces, piercing, pierced**) **1** make a hole in something with a sharp object 刺破；穿牙；刺透 **2** force or cut a way through 穿透；突破 **3** (**piercing**) very sharp, cold, or high-pitched 锐利的；刺骨的；刺耳的

piety /ˈpaɪəti/ **noun** (plural **pieties**) the quality of being religious in a respectful and serious way 虔诚；虔敬

piffle /ˈpɪfl/ **noun** informal 【非正式】 nonsense 废话；胡说八道

pig /pɪɡ/ **noun 1** an animal with a short, curly tail and a flat snout 猪 **2** informal 【非正式】 a greedy, dirty, or unpleasant person 猪一样的人(指贪婪、肮脏或令人讨厌的人) • **verb** (**pigs, pigging, pigged**) informal 【非正式】 eat too much food 贪婪地吃，大吃 □ **pig-headed** stupidly stubborn 固执的；愚蠢的 **pig iron** iron when it is first taken out of a smelting furnace 生铁 ■ **piggish** adjective **piglet** noun.

pigeon /ˈpɪdʒɪn/ **noun** a plump grey and white bird with a cooing voice 鸽子 □ **pigeon-toed** having the toes and feet turned inwards 足内翻的；内八字的

> ✔ **拼写指南** note that there is no *d*: p*i*geon. 注意 pigeon 中没有 d。

pigeonhole /ˈpɪdʒɪnhəʊl/ **noun 1** a small hole in a wall leading into a place where pigeons nest 鸽巢 **2** each of a set of small compartments in a workplace, college, etc. where letters or messages may be left for individuals (信件等的)鸽笼式分类架；文件格 **3** a category in which someone or something is put 分类 • **verb**

(**pigeonholes**, **pigeonholing**, **pigeonholed**) put into a particular category 把…归类

piggery /ˈpɪɡəri/ **noun** (plural **piggeries**) a place where pigs are kept 养猪场，猪圈

piggy /ˈpɪɡi/ **noun** (plural **piggies**) a child's word for a pig or piglet (儿语)猪，小猪 ▪ **adjective** like a pig 像猪的；猪似的 □ **piggy bank** a money box shaped like a pig (猪形)储蓄罐，扑满

piggyback /ˈpɪɡibæk/ **noun** a ride on someone's back and shoulders 背驮；肩扛 ▪ **adverb** on the back and shoulders of another person 在背上，在肩上

pigment /ˈpɪɡmənt/ **noun 1** the substance that gives natural colouring to animal or plant tissue (动植物的)天然色素，色质 **2** a coloured powder mixed with a liquid to make paints, crayons, etc. 颜料；涂料 ▪ **pigmentation** **noun** **pigmented** adjective.

pigmy /ˈpɪɡmi/ ⇒ 见 **PYGMY**.

pigskin /ˈpɪɡskɪn/ **noun** leather made from the hide of a pig 猪皮革

pigsty /ˈpɪɡstaɪ/ **noun** (plural **pigsties**) **1** an enclosure for a pig or pigs 猪圈；猪栏 **2** a very dirty or untidy place 肮脏地方；邋遢地方

pigswill /ˈpɪɡswɪl/ **noun** kitchen refuse and scraps fed to pigs (喂猪的)泔水

pigtail /ˈpɪɡteɪl/ **noun** a length of hair worn in a plait at the back or on each side of the head 辫子；发辫

pike¹ /paɪk/ **noun** (plural **pike**) a freshwater fish with a long body and sharp teeth 狗鱼，梭鱼(一种淡水鱼，体长，有尖利牙齿)

pike² **noun** (in the past) a weapon with a pointed metal head on a long wooden shaft (旧时的)长矛，长枪

pikestaff /ˈpaɪkstɑːf/ **noun** (**as plain as a pikestaff**) very obvious 显而易见的；一清二楚的

pilaster /pɪˈlæstə(r)/ **noun** a column that projects from a wall 壁柱；半露柱

pilchard /ˈpɪltʃəd/ **noun** a small fish of the herring family 沙丁鱼

pile¹ /paɪl/ **noun 1** a heap of things lying one on top of another 一堆，一叠 **2** informal 【非正式】 a large amount 大量 **3** a large and impressive building 高大建筑物；大厦 ▪ **verb** (**piles**, **piling**, **piled**) **1** place things one on top of the other 把…堆积起来 **2** (**pile up**) form a pile or very large quantity 堆积；大量积聚 **3** (**pile into** or **out of**) get into or out of a vehicle in a disorganized way 拥进，挤出(车辆) □ **pile-up** a crash involving a lot of vehicles 多车相撞，连环撞车

pile² **noun** the soft surface of a carpet or a fabric, consisting of the cut ends of many small threads (地毯或织物的)绒面，绒头

pile³ **noun** a heavy post driven into the ground to support foundations 桩；地桩

piledriver /ˈpaɪldraɪvə(r)/ **noun** a machine for driving piles into the ground 打桩机

piles /paɪlz/ **plural noun** haemorrhoids 痔；痔疮

pilfer /ˈpɪlfə(r)/ **verb** (**pilfers**, **pilfering**, **pilfered**) steal small items of little value 偷；小偷小摸

pilgrim /ˈpɪlɡrɪm/ **noun** a person who travels to a sacred place for religious reasons 朝圣者；香客

pilgrimage /ˈpɪlɡrɪmɪdʒ/ **noun** a pilgrim's journey 朝圣(旅程)

pill /pɪl/ **noun 1** a small round mass of solid medicine for swallowing whole 药丸；药片 **2** (**the Pill**) a contraceptive pill 口服避孕药

pillage /ˈpɪlɪdʒ/ **verb** (**pillages**, **pillaging**, **pillaged**) steal from a place in a rough and violent way 掠夺；洗劫 ▪ **noun** the action of pillaging

掠夺 | 洗劫

pillar /'pɪlə(r)/ *noun* **1** a tall upright structure used as a support for a building (建筑物的)柱子，支柱 **2** a source of help and support 支柱，中坚 □ **from pillar to post** from one place to another without achieving anything 四处奔走但到处碰壁 **pillar box** (in the UK) a red cylindrical public postbox (英国的)邮筒

pillbox /'pɪlbɒks/ *noun* **1** a small round hat with a flat top and no brim 圆筒形小帽 **2** a small concrete fort 掩机，碉堡

pillion /'pɪliən/ *noun* a seat for a passenger behind a motorcyclist 摩托车后座

pillory /'pɪləri/ *noun* (plural **pillories**) (in the past) a wooden framework with holes for the head and hands, in which people were locked and left on display as a punishment (旧时的)颈手枷(将示众的犯人的头和手夹住) • *verb* (**pillories**, **pillorying**, **pilloried**) criticize or ridicule someone publicly 公开谴责；公开嘲笑

pillow /'pɪləʊ/ *noun* a soft pad used to support the head when you lie down in bed 枕头 □ **pillow talk** intimate conversation between a couple in bed 枕边私房话

pillowcase /'pɪləʊkeɪs/ *noun* a removable cloth cover for a pillow 枕套

pilot /'paɪlət/ *noun* **1** a person who flies an aircraft 飞行员，飞机驾驶员 **2** a person qualified to take charge of a ship entering or leaving a harbour (船舶的)领航员，引水员 **3** something done or produced as a test before being introduced more widely 小规模试验；试用品 • *verb* (**pilots**, **piloting**, **piloted**) **1** act as a pilot of an aircraft or ship 驾驶(飞机)；为(船舶)导航 **2** test a scheme, project, etc. before introducing it more widely 试

行，试验(计划、方案等) □ **pilot light** a small gas burner that is kept alight permanently, used to fire a boiler (用于引燃火炉的)长燃小火，引火火苗

pimento *or* **pimiento** /pɪ'mentəʊ/ *noun* (plural **pimentos**) a sweet red pepper 灯笼椒；甜椒

pimp /pɪmp/ *noun* a man who controls prostitutes and takes part of their earnings 皮条客；为妓女拉客的人 • *verb* act as a pimp 拉皮条

pimple /'pɪmpl/ *noun* a small inflamed lump on the skin 丘疹；小脓疱 ■ **pimply** *adjective.*

PIN /pɪn/ *or* **PIN number** *abbreviation* personal identification number 个人身份识别码

pin /pɪn/ *noun* **1** a very thin pointed piece of metal with a round head, used to hold pieces of fabric together or as a fastener 别针；大头针；扣钉；栓 **2** a metal projection from an electric plug (电器插头的)插脚 **3** a small brooch 胸针；饰针 **4** a steel rod used to join the ends of broken bones while they heal (治疗骨折时固定用的)钢钉 **5** a metal peg in a hand grenade that prevents it exploding (手榴弹的)保险栓，保险销 **6** a skittle in bowling (撞柱游戏的)木柱，球柱 **7** (**pins**) informal 【非正式】 legs 腿 • *verb* (**pins**, **pinning**, **pinned**) **1** attach or fasten with a pin or pins (用别针等)固定，别住 **2** hold someone firmly so they are unable to move 按住；使不能动 **3** (**pin someone down**) force someone to be specific about their plans 使明确说明；使确切表态 **4** (**pin someone down**) trap an enemy by firing at them (用火力)压制(敌人) **5** (**pin something on**) fix blame or responsibility on 归罪于 □ **pin money** a small sum of money for spending on everyday items 零花钱 **pins and needles** a tingling sensation in a part of the body that is recovering from numbness (四肢的)

麻痹感;针刺感 **pin-up** a poster of an attractive person (钉在墙上的)漂亮人物招贴画

pinafore /'pɪnəfɔː(r)/ **noun** a collarless, sleeveless dress worn over a blouse or jumper 无领无袖连衣裙

pinball /'pɪnbɔːl/ **noun** a game in which balls are shot across a sloping board and score points by hitting targets 弹球游戏(将小金属球沿斜板弹击目标得分)

pince-nez /'pæns'neɪ/ **noun** a pair of glasses kept in place with a nose clip instead of parts that rest on the ears 夹鼻眼镜

pincer /'pɪnsə(r)/ **noun 1** (**pincers**) a metal tool with blunt inward-curving jaws for gripping and pulling things 钳子;镊子 **2** a front claw of a lobster or similar shellfish (龙虾等甲壳类动物的)螯

pinch /pɪntʃ/ **verb 1** grip flesh tightly between your finger and thumb 捏;掐;拧 **2** (of a shoe) hurt a foot by being too tight (鞋)夹痛,挤痛 **3** informal 【非正式】 steal 偷 • **noun 1** an act of pinching 捏;掐;拧 **2** an amount of an ingredient that can be held between your fingers and thumb (配料的)一小撮 □ **feel the pinch** experience financial hardship 感到手头拮据

pinched /pɪntʃt/ **adjective** (of a person's face) tight with cold or suffering (某人的脸因寒冷或痛苦)收紧的,皱起的

pincushion /'pɪnkʊʃn/ **noun** a small pad into which you stick pins to store them (插缝纫针用的)针垫

pine¹ /paɪn/ **noun** an evergreen tree that produces cones and has clusters of long needle-shaped leaves 松树 □ **pine nut** the edible seed of various pines 松子;松仁 **pine marten** an animal resembling a weasel that lives in trees 松貂

pine² **verb** (**pines**, **pining**, **pined**) **1** become very sad or weak because you miss someone so much (因思念而)消瘦, 憔悴 **2** (**pine for**) miss or long for 苦苦思念;想念

pineapple /'paɪnæpl/ **noun** a large juicy tropical fruit consisting of yellow flesh surrounded by a tough skin 凤梨;菠萝

ping /pɪŋ/ **noun** a short high-pitched ringing sound 砰;乓 • **verb** make such a sound 发出砰的声响 □ **ping-pong** (also US trademark 【美,商标】 **Ping-Pong**) informal 【非正式】 table tennis 乒乓球

pinion¹ /'pɪnjən/ **verb** tie or hold someone's arms or legs so that they cannot move 抓住,绑住(胳膊或腿) • **noun** the outer part of a bird's wing (鸟的)翼尖,前翼

pinion² **noun** a small cogwheel or spindle that engages with a large cogwheel 小齿轮,副齿轮

pink¹ /pɪŋk/ **adjective** of a colour midway between red and white 粉红色的 • **noun** a pink colour 粉红色 □ **in the pink** informal 【非正式】 in the best condition 状况极佳

pink² **noun** a plant with sweet-smelling pink or white flowers 石竹(开粉色或白色花, 花香宜人)

pinking shears /'pɪŋkɪŋ/ **plural noun** scissors with a thick serrated blade, used for cutting a zigzag edge on fabric to prevent it fraying (用于剪织物的)锯齿剪刀

pinky or **pinkie** /'pɪŋki/ **noun** informal 【非正式】 the little finger 小手指

pinnacle /'pɪnəkl/ **noun 1** the most successful point 顶点,顶峰;鼎盛时期 **2** a high pointed piece of rock 尖岩;兀立岩石 **3** a small pointed turret on a roof (屋顶的)小尖塔,尖顶

pinpoint /'pɪnpɔɪnt/ **verb** locate or identify something precisely 为…准确定位 • **adjective** absolutely precise 精确的 • **noun** a tiny dot 小点

pinprick /ˈpɪnprɪk/ **noun** a very small dot or amount 极小的点；极少的数量

pinstripe /ˈpɪnstraɪp/ **noun** a very narrow white stripe woven into dark material (深色织物上的)细线条，细条纹 ■ **pinstriped** adjective.

pint /paɪnt/ **noun 1** a unit of liquid or dry capacity equal to one eighth of a gallon, in Britain equal to 0.568 litre 品脱(液量或干量单位，等于1/8加仑，英制合0.568升) **2** Brit. 【英】a pint of beer 一品脱啤酒 □ **pint-sized** informal 【非正式】very small 极小的

pinwheel /ˈpɪnwiːl/ **noun** chiefly N. Amer. 【主北美】a Catherine wheel firework 五彩转轮

pioneer /ˌpaɪəˈnɪə(r)/ **noun 1** a person who explores or settles in a new region 拓荒者 **2** a developer of new ideas or techniques 先驱；先锋；创始人 • **verb** (**pioneers, pioneering, pioneered**) be a pioneer of a new idea or technique 开拓；开创；倡导

pious /ˈpaɪəs/ **adjective 1** religious in a very respectful and serious way 虔诚的；笃信的 **2** pretending to be moral and good in order to impress other people 伪善的；貌似虔诚的 **3** (of a hope) very much wanted, but unlikely to be achieved (希望)迫切但不大可能实现的 ■ **piously** adverb.

pip /pɪp/ **noun 1** a small hard seed in a fruit (水果的)籽 **2** Brit. 【英】a short, high-pitched sound used as a signal on the radio or in a telephone (广播或电话中的)信号 □ **pip someone at (or to) the post** Brit. informal 【英，非正式】defeat someone by a small margin or at the last moment 以微弱优势击败(某人)，在最后时刻战胜(某人)

pipe /paɪp/ **noun 1** a tube through which water, gas, oil, etc. can flow (输送水、煤气、石油等的)管，管道 **2** a device for smoking tobacco, consisting of a narrow tube that

opens into a small bowl in which the tobacco is burned 烟斗；烟袋 **3** a wind instrument consisting of a single tube with holes along its length that you cover with your fingers to produce different notes 笛子；(单管)管乐器 **4** each of the tubes by which notes are produced in an organ (管风琴的)音管，簧管 **5** (**pipes**) bagpipes 风笛 • **verb** (**pipes, piping, piped**) **1** send a liquid through a pipe 用管道输送(液体) **2** transmit music, a programme, a signal, etc. by wire or cable (用有线系统)广播(音乐、节目等)，传送(信号) **3** play a tune on a pipe (用管乐器)吹奏 **4** sing or say something in a high voice 尖声唱；尖声说 **5** decorate something with piping (用花饰)装点 □ **piped music** pre-recorded background music played through loudspeakers (预先录制好通过扬声器播放的)背景音乐 **pipe dream** a hope or plan that is impossible to achieve 白日梦；空想 **pipe down** informal 【非正式】be less noisy 安静下来 **pipe up** informal 【非正式】say something suddenly 突然说

pipeline /ˈpaɪplaɪn/ **noun** a long pipe for carrying oil, gas, etc. over a distance (长距离输送石油、煤气等的)管道，管线 □ **in the pipeline** in the process of being developed 在规划中；在进行中

piper /ˈpaɪpə(r)/ **noun** a person who plays a pipe or bagpipes 管乐器吹奏者；风笛吹奏者

pipette /pɪˈpet/ **noun** a thin tube used in a laboratory for transferring small quantities of liquid (实验室用)移液管，吸管

piping /ˈpaɪpɪŋ/ **noun 1** lengths of pipe 管道；管线 **2** lines of icing or cream used to decorate cakes and desserts (装饰蛋糕和甜品的)糖霜花饰，奶油花饰 **3** thin cord covered in fabric and used for decorating a garment or piece of furniture (服装或家具的)装饰缘边 □ **piping hot** (of food or water) very hot (食物或水)滚烫的

pipistrelle /ˌpɪpɪˈstrel/ **noun** a small insecteating bat 伏翼(一种小型蝙蝠)

pipit /ˈpɪpɪt/ **noun** a bird that lives on the ground in open country 鹨(栖息于空旷野外)

pippin /ˈpɪpɪn/ **noun** a sweet red and yellow apple (黄红色的)点心苹果

pipsqueak /ˈpɪpskwiːk/ **noun** informal 【非正式】 an unimportant person 无足轻重者;小人物

piquant /ˈpiːkənt/ **adjective** having a pleasantly strong and sharp taste 辛辣的;开胃的 ■ **piquancy** noun **piquantly** adverb.

pique /piːk/ **noun** a feeling of irritation mixed with hurt pride (因自尊心受伤害产生的)愤慨,不悦 • **verb** (**piques, piquing, piqued**) **1** (**be piqued**) feel both irritated and hurt 感到受伤害;恼怒 **2** stimulate someone's interest 引起,激起(兴趣)

piracy /ˈpaɪrəsi/ **noun 1** the attacking and robbing of ships at sea 海盗行为;海上劫掠 **2** the reproduction of a film or recording without permission and so as to make a profit (对他人作品的)盗版,非法复制

piranha /pɪˈrɑːnə/ **noun** a freshwater fish with very sharp teeth 锯齿鲑(有尖利牙齿的淡水鱼)

pirate /ˈpaɪrət/ **noun** a person who attacks and robs ships at sea 海盗 • **adjective 1** (of a film or recording) having been reproduced and used for profit without permission (电影或音像制品)非法复制的,盗版的 **2** (of an organization) broadcasting without permission (组织)非法广播的 • **verb** (**pirates, pirating, pirated**) reproduce a film or recording for profit without permission 非法复制;盗版

pirouette /ˌpɪruˈet/ **noun** a movement in ballet involving spinning on one foot (芭蕾舞中的)单脚尖旋转,单足着地旋转 • **verb** (**pirouettes, pirouetting, pirouetted**) perform a pirouette 作单脚尖(或单足着地)旋转

piscatorial /ˌpɪskəˈtɔːriəl/ **adjective** having to do with fish 渔业的

Pisces /ˈpaɪsiːz/ **noun** a sign of the zodiac (the Fish or Fishes), 21 February-19 March 双鱼宫(黄道十二宫之一)

pistachio /pɪˈstæʃiəʊ, pɪˈstɑːʃiəʊ/ **noun** (plural **pistachios**) a small pale green nut 阿月浑子;开心果

piste /piːst/ **noun** a course or run for skiing 滑雪道

pistil /ˈpɪstɪl/ **noun** Botany 【植物】 the female organs of a flower (the stigma, style, and ovary) 雌蕊;雌蕊群

pistol /ˈpɪstl/ **noun** a small gun designed to be held in one hand 手枪

piston /ˈpɪstən/ **noun** a sliding disc or cylinder fitting closely inside a tube in which it moves up and down as part of an engine or pump 活塞

pit[1] /pɪt/ **noun 1** a large hole in the ground (地面的)坑,洞 **2** a mine for coal, chalk, etc. 矿井,煤矿;窑 **3** a hollow in a surface (表面的)凹痕,凹陷 **4** a sunken area in a workshop floor where people can work on the underside of vehicles (汽车修理厂的)检修坑 **5** an area at the side of a track where racing cars are serviced and refuelled (赛车道旁的)检修加油站 **6** a part of a theatre where the orchestra plays (剧院舞台前的)乐池 **7** (**the pits**) informal 【非正式】 a very bad place or situation 糟糕的地方(或局面) • **verb** (**pits, pitting, pitted**) **1** (**pit someone/thing against**) test someone or something in a contest with 使与…竞争;使和…较量 **2** make a hollow in the surface of something 使有洞;使凹陷 □ **pit bull terrier** a fierce breed of bull terrier 斗兽场斗牛㹴狗 **the pit of the**

stomach an area low down in the stomach 胸口；心窝

pit² **noun** chiefly N. Amer.【主北美】the stone of a fruit 水果核 • **verb** (**pits**, **pitting**, **pitted**) remove the stone from a fruit 除去(水果的)核

pitch¹ /pɪtʃ/ **noun** **1** Brit.【英】an area of ground used for outdoor team games 户外球场；运动场 **2** the degree of highness or lowness in a sound or tone 音高 **3** a particular level of intensity 强度；程度 **4** a form of words used when trying to sell something 推销的话；广告语：*a sales pitch* 推销行话 **5** Brit.【英】a place on a street where someone performing or selling something has settled (街头艺人的)表演地点；(街头商贩的)摊位 **6** the steepness of a roof (屋顶的)倾斜，斜度 • **verb** **1** throw heavily or roughly 扔；掷；重重跌倒 **2** set your voice, a sound, or a piece of music at a particular pitch 为…定音高；为…定调 **3** aim something at a particular level, target, or audience 针对；面向 **4** set up a tent or camp 搭(帐篷)；扎(营) **5** (**pitch in**) informal【非正式】join in enthusiastically with an activity 热情参与 **6** (**pitch up**) informal【非正式】arrive 到达 **7** (of a moving ship, aircraft, or vehicle) rock up and down (行驶中的船只、飞行器或车辆)颠簸 **8** (**pitched**) (of a roof) sloping (屋顶)倾斜的，有坡度的 □ **pitched battle** a battle in which the time and place are decided beforehand (时间和地点预先确定的)战斗，激战

pitch² **noun** a sticky black substance made from tar or turpentine and used for waterproofing 沥青 □ **pitch-black** (or **pitch-dark**) completely dark 漆黑的

pitcher /ˈpɪtʃə(r)/ **noun** a large jug 大水罐

pitchfork /ˈpɪtʃfɔːk/ **noun** a farm tool with a long handle and two sharp metal prongs, used for lifting hay 干草叉，草耙

piteous /ˈpɪtiəs/ **adjective** deserving or arousing pity 可怜的；惹人怜悯的 ■ **piteously** adverb.

pitfall /ˈpɪtfɔːl/ **noun** a hidden danger or difficulty 陷阱；隐患；意想不到的困难

pith /pɪθ/ **noun** **1** spongy white tissue lining the rind of citrus fruits (柑橘类水果外皮的)海绵层，中果皮 **2** spongy tissue in the stems of many plants (植物的)木髓；树心 **3** the most important part of something 精髓；核心 □ **pith helmet** a lightweight hat made from the dried pith of a plant, used for protection from the sun 木髓遮阳帽

pithead /ˈpɪthed/ **noun** the top of a mineshaft and the area around it 矿井口；矿井口周围地区

pithy /ˈpɪθi/ **adjective** (**pithier**, **pithiest**) (of language) concise and clear (语言)简洁的，言简意赅的

pitiable /ˈpɪtiəbl/ **adjective** **1** deserving or arousing pity 可怜的；惹人怜悯的 **2** deserving contempt 可鄙的；卑劣的

pitiful /ˈpɪtɪfl/ **adjective** **1** deserving or arousing pity 可怜的；惹人怜悯的 **2** very small or inadequate 卑微的；不足的 ■ **pitifully** adverb.

pitiless /ˈpɪtiləs/ **adjective** showing no pity 无怜悯心的；无情的

piton /ˈpiːtɒn/ **noun** (in rock climbing) a peg or spike driven into a crack to support a climber or hold a rope (攀岩用的)钢锥，岩钉

pitta /ˈpiːtə/ **noun** a type of flat bread which can be split open to hold a filling 填馅面包

pittance /ˈpɪtns/ **noun** a very small or inadequate amount of money 少得可怜的钱

pitter-patter /ˈpɪtəpætə(r)/ **noun** the sound of quick light steps or taps 噼噼啪啪，啪嗒(轻快的脚步声或轻拍

声)

pituitary gland /pɪˈtjuːɪtəri/ **noun** a gland at the base of the brain which controls growth and development 垂体腺；脑垂体

pity /ˈpɪti/ **noun** (plural **pities**) **1** a feeling of sympathy and sadness caused by the suffering of other people 怜悯；同情 **2** a cause for regret or disappointment 遗憾；可惜 • **verb** (**pities**, **pitying**, **pitied**) feel pity for 怜悯；同情

pivot /ˈpɪvət/ **noun** the central point, pin, or shaft on which a mechanism turns or is balanced 支点；枢轴 • **verb** (**pivots**, **pivoting**, **pivoted**) **1** turn on or as if on a pivot 在枢轴上转动 **2** (**pivot on**) depend on 依靠；依赖

pivotal /ˈpɪvətl/ **adjective** of central importance 关键的；中枢的

pixel /ˈpɪksl/ **noun** any of the tiny areas of light on a computer screen which make up an image (计算机显示屏上构成图像的)像素，像点

pixie or **pixy** /ˈpɪksi/ **noun** (plural **pixies**) an imaginary being portrayed as a tiny man with pointed ears 小妖怪；小精灵

pizza /ˈpiːtsə/ **noun** a flat, round base of dough baked with a topping of tomatoes, cheese, and other ingredients 比萨饼；意大利饼

pizzeria /ˌpiːtsəˈriːə/ **noun** a pizza restaurant 比萨饼店

pizzicato /ˌpɪtsɪˈkɑːtəʊ/ **adverb & adjective** plucking the strings of a stringed instrument such as a violin with your finger 拨奏地(的)；弹拨地(的)

placard /ˈplækɑːd/ **noun** a large written sign fixed to a wall or carried during a demonstration 布告；海报；标语牌

placate /pləˈkeɪt/ **verb** (**placates**, **placating**, **placated**) make someone less angry or upset 使消气；安抚
■ **placatory** adjective.

place /pleɪs/ **noun 1** a particular position or location 位置；地点；地方 **2** an opportunity to study on a course or be a member of a team (修读课程的)机会，名额；队员资格 **3** a position in a sequence 名次；次序 **4** (in place names) a square or short street (用于地名)广场，街 • **verb** (**places**, **placing**, **placed**) **1** put something in a particular position or situation 放置；使处于(某种境地) **2** find an appropriate place or role for 为…找到合适位置；安排；安插 **3** remember where you have seen someone before 认出；想起 **4** make a reservation or order 下(订单) □ **take place** happen 发生

placebo /pləˈsiːbəʊ/ **noun** (plural **placebos**) a medicine given to a patient to make them feel happier or more confident rather than for any physical effect 安慰剂(仅在精神上起安慰作用)

placement /ˈpleɪsmənt/ **noun 1** the action of placing 放置；安排 **2** a temporary job undertaken to gain work experience (用于获取工作经验的)临时性工作，实习职位

placenta /pləˈsentə/ **noun** (plural **placentae** /pləˈsentiː/ or **placentas**) an organ that is formed in the womb during pregnancy and which supplies blood and nourishment to the fetus through the umbilical cord 胎盘

placid /ˈplæsɪd/ **adjective** not easily upset or excited 温和的；平和的
■ **placidity** noun **placidly** adverb.

placket /ˈplækɪt/ **noun** an opening in a garment, covering fastenings or giving access to a pocket (衣服的)开襟，开口

plagiarize or **plagiarise** /ˈpleɪdʒəraɪz/ **verb** (**plagiarizes**, **plagiarizing**, **plagiarized**) copy another person's words or ideas and pretend that they are your own 剽窃；

抄袭 ■ **plagiarism** noun **plagiarist** noun.

plague /pleɪg/ noun **1** an infectious disease causing fever and delirium 瘟疫；鼠疫 **2** an unusually large number of insects or animals (大批昆虫或兽类,动物造成的)灾害 • verb (**plagues**, **plaguing**, **plagued**) **1** cause continual trouble to (不断地)折磨,困扰 **2** pester someone 纠缠；骚扰

plaice /pleɪs/ noun (plural **plaice**) a flat brown fish with orange spots, used for food 鲽(一种棕色比目鱼,带有橙色斑点,可食用)

plaid /plæd/ noun fabric woven in a chequered or tartan design 彩格呢；格子花呢

plain /pleɪn/ adjective **1** simple or ordinary 简单的;平常的 **2** without a pattern 素的;无花纹的 **3** unmarked 空白的 **4** easy to understand; clear 明白的;清楚的 **5** (of a woman or girl) not attractive (女子)不好看的,相貌平平的 • noun a large area of flat land with few trees 平原 □ **plain chocolate** Brit. 【英】 dark, slightly bitter chocolate made without added milk (不加牛奶的)黑巧克力,纯巧克力 **plain clothes** ordinary clothes rather than uniform 便装;便服 **plain sailing** smooth and easy progress 一帆风顺;进展顺利 ■ **plainly** adverb **plainness** noun.

plainsong /pleɪnsɒŋ/ or **plainchant** /pleɪntʃɑːnt/ noun a kind of medieval church music that was sung by a number of voices without any accompanying instruments 单旋律圣歌;素歌(中世纪一种无伴奏的齐唱教堂音乐)

plaintiff /pleɪntɪf/ noun a person who brings a case against someone in a court of law 起诉人;原告

plaintive /pleɪntɪv/ adjective sounding sad and mournful (听起来)悲伤的, 哀怨的 ■ **plaintively** adverb.

plait /plæt/ noun Brit. 【英】 a length of hair or rope made up of strands woven together (由多股编成的)发辫,辫绳 • verb form into a plait or plaits 把…编成辫(或辫绳)

plan /plæn/ noun **1** a detailed proposal for doing or achieving something 计划;规划;方案 **2** an intention 打算;意图 **3** a map or diagram 平面图;示意图;图解 **4** a scheme for making regular payments towards a pension, insurance policy, etc. (退休金、保险单等的)偿付方案 • verb (**plans**, **planning**, **planned**) **1** decide on and arrange something in advance 计划;策划 **2** intend to do something 打算做 **3** (**plan for**) make preparations for 筹划 **4** make a plan of a building, town, garden, etc. 设计 ■ **planner** noun.

plane[1] /pleɪn/ noun **1** a completely flat surface 平面 **2** a level of existence or thought (生活)水平;(思想)层面,境界 • adjective **1** completely flat 平的;平坦的 **2** relating to two-dimensional surfaces or sizes 平面的 • verb (**planes**, **planing**, **planed**) **1** (of a bird) soar without moving its wings (鸟)滑翔 **2** skim over the surface of water 在水面滑行;掠过水面

plane[2] noun an aeroplane 飞机

plane[3] or **planer** /pleɪnə(r)/ noun a tool used to smooth a wooden surface by cutting thin shavings from it 刨子;平刨 • verb (**planes**, **planing**, **planed**) smooth a surface with a plane 刨平;刨光

plane[4] noun a tall tree with broad leaves and peeling bark 悬铃木(一种高大树木,叶宽阔,树皮易剥落)

planet /plænɪt/ noun a large round mass in space that orbits a star 行星 ■ **planetary** adjective.

planetarium /plænɪteəriəm/ noun (plural **planetariums** or **planetaria** /plænɪteəriə/) a building in which images of stars, planets, and constellations are projected on to a domed ceiling 天文馆；天象馆

plangent /'plændʒənt/ **adjective** (of a sound) loud and melancholy (声音) 凄切的，哀鸣的

plank /plæŋk/ **noun** a long, flat piece of timber 长木板

plankton /'plæŋktən/ **noun** tiny creatures living in the sea or fresh water 浮游生物

plant /plɑ:nt/ **noun 1** a living thing that absorbs substances through its roots and makes nutrients in its leaves by photosynthesis 植物 **2** a place where a manufacturing process takes place 工厂；车间 **3** machinery used in a manufacturing process 机械设备 **4** a person placed in a group as a spy 卧底；内线 • **verb 1** place a seed, bulb, or plant in the ground so that it can grow 种植；栽种；播种 **2** place in a particular position 放置；安置 **3** secretly place a bomb 偷偷安放(炸弹) **4** hide something among someone's belongings to make them appear guilty of something 栽(赃) **5** send someone to join a group to act as a spy 安插(某人)做间谍 **6** fix an idea in someone's mind 灌输(想法)，使(观念)扎根 ■ **planter** noun.

Plantagenet /plæn'tædʒənət/ **noun** a member of the English royal house which ruled 1154-1485 金雀花王朝成员(1154-1485年统治英国)

plantain /'plæntɪn/ **noun 1** a type of banana eaten as a vegetable 大蕉 **2** a wild plant with small green flowers and broad leaves that spread out near the ground 车前草(开绿色小花，叶宽大，近地蔓生)

plantation /plɑ:n'teɪʃn/ **noun 1** a large estate on which crops such as coffee, sugar, and tobacco are grown 种植园，大农场 **2** an area in which trees have been planted 林地；人工林

plaque /plæk/ **noun 1** an ornamental tablet fixed to a wall in memory of a person or event (纪念性的)饰板，匾 **2** a sticky deposit that forms on teeth and in which bacteria grow quickly (牙齿上的)噬斑，蚀斑

plasma /'plæzmə/ **noun 1** the clear fluid part of blood in which blood cells are suspended 血浆；淋巴浆；乳清 **2** a gas of positive ions and free electrons with little or no overall electric charge 等离子体

plaster /'plɑ:stə(r)/ **noun 1** a soft mixture of lime with sand or cement and water for spreading on walls and ceilings to form a smooth, hard surface when dried (涂抹墙壁和天花板的)灰泥，灰浆 **2** (also **plaster of Paris**) a hard white substance made by adding water to powdered gypsum, used for setting broken bones and making sculptures and casts 熟石膏(用于固定断骨或制作雕塑品、石膏模型) **3** a sticky strip of material for covering cuts and wounds 膏药；创可贴 • **verb** (**plasters**, **plastering**, **plastered**) **1** apply plaster to 在…上涂灰泥；在…上敷石膏 **2** coat something thickly 厚厚涂抹，覆盖 **3** make hair lie flat by applying liquid to it (用液体)使(头发)平顺 **4** (**plastered**) informal 【非正式】drunk 烂醉的，■ **plasterer** noun.

plasterboard /'plɑ:stəbɔ:d/ **noun** board made of plaster set between two sheets of paper, used to line interior walls and ceilings 石膏灰泥板

plastic /'plæstɪk/ **noun** a chemically produced material that can be moulded into shape while soft and then set into a hard or slightly flexible form 塑料；塑胶 • **adjective 1** made of plastic 塑料的；塑胶的 **2** easily shaped or formed 可塑的；有塑性的 □ **plastic surgery** surgery performed to repair or reconstruct parts of the body 整形手术 ■ **plasticity** noun

plasticky adjective.

plasticine /'plæstəsiːn/ **noun** trademark 【商标】 a soft modelling material 橡皮泥

plate /pleɪt/ **noun 1** a flat dish for holding food 盘 **2** bowls, cups, and other utensils made of gold or silver 金制(或银制)器具 **3** a thin, flat piece of metal, plastic, etc. (金属,塑料等的)薄板材 **4** a small, flat piece of metal with writing on it, fixed to a wall or door (写有文字的)金属牌,门牌 **5** a printed photograph or illustration in a book (书中的)插图,照片 **6** each of the several rigid pieces which together make up the earth's surface (地壳)板块 • **verb** (**plates**, **plating**, **plated**) cover a metal object with a thin coating of a different metal (以另一种金属)覆镀 □ **plate glass** thick glass used for shop windows and doors (用于商店橱窗或门的)平板玻璃

plateau /'plætəʊ/ **noun** (plural **plateaux** /'plætəʊz/ or **plateaus**) **1** an area of fairly level high ground 高原 **2** a state of little or no change after a period of activity or progress 平稳时期,停滞状态 • **verb** (**plateaus**, **plateauing**, **plateaued**) reach a plateau 达到稳定水平,进入停滞状态

platelet /'pleɪtlət/ **noun** a disc-shaped cell fragment found in large numbers in blood and involved in clotting 血小板

platen /'plætn/ **noun** a cylindrical roller in a typewriter against which the paper is held (打字机上的)压纸卷筒

platform /'plætfɔːm/ **noun 1** a raised level surface on which people or things can stand 平台;高台 **2** a raised structure along the side of a railway track where passengers get on and off trains (火车站的)站台, 月台 **3** a raised structure standing in the sea from which oil or gas wells can be drilled (海上)钻井平台 **4** the stated policy of a political party or group (政党的)政纲,宣言 **5** an opportunity for the expression or exchange of views (表达或交流观点的)机会 **6** a very thick sole on a shoe 厚鞋跟;厚鞋底

platinum /'plætɪnəm/ **noun** a precious silvery-white metallic element (贵重金属元素)铂;白金

platitude /'plætɪtjuːd/ **noun** a remark that has been used too often to be interesting 老生常谈;陈词滥调 ■ **platitudinous** adjective.

platonic /plə'tɒnɪk/ **adjective 1** (of love or friendship) intimate and affectionate but not sexual (爱情或友谊)柏拉图式的, 纯精神而无肉欲的 **2** (**Platonic**) having to do with the ideas of Plato, a philosopher of ancient Greece 柏拉图的;柏拉图哲学的

platoon /plə'tuːn/ **noun** a subdivision of a company of soldiers (部队连队的)排

platter /'plætə(r)/ **noun** a large flat serving dish 大平盘;大浅盘

platypus /'plætɪpəs/ or **duck-billed platypus** /'dʌkbɪld plætɪpəs/ **noun** (plural **platypuses**) an animal with a duck-like bill and webbed feet, which lays eggs 鸭嘴兽

plaudits /'plɔːdɪts/ **plural noun** praise 赞扬;称赞

plausible /'plɔːzəbl/ **adjective 1** seeming reasonable or probable 貌似合理的;似乎可能的 **2** skilled at making people believe something 能言善辩的;花言巧语的 ■ **plausibility** noun **plausibly** adverb.

play /pleɪ/ **verb 1** take part in games for enjoyment 玩,玩耍 **2** take part in a sport or contest 参加(体育运动或比赛) **3** compete against another player or team 与(另一选手或队伍)比赛 **4** act the role of a character in a play or film 扮演(角色) **5** perform on a musical instrument 演奏(乐器) **6** perform a piece of music 演奏(乐曲) **7** make a CD, tape, or record produce sounds 播放(CD、磁带、唱片等) **8** move a piece or display a playing card when it is your turn in a game (游戏中)走动(棋子)、出(牌) **9** move or flicker over a surface 变幻;晃动;摇曳 ▪ noun **1** a piece of writing performed by actors 剧本;戏剧 **2** games that people take part in for enjoyment 游戏;玩耍 **3** the performing of a sports match 体育比赛 **4** a move in a sport or game (体育运动中)的动作,(游戏中的)一步 **5** freedom of movement 活动的自由(或空间) **6** constantly changing movement 变幻;晃动;摇曳 □ **make a play for** informal 【非正式】 attempt to attract or gain 挖空心思吸引;想方设法得到 **play along** pretend to cooperate with someone 假装合作 **play something by ear 1** perform music without having seen a score 不看乐谱演奏(乐曲) **2** (play it by ear) informal 【非正式】proceed without having formed a plan 见机行事;随机应变 **play something down** disguise the importance of something 贬低…的重要性;对…轻描淡写 **playing card** each of a set of rectangular pieces of card with numbers and symbols on one side, used in various games (一张)纸牌,扑克牌 **play-off** an extra match played to decide the outcome of a contest 加时赛;延长赛 **play on** take advantage of someone's weak point 利用(某人的弱点) **play up** Brit. informal【英,非正式】cause problems 制造麻烦

playboy /'pleɪbɔɪ/ noun a wealthy man who spends his time enjoying himself 花花公子

player /'pleɪə(r)/ noun **1** a person taking part in a sport or game 运动员;选手;游戏者 **2** a person who plays a musical instrument (乐器的)

演奏者 **3** a device for playing CDs, cassettes, etc. (CD、磁带等的)播放机 **4** a person who has influence in a particular area (某一领域)有影响力的人 **5** an actor 演员

playful /'pleɪfl/ adjective **1** fond of games and amusement 爱玩的;爱嬉戏的 **2** light-hearted 闹着玩的;不当真的 ▪ **playfully** adverb.

playground /'pleɪɡraʊnd/ noun an outdoor area provided for children to play in (室外的)儿童游乐场;操场

playgroup /'pleɪɡruːp/ or **play-school** /'pleɪskuːl/ noun Brit.【英】a regular supervised play session for preschool children (家长组织的)学龄前幼儿游戏组

playhouse /'pleɪhaʊs/ noun **1** a theatre 剧场;戏院 **2** a toy house for children to play in 儿童游戏室

playmate /'pleɪmeɪt/ noun a friend with whom a child plays (儿童的)玩伴

playpen /'pleɪpen/ noun a small portable enclosure in which a baby or small child can play safely 便携式游戏围栏(供婴幼儿在内玩耍)

plaything /'pleɪθɪŋ/ noun **1** a person who is treated as amusing but unimportant 被玩弄者;玩物 **2** a toy 玩具

playwright /'pleɪraɪt/ noun a person who writes plays 剧作家;编剧

plaza /'plɑːzə/ noun **1** an open public space in a built-up area 广场 **2** N. Amer.【北美】a shopping centre 购物中心

plc or **PLC** /ˌpiː el 'siː/ abbreviation Brit.【英】public limited company.

plea /pliː/ noun **1** a request made in an urgent and emotional way 恳求;请求 **2** a formal statement made by or on behalf of a person charged with an offence in a law court (法庭上被告的)申诉,抗辩

plead /pliːd/ verb (**pleads**, **pleading**, **pleaded** or US & dialect【美和方】**pled**) **1** make an emotional appeal

悬求；请求 **2** argue in support of something 为…争辩；极力主张 **3** state formally in court whether you are guilty or not guilty of the offence with which you are charged (法庭上)承认(或否认)有罪，申辩 **4** present something as an excuse for doing or not doing something 提出…为借口 ■ **pleadingly** adverb.

pleasant /'pleznt/ **adjective 1** satisfactory and enjoyable 合意的；令人愉快的 **2** friendly and likeable 友善的；讨人喜欢的 ■ **pleasantly** adverb.

pleasantry /'plezntri/ **noun** (plural **pleasantries**) **1** an unimportant remark made as part of a polite conversation (礼貌性交谈中的)客套，客气话 **2** a mildly amusing joke 打趣的话；小玩笑

please /pliːz/ **verb** (**pleases, pleasing, pleased**) **1** make someone feel happy and satisfied 使高兴；使满意；讨好 **2** wish or choose to do something 愿意；喜欢做 **3** (**please yourself**) consider only your own wishes 愿意怎样就怎样 • **adverb** used in polite requests or questions, or to accept an offer (用于礼貌的请求或问句中)请，好吗；(用于接受别人的好意)行，谢谢

pleased /pliːzd/ **adjective** feeling or showing pleasure and satisfaction 高兴的；满意的

pleasurable /'pleʒərəbl/ **adjective** enjoyable 令人愉快的；舒适的 ■ **pleasurably** adverb.

pleasure /'pleʒə(r)/ **noun 1** a feeling of happy satisfaction and enjoyment 愉快；满足 **2** an event or activity which you enjoy 令人愉快的事；乐趣 • **verb** (**pleasures, pleasuring, pleasured**) give pleasure to 给…快乐；使高兴

pleat /pliːt/ **noun** a fold in fabric, held by stitching at the top or side (布料的)褶 • **verb** fold or form into pleats 使打褶

pleb /pleb/ **noun** informal, disapproving 【非正式，贬】 a member of the lower

social classes 下层平民；百姓

plebeian /pləˈbiːən/ **adjective** ordinary or unsophisticated 平民的；粗俗的 • **noun** a member of the ordinary people or the lower classes 下层平民；百姓

plebiscite /'plebɪsɪt/ **noun** a vote made by everyone entitled to do so on an important public question 公民投票

plectrum /'plektrəm/ **noun** (plural **plectrums** or **plectra**) a thin flat piece of plastic used to pluck the strings of a guitar (吉他的)拨子，琴拨

pled /pled/ US or dialect past participle of PLEAD.

pledge /pledʒ/ **noun 1** a solemn promise or undertaking 誓言；诺言 **2** something valuable promised as a guarantee that a debt will be paid or a promise kept 抵押品；典押物 **3** a thing given as a token of love or loyalty (爱情或忠诚的)信物，象征物 • **verb** (**pledges, pledging, pledged**) **1** solemnly undertake to do or give something 保证；发誓 **2** promise something as a pledge 以…抵押

plenary /'pliːnəri/ **adjective 1** (of a meeting at a conference or assembly) to be attended by all participants (会议)全体出席的 **2** full; complete 完全的；充分的

plenipotentiary /ˌplenɪpəˈtenʃəri/ **noun** (plural **plenipotentiaries**) a person given full power by a government to act on its behalf (政府的)全权代表，全权大使 • **adjective** having full power to take independent action 有全权的

plenitude /'plenɪtjuːd/ **noun** formal【正式】 a large amount of something 丰富；充足

plenteous /'plentiəs/ **adjective** literary 【文】 plentiful 丰富的；充足的

plentiful /'plentɪfl/ **adjective** existing in or producing great quantities 丰富的；充足的 ■ **plentifully** adverb.

plenty /'plenti/ **pronoun** as much as is wanted or needed; quite enough 大量;充足 • **noun** a situation in which food and other necessities are available in large enough quantities (食物等必需品的)丰富,充裕

plenum /'pli:nəm/ **noun** an assembly of all the members of a group or committee 全体会议

plethora /'pleθərə/ **noun** an excessive amount or number of something 过多,过剩

pleurisy /'pluərəsi/ **noun** inflammation of the membranes around the lungs, causing pain during breathing 胸膜炎

plexus /'pleksəs/ **noun** (plural **plexus** or **plexuses**) a complex network or web-like structure (错综复杂的)网络,网状结构

pliable /'plaɪəbl/ **adjective 1** easily bent 易弯的;柔韧的 **2** easily influenced or persuaded 易受影响的,顺从的 ■ **pliability** noun.

pliant /'plaɪənt/ **adjective** pliable 易弯的;易受影响的

pliers /'plaɪəz/ **plural noun** pincers having jaws with flat surfaces, used for gripping small objects and bending or cutting wire 钳子;镊子

plight[1] /plaɪt/ **noun** a dangerous or difficult situation 危境;困境

plight[2] **verb** (plight your troth) old use 【旧】promise to marry 订婚

plimsoll /'plɪmsəl/ **noun** Brit. 【英】a light rubber-soled canvas sports shoe 胶底帆布运动鞋

plinth /plɪnθ/ **noun** a heavy block or slab supporting a statue or forming the base of a column (雕像的)底座;柱基

PLO /pi: el 'əʊ/ **abbreviation** Palestine Liberation Organization 巴勒斯坦解放组织

plod /plɒd/ **verb** (plods, plodding, plodded) **1** walk slowly with heavy steps 沉重缓慢地走 **2** work slowly and steadily at a dull task 埋头苦干 (无趣的工作) • **noun** a slow, heavy walk 沉重缓慢的行走

plonk[1] /plɒŋk/ **verb** informal 【非正式】put something down heavily or carelessly 重重放下;随意放下

plonk[2] **noun** Brit. informal【英,非正式】cheap wine 廉价酒

plop /plɒp/ **noun** a sound like that of a small, solid object dropping into water without a splash (落入水中的)扑通声 • **verb** (plops, plopping, plopped) fall or drop with a plop 扑通落下;吧嗒一声掉下

plot /plɒt/ **noun 1** a secret plan to do something illegal or harmful 阴谋,密谋 **2** the main sequence of events in a play, novel, or film (戏剧、小说或电影的)情节 **3** a small piece of ground marked out for building, gardening, etc. (建筑、园艺等用的)小块土地 • **verb** (plots, plotting, plotted) **1** secretly make plans to carry out something illegal or harmful 密谋;策划 **2** mark a route or position on a chart or graph (在图表上)标绘出(路线或位置) ■ **plotter** noun.

plough /plaʊ/ (US spelling【美拼作】**plow**) **noun 1** a piece of farming equipment with one or more blades fixed in a frame, used to turn over soil 犁 **2** (the Plough) a formation of seven stars shaped like a simple plough, in the constellation Ursa Major (the Great Bear) 北斗七星 • **verb 1** turn earth with a plough 犁(地);耕(地) **2** move forward with difficulty or force 奋力前行 **3** (of a ship or boat) travel through an area of water (船只)破浪前行 **4** (plough something in) invest money in a business 把(资金)投入;投资于

ploughman's lunch /'plaʊmənz/ **noun** Brit. 【英】a meal of bread, cheese, and pickle 简便午餐,农夫午餐(有面包、干酪和泡菜)

plover /'plʌvə(r)/ **noun** a wading bird

with a short bill 鹬(一种短喙涉禽)

ploy /plɔɪ/ *noun* a cunning act performed to gain an advantage (为获得利益使用的)计策,手段

pluck /plʌk/ *verb* **1** take hold of something and quickly remove it from its place 拔;摘;采 **2** pull out a hair or feather 拔除(头发或羽毛) **3** pull the feathers from a bird's carcass to prepare it for cooking 拔去(死禽的)羽毛(以备烹调) **4** pull at 用力拉 **5** sound a stringed instrument with your fingers or a plectrum 弹、拨(弦乐器) • *noun* courage 勇气 □ **pluck up courage** summon up enough courage to do something frightening 鼓起勇气

plucky /ˈplʌki/ *adjective* (**pluckier**, **pluckiest**) having a lot of courage and determination 有勇气的;有胆量的 ■ **pluckily** *adverb*.

plug /plʌg/ *noun* **1** a piece of solid material that tightly blocks a hole 塞子;栓 **2** a device with metal pins that fit into holes in a socket to make an electrical connection 插头;插塞 **3** an electrical socket 插座 **4** *informal* 【非正式】a piece of publicity promoting a product or event 推销广告;推销;捧场 • *verb* (**plugs**, **plugging**, **plugged**) **1** block a hole 塞住;堵 **2** (**plug something in**) connect an appliance to an electric circuit 给⋯接通电源 **3** *informal* 【非正式】promote a product or event by mentioning it publicly 大肆宣传;为⋯大做广告 **4** (**plug away**) *informal* 【非正式】proceed steadily with a task 坚持不懈地干;稳步进行

plughole /ˈplʌɡhəʊl/ *noun* Brit. 【英】a hole at the bottom or end of a sink or bath, through which the water drains away (水池或浴缸的)排水孔

plum /plʌm/ *noun* **1** an oval fruit which is purple, reddish, or yellow when ripe 李子;梅子 **2** a reddish-purple colour 紫红色 • *adjective*

informal 【非正式】highly desirable 很值得拥有的;令人垂涎的: *a plum job* 美差

plumage /ˈpluːmɪdʒ/ *noun* a bird's feathers 羽毛

plumb[1] /plʌm/ *verb* **1** explore or experience something fully 探究;经受 **2** measure the depth of water 测量(水深) **3** test an upright surface to find out if it is vertical 检测(竖直面)是否垂直 • *noun* a heavy object attached to a plumb line 测深锤;铅锤 • *adverb* *informal* 【非正式】exactly 恰恰;正 • *adjective* vertical 垂直的 □ **plumb line** a line with a heavy object attached to it, used for measuring the depth of water or checking that a wall, post, etc. is vertical 铅垂线;重力线

plumb[2] *verb* (**plumb something in**) install a bath, washing machine, etc. and connect it to water and drainage pipes 把(浴缸、洗衣机等)与水管连接

plumber /ˈplʌmə(r)/ *noun* a person who fits and repairs the pipes and fittings used in the supply of water and heating in a building 管子工;水暖工

plumbing /ˈplʌmɪŋ/ *noun* the system of pipes and fittings required for the water supply and heating in a building (建筑物的)管道设备,水暖设备

plume /pluːm/ *noun* **1** a long, soft feather or group of feathers (长而柔软的)羽毛,大羽 **2** a long spreading cloud of smoke or vapour 烟柱;羽状云 ■ **plumed** *adjective*.

plummet /ˈplʌmɪt/ *verb* (**plummets**, **plummeting**, **plummeted**) **1** fall straight down very quickly 快速落下;陡直坠落 **2** decrease rapidly in value or amount 暴跌;锐减 • *noun* a steep and rapid fall or drop 骤然跌落;陡直坠落

plummy /ˈplʌmi/ *adjective* (**plummier**, **plummiest**) Brit. *informal* 【英、

非 正 式 】(of a person's voice) typical of the English upper classes (噪音)典型英国上层阶级的

plump¹ /plʌmp/ **adjective 1** rather fat 丰满的;胖乎乎的 **2** full and rounded in shape 圆鼓鼓的 • *verb* (**plump something up**) make something more full and rounded 使变得圆鼓鼓

plump² *verb* **1** set or sit down heavily 重重放下;沉重地坐下 **2** (**plump for**) decide in favour of one of two or more possibilities 选定;选择

plunder /'plʌndə(r)/ *verb* (**plunders**, **plundering**, **plundered**) force your way into a place and steal everything of value 劫掠 • *noun* **1** goods obtained by plundering 劫掠物;赃物 **2** the action of plundering 劫掠;抢劫

plunge /plʌndʒ/ *verb* (**plunges**, **plunging**, **plunged**) **1** fall or move suddenly and uncontrollably 骤然跌落(或移动) **2** jump or dive quickly 猛地一跃;纵身跳入 **3** push or thrust something quickly 猛推;猛力插入 **4** (**plunge in**) begin a course of action without thought or care 贸然行动 **5** (**be plunged into**) be suddenly brought into a particular state 突然陷入;一跃;贸然开始 □ **take the plunge** *informal* 【非正式】finally decide to do something difficult or challenging 最终决定冒险一试

plunger /'plʌndʒə(r)/ *noun* **1** a part of a device that works with a plunging or thrusting movement 柱塞;活塞 **2** a rubber cup on a long handle, used to clear blocked pipes by means of suction (疏通堵塞管道的)手压皮碗泵

pluperfect /,plu:'pɜːfɪkt/ *adjective* Grammar 【语法】(of a tense) referring to an action completed earlier than some past point of time, formed by *had* and the past participle (as in *he had gone by then*) (时态)过去完成时

的

plural /'plʊərəl/ *adjective* **1** more than one in number 多于一的;多数的 **2** Grammar 【语法】(of a word or form) referring to more than one (单词或形式)复数的 • *noun* Grammar 【语法】a plural word or form 复数单词;复数形式

pluralism /'plʊərəlɪzəm/ *noun* **1** a system in which power is shared among a number of political parties 多元政治 **2** the acceptance within a society of a number of groups with different beliefs or ethnic backgrounds 多元化;多元性 ■ **pluralist** *noun & adjective.*

plurality /plʊə'ræləti/ *noun* (plural **pluralities**) **1** the fact or state of being plural 复数;多数 **2** a large number of people or things (人或物的)大量,众多

plus /plʌs/ *preposition* **1** with the addition of 加…上 **2** together with; as well as 和,加上 • *adjective* **1** (after a number or amount) at least (用于数量后)至少,多于…的 **2** (after a grade) rather better than (用于等级后)好于…的,高于…的 **3** (before a number) above zero (用于数字前)大于零的,在零以上的 **4** having a positive electric charge (电极)正极的,阳性的 • *noun* **1** (also **plus sign**) the symbol +, indicating addition or a positive value 加号,正号(+) **2** *informal* 【非正式】an advantage 好处;有利因素 • *conjunction informal* 【非正式】also 也;并且 □ **plus fours** men's trousers that are cut wide over the thigh and are gathered in at mid-calf length 灯笼裤,宽大运动裤

plush /plʌʃ/ *noun* a fabric with a thick, velvety surface 长毛绒 • *adjective informal* 【非正式】luxurious 奢华的,豪华的

Pluto /'plu:təʊ/ *noun* a dwarf planet, once considered a planet 冥王星(一颗矮行星,曾被认为是行星)

plutocracy /pluːˈtɒkrəsi/ **noun** (plural **plutocracies**) **1** government by the richest people in a country 富豪统治; 财阀统治 **2** a society governed by the richest people in it 富豪(或财阀)统治的社会

plutocrat /ˈpluːtəkræt/ **noun** a person who is powerful because of their wealth 财阀; 有钱有势者

plutonium /pluːˈtəʊniəm/ **noun** a radioactive metallic element used as a fuel in nuclear reactors and as an explosive in atomic weapons (放射性金属元素)钚

ply[1] /plaɪ/ **noun** (plural **plies**) a thickness or layer of a material (材料的)厚度, 一层

ply[2] **verb** (**plies**, **plying**, **plied**) **1** (**ply someone with**) keep presenting someone with food or drink, or asking them questions 不断供应(食物或饮料); 不断问(问题) **2** (of a ship or vehicle) travel regularly over a route (船或车辆)定期往返于 **3** work steadily with a tool (用工具不停地)从事, 做 □ **ply your trade** do your job or business 做事; 做生意

plywood /ˈplaɪwʊd/ **noun** board consisting of layers of wood glued together 胶合板

PM /ˌpiː ˈem/ **abbreviation** Prime Minister.

p.m. **abbreviation** after noon 下午 [short for Latin 【缩写, 拉丁】 = *post meridiem*.]

pneumatic /njuːˈmætɪk/ **adjective** containing or operated by air or gas under pressure 充气的; 压缩空气推动的; 风动的

pneumonia /njuːˈməʊniə/ **noun** an infection causing inflammation in the lungs 肺炎

poach[1] /pəʊtʃ/ **verb** cook something by simmering it in a small amount of liquid (用少量水)煮, 炖, 煨

poach[2] **verb** **1** hunt game or catch fish illegally from private or protected areas 偷猎; 偷捕(鱼) **2** unfairly entice customers, workers, etc. away from someone else 挖走(顾客、员工等) ■ **poacher** noun.

pocked /ˈpɒkt/ **adjective** having pockmarks 有痘痕的; 有凹坑的

pocket /ˈpɒkɪt/ **noun** **1** a small bag sewn into or on clothing, used for carrying small articles 衣袋; 口袋; 兜 **2** a small area or group that is different from its surroundings (不同于周围事物的)小片区域, 小群体 **3** informal 【非正式】 the money that you have available 钱; 财力: *gifts to suit every pocket* 适合每个人经济能力的礼物 **4** an opening at the corner or on the side of a billiard table into which balls are struck (台球桌边的)球穴, 球袋 • **verb** (**pockets, pocketing, pocketed**) **1** put something into your pocket 把… 放入口袋 **2** take something that is not yours 把…据为己有; 窃取 □ **pocket money 1** a small amount of money given to children regularly by their parents (父母给孩子的)零花钱 **2** a small amount of money for minor expenses 零用钱

pockmark /ˈpɒkmɑːk/ **noun 1** a hollow scar or mark on the skin left by a spot 痘瘢; 麻子 **2** a mark or hollow area on a surface (表面的)凹痕, 凹坑 ■ **pockmarked** adjective.

pod[1] /pɒd/ **noun** a long seed case of a pea, bean, etc. 荚; 豆荚 • **verb** (**pods, podding, podded**) remove peas or beans from their pods before cooking 把(豆)剥出荚壳; 剥(豆)

pod[2] **noun** a small herd of whales or similar sea mammals (鲸等的)一小群

podgy /ˈpɒdʒi/ **adjective** (**podgier, podgiest**) Brit. informal 【英, 非正式】 rather fat 胖乎乎的

podium /ˈpəʊdiəm/ **noun** (plural **podiums** or **podia** /ˈpəʊdiə/) a small platform on which a person stands to conduct an orchestra or give a speech 乐队指挥台；讲台

poem /'pəʊɪm/ **noun** a piece of imaginative writing in verse 诗；韵文

poesy /'pəʊzi/ **noun** old use 【旧】 poetry 诗歌

poet /'pəʊɪt/ **noun** a person who writes poems 诗人 □ **Poet Laureate** (plural **Poets Laureate**) a poet appointed by the British king or queen, formerly responsible for writing poems for important occasions 桂冠诗人(由英国君主选定)

poetic /pəʊ'etɪk/ or **poetical** / pəʊ'etɪkl/ **adjective 1** having to do with poetry 诗的；韵文的 **2** expressed in a sensitive and imaginative way 充满诗意的 □ **poetic justice** a situation in which something bad happens to someone who has done something wrong 报应 **poetic licence** freedom to change facts or the normal rules of language to achieve a special effect in writing 诗的破格(指为追求艺术效果可违背语言常规或事实的自由) ■ **poetically** adverb.

poetry /'pəʊɪtri/ **noun 1** poems as a whole or as a form of literature (总称)诗，诗歌 **2** a quality of beauty and sensitivity 诗意，诗一般的感受

po-faced /'pəʊfeɪst/ **adjective** Brit. informal 【英，非正式】 serious and disapproving 板着脸的，不以为然的

pogo stick /'pəʊgəʊ/ **noun** a toy for bouncing around on, consisting of a pole on a spring, with a bar to stand on and a handle at the top 弹簧单高跷(下部装有弹簧和踏板、上端装有扶手的跳跃游戏器具)

pogrom /'pɒgrəm/ **noun** an organized massacre of an ethnic group, originally that of Jews in Russia or eastern Europe (有组织的)大屠杀，集体迫害

poignant /'pɔɪnjənt/ **adjective** making you feel sadness or regret 辛酸的；惨痛的 ■ **poignancy** noun **poignantly** adverb.

point /pɔɪnt/ **noun 1** the tapered, sharp end of a tool, weapon, or other object (工具、武器等的)尖，尖端 **2** a particular place or moment 地点；时间点；时刻 **3** an item, detail, or idea (事项、细节或想法的)点，项，条 **4** (**the point**) the most important part of what is being discussed (讨论的)重点，核心问题 **5** the advantage or purpose of something 好处；目的；意图 **6** a unit of scoring, value, or measurement 点，分，度(分数、价值或测量单位) **7** a small dot used as punctuation or in decimal numbers (标点符号中的)句点，(小数中的)小数点 **8** each of thirty two directions marked at equal distances round a compass (指南针上的)罗经点，方位点 **9** a narrow piece of land jutting out into the sea 岬角，海角 **10** (**points**) Brit. 【英】 a junction of two railway lines (铁路两轨相交处的)道轨，道岔 **11** (also **power point**) Brit. 【英】 an electrical socket 插座 **12** (**points**) a set of electrical contacts in the distributor of a motor vehicle (机动车辆的)接触点 • **verb 1** direct someone's attention by extending your finger (用手指)指向，指向 **2** aim, indicate, or face in a particular direction 瞄准；指向；朝向 **3** (**point something out**) make someone aware of something 指出 **4** (**point to**) indicate that something is likely to happen 显示(或表明)…有可能 **5** fill in the joints of brickwork or tiling with mortar or cement (以灰泥或水泥)勾缝，砌缝 □ **point of view** a particular attitude or opinion 态度；观点；见解 **point-to-point** (plural **point-to-points**) Brit. 【英】 a cross-country race for horses used in hunting 定点越野赛马

pointed /'pɔɪntɪd/ **adjective 1** having a sharpened or tapered tip or end 尖的；有尖头的 **2** (of a remark or look) directed towards a particular person and expressing a clear message (话语)有针对性的，尖锐的；(目光)敏锐的，犀利的

pointer /ˈpɔɪntə(r)/ **noun 1** a long, thin piece of metal on a scale or dial which moves to give a reading (天平或刻度表的)指针 **2** a hint or tip 暗示；提示 **3** a breed of dog that, when it scents game, stands rigid and looks towards it 指示猎犬(能嗅出并示意猎物位置)

pointless /ˈpɔɪntləs/ **adjective** having little or no sense or purpose 无意义的；无目的的 ∎ **pointlessly** adverb.

poise /pɔɪz/ **noun 1** a graceful way of holding your body (优雅的)体态，姿态 **2** a calm and confident manner 镇定；泰然自若 • **verb 1** cause to be balanced or suspended 使平衡；使悬着不动 **2** (**poised**) calm and confident 镇定的；泰然自若的 **3** (**be poised to do**) be ready to do 准备就绪做

poison /ˈpɔɪzn/ **noun 1** a substance that causes death or injury to a person or animal that swallows or absorbs it 毒药 **2** a harmful influence 毒害；有害影响 • **verb 1** harm or kill a person or animal with poison 毒害；毒死 **2** put poison on or in 在…上下毒；投毒于 **3** have a harmful effect on 毒害；危害 ∎ **poisoner** noun **poisonous** adjective.

poke /pəʊk/ **verb** (**pokes**, **poking**, **poked**) **1** prod with a finger or a sharp object (以手指或尖物)戳，捅 **2** (**poke about** or **around**) look or search around 搜寻；寻找 **3** push or stick out in a particular direction 探出；伸出 • **noun** an act of poking 戳；捅；探out

poker¹ /ˈpəʊkə(r)/ **noun** a metal rod used for prodding an open fire 拨火棒

poker² **noun** a card game in which the players bet on the value of the hands dealt to them 扑克牌戏 □ **poker face** a blank expression that hides

your true feelings 面无表情；不动声色

poky or **pokey** /ˈpəʊki/ **adjective** (**pokier**, **pokiest**) (of a room or building) uncomfortably small and cramped (房间或建筑物)狭小的，闷气的

polar /ˈpəʊlə(r)/ **adjective 1** relating to the North or South Poles or the regions around them 南(或北)极的；极地的 **2** having an electrical or magnetic field 磁极的 **3** completely opposite 截然相反的 □ **polar bear** a large white bear from the Arctic 北极熊

polarity /pəˈlærəti/ **noun** (plural **polarities**) **1** the state of having poles or opposites 极性；对立状态；截然相反 **2** the direction of a magnetic or electric field 磁极；电极

polarize or **polarise** /ˈpəʊləraɪz/ **verb** (**polarizes**, **polarizing**, **polarized**) **1** divide people into two sharply contrasting groups with different opinions 使两极化；使截然对立 **2** Physics 【物理】restrict the vibrations of a wave of light to one direction 使(光波)偏振 **3** give magnetic or electric polarity to 使极化；使有极性 ∎ **polarization** noun.

Polaroid /ˈpəʊlərɔɪd/ **noun** trademark 【商标】**1** a material that polarizes the light passing through it, used in sunglasses (用于太阳镜的)偏振片 **2** a camera that produces a finished print rapidly after each exposure 宝丽来(一次成像)照相机

Pole /pəʊl/ **noun** a person from Poland 波兰人

pole¹ /pəʊl/ **noun** a long, thin rounded piece of wood or metal, used as a support 杆；支杆 □ **pole position** the most favourable position at the start of a motor race 杆位(赛车起跑时的最有利位置) **pole vault** an athletic event in which competitors vault over a high bar with the aid of a long pole 撑竿跳高

pole² noun **1** either of the two points (**North Pole** or **South Pole**) at opposite ends of the earth's axis 地极, 极(指南极或北极) **2** each of the two opposite points of a magnet at which magnetic forces are strongest 磁极 **3** the positive or negative terminal of an electric cell or battery 电极(指正极或负极) □ **be poles apart** have nothing in common 截然相反; 大相径庭

poleaxe /'pəʊlæks/ (US spelling 【美拼作】**poleax**) verb (**poleaxes, poleaxing, poleaxed**) **1** kill or knock down with a heavy blow 砍杀; 击倒 **2** shock someone very much 使震惊

polecat /'pəʊlkæt/ noun **1** a dark brown weasel-like animal with an unpleasant smell 鸡貂 **2** N. Amer. 【北美】 a skunk 臭鼬

polemic /pə'lemɪk/ noun **1** a speech or piece of writing that argues strongly for or against something (口头或书面的)激烈争论, 论战 **2** (also **polemics**) the practice of using fierce argument or discussion 争辩; 辩论 • adjective (also **polemical**) having to do with fierce argument or discussion 争辩的; 辩论的 ■ **polemicist** noun.

police /pə'liːs/ noun an official body of people employed by a state to prevent and solve crime and keep public order 警力; 警察部门 • verb (**polices, policing, policed**) **1** keep law and order in an area 维持…的治安 **2** make sure that a particular set of rules is obeyed 管理; 监督 □ **police state** a state in which the government requires the police to watch people secretly and control their activities 警察国家; 极权国家

policeman /pə'liːsmən/ or **police-woman** /pə'liːswʊmən/ noun (plural **policemen** or **policewomen**) a member of a police force 警察

policy /'pɒləsi/ noun (plural **policies**) **1** a plan of action adopted by an organization or person 方针; 政策; 方法 **2** a contract of insurance 保险单

polio /'pəʊlɪəʊ/ or **poliomyelitis** /ˌpəʊlɪəʊˌmaɪə'laɪtɪs/ noun a disease that can cause temporary or permanent paralysis 脊髓灰质炎; 小儿麻痹症

Polish /'pəʊlɪʃ/ noun the language of Poland 波兰语 • adjective relating to Poland 波兰的

polish /'pɒlɪʃ/ verb **1** make something smooth and shiny by rubbing 擦光; 擦亮 **2** (**polish something up**) improve a skill 改进; 润色 **3** (**polish something off**) finish eating or doing something quickly 迅速吃光; 快速完成 • noun **1** a substance used to polish something 擦亮剂; 上光剂 **2** an act of polishing 擦光; 擦亮 **3** a shiny appearance produced by polishing (擦拭后)光亮的表面 **4** refinement or elegance 精致; 优雅 ■ **polisher** noun.

polite /pə'laɪt/ adjective (**politer, politest**) **1** respectful and considerate towards other people; courteous 有礼貌的; 客气的 **2** civilized or refined 有教养的; 优雅的 ■ **politely** adverb **politeness** noun.

politic /'pɒlɪtɪk/ adjective (of an action) sensible and wise in the circumstances (举动)明智的, 精明的

political /pə'lɪtɪkl/ adjective **1** relating to the government or public affairs of a country 政治的; 政府的; 国家公共事务的 **2** related to or interested in politics 与政治有关的; 对政治感兴趣的 □ **political correctness** the avoidance of language or behaviour that could offend certain groups of people 政治正确性(指言行上避免冒犯某些人群) **political prisoner** a person who is imprisoned for their beliefs rather than because they have committed a crime 政治犯 ■ **politically** adverb.

politician /ˌpɒləˈtɪʃn/ **noun** a person who holds an elected position within the government 政治家；从政者

politicize or **politicise** /pəˈlɪtɪsaɪz/ **verb** (politicizes, politicizing, politicized) **1** make someone interested in politics 使参与政治 **2** make something a political issue 使政治化 ■ **politicization** noun.

politics /ˈpɒlɪtɪks/ **noun 1** the activities concerned with governing a country or area 政治；政治活动 **2** a particular set of political beliefs 政见；政治主张 **3** activities concerned with gaining or using power within an organization or group 争权活动；手腕；权术: *office politics* 办公室权谋

polity /ˈpɒləti/ **noun** (plural **polities**) **1** a form of government 政体；国体 **2** a society as a politically organized state 有组织体制的社会；国家

polka /ˈpɒlkə/ **noun** a lively dance for couples 波尔卡舞 □ **polka dot** each of a number of dots that are evenly spaced to form a pattern 圆点花纹

poll /pəʊl/ **noun 1** the process of voting in an election 选举投票 **2** a record of the number of votes cast 选票数；投票结果 • **verb 1** record the opinion or vote of 记录…的意见；统计…的选票 **2** (of a candidate in an election) receive a particular number of votes (候选人)获得…票数 □ **poll tax** a tax paid at the same rate by every adult 人头税

pollard /ˈpɒləd/ **verb** cut off the top and side branches of a tree to encourage new growth (为促进树的生长)截去树梢和树枝，截树头

pollen /ˈpɒlən/ **noun** a powder produced by the male part of a flower, which is carried by bees, the wind, etc. and can fertilize other flowers 花粉 □ **pollen count** a measure of the amount of pollen in the air (空气中的)花粉量，花粉计数

pollinate /ˈpɒlɪneɪt/ **verb** (pollinates, pollinating, pollinated) carry pollen to and fertilize a flower or plant 给(花或植物)授粉 ■ **pollination** noun.

pollster /ˈpəʊlstə(r)/ **noun** a person who carries out opinion polls 民意调查者；民意测验者

pollutant /pəˈluːtənt/ **noun** a substance that causes pollution 污染物

pollute /pəˈluːt/ **verb** (pollutes, polluting, polluted) make something dirty or poisonous with unwanted or harmful substances 弄脏；污染 ■ **polluter** noun.

pollution /pəˈluːʃn/ **noun** the presence in the air, soil, or water of a substance with unpleasant or harmful effects 污染

polo /ˈpəʊləʊ/ **noun** a game similar to hockey, played on horseback with a long-handled mallet 马球(运动) □ **polo neck** Brit. 【英】 a high, tight, turned-over collar on a sweater (羊毛衫的)高圆翻领 **polo shirt** a casual short-sleeved shirt with a collar and two or three buttons at the neck (开领短袖式)马球衬衫

poltergeist /ˈpɒltəɡaɪst/ **noun** a kind of ghost that is said to make loud noises and throw objects around 捉弄人的鬼怪；促狭鬼

polychrome /ˈpɒlikrəʊm/ **adjective** consisting of several colours 多色的 ■ **polychromatic** adjective.

polyester /ˌpɒliˈestə(r)/ **noun** a synthetic fibre used to make fabric for clothes 聚酯纤维；涤纶

polygamy /pəˈlɪɡəmi/ **noun** the practice of having more than one wife or husband at the same time 多配偶(制)；一夫多妻(制)；一妻多夫(制) ■ **polygamist** noun **polygamous** adjective.

polyglot /ˈpɒliɡlɒt/ **adjective** knowing or using several languages 通晓多种语言的；使用多种语言的

polygon /ˈpɒliɡən/ **noun** a figure

with three or more straight sides and angles 多边形;多角形

polygraph /'pɒlɪgræf/ **noun** a lie detector 测谎器

polyhedron /ˌpɒlɪ'hiːdrən/ **noun** (plural **polyhedra** /ˌpɒlɪ'hiːdrə/ or **polyhedrons**) a solid figure with many sides 多面体

polymath /'pɒlɪmæθ/ **noun** a person with a wide knowledge of many subjects 博学者;学识渊博的人

polymer /'pɒlɪmə(r)/ **noun** a substance with a molecular structure formed from many identical small molecules bonded together 聚合物

polymorphic /ˌpɒlɪ'mɔːfɪk/ or **polymorphous** /ˌpɒlɪ'mɔːfəs/ **adjective** having several different forms 多种形式的;多态的

polyp /'pɒlɪp/ **noun 1** a simple sea creature which remains fixed in the same place, such as coral (水螅型)珊瑚虫 **2** Medicine 【医】a small lump sticking out from a mucous membrane 息肉

polyphony /pə'lɪfəni/ **noun** the combination of a number of musical parts, each forming an individual melody and harmonizing with each other 复调音乐 ■ **polyphonic** adjective.

polystyrene /ˌpɒlɪ'staɪriːn/ **noun** a light synthetic material 聚苯乙烯

polysyllabic /ˌpɒlɪsɪ'læbɪk/ **adjective** having more than one syllable 多音节的

polytechnic /ˌpɒlɪ'teknɪk/ **noun** (in the past in the UK) a college offering courses at degree level (now called a 'university') (旧时英国)理工学院,工艺专科学校(现称大学)

polytheism /'pɒlɪθiːɪzəm/ **noun** the worship of more than one god 多神论;多神主义 ■ **polytheistic** adjective.

polythene /'pɒlɪθiːn/ **noun** Brit. 【英】a tough, light, flexible plastic 聚乙烯

polyunsaturated /ˌpɒliʌn'sætʃəreɪtɪd/

adjective (of a fat) having a chemical structure that is thought not to lead to the formation of cholesterol in the blood (脂肪)多重不饱和的

polyurethane /ˌpɒlɪ'jʊərəθeɪn/ **noun** a synthetic material used in paints and varnishes 聚氨基甲酸乙酯;聚氨酯

Pom /pɒm/ **noun** Austral./NZ informal 【澳/新西兰,非正式】a British person 英国佬 ■ **Pommy** adjective & noun.

pomade /pə'meɪd, -mɑːd/ **noun** a scented oil or cream for making the hair glossy and smooth 头油;润发脂

pomander /pə'mændə(r)/ **noun** a ball or container of sweet-smelling substances used to perfume a room or cupboard 香球,香盒(置于房间或橱柜中散发香味)

pomegranate /'pɒmɪgrænɪt/ **noun** a round tropical fruit with a tough orange outer skin and red flesh containing many seeds 石榴

pommel /'pɒml/ **noun 1** the curving or projecting front part of a saddle (马鞍的)前鞍桥 **2** a rounded knob on the handle of a sword (剑柄的)圆头

pomp /pɒmp/ **noun** the special clothes, music, and customs that are part of a grand public ceremony (典礼山)盛况,宏伟壮观的景象

pompom /'pɒmpɒm/ **noun** a small woollen ball attached to a garment for decoration (衣服上用作装饰的)绒球,丝球

pompous /'pɒmpəs/ **adjective** showing in a rather solemn or arrogant way that you have a high opinion of yourself and your own views 自命不凡的;自负的;虚华的 ■ **pomposity** noun **pompously** adverb.

ponce /pɒns/ Brit. informal 【英,非正式】 **noun 1** a man who lives off a prostitute's earnings 靠妓女卖淫为生的男人;拉皮条的人 **2** 【贬】an effeminate man 脂粉气十足的男人 • **verb** (**ponces**, **poncing**, ponced) (**ponce about** or **around**) behave in a way that wastes time or looks silly 游手好闲，招摇 ■ **poncey** (or **poncy**) adjective.

poncho /ˈpɒntʃəʊ/ **noun** (plural **ponchos**) a garment made of a thick piece of cloth with a slit in the middle for the head 披风，斗篷(以厚毛料制成，中间开有领口)

pond /pɒnd/ **noun** a small area of still water 池塘

ponder /ˈpɒndə(r)/ **verb** (**ponders**, **pondering**, **pondered**) consider something carefully 仔细考虑，思索

ponderous /ˈpɒndərəs/ **adjective 1** moving slowly and heavily 笨拙的；行动迟缓的 **2** boringly solemn or long-winded 严肃而沉闷的；冗长的 ■ **ponderously** adverb.

pondweed /ˈpɒndwiːd/ **noun** a plant that grows in still or running water 水池草

pong /pɒŋ/ Brit. informal 【英，非正式】 **noun** a strong, unpleasant smell 强烈难闻的气味，臭味；恶臭 • **verb** smell strongly and unpleasantly 发出刺鼻的臭味 ■ **pongy** adjective.

pontiff /ˈpɒntɪf/ **noun** the Pope 教皇

pontifical /pɒnˈtɪfɪkl/ **adjective** having to do with a pope; papal 教皇的；教皇职位的

pontificate verb /pɒnˈtɪfɪkeɪt/ (**pontificates**, **pontificating**, **pontificated**) express your opinions in a pompous and overbearing way 武断地说话；自负地发表意见 • noun /pɒnˈtɪfɪkət/ (**the Pontificate**) the official position of a pope or bishop 教皇职位；主教职位

pontoon¹ /pɒnˈtuːn/ **noun** Brit. 【英】 a card game in which players try to obtain cards with a value totalling twenty-one 二十一点牌戏

pontoon² **noun 1** a flat-bottomed boat or hollow cylinder used with others to support a temporary bridge or floating landing stage (架设浮桥或浮码头用的)浮舟，浮筒 **2** a bridge or landing stage supported by pontoons 浮桥；浮码头

pony /ˈpəʊni/ **noun** (plural **ponies**) a small breed of horse, especially one below 15 hands (尤指低于15手之宽的)矮种马，小型马 □ **pony-trekking** Brit.【英】 the riding of ponies across country as a leisure activity 骑马旅行；骑马郊游

ponytail /ˈpəʊniteɪl/ **noun** a hairstyle in which the hair is drawn back and tied at the back of the head 马尾辫

pooch /puːtʃ/ **noun** informal 【非正式】 a dog 狗

poodle /ˈpuːdl/ **noun** a breed of dog with a curly coat that is usually clipped 卷毛狗；贵妇狗

poof¹ /puf/ or **poof²** /puːf/ **noun** Brit. informal 【英，非正式】 a homosexual man 男同性恋者

pooh-pooh /ˌpuːˈpuː/ **verb** informal 【非正式】 dismiss an idea as being silly or impractical 对(想法)嗤之以鼻

pool¹ /puːl/ **noun 1** a small area of still water 池塘；水塘 **2** (also **swimming pool**) an artificial pool for swimming in 游泳池 **3** a small, shallow patch of liquid on a surface (液体的)一片，一摊

pool² **noun 1** a supply of vehicles, goods, money, etc. that is shared between a number of people and available for use when needed 共用资源；集中备用资源 **2** (**the pools** or **football pools**) a form of gambling on the results of football matches 普尔(竞猜足球比赛结果的赌博方式) **3** a game played on a billiard table using sixteen balls (16球的)落袋台球戏 • **verb** put something into a common fund to be used by a number of people 把…投入共用基金使用；共用

poop /puːp/ or **poop deck** **noun** a raised deck at the back of a ship 舰

楼甲板

poor /pɔː(r), pʊə(r)/ **adjective 1** having very little money 贫穷的；困困的 **2** of a low standard or quality 差的，低劣的 **3** (**poor in**) not having enough of something 缺乏…的 **4** deserving pity or sympathy 可怜的；不幸的

poorhouse /'pɔːhaʊs, 'pʊə-/ **noun** Brit. 【英】a workhouse 济贫院；贫民所

poorly /'pɔːli, 'pʊə-/ **adverb** badly 恶劣地；糟糕地 ■ **adjective** chiefly Brit. 【主英】unwell 健康欠佳的

pootle /'puːtl/ **verb** (**pootles, pootling, pootled**) Brit. informal 【英，非正式】move or travel in a leisurely way 悠闲地走动(或旅行)

pop¹ /pɒp/ **verb** (**pops, popping, popped**) **1** make a sudden short explosive sound 发出砰的响声，噼啪作响 **2** go or come quickly or unexpectedly 迅速去；出其不意地出现 **3** put something somewhere quickly or for a short time 迅速放置 **4** (of a person's eyes) open wide and appear to bulge (人的眼睛)睁大凸出 ■ **noun 1** a sudden short explosive sound 砰的一声 **2** informal, dated 【非正式，废】a sweet fizzy drink 汽水

pop² **noun** (also **pop music**) modern popular music, usually with a strong melody and beat 流行音乐，流行歌曲 ■ **adjective 1** relating to pop music 流行音乐的 **2** often disapproving 【常贬】made easy for the general public to understand; popularized 通俗的，大众化的: *pop psychology* 通俗心理学 □ **pop art** a style of art that uses images taken from popular culture, such as advertisements or films 波普艺术，通俗艺术(以大众文化为基础、从广告、电影等中收集素材的艺术形式)

pop³ **noun** informal, chiefly US 【非正式，主美】father 爸爸

popcorn /'pɒpkɔːn/ **noun** a snack consisting of maize kernels which are heated until they burst open 爆(玉)米花

pope /pəʊp/ **noun** the Bishop of Rome as head of the Roman Catholic Church (罗马天主教会的)教皇

popery /'pəʊpəri/ **noun** disapproving 【贬】Roman Catholicism 罗马天主教教义 ■ **popish** adjective.

popinjay /'pɒpɪndʒeɪ/ **noun** old use 【旧】a person who is vain and dresses in a showy way 讲究衣着的人；纨绔子弟

poplar /'pɒplə(r)/ **noun** a tall, slender tree with soft wood 杨树

poplin /'pɒplɪn/ **noun** a cott on fabric with a finely ribbed surface 府绸；毛葛

poppadom /'pɒpədəm/ **noun** (in Indian cookery) a thin circular piece of spiced bread that is fried until crisp (印度烹饪中的)油煎薄饼

popper /'pɒpə(r)/ **noun** Brit. informal 【英，非正式】a press stud 按扣；子母扣

poppet /'pɒpɪt/ **noun** Brit. informal 【英，非正式】a pretty or charming child 宝宝；宝贝

poppy /'pɒpi/ **noun** a plant with bright flowers and small black seeds 罂粟

poppycock /'pɒpikɒk/ **noun** informal 【非正式】nonsense 胡扯；废话

populace /'pɒpjʊləs/ **noun** the general public 大众；老百姓

popular /'pɒpjʊlə(r)/ **adjective 1** liked or admired by many people 受欢迎的，流行的 **2** suited to the tastes of the general public 通俗的；大众化的 **3** connected with or carried out by ordinary people 公众的；民众的 ■ **popularly** adverb.

popularity /ˌpɒpjʊ'lærəti/ **noun** the state of being liked or supported by many people 流行；受欢迎；普及

popularize or **popularise** /'pɒpjʊləraɪz/ **verb** (**popularizes, popularizing, popularized**) **1** make something popular 使流行；

p

使受欢迎；推广 **2** make something understandable or interesting to the general public 使通俗化；普及 ■ **popularization** noun.

populate /ˈpɒpjuleɪt/ **verb (populates, populating, populated) 1** live in an area and form its population (大批)居位于…，生活于…，构成…的人口 **2** cause people to settle in an area 使居住于；向…移民

population /ˌpɒpjuˈleɪʃn/ **noun 1** all the people living in an area (某一地区的)全体居民，人口 **2** the number of people living in an area (某地区的)一群人，群体

populist /ˈpɒpjulɪst/ **adjective** aiming to appeal to ordinary people, especially in politics 平民主义的 • **noun** a populist politician 平民主义者 ■ **populism** noun.

populous /ˈpɒpjuləs/ **adjective** having a large population 人口众多的

porcelain /ˈpɔːsəlɪn/ **noun** a type of delicate china 瓷；瓷器

porch /pɔːtʃ/ **noun** a covered shelter at the entrance to a building (建筑物入口处有顶的)门廊，门厅

porcine /ˈpɔːsaɪn/ **adjective** relating to pigs, or like a pig 猪的；像猪的

porcupine /ˈpɔːkjupaɪn/ **noun** an animal with long protective spines on the body and tail 豪猪；箭猪

pore¹ /pɔː(r)/ **noun** each of many tiny openings in the skin or another surface (皮肤等表面的)毛孔，气孔

pore² /pɔː(r)/ **verb (pores, poring, pored) (pore over or through)** study or read something with close attention 钻研；专心阅读

> **！注意** don't confuse pore and pour: you **pore over** a book, not **pour over** it. 不要混淆 pore 和 pour，pore over a book (专心读一本书)是正确说法，不要误用 pour over。

pork /pɔːk/ **noun** the flesh of a pig used as food 猪肉

porker /ˈpɔːkə(r)/ **noun** a young pig raised and fattened for food 肉用猪；肥育小猪

porn /pɔːn/ **noun** informal【非正式】 pornography 色情作品

pornography /pɔːˈnɒɡrəfi/ **noun** pictures, writing, or films that are intended to arouse sexual excitement 色情作品 ■ **pornographic** adjective.

porous /ˈpɔːrəs/ **adjective** having tiny spaces through which liquid or air can pass 能渗透的；渗水的；透气的 ■ **porosity** noun.

porpoise /ˈpɔːpəs/ **noun** a type of small whale with a rounded snout 钝吻海豚；鼠海豚

porridge /ˈpɒrɪdʒ/ **noun** a dish consisting of oats or oatmeal boiled with water or milk 燕麦粥；麦片粥

port¹ /pɔːt/ **noun 1** a town or city with a harbour 港口城市；口岸 **2** a harbour 港；**port of call** a place where a ship or person stops on a journey (船只的)沿途停靠港口；(旅人的)沿途停留处

port² **noun** a strong, sweet dark red wine from Portugal 波尔图葡萄酒(葡萄牙的一种烈性甜葡萄酒，呈深红色)

port³ **noun** the side of a ship or aircraft that is on the left when you are facing forward (船舶或飞机的)左舷

port⁴ **noun 1** an opening in the side of a ship for boarding or loading (船舶的)舱门，上货口 **2** an opening in an aircraft or vehicle through which a gun can be fired (飞机或车辆的)射击孔，炮眼，枪眼 **3** a socket in a computer network into which a device can be plugged (计算机网络的)端口

portable /ˈpɔːtəbl/ **adjective** able to be carried or moved easily 便携的；手提式的 ■ **portability** noun.

portal /ˈpɔːtl/ **noun** a large and impressive doorway or gate (高大壮观的)大门，入口

portcullis /pɔːtˈkʌlɪs/ **noun** a strong,

heavy grating that can be lowered to block a gateway to a castle (城堡的) 吊门, 吊闸

portend /pɔː'tend/ *verb* be a sign or warning that something important or unpleasant is likely to happen 预示 (重要或不祥之事); 为…的前兆

portent /'pɔːtent/ *noun* a sign or warning that something important or unpleasant is likely to happen (重要事情的)前兆; 凶兆; 恶兆

portentous /pɔː'tentəs/ *adjective* **1** warning or showing that something important is likely to happen 预兆的; 前兆的 **2** very serious or solemn 煞有介事的; 装腔作势的 ■ **portentously** *adverb*.

porter /'pɔːtə(r)/ *noun* **1** a person employed to carry luggage and other loads 搬运工 **2** a hospital employee who moves equipment or patients (医院中的)勤杂工, 护工 **3** Brit.【英】an employee in charge of the entrance of a large building (大楼的)门房, 看门人 **4** dark brown bitter beer 黑啤酒

portfolio /pɔːt'fəʊliəʊ/ *noun* (plural **portfolios**) **1** a thin, flat case for carrying drawings, maps, etc. 文件夹; 公事包 **2** a set of pieces of creative work collected together to show someone's ability (个人的)代表作选集 **3** a range of investments held by a person or organization (个人或机构的)投资组合 **4** the position and duties of a government minister 部长职位; 大臣职位

porthole /'pɔːthəʊl/ *noun* a small window in the side of a ship or aircraft (船舶或飞机的)舷窗

portico /'pɔːtɪkəʊ/ *noun* (plural **porticoes** or **porticos**) a roof supported by columns, built over the entrance to a building (有柱子的)门廊; 柱廊

portion /'pɔːʃn/ *noun* **1** a part or share of something 部分; 份 **2** an amount of food for one person (食物的)一客,

一份 • *verb* share something out in portions 分配; 分担; 分享

portly /'pɔːtli/ *adjective* rather fat 肥胖的

portmanteau /pɔːt'mæntəʊ/ *noun* (plural **portmanteaus** or **portmanteaux** /pɔːt'mæntəʊz/) a large travelling bag that opens into two parts (两半合拢的)手提箱, 旅行箱

portrait /'pɔːtreɪt/ *noun* **1** a painting, drawing, or photograph of a particular person 肖像; 画像; 人像照片 **2** a piece of writing or film about a particular person (文字或影像)描写; 描绘

portraiture /'pɔːtrətʃə(r)/ *noun* the art of making portraits 肖像绘制法; 人像摄影法

portray /pɔː'treɪ/ *verb* **1** show or describe in a work of art or literature 描绘; 描述; 表现 **2** describe in a particular way 把…描绘为; 把…刻画成 ■ **portrayal** *noun*.

Portuguese /ˌpɔːtʃuˈɡiːz/ *noun* (plural **Portuguese**) **1** a person from Portugal 葡萄牙人 **2** the language of Portugal and Brazil 葡萄牙语 • *adjective* relating to Portugal 葡萄牙的

✔ 拼写指南 *-guese*, not *-gese*: Portu*guese*. Portuguese 中的 -guese 不要拼作 -gese.

---

pose /pəʊz/ *verb* (**poses**, **posing**, **posed**) **1** present a problem, question, etc. 提出(问题); 构成(难题等) **2** sit or stand in a particular position in order to be photographed, painted, or drawn (为拍照或画像)摆姿势 **3** (**pose as**) pretend to be 假装; 冒充 **4** behave in a way that is intended to impress people 装腔作势; 做作 • *noun* **1** a position adopted in order to be painted, drawn, or photographed (为画像或拍照摆出的)姿势, 造型 **2** a way of behaving that is intended to impress people 招摇; 装腔作势

poser /'pəʊzə(r)/ noun **1** a person who behaves in a way intended to impress other people 装模作样者；装模作样者 **2** a puzzling question or problem 棘手的问题；难题

poseur /pəʊ'zɜː(r)/ noun a person who poses in order to impress; a poser 装腔作势者；故作姿态者

posh /pɒʃ/ adjective informal【非正式】**1** very elegant or luxurious 优雅的；高档的；豪华的 **2** chiefly Brit.【主英】upper-class 上流社会的

posit /'pɒzɪt/ verb (posits, positing, posited) present something as a fact or as a basis for argument 假定；假设

position /pə'zɪʃn/ noun **1** a place where something is situated 位置；方位 **2** a way in which someone or something is placed or arranged (人的)姿势,(人或物的)安置方式,位置安排 **3** a situation or set of circumstances 处境；状况 **4** a job 职位；工作 **5** a person's place or importance in relation to others (相对于他人的)位置,地位,身份 **6** a point of view 态度；立场 • verb put or arrange in a particular position 放置；安置 ■ **positional** adjective.

positive /'pɒzətɪv/ adjective **1** indicating agreement with or support for something 肯定的；赞成的；积极的 **2** hopeful, favourable, or confident 乐观的；有信心的 **3** with no possibility of doubt; certain 有把握的；确信的 **4** (of the results of a test or experiment) showing the presence of something (测试或实验结果)证明存在的,阳性的 **5** (of a quantity) greater than zero (数量)正的,正数的 **6** having to do with the kind of electric charge opposite to that carried by electrons 正电的；阳极的 **7** (of an adjective or adverb) expressing the basic degree of a quality (e.g. *brave*) (形容词或副词)原级的 • noun a positive quality 肯定要素；阳性；正值 □ **positive discri-**

mination Brit.【英】the policy of giving jobs or other opportunities to people who belong to groups which suffer discrimination 积极区别对待政策(为受歧视群体提供工作等机会) ■ **positively** adverb **positivity** noun.

positivism /'pɒzətɪvɪzəm/ noun a system of philosophy that recognizes only things that can be scientifically or logically proved 实证主义；实证论 ■ **positivist** noun & adjective.

positron /'pɒzɪtrɒn/ noun a subatomic particle with the same mass as an electron and an equal but positive charge 正电子；阳电子

posse /'pɒsɪ/ noun **1** N. Amer.(in the past) a group of men summoned by a sheriff to enforce the law (旧时县治安官召集的)地方武装团队,民防团 **2** informal【非正式】a group of people 一群人；一伙人

possess /pə'zes/ verb **1** have or own something 持有；拥有 **2** (also be **possessed of**) have a particular ability or quality 具有；具备(能力或品质) **3** dominate or have complete power over someone 控制；支配 ■ **possessor** noun.

> ✔ 拼写指南 double s in the middle as well as at the end: po*ss*e*ss*. possess 的中间和末尾有两个 s。

possession /pə'zeʃn/ noun **1** the state of having or owning something 拥有；占有 **2** a thing owned 所有物；财产

possessive /pə'zesɪv/ adjective **1** demanding someone's total attention and love 要求悉心关爱的；占有欲强的 **2** unwilling to share your possessions 不愿与人分享的；独占欲强的 **3** Grammar【语法】(of a pronoun or determiner) showing that someone owns something (代词或限定词)所属关系的,所有格的 ■ **possessively** adverb.

possibility /ˌpɒsə'bɪləti/ noun (plural

possibilities) **1** a thing that is possible 可能的事 **2** the state of being possible 可能性 **3** (**possibilities**) qualities suggesting that something might be good or could be improved 潜在价值;潜力

possible /'pɒsəbl/ **adjective 1** capable of existing, happening, or being done 可能(存在、发生或实现)的 **2** that may be so 可能的;不能确定的 • **noun** a person or thing that may be chosen 可能人选;可能选择

possibly /'pɒsəbli/ **adverb 1** perhaps 可能;也许 **2** in accordance with what is possible (尽)可能地

possum /'pɒsəm/ **noun 1** a marsupial that lives in trees 袋貂(树栖有袋动物) **2** N. Amer. informal [北美,非正式] an opossum 负鼠

post[1] /pəʊst/ **noun 1** a strong, upright piece of timber or metal used as a support or a marker 柱;杆;标杆 **2** (**the post**) part marking the start or finish of a race (竞逐比赛中的)起点柱;终点柱 • **verb 1** display a notice in a public place 张贴(布告) **2** send a message to an Internet bulletin board or newsgroup (在因特网公告板或新闻组)发帖子

post[2] chiefly Brit. [主英] **noun 1** the official service or system that delivers letters and parcels 邮政;邮递 **2** letters and parcels delivered 邮件 **3** a single collection or delivery of post 一次投递;一次收信;邮展 • **verb** send something via the postal system 邮寄 □ **keep someone posted** keep someone up to date with the latest news about something 使(某人)掌握最新消息 **post office 1** the organization responsible for postal services 邮政部门 **2** a building where postal business is carried out 邮局

post[3] **noun 1** a place where someone is on duty or where an activity is carried out 岗位;哨所;驻地 **2** a job 工作;职位 • **verb 1** put a soldier,

police officer, etc. in a particular place 部署(士兵、警察等);设置(岗哨) **2** send someone to a place to take up a job 调派;委派

post- /pəʊst-/ **prefix** after 后: *post- graduate* 研究生

postage /'pəʊstɪdʒ/ **noun 1** the sending of letters and parcels by post 邮寄 **2** the charge for sending something by post 邮费;邮资

postal /'pəʊstl/ **adjective** relating to or carried out by post 邮政的;邮寄的 □ **postal order** Brit. [英] a document that can be bought from a post office and sent to someone who exchanges it for money 邮政汇票

postbox /'pəʊstbɒks/ **noun** a large public box into which letters are posted for collection by the post office 邮筒;邮箱

postcard /'pəʊstkɑːd/ **noun** a card for sending a message by post without an envelope 明信片

postcode /'pəʊstkəʊd/ **noun** Brit. [英] a group of letters and numbers added to a postal address to help in the sorting of mail 邮政编码

post-date /ˌpəʊst'deɪt/ **verb 1** put a date later than the actual one on a cheque or document 把(支票或文件)日期填迟(或签迟) **2** happen, exist, or be found later than 发生于…之后;晚于

poster /'pəʊstə(r)/ **noun** a large picture or notice used for decoration or advertisement 海报;招贴画;广告

poste restante /ˌpəʊst 'rest ɑːnt/ **noun** Brit. [英] a department in a post office that keeps people's letters until they are collected (邮局的)邮件寄存待领处

posterior /pɒ'stɪəriə(r)/ **adjective** at or near the rear (靠近)后部的 • **noun** humorous [幽默] a person's bottom 臀部;屁股

posterity /pɒ'sterəti/ **noun** all future generations of people 后代;子孙

postgraduate /ˌpəʊst'grædʒʊət/ **adjective** relating to study done after completing a first degree 研究生的 • **noun** a person taking a course of postgraduate study 研究生

post-haste /ˌpəʊst'heɪst/ **adverb** very fast 飞快地；急速地

posthumous /'pɒstjʊməs/ **adjective** happening or appearing after the person involved has died 死后的；身后的 ■ **posthumously** adverb.

posting¹ /'pəʊstɪŋ/ **noun** chiefly Brit. 【主英】an appointment to a job abroad 派驻国外

posting² **noun** a message sent to an Internet bulletin board or newsgroup (因特网公告板或新闻组的)帖子

postman /'pəʊstmən/ **noun** (plural **postmen**) Brit. 【英】a man employed to deliver or collect post 邮差；邮递员

postmark /'pəʊstmɑːk/ **noun** an official mark stamped on a letter or parcel, giving the date of posting and cancelling the postage stamp 邮戳 • **verb** stamp a letter or parcel with a postmark 盖邮戳于

postmaster /'pəʊstmɑːstə(r)/ or **postmistress** /'pəʊstmɪstrəs/ **noun** a person in charge of a post office 邮政局长

postmodernism /ˌpəʊst'mɒdənɪzəm/ **noun** a movement in the arts that features a deliberate mixing of different styles 后现代主义 ■ **postmodern** adjective **postmodernist** noun & adjective.

post-mortem /ˌpəʊst'mɔːtəm/ **noun** an examination of a dead body to find out the cause of death 验尸；尸体解剖

post-natal /ˌpəʊst'neɪtl/ **adjective** having to do with the period after childbirth 产后的；分娩后的

postpone /pə'spəʊn/ **verb** (**postpones, postponing, postponed**) arrange for something to take place

at a time later than that first planned 使延期；推迟 ■ **postponement** noun.

postscript /'pəʊstskrɪpt/ **noun** a remark added at the end of a letter (信末的)附言，又及

postulant /'pɒstjʊlənt/ **noun** a person who has recently entered a religious order (宗教职位的)候补人

postulate /'pɒstjʊleɪt/ **verb** (**postulates, postulating, postulated**) assume that something is true, as a basis for a theory or discussion 假定…为真；假设 ■ **postulation** noun.

posture /'pɒstʃə(r)/ **noun 1** a particular position of the body 姿势 **2** the usual way in which a person holds their body 仪态；姿态 **3** an approach or attitude towards something 态度；立场 • **verb** (**postures, posturing, postured**) behave in a way that is meant to impress or mislead other people 故作姿态；装腔作势 ■ **postural** adjective.

posy /'pəʊzi/ **noun** (plural **posies**) a small bunch of flowers 小花束

pot¹ /pɒt/ **noun** a rounded container used for storage or cooking 壶；罐；花盆 • **verb** (**pots, potting, potted**) **1** plant a young plant in a flowerpot 把…栽种在花盆里 **2** preserve food in a sealed pot or jar 把(食物)储存在密封罐中 **3** Billiards & Snooker【台球和斯诺克】hit a ball into a pocket 击(球)落袋 **4** informal 【非正式】hit or kill by shooting 射击；射杀 □ **go to pot** informal 【非正式】be ruined through neglect 荒疏；荒废 **pot belly** a large stomach that sticks out 罗汉肚；大肚子 **pot luck** a situation in which you take a chance that whatever is available will be acceptable 碰运气 **potting shed** a shed used for potting plants and storing garden tools 盆栽棚；园圃

pot² **noun** informal 【非正式】cannabis 大麻

potable /'pəʊtəbl/ **adjective** formal 【正

式】(of water) safe to drink (水)适合饮用的

potash /'pɒtæʃ/ *noun* a substance obtained from potassium, used in making soap and fertilizers 钾碱，碳酸钾(可用作制肥皂和肥料的原料)

potassium /pə'tæsɪəm/ *noun* a soft silvery-white metallic element (金属元素)钾

potato /pə'teɪtəʊ/ *noun* (plural **potatoes**) an oval vegetable with starchy white or yellow flesh and a brown skin, that grows underground as a tuber 马铃薯，土豆

✔ **拼写指南** the singular has no *e* on the end: pota*to*. 单数形式的 potato 词末没有 e。

potent /'pəʊtnt/ *adjective* **1** very powerful 强有力的 **2** (of a man) able to achieve an erection (男子)有性交能力的 ■ **potency** *noun*.

potentate /'pəʊtnteɪt/ *noun* a monarch or ruler 君主；统治者

potential /pə'tenʃl/ *adjective* capable of becoming or developing into something 潜在的；可能的 • *noun* **1** qualities or abilities that may be developed and lead to future success 潜力，潜能 **2** the possibility of something happening 潜在性；可能性 ■ **potentiality** *noun* **potentially** *adverb*.

pothole /'pɒthəʊl/ *noun* **1** a deep underground cave 锅穴；瓯穴；地壶 **2** a hole in the surface of a road (路面的)坑洼 ■ **potholed** *adjective*.

potholing /'pɒthəʊlɪŋ/ *noun* exploring potholes as a pastime 地下洞穴探险

potion /'pəʊʃn/ *noun* a drink with healing, magical, or poisonous powers 药水，魔水；毒液

potpourri /ˌpəʊpʊ'riː/ *noun* (plural **potpourris**) a mixture of dried petals and spices used to perfume a room 百花香(放在钵内的干花和香料

混合物，用于室内熏香)

potshot /'pɒtʃɒt/ *noun* a shot aimed unexpectedly or at random 任意射击；胡乱射击

pottage /'pɒtɪdʒ/ *noun* old use 【旧】soup or stew 汤；羹；炖菜

potted /'pɒtɪd/ *adjective* **1** preserved in a sealed pot 盆栽的；罐装的 **2** put into a short, easily understandable form 简略的，浓缩的

potter[1] /'pɒtə(r)/ *verb* (**potters, pottering, pottered**) **1** spend your time doing small tasks in a relaxed way 悠然地干些琐碎活 **2** move in an unhurried way 闲逛，慢条斯理地走

potter[2] *noun* a person who makes pottery 陶工

pottery /'pɒtəri/ *noun* (plural **potteries**) **1** articles made of fired clay 陶器 **2** the craft of making such articles 制陶工艺 **3** a place where pottery is made 陶器厂

potty[1] /'pɒti/ *adjective* (**pottier, pottiest**) Brit. informal 【英，非正式】**1** mad; crazy 发疯的 **2** very enthusiastic about someone or something 狂热的；着迷的

potty[2] *noun* (plural **potties**) a bowl for a child to sit on and use as a toilet (儿童用的)便盆

pouch /paʊtʃ/ *noun* **1** a small flexible bag 小袋；小包 **2** a pocket of skin in an animal's body, especially that in which animals such as kangaroos carry their young (袋鼠等的)育儿袋

pouf /puːf/ ⇒ 见 POOF OR POUFFE.

pouffe or **pouf** /puːf/ *noun* a large, firm cushion used as a seat or for resting your feet on (厚实的)坐垫，脚垫

poulterer /'pəʊltərə(r)/ *noun* Brit. 【英】a person who sells poultry 家禽商贩

poultice /'pəʊltɪs/ *noun* a soft, moist mass of flour or plant material that is put on the skin to reduce inflammation 泥罨剂；膏药

poultry /'pəʊltri/ noun chickens, turkeys, ducks, and geese 家禽

pounce /paʊns/ verb (**pounces**, **pouncing**, **pounced**) **1** suddenly spring to seize or attack something 猛扑；突然袭击 **2** (**pounce on**) quickly notice and criticize something that someone has said or done 抓住机会抨击 • noun an act of pouncing 猛扑；突然袭击

pound¹ /paʊnd/ noun **1** a unit of weight equal to 16 oz avoirdupois (0.4536 kg), or 12 oz troy (0.3732 kg) 磅(重量单位；常衡磅(合16盎司或0.4536千克)；金衡磅(合12盎司或0.3732千克) **2** (also **pound sterling**) the basic unit of money of the UK, equal to 100 pence 英镑(英国基本货币单位，等于100便士)

pound² /paʊnd/ verb **1** hit something heavily again and again 连续重击 **2** walk or run with heavy steps 脚步沉重地走(或跑) **3** beat or throb with a strong regular rhythm 剧烈跳动 **4** crush or grind something into a powder or paste 捣碎；舂烂

pound³ /paʊnd/ noun a place where stray dogs or illegally parked vehicles are officially taken and kept until claimed (走失犬的)待领场；(违规停放车辆的)临时扣押场

pour /pɔː(r)/ verb **1** flow or cause to flow in a steady stream 倒，流；(使)倾泻 **2** (of rain) fall heavily (雨)倾盆而下 **3** prepare and serve a drink 斟，倒(饮料) **4** come or go in large numbers 涌进；涌出 **5** (**pour something out**) express your feelings freely 倾诉，倾吐(感受)

> **！注意** don't confuse **pour** and **pore**: you **pore** over a book, not **pour over** it. 不要混淆 pour 和 pore，pore over a book (专心读一本书)是正确说法，不要误用 pour over。

pout /paʊt/ verb push your lips forward as a sign of sulking or to make yourself look sexually attractive (为表示生气或显得性感)撅起嘴，嘟起嘴 • noun a pouting expression 撅嘴 ■ **pouty** adjective.

poverty /'pɒvəti/ noun **1** the state of being very poor 贫穷；贫困 **2** the state of lacking in a particular quality 贫乏；不足

powder /'paʊdə(r)/ noun **1** a mass of fine dry particles 粉；粉末 **2** a cosmetic in this form applied to a person's face 化妆用粉 • verb (**powders**, **powdering**, **powdered**) **1** sprinkle powder over 撒粉；敷粉；以粉状物覆盖 **2** make something into a powder 使成粉末 □ **powder room** a women's toilet in a public building 女盥洗室；女洗手间 ■ **powdery** adjective.

power /'paʊə(r)/ noun **1** the ability to do something 能力；本领 **2** the ability to influence people or events 影响力；感染力 **3** the right or authority to do something 权利；职权；权限 **4** political authority or control (政治)权力；统治地位 **5** a country seen as having international influence and military strength 有影响力的国家；大国；(军事)强国 **6** strength, force, or energy 力量；强度；活力 **7** capacity or performance of an engine or other device (发动机等的)动力，工作性能 **8** energy that is produced by mechanical, electrical, or other means 机械力；动力，电力 **9** Physics 【物理】the rate of doing work, measured in watts or horse power 功率 **10** Maths 【数学】the product obtained when a number is multiplied by itself a certain number of times 幂；乘方 • verb (**powers**, **powering**, **powered**) **1** supply with power 为…提供动力 **2** move with speed or force 快速移动；奋力行进 □ **power cut** a temporary interruption in an electricity supply 供电中断；停电 **power station** a building where electrical power is generated 发电厂;发电站 **power steering** steering aided by power from a vehicle's engine (机动车辆的)动力转向装置

powerboat /'pauəbəut/ **noun** a fast motorboat 摩托艇;汽艇

powerful /'pauəfl/ **adjective** having power 强有力的;有势力的;有影响的 ■ **powerfully** adverb.

powerhouse /'pauəhaus/ **noun** a person or thing having great energy or power 精力充沛的人;具有影响力的人(或物);权势集团

powerless /'pauələs/ **adjective** without the power to take action 无能力的;无权力的;无效力的

powwow /'pauwau/ **noun 1** informal 【非正式】a meeting for discussion 会议;会谈 **2** a North American Indian ceremony involving feasting and dancing (北美印第安人的)帕瓦仪式(包括盛宴和舞蹈)

pox /pɒks/ **noun 1** any disease that produces a rash of pus-filled pimples that leave pockmarks on healing 痘;痘疹 **2** (**the pox**) informal 【非正式】syphilis 梅毒

poxy /'pɒksi/ **adjective** Brit. informal 【英,非正式】of bad quality 劣质的

pp or **p.p.** **abbreviation** used when signing a letter on someone else's behalf (用于代别人签署信件时)代表… [short for Latin 【缩写,拉丁】= *per procurationem*, literally 'through the agency of'.]

PR /ˌpiː 'ɑː(r)/ **abbreviation 1** proportional representation. **2** public relations.

practicable /'præktɪkəbl/ **adjective** able to be done successfully 可行的;行得通的 ■ **practicability** noun.

practical /'præktɪkl/ **adjective 1** relating to the actual doing or use of something rather than theory 实地的;实践的;实际的 **2** likely to be successful or useful 可行的;行得通的 **3** skilled at making or doing things

心灵手巧的;实干的 ● **noun** Brit. 【英】an exam or lesson in which students have to do or make things 实用技能考试;实验课;实习课 □ **practical joke** a trick played on someone to make them look silly 恶作剧

practicality /ˌpræktɪ'kæləti/ **noun** (plural **practicalities**) **1** the state of being practical 可行性;实用性;实际性 **2** (**practicalities**) the real facts or aspects of a situation 实际情况;实际问题

practically /'præktɪkli/ **adverb 1** almost; virtually 几乎,实质上 **2** in a practical way 实用地;实际地

practice /'præktɪs/ **noun 1** the actual doing of something rather than the theories about it 实践;实施 **2** the usual way of doing something 惯常做法,惯例 **3** the work, business, or place of work of a doctor, dentist, or lawyer (医生、牙医或律师的)工作,行业,诊所,事务所 **4** the doing of something repeatedly to improve your skill (反复的)练习 ● **verb** US spelling of PRACTISE. practise 的美式拼法

! 注意 do you mean **practice** or **practise**? **Practice** is the spelling for the noun, and in America for the verb as well; **practise** is the British spelling of the verb. 使用 practice 还是 practise 要看表达何种含义, practice 是用作名词时的拼法,在美式英语中,该词的动词形式也是practice;而在英式英语中,该词的动词形式为 practise.

practise /'præktɪs/ (US spelling 【美拼作】 **practice**) **verb** (**practises**, **practising**, **practised**) **1** do something repeatedly to improve your skill (反复)练习 **2** do something regularly as part of your normal behavior 经常做;养成…的习惯 **3** be working in a particular profession 从事(某一职业) **4** (**practised**) skilful as a result of experience 熟练的;内行的

5 follow the teaching and rules of a religion 遵循(宗教教义和准则)

practitioner /præk'tɪʃnə(r)/ **noun** a person who practises a profession or activity 从业者;从事者

pragmatic /præg'mætɪk/ **adjective** dealing with things in a sensible and realistic way 讲求实效的;务实的
■ **pragmatically** adverb.

pragmatism /'prægmətɪzəm/ **noun** a realistic and sensible attitude or approach to something 务实态度;实用主义 ■ **pragmatist** noun.

prairie /'preəri/ **noun** (in North America) a large open area of grassland (北美洲的)大草原

praise /preɪz/ **verb** (**praises, praising, praised**) **1** show approval of or admiration for 称赞;赞扬 **2** express thanks to or respect for God 赞美,赞颂(上帝) • **noun** words that show approval or admiration 称赞;赞扬

praiseworthy /'preɪzwɜːði/ **adjective** deserving praise 值得赞扬的

praline /'prɑːliːn/ **noun** a sweet substance made from nuts boiled in sugar 果仁糖

pram /præm/ **noun** Brit. 【英】a four-wheeled vehicle for a baby, pushed by a person on foot (四轮手推)婴儿车

prance /prɑːns/ **verb** (**prances, prancing, pranced**) walk with exaggerated steps 趾高气扬地走;昂首阔步

prang /præŋ/ **verb** Brit. informal 【英,非正式】crash a motor vehicle or aircraft 使(车辆)撞毁;使(飞机)坠毁

prank /præŋk/ **noun** a practical joke or mischievous act 恶作剧;欺骗行为

prankster /'præŋkstə(r)/ **noun** a person who is fond of playing pranks 爱搞恶作剧的人

prat /præt/ **noun** Brit. informal 【英,非正式】a stupid person 傻瓜;笨蛋

prate /preɪt/ **verb** (**prates, prating, prated**) talk too much in a silly or boring way 瞎扯;唠叨

prattle /'prætl/ **verb** (**prattles, prattling, prattled**) talk too much in a silly or trivial way 闲扯;喋喋不休 • **noun** foolish or silly talk 闲扯

prawn /prɔːn/ **noun** an edible shellfish like a large shrimp 对虾;明虾

pray /preɪ/ **verb 1** say a prayer 祈祷,祷告 **2** hope strongly for something 祈望;祈求 • **adverb** formal or old use 【正式或旧】please 请 □ **praying mantis** ⇒ 见 **MANTIS**.

prayer /preə(r)/ **noun 1** a request for help or expression of thanks made to God or a god 祷告;祈祷文 **2** (**prayers**) a religious service at which people gather to pray together 祈祷仪式 **3** an earnest hope or wish 祈望;愿望

pre- /priː-/ **prefix** before 前;在前;先于;预先 : *prearrange* 预先安排

preach /priːtʃ/ **verb 1** give a religious talk to a group of people 讲道;布道 **2** recommend a particular way of thinking or behaving 宣扬;鼓吹 **3** (**preach at**) tell someone how they should think or behave in a way that is boring or annoying 喋喋不休地灌输 ■ **preacher** noun.

preamble /priː'æmbl, 'priːæmbl/ **noun** an opening statement; an introduction 介绍;开场白;序言

prearrange /ˌpriːə'reɪndʒ/ **verb** (**prearranges, prearranging, prearranged**) arrange something in advance 预先安排

precarious /prɪ'keəriəs/ **adjective 1** likely to tip over or fall 不稳的,不牢靠的 **2** (of a situation) not safe or certain (局势)不安全的,不确定的 ■ **precariously** adverb.

precaution /prɪ'kɔːʃn/ **noun** something done to avoid problems or danger 预防措施 ■ **precautionary** adjective.

precede /prɪ'siːd/ **verb** (**precedes, preceding, preceded**) **1** happen before something in time or order 时间或顺序上)先于 **2 go somewhere in front of someone** 走在…之前

precedence /'presɪdəns/ **noun** the state of coming before others in order or importance (顺序或重要性上的)在先,居前

precedent /'presɪdənt/ **noun** an earlier event, action, or legal case that is taken as an example to be followed in similar situations (作为参照的)先例,前例

precept /'pri:sept/ **noun** a general rule about how to behave 行为准则;行为规范

precinct /'pri:sɪŋkt/ **noun 1** Brit. 【英】an area in a town that is closed to traffic (城镇中的)步行区 **2** an enclosed area around a place or building (建筑物等周围围起的)场地,院落 **3** N. Amer.【北美】each of the districts into which a city or town is divided for elections or policing (城镇中的)选区,警察分管区

precious /'preʃəs/ **adjective 1** rare and worth a lot of money 贵重的;珍贵的 **2** greatly loved or valued 珍爱的;珍视的 **3** sophisticated in a way that is artificial and exaggerated 矫揉造作的,做作的 □ **precious little** (or **few**) informal 【非正式】very little (or **few**) 非常少 **precious metal** a valuable metal such as gold, silver, or platinum 贵金属(如金、银或铂) **precious stone** an attractive and valuable piece of mineral, used in jewellery 宝石

precipice /'presəpɪs/ **noun** a tall and very steep rock face or cliff 悬崖;峭壁

precipitate verb /prɪ'sɪpɪteɪt/ (**precipitates, precipitating, precipitated**) **1** make something bad happen suddenly or sooner than it should 使(坏事)突然发生;加速(坏事)发生 **2** make something move or happen suddenly and with force 使猛然移动 **3** Chemistry 【化学】cause a substance to be deposited in solid form from a solution 使沉淀;使淀析 **4** cause moisture in the air to condense and fall as rain, snow, etc. 使(水汽)凝结成雨(或雪等) • **adjective** /prɪ'sɪpɪtət/ done or happening suddenly or without careful thought 仓促的;轻率的 • **noun** /prɪ'sɪpɪteɪt, -tət/ Chemistry 【化学】a substance precipitated from a solution 沉淀物

precipitation /prɪˌsɪpɪ'teɪʃn/ **noun 1** rain, snow, sleet, or hail 降水(包括雨、雪、冻雨或冰雹) **2** Chemistry 【化学】the action of precipitating a substance from a solution 沉淀;淀析

precipitous /prɪ'sɪpɪtəs/ **adjective** dangerously high or steep 陡峭的;险峻的

precis /'preɪsi:/ (also **précis**) **noun** (plural **precis** /'preɪsi:, -si:z/) a short summary 提要;梗概 • **verb** (**precises** /'preɪsi:z/, **precising** /'preɪsi:ɪŋ/, **precised** /'preɪsi:d/) make a precis of 写…的摘要

precise /prɪ'saɪs/ **adjective 1** presented in a detailed and accurate way 详细的;精确的 **2** taking care to be exact and accurate 严谨的;细致的 **3** particular 特定的 ■ **precisely** adverb.

precision /prɪ'sɪʒn/ **noun** the quality of being exact, accurate, and careful 准确;精确;细致

preclude /prɪ'klu:d/ **verb** (**precludes, precluding, precluded**) prevent something from happening 防止;阻止;使不可能

precocious /prɪ'kəʊʃəs/ **adjective** having developed certain abilities or tendencies at an earlier age than usual 早熟的 ■ **precocity** noun.

precognition /ˌpri:kɒg'nɪʃn/ **noun** knowledge of an event before it happens 预知;预见

preconceived /ˌpri:kən'si:vd/ **adjective** (of an idea or opinion) formed before full knowledge or evidence is available (想法或观点)预先形成的,先入为主的

preconception /ˌpriːkənˈsepʃn/ **noun** a preconceived idea or opinion 先入为主的想法(或观点);成见

precondition /ˌpriːkənˈdɪʃn/ **noun** something that must exist or happen before other things can happen or be done 前提;先决条件

precursor /priˈkɜːsə(r)/ **noun** a person or thing that comes before another of the same kind 先驱;先兆;前身

pre-date /ˌpriːˈdeɪt/ **verb** happen, exist, or be found earlier than 早于;先于

predator /ˈpredətə(r)/ **noun** an animal that hunts and kills others for food 食肉动物

predatory /ˈpredətri/ **adjective 1** (of an animal) killing other animals for food (动物)食肉的,捕食其他动物的 **2** taking advantage of weaker people 欺负弱小的

predecease /ˌpriːdɪˈsiːs/ **verb** (**predeceases, predeceasing, predeceased**) formal 【正式】 die before another person 比(另一人)先死

predecessor /ˈpriːdɪsesə(r)/ **noun 1** a person who held a job or office before the current holder 前任;前辈 **2** a thing that has been followed or replaced by another 原有事物;前身

predestination /ˌpriːdestɪˈneɪʃn/ **noun** the belief that everything that happens has been decided in advance by God or fate 宿命论

predestined /ˌpriːˈdestɪnd/ **adjective** already decided by God or fate 上天注定的;命定的

predetermine /ˌpriːdɪˈtɜːmɪn/ **verb** (**predetermines, predetermining, predetermined**) establish or decide in advance 预先确立;预先决定

predicament /prɪˈdɪkəmənt/ **noun** a difficult situation 困境

predicate noun /ˈpredɪkət/ Grammar 【语法】 the part of a sentence or clause containing a verb and stating something about the subject (e.g. *went home* in *she went home*) 谓语 ● **verb** /ˈpredɪkeɪt/ (**predicates, predicating, predicated**) (**predicate something on**) base something on 使基于;使取决于

predicative /prɪˈdɪkətɪv/ **adjective** Grammar 【语法】 (of an adjective) coming after a verb, as *old* in *the dog is old* (形容词)谓语性的,表语的

predict /prɪˈdɪkt/ **verb** state that an event will happen in the future 预言;预料;预告;预报 ■ **predictive** adjective **predictor** noun.

predictable /prɪˈdɪktəbl/ **adjective 1** able to be predicted 可预言的;可预料的;可预报的 **2** always behaving or happening in the way that you would expect 不出所料的;墨守成规的 ■ **predictability** noun **predictably** adverb.

prediction /prɪˈdɪkʃn/ **noun 1** a statement saying that something will happen; a forecast 预言;预报 **2** the action of predicting 预言行为

predilection /ˌpriːdɪˈlekʃn/ **noun** a preference or special liking for something 偏爱;偏好

predispose /ˌpriːdɪˈspəʊz/ **verb** (**predisposes, predisposing, predisposed**) make someone likely to be, do, or think something 使倾向于;使易于 ■ **predisposition** noun.

predominant /prɪˈdɒmɪnənt/ **adjective 1** present as the main part of something 主要的;显著的 **2** having the greatest power 占支配地位的;占主导地位的 ■ **predominance** noun **predominantly** adverb.

predominate /prɪˈdɒmɪneɪt/ **verb** (**predominates, predominating, predominated**) **1** be the main part of something 占主导地位 **2** have control or power 主宰;支配

pre-eminent /prɪ'emɪnənt/ **adjective** better than all others 卓越的；超群的 ■ **pre-eminence** noun.

pre-empt /prɪ'empt/ **verb 1** take action so as to prevent something happening 在…之前行动；预先阻止 **2** stop someone from saying something by speaking first 抢在(某人)之前说出 ■ **preemption** noun **pre-emptive** adjective.

preen /priːn/ **verb 1** (of a bird) tidy and clean its feathers with its beak (鸟)用啄整理羽毛 **2** attend to and admire your appearance 精心打扮 **3** (**preen yourself**) feel very pleased with yourself 洋洋得意；沾沾自喜

pre-existing /priːɪg'zɪstɪŋ/ **adjective** existing from an earlier time 先前存在的

prefab /'priːfæb/ **noun** informal 【非正式】 a prefabricated building 预制装配式房屋

prefabricated /priː'fæbrɪkeɪtɪd/ **adjective** (of a building) made in previously constructed sections that can be easily put together on site (建筑)预制好构件的

preface /'prefɪs/ **noun** an introduction to a book (书的)前言，序言 • **verb** (**prefaces, prefacing, prefaced**) (**preface something with or by**) say or do something to introduce a book, speech, or event 为(书)作序；作…的开场白；以…为(事件)的开端

prefect /'priːfekt/ **noun 1** Brit. 【英】 a senior pupil in a school who has some authority over younger pupils (学校中负责维持纪律的)级长，班长 **2** a chief officer or regional governor in certain countries (一些国家的)地方行政长官

prefecture /'priːfektʃə(r)/ **noun** (in certain countries) a district administered by a prefect (某些国家)地方行政长官的辖区

prefer /prɪ'fɜː(r)/ **verb** (**prefers, preferring, preferred**) like one

person or thing better than another 更喜欢

✔ **拼写指南** double the *r* when forming the past tense: pre**ferr**ed. prefer 的过去时形式要双写 r，拼作 preferred。

preferable /'prefrəbl/ **adjective** more desirable or suitable 更可取的；更合适的 ■ **preferably** adverb.

preference /'prefrəns/ **noun 1** a greater liking for one person or thing than another 偏爱；喜好 **2** a thing preferred 偏爱的事物 **3** favour shown to one person over another 优先(权)

preferential /prefə'renʃl/ **adjective** favouring a particular person or group 优待的；优惠的 ■ **preferentially** adverb.

preferment /prɪ'fɜːmənt/ **noun** formal 【正式】 promotion to a job or position 提升；晋升；升职

prefigure /priː'fɪgə(r)/ **verb** (**prefigures, prefiguring, prefigured**) be an early sign or version of 预示；预兆

prefix /'priːfɪks/ **noun 1** a letter or group of letters placed at the beginning of a word to alter its meaning (e.g. *non-*) 前缀 **2** a word, letter, or number placed before another 前置词；前置代号；前束 • **verb** add a prefix to 把…置于前面；给…加前缀

pregnancy /'pregnənsi/ **noun** (plural **pregnancies**) the state or period of being pregnant 怀孕(期)；妊娠(期)

pregnant /'pregnənt/ **adjective 1** (of a woman) having a baby developing inside her womb (女子)怀孕的，妊娠的 **2** full of meaning 意味深长的

prehensile /prɪ'hensaɪl/ **adjective** (of an animal's limb or tail) capable of grasping things (动物的四肢或尾巴)能抓住东西的，缠绕的

prehistoric /priːhɪ'stɒrɪk/ **adjective** relating to the period before written records of events were made 有文字

记载以前的;史前的

prehistory /ˌpriːˈhɪstri/ **noun 1** the period of time before written records were made (有文字记载以前的)史前阶段 **2** the early stages in the development of something 最初发展阶段

pre-industrial /ˌpriːɪnˈdʌstriəl/ **adjective** before the development of industries 工业化以前的

prejudge /ˌpriːˈdʒʌdʒ/ **verb** (**prejudges, prejudging, prejudged**) make a judgement before you have all the necessary information (未了解全部情况而)预约对…作出判断

prejudice /ˈpredʒʊdɪs/ **noun 1** an opinion that is not based on reason or experience 偏见;成见 **2** unfair reactions or behaviour based on such opinions (由偏见产生的)反感,歧视 • **verb** (**prejudices, prejudicing, prejudiced**) **1** influence someone so that they form an opinion that is not based on reason or experience 使有成见,使产生偏见;使歧视 **2** cause harm to 损害;侵害

prejudicial /ˌpredʒʊˈdɪʃl/ **adjective** harmful to someone or something 有害的;不利的

prelate /ˈprelət/ **noun** a bishop or other high-ranking minister in the Christian Church (基督教)高级教士

preliminary /prɪˈlɪmɪnəri/ **adjective** taking place before a main action or event 初步的;预备的 • **noun** (plural **preliminaries**) a preliminary action or event 初步行动;开端;准备工作

prelude /ˈprelju:d/ **noun 1** an action or event acting as an introduction to something more important 前奏;序幕 **2** a piece of music introducing a longer piece 前奏曲

premarital /ˌpriːˈmærɪtl/ **adjective** happening before marriage 婚前的

premature /ˈpremətʃə(r)/ **adjective 1** happening or done before the proper time 比正常时间早的;过早的 **2** (of a baby) born before the normal length of pregnancy is completed (婴儿)早产的 ■ **prematurely** adverb.

premeditated /ˌpriːˈmedɪteɪtɪd/ **adjective** (of a crime or other bad action) planned in advance (罪行或其他恶行)预谋的,预先策划的 ■ **premeditation** noun.

premenstrual /ˌpriːˈmenstruəl/ **adjective** happening or experienced in the days of the month before menstruation 经期前的;月经前的

premier /ˈpremiə(r)/ **adjective** first in importance, order, or position 首要的;首位的;最先的 • **noun** a Prime Minister or other head of government 总理;首相 ■ **premiership** noun.

premiere /ˈpremieə(r)/ **noun** the first performance or showing of a play, film, ballet, etc. (戏剧、芭蕾等的)首次公演,(电影的)首映

premise or Brit. 【英】**premiss** /ˈpremɪs/ **noun** a statement or idea that forms the basis for a theory or argument 前提

premises /ˈpremɪsɪz/ **plural noun** the building and land occupied by a business (企业的)房屋及土地,生产场所,经营场所

premium /ˈpriːmiəm/ **noun** (plural **premiums**) **1** an amount paid for an insurance policy 保险费 **2** an extra sum added to a basic price (基本价格等的)加付款,额外费用 • **adjective** of high quality and more expensive 质优价高的 □ **at a premium 1** scarce and in demand 奇缺的;紧俏的 **2** above the usual price 以高于一般价格

premonition /ˌpriːməˈnɪʃn/ **noun** a strong feeling that something is going to happen (对某事即将发生的)预感 ■ **premonitory** adjective.

prenatal /ˌpriːˈneɪtl/ **adjective** N. Amer. 【北美】before birth 产前的;出生前的

preoccupation /priˌɒkjuˈpeɪʃn/ **noun 1** the state of being preoccupied 全神贯注;入神 **2** a matter that preoccupies someone 使人全神贯注的事物;使人入神的事物

preoccupy /priˈɒkjupaɪ/ **verb** (**preoccupies**, **preoccupying**, **preoccupied**) completely fill someone's mind 使人入神;使全神贯注

preordained /ˌpriːɔːˈdeɪnd/ **adjective** decided or determined beforehand 预先决定的;注定的

prep /prep/ **noun** Brit. informal【英, 非正式】school work done outside lessons 家庭作业 □ **prep school** a preparatory school 私立小学

prepaid /priːˈpeɪd/ **adjective** paid for in advance 预先支付的

preparation /ˌprepəˈreɪʃn/ **noun 1** the process of getting ready for something 准备;预备 **2** something that is done to get ready for something 准备工作;筹备工作 **3** a substance prepared for use as a medicine, cosmetic, etc. (用作药品、化妆品等的)制剂, 混合剂

preparatory /prɪˈpærətri/ **adjective** done in order to prepare for something 预备性的;准备性的 □ **preparatory school** Brit.【英】a private school for pupils aged seven to thirteen (7至13岁儿童就读的)私立小学

prepare /prɪˈpeə(r)/ **verb** (**prepares**, **preparing**, **prepared**) **1** make something ready for use 准备;预备 **2** get ready to do or deal with something 作好准备;准备好应付 **3** (**be prepared to do**) be willing to do 愿意做

preparedness /prɪˈpeərɪdnəs/ **noun** readiness 准备就绪

preponderance /prɪˈpɒndərəns/ **noun** a greater number or incidence of something 优势;多数

preponderant /prɪˈpɒndərənt/ **adjective** greater in number or happening more often 占优势的;主要的

preposition /ˌprepəˈzɪʃn/ **noun** Grammar【语法】a word used with a noun or pronoun to show place, time, or method 介词 ■ **prepositional** adjective.

prepossessing /ˌpriːpəˈzesɪŋ/ **adjective** attractive or appealing in appearance 有吸引力的;动人的

preposterous /prɪˈpɒstərəs/ **adjective** completely ridiculous or outrageous 荒谬的;无法容忍的 ■ **preposterously** adverb.

prepubescent /ˌpriːpjuːˈbesnt/ **adjective** having to do with the period before puberty 青春期前的

prerequisite /ˌpriːˈrekwɪzɪt/ **noun** a thing that must exist or happen before something else can exist or happen 先决条件;前提

prerogative /prɪˈrɒgətɪv/ **noun** a right or privilege belonging to a particular person or group 独有权利;特权

presage /ˈpresɪdʒ/ **verb** (**presages**, **presaging**, **presaged**) be a sign or warning of 预示;预兆 • **noun** an omen 预示;预兆

Presbyterian /ˌprezbɪˈtɪəriən/ **adjective** relating to a Protestant Church governed by elders who are all of equal rank (新教)长老派的, 长老会的 • **noun** a member of a Presbyterian Church 长老会教徒 ■ **Presbyterianism** noun.

presbytery /ˈprezbɪtri/ **noun** (plural **presbyteries**) **1** an administrative body in a Presbyterian Church (长老会的)教务评议会 **2** the house of a Roman Catholic parish priest (罗马天主教的)堂区神父住宅 **3** the eastern part of a church near the altar (教堂圣坛东侧的)教堂圣所

prescient /ˈpresiənt/ **adjective** knowing about things before they happen 有预知能力的;有先见之明的 ■ **prescience** noun.

prescribe /prɪˈskraɪb/ **verb** (**prescribes**, **prescribing**, **prescribed**) **1** (of a doctor) state officially that someone should take a particular medicine or have a particular treatment (医生)开(药)，建议(疗法) **2** state officially that something should be done 规定；指定

prescription /prɪˈskrɪpʃn/ **noun 1** a piece of paper on which a doctor states that a patient may be supplied with a medicine or treatment (书面的)药方，处方 **2** the action of prescribing a medicine or treatment 开药方；开处方

prescriptive /prɪˈskrɪptɪv/ **adjective** stating what should be done 规定的；指定的

presence /ˈprezns/ **noun 1** the state of being in a particular place 在场；出席；存在 **2** a person's impressive manner or appearance 仪态；仪表；风度 **3** a person or thing that seems to be present but is not seen (看不见的)存在物(或人)；鬼怪；神灵 □ **presence of mind** the ability to remain calm and act sensibly in a difficult situation 镇定自若；处变不惊

present[1] /ˈpreznt/ **adjective 1** being or existing in a particular place 在场的；出席的；存在的 **2** existing or happening now 现存的；目前的 **3** Grammar 【语法】(of a tense of a verb) expressing an action or state happening or existing now (动词时态)现在时的 • **noun** the period of time happening now 现在；目前；如今 □ **present participle** Grammar 【语法】the form of a verb, ending in -ing, which is used in forming tenses describing continuous action (e.g. I'm thinking), as a noun (e.g. good thinking), and as an adjective (e.g. running water) 现在分词

present[2] **verb** /prɪˈzent/ **1** formally give someone something 正式递交；呈送；授予 **2** offer something for consideration or payment 提交，提出(以供考虑或付款) **3** formally introduce someone to someone else 引见；正式介绍 **4** produce a show, broadcast, etc. for the public 上演；演出 **5** introduce and take part in a television or radio show 主持(电视或广播节目) **6** be the cause of a problem 引起，导致(问题) **7** give a particular impression to other people 显示出；表现出：We must present a united front. 我们必须结成统一战线。 **8** (**present yourself**) appear at or attend a formal or official occasion 出席(正式场合)；到场 • **noun** /ˈpreznt/ a thing given to someone as a gift 礼物 ■ **presenter** noun.

presentable /prɪˈzentəbl/ **adjective** looking smart enough to be seen in public 像样的；体面的；拿得出手的

presentation /ˌprezn'teɪʃn/ **noun** the action of presenting something, or the way in which it is presented 授予；呈送；展示；外观 ■ **presentational** adjective.

presentiment /prɪˈzentɪmənt/ **noun** a feeling that something unpleasant is going to happen (不祥的)预感

presently /ˈprezntli/ **adverb 1** soon 很快；不久 **2** now 目前；现在

preservative /prɪˈzɜːvətɪv/ **noun** a substance used to prevent food or wood from decaying 防腐剂

preserve /prɪˈzɜːv/ **verb** (**preserves**, **preserving**, **preserved**) **1** keep something in its original state or in good condition 保持，维持(原样或良好状况) **2** keep someone safe from harm 保护；维护 **3** treat food to prevent it from decaying (为保鲜)腌制(食物)；使防腐 • **noun 1** a food preserved in sugar, salt, vinegar, alcohol, such as jam or pickle 腌制食品 **2** something reserved for a particular person or group (某人或某群体的)专有物 **3** a place where game is protected and kept for private hunting 私人狩猎区 ■ **preservation** noun **preserver** noun.

preset /priːˈset/ **verb** (**presets**,

presetting, preset) set the controls of an electrical device before it is used 预先设置,调试(电子设备)

preside /prɪˈzaɪd/ **verb** (**presides, presiding, presided**) lead or be in charge of a meeting or event 主持,主管(会议、活动等)

presidency /ˈprezɪdənsi/ **noun** (plural **presidencies**) the job of president, or the period of time it is held 总统(或总裁、校长等)职位;总统(或总裁、校长等)任期

president /ˈprezɪdənt/ **noun 1** the elected head of a republic 总统 **2** the head of an organization 主管人,总裁,会长,校长 ∎ **presidential** adjective.

presidium /prɪˈsɪdiəm/ **noun** a permanent decision-making committee within a political organization, especially a communist one 主席团;常务委员会

press¹ /pres/ **verb 1** (**press against** or **to**) move into contact with something by using steady force 压;挤;紧 贴 **2** push something that operates a device 按,揿(以启动设备) **3** apply pressure to something to flatten or shape it 压平,熨平,把…压成型 **4** move by pushing 挤着走 **5** (**press on** or **ahead**) continue in what you are doing 继续进行;坚持进行 **6** express or repeat an opinion or claim in a forceful way 竭力推行,坚持(意见或主张) **7** make strong efforts to persuade someone to do something 催促;敦促;竭力劝说 **8** (**be pressed for**) have too little of 紧缺,短缺 **9** (**be pressed to do**) have difficulty doing 勉强做 ∎ **noun 1** a device for crushing, flattening, or shaping something 压榨机,压平器,熨烫机 **2** a printing press 印刷机 **3** (**the press**) newspapers or journalists as a whole 报业,新闻界 □ **press conference** a meeting with journalists in order to make an announcement or answer questions

记者招待会 **press release** a statement or piece of publicity issued to journalists (向媒体发布的)新闻稿 **press stud** Brit.【英】a small fastener with two parts that fit together when pressed 揿扣;子母扣 **press-up** Brit.【英】an exercise in which you lie face down on the floor and push your body up by pressing down with your hands and arms 俯卧撑

press² **verb** (in the past) force someone to serve in the army or navy (旧时)强征(某人)入伍 □ **press gang** (in the past) a group of men employed to force men to serve in the army or navy (旧时)的征兵队,抓壮丁队 **press-gang** force someone into doing something 强迫做 **press someone/thing into service** use someone or something for a particular purpose as a temporary or emergency measure 暂时使用,临时凑合

pressing /ˈpresɪŋ/ **adjective 1** needing urgent action 紧迫的,迫切的 **2** strongly expressed and difficult to refuse or ignore 恳切的;坚持的 ∎ **noun** an object made by pressing 冲压件;模压制品

pressure /ˈpreʃə(r)/ **noun 1** steady force applied to an object by something that is in contact with it 压力 **2** the use of persuasion or threats to make someone do something 施压 **3** a feeling of stress caused by the need to do something (因要做某事产生的)压力,困扰 **4** the force per unit area applied by a fluid against a surface 压力;压强 ∎ **verb** (**pressures, pressuring, pressured**) persuade or force someone into doing something 对…施加压力;迫使;威逼 □ **pressure cooker** a large airtight saucepan in which food is cooked quickly in steam held under pressure 压力锅;高压锅 **pressure group** a group that tries to influence the government or public opinion in order to help a cause (试图影响政府政策或公众意见的)压力集团

pressurize or **pressurise** /'preʃəraɪz/ **verb** (**pressurizes, pressurizing, pressurized**) **1** persuade or force someone into doing something 对…施加压力;强迫;威逼 **2** keep the air pressure in an aircraft cabin the same as it is at ground level 使(飞机座舱)保持正常气压

prestige /pre'stiːʒ/ **noun** respect and admiration resulting from achievements or high quality 声望,名望;威信

prestigious /pre'stɪdʒəs/ **adjective** having or bringing prestige 有威望的;受人尊敬的

presto /'prestəʊ/ **adverb & adjective** Music【音乐】in a quick tempo 急板地(的)

prestressed /ˌpriː'strest/ **adjective** (of concrete) strengthened by means of rods inserted under tension before setting (混凝土)预应力的

presumably /prɪ'zjuːməblɪ/ **adverb** as may be supposed 据推测

presume /prɪ'zjuːm/ **verb** (**presumes, presuming, presumed**) **1** suppose that something is probably true 推测;假定;假设 **2** show a lack of respect by doing something that you do not have authority or permission to do 擅自行事;肆意妄为 **3** (**presume on**) take advantage of someone's kindness, friendship, etc. 利用,滥用(某人的善良、友情等)

presumption /prɪ'zʌmpʃn/ **noun** **1** something that is thought to be true or probable 假定的事物 **2** an act of presuming 假定;假设 **3** behaviour that is too confident 妄自尊大;傲慢无礼

presumptuous /prɪ'zʌmptʃuəs/ **adjective** behaving too confidently 妄自尊大的;傲慢无礼的 ■ **presumptuously** adverb.

✔ **拼写指南** *-uous*, not *-ious*: presumptuous. presumptuous 中的 -uous 不要拼作 -ious。

---

presuppose /ˌpriːsə'pəʊz/ **verb** (**presupposes, presupposing, presupposed**) **1** need something to have happened in order to exist or be true 以…为先决条件;预设 **2** assume, without knowing for sure, that something exists or is true and act on that basis 假定;假设 ■ **presupposition** noun.

pretence /prɪ'tens/ (US spelling【美拼作】**pretense**) **noun** **1** an act of pretending 假装;伪装 **2** a claim to have or be something 自称;自夸

pretend /prɪ'tend/ **verb** **1** make it seem that something is the case when in fact it is not 假装;佯称 **2** give the appearance of feeling or having an emotion or quality 假装具有(某种感情或品质) **3** (**pretend to**) claim to have a skill, quality, or title 自封;声称

pretender /prɪ'tendə(r)/ **noun** a person who claims a right to a title or position (头衔或职位的)觊觎者,妄求者

pretension /prɪ'tenʃn/ **noun** **1** the act of trying to appear more important or better than you actually are 做作;矫饰 **2** (also **pretensions**) a claim to have or be something 自命;声称

pretentious /prɪ'tenʃəs/ **adjective** trying to appear more important or better than you actually are so as to impress other people 做作的;矫饰的 ■ **pretentiousness** noun.

preternatural /ˌpriːtə'nætʃrəl/ **adjective** beyond what is normal or natural 异常的;超自然的 ■ **preternaturally** adverb.

pretext /'priːtekst/ **noun** a false reason used to justify an action 借口;托词

prettify /'prɪtɪfaɪ/ **verb** (**prettifies, prettifying, prettified**) try to make something look pretty 美化；粉饰

pretty /'prɪti/ **adjective (prettier, prettiest) 1** (of a woman or girl) having an attractive face (女子)漂亮的，俊俏的 **2** pleasant to look at 赏心悦目的；美观的 • **adverb** informal 【非正式】 to a certain extent; fairly 相当；颇 ■ **prettily** adverb **prettiness** noun.

pretzel /'pretsl/ **noun** a crisp salty biscuit in the shape of a knot or stick 椒盐卷饼/纽结状椒盐脆饼

prevail /prɪ'veɪl/ **verb 1** be widespread or current 流行 **2** (**prevail against** or **over**) be more powerful than 占优势；占上风 **3** (**prevail on**) persuade someone to do something 劝说；说服

prevalent /'prevələnt/ **adjective** widespread; common 流行的，普遍的 ■ **prevalence** noun.

prevaricate /prɪ'værɪkeɪt/ **verb** (**prevaricates**, **prevaricating**, **prevaricated**) avoid giving a direct answer to a question 搪塞；含糊其词 ■ **prevarication** noun.

prevent /prɪ'vent/ **verb 1** keep something from happening 防止，预防 **2** stop someone from doing something 阻止；妨碍 ■ **preventable** adjective **prevention** noun.

preventive /prɪ'ventɪv/ or **preventative** /prɪ'ventətɪv/ **adjective** designed to prevent something from happening 预防(性)的；防止的

preview /'priːvjuː/ **noun 1** a viewing or showing of something before it becomes generally available 预观，预演；预展 **2** a review of a forthcoming film, book, or performance (对即将上映或上演的电影或演出的)预告，预审(对即将出版图书的)预评

previous /'priːvɪəs/ **adjective 1** coming before something else in time or order 先前的；在先的 **2** (**previous to**) before 在…以前 ■ **previously** adverb.

prey /preɪ/ **noun 1** an animal that is hunted and killed by another for food 被捕食的动物；猎物 **2** a person who is harmed or deceived by someone or something 受害人；受骗者 • **verb** (**prey on**) **1** hunt and kill another animal for food 捕猎，捕食 **2** take advantage of or cause distress to someone 劫掠；折磨；使痛苦

price /praɪs/ **noun 1** the amount of money for which something is bought or sold 价格；价钱 **2** something unwelcome that must be done in order to achieve something 代价 **3** the odds in betting (赌博中的)投注赔率 • **verb** (**prices**, **pricing**, **priced**) decide the price of 给…定价

priceless /'praɪsləs/ **adjective 1** very valuable 贵重的；无价的 **2** informal 【非正式】 very amusing 极有趣的

pricey /'praɪsi/ **adjective** (**pricier, priciest**) informal 【非正式】 expensive 昂贵的

prick /prɪk/ **verb 1** make a small hole in something with a sharp point 在…上刺孔；戳 **2** cause someone to feel a small, sharp pain 刺痛；使有刺痛感 • **noun** a mark, hole, or pain caused by pricking 刺痕；刺孔；刺痛感 ◻ **prick up your ears 1** (of a horse or dog) raise the ears when alert (马或狗警觉时)竖起耳朵 **2** suddenly begin to pay attention 侧耳倾听

prickle /'prɪkl/ **noun 1** a small thorn on a plant or a pointed spine on an animal (动植物的)皮刺，刺，棘 **2** a tingling feeling on the skin (皮肤的)刺痛感 • **verb** (**prickles**, **prickling**, **prickled**) have a tingling feeling on the skin (皮肤)感到刺痛

prickly /'prɪkli/ **adjective 1** having prickles 有刺的；多刺的 **2** causing a prickling feeling 引起刺痛的；痒的 **3** easily offended or annoyed 易生气的；敏感的 ◻ **prickly pear** a cactus which produces prickly, pear-shaped fruits 仙人果；刺梨

pride /praɪd/ **noun 1** deep pleasure or satisfaction felt if you or people close to you have done something well 自豪(感) **2** a source of pride 引以为豪的人(或事物)；骄傲: *The team is the pride of the town.* 这个球队是该城的骄傲。 **3** self-respect 自尊(心) **4** the feeling that you are better than other people 骄傲；自负；自大 **5** a group of lions 狮群 • **verb** (**prides, priding, prided**) (**pride yourself on**) be especially proud of a quality or skill 以…为豪；为…感到骄傲 □ **pride of place** the most noticeable or important position 最引人注目的位置；最重要的地位

priest /priːst/ **noun 1** a person who is qualified to perform religious ceremonies in the Christian Church (基督教的)神父，牧师 **2** (also **priestess**) a person who performs ceremonies in a non-Christian religion (基督教以外宗教的)神职人员 ■ **priesthood** noun **priestly** adjective.

prig /prɪg/ **noun** a person who behaves as if they are morally superior to other people 一本正经的人；道学先生 ■ **priggish** adjective.

prim /prɪm/ **adjective** very formal and correct and disapproving of anything rude 一本正经的；古板的 ■ **primly** adverb.

prima ballerina /ˌpriːmə ˌbæləˈriːnə/ **noun** the chief female dancer in a ballet company 芭蕾舞团首席女演员

primacy /ˈpraɪməsi/ **noun** the fact of being most important 第一位；首位；首要

prima donna /ˌpriːmə ˈdɒnə/ **noun 1** the chief female singer in an opera 歌剧女主角 **2** a very temperamental and self-important person 妄自尊大爱发脾气的人

primaeval /praɪˈmiːvl/ ⇒ 见 PRIMEVAL.

prima facie /ˌpraɪmə ˈfeɪʃi/ **adjective & adverb** Law 【法律】 accepted as correct until proved otherwise 初步认定的；初步地

primal /ˈpraɪml/ **adjective** having to do with early human life; primeval 最初的；原始的

primarily /praɪˈmerəli/ **adverb** for the most part; mainly 主要地；根本上

primary /ˈpraɪməri/ **adjective 1** of chief importance 首要的 **2** earliest in time or order 最初的；原始的 **3** (of education) for children between the ages of about five and eleven (教育)初级的，小学的 • **noun** (plural **primaries**) (in the US) a preliminary election to appoint delegates to a party conference or to choose candidates for an election (美国政党选举的)初选 □ **primary colour** each of the colours blue, red, and yellow, from which all other colours can be obtained by mixing 原色, 基色(可用以调配出其他所有颜色的蓝、红、黄色之一)

primate /ˈpraɪmeɪt/ **noun 1** an animal belonging to the group that includes monkeys, apes, and humans 灵长目动物 **2** (in the Christian Church) an archbishop (基督教的)大主教，总主教

prime¹ /praɪm/ **adjective 1** of chief importance 首要的；主要的 **2** of the highest quality; excellent 一流的；最好的 **3** (of a number) that can be divided only by itself and one (e.g. 2, 3, 5) (数字)素数的, 质数的 • **noun** the time in a person's life when they are the strongest and most successful 壮年；全盛时期 □ **prime minister** the head of a government 首相, 总理 **prime time** the time at which a radio or television audience is greatest (收听广播或收看电视的)高峰时间, 黄金时段

prime² verb (**primes, priming, primed**) **1** prepare someone for a situation by giving them information (通过提供信息)使作好准备 **2** make something ready for use or action 使

可用；使就绪 **3** cover a surface with primer 涂底漆于(表面)

primer /ˈpraɪmə(r)/ **noun 1** a substance painted on a surface as a base coat 底层涂料；底漆 **2** a book for teaching children to read or giving a basic introduction to a subject 识字课本；入门读物

primeval or **primaeval** /praɪˈmiːvl/ **adjective** relating to the earliest times in history 原始的；远古的

primitive /ˈprɪmɪtɪv/ **adjective 1** relating to the earliest times in history or stages in development 原始的；早期的 **2** offering a very basic level of comfort 简陋的；简单的 **3** (of behaviour or emotion) not based on reason; instinctive (行为或情感)质朴的，本能的 ■ **primitively** adverb.

primordial /praɪˈmɔːdiəl/ **adjective** existing at the beginning of time 原始的；原生的

primp /prɪmp/ **verb** make small adjustments to your appearance 修饰，打扮(外表)

primrose /ˈprɪmrəʊz/ **noun** a plant of woods and hedges with pale yellow flowers 报春花(生长于林木或灌木丛中，开浅黄色花)

primula /ˈprɪmjələ/ **noun** a plant of a group that includes primroses and cowslips 报春花属植物(包括报春花、黄花九轮草等)

prince /prɪns/ **noun** a son or other close male relative of a king or queen 王子；亲王；王孙 □ **prince consort** the husband of a reigning queen who is himself a prince 女王丈夫；王夫 **Prince of Wales** the title given to the eldest son of a British king or queen 威尔士亲王(英国国王或女王长子的封号)

princeling /ˈprɪnslɪŋ/ **noun 1** the ruler of a small country (小国的)统治者；小诸侯 **2** a young prince 幼年王子；幼君

princely /ˈprɪnsli/ **adjective 1** relating to or suitable for a prince 王子的；王侯的；与王子(或王侯)地位相称的 **2** (of a sum of money) generous (钱)大笔的

princess /ˌprɪnˈses/ **noun 1** a daughter or other close female relative of a king or queen 公主 **2** the wife or widow of a prince 王妃 □ **Princess Royal** a title given to the eldest daughter of a British king or queen 大公主，长公主(英国授予国王或女王长女的封号)

principal /ˈprɪnsəpl/ **adjective** most important; main 最重要的；主要的 ● **noun 1** the most important person in an organization or group (组织或团体的)负责人，首领 **2** the head of a school or college 校长；院长 **3** a sum of money lent or invested, on which interest is paid 本金；资本 □ **principal boy** Brit. 【英】a woman who takes the leading male role in a pantomime 哑剧中扮演男主角的女演员 ■ **principally** adverb.

> **！注意** don't confuse the words **principal** and **principle**. Principal is usually an adjective meaning 'main or most important', whereas **principle** is a noun meaning 'a law, rule, or theory on which something is based'. 不要混淆单词 principal 和 principle。principal 通常用作形容词，意为"主要的，最重要的"，而 principle 是名词，意为"法则，原则，原理"。

principality /ˌprɪnsɪˈpæləti/ **noun** (plural **principalities**) **1** a state ruled by a prince 公国；侯国；封邑 **2** (**the Principality**) Brit. 【英】Wales 威尔士

principle /ˈprɪnsəpl/ **noun 1** a law, rule, or theory on which something is based 法则；原理 **2** (**principles**) rules or beliefs that govern the way you behave (行为)准则，原则 **3** a scientific theorem or natural law that explains why something happens or how it works 原理；法则 □ **in principle** in theory 理论上 **on principle** because of your moral principles 基于道德准则

principled /ˈprɪnsəpld/ *adjective* acting according to strong moral principles 原则性的；基于道德准则的

print /prɪnt/ *verb* **1** produce a book, newspaper, etc. by a process involving the transfer of words or pictures to paper 印刷，出版(书、报等) **2** produce a photographic print from a negative 印出，冲洗(照片) **3** write words clearly without joining the letters 用印刷体书写 **4** mark fabric with a coloured design 印(或烙)图案于 • *noun* **1** printed words in a book, newspaper, etc. (书、报纸等上)印出的文字 **2** a mark where something has pressed or touched a surface 印痕，印记 **3** a printed picture or design 印出的画(或图案) □ **in** (or **out of**) **print** (of a book) available (or no longer available) from the publisher (书)仍在售(或已绝版) ■ **printer** *noun*.

printing /ˈprɪntɪŋ/ *noun* **1** the transfer of words or pictures to paper in the production of books, newspapers, etc. 印刷 **2** handwriting in which the letters are written separately 印刷体 □ **printing press** a machine for printing books, newspapers, etc. by pressing an ink-covered surface on to paper 印刷机

printout /ˈprɪntaʊt/ *noun* a page of printed material from a computer's printer (电脑打印机的)打印件，打印稿

prion /ˈpriːɒn/ *noun* a protein particle believed to be the cause of brain diseases such as BSE and CJD 朊毒，朊病毒(一种据信可引起牛海绵状脑病和克-雅病等脑病的蛋白粒子)

prior¹ /ˈpraɪə(r)/ *adjective* **1** coming before in time, order, or importance 在前的；优先的；较重要的 **2** (**prior**

to) before 在…以前

prior² *noun* (feminine **prioress**) **1** (in an abbey) the person next in rank below an abbot or abbess (大修道院的)副院长 **2** the head of a house of friars or nuns 小修道院院长

prioritize or **prioritise** /praɪˈɒrɪtaɪz/ *verb* (**prioritizes, prioritizing, prioritized**) **1** decide the order of importance of a number of tasks 确定(事项)的优先顺序 **2** treat something as being more important than other things 优先考虑

priority /praɪˈɒrəti/ *noun* (plural **priorities**) **1** the condition of being more important than other things 优先；重点；优先权 **2** a thing seen as more important than others 优先考虑的事物 **3** Brit. 【英】the right to go before other traffic (车辆的)优先通行权

priory /ˈpraɪəri/ *noun* (plural **priories**) a monastery or nunnery governed by a prior or prioress 小修道院；小女修道院

prise /praɪz/ (US spelling 【美拼作】**prize**) *verb* (**prises, prising, prised**) force something open or apart 撬开；撬起

prism /ˈprɪzəm/ *noun* **1** a piece of glass or other transparent material with facets, used to separate white light into a spectrum of colours 棱镜 **2** a solid geometric figure whose two ends are parallel and of the same size and shape, and whose sides are parallelograms 棱柱(体) ■ **prismatic** *adjective*.

prison /ˈprɪzn/ *noun* a building where criminals are kept as a punishment 监狱；看守所

prisoner /ˈprɪznə(r)/ *noun* **1** a person who has been found guilty of a crime and sent to prison 囚徒；犯人 **2** a person who has been captured by someone and kept confined 被囚禁的人；囚徒 □ **prisoner of war** a person captured and imprisoned by the enemy in war 战俘

prissy /'prɪsi/ **adjective** too concerned with behaving in a correct and respectable way 谨小慎微的;拘谨的;刻板的

pristine /'prɪstiːn/ **adjective 1** in its original condition 原始状态的;完好无损的 **2** clean and fresh as if new 崭新的;新鲜如初的

privacy /'prɪvəsi/ **noun** a state in which you are not watched or disturbed by other people 独处;清静

private /'praɪvət/ **adjective 1** intended for or involving a particular person or group 私用的;个人的;私有的 **2** (of thoughts, feelings, etc.) that you do not tell other people about (想法、感情等)秘密的,非公开的 **3** not sharing thoughts and feelings with other people 喜欢独处的;不愿吐露心思的;内向的 **4** where you will not be disturbed; secluded (地方)清静的,僻静的 **5** (of a service or industry) provided by an individual or commercial company rather than the state (服务或产业)私人提供的,私营的 **6** not connected with a person's work or official role 私人的;与工作(或公职)无关的 • **noun** (also **private soldier**) a soldier of the lowest rank in the army 列兵;二等兵 □ **private company** Brit. 【英】a company whose shares may not be offered to the public for sale 私人公司,股权不公开公司(指股权不向公众发售的公司) **private detective** a detective who is not a police officer and who carries out investigations for clients 私家侦探 **private enterprise** business or industry managed by independent companies rather than the state 私营企业 **private eye** informal【非正式】a private detective 私家侦探 **private member** a member of parliament who does not hold a government office 无公职议员 **private**

parts a person's genitals 私处;阴部 **private practice** the work of a doctor, lawyer, etc. who is self-employed (医生、律师等的)私人开业 **private school** Brit.【英】an independent school financed mainly by the fees paid by pupils 私立学校 **private secretary 1** a secretary who deals with the personal matters of their employer 私人秘书 **2** a civil servant acting as an assistant to a senior government official (政府高级官员的)私人秘书,私人助理 **private sector** the part of the national economy not under direct state control (国民经济的)私营部分 ■ **privately** adverb.

privateer /ˌpraɪvə'tɪə(r)/ **noun** (in the past) an armed but privately owned ship, authorized by a government for use in war (旧时的)私掠船(战时政府授权的武装民船)

privation /praɪ'veɪʃn/ **noun** a state in which you do not have the basic things you need, such as food and warmth (生活必需品的)匮乏;贫困

privatize or **privatise** /'praɪvətaɪz/ **verb** (**privatizes**, **privatizing**, **privatized**) transfer a business or industry from ownership by the state to private ownership 使(国有产业)私有化 ■ **privatization** noun.

privet /'prɪvɪt/ **noun** a shrub with small white flowers 女贞(一种灌木,开白色小花)

privilege /'prɪvəlɪdʒ/ **noun 1** a special right or advantage for a particular person or group 特权;优惠;特殊待遇 **2** an opportunity to do something regarded as a special honour 殊荣;荣幸 **3** the advantages available to people who are rich and powerful (有钱有势者的)特权,特殊待遇

✔ 拼写指南 -il-, not -el-, and no d: privilege. privilege 中的 -il- 不要拼作 -el-,也没有 d 字母。

privileged /ˈprɪvəlɪdʒd/ **adjective 1** having a privilege or privileges 享有特权(的)的; 获得优待的 **2** (of information) protected from being made public (信息)保密的

privy /ˈprɪvi/ **adjective** (**privy to**) sharing in the knowledge of something secret (对秘密)知情的; 了解内情的 • **noun** (plural **privies**) a toilet in a small shed outside a house (房子外的)简易厕所 □ **Privy Council** a group of politicians appointed to advise a king or queen 枢密院

prize¹ /praɪz/ **noun 1** a thing given to someone who wins a competition or race or to mark an outstanding achievement 奖品; 奖项; 奖赏 **2** something that is worth struggling to achieve 值得追求的东西 • **adjective 1** having been awarded a prize 获奖的 **2** outstanding 第一流的; 优质的 • **verb** (**prizes, prizing, prized**) value highly 重视; 珍视

prize² US spelling of PRISE. prise 的美式拼法

pro¹ /prəʊ/ informal 【非正式】 **noun** (plural **pros**) a professional, especially in sport 专业人士; (尤指)职业运动员 • **adjective** professional 专业的; 职业的

pro² **noun** (plural **pros**) (usu. in 通常用于 **pros and cons**) an advantage of or argument in favour of something 赞成的立场; 赞成的论点

proactive /prəʊˈæktɪv/ **adjective** creating or controlling a situation rather than just responding to it 积极的; 主动的; 预先采取行动的 ■ **proactively** adverb.

probability /ˌprɒbəˈbɪləti/ **noun** (plural **probabilities**) **1** the extent to which something is probable 可能性 **2** an event that is likely to happen 很可能发生的事

probable /ˈprɒbəbl/ **adjective** likely to happen or be the case 很可能的

probably /ˈprɒbəbli/ **adverb** almost

certainly 很可能

probate /ˈprəʊbeɪt/ **noun** the official process of proving that a will is valid 遗嘱检验; 遗嘱认证

probation /prəˈbeɪʃn/ **noun 1** a system in which a person who has committed a crime does not have to go to prison if they behave well and report regularly to an official 缓刑 **2** a period of training and testing when you start a new job 试用期; 见习期 ■ **probationary** adjective **probationer** noun.

probe /prəʊb/ **noun 1** an investigation 探查; 调查 **2** a surgical instrument used to examine the body (医用)探针 **3** a small device for measuring or testing something 探测仪 **4** (also **space probe**) an unmanned spacecraft used for exploration (无人驾驶)航天探测器 • **verb** (**probes, probing, probed**) **1** physically explore or examine something 用探针探测(或检查) **2** investigate something closely 探究; 查查 ■ **probing** adjective.

probity /ˈprəʊbəti/ **noun** formal 【正式】 the quality of being honest and having high moral standards 诚实; 正直

problem /ˈprɒbləm/ **noun** a thing that is difficult to deal with or understand 棘手的事情; 问题; 困难

problematic /ˌprɒbləˈmætɪk/ or **problematical** /ˌprɒbləˈmætɪkl/ **adjective** difficult to deal with or understand 有问题的; 疑难的

proboscis /prəˈbɒsɪs/ **noun** (plural **probosces** /prəˈbɒsiːz/ or **proboscises**) **1** a mammal's long, flexible snout, e.g. an elephant's trunk (象等哺乳动物的)长鼻 **2** the long, thin mouth of some insects (某些昆虫的)长喙, 吻

procedure /prəˈsiːdʒə(r)/ **noun 1** an established or official way of doing something 常规; 惯例; (官方的)程序; 手续 **2** a series of actions done in a certain way 步骤；过程 ■ **procedural** adjective.

proceed /prə'si:d/ verb **1** begin a course of action 开展；开始进行 **2** go on to do something 进而做；接着做 **3** carry on or continue 继续进行

proceedings /prə'si:dɪŋz/ plural noun **1** an event or a series of actions 事件；(一连串)行动 **2** action taken in a law court to settle a dispute 诉讼

proceeds /'prəʊsi:dz/ plural noun money obtained from an event or activity 从某个事件或活动得到的收入，收益

process[1] /'prəʊses/ noun **1** a series of actions that are done to achieve a particular end 过程；步骤；程序 **2** a natural series of changes 自然进程；变化过程：*the ageing process* 衰老过程 • verb **1** perform a series of actions on something to change or preserve it 对…进行加工(或处理) **2** deal with someone or something using an established procedure (按照固定手续)处理，办理 ■ **processor** noun.

process[2] /prə'ses/ verb walk in procession 列队行进

procession /prə'seʃn/ noun **1** a number of people or vehicles moving forward in an orderly way (人或车辆的行进)行列，队列 **2** a large number of people or things that come one after another (一个接一个出现的)一大队人，大量事物

proclaim /prə'kleɪm/ verb **1** announce officially or publicly 正式宣告；公布；声明 **2** show something clearly 显示；表明 ■ **proclamation** noun.

proclivity /prə'klɪvəti/ noun (plural **proclivities**) a tendency to do something regularly 倾向；癖好

procrastinate /prəʊ'kræstɪneɪt/ verb (**procrastinates, procrastinating, procrastinated**) delay or postpone action 拖延；推迟 ■ **procrastination** noun.

procreate /'prəʊkrieɪt/ verb (pro-

creates, procreating, procreated) produce a baby or young animal 生育；生殖 ■ **procreation** noun.

proctor /'prɒktə(r)/ noun Brit. 【英】 an officer in charge of discipline at some universities (某些大学的)校监，学监

procurator fiscal /'prɒkjʊreɪtə 'fɪskl/ noun (plural **procurators fiscal** or **procurator fiscals**) (in Scotland) a local coroner and public prosecutor (苏格兰的)地方检察官

procure /prə'kjʊə(r)/ verb (**procures, procuring, procured**) obtain 获得；得到 ■ **procurement** noun.

prod /prɒd/ verb (**prods, prodding, prodded**) **1** push someone or something with a finger or pointed object (以手指或尖物)戳，刺，捅 **2** prompt or remind someone to do something 激励；敦促；提醒 • noun **1** an act of prodding 戳；刺；捅 **2** a prompt or reminder 刺激；激励；提醒物 **3** a pointed object like a stick 尖物；锥；刺针

prodigal /'prɒdɪgl/ adjective **1** using time, money, etc. in a wasteful way 挥霍的；浪费的 **2** lavish 非常慷慨的；大方的 • noun (also **prodigal son**) a person who leaves home and leads a wasteful life but is later sorry for their actions and returns 回头的浪子 ■ **prodigality** noun.

prodigious /prə'dɪdʒəs/ adjective impressively large 庞大的；巨大的 ■ **prodigiously** adverb.

prodigy /'prɒdədʒi/ noun (plural **prodigies**) a young person with exceptional abilities (年轻的)奇才，天才

produce verb /prə'dju:s/ (**produces, producing, produced**) **1** make, manufacture, or create 生产；制造；创造 **2** make something happen or exist 引起；导致；产生 **3** show or provide something for consideration 提出；出示 **4** be in charge of the

financial aspects of a film or the staging of a play 监制，制作(电影或戏剧) **5** supervise the making of a musical recording 制作(音乐唱片)
• **noun** /'prɒdjuːs/ things that have been produced or grown 产品；农产品 ■ **producer** noun.

product /'prɒdʌkt/ **noun 1** an article or substance manufactured for sale 产品；制品 **2** a result of an action or process 结果；结局 **3** a substance produced during a natural, chemical, or manufacturing process 产物 **4** Maths 【数学】 a quantity obtained by multiplying one number by another (乘)积

production /prə'dʌkʃn/ **noun 1** the action of producing something 生产；制造 **2** the amount of something produced 产量 □ **production line** an assembly line 生产线；装配线

productive /prə'dʌktɪv/ **adjective 1** producing large amounts of goods or crops 多产的；富饶的 **2** doing or achieving a lot 富有成效的；成果丰硕的 ■ **productively** adverb.

productivity /ˌprɒdʌk'tɪvəti/ **noun 1** the quality of being productive 多产；富饶 **2** the efficiency with which things are produced 生产率

profane /prə'feɪn/ **adjective 1** not religious; secular 非宗教的；世俗的 **2** not having respect for God or holy things 亵渎的；不敬神的 • **verb** (**profanes**, **profaning**, **profaned**) treat something holy with a lack of respect 亵渎(神圣物)

profanity /prə'fænəti/ **noun** (plural **profanities**) **1** language or behaviour that shows a lack of respect for God or holy thing 渎神言语(或行为) **2** a swear word 咒骂语

profess /prə'fes/ **verb 1** claim that something is true 自称；表明 **2** declare your faith in a religion 表明信奉(某宗教)

profession /prə'feʃn/ **noun 1** a job

that needs special training and a formal qualification (需要特殊培训和正式资格的)职业，专业 **2** all the people working in a particular profession 同业；同行 **3** a claim 声称 **4** a declaration of belief in a religion (对宗教信仰的)声明，表白

professional /prə'feʃənl/ **adjective 1** relating to or belonging to a profession 职业的，专业的 **2** doing something as a job rather than as a hobby 职业(性)的；非业余的 **3** having the skills or qualities of a professional person 专业化的；内行的 • **noun 1** a professional person 职业人员；专业人士 **2** a person who is very skilled in a particular activity 专家；内行 ■ **professionally** adverb.

✔ **拼写指南** only one *f*: professional. professional 中只有一个 f。

---

professionalism /prə'feʃənəlɪzəm/ **noun** the ability or skill that you expect from a professional person 专业素质；专业水平

professor /prə'fesə(r)/ **noun 1** a university teacher or scholar of the highest rank 教授 **2** N. Amer. 【北美】 a university teacher 大学教师 ■ **professorial** adjective **professorship** noun.

proffer /'prɒfə(r)/ **verb** (**proffers**, **proffering**, **proffered**) offer something for someone to accept 提供；提出

proficient /prə'fɪʃnt/ **adjective** competent; skilled 胜任的；熟练的 ■ **proficiency** noun.

profile /'prəʊfaɪl/ **noun 1** an outline of someone's face, seen from the side (面部的)侧影 **2** a short article that describes someone or something 人物简介；传略 **3** the extent to which someone attracts attention 公众形象，印象：*her high profile* 她的瞩目形象 • **verb** (**profiles**, **profiling**, **profiled**) describe in a short article 简要介绍；

概述 □ **keep a low profile** try not to attract attention 保持低调；保持低姿态

profit /ˈprɒfɪt/ **noun 1** a financial gain 利润；盈利 **2** advantage or benefit 好处；利益 • **verb** (**profits, profiting, profited**) benefit someone 使获益 □ **profit margin** the difference between the cost of producing something and the price at which it is sold 利润；利润幅度

> ✔ 拼写指南 note that the forms **profited** and **profiting** have a single rather than a double *t*. 注意 profited 和 profiting 只有一个 t，不需双写。

profitable /ˈprɒfɪtəbl/ **adjective 1** (of a business or activity) making a profit (生意或活动)盈利的 **2** useful 有用的；有益的 ■ **profitability** noun **profitably** adverb.

profiteering /prɒfɪˈtɪərɪŋ/ **noun** the making of a large profit in an unfair way 牟取暴利 ■ **profiteer** noun.

profiterole /prəˈfɪtərəʊl/ **noun** a small ball of choux pastry filled with cream and covered with chocolate 泡夫夹心酥球

profligate /ˈprɒflɪɡət/ **adjective 1** using money, in a wasteful or extravagant way 肆意挥霍的；浪费的 **2** indulging too much in physical pleasures 放荡的，荒淫的 • **noun** a profligate person 肆意挥霍者；放荡的人 ■ **profligacy** noun.

profound /prəˈfaʊnd/ **adjective** (**profounder, profoundest**) **1** very great 深远的，重大的 **2** showing great knowledge or understanding 渊博的；思想深邃的 **3** needing a lot of study or thought 深奥的 ■ **profoundly** adverb **profundity** noun.

profuse /prəˈfjuːs/ **adjective** produced or appearing in large quantities 大量的；丰富的 ■ **profusely** adverb.

profusion /prəˈfjuːʒn/ **noun** a very large quantity of something 丰富；大量

progenitor /prəʊˈdʒenɪtə(r)/ **noun 1** an ancestor or parent 祖先；父辈 **2** the person who started an artistic, political, or intellectual movement (艺术、政治或学术运动的)先驱，创始人

progeny /ˈprɒdʒəni/ **noun** offspring 后代

progesterone /prəˈdʒestərəʊn/ **noun** a hormone that stimulates the uterus to prepare for pregnancy 孕酮；黄体酮

prognosis /prɒɡˈnəʊsɪs/ **noun** (plural **prognoses** /prɒɡˈnəʊsiːz/) **1** an opinion about how an illness is likely to develop (对病情发展的)预断，预后 **2** the likely course of a situation 前景 ■ **prognostic** adjective.

programmatic /ˌprəʊɡrəˈmætɪk/ **adjective** having to do with or following a programme 计划性的；有关规划的；按计划的

programme /ˈprəʊɡræm/ (US spelling 【美拼作】 **program**) **noun 1** a plan of future events or things to be done 计划；规划；方案 **2** a radio or television broadcast (广播或电视)节目 **3** a sheet or booklet giving details about a play, concert, etc. (戏剧演出、音乐会等的)节目单 **4** (**program**) a series of software instructions to control the operation of a computer 程序 • **verb** (**programmes, programming, programmed**) **1** (**program**) provide a computer with a program 为(计算机)编写程序 **2** make something behave in a particular way 使按⋯方式工作；预设 **3** arrange something according to a plan 按计划安排 ■ **programmable** adjective **programmer** noun.

progress noun /ˈprəʊɡres/ **1** forward movement towards a place 前进；行进 **2** the process of improving or developing 改进；进展；进步 • **verb** /

prə'gres/ **1** move forwards 前进；行进 **2** improve or develop 改进；进步

progression /prə'greʃn/ **noun 1** a gradual movement from one place or state to another 前进；进展；发展 **2** a number of things coming one after another (事物的)一系列，连续

progressive /prə'gresɪv/ **adjective 1** proceeding gradually or in stages 逐渐的，循序渐进的 **2** favouring new ideas or social reform 进步的；改良的 • **noun** a person who is in favour of social reform 进步人士；革新派 ■ **progressively** adverb.

prohibit /prə'hɪbɪt/ **verb** (**prohibits, prohibiting, prohibited**) **1** formally forbid something by law (以法律)禁止 **2** prevent something from happening 使不可能；阻止

prohibition /prəʊɪ'bɪʃn/ **noun 1** the action of forbidding 禁止；阻止 **2** an order that forbids something 禁令；禁律

prohibitive /prə'hɪbɪtɪv/ **adjective 1** forbidding or restricting something 禁止的；限制的 **2** (of a price) too high (价格)过高的，高得令人望而却步的 ■ **prohibitively** adverb.

project noun /'prɒdʒekt/ **1** a piece of work that is carefully planned to achieve a particular aim 工程；项目；方案 **2** a piece of work by a school or college student in which they carry out their own research 科研项目；课题 • **verb** /prə'dʒekt/ **1** estimate or predict something based on what is happening now 预计；推断 **2** (**be projected**) be planned 计划；规划 **3** stick out beyond something else 伸出；凸出 **4** make light or an image fall on a surface or screen 使(光或影像)投射；放映 **5** present yourself to other people in a particular way 展现

projectile /prə'dʒektaɪl/ **noun** an object that is fired or thrown at a target 发射物；投射物

projection /prə'dʒekʃn/ **noun** a

prediction about something based on what is happening now 预计；推测 **2** the projecting of an image, sound, etc. (影像、声音等)的投射，投影，放映 **3** a thing that sticks out from something else 凸出物 ■ **projectionist** noun.

projector /prə'dʒektə(r)/ **noun** a device for projecting slides or film on to a screen 电影放映机；幻灯机；投影仪

prolapse /'prəʊlæps/ **noun** a condition in which an organ of the body has slipped forward or down from its normal position (身体器官的)脱垂，脱出

proletarian /prəʊlə'teəriən/ **adjective** relating to the proletariat 无产者的；无产阶级的 • **noun** a member of the proletariat 无产者；无产阶级的一员

proletariat /prəʊlə'teəriət/ **noun** workers or working-class people 无产阶级；工人阶级

proliferate /prə'lɪfəreɪt/ **verb** (**proliferates, proliferating, proliferated**) reproduce rapidly; increase rapidly in number (迅速)增殖，繁殖，猛增 ■ **proliferation** noun.

prolific /prə'lɪfɪk/ **adjective 1** (of a plant or animal) producing a lot of fruit, leaves, or young (动植物)多产的，多育的 **2** (of an artist, author, etc.) producing many works (艺术家、作家等)多产的 ■ **prolifically** adverb.

prolix /'prəʊlɪks/ **adjective** (of speech or writing) long and boring (讲话或写作)冗长的，啰唆的 ■ **prolixity** noun.

prologue /'prəʊlɒg/ **noun 1** a separate introductory part of a play, book, or piece of music (戏剧的)开场白，序幕，(书籍的)序言，(音乐作品的)序曲 **2** an event that leads to another 序幕；开端

prolong /prə'lɒŋ/ **verb** make something last longer 延长；拖延 ■ **prolongation** noun.

prolonged /prə'lɒŋd/ **adjective** continuing for a long time 持续时间久的

prom /prɒm/ **noun** informal 【非正式】 1 Brit. 【英】 a promenade by the sea 海滨人行道 2 Brit. 【英】 a promenade concert 逍遥音乐会 3 N. Amer. 【北美】 a formal dance at a high school or college (中学或大学的)正式舞会

promenade /ˌprɒmə'nɑːd/ **noun** 1 a paved walkway along a seafront (铺筑的)海滨人行道 2 a leisurely walk 散步 • **verb** (**promenades, promenading, promenaded**) go for a leisurely walk 散步 □ **promenade concert** Brit. 【英】 a concert of classical music at which part of the audience stands 逍遥音乐会,漫步音乐会(部分听众站立欣赏的古典音乐会)

prominence /'prɒmɪnəns/ **noun** the state of being prominent 突出;突出;显著

prominent /'prɒmɪnənt/ **adjective** 1 important; famous 重要的;著名的 2 sticking out 凸出的 3 particularly noticeable 显眼的;显著的 ■ **prominently** adverb.

promiscuous /prə'mɪskjʊəs/ **adjective** having a lot of sexual relationships 滥交的;淫乱的, ■ **promiscuity** noun.

promise /'prɒmɪs/ **noun** 1 an assurance that you will do something or that something will happen 承诺;保证 2 qualities or abilities that may lead to future success 前途;潜质 • **verb** (**promises, promising, promised**) 1 make a promise 承诺;保证 2 give good grounds for expecting something 有指望

promising /'prɒmɪsɪŋ/ **adjective** showing signs of future success 有前途的;大有希望的 ■ **promisingly** adverb.

promissory note /'prɒmɪsəri/ **noun** a signed document containing a written promise to pay a stated amount of money (书面承诺支付一定数额钱款的)本票,期票

promo /'prəʊməʊ/ **noun** (plural **promos**) informal 【非正式】 a promotional film, video, etc. 广告片

promontory /'prɒməntəri/ **noun** (plural **promontories**) a point of high land jutting out into the sea (伸入海中的)岬,海角

promote /prə'məʊt/ **verb** (**promotes, promoting, promoted**) 1 help something to happen 促进;推动 2 give publicity to a product, event, etc. in order to increase sales or make people aware of it 推广(产品);宣传(活动) 3 raise someone to a higher position or rank 提升;晋升 ■ **promoter** noun.

promotion /prə'məʊʃn/ **noun** 1 activity that supports or encourages a cause or aim 提倡;鼓励 2 the action of promoting a product, event, etc. (产品的)推广;(活动的)宣传 3 movement to a higher position or rank 提升;晋升 ■ **promotional** adjective.

prompt /prɒmpt/ **verb** 1 make something happen 导致;促使 2 (**prompt someone to**) make someone take a course of action 促使(某人)采取行动 3 encourage someone to speak 鼓励(讲话) 4 tell an actor a word that they have forgotten 为(演员)提词 • **noun** 1 a word or phrase used to prompt an actor (给演员的)提词,提白 2 a symbol on a computer screen to show that more input is needed (计算机屏幕上的)提示,提示符 • **adjective** done without delay 迅速的;及时的 • **adverb** Brit. 【英】 exactly or punctually 整;准时 ■ **prompter** noun **promptly** adverb.

promulgate /'prɒmlɡeɪt/ **verb** (**promulgates, promulgating, promulgated**) 1 make an idea widely known 推广;宣扬 **2** announce the official beginning of a new law 颁布,公布(法律) ∎ **promulgation** noun.

prone /prəʊn/ **adjective 1** (**prone to** or **to do**) likely to suffer from, do, or experience something unfortunate 易于遭受(不幸之事)的;有做(不幸之事)倾向的 **2** lying flat, especially face downwards 俯卧的

prong /prɒŋ/ **noun 1** each of two or more long pointed parts on a fork (叉子的)尖头, 尖齿 **2** each of the separate parts of an attack (进攻等的)方面 ∎ **pronged** adjective.

pronoun /'prəʊnaʊn/ **noun** a word used instead of a noun to indicate someone or something already mentioned or known, e.g. *I, this* 代词

pronounce /prə'naʊns/ **verb** (**pronounces**, **pronouncing**, **pronounced**) **1** make the sound of a word or part of a word 发(音) **2** declare or announce 宣称;宣言;宣布 **3** (**pronounce on**) pass judgement or make a decision on 对…作出判断(或表态);对…进行宣判 ∎ **pronouncement** noun.

pronounced /prə'naʊnst/ **adjective** very noticeable 明显的;显而易见的

pronto /'prɒntəʊ/ **adverb** informal【非正式】promptly 马上;即刻

pronunciation /prəˌnʌnsi'eɪʃn/ **noun** the way in which a word is pronounced 发音

> ✔ 拼写指南 **pronunciation** has no *o* in the middle. pronunciation 中间没有 o。

proof /pruːf/ **noun 1** evidence that shows that something is true 证据;证物;证词 **2** the process of finding out whether something is true 证明;证实 **3** a series of stages in the solving of a mathematical problem (数学问题的)验算, 求证, 证明 **4** a copy of printed material used for making

corrections before final printing 校样 **5** a standard used to measure the strength of alcohol (酒类的)标准酒精度 • **adjective** resistant to 防…的;抗…的: *damp-proof* 防潮的

proofread /'pruːfriːd/ **verb** read written or printed material and mark any mistakes 校对 ∎ **proofreader** noun.

prop¹ /prɒp/ **noun 1** a pole or beam used as a temporary support 支柱;支撑物 **2** a source of support or assistance 支柱;支持者 **3** (also **prop forward**) Rugby【英式橄榄球】a forward at either end of the front row of a scrum 支柱前锋 • **verb** (**props**, **propping**, **propped**) **1** support with a prop 支撑;支撑 **2** lean something against something else 倚靠 **3** (**prop something up**) help something that is in difficulty 支持;扶持

prop² **noun** a portable object used by actors during a play or film (戏剧或电影中的)道具

propaganda /ˌprɒpə'gændə/ **noun** false or exaggerated information, used to win support for a political cause or point of view (对政治目标或观点的)鼓吹, 宣传 ∎ **propagandist** noun.

> ✔ 拼写指南 *propa-*, not *propo-*: *propaganda*. propaganda 中的 propa- 不要拼作 propo-。

propagate /'prɒpəgeɪt/ **verb** (**propagates**, **propagating**, **propagated**) **1** grow a new plant from a parent plant 繁殖, 增殖(植物) **2** spread an idea or information widely 宣传, 传播(思想或知识) ∎ **propagation** noun.

propane /'prəʊpeɪn/ **noun** a flammable gas present in natural gas and used as fuel 丙烷(天然气中的可燃气体, 用作燃料)

propel /prə'pel/ **verb** (**propels**, **propelling**, **propelled**) drive or push forwards 推进;推动;驱动

propellant /prə'pelənt/ **noun** a gas which forces out the contents of an aerosol (喷雾装置中的)压缩气体

propeller or **propellor** /prə'pelə(r)/ **noun** a device which uses two or more angled blades to propel a ship or aircraft (轮船或航天器的)螺旋桨，推进器

propensity /prəʊ'pensəti/ **noun** (plural **propensities**) a tendency to behave in a particular way 行为倾向；习性

proper /'prɒpə(r)/ **adjective 1** truly what it is said to be; real 名副其实的；真正的 **2** in its true form 严格意义上的"世界杯" **3** appropriate or correct 合适的；恰当的 **4** (**proper to**) belonging exclusively to 为…专有(或特有)的 □ **proper fraction** a fraction that is less than one 真分数 **proper noun** (or **proper name**) a name of a person, place, or organization, written with a capital letter 专有名词 ■ **properly** adverb.

property /'prɒpəti/ **noun** (plural **properties**) **1** a thing or things belonging to someone 所有物；财产；资产 **2** a building and the land belonging to it 不动产；房地产 **3** a characteristic or quality 特性；性质

prophecy /'prɒfəsi/ **noun** (plural **prophecies**) **1** a prediction about what will happen in the future 预言 **2** the ability to predict the future 预言能力

prophesy /'prɒfəsaɪ/ **verb** (**prophesies**, **prophesying**, **prophesied**) predict that a particular thing will happen in the future 预言；预测

prophet /'prɒfɪt/ **noun 1** a person regarded as being sent by God to teach people 先知 **2** a person who predicts the future 预言家

prophetic /prə'fetɪk/ **adjective 1** accurately predicting the future 正确预见的 **2** having to do with a prophet or prophecy 预言家的；预言的

prophylactic /ˌprɒfɪ'læktɪk/ **adjective** intended to prevent disease 预防疾病的 • **noun** a medicine intended to prevent disease 预防药

propinquity /prə'pɪŋkwəti/ **noun** nearness in time or space (时间或空间上的)接近

propitiate /prə'pɪʃieɪt/ **verb** (**propitiates**, **propitiating**, **propitiated**) win or regain the favour of 讨好；重新赢得…的好感 ■ **propitiation** noun **propitiatory** adjective.

propitious /prə'pɪʃəs/ **adjective** indicating a good chance of success; favourable 吉利的；有利的

proponent /prə'pəʊnənt/ **noun** a person who proposes a theory or plan 提议者；倡导者

proportion /prə'pɔːʃn/ **noun 1** a part or share of a whole 部分；份额 **2** the relationship of one thing to another in terms of quantity or size 比例 **3** the correct relationship between one thing and another 均衡；协调 **4** (**proportions**) the size and shape of something 大小；形状

proportional /prə'pɔːʃənl/ or **proportionate** /prə'pɔːʃənət/ **adjective** corresponding in size or amount to something else (大小或数量)成比例的，相称的，均衡的 □ **proportional representation** an electoral system in which parties gain seats in proportion to the number of votes cast for them 比例代表制(各政党按其所获选票比例确定议员席位的选举制度) ■ **proportionally** adverb.

proposal /prə'pəʊzl/ **noun 1** a plan or suggestion 计划；建议；提案 **2** the action of proposing something 提出建议 **3** an offer of marriage 求婚

propose /prə'pəʊz/ **verb** (**proposes**, **proposing**, **proposed**) **1** put forward an idea or plan for consideration by other people 提议;建议 **2** nominate someone for an official position 提名,推荐(某人担任公职) **3** plan or intend to do something 计划;打算 **4** make an offer of marriage to someone 求婚

proposition /ˌprɒpə'zɪʃn/ **noun 1** a statement that expresses an opinion 主张,观点;见解 **2** a plan of action 提议;提案 **3** a problem to be dealt with 待处理的问题 • **verb** informal【非正式】offer to have sex with someone 向…提出性交要求;向…求欢

propound /prə'paʊnd/ **verb** put forward an idea or theory for consideration 提出(想法或理论)供考虑

proprietary /prə'praɪətri/ **adjective 1** having to do with an owner or ownership 所有的;所有权的 **2** (of a product) marketed under a registered trademark (产品)专卖的,专利的 □ **proprietary name** a name of a product or service registered as a trademark 专利商标名

proprietor /prə'praɪətə(r)/ **noun** the owner of a business 业主;老板

proprietorial /prəˌpraɪə'tɔːriəl/ **adjective** behaving as if you owned something; possessive 所有者的;业主的;所有的

propriety /prə'praɪəti/ **noun** (plural **proprieties**) **1** correctness of behaviour or morals (行为或道德规范的)得体,合乎规矩 **2** the condition of being right or appropriate 适当;妥当

propulsion /prə'pʌlʃn/ **noun** the action of propelling or driving something forward 推进;驱动 ■ **propulsive** adjective.

pro rata /ˌprəʊ 'rɑːtə/ **adjective** proportional 按比例的;成比例的 • **adverb** proportionally.

prosaic /prə'zeɪk/ **adjective** ordinary or unimaginative; dull 平庸的,缺乏想象力的;枯燥乏味的 ■ **prosaically** adverb.

proscenium /prə'siːniəm/ **noun** (plural **prosceniums** or **proscenia** /prə'siːniə/) **1** the part of a stage in front of the curtain (幕布前的)舞台部分;舞台前部 **2** (also **proscenium arch**) an arch framing the opening between the stage and the part of the theatre in which the audience sits 舞台前的拱形框架

proscribe /prə'skraɪb/ **verb** (**proscribes**, **proscribing**, **proscribed**) **1** forbid 禁止;取缔 **2** criticize or condemn 斥责;谴责

prose /prəʊz/ **noun** ordinary written or spoken language 散文;白话文

prosecute /'prɒsɪkjuːt/ **verb** (**prosecutes**, **prosecuting**, **prosecuted**) **1** take legal proceedings against someone 起诉;检控 **2** continue doing or taking part in something 继续进行;继续参与 ■ **prosecutor** noun.

prosecution /ˌprɒsɪ'kjuːʃn/ **noun 1** the action of prosecuting 起诉;指控 **2** (**the prosecution**) the party prosecuting someone in a lawsuit 控方;原告

proselyte /'prɒsɪlaɪt/ **noun** a person who has converted from one religion or belief to another 改变宗教信仰者

proselytize or **proselytise** /'prɒsələtaɪz/ **verb** (**proselytizes**, **proselytizing**, **proselytized**) convert someone from one religion or belief to another 改变…的宗教信仰

prosody /'prɒsədi/ **noun 1** the patterns of rhythm and sound used in poetry 诗体;韵律 **2** the study of these patterns 诗体学;韵律学

prospect /'prɒspekt/ **noun 1** a possibility of something happening (事情发生的)可能性,机会 **2** an idea about what will happen in the future 预期;展望 **3** (**prospects**) chances of being successful 前景;前途;前程 **4** a person who is likely to be successful 有前途的人 • **verb** search for mineral deposits 勘探，勘察(矿藏) ■ **prospector** noun.

prospective /prəˈspektɪv/ **adjective** expected or likely to happen or be something in the future 可能的；预期的 ■ **prospectively** adverb.

prospectus /prəˈspektəs/ **noun** (plural **prospectuses**) a printed booklet advertising a school, university, or business 学校简介，(企业)说明书

prosper /ˈprɒspə(r)/ **verb** (**prospers**, **prospering**, **prospered**) be successful, especially in making money 成功，繁荣(尤指)生意兴隆

prosperous /ˈprɒspərəs/ **adjective** rich and successful 成功的；兴旺的，繁荣的 ■ **prosperity** noun.

prostate /ˈprɒsteɪt/ **noun** a gland in men and male mammals that produces the fluid part of semen 前列腺

prostitute /ˈprɒstɪtjuːt/ **noun** a person who has sex for money 娼妓，妓女 • **verb** (**prostitutes**, **prostituting**, **prostituted**) (**prostitute yourself**) **1** work as a prostitute 卖淫 **2** put your talents to an unworthy use in order to earn money (为金钱而)滥用(才能) ■ **prostitution** noun.

prostrate **adjective** /ˈprɒstreɪt/ **1** lying stretched out on the ground with the face downwards 俯卧的，趴着的 **2** completely overcome or helpless 极为沮丧的；无助的 • **verb** /prɒsˈtreɪt/ (**prostrates**, **prostrating**, **prostrated**) **1** (**prostrate yourself**) throw yourself flat on the ground 俯卧；平躺 **2** (**be prostrated**) be completely overcome with stress or exhaustion 使沮丧；使筋疲力尽 ■ **prostration** noun.

protagonist /prəˈtæɡənɪst/ **noun** **1** the leading character in a drama, film, or novel (戏剧,电影或小说的)主角,主人公 **2** an important person in a real event (现实情境中的)重要人物

protean /ˈprəʊtiən/ **adjective** tending or able to change or adapt 变化多端的；多变的

protect /prəˈtekt/ **verb** keep someone or something safe from harm or injury 保护，保卫 ■ **protector** noun.

protection /prəˈtekʃn/ **noun** **1** the action of protecting 保护；保卫 **2** a person or thing that protects 防护物 **3** the payment of money to criminals so that they will not attack your property (付给犯罪分子的)保护费

protectionism /prəˈtekʃənɪzəm/ **noun** the practice of protecting a country's industries from foreign competition by taxing imported goods 贸易保护(主义) ■ **protectionist** noun & adjective.

protective /prəˈtektɪv/ **adjective** **1** protecting someone or something 保护的；防护的 **2** having a strong wish to protect someone 爱护的；关切的 ■ **protectively** adverb.

protectorate /prəˈtektərət/ **noun** a state that is controlled and protected by another 受保护国

protégé /ˈprɒtəʒeɪ/ **noun** (feminine **protégée**) a person who is guided and supported by an older and more experienced person 门生；门徒

protein /ˈprəʊtiːn/ **noun** a substance which forms part of body tissues and is an important part of the human diet 蛋白质

✔ 拼写指南 **protein** is an exception to the usual rule of *i* before *e* except after *c*. 通常的规则是 i 置于 e 前，在 c 后时除外，但 protein 是例外。

protest **noun** /ˈprəʊtest/ a statement or action expressing disapproval or objection to something 抗议；反对；异议 • **verb** /prəˈtest/ **1** express an objection to what someone has said or done 反对；表示异议 **2** take part in a public protest 参加抗议示威 **3** state something strongly in response to an accusation (对指控)申明，申辩: *She protested her innocence.* 她辩称自己是清白的。■ **protester** (or **protestor**) noun.

Protestant /'prɒtɪstənt/ **noun** a member or follower of any of the Western Christian Churches that are separate from the Roman Catholic Church 新教教徒 ● **adjective** relating to or belonging to any of the Protestant Churches 新教的；新教教徒的 ■ **Protestantism** noun.

protestation /ˌprɒtə'steɪʃn/ **noun 1** a firm declaration that something is or is not the case (坚决的)声明，断言 **2** an objection or protest 异议；抗议

proto- /'prəʊtəʊ-/ **combining form** original, primitive, or first 原始；初: *prototype* 原型 | *protozoan* 原生动物

protocol /'prəʊtəkɒl/ **noun 1** the system of rules governing formal occasions 礼仪；外交礼节 **2** the accepted way to behave in a particular situation 行为规范；礼节

proton /'prəʊtɒn/ **noun** a subatomic particle with a positive electric charge 质子

prototype /'prəʊtətaɪp/ **noun** a first form of something from which other forms are copied or developed 原型；样品；雏形

protozoan /ˌprəʊtə'zəʊən/ **noun** a microscopic animal that is made up of a single cell (单细胞的)原生动物

protracted /prə'træktɪd/ **adjective** lasting for a long time 延长的；拖延的

protractor /prə'træktə(r)/ **noun** an instrument for measuring angles, in the form of a flat semicircle marked with degrees 量角器；分度规

protrude /prə'truːd/ **verb** (**protrudes**, **protruding**, **protruded**) stick out from a surface 伸出；凸出 ■ **protrusion** noun.

protuberance /prə'tjuːbərəns/ **noun**

a thing that sticks out from a surface 凸出物；隆起物 ■ **protuberant** adjective.

> ✔ 拼写指南 there is no *r* immediately after the *t*: pro*tuberance*. protuberance 中紧接在 t 后没有 r。

proud /praʊd/ **adjective 1** feeling pleased or satisfied by your own or another's achievements 感到自豪的；引以为荣的 **2** having too high an opinion of yourself 骄傲的；自大的 **3** having respect for yourself 自尊的；自重的 **4** slightly sticking out from a surface 稍凸起的 ■ **proudly** adverb.

prove /pruːv/ **verb** (**proves**, **proving**, **proved**; past participle **proved** or **proven** /'pruːvn/) **1** use evidence to show that something is true or exists 证明；证实 **2** be found to be 表明；证明 **3** (**prove yourself**) show your abilities or courage 证明能力(或勇气) **4** (**proven**) found through experience to be effective or true 被证明的；已证实的 ■ **provable** adjective.

provenance /'prɒvənəns/ **noun** the place where something originally comes from 来源；出处

provender /'prɒvɪndə(r)/ **noun** old use 【旧】food or animal fodder 食物；(家畜的)饲料

proverb /'prɒvɜːb/ **noun** a short saying that gives advice or states something that is generally true 谚语；俗语

proverbial /prə'vɜːbɪəl/ **adjective 1** referred to in a proverb 谚语的；谚语所表达的 **2** well known 出名的 ■ **proverbially** adverb.

provide /prə'vaɪd/ **verb** (**provides**, **providing**, **provided**) **1** make something available for someone to use 供应；供给；提供 **2** (**provide for**) make enough preparation for a possible event 为…安排妥当；为…作

准备

provided /prəˈvaɪdɪŋ/ or **providing** /prəˈvaɪdɪŋ/ **conjunction** on the condition that 只要；除非

providence /ˈprɒvɪdəns/ **noun 1** the protective care of God or of nature 天佑；天意 **2** careful preparation for the future 远虑，远见

provident /ˈprɒvɪdənt/ **adjective** careful in preparing for the future 未雨绸缪的，有远见的

providential /ˌprɒvɪˈdenʃl/ **adjective** happening at a favourable time 适时的；凑巧的

province /ˈprɒvɪns/ **noun 1** a main administrative division of a country or empire 省；行政区 **2 (the provinces)** the whole of a country outside the capital city (首都以外的)外省，外地

provincial /prəˈvɪnʃl/ **adjective 1** relating to a province or the provinces 省的；外省的 **2** unsophisticated or narrow-minded 头脑简单的，偏狭的 • **noun** a person who lives in a province 外省人；外地人 ■ **provincialism** noun.

provision /prəˈvɪʒn/ **noun 1** the action of providing 供应；供给 **2** something supplied or provided 供应品；供给物 **3 (provision for** or **against)** arrangements for possible future events or needs 预先采取的措施；预备 **4 (provisions)** supplies of food, drink, or equipment (食物、饮料或装备等)储备物，必需品 **5** a condition or requirement in a legal document (法律文件中的)条文，条款 • **verb** supply with provisions 向…供应必需品

provisional /prəˈvɪʒənl/ **adjective** arranged for the present time only, possibly to be changed later 临时的；暂定的 ■ **provisionally** adverb.

proviso /prəˈvaɪzəʊ/ **noun** (plural **provisos**) a condition attached to an agreement 限制性条款；附文

provocation /ˌprɒvəˈkeɪʃn/ **noun**

action or speech that makes someone angry or causes a strong reaction 挑衅行为(或言论)

provocative /prəˈvɒkətɪv/ **adjective 1** intended to make someone annoyed or angry 挑衅的；意在激怒的 **2** intended to make someone sexually interested 挑逗的；勾引的 ■ **provocatively** adverb.

provoke /prəˈvəʊk/ **verb** (**provokes, provoking, provoked**) **1** cause a strong reaction 激起，引起(强烈反应) **2** deliberately make someone feel angry 挑衅；激怒 **3** stir someone up to do something 煽动

provost /ˈprɒvəst/ **noun 1** Brit. 【英】the head of certain university colleges and public schools (某些大学学院的)院长；(某些公学的)校长 **2** N. Amer. 【北美】a senior administrative officer in certain universities (某些大学的)教务长 **3** Scottish 【苏格兰】a mayor 市长

prow /praʊ/ **noun** the pointed front part of a ship 船首；船头

prowess /ˈpraʊəs/ **noun** skill or expertise 技艺；造诣

prowl /praʊl/ **verb** move about stealthily or restlessly 潜行；转悠 □ **on the prowl** moving about in a stealthy way 在潜行；在鬼鬼祟祟地转悠 ■ **prowler** noun.

proximity /prɒkˈsɪmətɪ/ **noun** nearness or closeness 靠近；临近 ■ **proximate** adjective.

proxy /ˈprɒksi/ **noun** (plural **proxies**) **1** the authority to represent someone else 代理权；代表权 **2** a person authorized to act on behalf of another 代理人，代表

prude /pruːd/ **noun** a person who is easily shocked by matters relating to sex (在性方面大惊小怪的人，过分正经的人 ■ **prudish** adjective.

prudent /ˈpruːdnt/ **adjective** acting in a cautious and sensible way 审慎的；精明的 ■ **prudence** noun **prudently**

adverb.

prudential /pru:'denʃl/ **adjective** prudent 谨慎的;小心的

prune¹ /pru:n/ **noun** a dried plum 李子干;西梅干

prune² **verb** (**prunes**, **pruning**, **pruned**) **1** trim a tree or bush by cutting away dead or overgrown branches 修剪,修整(树或灌木) **2** remove unwanted parts from 削减,删除(不需要的部分) • **noun** an instance of pruning 修剪;删除

prurient /'prʊəriənt/ **adjective** having too much interest in sexual matters 好色的;淫秽的 ■ **prurience** noun.

pry¹ /praɪ/ **verb** (**pries**, **prying**, **pried**) ask someone unwelcome questions about their private life 窥探,刺探(隐私)

pry² = PRISE.

PS /pi: 'es/ **abbreviation** postscript.

psalm /sɑːm/ **noun** a song or poem that praises God 赞美诗;圣歌

psalter /'sɔːltə(r)/ **noun** a copy of the Book of Psalms in the Bible (《圣经》的)诗篇歌集

pseudo /'suːdəʊ/ **adjective** informal 【非正式】 not genuine; false 假的;伪的

pseudonym /'suːdənɪm/ **noun** a false name, especially one used by an author 假名;(尤指作家的)笔名

PSHE /pi: es eɪtʃ 'i:/ **abbreviation** personal, social, and health education (as a school subject) (学校的)个人、社会及健康教育

psoriasis /sə'raɪəsɪs/ **noun** a condition in which patches of skin become red and itchy 牛皮癣;银屑病

psych /saɪk/ **verb 1** (**psych yourself up**) informal 【非正式】 prepare yourself mentally for a difficult task 作好心理准备 **2** (**psych someone out**) intimidate an opponent by appearing very confident or aggressive 用心理战使(对手)心虚

psyche /'saɪki/ **noun** the human soul, mind, or spirit 灵魂;心灵;精神

psychedelia /ˌsaɪkə'diːliə/ **noun** music or art based on the experiences produced by taking psychedelic drugs 迷幻作品(指迷幻药物作用下创作的音乐或艺术作品)

psychedelic /ˌsaɪkə'delɪk/ **adjective 1** (of drugs) producing hallucinations (药品)致幻的,引起幻觉的 **2** having a strong, vivid colour or a swirling abstract pattern 色彩绚烂的;有涡旋图案的

psychiatry /saɪ'kaɪətri/ **noun** the branch of medicine concerned with mental illness 精神病学 ■ **psychiatric** adjective **psychiatrist** noun.

psychic /'saɪkɪk/ **adjective 1** relating to or possessing abilities that cannot be explained by science, e.g. telepathy or clairvoyance 超自然的;通灵的;神视的 **2** relating to the mind 精神的;心灵的 • **noun** a person considered or claiming to have psychic powers 通灵的人 ■ **psychically** adverb.

psycho /'saɪkəʊ/ **noun** (plural **psychos**) informal 【非正式】 a psychopath 精神变态者;变态人格者

psychoanalyse /ˌsaɪkəʊ'ænəlaɪz/ (US spelling 【美拼作】 **psychoanalyze**) **verb** (**psychoanalyses**, **psychoanalysing**, **psychoanalysed**) treat someone using psychoanalysis 用精神分析法治疗

psychoanalysis /ˌsaɪkəʊə'næləsɪs/ **noun** a method of treating mental disorders by investigating the unconscious elements of the mind 精神分析(治疗法);心理分析(治疗法) ■ **psychoanalyst** noun **psychoanalytic** adjective.

psychological /ˌsaɪkə'lɒdʒɪkl/ **adjective 1** having to do with the mind 精神的;心理的 **2** relating to psychology 心理学的 ■ **psychologically** adverb.

psychology /saɪ'kɒlədʒi/ **noun 1** the

scientific study of the human mind 心理学 **2** the way in which someone thinks or behaves 心理；心理状态 ■ **psychologist** noun.

psychopath /ˈsaɪkəpæθ/ **noun** a person suffering from a serious mental illness which makes them behave violently 精神变态者；变态人格者 ■ **psychopathic** adjective.

psychosis /saɪˈkəʊsɪs/ **noun** (plural **psychoses** /saɪˈkəʊsiːz/) a serious mental illness in which a person loses contact with external reality 精神病；精神失常

psychosomatic /ˌsaɪkəʊsəˈmætɪk/ **adjective** (of a physical illness) caused or made worse by a mental factor such as stress (身体疾病)由精神压力引起(或加重)的

psychotherapy /ˌsaɪkəʊˈθerəpi/ **noun** the treatment of mental disorders by psychological rather than medical means 心理疗法；精神疗法 ■ **psychotherapist** noun.

psychotic /saɪˈkɒtɪk/ **adjective** relating to or suffering from a psychosis 精神病的；精神失常的

PT /ˌpiːˈtiː/ **abbreviation** physical training 体育锻炼

Pt abbreviation 1 Part. **2 (pt)** pint. **3** (in scoring) point (评分中的)分数

PTA /ˌpiːtiːˈeɪ/ **abbreviation** parent–teacher association 家长教师谊会

ptarmigan /ˈtɑːmɪɡən/ **noun** a grouse with grey and black feathers which change to white in winter 雷鸟(一种松鸡，羽毛灰黑色，冬季变为白色)

Pte abbreviation Private (in the army) 列兵；二等兵

pterodactyl /ˌterəˈdæktɪl/ **noun** a fossil flying reptile with a long, slender head and neck 翼手龙(一种头颈细长的翼龙)

PTO /ˌpiːtiːˈəʊ/ **abbreviation** please turn over 请看背面；见下页

pub /pʌb/ **noun** Brit. 【英】 a building in which beer and other drinks are served 酒馆；酒吧

puberty /ˈpjuːbəti/ **noun** the period during which adolescents reach sexual maturity 青春期；发育期

pubes /ˈpjuːbiːz/ **noun** the lower front part of the abdomen 阴部；阴阜

pubescence /pjuːˈbesns/ **noun** the time when puberty begins 青春期开始时期 ■ **pubescent** adjective & noun.

pubic /ˈpjuːbɪk/ **adjective** relating to the pubes or pubis 阴部的；耻骨的

pubis /ˈpjuːbɪs/ **noun** (plural **pubes** /ˈpjuːbiːz/) either of a pair of bones forming the two sides of the pelvis 耻骨

public /ˈpʌblɪk/ **adjective 1** having to do with the people as a whole 公众的；公用的；公共的 **2** involved in the affairs of the community 公众事务的：*a public figure* 公众人物 **3** intended to be seen or heard by people in general 公开的 **4** provided by the government rather than an independent company 国家的；政府的 • **noun 1 (the public)** ordinary people in general 公众；民众 **2** a group of people with a particular interest (具有共同兴趣的)一群人：*the reading public* 读者大众 □ **in public** when other people are present 公开地 **public address system** a system of microphones and loudspeakers used to amplify speech or music 有线广播系统；扩音系统 **public company** (or **public limited company**) a company whose shares are traded freely on a stock exchange 公开招股公司；股票上市公司 **public house** a pub 酒馆；酒吧 **public relations** the business of creating a good public image for an organization or famous person 公共关系；公关工作；公关活动 **public school** (in the UK) a private fee-paying secondary school (英国的)公学(指私立付费中学) **public sector** the part of an economy that is controlled by the state 国营部门；

国有部分 **public transport** buses, trains, and other forms of transport that are available to the public and run on fixed routes 公共交通 ■ **publicly** adverb.

publican /ˈpʌblɪkən/ **noun** Brit.【英】 a person who owns or manages a pub 酒馆老板

publication /ˌpʌblɪˈkeɪʃ n/ **noun 1** the action of publishing something 出版;发表 **2** a book or journal that is published 出版物

publicist /ˈpʌblɪsɪst/ **noun** a person responsible for publicizing a product or celebrity 宣传员;广告员;公关人员

publicity /pʌbˈlɪsəti/ **noun 1** attention given to someone or something by television, newspapers, etc. (电视、报纸等媒体的)关注,宣传 **2** information used for advertising or promoting a product, person, event, etc. 宣传信息;宣传资料

publicize or **publicise** /ˈpʌblɪsaɪz/ **verb** (**publicizes**, **publicizing**, **publicized**) **1** make something widely known 公开;宣传 **2** give out information about a product, person, event, etc. in order to advertise or promote them 做广告;推广

publish /ˈpʌblɪʃ/ **verb 1** produce a book, newspaper, etc., for public sale 出版,发行(书籍,报纸等) **2** print something in a book or newspaper 发表;刊载 ■ **publisher** noun.

puce /pjuːs/ **noun** a dark red or purple-brown colour 暗红色;紫褐色

puck /pʌk/ **noun** a black disc made of hard rubber, used in ice hockey (冰球运动中使用的)冰球

pucker /ˈpʌkə(r)/ **verb** (**puckers**, **puckering**, **puckered**) tightly gather into wrinkles or small folds 起皱纹;起褶 • **noun** a wrinkle or small fold 皱纹;皱褶

pudding /ˈpʊdɪŋ/ **noun** chiefly Brit.【主英】**1** a cooked sweet dish eaten at the end of a meal (餐末)甜点 **2** the dessert course of a meal (一餐中的)甜食 **3** a savoury dish made with suet and flour 布丁(由板油和面粉制成的开胃菜)

puddle /ˈpʌdl/ **noun** a small pool of liquid, especially of rain on the ground (地面上的)水坑;(尤指)雨水坑

pudgy /ˈpʌdʒi/ **adjective** (**pudgier**, **pudgiest**) informal【非正式】rather fat 肥胖的

puerile /ˈpjʊəraɪl/ **adjective** childishly silly 幼稚的;愚蠢的

Puerto Rican /ˌpwɜːtəʊ ˈriːkən/ **noun** a person from Puerto Rico 波多黎各人 • **adjective** relating to Puerto Rico 波多黎各的

puff /pʌf/ **noun 1** a small amount of air or smoke that is blown out from somewhere (空气或烟雾的)一阵,一股 **2** an act of breathing in smoke from a pipe, cigarette, or cigar (烟的)吸,抽 **3** a hollow piece of light pastry that is filled with cream or jam 泡夫,松饼 **4** informal【非正式】breath 呼吸: *out of puff* 气喘吁吁 • **verb 1** breathe in repeated short gasps 喘息,喘气 **2** move with short, noisy puffs of air or steam 喷着气(或蒸汽)移动 **3** smoke a pipe, cigarette, or cigar 吸,抽(烟) **4** (**be puffed** or **puffed out**) informal【非正式】be out of breath 气喘吁吁 **5** (**puff out** or **up**) swell 膨胀;肿胀 □ **puff pastry** light flaky pastry 做泡夫的酥皮面团

puffball /ˈpʌfbɔːl/ **noun** a fungus with a round head that bursts to release its seeds 马勃(菌)

puffin /ˈpʌfɪn/ **noun** a seabird with a large brightly coloured triangular bill 角嘴海雀(长有色彩鲜艳的巨大三角形喙)

puffy /ˈpʌfi/ **adjective** (**puffier**, **puffiest**) **1** (of a part of the body) swollen and soft (身体部位)浮肿的,肿胀的 **2** softly rounded 蓬松的;

puffy clouds 大团的云彩

pug /pʌg/ **noun** a very small breed of dog with a broad flat nose and a wrinkled face 哈巴狗

pugilist /ˈpjuːdʒɪlɪst/ **noun** chiefly humorous 【主幽默】 a boxer 拳击手 ■ **pugilistic** adjective.

pugnacious /pʌɡˈneɪʃəs/ **adjective** eager or quick to argue or fight 好争吵的；好斗的 ■ **pugnaciously** adverb **pugnacity** noun.

puke /pjuːk/ informal 【非正式】 **verb** (**pukes**, **puking**, **puked**) vomit 呕吐 • **noun** vomit 呕吐

pukka /ˈpʌkə/ informal 【非正式】 **adjective 1** genuine 真正的 **2** socially acceptable 社会认可的；体面的 **3** excellent 极好的

pulchritude /ˈpʌlkrɪtjuːd/ **noun** literary 【文】 beauty 美丽

pull /pʊl/ **verb 1** apply force to something so as to move it towards yourself 拉；扯；拽 **2** remove from a place by pulling 拉开；拖去 **3** move steadily (匀速)移动: *The bus pulled away.* 公交车开走了。**4** strain a muscle 拉伤(肌肉) **5** attract someone as a customer 吸引(顾客) **6** Brit. informal 【英，非正式】 attract a potential sexual partner 勾引 **7** informal 【非正式】 bring out a weapon or use 拔出，掏出(武器) • **noun 1** an act of pulling 拉；扯；拖 **2** a force, influence, or attraction 拉力；影响力；吸引力 **3** a deep drink of something or a deep breath of smoke from a cigarette, pipe, etc. 喝一大口(酒)；猛抽一口(烟) □ **pull back** retreat 撤退；撤回 **pull someone's leg** deceive someone for a joke 开(某人的)玩笑 **pull something off** informal 【非正式】 succeed in doing something difficult 完成，做成(困难的事) **pull out** withdraw 撤退 **pull strings** use your influence to gain an advantage 运用影响谋取好处；走后门 **pull yourself together** regain your self-control 克制自己；

重新振作 **pull your weight** do your fair share of work 尽本分

pullet /ˈpʊlɪt/ **noun** a young hen 小母鸡

pulley /ˈpʊli/ **noun** (plural **pulleys**) a wheel around which a rope or chain passes, used to raise heavy objects 滑轮；滑车

pullover /ˈpʊləʊvə(r)/ **noun** a knitted garment for the upper body 套衫

pulmonary /ˈpʌlmənəri/ **adjective** relating to the lungs 肺的；肺部的

pulp /pʌlp/ **noun 1** a soft, wet mass of crushed material 浆；糊 **2** the soft fleshy part of a fruit 果肉 • **verb** crush into a pulp 把…碾成糊状 • **adjective** (of writing) popular and badly written (文字作品)通俗的, 低级庸俗的: *pulp fiction* 低俗小说 ■ **pulpy** adjective.

pulpit /ˈpʊlpɪt/ **noun** a raised platform in a church from which the preacher gives a sermon (教堂中的)讲坛, 布道坛

pulsar /ˈpʌlsɑː(r)/ **noun** a star that gives off regular rapid pulses of radio waves 脉冲星

pulsate /pʌlˈseɪt/ **verb** (**pulsates**, **pulsating**, **pulsated**) **1** expand and contract with strong regular movements 搏动 **2** produce a regular throbbing sensation or sound (有规律地)振动, 颤动 ■ **pulsation** noun.

pulse[1] /pʌls/ **noun 1** the regular beat of the blood as it is pumped around the body 脉搏 **2** a single vibration or short burst of sound, electric current, light, etc. (声音、电流、光等的)脉冲 **3** a regular musical rhythm (音乐)节拍 • **verb** (**pulses**, **pulsing**, **pulsed**) pulsate 搏动,振动

pulse[2] **noun** the edible seeds of various plants, such as lentils or beans (可食用的)豆科植物种子；豆子

pulverize or **pulverise** /ˈpʌlvəraɪz/ **verb** (**pulverizes**, **pulverizing**, **pulverized**) **1** crush into fine particles 将…捣成粉末 **2** informal【非正式】completely defeat 彻底击败

puma /ˈpjuːmə/ **noun** a large American wild cat with a yellowish-brown or grey coat 美洲狮

pumice /ˈpʌmɪs/ **noun** a very light rock formed from lava 轻石；浮石

pummel /ˈpʌml/ **verb (pummels, pummelling, pummelled;** US spelling【美拼作】**pummels, pummeling, pummeled)** hit repeatedly with the fists (用拳头)连续捶

pump¹ /pʌmp/ **noun** a device used to move liquids and gases or to force air into inflatable objects 泵；抽水机；打气筒 • **verb 1** move with a pump, or with something that works like a pump (用泵等)抽取，抽吸 **2** fill something with liquid, gas, etc. 把(液体、气体等)注入 **3** move something up and down energetically 有力地上下运动 **4** informal【非正式】try to get information from someone 追问(以获取信息) □ **pump iron** informal【非正式】exercise with weights 举哑铃锻炼

pump² **noun 1** chiefly N. English【主英格兰北部】a plimsoll 胶底帆布运动鞋 **2** a light shoe for dancing 轻软舞鞋

pumpkin /ˈpʌmpkɪn/ **noun 1** a large round fruit with a thick orange skin and edible flesh 南瓜 **2** Brit.【英】= SQUASH².

pun /pʌn/ **noun** a joke that uses a word or words with more than one meaning 双关谐语语；双关语 • **verb (puns, punning, punned)** make a pun 使用双关语

punch¹ /pʌntʃ/ **verb 1** hit with the fist 用拳猛击 **2** press a button or key on a machine 用力按(机器按钮或按键) • **noun 1** a blow with the fist 一拳；殴打 **2** informal【非正式】the power to impress someone 力量 □ **punch-drunk 1** dazed by a series of punches (因受多次重击)眩晕的 **2** very con-

fused or shocked 极度困惑(或震惊)的 **punch-up** informal【非正式】a fight 打架；争斗

punch² **noun** a device for cutting holes in paper, metal, leather, etc. 打孔器；穿孔机 • **verb** pierce a hole in something 在…上打孔

punch³ **noun** a drink made from wine or spirits mixed with water, fruit juices, and spices 潘趣酒(以酒兑水、果汁、香料等调制)

punchbag /ˈpʌntʃbæg/ **noun** Brit.【英】a heavy bag hung on a rope, used for punching as exercise or training (练习拳击用的)吊袋，沙包

punchline /ˈpʌntʃlaɪn/ **noun** the final part of a joke that makes it funny (笑话最后抛出的)笑料，画龙点睛的妙语

punchy /ˈpʌntʃi/ **adjective (punchier, punchiest)** effective; forceful 有效的；强有力的

punctilious /pʌŋkˈtɪliəs/ **adjective** showing great attention to detail or correct behavior 注重细节的；一丝不苟的；拘礼的

punctual /ˈpʌŋktʃuəl/ **adjective** happening or doing something at the agreed or proper time 准时的；守时的 ■ **punctuality** **noun** **punctually** **adverb.**

punctuate /ˈpʌŋktʃueɪt/ **verb (punctuates, punctuating, punctuated) 1** interrupt something at intervals 不时打断 **2** add punctuation marks to a piece of writing 给…加标点

punctuation /ˌpʌŋktʃuˈeɪʃn/ **noun** the marks, such as full stop, comma, and brackets, used in writing to separate sentences and make meaning clear 标点符号

puncture /ˈpʌŋktʃə(r)/ **noun** a small hole caused by a sharp object (尖物刺成的)小孔 • **verb (punctures, puncturing, punctured)** make a puncture in 穿(孔)；刺破

pundit /ˈpʌndɪt/ **noun** a person who

frequently gives opinions about a subject in public 专家；权威

pungent /'pʌndʒənt/ **adjective** **1** having a sharply strong taste or smell 气味浓烈的 **2** (of remarks or humour) having a strong effect (言论或幽默)辛辣的，尖刻的 ■ **pungency** noun.

punish /'pʌnɪʃ/ **verb** **1** make someone experience something unpleasant because they have done something criminal or wrong 惩罚；处罚 **2** treat harshly or unfairly 严厉(或不公正)地对待 ■ **punishable** adjective.

punishment /'pʌnɪʃmənt/ **noun** **1** an unpleasant experience imposed on someone because they have done something criminal or wrong 受罚；刑罚 **2** the action of punishing 惩罚；处罚 **3** harsh or rough treatment 严酷对待

punitive /'pjuːnɪtɪv/ **adjective** intended as punishment 惩罚性的

Punjabi /pʌn'dʒɑːbi/ **noun** (plural **Punjabis**) **1** a person from Punjab, a region of NW India and Pakistan 旁遮普人 **2** the language of Punjab 旁遮普语

punk /pʌŋk/ **noun** **1** (also **punk rock**) a loud and aggressive form of rock music 朋克摇滚乐 **2** (also **punk rocker**) a person who likes or plays punk music 朋克摇滚乐迷(或摇滚乐手) **3** N. Amer. informal 【北美，非正式】a worthless person 不中用的人

punnet /'pʌnɪt/ **noun** Brit. 【英】a small container for fruit or vegetables (盛放水果或蔬菜的)小篮

punt¹ /pʌnt/ **noun** a long, narrow boat with a flat bottom, moved forward with a long pole (用篙撑的)方头平底船 ■ **verb** travel in a punt 乘方头平底船旅行

punt² **verb** kick a ball after it has dropped from the hands and before it reaches the ground 踢(悬空球) ■ **noun** a kick of this kind 踢悬空球

punt³ **noun** Brit. informal 【英，非正式】a bet 打赌

punt⁴ **noun** the former basic unit of money in the Republic of Ireland 爱尔兰镑(爱尔兰共和国旧时基本货币单位)

punter /'pʌntə(r)/ **noun** Brit. informal 【英，非正式】**1** a person who gambles 赌徒 **2** a customer or client 顾客；客户

puny /'pjuːni/ **adjective** (**punier**, **puniest**) **1** small and weak 弱小的；瘦弱的 **2** not very impressive 欠佳的；不足道的

pup /pʌp/ **noun** **1** a young dog 小狗 **2** a young wolf, seal, rat, or other animal (狼、海豹、老鼠等哺乳动物的)幼崽

pupa /'pjuːpə/ **noun** (plural **pupae** /'pjuːpiː/) an insect in the form between larva and adult (昆虫的)蛹 ■ **pupal** adjective.

pupate /pjuː'peɪt/ **verb** (**pupates**, **pupating**, **pupated**) become a pupa 化蛹

pupil¹ /'pjuːpl/ **noun** a person who is being taught 学生；弟子；门生

pupil² **noun** the dark circular opening in the centre of the iris of the eye 瞳孔

puppet /'pʌpɪt/ **noun** **1** a model of a person or animal which can be moved either by strings or by a hand inside it 木偶 **2** a person under the control of someone else 傀儡；受人操纵者 ■ **puppeteer** noun **puppetry** noun.

puppy /'pʌpi/ **noun** (plural **puppies**) a young dog 小狗；幼犬 □ **puppy fat** fat on a child's body that disappears as they grow up 儿时肥胖；婴儿肥 **puppy love** strong but short-lived love 短暂的爱情

purblind /'pɜːblaɪnd/ **adjective** literary 【文】**1** partially sighted 半盲的；视力模糊的 **2** lacking awareness or understanding 迟钝的；愚笨的

purchase /ˈpɜːtʃəs/ **verb** (**purchases, purchasing, purchased**) buy 购买 ■ **noun 1** the action of buying 购买 **2** a thing bought 购得物 **3** firm contact or grip 抓牢;紧握 ■ **purchaser** noun.

purdah /ˈpɜːdə/ **noun** the practice in certain Muslim and Hindu societies of screening women from men or strangers 深闺制度(一些伊斯兰教和印度教国家使女性在男性或陌生人面前以面纱遮面的制度)

pure /pjʊə(r)/ **adjective 1** not mixed with any other substance or material 纯的;纯粹的;不掺杂的;pure wool 纯羊毛 **2** not containing any harmful or polluting substances 纯净的;洁净的 **3** innocent or morally good 纯洁的;无瑕的 **4** sheer; nothing but 十足的;仅仅的;a shout of pure anger 愤怒至极的吼叫 **5** theoretical rather than practical 纯理论的;pure mathematics 理论数学 **6** (of a sound) perfectly in tune and with a clear tone (声音)纯净的,纯正的 ■ **purely** adverb.

purée /ˈpjʊəreɪ/ **noun** a mass of crushed fruit or vegetables (水果或蔬菜的)泥,酱 ■ **verb** (**purées, puréeing, puréed**) make a purée of 把…制成泥(或酱)

purgative /ˈpɜːɡətɪv/ **adjective** having a strong laxative effect 催泻的;通便的 ■ **noun** a laxative 泻药;泻剂

purgatory /ˈpɜːɡətri/ **noun** (plural **purgatories**) (in Roman Catholic belief) a place inhabited by the souls of sinners who are making up for their sins before going to heaven (罗马天主教信仰中的)炼狱 ■ **purgatorial** adjective.

purge /pɜːdʒ/ **verb** (**purges, purging, purged**) rid someone or something of undesirable or harmful people or things 清除;肃清 ■ **noun** an act of purging 清除(行动);肃清

purify /ˈpjʊərɪfaɪ/ **verb** (**purifies, purifying, purified**) make something pure 使纯净;净化 ■ **purification** noun.

✔ 拼写指南 i not e: purify. purify 中的 i 不要拼作 e。

purist /ˈpjʊərɪst/ **noun** a person who insists on following traditional rules, especially in language or style (尤指在语言和艺术风格方面的)纯粹主义者 ■ **purism** noun.

puritan /ˈpjʊərɪtən/ **noun 1** (Puritan) a member of a group of English Protestants in the 16th and 17th centuries who tried to simplify forms of worship 清教徒(16至17世纪主张简化宗教仪式的英格兰新教教派) **2** a person with strong moral beliefs who is critical of the behaviour of other people 清教徒似的人;恪守道德规范的人 ■ **puritanical** adjective.

purity /ˈpjʊərəti/ **noun** the state of being pure 纯净;纯粹;纯洁

purl /pɜːl/ **adjective** (of a knitting stitch) made by putting the needle through the front of the stitch from right to left (编织法)反针的 ■ **verb** knit with a purl stitch 用反针织

purlieus /ˈpɜːljuːz/ **plural noun** literary 【文】 the area around or near a place 邻近地区;外围地区

purloin /pɜːˈlɔɪn/ **verb** formal 【正式】 steal 偷窃

purple /ˈpɜːpl/ **adjective** of a colour between red and blue 紫色的 ■ **noun** a purple colour 紫色 ■ **purple patch** informal 【非正式】 a run of success or good luck 成功时期;一连串好运 **purple prose** prose that is too elaborate 风格过于华丽的散文

purport **verb** /pəˈpɔːt/ appear or claim to be or do 声称 ■ **noun** /ˈpɜːpɔːt/ the meaning or purpose of something 含义;要旨

purpose /ˈpɜːpəs/ **noun 1** the reason for which something is done or for which something exists 目的;意图 **2** strong determination 决心;意志 □ **on purpose** intentionally 故意地;

有意地

purposeful /'pɜːpəsfl/ **adjective**
1 having or showing determination
坚定的；果断的 **2** having a purpose
有目的的 ■ **purposefully** adverb.

purposely /'pɜːpəsli/ **adverb** on
purpose 特意地；故意地

purposive /'pɜːpəsɪv/ **adjective**
having or done with a purpose 有目
的的；故意的

purr /pɜː(r)/ **verb 1** (of a cat) make
a low continuous sound expressing
contentment (猫惬意时)发呼噜声
2 (of an engine) run smoothly while
making a similar sound (发动机)发
出轰隆声 ■ **noun** a purring sound (猫
的)呼噜声；(发动机的)轰隆声

purse /pɜːs/ **noun 1** chiefly Brit.【主
英】 a small pouch for carrying
money 小钱包；钱夹 **2** N. Amer.【北
美】 a handbag 手提包 **3** money for
spending 资金 **4** a sum of money
given as a prize 奖金 • **verb** (**purses,**
pursing, pursed) form the lips into
a tight round shape 撅起(嘴唇)

purser /'pɜːsə(r)/ **noun** a ship's officer
who keeps the accounts (轮船上的)
账目主管，事务长

pursuance /pə'sjuːəns/ **noun** formal
【正式】 the carrying out of a plan or
action (计划或行动的)执行，实行

pursuant /pə'sjuːənt/ **adverb**
(**pursuant to**) formal 【正式】 in
accordance with 按照；依据

pursue /pə'sjuː/ **verb** (**pursues,**
pursuing, pursued) **1** follow
someone or something in order to
catch or attack them 追踪；追捕，追
击 **2** try to achieve a goal 追求(目
标) **3** follow a course of action 从事；
继续进行 **4** continue to investigate
or discuss a topic 追查；继续讨论
■ **pursuer** noun.

✔ 拼写指南 *pur*-, not *per*-: *pursue*.
pursue 中的 pur- 不要排作 per-。

pursuit /pə'sjuːt/ **noun 1** the action of
pursuing someone or something 追
踪；追求；追逐 **2** a leisure or sporting
activity 消遣；体育活动

purulent /'pjʊərələnt/ **adjective** made
up of or giving out pus 化脓的；流脓
的

purvey /pə'veɪ/ **verb** formal 【正式】
provide or supply food or drink as a
business 供应(饮食) ■ **purveyor** noun.

purview /'pɜːvjuː/ **noun** formal 【正式】
the range of something's influence
or concerns 影响范围；权限

pus /pʌs/ **noun** a thick yellowish or
greenish liquid produced in infected
body tissue 脓

push /pʊʃ/ **verb 1** apply force to
something so as to move it away
from yourself 推；推开 **2** move part
of your body into a particular position
推进(身体部位) **3** move by using
force 挤开 **4** encourage someone to
work hard 催促；力劝 **5** (**push for**)
repeatedly demand something 一再
要求 **6** informal 【非正式】 promote the
use, sale, or acceptance of 推行；推
销；推荐 **7** informal 【非正式】 sell an
illegal drug 非法销售(药品) • **noun**
1 an act of pushing 推；挤 **2** a great
effort 奋斗；努力：*one last push* 最后
的努力 ■ **pusher** noun.

pushbike /'pʊʃbaɪk/ **noun** Brit.
informal 【英,非正式】 a bicycle 自行
车

pushchair /'pʊʃtʃeə(r)/ **noun** Brit.【英】
a folding chair on wheels, in which a
young child can be pushed along 折
叠式幼儿推车

pushover /'pʊʃəʊvə(r)/ **noun** informal
【非正式】 **1** a person who is easy to
influence or defeat 易受影响(或被击
败)的人 **2** a thing that is easily done
易如反掌的事

pushy /'pʊʃi/ **adjective** (**pushier,**
pushiest) too assertive or ambitious
固执己见的；咄咄逼人的

pusillanimous /ˌpjuːsɪ'lænɪməs/
adjective weak or cowardly 胆小的；

懦弱的 ■ **pusillanimity** noun.

pussy /ˈpusi/ or **puss** /pus/ **noun** (plural **pussies** or **pusses**) (also **pussycat**) informal 【非正式】 a cat 猫咪 □ **pussy willow** a willow with soft, fluffy catkins that appear before the leaves 褪色柳

pussyfoot /ˈpusifut/ **verb** (**pussyfoots**, **pussyfooting**, **pussyfooted**) act very cautiously 谨慎行事；畏首畏尾

pustule /ˈpʌstjuːl/ **noun** a small blister on the skin containing pus 脓疱 ■ **pustular** adjective.

put /put/ **verb** (**puts**, **putting**, **put**) 1 move something into a particular position 放；置 2 bring into a particular state or condition 使处于(某种状态或环境)：*She tried to put me at ease.* 她努力让我放松下来。 3 (**put something on** or **on to**) make a person or thing subject to something 施加 4 give a value, figure, or limit to 给…定价；估计(数字或限度) 5 express something in a particular way 表述；表达 6 (of a ship) go in a particular direction (船)驶向：*The boat put out to sea.* 船出海了。 7 throw a shot or weight as a sport 推(铅球)；投掷(铁饼) □ **put someone/thing down** 1 end a riot by using force 镇压(暴乱) 2 kill a sick, old, or injured animal 杀死(病、老或受伤的动物) 3 pay a sum as a deposit 付(定金) 4 informal 【非正式】 criticize someone in public (公开)指责，奚落 **put someone/thing off** 1 postpone something 推迟(某事) 2 make someone feel dislike or lose enthusiasm 使(某人)反感(或失去热情) 3 distract someone 使分心 **put something on** 1 organize an event 组织(活动) 2 gain weight 增加(体重) 3 adopt an expression, accent, etc. 装出(表情、口音等) **put someone out** cause someone trouble or inconvenience 使(某人)有麻烦(或不方便) **put someone/thing up**

1 present, provide, or offer something 推举(某人)；提出，提供(某事物) 2 give someone a place to stay 为(某人)提供住处 **put someone up to** informal 【非正式】 encourage someone to do something wrong 唆使(某人)做(坏事) **put up with** tolerate 忍受

putative /ˈpjuːtətɪv/ **adjective** formal 【正式】 generally considered to be 公认的；普遍认为的

putrefy /ˈpjuːtrɪfaɪ/ **verb** (**putrefies**, **putrefying**, **putrefied**) decay or rot and produce a very unpleasant smell 腐烂；腐败 ■ **putrefaction** noun.

putrid /ˈpjuːtrɪd/ **adjective** 1 decaying or rotting and producing a very unpleasant smell 腐烂的；腐臭的 2 informal 【非正式】 very unpleasant 令人不快的

putsch /putʃ/ **noun** a violent attempt to overthrow a government 起义；造反；政变

putt /pʌt/ **verb** (**putts**, **putting**, **putted**) hit a golf ball gently so that it rolls into or near a hole 〈高尔夫球运动中〉轻击，打推杆 ● **noun** a stroke of this kind 轻击球；推杆 □ **putting green** a smooth area of short grass surrounding a hole on a golf course 〈高尔夫球场的〉果岭，球洞区

putter[1] /ˈpʌtə(r)/ **noun** a golf club designed for putting 〈高尔夫球〉轻击棒

putter[2] **noun** the rapid irregular sound of a small petrol engine 〈小型汽油引擎的〉突突声 ● **verb** (**putters**, **puttering**, **puttered**) move with this sound 突突响着开动

putty /ˈpʌti/ **noun** a soft paste that hardens as it sets, used for sealing glass in window frames 〈嵌装玻璃的〉油灰；腻子

puzzle /ˈpʌzl/ **verb** (**puzzles**, **puzzling**, **puzzled**) 1 make someone feel confused because they cannot understand something 使困惑 2 think hard about something difficult to understand (为难题)伤脑筋, 苦思冥想 • noun 1 a game, toy, or problem designed to test mental skills or knowledge 智力游戏; 智力玩具; 智力题 2 a person or thing that is difficult to understand 令人迷惑的人; 难题 ■ **puzzlement** noun **puzzler** noun.

PVC /ˌpiː viː ˈsiː/ **abbreviation** polyvinyl chloride, a sort of plastic 聚氯乙烯 (一种塑料)

pygmy or **pigmy** /ˈpɪɡmi/ **noun** (plural **pygmies**) 1 (Pygmy) a member of a race of very short people living in parts of Africa 俾格米人(非洲地区一身材非常矮小的种族) 2 a very small person or thing 非常矮小的人(或物) • adjective very small 非常小的, 矮小的

pyjamas /pəˈdʒɑːməz/ (US spelling 【美拼作】**pajamas**) **plural noun** a loose jacket and trousers for sleeping in 睡衣裤

pylon /ˈpaɪlən/ **noun** a tall tower-like structure for carrying electricity cables 电缆塔

pyramid /ˈpɪrəmɪd/ **noun** a very large stone structure with a square or triangular base and sloping sides that meet in a point at the top 金字塔; (石块建造的)锥形塔, 方尖塔 ■ **pyramidal** adjective.

pyre /ˈpaɪə(r)/ **noun** a large pile of wood for the ritual burning of a dead body (火葬用的)柴堆

pyrites /paɪˈraɪtiːz/ or **pyrite** /ˈpaɪraɪt/ **noun** a shiny yellow mineral that is a compound of iron and sulphur 硫化铁矿; 黄铁

pyromania /ˌpaɪrəʊˈmeɪniə/ **noun** a strong urge to set fire to things 纵火狂 ■ **pyromaniac** noun.

pyrotechnics /ˌpaɪrəˈtekniks/ **plural noun** 1 a firework display 烟火燃放 2 the art of making fireworks or staging firework displays 烟火制造(术); 烟火施放(术) ■ **pyrotechnic** adjective.

pyrrhic /ˈpɪrɪk/ **adjective** (of a victory) won at too great a cost to have been worthwhile (胜利)得不偿失的, 代价惨重的

python /ˈpaɪθən/ **noun** a large snake which crushes its prey 蟒蛇; 蚺蛇

Qq

Q or **q** /kju:/ **noun** (plural **Qs** or **Q's**) the seventeenth letter of the alphabet 英语字母表的第17个字母 • **abbreviation** question.

QC /kju: 'si:/ **abbreviation** Law 【法律】 Queen's Counsel 王室法律顾问；御用大律师

QED /kju: i: 'di:/ **abbreviation** used to say that something proves the truth of your claim 证明完毕 [short for Latin 【缩写,拉丁】 = *quod erat demonstrandum* 'which was to be demonstrated'.]

qt abbreviation quarts.

qua /kweɪ/ **conjunction** formal 【正式】 in the role or capacity of 作为；以…身份

quack¹ /kwæk/ **noun** the harsh sound made by a duck (鸭子的)嘎嘎声,呱呱声 • **verb** make this sound 嘎嘎叫;呱呱叫

quack² **noun 1** an unqualified person who claims to have medical knowledge 冒牌医生;江湖郎中;庸医 **2** Brit. informal 【英,非正式】 a doctor 医生

quad /kwɒd/ **noun 1** a quadrangle 广场;方形庭院;四边形 **2** a quadruplet 四胞胎之一

quadrangle /'kwɒdræŋgl/ **noun 1** a square or rectangular courtyard enclosed by buildings (四周由建筑物围绕的)广场,方形庭院 **2** a four-sided geometrical figure 四边形 ■ **quadrangular** adjective.

quadrant /'kwɒdrənt/ **noun 1** a quarter of a circle or of a circle's circumference 四分之一圆(或圆周);象限 **2** historical 【历史】 an instrument for measuring angles in astronomy and navigation (天文和航海测量用的)象限仪,四分仪

quadraphonic or **quadrophonic** /ˌkwɒdrə'fɒnɪk/ **adjective** (of sound reproduction) using four channels (声音录放)四声道的

quadratic /kwɒ'drætɪk/ **adjective** Maths 【数学】 involving the second and no higher power of an unknown quantity 二次方的;平方的

quadriceps /'kwɒdrɪseps/ **noun** (plural **quadriceps**) a large muscle at the front of the thigh 四头肌

quadrilateral /ˌkwɒdrɪ'lætərəl/ **noun** a four-sided figure 四边形 • **adjective** having four straight sides 有四条直边的

quadrille /kwə'drɪl/ **noun** a square dance performed by four couples (四对男女构成方阵表演的)方阵舞,卡德利尔舞

quadriplegia /ˌkwɒdrɪ'pli:dʒə/ **noun** paralysis of all four limbs 四肢麻痹;四肢瘫痪 ■ **quadriplegic** adjective & noun.

quadruped /'kwɒdruped/ **noun** an animal which has four feet 四足动物

quadruple adjective /kwɒ'dru:pl/ **1** consisting of four parts 四部分组成的 **2** four times as much or as many 四倍的 • **verb** /kwɒ'dru:pl/ (**quadruples, quadrupling, quadrupled**) multiply by four (使)增长四倍

quadruplet /'kwɒdruplət/ **noun** each of four children born at one birth 四胞胎之一

quaff /kwɒf/ **verb** drink a large amount of something quickly 畅饮,痛饮

quagmire /'kwæɡmaɪə(r)/ **noun** a soft, wet area of land 沼泽;泥淖;潮地

quail¹ /kweɪl/ **noun** (plural **quail** or **quails**) a small short-tailed game bird 鹌鹑

quail² **verb** feel or show fear 畏惧;胆怯

quaint /kweɪnt/ **adjective** attractively unusual or old-fashioned 新奇的;古色古香的 ■ **quaintly** adverb.

quake /kweɪk/ **verb** (**quakes**, **quaking**, **quaked**) **1** (especially of the earth) shake or tremble (尤指地球)摇晃,震动 **2** shudder with fear (因恐惧而)颤抖,哆嗦 • **noun** informal 【非正式】 an earthquake 地震

Quaker /'kweɪkə(r)/ **noun** a member of the Religious Society of Friends, a Christian movement devoted to peaceful principles and rejecting set forms of worship 贵格会教徒,公谊会教徒(属于致力于和平原则的宗教运动,反对固有的礼拜仪式) ■ **Quakerism** noun.

qualification /ˌkwɒlɪfɪ'keɪʃn/ **noun** **1** the action of qualifying 取得资格 **2** a pass of an exam or an official completion of a course 学历证书;资格证明 **3** a quality that makes someone suitable for a job or activity 资格;条件 **4** a statement that limits the meaning of another statement 限定条件

qualify /'kwɒlɪfaɪ/ **verb** (**qualifies**, **qualifying**, **qualified**) **1** meet the necessary standard or conditions to be able to do or receive something 取得资格(或学历);合格 **2** become officially recognized as able to do a particular job 正式取得资格 **3** add something to a statement to limit its meaning 为(陈述)添加限制性说明 **4** Grammar 【语法】(of a word or phrase) give a quality to another word (词或短语)修饰,限定(另一词) ■ **qualifier** noun.

qualitative /'kwɒlɪtətɪv/ **adjective** relating to or measured by quality 质量的;性质的,定性的 ■ **qualitatively**

adverb.

quality /'kwɒləti/ **noun** (plural **qualities**) **1** the standard of something as measured against other similar things; how good or bad something is 质量;品质 **2** general excellence 优秀;卓越 **3** a distinctive characteristic 特点;特质,特征

qualm /kwɑːm/ **noun** a feeling of doubt about what you are doing (对自己行为的)顾虑,不安

quandary /'kwɒndəri/ **noun** (plural **quandaries**) a state of uncertainty 困惑;进退两难

quango /'kwæŋɡəʊ/ **noun** (plural **quangos**) disapproving 【贬】an organization that works independently but with support from the government (由政府赞助但独立运作的)半官方机构

quantify /'kwɒntɪfaɪ/ **verb** (**quantifies**, **quantifying**, **quantified**) express or measure the quantity of 用数量表示;量化 ■ **quantifiable** adjective.

quantitative /'kwɒntɪtətɪv/ **adjective** relating to or measured by quantity 数量的;量化的,定量性的 ■ **quantitatively** adverb.

quantity /'kwɒntəti/ **noun** (plural **quantities**) **1** a certain amount or number (一定的)数量,数目 **2** the property of something that can be measured in number, amount, size, or weight 量;数量 **3** a large number or amount 大量;大宗 □ **quantity surveyor** Brit. 【英】a person who calculates the amount and cost of materials needed for building work (建筑)估算员,估算师

quantum /'kwɒntəm/ **noun** (plural **quanta**) Physics 【物理】a distinct quantity of energy corresponding to that involved in the absorption or emission of energy by an atom 量子 □ **quantum leap** a sudden large increase or advance 巨增;飞跃 **quantum mechanics** the branch of physics concerned with describing the behaviour of subatomic particles in terms of quanta 量子力学

quarantine /'kwɒrəntiːn/ noun a period of time when an animal or person that may have a disease is kept in isolation (可能患病的人或动物的)隔离期，检疫期 • verb (**quarantines, quarantining, quarantined**) put in quarantine 对…进行隔离；对…检疫

quark /kwɑːk/ noun any of a group of subatomic particles which carry a very small electric charge and are believed to form protons, neutrons, and other particles 夸克(据信构成质子、中子等的微小粒子)

quarrel /'kwɒrəl/ noun 1 an angry argument or disagreement 争吵；口角；拌嘴 2 a reason for disagreement 不和的原因；吵闹的缘由 • verb (**quarrels, quarrelling, quarrelled**; US spelling 【美拼作】**quarrels, quarreling, quarreled**) 1 have a quarrel 吵架；争吵；吵嘴 2 (**quarrel with**) disagree with 不赞同，反对

quarrelsome /'kwɒrəlsəm/ adjective tending to quarrel with people 爱争吵的；好口角的

quarry[1] /'kwɒri/ noun (plural **quarries**) a place where stone or other materials are dug out of the earth 采石场 • verb (**quarries, quarrying, quarried**) dig out stone or other materials from a quarry 从(采石场)采(石等)

quarry[2] noun (plural **quarries**) an animal or person that is being hunted or chased 猎物；被追捕的人；被追逐的目标

quart /kwɔːt/ noun a unit of liquid capacity equal to a quarter of a gallon or two pints, in Britain equal to 1.13 litres and in the US to 0.94 litre 夸脱(液量单位，等于0.25加仑或2品脱，合英制1.13升和美制0.94升)

quarter /'kwɔːtə(r)/ noun 1 each of four equal parts of something 四分之一 2 a period of three months 季(度)；三个月时间 3 a quarter of an hour; fifteen minutes 一刻钟；十五分钟 4 one fourth of a pound weight, equal to 4 oz avoirdupois 四分之一磅(衡量等于4盎司) 5 a part of a town (城镇的)区，地区 6 a US or Canadian coin worth 25 cents (美国或加拿大的)二十五分硬币 7 one fourth of a hundredweight, in Britain equal to 28 lb and in the US equal to 25 lb 夸特，四分之一英担(合英制28磅和美制25磅) 8 (**quarters**) rooms to live in 住处；宿舍 9 a person or area seen as the source of something 视为某事物来源的人，区域：*help from an unexpected quarter* 意外得到的某个人的帮助 10 mercy shown to an opponent (对对手的)仁慈，怜悯，宽容 • verb (**quarters, quartering, quartered**) 1 divide into quarters 把…四等分 2 (**be quartered**) be provided with rooms to live in 住宿；居住 3 historical 【历史】cut the body of an executed person into four parts 将(被处死者)肢解为四块 **quarter-final** a match of a competition coming before the semi-final 四分之一决赛

quarterdeck /'kwɔːtədek/ noun the part of a ship's upper deck near the stern (船舶的)上层后甲板区

quarterly /'kwɔːtəli/ adjective & adverb produced or happening once every quarter of a year 按季度的(的)；每季度(的) • noun (plural **quarterlies**) a publication produced four times a year 季刊

quartermaster /'kwɔːtəmɑːstə(r)/ noun an army officer in charge of accommodation and supplies 军需官

quartet /kwɔː'tet/ noun 1 a group of four people playing music or singing together 四重奏乐团；四重唱组合 2 a piece of music for a quartet 四重奏(曲)；四重唱(曲) 3 a set of four 四件套；四人组；四部曲

quarto /'kwɔːtəʊ/ **noun** (plural **quartos**) a size of page for a book, resulting from folding a sheet into four leaves (书页的)四开

quartz /kwɔːts/ **noun** a hard mineral consisting of silica 石英

quasar /'kweizɑː(r)/ **noun** (in astronomy) a kind of galaxy which gives off enormous amounts of energy (天文学中的)类星体

quash /kwɒʃ/ **verb 1** officially declare that a legal decision is no longer valid 宣布(法律裁决)无效;撤销 **2** put an end to 结束;终止

quasi- /'kweizai-, -sai-/ **combining form** seemingly; as if 类似的;准: *quasis-cientific* 准科学的

quatrain /'kwɒtrein/ **noun** a poem or verse of four lines 四行诗

quaver /'kweivə(r)/ **verb** (**quavers**, **quavering**, **quavered**) (of a voice) tremble (嗓音)颤抖, 发颤 • **noun 1** a tremble in a voice 颤抖的嗓音 **2** chiefly Brit.【主英】a musical note that lasts as long as half a crotchet 八分音符 ■ **quavery** adjective.

quay /kiː/ **noun** a platform in a harbour for loading and unloading ships 码头;埠头

quayside /'kiː said/ **noun** a quay and the area around it 码头边;码头区

queasy /'kwiːzi/ **adjective** (**queasier**, **queasiest**) feeling sick 恶心的;欲吐的 ■ **queasiness** noun.

queen /kwiːn/ **noun 1** the female ruler of an independent state 女王;女酋长;女首领 **2** (also **queen consort**) a king's wife 王后 **3** the best or most important woman or thing in a particular group (某群体中的)王后,出类拔萃者,精华 **4** a playing card ranking next below a king (纸牌中的)王后(牌) **5** the most powerful chess piece, able to move in any direction (国际象棋中的)后 **6** a female that lays eggs for a colony of ants, bees, wasps, or termites (为群体产卵的)蚁后,蜂王,后蜂 **7** informal【非正式】a homosexual man who behaves like a woman 女性化的男同性恋者 □ **queen mother** the widow of a king who is also mother of the current king or queen 太后;皇太后;王太后 ■ **queenly** adjective.

Queensberry Rules /'kwiː nzbəri/ **plural noun** the standard rules of boxing (拳击的)昆斯伯里规则,标准规则

queer /kwiə(r)/ **adjective 1** strange; odd 奇异的;奇怪的;古怪的 **2** disapproving【贬】(of a man) homosexual (男子)同性恋的 • **noun** disapproving【贬】a homosexual man 男同性恋者

quell /kwel/ **verb 1** put an end to a rebellion by force 镇压,平息(叛乱) **2** suppress a feeling 抑制(不快情绪)

quench /kwentʃ/ **verb 1** satisfy thirst by drinking 解(渴) **2** put out a fire 扑灭(火)

querulous /'kwerələs/ **adjective** complaining in an irritable way 抱怨的;爱发牢骚的 ■ **querulously** adverb.

query /'kwiəri/ **noun** (plural **queries**) a question, especially one expressing a doubt about something 疑问;询问 • **verb** (**queries**, **querying**, **queried**) ask a question expressing doubt about something 提出疑问;质问

quest /kwest/ **noun** a long or difficult search 探索;寻找 • **verb** search for something 搜寻;探求

question /'kwestʃən/ **noun 1** a sentence worded so as to obtain information 问题 **2** doubt, or the raising of a doubt about something 疑问;质疑 **3** a problem needing to be solved (待解决的)问题 **4** a matter depending on stated conditions (取决于已知条件的)问题,事情: *It's only a question of time.* 这只是个时间问题。• **verb 1** ask someone questions 提问;质询;问 **2** express doubt about something 怀疑;表示疑问 □ **out of the question** not possible 不可能

的 **question mark** a punctuation mark (?) indicating a question 问号 ■ **questioner** noun.

questionable /ˈkwestʃənəbl/ **adjective** likely to be wrong 有问题的;可能不对的

questionnaire /ˌkwestʃəˈneə(r)/ **noun** a set of questions written for a survey 问卷;调查表

> ✔ **拼写指南** there are two *ns*: questionnaire. questionnaire 中有两个 n。

queue /kjuː/ **noun** a line of people or vehicles waiting their turn for something (人或车辆的)队,行列 • **verb** (**queues**, **queuing** or **queueing**, **queued**) wait in a queue 排队等候 □ **queue-jump** Brit. 【英】 move forward out of turn in a queue 插队;夹塞儿

quibble /ˈkwɪbl/ **noun** a minor objection 小意见;抱怨 • **verb** (**quibbles**, **quibbling**, **quibbled**) raise a minor objection (为小事)抱怨,吹毛求疵

quiche /kiːʃ/ **noun** a baked flan with a savoury filling thickened with eggs 鸡蛋馅饼

quick /kwɪk/ **adjective 1** moving fast 迅速的;快 **2** lasting or taking a short time 短暂的 **3** with little or no delay 迅速的;即时的 **4** intelligent 聪明的;敏锐的 **5** (of temper) easily roused (脾气)急的 • **noun** (**the quick**) the tender flesh below the growing part of a fingernail or toenail (指甲或趾甲下的)活肉 □ **cut someone to the quick** upset someone very much 深深伤害(某人) **quick-tempered** easily angered 急性子的;火爆脾气的 **quick-witted** able to think or respond quickly 机敏的;机智的 ■ **quickly** adverb.

quicken /ˈkwɪkən/ **verb 1** make or become quicker (使)加快;(使)变快 **2** make or become active or alive (使)变活跃;(使)有生气

quicklime /ˈkwɪklaɪm/ **noun** a white alkaline substance consisting of calcium oxide, obtained by heating limestone 石灰

quicksand /ˈkwɪksænd/ or **quicksands** /ˈkwɪksændz/ **noun** loose wet sand that sucks in anything resting on it 流沙

quicksilver /ˈkwɪksɪlvə(r)/ **noun** mercury 水银;汞 • **adjective** moving or changing rapidly 移动(或变化)迅速的;瞬息万变的

quickstep /ˈkwɪkstep/ **noun** a fast foxtrot 快(狐)步舞;活泼的舞步

quid /kwɪd/ **noun** (plural **quid**). Brit. informal 【英,非正式】 one pound sterling 一英镑

quid pro quo /ˌkwɪd prəʊ ˈkwəʊ/ **noun** (plural **quid pro quos**) a favour given in return for something 报偿;回报

quiescent /kwiˈesnt/ **adjective** not active 静止的;静态的 ■ **quiescence** noun.

quiet /ˈkwaɪət/ **adjective** (**quieter**, **quietest**) **1** making little or no noise 安静的;轻声的,不出声的 **2** free from activity or excitement 僻静的;寂静的;清静的 **3** without being disturbed 不受干扰的;平静的: *a quiet drink* 安安静静饮酒 • **adjective** 暗中的;秘密的: *a quiet word* 私下谈话 **5** (of a person) shy and not tending to talk very much (人)文静的,温和的,害羞的 • **noun** absence of noise or disturbance 安静;安宁 • **verb** N. Amer. 【北美】 make or become quiet (使)安静,(使)平静 ■ **quietly** adverb.

quieten /ˈkwaɪətn/ **verb** Brit. 【英】 make or become quiet and calm (使)安静下来,(使)平静下来

quietude /ˈkwaɪətjuːd/ **noun** a state of calmness and quiet 平静;寂静;宁静

quiff /kwɪf/ **noun** Brit. 【英】 a piece of hair brushed upwards and backwards from the forehead 额发(额前向上梳的一绺头发)

quill /kwɪl/ **noun 1** a main wing or tail

feather of a bird 翎(鸟的翅膀或尾部的大羽毛) **2** the hollow shaft of a feather 羽毛管 **3** a pen made from a quill 羽管笔;翎笔 **4** a spine of a porcupine or hedgehog (豪猪或刺猬的)刺

quilt /kwɪlt/ **noun** a warm bed covering made of padding enclosed between layers of fabric 加衬芯床罩 ■ **quilting** noun.

quilted /'kwɪltɪd/ **adjective** made of two layers of cloth filled with padding 絮棉的,加衬芯的

quin /kwɪn/ **noun** Brit. informal 【英,非正式】 a quintuplet 五胞胎之一

quince /kwɪns/ **noun** a hard yellow pear-shaped fruit 榅桲(黄色梨形果实)

quinine /kwɪ'niːn/ **noun** a bitter drug made from the bark of a South American tree 奎宁,金鸡纳霜(一种药物,味苦,提取自一种南美树木的树皮)

quintessence /kwɪn'tesns/ **noun 1** a perfect example of something 典范;范例 **2** the central and most important part or quality of something 精华;精髓

quintessential /ˌkwɪntɪ'senʃl/ **adjective** representing the most perfect example 典范的,最典型的 ■ **quintessentially** adverb.

quintet /kwɪn'tet/ **noun 1** a group of five people playing music or singing together 五重奏乐团;五重唱组合 **2** a piece of music for a quintet 五重奏(曲);五重唱(曲) **3** a set of five 五件套;五人组;五部曲

quintuple /'kwɪntjʊpl/ **adjective 1** consisting of five parts or elements 五部分组成的 **2** five times as much or as many 五倍的;五重的

quintuplet /'kwɪntjʊplət/ **noun** each of five children born at one birth 五胞胎之一

quip /kwɪp/ **noun** a witty remark 妙语;俏皮话 • **verb** (**quips**, **quipping**, **quipped**) make a witty remark 说俏

皮话;打趣

quire /'kwaɪə(r)/ **noun 1** four sheets of paper folded to form eight leaves 帖(对折成8页的4张纸) **2** 25 sheets of paper (纸的)一刀(25张)

quirk /kwɜːk/ **noun 1** a peculiar habit 古怪习惯;怪癖 **2** a strange thing that happens by chance (偶然发生的)怪事,奇事;巧合

quirky /kwɜːki/ **adjective** (**quirkier**, **quirkiest**) having peculiar or unexpected habits or qualities 有怪癖的;古怪的

quisling /'kwɪzlɪŋ/ **noun** a traitor who collaborates with an enemy force that has occupied their country 卖国贼;内奸

quit /kwɪt/ **verb** (**quits**, **quitting**, **quitted** or **quit**) **1** leave a place 离开(某地) **2** resign from a job 辞去(工作) **3** informal, chiefly N. Amer.【非正式,主北美】 stop doing something 停止,放弃(做某事) ■ **quitter** noun.

quite /kwaɪt/ **adverb 1** to a certain extent; fairly 相当,还算 **2** to the greatest degree; completely 极;十分;完全 • **exclamation** expressing agreement 是啊;对啦;没错

quits /kwɪts/ **adjective** on equal terms because a debt or score has been settled 互不相欠的;两清的

quiver[1] /'kwɪvə(r)/ **verb** (**quivers**, **quivering**, **quivered**) shake or vibrate slightly 颤抖;发抖 • **noun** a quivering movement 颤抖;抖动

quiver[2] **noun** a case for carrying arrows 箭囊;箭筒

quixotic /kwɪk'sɒtɪk/ **adjective** idealistic but impractical 堂吉诃德式的;异想天开的;不切实际的

quiz /kwɪz/ **noun** (plural **quizzes**) a competition in which people answer questions that test their knowledge 知识竞赛;智力游戏 • **verb** (**quizzes**, **quizzing**, **quizzed**) question someone 盘问;查问

quizzical /'kwɪzɪkl/ **adjective**

q.v.

showing mild or amused puzzlement 诧异的;感到好笑的 ■ **quizzically** adverb.

quoin /kɔɪn/ *noun* **1** an external angle of a wall or building (墙或建筑物的) 外角 **2** a cornerstone 墙角石;墙角砖

quoit /kɔɪt/ *noun* a ring that you throw over an upright peg in the game of quoits (掷环套桩游戏用的)环,圈

quorate /ˈkwɔːreɪt/ *adjective* Brit.【英】 (of a meeting) having a quorum (会议)达到法定人数的

quorum /ˈkwɔːrəm/ *noun* (plural **quorums**) the minimum number of people that must be present at a meeting to make its business valid (会议的)法定人数

quota /ˈkwəʊtə/ *noun* **1** a limited quantity of people or things that is officially allowed 定额;限额 **2** a share of something that you have to contribute 配额;分担部分

quotation /kwəʊˈteɪʃn/ *noun* **1** a passage or remark repeated by someone other than the person who originally said or wrote it 引文;引语;语录 **2** a formal statement of the estimated cost of a job or service 估价;报价 □ **quotation marks** a pair of punctuation marks, (' ') or (" "),

used to mark the beginning and end of a quotation or passage of speech 引号(指单引号''或双引号"")

quote /kwəʊt/ *verb* (**quotes**, **quoting**, **quoted**) **1** repeat a passage or remark by another person 引述;引用 **2** (**quote something as**) mention something as an example to support a point 举出…作为例证 **3** give someone an estimated price (向某人)报价,开价 **4** give a company a listing on a stock exchange 向(公司)提供股票报价 ● *noun* **1** a quotation 引文;引语;语录 **2** (**quotes**) quotation marks 引号 ■ **quotable** adjective.

quoth /kwəʊθ/ *verb* old use【旧】said 说过

quotidian /kwɒˈtɪdiən/ *adjective* formal【正式】 **1** daily 每日的;日常的 **2** ordinary or everyday 普通的;平常的;平凡的

quotient /ˈkwəʊʃnt/ *noun* Maths【数学】a result obtained by dividing one quantity by another 商

q.v. /kjuː ˈviː/ *abbreviation* used to direct a reader to another part of a book for further information 参阅;参见 [short for Latin【缩写,拉丁】 = *quod vide*, literally 'which see'.]

Rr

R or **r** /ɑ:(r)/ noun (plural **Rs** or **R's**) the eighteenth letter of the alphabet 英语字母表的第18个字母 • **abbreviation 1** Regina or Rex 女王；国王 **2** (R.) River.

rabbi /'ræbaɪ/ noun (plural **rabbis**) a Jewish religious leader or teacher of Jewish law 拉比(犹太教会领袖)；大师，夫子(对教授犹太律法教师的尊称) ■ **rabbinic** (or **rabbinical**) adjective.

rabbit /'ræbɪt/ noun a burrowing animal with long ears and a short tail 兔；穴 兔 • verb (**rabbits**, **rabbiting**, **rabbited**) Brit. informal【英，非正式】chatter 闲扯

rabble /'ræbl/ noun **1** a disorderly crowd of people 乌合之众 **2** (**the rabble**) disapproving【贬】ordinary people 平民百姓；下层民众 □ **rabble-rouser** a person who makes speeches intended to make people angry or excited, usually for political reasons 蛊惑人心的政客；暴民煽动者

rabid /'ræbɪd/ adjective **1** having extreme opinions; fanatical 极端的，狂热的 **2** having rabies 患狂犬病的 ■ **rabidly** adverb.

rabies /'reɪbi:z/ noun a dangerous disease of dogs and other animals, that can be transmitted through saliva to humans 狂犬病

raccoon or **racoon** /rə'ku:n/ noun a greyish-brown American animal with a black face and striped tail 浣熊(产于美洲，黑脸，尾巴有斑纹)

race¹ /reɪs/ noun **1** a competition to see who or which is fastest over a set course 速度竞赛；赛跑 **2** a strong current flowing through a narrow channel 急流 • verb (**races**, **racing**, **raced**) **1** compete against someone or something in a race 参加比赛；参加竞赛 **2** move or progress rapidly 快速运动；迅速推进 **3** (of an engine) operate at too high a speed (发动机)猛转 ■ **racer** noun.

race² noun **1** each of the major divisions of humankind 人种 **2** a group of people or things with a common feature 血 统；宗族；世系 **3** a subdivision of a species 类；属；种 □ **race relations** relations between members of different races within a country (一国内部的)种族关系

racecourse /'reɪskɔ:s/ noun a ground or track for horse or dog racing 赛马场；赛马场；赛马(或赛狗)跑道

racehorse /'reɪshɔ:s/ noun a horse bred and trained for racing 赛马

raceme /'ræsi:m, rə'si:m/ noun a flower cluster with separate flowers along a central stem 总状花序

racetrack /'reɪstræk/ noun **1** a racecourse 赛马(或赛 狗)跑道 **2** a track for motor racing 赛车跑道

racial /'reɪʃl/ adjective **1** having to do with race 人种的；种族的，民族的 **2** relating to relations or differences between races 与种族关系(或差异)相关的 ■ **racially** adverb.

racialism /'reɪʃəlɪzəm/ noun racism 种族主义；种族偏见 ■ **racialist** noun & adjective.

racism /'reɪsɪzəm/ **noun 1** the belief that certain races are better than others 种族主义；种族偏见 **2** discrimination against, or hostility towards, other races 种族歧视；种族对抗 ■ **racist** noun & adjective.

rack /ræk/ **noun 1** a framework for holding or storing things 架子；挂架；支架；搁架 **2** (**the rack**) (in the past) a frame on which people were tortured by being stretched (旧时的)肢刑架(牵拉犯人肢体的刑具) **3** a joint of meat that includes the front ribs (连带前肋的)颈脊肉 • **verb 1** (also **wrack**) cause great pain to 使受剧烈痛苦；折磨 **2** (**rack something up**) achieve a score or amount 得(分)；累计取得 □ **go to rack and ruin** fall into a bad condition 走向毁灭，变得一团糟 **rack** (**or wrack**) **your brains** think very hard 绞尽脑汁

racket[1] **or racquet** /'rækɪt/ **noun 1** a bat with a round or oval frame, used in tennis, badminton, and squash (网球、羽毛球和壁球运动中使用的)球拍 **2** (**rackets**) a ball game played with rackets in a four-walled court 墙网球(运动)

racket[2] **noun 1** a loud, unpleasant noise 喧嚣；吵闹；嘈杂 **2** informal 【非正式】 a dishonest scheme for making money 诈骗；敲诈勒索 ■ **rackety** adjective.

racketeer /ˌrækə'tɪə(r)/ **noun** a person who makes money through dishonest activities 诈骗者；敲诈勒索者 ■ **racketeering** noun.

raconteur /ˌrækɒn'tɜː(r)/ **noun** a person who tells stories in an interesting and amusing way 善于讲故事的人

racoon /rə'kuːn/ ⇒ 见 RACCOON.

racy /'reɪsi/ **adjective** lively and exciting 充满活力的；兴奋的

radar /'reɪdɑː(r)/ **noun** a system for detecting aircraft, ships, etc., by sending out radio waves which are reflected back off the object 雷达

raddled /'rædld/ **adjective** showing signs of age and tiredness 显老态的；露疲态的

radial /'reɪdiəl/ **adjective 1** arranged in lines coming out from a central point to the edge of a circle 辐射状的 **2** (of a tyre) in which the layers of fabric run at right angles to the circumference of the tyre (轮胎)径向帘布层的，辐射式的 ■ **radially** adverb.

radian /'reɪdiən/ **noun** an angle of 57.3 degrees, equal to the angle at the centre of a circle formed by an arc equal in length to the radius 弧度(1弧度为57.3度)

radiant /'reɪdiənt/ **adjective 1** shining or glowing brightly 明亮闪耀的；灿烂的 **2** glowing with joy, love, or health 喜气洋洋的；容光焕发的 **3** transmitted by radiation 辐射的；放射的 ■ **radiance** noun **radiantly** adverb.

radiate /'reɪdieɪt/ **verb** (**radiates, radiating, radiated**) **1** (of light, heat, or other energy) be sent out in rays or waves (光、热或其他能量)辐射，发散 **2** show a strong feeling or quality 流露(强烈感情)；显示(品质) **3** spread out from a central point 呈辐射状发出；从中心发出

radiation /ˌreɪdi'eɪʃn/ **noun** energy sent out as electromagnetic waves or subatomic particles 辐射能

radiator /'reɪdieɪtə(r)/ **noun 1** a metal device for heating a room, usually filled with hot water pumped in through pipes 暖气装置；电炉 **2** a cooling device in a vehicle or aircraft engine (车辆或飞机发动机的)散热器

radical /'rædɪkl/ **adjective 1** having to do with the basic nature of something; fundamental 根本的；基本的 **2** supporting complete political

R

or social reform 激进的；革命的 **3** departing from tradition; new 颠覆传统的；全新的 **4** Maths 【数学】 relating to the root of a number or quantity 根号的；根式的 • noun **1** a supporter of radical reform 激进分子；极端分子 **2** Chemistry 【化学】 a group of atoms behaving as a unit in a compound 基；原子团 ■ **radicalism** noun **radically** adverb.

radii /ˈreɪdiaɪ/ plural of RADIUS.

radio /ˈreɪdiəʊ/ noun (plural **radios**) **1** the sending and receiving of electromagnetic waves carrying sound messages 无线电发射接收 **2** the activity or medium of broadcasting in sound 无线电广播 **3** a device for receiving radio programmes, or for sending and receiving radio messages 收音机；无线电设备 • verb (**radioes**, **radioing**, **radioed**) send a message to someone by radio 用无线电发送

radioactive /ˌreɪdiəʊˈæktɪv/ adjective giving out harmful radiation or particles 放射性的；有辐射的

radioactivity /ˌreɪdiəʊæˈktɪvəti/ noun harmful radiation or particles sent out when atomic nuclei break up 放射线，辐射线；放射粒子

radiocarbon /ˌreɪdiəʊˈkɑːbən/ noun a radioactive isotope of carbon used in carbon dating 放射性碳（用于测定物年代）

radiogram /ˈreɪdiəʊɡræm/ noun Brit. dated 【英，废】a combined radio and record player 收音电唱两用机

radiography /ˌreɪdiˈɒɡrəfi/ noun the production of images by X-rays or other radiation X射线照相；射线照相 ■ **radiographer** noun.

radioisotope /ˌreɪdiəʊˈaɪsətəʊp/ noun a radioactive isotope 放射性同位素

radiology /ˌreɪdiˈɒlədʒi/ noun the science of X-rays and similar

radiation, especially as used in medicine (尤指应用于医疗的) 放射学，辐射学 ■ **radiologist** noun.

radiotherapy /ˌreɪdiəʊˈθerəpi/ noun the treatment of disease using X-rays or similar radiation 放射疗法；放射治疗

radish /ˈrædɪʃ/ noun a crisp, hot-tasting root vegetable, eaten raw in salads 萝卜

radium /ˈreɪdiəm/ noun a radioactive metallic element (放射性金属元素) 镭

radius /ˈreɪdiəs/ noun (plural **radii** /ˈreɪdiaɪ/ or **radiuses**) **1** a straight line from the centre to the edge of a circle or sphere (圆或球的)半径 **2** a stated distance from a centre in all directions 半径距离；半径范围 **3** the thicker and shorter of the two bones in the human forearm 桡骨

radon /ˈreɪdɒn/ noun a rare radioactive gas (放射性稀有气体元素)氡

RAF /ˌɑːr eɪ ˈef/ abbreviation Royal Air Force (英国)皇家空军

raffia /ˈræfiə/ noun fibre from the leaves of a tropical palm tree 酒椰叶纤维(提取自一种热带棕榈树的树叶)

raffish /ˈræfɪʃ/ adjective slightly disreputable, but in an attractive way 落拓不羁的

raffle /ˈræfl/ noun a lottery with goods as prizes 兑奖售物；抽彩 • verb (**raffles**, **raffling**, **raffled**) offer something as a prize in a raffle 提供…为兑奖奖品

raft /rɑːft/ noun **1** a flat structure used as a boat or floating platform 木筏；木排；浮台 **2** a small inflatable boat 充气橡皮艇 **3** a large amount 大量；许多

rafter /ˈrɑːftə(r)/ noun a beam forming part of the internal framework of a roof 椽；椽木

rag /ræg/ noun **1** a piece of old cloth 抹布；破布 **2** (**rags**) old or tattered clothes 破旧衣服 **3** informal 【非正

式 】 low-quality newspaper 劣质报纸 **4** Brit.【英】a programme of entertainments organized by students to raise money for charity (学生组织的)慈善募捐活动 **5** a piece of ragtime music 雷格泰姆音乐曲 □ **the rag trade** informal【非正式】the clothing or fashion industry 服装业；时装业

ragamuffin /'rægəmʌfɪn/ **noun** a person in ragged, dirty clothes 衣衫褴褛的人

ragbag /'ræɡbæɡ/ **noun** a collection of widely different things 杂七杂八的一堆；大杂烩

rage /reɪdʒ/ **noun** violent, uncontrollable anger 暴怒；盛怒 • **verb** (**rages**, **raging**, **raged**) **1** feel or express rage 感到愤怒；发火 **2** continue with great force 激烈进行 □ **all the rage** temporarily very popular or fashionable 风靡一时的；时尚的

ragged /'ræɡɪd/ **adjective 1** (of cloth or clothes) old and torn (衣服)破旧的，褴褛的 **2** rough or irregular 崎岖的，不规则的；参差不齐的 **3** not smooth or steady 不流畅的；不统一的；不协调的 ■ **raggedly** adverb.

ragout /ræˈɡuː/ **noun** a spicy stew of meat and vegetables 五香菜炖肉；五香杂烩

ragtag /'ræɡtæɡ/ **adjective** disorganized and made up of a mixture of different types of people 无秩序的；纷乱的

ragtime /'ræɡtaɪm/ **noun** an early form of jazz played especially on the piano 雷格泰姆音乐(一种早期爵士乐,尤用钢琴演奏)

ragwort /'ræɡwɜːt/ **noun** a plant with yellow flowers and ragged leaves 千里光，狗舌草(开黄花,叶边缘参差不齐)

raid /reɪd/ **noun 1** a sudden attack on an enemy, or on a building to commit a crime 突然袭击；侵袭；劫掠 **2** a surprise visit by police to arrest suspects or seize illegal goods (警方的)突击搜捕，突击查缉 • **verb** make a raid on (警方)突击搜捕，突击查缉 ■ **raider** noun.

rail /reɪl/ **noun 1** a fixed bar forming part of a fence or barrier or used to hang things on 横条；横杆；扶手；栏杆 **2** each of the two metal bars laid on the ground to form a railway track 铁轨；轨道 **3** railways as a means of transport 铁路 • **verb 1** enclose with a rail or railings 装栏杆；用栏杆围 **2** (**rail against** or **at**) complain strongly about 抱怨；申斥 □ **go off the rails** informal【非正式】behave in an uncontrolled way 行为古怪；神经错乱

railing /'reɪlɪŋ/ **noun** a fence or barrier made of rails 栏杆；围栏；栅栏

raillery /'reɪləri/ **noun** good-humoured teasing 善意的嘲笑；逗弄；戏谑

railroad /'reɪlrəʊd/ **noun** N. Amer.【北美】a railway 铁道，铁路系统 • **verb** informal【非正式】rush or force someone into doing something 使草率做(某事)；迫使做(某事)

railway /'reɪlweɪ/ **noun** Brit.【英】**1** a track made of rails along which trains run 铁路；铁道 **2** a system of tracks and trains 铁路系统；铁路部门

raiment /'reɪmənt/ **noun** old use or literary【旧或文】clothing 衣服；服装

rain /reɪn/ **noun 1** condensed moisture from the atmosphere falling in separate drops 雨水 **2** (**rains**) falls of rain 降雨；下雨 **3** a large quantity of things falling together (降雨般的)一阵；倾泻物 • **verb 1** (**it rains, it is raining, it rained**) rain falls 降雨；下雨 **2** (**be rained off**) (of an event) be prevented by rain from continuing or taking place (活动)因雨取消 **3** fall in large quantities 大量降下

rainbow /'reɪnbəʊ/ **noun** an arch of

colours in the sky, caused by the sun shining through water droplets in the atmosphere 彩虹

raincoat /'reɪnkəʊt/ *noun* a coat made from water-resistant fabric 雨衣

rainfall /'reɪnfɔːl/ *noun* the amount of rain falling (降)雨量

rainforest /'reɪnfɒrɪst/ *noun* a dense forest found in tropical areas with consistently heavy rainfall (热带)雨林

rainy /'reɪnɪ/ *adjective* (**rainier, rainiest**) having a lot of rain 多雨的 □ **a rainy day** a time in the future when money may be needed 未来可能需要用钱的日子;未来可能的穷困时期

raise /reɪz/ *verb* (**raises, raising, raised**) **1** lift or move upwards or into an upright position 竖起;扶直 **2** increase the amount, level, or strength of 提高;增大;提升 **3** express doubts, objections, etc. 提出;发出;表露 **4** collect money 筹集;招募;征集 **5** bring up a child 养育,培养(孩子) **6** breed or grow animals or plants 培育,培养(动物或植物) **7** (**raise something to**) Maths 【数学】multiply a quantity to a particular power 使自乘(特定次数) • *noun* N. Amer. 【北美】an increase in salary 加薪 □ **raise the roof** cheer very loudly 大声欢闹

raisin /'reɪzn/ *noun* a partially dried grape 葡萄干

raison d'être /ˌreɪzɒn 'detrə/ *noun* (plural **raisons d'être** /ˌreɪzɒn 'detrə/) the most important reason for someone or something's existence 存在的理由

Raj /rɑːdʒ/ *noun* (**the Raj**) the period of British rule in India 英国统治印度时期

raja or **rajah** /'rɑːdʒə/ *noun* historical 【历史】an Indian king or prince 拉甲(印度的国王或王子)

rake¹ /reɪk/ *noun* a pole with metal prongs at the end, used for drawing together leaves, smoothing soil, etc. (长柄)耙,搂耙,钉齿耙 • *verb* (**rakes, raking, raked**) **1** draw together or smooth with a rake 用耙耙集(或耙平) **2** scratch or sweep with a long broad movement 刮过;擦过;搔;抓 **3** search through 搜索;搜寻 □ **rake it in** informal 【非正式】make a lot of money 捞进大笔钱 **rake something up** bring up something that is best forgotten 重提(旧事等);揭(疮疤)

rake² *noun* a fashionable, rich, but immoral man 花花公子;淫逸浪子

rake³ *verb* (**rakes, raking, raked**) set something at a sloping angle 使倾斜 • *noun* the angle at which something slopes 斜度;斜角

rakish /'reɪkɪʃ/ *adjective* having a dashing, jaunty, or slightly disreputable appearance 潇洒的;漂亮的;放荡不羁的

rally /'rælɪ/ *noun* (plural **rallies**) **1** a mass meeting held as a protest or in support of a cause 群众集会;群众大会 **2** a long distance competition for motor vehicles over roads or rough ground 汽车公路赛;汽车拉力赛 **3** a quick or strong recovery 迅速复原;重新振作 **4** (in tennis and similar games) a long exchange of strokes between players (网球运动及类似运动的)连续对打,往返拍击 • *verb* (**rallies, rallying, rallied**) **1** (of troops) come together again to continue fighting (军队)重新集结,重整 **2** come together to support a person or cause 召集;集合;团结 **3** recover health or strength 恢复健康;复原 **4** (of shares or currency) increase in value after a fall (股票或货币价值)止跌反弹,降后复涨 **5** (rallying) the sport of taking part in a motor rally 汽车公路赛运动

ram /ræm/ *noun* **1** an adult male sheep

公羊 **2** a long, heavy object swung against a door to break it down 攻城槌 **3** a striking or plunging device in a machine (机器的)冲头,撞锤 • **verb (rams, ramming, rammed) 1** hit with force 夯(实),捣(实) **2** roughly force into place 猛压;用力推;硬塞 □ **ram raid** a robbery in which people ram a shop window with a vehicle to steal goods 破橱窗抢劫

Ramadan /ˈræmədæn/ **noun** the ninth month of the Muslim year, during which Muslims do not eat from dawn to sunset 斋月,莱麦丹月(伊斯兰教历9月,该月内教徒每日从黎明到日落禁食)

ramble /ˈræmbl/ **verb (rambles, rambling, rambled) 1** walk for pleasure in the countryside (在乡间)漫步,闲逛 **2** talk or write in a confused way 漫谈;瞎扯 • **noun** a country walk taken for pleasure (乡间的)漫步,闲逛 ■ **rambler noun.**

ramekin /ˈræmɪkɪn/ **noun** a small dish for baking and serving an individual portion of food 小盘子(用于烤制和盛放供单人食用的小份食物)

ramifications /ˌræmɪfɪˈkeɪʃnz/ **plural noun** complex results of an action or event (复杂的)结果,后果

ramp /ræmp/ **noun 1** a sloping surface joining two different levels 斜面;斜坡 **2** a set of steps for entering or leaving an aircraft (上下飞机用的)活动舷梯,轻便梯

rampage **verb** /ræmˈpeɪdʒ/ **(rampages, rampaging, rampaged)** rush around in a wild and violent way 横冲直撞 • **noun** /ˈræmpeɪdʒ/ a period of wild and violent behaviour 狂暴行径,横冲直撞

rampant /ˈræmpənt/ **adjective 1** flourishing or spreading in an uncontrolled way 猖獗的;肆虐的;无约束的 **2** Heraldry 【纹章】 (of an animal) shown standing on its left hind

foot with its forefeet in the air (动物)以后腿支撑跃立的

rampart /ˈræmpɑːt/ **noun** a wall defending a castle or town, having a broad top with a walkway (城堡或城镇的)防御墙,壁垒

ramrod /ˈræmrɒd/ **noun** a rod formerly used to ram down the charge of a firearm (枪的)送弹棍,输弹机

ramshackle /ˈræmʃækl/ **adjective** in a very bad condition 摇摇欲坠的;东歪西倒的;快要散架的

ran /ræn/ past of RUN.

ranch /rɑːntʃ/ **noun** a large farm in America where cattle or other animals are bred (美国的)大牧场 ■ **rancher** noun.

rancid /ˈrænsɪd/ **adjective** (of fatty or oily food) stale and smelling or tasting unpleasant (油脂食物)酸臭的,腐臭的,腐败变质的

rancour /ˈræŋkə(r)/ (US spelling 【美拼作】 **rancor**) **noun** bitter feeling or resentment 怨恨;憎恶 ■ **rancorous** adjective.

rand /rænd/ **noun** the basic unit of money of South Africa 兰特(南非的基本货币单位)

R & B /ˌɑːr ən ˈbiː/ **abbreviation 1** rhythm and blues. **2** a kind of pop music with soulful vocals (具有灵魂风格的)流行乐

random /ˈrændəm/ **adjective** done or happening without any plan, purpose, or regular pattern 任意的;随机的 □ **at random** without thinking or planning in advance 胡乱地;随便地 ■ **randomly** adverb **randomness** noun.

randy /ˈrændi/ **adjective (randier, randiest)** Brit. informal 【英,非正式】 sexually excited 性欲冲动的;性兴奋的

rang /ræŋ/ past of RING[2].

range /reɪndʒ/ **noun 1** the limits between which something varies 范

围;幅度 **2** a set of different things of the same general type 系列 **3** the distance over which a sound, missile, etc. can travel (声音的)传送距离;(导弹等的)射程 **4** a line of mountains or hills 山脉 **5** a large area of open land for grazing or hunting 放牧地,牧场;猎场 **6** an area for testing military equipment or practising shooting (军事设备的)试验场,靶场;射击场 **7** a large stove with several burners or hotplates 多眼炉灶 • verb **(ranges, ranging, ranged) 1** vary between particular limits (在特定范围内)变动,变化 **2** arrange things in a particular way 排列;把⋯排成行 **3 (be ranged against)** be in opposition to 处于反对⋯的行列 **4** travel over a wide area 四处漫游;走遍

ranger /'reɪndʒə(r)/ noun a keeper of a park, forest, or area of countryside 园林管理员;护林员

rangy /'reɪndʒi/ adjective (of a person) tall and slim with long limbs (人)细高的,四肢修长的

rank¹ /ræŋk/ noun **1** a position within the armed forces or an organization 军阶;职衔 **2** a row of people or things (人或事物的)排,行,列 **3** high social position 高级地位,显贵 **4 (the ranks)** (in the armed forces) those who are not commissioned officers (军队的)普通士兵 • verb **1** give a rank to 把⋯分等级;给⋯评等级 **2** hold a particular rank 占特定等级 **3** arrange in a row or rows 把⋯排成行;排列 □ **close ranks** unite to defend shared interests 紧密团结 **pull rank** use your higher rank to take advantage of someone 仗势欺人 **rank and file** the ordinary members of an organization (组织的)普通成员,基层人员

rank² adjective **1** having a very unpleasant smell 恶臭难闻的;腥臭的 **2** complete 十足的;彻头彻尾的,不

折不扣的: *a rank amateur* 十足的外行 **3** (of plants) growing too thickly (植物)过于繁茂的,疯长的

rankle /'ræŋkl/ verb **(rankles, rankling, rankled)** cause continuing annoyance or resentment 激起怨恨;引起烦恼

ransack /'rænsæk/ verb go hurriedly through a place stealing or searching for things 洗劫;劫掠

ransom /'rænsəm/ noun a sum of money demanded for the release of someone who is held captive 赎金 • verb cause someone to be released by paying a ransom 赎出,赎回(某人) □ **hold someone to ransom 1** hold someone captive and demand payment for their release 把(某人)扣作人质 **2** force someone to do something by threatening them 胁迫(某人);要挟(某人)

rant /rænt/ verb speak in a loud, angry, and forceful way 大叫大嚷;怒气冲冲地叫嚷

rap /ræp/ verb **(raps, rapping, rapped) 1** hit a hard surface several times (多次)叩,敲击 **2** hit sharply 急拍 **3** informal 【非正式】criticize sharply 严厉批评;尖锐批评 **4** say sharply or suddenly 厉声急促地说 • noun **1** a quick, sharp knock or blow 叩击;敲击 **2** a type of popular music in which words are spoken rhythmically over an instrumental backing 说唱(乐) □ **take the rap** informal 【非正式】be punished or blamed for something 受惩罚;被责备 ■ **rapper** noun.

rapacious /rə'peɪʃəs/ adjective very greedy 贪婪的,贪吃的

rapacity /rə'pæsəti/ noun greed 贪婪;贪吃

rape¹ /reɪp/ verb **(rapes, raping, raped) 1** (of a man) force someone to have sex with him against their will (男子)强奸 **2** spoil or destroy a place 破坏,蹂躏,摧毁(某场所) • noun an act of raping 强奸

rape² noun a plant with bright yellow flowers, grown for its oil-rich seed 芸苔，欧洲油菜(开黄花，种子用于榨油)

rapid /'ræpɪd/ adjective very fast 飞快的；迅速的 • noun (**rapids**) a part of a river where the water flows very fast 急流；湍流 ■ **rapidity** noun **rapidly** adverb.

rapier /'reɪpɪə(r)/ noun a thin, light sword 轻剑

rapist /'reɪpɪst/ noun a man who commits rape 强奸犯

rapport /ræ'pɔː(r)/ noun a close relationship in which people understand each other and communicate well 融洽关系；和睦关系

rapprochement /ræ'prɒʃmɒn/ noun a renewal of friendly relations between two countries or groups (两国或两组织间的)恢复友好，重建和睦

rapscallion /ræp'skælɪən/ noun old use 【旧】a rascal 坏蛋；无赖

rapt /ræpt/ adjective completely fascinated or absorbed 着迷的；痴迷的；全神贯注的

rapture /'ræptʃə(r)/ noun **1** great pleasure or joy 狂喜 **2** (**raptures**) the expression of great pleasure or enthusiasm 狂喜；兴高采烈，欢呼

rapturous /'ræptʃərəs/ adjective very pleased or enthusiastic 狂喜的，狂热的 ■ **rapturously** adverb.

rare /reə(r)/ adjective (**rarer, rarest**) **1** not happening or found very often 稀有的；罕见的 **2** unusually good 极好的，极度的 **3** (of red meat) lightly cooked, so that the inside is still red (红肉)煎得嫩的，半熟的 ■ **rarely** adverb.

rarebit /'reəbɪt/ = Welsh rarebit

rarefied /'reərɪfaɪd/ adjective **1** (of air) of lower pressure than usual; thin (空气)稀薄的 **2** understood by only a limited group of people 深奥的

✔ 拼写指南 -ref-, not -rif-: rarefied. rarefied中ref- 不要拼作rif-。

raring /'reərɪŋ/ adjective (**raring to do**) informal 【非正式】very eager to do something 急切的；渴望的

rarity /'reərəti/ noun (plural **rarities**) **1** the state of being rare 稀有；罕见，珍奇 **2** a rare thing 稀有物；珍品

rascal /'rɑːskl/ noun **1** a mischievous or cheeky person 淘气鬼；捣蛋鬼；无礼的人 **2** a dishonest man 无赖；恶棍；流氓 ■ **rascally** adjective.

rash¹ /ræʃ/ adjective acting or done without careful consideration of the possible results 轻率的；鲁莽的；仓促的 ■ **rashly** adverb.

rash² noun **1** an area of red spots or patches on a person's skin 疹；皮疹 **2** a series of unpleasant things happening within a short time (短时间内发生的)一连串坏事

rasher /'ræʃə(r)/ noun a thin slice of bacon 咸肉片；熏肉片

rasp /rɑːsp/ noun **1** a harsh, grating noise 锉磨声；刺耳声 **2** a tool with a rough edge, used for smoothing surfaces 锉刀，木锉 • verb **1** make a harsh, grating noise 发出刺耳声，发出擦刮声 **2** scrape roughly 粗锉；擦刮 **3** file with a rasp 用锉刀锉

raspberry /'rɑːzbəri/ noun (plural **raspberries**) **1** a reddish-pink soft fruit 悬钩子；覆盆子；山莓 **2** informal 【非正式】a rude sound made with the tongue and lips (粗鲁的)吓声

Rasta /'ræstə/ noun informal 【非正式】a Rastafarian 拉斯特法里派成员

Rastafarian /ˌræstə'feərɪən,-'fɑː-/ noun a member of a Jamaican religious movement which worships Haile Selassie, the former Emperor of Ethiopia 拉斯特法里派成员(牙买加宗教运动成员，信奉前埃塞俄比亚皇帝海尔·塞拉西是救世主) ■ **Rastafarianism** noun.

R

rat /ræt/ *noun* **1** a rodent resembling a large mouse 鼠；大家鼠 **2** informal【非正式】an unpleasant person 讨厌鬼；鼠辈；卑鄙小人 • *verb* (**rats**, **ratting**, **ratted**) (**rat on**) informal【非正式】**1** inform on someone 告发 **2** break an agreement or promise 背叛(协议或诺言) □ **the rat race** informal【非正式】a way of life which is a fiercely competitive struggle for money or power (财富或权力的)激烈竞争

ratatouille /ˌrætəˈtuːi, ˌrætəˈtwiː/ *noun* a vegetable dish of stewed onions, courgettes, tomatoes, etc. 普罗旺斯杂烩(以洋葱、胡瓜、西红柿等烹制)

ratchet /ˈrætʃɪt/ *noun* a device with a set of angled teeth in which a cog, tooth, or bar fits, allowing movement in one direction only 棘轮机构

rate[1] /reɪt/ *noun* **1** a measure, quantity, or frequency measured against another 比率；率 **2** the speed of something 速度；速率；进度 **3** a fixed price paid or charged for something 价格；费用 **4** (**rates**) (in the UK) a tax on land and buildings paid to a local authority by a business (英国的)不动产税，地方税 • *verb* (**rates**, **rating**, **rated**) **1** give something a standard or value according to a particular scale 评估；给…定级；给…估值 **2** consider to be of a certain quality or standard 把…看作，认为 **3** be worthy of; deserve 值得；应得 **4** informal【非正式】have a high opinion of 对…评价高 ■ **rateable** (or **ratable**) *adjective.*

rate[2] *verb* old use【旧】scold angrily 呵斥，严责

rather /ˈrɑːðə(r)/ *adverb* **1** (**would rather**) would prefer 宁愿；宁可 **2** to some extent; fairly 有几分；相当 **3** used to correct something you have said or to be more precise 更确切些 **4** instead of 代替

ratify /ˈrætɪfaɪ/ *verb* (**ratifies**, ratifying, ratified**)** make a treaty, contract, etc. valid by signing or agreeing to it 正式批准；认可 ■ **ratification** *noun.*

rating /ˈreɪtɪŋ/ *noun* **1** a classification based on quality, standard, or performance 等级；品级 **2** (**ratings**) the estimated audience size of a television or radio programme (电视节目的)收视率，(电台节目的)收听率 **3** Brit.【英】a sailor in the navy who does not hold a commission 水兵

ratio /ˈreɪʃɪəʊ/ *noun* (plural **ratios**) an indication of the relationship between two amounts, showing the number of times one contains the other 比；比率

ratiocination /ˌrætɪɒsɪˈneɪʃn/ *noun* formal【正式】the process of thinking in a logical way; reasoning 推理

ration /ˈræʃn/ *noun* **1** a fixed amount of food, fuel, etc. officially allowed to each person (粮食、燃料等供应的)配给量，定量 **2** (**rations**) a regular allowance of food supplied to members of the armed forces (军队的)给养，口粮 • *verb* limit the supply of food, fuel, etc. 定量供应(食物、燃料等)

rational /ˈræʃnəl/ *adjective* **1** based on reason or logic 基于理性的；合理的 **2** able to think sensibly or logically 理性的；理智的；神智健全的 ■ **rationality** *noun* **rationally** *adverb.*

rationale /ˌræʃəˈnɑːl/ *noun* the reasons for doing or believing something (行动或信仰的)全部理由，逻辑依据

rationalism /ˈræʃnəlɪzəm/ *noun* the belief that opinions and actions should be based on reason rather than on religious belief or emotions 理性主义；唯理论 ■ **rationalist** *noun.*

rationalize or **rationalise** /ˈræʃnəlaɪz/ *verb* (**rationalizes**, rationalizing, rationalized**)** **1** try to find a logical reason for an action or attitude 为(行动或态度)自圆其说；文饰 **2** reorganize a business, system, etc. to make it more efficient 使合理化；对⋯进行合理化改造 ■ **rationalization** noun.

rattan /ræˈtæn/ noun the thin stems of a tropical palm, used to make furniture 白藤茎(一种热带棕榈树的细茎，用于制作家具)

rattle /ˈrætl/ verb (**rattles**, **rattling**, **rattled**) **1** make a rapid series of short, sharp sounds 发连续短促的尖厉声音；发格格声 **2** informal【非正式】make someone nervous or irritated 使紧张，使窘迫，使恼怒 **3** (**rattle something off**) say or do something quickly and easily 脱口而出；雷厉风行地做(某事) • noun **1** a rattling sound 连续短促的尖厉声音；格格声 **2** a toy that makes a rattling sound 拨浪鼓

rattlesnake /ˈrætlsneɪk/ noun an American viper with horny rings on the tail that produce a rattling sound (美洲)响尾蛇

ratty /ˈræti/ adjective Brit. informal【英，非正式】irritable 暴躁易怒的

raucous /ˈrɔːkəs/ adjective sounding loud and harsh 嘶哑的，粗嘎的 ■ **raucously** adverb.

raunchy /ˈrɔːntʃi/ adjective (**raunchier**, **raunchiest**) informal【非正式】sexually exciting or explicit 淫秽的；下流的

ravage /ˈrævɪdʒ/ verb (**ravages**, **ravaging**, **ravaged**) cause great damage to 毁坏；蹂躏 • noun (**ravages**) the destruction caused by something 破坏；蹂躏

rave /reɪv/ verb (**raves**, **raving**, **raved**) **1** talk angrily or without making sense 生气地说；说胡话；语无伦次地说 **2** speak or write about someone or something with great enthusiasm 极力夸奖；热烈赞扬 • noun

a large event with dancing to loud, fast electronic music 狂欢热舞聚会

raven /ˈreɪvn/ noun a large black crow 渡鸦 • adjective (of hair) of a glossy black colour (头发)乌亮的，乌油油的

ravening /ˈrævənɪŋ/ adjective literary【文】very fierce and hungry 饥肠辘辘的

ravenous /ˈrævənəs/ adjective very hungry 饥肠辘辘的；饿极了的 ■ **ravenously** adverb.

raver /ˈreɪvə(r)/ noun informal【非正式】a person who has an exciting or wild social life 恣意作乐者；社交场常客

ravine /rəˈviːn/ noun a deep, narrow gorge 沟壑；冲沟

raving /ˈreɪvɪŋ/ noun (**ravings**) wild talk that makes no sense 胡言乱语；疯话 • adjective & adverb informal【非正式】used for emphasis (用于强调)绝顶；极其：raving mad 极度疯狂的

ravioli /ˌrævɪˈəʊli/ plural noun small pasta cases containing minced meat, cheese, or vegetables 意大利式小饺子(包有碎肉、乳酪或蔬菜)

ravish /ˈrævɪʃ/ verb **1** dated【废】rape 强奸 **2** (**ravishing**) very beautiful 美丽迷人的；令人销魂的

raw /rɔː/ adjective **1** (of food) not cooked (食物)生的，未经烹煮的 **2** (of a material) in its natural state (材料)自然状态的，未加工的 **3** (of the skin) red and painful from being rubbed or scraped (皮肤)因刮擦而发红刺痛的 **4** (of an emotion or quality) strong and undisguised (感情或品质)粗犷的，不加遮掩的 **5** (of the weather) cold and damp (天气)湿冷的，阴冷的 **6** new to an activity and lacking experience 生疏无知的；无阅历的；无经验的 □ **a raw deal** unfair treatment 不公平待遇 ■ **rawness** noun.

ray¹ /reɪ/ noun **1** a narrow line or beam of light or radiation 光线；射线 **2** a trace of something good 闪光；闪

现: *a ray of hope* 一线希望

ray² noun a broad flat fish with a long, thin tail 鳐鱼(身体扁宽,尾细长)

rayon /'reɪɒn/ noun a synthetic fabric made from viscose 人造纤维;人造丝

raze /reɪz/ verb (**razes, razing, razed**) completely destroy a building, town, etc. 彻底摧毁,夷平(建筑物、城市等)

razor /'reɪzə(r)/ noun an instrument used to shave hair 剃刀

razzle /'ræzl/ noun (**on the razzle**) Brit. informal 【英,非正式】out celebrating or enjoying yourself 外出欢闹;狂欢

razzmatazz or **razzamatazz** /ˌræzmə'tæz/ noun informal 【非正式】noisy and exciting activity designed to attract attention 吵嚷喧闹的活动;欢闹

RC /ɑː'siː/ abbreviation Roman Catholic.

re /riː, reɪ/ preposition with reference to 关于

reach /riːtʃ/ verb 1 stretch out an arm to touch or grasp something 伸手去够(或抓) 2 be able to touch something with an outstretched arm or leg (伸出手或腿)可触及,能碰到 3 arrive at; get as far as 到达;抵达;延伸到 4 come to a particular level or point 达到(某点或某状态) 5 make contact with 与…建立联系 • noun 1 the distance to which someone can stretch out their arm or arms to touch something 伸手可及的距离 2 a continuous stretch of river between two bends (河流两个弯道之间的)一段流域,直水道

react /ri'ækt/ verb 1 respond to something in a particular way 反应;作出反应 2 interact and undergo a chemical or physical change 起化学(或物理)反应 ▪ **reactive** adjective.

reaction /ri'ækʃn/ noun 1 something done or experienced as a result of an event 反应;回应 2 (**reactions**) a person's ability to respond to an event 反应能力;反应灵敏度 3 a bad

response by the body to a drug or substance (生理上的)过敏反应 4 a process in which substances interact causing chemical or physical change (化学)反应;(物理)作用 5 a force exerted in opposition to an applied force 反击;反攻

reactionary /ri'ækʃənri/ adjective opposing political or social progress or reform 反对政治(或社会)改革的;反动的 • noun (plural **reactionaries**) a person holding reactionary views 反动分子

reactivate /ri'æktɪveɪt/ verb (**reactivates, reactivating, reactivated**) bring something back into action 使恢复活动;使重新起作用 ▪ **reactivation** noun.

reactor /ri'æktə(r)/ noun an apparatus in which material is made to undergo a controlled nuclear reaction that releases energy 核反应堆

read /riːd/ verb (**reads, reading, read**) 1 understand the meaning of written or printed words or symbols 读懂,识读(书面文字或符号) 2 speak written or printed words aloud 朗读;宣读 3 have a particular wording 措词为;文字是 4 understand the nature or meaning of 懂得;理解 5 (**read something into**) think that something has a meaning that it may not possess 对…作过多的理解;无中生有地推断出 6 Brit. 【英】study a subject at a university (在大学)攻读,学习 7 (of an instrument) show a measurement or figure (仪器)读数为,标明 • noun informal 【非正式】a book that is interesting to read 读物 □ **take something as read** assume something 认定(某事物) ▪ **readable** adjective **reader** noun.

readership /'riːdəʃɪp/ noun the readers of a publication regarded as a group (某出版物的)读者群

readily /'redɪli/ adverb 1 willingly 乐意地;愿意地 2 easily 容易地;无困

难地

reading /'riːdɪŋ/ **noun 1** the action of reading 阅读 **2** something that is read 读物 **3** a figure recorded on a measuring instrument (仪器上的)读数,度数,指示数

readjust /ˌriːəˈdʒʌst/ **verb 1** adjust again 重新调节;再调整 **2** adapt to a changed situation 重新适应 ■ **re-adjustment** noun.

ready /'redi/ **adjective** (**readier**, **readiest**) **1** prepared for an activity or situation 准备就绪的 **2** made available for immediate use 立即可用的;现成的 **3** easily available or obtained 容易获得 **4** (**ready to do**) willing or eager to do 愿意做的;渴望做的 **5** immediate or quick 反应快的;机敏的 • **noun** (**readies** or **the ready**) Brit. informal 【英,非正式】 available money 现钱,现金 • **verb** (**readies**, **readying**, **readied**) prepare 作准备;使准备好 ■ **readiness** noun.

reagent /riˈeɪdʒənt/ **noun** a substance that produces a chemical reaction, used to detect the presence of another substance (化学)试剂

real /'riːəl/ **adjective 1** actually existing or happening 现实的;真实的 **2** not artificial; genuine 非人工的;真的 **3** worthy of the description; proper 名副其实的;真正的 • **adverb** N. Amer. informal 【北美,非正式】 really; very 真正地;确实地;很 □ **real estate** N. Amer. 【北美】 land or housing 房产 **real tennis** the original form of tennis, played with a solid ball on an enclosed court 庭院网球(运动)

realign /ˌriːəˈlaɪn/ **verb** change something to a different position or state 调整…的位置(或状态) ■ **re-alignment** noun.

realism /'riːəlɪzəm/ **noun 1** the acceptance of a situation as it is 务实作风,现实态度 **2** the presentation of things in a way that is accurate and

true to life 写实主义,现实主义 ■ **re-alist** noun.

realistic /ˌriːəˈlɪstɪk/ **adjective 1** having a sensible and practical idea of what can be achieved 现实的;注重实际的 **2** showing things in a way that is accurate and true to life 写实的;现实主义的 ■ **realistically** adverb.

reality /riˈæləti/ **noun** (plural **realities**) **1** the state of things as they actually exist 现实;实际 **2** a thing that is real 实体 **3** the state of being real 实在;真实;真实性 □ **reality TV** television programmes based on real people or situations, presented as entertainment 现实题材电视节目

realize or **realise** /'riːəlaɪz/ **verb** (**realizes**, **realizing**, **realized**) **1** become fully aware of a fact 意识到;认知;认识 **2** achieve or fulfil a wish or plan 实现(愿望或计划) **3** be sold for a particular amount 售得;卖得 **4** convert property, shares, etc. into money by selling them 把(财产,股票等)变现 ■ **realization** noun.

really /'riːəli/ **adverb 1** in actual fact 实际上,事实上 **2** very; thoroughly 很;十分;全然 • **exclamation** expressing interest, surprise, doubt, etc. 真的,是吗,真是的(表示感兴趣、吃惊、怀疑等)

realm /relm/ **noun 1** chiefly literary 【主文】 a kingdom 王国;国度 **2** an area of activity or interest 界;领域;范围

ream /riːm/ **noun 1** 500 sheets of paper 令(500张纸) **2** (**reams**) a large quantity 大量

reap /riːp/ **verb 1** gather in a crop or harvest 收割(庄稼) **2** receive a reward or benefit as a result of your actions 得到(回报);获(利)

reaper /'riːpə(r)/ **noun** a person or machine that harvests a crop 收割者;收割机 □ **the Grim Reaper** death, shown as a cloaked skeleton holding a scythe 死神(被描绘为手持长柄镰刀,身披斗篷的骷髅)

rear¹ /rɪə(r)/ **noun** the back part of something 后面;背部 • **adjective** at the back 后面的;背部的 □ **rear admiral** the naval rank above commodore 海军少将 ■ **rearmost** adjective **rearward** adjective & adverb **rearwards** adverb.

rear² **verb 1** bring up offspring 抚养,养育(子女) **2** breed animals 饲养(动物) **3** (of an animal) raise itself upright on its hind legs (动物)用后腿直立 **4** extend to a great height 高耸

rearguard /'rɪəɡɑːd/ **noun** a group of soldiers protecting the rear of the main force 后卫部队

rearm /riː'ɑːm/ **verb** provide with or obtain a new supply of weapons 重新装备;重新武装 ■ **rearmament** noun.

rearrange /ˌriː ə'reɪndʒ/ **verb** (**rearranges, rearranging, rearranged**) arrange again in a different way 重新整理;再排列 ■ **rearrangement** noun.

reason /'riː zn/ **noun 1** a cause or explanation 理由;原因 **2** good or obvious cause to do something (做某事的)充分理由 **3** the power to think and draw conclusions logically 判断力;推理力 **4** (**your reason**) your sanity 理智 **5** what is right, practical, or possible 道理;情理;明智 • **verb 1** think and draw conclusions logically 推理;推论 **2** (**reason with**) persuade someone by using logical arguments 和(某人)讲道理 □ **stand to reason** be logical 合情合理

reasonable /'riː znəbl/ **adjective 1** fair and sensible 公平的;公道的 **2** appropriate in a particular situation 适当的;正当的;合理的 **3** fairly good 尚可的;过得去的 **4** not too expensive 不太贵的 ■ **reasonably** adverb.

reassure /ˌriː ə'ʃʊə(r)/ **verb** (**reassures, reassuring, reassured**) make someone feel less worried or afraid 使减轻疑虑;使安心 ■ **reassurance** noun.

rebarbative /rɪ'bɑːbətɪv/ **adjective** unpleasant 讨厌的;令人不快的

rebate /'riː beɪt/ **noun 1** a partial refund to someone who has paid too much for tax, rent, etc. (税款、房租等的)部分退款 **2** a discount on a sum that is due 折扣

rebel **verb** /rɪ'bel/ (**rebels, rebelling, rebelled**) **1** refuse to obey the government or ruler 反叛;造反 **2** oppose authority, or refuse to behave conventionally 不服从;抗命;反对 • **noun** /'rebl/ a person who rebels 造反者;反抗者;反对者

rebellion /rɪ'beljən/ **noun 1** an act of rebelling 叛乱;反叛;造反 **2** opposition to authority or control 反抗;反对

rebellious /rɪ'beljəs/ **adjective** choosing to rebel 反叛的;造反的;反抗的 ■ **rebelliously** adverb.

rebirth /ˌriː'bɜːθ/ **noun** a return to life or activity 复活;复兴

reborn /ˌriː'bɔːn/ **adjective** brought back to life or activity 复活的;复兴的

rebound **verb** /rɪ'baʊnd/ **1** bounce back after hitting a hard surface 弹回;跳回 **2** increase again 反弹 **3** (**rebound on**) have an unexpected and unpleasant effect on 产生意想不到的不良结果 • **noun** /'riː baʊnd/ a ball or shot that rebounds 篮板球;反弹球 □ **on the rebound** while still upset after the ending of a romantic relationship (失恋后)在伤心失意之时

rebuff /rɪ'bʌf/ **verb** reject in an abrupt or unkind way 断然拒绝;粗暴回绝 • **noun** an abrupt or unkind rejection 断然拒绝;生硬的回绝

rebuke /rɪ'bjuːk/ **verb** (**rebukes, rebuking, rebuked**) sharply criticize or tell off 指责;叱责;训斥

• **noun** a sharp criticism 指責；叱責

rebus /ˈriːbəs/ **noun** (plural **rebuses**) a puzzle in which words are represented by combinations of pictures and letters 画谜

rebut /rɪˈbʌt/ **verb** (**rebuts, rebutting, rebutted**) claim or prove that something is false 驳斥；反驳 ■ **rebuttal** noun.

recalcitrant /rɪˈkælsɪtrənt/ **adjective** unwilling to cooperate; disobedient 不愿合作的；拒不服从的 ■ **recalcitrance** noun.

recall /rɪˈkɔːl/ **verb 1** remember 记得 **2** make someone think of; bring to mind 回想起；回忆起 **3** officially order someone to return 召回(某人) **4** (of a manufacturer) ask for faulty products to be returned (制造商)收回，召回(有缺陷产品) • **noun 1** the action of remembering 回忆；记忆力 **2** an official order for someone to return 召回令

recant /rɪˈkænt/ **verb** withdraw a former opinion or belief 撤回(观点)；放弃(信仰)

recap /ˈriːkæp/ **verb** (**recaps, recapping, recapped**) recapitulate 概述；概括

recapitulate /ˌriːkəˈpɪtʃuleɪt/ **verb** (**recapitulates, recapitulating, recapitulated**) give a summary of 概述；概括 ■ **recapitulation** noun.

recapture /ˌriːˈkæptʃə(r)/ **verb** (**recaptures, recapturing, recaptured**) **1** capture a person or animal that has escaped 再俘房；再捕获 **2** recover something taken or lost 夺回；收复 **3** bring back or experience again a past time or feeling 重温，再体验 • **noun** an act of recapturing 再俘房；夺回；重温

recast /ˌriːˈkɑːst/ **verb** (**recasts, recasting, recast**) present something in a different form 重新浇铸；改铸

recce /ˈreki/ **noun** Brit. informal 【英，非正式】 a reconnaissance 侦察

recede /rɪˈsiːd/ **verb** (**recedes, receding, receded**) **1** move back or further away 后退；远离 **2** gradually become weaker or smaller 逐渐变弱；渐渐变小 **3** (**receding**) (of part of the face) sloping backwards (脸的某部分)向后缩的

receipt /rɪˈsiːt/ **noun 1** a written statement confirming that something has been paid for or received 收据；收条 **2** the action of receiving something 接收；收到 **3** (**receipts**) the amount of money received over a period by a business (生意上的)收入，进款

receive /rɪˈsiːv/ **verb** (**receives, receiving, received**) **1** be given or paid 得到；领到 **2** accept something sent or offered 接受 **3** experience or meet with 经历；受到 **4** form an idea or impression from an experience (从经历中)获得(想法或印象) **5** entertain someone as a guest 接待；款待 **6** detect or pick up broadcast signals 接收(广播信号) **7** (**received**) widely accepted as true 被广泛接受的；公认的 □ **received pronunciation** the standard form of British English pronunciation, based on educated speech in southern England (英语的)标准发音

✔ 拼写指南 remember, the rule is *i* before *e* except after *c*: re*ceive*. 记住规则：*i* 置于 *e* 前，在 *c* 后时除外，如 re*ceive*.

receiver /rɪˈsiːvə(r)/ **noun 1** a radio or television apparatus that converts broadcast signals into sound or images 收音机；收报机；电视接收器 **2** the part of a telephone that converts electrical signals into sounds 电话听筒 **3** (also **official receiver**) a person appointed to manage the financial affairs of a bankrupt business (被指定管理破产

公司财务的)破产事务官,破产管理人
■ **receivership** noun.

recent /'ri:snt/ adjective having
happened or been done shortly
before the present 不久前的;新近的
■ **recently** adverb.

receptacle /rɪ'septəkl/ noun an
object used to contain something 容
器;贮藏器

reception /rɪ'sepʃn/ noun 1 the action
of receiving 接受;接纳 2 the way in
which people react to something 接
待;迎接 3 a formal social occasion
held to welcome someone or
celebrate an event 招待会;欢迎会;
庆祝会 4 the area in a hotel, office,
etc. where visitors are greeted 接待
处;接待室 5 the quality with which
broadcast signals are received (广播
信号的)接收

receptionist /rɪ'sepʃənɪst/ noun a
person who greets and deals with
visitors to an office, hotel, etc. 接待
员;迎宾员

receptive /rɪ'septɪv/ adjective 1 able
or willing to receive something
可以接受的;愿接受的 2 willing to
consider new ideas (对新思想)愿意
接受的 ■ **receptivity** noun.

receptor /rɪ'septə(r)/ noun a nerve
ending in the body that responds to a
stimulus such as light (生理)感受器,
受体

recess /rɪ'ses/ noun 1 a small space
set back in a wall or in a surface 凹
室;壁龛 2 a break between sessions
of a parliament, law court, etc. (议
会;会议;法庭等的)暂停,休息 3
(**recesses**) remote or hidden places
幽深处;隐秘处 • verb fit something
so that it is set back into a surface
把…嵌入墙面

recession /rɪ'seʃn/ noun a period
during which trade and industrial
activity in a country are reduced (经
济的)衰退

recessive /rɪ'sesɪv/ adjective (of a

gene) appearing in offspring only if
a contrary gene is not also inherited
(基因)隐性的

recharge /ˌriː'tʃɑːdʒ/ verb (re-
charges, recharging, recharged)
charge a battery or device
again 给(电池或充电设备)再充电
■ **rechargeable** adjective **recharger**
noun.

recherché /rə'ʃeəʃeɪ/ adjective
unusual and not easily understood 罕
见的;不平常的;鲜为人知的

recidivist /rɪ'sɪdɪvɪst/ noun a person
who constantly commits crimes 惯
犯;累犯 ■ **recidivism** noun.

recipe /'resəpi/ noun 1 a list of
ingredients and instructions for
preparing a dish 食谱 2 something
likely to lead to a particular outcome
因素;方法;秘诀: a recipe for disaster
导致灾难的因素

recipient /rɪ'sɪpiənt/ noun a person
who receives something 接受者;收受
者

reciprocal /rɪ'sɪprəkl/ adjective 1
given or done in return 相互的;交互
的 2 affecting two parties equally 互
惠的;对等的 ■ **reciprocally** adverb.

reciprocate /rɪ'sɪprəkeɪt/ verb
(**reciprocates, reciprocating,
reciprocated**) respond to an action
or emotion with a similar one 回应
(行动);回报(感情)

reciprocity /ˌresɪ'prɒsəti/ noun
a situation in which two parties
provide the same help to each other
互助;互惠

recital /rɪ'saɪtl/ noun 1 the
performance of a programme of
music by a soloist or small group
音乐独奏会;小型演奏会 2 a long
account of a series of facts or events
详述;叙述

recite /rɪ'saɪt/ verb (**recites, reciting,
recited**) 1 repeat a passage aloud
from memory 背诵(段落) 2 state
facts, events, etc. in order 历数;列举

(事实、事件等) ■ **recitation** noun.

reckless /ˈreklǝs/ **adjective** without thought or care for the results of an action 草率的；冒失的；鲁莽的 ■ **recklessly** adverb **recklessness** noun.

reckon /ˈrekǝn/ **verb 1** have an opinion about something; think 认为；以为 **2 (reckon on)** rely on or expect 依赖；指望；期待 **3** calculate 算；计算 **4 (reckon with** or **without)** take (or fail to take) something into account (未)考虑到；(未)预料到 **□ to be reckoned with** to be treated as important 被(认真)处理

reckoning /ˈrekǝnɪŋ/ **noun 1** the action of calculating or estimating something 计算；估计 **2** punishment for past actions 惩罚；报应

reclaim /rɪˈkleɪm/ **verb 1** get possession of something again 要求收回；恢复 **2** make land usable 开垦，开拓(荒地) ■ **reclamation** noun.

recline /rɪˈklaɪn/ **verb (reclines, reclining, reclined)** lean back in a relaxed position 斜倚；靠；躺

recluse /rɪˈkluːs/ **noun** a person who avoids other people and lives alone 隐士；遁世者 ■ **reclusive** adjective.

recognition /ˌrekǝɡˈnɪʃn/ **noun 1** the action of recognizing 认出；识别；认识 **2** appreciation or acknowledgement 赏识；承认

recognize or **recognise** /ˈrekǝɡnaɪz/ **verb (recognizes, recognizing, recognized)** **1** know someone or something from having come across them before 认出；识别；认识 **2** accept something as genuine, legal, or valid 认可；承认 **3** show official appreciation of 赏识；表彰 ■ **recognizable** adjective.

recoil **verb** /rɪˈkɔɪl/ **1** suddenly move back in fear, horror, or disgust 退缩；畏缩 **2** (of a gun) suddenly move backwards as a reaction on being fired (枪炮)产生后坐力，反冲 **3** (recoil

on) have an unpleasant effect on 报应；回报 • **noun** /ˈriː kɔɪl/ the action of recoiling 退缩；畏缩

recollect /ˌrekǝˈlekt/ **verb** remember 追忆；想起 ■ **recollection** noun.

recommend /ˌrekǝˈmend/ **verb 1** say that someone or something is suitable for a particular purpose or role 推荐；荐举 **2** make something seem appealing or desirable 使吸引人 ■ **recommendation** noun.

> ✔ 拼写指南 one *c* and two *m*s: re*c*o**mm**end. recommend 中有一个c和两个m。

recompense /ˈrekǝmpens/ **verb (recompenses, recompensing, recompensed) 1** compensate someone for loss or harm suffered 赔偿；补偿 **2** pay or reward someone for effort or work 酬报；酬谢 • **noun** compensation or reward 赔偿；补偿；报酬

reconcile /ˈrekǝnsaɪl/ **verb (reconciles, reconciling, reconciled) 1** make two people or groups friendly again 使和解；使和好 **2** find a satisfactory way of dealing with opposing facts, ideas, etc. 调和(相异事实、想法等) **3 (reconcile someone to)** make someone accept something unwelcome 使将就；使甘心接受

reconciliation /ˌrekǝnsɪliˈeɪʃn/ **noun 1** the end of a disagreement and the return to friendly relations 和解；和好，和好 **2** the action of reconciling opposing ideas, facts, etc. 调和；和谐

recondite /ˈrekǝndaɪt/ **adjective** not known about or understood by many people 鲜为人知的

recondition /ˌriː kǝnˈdɪʃn/ **verb** Brit. 【英】bring back to a good condition; renovate 修复；修补；更新

reconnaissance /rɪˈkɒnɪsns/ **noun** military observation of an area to gain information (军事)侦察

reconnoitre /ˌrekəˈnɔɪtə(r)/ (US spelling 【美拼作】 **reconnoiter**) **verb** (**reconnoitres**, **reconnoitring**, **reconnoitred**) make a military observation of an area (军事)侦察(一个地区)

reconsider /ˌriː kənˈsɪdə(r)/ **verb** (**reconsiders**, **reconsidering**, **reconsidered**) consider again, with the possibility of changing a decision 重新考虑;重新审议 ■ **reconsideration** noun.

reconstitute /ˌriːˈkɒnstɪtjuːt/ **verb** (**reconstitutes**, **reconstituting**, **reconstituted**) **1** change the form of an organization 改组,改编(机构) **2** restore dried food to its original state by adding water 使(脱水食品)复原 ■ **reconstitution** noun.

reconstruct /ˌriː kənˈstrʌkt/ **verb 1** construct again 重建;重建 **2** show how a past event happened by using the evidence that has been gathered 使(往事)重现;使再现 ■ **reconstruction** noun.

record noun /ˈrekɔːd/ **1** a permanent account of something, kept for evidence or information 记录;记载 **2** the previous behaviour or performance of a person or thing 履历;历史成绩 **3** (also **criminal record**) a list of a person's previous criminal convictions 前科记录 **4** the best performance of its kind that has been officially recognized 最高记录;最佳成绩 **5** a thin plastic disc carrying recorded sound in grooves on each surface 唱片 • **verb** /rɪˈkɔːd/ **1** make a record of something;记载 **2** convert sound or vision into a permanent form so that it can be reproduced later 录制(声音或图像)录音;录像 □ **off the record** not made as an official statement 非正式记录在案的 **record player** a device for playing records (电)唱机 ■ **recording** noun.

recorder /rɪˈkɔːdə(r)/ **noun 1** a device for recording sound, pictures, etc. 录音机;录像机 **2** a person who keeps records 录音师;录像师 **3** a musical instrument which you play by blowing through a mouthpiece and putting your fingers over holes 竖笛;八孔直笛

recount[1] /rɪˈkaʊnt/ **verb** describe something to someone 叙述;描述;讲述

recount[2] **verb** /ˌriːˈkaʊnt/ count again 重新计数;再清点 • **noun** /ˈriːkaʊnt/ an act of counting something again 重新计数;再清点

recoup /rɪˈkuːp/ **verb** recover an amount of money that has been lost or spent 挽回(损失);收回(成本)

recourse /rɪˈkɔːs/ **noun 1** a source of help in a difficult situation 求助对象;(困境中赖以得救的)手段,方法 **2** (**recourse to**) the use of a particular source of help 求助;依赖;依靠

recover /rɪˈkʌvə(r)/ **verb** (**recovers**, **recovering**, **recovered**) **1** return to a normal state of health or strength 恢复(健康或力气) **2** regain possession or control of 恢复对…的占有(或控制) **3** regain an amount of money that has been spent or lent 收回(成本或欠款) ■ **recoverable** adjective.

recovery /rɪˈkʌvəri/ **noun** (plural **recoveries**) the action or an act of recovering 恢复;收回

recreate /ˌriː kriˈeɪt/ **verb** (**recreates**, **recreating**, **recreated**) make or do again 再创造;再创作;再创建

recreation[1] /ˌrekriˈeɪʃn/ **noun** enjoyable leisure activity 娱乐(活动);消遣 ■ **recreational** adjective.

recreation[2] /ˌriː kriˈeɪʃn/ **noun** the action of recreating something 再创造;再创作;再创建

recrimination /rɪˌkrɪmɪˈneɪʃn/ **noun** an accusation made in response to one from someone else 反控;反诉

recrudescence /ˌriːkruːˈdesns/ **noun** formal 【正式】 a recurrence 一再发生;反复出现

recruit /rɪˈkruːt/ **verb** take on someone to serve in the armed forces or work for an organization 征募,招募(新兵);招收,招募(成员) • **noun** a newly recruited person 新兵;新人;新成员 ■ **recruitment** noun.

rectal /ˈrektəl/ **adjective** relating to or affecting the rectum (影响)直肠的

rectangle /ˈrektæŋɡl/ **noun** a flat shape with four right angles and four straight sides, two of which are longer than the others 长方形;矩形 ■ **rectangular** adjective.

rectify /ˈrektɪfaɪ/ **verb** (**rectifies**, **rectifying**, **rectified**) **1** put right; correct 矫正;纠正;改正 **2** convert alternating current to direct current 把(交流电)转化成直流电;整(流)流 ■ **rectification** noun **rectifier** noun.

rectilinear /ˌrektɪˈlɪniə(r)/ **adjective** having or moving in a straight line or lines 直线的,沿直线(运动)的

rectitude /ˈrektɪtjuːd/ **noun** morally correct behaviour 操行端正;正直

recto /ˈrektəʊ/ **noun** (plural **rectos**) a right-hand page of an open book, or the front of a loose document (书的)右页,奇数页

rector /ˈrektə(r)/ **noun 1** a Christian priest in charge of a parish (基督教的)教区长 **2** the head of certain universities, colleges, and schools (某些大学、学院的)校长,院长

rectory /ˈrektəri/ **noun** (plural **rectories**) the house of a rector 教区长住宅

rectum /ˈrektəm/ **noun** the final section of the large intestine, ending at the anus 直肠

recumbent /rɪˈkʌmbənt/ **adjective** lying down 躺着的

recuperate /rɪˈkuːpəreɪt/ **verb** (**recuperates**, **recuperating**, re-cuperated) **1** recover from illness or tiredness 康复;恢复体力 **2** get back something that has been lost or spent 挽回(损失);收回(成本) ■ **recuperation** noun.

recur /rɪˈkɜː(r)/ **verb** (**recurs**, **recurring**, **recurred**) happen again or repeatedly 再发生;复发,反复出现 ■ **recurrence** noun.

recurrent /rɪˈkʌrənt/ **adjective** happening often or repeatedly 一再发生的;反复出现的

recycle /ˌriːˈsaɪkl/ **verb** (**recycles**, **recycling**, **recycled**) **1** convert waste into a form in which it can be reused 回收利用(废物) **2** use something again 重新利用;再使用 ■ **recyclable** adjective.

red /red/ **adjective** (**redder**, **reddest**) **1** of the colour of blood or fire 血红的,火红的 **2** (of hair or fur) of a reddish-brown colour (头发或皮毛)红褐色的 • **noun 1** red colour 红;红色 **2** informal,chiefly disapproving 【非正式,主贬】 a communist or socialist 共产党人;社会主义者 □ **in the red** having spent more than is in your bank account 出现赤字;负债 **red blood cell** a blood cell which contains haemoglobin and carries oxygen to the tissues 红细胞 **red-blooded** (of a man) energetic and healthy (男子)血气方刚的,精力充沛的 **red-brick** (of a British university) founded in the late 19th or early 20th century(英国大学)红砖校舍的(建于19世纪末、20世纪初) **red card** (in soccer) a red card shown by the referee to a player being sent off the field (足球比赛中裁判罚球员出场的)红牌 **red-handed** in the act of doing something wrong 正在做坏事的 **red herring** a thing that takes people's attention away from something important 令人分心的事物;转移注意力的东西 **red-hot 1** so

R

hot that it glows red 炽热的；火热的 **2** very exciting 激动人心的 **Red Indian** dated, often offensive 【废，常冒犯】an American Indian 美洲印第安人 **red-letter day** an important or memorable day 重要日子；纪念日 **red-light district** an area with many brothels, strip clubs, etc. (妓院、脱衣舞夜总会等集中的)红灯区 **red pepper** a ripe sweet pepper 红辣椒 **red tape** complicated official rules which cause irritation because they take up your time (浪费时间的)官方复杂规定，繁琐手续 **see red** informal 【非正式】suddenly become very angry 火冒三丈；怒不可遏 ■ **reddish** adjective.

redcurrant /ˈredkʌrənt/ noun a small edible red berry 红醋栗；普通红茶子

redden /ˈredn/ verb make or become red (使)变红，染红

redeem /rɪˈdiːm/ verb **1** make up for the faults of 弥补…的过失，对…作补偿 **2** save someone from sin or evil 拯救；救赎 **3** fulfil a promise 履行(诺言) **4** pay a debt 偿还，偿付(债务) **5** exchange a coupon for goods or money 兑换，兑现(商品或钱款) **6** regain possession of something in exchange for payment 赎回；买回

Redeemer /rɪˈdiːmə(r)/ noun (the Redeemer) Jesus 耶稣基督；救世主

redemption /rɪˈdempʃn/ noun the action of redeeming 弥补；救赎；清偿

redeploy /ˌriːdɪˈplɔɪ/ verb move troops, resources, etc. to a new place or task 重新部署(军队)；重新调配(资源) ■ **redeployment** noun.

redhead /ˈredhed/ noun a person with red hair 红发人

redneck /ˈrednek/ noun US informal【美，非正式】a conservative working-class white person "红脖子"(观念保守的劳动阶层白人)

redolent /ˈredələnt/ adjective (redolent of or with) **1** making you think of a particular thing 使人想起…的 **2** literary【文】smelling of 散发强烈气味的 ■ **redolence** noun.

redouble /ˌriːˈdʌbl/ verb (redoubles, redoubling, redoubled) make or become greater or stronger (使)变得更大；(使)加强

redoubt /rɪˈdaʊt/ noun a small or temporary structure from which soldiers can defend a place under attack 棱堡，多面堡(小型或临时性防御工事)

redoubtable /rɪˈdaʊtəbl/ adjective worthy of respect or fear; formidable 可敬的；可畏的；值得敬畏的

redound /rɪˈdaʊnd/ verb (redound to) formal 【正式】be to someone's credit 对(某人的信誉)极有帮助

redress verb /ˌriːˈdres/ put right something that is unfair or wrong 平反，洗雪(冤屈)；纠正，矫正(错误) • noun /rɪˈdres/ payment or action to make amends for a wrong 补偿；平反；矫正

redskin /ˈredskɪn/ noun dated or offensive 【废或冒犯】an American Indian 美洲印第安人

reduce /rɪˈdjuːs/ verb (reduces, reducing, reduced) **1** make or become less (使)减少；(使)缩小；(使)降低 **2** (reduce something to) change something to a simpler form 使变成(更简单的形式) **3** (reduce someone to) bring someone to a particular state or condition 使处于(某种状态或状况) **4** boil a liquid so that it becomes thicker 煮浓，熬浓(液体) □ **reduced circumstances** a state in which you have become poorer than you were before (较富有之后的)穷困境遇 ■ **reducible** adjective.

reduction /rɪˈdʌkʃn/ noun **1** the action of reducing 缩小；减低；转换 **2** the amount by which something is reduced 缩减量；削减数

reductive /rɪˈdʌktɪv/ adjective presenting something in an oversimplified form 简化(法)的

redundant /rɪ'dʌndənt/ **adjective 1** Brit.【英】unemployed because your job is no longer needed 被解雇的；失业的 **2** no longer needed or useful 多余的；不需要的；无用的 ■ **redundancy** noun (plural **redundancies**)

redwood /'redwʊd/ **noun** a giant coniferous tree with reddish wood 红杉

reed /riːd/ **noun 1** a tall, slender plant that grows in water or on marshy ground 芦苇 **2** a piece of thin cane or metal in musical instruments such as the clarinet, which vibrates when air is blown over it and produces sound 簧片；簧舌

reedy /'riːdi/ **adjective 1** (of a sound or voice) high and thin in tone (声音或嗓音)尖细的，尖厉的 **2** full of reeds 多芦苇的

reef /riːf/ **noun 1** a ridge of jagged rock or coral just above or below the surface of the sea 礁，暗礁 **2** each of several strips across a sail that can be taken in when the wind is strong 缩帆部(帆的收缩部分) ■ **verb** make a sail smaller by taking in a reef 缩(帆) □ **reef knot** a type of secure knot 平结

reefer /'riːfə(r)/ **noun** informal【非正式】a cannabis cigarette 大麻烟卷

reefer jacket noun a thick close-fitting double-breasted jacket 双排纽厚呢短夹克

reek /riːk/ **verb** have a very unpleasant smell 散发恶臭 ■ **noun** a very unpleasant smell 恶臭

reel /riːl/ **noun 1** a cylinder on which film, thread, etc. can be wound (胶片、丝线等的)卷轴，卷筒，绕线轮 **2** a lively Scottish or Irish folk dance (苏格兰或爱尔兰的)里尔舞 ■ **verb 1** (**reel something in**) bring something towards you by turning a reel (转动卷轴)收绕 **2** (**reel something off**) recite something

quickly and with ease 一下子说出；轻而易举地背出 **3** stagger 踉跄；蹒跚 **4** feel giddy, shocked, or bewildered 感到震惊(或迷惑)；不知所措

re-entry /riː'entri/ **noun** (plural **re-entries**) **1** the action of entering again 重返 **2** the return of a spacecraft or missile into the earth's atmosphere (航天器的)重返大气层

refectory /rɪ'fektri/ **noun** (plural **refectories**) a room used for meals in an educational or religious institution (教育或宗教机构的)食堂，餐厅

refer /rɪ'fɜː(r)/ **verb** (**refers**, **referring**, **referred**) (**refer to**) **1** write or say something about; mention 写到；提及；谈到 **2** (of a word or phrase) describe (词或短语)指代，形容 **3** turn to a person, book, etc. for information 询问；咨询；查看 **4** (**refer someone/thing to**) pass a person or matter on to someone else for help or a decision 将…提交给

referee /ˌrefə'riː/ **noun 1** an official who supervises a game to ensure that players keep to the rules 裁判员 **2** Brit.【英】a person who is willing to provide a reference for a person applying for a job (求职者的)介绍人，推荐人 **3** a person who reads academic work before it is published (学术著作出版之前的)审阅人 ■ **verb** (**referees**, **refereeing**, **refereed**) be a referee of 担任…的裁判；审阅

reference /'refrəns/ **noun 1** the action of referring to something 提到；论及；查阅 **2** a mention of a source of information in a book or article 引文出处；参考书目 **3** a letter giving information about how suitable someone is for a new job (关于求职者能力的)证明文书，推荐信

✔ 拼写指南 one r in the middle, not two: reference. reference 中间只有一个r，而不是两个。

referendum /ˌrefəˈrendəm/ **noun** (plural **referendums** or **referenda**) a vote by the people of a country on a single political issue (就单个政治问题举行的)全民公投

referral /rɪˈfɜːrəl/ **noun** the action of referring someone or something to a specialist or higher authority 推荐；参考；引证

refine /rɪˈfaɪn/ **verb** (**refines, refining, refined**) **1** make something pure by removing unwanted substances 提炼，精炼 **2** improve something by making minor changes 改进；使完善 **3** (**refined**) well educated, elegant, and having good taste 有教养的；优雅的；高雅的

refinement /rɪˈfaɪnmənt/ **noun 1** the process of refining 提炼；精炼 **2** an improvement 改进；完善 **3** the quality of being well educated, elegant, and having good taste 有教养；优雅；高雅

refinery /rɪˈfaɪnəri/ **noun** (plural **refineries**) a factory where a substance such as oil is refined 提炼厂；精炼厂

refit **verb** /ˌriːˈfɪt/ (**refits, refitting, refitted**) replace or repair equipment and fittings in a ship, building, etc. 对(船、建筑物等)重新装备、改装、整修 • **noun** /ˈriːfɪt/ an act of refitting 重新装备；改装；整修

reflect /rɪˈflekt/ **verb 1** throw back heat, light, or sound from a surface 反射(热、光或声音) **2** (of a mirror) show an image of 映出 **3** show in a realistic or appropriate way 反映；表明；显示 **4** (**reflect well** or **badly on**) give a good or bad impression of 带来(荣誉)；招致(耻辱) **5** (**reflect on**) think seriously about 深思；考虑

reflection /rɪˈflekʃn/ **noun 1** the process of reflecting 反射 **2** a reflected image 映像；倒影 **3** a sign of something's true nature (本质的)反映 **4** something that brings discredit 招致羞耻(或责难)的事 **5** serious thought 深思；沉省

reflective /rɪˈflektɪv/ **adjective 1** providing a reflection 反射的；反照的；反映的 **2** thoughtful 思考的；沉思的 ■ **reflectively** adverb.

reflector /rɪˈflektə(r)/ **noun** a piece of glass or plastic on the back of a vehicle for reflecting light (车辆尾部的)反光玻璃(或塑料)

reflex /ˈriːfleks/ **noun** an action done without conscious thought as a response to something (生理的)反射，本能反应 • **adjective 1** done as a reflex 反射(性)的；本能反应的 **2** (of an angle) more than 180° (角度)优角(大于180°)

reflexive /rɪˈfleksɪv/ **adjective** Grammar 【语法】 referring back to the subject of a clause or verb, e.g. *myself* in I hurt myself 反身的

reflexology /ˌriːflekˈsɒlədʒi/ **noun** a system of massage used to relieve tension and treat illness 反射疗法(按摩以缓解紧张情绪、治疗疾病) ■ **reflexologist** noun.

refocus /ˌriːˈfəʊkəs/ **verb** (**refocuses, refocusing** or **refocussing, refocused** or **refocussed**) **1** adjust the focus of a lens or your eyes 重调焦距 **2** focus attention on something new or different 将(注意力)转于(新事物)；改变(关注)的重点

reform /rɪˈfɔːm/ **verb 1** change something to improve it 改良；改革；改进 **2** make someone improve their behaviour 改造；使改过自新 • **noun** an act of reforming 改良；改革；改造 ■ **reformer** noun.

reformation /ˌrefəˈmeɪʃn/ **noun 1** the action of reforming 改良；改革；改造 **2** (**the Reformation**) a 16th-century movement for reforming the Roman Catholic Church, leading to the establishment of the Protestant

Churches 宗教改革(16世纪改革罗马天主教会的运动,结果导致新教的建立)

reformist /rɪ'fɔːmɪst/ **adjective** supporting political or social reform 支持改革的;改良主义的 • **noun** a supporter of such reform 改革派;改良主义者 ■ **reformism** noun.

refract /rɪ'frækt/ **verb** (of water, air, or glass) make a ray of light change direction when it enters at an angle (水、空气或玻璃)使(光线)折射 ■ **refraction** noun **refractive** adjective.

refractory /rɪ'fræktəri/ **adjective 1** stubborn or difficult to control 执拗的;倔强的;难驾驭的 **2** (of an illness) not responding to treatment (疾病)顽固的,难治的

refrain¹ /rɪ'freɪn/ **verb** (**refrain from**) stop yourself from doing something 克制;抑制;忍住

refrain² **noun** a part of a song that is repeated at the end of each verse (歌曲每节末尾的)叠句

refresh /rɪ'freʃ/ **verb** make someone feel less tired or hot 使恢复活力;使凉爽

refresher /rɪ'freʃə(r)/ **noun** a course intended to improve or update your skills or knowledge 进修课程

refreshing /rɪ'freʃɪŋ/ **adjective 1** making you feel less tired or hot 解乏的;使人凉爽的 **2** pleasingly new or different 令人耳目一新的;别具一格的 ■ **refreshingly** adverb.

refreshment /rɪ'freʃmənt/ **noun 1** a snack or drink 小吃;便餐;饮料 **2** the giving of fresh energy 恢复活力;焕发精神

refrigerate /rɪ'frɪdʒəreɪt/ **verb** (**refrigerates, refrigerating, refrigerated**) make food or drink cold to keep it fresh 冷藏(食物或饮料) ■ **refrigeration** noun.

refrigerator /rɪ'frɪdʒəreɪtə(r)/ **noun** a fridge 冰箱;雪柜;冷藏室

✔ **拼写指南** no *d* in the middle: refrigerator, not -*ridg*-. refrigerator 中间没有d,不要拼作 -ridg-。

refuel /ˌriː'fjuːəl/ **verb** (**refuels, refuelling, refuelled**; US spelling【美拼作】**refuels, refueling, refueled**) supply with more fuel 给…加油;给…补充燃料

refuge /'refjuːdʒ/ **noun 1** shelter from danger or trouble 避难所;庇护 **2** a safe place 避难所;安全地带

refugee /ˌrefjuˈdʒiː/ **noun** a person who has been forced to leave their country because of a war or because they are being persecuted 流亡者;难民

refund **verb** /rɪ'fʌnd/ pay back money to 将(钱)退还(或偿还) • **noun** /'riː fʌnd/ a repayment of a sum of money 退款;偿还金额

refurbish /ˌriː'fɜːbɪʃ/ **verb** redecorate and improve a building or room 再装修;整修(建筑物或房间) ■ **refurbishment** noun.

refuse¹ /rɪ'fjuːz/ **verb** (**refuses, refusing, refused**) say that you are unwilling to do or accept something 拒绝 ■ **refusal** noun.

refuse² /'refjuːs/ **noun** things thrown away; rubbish 废物;废料

refute /rɪ'fjuːt/ **verb** (**refutes, refuting, refuted**) prove a statement or person to be wrong 驳斥;反驳 ■ **refutation** noun.

regain /rɪ'geɪn/ **verb 1** get something back after losing possession of it 收回;收复;恢复 **2** get back to a place 返回;回到

regal /'riːgl/ **adjective** having to do with a king or queen, especially in being magnificent or dignified 帝王的;(帝王般)奢华的,威严的 ■ **regally** adverb.

regale /rɪ'geɪl/ **verb** (**regales, regaling, regaled**) **1** entertain someone with anecdotes or stories

(以趣闻铁事等)使愉悦,使高兴 **2** supply someone generously with food or drink 宴请;款待

regalia /rɪˈgeɪlɪə/ **noun 1** objects such as the crown and sceptre used at coronations or other state occasions (王冠、权杖等)王位标志,王室器物 **2** the distinctive clothes and items worn or carried on official occasions by important people (重要人物在正式场合穿戴或携带的)特别服饰,特别物品

regard /rɪˈgɑːd/ **verb 1** think of in a particular way 认为;看待 **2** look steadily at 凝视;注视 • **noun 1** concern or care 关心,关心 **2** high opinion; respect 敬意;尊敬;尊重 **3 (regards)** best wishes 问候;(问候的)好意 □ **as regards (or with regard to)** concerning 关于;至于

regarding /rɪˈgɑːdɪŋ/ **preposition** about; concerning 关于;至于

regardless /rɪˈgɑːdləs/ **adverb 1 (regardless of)** without concern for 不顾;不考虑 **2** despite what is happening 无论如何,不管怎样

regatta /rɪˈgætə/ **noun** a sports event consisting of a series of boat or yacht races 赛船大会

regency /ˈriːdʒənsɪ/ **noun** (plural **regencies**) **1** a period of government by a regent 摄政期 **2 (the Regency)** the period when George, Prince of Wales, acted as regent in Britain (1811–1820) (英国1811至1820年由威尔士亲王乔治摄政的)摄政时期

regenerate /rɪˈdʒenəreɪt/ **verb** (**regenerates, regenerating, regenerated**) **1** bring new life or strength to 使新生,复兴;使恢复 **2** grow new tissue 生长出(新组织) ■ **regeneration** noun.

regent /ˈriːdʒənt/ **noun** a person appointed to rule a state because the king or queen is too young or ill to rule, or is absent 摄政者;摄政王

reggae /ˈregeɪ/ **noun** a style of popular music originating in Jamaica 雷盖(源于牙买加的流行音乐)

regicide /ˈredʒɪsaɪd/ **noun 1** the killing of a king 弑君 **2** a person who kills a king 弑君者

regime /reɪˈʒiːm/ **noun 1** a government, especially one that strictly controls a state (尤指专制的)政府,政权,政体 **2** an ordered way of doing something; a system 制度;体制;体系

regimen /ˈredʒɪmən/ **noun** a course of medical treatment, diet, or exercise 疗程;养生法

regiment /ˈredʒɪmənt/ **noun 1** a permanent unit of an army (军队的)团 **2** a large number of people (人的)大群,大批 ■ **regimental** adjective.

regimented /ˈredʒɪmentɪd/ **adjective** organized according to a strict system 系统化的;严格控制的

Regina /rɪˈdʒaɪnə/ **noun** the reigning queen (used in referring to lawsuits) 女王(用于诉讼文件中)

region /ˈriːdʒən/ **noun 1** an area of a country or the world 地区;区域 **2** an administrative district of a city or country (城市或国家的)行政区 **3 (the regions)** the parts of a country outside the capital (首都以外的)地方 **4** a part of the body (身体的)区,部,部位 □ **in the region of** approximately 接近;大约 ■ **regional** adjective **regionally** adverb.

register /ˈredʒɪstə(r)/ **noun 1** an official list or record (官方的)登记,注册 **2** a particular part of the range of a musical instrument or voice (乐器或声音的)音区,声区 **3** the level and style of a piece of writing or speech (e.g. informal, formal) (写作或讲话的)语域,使用域 • **verb** (**registers, registering, registered**) **1** enter in a register 注册 **2** put your name on a register 登记(姓名) **3** express an opinion or emotion 表

达(意见或情感) **4** become aware of 意识到；注意到 **5** (of a measuring instrument) show a reading (测量仪器)显示，指示 □ **register office** (in the UK) a government building where marriages are performed and births, marriages, and deaths are recorded (英国办理结婚手续、登记出生和死亡的)户籍登记处

registrar /ˌredʒɪˈstrɑː(r), ˈredʒɪstrɑː(r)/ **noun 1** an official responsible for keeping official records 登记员；户籍员 **2** Brit. 【英】 a hospital doctor who is training to be a specialist 专科住院医生

registration /ˌredʒɪˈstreɪʃn/ **noun 1** the action of registering 登记；注册 **2** (also **registration number**) Brit. 【英】 the series of letters and figures shown on a vehicle's number plate (车辆)登记号码，牌照号码

registry /ˈredʒɪstri/ **noun** (plural **registries**) a place where registers are kept 登记处；注册处 □ **registry office** a register office 户籍登记处

regress /rɪˈgres/ **verb** return to an earlier or less advanced state 退回；回归，退化 ■ **regression** noun.

regressive /rɪˈgresɪv/ **adjective 1** returning to a less advanced state 退回的；回归的，退化的 **2** (of a tax) taking a proportionally greater amount from those on lower incomes (税)递减的

regret /rɪˈgret/ **verb** (**regrets**, **regretting**, **regretted**) feel sorry or disappointed about something you have done or should have done 对…感到惋惜；对…感到遗憾 ● **noun** a feeling of regretting something 惋惜；遗憾

regretful /rɪˈgretfl/ **adjective** feeling or showing regret 遗憾的；懊悔的；感到惋惜的 ■ **regretfully** adverb.

regrettable /rɪˈgretəbl/ **adjective** causing regret 让人悔恨的；令人遗憾

的；可惜的 ■ **regrettably** adverb.

regular /ˈregjələ(r)/ **adjective 1** following or arranged in an evenly spaced pattern or sequence 定时的；定期的 **2** done or happening frequently 经常的 **3** doing the same thing often 习惯性的；固定的 **4** following an accepted standard 规则的；循常例的 **5** usual 通常的，平常的 **6** Grammar 【语法】 (of a word) following the normal pattern of inflection (词语)规则变化的，规则的 **7** belonging to the permanent professional armed forces of a country 常备军的；正规军的 **8** (of a geometrical figure) having all sides and angles equal (几何图形)等边等角的，正的 ● **noun** a regular customer, member of a team, etc. 常客；正式队员 ■ **regularity** noun **regularly** adverb.

regularize or **regularise** /ˈregjələraɪz/ **verb** (**regularizes**, **regularizing**, **regularized**) **1** make regular 使有规律；使条理化 **2** make a temporary situation legal or official 使合法化；使正式存在

regulate /ˈregjuleɪt/ **verb** (**regulates**, **regulating**, **regulated**) **1** control the rate or speed of a machine or process 调节；控制 **2** control or supervise by means of rules 控制；管理 ■ **regulator** noun **regulatory** adjective.

regulation /ˌregjuˈleɪʃn/ **noun 1** a rule made by an authority 规章，规则；条例 **2** the action of regulating 调节；控制；管理

regurgitate /rɪˈgɜːdʒɪteɪt/ **verb** (**regurgitates**, **regurgitating**, **regurgitated**) **1** bring swallowed food up again to the mouth 使(已吞咽的食物)返回口中 **2** repeat information without understanding it 机械刻板地重复(信息) ■ **re-gurgitation** noun.

rehabilitate /ˌriːəˈbɪlɪteɪt/ **verb**

(**rehabilitates**, **rehabilitating**, **rehabilitated**) **1** help someone who has been ill or in prison to return to normal life 使(病人)康复;使(服刑者)恢复正常生活 **2** restore the reputation of someone previously out of favour 恢复(某人)的名誉 ■ **rehabilitation** noun.

rehash /riːˈhæʃ/ verb reuse old ideas or material 重新使用(旧想法或旧材料) • noun a reuse of old ideas or material (旧想法或旧材料的)重新使用

rehearsal /rɪˈhɜːsl/ noun a trial performance of a play or other work for later public performance 排练;排演

rehearse /rɪˈhɜːs/ verb (**rehearses**, **rehearsing**, **rehearsed**) **1** practise a play, piece of music, etc. for later public performance 排练,排演(戏剧、音乐等) **2** state points that have been made many times before 反复讲

rehydrate /riː haɪˈdreɪt/ verb (**rehydrates**, **rehydrating**, **rehydrated**) add moisture to something dehydrated 使(脱水后)再水化;使复水 ■ **rehydration** noun.

Reich /raɪk/ noun the former German state, in particular the **Third Reich** (the Nazi regime,1933–1945) (德意志)帝国(尤指纳粹第三帝国)

reign /reɪn/ verb **1** rule as king or queen (君主)统治 **2** be the main quality or aspect 盛行;占优势: *Confusion reigned*. 局势一片混乱. **3** (**reigning**) currently holding a particular title in sport (在体育上)称雄的 • noun the period of rule of a king or queen 君主统治时期;君主在位期

reimburse /ˌriːɪmˈbɜːs/ verb (**reimburses**, **reimbursing**, **reimbursed**) repay money to 偿还;赔偿 ■ **reimbursement** noun.

rein /reɪn/ noun (**reins**) **1** long, narrow straps attached to a horse's

bit, used to control the horse (驾驶马的)缰绳 **2** the power to direct and control something 支配权;控制权 • verb **1** control a horse by pulling on its reins 用缰绳驾驭(马) **2** (**rein someone/thing in** or **back**) restrain someone or something 抑制;约束 □ **free rein** freedom of action 行动自由;无拘束

reincarnate /ˌriːɪnˈkɑːneɪt/ verb (**be reincarnated**) be born again in another body 转世化身 ■ **reincarnation** noun.

reindeer /ˈreɪndɪə(r)/ noun (plural **reindeer** or **reindeers**) a deer with large antlers, found in cold northern regions 驯鹿

reinforce /ˌriːɪnˈfɔːs/ verb (**reinforces**, **reinforcing**, **reinforced**) **1** make something stronger 加强,使更有力 **2** strengthen a military force with additional personnel 增强,充实(军力)

reinforcement /ˌriːɪnˈfɔːsmənt/ noun **1** the action of reinforcing 增强;加强;增援 **2** (**reinforcements**) extra personnel sent to strengthen a military force 援军;增援部队

reinstate /ˌriːɪnˈsteɪt/ verb (**reinstates**, **reinstating**, **reinstated**) restore to a former position 使恢复原职 ■ **reinstatement** noun.

reiterate /riˈɪtəreɪt/ verb (**reiterates**, **reiterating**, **reiterated**) say something again or repeatedly 重复讲;反复重申 ■ **reiteration** noun.

reject verb /rɪˈdʒekt/ **1** refuse to accept or agree to 拒绝接受;不同意 **2** fail to show proper affection or concern for 未能给予…应有的关爱(或关心) **3** (of the body) react against a transplanted organ or tissue (身体)排斥(移植的器官) • noun /ˈriː dʒekt/ a rejected person or thing 被拒绝者;被拒货品 ■ **rejection** noun.

rejig /riːˈdʒɪg/ **verb** (**rejigs, rejigging, rejigged**) Brit. 【英】rearrange 调整；重新安排

rejoice /rɪˈdʒɔɪs/ **verb** (**rejoices, rejoicing, rejoiced**) feel or show great joy 充满喜悦；极欢喜

rejoin[1] /riːˈdʒɔɪn/ **verb** join again 重新会合；重新加入

rejoin[2] /riːˈdʒɔɪn/ formal 【正式】say in reply; retort 回答；反驳

rejoinder /rɪˈdʒɔɪndə(r)/ **noun** a quick reply (迅速的)回答

rejuvenate /rɪˈdʒuːvəneɪt/ **verb** (**rejuvenates, rejuvenating, rejuvenated**) make more lively or youthful 使变得年轻；使恢复青春活力 ■ **rejuvenation** noun.

rekindle /riːˈkɪndl/ **verb** (**rekindles, rekindling, rekindled**) 1 revive a past feeling, relationship, etc. 重新激起(昔日情感等)；重新恢复(昔日关系等) 2 relight a fire 再点燃，重新燃起

relapse verb /rɪˈlæps/ (**relapses, relapsing, relapsed**) 1 become ill again after a period of improvement 旧病复发 2 (**relapse into**) return to a worse state 重新陷入，回复(糟糕的状况)；故态复萌 ● **noun** /ˈriːlæps/ a return to bad health after a temporary improvement (病的)复发

relate /rɪˈleɪt/ **verb** (**relates, relating, related**) 1 make or show a connection between (使)关联；(使)有联系 2 (**be related**) be connected by blood or marriage 有血缘(或婚姻)关系 3 (**relate to**) have to do with; concern 与…有关；涉及 4 (**relate to**) feel sympathy with 与…有共鸣；认同 5 give a spoken or written account of 讲述；叙述

relation /rɪˈleɪʃn/ **noun** 1 the way in which people or things are connected or related 关系；关联 2 (**relations**) the way in which people or groups behave towards each other (人际或团体之间的)关系，往来 3 a relative

亲戚；家属

relationship /rɪˈleɪʃnʃɪp/ **noun** 1 the way in which people or things are connected or related 关系；关联 2 the way in which people or groups behave towards each other (人际或团体之间的)关系 3 an emotional and sexual association between two people (两人间的)情感关系，性关系

relative /ˈrelətɪv/ **adjective** 1 considered in relation or in proportion to something else 比较的；比较而言的 2 existing or possessing a quality only in comparison to something else 相对的 3 Grammar 【语法】referring to an earlier noun, sentence, or clause 表示引导的，表示关系的 ● **noun** a person connected to another by blood or marriage 亲戚；亲属

relatively /ˈrelətɪvli/ **adverb** 1 in comparison or proportion to something else 比较而言地，相对地 2 quite 相当

relativism /ˈrelətɪvɪzəm/ **noun** the idea that truth, morality, etc. exist only in relation to other things and are not absolute (认为真理和道德仅是相对存在的)相对主义，相对论 ■ **relativist** noun.

relativity /ˌreləˈtɪvəti/ **noun** 1 the state of being relative; ability to be judged only in comparison with something else 相关性 2 Physics 【物理】a description of matter, energy, space, and time according to Albert Einstein's theories 相对论

relax /rɪˈlæks/ **verb** 1 become less tense, anxious, or rigid 松弛；放松 2 rest from work; do something recreational 休息；消遣 3 make a rule or restriction less strict 放宽(规定或限制) ■ **relaxation** noun.

relay noun /ˈriːleɪ/ 1 a group of people or animals carrying out a task for a time and then replaced by a similar group 接替的一组人(或动物)；替换

组 **2** a race between teams of runners, each team member in turn covering part of the total distance 接力赛 **3** an electrical device which opens or closes a circuit in response to a current in another circuit 继电器;替续器 **4** a device which receives, strengthens, and transmits a signal again (信号的)中继设备 • **verb 1** receive and pass on information 接转,转发(信息) **2** broadcast something by means of a relay 转播

release /rɪ'liːs/ **verb** (**releases**, **releasing**, **released**) **1** set someone free from a place where they have been kept or trapped 释放;解放 **2** free someone from a duty, responsibility, etc. 解除;免除 **3** allow to move freely 放开;使解脱 **4** allow information to be made available 发布(信息) **5** make a film or recording available to the public 公开发行(电影或唱片) • **noun 1** the action of releasing 释放;解除;发布 **2** a film or recording made available to the public 公开发行的影片(或唱片)

relegate /'relɪɡeɪt/ **verb** (**relegates**, **relegating**, **relegated**) **1** place in a lower rank or position 把…降级;把…置于次要地位 **2** Brit. 【英】transfer a sports team to a lower division of a league 使(运动队)降级 ■ **relegation** noun.

relent /rɪ'lent/ **verb 1** finally agree to something after first refusing it 最终同意 **2** become less severe or intense 减弱,变宽容;变温和

relentless /rɪ'lentləs/ **adjective 1** never stopping or ending 不间断的;持续的 **2** harsh or inflexible 残酷的;无情的;强硬的 ■ **relentlessly** adverb.

relevant /'reləvənt/ **adjective** closely connected or appropriate to the current subject 密切相关的;切题的;适宜的 ■ **relevance** noun.

✔ 拼写指南 *-ant*, not *-ent*: relev*ant*. relevant 中 -ant 不要拼作 -ent。

reliable /rɪ'laɪəbl/ **adjective** able to be depended on or trusted 可靠的;可信赖的 ■ **reliability** noun **reliably** adverb.

reliance /rɪ'laɪəns/ **noun** dependence on or trust in someone or something 依靠;信赖;信任 ■ **reliant** adjective.

relic /'relɪk/ **noun 1** an object or custom that survives from an earlier time 遗物;遗迹;遗俗 **2** a part of a holy person's body or belongings kept after their death 圣骨;圣徒遗物;圣物

relief /rɪ'liːf/ **noun 1** a feeling of reassurance and relaxation after anxiety or stress 轻松;宽心;解脱 **2** a cause of relief 宽慰的原因 **3** the action of relieving 缓解;减轻;解除 **4** (also **light relief**) a temporary break in a tense or boring situation (对紧张或单调的)调剂 **5** help given to people in need or difficulty 救助;救济;解救 **6** a person or group replacing others who have been on duty 换班人;接替者 **7** a way of carving in which the design stands out from the surface 浮雕 □ **relief map** a map that indicates hills and valleys by shading (用分层设色法表示地形高低的)地势图,地形图

relieve /rɪ'liːv/ **verb** (**relieves**, **relieving**, **relieved**) **1** lessen or remove pain, difficulty, etc. 减轻;缓解;缓和 **2** (**be relieved**) stop feeling anxious or stressed 宽心;宽慰 **3** replace someone who is on duty 接替;换下 **4** (**relieve someone of**) take a responsibility from someone 使摆脱(责任) **5** bring military support for a place which is surrounded by the enemy 解救,救援(被围之地) **6** make something less boring 使得到调剂;使不单调 **7** (**relieve yourself**) go to the toilet 方便;解手

✔ 拼写指南 remember, *i* before *e* except after *c*: reli*eve*. 记住 i 置于 e 前，在 c 后时除外，如 relieve。

religion /rɪˈlɪdʒən/ **noun 1** belief in and worship of a God or gods 宗教 信仰 **2** a particular system of faith and worship 宗教；教派

religious /rɪˈlɪdʒəs/ **adjective 1** concerned with or believing in a religion 宗教的；笃信宗教的；虔诚的 **2** very careful and regular 严谨的；有规律的 ■ **religiously** adverb.

✔ 拼写指南 reli*gious*, not *-gous*. religious 不要拼作 -gous。

relinquish /rɪˈlɪŋkwɪʃ/ **verb** give up something, especially unwillingly (尤指不情愿地)放弃

reliquary /ˈrelɪkwəri/ **noun** (plural **reliquaries**) a container for holy relics (盛放圣人遗物的)圣盒，圣骨盒

relish /ˈrelɪʃ/ **noun 1** great enjoyment or anticipation 享受；喜爱；兴趣 **2** a strongly flavoured sauce or pickle 调味品；佐料 • **verb** enjoy or look forward to 享受；期待；指望

relive /riːˈlɪv/ **verb** (**relives, reliving, relived**) live through an experience or feeling again in your mind (在想象中)再经历，重温

reload /riːˈləʊd/ **verb** load something, especially a gun, again 重新装载；(尤指给(枪炮)再装填弹药

relocate /riːləʊˈkeɪt/ **verb** (**relocates, relocating, relocated**) move your home or business to a new place 重新安置(家业)；搬迁 ■ **relocation** noun.

reluctant /rɪˈlʌktənt/ **adjective** unwilling and hesitant 不情愿的；勉强的 ■ **reluctance** noun **reluctantly** adverb.

rely /rɪˈlaɪ/ **verb** (**relies, relying, relied**) (**rely on**) **1** need or be dependent on 依靠；依赖 **2** have faith in; trust 信任；信赖；相信

remain /rɪˈmeɪn/ **verb 1** still be in the same place or condition 保持不变 **2** continue to be 继续；依然 **3** be left over 剩下；遗留

remainder /rɪˈmeɪndə(r)/ **noun 1** a part, number, or amount that is left over 剩余部分；剩余数；剩余量 **2** a part that is still to come 其余部分 **3** the number left over when one quantity does not exactly divide another 余数；差数

remains /rɪˈmeɪnz/ **plural noun 1** things that remain or are left 剩余物；剩余、残余 **2** historical or archaeological relics 遗迹；遗址 **3** a person's body after death 遗体；遗骸；遗骨

remand /rɪˈmɑːnd/ **verb** send a defendant to wait for their trial, either on bail or in jail 将(被告)交保候审(或还押候审) □ **on remand** in jail before being tried 在押候审

remark /rɪˈmɑːk/ **verb 1** say as a comment 评论；议论 **2** notice 注意；看到；觉察 • **noun** a comment 评论；意见

remarkable /rɪˈmɑːkəbl/ **adjective** extraordinary or striking 非凡的；卓越的；显著的 ■ **remarkably** adverb.

rematch /ˈriːmætʃ/ **noun** a second match between two teams or players 重赛；复赛

remedial /rɪˈmiːdiəl/ **adjective 1** intended as a remedy 治疗的；补救的；纠正的 **2** provided for children with learning difficulties (为学习有困难的孩子)补习的，辅导的

remedy /ˈremədi/ **noun** (plural **remedies**) **1** a medicine or treatment for a disease or injury 药物；治疗；治疗法 **2** a means of dealing with something undesirable 纠正方法；补救办法 • **verb** (**remedies, remedying, remedied**) put right an undesirable situation 纠正；补救

remember /rɪˈmembə(r)/ **verb** (**remembers, remembering,**

R

remembered) **1** have in your mind someone or something from the past 记得；回想起 **2** not forget to do something necessary or important 牢记；记住 **3** (**remember someone to**) pass on greetings from one person to another 代(某人)问候

remembrance /rɪˈmembrəns/ **noun 1** the action of remembering 回忆 **2** a memory 记忆力；记性 **3** a thing acting as a reminder of someone 纪念品，纪念物

remind /rɪˈmaɪnd/ **verb 1** help someone to remember something 使记起；提醒 **2** (**remind someone of**) make someone think of someone or something because of a resemblance 使想起；使联想起

reminder /rɪˈmaɪndə(r)/ **noun** a thing that makes someone remember something 提醒之物

reminisce /ˌremɪˈnɪs/ **verb** (**reminisces**, **reminiscing**, **reminisced**) think or talk about the past 缅怀，追忆(过去)

reminiscence /ˌremɪˈnɪsns/ **noun 1** an account of something that you remember 往事；旧事 **2** the enjoyable remembering of past events 回忆；怀旧

reminiscent /ˌremɪˈnɪsnt/ **adjective 1** (**reminiscent of**) tending to remind you of something 使人回想的；使人联想的 **2** absorbed in memories 沉浸在往事中的；怀旧的

remiss /rɪˈmɪs/ **adjective** not giving something proper attention or care 粗心的；大意的

remission /rɪˈmɪʃn/ **noun 1** a temporary period during which a serious illness becomes less severe (病情的)缓解，缓和 **2** Brit. 【英】the reduction of a prison sentence as a reward for good behaviour 刑期缩短；减刑 **3** the cancellation of a debt, penalty, etc. (债务、惩罚等的)免除

remit noun /ˈriːmɪt/ the task or area of activity officially given to a person or organization 委托的任务；委托权限 • **verb** /rɪˈmɪt/ (**remits**, **remitting**, **remitted**) **1** send money in payment 汇(款)；汇付 **2** cancel a debt or punishment 免除(债务或惩罚) **3** refer a matter to an authority for a decision 提交

remittance /rɪˈmɪtns/ **noun 1** a sum of money sent as payment 汇款额 **2** the action of remitting money 汇付

remix /ˌriːˈmɪks/ **verb** produce a different version of a musical recording by altering the balance of the separate parts 混和录制，合成(音乐唱片) • **noun** a remixed recording 混录音乐；合成音乐

remnant /ˈremnənt/ **noun** a small remaining quantity of something 残余；剩余

remonstrate /ˈremənstreɪt/ **verb** (**remonstrates**, **remonstrating**, **remonstrated**) complain or protest strongly 抱怨；抗议 ■ **remonstration noun.**

remorse /rɪˈmɔːs/ **noun** deep regret or guilt for something wrong that you have done 痛悔；悔恨 ■ **remorseful adjective.**

remorseless /rɪˈmɔːsləs/ **adjective 1** (of something unpleasant) never ending or improving (令人不快的事)无休止的，持续恶化的 **2** without remorse 无情的；冷酷的 ■ **remorselessly adverb.**

remote /rɪˈməʊt/ **adjective** (**remoter**, **remotest**) **1** far away in space or time 遥远的；久远的 **2** situated far from the main centres of population 边远的，偏远的；偏僻的 **3** having very little connection 联系少的 **4** (of a chance or possibility) unlikely to happen (机会或可能性)微小的，极小的 **5** unfriendly and distant in manner 冷淡的；冷漠的 **6** operating or operated by means of radio or infrared signals 遥控的

□ **remote control 1** control of a machine from a distance by means of signals transmitted from a radio or electronic device (无线电或电子)遥控 **2** a device that controls a machine in this way 遥控装置；遥控器 ■ **remotely** adverb **remoteness** noun.

removal /rɪ'muːvl/ **noun 1** the action of removing 消除；去除；免除 **2** Brit. 【英】 the transfer of furniture and other items when moving house (家具等的)搬运，搬迁

remove /rɪ'muːv/ **verb** (**removes, removing, removed**) **1** take something away from the position it occupies 拿去；移开；挪走 **2** abolish or get rid of 取消；消除；除去 **3** dismiss from a post 免除…的职务；开除 **4** (**be removed**) be very different from 与…迥然不同 **5** (**removed**) separated by a particular number of steps of descent 隔代的；隔辈的: *a second cousin once removed* 叔伯祖父(或姑婆)的曾孙(或曾孙女) • **noun** the amount by which things are separated 间距；差距 ■ **removable** adjective.

remunerate /rɪ'mjuːnəreɪt/ **verb** (**remunerates, remunerating, remunerated**) formal 【正式】 pay someone for work they have done 给(某人)报酬 ■ **remuneration** noun.

remunerative /rɪ'mjuːnərətɪv/ **adjective** formal 【正式】 paying a lot of money 报酬丰厚的

Renaissance /rɪ'neɪsns/ **noun 1** the revival of classical styles in art and literature in the 14th–16th centuries(14至16世纪的)文艺复兴 **2** (**renaissance**) a period of renewed interest in something 复萌；复兴

renal /'riːnl/ **adjective** technical 【术语】 having to do with the kidneys 肾脏的；肾的

rename /ˌriː'neɪm/ **verb** (**renames, renaming, renamed**) give a new name to 给…改名；给…重新起名

renascence /rɪ'næsns/ **noun** formal 【正式】 a revival or rebirth 复兴；复活 ■ **renascent** adjective.

rend /rend/ **verb** (**rends, rending, rent**) literary 【文】 tear something to pieces 撕裂；扯碎

render /'rendə(r)/ **verb** (**renders, rendering, rendered**) **1** provide or give a service, help, etc. 提供，给予(服务、帮助等) **2** hand over for inspection, consideration, or payment 提出；发出；呈交 **3** cause to be or become 使变得；使成为: *He was rendered speechless.* 他被弄得哑口无言。 **4** perform a piece of music or drama 演奏，表演 **5** melt down fat to separate out its impurities 将(脂肪)熬化 **6** cover a wall with a coat of plaster 给(墙壁)抹灰打底

rendezvous /'rɒndeɪvuː/ **noun** (plural **rendezvous** /'rɒndeɪvuːz; 'rɒndeɪvuːz/) **1** a meeting at an agreed time and place 约会；会面；会合 **2** a meeting place 约会地点；会面地点 • **verb** (**rendezvouses, rendezvousing** /'rɒndeɪvuːɪŋ/, **rendezvoused** /'rɒndeɪvuːd/) meet at an agreed time and place 约会；会面

rendition /ren'dɪʃn/ **noun** a performance or version of a piece of music or drama 演奏；表演

renegade /'renɪgeɪd/ **noun** a person who deserts and betrays an organization, country, or set of principles 变节者；叛徒；改变信仰者

renege /rɪ'neɪg, -'niːg/ **verb** (**reneges, reneging, reneged**) go back on an agreement or promise 违约；背信；食言

renew /rɪ'njuː/ **verb 1** start doing something again after an interruption 重新开始；(中断后)继续 **2** give fresh life or strength to 使获得新生；使恢复活力 **3** make a licence, subscription, etc. valid for a further period 延长…的有效期，续订(刊物)

R

4 replace something broken or worn out 更换(破旧物品) ■ **renewable** adjective **renewal** noun.

rennet /'renɪt/ noun a substance used to curdle milk in order to make cheese (用于制作干酪的)凝乳块

renounce /rɪ'naʊns/ verb (**renounces, renouncing, renounced**) **1** formally give up a title or possession 声明放弃(头衔或财产) **2** state that you no longer have a particular belief or allegiance 宣布抛弃(某信仰) **3** abandon a cause, habit, etc. 放弃(事业);摒弃(坏习惯等)

renovate /'renəveɪt/ verb (**renovates, renovating, renovated**) restore something old to a good state; repair 修复;整修(旧物)如新 ■ **renovation** noun.

renown /rɪ'naʊn/ noun the state of being famous 名望;声誉 ■ **renowned** adjective.

rent[1] /rent/ noun a regular payment made for the use of property or land 房租;地租;租金 • verb **1** regularly pay money to someone for the use of property or land 租借;租用 **2** let someone use property or land in return for payment 出租;出借

rent[2] past and past participle of REND. • noun a large tear in a piece of fabric (织物的)裂缝,破洞

rental /'rentl/ noun **1** an amount paid as rent 租费;租金 **2** the action of renting 租赁;出租

renunciation /rɪˌnʌnsɪ'eɪʃn/ noun the action of renouncing or giving up something 放弃;抛弃

reorganize or **reorganise** /riː'ɔːgənaɪz/ verb (**reorganizes, reorganizing, reorganized**) change the organization of 改组;改编 ■ **reorganization** noun.

rep /rep/ noun informal 【非正式】 **1** a representative 代表 **2** repertory 仓库

repaid /rɪ'peɪd/ past and past

participle of REPAY.

repair[1] /rɪ'peə(r)/ verb restore something damaged or worn to a good condition 修理;修补 • noun **1** an act of repairing something 修理 **2** the condition of an object 维修状态;保养状况: *in good repair* 维修状况良好 ■ **repairer** noun.

repair[2] verb (**repair to**) go to a place 去;赴;前往

reparable /'repərəbl/ adjective able to be repaired 可修理的;可修补的

reparation /ˌrepə'reɪʃn/ noun **1** something done to make up for a wrong 补偿;赔偿 **2** (**reparations**) compensation for war damage paid by a defeated country (战败国支付的)赔款

repartee /ˌrepɑː'tiː/ noun quick, witty comments or conversation 机智的评论(或对话)

repast /rɪ'pɑːst/ noun formal 【正式】 a meal 餐;饭菜

repatriate /riː'pætrieɪt/ verb (**repatriates, repatriating, repatriated**) send someone back to their own country 把(某人)遣送回国;遣返 ■ **repatriation** noun.

repay /rɪ'peɪ/ verb (**repays, repaying, repaid**) **1** pay back money owed to someone 偿还;清偿 **2** do something as a reward for a favour or kindness 报答;回报 **3** be worthy of investigation, attention, etc. 值得 ■ **repayment** noun.

repeal /rɪ'piːl/ verb make a law no longer valid 撤销;废止(法律) • noun the action of repealing 撤销;废止

repeat /rɪ'piːt/ verb **1** say or do again 重说;重做;重复 **2** (**repeat yourself**) say the same thing again 复述 **3** (**repeat itself**) happen again in the same way or form 再发生;再现 • noun **1** something that happens or is done again 再现之事;重做之事 **2** a repeated broadcast of a television or radio programme (电视或电台节目的)重播 ■ **repeatedly** adverb.

repel /rɪ'pel/ **verb (repels, repelling, repelled) 1** drive back or away 击退;逐回;赶走 **2** make someone feel disgust 使厌恶;使反感 **3** force away something with a similar magnetic charge 排斥;相斥

repellent /rɪ'pelənt/ **adjective 1** causing disgust or distaste 令人厌恶的;令人反感的 **2** able to keep a particular substance out 防…的;隔绝…的: *water-repellent nylon* 防水尼龙 • **noun 1** a substance that keeps insects away 驱虫剂 **2** a substance used to treat something so that water cannot pass through it 防水剂

repent /rɪ'pent/ **verb** feel sorry for something bad that you have done (对…)感到后悔(或自责) ■ **repentance** noun **repentant** adjective.

repercussions /ˌriːpə'kʌʃnz/ **plural noun** the consequences of an event or action (事件或行动的)后果,影响

repertoire /'repətwɑː(r)/ **noun** the material known or regularly performed by a performer or company (演员或剧团的)全部剧目,全部曲目,全部节目

repertory /'repətri/ **noun (plural repertories) 1** the performance by a company of various plays, operas, etc. at regular intervals 保留剧目轮演 **2** a repertoire 保留剧目

repetition /ˌrepə'tɪʃn/ **noun 1** the action of repeating 重复;重做;重说 **2** a repeat of something 复制品;副本

repetitious /ˌrepə'tɪʃəs/ **adjective** having too much repetition; repetitive 重复过多的;多次重复的

• **repetitive** /rɪ'petətɪv/ **adjective** involving repetition; repeated many or too many times 多次重复的;重复过多的 ■ **repetitively** adverb.

rephrase /ˌriː'freɪz/ **verb (re-**

phrases, rephrasing, rephrased) express something in an alternative way 重新措词;改用其他措词表述

repine /rɪ'paɪn/ **verb (repines, repining, repined)** literary 【文】 be unhappy or anxious 苦恼;发愁

replace /rɪ'pleɪs/ **verb (replaces, replacing, replaced) 1** take the place of 代替;替 **2** provide a substitute for 更换;调换 **3** put something back in its previous position 把…放回原处 ■ **replaceable** adjective.

replacement /rɪ'pleɪsmənt/ **noun 1** the action of replacing 代替;取代;更换 **2** a person or thing that takes the place of another 接替者;代替物;替换品

replay noun /'riːpleɪ/ **1** a match that is played again because the previous game was a draw (比赛打平后的)重赛 **2** an act of playing a recording again 重播;重放 • **verb** /ˌriː'pleɪ/ **1** play back a recording 重播,重放(录音) **2** play a match again 重新比赛

replenish /rɪ'plenɪʃ/ **verb** fill up a supply again after using some of it 补充(供给) ■ **replenishment** noun.

replete /rɪ'pliːt/ **adjective 1 (replete with)** filled or well supplied with 充满的;装满的 **2** very full with food 吃饱喝足的 ■ **repletion** noun.

replica /'replɪkə/ **noun** an exact copy or model of something 复制品;摹本

replicate /'replɪkeɪt/ **verb (replicates, replicating, replicated)** make an exact copy of 复制;摹写 ■ **replication** noun.

reply /rɪ'plaɪ/ **verb (replies, replying, replied) 1** say or write a response to something said or written 回答;答复;回应 **2** respond with a similar action 回击 • **noun (plural replies)** a spoken or written response 回答;答复;回应

report /rɪ'pɔːt/ **verb 1** give a spoken or written account of something 报

告；汇报 **2 (be reported)** be said or rumoured 传闻；传说 **3** make a formal complaint about 举报；告发 **4** tell someone in authority that you have arrived or are ready to do something 报到 **5 (report to)** be responsible to a manager 对···负责；隶属 • **noun 1** a spoken or written account of something 报告；报告书 **2** Brit.【英】a teacher's written assessment of a pupil's progress (学生的)学习情况报告单 **3** the sound of an explosion or a gun being fired 爆炸声；射击声

reportage /rɪ'pɔːtɪdʒ/ **noun** the reporting of news by the press and the broadcasting media 新闻报道

reporter /rɪ'pɔːtə(r)/ **noun** a person who reports news for a newspaper or broadcasting company 记者

repose /rɪ'pəʊz/ **noun** a state of restfulness, peace, or calm 平静；安静；安宁 • **verb (reposes, reposing, reposed)** lie or be kept in a particular place 安放；安置

repository /rɪ'pɒzɪtri/ **noun (plural repositories) 1** a place or container for storage 贮藏室；贮物器 **2** a place where a lot of something is found 仓库，库房

repossess /ˌriː pə'zes/ **verb** take possession of something when a buyer fails to make the required payments (购买者未能如期付款时)取回，收回 ■ **repossession** noun.

reprehensible /ˌreprɪ'hensəbl/ **adjective** deserving condemnation; bad 应受谴责的；应受指摘的；不道德的

represent /ˌreprɪ'zent/ **verb 1** act and speak on behalf of 代表 **2** amount to 意味着 **3** be a specimen or example of ···的典型(或范例) **4** show or describe in a particular way 展现，表现 **5** depict in a work of art (在艺术作品中)描绘 **6** signify or symbolize 象征

representation /ˌreprɪzen'teɪʃn/ **noun 1** the action of representing 代表；代理 **2** an image, model, etc. of something 图像；模型 **3 (representations)** statements made to an authority 陈述；诉说；抗议

representational /ˌreprɪzen'teɪʃnl/ **adjective 1** relating to representation 代表性的 **2** (of art) not abstract (美术)具象派的

representative /ˌreprɪ'zentətɪv/ **adjective 1** typical of a class or group 代表···的；典型的 **2** consisting of people chosen to act and speak on behalf of a wider group 由代表组成的；代议制的 **3** portraying or symbolizing something 描绘···的；象征···的 • **noun 1** a person chosen to act and speak for another or others 代表，代理人 **2** a person who travels around trying to sell their company's products 代理商 **3** an example of a class or group 代表；典型

repress /rɪ'pres/ **verb 1** bring under control by force 镇压；平息 **2** try not to have or show a thought or feeling 抑制，压制(想法或情感) **3 (repressed)** tending to keep your feelings or desires hidden 压抑的，克制的 ■ **repression** noun.

repressive /rɪ'presɪv/ **adjective** restricting personal freedom 压制的；强制性的

reprieve /rɪ'priːv/ **noun 1** the cancellation or postponement of a punishment, especially the death penalty (处罚)的取消；(尤指)死刑缓刑令 **2** a brief delay before something undesirable happens 暂时缓解 • **verb (reprieves, reprieving, reprieved)** give someone a reprieve 取消对(某人)的处罚；缓期执行(某人)的死刑

reprimand /'reprɪmɑːnd/ **verb** speak severely to someone because they have done something wrong 训斥；斥

责;谴责 • **noun** an act of reprimanding someone 训斥;斥责;谴责

reprint **verb** /ˌriːˈprɪnt/ print again 重印;再版 • **noun** /ˈriːprɪnt/ **1** an act of reprinting 重印;再版 **2** a copy of a book that has been reprinted 重印本;再版本

reprisal /rɪˈpraɪzl/ **noun** an act of retaliation 报复;报复行动

reprise /rɪˈpriːz/ **noun 1** a repeated passage in music (音乐中的)重奏,反复 **2** a further performance of something 重演;重复 • **verb** (**reprises, reprising, reprised**) repeat a piece of music or a performance 重奏;重演

reproach /rɪˈprəʊtʃ/ **verb** express disapproval of or disappointment with 批评;指责 • **noun** an expression of disapproval or disappointment 批评话;指责的言语 ■ **reproachful** adjective **reproachfully** adverb.

reprobate /ˈreprəbeɪt/ **noun** a person who behaves in an immoral way 堕落者;道德败坏者

reproduce /ˌriːprəˈdjuːs/ **verb** (**reproduces, reproducing, reproduced**) **1** produce a copy or representation of 复制;翻印 **2** recreate in a different medium or context 使重现 **3** produce young or offspring 生殖;繁殖

reproduction /ˌriːprəˈdʌkʃn/ **noun 1** the process of reproducing 复制;重现;繁殖 **2** a copy of a work of art (艺术品的)复制品 ■ **reproductive** adjective.

reproof /rɪˈpruːf/ **noun** a reprimand 责备;指摘;申斥

reprove /rɪˈpruːv/ **verb** (**reproves, reproving, reproved**) reprimand; tell off 责备;指摘;申斥

reptile /ˈreptaɪl/ **noun** a cold-blooded animal of a class that includes snakes, lizards, crocodiles, and tortoises 爬行动物 ■ **reptilian** adjective.

republic /rɪˈpʌblɪk/ **noun** a state in which power is held by the people and their representatives, and which has a president rather than a king or queen 共和国;共和政体

republican /rɪˈpʌblɪkən/ **adjective 1** belonging to or characteristic of a republic 共和国的;共和政体的 **2** in favour of republican government 拥护共和政体的 **3** (**Republican**) (in the US) relating to or supporting the Republican Party (美国)拥护共和党的 • **noun 1** a person in favour of republican government 拥护共和政体者;共和主义者 **2** (**Republican**) (in the US) a member or supporter of the Republican Party (美国)共和党党员 **3** (**Republican**) a person who wants Ireland to be one country 北爱尔兰共和主义者(主张统一爱尔兰) ■ **republicanism** noun.

repudiate /rɪˈpjuːdieɪt/ **verb** (**repudiates, repudiating, repudiated**) **1** refuse to accept or support 拒绝接受;拒绝支持 **2** deny that something is true or valid 否认…属实;否定…的有效性 ■ **repudiation** noun.

repugnance /rɪˈpʌɡnəns/ **noun** great disgust 强烈的反感;厌恶

repugnant /rɪˈpʌɡnənt/ **adjective** very unpleasant 令人厌恶的;使人反感的

repulse /rɪˈpʌls/ **verb** (**repulses, repulsing, repulsed**) **1** drive back by force 击退 **2** reject or refuse to accept 拒绝;拒绝接受 **3** give someone a feeling of strong disgust 使极端厌恶;使十分反感 • **noun** the action of repulsing 击退;拒绝

repulsion /rɪˈpʌlʃn/ **noun 1** a feeling of strong disgust 厌恶;憎恶;反感 **2** a force by which objects tend to push each other away 斥力;排斥力

repulsive /rɪˈpʌlsɪv/ **adjective** arousing a feeling of strong disgust 令人厌恶的;引起反感的

reputable /ˈrepjətəbl/ **adjective** having a good reputation 声誉好的;

享有声望的

reputation /ˌrepjuˈteɪʃn/ **noun** the beliefs or opinions that people generally hold about someone or something 名气；名声

repute /rɪˈpjuːt/ **noun 1** the opinion that people have of someone or something 名气；名声 **2** good reputation 美名；声誉；名望 • **verb 1** (**be reputed**) have a particular reputation 有…的名声 **2** (**reputed**) believed to exist 认为存在的 ■ **reputedly** adverb.

request /rɪˈkwest/ **noun 1** an act of asking politely or formally for something 请求；要求 **2** something that is asked for in this way 请求（或要求）的内容 • **verb** politely or formally ask for something, or ask someone to do something 请求；要求

requiem /ˈrekwiəm/ **noun 1** a Christian Mass for the souls of dead people (基督教的)追思弥撒，安魂弥撒 **2** a musical work based on such a Mass (做追思弥撒时奏的)追思曲，安魂曲

require /rɪˈkwaɪə(r)/ **verb** (**requires, requiring, required**) **1** need or want something for a purpose 需要 **2** instruct or expect someone to do something 指示；期望 **3** regard a particular thing as necessary or compulsory 要求；规定

requirement /rɪˈkwaɪəmənt/ **noun 1** something that you need or want 需要的东西；必需品 **2** something that is compulsory 要求的东西；规定

requisite /ˈrekwɪzɪt/ **adjective** necessary because of circumstances or regulations 必要的；需要的 • **noun** a thing that is needed for a particular purpose 必需品

requisition /ˌrekwɪˈzɪʃn/ **noun 1** an official order allowing property or materials to be taken or used 征用令 **2** the taking of goods for military or public use 征用 • **verb** officially take possession of something, especially during a war (尤指在战争期间)征用

rerun **verb** /ˌriːˈrʌn/ (**reruns, rerunning, reran;** past participle **rerun**) show, stage, or perform again 再播放；再上映；再上演 • **noun** /ˈriːrʌn/ a rerun event, competition, or programme 重新赛跑；重新比赛；(节目的)重新播放

resat /ˌriːˈsæt/ past and past participle of RESIT.

reschedule /ˌriːˈʃedjuːl/ **verb** (**reschedules, rescheduling, rescheduled**) change the timing of 改变…的时间安排

rescind /rɪˈsɪnd/ **verb** cancel or repeal a law, order, etc. 废除，撤销(法律、命令等)

rescue /ˈreskjuː/ **verb** (**rescues, rescuing, rescued**) save from danger or distress 营救；救援；挽救 • **noun** an act of rescuing or being rescued 营救行动 ■ **rescuer** noun.

research **noun** /rɪˈsɜːtʃ, ˈriːsɜːtʃ/ the study of materials and sources in order to establish facts and reach new conclusions 研究；调查 • **verb** /rɪˈsɜːtʃ/ carry out research into a subject, for a book, programme, etc. 研究；调查 ■ **researcher** noun.

resemblance /rɪˈzembləns/ **noun 1** the state of resembling 相像；形似 **2** a way in which things resemble each other 相似

resemble /rɪˈzembl/ **verb** (**resembles, resembling, resembled**) look or be like 像；与…相似

resent /rɪˈzent/ **verb** feel bitter towards 怨恨；对…愤恨不平

resentful /rɪˈzentfl/ **adjective** bitter about something you think is unfair 气愤的；怨恨的 ■ **resentfully** adverb.

resentment /rɪˈzentmənt/ **noun** a feeling of bitterness about something unfair 怨恨；不满

reservation /ˌrezəˈveɪʃn/ **noun 1** the action of reserving 留出；留存 **2** an arrangement for something to be reserved 预订 **3** an area of land set aside for a native people (土著居民的)居留地，保留地 **4** an expression of doubt about a statement 保留意见；存疑

reserve /rɪˈzɜːv/ **verb (reserves, reserving, reserved) 1** keep something to be used in the future 保留；留存；储备 **2** arrange for a seat, ticket, etc. to be kept for a particular person 预订(座位、票等) **3** have or keep a right or power 保留(权利或权力) • **noun 1** a supply of something available for use if required 储备(物) **2** money kept available by a bank, company, etc. 储备金；准备金 **3** a military force kept to reinforce others or for use in an emergency 后备军；预备队；预备役 **4** an extra player in a team, who can be called on to play if necessary 预备队员；替补队员 **5** (**the reserves**) the second-choice team 替补队伍；预备队 **6** an area of land set aside for wildlife or for a native people 自然保护区；专用地 **7** a lack of warmth or openness 矜持；内向；寡言

reserved /rɪˈzɜːvd/ **adjective** slow to reveal emotion or opinions 矜持的；寡言少语的

reservist /rɪˈzɜːvɪst/ **noun** a member of a military reserve force 预备役军人

reservoir /ˈrezəvwɑː(r)/ **noun 1** a large lake used as a source of water supply 水库 **2** a place where fluid collects 贮液器；贮液槽 **3** a supply or source of something 储藏；蓄积；宝库

reshuffle /ˌriːˈʃʌfl/ **verb (reshuffles, reshuffling, reshuffled) 1** change the roles or positions of government ministers 改组 **2** rearrange 重新安排 • **noun** an act of reshuffling 改组；重新安排

reside /rɪˈzaɪd/ **verb (resides, residing, resided)** formal 【正式】 **1** live in a particular place 居住；定居 **2** (**reside in** or **with**) (of a right or power) belong to a person or group (权利或权力)归属，属于 **3** (**reside in**) (of a quality) be naturally present in (性质)存在，在于

residence /ˈrezɪdəns/ **noun 1** the fact of living somewhere 居住；定居 **2** the place where a person lives 住所；居所

residency /ˈrezɪdənsi/ **noun** (plural **residencies**) the fact of living in a place 居住；定居

resident /ˈrezɪdənt/ **noun 1** a person who lives somewhere on a long-term basis 居民；定居者 **2** Brit. 【英】 a guest in a hotel (旅馆的)住客，寄宿者 • **adjective** living somewhere on a long-term basis 定居的；常驻的

residential /ˌrezɪˈdenʃl/ **adjective 1** involving residence 居住的 **2** providing accommodation 提供住宿的 **3** occupied by private houses 作住所用的

residual /rɪˈzɪdjuəl/ **adjective** remaining after the greater part has gone or been taken away 残余的；剩余的

residue /ˈrezɪdjuː/ **noun** a small amount of something that remains after the main part has gone or been taken 剩余物；残留物

resign /rɪˈzaɪn/ **verb 1** voluntarily leave a job or position of office 辞职；辞去 **2** (**be resigned**) accept that something bad cannot be avoided 听从；顺从

resignation /ˌrezɪɡˈneɪʃn/ **noun 1** an act of resigning 辞职 **2** a document stating that you intend to resign 辞职信；辞呈 **3** acceptance of something bad but inevitable 听任；顺从

resilient /rɪˈzɪliənt/ **adjective 1** able to spring back into shape after bending, stretching, or being compressed (弯曲、伸展或压缩后)能复原的;有弹性的 **2** able to withstand or recover quickly from difficult conditions 适应性强的;可迅速恢复的 ■ **resilience** noun.

resin /'rezɪn/ **noun 1** a sticky substance produced by some trees (某些树木分泌的)树脂 **2** a synthetic substance used as the basis of plastics, adhesives, etc. 合成树脂(用作塑料、黏合剂等的基本原料)

resist /rɪ'zɪst/ **verb 1** withstand the action or effect of 按捺;忍住;拒受…的影响 **2** try to prevent or fight against 试图阻止;试图对抗 **3** stop yourself having or doing something tempting 抵制,抗拒(诱惑)

resistance /rɪ'zɪstəns/ **noun 1** the action of resisting 对抗;抵制;抗拒 **2** a secret organization that fights against an occupying enemy 抵抗组织 **3** the ability not to be affected by something 抵抗力 **4** the degree to which a material or device resists the passage of an electric current 电阻 ■ **resistant** adjective.

resistor /rɪ'zɪstə(r)/ **noun** a device that resists the passage of an electric current 电阻器

resit /ˌriː'sɪt/ **verb (resits, resitting, resat)** Brit. 【英】take an exam again after failing (考试不及格后)重考,补考

resolute /'rezəluːt/ **adjective** determined 坚决的;坚定的;有决心的 ■ **resolutely** adverb.

resolution /ˌrezə'luːʃn/ **noun 1** a firm decision 决议 **2** a formal statement of opinion by a parliament (立法机关的)决议 **3** determination 决心;坚定 **4** the resolving of a problem or dispute (问题或争端的)解决 **5** the degree to which detail is visible in a photograph or an image on a computer or television screen (照片或电脑、电视屏幕的)分辨率

resolve /rɪ'zɒlv/ **verb (resolves, resolving, resolved) 1** find a solution to 解决 **2** decide firmly on a course of action 决定;决意 **3** take a decision by a formal vote (通过正式投票)决定 **4** (resolve into) separate into different parts 分解;解体 ● **noun** determination 决心;坚定信念

resonant /'rezənənt/ **adjective 1** (of sound) deep, clear, and ringing(声音)洪亮的,回响的 **2** having the power to bring images, memories, or feelings into your mind 激起回响的;引起共鸣的 ■ **resonance** noun.

resonate /'rezəneɪt/ **verb (resonates, resonating, resonated)** make a deep, clear, ringing sound 起鸣声;使回响

resort /rɪ'zɔːt/ **noun 1** a place visited for holidays 度假地;胜地 **2** a strategy or course of action 采取;诉诸 ● **verb (resort to)** turn to a strategy or course of action so as to resolve a difficult situation 采取(策略或行动);诉诸

resound /rɪ'zaʊnd/ **verb 1** make a ringing, booming, or echoing sound (使)回响;(使)回荡;(声音)鸣响 **2** (resounding) definite; unmistakable 肯定的;确定的;确凿无误的

resource /rɪ'sɔːs/ **noun 1** (resources) a stock or supply of materials or assets 资源;资产;资财 **2** something that can be used to help achieve an aim 有助于实现目标的东西 **3** (resources) personal qualities that help you to cope with difficult circumstances 才智 ● **verb (be resourced)** be provided with resources 获得资源

resourceful /rɪ'sɔːsfl/ **adjective** able to find quick and clever ways to overcome difficulties 机敏的;足智多谋的 ■ **resourcefully** adverb **resourcefulness** noun.

respect /rɪ'spekt/ **noun 1** a feeling of admiration for someone because of their qualities or achievements 尊敬;尊重 **2** consideration for the feelings or rights of other people 尊重；重视 **3** (**respects**) polite greetings 敬意；问候 **4** a particular aspect, point, or detail 方面；细节 • verb **1** have respect for 尊敬；尊重 **2** avoid harming or interfering with 顾及；避免伤害 **3** agree to observe a law, principle, etc. 遵守(法律、原则等)

respectable /rɪˈspektəbl/ adjective **1** regarded by society as being correct or proper 正派的；体面的；可敬的 **2** adequate or acceptable 还不错的；过得去的 ■ **respectability** noun **respectably** adverb.

respectful /rɪˈspektfl/ adjective feeling or showing respect 尊敬的；表示敬意的 ■ **respectfully** adverb.

respecting /rɪˈspektɪŋ/ preposition with reference to 关于；至于

respective /rɪˈspektɪv/ adjective belonging or relating separately to each of two or more people or things 各自的；各个的；分别的

respectively /rɪˈspektɪvli/ adverb individually and in the order already mentioned 各自地；各个地；分别地

respiration /ˌrespəˈreɪʃn/ noun the action of breathing 呼吸

respirator /ˈrespəreɪtə(r)/ noun **1** a device worn over the face to prevent you breathing in dust, smoke, etc. 口罩；防毒面具 **2** a device that enables someone to breathe when they cannot do so naturally (人工)呼吸器，呼吸机

respiratory /rəˈspɪrətri/ adjective relating to breathing 呼吸的

respire /rɪˈspaɪə(r)/ verb (**respires**, **respiring**, **respired**) technical 【术语】 breathe 呼吸

respite /ˈrespaɪt/ noun a short period of rest or relief from something difficult or unpleasant 短暂休息；喘息时间

resplendent /rɪˈsplendənt/ adjective attractive and impressive 灿烂的；辉

煌的；华丽的

respond /rɪˈspɒnd/ verb say or do something in reply or as a reaction 回答；作答；作出反应

respondent /rɪˈspɒndənt/ noun **1** Law 【法律】 a person against whom a petition is filed, especially one in a divorce case (尤指离婚案的)被告 **2** a person who responds to a questionnaire or advertisement (问卷或广告的)答卷人，回应者

response /rɪˈspɒns/ noun an answer or reaction 回答；答复；反应

responsibility /rɪˌspɒnsəˈbɪləti/ noun (plural **responsibilities**) **1** the state of being responsible 负责；有责任 **2** the opportunity to act independently 责任(能力) **3** a thing which you are required to do as part of a job, role, or obligation 任务；职责；义务

responsible /rɪˈspɒnsəbl/ adjective **1** obliged to do something or look after someone 有义务的；需负责任的 **2** being the cause of something and so able to be blamed or credited for it 有责任的；应受责备(或褒奖)的 **3** able to be trusted 可靠的；可信赖的 **4** (of a job) involving important duties or decisions (工作)责任重大的，重要的 **5** (**responsible to**) having to report to a senior person 对(上级)负责的；隶属(上级)的 ■ **responsibly** adverb.

> ✔ 拼写指南 respon*sible*, not -*able*. responsible 不要拼作 -able。

responsive /rɪˈspɒnsɪv/ adjective responding readily and positively 作出反应的；反应积极的

rest¹ /rest/ verb **1** stop working or moving in order to relax or recover your strength 休息；歇息 **2** place something so that it stays in a particular position 放；安放 **3** remain or be left in a particular condition 保持不变；*rest assured* 放心 **4** (**rest on**) depend or be based on 依靠；依赖 **5** (**rest**

with) (of power, responsibility, etc.) belong to (权力、责任等)归于，属于
• noun 1 a period of resting 休息期间 2 a motionless state 静止 3 an object that is used to hold or support something 撑架；支座；托垫 4 a brief interval of silence in a piece of music (音乐中的)休止

rest² noun the remaining part, people, or things 剩余部分；其余

restaurant /'restront/ noun a place where people pay to sit and eat meals that are cooked on the premises 餐馆；饭店

restaurateur /ˌrestərə'tɜ:(r)/ noun a person who owns and manages a restaurant 饭店老板

> ✔ 拼写指南 note that there is no *n*: restaura*teur*. 注意 restaurateur 中没有 n。

restful /'restfl/ adjective having a quiet and soothing quality 安闲宁静的

restitution /ˌrestɪ'tju:ʃn/ noun 1 the restoration of something lost or stolen to its proper owner 物归原主；归还 2 payment for injury or loss that has been suffered 伤害补偿；赔偿

restive /'restɪv/ adjective unable to keep still or silent: restless 焦躁不安的；不耐烦的

restless /'restləs/ adjective unable to rest or relax 焦躁不安的；烦躁的 ■ **restlessly** adverb.

restorative /rɪ'stɔ:rətɪv/ adjective able to restore health or strength 促使康复的；有助于恢复体力的

restore /rɪ'stɔ:(r)/ verb (**restores**, **restoring**, **restored**) 1 bring back a previous practice, situation, etc. 恢复(先前的做法、状况等) 2 return someone or something to a previous condition, place, position, etc. 使复原，使复位；使复职 3 repair or renovate a

building, work of art, etc. 修复，整修，修缮(建筑物、艺术品等) ■ **restoration** noun **restorer** noun.

restrain /rɪ'streɪn/ verb 1 keep under control or within limits 控制；限制；约束 2 stop someone moving or acting freely 管束；拘禁

restrained /rɪ'streɪnd/ adjective 1 reserved or unemotional 克制的；节制的；不露感情的 2 not richly decorated or brightly coloured; subtle 素淡的；婉约的

restraint /rɪ'streɪnt/ noun 1 the action of keeping someone or something under control 控制；限制；约束 2 a device which limits or prevents freedom of movement 约束装置 3 self-controlled behaviour 克制；节制

restrict /rɪ'strɪkt/ verb 1 put a limit on 限制；约束；限定 2 stop someone moving or acting freely 管束；拘禁

restricted /rɪ'strɪktɪd/ adjective 1 limited in extent, number, or scope (程度、数量或见识)受限制的，有限的 2 not open to the public; secret 保密的；秘密的

restriction /rɪ'strɪkʃn/ noun 1 a rule, law, etc. that prevents free movement or action 限制条件；制约措施 2 the action of restricting 限制；约束；限定

restrictive /rɪ'strɪktɪv/ adjective preventing freedom of action or movement 限制性的；约束性的

restroom /'restru:m/ noun N. Amer.【北美】 a toilet in a public building (公共建筑内的)厕所，洗手间

result /rɪ'zʌlt/ noun 1 a thing that is caused or produced by something else 结果；后果 2 a piece of information obtained by experiment or calculation (实验或计算的)结果，答案 3 a final score or mark in an exam or sports event (考试)成绩，(体育比赛)结果，比分 4 a satisfactory or favourable outcome 成果；好成绩 • verb 1 hap-

pen because of something else 由…
引起；由…造成 **2 (result in)** have a
particular outcome 导致(某种后果)

resultant /rɪˈzʌltənt/ **adjective**
happening or produced as a result 作
为结果的；因而发生的

resume /rɪˈzuːm/ **verb (resumes,
resuming, resumed)** begin again
or continue after a pause (中断后)重
新开始，继续 ■ **resumption** noun.

résumé /ˈrezjumeɪ/ **noun 1** a
summary 摘要；梗概 **2** N. Amer. 【北
美】a curriculum vitae 履历；简历

resurgent /rɪˈsɜːdʒənt/ **adjective**
becoming stronger or more popular
again 复兴的；再度流行的 ■ **resur-
gence** noun.

resurrect /ˌrezəˈrekt/ **verb 1** restore
to life 使复活 **2** start using or doing
again 重新使用；复兴

resurrection /ˌrezəˈrekʃn/ **noun 1**
the action of resurrecting 复活；重新
使用；复兴 **2 (the Resurrection)** (in
Christian belief) the time when Jesus
rose from the dead (基督教信仰中的)
耶稣复活

resuscitate /rɪˈsʌsɪteɪt/ **verb (resus-
citates, resuscitating, resus-
citated)** make someone conscious
again 使复活；使苏醒 ■ **resuscitation** noun.

✔ 拼写指南 note that it is -*susc*-, not
-*suss*-: re*susc*itate. 注意 resuscitate
中 -susc-不要拼作 -suss-。

retail /ˈriːteɪl/ **noun** the sale of goods
to the public 零售；售卖 • **verb 1** sell
goods to the public 零售，售卖(货
物) **2 (retail at or for)** be sold for a
particular price 以(某价格)出售 ■ **retailer** noun.

retain /rɪˈteɪn/ **verb 1** continue to
have; keep possession of 留住；保
存 **2** absorb and continue to hold a
substance 保存；保持 **3 (retaining)**
keeping something in place 固定的

retainer /rɪˈteɪnə(r)/ **noun 1** a fee paid

in advance to a barrister to secure
their services (聘请律师的)定金 **2** a
servant who has worked for a family
for a long time (服务多年的)家仆，仆
人

retake verb /riːˈteɪk/ **(retakes, retaking,
retook;** past participle **retaken) 1** take
a test or exam again 重测；重考 **2**
regain possession of 再夺走；再占有
• **noun** /ˈriːteɪk/ a test or exam that is
retaken 重测；重考

retaliate /rɪˈtælieɪt/ **verb (retaliates,
retaliating, retaliated)** make an
attack in return for a similar attack
报复；以牙还牙 ■ **retaliation** noun
retaliatory adjective.

retard /rɪˈtɑːd/ **verb** stop from
developing or progressing 阻滞；减
缓 ■ **retardation** noun.

retarded /rɪˈtɑːdɪd/ **adjective** offensive
【冒犯】less developed mentally than
is usual at a particular age 迟钝的；
弱智的

retch /retʃ/ **verb** make the sound and
movements of vomiting 干呕；作呕

retention /rɪˈtenʃn/ **noun** the action
of retaining, or the state of being
retained 保留；保持；留置

retentive /rɪˈtentɪv/ **adjective** (of a
person's memory) effective in retaining impressions (记忆力)强
的；能记住的

rethink /riːˈθɪŋk/ **verb (rethinks,
rethinking, rethought)** consider a
policy or course of action again 再
想；重新考虑 • **noun** an instance of
rethinking 重新考虑，反思

reticent /ˈretɪsnt/ **adjective** not
revealing your thoughts or feelings
readily 不愿表露想法的；内向的 ■ **reti-
cence** noun.

retina /ˈretɪnə/ **noun (plural retinas or
retinae** /ˈretɪniː/) a layer at the back
of the eyeball that is sensitive to
light and sends impulses to the brain
视网膜

R

retinue /'retɪnjuː/ **noun** a group of assistants accompanying an important person (要人的)随员;扈从

retire /rɪ'taɪə(r)/ **verb** (**retires, retiring, retired**) **1** leave your job and stop working, especially because you have reached a particular age (尤指因到某一年龄而)退休,退职 **2** withdraw from a race or match because of accident or injury (因意外或受伤)退出(比赛) **3** formal 【正式】 leave a place 离开 **4** (of a jury) leave the courtroom to decide the verdict of a trial (陪审团)退下(去考虑如何裁决) **5** go to bed 就寝;上床睡觉 ■ **retired** adjective.

retirement /rɪ'taɪəmənt/ **noun 1** the action of retiring 退休;退职 **2** the period of life after retiring from work 退休生涯;退休时期

retiring /rɪ'taɪərɪŋ/ **adjective** tending to avoid company; shy 离群索居的;羞怯的;害羞的

retook /riː'tʊk/ past of RETAKE.

retort[1] /rɪ'tɔːt/ **verb** say something sharp or witty in answer to a remark or accusation 反驳;回嘴 • **noun** a sharp or witty reply (尖锐或机智的)反驳,回嘴

retort[2] **noun** a glass container with a long neck, used for distilling liquids and heating chemicals 曲颈甑;蒸馏甑

retouch /riː'tʌtʃ/ **verb** make slight improvements to a painting, photograph, etc. 润色,修整(画作、照片等)

retrace /rɪ'treɪs/ **verb** (**retraces, retracing, retraced**) **1** go back over the route that you have just taken 沿(同一路线)折返;原路返回 **2** follow a route taken by someone else 追踪 **3** trace something back to its source 追溯;回溯

retract /rɪ'trækt/ **verb 1** draw something back 缩回;缩进 **2** with-draw a statement or accusation 撤回,收回(声明或指控) **3** go back on an undertaking 违背(承诺) ■ **retractable** adjective **retraction** noun.

retreat /rɪ'triːt/ **verb 1** (of an army) withdraw from confrontation with enemy forces (军队)撤退,退却 **2** move back from a difficult situation 退缩 **3** withdraw to a quiet or secluded place 退避;躲避 • **noun 1** an act of retreating 撤退;退缩;退避 **2** a quiet or secluded place 僻静处;隐居处 **3** a quiet place where people go for a time to pray and meditate 静养所

retrench /rɪ'trentʃ/ **verb** reduce costs or spending in times of economic difficulty (在经济困难时期)削减费用(或开支) ■ **retrenchment** noun.

retrial /riː'traɪəl/ **noun** a second or further trial 再审;复审

retribution /ˌretrɪ'bjuːʃn/ **noun** severe punishment inflicted as revenge 惩罚;报应

retrieve /rɪ'triːv/ **verb** (**retrieves, retrieving, retrieved**) **1** get or bring back 重新得到;取回;领回 **2** find or extract information stored in a computer 检索(计算机中存储的信息) **3** improve a bad situation 补救;挽救 ■ **retrieval** noun.

retriever /rɪ'triːvə(r)/ **noun** a breed of dog used for finding and bringing back game that has been shot (会衔回猎物的)寻回犬

retrograde /'retrəɡreɪd/ **adjective** directed or moving backwards or to a worse state 向后的;后退的;衰退的;恶化的

retrogressive /ˌretrəʊ'ɡresɪv/ **adjective** going back to an earlier and inferior state 倒退的;恶化的 ■ **retrogression** noun.

retrorocket /'retrəʊrɒkɪt/ **noun** a small rocket on a spacecraft or missile, fired in the direction of travel to slow it down (航天器或导

(弹上的)制动火箭,减速火箭

retrospect /'retrəspekt/ noun (**in retrospect**) when looking back on a past event 回想;回顾;追溯

retrospective /ˌretrəˈspektɪv/ adjective **1** looking back on or dealing with past events or situations 回顾的;回想的 **2** taking effect from a date in the past 有追溯效力的 ▪ noun an exhibition showing the development of an artist's work over a period of time (艺术家)作品回顾展 ▪ **retrospectively** adverb.

retroussé /rəˈtruːseɪ/ adjective (of a person's nose) turned up at the tip (鼻子)尖端上翘的

retsina /retˈsiːnə/ noun a Greek white wine flavoured with resin 松香味希腊白葡萄酒

return /rɪˈtɜːn/ verb **1** come or go back to a place 回;返回 **2** (**return to**) go back to a particular state or activity 复归(某状态);恢复(某活动) **3** give, send, or put back 送回;归还;放回 **4** feel, say, or do the same thing in response 回报;回应;报答 **5** (in tennis) hit the ball back to an opponent (网球运动中)回(球) **6** (of a judge or jury) give a verdict (法官或陪审团)作出, 宣布(裁决) **7** produce a profit 产生(收益) **8** elect someone to a political office 选举, 推举(政治家) ▪ noun **1** an act of returning 送回;归还;恢复 **2** a profit from an investment 收益;盈利 **3** Brit. 【英】a ticket that lets you travel to a place and back again 往返票

reunify /ˌriːˈjuːnɪfaɪ/ verb (**reunifies, reunifying, reunified**) make a place a united country again 使重新统一 ▪ **reunification** noun.

reunion /ˌriːˈjuːnɪən/ noun **1** the process of reuniting 再联合;再会合 **2** a gathering of people who have not seen each other for some time 团聚;团圆;重聚

reunite /ˌriːjuːˈnaɪt/ verb (**reunites, reuniting, reunited**) bring two or more people or things together again 使再联合;使重新结合

reuse /riːˈjuːz/ verb (**reuses, reusing, reused**) use something again 再使用;重新使用 ▪ **reusable** adjective.

Rev. or **Revd** abbreviation Reverend.

rev /rev/ informal 【非正式】noun (**revs**) the number of revolutions of an engine per minute (发动机的)每分钟转数 ▪ verb (**revs, revving, revved**) make an engine run quickly by pressing the accelerator 加快(发动机)的转速

revamp verb /ˌriːˈvæmp/ alter something so as to improve it 改进,翻新 ▪ noun /ˈriːvæmp/ a new and improved version of something 改进之物;翻新之物

reveal /rɪˈviːl/ verb **1** make previously unknown or secret information known 透露;揭露 **2** allow something hidden to be seen 使显露;展现,显示

revealing /rɪˈviːlɪŋ/ adjective **1** giving out interesting or significant information 透露信息的;有启迪性的 **2** (of a garment) allowing a lot of your body to be seen (衣服)过分暴露的

reveille /rɪˈvæli/ noun a signal sounded on a bugle, drum, etc. to wake up soldiers in the morning (军队的)起床号

revel /ˈrevl/ verb (**revels, revelling, revelled**; US spelling 【美拼作】**revels, reveling, reveled**) **1** spend time enjoying yourself in a lively, noisy way 作乐;狂欢 **2** (**revel in**) get great pleasure from 陶醉于;醉心于 ▪ noun (**revels**) lively, noisy celebrations 喧闹的庆祝活动 ▪ **reveller** noun **revelry** noun (plural **revelries**).

revelation /ˌrevəˈleɪʃn/ noun **1** the revealing of something previously unknown 揭露；揭示；透露 **2** a surprising or remarkable thing 出人意料的事；惊人的发现

revelatory /ˌrevəˈleɪtəri/ **adjective** revealing something previously unknown 揭露的；揭示的

revenge /rɪˈvendʒ/ **noun** something harmful done to someone in return for something bad that they did to you 复仇；报复 • **verb** (**revenges, revenging, revenged**) (**revenge yourself** or **be revenged**) harm someone in return for something bad that they did to you 报仇；报复

revenue /ˈrevənjuː/ **noun** the income received by an organization, or by a government from taxes (机构的)收入；(政府的)税收

reverberate /rɪˈvɜːbəreɪt/ **verb** (**reverberates, reverberating, reverberated**) **1** (of a loud noise) be repeated as an echo (巨大响声)回响 **2** have continuing serious effects 产生持续深刻的影响 ■ **reverberation** noun.

revere /rɪˈvɪə(r)/ **verb** (**reveres, revering, revered**) respect or admire deeply 尊敬；崇敬

reverence /ˈrevərəns/ **noun** deep respect 尊敬；崇敬

reverend /ˈrevərənd/ **adjective** a title given to Christian ministers 尊敬的，可敬的(对基督教神职人员的称呼)

reverent /ˈrevərənt/ **adjective** showing reverence; deeply respectful 恭敬的；非常尊敬的 ■ **reverential** adjective **reverently** adverb.

reverie /ˈrevəri/ **noun** a daydream 白日梦；幻想

reversal /rɪˈvɜːsl/ **noun** 1 a change to an opposite direction, position, or course of action 反向；倒转；颠倒 **2** a harmful change of fortune (命运的)逆转

reverse /rɪˈvɜːs/ **verb** (**reverses, reversing, reversed**) **1** move backwards 倒退 **2** make something the opposite of what it was 使彻底改变 **3** turn something the other way round 使反向；使翻转 **4** cancel a judgement by a lower court 撤销(下级法院的判决) • **adjective** **1** going in or turned towards the opposite direction 反向的；倒转的 **2** opposite to the usual way 颠倒的；反转的 • **noun** **1** a complete change of direction or action 彻底转向；大逆转 **2** (**the reverse**) the opposite or contrary 相反情况；对立面 **3** a setback or defeat 挫折；失败 **4** the opposite side of something to the observer 反面；背部；后部 ■ **reversible** adjective.

reversion /rɪˈvɜːʃn/ **noun** a return to a previous state, practice, etc. 恢复；回复；回归

revert /rɪˈvɜːt/ **verb** (**revert to**) return to a previous state, practice, etc. 恢复；回复；回归

review /rɪˈvjuː/ **noun** 1 an examination of something to decide whether changes are necessary 审核；审查 **2** a critical assessment of a book, play, etc. (书、戏剧等的)评论，评介 **3** a report of an event that has already happened 回顾；检讨 **4** a ceremonial display of military forces (军事)检阅；阅兵 • **verb** **1** examine or consider something again 复查；再思考 **2** write a review of 评论；写…的评论文章 ■ **reviewer** noun.

revile /rɪˈvaɪl/ **verb** (**reviles, reviling, reviled**) criticize in a rude or scornful way 辱骂；谩骂

revise /rɪˈvaɪz/ **verb** (**revises, revising, revised**) **1** examine and alter a piece of writing 修订，校订(文本) **2** reconsider and change an opinion 修改，修正(意见) **3** Brit. 【英】reread work in order to prepare for an exam (为准备考试)复习功课 ■ **revision** noun.

revisionism /rɪˈvɪʒənɪzəm/ **noun**

disapproving 【贬】 the changing of accepted theories or principles 修正主义 ■ **revisionist** noun & adjective.

revitalize or **revitalise** /ˌriːˈvaɪtəlaɪz/ verb (**revitalizes, revitalizing, revitalized**) give new life and vitality to 使恢复生机；使恢复兴旺 ■ **revitalization** noun.

revival /rɪˈvaɪvl/ noun 1 an improvement in the condition, strength, or popularity of something (条件、力量的)进步，振兴；(某事物的)重新流行 2 a new production of an old play (旧剧的)重演

revivalism /rɪˈvaɪvəlɪzəm/ noun 1 the process of trying to reawaken interest in a particular religious faith (宗教)信仰复兴 2 the practice of returning to former customs, fashions, etc. (旧风俗、旧风尚等的)复苏，复兴 ■ **revivalist** noun & adjective.

revive /rɪˈvaɪv/ verb (**revives, reviving, revived**) 1 make conscious, healthy, or strong again 使苏醒，使恢复(或精力) 2 start doing, using, or performing something again 恢复做；重新使用；重新上演

revivify /ˌriːˈvɪvɪfaɪ/ verb (**revivifies, revivifying, revivified**) formal 【正式】 revive 使苏醒；使恢复健康(或精力)；恢复做，重新使用；重新上演

revoke /rɪˈvəʊk/ verb (**revokes, revoking, revoked**) make a decree, law, etc. no longer valid 撤销，废除(法令、法律等) ■ **revocation** noun.

revolt /rɪˈvəʊlt/ noun an act of rebellion or defiance 反叛，叛乱，造反 • verb 1 rebel against an authority 反叛，叛乱，造反 2 make someone feel disgust 使生反感，使厌恶

revolting /rɪˈvəʊltɪŋ/ adjective very unpleasant; disgusting 使人反感的；令人作呕的

revolution /ˌrevəˈluːʃn/ noun 1 the overthrow of a government by force, in favour of a new system 革命 2 a dramatic and far-reaching change 巨大变革；巨变 3 a single circular movement around a central point 旋转；绕转

revolutionary /ˌrevəˈluːʃənəri/ adjective 1 involving or causing dramatic change 巨变的；引起巨大变革的 2 taking part in, or relating to, political revolution (参加)革命的 • noun (plural **revolutionaries**) a person who starts or supports a political revolution 革命家；革命者

revolutionize or **revolutionise** /ˌrevəˈluːʃənaɪz/ verb (**revolutionizes, revolutionizing, revolutionized**) change something completely or fundamentally 彻底变革；根本改变

revolve /rɪˈvɒlv/ verb (**revolves, revolving, revolved**) 1 move in a circle around a central point 转动；旋转 2 (**revolve around**) treat as the most important element 围绕；以…为中心

revolver /rɪˈvɒlvə(r)/ noun a pistol with revolving chambers that allow several shots to be fired without reloading 左轮手枪

revue /rɪˈvjuː/ noun a theatrical show with short sketches, songs, and dances 轻松歌舞剧；滑稽歌舞串演

revulsion /rɪˈvʌlʃn/ noun a sense of disgust and loathing 厌恶；强烈反感

reward /rɪˈwɔːd/ noun something given in recognition of service, effort, or achievement 报偿；酬劳 • verb 1 give a reward to 酬谢；报偿 2 show appreciation of an action or quality by giving a reward 奖赏

rewarding /rɪˈwɔːdɪŋ/ adjective providing satisfaction 给予报偿的

rewind /ˌriːˈwaɪnd/ verb (**rewinds, rewinding, rewound**) wind a film or tape back to the beginning 倒回(影片或磁带)

rewire /ˌriːˈwaɪə(r)/ verb (**rewires, rewiring, rewired**) provide with new wiring 给…重配新线

rework /riː'wɜːk/ **verb** alter something in order to improve or update it 修正；改进

rhapsodize or **rhapsodise** /'ræpsədaɪz/ **verb** (**rhapsodizes**, **rhapsodizing**, **rhapsodized**) express great enthusiasm about someone or something 狂热表达

rhapsody /'ræpsədi/ **noun** (plural **rhapsodies**) **1** an expression of great enthusiasm 狂热表达 **2** a piece of music in one extended movement 狂想曲 ■ **rhapsodic** adjective.

rheostat /'riːəstæt/ **noun** a device for varying the amount of resistance in an electrical circuit 变阻器

rhesus factor /'riːsəs/ **noun** a substance found in the red blood cells of many humans (很多人体内红细胞中含有的)猕因子，Rh因子

rhesus monkey **noun** a small monkey found in southern Asia 猕猴,恒河猴(产于南亚)

rhetoric /'retərɪk/ **noun** **1** effective or persuasive public speaking 有说服力的演讲；修辞 **2** persuasive but insincere language 华而不实的言语

rhetorical /rɪ'tɒrɪkl/ **adjective** **1** relating to rhetoric 修辞的，**2** intended to persuade or impress 言辞浮夸的，词藻华丽的 **3** (of a question) asked for effect or to make a statement rather than to obtain an answer (问题)反问的 ■ **rhetorically** adverb.

rheumatic /ruː'mætɪk/ **adjective** relating to, or suffering from, rheumatism (患)风湿病的

rheumatism /'ruːmətɪzəm/ **noun** a disease with inflammation and pain in the joints and muscles 风湿病

rheumy /'ruːmi/ **adjective** (of a person's eyes) watery (人眼)湿润的

rhinestone /'raɪnstəʊn/ **noun** an imitation diamond 莱茵石(一种钻石仿制品)

rhino /'raɪnəʊ/ **noun** (plural **rhino** or **rhinos**) informal 【非正式】 a rhinoceros 犀，犀牛

rhinoceros /raɪ'nɒsərəs/ **noun** (plural **rhinoceros** or **rhinoceroses**) a large plant-eating animal with one or two horns on the nose and thick skin, found in Africa and Asia 犀，犀牛(产于非洲和亚洲)

rhizome /'raɪzəʊm/ **noun** a horizontal underground plant stem producing both roots and shoots 根茎；根状茎

rhododendron /ˌrəʊdə'dendrən/ **noun** a shrub with large clusters of bright flowers 杜鹃花

rhombus /'rɒmbəs/ **noun** (plural **rhombuses** or **rhombi** /'rɒmbaɪ/) a flat shape with four straight sides of equal length 菱形

rhubarb /'ruːbɑːb/ **noun** the thick leaf stalks of a plant, cooked and eaten as fruit 大黄；大黄茎

rhumba /'rʌmbə/ ⇒ 见 **RUMBA**.

rhyme /raɪm/ **noun** **1** a word that has the same sound or ends with the same sound as another 同韵词；押韵词 **2** similarity of sound between words or the endings of words 韵；押韵 **3** a short poem with rhyming lines 押韵短诗 • **verb** (**rhymes**, **rhyming**, **rhymed**) have or end with the same sound as another word or line (词或诗行)和…同韵，押韵 □ **rhyming slang** slang in which you use words that rhyme with the word you mean (e.g. *butcher's*, short for *butcher's hook*, meaning 'look') 同韵俚语(以同韵的词语替代另一个词语，如用简写为butcher's 的 butcher's hook 代替look)

✔ 拼写指南 remember the first *h*, following the *r*, in *rhyme* and *rhythm*. 记住拼写rhyme 和rhythm中r 之后的第一个h。

rhythm /'rɪðəm/ **noun** **1** a strong, regular repeated pattern of sound or rhythm movement 节奏；律动 **2** a regularly recurring sequence of events or actions 规律 □ **rhythm and blues** a type of music that is a combination of blues and jazz 节奏布鲁斯(布鲁斯音乐与爵士乐的混合)

rhythmic /ˈrɪðmɪk/ **adjective 1** having or relating to rhythm 有节奏的；有韵律的 **2** happening regularly 有规律的 ■ **rhythmically** adverb.

rib /rɪb/ **noun 1** each of a series of bones that are attached to the spine and curve around the chest 肋骨 **2** a curved structure supporting an arched roof or forming part of a boat's framework (拱形屋顶或船体的)肋拱 • **verb (ribs, ribbing, ribbed)** informal 【非正式】 tease someone good-naturedly (善意地)取笑，戏弄

ribald /ˈrɪbld/ **adjective** referring to sex in a rude but humorous way 粗俗诙谐的 ■ **ribaldry** noun.

riband /ˈrɪbənd/ **noun** old use 【旧】 a ribbon 缎带；丝带

ribbed /rɪbd/ **adjective** having a pattern of raised bands 有螺纹的

ribbon /ˈrɪbən/ **noun 1** a long, narrow strip of fabric, used for tying something or for decoration (用于捆扎或装饰的)缎带，绒带，丝带 **2** a long, narrow strip 带状物 **3** a narrow strip of inked material used to produce the characters in some typewriters (打字机的)色带

ribcage /ˈrɪbkeɪdʒ/ **noun** the bony frame formed by the ribs 胸腔；胸廓

riboflavin /ˌraɪbəˈfleɪvɪn/ **noun** vitamin B2 维生素B2；核黄素

rice /raɪs/ **noun** grains of a cereal plant which is grown for food on wet land in warm countries 大米；稻米

ricepaper /ˈraɪspeɪpə(r)/ **noun** thin edible paper made from a type of plant, used in oriental painting and in baking biscuits and cakes 米纸(用于东方绘画和烘烤糕饼，可食用)

rich /rɪtʃ/ **adjective 1** having a lot of money, assets, or resources 富有的；有钱的 **2** made of expensive materials 贵重的；昂贵的 **3** plentiful 丰富的；充裕的 **4** having or producing something in large amounts 富含…的；盛产…的 **5** (of food) containing a lot of fat, sugar, etc. (食物)油腻的 **6** (of a colour, sound, or smell) pleasantly deep and strong (色彩)浓艳的；(声音)深沉的；(气味)浓烈的 **7** (of soil or land) fertile (土壤或土地)肥沃的 ■ **richness** noun.

riches /ˈrɪtʃɪz/ **plural noun 1** large amounts of money or valuable possessions 财富；财产 **2** valuable natural resources 宝藏；珍贵的自然资源

richly /ˈrɪtʃli/ **adverb 1** in a rich way 富裕地；丰富地 **2** fully; thoroughly 完全地；十足地

Richter scale /ˈrɪktə(r)/ **noun** a scale for measuring the severity of an earthquake 里氏震级(地震等级的一种数值标度)

rick¹ /rɪk/ **noun** a stack of hay, corn, or straw 柴垛；玉米垛；草堆

rick² Brit. 【英】 **verb** strain part of your body slightly 轻度扭伤 • **noun** a slight sprain or strain 轻度扭伤

rickets /ˈrɪkɪts/ **noun** a disease of children in which the bones are softened and distorted 佝偻病

rickety /ˈrɪkəti/ **adjective** badly made and likely to collapse 摇晃的；不牢靠的

rickshaw /ˈrɪkʃɔː/ **noun** a light two-wheeled vehicle pulled by a person walking or riding a bicycle 人力车；黄包车

ricochet /ˈrɪkəʃeɪ/ **verb (ricochets, ricocheting, ricocheted)** (of a bullet or other fast-moving object) rebound off a surface (子弹等快速移动物体)弹射，反弹出去 • **noun** a shot or hit that ricochets (射击或撞击的)

反弹，弹开

rictus /'rɪktəs/ **noun** a fixed grimace or grin (定格的)鬼脸，咧嘴笑

rid /rɪd/ **verb** (rids, ridding, rid) **1** (rid someone/thing of) free a person or place of something unwanted 使摆脱 **2** (be or get rid of) be or make yourself free of 摆脱，除去

riddance /'rɪdns/ **noun** (good riddance) said when expressing relief at getting rid of someone or something 谢天谢地(用于表示庆幸摆脱某人或某事物)

ridden /'rɪdn/ past participle of RIDE. • **adjective** full of a particular unpleasant thing 充满…的: *disease-ridden* 疾病缠身的

riddle¹ /'rɪdl/ **noun** **1** a cleverly worded question that is asked as a game 谜语 **2** a puzzling person or thing 谜一般的人，谜

riddle² **verb** (usu. be riddled with) **1** make a lot of holes in 使布满窟窿 **2** fill with something bad or unpleasant 充斥，布满 • **noun** a type of large sieve 粗筛，格筛

ride /raɪd/ **verb** (rides, riding, rode; past participle ridden) **1** sit on and control the movement of a horse, bicycle, or motorcycle 骑(马或自行车)，驾驶(摩托车) **2** travel in a vehicle 乘(车) **3** be carried or supported by 受承载 **4** (ride up) (of clothing) gradually move upwards out of its proper position (衣服)向上拱，往上皱起 **5** (ride on) depend on 依靠，依托 • **noun** **1** an act of riding 骑；乘；搭乘 **2** a roller coaster, roundabout, etc. ridden at a fair or amusement park (游乐场所中的)供骑乘的游乐设施 **3** a path for horse riding 骑马道 □ **take someone for a ride** informal 【非正式】 deceive someone 欺骗(某人)

rider /'raɪdə(r)/ **noun** **1** a person who rides a horse, bicycle, etc. 骑马(或自行车等)的人 **2** an added condition on an official document (正式文件的)附文

ridge /rɪdʒ/ **noun** **1** a long, narrow hilltop or mountain range 山脊，岭 **2** a narrow raised band on a surface 脊状凸起；隆起部分 **3** the edge formed where the two sloping sides of a roof meet at the top 屋脊 ■ **ridged** adjective.

ridicule /'rɪdɪkjuːl/ **noun** making fun of someone in an unkind way; mockery 嘲弄，讥笑 • **verb** (ridicules, ridiculing, ridiculed) make fun of 嘲弄；奚落

ridiculous /rɪ'dɪkjələs/ **adjective** very silly or unreasonable; absurd 愚蠢可笑的，荒谬的 ■ **ridiculously** adverb.

riding /'raɪdɪŋ/ **noun** each of three former administrative divisions of Yorkshire 区(约克郡过去所设三个行政区之一)

rife /raɪf/ **adjective** **1** (of something bad or unpleasant) widespread (坏事物)猖獗的，普遍的 **2** (rife with) full of something bad or unpleasant 充斥…的

riff /rɪf/ **noun** a short repeated phrase in pop music or jazz (流行音乐或爵士乐的)重复小段

riffle /'rɪfl/ **verb** (riffles, riffling, riffled) (riffle through) turn over the pages of a book quickly and casually 飞快翻动(书页)

riff-raff /'rɪfræf/ **noun** people who are considered socially undesirable 不三不四的人；地痞流氓

rifle /'raɪfl/ **noun** a gun with a long barrel 来复枪，步枪 • **verb** (rifles, rifling, rifled) **1** search through something hurriedly to find or steal something 搜寻；抢掠；偷走 **2** hit or kick a ball hard and straight 猛击(球)；猛踢(球)

rift /rɪft/ **noun** **1** a crack, split, or break 裂缝；裂口；裂隙 **2** a serious break in friendly relations (友好关系的)裂痕

rig /rɪg/ **verb** (**rigs, rigging, rigged**) **1** secretly arrange something in order to gain an advantage (秘密)操纵 **2** fit sails and rigging on a boat 给(船只)装配桅帆及索具 **3** (often **rig something up**) set up a device or structure 装配；搭建 **4** (**rig someone out**) provide with clothes of a particular type (为…提供(某类)服装 • **noun 1** a piece of equipment for a particular purpose (有特殊用途的)装置,设备,器械: *a lighting rig* 照明设备 **2** a large piece of equipment for extracting oil or gas from the ground (石油或天然气)钻塔

rigging /ˈrɪgɪŋ/ **noun** the system of ropes or chains supporting a ship's masts (船的)索具

right /raɪt/ **adjective 1** on or towards the side of a person or thing which is to the east when the person or thing is facing north 右边的；右面的；向右的 **2** justified or morally good 正当的；合乎道德的 **3** factually correct 正确的；对的 **4** most appropriate 合适的；恰当的 **5** satisfactory, sound, or normal 健全的；完好的；正常的 **6** right-wing 右翼的；右派的 • **adverb 1** on or to the right side 在右面；往右；向右 **2** completely; totally 彻底地；完全地 **3** exactly; directly 恰好；正好 **4** correctly or satisfactorily 正确地；令人满意地 • **noun 1** what is morally right 正当；正义 **2** an entitlement to have or do something 权利 **3** (**rights**) the authority to perform, publish, or film a work or event 版权；发行权 **4** (**the right**) the right-hand part, side, or direction 右边；右面 **5** a right turn 右转弯 **6** (often **the Right**) a right-wing group or party 右翼团体(或政党) • **verb 1** put something back in a normal or upright position 使复位；把…扶正 **2** correct or make up for a wrong 纠正；补救 □ **by rights** if things were fair or correct 根据正当

权利；按理 **in your own right** as a result of your own qualifications or efforts 凭本身的资格(或努力) **right angle** an angle of 90°, as in a corner of a square 直角 **right of way 1** the legal right to go through someone's property along a specific route (穿越私人地产的)通行权,穿行权 **2** a public path through someone's property (穿越私人地产的)公用通道 **3** the right to proceed before another vehicle (车辆的)先行权 **right wing** conservative or opposed to political or social change 右翼的；右派的 ■ **rightly adverb.**

righteous /ˈraɪtʃəs/ **adjective** morally right 正直的；正义的；正当的 ■ **righteously adverb.**

rightful /ˈraɪtfl/ **adjective 1** having a clear right to something 依法享有权利的；合法的 **2** proper; fitting 恰当的；合适的 ■ **rightfully adverb.**

rigid /ˈrɪdʒɪd/ **adjective 1** unable to bend or be put out of shape 刚硬的；坚硬的 **2** (of a person) stiff and unmoving (人)苛严的，坚定的 **3** not able to be changed or adapted 无法改变的；僵化的；刻板的 ■ **rigidity noun rigidly adverb.**

rigmarole /ˈrɪgmərəʊl/ **noun** a lengthy and complicated procedure 繁琐费时的程序

rigor mortis /ˌrɪgə ˈmɔːtɪs/ **noun** stiffening of the joints and muscles that happens a few hours after death 尸僵；死后强直

rigorous /ˈrɪgərəs/ **adjective 1** very thorough or accurate 严密的；精确的 **2** (of a rule, system, etc.) strictly applied or followed (规定、制度等)严格的 **3** harsh or severe 苛刻的；苛严的；严厉的 ■ **rigorously adverb.**

rigour /ˈrɪgə(r)/ (US spelling 【美拼作】 **rigor**) **noun 1** the quality of being rigorous 严格；严密；精确 **2** (**rigours**)

difficult or extreme conditions 艰苦；
严酷

rile /raɪl/ verb (**riles, riling, riled**)
informal 【非正式】 annoy or irritate
使恼火，激怒；使烦躁

rill /rɪl/ noun literary 【文】 a small
stream 小河；小溪

rim /rɪm/ noun **1** the upper or outer
edge of something circular (圆形物的)
边，缘 **2** a limit or boundary 界限，边
界 • verb (**rims, rimming, rimmed**)
provide with a rim on 装边(或框)

rime /raɪm/ noun literary 【文】 hoar frost
白霜；雾凇

rind /raɪnd/ noun a tough outer layer
or covering of fruit, cheese, bacon,
etc. (水果的)外皮，(干酪、熏肉等的)
硬皮

ring¹ /rɪŋ/ noun **1** a small circular
metal band worn on a finger 戒指；指
环 **2** a circular band, object, or mark
环形物；环圈 **3** an enclosed space in
which a sport, performance, or show
takes place 圆形竞技场，圆形表演
场；圆形展场 **4** each of the flat plates
on a cooker that are used for cooking
on (炊具的)圆盘 **5** a group of people
with a shared interest or goal 帮派；
团伙 • verb **1** surround 包围 **2** draw
a circle round 绕…画圆圈 □ **ring
binder** a binder with ring-shaped
clasps 活页夹，活页簿 **ring pull** Brit.
【英】 a ring on a can that you pull
to open it (易拉罐的)拉环 **ring road**
Brit. 【英】 a road encircling a town
环路，环城公路

ring² /rɪŋ/ verb (**rings, ringing, rang**;
past participle **rung**) **1** make a clear
and repeated or long-lasting sound
发出响亮持久的声音 **2** (**ring with**)
echo with such a sound 回响 **3** Brit.
【英】 telephone someone 给(某人)
打电话 **4** (**ring off**) Brit. 【英】 end
a telephone call by replacing the
receiver 挂断电话 **5** call for attention
by sounding a bell 以钟声宣告；按
铃召唤 **6** (of the ears) be filled with

a buzzing or humming sound (双耳)
鸣响，嗡嗡作响 **7** (**ring something
up**) record an amount on a cash
register 把(款额)记入现金出纳机
• noun **1** an act of ringing 鸣铃，敲钟；
按 铃 **2** a loud, clear sound or tone
清脆响亮的声音(或音调) **3** a quality
or feeling conveyed by words (言语
传达的)特质，感觉：*a ring of truth* 几
分真实性 □ **give someone a ring**
Brit. informal 【英，非正式】 telephone
someone 给(某人)打电话 ■ **ringer**
noun.

ringing /ˈrɪŋɪŋ/ adjective **1** having a
clear, resonant sound 清脆响亮的，银
铃般的 **2** forceful and clear 清晰有
力的；毫不含糊的

ringleader /ˈrɪŋliːdə(r)/ noun a person
who leads others in committing a
crime or causing trouble 头目；首恶；
元凶

ringlet /ˈrɪŋlət/ noun a corkscrew-
shaped curl of hair (螺旋形的)卷发

ringmaster /ˈrɪŋmɑːstə(r)/ noun
the person who directs a circus
performance 马戏演出领班

ringtone /ˈrɪŋtəʊn/ noun a sound
made by a mobile phone when an
incoming call is received (手机的)来
电铃声

ringworm /ˈrɪŋwɜːm/ noun a skin
disease that causes small, itchy
circular patches 癣；癣菌病

rink /rɪŋk/ noun **1** (also **ice rink**) an
enclosed area of ice for skating, ice
hockey, or curling (供滑冰、冰球或
冰壶运动用的)冰场 **2** the strip of a
bowling green used for a match 草地
滚球场

rinse /rɪns/ verb (**rinses, rinsing,
rinsed**) **1** wash with clean water
to remove soap or dirt 冲洗；漂洗 **2**
remove soap or dirt by rinsing 冲掉…
的皂液；漂净 • noun **1** an act of rinsing
冲洗；漂洗 **2** an antiseptic solution for
cleaning the mouth 漱口液 **3** a liquid
for conditioning or colouring the hair

染发剂

riot /'raɪət/ **noun 1** a violent disturbance caused by an angry crowd 骚动;暴乱;暴动 **2** a confused combination or display 杂乱;丰富;众多 **3** (a riot) informal 【非正式】 a very entertaining person or thing 非常有趣的人(或事物) • **verb** take part in a riot 参加暴乱 □ **run riot** behave in an uncontrolled way 撒野;胡作非为 ■ **rioter** noun.

riotous /'raɪətəs/ **adjective 1** wild and uncontrolled 放纵的;纵情的 **2** involving public disorder 暴乱的;聚众闹事的

RIP /ɑː aɪ 'piː/ **abbreviation** rest in peace 安息

rip /rɪp/ **verb** (**rips, ripping, ripped**) **1** suddenly tear or become torn 撕;扯;撕破 **2** pull forcibly away 猛力扯掉;猛力移去;猛力去除 • **noun** a long tear 大口子;长裂缝 □ **let rip** informal 【非正式】 move or act without restraint 无拘束地行动 **rip someone/thing off** informal 【非正式】 **1** cheat someone 欺骗(某人) **2** steal something 窃取(某物) **rip-roaring** very energetic and exciting 活力十足的;兴奋的 **rip tide** a stretch of fast-flowing rough water caused by currents meeting (水流交汇产生的)急流,激流潮

riparian /raɪ'peərɪən/ **adjective** technical 【术语】 relating to or on the banks of a river 河岸的;水边的

ripcord /'rɪpkɔːd/ **noun** a cord that you pull to open a parachute (降落伞的)开伞索

ripe /raɪp/ **adjective 1** ready for harvesting and eating 成熟(可食)的 **2** (of a cheese or wine) fully matured (干酪或葡萄酒)熟的,酿熟的 **3** (**ripe for**) having reached the right time for 时机成熟的 **4** (of a person's age) advanced (某人的年龄)高的,上年纪的 ■ **ripely** adverb **ripeness** noun.

ripen /'raɪpən/ **verb** become or make

ripe (使)成熟

riposte /rɪ'pɒst/ **noun** a quick reply 迅捷的回应

ripple /'rɪpl/ **noun 1** a small wave or series of waves 涟漪;微波;细浪 **2** a feeling, effect, or sound that spreads through someone or something 反响;波动 **3** ice cream with wavy lines of syrup running through it 彩条纹纹冰激凌 • **verb** (**ripples, rippling, rippled**) **1** form ripples 起涟漪;呈波状 **2** (of a sound, feeling, etc.) spread through a person or place (声音、感觉等)传开,扩散

rise /raɪz/ **verb** (**rises, rising, rose;** past participle **risen**) **1** come or go up 升起;上升 **2** get up after lying, sitting, or kneeling 起床;起立;起身 **3** increase in number, size, strength, etc. (数量、规模、力量等)扩大,增长 **4** (of land) slope upwards (土地)隆起,凸起 **5** (of the sun, moon, or stars) appear above the horizon (太阳、月亮或恒星)升起 **6** (**rise above**) manage not to be restricted by 超越(限制),克服(束缚) **7** (**rise to**) respond well to a difficult situation 对(困境)随机应变;成功应对(困境) **8** (**rise up**) rebel 反抗;反叛;起义 **9** (of a river) have its source (河流)发源 • **noun 1** an act of rising 升起;上升 **2** an upward slope or hill 坡;小山;丘 **3** Brit. 【英】 a pay increase 加薪

riser /'raɪzə(r)/ **noun 1** a person who gets up at a particular time (在特定时间)起床的人 **2** a vertical section between the treads of a staircase 楼梯踏步竖板

risible /'rɪzəbl/ **adjective** causing laughter 可笑的;滑稽的 ■ **risibly** adverb.

rising /'raɪzɪŋ/ **noun** a rebellion or revolt 反抗;起义;叛乱 • **adjective** approaching a particular age (年龄)将近…岁的 □ **rising damp** Brit. 【英】 moisture absorbed from the ground into a wall (从地面渗入墙壁

的)上升潮气

risk /rɪsk/ **noun 1** a situation that involves being exposed to danger 危险(情况) **2** the possibility that something bad will happen 风险 **3** a person or thing that causes a risk 引起危险的人(或事物) • **verb 1** expose to danger or loss 使遭受危险(或损失) **2** act in such a way that there is a chance of something bad happening 冒险；铤而走险

risky /'rɪski/ **adjective (riskier, riskiest)** involving the possibility of danger or a bad outcome 危险的；有风险的 ■ **riskily** adverb **riskiness** noun.

risotto /rɪ'zɒtəʊ/ **noun (plural risottos)** a dish of rice with meat, seafood, etc. (拌有肉、海鲜等的)意大利烩饭

> ✔ **拼写指南** only one s: risotto.
> risotto 中只有一个 s。

risqué /'rɪskeɪ/ **adjective** slightly indecent or rude 有伤风化的，不雅的

rissole /'rɪsəʊl/ **noun** Brit. 【英】 a small flat mass of chopped meat that is coated in breadcrumbs and fried 炸肉饼，炸肉丸

rite /raɪt/ **noun** a religious ceremony, or other solemn procedure 宗教仪式，典礼 □ **rite of passage** a ceremony or event that marks an important stage in someone's life (标志人生重大阶段的)通过仪式，重大事件

ritual /'rɪtʃʊəl/ **noun 1** a ceremony that involves a series of actions performed in a set order 仪式；程序；礼节 **2** something that is habitually done in the same way 习惯，例行公事 • **adjective** done as a ritual 作为仪式进行的 ■ **ritually** adverb.

ritzy /'rɪtsi/ **adjective (ritzier, ritziest)** informal 【非正式】 expensively stylish 豪华时尚的；时髦高贵的

rival /'raɪvl/ **noun 1** a person or thing competing with another for the same thing 竞争对手；敌手 **2** a person or thing equal to another in quality 相匹敌的人(或物) • **verb (rivals, rivalling, rivalled;** US spelling 【美拼作】 **rivals, rivaling, rivaled)** be comparable to 与…相匹敌；比得上 ■ **rivalry** noun (plural **rivalries**).

riven /'rɪvn/ **adjective** literary 【文】 torn apart; split 扯开的，裂开的；豁开的

river /'rɪvə(r)/ **noun 1** a large natural flow of water moving in a channel to the sea or another river 河，川 **2** a large quantity of a flowing substance 巨流；涌流

rivet /'rɪvɪt/ **noun** a short metal pin or bolt for holding together two metal plates 铆钉 • **verb (rivets, riveting, riveted) 1** fasten with a rivet or rivets 用铆钉固定 **2** (**be riveted**) be completely fascinated by something 被完全吸引住；入迷

riviera /rɪvi'eərə/ **noun** a coastal area of a warm country, especially in southern France and northern Italy (尤指法国南部和意大利北部的)海滨胜地

rivulet /'rɪvjələt/ **noun** a small stream 小河；小溪；细流

RN /ɑːr 'en/ **abbreviation** Royal Navy (英国)皇家海军

RNA /ɑːr en 'eɪ/ **noun** a substance in living cells which carries instructions from DNA 核糖核酸 [short for 【缩写】 = *ribonucleic acid*.]

roach¹ /rəʊtʃ/ **noun (plural roach)** a common freshwater fish of the carp family 拟鲤

roach² **noun** N. Amer. informal 【北美，非正式】 a cockroach 蟑螂

road /rəʊd/ **noun 1** a wide track with a hard surface for vehicles to travel on 道路；公路 **2** a way to achieving a particular outcome 方法；途径 □ **road rage** informal 【非正式】 violent anger caused by conflict with the driver of another vehicle 公路暴

力(指司机之间发生冲突时大动肝火)

road test a test of the performance of a vehicle or of other equipment (测试车辆或其他设备性能的)道路测试, 路试

roadblock /ˈrəʊdblɒk/ **noun** a barrier put across a road by the police or army to stop and examine traffic 路障, 关卡

roadholding /ˈrəʊdhəʊldɪŋ/ **noun** the ability of a moving vehicle to remain stable (车辆的)运行性能, 行驶稳定性

roadie /ˈrəʊdi/ **noun** informal【非正式】 a person who sets up equipment for a rock group (摇滚乐队的)随团技术员

roadshow /ˈrəʊdʃəʊ/ **noun 1** a show broadcast from a different place each day 巡回广播; 巡回演出 **2** a touring political or promotional campaign 巡回政治宣传; 巡回广告宣传

roadster /ˈrəʊdstə(r)/ **noun** an open-top sports car (双座)敞篷小汽车

roadway /ˈrəʊdweɪ/ **noun 1** a road面; 道路 **2** the part of a road intended for vehicles 车行道

roadworks /ˈrəʊdwɜːks/ **plural noun** Brit.【英】 repairs to roads or to pipes under roads 道路检修

roadworthy /ˈrəʊdwɜːði/ **adjective** (of a vehicle) fit to be used on the road (车辆)适合行驶的

roam /rəʊm/ **verb** travel aimlessly over a wide area 闲逛, 漫步

roaming /ˈrəʊmɪŋ/ **noun** the use of a mobile phone on another operator's network, typically while abroad (手机的)漫游功能

roan /rəʊn/ **adjective** (of a horse) having a bay, chestnut, or black coat mixed with hairs of another colour (马)杂色的

roar /rɔː(r)/ **noun** a loud, deep sound made by a lion, engine, etc., or by a person who is angry, amused, or in pain (狮的)吼声; (发动机的)轰鸣; (人的)咆哮声, 大笑声, 惨叫声 • **verb 1** make a roar 咆哮; 轰鸣 **2** laugh loudly 大笑 **3** move very fast 快速行进; 迅速行动 □ **a roaring trade** informal【非正式】 very good business 兴隆的生意

roast /rəʊst/ **verb 1** cook food in an oven or over a fire 烘, 炙, 烤(食物) **2** make or become very warm (使)受热发烫 • **adjective** (of food) having been roasted (食物)烤过的, 烘过的 • **noun** a joint of meat that has been roasted 烤肉

roasting /ˈrəʊstɪŋ/ informal【非正式】 **adjective** very hot and dry 火烫的; 灼热的 • **noun** a severe telling-off 严厉批评; 申斥

rob /rɒb/ **verb** (**robs, robbing, robbed**) **1** steal property from a person or place by using force or threatening violence 抢劫; 掠夺 **2** deprive someone of something 剥夺; 使丧失 ▪ **robber** noun.

robbery /ˈrɒbəri/ **noun** (plural **robberies**) the action of robbing a person or place 抢劫; 掠夺

robe /rəʊb/ **noun 1** a loose garment reaching to the ankles, worn on formal or ceremonial occasions (正式场合或仪式上穿着的)长袍, 礼袍 **2** a dressing gown 睡袍 • **verb** (**robes, robing, robed**) clothe someone in a robe 使穿上长袍(或礼袍、睡袍)

robin /ˈrɒbɪn/ **noun** a small bird with a red breast and brown back and wings 旅鸫, 知更鸟(胸部红色、背部和翅膀呈褐色的小鸟)

robot /ˈrəʊbɒt/ **noun** a machine capable of carrying out a complex series of actions automatically 机器人

robotic /rəʊˈbɒtɪk/ **adjective 1** relating to robots 机器人的 **2** mechanical, stiff, or unemotional 机械的; 呆板的; 不动感情的

robotics /rəʊˈbɒtɪks/ **plural noun** the

R

science of constructing and using robots 机器人科学

robust /rəʊˈbʌst/ **adjective 1** sturdy or able to withstand difficult conditions 坚固的；耐用的；结实的 **2** strong and healthy 强健的；强壮的 **3** determined and forceful 坚定的；坚决的；有力的 □ **robustly** adverb

rock¹ /rɒk/ **noun 1** the hard material that makes up the earth's crust (地球表层的)岩石，岩 **2** a projecting mass of rock 石山，礁石 **3** a boulder 大石，岩块 **4** Brit. 【英】a hard sweet in the form of a cylindrical stick 硬棒糖 **5** informal 【非正式】a diamond or other precious stone 钻石，宝石 □ **on the rocks** informal 【非正式】**1** in difficulties and likely to fail 处在困难的；濒于失败的 **2** (of a drink) served undiluted and with ice cubes (饮料)只加冰块(不掺水)的 **rock bottom** the lowest possible level 最低水平的；最低限度的 **rock salt** salt occurring naturally as a mineral 岩盐，石盐

rock² **verb 1** move gently to and fro or from side to side 摇摆；轻晃；来回摆动 **2** shake violently 剧烈震动 **3** shock or distress very much 使震惊；使苦恼 • **noun 1** (also **rock music**) a type of loud popular music with a heavy beat 摇滚乐 **2** a rocking movement 轻微摇摆；轻轻摇晃 □ **rock and roll** a type of popular music with simple melodies, originating in the 1950s 摇滚乐(起源于20世纪50年代，旋律简单的流行乐) **rocking chair** a chair mounted on curved bars 摇椅 **rocking horse** a model horse mounted on curved bars for a child to ride on (架在弧形弯脚上供儿童骑坐的)木马，弹簧马

rockabilly /ˈrɒkəbɪli/ **noun** music that combines rock and roll and country music 乡村摇滚乐

rocker /ˈrɒkə(r)/ **noun 1** a curved piece of wood on the bottom of a rocking chair (摇椅底部的)弧形弯脚 **2** a person who performs or likes rock music 摇滚歌手；摇滚乐迷 □ **off your rocker** informal 【非正式】mad 发疯的

rockery /ˈrɒkəri/ **noun** (plural **rockeries**) an arrangement of rocks in a garden with plants growing between them (花园中的)假山

rocket /ˈrɒkɪt/ **noun 1** a tube-shaped missile or spacecraft propelled by a stream of burning gases 火箭 **2** a firework that shoots high in the air and explodes (火箭式)焰火 **3** Brit. informal 【英，非正式】a severe telling-off 斥责；申斥 **4** a plant similar to lettuce, eaten in salads 芝麻菜；紫花南芥 • **verb** (**rockets, rocketing, rocketed**) move or increase very quickly and suddenly 迅速移动；猛涨

rocky /ˈrɒki/ **adjective** (**rockier, rockiest**) **1** consisting or formed of rock 岩石(形成)的 **2** full of rocks 多岩石的 **3** unsteady or unstable 摇动的；摇晃的；不稳的

rococo /rəˈkəʊkəʊ/ **adjective** (of furniture or architecture) in a highly decorated style popular in the 18th century (家具或建筑)洛可可风格的

rod /rɒd/ **noun 1** a thin straight bar of wood, metal, etc. 棒条，杆；竿 **2** (also **fishing rod**) a long stick with a line and hook attached, for catching fish 钓竿

rode /rəʊd/ past of RIDE.

rodent /ˈrəʊdnt/ **noun** a mammal of a large group including rats, mice, and squirrels, with large front teeth 啮齿动物(包括老鼠、松鼠等)

rodeo /ˈrəʊdiəʊ/ **noun** (plural **rodeos**) a contest or entertainment in which cowboys show their horse-riding and lassoing skills (牛仔)牧马骑术竞赛(或表演)

roe /rəʊ/ **noun** the eggs or sperm of a fish, used as food (可食用的)鱼卵，鱼子

roebuck /'rəʊbʌk/ **noun** a male roe deer 雄狍

roe deer **noun** a small deer with a coat that is reddish in summer 狍(一种小鹿,夏季毛呈红色)

roentgen /'rʌntjən/ **noun** a unit of radiation 伦琴(辐射单位)

rogue /rəʊg/ **noun 1** a dishonest or immoral man 无赖;流氓;恶棍 **2** a mischievous but likeable person 调皮鬼;捣蛋鬼 **3** an elephant that is living apart from the herd 离群象

roguish /'rəʊgɪʃ/ **adjective** mischievous 调皮的;淘气的

roister /'rɔɪstə(r)/ **verb** (**roisters**, **roistering, roistered**) old use 【旧】 enjoy yourself in a lively, noisy way 喧闹作乐;狂欢庆祝

role /rəʊl/ **noun 1** an actor's part in a play, film, etc. (戏剧、电影等中的)角色 **2** a person's or thing's function in a particular situation 作用;职责 □ **role model** a person that others look up to as an example to be imitated 角色模型;仿效榜样 **role play** the acting out of a role or situation 角色扮演

> **！注意** don't confuse **role** with **roll**, which mainly means 'move by turning over and over' or 'a rolling movement'. 不要混淆 role 和 roll, 后者主要含义为"翻滚"或"滚动;打滚"。

roll /rəʊl/ **verb 1** move by turning over and over 翻滚 **2** move forward on wheels or with a smooth motion (乘车)行进;平滑移动 **3** (of a moving ship, aircraft, etc.) sway from side to side (行进中的船、飞机等)左右摇晃 **4** (of a machine or device) begin operating (机器或设备)运转,启动 **5** (often **roll something up**) turn something flexible over and over on itself 卷;绕;裹 **6** (**roll up**) curl up tightly 卷起 **7** (**roll something out**)

officially launch a new product 推出(新产品) **8** flatten with a roller 滚平;碾平 **9** (of a loud, deep sound) reverberate (深沉响亮的声音)发出回声,回响 **10** (**roll up**) informal 【非正式】 arrive 到达 ● **noun 1** a cylinder formed by rolling flexible material 筒形物;卷状物 **2** a rolling movement 滚动;打滚 **3** a long, deep, reverberating sound 隆隆声;轰鸣声 **4** a very small loaf of bread 小面包条 **5** an official list or register of names 名单;花名册 □ **roll call** an occasion when a list of names is read out to discover who is present 点名 **rolling pin** a cylinder for rolling out dough 擀面杖 **rolling stock** locomotives, carriages, and other vehicles used on a railway (铁路上运行的)全部车辆 **roll neck** a high turned-over collar 翻领 **roll-on** applied by means of a rotating ball 滚揉式的;走珠式的

> **！注意** don't confuse **roll** with **role**, which means 'an actor's part in a play or film'. 不要混淆 roll 和 role, 后者意为"(戏剧或电影中的)角色"。

roller /'rəʊlə(r)/ **noun 1** a rotating cylinder used to move, flatten, or spread something 滚轴;滚轧机;碾压机 **2** a small cylinder on which you roll your hair to make it curly 卷发筒 **3** a long wave moving towards the shore 卷浪;巨浪 □ **roller coaster** a fairground attraction in which you ride in an open carriage on a steep, twisting track 过山车;云霄飞车 **roller skate** a boot with wheels on which you can glide across a hard surface 旱冰鞋

Rollerblade /'rəʊləbleɪd/ **noun** trademark 【商标】 a roller skate with wheels in a single line along the sole 一字轮旱冰鞋, 单排轮旱冰鞋 ■ **rollerblading** noun.

rollicking /'rɒlɪkɪŋ/ **adjective** cheerfully

lively and amusing 兴高采烈的；欢闹的 • noun Brit. informal【英，非正式】a severe telling-off 斥责；申斥

rollmop /'rɒlmɒp/ **noun** a rolled pickled herring fillet 醋泡鲱鱼卷

roly-poly /ˌrəʊli'pəʊli/ **adjective** informal【非正式】round and plump 矮胖的；圆滚滚的 • **noun** Brit.【英】a hot pudding made of suet pastry covered with jam and rolled up (果酱)布丁卷

Roman /'rəʊmən/ **adjective 1** relating to Rome or its ancient empire 罗马的；古罗马帝国的 **2** referring to the alphabet used for writing Latin, English, and most European languages 拉丁字母的 **3 (roman)** (of a typeface) plain and upright, used in ordinary print (字体)罗马体的，正体的 • **noun 1** an inhabitant of Rome 罗马人 **2 (roman)** roman type 正体字；罗马字体 □ **Roman Catholic 1** of the Christian Church which has the Pope as its head 罗马天主教的 **2** a member of the Roman Catholic Church 罗马天主教教徒 **Roman numeral** each of the letters, I, V, X, L, C, D, and M, used in ancient Rome to represent numbers 罗马数字

romance /rəʊ'mæns/ **noun 1** a pleasurable feeling of excitement associated with love 浪漫的爱情 **2** a love affair 恋爱；风流韵事 **3** a book or film that deals with love in a sentimental or idealized way 浪漫作品；爱情电影 **4** a feeling of mystery, excitement, and remoteness from everyday life 传奇性 **5 (Romance)** French, Spanish, Italian, and other languages descended from Latin (源自拉丁语的)法语、西班牙语、意大利语等)罗曼诸语言 • **verb (romances, romancing, romanced)** try to win the love of someone 向(某人)求爱；追求

Romanesque /ˌrəʊmə'nesk/ **adjective** relating to a style of architecture common in Europe c.900–1200 (建筑)罗马式的，罗马风格的

Romanian or **Rumanian** /ruː'meɪnɪən/ **noun 1** a person from Romania 罗马尼亚人 **2** the language of Romania 罗马尼亚语 • **adjective** relating to Romania 罗马尼亚的

romantic /rəʊ'mæntɪk/ **adjective 1** having to do with love or romance 浪漫的；有浪漫色彩的 **2** thinking about or showing life in an idealized rather than realistic way 不切实际的；空想的；幻想的 **3 (Romantic)** relating to the artistic and literary movement of Romanticism (艺术、文学)浪漫主义的，浪漫派的 • **noun 1** a person with romantic beliefs or attitudes 浪漫的人；好幻想的人 **2 (Romantic)** an artist or writer of the Romantic movement 浪漫主义艺术家(或作家) ■ **romantically** adverb.

Romanticism /rəʊ'mæntɪsɪzəm/ **noun** a literary and artistic movement which emphasized creative inspiration and individual feeling 浪漫主义(强调创造性灵感和个人情感的文学和艺术运动)

romanticize or **romanticise** /rəʊ'mæntɪsaɪz/ **verb (romanticizes, romanticizing, romanticized)** make something seem more attractive and inspiring than it really is 使浪漫化；使理想化

Romany /'rɒmənɪ/ **noun (plural Romanies) 1** the language of the Gypsies 罗姆语；吉卜赛语 **2** a Gypsy 吉卜赛人

Romeo /'rəʊmɪəʊ/ **noun (plural Romeos)** an attractive, passionate male lover 痴情相恋的男子

romp /rɒmp/ **verb 1** play about roughly and energetically 嬉戏欢闹 **2 (romp ahead** or **home)** easily lead or win a race 轻松领先；轻易取

R

胜 3 **(romp through)** informal【非正式】do or achieve something easily 轻松完成；轻易获得

rompers /'rɒmpəz/ or **romper suit** /'rɒmpə/ **plural noun** a young child's one-piece garment (小孩穿的)连裤外衣，连衫裤

rondo /'rɒndəʊ/ **noun** (plural **rondos**) a piece of music with a recurring leading theme 回旋曲

röntgen /'rʌntjən/ = ROENTGEN.

rood screen /ruːd/ **noun** a screen of wood or stone separating the nave from the chancel of a church (教堂的)圣坛屏风

roof /ruːf/ **noun** (plural **roofs**) **1** the upper covering of a building or vehicle 屋顶；屋面；车顶 **2** the top inner surface of a covered space (有顶空间的)内顶 • **verb** put a roof over 给⋯盖顶 □ **roof rack** a framework for carrying luggage on the roof of a vehicle 车顶行李架

roofer /'ruːfə(r)/ **noun** a person who builds or repairs roofs 盖(或修)屋顶的人

rook[1] /rʊk/ **noun** a crow that nests in colonies in treetops 秃鼻乌鸦(群居在树顶处)

rook[2] **noun** a chess piece that can move in any direction (国际象棋中的)车

rookery /'rʊkəri/ **noun** (plural **rookeries**) **1** a collection of rooks' nests high in a clump of trees 秃鼻乌鸦结巢处 **2** a breeding place of seabirds 海鸟繁殖地

rookie /'rʊki/ **noun** informal【非正式】a new recruit 新兵；新手；生手

room /ruːm, rʊm/ **noun 1** a part of a building enclosed by walls, a floor, and a ceiling 房间；室 **2** (**rooms**) a set of rooms rented out to a lodger (租用的)住所，寓所 **3** empty space in which you can do or put things 地盘；空间 • **verb** N. Amer.【北美】share a

rented room or flat 同住(公寓)

roomy /'ruːmi, rʊmi/ **adjective** (**roomier, roomiest**) having plenty of space 宽敞的；宽大的

roost /ruːst/ **noun** a place where birds regularly settle to rest (鸟类的)栖息处 • **verb** (of a bird or birds) settle or gather for rest (鸟)栖息

rooster /'ruːstə(r)/ **noun** N. Amer.【北美】a male chicken 公鸡

root[1] /ruːt/ **noun 1** the part of a plant that is normally below ground, which acts as a support and collects water and nourishment (植物的)根，根部 **2** the part of a hair, tooth, nail, etc. that is fixed in the body tissue (头发、牙齿、指甲等的)根 **3** the basic cause or origin of something 根由；原因；根源 **4** (**roots**) your family or origins (家族或种族的)根 **5** Maths【数学】a number that when multiplied by itself one or more times gives a particular number 方根；根 • **verb 1** (of a plant or cutting) grow roots (植物或插条)生根 **2** (**be rooted**) be firmly established 扎根；被牢固树立 **3** (**root something out**) find and get rid of something 根除；铲除 □ **root vegetable** a vegetable which grows as the root of a plant 块根类蔬菜

root[2] **verb 1** (of an animal) turn up the ground with its snout in search of food (动物)拱土觅食 **2** rummage 翻找；搜查 **3** (**root for**) informal【非正式】support someone enthusiastically 助威；声援

rootless /'ruːtləs/ **adjective** having nowhere where you feel settled and at home 无根的；漂泊的

rootstock /'ruːtstɒk/ **noun 1** a rhizome 根茎；根状茎 **2** a plant on to which another variety is grafted (嫁接用的)砧木

rope /rəʊp/ **noun 1** a length of thick cord made by twisting together thinner strands of fibre 粗绳；绳索 **2**

a number of objects strung together 一串(物体) **3 (the ropes)** the ropes enclosing a boxing or wrestling ring (拳击台或摔跤台四周的)围绳 **4 (the ropes)** informal 【非正式】 the established way of doing something 诀窍；方法 • verb **(ropes, roping, roped) 1** secure something with rope 用绳捆(或系) **2 (rope someone in** or **into)** informal 【非正式】 persuade someone to take part in something 说服(某人)参加

ropy or **ropey** /'rəʊpi/ **adjective** Brit. informal 【英, 非正式】 of bad quality, or in bad health 劣质的；体弱的

rosary /'rəʊzəri/ **noun** (plural **rosaries**) a string of beads used by some Roman Catholics for keeping count of how many prayers they have said (罗马天主教徒念经时用的)念珠

rose[1] /rəʊz/ **noun 1** a sweet-smelling flower that grows on a prickly bush 玫瑰花；蔷薇花 **2** a cap with holes in it attached to a spout, hose, shower, etc. to produce a spray 莲蓬式喷嘴 **3** a soft pink colour 玫瑰色；玫瑰红 □ **rose hip** the fruit of a rose 玫瑰果

rose[2] past of **RISE**.

rosé /'rəʊzeɪ/ **noun** light pink wine made from red grapes, coloured by only brief contact with the skins 玫瑰红葡萄酒

rosemary /'rəʊzməri/ **noun** an evergreen shrub with sweet-smelling leaves which are used as a herb in cooking 迷迭香(一种常绿灌木, 叶子气味芳香, 用于烹饪)

rosette /rəʊ'zet/ **noun 1** a rose-shaped decoration made of ribbon, worn by supporters of a sports team or political party or awarded as a prize 玫瑰花结(用丝带制成, 为运动队或政党支持者所佩戴, 亦可用作奖品) **2** a piece of decoration in the shape of a rose 玫瑰花形饰物

rosewood /'rəʊzwʊd/ **noun** the wood

of a tropical tree, used for making furniture and musical instruments 红木(热带树木材, 用于制作家具和乐器)

Rosh Hashana or **Rosh Hashanah** /ˌrɒʃ hə'ʃɑːnə/ **noun** the Jewish New Year festival 岁首节(犹太教岁首新年)

rosin /'rɒzɪn/ **noun** a kind of resin that is rubbed on the bows of stringed instruments 松香, 香脂(用于涂擦弦乐器)

roster /'rɒstə(r)/ **noun 1** a list of people's names and the jobs they have to do at a particular time 值勤人员表；勤务簿 **2** a list of sports players available for team selection (运动员)候选名单 • verb **(rosters, rostering, rostered)** put a person's name on a roster 将(某人姓名)列入值勤表中

rostrum /'rɒstrəm/ **noun** (plural **rostra** /'rɒstrə/ or **rostrums**) a platform on which a person stands to make a speech, receive a prize, or conduct an orchestra 演讲台；领奖台；(管弦乐队的)指挥台

rosy /'rəʊzi/ **adjective** (**rosier**, **rosiest**) **1** of a soft pink colour 玫瑰色的 **2** promising 有希望的；乐观的：*a rosy future* 乐观的前景

rot /rɒt/ **verb** (**rots**, **rotting**, **rotted**) gradually decay 腐烂；变质 • noun **1** the process of decaying 腐坏；变质 **2** informal 【非正式】 rubbish 废话；蠢话

rota /'rəʊtə/ **noun** Brit. 【英】 a list showing when each of a number of people has to do a particular job 勤务轮值表；花名册

rotary /'rəʊtəri/ **adjective 1** revolving around a centre or axis 轮转的；转动的 **2** having a rotating part or parts 有旋转部件的

rotate /rəʊ'teɪt/ **verb** (**rotates**, **rotating**, **rotated**) **1** move in a circle round an axis 旋转；转动 **2** (of a job) pass on a regular basis to each member of a group in turn (工作)轮流,轮换 **3** grow different crops one after the other on a piece of land 轮种 (作物) ▪ **rotation** noun **rotator** noun **rotatory** adjective.

rote /rəʊt/ **noun** regular repetition of something to be learned 死记硬背

rotisserie /rəʊˈtɪsəri/ **noun** a rotating spit for roasting meat 电热轮转烤肉器

rotor /ˈrəʊtə(r)/ **noun 1** the rotating part of a turbine, electric motor, or other device (涡轮的)旋转器;(电动机或其他装置的)转子 **2** a hub with a number of blades spreading out from it that is rotated to provide the lift for a helicopter (直升机的)旋翼

rotten /ˈrɒtn/ **adjective 1** decayed 腐烂的,腐朽的 **2** corrupt 腐败的,腐化的,堕落的 **3** informal 【非正式】very bad 卑劣的;极坏的

rotter /ˈrɒtə(r)/ **noun** informal, dated 【非正式，废】an unkind or unpleasant person 无赖;下流坯;坏蛋

Rottweiler /ˈrɒtwaɪlə(r)/ **noun** a large, powerful breed of dog 罗特韦尔狗(一种高大猛犬)

rotund /rəʊˈtʌnd/ **adjective** rounded and plump 圆滚滚的;丰满的

rotunda /rəʊˈtʌndə/ **noun** a round building or room 圆形建筑;圆形大厅

rouble or **ruble** /ˈruːbl/ **noun** the basic unit of money in Russia 卢布 (俄罗斯基本货币单位)

roué /ˈruːeɪ/ **noun** a man who leads an immoral life 浪荡子;酒色之徒

rouge /ruːʒ/ **noun** a red powder or cream used for colouring the cheeks 胭脂

rough /rʌf/ **adjective 1** not smooth or level 不平滑的;高低不平的;崎岖的 **2** not gentle 粗暴的;粗鲁的 **3** (of weather or the sea) wild and stormy (天气)有暴风雨的;(大海)汹涌的 **4** plain and basic 粗制的;未经琢磨的 **5** not worked out in every detail 粗略的;不精确的 **6** harsh in sound or taste (声音)刺耳的,不悦耳的;(味道)差的 **7** unsophisticated 单纯的;不谙世故的 **8** informal 【非正式】difficult and unpleasant 艰难的;不愉快的 ▪ **noun 1** a basic draft of a design, piece of writing, etc. 草稿;纲要 **2** (on a golf course) the area of longer grass around the fairway and the green (高尔夫球场上的)深草区 ▪ **verb 1** (**rough something out**) make a draft or first version of something 草拟;画…的草图 **2** (**rough it**) informal 【非正式】live with only very basic necessities 因陋就简地生活 **3** (**rough someone up**) informal 【非正式】beat someone up 殴打(某人) ▫ **rough diamond** Brit. 【英】a person who lacks good manners and education but has a good character 外粗内秀的人 **rough justice** treatment that is not fair or in accordance with the law 不公平的对待;不合法的处置 **sleep rough** Brit. 【英】sleep outside or without a bed 露宿在外 ▪ **roughness** noun.

roughage /ˈrʌfɪdʒ/ **noun** material in cereals, fruit, and vegetables that cannot be digested (谷物、水果和蔬菜中的)粗纤维

roughen /ˈrʌfn/ **verb** make or become rough 使粗糙;变粗糙

roughly /ˈrʌfli/ **adverb 1** in a rough way 粗糙地;粗暴地 **2** approximately 大致,大体;大约

roughneck /ˈrʌfnek/ **noun** informal 【非正式】**1** a rough, rude person 粗暴的人;粗鲁的人 **2** a person who works on an oil rig 钻井工,油井工人

roughshod /ˈrʌfʃɒd/ **adjective** (**ride roughshod over**) fail to consider someone's needs or wishes 粗暴对待;对(某人)恣意妄为

roulette /ruːˈlet/ **noun** a gambling

game in which a ball is dropped on to a revolving wheel 轮盘赌

round /raʊnd/ **adjective 1** shaped like a circle, sphere, or cylinder 圆形的；环形的；球形的；圆柱形的 **2** having a curved surface with no sharp projections 弧形的 **3** (of a person's shoulders) bent forward (人的肩膀)浑圆的 **4** (of a sound) rich and smooth(声音)圆润洪亮的 **5** (of a number) expressed in convenient units rather than exactly (数字)用约数表示的，大致的 • **noun 1** a circular shape or piece 圆形；环形；环状物；球状物 **2** a route by which you visit a number of people or places in turn 巡回路线 **3** a sequence of things that you do regularly 惯常活动 **4** each of a sequence of stages in a process (过程的)一轮，一场 **5** a single division of a boxing or wrestling match (拳击或摔跤比赛的)一个回合 **6** a song for three or more voices or parts, each singing the same theme but starting one after another 轮唱歌曲 **7** the amount of ammunition needed to fire one shot (弹药的)一发 **8** a set of drinks bought for all the members of a group (买给集体中所有成员的)一巡饮料 **9** Brit. 【英】the quantity of sandwiches made from two slices of bread (两片面包做的)三明治 • **adverb** 【英】**1** so as to rotate or cause rotation 环绕；旋转 **2** so as to cover the whole area surrounding a particular centre 四处；到处 **3** so as to turn and face in the opposite direction 调转方向；转过来 **4** used in describing the position of something (用于描述位置)：*the wrong way round* 弄反 **5** so as to surround someone or something 在周围；围绕 **6** so as to reach a new place or position 到某处；到某地 • **preposition** chiefly Brit. 【主英】**1** on every side of 在…的周围；在…的四面八方 **2** so as to encircle 围绕；环绕 **3** from or on the other side of 绕

过；在…的另一边 **4** so as to cover the whole area of 在…各处，到…各部分 • **verb 1** pass and go round 环行；围绕 **2** (**round something up** or **down**) make a figure less exact but easier to use in calculations 使成为整数 **3** make or become round in shape (使)丰满；(使)发胖 □ **round something off** complete in a suitable or satisfying way 圆满完成(某事) **round on** make a sudden attack on 突然攻击；突然袭击 **round robin 1** a tournament in which every player or team plays against every other player or team 循环赛 **2** a petition 联名信 **round trip** a journey to a place and back again 往返旅程；来回旅行 **round someone/thing up** collect a number of people or animals together 将…聚拢起来

roundabout /'raʊndəbaʊt/ **noun** Brit. 【英】**1** a road junction at which traffic moves in one direction round a central island to reach one of the roads leading off it 环岛；环形交通枢纽 **2** a large revolving device in a playground, for children to ride on (儿童游乐场的)大型旋转装置 **3** a merry-go-round 旋转木马 • **adjective** not following a direct route 兜圈子的；迂回的

rounded /'raʊndɪd/ **adjective 1** round or curved 圆形的；弧形的 **2** complete and balanced 完善的；全面的

roundel /'raʊndl/ **noun** a small disc or circular design 小圆盘；圆形设计图案

rounders /'raʊndəz/ **noun** a ball game in which players run round a circuit after hitting the ball with a cylindrical wooden bat 圆场棒球(运动)

Roundhead /'raʊndhed/ **noun** a supporter of the Parliamentary party in the English Civil War 圆颅党人(英格兰内战时期议会派支持者)

roundly /'raʊndlɪ/ **adverb** in a firm or

thorough way 有力地；全面地

roundworm /'raʊndwɜːm/ **noun** a parasitic worm found in the intestines of animals 线虫；蛔虫

rouse /raʊz/ **verb (rouses, rousing, roused) 1** wake someone up 唤醒；使醒来 **2** make someone move or take an interest in something 使活跃起来；使产生兴趣

rousing /'raʊzɪŋ/ **adjective** stirring 激动人心的

rout /raʊt/ **noun 1** a disorderly retreat of defeated troops (军队的)溃退，溃败 **2** a decisive defeat 大败 • **verb** defeat troops decisively and force them to retreat 击溃；使溃败

route /ruːt/ **noun** a way taken in getting from a starting point to a destination 路线,路途 • **verb (routes, routeing or routing, routed)** send along a particular route (按特定路线)发送

routine /ruːˈtiːn/ **noun 1** the order and way in which you regularly do things 惯常程序；惯例 **2** a set sequence in a stage performance (舞台表演的)一套固定动作 • **verb** **adjective 1** performed as part of a regular procedure 常规的；惯例的 **2** without variety 无变化的；平常的 ■ **routinely** adverb.

roux /ruː/ **noun (plural roux)** a mixture of butter and flour used in making sauces 黄油面粉糊(用于调味汁)

rove /rəʊv/ **verb (roves, roving, roved) 1** travel from place to place without a fixed destination 流浪；漫游 **2** (of eyes) look around in all directions (眼睛)环顾，环视 ■ **rover** noun.

row¹ /rəʊ/ **noun** a number of people or things in a more or less straight line 一排；一行；一列

row² /rəʊ/ **verb** move a boat through water with oars 划(船)

row³ /raʊ/ Brit. 【英】 **noun 1** an angry quarrel 吵架；争吵 **2** a loud noise 喧闹 • **verb** have an angry quarrel 吵架；争吵

rowan /'raʊən/ **noun** a small tree with

white flowers and red berries 花楸(树)；红果花楸

rowdy /'raʊdi/ **adjective (rowdier, rowdiest)** noisy and disorderly 吵嚷的；喧闹的 • **noun (plural rowdies)** a rowdy person 粗暴好争吵的人 ■ **rowdily** adverb **rowdiness** noun.

rowlock /'rɒlək/ **noun** a fitting on the side of a boat for holding an oar (船边缘的)桨架

royal /'rɔɪəl/ **adjective 1** having the status of a king or queen or a member of their family 皇家的；王室的 **2** having to do with a king or queen 国王的；女王的 **3** of a quality or size suitable for a king or queen 适于国王(或女王)的，盛大的，庄严的 • **noun** informal 【非正式】a member of a royal family 王室成员 □ **royal blue** a deep, vivid blue 品蓝；宝蓝 **royal jelly** a substance produced by worker bees and fed by them to larvae raised to be queen bees 蜂王浆 ■ **royally** adverb.

royalist /'rɔɪəlɪst/ **noun** a person who supports the principle of having a king or queen 君主主义者；保皇主义者

royalty /'rɔɪəlti/ **noun (plural royalties) 1** the members of a royal family 王室成员 **2** the status or power of a king or queen 王位；王权 **3** a sum of money paid for the use of a patent, to an author for each copy of a book sold, or to a composer for each performance of a work (专利权的)使用费；版税

RSPCA /ˌɑːr es piː siː ˈeɪ/ **abbreviation** Royal Society for the Prevention of Cruelty to Animals 皇家防止虐待动物协会

RSVP /ˌɑːr es viː ˈpiː/ **abbreviation** please reply 敬请赐复 [short for French 【缩写，法】 = *répondez s'il vous plaît*.]

Rt Hon. abbreviation Brit. 【英】 Right Honourable 阁下

rub /rʌb/ **verb (rubs, rubbing, rubbed)**

1 move your hand, a cloth, etc. over the surface while pressing down firmly 擦;摩;搓 **2** apply a substance with a rubbing action 涂;抹;搽 **3** (**rub off**) come off a surface through being rubbed 被擦掉;被抹掉 **4** (**rub something out**) erase pencil marks with a rubber (用橡皮)擦掉(笔迹) **5** (**rub something down**) dry, smooth, or clean something by rubbing 擦干;磨平;擦净 **6** (**rub it in**) informal【非正式】keep reminding someone of an embarrassing fact they would rather forget 反复提及令人尴尬的事;触及痛处 • noun **1** an act of rubbing 擦;摩;擦;抹;擦;按摩 **2** a substance for rubbing on the skin (涂擦皮肤的)药膏,油膏

rubber¹ /'rʌbə(r)/ noun **1** a tough stretchy waterproof substance obtained from a tropical plant or from chemicals 橡胶 **2** Brit.【英】a piece of this or a similar substance used for erasing pencil marks (擦铅笔字迹的)橡皮,橡皮擦 **3** N. Amer. informal【北美,非正式】a condom 避孕套 □ **rubber band** a stretchy loop of rubber for holding things together 橡皮筋 **rubber plant** an evergreen plant with large shiny leaves 橡胶植物(常绿植物,叶大有光泽) **rubber-stamp** approve something automatically without proper consideration (未经认真考虑而)批准 ■ **rubbery** adjective.

rubber² noun a unit of play in the card game bridge (桥牌比赛的)一盘

rubberneck /'rʌbənek/ verb informal【非正式】turn to look at something as you pass it 扭头观望

rubbing /'rʌbɪŋ/ noun **1** the action of rubbing 擦;摩擦 **2** an impression of a design on brass or stone, made by placing paper over it and rubbing it with chalk or pencil 拓印;摹拓

rubbish /'rʌbɪʃ/ Brit.【英】noun **1** waste material and discarded items 垃圾;废弃物 **2** something that has no value or makes no sense 无价值之物;无意义之物 • verb informal【非正式】say that something is bad 批评;抨击 ■ **rubbishy** adjective.

rubble /'rʌbl/ noun rough fragments of stone, brick, or concrete 碎石;碎砖;瓦砾

rubella /ruː'belə/ noun a disease with symptoms like mild measles 风疹

rubicund /'ruːbɪkənd/ adjective having a red complexion (面色)红润的

ruble /'ruːbl/ ⇒ 见 ROUBLE.

rubric /'ruːbrɪk/ noun **1** a heading on a document (文件的)标题 **2** a set of instructions 提示;说明

ruby /'ruːbi/ noun (plural **rubies**) **1** a deep red precious stone 红宝石 **2** a deep red colour 深红色 □ **ruby wedding** Brit.【英】the fortieth anniversary of a wedding 红宝石婚(结婚40周年纪念)

ruche /ruːʃ/ noun a frill or pleat of fabric 褶裥饰边 ■ **ruched** adjective.

ruck¹ /rʌk/ noun **1** Rugby【英式橄榄球】a loose scrum formed around a player with the ball on the ground 自由密集争球 **2** a crowd of people 一大群人

ruck² verb (often **ruck up**) form creases or folds 起皱褶 • noun a crease 皱褶

rucksack /'rʌksæk/ noun a bag with two shoulder straps, that you carry on your back 背包;旅行包

ruckus /'rʌkəs/ noun a row or commotion 争吵;喧闹;骚扰

ructions /'rʌkʃnz/ plural noun Brit. informal【英,非正式】angry reactions or protests 愤怒抗议

rudder /'rʌdə(r)/ noun a flat piece hinged in an upright position at the back of a boat, used for steering (船的)舵

ruddy /'rʌdi/ **adjective** (**ruddier, ruddiest**) **1** (of a person's face) having a healthy red colour (人的脸) 红润健康的 **2** reddish 红的；发红的

rude /ru:d/ **adjective 1** saying impolite things that offend and hurt someone 粗鲁的；粗野的 **2** referring to sex or the body in a way that people find offensive or embarrassing 下流的；猥亵的 **3** very abrupt 突然的；突如其来的 **4** Brit.【英】hearty 强健的；有活力的：*rude health* 十分健康 ■ **rudely adverb rudeness** noun.

rudimentary /ˌru:dɪ'mentri/ **adjective 1** involving only basic matters or facts 基本的；基础的 **2** undeveloped 尚未充分发展的

rudiments /'ru:dɪmənts/ **plural noun 1** the essential matters or facts relating to a subject 基本原理 **2** a basic form of something 雏形

rue /ru:/ **verb** (**rues, rueing** or **ruing, rued**) bitterly regret a past event or action 对…感到懊悔（或悔恨）

rueful /'ru:fʊl/ **adjective** expressing regret 悔恨的；遗憾的 ■ **ruefully adverb**.

ruff /rʌf/ **noun 1** a frill worn round the neck 轮状皱领 **2** a ring of feathers or hair round the neck of a bird or mammal (鸟或哺乳动物的) 翎领

ruffian /'rʌfiən/ **noun** a rough person 暴徒；恶棍

ruffle /'rʌfl/ **verb** (**ruffles, ruffling, ruffled**) **1** disturb the smooth surface of 使(表面)不平；弄皱 **2** upset or worry 搅扰；使焦虑 **3** (**ruffled**) gathered into a frill 打褶裥的；饰褶边的 ● **noun** a gathered frill on a garment (衣服上的)褶饰，花边

rug /rʌg/ **noun 1** a small carpet 小地毯 **2** Brit.【英】a thick woollen blanket 厚毛毯

rugby /'rʌgbi/ or **rugby football noun** a team game played with an oval ball that may be kicked, carried, and passed by hand (英式)橄榄球(运动)

rugged /'rʌgɪd/ **adjective 1** having a rocky surface 多岩石的；崎岖的 **2** tough and determined 坚强的；坚毅的 **3** (of a man) having attractively masculine features (男性)魁梧强健的 ■ **ruggedly adverb ruggedness** noun.

rugger /'rʌgə(r)/ **noun** Brit. informal 【英，非正式】rugby 英式橄榄球(运动)

ruin /'ru:ɪn/ **verb 1** completely spoil or destroy something 彻底毁灭；使成为废墟 **2** make someone bankrupt or very poor 使破产；使倾家荡产 ● **noun 1** the destruction or collapse of something 毁坏；破坏；毁灭 **2** (also **ruins**) a building that has been badly damaged 废墟；残垣断壁 **3** the complete loss of a person's money and property (钱和财产的)完全丧失

ruination /ˌru:ɪ'neɪʃn/ **noun** the process of ruining something 毁灭；毁灭

ruinous /'ru:ɪnəs/ **adjective 1** disastrous or destructive 灾难性的；毁灭性的；破坏性的 **2** in ruins 已成废墟的

rule /ru:l/ **noun 1** a statement saying what you must or must not do 规则；规章；条例 **2** authority and control over a people or country 统治；管制 **3** (**the rule**) the normal state of things 常规；一般情况 **4** a ruler (for measuring or drawing) 直尺；尺 ● **verb** (**rules, ruling, ruled**) **1** have authority and control over a people or country 统治 (人民或国家) **2** control or influence 控制；支配 **3** state with legal authority that something is the case 裁决；裁定 **4** (**rule something out**) say that something is not possible 排除…的可能性 **5** (**ruled**) (of paper) marked with thin horizontal lines (纸)有横格的 □ **rule of thumb** a rough guide 经验法则

ruler /'ru:lə(r)/ **noun 1** a person who has authority and control over a people or country 统治者 **2** a strip of rigid material marked with centimetres or inches, used to measure short distances or draw straight lines 尺；直尺

ruling /'ru:lɪŋ/ **noun** a decision or statement made by an authority 裁决；裁定；判决

rum¹ /rʌm/ **noun** a strong alcoholic drink made from sugar cane 郎姆酒（由甘蔗制成）

rum² **adjective** (**rummer**, **rummest**) Brit. informal, dated 【英，非正式，废】 peculiar 古怪的；奇特的

Rumanian /ru:'meɪnɪən/ ⇒ 见 **RO-MANIAN.**

rumba or **rhumba** /'rʌmbə/ **noun** a rhythmic dance with Spanish and African elements 伦巴舞（含有西班牙和非洲舞蹈元素，节奏感强）

rumble /'rʌmbl/ **verb** (**rumbles**, **rumbling**, **rumbled**) **1** make a continuous deep sound, like distant thunder 发出持续而低沉的声音；发出隆隆声 **2** (**rumble on**) (of a dispute) continue in a low-key way （争论）低调持续 **3** Brit. informal 【英，非正式】 discover that someone is doing something wrong 看穿；识破 • **noun** a continuous deep sound like that of distant thunder 持续而低沉的声音；隆隆声

rumbustious /rʌm'bʌstʃəs/ **adjective** Brit. informal 【英，非正式】 high-spirited or difficult to control 喧闹的；难控制的

ruminant /'ru:mɪnənt/ **noun** an animal that chews the cud, such as a cow or sheep (牛、羊等)反刍动物

ruminate /'ru:mɪneɪt/ **verb** (**ruminates**, **ruminating**, **ruminated**) **1** think deeply about something 沉思；认真思考 **2** (of an animal) chew the cud (动物)反刍

rummage /'rʌmɪdʒ/ **verb** (**rummages**, **rummaging**, **rummaged**) search for something by turning things over or moving them about in an untidy way 翻查；搜寻 • **noun** an act of rummaging 翻查；搜寻

rummy /'rʌmi/ **noun** a card game in which the players try to form sets and sequences of cards 拉米纸牌戏（游戏者要凑成某种组合）

rumour /'ru:mə(r)/ (US spelling 【美拼作】 **rumor**) **noun** a piece of information spread among a number of people which is not confirmed and may be false 谣言；传闻 • **verb** (**be rumoured**) be spread as a rumour 谣传；传说

rump /rʌmp/ **noun 1** the hind part of the body of a mammal (哺乳动物的)臀部 **2** a piece left over from something larger 残余部分；剩余部分

rumple /'rʌmpl/ **verb** (**rumples**, **rumpling**, **rumpled**) make something less smooth and neat 弄皱；弄乱

rumpus /'rʌmpəs/ **noun** (plural **rumpuses**) a noisy disturbance 喧闹；骚乱

run /rʌn/ **verb** (**runs**, **running**, **ran**; past participle **run**) **1** move at a speed faster than a walk, never having both feet on the ground at the same time 跑；奔跑 **2** be in charge of people or an organization 管理；掌管 **3** continue, operate, or proceed 继续 **4** function or cause to function (使)运行 **5** pass into or reach a particular state or level 达到…状态(或水平) **6** (of a liquid) flow (液体流、流动) **7** (**run in**) (of a quality) be common or lasting in (品质)常见于 **8** (of dye or colour) dissolve and spread when wet (染料或颜色)掉色、褪色 **9** stand as a candidate in an election 参加竞选；当候选人 **10** compete in a race 参加赛跑 **11** (of a bus or train) make a regular journey on a particular route (公共汽车或火车按某线路)行驶，往来 **12** take someone somewhere in a car 开车送 **13** publish a story in a newspaper (在报纸上)发表, 刊登 **14** smuggle goods 走私(货物) • *noun* **1** an act or period of running 跑; 奔跑 **2** a journey or route 旅程; 路线 **3** a course that is regularly used (固定使用的)道路, 跑道: *a ski run* 滑雪道 **4** a continuous period or sequence 持续时间; 一连串 **5** an enclosed area in which chickens or animals can run around 养鸡场; 饲养场 **6 (the run of)** unrestricted use of or access to a place 使用自由; 出入自由 **7** a point scored in cricket or baseball (板球或棒球的)一分 **8** a ladder in stockings or tights (长袜或紧身衣裤的)抽丝 □ **run across** meet or find by chance 偶遇; 偶然发现 **run down** gradually lose power 耗尽能量 **run someone down 1** knock someone down with a vehicle (车辆)把(某人)撞倒 **2** criticize someone unfairly or unkindly 恶意批评; 把…的坏话 **run-down 1** in a bad or neglected state 破败的; 失修的 **2** tired and rather unwell 疲惫的; 感到不适 **run-of-the-mill** ordinary 一般的; 普通的 **run into 1** collide with 和…相撞 **2** meet someone by chance 偶遇(某人) **run out 1** be used up 用完; 耗尽 **2** be no longer valid 到期; 失效 **run someone out** Cricket【板球】dismiss a batsman by hitting the bails with the ball while the batsman is still running 将(奔跑的击球员)截杀出局 **run someone over** knock someone down with a vehicle (车辆)把(某人)撞倒 **run through (or over)** go over something as a quick rehearsal or reminder (粗略地)排演; 浏览; 匆匆翻阅 **run something up 1** allow a bill to build up 积累(账单) **2** make something quickly 迅速做成(某物) **run-up** the period before an important event (重大活动的)准备阶段, 预备期

runaway /ˈrʌnəweɪ/ *noun* a person who has run away from their home or an institution 离家出走者; 逃跑者 • *adjective* **1** (of an animal or vehicle) running out of control (动物或车辆)失控的 **2** happening or done quickly or uncontrollably 迅速的; 失控的

rundown /ˈrʌndaʊn/ *noun* a brief summary 概要; 梗概

rune /ruːn/ *noun* **1** a letter of an ancient Germanic alphabet 如尼字母(古日耳曼语字母) **2** a symbol with mysterious or magical significance 神秘记号; 有魔力的符号 ■ **runic** *adjective*.

rung[1] /rʌŋ/ *noun* **1** a horizontal support on a ladder for the foot (梯子的)横档, 梯级 **2** a level or rank 水平; 等级

rung[2] past participle of RING[2].

runnel /ˈrʌnl/ *noun* **1** a gutter 沟; 水沟 **2** a stream 溪流; 小河

runner /ˈrʌnə(r)/ *noun* **1** a person who runs in a race or for exercise 赛跑(或跑步)的人 **2** a messenger 送信人; 跑腿的人 **3** a rod, groove, or blade on which something slides (滚杠、滑槽、冰刀等)条状滑行装置 **4** a shoot which grows along the ground and can take root at points along its length 纤匍枝 **5** a long, narrow rug 长条地毯 □ **runner bean** a climbing bean plant with long edible pods 红花菜豆 **runner-up** (plural **runners-up**) a competitor who comes second 第二名; 亚军

running /ˈrʌnɪŋ/ *noun* **1** the activity or movement of a runner 跑; 跑步 **2** the action of managing or operating something 掌管; 控制; 操纵 • *adjective* **1** (of water) flowing naturally or supplied through pipes and taps (水)流动的, 从龙头流出的 **2** producing liquid or pus 排出液体的; 流脓的 **3** continuous or recurring 持续的; 连续不断的 **4** done while

R

running 跑步时做的 **5 in succession** 接连的：*the third week running* 连续的第三周 □ **in (in or out of) the running** in (or no longer in) with a chance of success 有(或不再有)成功的机会 **running board** a board acting as a step which extends along the side of a vehicle (车辆的)踏板，脚蹬板 **running commentary** a description of events given as they happen 现场评述；实况报道

runny /'rʌni/ *adjective* (**runnier**, **runniest**) more liquid than is usual 水分过多的 **2** (of a person's nose) producing mucus (人的鼻子)流鼻涕的

runt /rʌnt/ *noun* the smallest animal in a litter (一窝中)最小的幼崽

runway /'rʌnwei/ *noun* a strip of hard ground where aircraft take off and land 飞机跑道

rupee /ruːˈpiː/ *noun* the basic unit of money of India and Pakistan 卢比(印度和巴基斯坦的基本货币单位)

rupture /'rʌptʃə(r)/ *verb* (**ruptures**, **rupturing**, **ruptured**) **1** break or burst suddenly (突然)断裂，破裂 **2** (**be ruptured** or **rupture yourself**) develop a hernia in the abdomen 发疝气 • *noun* **1** an instance of rupturing 破裂；裂开 **2** a hernia in the abdomen (腹部的)疝

rural /'rʊərəl/ *adjective* having to do with the countryside 农村的；乡村的 ■ **rurally** *adverb*.

ruse /ruːz/ *noun* something done to deceive or trick someone 诡计；骗术

rush¹ /rʌʃ/ *verb* **1** move or act very quickly, often too quickly 迅速移动；急速行动 **2** produce, deal with, or transport very quickly 很快制作；仓促行事；快速运输 **3** (of air or a liquid) flow strongly (空气或液体)急速流动，涌流 **4** dash towards a person or place as a form of attack 突然袭击(某人)；突然攻占(某地) • *noun* **1** a sudden quick movement

towards something 冲；奔 **2** a sudden period of hasty activity 繁忙时期；高峰时间 **3** a sudden strong demand for a product (对某产品的)大量急需，争购 **4** a sudden strong feeling (情感的)涌动，迸发 **5** *informal* 【非正式】 a sudden thrill experienced after taking certain drugs (吸毒后产生的)一阵快感 **6** (**rushes**) the first prints made of a film after a period of shooting (电影的)工作样片 □ **rush hour** a time at the start and end of the working day when traffic is at its heaviest (上下班时的)交通高峰期，交通拥挤时段

rush² /rʌʃ/ *noun* a water plant used in making mats, baskets, etc. 灯心草(可制作垫子、篮筐等)

rusk /rʌsk/ *noun* a dry biscuit or piece of baked bread 脆饼干

russet /'rʌsɪt/ *adjective* reddish brown 赤褐色的 • *noun* a kind of apple with a greenish-brown skin 青褐色粗皮苹果

Russian /'rʌʃn/ *noun* **1** a person from Russia 俄罗斯人 **2** the language of Russia 俄语 • *adjective* relating to Russia 俄罗斯的 □ **Russian roulette** a dangerous game of chance in which a person loads one bullet into a revolver, spins the cylinder, and then pulls the trigger while pointing the gun at their own head 俄罗斯轮盘赌(危险概率游戏，游戏者在左轮手枪中仅装一发子弹，然后转动旋转弹膛，举枪对准自己头部开枪)

rust /rʌst/ *noun* a brown flaky coating which forms on iron or steel when it is wet 锈；铁锈 • *verb* be affected by rust 生锈，锈蚀

rustic /'rʌstɪk/ *adjective* **1** having to do with life in the country 乡村的；乡居的 **2** simple and charming in a way seen as typical of the countryside 质朴的；淳朴的 • *noun* an unsophisticated country person 质朴的乡下人 ■ **rusticity** *noun*.

rustle /'rʌsl/ **verb 1** make a soft crackling sound 发出沙沙声,发出轻轻磨擦声 **2** round up and steal cattle, horses, or sheep 把(牛、马或羊)赶拢偷走 **rustle something up** informal 【非正式】produce food or a drink quickly 草草弄好(食物或饮料) • **noun** a rustling sound 沙沙声;轻轻磨擦声 ■ **rustler** noun.

rusty /'rʌsti/ **adjective 1** affected by rust 生锈的;锈蚀的 **2** of the colour of rust; reddish-brown 铁锈色的,黄褐色的 **3** (of knowledge or a skill) less good than it used to be because of a lack of recent practice (知识或技能)荒疏的,退步的

rut¹ /rʌt/ **noun 1** a long deep track made by the wheels of vehicles 车辙 **2** a way of living or working that has become routine and dull but is hard to change 刻板乏味的生活

rut² **noun** an annual period of sexual activity in deer and some other animals, during which the males fight each other for access to the females (动物的)发情期 • **verb** (**ruts**, **rutting**, **rutted**) be in such a period of activity 处于发情期

ruthless /'ru:θləs/ **adjective** hard, determined, and showing no sympathy 无情的;残酷的;残忍的 ■ **ruthlessly** adverb **ruthlessness** noun.

rye /raɪ/ **noun 1** a type of cereal plant 黑麦 **2** whisky made from rye 黑麦威士忌酒

ryegrass /'raɪgrɑːs/ **noun** a grass used for lawns and as food for farm animals 黑麦草(用于铺草坪和作饲料)

Ss

S or **s** /es/ *noun* (plural **Ss** or **S's**) the nineteenth letter of the alphabet 英语字母表的第 19 个字母 • **abbreviation** South or Southern

sabbath /ˈsæbəθ/ *noun* (often **the Sabbath**) a day for rest and religious worship 安息日;主日

sabbatical /səˈbætɪkl/ *noun* a period of paid leave for study or travel 带薪休假

sable /ˈseɪbl/ *noun* a marten native to Japan and Siberia, hunted for its dark brown fur 紫貂,黑貂(产于日本和西伯利亚)

sabotage /ˈsæbətɑːʒ/ *verb* (**sabotages**, **sabotaging**, **sabotaged**) deliberately damage or destroy 蓄意破坏 • *noun* the action of sabotaging 蓄意破坏

saboteur /ˌsæbəˈtɜː(r)/ *noun* a person who sabotages something 蓄意破坏者

sabre /ˈseɪbə(r)/ (US spelling 【美拼作】 **saber**) *noun* **1** a heavy sword with a curved blade (刀刃呈弧形的)马刀 **2** a light fencing sword with a thin blade 佩剑;长剑

sabretooth tiger /ˈseɪbətuːθ/ or **sabretoothed tiger** /ˈseɪbətuːθd/ *noun* a large extinct member of the cat family with massive curved upper canine teeth 剑齿虎(大型猫科动物,已灭绝,有巨大的上犬齿)

sac /sæk/ *noun* a hollow, flexible structure resembling a bag or pouch 囊;液囊

saccharin /ˈsækərɪn/ *noun* a sweet-tasting substance used as a low-calorie substitute for sugar 糖精

saccharine /ˈsækəriːn/ *adjective* too sweet or sentimental 过分甜蜜的;多愁善感的

sacerdotal /ˌsæsəˈdəʊtl/ *adjective* relating to priests 司祭的;司铎的

sachet /ˈsæʃeɪ/ *noun* Brit.【英】a small sealed bag or packet 小袋;小包

sack¹ /sæk/ *noun* **1** a large bag made of rough material or thick paper, used for storing and carrying goods (用于装运货物的)塑料袋,麻袋,硬纸袋 **2** (**the sack**) informal 【非正式】dismissal from employment 解雇;开除 **3** (**the sack**) informal 【非正式】bed 床 • *verb* informal 【非正式】dismiss someone from employment 解雇;开除;炒鱿鱼 ■ **sackable** *adjective*.

sack² *verb* violently attack, steal from, and destroy a town or city (used when talking about the past) (旧时)洗劫,劫掠(城镇) • *noun* the sacking of a town or city (对城镇的)洗劫

sackcloth /ˈsækklɒθ/ *noun* a rough fabric woven from flax or hemp 粗麻布

sacra /ˈseɪkrə/ plural of **SACRUM**.

sacrament /ˈsækrəmənt/ *noun* **1** (in the Christian Church) an important religious ceremony in which the people taking part are believed to receive the grace of God (基督教的)圣事，圣礼 **2** (also **the Blessed Sacrament** or **the Holy Sacrament**) (in Catholic use) the bread and wine used in the Mass (天主教的)圣餐 ■ **sacramental** adjective.

sacred /ˈseɪkrɪd/ **adjective 1** connected with God or a god or goddess, and treated as holy 神的；神圣的 **2** (of a piece of writing) containing the teachings of a religion (文本)传教的，神圣的 **3** religious 宗教性的 □ **sacred cow** a thing that people believe must not be criticized 不可批评的事物

sacrifice /ˈsækrɪfaɪs/ **noun 1** the killing of an animal or person or giving up of a possession as an offering to a god or goddess 祭祀；献祭 **2** an animal, person, or object offered in this way 献祭品；祭品 **3** an act of giving up something you value for the sake of something that is more important 牺牲；舍弃 ● **verb** (**sacrifices, sacrificing, sacrificed**) offer as a sacrifice 献祭；牺牲 ■ **sacrificial** adjective.

sacrilege /ˈsækrɪlɪdʒ/ **noun** an act of treating a sacred or highly valued thing without respect (对圣物或贵重物品的)亵渎 ■ **sacrilegious** adjective.

✔ 拼写指南 sacrilege, not -relige or -rilige. sacrilege 不要拼作 -relige 和 -rilige.

sacristan /ˈsækrɪstən/ **noun** a person in charge of a sacristy 祭衣室(或圣器室)管理员

sacristy /ˈsækrɪsti/ **noun** (plural **sacristies**) a room in a church where a priest prepares for a service (教堂的)祭衣室，圣器室

sacrosanct /ˈsækrəʊsæŋkt/ **adjective** too important or valuable to be changed 极其神圣的；神圣不容更改的

sacrum /ˈseɪkrəm/ **noun** (plural **sacra** /ˈseɪkrə/ or **sacrums**) a triangular bone in the lower back between the two hip bones 骶骨

sad /sæd/ **adjective** (**sadder, saddest**) **1** unhappy 不快乐的；悲伤的 **2** causing sorrow 可悲的；令人悲伤的 **3** informal 非正式 very inadequate or unfashionable 极不充分的，过时的 ■ **sadly** adverb **sadness** noun.

sadden /ˈsædn/ **verb** make someone unhappy 使不快；使悲伤

saddle /ˈsædl/ **noun 1** a seat with a raised ridge at the front and back, fastened on the back of a horse for riding 马鞍；鞍座 **2** a seat on a bicycle or motorcycle (自行车或摩托车的)车座 **3** a piece of meat from the back of an animal 里脊肉 ● **verb** (**saddles, saddling, saddled**) **1** put a saddle on a horse 给(马)装上鞍座 **2** (**saddle someone with**) give someone an unpleasant responsi-bility or task 使肩负重担

saddlebag /ˈsædlbæg/ **noun** a bag attached to a saddle (马鞍上的)鞍囊，马褡裢

saddler /ˈsædlə(r)/ **noun** a person who makes, sells, and repairs saddles and other equipment for horses 鞍匠；马具商 ■ **saddlery** (plural **saddleries**).

sadism /ˈseɪdɪzəm/ **noun** enjoyment felt in hurting or humiliating other people 施虐癖 ■ **sadist** noun **sadistic** adjective.

sadomasochism /ˌseɪdəʊ'mæsəkɪzəm/ **noun** enjoyment felt in hurting or being hurt by someone else, especially during sex 施虐受虐狂；(尤指)性施虐受虐狂 ■ **sadomasochist** noun **sadomasochistic** adjective.

safari /səˈfɑːri/ **noun** (plural **safaris**) an expedition to observe or hunt animals in their natural environment

(观察或猎捕野兽的)游猎 □ **safari park** an area of parkland where wild animals are kept in the open and may be observed by visitors 野生动物园

safe /seɪf/ **adjective 1** protected from danger or risk 平安的；无危险的 **2** not leading to harm or injury; not risky 无害的，无风险的 **3** (of a place) giving security or protection (场所)安全的，无危险的 **4** based on good reasons and not likely to be proved wrong 可靠的；有充分理由的 • **noun** a strong fireproof cabinet with a complex lock, used for storing valuable items 保险箱；保险柜 □ **safe house** a house in a secret location, used by people in hiding 安全房；藏身房 ■ **safely** adverb.

safeguard /'seɪfɡɑːd/ **noun** a thing done in order to protect or prevent something 保护措施；防护措施 • **verb** protect with a safeguard 保护，卫护；维护

safekeeping /seɪf'kiːpɪŋ/ **noun** the keeping of something in a safe place 妥善保管

safety /'seɪfti/ **noun** (plural **safeties**) the condition of being safe 安全；平安 □ **safety belt** a belt that secures a person to their seat in a vehicle or aircraft (车辆或飞机上的)安全带 **safety net** a net placed to catch an acrobat should they fall (杂技表演时用于防摔的)安全网 **2** something arranged as a safeguard 安全措施；保障 **safety pin** a pin with a point that is bent back to the head and held in a guard when closed 安全别针

saffron /'sæfrən/ **noun** a yellow spice made from the dried stigmas of a crocus 干藏红花粉(一种黄色调料，由干藏红花柱头制成)

sag /sæɡ/ **verb** (**sags**, **sagging**, **sagged**) **1** sink downwards gradually under weight or pressure or through weakness 下沉；下陷 **2** hang down loosely or unevenly 松散(或不均衡)地下垂 • **noun** an instance of sagging 下沉；下陷；松散(或不均衡)的下垂 ■ **saggy** adjective.

saga /'sɑːɡə/ **noun 1** a long traditional story describing brave acts 萨迦；英雄传奇故事 **2** a story covering a long period of time (时间跨度很大的)故事 **3** a long and complicated series of incidents (情节曲折的)长篇故事

sagacious /sə'ɡeɪʃəs/ **adjective** having good judgement; wise 有判断力的；睿智的 ■ **sagacity** noun.

sage[1] /seɪdʒ/ **noun** a sweet-smelling Mediterranean plant with greyish-green leaves, used as a herb in cookery 鼠尾草(地中海植物，叶片呈灰绿色，烹饪中用作香草调料)

sage[2] **noun** a very wise man 智者；圣人 • **adjective** wise 智慧的；明智的 ■ **sagely** adverb.

Sagittarius /ˌsædʒɪ'teəriəs/ **noun** a sign of the zodiac (the Archer), 22 November–20 December 人马宫(黄道十二宫之一)

sago /'seɪɡəʊ/ **noun** a pudding made with starchy granules obtained from a palm tree, cooked with milk 西谷米，西米(用提取自一种棕榈树的淀粉粒制作的布丁，可加牛奶烹制)

sahib /sɑːb, 'sɑːɪb/ **noun** Indian 【印度】a polite form of address for a man 先生；老爷

said /sed/ past and past participle of **SAY**. • **adjective** referring to someone or something already mentioned 所说的；已经论及的

sail /seɪl/ **noun 1** a piece of material spread on a mast to catch the wind and propel a boat or ship 船帆 **2** a trip in a sailing boat or ship (乘帆船)的航行，航程 **3** a flat board attached to the arm of a windmill (风车的)翼板 • **verb 1** travel in a sailing boat as a sport or pastime (作为体育运动或娱乐)驾驶帆船航行 **2** travel in a ship or boat using sails or engine power (乘帆船或发动机动力船)航行 **3** begin a voyage 启航 **4** direct or control a boat or ship 驾驶，控制(小船或轮船) **5** move smoothly or confidently 轻快(或自信)地移动 **6** (**sail through**) informal 【非正式】 succeed easily at 轻易取得…的成功 □ **sail close to the wind** take risks 铤而走险 **sailing boat** (N. Amer. 【北美】**sailboat**) a boat propelled by sails 帆船

sailboard /'seɪlbɔːd/ **noun** a board with a mast and a sail, used in windsurfing (冲浪)帆板

sailcloth /'seɪlklɒθ/ **noun** strong fabric used for making sails 帆布；制帆材料

sailor /'seɪlə(r)/ **noun 1** a member of the crew of a ship or boat 水手；海员 **2** a person who sails as a sport or pastime (作为运动或娱乐)驾船者 **3** (**a good** or **bad sailor**) a person who rarely (or often) becomes seasick 几乎不(或经常)晕船的人

saint /seɪnt/ **noun 1** a good person who Christians believe will go to heaven when they die (基督徒认为死后会进入天堂的)圣徒，圣人 **2** a person of great goodness who after their death is formally declared by the Church to be a saint, and to whom people offer prayers (死后由基督教会追封的)圣徒，圣者 **3** informal 【非正式】 a very good or kind person 圣徒般的人；非常好(或善良)的人 □ **saint's day** (in the Christian Church) a day each year when a particular saint is honoured (基督教的)圣徒节 ■ **sainthood** noun.

sainted /'seɪntɪd/ **adjective** dated 【废】 very good or kind, like a saint 圣人般的；非常好的；极善良的

St George's cross noun a red cross on a white background 白底红十字架

saintly /'seɪntli/ **adjective** very holy or good 神圣的；好的 ■ **saintliness**

noun.

sake[1] /seɪk/ **noun 1** (**for the sake of**) in the interest of 为了；为了…的利益 **2** (**for the sake of**) out of consideration for 出于…的考虑 **3** (**for old times' sake**) in memory of former times 看在往日的份上

sake[2] /'sɑːki/ **noun** a Japanese alcoholic drink made from rice (稻米酿制的)日本清酒

salaam /sə'lɑːm/ **noun** a low bow with the hand touching the forehead, used by Muslims as a gesture of respect 额首礼(伊斯兰教徒使用来表示敬意的礼节)；问候 ▪ **verb** make a salaam 行额首礼

salacious /sə'leɪʃəs/ **adjective** containing too much sexual detail 淫秽的；色情的

salad /'sæləd/ **noun** a cold dish of raw vegetables 色拉；凉拌生蔬菜 □ **your salad days** the time when you are young and inexperienced 年少欠阅历的时期；经验不足的青年时代

salamander /'sæləmændə(r)/ **noun 1** an animal like a newt that can live in water or on land 蝾螈(一种形似水蜥的两栖动物) **2** a mythical creature resembling a lizard, said to be able to stay alive in fire 火蜥蜴，火蛇(传说可生活在火中)

salami /sə'lɑːmi/ **noun** (plural **salami** or **salamis**) a type of spicy preserved sausage 萨拉米香肠

salary /'sæləri/ **noun** (plural **salaries**) a fixed payment made every month to an employee 薪水；薪俸 ■ **salaried** adjective.

sale /seɪl/ **noun 1** the exchange of something for money 卖；出售，销售 **2** (**sales**) the activity or profession of selling 销售活动；销售职业 **3** a period in which goods in a shop are sold at reduced prices 降价销售 **4** a public event at which goods are sold or auctioned 商贸会；拍卖会 ■ **saleable** (or **salable**) adjective.

saleroom /'seɪlruːm/ or **sales-room** /'seɪlzruːm/ **noun** a room in which auctions are held or cars are sold 拍卖行

salesman /'seɪlzmən/ or **sales-woman** /'seɪlzwʊmən/ **noun** (plural **salesmen** or **saleswomen**) a person whose job involves selling goods 售货员；推销员 ■ **salesmanship** noun.

salient /'seɪlɪənt/ **adjective** most noticeable or important 显著的；突出的；最重要的 ■ **salience** noun.

saline /'seɪlaɪn/ **adjective** containing salt 含盐的 ■ **salinity** noun.

saliva /sə'laɪvə/ **noun** a watery liquid in the mouth produced by glands, that helps chewing, swallowing, and digestion 涎；唾液 ■ **salivary** adjective.

salivate /'sælɪveɪt/ **verb** (**salivates**, **salivating**, **salivated**) have a lot of saliva in the mouth 垂涎的；渴望的 ■ **salivation** noun.

sallow /'sæləʊ/ **adjective** (of a person's skin) yellowish or pale brown in colour (人的皮肤)灰黄色的

sally /'sælɪ/ **noun** (plural **sallies**) **1** a sudden charge out of a place surrounded by an enemy 突击；突围 **2** a witty or lively reply 妙语；俏皮话 • **verb** (**sallies**, **sallying**, **sallied**) (**sally forth**) set out 出发；动身

salmon /'sæmən/ **noun** (plural **salmon** or **salmons**) a large fish with pink flesh, that matures in the sea and moves to freshwater streams to release eggs 鲑，大麻哈鱼(一种大鱼，肉色粉红，在海中发育成熟，游到淡水水域产卵)

salmonella /ˌsælmə'nelə/ **noun** a germ that can cause food poisoning 沙门氏菌(可引起食物中毒)

salon /'sælɒn/ **noun 1** a place where a hairdresser, beautician, or clothes designer works 美发厅；美容院；服装店 **2** a reception room in a large house 客厅；会客室 **3** (in the past)

a regular gathering of writers and artists held in someone's house (旧时的)沙龙(作家、艺术家定期参加的家庭社交聚会)

saloon /sə'luːn/ **noun 1** Brit. 【英】a car with a separate boot 箱式小客车 **2** Brit. 【英】a lounge bar in a pub (酒馆中的)雅座酒吧 **3** a large room for use as a lounge on a ship (船上的)休息室，交谊厅 **4** N. Amer. old use 【北美，旧】a bar 酒馆

salopettes /ˌsælə'pets/ **plural noun** padded trousers with a high waist and shoulder straps, worn for skiing 滑雪服

salsa /'sælsə/ **noun 1** a Latin American dance performed to music that combines jazz and rock 萨尔萨舞曲(一种拉丁美洲舞曲，融入了爵士乐和摇滚乐的成分) **2** a spicy sauce 辛香调味汁

salt /sɔːlt/ **noun 1** sodium chloride, a white substance in the form of crystals, used for flavouring or preserving food 氯化钠；食盐 **2** Chemistry 【化学】any compound formed by the reaction of an acid with a base 盐；酸碱化合物 • **verb 1** season or preserve food with salt 用盐加工处理；腌制 **2** sprinkle a road or path with salt in order to melt snow or ice 在(道路)上撒盐(以使雪或冰融化) □ **salt cellar** a container for salt 盐瓶 **the salt of the earth** a person who is very kind, reliable, or honest 世上的善良、诚实、可靠的人 **take something with a pinch** (or **grain**) **of salt** recognize that something may be exaggerated or untrue 对(某事)半信半疑

saltings /'sɔːltɪŋz/ **noun** Brit. 【英】an area of coastal land regularly covered by the tide 盐滩岸

saltpetre /ˌsɔːlt'piːtə(r)/ (US spelling 【美拼作】**saltpeter**) **noun** a white powder (potassium nitrate) used to make gunpowder and preserve meat

硝石,钾硝(用于制造火药和保存肉类)

salty /'sɔːlti/ **adjective (saltier, saltiest) 1** containing or tasting of salt 咸味的;含盐的 **2** (of language or humour) rather rude (语言或幽默)粗俗的 ■ **saltiness** noun.

salubrious /sə'luːbriəs/ **adjective 1** good for your health 有益健康的 **2** (of a place) well maintained and pleasant to be in (地方)环境宜人的,适宜居住的

salutary /'sæljətri/ **adjective** (with reference to something unpleasant) producing a good effect because it teaches you something (令人不快的事物)有益的,有利的

salutation /ˌsæljuː'teɪʃn/ **noun** a greeting 问候;招呼;致意

salute /sə'luːt/ **noun 1** a raising of a hand to the head, made as a formal gesture of respect by a member of a military force 行军礼,敬礼 **2** a gesture of admiration or respect 行礼;致敬 **3** the shooting of a gun or guns as a formal sign of respect or celebration 鸣礼炮;鸣枪致意 • **verb (salutes, saluting, saluted) 1** make a formal salute to 向…致敬 **2** greet 打招呼;问候 **3** express admiration and respect for 向…致敬;赞扬;颂扬

salvage /'sælvɪdʒ/ **verb (salvages, salvaging, salvaged) 1** rescue something that is in danger of being lost or destroyed 营救;挽救;抢救 **2** rescue a ship or its contents from being lost at sea 抢救(失事船只或其财物) • **noun 1** the action of salvaging 营救;救助 **2** contents rescued from a wrecked ship (从遇难船只上)抢救出的财物 □ **salvage yard** a place where disused machinery and vehicles are broken up so that the metal or parts can be used again (拆解废旧机器和车辆部件以回收利用的)回收站,废旧机械处理场

salvation /sæl'veɪʃn/ **noun 1** the

saving of a person from sin and its consequences, believed to be brought about by faith in Jesus (基督教信仰中的)得救,超度,救世 **2** the protecting or saving of someone or something from harm or loss 拯救;救助

salve /sælv/ **noun 1** an ointment that soothes the skin 软膏;油膏 **2** something that makes you feel less guilty 慰藉;安慰话 • **verb (salves, salving, salved)** reduce feelings of guilt 缓解;抚慰;宽慰

salver /'sælvə(r)/ **noun** a tray 托盘

salvo /'sælvəʊ/ **noun** (plural **salvos** or **salvoes**) **1** a shooting of a number of guns at the same time (枪炮的)齐发,同时开火 **2** a sudden series of aggressive statements or acts (言语攻击或攻击性行为的)一阵,一系列

salwar /sʌl'wɑː(r)/ (also **shalwar**) **noun** light, loose trousers that fit tightly around the ankles, worn by women from the Indian subcontinent (印度次大陆女子穿的)宽松裤

Samaritan /sə'mærɪtən/ **noun 1** (**good Samaritan**) a helpful person 助人为乐者;乐善好施者 **2** a member of a people living in Samaria, an ancient city and region of Palestine 撒马利亚人(撒马利亚为巴勒斯坦一古城及其周围地区)

samba /'sæmbə/ **noun** a Brazilian dance of African origin 桑巴舞(源于非洲的巴西舞蹈)

same /seɪm/ **adjective 1** exactly alike 相同的,一模一样的 **2** (**this** or **that same**) referring to a person or thing just mentioned (与提到的人或事物相同的,一样的 • **pronoun 1** (**the same**) the same thing as previously mentioned (与提到的事物)相同的事物 **2** (**the same**) identical people or things 同样的人(或事物) • **adverb** in the same way 同样地 ■ **sameness** noun.

samey /'seɪmi/ **adjective** Brit. informal

【英,非正式】lacking in variety 千篇一律的;单调的

samovar /'sæməvɑ:(r)/ noun a highly decorated Russian tea urn 俄式茶炊

sample /'sɑ:mpl/ noun **1** a small part or quantity of something intended to show what the whole is like 样品;式样 **2** a specimen taken for scientific testing (用于科学试验的)样品, 样本, 标本 • verb (samples, sampling, sampled) **1** take a sample of 从…中取样 **2** try out 品尝;体验 **3** take a short extract from one musical recording and reuse it as part of another recording 节录,选录(一段乐曲)

sampler /'sɑ:mplə(r)/ noun **1** a piece of fabric decorated with a number of different embroidery stitches 刺绣样本 **2** a device for sampling music (音乐)取样器

samurai /'sæmuraɪ/ noun (plural **samurai**) (in the past) a member of a powerful Japanese military class (旧时的)日本武士

sanatorium /ˌsænə'tɔ:riəm/ noun (plural **sanatoriums** or **sanatoria** /ˌsænə'tɔ:riə/) **1** a place like a hospital where people who have a long-term illness or who are recovering from an illness are treated 疗养院;修养院 **2** Brit.【英】a place in a boarding school for children who are ill (寄宿学校的)医务室,治疗室

sanctify /'sæŋktɪfaɪ/ verb (**sanctifies**, **sanctifying**, **sanctified**) **1** make something holy 使神圣化 **2** make something legal or right 使合法化；使正当 ■ **sanctification** noun.

sanctimonious /ˌsæŋktɪ'məʊniəs/ adjective disapproving 【贬】making a show of being morally superior to other people 假装圣洁的;道貌岸然的;伪善的

sanction /'sæŋkʃn/ noun **1** (**sanctions**) measures taken by a state to try to force another state to behave well 国际制裁 **2** a penalty for disobeying a law or rule (对违反法律、规定者的)制裁 **3** official permission or approval 批准;认可 • verb give official permission for 批准;认可

sanctity /'sæŋktəti/ noun (plural **sanctities**) **1** the state of being holy 神圣；圣洁 **2** the state of being very important 神圣;神圣性

sanctuary /'sæŋktʃuəri/ noun (plural **sanctuaries**) **1** a place of safety 庇护所;避难所 **2** a nature reserve 自然保护区 **3** a place where injured or unwanted animals are cared for 动物收容所 **4** a holy place 圣所;圣地 **5** the part of the chancel of a church containing the high altar (教堂里的)圣殿

sanctum /'sæŋktəm/ noun **1** a sacred place 圣所 **2** a private place 私室;密室

sand /sænd/ noun **1** a substance consisting of very fine particles resulting from the wearing down of rocks, found in beaches and deserts and on the seabed 沙;沙子 **2** (**sands**) a wide area of sand 沙滩;沙地 • verb smooth a surface with sandpaper or a sander (用砂纸或打磨机)擦净, 磨光

sandal /'sændl/ noun a shoe with a partly open upper part or straps attaching the sole to the foot 凉鞋;拖鞋

sandalwood /'sændlwʊd/ noun the sweet-smelling wood of an Asian tree (亚洲产的)檀香木,白檀木

sandbag /'sændbæg/ noun a bag of sand, used to protect or strengthen a structure or as a weight 沙袋;沙包

sandbank /'sændbæŋk/ noun a deposit of sand forming a shallow area in the sea or a river 沙洲;沙坝

sandbar /'sændbɑ:(r)/ noun a long, narrow sandbank (狭长的)沙洲

sandblast /'sændblɑ:st/ verb roughen or clean a surface with a jet of sand

喷砂(以磨粒粗或清洁表面)

sandcastle /ˈsændkɑːsl/ **noun** a model of a castle built out of sand 沙堡

sander /ˈsændə(r)/ **noun** a power tool used for smoothing a surface 打磨机

sandpaper /ˈsændpeɪpə(r)/ **noun** paper coated with sand or another rough substance, used for smoothing surfaces 砂纸 • **verb** smooth with sandpaper (用砂纸)磨光

sandpit /ˈsændpɪt/ **noun** Brit. 【英】a shallow box or hollow containing sand, for children to play in (供儿童玩耍的)沙坑

sandstone /ˈsændstəʊn/ **noun** rock formed from compressed sand 沉积砂岩

sandstorm /ˈsændstɔːm/ **noun** a strong wind in a desert carrying clouds of sand 沙尘暴

sandwich /ˈsænwɪtʃ/ **noun** two pieces of bread with a filling between them 三明治；夹心面包片 • **verb** (**sandwich someone/thing between**) squeeze someone or something between two people or things 把 … 插入(或夹入)… 之间 □ **sandwich board** a pair of boards hung in front of and behind a person's body as they walk around, used especially to advertise something 三明治式广告牌(带子系住挂在某人胸前及后背) **sandwich course** Brit. 【英】a course of study which includes periods working in business or industry 工读交替制课程

sandy /ˈsændi/ **adjective** (**sandier**, **sandiest**) **1** covered in or consisting of sand 覆盖的，含沙的 **2** light yellowish brown 沙褐色的；浅棕色的

sane /seɪn/ **adjective 1** not mad 心智健全的；神志正常的 **2** sensible 明智的；合理的

sang /sæŋ/ past of SING.

sangfroid /ˌsɒ̃ˈfrwɑː/ **noun** the ability to stay calm in difficult circumstances (在困境中保持的)冷静，镇定

sanguinary /ˈsæŋɡwɪnəri/ **adjective** old use【旧】involving a lot of bloodshed 血腥的；流血的

sanguine /ˈsæŋɡwɪn/ **adjective** cheerful and confident about things that are going to happen 乐观的；充满信心的

sanitarium /ˌsænəˈteəriəm/ US【美】= SANATORIUM.

sanitary /ˈsænətri/ **adjective 1** relating to sanitation 有关卫生设施的 **2** hygienic 卫生的 □ **sanitary towel** a pad worn by women to absorb blood during a menstrual period 卫生巾；月经垫

sanitation /ˌsænɪˈteɪʃn/ **noun** arrangements to protect public health, such as the provision of clean drinking water and the disposal of sewage 公共卫生设备；卫生设施体系

sanitize or **sanitise** /ˈsænɪtaɪz/ **verb** (**sanitizes, sanitizing, sanitized**) **1** make something hygienic 使卫生 **2** make something unpleasant seem more acceptable 使(令人不快的事物)更易于接受；净化

sanity /ˈsænəti/ **noun 1** the condition of being sane 神志清楚；精神健全 **2** reasonable behaviour 理智行为

sank /sæŋk/ past of SINK.

Sanskrit /ˈsænskrɪt/ **noun** an ancient language of India 梵语(印度古语)

Santa Claus /ˈsæntə klɔːz/ **noun** Father Christmas 圣诞老人

sap /sæp/ **noun** the liquid that circulates in plants, carrying food to all parts (植物的)汁液 • **verb** (**saps, sapping, sapped**) gradually weaken a person's strength 逐渐削弱

sapling /ˈsæplɪŋ/ **noun** a young tree 树苗；幼苗

sapphic /ˈsæfɪk/ **adjective** literary【文】relating to lesbians 女同性恋的

sapphire /ˈsæfaɪə(r)/ **noun 1** a transparent blue precious stone 蓝宝

石 2 a bright colour 宝石蓝；天蓝色

saprophyte /'sæprəfaɪt/ **noun** a plant or fungus that lives on decaying matter 腐生植物；腐生生物 ■ **saprophytic** adjective.

Saracen /'særəsən/ **noun** an Arab or Muslim at the time of the Crusades (十字军东征时的)阿拉伯人，穆斯林

sarcasm /'sɑːkæzəm/ **noun** the use of words which say the opposite of what you mean, as a way of hurting or mocking someone 讽刺；嘲笑；挖苦

sarcastic /sɑːˈkæstɪk/ **adjective** using sarcasm 讽刺的；嘲笑的；挖苦的 ■ **sarcastically** adverb.

sarcophagus /sɑːˈkɒfəgəs/ **noun** (plural **sarcophagi** /sɑːˈkɒfəgaɪ/) a stone coffin 石棺

sardine /sɑːˈdiːn/ **noun** a small edible sea fish 沙丁鱼

sardonic /sɑːˈdɒnɪk/ **adjective** mocking 嘲笑的；嘲讽的 ■ **sardonically** adverb.

sari /'sɑːri/ or **saree** /'sɑːriː/ **noun** (plural **saris** or **sarees**) a length of fabric draped around the body, worn by women from the Indian subcontinent (印度次大陆女子穿的) 莎丽(用以裹身披肩的整段织物)

sarky /'sɑːki/ **adjective** Brit. informal 【英，非正式】 sarcastic 讽刺的；嘲笑的；挖苦的 ■ **sarkily** adverb.

sarnie /'sɑːni/ **noun** Brit. informal 【英，非正式】a sandwich 三明治；夹心面包片

sarong /sə'rɒŋ/ **noun** a long piece of cloth wrapped round the body and tucked at the waist or under the armpits 莎笼，围裙(裹在身上并塞进腰间或腋下的一条长布)

sartorial /sɑːˈtɔːriəl/ **adjective** having to do with the way a person dresses 裁缝的、缝纫的 ■ **sartorially** adverb.

sash[1] /sæʃ/ **noun** a strip of fabric worn over one shoulder or round the waist 腰带；肩带

sash[2] **noun** a frame holding the glass in a window 窗框 □ **sash window** a window with two sashes which can be slid up and down to open it 上下推拉窗

sashay /'sæʃeɪ/ **verb** informal 【非正式】swing the hips from side to side when walking 大摇大摆地走

Sassenach /'sæsənæk/ Scottish & Irish disapproving 【苏格兰和爱尔兰，贬】 **noun** an English person 英格兰人 • **adjective** English 英格兰人的

sassy /'sæsi/ **adjective** (**sassier**, **sassiest**) informal 【非正式】 confident, spirited, and cheeky 自信的；大胆的；厚脸皮的

SAT /sæt/ **abbreviation** standard assessment task 标准会考；标准课业测试

sat /sæt/ past and past participle of SIT.

Satan /'seɪtn/ **noun** the Devil 撒旦，魔鬼

satanic /sə'tænɪk/ **adjective** having to do with Satan or the worship of Satan 撒旦的；撒旦崇拜的

satanism /'seɪtənɪzəm/ **noun** the worship of Satan 撒旦崇拜，魔鬼崇拜 ■ **satanist** noun & adjective.

satchel /'sætʃəl/ **noun** a bag with a long strap worn over one shoulder 书包；肩背书包

sated /'seɪtɪd/ **adjective** having had as much or more of something than you want 心满意足的；厌腻的

satellite /'sætəlaɪt/ **noun 1** a man-made device placed in orbit round the earth or another planet to collect information or for communication 人造卫星 **2** a celestial body that moves in orbit round a planet (行星的)卫星 **3** a thing that is separate from but controlled by something else 附属物；卫星组织 □ **satellite television** television in which the signals are broadcast via satellite 卫星电视

satiate /'seɪʃɪeɪt/ **verb** give someone as much or more of something than they want 充分满足;使饱足 ■ **satiation** noun.

satiety /sə'taɪəti, 'seɪʃəti/ **noun** the state of being fully satisfied or of having had too much of something 饱足;满足

satin /'sætɪn/ **noun** a smooth, glossy fabric 缎子 ■ **satiny** adjective.

satire /'sætaɪə(r)/ **noun 1** the use of humour, irony, exaggeration, or ridicule to reveal and criticize people's bad points 讽刺;讥讽 **2** a play or other piece of writing that uses satire 讽刺作品 ■ **satirist** noun.

satirical /sə'tɪrɪkl/ or **satiric** /sə'tɪrɪk/ **adjective** using satire 讽刺的;使用讽刺手法的 ■ **satirically** adverb.

satirize or **satirise** /'sætəraɪz/ **verb** (**satirizes, satirizing, satirized**) mock or criticize using satire 讽刺;讥讽

satisfaction /ˌsætɪs'fækʃn/ **noun** the feeling of pleasure that arises when you have the things you need or want or when the things you want to happen have happened 满意;满足

satisfactory /ˌsætɪs'fæktəri/ **adjective** acceptable 可接受的 ■ **satisfactorily** adverb.

satisfy /'sætɪsfaɪ/ **verb** (**satisfies, satisfying, satisfied**) **1** give someone the things they need or want or bring about the things they want to happen 使满意;使高兴;使满足 **2** meet a particular demand, desire, or need 满足(要求、欲望或需要)

satsuma /ˌsæt'su:mə/ **noun** a kind of tangerine with a loose skin 萨摩蜜橘 (果皮松软)

saturate /'sætʃəreɪt/ **verb** (**saturates, saturating, saturated**) **1** soak thoroughly with a liquid 浸透;渗透 **2** make a substance combine with, dissolve, or hold the greatest possible

quantity of another substance 使饱和 **3** put more than is needed of a particular product into the market 使(市场)饱和 ■ **saturation** noun.

saturated /'sætʃəreɪtɪd/ **adjective** Chemistry【化学】(of fats) having only single bonds between carbon atoms in their molecules and therefore being less easily processed by the body (脂肪)饱和的

Saturday /'sætədeɪ, -di/ **noun** the day of the week before Sunday and following Friday 星期六;周六

Saturn /'sætən/ **noun** the sixth planet from the sun in the solar system, circled by broad flat rings 土星

saturnine /'sætənaɪn/ **adjective 1** (of a person or their manner) gloomy (人或其举止)严肃的,阴郁的 **2** (of looks) dark and brooding (外表)阴沉的,忧郁的

satyr /'sætə(r)/ **noun** (in Greek mythology) a lecherous woodland god, with a man's face and body and a horse's or goat's ears, tail, and legs (希腊神话中的)萨梯(森林之神,好色,具人脸人身,有马或羊的耳、尾和腿)

sauce /sɔ:s/ **noun 1** a thick liquid served with food to add moistness and flavour 调味汁;酱;沙司 **2** informal【非正式】cheeky talk or behaviour 放肆言语(或行为) □ **sauce boat** a boat-shaped jug for serving sauce 船形调味碟

saucepan /'sɔ:spən/ **noun** a deep cooking pan, with one long handle and a lid (长柄有盖的)深平底锅

saucer /'sɔ:sə(r)/ **noun** a small shallow dish on which a cup stands 茶碟;茶托

saucy /'sɔ:si/ **adjective** (**saucier, sauciest**) informal【非正式】**1** sexually suggestive in a light-hearted way 有色情意味的;不雅的;荤的 **2** cheeky 放肆的;无礼的 ■ **saucily** adverb.

Saudi /ˈsaʊdi/ noun (plural **Saudis**) a person from Saudi Arabia 沙特阿拉伯人 • adjective relating to Saudi Arabia 沙特阿拉伯的

sauerkraut /ˈsaʊəkraʊt/ noun a German dish of pickled cabbage (德式)泡菜

sauna /ˈsɔːnə/ noun 1 a small room used as a hot-air or steam bath for cleaning and refreshing the body 桑拿浴室，蒸汽浴室 2 a session in a sauna 桑拿浴，蒸汽浴

saunter /ˈsɔːntə(r)/ verb (**saunters**, **sauntering**, **sauntered**) walk in a slow, relaxed way 闲逛；漫步 • noun a leisurely stroll 闲逛；漫步

sausage /ˈsɒsɪdʒ/ noun 1 a short tube of raw minced meat encased in a skin and grilled or fried before eating 香肠，腊肠 2 a tube of seasoned minced meat that is cooked or preserved and eaten cold in slices (切片冷食的)一段香肠(或腊肠) □ **sausage dog** Brit. informal 【英，非正式】a dachshund 腊肠狗 **sausage meat** minced meat used in sausages or as a stuffing 香肠肉馅 **sausage roll** a portion of sausage meat baked in a roll of pastry 香肠卷(香肠肉糜外裹面饼烤制而成)

sauté /ˈsəʊteɪ/ adjective fried quickly in shallow fat or oil 炒的；嫩煎的 • verb (**sautés**, **sautéing**, **sautéed** or **sautéd**) cook in such a way 炒；嫩煎

savage /ˈsævɪdʒ/ adjective 1 fierce and violent 凶猛的 2 cruel and vicious 残酷的，野蛮的 3 primitive and uncivilized 原始的，未开化的 • noun 1 a member of a people seen as primitive and uncivilized 野蛮人；原始人，未开化的人 2 a brutal person 残暴的人 • verb (**savages**, **savaging**, **savaged**) 1 attack ferociously; maul 猛烈攻击；撕咬 2 criticize severely 激烈抨击 ■ **savagely** adverb **savagery** noun.

savannah or **savanna** /səˈvænə/ noun a grassy plain in hot regions 热带稀树草原

savant or **savante** /ˈsævənt/ noun a wise and knowledgeable person 博学之士；学者；专家

save[1] /seɪv/ verb (**saves**, **saving**, **saved**) 1 rescue or protect someone or something from harm or danger 救助；搭救；挽救 2 prevent someone from dying 抢救 3 store or keep for future use 保存；积攒；储存 4 (in computing) store data(在计算机中)存储(数据) 5 avoid, lessen, or guard against 避免；节省；防止 6 prevent an opponent from scoring a goal 防止对手进(球) 7 (in Christian use) prevent a soul from being damned (基督教用语)拯救(灵魂) • noun an act of preventing an opponent's goal 扑救，救球 ■ **saver** noun.

save[2] preposition & conjunction formal 【正式】except 除了；除外

saveloy /ˈsævɪlɔɪ/ noun Brit. 【英】A smoked pork sausage 萨维罗熏猪肉肠

saving /ˈseɪvɪŋ/ noun 1 a reduction in money, time, or some other resource 节省；节约 2 (**savings**) money saved 储蓄金；存款 • preposition except 除…外 □ **saving grace** a good quality that makes up for someone or something's faults 可资弥补的优点，可取之处

saviour /ˈseɪvjə(r)/ (US spelling 【美拼作】 **savior**) noun 1 a person who saves someone or something from danger or harm 救助者；拯救者；救星 2 (**Saviour**) (in Christianity) God or Jesus (基督教的)上帝，耶稣基督，救世主

savoir faire /ˌsævwɑː ˈfeə(r)/ noun the ability to act appropriately in social situations 社交能力，处世才干

savour /ˈseɪvə(r)/ (US spelling 【美拼作】 **savor**) verb 1 eat or drink something slowly while enjoying its full flavour 品尝，细品(食物或饮

料) **2** enjoy a feeling or experience thoroughly 欣赏，品味；享受 • **noun** a characteristic flavour or smell 滋味；味道；气味

savoury /ˈseɪvəri/ (US spelling 【美拼作】**savory**) **adjective 1** (of food) salty or spicy rather than sweet (食物) 咸味的，辛辣的 **2** morally acceptable or respectable 品性优良的；可敬的 • **noun** (plural **savouries**) Brit. 【英】a savoury snack 开胃菜

savvy /ˈsævi/ informal 【非正式】**noun** intelligence and good judgement 智慧；知识；见识 • **adjective** having intelligence and good judgement 智慧的，有见识的

saw¹ /sɔː/ **noun** a tool with a long, thin jagged blade, used with a backwards and forwards movement to cut wood and other hard materials 锯 • **verb** (**saws, sawing, sawed**; past participle Brit. 【英】**sawn** or N. Amer. 【北美】**sawed**) cut through or cut off with a saw 用锯切割

saw² past of SEE¹.

saw³ /sɔː/ **noun** a proverb or wise saying 谚语；格言

sawdust /ˈsɔːdʌst/ **noun** powdery particles of wood produced by sawing 锯末；锯屑

sawmill /ˈsɔːmɪl/ **noun** a place where logs are sawn by machine 锯木厂

sawtooth /ˈsɔːtuːθ/ or **sawtoothed** /ˈsɔːtuːθt/ **adjective** shaped like the jagged teeth of a saw 锯齿状的

sawyer /ˈsɔːjə(r)/ **noun** a person who saws timber 锯工；锯木匠

sax /sæks/ **noun** informal 【非正式】a saxophone 萨克斯管

Saxon /ˈsæksn/ **noun** a member of a people from Germany that settled in southern England in the 5th and 6th centuries 撒克逊人(5、6 世纪在英格兰南部定居的日耳曼人)

saxophone /ˈsæksəfəʊn/ **noun** a metal wind instrument with a reed in the mouthpiece 萨克斯管 ■ **sax-**

ophonist noun.

say /seɪ/ **verb** (**says, saying, said**) **1** speak words to communicate something 说；讲 **2** (of a piece of writing or a symbol) convey information or instructions (文本或符号)传达，表达(信息或指令) **3** (of a clock or watch) indicate a time (钟表)指示，指明(时间) **4** (**be said**) be reported 据说；据传 **5** assume something in order to work out what its consequences would be 假定；假设；比如说 • **noun** an opportunity to state your opinion 发言机会；发言权

saying /ˈseɪɪŋ/ **noun** a well-known statement expressing a general truth 格言；警句；谚语

scab /skæb/ **noun 1** a crust that forms over a wound as it heals 痂 **2** informal, disapproving 【非正式，贬】a person who refuses to take part in a strike 拒绝参加罢工的人 ■ **scabby** adjective.

scabbard /ˈskæbəd/ **noun** a cover for the blade of a sword or dagger (剑或匕首的)鞘

scabies /ˈskeɪbiːz/ **noun** a skin disease that causes itching and small red spots 疥疮；疥螨病

scabrous /ˈskeɪbrəs/ **adjective 1** rough and covered with scabs 粗糙的；凹凸不平的 **2** indecent or sordid 猥亵的；下流的；淫秽的

scaffold /ˈskæfəʊld/ **noun 1** (in the past) a raised wooden platform on which people stood when they were to be executed (旧时的)断头台，绞刑台 **2** a structure made using scaffolding 脚手架

scaffolding /ˈskæfəldɪŋ/ **noun 1** a structure made of wooden planks and metal poles, for people to stand on when building or repairing a building 脚手架；鹰架 **2** the planks and poles used in such a structure (木板、杆柱等)搭建脚手架的材料

scald /skɔːld/ **verb 1** burn with very

hot liquid or steam 烫伤 **2** heat a liquid to near boiling point 把(液体)加热至接近沸腾 **3** dip something briefly in boiling water 烫洗 • **noun** an injury caused by hot liquid or steam 烫伤

scale¹ /skeɪl/ **noun 1** each of the small overlapping plates protecting the skin of fish and reptiles (鱼和爬行动物的)鳞，鳞片 **2** a dry flake of skin (皮肤的)鳞屑 **3** a white deposit which is left in a kettle, water pipe, etc. when water containing lime is heated (水壶、水管等的)水垢，水锈 **4** a hard deposit that forms on teeth 牙垢；牙石 • **verb (scales, scaling, scaled) 1** remove the scales from 除去…的鳞片(或水垢) **2** form or flake off in scales 形成鳞片(或水垢)；呈鳞片状剥落

scale² **noun 1** (usu. **scales**) an instrument for weighing 天平；秤；磅秤 **2** either of the dishes on a simple set of scales 天平盘；秤盘

scale³ **noun 1** a range of values forming a system for measuring or grading something 等级体系；衡量标准 **2** a measuring instrument based on such a system 标尺；刻度尺 **3** relative size or extent 大小；规模 **4** a ratio of size in a map, model, drawing, or plan 比例；比率 **5** Music 【音乐】an arrangement of notes in order of pitch 音阶 • **verb (scales, scaling, scaled) 1** climb up or over something high and steep 攀登；爬越 **2** (**scale something down** or **up**) reduce (or increase) something in size, number, or extent 按比例缩减(或增加)；相应缩减(或增加) **3** represent something in a size that is larger or smaller than the original but exactly in proportion to it 按比例绘制(或制作) □ **to scale** reduced or enlarged in proportion to something 按比例(缩小或扩大)

scallion /ˈskælɪən/ **noun** N. Amer. 【北

美】a spring onion 小洋葱；嫩洋葱

scallop /ˈskɒləp/ **noun 1** an edible shellfish with two hinged fan-shaped shells 扇贝 **2** each of a series of small curves like the edge of a scallop shell, forming a decorative edging 扇形饰边

scalloped /ˈskɒləpt/ **adjective** (of the edge of something) decorated with a series of small curves (某物边缘)用扇形边装饰的

scallywag /ˈskælɪwæɡ/ **noun** informal 【非正式】a mischievous person 调皮捣蛋的人；淘气鬼

scalp /skælp/ **noun 1** the skin covering the top and back of the head 头皮 **2** (in the past, among American Indians) the scalp and hair cut away from an enemy's head as a battle trophy (旧时美洲印地安人从敌人头上剥下作为战利品的)带发头皮 • **verb** historical 【历史】take the scalp of an enemy 剥下(敌人)的头皮

scalpel /ˈskælpəl/ **noun** a knife with a small sharp blade, used by a surgeon 解剖刀；手术刀

scaly /ˈskeɪli/ **adjective** (**scalier, scaliest**) **1** covered in scales 有鳞的 **2** (of skin) dry and flaking (皮肤)干燥粗糙的

scam /skæm/ **noun** informal 【非正式】a dishonest scheme for making money 诡计；阴谋

scamp /skæmp/ **noun** informal 【非正式】a mischievous person 淘气鬼；捣蛋鬼

scamper /ˈskæmpə(r)/ **verb** (**scampers, scampering, scampered**) run with quick light steps 奔跑；疾走

scampi /ˈskæmpi/ **plural noun** the tails of large prawns, covered in breadcrumbs or batter and fried 炸大虾

scan /skæn/ **verb** (**scans, scanning, scanned**) **1** look at something quickly in order to find the parts that are most relevant or important 粗略

地看;浏览;快读 **2** move a detector or beam across (用探测器或光束) 扫描,扫掠 **3** convert a document or picture into digital form for storing or processing on a computer 扫描 (文件或图片) **4** analyse the metre of a line of verse 分析诗歌格律 **5** (of poetry) follow metrical rules (诗歌) 符合格律 • **noun 1** an act of scanning 浏览;扫描;扫掠 **2** a medical examination using a scanner 扫描体检 **3** an image obtained by scanning 扫描图

scandal /'skændl/ **noun 1** an action or event that causes public outrage 丑行;丑事;丑闻 **2** outrage or gossip arising from such an action or event (丑闻引起的)愤慨,流言 **3** an action or situation that you find shocking and unacceptable 令人震惊(或无法接受)的行为(或局面)

scandalize or **scandalise** /'skændəlaɪz/ **verb** (**scandalizes**, **scandalizing**, **scandalized**) shock other people by acting in way that is considered shameful or immoral (因可耻或不道德行为)使震惊,使愤慨

scandalous /'skændələs/ **adjective 1** causing public outrage 令人愤慨的;使人反感的 **2** shocking and unacceptable 令人震惊的;不可接受的 ■ **scandalously** adverb.

Scandinavian /ˌskændɪ'neɪvɪən/ **adjective** relating to the countries of Scandinavia, especially Norway, Sweden, and Denmark 斯堪的纳维亚的 • **noun** a person from Scandinavia 斯堪的纳维亚人

scanner /'skænə(r)/ **noun 1** a machine that uses X-rays or ultrasound to record images, used by doctors to examine the inside of someone's body (使用 X 光或超声波等的)扫描器,扫描仪 **2** a device that scans documents or pictures and converts them into digital data (将文件或图片转化为数字数据的)扫描仪

scansion /'skænʃn/ **noun 1** the

action of scanning a line of verse to find out its rhythm (对诗的)韵律分析 **2** the rhythm of a line of verse (诗的)韵律

scant /skænt/ **adjective** barely reaching the amount specified or needed 不足的,缺乏的

scanty /'skænti/ **adjective** (**scantier**, **scantiest**) too little in size or amount for what is needed 少量的;不足的;缺乏的 ■ **scantily** adverb.

scapegoat /'skeɪpgəʊt/ **noun** a person who is blamed for the things other people do wrong 代人受过的人;替罪羊 • **verb** make a scapegoat of 使成为…的替罪羊

scapula /'skæpjʊlə/ **noun** the shoulder blade 肩;肩胛骨

scar¹ /skɑː(r)/ **noun 1** a mark left on the skin or in body tissue after the healing of a wound 疤;伤疤;创痕 **2** a lasting effect left after an unpleasant experience (不愉快的经历留下的)创伤 **3** a mark left at the point where a leaf or other part separates from a plant (植物枝叶等上的)痕,瘢痕 • **verb** (**scars**, **scarring**, **scarred**) mark or be marked with a scar (使)结疤;(使)留伤痕

scar² **noun** a steep high cliff or outcrop of rock 悬崖;峭壁

scarab /'skærəb/ **noun 1** a kind of large beetle, seen as sacred in ancient Egypt (古埃及人视为神圣的)圣甲虫 **2** an ancient Egyptian gem in the form of a scarab beetle (古埃及的)圣甲虫形宝石

scarce /skeəs/ **adjective 1** (of a resource) only available in small quantities that do not meet a demand (资源)不足的, 缺乏的, 供不应求的 **2** rarely found 难得的;稀有的;罕见的 ■ **scarcity** noun.

scarcely /'skeəsli/ **adverb 1** only just 刚刚;仅仅 **2** just moments before (时间)刚刚, 才 **3** definitely or very probably not 决不;不可能

scare /skeə(r)/ **verb** (**scares, scaring, scared**) **1** frighten or become frightened 使惊恐；受惊吓；害怕 **2** (**scare someone away** or **off**) drive or keep someone away by frightening them 吓走；吓跑 • **noun 1** a sudden attack of fright (突然的)惊吓，惊恐 **2** a period of general alarm (一阵)恐慌，恐惧

scarecrow /'skeəkrəʊ/ **noun** an object made to look like a person, set up to scare birds away from crops 稻草人

scarf /skɑːf/ **noun** (plural **scarves** or **scarfs**) a length or square of fabric worn around the neck or head 围巾；头巾

scarify /'skærɪfaɪ/ **verb** (**scarifies, scarifying, scarified**) **1** rake out unwanted material from a lawn 翻挖(草坪) **2** break up the surface of soil 翻松(土地) **3** make shallow cuts in the skin 划破(皮肤)

scarlatina or **scarletina** /ˌskɑːlə'tiːnə/ **noun** scarlet fever 猩红热

scarlet /'skɑːlət/ **noun** a bright red colour 猩红色；绯红色 □ **scarlet fever** an infectious disease that affects children, causing fever and a scarlet rash 猩红热

scarp /skɑːp/ **noun** a very steep slope 陡坡；悬崖

scarper /'skɑːpə(r)/ **verb** (**scarpers, scarpering, scarpered**) Brit. informal 【英,非正式】run away 逃跑；溜走

scarves /skɑːvz/ plural of SCARF.

scary /'skeəri/ **adjective** (**scarier, scariest**) informal 【非正式】frightening 恐怖的；吓人的 ■ **scarily** adverb

scathing /'skeɪðɪŋ/ **adjective** severely critical 尖刻的，严厉的 ■ **scathingly** adverb

scatological /ˌskætə'lɒdʒɪkl/ **adjective** obsessed with excrement and excretion 迷恋粪便的 ■ **scatology** noun.

scatter /'skætə(r)/ **verb** (**scatters, scattering, scattered**) **1** throw in various random directions 撒；撒播 **2** separate and move off in different directions 分散；驱散；散开 **3** (**be scattered**) be found at various places 散布在各处

scatty /'skæti/ or **scatterbrained** /'skætəbreɪnd/ **adjective** informal 【非正式】disorganized and rather silly 无条理的；傻乎乎的

scavenge /'skævɪndʒ/ **verb** (**scavenges, scavenging, scavenged**) **1** search through waste for anything that can be used again (从废物中)搜寻(可用之物) **2** (of an animal) search for and eat dead animals (动物)觅食(动物尸体) ■ **scavenger** noun.

scenario /sə'nɑːriəʊ/ **noun** (plural **scenarios**) **1** a possible sequence of events in the future (可能的)事态 **2** a written outline of a film, play, or novel 电影脚本；剧本梗概；小说情节大纲

scene /siːn/ **noun 1** the place where an incident happens (事件发生的)地点 **2** a view or landscape as seen by a spectator 景色；景象 **3** an incident 事件: *scenes of violence* 暴力事件 **4** a sequence of continuous action in a play, film, etc. (戏剧、电影等的)场景，片段，镜头 **5** an area of activity or interest 活动领域；兴趣领域；界；圈子: *the literary scene* 文学界 **6** a public display of emotion or anger 发脾气；当众吵闹 □ **behind the scenes** out of public view 在幕后；秘密地；不公开地

scenery /'siːnəri/ **noun 1** a landscape considered in terms of its appearance 风景；景色 **2** the background used to represent a place on a stage or film set 舞台布景

scenic /'siːnɪk/ **adjective** having beautiful natural scenery 自然风景优美的 ■ **scenically** adverb.

scent /sent/ **noun 1** a distinctive

smell, especially a pleasant one 香味;香气 **2** pleasant-smelling liquid worn on the skin; perfume 香水 **3** a trail left by an animal, indicated by its smell (动物的)遗臭, 臭迹 • verb **1** give a pleasant scent to 使…充满香气 **2** find or recognize something by using the sense of smell 闻到, 嗅出 **3** sense that something is about to happen 察觉;发觉 ■ **scented** adjective.

sceptic /ˈskeptɪk/ (US spelling 【美拼作】**skeptic**) noun a person who questions accepted opinions 怀疑(论)者 ■ **scepticism** noun.

sceptical /ˈskeptɪkl/ (US spelling 【美拼作】**skeptical**) adjective not easily convinced; having doubts 惯持怀疑态度的;有疑问的 ■ **sceptically** adverb.

sceptre /ˈseptə(r)/ (US spelling 【美拼作】**scepter**) noun a decorated rod carried by a king or queen on ceremonial occasions 国王或女王在典礼仪式上所持的)节杖, 权杖

schedule /ˈʃedjuːl/ noun **1** a plan for doing something, with a list of intended events and times 计划(表);日程安排(表) **2** a timetable 时间表 • verb (**schedules**, **scheduling**, **scheduled**) **1** plan for something to happen at a particular time 安排, 为…制定计划 **2** (**scheduled**) (of a flight) forming part of a regular service rather than specially chartered (航班)定期的

schema /ˈskiːmə/ noun (plural **schemata** /ˈskiːmɑːtə/ or **schemas**) technical 【术语】an outline of a plan or theory (计划或理论的)纲要, 概要

schematic /skiːˈmætɪk/ adjective **1** (of a diagram) simplified and using symbols (图表)简略的, 略图的 **2** presented according to a plan 纲要的;计划的 ■ **schematically** adverb.

scheme /skiːm/ noun **1** a careful plan for achieving something 计划;规划, 方案 **2** a secret or devious plan; a plot 阴谋;诡计 **3** a system or pattern 系统;体制;格式 • verb (**schemes**, **scheming**, **schemed**) make secret plans; plot 搞阴谋;密谋

scherzo /ˈskeətsəʊ/ noun (plural **scherzos** or **scherzi** /ˈskeətsiː/) a short, lively piece of music 谐谑曲

schism /ˈskɪzəm/ noun a disagreement or division between two groups or within an organization 分裂;不和 ■ **schismatic** adjective.

schist /ʃɪst/ noun a metamorphic rock which consists of layers of different minerals 片岩

schizoid /ˈskɪtsɔɪd/ adjective having a mental condition similar to schizophrenia 精神分裂般的;类精神分裂症的

schizophrenia /ˌskɪtsəˈfriːniə/ noun a mental disorder whose symptoms include a withdrawal from reality into fantasy 精神分裂症

schizophrenic /ˌskɪtsəˈfrenɪk/ adjective **1** suffering from schizophrenia 患精神分裂症的 **2** having contradictory elements 相互矛盾的;不一致的 • noun a schizophrenic person 精神分裂症患者

schmaltz /ʃmɔːlts/ noun informal 【非正式】the quality of being too sentimental 过分伤感 ■ **schmaltzy** adjective.

schnapps /ʃnæps/ noun a strong alcoholic drink 烈酒

scholar /ˈskɒlə(r)/ noun **1** a person who is studying at an advanced level 学者 **2** a student who has a scholarship 奖学金获得者

scholarly /ˈskɒləli/ adjective **1** relating to serious academic study 学术的 **2** very knowledgeable and keen on studying 有学问的;有学识的

scholarship /ˈskɒləʃɪp/ noun **1** academic work 学术;学术研究 **2** an amount of money given to a student to help pay for their education 奖学金

scholastic /skə'læstɪk/ **adjective** having to do with schools and education 学校的，教育的；学业的

school /sku:l/ **noun 1** a place where children are educated (中、小)学校 **2** a place where instruction is given in a particular subject 专科学校 **3** a group of artists, philosophers, etc. sharing similar ideas (艺术、哲学等的)流派，学派 **4** a large group of fish or sea mammals (鱼或海生哺乳动物的)群 ▪ **verb 1** formal or N. Amer. 【正式或北美】educate 教育 **2** train in a particular skill or activity 培养；训练 □ **school of thought** a particular way of thinking 思想流派

schooling /'sku:lɪŋ/ **noun** education received at school 学校教育

schooner /'sku:nə(r)/ **noun 1** a sailing ship with two or more masts (双桅或多桅)纵帆船 **2** Brit. 【英】a large glass for sherry 雪利酒杯

sciatic /saɪ'ætɪk/ **adjective** having to do with the hip or with the nerve which goes down the back of the thigh (the sciatic nerve) 髋部的；坐骨的；坐骨神经的

sciatica /saɪ'ætɪkə/ **noun** pain affecting the back, hip, and leg, caused by pressure on the sciatic nerve 坐骨神经痛

science /'saɪəns/ **noun 1** study or knowledge of the physical and natural world, based on observation and experiment 科学；自然科学 **2** a particular branch of science 学科；**3** a body of knowledge on any subject (一门学科的)系统知识；学 □ **science fiction** fiction set in the future and dealing with imagined scientific advances 科幻小说 **science park** an area where a number of science-based companies are located 科技园区

scientific /saɪən'tɪfɪk/ **adjective 1** relating to or based on science 科学

的；关于科学的 **2** systematic; methodical 系统的；有条理的 ▪ **scientifically** adverb.

scientist /'saɪəntɪst/ **noun** a person who studies or is an expert in science 科学家

sci-fi /'saɪfaɪ/ **noun** science fiction 科幻小说

scimitar /'sɪmɪtə(r)/ **noun** a short sword with a curved blade 短弯刀

scintillating /'sɪntɪleɪtɪŋ/ **adjective** very skilful and exciting 才华横溢的；激动人心的

scion /'saɪən/ **noun 1** a young shoot or twig of a plant (植物的)幼枝，接穗 **2** literary 【文】a descendant of a notable family (名门望族的)后裔，子孙

scissors /'sɪzəz/ **plural noun** a device for cutting cloth and paper, consisting of two crossing blades pivoted in the middle 剪刀；剪子

sclerosis /sklə'rəʊsɪs/ **noun 1** abnormal hardening of body tissue (人体组织的)硬化 **2** (also **multiple sclerosis**) a serious disease of the nervous system that can cause partial paralysis 多发性硬化(一种可导致部分瘫痪的严重神经系统疾病)

scoff¹ /skɒf/ **verb** speak about something in a scornful way 嘲笑；嘲弄；讥笑

scoff² **verb** informal 【非正式】eat something quickly and greedily 狼吞虎咽

scold /skəʊld/ **verb** angrily criticize or tell off 骂；呵斥；斥责

sconce /skɒns/ **noun** a candle holder attached to a wall 壁式烛台

scone /skɒn/ **noun** a small plain cake, usually eaten with butter (通常抹黄油食用的)烤饼，司康饼

scoop /sku:p/ **noun 1** an implement like a spoon, with a short handle and a deep bowl 勺，铲子 **2** the bowl-shaped part of a digging machine (挖掘机的)碗形铲凿 **3** informal 【非

正式】a piece of news printed by one newspaper before its rivals 抢先报道的新闻；独家新闻 • **verb 1** pick something up with a scoop 用勺舀；用铲子铲 **2** create a hollow or hole in something 挖空；挖出 **3** pick someone or something up in a quick, smooth movement (迅速)拣起，拿起 **4** informal【非正式】be quicker than other newspapers in printing a piece of news 抢先播出；抢先报道

scoot /skuːt/ **verb** informal【非正式】move or go quickly 飞奔；疾走

scooter /'skuːtə(r)/ **noun 1** (also **motor scooter**) a light motorcycle 轻便摩托车 **2** a child's vehicle with two wheels and a long steering handle, which you move by pushing one foot against the ground 踏板车；滑板车

scope /skəup/ **noun 1** the opportunity or possibility for doing something (做某事的)机会，可能性 **2** the extent of the area or subject matter that something deals with 范围

scorch /skɔːtʃ/ **verb 1** burn something on the surface or edges 把…烧焦 **2** (**scorched**) dried out and withered as a result of extreme heat 烤焦的，枯萎的

scorcher /'skɔːtʃə(r)/ **noun** informal【非正式】a very hot day 大热天

score /skɔː(r)/ **noun 1** the number of points, goals, etc. achieved by a person or team in a game (比赛中一方的)得分 **2** (plural **score**) a group or set of twenty 二十个【**3** (**scores of**) a lot of 许多；大量 **4** the written music for a composition 总乐谱；总谱 • **verb** (**scores, scoring, scored**) **1** win a point, goal, etc. in a game (在比赛中)得(分) **2** record the score during a game (在比赛中)记(分) **3** cut or scratch a mark on a surface 在(表面)作记号；划痕于；划线于 **4** (**score something out**) cross out a word or words 划掉，删去(文字) **5**

arrange a piece of music 改编(乐曲)

scoreline /'skɔːlaɪn/ **noun** Brit.【英】the final score in a game (比赛的)最终比分

scorn /skɔːn/ **noun** a strong feeling that someone or something is worthless; contempt 轻蔑，蔑视 • **verb 1** express scorn for 轻蔑；蔑视 **2** reject in a contemptuous way 轻蔑地拒绝

scornful /'skɔːnfl/ **adjective** showing or feeling scorn 轻蔑的；蔑视的 ■ **scornfully** adverb.

Scorpio /'skɔːpiəu/ **noun** a sign of the zodiac (the Scorpion), 23 October– 21 November 天蝎宫(黄道十二宫之一)

scorpion /'skɔːpiən/ **noun** a small creature with six legs, pincers, and a poisonous sting at the end of its tail 蝎；蝎子

Scot /skɒt/ **noun** a person from Scotland 苏格兰人

Scotch /skɒtʃ/ **noun** (also **Scotch whisky**) whisky distilled in Scotland 苏格兰威士忌 • **adjective** dated【废】Scottish 苏格兰的 □ **Scotch egg** Brit.【英】a hard-boiled egg enclosed in sausage meat 苏格兰香肠蛋

> **！注意** use **Scots** or **Scottish** rather than **Scotch** to refer to people or things from Scotland. 指称苏格兰的人或事物要用 Scots 或 Scottish，不要用 Scotch。

scotch /skɒtʃ/ **verb** decisively put an end to 结束；终止

scot-free /,skɒt'friː/ **adverb** without suffering any punishment or injury 免于受罚地；未受损害地；安然无恙地

Scots /skɒts/ **adjective** Scottish 苏格兰的；苏格兰人的 • **noun** the form of English used in Scotland 苏格兰英语

Scottish /'skɒtɪʃ/ **adjective** relating to Scotland or its people 苏格兰的；苏格兰人的

scoundrel /'skaʊndrəl/ noun old use 【旧】a dishonest or immoral person 无赖;恶棍

scour /'skaʊə(r)/ verb 1 clean by rubbing with rough material 擦净;擦亮 2 search a place thoroughly 细查;彻底搜查

scourge /skɜːdʒ/ noun 1 a cause of great suffering 祸根;灾难;祸患 2 old use 【旧】a whip 鞭子 • verb (scourges, scourging, scourged) 1 cause great suffering to 使蒙苦;折磨 2 old use 【旧】whip someone 鞭笞;鞭答

Scouse /skaʊs/ Brit. informal 【英,非正式】noun 1 the dialect or accent of people from Liverpool 利物浦方言;利物浦口音 2 (also **Scouser**) a person from Liverpool 利物浦人

scout /skaʊt/ noun 1 a person who is sent ahead to gather information about the enemy 侦察员 2 a member of the Scout Association, an organization for young people 童子军成员 3 (also **talent scout**) a person whose job is searching for talented performers 星探;人才发掘者 • verb 1 search a place to find something or gather information 搜索;搜寻 2 act as a scout 侦察;物色人才

scowl /skaʊl/ noun a bad-tempered expression 怒容;阴沉的脸色 • verb frown in an angry or bad-tempered way 皱眉;蹙额

scrabble /'skræbl/ verb (scrabbles, scrabbling, scrabbled) 1 grope around with your fingers to find or hold on to something 摸索着寻找;翻找 2 move quickly and awkwardly; scramble 快速而笨拙地移动;攀爬

scraggy /'skrægi/ adjective thin and bony 瘦的;皮包骨的

scram /skræm/ verb (scrams, scramming, scrammed) informal 【非正式】leave quickly 走开;滚开

scramble /'skræmbl/ verb (scrambles, scrambling, scrambled) 1 move quickly and awkwardly, using hands as well as feet (迅速而笨拙地)爬,攀爬 2 muddle 弄乱;搞乱 3 put a transmission into a form that can only be understood by using a decoding device 扰频,倒频(使传输信息只有通过译码装置才能获知其内容) 4 cook beaten eggs in a pan (用平底锅)炒(蛋) 5 (of fighter aircraft) take off immediately in an emergency (战斗机)紧急升空 • noun 1 an act of scrambling 攀爬;混乱;扰频 2 Brit. 【英】a motorcycle race over rough and hilly ground 摩托车越野赛

scrap¹ /skræp/ noun 1 a small piece or amount of something 小块;碎片;碎屑 2 (**scraps**) bits of uneaten food left after a meal 残羹剩饭 3 unwanted metal that can be used again (可回收利用的)废金属,废料 • verb (**scraps, scrapping, scrapped**) 1 abolish or cancel a plan, policy, etc. 废止,废除(计划,政策等) 2 remove from use 废弃;抛弃

scrap² noun a short fight or quarrel 打架;争吵 • verb (**scraps, scrapping, scrapped**) be involved in a scrap 打架;争吵

scrapbook /'skræpbʊk/ noun a book for sticking cuttings or pictures in 剪贴簿

scrape /skreɪp/ verb (scrapes, scraping, scraped) 1 drag something hard or sharp across a surface to remove dirt or waste matter 刮;刮净;刮光 2 rub against a rough or hard surface 刮擦 3 just manage to achieve, succeed, or pass 勉强实现(或通过) • noun 1 an act or sound of scraping 刮;刮擦声 2 an injury or mark caused by scraping 刮伤;擦痕 3 informal 【非正式】an awkward or difficult situation 窘境;困境

scrappy /'skræpi/ adjective disorganized, untidy, or incomplete 杂乱无章的;散乱的;不完整的

scrapyard /'skræpjɑːd/ noun a place

where scrap metal is collected 废料场;废旧金属回收站

scratch /skrætʃ/ verb **1** make a long mark or wound on a surface with something sharp or pointed (用尖物或利刃)刻,划(物体表面) **2** rub part of the body with your fingernails to relieve itching 搔,挠(痒处) **3** (**scratch something out**) cross out a word or words 删去;勾掉 **4** withdraw from a competition 退出比赛 **5** cancel or abandon a plan, project, etc. 取消,放弃(计划或方案) • noun **1** a mark or wound made by scratching 划痕;刮痕;抓痕 **2** informal 【非正式】a slight injury 微伤;小伤 • adjective put together from whatever is available 拼凑而成的: *a scratch squad* 临时凑成的一个小队 □ **from scratch** from the very beginning 从头开始; 从零开始 **up to scratch** up to the required standard 达到要求的标准; 合格 **scratch card** a card with a section which you scrape to reveal whether a prize has been won 刮奖卡 ■ **scratchy** adjective.

scrawl /skrɔːl/ verb write in a hurried, careless way 潦草地写;涂写 • noun scrawled handwriting 潦草的笔迹; 涂鸦

scrawny /ˈskrɔːni/ adjective (**scrawnier, scrawniest**) thin and bony 骨瘦如柴的;皮包骨的

scream /skriːm/ verb make a loud, piercing cry or sound 尖叫;惊呼 • noun **1** a loud, piercing cry or sound 尖叫(声) **2** (**a scream**) informal 【非正式】a very funny person or thing 极其滑稽可笑的人(或事物)

scree /skriː/ noun a mass of small loose stones on a mountain slope 碎石坡

screech /skriːtʃ/ noun a loud, harsh cry or sound 尖叫;尖锐刺耳的声音 • verb make a screech 尖叫;发出尖锐刺耳的声音

screed /skriːd/ noun **1** a long speech

or piece of writing 长篇演说;冗长的文章 **2** a layer of material applied to make a floor level (用来压平地面的)整平板

screen /skriːn/ noun **1** an upright partition used to divide a room or conceal something 帘;幕;帐;挡板 **2** the front part of a television or computer monitor, on which images and data are displayed 屏幕;荧光屏 **3** a blank surface on which films are projected (放映电影用的)银幕 **4** (**the screen**) films or television 电影;电视 • verb **1** conceal or protect with a screen (用遮蔽物)遮蔽,掩护,保护 **2** test a group of people for the presence of a disease (对疾病)检查,筛查 **3** show or broadcast a film or television programme 放映(影片); 播放(电视节目) □ **screen printing** a process in which ink is forced through a screen of fine material to create a picture or pattern 丝网印刷 **screen test** a filmed audition for a film part (挑选影片角色扮演者的)试镜

screenplay /ˈskriːnpleɪ/ noun the script of a film, including acting instructions 电影剧本

screenwriter /ˈskriːnraɪtə(r)/ noun a person who writes a screenplay 电影编剧

screw /skruː/ noun **1** a metal pin with a spiral thread running around it, which is turned and pressed into a surface to join things together 螺丝钉;螺丝 **2** a ship's or aircraft's propeller (船或飞机的)螺旋桨 **3** informal 【非正式】a prison warder 监狱看守 • verb **1** fasten or tighten with a screw or screws (用螺丝)固定,拧紧 **2** rotate something to attach or remove it 旋;拧 **3** informal 【非正式】cheat or swindle 欺骗 □ **screw someone/thing up 1** crush something into a tight mass 把…揉成一团 **2** informal 【非正式】make something fail or go wrong 弄糟；搞乱 **3** informal 【非正式】make someone emotionally disturbed 使紧张；使心烦意乱

screwdriver /ˈskruːdraɪvə(r)/ **noun** a tool with a tip that fits into the head of a screw to turn it 螺丝刀；螺丝起子

screwy /ˈskruːi/ **adjective** informal 【非正式】rather odd or eccentric 古怪的；怪诞的，异常的

scribble /ˈskrɪbl/ **verb** (**scribbles**, **scribbling**, **scribbled**) write or draw carelessly or hurriedly 潦草书写；乱画；涂鸦 • **noun** a scribbled picture or piece of writing 涂鸦；潦草字迹

scribe /skraɪb/ **noun** (in the past) a person who copied out documents (旧时的)抄写员，誊录者

scrimmage /ˈskrɪmɪdʒ/ **noun** a confused struggle or fight 扭打；混战

scrimp /skrɪmp/ **verb** be very careful with money; economize 吝啬；节俭；节约

script /skrɪpt/ **noun 1** the written text of a play, film, or broadcast (戏剧或电影的)剧本，广播稿 **2** handwriting as distinct from print 笔迹；手迹 • **verb** write a script for 为…写剧本

scripture /ˈskrɪptʃə(r)/ or **scriptures** /ˈskrɪptʃəz/ **noun 1** the sacred writings of Christianity contained in the Bible (基督教的)圣经 **2** the sacred writings of another religion (基督教以外其他宗教的)经文，经典 ■ **scriptural** adjective.

scrofula /ˈskrɒfjʊlə/ **noun** the name in the past for a form of tuberculosis 瘰疬(结核病的旧称) ■ **scrofulous** adjective.

scroll /skrəʊl/ **noun** a roll of parchment or paper for writing or painting on (用来写字或作画的)卷轴 • **verb** move data on a computer screen in order to view different parts of it 滚动，滚屏(以察看计算机屏幕上不同部分的数据)

Scrooge /skruːdʒ/ **noun** a person who is mean with money 吝啬鬼；守财奴

scrotum /ˈskrəʊtəm/ **noun** (plural **scrota** /ˈskrəʊtə/ or **scrotums**) the pouch of skin containing the testicles 阴囊

scrounge /skraʊndʒ/ **verb** (**scrounges**, **scrounging**, **scrounged**) informal 【非正式】try to get something from someone without having to pay or work for it 白要；白拿；擅取 ■ **scrounger** noun.

scrub[1] /skrʌb/ **verb** (**scrubs**, **scrubbing**, **scrubbed**) rub something hard to clean it (用力)擦净，擦洗 • **noun** an act of scrubbing.

scrub[2] **noun 1** vegetation consisting mainly of bushes and small trees 灌木丛；矮树丛 **2** land covered with such vegetation 灌木丛地带；矮树丛地带 ■ **scrubby** adjective.

scruff[1] /skrʌf/ **noun** the back of a person's or animal's neck (人或动物的)颈背，后颈

scruff[2] **noun** Brit. informal 【英，非正式】a scruffy person 邋遢鬼

scruffy /ˈskrʌfi/ **adjective** (**scruffier**, **scruffiest**) shabby and untidy or dirty 衣衫褴褛的；不整洁的；肮脏的 ■ **scruffiness** noun.

scrum /skrʌm/ **noun 1** (also **scrummage**) Rugby 【英式橄榄球】a formation in which players push against each other with heads down and try to gain possession of the ball when it is thrown in between them 并列争球 **2** Brit. informal 【英，非正式】a disorderly crowd 混乱的人群

scrummy /ˈskrʌmi/ **adjective** informal 【非正式】delicious 美味的；可口的

scrump /skrʌmp/ **verb** Brit. informal 【英，非正式】steal fruit from an orchard or garden (从果园或花园)偷(水果)

scrumptious /ˈskrʌmpʃəs/ **adjective** informal 【非正式】delicious 美味的；

可口的

scrumpy /'skrʌmpi/ **noun** strong cider made in the west of England (英格兰西部产的)苹果烈酒

scrunch /skrʌntʃ/ **verb** crush or squeeze into a tight mass 压(或挤)成一团

scruple /'skruːpl/ **noun** a feeling of doubt as to whether an action is morally right (道义上的)顾虑,不安 • **verb (not scruple to do)** formal 【正式】not hesitate to do something, even if it may be wrong 毫无顾忌地做

scrupulous /'skruːpjələs/ **adjective 1** very careful and thorough 一丝不苟的;认真细致的 **2** very concerned to avoid doing wrong 谨小慎微的 ■ **scrupulously** adverb.

scrutinize or **scrutinise** /'skruːtənaɪz/ **verb (scrutinizes, scrutinizing, scrutinized)** examine thoroughly 详细审查;仔细检查

scrutiny /'skruːtəni/ **noun (plural scrutinies)** close and critical examination 详细审查;仔细检查

scuba diving /'skuːbə/ **noun** swimming underwater using an aqualung 戴水肺潜水

scud /skʌd/ **verb (scuds, scudding, scudded)** move quickly, driven by the wind 飞奔;疾行

scuff /skʌf/ **verb 1** make a mark on the surface of something by scraping it against something rough 留擦痕(或刮痕) **2** drag your feet when walking 拖曳而行;拖着脚走 • **noun** a mark made by scuffing 擦痕;刮痕

scuffle /'skʌfl/ **noun** a short, confused fight or struggle 混战;扭打 • **verb (scuffles, scuffling, scuffled)** take part in a scuffle 混战;扭打

scull /skʌl/ **noun 1** each of a pair of small oars used by a single rower (单人双桨划船手使用的)短桨 **2** a light, narrow boat propelled by a single rower 单(或双)桨小艇 • **verb** propel a boat with sculls 用短桨划(船)

scullery /'skʌləri/ **noun (plural sculleries)** a small room in an old house, used for washing dishes and laundry (清洗碗碟、衣物的)洗涤室

sculpt /skʌlpt/ **verb** carve or shape 雕刻;雕塑

sculptor /'skʌlptə(r)/ **noun (feminine 【阴性】sculptress)** an artist who makes sculptures 雕塑家;雕刻家

sculpture /'skʌlptʃə(r)/ **noun 1** the art of making three-dimensional figures and shapes by carving or shaping wood, stone, metal, etc. 雕刻(艺术);雕塑(艺术) **2** a work of such a kind 雕刻品;雕塑品 • **verb (sculptures, sculpturing, sculptured) 1** make or represent by sculpture 雕刻;雕塑 **2 (sculptured)** pleasingly shaped, with strong, smooth lines 线条清晰平滑的 ■ **sculptural** adjective.

scum /skʌm/ **noun 1** a layer of dirt or froth on the surface of a liquid 浮渣;浮垢;浮沫 **2** informal 【非正式】a worthless person or group of people 无用之人;渣滓;败类 ■ **scummy** adjective.

scupper /'skʌpə(r)/ **verb (scuppers, scuppering, scuppered)** Brit. 【英】**1** informal 【非正式】stop something working or succeeding 破坏;使成泡影;使完蛋 **2** sink your own ship deliberately 故意使(船)沉没

scurf /skɜːf/ **noun** flakes of skin 皮屑;头皮屑

scurrilous /'skʌrələs/ **adjective** rude and insulting; slanderous 粗鲁谩骂的;恶言毁谤的

scurry /'skʌri/ **verb (scurries, scurrying, scurried)** move hurriedly with short, quick steps (小步)疾走,疾跑

scurvy /'skɜːvi/ **noun** a disease caused by a lack of vitamin C 坏血病

scut /skʌt/ **noun** the short tail of a hare, rabbit, or deer (兔或鹿的)短尾巴

S

scuttle¹ /'skʌtl/ **noun** a metal container used to store coal for a domestic fire 煤桶;煤斗

scuttle² **verb** (**scuttles, scuttling, scuttled**) run hurriedly or secretively with short, quick steps 小步急跑;逃奔

scuttle³ **verb** (**scuttles, scuttling, scuttled**) 1 cause a scheme to fail 使(计划)失败 2 sink your own ship deliberately 故意使(自己的船)沉没,凿沉

scythe /saɪð/ **noun** a tool with a long curved blade for cutting grass or corn 长柄大镰刀 • **verb** (**scythes, scything, scythed**) cut with a scythe 用长柄大镰刀割

SE **abbreviation** south-east or south-eastern.

sea /si:/ **noun** 1 the salt water that surrounds the land masses of the earth 海;海洋 2 a particular area of sea (特定区域的)海 3 a vast expanse or quantity 一大片;大量 □ **at sea** very confused and uncertain 茫然的;困惑的;不知所措的 **sea anemone** a sea creature with stinging tentacles that make it resemble a flower 海葵 **sea change** a great or remarkable change in a situation 巨变;突变 **sea cow** a manatee or other large planteating sea animal 海牛目哺乳动物 **sea horse** a small sea fish that swims upright and has a head rather like a horse's 海马 **sea level** the average level of the sea's surface, used in calculating the height of land 海平面 **sea lion** a large seal with a mane on the neck and shoulders 海狮(颈部和肩部有鬃毛) **sea urchin** a small sea creature with a shell covered in spines 海胆

seabird /'si:bɜːd/ **noun** a bird that lives near the sea 海鸟

seaboard /'si:bɔːd/ **noun** a region bordering the sea; the coastline 海岸;海滨地区

seafaring /'si:feərɪŋ/ **adjective & noun** travelling by sea 出海(的);航海(的) ■ **seafarer** noun.

seafood /'si:fu:d/ **noun** shellfish and sea fish as food 海鲜;海产食品

seafront /'si:frʌnt/ **noun** the part of a coastal town facing the sea (城镇的)滨海区,沿海地带

seagoing /'si:gəʊɪŋ/ **adjective** travelling on the sea 航海的

seagull /'si:gʌl/ **noun** a gull 海鸥

seal¹ /si:l/ **noun** 1 a device or substance used to join two things together or to stop fluid getting in 封口机;密封物 2 a piece of wax with a design stamped into it, attached to letters and documents to guarantee they are genuine 封记;印记;图章 3 a confirmation or guarantee 确认;批准;保证: *a seal of approval* 批准 • **verb** 1 fasten or close securely 密封 2 (**seal something off**) stop people entering and leaving an area 封锁(某地区) 3 coat a surface to stop fluid passing through it 加防渗涂层于(表面);封盖…的表面 4 conclude; make definite 达成;使明确;确定 ■ **sealer** noun.

seal² **noun** a sea mammal with flippers and a streamlined body 海豹

sealant /'si:lənt/ **noun** material used to make something airtight or watertight (不透气或不透水的)密封材料

seam /si:m/ **noun** 1 a line where two pieces of fabric are sewn together (缝在一起的两块织物的)缝,线缝 2 an underground layer of a mineral 矿层 ■ **seamed** adjective.

seaman /'si:mən/ **noun** (plural **seamen**) a sailor, especially one below the rank of officer 水手;海员

seamless /'si:mləs/ **adjective** smooth and without seams or obvious joins 平滑的;无缝的 ■ **seamlessly** adverb.

seamstress /'si:mstrəs/ **noun** a woman who sews, especially as a job 女裁缝；(尤指)女缝纫工

seamy /'si:mi/ **adjective** (**seamier**, **seamiest**) immoral and unpleasant 不道德的；丑恶的；卑鄙的

seance /'seɪɒns/ **noun** a meeting at which people attempt to make contact with the dead (人们试图与死者通话的)降神会

seaplane /'si:pleɪn/ **noun** an aircraft designed to land on and take off from water 水上飞机

sear /sɪə(r)/ **verb 1** scorch with a sudden intense heat 烫焦；烧蚀;灼伤 **2** (of pain) be experienced as a burning sensation (疼痛)突发,突然刺痛

search /sɜ:tʃ/ **verb 1** try to find something by looking carefully and thoroughly 搜寻;搜索 **2** examine something thoroughly in order to find something or someone 搜查 **3** look for information on the Internet by using a search engine (在因特网上)搜索(信息) **4** (**searching**) investigating very deeply 深入调查的;细察的;仔细探究的 • **noun** an act of searching 搜索;搜查;探究 ■ **search engine** a computer program that searches the Internet for web pages containing a specified word or words 搜索引擎(利用某个或几个特定词语在因特网上搜索网页的程序) **search warrant** a document authorizing a police officer to enter and search a place 搜查证 ■ **searcher** noun **searchingly** adverb.

searchlight /'sɜ:tʃlaɪt/ **noun** a powerful electric light with a concentrated beam that can be turned in any direction 探照灯

seascape /'si:skeɪp/ **noun** a view or picture of the sea 海景

seashell /'si:ʃel/ **noun** the shell of a marine shellfish 海贝壳

seashore /'si:ʃɔ:(r)/ **noun** an area of sandy, stony, or rocky land next to the sea 海滨;海岸

seasick /'si:sɪk/ **adjective** suffering from nausea caused by the motion of a ship at sea 晕船的 ■ **seasickness** noun.

seaside /'si:saɪd/ **noun** a place by the sea, especially a beach area or holiday resort 海滩;海滨度假地

season /'si:zn/ **noun 1** each of the four divisions of the year (spring, summer, autumn, and winter) 季节 **2** a part of the year with particular weather, or when a particular sport is played 时节;赛季 • **verb 1** add salt or spices to food 给(食物)加调料 **2** dry wood for use as timber 对(木材)作干燥处理;风干 **3** (**seasoned**) experienced 老练的;有经验的 ☐ **in season 1** (of food) available and ready to eat (食物)当令的, 应时的 **2** (of a female mammal) ready to mate (雌性哺乳动物)处在发情期的 **season ticket** a ticket that lets you travel within a particular period or gain admission to a series of events (旅行或系列活动的)季票, 长期票

seasonable /'si:znəbl/ **adjective** usual or appropriate for a particular season of the year 符合时令的;适时的

seasonal /'si:zənl/ **adjective 1** relating to or characteristic of a particular season of the year 季节的;季节性的 **2** changing according to the season 随季节变化的 ■ **seasonally** adverb.

seasoning /'si:zənɪŋ/ **noun** salt or spices added to food to improve the flavour 调味品;佐料

seat /si:t/ **noun 1** a thing made or used for sitting on 座;座位 **2** the part of a chair designed for sitting on (椅子的)坐部 **3** a place for a person to sit in a vehicle, theatre, etc. (乘客或观众的)座位 **4** a person's bottom (人的)臀部 **5** a place in an elected parliament or council (议会或委员会的)席位 **6** Brit.[英] a parliamentary

S

constituency (议会的)选区 **7** a site or location 地点；位置 **8** Brit. 【英】a large country house belonging to an aristocratic family (贵族之家的)乡村宅第 • **verb 1** arrange for someone to sit somewhere 使就座 **2** (**seat yourself** or **be seated**) formal 【正式】sit down 就座；坐下 **3** (of a place) have enough seats for (场所)可容纳…，坐得下 □ **seat belt** a belt used to secure someone in the seat of a motor vehicle or aircraft (机动车辆或飞机座椅上的)安全带

seaweed /'si:wi:d/ **noun** plants growing in the sea or on rocks by the sea 海藻；海草

seaworthy /'si:ˌwɜːði/ **adjective** (of a boat) in a good enough condition to sail on the sea (小船)适宜航海的，经得起风浪的

sebaceous /sɪ'beɪʃəs/ **adjective** technical 【术语】producing oil or fat 油脂的；分泌油脂的

secateurs /ˌsekə'tɜːz/ **plural noun** Brit. 【英】a cutting tool like a pair of strong scissors, used for pruning plants, bushes, etc. 整枝剪；修枝剪

secede /sɪ'si:d/ **verb** (**secedes**, **seceding**, **seceded**) withdraw formally from an alliance or federation of states 正式退出；脱离(联盟或联邦)

secession /sɪ'seʃn/ **noun** the action of seceding 退出；脱离

secluded /sɪ'klu:dɪd/ **adjective** (of a place) sheltered and private (场所)隐蔽的，僻静的

seclusion /sɪ'klu:ʒn/ **noun** the state of being private and away from other people 与世隔绝；隐居；隐退

second[1] /'sekənd/ **ordinal number 1** that is number two in a sequence; 2nd 第二的 **2** lower in position, rank, or importance 副的；从属的；次要的 **3** (**seconds**) goods that are not of perfect quality 二等货；二级品 **4** a person who helps someone fighting in a duel or boxing match (决斗或拳击比赛中的)助手 **5** Brit. 【英】a place in the second highest grade in an exam for a degree (学位考试的)第二等 • **verb 1** formally support a nomination or resolution before voting or discussion 支持，赞成(提案或决议) **2** express agreement with 赞成…的意见；对…表示同意 □ **second best** not quite as good as the best 次好的；居第二位的 **second class 1** the second-best accommodation in a train, ship, etc. (火车、轮船等的)二等舱 **2** of a lower standard or quality than the best 次等的；第二流的 **second-degree** (of burns) causing blistering but not permanent scars (烧伤)二度的 **second-guess** predict someone's actions or thoughts by guesswork (凭猜测)预测，预言(某人的行动或想法) **second-hand 1** having had a previous owner 二手的；旧的 **2** heard from another person 间接得知的 **second nature** a habit that has become instinctive 第二天性；习性 **second-rate** of bad quality (质量)次等的，二流的 **second sight** the supposed ability to know what will happen in the future 洞察力；先见之明 **second thoughts** a change of opinion after reconsidering something 重新考虑后的意见 **second wind** fresh energy gained during exercise after having been out of breath 恢复的精力；重振的精神 ■ **secondly** adverb.

second[2] /'sekənd/ **noun 1** a unit of time equal to one sixtieth of a minute 秒 **2** (**a second**) informal 【非正式】a very short time 瞬间；片刻 **3** a measure-ment of an angle equal to one sixtieth of a minute 秒(角度单位)

second[3] /sɪ'kɒnd/ **verb** Brit. 【英】temporarily move a worker to another position or role 临时调派 ■ **secondment** noun.

secondary /'sekəndri/ **adjective 1**

coming after, or less important than, something else 次要的；第二位的 **2** (of education) for children from the age of eleven to sixteen or eighteen (教育)中学教育的 ■ **secondarily** adverb.

secret /'si:krət/ **adjective 1** hidden from, or not known by, other people 秘密的；保密的 **2** secretive 隐秘的；守口如瓶的 ● **noun 1** something that other people do not know about 秘密；机密 **2** a method of achieving something that is not generally known 秘诀；诀窍；秘方 □ **secret agent** a spy 特工；特务 **secret police** a police force working in secret against a government's political opponents 秘密警察 **secret service** a government department concerned with spying 特工部门；特务机关 ■ **secrecy** noun **secretly** adverb.

secretariat /ˌsekrə'teəriət/ **noun** a government office or department 秘书处；书记处

secretary /'sekrətri/ **noun** (plural **secretaries**) **1** a person employed to type letters, keep records, etc. 秘书 **2** an official of a society or other organization (社团等的)干事，文书 □ **Secretary of State 1** (in the UK) the head of a major government department (英国的)国务大臣 **2** (in the US) the government official responsible for foreign affairs (美国的)国务卿 ■ **secretarial** adjective.

> **✔ 拼写指南** -*ary*, not -*ery*: secre-*tary*. secretary 中的 -ary 不要拼作 -ery。

secrete /sɪ'kri:t/ **verb** (**secretes**, **secreting**, **secreted**) **1** (of a cell, gland, or organ) produce a liquid substance (细胞、腺或器官)分泌 **2** hide an object 隐藏；隐匿 ■ **secretion** noun.

secretive /'si:krətɪv/ **adjective** inclined to hide your feelings or not

to give out information 遮遮掩掩的；隐秘的；守口如瓶的 ■ **secretively** adverb.

sect /sekt/ **noun** a small religious or political group with different beliefs from those of the larger group that they belong to (宗教内部的)派别，宗派，非正统教派；政治派别；党派

sectarian /sek'teəriən/ **adjective** having to do with a sect or group 宗派的；教派的；派性的 ■ **sectarianism** noun.

section /'sekʃn/ **noun 1** any of the parts into which something is divided 部分 **2** a distinct group within a larger body of people or things (大机构下属的)部门，处，科，股 **3** the shape that results from cutting through something 截面；断面；剖面 ● **verb** divide into sections 把…分成区(或段、组)

sector /'sektə(r)/ **noun 1** a distinct area or part 领域；部分 **2** a part of a circle between two lines drawn from its centre to its circumference 扇形；扇形面

secular /'sekjələ(r)/ **adjective** not religious or spiritual 世俗的；尘世的；非宗教的 ■ **secularism** noun.

secure /sɪ'kjʊə(r)/ **adjective 1** certain to remain safe 安全的；无危险的 **2** fixed or fastened so as not to give way or become loose 牢靠的；稳固的；紧固的 **3** free from fear or anxiety 安心的；不焦虑的；感觉安全的 ● **verb** (**secures, securing, secured**) **1** protect against danger or threat 保卫；掩护；使之安全 **2** firmly fix or fasten 牢牢固定；扣紧；关严 **3** succeed in obtaining 得到；弄到 ■ **securely** adverb.

security /sɪ'kjʊərəti/ **noun** (plural **securities**) **1** the state of being or feeling secure 安全；有安全感 **2** the safety of a state or organization (国家或组织的)安全 **3** a valuable item offered as a guarantee that you will repay a loan 担保物;抵押品

sedan /sɪˈdæn/ noun **1** an enclosed chair carried between two horizontal poles 轿子 **2** N. Amer.【北美】a car for four or more people (可供 4 人或更多人乘坐的)轿车

sedate /sɪˈdeɪt/ adjective **1** calm and unhurried 镇定的;稳重的 **2** respectable and rather dull 庄重的;沉闷的 • verb (**sedates, sedating, sedated**) give someone a sedative drug 给(某人)服镇静剂 ■ **sedately** adverb.

sedation /sɪˈdeɪʃn/ noun the action of sedating someone 施以镇静剂

sedative /ˈsedətɪv/ adjective having the effect of making someone calm or sleepy 镇静的,催眠的 • noun a sedative drug 镇静药

sedentary /ˈsedntri/ adjective **1** involving a lot of sitting and not much exercise 惯于久坐的,少动的 **2** sitting down a lot; taking little exercise 久坐的;少活动的

sedge /sedʒ/ noun a grass-like plant that grows in wet ground 莎草,苔

sediment /ˈsedɪmənt/ noun **1** matter that settles to the bottom of a liquid 沉淀物;沉渣 **2** material carried by water or wind and deposited on land 沉积物 ■ **sedimentary** adjective.

sedition /sɪˈdɪʃn/ noun things done or said to stir up rebellion against a ruler or government 煽动叛乱的行动(或言论) ■ **seditious** adjective.

seduce /sɪˈdjuːs/ verb (**seduces, seducing, seduced**) **1** persuade someone to do something unwise 使人入歧途;唆使 **2** persuade someone to have sex with you 勾引,诱奸 ■ **seduction** noun.

seductive /sɪˈdʌktɪv/ adjective tempting and attractive 诱人的,有吸引力的 ■ **seductively** adverb.

sedulous /ˈsedjələs/ adjective showing great care or effort; diligent 小心周到的;勤勉的

see¹ /siː/ verb (**sees, seeing, saw**;

past participle **seen**) **1** become aware of with the eyes 看见;见到 **2** experience or witness 经历;目睹 **3** realize something after thinking or getting information 领会;理解 **4** think of in a particular way 认为;看作 **5** meet someone socially or by chance 见面;会面;碰见 **6** meet someone regularly as a boyfriend or girlfriend (男女朋友)约会 **7** consult a specialist or professional 咨询(专家或专业人员) **8** guide or lead someone somewhere 引领;伴送 □ **see someone off** go with a person who is leaving to their point of departure 送别(某人) **see something through** carry on with a project until it is completed 把(某事)干到底,做完(某事) **see through** transparent or semitransparent 看穿;看透;看破 **see to** deal with 办理;处理

see² noun the district or position of a bishop or archbishop 教区;主教(或大主教)职务

seed /siːd/ noun **1** a small, hard object produced by a plant, from which a new plant may grow 种子 **2** the beginning of a feeling, process, etc. 开端;萌芽 **3** any of the stronger competitors in a sports tournament who are kept from playing each other in the early rounds 种子选手 **4** old use【旧】a man's semen (男子的)精液 • verb **1** sow land with seeds 给(土地)播种 **2** remove the seeds from 给……去籽 **3** (**be seeded**) be made a seed in a sports tournament 被确定为种子选手

seedling /ˈsiːdlɪŋ/ noun a young plant raised from seed 籽苗;幼苗

seedy /ˈsiːdi/ adjective (**seedier, seediest**) unpleasant because dirty or immoral 肮脏的;不道德的;下流的 ■ **seediness** noun.

seeing /ˈsiːɪŋ/ conjunction because; since 因为;既然;鉴于

seek /siːk/ verb (**seeks, seeking,**

sought 1 try to find or get 寻求;寻找 2 ask for 要求;请求 3 (seek to do) try or want to do 寻求 4 (seek someone/thing out) search for and find someone or something 找出;查出 ■ seeker noun.

seem /siːm/ verb 1 give the impression of being 好像;似乎 2 (cannot seem to do) be unable to do, despite having tried 做不到

seeming /ˈsiːmɪŋ/ adjective appearing to be real or true 看似…的;表面上的 ■ seemingly adverb.

seemly /ˈsiːmli/ adjective respectable or in good taste 合宜的;得体的;合乎礼仪的

seen /siːn/ past participle of SEE¹.

seep /siːp/ verb (of a liquid) flow or leak slowly through a substance (液体)渗出,渗漏 ■ seepage noun.

seer /sɪə(r)/ noun a person supposedly able to see visions of the future 预言家;先知

seersucker /ˈsɪəsʌkə(r)/ noun a fabric with a crinkled surface 绉条纹织物;泡泡纱

see-saw /ˈsiːsɔː/ noun a long plank supported in the middle, on each end of which children sit and move up and down by pushing the ground with their feet 跷跷板 • verb repeatedly change between two states or positions (状态或位置)摇摆不定,来回变动

seethe /siːð/ verb (seethes, seething, seethed) 1 be very angry but try not to show it 恼怒;生闷气 2 be filled with a crowd that is moving about 密集;云集;充满 3 (of a liquid) boil or churn (液体)沸腾,翻腾

segment noun /ˈsegmənt/ each of the parts into which something is divided 部分;段;片 • verb /segˈment/ divide into segments 分割;切分

segregate /ˈsegrɪgeɪt/ verb (segregates, segregating, segregated) 1 keep separate from the rest or from each

other 分开;分隔;隔离 2 keep people of different races, sexes, or religions separate (按种族、性别或宗教)使隔离,使分开 ■ segregation noun.

segue /ˈsegweɪ/ verb (segues, segueing or seguing, segued) move without interruption from one song or film scene to another (歌曲或电影场景)无间断继续,无间断转换

seine /seɪn/ noun a fishing net which hangs vertically in the water, with floats at the top (捕鱼的)围网

seismic /ˈsaɪzmɪk/ adjective 1 having to do with earthquakes 地震的 2 enormous in size or effect 巨大的;影响巨大的

seismology /saɪzˈmɒlədʒi/ noun the study of earthquakes 地震学 ■ seismologist noun.

seize /siːz/ verb (seized, seizing, seized) 1 take hold of suddenly and forcibly 猛抓;抓住 2 (of the police) officially take possession of (警方)没收, 扣留 3 take an opportunity eagerly and decisively 抓住(机会) 4 (seize on) take advantage of eagerly (急切地)利用 5 (often seize up) (of a machine) become jammed (机器)卡住,发生故障

> ✔ **拼写指南** seize is an exception to the usual rule of *i* before *e* except after *c*. 通常的规则是 *i* 置于 e 前,在 c 后时除外,但 seize 例外。

seizure /ˈsiːʒə(r)/ noun 1 the action of seizing 抓住;攻占;没收 2 a sudden attack of illness, especially a stroke or an epileptic fit 中风;癫痫

seldom /ˈseldəm/ adverb not often 不常;很少

select /sɪˈlekt/ verb carefully choose from a group 挑选;选择 • adjective 1 carefully chosen as being among the best 精选的;优等的 2 used by, or made up of, wealthy people 供富人阶层使用的;由有钱人组成的 □ select committee a small parliamentary committee appointed for a special purpose (为特殊目的而组建的)特别委员会 ■ **selector** noun.

selection /sɪˈlekʃn/ noun **1** the action of selecting 选择;挑选 **2** a number of selected things 挑选出的事物;精选品 **3** a range of things from which you can choose 供选择之物

selective /sɪˈlektɪv/ adjective **1** involving selection 挑选的;选择的 **2** choosing carefully 认真挑选的;挑剔的 **3** affecting some things and not others 选择性的 ■ **selectively** adverb **selectivity** noun.

selenium /sɪˈliːniəm/ noun a grey crystalline chemical element (化学元素)硒

self /self/ noun (plural selves) **1** a person's essential being that distinguishes them from other people 自己;自我;自身 **2** a person's particular nature or personality 本性;本质

self-absorbed /ˌselfəbˈsɔːbd/ adjective obsessed with your own emotions or interests 自我专注的;只关心自己的

self-addressed /ˌselfəˈdrest/ adjective (of an envelope) addressed to yourself (信封)写有回邮地址的

self-adhesive /ˌselfədˈhiːsɪv/ adjective sticking without needing to be moistened 自黏的;自动附着的

self-appointed /ˌselfəˈpɔɪntɪd/ adjective having taken up a position or role without the approval of other people 自己任命的;自封的

self-assessment /ˌselfəˈsesmənt/ noun **1** assessment of your own performance 自我评估 **2** a system in which you calculate yourself how much tax you owe 自行估税

self-assurance /ˌselfəˈʃʊərəns/ noun confidence in your own abilities or character 自信;胸有成竹 ■ **self-assured** adjective.

self-aware /ˌselfəˈweə(r)/ adjective knowledgeable about your own character, feelings, motives, etc. 自知的;自觉的 ■ **selfawareness** noun.

self-catering /ˌselfˈkeɪtərɪŋ/ adjective Brit. 【英】(of a holiday or accommodation) offering facilities for you to cook your own meals (假日或膳宿处)有自炊设备的,可自己做饭的

self-centred /ˌselfˈsentəd/ adjective obsessed with yourself and your affairs 自我中心的;自私的

self-confessed /ˌselfkənˈfest/ adjective admitting to having certain characteristics 自己承认的;自己坦白的

self-confidence /ˌselfˈkɒnfɪdəns/ noun a feeling of trust in your abilities and judgement 自信 ■ **self-confident** adjective.

self-conscious /ˌselfˈkɒnʃəs/ adjective nervous or awkward through being worried about what other people think of you 不自然的;忸怩的;难为情的

self-contained /ˌselfkənˈteɪnd/ adjective **1** complete in itself 自给的;自足的 **2** not depending on or influenced by other people 独立的;不受他人影响的

self-control /ˌselfkənˈtrəʊl/ noun the ability to control your emotions or behaviour 自我控制(力);自制(力) ■ **self-controlled** adjective.

self-defeating /ˌselfdɪˈfiːtɪŋ/ adjective making things worse rather than achieving the desired aim 有违初衷的;事与愿违的

self-defence /ˌselfdɪˈfens/ noun defence of yourself 自卫;自我保护

self-denial /ˌselfdɪˈnaɪəl/ noun not allowing yourself to have things that you want 克己

self-deprecating /ˌselfˈdeprəkeɪtɪŋ/ adjective modest about yourself 自谦的;自我贬低的 ■ **self-deprecation** noun.

self-destruct /ˌselfdɪˈstrʌkt/ verb explode or disintegrate automatically

自毁；自爆；自行解体

self-destructive /ˌselfdɪ'strʌktɪv/ **adjective** causing harm to yourself 自毁的

self-determination /ˌselfdɪˌtɜːmɪ'neɪʃn/ **noun** the right or ability of a country or person to manage their own affairs (国家或人的)自决权，自主权

self-discipline /ˌself 'dɪsɪplɪn/ **noun** the ability to control your feelings and actions 自我约束(力)；自律；自制(力) ■ **self-disciplined** adjective.

self-doubt /ˌself'daʊt/ **noun** lack of confidence in yourself and your abilities 自我怀疑；缺乏自信

self-effacing /ˌselfɪ'feɪsɪŋ/ **adjective** not wanting to attract attention 低调的；谦逊的

self-employed /ˌselfɪm'plɔɪd/ **adjective** working for yourself rather than for an employer 自由职业的；自雇的；个体经营的 ■ **self-employment** noun.

self-esteem /ˌselfɪ'stiːm/ **noun** confidence in your own worth or abilities 自尊(心)

self-evident /ˌself'evɪdnt/ **adjective** obvious 显而易见的

self-explanatory /ˌselfɪk'splænətri/ **adjective** not needing explanation; clearly understood 无须解释的；明白易晓的

self-expression /ˌselfɪk'spreʃn/ **noun** the expression of your feelings or thoughts 个性表现；自我表现

self-fulfilling /ˌselfful'fɪlɪŋ/ **adjective** (of a prediction) bound to come true because people behave in a way that makes it happen (预测)自我应验的

self-help /ˌself'help/ **noun** reliance on your own efforts and resources to achieve things 自助；自立

self-importance /ˌselfɪm'pɔːtns/ **noun** an exaggerated sense of your own value or importance 妄自尊大，自大 ■ **self-important** adjective.

self-indulgent /ˌselfɪn'dʌldʒənt/ **adjective** allowing yourself to have or do things that you like, especially to an excessive extent 自我放纵的 ■ **self-indulgence** noun.

self-interest /ˌself'ɪntrəst/ **noun** your personal interest or advantage 自身利益；私利

selfish /'selfɪʃ/ **adjective** concerned mainly with your own needs and wishes 自私的 ■ **selfishly** adverb **selfishness** noun.

selfless /'selfləs/ **adjective** concerned more with the needs and wishes of other people than with your own 无私的；为他人着想的

self-made /ˌself'meɪd/ **adjective** having become successful by your own efforts 白手起家的；靠自己努力成功的

self-pity /ˌself'pɪti/ **noun** too much sorrow and concern for yourself and your own problems 自我怜悯；自怜 ■ **self-pitying** adjective.

self-portrait /ˌself'pɔːtreɪt/ **noun** a portrait by an artist of himself or herself (艺术家的)自画像

self-possessed /ˌselfpə'zest/ **adjective** calm, confident, and in control of your feelings 坦然自若的；沉着镇定的 ■ **self-possession** noun.

self-raising flour /ˌself'reɪzɪŋ/ **noun** Brit.【英】flour that has baking powder already added (已加入发酵粉的)自发面粉

self-reliance /ˌselfrɪ'laɪəns/ **noun** reliance on your own powers and resources 自立；自主；自力更生 ■ **self-reliant** adjective.

self-respect /ˌselfrɪ'spekt/ **noun** pride and confidence in yourself 自尊(心)

self-righteous /ˌself'raɪtʃəs/ **adjective** certain that you are right or morally superior 自以为是的；自认为道德高尚的

self-sacrifice /ˌself'sækrɪfaɪs/ **noun** the giving up of your own needs or wishes to help other people 自我牺牲 ■ **self-sacrificing** adjective.

selfsame /'selfseɪm/ **adjective** (**the selfsame**) the very same (完全)相同的;同一的

self-satisfied /ˌself'sætɪsfaɪd/ **adjective** smugly pleased with yourself 自满的;沾沾自喜的;自鸣得意的 ■ **self-satisfaction** noun.

self-seeking /ˌself'siːkɪŋ/ or **self-serving** /ˌself'sɜːvɪŋ/ **adjective** concerned only with your own welfare and interests 追逐私利的

self-service /ˌself 'sɜːvɪs/ **adjective** (of a shop or restaurant) where customers choose goods for themselves and pay at a checkout (商店或饭店)自助的

self-styled /ˌself'staɪld/ **adjective** using a description or title that you have given yourself 自称的;自封的: *self-styled experts* 自封的专家

self-sufficient /ˌselfsə'fɪʃnt/ **adjective** able to satisfy your basic needs without outside help 自立的;自给自足的 ■ **self-sufficiency** noun.

self-worth /ˌself'wɜːθ/ **noun** self-esteem 自尊;自我价值感

sell /sel/ **verb** (**sells**, **selling**, **sold**) **1** hand over something in exchange for money 卖;出售 **2** (of goods) be bought (货物)出售 **3** (**sell up**) sell all your property or assets 全部出售,卖光(财产或资产) **4** persuade someone that something is good 推销;促销;推荐 □ **sell out 1** sell all your stock of something 售完,全部出售(存货) **2** (of tickets for an event) be all sold (门票)全部售完 **3** abandon your principles for reasons of convenience 放弃原则;屈服 ■ **seller** noun.

Sellotape /'seləteɪp/ **noun** Brit. trademark【英,商标】transparent adhesive tape 赛勒塔普透明胶带

selvedge /'selvɪdʒ/ **noun** an edge on woven fabric that prevents it from fraying or unravelling (布的)织边,镶边

selves /selvz/ plural of SELF.

semantic /sɪ'mæntɪk/ **adjective** having to do with meaning 语义的 ■ **semantically** adverb.

semantics /sɪ'mæntɪks/ **plural noun 1** the study of the meaning of words and phrases 语义学 **2** the meaning of words, phrases, etc. 语义

semaphore /'seməfɔː(r)/ **noun** a system of sending messages by holding the arms or two flags in positions that represent letters of the alphabet 信号;旗语

semblance /'sembləns/ **noun** the way that something looks or seems 外貌;外观

semen /'siːmen/ **noun** a fluid containing sperm that is produced by men and male animals 精液

semester /sɪ'mestə(r)/ **noun** a half-year term in a school or university (中、小学校或大学的)学期

semi /'semi/ **noun** (plural **semis**) informal【非正式】**1** Brit.【英】a semi-detached house 半独立式房子 **2** a semi-final 半决赛

semi-automatic /ˌsemiːɔː'mætɪk/ **adjective** (of a gun) able to load bullets automatically but not fire continuously (枪)半自动的

semibreve /'semibriːv/ **noun** Brit. 【英】a musical note that lasts as long as two minims or four crotchets 全音符

semicircle /'semiːsɜːkl/ **noun** a half of a circle 半圆;半圆弧 ■ **semicircular** adjective.

semicolon /ˌsemi'kəʊlən/ **noun** a punctuation mark (;) indicating a bigger pause than that indicated by a comma 分号

semiconductor /ˌsemikən'dʌktə(r)/ **noun** a solid which conducts electricity, but to a smaller extent than a metal 半导体

semi-detached /ˌsemɪdɪ'tætʃt/ **adjective** Brit.【英】(of a house) joined to another house on one side by a common wall (房屋)半独立式的

semi-final /ˌsemɪ'faɪnl/ **noun** (in sport) a match or round coming immediately before the final (体育运动中的)半决赛 ■ **semi-finalist** noun.

seminal /'semɪnl/ **adjective 1** strongly influencing later developments 有重大影响的 **2** referring to semen 精液的

seminar /'semɪnɑː(r)/ **noun 1** a meeting for discussion or training 研讨会;培训会 **2** a university class for discussion of topics with a teacher (大学的)研讨班

seminary /'semɪnəri/ **noun** (plural **seminaries**) a training college for priests or rabbis 神学院

semiotics /ˌsemi'ɒtɪks/ **plural noun** the study of signs and symbols 符号学 ■ **semiotic** adjective.

semi-precious /ˌsemi'preʃəs/ **adjective** (of minerals) used as gems but less valuable than precious stones (矿物)次贵重的,半宝石的

semiquaver /'semikweɪvə(r)/ **noun** Brit.【英】a musical note lasting half as long as a quaver 十六分音符

semi-skimmed /ˌsemi'skɪmd/ **adjective** Brit.【英】(of milk) having had some of the cream removed (奶)半脱脂的

semitone /'semɪtəʊn/ **noun** Brit.【英】a musical interval equal to half a tone 半音

semolina /ˌseməˈliːnə/ **noun** the hard grains left after flour has been milled, used to make puddings and pasta (做布丁、意大利面食用的)粗面粉

senate /'senət/ **noun 1** the smaller but higher law-making assembly in the US, France, etc. (美国、法国等国家的)参议院 **2** the governing body of a university or college (大学或学院的)理事会,评议会 **3** the state council of ancient Rome (古罗马的)元老院

senator /'senətə(r)/ **noun** a member of a senate 参议员

send /send/ **verb** (**sends, sending, sent**) **1** cause to go or be taken to a destination 运送;邮送 **2** cause to move sharply or quickly 推进;驱动 **3** put someone into a particular state 使处于…状态 □ **send someone down** Brit.【英】**1** expel a student from a university (大学)勒令(某学生)退学;开除(某学生) **2** informal【非正式】sentence someone to imprisonment 使(某人)入狱 **send-off** a gathering to say goodbye to someone who is leaving 话别(会);送别(会) **send someone up** informal【非正式】make fun of someone by imitating them (通过模仿)取笑(某人)

senile /'siːnaɪl/ **adjective** suffering a loss of mental faculties because of old age 衰老的;老态龙钟的;年老糊涂的 ■ **senility** noun.

senior /'siːniə(r)/ **adjective 1** having to do with older people 年高的;年长的 **2** Brit.【英】having to do with schoolchildren above the age of about eleven (约11岁以上的)学童的 **3** US【美】of the final year at a university or high school (大学或中学)毕业年级的 **4** (after a name) referring to the elder of two with the same name in a family 老(置于姓名后,表示同一家庭中名字相同的两人中较年长的一个) **5** high or higher in status (等级或地位高的,较高的 • **noun 1** a person who is a stated number of years older than someone else 年长者;资深者: *She was two years his senior* 她比他年长两岁。**2** a student at a senior school 中学生;高年级学生 **3** (in sport) a competitor of above a certain age or of the highest status (体育运动中的)老运动

员,顶尖运动员 □ **senior citizen** an old-age pensioner 老年人;长者 ■ **seniority** noun.

senna /'senə/ noun a laxative prepared from the dried pods of a tree (用树木的干荚果制成的)轻泻剂

sensation /sen'seɪʃn/ noun **1** a feeling resulting from something that happens to or comes into contact with the body 感觉;知觉 **2** the ability to have such feelings 感觉能力;知觉能力 **3** a vague awareness or impression 模糊感觉;模糊印象 **4** a widespread reaction of interest and excitement, or a person or thing that causes it 轰动;引起轰动的人(或事物)

sensational /sen'seɪʃənl/ adjective **1** causing or trying to cause great public interest and excitement 轰动性的;耸人听闻的 **2** informal 【非正式】very impressive or attractive 令人印象深刻的,有吸引力的 ■ **sensationalism** noun **sensationalist** noun & adjective **sensationally** adverb.

sensationalize or **sensationalise** /sen'seɪʃənəlaɪz/ verb (**sensationalizes, sensationalizing, sensationalized**) present information in an exaggerated way to make it seem more interesting 耸人听闻地夸张,大肆渲染

sense /sens/ noun **1** any of the powers of sight, smell, hearing, taste, and touch, which allow the body to perceive things 感觉官能;感官 **2** a feeling that something is the case 感觉;觉察 **3** (**sense of**) awareness of or sensitivity to 意识;敏感性 **4** a sensible and practical attitude or behaviour 理性;见识 **5** a meaning of a word or expression 意义;含义;意思 • verb (**senses, sensing, sensed**) **1** perceive by a sense or senses (通过感官)感觉到 **2** be vaguely aware of 意识到,觉察到 □ **make sense** be understandable or sensible 可理解;

合情合理;讲得通

senseless /'sensləs/ adjective **1** lacking meaning, purpose, or common sense 无意义的;无目的的;不省人事的 **2** unconscious 失去知觉的,不省人事的

sensibility /ˌsensə'bɪləti/ noun (plural **sensibilities**) **1** the ability to experience and understand emotion or art; sensitivity 鉴赏力;识别力;感受力 **2** (**sensibilities**) the degree to which a person can be offended or shocked (易生气或受触动的)情感

sensible /'sensəbl/ adjective **1** having or showing common sense 有常识的;合情合理的;切合实际的 **2** practical rather than decorative 实用的;不花哨的 ■ **sensibly** adverb.

sensitive /'sensətɪv/ adjective **1** quick to detect or be affected by slight changes (对细微变化)敏感的 **2** appreciating the feelings of other people 体察他人感受的;体贴的 **3** easily offended or upset 易生气的;易心烦的 **4** secret or controversial 机密的;有争议的;敏感的 ■ **sensitively** adverb.

sensitivity /ˌsensə'tɪvəti/ noun (plural **sensitivities**) **1** the quality of being sensitive 敏感(性) **2** (**sensitivities**) a person's feelings which might be offended or hurt 容易生气;敏感情感

sensitize or **sensitise** /'sensətaɪz/ verb (**sensitizes, sensitizing, sensitized**) make sensitive or aware 使敏感;使意识到

sensor /'sensə(r)/ noun a device which detects or measures a light, heat, pressure, etc. (光、热、压力等的)探测装置;传感器

sensory /'sensəri/ adjective relating to sensation or the senses 感觉的;感官的

sensual /'senʃuəl/ adjective relating to the physical senses as a source of pleasure 感官享受的 ■ **sensuality** noun **sensually** adverb.

sensuous /'senʃuəs/ **adjective 1** relating to or affecting the senses rather than the intellect 感官方面的 **2** attractive or pleasing physically 迷人的；愉悦感观的 ■ **sensuously** adverb.

sent /sent/ past and past participle of SEND.

sentence /'sentəns/ **noun 1** a set of words that is complete in itself, conveying a statement, question, exclamation, or command 句子；句 **2** the punishment given to someone found guilty by a court (法庭的)判决，宣判，判刑 • **verb** (**sentences, sentencing, sentenced**) say officially in a law court that an offender is to receive a particular punishment (法庭)宣判，判决

sententious /sen'tenʃəs/ **adjective** given to making pompous comments on moral issues 空洞说教的

sentient /'sentiənt/ **adjective** able to perceive or feel things 有感知力的；有知觉的

sentiment /'sentimənt/ **noun 1** an opinion or feeling 观点，感情 **2** exaggerated feelings of tenderness, sadness, or nostalgia (过度的)柔情，伤感；怀旧

sentimental /senti'mentl/ **adjective** having or causing exaggerated feelings of tenderness, sadness, or nostalgia 感伤的；多愁善感的 ■ **sentimentality** noun **sentimentally** adverb.

sentinel /'sentinl/ **noun** a guard whose job is to stand and keep watch 哨兵，岗哨；看守

sentry /'sentri/ **noun** (plural **sentries**) a soldier whose job is to guard or control access to a place 哨兵；岗哨

sepal /'sepl/ **noun** each of the leaf-like parts of a flower that surround the petals (花的)萼片

separable /'sepərəbl/ **adjective** able to be separated or treated separately 可分隔的；可分离的；可区分的

separate adjective /'sepərət/ **1** forming a unit by itself 单独的；独立的 **2** different; distinct 不同的；特别的 • **verb** /'sepəreit/ (**separates, separating, separated**) **1** move or come apart 分离；分开 **2** stop living together as a couple (夫妻)分居 **3** divide into distinct parts 分开 **4** form a distinction or boundary between 区分；划分；分隔 ■ **separately** adverb.

> ✔ 拼写指南 the middle is -*par*-, not -*per*-: separate. separate 中间的 -par- 不要拼作 -per-。

separation /sepə'reiʃn/ **noun 1** the action of separating 分离；分开 **2** the state in which a husband and wife remain married but live apart (夫妻的)分居

separatism /'sepərətizm/ **noun** separation of a group of people from a larger group 分离主义 ■ **separatist** noun & adjective.

sepia /'si:piə/ **noun** a reddish-brown colour 红褐色；深褐色

sepoy /'si:pɔi/ **noun** historical 【历史】 an Indian soldier who served the British (在英国军队服役的)印度兵

sepsis /'sepsis/ **noun** the infection of body tissues with harmful bacteria 脓毒病；脓毒症

September /sep'tembə(r)/ **noun** the ninth month of the year 九月

septet /sep'tet/ **noun** a group of seven people playing music or singing together 七重奏；七重唱

septic /'septik/ **adjective** (of a wound or a part of the body) infected with bacteria (伤口或身体部位)脓毒性的 □ **septic tank** an underground tank in which sewage is allowed to decompose before draining slowly into the soil 化粪池

septicaemia /septi'si:miə/ (US spelling 【美拼作】 **septicemia**) **noun**

blood poisoning caused by bacteria 败血症;败血病

septuagenarian /ˌseptjʊədʒə-'neəriən/ **noun** a person who is between 70 and 79 years old 70 至 79 岁的人

septum /'septəm/ **noun** (plural **septa** /'septə/) a partition separating two hollow areas in the body, such as that between the nostrils 中隔;隔片; 隔膜

sepulchral /sə'pʌlkrəl/ **adjective 1** having to do with a tomb or burial 坟墓的;埋葬的 **2** gloomy 阴沉的;阴郁的

sepulchre /'seplkə(r)/ (US spelling 【美拼作】**sepulcher**) **noun** a stone tomb(用石头砌成的)坟墓,墓穴

sequel /'si:kwəl/ **noun 1** a book, film, or programme that continues the story of an earlier one (书、电影或节目的)续篇,续集 **2** something that takes place after or as a result of an earlier event 后续;随之而来的事;后果;余波

sequence /'si:kwəns/ **noun 1** a particular order in which things follow each other 次序;顺序;先后 **2** a set of things that follow each other in a particular order (按特定顺序排列的)一组事物 • **verb** (**sequences, sequencing, sequenced**) arrange in a sequence 按顺序排列

sequential /sɪ'kwenʃl/ **adjective** following in a logical order or sequence 顺序的;序列的 ■ **sequentially** adverb.

sequester /sɪ'kwestə(r)/ **verb** (**sequesters, sequestering, sequestered**) **1** isolate or hide away 使隔绝;隐藏 **2** sequestrate 扣押

sequestrate /'si:kwəstreɪt/ **verb** (**sequestrates, sequestrating, sequestrated**) take legal possession of assets until a debt has been paid 扣押(债务人的资产) ■ **sequestration** noun.

sequin /'si:kwɪn/ **noun** a small, shiny disc sewn on to clothing for decoration (衣服上作装饰的)闪光小圆片 ■ **sequinned** (or **sequined**) adjective.

sequoia /sɪ'kwɔɪə/ **noun** a redwood tree 红杉

seraglio /se'rɑːlɪəʊ/ **noun** (plural **seraglios**) **1** the women's apartments in a Muslim palace (伊斯兰宫殿中的)闺房 **2** a harem 女眷;妻妾婢女

seraph /'serəf/ **noun** (plural **seraphim** /'serəfɪm/ or **seraphs**) an angelic being associated with light and purity 撒拉弗(象征光明和纯洁的天使) ■ **seraphic** adjective.

Serbian /'sɜːbiən/ **noun 1** the language of the Serbs 塞尔维亚语 **2** (also **Serb** /sɜːb/) a person from Serbia 塞尔维亚人 • **adjective** relating to Serbia 塞尔维亚的

serenade /ˌserə'neɪd/ **noun** a piece of music sung or played by a man for a woman he loves, outdoors and at night (男子夜间在其爱慕的女子屋外吟唱或演奏的)小夜曲 • **verb** (**serenades, serenading, serenaded**) perform a serenade for 唱(或演奏)小夜曲

serendipity /ˌserən'dɪpɪti/ **noun** the occurrence of something by chance in a fortunate way 巧事;机缘凑巧 ■ **serendipitous** adjective.

serene /sə'riːn/ **adjective** calm and peaceful 平静的;宁静的 ■ **serenely** adverb **serenity** noun.

serf /sɜːf/ **noun** (in the feudal system) an agricultural labourer who had to work on a particular estate and was not allowed to leave (封建制度下的)农奴 ■ **serfdom** noun.

serge /sɜːdʒ/ **noun** a hard-wearing woollen fabric 哔叽布料

sergeant /'sɑːdʒənt/ **noun 1** the rank of officer in the army or air force above corporal (陆军或空军的)中士 **2** Brit. 【英】a police officer just below the rank of inspector 警佐；巡佐 □ **sergeant major** an officer in the British army who helps with administrative duties (英国陆军的)准尉副官

serial /'sɪərɪəl/ **adjective 1** arranged in a series 按顺序排列的；连续的；系列的 **2** repeatedly committing the same offence or doing the same thing 连续作案的；多次的：*a serial killer* 连环杀手 ■ **noun** a story published or broadcast in regular instalments 连载小说；电视(或广播)连续剧 □ **serial number** an identification number given to a manufactured item (产品的)序列号，编号

serialize or **serialise** /'sɪərɪəlaɪz/ **verb** (**serializes, serializing, serialized**) **1** publish or broadcast a story in regular instalments 连载；连播 **2** arrange in a series 使连续；使系列化 ■ **serialization** noun.

series /'sɪəriːz/ **noun** (plural **series**) **1** a number of related things coming one after another 连续；接连；一系列 **2** a sequence of related television or radio programmes 电视(或广播)系列节目

serious /'sɪərɪəs/ **adjective 1** dangerous or very bad: 危险的；严重的：*serious injury* 重伤 **2** needing careful consideration or action 需认真考虑(或处理)的；重要的 **3** solemn or thoughtful 严肃的；认真思考的 **4** sincere and in earnest 真诚的；当真的 ■ **seriously** adverb **seriousness** noun.

sermon /'sɜːmən/ **noun** a talk on a religious or moral subject, especially one given during a church service (尤指教堂礼拜期间的)布道，讲道

serpent /'sɜːpənt/ **noun** literary 【文】a large snake 大蛇；巨蛇

serpentine /'sɜːpəntaɪn/ **adjective** winding or twisting like a snake (似蛇般)蜿蜒的，迂回的，弯曲的

serrated /sə'reɪtɪd/ **adjective** having a jagged edge like the teeth of a saw 锯齿状的

serration /se'reɪʃn/ **noun** a tooth or point of a serrated edge 锯齿；锯齿状突起

serried /'serɪd/ **adjective** (of rows of people or things) standing close together (一排排的人或物)密集的，密排的，靠拢的

serum /'sɪərəm/ **noun** (plural **sera** /'sɪərə/ or **serums**) a thin liquid which separates out when blood solidifies 血清

servant /'sɜːvənt/ **noun** a person employed to perform domestic duties in a household or for a person 仆人；用人

serve /sɜːv/ **verb** (**serves, serving, served**) **1** perform duties or services for 服务；伺候 **2** be employed as a member of the armed forces (在军队)服役 **3** spend a period in a job or in prison 任职；供职；服刑；坐牢 **4** present food or drink to 端上，摆出 (饭菜或饮料) **5** (of food or drink) be enough for (食物或饮料)对…足够，足够供给 **6** attend to a customer in a shop (在商店)接待(顾客) **7** fulfil a purpose 达到(目的) **8** treat in a particular way (以某种方式)对待 **9** (in tennis, badminton, etc.) hit the ball or shuttlecock to begin play for each point of a game (在网球、羽毛球等运动中)发球 ■ **noun** an act of serving in tennis, badminton, etc. (网球、羽毛球等运动中的)发球 □ **serve someone right** be someone's deserved punishment (某人)咎由自取；(某人)罪有应得

server /'sɜːvə/ **noun 1** a person or thing that serves 服务员；侍者；上菜用具 **2** a computer or program that controls or supplies information to a network of computers (计算机)服务器

service /'sɜːvɪs/ **noun 1** the action of serving 服务；接待 **2** a period of employment with an organization 供职;受雇期 **3** an act of assistance 帮助 **4** a ceremony of religious worship 宗教礼拜仪式 **5** a system supplying a public need such as water or electricity 公共设施 **6** a department or organization run by the state 国家机构;公务部门 **7** (**the services**) the armed forces 武装部队 **8** a set of matching crockery 整套餐具 **9** (in tennis, badminton, etc.) a serve (网球、羽毛球等运动中的)发球 **10** a routine inspection and maintenance of a vehicle or machine (对车辆或机器的)检修,维修,保养 **11** (**services** or **service area**) a roadside area with a petrol station, cafe, toilets, etc. for motorists (公路边为驾车者服务的)服务区,服务站(设有加油站、小餐馆、卫生间等) • verb (**services, servicing, serviced**) **1** perform routine maintenance or repair work on 保养;维修 **2** provide a service or services for someone 为(某人)服务 **3** pay interest on a debt 支付(债务)利息 □ **in service** dated 【废】 employed as a servant 做仆人 **service industry** a business that provides a service rather than manufacturing things 服务行业 **service station** a garage selling petrol, oil, etc. 加油站;服务站

serviceable /'sɜːvɪsəbl/ **adjective 1** in working order 可操作的;能用的 **2** useful and hard-wearing 耐用的

serviceman /'sɜːvɪsmən/ or **servicewoman** /'sɜːvɪswʊmən/ **noun** (plural **servicemen** or **servicewomen**) a member of the armed forces 军人

serviette /ˌsɜːvɪ'et/ **noun** Brit. 【英】 a table napkin 餐巾

servile /'sɜːvaɪl/ **adjective 1** too willing to serve or please other people 奴颜婢膝的;卑躬屈膝的 **2** of a slave or slaves 奴隶的 ■ **servility** noun.

serving /'sɜːvɪŋ/ **noun** a quantity of food for one person (食物的)一份,一客

servitude /'sɜːvɪtjuːd/ **noun** the state of being a slave, or of being under the complete control of someone more powerful 奴役(状态);被控制地位;屈从地位

servo /'sɜːvəʊ/ **noun** a device in a vehicle which converts a force into a larger force 伺服机构

sesame /'sesəmi/ **noun** a tropical plant grown for its oil-rich seeds 芝麻

session /'seʃn/ **noun 1** a period devoted to a particular activity 一段时间;一节;一场 **2** a meeting of a council, court, etc., or the period when such meetings are held (议会等的)会议,会期;(法庭的)开庭,开庭期

set /set/ **verb** (**sets, setting, set**) **1** put in a particular place or position 置;放;安放 **2** bring into a particular state 使…处于特定状态 **3** give someone a task 分派,指派(任务) **4** decide on or fix a time or limit 确定,决定(时间或限度) **5** establish as an example or record 树立(榜样);创立(纪录) **6** adjust a device as required 设置,调整(装置) **7** prepare a table for a meal 摆放餐具 **8** harden into a solid, semi-solid, or fixed state 硬化;凝固;凝结 **9** arrange damp hair into the required style 给(头发)定型 **10** put a broken or dislocated bone into the right position for healing 使(断裂或脱位的骨头)复位 **11** (of the sun, moon, etc.) appear to move towards and below the earth's horizon (太阳、月亮等)落,下沉 • **noun 1** a number of things or people grouped together 一群;一组;一副;一套 **2** the way in which something is set 姿势;姿态;样子 **3** a radio or television receiver 收音机;电视机 **4** (in tennis and similar games) a group of games counting as a unit towards a match (网球等比赛中的)盘 **5** a collection of scenery, furniture, etc., used for a scene in a play or film (戏剧或电影的)布景 • **adjective 1** fixed or arranged in advance 预先确定(或安排)的 **2** firmly fixed and unchanging 固定不变的 **3** having a conventional or fixed wording 习用的;老一套的 **4** ready, prepared, or likely to do something 准备就绪的 □**set about** start doing 开始做;着手 **set something aside 1** temporarily stop using land for growing crops 暂时停止使用(耕地);将(耕地)暂时旁置 **2** declare that a legal decision is no longer valid 撤销(判决);宣布(判决)无效 **set off** begin a journey 出发;启程 **set something off** make a bomb or alarm go off 使(炸弹)爆炸;使(警报器)鸣响 **set on** attack violently 猛烈攻击 **set out 1** begin a journey 出发;启程 **2** aim or intend to do something 打算;试图 **set piece 1** a formal or elaborate arrangement in a novel, film, etc. (小说、电影等的)固定套路,精心设计的片断 **2** Brit. 【英】a carefully organized move in a team game (团体比赛项目中的)精心安排的打法,攻防套路 **set square** a flat triangular piece of plastic or metal with a right angle, for drawing lines and angles (制图用的)三角板,三角尺 **set-top box** a device which converts a digital television signal into a form which can be viewed on an ordinary television (电视)机顶盒 (用于转换数字电视信号,使之可以在普通电视上播放) **set something up** establish a business or other organization 创立,开办(企业或其他组织)

setback /'setbæk/ **noun** a difficulty or problem that holds back progress 挫折

sett /set/ **noun** a badger's burrow 獾穴

settee /se'tiː/ **noun** Brit. 【英】a long padded seat for more than one person (有坐垫的)长椅,长靠椅

setter /'setə(r)/ **noun** a breed of dog trained to stand rigid when it scents game 塞特猎犬

setting /'setɪŋ/ **noun 1** the way or place in which something is set 设置方式;背景;场景;环境 **2** the metal in which a precious stone or gem is fixed to form a piece of jewellery (镶嵌宝石的)镶托,托底 **3** a piece of music composed for particular words (为歌词谱写的)配曲 **4** (also **place setting**) a complete set of crockery and cutlery for one person at a meal 一套餐具

settle[1] /'setl/ **verb** (**settles**, **settling**, **settled**) **1** resolve a dispute or difficulty 解决(纠纷或困难) **2** decide or arrange something finally 最终决定;最终安排 **3** make your home in a new place 定居;安家落户 **4** (often **settle down**) start to live in a more steady or secure way 过安定生活 **5** make or become calmer (使)镇定下来;(使)平静下来 **6** sit or rest comfortably or securely (舒适或安稳地)坐下,休息 **7** (often **settle in**) begin to feel comfortable in a new situation (在新环境中)安下心来,安顿下来 **8** pay a debt 结清(债务) **9** (**settle for**) accept after negotiation (经协商后)勉强接受 ■ **settler** noun.

settle[2] **noun** a wooden bench with a high back and arms 高背扶手木长椅

settlement /'setlmənt/ **noun 1** the process of settling 解决;处理 **2** an agreement that is intended to settle a dispute (解决纠纷的)协议,协定 **3** a place where people establish a community 定居点;社区

seven /'sevn/ **cardinal number** one more than six; 7 七 (Roman numeral 罗马数字: **vii** or **VII**.)

seventeen /ˌsevn'tiːn/ **cardinal number** one more than sixteen; 17 十七 (Roman numeral 罗马数字:

xvii or XVII.) ■ **seventeenth** ordinal number.

seventh /'sevnθ/ **ordinal number 1** at number seven in a sequence; 7th 第七 **2** (**a seventh** or **one seventh**) each of seven equal parts of something 七分之一

seventy /'sevntı/ **cardinal number** (plural **seventies**) ten less than eighty; 70 七十 (Roman numeral 罗马数字: **lxx** or **LXX**.) ■ **seventieth** ordinal number.

sever /'sevə(r)/ **verb** (**severs**, **severing**, **severed**) **1** cut off, or cut into two pieces 切断; 割断 **2** put an end to a connection or relationship 断绝, 中断(联系或关系)

several /'sevrəl/ **determiner & pronoun** more than two but not many 几个; 数个 • **adjective** separate or respective 各自的; 分别的; 各自的 ■ **severally** adverb.

severance /'sevərəns/ **noun 1** the ending of a connection, relationship, or period of employment (联系、关系或工作的)断绝, 中断 **2** the state of being separated or cut off 分离

severe /sı'vıə(r)/ **adjective 1** (of something bad or difficult) very great (不好或困难的事物)严重的, 剧烈的 **2** strict or harsh 严格的; 苛刻的 **3** very plain in style or appearance 朴素的; 简洁的 ■ **severely** adverb **severity** noun.

sew /səʊ/ **verb** (**sews**, **sewing**, **sewed**; past participle **sewn** or **sewed**) join or repair by making stitches with a needle and thread or a machine 缝, 缝合

sewage /'suːɪdʒ/ **noun** human waste and water carried away from drains in sewers (由下水道排放的)污水, 排泄物

sewer /'suːə(r)/ **noun** an underground channel for carrying away human waste and water from drains 下水道; 阴沟 ■ **sewerage** noun.

sex /seks/ **noun 1** either of the two main categories (male and female) into which humans and most other living things are divided 性; 性别 **2** the fact of being male or female 男性(或雄性); 女性(或雌性) **3** the group of all members of either sex (总称)男人, 女人, 雄性, 雌性 **4** sexual intercourse 性交 □ **sex symbol** a celebrity famous for being sexually attractive 性感偶像; 极具性魅力的人 **sex something up** informal 【非正式】present something in a more interesting way 使(某事)更有趣味

sexagenarian /ˌseksədʒə'neəriən/ **noun** a person between 60 and 69 years old 六十多岁的人

sexism /'seksızəm/ **noun** prejudice or discrimination on the basis of a person's sex 性别歧视; 性别偏见 ■ **sexist** adjective & noun.

sexless /'seksləs/ **adjective 1** not sexually attractive or active 不性感的; 性冷淡的 **2** neither male nor female 无性别的

sextant /'sekstənt/ **noun** an instrument for measuring angles and distances, used in navigation and surveying (导航及勘测用的)六分仪

sextet /seks'tet/ **noun 1** a group of six musicians 六重奏乐团; 六重唱组合 **2** a piece of music for a sextet 六重奏曲; 六重唱曲

sexton /'sekstən/ **noun** a person who looks after a church and churchyard (负责看管教堂和教堂墓地的)教堂司事

sextuple /'sekstjupl/ **adjective 1** made up of six parts or elements 六部分组成的 **2** six times as much or as many 六倍的

sextuplet /'sekstjuplət/ **noun** each of six children born at one birth 六胞胎之一

sexual /'sekʃuəl/ **adjective 1** relating to sex, or to physical attraction or contact between individuals 性

的;性欲的;性关系的 **2** connected with the state of being male or female 两性的;性别的 **3** (of reproduction) involving the fusion of male and female cells (繁殖)有性的 □ **sexual harassment** the making of unwanted sexual advances or remarks to someone, especially at work (尤指工作中的)性骚扰 **sexual intercourse** sexual contact in which the man inserts his erect penis into the woman's vagina 性交 ■ **sexually** adverb.

sexuality /ˌseksʃu'æləti/ noun (plural **sexualities**) **1** capacity for sexual feelings 性能力;性欲 **2** a person's sexual preference 性倾向

sexy /'seksi/ adjective (**sexier, sexiest**) **1** sexually attractive or exciting 性感的 **2** sexually aroused 引起性欲的 **3** informal 【非正式】exciting and interesting 富有魅力的;有吸引力的 ■ **sexily** adverb **sexiness** noun.

shabby /'ʃæbi/ adjective (**shabbier, shabbiest**) **1** worn out or scruffy 破烂的;破旧的;邋遢的 **2** mean and unfair 卑鄙的;不光彩的;不公正的 ■ **shabbily** adverb **shabbiness** noun.

shack /ʃæk/ noun a roughly built hut or cabin 棚屋;简陋木屋 • verb (**shack up with**) informal 【非正式】live with someone as a lover 和(情人)同居

shackle /'ʃækl/ noun (**shackles**) **1** rings connected by a chain, used to fasten a prisoner's wrists or ankles together 手铐;脚镣 **2** restraints or restrictions 束缚 • verb (**shackles, shackling, shackled**) **1** chain with shackles 用钩环扣住;给…戴上镣铐 **2** restrain; limit 束缚;羁绊

shade /ʃeɪd/ noun **1** relative darkness and coolness caused by shelter from direct sunlight 背阴,阴凉处 **2** a colour, especially in terms of how light or dark it is 色度;(色彩的)浓浅深度 **3** a variety 差别 **4** a slight amount 略微;

少许 **5** (**shades**) informal 【非正式】sunglasses 太阳镜;墨镜 **6** literary 【文】a ghost;幽灵 • verb (**shades, shading, shaded**) **1** screen from direct light 遮(光);挡(光) **2** cover or lessen the light of 荫蔽,为…遮光 **3** represent a darker area with pencil or a block of colour (用铅笔)给…涂阴影;(用色块儿)把…涂暗 **4** change gradually into something else 渐变

shadow /'ʃædoʊ/ noun **1** a dark area or shape produced by an object coming between light rays and a surface 影子;阴影 **2** partial or complete darkness 昏暗处;背光处 **3** sadness or gloom 悲哀;阴郁 **4** the slightest trace 丝毫 **5** a weak or less good version 弱(或差)的版本 **6** a person who constantly accompanies or secretly follows another 形影不离的伴侣;暗地跟踪者 • verb **1** cast a shadow over 在…上投下阴影 **2** follow and observe secretly 暗地跟踪;盯梢 □ **shadow-boxing** boxing against an imaginary opponent as a form of training (拳击中的)空拳练习 **Shadow Cabinet** Brit.【英】those members of the main opposition party who would become government ministers if their party won the next election 影子内阁(一旦在下次大选中获胜就将成为政府各部部长的主要反对党成员) ■ **shadowy** adjective.

shady /'ʃeɪdi/ adjective (**shadier, shadiest**) **1** giving, or situated in, shade 在阴处的;背阴的;成阴的 **2** informal 【非正式】seeming to be dishonest or illegal 可疑的;靠不住的;可能非法的

shaft /ʃɑːft/ noun **1** the long, narrow handle of a tool or club, body of a spear or arrow, etc. (工具、高尔夫球杆等的)柄;矛杆;箭杆 **2** a ray of light or bolt of lightning (光或闪电的)一束,一道 **3** a narrow vertical passage giving access to a mine, accommodating a lift, etc. 矿井；电梯井；通风井 **4** each of the pair of poles between which a horse is harnessed to a vehicle (马车的) 辕 **5** a rotating rod for transmitting mechanical power in a machine (机器的) 轴

shag¹ /ʃæg/ **noun** coarse tobacco 粗烟丝 • **adjective** (of pile on a carpet) long and rough (地毯的绒毛) 长而粗的

shag² **noun** a cormorant (seabird) with greenish-black feathers 欧鸬鹚 (羽毛墨绿色)

shaggy /ˈʃægi/ **adjective** (**shaggier**, **shaggiest**) **1** (of hair or fur) long, thick, and untidy (毛发) 长而厚的，蓬乱的 **2** having shaggy hair or fur 长着长而厚的杂乱毛发的

shah /ʃɑː/ **noun** (in the past) the title of the king of Iran 沙 (旧时伊朗国王的称号)

shake /ʃeɪk/ **verb** (**shakes**, **shaking**, **shook**; past participle **shaken**) **1** move quickly and jerkily up and down or to and fro 摇；摇动；抖动 **2** tremble 颤抖 **3** shock or upset 使震惊；使不安 **4** get rid of or put an end to 摆脱；结束；终止 • **noun 1** an act of shaking 摇动；振动；抖动；颤抖 **2** informal 【非正式】 a milkshake 奶昔 □ **shake hands** (**with someone**) clasp someone's right hand in your own when meeting or leaving them, to congratulate them, or as a sign of agreement (与某人) 握手 **shake someone/thing up 1** stir someone into action 使(某人)振作 **2** make major changes to an institution or system 彻底改组(机构或系统) ■ **shaker** noun.

Shakespearean or **Shakespearian** /ʃeɪkˈspɪərɪən/ **adjective** having to do with the English dramatist William Shakespeare or his works 莎士比亚的；莎士比亚作品的

shaky /ˈʃeɪki/ **adjective** (**shakier**, **shakiest**) **1** shaking; unsteady 摇晃的；不稳固的 **2** not safe or certain 不安全的，不可靠的；不确定的 ■ **shakily** adverb.

shale /ʃeɪl/ **noun** soft rock formed from compressed mud or clay 页岩

shall /ʃəl/ **modal verb** (3rd singular present **shall**) **1** used with *I* and *We* to express the future tense (与 I 和 We 连用，表示将来时) 将要，会 **2** expressing a strong statement, intention, or order (表示坚决立场、强烈意愿或强硬命令) 一定，必须，应该 **3** Brit.【英】 used in questions to make offers or suggestions (用于问句中表示提议或建议) 好吗，要不要：*Shall we go?* 我们要不要去？

> ! 注意 the traditional rule is that you should use **shall** when forming the future tense with **I** and **we** (*I shall be late*) and **will** with **you**, **he**, **she**, **it**, and **they** (*he will not be there*). 根据语法规则，在构成将来时态时，shall 应与 I 和 We 连用(如 I shall be late 我会迟到的)。而 will 则应与 you, he, she, it 及 they 连用(如 he will not be there 他不会去那儿)。

shallot /ʃəˈlɒt/ **noun** a vegetable like a small onion 青葱；大葱

shallow /ˈʃæləʊ/ **adjective 1** having a short distance between the top and the bottom; not deep 浅的；不深的 **2** not thinking or thought out seriously 肤浅的，浅薄的 • **noun** (**shallows**) a shallow area of water 浅水处；浅滩 ■ **shallowly** adverb.

shalwar /ˈʃælwɑː(r)/ = SALWAR.

sham /ʃæm/ **noun 1** a thing that is not what it appears to be or is not as good as it seems 仿造品；假冒物；赝品 **2** a person who pretends to be something they are not 假冒者 • **adjective** not genuine; false 虚假的；假装的；假冒的 • **verb** (**shams**,

shamming, shammed) pretend 假装;佯作

shaman /ˈʃeɪmən/ **noun** (plural **shamans**) (in some societies) a person believed to be able to contact good and evil spirits (某些社会中的)萨满教巫师 ■ **shamanic** adjective **shamanism** noun.

shamble /ˈʃæmbl/ **verb** (**shambles, shambling, shambled**) walk in a slow, shuffling, awkward way 蹒跚而行;跟跄而行;拖着脚走

shambles /ˈʃæmblz/ **noun** informal 【非正式】a state of complete disorder 混乱;一团糟

shambolic /ʃæmˈbɒlɪk/ **adjective** Brit. informal【英,非正式】very disorganized 混乱的;一团糟的

shame /ʃeɪm/ **noun 1** the feeling you have of embarrassment or distress when you know you have done something wrong or foolish 羞耻;羞辱;羞愧 **2** loss of respect; dishonour 耻辱;丢脸 **3** a cause of shame 令人羞辱的人(或事) **4** a cause for regret or disappointment 遗憾;憾事 • **verb** (**shames, shaming, shamed**) make someone feel shame 使感到羞耻 □ **put someone/thing to shame** be much better than someone or something 使…相形见绌

shamefaced /ˌʃeɪmˈfeɪst/ **adjective** showing shame 面带愧色的

shameful /ˈʃeɪmfl/ **adjective** causing a feeling of shame 可耻的;丢脸的 ■ **shamefully** adverb.

shameless /ˈʃeɪmləs/ **adjective** showing no shame 不知羞耻的;无羞耻心的 ■ **shamelessly** adverb.

shammy /ˈʃæmi/ **noun** (plural **shammies**) informal 【非正式】chamois leather 麂皮革

shampoo /ʃæmˈpuː/ **noun 1** a liquid soap for washing the hair 洗发液;洗发剂 **2** a similar substance for cleaning a carpet, car, etc. (清洗地毯、汽车等的)洗涤剂 **3** an act of washing with shampoo 用洗发液(或洗涤液)清洗 • **verb** (**shampoos, shampooing, shampooed**) wash or clean with shampoo 用洗发液(或洗涤液)清洗

shamrock /ˈʃæmrɒk/ **noun** a clover-like plant with three leaves on each stem, the national emblem of Ireland 三叶草,白花酢浆草(爱尔兰的国花)

shandy /ˈʃændi/ **noun** (plural **shandies**) beer mixed with lemonade or ginger beer 掺柠檬汁(或姜汁)的啤酒,香槟啤酒

shanghai /ˌʃæŋˈhaɪ/ **verb** (**shanghais, shanghaiing, shanghaied**) informal 【非正式】force or trick into doing something 强迫做;诱骗

shank /ʃæŋk/ **noun 1** the lower part of the leg 胫;小腿 **2** the shaft of a tool (工具的)长柄 □ **Shanks's pony** your own legs as a means of transport 自己的双腿;步行

shan't /ʃɑːnt/ **short form** shall not.

shantung /ˌʃænˈtʌŋ, -dʌŋ/ **noun** a type of silk fabric with a rough surface 山东绸

shanty¹ /ˈʃænti/ **noun** (plural **shanties**) a small roughly built hut 简陋小屋;棚屋 □ **shanty town** a settlement in or near a town where poor people live in shanties (市镇中或其附近的)棚户区,贫民区

shanty² **noun** (plural **shanties**) a song with alternating solo and chorus, sung by sailors when working (水手唱的)劳动号子,船歌

shape /ʃeɪp/ **noun 1** the form of something produced by its outline 外形;样子;形状 **2** a piece of material, paper, etc. cut in a particular form 特定形状的材料(或纸张等) **3** a particular condition or state 状况;条件 **4** well-defined structure or arrangement 有条理的结构(或安排) • **verb** (**shapes, shaping, shaped**) **1** give a shape to 使成形;使成…形状;塑造 **2** have a big influence on 对…

有巨大影响 □ **shape up 1** develop in a particular way (以特定方式) 形成，发展 **2** improve your fitness, behaviour, etc. 锻炼(身体)；改进(行为举止等)

shapeless /'ʃeɪpləs/ **adjective** lacking a definite or attractive shape 不定形的；无形状的；形状难看的

shapely /'ʃeɪpli/ **adjective** having an attractive shape 形状优美的

shard /ʃɑːd/ **noun** a sharp piece of broken pottery, glass, etc. (陶器、玻璃等的)碎片，碎块

share /ʃeə(r)/ **noun 1** a part of a larger amount which is divided among or contributed to by a number of people 一份；份儿；份额 **2** any of the equal parts into which a company's wealth is divided, which can be bought by people in return for a proportion of the profits 股份；股票 **3** an amount thought to be normal or acceptable (视为正常或可接受的)分额，分量 • **verb (shares, sharing, shared) 1** have or give a share of 分享，分担 **2** have, use, or experience jointly with others 共用，共享，共同经历 ■ **sharer** noun.

shareholder /'ʃeəhəʊldə(r)/ **noun** an owner of shares in a company 股票持有人，股东

shark[1] /ʃɑːk/ **noun** a large and sometimes aggressive sea fish with a triangular fin on its back 鲨鱼

shark[2] **noun** informal 【非正式】a person who dishonestly obtains money from other people 勒索者；诈骗者

sharp /ʃɑːp/ **adjective 1** having a cutting or piercing edge or point (刃或尖)锋利的，锐利的 **2** tapering to a point or edge 有尖的，有刃的 **3** sudden and noticeable 突然的，显而易见的，明显的 **4** clear and definite 清楚的，明确的，确切的 **5** producing a sudden, piercing feeling 剧烈的，猛烈的 **6** quick to understand, notice,

or respond 机智的，敏锐的，灵敏的 **7** (of a taste or smell) strong and slightly bitter (味道或气味)强烈的，刺鼻的 **8** (of a note or key) higher by a semitone than a stated note or key (音符或音调)升半音的 **9** (of musical sound) above true or normal pitch (音乐声)偏高的，高调的 • **adverb 1** precisely 正点地 **2** suddenly or abruptly 突然地，意外地 • **noun** a musical note raised a semitone above natural pitch, shown by the sign # 升半音号(以 # 表示) □ **sharp practice** dishonest business dealings 卑鄙交易；欺诈性交易 ■ **sharply** adverb **sharpness** noun.

sharpen /'ʃɑːpən/ **verb** make or become sharp 磨尖，磨快，变锋军，变尖锐 ■ **sharpener** noun.

sharpshooter /'ʃɑːpʃuːtə(r)/ **noun** a person skilled in shooting 神枪手，神射手

shatter /'ʃætə(r)/ **verb (shatters, shattering, shattered) 1** break suddenly and violently into pieces 砸碎，使破碎 **2** damage or destroy 破坏，损坏 **3** upset someone greatly 使心烦意乱 **4** (shattered) Brit. informal 【英，非正式】completely exhausted 极度疲劳的，筋疲力尽的

shave /ʃeɪv/ **verb (shaves, shaving, shaved) 1** remove hair by cutting it off close to the skin with a razor 刮，剃(胡须或毛发) **2** cut a thin slice or slices from something 削掉，刨去，切掉 **3** reduce something by a small amount (少量地)减去，削减 • **noun** an act of shaving 修面，刮脸，剃毛发

shaven /'ʃeɪvn/ **adjective** shaved 修过面的，剃过毛发的

shaver /'ʃeɪvə(r)/ **noun** an electric razor 电动剃须刀

shaving /'ʃeɪvɪŋ/ **noun** a thin strip cut off a surface (刨削下来的)薄片，刨花

shawl /ʃɔːl/ **noun** a large piece of fabric worn by women over the shoulders or head or wrapped round a baby (妇女的)披巾,披肩;(裹婴儿的)包巾,襁褓

she /ʃi:, ʃi/ **pronoun 1** used to refer to a female person or animal previously mentioned or easily identified 她 **2** used to refer to a ship, country, or other thing thought of as female 她, 它(指舰船、国家等被视为阴性的事物)

sheaf /ʃi:f/ **noun** (plural **sheaves**) **1** a bundle of papers (纸的)一叠,一沓 **2** a bundle of grain stalks tied together after reaping (谷物秸秆的)一捆,一束

shear /ʃɪə(r)/ **verb** (**shears, shearing, sheared**; past participle **shorn** or **sheared**) **1** cut the wool off a sheep 剪(羊毛) **2** cut off something such as wool or grass with shears (用剪刀)剪割,修剪 **3** (**be shorn of**) have something taken away from you 被剥夺;被褫夺 **4** (**shear off**) tear or break off under pressure (因压力而)折断,断裂 ■ **shearer** noun.

> **！注意** don't confuse **shear** with **sheer**, which is a verb meaning 'change course quickly' and also an adjective meaning 'nothing but; absolute'. 不要混淆 shear 和 sheer, 后者是动词,表示"急转向";亦可用作形容词,意为"完全;十足;绝对的"。

shears /ʃɪəz/ **plural noun** a cutting tool like very large scissors 大剪刀

sheath /ʃi:θ/ **noun** (plural **sheaths**) **1** a cover for the blade of a knife or sword (刀或剑的)鞘 **2** a condom 避孕套 **3** a close-fitting covering 覆盖层;护套;护层

sheathe /ʃi:ð/ **verb** (**sheathes, sheathing, sheathed**) **1** put a knife or sword into a sheath 把(刀或剑)装入鞘中 **2** encase something in a close-fitting or protective covering 给…加护套(或护层)

shebang /ʃɪˈbæŋ/ **noun** (**the whole shebang**) informal【非正式】the whole thing 整个事情

shed¹ /ʃed/ **noun** a simple building used for storage 货棚

shed² **verb** (**sheds, shedding, shed**) **1** allow leaves, hair, skin, etc. to fall off naturally 使(树叶、毛发、皮肤等)脱落 **2** get rid of 去除;摆脱 **3** take off clothes 脱下(衣服) **4** give off light 发出,散发(光亮) **5** (of a vehicle) accidentally drop what it is carrying (车辆)意外掉落(装载物品) □ **shed tears** cry 流眼泪

she'd /ʃi:d/ **short form** she had or she would.

sheen /ʃi:n/ **noun** a soft shine on a surface 光泽

sheep /ʃi:p/ **noun** (plural **sheep**) an animal with a thick woolly coat, kept in flocks for its wool or meat 羊;绵羊 □ **sheep dip** a liquid in which sheep are dipped to clean and disinfect their wool 浴羊药液(用于清洗羊毛和给羊毛消毒)

sheepdog /ʃi:pdɒg/ **noun** a breed of dog trained to guard and herd sheep 牧羊犬

sheepish /ʃi:pɪʃ/ **adjective** feeling embarrassed from shame or shyness 窘迫的;腼腆的;羞怯的 ■ **sheepishly** adverb.

sheepskin /ʃi:pskɪn/ **noun** a sheep's skin with the wool on (带毛的)羊皮

sheer¹ /ʃɪə(r)/ **adjective 1** nothing but; absolute 完全的;十足的;绝对的 **2** (of a cliff or wall) vertical or almost vertical (悬崖或墙壁)陡峭的,垂直的 **3** (of fabric) very thin (织物)极薄的

> **！注意** don't confuse **sheer** with **shear**: see the note at SHEAR. 不要混淆 sheer 和 shear, 见词条 shear 处注释。

sheer² **verb** (**sheers, sheering, sheered**) **1** (especially of a boat) change course quickly (尤指船只)急转向,急拐 **2** move away from an unpleasant topic 避开(令人不快的话题)

sheet¹ /ʃiːt/ **noun 1** a large rectangular piece of cotton or other fabric, used on a bed to lie on or under 被单;褥单 **2** a broad flat piece of metal or glass (金属或玻璃的)薄片,薄板 **3** a rectangular piece of paper (长方形的)一张纸 **4** a wide expanse or moving mass of water, flames, etc. (水、火焰等)移动的一大片 □ **sheet music** music printed on loose sheets of paper 活页乐谱

sheet² **noun** a rope attached to the lower corner of a sail (系帆用的)帆脚索,缭绳

sheikh or **sheik** /ʃeɪk/ **noun** a Muslim or Arab leader (伊斯兰教的)教长;(阿拉伯人的)酋长,首领

sheila /'ʃiːlə/ **noun** Austral./NZ informal 【澳/新西兰,非正式】a girl or woman 姑娘;妇女

shekel /'ʃekl/ **noun** the basic unit of money of modern Israel 谢克尔(现代以色列的基本货币单位)

shelf /ʃelf/ **noun** (plural **shelves**) **1** a flat length of wood or other rigid material, fixed horizontally and used to display or store things 架子;搁板 **2** a ledge of rock 岩脊;岩坡 □ **off the shelf** taken from existing supplies, not made to order 现货供应的 **on the shelf** (of a woman) past an age when she might expect to be married (女子)大龄而嫁不出去的 **shelf life** the length of time for which an item to be sold can be stored (产品的)货架期,保存期限

shell /ʃel/ **noun 1** the hard protective outer case of an animal such as a shellfish or turtle (有壳水生动物、海龟等的)硬壳 **2** the outer covering of an egg, nut kernel, or seed (鸡蛋、坚果或种子的)外壳 **3** a metal case filled with explosive, to be fired from a large gun 炮弹 **4** a hollow case 空壳 **5** an outer structure or framework 框架;骨架;壳体 • **verb 1** fire explosive shells at 炮轰 **2** remove the shell or pod from 去掉…的壳;剥去…的荚 **3** (**shell something out**) informal 【非正式】pay an amount of money 支付(钱款) □ **shell shock** a mental condition resembling a state of shock, that can affect soldiers who have been in battle for a long time 战斗疲劳症,炮弹休克(长期作战引起的一种精神疾病) **shell suit** Brit.【英】an outfit consisting of a top and trousers with a soft lining and shiny outer layer 贝壳装(包括上衣和裤子,衬里柔软而外层发亮)

she'll /ʃiːl/ **short form** she shall or she will.

shellfish /'ʃelfɪʃ/ **noun** a water animal that has a shell and that can be eaten, such as a crab or oyster 有壳水生动物(如蟹或牡蛎)

shelter /'ʃeltə(r)/ **noun 1** a place giving protection from bad weather or danger 躲避处;避难所 **2** a place providing food and accommodation for the homeless 为无家可归者提供食宿的收容所 **3** protection from danger or bad weather 保护;庇护;遮蔽 • **verb** (**shelters**, **sheltering**, **sheltered**) **1** provide with shelter 保护;庇护;遮蔽 **2** find protection or take cover 找到躲避处;躲起来 **3** (**sheltered**) protected from the more unpleasant aspects of life 免受(生活烦恼)困扰的 **4** (**sheltered**) Brit.【英】(of accommodation) designed for elderly or disabled people, and staffed by a warden (住房)为老人(或残疾人)提供的

shelve /ʃelv/ **verb** (**shelves**, **shelving**, **shelved**) **1** decide not to continue with a plan for the time being 搁置(计划) **2** place something on a shelf 把…放在架子(或搁板)上 **3** (of ground) slope downwards (地面)倾斜

shelves /ʃelvz/ plural of SHELF.

shenanigans /ʃɪˈnænɪɡənz/ **plural noun** informal 【非正式】mischievous behaviour 诡计;鬼把戏;欺骗行为

shepherd /ˈʃepəd/ **noun** a person who looks after sheep 牧羊人
• **verb** guide or direct someone 带领;引导 □ **shepherd's pie** Brit. 【英】a dish of minced meat under a layer of mashed potato 肉馅土豆泥饼 ◼ **shepherdess** noun.

sherbet /ˈʃɜːbət/ **noun 1** Brit. 【英】a sweet fizzing powder eaten alone or made into a drink 果味甜粉;冒泡部饮料 **2** (in Arab countries) a drink of sweet diluted fruit juices (阿拉伯国家的)果子露

sheriff /ˈʃerɪf/ **noun 1** (also **high sheriff**) (in England and Wales) the chief executive officer in a county, working on behalf of a king or queen (英格兰和威尔士的)郡长 **2** (in Scotland) a judge (苏格兰的)法官 **3** (in the US) an elected officer in a county, responsible for keeping the peace (美国的)县治安官

Sherpa /ˈʃɜːpə/ **noun** (plural **Sherpa** or **Sherpas**) a member of a Himalayan people living on the borders of Nepal and Tibet, China 夏尔巴人(喜马拉雅山脉地区的一个民族,居住在尼泊尔和中国西藏的交界处)

sherry /ˈʃeri/ **noun** (plural **sherries**) a strong wine from southern Spain 雪利酒(原产于西班牙南部的一种烈性葡萄酒)

she's /ʃiːz/ **short form** she is or she has.

Shetland pony /ˈʃetlənd/ **noun** a small breed of pony with a rough coat 设得兰矮种马;设得兰小型马

Shia /ˈʃiə/ **noun** (plural **Shia** or **Shias**) **1** one of the two main branches of Islam. The other is **Sunni**. 什叶派(伊斯兰教两大教派之一,另一派为逊尼派) **2** a Muslim who follows the Shia branch of Islam 什叶派教徒

shiatsu /ʃiˈætsuː/ **noun** a medical treatment from Japan in which pressure is applied with the hands to points on the body 指压按摩(源自日本的一种疗法,以双手按压身体穴位)

shibboleth /ˈʃɪbəleθ/ **noun** a long-standing belief or principle held by a group of people 信仰;准则

shied /ʃaɪd/ past and past participle of SHY².

shield /ʃiːld/ **noun 1** a broad piece of armour held for protection against blows or missiles 盾牌;盾牌 **2** a person or thing that acts as a protective barrier or screen 保护者;庇护者;防护屏障;保护屏 **3** a sports trophy consisting of an engraved metal plate mounted on a piece of wood (体育比赛的)盾形奖牌 **4** a drawing or model of a shield used for displaying a coat of arms 盾形徽章 • **verb** protect or hide 保护;隐藏;遮蔽

shift /ʃɪft/ **verb 1** move or change from one position to another 转移;挪动 **2** transfer blame or responsibility to someone else 转嫁,推诿(过错或责任) **3** Brit. informal 【英,非正式】move quickly 迅速移动 • **noun 1** a slight change in position or direction (位置或方向微小的)变动,改变 **2** a period of time worked by someone who starts work as another finishes 班;轮班 **3** a straight dress without a fitted waist 宽松直筒连衣裙 **4** a key used to switch between two sets of characters or functions on a keyboard (键盘上在两种字型或功能之间转换的)切换键

shiftless /ˈʃɪftləs/ **adjective** lazy and lacking ambition 偷懒的;无志气的;得过且过的

shifty /ˈʃɪfti/ **adjective** informal 【非正式】seeming dishonest or untrustworthy 诡诈的;显得不可靠的

Shiite /ˈʃiːaɪt/ **noun** a follower of the Shia branch of Islam (伊斯兰教的)什叶派教徒

shilling /ˈʃɪlɪŋ/ **noun 1** a former British coin worth one twentieth of a pound or twelve old pence (five p) 先令(英国旧币，合1/20英镑或 12 旧便士) **2** the basic unit of money of Kenya, Tanzania, and Uganda 先令 (肯尼亚、坦桑尼亚和乌干达的基本货币单位)

shilly-shally /ˈʃɪlɪʃælɪ/ **verb** (**shilly-shallies, shilly-shallying, shilly-shallied**) be unable to make up your mind 犹豫不决；踌躇

shimmer /ˈʃɪmə(r)/ **verb** (**shimmers, shimmering, shimmered**) shine with a soft wavering light 发微光；闪光 • **noun** a soft wavering light or shine 微光；闪光 ■ **shimmery** adjective.

shimmy /ˈʃɪmɪ/ **verb** (**shimmies, shimmying, shimmied**) move quickly and smoothly 迅速顺畅地移动

shin /ʃɪn/ **noun** the front of the leg below the knee 胫；胫部 • **verb** (**shins, shinning, shinned**) (**shin up** or **down**) climb quickly up or down by gripping with your arms and legs 攀；爬

shindig /ˈʃɪndɪg/ **noun** informal【非正式】a lively party 热闹的聚会

shine /ʃaɪn/ **verb** (**shines, shining**, past and past participle **shone** or **shined**) **1** give out or reflect light 发光；发亮；照耀；反光 **2** direct a torch or other light somewhere 用(手电筒等)照射 **3** (of a person's eyes) be bright with an emotion (人的眼睛因表达某种情感而)闪光，发亮 **4** be very good at something (在某方面)干得出色 **5** (past and past participle **shined**) polish 擦亮 • **noun** a quality of brightness 光亮；光泽；光彩 □ **take a shine to** informal【非正式】develop a liking for 喜欢；喜爱

shiner /ˈʃaɪnə(r)/ **noun** informal【非正式】a black eye 黑眼圈

shingle¹ /ˈʃɪŋgl/ **noun** a mass of small rounded pebbles on a seashore (海滨的)小卵石

shingle² **noun** a wooden tile used on walls or roofs (墙上或屋顶的)木瓦 ■ **shingled** adjective.

shingles /ˈʃɪŋglz/ **noun** a disease in which painful blisters form along the path of a nerve 带状疱疹

shiny /ˈʃaɪnɪ/ **adjective** (**shinier, shiniest**) reflecting light 反光的；有光亮的

ship /ʃɪp/ **noun** a large boat for transporting people or goods by sea 海船；轮船 • **verb** (**ships, shipping, shipped**) **1** transport goods on a ship or by other means 用船运；运输；运送 **2** (of a boat) take in water over the side (小船)在舷侧进(水)

shipbuilder /ˈʃɪpbɪldə(r)/ **noun** a person or company that designs and builds ships 造船者；造船公司 ■ **shipbuilding** noun.

shipment /ˈʃɪpmənt/ **noun** **1** the action of transporting goods 运送；装运；装载 **2** an amount of goods shipped 装货量；运货量

shipping /ˈʃɪpɪŋ/ **noun** **1** ships as a whole 船舶 **2** the transport of goods 运送；装运；运输

shipshape /ˈʃɪpʃeɪp/ **adjective** orderly and neat 整齐的，整洁的，井井有条的

shipwreck /ˈʃɪprek/ **noun** **1** the sinking or breaking up of a ship at sea 船舶失事；海难 **2** a ship that has been lost or destroyed at sea 失事船只；沉船 • **verb** (**be shipwrecked**) suffer a shipwreck 遭遇船难；失事

shipyard /ˈʃɪpjɑːd/ **noun** a place where ships are built and repaired 造船厂，修船厂；船坞

shire /ˈʃaɪə(r)/ **noun** **1** Brit.【英】a county in England (英格兰的)郡 **2** (**the Shires**) country areas of England regarded as strongholds of traditional country life (被认为是依旧过着传统乡村生活的)英格兰乡村地区 □ **shire horse** a heavy, powerful breed of horse 夏尔马

shirk /ʃɜːk/ **verb** avoid work or a duty 逃避(工作或职责) ■ **shirker** noun.

shirred /ʃɜːd/ **adjective** (of fabric) gathered by means of threads in parallel rows (织物)抽褶的

shirt /ʃɜːt/ **noun** a garment for the upper body, with a collar and sleeves and buttons down the front 衬衫

shirtsleeves /ˈʃɜːtsliːvz/ **plural noun** (**in your shirtsleeves**) wearing a shirt without a jacket 只穿衬衫(未穿外衣)的

shirty /ˈʃɜːti/ **adjective** Brit. informal 【英,非正式】irritated or annoyed 脾气坏的,发怒的,烦恼的

shish kebab /ˈʃɪʃ kɪbæb/ **noun** a dish of pieces of meat and vegetables cooked and served on skewers 烤肉串

shiver /ˈʃɪvə(r)/ **verb** (**shivers, shivering, shivered**) shake slightly from fear, cold, or excitement (因恐惧,寒冷或激动而)发抖,颤抖,哆嗦 • **noun** a trembling movement 发抖;颤抖 ■ **shivery** adjective.

shoal¹ /ʃəʊl/ **noun** a large number of fish swimming together 鱼群

shoal² **noun 1** an area of shallow water 浅水域 **2** a submerged sandbank that can be seen at low tide 浅滩;沙洲

shock¹ /ʃɒk/ **noun 1** a sudden upsetting or surprising event or experience 令人苦恼(或震惊)的事 **2** an unpleasant feeling of sudden surprise and distress 震惊;悲痛 **3** a serious medical condition associated with a fall in blood pressure, caused by loss of blood, severe burns, etc. (失血,重度烧伤等引起的)虚脱,休克 **4** a violent shaking movement caused by an impact, explosion, or earthquake (撞击,爆炸或地震引起的)震动,震荡 **5** an electric shock 电击 • **verb 1** greatly surprise and upset someone 使震惊;使心烦意乱 **2** make

someone feel outraged or disgusted 使愤慨;使厌恶 □ **shock absorber** a device for absorbing jolts and vibrations on a vehicle (汽车的)减震器,缓冲器 **shocking pink** a very bright shade of pink 艳粉红色 **shock troops** troops trained to carry out sudden attacks 奇袭部队;突击部队 **shock wave** a moving wave of very high pressure caused by an explosion or by something travelling faster than sound 冲击波;爆炸反应

shock² **noun** an untidy or thick mass of hair 蓬乱(或浓密)的头发

shocking /ˈʃɒkɪŋ/ **adjective 1** causing shock or disgust 令人震惊的;令人厌恶的 **2** Brit. informal 【英,非正式】very bad 极其恶劣的 ■ **shocker** noun **shockingly** adverb.

shoddy /ˈʃɒdi/ **adjective** (**shoddier, shoddiest**) **1** badly made or done 粗制滥造的;劣质的 **2** dishonest or unfair 不诚实的;不公平的;卑鄙的 ■ **shoddily** adverb.

shoe /ʃuː/ **noun 1** a covering for the foot with a stiff sole 鞋 **2** a horseshoe 马蹄铁;马掌 • **verb** (**shoes, shoeing, shod**) **1** fit a horse with a shoe or shoes 给(马)钉蹄铁 **2** (**be shod**) be wearing shoes of a particular kind 穿…鞋 □ **shoe tree** a shaped block put into a shoe when it is not being worn, to keep it in shape 鞋楦(可使鞋在不穿时保持鞋形)

shoehorn /ˈʃuːhɔːn/ **noun** a curved piece of metal or plastic, used for easing your heel into a shoe 鞋拔 • **verb** force into a tight space 挤进;塞进

shoelace /ˈʃuːleɪs/ **noun** a cord passed through holes or hooks on opposite sides of the opening in a shoe to fasten it 鞋带

shoestring /ˈʃuːstrɪŋ/ **noun** (**on a shoestring**) informal 【非正式】with only a very small amount of money 以小额资本;小本经营

S

shogun /'ʃəʊgən/ **noun** (in the past, in Japan) a hereditary leader of the army (旧时日本世袭的)幕府将军

shone /ʃɒn/ past and past participle of SHINE.

shook /ʃʊk/ past of SHAKE.

shoot /ʃuːt/ **verb** (**shoots, shooting, shot**) **1** kill or wound someone with a bullet, arrow, etc. (用子弹、箭等)射死,射伤 **2** fire a gun 开枪;射击 **3** move suddenly and rapidly 飞驰;急冲 **4** direct a glance, question, or remark at someone 抛出(一瞥);(向某人)提出(问题),说出(看法) **5** (in sport) kick, hit, or throw the ball in an attempt to score a goal (体育运动中)射门,投球 **6** photograph or film a scene or film 拍摄(场景或影片) **7** (**shooting**) (of a pain) sudden and piercing (疼痛)钻心般的 **8** (of a boat) travel quickly down rapids (小船)迅速驶过(急流) **9** move a bolt to fasten a door 插上(门闩) **10** send out buds or shoots 吐 芽;绽 蕾 **11** (**shoot up**) informal【非正式】inject yourself with an illegal drug 注射毒品 ▪ **noun 1** a new part growing from a plant 芽;苗;新枝 **2** an occasion of taking photographs or making a film 摄影;拍照;拍摄 **3** an occasion when a group of people hunt and shoot animals or birds as a sport 打猎;狩猎 □ **shooting star** a small rapidly moving meteor that burns up on entering the earth's atmosphere 流星;陨星 **shooting stick** a walking stick with a handle that unfolds to form a seat 折叠座手杖

shooter /'ʃuːtə(r)/ **noun 1** a person who uses a gun 使用枪者;射手 **2** informal【非正式】a gun 枪

shop /ʃɒp/ **noun 1** a building or part of a building where goods are sold 商店;店铺 **2** a place where things are manufactured or repaired; a workshop 工场;作坊;车间 ▪ **verb** (**shops, shopping, shopped**) **1** go to a shop or shops to buy goods 购物 **2** (**shop around**) look for the best available price or rate for something 逐店选购 **3** Brit. informal【英,非正式】inform on 告发 □ **shop floor** Brit.【英】the area in a factory where things are made or put together by the workers (工厂中的)生产区 **shop-soiled** Brit.【英】(of an article) dirty or damaged from being displayed or handled in a shop (物品)在商店陈设变旧(或损坏)了的 **shop steward** Brit.【英】a person elected by workers in a factory to represent them in dealings with the management (代表工人与管理层交涉的)工会代表 **talk shop** discuss work matters with a colleague when you are not at work (在工作时间外)谈论工作,三句话不离本行 ▪ **shopper** noun **shopping** noun.

shopkeeper /'ʃɒpkiːpə(r)/ **noun** the owner and manager of a shop 店主;商店经理

shoplifting /'ʃɒplɪftɪŋ/ **noun** the stealing of goods from a shop 入店行窃 ▪ **shoplifter** noun.

shore[1] /ʃɔː(r)/ **noun 1** the land along the edge of a sea or other stretch of water (海、湖等的)滨,岸 (**shores**) literary【文】a foreign country or region 外国;异域 □ **on shore** on land 在岸上

shore[2] **verb** (**shores, shoring, shored**) (**shore something up**) **1** support or strengthen something 支持;巩固;加强 **2** hold something up with a prop or beam 用支撑物(或梁)支撑

shoreline /'ʃɔːlaɪn/ **noun** the line along which a sea or other stretch of water meets the land 海岸线;湖滨线

shorn /ʃɔːn/ past participle of SHEAR.

short /ʃɔːt/ **adjective 1** of a small length in space or time (距离)短的;(时间)短的 **2** small in height 矮的;低的 **3** smaller than is usual or expected 简短的 **4** (**short of** or **on**) not having enough of 不足的 **5** not available in large enough quantities; scarce 缺乏的;短缺的 **6** rude and abrupt 粗鲁的;简慢无礼的;唐突的 **7** (of odds in betting) reflecting a high level of probability (赌注赔率)低的 **8** (of pastry) containing a high proportion of fat to flour and therefore crumbly (糕点)酥脆的 • adverb not as far as expected or required 未达到;不及 • noun Brit.【英】a small drink of spirits 一口烈酒 • verb have a short circuit 短路 □ **short-change** cheat someone by giving them less than the correct change 少找零头以欺骗 **short circuit** a faulty connection in an electrical circuit in which the current flows along a shorter route than it should do (电路的)短路 **short-circuit** cause a short circuit in 使短路 **short cut** a way of going somewhere or doing something that is quicker than usual 捷径 **short-handed** (or **short-staffed**) having fewer staff than you need or than is usual 人手短缺的 **short-lived** lasting only a short time 短命的;短暂的 **short shrift** abrupt and unsympathetic treatment 草率对待;淡漠处置 **short-sighted** Brit.【英】**1** unable to see things clearly unless they are close to your eyes 近视的 **2** not thinking carefully about the consequences of something 目光短浅的 **short-tempered** losing your temper quickly 急性子的;火爆脾气的 **stop short** suddenly stop 突然停住 ■ **shortness** noun.

shortage /ˈʃɔːtɪdʒ/ noun a lack of something needed 缺少;不足

shortbread /ˈʃɔːtbred/ or **shortcake** /ˈʃɔːtkeɪk/ noun a rich, crumbly type of biscuit made with butter, flour, and sugar (用黄油、面粉和糖做成的)白脱甜酥饼

shortcoming /ˈʃɔːtkʌmɪŋ/ noun a

fault in someone's character or in a system 缺点;短处

shortcrust pastry /ˈʃɔːtkrʌst/ noun Brit.【英】crumbly pastry made with flour, fat, and a little water 松脆糕点

shorten /ˈʃɔːtn/ verb make or become shorter (使)缩短;(使)变短

shortening /ˈʃɔːtnɪŋ/ noun fat used for making pastry (做糕点用的)起酥油

shortfall /ˈʃɔːtfɔːl/ noun a situation in which something amounts to less than is required 不足;差额;亏空

shorthand /ˈʃɔːthænd/ noun a way of writing very quickly when recording what someone is saying, by using abbreviations and symbols 速记法

shortlist /ˈʃɔːtlɪst/ noun a list of selected candidates from which a final choice is made 最终候选名单;入围名单 • verb put on a shortlist 列入最终候选名单

shortly /ˈʃɔːtli/ adverb **1** in a short time; soon 马上;不久 **2** abruptly or sharply 唐突地;突然地

shorts /ʃɔːts/ plural noun short trousers that reach to the thighs or knees 短裤

shot¹ /ʃɒt/ noun **1** the firing of a gun, arrow, etc. 开枪;开炮;射箭 **2** (in sport) a hit, stroke, or kick of the ball as an attempt to score (体育运动中的)射球,踢球 **3** informal【非正式】an attempt 尝试 **4** a photograph 照片 **5** a film sequence photographed continuously by one camera 一段镜头;一段影片 **6** a person with a particular level of ability in shooting 射手 **7** (also **lead shot**) tiny lead pellets used in a shotgun (猎枪用的)铅砂弹 **8** a heavy ball thrown in the sport of shot put 铅球 **9** the launch of a rocket (火箭的)发射 **10** informal【非正式】a small drink of spirits 少量烈酒 **11** informal【非正式】an injection of a drug or vaccine (麻醉品或疫苗的)注射 □ **like a shot**

informal 【非正式】without hesitation 毫不迟疑 **shot put** an athletic contest in which a very heavy round ball is thrown as far as possible 推铅球；掷铅球

shot² /ʃɒd/ past and past participle of SHOOT. **adjective** woven with a warp and weft of different colours, giving a contrasting effect (彩色布料)杂色的 □ **shot through with** filled with a quality 充满(某种品质)

shotgun /'ʃɒtgʌn/ **noun** a gun for firing small bullets at short range 猎枪；滑膛枪 □ **shotgun wedding** informal 【非正式】a wedding arranged quickly because the bride is pregnant (由于新娘已有身孕的)仓促结婚，奉子成婚

should /ʃəd, ʃud/ **modal verb** (3rd singular **should**) **1** used to indicate what is right or ought to be done (表示恰当的行为或义务)应该，应当 **2** used to indicate what is probable (表示可能性)应该会，可能 **3** formal 【正式】used to state what would happen if something else was the case (表示假设)假如，万一：*If you should change your mind, I'll be at the hotel.* 如果你改变主意的话，我会在旅馆等你。**4** used with *I* and *we* to express a polite request, opinion, or hope (与 I 和 we 连用，表示礼貌的请求、看法或希望)倒，吧

shoulder /'ʃəʊldə(r)/ **noun** the joint between the upper arm and the main part of the body 肩；肩膀 • **verb** (**shoulders, shouldering, shouldered**) **1** take on a responsibility 承担(责任) **2** push aside with your shoulder 用肩推开 **3** carry on your shoulder 肩负；扛起；挑起 □ **shoulder blade** either of the triangular bones at the top of the back 肩胛骨

shouldn't /'ʃudnt/ **short form** should not.

shout /ʃaʊt/ **verb 1** speak or call out very loudly 呼喊声；叫喊 **2** (**shout someone down**) prevent someone from being heard by shouting 大声叫叫使某人声音被盖住 • **noun 1** a loud cry or call 呼喊声；大叫 **2** (**your shout**) Brit. informal 【英，非正式】your turn to buy a round of drinks 轮到某人请客(喝酒)

shove /ʃʌv/ **verb** (**shoves, shoving, shoved**) **1** push roughly 猛推；搡 **2** place carelessly or roughly 乱放；乱扔 **3** (**shove off**) informal 【非正式】go away 离开 • **noun** a strong push 猛推；搡

shovel /'ʃʌvl/ **noun** a tool resembling a spade with a broad blade and upturned sides, used for moving earth, snow, etc. 铲；铁锹 • **verb** (**shovels, shovelling, shovelled**; US spelling 【美拼作】**shovels, shoveling, shoveled**) move earth, snow, etc. with a shovel (用铁锹)铲起

show /ʃəʊ/ **verb** (**shows, showing, showed**; past participle **shown** or **showed**) **1** be or make visible (使)显现，(使)显露，(使)出现 **2** offer for inspection or viewing 出示；展示 **3** present an image of 描绘；描述 **4** lead or guide 引领；带领 **5** behave in a particular way towards someone (以某种方式)对待(某人) **6** be evidence of; prove 证明；证实；表明 **7** make someone understand something by explaining it or doing it yourself 向(某人)阐明；向(某人)说明；(通过示范)教 **8** (also **show up**) informal 【非正式】arrive for an appointment 来到；出席；露面 • **noun 1** a stage performance involving singing and dancing 歌舞演出 **2** an entertainment programme on television or radio (电视或广播的)娱乐节目 **3** an event or competition in which animals, plants, or products are displayed 展览；展览会 **4** an impressive or pleasing sight 景象；奇观 **5** a display of a quality or feeling (品质或感情的)显示，表露 **6** a display intended to give a false impression 假装;假象;做样子 □ **show business** the world of theatre, films, television, and pop music as a profession or industry 娱乐业 **show off** try to impress other people by talking about your abilities or possessions 卖弄(能力);夸耀(财富) **show something off** display something that you are proud of 展示,炫耀(引以为傲的事物) **show-off** a person who tries to impress other people by showing off 爱卖弄(或炫耀)的人 **show trial** a public trial held to influence or please people, rather than to ensure that justice is done 摆样子公审(用以影响或迎合民意而非确保公正的审判) **show someone/thing up 1** reveal someone or something to be bad or at fault 揭露,暴露(坏处或缺陷) **2** informal 【非正式】humiliate someone 使(某人)蒙受羞辱

showbiz /ˈʃəʊbɪz/ **noun** informal 【非正式】show business 娱乐业

showcase /ˈʃəʊkeɪs/ **noun 1** an occasion for presenting someone or something to their best advantage 供亮相的场合(或机会) **2** a glass case used for displaying articles 玻璃橱窗;玻璃陈列柜

showdown /ˈʃəʊdaʊn/ **noun** a final argument, fight, or test, to settle a dispute (旨在解决冲突的)最后的较量;摊牌

shower /ˈʃaʊə(r)/ **noun 1** a short period of rain or snow 阵雨;阵雪 **2** a large number of things that fall or arrive together 一大批;一阵;一连串 **3** a device that creates a spray of water under which you stand to wash yourself 淋浴头的喷头;淋浴器 **4** an act of washing yourself in a shower 洗淋浴 • **verb** (**showers**, **showering**, **showered**) **1** fall or make things fall in a shower (阵雨般地)落下(或投掷) **2** (**shower someone with**) give large quantities

of something to someone 大量地给;倾注 **3** wash yourself in a shower 给(自己)洗淋浴 ■ **showery** adjective

showgirl /ˈʃəʊgɜːl/ **noun** an actress who sings and dances in a musical or variety show (在音乐剧、综艺演出中表演的)歌舞女演员

showjumping /ˈʃəʊdʒʌmpɪŋ/ **noun** the competitive sport of riding horses over a course of obstacles in an arena (赛马运动中的)跨越障碍比赛

shown /ʃəʊn/ past participle of **SHOW**.

showpiece /ˈʃəʊpiːs/ **noun** an outstanding example of something 范例

showroom /ˈʃəʊruːm/ **noun** a room used to display cars, furniture, or other goods for sale (汽车、家具等商品的)展销室,陈列室

showy /ˈʃəʊi/ **adjective** very bright or colourful and attracting a lot of attention 艳丽的;鲜艳的;引人注目的

shrank /ʃræŋk/ past of **SHRINK**.

shrapnel /ˈʃræpnəl/ **noun** small metal fragments from an exploding shell or bomb (炮弹或炸弹的)碎片

shred /ʃred/ **noun 1** a strip of material that has been torn, cut, or scraped from something 撕下、割下或刮掉的)细条,碎片 **2** a very small amount 微量;些许 • **verb** (**shreds**, **shredding**, **shredded**) tear or cut into shreds 撕碎;切碎 ■ **shredder** noun.

shrew /ʃruː/ **noun 1** a small mouse-like animal with a long pointed snout 鼩鼱(一种小型哺乳动物,似老鼠,口鼻部长而尖) **2** a bad-tempered woman 悍妇;泼妇

shrewd /ʃruːd/ **adjective** having or showing good judgement 敏锐的;精明的 ■ **shrewdly** adverb **shrewdness** noun.

shrewish /ˈʃruːɪʃ/ **adjective** (of a woman) bad-tempered or nagging (女子)脾气暴躁的,唠叨不休的

shriek /ʃriːk/ **verb** make a piercing cry 尖叫 ▪ **noun** a piercing cry 尖叫(声);尖声

shrike /ʃraɪk/ **noun** a songbird with a strong hooked bill 伯劳(一种鸣禽,有钩状硬喙)

shrill /ʃrɪl/ **adjective** high-pitched and piercing 尖声的;尖锐的 • **verb** make a shrill noise 发出尖锐刺耳的声音;尖叫 ▪ **shrilly** adverb.

shrimp /ʃrɪmp/ **noun** (plural **shrimp** or **shrimps**) a small edible shellfish 小虾

shrine /ʃraɪn/ **noun 1** a place connected with a holy person or event, where people go to pray 神龛;圣坛 **2** a place containing a religious statue or object 圣地;神龛

shrink /ʃrɪŋk/ **verb** (**shrinks, shrinking, shrank**; past participle **shrunk** or (especially as adjective) **shrunken**) **1** become or make smaller (使)变小;(使)收缩 **2** move back or away in fear or disgust (因恐惧或厌恶而)退缩,离开 **3** (**shrink from**) be unwilling to do 不愿做;回避做 • **noun** informal【非正式】a psychiatrist 精神病医生;精神病学家 □ **shrinking violet** informal【非正式】a very shy person 羞怯的人;腼腆的人 **shrink-wrap** wrap in clinging plastic film 用收缩薄膜包装 ▪ **shrinkage** noun.

shrivel /ˈʃrɪvl/ **verb** (**shrivels, shrivelling, shrivelled**; US spelling【美作拼】**shrivels, shriveling, shriveled**) wrinkle and shrink through loss of moisture (因失水而)干枯,枯萎,皱缩

shroud /ʃraʊd/ **noun 1** a length of cloth in which a dead person is wrapped for burial 裹尸布;寿衣 **2** a thing that closely surrounds or hides something 罩;遮蔽物 **3** (**shrouds**) a set of ropes supporting the mast of a sailing boat (桅)的左右支索,侧支索 • **verb 1** wrap in a shroud 用裹尸布

裹 **2** cover or hide 覆盖;遮蔽;隐藏

shrub /ʃrʌb/ **noun** a woody plant which is smaller than a tree and divided into separate stems from near the ground 灌木 ▪ **shrubby** adjective.

shrubbery /ˈʃrʌbəri/ **noun** (plural **shrubberies**) an area planted with shrubs 灌木丛

shrug /ʃrʌg/ **verb** (**shrugs, shrugging, shrugged**) **1** raise your shoulders slightly and briefly as a sign that you do not know or care about something (为表示不知道或不在乎)耸(肩) **2** (**shrug something off**) treat something as unimportant 对…满不在乎;对…不屑一顾 • **noun** an act of shrugging your shoulders 耸肩

shudder /ˈʃʌdə(r)/ **verb** (**shudders, shuddering, shuddered**) tremble or shake violently 打战;战栗;发抖 • **noun** an act of shuddering 打战;战栗;发抖

shuffle /ˈʃʌfl/ **verb** (**shuffles, shuffling, shuffled**) **1** walk without lifting your feet completely from the ground 拖着脚走 **2** move about restlessly while sitting or standing 不断改变坐姿(或站姿);坐立不安 **3** rearrange a pack of cards by sliding them over and under each other quickly 洗(牌) **4** rearrange people or things 重新安排(人);重新整理,改组(某事物) • **noun** an act of shuffling 洗牌

shun /ʃʌn/ **verb** (**shuns, shunning, shunned**) avoid or reject 避开;回避

shunt /ʃʌnt/ **verb 1** push or pull a railway vehicle from one set of tracks to another 将(火车等)拖(或拉)入另一轨道;使(车辆)转轨 **2** move something around or along 移开;转向 **3** move someone to a less important position 闲置(某人) ▪ **shunter** noun.

shut /ʃʌt/ **verb** (**shuts, shutting, shut**) **1** move something into position to block an opening 关；闭；合上 **2** (**shut someone/thing in or out**) keep a person or animal in or out by closing a door, gate, etc. 将…关在…内(或外) **3** prevent access to a place or along a route 封住…的入口；封锁 **4** (with reference to a shop or other business) stop operating for business (商店等)停止营业 **5** close a book, curtains, etc. 合上, 闭拢(书、窗帘等) □ **shut down** stop opening for business, or stop operating 倒闭；停业；停止运行 **shut up** informal【非正式】stop talking 闭嘴

shutter /ˈʃʌtə(r)/ **noun 1** each of a pair of hinged panels inside or outside of a window that can be closed for security or to keep out the light (窗户的)活动遮板，百叶窗 **2** a device that opens and closes to expose the film in a camera (照相机的)快门 • **verb** (**shutters, shuttering, shuttered**) close the shutters of a window or building 关上, 合上(窗户或建筑物)的活动遮板(或百叶窗)

shuttle /ˈʃʌtl/ **noun 1** a form of transport that travels regularly between two places (在两地之间定期往返的)交通工具 **2** (in weaving) a bobbin for carrying the weft thread across the warp (用于编织的)梭，梭子 • **verb** (**shuttles, shuttling, shuttled**) **1** travel regularly between places (定期)往返，穿梭 **2** transport in a shuttle 往返运送

shuttlecock /ˈʃʌtlkɒk/ **noun** a light coneshaped object that is struck with rackets in the game of badminton 羽毛球

shy[1] /ʃaɪ/ **adjective** (**shyer, shyest**) nervous about meeting or talking to other people 害羞的，腼腆的 • **verb** (**shies, shying, shied**) **1** (of a horse) turn aside in fright (马)惊逸，惊退 **2** (**shy away from**) avoid doing something through lack of confidence (因紧张或信心不足而)躲

避，避开；畏缩 ■ **shyly** adverb.

shy[2] **verb** (**shies, shying, shied**) throw something at a target 投掷；扔

shyster /ˈʃaɪstə(r)/ **noun** informal【非正式】a dishonest person, especially a lawyer 奸诈之徒；(尤指)不择手段的律师

SI /ˌes ˈaɪ/ **abbreviation** Système International, the international system of units of measurement 国际单位制

Siamese /ˌsaɪəˈmiːz/ **adjective** relating to Siam (the old name for Thailand) 暹罗(泰国的旧称)的 □ **Siamese cat** a breed of cat that has short pale fur with darker face, ears, feet, and tail 暹罗猫(毛短，呈灰白色、面、耳、足及尾部颜色较深) **Siamese twins** twins whose bodies are joined at birth 暹罗孪生子，连体双胞胎

sibilant /ˈsɪbɪlənt/ **adjective** making a hissing sound 发咝咝声的 ■ **sibilance** noun.

sibling /ˈsɪblɪŋ/ **noun** a brother or sister 兄；弟；姐；妹

sibyl /ˈsɪbl/ **noun** (in ancient Greece and Rome) a woman supposedly able to pass on messages from a god (古希腊和古罗马的)女预言家(被认为可传达神谕) ■ **sibylline** adjective.

sic /sɪk/ **adverb** (after a copied word that seems odd or wrong) written exactly as it stands in the original 原文如此(注于抄录的古怪词语或错误词语之后)

sick /sɪk/ **adjective 1** physically or mentally ill 患病的；有病的 **2** wanting to vomit 要恶心的 **3** (**sick of**) bored by or annoyed about 对…厌恶(或厌倦、腻烦)的 **4** informal【非正式】behaving in an abnormal or cruel way 病态的；不正常的；残忍的 **5** informal【非正式】(of humour) dealing with unpleasant subjects in a way that is offensive (幽默)可怕的，恐怖的 • **noun** Brit. informal【英,非正式】vomit 呕吐 □ **be sick 1** be ill 患病；生病 **2** Brit.【英】vomit 呕吐

sickbay /'sɪkbeɪ/ **noun** a room set aside for sick people 病室；病房

sickbed /'sɪkbed/ **noun** the bed of a person who is ill 病床

sicken /'sɪkən/ **verb 1** disgust or shock 使厌恶；使震惊 **2** (**be sickening for**) start to develop an illness 初显(疾病)的症状

sickle /'sɪkl/ **noun** a tool for cutting corn, with a semicircular blade and a short handle (用来收割谷物的)镰刀

sickly /'sɪkli/ **adjective** (**sicklier, sickliest**) **1** often ill 多病的 **2** looking or seeming unhealthy 有病容的；缺乏生气的 **3** (of flavour, colour, etc.) so bright or sweet as to cause sickness (味道、颜色等)令人作呕的，使人不舒服的

sickness /'sɪknəs/ **noun 1** the state of being ill 生病；患病 **2** a particular type of illness or disease 疾病 **3** nausea or vomiting 恶心；呕吐

side /saɪd/ **noun 1** a position to the left or right of an object, place, or central point 边；侧；缘 **2** either of the two halves into which something can be divided (划分为两部分物体的)一边，一侧 **3** an upright or sloping surface of something that is not the top, bottom, front, or back 侧面 **4** each of the flat surfaces of a solid object, or either of the two surfaces of something flat and thin, e.g. paper (物体的)面；(纸等两面中的)一面 **5** either of the two surfaces of a record or the corresponding parts of a cassette tape (磁带两面中的)一面 **6** a part near the edge of something 边；旁 **7** a person or group opposing another in a dispute or contest (辩论或竞赛中的)一方，一队 **8** a sports team 运动队 **9** a particular aspect 方面 **10** Geometry 【几何】each of the lines forming the boundary of a plane figure 边 • **adjective** additional or less important 附带的；次要的 • **verb** (**sides, siding, sided**) (**side with** or **against**) support or oppose in a conflict or dispute (在冲突或辩论中)支持(或反对) □ **side effect** a secondary effect of a drug (药物的)副作用 **side road** (or **street**) a minor road 旁路 **side-saddle** (of a rider) sitting with both feet on the same side of the horse (骑马者)侧坐 **take sides** support one person or cause against another 支持一方；袒护

sideboard /'saɪdbɔːd/ **noun 1** a piece of furniture with cupboards and drawers, used for storing crockery, glasses, etc. 餐具柜 **2** (**sideboards**) Brit.【英】sideburns 连鬓胡子

sideburns /'saɪdbɜːnz/ **plural noun** a strip of hair growing down each side of a man's face in front of his ears 连鬓胡子，鬓角

sidecar /'saɪdkɑː(r)/ **noun** a small, low vehicle attached to the side of a motorcycle for carrying passengers (摩托车的)侧车，边斗

sidekick /'saɪdkɪk/ **noun** informal 【非正式】a person's assistant 助手；助理

sidelight /'saɪdlaɪt/ **noun** Brit.【英】a small additional light on either side of a motor vehicle's headlights (机动车的)侧灯

sideline /'saɪdlaɪn/ **noun 1** something you do in addition to your main job 兼职；副业 **2** either of the two lines along the longer sides of a sports field or court (球场的)边线 **3** (**the sidelines**) a position of watching a situation rather than being directly involved in it 旁观者的地位 • **verb** (**sidelines, sidelining, sidelined**) remove from a team, game, or influential position 使退出比赛；使下场；使降格

sidelong /'saɪdlɒŋ/ **adjective & adverb** to or from one side; sideways 倾斜的(地)；向一侧的(地)

sidereal /saɪ'dɪəriəl/ **adjective** relating to the distant stars or their apparent positions in the sky 星的;星座的;恒星的

sideshow /'saɪdʃəʊ/ **noun** a small show or stall at an exhibition, fair, or circus (展览、集市上的)小型展示,小货摊,(马戏中的)穿插表演

sidestep /'saɪdstep/ **verb** (**sidesteps**, **sidestepping**, **sidestepped**) **1** avoid dealing with a difficult issue 回避,规避(难题) **2** avoid someone or something by stepping sideways 横跨一步避开;侧移一步躲过

sideswipe /'saɪdswaɪp/ **noun** a critical or harsh remark made while discussing another matter 借机抨击;附带贬损

sidetrack /'saɪdtræk/ **verb** distract someone from the main issues of what they are discussing or doing 使转移话题;使离题

sidewalk /'saɪdwɔːk/ **noun** N. Amer. 【北美】 a pavement 人行道

sideways /'saɪdweɪz/ **adverb & adjective** to, towards, or from the side 向一边的(地);朝一旁(的);来自一侧(的);从一边的(地)

siding /'saɪdɪŋ/ **noun** a short track beside a main railway line, where trains are left (铁路的)侧线,岔线

sidle /'saɪdl/ **verb** (**sidles**, **sidling**, **sidled**) walk in a secretive or timid way 偷偷地走;羞怯地走

siege /siːdʒ/ **noun 1** a military operation in which forces surround a town and cut off its supplies 围城;围困,围攻 **2** a similar operation by a police team to force an armed person to surrender (警察对武装分子的)包围

✔ 拼写指南 remember, i before e in **siege** and **sieve**. 记住,在 siege 和 sieve 中,i 在 e 前。

sienna /si'enə/ **noun** a kind of earth used as a brown colouring in painting 黄土,褐土(用作颜料)

siesta /si'estə/ **noun** an afternoon rest

or nap 午睡;午休

sieve /sɪv/ **noun** a piece of mesh held in a frame, used for straining solids from liquids or separating coarser from finer particles 筛;筛网;滤器 • **verb** (**sieves**, **sieving**, **sieved**) put a substance through a sieve (用筛网、滤器等)筛,滤

sift /sɪft/ **verb 1** put a substance through a sieve 筛;过滤 **2** examine something thoroughly to sort out what is important or useful 精选;挑拣

sigh /saɪ/ **verb** let out a long, deep breath expressing sadness, relief, etc. 叹气,叹息 • **noun** such a breath 叹气;叹息

sight /saɪt/ **noun 1** the ability to see 视力;视觉 **2** the act of seeing something 看到;见到 **3** the area or distance within which you can see something 视域;视野 **4** a thing that you see 看见的事物;情景;景象 **5** (**sights**) places of interest to tourists 名胜;景点 **6** (**a sight**) informal 【非正式】 a person or thing that looks ridiculous or unattractive 滑稽可笑(或无吸引力)的人(或物) **7** (also **sights**) a device that you look through to aim a gun or see something with a telescope (枪的)瞄准器;(望远镜的)观测器 • **verb** see or glimpse 看到;见到;瞥见 □ **raise** (or **lower**) **your sights** increase (or lower) your expectations 提高(或降低)期望 **set your sights on** have something as an ambition 以…为奋斗目标 **sight-read** read a musical score and play it without preparation 视奏(无事先演练地见谱即奏)

!注意 don't confuse **sight** with **site**, which means 'a place where something is located or happens'. 不要混淆 sight 和 site,后者意为"地点;现场"。

sighted /'saɪtɪd/ **adjective 1** having

the ability to see; not blind 看得见的;不盲的 **2** having a particular kind of sight 有视力(或视觉)的

sightless /'saɪtləs/ **adjective** blind 盲的;无视力的

sightseeing /'saɪtsiːɪŋ/ **noun** the activity of visiting places of interest 观光;旅游 ■ **sightseer** noun.

sign /saɪn/ **noun 1** an indication that something exists, is happening, or may happen 迹象;征兆;预兆 **2** a signal, gesture, or notice giving information or an instruction 信号;手势;指示牌;招牌 **3** a symbol used to represent something in algebra, music, or other subjects (代数、音乐或其他科目中的)符号,记号 **4** each of the twelve divisions of the zodiac (黄道十二宫中的)宫 • **verb 1** write your name on something to show that you have written it, or to authorize it 签署;署名于 **2** recruit a sports player, musician, etc. by signing a contract 和(运动员、音乐家等)签约 **3** use gestures to give information or instructions 用手势示意 □ **sign language** a system of hand movements and facial expressions used to communicate with people who are deaf (聋人使用的)手势语,手语 **sign off** end a letter, broadcast, or other message 结束写信件,终止广播;停止讲话 **sign on 1** commit yourself to a job 签约入职 **2** Brit. 【英】register as unemployed 登记失业 **sign someone on** employ someone 雇用(某人) **sign up** commit yourself to a course, job, etc. 报名(参加课程);签约受雇 ■ **signer** noun.

signal /'sɪɡnəl/ **noun 1** a gesture, action, or sound giving information or an instruction 信号;暗号 **2** a sign indicating a particular situation 征兆;迹象 **3** a device that uses lights or a movable arm to tell drivers to stop or beware on a road or railway 交通

指示灯;交通信号装置 **4** an electrical impulse or radio wave that is sent or received (电子脉冲或无线电波)信号 • **verb** (**signals**, **signalling**, **signalled**; US spelling 【美拼作】 **signals**, **signaling**, **signaled**) give a signal 发信号 • **adjective** noteworthy 显著的;引人注目的 □ **signal box** Brit. ■ a building beside a railway track from which signals and points are controlled (铁路边的)信号所,信号塔

signatory /'sɪɡnətri/ **noun** (plural **signatories**) a person who has signed an agreement (协议的)签署者,签署人

signature /'sɪɡnətʃə(r)/ **noun 1** a person's name written in a distinctive way, used in signing something 署名;签名 **2** a distinctive product or quality by which someone or something can be recognized 标志性产品或特征 **signature tune** a tune announcing a particular television or radio programme (某个电视或广播节目的)信号曲

signet /'sɪɡnət/ **noun** (in the past) a small seal used to authorize an official document (旧时的)小图章,小公章 □ **signet ring** a ring with letters or a design set into it 图章戒指

significance /sɪɡ'nɪfɪkəns/ **noun 1** importance 重要性 **2** the meaning of something 含义;意义

significant /sɪɡ'nɪfɪkənt/ **adjective 1** important or large enough to have an effect or be noticed 重要的;重大的;影响深远的 **2** having a particular or secret meaning 别有含义的;意味深长的 ■ **significantly** adverb.

signify /'sɪɡnɪfaɪ/ **verb** (**signifies**, **signifying**, **signified**) **1** be a sign of; mean 表示;意味着 **2** make a feeling or intention known 表达,显示(感情或意图) ■ **signification** noun.

signing /'saɪnɪŋ/ **noun 1** Brit. 【英】

a person who has recently been recruited to a sports team, record company, etc. (运动队、唱片公司等的)签约队员，签约受雇者 **2** an event at which an author signs copies of their book (图书作者的)签名活动，签名售书 **3** the use of sign language 手语的使用

signpost /'saɪnpəʊst/ **noun** a sign on a post, giving information such as the direction and distance to a nearby place 指向标；指示牌；路标

Sikh /siːk/ **noun** a follower of a religion that developed from Hinduism 锡克教信徒 ■ **Sikhism** noun.

silage /'saɪlɪdʒ/ **noun** grass or other green crops that are stored in a silo without being dried, used as animal feed in the winter 青贮饲料

silence /'saɪləns/ **noun 1** complete lack of sound 寂静；无声 **2** a situation in which someone is unwilling to speak or discuss something 默不作声；沉默 ▪ **verb** (**silences, silencing, silenced**) **1** stop someone from speaking 使沉默；使 ··· 缄默 **2** make something remain silent 使安静

silencer /'saɪlənsə(r)/ **noun** a device for reducing the noise made by a gun or exhaust system (枪或排气系统的)消音器，消声器

silent /'saɪlənt/ **adjective 1** without any sound 安静的；寂静无声的 **2** not speaking or not spoken aloud 沉默的；不说话的；轻声的 ■ **silently** adverb.

silhouette /ˌsɪluˈet/ **noun** a dark shape and outline seen against a lighter background (浅色背景上的)暗色轮廓，剪影 ▪ **verb** (**silhouettes, silhouetting, silhouetted**) show as a silhouette 使现出暗色轮廓(或影像)

silica /'sɪlɪkə/ **noun** a hard substance formed from silicon and oxygen that occurs as quartz in sandstone and other rocks 硅石；二氧化硅

silicon /'sɪlɪkən/ **noun** a chemical element that is a semiconductor and is used to make electronic circuits (化学元素)硅 □ **silicon chip** a microchip 硅片

silicone /'sɪlɪkəʊn/ **noun** a synthetic substance made from silicon 硅酮；硅树脂

silk /sɪlk/ **noun** a fine, soft shiny fibre produced by silkworms, made into thread or fabric 丝；蚕丝

silken /'sɪlkən/ **adjective 1** smooth and shiny like silk 丝般柔软的；有丝般光泽的 **2** made of silk 丝制的；丝绸的

silkworm /'sɪlkwɜːm/ **noun** a caterpillar that spins a silk cocoon from which silk fibre is obtained 蚕

silky /'sɪlki/ **adjective** (**silkier, silkiest**) smooth and shiny like silk 丝般的；柔软有光泽的

sill /sɪl/ **noun** a shelf or slab at the foot of a window or doorway 窗台；门槛

silly /'sɪli/ **adjective** (**sillier, silliest**) showing a lack of good judgement or common sense 缺乏常识的；不明智的；愚蠢的 ■ **silliness** noun.

silo /'saɪləʊ/ **noun** (plural **silos**) **1** a tower used to store grain (贮藏谷物的)筒仓 **2** a pit or airtight structure for storing silage 青贮窖 **3** an underground chamber in which a guided missile is kept ready for firing (导弹的)地下发射井

silt /sɪlt/ **noun** fine sand or clay carried by running water and deposited as a sediment (水流夹带或水底沉积的)泥沙，淤泥，淤沙 ▪ **verb** (**silt up**) fill or block with silt 使淤塞 ■ **silty** adjective.

silver /'sɪlvə(r)/ **noun 1** a shiny greyish-white precious metal (贵重金属)银 **2** a shiny grey-white colour 银白色 **3** coins made from silver or from a metal that looks like silver 银币；镍币 **4** silver dishes, containers, or cutlery 银器 ▪ **verb** (**silvers, silvering, silvered**) cover or plate with silver 给 ··· 包银；给 ···

镀银 □ **silver birch** a birch tree with silver-grey bark 白桦(树) **silver jubilee** the twenty-fifth anniversary of an important event (重要事件的)二十五周年纪念 **silver medal** a medal awarded for second place in a race or competition 银质奖章；银牌 **silver plate 1** a thin layer of silver applied as a coating to another metal 镀银层 **2** plates, dishes, etc. made of or plated with silver 银器；镀银器 **silver wedding** Brit. 【英】the twentyfifth anniversary of a wedding 银婚(结婚25周年纪念) ■ **silvery** adjective.

silverfish /'sɪlvəfɪʃ/ *noun* (plural **silverfish**) a small silvery wingless insect that lives in buildings 蠹鱼(生活在建筑物中的一种银色无翅小昆虫)

silverside /'sɪlvəsaɪd/ *noun* the upper side of a cut of beef from the outside of the leg 牛臀肉

silversmith /'sɪlvəsmɪθ/ *noun* a person who makes silver articles 银匠

SIM card /sɪm/ *noun* a small card inside a mobile phone that stores information such as details of calls made and received (手机的) SIM 卡，用户识别模块

simian /'sɪmiən/ *adjective* relating to or like apes or monkeys 类人猿的；猴的 • *noun* an ape or monkey 类人猿；猴

similar /'sɪmələ(r)/ *adjective* like something but not exactly the same 类似的；相像的 ■ **similarity** *noun* (plural **similarities**) **similarly** adverb.

simile /'sɪməli/ *noun* a word or phrase that compares one thing to another of a different kind (e.g. *the family was as solid as a rock*)明喻

simmer /'sɪmə(r)/ *verb* (**simmers**, **simmering**, **simmered**) **1** stay or cause to stay just below boiling point 煨，炖 **2** be in a state of anger

or excitement which you only just keep under control 按捺,压抑(愤怒或激动的情绪) **3** (**simmer down**) become calmer and quieter 冷静下来

simper /'sɪmpə(r)/ *verb* (**simpers**, **simpering**, **simpered**) smile in a coy and silly way 忸怩地笑；傻笑 • *noun* a coy and silly smile 忸怩的笑；傻笑

simple /'sɪmpl/ *adjective* (**simpler**, **simplest**) **1** easily understood or done 简单的；简易的；简明的 **2** plain and basic 一般的；普通的 **3** composed of a single element; not compound 非复合的；单一的 **4** of very low intelligence 弱智的，无知的，愚蠢的 □ **simple fracture** a fracture of a bone without any breaking of the skin 单纯骨折；无创骨折

simpleton /'sɪmpltən/ *noun* a foolish or unintelligent person 傻瓜；笨蛋；易上当受骗的人

simplicity /sɪm'plɪsəti/ *noun* the quality of being simple 简单；简易；简明

simplify /'sɪmplɪfaɪ/ *verb* (**simplifies**, **simplifying**, **simplified**) make easier to do or understand 简化；使简易；使简明 ■ **simplification** noun.

simplistic /sɪm'plɪstɪk/ *adjective* treating complex issues as more simple than they really are 过分简单化的 ■ **simplistically** adverb.

simply /'sɪmpli/ *adverb* **1** in a simple way 简单地；简易地；简明地 **2** just; merely 仅仅；只不过 **3** absolutely 完全地；非常；极其

simulacrum /ˌsɪmju'leɪkrəm/ *noun* (plural **simulacra** /ˌsɪmju'leɪkrə/ or **simulacrums**) something that is similar to something else 类似物；幻影；假象

simulate /'sɪmjuleɪt/ *verb* (**simulates**, **simulating**, **simulated**) **1** imitate the appearance or nature of 模仿 **2** use a computer to create a model of something or conditions that are like those in real life (用计算机)模拟 **3** pretend to have or feel a particular emotion 假装; 装作 ■ **simulation** noun **simulator** noun.

simultaneous /ˌsɪml'teɪnɪəs/ **adjective** happening or done at the same time 同时发生的; 同时进行的; 同步的 ■ **simultaneity** noun **simultaneously** adverb.

✔ **拼写指南** the ending is -eous, not -ious: simultaneous. simultaneous 词末的 -eous 不要拼作 -ious。

---

sin /sɪn/ **noun 1** an act that breaks a religious or moral law (违反宗教戒律或道德规范的)罪, 罪孽 **2** an act that causes strong disapproval 过错; 过失 • **verb** (**sins, sinning, sinned**) commit a sin 犯罪; 犯过失

since /sɪns/ **preposition** in the period between a time in the past and the present 从…以后; 自…以来 • **conjunction 1** during or in the time after 自…以来; 从…以后 **2** because 因为; 既然 • **adverb 1** from the time mentioned until the present 从那以后; 此后; 后来 **2** ago 之前; 以前

sincere /sɪn'sɪə(r)/ **adjective** (**sincerer, sincerest**) not pretending anything or deceiving anyone; genuine and honest 诚恳的; 真诚的; 诚实的 ■ **sincerely** adverb **sincerity** noun.

sine /saɪn/ **noun** Maths【数学】(in a right-angled triangle) the ratio of the side opposite a particular acute angle to the hypotenuse (直角三角形的)正弦

sinecure /'sɪnɪkjʊə(r)/ **noun** a job for which you are paid but which requires little or no work 闲职; 挂名差事

sine qua non /ˌsiː neɪ kwɑː 'nəʊn/ **noun** a thing that is absolutely necessary 必要条件

sinew /'sɪnjuː/ **noun** a band of strong tissue that joins a muscle to a bone

腱; 肌腱 ■ **sinewy** adjective.

sinful /'sɪnfl/ **adjective 1** wicked 坏的; 邪恶的; 罪恶的 **2** disgraceful 可耻的; 丢脸的; 不光彩的 ■ **sinfully** adverb **sinfulness** noun.

sing /sɪŋ/ **verb** (**sings, singing, sang**; past participle **sung**) **1** make musical sounds with your voice; perform a song 唱; 唱歌 **2** make a whistling sound 呜呜作响; 发嗖嗖声 □ **sing-song 1** a rising and falling sound in someone's voice 声调起伏的嗓音 **2** informal【非正式】an informal gathering for singing 歌咏会 ■ **singer** noun.

singalong /'sɪŋəlɒŋ/ **noun** an informal occasion when people sing together 跟唱歌咏会; 自娱歌咏会

singe /sɪndʒ/ **verb** (**singes, singeing, singed**) burn the surface of something slightly (轻微)烧焦 • **noun** a slight burn 烧焦; 烧灼

single /'sɪŋgl/ **adjective 1** one only 唯一的; 单个的 **2** designed for one person 单人的; 供一人用的 **3** consisting of one part 单一的 **4** taken separately from others 分别的; 个别的 **5** not involved in a romantic or sexual relationship 单身的; 未婚的 **6** Brit.【英】(of a ticket) for an outward journey only (车票)单程的 • **noun 1** a single person or thing 单个人(或事物), 一个 **2** a short record or CD 单曲唱片 **3** (**singles**) a game or competition for individual players 单打比赛 • **verb** (**singles, singling, singled**) (**single someone/thing out**) choose someone or something from a group for special treatment 挑出; 选出 □ **single-breasted** (of a jacket or coat) fastened by one row of buttons at the centre of the front (夹克或大衣)单排扣的 **single file** a line of people moving one behind another 单行; 一路纵队 **single-handed** done without help from other people 独自; 单枪匹马

地 **single-minded** determined to concentrate on one particular aim 专一的;一心一意的；专心致志的

single parent a person bringing up a child or children without a partner 单亲 ■ **singly** adverb.

singlet /'sɪŋɡlət/ noun Brit. 【英】a vest or similar sleeveless garment 背心;(无袖)汗衫

singleton /'sɪŋɡltən/ noun a single person or thing 单独的人(或物)

singular /'sɪŋɡjələ(r)/ adjective 1 Grammar 【语法】(of a word or form) referring to just one person or thing (词或词的形式)单数的 2 very good or interesting; remarkable 出色的;非凡的；突出的 • noun Grammar 【语法】 the singular form of a word (词的)单数形式 ■ **singularity** noun **singularly** adverb.

sinister /'sɪnɪstə(r)/ adjective seeming evil or dangerous 邪恶的;凶险的

sink /sɪŋk/ verb (**sinks, sinking, sank**; past participle **sunk**) 1 go down below the surface of liquid 下沉;沉没 2 go or cause to go to the bottom of the sea (使)下沉;(使)沉没 3 move slowly downwards (缓缓地)下落,沉 4 gradually decrease in amount or strength 减少；降低;减弱 5 (**sink something into**) force something sharp through a surface 使(尖利物)插入;在(表面)凿(或钻) 6 (**sink in**) become fully understood 被理解了 7 pass into a particular state 进入,陷入 (某种状态) 8 (**sink something into**) put money or resources into 投入(资金或资源) • noun a fixed basin with a water supply and a drainage pipe 洗涤槽

sinker /'sɪŋkə(r)/ noun a weight used to keep a fishing line beneath the water (钓鱼线上的)铅锤

sinner /'sɪnə(r)/ noun a person who sins 罪人；有错者；有过失者

sinuous /'sɪnjuəs/ adjective 1 having many curves and turns 弯曲的；蜿蜒

的;起伏的 2 moving in a graceful, swaying way 动作柔美的 ■ **sinuously** adverb.

sinus /'saɪnəs/ noun a hollow space within the bones of the face that connects with the nostrils 窦;鼻窦

sinusitis /ˌsaɪnə'saɪtɪs/ noun inflammation of a sinus (鼻)窦炎

sip /sɪp/ verb (**sips, sipping, sipped**) drink something in small mouthfuls 呷,啜;抿 • noun a small mouthful of liquid 一呷之量；一小口

siphon or **syphon** /'saɪfn/ noun a tube used to move liquid from one container to another, using air pressure to maintain the flow 虹吸管 • verb 1 draw off or move liquid by means of a siphon 用虹吸管吸出(或输送) 2 (**siphon something off**) take small amounts of money over a period of time 抽取,撤走(小额款项)

sir /sɜː(r)/ noun 1 a polite form of address to a man 先生,长官,阁下(对男子的尊称) 2 used as a title for a knight or baronet 爵士(对爵士或准男爵的称呼)

sire /'saɪə(r)/ noun 1 the male parent of an animal 雄性种兽 2 literary 【文】 a father 父亲 3 old use 【旧】a respectful form of address to a king 陛下 (对国王的尊称) • verb (**sires, siring, sired**) be the male parent of 做…的父亲

siren /'saɪrən/ noun 1 a device that makes a loud prolonged warning sound 汽笛；警报器 2 Greek Mythology 【希腊神话】each of a group of creatures who were part woman, part bird, whose singing lured sailors on to rocks 塞壬(半人半鸟的女海妖,以歌声诱惑海员而使船只触礁沉没) 3 a woman whose attractiveness is regarded as dangerous to men 危险的美人；妖妇

sirloin /'sɜːlɔɪn/ noun the best part of a loin of beef 牛上腰肉；牛里脊肉

sirup /'sɪrəp/ US spelling of SYRUP.

syrup 的美式拼法

sisal /ˈsaɪsl/ **noun** fibre made from the leaves of a tropical Mexican plant, used for ropes or matting 西沙尔麻，剑麻(一种热带墨西哥植物叶子制成的纤维，用于制绳或织席子)

sissy /ˈsɪsi/ **noun** (plural **sissies**) informal【非正式】a weak or cowardly person 柔弱的人；懦弱的人

sister /ˈsɪstə(r)/ **noun 1** a woman or girl in relation to other children of her parents 姐；妹 **2** a female friend or colleague 女性朋友；女同事 **3** a member of a religious order of women 女教友；修女 **4** Brit.【英】a senior female nurse 女护士长 ■ **sister-in-law** (plural **sisters-in-law**) **1** the sister of a person's wife or husband 姑子；姨子 **2** the wife of a person's brother or brother-in-law 嫂子；弟媳；妯娌 ■ **sisterly** adjective.

sisterhood /ˈsɪstəhʊd/ **noun 1** the relationship between sisters 姐妹关系 **2** a bond of friendship and understanding between women 姐妹情谊 **3** a group of women linked by a shared interest 妇女团体

sit /sɪt/ **verb** (**sits**, **sitting**, **sat**) **1** rest your weight on your bottom with your back upright 坐；就座 **2** be in a particular position or state 位于(某一位置)；处于(某种状态) **3** serve as a member of a council, jury, or other official body (在议会、陪审团或其他官方机构中)任职 **4** (of a parliament, committee, or court of law) be carrying on its business (议会、委员会或法庭)开会，开庭 **5** Brit.【英】take an exam 参加(考试)；应试 **6** (**sit for**) pose for an artist or photographer 为(艺术家或摄影师)当模特儿 □ **sit-in** the occupation of a college or workplace as a form of protest (大学或工作场所的)室内静坐抗议

❗ **注意** use **sitting** rather than **sat** with the verb 'to be': say we were sitting there for hours rather than we were sat there for hours. 与动词 to be 连用时，应使用 sitting 而不是 sat：如应说 we were sitting there for hours (我们在那儿坐了数个小时)，而不说 we were sat there for hours。

sitar /sɪˈtɑː(r)/ **noun** an Indian lute with a long neck (印度的)锡塔尔琴

sitcom /ˈsɪtkɒm/ **noun** a situation comedy 情景喜剧

site /saɪt/ **noun 1** a place where something is located or happens 地点；现场 **2** a website (因特网)网站 • **verb** (**sites**, **siting**, **sited**) build or establish something in a particular place 使坐落在；为…选址

❗ **注意** don't confuse **site** with **sight**, which means 'the ability to see'. 不要混淆 site 和 sight，后者意为"视力；视觉"。

sitter /ˈsɪtə(r)/ **noun 1** a person who sits for a portrait 坐着让人画像的人 **2** a person who looks after children, pets, or a house while the parents or owners are away 代人临时照看孩子(或宠物、房子)的人

sitting /ˈsɪtɪŋ/ **noun 1** a period of time during which a court of law, committee, or parliament is carrying on its business (法院的)开庭期间；(委员会或议会的)开会期间 **2** a period of time when a group of people are served a meal 供餐(时间) **3** a period of posing for a portrait 摆姿势让人画像的时间 □ **sitting duck** informal【非正式】a person or thing that is easy to attack 易受攻击者；容易击中的目标 **sitting room** a room for sitting and relaxing in 起居室；会客室 **sitting tenant** Brit.【英】a tenant who has the legal right to remain living in a property 已租住房子的人；现有房客

situate /ˈsɪtʃueɪt/ **verb** (**situates**, **situating**, **situated**) **1** put in a particular place 使位于(某一位置) **2**

(**be situated**) be in a particular set of circumstances 处于(某境地)

situation /ˌsɪtʃʊˈeɪʃn/ **noun 1** a set of circumstances 状况；处境 **2** the location and surroundings of a place 位置；地点；环境 **3** a job 职业；职务；工作 □ **situation comedy** a comedy series in which the same characters are involved in various amusing situations 情景喜剧 ■ **situational** adjective.

six /sɪks/ **cardinal number 1** one more than five; 6 六 (Roman numeral 罗马数字：**vi** or **VI**.) **2** Cricket【板球】a hit that reaches the boundary without first hitting the ground, scoring six runs 得六分的击球；以六分计算的击球 □ **at sixes and sevens** in a state of confusion 乱七八糟 **knock someone for six** Brit. informal【英，非正式】take someone completely by surprise 使(某人)大吃一惊

sixpence /ˈsɪkspəns/ **noun** Brit.【英】(in the past) a coin worth six old pence (2½ p)(旧时的)六便士硬币

sixteen /sɪksˈtiːn/ **cardinal number** one more than fifteen; 16 十六 (Roman numeral 罗马数字：**xvi** or **XVI**.) ■ **sixteenth** ordinal number.

sixth /sɪksθ/ **ordinal number 1** being number six in a sequence; 6th 第六 **2** (**a sixth** or **one sixth**) each of six equal parts of something 六分之一 □ **sixth-form college** Brit.【英】a college for students aged 16 to 18 第六学级学院 **sixth sense** a supposed ability to know things by intuition rather than using your sight, hearing, etc. 第六感觉；直觉

sixty /ˈsɪksti/ **cardinal number** (plural **sixties**) ten more than fifty; 60 六十 (Roman numeral 罗马数字：**lx** or **LX**.) ■ **sixtieth** ordinal number.

size¹ /saɪz/ **noun 1** the overall measurements or extent of something 大小；尺寸；规模 **2** each of the series of standard measurements in which clothes, shoes, and other goods are made 号；尺码 • **verb** (**sizes, sizing, sized**) **1** group things according to size 按大小(或尺码)分类 **2** (**size someone/thing up**) informal【非正式】form a judgement of a person or thing 判断；估计

size² **noun** a sticky solution used to glaze paper, stiffen textiles, and prepare plastered walls for decoration (使纸张光亮或使织物坚挺的)胶料，浆料；(贴装饰壁纸的)涂料 • **verb** (**sizes, sizing, sized**) treat with size 给…上胶

sizeable or **sizable** /ˈsaɪzəbl/ **adjective** fairly large 相当大的

sizzle /ˈsɪzl/ **verb** (**sizzles, sizzling, sizzled**) **1** (of food) make a hissing sound when being fried (食物油炸时)发出咝咝声 **2** (**sizzling**) informal【非正式】very hot or exciting 酷热的；热烈的

skate¹ /skeɪt/ **noun** an ice skate or roller skate 冰鞋；冰刀；旱冰鞋；溜冰鞋 • **verb** (**skates, skating, skated**) **1** move on skates 滑冰；溜冰 **2** (**skate over** or **round**) pass over or refer only briefly to 回避，避免涉及；一带而过 ■ **skater** noun.

skate² **noun** (plural **skate** or **skates**) an edible sea fish with a diamond-shaped body 鳐鱼(一种可食用的菱形海鱼)

skateboard /ˈskeɪtbɔːd/ **noun** a short narrow board fitted with two small wheels at either end, on which a person can ride 滑板 ■ **skateboarder** noun **skateboarding** noun.

skedaddle /skɪˈdædl/ **verb** (**skedaddles, skedaddling, skedaddled**) informal【非正式】leave quickly 迅速离开；匆匆离去

skein /skeɪn/ **noun** a length of yarn held in a loose coil or knot (线或纱的)一绞，一束

skeletal /ˈskelɪtl/ **adjective 1** having to do with a skeleton 骨骼的 **2** very thin 骨瘦如柴的

skeleton /'skelɪtn/ **noun 1** a framework of bone or cartilage supporting or containing the body of an animal (动物的)骨骼, 骸骨 **2** a supporting framework or structure 骨架; 框架 • **adjective** referring to an essential or minimum number of people (人员)最基本的, 最起码的: *a skeleton staff* 基本人员 □ **skeleton in the cupboard** a shocking or embarrassing fact that someone wishes to keep secret (不可外扬的)家丑, 隐情 **skeleton key** a key designed to fit a number of locks 万能钥匙

skeptic /'skeptɪk/ US spelling of SCEPTIC. sceptic 的美式拼法

skeptical /'skeptɪkl/ US spelling of SCEPTICAL. sceptical 的美式拼法

sketch /sketʃ/ **noun 1** a rough drawing or painting 草图; 略图; 速写; 素描 **2** a short humorous scene in a comedy show (喜剧性)短剧, 独幕剧 **3** a brief written or spoken account (书面或口头的)概述, 概要 • **verb 1** make a sketch of 画…的略图 or 概述; 简述 **2** give a brief account of

sketchbook /'sketʃbʊk/ **noun** a pad of drawing paper for sketching on 写生簿; 素描册; 速写本

sketchy /'sketʃi/ **adjective** (**sketchier**, **sketchiest**) not thorough or detailed; rough 简略的; 粗略的 ■ **sketchily** adverb

skew /skjuː/ **verb 1** suddenly change direction or move at an angle (突然)改变方向; 偏斜; 扭转 **2** make something biased or distorted 使有偏见; 使曲解; 使歪曲 • **noun** a bias towards one particular group or subject 偏爱; 偏好; 偏祖 **skew-whiff** Brit. informal 【英, 非正式】 not straight; askew 不直的; 歪斜的

skewbald /'skjuːbɔːld/ **adjective** (of a horse) having patches of white and brown (马)白色与棕色夹杂的, 杂色的, 花斑的

skewer /'skjuːə(r)/ **noun** a long piece of metal or wood used for holding pieces of food together during cooking (串食物用的)扦, 棒 • **verb** (**skewers**, **skewering**, **skewered**) hold or pierce with a pin or skewer 用大头针别住; 用扦子串住

ski /skiː/ **noun** (plural **skis**) each of a pair of long, narrow pieces of wood, metal, or plastic, attached to boots for travelling over snow 滑雪板 • **verb** (**skis**, **skiing**, **skied**) travel on skis 滑雪 □ **ski jump** a steep slope levelling off before a sharp drop to allow a skier to leap through the air 跳台滑雪助滑道 **ski lift** a system of moving seats attached to an overhead cable, used for taking skiers to the top of a run (运送滑雪者上坡的)上山吊椅 ■ **skier** noun.

✔ 拼写指南 the plural of the noun is **skis**, without an e. ski 的复数为 skis, 没有 e。

skid /skɪd/ **verb** (**skids**, **skidding**, **skidded**) **1** (of a vehicle) slide sideways in an uncontrolled way (车辆)打滑, 滑向一侧 **2** slip; slide 滑倒; 滑行 • **noun 1** an act of skidding 打滑; 滑行 **2** a runner attached to the underside of a helicopter and some other aircraft (直升机等)起落撬, 滑橇 □ **skid row** N. Amer. informal 【北美, 非正式】 a run-down part of a town or city where homeless people and alcoholics live (城镇中流浪汉、酗酒者聚居的)贫民窟, 贫民区

skiff /skɪf/ **noun** a light rowing boat 划艇

skilful /'skɪlfl/ US spelling 【美式作】 **skillful** adjective having or showing skill 有技术的; 熟练的 ■ **skilfully** adverb

✔ 拼写指南 there is only one *l* in the middle: skilful. The spelling with two ls is American. skilful 中间只有一个 l。有两个 l 是美式拼法。

skill /skɪl/ **noun 1** the ability to do something well 技能；技艺 **2** a particular ability (专门)技术，技能

skilled /skɪld/ **adjective 1** having or showing skill 有技能的；熟练的 **2** (of work) needing special abilities or training (工作)技术性的，需要接受专门训练的

skillet /ˈskɪlɪt/ **noun** N. Amer.【北美】a frying pan 平底煎锅

skim /skɪm/ **verb** (**skims, skimming, skimmed**) **1** remove a substance from the surface of a liquid (从液体上)撇去(浮物) **2** move quickly and lightly over a surface or through the air 轻掠过；轻擦过 **3** read through quickly 略读；浏览 **4** (**skim over**) deal with briefly 敷衍；应付 □ **skimmed milk** milk from which the cream has been removed 脱脂奶；脱脂乳

skimp /skɪmp/ **verb** spend less money or use less of something than is really needed in an attempt to economize 吝惜；节省

skimpy /ˈskɪmpi/ **adjective** (**skimpier, skimpiest**) **1** not large enough in amount or size (数量或尺寸)不足的 **2** (of clothes) short and revealing (衣服)短而暴露的

skin /skɪn/ **noun 1** the thin layer of tissue forming the outer covering of the body 皮；皮肤 **2** the skin of a dead animal used for clothing or other items 兽皮；皮张 **3** the peel or outer layer of a fruit or vegetable 果皮；(蔬菜的)外皮 • **verb** (**skins, skinning, skinned**) **1** remove the skin from 剥皮 **2** graze a part of your body 擦破(身体某部位)的皮肤 □ **by the skin of your teeth** only just 仅仅；刚好；勉强 **have a thick skin** be unaffected by criticism or insults (对待批评或侮辱)脸皮厚 **skin-deep** not deep or lasting; superficial 表皮的；表面的；肤浅的 **skin-diving** swimming underwater without a diving suit, using an aqualung and

flippers 赤身潜水，裸潜(使用水中呼吸器和脚蹼，不穿潜水服)

skinflint /ˈskɪnflɪnt/ **noun** informal【非正式】a very mean person 吝啬鬼；一毛不拔的人

skinhead /ˈskɪnhed/ **noun** a young person of a group with very short shaved hair 光头仔(剃光头的青年群体)

skinny /ˈskɪni/ **adjective** (**skinnier, skinniest**) **1** (of a person) very thin (人)极瘦的，皮包骨的 **2** (of a garment) tight-fitting (衣服)紧绷的，紧身的

skint /skɪnt/ **adjective** Brit. informal【英，非正式】having little or no money 身无分文的；不名一文的

skintight /ˈskɪnˈtaɪt/ **adjective** (of a garment) very tight-fitting (衣服)紧身的

skip¹ /skɪp/ **verb** (**skips, skipping, skipped**) **1** move along lightly, stepping from one foot to the other with a little jump 蹦跳着走 **2** Brit.【英】jump repeatedly over a rope turned over the head and under the feet 跳绳 **3** leave out or move quickly over 跳读；略读 **4** fail to attend or deal with 略过；跳过；漏掉 • **noun** a skipping movement 蹦跳；跳跃

skip² **noun** Brit.【英】a large open-topped container for holding and carrying away large unwanted items, builders' rubbish, etc. (盛装废弃物品、建筑垃圾等的)废料桶

skipper /ˈskɪpə(r)/ informal【非正式】**noun 1** the captain of a ship, boat, or aircraft 船长；(飞机的)机长 **2** the captain of a sports team (运动队的)队长 • **verb** (**skippers, skippering, skippered**) be captain of 当…的船长(或机长)；当(运动队)的队长

skirl /skɜːl/ **noun** a shrill sound made by bagpipes (尖厉的)风笛声 • **verb** make such a sound 发出尖厉的声音

skirmish /ˈskɜːmɪʃ/ **noun** a short period of fighting 小冲突 • **verb** take part in a skirmish 发生小冲突

skirt /skɜːt/ **noun** a woman's garment that hangs from the waist and surrounds the lower body and legs 女裙 • **verb 1** go round or past the edge of 绕…的边缘走 **2** (also **skirt round**) avoid dealing with 绕开；避开

skirting /'skɜːtɪŋ/ or **skirting board** **noun** Brit. 【英】a wooden board running along the base of the walls of a room (内墙底部的)踢脚板，壁脚板

skit /skɪt/ **noun** a short comedy sketch that makes fun of something by imitating it 讽刺小品；滑稽短剧

skitter /'skɪtə(r)/ **verb** (**skitters**, **skittering**, **skittered**) move lightly and quickly 轻快地跑；飞掠

skittish /'skɪtɪʃ/ **adjective 1** (of a horse) nervous and tending to shy (马)易惊的 **2** lively or changeable 活泼的；易变的 ■ **skittishly** **adverb**.

skittle /'skɪtl/ **noun 1** (**skittles**) a game played with wooden pins set up to be bowled down with a ball 撞柱游戏(用木球将木柱击倒的游戏) **2** a pin used in the game of skittles (撞柱游戏中用的)木柱

skive /skaɪv/ **verb** (**skives**, **skiving**, **skived**) Brit. informal 【英，非正式】avoid work or a duty by staying away or leaving early 逃避(工作或责任) ■ **skiver** **noun**.

skivvy /'skɪvi/ **noun** (plural **skivvies**) Brit. informal 【英，非正式】a female domestic servant 女佣；女仆

skua /'skjuːə/ **noun** a large seabird like a gull 贼鸥(似海鸥的巨大海鸟)

skulduggery or **skullduggery** /skʌl'dʌɡəri/ **noun** underhand behaviour 欺诈；欺骗

skulk /skʌlk/ **verb** hide or move around in a secretive way 藏；躲避；偷偷摸摸地走动

skull /skʌl/ **noun** the bony framework that surrounds and protects the brain 头骨；颅骨 □ **skull and crossbones** a picture of a skull with two thigh bones crossed below it, used in the past by pirates and now as a sign of danger 骷髅图(由一个骷髅和两根交叉的大腿骨组成，旧时为海盗所用，现在是警示标志)

skullcap /'skʌlkæp/ **noun** a small close-fitting cap without a peak 无檐便帽

skunk /skʌŋk/ **noun** an animal with black and white stripes that can spray foul-smelling liquid at attackers 臭鼬(身体有黑白条纹，遇到攻击会喷出恶臭液体)

sky /skaɪ/ **noun** (plural **skies**) the region of the upper atmosphere seen from the earth 天；天空

skydiving /'skaɪdaɪvɪŋ/ **noun** the sport of jumping from an aircraft and performing movements in the air before landing by parachute 高空跳伞运动 ■ **skydiver** **noun**.

skylark /'skaɪlɑːk/ **noun** a lark that sings while flying 云雀 • **verb** behave in a playful and mischievous way 开玩笑；胡闹

skylight /'skaɪlaɪt/ **noun** a window set in a roof 天窗

skyline /'skaɪlaɪn/ **noun** an outline of land and buildings seen against the sky (陆地和建筑物在天空映衬下的)空中轮廓线，天际线

skyrocket /'skaɪrɒkɪt/ **verb** (**skyrockets**, **skyrocketing**, **skyrocketed**) informal 【非正式】(of a price or amount) increase rapidly (价格或数量)猛涨，猛升

skyscraper /'skaɪskreɪpə(r)/ **noun** a very tall building 摩天大楼

slab /slæb/ **noun 1** a large, thick, flat piece of stone or concrete (石头或混凝土制的)厚板，平板 **2** a thick slice of cake, bread, etc. (蛋糕、面包等的)大块，大片

slack /slæk/ **adjective 1** not taut or held tightly 不紧的；松的 **2** (of business or trade) quiet (商业或贸易)不活跃的，不景气的，萧条的 3 careless or lazy 不认真的；马虎的，懒散的 4 (of a tide) between the ebb and the flow (潮水)无涨落的 • noun 1 the part of a rope or line which is not held taut (绳索或线的)松弛部分 2 (slacks) casual trousers 便裤；宽松长裤 • verb 1 (slack off or up) become slower or less intense 减缓；放松；松弛 2 Brit. informal 【英，非正式】 work slowly or lazily 懈怠；懒散 ■ slacker noun slackly adverb slackness noun.

slacken /ˈslækən/ verb 1 make or become less active or intense (使)松懈；(使)松弛；(使)放松 2 make or become less tight 使放松；变松弛

slag /slæɡ/ noun 1 stony waste matter left when metal has been separated from ore by smelting or refining 矿渣，熔渣；炉渣 2 Brit. informal, disapproving 【英，非正式，贬】 a woman who has many sexual partners 荡妇 • verb (slags, slagging, slagged) (slag someone/thing off) Brit. informal 【英，非正式】 criticize someone or something rudely 责难；辱骂 □ slag heap a mound of waste material from a mine 矿渣堆.

slain /sleɪn/ past participle of SLAY.

slake /sleɪk/ verb (slakes, slaking, slaked) satisfy a desire, thirst, etc. 满足；消解

slalom /ˈslɑːləm/ noun a skiing or canoeing race following a winding course marked out by poles (滑雪)回转赛，障碍赛；(划艇)回旋赛

slam /slæm/ verb (slams, slamming, slammed) 1 shut forcefully and loudly 使劲关上；砰地关上 2 put down with great force 使劲摔；砰地放下 3 hit a ball with great force 猛击(球) 4 informal 【非正式】 criticize severely 抨击；谴骂 • noun a loud bang caused when a door is slammed (猛关门时的)砰声

slander /ˈslɑːndə(r)/ noun the crime of saying something untrue that harms a person's reputation 诽谤；诋毁 • verb (slanders, slandering, slandered) say something untrue and damaging about 诽谤；诋毁 ■ slanderous adjective.

slang /slæŋ/ noun very informal words and phrases that are more common in speech than in writing and are used by a particular group of people 俚语 □ slanging match Brit. 【英】 an angry argument in which people insult each other 互相谩骂 ■ slangy adjective.

slant /slɑːnt/ verb 1 slope or lean 倾斜；歪斜 2 present information from a particular point of view 有倾向性地报道；有倾向性地陈述 • noun 1 a sloping position 斜面；斜坡 2 a point of view 观点，看法

slap /slæp/ verb (slaps, slapping, slapped) 1 hit with the palm of your hand or a flat object (用手掌或扁平物)掴，打，拍打 2 hit against a surface with a slapping sound 啪地击打(或撞上) 3 (slap something on) put something on a surface quickly or carelessly 随意扔放 • noun an act or sound of slapping 掴；打 • adverb (also slap bang) informal 【非正式】 suddenly and with great force 突然；猛然 □ slap-up Brit. informal 【英，非正式】 (of a meal) large and extravagant (饭菜)丰盛的，高档的，讲究的

slapdash /ˈslæpdæʃ/ adjective done too hurriedly and carelessly 仓促的；草率的

slapstick /ˈslæpstɪk/ noun comedy consisting of deliberately clumsy actions and embarrassing situations 粗俗滑稽剧；打闹剧

slash /slæʃ/ verb 1 cut with a violent sweeping movement 砍杀 2 informal 【非正式】 greatly reduce a price or quantity 大幅削减(价格或数量)

• **noun 1** a cut made with a wide sweeping stroke 切口;砍痕 **2** a slanting stroke (/) used between alternatives and in fractions and ratios 斜线号;斜杠

slat /slæt/ **noun** each of a series of thin, narrow pieces of wood or other material, arranged so as to overlap or fit into each other (木头等材料制成的)板条, 狭板 ■ **slatted** adjective.

slate /sleɪt/ **noun** a dark grey rock that is easily split into smooth, flat plates, used in building and in the past for writing on 板岩;石板 • **verb** (**slates, slating, slated**) Brit. informal【英,非正式】 severely criticize 抨击;谴责

slather /'slæðə(r)/ **verb** (**slathers, slathering, slathered**) informal【非正式】 spread or smear thickly over 厚厚地涂抹

slattern /'slætən/ **noun** old use【旧】a dirty, untidy woman 不整洁的女人;邋遢女人 ■ **slatternly** adjective

slaughter /'slɔːtə(r)/ **noun 1** the killing of farm animals for food 屠宰;宰杀 **2** the killing of a large number of people in a cruel or violent way 屠杀;残杀 • **verb** (**slaughters, slaughtering, slaughtered**) **1** kill animals for food 屠宰;宰杀(动物) **2** kill a number of people in a cruel or violent way 屠杀;残杀(人)

slaughterhouse /'slɔːtəhaʊs/ **noun** a place where animals are killed for food (动物的)屠宰场

Slav /slɑːv/ **noun** a member of a group of peoples in central and eastern Europe 斯拉夫人 ■ **Slavic** adjective.

slave /sleɪv/ **noun 1** (in the past) a person who was the legal property of another and was forced to obey them (旧时的)奴隶 **2** a person who is strongly influenced or controlled by something 奴隶般受控制的人;痴迷者;沉迷者 • **verb** (**slaves, slaving, slaved**) work very hard 拼命工作;苦干 □ **slavedriver** informal

【非正式】a person who makes other people work very hard 逼迫他人拼命工作的人;苛刻的工头 **slave labour** very demanding work that is very badly paid 苦工

slaver /'sleɪvə(r)/ **verb** (**slavers, slavering, slavered**) let saliva run from the mouth 淌口水;垂涎 • **noun** saliva running from the mouth 口水;涎水

slavery /'sleɪvəri/ **noun 1** the state of being a slave 奴隶身份 **2** the practice or system of owning slaves 蓄奴;奴隶制

slavish /'sleɪvɪʃ/ **adjective** showing no attempt to be original or do something in a new way 盲目的;无新意的;缺乏独创性的 ■ **slavishly** adverb.

slay /sleɪ/ **verb** (**slays, slaying, slew; past participle slain**) old use or N. Amer.【旧或北美】violently kill 残杀;杀戮

sleaze /sliːz/ **noun** informal【非正式】immoral or dishonest behaviour 卑劣行径

sleazy /'sliːzi/ **adjective** (**sleazier, sleaziest**) **1** immoral or dishonest 不道德的;卑鄙的 **2** (of a place) dirty and seedy (地方)肮脏的, 邋遢的, 污秽的

sled /sled/ **noun & verb** (**sleds, sledding, sledded**) N. Amer.【北美】= **SLEDGE**.

sledge /sledʒ/ **noun 1** a vehicle on runners for travelling over snow or ice, sometimes pulled by dogs (有时由狗拉的)雪橇(车) **2** Brit.【英】a toboggan 平底雪橇 • **verb** (**sledges, sledging, sledged**) ride or carry on a sledge 乘雪橇

sledgehammer /'sledʒhæmə(r)/ **noun** a large, heavy hammer 大锤

sleek /sliːk/ **adjective 1** smooth and glossy 光滑的;光亮的 **2** having a wealthy and smart appearance 有钱的;衣冠楚楚的 **3** elegant and stream-lined 造型优美的;流线型的;线条明快的 ■ **sleekly** adverb.

sleep /sliːp/ **noun** a condition of rest in which the eyes are closed, the muscles are relaxed, and the mind is unconscious 睡眠；睡觉 • **verb (sleeps, sleeping, slept) 1** be asleep 入睡；睡觉 **2 (sleep in)** remain asleep or in bed later than usual in the morning 迟起；睡过头；睡懒觉 **3** provide a particular number of people with beds 为…提供住宿 **4 (sleep with)** have sex or be involved in a sexual relationship with 与…睡觉；和…发生性关系 **5 (sleep around)** have many sexual partners 到处跟人睡觉；乱搞男女关系 □ **put something to sleep** kill an animal painlessly 使(动物)无痛苦地死去 **sleeping bag** a warm padded bag for sleeping in when camping or travelling (露营或旅游时用的)睡袋 **sleeping car** a railway carriage fitted with beds or berths (火车的)卧铺车厢 **sleeping partner** Brit. 【英】a partner who puts money into a business but is not involved in running it 不参与公司具体经营的合伙人 **sleeping policeman** Brit. 【英】a hump in the road for slowing down traffic 减速垄 ■ **sleepless** adjective.

sleeper /'sliːpə(r)/ **noun 1** Brit. 【英】each of the wooden supports on which a railway track rests (铁轨的)枕木 **2** Brit. 【英】a ring or bar worn in a pierced ear to keep the hole from closing (为保持耳孔穿通而戴的)小耳环 **3** a train carrying sleeping cars 卧铺列车

sleepover /'sliːpəʊvə(r)/ **noun** a night spent by children at another person's house (小孩的)在外过夜，在外住宿

sleepwalk /'sliːpwɔːk/ **verb** walk around while asleep 梦游 ■ **sleep-walker** noun.

sleepy /'sliːpi/ **adjective (sleepier, sleepiest) 1** ready for, or needing, sleep 昏昏欲睡的；瞌睡的；困倦的 **2**

(of a place) without much activity (地方)寂静的，冷清的 ■ **sleepily** adverb **sleepiness** noun.

sleet /sliːt/ **noun** rain containing some ice, or snow melting as it falls 雨夹雪；冻雨 • **verb (it sleets, it is sleeting, it sleeted)** sleet falls 下雨夹雪；下冻雨

sleeve /sliːv/ **noun 1** the part of a garment covering a person's arm 袖子 **2** a protective cover for a record 唱片套 **3** a tube fitting over a rod or smaller tube 套筒；套管 □ **up your sleeve** kept secret and ready for use when needed 留有一招；留有锦囊妙计 ■ **sleeveless** adjective.

sleigh /sleɪ/ **noun** a sledge pulled by horses or reindeer (由马或驯鹿拖拉的)雪橇，雪车

sleight /slaɪt/ **noun (sleight of hand) 1** skilful use of the hands when performing magic tricks (表演魔术时的)敏捷手法 **2** skilful deception 诡计；把戏

slender /'slendə(r)/ **adjective (slenderer, slenderest) 1** gracefully thin 修长的；苗条的；纤细的 **2** barely enough 不足的；微薄的

slept /slept/ past and past participle of SLEEP.

sleuth /sluːθ/ **noun** informal 【非正式】a detective 侦探 ■ **sleuthing** noun.

slew[1] /sluː/ **verb** turn or slide violently or uncontrollably 紧急转向；急转

slew[2] past of SLAY.

slice /slaɪs/ **noun 1** a thin, broad piece of food cut from a larger portion (从大块食物上切下的)薄片，片 **2** a portion or share 一份；一部分 **3** a kitchen implement with a broad, flat blade for lifting cake, fish, etc. 锅铲；炒铲 **4** (in sports) a sliced stroke or shot (体育运动中的)斜切球，削球 • **verb (slices, slicing, sliced) 1** cut into slices 切成(薄)片 **2** cut with something sharp (用锋利工具)切，削 **3** (in sport) hit the ball so that it spins or curves away to the side (在体育运动中)打侧旋球;削球

slick /slɪk/ **adjective 1** impressively smooth and efficient 熟练的;灵巧的 **2** self-confident but insincere 圆滑的;油滑的 **3** (of a surface) smooth, glossy, or slippery (表面)油光发亮的 • **noun** a smooth patch of oil 浮油 • **verb** make hair smooth and glossy with water, oil, or cream 使(头发)变顺;使(头发)变光滑 ■ **slickly** adverb.

slide /slaɪd/ **verb** (**slides**, **sliding**, **slid**) **1** move along a smooth surface while remaining in contact with it 滑行;滑动 **2** move smoothly, quickly, or without being noticed 快捷而悄声地移动;潜行 **3** become gradually lower or worse 逐渐降低;逐渐恶化 • **noun 1** a structure with a smooth sloping surface for children to slide down (供儿童玩耍的)滑梯 **2** an act of sliding 滑行;滑动 **3** a piece of glass which you place an object on to look at it through a microscope (显微镜的)载玻璃片 **4** a small piece of photographic film which you view using a projector 幻灯片 □ **slide rule** a ruler with a sliding central strip, used for making calculations quickly (用于快速计算的)计算尺, 滑尺 **sliding scale** a scale of fees, wages, etc. that varies according to some other factor (根据某些情况的变化而对收费、工资等进行调整的)浮动计算(法)

slight /slaɪt/ **adjective 1** small in degree 轻微的;细微的 **2** not sturdy or strongly built 纤弱的;不结实的 **3** lacking depth; trivial 缺乏深度的;肤浅的;琐碎的 • **verb** insult someone by treating them without proper respect or attention 轻视;怠慢;冷落 • **noun** an insult 侮辱;侮慢 ■ **slightly** adverb.

slim /slɪm/ **adjective** (**slimmer**, **slimmest**) **1** gracefully thin 修长的;

苗条的 **2** small in width and long and narrow in shape 细长的;纤细的 **3** very small 微小的;微薄的;极少的: a slim chance 渺茫的机会 • **verb** (**slims, slimming, slimmed**) Brit. 【英】make or become thinner (使)变苗条;(使)瘦身 ■ **slimmer** noun.

slime /slaɪm/ **noun** an unpleasantly moist, soft, and slippery substance (令人厌恶的)黏质物, 黏液

slimy /ˈslaɪmi/ **adjective** (**slimier, slimiest**) **1** like or covered by slime 似黏液的; 粘有黏液的 **2** informal【非正式】polite and flattering in a way that is not sincere 讨好的; 谄媚的; 假惺惺的

sling /slɪŋ/ **noun 1** a loop of fabric used to support or raise a hanging weight 吊索;吊链;吊具 **2** a strap or loop used to hurl small missiles (用来发射小块发射物的)投石器, 弹弓 • **verb** (**slings, slinging, slung**) **1** hang or carry with a sling or strap 吊挂;悬挂 **2** informal【非正式】throw 抛;投;掷

slingback /ˈslɪŋbæk/ **noun** a shoe held in place by a strap around the ankle 后祥带女鞋

slingshot /ˈslɪŋʃɒt/ **noun** a hand-held catapult 弹弓

slink /slɪŋk/ **verb** (**slinks, slinking, slunk**) move quietly in a secretive way 偷偷摸摸地走;潜行

slinky /ˈslɪŋki/ **adjective** (**slinkier, slinkiest**) informal【非正式】(of a woman's garment) close-fitting and sexy (女性服装)紧身的, 性感的

slip¹ /slɪp/ **verb** (**slips, slipping, slipped**) **1** lose your balance and slide for a short distance 失足;滑跤;溜 **2** accidentally slide out of position or from someone's grasp 滑倒;滑落;滑脱 **3** fail to grip a surface 打滑 **4** get gradually worse 变坏;变差 **5** (usu. **slip up**) make a careless mistake 疏漏;出错 **6** move or place quietly, quickly, or secretly

溜;悄悄地走;偷偷地放置 **7 get free from** 挣脱;摆脱 • **noun 1** an act of slipping 滑;溜;滑倒;滑跤 **2** a minor or careless mistake 疏漏;差错 **3** a loose-fitting short petticoat (宽松的)衬裙 **4** Cricket 【板球】a fielding position close behind the batsman to one side (击球员后侧的)守场员防守位置 □ **slip knot** a knot that can be undone by a pull, or that can slide along the rope on which it is tied 活结;滑结 **slip-on** (of shoes or clothes) having no fastenings (鞋或衣服)无揿扣的,穿脱方便的 **slipped disc** a displaced disc in the spine that presses on nearby nerves and causes pain 椎间盘突出 **slip road** Brit. 【英】a road entering or leaving a motorway or dual carriageway (进出高速公路的)支路,岔道 ■ **slippage** noun.

slip² noun **1** a small piece of paper 纸片;纸条 **2** a cutting from a plant (植物的)接枝,插条

slipper /ˈslɪpə(r)/ **noun** a comfortable slip-on shoe worn indoors 拖鞋

slippery /ˈslɪpəri/ **adjective 1** difficult to hold firmly or stand on through being smooth, wet, or slimy 滑的;滑溜的 **2** (of a person) difficult to pin down (人)不可靠的,狡猾的 ■ **slipperiness** noun.

slippy /ˈslɪpi/ **adjective** (slippier, slippiest) informal 【非正式】slippery 滑的;滑溜的

slipshod /ˈslɪpʃɒd/ **adjective** careless, thoughtless, or disorganized 马虎的;轻率的;缺乏组织的;杂乱无章的

slipstream /ˈslɪpstriːm/ **noun 1** a current of air or water driven back by a propeller or jet engine (螺旋桨或喷气式发动机的)向后气流,滑流 **2** the partial vacuum created in the wake of a moving vehicle (行驶的车辆后部形成的部分真空状态)

slipway /ˈslɪpweɪ/ **noun** a slope leading into water, used for launching and landing boats and ships 船台;滑台;下水滑道

slit /slɪt/ **noun** a long, narrow cut or opening 狭长切口(或裂口、裂缝) • **verb** (slits, slitting, slit) make a slit in 切开;割开;撕开;撕裂

slither /ˈslɪðə(r)/ **verb** (slithers, slithering, slithered) **1** move smoothly over a surface with a twisting motion 蜿蜒滑行;蛇行 **2** slide unsteadily on a loose or slippery surface (摇晃着)滑动,滑行 • **noun** a slithering movement 滑行;滑动 ■ **slithery** adjective.

sliver /ˈslɪvə(r)/ **noun** a small, narrow, sharp piece cut or split off a larger piece 狭长片;裂片;小片

slob /slɒb/ Brit. informal 【英,非正式】**noun** a lazy, untidy person 懒惰而邋遢的人 • **verb** (slobs, slobbing, slobbed) behave in a lazy, untidy way 懒散;不修边幅

slobber /ˈslɒbə(r)/ **verb** (slobbers, slobbering, slobbered) have saliva dripping from the mouth 淌口水;流涎 • **noun** saliva dripping from the mouth 口水 ■ **slobbery** adjective.

sloe /sləʊ/ **noun** the small bluish-black fruit of the blackthorn 黑刺李果实

slog /slɒg/ **verb** (slogs, slogging, slogged) **1** work hard over a period of time (一段时间内)艰苦工作,努力苦干 **2** move with difficulty or effort 艰难地移动;费劲儿地行进 **3** hit forcefully 猛击;狠打 **4** (slog it out) fight or compete fiercely 激烈打斗(或竞争) • **noun** a period of difficult, tiring work or travelling 一阵苦干;一段跋涉

slogan /ˈsləʊgən/ **noun** a short, memorable phrase used in advertising or associated with a political group (宣传用的)广告语;(政治)口号,标语

sloop /sluːp/ **noun** a type of sailing

boat with one mast 单桅小帆船

slop /slɒp/ **verb (slops, slopping, slopped) 1** (of a liquid) spill over the edge of a container (液体)溅出, 溢出 **2** (**slop about** or **around**) Brit. informal 【英,非正式】spend time relaxing in casual or scruffy clothes (穿着随意或邋遢地)休息, 放松 • **noun** (**slops**) **1** waste liquid that has to be emptied by hand (需人工倾倒的)液体废物;污水 **2** unappetizing semi-liquid food (难吃的)半流质食物

slope /sləʊp/ **noun 1** a surface with one end at a higher level than another 斜面 **2** a part of the side of a hill or mountain 山丘;斜坡 • **verb (slopes, sloping, sloped) 1** slant up or down 倾斜 **2** (**slope off**) informal 【非正式】 leave without attracting attention 溜走

sloppy /ˈslɒpi/ **adjective (sloppier, sloppiest) 1** careless and disorganized 马虎的;粗心的 杂乱无章的 **2** containing too much liquid (物)含水分太多的, 稀薄的 **3** too sentimental 过分多愁善感的 ■ **sloppily** adverb **sloppiness** noun.

slosh /slɒʃ/ **verb 1** (of liquid in a container) move around with a splashing sound (容器中的液体)泼溅, 晃荡 **2** move through liquid with a splashing sound 溅着水行进 **3** pour liquid clumsily 笨拙地倒(液体)

sloshed /slɒʃt/ **adjective** informal 【非正式】drunk 喝醉的

slot /slɒt/ **noun 1** a long, narrow opening into which something may be inserted 狭长孔;狭缝;狭槽 **2** a place in an arrangement or scheme (安排或计划表中的)位置, 时间段 • **verb (slots, slotting, slotted) 1** place into a slot 把…放入狭长孔(或狭缝, 狭槽) **2** (**slot in** or **into**) fit easily into a new role or situation 顺利地适应(新角色或新情况) □ **slot machine** a fruit machine or (Brit.

【英】) vending machine 吃角子老虎机;(英国的)投币自动售货机

sloth /sləʊθ/ **noun 1** laziness 怠惰 懒散 **2** a slow-moving animal that hangs upside down 树懒(行动迟缓, 常常倒挂身体) ■ **slothful** adjective.

slouch /slaʊtʃ/ **verb** stand, move, or sit in a lazy, drooping way 没精打采地站(或走、坐) • **noun** a lazy, drooping posture 没精打采的姿势 □ **be no slouch** informal 【非正式】be fast or good at something 做…很快;擅长

slough[1] /slaʊ/ **noun 1** a swamp 沼泽; 泥潭;泥坑 **2** a situation without progress or activity 困境;绝境

slough[2] /slʌf/ **verb** (of an animal) cast off an old skin (动物)蜕皮, 脱皮

Slovakian /sləˈvækiən/ (also **Slovak**) **noun** a person from Slovakia 斯洛伐克人 • **adjective** relating to Slovakia 斯洛伐克的

Slovene /ˈsləʊviːn/ **noun 1** a person from Slovenia 斯洛文尼亚人 **2** the language of Slovenia 斯洛文尼亚语 ■ **Slovenian** noun & adjective.

slovenly /ˈslʌvnli/ **adjective** untidy and dirty 邋遢的;不修边幅的 **2** careless 马虎的;粗心的;轻率的 ■ **slovenliness** noun.

slow /sləʊ/ **adjective 1** moving or capable of moving only at a low speed 缓慢的;迟缓的 **2** taking a long time 费事的 **3** (of a clock or watch) showing a time earlier than the correct time (钟表)慢了的 **4** not quick to understand, think, or learn 反应慢的;迟钝的 • **verb** (often **slow down** or **up**) **1** reduce speed 减速;慢下来 **2** be less busy or active 闲散;不忙 □ **slow motion** the showing of film or video more slowly than it was made or recorded (电影或录像中的)慢动作, 慢镜头 **slow-worm** a small snake-like lizard 慢蚰蜥蜴 (一种似蛇的小蜥蜴) ■ **slowly** adverb **slowness** noun.

slowcoach /'sləʊkəʊtʃ/ **noun** Brit. informal【英，非正式】a person who acts or moves slowly 动作(或行动)迟缓的人

sludge /slʌdʒ/ **noun** thick, soft, wet mud or a similar mixture 软泥；淤泥；烂泥状混合物 ■ **sludgy** adjective.

slug[1] /slʌg/ **noun 1** a small creature like a snail without a shell 蛞蝓；鼻涕虫 **2** informal【非正式】a small amount of an alcoholic drink 少量酒 **3** informal【非正式】a bullet 子弹 • **verb** (**slugs**, **slugging**, **slugged**) informal【非正式】gulp a drink 大喝；痛饮

slug[2] informal【非正式】 **verb** (**slugs**, **slugging**, **slugged**) **1** hit with a hard blow 猛击；重击 **2** (**slug it out**) settle a dispute by fighting or competing fiercely 决一雌雄；比出高下

sluggard /'slʌgəd/ **noun** a lazy, inactive person 懒人；懒汉；懒鬼

sluggish /'slʌgɪʃ/ **adjective 1** slow-moving or inactive 迟缓的；行动迟缓的；怠惰的 **2** not energetic or alert 缺乏活力的；不活泼的；呆滞的 ■ **sluggishly** adverb.

sluice /sluːs/ **noun 1** (also **sluice gate**) a sliding device for controlling the flow of water 水闸；闸门 **2** a channel for carrying off surplus water (用来排放多余的水的)人工水道，泄水道 • **verb** (**sluices**, **sluicing**, **sluiced**) wash or rinse with water (用水)洗涤，冲洗

slum /slʌm/ **noun 1** a rundown area of a city or town inhabited by very poor people (城镇中的)贫民窟，贫民区 **2** a house or building unfit to be lived in (不适合居住的)破旧房子 • **verb** (**slums**, **slumming**, **slummed**) (**slum it**) informal【非正式】choose to spend time in uncomfortable conditions or at a low social level 将就(较差的条件)；屈就过贫民生活

slumber /'slʌmbə(r)/ **verb** (**slumbers**, **slumbering**, **slumbered**) sleep 睡；睡眠 • **noun** a sleep 睡眠

slump /slʌmp/ **verb 1** sit, lean, or fall heavily and limply (沉重而无力地)坐下，倚靠，倒下 **2** fall in price, value, number, etc. suddenly and by a large amount (在价格、价值、数量等方面)大幅下降 • **noun** an instance of slumping 消沉；衰退；暴跌

slung /slʌŋ/ past and past participle of SLING.

slunk /slʌŋk/ past and past participle of SLINK.

slur /slɜː(r)/ **verb** (**slurs**, **slurring**, **slurred**) **1** speak in a way that is difficult to understand 含糊不清地说 **2** perform a group of musical notes in a smooth, flowing way 连奏；连唱 • **noun 1** an insult or accusation intended to damage someone's reputation 诽谤；诋毁 **2** a curved line indicating that notes are to be slurred (标示需连唱或连奏音符的)连线

slurp /slɜːp/ **verb** eat or drink with a loud sucking sound 出声地吃(或喝) • **noun** a slurping sound (吃喝时的)吧嗒声，咕咚声

slurry /'slʌri/ **noun** (plural **slurries**) a semi-liquid mixture of water and manure, cement, or coal (由水、粪肥、水泥或煤末混合而成的)泥浆，灰浆

slush /slʌʃ/ **noun 1** partially melted snow or ice 半融化的雪(或冰)；雪泥；软冰 **2** informal【非正式】very sentimental talk or writing 极其动人的话(或文字) □ **slush fund** a reserve of money used for something illegal 用于非法目的的基金 ■ **slushy** adjective.

slut /slʌt/ **noun** disapproving【贬】a woman who has many sexual partners, or who is untidy and lazy 荡妇；邋遢女人 ■ **sluttish** adjective.

sly /slaɪ/ **adjective** (**slyer**, **slyest**) **1** cunning and deceitful 狡猾的；诡诈的；阴险的 **2** (of a remark, glance, or expression) suggesting secret knowledge (话语、目光或表情)诡秘的 ■ **slyly** adverb.

smack¹ /smæk/ **noun 1** a sharp blow with the palm of the hand 掌掴；用手扇；猛拍 **2** a loud, sharp sound 尖厉声 **3** a loud kiss 响吻 • **verb 1** give someone a smack 掴，扇(某人) **2** smash or drive into 猛击；撞进 **3** part your lips noisily 咂(嘴) • **adverb** informal【非正式】exactly or directly 恰好；正好；直接

smack² **verb** (**smack of**) **1** seem to contain or involve something wrong or unpleasant 带有(错误或令人不快之事)的意味 **2** smell or taste of 有…的气味(或味道)

smack³ **noun** Brit.【英】a sailing boat with one mast 单桅小帆船

smack⁴ **noun** informal【非正式】heroin 海洛因

smacker /'smækə(r)/ **noun** informal【非正式】**1** a loud kiss 响吻 **2** Brit.【英】one pound sterling 一英镑

small /smɔːl/ **adjective 1** of less than normal size 小的 **2** not great in amount, number, strength, or power (数量、数字、力量或权力)小的，少的 **3** young 年幼的；幼小的 □ **small arms** guns that can be carried in the hands 轻武器 **small beer** Brit.【英】something unimportant 小事；琐事 **small fry** young or unimportant people or things 小人物；不重要的东西 **the small hours** the early hours of the morning after midnight 凌晨时分 **the small of the back** the lower part of a person's back where the spine curves in (人的)腰背部 **small print** details printed so small that they are not easily noticed in an agreement or contract (协议或合同中不容易注意到的)附属细则 **small talk** polite conversation about unimportant things 聊天；闲谈 ■ **smallness** noun.

smallholding /'smɔːlhəʊldɪŋ/ **noun** Brit.【英】a piece of agricultural land that is smaller than a farm 小片耕地；小片农田 ■ **smallholder** noun.

smallpox /'smɔːlpɒks/ **noun** a serious disease which causes blisters that usually leave permanent scars 天花

smarmy /'smɑːmi/ **adjective** Brit. informal【英，非正式】friendly or flattering in an unpleasant and insincere way 奉承的，谄媚的

smart /smɑːt/ **adjective 1** clean, tidy, and stylish 整齐的；时髦的 **2** bright and fresh in appearance 外表光鲜的；亮丽的 **3** (of a place) fashionable and upmarket (场所)时尚的，高档的 **4** informal【非正式】quick-witted 机智的；机敏的 **5** chiefly N. Amer.【主北美】cheekily clever 聪明的 **6** quick 快速的 • **verb 1** give a sharp, stinging pain 刺痛；引起剧痛 **2** feel upset and annoyed 感到烦乱；感到痛苦 □ **smart card** a plastic card on which information is stored in electronic form (电子)智能卡 ■ **smartish** adjective **smartly** adverb **smartness** noun.

smarten /'smɑːtn/ **verb** (**smarten up**) make or become smarter (使)变得更漂亮；(使)变得更聪明

smash /smæʃ/ **verb 1** break violently into pieces 打碎；粉碎 **2** hit or collide forcefully 猛击(或碰)；猛撞 **3** (in sport) hit the ball hard (体育运动中)杀(球)，扣(球) **4** completely defeat or destroy 击溃；摧毁；挫败 • **noun 1** an act or sound of smashing 打碎；粉碎 **2** (also **smash hit**) informal【非正式】a very successful song, film, or show 十分走红的歌曲(或电影、节目)

smashing /'smæʃɪŋ/ **adjective** Brit. informal【英，非正式】excellent 极好的；出色的 ■ **smasher** noun.

smattering /'smætərɪŋ/ **noun 1** a small amount 少数；些许 **2** a slight knowledge of a language (对某一语言的)略知，浅知

smear /smɪə(r)/ **verb 1** coat or mark with a greasy or sticky substance (用油脂或黏性物质)涂抹，抹上 **2** blur or smudge 弄污；弄脏 **3** make false accusations about someone so as to damage their reputation 诽谤;诬蔑 • noun 1 a greasy or sticky mark 污迹;污斑 2 a false accusation 诽谤;诋毁 □ **smear test** Brit.【英】a test to detect signs of cervical cancer 巴氏试验(用于探查子宫颈癌)

smell /smel/ **noun** 1 the ability to sense different things by means of the organs in the nose 嗅觉 2 something sensed by the organs in the nose; an odour 气味 3 an act of smelling 闻;嗅 • **verb (smells, smelling, smelt** or **smelled) 1** sense by means of the organs in the nose 闻到;嗅到 2 sniff at something to find out its smell 嗅、闻(某物) 3 send out a smell 散发气味 4 have a strong or unpleasant smell 有(或散发)强烈(或难闻)的气味 5 sense or detect 察觉到;感觉到 □ **smell a rat** informal【非正式】suspect a trick 觉得可疑;感觉不妙 **smelling salts** a strong-smelling liquid formerly sniffed by people who felt faint 嗅盐 (一种有强烈气味的液体,旧时感觉眩晕的人用来嗅闻)

smelly /ˈsmeli/ **adjective (smellier, smelliest)** having a strong or unpleasant smell 有强烈气味的;发臭的

smelt[1] /smelt/ **verb** extract metal from its ore by heating and melting it 熔炼,提炼(金属)

smelt[2] past and past participle of SMELL.

smidgen or **smidgeon** /ˈsmɪdʒən/ **noun** informal【非正式】a tiny amount 少量;一点点

smile /smaɪl/ **verb (smiles, smiling, smiled)** form your features into a pleased, friendly, or amused expression, with the corners of the mouth turned up 笑;微笑 • **noun** an act of smiling 笑;微笑

smirk /smɜːk/ **verb** smile in a smug or silly way 得意地笑;痴笑;傻笑 • **noun**

a smug or silly smile 得意的笑;痴笑;傻笑

smite /smaɪt/ **verb (smites, smiting, smote; past participle smitten) 1** old use【旧】hit with a hard blow 猛击;重打 2 (**be smitten**) be strongly attracted to someone 被(某人)迷住 3 (**be smitten**) be severely affected by a disease (疾病)袭击,侵袭

smith /smɪθ/ **noun 1** a person who works in metal 锻工 2 a blacksmith 铁匠

smithereens /ˌsmɪðəˈriːnz/ **plural noun** informal【非正式】small pieces 碎片;小片

smithy /ˈsmɪði/ **noun (plural smithies)** a blacksmith's workshop 铁匠铺;打铁工场;锻工车间

smock /smɒk/ **noun 1** a loose dress or blouse with the upper part gathered into decorative stitched pleats (上部有褶饰的)宽腰身女服,宽松舒适的上衣 2 a loose overall worn to protect your clothes 罩衣;工作服

smog /smɒg/ **noun** fog or haze made worse by pollution in the atmosphere (大气污染物形成的)烟雾

smoke /sməʊk/ **noun 1** a visible vapour in the air produced by a burning substance 烟 2 an act of smoking tobacco 抽烟 3 informal【非正式】a cigarette or cigar 香烟;雪茄烟 4 (**the Smoke** or **the Big Smoke**) Brit.【英】a big city 大城市 • **verb (smokes, smoking, smoked) 1** give out smoke 冒烟 2 breathe smoke from a cigarette, pipe, etc. in and out again 抽烟;吸烟 3 preserve meat or fish by exposing it to smoke 熏制(肉或鱼) 4 (**smoke someone/thing out**) drive someone or something out of a place by using smoke 用烟熏出 5 (**smoked**) (of glass) darkened (玻璃)熏黑的, ■ **smokeless** adjective **smoker** noun.

smokescreen /ˈsməʊkskriːn/ **noun 1** something designed to disguise your real intentions or activities (用来掩盖真实意图或活动的)障眼法 **2** a cloud of smoke created to conceal military operations (用来掩蔽军事行动的)烟幕

smokestack /'sməʊkstæk/ **noun** a chimney or funnel which takes away smoke produced by a locomotive, ship, factory, etc. (火车机车、轮船、工厂等的)烟囱

smoky /'sməʊki/ **adjective** (**smokier, smokiest**) producing, filled with, or like smoke 冒烟的；多烟的；烟雾弥漫的；烟状的

smolder /'sməʊldə(r)/ US spelling of **SMOULDER**. smoulder 的美式拼法

smooch /smuːtʃ/ **verb** informal【非正式】 kiss and cuddle 搂抱亲吻；拥吻

smooth /smuːð/ **adjective 1** having an even and regular surface 平滑的，光滑的；平坦的 **2** (of a liquid) without lumps (液体)调匀的，无颗粒的 **3** (of movement) without jerks (动作)平稳的，不摇晃的；无颠簸的 **4** without difficulties 顺利的；无阻滞的 **5** charming in a very confident or flattering way 圆滑的；逢迎的；八面玲珑的 **6** (of a flavour) not harsh or bitter (味道)醇和的，不苦的 • **verb** (also **smoothe**) (**smooths** or **smoothes, smoothing, smoothed**) **1** make something smooth 使光滑；使平坦 **2** (**smooth something over**) deal successfully with a problem 顺利地解决(问题) □ **smooth-talking** informal【非正式】using very persuasive or flattering language 口若悬河的；花言巧语的；巧舌如簧的 ■ **smoothly adverb** **smoothness** noun.

smoothie /'smuːði/ **noun 1** a thick, smooth drink of fresh fruit with milk, yogurt, or ice cream (加入牛奶、酸奶或冰激凌制成的)鲜浓果汁 **2** informal【非正式】a man with a charming, confident manner 圆滑的人；八面玲珑的人

smorgasbord /'smɔːɡəsbɔːd/ **noun** a meal at which you choose from a range of open sandwiches and savoury items 斯堪的纳维亚式自助餐(包括各种单片三明治和开胃菜)；丰盛的自助餐

smote /sməʊt/ past of **SMITE**.

smother /'smʌðə(r)/ **verb** (**smothers, smothering, smothered**) **1** suffocate someone by covering their nose and mouth 使窒息；把…闷死 **2** (**smother someone/thing in** or **with**) cover someone or something thickly with 用…完全覆盖 **3** be oppressively protective or loving towards someone 溺爱

smoulder /'sməʊldə(r)/ (US spelling【美拼作】**smolder**) **verb** (**smoulders, smouldering, smouldered**) **1** burn slowly with smoke but no flame (有烟而无火苗地)闷燃，阴燃 **2** feel strong and barely hidden anger, hatred, lust, etc. 愤愤不平；流露出仇恨(或欲望等)

SMS abbreviation Short Message (or Messaging) Service, a system for sending and receiving text messages 短信(或短信传递)服务 • **noun** a message sent by SMS 短信；短信息

smudge /smʌdʒ/ **verb** (**smudges, smudging, smudged**) make or become blurred or smeared 使模糊；弄脏；变脏 • **noun** a smudged mark or image 污点；污斑；污迹 ■ **smudgy** adjective.

smug /smʌɡ/ **adjective** (**smugger, smuggest**) irritatingly pleased with yourself 自满的；沾沾自喜的；自鸣得意的 ■ **smugly adverb** **smugness** noun.

smuggle /'smʌɡl/ **verb** (**smuggles, smuggling, smuggled**) **1** move goods illegally into or out of a country 走私；非法私运(货物) **2** secretly convey 偷运；偷带；偷放 ■ **smuggler** noun.

smut /smʌt/ **noun 1** a small flake of

soot or dirt 煤烟；煤炱；污泥 **2** indecent talk, writing, or pictures 下流的言语(或文字、图片) ■ **smutty** adjective.

snack /snæk/ **noun** a small quantity of food eaten between meals or in place of a meal 小吃；快餐；便餐 • **verb** eat a snack 吃快餐；吃小吃

snaffle /'snæfl/ **noun** a bit on a horse's bridle 马嚼子；马衔铁 • **verb** (**snaffles, snaffling, snaffled**) Brit. informal【英, 非正式】quickly take for yourself 偷盗；攫取；盗用

snag /snæg/ **noun 1** an unexpected difficulty (意外的)困难, 障碍 **2** a sharp or jagged projection 尖利(或锯齿状)的凸出物；尖齿；尖刺 **3** a small tear 细小的裂口；细缝 • **verb** (**snags, snagging, snagged**) catch or tear on a snag (在尖利物上)勾住, 刺破

snail /sneɪl/ **noun** a small, slow-moving creature with a spiral shell into which it can withdraw its whole body 蜗牛

snake /sneɪk/ **noun** a reptile with no legs and a long slender body 蛇 • **verb** (**snakes, snaking, snaked**) move with the twisting motion of a snake 蛇行；蜿蜒行进 □ **snake in the grass** a person who pretends to be someone's friend but is secretly working against them 暗藏的敌人；(伪装成朋友的)阴险的人 ■ **snaky** adjective.

snap /snæp/ **verb** (**snaps, snapping, snapped**) **1** break with a sharp cracking sound 喀嚓折断 **2** open or close with a brisk movement or sharp sound 轻快地(或啪地)打开(或关闭) **3** (of an animal) make a sudden bite (动物)突然咬, 猛咬 **4** say something quickly and irritably 急促地说；厉声说 **5** suddenly lose self-control 突然失去自控力；突然崩溃；突然支持不住 **6** take a snapshot of 给…拍快照 • **noun 1** an act or sound of snapping 噼啪作响；噼啪声 **2** a snapshot 快照；抓拍 **3** Brit.【英】a

card game in which players compete to call 'snap' as soon as two cards of the same type are exposed "对儿"牌游戏(在牌戏中遇到两张相同扑克牌时, 游戏者抢喊"对儿") • **adjective** done on the spur of the moment 仓促的；匆忙的；突然的：a snap decision 仓促的决定 □ **snap something up** quickly buy something that is in short supply 迅速购买, 抢购(短缺物品) **snap out of** informal【非正式】get out of a bad mood by a sudden effort 迅速努力摆脱(坏心情)

snapdragon /'snæpdrægən/ **noun** a plant with brightly coloured flowers which have a mouth-like opening 金鱼草

snapper /'snæpə(r)/ **noun** a sea fish noted for snapping its jaws 笛鲷(一种海鱼)

snappy /'snæpi/ **adjective** (**snappier, snappiest**) informal【非正式】**1** short and clever or amusing 短小精悍的；简明巧妙的；有趣的：snappy slogans 精炼的口号 **2** neat and stylish 整洁的；时髦的 **3** irritable; speaking sharply 易躁的；易怒的；厉声说话的 □ **make it snappy** do it quickly 赶快；快点儿

snapshot /'snæpʃɒt/ **noun** an informal photograph, taken quickly 快照

snare /sneə(r)/ **noun 1** a trap for catching animals, consisting of a loop of wire that pulls tight (捕兽的)陷阱, 罗网, 套索 **2** a thing likely to lure someone into trouble 陷阱；圈套；骗局 **3** (also **snare drum**) a drum with a length of wire stretched across the head to produce a rattling sound 有响弦的小鼓 • **verb** (**snares, snaring, snared**) catch in a snare or trap (用罗网或陷阱)捕捉

snarl /snɑːl/ **verb 1** growl with bared teeth 龇牙吼叫 **2** say something aggressively 厉声喊叫；咆哮 **3** (**snarl something up**) make something

tangled 使混乱;使错综复杂;使纠结
• **noun** an act of snarling 狂吠;嗥叫
□ **snarl-up** Brit. informal【英,非正式】
a traffic jam 交通阻塞

snatch /snætʃ/ **verb 1** seize quickly in a rude or eager way 一把抓起;攫取;抢 **2** informal【非正式】steal or kidnap 偷窃;抢走;绑架 **3** quickly take the chance to have 抓住机会获取 • **noun 1** an act of snatching 抢夺;抓住;攫取 **2** a fragment of music or talk 音乐(或谈话)片段

snazzy /'snæzi/ **adjective** (**snazzier**, **snazziest**) informal【非正式】smart and stylish 漂亮的;时髦的

sneak /sniːk/ **verb** (**sneaks**, **sneaking**, **sneaked** or N. Amer. informal【北美,非正式】**snuck**) **1** move or take in a secretive way 潜行;溜;偷 **2** Brit. informal【英,非正式】tell someone in authority of a person's wrong-doings 打小报告;告密 **3** (**sneaking**) (of a feeling) remaining persistently in the mind (感情)萦绕在心的,暗暗扰人不止的 • **noun** Brit. informal【英,非正式】a telltale 告密者 • **adjective** secret or unofficial 偷偷摸摸的;暗中进行的;秘密的: *a sneak preview* 秘密的预审

sneaker /'sniːkə(r)/ **noun** chiefly N. Amer.【主北美】a soft shoe worn for sports or casual occasions 帆布软底运动鞋;旅游鞋

sneaky /'sniːki/ **adjective** (**sneakier**, **sneakiest**) secretive in a sly or dishonest way 偷偷摸摸的;鬼鬼祟祟的 ■ **sneakily** adverb.

sneer /snɪə(r)/ **noun** a scornful or mocking smile or remark 嘲笑;嗤笑;讥笑 • **verb** (**sneers**, **sneering**, **sneered**) smile or speak in a scornful or mocking way 嘲笑;讥笑;嗤笑;嘲笑(或讥笑、嗤笑)着说

sneeze /sniːz/ **verb** (**sneezes**, **sneezing**, **sneezed**) suddenly expel air from the nose and mouth due to irritation of the nostrils 打喷嚏 • **noun**

an act of sneezing 喷嚏 □ **not to be sneezed at** informal【非正式】worth having or considering 不可轻视;值得考虑

snick /snɪk/ **verb** cut a small notch in 刻凹痕于 • **noun** a small notch or cut 刻痕;切口

snicker /'snɪkə(r)/ **verb** (**snickers**, **snickering**, **snickered**) **1** snigger 窃笑;暗笑;傻笑 **2** (of a horse) make a gentle high-pitched neigh (马)嘶鸣 • **noun** a sound of snickering 窃笑;暗笑;(马的)嘶鸣

snide /snaɪd/ **adjective** disrespectful or mocking in an indirect way 讽刺的;挖苦的

sniff /snɪf/ **verb 1** draw in air audibly through the nose (吸着气)嗅,闻 **2** (**sniff around** or **round**) informal【非正式】investigate secretly 暗中调查 **3** (**sniff something out**) informal【非正式】discover something by investigation (通过调查)发现,觉察出 • **noun** an act of sniffing 嗅;闻 □ **not to be sniffed at** informal【非正式】worth having or considering 不可轻视;值得考虑 **sniffer dog** a dog trained to find drugs or explosives by smell (经过训练能嗅出毒品或炸药的)嗅犬 ■ **sniffer** noun **sniffy** adjective.

sniffle /'snɪfl/ **verb** (**sniffles**, **sniffling**, **sniffled**) sniff slightly or repeatedly (轻微或不停地)抽鼻子,吸鼻子 • **noun 1** an act of sniffling 抽鼻子;吸鼻子 **2** a slight cold (轻微的)伤风,感冒 ■ **sniffly** adjective.

snifter /'snɪftə(r)/ **noun** Brit. informal【英,非正式】a small quantity of an alcoholic drink 一小杯酒;一口酒

snigger /'snɪgə(r)/ **verb** (**sniggers**, **sniggering**, **sniggered**) give a half-suppressed laugh 窃笑;暗笑 • **noun** a half-suppressed laugh 哧哧的笑;窃笑

snip /snɪp/ **verb** (**snips**, **snipping**, **snipped**) cut with small, quick strokes (快速)剪,剪断 • noun 1 an act of snipping 剪,剪断 2 Brit. informal【英,非正式】a bargain 廉价物;便宜货

snipe /snaɪp/ verb (snipes, sniping, sniped) 1 shoot at someone from a hiding place at long range 狙击;打冷枪 2 criticize someone in an unpleasant or petty way 诽谤;中伤 • noun (plural snipe or snipes) a wading bird with brown feathers and a long straight bill 鹬,沙锥鸟(一种涉禽,羽毛棕色,喙长而直) ■ sniper noun.

snippet /ˈsnɪpɪt/ noun a small piece or brief extract 小片;碎片;小段摘录

snitch /snɪtʃ/ informal【非正式】verb 1 steal 偷窃 2 inform on someone 告发 • noun an informer 告发者;告密者

snivel /ˈsnɪvl/ verb (snivels, snivelling, snivelled; US spelling【美拼式】snivels, sniveling, sniveled) cry or complain in a whining way 啜泣;呜咽

snob /snɒb/ noun 1 a person who has great respect for people with social status or wealth and looks down on lower-class people 势利小人 2 a person who believes that they have superior taste in a particular area 自命不凡者;假行家: a wine snob 自以为懂葡萄酒的人 ■ snobbery noun snobbish adjective snobby adjective.

snog /snɒɡ/ Brit. informal【英,非正式】verb (snogs, snogging, snogged) kiss 亲吻 • noun an act or period of kissing 亲吻;一段时间的亲吻

snood /snuːd/ noun a hairnet worn at the back of a woman's head (女性的)发网,发套

snook /snuːk/ noun (cock a snook at) Brit. informal【英,非正式】openly show contempt or disrespect for 瞧不起;蔑视

snooker /ˈsnuːkə(r)/ noun 1 a game played with cues on a billiard table 斯诺克台球 2 a position in a game of snooker or pool in which a player cannot make a direct shot at any permitted ball (斯诺克台球或落袋台球中)无法打直线球的位置 • verb (snookers, snookering, snookered) 1 (in snooker or pool) put your opponent in a snooker (斯诺克或落袋台球中)设障碍球,给(对手)做成斯诺克 2 (be snookered) Brit. informal【英,非正式】be placed in an impossible position 陷入绝境

snoop /snuːp/ informal【非正式】verb look around or investigate secretly in order to find out something 窥探;秘密调查 • noun an act of snooping 窥探;秘密调查;暗中调查 ■ snooper noun.

snooty /ˈsnuːti/ adjective (snootier, snootiest) informal【非正式】behaving as if you are better or more important than other people 傲慢的;目中无人的 ■ snootily adverb.

snooze /snuːz/ informal【非正式】noun a short, light sleep 小睡;打盹 • verb (snoozes, snoozing, snoozed) have a snooze 小睡;打盹

snore /snɔː(r)/ noun a snorting sound in a person's breathing while they are asleep 打鼾(声);打呼噜(声) • verb (snores, snoring, snored) make a snorting sound while asleep 打鼾;打呼噜

snorkel /ˈsnɔːkl/ noun a tube for a swimmer to breathe through while underwater (潜水者用的)水下呼吸管 ■ snorkelling (US spelling【美拼式】snorkeling) noun.

snort /snɔːt/ verb 1 make a loud explosive sound by forcing breath out through the nose 哼;喷鼻息 2 informal【非正式】inhale cocaine 吸入可卡因 • noun a snorting sound 哼;喷鼻息

snot /snɒt/ noun informal【非正式】mucus in the nose 鼻涕

snotty /ˈsnɒti/ adjective informal【非正

式】**1** full of, or covered with, mucus from the nose 流鼻涕的；满是鼻涕的 **2** superior or arrogant 傲慢的；目中无人的

snout /snaʊt/ **noun 1** the projecting nose and mouth of an animal (动物的)口鼻部，吻 **2** the projecting front or end of something such as a pistol (手枪等物品的)突出部分，凸端

snow /snəʊ/ **noun 1** frozen water vapour in the atmosphere that falls in light white flakes 雪 **2** (**snows**) falls of snow 降雪(量) • **verb 1** (**it snows, it is snowing, it snowed**) snow falls下雪 **2** (**be snowed in** or **up**) be unable to leave a place because of heavy snow 被雪困住 **3** (**be snowed under**) be overwhelmed with a large quantity of something, especially work (尤指因工作太多)应接不暇，忙得不可开交

snowball /snəʊbɔːl/ **noun** a ball of packed snow 雪球 • **verb** increase rapidly in size, strength, or importance (规模、力量或重要性)滚雪球般迅速增大

snowboard /ˈsnəʊbɔːd/ **noun** a board that resembles a short, broad ski, used for sliding downhill on snow 滑雪板 ■ **snowboarder** noun **snowboarding** noun.

snowbound /ˈsnəʊbaʊnd/ **adjective 1** unable to travel or go out because of snow 被雪困住的；因大雪而受阻的 **2** (of a place) cut off by snow (地方)被雪阻断的

snowdrift /ˈsnəʊdrɪft/ **noun** a bank of deep snow heaped up by the wind (风吹成的)雪堆

snowdrop /ˈsnəʊdrɒp/ **noun** a plant with drooping white flowers that appear during late winter 雪花莲(一种植物，在晚冬时节开白色悬垂花)

snowfall /ˈsnəʊfɔːl/ **noun 1** a fall of snow 下雪；降雪 **2** the quantity of snow falling within a certain area in a given time 降雪量

snowflake /ˈsnəʊfleɪk/ **noun** each of the many ice crystals that fall as snow 雪花；雪片

snowline /ˈsnəʊlaɪn/ **noun** the altitude above which some snow remains on the ground throughout the year 雪线(积雪终年不化的海拔高度)

snowman /ˈsnəʊmæn/ **noun** (plural **snowmen**) a model of a human figure made with compressed snow 雪人

snowplough /ˈsnəʊplaʊ/ (US spelling 【美拼作】**snowplow**) **noun** a device or vehicle for clearing roads of snow 雪犁；扫雪机

snowshoe /ˈsnəʊʃuː/ **noun** a flat device attached to the sole of a boot and used for walking on snow (用于雪地行走的)雪鞋

snowy /ˈsnəʊi/ **adjective** (**snowier, snowiest**) **1** having a lot of snow 下雪多的；积雪覆盖的 **2** pure white 纯白的；雪白的

snub /snʌb/ **verb** (**snubs, snubbing, snubbed**) **1** insult someone by ignoring them when you meet 冷落；怠慢 **2** refuse to attend or accept something 拒不出席；拒绝接受；抵制 • **noun** an act of snubbing 冷落；怠慢；抵制 □ **snub nose** a nose that is short and turned up at the end 短而翘的鼻子

snuck /snʌk/ N. Amer. informal【北美，非正式】past and past participle of SNEAK.

snuff¹ /snʌf/ **verb 1** put out a candle 掐灭，熄灭(蜡烛) **2** (**snuff something out**) abruptly put an end to something 扼杀；消灭 **3** (**snuff it**) Brit. informal【英，非正式】die 断气；死去

snuff² **noun** powdered tobacco that is sniffed up the nostril 鼻烟 • **verb** sniff at 嗅，闻

snuffle /ˈsnʌfl/ **verb** (**snuffles, snuffling, snuffled**) **1** breathe noisily through a partially blocked nose (鼻塞时)鼻子呼哧出声;抽鼻子 **2** (of an animal) make repeated sniffing sounds (动物)不断地哧哧嗅 • **noun** a snuffling sound 抽鼻子声

snug /snʌɡ/ **adjective** (**snugger**, **snuggest**) **1** warm and cosy 温暖舒适的 **2** close-fitting 紧身的 • **noun** Brit. 【英】a small, cosy bar in a pub or hotel (酒馆或宾馆中的)包间,雅座 ■ **snugly** adverb.

snuggle /ˈsnʌɡl/ **verb** (**snuggles**, **snuggling**, **snuggled**) settle into a warm, comfortable position 蜷伏;依偎;紧贴

so /səʊ/ **adverb** **1** to such a great extent (表示程度)这么 **2** extremely; very much 极;很 **3** to the same extent; as 那么;那样;如此 **4** that is the case 这样 **5** similarly 相似地;类似地 **6** thus 因此;所以 • **conjunction** **1** therefore 因此;所以 **2** (**so that**) with the result or aim that 以至;为了 **3** and then 接着;然后 **4** in the same way 同样地 □ **or so** approximately 大约 **so-and-so** (plural **so-and-sos**) informal【非正式】**1** a person whose name you do not know 某某人 **2** a person that you do not like 恼人的家伙;讨厌鬼 **so-called** wrongly or inappropriately called a particular thing 称呼错误(或不适当)的;所谓的 **so long!** informal【非正式】goodbye 再见 **so-so** neither very good nor very bad 不好不坏的;还过得去的;一般的

soak /səʊk/ **verb** **1** make something thoroughly wet by leaving it in liquid 浸泡;湿透;浸湿 **2** (of a liquid) spread completely throughout (液体)渗透,渗入 **3** (**soak something up**) absorb a liquid 吸收,吸掉(液体) **4** (**soak something up**) expose yourself to something enjoyable 吸收,沉浸于(令人愉悦的事物) • **noun** **1** a period of soaking (一段时间的)浸,泡 **2** informal【非正式】a heavy drinker 酒鬼;醉汉 ■ **soaking** adjective.

soap /səʊp/ **noun** **1** a substance used with water for washing and cleaning 肥皂 **2** informal【非正式】a soap opera 肥皂剧 • **verb** wash with soap 用肥皂洗 □ **soap opera** a television or radio serial that deals with the daily lives of a group of characters 肥皂剧 ■ **soapy** adjective.

soapbox /ˈsəʊpbɒks/ **noun** a box that someone stands on to speak in public 临时演讲台

soapstone /ˈsəʊpstəʊn/ **noun** a soft rock used for making ornaments 皂石(质软,可作装饰材料)

soar /sɔː(r)/ **verb** **1** fly or rise high into the air 高飞;翱翔 **2** increase rapidly 骤升;飞涨;猛增

sob /sɒb/ **verb** (**sobs**, **sobbing**, **sobbed**) **1** cry with loud gasps 抽噎;啜泣 **2** say while sobbing 抽噎着说;哭诉 • **noun** a sound of sobbing 抽噎(声);啜泣(声)

sober /ˈsəʊbə(r)/ **adjective** (**soberer**, **soberest**) **1** not drunk 未醉的 **2** serious 持重的;冷静的 **3** (of a colour) not bright or likely to attract attention (色彩)素净的,淡素的 • **verb** (**sobers**, **sobering**, **sobered**) **1** (**sober up**) make or become sober after being drunk (使)醒酒,(使)清醒 **2** make or become serious (使)变得持重,(使)变得冷静 ■ **soberly** adverb.

sobriety /səˈbraɪəti/ **noun** the state of being sober 未醉;持重;冷静

sobriquet /ˈsəʊbrɪkeɪ/ or **soubriquet** /ˈsuːbrɪkeɪ/ **noun** a person's nickname 外号;绰号

soccer /ˈsɒkə(r)/ **noun** a form of football played with a round ball which may not be handled during play except by the goalkeepers 足球

sociable /ˈsəʊʃəbl/ **adjective** **1** liking to talk to and do things with other people 爱交际的;合群的 **2** friendly and welcoming 友好的 ■ **sociability** noun **sociably** adverb.

social /ˈsəʊʃl/ **adjective** **1** having to

do with society and its organization 社会的 **2** needing the company of other people (人)过社会生活的 **3** (of an activity) in which people meet each other for pleasure (活动)社交的,交际的 **4** (of animals) breeding or living in organized communities (动物)群居的 • **noun** an informal social gathering 联谊会;联欢会 □ **social science 1** the study of human society and social relationships 社会科学 **2** a subject within this field, such as economics 社会科学学科 **social security** (in the UK) money provided by the state for poor or unemployed people (英国的)社会保障金(国家为穷人或失业者提供的资金) **social services** services provided by the state such as education and medical care 社会福利事业(国家为全体国民提供的教育、医疗等服务) **social worker** a person whose job is to help improve the conditions of the poor, the old, etc. 社会福利工作者(帮助改善穷人、老人等生活境况的人) ■ **socially** adverb.

socialism /ˈsəʊʃəlɪzm/ **noun** the theory that a country's land, transport, industries, etc. should be owned or controlled by the community as a whole 社会主义 ■ **socialist** noun & adjective.

socialite /ˈsəʊʃəlaɪt/ **noun** a person who mixes in fashionable society 社交名流

socialize or **socialise** /ˈsəʊʃəlaɪz/ **verb** (**socializes**, **socializing**, **socialized**) **1** mix socially with other people (和他人)交际,交往 **2** make someone behave in a socially acceptable way 使适应社会

society /səˈsaɪəti/ **noun** (plural **societies**) **1** people living together in an ordered community 社会(生活在一个有序社区里的人) **2** a community of people 社会;群体 **3** (also **high society**) people who are fash-ionable, wealthy, and influential 上流社会;社会名流;名人圈子 **4** an organization formed for a particular purpose 社团;学会;协会 **5** the situation of being in the company of other people 交往;相伴 ■ **societal** adjective.

sociology /ˌsəʊsiˈɒlədʒi/ **noun** the study of human society 社会学 ■ **sociological** adjective **sociologist** noun.

sock /sɒk/ **noun 1** a knitted garment for the foot and lower part of the leg 短袜 **2** informal 【非正式】a hard blow 猛击;重击 • **verb** informal 【非正式】hit forcefully 狠打;猛击 □ **pull your socks up** informal 【非正式】make an effort to improve 努力改进(或提高)

socket /ˈsɒkɪt/ **noun 1** a hollow in which something fits or revolves 窝;孔;洞;槽 **2** an electrical device which a plug or light bulb fits into (电源)插座,插口

sod /sɒd/ **noun 1** grass-covered ground 草地 **2** a piece of turf 草皮

soda /ˈsəʊdə/ **noun 1** (also **soda water**) carbonated water 苏打水 **2** N. Amer. 【北美】a sweet fizzy drink 甜苏打饮料 **3** a compound of sodium 苏打;含钠化合物;无水碳酸钠

sodden /ˈsɒdn/ **adjective 1** soaked through 湿透的;湿漉漉的 **2** having drunk too much alcohol 饮酒过量的: *whisky-sodden* 喝威士忌过量的

sodium /ˈsəʊdiəm/ **noun** a soft silver-white metallic element (金属元素)钠 □ **sodium bicarbonate** a white powder used in fizzy drinks and as a raising agent in baking 碳酸氢钠;小苏打 **sodium chloride** the chemical name for salt 氯化钠;食盐 **sodium hydroxide** a strongly alkaline white compound; caustic soda 氢氧化钠;烧碱

sodomite /ˈsɒdəmaɪt/ **noun** a person who engages in sodomy 鸡奸者

sodomy /ˈsɒdəmi/ **noun** anal

intercourse 肛交；鸡奸

sofa /'səʊfə/ *noun* a long padded seat with a back and arms 长沙发

soft /sɒft/ *adjective* **1** easy to mould, cut, compress, or fold 软的，柔软的 **2** not rough in texture (质地)细腻的，柔滑的 **3** quiet and gentle 温柔的；温和的；和蔼的 **4** (of light or colour) not harsh (光线或色彩)柔和的，悦目的，**5** not strict enough 不(够)严厉的；态度偏软的 **6** *informal* 【非正式】 not needing much effort 轻松的；安逸的 **7** *informal* 【非正式】 foolish 愚蠢的；头脑简单的 **8** (soft on) *informal* 【非正式】 having romantic feelings for 喜欢…的；钟情于…的 **9** (of a drink) not alcoholic (饮料)不含酒精的 **10** (of a drug) not likely to cause addiction (药物)不易成瘾的 **11** (of water) free from mineral salts (水)软性的，无矿盐的 □ **have a soft spot for** be fond of 喜欢；喜爱 **soft focus** deliberate slight blurring in a photograph or film 软聚焦(有意使照片或胶片有点模糊) **soft-hearted** kind and sympathetic 善良的；富同情心的；心肠软的 **softly-softly** *Brit.* 【英】 cautious and patient 小心谨慎的 **soft-pedal** play down the unpleasant aspects of 低调处理；轻描淡写 **soft sell** the selling of something in a gently persuasive way 劝诱推销；软推销 **soft-soap** *informal* 【非正式】 use flattery to persuade someone 奉承；劝诱；说好听的 **soft top** a car with a roof that can be folded back 软顶篷汽车 **soft touch** *informal* 【非正式】 a person who is easily persuaded 耳根子软的人 ■ **softly** *adverb* **softness** *noun*.

softball /'sɒftbɔːl/ *noun* a form of baseball played with a larger, softer ball 垒球(运动)

soften /'sɒfn/ *verb* **1** make or become soft or softer (使)变软；(使)软化；(使)缓和 **2** (soften someone up) make someone more likely to do or agree to something 使易于做(或同意)；诱导；打动

software /'sɒftweə(r)/ *noun* programs and other operating information used by a computer (计算机)软件

softwood /'sɒftwʊd/ *noun* the wood from a conifer as opposed to that from a broadleaved tree 软质木，软木(指针叶材，非阔叶树材)

soggy /'sɒgi/ *adjective* (**soggier, soggiest**) very wet and soft 湿软的

soil /sɔɪl/ *noun* **1** the upper layer of earth, in which plants grow 土壤 **2** the territory of a particular nation 国土；领土 ● *verb* **1** make dirty 弄脏；弄污 **2** bring discredit to 玷污；败坏

soirée /'swɑːreɪ/ *noun* an evening social gathering 社交晚会

sojourn /'sɒdʒən/ *literary* 【文】 *noun* a temporary stay 旅居；逗留；暂住 ● *verb* stay temporarily 旅居；逗留；暂住

solace /'sɒləs/ *noun* comfort in a difficult time 安慰；慰藉 ● *verb* (**solaces, solacing, solaced**) give comfort to 安慰；抚慰

solar /'səʊlə(r)/ *adjective* having to do with the sun or its rays 太阳的；日光的 □ **solar eclipse** an eclipse in which the sun is hidden by the moon 日食 **solar plexus** a network of nerves at the pit of the stomach 腹腔神经丛 **solar system** the sun together with the planets, asteroids, comets, etc. in orbit around it 太阳系

solarium /sə'leəriəm/ *noun* a room equipped with sunlamps or sunbeds (装有太阳灯或日光浴浴床的)日光浴室，日光浴室

sold /səʊld/ past and past participle of SELL.

solder /'səʊldə(r)/ *noun* a soft alloy used for joining metals 焊料；焊锡 ● *verb* (**solders, soldering, soldered**) join with solder 焊合；焊接 □ **soldering iron** an electrical tool for melting and applying solder 烙铁

soldier /ˈsəuldʒə(r)/ **noun 1** a person who serves in an army 军人 **2** a private in an army 士兵；列兵 **3** Brit. informal【英,非正式】a strip of bread or toast for dipping into a boiled egg (蘸煮鸡蛋吃的)一片(烤)面包 • **verb** (**soldiers, soldiering, soldiered**) **1** serve as a soldier 当兵；从军 **2** (**soldier on**) informal【非正式】keep trying or working 坚持；硬挺着 □ **soldier of fortune** a mercenary 雇佣兵 ■ **soldierly** adjective.

soldiery /ˈsəuldʒəri/ **noun** soldiers as a group 军队；队伍

sole[1] /səul/ **noun 1** the underside of the foot 脚底；脚掌 **2** the underside of a piece of footwear 鞋底；袜底 • **verb** (**soles, soling, soled**) put a new sole on a shoe 给(鞋)换底

sole[2] **noun** (plural **sole**) a kind of edible flatfish 鳎(一种可食用比目鱼)

sole[3] **adjective 1** one and only 唯一的；仅有的 **2** belonging or restricted to one person or group 专有的；独占的 ■ **solely** adverb.

solecism /ˈsɒlɪsɪzəm/ **noun 1** a grammatical mistake 语法错误；语病 **2** an example of bad manners or incorrect behaviour 失礼；粗俗的举止

solemn /ˈsɒləm/ **adjective 1** formal and dignified 正式的；庄严的；郑重的；严正的 **2** serious 冷峻的；严肃的 **3** deeply sincere 认真的；一本正经的 ■ **solemnly** adverb.

solemnity /səˈlemnəti/ **noun** (plural **solemnities**) **1** the quality of being solemn 庄严；严肃；庄重 **2** (**solemnities**) solemn rites or ceremonies 庄重的仪式；礼仪

solemnize or **solemnise** /ˈsɒləmnaɪz/ **verb** (**solemnizes, solemnizing, solemnized**) **1** perform a ceremony 举行仪式 **2** mark an occasion with a ceremony 举行仪式庆祝

solenoid /ˈsəʊlənɔɪd/ **noun** a coil of wire which becomes magnetic when an electric current is passed through it 螺线管

solicit /səˈlɪsɪt/ **verb** (**solicits, soliciting, solicited**) **1** try to obtain something from someone 乞求；讨要；请求；恳求 **2** (of a prostitute) approach someone and offer sex for money (妓女)拉(客),招徕(嫖客) ■ **solicitation** noun.

solicitor /səˈlɪsɪtə(r)/ **noun** Brit. 【英】a lawyer qualified to advise on property, wills, etc., instruct barristers, and represent clients in lower courts 诉讼律师,事务律师(提供财产、遗嘱等咨询,为高级法院出庭律师准备案件相关信息,代表当事人在初级法院出庭)

solicitous /səˈlɪsɪtəs/ **adjective** showing interest or concern about a person's well-being (对某人的健康)关心的,关切的 ■ **solicitously** adverb.

solicitude /səˈlɪsɪtjuːd/ **noun** care or concern 关心；关切；牵挂

solid /ˈsɒlɪd/ **adjective** (**solider, solidest**) **1** firm and stable in shape 固态的；固体的 **2** strongly built or made 结实的；坚固的；牢固的 **3** not hollow or having spaces or gaps 实心的 **4** consisting of the same substance throughout 纯质的；纯…的 **5** (of time) uninterrupted (时间)不间断的,连续的 **6** three-dimensional 三维的；立体的 • **noun 1** a solid substance or object 固体 **2** (**solids**) food that is not liquid 固体食物 □ **solid-state** (of an electronic device) using solid semiconductors, e.g. transistors, as opposed to valves (电子装置)固态的(有别于电子管) ■ **solidity** noun **solidly** adverb.

solidarity /ˌsɒlɪˈdærəti/ **noun** agreement and support resulting from shared interests, feelings, or opinions 团结；齐心协力；同心同德

solidify /səˈlɪdɪfaɪ/ **verb** (**solidifies,**

solidifying, solidified) make or become hard or solid (使)变硬;(使)凝固;(使)变得结实 ■ **solidification** noun.

soliloquy /sə'lɪləkwi/ **noun** (plural **soliloquies**) a speech in which a character speaks their thoughts aloud when alone on stage (舞台上剧中角色的)独白

solipsism /'sɒlɪpsɪzəm/ **noun** the view that the self is all that can be known to exist 唯我论 ■ **solipsist** noun **solipsistic** adjective.

solitaire /ˌsɒlɪ'teə(r)/ **noun 1** Brit. 【英】a game for one player played by removing pegs from a board by jumping others over them 单人跳棋 **2** N. Amer. 【北美】the card game patience 单人纸牌戏 **3** a single gem in a piece of jewellery 独粒宝石

solitary /'sɒlətri/ **adjective 1** done or existing alone 单独的;独自的 **2** (of a place) secluded or isolated (地方)偏僻的,孤零零的 **3** single 单个的;唯一的 □ **solitary confinement** the isolating of a prisoner in a separate cell as a punishment 单独监禁;单独禁闭

solitude /'sɒlɪtjuːd/ **noun** the state of being alone 独居;独处

solo /'səʊləʊ/ **noun** (plural **solos**) **1** a piece of music or dance for one performer 独奏曲;独舞 **2** a flight undertaken by a single pilot 单independ飞行 • **adjective & adverb** for or done by one person 单人(的);单独(的) • **verb** (**soloes, soloing, soloed**) perform a solo 独奏;单独表演;独舞 ■ **soloist** noun.

solstice /'sɒlstɪs/ **noun** each of the two times in the year when the sun reaches its highest or lowest point in the sky at noon, marked by the longest and shortest days 冬至(或夏至);至(点)

soluble /'sɒljəbl/ **adjective 1** (of a substance) able to be dissolved (物质)可溶的 **2** (of a problem) able to be solved (问题)能解决的,能解答的,能解答的 ■ **solubility** noun.

solution /sə'luːʃn/ **noun 1** a way of solving a problem (问题的)解决办法 **2** the correct answer to a puzzle 谜底;答案 **3** a mixture formed when a substance is dissolved in a liquid 溶液 **4** the process of dissolving 溶解;消散

solve /sɒlv/ **verb** (**solves, solving, solved**) find an answer to, or way of dealing with, a problem or mystery 解答(问题);解释,解决(谜团)

solvency /'sɒlvənsi/ **noun** the state of having more money than you owe (债务的)清偿能力

solvent /'sɒlvənt/ **adjective 1** having more money than you owe 有偿付能力的 **2** able to dissolve other substances 有溶解力的;可溶的 • **noun** the liquid in which another substance is dissolved to form a solution 溶剂

Somali /sə'mɑːli/ **noun** (plural **Somali** or **Somalis**) **1** a person from Somalia 索马里人 **2** the language of the Somali 索马里语 • **adjective** relating to Somalia 索马里的

sombre /'sɒmbə(r)/ (US spelling 【美拼作】**somber**) **adjective 1** dark or dull 昏暗的;阴沉的 **2** very solemn or serious 严峻的;严肃的 ■ **sombrely** adverb.

sombrero /sɒm'breərəʊ/ **noun** (plural **sombreros**) a broad-brimmed felt or straw hat 阔边毡帽(或草帽)

some determiner /sʌm, səm/ **1** an unspecified amount or number of 若干;一些 **2** unknown or unspecified 某些;有的 **3** approximately 大约;大概 **4** a considerable amount or number of 相当多;大量 **5** used to express admiration (表示赞美)极好的 • **pronoun** /sʌm/ a certain amount or number of people or things 某些人(或事物)

somebody /'sʌmbədi/ **pronoun** someone or anyone 有人

some day or **someday** /'sʌmdeɪ/ **adverb** at some time in the future 将来;总有一天;有朝一日

somehow /'sʌmhaʊ/ **adverb 1** by one means or another 用某种方式(或方法) **2** for an unknown or unspecified reason 由于某种原因;不知为何

someone /'sʌmwʌn/ **pronoun 1** an unknown or unspecified person 某人;有人 **2** an important or famous person 大人物;名人

someplace /'sʌmpleɪs/ **adverb & pronoun** N. Amer. informal【北美,非正式】somewhere (在)某处;(到)某处

somersault /'sʌməsɔːlt/ **noun** a movement in which a person turns head over heels and finishes on their feet 滚翻;筋斗 • **verb** perform a somesault 翻筋斗;做空翻

something /'sʌmθɪŋ/ **pronoun** an unspecified or unknown thing or amount 某物;某事;某数量

sometime /'sʌmtaɪm/ **adverb** at some unspecified or unknown time in 某时;有朝一日 • **adjective** former 从前的;以前的

sometimes /'sʌmtaɪmz/ **adverb** occasionally 有时;间或

somewhat /'sʌmwɒt/ **adverb** to some extent 稍微;有点;有些

somewhere /'sʌmweə(r)/ **adverb** in or to an unspecified or unknown place 在某处;到某处 • **pronoun** some unspecified place 某处

somnambulism /sɒm'næm-bjəlɪzəm/ **noun** formal【正式】sleep-walking 梦游(症) ■ **somnambulist** noun.

somnolent /'sɒmnələnt/ **adjective** sleepy or drowsy 瞌睡的;困倦的;睡意蒙眬的 ■ **somnolence** noun.

son /sʌn/ **noun 1** a boy or man in relation to his parents 儿子 **2** a male descendant 子孙;男性后裔 **3** (**the Son**) Jesus 耶稣 □ **son-in-law**

(plural **sons-in-law**) the husband of a person's daughter 女婿

sonar /'səʊnɑː(r)/ **noun** a system for detecting objects underwater by giving out sound pulses 声呐(利用传送声脉冲探测水下物体的系统)

sonata /sə'nɑːtə/ **noun** a piece of music for a solo instrument, sometimes with piano accompaniment 奏鸣曲

song /sɒŋ/ **noun 1** a set of words set to music 歌;歌曲 **2** singing 歌唱 **3** the musical phrases uttered by some birds, whales, and insects (鸟的)鸣唱,啼啭;(鲸和虫的)鸣声 **4** literary【文】a poem 诗歌 □ **for a song** informal【非正式】very cheaply 非常便宜;以低价 **on song** Brit. informal【英,非正式】performing well 性能良好;运转顺畅

songbird /'sɒŋbɜːd/ **noun** a bird with a musical song 鸣禽

songster /'sɒŋstə(r)/ **noun** (feminine【阴性】**songstress**) a person who sings 歌唱家;歌手

sonic /'sɒnɪk/ **adjective** relating to or using sound waves 声波的 □ **sonic boom** an explosive noise caused by the shock wave from an object travelling faster than the speed of sound 轰声,声震(物体超音速飞行时发出的巨大声响) ■ **sonically** adverb.

sonnet /'sɒnɪt/ **noun** a poem of fourteen lines using a fixed rhyme scheme 十四行诗;商籁体

sonorous /'sɒnərəs/ **adjective 1** (of a sound) deep and full (声音)洪亮的,浑厚的 **2** (of speech) using powerful language (讲话)铿锵有力的 ■ **sonority** noun **sonorously** adverb.

soon /suːn/ **adverb 1** in or after a short time 马上;不久 **2** early 早 **3** (**would sooner**) would rather 宁可;宁愿

soot /sʊt/ **noun** a black powdery substance produced when wood, coal, etc. is burned 煤烟;烟灰 ■ **sooty**

adjective.

soothe /suːð/ **verb** (**soothes, soothing, soothed**) **1** gently calm 安慰；劝慰 **2** relieve pain or discomfort 缓和，减轻(痛苦或不适)

soothsayer /'suːθseɪə(r)/ **noun** a person supposed to be able to foresee the future 占卜者；预言家

sop /sɒp/ **noun** a thing given or done to calm or please someone who is angry or disappointed (为缓和某人愤怒或失望情绪而给予的)抚慰品，小礼物 • **verb** (**sops, sopping, sopped**) (**sop something up**) soak up liquid 吸干(液体)

sophism /'sɒfɪzəm/ **noun** a false argument 诡辩；谬论

sophist /'sɒfɪst/ **noun** a person who uses clever but false arguments 诡辩者；诡辩家 ■ **sophistry** noun.

sophisticate /sə'fɪstɪkeɪt/ **noun** a sophisticated person 老于世故的人，见多识广的人

sophisticated /sə'fɪstɪkeɪtɪd/ **adjective 1** having experience and taste in matters of culture or fashion 老于世故的，见多识广的 **2** highly developed and complex 先进的，精密的；复杂巧妙的 ■ **sophistication** noun.

sophomore /'sɒfəmɔː(r)/ **noun** N. Amer. 【北美】 a second-year university or high-school student (大学或中学的)二年级学生

soporific /sɒpə'rɪfɪk/ **adjective** causing drowsiness or sleep 催眠的，让人瞌睡的

sopping /'sɒpɪŋ/ **adjective** wet through 湿透的，浸透的

soppy /'sɒpi/ **adjective** (**soppier, soppiest**) Brit. informal 【英，非正式】 **1** too sentimental 感情过于丰富的，多愁善感的 **2** feeble 虚弱的，无力的 ■ **soppily** adverb.

soprano /sə'prɑːnəʊ/ **noun** (plural **sopranos**) the highest singing voice 最高音

sorbet /'sɔːbeɪ/ **noun** a water ice 雪糕；冰糕

sorcerer /'sɔːsərə(r)/ **noun** (feminine 【阴性】 **sorceress**) a person who practises magic 巫师；术士 ■ **sorcery** noun.

sordid /'sɔːdɪd/ **adjective 1** dishonest or immoral 卑鄙的；不道德的；无耻的 **2** very dirty and unpleasant 肮脏的；污秽的 ■ **sordidly** adverb.

sore /sɔː(r)/ **adjective 1** painful or aching 疼痛的；引起痛苦的 **2** urgent 急迫的；紧要的：in sore need 急需 **3** N. Amer. informal 【北美，非正式】 upset and angry 心烦的；恼怒的 • **noun** a raw or painful place on the body (身体上的)伤处，痛处 • **adverb** old use 【旧】 very 很；非常：sore afraid 非常害怕 □ **sore point** an issue about which someone feels distressed or annoyed 心病；痛处；伤心事 ■ **soreness** noun.

sorely /'sɔːli/ **adverb** extremely; badly 严重地；非常

sorghum /'sɔːgəm/ **noun** a cereal plant found in warm regions, grown for grain and animal feed 蜀黍；高粱

sorority /sə'rɒrəti/ **noun** (plural **sororities**) N. Amer. 【北美】 a society for female students in a university or college (大学里的)女生联谊会

sorrel /'sɒrəl/ **noun 1** an edible plant with a bitter flavour 酸模(可食用植物，有苦味) **2** a light reddish-brown colour 红褐色；栗色

sorrow /'sɒrəʊ/ **noun 1** deep distress caused by loss or disappointment 悲痛；悲伤；悲哀 **2** a cause of sorrow 伤心事；悲伤的事；不幸

sorrowful /'sɒrəfʊl/ **adjective** feeling or showing sorrow 伤心的；悲痛的 ■ **sorrowfully** adverb.

sorry /'sɒri/ **adjective** (**sorrier, sorriest**) **1** feeling sympathy for someone else's misfortune (为别人的不幸)感到难过的，怜悯的，同情的 **2** feeling or expressing regret 抱歉的；

遗憾的;懊悔的 3 in a bad or pitiful state 可怜的;悲惨的 4 unpleasant and regrettable 令人不快的;讨厌的;令人遗憾的

sort /sɔːt/ **noun 1** a category of people or things with a common feature or features 种类;类别;品种 **2** informal 【非正式】a person 某一种人:*a friendly sort* 一个友好的人 • **verb 1** arrange systematically in groups 整理 **2** (often **sort someone/thing out**) separate someone or something from a mixed group 把…分类 **3** (**sort something out**) deal with a problem or difficulty 解决(问题或困难) □ **out of sorts** slightly unwell or unhappy 身体不适;心情不佳

> **! 注意** use **this sort of** to refer to a singular noun (e.g. *this sort of job*), and **these sorts of** to refer to a plural noun (e.g. *these sorts of questions*). 修饰单数名词时用 this sort of (如 this sort of job 这种工作),后接复数名词用 these sorts of (如 these sorts of questions 这些问题)。

sorted /ˈsɔːtɪd/ **adjective** Brit. informal 【英,非正式】**1** organized; arranged 井然有序的;有条理的 **2** emotionally stable 情绪稳定的

sortie /ˈsɔːtiː/ **noun 1** an attack made by troops from a position of defence (从防御处)出击 **2** a flight by an aircraft on a military operation (军事行动中飞机的)出动架次 **3** a short trip 短程旅行

SOS /ˌes əʊ ˈes/ **noun 1** an international signal sent when in great trouble (国际通用的)紧急呼救信号 **2** an urgent appeal for help [letters chosen to be easily transmitted and recognized in Morse code, but often thought to be short for *save our souls*] 紧急求救(字母选自容易传输和识别的摩尔斯代码,但往往被认为是 save our souls 的缩写)

sot /sɒt/ **noun** old use 【旧】a person who is regularly drunk 酒鬼;醉鬼 ■ **sottish** adjective.

sotto voce /ˌsɒtəʊ ˈvəʊtʃi/ **adverb & adjective** in a quiet voice 小声地(的);轻声地(的)

soubriquet /ˈsuːbrɪkeɪ/ ⇒ 见 SOBRIQUET.

soufflé /ˈsuːfleɪ/ **noun** a light, spongy dish made by mixing egg yolks with beaten egg whites 蛋奶酥

sought /sɔːt/ past and past participle of SEEK. □ **sought after** in great demand 很吃香的,广受欢迎的

souk /suːk/ **noun** an Arab market (阿拉伯国家的)露天市场

soul /səʊl/ **noun 1** the spiritual element of a person, believed by some to be immortal 灵魂 **2** a person's inner nature (人的)内在,心性,心灵 **3** emotional energy or power 强烈感情;气魄 **4** (**the soul of**) a perfect example of a particular quality 典范,化身 **5** an individual人;家伙:*Poor soul!* 可怜的家伙! **6** a kind of music that expresses strong emotions, made popular by black Americans (由美国黑人普及开来的表达强烈情感的)灵歌,灵乐 □ **soul-destroying** unbearably dull and repetitive 消磨精神的;极度乏味的 **soul-searching** close examination of your emotions and motives 内省;反省

soulful /ˈsəʊlfl/ **adjective** expressing deep feeling 深情的 ■ **soulfully** adverb.

soulless /ˈsəʊlləs/ **adjective 1** lacking character or interest 缺乏特色的;乏味的 **2** lacking human feelings 冷漠无情的;无动于衷的

soulmate /ˈsəʊlmeɪt/ **noun** a person ideally suited to another 知心朋友;知己

sound¹ /saʊnd/ **noun 1** vibrations which travel through the air and are sensed by the ear 声音;响声 **3** an impression given by words 印象;感觉 • **verb 1** make sound 发音;

发声 **2** make a sound to show or warn of something 发出声音(以传达某种含义或表示警告) **3** give a particular impression 听起来好像 **4** (**sound off**) express your opinions loudly or forcefully 高谈阔论；夸夸其谈 □ **sound barrier** the point at which an aircraft approaches the speed of sound 音障；声障 **sound bite** a short, memorable extract from a speech or interview (演说或访谈的)声音片段 **sound effect** a sound other than speech or music that is used in a play, film, etc. (戏剧、电影等中人工合成的)音响效果 **sound wave** a wave by which sound travels through water, air, etc. 声波 ■ **soundless** adjective.

sound² adjective 1 in good condition 健康的；健全的；完好的 **2** based on solid judgement 合理的；明智的；正确的 **3** financially secure 资金充足的；殷实的 **4** competent or reliable 有能力的；能胜任的；可靠的；可信赖的 **5** (of sleep) deep and unbroken (睡眠)香甜的，酣畅的 **6** severe or thorough 剧烈的；彻底的；完全的 ■ **soundly** adverb.

sound³ verb 1 find out the depth of water using a line, pole, or sound echoes (用绳、竿或回波)测量(水)的深度 **2** (**sound someone out**) question someone about their opinions or feelings 试探(某人)的看法；探口风

sound⁴ noun a narrow stretch of water connecting two larger areas of water 海峡；海湾

sounding /ˈsaʊndɪŋ/ **noun 1** a measurement of the depth of water 水深测量 **2** (**soundings**) information found out before taking action 调查收集的信息 □ **sounding board** a person or group that you talk to in order to test out new ideas 受征询探测新想法是否可行的)被咨询人群

soundproof /ˈsaʊndpruːf/ **adjective** preventing sound getting in or out 隔

音的 • **verb** make soundproof 使隔音

soundtrack /ˈsaʊndtræk/ **noun** the sound accompaniment to a film (电影)的声带，声迹

soup /suːp/ **noun** a savoury liquid dish made by boiling meat, fish, or vegetables 汤，羹 • **verb** (**soup something up**) informal 【非正式】make a car more powerful 加大(汽车)马力 □ **soup kitchen** a place where free food is served to homeless or very poor people (救济无家可归者或穷人的)施食处，施粥所

soupçon /ˈsuːpsɒn/ **noun** a very small quantity of something 微量；一点儿

sour /ˈsaʊə(r)/ **adjective 1** having a sharp taste like lemon or vinegar 酸的；有酸味的 **2** (especially of milk) stale and unpleasant (尤指奶)馊的，酸腐的 **3** resentful or angry 尖酸的，不满的；愤怒的 • **verb** make or become sour (使)变酸 □ **sour cream** cream that has been made sour by adding bacteria 酸奶油 **sour grapes** an attitude of pretending that something is worthless or undesirable because you cannot have it yourself 酸葡萄心理(对得不到的东西进行贬低) ■ **sourly** adverb **sourness** noun.

source /sɔːs/ **noun 1** a place, person, or thing from which something originates 发源地；创始人；来源 **2** a place where a river or stream starts 源头；水源 **3** a person, book, or document that provides information 消息来源；原始资料 • **verb** (**sources, sourcing, sourced**) obtain from a particular source 从(某一来源)获得

sourpuss /ˈsaʊəpʊs/ **noun** informal 【非正式】a bad-tempered or sulky person 性情乖戾的人；尖酸刻薄的人

souse /saʊs/ **verb** (**souses, sousing, soused**) **1** soak in liquid 把…浸入液体中 **2** (**soused**) pickled or marinaded 腌制的；腌渍的

south /saʊθ/ **noun 1** the direction which is on your right-hand side when you are facing east 南；南方 **2** the southern part of a place 南部；南部地区 • **adjective 1** lying towards or facing the south 向南的；朝南的 **2** (of a wind) blowing from the south (风)从南面吹来的 • **adverb** to or towards the south 向南；朝南 ■ **southward** adjective & adverb **southwards** adverb.

south-east /ˌsaʊθˈiːst/ **noun** the direction or region halfway between south and east 东南；东南方；东南地区 • **adjective & adverb 1** towards or facing the south-east 向东南的；朝东南的 **2** (of a wind) blowing from the south-east (风)从东南面吹来的 ■ **south-eastern** adjective.

south-easterly /ˌsaʊθˈiːstəli/ **adjective & adverb 1** in or towards the south-east 在东南的；向东南的 **2** (of a wind) blowing from the south-east (风)从东南面吹来，从东南面

southerly /ˈsʌðəli/ **adjective & adverb 1** facing or moving towards the south 朝南的；向南的 **2** (of a wind) blowing from the south (风)从南面吹来的，从南面

southern /ˈsʌðən/ **adjective 1** situated in or facing the south 南方的；朝南的 **2** coming from or characteristic of the south 来自南面的；南部特有的

southerner /ˈsʌðənə(r)/ **noun** a person from the south of a region 南方人

south-west /ˌsaʊθˈwest/ **noun** the direction or region halfway between south and west 西南 • **adjective & adverb 1** towards or facing the south-west 向西南的；朝西南的 **2** (of a wind) blowing from the south-west (风)从西南面吹来的 ■ **south-western** adjective.

south-westerly /ˌsaʊθˈwestəli/ **adjective & adverb 1** in or towards

the south-west 在西南(的)；向西南(的) **2** (of a wind) blowing from the south-west (风)从西南面吹来的(的)

souvenir /ˌsuːvəˈnɪə(r)/ **noun** a thing that is kept as a reminder of a person, place, or event 纪念品；纪念物

sou'wester /ˌsaʊˈwestə(r)/ **noun** a waterproof hat with a brim that covers the back of the neck 防水帽 (后檐宽以护颈)

sovereign /ˈsɒvrɪn/ **noun 1** a king or queen who is the supreme ruler of a country 君主；国王；女王 **2** a former British gold coin worth one pound sterling 沙弗林(旧时英国面值1英镑的金币) • **adjective 1** possessing supreme power 拥有至高无上权力的 **2** (of a country) independent (国家)有主权的，独立自主的

sovereignty /ˈsɒvrənti/ **noun** (plural **sovereignties**) **1** supreme power or authority 主权；至高无上的权威；最高统治权 **2** a self-governing state 独立自主

Soviet /ˈsəʊviət/ **noun 1** a citizen of the former Soviet Union (前)苏联公民 **2** (**soviet**) an elected council in the former Soviet Union 苏维埃(前苏联的代表会议) • **adjective** having to do with the former Soviet Union (前)苏联的

sow[1] /səʊ/ **verb** (past **sowed**; past participle **sown** or **sowed**) **1** plant seed by scattering it on or in the earth 播种；种 **2** spread or introduce something unwelcome 传播；散布；煽动

sow[2] /saʊ/ **noun** an adult female pig 母猪

soy sauce /sɔɪ/ **noun** a sauce made with fermented soya beans, used in Chinese and Japanese cooking (中国和日本烹饪用的)酱油

soya bean /ˈsɔɪə/ **noun** an edible bean that is high in protein 大豆；黄豆

sozzled /'sɒzld/ **adjective** informal【非正式】very drunk 大醉的；烂醉的

spa /spɑː/ **noun 1** a mineral spring considered to have health-giving properties 矿泉 **2** a place with a mineral spring 矿泉疗养地

space /speɪs/ **noun 1** unoccupied ground or area 空地；空间 **2** a blank between typed or written words or characters 空行；间隔；空格 **3** the dimensions of height, depth, and width within which all things exist and move 空间 **4** (also **outer space**) the universe beyond the earth's atmosphere 太空；外层空间 **5** an interval of time (时间上的)间隔；期间 **6** freedom to live and develop as you wish 自我支配的自由；属于自我的空间 • **verb** (**spaces**, **spacing**, **spaced**) **1** position items at a distance from one another 以一定间隔放置 **2** (**be spaced out**) informal【非正式】be confused or not completely conscious 精神恍惚；神志不清 □ **space shuttle** a spacecraft used for journeys between earth and craft which are orbiting the earth 航天飞机 **space station** a large spacecraft used as a base for manned operations in space 宇宙空间站；航天站

spacecraft /'speɪskrɑːft/ **noun** (plural **spacecraft** or **spacecrafts**) a vehicle used for travelling in space 航天器；宇宙飞船

spaceman /'speɪsmæn/ **noun** (plural **spacemen**) a male astronaut 字航员；航天员

spaceship /'speɪsʃɪp/ **noun** a manned spacecraft 宇宙飞船

spacesuit /'speɪssuːt/ **noun** a pressurized suit covering the whole body that allows you to survive in space 航天服；字航服

spacious /'speɪʃəs/ **adjective** (of a room or building) having plenty of space (房间或建筑物)宽敞的

spade /speɪd/ **noun** a tool with a rectangular metal blade and a long handle, used for digging 铲；锹 □ **call a spade a spade** speak plainly and frankly 直言不讳

spades /speɪdz/ **noun** one of the four suits in a pack of playing cards, represented by a black heart-shaped figure with a small stalk (纸牌中的)黑桃 □ **in spades** informal【非正式】in large amounts or to a high degree 大量；非常；极度

spadework /'speɪdwɜːk/ **noun** hard or routine work done to prepare for something 艰苦的准备工作；例行准备工作

spaghetti /spə'geti/ **plural noun** pasta made in long, thin strands 意大利式细面条

spake /speɪk/ old-fashioned past of SPEAK. speak 过去式的旧式拼法

spam /spæm/ **noun 1** (**Spam**) trademark【商标】a canned meat product made mainly from ham (斯帕姆)午餐肉 **2** unwanted email sent to many Internet users (因特网)垃圾邮件

span /spæn/ **noun 1** the length of time for which something lasts 持续时间 **2** width or extent from side to side 跨度；宽度 **3** a part of a bridge between the uprights supporting it (桥墩间的)墩距，跨距 **4** the maximum distance between the tips of the thumb and little finger 掌距(拇指尖至小指尖的最大距离) • **verb** (**spans**, **spanning**, **spanned**) extend across or over 延伸；贯穿；横跨

spangle /'spæŋgl/ **noun 1** a small piece of decorative glittering material 亮晶晶的饰片 **2** a spot of bright colour or light 发亮的斑点；色彩鲜艳的斑点 ■ **spangled** adjective **spangly** adjective.

Spaniard /'spænjəd/ **noun** a person from Spain 西班牙人

spaniel /'spænjəl/ **noun** a breed of dog with a long silky coat and drooping ears 獚(皮毛柔软光洁，耳朵下垂)

Spanish /'spænɪʃ/ **noun** the main language of Spain and of much of Central and South America 西班牙语(通行于西班牙和中南美洲许多地区) • **adjective** relating to Spain or Spanish 西班牙的；西班牙语的

spank /spæŋk/ **verb** slap someone on the buttocks with your hand or a flat object 打(某人)的屁股 • **noun** a slap on the buttocks 打屁股

spanking /'spæŋkɪŋ/ **adjective 1** brisk 轻快的；飞快的 **2** informal 【非正式】impressive or pleasing 给人深刻印象的；令人愉快的；极好的 • **noun** a series of spanks 打屁股

spanner /'spænə(r)/ **noun** Brit. 【英】a tool for gripping and turning a nut or bolt 扳钳；扳手 □ **spanner in the works** something that prevents a plan being carried out successfully 困难；障碍

spar[1] /spɑː(r)/ **noun 1** a thick, strong pole used to support the sails on a ship (船上用作桅杆的)圆材 **2** the main supporting structure of an aircraft's wing (飞机的)翼梁

spar[2] **verb** (**spars**, **sparring**, **sparred**) **1** make the motions of boxing without landing heavy blows, as a form of training 练习拳击；虚晃一拳 **2** argue in a friendly way (在友好的气氛中)争论，辩论

spare /speə(r)/ **adjective 1** additional to what is required for ordinary use 多余的；剩余的 **2** not being used or occupied 不用的；闲置的 **3** thin 瘦的 • **noun** an item kept in case another is lost, broken, or worn out 备件；备用品 • **verb** (**spares**, **sparing**, **spared**) **1** let someone have something that you have enough of 匀出；留出；抽出 **2** refrain from killing or harming 饶恕；赦免；使不受伤害 **3** protect from

something unpleasant 使免遭，省得，免去(令人不快的事) □ **go spare** Brit. informal 【英，非正式】become very angry 极其愤怒；极为恼火 **spare no expense** be prepared to pay any amount 不惜一切代价 **spare ribs** trimmed ribs of pork 猪排骨 **spare tyre** informal 【非正式】a roll of fat around a person's waist (人体腰部的)多余脂肪

sparing /'speərɪŋ/ **adjective** not wasteful; economical 节俭的；节约的 ■ **sparingly** adverb.

spark /spɑːk/ **noun 1** a small fiery particle produced by burning or caused by friction 火花；火星 **2** a flash of light produced by an electrical discharge 电火花 **3** a small amount of a quality or feeling (品质或情感的)一星，一点 **4** a sense of liveliness and excitement 生气；活力；热情 • **verb 1** give out or produce sparks 冒火花；飞火星 **2** ignite a fire 点燃；点火 **3** (usu. spark something off) cause something 引发；触发 □ **spark plug** a device that produces a spark to ignite the fuel in a vehicle engine (内燃机的)火花塞 ■ **sparky** adjective.

sparkle /'spɑːkl/ **verb** (**sparkles**, **sparkling**, **sparkled**) **1** shine brightly with flashes of light 闪烁；闪耀 **2** be attractively lively and witty 神采飞扬；生气勃勃；才华横溢 **3** (**sparkling**) (of a drink) fizzy (饮料)发泡的，起泡沫的 • **noun 1** a glittering flash of light 闪光；闪耀；火花；火星 **2** attractive liveliness and wit 机智活泼；敏锐 ■ **sparkly** adjective.

sparkler /'spɑːklə(r)/ **noun** a hand-held firework that gives out sparks 烟花棒

sparrow /'spærəʊ/ **noun** a small bird with brown and grey feathers 麻雀

sparrowhawk /'spærəʊhɔːk/ **noun** a small hawk that preys on small birds 雀鹰(一种捕食小鸟的小鹰)

sparse /spɑːs/ **adjective** thinly scattered 稀少的；稀疏的；零星的 ■ **sparsely** adverb **sparsity** noun.

spartan /'spɑːtn/ **adjective** not comfortable or luxurious 斯巴达式的；简朴的，艰苦的

spasm /'spæzəm/ **noun 1** a sudden involuntary contraction of a muscle 痉挛；抽搐 **2** a sudden period of an activity or sensation 一阵阵发作；阵发

spasmodic /spæz'mɒdɪk/ **adjective** happening or done in brief, irregular bursts 间歇性的；阵发性的 ■ **spasmodically** adverb.

spastic /'spæstɪk/ **adjective 1** relating to or affected by muscle spasm 由肌肉痉挛引起的；痉挛性的 **2** offensive 【冒犯】 having to do with cerebral palsy 患大脑性麻痹的 • **noun** offensive 【冒犯】 a person with cerebral palsy 大脑性麻痹患者 ■ **spasticity** noun.

> **！注意** say *person with cerebral palsy* rather than **spastic**, which many people find offensive. 可以用 person with cerebral palsy 来代替让人觉得受到冒犯的 spastic。

spat¹ /spæt/ past and past participle of **spit**¹.

spat² **noun** informal 【非正式】 a quarrel about something unimportant 口角；小争吵

spat³ **noun** a cloth covering formerly worn by men over their ankles and shoes (旧时男子的)鞋罩

spate /speɪt/ **noun 1** a large number of similar things coming quickly one after another 一连串；接二连三 **2** a sudden flood in a river (河水的)猛涨，发洪水

spathe /speɪð/ **noun** a large sheath enclosing the flower cluster of certain plants 佛焰苞(一种包裹花簇的大型苞叶)

spatial /'speɪʃl/ **adjective** having to do with space 空间的 ■ **spatially** adverb.

spatter /'spætə(r)/ **verb** (**spatters**, **spattering**, **spattered**) cover something with drops or spots of a liquid 溅；洒 ；溅污；喷溅；洒 • **noun** a spray or splash 溅；喷溅；洒

spatula /'spætʃələ/ **noun** an object with a broad, flat, blunt blade, used for mixing or spreading (搅拌或涂抹用的)抹刀，刮刀，刮勺

spawn /spɔːn/ **verb 1** (of a fish, frog, etc.) release or deposit eggs (鱼、青蛙等)产卵 **2** give rise to 引起；造成；导致 • **noun** the eggs of fish, frogs, etc.(鱼、青蛙等产下的)卵

spay /speɪ/ **verb** sterilize a female animal by removing the ovaries 切除(雌兽)的卵巢

speak /spiːk/ **verb** (**speaks**, **speaking**, **spoke**; past participle **spoken**) **1** say something 说话；讲话 **2** communicate, or be able to communicate, in a particular language (会)讲(某种语言) **3** (**speak up**) speak more loudly 更大声地说 **4** (**speak out** or **up**) express your opinions frankly and publicly 坦率地说；大胆地讲 □ **speak in tongues** speak in an unknown language during religious worship (在宗教仪式中)讲不为人知的语言 **speak volumes** convey a great deal without using words 清楚说明；充分表明

speakeasy /'spiːkiːzi/ **noun** (plural **speakeasies**) (in the US during Prohibition) a secret illegal drinking club (美国禁酒时期)非法经营的酒店

speaker /'spiːkə(r)/ **noun 1** a person who speaks 说话者 **2** (**Speaker**) the person who is in charge of proceedings in a parliament (议会的)议长 **3** a loudspeaker 扬声器

spear /spɪə(r)/ **noun 1** a weapon with a pointed metal tip and a long shaft 矛；标枪；梭镖 **2** a pointed stem of asparagus or broccoli (芦笋或花椰菜

的)嫩茎 • **verb** pierce with a spear or other pointed object (用有尖头的东西)刺，戳

spearhead /'spɪəhed/ **verb** lead a campaign or attack 领导(运动或进攻)；当 … 的 先锋；带 头 做 • **noun** a person or group that leads a campaign or attack 先锋；前锋；先头部队

spearmint /'spɪəmɪnt/ **noun** a type of garden mint, used in cooking 留兰香，绿薄荷(用于烹调)

spec /spek/ **noun** informal【非正式】 1 (**on spec**) without any specific preparation or plan 碰运气；投机；冒险 2 a detailed working description 操作指南；说明书

special /'speʃl/ **adjective** 1 better or different from what is usual 特别的；特殊的 2 designed for or belonging to a particular person, place, or event 特用的；特设的，专门针对…的 • **noun** 1 something designed or organized for a particular occasion or purpose 特别产品；特别活动 2 a dish not on the regular menu but served on a particular day (在特定日子供应的)特色菜 □ **spe·cial constable** a person trained to act as a police officer on particular occasions (非 常 时 期 的)临时警察 **special effects** illusions created for films and television by camerawork, computer graphics, etc. (电影和电视中的)特技效果

specialist /'speʃəlɪst/ **noun** an expert in a particular subject, area of activity, etc. 专家 • **adjective** involving detailed knowledge within a subject, area of activity, etc. 专业的，专科的，专门学科的 ■ **specialism** noun.

speciality /ˌspeʃi'æləti/ (US spelling 【美拼作】**specialty**) **noun** (plural **specialities**) 1 a skill or area of study in which someone is an expert 专业；专长 2 a product for which a person or region is famous 特产；名产 3 (usu. **specialty**) a branch of

medicine or surgery (内科或外科的)科

specialize or **specialise** /'speʃəlaɪz/ **verb** (**specializes, specializing, specialized**) 1 concentrate on and become expert in a particular skill or area 专门研究(或从事)；专攻 2 (**specialized**) adapted or designed for a particular purpose or area of activity 专用的；专业的；专门的 ■ **specialization** noun.

specially /'speʃəli/ **adverb** 1 for a special purpose 特意；专门地 2 particularly 格外；尤其

species /'spiːʃiːz/ **noun** (plural **species**) a group of animals or plants that are capable of breeding with each other 物种，种 2 a kind 种类

specific /spə'sɪfɪk/ **adjective** 1 clearly defined or identified 明确的；具体的 2 precise and clear 确切的 3 (**specific to**) belonging or relating only to 特有的；特定的；特种的，独特的 • **noun** (**specifics**) precise details 详情；细节 ■ **specifically** adverb.

specification /ˌspesɪfɪ'keɪʃn/ **noun** 1 the action of specifying 指定；指明；详述；说明 2 (usu. **specifications**) a detailed description of the design and materials used to make something 说明书；明细单 3 the standard of workmanship and materials in a piece of work (工艺和材料的)规格，标准，规范

specify /'spesɪfaɪ/ **verb** (**specifies, specifying, specified**) state, identify, or require clearly and definitely 具体指定；详细指明；明确说明

specimen /'spesɪmən/ **noun** 1 an example of an animal, plant, object, etc. used for study or display (用于研究或陈列的)样本，标本，样品 2 a sample for medical testing (用于医学实验的)抽样，标本 3 a typical example of something (某事物的)范例 4 informal【非正式】a person of a specific type 某类人；*a sorry specimen* 可怜的人

specious /'spi:ʃəs/ **adjective** seeming right or reasonable, but actually wrong 似是而非的；貌似有理的

speck /spek/ **noun** a tiny spot or particle 斑点；污点；瑕疵 • **verb** mark with small spots 使产生斑点(或污点、瑕疵)

speckle /'spekl/ **noun** a small spot or patch of colour 小斑点；斑纹；色斑 • **verb** (**speckles**, **speckling**, **speckled**) mark with speckles 使产生斑点(或斑纹)

specs /speks/ **plural noun** informal 【非正式】 spectacles 眼镜

spectacle /'spektəkl/ **noun** a visually striking performance or display 惊人的表演(或展示)；壮观

spectacles /'spektəklz/ **plural noun** Brit. 【英】 a pair of glasses 一幅眼镜

spectacular /spek'tækjələ(r)/ **adjective** very impressive, striking, or dramatic 令人惊叹的；壮观的；突出的 • **noun** a spectacular performance or event 壮观的场面；引人注目的事件 ■ **spectacularly** adverb.

spectate /spek'teit/ **verb** (**spectates**, **spectating**, **spectated**) be a spectator 出席观看

spectator /spek'teitə(r)/ **noun** a person who is watching a show, game, etc. (表演、运动等的)观众，观看者

spectral /'spektrəl/ **adjective 1** like a spectre (似)鬼怪的；幽灵(般)的 **2** having to do with the spectrum 谱的；光谱的

spectre /'spektə(r)/ (US spelling 【美拼作】 **specter**) **noun 1** a ghost 鬼怪；幽灵 **2** a possible unpleasant or dangerous occurrence 恐惧；恐慌；忧虑

spectrum /'spektrəm/ **noun** (plural **spectra** /'spektrə/) **1** a band of colours produced by separating light into elements with different wavelengths, e.g. in a rainbow 光谱 **2** the entire range of wavelengths of light 波长的全部范围 **3** a range of sound waves or different types of wave 声谱；波谱 **4** an entire range of beliefs, ideas, etc. 范围；各层次：*the political spectrum* 政治派别

speculate /'spekjuleit/ **verb** (**speculates**, **speculating**, **speculated**) **1** form a theory without firm evidence 推测；猜测 **2** invest in stocks, property, etc. in the hope of gain but with the risk of loss 投机；做投机买卖 ■ **speculation** noun **speculator** noun.

speculative /'spekjələtɪv/ **adjective 1** based on theory or guesswork rather than knowledge 理论上的；推测的；猜测的 **2** (of an investment) risky 投机性的，风险性的 ■ **speculatively** adverb.

speech /spi:tʃ/ **noun 1** the expression of thoughts and feelings using spoken language 说话；谈话 **2** a formal talk given to an audience 演讲；发言 **3** a sequence of lines meant for one character in a play (戏剧中演员的)台词 □ **speech therapy** treatment to help people with speech problems 言语矫治 **speech marks** inverted commas 引号

speechify /'spi:tʃɪfaɪ/ **verb** (**speechifies**, **speechifying**, **speechified**) deliver a speech in a boring or pompous way 枯燥乏味地讲话；装腔作势地演讲

speechless /'spi:tʃləs/ **adjective** unable to speak due to shock or strong emotion (因震惊或激动而)说不出话的

speed /spi:d/ **noun 1** the rate at which someone or something moves or operates 速率；速度 **2** a fast rate of movement or action 快速；迅速 **3** each of the possible gear ratios of a vehicle or bicycle (车辆的)排挡，变速器 **4** the sensitivity of photographic film to light (胶卷的)感光度 **5** informal 【非正式】 an amphetamine drug 安非他明 • **verb** (**speeds**, **speeding**, **speeded** or **sped**) **1** move quickly 快走；迅速行进；疾驰 **2** (**speed up**) move or work more quickly 加速；增速 **3** (of a motorist) travel at a speed greater than the legal limit (驾车者)违章驾驶 **4** old use 【旧】 make prosperous or successful 使兴旺发达；使成功

speedboat /ˈspiːdbəʊt/ **noun** a motorboat designed for high speed 快艇

speedometer /spiːˈdɒmɪtə(r)/ **noun** an instrument that indicates a vehicle's speed (车辆的)速度计

speedway /ˈspiːdweɪ/ **noun** Brit. 【英】 a form of motorcycle racing in which the riders race around an oval dirt track (摩托车)赛车运动

speedy /ˈspiːdi/ **adjective** (**speedier**, **speediest**) done, happening, or moving quickly 快速的；迅速的 ■ **speedily** adverb.

spell[1] /spel/ **verb** (**spells**, **spelling**, **spelled** or chiefly Brit. 【主英】 **spelt**) **1** write or name the letters that form a word in correct sequence 用字母拼；拼写 **2** (of letters) form a word (字母)拼作，拼成 **3** be a sign of 意味 **4** (**spell something out**) explain something clearly and in detail 详细解释；清楚说明

spell[2] **noun 1** a form of words with magical power 符咒；咒语 **2** a state of enchantment caused by a spell 着魔状态 **3** an ability to control or influence other people (控制或影响他人的)魔力，魅力

spell[3] **noun** a short period of time 一段时间；一会儿

spellbound /ˈspelbaʊnd/ **adjective** with your attention completely held by something 入迷的；出神的 ■ **spellbinding** adjective.

spellchecker /ˈspeltʃekə(r)/ **noun** a computer program which checks the spelling of words in an electronic document 拼写检查程序

spelling /ˈspelɪŋ/ **noun 1** the process of spelling a word 拼写 **2** the way in which a word is spelled 拼法

spend /spend/ **verb** (**spends**, **spending**, **spent**) **1** pay out money to buy or hire goods or services 花(钱)；花费 **2** pass time in a particular way 度过，消磨(时间) **3** use up energy or resources 消耗，用尽，耗尽(精力或资源) ■ **spender** noun.

spendthrift /ˈspendθrɪft/ **noun** a person who spends too much money or wastes money 挥霍者；浪费者

sperm /spɜːm/ **noun** (plural **sperm** or **sperms**) **1** semen 精液 **2** a spermatozoon 精子 □ **sperm whale** a toothed whale that feeds largely on squid 抹香鲸(一种有齿鲸，主要以鱿鱼为食)

spermatozoon /ˌspɜːmətəˈzəʊən/ **noun** (plural **spermatozoa** /ˌspɜːmətəˈzəʊə/) the male sex cell of an animal, that fertilizes the egg 精子

spermicide /ˈspɜːmɪsaɪd/ **noun** a contraceptive substance that kills spermatozoa 杀精子剂

spew /spjuː/ **verb 1** pour out in large quantities 倾泻而出；喷出；涌 **2** informal 【非正式】 vomit 呕吐

sphagnum /ˈsfægnəm/ **noun** a kind of moss that grows in boggy areas 泥炭藓(生长于多沼泽地区)

sphere /sfɪə(r)/ **noun 1** a round solid figure in which every point on the surface is at an equal distance from the centre 球；球体；球形 **2** an area of activity or interest (行动或兴趣的)范围，领域

spherical /ˈsferɪkl/ **adjective** shaped like a sphere 球形的；球状的 ■ **spherically** adverb.

sphincter /ˈsfɪŋktə(r)/ **noun** a ring of muscle surrounding an opening such as the anus 括约肌

sphinx /sfɪŋks/ **noun** an ancient Egyptian stone figure having a lion's body and a human or animal head 斯芬克斯(古埃及狮身人面石像)

spice /spaɪs/ **noun 1** a strong-tasting substance used to flavour food (调味)香料 **2** an element that provides interest and excitement 趣味;情趣 • **verb** (**spices, spicing, spiced**) **1** flavour with spice 加香料于;用香料给…调味 **2** (**spice something up**) make something more exciting or interesting 让…变得刺激;给…增添趣味

spick and span adjective neat, clean, and well looked after 干净整洁的;清洁爽净的

spicy /spaɪsi/ **adjective** (**spicier, spiciest**) **1** strongly flavoured with spice 加香料的;用香料调味的 **2** mildly indecent 粗俗的;下流的 ■ **spiciness noun.**

spider /spaɪdə(r)/ **noun** a small insect-like creature (an arachnid) with eight legs 蜘蛛 ■ **spidery adjective.**

spiel /ʃpiːl/ **noun** informal 【非正式】an elaborate and insincere speech made in an attempt to persuade someone 油嘴滑舌地游说

spigot /spɪɡət/ **noun 1** a small peg or plug 塞栓;塞子 **2** the end of a section of a pipe that fits into the socket of the next one (管子的)插端

spike /spaɪk/ **noun 1** a thin, pointed piece of metal or wood (金属或木头的)尖端 **2** each of several metal points set into the sole of a sports shoe to prevent slipping (防滑)跑鞋钉 **3** a cluster of flower heads attached directly to a long stem 穗状花序 • **verb** (**spikes, spiking, spiked**) **1** impale on or pierce with a spike 用尖物刺入(或扎破) **2** cover with sharp points 用尖刺覆盖 **3** informal 【非正式】secretly add alcohol or a drug to drink or food 在(饮料或食物中)偷偷掺入烈性酒(或毒品) ■ **spiky adjective.**

spill[1] /spɪl/ **verb** (**spills, spilling, spilt** or **spilled**) **1** flow, or allow to flow, over the edge of a container (使)溢出;(使)溅出;(使)泼出 **2** move or empty out from a place 从(某地)搬出,腾出,倒出 • **noun 1** a quantity of liquid spilt 溢出量 **2** informal 【非正式】a fall from a horse or bicycle (从马或自行车上)摔下,跌下 □ **spill the beans** informal 【非正式】disclose confidential information 泄漏秘密 **spill blood** kill or wound someone 杀害,伤害(某人) ■ **spillage noun.**

spill[2] **noun** a thin strip of wood or paper used for lighting a fire (用于点火的)木片,纸捻

spin /spɪn/ **verb** (**spins, spinning, spun**) **1** turn round quickly 快速旋转 **2** (of a person's head) have a dizzy sensation (人的头)眩晕 **3** (of a ball) move through the air with a revolving motion (球)在空中旋转 **4** draw out and twist the fibres of wool, cotton, etc. to convert them into yarn 纺(羊毛、棉花等) **5** (of a spider, silkworm, etc.) produce silk or a web by forcing out a fine thread from a special gland (蜘蛛、蚕等)结(网),吐(丝),作(茧) **6** (**spin something out**) make something last as long as possible 拖长;拉长 • **noun 1** a spinning motion 旋转 **2** informal 【非正式】a brief trip in a vehicle for pleasure 乘车短途游览;兜风 **3** a favourable slant given to a news story (新闻报道有利于某人的)有倾向的陈述,粉饰,美化 □ **spin doctor** informal 【非正式】a person employed by a political party to give a favourable interpretation of events to the media (某一政党雇用的)舆论导向专家 **spin dryer** a machine that removes water from washed clothes by spinning them in a drum 旋转式脱水机 **spinning wheel** a piece of equipment for spinning yarn or thread with a spindle driven by a wheel operated by hand or foot 纺车 **spin-off** something unexpected but useful resulting from an activity (出乎意料但有用的)派生物, 副产品 ■ **spinner** noun.

spina bifida /ˌspaɪnə ˈbɪfɪdə/ noun a condition in which part of the spinal cord is exposed, sometimes causing paralysis 脊柱裂(椎骨背侧闭合不全,可导致瘫痪)

spinach /ˈspɪnɪtʃ/ noun a plant with large dark green leaves which are eaten as a vegetable 菠菜

spinal /ˈspaɪnl/ adjective relating to the spine 脊的; 脊柱的; 脊髓的 □ **spinal column** the spine 脊柱 **spinal cord** the nerve fibres enclosed in the spine and connected to the brain 脊髓

spindle /ˈspɪndl/ noun 1 a slender rod with tapered ends used for spinning wool, flax, etc. by hand (手纺羊毛、羊毛织物、亚麻布等用的)绕线杆 2 a rod around which something revolves 轴; 心轴

spindly /ˈspɪndli/ adjective long or tall and thin 细长的; 瘦长的

spindrift /ˈspɪndrɪft/ noun spray blown from the sea by the wind (被大风吹起的)海浪溅沫

spine /spaɪn/ noun 1 a series of bones extending from the skull to the small of the back, enclosing the spinal cord; the backbone 脊椎; 脊柱 2 the part of a book that encloses the inner edges of the pages 书脊 3 a hard pointed projection found on certain plants and animals (植物的)刺, (动物的)刺, 刺毛 □ **spine-chiller** a story or film that causes terror and excitement 恐怖故事(或电影) ■ **spiny** adjective.

spineless /ˈspaɪnləs/ adjective 1 lacking courage and determination 没有骨气的; 怯懦的; 软弱的 2 having no backbone; invertebrate 无脊椎的 3 having no spines 无脊柱的

spinet /spɪˈnet/ noun a kind of small harpsichord 斯皮内琴(一种小型拨弦键琴)

spinnaker /ˈspɪnəkə(r)/ noun a large threecornered sail used on a racing yacht when the wind is coming from behind (赛艇的)大三角帆(顺风时使用)

spinney /ˈspɪni/ noun (plural spinneys) Brit. 【英】a small area of trees and bushes 小树林; 灌木丛

spinster /ˈspɪnstə(r)/ noun disapproving 【贬】a single woman beyond the usual age for marriage 老处女 ■ **spinsterhood** noun.

spiral /ˈspaɪrəl/ adjective winding in a continuous curve around a central point or axis 螺旋形的; 螺旋式的 • noun 1 a spiral curve, shape, or pattern 螺旋(形) 2 a continuous rise or fall of prices, wages, etc. (价格、工资等的)不断上升(或下降) • verb (spirals, spiralling, spiralled; US spelling 【美拼作】spirals, spiraling, spiraled) 1 follow a spiral course 螺旋形升降; 盘旋升降 2 show a continuous increase or decrease 不断地上升(或下降) ■ **spirally** adverb.

spire /ˈspaɪə(r)/ noun a pointed structure on the top of a church tower (教堂的)尖塔, 尖顶

spirit /ˈspɪrɪt/ noun 1 the part of a person that consists of their character and feelings rather than their body 心灵; 精神 2 a supernatural being 鬼魂; 幽灵 3 typical character, quality, or mood 性格; 本质; 精神 4 (spirits) a person's mood or state of mind 心境; 情绪 5 courage, energy, and determination 勇气; 活力; 决心 6 the real meaning of something as opposed to its strict interpretation 本质; 精髓; 实质 7 (also spirits) chiefly Brit. 【主英】strong alcoholic drink, e.g. rum 烈酒 8 purified distilled alcohol, e.g. methylated spirit 蒸

馏酒精 • verb (**spirits**, **spiriting**, **spirited**) (**spirit someone/thing away**) take someone or something away quickly and secretly 迅速秘密地带走；偷偷运送 □ **spirit level** a glass tube partially filled with a liquid, containing an air bubble whose position reveals whether a surface is perfectly level (气泡)水准仪

spirited /'spiritid/ **adjective** energetic and determined 精神饱满的；坚定的；果断的 ■ **spiritedly** adverb.

spiritual /'spiritʃuəl/ **adjective 1** having to do with the human spirit as opposed to material or physical things 精神的；心灵的 **2** having to do with religion or religious belief 宗教的；宗教信仰的 • **noun** a religious song of a kind associated with black Christians of the southern US (美国南部黑人基督徒的)灵歌 ■ **spirituality noun spiritually** adverb.

spiritualism /'spiritʃuəlizəm/ **noun** the belief that the spirits of the dead can communicate with the living 招魂说(认为死者的亡魂可与活人互通信息) ■ **spiritualist** noun.

spirogyra /ˌspaiərə'dʒaiərə/ **noun** a type of algae consisting of long green threads 水绵(一种丝状绿色海藻)

spit¹ /spit/ **verb** (**spits**, **spitting**, **spat** or **spit**) **1** forcibly eject saliva, or food, liquid, etc., from the mouth 吐、唾(唾沫、食物、液体等) **2** say in a hostile way 厉声说出；怒斥 **3** give out small bursts of sparks or hot fat 爆出火花；噼噼地溅油 **4** (**it spits, it is spitting**) Brit. 【英】light rain falls 下小雨 • **noun 1** saliva 口水；唾液 **2** an act of spitting 啐；唾沫；吐痰；吐食物 □ **be the spitting image of** informal 【非正式】look exactly like 和…一模一样；酷似

spit² **noun 1** a metal rod pushed through meat in order to hold and

turn it while it is roasted 烤肉叉；炙叉 **2** a narrow point of land sticking out into the sea 岬

spite /spait/ **noun** a desire to hurt, annoy, or offend someone 恶意 • **verb** (**spites**, **spiting**, **spited**) deliberately hurt, annoy, or offend someone 存心伤害；故意使烦恼；故意冒犯 □ **in spite of** without being affected by 不管；不顾

spiteful /'spaitfl/ **adjective** deliberately hurtful; malicious 恶意的 ■ **spitefully** adverb.

spitfire /'spitfaiə(r)/ **noun** a person with a fierce temper 脾气暴躁的人

spittle /'spitl/ **noun** saliva 唾沫；口水

spittoon /spi'tu:n/ **noun** a container for spitting into 痰盂

spiv /spiv/ **noun** Brit. informal 【英，非正式】a flashily dressed man who makes a living by dishonest business dealings 衣冠楚楚的奸商

splash /splæʃ/ **verb 1** (of a liquid) fall in scattered drops (液体)溅，泼 **2** make wet with scattered drops 溅湿；溅污 **3** move around in water, causing it to fly about (在水里)溅着水花走动，拍起水花游 **4** (**splash down**) (of a spacecraft) land on water (航天器)溅落 **5** prominently display a story or photograph in a newspaper or magazine (在报纸或杂志上)以显著位置刊登，显眼地展示(新闻报道或照片) **6** (**splash out**) Brit. informal 【英，非正式】spend money freely 随意花钱；大肆挥霍 • **noun 1** an instance of splashing 溅；泼 **2** a small quantity of liquid splashed on to a surface 溅上的液体；溅落后留下的水迹 **3** a small quantity of liquid added to a drink (掺入饮料中的)少量液体 **4** a bright patch of colour (鲜艳的)色块 **5** informal 【非正式】a prominent news story 受人瞩目的新闻报道 □ **make a splash** informal 【非正式】attract a lot of attention 引起轰动；惹人注目

splatter /'splætə(r)/ **verb** (**splatters, splattering, splattered**) splash with a sticky or thick liquid 用(黏性的或浓稠的液体)溅泼, 溅湿, 溅污 • **noun** a splash of a sticky or thick liquid 溅(黏性或浓稠液体的)溅泼, 溅湿, 溅污

splay /spleɪ/ **verb** spread out wide apart 展开; 张开

spleen /spliːn/ **noun 1** an organ involved in producing and removing blood cells 脾(脏) **2** bad temper 坏脾气

splendid /'splendɪd/ **adjective 1** magnificent; very impressive 华丽的; 给人深刻印象的 **2** informal 【非正式】excellent 极好的; 杰出的 ■ **splendidly** adverb.

splendour /'splendə(r)/ (US spelling 【美拼作】**splendor**) **noun** magnificent and impressive appearance 壮丽; 壮观

splenetic /splə'netɪk/ **adjective** bad-tempered or spiteful 脾气坏的; 恶意的

splice /splaɪs/ **verb** (**splices, splicing, spliced**) **1** join ropes by weaving together the strands at the ends 编接; 接合(绳子) **2** join pieces of film, tape, etc. at the ends 拼接, 叠接(电影胶片或磁带等) • **noun** a spliced join 编接; 拼接

spliff /splɪf/ **noun** informal 【非正式】a cannabis cigarette 大麻烟卷

splint /splɪnt/ **noun** a rigid support for a broken bone (用于固定断骨的)夹板

splinter /'splɪntə(r)/ **noun** a small, thin, sharp piece of wood, glass, etc. broken off from a larger piece (木头、玻璃等的)碎片, 裂片 • **verb** (**splinters, splintering, splintered**) break into splinters 裂成碎片 □ **splinter group** a small breakaway group (从大集团里分出来的)小集团, 小派别

split /splɪt/ **verb** (**splits, splitting, split**) **1** break into parts by force 使裂开; 劈开 **2** divide into parts or groups 划分; 使分组 **3** (often **split up**) end a marriage or other relationship 离婚; 分手; 绝交 **4** (**be splitting**) informal 【非正式】(of a person's head) be suffering from a bad headache (人的头部)头痛欲裂 • **noun 1** a tear or crack 裂口; 裂缝 **2** an instance of splitting 裂开; 分裂 **3** (**the splits**) a leap or seated position with the legs straight and at right angles to the body 劈叉 □ **split infinitive** Grammar 【语法】an infinitive construction in which an adverb or other word is placed between to and the verb (e.g. *she used to secretly admire him*), traditionally regarded as bad English 分裂不定式(在 to 和动词之间有副词或其他词插入的结构) **split-level** (of a room or building) having the floor divided into two levels (房间或建筑物)错层式的 **split second** a very brief moment of time 瞬间; 霎那间

splodge /splɒdʒ/ or **splotch** /splɒtʃ/ **noun** Brit. 【英】a spot, splash, or smear 污点; 污迹; 污渍

splosh /splɒʃ/ informal 【非正式】**verb** make a soft splashing sound 溅泼着前行; 使发出溅泼声 • **noun** a splashing sound 溅(或泼)的声音

splurge /splɜːdʒ/ **noun** informal 【非正式】**verb** (**splurges, splurging, splurged**) spend extravagantly 挥霍 • **noun** a sudden burst of extravagance 挥霍

splutter /'splʌtə(r)/ **verb** (**splutters, spluttering, spluttered**) **1** make a series of short explosive spitting or choking sounds 发出噼啪(或毕剥)声 **2** say in a rapid, unclear way 急促含混地说; 语无伦次地说 • **noun** a spluttering sound 噼啪声; 毕剥声

spoil /spɔɪl/ **verb** (**spoils, spoiling**, past and past participle **spoilt** (chiefly Brit. 【主英】) or **spoiled**) **1** make something less good or enjoyable 破坏; 损害; 糟蹋 **2** (of food) become unfit for eating (食物)变坏, 变质, 腐败 **3** harm the character of a child by not being strict enough 宠坏, 娇惯, 溺爱(孩子) **4** treat with great or excessive kindness 友好对待; 悉心照料; 娇纵 **5** (be spoiling for) be very eager for 极想 • noun (spoils) stolen goods 赃物

spoiler /ˈspɔɪlə(r)/ noun **1** a flap on an aircraft wing which can be raised to create drag and slow it down (航空器机翼上的)扰流器, 阻流板 **2** a similar device on a car intended to improve roadholding at high speeds (汽车上的)气流偏导器

spoilsport /ˈspɔɪlspɔːt/ noun a person who spoils the pleasure of other people 扫兴的人; 败兴者

spoke[1] /spəʊk/ noun each of the rods connecting the centre of a wheel to its rim 轮辐; 辐条

spoke[2] past of SPEAK.

spoken /ˈspəʊkən/ past participle of SPEAK. ■ adjective speaking in a particular way 说话有…特点的: a soft-spoken man 说话柔声细气的男子 □ be spoken for be already claimed 已认领的; 已有人索取的

spokesman /ˈspəʊksmən/ or **spokeswoman** /ˈspəʊkswʊmən/ noun (plural spokesmen or spokeswomen) a person who makes statements on behalf of a group 代言人; 发言人

sponge /spʌndʒ/ noun **1** a simple sea creature with no backbone and a soft porous body 海绵(一种水生无脊椎动物, 身体柔软多孔) **2** a piece of a light, absorbent substance used for washing, as padding, etc. (用于清洗或作填塞物的)海绵状物 **3** Brit. 【英】a cake made with little or no fat 海绵蛋糕, 松糕(含有极少量或不含脂肪) • verb (sponges, sponging or spongeing, sponged) **1** wipe or clean with a wet sponge or cloth 用湿海绵(或布)擦(或揩) **2** informal 【非正式】obtain money or food from other people without giving

anything in return 白要; 白拿; 白吃; 揩油 □ sponge bag Brit. 【英】a toilet bag 盥洗用品袋 ■ sponger noun spongy adjective.

sponsor /ˈspɒnsə(r)/ noun **1** a person or organization that helps pays for an event in return for advertising (以宣传为目的的)赞助人, 赞助组织 **2** a person who promises to give money to a charity if another person completes a task or activity (以他人完成某项任务或活动为条件而承诺作慈善捐款的)赞助人 **3** a person who proposes a new law (新法案的)提出者, 倡议人 • verb be a sponsor for 发起; 举办; 主办; 赞助 ■ sponsorship noun.

✔ 拼写指南 -or, not -er: sponsor. sponsor 中的 -or 不要拼作 -er。

spontaneous /spɒnˈteɪniəs/ adjective **1** done or happening as a result of an impulse 自发的; 自然产生的 **2** open, natural, and relaxed 天真率直的; 自然的; 放松随意的 **3** happening without apparent external cause 自发的, 自然发生的, 非外力诱发的 ■ spontaneity noun spontaneously adverb.

spoof /spuːf/ noun informal 【非正式】a humorous imitation of something 滑稽模仿

spook /spuːk/ informal 【非正式】noun **1** a ghost 鬼; 幽灵 **2** N. Amer. 【北美】a spy 间谍; 暗探 • verb frighten 吓唬

spooky /ˈspuːki/ adjective (spookier, spookiest) informal 【非正式】sinister or ghostly 恶意的; 阴险的; 鬼的; 鬼一般的 ■ spookily adverb

spool /spuːl/ noun a cylindrical device onto which thread, film, etc. can be wound (线、胶片等的)卷盘, 卷轴 • verb wind on to a spool 把…缠绕在卷轴上

spoon /spuːn/ noun an implement consisting of a small, shallow bowl on a long handle, used for eating and serving food 勺;匙;调羹 • **verb** transfer food with a spoon 用匙舀取 □ **spoon-feed 1** feed someone with a spoon 用匙喂(某人) **2** provide someone with so much help that they do not need to think for themselves 对(某人)填鸭式灌输 ■ **spoonful** noun.

spoonbill /ˈspuːnbɪl/ **noun** a tall wading bird that has a long bill with a very broad flat tip 琵鹭(一种高大涉禽,喙长,端部宽扁)

spoonerism /ˈspuːnərɪzəm/ **noun** a mistake in speech in which the initial sounds or letters of two or more words are accidentally swapped around, as in *you have hissed the mystery lectures* 斯本内现象,首音误置(说话时误把几个单词的首音或首字母换掉)

sporadic /spəˈrædɪk/ **adjective** happening at irregular intervals or only in a few places 不时发生的;断断续续的;零散的;分散的 ■ **sporadically** adverb.

spore /spɔː(r)/ **noun** a tiny reproductive cell produced by fungi and plants such as mosses and algae (真菌或苔藓、海藻等植物所产生的)孢子

sporran /ˈspɒrən/ **noun** a small pouch worn around the waist as part of men's Scottish Highland dress (苏格兰高地男子系在腰间的)毛皮袋

sport /spɔːt/ **noun 1** a competitive activity involving physical effort and skill 体育运动;竞技运动 **2** informal 【非正式】a person who behaves well when teased or defeated 大度的人;输得起的人 • **verb 1** wear a distinctive item 穿戴(独特的衣物) **2** literary 【文】amuse yourself or play in a lively way 娱乐;消遣;嬉戏 □ **sports car** a small, fast car 跑车 **sports jacket** a man's informal jacket resembling a suit jacket (男子在非正式场合穿的)粗花呢夹克

sporting /ˈspɔːtɪŋ/ **adjective 1** connected with or interested in sport 体育运动的;爱好体育运动的 **2** fair and generous 公正的;宽宏大量的;大度的 □ **sporting chance** a reasonable chance of winning or succeeding 合理的成功机会 ■ **sportingly** adverb.

sportive /ˈspɔːtɪv/ **adjective** playful; lighthearted 嬉戏的;爱闹着玩的;轻松愉快的;无忧无虑的

sportsman /ˈspɔːtsmən/ or **sportswoman** /ˈspɔːtswʊmən/ **noun** (plural **sportsmen** or **sportswomen**) **1** a person who takes part in a sport 体育运动爱好者;运动员 **2** a person who behaves in a fair and generous way 具有体育道德的人;有运动员风范的人 ■ **sportsmanship** noun.

sporty /ˈspɔːti/ **adjective** (**sportier**, **sportiest**) informal 【非正式】**1** fond of or good at sport 爱好运动的;擅长体育运动的 **2** (of clothing) suitable for sport or casual wear (衣服)适合运动时穿的,休闲的 **3** (of a car) compact and fast (汽车)竞赛车型的,车型紧凑且速度快的

spot /spɒt/ **noun 1** a small round mark on a surface (物体表面的)小圆点,斑点 **2** a pimple 丘疹;小脓疱 **3** a particular place, point, or position 地点;位置 **4** a small amount of something 少量;少许 • **verb** (**spots**, **spotting**, **spotted**) **1** notice or recognize, especially with difficulty or effort 注意到;认出;发现 **2** mark with spots 用点标记 □ **on the spot 1** immediately 立即;马上 **2** at the scene of an action or event 当场;当场 **spot check** a test made without warning on a person or thing selected at random 突击抽检;抽查 **spot on** completely accurate 完全正确的;准确的 ■ **spotted** adjective **spotter** noun **spotty** adjective.

spotless /ˈspɒtləs/ **adjective** absolutely clean or pure 一尘不染的;没有污点的;完美的;纯洁的 ■ **spotlessly** adverb.

spotlight /'spɒtlaɪt/ **noun 1** a lamp projecting a narrow, strong beam of light directly on to a place or person 聚光灯 **2** (**the spotlight**) intense public attention 公众注意中心 • **verb** (**spotlights, spotlighting,** past and past participle **spotlighted** or **spotlit**) light up with a spotlight 用聚光灯照明

spouse /spaʊs/ **noun** formal【正式】a husband or wife 配偶

spout /spaʊt/ **noun 1** a projecting tube or lip through or over which liquid can be poured from a container 壶嘴；口；喷嘴 **2** a stream of liquid flowing out (喷射出的)水柱，水流 • **verb 1** send out or flow in a stream 喷出；喷射 **2** express your views in a lengthy and forceful way 滔滔不绝地讲；喋喋不休地强调 □ **up the spout** Brit. informal【英，非正式】useless or ruined 无用的，毁坏了的；无可救药的

sprain /spreɪn/ **verb** wrench a joint violently so as to cause pain and swelling 扭伤(关节) • **noun** an instance of wrenching a joint 关节扭伤

sprang /spræŋ/ past of SPRING.

sprat /spræt/ **noun** a small sea fish of the herring family 黍鲱，西鲱(一种小海鱼)

sprawl /sprɔːl/ **verb 1** sit, lie, or fall with your arms and legs spread out awkwardly (笨拙地)伸开四肢坐(或躺、倒)下 **2** spread out irregularly over a large area 无规则地扩展(或延伸)；蔓延；丛生 • **noun 1** a sprawling position or movement 四肢伸开的姿势(或动作) **2** the disorganized expansion of a town or city (城市的)无序扩展

spray /spreɪ/ **noun 1** liquid sent through the air in tiny drops 喷雾；水沫；飞沫 **2** a liquid which can be forced out of an aerosol or other container in a spray 喷剂 **3** a stem or small branch with flowers and leaves 小花枝；小树枝 **4** a small bunch of cut flowers worn on clothing (戴在衣服上的)小花枝，枝状花饰 • **verb 1** apply a spray of liquid to something 喷；喷射 **2** scatter something over an area with great force (用力)喷洒

spread /spred/ **verb** (**spreads, spreading, spread**) **1** open out fully 摊开；铺开；展开 **2** stretch out hands, fingers, wings, etc. 伸开，张开，展开(手、手指或翅膀等) **3** extend over a wide area or a specified period of time 伸展；扩展；延长；延续 **4** apply a substance in an even layer 涂；敷 • **noun 1** the process of spreading 展开；伸展；张开 **2** the extent, width, or area covered by something 界限；跨度；幅员 **3** the range of something 范围；幅度 **4** a soft paste that can be spread on bread 涂抹面包的酱 **5** an article covering several pages of a newspaper or magazine (报刊上的)跨版(或跨页)的文章 **6** informal【非正式】a large and elaborate meal 丰盛的饭菜 ■ **spreader** noun.

spreadeagle /spred'iːɡl/ **verb** (**be spreadeagled**) be stretched out with the arms and legs extended 四肢伸开

spreadsheet /'spredʃiːt/ **noun** a computer program in which figures are arranged in a grid and used in calculations (计算机)电子表格程序

spree /spriː/ **noun** a short period of time spent doing a lot of a particular thing 无节制的狂热；纵乐: *a shopping spree* 疯狂购物

sprig /sprɪɡ/ **noun** a small stem with leaves or flowers, taken from a bush or plant (从灌木丛或某植株上取下带叶或花的)小枝

sprightly /'spraɪtli/ **adjective** (**sprightlier, sprightliest**) (of an old person) lively; energetic (年长者)精神矍铄的，精力充沛的 ■ **sprightliness** noun.

spring /sprɪŋ/ **verb** (**springs,**

springing, sprang or **sprung**; past participle **sprung**) **1** move suddenly upwards or forwards 跳、跃 **2** (**spring from**) come or appear from 来自；起源于；从…中涌现 **3** (**spring up**) suddenly develop or appear 迅速出现；突然兴起 **4** (**sprung**) having springs 装弹簧的 • **noun 1** the season after winter and before summer 春天；春季 **2** a spiral metal coil that returns to its former shape after being pressed or pulled 弹簧；发条 **3** a sudden jump upwards or forwards 反弹；弹回 **4** a place where water wells up from an underground source 泉；源泉 **5** the quality of being elastic 弹性；弹力 **spring-clean** clean a house or building thoroughly 彻底打扫 **spring-loaded** containing a spring that presses one part against another 装有弹簧的；弹簧承载的 **spring onion** Brit.【英】an onion taken from the ground before the bulb has formed 小葱；春葱 ■ **springy** adjective.

springboard /'sprɪŋbɔːd/ noun **1** a flexible board from which a diver or gymnast jumps in order to push off more powerfully (跳水或体操运动中的)跳板 **2** something that starts off an activity or enterprise (开展活动或事业的)助推物，基础，出发点

springbok /'sprɪŋbɒk/ noun a southern African gazelle which leaps when disturbed 跳羚(产于非洲南部，受到惊扰时跳跃)

sprinkle /'sprɪŋkl/ verb (**sprinkles, sprinkling, sprinkled**) **1** scatter or pour small drops or particles over an object or surface 撒；洒 **2** distribute something randomly throughout 用…点缀；使…星星点点地分布 • **noun** a small amount that is sprinkled 少量

sprinkler /'sprɪŋklə(r)/ noun **1** a device for watering lawns (浇草坪的)洒水器，喷洒器 **2** an automatic fire extinguisher installed in a ceiling (天花板上安装的)自动喷淋灭火装置

sprint /sprɪnt/ verb run at full speed over a short distance 短距离快速奔跑；冲刺 • **noun 1** a period of sprinting 冲刺 **2** a short, fast race 短距离赛跑 ■ **sprinter** noun.

sprite /spraɪt/ noun an elf or fairy 小精灵；仙子

spritzer /'sprɪtsə(r)/ noun a mixture of wine and soda water 斯普瑞兹(由葡萄酒加苏打水混合而成)

sprocket /'sprɒkɪt/ noun each of several projections on the rim of a wheel that engage with the links of a chain or with holes in film, paper, etc. 链齿，链轮齿

sprout /spraʊt/ verb produce shoots; begin to grow 发芽；抽条；长出 • **noun 1** a shoot of a plant 新芽；嫩枝 **2** a Brussels sprout 汤菜；孢子甘蓝；球芽甘蓝

spruce[1] /spruːs/ adjective neat and smart 整洁漂亮的 • **verb** (**spruces, sprucing, spruced**) (**spruce someone/thing up**) make someone or something smarter 使…整洁漂亮，把…打扮得整洁漂亮

spruce[2] noun an evergreen tree with hanging cones 云杉

sprung /sprʌŋ/ past and past participle of SPRING.

spry /spraɪ/ adjective (of an old person) lively (年长者)精力旺盛的，充满活力的

spud /spʌd/ noun informal【非正式】a potato 土豆

spume /spjuːm/ noun literary【文】froth or foam 泡沫

spun /spʌn/ past and past participle of SPIN.

spunk /spʌŋk/ noun informal【非正式】courage and determination 勇气；决心 ■ **spunky** adjective.

spur /spɜː(r)/ noun **1** a spiked device worn on a rider's heel for urging a horse forward 马刺，靴刺 **2** encouragement 激励；鼓舞 **3** an area of high ground that sticks out from a mountain 尖坡；山鼻子 **4** a short branch road or railway line (公路或铁路的)支线，岔线 • verb (**spurs, spurring, spurred**) **1** encourage someone to do something, or make something happen faster or sooner 鼓励；激励；促进；使加速 **2** urge a horse forward with spurs 用马刺踢(马) □ **on the spur of the moment** on a sudden impulse; without planning in advance 一时冲动之下；即兴

spurious /'spjʊəriəs/ **adjective 1** false or fake 假的；伪造的；欺骗性的 **2** (of reasoning) apparently but not actually correct (推理)似是而非的 ■ **spuriously** adverb.

spurn /spɜːn/ **verb** reject in a contemptuous way 轻蔑拒绝；唾弃

spurt /spɜːt/ **verb 1** gush out in a stream 喷出；冒出 **2** move with a sudden burst of speed 突然加速行进；冲，冲刺 • **noun 1** a gushing stream 喷射流 **2** a sudden burst of activity or speed (活动的)突然性进展，突然加速

sputter /'spʌtə(r)/ **verb** (**sputters, sputtering, sputtered**) make a series of soft explosive sounds 发出劈啪声 • **noun** a sputtering sound 劈啪声

sputum /'spjuːtəm/ **noun** saliva and mucus that is coughed up 痰

spy /spaɪ/ **noun** (plural **spies**) a person who secretly collects information about an enemy or competitor 间谍；密探 • **verb** (**spies, spying, spied**) **1** be a spy 从事间谍活动 **2** (**spy on**) watch secretly 暗中监视；暗中侦查 **3** see or notice 看见；注意到

spyglass /'spaɪglɑːs/ **noun** a small telescope 小型望远镜

spyhole /'spaɪhəʊl/ **noun** Brit. 【英】a peephole 窥视孔

sq. /skweə/ **abbreviation** square.

squab /skwɒb/ **noun** a young pigeon that has not yet left the nest 雏鸽

squabble /'skwɒbl/ **noun** a noisy quarrel about something unimportant 争吵；口角 • **verb** (**squabbles, squabbling, squabbled**) have a squabble 争吵

squad /skwɒd/ **noun 1** a division of a police force 警队；办案组 **2** a group of sports players from which a team is chosen 运动队 **3** a small group of soldiers (军队的)班

squaddie /'skwɒdi/ **noun** (plural **squaddies**) Brit. informal【英，非正式】a private soldier 列兵；陆军二等兵

squadron /'skwɒdrən/ **noun** a unit of an air force (空军的)中队 **2** a group of warships 舰队

squalid /'skwɒlɪd/ **adjective 1** very dirty and unpleasant 污秽的；肮脏的 **2** immoral or dishonest 道德败坏的；卑鄙的；不诚实的

squall /skwɔːl/ **noun 1** a sudden violent gust of wind 暴风；狂风 **2** a loud cry 大喊；大叫 • **verb** (of a baby) cry noisily and continuously (婴儿)不停地大声啼哭

squalor /'skwɒlə(r)/ **noun** the state of being squalid 污秽；肮脏

squander /'skwɒndə(r)/ **verb** (**squanders, squandering, squandered**) waste time, money, etc. in a reckless or foolish way 浪费，挥霍(时间、金钱等)

square /skweə(r)/ **noun 1** a flat shape with four equal straight sides and four right angles 四方形；正方形 **2** an open area surrounded by buildings (建筑物围绕的)方形广场 **3** the product of a number multiplied by itself 平方 **4** an L-shaped or T-shaped instrument used for obtaining or testing right angles 直角尺；丁字尺 **5** informal【非正式】an old-fashioned or boring person 古板守旧之人；无聊乏味之人 • **adjective 1** having the shape of a square 正方形的 **2** having or forming a right angle 有方角的；构成方角的 **3** (of a unit of measurement) equal to the area of a square whose side is of the unit specified (计量单位)平方…的: *2,000 square feet* 2,000 平方英尺 **4** referring to the length of each side of a square shape or object (正方形或正方体)各边长…的: *ten metres square* 10 米见方 **5** level or parallel 水平的；平行的 **6** broad and solid in shape 宽阔结实的；魁梧的 **7** fair or honest 公平的；公正的；诚实的 **8** informal 【非正式】old-fashioned or boringly conventional 古板守旧的；保守的；安分守己的 • adverb directly; straight 直接地；直截了当地 • verb (squares, squaring, squared) **1** make something square or rectangular 使成正方形(或矩形) **2** (squared) marked out in squares 用方形标出的 **3** multiply a number by itself 使(某数)成平方 **4** (square with) make or be consistent with 使与…相符或与…一致 **5** settle a bill or debt 结清，付清(账单或债务) **6** make the score of a game even 使(比分)成平局 **7** (square up) take up the position of a person about to fight 摆好打架的姿势 □ **square dance** a country dance that starts with four couples facing one another in a square (四对男女面对面围成方形跳的)方形舞 **square meal** a large and balanced meal 美餐；丰盛的一餐 ■ **squarely** adverb.

squash[1] /skwɒʃ/ verb **1** crush or squeeze something so that it becomes flat or distorted 压扁；挤扁；压烂；挤烂 **2** force into a restricted space 挤入；挤进；塞入 **3** stop something from continuing or developing 制止；打断；压制 • noun **1** a state of being squashed 挤压；压紧 **2** Brit. 【英】a concentrated liquid mixed with water to make a fruit-flavoured drink 果汁饮料 **3** (also **squash rackets**) a game in which two players use rackets to hit a small rubber ball against the walls of a closed court 壁球(运动)(在封闭球场内用球拍将小橡皮球向墙上击打的运动) ■ **squashy** adjective.

squash[2] noun a type of vegetable like a marrows 笋瓜；西葫芦

squat /skwɒt/ verb (squats, squatting, squatted) **1** crouch or sit with the knees bent and the heels close to the thighs 蹲；蹲坐；盘腿坐 **2** unlawfully occupy an uninhabited building or area of land 非法占用(建筑物或土地) • adjective short or low and wide 矮胖的；粗短的；低矮的；矮而宽的 • noun **1** a squatting position 蹲；蹲坐 **2** a building occupied by squatters 擅自占用的建筑物 ■ **squatter** noun.

squaw /skwɔː/ noun offensive 【冒犯】an American Indian woman or wife 美洲印第安女人(或老婆)

squawk /skwɔːk/ verb **1** (of a bird) make a loud, harsh noise (鸟)发出刺耳尖叫 **2** say something in a loud, ugly tone 叫嚷；声嘶力竭地叫 • noun a squawking sound 刺耳的尖叫声

squeak /skwiːk/ noun a short, high-pitched sound or cry 短促的尖叫声 • verb **1** make a squeak 尖叫 **2** say something in a highpitched tone 尖声说出 ■ **squeaky** adjective.

squeal /skwiːl/ noun a long, high-pitched cry or noise 长而尖的叫声 • verb **1** make a squeal 发出长而尖的叫声 **2** say something in a high-pitched tone 尖着声音说话 **3** (squeal on) informal 【非正式】inform on 告发；告密

squeamish /ˈskwiːmɪʃ/ adjective **1** easily disgusted or made to feel sick 易产生厌恶感的；神经质的；易恶心的 **2** having very strong moral views 道德观念很强的

squeegee /ˈskwiːdʒiː/ noun a scraping tool with a rubber-edged blade, used for cleaning windows (用

于擦窗户的)橡皮刷帚

squeeze /skwiːz/ **verb (squeezes, squeezing, squeezed) 1** firmly press from opposite sides 用力挤压 **2** extract liquid from something by squeezing 榨取;挤取 **3** manage to get into or through a restricted space 硬挤进,硬塞入(狭小的空间) • **noun 1** an act of squeezing 榨取;挤压 **2** a hug 拥抱;紧抱 **3** a small amount of liquid extracted by squeezing 榨出物;挤出物 **4** a strong financial demand or pressure 拮据;经济困难;银根紧缩 ■ **squeezy** adjective.

squelch /skweltʃ/ **verb** make a soft sucking sound, e.g. by treading in thick mud 发嘎吱声;发吧唧唧声 • **noun** a squelching sound 吧唧声;扑哧声 ■ **squelchy** adjective.

squib /skwɪb/ **noun** a small firework 小爆竹;小鞭炮

squid /skwɪd/ **noun** (plural **squid** or **squids**) a sea creature with a long body, eight arms, and two long tentacles 枪乌贼;鱿鱼

squiffy /ˈskwɪfi/ **adjective** Brit. informal 【英,非正式】 slightly drunk 微醉的

squiggle /ˈskwɪɡl/ **noun** a short line that curls and loops irregularly 弯曲的短线条;波形曲线 ■ **squiggly** adjective.

squint /skwɪnt/ **verb 1** look at someone or something with your eyes partly closed 眯着眼看 **2** have a squint affecting one eye 斜视 • **noun 1** a condition in which one eye looks in a different direction from the other 斜视 **2** informal 【非正式】 a quick or casual look 斜眼一瞥;一瞥

squire /ˈskwaɪə(r)/ **noun 1** a country gentleman 乡绅 **2** (in the past) a young nobleman who acted as an attendant to a knight (旧时骑士的)随从

squirm /skwɜːm/ **verb 1** wriggle or twist the body from side to side 扭动;蠕动 **2** be embarrassed or ashamed 局促不安;感到惭愧 • **noun** a

wriggling movement 扭动;蠕动

squirrel /ˈskwɪrəl/ **noun** a bushy-tailed rodent which lives in trees 松鼠 • **verb** (**squirrels, squirrelling, squirrelled**; US spelling 【美拼作】 **squirrels, squirreling, squirreled**) (**squirrel something away**) hide money or valuables in a safe place 把…藏起来;把…储藏好

squirt /skwɜːt/ **verb 1** force liquid out in a thin jet from a small opening 使(液体)喷;使喷射 **2** wet with a jet of liquid 被(一股液体)喷溅 • **noun 1** a thin jet of liquid 喷流;射流 **2** informal 【非正式】 a weak or insignificant person 懦弱的人;无足轻重的人

squish /skwɪʃ/ **verb 1** make a soft squelching sound 嘎吱作响;发吧唧声 **2** informal 【非正式】 squash 挤压;压扁 • **noun** a soft squelching sound 嘎吱声;吧唧声 ■ **squishy** adjective.

Sri Lankan /sri ˈlæŋkən/ **noun** a person from Sri Lanka 斯里兰卡人 • **adjective** relating to Sri Lanka 斯里兰卡的

SS /es ˈes/ **abbreviation 1** Saints 圣人;圣徒 **2** steamship. • **noun** the Nazi special police force 党卫军

St abbreviation 1 Saint. **2** Street. **3** (**st**) stone (in weight).

stab /stæb/ **verb** (**stabs, stabbing, stabbed**) **1** thrust a knife or other pointed weapon into (用刀或其他利器)刺,戳,刺伤,戳伤 **2** thrust a pointed object at 用尖利物刺(或捅、戳) **3** (of a pain) cause a sudden sharp feeling 使有刺痛感 • **noun 1** an act of stabbing 刺;戳;刺伤;戳伤 **2** a sudden sharp feeling or pain 一阵剧痛 **3** (**a stab at**) informal 【非正式】 an attempt to do 尝试

stability /stəˈbɪləti/ **noun** the state of being stable 稳定;稳定性

stabilize or **stabilise** /ˈsteɪbəlaɪz/ **verb** (**stabilizes, stabilizing, stabilized**) make or become stable (使)稳定;(使)稳固 ■ **stabilization** noun

stabilizer noun.

stable[1] /'steɪbl/ **adjective 1** not likely to give way or overturn; firmly fixed 稳固的；牢固的，稳定的 **2** not worsening in health after an injury or operation (受伤或手术后)病情稳定的 **3** emotionally well balanced (感情或情绪)稳定的，持重的，稳重的 **4** not likely to change or fail 不可能发生改变(或失去作用)的，稳定的
■ **stably** adverb.

stable[2] **noun 1** a building in which horses are kept 马厩；马棚 **2** an establishment where racehorses are kept and trained 赛马训练场 • **verb** (**stables, stabling, stabled**) put or keep a horse in a stable 使(马)入厩，把(马)拴在马厩

stablemate /'steɪblmeɪt/ **noun** a horse from the same stable as another 同厩之马

staccato /stə'kɑːtəʊ/ **adjective** Music 【音乐】 with each sound or note sharply separated from the others 断音的；断奏的

stack /stæk/ **noun 1** a neat pile of objects (整齐的)一堆，一叠 **2** a rectangular or cylindrical pile of hay, straw, etc. (稻草、麦秆等的)堆，垛 **3** informal 【非正式】 a large quantity 大量；许多 **4** a chimney 烟囱 • **verb 1** arrange in a stack 堆成堆；堆成垛 **2** fill or cover with stacks of things 用(大堆东西)堆满(或覆盖) **3** cause aircraft to fly at different altitudes while waiting to land 使(飞机)分层盘旋等待着陆 **4** arrange a pack of cards dishonestly 洗(牌)作弊

stadium /'steɪdɪəm/ **noun** (plural **stadiums** or **stadia** /'steɪdɪə/) a sports ground with rows of seats for spectators (设有看台的)露天体育场

staff /stɑːf/ **noun 1** the employees of an organization 全体职员；全体雇员 **2** a group of military officers assisting an officer in command (军队的)全体参谋人员 **3** a long stick used as a support or weapon 拐杖；警棍 **4** a rod or sceptre held as a symbol of authority 权杖；官杖；指挥棒 **5** Music 【音乐】 a stave 五线谱 • **verb** provide an organization with staff 为(组织)配备人员 □ **staff nurse** Brit.【英】 an experienced nurse less senior than a sister (有经验的)医院护士(比护士长低一级)

stag /stæg/ **noun** a fully adult male deer 成年雄鹿 □ **stag night** an all-male celebration held for a man who is about to get married (为即将结婚的男子举行的)男子聚会

stage /steɪdʒ/ **noun 1** a point or step in a process or development 阶段；时期 **2** a raised platform on which actors, entertainers, or speakers perform 舞台；高台 **3** (**the stage**) the acting profession 戏剧表演，戏剧工作；演员职业 **4** a platform on to which passengers or cargo can be landed from a boat 浮码头 • **verb** (**stages, staging, staged**) **1** present a performance of a play 演出(剧本) **2** organize an event 组织(活动) □ **stage fright** nervousness before or during a performance (演员上场前后的)怯场 **stage-manage** arrange something carefully to create a certain effect (为达到某种效果而)周密安排 **stage manager** the person responsible for lighting and other technical arrangements for a play 舞台监督 **stage-struck** having a strong desire to become an actor 渴望当演员的 **stage whisper** a loud whisper by an actor on stage, intended to be heard by the audience (演员有意让观众听见的)舞台低语，低声旁白 **staging post** a regular stop on a journey (旅途中的)驿站

stagecoach /'steɪdʒkəʊtʃ/ **noun** a horse-drawn vehicle formerly used to carry passengers along a regular route (旧时在两地之间沿固定路线往返运送乘客的)驿站马车

stagehand /'steɪdʒhænd/ **noun** a person who deals with the scenery or props for a play (演出中负责布景或道具的)舞台工作人员

stagger /'stægə(r)/ **verb** (staggers, staggering, staggered) 1 walk or move unsteadily 蹒跚;摇晃;跟跄 2 astonish 使吃惊 3 spread over a period of time 使(时间)错开 • **noun** an unsteady walk 蹒跚;摇晃;跟跄

stagnant /'stægnənt/ **adjective** 1 (of water or air) not moving and having an unpleasant smell (水或空气)不流动的,污浊的 2 showing little activity 不活跃的;死气沉沉的;不发展的,停滞的

stagnate /stæg'neɪt/ **verb** (stagnates, stagnating, stagnated) become stagnant 不流动;变得污浊;变得死气沉沉;停滞;不发展 ■ **stagnation** noun.

stagy or **stagey** /'steɪdʒi/ **adjective** very theatrical or exaggerated 演戏似的;做作的;装腔作势的

staid /steɪd/ **adjective** respectable and unadventurous 端庄的;稳重的;古板的

stain /steɪn/ **verb** 1 mark or discolour with something that is not easily removed 沾污;污染 2 damage someone's reputation 玷污,败坏,损害(名声) 3 colour with a dye or chemical 给⋯染色;给⋯着色 • **noun** 1 a discoloured patch or mark 色斑;污点;污迹 2 a thing that damages someone's reputation (名声上的)污点 3 a dye or chemical used to colour materials 染色剂;着色剂 □ **stained glass** coloured glass used to form pictures or designs (拼成图画或装饰性图案的)着色玻璃,彩色玻璃 **stainless steel** a form of steel containing chromium, resistant to tarnishing and rust 不锈钢 ■ **stainless** adjective.

stair /steə(r)/ **noun** 1 each of a set of fixed steps 梯级 2 (stairs) a set of steps leading from one floor of a building to another 楼梯

staircase /'steəkeɪs/ or **stairway** /'steəweɪ/ **noun** a set of stairs and its surrounding structure 楼梯

stairwell /'steəwel/ **noun** a shaft in which a staircase is built 楼梯井

stake¹ /steɪk/ **noun** a strong post driven into the ground to support a tree, form part of a fence, etc. 桩;标桩;篱笆桩 • **verb** (stakes, staking, staked) 1 support with a stake 用桩支撑 2 (stake something out) mark an area with stakes to claim ownership 用桩把⋯围起(以宣布其所有权) 3 (stake someone/thing out) informal 【非正式】keep a place or person under observation 监视

stake² **noun** 1 a sum of money gambled 赌金;赌本;赌注 2 a share or interest in a business or situation (生意的)股本,股份;利害关系 3 (stakes) prize money 奖金 4 (stakes) a competitive situation 有奖比赛;争夺赛 • **verb** (stakes, staking, staked) gamble money or valuables 以(钱或贵重物品)打赌 □ **at stake** 1 at risk 在危险中;在危急关头 2 in question 成问题地;有疑问地

stalactite /'stæləktaɪt/ **noun** a tapering structure hanging from the roof of a cave, formed of calcium salts deposited by dripping water 钟乳石

stalagmite /'stæləgmaɪt/ **noun** a tapering column rising from the floor of a cave, formed of calcium salts deposited by dripping water 石笋

stale /steɪl/ **adjective** 1 (of food) no longer fresh (食物)不新鲜的,走味的 2 no longer new and interesting 陈腐的;没有新意的;无趣味的 3 no longer interested or motivated 厌倦的;乏味的;没精打采的 ■ **staleness** noun.

stalemate /'steɪlmeɪt/ **noun** 1 a situation in which further progress

by opposing sides seems impossible
僵持；僵局 **2** Chess【象棋】a position in which a player is not in check but can only move into check 王棋受困；僵局

stalk¹ /stɔ:k/ **noun 1** the stem of a plant or support of a leaf, flower, or fruit (植物的)茎，秆；(叶)柄；(花或果的)梗 **2** a slender support or stem 肉柄；肉茎

stalk² **verb 1** follow or approach stealthily 暗中跟踪；暗中靠近 **2** obsessively follow, watch, or try to communicate with a particular person 过分关注；不断纠缠 **3** walk in a proud, stiff, or angry way (高傲或气愤地)大步走 ■ **stalker** noun.

stall /stɔ:l/ **noun 1** a stand or booth where goods are sold in a market (市场的)货摊，摊位 **2** a compartment for an animal in a stable or cowshed (马厩或牛棚内的)隔栏，分隔间 **3** a compartment in which a horse is held before the start of a race (赛马开始前各匹马站位的)单间马房 **4** a compartment in a set of toilets (洗手间的)分隔间 **5** (**stalls**) Brit.【英】the ground-floor seats in a theatre (剧院内的)正厅前排座位 **6** a seat in the choir or chancel of a church (教堂内唱诗班或圣坛上的)牧师席位 • **verb 1** (of a vehicle's engine) suddenly stop running (车辆的发动机)熄火，抛锚 **2** stop making progress 停滞不前；停止 **3** be vague or indecisive so as to gain more time to deal with something 有意拖延；有意推迟 **4** (of an aircraft) be moving too slowly to be controlled effectively (飞机)失速

stallion /'stælɪən/ **noun** an adult male horse that has not been castrated 牡马；种马

stalwart /'stɔ:lwət/ **adjective** loyal, reliable, and hard-working 忠诚的；可靠的；勤勉的 • **noun** a stalwart supporter or member of an organiza-tion (某一组织的)坚定分子

stamen /'steɪmən/ **noun** a male fertilizing organ of a flower 雄蕊

stamina /'stæmɪnə/ **noun** the ability to keep up effort over a long period 精力；耐力；持久力

stammer /'stæmə(r)/ **verb** (**stammers, stammering, stammered**) speak or say with difficulty, making sudden pauses and repeating the first letters of words 结巴；口吃 • **noun** a tendency to stammer 结巴；口吃

stamp /stæmp/ **verb 1** bring down your foot heavily 踩(脚)；猛踩；猛踩 **2** walk with heavy, forceful steps 重步走 **3** (**stamp something out**) decisively put an end to something 消灭；粉碎；毁灭 **4** press with a device that leaves a mark or pattern 在…上压印标记(或图案) • **noun 1** a small piece of paper stuck to a letter or parcel to record payment of postage 邮票 **2** an instrument for stamping a pattern or mark 印章；图章 **3** a mark or pattern made by a stamp 印记；戳记 **4** a characteristic impression or quality 不可磨灭的印象；特征 **5** an act of stamping the foot 跺脚；踩踏 □ **stamp duty** a tax on some legal documents 印花税 **stamping ground** a place you regularly visit or spend time in 常去的场所；经常出没之处

stampede /stæm'pi:d/ **noun 1** a sudden panicked rush of a number of horses, cattle, etc. (马、牛等的)惊跑，惊逃 **2** a sudden mass movement or reaction due to interest or panic 蜂拥；涌向；惊跑；逃窜 • **verb** (**stampedes, stampeding, stampeded**) take part in a stampede 蜂拥；惊跑；逃窜

stance /stæns/ **noun 1** the way in which someone stands 站姿 **2** an attitude or standpoint 态度；立场；姿态

stanch /stɔ:ntʃ/ US spelling of

STAUNCH², staunch² 的美式拼法

stanchion /ˈstænʃən/ *noun* an upright bar, post, or frame forming a support or barrier 栅柱；支柱；框架

stand /stænd/ *verb* (**stands, standing, stood**) **1** be or become upright, supported by the feet 站立；起立 **2** place or be situated in a particular position 放置；位于；坐落 **3** remain stationary, undisturbed, or unchanged 固定；静止；保持不变 **4** be in a particular state or condition 处于(某种状态或境况) **5** tolerate or like 忍受；容忍；喜欢 **6** Brit. 【英】be a candidate in an election 候选；竞选 • *noun* **1** an attitude towards an issue 态度；立场；观点 **2** a determined effort to hold your ground or resist something 捍卫；坚决反抗；抵御；抵制 **3** a structure for holding or displaying something (盛放或陈列物品的)架，座，几，台 **4** a large structure for spectators to sit or stand in 看台 **5** a raised platform for a band, orchestra, or speaker 舞台；讲台 **6** a stall from which goods are sold or displayed 售货处；货摊；展台 **7** (**the stand**) the witness box in a law court (法庭上的)证人席 **8** a stopping of motion or progress 停止；中断 ☐ **stand by 1** look on without becoming involved 袖手旁观 **2** support or remain loyal to 支持；忠于 **3** be ready to take action if needed 做好准备；准备行动 **stand down** (or **aside**) resign from a position or office 辞职 **stand for 1** be an abbreviation of or symbol for 代表；象征 **2** put up with 忍受；容忍 **stand in** deputize for someone 代表；代理 **stand-off** a deadlock between two opponents (对立双方的)僵持局面 **stand-offish** informal 【非正式】distant and cold in manner 冷漠的；冷淡的 **stand out 1** stick out or be easily noticeable 突出；显眼；引人注目 **2** be clearly better 突出；出色；

杰出 **stand someone up** informal 【非正式】fail to keep a date with someone 对(某人)失约；未如约与(某人)见面 **stand up for** speak or act in support of 支持；维护

> **! 注意** use **standing** rather than **stood** with the verb 'to be': say *we were standing in a line for hours* rather than *we were stood in a line for hours.* 与动词 to be 连用时，要用 standing，而不要用 stood。例如，应该说 we were standing there for hours (我们在那儿排队排了好几个小时)，而不说 we were stood there for hours。

standard /ˈstændəd/ *noun* **1** a level of quality or achievement 标准；水平 **2** a measure or model used to make comparisons (用来作比较的)标准，规范 **3** (**standards**) principles of good behaviour 行为准则；行为规范 **4** a military or ceremonial flag 军旗；彩旗 • *adjective* used or accepted as normal or average 标准的；符合标准的，规范的 ☐ **standard-bearer 1** a leading figure in a cause or movement 领袖 **2** a soldier who carries a military or ceremonial flag 掌旗兵；旗手 **standard English** 标准英语 **standard lamp** a tall lamp that is placed on the floor 落地灯 **standard of living** the degree of comfort that a person or community has 生活水平

standardize or **standardise** /ˈstændədaɪz/ *verb* (**standardizes, standardizing, standardized**) make something fit in with a standard 使标准化；使合乎标准 ∎ **standardization** *noun*.

standby /ˈstændbaɪ/ *noun* (plural **standbys**) **1** readiness for duty or action 随时待命 **2** a person or thing ready to be used in an emergency 后备人员；备用物资 • *adjective* (of tickets) sold only at the last minute

(票)机动的,备用的

standing /ˈstændɪŋ/ **noun 1** position, status, or reputation 地位;身份;名声 **2** duration or length 持续时间 • **adjective** remaining in force or use 长期存在的;长期有效的;持久的: *a standing invitation* 长期有效的邀请 □ **standing joke** something that regularly causes amusement 老笑话 **standing order** Brit. 【英】an instruction to a bank to make regular fixed payments to someone 委托银行定期付款的)按期付款委托书 **standing ovation** a long period of applause during which the audience rise to their feet 长时间起立鼓掌

standpoint /ˈstændpɔɪnt/ **noun** an attitude towards a particular issue 立场;观点

standstill /ˈstændstɪl/ **noun** a situation or condition without movement or activity 停顿;停滞

stank /stæŋk/ past of STINK.

stanza /ˈstænzə/ **noun** a group of lines forming the basic unit in a poem 诗节

staple[1] /ˈsteɪpl/ **noun 1** a small piece of wire used to fasten papers together 订书钉 **2** a small U-shaped metal bar driven into wood to hold things in place U 形钉 • **verb** (**staples**, **stapling**, **stapled**) secure with a staple or staples 用订书钉钉;用 U 形钉固定 ■ **stapler** noun.

staple[2] **noun 1** a main item of trade or production 主要商品;主要产品 **2** a main or important element 主要成分;主要内容 • **adjective** main or important 主要的;重要的

star /stɑː(r)/ **noun 1** a large ball of burning gas which appears as a glowing point in the night sky 恒星;星 **2** a simplified representation of a star with five or six points 星号;星级 **3** a famous entertainer or sports player (娱乐界或体育界的)明星 • **verb** (**stars**, **starring**, **starred**)

1 have someone as a leading performer 由…主演;由…担任主角 **2** have a leading role in a film, play, etc. 主演;担任主角 □ **Stars and Stripes** the national flag of the US 美国国旗,星条旗 **star sign** a sign of the zodiac 星座 ■ **stardom** noun.

starboard /ˈstɑːbəd/ **noun** the side of a ship or aircraft that is on the right when you are facing forward (船或飞机的)右舷,右侧

starch /stɑːtʃ/ **noun 1** a carbohydrate which is obtained from potatoes, flour, rice, etc. and is an important part of the human diet 淀粉 **2** powder or spray used to stiffen fabric (浆织物用的)淀粉浆 • **verb** stiffen with starch 用淀粉上浆

starchy /ˈstɑːtʃi/ **adjective** (**starchier**, **starchiest**) **1** containing a lot of starch 淀粉多的;高淀粉的 **2** informal 【非正式】stiff and formal in manner 古板的;拘谨的

stare /steə(r)/ **verb** (**stares**, **staring**, **stared**) look with concentration and the eyes wide open 凝视;注视;目不转睛地看 • **noun** an act of staring 凝视;注视

starfish /ˈstɑːfɪʃ/ **noun** (plural **starfish** or **starfishes**) a sea creature having five or more arms extending from a central point 海星(一种海洋生物)

stark /stɑːk/ **adjective 1** severe or bare in appearance 朴素的;不加装饰的;赤裸的;一丝不挂的 **2** unpleasantly or sharply clear 突出的;明显的 **3** complete; sheer 完全的;十足的: *stark terror* 极端的恐惧 □ **stark naked** completely naked 一丝不挂的;赤裸的 ■ **starkly** adverb.

starkers /ˈstɑːkəz/ **adjective** Brit. informal 【英,非正式】completely naked 一丝不挂的;赤裸的

starlet /ˈstɑːlət/ **noun** informal 【非正式】a promising young actress or performer 有前途的年轻女演员(或表演者)

starling /'stɑːlɪŋ/ **noun** a bird with shiny dark speckled feathers 椋鸟

starry /'stɑːri/ **adjective** (**starrier, starriest**) full of or lit by stars 布满星星的；星光照耀的 □ **starry-eyed** full of unrealistic hopes or dreams 不切实际的；充满幻想的；空想的

starship /'stɑːʃɪp/ **noun** (in science fiction) a spaceship for travel between stars (科幻小说中的)星际飞船

start /stɑːt/ **verb 1** begin to do or happen 开始 **2** begin to operate or start working 开始做；着手 **3** make something happen or start working 使发生；使开始；使启动 **4** begin to move or travel 出发；动身；启程 **5** (**start out** or **up**) begin a project or undertaking 开始(某工程)；开始从事(某项工作) **6** jump or jerk from surprise 惊起；吓一跳 • **noun 1** an act of beginning 开始 **2** the point at which something begins 开端；起点 **3** an advantage given to a competitor at the beginning of a race (比赛中的)先起跑的优势，抢先的优势 **4** a sudden movement of surprise 突然跳起；吃惊

starter /'stɑːtə(r)/ **noun 1** a person or thing that starts 起始者；启动者；启动装置 **2** the first course of a meal 第一道菜，开胃品

startle /'stɑːtl/ **verb** (**startles, startling, startled**) make someone feel sudden shock or alarm 惊吓，使吃惊；使惊奇

startling /'stɑːtlɪŋ/ **adjective** very surprising 令人吃惊的；令人震惊的 ■ **startlingly** adverb.

starve /stɑːv/ **verb** (**starves, starving, starved**) **1** suffer or die from hunger 挨饿；饿死 **2** make someone starve 使挨饿；使饿死 **3** (**be starving** or **starved**) informal 【非正式】feel very hungry 饿得慌；饿得要死 **4** (**be starved of**) be deprived of 匮乏；急需 ■ **starvation** noun.

stash /stæʃ/ informal 【非正式】**verb** store safely in a secret place 隐藏；藏匿 • **noun** a secret store 隐藏；藏匿

stasis /'steɪsɪs/ **noun** formal 【正式】a period or state when there is no activity or change 静止；停滞

state /steɪt/ **noun 1** the condition of someone or something at a particular time 状况；情况，状态 **2** a country considered as an organized political community 国家 **3** an area forming part of a federal republic 州；邦 **4** (**the States**) the United States of America 美国 **5** the government of a country 政府 **6** the ceremonial procedures associated with monarchy or government (君主国或政府的)礼仪，仪式 **7** (**a state**) informal 【非正式】an agitated, untidy, or dirty condition 零乱；不整洁 • **verb** (**states, stating, stated**) express definitely in speech or writing 陈述；说明；声明 □ **state-of-the-art** up to date 最新的；最新式的；最先进的 ■ **stateless** adjective.

stately /'steɪtli/ **adjective** (**statelier, stateliest**) dignified, imposing, or grand 威严的；庄重的，堂皇的 □ **stately home** Brit.【英】a large and fine house occupied or formerly occupied by an aristocratic family (旧时贵族居住的)豪华住宅

statement /'steɪtmənt/ **noun 1** a clear expression of something in speech or writing 陈述；叙述；说明 **2** an account of events given to the police or in court (提供给警察或法庭的)陈述，供述 **3** a list of amounts paid into and out of a bank account (银行的)账户记录，报表，结算单

stateside /'steɪtsaɪd/ **adjective & adverb** informal 【非正式】relating to or towards the US 美国的；去美国(的)，向美国的

statesman /'steɪtsmən/ or **stateswoman** /'steɪtswʊmən/ **noun** (plural **statesmen** or **stateswomen**) an experienced and respected political leader 政治家

static /'stætɪk/ **adjective** not moving, acting, or changing 静止的；静态的；不变的 • **noun 1** (also **static electricity**) an electric charge acquired by an object that is not a conductor of electricity 静电 **2** crackling or hissing on a telephone, radio, etc. (电话、电台等的)静电噪声，静电干扰 ■ **statically** adverb.

station /'steɪʃn/ **noun 1** a place where passenger trains stop on a railway line 火车站 **2** a place where an activity or service is based (进行某项活动或提供某种服务的)站，局，所 **3** a broadcasting company 广播电台；电视台 **4** the place where someone or something stands or is placed 岗位；驻地；位置 **5** dated【废】a person's social rank or position 地位；身份 • **verb** put someone in a particular place or position 安置；配置；派驻；使驻扎 ▢ **station wagon** N. Amer. & Austral./NZ【北美和澳/新西兰】an estate car 客货两用轿车；旅行轿车

stationary /'steɪʃənri/ **adjective** not moving or changing 静止的；停滞的；不变的；稳定的

> **！注意** don't confuse **stationary** and **stationery**: **stationary** means 'not moving or changing', whereas **stationery** means 'paper and other writing materials'. 不要混淆 stationary 和 stationery: stationary 是形容词，表示"静止的，不变的"；而 stationery 是名词，意为"文具"。

stationer /'steɪʃənə(r)/ **noun** a person who sells stationery 文具商

stationery /'steɪʃənri/ **noun** paper and other materials needed for writing 文具

stationmaster /'steɪʃnmɑːstə(r)/ **noun** a person in charge of a railway station (火车站)站长

statistic /stə'tɪstɪk/ **noun 1** (**statistics**) the collection and analysis of large amounts of information shown in numbers 统计值；统计量 **2** a fact or piece of data obtained from a study of statistics 统计资料；统计数据 ■ **statistician** noun.

statistical /stə'tɪstɪkl/ **adjective** having to do with statistics 统计的；统计学的 ■ **statistically** adverb.

statuary /'stætʃuəri/ **noun** statues 雕像；塑像；铸像

statue /'stætʃuː/ **noun** a model of a person or animal made of stone, metal, etc. 雕像；塑像；铸像

statuesque /ˌstætʃu'esk/ **adjective** (of a woman) attractively tall and dignified (女子)高挑的，端庄优雅的

statuette /ˌstætʃu'et/ **noun** a small statue 小雕像，小塑像，小铸像

stature /'stætʃə(r)/ **noun 1** a person's height when they are standing 身高；个子 **2** importance or reputation 重要地位；声望；名望

status /'steɪtəs/ **noun 1** a person's social or professional position 地位；身份 **2** high rank or social standing 重要地位；高位 **3** the situation at a particular time 情形；状况；状态 ▢ **status symbol** a possession intended to show a person's wealth or high status 地位象征

status quo /ˌsteɪtəs 'kwəʊ/ **noun** the existing situation 现状

statute /'stætʃuːt/ **noun 1** a written law 成文法；法令；法规 **2** a rule of an organization or institution 规章；条约

statutory /'stætʃətri/ **adjective 1** required or permitted by law 依照法令的；法定的；法令的 **2** done or happening regularly and therefore expected 规律的；可以预期的

staunch¹ /stɔːntʃ/ **adjective** very loyal and committed 忠实的；可靠的 ■ **staunchly** adverb.

staunch² (US spelling【美拼作】**stanch**) **verb** stop or slow down a flow of blood 止(血)

stave /steɪv/ **noun 1** any of the lengths of wood fixed side by side to make a barrel, bucket, etc. (木桶、提桶等的)桶板，桶材 **2** a strong stick, post or pole 棒；杖 **3** (also **staff**) Music【音乐】a set of five parallel lines which notes are written on or between 五线谱 • verb (**staves, staving**, past and past participle **staved** or **stove**) **1** (**stave something in**) break something by forcing it inwards 压坏；击破 **2** (past and past participle **staved**) (**stave something off**) stop or delay something bad or dangerous 阻止；制止，推迟(不好的或危险的事物)

stay /steɪ/ **verb 1** remain in the same place 停留；逗留 **2** remain in a particular state or position 保持；维持 **3** live somewhere temporarily as a visitor or guest 逗留；暂住 **4** stop, delay, or prevent 停下；中止；延迟，延缓；制止，阻止 • **noun 1** a period of staying somewhere 逗留；停留 **2** a brace or support 支架；支撑物；依靠 **3** (**stays**) historical【历史】a corset stiffened by strips of whalebone 紧身褡；胸衣 □ **staying power** informal【非正式】endurance or stamina 耐久力，持久力 **stay of execution** a delay in carrying out the orders of a law court 缓期执行

stead /sted/ **noun** (**in someone's** or **something's stead**) instead of someone or something 代替(某人或某物) □ **stand someone in good stead** be useful to someone over time 将来对(某人)有用

steadfast /stedfɑːst/ **adjective** not changing in your attitudes or aims 坚定的；坚决的 ▪ **steadfastly** adverb.

steady /stedi/ **adjective** (**steadier, steadiest**) **1** firmly fixed, supported, or balanced 固定的；平稳的 **2** not faltering or wavering 不摇晃的；稳的 **3** sensible and reliable 稳重的；持重的；可靠的 **4** regular, even, and continuous 有规律的；稳定的；持续的 • **verb** (**steadies, steadying, steadied**) make steady 使稳；使平稳；使不摇晃 ▪ **steadily** adverb **steadiness** noun.

steak /steɪk/ **noun 1** high-quality beef cut into thick slices for grilling or frying (用来烤或煎的上好的)牛排 **2** a thick slice of other meat or fish 肉块，块肉 **3** poorer-quality beef for stewing (用来炖的质量欠佳的)牛肉

steal /stiːl/ **verb** (**steals, stealing, stole**; past participle **stolen**) **1** take something without permission and without intending to return it 偷窃；偷 盗 **2** move quietly or secretively 悄悄移动；偷偷移动 • **noun** informal【非正式】a bargain 便宜货 □ **steal the show** attract the most attention and praise 抢风头

stealth /stelθ/ **noun** cautious and secretive action or movement 秘密行动；暗中行动

stealthy /stelθi/ **adjective** (**stealthier, stealthiest**) cautious and secretive 不声张的，秘密的 ▪ **stealthily** adverb.

steam /stiːm/ **noun 1** the hot vapour into which water is converted when heated 蒸汽，水蒸气 **2** power produced by steam under pressure 蒸汽动力 **3** momentum 势头，声势 • **verb 1** give off or produce steam 散发出蒸汽；冒水汽 **2** (**steam up**) mist over with steam 蒙上水汽；蒙上汽雾 **3** cook food by heating it in steam from boiling water 蒸煮，蒸(食物) **4** (of a ship or train) travel under steam power (轮船或火车)靠蒸汽动力行驶 **5** informal【非正式】move quickly or forcefully 高速前进；奋力前进 ▪ **steamer** noun.

steamroller /stiːmrəʊlə(r)/ **noun** a heavy, slow vehicle with a roller, used to flatten the surfaces of roads 蒸汽压路机 • **verb** (**steamrollers, steamrollering, steamrollered**) **1**

force someone into doing or accepting something 强迫使 **2** forcibly pass a law 强行通过(法律)

steamy /ˈstiːmi/ **adjective (steamier, steamiest) 1** producing or filled with steam 冒出蒸汽的;充满蒸汽的 **2** informal 【非正式】involving passionate sexual activity 色情的

steed /stiːd/ **noun** literary【文】a horse 马

steel /stiːl/ **noun 1** a hard, strong metal that is a mixture of iron and carbon 钢;钢铁 **2** strength and determination 坚毅;刚强;坚强 • **verb** mentally prepare yourself for something difficult 下决心应付 □ **steel band** a band that plays music on drums made from empty oil containers 钢鼓乐队

steelworks /ˈstiːlwɜːks/ **plural noun** a factory where steel is produced 炼钢厂;钢铁厂

steely /ˈstiːli/ **adjective (steelier, steeliest) 1** like steel 似钢的;钢铁般的 **2** coldly determined 冷酷的;强硬的

steep[1] /stiːp/ **adjective 1** rising or falling sharply 陡的;陡峭的 **2** (of a rise or fall in an amount) very large or rapid (数量的涨落)巨大的,急剧的 **3** informal【非正式】(of a price or demand) too great (价格或要求)过高的,不合理的 ■ **steepen** verb **steeply** adverb.

steep[2] **verb 1** soak in water or other liquid 泡;浸 泡 **2** (**be steeped in**) have a lot of a particular quality or atmosphere 深深浸湿;沉湎于

steeple /ˈstiːpl/ **noun** a church tower and spire (教堂顶上的)尖塔

steeplechase /ˈstiːpltʃeɪs/ **noun 1** a horse race with ditches and hedges as jumps 障碍赛马 **2** a race in which runners must clear hurdles and water jumps 障碍赛跑 ■ **steeplechaser** noun.

steeplejack /ˈstiːpldʒæk/ **noun** a

person who climbs tall structures such as chimneys and steeples to repair them 高空修理工

steer[1] /stɪə(r)/ **verb 1** guide or control the movement of a vehicle, ship, etc. 驾驶(车辆、船等) **2** direct or guide 指导;带领;操纵 □ **steer clear of** take care to avoid 绕开;避开 **steering wheel** a wheel that a driver turns in order to steer a vehicle 舵轮;方向盘

steer[2] **noun** a bullock 阉牛;小公牛

steerage /ˈstɪərɪdʒ/ **noun** (in the past) the cheapest accommodation in a ship (旧时客轮上价格最便宜的)统舱

steersman /ˈstɪəzmən/ **noun (plural steersmen)** a person who steers a boat or ship 舵手;操舵员

stegosaurus /ˌstegəˈsɔːrəs/ **noun** a plant-eating dinosaur with large bony plates along the back 剑龙(一种食草恐龙)

stellar /ˈstelə(r)/ **adjective** having to do with a star or stars 恒星的;与恒星(或星群)相关的

stem[1] /stem/ **noun 1** the long, thin main part of a plant or shrub, or support of a fruit, flower, or leaf (草本植物、灌木的)茎,干;(果实、花或叶的)梗,柄 **2** a long, thin supporting part of a wine glass, tobacco pipe, etc. (葡萄酒杯、烟斗等的)柄,柄脚 **3** a vertical stroke in a letter or musical note (字母的)直立笔划;(音符的)符干 **4** the root or main part of a word 词干 • **verb (stems, stemming, stemmed) (stem from)** come from or be caused by 起源于;由…造成

stem[2] **verb (stems, stemming, stemmed)** stop or slow down the flow or progress of something 堵住,阻止,阻拦,制止(流动或进展);使缓下来;使减速

stench /stentʃ/ **noun** a strong and very unpleasant smell 恶臭;臭气

stencil /ˈstensl/ **noun** a thin sheet with a pattern or letters cut out of it, used to produce a design by applying ink or paint through the holes (印刷图案或文字用的)模版, 蜡纸 • verb (stencils, stencilling, stencilled; US spelling【美拼作】stencils, stenciling, stenciled) decorate or form something with a stencil 用模版制作;用蜡纸印

stenographer /stə'nɒɡrəfə(r)/ noun N. Amer.【北美】a shorthand typist 速记员

stentorian /sten'tɔːriən/ adjective (of a person's voice) loud and powerful (人的嗓音)洪亮的

step /step/ noun 1 an act of lifting and putting down the foot or feet in walking 迈步 2 the distance covered by a step 一步的距离;步长 3 a flat surface on which to place the feet when moving from one level to another 梯级;台阶 4 a position or grade in a scale or ranking 级别;等级 5 a measure or action taken to deal with something 措施,步骤;办法 • verb (steps, stepping, stepped) lift and put down your foot or feet 迈步;跨步;举步 step down resign from a job or post 辞职;让位;下台 step in become involved in a difficult situation 牵涉进,插入(某一困境) stepping stone 1 a raised stone which you can step on when crossing a stream (小溪中的)踏脚石,垫脚石 2 something that helps you make progress towards a goal (借以达到目的的)跳板,进身之阶 step something up increase the amount, speed, or strength of 增加(数量或速度);增强(力量)

stepbrother /'stepbrʌðə(r)/ noun a son of a person's stepfather or stepmother 同父异母(或同母异父)的兄弟

stepchild /'steptʃaɪld/ noun (plural stepchildren) a child of a person's husband or wife from a previous marriage 继子女(前夫或前妻所生的孩子)

stepdaughter /'stepdɔːtə(r)/ noun a daughter of a person's husband or wife from a previous marriage 继女

stepfather /'stepfɑːðə(r)/ noun a man who is married to a person's mother but is not his or her father 继父

stepladder /'steplædə(r)/ noun a short freestanding folding ladder 活梯;梯凳

stepmother /'stepmʌðə(r)/ noun a woman who is married to a person's father but is not his or her mother 继母

steppe /step/ noun a large area of flat unforested grassland in SE Europe and Siberia (东南欧和西伯利亚没有树木的)干草原

stepsister /'stepsɪstə(r)/ noun a daughter of a person's stepfather or stepmother 同父异母(或同母异父)姐(妹);继姐(妹)

stepson /'stepsʌn/ noun a son of a person's husband or wife from a previous marriage 继子

stereo /'steriəʊ/ noun (plural stereos) 1 music or sound that come from two or more speakers and seems to surround you 立体声 2 a CD player, record player, etc. that has two or more speakers 立体声音响器材 • adjective (also stereophonic) relating to this kind of sound 立体声的

stereotype /'steriətaɪp/ noun an oversimplified idea of the typical characteristics of a person or thing 陈规,模式化观念;刻板模式 • verb (stereotypes, stereotyping, stereotyped) represent as a stereotype 使陈规化,使僵化,使模式化 ■ stereotypical adjective

sterile /'steraɪl/ adjective 1 not able to produce children, young, crops, or fruit 不育的;不结果实的;贫瘠的 2 not imaginative, creative, or exciting 缺乏想象力的;缺乏新意的;

枯燥乏味的；无生气的 **3** free from bacteria 无菌的 ■ **sterility** noun.

sterilize or **sterilise** /'sterəlaɪz/ **verb** (sterilizes, sterilizing, sterilized) make sterile 给…杀菌；给…消毒 ■ **sterilization** noun.

sterling /'stɜːlɪŋ/ **noun** British money (英国货币)英镑 • **adjective 1** excellent 优秀的；出色的 **2** (of silver) of at least 92¼ per cent purity (银)标准成分的；纯银的

stern¹ /stɜːn/ **adjective 1** grimly serious or strict 严格的；严厉的 **2** severe 严肃的 ■ **sternly** adverb.

stern² **noun** the rear end of a ship or boat 船尾

sternum /'stɜːnəm/ **noun** the breastbone 胸骨

steroid /'stɪərɔɪd/ **noun 1** any of a class of substances that includes certain hormones and vitamins 甾类化合物；类固醇 **2** an anabolic steroid 促蛋白合成甾类；促蛋白合成类固醇

stertorous /'stɜːtərəs/ **adjective** (of breathing) noisy and laboured (呼吸)发鼾声的，打鼾的

stethoscope /'steθəskəʊp/ **noun** a device used by doctors for listening to the sound of a person's heart or breathing 听诊器

Stetson /'stetsn/ **noun** (trademark in the US 【美国商标】) a hat with a high crown and a very wide brim, worn by cowboys and ranchers in the US 斯泰森毡帽(牛仔所戴的阔边高顶毡帽)

stevedore /'stiːvədɔː(r)/ **noun** a person employed at a dock to load and unload ships 码头装卸工

stew /stjuː/ **noun 1** a dish of meat and vegetables cooked slowly in a closed dish (肉与蔬菜一起炖的)炖菜，焖菜 **2** informal 【非正式】 a state of anxiety or agitation 不安；担忧；激动 • **verb 1** cook slowly in a closed dish 炖；煨；焖 **2** Brit. 【英】 (of tea) become strong and bitter with prolonged

brewing (茶因久泡)变得浓苦 **3** informal 【非正式】 be anxious or agitated 不安；忧虑；激动

steward /'stjuːəd/ **noun 1** a person who looks after the passengers on a ship or aircraft (轮船或飞机上的)乘务员，服务员 **2** an official who supervises arrangements at a large public event (大型公共活动的)管事，干事 **3** a person employed to manage a large house or estate (大型房舍或地产的)管家，管事 **4** a person responsible for supplies of food to a college, club, etc. (学院、俱乐部等的)伙食管理员 ■ **stewardship** noun.

stewardess /ˌstjuːəˈdes/ **noun** a woman who looks after the passengers on a ship or aircraft (轮船或飞机上的)女乘务员，女服务员

stick¹ /stɪk/ **noun 1** a thin piece of wood that has fallen or been cut from a tree 枝条；木枝 **2** a piece of wood for support in walking or as a weapon 手杖；拐杖；(用作武器的)棍，棒 **3** a long, thin implement used in hockey, polo, etc. to hit the ball or puck 球棍；球棒 **4** a long, thin object or piece 条状物；棒状物 **5** Brit. informal 【英，非正式】 severe criticism or treatment 严厉批评；谴责 **6** (**the sticks**) informal 【非正式】 remote country areas 穷乡僻壤；偏远的乡村 □ **stick insect** a long, slender insect that resembles a twig 竹节虫(一种昆虫，身体细长，形似小树枝)

stick² **verb** (sticks, sticking, stuck) **1** push something pointed into or through something (用尖物)刺入，插入，戳入 **2** be fixed with its point embedded in something 被刺入；被插入；被戳入 **3** protrude or extend 使突出；伸出 **4** informal 【非正式】 put something somewhere carelessly or carelessly (指迅速或随意地)放置 **5** cling firmly to a surface; adhere 粘住；贴住 **6** (**be stuck**) be fixed or unable to move 卡住；动不了 **7** (**be**

stuck) be unable to complete a task 无法进展；处于困境 **8 (be stuck with)** informal【非正式】 be unable to get rid of or escape from 摆脱不了；解脱不了 **9 (stick around)** informal【非正式】 remain in or near a place 呆在某处；呆在附近；不走远 **10 (stick to)** continue doing or using 坚持(做或使用) **11 (stick up for)** informal【非正式】 support 支持；维护；拥护

sticker /'stɪkə(r)/ **noun** a sticky label or notice 有粘胶的标签(或通知)

stickleback /'stɪklbæk/ **noun** a small fish with sharp spines along its back 刺鱼

stickler /'stɪklə(r)/ **noun** a person who insists on people behaving in a particular way 固执己见的人；坚持(或拘泥于)某种做法的人

sticky /'stɪki/ **adjective (stickier, stickiest) 1** designed or able to stick 黏(性)的；涂有黏胶物质的 **2** like glue in texture 似黏胶的 **3** (of the weather) hot and humid (天气)湿热的

stiff /stɪf/ **adjective 1** not easily bent 不易弯曲的；僵硬的；僵直的 **2** difficult to turn or operate 难转向的；活动不自如的 **3** unable to move easily and without pain 难以活动的；活动时疼痛的 **4** not relaxed or friendly 拘谨的；不自然的；生硬的；不友好的 **5** severe or strong 严厉的；严格的；强烈的；有力的 • **noun** informal【非正式】 a dead body 尸体 □ **stiff upper lip** the tendency to hide your feelings and not complain 坚忍；刚毅 ■ **stiffly** adverb **stiffness** noun.

stiffen /'stɪfn/ **verb 1** make or become stiff (使)变硬；(使)难以弯曲 **2** make or become stronger 使顽强；使坚定；加强；提高

stifle /'staɪfl/ **verb (stifles, stifling, stifled) 1** prevent from breathing freely; suffocate 使窒息；闷死 **2** restrain or suppress 遏止；阻止；抑制

stifling /'staɪflɪŋ/ **adjective** unpleasantly hot and stuffy 闷热的；气闷的；令人窒息的

stigma /'stɪɡmə/ **noun (plural stigmas or stigmata** /'stɪɡmətə/**) 1** a mark or sign of disgrace 耻辱；污名 **2 (stigmata)** marks on a person's body believed by some Christians to correspond to those left on Jesus's body by the Crucifixion 圣伤；圣痕(据信出现在某些圣徒身上，与耶稣在十字架上钉死后身上所留下的伤痕位置一致) **3** the part of a plant that receives the pollen during pollination 柱头

stigmatize or stigmatise /'stɪɡmətaɪz/ **verb (stigmatizes, stigmatizing, stigmatized)** regard or treat as shameful 视…为可耻；污蔑

stile /staɪl/ **noun** an arrangement of steps in a fence or wall that allows people to climb over 供在篱笆或墙边供人爬越的)台阶，阶梯

stiletto /str'letəʊ/ **noun (plural stilettos) 1** a thin, high heel on a woman's shoe (女鞋的)细高跟 **2** a short dagger with a tapering blade 短剑；匕首

still /stɪl/ **adjective 1** not moving 静止的；不动的 **2** Brit.【英】 (of a drink) not fizzy (饮料)不起泡的 • **noun 1** deep, quiet calm 寂静；安静 **2** a photograph or a single shot from a cinema film (电影)剧照 **3** a piece of equipment for distilling alcoholic drinks such as whisky (蒸馏威士忌等含酒精饮料用的)蒸馏器 • **adverb 1** even now or at a particular time 仍然；还是 **2** nevertheless 然而 **3** even 甚至更；还要 • **verb** make or become still (使)静止；(使)平静；(使)安静 □ **still life** (plural **still lifes**) a painting or drawing of an arrangement of objects such as flowers or fruit (花、水果等的)静物画 ■ **stillness** noun.

stillborn /'stɪlbɔːn/ **adjective** (of a baby) born dead (胎儿)死产的 ■ stillbirth noun.

stilt /stɪlt/ **noun 1** either of a pair of upright poles that are used to walk raised above the ground 高跷 **2** each of a set of posts supporting a building (支撑建筑物的)支柱,支材

stilted /ˈstɪltɪd/ **adjective** (of speech or writing) stiff and unnatural (言语或文字)矫揉造作的,生硬的

Stilton /ˈstɪltən/ **noun** trademark 【商标】a kind of strong, rich blue cheese 斯提尔顿干酪

stimulant /ˈstɪmjələnt/ **noun** something that stimulates 兴奋剂;刺激物

stimulate /ˈstɪmjuleɪt/ **verb** (**stimulates, stimulating, stimulated**) **1** cause a reaction in the body 刺激 **2** make more active or interested 激发;激励;鼓舞 ■ **stimulation** noun.

stimulus /ˈstɪmjələs/ **noun** (plural **stimuli** /ˈstɪmjəlaɪ/) something that stimulates 刺激物;激励物;引起兴奋的事物

sting /stɪŋ/ **noun 1** a sharp-pointed part of an insect, capable of inflicting a wound by injecting poison (昆虫的)螫针,螫刺,刺 **2** a wound from a sting 刺伤处;刺痛处 **3** a sharp tingling sensation 刺痛;剧痛 • **verb** (**stings, stinging, stung**) **1** wound with a sting 螫;叮 **2** produce a stinging sensation 引起刺痛 **3** upset someone 使痛苦;使苦恼

stingray /ˈstɪŋreɪ/ **noun** a ray (fish) with a poisonous spine at the base of the tail 刺虹(一种扁平海鱼,尾部长有毒刺)

stingy /ˈstɪndʒi/ **adjective** (**stingier, stingiest**) informal 【非正式】mean 吝啬的,小气的

stink /stɪŋk/ **verb** (**stinks, stinking, stank** or **stunk**; past participle **stunk**) **1** have a strong, unpleasant smell 发出恶臭,发出异味 **2** informal 【非正式】be very bad or unpleasant 很糟糕,令人讨厌 • **noun 1** a strong, unpleasant smell 恶臭;异味 **2** informal 【非正式】

a row or fuss 争吵;喧闹;大吵大闹 ■ **stinker** noun.

stinking /ˈstɪŋkɪŋ/ **adjective 1** foul-smelling 臭的;发恶臭的 **2** informal 【非正式】very unpleasant or bad 令人讨厌的;糟糕的 • **adverb** informal 【非正式】very 极度地;十分;非常: stinking rich 极其富有的

stint /stɪnt/ **verb** (**stint on**) be very economical or mean about spending or providing something 吝惜;限量供给 • **noun** a period of work 分配的任务;工作期限

stipend /ˈstaɪpend/ **noun** a fixed regular sum paid as a salary to a priest, teacher, or official (发给牧师、教师或公职人员的)薪金,俸给

stipendiary /staɪˈpendɪəri/ **adjective** receiving a stipend; working for pay 领薪金的;有俸给的;为俸给而工作的

stipple /ˈstɪpl/ **verb** (**stipples, stippling, stippled**) mark a surface with many small dots or specks 点缀;在…上点彩

stipulate /ˈstɪpjuleɪt/ **verb** (**stipulates, stipulating, stipulated**) demand or specify as part of an agreement 要求;规定 ■ **stipulation** noun.

stir /stɜː(r)/ **verb** (**stirs, stirring, stirred**) **1** move an implement round and round in a liquid or soft substance to mix it 搅动;搅拌;搅和 **2** move slightly 使微动 **3** wake or get up 唤醒;唤起 **4** (often **stir something up**) arouse a strong feeling in someone 唤起,激起(强烈感情) **5** Brit. informal 【英,非正式】deliberately cause trouble by spreading rumours or gossip 煽动;挑起(麻烦) • **noun 1** an act of stirring 搅动;搅拌;搅和 **2** a disturbance or commotion 扰乱;骚乱;骚动;混乱 □ **stir-fry** fry quickly over a high heat while stirring (用旺火)煸炒 ■ **stirrer** noun.

stirring /ˈstɜːrɪŋ/ **adjective** causing great excitement or strong emotion 激动人心的；令人兴奋的；令人振奋的

stirrup /ˈstɪrəp/ **noun** each of a pair of loops attached to a horse's saddle to support the rider's foot 马镫

stitch /stɪtʃ/ **noun 1** a loop of thread made by a single pass of the needle in sewing or knitting (缝纫或针织的)一针，针脚，针迹 **2** a method of sewing or knitting that produces a particular pattern (缝纫或针织的)针法，编结法 **3** a sudden sharp pain in the side of the body, caused by strenuous exercise (剧烈运动引起的)肋部的突然剧痛 • **verb** make or mend with stitches 缝；缝缀；缝补；绣；编结 □ **in stitches** informal【非正式】laughing uncontrollably 忍俊不禁 **stitch someone up** Brit. informal【英，非正式】make someone appear to be guilty of something that they did not do 诬陷(某人)；陷害(某人)；算计(某人)

stoat /stəʊt/ **noun** a small meat-eating animal of the weasel family 白鼬

stock /stɒk/ **noun 1** a supply of goods or materials available for sale or use 库存物；储备物；备用物 **2** farm animals; livestock 家畜 **3** money raised by selling shares in a company 资本 **4** (**stocks**) shares in a company 股份；股票 **5** water in which bones, meat, fish, or vegetables have been simmered (由骨头、肉、鱼或蔬菜炖成的)汤计，原汤 **6** a person's ancestry 祖先；家系；血统 **7** a breed, variety, or population of an animal or plant (动植物的)种，属，品种，种群 **8** the trunk or stem of a tree or shrub (树或灌木的)主干 **9** a plant with sweet-smelling lilac, pink, or white flowers 紫罗兰属植物 **10** (**the stocks**) (in the past) a wooden structure in which criminals were locked as a public punishment (旧时

惩罚罪犯用的)手枷和足枷 • **adjective** common or conventional 通常的；老套的；死板的；*stock characters* 死板的人 • **verb 1** have or keep a stock of 备货，储备 **2** provide or fill with a stock of something 供应；为…备货；囤积 **3** (**stock up**) collect stocks of something 备货 □ **stock car** a car used in a type of racing in which cars collide with each other (改装的)赛车 **stock exchange** (or **stock market**) a place where stocks and shares are bought and sold 股票(或证券)交易所；股票(或证券)市场 **stock-in-trade** the typical thing a person or company uses or deals in (某人或某公司的)必备用具，所需材料，营业用品 **stock-still** completely still 静止；纹丝不动地 **take stock** assess your situation 估计；估计

stockade /stɒˈkeɪd/ **noun** a barrier or enclosure formed from wooden posts (用木桩围成的)栅栏，围栏

stockbroker /ˈstɒkbrəʊkə(r)/ **noun** a person who buys and sells stocks and shares on behalf of clients 股票(或证券)经纪人

stocking /ˈstɒkɪŋ/ **noun 1** either of a pair of women's close-fitting nylon garments covering the foot and leg 长筒袜 **2** US or old use【美或旧】a long sock 长袜 ■ **stockinged** adjective.

stockist /ˈstɒkɪst/ **noun** Brit.【英】a retailer that sells goods of a particular type (某类产品的)专营零售商

stockpile /ˈstɒkpaɪl/ **noun** a large stock of goods or materials 储备物资 • **verb** (**stockpiles, stockpiling, stockpiled**) gather together a large stock of 储备；贮存；积累

stocktaking /ˈstɒkteɪkɪŋ/ **noun** the process of listing all the stock held by a business (商店的)存货盘点，清点存货

stocky /ˈstɒki/ **adjective** (**stockier, stockiest**) (of a person) short and sturdy (人)矮壮的,粗壮的

stodge /stɒdʒ/ **noun** Brit. informal 【英,非正式】food that is heavy and filling 油腻的食物;易使人饱的食物 ▪ **stodgy** adjective.

stoic /ˈstəʊɪk/ **noun** a stoical person 坚忍的人 ▪ **adjective** stoical 坚忍的

stoical /ˈstəʊɪkl/ **adjective** enduring pain and hardship without complaining 坚忍的 ▪ **stoically** adverb **stoicism** noun.

stoke /stəʊk/ **verb** (**stokes, stoking, stoked**) **1** add coal to a fire, furnace, etc. 添煤拨旺(炉火等);给(火炉等)添煤;司(炉) **2** encourage a strong emotion 煽起,激起(某种强烈感情) ▪ **stoker** noun.

stole¹ /stəʊl/ **noun** a woman's long scarf or shawl 女用披肩;女用长围巾

stole² past of STEAL.

stolen /ˈstəʊlən/ past participle of STEAL.

stolid /ˈstɒlɪd/ **adjective** calm, dependable, and unemotional 不动感情的;淡漠的 ▪ **stolidly** adverb.

stomach /ˈstʌmək/ **noun 1** the internal organ in which the first part of digestion occurs 胃 **2** the front part of the body below the chest; the belly 腹部;肚子 **3** inclination or desire 爱好;欲望 ▪ **verb 1** consume food or drink without feeling ill 吃得下;喝得下 **2** accept or approve of something 接受;赞成

stomp /stɒmp/ **verb 1** tread heavily and noisily 跺脚;重踩;重踏 **2** dance with stamping steps 迈着重重的步子跳舞

stone /stəʊn/ **noun 1** the hard material that rock is made of 石头;石料 **2** a small piece of stone found on the ground 石块;石子 **3** a piece of stone shaped as a memorial, a boundary marker, etc. 纪念碑;界石;界石牌 **4** a gem 宝石;钻石 **5** the hard seed of certain fruits (某些水果硬质的)种子,果核 **6** (plural **stone**) Brit.

【英】a unit of weight equal to 14 lb (6.35 kg)英石(英制重量单位,等于14磅,即 6.35 千克)▪ **verb** (**stones, stoning, stoned**) **1** throw stones at 向…扔石块;用石头砸 **2** remove the stone from a fruit 去掉…的果核 ▪ **adverb** extremely or totally 完全地;十足地: *stone cold* 极其寒冷的 □ **Stone Age** the prehistoric period when tools were made of stone 石器时代(工具为石制的时代) **a stone's throw** a short distance 近距离

stoned /stəʊnd/ **adjective** informal 【非正式】strongly affected by drugs or alcohol (受毒品)麻醉的;醉酒的

stonewall /ˈstəʊnˈwɔːl/ **verb 1** refuse to answer questions, or give evasive replies 拒绝回答(问题);模棱两可地回答 **2** Cricket【板球】bat very defensively 防守挡击

stony /ˈstəʊni/ **adjective** (**stonier, stoniest**) **1** full of stones 多石的;铺石头的 **2** made of or like stone 石头的;坚硬如石的;极坚硬的 **3** cold and unfeeling 冷酷的;无情的;铁石心肠的 ▪ **stonily** adverb.

stood /stʊd/ past and past participle of STAND.

stooge /stuːdʒ/ **noun** disapproving 【贬】a less important person used by someone to do routine or unpleasant work 下手;帮手;跟班 **2** a performer whose act involves being the butt of a comedian's jokes (喜剧中充当主角打趣对象的)丑角

stool /stuːl/ **noun 1** a seat without a back or arms 凳子 **2** Medicine【医】a piece of faeces 大便;粪便 □ **stool pigeon** informal 【非正式】a police informer (警方的)眼线,内线

stoop /stuːp/ **verb 1** bend the head or body forwards and downwards 俯首;弯腰 **2** lower your standards to do something wrong 屈尊,自贬,堕落(去做某事)▪ **noun** a stooping posture 俯首;弯腰;曲背

stop /stɒp/ **verb** (**stops, stopping,**

stopped) **1** come or bring to an end (使)停下;(使)停止 **2** prevent from happening or from doing something 阻止;制止 **3** no longer move or operate 中止 **4** (of a bus or train) call at a place to pick up or let off passengers (公共汽车或火车)停下;填塞(洞或缝隙) • noun **1** an act of stopping 停止;中止 **2** a place for a bus or train to stop at (汽车或火车的)车站 **3** an object or part of a mechanism which prevents movement 定位器;止动器 **4** a set of organ pipes (管风琴的)音管 □ **pull out all the stops** make a very great effort to achieve something 竭尽全力;全力以赴 **stop press** Brit.【英】news added to a newspaper at the last minute (报纸付印时临时插入的)最新消息

stopcock /'stɒpkɒk/ noun a valve which controls the flow of a liquid or gas through a pipe (调节管子中液体或气体流量的)管口, 活塞

stopgap /'stɒpgæp/ noun a temporary solution or substitute 权宜之计;补缺者;临时替代人(或物)

stoppage /'stɒpɪdʒ/ noun **1** an instance of being stopped 停止;中止;中断 **2** an instance of industrial action (工厂的)停工, 罢工 **3** a blockage 阻塞;阻塞 **4** (stoppages) Brit.【英】deductions from wages for tax, National Insurance, etc. (从工资中扣除的税款、国民保险金等)扣除款

stopper /'stɒpə(r)/ noun a plug for sealing a hole 阻塞物;塞子;栓 • verb (stoppers, stoppering, stoppered) seal with a stopper 用阻塞物塞住

stopwatch /'stɒpwɒtʃ/ noun a watch with buttons that start and stop the display, used to time races (赛跑时用的)秒表;跑表

storage /'stɔːrɪdʒ/ noun **1** the action of storing 贮藏;贮存 **2** space avail-

able for storing 贮藏空间;贮存场地 □ **storage heater** Brit.【英】an electric heater that stores up heat during the night and releases it during the day 电蓄热器

store /stɔː(r)/ noun **1** an amount or supply kept to be used when needed 储备;贮存物;储藏 **2** (stores) equipment and food kept for use by an army, navy, etc. (陆军、海军等的)储存品, 备用品, 补给品 **3** a place where things are kept for future use or sale 仓库;栈房;贮藏所 **4** Brit.【英】a large shop selling different types of goods 百货商店 **5** N. Amer.【北美】a shop 商店;店铺 • verb (stores, storing, stored) **1** keep for future use 储备;贮存 **2** enter information in the memory of a computer (在计算机里)存储(信息) □ **in store** about to happen 即将发生 **set store by** consider to be important 重视

storey /'stɔːri/ (US spelling【美拼作】story) noun (plural storeys or stories) a particular level of a building 楼层

> **!** 注意 don't confuse **storey** with **story**, which means 'an account of events told for entertainment'. In American English, the spelling **story** is used for both senses. 不要混淆 storey 和 story, 后者意为"故事, 小说"。在美国英语中, story 用于表示"楼层"和"故事"两种含义。

stork /stɔːk/ noun a tall long-legged bird with a long, heavy bill 鹳(一种高大禽鸟, 腿长, 喙大而长)

storm /stɔːm/ noun **1** a violent disturbance of the atmosphere with strong winds and rain, thunder, etc. 风暴;暴风雨;暴风雪;暴雷天气 **2** an uproar or controversy 骚乱, 激动;争议;辩论 • verb **1** move angrily or forcefully 横冲直撞;怒闯;猛冲 **2** (of troops) suddenly attack and capture a place (军队)猛攻, 突袭, 强击 **3** shout angrily 怒吼;大发雷霆 □ **a storm in a teacup** Brit.【英】great anger or excitement about something that is not very important 茶壶里掀起的大风暴;小事引起的轩然大波;小题大做

stormy /'stɔːmi/ **adjective** (**stormier, stormiest**) **1** affected by a storm 有暴风雨的;多暴风雨的 **2** full of angry or violent outbursts of feeling 狂怒的;暴躁的

story¹ /'stɔːri/ **noun** (plural **stories**) **1** an account of imaginary or real events told for entertainment 叙述;描述;故事;小说 **2** an item of news 新闻报道 **3** (also **storyline**) the plot of a novel, film, etc. (小说、电影等的)故事情节 **4** informal【非正式】a lie 谎言;假话

! 注意 don't confuse **story** with **storey**: see the note at **STOREY**. 不要混淆 story 和 storey：见词条 storey 处注释。

story² US spelling of **STOREY**. storey 的美式拼法

stoup /stuːp/ **noun** a basin for holy water in a church (教堂的)圣水钵

stout /staʊt/ **adjective** **1** rather fat or heavily built 肥胖的;粗壮的 **2** sturdy and thick 结实的;厚厚的 **3** brave and determined 勇敢的;顽强的 ■ **noun** a kind of strong, dark beer 烈性黑啤酒 ■ **stoutly** adverb.

stove¹ /stəʊv/ **noun** a device for cooking or heating (烹饪或取暖用的)炉,火炉,电炉

stove² past and past participle of **STAVE**.

stow /stəʊ/ **verb** **1** pack or store an object tidily 堆放;妥善放置;收藏;贮藏 **2** (**stow away**) hide on a ship, aircraft, etc. to travel secretly and without paying 偷乘,无票偷乘(船、飞机等)

stowaway /'stəʊəweɪ/ **noun** a person who stows away 逃票乘客;偷乘者;

偷渡者

straddle /'strædl/ **verb** (**straddles, straddling, straddled**) **1** sit or stand with one leg on either side of 骑;跨坐;分开腿站立 **2** extend across both sides of 跨越;横跨

strafe /strɑːf/ **verb** (**strafes, strafing, strafed**) attack with gunfire or bombs from a low-flying aircraft (从低飞的飞机上)扫射,轰炸

straggle /'strægl/ **verb** (**straggles, straggling, straggled**) **1** trail slowly behind the person or people in front 掉队,落伍 **2** grow or spread out in an untidy way 蔓生;散布 ■ **straggler** noun **straggly** adjective.

straight /streɪt/ **adjective** **1** extending in one direction only; without a curve or bend 直的;笔直的;直线的 **2** level, upright, or symmetrical 端正的;水平的;竖直的;均衡的 **3** in proper order or condition 整齐的;井井有条的 **4** honest and direct 诚实的;坦率的;直截了当的 **5** in continuous succession 连续的;不间断的 **6** (of an alcoholic drink) undiluted (含酒精饮料)未掺水的,纯的 **7** informal【非正式】conventional or respectable 传统的;体面的 **8** informal【非正式】heterosexual 异性恋的 ■ **adverb** **1** in a straight line or in a straight way 成直线地;直接地;径直地 **2** without delay 立即;马上 **3** clearly and logically 清楚地;有条理地 □ **straight away** immediately 立即;马上 **straight-faced** having a serious expression 表情严肃的 **straight-laced** ⇨ 见 **STRAIT-LACED**.

straighten /'streɪtn/ **verb** make or become straight (使)笔直,(使)变直

straightforward /ˌstreɪt'fɔːwəd/ **adjective** **1** easy to do or understand 简单的;易懂的 **2** honest and open 坦诚的;坦率的 ■ **straightforwardly** adverb.

straightjacket /'streɪtdʒækɪt/ ⇨ 见 **STRAITJACKET**.

strain¹ /streɪn/ **verb 1** make an unusually great effort 努力 **2** injure a muscle, limb, etc. by making it work too hard (因过度用力而)损伤,扭伤(肌肉、四肢等) **3** make great or excessive demands on 过度要求;苛求 **4** pour a mainly liquid substance through a sieve to separate out solid matter 过滤;滤出;滤掉 • **noun 1** a force tending to strain something to an extreme degree 拉力;张力;应力 **2** an injury caused by straining a muscle, limb, etc. 损伤;劳损;扭伤 **3** a severe demand on strength or resources (对体力或资源的)严格要求,苛求 **4** a state of tension or exhaustion 极度紧张;筋疲力尽 **5** the sound of a piece of music 旋律;曲调 ■ **strainer** noun.

strain² **noun 1** a breed or variety of an animal or plant (动植物的)系,品种,种类 **2** a tendency in a person's character (人的)气质,性格,性格

strained /streɪnd/ **adjective 1** not relaxed or comfortable; showing signs of strain 勉强的,不自然的 **2** produced by deliberate effort; not graceful or spontaneous 牵强附会的;做作的

strait /streɪt/ **noun 1** (also **straits**) a narrow passage of water connecting two other large areas of water 海峡 **2** (**straits**) trouble or difficulty 窘境;困境；*in dire straits* 处于极度的困境

straitened /ˈstreɪtnd/ **adjective** without enough money; poor 贫困的

straitjacket or **straightjacket** /ˈstreɪtdʒækɪt/ **noun** a strong garment with long sleeves which can be tied together to confine the arms of a violent person (束缚狂暴者双臂用的)约束衣

strait-laced or **straight-laced** /ˌstreɪtˈleɪst/ **adjective** very strictly moral and conventional 极严谨的;古板的;极拘谨的

strand¹ /strænd/ **verb 1** drive or leave a ship, whale, etc. aground on a shore (使船只、鲸等)搁浅 **2** leave someone or something without the means to move from a place 使处于困境;使滞留 • **noun** literary【文】a beach or shore 海滩;海岸;湖滨

strand² **noun 1** a single thin length of thread, wire, etc. (线、金属丝等的)股,缕 **2** an element that forms part of a complex whole (构成整体的)成分,部分

strange /streɪndʒ/ **adjective 1** unusual or surprising 不寻常的;奇异的;不可思议的 **2** not previously visited or encountered 陌生的;生疏的 ■ **strangely** adverb.

stranger /ˈstreɪndʒə(r)/ **noun 1** a person that you do not know 陌生人 **2** a person who does not know a particular place 外地人;新来者

strangle /ˈstræŋɡl/ **verb** (**strangles**, **strangling**, **strangled**) **1** kill or injure someone by squeezing their neck 扼死;勒死;扼住(脖子) **2** prevent from growing or developing 抑制;压制 ■ **strangler** noun.

stranglehold /ˈstræŋɡlhəʊld/ **noun 1** a firm grip around a person's neck that deprives them of oxygen (致命的)紧扼 **2** complete or overwhelming control 遏制;箝制

strangulation /ˌstræŋɡjuˈleɪʃn/ **noun** the action of strangling 紧扼;紧勒;扼死;勒死

strap /stræp/ **noun** a strip of flexible material used for fastening, carrying, or holding on to (用来固定、携带或支撑的)带,皮带,布带 • **verb** (**straps**, **straping**, **strapped**) fasten or secure with a strap 用带系劳;束牢 ■ **strapless** adjective **strappy** adjective.

strapping /ˈstræpɪŋ/ **adjective** (of a person) big and strong (人)魁梧的,高大强壮的

stratagem /ˈstrætədʒəm/ **noun** a plan or scheme intended to outwit an opponent 策略；计策；计谋

strategic /strə'tiːdʒɪk/ **adjective 1** forming part of a long-term plan to achieve something 战略的；具有战略意义的 **2** relating to the gaining of long-term military advantage 战略性的；服务于长远军事目标的 **3** (of weapons) for use against enemy territory rather than in battle (武器) 战略上的，战略上有用的 ■ **strategically** adverb.

strategy /'strætɪdʒi/ **noun** (plural **strategies**) **1** a plan designed to achieve a long-term aim 策略；计谋；行动计划 **2** the planning and directing of military activity in a war or battle 战略；战略部署 ■ **strategist** noun.

stratify /'strætɪfaɪ/ **verb** (**stratifies**, **stratifying**, **stratified**) form or arrange into strata 使成层；使分层 ■ **stratification** noun.

stratosphere /'strætəsfɪə(r)/ **noun 1** the layer of the earth's atmosphere above the lowest layer, at a height of about 10–50 km 平流层【非正式】 **2** informal the very highest levels of something 最高档；最上层；最高部位 ■ **stratospheric** adjective.

stratum /'strɑːtəm/ **noun** (plural **strata** /'streɪtə/) **1** a layer or series of layers of rock 地层；岩层 **2** a level or class of society 社会阶层

straw /strɔː/ **noun 1** dried stalks of grain 禾秆；稻草；麦秆 **2** a single dried stalk of grain (单根的) 麦秆，稻草，禾秆 **3** a thin hollow tube used for sucking drink from a container (喝饮料用的) 吸管 **4** a pale yellow colour 浅黄色 □ **clutch at straws** turn to something in desperation 抓救命稻草；作最后挣扎 **draw the short straw** be chosen to do something unpleasant 被分配做乏味的工作 **the last** (or **final**) **straw** the final difficulty that makes a situation unbearable 最终使人无法忍受的

事 **straw poll** an unofficial test of opinion (作为民意调查的) 非正式投票

strawberry /'strɔːbəri/ **noun** (plural **strawberries**) a sweet red fruit with seeds on the surface 草莓 □ **strawberry blonde** (of hair) light reddish-blonde (头发) 粉红金色的，草莓红的

stray /streɪ/ **verb** move away aimlessly from a group or from the right course or place 走失；离群；迷路；走离 • **adjective 1** not in the right place; separated from a group 迷路的；走失的；离群的 **2** (of a domestic animal) having no home or having wandered away from home (家畜) 无主的，走失的 • **noun** a stray person or thing 迷路者；流浪者；走失的家畜；离群的动物

streak /striːk/ **noun 1** a long, thin mark 条纹；条痕 **2** an element in someone's character 个性特征：*a ruthless streak* 残忍的天性 **3** a period of success or luck of a certain kind (指成功或运气)一段时间，一阵子，一系列：*a winning streak* 连连获胜 • **verb 1** mark with streaks 在…上加条纹；在…上留下条痕 **2** move very fast 飞跑；急驰 **3** informal 【非正式】run naked in a public place to shock or amuse people (为吓人或逗乐而在公共场所)裸奔 ■ **streaker** noun **streaky** adjective.

stream /striːm/ **noun 1** a small, narrow river 小河；溪流 **2** a continuous flow of liquid, air, people, etc. (指液体、空气或人等的)一connect串，源源不断，川流不息 **3** Brit. 【英】a group in which schoolchildren of the same age and ability are taught (年龄、能力相仿的儿童被分在一起的)能力小组 • **verb 1** move in a continuous flow 流；流动；涌 **2** run with tears, sweat, etc.(眼泪、汗等)流淌，泪涟涟，汗淋淋 **3** float out in the wind 飘扬；招展 **4** Brit.【英】put schoolchildren in streams 把(学生)分成能力小组 □ **on**

stream in operation or existence 在运行；在生产；存在

streamer /'striːmə(r)/ **noun** a long, narrow flag or strip of decorative material 长旗，幡；(用作装饰品的)横幅

streamline /'striːmlaɪn/ **verb** (**streamlines, streamlining, streamlined**) 1 (**be streamlined**) have a shape that allows quick, easy movement through air or water 把…设计成流线型；使…成流线型 2 make an organization or system more efficient 使(某一组织或系统)效率更高；提高…的效率

street /striːt/ **noun** a public road in a city, town, or village 街，街道 □ **street value** the price something, especially drugs, would fetch if sold illegally (尤指毒品的)街头黑市价

streetcar /'striːtkɑː(r)/ **noun** N. Amer. 【北美】a tram 有轨电车

streetwalker /'striːtwɔːkə(r)/ **noun** a prostitute who seeks clients in the street 街头拉客妓女

streetwise /'striːtwaɪz/ **adjective** informal 【非正式】able to deal with the difficulties and dangers of life in a big city 适应都市生活的；有都市生活技能的

strength /streŋθ/ **noun** 1 the quality or state of being strong 力；力量 2 a good or useful quality or attribute 优点；长处 3 the number of people making up a group (构成某一团体的)人数 □ **on the strength of** on the basis of 基于；依据

> ✔ **拼写指南** remember the g before the -th: streng*th*. 记住拼写 strength 中 -th 前的 g。

strengthen /'streŋθn/ **verb** make or become stronger 加强；巩固；(使)变强

strenuous /'strenjuəs/ **adjective** needing or using a lot of effort or exertion 艰苦的；繁重的 ■ **strenuously** adverb.

stress /stres/ **noun** 1 pressure or tension exerted on an object 压力；重压 2 mental or emotional strain or tension (精神或情绪上的)压力，紧张 3 particular emphasis given to a syllable or word in speech 重音；重读 • **verb** 1 emphasize 强调；着重 2 subject to pressure, tension, or strain 使受到压力；使紧张

stressful /'stresfl/ **adjective** causing mental or emotional stress 有压力的；紧张的 ■ **stressfully** adverb.

stretch /stretʃ/ **verb** 1 be able to be made longer or wider without tearing or breaking 拉长；撑大 2 extend something without tearing or breaking it 延伸；延展 3 extend part of the body to its full length 舒展；伸直 4 extend over an area or period of time 延伸；绵延；延续 5 make demands on 对…提出要求 • **noun** 1 an act of stretching 伸展；伸展 2 the capacity to stretch or be stretched; elasticity 伸展力；弹性 3 a continuous expanse or period 延伸；连绵；连续 ■ **stretchy** adjective.

stretcher /'stretʃə(r)/ **noun** a long framework covered with canvas, used for carrying sick, injured, or dead people (运送病人、伤员或死者的)担架 • **verb** (**stretchers, stretchering, stretchered**) carry on a stretcher 用担架抬送

strew /struː/ **verb** (**strews, strewing**, past participle **strewn** or **strewed**) 1 scatter untidily over a surface or area 撒；散播 2 (**be strewn with**) be covered with untidily scattered things 撒满；散布

striated /straɪ'eɪtɪd/ **adjective** marked with ridges or furrows 有条纹的；有条痕的 ■ **striation** noun.

stricken /'strɪkən/ North American or old-fashioned past participle of STRIKE. (strike 过去分词的北美或旧式拼法) • **adjective** 1 seriously affected by something unpleasant 遭受(不快之事)打击的;受…侵袭的 **2** showing great distress 痛苦的;悲伤的;苦恼的

strict /strɪkt/ **adjective 1** demanding that rules are obeyed 严厉的 **2** following rules or beliefs exactly 完全的;绝对的;不折不扣的 ■ **strictly** adverb **strictness** noun.

stricture /ˈstrɪktʃə(r)/ **noun 1** a rule restricting behaviour or action 限制;束缚;约束 **2** a sternly critical remark 指责;非难;苛评

stride /straɪd/ **verb** (**strides, striding, strode;** past participle **stridden**) walk with long, decisive steps 阔步行进;大踏步走 ● **noun 1** a long, decisive step 大步;跨步 **2** a step made towards an aim 进展;进步 □ **take something in your stride** deal calmly with something difficult 从容处理(某事);毫不费力地做(某事)

strident /ˈstraɪdnt/ **adjective 1** loud and harsh 尖声的;刺耳的 **2** presenting a point of view in a way that is too forceful 强有力的;有说服力的 ■ **stridency** noun **stridently** adverb.

strife /straɪf/ **noun** angry or bitter disagreement 冲突;纠纷;争论

strike /straɪk/ **verb** (**strikes, striking, struck**) **1** hit someone or something with force 打;击;击打 **2** attack suddenly 突然攻击(或袭击) **3** (of a disaster) happen suddenly and have harmful effects on (灾难)突然侵袭,爆发 **4** refuse to work as a form of organized protest 罢工;罢工抗议 **5** discover gold, oil, etc. by digging or drilling (通过挖掘)发现(金矿、石油等) **6** light a match by rubbing it against a rough surface 划(火柴) **7** (of a clock) show the time by sounding a chime or stroke (时钟)敲,报时 **8** reach an agreement or deal (协议) ● **noun 1** an act of striking by employees 罢工 **2** a sudden attack 突然袭击 **3** an act of hitting a ball 击

球 □ **strike someone off** officially expel someone from a professional group 把(某人)从(专业团体)中除名 **strike out** start out on a new course 独立闯新路;开辟新道路 **strike up** begin to play a piece of music 开始演奏(乐曲) **strike something up** begin a friendship or conversation with someone 结识(某人);开始(交谈)

striker /ˈstraɪkə(r)/ **noun 1** an employee who is on strike 罢工者 **2** (in soccer) a forward (足球运动中的)前锋

striking /ˈstraɪkɪŋ/ **adjective 1** noticeable 惹人注目的;显著的;突出的 **2** dramatically good-looking 美丽的;漂亮的 ■ **strikingly** adverb.

string /strɪŋ/ **noun 1** material consisting of threads twisted together to form a thin length 细绳 **2** a length of catgut or wire on a musical instrument, producing a note when it is made to vibrate (乐器的)弦 **3** (**strings**) the stringed instruments in an orchestra (管弦乐团的)弦乐器 **4** a sequence of similar items or events 一连串;一系列 ● **verb** (**strings, stringing, strung**) **1** thread things together on a string 使连成一串;用线串 **2** (**be strung** or **be strung out**) be arranged in a long line 被排成一行 **3** fit strings to a musical instrument, bow, etc. 给(乐器、弓等)上弦 □ **with no strings attached** informal【非正式】with no special conditions or restrictions 无附带条件,无特别限制 **string someone along** informal【非正式】deliberately mislead someone 故意误导(某人) **string bean** any of various beans eaten in their pods 刀豆;食荚菜豆 **string quartet** a chamber music group consisting of two violinists and a viola and cello player 弦乐四重奏 ■ **stringed** adjective.

stringent /ˈstrɪndʒənt/ **adjective** (of

regulations or requirements) strict and precise (规章或要求)严格的，严厉的 ■ **stringency** noun **stringently** adverb.

stringy /ˈstrɪŋi/ **adjective 1** like string 细绳状的；线状的；弦状的 **2** (of meat) containing tough fibres that are difficult to chew (肉)多纤维的，多筋的

strip¹ /strɪp/ **verb** (**strips, stripping, stripped**) **1** remove all coverings or clothes from 除去…的覆盖物；脱衣服 **2** take off your clothes 脱衣 **3** remove all the contents or fittings of a room, vehicle, etc. 拆除，拆散(房间的陈设、交通工具等) **4** remove paint from a surface (从表面)除去，刮掉(油漆) **5** (**strip someone of**) deprive someone of rank, power, or property 剥夺，夺走(某人的职位、权力或财产) ● **noun 1** an act of undressing 脱衣 **2** Brit.【英】the identifying outfit worn by a sports team (运动队的)队服

strip² noun **1** a long, narrow piece of cloth, paper, etc. 条，狭条，带状物(如布条、纸条等) **2** a long, narrow area of land 狭长地带 □ **strip light** Brit. 【英】a fluorescent lamp in the shape of a tube 带形日光灯

stripe /straɪp/ noun **a** long, narrow band or strip of a different colour or texture from the areas next to it 条纹；长条；纹 ● **verb** (**stripes, striping, striped**) mark with stripes 给…加条纹(或线条)；使有条纹(或线条) ■ **stripy** (or **stripey**) adjective.

stripling /ˈstrɪplɪŋ/ noun old use【旧】a young man 青年；小伙子

stripper /ˈstrɪpə(r)/ noun **1** a strip-tease performer 脱衣舞表演者 **2** a device or substance for stripping paint, varnish, etc. off a surface 剥离器；剥皮器

striptease /ˈstrɪptiːz/ noun a form of entertainment in which a performer gradually undresses to music in an erotic way 脱衣舞

strive /straɪv/ **verb** (**strives, striving, strove** or **strived**; past participle **striven** or **strived**) try very hard to do or achieve something 努力；力争

strobe /strəʊb/ noun a bright light which shines at rapid intervals 频闪闪光灯

strode /strəʊd/ past of STRIDE.

stroke /strəʊk/ noun **1** an act of hitting 敲；打；击 **2** a sound made by a striking clock (时钟发出的)敲击声，鸣声 **3** an act of stroking with the hand 抚；摩；捋 **4** a mark made by drawing a pen, pencil, etc. across paper or canvas (钢笔、铅笔等的)一笔，一画 **5** a short diagonal line separating characters or figures (分隔字符的)斜线号，斜号 **6** each of a series of repeated movements, e.g. in rowing or swimming (一系列重复动作中的)一举，一动 **7** a style of moving the arms and legs in swimming 游泳姿势；泳姿 **8** a sudden disabling attack caused by an interruption in the flow of blood to the brain 中风 ● **verb** (**strokes, stroking, stroked**) gently move your hand over (用手)轻抚，抚摩

stroll /strəʊl/ **verb** walk in a leisurely way 漫步；溜达；闲逛 ● **noun** a short leisurely walk 漫步；溜达；闲逛

strong /strɒŋ/ **adjective** (**stronger, strongest**) **1** physically powerful 强壮的；强健的 **2** done with or supplying great force 强有力的；强大的 **3** able to withstand great force or pressure 坚固的；牢固的，坚定的；坚强的 **4** secure or stable 牢固的；稳固的 **5** great in power, influence, or ability 有权力的；有影响力的；精通的；擅长的 **6** great in intensity or degree 强烈的；浓烈的 **7** having a lot of flavour (味道)浓郁的 **8** (of a solution or drink) containing a large proportion of a substance (溶液或饮料)浓的 **9** used after a number to indicate the size of a group (与数字连用)多达…的

□ **going strong** informal【非正式】continuing to be healthy, active, or successful 保持健康;活跃依旧;兴盛不衰 ■ **strongly** adverb.

strongbox /ˈstrɒŋbɒks/ **noun** a small metal box in which valuables are kept 保险箱;保险柜

stronghold /ˈstrɒŋhəʊld/ **noun 1** a place of strong support for a cause or political party (事业或政党的)根据地,大本营 **2** a place that has been strengthened against attack 堡垒,要塞

strongroom /ˈstrɒŋruːm/ **noun** a room designed to protect valuable items against fire and theft 保险库

strontium /ˈstrɒntiəm/ **noun** a soft silver-white metallic element (金属元素)锶

stroppy /ˈstrɒpi/ **adjective** Brit. informal【英,非正式】bad-tempered or argumentative 脾气坏的;性子暴躁的,好争吵的

strove /strəʊv/ past of STRIVE.

struck /strʌk/ past and past participle of STRIKE.

structural /ˈstrʌktʃərəl/ **adjective** relating to or forming part of a structure 结构的;构造的 ■ **structurally** adverb.

structure /ˈstrʌktʃə(r)/ **noun 1** the putting together of different parts to form a whole 构造;结构 **2** a building or other object constructed from several parts 构造物;机构;组织;体系 **3** good organization 条理(性) • **verb** (**structures**, **structuring**, **structured**) put parts together to form a whole 建造;建筑

strudel /ˈstruːdl/ **noun** a dessert of thin pastry rolled up round a fruit filling and baked 果馅卷

struggle /ˈstrʌɡl/ **verb** (**struggles**, **struggling**, **struggled**) **1** make great efforts to get free 挣扎;斗争 **2** try hard to do something 奋斗;努力;拼搏 **3** make your way with dif-

ficulty 艰难地行进 • **noun 1** an act of struggling 挣扎;斗争 **2** a very difficult task 难事 ■ **struggler** noun.

strum /strʌm/ **verb** (**strums**, **strumming**, **strummed**) play a guitar or similar instrument by sweeping the thumb or a plectrum up or down the strings 弹奏(吉他等) • **noun** an instance of strumming 弹拨

strumpet /ˈstrʌmpɪt/ **noun** old use【旧】a woman who has a lot of sexual partners 妓女;淫妇

strung /strʌŋ/ past and past participle of STRING.

strut /strʌt/ **noun 1** a bar used to support or strengthen a structure 支柱;支杆;支撑;撑杆 **2** a proud, confident walk 趾高气扬的步态 • **verb** (**struts**, **strutting**, **strutted**) walk in a proud and confident way 趾高气扬地走;高视阔步

strychnine /ˈstrɪkniːn/ **noun** a bitter and highly poisonous substance obtained from an Asian tree 士的宁,马钱子碱(一种具有苦极毒的物质,取自一种亚洲树木的果实)

Stuart or **Stewart** /ˈstjuːət/ **adjective** relating to the royal family ruling Scotland 1371 – 1714 and Britain 1603 – 1714 斯图亚特王室的;与斯图亚特王室相关的

stub /stʌb/ **noun 1** the remaining part of a pencil, cigarette, etc. after use 铅笔头;烟蒂;残余部分 **2** the counterfoil of a cheque, ticket, etc. (支票、车票等的)存根;票根 • **verb** (**stubs**, **stubbing**, **stubbed**) **1** accidentally bump your toe against something 不小心把脚趾碰到⋯上 **2** (often **stub something out**) put out a cigarette by pressing the lighted end against something 掐灭(香烟) ■ **stubby** adjective.

stubble /ˈstʌbl/ **noun 1** short, stiff hairs growing on a man's face when he has not shaved for a while 胡子茬 **2** the cut stalks of cereal plants left in the ground after harvesting (谷物收割后遗留的)茬 ■ **stubbly** adjective.

stubborn /ˈstʌbən/ **adjective 1** determined not to change your attitude or position 顽固的;执拗的;倔强的 **2** difficult to move or remove 难移动的;难去除的 ■ **stubbornly** adverb **stubbornness** noun.

stucco /ˈstʌkəʊ/ **noun** plaster used for coating wall surfaces or moulding into decoration (刷墙或建筑物装饰用的)灰泥,粉饰灰泥 ■ **stuccoed** adjective.

stuck /stʌk/ past participle of STICK². □ **stuck-up** informal 【非正式】having snobbish views and thinking that you are better than other people 高傲自大的;自命不凡的;势利的

stud¹ /stʌd/ **noun 1** a piece of metal with a large head that projects from a surface 大头钉;饰钉;嵌钉 **2** Brit. 【英】a small projection fixed to the base of a shoe or boot to provide better grip (鞋底或靴底的)防滑钉 **3** a small piece of jewellery which is pushed through a pierced ear or nostril (饰有珠宝的)钉状首饰,耳钉,鼻插 **4** a fastener consisting of two buttons joined with a bar 领扣 • **verb** (**studs, studding, studded**) decorate with studs or similar small objects 用饰钉(或嵌钉等)装饰

stud² **noun 1** an establishment where horses are kept for breeding 种马场 **2** a stallion 种马 **3** informal 【非正式】a man who has many sexual partners 乱搞性关系的男子

student /ˈstjuːdnt/ **noun 1** a person studying at a university or college (大学或学院的)学生 **2** a school pupil (中学的)学生

studio /ˈstjuːdiəʊ/ **noun** (plural **studios**) **1** a room from which television or radio programmes are broadcast (电视或广播的)演播室,播音室,录像室 **2** a place where

film or sound recordings are made 电影制片厂;电影摄影棚;录音棚 **3** a room where an artist works or where dancers practise (艺术家的)工作室;画室;(舞蹈的)排练房 □ **studio flat** Brit. 【英】a flat containing one main room 单间公寓

studious /ˈstjuːdiəs/ **adjective 1** spending a lot of time studying or reading 勤奋的;用功的 **2** done with careful effort 故意的;小心的;仔细的 ■ **studiously** adverb.

study /ˈstʌdi/ **noun** (plural **studies**) **1** the reading of books or examination of other materials to gain knowledge 学习;攻读 **2** a detailed investigation into a subject or situation 研究;研析;调查 **3** a room used for reading and writing 书房;书斋 **4** a piece of work done for practice or as an experiment 习作 • **verb** (**studies, studying, studied**) **1** learn about something 学习;攻读 **2** investigate a subject or situation in detail 仔细调查 **3** look at something closely in order to observe or read it 观察;研究 **4** (**studied**) done with careful effort 故意的;有意的;刻意的

stuff /stʌf/ **noun 1** material, articles, or activities of a particular kind, or of a mixed or unspecified kind 东西;物品;玩意儿 **2** basic characteristics 要素;特质;本质;素质 **3** (**your stuff**) informal 【非正式】the things that you are good at or responsible for 擅长;特长 • **verb 1** fill a container or space tightly with something 把…塞满(或装满,塞满) **2** fill out the skin of a dead animal or bird with material to restore its original appearance 制作(动物或鸟的)标本

stuffing /ˈstʌfɪŋ/ **noun 1** a mixture used to stuff poultry or meat before cooking (烹制前塞入家禽腔内或肉中的)填料 **2** padding used to fill cushions, furniture, or soft toys (垫子,家具或布绒玩具的)填塞物

stuffy /'stʌfi/ **adjective** (**stuffier**, **stuffiest**) **1** lacking fresh air or ventilation 缺乏新鲜空气的；不通风的，闷的 **2** conventional and narrow-minded 古板的；守旧的 **3** (of a person's nose) blocked up (鼻子)堵塞的，不通的

stultify /'stʌltɪfaɪ/ **verb** (**stultifies**, **stultifying**, **stultified**) make someone feel bored or drained of energy 使感觉无聊；使精疲力竭的

stumble /'stʌmbl/ **verb** (**stumbles**, **stumbling**, **stumbled**) **1** trip and momentarily lose your balance 绊脚，绊跌；绊倒 **2** walk unsteadily 跌跌撞撞地走；蹒跚而行 **3** make a mistake in speaking 说错话；口误 **4** (**stumble across** or **on**) find by chance 偶然发现 • **noun** an act of stumbling 绊脚，绊跌；绊倒 □ **stumbling block** an obstacle 障碍物；绊脚石

stump /stʌmp/ **noun 1** the part of a tree trunk left sticking out of the ground after the rest has fallen or been cut down 树墩；树桩 **2** a remaining piece 残余部分 **3** Cricket【板球】each of the three upright pieces of wood which form a wicket (三柱门的)柱 • **verb** informal【非正式】baffle 使为难；把…难住

stumpy /'stʌmpi/ **adjective** (**stumpier**, **stumpiest**) short and thick; squat 粗短的；矮胖的

stun /stʌn/ **verb** (**stuns**, **stunning**, **stunned**) **1** knock someone into a dazed or unconscious state 把…打昏；使昏迷 **2** greatly astonish or shock someone 使震惊；使目瞪口呆

stung /stʌŋ/ past and past participle of STING.

stunk /stʌŋk/ past and past participle of STINK.

stunner /'stʌnə(r)/ **noun** informal【非正式】a strikingly attractive or impressive person or thing 极漂亮的人；给人深刻印象的人(或物)；绝妙的事物

stunning /'stʌnɪŋ/ **adjective** very impressive or attractive 给人以深刻印象的；极吸引人的 ■ **stunningly** adverb.

stunt[1] /stʌnt/ **verb** slow down the growth or development of 阻碍生长，妨碍发展

stunt[2] **noun 1** an action displaying spectacular skill and daring 惊险动作；特技；惊人的表演 **2** something unusual done to attract attention 意在引人注意的举动；引人注目的花招；噱头

stuntman /'stʌntmæn/ **noun** (plural **stuntmen**) a person taking an actor's place in performing dangerous stunts 特技替身演员

stupefy /'stjuːpɪfaɪ/ **verb** (**stupefies**, **stupefying**, **stupefied**) make someone unable to think properly 使茫然；使麻木；使神志不清 ■ **stupefaction** noun.

stupendous /stjuː'pendəs/ **adjective** very impressive 使人印象极其深刻的；令人惊叹的，惊人的 ■ **stupendously** adverb.

stupid /'stjuːpɪd/ **adjective 1** lacking intelligence or common sense 愚蠢的，迟钝的；笨的 **2** dazed and unable to think clearly 恍惚的，迷糊的 ■ **stupidity** noun **stupidly** adverb.

stupor /'stjuːpə(r)/ **noun** a state of being very dazed or nearly unconscious 昏迷；麻木；恍惚

sturdy /'stɜːdi/ **adjective** (**sturdier**, **sturdiest**) **1** strong and solidly built or made 强壮的；结实的 **2** confident and determined 坚定的；刚毅的，坚强的 ■ **sturdily** adverb **sturdiness** noun.

sturgeon /'stɜːdʒən/ **noun** a very large fish with bony plates on the body, from whose roe (eggs) caviar is made 鲟鱼(一种体侧生长有骨板的大鱼，卵可做鱼子酱)

stutter /'stʌtə(r)/ **verb** (**stutters**, **stuttering**, **stuttered**) **1** have difficulty talking because you are sometimes unable to stop repeating the first sounds of a word 口吃;结结巴巴地说 **2** (of a machine or gun) produce a series of short, sharp sounds (机器或枪)突突地响 • **noun** a tendency to stutter while speaking 结巴;口吃 ∎ **stutterer** noun.

sty¹ /staɪ/ **noun** (plural **sties**) a pigsty 猪舍;猪栏

sty² or **stye** **noun** (plural **sties** or **styes**) an inflamed swelling on the edge of an eyelid 睑腺炎;麦粒肿

Stygian /ˈstɪdʒɪən/ **adjective** literary 【文】 very dark 漆黑的

style /staɪl/ **noun 1** a way of doing something 方式;方法;作风 **2** a particular appearance, design, or arrangement 样式;款式 **3** a way of painting, writing, etc. characteristic of a particular period or person (绘画,文学作品等的)风格;文体 **4** elegance and sophistication 派头;气派;风度;仪态 **5** Botany【植物】 a narrow extension of the ovary, carrying the stigma 花柱 • **verb** (**styles**, **styling**, **styled**) **1** design, make, or arrange in a particular form (根据某种样式)设计;制作 **2** give a particular name, description, or title to 称呼;叫

stylish /ˈstaɪlɪʃ/ **adjective** having a good sense of style; fashionably elegant 时髦的;雅致的 ∎ **stylishly** adverb.

stylist /ˈstaɪlɪst/ **noun** a person who designs fashionable clothes or cuts hair 时装设计师;发型师

stylistic /staɪˈlɪstɪk/ **adjective** relating to style 风格上的 ∎ **stylistically** adverb.

stylized or **stylised** /ˈstaɪlaɪzd/ **adjective** represented in an artificial style 程式化的;非写实的

stylus /ˈstaɪləs/ **noun** (plural **styli** /ˈstaɪlaɪ/) **1** a hard point that follows a groove in a gramophone record and transmits the recorded sound for reproduction (留声机的)唱针;(灌录唱片的)录音针 **2** a pointed implement used for scratching or tracing letters or engraving (用于刻字或雕刻的)尖笔

stymie /ˈstaɪmi/ **verb** (**stymies**, **stymying** or **stymieing**, **stymied**) informal 【非正式】 prevent or slow down the progress of 阻拦;阻碍

styptic /ˈstɪptɪk/ **adjective** able to make bleeding stop 止血的

suave /swɑːv/ **adjective** (of a man) charming, confident, and elegant (男子)文雅的,文绉绉的 ∎ **suavely** adverb **suavity** noun.

sub /sʌb/ informal 【非正式】 **noun 1** a submarine 潜艇;潜水艇 **2** a subscription 捐助 **3** a substitute in a sports team (运动队的)替补 • **verb** (**subs**, **subbing**, **subbed**) act as a substitute 替补;替代

subaltern /ˈsʌbltən/ **noun** an officer in the British army below the rank of captain (英军的)陆军中尉

subatomic /ˌsʌbəˈtɒmɪk/ **adjective** smaller than or occurring within an atom 亚原子的;原子内的

subconscious /sʌbˈkɒnʃəs/ **adjective** concerning the part of the mind which you are not aware of but which influences your actions and feelings 下意识的;潜意识的 • **noun** this part of the mind 下意识;潜意识 ∎ **subconsciously** adverb.

subcontinent /ˌsʌbˈkɒntɪnənt/ **noun** a large part of a continent considered as a particular area, such as North America or southern Africa 次大陆

subcontract /ˌsʌbkənˈtrækt/ **verb** employ a firm or person outside your company to do work 分包;转包(工作) ∎ **subcontractor** noun.

subculture /ˈsʌbkʌltʃə(r)/ **noun** a distinct group within a society or class, having beliefs or interests that are different from those of the larger group 亚文化群(拥有与更大文化群体不同的信仰或利益)

subcutaneous /ˌsʌbkjuˈteɪnɪəs/

adjective situated or applied under the skin 皮下的

subdivide /ˌsʌbdɪˈvaɪd/ **verb** (**subdivides, subdividing, subdivided**) divide a part into smaller parts 将(某物)再分；细分 ■ **subdivision** noun.

subdue /səbˈdjuː/ **verb** (**subdues, subduing, subdued**) **1** overcome, quieten, or control 战胜；制服；平息；控制 **2** bring a group or country under control by force 武力征服，慑服(某集团或国家)

subdued /səbˈdjuːd/ **adjective 1** quiet and thoughtful or depressed 默不作声的；抑郁的 **2** (of colour or lighting) soft; muted (颜色或照明)柔和的，暗淡的

subedit /ˌsʌbˈedɪt/ **verb** (**subedits, subediting, subedited**) check and correct newspaper or magazine text before printing 审阅(文稿)；对(文稿)进行文字加工 ■ **subeditor** noun.

subhuman /ˌsʌbˈhjuːmən/ **adjective** not behaving like a human being (行为)不齿于人类的

subject noun /ˈsʌbdʒɪkt/ **1** a person or thing that is being discussed, studied, or dealt with (讨论、研究或处理的)题目，问题，主题 **2** a branch of knowledge that is studied or taught 学科；科目 **3** Grammar【语法】the word or words in a sentence that come before the verb and which the verb says something about, e.g. *Joe* in *Joe ran home* 主语 **4** each of the people in a population ruled by a king or queen (国王或女王统治下的)臣民，国民 • **adjective** /ˈsʌbdʒekt/ (**subject to**) **1** able to be affected by 可能受…影响的；易遭受…的 **2** dependent or conditional on 由…决定的；视…而定的；取决于…的 **3** under the control or authority of 受支配的；听命于…的；隶属的 • **adverb** /ˈsʌbdʒɪkt/ (**subject to**) if certain conditions are fulfilled 取决于；视…而定 • **verb** /səbˈdʒekt/

(**subject someone/thing to**) make someone or something undergo an unpleasant experience 使经受；使遭受 ■ **subjection** noun.

subjective /səbˈdʒektɪv/ **adjective** based on or influenced by personal opinions 主观的 ■ **subjectively** adverb **subjectivity** noun.

sub judice /ˌsʌb ˈdʒuːdəsi/ **adjective** being considered by a court of law and therefore not to be publicly discussed elsewhere 在审理中的；尚未裁决的

subjugate /ˈsʌbdʒʊɡeɪt/ **verb** (**subjugates, subjugating, subjugated**) bring someone under your control by force 征服；制服；使屈服 ■ **subjugation** noun.

subjunctive /səbˈdʒʌŋktɪv/ **adjective** Grammar【语法】(of a verb) expressing what is imagined or wished or possible (动词)虚拟式的

sublet /ˌsʌbˈlet/ **verb** (**sublets, subletting, sublet**) let a property or part of a property that you are already renting to someone else 将(租借的房产)转租

sublimate /ˈsʌblɪmeɪt/ **verb 1** direct energy, especially sexual energy, into socially acceptable activities such as exercise, work, or art 升华；使高尚化 **2** Chemistry【化学】= SUBLIME. ■ **sublimation** noun.

sublime /səˈblaɪm/ **adjective 1** of great beauty or excellence 壮丽的；品质超群的 **2** extreme 极端的；十足的：*sublime confidence* 十足的信心 • **verb** (**sublimes, subliming, sublimed**) Chemistry【化学】(of a solid substance) change directly into vapour when heated (固态物质)升华 ■ **sublimely** adverb.

subliminal /ˌsʌbˈlɪmɪnl/ **adjective** affecting your mind without your being aware of it 下意识的；潜意识的 ■ **subliminally** adverb.

sub-machine gun /ˌsʌbməˈʃiːn/

noun a hand-held lightweight machine gun 冲锋枪；轻型自动(或半自动)枪

submarine /ˌsʌbməˈriːn/ **noun** a streamlined warship designed to operate completely submerged in the sea 潜艇；潜水艇 • **adjective** existing, occurring, or used under the surface of the sea 水下的；海中的；水下(或海中)使用的 ■ **submariner** noun.

submerge /səbˈmɜːdʒ/ **verb** (**submerges, submerging, submerged**) **1** push or hold something underwater 浸没，淹没；使没入水中 **2** go down below the surface of water 没入水中；潜入水中 **3** completely cover or hide 淹没；湮灭

submerse /səbˈmɜːs/ **verb** submerge 浸没；淹没 ■ **submersion** noun.

submersible /səbˈmɜːsəbl/ **adjective** designed to operate while submerged 可潜水的；可浸入水中的

submicroscopic /ˌsʌbmaɪkrəˈskɒpɪk/ **adjective** too small to be seen by a microscope 亚微观的(普通显微镜看不见的)

submission /səbˈmɪʃn/ **noun 1** the action of submitting 递交；呈递 **2** a proposal or application submitted for consideration 呈递书；提案

submissive /səbˈmɪsɪv/ **adjective** very obedient or passive 谦恭的；恭顺的 ■ **submissively** adverb.

submit /səbˈmɪt/ **verb** (**submits, submitting, submitted**) **1** give in to the authority, control, or greater strength of someone or something 屈服，服从；投降 **2** present a proposal or application for consideration 提交，呈递(提案或申请表) **3** subject to a particular process or treatment 使接受(流程或治疗)

subordinate adjective /səˈbɔːdɪnət/ **1** lower in rank or position 下级的；级别低的 **2** of less importance 次要的；第二位的 • **noun** /səˈbɔːdɪnət/ a person who is under the authority of someone else 部属；下级 • **verb** /səˈbɔːdɪneɪt/ (**subordinates, subordinating, subordinated**) treat someone or something as less important than another 把…置于次要地位；使从属于 ■ **subordination** noun.

subplot /ˈsʌbplɒt/ **noun** a secondary plot in a play, novel, etc. (剧本、小说等的)次要情节

subpoena /səˈpiːnə/ Law 【法律】 **noun** a written order instructing someone to attend a court (传唤出庭作证的)传票 • **verb** (**subpoenas, subpoenaing, subpoenaed**) summon someone with a subpoena (用传票)传唤

subscribe /səbˈskraɪb/ **verb** (**subscribes, subscribing, subscribed**) **1** (often **subscribe to**) arrange to receive something regularly by paying in advance 订购；订阅 **2** (**subscribe to**) contribute a sum of money to a project or cause 认捐，捐助，赞助(一定款项) **3** (**subscribe to**) say you agree with an idea or proposal 同意，赞成，赞许(想法或建议) ■ **subscriber** noun.

subscript /ˈsʌbskrɪpt/ **adjective** (of a letter, figure, or symbol) printed below the line (字母、数字或符号)印在下方的，下标的，角注的

subscription /səbˈskrɪpʃn/ **noun 1** money paid to subscribe to something 订阅费；订购费 **2** the action of subscribing 订阅；订购；认捐；捐助

subsection /ˈsʌbsekʃn/ **noun** a division of a section 分支；分段；分区；分部

subsequent /ˈsʌbsɪkwənt/ **adjective** coming after something 随后的；后来的 ■ **subsequently** adverb.

subservient /səbˈsɜːviənt/ **adjective** too ready to obey other people 卑躬屈膝的；恭顺的；驯服的 ■ **subservience** noun.

subside /səbˈsaɪd/ **verb** (**subsides, subsiding, subsided**) **1** become less strong, violent, or severe 减弱;减退;平静;平息 **2** (of water) go down to a lower level (水)回落,消退 **3** (of a building) sink lower into the ground (建筑物)下陷,下沉,塌陷 **4** (of the ground) cave in; sink (地面)下陷,下沉 **5** (**subside into**) give way to a strong feeling 陷于(强烈感情);禁不住…起来

subsidence /səb'saɪdns/ **noun** the gradual caving in or sinking of an area of land (地面)下陷,下沉,沉降

subsidiary /səb'sɪdiəri/ **adjective 1** related but less important 辅助的;附带的;从属的;次要的 **2** (of a company) controlled by another company (公司)隶属(另一公司)的 • **noun** (plural **subsidiaries**) a subsidiary company 附属公司;子公司

subsidize or **subsidise** /'sʌbsɪdaɪz/ **verb** (**subsidizes, subsidizing, subsidized**) **1** support an organization or activity financially 补助,资助(机构或活动) **2** pay part of the cost of producing something to reduce its price 给…发津贴(或补贴)

subsidy /'sʌbsədi/ **noun** (plural **subsidies**) a sum of money given to help keep the price of a product or service low (用以保持产品或服务低价格的)补贴,补助金,津贴

subsist /səb'sɪst/ **verb** maintain or support yourself at a basic level 生存;维持生计

subsistence /səb'sɪstəns/ **noun** the action or fact of subsisting 活命;存活;生存 • **adjective** (of production) at a level which is enough only for your own use, without any surplus for trade (产量)仅够自身用的,没有贸易余量的

subsoil /'sʌbsɔɪl/ **noun** soil lying under the surface soil (土壤的)底土,心土

subsonic /sʌb'sɒnɪk/ **adjective** relating to or flying at a speed less than that of sound 亚声速(飞行)的

substance /'sʌbstəns/ **noun 1** a type of solid, liquid, or gas that has particular qualities (具有某一特性的)物质,物品 **2** the real physical matter of which a person or thing consists (构成人或事物的)物质;材料 **3** solid basis in reality or fact 事实基础;根据 **4** the quality of being important, valid, or significant 重要性;有效性 **5** the most important or essential part or meaning 实质;本质;主旨

substandard /sʌb'stændəd/ **adjective** below the usual or required standard 不够标准的;不合格的

substantial /səb'stænʃl/ **adjective 1** of considerable importance, size, or value 重大的;相当大的;价值巨大的 **2** strongly built or made 结实的;坚固的 **3** concerning the essential points of something 实质的;本质的;基本的

substantially /səb'stænʃəli/ **adverb 1** to a great extent 非常;相当大地;在很大程度上 **2** for the most part; mainly 多半;大部分地;主要地

substantiate /səb'stænʃieɪt/ **verb** (**substantiates, substantiating, substantiated**) provide evidence to support or prove the truth of something 证明;证实

substantive /'sʌbstəntɪv/ **adjective** real and meaningful 实质性的;重大的 ■ **substantively** adverb.

substitute /'sʌbstɪtjuːt/ **noun** a person or thing that does something in place of someone or something else 替代者;替代物;代用品 • **verb** (**substitutes, substituting, substituted**) make someone or something act as a substitute for (用…)取代,代替 ■ **substitution** noun.

subsume /səb'sjuːm/ **verb** (**subsumes, subsuming, subsumed**) include or absorb something in something else 把…包括在内;将…纳入

subterfuge /'sʌbtəfjuːdʒ/ **noun** secretive or dishonest actions 花招;

佽俩

subterranean /ˌsʌbtə'reɪnɪən/ **adjective** existing or happening under the earth's surface 存在于地表下的;在地下进行的;地表下发生的

subtext /'sʌbtekst/ **noun** an underlying theme in a piece of writing or speech (作品或谈话中的)潜台词

subtitle /'sʌbtaɪtl/ **noun 1** (**subtitles**) words displayed at the bottom of a cinema or television screen that translate what is being said (电影或电视屏幕下方的翻译)字幕 **2** a secondary title of a published work (图书等的)副标题, 小标题 • **verb** (**subtitles, subtitling, subtitled**) provide something with a subtitle or subtitles 给…加副标题(或小标题);给…配字幕

subtle /'sʌtl/ **adjective** (**subtler, subtlest**) **1** so delicate or precise as to be difficult to analyse or describe 微妙的;玄妙的;难以捉摸的 **2** capable of making fine distinctions 细心的;敏锐的 **3** making use of clever and indirect methods to achieve something 精巧的;精致的;技艺精湛的 ■ **subtlety noun subtly** adverb.

subtotal /'sʌbtəʊtl/ **noun** the total of one set within a larger set of figures 小计;部分和

subtract /səb'trækt/ **verb** take away a number or amount from another to calculate the difference 减, 减去(数字或数量) ■ **subtraction** noun.

suburb /'sʌbɜːb/ **noun** a residential district that is outside the central part of a city 市郊;郊区 ■ **suburban** adjective.

suburbia /sə'bɜːbɪə/ **noun** suburbs, and the way of life of the people who live in them 郊区及其居民的生活方式

subversive /səb'vɜːsɪv/ **adjective** trying to damage or weaken the power of an established system or institution 企图颠覆(现存体制或机构)的 • **noun** a subversive person 颠覆分子;破坏分子 ■ **subversively** adverb.

subvert /səb'vɜːt/ **verb** damage or weaken the power of an established system or institution 破坏,颠覆(现有体制或机构) ■ **subversion** noun.

subway /'sʌbweɪ/ **noun 1** Brit. [英] a passage under a road for use by pedestrians (马路下面供行人穿越的)地下通道 **2** N. Amer. [北美] an underground railway 地铁

sub-zero /ˌsʌb'zɪərəʊ/ **adjective** (of temperature) lower than zero; below freezing (温度)低于零度的,零下的

succeed /sək'siːd/ **verb 1** achieve an aim or purpose 达到目的,实现目标 **2** gain wealth or status 发财;升迁 **3** take over a job, role, or title from someone else 接替(某人)的工作(或职位);继承(某人)的头衔 **4** come after and take the place of 接替;继任;随后出现

success /sək'ses/ **noun 1** the achievement of an aim or purpose 成功;胜利 **2** the gaining of wealth or status 发财;升迁 **3** a person or thing that achieves success 成功的人(或事物)

✔ 拼写指南 double c and double s in success, successful, and succession, and successive. success, successful, succession 和 successive 中有两个 c 和两个 s。

successful /sək'sesfl/ **adjective 1** having achieved an aim or purpose 成功的;有成效的;胜利的 **2** having gained wealth or status 富有的;有地位的 ■ **successfully** adverb.

succession /sək'seʃn/ **noun 1** a number of people or things following one after the other (人或事的)一连串,一系列 **2** the action, process, or right of inheriting a position or title (职位的)继任(权);(头衔的)继承(权)

successive /sək'sesɪv/ **adjecti**

following one another or following others 接连的；依次的；连续的 ■ **successively** adverb.

successor /sək'sesə(r)/ **noun** a person or thing that succeeds another 继承人(或物)；继任人(或物)

succinct /sək'sɪŋkt/ **adjective** briefly and clearly expressed 简要的；简明的；简洁的 ■ **succinctly** adverb.

succour /'sʌkə(r)/ (US spelling【美拼作】**succor**) **noun** help and support in difficult times (困难时的)帮助，援助，救助 ■ **verb** give help and support to 援助；救助

succulent /'sʌkjələnt/ **adjective 1** (of food) tender, juicy, and tasty (食物)汁多味美的 **2** (of a plant) having thick fleshy leaves or stems that store water (植物)肉质的,多汁的 ● **noun** a succulent plant 肉质植物；多汁植物 ■ **succulence** noun.

succumb /sə'kʌm/ **verb 1** give in to pressure or temptation 屈从(于压力)；抵挡不住(诱惑) **2** die from the effect of a disease or injury (因病或受伤而)死亡

such /sʌtʃ/ **determiner & pronoun 1** of the type previously mentioned or about to be mentioned 这样的；这种的；此类的 **2** to so high a degree; so great 如此程度的；非常的；那么的 □ **such as 1** for example 例如 **2** of a kind that; like 诸如此类的；像…这种的

suchlike /'sʌtʃlaɪk/ **pronoun** things of the type mentioned 诸如此类的事物

suck /sʌk/ **verb 1** draw something into your mouth by tightening your lip muscles to make a partial vacuum 吸；吮；嘬；咂 **2** hold something in your mouth and draw at it by tightening your lip and cheek muscles 吮吸；吸食；将(某物)含在嘴里舔食 **3** draw something in a particular direction by creating a vacuum 卷入；吸入；吞没 **4** (**suck someone in** or **into**) involve someone in a situation or activity without them being able to choose or resist it 使(某人)卷入(不想做的事) **5** (**suck up to**) informal【非正式】do things to please someone in authority in order to gain advantage for yourself 巴结；奉承 **6** N. Amer. informal【北美,非正式】be very bad or unpleasant 极糟的;恶心 ● **noun** an act of sucking 吸；吮；嘬；咂

sucker /'sʌkə(r)/ **noun 1** a rubber cup that sticks to a surface by suction 橡皮吸盘 **2** an organ that allows an animal to cling to a surface by suction (动物的)吸盘 **3** informal【非正式】a person who is easily fooled 容易受骗的人 **4** (**a sucker for**) informal【非正式】a person who is very fond of a particular thing 对…着迷的人；酷爱…的人 **5** a shoot springing from the base of a tree or other plant (树或其他植物的)根出条,吸枝

suckle /'sʌkl/ **verb** (**suckles, suckling, suckled**) feed at the breast or a teat 给…喂奶；给…哺乳

suckling /'sʌklɪŋ/ **noun** a young child or animal that is still feeding on its mother's milk 乳儿；乳畜；乳兽

sucrose /'su:krəʊs/ **noun** the main substance in cane or beet sugar (从甘蔗或甜菜中榨取的)蔗糖

suction /'sʌkʃn/ **noun** the force produced when a partial vacuum is created by the removal of air (因抽气形成真空状态而产生的)吸力

Sudanese /ˌsu:dən'i:z/ **noun** a person from Sudan 苏丹人 ● **adjective** relating to Sudan 苏丹的

sudden /'sʌdn/ **adjective** happening or done quickly and unexpectedly 突然的；出乎意料的 ■ **suddenly** adverb **suddenness** noun.

sudoku /su'dəʊku:/ **noun** a type of number puzzle 数独游戏

suds /sʌdz/ **plural noun** froth made from soap and water 肥皂泡沫

sue /suː/ verb (**sues, suing, sued**) **1** start legal proceedings against someone that you claim has harmed you 控告；对…提起诉讼 **2** (**sue for**) formal【正式】appeal formally to a person for 请求，恳求；要求

suede /sweɪd/ noun leather with the flesh side rubbed to give it a velvety surface 绒面革

suet /ˈsuːɪt/ noun hard white fat obtained from cattle, sheep, and other animals, used in cooking (牛、羊等动物的)板油

suffer /ˈsʌfə(r)/ verb (**suffers, suffering, suffered**) **1** experience something bad 经受；遭受 **2** (**suffer from**) be affected by an illness or condition 受(疾病或状况)侵袭；患…病；受…苦 **3** become worse in quality 变差；变糟 **4** old use【旧】tolerate 忍受；容忍 ■ **sufferer** noun.

sufferance /ˈsʌfərəns/ noun toleration, rather than genuine approval 忍受；忍耐；容忍

suffice /səˈfaɪs/ verb (**suffices, sufficing, sufficed**) be enough or adequate 足够；足以

sufficiency /səˈfɪʃnsi/ noun (plural **sufficiencies**) **1** the quality of being enough or adequate 足够 **2** an adequate amount 足量；充足

sufficient /səˈfɪʃnt/ adjective enough; adequate 足够的；充足的；充分的 ■ **sufficiently** adverb.

suffix /ˈsʌfɪks/ noun a part added on to the end of a word (e.g. *-ly, -ation*) 后缀；词尾

suffocate /ˈsʌfəkeɪt/ verb (**suffocates, suffocating, suffocated**) die or cause to die from lack of air or being unable to breathe (使)窒息而死；(使)闷死 ■ **suffocation** noun.

suffrage /ˈsʌfrɪdʒ/ noun the right to vote in political elections (政治选举中的)选举权，投票权

suffragette /ˌsʌfrəˈdʒet/ noun (in the past, when only men could vote) a woman who campaigned for the right to vote in an election (旧时只有男子可以投票选举时)争取妇女选举权的女子

suffuse /səˈfjuːz/ verb (**suffuses, suffusing, suffused**) gradually spread through or over (逐渐)弥漫于，布满，充满 ■ **suffusion** noun.

sugar /ˈʃʊɡə(r)/ noun **1** a sweet substance obtained from sugar cane or sugar beet (从甘蔗或甜菜中榨取的)糖 **2** a type of sweet soluble carbohydrate found in plant and animal tissue 糖(指见于植物和动物组织中的任何一种可溶的甜味碳水化合物) ▪ verb sweeten, sprinkle, or coat with sugar 在…中加糖；在…上撒糖；在…外裹糖衣 □ **sugar beet** a type of beet from which sugar is extracted 甜菜 **sugar cane** a tropical grass with tall thick stems from which sugar is extracted 甘蔗 **sugar daddy** informal【非正式】a rich older man who gives presents and money to a much younger woman 甜爹(指给年轻女子滥送礼物的老富翁) ■ **sugary** adjective.

suggest /səˈdʒest/ verb **1** put forward an idea or plan for people to consider 建议，提议，提出 **2** make you think that something exists or is the case 使人想到；使人联想到 **3** say or indicate something indirectly (间接地)表明，暗示 **4** (**suggest itself**) (of an idea) come into your mind (想法)出现在脑海中

suggestible /səˈdʒestəbl/ adjective quick to accept other people's ideas or suggestions 易受影响的；易受暗示影响的

suggestion /səˈdʒestʃən/ noun **1** an idea or plan put forward for people to consider (提出的)建议，意见，提议 **2** a thing that suggests that something is the case 暗示；提示 **3** a slight trace or indication 痕迹；细微的迹象

suggestive /səˈdʒestɪv/ adjectiv

1 making you think of a particular thing 提示的；暗示的；引起联想的 **2** hinting at sexual matters 性暗示的；性挑逗的；猥亵的 ■ **suggestively** adverb.

suicide /'suːɪsaɪd/ noun **1** the action of killing yourself intentionally 自杀 **2** a person who commits suicide 自杀者 ■ **suicidal** adjective **suicidally** adverb.

suit /suːt/ noun **1** a set of clothes made of the same fabric, consisting of a jacket and trousers or a skirt 一套衣服(由同一质地的上衣、裤子或裙子组成) **2** a set of clothes for a particular activity 为某项特殊活动所穿的)套装，套服 **3** any of the sets into which a pack of playing cards is divided (spades, hearts, diamonds, and clubs) (扑克牌中)任何花色的一套牌(指黑桃、红心、方块和梅花) **4** a lawsuit 诉讼 • verb **1** be right or good for 便于；有利于 **2** (of clothes, colours, etc.) be right for someone's features or figure (衣服、颜色等)适合于，适宜于(某人的特点或身材) **3** (suit yourself) do as you wish 按自己的意愿行事

suitable /'suːtəbl/ adjective right or good for a particular person or situation 合适的；适合的；适宜的；适当的 ■ **suitability** noun **suitably** adverb.

suitcase /'suːtkeɪs/ noun a case with a handle and a hinged lid, used for carrying clothes and other possessions 手提箱

suite /swiːt/ noun **1** a set of rooms 套间；套房 **2** a set of furniture 一套家具 **3** (in music) a set of instrumental compositions to be played one after the other (音乐中的)组曲

suitor /'suːtə(r)/ noun dated 【废】a man who pays attention to a woman because he wants to marry her 求婚者

sulfur /'sʌlfə(r)/ US spelling of

SULPHUR. sulphur 的美式拼法

sulk /sʌlk/ verb be quietly bad-tempered and resentful because you are annoyed 生闷气；愠怒 • noun a period of sulking 生闷气；愠怒

sulky /'sʌlki/ adjective quietly bad-tempered and resentful 闷闷不乐的；愠怒的；阴郁的 ■ **sulkily** adverb.

sullen /'sʌlən/ adjective silent and bad-tempered 闷闷不乐的；生闷气的；愠怒的 ■ **sullenly** adverb.

sully /'sʌli/ verb (**sullies**, **sullying**, **sullied**) literary 【文】spoil the purity or cleanness of something 玷污；弄脏

sulphur /'sʌlfə(r)/ (US spelling 【美拼作】**sulfur**) noun a chemical element in the form of yellow crystals, which easily catches fire 硫；硫磺 □ **sulphur dioxide** a poisonous gas formed by burning sulphur 二氧化硫

sulphuric /sʌl'fjʊərɪk/ (US spelling 【美拼作】**sulfuric**) adjective containing sulphur 含硫的；含硫酸的 □ **sulphuric acid** a strong corrosive acid 硫酸

sulphurous /'sʌlfərəs/ (US spelling 【美拼作】**sulfurous**) adjective containing or obtained from sulphur 含硫的；含硫磺的

sultan /'sʌltən/ noun a Muslim king or ruler 苏丹(伊斯兰国家的最高统治者)

sultana /sʌl'tɑːnə/ noun **1** Brit.【英】a light brown seedless raisin 无核葡萄干 **2** the wife of a sultan 苏丹女眷(指王后或王妃)

sultry /'sʌltri/ adjective **1** (of the weather) hot and humid (天气)闷热的，湿热的 **2** suggesting sexual passion 性感的；风情万种的

sum /sʌm/ noun **1** a particular amount of money 款额；金额 **2** (also **sum total**) the total amount resulting from the addition of two or more numbers or amounts 总数；总计；总和 **3** a calculation in arithmetic 算术 • verb (**sums**, **summing**, **summed**) (**sum someone/thing up**) **1** describe the nature or character of someone or something concisely 概述···的性格(或特征) **2** summarize something briefly 总结;概括

summarize or **summarise** /'sʌməraɪz/ **verb** (**summarizes, summarizing, summarized**) give a summary of 概述;概括

summary /'sʌməri/ **noun** (plural **summaries**) a brief statement of the main points of something 总结;摘要;概要 • **adjective 1** not including many details; brief 概括的;扼要的;总结性的 **2** (of a legal process or judgement) done or made immediately and without following the normal procedures (司法程序或判决)即决的,简易的 ■ **summarily** adverb.

summation /sʌ'meɪʃn/ **noun 1** the process of adding things together 求和;相加 **2** the action of summing up 总结 **3** a summary 总结;摘要;概要

summer /'sʌmə(r)/ **noun** the season after spring and before autumn 夏天;夏季 □ **summer house** a small building in a garden, used for relaxing in during hot weather (花园中的)凉亭 ■ **summery** adjective.

summit /'sʌmɪt/ **noun 1** the highest point of a hill or mountain (小山或山岳的)峰顶,最高点,绝顶 **2** the highest possible level of achievement (成就的)顶峰,极点 **3** a meeting between heads of government (政府首脑间的)最高级会议,峰会

summon /'sʌmən/ **verb 1** order someone to be present 传讯;传唤 **2** urgently ask for help (紧急地)请求, 吁求(帮助) **3** call people to attend a meeting 召集(会议) **4** make an effort to produce a quality or reaction from within yourself 鼓起;振作;使出

summons /'sʌmənz/ **noun** (plural **summonses**) **1** an order to appear in a law court (法庭的)传唤,传讯 **2** an

act of summoning 召唤;命令

sumo /'suːməʊ/ **noun** a Japanese form of wrestling (日本)相扑

sump /sʌmp/ **noun** the base of an internal-combustion engine, in which a reserve of oil is stored (润滑系统的)油底壳,集油槽

sumptuous /'sʌmptʃuəs/ **adjective** splendid and expensive-looking 豪华的;奢侈的;奢华的 ■ **sumptuously** adverb.

sun /sʌn/ **noun 1** (also **Sun**) the star round which the earth orbits 太阳 **2** any similar star 恒星 **3** the light or warmth received from the sun 阳光;日光;太阳热 • **verb** (**suns, sunning, sunned**) (**sun yourself**) sit or lie outside in the heat of the sun 晒太阳

sunbathe /'sʌnbeɪð/ **verb** (**sunbathes, sunbathing, sunbathed**) sit or lie outside in the sun to get a suntan (为晒黑皮肤而)晒太阳,沐日光浴

sunbeam /'sʌnbiːm/ **noun** a ray of sunlight 日光光束

sunbed /'sʌnbed/ **noun** Brit. [英] **1** a long chair that you lie on when sunbathing 日光浴浴床 **2** a bed between two banks of sunlamps, which you lie on to get an artificial suntan 太阳灯浴浴床

sunblock /'sʌnblɒk/ **noun** a cream or lotion used on the skin for complete protection from sunburn 防晒膏(或霜)

sunburn /'sʌnbɜːn/ **noun** inflammation of the skin caused by too much exposure to the ultraviolet rays of the sun 晒伤;晒斑 ■ **sunburned** (or **sunburnt**) adjective.

sundae /'sʌndeɪ/ **noun** a dish of ice cream with added fruit and syrup 圣代冰激凌(加有水果和糖浆)

✔ 拼写指南 -ae, not -ay: sund*ae* suanda*e* 中的 -ae 不要拼作 -ay.

Sunday /'sʌndeɪ, -di/ **noun** the da

of the week before Monday and following Saturday, observed by Christians as a day of worship 星期日;星期天 □ **Sunday school** a class held on Sundays to teach children about Christianity or Judaism (在星期日对儿童进行基督教或犹太教教育的)主日学校

sunder /'sʌndə(r)/ **verb** (**sunders, sundering, sundered**) literary【文】split apart 分开;隔开;撕裂

sundial /'sʌndaɪəl/ **noun** an instrument showing the time by the shadow cast by a pointer 日晷(仪);日规

sundry /'sʌndri/ **adjective** of various kinds 各种各样的;杂七杂八的 • **noun** (**sundries**) various items not important enough to be mentioned individually 杂项(物品)

sunflower /'sʌnflaʊə(r)/ **noun** a tall plant with very large yellow flowers 向日葵;葵花

sung /sʌŋ/ past participle of SING.

sunglasses /'sʌnglɑːsɪz/ **plural noun** glasses tinted to protect the eyes from sunlight 太阳镜;墨镜

sunk /sʌŋk/ past participle of SINK.

sunken /'sʌŋkən/ **adjective 1** having sunk 沉没的;下陷的 **2** at a lower level than the surrounding area 低洼的;凹陷的

sunlamp /'sʌnlæmp/ **noun** a lamp giving off ultraviolet rays, under which you lie to get an artificial suntan 太阳灯

sunlight /'sʌnlaɪt/ **noun** light from the sun 阳光;日光 ■ **sunlit** adjective.

Sunni /'sʊni/ **noun** (plural **Sunni** or **Sunnis**) **1** one of the two main branches of Islam. The other is Shia 逊尼派(伊斯兰教两大派别之一,另一派为什叶派) **2** a Muslim who follows the Sunni branch of Islam 逊尼派教徒

sunny /'sʌni/ **adjective** (**sunnier, sunniest**) **1** bright with or receiving a lot of sunlight 阳光明媚的;阳光充足的 **2** cheerful 愉快的;高兴的

sunrise /'sʌnraɪz/ **noun 1** the time when the sun rises 日出(时分) **2** the colours and light visible in the sky at sunrise 晨曦;朝霞

sunroof /'sʌnruːf/ **noun** a panel in the roof of a car that can be opened to let air in (汽车车顶可开启的)遮阳篷顶,天窗

sunscreen /'sʌnskriːn/ **noun** a cream or lotion rubbed on to the skin to protect it from the sun 防晒霜;防晒油

sunset /'sʌnset/ **noun 1** the time when the sun sets 日落,日没(时分) **2** the colours and light visible in the sky at sunset 晚霞

sunshade /'sʌnʃeɪd/ **noun** a light umbrella or awning giving protection from the sun 遮阳伞;遮阳篷

sunshine /'sʌnʃaɪn/ **noun** sunlight unbroken by cloud 日光;日照;阳光;晴朗

sunspot /'sʌnspɒt/ **noun** a temporary darker and cooler patch on the sun's surface 太阳黑子

sunstroke /'sʌnstrəʊk/ **noun** heatstroke brought about by staying in the sun for too long 日射病;中暑

suntan /'sʌntæn/ **noun** a golden-brown colouring of the skin caused by spending time in the sun (皮肤的)晒黑;晒成的棕褐肤色 ■ **suntanned** adjective.

sup¹ /sʌp/ **verb** (**sups, supping, supped**) dated or N. English【旧或英格兰北部】take drink or liquid food by sips or spoonfuls 小口地喝;用汤匙喝；呷,啜(饮料或液体食物) • **noun** a sip 一小口;一啜

sup² **verb** (**sups, supping, supped**) old use【旧】eat supper 吃晚饭

super /'suːpə(r)/ **adjective** informal【非正式】excellent 极好的;绝妙的

superannuate /ˌsuːpər'ænjueɪt/ **verb** (**superannuates, superannuating,**

superannuated) 1 arrange for someone to retire with a pension 使(某人)领取养老金退休 **2 (superannuated)** humorous【谐默】too old to be effective or useful 老朽的；老弱无能的

superannuation /ˌsuːpərænjuˈeɪʃn/ **noun** regular payment made by an employee into a fund from which a future pension will be paid (雇员为得到退休金而需按期支付的)养老金

superb /suːˈpɜːb/ **adjective 1** very good; excellent 优秀的，极好的 **2** magnificent or splendid 壮丽的，豪华的 ■ **superbly** adverb.

supercharger /ˈsuːpətʃɑːdʒə(r)/ **noun** a device that makes an engine more efficient by forcing extra air or fuel into it 增压器(通过增加内燃机内空气或燃料以提高效率的装置) ■ **supercharged** adjective.

supercilious /ˌsuːpəˈsɪliəs/ **adjective** having a manner that shows you think you are better than other people 目空一切的，傲慢的，自大的

superficial /ˌsuːpəˈfɪʃl/ **adjective 1** existing or happening at or on the surface 表面的，表层的 **2** apparent rather than real 表面上的，外表的 **3** not thorough 粗略的，草率的 **4** lacking the ability to think deeply about things 肤浅的，浅薄的 ■ **superficiality** noun **superficially** adverb.

superfluous /suːˈpɜːfluəs/ **adjective** more than what is needed 过多的，过剩的，多余的 ■ **superfluity** noun.

superglue /ˈsuːpəgluː/ **noun** a very strong quick-setting glue 超级胶，强力胶

supergrass /ˈsuːpəgrɑːs/ **noun** Brit. informal【英，非正式】a person who secretly gives the police information about the criminal activities of a large number of people (告发多人犯罪活动的)向警方告密者

superhuman /ˌsuːpəˈhjuːmən/ **adjective** having exceptional ability or

powers 超人的；神奇的；非凡的

superimpose /ˌsuːpərɪmˈpəʊz/ **verb (superimposes, superimposing, superimposed)** lay one thing over another 把(某物)放在(或堆在)另一物之上 ■ **superimposition** noun.

superintend /ˌsuːpərɪnˈtend/ **verb** manage or oversee 主管；监督；监管

superintendent /ˌsuːpərɪnˈtendənt/ **noun 1** a person who supervises and controls a group or activity (团体或活动的)主管，负责人 **2** a senior police officer (较高等级的)警官，警司

superior /suːˈpɪəriə(r)/ **adjective 1** higher in status, quality, or power (地位、品质或权力)较高的 **2** of high quality (质量)高的，优秀的，优良的 **3** arrogant and conceited 高傲的，自负的 • **noun** a person of higher rank or status 上级，长官

superiority /suːˌpɪəriˈɒrəti/ **noun** the state of being superior 优秀；优良；优越

superlative /suːˈpɜːlətɪv/ **adjective 1** of the highest quality or degree (质量或程度)最高的，最好的 **2** (of an adjective or adverb) expressing the highest degree of a quality (e.g. *bravest*) (形容词或副词)最高级的 • **noun** an exaggerated expression of praise (用于赞美的)极端话，夸大话

superman /ˈsuːpəmæn/ **noun** (plural **supermen**) informal【非正式】a man who is unusually strong or intelligent (具有非凡体力或脑力的)超人

supermarket /ˈsuːpəmɑːkɪt/ **noun** a large self-service shop selling foods and household goods 超级市场；超市

supermodel /ˈsuːpəmɒdl/ **noun** a very successful and famous fashion model 超级模特

supernatural /ˌsuːpəˈnætʃrəl/ **adjective** not able to be explained by the laws of nature 超自然的 • **noun (the supernatural)** supernatural events 超自然现象 ■ **supernaturally** adverb.

supernova /ˌsuːpəˈnəʊvə/ **noun**

(plural **supernovae** /ˌsuːpəˈnəʊviː/ or **supernovas**) a star that undergoes an explosion, becoming suddenly very much brighter 超新星(因爆炸而突然亮度大增的星体)

supernumerary /ˌsuːpəˈnjuːmərəri/ **adjective 1** present in more than the required number 过剩的；额外的；多余的 **2** not belonging to a regular staff but employed for extra work 打杂的

superpower /ˈsuːpəpaʊə(r)/ **noun** a very powerful and influential country 超级大国

superscript /ˈsuːpəskrɪpt/ **adjective** (of a letter, figure, or symbol) printed above the line (字母、数字或符号)印在上方的，上角标的

supersede /ˌsuːpəˈsiːd/ **verb** (**supersedes**, **superseding**, **superseded**) take the place of 替代；取代

✔ 拼写指南 *-sede*, not *-cede*: super*sede*. supersede 中的 *-sede* 不要拼作 *-cede*.

supersonic /ˌsuːpəˈsɒnɪk/ **adjective** involving or flying at a speed greater than that of sound 超音速的；超声速的

superstar /ˈsuːpəstɑː(r)/ **noun** a very famous and successful performer or sports player 超级明星(指非常著名、成功的表演者或运动员)

superstition /ˌsuːpəˈstɪʃn/ **noun** a belief in the supernatural, especially that particular things bring good or bad luck 迷信；迷信观念

superstitious /ˌsuːpəˈstɪʃəs/ **adjective** believing in the supernatural and in the power of particular things to bring good or bad luck 有迷信观念的；迷信的 ■ **superstitiously** adverb.

superstore /ˈsuːpəstɔː(r)/ **noun** a very large out-of-town supermarket (城外的)大型超级市场

superstructure /ˈsuːpəstrʌktʃə(r)/ **noun 1** a structure built on top of something else (建于他物之上的)上层结构，上层建筑 **2** the part of a structure that is built above a supporting base or foundation 上部建筑(建筑物高于地基的部分)

supervene /ˌsuːpəˈviːn/ **verb** happen so as to interrupt or change an existing situation 意外发生；随后发生

supervise /ˈsuːpəvaɪz/ **verb** be in charge of the carrying out of a task or the work done by a person, ensuring that everything is done correctly 监督，管理，指导(任务或某人的工作) ■ **supervision** noun **supervisor** noun **supervisory** adjective.

supine /ˈsuːpaɪn/ **adjective 1** lying face upwards 仰卧的；平躺着的 **2** failing to act as a result of laziness or weakness 懒散的；倦怠的；软弱的；缺乏勇气的

supper /ˈsʌpə(r)/ **noun** a light or informal evening meal (简单或非正式的)晚饭，晚餐

supplant /səˈplɑːnt/ **verb** take the place of 取代；替代

supple /ˈsʌpl/ **adjective** (**suppler**, **supplest**) able to bend and move parts of your body easily; flexible (身体)灵活的，柔软的，柔韧的，易弯曲的

supplement noun /ˈsʌplɪmənt/ **1** a thing added to something else to improve or complete it 增补(物)；补充(物) **2** a separate section added to a newspaper or magazine (报纸或杂志的)副刊，增刊 **3** an additional charge payable for an extra service or facility (为额外服务或设施而支付的)附加费 • verb /ˈsʌplɪment/ add an extra thing or amount to 增补；补充 ■ **supplemental** adjective.

supplementary /ˌsʌplɪˈmentri/ **adjective** completing or improving something 补充的；增补的；改进的

suppliant /ˈsʌplɪənt/ **noun** a person who makes a humble request 恳求者；哀求者 • adjective making a humble request 恳求的；哀求的

supplicate /ˈsʌplɪkeɪt/ **verb** (**supplicates, supplicating, supplicated**) humbly ask for something 恳求;央求 ■ **supplicant** noun **supplication** noun.

supply /səˈplaɪ/ **verb** (**supplies, supplying, supplied**) provide someone with something that is needed or wanted (为…)提供所需物;供给;供应 • **noun** (plural **supplies**) **1** a stock or amount of something supplied or available 供给品;供给量;储备物 **2** the action of supplying 供给;供应 **3** (**supplies**) provisions and equipment necessary for a large group of people or for an expedition (大群人或探险队的)必需品,补给品 ■ **supplier** noun.

support /səˈpɔːt/ **verb 1** carry all or part of the weight of 支撑;支承 **2** give help, encouragement, or approval to 支援;鼓励;赞成 **3** confirm or back up 证实;证明 **4** provide someone with a home and the things they need in order to live 供养;赡养;养活 **5** like a particular sports team and watch or go to their matches 支持,喜爱(某支运动队) • **noun 1** help, encouragement, or approval 支援;支持;鼓励;赞成 **2** a person or thing that supports 支援者;支持者;拥护者;资助者;支撑物 **3** the action of supporting 支撑;支承 ■ **supporter** noun.

supportive /səˈpɔːtɪv/ **adjective** providing encouragement or emotional help 支持的;援助的;鼓励的

suppose /səˈpəʊz/ **verb** (**supposes, supposing, supposed**) **1** think that something is true or likely, but lack proof 猜想;料想 **2** consider something as a possibility 假定;假设 **3** (**be supposed to do**) be required or expected to do 须;应当;应该

supposedly /səˈpəʊzɪdli/ **adverb** according to what is generally believed 据称;据猜测

supposition /ˌsʌpəˈzɪʃn/ **noun** a belief that something is likely to be true 假定;猜测

suppository /səˈpɒzɪtri/ **noun** (plural **suppositories**) a solid medical preparation designed to dissolve after being inserted into the rectum or vagina 栓剂(放入直肠或阴道溶解的小块药物)

suppress /səˈpres/ **verb 1** forcibly put an end to 压制;镇压 **2** prevent from acting or developing 阻止…发生(或发展) **3** stop something from being stated or published 抑制(言论);阻止(某物的出版) ■ **suppressant** noun **suppression** noun.

> ✔ 拼写指南 two *p*s: su*pp*ress.
> suppress 中有两个 p。

suppurate /ˈsʌpjʊreɪt/ **verb** (**suppurates, suppurating, suppurated**) form pus 化脓 ■ **suppuration** noun.

supremacist /suːˈpreməsɪst/ **noun** a person who believes that a particular group is superior to all others 至上主义者;优越论者

supremacy /suːˈpreməsi/ **noun** the state of being superior to all others 至高无上;最高地位;优势

supreme /suːˈpriːm/ **adjective 1** highest in authority or rank (权力或地位)最高的,至上的 **2** very great or greatest; most important 极大的,极度的,最大(程度)的;最重要的 □ **supreme court** the highest law court in a country or state (某国或某州的)最高法院 ■ **supremely** adverb.

supremo /suːˈpriːməʊ/ **noun** (plural **supremos**) Brit. informal【英,非正式】a person in overall charge 最高统治者;最高领导人;总管;总指挥

surcharge /ˈsɜːtʃɑːdʒ/ **noun** an extra charge or payment 附加费;增收费

surd /sɜːd/ **noun** Maths【数学】a number which cannot be expressed as a ratio of two whole numbers 无理数;不尽根

sure /ʃʊə(r)/ **adjective 1** completely

confident that you are right 确信的；肯定的 **2** (**sure of** or **to do**) certain to receive, get, or do 一定；必定；肯定 **3** undoubtedly true 无可置疑的；毫无疑问的 **4** steady and confident 可靠的；稳妥的；有把握的；有信心的 • adverb informal【非正式】certainly 当然 ■ **sureness** noun.

surely /'ʃʊəli/ **adverb 1** it must be true that 确实；无疑 **2** certainly 当然

surety /'ʃʊərəti/ noun (plural **sureties**) **1** a person who guarantees that somebody else will do something or pay a debt 担保人；保证人 **2** money given as a guarantee that someone will do something 担保金；保证金

surf /sɜːf/ noun the breaking of large waves on a seashore or reef (拍打海岸或暗礁的)碎波，激浪 • verb **1** stand or lie on a surfboard and ride on the crest of a wave towards the shore 冲浪；进行冲浪运动 **2** move from site to site on the Internet (在因特网上)浏览 ■ **surfer** noun **surfing** noun.

surface /'sɜːfɪs/ noun **1** the outside or top layer of something (某物的)外部，表面，表层 **2** outward appearance 外表，外观 • verb (**surfaces**, **surfacing**, **surfaced**) **1** rise to the surface 升到地面(或水面) **2** become apparent 显露；显现 **3** provide a road, floor, etc. with a top layer 给(道路、地板等)铺设某种面层

surfboard /'sɜːfbɔːd/ noun a long, narrow board used in surfing 冲浪板

surfeit /'sɜːfɪt/ noun an amount that is more than is needed or wanted 过量；过度

surge /sɜːdʒ/ noun **1** a sudden powerful movement forwards or upwards 汹涌，澎湃 **2** a sudden increase 激增；急剧上升 **3** a powerful rush of an emotion or feeling (感情)的一阵激动 • verb (**surges**, **surging**, **surged**) **1** move in a surge 汹涌；澎湃 **2** increase suddenly and powerfully 激增；急剧上升

surgeon /'sɜːdʒən/ noun a doctor who is qualified to practise surgery 外科医生

surgery /'sɜːdʒəri/ noun (plural **surgeries**) **1** medical treatment that involves cutting open the body and repairing or removing parts 外科手术 **2** Brit.【英】a place where a doctor or nurse sees patients 诊所；诊室

surgical /'sɜːdʒɪkl/ adjective relating to or used in surgery 外科的；外科手术的 □ **surgical spirit** Brit.【英】methylated spirit used for cleaning the skin before injections or surgery (注射或手术前清洗皮肤用的)消毒用酒精 ■ **surgically** adverb.

surly /'sɜːli/ adjective (**surlier**, **surliest**) bad-tempered and unfriendly 脾气坏的；乖戾的；不友好的

surmise /sə'maɪz/ verb (**surmises**, **surmising**, **surmised**) suppose something without having evidence 猜测；臆测 • noun a guess 猜测；推测；臆测

surmount /sə'maʊnt/ verb **1** overcome a difficulty or obstacle 克服，战胜(困难或障碍) **2** stand or be placed on top of 位于(或置于)…顶端

surname /'sɜːneɪm/ noun an inherited name used by all the members of a family 姓；姓氏

surpass /sə'pɑːs/ verb be greater or better than 超过；胜过；优于

surplice /'sɜːplɪs/ noun a white robe worn over a cassock by Christian ministers and people singing in church choirs (教士和唱诗班成员做礼拜时穿的)白色罩袍，白色法衣

surplus /'sɜːpləs/ noun an amount left over 过剩；剩余量 • adjective more than what is needed or used 过剩的；剩余的

surprise /sə'praɪz/ noun **1** a feeling of mild astonishment or shock caused by something unexpected 惊奇；诧异 **2** an unexpected or astonishing thing 意想不到的事；令人惊奇

的事 • **verb** (**surprises**, **surprising**, **surprised**) **1** make someone feel surprise 使惊讶；使惊奇；使感到意外 **2** attack or discover suddenly and unexpectedly 突然袭击；意外地发现

✔ 拼写指南 don't forget the first *r*, and note also that **surprise** can't be spelled with an *-ize* ending: su*r*p*r*ise. 不要忘记拼写 surprise 中的第一个 r，并要注意词末不能拼作 -ize。

surreal /sə'ri:əl/ **adjective** strange and having the qualities of a dream 离奇的；荒诞不经的；梦幻般的 ■ **surreally** adverb.

surrealism /sə'ri:əlɪzəm/ **noun** an artistic movement which combined normally unrelated images in a bizarre way 超现实主义 ■ **surrealist** noun & adjective.

surrender /sə'rendə(r)/ **verb** (**surrenders**, **surrendering**, **surrendered**) **1** give in to an opponent 屈服；让步 **2** give up a right or possession 放弃，交出(权利或财产) **3** (**surrender yourself to**) abandon yourself to a powerful emotion or influence 听任(某种强烈感情或影响的)摆布 • **noun** an act of surrendering 投降；屈服；放弃；交出

surreptitious /ˌsʌrəp'tɪʃəs/ **adjective** done secretly 偷偷的；秘密的；保密的 ■ **surreptitiously** adverb.

surrogate /'sʌrəgət/ **noun** a person who stands in for someone else (某人的)替代者，代理人 □ **surrogate mother** a woman who gives birth to a child on behalf of another woman 代孕母亲(代替他人生育的妇女) ■ **surrogacy** noun.

surround /sə'raʊnd/ **verb 1** be all round someone or something 包围；环绕；围住；圈住 **2** be associated with 与…有联系；与…有关 • **noun 1** a border or edging 边，缘 **2** (**surrounds** or **surroundings**) the conditions or

area around a person or thing 周围的情况；环境

surtax /'sɜ:tæks/ **noun** an extra tax on something already taxed 附加税

surtitle /'sɜ:taɪtl/ **noun** a caption projected on a screen above the stage in an opera, translating the words that are being sung (歌剧演出时投射在舞台上方屏幕上的)歌词字幕

surveillance /sɜ:'veɪləns/ **noun** close observation, especially of a suspected spy or criminal (尤指对间谍嫌疑者或疑犯的)监视

survey verb /sə'veɪ/ (**surveys**, **surveying**, **surveyed**) **1** look carefully and thoroughly at 审视；查看；审查 **2** examine and record the features of an area of land in order to produce a map or description 勘测，测绘(土地) **3** Brit. [英] examine and report on the condition of a building 考察，检查，鉴定(建筑物) **4** question a group of people to find out their opinions 对(一群人)进行民意调查(或民意测验) • **noun** /'sɜ:veɪ/ **1** an investigation into the opinions or experience of a group of people, based on a series of questions 民意调查；民意测验 **2** a general view, examination, or description 通观；概论；概略；总体研究；全面述评 **3** an act of surveying 审视，考察，调查；测绘，鉴定 **4** a map or report obtained by surveying 测量图；测量报告 ■ **surveyor** noun.

survival /sə'vaɪvl/ **noun 1** the state or fact of surviving 幸存；存活 **2** an object or practice that has survived from an earlier time 幸存者；幸存物；残存物

survive /sə'vaɪv/ **verb** (**survives**, **surviving**, **survived**) **1** continue to live or exist 继续生存(或存在) **2** remain alive after an accident or ordeal 生存，存活；幸免于难 **3** remain alive after someone has died 比…活得长；比…存在得久 ■ **survivor** noun.

susceptibility /səˌseptə'bɪləti/ **noun**

(plural **susceptibilities**) the quality of being easily influenced or hurt 敏感性；过敏性

susceptible /sə'septəbl/ **adjective 1** (**susceptible to**) likely to be influenced or harmed by 易受影响的；易受伤害的 **2** easily influenced by feelings or emotions 感情丰富的；易动感情的；善感的

sushi /'suːʃi/ **noun** a Japanese dish consisting of balls of cold rice with raw seafood, vegetables, etc. 寿司(一种日本食物，以冷米饭团配生海鲜、蔬菜等)

suspect **verb** /sə'spekt/ **1** believe something to be likely or possible 推测，猜想，料想···有可能 **2** believe that someone is guilty of a crime or offence, without having definite proof 怀疑(某人)有罪(或有过错) **3** feel that something may not be genuine or true 怀疑···的真实性 • **noun** /'sʌspekt/ a person suspected of a crime or offence 嫌疑犯，嫌疑分子 • **adjective** /'sʌspekt/ possibly dangerous or false 可疑的；可能有危险的；不可信的

suspend /sə'spend/ **verb 1** temporarily bring a stop to something 暂停；中止 **2** temporarily stop someone from doing their job or attending school, as a punishment or during an investigation (作为惩罚或在调查期间)暂时解除(某人)的职务，使暂时停学 **3** postpone or delay an action, event, or judgement 延缓，推迟(行动或事件)；暂不作出(判决或判断) **4** (**suspended**) (of a sentence given by a court) not enforced as long as no further offence is committed (判决)暂缓执行 **5** hang something in the air 挂起；吊起

suspender /sə'spendə(r)/ **noun 1** Brit. 【英】an elastic strap attached to a belt and fastened to the top of a stocking to hold it up 吊袜带 **2** (**suspenders**) N. Amer. 【北美】braces for

holding up trousers 吊裤带；背带

suspense /sə'spens/ **noun** a state or feeling of excited or anxious uncertainty about what may happen 悬念；挂虑；担心

suspension /sə'spenʃn/ **noun 1** the action of suspending or the state of being suspended 暂停(状态)；暂缓(状态) **2** a system of springs and shock absorbers which supports a vehicle on its wheels and makes it more comfortable to ride in (装在车轮上减震用的)悬架 **3** a mixture in which particles are spread throughout a fluid 悬浮液 □ **suspension bridge** a bridge which is suspended from cables running between towers 吊桥；悬索桥

suspicion /sə'spiʃn/ **noun 1** an idea that something is possible or likely or that someone has done something wrong 怀疑；嫌疑 **2** a feeling of distrust 不信任 **3** a very slight trace 一点儿；少量

suspicious /sə'spiʃəs/ **adjective 1** having a feeling that someone has done something wrong 感觉可疑的；怀疑的 **2** making you feel that something is wrong 令人怀疑的；可疑的 **3** not able to trust other people 对(某人)表示怀疑(或起疑心)的 ▪ **suspiciously** adverb.

suss /sʌs/ **verb** (**susses, sussing, sussed**) (often **suss someone/thing out**) Brit. informal 【英，非正式】realize or understand the true character or nature of 意识到，认识到(···的特性或本质)

sustain /sə'stein/ **verb 1** strengthen or support someone physically or mentally 给(某人)以力量；支持，鼓励(某人) **2** keep something going over time or continuously 使持续，使保持 **3** experience something unpleasant 遭受，经受，蒙受(令人不快的事物) **4** carry the weight of an object 支撑，

承受(某物的重量)

sustainable /sə'steɪnəbl/ **adjective 1** able to be sustained 能承受的; 支撑得住的;能维持的;能保持的 **2** (of industry, development, or agriculture) avoiding using up natural resources (工业、发展或农业)避免耗尽自然资源的,可持续的 ■ **sustainability** noun **sustainably** adverb.

sustenance /'sʌstənəns/ **noun 1** the food needed to keep someone alive 生活资料;食物;粮食 **2** the process of keeping something going 支持;维持;供养

suture /'suːtʃə(r)/ **noun** a stitch holding together the edges of a wound or surgical cut (伤口或手术切口的)缝合针脚,缝线 • **verb** (**sutures, suturing, sutured**) stitch up a wound or cut 缝合

suzerainty /'suːzəreɪnti/ **noun** the right of one country to rule over another country which has its own ruler but is not fully independent 宗主权

svelte /svelt/ **adjective** slender and elegant 苗条的

SW **abbreviation** southwest or southwestern.

swab /swɒb/ **noun 1** a pad used for cleaning a wound or taking liquid from the body for testing (用来清洗伤口或从人体采集化验标本时用的)药棉块,纱布垫,拭子 **2** a sample of liquid taken with a swab (用拭子取下的)化验标本 • **verb** (**swabs, swabbing, swabbed**) **1** clean or take liquid from a wound or part of the body with a swab 用拭子清洗(伤口);用拭子对(人体)化验标本进行采集 **2** wash down a surface with water and a cloth or mop 用布(或拖布)擦洗(表面)

swaddle /'swɒdl/ **verb** (**swaddles, swaddling, swaddled**) wrap in clothes or a cloth (用衣服或布片)

包裹 □ **swaddling clothes** (in the past) strips of cloth wrapped round a baby to calm it (旧时的)襁褓

swag /swæg/ **noun 1** a curtain hanging in a drooping curve 垂帘 **2** informal 【非正式】property stolen by a burglar (窃贼偷来的)赃物

swagger /'swægə(r)/ **verb** (**swaggers, swaggering, swaggered**) walk or behave in a very confident or arrogant way 昂首阔步;大摇大摆地走 • **noun** a swaggering walk or way of behaving 昂首阔步;(走路)大摇大摆;(行为)趾高气扬

swain /sweɪn/ **noun** old use 【旧】 **1** a young male lover 情郎 **2** a country youth 乡村青年

swallow¹ /'swɒləʊ/ **verb 1** contract the muscles of the mouth and throat so that food, drink, or saliva pass down the throat 吞,咽(食物、饮料或唾液) **2** (**swallow someone/thing up**) surround or cover someone or something so that they disappear 吞没;淹没 **3** believe an untrue statement without question 轻信(不真实的说法) • **noun** an act of swallowing 吞;咽

swallow² **noun** a fast-flying bird with a forked tail 燕子

swam /swæm/ past of SWIM.

swamp /swɒmp/ **noun** an area of boggy or marshy land 沼泽;湿地 • **verb 1** flood an area with water 淹没;浸没 **2** overwhelm with too much of something (以极大的数量或数目)压倒,充斥,吞没 ■ **swampy** adjective.

swan /swɒn/ **noun** a large white waterbird with a long flexible neck 天鹅 • **verb** (**swans, swanning, swanned**) Brit. informal 【英,非正式】 go around enjoying yourself in a way that makes other people jealous or annoyed (让人羡慕或气恼的)闲游,悠然闲逛

swank /swæŋk/ informal 【非正式】 **verb** show off your achievements, knowledge, or wealth 炫耀，显摆 (成就、知识或财富) • **noun** the act of showing off 炫耀；显摆

swanky /'swæŋki/ **adjective** (**swankier, swankiest**) informal 【非正式】 stylishly luxurious and expensive 时髦且奢华的

swansong /'swɒnsɒŋ/ **noun** the final performance or activity of a person's career 天鹅绝唱 (某人事业生涯的) 最后演出 (或活动)

swap or **swop** /swɒp/ **verb** (**swaps, swapping, swapped**) exchange or substitute something for something else 交换；替代 • **noun** an act of swapping 交换；替代

sward /swɔːd/ **noun** literary 【文】 an area of grass 草地；草皮

swarm /swɔːm/ **noun 1** a large group of insects flying closely together 密密麻麻的一大群飞虫 **2** a large number of honeybees that leave a hive with a queen in order to form a new colony (为建立新巢而跟随蜂王迁出的) 蜂群 **3** a large group of people or things 一大群人 (或事物) • **verb 1** move in or form a swarm 成群地移动；聚集成群 **2** (**swarm with**) be crowded or overrun with 挤满，充满 **3** (**swarm up**) climb something rapidly by gripping with your hands and feet (快速地) 攀，爬

swarthy /'swɔːði/ **adjective** (**swarthier, swarthiest**) having a dark skin 深肤色的；黝黑的

swashbuckling /'swɒʃbʌklɪŋ/ **adjective** having many daring and romantic adventures 充满传奇冒险经历的，■ **swashbuckler** noun.

swastika /'swɒstɪkə/ **noun** an ancient symbol in the form of a cross with its arms bent at a right angle, used in the 20th century as the emblem of the Nazi party 万字饰，万字形符号 (古代的一种象征标志，20 世纪时曾用作纳粹党的党徽)

swat /swɒt/ **verb** (**swats, swatting, swatted**) hit or crush something with a sharp blow from a flat object (用扁平物重拍) 重击，重击

swatch /swɒtʃ/ **noun** a piece of fabric used as a sample (织物的) 样品，布样

swathe[1] /sweɪð/ (US spelling 【美拼作】 **swath** /swɒθ/) **noun** (plural **swathes** or **swaths** /sweɪðz/) **1** a broad strip or area 长而宽的一条；长而宽的地带 **2** a row or line of grass, corn, etc. as it falls when cut down (割下的) 一行草 (或谷物等)

swathe[2] /sweɪð/ **verb** (**swathes, swathing, swathed**) wrap in several layers of fabric (用多层织物) 缠裹，绑，捆

sway /sweɪ/ **verb 1** move slowly and rhythmically backwards and forwards or from side to side 摇摆；摆动；摇晃 **2** make someone change their opinion 使 (某人) 改变看法 (或主意)；使动摇 • **noun 1** a swaying movement 摇摆；摆动；摇晃 **2** influence or control over people (对人的) 影响，控制 □ **hold sway** have power or influence 有权力；有影响力

swear /sweə(r)/ **verb** (**swears, swearing, swore**; past participle **sworn**) **1** promise something solemnly or on oath 发誓；宣誓 **2** use offensive or obscene language 咒骂；辱骂 □ **swear by** informal 【非正式】 have or express great confidence in 对…极其信赖；对…推崇备至 **swear someone in** admit someone to a new post by making them take a formal oath 使 (某人) 宣誓就职 **swear word** an offensive or obscene word 骂人话；脏字

sweat /swet/ **noun** moisture that comes out through the pores of the skin when you are hot, making a physical effort, or anxious (指由于炎热、劳作或焦虑而出的) 汗 • **verb** (**sweats, sweating**, past and past participle **sweated** or N. Amer. 【北美】

sweat) 1 give off sweat 出汗;流汗 **2 (sweat over)** make a lot of effort in doing something 尽力;拼搏;辛苦地干 **3** be very anxious 焦虑;担心 ■ **sweaty** adjective.

sweatband /'swetbænd/ **noun** a band of absorbent material worn round the head or wrists to soak up sweat 汗巾;吸汗带

sweater /'swetə(r)/ **noun** a pullover with long sleeves 长袖套衫

sweatshirt /'swetʃɜːt/ **noun** a loose, warm cotton sweater 棉质针织运动衫

sweatshop /'swetʃɒp/ **noun** a factory or workshop employing workers for long hours in bad conditions 血汗工厂,血汗工场(指工作条件恶劣,工作时间长的工厂)

swede /swiːd/ **noun 1 (Swede)** a person from Sweden 瑞典人 **2** Brit. 【英】a round yellow root vegetable 芜菁甘蓝,瑞典芜菁,洋大头菜(一种生有黄色块根的蔬菜)

Swedish /'swiːdɪʃ/ **noun** the language of Sweden 瑞典语 • **adjective** relating to Sweden 瑞典的

sweep /swiːp/ **verb (sweeps, sweeping, swept) 1** clean an area by brushing away dirt or litter 打扫,清扫(某一地区) **2** move quickly or forcefully 猛力移动;猛力推进 **3 (sweep something away** or **aside)** remove or abolish something quickly and suddenly 迅速消除;肃清;消灭 **4** search an area 搜寻,搜查(某一地区) • **noun 1** an act of sweeping 扫;拂;清扫;打扫 **2** a long, swift, curving movement 扫掠;拂拭 **3** a long curved stretch of road, river, etc. 弯曲的道路(或河流等) **4** the range or scope of something 连绵的一片;范围;广度 **5 (also chimney sweep)** a person who cleans out the soot from chimneys 烟囱清扫工 ■ **sweeper** noun.

sweeping /'swiːpɪŋ/ **adjective 1** ex-tending or performed in a long, continuous curve 大幅度弯曲的;弧线的 **2** wide in range or effect 大范围的;影响广泛的 **3** (of a statement) too general (陈述)过分笼统的

sweepstake /'swiːpsteɪk/ or **sweepstakes** /'swiːpsteɪks/ **noun** a form of gambling in which the winner receives all the money bet by the other players 赌金全赢制(比赛)(胜者可获得所有赌注的赌博形式)

sweet /swiːt/ **adjective 1** having the pleasant taste characteristic of sugar 甜的 **2** having a pleasant smell 芬芳的;芳香的 **3** pleasing or satisfying 令人愉快的;满足的;惬意的 **4** charming and endearing 可爱的;迷人的 **5** kind and thoughtful 善良的;体贴的 • **noun** Brit.【英】**1** a small item of sweet food made with sugar, chocolate, etc. 糖果 **2** a sweet dish forming a course of a meal 甜点 □ **sweet-and-sour** cooked with both sugar and vinegar 糖醋的;甜酸的 **sweet pea** a climbing plant of the pea family with colourful, sweet-smelling flowers 香豌豆 **sweet pepper** a large pepper with a mild or sweet flavour 甜椒;柿子椒 **sweet potato** the pinkish-orange tuber of a tropical climbing plant, eaten as a vegetable 甘薯;白薯;红薯 **sweet-talk** informal 【非正式】use charming or flattering words to persuade someone to do something 甜言蜜语 **sweet tooth** a great liking for sweet-tasting foods 对甜食的极其喜爱 ■ **sweetly** adverb **sweetness** noun.

sweetbread /'swiːtbred/ **noun** an animal's pancreas, eaten as food (供食用的)动物胰脏

sweetcorn /'swiːtkɔːn/ **noun** a kind of maize with sweet-tasting yellow kernels which are eaten as a vegetable 甜玉米

sweeten /'swi:tn/ verb 1 make or become sweet or sweeter (使)变甜;加糖于 2 make more pleasant or acceptable 使舒适;使更易接受;缓和

sweetener /'swi:tnə(r)/ noun 1 a substance used to sweeten food or drink (食品或饮料的)甜味剂,增甜剂 2 informal 【非正式】a bribe 贿赂

sweetheart /'swi:thɑ:t/ noun a person you are in love with 心上人;恋人

sweetmeat /'swi:tmi:t/ noun old use 【旧】a sweet or other item of sweet food 糖果;甜点

swell /swel/ verb (swells, swelling, swelled; past participle swollen or swelled) 1 become larger or more rounded 变大;膨胀;隆起 2 increase in strength, amount, or loudness (力量、数量或声音)增加,增大,扩大 • noun 1 a slow, regular, rolling movement of the sea 海浪的涌动;涌涛 2 a full or gently rounded form 隆起;凸起 3 a gradual increase in strength, amount, or loudness (力量、数量或声音的)渐强,渐增 • adjective N. Amer. informal, dated 【北美,非正式,废】excellent 极好的;杰出的

swelling /'swelɪŋ/ noun a place on the body that has swollen as a result of illness or an injury (疾病或受伤导致的)肿块;肿胀

swelter /'sweltə(r)/ verb (swelters, sweltering, sweltered) be uncomfortably hot 闷热;酷热;热得难受

swept /swept/ past and past participle of SWEEP.

swerve /swɜːv/ verb (swerves, swerving, swerved) abruptly go off from a straight course 突然转向;急转弯 • noun an abrupt change of course 突然转向;急转弯

swift /swɪft/ adjective 1 happening quickly or promptly 迅即发生的;迅速的;快速的 2 moving or able to move very fast 速度快的;敏捷的;矫健的 • noun a fast-flying bird with long, slender wings 雨燕 ■ **swiftly** adverb **swiftness** noun.

swig /swɪg/ verb (swigs, swigging, swigged) drink deeply and quickly 畅饮;痛饮 • noun a quick, deep drink 畅饮;痛饮

swill /swɪl/ verb Brit. 【英】1 rinse something out with large amounts of water (用水)浇洗,冲洗,冲刷 2 (of liquid) swirl round in a container or cavity (液体)(在容器或腔内)晃荡 • noun waste food mixed with water for feeding to pigs (喂猪的)泔水,泔脚饲料

swim /swɪm/ verb (swims, swimming, swam; past participle swum) 1 move through water using your arms and legs 游泳 2 be covered with liquid 被淹没;被浸没 3 experience a dizzy, confusing feeling 眩晕 • noun a period of swimming 游泳 ■ **swimmer** noun.

swimmingly /'swɪmɪŋli/ adverb informal 【非正式】smoothly and satisfactorily 顺利地;顺畅地

swimsuit /'swɪmsuːt/ noun a woman's one-piece garment for swimming (女式)连体泳衣

swindle /'swɪndl/ verb (swindles, swindling, swindled) cheat someone in order to get money from them 诈取,诈骗(某人金钱) • noun a dishonest scheme to get money from someone 骗局;骗术 ■ **swindler** noun.

swine /swaɪn/ noun 1 (plural swine) a pig 猪 2 (plural swine or swines) informal 【非正式】an unpleasant person 讨厌鬼;猪猡 ■ **swinish** adjective.

swing /swɪŋ/ verb (swings, swinging, swung) 1 move backwards and forwards or from side to side while suspended 摇晃;摇摆 2 move by grasping a support and leaping (抓住某一支撑点)摆荡 3 move in a smooth, curving line 作弧线动 4 (swing at) attempt to hit 朝…

打去 **5** change from one opinion, mood, or situation to another (在 观点、情绪或态度上)摇摆、转变 **6** have a decisive influence on a vote or opinion 左右,改变(表决结果、意见等) **7** informal 【非正式】 succeed in bringing something about 办成；做成 • **noun 1** a seat suspended by ropes or chains, on which you can sit and swing backwards and forwards 秋千 **2** an act of swinging 摇晃；摆动；荡秋千 **3** a clear change in public opinion (民意的)显著变化,剧变 **4** a style of jazz or dance music with an easy flowing rhythm 摇摆乐(轻快且节奏强劲的爵士乐或舞曲)

swingeing /ˈswɪndʒɪn/ **adjective** Brit. 【英】 extreme or severe 极度的；严重的

swinging /ˈswɪŋɪn/ **adjective** informal 【非正式】 lively, exciting, and fashionable 活跃而赶时髦的

swipe /swaɪp/ informal 【非正式】 **verb** (**swipes**, **swiping**, **swiped**) **1** hit or try to hit something with a swinging blow 挥击；重掴 **2** steal 偷窃；扒窃 **3** pass a swipe card through an electronic reader 刷,打(卡) • **noun** a swinging blow 挥击；重掴 □ **swipe card** a plastic card carrying coded information which is read when the card is slid through an electronic device 磁卡(载有加密信息的塑料卡,划过电子仪器时读取信息)

swirl /swɜːl/ **verb** move in a twisting or spiralling pattern 打旋；打转；涡动 • **noun** a swirling movement or pattern 打旋;打转;涡动;漩涡 ■ **swirly** adjective.

swish /swɪʃ/ **verb** move with a soft rushing sound 嗖嗖(或嗖嗖)地移动 • **noun** a soft rushing sound or movement 嗖嗖声,嗖嗖声,伴有嗖嗖声(或嗖嗖声)的运动 • **adjective** Brit. informal 【英,非正式】 impressively smart 漂亮的;时髦的;高档的

Swiss /swɪs/ **adjective** relating to

Switzerland 瑞士的 • **noun** (plural **Swiss**) a person from Switzerland 瑞士人 □ **Swiss roll** Brit.【英】a thin sponge cake spread with jam or cream and rolled up 卷筒蛋糕;瑞士卷

switch /swɪtʃ/ **noun 1** a device for making and breaking an electrical connection 开关,电闸 **2** a change or exchange 变化;转变,交换 **3** a flexible shoot cut from a tree (树木的)柔软枝条 • **verb 1** change in position, direction, or focus (位置、方向或焦点)改变,转移 **2** exchange one thing for another 交换 **3** (**switch something off** or **on**) turn an electrical device off or on 关(或开)(电器) **4** (**switch off**) informal 【非正式】 stop paying attention 不再注意

switchback /ˈswɪtʃbæk/ **noun** Brit. 【英】a road that alternately slopes up and down very steeply (道路的)之字形路线,上下起伏的路线

switchblade /ˈswɪtʃbleɪd/ **noun** N. Amer.【北美】a flick knife 弹簧刀

switchboard /ˈswɪtʃbɔːd/ **noun** a device for putting phone calls made to an organization through to the right person (电话的)交换台,总机

swivel /ˈswɪvl/ **verb** (**swivels**, **swivelling**, **swivelled**; US spelling 【美拼作】 **swivels**, **swiveling**, **swiveled**) turn around a central point 旋转;转动 • **noun** a connecting device between two parts enabling one to revolve without turning the other 转节;转环; 旋转接头

swizz /swɪz/ **noun** Brit. informal 【英,非正式】an instance of being mildly cheated or disappointed 上当;受骗;令人失望的事

swollen /ˈswəʊlən/ past participle of **SWELL**.

swoon /swuːn/ literary 【文】 **verb** faint, especially from strong emotion (尤指因感情过于强烈而)昏厥,昏倒 • **noun** an act of fainting 昏厥,昏倒

swoop /swuːp/ **verb 1** move rapidly downwards through the air 猝然下降；突然下落 **2** carry out a sudden raid 突袭 ▪ **noun** an act of swooping 猝然下降；突袭

swop /swɒp/ ⇒ 见 SWAP.

sword /sɔːd/ **noun** a weapon with a long, sharp metal blade 剑；刀

swordfish /'sɔːdfɪʃ/ **noun** (plural **swordfish** or **swordfishes**) a large sea fish with a sword-like snout 剑鱼；箭鱼

swore /swɔː(r)/ past of SWEAR.

sworn /swɔːn/ past participle of SWEAR. ▪ **adjective 1** made after having sworn to tell the truth 宣过誓的；宣誓证明的 **2** determined to remain so 发誓要保持…的：*sworn enemies* 不共戴天的仇敌

swot /swɒt/ Brit. informal【英，非正式】 **verb** (**swots**, **swotting**, **swotted**) study hard 死用功；刻苦学习 ▪ **noun** a person who spends a lot of time studying 死用功的人；书呆子

swum /swʌm/ past participle of SWIM.

swung /swʌŋ/ past and past participle of SWING.

sybarite /'sɪbəraɪt/ **noun** a person who is very fond of luxury 爱奢侈享乐的人；骄奢淫逸者 ▪ **sybaritic** adjective.

sycamore /'sɪkəmɔː(r)/ **noun 1** a tree with five-pointed leaves and seeds shaped like wings 西克莫；西克莫无花果 **2** N. Amer.【北美】a plane tree 悬铃木

sycophant /'sɪkəfænt/ **noun** a person who tries to gain favour with someone important by saying flattering things to them 马屁精；谄媚者 ▪ **sycophancy** noun **sycophantic** adjective.

syllable /'sɪləbl/ **noun** a unit of pronunciation having one vowel sound and forming all or part of a word 音节 ▪ **syllabic** adjective.

syllabus /'sɪləbəs/ **noun** (plural **syllabuses** or **syllabi** /'sɪləbaɪ/) all the things covered in a course of study or teaching 教学大纲；课程大纲

syllogism /'sɪlədʒɪzəm/ **noun** a form of reasoning in which a conclusion is drawn from two propositions (由两个前提得出结论的)三段论，三段论推理法

sylph /sɪlf/ **noun 1** a slender woman or girl 苗条的女子(或女孩) **2** an imaginary spirit of the air 气精；气仙 ▪ **sylphlike** adjective.

sylvan /'sɪlvən/ **adjective** literary【文】 having to do with woods and trees 森林的；与森林有关的

symbiosis /ˌsɪmbaɪ'əʊsɪs/ **noun** (plural **symbioses** /ˌsɪmbaɪ'əʊsiːz/) Biology【生物】a situation in which two living things are connected with and dependent on each other to the advantage of both 共生 ▪ **symbiotic** adjective.

symbol /'sɪmbl/ **noun 1** an object, person, or event that represents something else 象征；标志 **2** a letter, mark, or character used as a representation of something 符号；记号

symbolic /sɪm'bɒlɪk/ **adjective 1** acting as a symbol 作为象征的；象征性的 **2** involving the use of symbols or symbolism 使用象征的，象征主义的，使用象征手法的 ▪ **symbolically** adverb.

symbolism /'sɪmbəlɪzəm/ **noun** the use of symbols to represent ideas or qualities 象征主义；象征手法 ▪ **symbolist** noun & adjective.

symbolize or **symbolise** /'sɪmbəlaɪz/ **verb** (**symbolizes**, **symbolizing**, **symbolized**) **1** be a symbol of 是…的象征；象征；标志 **2** represent something by means of symbols 用符号代表

symmetrical /sɪ'metrɪkl/ **adjective** exactly the same on each side 对称

的 ■ **symmetrically** adverb.

symmetry /'sɪmɪtri/ **noun** (plural **symmetries**) **1** the exact match in size or shape between two halves, parts, or sides of something 对称 **2** the quality of being exactly the same or very similar 匀称；整齐；相似；相仿

sympathetic /ˌsɪmpə'θetɪk/ **adjective 1** feeling or showing sympathy 同情的；表示同情的 **2** showing approval of an idea or action 赞同的；支持的 **3** pleasing or likeable 令人愉快的；可爱的 ■ **sympathetically** adverb.

sympathize or **sympathise** /'sɪmpəθaɪz/ **verb** (**sympathizes**, **sympathizing**, **sympathized**) **1** feel or express sympathy 同情；表示同情 **2** agree with an opinion 赞同；支持

sympathy /'sɪmpəθi/ **noun** (plural **sympathies**) **1** the feeling of being sorry for someone 同情 **2** support for or approval of something 支持；赞同 **3** understanding between people 意气相投；投契；同感 □ **in sympathy** fitting in; in keeping 一致；协调；统一

symphonic /sɪm'fɒnɪk/ **adjective** having the form of a symphony 交响乐(式)的

symphony /'sɪmfəni/ **noun** (plural **symphonies**) a long, elaborate piece of music for a full orchestra 交响乐；交响曲

symposium /sɪm'pəʊziəm/ **noun** (plural **symposia** /sɪm'pəʊziə/ or **symposiums**) a conference to discuss a particular academic subject 研讨会；专题讨论会

symptom /'sɪmptəm/ **noun 1** a change in the body or mind which is the sign of a disease (疾病的)症状 **2** a sign of an undesirable situation (指令人不快的情况的)征兆，症候 ■ **symptomatic** adjective.

synagogue /'sɪnəgɒg/ **noun** a building where Jews meet for worship and teaching 犹太会堂；犹太教堂

synapse /'saɪnæps/ **noun** a connection between two nerve cells (神经元的)突触 ■ **synaptic** adjective.

sync or **synch** /sɪŋk/ **noun** informal 【非正式】 synchronization 同时性 □ **in** (or **out of**) **sync** working well (or badly) together 同步(或不同步)的；协调(或不协调)的

synchromesh /'sɪŋkrəʊmeʃ/ **noun** a system of gear changing in which the gearwheels are made to revolve at the same speed during engagement 同步齿轮系

synchronize or **synchronise** /'sɪŋkrənaɪz/ **verb** (**synchronizes**, **synchronizing**, **synchronized**) make things happen or operate at the same time or rate 使同时发生；使同步 ■ **synchronization** noun.

synchronous /'sɪŋkrənəs/ **adjective** existing or happening at the same time 同时存在的；同时发生的；同步的

syncopate /'sɪŋkəpeɪt/ **verb** (**syncopates**, **syncopating**, **syncopated**) alter the beats or accents of music so that strong beats become weak and vice versa (对音乐中的节奏或重音进行)切分(使节拍强弱弱倒置) ■ **syncopation** noun.

syndicate noun /'sɪndɪkət/ a group of people or organizations who get together to promote a common interest (为促进共同利益而结成的)辛迪加，私人联合会，企业联合组织 ● **verb** /'sɪndɪkeɪt/ (**syndicates**, **syndicating**, **syndicated**) **1** control or manage an operation through a syndicate 把…置于辛迪加的管理之下 **2** publish or broadcast something in a number of different ways at the same time (通过多种方式)同时发表(或播出) ■ **syndication** noun.

syndrome /'sɪndrəʊm/ **noun** a set of medical symptoms which tend to occur together 综合症状；综合征

synergy /'sɪnədʒi/ **noun** the working

together of two or more people or things to produce a combined effect that is greater than the sum of their separate effects (两个或两个以上的人或事物共同作用的效果大于各单独作用之和的)协同作用,协同增效作用

synod /'sɪnəd/ *noun* an official meeting of Church ministers and members 教会会议

synonym /'sɪnənɪm/ *noun* a word or phrase that means the same as another word or phrase in the same language 同义词

synonymous /sɪ'nɒnɪməs/ *adjective* **1** (of a word or phrase) having the same meaning as another word or phrase in the same language (单词或短语)同义的 **2** closely associated 紧密关联的

synopsis /sɪ'nɒpsɪs/ *noun* (plural **synopses**) a brief summary or survey 概要;大纲

syntax /'sɪntæks/ *noun* the way in which words and phrases are put together to form sentences 句法 ■ **syntactic** *adjective* **syntactical** *adjective*.

synthesis /'sɪnθəsɪs/ *noun* (plural **syntheses** /'sɪnθəsiːz/) **1** the combination of parts to form a connected whole 综合;合成 **2** the production of chemical compounds from simpler materials (化学)合成

synthesize or **synthesise** /'sɪnθəsaɪz/ *verb* (**synthesizes, synthesizing, synthesized**) **1** combine parts into a connected whole 综合;合成 **2** make something by chemical synthesis (化学)合成 **3** produce sound with a synthesizer 合成(声音)

synthesizer or **synthesiser** /'sɪnθəsaɪzə(r)/ *noun* an electronic musical instrument that produces sounds by generating and combining signals of different frequencies (音响)合成器(一种电子乐器)

synthetic /sɪn'θetɪk/ *adjective* **1** made by chemical synthesis, especially to imitate a natural product 人造的;(人工)合成的 **2** not genuine 假的 ■ **synthetically** *adverb*.

syphilis /'sɪfɪlɪs/ *noun* a disease caused by bacteria that are passed on during sex 梅毒 ■ **syphilitic** *adjective*.

syphon /'saɪfn/ ⇒ 见 SIPHON.

Syrian /'sɪriən/ *noun* a person from Syria 叙利亚人 • *adjective* relating to Syria 叙利亚的

syringe /sɪ'rɪndʒ/ *noun* a tube with a nozzle and a piston that is fitted with a hollow needle for injecting drugs or withdrawing blood 注射器

syrup /'sɪrəp/ (US spelling 【美拼法】 **sirup**) *noun* **1** a thick sweet liquid made by dissolving sugar in boiling water 糖水 **2** a thick sweet liquid containing medicine or diluted to make a drink (含有药物或用作饮料的)糖浆

syrupy /'sɪrəpi/ (US spelling 【美拼法】 **sirupy**) *adjective* **1** like syrup 糖浆似的;像糖浆的 **2** too sentimental 过于多愁善感的;过分多情感伤的

system /'sɪstəm/ *noun* **1** a set of things that are connected or that work together 系统 **2** an organized scheme or method 体系;体制;方法 **3** (**the system**) the laws and rules that govern society (社会)制度

systematic /ˌsɪstə'mætɪk/ *adjective* done according to a system 系统的;有条理的 ■ **systematically** *adverb*.

systematize or **systematise** /'sɪstəmətaɪz/ *verb* (**systematizes, systematizing, systematized**) arrange things according to an organized system 使系统化

systemic /sɪ'stemɪk/ *adjective* affecting the whole of a system 系统的

Tt

T or **t** /tiː/ **noun** (plural **Ts** or **T's**) the twentieth letter of the alphabet 英语字母表的第20个字母 □ **to a T** informal【非正式】to perfection 丝毫不差；完美地 **T-bone** a large piece of steak containing a T-shaped bone T 字骨牛排 **T-shirt** a short-sleeved casual top 体恤衫；短袖休闲汗衫 **T-square** a T-shaped instrument for drawing or testing right angles 丁字尺；曲尺

TA /tiː 'eɪ/ **abbreviation** Territorial Army.

ta /tɑː/ **exclamation** Brit. informal【英，非正式】thank you 谢谢

tab¹ /tæb/ **noun 1** a small flap or strip of material attached to something 标签；签条 **2** informal, chiefly N. Amer.【非正式，主北美】a restaurant bill 餐厅账单 □ **keep tabs on** informal【非正式】keep a watch on 监视；密切注意

tab² = TABULATOR.

tab³ **noun** informal【非正式】a tablet containing an illegal drug (含违禁药物成分的)药片

tabby /'tæbi/ **noun** (plural **tabbies**) a grey or brownish cat with dark stripes 斑猫(毛皮呈灰色或棕色，带有深色斑纹)

tabernacle /'tæbənækl/ **noun 1** a place of worship for some religions (某些宗教的)礼拜堂，教堂 **2** (in the Bible) a tent in which the Israelites kept the Ark of the Covenant during the Exodus. (《圣经》中记载的)帐篷，会幕(古犹太人出埃及途中存放约柜的帐篷)

table /'teɪbl/ **noun 1** a piece of furniture with a flat top and legs, for eating, writing, or working at 桌子；台子；餐桌 **2** a set of facts or figures arranged in rows and columns 表；

表格 **3** (**tables**) multiplication sums arranged in sets 乘法口诀 • **verb** (**tables, tabling, tabled**) Brit.【英】present something for discussion at a meeting (正式)提出；把⋯列入议事日程 □ **table tennis** a game played with small round bats and a small hollow ball which is hit across a table over a net 乒乓球(运动) **turn the tables** reverse a situation 扭转形势；转变局面

tableau /'tæbləʊ/ **noun** (plural **tableaux** /'tæbləʊz/) a group of models or motionless figures representing a scene 舞台造型；静态画面

tablecloth /'teɪblklɒθ/ **noun** a cloth spread over a table 桌布；台布

table d'hôte /ˌtɑːbl 'dəʊt/ **noun** a restaurant menu or meal offered at a fixed price and with limited choices 定餐菜单；套餐

tablespoon /'teɪblspuːn/ **noun** a large spoon for serving food (用于分食物的)餐匙，汤匙

tablet /'tæblət/ **noun 1** a pill 药片；片剂 **2** a slab of stone or other hard material on which an inscription is written (铭刻文字的)匾，牌，碑

tabloid /'tæblɔɪd/ **noun** a newspaper that has small pages and is written in a popular style(版面小的)小报，通俗小报

taboo /tə'buː/ **noun** (plural **taboos**) a social custom that prevents people from doing or talking about something 禁忌；忌讳 • **adjective** banned or restricted by social custom 禁忌的；忌讳的

tabular /'tæbjələ(r)/ **adjective** (of facts or figures) arranged in columns or tables (数据) 制成表的，表格式的

tabulate /'tæbjuleɪt/ **verb** (**tabulates, tabulating, tabulated**) arrange facts or figures in columns or tables. 列表显示 (数据) ■ **tabulation** noun.

tabulator /'tæbjuleɪtə(r)/ **noun** a facility in a wordprocessing program, or a device on a typewriter, used for moving to fixed positions in a document when creating tables or columns (文字处理程序或打字机的) 制表符，跳格键

tachograph /'tækɡrɑːf/ **noun** an instrument used in commercial road vehicles to provide a record of their speed and the distance travelled 转速计(用于记录商用车辆速度和里程)

tachometer /tæ'kɒmɪtə(r)/ **noun** an instrument which measures the working speed of an engine (发动机) 转速表，流速计

tachycardia /ˌtækɪ'kɑːdɪə/ **noun** an abnormally fast heart rate 心动过速

tacit /'tæsɪt/ **adjective** understood or meant without being stated 不言而喻的，心照不宣的 ■ **tacitly** adverb.

taciturn /'tæsɪtɜːn/ **adjective** not saying very much 沉默寡言的 ■ **taciturnity** noun.

tack¹ /tæk/ **noun 1** a small broad-headed nail 平头钉；大头钉 **2** N. Amer. 【北美】a drawing pin 图钉 **3** a long stitch used to fasten fabrics together temporarily 绷；粗线缝缝 **4** a course of action 行动方针；策略 **5** Sailing 【航行】a sailing boat's course relative to the direction of the wind 戗风调向；戗风行驶 • **verb 1** fasten or fix with tacks (用平头钉) 钉住 **2** (**tack something on**) casually add something to something else (漫不经心地) 附加，增补 **3** change course by turning a boat's head into and through the wind 戗风行驶 **4** make a series of such changes of course while sailing 换戗；作之字形

航行

tack² **noun** equipment used in horse riding 马具；鞍辔

tackle /'tækl/ **verb** (**tackles, tackling, tackled**) **1** start to deal with a problem or task 着手处理；应付 **2** confront someone about a difficult issue. 与(某人)交涉 **3** (in soccer, hockey, rugby, etc.) try to take the ball from or prevent the movement of an opponent (足球、曲棍球、橄榄球等运动中)阻截，拦截，擒抱(对方持球队员) • **noun 1** the equipment needed for a task or sport 用具；体育器械 **2** a mechanism consisting of ropes, pulley blocks, and hooks for lifting heavy objects 滑轮 **3** (in sport) an act of tackling an opponent (体育运动中的)阻截，拦截，擒抱 ■ **tackler** noun.

tacky /'tæki/ **adjective** (**tackier, tackiest**) **1** (of glue, paint, etc.) not fully dry (胶水、油漆等)未干透的，发黏的 **2** informal 【非正式】showing bad taste and quality 俗气的；低劣的

taco /'tɑːkəʊ/ **noun** (plural **tacos**) (in Mexican cookery) a folded tortilla filled with spicy meat or beans (墨西哥烹饪中裹有辣味肉馅或豆馅的)炸玉米面卷

tact /tækt/ **noun** sensitivity and skill in dealing with other people (为人处世的)机敏，圆通，乖巧

tactful /'tæktfl/ **adjective** having or showing tact 机敏的；圆通的；乖巧的 ■ **tactfully** adverb.

tactic /'tæktɪk/ **noun 1** the method you use to achieve something 手段；策略 **2** (**tactics**) the art of organizing and directing the movement of soldiers and equipment during a war 战术；兵法 ■ **tactician** noun.

tactical /'tæktɪkl/ **adjective 1** planned in order to achieve a particular end 策略上的 **2** (of weapons) for use in direct support of military or naval

operations (武器)战术的，作战的
3 (of voting) done to prevent the strongest candidate from winning, rather than indicating your true political choice (选举投票)策略性的 (指为防止最强候选者获胜而不顾自己的政治倾向转而支持仅居其后的候选人) ■ **tactically** adverb.

tactile /ˈtæktaɪl/ **adjective 1** having to do with the sense of touch (有)触觉的；能触知的 **2** liking to touch other people in a friendly way 喜欢触碰他人的

tactless /ˈtæktləs/ **adjective** thoughtless and insensitive 欠考虑的；不得体的；不圆通的 ■ **tactlessly** adverb.

tad /tæd/ **adverb (a tad)** informal 【非正式】 to a small extent 少许，稍微

tadpole /ˈtædpəʊl/ **noun** the larva of a frog or toad, which lives in water and has gills, a large head, and a tail 蝌蚪

taffeta /ˈtæfɪtə/ **noun** a crisp shiny fabric 塔夫绸

tag /tæɡ/ **noun 1** a label giving information about something 标签，标牌 **2** an electronic device attached to someone to monitor their movements 监视器；追踪器 **3** a nickname or commonly used description 绰号；诨名 **4** a nickname or identifying mark written as the signature of a graffiti artist (街头涂鸦艺术家当作签名所书写的)绰号，识别标志 **5** a frequently repeated phrase 套话；口头禅 **6** a metal or plastic point at the end of a shoelace (鞋带的)金属(或塑料)包头 **7** a chasing game played by children 捉人(儿童游戏) ● **verb (tags, tagging, tagged) 1** attach a tag to 给…加标签 **2** (**tag something on**) add something to the end of something else as an afterthought 事后附加 **3** (**tag along**) accompany someone without being invited (未经邀请)擅自尾随，跟随

tagliatelle /ˌtæljəˈteli/ **plural noun**

pasta in narrow ribbon 意大利细面条

tail /teɪl/ **noun 1** the part at the rear of an animal that sticks out and can be moved 尾；尾巴 **2** the rear part of an aircraft, with the tailplane and rudder (飞机的)尾部 **3** the final, more distant, or weaker part 末端，末尾 **4** (**tails**) the side of a coin without the image of a head on it 硬币的反面 **5** (**tails**) informal 【非正式】a tailcoat 燕尾服 ● **verb 1** informal 【非正式】secretly follow someone 盯梢，跟踪 **2** (**tail off** or **away**) gradually become smaller or weaker 逐渐减少，渐渐变弱

tailback /ˈteɪlbæk/ **noun** Brit. 【英】a long queue of stationary traffic (交通阻塞造成的)车辆长龙

tailcoat /ˈteɪlkəʊt/ **noun** Brit. 【英】a man's formal jacket with a long skirt divided at the back and cut away in front 燕尾服；男士晚礼服

tailgate /ˈteɪlɡeɪt/ **noun 1** a hinged flap at the back of a truck (卡车的)后挡板，后栏板 **2** the door at the back of an estate or hatchback car (旅行车或掀背车的)舱盖式后门，尾门

tailor /ˈteɪlə(r)/ **noun** a person who makes men's clothing for individual customers (为个别顾客制作男装的)裁缝 ● **verb 1** make clothes to fit individual customers 专门制作，订做(服装) **2** make or adapt for a particular purpose or person (为某目的或某人)定制，修改 □ **tailor-made** made for a particular purpose 专门订做的；特制的

tailored /ˈteɪləd/ **adjective** (of clothes) smart, fitted, and well cut (衣服)考究的，剪裁合体的

tailplane /ˈteɪlpleɪn/ **noun** Brit. 【英】a small wing at the tail of an aircraft (飞机尾部的)水平尾翼

tailspin /ˈteɪlspɪn/ **noun** a fast spinning motion made by a rapidly descending aircraft (飞机的)尾旋

tailwind /ˈteɪlwɪnd/ **noun** a wind

blowing from behind 顺风

taint /teɪnt/ **verb 1** contaminate or pollute 弄脏;污染 **2** affect with a bad or unpleasant quality 玷污;败坏 • **noun** a trace of something bad or unpleasant 污点;瑕疵

Taiwanese /taɪwɑːˈniːz/ **noun** (plural **Taiwanese**) a person from Taiwan, China 台湾人 • **adjective** relating to Taiwan 台湾的;台湾人的

take /teɪk/ **verb** (**takes**, **taking**, **took**; past participle **taken**) **1** reach for and hold 拿;取;抓住 **2** occupy a place or position 占用,占据(地方或位置) **3** gain possession of by force 攻取;夺取 **4** carry or bring with you 带着;携带 **5** remove from a place 拿走;取走 **6** subtract 减去 **7** consume 吃;喝;服用 **8** bring into a particular state 使处于…状态 **9** experience or be affected by 经受;遭受;受…的影响 **10** use as a route or a means of transport 走…路线;乘坐;搭乘 **11** accept or receive 接受;收到 **12** require or use up 需要;花费 **13** act on an opportunity 抓住(机会) **14** see or deal with in a particular way 认为;以…方式处理 **15** tolerate or endure 容忍;忍受 **16** study a subject 修读(科目) **17** do an exam or test 参加(考试) • **noun 1** a sequence of sound or vision photographed or recorded continuously 一组连拍镜头;一段连续录音 **2** a particular approach to something 看法;态度 **3** an amount gained 收获量;进项 □ **take after** look or behave like a parent or ancestor 长得像(父母或祖辈) **take someone/thing for granted 1** be too familiar with someone or something to appreciate them properly 对…想当然,对…习以为常 **2** assume that something is true 认为…正确 **take someone/thing in 1** cheat or deceive someone 欺骗(某人) **2** make a garment tighter by altering its seams 把(衣服)改小 **3** understand

something 理解;领会 **take off 1** become airborne 升空;起飞 **2** leave hastily 匆匆离开 **take someone/thing off 1** remove clothing 脱下(衣服) **2** informal mimic someone 模仿(某人) **take-off** an act of taking off 起飞;升空 **take someone/thing on 1** employ someone 雇用(某人) **2** undertake a task 承担(任务) **3** begin to have a meaning or quality 获得(意义);呈现出(特性) **take over** begin to have control of or responsibility for something, in place of someone else 接收;接管 **take to 1** get into the habit of 形成…习惯,开始沉迷于 **2** start liking someone 开始对…产生好感 **3** go to a place to escape danger 逃到(某地) **take something up 1** start to do something 开始从事,着手处理 **2** occupy time, space, or attention 占据(时间、空间或注意力) **3** pursue a matter further 继续进行

takeaway /ˈteɪkəweɪ/ **noun** Brit. 【英】**1** a restaurant or shop selling cooked food to be eaten elsewhere 外卖餐馆(或商店) **2** a meal of such food 外卖食品

takeout /ˈteɪkaʊt/ **noun** N. Amer. 【北美】a takeaway 外卖餐馆(或商店);外卖食品

takeover /ˈteɪkəʊvə(r)/ **noun** an act of taking control of something from someone else 接收;接管

takings /ˈteɪkɪŋz/ **plural noun** money received by a shop for goods sold (商店的)营业额,进账

talc /tælk/ **noun 1** talcum powder 滑石粉;爽身粉 **2** a soft mineral 滑石

talcum powder /ˈtælkəm/ **noun** a powder used to make the skin feel smooth and dry 滑石粉;爽身粉

tale /teɪl/ **noun 1** a story 故事 **2** a lie 谎言

talent /ˈtælənt/ **noun 1** natural ability or skill 天赋;才能 **2** people possessing natural ability or skill 天才;人才 **3** an ancient weight and unit of currency 塔兰特(古代重量及货币单位) ∎ **talented** adjective.

talisman /'tælɪzmən/ noun (plural **talismans**) an object thought to have magic powers and to bring good luck 护身符;避邪物 ∎ **talismanic** adjective.

talk /tɔːk/ verb **1** speak in order to give information or express ideas or feelings 讲话;谈论 **2** be able to speak 说话 **3** (**talk something over or through**) discuss something thoroughly 彻底地讨论 **4** (**talk back**) reply in a defiant or cheeky way 反唇相讥;顶嘴 **5** (**talk down to**) speak to someone in a superior way 以高人一等的口气对(某人)说话 **6** (**talk someone round**) persuade someone to accept or agree to something 说服;使同意 **7** (**talk someone into or out of**) persuade someone to do or not to do something 说服(某人)做(或不做) • noun **1** conversation 谈话;交谈 **2** a speech or lecture 演讲;讲座;报告 **3** (**talks**) formal discussions 正式会谈 □ **talking-to** informal【非正式】a telling-off 斥责

talkative /'tɔːkətɪv/ adjective fond of talking 健谈的;爱说话的

tall /tɔːl/ adjective **1** of great or more than average height 高的;高大的 **2** measuring a stated distance from top to bottom 有…高的;高度达…的 □ **a tall order** a difficult challenge 苛刻的要求;艰巨挑战 **tall ship** a sailing ship with high masts 高桅横帆船 **a tall story** an account of something that seems unlikely to be true 无稽之谈;荒诞故事

tallow /'tæləʊ/ noun a hard substance made from animal fat, used in making candles and soap 动物脂油(用于制蜡烛和肥皂)

tally /'tæli/ noun (plural **tallies**) **1** a current score or amount 得分;计数;账目 **2** a record of a score or amount 计分卡;技术牌;记账单 • verb (**tal-**

lies, **tallying**, **tallied**) **1** agree or correspond 符合;吻合 **2** calculate the total number of 计算(总数)

tally-ho /ˌtæli'həʊ/ exclamation a huntsman's cry to the hounds on sighting a fox 呔嗬(猎人发现狐狸时呼唤猎犬的声音)

Talmud /'tælmʊd/ noun a collection of ancient writings on Jewish law and legend《塔木德》(记载犹太人律法和传说的古代文献集)

talon /'tælən/ noun a curved claw (猛禽的)利爪

tamarind /'tæmərɪnd/ noun a fruit with sticky brown pulp used in Asian cookery 罗望子果实,酸荚(用于亚洲烹饪)

tamarisk /'tæmərɪsk/ noun a small tree with tiny leaves on slender branches 柽柳(小型乔木,叶小,枝条细长)

tambourine /ˌtæmbə'riːn/ noun a shallow drum with metal discs around the edge, which you play by shaking or hitting with your hand (边像有小金属片的)铃鼓

tame /teɪm/ adjective **1** (of an animal) not dangerous or frightened of people (动物)驯服的;驯养的 **2** not exciting, adventurous, or controversial 沉闷的;平淡的;无争议的 • verb (**tames**, **taming**, **tamed**) **1** make an animal tame 驯服,驯养(动物) **2** make less powerful and easier to control 控制;驾驭 ∎ **tamely** adverb.

tamp /tæmp/ verb firmly ram or pack a substance into something 夯实;压实;填塞

tamper /'tæmpə(r)/ verb (**tampers**, **tampering**, **tampered**) (**tamper with**) interfere with something without permission (未经允许)擅自插手,干扰

tampon /'tæmpɒn/ noun a plug of soft material that a woman puts into her vagina to absorb blood during a period 月经棉拴

tan /tæn/ **noun 1** a golden-brown shade of skin developed by pale-skinned people after being in the sun (日晒后的)棕褐色肤色 **2** a yellowish-brown colour 棕黄色；黄褐色 • **verb** (**tans, tanning, tanned**) **1** become golden-brown from being in the sun (肤色)晒成棕褐色 **2** convert animal skin into leather 把(兽皮)制成皮革

tandem /'tændəm/ **noun** a bicycle for two riders, one sitting behind the other 双人自行车 • **adverb** one behind another 一前一后地；以纵列 □ **in tandem** together or at the same time 共同；一起；同时

tandoori /tæn'dʊəri/ **adjective** (of Indian food) cooked in a clay oven called a **tandoor** (印度食品)用泥炉炭火烹制的，用唐杜里泥炉烹饪法制作的

tang /tæŋ/ **noun 1** a strong flavour or smell 浓烈的味道(或气味) **2** the projection on the blade of a tool that holds it firmly in the handle 带柄工具的)柄脚，柄舌 ■ **tangy** adjective.

tangent /'tændʒənt/ **noun 1** a straight line that touches a curve but does not cross it at that point 切线 **2** Maths 【数学】(in a right-angled triangle) the ratio of the sides opposite and adjacent to a particular angle (直角三角形的)正切 **3** a completely different line of thought or action 离题；完全无关的行为

tangential /tæn'dʒenʃl/ **adjective 1** only slightly relevant 稍相关的；离题的 **2** relating to or along a tangent 切线的；正切的

tangerine /tændʒə'riːn/ **noun** a small citrus fruit with a loose skin 柑橘

tangible /'tændʒəbl/ **adjective 1** able to be perceived by touch 可触知的；有形的 **2** real 明确的；确凿的 ■ **tangibility** noun **tangibly** adverb.

tangle /'tæŋgl/ **verb** (**tangles, tangling, tangled**) **1** twist together into a knotted mass 使纠结；使乱成一团 **2** (**tangle with**) informal 【非正式】come into conflict with 与…发生冲突 • **noun 1** a twisted, knotted mass 纠结的一团 **2** a muddle 困惑；混乱

tango /'tæŋgəʊ/ **noun** (plural **tangos**) a South American ballroom dance with abrupt pauses 探戈舞 • **verb** (**tangoes, tangoing, tangoed**) dance the tango 跳探戈舞

tank /tæŋk/ **noun 1** a large container for liquid or gas 箱；罐 **2** the container holding the fuel supply in a vehicle (汽车的)油箱 **3** a clear container for keeping pet fish (饲养观赏鱼的)鱼缸 **4** a heavy armoured fighting vehicle that moves on a continuous metal track 坦克 □ **tank engine** a steam locomotive carrying fuel and water holders in its own frame, not in a separate wagon 水柜机车 **tank top** a sleeveless top worn over a shirt or blouse 紧身短背心；背心装

tankard /'tæŋkəd/ **noun** a large beer mug sometimes with a hinged lid 带铰链盖的大啤酒杯

tanker /'tæŋkə(r)/ **noun** a ship, road vehicle, or aircraft for carrying liquids in bulk 油船；油罐车；空中加油机

tannin /'tænɪn/ **noun** a bitter-tasting substance present in tea, grapes, etc. 丹宁(酸)；鞣酸

tannoy /'tænɔɪ/ **noun** Brit. trademark 【英,商标】a type of public address system 坦诺伊扩音系统；公共广播系统

tantalize or **tantalise** /'tæntəlaɪz/ **verb** (**tantalizes, tantalizing, tantalized**) tease someone by showing or promising them something that they cannot have 使干着急；逗弄

tantamount /'tæntəmaʊnt/ **adjective** (**tantamount to**) equivalent in seriousness to (严重性)等同的

tantrum /'tæntrəm/ noun an uncontrolled outburst of anger and frustration 发脾气

Tanzanian /ˌtænzə'nɪən/ noun a person from Tanzania 坦桑尼亚人 • adjective relating to Tanzania 坦桑尼亚的

Taoiseach /'tiːʃəkh/ noun the Prime Minister of the Irish Republic (爱尔兰共和国的)总理

tap¹ /tæp/ noun a device for controlling the flow of liquid or gas from a pipe or container 龙头；阀门；旋塞 • verb (taps, tapping, tapped) 1 make use of a supply or resource 开发，利用(资源) 2 connect a device to a telephone so as to listen to conversations secretly 在(电话)上装窃听器；窃听(电话) 3 draw liquid from a cask, barrel, etc. 从(桶等)中放出液体 4 draw sap from a tree by cutting into it 在(树)上开口引出液体 □ on tap 1 ready to be poured from a tap 装有龙头(或旋塞)可随时取用的 2 informal 【非正式】 freely available whenever needed 可随时取用的

tap² verb (taps, tapping, tapped) hit with a quick, light blow 轻敲；轻拍 • noun a quick, light blow 轻敲；轻拍 □ tap dancing a style of dancing performed in shoes with metal pieces on the toes and heels 踢踏舞

tapas /'tæpəs/ plural noun small Spanish savoury dishes served with drinks at a bar (西班牙酒吧的)餐前小吃，下酒菜

tape /teɪp/ noun 1 light, flexible material in a narrow strip, used to hold, fasten, or mark off something 带子；线带 2 tape with magnetic properties, used for recording sound, pictures, or computer data (录音、录像或记录电脑数据的)磁带 3 a cassette or reel containing magnetic tape 盒式磁带；磁带盘 • verb (tapes, taping, taped) 1 record sound or pictures on magnetic tape (用磁带)录音，录像 2 fasten,

attach, or mark off with tape (用带子)固定，捆扎，标记 □ tape measure a strip of tape marked for measuring the length of things 卷尺；标尺 tape recorder a device for recording and then reproducing sounds on magnetic tape (磁带)录音机

taper /'teɪpə(r)/ verb (tapers, tapering, tapered) 1 reduce in thickness towards one end 一端逐渐变细 2 (taper off) gradually lessen 逐渐减少 • noun a thin candle 细蜡烛

tapestry /'tæpəstri/ noun (plural tapestries) a piece of thick fabric with a design woven or embroidered on it 花毯；织锦

tapeworm /'teɪpwɜːm/ noun a long ribbon-like worm which lives as a parasite in the intestines of a person or animal 绦虫(一肠肠寄生虫)

tapioca /ˌtæpi'əukə/ noun hard white grains of cassava, used for making puddings 木薯淀粉(用于做布丁)

tapir /'teɪpə(r)/ noun a piglike animal with a short flexible snout 貘(外形似猪，有可伸缩短鼻)

tappet /'tæpɪt/ noun a moving part in a machine which transmits motion between a cam and another part (机器上的)挺杆，推杆

tar /tɑː(r)/ noun 1 a dark, thick liquid distilled from wood or coal 柏油；沥青 2 a similar substance formed by burning tobacco (烟草燃烧产生的)烟碱，焦油，尼古丁 • verb (tars, tarring, tarred) cover with tar 用柏油铺；用沥青覆盖

taramasalata /ˌtærəməsə'lɑːtə/ noun a dip made from the roe (eggs) of certain fish 鱼子酱

tarantula /tə'ræntjələ/ noun 1 a very large hairy spider found in warm parts of America 鸟蛛(一种有毛的巨型蜘蛛，见于美洲温暖地区) 2 a large black spider of southern Europe 塔兰托毒蛛，狼蛛(欧洲南部的一种黑色大蜘蛛)

tardy /'tɑːdi/ adjective (tardier,

tardiest) formal【正式】**1** late 迟到的 **2** slow to act or respond 行动迟缓的；拖沓的 ▪ **tardily** adverb **tardiness** noun.

tare /teə(r)/ noun the weight of a vehicle without its fuel or load 空车重量；车身自重；车皮重

target /ˈtɑːgɪt/ noun **1** a person, object, or place that is aimed at in an attack (攻击的)目标，对象 **2** a board marked with a series of circles that you aim at in archery or shooting 靶子 **3** something that you aim to achieve 目标；指标 ▪ verb (**targets, tar-geting, targeted**) **1** select as an object of attention or attack 把…作为攻击目标；针对 **2** aim or direct 瞄准；指向

✔ 拼写指南 **targeted** and **targeting** have a single *t* in the middle. targeted和targeting 中间位置只有一个t。

tariff /ˈtærɪf/ noun **1** a tax to be paid on a particular class of imports or exports 关税 **2** a list of the charges made by a hotel, restaurant, etc. (旅馆、酒店等的)价目表，收费表

✔ 拼写指南 one *r*, double *f*: tariff. tariff 有一个r和两个f。

tarmac /ˈtɑːmæk/ noun **1** (trademark in the UK【英国商标】) a mixture of broken stone and tar used for making road surfaces 塔马克柏油碎石(用于铺筑路面) **2** (**the tarmac**) a runway or other area with a tarmac surface 柏油碎石跑道(或路面) ▪ verb (**tarmacs, tarmacking, tarmacked**) give a road or runway a tarmac surface 用柏油碎石铺筑(路面或跑道)

tarn /tɑːn/ noun a small mountain lake 冰斗湖；山中小湖

tarnish /ˈtɑːnɪʃ/ verb **1** make metal lose its shine by exposure to air or damp 使(金属)失去光泽，使变暗 **2** make something less respected 败坏；玷污 ▪ noun a film or stain formed on

the exposed surface of metal (金属表面的)失泽膜，暗锈

tarot /ˈtærəʊ/ noun a set of cards used for fortune telling 塔罗纸牌(用于算命)

tarpaulin /tɑːˈpɔːlɪn/ noun a sheet of heavy waterproof cloth (防水)帆布，油布

tarragon /ˈtærəgən/ noun a herb with narrow strong-tasting leaves 龙蒿(叶窄，有强烈气味)

tarry /ˈtæri/ verb (**tarries, tarrying, tarried**) literary【文】stay longer than intended 逗留；耽搁

tarsus /ˈtɑːsəs/ noun (plural **tarsi** /ˈtɑːsaɪ/) the group of small bones in the ankle and upper foot 踝；跗骨

tart[1] /tɑːt/ noun an open pastry case containing a sweet or savoury filling 果馅饼 ▪ **tartlet** noun.

tart[2] informal【非正式】noun disapproving【贬】a woman who has many sexual partners 荡妇；淫妇 ▪ verb Brit.【英】**1** (**tart yourself up**) make yourself look attractive with clothes or make-up 打扮得花枝招展；浓妆艳抹 **2** (**tart something up**) improve the appearance of something 装饰；打扮 ▪ **tarty** adjective.

tart[3] adjective **1** sharp or acid in taste 酸的，酸涩的 **2** (of a remark or tone of voice) sharp or hurtful (话语或口气)尖酸的，刻薄的 ▪ **tartly** adverb.

tartan /ˈtɑːtn/ noun **1** a pattern of coloured checks and intersecting lines 格子花呢 **2** cloth with a tartan pattern 格子花呢

tartar[1] /ˈtɑːtə(r)/ noun a person who is fierce or difficult to deal with 凶悍的人；难对付的人

tartar[2] noun **1** a hard deposit that forms on the teeth 牙石；牙垢 **2** a deposit formed during the fermentation of wine 酒石(葡萄酒发酵形成的沉淀物)

tartare sauce /ˈtɑːtə(r)/ noun a sauce consisting of mayonnaise mixed with chopped onions, gherkins, and capers 鲑粗酱，蛋黄沙司(由蛋黄酱、洋葱末、小黄瓜和刺山柑调制而成)

task /tɑːsk/ **noun** a piece of work to be done 任务 □ **task force 1** an armed force organized for a special operation 特遣部队 **2** a group of people specially organized to deal with a particular problem 特别工作组；专门小组 **take someone to task** criticize or reprimand someone 申斥(某人)；斥责(某人)

taskmaster /ˈtɑːskmɑːstə(r)/ **noun** a person who gives someone a lot of difficult tasks 工头；监工

tassel /ˈtæsl/ **noun** a tuft of threads that are knotted together at one end 流苏；穗 ■ **tasselled** (US spelling【美拼作】**tasseled**) **adjective**.

taste /teɪst/ **noun 1** the sensation of flavour produced in the mouth when it comes into contact with a particular substance 味道；滋味 **2** the sense by which taste is perceived 味觉 **3** a small sample of food or drink 少量品尝的东西；一口；一点儿 **4** a brief experience of something (短暂的)感受，体验 **5** a liking for something 爱好；兴趣 **6** the ability to pick out things that are of good quality or appropriate 鉴赏力；审美力，品位 • **verb** (**tastes, tasting, tasted**) **1** have a particular flavour 有…的味道 **2** perceive or recognize the flavour of 品味；辨别 **3** test the flavour of 尝；品 **4** have a brief experience of 感受；体验 □ **taste bud** any of the clusters of nerve endings on the tongue and in the mouth which provide the sense of taste 味蕾 ■ **taster noun**.

tasteful /ˈteɪstfl/ **adjective** showing good judgement of quality, appearance, or appropriate behaviour 有品位的；高雅的；得体的 ■ **tastefully** adverb.

tasteless /ˈteɪstləs/ **adjective 1** having little or no flavour 无味的；不可口的 **2** not showing good judge-

ment of quality, appearance, or appropriate behaviour 无品位的；庸俗的；不得体的 ■ **tastelessly** adverb.

tasty /ˈteɪsti/ **adjective** (**tastier, tastiest**) **1** (of food) having a pleasant flavour (食物)美味的，好吃的 **2** Brit. informal【英，非正式】attractive; appealing 有吸引力的

tat /tæt/ **noun** Brit. informal【英，非正式】tasteless or badly made articles 劣质东西；破烂

tattered /ˈtætəd/ **adjective** old and torn 破旧的；破烂的

tatters /ˈtætəz/ **plural noun** torn pieces of cloth, paper, etc. 破布；碎纸条；破烂东西 □ **in tatters 1** torn in many places 破破烂烂的 **2** destroyed; ruined 毁掉的；破坏的

tattle /ˈtætl/ **noun** gossip 闲谈；说长道短 • **verb** (**tattles, tattling, tattled**) engage in gossip 闲谈；说长道短

tattoo¹ /təˈtuː/ **noun** (plural **tattoos**) a permanent design made on the skin with a needle and ink 文身；刺青 • **verb** (**tattoos, tattooing, tattooed**) give someone a tattoo 给…刺文身 ■ **tattooist noun**.

tattoo² **noun** (plural **tattoos**) **1** Brit. 【英】a military display with music and marching 野外军事表演(包括音乐和齐步行进) **2** a rhythmic tapping or drumming 有节奏的敲击

tatty /ˈtæti/ **adjective** (**tattier, tattiest**) informal【非正式】worn and shabby 破旧的；褴褛的

taught /tɔːt/ past and past participle of TEACH.

taunt /tɔːnt/ **noun** a remark made in order to anger or upset someone 嘲弄；奚落 • **verb** anger or upset with taunts 嘲弄；奚落

Taurus /ˈtɔːrəs/ **noun** a sign of the zodiac (the Bull), 21 April–20 May 金牛宫(黄道十二宫之一)

taut /tɔːt/ **adjective 1** stretched or pulled tight 绷紧的；拉紧的 **2** (of muscles or nerves) tense (肌肉)紧绷

的;(神经)紧张的 ■ **tauten** verb **tautly** adverb.

tautology /tɔːˈtɒlədʒi/ **noun** (plural **tautologies**) the saying of the same thing twice in different words (e.g. They arrived one after the other in succession.) 同义反复;赘述 ■ **tautological** adjective **tautologous** adjective.

tavern /ˈtævən/ **noun** old use 【旧】 an inn or pub 小旅店;小酒馆

tawdry /ˈtɔːdri/ **adjective 1** showy but cheap and of bad quality 俗丽而不值钱的;花哨的 **2** sleazy or unpleasant 粗俗的;令人厌恶的 ■ **tawdriness** noun.

tawny /ˈtɔːni/ **adjective** of an orange-brown or yellowish-brown colour 黄褐色的;茶色的

tax /tæks/ **noun** money that must be paid to the state, charged as a proportion of income and profits or added to the cost of some goods and services 税;款 • verb **1** impose a tax on 对 … 征税 **2** pay tax on a vehicle 缴纳车辆牌照税 **3** make heavy demands on 使负重担;使受压力 **4** accuse someone of doing something wrong 指责;谴责 □ **tax-deductible** allowed to be deducted from income before the amount of tax to be paid is calculated 可减免课税的 **tax exile** a rich person who chooses to live somewhere with low rates of taxation 跨境避税者(指选择居住在税率较低地区的富人) **tax haven** a country or independent area where low rates of taxes are charged (税率低的)避税地,避税港 **tax return** a form on which a person states their income, used to assess how much tax they should pay 纳税申报单 ■ **taxable** adjective.

taxation /tækˈseɪʃn/ **noun 1** the imposing of tax 征税;课税 **2** money paid as tax 税款;税收

taxi /ˈtæksi/ **noun** (plural **taxis**) a vehicle which takes fare-paying passengers to the place of their choice 出租车;计程车;的士 • verb (**taxies**, **taxiing** or **taxying**, **taxied**) (of an aircraft) move slowly along the ground before take-off or after landing (飞机起飞前或降落后)滑行 □ **taxi rank** Brit. 【英】 a place where taxis wait to be hired 出租汽车候客站

taxicab /ˈtæksikæb/ **noun** a taxi 出租车

taxidermy /ˈtæksidɜːmi/ **noun** the art of preparing and stuffing the skins of dead animals so that they look like living ones 动物标本剥制术 ■ **taxidermist** noun.

taxing /ˈtæksɪŋ/ **adjective** physically or mentally demanding 繁重的;伤脑筋的

taxonomy /tækˈsɒnəmi/ **noun 1** the branch of science concerned with classification 分类学 **2** a system of classifying things 分类系统 ■ **taxonomic** adjective.

TB /tiː ˈbiː/ **abbreviation** tuberculosis.

tbsp or **tbs** **abbreviation** tablespoonful 一汤匙的量

tea /tiː/ **noun 1** a hot drink made by soaking the dried leaves of an evergreen Asian shrub in boiling water 茶;茶水 **2** the dried leaves used to make tea 茶叶 **3** Brit. 【英】 a light afternoon meal of sandwiches, cakes, etc., with tea to drink 下午茶;午后茶点 **4** Brit. 【英】 a cooked evening meal 晚餐;晚饭 □ **tea bag** a sachet of tea leaves on to which boiling water is poured to make tea 茶包;袋泡茶 **tea room** a cafe serving tea, cakes, etc. (供应茶、点心等的)茶馆,茶室 **tea towel** (or **tea cloth**) Brit. 【英】 a cloth for drying washed crockery, cutlery, etc. 茶巾;抹布 **tea tree** a shrub of Australia and New

Zealand that produces an oil with antiseptic qualities 茶树(一种灌木，产于澳大利亚和新西兰，其油可以杀菌)

teacake /'tiːkeɪk/ noun Brit. 【英】a kind of bun which contains currants 茶点,茶点饼(内含无核小葡萄干)

teach /tiːtʃ/ verb (**teaches, teaching, taught**) 1 give lessons in a particular subject to a class or pupil 教授;讲授 2 show someone how to do something 教;训练 3 make someone realize or understand something 教导;教育 ■ **teacher** noun.

teacup /'tiːkʌp/ noun a cup from which you drink tea 茶杯

teak /tiːk/ noun hard wood obtained from a tree native to India and SE Asia 柚木(硬质木材,原产于印度和东南亚)

teal /tiːl/ noun (plural **teal** or **teals**) a small freshwater duck 短颈野鸭

team /tiːm/ noun 1 a group of players forming one side in a game or sport (游戏或体育运动的)队 2 two or more people working together (一起工作的)团队,组 3 two or more horses harnessed together to pull something (同拉一辆车的)一组马 ▪ verb 1 (**team up**) work together to achieve a shared goal 组成团队;合作 2 (**team something with**) wear an item of clothing with another 将…与…搭配着穿 □ **team spirit** trust and cooperation among the members of a team 团队精神;合作精神

teammate /'tiːmmeɪt/ noun a fellow member of a team 队友

teamwork /'tiːmwɜːk/ noun organized effort as a group 协作;配合

teapot /'tiːpɒt/ noun a pot with a handle, spout, and lid, in which tea is made 茶壶

tear[1] /teə(r)/ verb (**tears, tearing, tore**; past participle **torn**) 1 rip a hole or split in 戳破;撕破 2 (usu. **tear something up**) pull something apart or to pieces 撕开;撕碎 3 damage a muscle or ligament by overstretching it 撕裂;拉伤(肌肉或韧带) 4 (**tear something down**) demolish or destroy something 毁坏;拆除 5 (**be torn**) be unsure about which of two options to choose 左右为难;难以抉择 6 informal 【非正式】move very quickly 飞奔;疾驰 7 (**tear into**) attack verbally 抨击;斥责 ▪ noun a hole or split caused by tearing 裂口;裂缝

tear[2] /tɪə(r)/ noun a drop of clear salty liquid produced in a person's eye when they are crying or when the eye is irritated 眼泪;泪水 □ **tear gas** gas that causes severe irritation to the eyes, used in warfare and riot control 催泪瓦斯 **tear-jerker** /'tɪədʒɜːkə(r)/ informal 【非正式】a very sad book, film, or song 催人泪下的书(或电影、歌曲)

tearaway /'teərəweɪ/ noun Brit. 【英】a person who behaves in a wild or reckless way 放荡不羁的人;野性难驯的人

teardrop /'tɪədrɒp/ noun a single tear 泪滴;泪珠

tearful /'tɪəfl/ adjective 1 crying or about to cry 哭泣的;眼泪汪汪的 2 causing tears 催人泪下的 ■ **tearfully** adverb.

tease /tiːz/ verb (**teases, teasing, teased**) 1 playfully make fun of or attempt to provoke 取笑;戏弄;揶揄 2 tempt sexually 挑逗;调情 3 (**tease something out**) find out something by searching through a mass of information 理清;梳理清楚 4 gently pull tangled wool, hair, etc. into separate strands 梳理,梳通(缠绕的毛线、头发等) ▪ noun a person who teases 爱戏弄人者 ■ **teaser** noun.

teasel or **teazle** /'tiːzl/ noun a prickly plant with spiny flower heads 川续断;起绒草(高大多刺植物,具有刺头状花序)

teaspoon /'tiːspuːn/ *noun* a small spoon for adding sugar to hot drinks 茶匙；小勺

teat /tiːt/ *noun* **1** a nipple on an animal's udder or similar organ (动物的)乳头 **2** Brit.【英】a plastic nipple-shaped device for sucking milk from a bottle 塑料奶嘴

technical /'teknɪkl/ *adjective* **1** having to do with the techniques of a particular subject, art, or craft 专门技术的；技巧的，工艺的 **2** needing specialized knowledge 专科的；专业的 **3** having to do with the practical use of machinery and methods in science and industry 技术的；技能的 **4** according to the law or rules when applied strictly 严格依据法律（或规则）的；技术性的 □ **technical college** a college specializing in applied sciences and other practical subjects 工学院 ■ **technically** *adverb.*

technicality /ˌteknɪ'kælətɪ/ *noun* (plural **technicalities**) **1** a small formal detail in a set of rules 技术性细则 **2** (**technicalities**) small details of how something works or is done 技术细节 **3** the use of technical terms or methods 术语使用；技术应用

technician /tek'nɪʃn/ *noun* **1** a person who looks after equipment or does practical work in a laboratory 技术员；技师 **2** a person skilled in the technique of an art, science, craft, or sport (艺术、科学、手艺或体育的)技艺精湛者

Technicolor /'teknɪkʌlə(r)/ *noun* trademark【商标】a process of producing cinema films in colour (电影的)彩色印片法

technique /tek'niːk/ *noun* **1** a particular way of carrying out a task 技术；工艺 **2** a person's level of skill in doing something 技术水平；技巧

techno /'teknəʊ/ *noun* a style of fast, loud electronic dance music 高技术

音乐，泰克诺音乐(节奏快、高音量的电子舞曲)

technology /tek'nɒlədʒɪ/ *noun* (plural **technologies**) **1** the application of scientific knowledge for practical purposes 技术；工艺；工业技术 **2** machinery or equipment developed from this knowledge 技术性机器(或设备) **3** the branch of knowledge concerned with applied sciences 应用技术 ■ **technological** *adjective* **technologically** *adverb* **technologist** *noun.*

tectonic /tek'tɒnɪk/ *adjective* Geology【地质】having to do with the earth's crust 地壳构造的

teddy /'tedɪ/ or **teddy bear** *noun* (plural **teddies**) a soft toy bear 泰迪熊；玩具熊

Teddy boy *noun* (in Britain during the 1950s) a young man of a group who had their hair slicked up in a quiff and liked rock-and-roll music (英国20世纪50年代的)男阿飞(头发光洁平整，额前一绺头发上梳，喜欢摇滚乐)

tedious /'tiːdɪəs/ *adjective* too long, slow, or dull 冗长的；乏味的 ■ **tediously** *adverb*

tedium /'tiːdɪəm/ *noun* the state of being tedious 冗长；乏味

tee /tiː/ *noun* **1** a place on a golf course from which the ball is struck at the beginning of each hole (高尔夫球场的)发球区，开球处 **2** a small peg placed in the ground to support a golf ball before it is struck from a tee (高尔夫球的)球座 **3** a mark aimed at in bowls (滚木球戏中的)目标 • *verb* (**tees**, **teeing**, **teed**) Golf【高尔夫】**1** (**tee up**) place the ball on a tee ready to begin a round or hole 把(高尔夫球)置于球座上；准备开球 **2** (**tee off**) begin a round or hole 开球；发球

teem /tiːm/ *verb* **1** (**teem with**) be

swarming with 充满；密集 **2** (of rain) fall heavily (雨)倾泻，倾注

teen /tiːn/ informal 【非正式】 **adjective** having to do with teenagers 青少年的；十几岁的 • **noun** a teenager 少年；青少年

teenage /ˈtiːneɪdʒ/ **adjective** having to do with teenagers 青少年的；十几岁的 ■ **teenaged** adjective.

teenager /ˈtiːneɪdʒə(r)/ **noun** a person aged between 13 and 19 years 少年，青少年(年龄在13至19岁之间)

teens /tiːnz/ **plural noun** the years of a person's age from 13 to 19 十几岁(指13至19岁之间)

teeny /ˈtiːni/ or **teensy** /ˈtiːnzi/ **adjective** (**teenier**, **teeniest**) informal 【非正式】 tiny 很小的；小小的

teepee /ˈtiːpiː/ ⇒ TEPEE.

tee shirt **noun** a T-shirt T恤衫

teeter /ˈtiːtə(r)/ **verb** (**teeters**, **teetering**, **teetered**) move or sway unsteadily 蹒跚；踉跄；摇摇欲坠

teeth /tiːθ/ **plural of** TOOTH.

teethe /tiːð/ **verb** (**teethes**, **teething**, **teethed**) (of a baby) develop its first teeth (幼儿)出牙，长牙 □ **teething troubles** problems that occur in the early stages of a new project 初期困难；开始阶段的问题

teetotal /ˌtiːˈtəʊtl/ **adjective** choosing not to drink alcohol 不饮酒的；滴酒不沾的 ■ **teetotaller** noun.

telecommunications /ˌtelikəˌmjuːnɪˈkeɪʃnz/ **noun** the technology concerned with long distance communication by means of cable, telephone, broadcasting, satellite, etc. 电信；电讯

telegram /ˈtelɪɡræm/ **noun** a message sent by telegraph and delivered in written or printed form 电报

telegraph /ˈtelɪɡrɑːf/ **noun** a system or device for transmitting messages from a distance along a wire 电报；电报机 • **verb** send a message to someone by telegraph 发电报；用电报发

送 □ **telegraph pole** a tall pole used to carry telegraph or telephone wires (电报或电话线路的)电线杆 ■ **telegraphic** adjective.

telekinesis /ˌtelɪkɪˈniːsɪs/ **noun** the movement of objects supposedly as a result of using mental power 心灵致动；心灵遥感 ■ **telekinetic** adjective.

telepathy /təˈlepəθi/ **noun** the supposed communication of thoughts or ideas by means other than the known senses 心灵感应；通灵 ■ **telepathic** adjective.

telephone /ˈtelɪfəʊn/ **noun 1** a system for transmitting voices over a distance using wire or radio 电话 **2** an instrument used in a telephone system for speaking into 电话机 • **verb** (**telephones**, **telephoning**, **telephoned**) contact someone by telephone 给(某人)打电话

telephonist /təˈlefənɪst/ **noun** Brit. 【英】 an operator of a telephone switchboard 电话接线员；话务员

telephony /təˈlefəni/ **noun** the working or use of telephones 电话通讯

telephoto lens /ˈtelɪfəʊtəʊ/ **noun** a lens that produces a magnified image of a distant object 摄远镜头

teleprinter /ˈtelɪprɪntə(r)/ **noun** Brit. 【英】 a device for transmitting telegraph messages as they are keyed 电传打印机

telesales /ˈtelɪseɪlz/ **plural noun** the selling of goods or services over the telephone 电话销售

telescope /ˈtelɪskəʊp/ **noun** an instrument designed to make distant objects appear nearer 望远镜 • **verb** (**telescopes**, **telescoping**, **telescoped**) **1** (of an object made up of several tubes) slide into itself so as to become smaller (由相互嵌套的管子组成的物体)叠套缩短 **2** condense or combine to occupy less space or time 压缩；精简；缩短 ■ **telescopic** adjective.

teletext /'telitekst/ *noun* an information service transmitted to televisions 图文电视；电视文字广播

telethon /'teləθɒn/ *noun* a long television programme broadcast to raise money for a charity (为募捐播放的)长时间电视节目，马拉松式电视节目

televise /'telɪvaɪz/ *verb* (**televises, televising, televised**) show on television 用电视播放

television /'telɪvɪʒn/ *noun* **1** a system for transmitting visual images with sound and displaying them electronically on a screen 电视 **2** (also **television set**) a device with a screen for receiving television signals 电视机 **3** the activity or medium of broadcasting on television 电视广播事业；电视行业 ■ **televisual** adjective.

telex /'teleks/ *noun* **1** an international system in which printed messages are transmitted and received by teleprinters 电传系统 **2** a message sent by telex 电传；用户电报 ● *verb* send a message to someone by telex 以电传发出(电文)

tell /tel/ *verb* (**tells, telling, told**) **1** communicate information to 告诉；告知 **2** say that someone must do something 吩咐；指示 **3** relate a story 讲述(故事) **4** (**tell on**) *informal* 【非正式】 inform someone about a person's wrongdoings 告发(某人) **5** (**tell someone off**) reprimand someone 责备；数落 **6** establish that something is true 确定；证实 **7** have a noticeable effect on someone 产生显著效果 □ **telling-off** (plural **tellings-off**) *informal* 【非正式】a reprimand 责备；数落

teller /'telə(r)/ *noun* **1** chiefly N. Amer. 【主北美】a person who deals with customers' transactions in a bank (银行)出纳员 **2** a person who counts votes (选举的)计票员 **3** a person who tells something 讲述者

telling /'telɪŋ/ *adjective* having a striking or revealing effect 有明显效果的；显著的 ■ **tellingly** adverb.

telltale /'telteɪl/ *adjective* revealing or betraying something 暴露内情的；能说明问题的：*telltale signs of stress* 紧张的明显表现 ● *noun informal* 【非正式】a person who reports things that other people have done wrong 告密者；搬弄是非者

telly /'teli/ *noun informal* 【非正式】television 电视

temerity /tə'merəti/ *noun* very confident behaviour that other people are likely to consider rude or disrespectful 鲁莽；冒失

temp /temp/ *informal* 【非正式】*noun* a person who is employed on a temporary basis 临时雇员 ● *verb* work as a temp 做临时雇员

temper /'tempə(r)/ *noun* **1** a person's state of mind 心情；情绪 **2** a tendency to become angry easily 坏脾气；易怒的性情 **3** an angry state of mind 怒气；火气 **4** the degree of hardness of a metal (金属)的硬度，强度 ● *verb* (**tempers, tempering, tempered**) **1** make something less extreme 使缓和；使温和 **2** harden metal by heating and then cooling it 使(金属)回火

tempera /'tempərə/ *noun* a method of painting with powdered colours mixed with egg yolk 蛋彩画法

temperament /'temprəmənt/ *noun* a person's nature in terms of the way it affects their behaviour 气质；性情；性格

temperamental /ˌtemprə'mentl/ *adjective* **1** tending to have sudden or unreasonable changes of mood 喜怒无常的；情绪化的 **2** relating to or caused by temperament 气质的；性情的；性格的 ■ **temperamentally** adverb.

temperance /'tempərəns/ **noun** the practice of never drinking alcohol 戒酒;滴酒不沾

temperate /'tempərət/ **adjective 1** (of a region or climate) having mild temperatures (地区或气候)温带的 **2** showing selfcontrol 温和的;自我克制的

temperature /'temprətʃə(r)/ **noun 1** the degree of heat in a place, substance, or object 温度;气温 **2** a body temperature above the normal 发烧

✔ 拼写指南 -era- in the middle: temp*era*ture. temperature 中间应拼作 -era-。

tempest /'tempɪst/ **noun** a violent windy storm 暴风雨;大风暴

tempestuous /tem'pestʃuəs/ **adjective 1** very stormy 狂风暴雨的 **2** full of strong and changeable emotions 骚动的;狂暴的;剧烈的

template /'templət/ **noun 1** a shaped piece of rigid material used as a pattern for cutting out, shaping, or drilling (用于切割、成型或钻孔的)样板,模板,型板 **2** a model for others to copy 样板;榜样

temple[1] /'templ/ **noun** a building for the worship of a god or gods 庙宇;寺院;神殿

temple[2] **noun** the flat part either side of the head between the forehead and the ear 太阳穴;鬓角

tempo /'tempəʊ/ **noun** (plural **tempos** or **tempi** /'tempiː/) **1** the speed at which a passage of music is played (乐曲的)速度,节拍 **2** the pace of an activity or process (活动或进程的)速度,进度

temporal /'tempərəl/ **adjective 1** relating to time 时间的 **2** having to do with the physical world rather than spiritual matters 尘世的;世俗的 ■ **temporally** adverb.

temporary /'temprəri/ **adjective** lasting for only a limited period 暂时的;临时性的 ■ **temporarily** adverb.

temporize or **temporise** /'tempəraɪz/ **verb** (**temporizes**, **temporizing**, **temporized**) delay making a decision 拖延(做决定)

tempt /tempt/ **verb 1** try to persuade someone to do something appealing but wrong 劝诱;怂恿 **2** (**be tempted to do**) have an urge or inclination to do 很想做;有做…的冲动 □ **tempt fate** do something risky or dangerous 玩命;冒险 ■ **tempting** adjective **temptingly** adverb.

temptation /temp'teɪʃn/ **noun 1** the action of tempting 引诱;诱惑 **2** a tempting thing 诱惑物

temptress /'temptrəs/ **noun** a woman who sets out to make a man desire her 引诱人的女子;尤物

ten /ten/ **cardinal number** one more than nine; 10 十 (Roman numeral 罗马数字: **x** or **X**.) □ **Ten Commandments** (in the Bible) the ten rules of conduct given by God to Moses 《圣经》中的)十诫 ■ **tenfold** adjective & adverb.

tenable /'tenəbl/ **adjective 1** able to be defended against attack or objection 站得住脚的;守得住的 **2** (of an academic post, grant, etc.) able to be held or used for a stated period (学术职位、津贴等)可担任(或保有)一段时间的

tenacious /tə'neɪʃəs/ **adjective 1** firmly holding on to something 紧握的;坚持的 **2** continuing to exist or do something for longer than might be expected 顽强的;坚忍不拔的 ■ **tenaciously** adverb **tenacity** noun.

tenancy /'tenənsi/ **noun** (plural **tenancies**) possession of land or property as a tenant (土地或房产的)租赁,租用

tenant /'tenənt/ **noun** a person who rents land or property from a landlord 租户;佃户;房客 ▪ **verb**

occupy property as a tenant (作为租赁者)居住，租用

tench /tentʃ/ **noun** (plural **tench**) a freshwater fish of the carp family 丁鱥(一种鲤科淡水鱼)

tend¹ /tend/ **verb 1** frequently behave in a particular way or have certain characteristics 倾向；易于 **2** go or move in a particular direction 趋向；走向

tend² **verb** care for or look after 照料；照顾

tendency /'tendənsi/ **noun** (plural **tendencies**) an inclination to act in a particular way (行为的)倾向，偏好

tendentious /ten'denʃəs/ **adjective** formal 【正式】expressing a strong, often controversial, opinion 有倾向的；有偏见的

tender¹ /'tendə(r)/ **adjective** (**tenderer**, **tenderest**) **1** gentle and sympathetic 温柔的；怜爱的 **2** (of food) easy to cut or chew (食物)嫩的，软的 **3** (of a part of the body) sensitive (身体部位)敏感的，一触即痛的 **4** young and vulnerable 幼小娇弱的 **5** (of a plant) easily damaged by severe weather (植物)脆弱的，娇嫩的 ■ **tenderly** adverb **tenderness** noun.

tender² **verb** (**tenders**, **tendering**, **tendered**) **1** offer or present formally (正式)提供，提出 **2** make a formal written offer to do work, supply goods, etc. for a stated fixed price 投标 **3** offer money as payment 付(款)；偿还 • **noun** a tendered offer 投标

tender³ **noun 1** a vehicle used by a fire service or the armed forces for carrying supplies (消防队或军队的)补给车 **2** a wagon attached to a steam locomotive to carry fuel and water (蒸汽机车的)煤水车 **3** a boat used to ferry people and supplies to and from a ship (向大船运送人员和补给的)附属船，供应船

tendon /'tendən/ **noun** a strong band or cord of tissue attaching a muscle to a bone 腱

tendril /'tendrəl/ **noun 1** a thin curling stem of a climbing plant, which twines round a support (攀援植物的)卷须 **2** a slender ringlet of hair 卷发

tenebrous /'tenɪbrəs/ **adjective** literary 【文】dark; shadowy 暗的；阴暗的

tenement /'tenəmənt/ **noun** a building divided into flats 经济住房；公寓房

tenet /'tenɪt/ **noun** a central principle or belief 原则；宗旨；信条

tenner /'tenə(r)/ **noun** Brit. informal 【英，非正式】a ten-pound note 十英镑钞票

tennis /'tenɪs/ **noun** a game in which players use rackets to hit a ball over a net stretched across a grass or clay court 网球(运动) □ **tennis elbow** inflammation of the tendons of the elbow caused by overuse of the forearm muscles 网球肘

tenon /'tenən/ **noun** a projecting piece of wood that fits into a slot in another piece of wood 雄榫；凸榫；榫舌

tenor¹ /'tenə(r)/ **noun** the male singing voice below alto or countertenor 男高音

tenor² **noun** the general meaning or character of something 大意；要旨

tenpin bowling /'tenpɪn/ **noun** a game in which ten skittles are bowled down with hard balls 十柱保龄球戏

tense¹ /tens/ **adjective 1** feeling, causing, or showing anxiety and nervousness 担心的，紧张的 **2** stretched tight or rigid 拉紧的；绷紧的 • **verb** (**tenses**, **tensing**, **tensed**) make or become tense (使)绷紧，(使)紧张 ■ **tensely** adverb.

tense² **noun** Grammar 【语法】a set of forms of a verb that indicate the time or completeness of the action referred to (动词的)时态

tensile /'tensaɪl/ **adjective 1** relating to tension 张力的;拉力的 **2** capable of being drawn out or stretched 可拉长的;可伸展的

tension /'tenʃn/ **noun 1** a situation that is strained because of differing views or aims 紧张状况;紧张局势 **2** mental or emotional strain (精神或情绪上的)紧张 **3** the state of being stretched tight 拉紧;绷紧 **4** voltage of a particular magnitude 电压: *high tension* 高电压

tent /tent/ **noun** a portable shelter made of cloth and supported by poles and cords 帐篷 ■ **tented** adjective.

tentacle /'tentəkl/ **noun** a long, thin, flexible part extending from the body of certain animals, used for feeling or holding things or moving about 触角;触手;触须

tentative /'tentətɪv/ **adjective 1** done without confidence 踌躇的;犹豫的 **2** not certain or fixed 不确定的;暂时的 ■ **tentatively** adverb.

tenterhook /'tentəhʊk/ **noun** (on tenterhooks) in a state of nervous suspense 焦虑不安;如坐针毡

tenth /tenθ/ **ordinal number 1** that is number ten in a sequence; 10th 第十 **2** (a tenth or one tenth) each of ten equal parts into which something is divided 十分之一

tenuous /'tenjuəs/ **adjective** very slight or weak 微弱的;脆弱的 ■ **tenuously** adverb.

tenure /'tenjə(r)/ **noun 1** the conditions under which land or buildings are held or occupied (房地产的)保有条件 **2** the period of time when someone holds a job or position (职务的)任期 **3** the right to stay permanently in a particular job 终身职位

tenured /'tenjəd/ **adjective** having permanent employment in a particular job (职位)终身的, 长期保有的

tepee or **teepee** /'ti:pi:/ **noun** a cone-shaped tent used by American Indians (美洲印第安人使用的)圆锥形帐篷

tepid /'tepɪd/ **adjective 1** lukewarm 微温的;温吞的 **2** unenthusiastic 不热烈的;不热情的

tequila /tə'ki:lə/ **noun** a clear Mexican alcoholic spirit 龙舌兰酒

tercentenary /ˌtɜ:sen'ti:nəri/ **noun** (plural **tercentenaries**) a three-hundredth anniversary 三百周年纪念

term /tɜ:m/ **noun 1** a word or phrase used to describe a thing or to express an idea 词语;术语;措词 **2** (terms) requirements or conditions 条件;条款 **3** (terms) relations between people 关系;交谊;交情: *We're on good terms.* 我们交情很好。 **4** a period for which something lasts 期间;期限 **5** each of the periods in the year during which teaching is given in a school or college 学期 **6** (also **full term**) the completion of a normal length of pregnancy 足月(分娩) **7** Maths 【数学】 each of the quantities in a ratio, equation, etc. (比率、方程式等的)项 • **verb** call by a particular term 把…称为;把…叫做 □ **come to terms with** become able to accept or deal with 与…妥协;接受 ■ **termly** adjective & adverb.

termagant /'tɜ:məgənt/ **noun** a bossy woman 悍妇;泼妇

terminal /'tɜ:mɪnl/ **adjective 1** having to do with or situated at the end 末端的;终点的;结尾的 **2** (of a disease) predicted to lead to death (疾病)致命的,不治的 • **noun 1** the station at the end of a railway or bus route (铁路或公共汽车路线的)终点站 **2** a departure and arrival building for passengers at an airport 航空站;机场大楼 **3** a point at which connection can be made in an electric circuit (电路的)端子,接头 **4** a keyboard and screen joined to a central computer system (计算机系统的)终端,终端设备 ■ **terminally** adverb.

terminate /'tɜːmɪneɪt/ **verb** (**terminates, terminating, terminated**) **1** bring or come to an end (使)终止;(使)结束 **2** (of a train or bus service) end its journey (火车或公共汽车)到达终点站

termination /ˌtɜːmɪ'neɪʃn/ **noun 1** the ending of something 结局;结束 **2** a medical procedure to end a pregnancy at an early stage 终止妊娠

terminology /ˌtɜːmɪ'nɒlədʒi/ **noun** (plural **terminologies**) a set of terms relating to a subject (学科)术语,专门用语 ■ **terminological** adjective.

terminus /'tɜːmɪnəs/ **noun** (plural **termini** /'tɜːmɪnaɪ/ or **terminuses**) **1** Brit. 【英】a railway or bus terminal (铁路或公共汽车路线的)终点站 **2** a final point or end 目标;目的地

termite /'tɜːmaɪt/ **noun** a small insect which eats wood and lives in colonies in large nests of earth 白蚁

tern /tɜːn/ **noun** a white seabird with long pointed wings and a forked tail 燕鸥

ternary /'tɜːnəri/ **adjective** composed of three parts 由三部分组成的

terpsichorean /ˌtɜːpsɪkə'riːən/ **adjective** relating to dancing 舞蹈的

terrace /'terəs/ **noun 1** a paved area next to a house; a patio (房屋的)露天平台,阳台 **2** Brit. 【英】a row of houses built in one block (同一街区内的)排屋 **3** each of a series of flat areas on a slope, used for growing plants and crops 梯田;阶地 **4** Brit. 【英】a flight of wide, shallow steps for standing spectators in a stadium (体育场的)阶梯看台 • **verb** (**terraces, terracing, terraced**) make sloping land into terraces 使成梯田;使成阶地 ■ **terraced** adjective **terracing** noun.

terracotta /ˌterə'kɒtə/ **noun** brownish-red earthenware that has

not been glazed (无釉的)赤土陶器

terra firma /ˌterə 'fɜːmə/ **noun** dry land; the ground 陆地;大地

terrain /tə'reɪn/ **noun** a stretch of land seen in terms of its physical features 地带;地形;地势

terrapin /'terəpɪn/ **noun** a small freshwater turtle 水龟

terrestrial /tə'restrɪəl/ **adjective 1** having to do with the earth or dry land 地球上的;陆地的 **2** (of an animal or plant) living on or in the ground (动植物)陆栖的,陆生的 **3** (of television broadcasting) not using a satellite (电视广播系统)非卫星传送的,地面上的

terrible /'terəbl/ **adjective 1** very bad, serious, or unpleasant 糟糕的;非常严重的;非常讨厌的 **2** troubled or guilty 烦恼的;不快的;内疚的 **3** causing terror 可怕的;骇人的

terribly /'terəbli/ **adverb 1** extremely 非常;极其 **2** very badly 很厉害地

terrier /'teriə(r)/ **noun** a small, lively breed of dog 狸(一种活泼的小狗)

terrific /tə'rɪfɪk/ **adjective 1** of great size, amount, or strength 尺寸、数量或力量极大的,异乎寻常的 **2** informal 【非正式】excellent 极棒的;非常好的 ■ **terrifically** adverb.

terrify /'terɪfaɪ/ **verb** (**terrifies, terrifying, terrified**) make someone feel very frightened 使惊恐;使十分害怕

terrine /te'riːn/ **noun** a mixture of chopped savoury food that is pressed into a container and served cold (切成碎末、冷食的)罐装风味食品

territorial /ˌterə'tɔːrɪəl/ **adjective 1** relating to a territory or area 领土的 **2** (of an animal) having a territory which it defends (动物)地盘性的 □ **Territorial Army** (in the UK) a military reserve force of volunteers (英国的)本土防卫义勇军 ■ **territorially** adverb.

territory /'terətri/ **noun** (plural **territories**) **1** an area controlled by a ruler or state 领土;版图;领地 **2** a division of a country 州州;地方;区 **3** an area defended by an animal against others (动物的)地盘 **4** an area in which a person has special rights, responsibilities, or knowledge (某人的)地盘,管辖区域;(知识)领域

terror /'terə(r)/ **noun 1** extreme fear 惊恐,恐惧 **2** a cause of terror 恐惧的缘由;令人恐惧的人(或事物) **3** the use of terror to intimidate people 恐怖行动 **4** informal 【非正式】a person causing trouble or annoyance 招惹麻烦的人;讨厌鬼

terrorism /'terərɪzəm/ **noun** the unofficial or unauthorized use of violence and intimidation in the attempt to achieve political aims 恐怖主义;恐怖统治;恐怖行动 ■ **terrorist** noun & adjective.

terrorize or **terrorise** /'terəraɪz/ **verb** (**terrorizes, terrorizing, terrorized**) threaten and frighten over a period of time 恐吓;威胁

terry /'teri/ **noun** a towelling fabric 毛圈织物;厚绒布

terse /tɜːs/ **adjective** (**terser, tersest**) using few words 简短的;简洁的 ■ **tersely** adverb.

tertiary /'tɜːʃəri/ **adjective 1** third in order or level 第三的;第三级的 **2** Brit. 【英】relating to university education 大学层次的;高等教育的

tessellated /'tesɪleɪtɪd/ **adjective** decorated with mosaics 镶嵌马赛克的 ■ **tessellation** noun.

test /test/ **noun 1** a procedure intended to establish how reliable or good something is, or whether something is present 测试;检测;试验 **2** a short examination of skill or knowledge 测验;小考 **3** a medical examination of part of the body (医疗)化验,检查 **4** a difficult situation 考验 **5** (**Test** or **Test match**) an international cricket

or rugby match (板球或橄榄球的)国际比赛 • **verb 1** subject someone or something to a test 测验;检验 **2** make great demands on someone's endurance or patience 考验 □ **test case** Law 【法律】a case that sets an example for future cases 判例 **test tube** a thin glass tube used to hold material in laboratory tests 试管 **test-tube baby** informal 【非正式】a baby conceived by in vitro fertilization 试管婴儿 ■ **tester** noun.

testament /'testəmənt/ **noun 1** a person's will 遗嘱 **2** evidence or proof 证据;证明 **3** (**Testament**) each of the two divisions of the Bible 圣经旧约;圣经新约 ■ **testamentary** adjective.

testate /'testeɪt/ **adjective** having made a valid will before dying 留下遗嘱的

testicle /'testɪkl/ **noun** either of the two oval organs that produce sperm in male mammals, enclosed in the scrotum 睾丸 ■ **testicular** adjective.

testify /'testɪfaɪ/ **verb** (**testifies, testifying, testified**) **1** give evidence as a witness in a law court (出庭)作证 **2** (**testify to**) be evidence or proof of 表明;证实

testimonial /ˌtestɪ'məʊniəl/ **noun 1** a formal statement of a person's good character and qualifications 推荐信;介绍信 **2** a public tribute to someone 感谢信;奖状;奖品

testimony /'testɪməni/ **noun** (plural **testimonies**) **1** a formal statement, especially one given in a court of law (尤指法庭上的)证词,证言 **2** (**testimony to**) evidence or proof of 证据;证明

testis /'testɪs/ **noun** (plural **testes** /'testiːz/) a testicle 睾丸

testosterone /te'stɒstərəʊn/ **noun** a hormone that stimulates the development of male physical characteristics 睾酮;睾丸素

testy /ˈtesti/ **adjective** (**testier**, **testiest**) easily irritated 易怒的；暴躁的 ■ **testily** adverb.

tetanus /ˈtetənəs/ **noun** a disease that causes the muscles to stiffen and go into spasms 破伤风

tetchy /ˈtetʃi/ **adjective** (**tetchier**, **tetchiest**) bad-tempered and irritable 易怒的；暴躁的 ■ **tetchily** adverb.

tête-à-tête /ˌteɪtɑːˈteɪt/ **noun** a private conversation between two people 两人密谈；促膝谈心 • **adjective & adverb** happening privately between two people 亲密的(地)；仅仅两人的(地)

tether /ˈteðə(r)/ **verb** (**tethers**, **tethering**, **tethered**) tie an animal to a post with a rope or chain (用绳或链)拴(动物) • **noun** a rope or chain used to tether an animal (拴动物的)拴绳，拴链

tetrahedron /ˌtetrəˈhiːdrən/ **noun** (plural **tetrahedra** /ˌtetrəˈhiːdrə/ or **tetrahedrons**) a solid figure with four triangular faces 四面体

Teutonic /tjuːˈtɒnɪk/ **adjective** often disapproving 【常贬】German 德意志民族特点的；日耳曼人风格的

text /tekst/ **noun 1** a book or other written or printed work 文稿；文字作品 **2** the main part of a work as distinct from illustrations, notes, etc. (文字作品的)正文 **3** written or printed words or computer data 文本；文档 **4** a text message 短信 • **verb** send someone a text message 给(某人)发短信 ■ **text message** an electronic message sent and received via mobile phone 短信；短消息 ■ **textual** adjective.

textbook /ˈtekstbʊk/ **noun** a book used for the study of a subject 课本；教科书 • **adjective** done in exactly the recommended way 标准的；规范的

textile /ˈtekstaɪl/ **noun** any type of cloth or fabric 布料；纺织品

texture /ˈtekstʃə(r)/ **noun** the feel, appearance, or consistency of a surface, substance, or fabric 质地；手感；纹理 • **verb** (**textures**, **texturing**, **textured**) give a rough or raised texture to 使有纹理；使质地不平 ■ **textural** adjective.

Thai /taɪ/ **noun** (plural **Thai** or **Thais**) **1** a person from Thailand 泰国人 **2** the official language of Thailand 泰国语

thalidomide /θəˈlɪdəmaɪd/ **noun** a sedative drug which was found to cause abnormalities in the fetus when taken by pregnant women 沙利度胺，反应停(一种镇静药物，后发现孕妇服用可导致婴儿畸形)

than /ðæn, ðən/ **conjunction & preposition 1** used to introduce the second part of a comparison (用于引出比较的第二部分)比 **2** used to introduce an exception or contrast (用于引出例外或对比)除，与其 **3** used in expressions indicating one thing happening immediately after another (用于表示一事紧接着另一事发生)就

thane /θeɪn/ **noun** an Anglo-Saxon or medieval Scottish landowner or nobleman (盎格鲁-撒克逊时代或中世纪苏格兰的)大乡绅，领主

thank /θæŋk/ **verb 1** express gratitude to 感谢；向⋯道谢 **2** ironic 【讽】blame or hold responsible 责备；由⋯负责 ■ **thank you** a polite expression of Gratitude 多谢；谢谢

✔ 拼写指南 **thank you** is a two-word phrase: don't spell it as one word. thank you 是由两个词构成的短语，不要写成一个词。

thankful /ˈθæŋkfl/ **adjective** pleased and relieved 欣慰的 ■ **thankfulness** noun.

thankfully /ˈθæŋkfəli/ **adverb 1** in a

thankful way 感激地 **2** fortunately 幸亏;好在

thankless /'θæŋkləs/ **adjective 1** (of a job or task) unpleasant and unlikely to be appreciated by other people (工作或任务)吃力不讨好的, 徒劳的 **2** not showing or feeling gratitude 不领情的;不知感激的

thanks /θæŋks/ **plural noun 1** an expression of gratitude 感谢;谢谢 **2** = thank you. □ **thanks to** due to 幸亏;由于

thanksgiving /,θæŋks'gɪvɪŋ/ **noun 1** the expression of gratitude to God (对上帝的)感恩 **2** (Thanksgiving) (in North America) a national holiday held in November in the US and October in Canada (北美的)感恩节(美国定在11月,加拿大定在10月)

that /ðæt, ðət/ **pronoun & determiner 1** (plural those) used to refer to a person or thing seen or heard or already mentioned or known (指看到、听到、已提及或已知的人或事物)那,那个 **2** (plural those) referring to the more distant of two things (指较远的事物)那,那个 • **pronoun** used instead of which, who, when, etc. to introduce a clause that defines or identifies something (代替which, who, when等引导从句,用于限定或说明某事物) • **adverb** to such a degree; so 那样,那么 • **conjunction** introducing a statement or suggestion (用于引出陈述或建议)

thatch /θætʃ/ **noun** a roof covering of straw, reeds, etc. 茅草屋顶 • **verb** cover with thatch 用茅草盖 ■ **thatcher** noun.

thaw /θɔː/ **verb 1** make or become liquid or soft after being frozen (结冰后)解冻, 融化 **2** make or become friendlier (使)变得缓和, (使)变得友好 • **noun 1** a period of warmer weather that thaws ice and snow 解冻期;融冰期 **2** an increase in friendliness 关系缓和;关系改善

the /ðiː, ðə, ðɪ/ **determiner 1** used to refer to one or more people or things already mentioned or easily understood; the definite article (用作定冠词,指已提及或易领会的人或事物) **2** used to refer to someone or something that is the only one of its kind (指独一无二的人或事物) **3** used to refer to something in a general rather than specific way (用以泛指)

theatre /'θɪətə(r)/ (US spelling 【美拼写】 **theater**) **noun 1** a building in which plays are Performed 戏院;剧场 **2** the writing and production of plays 戏剧写作;戏剧表演 **3** the dramatic quality of a play or event 戏剧性;戏剧效果 **4** a room where specific things are done (特定事情发生的)房间: *an operating theatre* 手术室 **5** the area in which something happens (事件发生的)场所: *a theatre of war* 战场

theatrical /θɪ'ætrɪkl/ **adjective 1** having to do with acting or the theatre 戏剧的;演剧的;剧场的 **2** exaggerated and too dramatic 夸张的;戏剧性的 • **noun (theatricals)** theatrical performances or behaviour 戏剧演出;戏剧化动作 ■ **theatricality** noun **theatrically** adverb.

theatrics /θɪ'ætrɪks/ **noun** theatricals 戏剧演出;戏剧化动作

thee /ðiː, ðɪ/ old-fashioned or dialect form of **you**, as the singular object of a verb or preposition. you 的过时或方言形式(作单数宾语)

theft /θeft/ **noun** the action or crime of stealing 偷盗;盗窃罪

their /ðeə(r)/ **possessive determiner 1** belonging to or associated with the people or things previously mentioned or easily identified 他们的;她们的;它们的 **2** belonging to or associated with a person whose sex is not specified (指性别不详的)

! 注意 don't confuse **their** with **there**, which means 'in or to that place' or **they're**, which is short for 'they are'. 不要混淆their、there和they're，there 意为"在那里，到那里"，they're是they are的缩写形式。

theirs /ðeəz/ **possessive pronoun** used to refer to something belonging to or associated with two or more people or things previously mentioned 他们的，她们的，它们的(所有物)

✔ 拼写指南 no apostrophe: **theirs**. theirs 没有撇号。

them /ðem, ðəm/ **pronoun 1** used as the object of a verb or preposition to refer to two or more people or things previously mentioned or easily identified (用作宾语)他们，她们，它们 **2** referring to a person whose sex is not specified (指性别不详的人)

thematic /θɪ'mætɪk/ **adjective** arranged according to subject, or connected with a subject 主题的，专题的 ■ **thematically** adverb.

theme /θiːm/ **noun 1** a subject which a person speaks, writes, or thinks about (讲话，写作或思考的)题目，主题 **2** a prominent or recurring melody in a piece of music (乐曲的)主调，主旋律 **3** an idea that is often repeated in a work of art or literature (艺术或文学作品的)主题，主题思想 **4** (also **theme tune** or **music**) a piece of music played at the beginning and end of a film or programme (电影或节目的)主题音乐 □ **theme park** a large amusement park based around a particular idea 主题公园；主题乐园 ■ **themed** adjective.

themselves /ðəm'selvz, ðem-/ **pronoun 1** used as the object of a verb or preposition to refer to a group of people or things previously mentioned as the subject of the clause 他们自己；她们自己；它们自己 **2** they or them personally 他们(或她们)、它们)亲自 **3** used instead of 'himself' or 'herself' to refer to a person whose sex is not specified (指性别不详的人用以代替himself 或 herself)

! 注意 note that you should use **themselves** rather than **themself** to refer to a person whose sex is not specified, e.g. *helping someone to help themselves*, not *helping someone to help themself*. 注意当指代性别不详的人时，应使用themselves而不是themself，例如，应该用helping someone to help themselves (帮助某人自救)，而不是 helping someone to help themself。

then /ðen/ **adverb 1** at that time 当时；那时 **2** after that 接着，然后 **3** also 还有；再者 **4** therefore 那么；既然如此

thence /ðens/ **or from thence** **adverb** formal 【正式】**1** from a place or source previously mentioned 从那里；从那 **2** as a consequence 因此；所以

thenceforth /ðens'fɔːθ/ **or thenceforward** /ðens'fɔːwəd/ **adverb** formal 【正式】from that time, place, or point onward 从那时起；从那开始；此后

theocracy /θɪ'ɒkrəsi/ **noun** (plural **theocracies**) a system of government by priests 神权政治；僧侣政治 ■ **theocratic** adjective.

theodolite /θɪ'ɒdəlaɪt/ **noun** an instrument used in surveying for measuring horizontal and vertical angles 经纬仪

theologian /ˌθiːə'ləʊdʒən/ **noun** a person who is an expert in or is studying theology 神学家；神学研究者

theology /θɪ'ɒlədʒi/ **noun** (plural **theologies**) **1** the study of God and religious belief 神学 **2** a system of religious beliefs and theory 宗教信仰(体系)；神学理论系统 ■ **theological** adjective **theologist** noun.

theorem /ˈθɪərəm/ noun a scientific or mathematical rule or proposition that can be proved by reasoning 定理

theoretical /ˌθɪəˈretɪkl/ adjective **1** concerned with the theory of a subject rather than its practical application 理论的，原理的 **2** based on theory rather than experience or practice 基于理论的 ■ **theoretically** adverb.

theoretician /ˌθɪərəˈtɪʃn/ noun a person who develops or studies the theoretical framework of a subject 理论家

theorist /ˈθɪərɪst/ noun a theoretician 理论家

theorize or **theorise** /ˈθɪəraɪz/ verb (**theorizes, theorizing, theorized**) form a theory or theories about something 形成理论，(使)理论化

theory /ˈθɪəri/ noun (plural **theories**) **1** an idea or system of ideas intended to explain something 学说，论，说 **2** a set of principles on which an activity is based 理论，原理

therapeutic /ˌθerəˈpjuːtɪk/ adjective **1** relating to the healing of disease 治疗的，治病的 **2** having a good effect on the body or mind 有益身心健康的 ■ **therapeutically** adverb.

therapy /ˈθerəpi/ noun (plural **therapies**) **1** treatment of a physical problem or illness 治疗，疗法 **2** treatment of mental or emotional problems using psychological methods 心理治疗，精神疗法 ■ **therapist** noun.

there /ðeə(r)/ adverb **1** in, at, or to that place or position 在那里，到那里，往那里 **2** on that issue 在那件事上 □ **there is** (or **there are**) used to indicate that something exists or is true 有，存在

!注意 don't confuse **there** with **their** or **they're**: see the note at THEIR. 不要混淆 there，their 和 they're，见词条 their 处的注释。

thereabouts /ˈðeərəbaʊts/ adverb near that place, time, or amount 在那附近；大约；左右

thereafter /ˌðeərˈɑːftə(r)/ adverb after that time 之后；此后

thereby /ˌðeəˈbaɪ/ adverb by that means; as a result of that 因此；由此

therefore /ˈðeəfɔː(r)/ adverb for that reason 因此；因而

therein /ˌðeərˈɪn/ adverb formal 【正式】in that place, document, or respect 在那里，在其中，在那点上

thereof /ˌðeərˈɒv/ adverb formal 【正式】of the thing just mentioned 在其中，其

there's /ðeəz/ short form **1** there is. there has.

thereupon /ˌðeərəˈpɒn/ adverb formal 【正式】immediately or shortly after that 立即；随即

therewith /ˌðeəˈwɪð/ adverb old use or formal 【旧或正式】**1** with or in the thing mentioned 与此；与之 **2** immediately after that 随即；立即

thermal /ˈθɜːml/ adjective **1** relating to heat 热的；热量的 **2** (of a garment) designed to keep the body warm by stopping heat from escaping (衣服)保暖的 • noun an upward current of warm air 上升的热气流 ■ **thermally** adverb.

thermodynamics /ˌθɜːməʊdaɪˈnæmɪks/ noun the study of the relationship between heat and other forms of energy 热力学 ■ **thermodynamic** adjective.

thermometer /θəˈmɒmɪtə(r)/ noun an instrument for measuring temperature, usually containing mercury or alcohol which expands when heated 温度计

thermonuclear /ˌθɜːməʊˈnjuːkliə(r)/

adjective relating to or using nuclear fusion reactions that occur at very high temperatures 热核的

Thermos /'θɜːməs/ **noun** trademark 【商标】 a vacuum flask 瑟姆斯保温瓶；真空瓶

thermostat /'θɜːməʊstæt/ **noun** a device that automatically controls temperature or activates a device at a set temperature 温度自动调节器；恒温器 ■ **thermostatic** adjective **thermostatically** adverb.

thesaurus /θɪ'sɔːrəs/ **noun** a book containing lists of words which have the same or a similar meaning 同义词词典；分类词汇编

these /ðiːz/ plural of THIS.

thesis /'θiːsɪs/ **noun** (plural **theses** /'θiːsiːz/) **1** a statement or theory that is put forward to be supported or proved 论点；论题；命题 **2** a long piece of work involving research, written as part of a university degree 论文；学位论文

thespian /'θespɪən/ **noun** an actor or actress 演员 • **adjective** relating to drama and the theatre 戏剧的；剧院的

they /ðeɪ/ **pronoun 1** used to refer to two or more people or things previously mentioned or easily identified 他们；她们；它们 **2** people in general (泛指)人们，众人 **3** used to refer to a person whose sex is not specified (in place of either 'he' or 'he or she') (指性别不详的人，用以代替he或he or she)

they'd /ðeɪd/ **short form 1** they had. **2** they would.

they'll /ðeɪl/ **short form 1** they shall. **2** they will.

they're /ðeə(r)/ **short form** they are.

> **! 注意** don't confuse they're with their or there: see the note at THEIR. 不要混淆they're，their 和there，见词条 their 处注释。

they've /ðeɪv/ **short form** they have.

thiamine /'θaɪəmiːn/ or **thiamin** /'θaɪəmɪn/ **noun** vitamin B₁, found in grains, nuts, beans, and liver 维生素 B₁；硫胺素

thick /θɪk/ **adjective 1** with opposite sides or surfaces relatively far apart 厚的；粗的 **2** (of a garment or fabric) made of heavy material (衣服或织物)厚重的，厚实的 **3** made up of a large number of things or people close together 密的；茂密的；密集的 **4** (**thick with**) filled or covered with 充满的；密布的 **5** (of the air or atmosphere) difficult to see through or breathe (空气或大气)浓密的，能见度低的 **6** (of something liquid or semi-liquid) relatively firm in consistency (液体或液状物)浓的，黏稠的 **7** informal 【非正式】 stupid 蠢笨的 **8** (of a voice) hoarse or husky (嗓音)沙哑的，嘶哑的 **9** (of an accent) strong and difficult to understand (口音)浓重的 **10** informal 【非正式】 having a very close, friendly relationship 亲密的；十分友好的 • **noun** (**the thick**) the middle or the busiest part 中心部分；最繁忙部分 □ **through thick and thin** under all circumstances 同甘共苦；患难与共 ■ **thickly** adverb.

thicken /'θɪkən/ **verb** make or become thick or thicker (使)变厚，(使)变浓，(使)变稠

thicket /'θɪkɪt/ **noun** a dense group of bushes or trees 灌木丛；树丛

thickness /'θɪknəs/ **noun 1** the distance through an object, as distinct from width or height 厚度 **2** the state or quality of being thick 厚，稠，浓 **3** a layer of material (一)层

thickset /θɪk'set/ **adjective** heavily built 体格粗壮的；膀阔腰圆的

thief /θiːf/ **noun** (plural **thieves**) a person who steals another person's property 小偷；贼

✔ 拼写指南 *i* before *e* except after *c*: thief. i置于e前，在c后时除外，如 thief.

thieve /θiːv/ **verb** (**thieves, thieving, thieved**) steal things 偷盗；偷窃 ■ **thievery** noun.

thigh /θaɪ/ **noun** the part of the leg between the hip and the knee 股；大腿

thimble /'θɪmbl/ **noun** a small covering that you wear to protect the end of the finger and push the needle in sewing 顶针；针箍

thin /θɪn/ **adjective** (**thinner, thinnest**) **1** having opposite surfaces or sides close together 薄的；细的 **2** (of a garment or fabric) made of light material (衣服或织物)轻的，薄的 **3** having little flesh or fat on the body 瘦的 **4** having few parts or members in relation to the area covered or filled 稀疏的；稀少的 **5** not dense or heavy 稀薄的；淡薄的 **6** containing a lot of liquid and not much solid substance 稀薄的，淡的 **7** (of a sound) faint and high-pitched (声音)微弱的，尖细的 **8** weak and inadequate 不能令人信服的；不充足的 • **verb** (**thins, thinning, thinned**) (often **thin out**) make or become less thick or dense (使)变薄；(使)变稀少；(使)变淡 ■ **thinly** adverb **thinness** noun.

thine /ðaɪn/ **pronoun & possessive determiner** old use 【旧】 your or yours 你的(所有物)；你们的(所有物)

thing /θɪŋ/ **noun 1** an inanimate object (无生命的)物体，物品 **2** an unspecified object, action, activity, etc. (未明的)东西，行为，活动 **3** (**your things**) personal belongings (个人的)所有物，用品，用具 **4** (**the thing**) informal 【非正式】 what is needed or required 所需之物 **5** (**your thing**) informal 【非正式】 your special interest 特殊兴趣

think /θɪŋk/ **verb** (**thinks, thinking,**

thought) **1** have a particular opinion, belief, or idea 认为；以为 **2** use or direct your mind 想；思考；思索 **3** (**think of** or **about**) take into account or consideration 考虑到；关心 **4** intend 打算；计划 **5** (**think something over**) consider something carefully 仔细考虑 **6** (**think something up**) informal 【非正式】 invent something 发明；想出 • **noun** an act of thinking 想，思索 □ **think better of** reconsider and decide not to do 重新考虑后决定不做 **think tank** a group of experts providing advice and ideas 智囊团；专家小组 ■ **thinker** noun.

thinner /'θɪnə(r)/ **noun** a solvent used to thin paint or other solutions (油漆等的)稀释剂

third /θɜːd/ **ordinal number 1** that is number three in a sequence; 3rd 第三 **2** (**a third** or **one third**) each of three equal parts into which something is divided 三分之一 **3** Brit. 【英】 a place in the third grade in an exam for a degree 三等学位 □ **third-degree** (of burns) of the most severe kind, affecting tissue below the skin (烧伤)三度的 **the third degree** lengthy and harsh questioning (长时间的)盘问，逼供 **third party 1** a person besides the two main ones involved in a situation (当事双方之外的)第三者，第三方 **2** Brit. 【英】 (of insurance) covering damage or injury suffered by someone other than the person who is insured (保险)第三方责任的 **Third World** the developing countries of Asia, Africa, and Latin America 第三世界(指亚洲、非洲和拉丁美洲的发展中国家) ■ **thirdly** adverb.

thirst /θɜːst/ **noun 1** a feeling of needing or wanting to drink 渴；口渴 **2** the state of not having enough water to drink 干渴 **3** (**thirst for**) a strong desire for 渴望；渴求 • **verb 1** (**thirst for** or **after**) have a strong desire for 渴望；渴求 **2** old use 【旧】 feel a need to drink 感到口渴；想喝水

thirsty /'θɜːsti/ *adjective* (**thirstier, thirstiest**) **1** feeling or causing thirst 口渴的；使人口渴的 **2** (**thirsty for**) having a strong desire for 渴望的；渴求的 ■ **thirstily** *adverb*.

thirteen /θɜːˈtiːn/ *cardinal number* one more than twelve; 13 十三 (Roman numeral 罗马数字：**xiii** or **XIII**.) ■ **thirteenth** *ordinal number*.

thirty /'θɜːti/ *cardinal number* (plural **thirties**) ten less than forty; 30 三十 (Roman numeral 罗马数字：**xxx** or **XXX**.) ■ **thirtieth** *ordinal number*.

this /ðɪs/ *pronoun & determiner* (plural **these**) **1** used to identify a specific person or thing close at hand, just mentioned, or being indicated or experienced 这；这个 **2** referring to the nearer of two things close to the speaker (两者中距离说话者较近的一个)这，这个 • *adverb* to the degree or extent indicated 这样，这么

thistle /'θɪsl/ *noun* a plant with a prickly stem and leaves and purple flowers 蓟(茎叶带刺，开紫色花)

thistledown /'θɪsldaʊn/ *noun* the light fluffy down of thistle seeds 蓟种子冠毛

thither /'ðɪðə(r)/ *adverb* old use 【旧】 to or towards that place 到那里；向那里

tho' or **tho** /ðəʊ/ *informal spelling of* THOUGH. though 的非正式拼法

thong /θɒŋ/ *noun* **1** a narrow strip used as a fastening or as the lash of a whip 皮条；皮带 **2** a pair of knickers like a G-string G带型女衬裤

thorax /'θɔːræks/ *noun* (plural **thoraces** /'θɔːrəsiːz/ or **thoraxes**) **1** the part of the body between the neck and the abdomen 胸；胸部 **2** the middle section of an insect's body, to which the legs and wings are attached (昆虫的)胸，胸部 ■ **thoracic** *adjective*.

thorn /θɔːn/ *noun* **1** a stiff sharp-pointed projection on a plant (植物的)刺，棘刺 **2** a thorny bush, shrub, or tree 带刺小灌木，荆棘 □ **a thorn in someone's side** (or **flesh**) a source of continual annoyance or trouble 使人苦恼(或招来麻烦)的人(或事)；眼中钉；肉中刺

thorny /'θɔːni/ *adjective* (**thornier, thorniest**) **1** having many thorns 带刺的；多刺的 **2** 荆棘丛生的 **2** causing difficulty 棘手的，麻烦的

thorough /'θʌrə/ *adjective* **1** complete with regard to every detail 彻底的，完全的 **2** 细致的 **2** very careful and complete 仔细周到的，缜密的 **3** absolute; utter 十足的；彻头彻尾的 ■ **thoroughly** *adverb*.

thoroughbred /'θʌrəbred/ *adjective* descended from animals that were all of the same breed 纯种的 • *noun* a thoroughbred animal 纯种动物

thoroughfare /'θʌrəfeə(r)/ *noun* a road or path between two places 大街；大道；通衢

thoroughgoing /θʌrəˈgəʊɪŋ/ *adjective* **1** thorough 彻底的 **2** complete; absolute 彻头彻尾的；十足的.

those /ðəʊz/ *plural of* THAT.

thou /ðaʊ/ *pronoun* old use 【旧】 you (as the singular subject of a verb) 你，汝，尔(用作单数宾语)

though /ðəʊ/ *conjunction* **1** despite the fact that; although 尽管；虽然 **2** however; but 然而；不过；但是 • *adverb* however 然而；不过

thought¹ /θɔːt/ *noun* **1** an idea or opinion produced by thinking, or occurring suddenly in the mind 想法；看法；主意 **2** the process of thinking 思考；思维 **3** (**thought of**) intention, hope, or idea of 意图；希望；打算 **4** the forming of opinions, or the opinions so formed 思潮，思想

thought² past and past participle of THINK.

thoughtful /'θɔːtfl/ *adjective* **1**

absorbed in thought 沉思的；思考的
2 showing careful consideration 深思熟虑的 **3** showing consideration for other people 考虑周到的；体贴的
■ **thoughtfully** adverb.

thoughtless /'θɔːtləs/ **adjective**
1 not showing consideration for other people 不为他人着想的；不顾及他人的 **2** without considering the consequences 欠考虑的；轻率的
■ **thoughtlessly** adverb.

thousand /'θaʊzənd/ **cardinal number**
1 the product of a hundred and ten; 1,000 一千 (Roman numeral 罗马数字：m or M.) **2** (**thousands**) informal【非正式】an unspecified large number 数以千计；成千上万
■ **thousandth** ordinal number.

thrall /θrɔːl/ **noun** the state of being in another person's power 奴役；束缚；控制

thrash /θræʃ/ **verb 1** beat repeatedly with a stick or whip (用棍或鞭)痛打，毒打 **2** move in a violent or uncontrolled way 激烈扭动；翻来覆去 **3** informal【非正式】defeat heavily 重创；彻底击败
4 thrash something out discuss an issue frankly and thoroughly 开诚布公地商讨；彻底讨论

thread /θred/ **noun 1** a thin strand of cotton or other fibres used in sewing or weaving (缝衣服或编织用的)线，细线 **2** a spiral ridge on the outside of a screw or bolt or on the inside of a hole, to allow two parts to be screwed together 螺纹 **3** a theme running through a situation or piece of writing 线索；脉络 • **verb 1** pass a thread through 穿(针)；给…穿线 **2** weave in and out of obstacles 穿过；绕行

threadbare /'θredbeə(r)/ **adjective**
thin and tattered with age 磨薄的；破旧的

threat /θret/ **noun 1** a stated intention to inflict harm on someone 威胁；恐吓 **2** a person or thing likely to cause harm 可能带来威胁的人(或事物) **3**

the possibility of trouble or danger 凶兆；坏事发生的可能

threaten /'θretn/ **verb 1** make a threat to 威胁；恐吓 **2** put at risk 危及；对…构成威胁 **3** seem likely to produce an unwelcome result (不利情况)逼近，将要发生
■ **threatening** adjective **threateningly** adverb.

three /θriː/ **cardinal number** one more than two; 3 三 (Roman numeral 罗马数字：iii or III.) □ **three-dimensional** having or appearing to have length, breadth, and depth 三度空间的，立体的 ■ **threefold** adjective & adverb.

threepence /'θrepəns/ **noun** Brit.【英】the sum of three old pence before decimalization (1971) (1971年采用十进制货币前的)三便士 ■ **threepenny** adjective.

threesome /'θriːsəm/ **noun** a group of three people 三人一组；三人小组

threnody /'θrenədi/ **noun** (plural **threnodies**) a song, piece of music, or poem expressing grief or regret 哀歌；挽歌

thresh /θreʃ/ **verb 1** separate grains of corn from the rest of the plant (使)脱粒 **2** move in an uncontrolled way 猛烈摆动；颠簸；翻滚 ■ **thresher** noun.

threshold /'θreʃhəʊld/ **noun 1** a strip of wood or stone forming the bottom of a doorway 门槛；门口 **2** a level or point marking the start of something 开端；起点，临界点

✔ **拼写指南** there is only one *h* in the middle: thres*h*old. threshold 中只有一个 h.

threw /θruː/ past of THROW.

!注意 don't confuse **threw** with **through**, which means 'in one side of an opening or place and out of the other'. 不要混淆 threw 和 through，

后者意为"从…一端到另一端；穿过；贯穿"。

thrice /θraɪs/ **adverb** old use【旧】three times 三次；三倍

thrift /θrɪft/ **noun** the quality of spending money very carefully, so that none is wasted 节约；节俭 ■ **thrifty** adjective

thrill /θrɪl/ **noun 1** a sudden feeling of excitement and pleasure 狂喜；兴奋；激动 **2** an exciting or enjoyable experience 令人兴奋的经历 **3** a wave of emotion or sensation 震颤感；兴奋感 • **verb 1** give someone a thrill 使感到非常兴奋(或激动) **2** (**thrill to**) experience something exciting 对…感到兴奋(或激动) ■ **thrilling** adjective

thriller /'θrɪlə(r)/ **noun** a novel, play, or film with an exciting plot, typically involving crime or spying (一般包含有犯罪或间谍内容的)惊险小说(或戏剧、电影)

thrive /θraɪv/ **verb** (**thrives**, **thriving**, **thrived** or **throve**; past participle **thrived** or **thriven**) **1** grow or develop well 茁壮成长；蓬勃发展 **2** be successful; flourish 繁荣；兴旺

throat /θrəʊt/ **noun 1** the passage which leads from the back of the mouth to the lungs and stomach 喉咙；咽喉 **2** the front part of the neck 颈前部

throaty /'θrəʊti/ **adjective** (**throatier**, **throatiest**) sounding deep and husky 声音低沉的；沙哑 ■ **throatily** adverb

throb /θrɒb/ **verb** (**throbs**, **throbbing**, **throbbed**) **1** beat or sound with a strong, regular rhythm (强烈而有节奏的)跳动，搏动 **2** feel pain in a series of pulsations 抽痛；跳动着作痛 • **noun** a strong, regular beat or sound (强烈而有节奏的)跳动，搏动；震响

throes /θrəʊz/ **plural noun** severe or violent pain and struggle 剧痛，痛苦挣扎 □ **in the throes of** in the middle of doing or dealing with something 挣扎于…之中，处于…的困苦之中

thrombosis /θrɒm'bəʊsɪs/ **noun** (plural **thromboses** /θrɒm'bəʊsiːz/) the formation of a blood clot in a blood vessel or the heart 血栓形成

throne /θrəʊn/ **noun 1** a chair for a king or queen, used during ceremonies (君王的)宝座，御座 **2** (**the throne**) the power or rank of a king or queen 王权；君权；王位

throng /θrɒŋ/ **noun** a large, densely packed crowd 聚集的人群；一大群人 • **verb** gather somewhere in large numbers 聚集；蜂拥；挤满

throttle /'θrɒtl/ **noun** a device controlling the flow of fuel or power to an engine (控制发动机燃料或动力的)节流阀，节流杆，风门，油门 • **verb** (**throttles**, **throttling**, **throttled**) **1** attack or kill by choking or strangling 使窒息；掐死；扼死 **2** control an engine or vehicle with a throttle 通过油门控制(发动机或车辆)；调节油门

through /θruː/ **preposition & adverb 1** in one side and out of the other side of an opening or place 从…一端到另一端；穿过；贯穿 **2** continuing in time towards 直到；一直到 **3** from beginning to end 至始至终；从头到尾 **4** by means of 以；凭借 • **adjective 1** (of public transport) continuing to the final destination (公共交通工具)直通的，直达的 **2** (of traffic, roads, etc.) passing straight through a place (交通、道路等)直通的 **3** having successfully reached the next stage of a competition (竞赛)成功进入下一阶段的，晋级的 **4** informal【非正式】having finished an activity, relationship, etc. (活动等)完结的；(关系)完结的

! 注意 don't confuse **through** with **threw**, which is the past of **throw**. 不要混淆 through 和 threw，后者是 throw 的过去式。

throughout /θru:'aʊt/ **preposition & adverb** all the way through 贯穿，遍及

throughput /'θru:pʊt/ **noun** the amount of material or number of items passing through a process (系统或流程的)通过量，吞吐量

throve /θrəʊv/ past of THRIVE.

throw /θrəʊ/ **verb** (**throws**, **throwing**, **threw**; past participle **thrown**) **1** send through the air with a rapid movement of the arm and hand 投，扔，抛 **2** move or place hurriedly or roughly 猛推；摔；丢；扔 **3** project, direct, or cast light, an expression, etc. in a particular direction 发出，投射(光线等)；作出(表情等) **4** send suddenly into a particular position or condition 使突然陷入(某种状态) **5** upset or confuse 使困惑；使心烦意乱 • **noun 1** an act of throwing 投；掷；扔；抛 **2** a small rug or light cover for furniture 小毯子；(家具的)罩，套 □ **throw something away** (or **out**) get rid of something 扔掉(某物)；摆脱(某事物) **throw up** informal 【非正式】 vomit 呕吐

throwaway /'θrəʊəweɪ/ **adjective 1** intended to be thrown away after use 用后即扔的；一次性的 **2** (of a remark) said without careful thought (话语)脱口而出的，顺口说的

throwback /'θrəʊbæk/ **noun** a person or thing that resembles someone or something that existed in the past 返祖者；返祖型的东西

thrum /θrʌm/ **verb** (**thrums**, **thrumming**, **thrummed**) make a continuous rhythmic humming sound 低沉地嗡嗡作响 • **noun** a thrumming sound 持续的嗡嗡声

thrush¹ /θrʌʃ/ **noun** a bird with a brown back and spotted breast 鸫(一种鸟，背部棕色，胸部有斑点)

thrush² **noun** an infection of the mouth and throat or the genitals 鹅口疮；真菌性口炎；念珠菌性阴道炎

thrust /θrʌst/ **verb** (**thrusts**, **thrusting**, **thrust**) **1** push suddenly or violently 推，塞 **2** make your way forcibly 冲；挤；搡 • **noun 1** a sudden or violent lunge or attack 刺，戳 **2** the main point of an argument (论证的)要点，要旨，重点 **3** the force produced by an engine to push forward a jet, rocket, etc. (发动机推动喷气机，火箭等的)推力，动力

thrusting /'θrʌstɪŋ/ **adjective** aggressively ambitious 过于积极进取的；盛气凌人的

thud /θʌd/ **noun** a dull, heavy sound 砰的一响；闷响 • **verb** (**thuds**, **thudding**, **thudded**) move, fall, or strike with a thud 咚咚地跑(或走)；砰地落下(或击中)

thug /θʌg/ **noun** a violent man 恶棍；暴徒 ■ **thuggery** noun **thuggish** adjective.

thumb /θʌm/ **noun** the short, thick first digit of the hand 拇指 • **verb 1** turn over pages with your thumb 拇指翻(页) **2** ask for a free ride in a passing vehicle by signalling with your thumb 竖起拇指请求(搭便车) □ **thumb index** lettered notches cut into the side of a book to help you find the section you want 拇指索引；书边挖月索引 **thumbs up** (or **down**) informal 【非正式】 an indication of approval (or disapproval) 竖起大拇指(表示满意或赞成)；拇指朝下(表示拒绝或失败) **under someone's thumb** under someone's control 完全受(某人)支配；受制于(某人)

thumbnail /'θʌmneɪl/ **noun** the nail of the thumb 拇指甲 □ **thumbnail sketch** a brief, concise description 简略描述

thumbscrew /ˈθʌmskruː/ **noun** an instrument of torture that crushes the thumbs 拇指夹(一种刑具)

thump /θʌmp/ **verb 1** hit heavily with your fist or a blunt object (用拳或钝器)捶击,重击 **2** put down forcefully 重重放下 **3** (of a person's heart) beat strongly (人的心脏)砰然跳动,有力地跳动 **• noun** a dull, heavy blow or noise 重击(声);砰的一声

thumping /ˈθʌmpɪŋ/ **adjective** informal 【非正式】 very big 巨大的;非常大的

thunder /ˈθʌndə(r)/ **noun 1** a loud rumbling or crashing noise heard after a lightning flash due to the expansion of rapidly heated air 雷;雷声 **2** a loud, deep noise 雷鸣般的响声;轰隆声 **• verb 1** (it thunders, it is thundering, it thundered) thunder is sounding 打雷 **2** make a loud, deep noise 轰鸣;发出雷鸣般的响声 **3** speak loudly and angrily 吼喝;大声斥责

thunderbolt /ˈθʌndəbəʊlt/ **noun** a flash of lightning with a crash of thunder at the same time 雷电;霹雳

thunderclap /ˈθʌndəklæp/ **noun** a sudden crash of thunder 雷鸣;雷声;霹雳

thundercloud /ˈθʌndəklaʊd/ **noun** a cloud charged with electricity and producing thunder and lightning 雷雨云

thunderous /ˈθʌndərəs/ **adjective 1** very loud 雷鸣般的;响声极大的 **2** (of a person's expression) very angry or threatening 怒容满面的;面色阴沉的

thunderstorm /ˈθʌndəstɔːm/ **noun** a storm with thunder and lightning 雷暴

thunderstruck /ˈθʌndəstrʌk/ **adjective** very surprised or shocked 极为吃惊的;惊得目瞪口呆的

Thursday /ˈθɜːzdeɪ, -di/ **noun** the day of the week before Friday and following Wednesday 星期四;周四

thus /ðʌs/ **adverb** formal 【正式】 **1** as a result or consequence of this; therefore 因此;从而 **2** in this way 以此方式;这样 **3** to this point; so 到如此程度;如此地

thwack /θwæk/ **verb** hit with a sharp blow (啪地)重击,使劲打 **• noun** a sharp blow 拍打声;重击声

thwart /θwɔːt/ **verb** prevent someone from accomplishing something 阻挠;使受挫折;挫败

thy /ðaɪ/ or (before a vowel) **thine** /ðaɪn/ **possessive determiner** old use 【旧】 your 你的

thyme /taɪm/ **noun** a low-growing, sweet-smelling plant used in cooking 百里香(一种植株低矮的香草,用于烹饪)

thymus /ˈθaɪməs/ **noun** (plural **thymi** /ˈθaɪmaɪ/) a gland in the neck which produces white blood cells for the immune system 胸腺

thyroid /ˈθaɪrɔɪd/ **noun** a large gland in the neck which produces hormones regulating growth and development 甲状腺

tiara /tiˈɑːrə/ **noun** a jewelled ornamental band worn above the forehead 冠状头饰

Tibetan /tɪˈbetən/ **noun** a person from Tibet, China 西藏人;藏族人 **• adjective** relating to Tibet 西藏的;藏族的

tibia /ˈtɪbiə/ **noun** (plural **tibiae** /ˈtɪbiiː/ or **tibias**) the inner of the two bones between the knee and the ankle 胫骨

tic /tɪk/ **noun** a recurring spasm in the muscles of the face (面部肌肉的)抽搐,痉挛

tick¹ /tɪk/ **noun 1** Brit. 【英】 a mark (✔) used to show that something is correct or has been chosen or checked 钩号;对号;记号 **2** a regular short, sharp sound 嘀嗒声 **3** Brit. informal 【英,非正式】 a moment 一会儿;一刹那 **• verb 1** Brit. 【英】 mark with a tick 打钩;标记号 **2**

make regular ticking sounds 发出嘀嗒声 **3** (**tick away** or **by** or **past**) (of time) keep passing (时间)嘀嘀嗒嗒过去, 流逝 **4** (**tick over**) (of an engine) run slowly while the vehicle is not moving (发动机)空转, 慢转 **5** (**tick someone off**) Brit. informal【英, 非正式】tell someone off 责备; 斥责

tick² noun a tiny insect-like creature which attaches itself to the skin and sucks blood 蜱, 壁虱(一种形似昆虫的小虫, 附着于皮肤上吸血)

ticker /'tɪkə(r)/ noun **1** informal【非正式】a person's heart (人的)心脏 **2** N. Amer.【北美】a machine that prints out data on a strip of paper 纸带打印机 □ **ticker tape** strips of paper on which data is printed by a machine (机器打印数据用的)纸带

ticket /'tɪkɪt/ noun **1** a piece of paper or card giving you the right to travel on public transport or letting you in to a place or an event 票; 入场券; 车票 **2** an official notice that you have committed a parking or driving offence (交通违章)通知单, 罚款单 **3** a label attached to a product, giving its price, size, etc. (产品上的)标签, 价格牌

ticking /'tɪkɪŋ/ noun a hard-wearing material used to cover mattresses (做垫套, 褥套等的)结实布料

tickle /'tɪkl/ verb (**tickles, tickling, tickled**) **1** lightly touch in a way that causes itching or twitching and often laughter 胳肢, 搔…的痒痒 **2** be appealing or amusing to 使感兴趣; 使高兴; 逗乐 • noun an act of tickling, or the sensation of being tickled 搔; 胳肢; 痒; 痒感 ■ **tickly** adjective.

ticklish /'tɪklɪʃ/ adjective **1** sensitive to being tickled 怕痒的; 易痒的 **2** needing care and tact 棘手的; 需要小心从事的

tidal /'taɪdl/ adjective relating to or affected by tides 潮汐的; 受潮汐影响的 □ **tidal wave** a huge sea wave caused by an earthquake, storm, etc. 潮汐波; 海啸 ■ **tidally** adverb.

tidbit /'tɪdbɪt/ US spelling of TITBIT. titbit 的美式拼法

tiddler /'tɪdlə(r)/ noun Brit. informal【英, 非正式】a small fish 小鱼

tiddly /'tɪdli/ adjective informal【非正式】**1** slightly drunk 有醉意的; 微醉的 **2** Brit.【英】little; tiny 小的; 微小的

tiddlywinks /'tɪdliwɪŋks/ plural noun a game in which small plastic counters are flicked into a cup 挑塑料圆片游戏

tide /taɪd/ noun **1** the alternate rising and falling of the sea due to the attraction of the moon and sun 潮汐; 海潮 **2** a powerful surge of feeling or trend of events (一阵)强烈感情; 浪潮; 潮流 • verb (**tides, tiding, tided**) (**tide someone over**) help someone through a difficult period 使度过困难时期

tidings /'taɪdɪŋz/ plural noun literary【文】news; information 消息; 音讯

tidy /'taɪdi/ adjective (**tidier, tidiest**) **1** arranged neatly and in order 整齐的; 井然有序的 **2** liking to keep yourself and your possessions neat and in order 爱整洁的; 有条理的 **3** informal【非正式】(of a sum of money) large (钱数)可观的, 高额的 • verb (**tidies, tidying, tidied**) (often **tidy up**) make a place tidy 使整洁; 使有条理 • noun (plural **tidies**) **1** an act of tidying 整理; 收拾 **2** a container for holding small objects 杂物箱; 整理箱 ■ **tidily** adverb **tidiness** noun.

tie /taɪ/ verb (**ties, tying, tied**) **1** attach or fasten with string, cord, ribbon, etc. (用线、绳、带等)系, 拴, 捆扎 **2** form into a knot or bow 打结; 系扣 **3** restrict to a particular situation or place 束缚; 限制 **4** connect; unite 连接; 联合 **5** achieve the same score or ranking as another competitor 打成平局; 得分相同 • noun (plural **ties**)

1 a strip of material worn beneath a collar and tied in a knot at the front 领带;领结 **2** a thing that ties 绳;线 **3** a result in a game or match in which two or more competitors are equal 平局;得分相同 **4** Brit. 【英】 a sports match in which the winners go on to the next round 淘汰赛 □ **tie-dye** produce patterns on fabric by tying knots in it before it is dyed 扎染 **tie in** fit or be in harmony 与…相符;与…协调 □ **tie someone/thing up 1** restrict someone's movement by tying their arms or legs 把(某人)捆绑起来 **2** bring something to a conclusion 得出(结论) **3** informal 【非正式】 occupy someone so that they have no time for other activities 把(某人)缠住;使(某人)不能分身

tiebreaker /ˈtaɪbreɪkə/ (also **tiebreak** /ˈtaɪbreɪk/) **noun** a means of deciding a winner from competitors who are equal at the end of a game or match 平局决胜制

tied /taɪd/ **adjective** Brit. 【英】 **1** (of accommodation) rented by someone on condition that they work for the owner (住处)只租给雇工居住的 **2** (of a pub) owned and controlled by a brewery (酒馆)酒厂专营的

tiepin /ˈtaɪpɪn/ **noun** an ornamental pin for holding a tie in place 领带扣针;领带别针;领带夹

tier /tɪə(r)/ **noun** one of a series of rows or levels placed one above and behind the other 排;层 ■ **tiered** adjective.

tiff /tɪf/ **noun** informal 【非正式】 a quarrel about something unimportant 争执;口角

tiger /ˈtaɪgə(r)/ **noun** a large cat with a yellow coat striped with black, native to the forests of Asia 虎;老虎

tight /taɪt/ **adjective 1** firmly fixed, closed, or fastened 紧的;牢固的;不松动的 **2** (of clothes) fitting closely (衣服)紧身的,贴身的 **3** well sealed against water or air 密封的;不漏的;不透的 **4** (of rope, fabric, or surface) stretched so as to leave no slack (绳、织物或表面)拉紧的,绷紧的 **5** (of an area or space) allowing little room for movement (场地或空间)狭小的,无回旋余地的 **6** closely packed together 塞得紧的;密集的 **7** (of a form of control) very strict (控制)严厉的,严格的 **8** (of money or time) limited (钱或时间)紧的,不宽裕的 • **adverb** very closely or firmly 紧紧地;牢固地 □ **tight-fisted** informal 【非正式】 not willing to spend your money 小气的;吝啬的 **tight-knit** (or **tightly knit**) (of a group of people) closely connected to each other through family or social relationships (一群人)紧密团结的 **tight-lipped** unwilling to express emotion or give away information (因不愿表露感情或透露信息)嘴唇紧闭的,一言不发的 ■ **tightly** adverb **tightness** noun.

tighten /ˈtaɪtn/ **verb** make or become tight or tighter (使)变紧;(使)变得更牢固

tightrope /ˈtaɪtrəʊp/ **noun** a rope or wire stretched high above the ground, on which acrobats balance (杂技演员表演用的)绷紧的钢丝(或绳索)

tights /taɪts/ **plural noun** a close-fitting garment made of stretchy material, covering the hips, legs, and feet 紧身裤袜

tigress /ˈtaɪgrəs/ **noun** a female tiger 母虎

tikka /ˈtɪkə/ **noun** an Indian dish of meat or vegetables marinated in spices 蒂卡(印度菜,由肉或蔬菜配辣酱腌制而成)

tilde /ˈtɪldə/ **noun** an accent (˜) placed over the Spanish *n* or Portuguese *a* or *o* to change the way they are pronounced 腭化符号(即˜,置于西班

牙语的n或者葡萄牙语的a或o之上)

tile /taɪl/ **noun** a thin square or rectangular piece of fired clay, concrete, cork, etc., used for covering roofs, floors, or walls (铺屋顶的)瓦，瓦片;(铺地或贴墙用的)地砖，瓷砖 •**verb (tiles, tiling, tiled)** cover with tiles 用瓦盖;铺地砖于，贴瓷砖于 ■ **tiler** noun.

till[1] /tɪl/ **verb** less formal way of saying UNTIL. until的不太正式的说法

till[2] **noun** a cash register or drawer for money 现金出纳机;钱柜;钱箱

till[3] **verb** prepare and cultivate land for crops 耕作;犁

tiller /'tɪlə(r)/ **noun** a horizontal bar fitted to a boat's rudder and used for steering (小船的)舵柄

tilt /tɪlt/ **verb 1** slip or move into a sloping position 倾斜;倾侧 **2 (tilt at)** (in the past, in jousting) thrust at someone with a lance (旧时在马上比武中)持矛冲刺 • **noun 1** a tilting position or movement 倾斜;倾侧 **2** a leaning or bias 倾向;偏向 **3** (in the past) a joust (旧时的)马上持矛比武 **4 (tilt at)** an attempt at winning something (为赢得某物发起的)冲刺，冲击 □ **(at) full tilt** with maximum speed or force 全速;全力

tilth /tɪlθ/ **noun** soil that has been prepared for crops 耕地

timber /'tɪmbə(r)/ **noun 1** wood prepared for use in building and carpentry 木材;木料 **2** a wooden beam used in building 大梁;栋木

timbre /'tæmbə(r)/ **noun** the quality of the sound in a voice or piece of music 音质;音色

time /taɪm/ **noun 1** the continuing and unlimited progress of existence and events 时间 **2** a past, present, and future 时间 **3** a point or period within this 钟点;一段时间 **3** a point of time as measured in hours and minutes past midnight or noon (以小时和分钟表示的)时间，时刻 **4** the right

or agreed moment to do something 合适时候;规定时间 **5** time as a resource to be used (可用的)时间 **6** an instance of something happening or being done 次;回 **7 (times)** (following a number) expressing multiplication (用于数字后)乘以，…倍 **8** the rhythmic pattern or tempo of a piece of music (音乐的)节拍，拍子 • **verb (times, timing, timed) 1** arrange a time for 为…安排时间;定时 **2** do at a particular time 在特定时间做 **3** measure the time taken by 测定…所需时间;为…计时 □ **behind the times** not using the latest ideas or techniques (观念或技术)落伍，过时，陈旧 **for the time being** until some other arrangement is made 暂时 **in time 1** not late 不迟;来得及 **2** eventually 最终;终于 **on time** punctual, or punctually 按时;准时 **time-honoured** (of a custom or tradition) respected or valued because it has existed for a long time (习俗或传统)因古老而受尊重的，经久不衰的 **time off** time spent away from your usual work or studies 休假时间;业余时间 **time-server** a person who makes little effort at work because they are waiting to leave or retire (等待离职或退休的)得过且过的人,当一天和尚撞一天钟 **time signature** a sign at the start of a piece of music showing the number of beats in a bar (乐曲小结中表示节拍数的)拍号

timekeeper /'taɪmkiːpə(r)/ **noun 1** a person who records the amount of time taken by a process or activity 计时员 **2** a person regarded in terms of their punctuality 守时的人 ■ **time-keeping** noun.

timeless /'taɪmləs/ **adjective** not affected by the passing of time 不受时间影响的;永不过时的;永恒的

timely /'taɪmli/ **adjective** done or happening at a good or appropriate time 及时的；适时的 ■ **timeliness** noun.

timepiece /ˈtaɪmpiːs/ noun a clock or watch 钟；表

timer /ˈtaɪmə(r)/ noun 1 a device that records how long something is taking 计时器 2 a device that stops or starts a machine at a preset time 定时器

timescale /ˈtaɪmskeɪl/ noun the time allowed for or taken by a process or events (某一过程或系列事件所需的)时段，时间

timeshare /ˈtaɪmʃeə(r)/ noun an arrangement in which joint owners use a property as a holiday home at different times 分时享用度假住房

timetable /ˈtaɪmteɪbl/ noun a list or plan of times at which events are scheduled to take place 时间表；时刻表 • verb (timetables, timetabling, timetabled) schedule events to take place at particular times 为…安排时间；给…定时间表

timid /ˈtɪmɪd/ adjective not brave or confident 胆怯的，缺乏自信的 ■ **timidity** noun **timidly** adverb.

timorous /ˈtɪmərəs/ adjective easily frightened 胆怯的，易受惊的；战战兢兢的

timpani or **tympani** /ˈtɪmpəni/ plural noun kettledrums 定音鼓

tin /tɪn/ noun 1 a silvery-white metal (金属元素)锡 2 an airtight container with a lid, made of tinplate or aluminium (马口铁或铝制的)有盖密封罐 3 Brit. 【英】a sealed tinplate or aluminium container for preserving food (马口铁或铝制的)食物密封罐；听，罐头 4 Brit. 【英】an open metal container for baking food 烤模 • verb (tins, tinning, tinned) 1 cover another metal with a thin layer of tin 在…上镀锡(或包锡) 2 (tinned) Brit. 【英】(of food) preserved in a tin (食物)罐装的，听装的 □ **tin whistle** a metal musical instrument like a

small flute 六孔小笛；六孔哨

tincture /ˈtɪŋktʃə(r)/ noun 1 a medicine made by dissolving a drug in alcohol 酊；酊剂 2 a slight trace 一丝；一毫

tinder /ˈtɪndə(r)/ noun dry material used in lighting a fire 引火物；火绒；火种

tinderbox /ˈtɪndəbɒks/ noun (in the past) a box containing tinder, flint, and other items for lighting fires (旧时的)引火盒，火绒盒

tine /taɪn/ noun a prong or sharp point 叉子头；尖头；尖齿

tinfoil /ˈtɪnfɔɪl/ noun metal foil used for covering or wrapping food (包裹食物的)锡纸

tinge /tɪndʒ/ noun a slight trace of a colour, feeling, or quality (颜色、感情或性质的)些许，一点，几分 • verb (tinges, tinging or tingeing, tinged) give a tinge to 给…着色；使略带…色彩(或感情，性质)

tingle /ˈtɪŋgl/ verb (tingles, tingling, tingled) have a slight prickling or stinging feeling 感到刺痛 • noun a slight prickling or stinging sensation 刺痛感 ■ **tingly** adjective.

tinker /ˈtɪŋkə(r)/ noun (in the past) a person who travelled from place to place mending pots, kettles, etc. (旧时流动做活儿的)小炉匠，补锅匠 • verb (tinkers, tinkering, tinkered) (tinker with) casually try to repair or improve (马虎地)修补，修理

tinkle /ˈtɪŋkl/ verb (tinkles, tinkling, tinkled) make or cause to make a light, clear ringing sound 发出叮当声(或丁零声) • noun a tinkling sound 叮当声；丁零声

tinnitus /ˈtɪnɪtəs/ noun a ringing or buzzing in the ears 耳鸣

tinny /ˈtɪni/ adjective 1 having a thin, metallic sound (声音)尖细的，细声细气的 2 made of thin or poor-quality metal 薄金属制的；劣质金属制的

tinplate /ˈtɪnpleɪt/ noun thin sheets of

steel or iron coated with a layer of tin 镀锡铁皮；马口铁

tinpot /'tɪnpɒt/ **adjective** informal 【非正式】 not important or effective 无足轻重的；不起作用的

tinsel /'tɪnsl/ **noun** thin strips of shiny metal foil attached to a length of thread, used to decorate a Christmas tree 金属丝，金属箔(用于装饰圣诞树)

tint /tɪnt/ **noun 1** a shade of a colour 色调 **2** a dye for colouring the hair 染发剂 • **verb 1** colour something slightly 为…轻微着色 **2** dye hair with a tint 轻度染(发)

tintinnabulation /ˌtɪntɪnæbju'leɪʃn/ **noun** a ringing or tinkling sound 铃声，叮当声；丁零声

tiny /'taɪni/ **adjective** (**tinier**, **tiniest**) very small 微小的，极小的

tip¹ /tɪp/ **noun 1** the pointed or rounded end of something slender or tapering 尖端，顶端；末梢 **2** a small part fitted to the end of an object (装在顶端的)小部件 □ **tip-top** of the very best quality 一流的，质量上乘的 ■ **tipped** adjective.

tip² **verb** (**tips**, **tipping**, **tipped**) **1** overbalance so as to fall or turn over (使)倾倒，(使)倾斜 **2** be or put in a sloping position (使)倾斜，(使)倾斜 **3** empty out the contents of a container by holding it at an angle 倒出，倾倒 • **noun 1** Brit. 【英】 a place where rubbish is left 垃圾场，垃圾堆 **2** informal 【非正式】 a dirty or untidy place 脏乱的地方

tip³ **noun 1** a small extra amount of money that you give to someone for their good service in a restaurant, taxi, etc. 小费 **2** a piece of practical advice 指点，小建议 **3** a prediction about the likely winner of a race or contest (比赛的)内幕消息，指点 • **verb** (**tips**, **tipping**, **tipped**) **1** give a tip to 给…小费 **2** Brit. 【英】 predict that a particular horse, competitor, etc.

is likely to win something 预言…获胜；预测…会成功 **3** (**tip someone off**) informal 【非正式】 give someone secret information 向(某人)透露消息

tipple /'tɪpl/ informal 【非正式】 **noun** an alcoholic drink 酒精饮料；酒 • **verb** (**tipples**, **tippling**, **tippled**) drink alcohol regularly (经常性地)饮酒 ■ **tippler** noun.

tipster /'tɪpstə(r)/ **noun** a person who gives tips as to the likely winner of a race or contest (比赛的)提供内幕消息者，情报贩子

tipsy /'tɪpsi/ **adjective** slightly drunk 微醺的；略有醉意的 ■ **tipsily** adverb.

tiptoe /'tɪptəʊ/ **verb** (**tiptoes**, **tiptoeing**, **tiptoed**) walk quietly and carefully with your heels raised 踮起脚尖走；蹑手蹑脚地走 □ **on tiptoe** (or **tiptoes**) with your heels raised 踮着脚，蹑手蹑脚地

tirade /taɪ'reɪd/ **noun** a long angry speech 激愤的长篇演说

tire¹ /'taɪə(r)/ **verb** (**tires**, **tiring**, **tired**) **1** make or become in need of rest or sleep 使疲劳，感到困倦 **2** (**tire of**) become impatient or bored with 厌烦；厌倦

tire² US spelling of TYRE. tyre 的美式拼法

tired /'taɪəd/ **adjective 1** in need of sleep or rest 疲倦的，困倦的 **2** (**tired of**) bored with 厌倦的；厌烦的 **3** (of a statement or idea) boring because it has been said or used too often (表述或想法)陈旧的，陈腐 ■ **tiredness** noun.

tireless /'taɪələs/ **adjective** having or showing great effort or energy 不懈的；不倦的，精力充沛的 ■ **tirelessly** adverb.

tiresome /'taɪəsəm/ **adjective** making you feel impatient or bored 令人厌烦的；讨厌的 ■ **tiresomely** adverb.

'tis /tɪz/ **short form** literary 【文】 it is.

tissue /'tɪʃuː, -sjuː/ **noun 1** any of

the distinct types of material of which animals or plants are made (动植物的)组织 **2** a disposable paper handkerchief 纸巾；手巾纸巾 □ **a tissue of lies** a story that is full of lies 一派谎言 **tissue paper** a very thin, soft paper 薄纸；绵纸

tit¹ /tɪt/ **noun** a small bird that searches for food among leaves and branches 山雀

tit² **noun** (**tit for tat**) a situation in which you insult or hurt someone because they have done the same to you 以牙还牙；还击

Titan /ˈtaɪtn/ **noun 1** any of a family of giant gods in Greek mythology 提坦神(希腊神话中的巨神) **2** (**titan**) a person of very great strength, intelligence, or importance 巨人；能人；伟人

titanic /taɪˈtænɪk/ **adjective** of exceptional strength, size, or power 强有力的；巨大的；强大的

titanium /tɪˈteɪniəm/ **noun** a silver-grey metal used in making strong alloys (金属元素)钛

titbit /ˈtɪtbɪt/ (US spelling 【美拼作】 **tidbit**) **noun 1** a small piece of tasty food 少量的)可口美食 **2** a small item of very interesting information 花絮；趣闻

titch /tɪtʃ/ **noun** Brit. informal 【英，非正式】 a small person 小不点儿；小个子 ■ **titchy** adjective.

tithe /taɪð/ **noun** (in the past) one tenth of what people produced or earned in a year, taken as a tax to support the Church (旧时将个人年收入的十分之一纳给教会的)什一税

titillate /ˈtɪtɪleɪt/ **verb** (**titillates**, **titillating**, **titillated**) make someone feel interested or mildly excited, especially sexually 使兴奋；(尤指)煽动情欲 ■ **titillation** noun.

✔ 拼写指南 one *t*, two *l*s: ti*till*ate. Also, don't confuse **titillate** with

titivate, which means 'make smarter or more attractive'. titillate中间有一个t和两个l。另外，不要混淆titillate和titivate，后者意为"修饰；打扮"。

titivate /ˈtɪtɪveɪt/ **verb** (**titivates**, **titivating**, **titivated**) informal 【非正式】 make smarter or more attractive 修饰；打扮 ■ **titivation** noun.

title /ˈtaɪtl/ **noun 1** the name of a book, piece of music, or other work (书、乐曲等的)名称，标题 **2** a name that describes someone's position or job 职称；职务 **3** a word, such as *Dr*, *Mrs*, or *Lord*, used before or instead of someone's name to indicate their rank or status (用于人名前或代替人名表示职衔或职业的)头衔，称谓 **4** a descriptive name that someone has earned or chosen 称号 **5** the position of being the champion of a major sports competition (重要体育比赛的)冠军 **6** a caption or credit in a film or broadcast (电影或电视中的)字幕 • **verb** (**titles**, **titling**, **titled**) give a title to 给…加标题；授予…职称(或头衔，称号) □ **title deed** a legal document giving evidence of someone's right to own a property 产权凭证；所有权凭证 **title role** the part in a play or film from which the title is taken (喜剧或电影中的)剧名角色，片名角色

titled /ˈtaɪtld/ **adjective** having a title indicating nobility e.g. Lord or Lady 有爵位的；有贵族头衔的

titration /taɪˈtreɪʃn/ **noun** the calculation of the amount of a substance in a solution by measuring the volume of a reagent required to react with it (化学)滴定法

titter /ˈtɪtə(r)/ **verb** (**titters**, **tittering**, **tittered**) laugh quietly 嗤嗤笑；窃笑 • **noun** a short, quiet laugh 嗤嗤的笑；窃笑

tittle-tattle /ˈtɪtltætl/ **noun** gossip 闲聊；飞短流长

titular /'tɪtjʊlə(r)/ **adjective 1** holding a formal position or title without any real authority 名义上的；有名无实的 **2** relating to a title 标题的；书名的

tizzy /'tɪzi/ **noun** (plural **tizzies**) informal 【非正式】 a state of nervous excitement or worry 紧张；焦虑

TNT /ˌti: en 'ti:/ **abbreviation** trinitrotoluene, a high explosive 三硝基甲苯；梯恩梯炸药

to /tə, tu, tu:/ **preposition 1** expressing direction or position in relation to a particular location, point, or condition (表示方向或位置)朝、向、往 **2** Brit.【英】 (in telling the time) before the hour mentioned (用于说明时间)在…之前，离，差 **3** identifying the person or thing affected by an action (确定受事者或受体)关于，对于 **4** identifying a particular relationship between one person or thing and another (确定人或事物之间的关系)关于，对于，属于 **5** indicating a rate of return on something (表示比率)等于，每：*ten miles to the gallon* 每加仑可行驶10英里 **6** indicating that two things are attached (表示两事物关联在一起)伴随，随同 • **infinitive** marker used with the base form of a verb to indicate that the verb is in the infinitive (用在动词原形前表示该动词为不定式) • **adverb** so as to be closed or nearly closed 关着；虚掩着 □ **to and fro** backwards and forwards or from side to side 来回地；往复地 **to-do** informal 【非正式】 a commotion or fuss 喧嚷；大惊小怪

❗ 注意 don't confuse **to** with **too** or **two**. **To** mainly means 'in the direction of' (as in *the next train to London*), while **too** means 'excessively' (as in *she was driving too fast*) or 'in addition', and **two** is the number meaning 'one less than three'. 不要混淆to，too 和two，to主要含义为"向，朝，往"，而too意为"太，过于"，

如she was driving too fast (她车开得太快了)，或者表示"也"，而two指数量，意为"二"。

toad /təʊd/ **noun** an amphibian with a short body, short legs, and no tail 蟾蜍；癞蛤蟆

toadstool /'təʊdstu:l/ **noun** a fungus with a rounded cap on a stalk 伞菌；毒菌；毒蕈

toady /'təʊdi/ **noun** (plural **toadies**) a person who is too polite and respectful to someone in order to gain their favour 谄媚的人；马屁精 • **verb** (**toadies, toadying, toadied**) act in a way that is too polite and respectful 拍马；谄媚

toast /təʊst/ **noun 1** sliced bread that has been held against a source of heat until it is brown and crisp 烤面包片，吐司 **2** an act of raising glasses at a gathering and drinking together in honour of a person or thing 祝酒；敬酒；干杯 **3** a person who is greatly respected or admired 备受尊崇的人 • **verb 1** make bread brown and crisp by holding it against a source of heat 烤(面包)，把(面包)烤至焦黄 **2** drink a toast to 为…敬酒；为…干杯

toaster /'təʊstə(r)/ **noun** an electrical device for making toast 烤面包机

tobacco /tə'bækəʊ/ **noun** (plural **tobaccos**) a preparation of the dried nicotine-rich leaves of an American plant, used for smoking or chewing 烟草；烟叶

tobacconist /tə'bækənɪst/ **noun** Brit.【英】 a shopkeeper who sells cigarettes and tobacco 烟草零售商；烟草商

toboggan /tə'bɒgən/ **noun** a light, narrow vehicle on runners, used for sliding downhill over snow or ice 长雪橇；平底雪橇 ■ **tobogganist** noun.

toccata /tə'kɑ:tə/ **noun** a piece of music for a keyboard instrument designed to show the performer's skill and technique 托卡塔(用键盘乐器演奏的乐曲,旨在显示演奏者弹奏技巧)

tod /tɒd/ **noun (on your tod)** Brit. informal 【英,非正式】on your own 独自;单独

today /tə'deɪ/ **adverb 1** on or in the course of this present day 在(今天;(在)今日 **2** at the present period of time 当今;如今 • **noun 1** this present day 今天;今日 **2** the present period of time 现在;眼下;当代

toddle /'tɒdl/ **verb (toddles, toddling, toddled) 1** (of a young child) move with short unsteady steps while learning to walk (幼儿学步时)摇摆摆地走,蹒跚而行 **2** informal【非正式】walk or go about in a leisurely way 信步而行;溜达

toddler /'tɒdlə(r)/ **noun** a young child who is just beginning to walk 学步幼儿;刚学走路的孩子

toddy /'tɒdi/ **noun (plural toddies)** a drink of spirits mixed with hot water 托迪酒(加热水调制的烈酒)

toe /təʊ/ **noun 1** any of the five digits at the end of the foot 脚趾 **2** the lower end, tip, or point of something (物体的)较低端,尖端 □ **on your toes** ready and alert 做好准备的;警觉的 **toe the line** be obedient 顺从;服从

toecap /'təʊkæp/ **noun** a piece of steel or leather fitted over the front part of a boot or shoe (靴或鞋尖的)外包头

toehold /'təʊhəʊld/ **noun** a small foothold 立小足点,小支点

toenail /'təʊneɪl/ **noun** a nail on the upper surface of the tip of each toe 趾甲

toff /tɒf/ **noun** Brit. informal, disapproving 【英,非正式,贬】a rich, upper-class person 富家子弟;花花公子

toffee /'tɒfi/ **noun** a kind of firm sweet which softens when sucked or chewed, made by boiling together sugar and butter 太妃糖,奶脂糖 □ **toffee-nosed** Brit. informal 【英,非

正式】snobbish 势利的;目空一切的

tofu /'təʊfuː/ **noun** a soft white substance made from mashed soya beans 豆腐

tog[1] /tɒg/ informal【非正式】**noun (togs)** clothes 衣服;服装 • **verb (be togged up)** be fully dressed for a particular occasion or activity 穿上(适合某一场合或活动的)全套服装;着盛装

tog[2] **noun** Brit.【英】a unit for measuring the warmth of duvets or quilts 托克(被褥保暖性的热阻计量单位)

toga /'təʊgə/ **noun** a loose outer garment made of a single piece of cloth, worn in ancient Rome (古罗马人穿的宽松的)托加袍

together /tə'geðə(r)/ **adverb 1** with or near to another person or people 在一起;共同 **2** so as to touch, combine, or be united 以便接触;结合起来;到一起 **3** regarded as a whole 公共地,整体地 **4** (of two people) married or in a sexual relationship (两个人)有婚姻关系,有性关系 **5** at the same time 同时;一起;一齐 **6** without interruption 连续地;不间断地 • **adjective** informal 【非正式】level-headed and well organized 镇静自若的;稳健妥当的 ■ **togetherness** noun.

toggle /'tɒgl/ **noun** a narrow piece of wood or plastic attached to a garment, pushed through a loop to act as a fastener (外衣上木质或塑料的)棒形纽扣,套索扣

toil /tɔɪl/ **verb 1** work very hard 苦干;辛勤工作 **2** move somewhere slowly and with difficulty 艰难缓慢地移动;跋涉 • **noun** exhausting work 劳累的工作;苦活

toilet /'tɔɪlət/ **noun 1** a large bowl for urinating or defecating into 坐便器;抽水马桶 **2** old use 【旧】the process of washing yourself, dressing, brushing your hair, etc. 梳妆;打扮 □ **toilet bag** Brit.【英】a waterproof bag for toothpaste, soap, etc., used when traveling 盥洗用品袋；洗漱包 **toilet-train** teach a young child to use the toilet 训练(幼儿)上厕所 **toilet water** a diluted form of perfume 花露水

toiletries /ˈtɔɪlətrɪz/ **plural noun** articles used in washing and taking care of your body, such as soap and shampoo 洗漱用品

token /ˈtəʊkən/ **noun 1** a thing that represents a feeling, fact, or quality (感情、事实或品质的)象征，标志 **2** a voucher that can be exchanged for goods or services (可兑换商品或服务的)代金券，优惠券 **3** a disc used to operate a machine (用于启动机器的)代币 • **adjective** involving little effort or commitment and done only for show 装样子的；敷衍的

told /təʊld/ past and past participle of TELL.

tolerable /ˈtɒlərəbl/ **adjective 1** able to be tolerated 可接受的；可容忍的 **2** fairly good 尚好的；过得去的 ■ **tolerably** adverb.

tolerance /ˈtɒlərəns/ **noun 1** the ability to accept things you do not like or agree with 容忍(力)；宽容 **2** an allowable amount of variation in the dimensions of a machine or part 公差；容限

tolerant /ˈtɒlərənt/ **adjective 1** able to accept things you do not like or agree with 容忍的；宽容的 **2** able to cope with particular conditions 耐受的；耐…的

tolerate /ˈtɒləreɪt/ **verb** (**tolerates**, **tolerating**, **tolerated**) **1** allow someone to do something you do not like or agree with 容许，容忍(不喜欢或不同意的事物) **2** patiently accept something unpleasant 容忍，包容 **3** be able to be exposed to a drug, toxin, etc. without a bad reaction 对(药物、毒素等)有耐受性 ■ **toleration** noun.

toll¹ /təʊl/ **noun 1** a charge you have to pay for the use of certain roads or bridges (道路或桥梁的)通行费 **2** the number of deaths or casualties arising from an accident, war, etc. (事故、战争等的)伤亡人数 **3** the cost or damage resulting from something 代价；损失

toll² **verb** (of a bell) sound with slow, even strokes, especially as a sign that someone has died (钟)缓慢而有规律地敲响；(尤指)鸣(丧钟) • **noun** a single ring of a bell 钟声

tom /tɒm/ or **tomcat** /ˈtɒmkæt/ **noun** a male domestic cat 雄猫

tomahawk /ˈtɒməhɔːk/ **noun** a light axe used in the past by American Indians (旧时美洲印第安人用的)轻型斧头

tomato /təˈmɑːtəʊ/ **noun** (plural **tomatoes**) a red fruit eaten as a vegetable or in salads 番茄；西红柿

✔ 拼写指南 no *e* on the end: tomato. tomato 词末没有 e。

tomb /tuːm/ **noun 1** a burial place consisting of a stone structure built above ground, or an underground vault 坟墓；冢 **2** a monument to a dead person, built over their burial place 墓碑

tombola /tɒmˈbəʊlə/ **noun** Brit. 【英】 a game in which tickets are drawn from a revolving drum to win prizes (将彩票放入旋转的鼓中抽奖的)"翻筋斗"赌戏

tomboy /ˈtɒmbɔɪ/ **noun** a girl who enjoys rough, noisy activities traditionally associated with boys 假小子；野丫头 ■ **tomboyish** adjective.

tombstone /ˈtuːmstəʊn/ **noun** a flat stone with an inscription, standing or laid over a grave 墓碑；墓石

tome /təʊm/ **noun** a large, serious book 大部头书；巨著

tomfoolery /tɒmˈfuːləri/ **noun** silly behaviour 愚蠢的行为

tomography /təˈmɒɡrəfi/ **noun** a technique for seeing a cross section through a human body or other solid object using X-rays or ultrasound X 射线断层显像术；X射线断层照相术 ■ **tomographic** adjective.

tomorrow /təˈmɒrəʊ/ **adverb** on the day after today (在)明天；(在)明日 •**noun 1** the day after today 明天；明日 **2** the future 来日；将来

✔ 拼写指南 one m, two *r*s: tomorrow. tomorrow 中有一个 m 和两个 r。

tom-tom /ˈtɒmtɒm/ **noun** a drum beaten with the hands 长筒鼓

ton /tʌn/ **noun 1** (also **long ton**) a unit of weight equal to 2,240 lb avoirdupois (1016.05 kg) 吨，长吨(等于2,240磅，合1016.05千克) **2** (also **short ton**) N. Amer.【北美】a unit of weight equal to 2,000 lb avoirdupois (907.19 kg) 短吨(等于2,000磅，合907.19千克) **3** a metric ton 公吨 **4** a unit of measurement of a ship's weight equal to 2,240 lb or 35 cubic feet (0.99 cubic metres) 排水吨，吨位(船舶重量单位，等于2,240磅或35立方英尺，即0.99立方米) **5** (also **tons**) informal 【非正式】a large number or amount 大量；许多 **6** Brit. informal 【英，非正式】a speed of one hundred miles per hour 一百英里的时速

tonal /ˈtəʊnl/ **adjective 1** relating to tone 音调的；声调的 **2** (of music) written using traditional keys and harmony (音乐)调性的 ■ **tonality** noun **tonally** adverb.

tone /təʊn/ **noun 1** the quality of a musical sound 音质；乐音；音色 **2** the feeling or mood expressed in a person's voice 语气；口吻 **3** general character 风格；特色；情调 **4** a particular brightness, deepness, or shade in a colour 色调；明暗；彩调 **5** firmness in a resting muscle (肌肉的)结实，有力 **6** a basic interval in classical Western music, equal to two semitones 全音 •**verb** (**tones, toning, toned**) **1** (often **tone something up**) give greater strength or firmness to a part of your body 使(身体)更健壮；使更结实 **2** (**tone something down**) make a statement or piece of writing less harsh, extreme, or strong 使(陈述或文字)缓和，使温和 □ **tone deaf** unable to hear differences in musical pitch 不能辨别音高的

toner /ˈtəʊnə(r)/ **noun 1** a liquid applied to the skin to reduce oiliness 润肤水 **2** a type of powder or ink used in photocopiers 墨粉

tongs /tɒŋz/ **plural noun** a tool with two arms that are joined at one end, used for picking up and holding things 夹剪；夹具；钳子

tongue /tʌŋ/ **noun 1** the fleshy organ in the mouth, used for tasting, licking, swallowing, and speaking 舌；舌头 **2** a person's way of speaking 说话方式：*a sharp tongue*话语尖刻 **3** a language 语言 **4** a strip of leather or fabric under the laces in a shoe 鞋舌 □ **tongue and groove** wooden boards which are joined by means of interlocking ridges and grooves down their sides 舌榫；榫槽接合 **tongue-tied** too shy or embarrassed to speak (因害羞或尴尬)张口结舌的，说不出话的 **tongue-twister** a sequence of words that are difficult to pronounce 绕口令 **with tongue in cheek** not seriously meaning what you are saying 说说而已；半开玩笑地

tonic /ˈtɒnɪk/ **noun 1** a drink taken as a kind of medicine, to make you feel energetic and healthy 补药，滋补剂 **2** something that makes you feel happier or healthier 振奋精神的东西，增进健康的东西 **3** (also **tonic water**) a fizzy drink with a slightly bitter flavour, often mixed with gin 奎宁水(一种起泡饮料，味微苦，常加于杜松子酒中)

tonight /tə'naɪt/ **adverb** on the evening or night of the present day (在)今晚;(在)今夜 • **noun** the evening or night of the present day 今晚;今夜

tonnage /'tʌnɪdʒ/ **noun 1** weight in tons 吨位 **2** the size or carrying capacity of a ship measured in tons (表示船舶大小或载重量的)船舶吨位

tonne /tʌn/ **noun** a metric ton 公吨

tonsil /'tɒnsl/ **noun** each of two small masses of tissue in the throat 扁桃体

tonsillectomy /ˌtɒnsə'lektəmi/ **noun** (plural **tonsillectomies**) an operation to remove the tonsils 扁桃体切除术

tonsillitis /ˌtɒnsə'laɪtɪs/ **noun** inflammation of the tonsils 扁桃体炎

tonsure /'tɒnʃə(r)/ **noun** a circular area on a monk's or priest's head where the hair is shaved off (僧侣或教士的)头顶剃光部位

too /tuː/ **adverb 1** to a higher degree than is desirable, allowed, or possible; excessively 太;过于 **2** in addition 也;又;还

!注意 don't confuse **too** with **to** or **two**: see the note at **to**. 不要混淆 too, 和 two, 见词条 to 处注释。

took /tʊk/ past of TAKE.

tool /tuːl/ **noun 1** an object or device used to carry out a particular function 工具;器具 **2** a thing that helps you to do your job or achieve something (有助于做工作或完成某事的)用具,手段,方法 • **verb 1** impress a design on leather with a heated tool (用加热的工具在皮革制品上)压印图案 **2** equip an organization with tools for industrial production 给…配备生产设备

toot /tuːt/ **noun** a short sound made by a horn, trumpet, or similar instrument (号角、喇叭等发出的)短而尖锐的声音,嘟嘟声 • **verb** make a toot 发出嘟嘟声

tooth /tuːθ/ **noun** (plural **teeth**) **1** each of the hard white projections in the mouth, used for biting and chewing 牙;齿 **2** a projecting part such as a cog on a gearwheel or a point on a saw or comb (齿轮锯、梳子等的)齿状物 ■ **toothed** adjective **toothless** adjective.

toothache /'tuːθeɪk/ **noun** pain in a tooth 牙痛;牙疼

toothbrush /'tuːθbrʌʃ/ **noun** a small long-handled brush for cleaning your teeth 牙刷

toothpaste /'tuːθpeɪst/ **noun** a paste for cleaning the teeth 牙膏

toothpick /'tuːθpɪk/ **noun** a thin, pointed piece of wood or plastic for removing bits of food from between your teeth 牙签

toothsome /'tuːθsəm/ **adjective 1** (of food) appetizing or tasty (食物)美味的,可口的 **2** informal 【非正式】attractive 诱人的,有吸引力的

toothy /'tuːθi/ **adjective** having large or prominent teeth 露齿的;有凸牙的

tootle /'tuːtl/ **verb** (**tootles**, **tootling**, **tootled**) **1** make a series of sounds on a horn, trumpet, etc. 连续吹响(号角、喇叭等) **2** walk or drive somewhere without hurrying 悠闲地走;闲逛

top¹ /tɒp/ **noun 1** the highest or uppermost point, part, or surface 顶部;顶端 **2** a thing placed on, fitted to, or covering the upper part of something 盖;顶盖;篷 **3** (**the top**) the highest or most important level or position 最高水平;最高职位 **4** the utmost degree 顶点;最高程度 **5** a garment covering the upper part of the body 上装 • **adjective** highest in position, status, or degree (位置、地位或程度)最高的 • **verb** (**tops, topping, topped**) **1** be more, better, or taller than 超过;优于;高过 **2** be at the highest place or rank in 居…之首;为…之冠 **3** reach the top of a hill or rise 到达山顶;到达…顶点 **4** provide with a top or topping 加盖的;加顶的;有装饰层

的;有保护层的 □ **on top of 1** so as to cover 覆盖;盖住 **2** in command or control of 控制着;掌握着 **3** in addition to 除…之外 **over the top** Brit. informal【英,非正式】excessive or exaggerated 过分的;夸张的 **top hat** a man's tall formal black hat (男士)高顶黑礼帽 **top-heavy** too heavy at the top and therefore likely to fall 头重脚轻的,不稳的 **top something up 1** add to a number or amount to bring it up to a certain level 添加(数字或数额)以达到(某水平) **2** fill up a partly full container 装满,注满(未满的容器)

top² noun a toy shaped like a cone with a point at the base, that can be made to spin 陀螺

topaz /'təʊpæz/ noun a colourless yellow or pale blue precious stone 黄玉;黄宝石

topcoat /'tɒpkəʊt/ noun **1** an overcoat 大衣;外套 **2** an outer coat of paint (油漆的)外涂层

topiary /'təʊpiəri/ noun (plural **topiaries**) **1** the art of clipping evergreen shrubs into interesting shapes 灌木修剪术 **2** shrubs clipped in this way (修剪过的)灌木,整形灌木丛

topic /'tɒpɪk/ noun a subject that you talk, write, or learn about 主题;题目;话题

topical /'tɒpɪkl/ adjective **1** relating to or dealing with current affairs 有关时事的;时下关注的 **2** relating to a particular subject 专题的 ■ **topicality** noun **topically** adverb.

topknot /'tɒpnɒt/ noun a knot of hair arranged on the top of the head 顶髻;头饰

topless /'tɒpləs/ adjective having the breasts uncovered 胸部裸露的;袒胸的

topography /tə'pɒɡrəfi/ noun **1** the arrangement of the physical features

of an area of land 地形;地貌;地势 **2** the representation of these features on a map 地图地形描绘 ■ **topographical** (or **topographic**) adjective.

topple /'tɒpl/ verb (**topples**, **toppling**, **toppled**) **1** overbalance and fall down 失去平衡而倒下 **2** remove a government or leader from power 推翻(政府或当权者)

topsoil /'tɒpsɔɪl/ noun the top layer of soil 表土;表层土

topspin /'tɒpspɪn/ noun a fast forward spin given to a moving ball (球的)上旋

topsy-turvy /ˌtɒpsi'tɜːvi/ adjective & adverb **1** upside down 上下颠倒的(地) **2** in a state of confusion 乱七八糟的(地);颠三倒四的(地)

tor /tɔː(r)/ noun a small steep hill or rocky peak 小山;岩丘

Torah /'tɔːrɑː/ noun (in Judaism) the law of God as revealed to Moses and recorded in the Pentateuch 犹太教记载于《摩西五经》中的托拉,律法书

torch /tɔːtʃ/ noun **1** Brit.【英】a portable lamp powered by a battery 手电筒 **2** (in the past) a piece of wood or cloth soaked in fat and set on fire (旧时的)火炬,火把 • verb informal【非正式】set fire to 放火烧

tore /tɔː(r)/ past of TEAR¹.

toreador /'tɒrɪədɔː(r)/ noun a bullfighter 斗牛士

torment noun /'tɔːment/ **1** great suffering 折磨;痛苦 **2** a cause of suffering 使人痛苦的东西(或人) • verb /tɔː'ment/ **1** make someone suffer very much 折磨,使痛苦 **2** annoy or tease in a cruel or unkind way 戏弄;捉弄 ■ **tormentor** noun.

torn /tɔːn/ past participle of TEAR¹.

tornado /tɔː'neɪdəʊ/ noun (plural **tornadoes** or **tornados**) a violent rotating wind storm 龙卷风;飓风

torpedo /tɔː'piːdəʊ/ noun (plural **torpedoes**) a long narrow underwater missile 鱼雷 • verb (torpedoes, torpedoing, torpedoed) attack using torpedoes 用鱼雷袭击

torpid /'tɔːpɪd/ adjective inactive and having no energy 不活泼的;有气无力的 ■ torpidity noun.

torpor /'tɔːpə(r)/ noun the state of being inactive and having no energy 迟钝;呆滞;死气沉沉

torque /tɔːk/ noun a force causing rotation 扭转力

torrent /'tɒrənt/ noun 1 a strong, fast-moving stream of water or other liquid 激流;湍流;洪流 2 a large outpouring 迸发;狂潮

torrential /tə'renʃl/ adjective (of rain) falling rapidly and heavily (雨水)倾泻的,如注的

torrid /'tɒrɪd/ adjective 1 very hot and dry 炎热而干燥的;灼热的 2 full of sexual passion (情爱)热烈的,狂热的 3 full of difficulty 充满艰辛的;艰难的

torsion /'tɔːʃn/ noun the state of being twisted 扭转

torso /'tɔːsəʊ/ noun (plural torsos) the trunk of the human body (人体的)躯干

tort /tɔːt/ noun Law【法律】a wrongful act or a violation of a right 侵权行为

tortellini /ˌtɔːtə'liːni/ plural noun stuffed pasta parcels rolled into small rings 意大利式饺子

tortilla /tɔː'tiːə/ noun 1 (in Mexican cookery) a thin, flat maize pancake (墨西哥烹饪中的)玉米粉薄饼 2 (in Spanish cookery) an omelette (西班牙烹饪中的)马铃薯煎蛋

tortoise /'tɔːtəs/ noun a slow moving reptile with a hard, round shell into which it can draw its head and legs 龟;陆龟;乌龟

tortoiseshell /'tɔːtəsʃel/ noun 1 the semitransparent mottled yellow and brown shell of certain turtles, used to make jewellery or ornaments 龟甲;龟板;玳瑁壳 2 a domestic cat with

markings resembling tortoiseshell 花斑家猫 3 a butterfly with mottled orange, yellow, and black markings (带有花黑斑纹的)蛱蝶

tortuous /'tɔːtʃuəs/ adjective 1 full of twists and turns 弯弯曲曲的;曲折的;蜿蜒的 2 very long and complicated 冗长费解的;拐弯抹角的 ■ tortuously adverb.

torture /'tɔːtʃə(r)/ noun 1 severe pain inflicted on someone, especially to make them say something 拷打;拷问;酷刑 2 great suffering or anxiety 折磨;痛苦;苦恼 • verb (tortures, torturing, tortured) subject someone to torture 拷打;拷问;折磨 ■ torturer noun torturous adjective.

Tory /'tɔːri/ noun (plural Tories) a member or supporter of the British Conservative Party 托利党党员;英国保守党成员

toss /tɒs/ verb 1 throw lightly or casually (轻轻或随意地)扔,抛,掷 2 move something from side to side or backwards and forwards 摇动;摆动;颠簸 3 jerk your head or hair backwards 向后甩(头或头发) 4 throw a coin into the air and see which side is facing upwards when it lands, using this to help decide something 掷硬币(看其正反)来决定 5 shake or turn food in a liquid to coat it lightly 摇匀,翻动,搅拌(食物以使其沾裹某物) • noun an act of tossing 投掷;掷硬币决定;甩头 □ toss-up 1 a situation in which any of two or more outcomes is equally possible (几种结果的)相等机会;难以定夺之事 2 the tossing of a coin to make a decision (为作出选择而进行的)掷硬币

tot¹ /tɒt/ noun 1 a very young child 幼儿 2 Brit.【英】a small drink of spirits 小杯烈酒

tot² verb (tots, totting, totted) (tot something up) Brit.【英】add up numbers or amounts 计算…的总和

total /ˈtəʊtl/ **adjective 1** consisting of the whole number or amount 总的;总计的;全部的 **2** complete 完全的;彻底的 • **noun** a total number or amount 总数;合计 • **verb (totals, totalling, totalled;** US spelling 【美拼作】**totals, totaling, totaled) 1** amount to a total number 总数达;共计 **2** find the total of…的总和 ■ **totality** noun **totally** adverb.

totalitarian /təʊˌtælɪˈteəriən/ **adjective** (of a system of government) consisting of only one leader or party and having complete power and control over the people (政府制度)极权主义的 ■ **totalitarianism** noun.

totalizator or **totalisator** /ˈtəʊtəlaɪzeɪtə(r)/ **noun 1** a device showing the number of bets and amount of money staked on a race (赌马用的)赌金计算器 **2** the system of betting based on this; the tote (赌马用的)赌金计算系统

tote[1] /təʊt/ **noun (the tote)** informal【非正式】 a system of betting based on the use of the totalizator, in which winnings are calculated according to the amount staked rather than odds offered (赛马赌博用的)赌金计算系统

tote[2] **verb (totes, toting, toted)** informal【非正式】 carry 携带;搬运

totem /ˈtəʊtəm/ **noun** a natural object or animal believed to have spiritual meaning and adopted as an emblem by a particular society 图腾 □ **totem pole** a pole on which totems are hung or on which images of totems are carved 图腾柱 ■ **totemic** adjective.

totter /ˈtɒtə(r)/ **verb (totters, tottering, tottered) 1** move in an unsteady way 跌跌撞撞;踉跄 **2** shake or rock as if about to collapse 摇摇欲坠

toucan /ˈtuːkæn/ **noun** a tropical bird with a massive bill and brightly coloured feathers 巨嘴鸟(产于热带地区,喙极大,羽色鲜艳)

touch /tʌtʃ/ **verb 1** bring your fingers or another part of your body into contact with 触摸;碰 **2** come into or be in physical contact with (身体上)接触 **3** have an effect on 影响 **4** (**be touched**) feel moved with gratitude or sympathy because of someone's actions or situation 感激;受感动 **5** harm or interfere with 伤害;干预 **6** use or consume 使用;吃;喝 **7** (**touched**) informal【非正式】 mad 疯疯颠颠的;精神失常的 • **noun 1** an act or way of touching 触摸;碰 **2** the ability to become aware of something and learn what it is like through physical contact, especially with the fingers 触觉 **3** a small amount 一点儿;少许 **4** a distinctive detail or feature 细节 特征;特色 **5** a distinctive or skilful way of dealing with something 作风;风格;手法 □ **in touch 1** in or into communication 联系;接触 **2** having up-to-date knowledge 掌握最新知识 **out of touch** lacking up-to-date knowledge or awareness 缺乏最新知识(或认识) **touch-and-go** (of a particular outcome) possible but very uncertain (结果)不确定的,很难说的 **touch down** (of an aircraft or spacecraft) land (飞机或航天器)着陆,降落 **touch on** deal briefly with 谈及;涉及 **touch-type** type using all of your fingers and without needing to look at the keys (不看键盘)按指法打字,盲打 **touch something up** make small improvements to something 对…稍作修改;润色

touchdown /ˈtʌtʃdaʊn/ **noun 1** the moment at which an aircraft touches down (飞机的)着陆,触地 **2** (in rugby) an act of scoring by touching the ball down behind the opponents' goal line (英式橄榄球运动中)(在对

方球门线后)持续触地得分

touché /ˈtuːʃeɪ/ **exclamation** used to acknowledge a good point made at your own expense (用于承认对方言之有理)一针见血，说的对

touching /ˈtʌtʃɪŋ/ **adjective** making you feel gratitude or sympathy; moving 令人同情的；感人的

touchline /ˈtʌtʃlaɪn/ **noun** (in football) the boundary line on each side of the field (足球场的)边线

touchstone /ˈtʌtʃstəʊn/ **noun** a standard by which something is judged (检验)标准，试金石

touchy /ˈtʌtʃi/ **adjective 1** quick to take offence 易怒的；易生气的 **2** (of a situation or issue) needing careful treatment (局面或问题)需小心处理的，棘手的

tough /tʌf/ **adjective 1** strong enough to withstand wear and tear 坚固的；不易磨损(或撕破)的 **2** able to deal with pain or difficulty 坚强的；坚忍不拔的；能吃苦耐劳的 **3** strict 严厉的，严格的 **4** involving problems or difficulties 艰难的，棘手的；艰苦的 **5** (of a person) rough or violent (人)粗暴的，粗野的 • **noun** informal【非正式】a rough or violent man 粗暴的人；暴徒 ■ **toughness** noun.

toughen /ˈtʌfn/ **verb** make or become tough (使)变坚固；(使)变坚韧

toupee /ˈtuːpeɪ/ **noun** a small wig or hairpiece worn to cover a bald spot 小型遮秃假发

tour /tʊə(r)/ **noun 1** a journey for pleasure in which several different places are visited 旅行；观光；游览 **2** a short trip to view or inspect something 视察 **3** a series of plays, matches, etc. performed in several different places 巡回演出(或比赛等) • **verb** make a tour of 在…旅行，在…巡回演出(或比赛)

tour de force /ˌtʊə də ˈfɔːs/ **noun** (plural **tours de force** /ˌtʊə də ˈfɔːs/) a performance or achievement accomplished with great skill 绝技；壮举；杰作

tourism /ˈtʊərɪzəm/ **noun** the business of organizing and operating holidays and visits to places of interest 旅游业；观光业

tourist /ˈtʊərɪst/ **noun 1** a person who travels for pleasure 游客；观光者 **2** Brit. 【英】a member of a touring sports team 巡回比赛运动队队员

touristy /ˈtʊərɪsti/ **adjective** informal 【非正式】visited by a lot of tourists 吸引很多游客的；游客熙熙攘攘的

tournament /ˈtʊənəmənt/ **noun 1** a series of contests between a number of competitors 锦标赛；联赛 **2** a medieval sporting event in which knights jousted with blunted weapons (中世纪的)马上比武

tourney /ˈtʊəni/ **noun** (plural **tourneys**) a joust or tournament (中世纪的)马上比武，锦标赛

tourniquet /ˈtʊənɪkeɪ/ **noun** a cord or tight bandage tied round a limb to stop the flow of blood through an artery 止血带；压脉器

tousle /ˈtaʊzl/ **verb** (**tousles, tousling, tousled**) make someone's hair untidy 弄乱(头发)；使蓬乱

tout /taʊt/ **verb 1** try to sell 兜售；推销 **2** try to persuade people of something's value 吹捧；吹嘘 **3** Brit. 【英】resell a ticket for a popular event at a higher price than you paid for it 倒卖高价票 • **noun** a person who buys up tickets for an event to resell them at a profit 票贩子；"黄牛"

tow /təʊ/ **verb** use a vehicle or boat to pull another vehicle or boat along 拖，拉，牵引(车辆或小船) • **noun** an act of towing (车辆或小船的)拖，拉，牵引口 **in tow 1** (also **on tow**) being towed 被拖着 **2** accompanying or following someone 陪伴着；随着

towards /təˈwɔːdz/ or **toward** /təˈwɔːd/ **preposition 1** in the direction of 向；朝；对着 **2** getting nearer to 接近；快

到…的时候 **3** in relation to 对;对于 **4** contributing to the cost of 有助于;用于

towel /'taʊəl/ **noun** a piece of absorbent cloth used for drying 毛巾 • **verb** (**towels**, **towelling**, **towelled**; US spelling【美拼作】**towels**, **toweling**, **toweled**) dry someone or something with a towel 用毛巾把…擦干

towelling /'taʊəlɪŋ/ (US spelling【美拼作】**toweling**) **noun** absorbent cloth used for towels 毛巾布;毛巾料

tower /'taʊə(r)/ **noun 1** a tall, narrow building or part of a building, especially of a church or castle (尤指教堂或城堡的)塔,塔楼 **2** a tall structure containing special equipment 高大结构;高架 • **verb** (**towers**, **towering**, **towered**) **1** rise to or reach a great height 高耸;屹立 **2** (**towering**) very important or influential 极重要的;有很大影响的 **3** (**towering**) very great 极度的;激烈的: *a towering rage* 怒不可遏 □ **tower block** Brit.【英】a tall modern building containing many floors of offices or flats 高层建筑;办公(或公寓)大楼

town /taʊn/ **noun 1** a settlement larger than a village and generally smaller than a city 镇;市镇;城镇 **2** the central part of a town or city containing its shopping area 市中心;商业区 □ **go to town** informal【非正式】do something thoroughly or enthusiastically 大干一番;满腔热情地干 **town crier** (in the past) a person employed to shout out public announcements in the streets (旧时受雇在街头宣读公告的)衔头公告员 **town hall** the building where local government offices are located 镇公所;市政厅

township /'taʊnʃɪp/ **noun** (in South Africa) a suburb or city occupied chiefly by black people (南非的)黑人城镇,黑人居住区

towpath /'taʊpɑːθ/ **noun** a path beside a river or canal, originally used as a pathway for horses towing barges 纤道,纤路(原为河流沿岸马拉驳船所行之路)

toxic /'tɒksɪk/ **adjective 1** poisonous 有毒的,有害的 **2** relating to or caused by poison 有毒物的;由毒物引起的 ■ **toxicity** noun.

toxicology /ˌtɒksɪ'kɒlədʒi/ **noun** the branch of science concerned with how poisons work 毒理学;毒物学 ■ **toxicologist** noun.

toxin /'tɒksɪn/ **noun** a poison caused by a germ, to which the body reacts by producing antibodies 毒素

toy /tɔɪ/ **noun** an object for a child to play with (儿童)玩具 • **verb** (**toy with**) **1** casually consider an idea 不太认真地考虑 **2** fiddle with something 玩弄;摆弄 • **adjective** (of a breed of dog) very small (狗)体型极小的,个头小的 □ **toy boy** Brit. informal【英,非正式】a male lover who is much younger than his partner (比对方年轻很多的)小情夫,玩具男伴

trace /treɪs/ **verb** (**traces**, **tracing**, **traced**) **1** find by careful investigation 查出;找到,发现;追踪到 **2** find or describe the origin or development of 追溯,追究,追述(起源或发展) **3** follow the course or position of something with your eye or finger (用眼睛或手指)追踪,追寻(路线或位置) **4** copy something by drawing over its lines on a piece of transparent paper placed on top of it (用透明纸覆盖在某物上面)映描,描摹 **5** draw a pattern or outline 绘出,勾出(图案或轮廓) • **noun 1** a mark or other sign of the existence or passing of something 痕迹;踪迹,遗迹 **2** a very small amount 微量;少许 **3** a barely noticeable indication 一丝 **4**

a line or pattern on paper or a screen showing information recorded by a machine 轨迹;迹线;描记图 □ **trace element** a chemical element that is present in tiny amounts 痕量元素;微量元素

tracer /'treɪsə(r)/ *noun* a bullet or shell whose course is made visible by a trail of flames or smoke 曳光弹

tracery /'treɪsəri/ *noun* (plural **traceries**) **1** a decorative design of holes and outlines in stone 窗花格子 **2** a delicate branching pattern 精美花饰图案

trachea /trə'kiːə, 'treɪkiə/ *noun* (plural **tracheae** /trə'kiːiː, 'treɪkiiː/ or **tracheas**) the tube carrying air between the larynx and the lungs; the windpipe 气管

tracheotomy /ˌtrækɪ'ɒtəmi/ or **tracheostomy** /ˌtrækɪ'ɒstəmi/ *noun* (plural **tracheotomies**) a surgical cut in the windpipe, made to enable someone to breathe when their windpipe is blocked 气管切开术

track /træk/ *noun* **1** a rough path or small road 小径;小道 **2** a course or circuit for racing 跑道 **3** a line of marks left on the ground by a person, animal, or vehicle as they move along 迹,车辙 **4** a continuous line of rails on a railway 铁路轨道 **5** a section of a CD, record, or cassette tape containing one song or piece of music 唱片、光盘或磁带的)一段录音,一首歌曲(或乐曲) **6** a strip or rail along which something may be moved 滑轨;滑道 • *verb* **1** follow the trail or movements of 跟踪;追踪 **2** (**track someone/thing down**) find someone or something after a thorough search 搜寻到;追查到 **3** follow a particular course 跟踪,追寻(特定的轨迹) **4** (of a camera) move along with the subject being filmed 追踪拍摄;移动拍摄 □ **keep** (or **lose**) **track of** keep (or fail to keep) fully aware of or informed about 保持(或失去)对…的了解 **on the right** (or **wrong**) **track** following a course that is likely to result in success (or failure) 有正确(或错误)的路线,做法对头(或不对路) **track events** athletic events that take place on a running track 径赛 **track record** someone's past achievements 业绩记录 ■ **tracker** *noun*.

tracksuit /'træksuːt/ *noun* an outfit consisting of a sweatshirt and loose trousers 宽松保暖裤;运动衣

tract[1] /trækt/ *noun* **1** a large area of land 大片土地;地带 **2** a system of connected organs or tissues in the body along which something passes (人体内的)道,管,束

tract[2] *noun* a short piece of religious writing in the form of a pamphlet (宗教宣传的)小册子,传单

tractable /'træktəbl/ *adjective* **1** (of a person) easy to control or influence (人)易驾驭的,易受影响的 **2** (of a difficulty) easy to resolve (困难)易处理的

traction /'trækʃn/ *noun* **1** the action of pulling a thing along a surface 牵引;拖拉 **2** the power used in pulling 牵引力;拉力 **3** a way of treating a broken bone by gradually pulling it back into position 牵引(使断骨复位的方法) **4** the grip of a tyre on a road or a wheel on a rail 车轮对地面轨道的)附着摩擦力 □ **traction engine** a steam or diesel-powered road vehicle used for pulling heavy loads (用于拖重物的)牵引机车,牵引车

tractor /'træktə(r)/ *noun* a powerful motor vehicle with large rear wheels, used for pulling farm machinery 拖拉机;牵引机

trade /treɪd/ *noun* **1** the buying and selling of goods and services 贸

易;买卖;商业;交易 **2** a particular area of commercial activity 行业;生意 **3** a job requiring special skills and training (需特殊技能和训练的)职业,手艺,行当 • verb (**trades, trading, traded**) **1** buy and sell goods and services 做生意;从事贸易 **2** exchange 交换 **3** (**trade something in**) exchange a used article as part of the payment for another 以旧物折价换新物;折价贴息 **4** (**trade on**) take advantage of 利用 **5** (**trade something off**) exchange something of value as part of a compromise 用(有价之物)交换 □ **trade union** (or Brit. 【英】 **trades union**) an association formed within an industry or particular workplace to protect the rights of the workers 工会 ■ **trader** noun.

trademark /'treɪdmɑːk/ noun **1** a symbol, word, or words chosen to represent a company or product 商标 **2** a distinctive characteristic 特征;标记

tradesman /'treɪdzmən/ noun (plural **tradesmen**) **1** a person who has a small shop 商人;店主 **2** a person working at a skilled trade 工匠

tradition /trə'dɪʃn/ noun **1** the passing on of customs or beliefs from generation to generation (风俗或信仰的)传承,传袭 **2** a long-established custom or belief passed on in this way 传统,惯例;传统的风俗(或信仰) **3** a method or style established by an artist, writer, or movement, and followed by others (艺术家、作家、或运动建立的)传统,风格

traditional /trə'dɪʃənl/ adjective having to do with or following tradition 传统的;习俗的;因袭的 ■ **traditionally** adverb.

traditionalism /trə'dɪʃənəlɪzəm/ noun the upholding of tradition, especially so as to resist change (主张保留传统、反对变革的)传统主义

■ **traditionalist** noun & adjective.

traduce /trə'djuːs/ verb (**traduces, traducing, traduced**) formal 【正式】 say things about someone that are unpleasant or untrue 诽谤;中伤

traffic /'træfɪk/ noun **1** vehicles moving on public roads (道路上的)行驶车辆;交通 **2** the movement of ships or aircraft 航行;行驶;飞行 **3** the commercial transportation of goods or passengers 运输;人流;货流 **4** the messages or signals that are sent through a communications system (通过通信传递的)信息;通信 **5** the action of trading in something illegal 非法交易;非法买卖 • verb (**traffics, trafficking, trafficked**) buy or sell something illegal 非法进行…交易;非法买卖 □ **traffic jam** a congestion in the flow of traffic so that it is at or almost at a standstill 堵车;交通阻塞 **traffic lights** a set of automatically operated lights for controlling the flow of traffic 交通信号灯 **traffic warden** Brit. 【英】 an official who locates and reports on cars breaking parking regulations (处理违章停车的)交通管理员 ■ **trafficker** noun.

tragedian /trə'dʒiːdiən/ noun **1** a person who writes tragedies for the theatre 悲剧作家 **2** a person who acts in tragedies 悲剧演员

tragedy /'trædʒədi/ noun (plural **tragedies**) **1** a very sad event or situation 悲惨的事、不幸;惨案 **2** a serious play with an unhappy ending 悲剧;悲剧作品

tragic /'trædʒɪk/ adjective **1** very sad 悲痛的;悲哀的 **2** relating to tragedy in a literary work 悲剧的 ■ **tragically** adverb.

tragicomedy /ˌtrædʒi'kɒmədi/ noun (plural **tragicomedies**) a play or novel containing elements of both comedy and tragedy 悲喜剧;悲喜剧小说 ■ **tragicomic** adjective.

trail /treɪl/ **noun 1** a line of marks or signs left behind by someone or something as it moves along 痕迹;踪迹;足迹 **2** a track or scent used in following someone or hunting an animal (追踪或狩猎时跟随的)踪迹,足迹,臭迹 **3** a path through rough country (荒野中踩出的)小路,小径 **4** a route planned or followed for a particular purpose (特定的)路线,路径 **5** a long thin part stretching behind or hanging down from something 拖曳物;尾部 • **verb 1** draw or be drawn along behind (被)拖,拉 **2** follow the trail of 跟踪;追踪 **3** walk or move slowly or wearily 慢走;磨蹭;疲惫地走 **4** (**trail away** or **off**) become gradually quieter and then stop 逐渐减弱;声音越来越小 **5** be losing to an opponent in a contest (竞赛中)落后,失利 **6** (of a plant) grow along the ground or so as to hang down (植物)蔓生,蔓延

trailblazer /'treɪlbleɪzə(r)/ **noun 1** a person who is the first to do something new 创始人;先驱 **2** a person who finds a new way through wild country 拓荒者;开路先锋 ■ **trailblazing** adjective.

trailer /'treɪlə(r)/ **noun 1** an unpowered vehicle pulled by another 拖车;挂车 **2** the rear section of an articulated truck (铰接式卡车的)载货挂车 **3** N. Amer. 【北美】 a caravan 旅行拖车 **4** an extract from a film or programme used to advertise it (电影或电视节目的)预告片

train /treɪn/ **verb 1** teach a person or animal a particular skill or type of behaviour 训练(人或动物);培训 **2** be taught a particular skill 接受训练 **3** make or become physically fit through a course of exercise (通过运动)强身健体,使保持良好身体状态 **4** (**train something on**) point something at 把……瞄准;把……对准 **5** make a plant grow in a particular

direction or into a required shape 使(植物)朝特定方向生长;给(植物)修枝整形 • **noun 1** a series of railway carriages or wagons drawn by a locomotive 火车;列车 **2** a number of vehicles or animals moving in a line 列队行进的车辆(或驮畜);行列;队列 **3** a series of connected events, thoughts, etc. 一连串事件(或想法) **4** a long piece of trailing material attached to the back of a formal dress or robe (礼服的)裙裾,拖裾 □ **in train** in progress 在进行中

trainee /ˌtreɪ'niː/ **noun** a person undergoing training for a job or profession 接受培训者;实习生,见习生

trainer /'treɪnə(r)/ **noun 1** a person who trains people or animals 教练员,驯兽师 **2** Brit. 【英】 a soft shoe for sports or casual wear 运动鞋;便鞋

trainspotter /'treɪnspɒtə(r)/ **noun** Brit. 【英】 a person who collects locomotive numbers as a hobby (爱好)收集机车号码者 ■ **trainspotting** noun.

traipse /treɪps/ **verb** (**traipses, traipsing, traipsed**) walk or move wearily or reluctantly 疲惫地走;拖沓地走,磨蹭 • **noun** a boring walk 疲惫的步行;长途跋涉

trait /treɪt/ **noun** a distinguishing quality or characteristic 特征,特性

traitor /'treɪtə(r)/ **noun** a person who betrays their country, an organization, or a cause 卖国贼;背叛者 ■ **traitorous** adjective.

trajectory /trə'dʒektəri/ **noun** (plural **trajectories**) the path followed by a moving object (移动物体的)轨道,轨迹

tram /træm/ or **tramcar** /'træmkɑː/ **noun** Brit. 【英】 a passenger vehicle powered by electricity and running on rails laid in a road 有轨电车

tramlines /'træmlaɪnz/ **plural noun** rails for a tram 电车轨道

trammel /'træml/ **noun** (**trammels**) literary【文】restrictions on someone's freedom (对自由的)限制，束缚 • **verb** (**trammels, trammelling, trammelled**; US spelling【美拼作】**trammels, trammeling, trammeled**) restrict or limit 限制；束缚

tramp /træmp/ **noun 1** a homeless person who travels around and lives by begging or doing casual work 流浪汉；流浪乞丐；流浪工人 **2** the sound of heavy steps 沉重的脚步声 **3** a long walk 长途步行；长途跋涉 **4** N. Amer. informal【北美，非正式】a woman who has a lot of sexual partners 淫妇；荡妇 • **verb 1** walk heavily or noisily 踏着沉重的脚步走 **2** walk over a long distance 长途跋涉

trample /'træmpl/ **verb** (**tramples, trampling, trampled**) **1** tread on and crush 踩碎；践踏 **2** (**trample on** or **over**) treat with contempt 无视；践踏

trampoline /'træmpəli:n/ **noun** a strong fabric sheet connected by springs to a frame, used as a springboard and landing area in doing acrobatic or gymnastic exercises (杂技表演或体操运动用的)弹床，蹦床 ■ **trampolining** noun.

trance /trɑːns/ **noun** a half-conscious state in which someone does not respond to things happening around them 昏睡状态；催眠状态

tranche /trɑːnʃ/ **noun** one of the parts into which something is divided, especially an amount of money (款额或股份的)一份，一部分

tranquil /'træŋkwɪl/ **adjective** free from disturbance; calm 平静的，安宁的 ■ **tranquillity** (or **tranquility**) noun **tranquilly** adverb.

tranquillize or **tranquillise** /'træŋkwəlaɪz/ (US spelling【美拼作】**tranquilize**) **verb** (**tranquillizes,**

tranquillizing, tranquillized) give a calming or sedative drug to (使用镇静剂)使镇静，使平静

tranquillizer or **tranquilliser** /'træŋkwəlaɪzə(r)/ (US spelling【美拼作】**tranquilizer**) **noun** a drug taken to reduce tension or anxiety 安定药；镇静剂

transact /træn'zækt/ **verb** conduct or carry out business 做业务；进行交易

transaction /træn'zækʃn/ **noun 1** an act of buying or selling 交易；业务；买卖 **2** the process of carrying out business 处理业务；交易

transatlantic /ˌtrænzət'læntɪk/ **adjective 1** crossing the Atlantic 横渡大西洋的 **2** concerning countries on either side of the Atlantic 大西洋两岸国家的

transcend /træn'send/ **verb 1** be or go beyond the range or limits of 超出，超越(限度) **2** be superior to 胜过；优于

transcendent /træn'sendənt/ **adjective 1** going beyond normal or physical human experience 超凡的；玄妙的 **2** (of God) existing apart from the material world (指超然存在于物质世界之外的) ■ **transcendence** noun.

transcendental /ˌtrænsen'dentl/ **adjective** going beyond the limits of human knowledge in a religious or spiritual context 超凡的；玄奥的 ■ **transcendentally** adverb.

transcontinental /ˌtrænzkɒntɪ'nentl/ **adjective** crossing or extending across a continent or continents 穿越大陆的；横贯大陆的

transcribe /træn'skraɪb/ **verb** (**transcribes, transcribing, transcribed**) **1** put thoughts, speech, or data into written form, or into a different written form 抄写，记录(想法、讲话或数据)；把…写成(另一种书写形式) **2** arrange a piece of music for a different instrument or voice (为适合另一种乐器或声部)改编(乐曲)

transcript /'trænskrɪpt/ **noun** a written or printed version of material that was originally spoken or presented in another form (口头或其他材料形式的)抄本，誊本，打印本

transcription /træn'skrɪpʃn/ **noun 1** a transcript 抄本，誊本，打印本 **2** the process of transcribing 抄写，誊写，打印 **3** a transcribed piece of music (乐曲的)改编版

transept /'trænsept/ **noun** (in a cross-shaped church) either of the two parts extending at right angles from the nave (十字形教堂的)耳堂

transfer /træns'fɜː(r)/ **verb** (**transfers, transferring, transferred**) **1** move someone or something from one place to another 使转移;使搬迁 **2** move to another department, job, etc. 调动;转职;转换(工作) **3** change to another place, route, or means of transport during a journey 转乘;换乘;倒车 **4** pass a property, right, or responsibility to another person 让与，转移(财产、权利或责任) • **noun 1** an act of transferring 转移;搬迁;调动;中转;换乘;转让 **2** Brit.【英】 a small coloured picture or design on paper, which can be transferred to another surface by being pressed or heated (可利用挤压或加热印到表面上的)转印图画，转印图案 ■ **transference** noun.

transfigure /træns'fɪɡə(r)/ **verb** (**be transfigured**) be transformed into something more beautiful or spiritual 使改观;使美化;使变得崇高 ■ **transfiguration** noun.

transfix /træns'fɪks/ **verb 1** make motionless with horror, wonder, or astonishment (因恐惧、惊愕等)呆立不得，惊呆 **2** pierce with a sharp object 刺穿;戳破

transform /træns'fɔːm/ **verb 1** change or be changed in nature, form, or appearance (使)改变性质(或形状、外观) **2** change the voltage of an electric current 变换(电压) ■ **transformation** noun.

transformer /træns'fɔːmə(r)/ **noun** a device for changing the voltage of an electric current 变压器

transfusion /træns'fjuːʒn/ **noun** a medical process in which someone is given a supply of someone else's blood 输血

transgress /trænz'ɡres/ **verb** go beyond the limits of what is morally, socially, or legally acceptable 违背(道德原则或标准);违犯(法律);越轨 ■ **transgression** noun **transgressor** noun.

transient /'trænziənt/ **adjective 1** lasting only for a short time 转瞬即逝的;倏忽的 **2** staying or working in a place for a short time only 暂住的;流动的;临时的 • **noun** a transient person 暂住者;流浪者;临时工 ■ **transience** noun **transiently** adverb.

transistor /træn'zɪstə(r)/ **noun 1** a silicon-based device which is able to amplify or rectify electric currents 晶体管 **2** (also **transistor radio**) a portable radio using circuits containing transistors 晶体管收音机

transit /'trænzɪt/ **noun 1** the carrying of people or things from one place to another 运输;运送;搬运;载运 **2** an act of passing through or across a place 通过;经过;过境;中转

transition /træn'zɪʃn/ **noun 1** the process of changing from one state or condition to another 过渡;转变;变革 **2** a period of such change 过渡时期 ■ **transitional** adjective.

transitive /'trænsətɪv/ **adjective** (of a verb) able to take a direct object, e.g. *saw* in *he saw the donkey* (动词)及物的 ■ **transitivity** noun.

transitory /'trænsətri/ **adjective** lasting for only a short time 暂时的;

转瞬即逝的

translate /træns'leɪt/ **verb**
(translates, translating, translated) 1 express the sense of words or a piece of writing in another language 翻译;译 **2 (translate into)** change or be changed into another form (使)转变;(使)变成

translation /træns'leɪʃn/ **noun 1** the action of translating 翻译;译 **2** a piece of writing or word that is translated 译文;译本

translator /træns'leɪtə(r)/ **noun** a person who translates writing or speech from one language into another 翻译;译者;翻译家

transliterate /træns'lɪtəreɪt/ **verb** **(transliterates, transliterating, transliterated)** write a letter or word using the corresponding letters of a different alphabet or language (按另一种字母表或语言)写出(字母或词语) 移译;音译 ■ **transliteration** noun.

translucent /trænz'lu:snt/ **adjective** allowing light to pass through partially; semitransparent 半透明的 ■ **translucence** (or **translucency**) noun.

transmission /trænz'mɪʃn/ **noun 1** the passing of something from one place or person to another 传输;输送;传送;传播;传染 **2** a transmitted programme or signal (播送的)节目;(发送的)电子信号 **3** the mechanism by which power is passed from an engine to the axle in a motor vehicle (机动车的)传动装置,变速器

transmit /træns'mɪt/ **verb (transmits, transmitting, transmitted) 1** cause to pass from one place or person to another 传输;输送;传播;传染 **2** broadcast or send out an electrical signal or a radio or television programme 播送(广播或电视节目);发射(电子信号) **3** allow heat, light, etc.

to pass through a material 传(热);透(光)

transmitter /træns'mɪtə(r)/ **noun** a device used to produce and transmit electromagnetic waves carrying messages or signals, especially those of radio or television (尤指广播或电视信号的)发射机,发射台,发报台

transmogrify /trænz'mɒɡrɪfaɪ/ **verb** **(transmogrifies, transmogrifying, transmogrified)** humorous【幽默】 change into something completely different 使完全改变

transmute /trænz'mju:t/ **verb** **(transmutes, transmuting, transmuted)** change in form, nature, or substance 变化;变形;变质 ■ **transmutation** noun.

transom /'trænsəm/ **noun 1** the flat surface forming the stern of a boat 艉横材;艉构架 **2** a strengthening crossbar 横档;横楣

transparency /træns'pærənsi/ **noun** (plural **transparencies**) **1** the condition of being transparent 透明 **2** a positive transparent photograph printed on plastic or glass, and viewed using a slide projector 透明正片;幻灯片

transparent /træns'pærənt/ **adjective 1** allowing light to pass through so that objects behind can be distinctly seen 透明的;清澈的 **2** obvious or evident 明显的;显而易见的 ■ **transparently** adverb.

transpire /træn'spaɪə(r)/ **verb** **(transpires, transpiring, transpired) 1** come to be known 公开了;为人所知 **2** take place; happen 发生 **3** (of a plant or leaf) give off water vapour through pores in the surface layer (植物或树叶)水分蒸发,蒸腾 ■ **transpiration** noun.

transplant **verb** /træns'plɑ:nt/ **1** take living tissue or an organ and implant it in another part of the body or in another body 移植(器官或组织) **2** transfer to another place or situation 移居;迁移 • noun /'trænsplɑ:nt/ **1** an operation in which an organ or tissue is transplanted (器官或组织)的移植 **2** a person or thing that has been transplanted 移居者;移植器官(或组织) ■ **transplantation** noun.

transport verb /træn'spɔ:t/ **1** carry people or goods from one place to another by means of a vehicle, aircraft, or ship (用交通工具)运输,运送,输送(人或货物) **2** (be transported) be overwhelmed with a strong emotion 感到万分激动 **3** (in the past) send someone to a distant place as a punishment (旧时)流放(犯人) • noun /'trænspɔ:t/ **1** a system or method of carrying people or goods from one place to another 交通运输系统;交通(或运输)工具 **2** the action of transporting 运输;输送;运送 **3** a large vehicle, ship, or aircraft for carrying troops or stores (送军队或给养的)运输车,运输船,运输机 **4** (transports) very strong emotions 强烈情感;激动;激情 ■ **transportation** noun **transporter** noun.

transpose /træn'spəuz/ verb (**transposes**, **transposing**, **transposed**) **1** cause two or more things to change places with each other 使换位,使互换位置 **2** move something to a different place or context 转移地点;改变处置 **3** write or play music in a different key from the original 使(音乐)变调,使移调 ■ **transposition** noun.

transsexual or **transexual** /trænz'sekʃuəl/ noun a person who emotionally and psychologically feels that they belong to the opposite sex 易性癖者

transubstantiation /ˌtrænsəbˌstænʃi'eɪʃn/ noun (in Christian thinking) the doctrine that the bread and wine served in the service of Holy Communion become the actual body and blood of Jesus after they have been blessed (基督教信仰中的)圣餐变体(指圣餐中的面饼和葡萄酒经祝圣后变成基督的身体和血)

transverse /'trænzvɜ:s/ adjective placed or extending across something 横向的;横断的;横切的 ■ **transversely** adverb.

transvestite /trænz'vestaɪt/ noun a person, especially a man, who likes to dress in clothes worn by the opposite sex (尤指男性)异装癖者 ■ **transvestism** noun.

trap /træp/ noun **1** a device, pit, or enclosure designed to catch and hold animals (捕捉动物的)夹子,陷阱,捕捉器 **2** an unpleasant situation from which you cannot escape (无法逃脱的)困境,牢笼 **3** a trick causing someone to say or do something which they do not intend 圈套;诡计 **4** a container or device used to collect a particular thing (用于收集特定物品的)容器(或装置) **5** a light, two-wheeled carriage pulled by a horse or pony (单马)双轮轻便马车 • verb (**traps**, **trapping**, **trapped**) **1** catch and hold in a trap 设陷阱捕捉;使陷入困境 **2** trick into doing something 使落入圈套;使上当

trapdoor /'træpdɔ:(r)/ noun a hinged or removable panel in a floor, ceiling, or roof 地板门;(天花板上的)活板门,通气门;(屋顶的)活动天窗

trapeze /trə'pi:z/ noun a horizontal bar hanging on two ropes high above the ground, used by acrobats in a circus (杂技演员使用的)高空秋千,吊架

trapezium /trə'pi:ziəm/ noun (plural **trapezia** /trə'pi:ziə/ or **trapeziums**) (in geometry) a quadrilateral with one pair of sides parallel (几何中的)梯形

trapper /'træpə(r)/ noun a person who traps wild animals 捕猎野生动物者

trappings /ˈtræpɪŋz/ **plural noun 1** the signs or objects associated with a particular situation or role (与某一处境或作用有关的)标志，相关物品 **2** a horse's ornamental harness 马饰

Trappist /ˈtræpɪst/ **noun** a monk belonging to an order that speaks only at certain times (天主教西多会的)特拉普派僧侣(此派信徒只在特定时间讲话)

trash /træʃ/ **noun 1** N. Amer.【北美】waste material 废物；垃圾 **2** poor-quality writing, art, etc. 拙劣的文学(或艺术等)作品 **3** N. Amer.【北美】a person or people of very low social status 窝囊废；没出息的人 • **verb** informal【非正式】wreck or destroy 损坏；破坏 □ **trash can** N. Amer.【北美】a dustbin 垃圾桶 ■ **trashy** adjective.

trauma /ˈtrɔːmə/ **noun** (plural **traumas**) **1** a deeply disturbing experience 痛苦经历；挫折 **2** emotional shock following a stressful event 精神创伤；心理创伤 **3** (in medicine) physical injury (医学)创伤，外伤 ■ **traumatic** adjective.

traumatize or **traumatise** /ˈtrɔːmətaɪz/ **verb** (be **traumatized**) suffer lasting shock as a result of a disturbing experience or injury 使(某人)受精神创伤

travail /ˈtræveɪl/ or **travails** /ˈtræveɪlz/ **noun** old use【旧】a situation involving a lot of hard work or difficulty 艰苦劳动；艰辛，煎熬

travel /ˈtrævl/ **verb** (**travels**, **travelling**, **travelled**; US spelling【美拼作】**travels**, **traveling**, **traveled**) **1** go from one place to another, especially over a long distance (尤指)长途行走；旅行；游历 **2** journey along a particular road or through a particular region 沿(公路)行进；穿过；经过(地区) • **noun 1** the action of travelling 旅行；游历 **2** (**travels**) journeys over a long distance 长途旅行

□ **travel agent** a person or agency that makes the necessary arrangements for travelers 旅行社办人；旅行代理人

traveller /ˈtrævələ(r)/ (US spelling【美拼作】**traveler**) **noun 1** a person who is travelling or who often travels 旅行者；旅游者；游客 **2** Brit.【英】a Gypsy or other travelling person 吉普赛人；旅行者 □ **traveller's cheque** a cheque for a fixed amount that can be exchanged for cash in foreign countries 旅行支票

travelogue /ˈtrævəlɒg/ **noun** a film, book, or talk about a person's travels 旅行记录片；游记；旅行见闻讲座

traverse /trəˈvɜːs/ **verb** (**traverses**, **traversing**, **traversed**) travel or extend across or through 穿过；横过；横越

travesty /ˈtrævəsti/ **noun** (plural **travesties**) a ridiculous or shocking version of something 嘲弄；歪曲

trawl /trɔːl/ **verb 1** catch fish with a trawl net 用拖网捕(鱼) **2** search through something thoroughly 搜罗；网罗 • **noun 1** an act of trawling 搜罗；网罗 **2** a large wide-mouthed fishing net dragged by a boat along the bottom of the sea (捕鱼的)拖网

trawler /ˈtrɔːlə(r)/ **noun** a fishing boat used for trawling 拖网渔船

tray /treɪ/ **noun** a flat container with a raised rim, used for carrying plates, cups, etc. (浅)盘；托盘；碟

treacherous /ˈtretʃərəs/ **adjective 1** guilty of or involving betrayal 背叛的；不忠的 **2** having hidden or unpredictable dangers 有潜在危险的；凶险的 ■ **treacherously** adverb **treachery** noun.

treacle /ˈtriːkl/ **noun** Brit.【英】**1** mo-lasses 糖蜜 **2** golden syrup 金黄色糖浆 ■ **treacly** adjective.

tread /tred/ **verb** (**treads**, **treading**, **trod**; past participle **trodden** or **trod**)

1 walk in a particular way (以某种方式)走，行走 **2** press down or crush with your feet 踩；踏；践踏 **3** walk on or along 在…走；沿着…走 • **noun 1** a way or the sound of walking 步法；步态；脚步声 **2** the top surface of a step or stair (台阶或楼梯的)踏步板，梯面 **3** the part of a vehicle tyre that grips the road (车胎的)胎面，着地面 **4** the part of the sole of a shoe that touches the ground 鞋底；鞋掌 □ **tread water** stay in an upright position in deep water by moving the feet with a walking movement 踩水

treadle /'tredl/ **noun** a lever which you work with your foot to operate a machine (驱动机器的)踏板

treadmill /'tredmɪl/ **noun 1** a job or situation that is tiring or boring and difficult to escape from 枯燥无味的工作(或状况) **2** a large wheel turned by the weight of people or animals treading on steps fitted into it, used in the past to drive machinery (旧时由人或牲畜踩动踏板，用以驱动机器的)踏车 **3** a device used for exercise consisting of a continuous moving belt on which you walk or run 走步机，跑步机

treason /'triːzn/ or **high treason** **noun** the crime of betraying your country 叛国罪 ■ **treasonable** adjective.

treasure /'treʒə(r)/ **noun 1** a quantity of precious coins, gems, or other valuable objects 财宝；财富 **2** a very valuable object 极贵重的物品；珍宝；珍品 **3** informal 【非正式】 a much loved or highly valued person 宠儿；心肝宝贝 • **verb** (**treasures**, **treasuring**, **treasured**) **1** look after carefully 珍藏 **2** value highly 珍视；珍爱；珍重 □ **treasure hunt** a game in which players search for hidden objects by following a trail of clues (根据线索寻找隐藏物品的)寻宝游戏 **treasure trove** a store of valuable or pleasant things 宝藏；宝库

treasurer /'treʒərə(r)/ **noun** a person appointed to manage the finances of a society, company, etc. (社团、公司等的)司库，出纳，财务主管

treasury /'treʒəri/ **noun** (plural **treasuries**) **1** the funds or revenue of a state, institution, or society 国库；(机构或社团的)资金，财政收入 **2** (**Treasury**) (in some countries) the government department responsible for the overall management of the economy (一些国家的)财政部

treat /triːt/ **verb 1** behave towards or deal with in a certain way (以…方式)对待 **2** give medical care or attention to 治疗；医治 **3** use a substance or process to protect or preserve something, or give it particular properties (利用某物质或通过某过程)处理，保护，保存 **4** present or discuss a subject 表现，讨论，探讨(主题) **5** (**treat someone to**) provide someone with food, drink, or entertainment that you have paid for 款待；招待；请(客) **6** (**treat yourself**) do or have something very enjoyable 犒劳自己；买令人中意之物；享受(令人愉悦之物) • **noun** a gift or event that gives someone great pleasure 乐趣；乐事；给人带来快乐的礼物(或事情)

treatise /'triːtɪz/ **noun** a formal piece of writing on a subject (专题)论文；专著

treatment /'triːtmənt/ **noun 1** a way of behaving towards someone or dealing with something 对待；待遇 **2** medical care for an illness or injury 治疗；诊治 **3** the use of a substance or process to preserve or give particular properties to something (利用某物质或通过某过程进行的)处理，加工，保存 **4** the presentation or discussion of a subject 论述；讨论

treaty /'triːti/ **noun** (plural **treaties**) a formal agreement between states (国家间的)条约，协定

treble[1] /'trebl/ **adjective 1** consisting

of three parts 有三部分的 **2** multiplied or occurring three times 三倍的；三重 • **pronoun** an amount which is three times as large as usual 三倍；三重 • **verb** (**trebles**, **trebling**, **trebled**) make or become treble (使)成三倍；(使)增加两倍

treble² **noun 1** a high-pitched voice, especially a boy's singing voice 高音；(尤指男孩的)童声高音 **2** the high-frequency output of a radio or audio system (收音机或音响系统的)高音部 □ **treble clef** (in music) a clef placing G above middle C on the second-lowest line of the stave (乐曲中的)高音谱号

tree /triː/ **noun** a plant consisting of a thick wooden stem and a number of branches, that can grow to a great height and live for many years 树；树木；乔木 □ **tree diagram** a diagram with a structure of branching lines 树形图 **tree house** a structure built in the branches of a tree for children to play in (搭建在树枝之间供儿童玩耍的)树上小屋

treeline /ˈtriːlaɪn/ **noun** a height up a mountain above which trees do not grow 树木线(指山区树木生长的上限)

trefoil /ˈtrefɔɪl/ **noun 1** a small plant with yellow flowers and clover-like leaves 三叶草；三叶植物 **2** a shape or design in the form of three rounded lobes like a clover leaf 三叶形装饰(或设计)

trek /trek/ **noun** a long, difficult journey, especially one made on foot 长途旅行；艰难的旅程；(尤指)徒步跋涉 • **verb** (**treks**, **trekking**, **trekked**) go on a trek 长途跋涉 ■ **trekker** noun.

trellis /ˈtrelɪs/ **noun** a framework of bars used as a support for climbing plants (支撑攀援植物的)棚，架子

tremble /ˈtrembl/ **verb** (**trembles**, **trembling**, **trembled**) **1** shake in a way that you cannot control, usually as a result of fear, excitement, or weakness (因恐惧、激动或虚弱)颤抖，哆嗦，战栗 **2** be in a state of great worry or fear 焦虑；恐惧 • **noun** a trembling feeling, movement, or sound 颤抖；战栗；摇动

tremendous /trəˈmendəs/ **adjective 1** very great in amount, scale, or force (数量、规模或强度)巨大的，极大的 **2** informal 【非正式】 very good or impressive 精彩的；了不起的 ■ **tremendously** adverb.

tremolo /ˈtremələʊ/ **noun** (plural **tremolos**) a wavering effect in singing or created in certain musical instruments (演唱或乐器演奏的)颤音，震音

tremor /ˈtremə(r)/ **noun 1** a quivering movement that cannot be controlled 颤抖；哆嗦；战栗 **2** (also **earth tremor**) a slight earthquake 轻微地震；微震 **3** a sudden feeling of fear or excitement (突然的)恐惧，激动

tremulous /ˈtremjələs/ **adjective 1** shaking or quivering slightly 颤抖的；战栗的；打战的 **2** nervous 紧张的

trench /trentʃ/ **noun 1** a long, narrow ditch 沟；沟渠 **2** a ditch dug by troops to provide shelter from enemy fire 战壕；堑壕 **3** (also **ocean trench**) a long, deep depression in the ocean bed 海沟 □ **trench coat** a belted, double-breasted raincoat (有腰带的)双排扣雨衣

trenchant /ˈtrentʃənt/ **adjective** (of something said or written) expressed strongly and clearly (言辞或文章)尖锐的，犀利的，鲜明的 ■ **trenchantly** adverb.

trencher /ˈtrentʃə(r)/ **noun** (in the past) a flat piece of wood from which food was served or eaten (旧时盛食物的)木盘，木碟

trend /trend/ **noun 1** a general direction in which something is developing or changing 趋势；倾向；动态 **2** a fashion

潮流；时尚

trendsetter /'trendsetə(r)/ **noun** a person who leads the way in fashion or ideas 引领时尚的人；创新风的人；标新立异者

trendy /'trendi/ **adjective (trendier, trendiest)** informal 【非正式】very fashionable 时髦的；新潮的

trepidation /ˌtrepɪ'deɪʃn/ **noun** a feeling of fear or nervousness 惊恐、不安

trespass /'trespəs/ **verb 1** enter someone's land or property without their permission 擅自进入，非法侵入(他人的土地或房产) **2 (trespass on)** take advantage of someone's time, good nature, etc. 占用；滥用 **3 (trespass against)** old use 【旧】do wrong or harm to 冒犯；伤害 • **noun 1** Law 【法律】the entering of someone's land or property without their permission (对他人土地或房产的)非法侵入 **2** old use 【旧】a bad or wrongful act 罪过，过失 ■ **trespasser** noun.

tress /tres/ **noun** literary 【文】a long lock of hair 一绺长发

trestle /'tresl/ **noun** a structure consisting of a horizontal bar on sloping legs, used in pairs to support a surface such as a table top (支撑桌面等成对的)支架，条凳

triad /'traɪæd/ **noun 1** a group of three people or things 三人组合；三件一套 **2** a Chinese secret society involved in criminal activity 三合会

trial /'traɪəl/ **noun 1** a formal examination in a court of law to decide if someone is guilty of a crime 审判；审讯 **2** a test of performance, qualities, or suitability (对性能、质量或适宜性的)试验，试用 **3 (trials)** an event in which horses or dogs compete or perform (马或狗的)比赛，表演 **4** something that tests a person's endurance or patience 考验；磨难 • **verb** (**trials, trialling, trialled**; US spelling 【美拼作】**trials, trialing, trialed**) test

something to assess its suitability or performance 测试，试验(适宜性或性能) □ **on trial 1** being tried in a court of law 受审 **2** undergoing tests 处于测试中；实验性的 **trial and error** the process of trying out various methods until you find one that works well 不断摸索；反复试验

triangle /'traɪæŋgl/ **noun 1** a figure with three straight sides and three angles 三角形 **2** a musical instrument consisting of a steel rod bent into a triangle, sounded with a rod 三角铁(一种打击乐器) **3** an emotional relationship involving a couple and a third person 三角关系 ■ **triangular** adjective.

triangulation /traɪˌæŋgjʊ'leɪʃn/ **noun** the division of an area into a series of triangles in order to determine distances and relative positions 三角测量；三角剖分

triathlon /traɪ'æθlɒn/ **noun** an athletic contest involving three different events, typically swimming, cycling, and long-distance running 铁人三项赛；三项全能赛 ■ **triathlete** noun.

tribalism /'traɪbəlɪzəm/ **noun** behaviour and attitudes that result from a system in which people belong to tribes 部落习性；部落主义；种族意识

tribe /traɪb/ **noun 1** a group of people within a traditional society sharing customs and beliefs and led by a chief 部落；部族 **2** informal 【非正式】a large number of people 大群；大帮 ■ **tribal** adjective.

tribesman /'traɪbzmən/ **noun** (plural **tribesmen**) a member of a tribe in a traditional society 部落成员

tribulation /ˌtrɪbjʊ'leɪʃn/ **noun** trouble, suffering, or difficulty 忧患，困难，磨难

tribunal /traɪ'bjuːnl/ **noun 1** Brit. 【英】a group of people established to settle disputes 仲裁机构；仲裁委员会 **2** a court of justice 法庭

tribune /'trɪbjuːn/ **noun** (in ancient Rome) an official chosen by the ordinary people to protect their interests (古罗马由平民选出的)保民官

tributary /'trɪbjətri/ **noun** (plural **tributaries**) a river or stream that flows into a larger river or lake 支流

tribute /'trɪbjuːt/ **noun 1** an act, statement, or gift intended to show respect or admiration for someone (表示敬意或爱慕的)行动, 颂词, 礼品 **2** historical 【历史】 payment made by a state to a more powerful one 贡金;贡品

trice /traɪs/ **noun** (**in a trice**) in a moment 转眼之间;瞬间

tricentenary /traɪsen'tiːnəri/ **noun** (plural **tricentenaries**) a three-hundredth anniversary 三百周年纪念

triceps /'traɪseps/ **noun** (plural **triceps**) the large muscle at the back of the upper arm (手臂上的)三头肌

triceratops /traɪ'serətɒps/ **noun** a large plant-eating dinosaur with two large horns 三角龙(长有两只巨型角、食草的大型恐龙)

trichology /trɪ'kɒlədʒi/ **noun** the branch of medicine concerned with the hair and scalp 毛发学 ▪ **trichologist** noun.

trick /trɪk/ **noun 1** something intended to deceive or outwit someone 诡计;花招;计谋 **2** a skilful act performed to entertain people 戏法;把戏 **3** an illusion 错觉;假象 **4** a habit or mannerism 习惯;习气;特点 **5** (in card games) a single round of play(纸牌游戏中的)一圈, 一墩 • **verb** cunningly deceive or outwit someone 欺骗;哄骗;算计 ▪ **trickery** noun.

trickle /'trɪkl/ **verb** (**trickles, trickling, trickled**) **1** (of a liquid) flow in a small stream (液体)滴, 淌, 小股流淌 **2** come or go slowly or gradually 慢慢移动;逐渐消散 • **noun 1** a small

flow of liquid 细流;涓流 **2** a small number of people or things moving slowly 少量缓慢移动的人(或物)

trickster /'trɪkstə(r)/ **noun** a person who cheats or deceives people

tricksy /'trɪksi/ **adjective** clever or mischievous 诡计多端的;顽皮的

tricky /'trɪki/ **adjective** (**trickier, trickiest**) **1** difficult or awkward 难处理的;棘手的;微妙的 **2** likely to deceive you; crafty 欺骗的;诡计多端的

tricolour /'trɪkələ(r)/ (US spelling 【美拼作】 **tricolor**) **noun** a flag with three bands of different colours, especially the French national flag 三色旗;(尤指)法国国旗

tricycle /'traɪsɪkl/ **noun** a vehicle similar to a bicycle but having three wheels 三轮(脚踏)车

trident /'traɪdnt/ **noun** a three-pronged spear 三叉戟

tried /traɪd/ past and past participle of TRY.

triennial /traɪ'eniəl/ **adjective** lasting for or happening every three years 持续三年的;三年一次的

trier /'traɪə(r)/ **noun** a person who always tries hard 坚持不懈者;勤勤恳恳的人

trifle /'traɪfl/ **noun 1** something of little value or importance 不值钱的东西;琐事;小事 **2** a small amount 少许、一点 **3** Brit. 【英】 a cold dessert of sponge cake and fruit with layers of custard, jelly, and cream 乳脂松糕, 酒浸果酱松糕(海绵水果蛋糕敷以蛋奶沙司、果冻和奶油的冷甜点) • **verb** (**trifles, trifling, trifled**) (**trifle with**) treat without seriousness or respect 怠慢;轻视;小看

trifling /'traɪflɪŋ/ **adjective** unimportant; trivial 不重要的;琐碎的

trigger /'trɪgə(r)/ **noun 1** a small lever that sets off a gun or other mechanism when pulled (枪的)扳机;启动装置

2 an event that causes something to happen (引发事件的)起因，诱因 • verb (**triggers**, **triggering**, **triggered**) **1** cause a device to function 开动，启动 **2** make something happen 触发；引发 □ **triggerhappy** tending to fire a gun on the slightest provocation 以开枪为乐的；动辄开枪的；好斗的

trigonometry /ˌtrɪɡəˈnɒmətri/ noun the branch of mathematics concerned with the relationships between the sides and angles of triangles 三角学

trilby /ˈtrɪlbi/ noun (plural **trilbies**) Brit. 【英】 a man's soft felt hat with a narrow brim (男式)窄边软毡帽

trill /trɪl/ noun a high warbling sound 颤声；颤音；鸟鸣 • verb make a high warbling sound 发颤音；发鸟啭鸣般的声音

trillion /ˈtrɪljən/ cardinal number **1** a million million (1,000,000,000,000 or 10^{12}) 万亿；百万兆 **2** Brit. dated 【英，废】 a million million million (1,000,000,000,000,000,000 or 10^{18}) 百亿亿；万亿兆 ■ **trillionth** ordinal number.

trilobite /ˈtraɪləbaɪt/ noun a fossil sea creature with a rear part divided into segments 三叶虫

trilogy /ˈtrɪlədʒi/ noun (plural **trilogies**) a group of three related novels, plays, or films (小说、戏剧或电影的)三部曲

trim /trɪm/ verb (**trims**, **trimming**, **trimmed**) **1** cut away unwanted parts from something 修剪；修整 **2** reduce the size, amount, or number of 削减；缩小；减少 **3** decorate something along its edges 装饰；点缀(某物)的边缘 **4** adjust a sail 调整(船帆) • noun **1** decoration along the edges of something 边饰；镶边 **2** the upholstery or interior lining of a car (汽车的)内部装潢，装潢配件 **3** an act of trimming 修剪；修整 **4**

good condition 井然有序；健康适宜 • adjective (**trimmer**, **trimmest**) neat and smart 整齐的；整洁的 □ **in trim** slim and fit 苗条健康的

trimaran /ˈtraɪməræn/ noun a yacht with three hulls side by side 三体帆船

trimming /ˈtrɪmɪŋ/ noun **1** (**trimmings**) small pieces trimmed off 修剪下来的东西；剪屑 **2** decoration or accompaniments 装饰；配饰；配料

trinity /ˈtrɪnəti/ noun (plural **trinities**) **1** (**the Trinity** or **the Holy Trinity**) (in Christian belief) the three persons (Father, Son, and Holy Spirit) that make up God (指基督教信仰中的)三位一体(指圣父、圣子和圣灵合为上帝) **2** a group of three people or things 三人一组；三件一套；三合一

trinket /ˈtrɪŋkɪt/ noun a small inexpensive ornament or item of jewel-lery 小装饰物；廉价首饰

trio /ˈtriːəʊ/ noun (plural **trios**) **1** a set or group of three 三人一组；三件一套；三合一 **2** a group of three musicians 三重奏乐团；三重唱组合

trip /trɪp/ verb (**trips**, **tripping**, **tripped**) **1** catch your foot on something and stumble or fall 绊；绊倒 **2** (**trip up**) make a mistake 犯错误 **3** walk, run, or dance with quick, light steps 脚步轻快地走(或跑、跳舞) **4** make a mechanism start working 开动(机械装置) **5** informal 【非正式】 experience hallucinations as a result of taking a drug such as LSD (服用毒品后)产生幻觉 • noun **1** a journey to a place and back again, especially for pleasure (尤指娱乐性的)旅行 **2** an instance of tripping or falling 绊；绊倒 **3** informal 【非正式】 a period of hallucinations caused by taking a drug such as LSD (服用毒品后的)幻觉，迷幻感受 **4** a device that trips a mechanism (机械装置的)启动装置；脱扣(装置)

tripartite /traɪˈpɑːtaɪt/ **adjective 1** consisting of three parts 包括三部分的 **2** shared by or involving three parties 三方参与的；涉及三方的

tripe /traɪp/ **noun 1** the stomach of a cow or sheep used as food 食用牛肚(或羊肚) **2** informal 【非正式】 nonsense 废话；胡说

triplane /ˈtraɪpleɪn/ **noun** an early type of aircraft with three pairs of wings, one above the other (早期的)三翼飞机

triple /ˈtrɪpl/ **adjective 1** consisting of three parts, things, or people 三部分的；三组的；三人的 **2** having three times the usual size, value, or strength 三倍的；三重的 • **noun** a thing that is three times as large as usual or is made up of three parts 三倍之物；三个一组之物 • **verb** (**triples**, **tripling**, **tripled**) make or become triple (使)成三倍；增至三倍 ☐ **triple jump** an athletic event in which competitors perform a hop, a step, and a jump from a running start 三级跳远 ■ **triply** adverb.

triplet /ˈtrɪplɪt/ **noun 1** each of three children born at the same birth 三胞胎之一 **2** a group of three musical notes to be performed in the time of two or four 三连音符

triplicate adjective /ˈtrɪplɪkət/ existing in three copies or examples 三联的；一式三份的 • **verb** /ˈtrɪplɪkeɪt/ (**triplicates**, **triplicating**, **triplicated**) **1** make three copies of 把…制成一式三份 **2** multiply by three 乘以三

tripod /ˈtraɪpɒd/ **noun** a three-legged stand for a camera or other device (照相机等的)三脚架

tripper /ˈtrɪpə(r)/ **noun** Brit. informal 【英，非正式】 a person who goes on a pleasure trip 旅游者；远足者

triptych /ˈtrɪptɪk/ **noun** a picture or carving on three panels 三幅相连的图画；三联浮雕

tripwire /ˈtrɪpwaɪə(r)/ **noun** a wire that is stretched close to the ground and sets off a trap or alarm when disturbed 绊索；地雷拉线；警报拉线

trite /traɪt/ **adjective** (of a remark or idea) unoriginal and dull (评论或观点)非独创的，陈腐的，老套的

triumph /ˈtraɪəmf/ **noun 1** a great victory or achievement 巨大成功；非凡成就 **2** joy or satisfaction resulting from a success or victory (成功或胜利带来的)喜悦，心满意足 **3** a very successful example of something (成功的)典范，楷模 • **verb** be successful or victorious 获胜；成功 ■ **triumphal** adjective.

triumphant /traɪˈʌmfənt/ **adjective 1** having won a battle or contest 战胜的；获胜的 **2** joyful after a victory or achievement (获胜后)欢欣鼓舞的，洋洋得意的 ■ **triumphantly** adverb.

triumvirate /traɪˈʌmvərət/ **noun** a group of three powerful or important people or things 三巨头；三人统治集团；三方执政集团

trivet /ˈtrɪvɪt/ **noun** a metal stand on which hot dishes are placed (垫热菜盘用的)金属架，隔热架

trivia /ˈtrɪvɪə/ **plural noun** unimportant details or pieces of information 琐事；细枝末节

trivial /ˈtrɪvɪəl/ **adjective** of little value or importance 琐碎的；不重要的 ■ **triviality** noun (plural **trivialities**) **trivially** adverb.

trivialize or **trivialise** /ˈtrɪvɪəlaɪz/ **verb** (**trivializes**, **trivializing**, **trivialized**) make something seem less important or complex than it really is 使显得不重要(或不复杂)；轻视 ■ **trivialization** noun.

trod /trɒd/ past and past participle of TREAD.

trodden /ˈtrɒdn/ past participle of TREAD.

troglodyte /ˈtrɒɡlədaɪt/ **noun** a

person who lives in a cave 穴居人

troika /'trɔɪkə/ **noun 1** a Russian vehicle pulled by a team of three horses side by side (俄罗斯的)三驾马车 **2** a group of three people working together 三人团体

Trojan /'trəʊdʒən/ **noun** an inhabitant of ancient Troy in Asia Minor (present-day Turkey) (古代小亚细亚、今土耳其的)特洛伊人 • **adjective** relating to Troy 特洛伊的 □ **Trojan Horse** something intended to weaken or defeat an enemy secretly 特洛伊木马；颠覆阴谋

troll¹ /trɒl/ **noun** (in stories) an ugly giant or dwarf (传说中)丑陋的巨人(或侏儒)

troll² **verb** fish by trailing a baited line along behind a boat 用曳绳钓(鱼)

trolley /'trɒli/ **noun** (plural **trolleys**) **1** Brit. 【英】 a large metal basket with wheels, for transporting heavy or bulky items (装有脚轮的)手推车、手拉车 **2** a small table on wheels (装有脚轮的)台车

trolleybus /'trɒlibʌs/ **noun** Brit. 【英】 a bus powered by electricity obtained from overhead wires 无轨电车

trollop /'trɒləp/ **noun** dated or humorous 【废或幽默】 a woman who has a lot of sexual partners 荡妇；娼妇

trombone /trɒm'bəʊn/ **noun** a large brass wind instrument with a sliding tube which you move to produce different notes 长号；伸缩长号 ■ **trombonist** noun.

troop /truːp/ **noun 1** (**troops**) soldiers or armed forces 军队；部队 **2** a unit of troops (军队的)连队，作战单位 **3** a group of people or animals (人或动物的)一群，一伙 • **verb** come or go as a group 成群结队而行

trooper /'truːpə(r)/ **noun 1** a soldier in a cavalry or armoured unit 骑兵，装甲兵 **2** US 【美】 a state police officer 州警察

trophy /'trəʊfi/ **noun** (plural **trophies**) **1** a cup or other object awarded as a prize (作为奖励颁发的)奖杯，奖品 **2** a souvenir of an achievement 战利品；胜利纪念品

tropic /'trɒpɪk/ **noun 1** the line of latitude 23°26´ north (**tropic of Cancer**) or south (**tropic of Capricorn**) of the equator 北(或南)回归线 **2** (**the tropics**) the region between the tropics of Cancer and Capricorn 热带地区

tropical /'trɒpɪkl/ **adjective 1** having to do with the tropics 热带的 **2** very hot and humid 炎热的；湿热的 ■ **tropically** adverb.

trot /trɒt/ **verb** (**trots, trotting, trotted**) **1** (of a horse) move at a pace faster than a walk (马)小跑，疾走 **2** run at a moderate pace with short steps (人)小步跑，碎步疾走 **3** (**trot something out**) informal 【非正式】 repeat something that has been said many times before 重复，翻出(老一套的解释) • **noun 1** a trotting pace 小跑；疾走 **2** a period of trotting 小跑的一段时间 □ **on the trot** Brit. informal 【英，非正式】 one after another 接连地；接二连三地

troth /trəʊθ/ **noun** (**plight your troth**) old use 【旧】 promise to marry 答应结婚；订婚

trotter /'trɒtə(r)/ **noun** a pig's foot 猪蹄；猪爪

troubadour /'truːbədɔː(r)/ **noun** a travelling singer and poet in medieval France (中世纪法国的)游吟诗人，行吟诗人

trouble /'trʌbl/ **noun 1** difficulty or problems 困难；问题 **2** effort that you make to do something 功夫；力气 **3** a cause of worry or inconvenience 苦恼；麻烦；困扰 **4** a situation in which you can be punished or blamed 过错；被批评的情形 **5** a situation in which people are angry or violent 动乱：骚乱。• verb (**troubles**, **troubling**, **troubled**) **1** cause distress or inconvenience to 使忧虑：使苦恼：给…带来麻烦 **2** (**troubled**) feeling anxious or experiencing problems 有困难的：苦恼的：忧虑的 **3** (**trouble to do**) make the effort required to do 费神去做；费事去做

troublemaker /'trʌblmeɪkə(r)/ **noun** a person who regularly causes trouble 惹是生非者；捣乱者

troubleshooter /'trʌblʃuːtə(r)/ **noun** a person who investigates and solves problems or faults 解决困难者；纠纷调停人 ■ **troubleshooting** noun.

troublesome /'trʌblsəm/ **adjective** causing difficulty or problems 棘手的；讨厌的

trough /trɒf/ **noun 1** a long, narrow open container for animals to eat or drink out of 饮水槽；饲料槽 **2** (in weather forecasting) a long region of low atmospheric pressure (天气预报中)低压槽，槽型低压 **3** a point of low activity or achievement 低谷；低潮

trounce /traʊns/ **verb** (**trounces**, **trouncing**, **trounced**) defeat heavily 彻底打败；击溃

troupe /truːp/ **noun** a touring group of entertainers (巡回演出的)表演班子，演出团

trouper /'truːpə(r)/ **noun 1** an entertainer with many years of experience 经验丰富的演员；台柱演员 **2** a reliable and uncomplaining person 可靠的人；任劳任怨者

trousers /'traʊzəz/ **plural noun** an outer garment that covers the body from the waist down and has a separate part for each leg 长裤；裤子

trousseau /'truːsəʊ/ **noun** (plural **trousseaux** or **trousseaus** /'truːsəʊz/) clothes and other belongings collected by a bride for her marriage 嫁妆；妆奁

trout /traʊt/ **noun** (plural **trout** or **trouts**) an edible fish of the salmon family 鲑；鲑鳟鱼；鳟鱼

trove /trəʊv/ **noun** a store of valuable things 宝藏；宝库

trowel /'traʊəl/ **noun 1** a small tool with a curved scoop for lifting plants or earth (移植树苗或挖土的)小铲子 **2** a small tool with a flat blade for applying mortar or plaster 镘刀；泥刀；抹子

troy /trɔɪ/ **noun** a system of weights used mainly for precious metals and gems, with a pound of 12 ounces 金衡，金衡制(贵重金属和宝石的衡量制，每金衡磅等于12金衡盎司)

truant /'truːənt/ **noun** a pupil who stays away from school without permission or explanation 逃学者；旷课的小学生 • **verb** (also **play truant**) stay away from school without permission or explanation 逃学；旷课 ■ **truancy** noun.

truce /truːs/ **noun** an agreement between enemies to stop fighting for a certain time 停战协定

truck¹ /trʌk/ **noun 1** a large road vehicle for carrying goods 卡车；运货汽车；载重汽车 **2** Brit. 【英】an open railway vehicle for carrying goods (铁路上运送货物的)敞篷车，无盖车皮 ■ **trucker** noun.

truck² **noun** (**have no truck with**) refuse to have any dealings or association with 拒不与…打交道

truculent /'trʌkjələnt/ **adjective** quick to argue or fight 爱争吵的；好斗的 ■ **truculence** noun **truculently** adverb.

trudge /trʌdʒ/ **verb** (**trudges**, **trudging**, **trudged**) walk slowly and with heavy steps 缓慢地走；步履沉重地走；拖着脚走 • **noun** a difficult or long and tiring walk 徒步跋涉；疲惫的长途步行

true /truː/ **adjective (truer, truest) 1** in accordance with fact or reality 合乎事实的；确实的 **2** rightly so called 名副其实的；真正的: *true love* 真爱 **3** real or actual 真正的；实质的；实际的 **4** accurate and exact 精确的；完全符合的 **5** (**true to**) in keeping with what is usual or expected 合乎(标准)的；符合(期望)的 **6** loyal or faithful 忠实的；虔诚的 **7** upright or level 正直的；垂直的；平的 ■ **truly** adverb.

✔ 拼写指南 note that there's no *e* in **truly**. 注意 truly 中没有e。

truffle /'trʌfl/ **noun 1** an underground fungus that is eaten as a delicacy 块菌，块菰(生长于地下的味美食用菌) **2** a soft chocolate sweet 巧克力软糖

trug /trʌg/ **noun** 【英】 a wooden basket for carrying flowers, fruit, and vegetables (装鲜花、水果或蔬菜用的)浅筐

truism /'truːɪzəm/ **noun** a statement that is obviously true and says nothing new or interesting 不言而喻的道理；老生常谈

trump /trʌmp/ **noun** (in card games) a card of the suit chosen to rank above the others (纸牌游戏中)王牌，主牌，将牌 • **verb 1** play a trump on a card of another suit 出王牌压掉(他人的牌) **2** beat by saying or doing something better 胜过；打败 **3** (**trump something up**) invent a false accusation or excuse 诬陷；捏造；编造 □ **come** (or **turn**) **up trumps** Brit. informal 【英，非正式】**1** unexpectedly do very well 结果出乎预料的好；意外地顺利 **2** be especially generous or helpful 特别友善；格外有帮助

trumpery /'trʌmpəri/ **adjective** old use 【旧】showy but worthless 虚有其表的；花哨而无价值的

trumpet /'trʌmpɪt/ **noun 1** a brass musical instrument with a flared end 小号，喇叭 **2** the loud cry of an ele-phant (大象的)吼声 • **verb (trumpets, trumpeting, trumpeted) 1** announce widely or enthusiastically 宣扬；鼓吹 **2** (of an elephant) make its characteristic loud cry (大象)吼叫 **3** play a trumpet 吹奏喇叭，吹小号 □ **blow your own trumpet** talk boastfully about your achievements 自吹自擂；自我吹嘘 ■ **trumpeter** noun.

truncate /trʌŋ'keɪt/ **verb (truncates, truncating, truncated)** shorten by cutting off the top or end 截去…的顶端(或尾端)；截短 ■ **truncation** noun.

truncheon /'trʌntʃən/ **noun** Brit. 【英】 a short, thick stick carried as a weapon by a police officer 警棍

trundle /'trʌndl/ **verb (trundles, trundling, trundled)** move or roll slowly and heavily (缓慢沉重地)移动，滚动

trunk /trʌŋk/ **noun 1** the main woody stem of a tree 树干 **2** a person's or animal's body apart from the limbs and head (人或动物的)躯干 **3** the long nose of an elephant 象鼻 **4** a large box for storing or transporting articles 大箱子 **5** N. Amer. 北美 the boot of a car (汽车)行李箱 □ **trunk call** Brit. dated 【英，废】a long-distance telephone call 长途电话 **trunk road** an important main road 干道

trunks /trʌŋks/ **plural noun** men's shorts worn for swimming or boxing (男士)游泳短裤，拳击短裤

truss /trʌs/ **noun 1** a framework which supports a roof, bridge, or other structure (支持屋顶、桥梁等的)构架，桁架 **2** a padded belt worn to support a hernia 疝带 • **verb 1** tie someone up tightly 捆紧；绑牢；扎；缚 **2** tie up the wings and legs of a bird before cooking (烹煮前)把(禽类的)翅膀和腿捆牢

trust /trʌst/ **noun 1** firm belief in the truth, reliability, or ability of someone or something 信任；信赖

2 responsibility for someone or something (对…的)责任，义务 **3** an arrangement by which someone manages property for the benefit of another person or people 委托，信托 **4** an organization or company managed by trustees 信托基金机构，托管机构 • **verb 1** have trust in 信赖；信任 **2** (**trust someone with**) allow someone to have, use, or look after 托交；托付；把…委托给(某人)照管 **3** (**trust someone/thing to**) give someone or something to another person for safekeeping 把…托付给 **4** (**trust to**) rely on luck, fate, etc. 依赖，依靠(运气、命运等) **5** expect or hope 希望；期望 □ **trust fund** a fund of money or property that is held for someone by a trust 信托基金

trustee /trʌsˈtiː/ **noun** a person who is given legal powers to manage property for the benefit of others (财产的)托管人

trustful /ˈtrʌstfl/ **adjective** having total trust in someone 完全信赖(他人)的 ■ **trustfully** adverb.

trusting /ˈtrʌstɪŋ/ **adjective** tending to trust other people；not suspicious 轻易相信人的；不猜疑的 ■ **trustingly** adverb.

trustworthy /ˈtrʌstwɜːðɪ/ **adjective** honest and reliable 可信赖的，可靠的 ■ **trustworthiness** noun.

trusty /ˈtrʌstɪ/ **adjective** (**trustier**, **trustiest**) old use or humorous 【旧或幽默】 reliable or faithful 可信赖的；忠实的

truth /truːθ/ **noun** (plural **truths**) **1** the quality or state of being true 真实，真实性 **2** true facts 真相；实情；事实 **3** a fact or belief that is accepted as true 真理

truthful /ˈtruːθfl/ **adjective 1** telling or expressing the truth 诚实的；讲真话的 **2** accurate；true to life 真实的；如实的 ■ **truthfully** adverb **truthfulness**

noun.

try /traɪ/ **verb** (**tries**, **trying**, **tried**) **1** make an attempt to do something 试图；设法，努力 **2** (also **try something out**) test something new or different 尝试；试用；试验 **3** attempt to open a door 试着开(门) **4** (**try something on**) put on an item of clothing to see if it fits or looks good 试穿(衣服) **5** put someone on trial 使(某人)受审 • **noun** (plural **tries**) **1** an attempt 尝试；努力 **2** an act of testing something new or different 试验；试用 **3** Rugby【英式橄榄球】an act of touching the ball down behind the opposing goal line to score points 在对方球门线后带球触地得分 □ **try someone's patience** make someone feel irritated or annoyed 使(某人)忍无可忍

> **! 注意** when writing, it is better to use **try to** rather than **try and** (*we should try to help them* rather than *we should try and help them*). 在书面语中最好使用try to，而不是try and，例如应该说 we should try to help them (我们应尽量帮助他们)，而不要说 we should try and help them。

trying /ˈtraɪɪŋ/ **adjective** difficult or annoying 难对付的；令人厌烦的

tryst /trɪst/ **noun** literary 【文】 a private, romantic meeting between lovers (情人间的)约会，幽会

tsar, czar, or **tzar** /zɑː(r)/ **noun** an emperor of Russia before 1917 (1917年前俄国的)沙皇 ■ **tsarist** adjective.

tsetse fly /ˈtsetsi/ **noun** an African bloodsucking fly which transmits diseases 舌蝇，采采蝇(产于非洲，吸血并传染疾病)

tsp abbreviation teaspoonful 一茶匙的量；一小勺的量

tsunami /tsuːˈnɑːmi/ **noun** a tidal wave caused by an underwater earthquake or other disturbance 海啸

tub /tʌb/ **noun 1** a low, wide, open container with a flat bottom (浅而宽、敞口平底的)桶,盆 **2** a small plastic or cardboard container for food (塑料或纸质)饭盒,食品盒 □ **tub-thumping** informal【非正式】loud, aggressive expression of opinions 大吹大擂的宣扬;叫嚣

tuba /'tjuːbə/ **noun** a large low-pitched brass wind instrument 大号(低音铜管乐器)

tubby /'tʌbi/ **adjective (tubbier, tubbiest)** informal【非正式】(of a person) short and rather fat (人)矮胖的

tube /tjuːb/ **noun 1** a long, hollow cylinder for conveying or holding something 管;管子 **2** a flexible container sealed at one end and having a cap at the other (一端密封一端带盖的)软管 **3 (the Tube)** Brit. trademark【英,商标】the underground railway system in London 伦敦地下铁道;伦敦地铁

tuber /'tjuːbə(r)/ **noun** a thick underground part of the stem or root of some plants, from which new plants grow 块茎

tubercular /tjuː'bɜːkjələ(r)/ **adjective** relating to, or suffering from, tuberculosis 结核病的;患结核病的

tuberculosis /tjuːˌbɜːkjuˈləʊsɪs/ **noun** a serious infectious disease in which small swellings (tubercles) appear, especially in the lungs 结核病;(尤指)肺结核

tubular /'tjuːbjələ(r)/ **adjective 1** long, round, and hollow like a tube 管状的;管式的 **2** made from a tube or tubes 管子构成的

TUC /ˌtiː juː 'siː/ **abbreviation** Trades Union Congress (英国)职工大会

tuck /tʌk/ **verb 1** push, fold, or turn between two surfaces 把…塞进,把…卷进,把…叠折进(两个平面之间) **2** put neatly into a small space 把…塞进狭窄空间;收藏起 **3 (tuck someone in** or **up)** settle someone in bed by pulling the edges of the bedclothes under the mattress 把(某人)的被子掖好 **4 (tuck in** or **into)** informal【非正式】eat food heartily 痛快地吃;狼吞虎咽 ● **noun 1** a flattened, stitched fold in a garment or material (衣服或布料上的)褶,裥 **2** Brit. informal【英,非正式】food eaten by children at school as a snack (儿童在学校吃的)零食,小吃

tucker /'tʌkə(r)/ **noun** Austral./NZ informal【澳/新西兰,非正式】food 食物

Tudor /'tjuːdə(r)/ **adjective** relating to the royal family which ruled England 1485–1603 (从1485年至1603年统治英格兰的)都铎王朝的,都铎王室的

Tuesday /'tjuːzdeɪ, -di/ **noun** the day of the week before Wednesday and following Monday 星期二;周二

tufa /'tjuːfə/ **noun 1** rock formed as a deposit from mineral springs 泉华 **2** rock formed from volcanic ash 石灰华

tuffet /'tʌfɪt/ **noun 1** a tuft or clump 一绺毛发;一丛草 **2** a footstool or low seat 脚凳,矮凳

tuft /tʌft/ **noun** a bunch of threads, grass, or hair held or growing together at the base (线、草、头发等的)一束,一簇,一丛 ■ **tufted** adjective **tufty** adjective.

tug /tʌg/ **verb (tugs, tugging, tugged)** pull hard or suddenly 猛拉;使劲拉;用力拖 ● **noun 1** a hard or sudden pull 猛拉;使劲扯(或拽) **2 (also tug-boat)** a small, powerful boat for towing larger boats and ships 拖船 □ **tug of war** a contest in which two teams pull at opposite ends of a rope 拔河

tuition /tjuː'ɪʃn/ **noun** teaching or instruction 教学;讲授;指导

tulip /'tju:lɪp/ *noun* a plant with brightly coloured cup-shaped flowers 郁金香

tulle /tju:l/ *noun* a soft, fine net material, used for making veils and dresses (用于制作面纱和连衣裙的) 绢网, 薄纱, 丝网眼纱

tumble /'tʌmbl/ *verb* (**tumbles, tumbling, tumbled**) **1** fall suddenly or clumsily 突然跌倒; 栽倒; 滚下 **2** move in a headlong way 跌跌撞撞地走; 莽撞地行动 **3** decrease rapidly in amount or value (数量或价值)骤降, 骤跌 • *noun* **1** a sudden or clumsy fall 跌倒; 栽倒; 滚下 **2** an untidy or confused arrangement 混乱; 杂乱 □ **tumble dryer** a machine that dries washed clothes by turning them in hot air inside a revolving drum 滚筒式干衣机

tumbledown /'tʌmbldaʊn/ *adjective* (of a building) ruined or falling into ruin (建筑物)摇摇欲坠的, 破败不堪的

tumbler /'tʌmblə(r)/ *noun* **1** a drinking glass with straight sides and no handle or stem (直壁无柄的)玻璃杯 **2** an acrobat 杂技演员 **3** a part of a lock that holds the bolt until lifted by a key (锁的)制栓

tumbril /'tʌmbrɪl/ *noun* an open cart of a kind used to take prisoners to the guillotine during the French Revolution (法国大革命期间押送囚犯去断头台的)死囚车

tumescent /tju:'mesnt/ *adjective* swollen or becoming swollen 肿大的; 肿胀的

tumid /'tju:mɪd/ *adjective* (of a part of the body) swollen (身体部位)肿大的, 肿胀的

tummy /'tʌmi/ *noun* (plural **tummies**) informal 【非正式】 a person's stomach or abdomen 胃; 肚子 □ **tummy button** the navel 肚脐

tumour /'tju:mə(r)/ (US spelling 【美

拼作】 **tumor**) *noun* an abnormal growth of tissue in the body 肿瘤; 肿块

tumult /'tju:mʌlt/ *noun* **1** a loud, confused noise 喧哗; 嘈杂 **2** confusion or disorder 混乱; 骚乱

tumultuous /tju:'mʌltʃuəs/ *adjective* **1** very loud and showing strong feelings 喧闹的; 嘈杂的: *tumultuous applause* 喧闹的喝彩声 **2** excited, confused, or disorderly 骚动的; 混乱的; 动荡的

tumulus /'tju:mjələs/ *noun* (plural **tumuli** /'tju:mjəlaɪ/) an ancient burial mound 冢; 古坟

tun /tʌn/ *noun* a large beer or wine cask (装啤酒或葡萄酒的)大酒桶

tuna /'tju:nə/ *noun* (plural **tuna** or **tunas**) a large edible fish of warm seas 金枪鱼

tundra /'tʌndrə/ *noun* the vast, flat, treeless regions of Europe, Asia, and North America in which the soil under the surface is permanently frozen 冻原, 苔原(欧洲、亚洲和北美洲的一些地区, 树木不生、底土永久冻灭)

tune /tju:n/ *noun* **1** a sequence of notes that form a piece of music; a melody 曲调; 曲子 **2** correct musical pitch 合调; 正确的音准 • *verb* (**tunes, tuning, tuned**) **1** adjust a musical instrument to the correct pitch 为(乐器)调音; 为…校音 **2** adjust a radio or television to a particular frequency 调(收音机)频率; 调(电视机)频道 **3** adjust an engine so that it runs smoothly and efficiently 调节, 调整(发动机) **4** adjust or adapt to a purpose or situation 调整; 使适应; 使适合 □ **tuning fork** a two-pronged steel device which produces a specific note when hit against a surface 音叉

tuneful /'tju:nfl/ *adjective* having a pleasing tune 音调优美的; 声音悦耳

的 ■ **tunefully** adverb.

tuneless /'tju:nləs/ **adjective** not having a pleasing tune 不成曲调的；不悦耳的 ■ **tunelessly** adverb.

tuner /'tju:nə(r)/ **noun 1** a person or device that tunes musical instruments 调音师；调音器 **2** a part of a stereo system that receives radio broadcasts (立体声音响中接收无线电信号的)调谐器

tungsten /'tʌŋstən/ **noun** a hard grey metal used to make electric light filaments (金属)钨

tunic /'tju:nɪk/ **noun 1** a loose sleeveless garment reaching to the thighs or knees (长及大腿或膝盖的)宽松无袖外衣 **2** a close-fitting short coat worn as part of a uniform 紧身制服上衣

Tunisian /tju:'nɪziən/ **noun** a person from Tunisia 突尼斯人 • **adjective** relating to Tunisia 突尼斯的

tunnel /'tʌnl/ **noun** a passage built underground for a road or railway or by a burrowing animal 地下通道；隧道; (穴居动物的)洞穴 • **verb** (**tunnels, tunnelling, tunnelled**; US spelling【美拼作】**tunnels, tunneling, tunneled**) dig a tunnel 开掘隧道;挖地道 □ **tunnel vision 1** a condition in which things cannot be seen properly if they are not straight ahead 管状视;视野狭窄 **2** informal【非正式】the tendency to focus only on a single aspect of a situation 一孔之见,井蛙之见

tunny /'tʌni/ **noun** (plural **tunny** or **tunnies**) a tuna 金枪鱼

tuppence /'tʌpəns/ ⇒ 见 TWOPENCE.

turban /'tɜ:bən/ **noun** a long length of material worn wound round the head by Muslim and Sikh men (穆斯林或锡克男教徒的)包头巾 ■ **turbaned** (or **turbanned**) adjective.

turbid /'tɜ:bɪd/ **adjective** (of a liquid) cloudy or muddy; not clear (液体)混浊的,污浊不清的

turbine /'tɜ:baɪn/ **noun** a machine in which a wheel or rotor is made to revolve by a fast-moving flow of water, air, etc. 涡轮机;汽轮机

turbocharger /'tɜ:bəʊtʃɑ:dʒə(r)/ or **turbo** /'tɜ:bəʊ/ **noun** a supercharger driven by a turbine powered by the engine's exhaust gases 涡轮增压器;透平增压器 ■ **turbocharged** adjective.

turbofan /'tɜ:bəʊfæn/ **noun** a jet engine in which a turbine-driven fan provides additional thrust 涡轮风扇发动机

turbojet /'tɜ:bəʊdʒet/ **noun** a jet engine in which the exhaust gases also operate a device for compressing the air drawn into the engine (飞机)涡轮喷气发动机

turboprop /'tɜ:bəʊprɒp/ **noun** a jet engine in which a turbine is used to drive a propeller (飞机)涡轮螺旋桨发动机

turbot /'tɜ:bət/ **noun** (plural **turbot** or **turbots**) an edible flatfish 大菱鲆(一种可食用的比目鱼)

turbulence /'tɜ:bjələns/ **noun 1** violent or unsteady movement of air or water (空气、水流等的)湍流,涡流,紊流 **2** conflict or confusion 冲突;骚乱;混乱

turbulent /'tɜ:bjələnt/ **adjective 1** involving a lot of conflict, disorder, or confusion 动荡的;骚乱的;混乱的 **2** (of air or water) moving unsteadily or violently (空气或水流)汹涌的,湍流的,猛烈的 ■ **turbulently** adverb.

tureen /tjʊ'ri:n/ **noun** a deep covered dish from which soup is served (盛汤的)大盖碗,带盖汤碗

turf /tɜ:f/ **noun** (plural **turfs** or **turves**) **1** grass and earth held together by its roots 草皮 **2** a piece of turf cut from the ground 草皮块 **3** (**the turf**) horse racing 赛马 **4** (**your turf**) informal【非正式

正式】your territory 地盘；势力范围 • **verb 1 (turf someone out)** Brit. informal【英，非正式】force someone to leave 驱走，驱逐(某人) **2** cover with turf 用草皮覆盖 □ **turf accountant** Brit.【英】a bookmaker (赛马场的)赌注纪人

turgid /'tɜːdʒɪd/ **adjective 1** (of language) pompous and boring (语言)浮夸而乏味的 **2** swollen or full 肿胀的；膨胀的；饱满的

Turk /tɜːk/ **noun** a person from Turkey 土耳其人

turkey /'tɜːki/ **noun** (plural **turkeys**) a large game bird bred for food 吐绶鸡，火鸡

Turkish /'tɜːkɪʃ/ **noun** the language of Turkey 土耳其语 • **adjective** relating to Turkey or its language 土耳其的；土耳其语的 □ **Turkish bath** a period of sitting in a room filled with very hot air or steam, followed by washing and massage 土耳其浴；蒸汽浴 **Turkish delight** a sweet consisting of flavoured gelatin coated in icing sugar 土耳其软糖，拌奶软糖(一种外裹糖粉的胶质软糖)

turmeric /'tɜːmərɪk/ **noun** a bright yellow powder obtained from a plant, used in Asian cookery 姜黄根粉(亚洲烹饪中用作调料)

turmoil /'tɜːmɔɪl/ **noun** a state of great disturbance, confusion, or uncertainty 骚动；混乱；焦虑

turn /tɜːn/ **verb 1** move around a central point 转动；旋转 **2** move so as to face or go in a different direction 转弯，转向 **3** make or become (使)变成，(使)成为：*She turned pale.* 她脸色变得苍白。**4** shape on a lathe (在车床上)车削 **5** twist or sprain an ankle 扭伤(脚踝) • **noun 1** an act of turning 转动；旋转 **2** a bend in a road, river, etc. (道路、河流等的)转弯处，弯道，河曲 **3** a place where a road meets or branches off another 转

弯处；岔路口；拐角 **4** the time when a member of a group must or is allowed to do something (依次轮到的)机会 **5** a time when one period of time ends and another begins (年代的)交替时期 **6** a short walk or ride 散步；(驾车、骑马等的)兜一圈 **7** a brief feeling of illness (疾病的)一阵发作；短暂的不适感 **8** a short performance 短节目 □ **be turned out** be dressed in a particular way 打扮成，装扮成 **do someone a good turn** do something that is helpful for someone 做有助于(某人)的事 **to a turn** to exactly the right degree 正好；恰好 **turn someone/ thing down 1** reject an offer made by someone 拒绝 **2** reduce the volume or strength of sound, heat, etc. produced by a device 把(音量、暖气等)调低 **turn in** informal【非正式】go to bed 上床睡觉 **turn someone in** hand someone over to the authorities 把(某人)扭送(官方)；使(某人)自首 **turn something off** switch something off 关掉；截掉 **turn on** suddenly attack 突然攻击 **turn someone/thing on 1** switch something on 打开；接通 **2** informal【非正式】excite sexually 使性兴奋 **turn out 1** prove to be the case 证明是；结果是 **2** be present at an event 出席(活动)，在场 **turn something out** switch off an electric light 关掉(电灯) **turn over** (of an engine) start to run (发动机)发动，转动 **turn up 1** be found 被发现；被找到 **2** arrive 出现，露面；到场 **turn something up** increase the volume or strength of sound, heat, etc. produced by a device 把(音量)调高，把(暖气等)开大 **turn-up** Brit.【英】**1** the end of a trouser leg folded upwards on the outside (裤脚的)翻边，外卷边 **2** informal【非正式】an unusual or unexpected event 奇异之事；出乎意料之事

turncoat /'tɜːnkəʊt/ **noun** a person

who deserts one party or cause in order to join an opposing one 叛徒；变节者；叛逆

turning /'tɜːnɪŋ/ **noun** a place where a road branches off another 岔路口；转弯处

turnip /'tɜːnɪp/ **noun** a round root which is eaten as a vegetable 蔓菁；芜菁

turnkey /'tɜːnkiː/ **noun** (plural **turnkeys**) old use【旧】a jailer 监狱看守；狱吏

turnout /'tɜːnaʊt/ **noun** the number of people attending or taking part in an event 出席人数；到场人数

turnover /'tɜːnəʊvə(r)/ **noun 1** the amount of money taken by a business in a particular period (一定时期的)营业额，成交额 **2** the rate at which employees leave a workforce and are replaced 人事变更率；人员调整率 **3** the rate at which goods are sold and replaced in a shop (商店的)货物周转率，销售比率 **4** a small pie made by folding a piece of pastry over on itself to enclose a filling 三角馅饼；半圆馅饼

turnpike /'tɜːnpaɪk/ **noun** US & historical【美和历史】a road on which a toll is charged 收费公路；收通行税的公路

turnstile /'tɜːnstaɪl/ **noun** a gate with revolving arms allowing only one person at a time to pass through (每次只允许一人通过的)旋转栅门

turntable /'tɜːnteɪbl/ **noun** a circular revolving platform or support, e.g. for the record in a record player (圆形的)转台；旋转托盘；(唱机上的)唱盘

turpentine /'tɜːpəntaɪn/ **noun** a liquid obtained from certain trees, used to thin paint and clean brushes 松脂；松节油

turpitude /'tɜːpɪtjuːd/ **noun** formal【正式】wickedness 卑鄙；邪恶

turps /tɜːps/ **noun** informal【非正式】

turpentine 松脂；松节油

turquoise /'tɜːkwɔɪz/ **noun 1** a greenish-blue or sky-blue semi-precious stone 绿松石 **2** a greenish-blue colour 绿松石色；青绿色

turret /'tʌrət/ **noun 1** a small tower at the corner of a building or wall (位于建筑物拐角或墙角的)塔楼，角楼 **2** an armoured tower for a gun in a ship, aircraft, or tank (战舰、飞机或坦克上的)炮塔，旋转枪架 ■ **turreted** adjective.

turtle /'tɜːtl/ **noun** a reptile with a bony or leathery shell, that lives in the sea 海龟 □ **turn turtle** (of a boat) turn upside down (船)倾覆，翻 **turtle dove** a small dove with a soft call 斑鸠

turtleneck /'tɜːtlnek/ **noun 1** Brit.【英】a high, round, close-fitting neck on a garment 圆翻领；高翻领 **2** N. Amer.【北美】a polo neck 圆高领

turves /tɜːvz/ plural of TURF.

tusk /tʌsk/ **noun** a long, pointed tooth which protrudes from the closed mouth of an elephant, walrus, or wild boar (象、海象或野猪的)长牙，獠牙

tussle /'tʌsl/ **noun** a short struggle or scuffle 扭打；打斗 ▪ **verb** (**tussles**, **tussling**, **tussled**) be involved in a tussle 扭打；打斗

tussock /'tʌsək/ **noun** a dense clump or tuft of grass (茂密的)草丛，(草)簇 一簇，一丛

tutelage /'tjuːtɪlɪdʒ/ **noun** formal【正式】**1** protection or authority 保护；监护；托管 **2** instruction 教导；指导；辅导

tutelary /'tjuːtələri/ **adjective** formal【正式】acting as a protector, guardian, or patron 守护的；监护的

tutor /'tjuːtə(r)/ **noun 1** a person who teaches a single pupil or a very small group 家庭教师；私人教师 **2** Brit.【英】a university or college teacher with extra responsibility for students (大学的)导师，指导教师 • **verb** act as a tutor to 担任…的私人教师；指导；辅导

tutorial /tjuːˈtɔːrɪəl/ **noun** a period of teaching by a university or college tutor (大学导师的)个别指导时间，辅导课 • **adjective** relating to a tutor 导师的；私人教师的

tutu /ˈtuːtuː/ **noun** a female ballet dancer's very short, stiff skirt that sticks out from the waist 芭蕾舞裙

tuxedo /tʌkˈsiːdəʊ/ **noun** (plural **tuxedos** or **tuxedoes**) chiefly N. Amer.【主北美】a man's dinner jacket (男子的)晚宴服，无尾礼服

TV /ˌtiː ˈviː/ **abbreviation** television.

twaddle /ˈtwɒdl/ **noun** informal【非正式】silly talk or writing 蠢话；胡说八道；拙劣的文字

twain /tweɪn/ old-fashioned form of TWO.

twang /twæŋ/ **noun 1** a strong ringing sound made by the plucked string of a musical instrument (乐器等的)拨弦声 **2** a distinctive nasal way of speaking (明显的)鼻音 • **verb** make a twang 弹拨；发出拨弦声 ■ **twangy** adjective.

tweak /twiːk/ **verb 1** twist or pull with a small but sharp movement 拧；扭；扯 **2** informal【非正式】improve by making small adjustments 稍微调整 • **noun** an act of tweaking 拧；扭

twee /twiː/ **adjective** Brit.【英】too sentimental or sweet 过分讲究的；矫揉造作的；故作多情的

tweed /twiːd/ **noun** a rough woollen cloth flecked with mixed colours 杂色粗花呢 ■ **tweedy** adjective.

tweet /twiːt/ **noun** the chirp of a small or young bird (小鸟的)啁啾，叽喳 • **verb** make a chirping noise 啁啾，叽叽喳喳叫

tweeter /ˈtwiːtə(r)/ **noun** a loudspeaker that reproduces high frequencies 高频扬声器

tweezers /ˈtwiːzəz/ **plural noun** a small pair of pincers for plucking out hairs and picking up small objects 镊子，小钳子

twelfth /twelfθ/ **ordinal number** being number twelve in a sequence; 12th 第十二

twelve /twelv/ **cardinal number** two more than ten; 12 十二 (Roman numeral 罗马数字: **xii** or **XII**.)

twenty /ˈtwenti/ **cardinal number** (plural **twenties**) ten less than thirty; 20 二十 (Roman numeral 罗马数字: **xx** or **XX**.) □ **twenty-twenty vision** normal vision 正常视力 ■ **twentieth** ordinal number.

twerp /twɜːp/ **noun** informal【非正式】a silly person 笨蛋，蠢人

twice /twaɪs/ **adverb 1** two times 两次，两遍 **2** double in degree or quantity 两倍

twiddle /ˈtwɪdl/ **verb** (**twiddles**, **twiddling**, **twiddled**) fiddle with something in an aimless or nervous way (漫无目的或紧张地)旋弄，摆弄 □ **twiddle your thumbs** have nothing to do 无所事事 ■ **twiddly** adjective.

twig[1] /twɪg/ **noun** a slender woody shoot growing from a branch or stem of a tree or shrub 细枝；嫩枝

twig[2] **verb** (**twigs**, **twigging**, **twigged**) Brit. informal【英，非正式】understand or realize something 明白；意识到

twilight /ˈtwaɪlaɪt/ **noun 1** the soft glowing light from the sky when the sun is below the horizon 暮色；薄暮；曙光；晨曦 **2** a period or state of gradual decline 没落(时期)；衰落(期) ■ **twilit** adjective.

twill /twɪl/ **noun** a fabric with a slightly ridged surface 斜纹织物；斜纹布；哔叽

twin /twɪn/ **noun 1** each of two children born at the same birth 孪生

儿之一；双胞胎之一 **2** a thing that is exactly like another 相似的人(或物) • **adjective** forming or being one of a pair of twins 孪生的；双胞胎的；孪生儿之一的；双胞胎之一的 • **verb** (**twins, twinning, twinned**) link or combine as a pair (使)相连；(使)成对；(使)成双

twine /twaɪn/ noun strong string consisting of strands twisted together 合股绳；麻线 • verb (**twines, twining, twined**) wind round something 缠绕；盘绕

twinge /twɪndʒ/ noun **1** a sudden, sharp pain (一阵)剧痛，刺痛 **2** a brief, sharp pang of emotion (一阵)痛苦，难过

twinkle /ˈtwɪŋkl/ verb (**twinkles, twinkling, twinkled**) **1** shine with a gleam that changes constantly from bright to faint 闪耀；闪烁 **2** (of a person's eyes) sparkle with amusement or liveliness (眼睛因欣喜或快活而)发亮，闪光 • noun a twinkling sparkle or gleam 闪耀；闪烁；闪光 ■ twinkly adjective.

twinset /ˈtwɪnset/ noun a woman's matching cardigan and jumper 女式套装毛衣

twirl /twɜːl/ verb spin quickly and lightly round 轻快地旋转；快速转动 • noun an act of twirling (轻快的)旋转，转动 ■ twirly adjective.

twist /twɪst/ verb **1** bend, curl, or distort 使弯曲；使扭曲 **2** force out of the natural position 使弯曲变形；使扭曲变形；使成畸形 **3** have a winding course 曲折地走(路)；曲折；蜿蜒 **4** deliberately change the meaning of 歪曲；曲解 **5** (**twisted**) unpleasantly abnormal; perverted 怪癖的；反常的；偏执的 • noun **1** an act of twisting 扭转；转动；拧 **2** a thing with a spiral shape 螺旋状物 **3** a new or unexpected development or treatment 转折；(意料不到的)转变 **4** (**the twist**)

a dance with a twisting movement of the body, popular in the 1960s (流行于20世纪60年代的)扭摆舞 □ twist someone's arm informal 【非正式】 forcefully persuade someone to do something 生拉硬拽；强迫(某人)做某事 ■ twister noun.

twit[1] /twɪt/ noun Brit. informal 【英，非正式】 a silly person 傻瓜；笨蛋

twit[2] verb (**twits, twitting, twitted**) informal 【非正式】 tease good-humouredly (善意地)揶揄，戏弄

twitch /twɪtʃ/ verb make a short jerking movement 痉挛；抽搐 • noun a twitching movement 痉挛；抽搐

twitcher /ˈtwɪtʃə(r)/ noun Brit. informal 【英，非正式】 a keen birdwatcher 狂热观鸟者；追鸟族

twitchy /ˈtwɪtʃi/ adjective informal 【非正式】 nervous 紧张的；焦虑不安的

twitter /ˈtwɪtə(r)/ verb (**twitters, twittering, twittered**) **1** (of a bird) make a series of short, high sounds (鸟)啁啾，叽喳 **2** talk rapidly in a nervous or silly way (因紧张而)叽叽喳喳地说，絮絮叨叨的说 • noun a twittering sound 啁啾声；叽叽喳喳声

two /tuː/ cardinal number one less than three; 2 二 (Roman numeral 罗马数字：ii 或 II.) □ put two and two together draw a conclusion from what is known or evident 根据已知(或明显)的情况得出显而易见的结论

two-dimensional having or appearing to have length and breadth but no depth 平面的，二维的；没有深度的 **two-faced** insincere and deceitful 两面派的；虚伪的 **two-time** be unfaithful to a husband, wife, or lover (对情人或配偶)不忠；对…用情不专 ■ two-fold adjective & adverb.

> **! 注意** don't confuse **two** with **to** or **too**: see the note at **to**. 不要混淆 two, to 和too，见词条 to 处注释。

twopence or **tuppence** /ˈtʌpəns/

noun Brit. 【英】 the sum of two pence before decimalization (1971) (1971 年英国采用货币十进制之前使用的) 两便士硬币 ■ **twopenny** (or **tuppenny**) adjective.

twosome /'tuːsəm/ **noun** a set of two people or things 两人一组；两件一套

tycoon /taɪ'kuːn/ **noun** a wealthy, powerful person in business or industry (商界或企业界的)巨头，大亨

tying /'taɪɪŋ/ present participle of TIE.

tyke or **tike** /taɪk/ **noun** informal 【非正式】 a mischievous child 小淘气；小捣蛋鬼

tympani /'tɪmpəni/ ⇒ 见 TIMPANI.

tympanum /'tɪmpənəm/ **noun** (plural **tympanums** or **tympana** /'tɪmpənə/) the eardrum 鼓膜

type /taɪp/ **noun 1** a category of people or things that share particular qualities or features 类型；种类；品种 **2** informal 【非正式】 a person of a particular nature 具有某种特点的人：*a sporty type* 运动型的人 **3** printed characters or letters 印刷文字；(印刷的)字体，字符 ■ **verb** (**types**, **typing**, **typed**) write using a typewriter or computer (用打字机或计算机)打(字) ■ **typist** noun.

typecast /'taɪpkɑːst/ **verb** (**be typecast**) (of an actor) always be cast in the same type of role (演员)重复扮演同一类型角色的，定型的，类型化的

typeface /'taɪpfeɪs/ **noun** a particular design of printed letters or numbers 字体

typescript /'taɪpskrɪpt/ **noun** a typed copy of a written work (打印出的)文稿，打字稿

typeset /'taɪpset/ **verb** (**typeset**, **typesetting**, **typeset**) arrange or generate the data or type for text to be printed 对(待印文本)进行排版 ■ **typesetter** noun.

typewriter /'taɪpraɪtə(r)/ **noun** a machine with keys that are pressed to produce characters similar to printed ones 打字机 ■ **typewriting** noun **typewritten** adjective.

typhoid /'taɪfɔɪd/ **noun** an infectious fever that causes red spots on the chest and severe pain in the intestines 伤寒

typhoon /taɪ'fuːn/ **noun** a tropical storm with very high winds 台风

typhus /'taɪfəs/ **noun** an infectious disease that causes a purple rash, headaches, fever, and usually delirium 斑疹伤寒

typical /'tɪpɪkl/ **adjective 1** having the distinctive qualities of a particular type of person or thing 典型的，有代表性的 **2** characteristic of a particular person or thing 特有的，独特的 ■ **typically** adverb.

typify /'tɪpɪfaɪ/ **verb** (**typifies**, **typifying**, **typified**) be typical of 为…的典型；是…的典范

typo /'taɪpəʊ/ **noun** (plural **typos**) informal 【非正式】 a small error in typed or printed writing 打字(或排印)文稿中的小错误

typography /taɪ'pɒɡrəfi/ **noun 1** the setting and arrangement of printed characters 排印；版式设计 **2** the style and appearance of printed material (印刷)版式 ■ **typographer** noun **typographical** (or **typographic**) adjective.

tyrannical /tɪ'rænɪkl/ **adjective** using power in a cruel or unfair way 暴君的；残暴的；专横的 ■ **tyrannically** adverb.

tyrannize or **tyrannise** /'tɪrənaɪz/ **verb** (**tyrannizes**, **tyrannizing**, **tyrannized**) rule or dominate in a cruel or unfair way 对…施行暴政；专横地对待

tyrannosaurus rex /tɪˌrænə'sɔːrəs 'reks/ **noun** a large meat-eating dinosaur that walked on its strong hind legs 霸王龙(大型食肉恐龙)

tyranny /ˈtɪrəni/ **noun** (plural **tyrannies**) cruel and oppressive government or rule 暴虐；苛政；专制

✔ 拼写指南 one *r*, two *ns* : *tyranny*. *tyranny* 中有一个r和两个n。

tyrant /ˈtaɪrənt/ **noun** a cruel and oppressive ruler 暴君；专制君主

tyre /ˈtaɪə(r)/ (US spelling 【美拼作】 **tire**) **noun** a rubber covering, usually inflated, that fits round a wheel 轮胎

tyro /ˈtaɪrəʊ/ **noun** (plural **tyros**) a beginner or novice 初学者；新手

tzar /zɑː(r)/ ⇒ 见 TSAR.

tzatziki /tsæˈtsiːki/ **noun** a Greek side dish of yogurt with cucumber and garlic (希腊的)酸奶黄瓜

Uu

U or **u** /juː/ **noun** (plural **Us** or **U's**) the twenty-first letter of the alphabet 英语字母表的第21个字母 • **abbreviation** Brit. 【英】(in film classification) universal (电影分级)适合各个年龄段观众观看的，U级的 □ **U-boat** a German submarine of the First or Second World War (第一次或第二次世界大战时德国的)U-潜艇 **U-turn 1** the turning of a vehicle in a U-shaped course so as to face the opposite way (车辆的)U形转弯 **2** a complete change in policy (政策的)180度转变

ubiquitous /juːˈbɪkwɪtəs/ **adjective** appearing or found everywhere 普遍存在的；无处不在的 ■ **ubiquitously** adverb **ubiquity** noun.

udder /ˈʌdə(r)/ **noun** the bag-like milk-producing organ of female cattle, sheep, horses, etc. (母牛、母羊、母马等的)乳房，乳

UFO /juː ef ˈəʊ/ **noun** (plural **UFOs**) a mysterious object seen in the sky that some people believe is carrying beings from outer space (short for unidentified flying object) 不明飞行物；飞碟

Ugandan /juːˈɡændən/ **noun** a person from Uganda 乌干达人 • **adjective** relating to Uganda 乌干达的

ugly /ˈʌɡli/ **adjective** (**uglier**, **ugliest**) **1** unpleasant or unattractive in appearance 难看的；丑陋的 **2** hostile or threatening 有敌意的；凶险的 □ **ugly duckling** a person who unexpectedly turns out to be beautiful or talented "丑小鸭" (指出人意料地变得漂亮或才华横溢的人) ■ **ugliness** noun.

UK /juː ˈkeɪ/ **abbreviation** United Kingdom 联合王国；英国

ukulele or **ukelele** /ˌjuːkəˈleɪli/ **noun** a small four-stringed guitar 尤克里里琴(小型四弦琴)

ulcer /ˈʌlsə(r)/ **noun** an open sore on the body or on an internal organ 溃疡 ■ **ulcerated** adjective **ulceration** noun.

ulna /ˈʌlnə/ **noun** (plural **ulnae** /ˈʌlniː/ or **ulnas**) the thinner and longer of the two bones in the human forearm 尺骨

ulterior /ʌlˈtɪəriə(r)/ **adjective** other than what is obvious or admitted 有意隐瞒的；矢口否认的：*She had an ulterior motive.* 她别有用心。

ultimate /ˈʌltɪmət/ **adjective 1** happening at the end of a process 最后的；最终的 **2** being the best or most extreme example of its kind 最好的；绝顶的；终极的 **3** basic or fundamental 基本的；根本的 • **noun** (**the ultimate**) the best of its kind that is imaginable 极品；精华 ■ **ultimately** adverb.

ultimatum /ˌʌltɪˈmeɪtəm/ **noun** a final warning that action will be taken against you if you do not agree to another party's demands 最后通牒

ultramarine /ˌʌltrəməˈriːn/ **noun** a brilliant deep blue colour or pigment 群青色(颜料)；佛青色(颜料)

ultrasonic /ˌʌltrəˈsɒnɪk/ **adjective** involving sound waves with a frequency above the upper limit of human hearing 超声(波)的；超音速的

ultrasound /ˈʌltrəsaʊnd/ **noun** sound or other vibrations with an ultrasonic frequency, used in medical scans 超声；超声波

ultraviolet /ˌʌltrəˈvaɪələt/ **adjective** (of electromagnetic radiation) having a wavelength just shorter than that of violet light (电磁辐射)紫外的，紫外线的

ululate /'juːljʊleɪt/ **verb** (ululates, ululating, ululated) howl or wail 嚎叫；嗥叫；哀号 ■ **ululation** noun.

umber /'ʌmbə(r)/ **noun** a dark brown or yellowish-brown colour 棕土色

umbilical /ʌm'bɪlɪkl/ **adjective** relating to the navel or umbilical cord 脐的；脐带的 □ **umbilical cord** a flexible tube which connects a developing fetus with the placenta while it is in the womb 脐带

umbilicus /ʌm'bɪlɪkəs/ **noun** the navel 脐

umbra /'ʌmbrə/ **noun** (plural **umbras** or **umbrae** /'ʌmbriː/) the shadow cast by the earth or the moon in an eclipse (发生日食或月食时地球或月球投下的)本影，暗影

umbrage /'ʌmbrɪdʒ/ **noun** (**take umbrage**) take offence; become annoyed 生气；不快

umbrella /ʌm'brelə/ **noun** a folding device used as protection against rain 伞；雨伞 •**adjective** including or containing many different parts 包含许多不同部分的

umlaut /'ʊmlaʊt/ **noun** a mark (¨) placed over a vowel in some languages to indicate how it should sound (加在元音上的)变音符

umpire /'ʌmpaɪə(r)/ **noun** (in certain sports) an official who supervises a game to make sure that players keep to the rules (某些体育运动中的)裁判 •**verb** (umpires, umpiring, umpired) be the umpire of 担任…的裁判

umpteen /ʌmp'tiːn/ **cardinal number** informal 【非正式】very many 许多；无数；大量 ■ **umpteenth** ordinal number.

UN /juː 'en/ **abbreviation** United Nations 联合国

unabashed /ˌʌnə'bæʃt/ **adjective** not embarrassed or ashamed 不害臊的；不怕羞的

unabated /ˌʌnə'beɪtɪd/ **adjective** not reduced in intensity or strength 不减弱的；不减退的

unable /ʌn'eɪbl/ **adjective** not able to do something 不会的；不能的

unacceptable /ˌʌnək'septəbl/ **adjective** not satisfactory or allowable 不合意的；不能允许的 ■ **unacceptably** adverb.

unaccountable /ˌʌnə'kaʊntəbl/ **adjective 1** unable to be explained 无法解释的；难以说明的 **2** not having to explain your actions or decisions 无须解释的；不负责任的 ■ **unaccountably** adverb.

unaccustomed /ˌʌnə'kʌstəmd/ **adjective 1** not usual 不寻常的 **2** (unaccustomed to) not familiar with or used to 不熟悉的；不习惯的

unadulterated /ˌʌnə'dʌltəreɪtɪd/ **adjective** not mixed with any different or extra elements 未掺杂的；无杂质的

unaided /ʌn'eɪdɪd/ **adjective** without any help 独力的；无助的

unalloyed /ˌʌnə'lɔɪd/ **adjective** complete; total 完全的；十足的：*unalloyed delight* 纯粹的快乐

unambiguous /ˌʌnæm'bɪgjuəs/ **adjective** not open to more than one interpretation 不含糊的；明确的；切的 ■ **unambiguously** adverb.

unanimous /juː'nænɪməs/ **adjective 1** fully in agreement 一致同意的；无异议的 **2** (of an opinion, decision, or vote) held or carried by everyone involved (意见、决定或投票)全体一致的 ■ **unanimity** noun **unanimously** adverb.

unannounced /ˌʌnə'naʊnst/ **adjective** without warning or notice 未通知的，未通告的

unappetizing or **unappetising** /ʌn'æpɪtaɪzɪŋ/ **adjective** not inviting or attractive 引不起食欲的；索然无味

的；无吸引力的

unapproachable /ˌʌnə'prəʊtʃəbl/ **adjective** not welcoming or friendly 不欢迎的；不友好的

unarguable /ʌn'ɑːgjuəbl/ **adjective** not able to be disagreed with 不容争辩的；无可辩驳的 ■ **unarguably** adverb.

unarmed /ʌn'ɑːmd/ **adjective** not equipped with or carrying weapons 未武装的；无武器的

unassailable /ˌʌnə'seɪləbl/ **adjective** unable to be attacked, questioned, or defeated 难以攻击的；不容置疑的；无懈可击的

unassuming /ˌʌnə'sjuːmɪŋ/ **adjective** not drawing attention to yourself or your abilities 不招摇的；谦逊的

unattached /ˌʌnə'tætʃt/ **adjective** without a husband or wife or established lover 单身的；未婚的；无确定伴侣的

unattended /ˌʌnə'tendɪd/ **adjective** not being supervised or looked after 无人看管的；无人照料的

unauthorized or **unauthorised** /ʌn'ɔːθəraɪzd/ **adjective** not having official permission or approval 未经批准的；未经许可的

unavailing /ˌʌnə'veɪlɪŋ/ **adjective** achieving little or nothing 一事无成的；徒劳的

unavoidable /ˌʌnə'vɔɪdəbl/ **adjective** not able to be avoided or prevented 不可避免的；必然的 ■ **unavoidably** adverb.

unaware /ˌʌnə'weə(r)/ **adjective** having no knowledge of a situation or fact 未意识到的；不知道的

unawares /ˌʌnə'weəz/ **adverb** so as to surprise someone; unexpectedly 出其不意地；冷不防地；突然地

unbalanced /ʌn'bælənst/ **adjective** emotionally or mentally disturbed 精神错乱的；情绪失常的

unbearable /ʌn'beərəbl/ **adjective** not able to be endured 无法忍受的；

不能容忍的 ■ **unbearably** adverb.

unbeknown /ˌʌnbɪ'nəʊn/ or **unbeknownst** /ˌʌnbɪ'nəʊnst/ **adjective** (**unbeknown** to) without the knowledge of 未知的；不为…所知的

unbelievable /ˌʌnbɪ'liːvəbl/ **adjective** **1** unlikely to be true 难以置信的；不可思议的 **2** extraordinary 非常的，特别的；非凡的 ■ **unbelievably** adverb.

unbeliever /ˌʌnbɪ'liːvə(r)/ **noun** a person without religious belief 无宗教信仰者

unbending /ʌn'bendɪŋ/ **adjective** unwilling to compromise or change your mind 坚定的；顽固的

unbiased or **unbiassed** /ʌn'baɪəst/ **adjective** showing no prejudice 无偏见的；不偏不倚的，公正的

unbidden /ʌn'bɪdn/ **adjective** without having been invited 未受邀请的；自发的

unborn /ʌn'bɔːn/ **adjective** not yet born 未出生的；未诞生的

unbounded /ʌn'baʊndɪd/ **adjective** having no limits 无边的；无涯的；无限的

unbowed /ʌn'baʊd/ **adjective** not having given in or been defeated 不低头的；不屈服的

unbridgeable /ʌn'brɪdʒəbl/ **adjective** (of a gap or difference between people) not able to be made smaller or less significant (隔阂或差异)无法弥合的，不可逾越的

unbridled /ʌn'braɪdld/ **adjective** uncontrolled 无法控制的；不受约束的；放纵的；*unbridled lust* 无法控制的强烈欲望

unburden /ʌn'bɜːdn/ **verb** (**unburden yourself**) confide in someone about your worries or problems 倾诉；诉苦

uncalled /ʌn'kɔːld/ **adjective** (**uncalled for**) not fair or appropriate; unnecessary 不公允的；不合适的；不必要的

uncanny /ʌn'kæni/ **adjective** (**uncannier, uncanniest**) strange or mysterious 奇怪的；怪异的；神秘的 ■ **uncannily** adverb.

unceasing /ʌnˈsiːsɪŋ/ **adjective** not ceasing; continuous 不停的；连续的；持续的 ■ **unceasingly** adverb.

unceremonious /ˌʌnˌserəˈməʊniəs/ **adjective** rude or abrupt 粗鲁的；唐突的 ■ **unceremoniously** adverb.

uncertain /ʌnˈsɜːtn/ **adjective 1** not known, reliable, or definite 不确知的；不可靠的确定的 **2** not completely confident or sure 不十分自信的；无把握的 □ **in no uncertain terms** clearly and forcefully 清清楚楚地；毫不含糊地 ■ **uncertainly** adverb **uncertainty** noun.

uncharitable /ʌnˈtʃærɪtəbl/ **adjective** unkind or unsympathetic to other people 不仁爱的；无同情心的；冷漠的 ■ **uncharitably** adverb.

uncharted /ʌnˈtʃɑːtɪd/ **adjective** (of an area of land or sea) not mapped or surveyed (陆地或海洋区域)图上未标明的，未经探测的

unchristian /ʌnˈkrɪstʃən/ **adjective 1** not in line with the teachings of Christianity 不合基督教教义的 **2** not generous or fair 心胸狭隘的；不公平的

uncle /ˈʌŋkl/ **noun** the brother of your father or mother or the husband of your aunt 伯父；叔父；舅父；姑父；姨父 □ **Uncle Sam** the United States 美国

unclean /ʌnˈkliːn/ **adjective 1** dirty 肮脏的；不干净的 **2** immoral 不道德的；猥亵的 **3** (of food) forbidden by a religion （食物）(宗教上认为)不洁净的

uncomfortable /ʌnˈkʌmftəbl/ **adjective 1** not physically comfortable (身体)不舒服的 **2** uneasy or awkward 不安的；不自在的；尴尬的 ■ **uncomfortably** adverb.

uncommon /ʌnˈkɒmən/ **adjective 1** out of the ordinary; unusual 不平常的；异乎寻常的 **2** remarkably great 极大的；超出一般的 ■ **uncommonly** adverb.

uncomprehending /ˌʌnˌkɒmprɪˈhendɪŋ/ **adjective** unable to understand something 不理解的；不领会的；不明白的 ■ **uncomprehendingly** adverb.

uncompromising /ʌnˈkɒmprəmaɪzɪŋ/ **adjective** unwilling to compromise 不妥协的；不让步的 ■ **uncompromisingly** adverb.

unconcern /ˌʌnkənˈsɜːn/ **noun** a lack of worry or interest 无忧虑；漠不关心；不感兴趣 ■ **unconcerned** adjective.

unconditional /ˌʌnkənˈdɪʃənl/ **adjective** not subject to any conditions 无条件的；不受条件制约的 ■ **unconditionally** adverb.

unconfined /ˌʌnkənˈfaɪnd/ **adjective 1** not confined to a limited space 未受限制的；自由的 **2** (of joy or excitement) very great (快乐或兴奋)巨大的，强烈的

unconscionable /ʌnˈkɒnʃənəbl/ **adjective** formal 【正式】 not right or reasonable 不合理的；不正当的 ■ **unconscionably** adverb.

unconscious /ʌnˈkɒnʃəs/ **adjective 1** not awake and aware of your surroundings 失去知觉的；神志不清的；无意识的 **2** done or existing without you realizing 下意识的；潜意识的 **3** (**unconscious of**) unaware of 未察觉到的；未意识到的 • **noun** the part of the mind which you are not aware of but which affects behaviour and emotions 潜意识 ■ **unconsciously** adverb **unconsciousness** noun.

unconstitutional /ˌʌnˌkɒnstɪˈtjuːʃənl/ **adjective** not allowed by the constitution of a country or the rules of an organization 违反宪法的；不符合宪法的；不符合章程的 ■ **unconstitutionally** adverb.

unconstrained /ˌʌnkənˈstreɪnd/

adjective not restricted or limited 不受限制的；不受约束的

uncontrollable /ˌʌnkənˈtrəʊləbl/ **adjective** not able to be controlled 无法控制的；控制不住的 ■ **uncontrollably** adverb.

unconventional /ˌʌnkənˈvenʃənl/ **adjective** not fitting in with what is generally done or believed 不依惯例的；不遵循传统的 ■ **unconventionally** adverb.

unconvincing /ˌʌnkənˈvɪnsɪŋ/ **adjective** failing to convince or impress 令人不信服的；未留下印象的 ■ **unconvincingly** adverb.

uncooperative /ˌʌnkəʊˈɒpərətɪv/ **adjective** unwilling to help other people or do what they ask 不合作的；不抱合作态度的

uncoordinated /ˌʌnkəʊˈɔːdɪneɪtɪd/ **adjective 1** clumsy 不协调的；笨拙的 **2** badly organized 组织不善的；不缜密的

uncouth /ʌnˈkuːθ/ **adjective** lacking good manners 无教养的；粗鲁的

uncover /ʌnˈkʌvə(r)/ **verb** (**uncovers, uncovering, uncovered**) **1** remove a cover or covering from 揭开…的盖子；移去…的覆盖物 **2** discover something previously secret or unknown 发现；揭示；揭露

unction /ˈʌŋkʃn/ **noun** formal 【正式】 the smearing of someone with oil or ointment as part of a religious ceremony 敷擦圣油礼 **2** excessive politeness or flattery 虚情假意；奉承拍马

unctuous /ˈʌŋktjuəs/ **adjective** excessively polite or flattering 虚情假意的；奉承拍马的 ■ **unctuously** adverb.

undaunted /ʌnˈdɔːntɪd/ **adjective** not discouraged by difficulty or danger 无畏的；大胆的；勇敢的

undeceive /ˌʌndɪˈsiːv/ **verb** tell someone that an idea or belief is mistaken 使醒悟；使不受蒙蔽

undecided /ˌʌndɪˈsaɪdɪd/ **adjective 1** not having made a decision 犹豫不决的；优柔寡断的 **2** not yet settled or resolved 未定的；未决的

undemonstrative /ˌʌndɪˈmɒnstrətɪv/ **adjective** not tending to express feelings openly 含蓄的；感情不外露的

undeniable /ˌʌndɪˈnaɪəbl/ **adjective** unable to be denied or disputed 不可否认的；无可争辩的；确凿无疑的 ■ **undeniably** adverb.

under /ˈʌndə(r)/ **preposition 1** extending or directly below 在…下面；在…正下方 **2** at a lower level or grade than 次于；低于；在…以下 **3** expressing control by another person 在…控制之下 **4** in accordance with rules 根据，按照(规则) **5** used to express grouping or classification 属于；在…分类中 **6** undergoing a process 在…过程中 **4** in…期间 • **adverb** extending or directly below something 在下面；在正下方 □ **under way 1** having started and making progress 已经开始；正在进行中 **2** (of a boat) moving through the water (小船)在水中前进

underachieve /ˌʌndərəˈtʃiːv/ **verb** (**underachieves, underachieving, underachieved**) do less well than is expected 成绩不佳；未能取得理想成绩

underarm /ˈʌndərɑːm/ **adjective & adverb** done with the arm or hand below shoulder level 低手的(地)；下手的(地)

undercarriage /ˈʌndəkærɪdʒ/ **noun** the wheeled structure which supports an aircraft when it is on the ground (飞机的)起落架

underclass /ˈʌndəklɑːs/ **noun** the lowest social class, consisting of very poor and unemployed people 下层阶级；下层社会

underclothes /ˈʌndəkləʊðz/ **plural noun** underwear 内衣；衬衣

undercoat /ˈʌndəkəʊt/ **noun** a layer of paint applied before the top layer 内涂层;底涂层

undercover /ˌʌndəˈkʌvə(r)/ **adjective & adverb** involving secret work for investigation or spying 从事秘密工作(的),在做卧底(的)

undercurrent /ˈʌndəkʌrənt/ **noun** an underlying feeling or influence (感情或影响的)暗流,潜流

undercut /ˌʌndəˈkʌt/ **verb** (**undercuts, undercutting, undercut**) **1** offer products or services at a lower price than a competitor 以低于(对手)的价格出售(或提供服务);削价竞争 **2** weaken or undermine 削弱;暗中破坏

underdog /ˈʌndədɒg/ **noun** a competitor thought to have little chance of winning a fight or contest (拼斗或竞赛中的)不被看好者

underdone /ˌʌndəˈdʌn/ **adjective** not cooked enough 夹生的;半生不熟的

underdressed /ˌʌndəˈdrest/ **adjective** wearing clothes that are too plain or casual 穿着过分简朴(或随便)的

underestimate verb /ˌʌndərˈestɪmeɪt/ (**underestimates, underestimating, underestimated**) **1** estimate something to be smaller or less important than it really is 对…估计不足;对…估价过低 **2** think of someone as less capable than they really are 低估,轻视(某人) • **noun** /ˌʌndərˈestɪmət/ an estimate that is too low 估价过低;估计不足 ■ **under-estimation noun**.

underfoot /ˌʌndəˈfʊt/ **adverb 1** on the ground 在地上 **2** constantly present and in the way 挡道path;碍手碍脚地

undergarment /ˈʌndəgɑːmənt/ **noun** a piece of underwear 内衣;衬衣

undergo /ˌʌndəˈgəʊ/ **verb** (**undergoes, undergoing, underwent**; past participle **undergone**) experience something unpleasant or difficult 经历,遭遇(令人不快的事或困境)

undergraduate /ˌʌndəˈgrædʒuət/ **noun** a student at a university who has not yet taken a first degree (尚未获得学士学位的)大学生,大学本科生

underground /ˈʌndəgraʊnd/ **adjective & adverb 1** beneath the surface of the ground 在地下(的) **2** in secrecy or hiding 秘密的(地);不公开的(地) • **noun 1** Brit. 【英】an underground railway 地下铁路;地铁 **2** a secret group working against the government or an enemy 地下组织

undergrowth /ˈʌndəgrəʊθ/ **noun** a mass of shrubs and other plants growing closely together 下层灌木丛

underhand /ˌʌndəˈhænd/ **adjective** done in a secret or dishonest way 偷偷摸摸的;秘密的;不光彩的

underlay /ˈʌndəleɪ/ **noun** material laid under a carpet 地毯衬垫

underlie /ˌʌndəˈlaɪ/ **verb** (**underlies, underlying, underlay**; past participle **underlain**) lie or be situated under 位于…之下

underline /ˌʌndəˈlaɪn/ **verb** (**underlines, underlining, underlined**) **1** draw a line under 在…下面画线 **2** emphasize 强调;突出

underling /ˈʌndəlɪŋ/ **noun** disapproving 【贬】a person of lower status 下手;下属;走卒

undermine /ˌʌndəˈmaɪn/ **verb** (**undermines, undermining, undermined**) **1** damage or weaken 损害;削弱 **2** wear away the base or foundation of 侵蚀…的基础(或根基)

underneath /ˌʌndəˈniːθ/ **preposition & adverb 1** situated directly below 在(…)正下方 **2** so as to be concealed by 在(…)掩盖下;在(…)隐藏下 • **noun** the part or side facing towards the ground 底面;底部;下部

underpants /ˈʌndəpænts/ **plural noun** a piece of underwear covering the lower part of the body and having two holes for the legs 内裤;衬裤

underpart /ˈʌndəpɑːt/ **noun** a lower

part 下部

underpass /ˈʌndəpɑːs/ **noun** a road or tunnel passing under another road or a railway 下层通道；地下通道(在另一条道路或铁路下)

underpin /ˌʌndəˈpɪn/ **verb** (**underpins, underpinning, underpinned**) **1** support or form the basis for an argument, claim, etc. 加强（或巩固、构成）(论点、主张等)的基础 **2** support a structure from below 加固…的基础

underplay /ˌʌndəˈpleɪ/ **verb** represent something as being less important than it really is 对…轻描淡写；贬低…的重要性

underprivileged /ˌʌndəˈprɪvəlɪdʒd/ **adjective** not having the same rights or standard of living as the majority of the population 社会地位低下的；生活水平低下的

underrated /ˌʌndəˈreɪtɪd/ **adjective** rated less highly than is deserved 评价过低的；低估的

underscore /ˌʌndəˈskɔː(r)/ **verb** underline 强调；突出

undersea /ˈʌndəsiː/ **adjective** found or situated below the surface of the sea 海底的；海面下的

undersecretary /ˌʌndəˈsekrətri/ **noun** (plural **undersecretaries**) (in the UK) a junior minister or senior civil servant (英国的)副大臣，次长

undersell /ˌʌndəˈsel/ **verb** (**undersells, underselling, undersold**) sell something at a lower price than a competitor 以低于(竞争者)的价格出售；竞价销售

underside /ˈʌndəsaɪd/ **noun** the bottom or lower side or surface of something 底面；下面；下侧

undersigned /ˌʌndəˈsaɪnd/ **noun** formal 【正式】the person or people who have signed the document in question (文件的)签名者，署名人

undersized /ˌʌndəˈsaɪzd/ or **undersize** /ˌʌndəˈsaɪz/ **adjective** of less than the usual size 比一般尺寸小

的；小尺寸的

understaffed /ˌʌndəˈstɑːft/ **adjective** having too few members of staff 人员配备不足的；人手不够的

understand /ˌʌndəˈstænd/ **verb** (**understands, understanding, understood**) **1** know or realize the real or intended meaning or cause of 了解；意识到 **2** know how someone feels or why they behave in a particular way 理解；谅解 **3** interpret or view in a particular way 阐释；以为 **4** believe that something is the case because of information that you have received 推断；猜想

understandable /ˌʌndəˈstændəbl/ **adjective 1** able to be understood 可理解的；可了解的 **2** natural, reasonable, or forgivable 正常的；合理的 ■ **understandably** adverb.

understanding /ˌʌndəˈstændɪŋ/ **noun 1** the ability to understand something 理解力；领悟力 **2** a person's intellect 智力 **3** the way in which a person looks at a situation 判断力；洞察力 **4** sympathetic awareness or tolerance 同情；谅解 **5** an informal or unspoken agreement or arrangement (非正式的)协定；默契 ● **adjective** sympathetically aware of other people's feelings 能谅解的；通情达理的 ■ **understandingly** adverb.

understate /ˌʌndəˈsteɪt/ **verb** (**understates, understating, understated**) represent something as being smaller or less significant than it really is 轻描淡写地陈述 ■ **understatement** noun.

understated /ˌʌndəˈsteɪtɪd/ **adjective** pleasingly subtle 轻描淡写的；低调的

understudy /ˈʌndəstʌdi/ **noun** (plural **understudies**) an actor who learns another's role in order to take their place if necessary 候补演员；替角 ● **verb** (**understudies, understudying, understudied**) be an understudy for 给…当替角

undertake /ˌʌndəˈteɪk/ **verb (undertakes, undertaking, undertook;** past participle **undertaken) 1** begin an activity 着手做;开始进行 **2** formally guarantee or promise 保证;承诺

undertaker /ˈʌndəteɪkə(r)/ **noun** a person whose job is preparing dead bodies for burial or cremation and making arrangements for funerals 丧事承办人;殡仪员

undertaking /ˌʌndəˈteɪkɪŋ/ **noun 1** a formal promise to do something 保证;承诺 **2** a task 任务;工作

undertone /ˈʌndətəʊn/ **noun 1** a subdued or muted tone 低音;低声 **2** an underlying quality or feeling 本质;蕴含的感情

undertow /ˈʌndətəʊ/ **noun** a current under the surface of water 潜流;底流;暗流

underused /ˌʌndəˈjuːzd/ **adjective** not used as much as it could or should be 未充分利用的;使用不当的 ■ **underuse** noun.

underwater /ˌʌndəˈwɔːtə(r)/ **adjective & adverb** situated, happening, or used beneath the surface of the water 在水下(的);在水下使用(的)

underwear /ˈʌndəweə(r)/ **noun** clothing worn under other clothes next to the skin 衬衣;内衣

underweight /ˌʌndəˈweɪt/ **adjective** below a normal or desirable weight 重量不足的;未达到标准(或理想)重量的

underwent /ˌʌndəˈwent/ past of **UNDERGO.**

underwhelmed /ˌʌndəˈwelmd/ **adjective** humorous 【幽默】 not very impressed 未留下深刻印象的

underworld /ˈʌndəwɜːld/ **noun 1** the world of criminals or of organized crime 黑社会 **2** (in myths and legends) the home of the dead, imagined as being under the earth (神话传说中的)

阴间, 地狱

underwrite /ˌʌndəˈraɪt/ **verb (underwrites, underwriting, underwrote;** past participle **underwritten) 1** accept legal responsibility for an insurance policy 承担保险责任 **2** accept financial responsibility for an undertaking 负担…的费用;资助 ■ **underwriter** noun.

undesirable /ˌʌndɪˈzaɪərəbl/ **adjective** harmful, offensive, or unpleasant 有害的;令人不快的;不受欢迎的 • **noun** an unpleasant or offensive person 不良分子;令人讨厌的人;不受欢迎的人

undeterred /ˌʌndɪˈtɜːd/ **adjective** persevering despite setbacks 不气馁的;不灰心丧气的

undeviating /ʌnˈdiːvieɪtɪŋ/ **adjective** constant and steady 始终如一的;不背离的

undies /ˈʌndiz/ **plural noun** informal 【非正式】 pieces of underwear 内衣

undisputed /ˌʌndɪˈspjuːtɪd/ **adjective** not disputed or called into question 无可争辩的;毫无异议的

undistinguished /ˌʌndɪˈstɪŋɡwɪʃt/ **adjective** not particularly good or successful 普通的;平凡的;平庸的

undivided /ˌʌndɪˈvaɪdɪd/ **adjective 1** not divided or broken into parts 未分离的;未分割的 **2** complete; total 完全的;全部的: my undivided attention 专心致志

undo /ʌnˈduː/ **verb (undoes, undoing, undid;** past participle **undone) 1** unfasten or loosen 解开;松开 **2** reverse the effects of something previously done 撤销;消除 **3** formal 【正式】 cause the downfall or ruin of 使垮台;使毁灭

undoing /ʌnˈduːɪŋ/ **noun** formal 【正式】 a person's ruin or downfall 毁灭;垮台;崩溃

undoubted /ʌnˈdaʊtɪd/ **adjective** not questioned or doubted 毋庸置疑的;无可争辩的 ■ **undoubtedly** adverb.

undreamed /ʌnˈdriːmd/ or Brit.【英】 **undreamt** /ʌnˈdriːmt/ adjective (**undreamed of**) not previously thought to be possible 想象不到的; 梦想不到的

undress /ʌnˈdres/ verb 1 (also **get undressed**) take off your clothes 脱 衣 服 2 take the clothes off someone else 脱去(某人)的衣服 • noun formal 【正式】 the state of being naked or only partially clothed 全裸(或半裸) 状态

undue /ʌnˈdjuː/ adjective more than is reasonable or necessary 不合理的; 过度的 ■ **unduly** adverb.

undulate /ˈʌndjuleɪt/ verb (**undulates, undulating, undulated**) 1 move with a smooth wave-like motion 起伏; 起伏 2 have a wavy form or outline 呈波浪形 ■ **undulation** noun.

undying /ʌnˈdaɪɪŋ/ adjective lasting forever 不朽的; 永恒的

unearth /ʌnˈɜːθ/ verb 1 find in the ground by digging 发掘; 掘出 2 discover by investigation or searching 发现; 找到

unearthly /ʌnˈɜːθli/ adjective 1 unnatural or mysterious 非自然的; 神秘的 2 informal 【非正式】 very early and therefore inconvenient or annoying 很早的; 过分早的

unease /ʌnˈiːz/ noun anxiety or discontent 焦虑; 忧虑; 不满

uneasy /ʌnˈiːzi/ adjective (**uneasier, uneasiest**) anxious or uncomfortable 心神不宁的; 忧虑的; 不舒服的 ■ **uneasily** adverb **uneasiness** noun.

unedifying /ʌnˈedɪfaɪɪŋ/ adjective distasteful or unpleasant 令人厌恶的; 使人不快的

unemployable /ˌʌnɪmˈplɔɪəbl/ adjective not having enough skills or qualifications to get paid employment (因缺乏技能或资质不足)不能被雇用的

unemployed /ˌʌnɪmˈplɔɪd/ adjective without a paid job but available to work 未被雇用的; 待业的

unemployment /ˌʌnɪmˈplɔɪmənt/ noun 1 the state of being unemployed 失业(状态) 2 the number or proportion of unemployed people 失业人数; 失业 率

unencumbered /ˌʌnɪnˈkʌmbəd/ adjective not burdened or held back 没有负担的; 没有拖累的; 没有阻碍 的

unending /ʌnˈendɪŋ/ adjective seeming to last forever 永无止境的; 永恒的

unenviable /ʌnˈenvɪəbl/ adjective difficult, undesirable, or unpleasant 艰难的; 不受欢迎的; 令人不快的

unequal /ʌnˈiːkwəl/ adjective 1 not equal 不 相 等 的 2 not fair or even 不平等的; 不公平的; 不对称的 3 (**unequal to**) not having the ability to meet a challenge 无力方面对(挑战) 的 ■ **unequally** adverb.

unequalled /ʌnˈiːkwəld/ (US spelling 【美拼作】 **unequaled**) adjective better or greater than all others 无与 伦比的; 无双的

unequivocal /ˌʌnɪˈkwɪvəkl/ adjective leaving no doubt; unambiguous 毫无 疑问的; 清楚明白的; 毫不含糊的 ■ **unequivocally** adverb.

unerring /ʌnˈɜːrɪŋ/ adjective always right or accurate 一贯正确的; 一贯准 确的 ■ **unerringly** adverb.

uneven /ʌnˈiːvn/ adjective 1 not level or smooth 不平的; 崎岖的 2 not regular or equal 不规则的; 不平 衡的; 不均等的 ■ **unevenly** adverb **unevenness** noun.

uneventful /ˌʌnɪˈventfl/ adjective not marked by interesting or exciting events 平凡的; 平静的 ■ **uneventfully** adverb.

unexceptionable /ˌʌnɪkˈsepʃənəbl/ adjective not able to be objected to, but not particularly new or exciting 无懈可击的; 不新奇的; 不刺激的

unexceptional /ˌʌnɪkˈsepʃənl/

adjective not out of the ordinary; usual 无特色的；平常的；普通的 ■ **unexceptionally** adverb.

unexpected /ˌʌnɪkˈspektɪd/ **adjective** not expected or thought likely to happen 意外的；突如其来的 ■ **unexpectedly** adverb.

unexpurgated /ʌnˈekspəgeɪtɪd/ **adjective** (of a written work) complete and containing all the original material (书面作品)完整的，未经删节的

unfailing /ʌnˈfeɪlɪŋ/ **adjective** reliable or never changing 可信赖的；始终如一的 ■ **unfailingly** adverb.

unfair /ʌnˈfeə(r)/ **adjective** not fair or just 不公正的；不公平的 ■ **unfairly** adverb **unfairness** noun.

unfaithful /ʌnˈfeɪθfl/ **adjective 1** having sex with someone who is not your husband, wife, or usual partner 不贞的；有通奸行为的 **2** disloyal 不忠实的；不忠诚的

unfathomable /ʌnˈfæðəməbl/ **adjective** incapable of being fully understood 高深莫测的；不可理解的

unfavourable /ʌnˈfeɪvərəbl/ (US spelling 【美拼作】 **unfavorable**) **adjective 1** not approving 反对的；不赞成的 **2** not good or likely to lead to success 不利的；有害的 ■ **unfavourably** adverb.

unfazed /ʌnˈfeɪzd/ **adjective** informal 【非正式】 not worried or confused by something unexpected 不惊慌的，镇定的

unfeasible /ʌnˈfiːzəbl/ **adjective** not able to be done or achieved 不切实际的；行不通的 ■ **unfeasibly** adverb.

unfit /ʌnˈfɪt/ **adjective 1** unsuitable 不合适的 **2** not in good physical condition 不健康的；不强健的

unflagging /ʌnˈflæɡɪŋ/ **adjective** not becoming weak or tired 不屈不挠的；不疲倦的

unflappable /ʌnˈflæpəbl/ **adjective** informal 【非正式】 calm in a crisis 沉着冷静的；镇定自若的

unflinching /ʌnˈflɪntʃɪŋ/ **adjective** not afraid or hesitant 不畏缩的；坚定的；不犹豫的 ■ **unflinchingly** adverb.

unfold /ʌnˈfəʊld/ **verb 1** open or spread out from a folded position 展开；打开；摊开 **2** reveal or be revealed (使)展现；(使)呈现；(被)揭露

unforeseen /ʌnfɔːˈsiːn/ **adjective** not anticipated or predicted; unexpected 未预见到的；意料之外的 ■ **unforeseeable** adjective.

✔ 拼写指南 remember the *e* after the r: unforeseen. 记住拼写 unforeseen 中 r 之后的 e。

unforgettable /ˌʌnfəˈɡetəbl/ **adjective** very memorable 难忘的 ■ **unforgettably** adverb.

unforgivable /ˌʌnfəˈɡɪvəbl/ **adjective** so bad as to be unable to be forgiven 不可饶恕的；不可原谅的 ■ **unforgivably** adverb.

unforgiving /ˌʌnfəˈɡɪvɪŋ/ **adjective 1** not willing to forgive 不肯原谅人的；不宽容的 **2** (of conditions) harsh (条件)严苛的，严酷的

unforthcoming /ˌʌnfɔːθˈkʌmɪŋ/ **adjective 1** not willing to give out information 口风紧的；不愿提供消息的 **2** not available when needed 不予人帮助的；不乐于助人的

unfortunate /ʌnˈfɔːtʃənət/ **adjective 1** unlucky 不幸的，倒霉的 **2** regrettable or inappropriate 令人遗憾的；可叹的；不合适的 • **noun** a person who suffers bad luck 不幸的人；倒霉的人 ■ **unfortunately** adverb.

unfounded /ʌnˈfaʊndɪd/ **adjective** having no basis in fact 无事实根据的；站不住脚的

unfurl /ʌnˈfɜːl/ **verb** open something that is rolled or folded 打开，展开(卷起或折起之物)

ungainly /ʌnˈɡeɪnli/ **adjective** clumsy; awkward 不利索的；笨拙的 ■ **ungainliness** noun.

ungodly /ʌnˈgɒdli/ **adjective 1** immoral or disrespectful to God 不敬神的；亵渎神灵的 **2** informal 【非正式】 very early or late, and therefore annoying (因时间过早或过晚)十分不便的

ungovernable /ʌnˈgʌvənəbl/ **adjective** impossible to control or govern 无法控制的；难以治理的

ungrateful /ʌnˈgreɪtfl/ **adjective** not grateful 不领情的；忘恩负义的 ■ **ungratefully** adverb.

unguarded /ʌnˈgɑːdɪd/ **adjective 1** without protection 无保护的；没有防卫的 **2** not well considered; careless 轻率的；不谨慎的；粗心大意的：*an unguarded remark* 轻率的话

unguent /ˈʌŋgwənt/ **noun** a soft greasy or thick substance used as ointment or for lubrication 油膏；软膏；润滑油

ungulate /ˈʌŋgjʊlɪt/ **noun** the name in zoology for a hoofed mammal 有蹄类哺乳动物

unhappy /ʌnˈhæpi/ **adjective** (**unhappier, unhappiest**) **1** not happy 不幸福的；不愉快的；不快乐的 **2** unfortunate 不幸的；倒霉的 ■ **unhappily** adverb **unhappiness** noun.

unharmed /ʌnˈhɑːmd/ **adjective** not harmed 未受伤害的；安然无恙的

unhealthy /ʌnˈhelθi/ **adjective** (**unhealthier, unhealthiest**) **1** not having good health 不健康的；健康状况不佳的 **2** not good for your health 有害健康的 ■ **unhealthily** adverb.

unheard /ʌnˈhɜːd/ **adjective 1** not heard or listened to 未听到的 **2** (**unheard of**) previously unknown 前所未闻的；空前的

unhelpful /ʌnˈhelpfl/ **adjective** not helpful 不愿帮忙的；无用的；无益的 ■ **unhelpfully** adverb.

unheralded /ʌnˈherəldɪd/ **adjective** not previously announced, expected, or recognized 未曾提及的；未预料到的；突如其来的

unhesitating /ʌnˈhezɪteɪtɪŋ/ **adjective** without doubt or hesitation 不迟疑的；不犹豫的；坚定的 ■ **unhesitatingly** adverb.

unhinged /ʌnˈhɪndʒd/ **adjective** mentally ill or unbalanced 精神错乱的；心理失衡的

unholy /ʌnˈhəʊli/ **adjective 1** sinful; wicked 邪恶的；罪恶的 **2** unnatural and likely to be harmful 不正常的；有害的 **3** informal 【非正式】 dreadful 可怕的

unhurried /ʌnˈhʌrid/ **adjective** moving or doing things in a leisurely way 从容不迫的；不慌不忙的 ■ **unhurriedly** adverb.

unhurt /ʌnˈhɜːt/ **adjective** not hurt or harmed 没有受伤的；未受伤害的

unicameral /ˌjuːnɪˈkæmərəl/ **adjective** (of a parliament) consisting of only one main part (议会)一院的，单院的

unicorn /ˈjuːnɪkɔːn/ **noun** (in stories) a creature like a horse with a single long horn on its forehead (传说中的)独角兽(外形像马、前额长有一只角的动物)

unicycle /ˈjuːnɪsaɪkl/ **noun** a cycle with a single wheel 独轮脚踏车 ■ **unicyclist** noun.

unidentified /ˌʌnaɪˈdentɪfaɪd/ **adjective** not recognized or identified 未被认出的；未被识别的；身份不明的

unification /ˌjuːnɪfɪˈkeɪʃn/ **noun** the process of uniting or of being united 联合；统一；一体化

uniform /ˈjuːnɪfɔːm/ **noun** the distinctive clothing worn by members of the same organization or school 制服；校服 • **adjective** not varying; the same in all cases and at all times 无变化的；始终如一的；一律的 ■ **uniformed** adjective **uniformity** noun **uniformly** adverb.

unify /ˈjuːnɪfaɪ/ **verb** (**unifies, unifying, unified**) make or become united (使)成一体；(使)联合；(使)统一

unilateral /ˌjuːnɪˈlætrəl/ **adjective** done by or affecting only one person or group 单方的;单边的 ■ **unilaterally** adverb.

unimaginable /ˌʌnɪˈmædʒɪnəbl/ **adjective** impossible to imagine or understand 不可想象的;不可思议的 ■ **unimaginably** adverb.

unimaginative /ˌʌnɪˈmædʒɪnətɪv/ **adjective** not using or showing imagination or new ideas; dull 缺乏想象力的;无创意的;乏味的 ■ **unimaginatively** adverb.

unimpeachable /ˌʌnɪmˈpiːtʃəbl/ **adjective** not able to be doubted or criticized 无可怀疑的;无可指责的

unimportant /ˌʌnɪmˈpɔːtnt/ **adjective** not important 不重要的;微不足道的 ■ **unimportance** noun.

uninhabited /ˌʌnɪnˈhæbɪtɪd/ **adjective** having no people living there 杳无人迹的;无人居住的 ■ **uninhabitable** adjective.

uninhibited /ˌʌnɪnˈhɪbɪtɪd/ **adjective** saying or doing things without concern about what other people think 无拘无束的;随心所欲的

uninitiated /ˌʌnɪˈnɪʃieɪtɪd/ **adjective** without knowledge or experience of something 外行的;缺乏专门知识(或经验)的

uninspired /ˌʌnɪnˈspaɪəd/ **adjective** **1** not original or exciting; dull 无创意的,无生气的;乏味的 **2** feeling no excitement 没有生气的;沉闷的 ■ **uninspiring** adjective.

unintelligible /ˌʌnɪnˈtelɪdʒəbl/ **adjective** impossible to understand 不可理解的;晦涩难懂的 ■ **unintelligibility** noun **unintelligibly** adverb.

unintentional /ˌʌnɪnˈtenʃənl/ **adjective** not done on purpose 非故意的;非存心的 ■ **unintentionally** adverb.

uninterested /ʌnˈɪntrəstɪd/ **adjective** not interested or concerned 不感兴趣的;不关心的;漠然的

! **注意** don't confuse **uninterested** and **disinterested**. **Disinterested** means 'impartial', while **uninterested** means 'not interested'. 不要混淆 **uninterested** 和 **disinterested**, **disinterested** 意为 "不偏不倚的", 而 **uninterested** 意为 "不感兴趣的"。

uninterrupted /ˌʌnɪntəˈrʌptɪd/ **adjective** not interrupted; continuous 连续不断的;不间断的

union /ˈjuːniən/ **noun** **1** the act of uniting two or more things 结合;联合;合并 **2** a trade union 工会 **3** a club, society, or association 俱乐部;协会;社团 **4** (also **Union**) a political unit consisting of a number of states or provinces with the same central government 联邦;联盟 **5** a state of harmony or agreement 和谐;一致;融洽 **6** a marriage 结婚;婚姻 □ **Union Jack** (or **Union Flag**) the national flag of the United Kingdom 联合王国国旗;英国国旗

unionist /ˈjuːniənɪst/ **noun** **1** a member of a trade union 工会会员 **2** (**Unionist**) a person in favour of the union of Northern Ireland with Great Britain 统一派(支持北爱尔兰仍为英国一部分)

unionize or **unionise** /ˈjuːniənaɪz/ **verb** (**unionizes**, **unionizing**, **unionized**) make or become members of a trade union (使)成为工会成员;(使)加入工会 ■ **unionization** noun.

unique /juːˈniːk/ **adjective** **1** being the only one of its kind 独一无二的;唯一的 **2** (**unique to**) belonging or connected to one particular person, group, or place (某人、某群体或某地)特有的,独具的 **3** very special or unusual 非常特殊的;极不寻常的 ■ **uniquely** adverb.

unisex /ˈjuːnɪseks/ **adjective** designed to be suitable for both sexes 男女皆宜的;不分男女的

unison /ˈjuːnɪsn/ **noun (in unison)** at the same time; together 一起；共同

unit /ˈjuːnɪt/ **noun 1** a single thing or group that is complete in itself but can also form part of something larger 单位；单元 **2** a device, part, or item of furniture with a particular function 部件；构件：*a sink unit* 洗涤台 **3** a self-contained section of a building or group of buildings (大楼的)单元；楼区 **4** a subdivision of a larger military grouping (军队的)小队，分队 **5** a quantity used as a standard measure (作为计量标准的)单位 □ **unit trust** Brit.【英】a company that invests money in various different businesses on behalf of individuals, who can buy small units 单位信托投资公司

Unitarian /ˌjuːnɪˈteəriən/ **noun** a member of a Christian Church that believes that God is one being and rejects the idea of the Trinity 神体一位派基督徒(不信仰三位一体)

unitary /ˈjuːnɪtəri/ **adjective 1** forming a single unit or entity 单一的；个体的 **2** relating to a unit or units 单位的；单元的

unite /juːˈnaɪt/ **verb (unites, uniting, united) 1** join together with others in order to do something as a group (使)联合 **2** bring people or things together to form a unit or whole (使)统一；(使)团结 ■ **united** adjective.

unity /ˈjuːnəti/ **noun (plural unities) 1** the state of being united or forming a whole 联合；团结；统一 **2** a thing forming a complex whole 统一体；整体 **3** Maths【数学】the number one (数字)一

universal /ˌjuːnɪˈvɜːsl/ **adjective 1** affecting or done by all people or things in the world or in a particular group 全体的；全世界的；共同的 **2** true or right in all cases 万有的；普遍适用的 ■ **universality** noun **universally** adverb.

universe /ˈjuːnɪvɜːs/ **noun** the whole of space and everything in it 宇宙；天地万物；万象

university /ˌjuːnɪˈvɜːsəti/ **noun (plural universities)** an institution where students study for a degree, and where academic research is done (综合性)大学

unjust /ʌnˈdʒʌst/ **adjective** not just; unfair 不公平的；不合理的；不公正的 ■ **unjustly** adverb.

unjustifiable /ʌnˈdʒʌstɪfaɪəbl/ **adjective** impossible to justify 无法证明正确的；不合理的 ■ **unjustifiably** adverb.

unjustified /ʌnˈdʒʌstɪfaɪd/ **adjective** not justified; unfair 未证明正确的；不合理的

unkempt /ʌnˈkempt/ **adjective** having an untidy appearance 不整洁的；凌乱的

unkind /ʌnˈkaɪnd/ **adjective** not caring or kind 无同情心的；不和蔼的；刻薄的 ■ **unkindly** adverb **unkindness** noun.

unknowing /ʌnˈnəʊɪŋ/ **adjective** not knowing or aware 不知道的；没察觉的 ■ **unknowingly** adverb.

unknown /ʌnˈnəʊn/ **adjective** not known or familiar 未知的；不熟悉的；陌生的 • **noun** an unknown person or thing 无名者；未知的人(或事物) □ **unknown quantity** a person or thing that is not known about and whose actions or effects are unpredictable 未知数(指行为或效果不可预测的人或事物) **Unknown Soldier** an unidentified member of a country's armed forces killed in war, buried in a national memorial to represent all those killed but unidentified 无名战士

unladylike /ʌnˈleɪdilaɪk/ **adjective** not typical of a well-mannered woman or girl (女子)不端庄的，不娴雅的

unlawful /ʌnˈlɔːfl/ **adjective** not

obeying or allowed by law or rules
违法的;非法的;不法的 ■ **unlawfully**
adverb.

unleaded /ʌnˈledɪd/ **adjective** (of
petrol) without added lead (汽油)无
铅的

unleash /ʌnˈliːʃ/ **verb** release
something from a leash or restraint;
set free 放开;释放

unleavened /ʌnˈlevnd/ **adjective**
(of bread) flat because made without
yeast (面包)未发酵的,未用酵母的

unless /ənˈles/ **conjunction** except
when; if not 除非;若非

unlike /ʌnˈlaɪk/ **preposition 1**
different from; not like 和…不同,
不像 **2** in contrast to 和…形成对比
3 not characteristic of 非…的特点
■ **adjective** different from each other
相异的;彼此不同的

unlikely /ʌnˈlaɪkli/ **adjective**
(unlikelier, unlikeliest) **1** not likely
to happen 不大可能的 **2** not what you
would expect 未必的 ■ **unlikelihood**
noun.

unlimited /ʌnˈlɪmɪtɪd/ **adjective** not
limited or restricted 无限制的;无约
束的

unload /ʌnˈləʊd/ **verb** remove goods
from a vehicle, ship, aircraft, or
container (从车辆、船只、飞机或容器
等)卸下,取下(货物)

unlock /ʌnˈlɒk/ **verb** undo the lock of
a door, container, etc. using a key 用
钥匙开(门、容器等)的锁

unlooked /ʌnˈlʊkt/ **adjective**
(unlooked for) not planned or
expected 未计划的;意外的

unloose /ʌnˈluːs/ or **unloosen**
/ʌnˈluːsn/ **verb** (unlooses, unloosing,
unloosed) release something 解开;
松开;释放

unlucky /ʌnˈlʌki/ **adjective** (unluckier,
unluckiest) having, bringing, or
resulting from bad luck 不幸的;倒霉
的 ■ **unluckily** adverb.

unmade /ʌnˈmeɪd/ **adjective** Brit.【英】

(of a road) without a hard, smooth
surface (道路)未铺硬化路面的

unmanageable /ʌnˈmænɪdʒəbl/
adjective difficult or impossible to
manage or control 难管理的;无法控
制的

unmanned /ʌnˈmænd/ **adjective** not
having or needing a crew or staff 无
人的;无人驾驶的

unmarked /ʌnˈmɑːkt/ **adjective 1** not
marked 无记号的;没有标志的 **2** not
noticed 未注意到的

unmarried /ʌnˈmærid/ **adjective** not
married 未婚的;独身的

unmask /ʌnˈmɑːsk/ **verb** reveal the
true character of 使露出真面目;揭露

unmatched /ʌnˈmætʃt/ **adjective** not
matched or equalled 不相配的;无与
伦比的

unmentionable /ʌnˈmenʃənəbl/
adjective too embarrassing or
shocking to be spoken about 不宜提
及的;说不出口的

unmerciful /ʌnˈmɜːsɪfl/ **adjective**
showing no mercy 不仁慈的;冷酷无
情的 ■ **unmercifully** adverb.

unmetalled /ʌnˈmetld/ **adjective** Brit.
【英】(of a road) not having a hard
surface (道路)无硬化路面的

unmindful /ʌnˈmaɪndfl/ **adjective**
(unmindful of) not conscious or
aware of 不注意的;未意识到的

unmissable /ʌnˈmɪsəbl/ **adjective**
that should not or cannot be missed
不应错过的;不可忽略的

unmistakable or **unmistakeable**
/ˌʌnmɪˈsteɪkəbl/ **adjective** not able to
be mistaken for anything else 不会弄
错的 ■ **unmistakably** adverb.

unmitigated /ʌnˈmɪtɪɡeɪtɪd/ **adjective**
complete 全然的;十足的: *an un-
mitigated disaster* 彻头彻尾的灾难

unmoved /ʌnˈmuːvd/ **adjective** not
affected by emotion or excitement
无动于衷的;平静的;冷静的

unnameable /ʌnˈneɪməbl/ **adjective**
too bad or frightening to mention 不

宜提及的；说不出口的

unnatural /ʌnˈnætʃrəl/ **adjective**
1 different from what is found in
nature or what is normal in society
反自然的；与自然相异的 **2** not
spontaneous 反常的；怪异的 ■ **unnaturally** adverb.

unnecessary /ʌnˈnesəsəri/ **adjective**
not necessary, or more than is
necessary 不必要的；多余的 ■ **unnecessarily** adverb.

unnerve /ʌnˈnɜːv/ **verb** (**unnerves,
unnerving, unnerved**) make
someone feel fearful or lacking in
confidence 使恐惧；使心慌意乱

unnoticeable /ʌnˈnəʊtɪsəbl/
adjective not easily seen or noticed
不易发现的；不易察觉的

unnoticed /ʌnˈnəʊtɪst/ **adjective** not
being or having been seen or noticed
未被察觉的；被忽视的

unobtainable /ʌnəbˈteɪnəbl/
adjective not able to be obtained 弄
不到的；难获得的

unobtrusive /ʌnəbˈtruːsɪv/ **adjective**
not conspicuous or attracting
attention 不显眼的；不引人注目的
■ **unobtrusively** adverb.

unofficial /ʌnəˈfɪʃl/ **adjective** not
officially authorized or confirmed 未
经官方批准(或证实)的 ■ **unofficially**
adverb.

unopposed /ʌnəˈpəʊzd/ **adjective**
not opposed or challenged 未遭到反
对的；未受到挑战的

unorthodox /ʌnˈɔːθədɒks/ **adjective**
different from what is usual,
traditional, or accepted 非正统的；非
传统的；异端的

unpack /ʌnˈpæk/ **verb** take things out
of a suitcase, bag, or package 打开
(手提箱、袋子或包裹)取出东西

unpaid /ʌnˈpeɪd/ **adjective 1** (of a
debt) not yet paid (债务)未偿的，未付
的 **2** done without payment 无偿的 **3**
not receiving payment for work done
(工作)没有报酬的，不支付薪水的

unpalatable /ʌnˈpælətəbl/ **adjective**
1 not pleasant to taste 不好吃的；不
可口的 **2** difficult to accept 难以接
受的；不合意的

unparalleled /ʌnˈpærəleld/ **adjective**
having no equal; exceptional 无比的；
无双的；非凡的

unpardonable /ʌnˈpɑːdnəbl/
adjective (of a fault or offence)
unforgivable (过错或罪行)不可宽
恕的，不可原谅的 ■ **unpardonably**
adverb.

unperturbed /ʌnpəˈtɜːbd/ **adjective**
not concerned or worried about
something 不担忧的；泰然自若的

unpick /ʌnˈpɪk/ **verb 1** undo the
sewing of stitches or a garment 拆
去(缝线、针脚)；拆去(衣服)上的缝
线(或针脚) **2** carefully analyse the
different elements of something 仔细
分析…的不同要素

unpleasant /ʌnˈpleznt/ **adjective 1**
not pleasant or comfortable 令人不快
的；不舒服的 **2** not friendly or kind
不友好的；不亲切的 ■ **unpleasantly**
adverb **unpleasantness** noun.

unplug /ʌnˈplʌg/ **verb** (**unplugs,
unplugging, unplugged**) disconnect
an electrical device from a socket 拔
去(电器)的电源插头

unpopular /ʌnˈpɒpjələ(r)/ **adjective**
not liked or popular 不受欢迎的；不
流行的 ■ **unpopularity** noun.

unprecedented /ʌnˈpresɪdentɪd/
adjective never done or known before
无先例的；空前的；前所未闻的

unpredictable /ʌnprɪˈdɪktəbl/
adjective not able to be predicted;
changeable 不可预测的；无法预言
的；多变的 ■ **unpredictability** noun
unpredictably adverb.

unprejudiced /ʌnˈpredʒədɪst/
adjective without prejudice; unbiased
无偏见的；无成见的；公正的

unpremeditated /ʌnpriːˈmedɪteɪtɪd/
adjective not planned beforehand 未
预先计划的

unprepared /ˌʌnprɪˈpeəd/ **adjective** not ready or able to deal with something 无准备的

unprepossessing /ˌʌnpriːpəˈzesɪŋ/ **adjective** not attractive or interesting 不吸引人的；无趣的

unprincipled /ʌnˈprɪnsəpld/ **adjective** without moral principles 不道德的；不正直的

unprintable /ʌnˈprɪntəbl/ **adjective** (of words or comments) too rude or offensive to be published (言语或评论)不可刊印的

unproductive /ˌʌnprəˈdʌktɪv/ **adjective** 1 not able to produce the required quantity of goods or crops 不多产的；不丰饶的 2 not achieving much; not very useful 成效不大的；徒劳的

unprofessional /ˌʌnprəˈfeʃənl/ **adjective** not in accordance with professional standards or behaviour 违反职业道德的；不符合职业行为规范的 ■ **unprofessionally** adverb.

unprofitable /ʌnˈprɒfɪtəbl/ **adjective** 1 not making a profit 无利可图的 2 not helpful or useful 无益的；无用的

unprompted /ʌnˈprɒmptɪd/ **adjective** without being prompted; spontaneous 自发的；自动的

unpronounceable /ˌʌnprəˈnaʊnsəbl/ **adjective** too difficult to pronounce 难发音的

unproven /ʌnˈpruːvn/ or **unproved** /ʌnˈpruːvd/ **adjective** not proved or tested 未经证实的；未经检验的

unprovoked /ˌʌnprəˈvəʊkt/ **adjective** (of an attack or crime) not directly provoked (攻击或犯罪)未受挑衅的，无端的

unqualified /ʌnˈkwɒlɪfaɪd/ **adjective** 1 not having the necessary qualifications or requirements 无资格的；不合格的；不胜任的 2 complete 绝对的；全然的

unquantifiable /ˌʌnkwɒntɪˈfaɪəbl/ **adjective** impossible to express or measure in terms of quantity 无法计量的；不可测量的

unquestionable /ʌnˈkwestʃənəbl/ **adjective** not able to be denied or doubted 无可否认的；无可置疑的 ■ **unquestionably** adverb.

unquestioned /ʌnˈkwestʃənd/ **adjective** not denied or doubted 不被否认的；不被怀疑的

unravel /ʌnˈrævl/ **verb** (unravels, unravelling, unravelled; US spelling 【美拼作】unravels, unraveling, unraveled) 1 undo twisted, knitted, or woven threads 拆开，解开(扭结或编织的线) 2 (of threads) become undone (线)解开，松开 3 solve a mystery or puzzle 解开(谜或难题)

unreadable /ʌnˈriːdəbl/ **adjective** 1 not clear enough to read 难以辨认的；模糊不清的 2 too dull or difficult to be worth reading 无可读性的；难读的

unreal /ʌnˈrɪəl/ **adjective** 1 strange and not seeming real 离奇的；奇异的 2 not related to reality; unrealistic 不真实的；虚构的；不现实的 ■ **unreality** noun.

unrealistic /ˌʌnrɪəˈlɪstɪk/ **adjective** 1 not showing things in a way that is accurate and true to life 非现实的 2 not having a sensible understanding of what can be achieved 不切实际的 ■ **unrealistically** adverb.

unreasonable /ʌnˈriːznəbl/ **adjective** 1 not based on good sense 不理性的；缺乏理智的 2 beyond what is achievable or acceptable 过分的；无法接受的 ■ **unreasonably** adverb.

unrecognizable or **unrecognisable** /ˌʌnrekəɡˈnaɪzəbl/ **adjective** not able to be recognized 认不出的；不能识别的

unrelenting /ˌʌnrɪˈlentɪŋ/ **adjective** 1 not stopping or becoming less severe 持续的；严厉的；冷酷的 2 not giving in to requests 不退让的；不屈服的 ■ **unrelentingly** adverb.

unreliable /ˌʌnrɪˈlaɪəbl/ **adjective** not able to be relied on 不可靠的；不可信赖的 ■ **unreliability** noun **unreliably** adverb.

unrelieved /ˌʌnrɪˈliːvd/ **adjective** lacking variation or change 无变化的；单调的

unremarkable /ˌʌnrɪˈmɑːkəbl/ **adjective** not particularly interesting or surprising 平凡的；不出色的；不显著的

unremitting /ˌʌnrɪˈmɪtɪŋ/ **adjective** never stopping or easing 不松懈的；不放松的

unrepeatable /ˌʌnrɪˈpiːtəbl/ **adjective** **1** not able to be repeated 不能重复的 **2** too offensive or shocking to be said again 粗俗难听的；再说不出口的

unrepentant /ˌʌnrɪˈpentənt/ **adjective** showing no shame or regret for your actions 不悔悟的；不悔改的

unrequited /ˌʌnrɪˈkwaɪtɪd/ **adjective** (of love) not given in return (爱)无回报的，单相思的

unreserved /ˌʌnrɪˈzɜːvd/ **adjective** **1** without any doubts or reservations 无怀疑的；无保留的 **2** not set apart or booked in advance 非保留的；未预订的 ■ **unreservedly** adverb.

unrest /ʌnˈrest/ **noun** **1** a situation in which people are feeling discontented and rebellious 不满 **2** a state of uneasiness 不安宁；动荡

unrivalled /ʌnˈraɪvld/ (US spelling【美拼作】**unrivaled**) **adjective** greater or better than all others 无比的；无双的

unroll /ʌnˈrəʊl/ **verb** open out something that is rolled up 铺开，展开(卷起之物)

unruffled /ʌnˈrʌfld/ **adjective** calm and undisturbed 泰然自若的；沉着的；平静的

unruly /ʌnˈruːli/ **adjective** (**unrulier**, **unruliest**) difficult to control; disorderly 难控制的；不守秩序的 ■ **unruliness** noun.

unsafe /ʌnˈseɪf/ **adjective** **1** not safe; dangerous 不安全的；危险的 **2** (of a decision in a court of law) not based on good evidence (法庭裁决)证据不足的，缺乏确凿证据的

unsatisfactory /ˌʌnsætɪsˈfæktəri/ **adjective** not good enough 不能令人满意的；差强人意的 ■ **unsatisfactorily** adverb.

unsaturated /ʌnˈsætʃəreɪtɪd/ **adjective** Chemistry【化学】(of fats) having double or triple bonds between carbon atoms in their molecules and therefore being more easily processed by the body (脂肪)不饱和的

unsavoury /ʌnˈseɪvəri/ (US spelling【美拼作】**unsavory**) **adjective** **1** unpleasant to taste, smell, or look at 难吃的；难闻的；难看的 **2** not respectable 品德败坏的；不道德的

unscathed /ʌnˈskeɪðd/ **adjective** without suffering any injury, damage, or harm 未受伤的；未受损的

unschooled /ʌnˈskuːld/ **adjective** lacking schooling or training 未受过学校教育的；未受过训练的

unscientific /ˌʌnsaɪənˈtɪfɪk/ **adjective** not using proper scientific methods 不科学的 ■ **unscientifically** adverb.

unscrew /ʌnˈskruː/ **verb** unfasten something by twisting it or undoing screws 旋出卸下；拧松

unscrupulous /ʌnˈskruːpjələs/ **adjective** without moral principles; dishonest or unfair 无道德原则的；无耻的；不公正的 ■ **unscrupulously** adverb.

unseasonable /ʌnˈsiːznəbl/ **adjective** (of weather) unusual for the time of year (天气)反常的，不合季节的 ■ **unseasonably** adverb.

unseasonal /ʌnˈsiːzənl/ **adjective** unusual or inappropriate for the time of year 不合时令(或季节)的

unseat /ʌnˈsiːt/ **verb** **1** make someone fall from a saddle or seat 使从马鞍(或座位)上摔下 **2** remove someone from a position of power 使下台(或退位，退职)

unseeing /ʌnˈsiː ɪŋ/ **adjective** having your eyes open but not noticing anything 视而不见的

unseemly /ʌnˈsiːmli/ **adjective** (of behaviour or actions) not proper or appropriate (行为或行动)不妥当的，不适宜的

unseen /ʌnˈsiːn/ **adjective 1** not seen or noticed 未被看见的；未被觉察的 **2** (of a passage for translation in an exam) not previously read or prepared (考试中的翻译段落)未读过的，事先无准备的

unselfconscious /ˌʌnselfˈkɒnʃəs/ **adjective** not selfconscious; not shy or embarrassed 不扭捏的；不拘束的；自然的 ■ **unselfconsciously** adverb.

unselfish /ʌnˈselfɪʃ/ **adjective** putting other people's needs before your own 不自私的；无私(心)的 ■ **unselfishly** adverb.

unserviceable /ʌnˈsɜːvɪsəbl/ **adjective** not in working order; unfit for use 不能使用的；不适用的

unsettle /ʌnˈsetl/ **verb** (**unsettles, unsettling, unsettled**) make someone anxious or uneasy 使不安；扰乱

unsettled /ʌnˈsetld/ **adjective 1** frequently changing, or likely to change 不稳定的；易变的 **2** anxious or uneasy 不安的；心神不宁的 **3** not yet resolved 悬而未决的；尚未解决的

unshakeable or **unshakable** /ʌnˈʃeɪkəbl/ **adjective** (of a belief or feeling) firm and unable to be changed (信仰或感情)坚定不移的，不可动摇的

unshaven /ʌnˈʃeɪvn/ **adjective** not having shaved 未剃须的；未修面的；未刮脸的

unsightly /ʌnˈsaɪtli/ **adjective** unpleasant to look at; ugly 不悦目的；难看的；丑陋的

unskilled /ʌnˈskɪld/ **adjective** not having or needing special skill or training 不熟练的；未受专门训练的；无需(特殊)技能(或训练)的

unsociable /ʌnˈsəʊʃəbl/ **adjective** not enjoying the company of other people 不爱交际的；不善交际的；不合群的

unsocial /ʌnˈsəʊʃl/ **adjective** (of hours of work) not falling within the normal working day (工作时间)正常工作日以外的，加班的

unsolicited /ˌʌnsəˈlɪsɪtɪd/ **adjective** not asked for 未经请求的

unsophisticated /ˌʌnsəˈfɪstɪkeɪtɪd/ **adjective 1** not having much experience in matters of culture or fashion 阅历浅的；不谙世故的 **2** not complicated or highly developed; basic 不复杂的；简单的；基本的

unsound /ʌnˈsaʊnd/ **adjective 1** not safe or strong; in bad condition 不安全的；不牢固的；情况不佳的 **2** not based on reliable evidence or reasoning 无根据的；不合逻辑的

unsparing /ʌnˈspeərɪŋ/ **adjective 1** very severe or harsh 严厉的；无情的 **2** giving generously 慷慨的

unspeakable /ʌnˈspiːkəbl/ **adjective** too bad or horrific to express in words 不堪入耳的；恐怖得无法形容的 ■ **unspeakably** adverb.

unspoilt or **unspoiled** /ʌnˈspɔɪlt/ **adjective** (of a place) beautiful because it has not been changed or built on (场所)未丧失原有自然美的，未受破坏的

unstable /ʌnˈsteɪbl/ **adjective 1** likely to fall or collapse 可能失败的；可能崩溃的 **2** likely to change; unsettled 易变的；动荡不定的；不稳当的 **3** tending to experience mental health problems or sudden changes of mood (情绪等)不稳定的，多变的，波动的

unsteady /ʌnˈstedi/ **adjective 1** liable to fall or shake; not firm 不稳固的；摇晃的；不坚固的 **2** not uniform or even 无规律的；反复无常的 ■ **unsteadily** adverb.

unstick /ʌnˈstɪk/ **verb (unsticks, unsticking, unstuck)** separate things that have been stuck together 扯开，松开(粘着的东西) □ **come unstuck** informal 【非正式】 fail 失败

unstinting /ʌnˈstɪntɪŋ/ **adjective** given or giving freely or generously 无限制的；慷慨的

unsuccessful /ˌʌnsəkˈsesfl/ **adjective** not successful 不成功的；失败的 ■ **unsuccessfully** adverb.

unsuitable /ʌnˈsuːtəbl/ **adjective** not right or appropriate for a particular purpose or occasion 不适当的；不适宜的；不相称的 ■ **unsuitability** noun **unsuitably** adverb.

unsung /ˌʌnˈsʌŋ/ **adjective** not celebrated or praised 未被歌颂的；未受赞美的

unsure /ʌnˈʃʊə(r)/ **adjective** having doubts about something; not certain 有疑虑的；不确定的

unsurpassed /ˌʌnsəˈpɑːst/ **adjective** better or greater than any other 超群的；无与伦比的

unsurprising /ˌʌnsəˈpraɪzɪŋ/ **adjective** expected and so not causing surprise 意料之中的；不令人惊讶的 ■ **unsurprisingly** adverb.

unsuspecting /ˌʌnsəˈspektɪŋ/ **adjective** not aware of the presence of danger 无戒心的；意识不到危险的

unsustainable /ˌʌnsəˈsteɪnəbl/ **adjective 1** not able to be maintained at the current level 无法维持的 **2** upsetting the ecological balance by using up natural resources 扰乱生态平衡的，不可持续的

unswerving /ʌnˈswɜːvɪŋ/ **adjective** not changing or becoming weaker (坚持)不懈的；坚定(不移)的

unsympathetic /ˌʌnˌsɪmpəˈθetɪk/ **adjective 1** not feeling or showing sympathy 不同情的；冷漠无情的 **2** not showing approval of an idea or action 不支持的；不赞同的 **3** not likeable 不可爱的；不讨人喜欢的 ■ **unsympathetically** adverb.

unsystematic /ˌʌnˌsɪstəˈmætɪk/ **adjective** not done or acting according to a fixed plan 无系统的；无条理的 ■ **unsystematically** adverb.

untapped /ʌnˈtæpt/ **adjective** (of a resource) available but not yet used (资源)尚未开发的，尚未使用的

untenable /ʌnˈtenəbl/ **adjective** (of a theory or view) not able to be defended against criticism or attack (理论或观点)站不住脚的，不堪一击的

unthinkable /ʌnˈθɪŋkəbl/ **adjective** too unlikely or unpleasant to be considered a possibility 不予考虑的；不能想象的；难以置信的

unthinking /ʌnˈθɪŋkɪŋ/ **adjective** not thinking about the effects of what you do or say 欠考虑的；考虑不周的 ■ **unthinkingly** adverb.

untidy /ʌnˈtaɪdi/ **adjective (untidier, untidiest) 1** not arranged tidily 混乱的；无条理的 **2** not inclined to be neat 不整齐的；凌乱的 ■ **untidily** adverb **untidiness** noun.

untie /ʌnˈtaɪ/ **verb (unties, untying, untied)** undo or unfasten something that is tied 解开，松开(打结之物)

until /ənˈtɪl/ **preposition & conjunction** up to the time or event mentioned 直到(某个时间点或所提及的事件)

✔ 拼写指南 just one *l* at the end: unti*l*. until 词尾只有一个 l。

untimely /ʌnˈtaɪmli/ **adjective 1** happening or done at an unsuitable time 不适时的；不是时候的 **2** (of a death or end) happening too soon or sooner than normal (死亡或结束)过早的

unto /ˈʌntə, ˈʌntu/ **preposition** old use 【旧】 **1** to 向；到 **2** until 直到；到……为止

untold /ˌʌnˈtəʊld/ **adjective 1** too much or too many to be counted 数不清的；无数的 **2** (of a story) not told to anyone (故事)未讲述的

untouchable /ʌnˈtʌtʃəbl/ **adjective 1**

not able to be touched 不可触摸的；不能触及的 **2** not able to be criticized or rivaled 不可批评的；不能匹敌的 • **noun** offensive【冒犯】a member of the lowest Hindu caste (social class) (印度社会中的)贱民，不可接触者

！注意 the official term today for the lowest Hindu social class is **scheduled caste**. 现在指印度社会最底层的正式用词为 scheduled caste。

untouched /ʌnˈtʌtʃt/ **adjective 1** not handled, used, or consumed 未碰过的；未使用的，未消耗的 **2** not affected, changed, or damaged 未受影响的；未改变的；未受损伤的

untoward /ˌʌntəˈwɔːd/ **adjective** unexpected and unwanted 意外的；不幸的；倒霉的

untrammelled /ʌnˈtræmld/ (US spelling【美拼作】**untrammeled**) **adjective** not restricted or hampered 不受限制的；自由自在的

untrue /ʌnˈtruː/ **adjective 1** false 假的；虚伪的 **2** not faithful or loyal 不忠实的；不忠诚的

untrustworthy /ʌnˈtrʌstwɜːðɪ/ **adjective** unable to be trusted 不能信任的；不可信赖的

unused /ʌnˈjuːzd/ **adjective 1** not used 未使用的 **2** (**unused to**) not accustomed to 不习惯…的

unusual /ʌnˈjuːʒuəl/ **adjective 1** not often done or happening 不平常的；少有的 **2** exceptional 与众不同的；非凡的 ▪ **unusually** adverb.

unutterable /ʌnˈʌtərəbl/ **adjective** too great or bad to describe 难以言表的 ▪ **unutterably** adverb.

unvarnished /ʌnˈvɑːnɪʃt/ **adjective 1** not varnished 未上清漆的；未加修饰的 **2** plain and straightforward 清楚明白的；坦率的

unveil /ˌʌnˈveɪl/ **verb 1** show or announce something publicly for the first time 揭示；公布 **2** remove a veil or covering from 揭去…的面纱(或遮盖物)

unwaged /ʌnˈweɪdʒd/ **adjective** Brit.【英】unemployed or doing unpaid work 失业的，没有工资收入的

unwanted /ʌnˈwɒntɪd/ **adjective** not wanted 不需要的；多余的

unwarrantable /ʌnˈwɒrəntəbl/ **adjective** not reasonable or justifiable 不合理的；无法证明的

unwarranted /ʌnˈwɒrəntɪd/ **adjective** not justified 无理的；未证实的

unwavering /ʌnˈweɪvərɪŋ/ **adjective** not changing or becoming weaker 不动摇的；坚定的

unwelcome /ʌnˈwelkəm/ **adjective** not wanted 不受欢迎的；讨厌的

unwell /ʌnˈwel/ **adjective** ill 不适的；生病的

unwholesome /ʌnˈhəʊlsəm/ **adjective 1** harmful to health 不健康的；有损健康的 **2** unpleasant or unnatural 令人生厌的；不自然的

unwieldy /ʌnˈwiːldɪ/ **adjective** hard to move or manage because of its size, shape, or weight (因大小、形状或重量而)难移动的，难操作的

unwilling /ʌnˈwɪlɪŋ/ **adjective** not willing 不愿意的；不乐意的 ▪ **unwillingly** adverb **unwillingness** noun.

unwind /ˌʌnˈwaɪnd/ **verb** (**unwinds**, **unwinding**, **unwound**) **1** undo something that has been wound or twisted 松开，解开(缠绕之物) **2** relax after a period of work or tension 放松；松弛

unwise /ʌnˈwaɪz/ **adjective** foolish 愚蠢的 ▪ **unwisely** adverb.

unwitting /ʌnˈwɪtɪŋ/ **adjective 1** not aware of the full facts 不知实情的 **2** unintentional 非故意的；无心的 ▪ **unwittingly** adverb.

unwonted /ʌnˈwəʊntɪd/ **adjective** not usual or expected 不寻常的；异常的

unworldly /ʌnˈwɜːldlɪ/ **adjective**

1 having little awareness of the realities of life 脱俗的；不谙世事的 **2** not seeming to belong to this world 非尘世的；非今世的

unworthy /ʌn'wɜːði/ **adjective** not deserving effort, attention, or respect 不值得的；可鄙的 ■ **unworthiness** noun.

unwrap /ʌn'ræp/ **verb** (**unwraps, unwrapping, unwrapped**) remove the wrapping from 去掉…的包装

unwritten /ʌn'rɪtn/ **adjective** (of a rule or law) generally known about and accepted, although not made official (法规)非书面的，不成文的

unyielding /ʌn'jiːldɪŋ/ **adjective 1** not bending or breaking; firm 不弯曲的；坚固的 **2** (of a person) not changing their mind (人)不让步的，不屈服的

unzip /ʌn'zɪp/ **verb** (**unzips, unzipping, unzipped**) **1** unfasten the zip of 拉开…的拉链 **2** Computing【计】 decompress a file 解开(压缩文件)

up /ʌp/ **adverb 1** towards a higher place or position 向上；向较高处 **2** to the place where someone is 靠近(某人) **3** at or to a higher level or value (水平或价值)较高地，从低到高地 **4** into the desired condition or position 处于理想境况(或位置) **5** out of bed 起床 **6** (of the sun) visible in the sky (太阳)升起 • **preposition 1** from a lower to a higher point of 从…的低处到高处 **2** from one end of a street to another 从(街道)的一端到另一端 • **adjective 1** directed or moving towards a higher place or position 朝上的；向上的 **2** at an end 在一端的 • **verb** (**ups, upping, upped**) increase a level or an amount 提高(水平或数量) □ **up-and-coming** likely to be successful 很有前途的；可能成功的 **up to date** using or aware of the latest developments and trends 使用最新信息的；与时俱进的

upbeat /'ʌpbiːt/ **adjective** positive and cheerful or enthusiastic 快乐的；活泼的

upbraid /ʌp'breɪd/ **verb** scold or criticize 责骂；训斥；批评

upbringing /'ʌpbrɪŋɪŋ/ **noun** the way in which a person is taught and looked after as a child 教养；养育

upcoming /'ʌpkʌmɪŋ/ **adjective** forthcoming 即将到来的；即将出现的

update verb /ʌp'deɪt/ (**updates, updating, updated**) **1** make something more modern 使现代化；更新 **2** give someone the latest information on something 给…提供最新信息 • **noun** /'ʌpdeɪt/ an act of updating, or an updated version of something 更新；升级版

upend /ʌp'end/ **verb** set something on its end or upside down 颠倒；倒放

upfront /ʌp'frʌnt/ informal【非正式】 **adjective 1** not trying to hide your thoughts or intentions; frank 率直的；坦率的 **2** (of a payment) made in advance (付款)预付的 • **adverb** (usu. **up front**) (of a payment) in advance (付款)预付地

upgrade /ʌp'greɪd/ **verb** (**upgrades, upgrading, upgraded**) raise something to a higher standard or rank 升级；提高；提升 • **noun** an act of upgrading, or an upgraded version of something 升级；提升；升级版

upheaval /ʌp'hiːvl/ **noun** a big change that causes a lot of upset or disruption 激变；剧变；动乱

uphill /ʌp'hɪl/ **adverb** towards the top of a slope 上坡地；向上 • **adjective 1** sloping upwards 上坡的；向上的 **2** difficult 艰难的；费力的：*an uphill struggle* 艰苦的斗争

uphold /ʌp'həʊld/ **verb** (**upholds, upholding, upheld**) **1** confirm or support something which has been questioned 赞成；认可；支持 **2** maintain a custom or practice 维持，

保持(风俗或惯例)

upholster /ʌpˈhəʊlstə(r)/ **verb** (**upholsters, upholstering, upholstered**) provide an armchair, sofa, etc. with a soft, padded covering 为(扶手椅、沙发等)配软垫(或套子等) ■ **upholsterer** noun.

upholstery /ʌpˈhəʊlstəri/ **noun 1** the soft, padded covering on an armchair, sofa, etc. 家具装饰材料 **2** the art of upholstering furniture 家具装饰艺术

upkeep /ˈʌpkiːp/ **noun** the process or cost of keeping something in good condition or of supporting a person 保养(费);维修(费)

upland /ˈʌplənd/ or **uplands** /ˈʌpləndz/ **noun** an area of high or hilly land 高地;高原;山地

uplift verb /ʌpˈlɪft/ make someone feel hope or happiness 使振奋;使振作 • noun /ˈʌplɪft/ **1** an act of lifting or raising something 抬起;提起;举起 **2** a feeling of hope or happiness 振作;振奋 ■ **uplifting** adjective.

upload /ʌpˈləʊd/ **verb** transfer data to a larger computer system 上传(数据)

upmarket /ʌpˈmɑːkɪt/ **adjective** chiefly Brit. 【主英】expensive or of high quality 昂贵的;高档的

upon /əˈpɒn/ more formal term for **on**. on 更加正式的说法

upper /ˈʌpə(r)/ **adjective 1** situated above another part 较高的;上部的;较上的 **2** higher in position or status (地位或身份)较高的 **3** situated on higher ground 地势高的 • noun the part of a boot or shoe above the sole 靴面;鞋帮 □ **have the upper hand** have an advantage or control over someone 占优势;占上风 **upper case** capital letters 大写字母 **upper class** the social group with the highest status 上层阶级;上流社会 **the Upper House** (in the UK) the House of Lords (英国的)上(议)院

uppercut /ˈʌpəkʌt/ **noun** a punch delivered with an upward motion and the arm bent 上钩拳

uppermost /ˈʌpəməʊst/ **adjective & adverb** highest in place, rank, or importance (位置、级别或重要性)处于最高的(地)

uppity /ˈʌpəti/ **adjective** informal 【非正式】behaving as if you are more important than you really are 妄自尊大的;自大的

upright /ˈʌpraɪt/ **adjective 1** in a vertical position 直立的;挺直的;竖立的 **2** greater in height than breadth 立式的 **3** strictly honest and respectable 诚实的;正直的;正派的 **4** (of a piano) having vertical strings (钢琴)有竖弦的,立式的 • adverb in or into an upright position 直立地;竖立地 • noun a vertical post, structure, or line 直柱;立式结构;竖线

uprising /ˈʌpraɪzɪŋ/ **noun** a rebellion 起义;暴动

upriver /ʌpˈrɪvə(r)/ ⇒ 见 UPSTREAM.

uproar /ˈʌprɔː(r)/ **noun 1** a loud noise or disturbance made by people who are angry or upset about something 吵闹;喧哗 **2** a public expression of outrage 骚动;骚乱

uproarious /ʌpˈrɔːriəs/ **adjective 1** very noisy and lively 喧嚣的;骚动的 **2** very funny 引人捧腹的;非常有趣的 ■ **uproariously** adverb.

uproot /ʌpˈruːt/ **verb 1** pull a tree or other plant out of the ground 将(树或其他植物)连根拔除 **2** move someone from their home or usual surroundings 使(某人)离开家园

upscale /ʌpˈskeɪl/ **adjective** N. Amer. 【北美】upmarket 昂贵的;高档的

upset verb /ʌpˈset/ (**upsets, upsetting, upset**) **1** make someone unhappy, disappointed, or worried 使不快;使失望;使担忧 **2** knock something over 弄翻;打翻 **3** disrupt or disturb a situation or arrangement 破坏;扰乱;打乱 • noun /ˈʌpset/ **1** a difficult or unexpected result or situation 意外结

果；意外状况 **2** a state of being upset 不快；失望；担忧 • adjective **1** /ʌpˈset/ unhappy, disappointed, or worried 不快的；失望的；担忧的 **2** /ˈʌpset/ (of a person's stomach) not digesting food normally (人的胃部)不适的

upshot /ˈʌpʃɒt/ noun the eventual outcome or conclusion of something 结果；结局

upside /ˈʌpsaɪd/ noun the positive aspect of something (某事物)好的一面，积极面 □ **upside down** with the upper part where the lower part should be 上下颠倒地(的)

upstage /ʌpˈsteɪdʒ/ verb (**upstages**, **upstaging**, **upstaged**) draw attention away from someone so that people notice you instead 使注意力从(某人)转移到自己身上 • adverb & adjective at or towards the back of a stage 在舞台后部的(的)；靠近舞台后部的(的)

upstairs /ʌpˈsteəz/ adverb & adjective on or to an upper floor 在楼上的(的)；往楼上的(的) • noun an upper floor 楼上

upstanding /ʌpˈstændɪŋ/ adjective very respectable and responsible 正直的，正派的

upstart /ˈʌpstɑːt/ noun disapproving 【贬】a person who thinks they are more important than they really are 自命不凡的人

upstate /ʌpˈsteɪt/ adjective & adverb US 【美】in or to a part of a state remote from its large cities 在边远地区(的)；往边远地区(的)

upstream /ʌpˈstriːm/ or **upriver** /ʌpˈrɪvə(r)/ adverb & adjective at or to a point nearer the source of a stream or river 逆流的(的)；往上游的(的)

upsurge /ˈʌpsɜːdʒ/ noun an increase 上升；增长

uptake /ˈʌpteɪk/ noun the action of taking up or making use of something 举起；拿起；使用 □ **be quick (or slow) on the uptake** informal 【非正

式】be quick (or slow) to understand something 理解力强(或弱)

uptight /ʌpˈtaɪt/ adjective informal 【非正式】nervously tense or angry, and unable to express your feelings 紧张不安的；生气的；局促的

upturn /ˈʌptɜːn/ noun an improvement or upward trend 好转；上升趋势 • verb (**be upturned**) be turned upwards or upside down 朝上；颠倒

upward /ˈʌpwəd/ adjective & adverb towards a higher level 向上的(地) ■ **upwards** adverb.

upwind /ʌpˈwɪnd/ adverb & adjective into the wind 迎风地(的)；逆风地(的)

uranium /juˈreɪniəm/ noun a radioactive metallic element used as a fuel in nuclear reactors (放射性金属元素)铀

Uranus /ˈjuːrənəs, juˈreɪnəs/ noun the seventh planet from the sun in the solar system 天王星

urban /ˈɜːbən/ adjective having to do with a town or city 城镇的

urbane /ɜːˈbeɪn/ adjective (of a man) confident, polite, and sophisticated (男子)自信的，彬彬有礼的，温文尔雅的 ■ **urbanity** noun.

urchin /ˈɜːtʃɪn/ noun a poor child dressed in ragged clothes 衣衫褴褛的孩子

Urdu /ˈʊəduː, ˈɜː-/ noun a language of Pakistan and India 乌尔都语(巴基斯坦及印度的一种语言)

ureter /juˈriːtə(r)/ noun the duct by which urine passes from the kidney to the bladder 输尿管

urethra /juˈriːθrə/ noun the duct by which urine passes out of the body, and which in males also carries semen 尿道 ■ **urethral** adjective.

urge /ɜːdʒ/ verb (**urges**, **urging**, **urged**) **1** encourage or earnestly ask someone to do something 鼓励；恳求 **2** strongly recommend 强烈推荐；极力主张 • noun a strong desire or impulse 强烈欲望；冲动

urgent /ˈɜːdʒənt/ **adjective** needing immediate action or attention 紧急的；急迫的；紧要的 ■ **urgency** noun **urgently** adverb.

urinal /juˈraɪnl/ **noun** a container into which men urinate, attached to the wall in a public toilet 尿池；小便处

urinate /ˈjʊərɪneɪt/ **verb** (**urinates, urinating, urinated**) pass urine out of the body 排尿 ■ **urination** noun.

urine /ˈjʊərɪn/ **noun** a yellowish liquid that is stored in the bladder and which contains waste substances that are passed with it out of the body 尿；小便 ■ **urinary** adjective.

URL /ˌjuː ɑː(r) ˈel/ **abbreviation** uniform (or universal) resource locator, the address of a World Wide Web page 统一资源定位器；网址

urn /ɜːn/ **noun 1** a container for storing a cremated person's ashes 骨灰瓮 **2** a metal container with a tap, in which tea or coffee is made and kept hot (带龙头的)大茶水壶，大咖啡壶

ursine /ˈɜːsaɪn/ **adjective** having to do with bears 熊的

Uruguayan /ˌjʊərəˈɡwaɪən/ **noun** a person from Uruguay 乌拉圭人 ● **adjective** relating to Uruguay 乌拉圭的

US /ˌjuː ˈes/ **abbreviation** United States

us /əs/ **pronoun** used by a speaker to refer to himself or herself and one or more other people as the object of a verb or preposition 我们(作动词或介词宾语)

USA /ˌjuː es ˈeɪ/ **abbreviation** United States of America 美利坚合众国；美国

usable or **useable** /ˈjuːzəbl/ **adjective** able to be used 可用的，能用的 ■ **usability** noun.

usage /ˈjuːsɪdʒ/ **noun** the using of something 使用

use verb /juːz/ (**uses, using, used**) **1** do something with an object or adopt a method in order to achieve

a purpose 运用；使用；采用 **2** (**use something up**) consume all of something 用完；耗尽 **3** take unfair advantage of a person or situation 剥削；利用 **4** (**used to**) did something repeatedly in the past, or existed or happened in the past 过去常常 **5** (**be** or **get used to**) be or become familiar with something through experience 习惯于 **6** (**used**) secondhand 二手的；旧的 ● **noun** /juːs/ **1** the using of something 用；使用 **2** the ability to use a part of the body 使用能力 **3** a purpose for something, or a way in which something can be used 效用；功用 **4** value 价值

useful /ˈjuːsfl/ **adjective** able to be used for a practical purpose or in several ways 实用的；有用的 ■ **usefully** adverb **usefulness** noun.

useless /ˈjuːsləs/ **adjective 1** serving no purpose 无用的 **2** informal 【非正式】having no ability or skill 无能的，差劲的 ■ **uselessly** adverb.

user /ˈjuːzə(r)/ **noun** a person who uses or operates something 使用者；用户 ☐ **user-friendly** easy for people to use or understand 容易使用的；易于掌握的

usher /ˈʌʃə(r)/ **noun 1** a person who shows people to their seats in a theatre or cinema or in church (剧院、影院或教堂的)引座员，招待员 **2** an official in a law court who swears in jurors and generally keeps order 法庭差警 ● **verb** (**ushers, ushering, ushered**) guide someone somewhere 引；领

usherette /ˌʌʃəˈret/ **noun** a woman who shows people to their seats in a cinema or theatre (影院或剧院的)女引座员

USSR /ˌjuː es es ˈɑː(r)/ **abbreviation** historical 【历史】Union of Soviet Socialist Republics 苏维埃社会主义共和国联盟；苏联

usual /ˈjuːʒuəl/ **adjective** happening or done typically, regularly, or frequently 通常的；惯常的 ■ **usually** adverb.

✔ 拼写指南 remember that **usually** is spelled with a double *l*. 记住 usually 拼写时双写 l。

usurp /juːˈzɜːp/ **verb** take over someone's position or power without having the right to do so 抢夺(当权者)的位置 ■ **usurper** noun.

usury /ˈjuːʒəri/ **noun** formal 【正式】 the practice of lending money at unreasonably high rates of interest 放高利贷 ■ **usurer** noun.

utensil /juːˈtensl/ **noun** a tool or container, especially for household use (尤指家用的)器皿，器具

uterus /ˈjuːtərəs/ **noun** the womb 子宫 ■ **uterine** adjective.

utilitarian /ˌjuːtɪlɪˈteəriən/ **adjective** useful or practical rather than attractive 有用的；实用的

utilitarianism /ˌjuːtɪlɪˈteəriənɪzəm/ **noun** the doctrine that the right course of action is the one that will lead to the greatest happiness of the greatest number of people 实用主义；功利主义

utility /juːˈtɪləti/ **noun** (plural **utilities**) **1** the state of being useful or profitable 效用；实用；功利 **2** an organization supplying electricity, gas, water, or sewerage to the public 公用事业 □ **utility room** a room where a washing machine and other domestic equipment are kept (放置洗衣机及其他家用器具的)存储间，杂物间

utilize or **utilise** /ˈjuːtɪlaɪz/ **verb** (**utilizes, utilizing, utilized**) make practical and effective use of 利用；有效地用 ■ **utilization** noun.

utmost /ˈʌtməʊst/ **adjective** most extreme; greatest 极度的；最大的 ● **(the utmost)** the greatest or most extreme extent or amount 极度；最大程度；最大量

Utopia /juːˈtəʊpiə/ **noun** an imagined world or society where everything is perfect 乌托邦(指想象中的完美社会)

utopian /juːˈtəʊpiən/ **adjective** idealistic 理想主义的；空想的

utter¹ /ˈʌtə(r)/ **adjective** complete; absolute 完全的；彻底的；绝对的 ■ **utterly** adverb.

utter² **verb** (**utters, uttering, uttered**) make a sound, or say something 发出(声音)；说；讲

utterance /ˈʌtərəns/ **noun 1** a word, statement, or sound uttered 言语；言论；声音 **2** the action of saying or uttering something 发声；吐露；表达

uttermost /ˈʌtəməʊst/ **noun** = UTMOST.

uvula /ˈjuːvjələ/ **noun** (plural **uvulae** /ˈjuːvjəli /) a small piece of flesh that hangs down at the top of the throat 悬雍垂；小舌

uxorious /ʌkˈsɔːriəs/ **adjective** (of a man) very fond of his wife (男子)疼爱妻子的

Vv

V or **v** /viː/ *noun* (plural **Vs** or **V's**)
1 the twenty-second letter of the alphabet 英语字母表的第22个字母
2 the Roman numeral for five (罗马数字)五 • *abbreviation* **1** volts.
2 (v) versus. □ **V-neck** a V-shaped neckline V形领;V字领 **V-sign 1** an insulting gesture made with the first two fingers pointing up and the back of the hand facing outwards V字手势(手背向外, 竖起食指和中指, 表示羞辱) **2** a similar sign made with the palm facing outwards, used as a symbol of victory V字手势(手掌向外, 竖起食指和中指, 表示胜利)

vacancy /'veɪkənsi/ *noun* (plural **vacancies**) **1** a job or position that is available 空缺;空职 **2** an available room in a hotel, guest house, etc. (宾馆, 家庭旅馆等的)空房 **3** empty space 空间;空处

vacant /'veɪkənt/ *adjective* **1** empty 空的;空白的 **2** (of a job or position) available (职位或位置)空缺的, 空着的 **3** showing no intelligence or interest 呆傻的;无兴趣的 ■ **vacantly** *adverb*.

vacate /və'keɪt/ *verb* (**vacates**, **vacating**, **vacated**) **1** go out of a place, leaving it empty 离开(某地) **2** give up a position 让(位);辞(职)

vacation /və'keɪʃn/ *noun* **1** a period when universities, law courts, etc. are closed (大学的)假期;(法庭的)休庭期 **2** N. Amer.【北美】a holiday 假日;休息日 **3** the action of vacating a place 搬出, 腾出(某处) • *verb* N. Amer.【北美】take a holiday 度假

vaccinate /'væksɪneɪt/ *verb* (**vaccinates**, **vaccinating**, **vaccinated**) give a person or animal an injection of a vaccine to protect them against a disease 给…接种疫苗 ■ **vaccination** *noun*.

vaccine /'væksiːn/ *noun* a substance injected into the body that causes the production of antibodies and so provides immunity against a disease 疫苗;菌苗

vacillate /'væsəleɪt/ *verb* (**vacillates**, **vacillating**, **vacillated**) keep changing your mind about something 犹豫不决;举棋不定 ■ **vacillation** *noun*.

vacuous /'vækjuəs/ *adjective* showing a lack of thought or intelligence 没有思想的;愚蠢的;无知的 ■ **vacuity** *noun*.

vacuum /'vækjuəm/ *noun* (plural **vacuums** or **vacua** /'vækjuə/) **1** a completely empty space in which there is no air or other matter 真空 **2** a gap left by the loss of someone or something important (因失去某重要的人或某重要物件造成的)真空状态, 空白, 空虚 • *verb* clean a surface using a vacuum cleaner 用真空吸尘器打扫 □ **vacuum cleaner** an electrical machine that collects dust by means of suction 真空吸尘器 **vacuum flask** a container with a double wall enclosing a vacuum, used for keeping drinks hot or cold 真空瓶;保温瓶

vagabond /'vægəbɒnd/ *noun* a person who has no settled home or job 流浪汉;无业游民

vagary /'veɪɡəri/ *noun* (plural **vagaries**) a change that is difficult to predict or control 难以预测的变化;变幻莫测

vagina /və'dʒaɪnə/ *noun* (in a woman or girl) a tube leading from an outer opening to the womb (女子的)阴道

■ **vaginal** adjective.

vagrant /'veɪgrənt/ **noun** a person who has no settled home or job 流浪者；无业游民 • **adjective** having no settled home or job 流浪的；漂泊的
■ **vagrancy** noun.

vague /veɪg/ **adjective 1** not certain or definite 含糊的；不确定的 **2** saying things or thinking in a way that is not clear 不确切的；不具体的 ■ **vaguely** adverb **vagueness** noun.

vain /veɪn/ **adjective 1** having too high an opinion of yourself 自负的；自视过高的 **2** useless or meaningless 无用的；无意义的 □ **in vain** without success 徒劳；白费劲 ■ **vainly** adverb.

vainglorious /veɪn'glɔːriəs/ **adjective** literary【文】boastful or vain 自负的；虚荣的 ■ **vainglory** noun.

valance /'væləns/ **noun** a length of fabric fitted over the base of the bed under the mattress (床架周围的)短帷幔，挂布

vale /veɪl/ **noun** literary【文】a valley 谷；山谷

valediction /ˌvælɪ'dɪkʃn/ **noun 1** the action of saying farewell 告别；道别 **2** a farewell statement 告别辞；临别赠言

valedictory /ˌvælɪ'dɪktəri/ **adjective** (especially of a speech) saying farewell (尤指讲话)告别的，告别性质的

valency /'veɪlənsi/ or **valence** /'veɪləns/ **noun** (plural **valencies**) Chemistry【化学】the combining power of an element, especially as measured by the number of hydrogen atoms it can displace or combine with 化合价；原子价

valentine /'væləntaɪn/ **noun 1** a card that you send to a person you love on St Valentine's Day (14 February) 情人节贺卡 **2** a person to whom you send such a card (收受情人节贺卡的)情人

valerian /və'lɪəriən/ **noun 1** a plant with small pink, red, or white flowers 缬草(开粉色、红色或白色小花) **2** a sedative drug obtained from valerian roots 缬草根(一种镇静药)

valet /'vælɪt/ **noun 1** a person who looks after a man's clothes and other personal needs (照料男主人着装等的)仆人，仆从 **2** N. Amer.【北美】a person employed to clean or park cars 洗车者；泊车者 • **verb** (**valets**, **valeting**, **valeted**) **1** clean a car as a professional service (专业)清洗(汽车) **2** act as a valet to 伺候；服侍

valetudinarian /ˌvælɪtjuːdɪ'neəriən/ **noun** a person who is in bad health, or worries too much about their health 体弱者；过分担忧自己健康的人

valiant /'væliənt/ **adjective** showing courage or determination 英勇的；坚定的 ■ **valiantly** adverb.

valid /'vælɪd/ **adjective 1** (of a reason, argument, etc.) sound or logical (理由、论据等)有理的，合乎逻辑的 **2** legally binding or acceptable (法律上)有约束力的，有效的 ■ **validity** noun.

validate /'vælɪdeɪt/ **verb** (**validates**, **validating**, **validated**) make valid, or show to be valid 使有效；证实…的有效性 ■ **validation** noun.

valise /və'liːz/ **noun** a small travelling bag or suitcase 小旅行包；小旅行箱

Valium /'væliəm/ **noun** trademark【商标】a tranquillizing drug used to relieve anxiety 安定(一种镇静药)

valley /'væli/ **noun** (plural **valleys**) a low area between hills or mountains 谷；山谷

valour /'vælə(r)/ (US spelling【美拼作】valor) **noun** great courage in the face of danger 勇气；英勇 ■ **valorous** adjective.

valuable /'væljuəbl/ **adjective 1** worth a lot of money 贵重的；值钱的 **2** very useful or important 很有用的；很重要的 • **noun** (**valuables**)

valuable items 贵重物品

valuation /ˌvæljuˈeɪʃn/ *noun* an estimation of how much something is worth 估价；评估

value /ˈvælju:/ *noun* **1** the importance or usefulness of something 重要性；有用性；价值 **2** the amount of money that something is worth (物品的)价值 **3** (**values**) standards of behaviour 行为标准；价值观 **4** Maths 【数学】 the amount represented by a letter or symbol (数)值 **5** the relative length of the sound represented by a musical note 时值(指音符的长度) • *verb* (**values, valuing, valued**) **1** estimate how much something is worth 评估；给…估价 **2** consider something to be important or useful 重视；珍视 □ **value added tax** a tax on the amount by which goods rise in value at each stage of production 增值税

valve /vælv/ *noun* **1** a device for controlling the flow of a liquid or gas through a pipe or duct 阀；活门；气门 **2** a mechanism that varies the length of the tube in a brass musical instrument (铜管乐器上的)活瓣，阀键 **3** a structure in the heart or a vein which allows blood to flow in one direction only (心脏或血管的)瓣，瓣膜

vamp¹ /væmp/ *verb* (**vamp something up**) informal 【非正式】 improve something by adding something more interesting to it (通过添加新奇元素)改善，翻新

vamp² *noun* informal 【非正式】 a woman who uses her sexual attractiveness to control men (以色相勾引并控制男子的)荡妇，妖妇 ■ **vampish** *adjective*.

vampire /ˈvæmpaɪə(r)/ *noun* **1** (in stories) a dead person that leaves their grave at night to drink the blood of living people (传说中的)吸血鬼 **2** (also **vampire bat**) a bloodsucking bat found mainly in tropical America 吸血蝙蝠(主要见于美洲热带地区) ■ **vampirism** *noun*.

van¹ /væn/ *noun* **1** a motor vehicle used for moving goods or a group of people 客货车 **2** Brit. 【英】 a railway carriage used for large luggage, mail, etc. (火车)行李车

van² *noun* (**the van**) the leading part of an advancing group of people 前锋；前驱

vanadium /vəˈneɪdiəm/ *noun* a hard grey metallic chemical element, used to make some types of steel (金属元素)钒

vandal /ˈvændl/ *noun* a person who deliberately destroys or damages property 蓄意破坏财物者 ■ **vandalism** *noun*.

vandalize or **vandalise** /ˈvændəlaɪz/ *verb* (**vandalizes, vandalizing, vandalized**) deliberately destroy or damage property 蓄意毁坏，故意破坏(财物)

vane /veɪn/ *noun* a broad blade that is moved by wind or water, forming part of a windmill, propeller, or turbine (风车、螺旋桨或涡轮的)翼，叶片，轮片

vanguard /ˈvænɡɑːd/ *noun* **1** the leading part of an advancing army 先头部队 **2** a group of people leading the way in new developments or ideas 先锋；先驱；先驱者

vanilla /vəˈnɪlə/ *noun* a substance obtained from the pods of a tropical plant, used as a flavouring or scent 香草兰，香草(从热带植物香子兰荚中提取的物质,用作调味品或香料)

vanish /ˈvænɪʃ/ *verb* **1** disappear suddenly and completely 突然不见；消失 **2** gradually cease to exist 逐渐消失；消亡

vanity /ˈvænəti/ *noun* (plural **vanities**) **1** too much pride in your own appearance or achievements 自负；自大 **2** the quality of being pointless

or futile 无意义；无用；无价值

vanquish /'væŋkwɪʃ/ **verb** literary 【文】defeat completely 战胜；击败；征服

vantage /'vɑːntɪdʒ/ or **vantage point** **noun** a place or position giving the best view 有利地形；有利位置

vapid /'væpɪd/ **adjective** offering no stimulation or challenge 无趣的，枯燥的，平淡的 ■ **vapidity** noun.

vaporize or **vaporise** /'veɪpəraɪz/ **verb** (**vaporizes, vaporizing, vaporized**) convert something into vapour (使)汽化，(使)蒸发 ■ **vaporization** noun **vaporizer** noun.

vapour /'veɪpə(r)/ (US **spelling** 【美拼作】**vapor**) **noun 1** moisture suspended in the air 蒸气；汽；雾 **2** Physics 【物理】a gaseous substance that can be made into liquid by pressure alone 气态物质

variable /'veəriəbl/ **adjective 1** not consistent or having a fixed pattern 多变的，易变的；反复无常的 **2** able to be changed or adapted 可变的；可调整的 • **noun** a variable element, feature, or quantity 可变因素；可变性；变量 ■ **variability** noun **variably** adverb.

variance /'veəriəns/ **noun 1** the fact or quality of being different or inconsistent 变化；差异 **2** the state of disagreeing or quarrelling 存在分歧，争吵

variant /'veəriənt/ **noun** a version that varies from other forms of the same thing 变体；变形

variation /ˌveəri'eɪʃn/ **noun 1** a change or slight difference in condition, amount, or level (条件、数量或水平的)变化，差异 **2** a different or distinct form or version 变异；变种 **3** a new but still recognizable version of a musical theme (乐曲的)变奏

varicose /'værɪkəʊs/ **adjective** (of a vein) swollen, twisted, and lengthened,

as a result of bad circulation (静脉)曲张的

varied /'veərid/ **adjective** involving a number of different types or elements 各种各样的；形形色色的

variegated /'veərigeɪtɪd/ **adjective** having irregular patches or streaks of a different colour or colours 斑驳的；杂色的 ■ **variegation** noun.

> ✔ **拼写指南** remember the *e* in the middle: variegated. 记住拼写 variegated 中间的 e。

variety /və'raɪəti/ **noun** (plural **varieties**) **1** the quality of being varied 多变(性)；多样(性) **2** (**a variety of**) a number of things of the same type that are distinct in character 种种 **3** a thing which differs in some way from others of the same general class 种类；变种 **4** a form of entertainment involving singing, dancing, and comedy (包括演唱、舞蹈和喜剧表演的)综合演出，综艺节目

various /'veəriəs/ **adjective** of different kinds or sorts 各种各样的；五花八门的 • **determiner & pronoun** more than one; individual and separate 不止一个的；许多的；单个，各个 ■ **variously** adverb.

varnish /'vɑːnɪʃ/ **noun** a liquid applied to wood to give a hard, clear, shiny surface when dry 清漆；罩光漆 • **verb** put varnish on 给…涂清漆；使光亮

vary /'veəri/ **verb** (**varies, varying, varied**) **1** differ in size, degree, or nature from something else of the same general class 不同；有差异 **2** change from one form or state to another 变化 **3** alter something to make it less uniform 使不同；更改；改变

vascular /'væskjələ(r)/ **adjective** referring to the system of vessels for carrying blood or (in plants) the tissues carrying sap, water, and nutrients 血管的;(植物)维管的

vas deferens /ˌvæs ˈdefərenz/ noun (plural **vasa deferentia** /ˌveɪsə defəˈrenʃiə/) the duct carrying sperm from a testicle to the urethra 输精管

vase /vɑːz/ noun a container for displaying cut flowers 装饰瓶;花瓶

vasectomy /vəˈsektəmi/ noun (plural **vasectomies**) the surgical cutting and sealing of part of each vas deferens as a means of sterilization 输精管切除术

Vaseline /ˈvæsəliːn/ noun trademark【商标】a type of petroleum jelly used as an ointment and lubricant 凡士林 (一种提炼自石油的胶状物质,用作药膏或润滑剂)

vassal /ˈvæsl/ noun (in the feudal system) a man who promised to support and fight for a king or lord in return for holding a piece of land (封建制度下的)封臣,家臣

vast /vɑːst/ adjective of very great extent or quantity; immense 大量的;巨大的;庞大的 ■ **vastly** adverb **vastness** noun.

VAT /ˌviː eɪ ˈtiː, væt/ abbreviation value added tax.

vat /væt/ noun a large tank or tub used to hold liquid (盛液体用的)大桶,大盆

Vatican /ˈvætɪkən/ noun the official residence of the Pope in Rome 梵蒂冈(罗马教皇的居住地)

vaudeville /ˈvɔːdəvɪl/ noun a type of entertainment featuring a mixture of musical and comedy acts 杂耍;轻歌舞剧

vault[1] /vɔːlt/ noun **1** a large room used for storage, especially in a bank 储藏室;(尤指银行的)金库,保险库 **2** a chamber beneath a church or in a graveyard, used for burials (教堂或墓地的)墓穴 **3** a roof in the form of an arch or a series of arches 拱顶 ■ **vaulted** adjective.

vault[2] verb leap or spring using your hands or a pole to push yourself (双手支撑)跳(过);撑杆跳(过) ● noun an act of vaulting 跳跃;撑杆跳

vaunted /ˈvɔːntɪd/ adjective praised or boasted about 过度吹嘘的;过度夸耀的

VC /ˌviː ˈsiː/ abbreviation Victoria Cross 维多利亚十字勋章

VCR /ˌviː siː ˈɑː(r)/ abbreviation video cassette recorder 盒式磁带录像机

VDU /ˌviː diː ˈjuː/ abbreviation Brit.【英】visual display unit.

veal /viːl/ noun meat from a young calf 小牛肉;牛犊肉

vector /ˈvektə(r)/ noun **1** Maths【数学】a quantity having direction as well as magnitude 矢量;向量 **2** the carrier of a disease or infection 传病媒介;带菌者

Veda /ˈveɪdə/ noun the most ancient Hindu scriptures 吠陀经(印度最古老的宗教文献)

veer /vɪə(r)/ verb (veers, veering, veered) **1** change direction suddenly 突然转向 **2** (of the wind) change direction clockwise around the points of the compass (风)(顺时针地)改变方向

vegan /ˈviːgən/ noun a person who does not eat or use any animal products 严格的素食主义者;纯素食者

vegetable /ˈvedʒtəbl/ noun **1** a plant used as food 蔬菜 **2** offensive【冒犯】a person who is incapable of normal mental or physical activity as a result of brain damage 植物人

> ✔ 拼写指南 vege-, not vega-: vegetable. vegetable 中 vege- 不要拼作 vega-。

vegetal /ˈvedʒətl/ adjective relating to plants 植物的

vegetarian /ˌvedʒəˈteəriən/ noun a person who does not eat meat or fish 素食主义者 ● adjective eating or including no meat or fish 食素的;素食的 ■ **vegetarianism** noun.

vegetate /'vedʒəteɪt/ **verb (vegetates, vegetating, vegetated)** spend your time in a dull way that involves little mental stimulation 过无聊生活

vegetation /ˌvedʒə'teɪʃn/ **noun** plants 植物

vegetative /'vedʒɪtətɪv/ **adjective 1** relating to vegetation 植物的 **2** Medicine【医】alive but showing no sign of brain activity or responsiveness 植物人状态的

vehement /'viːəmənt/ **adjective** showing strong feeling 有激情的；热情的 ■ **vehemence** noun **vehemently** adverb.

vehicle /'viːəkl/ **noun** a car, lorry, truck, etc. used for transporting people or goods on land (陆上)交通工具,车辆 ■ **vehicular** /və'hɪkjələ(r)/ adjective.

veil /veɪl/ **noun 1** a piece of thin material worn to protect or hide the face 面纱；面罩 **2** the part of a nun's headdress that covers the head and shoulders (修女的)头巾 **3** a thing that hides or disguises 掩饰物；遮蔽物 • **verb 1** cover with a veil 遮掩；掩盖 **2** (veiled) partially hidden or disguised 隐藏的；掩饰的

vein /veɪn/ **noun 1** any of the tubes that carry blood from all parts of the body towards the heart 静脉 **2** a blood vessel 血管 **3** (in plants) a thin rib running through a leaf (植物的)叶脉 **4** (in insects) a hollow rib forming part of the supporting framework of a wing (昆虫的)翅脉 **5** a streak of a different colour in wood, marble, cheese, etc. (木材、大理石、干酪等的)纹理;纹路,条纹 **6** a fracture in rock containing a deposit of minerals or ore 矿脉;矿床 **7** a source of a particular quality 情绪;特性: *a vein of humour* 幽默意味 ■ **veined** adjective.

Velcro /'velkrəʊ/ **noun** trademark【商标】a fastener consisting of two strips

of fabric covered with tiny hooks 维可牢(一种尼龙搭扣)

veld or **veldt** /velt/ **noun** open uncultivated country or grassland in southern Africa (非洲南部的)旷野,草原

vellum /'veləm/ **noun** fine parchment made from animal skin 犊皮纸；羊皮纸

velociraptor /və'lɒsɪræptə(r)/ **noun** a small meat-eating dinosaur 速龙,迅捷龙(小型食肉恐龙)

velocity /və'lɒsəti/ **noun (plural velocities)** speed in a particular direction 速度

velour /və'lʊə(r)/ **noun** a thick, soft fabric resembling velvet 丝绒；维罗绒

velvet /'velvɪt/ **noun** a fabric with a soft, short pile on one side 丝绒；平绒；天鹅绒 ■ **velvety** adjective.

velveteen /ˌvelvə'tiːn/ **noun** a cotton fabric resembling thin velvet 棉绒；纬绒

venal /'viːnl/ **adjective** open to bribery 可贿赂的；可贿买的 ■ **venality** noun.

vend /vend/ **verb** sell small items 出售(小件商品) □ **vending machine** a machine from which you can buy drinks, snacks, etc. by inserting coins 投币式自动售货机

vendetta /ven'detə/ **noun 1** a feud in which the family of a murdered person seeks vengeance on the murderer or the murderer's family 家族仇杀；家族血仇 **2** a long and bitter quarrel 宿怨；世仇

vendor /'vendə(r)/ **noun (US spelling【美拼作】vender) noun 1** a person selling small items 小贩；摊贩 **2** Law【法律】a person who is selling a property 卖方；卖主

veneer /və'nɪə(r)/ **noun 1** a thin covering of fine wood applied to a cheaper wood or other material 饰面薄板；镶板 **2** an outward appearance that hides the true nature of a person or thing 虚饰；伪装 ■ **veneered**

adjective.

venerable /'venərəbl/ **adjective** given great respect because of age, wisdom, or character (因高龄、智慧或品德)令人敬畏的，令人崇敬的

venerate /'venəreɪt/ **verb** (**venerates**, **venerating**, **venerated**) respect someone highly 尊重，尊敬；敬重 ∎ **veneration** noun.

venereal disease /və'nɪəriəl/ **noun** a disease caught by having sex with an infected person 性病，花柳病

Venetian /və'niːʃn/ **adjective** relating to Venice 威尼斯的 ∎ **venetian blind** a window blind consisting of horizontal slats which can be turned to control the amount of light that passes through 百叶窗帘

Venezuelan /ˌveni'zweɪlən/ **noun** a person from Venezuela 委内瑞拉人 ∎ **adjective** relating to Venezuela 委内瑞拉的

vengeance /'vendʒəns/ **noun** an act of harming or punishing someone in return for what they have done to you or someone close to you 报复；复仇；报仇 □ **with a vengeance** with great intensity 激烈地；猛烈地

vengeful /'vendʒfl/ **adjective** wanting to punish or harm someone in return for something they have done 图谋报复的

venial /'viːniəl/ **adjective** (of a fault or offence) slight and able to be forgiven (错误或过失)轻微的，可原谅的

venison /'venɪsn, -zn/ **noun** meat from a deer 鹿肉

Venn diagram /ven/ **noun** a diagram representing mathematical sets as circles, with overlapping sections representing elements shared between sets (用圆表示集与集之间关系的)维恩图

venom /'venəm/ **noun 1** the poisonous liquid produced by some animals that bite or sting, such as snakes and scorpions (蛇、蝎等分泌的)毒液 **2** a strong feeling of hatred or bitterness 恶毒；怨恨

venomous /'venəməs/ **adjective 1** producing venom 分泌毒液的 **2** full of hatred or bitterness 充满怨恨的；恶毒的 ∎ **venomously** adverb.

venous /'viːnəs/ **adjective** relating to a vein or the veins 静脉的

vent[1] /vent/ **noun** an opening that allows air, gas, or liquid to pass out of or into a confined space (空气、气体或液体进出的)孔，口 ∎ **verb 1** allow yourself to express a strong emotion 尽情表达，发泄(感情) **2** let air, gas, or liquid pass through a vent 排放(空气、气体或液体)

vent[2] **noun** a slit in a garment (衣服的)开口，开衩

ventilate /'ventɪleɪt/ **verb** (**ventilates**, **ventilating**, **ventilated**) cause air to enter and circulate freely in a room or building 使通风；使空气流通 ∎ **ventilation** noun.

ventilator /'ventɪleɪtə(r)/ **noun 1** an opening or a machine for ventilating a room or building (房间或建筑物的)通风口，通风设备 **2** a machine that pumps air in and out of a person's lungs to help them to breathe 呼吸器

ventral /'ventrəl/ **adjective** having to do with the underside or abdomen 向下一面的；内面的；腹部的

ventricle /'ventrɪkl/ **noun** each of the two larger and lower cavities of the heart (心脏的)心室

ventriloquist /ven'trɪləkwɪst/ **noun** an entertainer who can make their voice seem to come from elsewhere 腹语术表演者；口技表演者 ∎ **ventriloquism** noun.

venture /'ventʃə(r)/ **noun 1** a business enterprise involving considerable risk (有风险的)企业 **2** a risky or daring journey or undertaking 冒险旅行；冒险行动 ∎ **verb** (**ventures**, **venturing**,

ventured) 1 dare to do something dangerous or risky 敢于冒险;敢做 **2** dare to say something 敢于提出;大胆提出

venturesome /'ventʃəsəm/ **adjective** literary 【文】 willing to take on something risky or difficult 愿意冒险的

venue /'venju:/ **noun** the place where an event or meeting is held (举办活动或召开会议的)地点,场所

Venus /'vi:nəs/ **noun** the second planet from the sun in the solar system 金星 □ **Venus flytrap** a plant with hinged leaves that spring shut on and digest insects which land on them 捕蝇草(铰链状叶子可突然闭合并消化掉包住的昆虫)

veracious /və'reɪʃəs/ **adjective** formal 【正式】 truthful 说实话的;诚实的

veracity /və'ræsəti/ **noun** the quality of being truthful and accurate 真实(性);精确(性)

veranda or **verandah** /və'rændə/ **noun** a roofed structure with an open front along the outside of a house 游廊;走廊

verb /vɜːb/ **noun** a word expressing an action or occurrence 动词

verbal /'vɜːbl/ **adjective 1** relating to or in the form of words 词语的;言语的;文字的 **2** spoken rather than written 口头的;非书面的 **3** relating to a verb 动词的 ■ **verbally** adverb

verbalize or **verbalise** /'vɜːbəlaɪz/ **verb** (**verbalizes, verbalizing, verbalized**) express something in words 用文字(或言语)表达

verbatim /vɜː'beɪtɪm/ **adverb & adjective** in exactly the same words as were used originally 一字不差地(的);逐字逐句地(的)

verbiage /'vɜːbiɪdʒ/ **noun** speech or writing that is too long or detailed 冗词;赘语

verbose /vɜː'bəʊs/ **adjective** using more words than are needed 啰唆的;

冗长的 ■ **verbosity** noun.

verdant /'vɜːdnt/ **adjective** green with grass or other lush vegetation 青翠的;碧绿的

verdict /'vɜːdɪkt/ **noun 1** a decision made by a jury in a court of law about whether someone is innocent or guilty (陪审团的)裁决,判决 **2** an opinion or judgement formed after trying or testing something 判断性意见;定论

verdigris /'vɜːdɪɡrɪs/ **noun** a bright bluish-green substance formed on copper or brass by oxidation 铜绿;铜锈

verdure /'vɜːdʒə(r)/ **noun** literary 【文】 lush green vegetation 青葱的草木

verge /vɜːdʒ/ **noun 1** Brit. 【英】 a grass edging by the side of a road or path 路边草地 **2** a limit beyond which a particular thing will happen 临界点;界限 □ *I was on the verge of tears.* 我的眼泪几乎夺眶而出。■ **verb** (**verges, verging, verged on**) be very close or similar to 接近;与……类似

verger /'vɜːdʒə(r)/ **noun** an official in a church who acts as a caretaker and attendant 教堂司事

verify /'verɪfaɪ/ **verb** (**verifies, verifying, verified**) make sure or show that something is true and accurate 核实;证明;证实 ■ **verifiable** adjective **verification** noun.

verily /'verɪli/ **adverb** old use 【旧】 truly; certainly 真实地;真正地;肯定地

verisimilitude /ˌverɪsɪ'mɪlɪtjuːd/ **noun** the appearance of being true or real 貌似真实;逼真

veritable /'verɪtəbl/ **adjective** genuine 名副其实的;真正的 ■ **veritably** adverb.

verity /'verəti/ **noun** (plural **verities**) formal 【正式】 truthfulness, or a truth 真实;事实

vermicelli /ˌvɜːmɪ'tʃeli/ **plural noun 1**

pasta made in long thin threads 细面条；线面 **2** Brit. 【英】shreds of chocolate used to decorate cakes (糕点上的)巧克力装饰线条

vermilion /vəˈmɪlɪən/ *noun* a bright red colour 朱红色；鲜红色

vermin /ˈvɜːmɪn/ *noun* wild animals or birds which carry disease or harm crops 害兽；害鸟 ■ **verminous** *adjective*.

vermouth /ˈvɜːməθ/ *noun* a red or white wine flavoured with herbs 苦艾酒；味美思酒

vernacular /vəˈnækjələ(r)/ *noun* the language or dialect spoken by the ordinary people of a country or region 本国语；本地话；方言

vernal /ˈvɜːnl/ *adjective* relating to the season of spring 春天的

verruca /vəˈruːkə/ *noun* a contagious wart on the sole of the foot (脚底生的)疣，肉赘

versatile /ˈvɜːsətaɪl/ *adjective* able to adapt or be adapted to many different functions or activities 多功能的；多才多艺的 ■ **versatility** *noun*.

verse /vɜːs/ *noun* **1** writing arranged with a metrical rhythm 诗；诗歌；韵文 **2** a group of lines that form a unit in a poem or song 诗节；诗行；歌曲段落 **3** each of the short numbered divisions of a chapter in the Bible (《圣经》的)节

versed /vɜːst/ *adjective* (**versed in**) experienced or skilled in 熟练的；精通的

versify /ˈvɜːsɪfaɪ/ *verb* (**versifies, versifying, versified**) write verse, or turn a piece of writing into verse 作诗；把…改写成诗 ■ **versification** *noun*.

version /ˈvɜːʃn/ *noun* **1** a particular form of something which differs from other forms of the same type of thing (一事物的)变化形式，变体 **2** an account of something told from a particular person's point of view (个

人的)描述，说法

verso /ˈvɜːsəʊ/ *noun* (plural **versos**) a left-hand page of an open book, or the back of a loose document (书的)左页，偶数页；(散页的)背面

versus /ˈvɜːsəs/ *preposition* **1** against 以…为对手；对 **2** as opposed to 与…相对；与…相比

vertebra /ˈvɜːtɪbrə/ *noun* (plural **vertebrae** /ˈvɜːtɪbriː/) each of the series of small bones forming the backbone 椎骨；脊椎骨

vertebrate /ˈvɜːtɪbrət/ *noun* an animal having a backbone, e.g. a mammal, bird, reptile, amphibian, or fish 脊椎动物

vertex /ˈvɜːteks/ *noun* (plural **vertices** /ˈvɜːtɪsiːz/ or **vertexes**) **1** the highest point 顶点；最高点 **2** a meeting point of two lines that form an angle (角的)顶点

vertical /ˈvɜːtɪkl/ *adjective* going straight up or down, at a right angle to a horizontal line or surface 垂直的；竖的；立式的 ● *noun* a vertical line or surface 垂直线；垂直面 ■ **vertically** *adverb*.

vertiginous /vɜːˈtɪdʒɪnəs/ *adjective* very high or steep 引起眩晕的；陡峭的

vertigo /ˈvɜːtɪɡəʊ/ *noun* a feeling of giddiness caused by looking down from a great height (从高处俯视时引起的)眩晕

verve /vɜːv/ *noun* energy, spirit, and style 精力；生气；激情

very /ˈveri/ *adverb* in a high degree 极其；非常 ● *adjective* **1** actual; precise 真正的；正是的 **2** extreme 极端的；十足的 **3** mere 仅仅的

vespers /ˈvespəz/ *noun* a Christian service of evening prayer (基督教的)晚课

vessel /ˈvesl/ *noun* **1** a ship or large boat 船；舰 **2** a tube or duct carrying a liquid within the body, or within a plant (动物体内的)血管，脉管；(植物

的)导管 **3** old use 【旧】 a bowl, cup, or other container for liquids (盛液体的)容器,器皿

vest /vest/ **noun 1** Brit. 【英】 a sleeveless garment or undergarment worn on the upper part of the body 汗背心 **2** N. Amer. & Austral. 【北美和澳】 a waistcoat or sleeveless jacket 背心;马甲 • **verb** (**vest something in**) give someone power or property, or the legal right to hold power or own property (权力或财产)给予(某人) □ **vested interest** a personal reason for wanting something to happen 既得利益

vestibule /'vestɪbjuːl/ **noun** a room or hall just inside the outer door of a building (建筑物的)门厅,前厅

vestige /'vestɪdʒ/ **noun 1** a last remaining trace of something 残余;遗迹 **2** the smallest amount 丝毫;一点儿 ■ **vestigial** adjective.

vestment /'vestmənt/ **noun** a robe worn by ministers or members of the choir during church services (牧师或唱诗班成员在礼拜仪式上穿的)法衣,祭服

vestry /'vestri/ **noun** (plural **vestries**) a small room in a church, used as an office and for changing into ceremonial robes (教堂的)法衣室,祭服室

vet /vet/ **noun** a person qualified to treat sick or injured animals 兽医 • **verb** (**vets, vetting, vetted**) find out about someone's background and past before employing them 调查,审查(某人的背景和过去经历)

vetch /vetʃ/ **noun** a plant of the pea family grown as food for farm animals 巢菜,野豌豆(用作饲料)

veteran /'vetərən/ **noun 1** a person who has had many years of experience in a particular field 老手;经验丰富的人 **2** a person who used to serve in the armed forces 退伍军人;老兵

veterinarian /ˌvetərɪ'neərɪən/ **noun** N.

Amer. 【北美】 a vet 兽医

veterinary /'vetnri, 'vetrənəri/ **adjective** relating to the treatment of diseases and injuries in animals 兽医的 □ **veterinary surgeon** a vet 兽医

> ✔ 拼写指南 note the -er- before the -in-: veterinary. 注意拼写 veterinary 中 -in- 前的 -er-。

veto /'viːtəʊ/ **noun** (plural **vetoes**) **1** the right or power to reject a ruling or decision made by others 否决权 **2** a refusal to allow something 禁止;反对 • **verb** (**vetoes, vetoing, vetoed**) use a veto against, or refuse to allow 否决;禁止;反对

vex /veks/ **verb** make someone annoyed or worried 使恼火,使恼怒 ■ **vexation** noun **vexatious** adjective.

vexed /vekst/ **adjective 1** (of an issue) difficult to deal with and causing a lot of debate (问题)难解决的,争论不休的 **2** annoyed or worried 恼火的;忧恼的

VHF /ˌviː eɪtʃ 'ef/ **abbreviation** very high frequency 甚高频

VHS /ˌviː eɪtʃ 'es/ **abbreviation** trademark 【商标】 video home system 家用录像系统;VHS 制式

via /'vaɪə/ **preposition 1** travelling through a particular place on the way to a destination 途经 **2** by way of; through 经由;经过 **3** by means of 通过;凭借

viable /'vaɪəbl/ **adjective 1** capable of working successfully 切实可行的,可实施的 **2** (of a plant, animal, or cell) able to live (植物、动物或细胞)能存活的,能生长发育的 ■ **viability** noun.

viaduct /'vaɪədʌkt/ **noun** a long bridge-like structure carrying a road or railway across a valley or other low ground 高架桥;高架道路;高架铁路

vial /'vaɪəl/ **noun** a small cylindrical glass bottle for medicine etc. (盛药品等的)小玻璃瓶

viands /'vaɪəndz/ **plural noun** old use 【旧】food 食品

vibe /vaɪb/ or **vibes** /vaɪbz/ **noun** informal 【非正式】the atmosphere of a place, or a feeling passing between people (某地的)气氛, 氛围;(人们共有的)情绪

vibrant /'vaɪbrənt/ **adjective** 1 full of energy and enthusiasm 充满生气的;活跃的;热情洋溢的 2 (of sound) strong or resonant (声音)响亮的, 回荡的 3 (of colour) bright (色彩)鲜明的, 明快的 ■ **vibrancy** noun **vibrantly** adverb.

vibraphone /'vaɪbrəfəʊn/ **noun** an electrical percussion instrument giving a vibrato effect 电颤琴

vibrate /vaɪ'breɪt/ **verb** (**vibrates**, **vibrating**, **vibrated**) 1 move with rapid small movements to and fro 颤动;振动;抖动 2 (of a sound) resonate (声音)萦绕, 回荡 ■ **vibration** noun.

vibrato /vɪ'brɑːtəʊ/ **noun** a rapid, slight variation in pitch in singing or playing some musical instruments (演唱或演奏的)颤音

vicar /'vɪkə(r)/ **noun** (in the Church of England) a minister in charge of a parish (英格兰国教的)教区牧师

vicarage /'vɪkərɪdʒ/ **noun** a vicar's house 教区牧师住所

vicarious /vɪ'keərɪəs/ **adjective** experienced in the imagination rather than directly 通过他人经历感受到的;从他人经历间接获得的: *a vicarious thrill* 间接感受到的刺激 ■ **vicariously** adverb.

vice[1] /vaɪs/ **noun** 1 immoral or wicked behaviour 道德败坏行为;罪恶行为 2 criminal activities that involve sex or drugs (与性或毒品有关的)犯罪活动 3 a bad personal characteristic 堕落;邪恶 4 a bad habit 恶习;不良习气

vice[2] (US spelling 【美拼法】**vise**) **noun** a metal tool with movable jaws which are used to hold an object firmly in place while work is done on it 台钳;老虎钳

vice- /vaɪs-/ **combining form** next in rank to; deputy 副;代理: *vice-president* 副总统

viceroy /'vaɪsrɔɪ/ **noun** a person sent by a king or queen to govern a colony (由国王或女王派遣管辖殖民地的)总督

vice versa /ˌvaɪs 'vɜːsə/ **adverb** reversing the order of the items just mentioned 反之亦然;反过来也一样

vicinity /və'sɪnəti/ **noun** (plural **vicinities**) the area near or surrounding a place 邻近地区

vicious /'vɪʃəs/ **adjective** 1 cruel or violent 恶毒的;凶残的 2 (of an animal) wild and dangerous (动物)凶猛的, 危险的 □ **vicious circle** a situation in which one problem leads to another, which then makes the first one worse 恶性循环 ■ **viciously** adverb **viciousness** noun.

✔ 拼写指南 no *s* in the middle: vicious. vicious 中间没有 s.

vicissitudes /vɪ'sɪsɪtjuːdz/ **plural noun** the ups and downs and changes in your life (人生的)多变, 变化无常

victim /'vɪktɪm/ **noun** a person who is harmed or killed as a result of a crime, injustice, or accident 受害者;牺牲者;罹难者

victimize or **victimise** /'vɪktɪmaɪz/ **verb** (**victimizes**, **victimizing**, **victimized**) single someone out for cruel or unfair treatment 使牺牲;使受害;使受苦 ■ **victimization** noun.

victor /'vɪktə(r)/ **noun** a person who defeats an opponent in a battle, game or competition 胜利者;战胜者;获胜者

Victorian /vɪk'tɔːrɪən/ **adjective** relating to the reign of Queen Victoria (1837–1901) (英国)维多利亚时代的

victorious /vɪk'tɔːrɪəs/ **adjective**

having won a victory 胜利的；战胜
的；获胜的

victory /'vɪktəri/ **noun** (plural **victories**)
an act of defeating an opponent 胜利；
战胜；获胜

victuals /'vɪtlz/ **plural noun** old use
【旧】food and provisions 食品；粮食

video /'vɪdiəʊ/ **noun** (plural **videos**) **1**
a system of recording and reproducing
moving images using magnetic tape
(用磁带进行的)录制，录像，录影 **2** a
film or other recording on magnetic
tape (录制于磁带上的)录影，录像 **3**
Brit.【英】a video recorder 磁带录
像机 • **verb** (**videoes**, **videoing**,
videoed) film or make a video
recording of 录影；制作…的录像
□ **video game** a computer game
played on a television screen 电子游
戏 **video recorder** a machine linked
to a television, used for recording
programmes and playing videotapes
磁带录像机

videotape /'vɪdiəʊteɪp/ **noun 1**
magnetic tape for recording and
reproducing visual images and sound
录像(磁)带 **2** a cassette on which
this magnetic tape is held 盒式录像
带 • **verb** (**videotapes**, **videotaping**,
videotaped) record on videotape
把…录在录像带上，录制…的图像

vie /vaɪ/ **verb** (**vies**, **vying**, **vied**)
compete eagerly with others in order
to do or achieve something 竞争；相
争

Vietnamese /ˌviːetnəˈmiːz/ **noun** (plural
Vietnamese) **1** a person from
Vietnam 越南人 **2** the language of
Vietnam 越南语 • **adjective** relating
to Vietnam 越南的

view /vjuː/ **noun 1** the ability to see
something or to be seen from a
particular position 视力；视野；视线
2 something seen from a particular
position, especially natural scenery
风景；景色 **3** an attitude or opinion
态度；意见；观点 • **verb 1** look at or

inspect 察看；观察 **2** have a particular
attitude towards (以某种方式)看待，
考虑 □ **in view of** because or as a
result of 由于；鉴于 **with a view to**
with the intention of 指望；为了
■ **viewer noun**.

viewfinder /'vjuːfaɪndə(r)/ **noun** a
device on a camera that you look
through to see what will appear in
the picture (相机的)取景器

viewpoint /'vjuːpɔɪnt/ **noun** an opinion
观点；看法；见解

vigil /'vɪdʒɪl/ **noun** a period of staying
awake through the night to keep
watch or pray (夜间的)警戒；值夜；守
夜(祈祷)

vigilant /'vɪdʒɪlənt/ **adjective** keeping
careful watch for possible danger or
difficulties 警觉的，警惕的；警戒的
■ **vigilance noun vigilantly adverb**.

vigilante /ˌvɪdʒɪˈlænti/ **noun** a member
of a group of people who take it
on themselves to prevent crime
or punish criminals without legal
authority (自发组织的)治安维持会
会员 ■ **vigilantism noun**.

vignette /vɪnˈjet/ **noun 1** a brief, vivid
description or episode (生动的)短
文，花边文字 **2** a small illustration
or photograph which fades into its
background without a definite border
小插图；小装饰图案；虚光照

vigorous /'vɪɡərəs/ **adjective 1**
strong, healthy, and full of energy 精
力充沛的；充满活力的 **2** involving
physical strength, effort, or energy
有力的；强劲的 ■ **vigorously adverb**.

vigour /'vɪɡə(r)/ (US spelling 【美拼
作】**vigor**) **noun 1** physical strength
and good Health 体力；强健 **2** effort,
energy, and enthusiasm 精力；活力；
热情

Viking /'vaɪkɪŋ/ **noun** a member of
the Scandinavian people who settled
in parts of Britain and elsewhere in
NW Europe between the 8th and
11th centuries (8—11世纪定居在英

国和欧洲西北部地区的)北欧海盗,维
金人

vile /vaɪl/ **adjective 1** very unpleasant
令人作呕的;极令人讨厌的 **2** wicked
邪恶的;恶劣的 ■ **vilely** adverb.

vilify /ˈvɪlɪfaɪ/ **verb** (**vilifies, vilifying,
vilified**) speak or write about
someone in a very unpleasant way
诋毁;诽谤;中伤 ■ **vilification** noun.

villa /ˈvɪlə/ **noun 1** Brit. 【英】 a rented
holiday home abroad (在国外租
赁的)度假别墅 **2** (especially in
southern Europe) a large country
house in its own grounds (尤指欧洲
南部的)乡村房地产 **3** a large house
in ancient Rome (古罗马的)庄园

village /ˈvɪlɪdʒ/ **noun** a small community
of streets and houses in a country area
乡村;村庄 ■ **villager** noun.

villain /ˈvɪlən/ **noun 1** a bad person 恶
棍;流氓 **2** a bad character in a novel
or play whose actions are important
to the plot (小说或戏剧中的)反面角
色,反面人物 ■ **villainous** adjective
villainy noun.

villein /ˈvɪlən, -leɪn/ **noun** (in medieval
England) a poor man who had to
work for a lord in return for a small
piece of land on which to grow food
(中世纪英格兰的)隶农

vim /vɪm/ **noun** informal 【非正式】
energy; enthusiasm 活力;精力;热情

vinaigrette /ˌvɪnɪˈgret, -neɪ-/ **noun**
a salad dressing consisting of oil
mixed with vinegar 醋油沙司(一种
用油,醋混合调制的色拉调料)

vindicate /ˈvɪndɪkeɪt/ **verb** (**vindicates,
vindicating, vindicated**) **1** clear
someone of blame or suspicion 澄清
责难(或嫌疑) **2** show something to
be right or justified 证明…有理(或正当)
■ **vindication** noun.

vindictive /vɪnˈdɪktɪv/ **adjective**
having or showing a strong or
inappropriate desire for revenge 有
强烈复仇欲望的;想复仇的 ■ **vindic-
tiveness** noun.

vine /vaɪn/ **noun** a climbing plant,
especially one that produces grapes
藤本植物;(尤指)葡萄藤

vinegar /ˈvɪnɪgə(r)/ **noun** a sour liquid
made from wine, cider, or beer, used
as a seasoning or for pickling 醋
■ **vinegary** adjective.

vineyard /ˈvɪnjəd/ **noun** a plantation
of grapevines producing grapes used
in winemaking (种植酿酒葡萄的)葡
萄园

vintage /ˈvɪntɪdʒ/ **noun 1** the year or
place in which wine was produced
(酒的)酿制年份(或产地) **2** a wine
of high quality made from the crop
of a single identified district in a
good year (特定地方、优良年份酿
制的)佳酿酒 **3** the harvesting of
grapes for winemaking 采收葡萄
酿酒(季节) **4** the grapes or wine
of a particular season (特定季节产
的)葡萄,葡萄酒 **5** the time that
something was produced (某物的)
生产日期 • **adjective 1** referring to
vintage wine (酒上等的,佳酿的 **2**
referring to something from the past
of high quality (过去某时期)优质的

vintner /ˈvɪntnə(r)/ **noun** a wine
merchant 葡萄酒商

vinyl /ˈvaɪnl/ **noun** a type of strong
flexible plastic, used in making floor
coverings, paints, and gramophone
records 乙烯基(一种高强度弹性塑
料,用于制作地板、涂料和留声机唱
片)

viol /ˈvaɪəl/ **noun** an early instrument
like a violin, but with six strings 六
弦提琴(一种早期弦乐器)

viola¹ /viˈəʊlə/ **noun** an instrument
of the violin family, larger than the
violin and tuned to a lower pitch 中
提琴

viola² /ˈvaɪələ/ **noun** a plant of a group
that includes pansies and violets 堇
菜;簇生堇菜

violate /ˈvaɪəleɪt/ **verb** (**violates,
violating, violated**) **1** break a rule

or formal agreement 违反，违背(规定或正式协议) **2** treat something with disrespect 侵犯；亵渎 **3** rape or sexually assault someone 强奸；性侵犯 ■ **violation** noun.

violence /'vaɪələns/ **noun 1** actions using physical force and intended to hurt or kill someone or to cause damage 暴力；暴行 **2** an unpleasant or destructive natural force 猛劲；猛力 **3** strength of emotion 狂热；激情

violent /'vaɪələnt/ **adjective 1** using or involving violence 使用暴力的；暴力的 **2** very forceful or powerful 猛烈的；剧烈的 ■ **violently** adverb.

violet /'vaɪələt/ **noun 1** a small plant with purple or blue flowers 堇菜；紫罗兰 **2** a bluish-purple colour 紫罗兰色；紫色

violin /ˌvaɪə'lɪn/ **noun** a musical instrument with four strings, that you play with a bow 小提琴 ■ **violinist** noun.

violoncello /ˌvaɪələn'tʃeləʊ/ formal term for CELLO. cello 的正式说法

VIP /ˌviː aɪ 'piː/ **noun** a very important person 要人；贵宾

viper /'vaɪpə(r)/ **noun** a poisonous snake with large fangs and a patterned body 蝰蛇(一种毒蛇，毒牙巨大，身体有斑纹)

virago /vɪ'rɑːgəʊ/ **noun** (plural **viragos** or **viragoes**) a domineering, violent, or bad-tempered woman 悍妇；泼妇

viral /'vaɪrəl/ **adjective** having to do with a virus or viruses 病毒(性)的

virgin /'vɜːdʒɪn/ **noun 1** a person who has never had sex 处子；处女 **2** (**the Virgin**) the Virgin Mary, mother of Jesus 圣母马利亚 • **adjective 1** having had no sexual experience 无性经验的；贞洁的 **2** not yet used, touched, or spoiled 未使用过的；未遭破坏的；*virgin forest* 原始森林 **3** (of olive oil) made from the first pressing of olives (橄榄油)初榨的 ■ **virginal** adjective **virginity** noun.

Virgo /'vɜːgəʊ/ **noun** a sign of the zodiac (the Virgin), 23 August–22 September 室女宫(黄道十二宫之一)

virile /'vɪraɪl/ **adjective** (of a man) having strength, energy, and a strong sex drive (男子)阳刚的，精力充沛的，性欲强的 ■ **virility** noun.

virtual /'vɜːtʃuəl/ **adjective 1** almost or nearly the thing described, but not completely 几乎的；差不多的 **2** not existing in reality but made by computer software to appear to do so (计算机)虚拟的 □ **virtual reality** a system in which images that look like real objects are created by computer (计算机创造的)虚拟现实 ■ **virtually** adverb.

virtue /'vɜːtjuː/ **noun 1** behaviour showing high moral standards 高尚行为；正直品性 **2** a good or useful quality 美德；德行 **3** old use 【旧】virginity or chastity 童贞；贞操 □ **by virtue of** because or as a result of 因为；由于

virtuoso /ˌvɜːtʃu'əʊsəʊ/ **noun** (plural **virtuosi** /ˌvɜːtʃu'əʊsiː/ or **virtuosos**) a person highly skilled in music or another art (音乐或其他艺术的)大师，名家 ■ **virtuosity** noun.

virtuous /'vɜːtʃuəs/ **adjective 1** having high moral standards 道德高尚的；品性正直的 **2** old use 【旧】chaste 贞洁的 ■ **virtuously** adverb.

virulent /'vɪrələnt/ **adjective 1** (of a disease or poison) very harmful in its effects (疾病)恶性的；(毒药)剧毒的，致命的 **2** bitterly hostile or critical 恶毒的；狠毒的 ■ **virulence** noun **virulently** adverb.

virus /'vaɪrəs/ **noun 1** a submicroscopic organism which can cause disease 病毒 **2** an infection or disease caused by a virus 病毒感染；病毒性疾病 **3** a piece of code introduced secretly into a computer system in order to damage or destroy data 计算机病毒

visa /'viːzə/ **noun** a note on your

passport indicating that you are allowed to enter, leave, or stay in a country 签证

visage /ˈvɪzɪdʒ/ **noun** literary 【文】a person's facial features or expression 面容；容貌

vis-à-vis /ˌviːzɑːˈviː/ **preposition** in relation to 关于；对于

viscera /ˈvɪsərə/ **plural noun** the internal organs of the body 内脏；脏器

visceral /ˈvɪsərəl/ **adjective 1** relating to deep inward feelings rather than to the intellect 出自内心的；发自肺腑的 **2** relating to the viscera 内脏的；脏器的 ■ **viscerally** adverb.

viscose /ˈvɪskəʊz/ **noun** a smooth synthetic fabric made from cellulose 黏胶纤维织物

viscosity /vɪˈskɒsəti/ **noun** the state of being viscous 黏稠；黏性

viscount /ˈvaɪkaʊnt/ **noun** a British nobleman ranking above a baron and below an earl（英国的）子爵 ■ **viscountess** noun.

viscous /ˈvɪskəs/ **adjective** having a thick, sticky consistency between solid and liquid 黏稠的；黏性的

vise /vaɪs/ US spelling of VICE². vice² 的美式拼法

visibility /ˌvɪzəˈbɪləti/ **noun 1** the state of being able to see or be seen 可见性 **2** the distance you can see, as determined by light and weather conditions（取决于光线和天气状况的）能见距离，能见度；视程

visible /ˈvɪzəbl/ **adjective** able to be seen or noticed 看得见的；可见的 ■ **visibly** adverb.

vision /ˈvɪʒn/ **noun 1** the ability to see 视力；视觉 **2** the ability to think about the future with imagination or wisdom 想象力；幻想力；眼光 **3** an experience of seeing something in a dream, trance, etc. 幻觉；幻象 **4** the images seen on a television screen（电视）图像 **5** a person or sight of

unusual beauty 绝色美人；绝美之景

visionary /ˈvɪʒənri/ **adjective 1** thinking about the future with imagination or wisdom 幻想的；想象的；有眼光的 **2** relating to supernatural or dreamlike visions 幻觉的；幻象的 ● **noun** (plural **visionaries**) a person with imaginative and original ideas about the future 幻想家；有眼光的人，有预见的人

visit /ˈvɪzɪt/ **verb** (**visits**, **visiting**, **visited**) **1** go to spend time with a person or in a place 拜访；访问；参观 **2** view a website or web page 浏览（网页） **3** (**visit with**) N. Amer. 【北美】chat with someone 与（某人）聊天 **4** (**visit something on**) literary 【文】cause something harmful or unpleasant to affect someone 对（某人）施加(有害或令人不快的影响) ● **noun** an act of visiting 访问；参观；游览 ■ **visitor** noun.

visitation /ˌvɪzɪˈteɪʃn/ **noun 1** an official or formal visit（官方或正式的）访问，视察 **2** the appearance of a god, goddess, etc.（神仙等的）显现，现身 **3** a disaster or difficulty seen as a punishment from God 天谴；天祸

visor or **vizor** /ˈvaɪzə(r)/ **noun 1** a movable part of a helmet that can be pulled down to cover the face（头盔上可移动的）面甲，面罩，护面 **2** a screen for protecting the eyes from light（遮光）眼罩

vista /ˈvɪstə/ **noun** a pleasing view 景色；美景

visual /ˈvɪʒuəl/ **adjective** relating to seeing or sight 视觉的；视力的 ● **noun** a picture, piece of film, or display used to illustrate or accompany something（图片、影片、陈列品等）视觉资料 □ **visual display unit** Brit. 【英】a device that displays information from a computer on a screen（计算机的）视频显示器 ■ **visually** adverb.

visualize or **visualise** /ˈvɪʒuəlaɪz/ **verb** (**visualizes**, **visualizing**, visualized) form an image of something in the mind 使形象化;想象;设想 ■ **visualization** noun.

vital /'vaɪtl/ **adjective 1** absolutely necessary 必不可少的;不可或缺的 **2** essential for life 维持生命所必需的 **3** full of energy 充满生机的;生气勃勃的 • noun (**vitals**) the body's important internal organs 重要器官 □ **vital statistics** informal【非正式】the measurements of a woman's bust, waist, and hips 女子三围;女性形体尺寸 ■ **vitally** adverb.

vitality /vaɪ'tæləti/ noun the state of being strong and active 生命力;活力

vitalize or **vitalise** /'vaɪtlaɪz/ verb (**vitalizes**, **vitalizing**, **vitalized**) give strength and energy to 使有生机;使有活力

vitamin /'vɪtəmɪn/ noun any of a group of natural substances which are present in many foods and are essential for normal nutrition 维生素

vitiate /'vɪʃieɪt/ verb (**vitiates**, **vitiating**, **vitiated**) formal【正式】make something less good or effective 使削弱;使降低效能

viticulture /'vɪtɪkʌltʃə(r)/ noun the cultivation of grapevines 葡萄栽培

vitreous /'vɪtriəs/ adjective containing or like glass 含玻璃的;玻璃状的 □ **vitreous humour** the transparent jelly-like tissue that fills the eyeball (眼球的)玻璃体

vitrify /'vɪtrɪfaɪ/ verb (**vitrifies**, **vitrifying**, **vitrified**) convert into glass or a glass-like substance by exposure to heat (使)玻璃化;(使)成玻璃状

vitriol /'vɪtrɪɒl/ noun **1** very cruel or bitter remarks 刻薄话;恶语 **2** old use【旧】sulphuric acid 矾油;硫酸 ■ **vitriolic** adjective.

vituperation /vɪˌtjuːpə'reɪʃn/ noun bitter and abusive language 骂人话;污言 ■ **vituperative** adjective.

viva¹ /'viːvə/ exclamation long live!

万岁!

viva² /'vaɪvə/ or **viva voce** /ˌvaɪvə 'vəʊtʃi/ noun Brit.【英】an oral exam for an academic qualification 口试

vivacious /vɪ'veɪʃəs/ adjective attractively lively 活泼的;快活的 ■ **vivaciously** adverb **vivacity** noun.

vivarium /vaɪ'veəriəm, vɪ-/ noun (plural **vivaria** /vaɪ'veəriə, vɪ-/) a place for keeping animals in natural conditions for study or as pets (模拟自然环境的)动物饲养室

vivid /'vɪvɪd/ adjective **1** producing powerful feelings or strong, clear images in the mind 生动的;逼真的;清晰的 **2** (of a colour) very deep or bright (色彩)强烈的,鲜艳的,鲜明的 ■ **vividly** adverb **vividness** noun.

vivify /'vɪvɪfaɪ/ verb (**vivifies**, **vivifying**, **vivified**) formal【正式】make more lively or interesting; enliven 使更活跃;使更有趣;使生气勃勃

viviparous /vɪ'vɪpərəs/ adjective (of an animal) giving birth to live young (动物)胎生的

vivisection /ˌvɪvɪ'sekʃn/ noun the performance of operations on live animals for scientific research 活体解剖

vixen /'vɪksn/ noun **1** a female fox 雌狐 **2** a spirited or hot-tempered woman 悍妇;泼妇

viz. /vɪz/ adverb namely; in other words 即;也就是;换言之 [short for Latin【缩写,拉丁】= *videlicet*.]

vizor /'vaɪzə(r)/ ⇒ 见 VISOR.

vocabulary /və'kæbjələri/ noun (plural **vocabularies**) **1** all the words used in a particular language or activity 词汇 **2** all the words known to a person 词汇量 **3** a list of words and their meanings, provided with a piece of technical or foreign writing 词汇表

vocal /'vəʊkl/ adjective **1** relating to the human voice 嗓音的;发声的

2 expressing opinions or feelings freely or loudly 畅所欲言的;大声表达意见的 **3** (of music) consisting of or including singing (音乐)歌唱的 • **noun** (also **vocals**) a part of a piece of music that is sung 声乐作品 □ **vocal cords** strips of muscle in the throat that vibrate to produce the voice 声带 ■ **vocally** adverb.

vocalist /'vəʊkəlɪst/ **noun** a singer 歌唱家;声乐家;歌唱者

vocalize or **vocalise** /'vəʊkəlaɪz/ **verb** (**vocalizes, vocalizing, vocalized**) **1** make a sound or say a word 发出(声音);说(话) **2** express something with words 用语言表达 ■ **vocalization** noun.

vocation /vəʊ'keɪʃn/ **noun 1** a strong feeling that you ought to pursue a particular career or occupation (追求某种事业或从事某职业的)强烈愿望,使命感 **2** a person's career or occupation 事业;工作;职业 ■ **vocational** adjective.

vocative /'vɒkətɪv/ **noun** Grammar【语法】 the case of nouns, pronouns, and adjectives used in addressing a person or thing 呼格

vociferous /və'sɪfərəs/ **adjective** expressing opinions in a loud and forceful way 喧嚷的;言辞激烈的 ■ **vociferously** adverb.

vodka /'vɒdkə/ **noun** a clear alcoholic spirit, originally from Russia 伏特加(原产于俄罗斯的烈酒)

vogue /vəʊɡ/ **noun** the fashion or style current at a particular time 流行;时尚 ■ **voguish** adjective.

voice /vɔɪs/ **noun 1** the sound produced in a person's larynx and uttered through the mouth, as speech or song 说话声;嗓音 **2** the ability to speak or sing 发声能力 **3** a vocal part in a piece of music 声部 **4** Grammar【语法】 a form of a verb showing the relation of the subject to the action (动词的)语态 • **verb** (**voices, voicing,** voiced) express something in words 用言语表达 □ **voice box** the larynx 喉 **voice-over** a piece of speech in a film or broadcast that is spoken by a person who is not seen on the screen (电影或电视广播的)画外音,旁白 ■ **voiceless** adjective.

voicemail /'vɔɪsmeɪl/ **noun** an electronic system which can store messages from telephone callers 语音信箱

void /vɔɪd/ **adjective 1** not valid or legally binding 无(法律)效力的 **2** completely empty 空的;空空如也的 **3** (**void of**) free from; lacking 没有的;缺乏的 • **noun** a completely empty space 空白;真空 • **verb 1** empty waste matter from the bladder or bowels 排出,清空(废物) **2** declare to be not valid or legally binding 宣布…作废;取消

voile /vɔɪl/ **noun** a thin, semi-transparent fabric 巴里纱(一种半透明薄纱)

volatile /'vɒlətaɪl/ **adjective 1** liable to change rapidly and unpredictably 多变的,易变的;易变的 **2** (of a substance) easily evaporated at normal temperatures (物质)易挥发的,易散发的 ■ **volatility** noun.

vol-au-vent /'vɒləʊvɒn/ **noun** a small round case of puff pastry filled with a savoury mixture (填有美味馅料的)酥皮馅饼

volcanic /vɒl'kænɪk/ **adjective** relating to or produced by a volcano or volcanoes 火山的;火山产生的

volcano /vɒl'keɪnəʊ/ **noun** (plural **volcanoes** or **volcanos**) a mountain with an opening through which lava, rock, and gas are forced from the earth's crust 火山

vole /vəʊl/ **noun** a small mouse-like rodent 田鼠;仓鼠

volition /və'lɪʃn/ **noun** a person's will or power of independent action 意志力;决断

volley /'vɒli/ **noun** (plural **volleys**)

1 a number of bullets, arrows, etc. fired at one time (子弹、箭等的)群射，齐发 **2** a series of questions, insults, etc. directed rapidly at someone (针对某人的问题、侮辱等的)接连发出，迸发 **3** (in sport) an act of hitting the ball before it touches the ground (体育中球落地前的)截击，托球，凌空踢 • verb (volleys, volleying, volleyed) hit the ball before it touches the ground 截击(空中球)；凌空踢(球)

volleyball /ˈvɒlibɔːl/ noun a team game in which a ball is hit by hand over a net and must be kept from touching the ground 排球(运动)

volt /vəʊlt/ noun the basic unit of electric potential 伏特,伏(电压单位)

voltage /ˈvəʊltɪdʒ/ noun an electrical force expressed in volts 电压

volte-face /ˌvɒltˈfɑːs/ noun an abrupt and complete change of attitude or policy (态度或政策的)完全改变,大转变

voluble /ˈvɒljʊbl/ adjective talking easily and at length 健谈的;善辞令的;滔滔不绝的 ■ **volubility** noun **volubly** adverb.

volume /ˈvɒljuːm/ noun **1** the amount of space occupied by something or enclosed within a container 体积;容积;容量 **2** the amount or quantity of something 量;额 **3** degree of loudness 音量;响度 **4** a book, especially one forming part of a larger work or series (尤指大型著作的)卷,册

voluminous /vəˈluːmɪnəs/ adjective **1** (of clothing) loose and full (衣服)宽松的,宽大的 **2** (of writing) very lengthy (文字作品)浩繁的,冗长的

voluntary /ˈvɒləntri/ adjective **1** done or acting of your own free will 自愿的;志愿的 **2** working or done without payment 义务的;无偿的 • noun (plural **voluntaries**) an organ solo played before, during, or after a church service (教堂礼拜仪式前后或期间演奏的)管风琴独奏曲 ■ **voluntarily** adverb.

volunteer /ˌvɒlənˈtɪə(r)/ noun **1** a person who freely offers to do something 自告奋勇者 **2** a person who does work without being paid (无偿工作的)志愿者 **3** a person who freely joins the armed forces 志愿兵 • verb (**volunteers**, **volunteering**, **volunteered**) **1** freely offer to do something 自愿做;自愿效劳 **2** say or suggest something without being asked 自愿说出;主动建议

voluptuary /vəˈlʌptʃuəri/ noun (plural **voluptuaries**) a person who loves luxury and pleasure 骄奢淫逸者;酒色之徒

voluptuous /vəˈlʌptʃuəs/ adjective **1** (of a woman) curvaceous and sexually attractive (女子)肉感的,丰满的,性感的 **2** giving sensual pleasure 给感官以快感的 ■ **voluptuously** adverb.

vomit /ˈvɒmɪt/ verb (**vomits**, **vomiting**, **vomited**) **1** bring up food from the stomach through the mouth 呕吐 **2** send out in an uncontrolled stream 喷;喷出 • noun food vomited from the stomach 呕吐物

voodoo /ˈvuːduː/ noun a religious cult practised mainly in the Caribbean and involving sorcery and possession by spirits 伏都教(主要见于加勒比海的一种宗教仪式,涉及巫术和灵魂附体)

voracious /vəˈreɪʃəs/ adjective **1** wanting or eating great quantities of food 贪吃的;狼吞虎咽的 **2** doing something eagerly and enthusiastically 贪婪的;饥渴的;渴求的 ■ **voraciously** adverb **voracity** noun.

vortex /ˈvɔːteks/ noun (plural **vortexes** or **vortices** /ˈvɔːtɪsiːz/) a whirling mass of water or air 漩涡;旋风

votary /ˈvəʊtəri/ noun (plural **votaries**) **1** a person who has dedicated themselves to God or religious service

(宗教)献身者 **2** a devoted follower or supporter 忠实拥护者(或支持者)

vote /vəʊt/ **noun 1** a formal choice made between two or more candidates or courses of action 投票;选举;表决 **2 (the vote)** the right to take part in an election 投票权;选举权;表决权 • **verb** (**votes, voting, voted**) give or register a vote 投票;表决 ■ **voter** noun.

votive /ˈvəʊtɪv/ **adjective** offered to a god as a sign of thanks (对上帝)谢恩的,还愿的

vouch /vaʊtʃ/ **verb** (**vouch for**) **1** state that something is true or accurate 声明…属实(或准确) **2** state that someone is who they claim to be, or that they are of good character 为(某人)作担保

voucher /ˈvaʊtʃə(r)/ **noun** a piece of paper that entitles you to a discount, or that may be exchanged for goods or services 折扣券;代金券;票券

vouchsafe /ˌvaʊtʃˈseɪf/ **verb** (**vouchsafes, vouchsafing, vouchsafed**) formal 【正式】 give or say in a gracious or superior way 惠赐;赐予;恩准

vow /vaʊ/ **noun** a solemn promise 誓言;誓约 • **verb** solemnly promise to do something (庄严地)立誓,起誓

vowel /ˈvaʊəl/ **noun** a letter of the alphabet representing a sound in which the mouth is open and the tongue is not touching the top of the mouth, the teeth, or the lips (in English *a, e, i, o,* and *u*) 元音字母

voyage /ˈvɔɪdʒ/ **noun** a long journey by sea or in space 航海;航空;航行 • **verb** (**voyages, voyaging, voyaged**) go on a voyage 航海;航空;航行 ■ **voyager** noun.

voyeur /vwaɪˈɜː(r)/ **noun 1** a person who gains sexual pleasure from watching other people when they are naked or having sex 窥淫癖者;窥淫狂者 **2** a person who enjoys seeing the pain or distress of other people 喜欢目睹他人痛苦(或悲伤)的人 ■ **voyeurism** noun **voyeuristic** adjective.

vs abbreviation versus.

vulcanized or **vulcanised** /ˈvʌlkənaɪzd/ **adjective** (of rubber) hardened by being treated with sulphur at a high temperature (橡胶)硬化的,硫化的

vulgar /ˈvʌlgə(r)/ **adjective 1** lacking sophistication or good taste 庸俗的;粗俗的;不雅的 **2** referring to sex or bodily functions in a rude or inappropriate way 猥亵的;下流的 □ **vulgar fraction** Brit. 【英】 a fraction shown by numbers above and below a line, not decimally 普通分数 ■ **vulgarity** noun **vulgarly** adverb.

vulgarize or **vulgarise** /ˈvʌlgəraɪz/ **verb** (**vulgarizes, vulgarizing, vulgarized**) spoil something by making it less refined or exclusive 使庸俗化;使平庸

vulnerable /ˈvʌlnərəbl/ **adjective** able to be attacked or harmed 易受攻击的;易受伤的 ■ **vulnerability** noun **vulnerably** adverb.

vulpine /ˈvʌlpaɪn/ **adjective** having to do with foxes, or like a fox 狐狸的;狐狸似的

vulture /ˈvʌltʃə(r)/ **noun** a large bird of prey that feeds mainly on dead animals 兀鹫(大型猛禽,主要以动物死尸为食)

vulva /ˈvʌlvə/ **noun** the female external genitals 女阴;外阴

vying /ˈvaɪɪŋ/ present participle of VIE.

Ww

W or **w** /ˈdʌbljuː/ **noun** (plural **Ws** or **W's**) the twenty-third letter of the alphabet 英语字母表的第23个字母 • **abbreviation 1** watts. **2** West or Western.

wacky or **whacky** /ˈwæki/ **adjective** (**wackier**, **wackiest**) informal 【非正式】 funny or amusing in a slightly odd way 古怪的，滑稽可笑的

wad /wɒd/ **noun 1** a lump or bundle of a soft material 〔柔软的〕块状，填料，填絮 **2** a bundle of paper or banknotes 〔纸或钞票的〕捆，沓，叠 • **verb** (**wads**, **wadding**, **wadded**) **1** press a soft material into a wad 把〔软材料〕压缩成一团 **2** line or fill with soft material 用软材料加衬（或填充）

waddle /ˈwɒdl/ **verb** (**waddles**, **waddling**, **waddled**) walk with short steps and a clumsy swaying motion 蹒跚行走；摇摇摆摆地行走 • **noun** a waddling way of walking 蹒跚；摇摇摆摆的行走

wade /weɪd/ **verb** (**wades**, **wading**, **waded**) **1** walk through water or mud 涉，蹚〔水或泥浆〕 **2** (**wade through**) read or deal with something that is boring or takes a long time 读完，处理〔乏味或耗时的事物〕 **3** (**wade in** or **into**) informal 【非正式】 attack or intervene in a forceful way 猛烈攻击；强行介入；硬性干预

wader /ˈweɪdə(r)/ **noun 1** a long-legged bird that feeds in shallow water 涉水鸟；涉禽 **2** (**waders**) high waterproof boots 〔钓鱼者穿的〕长筒靴

wafer /ˈweɪfə(r)/ **noun 1** a very thin, light, sweet biscuit 薄酥饼；薄脆饼；华夫饼干 **2** a thin disc of unleavened bread used in the Christian service of Holy Communion 圣饼〔圣餐时用的未发酵的小圆饼〕

waffle[1] /ˈwɒfl/ Brit. informal 【英，非正式】 **verb** (**waffles**, **waffling**, **waffled**) speak or write at length without saying anything interesting or important 瞎扯；夸夸其谈；废话连篇 • **noun** lengthy talk or writing that does not say anything interesting or important 胡扯；空话；废话

waffle[2] **noun** a small, crisp batter cake, eaten hot with butter or syrup 蛋奶烘饼，华夫饼〔涂以奶油或糖浆趁热吃〕

waft /wɒft/ **verb** pass easily or gently through the air 随风传送；飘浮 • **noun** a gentle movement of air 吹拂；轻吹

wag /wæg/ **verb** (**wags**, **wagging**, **wagged**) move rapidly to and fro 摇动；摆动 • **noun 1** a wagging movement 摇动；摆动 **2** informal 【非正式】 a person who likes making jokes 爱说笑打趣的人 ■ **waggish** adjective.

wage /weɪdʒ/ **noun** (also **wages**) a fixed regular payment for work 工资；工钱 • **verb** (**wages**, **waging**, **waged**) carry on a war or campaign 发动〔战争〕；开展〔运动〕

wager /ˈweɪdʒə(r)/ more formal term for bet 〔正式用语〕打赌

waggle /ˈwægl/ **verb** (**waggles**, **waggling**, **waggled**) move with short, quick movements from side to side or up and down 来回（或上下）摇动（或摆动）

wagon or Brit. 【英】 **waggon** /ˈwægən/ **noun 1** a vehicle, especially a horse-drawn one, for transporting goods 运货车，（尤指）运货马车 **2** Brit. 【英】 a railway vehicle for carrying goods in bulk 铁路货车 □ **on the wagon** informal【非正式】not drinking alcohol 戒酒

wagtail /ˈwæɡteɪl/ **noun** a slender bird with a long tail that it frequently wags up and down 鹡鸰

waif /weɪf/ **noun 1** a poor, helpless person, especially a child 流浪者；(尤指)流浪儿 **2** a person who is thin and pale 消瘦而苍白的人

wail /weɪl/ **noun 1** a long high-pitched cry of pain, grief, or anger 恸哭；嚎 **2** a sound resembling this 呼啸(声)；尖啸(声) • **verb** make a wail 恸哭；嚎啕；呼啸

wain /weɪn/ **noun** old use【旧】a wagon or cart 四轮运货马车；大车

wainscot /ˈweɪnskət, -skɒt/ **noun** an area of wooden panelling on the lower part of the walls of a room 护壁板；护壁板；墙裙

waist /weɪst/ **noun 1** the part of the human body below the ribs and above the hips 腰；腰部 **2** a narrow part in the middle of something (某物的)中间细部

waistband /ˈweɪstbænd/ **noun** a strip of cloth forming the waist of a skirt or pair of trousers 裙带；裤腰

waistcoat /ˈweɪskəʊt/ **noun** Brit.【英】a waist-length garment with buttons down the front and no sleeves or collar 西装背心；马甲

waistline /ˈweɪstlaɪn/ **noun** the measurement around a person's body at the waist 腰围

wait /weɪt/ **verb 1** stay in a particular place or delay doing anything until a particular time or event 等候；等待 **2** be delayed or postponed 推迟；耽搁 **3** (**wait on**) act as an attendant to 给…当侍者；服侍 **4** serve people at a meal or in a restaurant (当侍者)侍候进餐 • **noun** a period of waiting 等待的时间

waiter /ˈweɪtə(r)/ or **waitress** /ˈweɪtrɪs/ **noun** a person whose job is

to serve customers at their tables in a restaurant 侍者；服务员

waive /weɪv/ **verb** (**waives, waiving, waived**) choose not to insist on a claim or right 不坚持，放弃(权利或要求)

waiver /ˈweɪvə(r)/ **noun** an instance of waiving a right or claim, or a document recording this (对权利或要求的)放弃；弃权声明书

wake¹ /weɪk/ **verb** (**wakes, waking, woke;** past participle **woken**) **1** (often **wake up**) stop sleeping 醒来 **2** bring to life, or make more alert 使复苏；使警惕 **3** (**wake up to**) become aware of 意识到 • **noun 1** a party held after a funeral (葬礼后的)守灵聚会 **2** a gathering held beside the body of someone who has died 守夜；守灵

wake² **noun** a trail of disturbed water or air left by a ship or aircraft (船舶或飞机留下的)伴流，尾流 □ **in the wake of** following as a result of 随着…而来；作为…的结果

wakeful /ˈweɪkfl/ **adjective 1** not sleeping 失眠的，不眠的 **2** alert and aware of possible dangers 警觉的，戒备的 ■ **wakefulness noun.**

waken /ˈweɪkən/ **verb** wake from sleep 醒来；唤醒

walk /wɔːk/ **verb 1** move fairly slowly using the legs 走；步行；散步 **2** travel over a route or area on foot 走过(某路线或地区) **3** accompany someone on foot 陪(某人)走 **4** take a dog out for exercise 牵着(狗)走；遛(狗) • **noun 1** a journey on foot 步行；徒步旅行 **2** a fairly slow rate of movement on foot 散步；慢走 **3** a person's way of walking 走路的姿态；步态 **4** a path for walking 人行道 □ **walking stick** a stick used for support when walking 手杖 **walk of life** the position in society that someone holds 职业；社会地位 ■ **walker noun.**

walkabout /ˈwɔːkəbaʊt/ **noun 1** chiefly Brit.【主英】an informal stroll among a crowd by an important visitor (来访的要人)在人群中漫步, 出巡 **2** Austral. 【澳】a journey (originally on foot) made by an Australian aboriginal in order to live in the traditional way (澳大利亚土著居民回归传统生活方式的)漫游, 流浪(最初为徒步漫游)

walkie-talkie /ˌwɔːkiˈtɔːki/ **noun** a portable two-way radio 步话机; 对讲机

Walkman /ˈwɔːkmən/ **noun** (plural **Walkmans** or **Walkmen**) trademark 【商标】a personal stereo "随身听"

walkout /ˈwɔːkaʊt/ **noun** a sudden angry departure as a protest or strike (作为抗议或罢工而突然愤怒的)离开, 退场, 退席

walkover /ˈwɔːkəʊvə(r)/ **noun** an easy victory 轻易取得的胜利; 轻易获胜

walkway /ˈwɔːkweɪ/ **noun** a raised passageway or a wide path (高出地面的)过道, 人行道; (宽阔的)道路

wall /wɔːl/ **noun 1** a continuous upright structure forming a side of a building or room, or enclosing or dividing an area of land 墙; 壁; 围墙 **2** a barrier 屏障; 隔阂 **3** the outer layer or lining of an organ or cavity in the body (人体器官或体腔的)外壁 • **verb** enclose or block with walls 用墙围住(或堵住) □ **go to the wall** informal 【非正式】(of a business) fail (企业)失败, 破产 **wall-eyed** informal 【非正式】having an eye that squints outwards 斜白眼的

wallaby /ˈwɒləbi/ **noun** (plural **wallabies**) an Australian animal like a small kangaroo (澳大利亚)沙袋鼠

wallet /ˈwɒlɪt/ **noun** a small flat, folding holder for money and plastic cards (放钱和信用卡的)皮夹, 钱夹

wallflower /ˈwɔːlflaʊə(r)/ **noun 1** a plant with sweet-smelling flowers that bloom in early spring 墙头花, 桂竹香(早春开花, 花香馥郁) **2** informal 【非正式】a girl who has no one to

dance with at a party "壁花"(聚会上没人邀舞的女孩)

wallop /ˈwɒləp/ informal 【非正式】**verb** (**wallops**, **walloping**, **walloped**) hit very hard 猛击; 重击 • **noun** a heavy blow 猛击; 重击

wallow /ˈwɒləʊ/ **verb 1** roll about or lie in mud or water (在泥或水中)打滚 **2** (of a boat or aircraft) roll from side to side (船或飞机)颠簸, 摇摆 **3** (**wallow in**) indulge in 沉湎于; 沉迷于; 纵乐于 • **noun 1** an act of wallowing 打滚; 翻滚 **2** an area of mud or shallow water where animals go to wallow (哺乳动物打滚的)泥沼, 水坑

wallpaper /ˈwɔːlpeɪpə(r)/ **noun 1** paper pasted in strips over the walls of a room as decoration 墙纸; 壁纸 **2** a background pattern or picture on a computer screen (计算机屏幕上的)壁纸, 桌面背景

wally /ˈwɒli/ **noun** (plural **wallies**) Brit. informal 【英, 非正式】a stupid person 笨蛋; 傻瓜

walnut /ˈwɔːlnʌt/ **noun** an edible nut with a wrinkled shell 核桃; 胡桃

walrus /ˈwɔːlrəs/ **noun** a large sea mammal with downward-pointing tusks 海象

waltz /wɔːlts, wɒlts/ **noun** a ballroom dance in triple time performed by a couple 华尔兹舞 • **verb 1** dance a waltz 跳华尔兹舞 **2** move in a casual or inconsiderate way 无拘无束地走动; 轻快地走动

waltzer /ˈwɔːlsə(r)/ **noun** a fairground ride in which cars are carried round a track that moves up and down (游乐场的)浪卷珍珠

wan /wɒn/ **adjective 1** (of a person) pale and appearing ill or exhausted (人)苍白憔悴的, 倦怠的 **2** (of light) pale or weak (光线)暗淡的, 微弱的 **3** (of a smile) lacking enthusiasm; strained (微笑)淡漠的, 勉强的 ■ **wanly** adverb.

wand /wɒnd/ **noun** a long, thin rod, especially one used in casting magic spells or performing tricks 魔杖

wander /'wɒndə(r)/ **verb** (**wanders, wandering, wandered**) **1** move in a leisurely, casual, or aimless way 漫步;闲逛;游荡 **2** move slowly away from the correct place 渐渐偏移,偏离(正确位置) ■ **noun** a period of wandering 漫步;闲逛;游荡 ■ **wanderer noun.**

wanderlust /'wɒndəlʌst/ **noun** a strong desire to travel 旅行癖;漫游癖

wane /weɪn/ **verb** (**wanes, waning, waned**) **1** (of the moon) appear to decrease in size day by day (月亮)亏,缺 **2** become weaker 衰落;败落;减弱 □ **on the wane** becoming weaker 日渐衰落;日益减弱

wangle /'wæŋgl/ **verb** (**wangles, wangling, wangled**) informal 【非正式】 get something by using persuasion or a clever plan (通过说服或妙计)获得,弄到

want /wɒnt, wɔːnt/ **verb** **1** have a desire to possess or do 想要;希望 **2** (**be wanted**) (of a suspected criminal) be searched for by the police (嫌疑犯)被缉拿,被追捕 **3** (also **want for**) lack or be short of 缺乏,缺少 **4** feel sexual desire for 想与…发生性关系 ■ **noun** **1** lack or shortage 缺乏;不足 **2** poverty 贫困;贫穷 **3** a desire for something 需要;渴望

wanting /'wɒntɪŋ/ **adjective** **1** not having something required or desired 缺少的;缺乏的 **2** not good enough 不够好的,不足以令人满意的

wanton /'wɒntən/ **adjective** **1** (of a cruel or violent action) deliberate and unprovoked (残忍或暴力行为)恶意的,恣意的 **2** having many sexual partners 淫荡的;淫乱的 ■ **wantonly adverb.**

WAP /wæp/ **abbreviation** Wireless Application Protocol, a means of enabling a mobile phone to browse the Internet 无线应用协议(一种能使手机浏览因特网的方法)

wapiti /'wɒpɪti/ **noun** (plural **wapitis**) a large North American red deer 北美赤鹿

war /wɔː(r)/ **noun** **1** a state of armed conflict between different nations, states, or groups 战争 **2** a long contest between rivals or campaign against something 斗争;竞争;对抗 ■ **verb** (**wars, warring, warred**) be involved in a war 打仗;进行战争 □ **be on the warpath** be very angry with someone 怒气冲冲;怒不可遏 **war crime** an action that breaks accepted international rules of war (违反国际战争法的)战争罪行

warble /'wɔːbl/ **verb** (**warbles, warbling, warbled**) sing in a trilling or quavering voice (用颤音高声)唱,(鸟)啭鸣

warbler /'wɔːblə(r)/ **noun** a small songbird with a warbling song 刺嘴莺

ward /wɔːd/ **noun** **1** a room in a hospital for one or more patients 病房;病室 **2** a division of a city or borough that is represented by a councillor or councilors 行政区;选区 **3** a young person looked after by a guardian appointed by their parents or a court (年轻的)被监护人 **4** a ridge or bar in a lock that engages with grooves on a key (锁中与钥匙齿凹相应的)圆形凸挡 ■ **verb** (**ward someone/thing off**) prevent someone or something from harming you 避开;挡开;避免

warden /'wɔːdn/ **noun** **1** a person supervising a place or procedure 保管人;管理人;看守人 **2** Brit. 【英】 the head of certain schools, colleges, etc. (某些学校、学院等的)校长、院长 **3** N. Amer. 【美义】 a prison governor 典狱长;监狱长

warder /'wɔːdə(r)/ **noun** (feminine 【阴

性】 **wardress**) Brit. 【英】 a prison guard 监狱看守;狱吏

wardrobe /ˈwɔːdrəub/ **noun 1** a large, tall cupboard for hanging clothes in 衣柜;衣橱 **2** a person's entire collection of clothes (个人的)全部服装 **3** the costume department of a theatre or film company (剧院或电影公司的)服装部,戏装保管室

wardroom /ˈwɔːdrʊm/ **noun** the room on a warship where the officers eat (军舰上的)军官食堂

ware /weə(r)/ **noun 1** pottery of a particular type (特定种类的)陶器,瓷器 **2** manufactured articles 器皿,制品 **3** (**wares**) articles offered for sale 商品;货物

warehouse /ˈweəhaʊs/ **noun 1** a large building for storing raw materials or manufactured goods 仓库;货栈 **2** a large wholesale or retail store 批发店;大型零售商店

warfare /ˈwɔːfeə(r)/ **noun** the activity of fighting a war 交战;作战

warhead /ˈwɔːhed/ **noun** the explosive head of a missile, torpedo, etc. (导弹、鱼雷等的)弹头

warhorse /ˈwɔːhɔːs/ **noun** informal 【非正式】 a very experienced soldier, politician, etc. 久经沙场的老兵;老练的政客

warlike /ˈwɔːlaɪk/ **adjective 1** hostile 有敌意的;好战的 **2** intended for war 准备战斗的

warlock /ˈwɔːlɒk/ **noun** a man who practises witchcraft 魔术师

warlord /ˈwɔːlɔːd/ **noun** a military commander, especially one controlling a region (尤指控制某一地区的)军阀,军阀首脑

warm /wɔːm/ **adjective 1** at a fairly high temperature 温暖的;暖和的 **2** helping the body to stay warm 保暖的 **3** enthusiastic, affectionate, or kind 热情的;充满深情的;友善的 **4** (of a colour) containing red, yellow, or orange tones (颜色)暖色

的(包含红色、黄色或橙色调) **5** (of a scent or trail) fresh and easy to follow (气味或痕迹)新鲜的,强烈的 • **verb 1** make or become warm (使)变温暖;(使)变暖和 **2** (**warm to** or **towards**) become more interested in or enthusiastic about 变得感兴趣;变得热情 • **noun** (**the warm**) a warm place or area 暖和的地方(或地区) □ **warm-blooded** (of animals) keeping a constant body temperature by their body's chemical processes (动物)温血的,恒温的 **warm up** prepare for physical exertion by doing gentle stretches and exercises 热身;做热身活动 **warm something up** entertain an audience before the arrival of the main act (在主要节目开始之前)使(观众)充满热情,使活跃 ■ **warmly** adverb.

warmonger /ˈwɔːmʌŋgə(r)/ **noun** a person who tries to bring about war 好战者;主战论者;战争贩子

warmth /wɔːmθ/ **noun 1** the quality of being warm 暖和;温暖 **2** enthusiasm, affection, or kindness 热情;亲切;善意 **3** strength of emotion 激动;生气

warn /wɔːn/ **verb 1** tell someone of a possible danger or problem 警告;提醒 **2** advise someone not to do something 告诫 **3** (**warn someone off**) order someone to keep away 告诫(某人)离开

warning /ˈwɔːnɪŋ/ **noun 1** a statement or event that indicates a possible danger or problem 警告;预兆 **2** advice against wrong or foolish behaviour 告诫 **3** advance notice 预先通知;预告

warp /wɔːp/ **verb 1** make or become bent or twisted (使)变弯;(使)变形 **2** make abnormal or strange 使反常;使奇怪 • **noun 1** a distortion or twist in shape 变形;扭曲 **2** the lengthwise threads on a loom over and under which the weft threads are passed to make cloth 经线;经纱

warrant /ˈwɒrənt/ **noun 1** an official authorization allowing police, soldiers, etc. to make an arrest, search premises, etc. 逮捕状;搜查令 **2** a document that entitles you to receive goods, money, or services (使持有者有资格得到货物、金钱或服务的)收款凭单 **3** justification or authority 理由;根据 • **verb 1** justify or make necessary 证明…正当(或有理);使成为必要 **2** officially state or guarantee 批准;保证 □ **warrant officer** a rank of military officer below the commissioned officers 准尉

warranty /ˈwɒrənti/ **noun** (plural **warranties**) a written guarantee promising to repair or replace an article if necessary within a stated period (商品的)保修单,担保书

warren /ˈwɒrən/ **noun 1** a network of interconnecting rabbit burrows 交错的兔穴网 **2** a complex network of paths or passages 复杂交错的小路(或通道)

warrior /ˈwɒriə(r)/ **noun** a brave or experienced soldier or fighter 勇士;(经验丰富的)战士,斗士

warship /ˈwɔːʃɪp/ **noun** an armed ship designed to take part in warfare at sea 军舰;舰艇

wart /wɔːt/ **noun** a small, hard growth on the skin 疣;肉赘 ■ **warty** adjective.

warthog /ˈwɔːthɒɡ/ **noun** an African wild pig with warty lumps on the face 疣猪(产于非洲,脸部有肉疣)

wary /ˈweəri/ **adjective** (**warier**, **wariest**) cautious about possible dangers or problems 谨慎的;小心翼翼的;警惕的 ■ **warily** adverb **wariness** noun.

was /wɒz, wəz/ 1st and 3rd person singular past of BE.

wash /wɒʃ/ **verb 1** clean with water and usually soap or detergent (通常指用肥皂或清洁剂)洗,洗涤 **2** (water) flow freely in a particular direction (水)冲蚀,冲击 **3** (**wash over**) happen all around someone without affecting them very much (周围发生的事)对…无多大影响 **4** informal 【非正式】 seem convincing or genuine 站得住脚;经得起考验;可靠 • **noun 1** an act of washing 洗涤;冲洗 **2** a quantity of clothes needing to be washed 要洗的衣物 **3** the water or air disturbed by a moving boat or aircraft (船或飞机驶过后的)尾流,涡流 **4** a medicinal or cleansing solution 药水;药剂;洗涤剂 **5** a thin coating of paint (涂料的)涂层 □ **be washed out 1** be postponed or cancelled because of rain (因下雨而)延迟,取消 **2** (**washed out**) pale and tired 苍白而疲惫的;精疲力竭的 **wash your hands of** take no further responsibility for 洗手不干;不再负责 **wash up 1** Brit. 【英】 wash crockery and cutlery after use 洗餐具 **2** (**washed up**) informal 【非正式】 no longer effective or successful 无效的;失败的

washbasin /ˈwɒʃbeɪsn/ **noun** a basin for washing your hands and face 洗脸盆

washboard /ˈwɒʃbɔːd/ **noun** a ridged or corrugated board formerly used for scrubbing clothes when washing them 洗衣板;搓板

washer /ˈwɒʃə(r)/ **noun 1** a person or device that washes 洗衣人;洗衣机 **2** a small flat ring fixed between a nut and bolt (螺母或螺钉之间的)垫圈

washing /ˈwɒʃɪŋ/ **noun** clothes, sheets, towels, etc. that need washing or have just been washed 待洗(或刚洗过的)衣物 □ **washing-up** Brit. 【英】 crockery, cutlery, etc. that need washing 待洗餐具

washout /ˈwɒʃaʊt/ **noun** informal 【非正式】 a disappointing failure 惨败

washroom /ˈwɒʃruːm, -rom/ **noun** N. Amer. 【北美】 a room with washing and toilet facilities 盥洗室

washstand /'wɒʃstænd/ **noun** a piece of furniture formerly used to hold a bowl or basin for washing the hands and face 脸盆架

wasn't /'wɒznt/ **short form** was not.

wasp /wɒsp/ **noun** a stinging winged insect with a black and yellow striped body 黄蜂；胡蜂 □ **wasp waist** a very narrow waist 蜂腰；细腰

waspish /'wɒspɪʃ/ **adjective** sharply irritable 易怒的；暴躁的 ■ **waspishly** adverb.

wassail /'wɒseɪl/ old use【旧】**noun** lively festivities involving the drinking of a lot of alcohol 狂欢酒宴；纵酒欢庆 • **verb 1** celebrate with a lot of alcohol 欢宴 **2** go carol-singing at Christmas (挨家挨户)唱圣诞颂歌

wastage /'weɪstɪdʒ/ **noun 1** the process of wasting 浪费；耗费；损耗 **2** an amount wasted 浪费(或耗费、损耗)量 **3** (also **natural wastage**) Brit.【英】the reduction in the size of a workforce through people resigning or retiring (由于辞职或退休引起的)减员

waste /weɪst/ **verb** (**wastes, wasting, wasted**) **1** use more of something than is necessary 浪费；滥用 **2** fail to make good use of 未充分(或很好)利用 **3** (**be wasted on**) not be appreciated by 未被…欣赏 **4** (often **waste away**) gradually become weaker and thinner 变衰弱；变消瘦 **5** (**wasted**) informal【非正式】under the influence of alcohol or illegal drugs 醉酒的；毒瘾发作的 • **adjective 1** discarded because no longer useful or required 丢弃的；废弃的；无用的 **2** (of land) uncultivated, or built on (土地)未被利用的，未开垦的，荒无人烟的 • **noun 1** an instance of wasting 浪费；滥用；糟蹋 **2** material that is not wanted or useful 废料；废弃物 **3** a large area of barren, uninhabited land 不毛之地；荒无人烟之地 □ **lay waste to** completely destroy 彻底破坏；摧毁 ■ **waster** noun.

wasteful /'weɪstfl/ **adjective** using more of something than is necessary 浪费的；挥霍的 ■ **wastefully** adverb.

wasteland /'weɪstlænd/ **noun** a barren or empty area of land 荒地；荒漠

wastrel /'weɪstrəl/ **noun** literary【文】a lazy person who spends their time or money wastefully 挥霍无度的人；败家子

watch /wɒtʃ/ **verb 1** look at attentively 注视；观看 **2** keep under careful observation 仔细观察；监视 **3** be cautious about 小心；留意 **4** (**watch for**) look out for 警惕；提防；戒备 **5** (**watch out**) be careful 当心；注意 • **noun 1** a small clock worn on a strap on your wrist 手表 **2** an instance of watching 注视；观察；监视 **3** a period of keeping watch during the night 值夜班 **4** a shift worked by firefighters or police officers (消防队员或警察的)轮班 □ **keep watch** be alert for danger or trouble 留意；警惕；提防(危险或困难) ■ **watchable** adjective **watcher** noun.

watchdog /'wɒtʃdɒg/ **noun 1** a dog kept to guard property 看门狗 **2** a person or group that monitors the practices of companies providing a particular service (对提供特定服务的公司的业务进行监督的)监察人员，监察团体

watchful /'wɒtʃfl/ **adjective** alert to possible difficulty or danger 警惕的；戒备的 ■ **watchfully** adverb **watchfulness** noun.

watchman /'wɒtʃmən/ **noun** (plural **watchmen**) a man employed to look after an empty building (受雇看守无人建筑物的)看守人，警卫

watchtower /'wɒtʃtaʊə(r)/ **noun** a

W

tower built as a high observation point 瞭望塔；岗楼

watchword /ˈwɒtʃwɜːd/ noun a word or phrase expressing a central aim or belief 口号；标语；格言

water /ˈwɔːtə(r)/ noun **1** the liquid which forms the seas, lakes, rivers, and rain 水 **2** (**waters**) an area of sea under the authority of a particular country 领海 **3** (**waters**) fluid that passes from a woman's body shortly before she gives birth (即将分娩前流出的)羊水 • verb (**waters, watering, watered**) **1** pour water over a plant 给(植物)浇水；灌溉 **2** give a drink of water to an animal 给(动物)喂水 **3** (of the eyes or mouth) produce tears or saliva 流泪；流口水 **4** dilute a drink with water 掺水冲淡；加水稀释 **5** (**water something down**) make something less forceful or controversial 削弱；缓解 □ **hold water** (of a theory) seem valid or reasonable (理论)符合逻辑，站得住脚 **water buffalo** a kind of Asian buffalo used for carrying heavy loads 水牛 **water cannon** a device that sends out a powerful jet of water, used to make a crowd disperse (用来疏散人群的)高压水炮 **water closet** dated 【废】 a flush toilet 抽水马桶 **water ice** a frozen dessert consisting of fruit juice or purée in a sugar syrup (用果汁或果泥加糖水制成的)冰糕 **watering can** a portable container with a long spout, used for watering plants 喷壶；洒水壶 **watering hole** informal 【非正式】 a pub or bar 酒吧 **water lily** a plant that grows in water, with large round floating leaves 睡莲 **water meadow** a meadow that is periodically flooded by a stream or river (因周期性被河水淹而保持肥沃的)浸水草地，草甸 **water polo** a game played by swimmers in a pool, who try to throw the ball into

their opponents' net 水球 **water table** the level below which the ground is saturated with water 地下水面；潜水面 **water tower** a tower that raises up a water tank to create enough pressure to distribute the water through pipes (自来水)水塔 ■ **waterless** adjective **watery** adjective.

waterbed /ˈwɔːtəbed/ noun a bed with a water-filled mattress (带有充水床垫的)水床

watercolour /ˈwɔːtəkʌlə(r)/ (US spelling 【美拼作】 **watercolor**) noun **1** artists' paint that is thinned with water 水彩(颜料) **2** a picture painted with watercolours 水彩画

watercourse /ˈwɔːtəkɔːs/ noun a stream or artificial water channel 溪流；河道；沟渠

watercress /ˈwɔːtəkres/ noun a kind of cress which grows in running water 水田芥

waterfall /ˈwɔːtəfɔːl/ noun a place where a stream of water falls from a height 瀑布

waterfowl /ˈwɔːtəfaʊl/ plural noun ducks, geese, or other large birds living in water 水鸟；水禽

waterfront /ˈwɔːtəfrʌnt/ noun a part of a town or city alongside an area of water (城镇的)滨水区，码头区

waterhole /ˈwɔːtəhəʊl/ noun a water-filled hollow where animals drink (尤指动物饮水的)水坑，水池

waterline /ˈwɔːtəlaɪn/ noun the level normally reached by the water on the side of a ship (船的)水(平)线，吃水线

waterlogged /ˈwɔːtəlɒgd/ adjective saturated with water 浸透水的；充满水的

watermark /ˈwɔːtəmɑːk/ noun a faint design made in some paper that can be seen when held against the light 水印

watermelon /ˈwɔːtəmelən/ noun a very large fruit with smooth green

skin, red pulp, and watery juice 西瓜

watermill /'wɔːtəmɪl/ **noun** a mill worked by a waterwheel 水磨；水力磨粉机

waterproof /'wɔːtəpruːf/ **adjective** unable to be penetrated by water 防水的；不透水的 • **noun** Brit. 【英】a waterproof garment 雨衣 • **verb** make waterproof 使防水；使不透水

watershed /'wɔːtəʃed/ **noun 1** an area of land that separates waters flowing to different rivers, seas, etc. 分水岭 **2** a turning point in a situation 转折点

waterski /'wɔːtəskiː/ **noun** (plural **waterskis**) each of a pair of skis that let you skim the surface of the water when towed by a motorboat (由快艇拖曳的)滑水橇 • **verb** (**waterskis**, **waterskiing**, **waterskied**) travel on waterskis 乘水橇滑水 ■ **waterskier** noun.

waterspout /'wɔːtəspaʊt/ **noun** a column of water formed by a whirlwind over the sea (海上旋风引起的)水龙卷，海龙卷

watertight /'wɔːtətaɪt/ **adjective 1** not allowing any water to pass through 水密的；防水的；不透水的 **2** unable to be called into question 无懈可击的；天衣无缝的

waterway /'wɔːtəweɪ/ **noun** a river, canal, or other route for travel by water 水路；航道

waterwheel /'wɔːtəwiːl/ **noun** a large wheel driven by flowing water, used to work machinery or to raise water to a higher level (水力推动的)水车，水轮；(汲水用的)辐轳

waterworks /'wɔːtəwɜːks/ **noun** a place with equipment for managing a water supply 自来水厂；供水系统

watt /wɒt/ **noun** the basic unit of power 瓦(特)(功率基本单位)

wattage /'wɒtɪdʒ/ **noun** an amount of electrical power expressed in watts 瓦(特)数

wattle¹ /'wɒtl/ **noun** rods interlaced with twigs or branches, used for making fences, walls, etc. (编筑篱笆、围墙等用的)枝条构架，编条结构 □ **wattle and daub** wattle covered with mud or clay, formerly used in building walls (旧时用来筑墙的)抹灰篱笆

wattle² **noun** a fleshy part hanging from the head or neck of the turkey and some other birds (火鸡等鸟类头部或颈部的)肉垂

wave /weɪv/ **verb** (**waves**, **waving**, **waved**) **1** move your hand, or something held in it, to and fro, especially when greeting someone 挥手打招呼(或示意) **2** move to and fro with a swaying motion 摇动；飘动 • **noun 1** a ridge of water moving along the surface of the sea or breaking on the shore 波涛；波浪 **2** a sudden increase in a phenomenon or emotion (现象的)突发，(情感的)高涨 **3** a gesture made by waving your hand 挥手 **4** a slightly curling lock of hair 卷发；波浪形头发 **5** a regular to-and-fro motion of particles of matter involved in transmitting sound, light, heat, etc. (声、光、热等的)波状运动

waveband /'weɪvbænd/ **noun** a range of wavelengths in radio transmission (用于无线电传输的)波段

wavelength /'weɪvleŋθ/ **noun 1** the distance between successive crests of a wave of sound, light, radio, etc (尤指声、光、无线电波等的)波长 **2** a person's way of thinking 观点

wavelet /'weɪvlɪt/ **noun** a small wave 小波浪；子波

waver /'weɪvə(r)/ **verb** (**wavers**, **wavering**, **wavered**) **1** move in a quivering way; flicker 摇晃；摇摆；闪烁 **2** begin to weaken; falter 开始变弱；动摇 **3** be indecisive 犹豫不决；举棋不定

wavy /'weɪvi/ **adjective** (**wavier, waviest**) having a series of wave-like curves 波浪式的；波状的

wax¹ /wæks/ **noun 1** a soft solid substance used for making candles or polishes (用于制蜡烛或上光的) 蜡 **2** a substance produced by bees to make honeycombs; beeswax 蜂蜡 • **verb** polish or treat with wax 用蜡上光(或处理) ▪ **waxen** adjective **waxy** adjective.

wax² **verb 1** (of the moon) gradually appear to increase in size (月亮)渐圆，渐满 **2** literary 【文】become larger or stronger 变大；增强 **3** literary 【文】speak or write in a particular way (以特定方式)说，写：*They waxed lyrical.* 他们越说越来劲。

waxwork /'wækswɜːk/ **noun 1** a lifelike dummy made of wax 蜡像 **2** (**waxworks**) an exhibition of waxworks 蜡像展览

way /weɪ/ **noun 1** a method, style, or manner of doing something 方法；风格；方式 **2** a road, track, or path 道；径；路；街 **3** a route or means taken in order to reach, enter, or leave a place (到达、进入或离开某地的)路线，途径，手段 **4** a direction 方向 **5** the distance in space or time between two points (空间或时间上两点之间的)距离 **6** condition or state 情况；状态 **7** (**ways**) parts into which something divides (分成的)部分 • **adverb** informal 【非正式】at or to a considerable distance or extent 远远地；大大地；非常 □ **by the way** used to introduce a comment that is not connected to the current subject of conversation 顺便提一下 **give way** yield 让步；屈服 **2** collapse or break under pressure 坍塌；折断 **3** (**give way to**) be replaced by 被⋯取代(或代替) **in the way** obstructing someone's progress 挡道的；妨碍人的 **make way** allow room for someone or something

else 让路；腾出地方 **way-out** informal 【非正式】very unconventional 非传统的；不寻常的

wayfarer /'weɪfeərə(r)/ **noun** literary 【文】a person who travels on foot 徒步旅行者

waylay /weɪ'leɪ/ **verb** (**waylays, waylaying, waylaid**) **1** intercept someone in order to attack them 袭击；伏击 **2** stop someone and talk to them 拦住询问；(为谈话而)拦截

wayside /'weɪsaɪd/ **noun** the edge of a road 路边；路旁

wayward /'weɪwəd/ **adjective** unpredictable and hard to control 反复无常的，难以控制的，任性的

WC /dʌblju: 'si:/ **abbreviation** Brit. 【英】water closet 盥洗室；厕所

we /wi:, wi/ **pronoun 1** used by a speaker to refer to himself or herself and one or more other people considered together 我们；咱们 **2** people in general (泛指)人们

weak /wi:k/ **adjective 1** lacking strength and energy (体力和精力)弱的，差的 **2** likely to break or give way under pressure 易破的，易倒塌的 **3** not secure or stable 不稳固的；不牢固的 **4** lacking power, influence, or ability 无权力的，无影响力的，无能力的 **5** (of a liquid or solution) heavily diluted (液体或溶液)稀薄的 ▪ **weakly** adverb.

weaken /'wi:kən/ **verb** make or become weak 削弱；(使)变弱

weakling /'wi:klɪŋ/ **noun** a weak person or animal 瘦弱的人；弱小的动物

weakness /'wi:knɪs/ **noun 1** the state of being weak 虚弱；衰弱 **2** a fault 弱点；缺点 **3** (**weakness for**) a liking for something that you find difficult to resist (对⋯的)嗜好，癖好

weal /wi:l/ **noun** a red swollen mark left on flesh by a blow or pressure (皮肤受击打或挤压后留下的)红肿的伤痕

wealth /welθ/ **noun 1** a large amount of money, property, or possessions 财富 **2** the state of being rich 富有；富裕 **3** a large amount of something desirable 大量；丰富；充裕

wealthy /ˈwelθi/ **adjective (wealthier, wealthiest)** rich 富有的；有钱的

wean /wi:n/ **verb 1** make a young mammal used to food other than its mother's milk 使(幼小的哺乳动物)断奶 **2 (wean someone off)** make someone give up a habit or addiction 使戒掉(某一习惯) **3 (be weaned on)** be strongly influenced by something from an early age 从小就深受(某事物)的影响

weapon /ˈwepən/ **noun 1** a thing used to cause physical harm or damage 武器；兵器；凶器 **2** a means of gaining an advantage or defending yourself 斗争的工具(或手段) ▪ **weaponry** noun.

wear /weə(r)/ **verb (wears, wearing, wore;** past participle **worn) 1** have something on your body as clothing, decoration, or protection 穿；戴 **2** have a particular facial expression 面露；面带 **3** damage something by continuous use or rubbing 用旧；穿破；磨损 **4 (wear off)** stop being effective or strong 失去效力(或力量) **5 (wear someone out)** exhaust someone 使筋疲力竭 **6 (wearing)** mentally or physically tiring 使人疲倦的；令人厌倦的 **7 (wear on)** (of time) pass in a slow or boring way (时间)逐渐消逝，慢慢过去 ▪ **noun 1** clothing of a particular type (特定类型的)服装 **2** damage caused by continuous use 磨损；用坏 ▪ **wearer** noun.

wearisome /ˈwɪərɪsəm/ **adjective** making you feel tired or bored 令人疲倦的；令人厌烦的

weary /ˈwɪəri/ **adjective (wearier, weariest) 1** tired 疲劳的；疲倦的 **2** causing tiredness 令人疲倦的；令人厌烦的 **3 (weary of)** bored with (对…)感到厌倦的 ▪ **verb (wearies, wearying, wearied) 1** make someone weary 使疲劳；使厌倦 **2 (weary of)** grow bored with (对…)感到厌倦 ▪ **wearily** adverb **weariness** noun.

weasel /ˈwi:zl/ **noun** a small, slender meat-eating animal with reddish-brown fur 鼬鼠；黄鼠狼

weather /ˈweðə(r)/ **noun** the state of the atmosphere in terms of temperature, wind, rain, etc. 天气；气象 ▪ **verb (weathers, weathering, weathered) 1** wear something away by long exposure to the weather (经长期风吹日晒而)风化，风干 **2** come safely through a difficult or dangerous situation 平安度过；经受住 □ **make heavy weather of** informal 【非正式】 have unnecessary difficulty in dealing with 夸大…的困难；对…小题大做 **under the weather** informal 【非正式】 slightly unwell 略感不适的

weathercock /ˈweðəkɒk/ **noun** a weathervane in the form of a cockerel (公鸡形)风向标，风信鸡

weatherman /ˈweðəmæn/ **noun** (plural **weathermen**) a man who gives a description and forecast of weather conditions on television or radio 气象预报员

weathervane /ˈweðəveɪn/ **noun** a revolving pointer that shows the direction of the wind 风向标

weave¹ /wi:v/ **verb (weaves, weaving, wove;** past participle **woven** or **wove) 1** make fabric by interlacing long threads with others 编制，编织(织物) **2** make facts, events, etc. into a story 编造；将…编成(故事) ▪ **noun** a particular way in which fabric is woven 织法；编织式样 ▪ **weaver** noun.

weave² **verb (weaves, weaving, weaved)** move from side to side to get around obstructions (为避开障碍物)迂回前进，穿插行进

web /web/ **noun 1** a network of fine threads made by a spider to catch its prey (蜘蛛结的)网 **2** a complex system of interconnected elements 一系列(相互关联的)复杂要素；错综复杂的事物 **3** (**the Web**) the World Wide Web 万维网 **4** the skin between the toes of a bird or animal living in water (水禽或水生动物的)蹼 □ **web page** a document that can be accessed via the Internet 网页

webbed /webd/ **adjective** (of an animal's feet) having the toes connected by a web (动物)蹼足的

webbing /'webɪŋ/ **noun** strong fabric used for making straps, belts, etc. (用于做带子、皮带等的)结实织物

webcam /'webkæm/ **noun** (trademark in the US【美国商标】) a video camera connected to a computer, so that the film produced may be viewed on the Internet (与电脑相连、所拍摄画面能在互联网上观看的)网络摄像机

weblog /'weblɒg/ **noun** a personal website on which someone regularly writes about their interests, experiences, etc. 网络博客

website /'websaɪt/ **noun** a location on the Internet that maintains one or more web pages 网站；站点

wed /wed/ **verb** (**weds**, **wedding**, **wedded** or **wed**) **1** formal or literary【正式或文】marry 结婚；嫁；娶 **2** (**wedded**) having to do with marriage 婚姻的 **3** combine two desirable factors or qualities 使(两种有利因素或特性)结合起来 **4** (**be wedded to**) be entirely devoted to a particular activity or belief 执著于，献身于(特定活动、信仰)

we'd /wiːd, wɪd/ **short form 1** we had. **2** we should or we would.

wedding /'wedɪŋ/ **noun** a marriage ceremony 婚礼，结婚庆典

wedge /wedʒ/ **noun 1** a piece of wood, metal, etc. with a thick end that tapers to a thin edge (木头、金属等的)楔子，尖劈 **2** a golf club for hitting the ball as high as possible into the air 带楔形头的高尔夫球杆 **3** a shoe with a fairly high heel forming a solid block with the sole 楔形后跟鞋；坡跟鞋 • **verb** (**wedges**, **wedging**, **wedged**) **1** fix in position using a wedge 把…楔住，把…楔牢 **2** force into a narrow space 楔入；挤入；塞入 □ **the thin end of the wedge** informal【非正式】something unimportant in itself which is likely to lead to a more serious or unpleasant situation 可能引起大变动(或糟糕局面)的小事

wedlock /'wedlɒk/ **noun** formal【正式】the state of being married 已婚状态

Wednesday /'wenzdeɪ, -dɪ/ **noun** the day of the week before Thursday and following Tuesday 星期三；周三

✔ 拼写指南 Remember the *d* before the *n*: We**d**nesday. 记住拼写 Wednesday 中 n 前的 d。

wee /wiː/ **adjective** Scottish【苏格兰】little 小的；一丁点儿的

weed /wiːd/ **noun 1** a wild plant growing where it is not wanted 杂草；野草 **2** informal【非正式】cannabis 大麻 **3** (**the weed**) informal【非正式】tobacco 烟草 **4** Brit. informal【英，非正式】a weak or skinny person 虚弱的人；极瘦的人 **5** (**weeds**) old use【旧】black clothes worn by a widow in mourning for her husband (寡妇穿的)丧服 • **verb 1** remove weeds from 给…除杂草 **2** (**weed someone/thing out**) remove unwanted members or items 清除，剔除，淘汰(无用的成员或东西)

weedkiller /'wiːdkɪlə(r)/ **noun** a substance used to destroy weeds 除草剂；除莠剂

weedy /'wiːdi/ **adjective** (**weedier**, **weediest**) **1** Brit. informal【英，非正**

式】 thin and weak 瘦弱的；虚弱无力的 **2** containing or covered with many weeds 杂草丛生的；长满杂草的

week /wiːk/ **noun 1** a period of seven days 星期；周；礼拜 **2** the five days from Monday to Friday, when many people work (从周一到周五的)五天，工作周 **3** Brit.【英】a week after a stated day (特定某一天之后的)一星期，一周

weekday /ˈwiːkdeɪ/ **noun** a day of the week other than Saturday or Sunday 工作日(指星期六、星期日以外的某一天)

weekend /ˌwiːkˈend/ **noun** Saturday and Sunday 周末(星期六和星期日)

weekly /ˈwiːkli/ **adjective & adverb** happening or produced once a week 一周一次的

weeny /ˈwiːni/ **adjective (weenier, weeniest)** informal【非正式】tiny 极小的，极小的

weep /wiːp/ **verb (weeps, weeping, wept) 1** shed tears; cry 哭泣；流泪 **2** (of a wound) produce liquid (伤口)流脓 • **noun** a period of shedding tears 一阵哭泣

weepy /ˈwiːpi/ **adjective (weepier, weepiest)** informal【非正式】**1** tearful 流泪的；泪汪汪的 **2** sentimental 感伤的；多愁善感的

weevil /ˈwiːvl/ **noun** a small beetle which eats crops or stored food 象甲；象鼻虫

weft /weft/ **noun** (in weaving) the threads that are passed over and under the warp threads to make cloth (编织中的)纬线，纬纱

weigh /weɪ/ **verb 1** find out how heavy someone or something is 称…的重量 **2** have a particular weight 重；重量为… **3** (**weigh something out**) measure and take out a portion of a particular weight 按(一定重量)分发 **4** (**weigh someone down**) be a burden to someone 使负重；

成为…的负担 **5** (**weigh on**) be depressing or worrying to 使压抑；使烦恼 **6** (**weigh in**) (of a boxer or jockey) be officially weighed before or after a contest (拳击手或赛马骑师)赛前(或赛后)称体重 **7** (often **weigh something up**) consider something carefully 权衡；斟酌 **8** (often **weigh against**) influence a decision or action 影响(决定或行为) **9** (**weigh in**) informal【非正式】join in something enthusiastically or forcefully 热情参与；充分发挥

weighbridge /ˈweɪbrɪdʒ/ **noun** a machine on to which vehicles are driven to be weighed (称车辆重量的)桥秤，地磅

weight /weɪt/ **noun 1** the heaviness of a person or thing 体重；重量 **2** the quality of being heavy 重 **3** a unit used for expressing how much something weighs 重量单位；衡制 **4** a piece of metal known to weigh a definite amount and used on scales to find out how heavy something is 砝码；秤砣；秤锤 **5** a heavy object 重体；重物 **6** ability to influence decisions 影响力 **7** the importance attached to something 重要(性) • **verb 1** make heavier or keep in place with a weight 使变重；加重量于(以使其稳固) **2** (**be weighted**) be arranged so as to give one party an advantage 对…有利 ■ **weightless** adjective.

weighting /ˈweɪtɪŋ/ **noun 1** adjustment made to take account of special circumstances (考虑到特殊情况而作的)调整，调节 **2** Brit.【英】additional wages paid to allow for a higher cost of living in a particular area (因某地区生活费用较高而发放的)额外津贴，额外补贴

weightlifting /ˈweɪtlɪftɪŋ/ **noun** the sport or activity of lifting heavy weights 举重(运动) ■ **weightlifter** noun.

weighty /'weɪti/ **adjective (weightier, weightiest)** 1 heavy 重的；沉重的；繁重的 2 very serious and important 重要的；重大的 3 very influential 有影响的；举足轻重的

weir /wɪə(r)/ **noun** a low dam built across a river to control its flow 堰；拦河坝

weird /wɪəd/ **adjective** 1 informal【非正式】very strange 奇特的；不可思议的 2 mysterious or strange in a frightening way; eerie 神秘的；奇怪的；怪异的 ■ **weirdly** adverb **weirdness** noun.

✔ 拼写指南 weird is an exception to the usual rule of i before e except after c. 通常的规则是 i 置于 e 前，在 c 后则除外，但 weird 例外。

weirdo /'wɪədəʊ/ **noun (plural weirdos)** informal【非正式】a strange or eccentric person 怪人

welch /weltʃ/ ⇨ see WELSH.

welcome /'welkəm/ **noun** 1 an instance or way of greeting someone 欢迎；(特定方式的)迎接 2 a pleased or approving reaction 欢迎；接受 • **verb (welcomes, welcoming, welcomed)** 1 greet someone in a polite or friendly way when they arrive somewhere 欢迎(到达者)；礼貌(或友好)地迎接 2 be glad to receive or hear of 欣然接受(或得知) • **adjective** 1 gladly received 受欢迎的 2 very pleasing because much needed or wanted (因被需要而)令人愉快的 3 allowed or invited to do a particular thing 被允许的；受邀请的

weld /weld/ **verb** 1 join together metal parts by heating the surfaces and pressing or hammering them together 焊接，煅接(金属零件) 2 make two things combine into a whole 使融为一体；使紧密结合 • **noun** a welded joint 焊接点(或处) ■ **welder** noun.

welfare /'welfeə(r)/ **noun** 1 the general health, happiness, and safety of a person or group 健康；幸福；运气 2 organized help given to people in need 福利；福利救济 □ **welfare state** a system under which the state provides pensions, health care, etc. 福利制度(国家提供养老金、医疗保健等的制度)

well[1] /wel/ **adverb** 1 in a good way 好地；令人满意地 2 thoroughly 彻底地；完全地；充分地 3 to a great extent or degree 相当 4 very probably 十有八九 5 without difficulty 顺利地；轻而易举地 6 with good reason 正当地；合理地 • **exclamation** used to express surprise, anger, resignation, etc. 嗯，咳，哟，好吧(用来表示惊讶、愤怒、无可奈何等) □ **as well** 1 in addition 也；还；而且 2 with equal reason or an equally good result 正好；同样地，也 **well advised** sensible; wise 合情理的；切合实际的；明智的 **well appointed** having a high standard of equipment or furnishing 设备高档(或上等)的；陈设一流的 **well-being** the state of being comfortable, healthy, or happy 舒适；安康；康乐 **well disposed** having a sympathetic or friendly attitude 好心好意的；友好的 **well heeled** informal【非正式】wealthy 有钱的；富裕的 **well nigh** almost 几乎 **well off** 1 wealthy 富有的 2 in a good situation 境况好的 **well read** having read widely 博览群书的；博学的 **well spoken** having an educated and refined voice 说话客气的；谈吐文雅的 **well-to-do** wealthy 富有的；宽裕的 **well-wisher** a person who wants someone else to be happy or successful 表示良好祝愿的人

! 注意 well is often used with a past participle such as *known* or *dressed* to form adjectives such as **well known, well dressed**, etc. Write these adjectives without a hyphen when they come after a noun or pronoun (*she is well known*) but with a hyphen when they come directly in front of a noun (*a well-known writer*). well 常与过去分词(如 known 或 dressed)连用构成形容词, 如 known well, well dressed 等。这些形容词用在名词或代词之后时不用连字符(如 she is well known 她很有名), 但当它们直接用于名词之前时则要用连字符(如 a well-known writer 著名的作家)。

well² *noun* **1** a shaft sunk into the ground to obtain water, oil, or gas 井; 水井; 油井; 气井 **2** a hollow made to hold liquid (用来盛液体的)坑, 槽 **3** a space in the middle of a building for stairs, a lift, etc. 楼梯(或电梯)井道 • *verb* (often **well up**) **1** (of a liquid) rise up to the surface (液体)溢出, 涌出, 冒出 **2** (of an emotion) develop and become stronger (情感)涌起, 涌上

we'll /wiːl, wɪl/ *short form* we shall or we will

wellington /'welɪŋtən/ *noun* Brit.【英】 a knee-length waterproof rubber or plastic boot (长及膝部的橡胶或塑料的)威灵顿长筒靴

welly or **wellie** /'weli/ *noun* Brit. informal【英, 非正式】 a wellington boot 威灵顿长筒靴

Welsh /welʃ/ *noun* the language of Wales 威尔士语 • *adjective* relating to Wales 威尔士的 □ **Welsh rarebit** (or **Welsh rabbit**) a dish of melted cheese on toast 威尔士乳酪面包(干酪化开后浇在烤面包上)

welsh or **welch** /welʃ/ *verb* (**welsh on**) fail to repay a debt or fulfil an obligation 赖账; 说话不算数

welt /welt/ *noun* **1** a leather rim to which the sole of a shoe is attached (鞋底与鞋帮间的)沿条 **2** a red swollen mark left on the skin by a blow or pressure (皮肤受击打或压力形成的)痕迹, 血印

welter /'weltə(r)/ *noun* a large and confused or disorganized number of items 杂乱的一大堆

welterweight /'weltəweɪt/ *noun* a weight in boxing between lightweight and middleweight (拳击及其他运动中的)次重量级

wench /wentʃ/ *noun* old use or humorous【旧或幽默】 a girl or young woman 姑娘; 少女

wend /wend/ *verb* (**wend your way**) go slowly or by an indirect route 缓慢行进; 迂回行进

Wendy house /'wendi/ *noun* Brit.【英】 a toy house large enough for children to play in 温迪屋(供儿童玩耍的游戏室)

went /went/ past of GO.

wept /wept/ past and past participle of WEEP.

were /wɜː(r), wə(r)/ 2nd person singular past, plural past, and past subjunctive of BE.

we're /wɪə(r)/ *short form* we are.

weren't /wɜːnt/ *short form* were not.

werewolf /'weəwʊlf/ *noun* (plural **werewolves**) (in stories) a person who periodically changes into a wolf, especially when there is a full moon (尤指民间传说中月圆时出现的)狼人

west /west/ *noun* **1** the direction in which the sun sets 西; 西方 **2** the western part of a place (地方的)西部 **3** (**the West**) Europe and North America 西方(指欧洲和北美洲) • *adjective & adverb* **1** towards or facing the west 向西(的); 朝西(的) **2** (of a wind) blowing from the west (风)来自西方(的) ■ **westward** *adjective & adverb* **westwards** *adverb*.

westerly /'westəli/ **adjective & adverb**
1 facing or moving towards the west 向西的(的);朝西(的) **2** (of a wind) blowing from the west (风)来自西方的,从西方

western /'westən/ **adjective 1** situated in or facing the west 位于西方的;朝西的 **2** (Western) having to do with the west, in particular Europe and North America 西方的;(尤指)欧美国家的 • **noun** a film or novel about cowboys in western North America (有关北美洲西部牛仔生活的)西部影片(或小说)

westerner /'westənə(r)/ **noun** a person from the west of a region 西部人;西方人

westernize or **westernise** /'westənaɪz/ **verb** (**westernizes**, **westernizing**, **westernized**) bring under the influence of Europe and North America 使西方化;使西化

wet /wet/ **adjective** (**wetter**, **wettest**) **1** covered or soaked with liquid (用液体)浸湿的,浸泡的 **2** (of the weather) rainy (天气)下雨的,多雨的 **3** not yet having dried or hardened 尚未干的;尚未硬化的 **4** Brit. informal 【英,非正式】 feeble 软弱的;脆弱的 • **verb** (**wets**, **wetting**, **wet** or **wetted**) **1** cover or touch with liquid 把…浸湿(或弄湿) **2** urinate in or on 尿湿;撒尿于 • **noun 1** (**the wet**) rainy weather 雨天 **2** liquid that makes something damp (弄湿东西的)液体 **3** Brit. informal 【英,非正式】 a feeble person 笨蛋;窝囊废 □ **wet blanket** informal 【非正式】 a person who spoils other people's enjoyment by being disapproving or unenthusiastic 扫人兴的人 **wet nurse** a woman employed to breastfeed another woman's child 奶妈;乳母 ■ **wetly adverb wetness noun.**

wether /'weðə(r)/ **noun** a castrated ram 阉羊;去势公羊

wetsuit /'wetsjuːt/ **noun** a close-fitting rubber garment covering the entire body, worn in water sports or diving 湿式潜水服(一种用橡胶制成的紧身潜水衣)

we've /'wiːv, wiv/ **short form** we have.

whack /wæk/ informal 【非正式】 **verb 1** hit forcefully 重打;猛击 **2** (**whacked**) Brit. 【英】 completely exhausted 筋疲力尽的;累极了的 **3** (**whacking**) Brit. 【英】 very large 极大的;巨大的 • **noun 1** a sharp blow 重击 **2** Brit. 【英】 a share or contribution 份儿;一份

whacky /'wæki/ ⟹ 见 **WACKY**.

whale /weɪl/ **noun** (plural **whales**) a very large sea mammal with a blowhole on top of the head for breathing 鲸(大型海洋哺乳动物,靠头顶的喷水孔呼吸) □ **have a whale of a time** informal 【非正式】 enjoy yourself very much 玩得痛快

whalebone /'weɪlbəʊn/ **noun** a hard substance growing in plates in the upper jaw of some whales, used by them to strain plankton from the seawater 鲸须

whaler /'weɪlə(r)/ **noun 1** a ship used for hunting whales 捕鲸船 **2** a sailor who hunts and kills whales 捕鲸人

whaling /'weɪlɪŋ/ **noun** the practice of hunting and killing whales 捕鲸;捕鲸业

whammy /'wæmi/ **noun** (plural **whammies**) informal 【非正式】 an event with a powerful and unpleasant effect 猛烈打击;致命打击

wharf /wɔːf/ **noun** (plural **wharves** or **wharfs**) a level area where ships are moored to load and unload 码头

what /wɒt/ **pronoun & determiner 1** asking for information about something (用于询问信息)什么 **2** whatever 不管什么;无论什么 **3** used to emphasize something surprising or remarkable (用于强调令人惊讶或异常的事物)什么 • **pronoun 1** asking someone to repeat something (用于请求重复某事物)什么 **2** the thing or

■ **W**

things that …的事物 • **adverb** to what extent 到何种程度

whatever /wɒt'evə(r)/ or **whatsoever** /ˌwɒtsəʊ'evə(r)/ **pronoun & determiner** everything or anything that; no matter what 凡是…的事物；不管什么 • **pronoun** used for emphasis instead of 'what' in questions (在疑问句中代替what表示强调)到底是什么，究竟是什么 • **adverb** at all; of any kind 任何；丝毫

whatnot /'wɒtnɒt/ **noun** informal 【非正式】an unspecified item or items 不可名状的事物

wheat /wiːt/ **noun** a cereal crop whose grain is ground to make flour 小麦

wheatear /'wiːtɪə(r)/ **noun** a small songbird 穗鹛(一种小鸣禽)

wheatgerm /'wiːtdʒɜːm/ **noun** a nutritious food consisting of the centre parts of grains of wheat 小麦胚芽

wheatmeal /'wiːtmiːl/ **noun** flour made from wheat from which some of the bran and germ has been removed 粗粉；小麦粉

wheedle /'wiːdl/ **verb** (**wheedles**, **wheedling**, **wheedled**) try to persuade someone to do something by flattering them or saying nice things that you do not mean (通过亲近或奉承对方)哄

wheel /wiːl/ **noun** 1 a revolving circular object that is fixed below a vehicle to enable it to move along, or that forms part of a machine 轮子；车轮；机轮 2 (**the wheel**) a steering wheel 方向盘 3 a turn or rotation 旋转(运动) • **verb** 1 push or pull a vehicle with wheels 推动，拉动(带轮车辆) 2 carry on a vehicle with wheels 用车轮车辆运送 3 fly or turn in a wide curve 盘旋；旋转 4 turn round quickly (迅速地)转身，改变方向 5 (**wheel something out**) informal 【非正式】resort to something that has been frequently seen or heard before 老

调重弹 □ **wheel and deal** take part in commercial or political scheming (在商界或政界)搞阴谋诡计，要手段

wheelbarrow /'wiːlbærəʊ/ **noun** a small cart with a wheel at the front and two handles at the rear 独轮手推车

wheelbase /'wiːlbeɪs/ **noun** the distance between the front and rear axles of a vehicle 轴距(车辆前后轮轴之间的距离)

wheelchair /'wiːltʃeə(r)/ **noun** a chair on wheels for a person who is ill or disabled (病人或残疾人用的)轮椅

wheeler-dealer /ˌwiːlə'diːlə(r)/ **noun** a person who wheels and deals 搞阴谋的人；要手腕的人

wheeze /wiːz/ **verb** (**wheezes**, **wheezing**, **wheezed**) 1 breathe with a whistling or rattling sound in the chest 喘；喘息 2 make a rattling or spluttering sound 气喘似地响；呼哧作响 • **noun** 1 a sound of wheezing 喘息声；气喘声 2 Brit. informal 【英，非正式】a clever or amusing scheme or trick 妙计；计谋 ■ **wheezy** adjective.

whelk /welk/ **noun** a shellfish with a pointed spiral shell 海螺，蛾螺

whelp /welp/ **noun** old use 【旧】1 a puppy 小狗 2 disapproving 【贬】a boy or young man 男孩；年轻男子 • **verb** give birth to a puppy (母狗)下(崽)，产(崽)

when /wen/ **adverb** 1 at what time? 什么时候？何时 2 in what circumstances? 在何种情况下 3 at which time or in which situation 哪一次；在哪种情况下 • **conjunction** 1 at or during the time that 在…时；当…时 2 at any time that; whenever 每当；无论何时；随时 3 in view of the fact that 既然 4 although; whereas 虽然；尽管

whence /wens/ or **from whence** **adverb** formal 【正式】1 from what place or source? 从何处；从哪里 2 from which or from where 从那个；

从那里 **3** to the place from which 到…来的地方 **4** as a consequence of which 因此；据此

whenever /wen'evə(r)/ or formal 【正式】 **whensoever** /ˌwensəu'evə(r)/ **conjunction 1** at whatever time or on whatever occasion 无论什么时候；在任何时机(或场合) **2** every time that 每当 • **adverb** used for emphasis instead of 'when' in questions (在问句中代替 when 表示强调)究竟什么时候

where /weə(r)/ **adverb 1** in or to what place or position? 在哪里；在何处；到哪里；向何处 **2** in what direction or respect? 在什么方向，在什么方面 **3** at, in, or to which 在那里；向那里；到那里 **4** in or to a place or situation in which 在(或向、到)…地方；在…情况下

whereabouts /ˌweərə'bauts/ **adverb** where or approximately where? 哪里，大概在何处 • **noun** the place where someone or something is 行踪；下落；所在

whereas /ˌweər'æz/ **conjunction 1** in contrast or comparison with the fact that 然而；尽管 **2** taking into consideration the fact that 考虑到，鉴于

whereby /weə'baɪ/ **adverb** by which 靠那个；凭借那个；借以

wherefore /'weəfɔː(r)/ old use 【旧】 **adverb** for what reason? 为什么，为何 • **adverb & conjunction** as a result of which 为此；因此；所以

wherein /weər'ɪn/ **adverb** formal 【正式】 **1** in which 在其中；在那里；在那方面 **2** in what place or respect? 在何处；在哪方面

whereof /weər'ɒv/ **adverb** formal 【正式】 of what or which 关于那个；关于那事；关于那人

whereupon /ˌweərə'pɒn/ **conjunction** immediately after which 随即；于是；马上

wherever /weər'evə(r)/ or formal 【正式】 **wheresoever** /ˌweəsəu'evə(r)/ **adverb 1** in or to whatever place 无论在何处；无论去何处 **2** used for emphasis instead of 'where' in questions (在问句中代替 where 表示强调)究竟在(或到)哪里 • **conjunction** in every case when 无论什么情况下

wherewithal /'weəwɪðɔːl/ **noun** the money or other resources needed for something (某事的)所需资金(或其他资源)

wherry /'weri/ **noun** (plural **wherries**) a light rowing boat or barge 浅水划桨船；浅水客货船

whet /wet/ **verb** (**whets**, **whetting**, **whetted**) **1** sharpen a blade 磨；磨快 **2** stimulate someone's interest or appetite 刺激，促进(某人的兴趣或胃口)

whether /'weðə(r)/ **conjunction 1** expressing a doubt or choice between alternatives (表示疑问或在两者之间选择)是否，是…(还是…)，或者…(或者…) **2** indicating that a statement applies whichever of the alternatives mentioned is the case (表示所说情况均适用)无论是…(还是…)

whetstone /'wetstəun/ **noun** a stone used for sharpening cutting tools 磨刀石

whey /wei/ **noun** the watery part of milk that remains after curds have formed 乳清，乳水(牛奶凝结时形成的澄清液体)

which /wɪtʃ/ **pronoun & determiner 1** asking for information specifying one or more people or things from a set 哪个；哪些 **2** used to refer to something previously mentioned when introducing a clause giving further information 那个，那些(引导非限定性从句，指代前面所提事物)

whichever /wɪtʃ'evə(r)/ **determiner & pronoun 1** any which; that or those which 任何一个 **2** regardless of which 无论哪个；无论哪些

whiff /wɪf/ **noun 1** a smell that is smelt only briefly or faintly (微弱的) 一股气味 **2** Brit. informal 【英，非正式】an unpleasant smell 难闻的气味；臭味 **3** a trace or hint of something bad or exciting 一点点，些许(坏事或令人激动的事) **4** a puff or breath of air or smoke (空气或烟的)一喷，一吹，一阵

Whig /wɪɡ/ **noun** historical 【历史】a member of a British political party that became the Liberal Party (英国自由党的前身)辉格党党员

while /waɪl/ **noun 1** (a while) a period of time 一段时间 **2** (a while) for some time 一会儿 **3** (the while) meanwhile 同时 • **conjunction 1** at the same time as 当…的时候；与…同时 **2** whereas 然而，(表示对照) **3** although 尽管 • **adverb** during which 在那期间 • **verb** (whiles, whiling, whiled) (while something away) pass time in a leisurely way 消磨，逍遥地打发(时间) □ **worth while** (or **worth your while**) worth the time or effort spent 值得花费的时间或精力

whilst /waɪlst/ **conjunction & adverb** chiefly Brit 【主英】while 当…的时候；在那期间

whim /wɪm/ **noun** a sudden desire or change of mind 冲动；突然改变主意

whimper /ˈwɪmpə(r)/ **verb** (whimpers, whimpering, whimpered) make low, feeble sounds expressing fear, pain, or discontent 抽泣，呜咽(表达恐惧、疼痛或不满) • **noun** a whimpering sound 呜咽声；呜咽声

whimsical /ˈwɪmzɪkl/ **adjective 1** playfully unusual 异想天开的；想入非非的 **2** showing sudden changes of mood or behaviour 随心所欲的；反复无常的 ■ **whimsically** adverb.

whimsy /ˈwɪmzi/ **noun** (plural whimsies) **1** playfully unusual behaviour or humour 奇怪的行为；离奇的幽默 **2** an odd or unusual thing 稀奇古怪的东西 **3** a whim 怪念头；

离奇的想法

whin /wɪn/ **noun** chiefly N. English 【主英格兰北部】gorse 荆豆

whine /waɪn/ **noun 1** a long, high-pitched complaining cry 哀叫声；哀诉声 **2** a long, high-pitched sound 长而尖锐的声音 • **verb** (whines, whining, whined) give or make a whine 哀叫；哀诉 ■ **whiny** adjective.

whinge /wɪndʒ/ Brit. informal 【英，非正式】 **verb** (whinges, whingeing, whinged) complain persistently and irritably 哼哼唧唧地抱怨(或哀诉) • **noun** an act of whingeing 抱怨；哀诉

whinny /ˈwɪni/ **noun** (plural whinnies) a gentle, high-pitched neigh (马的)嘶叫声 • **verb** (whinnies, whinnying, whinnied) (of a horse) make a whinny (马)嘶叫

whip /wɪp/ **noun 1** a length of leather or cord fastened to a handle, used for beating a person or urging on an animal 鞭子 **2** an official of a political party who is appointed to keep parliamentary discipline among its members 政党纪律委员，组织秘书(负责监督该党议员在议会中的纪律) **3** a written notice from a party whip telling members how to vote in a debate (政党组织秘书发给本党议员要求出席议会投票的)书面通知 **4** a dessert made from cream or eggs beaten into a light fluffy mass (用奶油或鸡蛋搅拌制成的)甜食 • **verb** (whips, whipping, whipped) **1** hit a person or animal with a whip 鞭打；鞭抽 **2** beat or move violently (猛烈地)鞭打，抽打，拍打 **3** move or take out fast or suddenly (迅速或突然地)移动，拿出，取出 **4** beat cream, eggs, etc. into a froth 将(奶油、鸡蛋等)搅拌成泡沫状 □ **the whip hand** a position of power or control over someone 支配地位 □ **whipping boy** a person who is blamed or punished for other people's faults 替罪羊；替死鬼；代人受过者 **whip-**

round Brit. informal 【英,非正式】a collection of money 募捐;凑份子
whip someone/thing up 1 make or prepare something very quickly 迅速制成(或准备好) **2** deliberately excite or provoke someone 煽动;鼓动

whiplash /'wɪplæʃ/ **noun 1** injury caused by a severe jerk to the head 颈椎过度屈伸损伤 **2** the flexible part of a whip 鞭索;鞭子的皮条

whippersnapper /'wɪpəsnæpə(r)/ **noun** informal 【非正式】a young and inexperienced but overconfident person 妄自尊大的年轻人

whippet /'wɪpɪt/ **noun** a small, slender breed of dog 小灵狗(体型小巧修长)

whippoorwill /'wɪpuːwɪl/ **noun** an American bird with a distinctive call (美洲产鸣叫声特别的)三声夜鹰

whirl /wɜːl/ **verb 1** move rapidly round and round (使)回旋;(使)旋转 **2** (of the head or mind) seem to spin round (头或头脑)眩晕 • **noun 1** a rapid movement round and round 旋转;回旋 **2** busy or hurried activity 忙乱;纷乱

whirligig /'wɜːlɪɡɪɡ/ **noun 1** a toy that spins round 旋转式玩具(如陀螺或风车) **2** a roundabout at a fair (游乐场的)旋转木马

whirlpool /'wɜːlpuːl/ **noun** a current of water that whirls in a circle 漩涡

whirlwind /'wɜːlwɪnd/ **noun 1** a column of air moving rapidly round and round 旋风;龙卷风 **2** a situation in which many things happen very quickly 纷乱;匆忙 • **adjective** very quick and unexpected 快速的;旋风似的: *a whirlwind romance* 旋风式爱情

whirr or **whir** /wɜː(r)/ **verb** (**whirs** or **whirrs**, **whirring**, **whirred**) (of something rapidly rotating or moving) make a low, continuous, regular sound (快速旋转或运动的物体)呼呼(或嗡嗡)作响 • **noun** a

whirring sound 呼呼声;嗡嗡声

whisk /wɪsk/ **verb 1** beat eggs, cream, etc. with a light, rapid movement 搅打(鸡蛋、奶油等) **2** move or take suddenly and quickly 迅速移动;飞奔;飞快(或突然)地带走 • **noun 1** a device for whisking eggs, cream, etc. 打蛋器;搅打器 **2** a bunch of grass, twigs, etc. for flicking away dust or flies 掸子;小笤帚

whisker /'wɪskə(r)/ **noun 1** each of the long hairs or bristles growing from the face of an animal (动物的)须 **2** (**whiskers**) the hair growing on a man's face (人的)胡须,髯 **3** (**a whisker**) informal 【非正式】a very small amount 一丝儿;一点

whisky /'wɪski/ (Irish & US spelling 【爱尔兰和美拼作】**whiskey**) **noun** (plural **whiskies**) a strong alcoholic drink distilled from malted grain 威士忌酒

> ✔ **拼写指南** Scotch whis*ky*, but Irish whis*key*. 苏格兰拼作 whisky, 而爱尔兰拼作 whiskey。

whisper /'wɪspə(r)/ **verb** (**whispers**, **whispering**, **whispered**) **1** speak very softly 低语;耳语 **2** literary 【文】rustle or murmur softly 发出沙沙声(或飒飒声、潺潺声) • **noun 1** something whispered 私下谈论的话 **2** a very soft voice 低语;耳语 **3** literary 【文】a soft rustling or murmuring 沙沙声,飒飒声,潺潺声 **4** a rumour or piece of gossip 传闻;谣传 **5** a slight trace 微量;些许

whist /wɪst/ **noun** a card game in which points are scored according to the number of tricks won 惠斯特(根据所赢牌的圈数来计分的一种牌戏)

whistle /'wɪsl/ **noun 1** a clear, high-pitched sound made by forcing breath between the lips or teeth 口哨声 **2** any similar high-pitched sound 类似哨声的声音 **3** a device used to produce a whistling sound 哨子;汽笛 • **verb**

(whistles, whistling, whistled) 1 give out a whistle 吹口哨 **2** move rapidly with a whistling sound 呼啸而行 **3** blow a whistle 吹哨子 □ **whistle-stop** very fast and with only brief pauses 飞快的;仅作短暂停留的

Whit /wɪt/ **noun** Whitsun 圣灵降临周 □ **Whit Sunday** a Christian festival held on the seventh Sunday after Easter (基督教的)圣灵降临节(复活节后的第七个星期日)

whit /wɪt/ **noun** a very small part or amount 一点点;丝毫

white /waɪt/ **adjective 1** having the colour of milk or fresh snow 白色的;乳白的;雪白的 **2** very pale 苍白的 **3** relating to people with light-coloured skin 白种人的 **4** Brit.【英】(of coffee or tea) with milk (咖啡或茶)加牛奶的 **5** (of wine) yellowish in colour (葡萄酒)淡黄色的 **6** innocent and pure 天真无邪的;纯洁的 ▪ **noun 1** white colour 白色 **2** the visible pale part of the eyeball around the iris 眼白 **3** the outer part which surrounds the yolk of an egg; the albumen (鸡蛋的)蛋清,蛋白 **4** a white person 白种人 □ **white blood cell** a cell in the blood or lymph which acts against foreign substances and disease 白细胞 **white-collar** relating to work in an office or other professional environment 白领的;白领阶层的 **white elephant** a useless or troublesome possession 无用之物;累赘的东西 **white flag** a flag waved as a symbol of surrender or truce 白旗,白布(表示投降、休战或请求谈判) **white-hot** so hot that it glows white 白热的;极热的 **white lie** a harmless lie told to avoid hurting someone's feelings (善意的)谎话 **white magic** magic used only for good purposes 白法术(仅用于行善目的的法术) **White Paper** (in the UK) a government report giving information or proposals on an issue (英国)白皮书(政府就某一问题发表的官方报告) **white sauce** a sauce made with flour, butter, and milk or stock (由面粉和黄油、牛奶等混合制成的)白汁沙司,白汁 **white spirit** Brit.【英】a colourless liquid distilled from petroleum, used as a paint thinner and solvent 石油溶剂油(一种由石油蒸馏而成的无色液体,用作涂料稀释剂和溶剂) ▪ **whiteness** noun.

whitebait /'waɪtbeɪt/ **noun** the young of various sea fish used as food 小鲱鱼,银鱼(海鱼的幼鱼,可食用)

whiten /'waɪtn/ **verb** make or become white (使)变白 ▪ **whitener** noun.

whitewash /'waɪtwɒʃ/ **noun 1** a solution of lime or chalk and water, used for painting walls white 石灰水;白涂料 **2** a deliberate concealment of mistakes or faults (对错误或缺点的)粉饰,掩饰 ▪ **verb 1** paint with whitewash 用石灰水把…刷白;粉刷 **2** conceal mistakes or faults 粉饰,掩盖(错误或缺点)

whither /'wɪðə(r)/ **adverb** formal or old use【正式或旧】**1** to what place or state 往何处;去何处;至何种情况 **2** what is the likely future of 怎样的前途;怎样的结果

whiting /'waɪtɪŋ/ **noun** (plural **whiting**) a sea fish with white flesh eaten as food 牙鳕(一种海鱼,肉白,可食用)

Whitsun /'wɪtsn/ or **Whitsuntide** /'wɪtsntaɪd/ **noun** the weekend or week including Whit Sunday 圣灵降临周(包括圣灵降临节在内的周末或一周)

whittle /'wɪtl/ **verb** (**whittles, whittling, whittled**) **1** carve wood by cutting small slices from it 削(木头) **2** (**whittle something away** or **down**) gradually reduce something 削减;削弱

whizz /wɪz/ **verb** (**whizzes, whizzing, whizzed**) **1** move quickly through the air 嗖嗖(或呼呼、嘶嘶、嘘嘘)作响 **2** move or go fast 迅速移动;飞驰,嗖嗖地疾驰 • noun informal 【非正式】 a person who is very clever at something 能手;善于…的人 □ **whizz-kid** informal 【非正式】 a young person who is very successful or skilful 非常成功的人;有特长的人

who /hu:/ **pronoun 1** what or which person or people 谁;什么人 **2** introducing a clause giving further information about a person or people previously mentioned (引导从句,对前面所提到的人作进一步的解释说明)

！注意 the rule is that you should use **who** as the subject of a verb (*Who decided this?*) and **whom** as the object of a verb or preposition (*Whom do you think we should support?*). When speaking, however, it's acceptable to use **who** instead of **whom**, as in *who do you think we should support?* 根据规则,who 应用作动词的主语(Who decided this? 这是谁作的决定?), whom 则应用作动词或介词的宾语(Whom do you think we should support? 你认为我们应该支持谁?)。然而,在口语中,用 who 代替 whom 也是可以接受的,如 Who do you think we should support?(你认为我们应该支持谁?)。

whoa /wəʊ/ **exclamation** used as a command to a horse to stop or slow down 吁(用于吆喝马停住或慢行)

who'd /hu:d/ **short form 1** who had. **2** who would.

whodunnit /ˌhu:ˈdʌnɪt/ (US spelling 【美拼作】 **whodunit**) **noun** informal 【非正式】 a crime story in which the identity of the murderer is not revealed until the end (凶手身份到故事结尾才被揭晓的)侦探故事

whoever /huːˈevə(r)/ or formal 【正式】 **whosoever** /ˌhuːsəʊˈevə(r)/

pronoun 1 the person or people who; any person who 那个…的人;任何…的人 **2** regardless of who 无论谁;不管谁 **3** used for emphasis instead of 'who' in questions (在疑问句中代替 who,用于强调)到底是谁,究竟是谁

whole /həʊl/ **adjective 1** complete; entire 完全的;全部的 **2** in one piece 完整的;整个的 • noun **1** a thing that is complete in itself 整个;整体 **2 (the whole)** all of something 全部;全体 □ **on the whole** taking everything into account; in general 总的说来;大体上;一般来说 ■ **wholeness** noun.

wholefood /ˈhəʊlfuːd/ **noun** Brit. 【英】 food that has been processed as little as possible and is free from additives (几乎未经加工且不含添加剂的)全营养食品

wholehearted /ˌhəʊlˈhɑːtɪd/ **adjective** completely sincere and committed 全心全意的;全身心投入的 ■ **wholeheartedly** adverb.

wholemeal /ˈhəʊlmiːl/ **adjective** Brit. 【英】 (of flour or bread) made from whole grains of wheat including the husk (面粉或面包)全麦的

wholesale /ˈhəʊlseɪl/ **noun** the selling of goods in large quantities to be sold to the public by others 批发;趸售;趸卖 • adjective & adverb **1** being sold in such a way 用批发方式(的) **2** done to a very large number of people or things 大规模的(地) • verb (**wholesales, wholesaling, wholesaled**) sell goods wholesale 批发,成批出售(货物) ■ **wholesaler** noun.

wholesome /ˈhəʊlsəm/ **adjective 1** good for health or well-being 有益于(身心)健康的;增进健康的 **2** morally good 道德高尚的

wholly /ˈhəʊlli/ **adverb** entirely; fully 完全地;全然地

✔ **拼写指南** two *l*s, no *e*: wholly, not *-ely*. wholly 中有两个 l，没有 e，不要拼作 -ely.

whom /huːm/ *pronoun* used instead of 'who' as the object of a verb or preposition (代替 who 用作动词或介词的宾语)谁，什么人

whoop /huːp, wuːp/ *noun* a loud cry of joy or excitement (高兴或激动时的)高喊，高呼 • *verb* give or make a whoop 高喊；高呼 □ **whooping cough** an illness which mainly affects children, marked by coughs followed by a noisy drawing in of breath 百日咳

whoopee /wʊˈpiː/ *exclamation* informal 【非正式】expressing excitement or joy (表示兴奋或高兴)哎哟

whoosh /wʊʃ/ *verb* move quickly with a rushing sound 嗖嗖(或呼呼)地移动 • *noun* a whooshing movement 嗖嗖(或呼呼)的移动

whopper /ˈwɒpə(r)/ *noun* informal 【非正式】**1** something that is very large 庞然大物；特大者 **2** a blatant lie 弥天大谎

whopping /ˈwɒpɪŋ/ *adjective* informal 【非正式】very large 巨大的；庞大的

whore /hɔː(r)/ *noun* **1** a prostitute 妓女 **2** disapproving 【贬】a woman who has many sexual partners 荡妇；淫妇

whorl /wɜːl/ *noun* **1** each of the turns in a spiral or coil (螺旋形外壳的)壳阶，螺层 **2** a spiral or coil 螺旋状物；卷状物 **3** a coil of leaves, flowers, or branches encircling a stem (植物茎部的)轮，轮生体

who's /huːz/ *short form* **1** who is. **2** who has.

! **注意** don't confuse **who's** with **whose**. Who's is short for either **who is** or **who has**, as in *he has a son who's a doctor* or *who's done the reading?*, whereas **whose** means 'belonging to which person' or 'of whom or which', as in *whose is*

this? or *he's a man whose opinion I respect.* who's 是 who is 或 who has 的缩写形式，如 he has a son who's a doctor(他有个儿子是医生)或 who's done the reading (谁 读 完 了)，而 whose 则表示 "属于或关于谁的"，如 whose is this (这是谁的)或 he's a man whose opinion I respect (他 是 一个我尊重其意见的人)。

whose /huːz/ *possessive determiner & pronoun* **1** belonging to or associated with which person 谁的 **2** of whom or which 哪个人的；谁的；哪个的

why /waɪ/ *adverb* **1** for what reason or purpose 为什么；为何 **2** on account of which; the reason that 为什么，之所以 • *exclamation* expressing surprise, annoyance, etc. (表示惊讶、恼怒等)哎呀，哟

wick /wɪk/ *noun* a length of cord in a candle, lamp, or lighter which carries liquid fuel to the flame 烛芯；灯芯

wicked /ˈwɪkɪd/ *adjective* **1** very bad; evil 邪恶的 **2** playfully mischievous 淘气的；顽皮的；恶作剧的 **3** informal 【非正式】excellent; wonderful 极好的；绝妙的 ■ **wickedly** *adverb* **wickedness** *noun*.

wicker /ˈwɪkə(r)/ *noun* twigs plaited or woven to make items such as furniture and baskets 枝条(用来编制家具、篮子等) ■ **wickerwork** *noun*.

wicket /ˈwɪkɪt/ *noun* 1 Cricket【板球】each of the two sets of three stumps with two bails across the top that are defended by a batsman 三柱门 **2** a small door or gate 小门，边门；便门

wicketkeeper /ˈwɪkɪtkiːpə(r)/ *noun* Cricket【板球】a fielder positioned close behind a batsman's wicket 三柱门守门员；捕手

wide /waɪd/ *adjective* (**wider, widest**) **1** of great or more than average width 宽的；宽阔的 **2** having a

particular width …宽的;宽度为…的
3 open to the full extent 广大的;渊博的;广泛的 **4** including a great variety of people or things 各式各样的;种类繁多的 **5** spread among a large number or over a large area 普遍的;范围大的;广泛的 **6** at a distance from a point or mark 远离某个点(或目标)的 **7** (in football) at or near the side of the field (足球运动中)在球场边线上(或附近)的 • adverb **1** to the full extent 充分地;全部地 **2** far from the target 远离目标地 □ **wide awake** fully awake 完全醒着的 **wide boy** Brit. informal 【英,非正式】a man involved in petty criminal activities 混混儿;痞子
■ **widely** adverb.

widen /ˈwaɪdn/ verb make or become wider 加宽;(使)变宽

widespread /ˈwaɪdspred/ adjective spread among a large number or over a large area 普遍的;分布广泛的

widgeon /ˈwɪdʒən/ ⇒ 见 WIGEON.

widget /ˈwɪdʒɪt/ noun informal 【非正式】a small gadget or mechanical device 小装置;小机械

widow /ˈwɪdəʊ/ noun a woman whose husband has died and who has not married again 寡妇 • verb (**be widowed**) become a widow or widower 成为寡妇(或鳏夫)

widower /ˈwɪdəʊə(r)/ noun a man whose wife has died and who has not married again 鳏夫

width /wɪdθ/ noun **1** the measurement or extent of something from side to side 宽度;阔度 **2** wide range or extent 广度;广阔;大范围

widthways /ˈwɪdθweɪz/ or **widthwise** /ˈwɪdθwaɪz/ adverb in a direction parallel with a thing's width 横向地;横着

wield /wiːld/ verb **1** hold and use a weapon or tool 挥,操,使用,掌握(武器或工具) **2** have power or influence 掌握,行使,运用(权力或影响力)

wife /waɪf/ noun (plural **wives**) the woman a man is married to 妻子;夫人 ■ **wifely** adjective.

wig /wɪg/ noun a covering for the head made of real or artificial hair 假发

wigeon or **widgeon** /ˈwɪdʒən/ noun a duck with mainly reddish-brown and grey feathers 赤颈鸭(羽毛以红褐色和灰色为主)

wiggle /ˈwɪgl/ verb (**wiggling, wiggled**) move with short movements up and down or from side to side 扭动;摆动 • noun a wiggling movement 扭动;摆动 ■ **wiggly** adjective.

wigwam /ˈwɪgwæm/ noun a tent consisting of animal skins fixed over a framework of poles, formerly lived in by some North American Indian peoples (旧时一些北美印第安人居住的)棚屋,帐篷

wild /waɪld/ adjective **1** (of animals or plants) living or growing in their natural environment (动植物)野生的,自然生长的 **2** (of scenery or a region) not lived in or changed by people (风景或地区)荒凉的,杳无人迹的,荒芜的 **3** lacking discipline or control 无节制的;不受控制的 **4** not based on reason or evidence 不合常理的;毫无根据的 **5** informal 【非正式】very enthusiastic or excited 满腔热情的;极为激动的 • noun **1** (**the wild**) a natural state 野生(状态);自然(状态) **2** (**the wilds**) a remote area 偏僻地区;荒地;荒野 □ **wild card 1** a playing card which can take on any value, suit, or colour that the player holding it needs (由持牌人自由决定大小、花色等的)百搭牌,变牌 **2** Computing 【计】a character that will match any character or sequence of characters in a search 通配符 **3** an opportunity to enter a sports competition without having qualified in the usual way "外卡"参赛(指没有正常参赛资格而参赛) **wild goose chase** a hopeless search for something that you will never find 毫无希望的追寻;徒劳的寻找 ■ **wildly** adverb 正常 **wildness** noun.

wildcat /'waɪldkæt/ **adjective** (of a strike) sudden and unofficial (罢工)突然且未经官方(或工会)同意的

wildebeest /'wɪldəbiːst/ **noun** a gnu (a kind of antelope) 牛羚;角马

wilderness /'wɪldənɪs/ **noun** a wild, uninhabited, and unwelcoming region 荒野;旷野

wildfire /'waɪldfaɪə(r)/ **noun** (**spread like wildfire**) spread very fast 野火般蔓延;飞速传播

wildfowl /'waɪldfaʊl/ **plural noun** birds that are hunted for sport or food (被人猎食的)野禽,猎鸟

wildlife /'waɪldlaɪf/ **noun** all the animals, birds, and insects that naturally inhabit a particular region 野生动物

wiles /waɪlz/ **plural noun** cunning methods used by someone to get what they want 诡计;奸计;花招

wilful /'wɪlfl/ (US spelling 【美拼作】 **willful**) **adjective 1** (of a bad act) deliberate (恶行)故意的,蓄意的 **2** stubborn and determined 固执的;执拗的;倔强的 ■ **wilfully** adverb **wilfulness** noun.

will[1] /wɪl/ **modal verb** (3rd singular present **will**; past **would**) **1** expressing the future tense (表示将来时态) **2** expressing a request (表示请求) **3** expressing desire, consent, or willingness (表示愿望、赞同或愿意) **4** expressing facts about ability or capacity (表示能力或容量)

!注意 the traditional rule is that you should use **shall** when forming the future tense with **I** and **we** (*I shall be late*) and **will** with **you, he, she, it,** and **they** (*he will not be there*). Nowadays, people do not follow this rule so strictly and are more likely to use the shortened forms **I'll, she'll**, etc. 按照传统规则，shall 必须与 I 和 we 连用构成将来时态(如 I shall be late 我会迟到)，而 will 则与 you, he, she, it 和 they 连用(如 he will not be here 他不会来这里)。如今，人们不再严格遵循这一规则，而是更多地使用缩写形式 I'll, she'll 等。

will[2] **noun 1** the power you have to decide on something and take action 意志 **2** (also **willpower**) the ability to control your thoughts and actions in order to achieve something 毅力;意志力;自制力 **3** a desire or intention 意愿;意图 **4** a legal document in which someone gives instructions about what should be done with their money and property after their death (书面的)遗嘱 • **verb 1** intend or desire that something should happen 想要;愿 **2** bring something about by using your mental powers 决意;立志 **3** leave money or property to someone in a will 遗赠 □ **at will** whenever or in whatever way you like 任意;随意

willing /'wɪlɪŋ/ **adjective 1** ready, eager, or prepared to do something 愿意的,乐意的 **2** given or done readily 出于自愿的;志愿的 ■ **willingly** adverb **willingness** noun.

will-o'-the-wisp /ˌwɪləðə'wɪsp/ **noun 1** a thing that is impossible to obtain 捉摸不透的事物 **2** a faint flickering light seen at night over marshy ground, thought to result from natural gases burning (夜晚沼泽地可见的)磷火,鬼火(由沼气燃烧引起)

willow /'wɪləʊ/ **noun** a tree which has

W

narrow leaves and produces catkins 柳；柳树

willowy /ˈwɪləʊi/ **adjective** tall and slim 高而苗条的；瘦高的

willy-nilly /ˌwɪliˈnɪli/ **adverb 1** whether you like it or not 不管愿不愿意；无可奈何地 **2** without any direction or plan 没有方向（或计划）地；乱糟糟地；杂乱无章地

wilt /wɪlt/ **verb 1** (of a plant) become limp through heat or lack of water （植物因受热或缺水而）枯萎，蔫 **2** feel tired and weak 萎靡不振

wily /ˈwaɪli/ **adjective** clever in a cunning or crafty way 老谋深算的；诡计多端的

wimp /wɪmp/ **noun** informal 【非正式】a person who is not strong, brave, or confident 怯懦无能的家伙；废物；软蛋 ■ **wimpish** adjective **wimpy** adjective.

wimple /ˈwɪmpl/ **noun** a cloth headdress covering the head, neck, and sides of the face, worn in the past by women and still today by some nuns （旧时妇女和现今有些修女戴的）头巾

win /wɪn/ **verb** (**wins**, **winning**, **won**) **1** be the most successful in a contest or conflict 获胜；赢 **2** gain something as a result of success in a contest or conflict （在竞争、冲突中）赢得，夺得 **3** gain someone's attention, support, or love 获得（注意、支持或喜爱） **4** (**win someone over**) gain someone's agreement or support by persuading them that you are right 赢得（某人）的赞同（或支持） • **noun** a victory in a game or contest （在比赛或竞争中的）胜利，赢

wince /wɪns/ **verb** (**winces**, **wincing**, **winced**) flinch slightly on feeling pain or distress （因疼痛或痛苦而）面部抽搐，退缩 • **noun** an act of wincing 皱眉蹙额，退缩

winceyette /ˌwɪnsiˈet/ **noun** Brit. 【英】a soft brushed cotton fabric 色织棉法兰绒

winch /wɪntʃ/ **noun** a hauling or lifting device consisting of a rope or chain winding around a rotating drum 绞车；起扬机 • **verb** hoist or haul something with a winch 用卷扬机吊（或拖）

wind¹ /wɪnd/ **noun 1** a natural movement of the air 风 **2** breath needed to play an instrument or do exercise （吹奏乐器或锻炼时需要的）气流，气息 **3** wind or woodwind instruments forming a band or section of an orchestra （组成乐队或管弦乐队中管乐器部的）管乐器 **4** Brit. 【英】air or gas in the stomach or intestines 胃气；肠气 • **verb 1** make someone unable to breathe easily for a short time 使气急；使喘不上气 **2** Brit. 【英】pat a baby on its back to help it bring up air swallowed while feeding （用轻拍背的方法）使（婴儿）进食后打嗝 □ **get wind of** informal 【非正式】hear a rumour of 风闻…的传闻 **put the wind up** Brit. informal 【英，非正式】alarm or frighten 使惊慌；使害怕 **wind instrument 1** a musical instrument which you play by blowing into it 管乐器；吹奏乐器 **2** a woodwind instrument as distinct from a brass instrument 木管乐器（有别于铜管乐器） **wind tunnel** a tunnel-like structure in which a strong current of air is created, to test the effect of wind and air flow on vehicles 风道，风洞（一种能产生空气气流的装置，用来观测气流或风对车辆的影响）

wind² /waɪnd/ **verb** (**winds**, **winding**, **wound**) **1** move in or take a twisting or spiral course 弯曲前行；曲折而行；迂回 **2** pass something around a thing or person so as to encircle or enfold them 包；裹；缠绕；卷绕 **3** (with reference to something long) twist or be twisted around itself or a central thing （长物）卷绕，缠绕 **4** make a clockwork device work by ■ **windy** adjective.

turning a key or handle 给(钟表装置)上发条 **5** turn a key or handle repeatedly 反复转动(钥匙或把手) **6** move an audio tape, videotape, or film backwards or forwards 将(录音带、录像带或胶片)倒回去(或向前快进) □ **wind down 1** (of a clockwork mechanism) gradually lose power (钟表机械装置)逐渐停转 **2** (also **wind something down**) draw or bring something gradually to an end 使逐渐结束 **3** informal【非正式】relax 放松 **wind up** informal【非正式】end up in a particular situation or place 以…告终(或告结)**wind someone/thing up 1** gradually bring something to an end 使逐渐结束 **2** Brit. informal【英,非正式】tease or irritate someone 取笑；嘲弄；激怒

windbag /'wɪndbæg/ **noun** informal【非正式】a person who talks a lot but without saying anything interesting or important 空话连篇的人

windbreak /'wɪndbreɪk/ **noun** a screen providing shelter from the wind 风障

windcheater /'wɪndtʃiːtə(r)/ **noun** Brit.【英】a wind-resistant jacket with a close-fitting neck and cuffs 风衣，防风夹克(其领口和袖口处有松紧带)

windfall /'wɪndfɔːl/ **noun 1** a piece of unexpected good fortune 意外收获；横财 **2** an apple or other fruit blown from a tree by the wind 被风吹落的果子

windlass /'wɪndləs/ **noun** a winch used on a ship or in a harbour (船上或海港中的)绞盘，绞车

windmill /'wɪndmɪl/ **noun** a building with sails or vanes that turn in the wind and generate power to grind corn, generate electricity, or draw water 风车房

window /'wɪndəʊ/ **noun 1** an opening in a wall, fitted with glass to let in light and allow people to see out 窗；窗户；窗口 **2** a framed

area on a computer screen for viewing information (计算机屏幕上用以查看信息的)视窗 □ **window dressing 1** the arrangement of a display in a shop window (商店的)橱窗布置,橱窗设计 **2** the presentation of something in a superficially attractive way to give a good impression 装饰门面(使表面上给人以良好印象)**window-shop** spend time looking at the goods displayed in shop windows 浏览商店橱窗

windowpane /'wɪndəʊpeɪn/ **noun** a pane of glass in a window (一块)窗玻璃

window sill **noun** a ledge or sill at the bottom of a window 窗沿，窗台

windpipe /'wɪndpaɪp/ **noun** the tube carrying air down the throat and into the lungs; the trachea 气管

windscreen /'wɪndskriːn/ **noun** Brit.【英】a glass screen at the front of a motor vehicle (机动车前面的)挡风玻璃

windshield /'wɪndʃiːld/ **noun** N. Amer.【北美】a windscreen (机动车前面的)挡风玻璃

windsock /'wɪndsɒk/ **noun** a light, flexible cone mounted on a mast to show the direction and strength of the wind 风向袋；套筒风标

windsurfing /'wɪndsɜːfɪŋ/ **noun** the sport of riding on a sailboard on water 帆板冲浪运动 ■ **windsurf** verb **windsurfer** noun.

windswept /'wɪndswept/ **adjective** exposed to strong winds 当风的；受大风侵袭的

windward /'wɪndwəd/ **adjective & adverb** facing the wind, or on the side facing the wind 向风(的)；迎风(的)；顶风(的)

wine /waɪn/ **noun** an alcoholic drink made from fermented grape juice 葡萄酒

winery /'waɪnəri/ **noun** (plural **wineries**) an establishment where

wine is made 酿酒厂；葡萄酒厂

wing /wɪŋ/ **noun 1** a kind of limb used by a bird, bat, or insect for flying (鸟、蝙蝠或昆虫的)翅，翼，翼状器官 **2** a rigid structure projecting from both sides of an aircraft and supporting it in the air 机翼 **3** a part of a large building (大型建筑物中的)侧翼部分，侧厅，厢房 **4** a group or faction within an organization (某一组织内的)派系，宗派 **5** (**the wings**) the sides of a theatre stage out of view of the audience (观众看不见的)剧院舞台)侧面 **6** the part of a soccer or rugby field close to the sidelines (足球、橄榄球运动的)边锋位置 **7** Brit.【英】the part of a car above and extending slightly over a wheel (车辆的)挡泥板，翼子板 **8** an air force unit of several squadrons (空军的)联队 • **verb 1** fly, or move quickly as if flying 飞越；飞过 **2** shoot a bird so as to wound it in the wing 射伤(鸟)的翅膀 **3** (**wing it**) informal【非正式】speak or act without preparation 即兴演讲；即兴表演 □ **wing nut** a nut with a pair of projections for the fingers to turn it on a screw 蝶形螺母；翼形螺帽 ■ **winged** adjective.

winger /ˈwɪŋə(r)/ **noun** an attacking player on the wing in soccer, hockey, etc. (足球、曲棍球等运动中的)边锋队员

wingspan /ˈwɪŋspæn/ **noun** the full extent from tip to tip of the wings of an aircraft, bird, etc. (飞机、鸟等的)翼展，翼幅

wink /wɪŋk/ **verb 1** close and open one eye quickly as a private signal 眨(一只)眼示意 **2** shine with an unsteady light; flash on and off 闪烁；闪亮 • **noun** an act of winking 眨眼；眨眼示意

winkle /ˈwɪŋkl/ **noun** a small edible shellfish with a spiral shell 食用蛾螺；玉黍螺；滨螺 • **verb** (**winkles**, **winkling**, **winkled**) (**winkle** something out) Brit.【英】**1** extract something with difficulty 费劲地取出 **2** get information from someone who is reluctant to give it 设法搞到(信息)

winning /ˈwɪnɪŋ/ **adjective** attractive 吸引人的，迷人的 • **noun** (**winnings**) money won by gambling (通过赌博)赢得的钱 ■ **winningly** adverb.

winnow /ˈwɪnəʊ/ **verb 1** remove people or things from a group until only the best ones are left 筛选，选拔(人或物) **2** blow air through grain in order to remove the chaff 簸，扬(谷)

wino /ˈwaɪnəʊ/ **noun** (plural **winos**) informal【非正式】a person who sits all day in the streets drinking alcohol 醉鬼；酒鬼

winsome /ˈwɪnsəm/ **adjective** appealing 吸引人的，动人的

winter /ˈwɪntə(r)/ **noun** the coldest season of the year, after autumn and before spring 冬季；冬天 • **verb** (**winters**, **wintering**, **wintered**) spend the winter in a particular place 过冬

wintry /ˈwɪntri/ **adjective** cold or bleak 寒冷的，凄凉的

wipe /waɪp/ **verb** (**wipes**, **wiping**, **wiped**) **1** clean or dry something by rubbing it with a cloth or your hand (用布或手)擦净，抹干 **2** remove something from a surface in this way 擦去；抹去 **3** erase data from a computer, tape, etc. 删除，掉掉(计算机、磁带等上的)数据或信息) • **noun 1** an act of wiping 擦；抹 **2** an absorbent cleaning cloth 毛巾，手帕，抹布 □ **wipe someone/thing out 1** remove or eliminate something 消除；消灭 **2** kill a large number of people 大规模杀死(人) ■ **wiper** noun.

wire /ˈwaɪə(r)/ **noun 1** metal in the form of a thin flexible strand 金属丝；金属线 **2** a length of wire used for fencing, to carry an electric current, etc. 铁丝网；电线；导线 **3** a concealed listening device 窃听器 **4** informal 【非正式】 a telegram 电报 • **verb (wires, wiring, wired) 1** install electric circuits or wires in a room or building 给(房间或建筑物)安装电线,接电源 **2** fasten or reinforce with wire 用金属丝捆扎(或加固) **3** informal 【非正式】 send a telegram to someone 向···发电报

wireless /ˈwaɪələs/ **adjective** using radio, microwaves, etc. (as opposed to wires) to transmit signals 无线电的 • **noun** dated 【废】 **1** a radio 无线电收音机 **2** broadcasting using radio signals 无线电广播

wiretapping /ˈwaɪətæpɪŋ/ **noun** the secret tapping of telephone lines in order to listen to other people's conversations (对电话的)搭线窃听

wiring /ˈwaɪərɪŋ/ **noun** a system of wires providing electric circuits for a device or building 供电系统;供电线路

wiry /ˈwaɪəri/ **adjective 1** resembling wire 金属丝般坚硬的 **2** lean, tough, and sinewy 瘦而结实的

wisdom /ˈwɪzdəm/ **noun 1** the quality of being wise 智慧 **2** the knowledge that a particular society or culture has gained over a period of time 知识;学问 □ **wisdom tooth** each of the four molars at the back of the mouth which usually appear at about the age of twenty 智齿

wise¹ /waɪz/ **adjective 1** having or showing experience, knowledge, and good judgement 智慧的,足智多谋的;有学问的,英明的 **2 (wise to)** informal 【非正式】 aware of 知道的,明白的;意识到的 • **verb (wises, wising, wised) (wise up)** informal 【非正式】 become aware of something 发觉;明白;知道 ■ **wisely** adverb.

wise² **noun** old use 【旧】 the manner or extent of something 方式;方法;程度

wisecrack /ˈwaɪzkræk/ informal 【非正式】 • **noun** a witty remark or joke 妙语;俏皮话 • **verb** make a wisecrack 说妙语;说俏皮话

wish /wɪʃ/ **verb 1** feel a strong desire for something 想要(得到某物) **2** silently express a hope that something will happen 希望(某事发生) **3** say that you hope that someone will be happy, successful, etc. 祝;祝愿(幸福,成功等) • **noun 1** a desire or hope 渴望;愿望;希望 **2 (wishes)** an expression of hope that someone will be happy, successful, etc. 祝愿;祝福 **3** a thing wished for 希望的事;想要的东西

wishbone /ˈwɪʃbəʊn/ **noun** a forked bone between the neck and breast of a bird (禽鸟颈和胸之间的)叉骨,如愿骨

wishful /ˈwɪʃfl/ **adjective** wishing for something to happen 渴望的;希望的 □ **wishful thinking** expectations that are based on optimistic wishes rather than facts 痴心妄想

wishy-washy /ˈwɪʃiˌwɒʃi/ **adjective** not firm or forceful; feeble 软弱无力的

wisp /wɪsp/ **noun** a small, thin bunch or strand of something 小捆;小把;小缕 ■ **wispy** adjective.

wisteria /wɪˈstɪəriə/ **noun** a climbing plant with hanging clusters of bluish-lilac flowers 紫藤

wistful /ˈwɪstfl/ **adjective** having a feeling of vague or regretful longing 渴望的;徒然神往的;伤感的 ■ **wistfully** adverb **wistfulness** noun.

wit /wɪt/ **noun 1 (also wits)** the ability to think quickly and make good decisions 悟性;理解力;智慧 **2** a natural talent for using words and ideas in a quick and funny way 才思敏捷;风趣 **3** a witty person 机智幽默的人 □ **at your wits' end** not knowing what to do 智穷计尽

witch /wɪtʃ/ **noun** a woman believed

to have evil magic powers 女巫；巫婆 □ **witch doctor** a person believed to have magic powers that cure illness 巫医(被认为具有治愈疾病的魔力) **witch hazel** a lotion made from the bark and leaves of a shrub, used for treating injuries on the skin (从金缕梅树皮和树叶中提取的)金缕梅酊剂 **witch-hunt** a campaign against a person who holds unpopular views (对持异见者的)迫害

witchcraft /'wɪtʃkrɑːft/ **noun** the use of evil magic powers 巫术；魔法

with /wɪð, wɪθ/ **preposition 1** accompanied by 和…一起；同 **2** in the same direction as 和…方向相同；顺着 **3** possessing; having 拥有；具有 **4** indicating the instrument used to perform an action or the material used for a purpose 用，以，借(表示执行某种动作所使用的器具或用于某种目的的材料) **5** in opposition to or competition with 与…对立(或竞争) **6** indicating the way or attitude in which a person does something (表示行为方式或态度) **7** in relation to 关于；涉及 □ **with it** informal 【非正式】 **1** up to date or fashionable 时新的；时髦的 **2** alert and able to understand 机灵的；有领悟力的

withdraw /wɪð'drɔː, wɪθ-/ **verb** (**withdraws, withdrawing, withdrew; past participle withdrawn**) **1** remove or take away 拿走 **2** leave or cause to leave a place (使)离开；(使)撤退 **3** stop taking part in an activity 退出(活动) **4** take back something you have said 收回(所说的话) **5** take money out of an account 提，取(钱) **6** go away to another place in search of quiet or privacy 离群索居；遁世 **7** stop taking an addictive drug 戒毒 **8** (**withdrawn**) very shy or reserved 害羞的；沉默寡言的；内向的 ■ **withdrawal** noun.

wither /'wɪðə(r)/ **verb** (**withers,**

withering, withered) **1** (of a plant) become dry and shriveled (植物)干枯，枯萎 **2** become shrunken or wrinkled from age or disease (因衰老或疾病而)形容枯槁 **3** become weaker; decline 衰败；衰退 **4** (**withering**) scornful 轻蔑的

withers /'wɪðəz/ **plural noun** the highest part of a horse's back, at the base of the neck 鬐甲，马肩隆(马颈部的隆起部位)

withhold /wɪð'həʊld, wɪθ-/ **verb** (**withholds, withholding, withheld**) **1** refuse to give 拒绝给予 **2** hold back an emotion or reaction 抑制，克制(情绪或反应)

✔ **拼写指南** remember to double the *h*: with**h**old. 记住 withhold 中要双写 h。

within /wɪ'ðɪn/ **preposition 1** before a particular period of time has passed 在(时间段)以内 **2** inside the range or bounds of something 在…范围(或限度)之内 **3** inside something 在…里面；在…内部 • **adverb** inside 在里面；在内部

without /wɪ'ðaʊt/ **preposition** not accompanied by, using, or having 无；没有 • **adverb** old use 【旧】 outside 在外面；向外；在户外

withstand /wɪð'stænd, wɪθ-/ **verb** (**withstands, withstanding, withstood**) remain undamaged by; resist 经受；顶住；抵住

witless /'wɪtləs/ **adjective** foolish; stupid 愚蠢的；笨的

witness /'wɪtnəs/ **noun 1** a person who sees an event take place 目击者；见证人 **2** a person who gives evidence in a court of law (在法庭提供证词的)证人 **3** a person who is present at the signing of a document and signs it themselves to confirm this (文件的)连署人 • **verb 1** be a witness to 目击；当场看到 **2** be the place, period, etc. in which an event takes place 是(事

件)的发生地点(或时期等)

witter /'wɪtə(r)/ **verb (witters, wittering, wittered)** Brit. informal【英,非正式】talk for a long time about unimportant things 唠叨,絮叨

witticism /'wɪtɪsɪzəm/ **noun** a witty remark 妙语;俏皮话

witty /'wɪti/ **adjective (wittier, wittiest)** able to say clever and amusing things 有幽默感的;妙趣横生的;机智的 ■ **wittily** adverb.

wives /waɪvz/ plural of **WIFE**.

wizard /'wɪzəd/ **noun 1** a man who has magical powers 男巫;神汉;术士 **2** a person who is very skilled in something 能手;行家;奇才 ■ **wizardry** noun.

wizened /'wɪznd/ **adjective** shrivelled or wrinkled with age (因衰老而)干枯的,干瘪的

WMD /ˌdʌbljuː em 'diː/ **abbreviation** weapon (or weapons) of mass destruction 大规模杀伤性武器

woad /wəʊd/ **noun** a plant whose leaves were used in the past to make blue dye 菘蓝(一种植物,其叶曾被用来制造蓝色染料)

wobble /'wɒbl/ **verb (wobbles, wobbling, wobbled) 1** move unsteadily from side to side 来回摆动;摇晃 **2** (of the voice) tremble (嗓音)颤抖,振动 • **noun** a wobbling movement or sound 摆动;摇摆 ■ **wobbly** adjective.

woe /wəʊ/ **noun** literary【文】**1** great sadness or distresss 悲哀;悲伤;痛苦 **2** (**woes**) troubles 困难,不幸;灾难 ◻ **woe betide someone** a person will be in trouble if they do a particular thing (某人)要倒霉(或遭殃)

woebegone /'wəʊbɪɡɒn/ **adjective** looking sad or miserable (神情)悲伤的,忧愁的

woeful /'wəʊfl/ **adjective 1** very sad 悲哀的,悲伤的 **2** very bad 糟糕的;悲惨的 ■ **woefully** adverb.

wok /wɒk/ **noun** a bowl-shaped frying pan used in Chinese cookery (中国式的)炒菜锅,炒锅

woke /wəʊk/ past of **WAKE**[1].

woken /'wəʊkn/ past participle of **WAKE**[1].

wold /wəʊld/ **noun** an area of high, open land 丘陵地带

wolf /wʊlf/ **noun** (plural **wolves**) a wild animal of the dog family, that lives and hunts in packs 狼 • **verb** (**wolfs, wolfing, wolfed**) eat food quickly and greedily 狼吞虎咽;贪婪地吃 ◻ **cry wolf** keep raising false alarms, so that when you really need help you are ignored 喊"狼来了";发假警报 **wolf whistle** a whistle with a rising and falling note, used by a man to show that he finds a woman sexually attractive 挑逗性口哨 ■ **wolfish** adjective.

wolfhound /'wʊlfhaʊnd/ **noun** a large breed of dog originally used to hunt wolves 猎狼犬

wolfram /'wʊlfrəm/ **noun** tungsten or its ore 钨;钨矿石

wolverine /'wʊlvəriːn/ **noun** a heavily built meat-eating animal found in cold northern areas 狼獾(食肉动物,体形粗壮,见于北部寒冷地区)

woman /'wʊmən/ **noun** (plural **women**) an adult human female 成年女子;妇女 ■ **womanhood** noun **womanly** adjective.

womanize or **womanise** /'wʊmənaɪz/ **verb (womanizes, womanizing, womanized)** (of a man) have a lot of casual affairs with women (男子)沉溺于女色的,玩弄女性的 ■ **womanizer** noun.

womankind /'wʊmənkaɪnd/ **noun** women as a whole (总称)女人,妇女,女性

womb /wuːm/ **noun** the organ in a woman's body in which a baby develops before it is born 子宫

wombat /'wɒmbæt/ **noun** an Australian animal resembling a small bear with

short legs 毛鼻袋熊(澳大利亚动物,似小熊,腿短)

won /wʌn/ past and past participle of **WIN**.

wonder /'wʌndə(r)/ **verb (wonders, wondering, wondered) 1** be interested to know about something 想要知道,感到好奇 **2** feel doubt 感到疑惑 **3** feel amazement and admiration 惊叹,感到惊奇,觉得诧异 • **noun 1** a feeling of amazement and admiration 惊奇,惊讶,诧异 **2** a person or thing that causes such a feeling 奇才,奇物,奇迹,奇事 □ **no wonder** it is not surprising 难怪,不足为奇

wonderful /'wʌndəfl/ **adjective** very good or remarkable 极好的,绝妙的 ■ **wonderfully adverb.**

wonderland /'wʌndəlænd/ **noun** a place full of wonderful things 仙境,奇境

wondrous /'wʌndrəs/ **adjective** literary 【文】inspiring wonder 令人惊奇的,令人赞叹的,奇妙的

wonky /'wɒŋki/ **adjective** informal 【非正式】**1** crooked 歪斜的,弯曲的 **2** unsteady or faulty 不稳的,摇晃的,有差错的

wont /wəʊnt/ **noun (your wont)** formal 【正式】your normal behaviour 惯常行为,习惯 • **adjective (wont to)** literary 【文】in the habit of doing something 习惯的

won't /wəʊnt/ **short form** will not.

wonted /'wəʊntɪd/ **adjective** literary 【文】usual 习惯的,惯例的

woo /wu:/ **verb (woos, wooing, wooed) 1** (of a man) try to make a woman love him (男子)追求(女子),向…求爱 **2** try to get someone's support or custom 争取…的支持,拉拢,招徕

wood /wʊd/ **noun 1** the hard material forming the trunk and branches of a tree 木头,木柴,木材 **2** (also **woods**) a small forest 树林,林地

■ **woody** adjective.

woodcut /'wʊdkʌt/ **noun** a print made with a block of wood in which a design has been cut 木版画

woodcutter /'wʊdkʌtə(r)/ **noun** a person who cuts down trees for wood 伐木人,樵夫

wooded /'wʊdɪd/ **adjective** (of land) covered with woods (土地)长满树木的,树木覆盖的

wooden /'wʊdn/ **adjective 1** made of wood 木制的 **2** acting or speaking in a stiff and awkward way 僵硬的,呆板的 ■ **woodenly adverb.**

woodland /'wʊdlənd/ or **woodlands** /'wʊdlændz/ **noun** land covered with trees 林地,林区

woodlouse /'wʊdlaʊs/ **noun** (plural **woodlice**) a small insect-like creature with a grey segmented body 潮虫,鼠虫

woodpecker /'wʊdpekə(r)/ **noun** a bird with a strong bill that pecks at tree trunks to find insects 啄木鸟

woodturning /'wʊdtɜːnɪŋ/ **noun** the activity of shaping wood with a lathe 木工车床加工

woodwind /'wʊdwɪnd/ **noun** wind instruments other than brass instruments forming a section of an orchestra (管弦乐队的)木管乐器

woodwork /'wʊdwɜːk/ **noun 1** the wooden parts of a room, building, or other structure (房屋、建筑物或其他结构的)木建部分,木构件 **2** the activity of making things from wood 木工活,木工手艺 ■ **woodworker** noun.

woodworm /'wʊdwɜːm/ **noun** the larva of a kind of beetle, that bores into wood 木蛀虫,木蠹

woof¹ /wʊf/ **noun** the barking sound made by a dog 汪汪(狗叫声) • **verb** bark (狗)汪汪叫,发出吠声

woof² = WEFT.

woofer /'wu:fə(r)/ **noun** a loudspeaker that reproduces low frequencies 低

音扬声器；低音喇叭

wool /wʊl/ **noun** the fine, soft hair forming the coat of a sheep (绵羊的)绒，毛

woollen /ˈwʊlən/ (US spelling 【美拼写】 **woolen**) **adjective 1** made of wool 毛料的；毛制的 **2** relating to the production of wool 毛纺的；毛纺业的 • **noun** (**woollens**) woollen clothes 毛料衣服

woolly /ˈwʊli/ **adjective 1** made of wool 毛料的；毛制的 **2** covered with wool or hair resembling wool 有毛(或毛状物)覆盖的；毛茸茸的 **3** resembling wool 似毛的 **4** confused or unclear 混乱的；模糊的 • **noun** (plural **woollies**) informal 【非正式】 a woollen jumper or cardigan 毛料衣服；套头毛衣

woozy /ˈwuːzi/ **adjective** informal 【非正式】 unsteady, dizzy, or dazed 不稳的；眩晕的；头昏眼花的 ■ **woozily** adverb.

word /wɜːd/ **noun 1** a unit of language which has meaning and is used with others to form sentences 词；单词 **2** a remark or statement 言语；言论 **3** (**words**) angry talk 争论；口角 **4** (**the word**) a command, slogan, or signal 命令；口号；信号 **5** (**your word**) your account of the truth of something that happened 说法；描述 **6** (**your word**) a thing that you promise 诺言；保证 **7** news 新闻；消息 • **verb** express something in particular words 用词；措词 □ **in a word** briefly 一句话，总而言之 **word of mouth** talking as a way of passing on information 口头传播；口头传达 **word processor** a computer or program for creating and printing a document or piece of text 文字处理机；文字处理软件 **word class** a category in which a word is placed according to its function in grammar; a part of speech 词性

wording /ˈwɜːdɪŋ/ **noun** the way in which something is worded 措词；用语

wordy /ˈwɜːdi/ **adjective** using too many words 冗长的；啰唆的

wore /wɔː(r)/ past of WEAR.

work /wɜːk/ **noun 1** activity involving mental or physical effort done in order to achieve a result 工作；劳动 **2** the activity or job that a person does in order to earn money (作为谋生手段的)工作，职业 **3** a task or tasks to be done 任务；工作 **4** a thing or things done or made 工作成果；产品；作品 **5** (**works**) a place where industrial or manufacturing processes are carried out 工厂 **6** (**works**) activities involving the building or repair of something 建筑；修建 **7** (**works**) the mechanism of a clock or other machine (钟表或其他机器的)机械装置 • **verb 1** do work as your job 工作 **2** make someone do work 使(某人)工作 **3** (of a machine or system) function properly (机器或系统)正常运行 **4** (of a machine) be in operation (机器)在运转(或操作)中 **5** have the desired result 起作用；奏效 **6** bring a material or mixture to a desired shape or consistency 使(材料或混合物)成形，使定形 **7** cultivate land, or extract materials from a mine or quarry 耕种(土地)；从(矿山)采矿 **8** move something gradually or with difficulty into another position 逐渐(或费力地)移动 □ **get worked up** become stressed or angry 逐渐变得焦虑(或愤怒) **work out 1** develop in the desired way 成功地发展 **2** do energetic physical exercise 锻炼；训练 **work something out 1** solve something 解决 **2** plan something in detail 详细计划 **work permit** an official document giving a foreigner permission to take a job in a country (准许外国人就业的)工作许可证 **work-to-rule** a situation in which people refuse to do overtime or extra work, as a form of protest 按章工作(作为抗议而拒绝做额外的工作) **work up to** proceed gradually towards something more demanding or advanced 逐步发展到,逐渐达到(更高级的事物)

workaday /'wɜːkədeɪ/ **adjective** ordinary 普通的,平常的

workbench /'wɜːkbentʃ/ **noun** a bench at which carpentry and other work is done (木工等的)工作台

worker /'wɜːkə(r)/ **noun 1** a person who works 工人;工作者;劳动者 **2** a neuter or undeveloped female bee, wasp, ant, etc., large numbers of which perform the basic work of a colony 职虫(指工蜂、工蚁等)

workforce /'wɜːkfɔːs/ **noun** the people working or available for work in a particular area, firm, or industry 劳动力;劳动人口

workhouse /'wɜːkhaʊs/ **noun** (in the past in the UK) a place where poor people were given accommodation and food in return for work (旧时英国的)济贫院,劳动救济所

working /'wɜːkɪŋ/ **adjective 1** having paid employment 有工作的 **2** doing manual work 从事体力劳动的;做工的 **3** functioning or able to function 能运转的;可起作用的 **4** used as a basis for work or discussion and likely to be changed later 初步的;暂定的 • **noun 1** a mine from which minerals are being extracted (开采矿石的)矿区 **2** (**workings**) the way in which a machine, organization, or system operates (机器、系统、组织的)运作方式,工作方法 □ **working class** the social group consisting mainly of people who do manual or industrial work 工人阶级 **working party** a group set up to study and report on a particular question and make recommendations (专题)调查委员会

workload /'wɜːkləʊd/ **noun** the amount of work to be done by someone or something 工作量

workman /'wɜːkmən/ **noun** (plural **workmen**) a man employed to do manual work 工人

workmanlike /'wɜːkmənlaɪk/ **adjective** showing efficient skill 技术娴熟的

workout /'wɜːkaʊt/ **noun** a session of energetic physical exercise 锻炼;训练

workshop /'wɜːkʃɒp/ **noun 1** a room or building in which things are made or repaired 车间;工场 **2** a meeting for discussion and activity on a particular subject or project 研讨会;讲习班

workstation /'wɜːksteɪʃn/ **noun** a desktop computer that is part of a network (计算机)工作站

worktop /'wɜːktɒp/ **noun** Brit. 【英】a flat surface for working on in a kitchen (厨房的)操作台

world /wɜːld/ **noun 1** (**the world**) the earth with all its countries and peoples 世界;地球;天下 **2** all that belongs to a particular region, period, or area of activity 领域;界 □ **world-weary** bored with or cynical about life 厌世的;厌弃人生的 **World Wide Web** an information system on the Internet which allows documents to be connected to each other using hypertext links 万维网

worldly /'wɜːldli/ **adjective 1** relating to material things rather than spiritual ones 物质的;非精神的 **2** experienced and sophisticated 精明老练的;久经世故的 □ **worldly-wise** having a lot of experience of life 精明老练的;老于世故的

worldwide /'wɜːldwaɪd/ **adjective & adverb** throughout the world 在全世界的(的);遍布世界各地的(的)

worm /wɜːm/ **noun 1** an earthworm or other creeping or burrowing creature with a long, thin body and no limbs 蚯蚓;(细长、无脊椎的)软体虫,蠕虫 **2** (**worms**) long, thin creatures that live as parasites in a person's or animal's intestines 肠虫;寄生虫 • **verb 1** move by crawling or wriggling 蠕动;蠕行 **2** (**worm your way into**) gradually move into 慢慢地进入;潜入 **3** (**worm something out of**) cleverly obtain information from someone who is reluctant to give it 从(某人口中)套出(信息) □ **worm cast** a small spiral of earth or sand thrown up at the surface by a burrowing worm 蚯蚓粪

wormwood /ˈwɜːmwʊd/ **noun** a plant with a bitter flavour, used in drinks such as vermouth 蒿属,苦艾(有苦味用于苦艾酒等饮料中)

worn /wɔːn/ past participle of WEAR. • **adjective** thin or damaged as a result of wear 磨薄的;用(或穿)坏的 □ **worn out 1** exhausted 疲惫不堪的;筋疲力尽的 **2** damaged by wear, and no longer usable 破旧的;不能再用的

worried /ˈwʌrɪd/ **adjective** feeling anxiety or concern 担心的;焦虑的 ■ **worriedly** adverb.

worrisome /ˈwʌrɪsəm/ **adjective** causing anxiety or concern 令人忧虑的;令人发愁的

worry /ˈwʌri/ **verb** (**worries, worrying, worried**) **1** feel or cause to feel troubled over unwelcome things that have happened or may happen (使)担心;(使)忧虑 **2** annoy or disturb 使烦恼;使不安;困扰 **3** (of a dog) repeatedly push at and bite something (狗)攻击,撕咬 **4** (of a dog) chase and attack livestock (狗)追咬(家畜) • **noun** (plural **worries**) **1** the state of being worried 担心;忧虑 **2** a source of anxiety 担心(或忧虑)的缘由 ■ **worrier** noun.

worse /wɜːs/ **adjective 1** less good, satisfactory, or pleasing 更坏的;更差的;更糟的 **2** more serious or severe 更严重的;更剧烈的 **3** more ill or unhappy 病情更重的;更不幸的 • **adverb 1** less well 更坏,更糟;病情更重地 **2** more seriously or severely 更严重地;更剧烈地 • **noun** a worse event or circumstance 更坏的事;更糟的情况

worsen /ˈwɜːsn/ **verb** make or become worse (使)变得更坏(或更糟);(使)恶化

worship /ˈwɜːʃɪp/ **noun 1** the practice of praising and praying to God or a god or goddess (对上帝的)崇拜,崇敬 **2** religious rites and ceremonies 宗教仪式;敬神活动 **3** a strong feeling of admiration and respect for someone 爱慕;热爱;挚爱 • **verb** (**worships, worshipping, worshipped**; US spelling 【美拼作】**worships, worshiping, worshiped**) **1** offer praise and prayers to God or a god or goddess 敬奉(上帝或神) **2** feel great admiration and respect for 崇拜;敬重 ■ **worshipper** noun.

worshipful /ˈwɜːʃɪpfl/ **adjective 1** feeling or showing great respect and admiration 崇敬的;敬重的 **2** (**Worshipful**) Brit. 【英】a title given to Justices of the Peace (对治安法官的尊称)尊敬的

worst /wɜːst/ **adjective** most bad, severe, or serious 最坏的;最差的;最糟的 • **adverb 1** most severely or seriously 最剧烈地;最严重地 **2** least well 最坏地;最差地 • **noun** the worst part, event, or circumstance 最差的部分;最坏的事情;最糟的情况

worsted /ˈwʊstɪd/ **noun** a smooth woollen fabric of good quality 精纺毛纱

worth /wɜːθ/ **adjective 1** equivalent in value to a particular sum or item 相当于…价值的;值…钱的 **2** deserving to be treated in a particular way 具有…的价值的;值得…的 • **noun 1** the value of someone or something 长

处；价值 **2** an amount of something that is equivalent to a particular sum of money 值一定金额的东西

worthless /'wɜːθləs/ **adjective 1** having no practical or financial value 无价值的；不值钱的，没用处的 **2** having no good qualities （品质）低劣的，卑鄙的

worthwhile /wɜːθ'waɪl/ **adjective** worth the time, money, or effort spent 值得花费时间(或金钱，精力)的

worthy /'wɜːði/ **adjective** (**worthier**, **worthiest**) **1** deserving effort, attention, or respect 值得花费精力的；值得注意的，值得敬重的 **2** (**worthy of**) deserving or good enough for 值得…的；应得…的，优秀得足以…的 **3** well intended but too serious and dull 好心但过分严肃(或枯燥)的 • **noun** (plural **worthies**) humorous【幽默】an important person 重要人士 ■ **worthily** adverb **worthiness** noun.

would /wʊd, wəd/ **modal verb** (3rd singular present **would**) **1** past of **WILL**[1]. **2** indicating the consequence of an imagined event (表示假想事件的后果)会，将 **3** expressing a desire or inclination (表示愿望或爱好)要，肯，会 **4** expressing a polite request (表示礼貌的请求)请 **5** expressing an opinion or assumption (表示看法或推测)也许，大概 **6** literary【文】expressing a wish or regret (表示愿望或遗憾)要是 □ **would-be** wishing to be a particular type of person 希望成为…的: *a would-be actress* 想要成为女演员的人

wouldn't /'wʊdnt/ **short form** would not.

wound[1] /wuːnd/ **noun 1** an injury to the body caused by a cut, blow, or bullet (身体上的)创伤，伤口 **2** an injury to a person's feelings (感情上的)伤害 • **verb 1** inflict a wound on 打伤，使受伤 **2** injure someone's feelings 伤害(某人的感情)

wound[2] /waʊnd/ past and past participle of **WIND**[2].

wove /wəʊv/ past of **WEAVE**[1].

woven /'wəʊvn/ past participle of **WEAVE**[1].

wow /waʊ/ informal【非正式】**exclamation** expressing great surprise or admiration (表示惊讶或羡慕)哇，呀 • **verb** impress someone very much 使叫绝；使喝彩

WPC /ˌdʌbljuː piː 'siː/ **abbreviation** woman police constable 女警察

wrack[1] /ræk/ ⇒ **RACK**.

wrack[2] **noun** a brown seaweed 海藻；海草

wraith /reɪθ/ **noun** a ghost 灵魂；鬼魂

wrangle /'ræŋgl/ **noun** a long dispute or argument (长时间的)争吵，争论 • **verb** (**wrangles**, **wrangling**, **wrangled**) be involved in a wrangle 争吵；争论

wrap /ræp/ **verb** (**wraps**, **wrapping**, **wrapped**) **1** enclose something in paper or soft material (用纸或柔软材料)包，裹 **2** encircle or wind round 环绕；缠绕；包围 • **noun 1** a loose outer garment or piece of material 宽松外衣；宽松材料 **2** paper or material used for wrapping 包装纸；包装材料 □ **under wraps** kept secret 保密地 **wrap someone/thing up 1** (also **wrap up**) dress someone in or put on warm clothes (使)穿得暖和 **2** bring a meeting or deal to a close 结束，完成(会议或交易) ■ **wrapper** noun.

wrasse /ræs/ **noun** (plural **wrasse** or **wrasses**) a brightly coloured sea fish with thick lips and strong teeth 隆头鱼(长有厚嘴唇和利齿的颜色鲜艳的海鱼)

wrath /rɒθ/ **noun** extreme anger 盛怒；暴怒 ■ **wrathful** adjective.

wreak /riːk/ **verb 1** cause a lot of damage or harm 造成(巨大破坏或伤害) **2** take revenge on someone 实施(报复)

wreath /riːθ/ **noun** (plural **wreaths**) **1** an arrangement of flowers or leaves fastened in a ring 花圈；花环 **2** a curl or ring of smoke or cloud 烟圈；云环

wreathe /riːð/ *verb* (**wreathes, wreathing, wreathed**) **1** (be **wreathed**) be surrounded or encircled 包围；环绕 **2** move with a curling motion 萦绕；盘绕

wreck /rek/ *noun* **1** the destruction of a ship at sea (船只在海上的)失事，遇难 **2** a ship destroyed at sea (海上的)失事船只，遇难船只 **3** a building, vehicle, etc. that has been destroyed or badly damaged 遭毁坏(或严重破坏)的建筑(或车辆等) **4** N. Amer. 【北美】 a road or rail crash (汽车或火车)车祸 **5** a person in a very bad state 身体(或精神)状态极差的人 • *verb* **1** destroy or badly damage 毁坏；严重损坏 **2** spoil a plan 破坏(计划) **3** cause a ship to sink or break up 使(船只)沉没(或失事)

wreckage /ˈrekɪdʒ/ *noun* the remains of something that has been badly damaged 残骸

wren /ren/ *noun* **1** a very small bird with a cocked tail 鹪鹩(一种体型极小的禽鸟，尾巴上翘) **2** (in the UK) a member of the former Women's Royal Naval Service (英国的)前皇家海军妇女服务队队员

wrench /rentʃ/ *verb* **1** pull or twist something suddenly and violently 猛拉；猛扭；猛拧 **2** twist and injure a part of the body 扭伤(身体部位) • *noun* **1** a sudden violent twist or pull 猛拉；猛扭；猛拧 **2** a feeling of sadness on leaving a place or person (离别的)痛苦，悲伤 **3** an adjustable tool used for gripping and turning nuts or bolts 扳钳；扳手

wrest /rest/ *verb* **1** forcibly pull something from someone's grasp 抢；夺 **2** succeed in taking power or control from someone after a struggle 攫取，抢夺(权力或控制权)

wrestle /ˈresl/ *verb* (**wrestles, wrestling, wrestled**) **1** take part in a fight or contest that involves close grappling with your opponent 摔跤；参加摔跤比赛 **2** struggle with a difficulty or problem 全力应对，努力解决(难题) **3** struggle to move an object 用力搬动(或移动) • *noun* **1** a wrestling bout or contest 摔跤比赛 **2** a hard struggle 奋斗；斗争；搏斗 ■ **wrestler** *noun* **wrestling** *noun*.

wretch /retʃ/ *noun* **1** an unfortunate person 不幸的人；苦命的人 **2** informal 【非正式】 an unpleasant person 无耻之徒；恶棍；坏蛋

wretched /ˈretʃɪd/ *adjective* **1** in a very unhappy or unfortunate state 悲惨的；不幸的；可怜的 **2** of bad quality 劣质的，拙劣的 ■ **wretchedly** *adverb*.

wriggle /ˈrɪɡl/ *verb* (**wriggles, wriggling, wriggled**) **1** twist and turn with quick short movements 扭动；蠕动 **2** (wriggle out of) use excuses to avoid doing something (施诡计)逃避 • *noun* a wriggling movement 扭动；蠕动 ■ **wriggly** *adjective*.

wring /rɪŋ/ *verb* (**wrings, wringing, wrung**) **1** squeeze and twist something to force water out of it 绞，拧绞，拧，拧出(水) **2** twist and break an animal's neck 拧断，扭断(动物的)脖子 **3** squeeze someone's hand tightly 拧，搢(某人的)手 **4** (wring something from or out of) obtain something from someone with difficulty 从…处费力获得 ■ **wringer** *noun*.

wringing /ˈrɪŋɪŋ/ *adjective* very wet 湿透的；湿淋淋的

wrinkle /ˈrɪŋkl/ *noun* a slight line or fold, especially in fabric or a person's skin (尤指织物或人脸上的)褶皱，皱纹 • *verb* (**wrinkles, wrinkling, wrinkled**) make or become covered with wrinkles (使)起皱纹；(使)起褶皱 ■ **wrinkly** *adjective*.

wrist /rɪst/ *noun* the joint connecting

the hand with the lower part of the arm 手腕；腕关节

wristwatch /ˈrɪstwɒtʃ/ noun a watch worn on a strap round the wrist 手表

writ[1] /rɪt/ noun an official document from a court or other legal authority, ordering someone to do or not to do something (法院或其他法定权力机构发出的)令状，书面命令

writ[2] old-fashioned past participle of WRITE. □ **writ large** in an obvious or exaggerated form 显而易见，夸张

write /raɪt/ verb (**writes, writing, wrote;** past participle **written**) 1 mark letters, words, or other symbols on a surface with a pen, pencil, etc. 写字，书写 2 write and send a letter to someone 写信 3 compose a written or musical work 撰写(文章)，作(曲) 4 fill out a cheque or similar document 填写(支票或类似文件) □ **write something off** decide that something is useless or a failure 认为(无用或失败) 2 decide not to pursue a debt 注销，勾销(债务) **write-off** Brit. 【英】a vehicle that is too badly damaged to be repaired 报废车辆 **write-up** a newspaper review of a recent event, performance, etc. (报刊上的)评论，评述 ■ **writer** noun.

writhe /raɪð/ verb (**writhes, writhing, writhed**) twist or squirm in pain or embarrassment (痛苦或尴尬地)挣扎，扭动

writing /ˈraɪtɪŋ/ noun 1 the activity or skill of writing 写作，写作技巧 2 a sequence of letters or symbols forming words 文字 3 (**writings**) books or other written works 著作，作品

wrong /rɒŋ/ adjective 1 not correct or true; mistaken or in error 不正确的，错误的 2 unjust, dishonest, or immoral 不公正的，不诚实的；不道德的 3 in a bad or abnormal condition 坏的，出故障的 ● adverb 1 in a mistaken or unwelcome way or direction (方式或方向)错误地，不得人心地 2 with an incorrect result (结果)不正确地，错误地 ● noun an unjust, dishonest, or immoral action 不公正行为；欺诈行径；不道德行为 ● verb treat someone unfairly 不公正地对待 □ **wrong-foot 1** (in a game) catch an opponent off balance (比赛中)打乱(对手的)阵脚 2 place someone in a difficult situation by saying or doing something unexpected 使措手不及，使窘态毕露 **wrong-headed** having bad judgement 执迷不悟的，判断错误的 ■ **wrongly** adverb **wrongness** noun.

wrongdoing /ˈrɒŋduːɪŋ/ noun illegal or dishonest behaviour 不法行为，欺诈行径 ■ **wrongdoer** noun.

wrongful /ˈrɒŋfl/ adjective not fair, just, or legal 不公平的，不公正的；不合法的 ■ **wrongfully** adverb.

wrote /rəʊt/ past tense of WRITE.

wrought /rɔːt/ old-fashioned 【过时】past and past participle of WORK. ● adjective 1 (of metals) beaten out or shaped by hammering (金属)锻造的 2 made in a particular way 以某种方式制成的：*well wrought* 精制的 □ **wrought iron** tough iron suitable for forging or rolling 锻铁；熟铁

wrung /rʌŋ/ past and past participle of WRING.

wry /raɪ/ adjective (**wryer, wryest** or **wrier, wriest**) 1 using dry, mocking humour 嘲弄的，挖苦的 2 (of a person's face) twisted into an expression of disgust, disappointment, or annoyance (人脸)扭曲的 3 bending or twisted to one side 扭曲的，歪斜的 ■ **wryly** adverb.

wunderkind /ˈwʊndəkɪnd/ noun a person who is very successful at a young age 极成功的青年人，少年得志者

Wurlitzer /ˈwɜːlɪtsə(r)/ noun trademark

【商标】a large pipe organ or electric organ 沃利策(电)管风琴

WWI *abbreviation* World War I 第一次世界大战

WWII *abbreviation* World War II 第二次世界大战

WWW /ˌdʌbljuː dʌbljuː ˈdʌbljuː/ *abbreviation* World Wide Web.

Xx

X or **x** /eks/ **noun** (plural **Xs** or **X's**) **1** the twenty-fourth letter of the alphabet 英语字母表的第24个字母 **2** an X-shaped written symbol, used to show that an answer is wrong, or to symbolize a kiss (用于表示错误或亲吻的)X形符号 **3** the Roman numeral for ten (罗马数字)十 □ **X chromosome** a sex chromosome, two of which are normally present in female cells and one in male cells X染色体(一种性染色体, 通常雌性细胞中含两个, 雄性细胞中含一个) **X certificate** (in the past) a classification of a film as suitable for adults only (旧时的) X级电影, 只适合成人看的电影 **x-rated** pornographic or indecent 色情的;下流的;猥亵的 **X-ray 1** an electromagnetic wave of very short wavelength, which is able to pass through many solids and so make it possible to see into or through them X射线;X光;伦琴射线

2 an image of the internal structure of an object produced by passing X-rays through it X光照片

xenon /'zenɒn, 'zi:-/ **noun** an inert gaseous element, present in small amounts in the air (惰性气体元素)氙

xenophobia /ˌzenə'fəʊbiə/ **noun** dislike or fear of people from other countries 仇外, 恐外(对外国人的憎恶或畏惧) ■ **xenophobic** adjective.

Xerox /'zɪərɒks, 'ze-/ **noun** trademark 【商标】 **1** a process for copying documents using an electric charge and dry powder 施乐复印;复印 **2** a copy made using such a process 施乐复印件;复印件 • **verb** (**xerox**) copy a document by such a process 静电复印(文件)

Xmas /'krɪsməs, 'eksməs/ **noun** informal 【非正式】 Christmas 圣诞节

xylophone /'zaɪləfəʊn/ **noun** a musical instrument consisting of a row of bars which you hit with small hammers 木琴

Y or **y** /waɪ/ **noun** (plural **Ys** or **Y's**) the twenty-fifth letter of the alphabet 英语字母表的第25个字母口 **Y chromosome** a sex chromosome which is normally present only in male cells Y染色体 (一种性染色体，通常仅存在于雄性细胞中) **Y-fronts** Brit. trademark【英，商标】men's or boys' under pants with a seam at the front in the shape of an upside-down Y (前缝呈倒Y形的) 紧身男短裤

yacht /jɒt/ **noun 1** a medium-sized sailing boat 中型游艇 **2** a boat with an engine, equipped for cruising (机动) 快艇，游艇 ■ **yachting** noun **yachtsman** noun (plural **yachtsmen**) **yachtswoman** noun (plural **yachtswomen**).

yahoo /ˈjɑːhuː, jəˈhuː/ **noun** informal【非正式】a rude or bad-mannered person 莽汉；粗人；野蛮人

yak¹ /jæk/ **noun** a large ox with shaggy hair and large horns, found in Tibet of China and central Asia 牦牛

yak² or **yack** verb (**yaks**, **yakking**, **yakked**) informal【非正式】talk continuously about something unimportant 闲扯；喋喋不休

yam /jæm/ **noun** the tuber of a tropical plant, eaten as a vegetable 薯蓣，山药(热带攀缘植物，可食用)

yang /jæŋ/ **noun** (in Chinese philosophy) the active male force in the universe (中国哲学中的) 阳

Yank /jæŋk/ **noun** informal【非正式】an American 美国佬

yank /jæŋk/ informal【非正式】**verb** pull quickly and hard 猛拉；使劲拉 ■ **noun** a sudden hard pull 猛拉；猛拽

Yankee /ˈjæŋki/ **noun** informal **1** an

American 美国佬 **2** US【美】a person from New England or one of the northern states 新英格兰人，北方人 **3** historical【历史】a Federal soldier in the Civil War (美国南北战争时期的) 联邦军队士兵，北军士兵

yap /jæp/ **verb** (**yaps**, **yapping**, **yapped**) give a sharp, high-pitched bark 狂吠 ■ **noun** a sharp, high-pitched bark 狂吠

yard¹ /jɑːd/ **noun 1** a unit of length equal to 3 feet (0.9144 metre) 码(长度单位，等于3英尺，合0.9144米) **2** a square or cubic yard 平方码；立方码 **3** a long piece of wood slung across a ship's mast for a sail to hang from (船桅杆上的)帆桁

yard² **noun 1** Brit.【英】a piece of enclosed ground next to a building (紧邻建筑物的) 围起的空地，院子 **2** an area of land used for a particular purpose (用于特定目的的) 场地 **3** N. Amer.【北美】the garden of a house 庭院花园

yardarm /ˈjɑːdɑːm/ **noun** either end of a ship's yard supporting a sail 帆桁端

Yardie /ˈjɑːdi/ **noun** informal【非正式】a member of a Jamaican gang of criminals 牙买加犯罪团伙成员

yardstick /ˈjɑːdstɪk/ **noun** a standard used for judging how good or successful something is 衡量标准；准绳

yarmulke or **yarmulka** /ˈjɑːmʊlkə/ **noun** a skullcap worn by Jewish men (犹太男子戴的) 亚莫克便帽，圆顶无檐小帽

yarn /jɑːn/ **noun 1** thread used for knitting, weaving, or sewing 纱；纱线 **2** informal【非正式】a long story 长

故事;漫谈

yashmak /ˈjæʃmæk/ *noun* a veil concealing all of the face except the eyes, worn by some Muslim women (穆斯林妇女戴的) 面纱

yaw /jɔː/ *verb* (of a moving ship or aircraft) turn unsteadily from side to side (航行中的船或飞机) 偏航,偏向 • *noun* a yawing movement 偏航;偏向

yawn /jɔːn/ *verb* **1** open your mouth wide and take a deep breath, usually when tired or bored (通常因疲劳或无聊) 打哈欠 **2 (yawning)** wide open 张开的;裂开的 • *noun* an act of yawning 打哈欠

yd *abbreviation* yard.

ye[1] /jiː/ *plural of* THOU.

ye[2] old use 【旧】 = the.

yea /jeɪ/ *adverb* old use 【旧】 yes 是

year /jɪə(r), jɜː(r)/ *noun* **1** the period of 365 days (or 366 days in leap years) starting from January 1 年;日历年 **2** a period of this length starting at a different point 一年时间 **3** the time taken by the earth to go around the sun 年(地球绕太阳旋转一周的时间) **4 (your years)** your age or time of life 年纪;年龄;年岁 **5 (years)** informal 【非正式】 a very long time 很久 **6** a set of students who enter and leave a school or college at the same time (学生的) 年级

yearling /ˈjɪəlɪŋ/ *noun* an animal between one and two years old 一两岁的动物

yearly /ˈjɪəli/ *adjective & adverb* happening or produced once a year or every year 一年一次(的);每年(的)

yearn /jɜːn/ *verb* have a strong feeling of longing for something 渴望;切盼 ■ **yearning** *noun & adjective*.

yeast /jiːst/ *noun* **1** a fungus which can convert sugar into alcohol and carbon dioxide 酵母菌 **2** a substance formed from this, used to make bread dough

rise and to ferment beer and wine 酵母;发酵粉 ■ **yeasty** *adjective*.

yell /jel/ *noun* a loud, sharp call or cry 叫喊;吼叫 • *verb* shout loudly 叫嚷;喊叫

yellow /ˈjeləʊ/ *adjective* **1** of the colour of egg yolks or ripe lemons 蛋黄色的;黄色的 **2** informal 【非正式】 cowardly 胆小的 • *noun* a yellow colour 黄色 • *verb* (of paper, fabric, etc.) become slightly yellow with age (纸张,织物等)变黄,发黄 □ **yellow card** (in soccer) a yellow card shown by the referee to a player being cautioned (足球运动中的) 黄牌 **yellow fever** a tropical disease that causes fever and jaundice and often death 黄热病(热带疾病,引起高烧,黄疸症状,常致命) ■ **yellowish** *adjective*.

yellowhammer /ˈjeləʊhæmə(r)/ *noun* a bird with a yellow head, neck, and breast 黄鹀(头、颈及胸部呈黄色)

yelp /jelp/ *noun* a short, sharp cry 尖叫 • *verb* give a yelp or yelps 发出尖叫声

yen[1] /jen/ *noun* (plural **yen**) the basic unit of money of Japan 日元(日本的基本货币单位)

yen[2] *noun* informal 【非正式】 a strong desire to have or do something 渴望;热望

yeoman /ˈjəʊmən/ *noun* (plural **yeomen**) (in the past) a man having his own house and small area of farming land (旧时的) 自耕农 □ **Yeoman of the Guard** a member of the British king or queen's ceremonial bodyguard (仪式上英国国王或女王的) 卫士

yes /jes/ *exclamation* **1** used to give a response in favour of something (用于表示肯定的回应) 是,是的,好的 **2** used to respond to someone who is talking to you (用于应答) 嗳,噢,嗯 • *noun* (plural **yeses** or **yesses**) a decision or vote in favour of something 同意；赞成；赞成票 □ **yesman** a person who always agrees with people in authority 唯唯诺诺的人；对上级唯命是从的人

yesterday /'jestədei, -di/ adverb on the day before today 在昨天；在昨日 • noun **1** the day before today 昨天 **2** the recent past 日前；不久前

yesteryear /'jestəjiə(r)/ noun literary 【文】last year or the recent past 去年；近年

yet /jet/ adverb **1** up until now or then 迄今；至此；到那时 **2** as soon as this 马上；立刻 **3** from now into the future 到将来某个时候 **4** referring to something that will or may happen 迟早；终将 **5** still; even 仍然；甚至；更 **6** in spite of that 不管；不顾 • **conjunction** but at the same time 然而；可是

yeti /'jeti/ noun a large hairy creature like a bear or a man, said to live in the highest part of the Himalayas 雪人(一种似熊或人的巨大长毛动物，据说居住在喜马拉雅山脉顶部)

yew /juː/ noun an evergreen tree with poisonous red fruit 紫杉(常绿树木，结红色有毒果实)

Yiddish /'jidiʃ/ noun a language used by Jews from central and eastern Europe 依地语，意第绪语(中欧及东欧犹太人使用的一种语言) • **adjective** relating to Yiddish 依地语的；意第绪语的

yield /jiːld/ verb **1** produce or provide a natural or industrial product 出产(自然物产或工业产品) **2** produce a result or financial gain 产生(结果或经济收益) **3** give way to demands or pressure 让步；屈服 **4** give up possession of 放弃…的所有权 **5** give way under force or pressure 屈曲；塌 • **noun** an amount or result yielded 产量；产物

✔ **拼写指南** remember, i before e except after c: yield. 记住 i 置于 e 前，在 c 后时除外，如 yield。

yin /jin/ noun (in Chinese philosophy) the passive female presence in the universe (中国哲学中的)阴

yob /jɒb/ or **yobbo** /'jɒbəʊ/ noun (plural **yobs** or **yobbos**) Brit. Informal 【英，非正式】a rude and aggressive young man 粗鲁的年轻人；小无赖；小流氓 ■ **yobbish** adjective.

yodel /'jəʊdl/ verb (**yodels**, **yodelling**, **yodelled**; US spelling 【美拼作】**yodels**, **yodeling**, **yodeled**) sing or call in a style that alternates rapidly between a normal voice and a very high voice 用真假嗓音反复变换地唱；用约德尔唱法歌唱 • **noun** a song or call of this type 真假嗓音交替唱出的歌曲(或发出的叫喊)；约德尔歌曲 ■ **yodeller** noun.

yoga /'jəʊgə/ noun a system involving breathing exercises and the holding of particular body positions, followed for fitness and relaxation and based on Hindu philosophy 瑜伽 ■ **yogic** adjective.

yogi /'jəʊgi/ noun (plural **yogis**) a person who is skilled in yoga 瑜伽术专家；瑜伽师

yogurt, **yoghurt**, or **yoghourt** /'jɒgət/ noun a thick liquid food made from milk with bacteria added 酸奶；酸酪

yoke /jəʊk/ noun **1** a piece of wood fastened over the necks of two animals and attached to a plough or cart in order for them to pull it 轭 **2** a frame fitting over a person's neck and shoulders, used for carrying buckets or baskets 轭形扁担 **3** something that limits freedom or is difficult to bear 枷锁；束缚；桎梏 **4** a part of a garment that fits over the shoulders and to which the main part of the garment is attached 上衣抵肩

Y

• **verb** (**yokes, yoking, yoked**) join together or attach to a yoke (用 轭) 连接

yokel /ˈjəʊkl/ **noun** an unsophisticated country person 乡巴佬；土包子

yolk /jəʊk/ **noun** the yellow part in the middle of an egg 蛋黄

Yom Kippur /ˌjɒm ˈkɪpə(r)/ **noun** an important day in the Jewish religion in which people pray and fast (犹太教的) 赎罪日

yon /jɒn/ old use or dialect 【旧或方】 **determiner & adverb** that (在)那边的
• **pronoun** that person or thing 那边的人(或事物)

yonder /ˈjɒndə(r)/ old use or dialect 【旧或方】 **adverb** over there 在那边
• **determiner** that or those 那边的；那些的

yonks /jɒŋks/ plural noun Brit. informal 【英，非正式】 a very long time 很久；很长时间

yore /jɔː(r)/ **noun** (**of yore**) literary 【文】 in the past; long ago 昔日；往昔

you /juː, jʊ, jə/ **pronoun 1** used to refer to the person or people that the speaker is talking to 您；你；你们 **2** used to refer to any person in general (泛指) 任何人

you'd /juːd, jʊd, jəd/ **short form 1** you had. **2** you would.

you'll /juːl, jʊl, jəl/ **short form** you will or you shall.

young /jʌŋ/ **adjective** (**younger, youngest**) **1** having lived or existed for only a short time 年轻的；幼小的；初期的；新兴的 **2** relating to or characteristic of young people 青年人的，年轻人特有的 • **plural noun** young children or animals; offspring 小孩；幼小动物；后代

youngster /ˈjʌŋstə(r)/ **noun** a young person 小孩；儿童；年轻人

your /jɔː(r)/ **possessive determiner 1** belonging to or associated with the person or people that the speaker

is talking to 您的；你的；你们的 **2** belonging to or associated with any person in general (泛指) 任何人的

! 注意 don't confuse **your** meaning 'belonging to you' (as in *let me talk to your daughter*) with the form **you're**, which is short for **you are** (as in *you're a good cook*). your意为"属于你(们) 的" (如 let me talk to your daughter 让我跟你的女儿谈谈)；而you're是you are的缩略形式 (如 you're a good cook 你是个好厨师)。不要混淆两者的用法。

you're /jʊə(r), jɔː(r), jə(r)/ **short form** you are.

yours /jɔːz, jʊəz/ **possessive pronoun** used to refer to something belonging to or associated with the person or people that the speaker is talking to 您的，你的，你们的(所有物或相关的人)

✔ 拼写指南 no apostrophe: **yours**. yours没有撇号。

yourself /jɔːˈself, jʊə-, jə-/ **pronoun** (plural **yourselves**) **1** used as the object of a verb or preposition when this is the same as the subject of the clause and the subject is the person or people being spoken to 你自己 **2** you personally 你亲自；你本人

youth /juːθ/ **noun** (plural **youths**) **1** the period between childhood and adult age 青(少) 年时代；青春时期 **2** the qualities of energy, freshness, etc. associated with being young 青春；青年时代(所具有) 的特点 **3** a young man 男青年；小伙子 **4** young people 年轻人；青年 □ **youth club** a club where young people can meet and take part in various activities 青年俱乐部 **youth hostel** a place providing cheap overnight accommodation, especially for young people 青年招待所；青年旅舍

youthful /'ju:θfl/ *adjective* **1** young or seeming young 年轻的；似青年的 **2** characteristic of young people 具有青年特性的 ■ **youthfully** *adverb* **youthfulness** *noun*.

you've /ju:v, juv, jəv/ *short form* you have.

yowl /jaul/ *noun* a loud wailing cry of pain or distress 哀号；惨叫 ■ *verb* make such a cry 发惨叫；哀叫

yo-yo /'jəuʃəu/ *noun* (plural **yo-yos**) (trademark in the UK【英国商标】) a toy consisting of a pair of joined discs with a groove between them in which string is attached and wound, which can be spun down and up as the string unwinds and rewinds 悠悠球(一种玩具，由两个相连的圆盘组成，一条细绳连接并缠绕在圆盘之间的凹槽处，细绳展开绕回同时，圆盘依靠自身重量随之上下移动) • *verb* (yo-

yoes, yoyoing, yo-yoed) move up and down repeatedly 反复上下起落

yucca /'jʌkə/ *noun* a plant with long, stiff pointed leaves, native to the southern US and Mexico 丝兰(一种生长于美国南部和墨西哥的植物，有剑形坚挺长叶)

Yugoslav /ju:gəuslɑ:v/ *noun* a person from any of the states of the former Yugoslavia 南斯拉夫人 ■ **Yugoslavian** *noun & adjective*.

Yule /ju:l/ or **Yuletide** /'ju:ltaɪd/ *noun* old use【旧】Christmas 圣诞节

yummy /'jʌmi/ *adjective* (**yummier**, **yummiest**) *informal*【非正式】delicious 美味的；可口的；好吃的

yuppie or **yuppy** /'jʌpi/ *noun* (plural **yuppies**) *informal*【非正式】a young middle class professional person who earns a lot of money 雅皮士(在城市中收入丰厚、年轻有为的中产阶级专业人士)

Zz

Z or **z** /zed/ noun (plural **Zs** or **Z's**) the twenty-sixth letter of the alphabet 英语字母表的第26个字母

zany /'zeɪni/ adjective (**zanier**, **zaniest**) amusingly unconventional or unusual 荒谬可笑的；滑稽古怪的

zap /zæp/ informal 【非正式】 verb (**zaps**, **zapping**, **zapped**) **1** destroy completely 除掉；消灭 **2** move very fast 迅疾地移动 **3** use a remote control to change television channels 用遥控器变换电视频道

zeal /ziːl/ noun great energy and enthusiasm for a cause or aim (对事业或目标的) 热忱，热情

zealot /'zelət/ noun a person who follows a religion, cause, or policy very strictly and enthusiastically (宗教) 狂热分子；(支持某事业或政策的) 极端分子 ■ **zealotry** noun.

zealous /'zeləs/ adjective showing great energy and enthusiasm for a cause or aim (对某事业或目标) 热忱的，热情的 ■ **zealously** adverb.

zebra /'ziːbrə, 'ze-/ noun an African wild horse with black and white stripes 斑马 (一种非洲野马，有黑白相间条纹) □ **zebra crossing** Brit. 【英】 an area of road marked with broad white stripes, where pedestrians can cross 斑马线；人行横道线

zeitgeist /'zaɪtɡaɪst/ noun the general spirit or mood of a particular period of history 时代精神

Zen /zen/ noun a type of Buddhism that emphasizes the value of meditation and intuition 禅，禅宗 (一

种佛教宗派，注重静坐冥想和直觉领悟)

zenith /'zenɪθ/ noun **1** the time at which someone or something is most powerful or successful 鼎盛时期；顶峰 **2** the point in the sky directly overhead 头顶的天空 **3** the highest point in the sky reached by the sun or moon 天顶 (太阳或月亮在天空中的最高点)

zephyr /'zefə(r)/ noun literary 【文】 a soft, gentle breeze 和风，微风

Zeppelin /'zepəlɪn/ noun a large German airship of the early 20th century 齐柏林飞艇 (德国20世纪早期的大型飞艇)

zero /'zɪərəʊ/ cardinal number (plural **zeros**) **1** the figure 0; nought (数字) 零；无 **2** a temperature of 0°C (32°F), marking the freezing point of water (气温的) 零度 **3** a point on a scale of measurement from which a positive or negative quantity is reckoned (量度表的) 零点，零位 • verb (**zeroes**, **zeroing**, **zeroed**) (**zero in on**) take aim at or focus attention on 对准目标；集中注意力于 □ **zero hour** the time at which a military operation or important event is set to begin (军事行动或重大事件的) 开始时刻

zest /zest/ noun **1** great enthusiasm and energy 热情；激情 **2** excitement or stimulation 兴奋；激动 **3** the outer coloured part of the peel of an orange or lemon 柑橘属水果的外皮

zigzag /'zɪɡzæɡ/ noun a line or course having sharp alternate right and left turns 锯齿形(或之字形)的线(或路线) • **adjective & adverb** veering to right and left alternately 之字形的(地);锯齿形的(地);左拐右拐的(地) • **verb** (**zigzags**, **zigzagging**, **zigzagged**) move in a zigzag 呈之字形移动;曲折行进

zilch /zɪltʃ/ **pronoun** informal【非正式】nothing 什么也没有;无

zillion /'zɪljən/ **cardinal number** informal【非正式】a very large number of people or things 无限多的人(或事物) ■ **zillionth** ordinal number.

Zimbabwean /zɪm'bɑːbweɪən/ **noun** a person from Zimbabwe 津巴布韦人 • **adjective** relating to Zimbabwe 津巴布韦的

Zimmer frame /'zɪmə(r)/ **noun** trademark【商标】a metal frame that people use to help them walk 齐默式助行架

zinc /zɪŋk/ **noun** a silvery-white metallic element used in making brass and to coat iron and steel (金属元素)锌

zing /zɪŋ/ **noun** informal【非正式】energy, enthusiasm, or liveliness 精力;热情;活力 ■ **zingy** adjective.

Zionism /'zaɪənɪzəm/ **noun** a movement for the development of a Jewish nation in Israel 犹太复国运动;犹太复国主义 ■ **Zionist** noun & adjective.

zip /zɪp/ **noun 1** Brit【英】a fastener consisting of two flexible interlocking strips of metal or plastic, closed or opened by pulling a slide along them 拉链 **2** informal【非正式】energy; liveliness 精力;活力 • **verb** (**zips**, **zipping**, **zipped**) **1** fasten with a zip 用拉链拉上 **2** informal【非正式】move quickly 迅速移动 **3** Computing【计】compress a file so that it takes up less space 压缩(文档) □ **zip code** US【美】a postcode 邮政编码

zipper /'zɪpə(r)/ **noun** chiefly N. Amer.

【主北美】a zip fastener 拉链;拉锁

zippy /'zɪpi/ **adjective** informal【非正式】**1** speedy 敏捷的;迅速的 **2** bright, fresh, or lively 机灵的;振奋的;活泼的

zircon /'zɜːkɒn/ **noun** a brown or semitransparent mineral 锆石(棕色或半透明矿石)

zit /zɪt/ **noun** informal【非正式】a spot on the skin 丘疹

zither /'zɪðə(r)/ **noun** a musical instrument with numerous strings stretched across a flat box, which you hold horizontally and play with your fingers and a plectrum 齐特琴(琴体呈扁平的匣状,多弦,水平放置,用手指及拨子拨奏)

zodiac /'zəʊdiæk/ **noun** an area in the sky in which the sun, moon, and planets appear to lie, divided by astrologers into twelve equal divisions or signs 黄道带(日、月、行星都出现其中的带形天区,由占星家分为相等的十二区或宫) ■ **zodiacal** /zəʊ'daɪəkl/ adjective.

zombie /'zɒmbi/ **noun 1** informal【非正式】a person who seems to be only partly alive 毫无生气的人;木讷呆板的人 **2** (in stories) a dead body that has been brought back to life by magic (传说中的)还魂尸(靠魔法起死回生)

zone /zəʊn/ **noun 1** an area that has particular characteristics or a particular use (有某种特点或用途的)区域 **2** (also **time zone**) an area where a common standard time is used 时区 • **verb** (**zones**, **zoning**, **zoned**) divide something into zones 把…分成区(或划成带) ■ **zonal** adjective.

zoo /zuː/ **noun** a place where wild animals are kept for study, conservation, or display to the public 动物园

zookeeper /'zuːkiːpə(r)/ **noun** a

person employed to look after the animals in a zoo (动物园的) 动物饲养员

zoology /zəʊˈɒlədʒɪ, zu-/ **noun 1** the scientific study of animals 动物学 **2** the animal life of a particular area or time 动物区系(某地区或时期的)动物种群) ■ **zoological** adjective **zoologist** noun.

zoom /zuːm/ **verb 1** move or travel very quickly 快速移动;疾行 **2** (of a camera) change smoothly from a long shot to a close-up or vice versa

(照相机或摄像机) 推近, 拉远 □ **zoom lens** a lens allowing a camera to zoom 变焦距镜头

zucchini /zʊˈkiːnɪ/ **noun** (plural **zucchini** or **zucchinis**) N. Amer. 【北美】a courgette 绿皮密生西葫芦

Zulu /ˈzuːluː/ **noun 1** a member of a South African people (南非的) 祖鲁人 **2** the language of the Zulus 祖鲁语

zygote /ˈzaɪɡəʊt/ **noun** Biology 【生物】 a cell resulting from the joining of two gametes 合子;接合体

Factfinder
资料速查

This section provides a wide range of information, giving you quick access to a variety of facts that will be useful for quizzes and crosswords, or just to remind yourself of something you have forgotten (for example: what is the capital of Peru?; when did Queen Victoria come to the throne?; how many pints are there in a litre?). 本部分提供了一系列内容广泛的知识信息,可以从中迅速查索各类资料,帮助完成知识竞赛和字谜游戏题目,亦可为忘记某些常识(如:秘鲁首都是哪个城市? 维多利亚女王何时即位? 一升合多少品脱?)的读者提供现成答案。

Countries of the World
世界各国

Country 国家	Capital 首都	Currency unit 货币单位
Afghanistan 阿富汗	Kabul 喀布尔	afghani = 100 puls 1阿富汗尼＝100普尔
Albania 阿尔巴尼亚	Tirana 地拉那	lek = 100 quintars 1列克＝100昆塔
Algeria 阿尔及利亚	Algiers 阿尔及尔	dinar = 100 centimes 1第纳尔＝100分
Andorra 安道尔	Andorra la Vella 安道尔城	euro = 100 cents 1欧元＝100分
Angola 安哥拉	Luanda 罗安达	kwanza = 100 lwei 1宽扎＝100勒韦
Antigua and Barbuda 安提瓜和巴布达	St John's 圣约翰	dollar = 100 cents 1元＝100分
Argentina 阿根廷	Buenos Aires 布宜诺斯艾利斯	peso = 100 centavos 1比索＝100分
Armenia 亚美尼亚	Yerevan 埃里温	dram = 100 luma 1德拉姆＝100卢马
Australia 澳大利亚	Canberra 堪培拉	dollar = 100 cents 1元＝100分
Austria 奥地利	Vienna 维也纳	euro = 100 cents 1欧元＝100分
Azerbaijan 阿塞拜疆	Baku 巴库	manat = 100 gopik 1纳特＝100戈比克
Bahamas 巴哈马	Nassau 拿骚	dollar = 100 cents 1元＝100分
Bahrain 巴林	Manama 麦纳麦	dinar = 1,000 fils 1第纳尔＝1,000费尔
Bangladesh 孟加拉国	Dhaka 达卡	taka = 100 poisha 1塔卡＝100波依夏
Barbados 巴巴多斯	Bridgetown 布里奇敦	dollar = 100 cents 1元＝100分
Belarus 白俄罗斯	Minsk 明斯克	Belarusian rouble 白俄罗斯卢布
Belgium 比利时	Brussels 布鲁塞尔	euro = 100 cents 1欧元＝100分
Belize 伯利兹	Belmopan 贝尔莫潘	dollar = 100 cents 1元＝100分

Country 国家	Capital 首都	Currency unit 货币单位
Benin 贝宁	Porto Novo 波多诺伏	franc = 100 centimes 1法郎=100分
Bhutan 不丹	Thimphu 廷布	ngultrum = 100 chetrum, Indian rupee 1努扎姆 = 100切扎姆,印度卢比
Bolivia 玻利维亚	La Paz 拉巴斯	boliviano =100 centavos 1玻利维亚诺=100分
Bosnia-Herzegovina 波斯尼亚和黑塞哥维那	Sarajevo 萨拉热窝	dinar = 100 paras 1第纳尔=100帕拉
Botswana 博茨瓦纳	Gaborone 哈博罗内	pula = 100 thebe 1普拉=100西比
Brazil 巴西	Brasilia 巴西利亚	real = 100 centavos 1雷亚尔=100分
Brunei 文莱	Bandar Seri Begawan 斯里巴加湾市	dollar = 100 sen 1元=100分
Bulgaria 保加利亚	Sofia 索非亚	lev = 100 stotinki 1列弗=100斯托丁基
Burkina Faso 布基纳法索	Ouagadougou 瓦加杜古	franc = 100 centimes 1法郎=100分
Burma (Myanmar) 缅甸	Nay Pyi Taw 内比都	kyat = 100 pyas 1缅元=100分
Burundi 布隆迪	Bujumbura 布琼布拉	franc = 100 centimes 1法郎=100分
Cambodia 柬埔寨	Phnom Penh 金边	riel = 100 sen 1瑞尔=100仙
Cameroon 喀麦隆	Yaoundé 雅温得	franc = 100 centimes 1法郎=100分
Canada 加拿大	Ottawa 渥太华	dollar = 100 cents 1元=100分
Cape Verde Islands 佛得角	Praia 普拉亚	escudo = 100 centavos 1埃斯库多=100分
Central African Republic 中非共和国	Bangui 班吉	franc = 100 centimes 1法郎=100分
Chad 乍得	N'Djamena 恩贾梅纳	franc = 100 centimes 1法郎=100分
Chile 智利	Santiago 圣地亚哥	peso = 100 centavos 1比索=100分
China 中国	Beijing 北京	yuan = 10 jiao or 100 fen 1元=10角或100分
Colombia 哥伦比亚	Bogotá 波哥大	peso = 100 centavos 1比索=100分

Country 国家	Capital 首都	Currency unit 货币单位
Comoros	Moroni	franc = 100 centimes
科摩罗	莫罗尼	1法郎=100分
Congo	Brazzaville	franc = 100 centimes
刚果(布)	布拉柴维尔	1法郎=100分
Congo, Democratic Republic of (Zaire)	Kinshasa	franc = 100 centimes
刚果(金)	金沙萨	1法郎=100分
Costa Rica	San José	colón = 100 centimos
哥斯达黎加	圣何塞	1科朗=100分
Cote d'Ivoire	Yamoussoukro	franc = 100 centimes
科特迪瓦	亚穆苏克罗	1法郎=100分
Croatia	Zagreb	kuna = 100 lipa
克罗地亚	萨格勒布	1库纳=100里帕
Cuba	Havana	peso = 100 centavos
古巴	哈瓦那	1比索=100分
Cyprus	Nicosia	euro = 100 cents
塞浦路斯	尼科西亚	1欧元=100分
Czech Republic	Prague	koruna = 100 halers
捷克共和国	布拉格	1克朗=100赫勒
Denmark	Copenhagen	krone = 100 øre
丹麦	哥本哈根	1克朗=100欧尔
Djibouti	Djibouti	franc = 100 centimes
吉布提	吉布提	1法郎=100分
Dominica	Roseau	dollar = 100 cents
多米尼克国	罗索	1元=100分
Dominican Republic	Santo Domingo	peso = 100 centavos
多米尼加共和国	圣多明各	1比索=100分
Ecuador	Quito	sucre = 100 centavos
厄瓜多尔	基多	1苏克雷=100分
Egypt	Cairo	pound = 100 piastres or 1,000 milliemes
埃及	开罗	1镑=100皮阿斯特或1,000米利姆
El Salvador	San Salvador	colón = 100 centavos
萨尔瓦多	圣萨尔瓦多	1科朗=100分
Equatorial Guinea	Malabo	franc = 100 centimes
赤道几内亚	马拉博	1法郎=100分
Eritrea	Asmara	nakfa; Ethiopian birr
厄立特里亚	阿斯马拉	纳克法；埃塞俄比亚比尔
Estonia	Tallinn	kroon = 100 sents
爱沙尼亚	塔林	1克朗=100分

Country 国家	Capital 首都	Currency unit 货币单位
Ethiopia 埃塞俄比亚	Addis Ababa 亚的斯亚贝巴	birr = 100 cents 1比尔 = 100分
Fiji 斐济	Suva 苏瓦	dollar = 100 cents 1元 = 100分
Finland 芬兰	Helsinki 赫尔辛基	euro = 100 cents 1欧元 = 100分
France 法国	Paris 巴黎	euro = 100 cents 1欧元 = 100分
Gabon 加蓬	Libreville 利伯维尔	franc = 100 centimes 1法郎 = 100分
Gambia 冈比亚	Banjul 班珠尔	dalasi = 100 butut 1达拉西 = 100布图
Georgia 格鲁吉亚	Tbilisi 第比利斯	lari = 100 tetri 1拉里 = 100特特里
Germany 德国	Berlin 柏林	euro = 100 cents 1欧元 = 100分
Ghana 加纳	Accra 阿克拉	cedi = 100 pesewas 1塞地 = 100比塞瓦
Greece 希腊	Athens 雅典	euro = 100 cents 1欧元 = 100分
Grenada 格林纳达	St George's 圣乔治	dollar = 100 cents 1元 = 100分
Guatemala 危地马拉	Guatemala City 危地马拉城	quetzal = 100 centavos 1格查尔 = 100分
Guinea 几内亚	Conakry 科纳克里	franc = 100 centimes 1法郎 = 100分
Guinea-Bissau 几内亚比绍	Bissau 比绍	peso = 100 centavos 1比索 = 100分
Guyana 圭亚那	Georgetown 乔治敦	dollar = 100 cents 1元 = 100分
Haiti 海地	Port-au-Prince 太子港	gourde = 100 centimes 1古德 = 100分
Holland (*see* 见 **Netherlands**)		
Honduras 洪都拉斯	Tegucigalpa 特古西加尔巴	lempira = 100 centavos 1伦皮拉 = 100分
Hungary 匈牙利	Budapest 布达佩斯	forint = 100 filler 1福林 = 100菲勒
Iceland 冰岛	Reykjavik 雷克雅未克	krona = 100 aurar 1克朗 = 100奥拉
India 印度	New Delhi 新德里	rupee = 100 paisa 1卢比 = 100派沙

Factfinder

Country 国家	Capital 首都	Currency unit 货币单位
Indonesia 印度尼西亚	Djakarta 雅加达	rupiah = 100 sen 1盾＝100仙
Iran 伊朗	Tehran 德黑兰	rial = 100 dinars 1里亚尔＝100第纳尔
Iraq 伊拉克	Baghdad 巴格达	dinar = 1,000 fils 1第纳尔＝1,000费尔
Ireland, Republic of 爱尔兰共和国	Dublin 都柏林	euro = 100 cents 1欧元＝100分
Israel 以色列	Tel Aviv 特拉维夫	shekel = 100 agora 1谢克尔＝100阿高洛
Italy 意大利	Rome 罗马	euro = 100 cents 1欧元＝100分
Jamaica 牙买加	Kingston 金斯敦	dollar = 100 cents 1元＝100分
Japan 日本	Tokyo 东京	yen = 100 sen 1日元＝100钱
Jordan 约旦	Amman 安曼	dinar = 1,000 fils 1第纳尔＝1,000费尔
Kazakhstan 哈萨克斯坦	Astana 阿斯塔纳	tenge = 100 teins 1坚戈＝100提因
Kenya 肯尼亚	Nairobi 内罗毕	shilling = 100 cents 1先令＝100分
Kiribati 基里巴斯	Bairiki 拜里基	Australian dollar 澳大利亚元
Korea, the Democratic People's Republic of 朝鲜	Pyongyang 平壤	won = 100 jun 1朝鲜元＝100钱
Korea, the Republic of 韩国	Seoul 首尔	won = 100 jeon 1韩元＝100钱
Kuwait 科威特	Kuwait City 科威特城	dinar = 1,000 fils 1第纳尔＝1,000费尔
Kyrgyzstan 吉尔吉斯斯坦	Bishkek 比什凯克	som = 100 tiyin 1索姆＝100提因
Laos 老挝	Vientiane 万象	kip = 100 ats 1基普＝100阿特
Latvia 拉脱维亚	Riga 里加	lat = 100 santims 1拉特＝100桑地姆
Lebanon 黎巴嫩	Beirut 贝鲁特	pound = 100 piastres 1镑＝100皮阿斯特
Lesotho 莱索托	Maseru 马塞卢	loti = 100 lisente 1洛蒂＝100黎森特

Country 国家	Capital 首都	Currency unit 货币单位
Liberia 利比里亚	Monrovia 蒙罗维亚	dollar = 100 cents 1元=100分
Libya 利比亚	Tripoli 的黎波里	dinar = 1,000 dirhams 1第纳尔=1,000迪拉姆
Liechtenstein 列支敦士登	Vaduz 瓦杜兹	franc = 100 centimes 1法郎=100分
Lithuania 立陶宛	Vilnius 维尔纽斯	litas = 100 centas 1立特=100立分
Luxembourg 卢森堡	Luxembourg 卢森堡	euro = 100 cents 1欧元=100分
Macedonia 马其顿	Skopje 斯科普里	denar = 100 deni 1代纳尔=100代尼
Madagascar 马达加斯加	Antananarivo 塔那那利佛	franc = 100 centimes 1法郎=100分
Malawi 马拉维	Lilongwe 利隆圭	kwacha = 100 tambala 1克瓦查=100坦布拉
Malaysia 马来西亚	Kuala Lumpur 吉隆坡	ringgit = 100 sen 1林吉特=100分
Maldives 马尔代夫	Male 马累	rufiyaa = 100 laris 1拉菲亚=100拉雷
Mali 马里	Bamako 巴马科	franc = 100 centimes 1法郎=100分
Malta 马耳他	Valletta 瓦莱塔	euro = 100 cents 1欧元=100分
Marshall Islands 马绍尔群岛	Majuro 马朱罗	US dollar 美元
Mauritania 毛里塔尼亚	Nouakchott 努瓦克肖特	ouguiya = 5 khoums 1乌吉亚=5库姆斯
Mauritius 毛里求斯	Port Louis 路易港	rupee = 100 cents 1卢比=100分
Mexico 墨西哥	Mexico City 墨西哥城	peso = 100 centavos 1比索=100分
Micronesia 密克罗尼西亚	Kolonia 科洛尼亚	US dollar 美元
Moldova 摩尔多瓦	Chisinau 基希讷乌	leu = 100 bani 1列伊=100巴尼
Monaco 摩纳哥	–	euro = 100 cents 1欧元=100分
Mongolia 蒙古	Ulan Bator 乌兰巴托	tugrik = 100 mongos 1图格里克=100蒙戈

Factfinder

Country 国家	Capital 首都	Currency unit 货币单位
Montenegro 黑山	Podgorica 波德戈里察	euro = 100 cents 1欧元＝100分
Morocco 摩洛哥	Rabat 拉巴特	dirham = 100 centimes 1迪拉姆＝100分
Mozambique 莫桑比克	Maputo 马普托	metical = 100 centavos 1梅蒂卡尔＝100分
Myanmar (*see* 见 **Burma**)		
Namibia 纳米比亚	Windhoek 温得和克	dollar = 100 cents 1元 ＝100分
Nauru 瑙鲁	– 	Australian dollar 澳大利亚元
Nepal 尼泊尔	Kathmandu 加德满都	rupee = 100 paisa 1卢比＝100派士
Netherlands 荷兰	Amsterdam 阿姆斯特丹	euro = 100 cents 1欧元＝100分
New Zealand 新西兰	Wellington 惠灵顿	dollar = 100 cents 1元＝100分
Nicaragua 尼加拉瓜	Managua 马那瓜	cordoba = 100 centavos 1科多巴＝100分
Niger 尼日尔	Niamey 尼亚美	franc = 100 centimes 1法郎＝100分
Nigeria 尼日利亚	Abuja 阿布贾	naira = 100 kobo 1奈拉＝100考包
Norway 挪威	Oslo 奥斯陆	krone = 100 øre 1克朗＝100欧尔
Oman 阿曼	Muscat 马斯喀特	rial = 1,000 baiza 1里亚尔＝1,000派沙
Pakistan 巴基斯坦	Islamabad 伊斯兰堡	rupee = 100 paisa 1卢比＝100派沙
Panama 巴拿马	Panama City 巴拿马城	balboa = 100 centésimos 1巴波亚＝100分
Papua New Guinea 巴布亚新几内亚	Port Moresby 莫尔兹比港	kina = 100 toea 1基那＝100托伊
Paraguay 巴拉圭	Asunción 亚松森	guarani = 100 centimos 1瓜拉尼＝100分
Peru 秘鲁	Lima 利马	sol = 100 cents 1索尔＝100分
Philippines 菲律宾	Manila 马尼拉	peso = 100 centavos 1比索＝100分
Poland 波兰	Warsaw 华沙	zloty = 100 groszy 1兹罗提＝100格罗什

Country 国家	Capital 首都	Currency unit 货币单位
Portugal	Lisbon	euro = 100 cents
葡萄牙	里斯本	1欧元＝100分
Qatar	Doha	riyal = 100 dirhams
卡塔尔	多哈	1里亚尔＝100迪拉姆
Romania	Bucharest	leu = 100 bani
罗马尼亚	布加勒斯特	1列伊＝100巴尼
Russia	Moscow	rouble = 100 copecks
俄罗斯	莫斯科	1卢布＝100戈比
Rwanda	Kigali	franc = 100 centimes
卢旺达	基加利	1法郎＝100分
St Kitts and Nevis	Basseterre	dollar = 100 cents
圣基茨和尼维斯	巴斯特尔	1元＝100分
St Lucia	Castries	dollar = 100 cents
圣卢西亚	卡斯特里	1元＝100分
St Vincent and the Grenadines	Kingstown	dollar = 100 cents
圣文森特和格林纳丁斯	金斯敦	1元＝100分
Samoa	Apia	tala = 100 sene
萨摩亚	阿皮亚	1塔拉＝100分
San Marino	San Marino	euro = 100 cents
圣马力诺	圣马力诺	1欧元＝100分
São Tomé and Principe	São Tomé	dobra = 100 centavos
圣多美和普林西比	圣多美	1多布拉＝100分
Saudi Arabia	Riyadh	riyal = 20 qursh or 100 halalas 1里亚尔＝20库什或100哈拉拉
沙特阿拉伯	利雅得	
Senegal	Dakar	franc = 100 centimes
塞内加尔	达喀尔	1法郎＝100分
Serbia	Belgrade	dinar = 100 paras
塞尔维亚	贝尔格莱德	1第纳尔＝100帕拉
Seychelles	Victoria	rupee = 100 cents
塞舌尔	维多利亚	1卢比＝100分
Sierra Leone	Freetown	leone = 100 cents
塞拉利昂	弗里敦	1利昂＝100分
Singapore	Singapore City	dollar = 100 cents
新加坡	新加坡市	1元＝100分
Slovakia	Bratislava	koruna = 100 haliers
斯洛伐克	布拉迪斯拉发	1克朗＝100赫勒

Country 国家	Capital 首都	Currency unit 货币单位
Slovenia 斯洛文尼亚	Ljubljana 卢布尔雅那	euro = 100 cents 1欧元=100分
Solomon Islands 所罗门群岛	Honiara 霍尼亚拉	dollar = 100 cents 1元=100分
Somalia 索马里	Mogadishu 摩加迪沙	shilling = 100 cents 1先令=100分
South Africa 南非	Pretoria 比勒陀利亚	rand = 100 cents 1兰特=100分
Spain 西班牙	Madrid 马德里	euro = 100 cents 1欧元=100分
Sri Lanka 斯里兰卡	Colombo 科伦坡	rupee = 100 cents 1卢比=100分
Sudan 苏丹	Khartoum 喀土穆	dinar = 10 pounds 1第纳尔=10镑
Suriname 苏里南	Paramaribo 帕拉马里博	guilder = 100 cents 1盾=100分
Swaziland 斯威士兰	Mbabane 姆巴巴内	lilangeni = 100 cents 1里兰吉尼=100分
Sweden 瑞典	Stockholm 斯德哥尔摩	krona = 100 öre 1克朗=100欧尔
Switzerland 瑞士	Berne 伯尔尼	franc = 100 centimes 1法郎=100分
Syria 叙利亚	Damascus 大马士革	pound = 100 piastres 1镑=100皮阿斯特
Tajikistan 塔吉克斯坦	Dushanbe 杜尚别	somoni = 100 dirams 1索莫尼=100迪拉姆
Tanzania 坦桑尼亚	Dodoma 多多马	shilling = 100 cents 1先令=100分
Thailand 泰国	Bangkok 曼谷	baht = 100 satangs 1铢=100萨当
Togo 多哥	Lomé 洛美	franc = 100 centimes 1法郎=100分
Tonga 汤加	Nuku'alofa 努库阿洛法	pa'anga = 100 seniti 1潘加=100分
Trinidad and Tobago 特立尼达和多巴哥	Port-of-Spain 西班牙港	dollar = 100 cents 1元=100分
Tunisia 突尼斯	Tunis 突尼斯	dinar = 1,000 milliemes 1第纳尔=1,000米利姆
Turkey 土耳其	Ankara 安卡拉	lira = 100 kurus 1里拉=100库鲁

Country 国家	Capital 首都	Currency unit 货币单位
Turkmenistan 土库曼斯坦	Ashgabat 阿什哈巴德	manat = 100 tenesi 1马纳特 = 100 捷涅西
Tuvalu 图瓦卢	Funafuti 富纳富提	dollar = 100 cents 1元 = 100分
Uganda 乌干达	Kampala 坎帕拉	shilling = 100 cents 1先令 = 100分
Ukraine 乌克兰	Kiev 基辅	hryvna = 100 kopiykas 1格里夫纳 = 100戈比克斯
United Arab Emirates 阿拉伯联合酋长国	Abu Dhabi 阿布扎比	dirham = 100 fils 1迪拉姆 = 100费尔
United Kingdom 联合王国, 英国	London 伦敦	pound = 100 pence 1英镑 = 100便士
United States 美利坚合众国, 美国	Washington DC 华盛顿	dollar = 100 cents 1美元 = 100分
Uruguay 乌拉圭	Montevideo 蒙得维的亚	peso = 100 centésimos 1比索 = 100分
Uzbekistan 乌兹别克斯坦	Tashkent 塔什干	som = 100 tiyin 1苏姆 = 100提因
Vanuatu 瓦努阿图	Vila 维拉	vatu = 100 centimes 1瓦图 = 100分
Vatican City 梵蒂冈	– 	euro = 100 cents 1欧元 = 100分
Venezuela 委内瑞拉	Caracas 加拉加斯	bolivar = 100 centimos 1玻利瓦尔 = 100分
Vietnam 越南	Hanoi 河内	dong = 100 xu 1盾 = 100分
Yemen 也门	Sana'a 萨那	riyal = 100 fils 1里亚尔 = 100费尔
Zambia 赞比亚	Lusaka 卢萨卡	kwacha = 100 ngwee 1克瓦查 = 100恩韦
Zimbabwe 津巴布韦	Harare 哈拉雷	dollar = 100 cents 1元 = 100分

Factfinder

Kings and Queens of England and United Kingdom
英格兰及联合王国历代君主

Ruler 君主	Dates of reign 在位时间	Ruler 君主	Dates of reign 在位时间
Saxon Line 撒克逊世系		**House of Plantagenet 金雀花王室**	
Edwy 埃德威	955–957	Henry II 亨利二世	1154–1189
Edgar 埃德加	959–975	Richard I 理查一世	1189–1199
Edward the Martyr 爱德华(殉道者)	975–978	John 约翰	1199–1216
Ethelred the Unready 艾特尔雷德(迟钝的)	978–1016	Henry III 亨利三世	1216–1272
Edmund Ironside 埃德蒙(勇敢者)	1016	Edward I 爱德华一世	1272–1307
Danish Line 丹麦世系		Edward II 爱德华二世	1307–1327
Canute (Cnut) 克努特	1017–1035	Edward III 爱德华三世	1327–1377
Harold I 哈罗德一世	1037–1040	Richard II 理查二世	1377–1399
Hardecanute 哈迪克努特	1040–1042	**House of Lancaster 兰开斯特王室**	
Saxon Line 撒克逊世系		Henry IV 亨利四世	1399–1413
Edward the Confessor 爱德华(忏悔者)	1042–1066	Henry V 亨利五世	1413–1422
Harold II 哈罗德二世	1066	Henry VI 亨利六世	1422–1461, 1470–1471
House of Normandy 诺曼底王室		**House of York 约克王室**	
William I (the Conqueror) 威廉一世(征服者)	1066–1087	Edward IV 爱德华四世	1461–1483
William II 威廉二世	1087–1100	Edward V 爱德华五世	1483
Henry I 亨利一世	1100–1135	Richard III 理查三世	1483–1485
Stephen 斯蒂芬	1135–1154		

Ruler 君主	Dates of reign 在位时间	Ruler 君主	Dates of reign 在位时间
House of Tudor 都铎王室		Anne 安妮	1702–1714
Henry VII 亨利七世	1485–1509	**House of Hanover 汉诺威王室**	
Henry VIII 亨利八世	1509–1547	George I 乔治一世	1714–1727
Edward VI 爱德华六世	1547–1553	George II 乔治二世	1727–1760
Mary I 玛丽一世	1553–1558	George III 乔治三世	1760–1820
Elizabeth I 伊丽莎白一世	1558–1603	George IV 乔治四世	1820–1830
House of Stuart 斯图亚特王室		William IV 威廉四世	1830–1837
James I 詹姆斯一世	1603–1625	Victoria 维多利亚	1837–1901
Charles I 查理一世	1625–1649	**House of Saxe-Coburg-Gotha 萨克森—科堡—哥达王室**	
Commonwealth (declared 1649) 共和国时期（1649年宣布）		Edward VII 爱德华七世	1901–1910
Oliver Cromwell, Lord Protector 奥利弗·克伦威尔 （护国主）	1653–1658	**House of Windsor 温莎王室**	
Richard Cromwell 理查·克伦威尔	1658–1659	George V 乔治五世	1910–1936
House of Stuart 斯图亚特王室		Edward VIII 爱德华八世	1936
Charles II 查理二世	1660–1685	George VI 乔治六世	1936–1952
James II 詹姆斯二世	1685–1688	Elizabeth II 伊丽莎白二世	1952–
William III and Mary II 威廉三世和玛丽二世	1689–1702		

Factfinder

Prime Ministers and Presidents
首相、总理和总统

Prime Ministers of Great Britain and of the United Kingdom 大不列颠及联合王国历任首相

[1721]–1742	Sir Robert Walpole 罗伯特·沃波尔爵士	1801–1804	Henry Addington 亨利·阿丁顿
1742–1743	Earl of Wilmington 威尔明顿伯爵	1804–1806	William Pitt the Younger 小威廉·皮特
1743–1754	Henry Pelham 亨利·佩勒姆	1806–1807	Lord William Grenville 威廉·格伦维尔勋爵
1754–1756	Duke of Newcastle 纽卡斯尔公爵		
1756–1757	Duke of Devonshire 德文希尔公爵	1807–1809	Duke of Portland 波特兰公爵
1757–1762	Duke of Newcastle 纽卡斯尔公爵	1809–1812	Spencer Perceval 斯潘塞·珀西瓦尔
1762–1763	Earl of Bute 比特伯爵	1812–1827	Earl of Liverpool 利物浦伯爵
1763–1765	George Grenville 乔治·格伦维尔	1827	George Canning 乔治·坎宁
1765–1766	Marquess of Rockingham 罗金厄姆侯爵	1827–1828	Viscount Goderich 戈德里奇子爵
1766–1768	William Pitt the Elder 老威廉·皮特	1828–1830	Duke of Wellington 威灵顿公爵
1768–1770	Duke of Grafton 格拉夫顿公爵	1830–1834	Earl Grey 格雷伯爵
1770–1782	Lord North 诺思勋爵	1834	Viscount Melbourne 梅尔本子爵
1782	Marquess of Rockingham 罗金厄姆侯爵	1834	Duke of Wellington 威灵顿公爵
1782–1783	Earl of Shelburne 谢尔本伯爵	1834–1835	Sir Robert Peel 罗伯特·皮尔爵士
1783	Duke of Portland 波特兰公爵	1835–1841	Viscount Melbourne 梅尔本子爵
1783–1801	William Pitt the Younger 小威廉·皮特	1841–1846	Sir Robert Peel 罗伯特·皮尔爵士
		1846–1852	Lord John Russell 约翰·罗素勋爵

1852	Earl of Derby 德比伯爵	1902–1905	Arthur James Balfour 阿瑟·詹姆斯·贝尔福
1852–1855	Earl of Aberdeen 阿伯丁伯爵	1905–1908	Sir Henry Campbell-Bannerman 亨利·坎贝尔-班纳曼爵士
1855–1858	Viscount Palmerston 帕默斯顿子爵	1908–1916	Herbert Henry Asquith 赫伯特·亨利·阿斯奎斯
1858–1859	Earl of Derby 德比伯爵	1916–1922	David Lloyd George 戴维·劳合·乔治
1859–1865	Viscount Palmerston 帕默斯顿子爵	1922–1923	Andrew Bonar Law 安德鲁·博纳·劳
1865–1866	Earl Russell 罗素伯爵	1923–1924	Stanley Baldwin 斯坦利·鲍德温
1866–1868	Earl of Derby 德比伯爵	1924	James Ramsay MacDonald 詹姆斯·拉姆齐·麦克唐纳
1868	Benjamin Disraeli 本杰明·迪斯累里	1924–1929	Stanley Baldwin 斯坦利·鲍德温
1868–1874	William Ewart Gladstone 威廉·尤尔特·格莱斯顿	1929–1935	James Ramsay MacDonald 詹姆斯·拉姆齐·麦克唐纳
1874–1880	Benjamin Disraeli 本杰明·迪斯累里	1935–1937	Stanley Baldwin 斯坦利·鲍德温
1880–1885	William Ewart Gladstone 威廉·尤尔特·格莱斯顿	1937–1940	Neville Chamberlain 内维尔·张伯伦
1885–1886	Marquess of Salisbury 索尔兹伯里侯爵	1940–1945	Winston Churchill 温斯顿·丘吉尔
1886	William Ewart Gladstone 威廉·尤尔特·格莱斯顿	1945–1951	Clement Attlee 克莱门特·艾德礼
1886–1892	Marquess of Salisbury 索尔兹伯里侯爵	1951–1955	Sir Winston Churchill 温斯顿·丘吉尔爵士
1892–1894	William Ewart Gladstone 威廉·尤尔特·格莱斯顿	1955–1957	Sir Anthony Eden 安东尼·艾登爵士
1894–1895	Earl of Rosebery 罗斯伯里伯爵	1957–1963	Harold Macmillan 哈罗德·麦克米伦
1895–1902	Marquess of Salisbury 索尔兹伯里侯爵	1963–1964	Sir Alec Douglas-Home 亚历克·道格拉斯-霍姆爵士
		1964–1970	Harold Wilson 哈罗德·威尔逊
		1970–1974	Edward Heath 爱德华·希思

1974–1976	Harold Wilson 哈罗德·威尔逊	1990–1997	John Major 约翰·梅杰
1976–1979	James Callaghan 詹姆斯·卡拉汉	1997–2007	Tony Blair 托尼·布莱尔
1979–1990	Margaret Thatcher 玛格丽特·撒切尔	2007–	Gordon Brown 戈登·布朗

Prime Ministers of Canada 加拿大历任总理

1867–1873	John A. Macdonald 约翰·A.麦克唐纳	1935–1948	W. L. Mackenzie King W. L.麦肯齐·金
1873–1878	Alexander Mackenzie 亚历山大·麦肯齐	1948–1957	Louis Stephen St Laurent 路易斯·斯蒂芬·圣劳伦特
1878–1891	John A. Macdonald 约翰·A.麦克唐纳	1957–1963	John George Diefenbaker 约翰·乔治·迪芬贝克
1891–1892	John J. C. Abbott 约翰·J.C.艾博特		
1892–1894	John S. D. Thompson 约翰·S.D.汤普森	1963–1968	Lester B. Pearson 莱斯特·B.皮尔逊
1894–1896	Mackenzie Bowell 麦肯齐·鲍威尔	1968–1979	Pierre Trudeau 皮埃尔·特鲁多
1896	Charles Tupper 查尔斯·塔珀	1979–1980	Joseph Clark 约瑟夫·克拉克
1896–1911	Wilfrid Laurier 威尔弗里德·洛里埃	1980–1984	Pierre Trudeau 皮埃尔·特鲁多
1911–1920	Robert L. Borden 罗伯特·L.博登	1984	John Turner 约翰·特纳
1920–1921	Arthur Meighen 阿瑟·米恩	1984–1993	Brian Mulroney 布莱恩·马尔罗尼
1921–1926	W. L. Mackenzie King W. L.麦肯齐·金	1993	Kim Campbell 金·坎贝尔
1926	Arthur Meighen 阿瑟·米恩	1993–2003	Jean Chrétien 让·克雷蒂安
1926–1930	W. L. Mackenzie King W. L.麦肯齐·金	2003–2006	Paul Martin 保罗·马丁
1930–1935	Richard B. Bennett 理查德·B.贝内特	2006–	Stephen Harper 斯蒂芬·哈珀

Prime Ministers of Australia 澳大利亚历任总理

| 1901–1903 | Edmund Barton 埃德蒙·巴顿 | 1903–1904 | Alfred Deakin 阿尔弗雷德·迪金 |

1904	John C. Watson 约翰·C.瓦斯顿	1941–1945	John Curtin 约翰·柯廷
1904–1905	George Houstoun Reid 乔治·胡斯顿·里德	1945–1949	Joseph Benedict Chifley 约瑟夫·贝尼迪克特·奇夫利
1905–1908	Alfred Deakin 阿尔弗雷德·迪金	1949–1966	Robert Gordon Menzies 罗伯特·戈登·孟席斯
1908–1909	Andrew Fisher 安德鲁·费希尔	1966–1967	Harold Edward Holt 哈罗德·爱德华·霍尔特
1909–1910	Alfred Deakin 阿尔弗雷德·迪金		
1910–1913	Andrew Fisher 安德鲁·费希尔	1967–1968	John McEwen 约翰·麦克尤恩
1913–1914	Joseph Cook 约瑟夫·库克	1968–1971	John Grey Gorton 约翰·格雷·戈顿
1914–1915	Andrew Fisher 安德鲁·费希尔	1971–1972	William McMahon 威廉·麦克马洪
1915–1923	William M. Hughes 威廉·M.休斯	1972–1975	Gough Whitlam 高夫·惠特拉姆
1923–1929	Stanley M. Bruce 斯坦利·M.布鲁斯	1975–1983	Malcolm Fraser 马尔科姆·弗雷泽
1929–1932	James H. Scullin 詹姆斯·H.斯卡伦	1983–1991	Bob Hawke 鲍勃·霍克
1932–1939	Joseph A. Lyons 约瑟夫·A.莱昂斯	1991–1996	Paul Keating 保罗·基廷
1939–1941	Robert Gordon Menzies 罗伯特·戈登·孟席斯	1996–2007	John Howard 约翰·霍华德
1941	Arthur William Fadden 阿瑟·威廉·法登	2007–	Kevin Rudd 陆克文

Factfinder

Prime Ministers of New Zealand 新西兰历任总理

1891–1893	John Ballance 约翰·巴兰斯	1912	Thomas Mackenzie 托马斯·麦肯齐
1893–1906	Richard John Seddon 理查德·约翰·塞登	1912–1925	William Ferguson Massey 威廉·弗格森·梅西
1906	William Hall-Jones 威廉·霍尔-琼斯		
1906–1912	Joseph George Ward 约瑟夫·乔治·沃德	1925	Francis Henry Dillon Bell 弗朗西斯·亨利·狄龙·贝尔

1925–1928	Joseph Gordon Coates 约瑟夫・戈登・科茨
1928–1930	Joseph George Ward 约瑟夫・乔治・沃德
1930–1935	George William Forbes 乔治・威廉・福布斯
1935–1940	Michael J. Savage 迈克尔・J. 萨维奇
1940–1949	Peter Fraser 彼得・弗雷泽
1949–1957	Sidney G. Holland 悉尼・G.霍兰
1957	Keith J. Holyoake 基思・J. 霍利约克
1957–1960	Walter Nash 沃尔特・纳什
1960–1972	Keith J. Holyoake 基思・J. 霍利约克
1972	John R. Marshall 约翰・R.马歇尔
1972–1974	Norman Kirk 诺曼・柯克
1974–1975	Wallace Rowling 华莱士・罗林
1975–1984	Robert D. Muldoon 罗伯特・D.马尔登
1984–1989	David Lange 戴维・兰格
1989–1990	Geoffrey Palmer 杰弗里・帕尔默
1990	Mike Moore 迈克・穆尔
1990–1997	James B. Bolger 詹姆斯・B.博尔杰
1997–1999	Jenny Shipley 珍妮・希普利
1999–	Helen Clark 海伦・克拉克

Presidents of the United States of America
美国历任总统

1789–1797	1. George Washington 乔治・华盛顿
1797–1801	2. John Adams 约翰・亚当斯
1801–1809	3. Thomas Jefferson 托马斯・杰斐逊
1809–1817	4. James Madison 詹姆斯・麦迪逊
1817–1825	5. James Monroe 詹姆斯・门罗
1825–1829	6. John Quincy Adams 约翰・昆西・亚当斯
1829–1837	7. Andrew Jackson 安德鲁・杰克逊
1837–1841	8. Martin Van Buren 马丁・范布伦
1841	9. William H. Harrison 威廉・H.哈里森
1841–1845	10. John Tyler 约翰・泰勒
1845–1849	11. James K. Polk 詹姆斯・K波尔克
1849–1850	12. Zachary Taylor 扎卡里・泰勒
1850–1853	13. Millard Fillmore 米勒德・菲尔莫尔
1853–1857	14. Franklin Pierce 富兰克林・皮尔斯
1857–1861	15. James Buchanan 詹姆斯・布坎南
1861–1865	16. Abraham Lincoln 亚布拉罕・林肯
1865–1869	17. Andrew Johnson 安德鲁・约翰逊
1869–1877	18. Ulysses S. Grant 尤利西斯・S.格兰特
1877–1881	19. Rutherford B.

	Hayes 拉瑟福德·B.海斯
1881	20. James A. Garfield 詹姆斯·A.加菲尔德
1881–1885	21. Chester A. Arthur 切斯特·A.阿瑟
1885–1889	22. Grover Cleveland 格罗弗·克利夫兰
1889–1893	23. Benjamin Harrison 本杰明·哈里森
1893–1897	24. Grover Cleveland 格罗弗·克利夫兰
1897–1901	25. William McKinley 威廉·麦金利
1901–1909	26. Theodore Roosevelt 西奥多·罗斯福
1909–1913	27. William H. Taft 威廉·H塔夫脱
1913–1921	28. Woodrow Wilson 伍德罗·威尔逊
1921–1923	29. Warren G. Harding 沃伦·G.哈定
1923–1929	30. Calvin Coolidge 卡尔文·柯立芝
1929–1933	31. Herbert Hoover 赫伯特·胡佛
1933–1945	32. Franklin D. Roosevelt 富兰 克林·D.罗斯福
1945–1953	33. Harry S. Truman 哈里·S.杜鲁门
1953–1961	34. Dwight D. Eisenhower 德怀 特·D.艾森豪威尔
1961–1963	35. John F. Kennedy 约翰·F.肯尼迪
1963–1969	36. Lyndon B. Johnson 林 登·B.约翰逊
1969–1974	37. Richard Nixon 理查德·尼克松
1974–1977	38. Gerald Ford 杰拉尔德·福特
1977–1981	39. Jimmy Carter 吉米·卡特
1981–1989	40. Ronald Reagan 罗纳德·里根
1989–1993	41. George Bush 乔治·布什
1993–2001	42. Bill Clinton 比尔·克林顿
2001–	43. George W. Bush 乔治·W.布什

Factfinder

Commonwealth Countries
英联邦成员国

Antigua and Barbuda
安提瓜和巴布达
Australia 澳大利亚
Bahamas 巴哈马
Bangladesh 孟加拉国
Barbados 巴巴多斯
Belize 伯利兹
Botswana 博茨瓦纳
Brunei 文莱
Cameroon 喀麦隆
Canada 加拿大
Cyprus 塞浦路斯
Dominica 多米尼克
Fiji 斐济
Gambia 冈比亚
Ghana 加纳
Grenada 格林纳达
Guyana 圭亚那
India 印度
Jamaica 牙买加
Kenya 肯尼亚
Kiribati 基里巴斯
Lesotho 莱索托

Malawi 马拉维
Malaysia 马来西亚
Maldives 马尔代夫
Malta 马耳他
Mauritius 毛里求斯
Mozambique
莫桑比克
Namibia 纳米比亚
Nauru 瑙鲁
New Zealand 新西兰
Nigeria 尼日利亚
Pakistan 巴基斯坦
Papua New Guinea
巴布亚新几内亚
St Kitts and Nevis
圣基茨和尼维斯
St Lucia 圣卢西亚
St Vincent and the
Grenadines
圣文森特和格林纳丁斯
Samoa 萨摩亚
Seychelles, the
塞舌尔

Sierra Leone
塞拉利昂
Singapore 新加坡
Solomon Islands
所罗门群岛
South Africa 南非
Sri Lanka 斯里兰卡
Swaziland 斯威士兰
Tanzania 坦桑尼亚
Tonga 汤加
Trinidad and Tobago
特立尼达和多巴哥
Tuvalu 图瓦卢
Uganda 乌干达
United Kingdom
联合王国，英国
Vanuatu 瓦努阿图
Zambia 赞比亚
Zimbabwe 津巴布韦
(withdrew in 2003
2003年退出)

Provinces and Territories of Canada
加拿大诸省及地区

Province 省份	Capital 首府
Alberta 艾伯塔	Edmonton 埃德蒙顿
British Columbia 不列颠哥伦比亚	Victoria 维多利亚
Manitoba 马尼托巴	Winnipeg 温尼伯
New Brunswick 新不伦瑞克	Fredericton 弗雷德里克顿
Newfoundland and Labrador 纽芬兰-拉布拉多	St. John's 圣约翰斯
Nova Scotia 新斯科舍	Halifax 哈利法克斯
Ontario 安大略	Toronto 多伦多
Prince Edward Island 爱德华王子岛	Charlottetown 夏洛特敦
Quebec 魁北克	Quebec 魁北克
Saskatchewan 萨斯喀彻温	Regina 雷日纳
Northwest Territories 西北地区	Yellowknife 耶洛奈夫
Nunavut 努纳武特地区	Iqaluit 伊卡卢伊特
Yukon Territory 育空地区	Whitehorse 怀特霍斯

Factfinder

Factfinder

States and Territories of Australia
澳大利亚诸州及地区

State 州	Capital 首府	State 州	Capital 首府
New South Wales 新南威尔士	Sydney 悉尼	Australian Capital Territory 澳大利亚首都直辖区	Canberra, (federal capital) 堪培拉 (联邦首都)
Northern Territory 北部地方	Darwin 达尔文	Tasmania 塔斯马尼亚	Hobart 霍巴特
Queensland 昆士兰	Brisbane 布里斯班	Victoria 维多利亚	Melbourne 墨尔本
South Australia 南澳大利亚	Adelaide 阿德莱德	Western Australia 西澳大利亚	Perth 珀斯

States and Union Territories of India
印度诸邦和中央直辖区

State 邦	Capital 首府	State 邦	Capital 首府
Andhra Pradesh 安得拉	Hyderabad 海得拉巴	Himachal Pradesh 喜马偕尔	Shimla 西姆拉
Assam 阿萨姆	Dispur 迪斯普尔	Jharkand 贾坎德	Ranchi 兰契
Bihar 比哈尔	Patna 巴特那	Karnataka 卡纳塔克	Bangalore 班加罗尔
Chhattisgarh 查提斯加尔	Raipur 赖布尔	Kerala 喀拉拉	Thiruvananthapuram (Trivandrum) 特里凡得琅
Goa 果阿	Panaji 帕纳吉		
Gujarat 古吉拉特	Gandhinagar 甘地讷格尔		
Haryana 哈里亚纳	Chandigarh 昌迪加尔		

State 邦	Capital 首府	State 邦	Capital 首府
Madhya Pradesh	Bhopal	Uttaranchal	Dehra Dun
中央	博帕尔	北安查尔	德拉敦
Maharashtra	Mumbai (Bombay)	Uttar Pradesh	Lucknow
马哈拉施特拉	孟买	北方	勒克瑙
Manipur	Imphal	West Bengal	Kolkata (Calcutta)
曼尼普尔	英帕尔	西孟加拉	加尔各答
Meghalaya	Shillong		
梅加拉亚	西隆		

Union Territory 中央直辖区

State 邦	Capital 首府
Mizoram	Aizawl
米佐拉姆	艾藻尔
Nagaland	Kohima
那加兰	科希马
Orissa	Bhubaneswar
奥里萨	布巴内斯瓦尔
Punjab	Chandigarh
旁遮普	昌迪加尔
Rajasthan	Jaipur
拉贾斯坦	斋浦尔
Sikkim	Gangtok
锡金	甘托克
Tamil Nadu	Chennai (Madras)
泰米尔纳德	钦奈 (马德拉斯)
Tripura	Agartala
特里普拉	阿加尔塔拉

Andaman and Nicobar Islands	Port Blair
安达曼–尼科巴群岛	布莱尔港
Chandigarh	Chandigarh
昌迪加尔	昌迪加尔
Dadra and Nagar Haveli	Silvassa
达德拉–加纳尔哈维利	锡尔瓦萨
Daman and Diu 达曼–第乌	Daman 达曼
Delhi	Delhi
德里	德里
Lakshadweep	Kavaratti
拉克沙群岛	卡瓦拉蒂岛
Pondicherry	Pondicherry
本地治里	本地治里

Factfinder

States of the United States of American
美国各州

State 州	Capital 首府	Popular name 俗名
Alabama 亚拉巴马	Montgomery 蒙哥马利	Yellowhammer State, Heart of Dixie, Cotton State 黄鹂州，迪克西中心，棉花州
Alaska 阿拉斯加	Juneau 朱诺	Great Land 大地方
Arizona 亚利桑那	Phoenix 菲尼克斯	Grand Canyon State 大峡谷州
Arkansas 阿肯色	Little Rock 小石城	Land of Opportunity 机会之乡
California 加利福尼亚	Sacramento 萨克拉门托	Golden State 黄金州
Colorado 科罗拉多	Denver 丹佛	Centennial State 百年州
Connecticut 康涅狄格	Hartford 哈特福德	Constitution State, Nutmeg State 宪法州，肉豆蔻州
Delaware 特拉华	Dover 多佛	First State, Diamond State 第一州，钻石州
Florida 佛罗里达	Tallahassee 塔拉哈西	Sunshine State 阳光州
Georgia 佐治亚	Atlanta 亚特兰大	Empire State of the South, Peach State 南方帝国州，桃树州
Hawaii 夏威夷	Honolulu 火奴鲁鲁	Aloha State 阿洛哈州
Idaho 爱达荷	Boise 博伊西	Gem State 宝石州
Illinois 伊利诺伊	Springfield 斯普林菲尔德	Prairie State 大草原州
Indiana 印第安纳	Indianapolis 印第安纳波利斯	Hoosier State 胡西儿州
Iowa 艾奥瓦	Des Moines 得梅因	Hawkeye State 鹰眼州
Kansas 堪萨斯	Topeka 托皮卡	Sunflower State 向日葵州

State 州	Capital 首府	Popular name 俗名
Kentucky 肯塔基	Frankfort 法兰克福	Bluegrass State 蓝色牧草州
Louisiana 路易斯安那	Baton Rouge 巴吞鲁日	Pelican State 鹈鹕州
Maine 缅因	Augusta 奥古斯塔	Pine Tree State 松树州
Maryland 马里兰	Annapolis 安纳波利斯	Old Line State, Free State 老分界线州，自由州
Massachusetts 马萨诸塞	Boston 波士顿	Bay State, Old Colony 海湾州，老殖民地
Michigan 密歇根	Lansing 兰辛	Great Lake State, Wolverine State 大湖州，狼獾州
Minnesota 明尼苏达	St Paul 圣保罗	North Star State, Gopher State 北极星州，金花鼠州
Mississippi 密西西比	Jackson 杰克逊	Magnolia State 木兰花州
Missouri 密苏里	Jefferson City 杰斐逊城	Show Me State 眼见为实州
Montana 蒙大拿	Helena 海伦娜	Treasure State 珍宝州
Nebraska 内布拉斯加	Lincoln 林肯	Cornhusker State, Sagebrush State 玉米剥皮人州，艾草州
Nevada 内华达	Carson City 卡森城	Battleborn State, Silver State 战斗诞生州，银州
New Hampshire 新罕布什尔	Concord 康科德	Granite State 花岗岩州
New Jersey 新泽西	Trenton 特伦顿	Garden State 花园州
New Mexico 新墨西哥	Santa Fe 圣菲	Land of Enchantment 迷人之乡
New York 纽约	Albany 奥尔巴尼	Empire State 帝国州
North Carolina 北卡罗来纳	Raleigh 罗利	Tar Heel State, Old North State 塔希尔州，老北方州
North Dakota 北达科他	Bismarck 俾斯麦	Peace Garden State 和平花园州
Ohio 俄亥俄	Columbus 哥伦布	Buckeye State 七叶树州
Oklahoma 俄克拉何马	Oklahoma City 俄克拉何马城	Sooner State 捷足者州

Factfinder

State 州	Capital 首府	Popular name 俗名
Oregon 俄勒冈	Salem 塞勒姆	Beaver State 河狸州
Pennsylvania 宾夕法尼亚	Harrisburg 哈里斯堡	Keystone State 基石州
Rhode Island 罗得岛	Providence 普罗维登斯	Little Rhody, Ocean State 小罗德，海洋州
South Carolina 南卡罗来纳	Columbia 哥伦比亚	Palmetto State 棕榈树州
South Dakota 南达科他	Pierre 皮尔	Coyote State, Sunshine State 郊狼州，阳光州
Tennessee 田纳西	Nashville 纳什维尔	Volunteer State 志愿军州
Texas 得克萨斯	Austin 奥斯汀	Lone Star State 孤星州
Utah 犹他	Salt Lake City 盐湖城	Beehive State 蜂房州
Vermont 佛蒙特	Montpelier 蒙彼利埃	Green Mountain State 青山州
Virginia 弗吉尼亚	Richmond 里士满	Old Dominion 老自治领
Washington 华盛顿	Olympia 奥林匹亚	Evergreen State 常青州
West Virginia 西弗吉尼亚	Charleston 查尔斯顿	Mountain State 山峦州
Wisconsin 威斯康辛	Madison 麦迪逊	Badger State 獾州
Wyoming 怀俄明	Cheyenne 夏延	Equality State 平权州

Members of the European Union
欧盟成员国

Founder members (1957) 创始成员国
Belgium
比利时
France
法国
Italy
意大利
Luxembourg
卢森堡
Netherlands
荷兰
West Germany
西德

Joined 1973 1973年加入
Denmark
丹麦
Republic of Ireland
爱尔兰共和国
UK
联合王国, 英国

Joined 1981 1981年加入
Greece
希腊

Joined 1986 1986年加入
Portugal
葡萄牙
Spain
西班牙

Joined 1995 1995年加入
Austria
奥地利
Finland
芬兰
Sweden
瑞典

Joined 2004 2004年加入
Cyprus*
塞浦路斯
Czech Republic
捷克共和国
Estonia

爱沙尼亚
Hungary
匈牙利
Latvia
拉脱维亚
Lithuania
立陶宛
Malta
马耳他
Poland
波兰
Slovakia
斯洛伐克
Slovenia
斯洛文尼亚

Joined 2007 2007年加入
Bulgaria
保加利亚
Romania
罗马尼亚

*excluding the Turkish Republic of Northern Cyprus 不包括北塞浦路斯土耳其共和国

Factfinder

Chemical Elements and Symbols
化学元素及符号

Actinium 锕	Ac	Gold 金	Au	Potassium 钾	K
Aluminium 铝	Al	Hafnium 铪	Hf	Praseodymium 镨	Pr
Americium 镅	Am	Hassium 𬭶	Hs	Promethium 钷	Pm
Antimony 锑	Sb	Helium 氦	He	Protactinium 镤	Pa
Argon 氩	Ar	Holmium 钬	Ho	Radium 镭	Ra
Arsenic 砷	As	Hydrogen 氢	H	Radon 氡	Rn
Astatine 砹	At	Indium 铟	In	Rhenium 铼	Re
Barium 钡	Ba	Iodine 碘	I	Rhodium 铑	Rh
Berkelium 锫	Bk	Iridium 铱	Ir	Rubidium 铷	Rb
Beryllium 铍	Be	Iron 铁	Fe	Ruthenium 钌	Ru
Bismuth 铋	Bi	Krypton 氪	Kr	Rutherfordium 𬬻	Rf
Bohrium 𬭛	Bh	Lanthanum 镧	La	Samarium 钐	Sm
Boron 硼	B	Lawrencium 铹	Lr	Scandium 钪	Sc
Bromine 溴	Br	Lead 铅	Pb	Seaborgium 𬭳	Sg
Cadmium 镉	Cd	Lithium 锂	Li	Selenium 硒	Se
Caesium 铯	Cs	Lutetium 镥	Lu	Silicon 硅	Si
Calcium 钙	Ca	Magnesium 镁	Mg	Silver 银	Ag
Californium 锎	Cf	Manganese 锰	Mn	Sodium 钠	Na
Carbon 碳	C	Meitnerium 𨭆	Mt	Strontium 锶	Sr
Cerium 铈	Ce	Mendelevium 钔	Md	Sulphur 硫	S
Chlorine 氯	Cl	Mercury 汞	Hg	Tantalum 钽	Ta
Chromium 铬	Cr	Molybdenum 钼	Mo	Technetium 锝	Tc
Cobalt 钴	Co	Neodymium 钕	Nd	Tellurium 碲	Te
Copper 铜	Cu	Neon 氖	Ne	Terbium 铽	Tb
Curium 锔	Cm	Neptunium 镎	Np	Thallium 铊	Tl
Dubnium 𬭊	Db	Nickel 镍	Ni	Thorium 钍	Th
Dysprosium 镝	Dy	Niobium 铌	Nb	Thulium 铥	Tm
Einsteinium 锿	Es	Nitrogen 氮	N	Tin 锡	Sn
Erbium 铒	Er	Nobelium 锘	No	Titanium 钛	Ti
Europium 铕	Eu	Osmium 锇	Os	Tungsten 钨	W
Fermium 镄	Fm	Oxygen 氧	O	Uranium 铀	U
Fluorine 氟	F	Palladium 钯	Pd	Vanadium 钒	V
Francium 钫	Fr	Phosphorus 磷	P	Xenon 氙	Xe
Gadolinium 钆	Gd	Platinum 铂	Pt	Ytterbium 镱	Yb
Gallium 镓	Ga	Plutonium 钚	Pu	Yttrium 钇	Y
Germanium 锗	Ge	Polonium 钋	Po	Zinc 锌	Zn
				Zirconium 锆	Zr

Weights and Measures
度量衡

Imperial, with metric equivalents 英制与公制换算表

Linear measure 长度单位

1 inch (英寸) = 25.4 millimetres (毫米) exactly (精确值)

1 foot (英尺) = 12 inches (英寸) = 0.3048 metre (米) exactly (精确值)

1 yard (码) = 3 feet (英尺) = 0.9144 metre (米) exactly (精确值)

1 (statute) mile (法定英里) = 1,760 yards (码) = 1.609 kilometres (公里)

1 international nautical mile (国际海里) = 1.150779 miles (英里) = 1.852 kilometres (公里) exactly (精确值)

Square measure 面积单位

1 square inch (平方英寸) = 6.45 square centimetres (平方厘米)

1 square foot (平方英尺) = 144 square inches (平方英寸) = 9.29 square decimetres (平方分米)

1 square yard (平方码) = 9 square feet (平方英尺) = 0.836 square metre (平方米)

1 acre (英亩) = 4,840 square yards (平方码) = 0.405 hectare (公顷)

1 square mile (平方英里) = 640 acres (英亩) = 259 hectares (公顷)

Cubic measure 体积单位

1 cubic inch (立方英寸) = 16.4 cubic centimetres (立方厘米)

1 cubic foot (立方英尺) = 1,728 cubic inches (立方英寸) = 0.0283 cubic metres (立方米)

1 cubic yard (立方码) = 27 cubic feet (立方英尺) = 0.765 cubic metres (立方米)

Capacity measure 容积单位

British 英制

1 fluid ounce (液盎司) = 1.7339 cubic inches (立方英寸) = 0.0284 litre (升)

1 gill (吉耳) = 5 fluid ounces (液盎司) = 0.1421 litre (升)

1 pint (品脱) = 20 fluid ounces (液盎司) = 34.68 cubic inches (立方英寸) = 0.568 litre (升)

1 quart (夸脱) = 2 pints (品脱) = 1.136 litres (升)

1 gallon (加仑) = 4 quarts (夸脱) = 4.546 litres (升)

1 peck (配克) = 2 gallons(加仑) = 9.092 litres (升)

1 bushel (蒲式耳) = 4 pecks (配克) = 36.4 litres (升)

American dry 美制干量

1 pint (品脱) = 33.60 cubic inches (立方英寸) = 0.550 litre (升)

1 quart (夸脱) = 2 pints (品脱) = 1.101 litres (升)

Factfinder

1 peck (配克) = 8 quarts (夸脱)
= 8.81 litres (升)

1 bushel (蒲式耳) = 4 pecks (配克)
= 35.3 litres (升)

American liquid 美制液量

1 pint (品脱) = 16 fluid ounces (液
盎司) = 28.88 cubic inches (立
方英寸) = 0.473 litre (升)

1 quart (夸脱) = 2 pints (品脱)
= 0.946 litre (升)

1 gallon (加仑) = 4 quarts (夸脱)
= 3.785 litres (升)

Avoirdupois weight 常衡

1 grain (格令) = 0.065 gram (克)

1 dram (打兰) = 1.772 grams (克)

1 ounce (盎司) = 16 drams (打兰)
= 28.35 grams (克)

1 pound (磅) = 16 ounces (盎司)
= 7,000 grains (格令)
= 0.4536 kilogram (千克)
(0.45359237 exactly 精确值)

1 stone (英石) = 14 pounds (磅)
= 6.35 kilograms (千克)

1 hundredweight (英担)
= 112 pounds (磅)
= 50.80 kilograms (千克)

1 short ton (短吨)
= 2,000 pounds (磅)
= 0.907 tonne (公吨)

1 (long) ton (长吨)
= 20 hundredweight (英担)
= 1.016 tonnes (公吨)

Metric, with Imperial equivalents 公制与英制换算表

Linear measure 长度单位

1 millimetre (毫米) = 0.039 inch (英
寸)

1 centimetre (厘米)
= 10 millimetres (毫米)
= 0.394 inch (英寸)

1 decimetre (分米) = 10 centimetres
(厘米) = 3.94 inches (英寸)

1 metre (米) = 100 centimetres (厘
米) = 1.094 yards (码)

1 kilometre (公里) = 1,000 metres
(米) = 0.6214 mile (英里)

Square measure 面积单位

1 square centimeter (平方厘米)
= 0.155 square inch (平方英寸)

1 square metre (平方米) = 10,000
square centimetres (平方厘米)
= 1.196 square yards (平方码)

1 are (公亩) = 100 square metres
(平方米) = 119.6 square yards
(平方码)

1 hectare (公顷) = 100 ares (公亩)
= 2.471 acres (英亩)

1 square kilometre (平方公里)
= 100 hectares(公顷)
= 0.386 square mile (平方英里)

Cubic measure 体积单位

1 cubic centimetre (立方厘米)
= 0.061 cubic inch (立方英寸)

1 cubic metre (立方米) = 1,000,000
cubic centimetres (立方厘米)
= 1.308 cubic yards (立方码)

Capacity measure 容积单位

1 millilitre (毫升) = 0.002 pint
(British) 品脱(英制)

1 centilitre(厘升) = 10 millilitres (毫
升) = 0.018 pint (品脱)

1 decilitre (分升) = 10 centilitres (厘
升) = 0.176 pint (品脱)

1 litre (升) = 1,000 millilitres (毫升)
= 1.76 pints (品脱)

1 decalitre (十升) = 10 litres (升)
= 2.20 gallons (加仑)

1 hectolitre (百升) = 100 litres (升)
= 2.75 bushels (蒲式耳)

1 kilolitre (千升) = 1,000 litres (升)
= 3.44 quarters (夸脱)

Weight 重量

1 milligram (毫克) = 0.015 grain (格令)

1 centigram (厘克) = 10 milligrams (毫克) = 0.154 grain (格令)

Temperature 温度

Fahrenheit: water boils (under standard conditions) at 212° and freezes at 32°. 华氏温标:(在标准条件下)水的沸点为212华氏度,冰点为32华氏度。

Celsius or Centigrade: water boils at 100° and freezes at 0°. 摄氏温标:水的沸点为100摄氏度,冰点为0摄氏度。

Kelvin: water boils at 373.15 K and freezes at 273.15 K. 开氏温标:水的沸点为373.15开,冰点为273.15开。

To convert Celsius into Fahrenheit: multiply by 9, divide by 5, and add 32. 将摄氏温标换算成华氏温标:先乘以9,再除以5,然后加上32。

To convert Fahrenheit into Celsius: subtract 32, multiply by 5, and divide by 9. 将华氏温标换算成摄氏温标:先减去32,再乘以5,然后除以9。

To convert Celsius into Kelvin: add 273.15. 将摄氏温标换算成开氏温标:加上273.15。

1 decigram (分克) = 100 milligrams (毫克) = 1.543 grains (格令)

1 gram (克) = 1,000 milligrams (毫克) = 15.43 grains (格令)

1 decagram (十克) = 10 grams (克) = 5.64 drams (打兰)

1 hectogram (百克) = 100 grams (克) = 3.527 ounces (盎司)

1 kilogram (千克) = 1,000 grams (克) = 2.205 pounds (磅)

1 tonne (metric ton) 吨(公吨) = 1,000 Kilograms (千克) = 0.984 (long) ton (长)吨

F 华氏温标 (度)	C 摄氏温标 (度)	C 摄氏温标 (度)	F 华氏温标 (度)
-40°	-40°	-40°	-40°
-10°	-23°	-10°	14°
0°	-18°	0°	32°
10°	-12°	10°	50°
20°	-7°	20°	68°
30°	-1°	30°	86°
40°	4°	40°	104°
50°	10°	50°	122°
60°	16°	60°	140°
70°	21°	70°	158°
80°	27°	80°	176°
90°	32°	90°	194°
100°	38°	100°	212°

Some figures are approximate
有些数字为近似值

Factfinder

The Phonetic Alphabet
语音字母表

This alphabet was devised by NATO (the North Atlantic Treaty Organization) in the mid 1950s, and represents a development of earlier systems in use in the British and American armed forces. Approved by aviation and telecommunications bodies, it is now in widespread use in the English-speaking world, although amateur radio users and others have devised other systems. Similar systems are used by speakers of other languages. 本字母表由北约(北大西洋公约组织)于20世纪50年代中期制定，代表了英美武装部队早期应用系统的发展。尽管业余无线电爱好者和其他人设计了另外的系统，但是这个字母表得到了航空和电讯机构批准，现广泛应用于英语国家。类似的系统也被讲其他语言的人所使用。

Factfinder

A	Alpha	J	Juliet	S	Sierra
B	Bravo	K	Kilo	T	Tango
C	Charlie	L	Lima	U	Uniform
D	Delta	M	Mike	V	Victor
E	Echo	N	November	W	Whisky
F	Foxtrot	O	Oscar	X	X-ray
G	Golf	P	Papa	Y	Yankee
H	Hotel	Q	Quebec	Z	Zulu
I	India	R	Romeo		

Wedding Anniversaries
结婚周年纪念

References to golden and silver weddings date from the middle of the 19th century, with diamond weddings following soon afterwards. From these there developed a tradition of associating significant anniversaries with particular materials, and then to the giving of gifts made from these materials. 金婚和银婚的说法起源于19世纪中期，此后不久又出现了钻石婚的说法。据此，形成了一个把重要结婚纪念日与特定材料联系起来的传统，进而又形成了赠送由这些材料制成的礼物的传统。

Year 年数	name 惯称	Year 年数	name 惯称	Year 年数	name 惯称
1st 第1年	Paper 纸婚	9th 第9年	Pottery (China) 陶(瓷)婚	25th 第25年	Silver 银婚
2nd 第2年	Cotton 布婚	10th 第10年	Tin (Aluminium) 锡(铝)婚	30th 第30年	Pearl 珍珠婚
3rd 第3年	Leather 皮婚	11th 第11年	Steel 钢婚	35th 第35年	Coral (Jade) 珊瑚(玉石)婚
4th 第4年	Linen (Silk) 亚麻(丝)婚	12th 第12年	Silk 丝婚	40th 第40年	Ruby 红宝石婚
5th 第5年	Wood 木婚	13th 第13年	Lace 花边婚	45th 第45年	Sapphire 蓝宝石婚
6th 第6年	Iron 铁婚	14th 第14年	Ivory 象牙婚	50th 第50年	Gold 金婚
7th 第7年	Wool (Copper) 毛(铜)婚	15th 第15年	Crystal 水晶婚	55th 第55年	Emerald 翡翠婚
8th 第8年	Bronze 青铜婚	20th 第20年	China 瓷婚	60th 第60年	Diamond 钻石婚

Factfinder

Roman Numerals
罗马数字

1	I	40	XL
2	II	50	L
3	III	60	LX
4	IV	70	LXX
5	V	80	LXXX
6	VI	90	XC
7	VII	100	C
8	VIII	101	CI
9	IX	144	CXLIV
10	X	200	CC
11	XI	400	CD (or CCCC)
12	XII	500	D
13	XIII	900	CM (or DCCCC)
14	XIV	1000	M
15	XV	1900	MCM (or MDCCCC)
16	XVI	1995	MCMXCV
17	XVII	1999	MCMXCIX
18	XVIII	2000	MM
19	XIX	2001	MMI
20	XX	2002	MMII
21	XXI		
30	XXX